A KENTISH LAD

The Autobiography of
Frank Muir

A KENTISH LAD

The Autobiography of Frank Muir

CORGI BOOKS

A KENTISH LAD
A CORGI BOOK : 0 552 14137 2

Originally published in Great Britain by Bantam Press,
a division of Transworld Publishers Ltd

PRINTING HISTORY
Bantam Press edition published 1997
Corgi edition published 1998

Set in 11/12pt Bembo by Falcon Oast Graphic Art

Corgi Books are published by Transworld Publishers Ltd,
61–63 Uxbridge Road, London W5 5SA,
in Australia by Transworld Publishers (Australia) Pty Ltd,
15–25 Helles Avenue, Moorebank, NSW 2170
and in New Zealand by Transworld Publishers (NZ) Ltd,
3 William Pickering Drive, Albany, Auckland.

Reproduced, printed and bound in Great Britain by
Cox & Wyman Ltd, Reading, Berks.

For the grandchildren.

Abigail and Gabriel Wheatcroft
Isobel Muir

To give them a whiff of how kind and colourful life
has been to Bummer.

Contents

Unless otherwise stated, photographs are from the author's collection.

Chapter 1

SMALL PLEASURES

Good holidays stick in the memory and I have complete recall of one trip which turned out to be quite perfect. I was travelling alone and I packed fussily with care and precision, emptying out my case and beginning again until all my holiday things lay in neat, unruffled order.

When the day of departure came at last I bade farewell to my loved ones, picked up my heavy case and off I went. I had three days of good food, late nights, sing-songs, games and laughter and then returned home with happy memories.

I was aged six. I had spent the holiday at the Derby Arms Hotel, Ramsgate, Kent, the pub in which I was born, which was 100 yards down the road and kept by my granny.

A pub is an excellent place for a holiday when you are young and impressionable. The Derby Arms was excitingly crowded and noisy on Friday and Saturday nights with a penny-in-the-slot mechanical piano plonking away and a great deal of loud singing of sad songs; the favourites in the public bar were 'Way Down Upon the Swanee River' and 'There's a Long, Long Trail A-Winding', both sung slowly and sorrowfully with deep feeling. The favourite tipples were pints of mild and bitter (a mixture of the two draught beers), stout, and, for ladies in funds, port and lemon (a tot of tawny port topped up with fizzy lemonade).

My brother Chas and I were not supposed to go into the bar, but we could see in and we would sneak in whenever possible to be nearer the action.

At weekends the bars were packed with sailors from the boarding houses up the hill and miners from Chislet colliery and Irish navvies working on the new railway line; there must have been some outbreaks of rowdyism and violent behaviour

9

but I cannot remember seeing or hearing any in the years when I grew up there. Perhaps because the working man had just survived a war and was not taking his pleasure in a fight but in a bit of fun; the local pub was his equivalent of radio, TV, theatre, music hall and bingo – and his wife was usually with him. Another factor was that our granny had a glittering eye like the ancient mariner and a very powerful, indeed awesome personality when provoked.

The Derby Arms Hotel was well positioned for a pub, being on the outskirts of Ramsgate on the main road to Margate. Just along the road, McAlpine's built a huge brick viaduct to carry the express trains from London over the Margate road to the new Ramsgate station and my brother Chas and I watched it being built.

Better still, we watched when the viaduct was tested by a convoy of six enormous railway engines which, like a family of elephants, huffed and puffed backwards and forwards across the viaduct, hissing steam and blowing their whistles triumphantly. For two small boys – very heaven.

On the far side of the road to the pub stood a grey, granite horse trough, much appreciated in summertime by the huge shire-horses in the brewer's dray when the pub's beer was delivered. It was a long pull from the town. In the granite on the front of the trough a message was chiselled saying that it had been donated by a local resident, the creator of *The Scarlet Pimpernel*, Baroness Orczy.

To my delight, a beer delivery took place on the Saturday morning of my perfect holiday. The dray was backed up to the front of the pub and two enormous draymen, not so much born as drawn by Beryl Cooke, jumped down and hooked back the huge trapdoors in the pavement. A special squat and very strong ladder was then lowered into the cellar; this ladder did not have normal wooden rungs but curved iron bars, which allowed the heavy wooden barrels to be safely slid down.

In the cellar where I crouched, overexcited and probably half drunk from the heavy fumes of beer which permanently hung in the cellar air, all was cobwebs, bent lead piping running from the barrels to holes in the ceiling, wooden spigots and mallets, and a lot of dust.

The massive draymen rolled a barrel off their dray and slid it down the ladder where it thudded onto a sandbag at the bottom. Granny's cellarman Fred then manhandled the barrel up a little ramp onto its rack. Four full barrels were delivered and then the four empties were pulled up the ladder by Spanish windlass (a rope looped round the barrel's tummy with one of its ends fastened to the top of the ladder and the other hauled upon).

During my holiday the weather was warm and sunny and I was taken for walks. Facing the Derby Arms was an old sunken country lane which was my favourite walk. It led through cornfields gashed with scarlet poppies ('Don't lie down and fall asleep near the poppies or you'll be drugged by opium and never wake up'), past St Lawrence College, Ramsgate's public school, eventually coming out on the main road near the Brown Jug pub, Dumpton Park, nearly at Broadstairs. The lane had the ancient and melodious name of Hollicondane.

At the side of the Derby Arms was a road leading uphill to where the new railway station was being built with the help of my father, who had a little wooden hut all to himself and was putting up a mile stretch of iron railings alongside the station's approach road. The hilly road up which my father walked to work every morning went past what was, in the last century, a rough and quite dangerous conglomeration of lowly boarding houses, slop shops and grocers called the Blue Mountains – a nickname almost certainly bestowed by Australian seamen from Sydney, which has a range of hills behind the city known as the Blue Mountains.

Until recently most pubs were called hotels and years ago they probably did provide accommodation of a modest 'commercial gentleman' nature. The Derby Arms Hotel could well have been built for that kind of trade.

Upstairs on the first floor there was a penny-in-the-slot loo for ladies, and my brother Chas and I, on our way up to bed or bath, grew used to making our way up the stairs alongside cheery ladies breathing out fumes of Mackeson's milk stout and hauling themselves up by the bannisters towards comfort.

One afternoon I crept into the ladies' loo – utterly forbidden territory – to find out what mysteries lurked there, and managed to lock myself in. As the pub was closed and my granny was resting, I had to cry myself hoarse before rescue arrived.

On the floor above were some small chill bedrooms where commercial gentlemen might once have been thriftily accommodated. At the age of six I thought there were about fifty bedrooms up there, but as I grew older the number shrank to more realistic estimates, until one day I counted them and found that there were three bedrooms, plus a couple of tinier rooms which had a bath and a loo.

In these bathrooms, above each enamelled iron bath crouched a Ewart's 'Victor' geyser, a gas-fired engine of copper and brass which had to be operated with caution and bravery.

The lighting operation was an act of faith. It required a good supply of matches and an iron nerve. An arm had to be swung out from the belly of the machine and the pilot light on the end of it lit. It was reluctant to go 'plop' and produce its tiny blue flame and often had to be warmed up first, which might take half a box of Union Jack matches, though there was some compensation in that the matchbox had a joke on the back. (Sample joke on the back of a Union Jack matchbox: 'Mummy, mummy! Johnny's swallowed a sixpence!' Mother: 'That's all right, it's his dinner money.')

Then the lit pilot light had to be swung back into the stomach of the engine. This action opened up all the main gas jets which hissed threateningly for a moment and then, touched by the pilot flame, exploded with a great 'WHOOSH!' If you swung the arm in too slowly or – and I've never understood the scientific reason for this – if you swung the arm in too swiftly there could be an explosion which charred the eyebrows. Ever since those days I have never been happy putting a match to gas.

After a few minutes of gestation the geyser's nozzle began to deliver a thin trickle of steamy water at a temperature of about 2,000 degrees centigrade.

A huge room which must once have been the function room of the 'hotel' took up most of the first floor. It had a faintly Far Eastern smell to it, probably from the Chinese bits and pieces of furniture with which the room was stuffed: brass gong-like tables on fretworked teak folding legs; huge black-lacquered screens with mother-of-pearl cockatoos flying across them; faded little framed watercolours of junks on the Yellow River and distant mountains capped with snow. The oriental smell probably lasted because the windows seemed to be kept tightly shut even in mid-summer. During the ten years or so when I more or less lived in the Derby Arms I had the feeling that I was the only person who ever went into that room.

I loved the place. When I walked across the floor the joists creaked and the floorboards floated up and down beneath me like a stiffish trampoline. I found all sorts of treasures stacked away in cupboards. There was a fine large musical box which still worked beautifully. It was cranked up by a ratchet handle and offered six tunes, changeable by working a lever which urged the cylinder sideways a tenth of an inch so that a differently arranged set of pins was presented to the musical teeth.

One of the machine's sophisticated extras was a set of large graduated bells. When I had forgotten all about the bells and the box was delicately tinkling away delineating a waltz, a pin on the revolving cylinder would lift a bar of heavy clappers and drop them down onto the bells with a terrific jangle.

I found four enormous volumes of *A Pictorial History of the Great War*. Terribly gripping photographs of Somme trenches and howitzers and mud and early tanks shaped like rectangles squashed sideways.

I unearthed several albums of cigarette-card collections, depicting such excitements as famous British footballers with haircuts like Dr Crippen and long shorts down to mid-shin, and British racing cars painted racing green with spare cans of petrol clamped to their ample running-boards and bonnets buckled down with leather straps.

I came upon albums of early picture postcards, each card held in place by having its corners tucked into oblique slits in the album's black pages. The favourite subjects for the photographers and watercolourists seem to have been pretty girls with their hair piled high, Canterbury Cathedral, cottages with heavily floral front gardens and sailing ships crowded together in Ramsgate's inner harbour, their bare masts and complicated rigging making patterns as delicate as spiders' webs.

It was a mystery how Granny came to amass this odd

collection of oriental oddments and local semi-collectibles and I suggested to my mother that they were bestowed by sailors in lieu of bar debts. For some reason my mother was horrified by this and pointed out that Granny's then current husband, known as Pop, was the engineer of a trading vessel plying the China Seas, and Pop had probably brought the Chinese bits home. Seemed a long way to transport furniture.

Pop turned up once or twice when he was a widower and my mother looked after him. He was a very fat man in a pale and crumpled tropical suit. I was greatly impressed by his revelation that he sweated so much in the Mystic East that an expensive leather watch strap rotted on his wrist in a few weeks, so he switched to knicker elastic.

He looked like the American movie villain Sidney Greenstreet, but I did not find him at all sinister. Like so many salts when ashore he flung money around freely, behaviour guaranteed to win the affection of any normally venal small boy.

If the character and shape of a growing lad is determined by a mixture of heredity and environment, then heredity from the maternal side of my family could have played only a small part. I am tall. I was once, some years ago, before I began to acquire a literary stoop, 6 feet 6 inches tall, and my son Jamie is even taller, and my daughter Sal is a good height, whereas my mother's side of the family were (except for my mother) short-ish and on the plump side.

Granny was a splendid lady of great character but she was small and stout and she waddled. She had a remarkable goitre like a small dumpling poised on her shoulder, so impressive that it took considerable will-power not to keep looking at it. Granny was not a great eater or drinker but every evening she sipped a half-pint glass of fresh milk – only one – which she had previously spiked with an unspecified quantity of whisky.

Granny was a Cowie from Peterhead in Scotland. The Cowies had always been connected with the sea and sea-going folk. Granny's mother had kept a kind of up-market boarding house in Barking High Street, East London, where she accepted as guests only ships' captains and chief engineers, and our granny continued the maritime tradition, although the life of a sailor was frequently brief in those days. Granny's father, a ship's carpenter, was drowned when the *Union Castle* went down in May 1896. He left six Cowie children, four of them girls. Besides Granny, whose name was Elizabeth Jane, there was her sister Susan, also short and stout, who stayed with Granny most of her life and helped her run the Derby Arms.

During the First World War Susan became engaged to a Canadian who then took himself off to live in Tiverton, Devon. He exchanged letters with Susan regularly for many years, but Mr Green behaved more like a pen pal than an ardent suitor, which was probably just as well as after forty years of correspondence it emerged that he had been married all the time.

Then there was Vera, charmingly bulky, who married a chap with the splendid name of Captain Helmer Augustus Dilner and went off with him to make a home in New Zealand.

And finally there was Adelaide, known as Addie, a jolly lady and nice to have for a great-aunt. Like her bulky sisters, Addie was not avoirdupois-deprived; indeed she was immensely proportioned, with a one-piece bosom which was a cross between a French provincial hotel bolster and a sandbag. In the garden she would lie back in her deckchair and park her cup of tea on nature's shelf; no hands. Addie married Jack Turnage, an Anglo-Indian who was a foreman in a gun and shell factory in Calcutta and they went off to live in India.

Jack Turnage was amiable and kind and Chas and I were fascinated by his ear lobes, which were long and dangly like an elephant's. When I was grown up, Addie and Jack retired from India to a modest house they had built on Ramsgate's West Cliff and here Jack was able to go quietly doolally in comfort (when we called, he would take us aside and whisper that they were coming up through the cavity walls to get him).

Our granny, when aged twenty-one, married a ship's carpenter, aged twenty-four, named Harry Harding, who was a breakaway member of an ancient West Country family which had farmed at Cranmore, Somerset, since before the Norman invasion. The union produced my mother, Margaret (Madge), and then poor Harry Harding, like Granny's father, was lost at sea.

Granny did not languish long as a young widow. She soon married the son of an inspector of lighthouses for Trinity House, Frank Herbert Webber, after whom I was christened (I could have done without the Herbert). In fact Granny and Frank Herbert could not have been legally married as poor Harry Harding's whereabouts and death could never be established. But in 1909 the Webbers moved to Ramsgate and Frank Herbert became the licensee of the Derby Arms Hotel, and there they produced a half-sister and two half-brothers for my mother: my Aunt Mary, Uncle Jack and Uncle Alex (my favourite of them all). All went well for ten years until in 1919, in the middle of the Spanish flu epidemic, Frank Herbert rather unwisely tried to shovel snow whilst wearing only trousers, shoes and a singlet. He caught flu and died.

Granny persuaded the magistrates that she, widow of the ex-licensee, was quite capable of running a decent, law-abiding public house by herself and she took over the Derby Arms and ran it trouble-free for twenty-two years, assisted in the bars by my mother, Margaret − known as Madge − my great-aunt Susan, and two employees, a French slave-of-all-works named Eugenie and, for the heavy work, a newly demobbed naval petty officer named Fred Pearce.

Meanwhile, in the superior boarding-house in Barking High Street, a young marine engineer from New Zealand booked in. His name was Charles James Muir and he was my father. He and his sister Rose had been orphaned in New Zealand when they were quite young and had to strike out for themselves. My father went to sea as a ship's engineer (a profession which at that time seemed to have consisted almost entirely of Scotsmen), and my Aunt Rose went to work in Christchurch Hospital in a lowly capacity, probably heaving a bumper across the ward lino to bring up a polish. She ended up Superintendent of the Hospital MBE, remembered by the Rose Muir Society for Nurses, which she founded, and a stained-glass window in the hospital chapel celebrating her contribution to nursing in New Zealand.

In the boarding house in Barking, young C. J. Muir caught a glimpse of the landlady's granddaughter, Margaret Harding, and that was that. He pursued her to the Derby Arms in Ramsgate, wooed her between voyages to and from New Zealand and they were married in St Luke's Church, Ramsgate, in 1916. Chas was born in 1918 and I in 1920.

Dad was tall. He was a lean 6 feet 1½ inches and he was gifted with accomplishments that were dazzlingly impressive to a small son: he could cut hair, repair socks, name the stars, do a little tap-dancing and he never lost his temper or shouted or complained. He was also rather good-looking, as was my mother. I am allowed to say this because physical traits notoriously jump a generation.

Dad found that life with his family was infinitely preferable to life on the ocean wave and he left the sea.

The Muir family moved out of the Derby Arms and along the road into Thanet Lodge, a pleasant but elderly and inconvenient little house, though with a garden. My mother had to cook on a neurotic kitchen range of great age which needed frequent stoking, and there was an old-fashioned 'copper' in a corner which had to be filled by saucepans and was heated from beneath by a small bonfire. On laundry days, or when a pudding needed a boil-up, a match was put to the bonfire. About an hour later the water began to hubble and bubble, all the windows steamed up and the whole house dripped with condensation.

On the opposite corner of the road to the Derby Arms stood a tiny sweetshop which was owned by my mother, bought with help from Granny. This yielded a small but steady income, very welcome as the depression of the Thirties built up.

It was a bad time for my father to have made his move away from the sea. Jobs on land were increasingly difficult to find and the only work available to him was in unskilled occupations like working on Ramsgate's new railway extension or loading stores onto naval vessels lying off-shore from the First World War 'mystery port' of Richborough. It was called the 'mystery port' (a military secret known to everyone in Ramsgate) because it was the main port from which ammunition, guns and tanks were shipped to France.

For Chas and me those were happy days. One of our occasional pleasant chores was to walk up the hill past the Blue Mountains to the railway site where Dad was putting up his railings and take him his tea makings. This was a spill of grease-proof paper containing a stiffish, unlovely-looking pudding of tea leaves, sugar and condensed milk. In his little hut Dad would boil up an enormous iron kettle, scrape the mixture into a large mug, add boiling water from the kettle and stir the brew into fragrant life.

I have never drunk tea since.

Mother was busy working in the pub and the sweetshop, so she would occasionally hire a very sweet, plump, young local girl named Edie Budd as a minder for Chas and me. Edie would take us for walks along Hollicondane ('I keep telling you, don't lie down near the poppies') or a splash about in the sea from a bathing machine on Ramsgate sands. It was all a bit Dickensian – a family with hardly any money hiring a girl for a few coppers who had no money at all, but it worked amiably.

Edie was a member of a fervent Pentecostal sect in Ramsgate and asked Mother whether she could take Chas and me to a service one Sunday morning. Mother was delighted to get us out of the house so that she could get on with cooking Sunday lunch, so off we went with Edie.

The vocal enthusiasm of the congregation and the charismatic nature of the service made a deep impression on Chas and me. So much so that back home, halfway through lunch, Chas suddenly leaped to his feet and declaimed very loudly, 'Alleluia!' Then he sat down leaving our two stunned parents looking at each other.

Not to be outdone and now well in the mood of the meeting, a few minutes later I too leaped to my feet, eyes shining with zeal. 'God be praised!' I announced ringingly. 'Can I have another potato?'

On non-Edie days the railway construction depot up the hill provided excellent play facilities; there were tall heaps of sand to run up and down and flatten, bags of cement to jump on and kick into grey clouds, heavy nuts and bolts to hurl at the watchman's hut, and, best of all, an old, slow-moving and bad-tempered watchman to provoke.

One evening Mother asked us what plans we had for the morning. We said, 'We're going to the builders' depot to play with the Bugger-Off Man.'

So much for the influence of heredity. Not much influence, really, or I should be walking with a waddle, sporting a goitre, or at least be able to break into a tap-dance, but all these accomplishments are alien, so perhaps the stronger influence on me when a toddler was environmental; it was being a Kentish lad growing up in Ramsgate and Broadstairs which did the damage.

Towns, like strangers, often seem dull and unattractive at first but become interesting the more one learns about them. Ramsgate is like that. Nowadays one thinks of it as vaguely sea-side, something to do with cross-Channel ferries and hovercraft, with a good harbour (some may perhaps even remember that this was a rallying point for the Dunkirk 'little ship' armada), on the whole not a very exciting place. But it was quite a town in its day.

In Tudor times it was a humble fishing village of about two dozen hovels clustered, as with most of the East Kent towns, round the sea end of a natural cleft in the chalk cliffs. This cleft was enlarged to allow carts first to haul catches of fish inland and later to carry into the hinterland much more lucrative goods.

By the eighteenth century the town was beginning to grow and to prosper modestly, due to the development of trade with the Baltic, Europe and Russia, to good fishing, but mostly to the most profitable trade of all – smuggling.

Everybody seemed to be in on smuggling. The gentry, farmers, professionals and tradesmen put up the working capital and they (with the clergy) were the customers. It was a good investment; it has been said that almost every house of any size built along the coast of Thanet in those days was paid for with the profits of smuggling. The actual heavy work on the beach at night – loading the casks and cases onto packhorses, avoiding the occasional officer of the Preventive Service, leading the train of horses up the steep cleft and on to an inland hiding place – was done by farm labourers only too happy to oblige at the going rate of three times their day wage.

A kind of highly profitable reverse smuggling also went on around Ramsgate and the Romney Marshes area in which high-quality, raw English wool, a carefully controlled export much sought after by continental weavers, was smuggled *out* by specialist wool smugglers known as 'owlers'.

There were two extraordinary things about this nationwide

criminal activity; firstly it seemed to carry with it no pangs of guilt; almost everybody who could afford to drink tea, which was heavily taxed in England, bought smuggled tea. And secondly, although smuggling was losing the government enormous sums in revenue, the politicians of the day never bothered to tackle the problem seriously. In the eighteenth century there were only fifty mounted revenue officers to patrol the whole length of the Kent coast, ludicrously few when the smugglers could assemble pony trains of 200 armed men.

In the eighteenth century the business of smuggling was called, without irony, 'free trade'. A rather more legitimate source of prosperity enjoyed by Ramsgate in the middle of the eighteenth century came with the invention of the British seaside holiday.

Until the middle 1700s, waves and mountains were not regarded as objects of natural beauty but as dangerous and boring obstructions which the traveller had to endure to get where he wanted to go. Then all this changed. The grand tourists began to enjoy the 'picturesque view' and the medical profession invented the seaside.

Up to the 1750s, citizens suffering from scrofula and various other unsightly diseases were prescribed a course of the waters, which meant taking rooms at a fashionable spa such as Bath or Royal Tunbridge Wells and enjoying a regime of dunking the unsightly body in a public bath of hot spring water claimed to be 'chalybeate' (not a word which passes the lips daily, meaning 'containing iron') and reeking of sulphurous salts, and then drinking a pint or so of the revolting stuff from a fountain.

The trouble with going to a fashionable spa for treatment was that it was like going to a modern health farm: far too expensive for the average citizen with a spotty back. But the sea was free and much more hygienic than cruising around in a hot bath with a batch of other skin diseases.

So wallowing in the briny, which began at Brighton as remedial treatment for the afflicted, became fun for the whole family. The great British seaside holiday was born.

The Isle of Thanet became London's seaside; its three key resorts being Margate, Broadstairs and Ramsgate. The pioneer town of the three was Margate, England's first seaside resort of any consequence. It was the nearest of the three towns to London, so it appealed to rich Londoners travelling by coach and to the poorer East Enders who arrived by the cheapest form of transport, boat. Margate was on the Thames estuary side of the North Foreland and so holidaymakers did not have to endure the boisterous seas which visitors sailing round the headland to Broadstairs and Ramsgate had to endure.

Large, pleasant houses were built at Margate for the *ton*, the town had (and still has) England's second oldest theatre, and bookshops and concert halls abounded. It had a long sandy beach, a sea-bathing infirmary, and it was a Margate Quaker, Benjamin Beale, who invented the 'modesty hood' to fit onto bathing machines. Bathing machines were a breakthrough in seaside decorum, consisting of a horse-drawn changing hut on wheels with Mr Beale's canvas hood at the back. The thing was towed by its horse into the shallows, enabling the lady within to change into her bathing costume, climb down a short ladder and cavort discreetly beneath Mr Beale's canopy in her own little bit of sea without the embarrassment of her wet flannel costume clinging to her form and revealing her intimate bumps and dents.

Gentlemen bathed stark naked further along the beach.

By the early nineteenth century Margate had changed considerably, moving firmly downmarket; perhaps because the new railways were demonstrating that the big profits came not from milord in his own coach strapped to a wagon, but in the masses crammed onto wooden benches in trucks. Much cheaper accommodation was built and Margate became the seaside success story for the working man and his family.

East End Londoners mostly travelled to Margate by the cheapest and most uncomfortable of small packet-boats, the common hoy (hoy polloi?).

Charles Lamb, aged fifteen, went for a happy week's holiday to Margate with his cousin and later recalled the humble voyage (fare – 2 shillings 6 pence) in his essay, 'The Old Margate Hoy' ('Can I forget thee, thou old Margate Hoy, with thy weather-beaten, sun-burnt captain, and his rough accommodations – ill-exchanged for the foppery and fresh-water niceness of the modern steam packet? . . . Not many rich, not many wise, or learned, composed at that time the common stowage of a Margate packet').

Broadstairs was the permanently genteel town of the three Thanet resorts, appealing strongly to the middle classes and those who wanted to be thought of as middle class, like Mr Pooter who referred affectionately to the town in *Diary of a Nobody* as 'good old Broadstairs'.

It was hardly a resort – no fairground with big dipper, or on the other social level no golf links either – but it did have a Grand Hotel and a pleasant, curved bay and a bandstand and a bit of a pier and a minstrel show on the beach, and it developed a reputation for its healthy sea air so it became a popular site for convalescent homes and expensive preparatory schools; many a union leader recovered his voice in his union's red-brick, neo-Gothic convalescent home on a Broadstairs cliff top, and many a minor royal and future duke began his schooling being walloped in a Broadstairs prep school.

Further lustre was added to the town's reputation when Charles Dickens found it a placid place in which to write. He frequently stayed and worked at the Royal Albion Hotel (still going strong) and at Bleak House, an odd building like a small Scottish baronial castle which overlooked the harbour. At the time it was called Fort House but the name was changed to Bleak House when the novel became successful. It is now a Dickens museum.

Of the three Thanet resorts serving London it was Ramsgate which managed to be the most comprehensive socially, offering an *Upstairs, Downstairs* arrangement of suitable holidays for both the rich and the non-rich.

The less well-off were tempted with a long, safe, free beach, an army of bathing machines, Punch and Judy shows, donkeys for children to ride, lots of pubs, bracing sea air, inexpensive boarding houses and a view of sailing ships constantly beating up and down the busy Downs (the slightly sheltered waters between the seashore and Goodwin Sands). And early in the century the uncomfortable voyage by hoy was superseded by the railway. Trains from London emerged dramatically from a tunnel cut in the chalk cliffs and disgorged their holidaymakers a few yards from the seafront. Later a new station was built on the edge of the town and the old seashore terminus became a funfair, Merrie England.

Unlike Margate, Ramsgate kept its hold on the affections of the wealthy. Elegant Georgian terraces were built on the East Cliff top, Nelson Crescent, Albion Place, Paragon Place, and well-to-do London merchants took to wintering in fashionable Ramsgate. And during the summer season their good ladies, after a discreet dip from their bathing machine, could drink their (smuggled) tea, tuck up their (smuggled) lace cuffs and enjoy their game of whist far away from both the citizens of Ramsgate, described by a lady visitor from London in a letter home as 'the smelly inhabitants', and the seething crowd of holidaymaking 'Arry and 'Arriets on the beach below, a busy scene captured by Frith in his hugely popular painting of 1853, *Ramsgate Sands*.

It was claimed that King George IV actually deserted his beloved Brighton one summer for a holiday at Ramsgate but I can find no proof of that; however, the monarch did graciously condescend to visit Ramsgate in 1821 when he disembarked from a visit to Hanover. The town fathers, in ecstasies, had 100 tons of Dublin granite fashioned into a copy of a classical obelisk and erected to commemorate this widely unpopular king's gouty foot touching down on Ramsgate soil. Local townspeople referred to the obelisk as the 'Royal Toothpick'.

During my childhood, trams used to grind noisily up and clatter noisily down Madeira Walk, the steep winding hill which descended rapidly from the rich terraces of the East Cliff through an ornamental chine to the harbour. I remember when very young being shown the sharp corner where, I was told, a tram had once jumped the tramlines, tipped over the edge and plunged down into somebody's back garden. I could never pass that corner again without an enjoyable little frisson.

Other frisson-inducers in my early years included the unhygienic-looking iron mug chained to the drinking fountain in Ellington Park, from which, I was informed, a boy of my age had recently caught the Black Death; a synagogue – actually a Jewish seminary and college set up by the Montefiore family – lying behind high walls on the road to Broadstairs where, my brother Chas told me, Jews used to be flogged until they agreed to give all their money to the roller-skating rink along the road and become Christians; and being christened at the age of seven, the ceremony having been postponed because my father was at sea when I was born. I was a bit old to be christened, but queuing up with the babies at the font was not so embarrassing in retrospect as was my appearance. The solemn ceremony marked the first occasion on which I faced the world with my hair stiff and glossy from a generous handful of Field's Lavender Solidified Brilliantine.

King George IV was not the only person of high consequence to enjoy the pleasures of Ramsgate. In AD 449, Hengist and Horsa (their names translate as 'The Horse Brothers') led the first Teutonic invasion of the island, setting sail from Jutland and landing on a beach, Ebbsfleet, to the west of Ramsgate. The Horse Brothers were followed in AD 597 by Augustine (later St Augustine), sent by Pope Gregory to bring Christianity and Latin verbs to our Isles. Augustine and forty monks managed to achieve this peacefully and he became the first Archbishop of Canterbury.

Princess Victoria, before becoming Queen Victoria, enjoyed a number of visits to Ramsgate, staying at many of the fine houses and meeting everyone of substance. The town also had its odd eccentric resident, such as Sir William Curtis, Bt, who built his estate, Cliff House, on Sion Hill, a splendid site overlooking the harbour. Sir William, a 'very badly educated Tory', made a huge fortune from manufacturing sea biscuits in Wapping. He became Lord Mayor of London and was famous in his day, rather like Lord and Lady Docker were in the 1960s, for his conspicuous wealth. His sumptuously fitted yacht was particularly marked out for mockery by Whig wits. King George IV, though, enjoyed many a luxurious cruise with his rich friend and stayed at Cliff House, Ramsgate, in 1821 when he returned from Hanover.

Another resident, less noble and rich, who made his mark on Ramsgate was the great Gothic revival architect and designer, Augustus Pugin, perhaps most famous for working with Barry as designer of decorations and statues for the Houses of Parliament. Pugin built himself a Gothic house in Ramsgate with its own little church. He was converted to Roman Catholicism in 1833 and made his church into a kind of abbey. His house and the church – St Augustine's, Ramsgate's first Roman Catholic church – are still there, faced with glistening black flints. Pugin died at his house in Ramsgate, insane.

And then there was young Vincent Van Gogh. In 1876 the somewhat muddled young Dutchman, aged twenty-three, recovering from unrequited love for his London landlady's daughter and uncertain whether to become a pastor like his father or an evangelist amongst the working classes, moved to Ramsgate and was taken on as a teacher in a small impoverished school with twenty-eight pupils, run by a Mr Stokes. For four months Van Gogh taught some of the young of Ramsgate their mathematics, French and geography.

My friend Michael Meyer pointed out to me that Mr Stokes almost certainly could not have afforded atlases for the geography lessons, so somewhere in Ramsgate there is probably an old gentleman whose father tucked away in the attic a sketch map of Mesopotamia drawn by Vincent Van Gogh.

Before he left England and went back to Holland leaving school-teaching for more creative pursuits, Van Gogh drew a charming little pen-and-ink sketch entitled *Vue de la fenêtre de l'École*. Ramsgate, 31 mai 1876.

The first school my brother and I went to was not unlike Mr Stokes's academy. Ours was about the same size, was called Thyra House School and its proprietor, headmaster and 50 per cent of its staff was a Mr Rule. Mr Rule, a heavily built man with a Bavarian accent, had a look about him of Field Marshal von Hindenburg, so when the First World War broke out he prudently changed the spelling of his name from Ruhl to Rule.

Chas and I used to walk to school, and a fair way away it was, too, for a couple of ex-toddlers. We would toil up the hill from the Derby Arms to what was the flour mill at the top and down the other side to South Eastern Road where Thyra House was, pausing to hurl a potato in a desultory sort of way at the front door of an old lady who lived in a row of houses on the left pavement. If we scored a hit the lady would hurtle out of her door shaking her fist at us and screeching. It was the kind of mindless bad behaviour which most children seem to enjoy for a while. Perhaps she, too, came to enjoy it as part of life's rich pattern because she never seriously tried to catch us.

The other 50 per cent of Thyra House School's staff was a thin, almost transparent lady who pedalled the harmonium with spirit and taught us to sing hymns, her favourite being 'You in Your Small Corner and I in Mine'. Chas was good at hymns and was nominated Best Singer. I was nominated Best Opener (opening the mouth wide was a much-esteemed virtue in Thyra House hymn-singing). Years later I was delighted to find that the French for 'small corner', *petit coin*, was a popular euphemism in France for the lavatory.

It was in the middle of an arithmetic lesson at Thyra House, taken by the headmaster himself, that I discovered the enormous satisfaction that came from creating laughter and it became the main aim of my working life.

I was sitting at a double desk with a plump fellow scholar who was almost asleep with boredom. To cheer him up I made a humorous remark. He sniggered and whispered what I had said to the boy behind him and he sniggered too.

Mr Rule's fat hairy forefinger bent in a beckoning movement and I slid out from my desk and stood next to him, clutching my pencil, knuckles white with fear.

'Muir, you were talking in class again. That is not permitted, heh? Vill you kindly repeat aloud vat you said to Leatherbarrow? It is fair, is it not, that you share your vit vith all of us?'

'Please, sir,' I mumbled, 'I said, "This pencil top is sir's bum."'

The roomful of children erupted in joyful mirth. It was an intoxicating moment. I had made the whole school laugh.

It might be thought that it was not really much of a joke on which to base a career. It was not even remotely witty, and it was hardly comedy of observation; my pencil top was only half a centimetre in diameter and held one of those useless pink rubbers which smear pencil marks without erasing them, whilst sir was what Americans call a 'lardbutt'; his behind was about a metre wide. But the roomful of children laughed at what I had said and my destiny was fixed.

Chapter 2

BEACH BOY

The parents suddenly upped sticks from Ramsgate and moved to Broadstairs, settling into a pleasant rented house named Fernbank. The move probably came about because Dad had been offered a reasonably good job with McAlpine's, helping to build a factory up in Selby, Yorkshire.

Then things began to go wrong. My father caught pneumonia rather seriously and my mother went up to Yorkshire to nurse him. My brother and I were looked after by Mother's sister Mary and her husband Len (Chas and I were pages in daffodil-coloured satin at their wedding. Yellow Pages?).

Mother was away for months and when she and Dad returned to Broadstairs their savings had all gone and Dad was none too strong. Uncle Len came to the rescue. He had opened a shop near Broadstairs railway station selling electrical goods and was building a business based on the new craze – listening to the wireless.

Dad became an installer of sets and aerials for Uncle Len. He rode around Broadstairs on a curious vehicle called a 'Ner-a-Car', not unlike the outcome of a liaison between a motor scooter and a sway-backed motorbike. Its main feature was a large storage box under the rider's legs, large enough to hold tools and bits of wireless sets.

Wireless was a growth industry and for years things went well for Uncle Len and Dad. One weekend Dad brought home the makings of a crystal set and put it together. I remember moveable coils like a pair of ears, glowing valves, the 'cat's whisker' (very important component), which was a piece of fine wire moved about by a little lever, and the 'mighty atom', a tiny lump of quartz glinting in the light. The quartz was probed by the 'cat's whisker' until a station was located and we could listen to it through the heavy black earphones (two members of the family per headset).

The excitement when Dad first tuned in and we heard sounds coming to us through the air *without wires* was terrific. Never mind that we knew perfectly well the transmission came from the North Foreland Lighthouse a mile up the road and was only a few dots and dashes of morse code – it was magic to us.

We moved to a newish rented bungalow, Adstone, on Linden Avenue, where Mother was able to take in lodgers during the summer season. Chas and I much enjoyed our lodgers, who made a change to our routine. We particularly liked a Mr Sumner and family who were most amiable and came year after year.

With the extra money coming in from the guests, Mother was able to cover the bungalow's floors (almost but not quite wall to wall) with grey haircord, an inexpensive form of carpet which was attractive enough to look at and hard-wearing. Walking on it in bare feet was like strolling across Brillo pads, but the carpet was my mother's pride: people like us – I suppose lower middle class hoping to become middle middle class – did not have carpets in those days, we had bare floorboards, varnished, or lino and rugs.

In keeping with my new role as the family jester, Chas gave me for my birthday a joke ink blot, a piece of metal pressed into the shape of a large shiny blot of Stephen's blue-black ink and suitably coloured. It was startlingly realistic.

Sniggering with excitement I laid it on Mother's new carpet, put an empty ink bottle on its side beside the blot and called out, 'Quick, Mother! I've had an accident!'

Mother shot in from the kitchen, took in the sight of the ink bottle on its side and the large blot on her beautiful new carpet and gave me a whack round the back of my head with her wedding-ring finger which sent me ricocheting off three walls.

This would probably have won her fourteen days hard labour in Holloway Prison in these enlightened times but it was exactly the right treatment then. I have hated the lurking sadism of practical joking ever since.

Adstone had a brick shed at the end of the garden where we could make things. I built a writing desk from plywood with a sloping front, but I was never able to use it: I unthinkingly painted it with a particularly pungent creosote and nobody was ever able to get closer than 6 feet to it.

Our real life was the beach. Or rather 'the sands'; it was rarely called 'the beach' in those days. When we were not at school we were playing on the sands, and swimming. Well-off visitors hired tents for changing and we soon knew which tents were not hired and could be used free by us, though they were hardly luxury accommodation; the green canvas tents were, whatever the weather, oddly airless and smelled heavily of linseed oil and pee.

Swimming costumes were not chic in the late 1920s. Chaps wore a black affair or one with a horizontally striped upper half and a black lower half with an imitation belt with a rusty buckle in between. A semi-exciting design innovation was large decorative holes below the normal armholes. In those days it was the chaps, not the girls, who wore a tiny modesty skirt on the front of their costumes. Made more sense, really.

Swimming caps were definitely *de rigueur*. If you were a swift swimmer, played water polo and were proud of your crawl, you wore a brightly coloured rubber skullcap like half a football bladder. If you were a distance man you wore a heavy black rubber helmet, about a quarter of an inch thick, which had black rubber earpieces vulcanized on. The difficulty was that you really had to be fitted for these. I occasionally found such a helmet abandoned in the sand, but the earpieces never quite coincided with my ears and agony ensued.

The quality of the bathing was hardly Cap Ferrat standard, not that we minded or even noticed (or had even heard of Cap Ferrat). The water normally had a healthy English Channel chill to it and was grey and semi-opaque with bits of dead seaweed and grains of sand swirling about in it.

If you were unlucky enough to be swimming when the *Perseverence*, a large, open, ex-fishing boat, moved away from the jetty in a wide sweep taking visitors on a shilling sick-round-the-bay, for the rest of the morning you swam in and swallowed petrol-flavoured sea water.

I was never a fast swimmer. I developed a labour-saving technique based on an ancient stroke called the 'trudgeon' which seems to have disappeared from the seaside swimmer's repertoire. In my version I lay floating on top of the water face down, occasionally giving little frog-like twitches of the legs as in the breaststroke whilst performing a lazy arm movement on my side as in the sidestroke. These dabs at propulsion through the water occurred only every few minutes and then in as gentle and energy-conserving a manner as possible. Although not yet in my teens, and thin with it, I could swim like this non-stop for an impressive three or four hours at a go. Unless there was a current running I hardly moved from the same spot.

I had lots of friends on the sands and after a swim we would dry off, throw ourselves face down on our towels in a star formation, heads together, and natter away for hours. I would try to make the others laugh, not with comical voices and jokes but with comical notions. I cannot remember these being very successful but neither can I remember any of my friends actually hitting me.

A large proportion of our chat was concerned with sex. We all knew with rough accuracy what happened in the process which Alan Bennett described in a play as 'the docking manoeuvre', but like most boys of our age we spoke out on all the more intricate and subtle nuances of lovemaking with the bold authority assumed by those anxious to hide their pig-ignorance.

One cherished fragment of sex-lore amongst our group was that any Belgian or French girl student who wore a gold cross on a chain was easy game. Easy game for *what* was not clear to us younger members of the group, but we cried, 'Yes, aren't they!' and leered along with the big boys.

The only one of us who achieved an, as it were, 'hands on' experience with a girl student was a senior member of our group. He had taken a French girl to the concert party at the Bohemia theatre in the High Street, which must have been a baffling enough experience for her, during which he established some sort of fleshly contact. He started out telling us the story of his achievement with a kind of boastful enthusiasm, but then this tailed off into a slightly embarrassed mumbling. He had become fond of the girl.

One chilly morning I rose enormously in my group's estimation by becoming the first of us to see a female nipple. Both of the pair, what is more, and only inches away from my nose.

Speculation as to what a girl's bosom actually looked like has fascinated growing lads all over the world, it seems. A few years ago I was on a plane to Mauritius with my wife Polly, who was born there, when an elderly American leaped to his feet, his brow knotted with worry, and shouted above the engines, 'Does anybody here know the lines which follow ''Twas brillig, and the slithy toves . . .'?

I did know ('Did gyre and gimble in the wabe; All mimsy were the borogoves, And the mome raths outgrabe'). So I bawled the rest of Lewis Carroll's extremely odd little verse to him and he sank back in his seat, at peace with the world again. I met him later on a beach in Mauritius and learned that his name was Dillon Ripley and he was Secretary Emeritus of the Smithsonian Institution in Washington and probably America's most distinguished ornithologist.

At the time Mr Ripley and I were sitting under one of those thatched parasols on a Mauritian beach, contemplating with aesthetic pleasure a very pretty Italian girl bouncing and jiggling along the beach, dressed entirely in what appeared to be a short piece of string.

'When I was a schoolboy at the beginning of this century,' Mr Ripley said reflectively, 'the entire boyhood of America thought that female breasts were brown.'

'Brown?' I ventured.

'Dark brown,' said Mr Ripley. 'You see, the only breasts American boys ever got to look at in those days were photographs of Far-Eastern tribes in the dentist's waiting-room copy of the *National Geographic* magazine.'

My own first glimpse of the erotic zones happened at Broadstairs when I was busy saving their owner's life.

There were two life-saving measures in force at that time for the preservation of Broadstairs bathers. Somewhere in the bay a small ancient rowing boat was anchored, with a retired salt of great age slumped asleep over the oars. This was known as the safety boat. There was also an anchored raft in the middle of the bay which not only provided a useful resting place for tired swimmers, but also gave purpose to a quick dip; one swam out to the raft, dragged oneself aboard, got one's breath back and then dived off again and swam back to the shore.

On that fateful morning there was a cool breeze blowing across the bay and the water was choppy and chilly. The rest of our group did not fancy swimming so wandered off and busied themselves with another healthy boyish activity on dry land, namely filling empty Andrews Liver Salts tins with thin strips of cordite, used during the war for projecting naval shells and still being washed up on the sands, and sealing the tins to make bombs which exploded most satisfactorily when thrown on somebody else's bonfire.

I was gazing vaguely at the horizon, the way you do when you are at the seaside and cannot think of anything better to do, when I noticed the head of a swimmer bobbing up and down in the choppy water. The bobbing head was making for the raft and seemed to be at the end of a long swim round the jetty. I heard a faint feminine cry for help in a foreign tongue and the head disappeared for a moment or two.

I swiftly removed my shirt and shorts, and now clad only in my swimming costume with the chic four armholes and the rusty buckle, I sprinted to the water's edge. I then sprinted back, took off my wristwatch and laid it on my towel. I went through the same routine with my leather sandals and then I plunged into the cold water and made for the struggling swimmer. In no time at all I had reached the raft. This speed through the water was not because I had up-graded my style from the trudgeon to the crawl, but because the tide was out, the raft was only in 4 feet of water and I could wade to it.

The swimmer was a girl and she really was a bit distressed, gasping for breath, uttering little foreign whimpers and clearly tired. Quite pretty.

'It's all right, madame,' I said, speaking very loudly because I thought she was probably French, 'you're safe now, I've got you.' I swivelled her face-up in the water and held her under the armpits as I had seen the Sea Scouts do in life-saving practice. 'Upsy-daisy!' I cried, trying to get her up onto the raft.

I don't know exactly what happened, but in the course of trying to pull and push her across the edge of the raft her swimming costume was rolled down to her waist.

I stared, goggle-eyed, I am afraid, at this revelation of secret feminine anatomy. My knowledge of what a nipple looked like had been until then largely conjectural, based on saucy stories in furtive American collegiate magazines ('Greg took off his catcher's mitt and slid his hand inside Fran's bra. Her erect nipple bored into the palm of his hand like a flint arrowhead. "Greg, no!" she hissed urgently . . .'). Suddenly I was unexpectedly face to face with the naked reality.

Her breasts (smallish, both about the same size) were not brown like those in the *National Geographic*, but extremely white with a touch of blue due to the cold, and they were slightly puckered from being too long in the water. Her nipples were, rather surprisingly, not brown either but a bluish-greenish colour and wrinkled by the cold water. They were not unlike dried olives.

Teeth chattering but rested, she thanked me charmingly in French for helping her (at least I think she did), pulled up her costume without any self-consciousness, slipped back into the water and swam competently towards the shore.

I waded to the shore, mind spinning, determined not to share with the others my warm and wonderful, very personal experience. Though I eventually gave them an edited version.

One thing about growing up at the seaside in Broadstairs was that come summertime there was little point in going elsewhere for a holiday. I did not 'go away' for a holiday until I was married; up until then there seemed no better place to be on holiday than Broadstairs sands.

Early on in my years as a beach boy I was wrenched away from the sands and taken into the countryside for a day's outing; it was my first close encounter with nature and I was not happy with it.

The occasion was part of a money-making scheme I had going. Our local parish church needed choirboys; it seems they

33

were constantly defecting or metamorphosing into baritones, and the going rate for the job was 5s. a quarter (£1 a year!) so I rushed to join. I have no singing voice as listeners to radio's *My Music* will sympathetically agree, but my proven skill at opening impressed the organist and I was taken on. I turned up religiously (an entirely inappropriate adverb) and hung on to my financial bonanza by lurking in the shadows a lot in church and, during hymn and anthem singing, miming.

But nobody warned me that there was an annual choir outing into the countryside.

For this the vicar traditionally hired a brake, an ancient, Edwardian, horse-drawn, bus-like vehicle which had plodded along for many years between Ramsgate and Pegwell Bay, carrying passengers who were in no hurry, until it became so unroadworthy that no horse could be persuaded to pull it on a regular basis. I sat on a plank seat on the uncovered top deck, well away from authority, happy to be lumbering slowly towards the Kent village of Pluck's Gutter (what magical names these old hamlets have, to be sure).

We arrived late at the meadow where we were to have our picnic lunch because the elderly horse turned bolshie just north of Deal and slowed down to about 1 m.p.h., but the vicar soon had us debussed and sitting in a circle round him on the meadow grass, clutching our official-issue brawn sandwiches.

'Choir!' he cried, ringingly, revolving slowly like a lighthouse so that his words would reach us all in turn. 'Most of your days are spent in the town or playing about on ugly sand. Today is your holiday from all that. Today, Choir, you are in the heart of Beautiful Nature!' In which case, one fake chorister's unspoken thought was, the sooner the holiday is over and we are back to ugly sand the better.

If you are uncomfortable sitting on sand you just wiggle a bit and the sand adjusts itself to the shape of your bottom. Nature does not do this. You sit on a tussock in a Pluck's Gutter meadow and what happens? You wiggle a bit and a needle-sharp piece of long grass goes up the leg of your shorts. You shift sideways to assuage the agony and the suspiciously warm patch on which you are now sitting is a reminder that this is a pasture on which sheep have safely grazed.

Nature, of which the countryside unfortunately has a lot, is not only carpeted with needle-sharp grass and prickly flora which scratches your ankles and becomes lodged in the buckles of your sandals, but is also full of dangerous fauna. The seaside has its little bits of fauna too, but these are harmless and frequently edible, e.g., shrimps.

At the seaside insect life is benign, just a few little hopping things in the sand. Nature, on the other hand, harbours whole regiments of malevolent predators whose teeth cause damage and pain far in excess of the tiny beasts' size and fighting weight.

For anybody collecting this kind of scientific data I am able to report that during about seventy minutes spent in a Kent meadow (the Garden of England) sitting unknowingly on firmish sheep droppings, the following occurred: a very large and shiny black bug, seemingly in drink, flew erratically backwards and forwards in front of me and then thudded into my forehead. A weal arose. A colony of ants invaded my lower legs and scurried about, biting; about 200,000 very small red marks appeared. A cricket levitated in front of me and dropped down the front of my shirt, causing me to utter a thin girlish scream. A squadron of large horseflies with hairy legs and metallic-blue tummies settled on my lunch. I threw away my brawn sandwich.

Soon after that hapless outing, to prevent recurrences I sought out the vicar and resigned from the choir, which came as a surprise to the vicar as he had no idea that I was in it. I did not sever all my connections with the church, though. I contributed 'The Mystery of the Tree Trunk, an Exciting Adventure Serial', to the parish magazine. Like all parish magazines of those days it had a properly printed section dealing with Christian issues, and another inserted section of local interest produced in purple ink on a jellygraph by a church-warden. This latter section was where my serial appeared, although 'appeared' is hardly the word, as in most issues, due to hot weather hardening the jelly, my contribution was partly or wholly illegible.

It was all rather sad because I much enjoyed writing the serial. It was an ordinary kind of story; some children fell down a hole in a hollow tree trunk and happened upon some Chinese airmen who were villainous dope-smugglers (to me 'dope' meant the pungent spirit which the RAF used to spray on their Sopwith fighter planes to tighten the fabric). I did not plan the story ahead, it just lurched from episode to episode. Unfortunately I never found out how it ended. Owing to lack of support in the parish, the magazine went out of business after four issues, the only time I have ever heard of a parish magazine going bust.

My interest in both reading and trying to write was awakened back in the Ramsgate days when I did well in an exam at Thyra House School and my granny gave me a book prize, the first book I had ever wholly owned. It was a highly popular volume in its day with well-drawn, sensitive illustrations: *The Story of a Red Deer* (1897) by the Hon. Sir John Fortescue KCVO.

As the title suggests, it was the story of a red deer. I read it very slowly, almost learning it by heart as I went, savouring every twist of the story, every description, and believing totally in the reality of the animal. Unfortunately Sir John did a Walt Disney and killed off the deer at the end. I did not actually blub because I was getting on a bit by then, rising seven, but I had a painful lump in my throat for about three weeks afterwards whenever I remembered the noble beast's sad end.

Two or three years later, when we moved to Broadstairs, I was given pocket money lavish enough to buy a weekly comic (3*d*.). The importance of this step to this young reader cannot be exaggerated. A comic once a week gave me entry into a syndicate of eight other comic-fanciers at school, each of whom bought a different comic. Then once a week we all swapped comics on a carefully worked-out rota system. So for threepence I enjoyed eight new comics a week.

I quite liked the *Champion*, which had stirring war stories such as the exploits of His Majesty's torpedo boat, HMTB *Battler*, but my favourite by a mile was the *Magnet*, stories set in a public school, Greyfriars, and featuring Billy Bunter the Fat Owl of the Remove, the peerless Bob Cherry and a cast of a hundred other regulars.

The weekly *Magnet*, usually about 20,000 words, was almost wholly written by Charles St John Hamilton under the pseudonym Frank Richards. Hamilton is in the *Guinness Book of Records* as the world's most prolific author, with a total output of boy's magazine prose equal to a thousand novels. And he lived just up the road from us in a large villa at Kingsgate, a frail old bachelor in his eighties, occasionally to be glimpsed through the front gate pottering about his garden dressed in a skullcap, dressing gown, pyjamas and bicycle clips.

Another local author was Countess Barcynska, a writer of fragrantly romantic novels (*Pretty Dear*, 1920; *Love's Last Reward*, 1921; *He Married His Parlourmaid*, 1929; and many more). The countess, originally from Poland, wintered in the south of France but summered in a modest house on the front at Broadstairs which was proudly pointed out to visitors. She was a sad-looking, rouged old lady in a large and floppy straw hat. I saw her from time to time doing unPolish, non-literary things like buying a dressed crab in the fish shop opposite Marchesi's restaurant in Albion Street.

It was the closest I had ever been to a real writer and I desperately wanted to talk to the countess and seek her advice on professional problems of authorship, like did she happen to know a publisher who might be interested in buying four episodes of a serial about dope-smuggling Chinese airmen who lived under a tree, and would a really good publisher print my work on a jellygraph efficient enough to deliver at least *part* of it in a legible state. But (thank God) I never plucked up enough courage to approach Countess Barcynska with my problems and she died in 1930.

The family move from Ramsgate meant, of course, that Chas and I had to bid farewell to Mr Rule and Thyra House School and start again at a school in Broadstairs. It has always been a matter of wonder to me (and profound gratitude) that Mother and Dad, neither of whom had much formal education, were absolutely committed to giving Chas and me the best education they could afford. They could not really afford *any*, but somehow each term they managed to save and scrape enough pounds and shillings together to pay the fees and keep us at one of the small private schools which existed (rather than prospered) in Thanet. I think they probably managed to do some sort of deal with the depression-hit proprietors but I have no idea what sort of deal it could have been.

In Broadstairs we became pupils of Stone House School, Stone Road. This was one up from Thyra House School because it took in a few boarders. I cannot think that it was a very agreeable place to board because Chas and I stayed there for just one night when our parents had to go away and we found the food most peculiar. For dinner we had liver which was overcooked to the point of being bone dry. Cutting into the liver was like sawing away at a leather purse, and when I finally made an incision the inside poured out onto the plate like sawdust.

We had several teachers, all faintly odd. One was a rather nervous old man who instituted weekly tests. To avoid mutiny he gave a penny to any boy who answered a question correctly.

Another unlikely pedagogue was Mr Murphy, a teenager who was not really a teacher at all. He had been accepted as a potential steward on the Ramsgate cross-Channel ferry and was filling in his time at Stone House School until a vacancy on the ferry occurred.

Mr Murphy was a cheerful young man and we all liked him, but the learning he imparted to us was mostly off-the-top-of-the-head rubbish. For instance, he taught us in a geography lesson that the west coast of Ireland was rough and rocky because it had been pounded for centuries by Atlantic waves. A moment's reflection might have reminded him that pounding waves tend to smooth out knobbly coastlines rather than roughen them, wearing away the headlands and silting up the inlets.

But we were all sad when Mr Murphy's job as a ferry steward came through and he departed to richer pickings, if only because he was young and amiable and most teachers in our sort of school were old and sarcastic.

Besides French and Belgian girls (with or without gold crosses round their necks) Broadstairs schools attracted children from further afield, particularly from rich Middle-Eastern families who wanted their sons to be able to speak conversational English.

Latterly I had a friend at the school who was Persian (now Iranian, I suppose) whose name I never saw written down so I can only guess at its spelling; it sounded like 'Mossen Sadri'. He had a great sense of humour and we got along very well. I thought I owed it to him to spell his name correctly in these pages so I telephoned a very nice jolly man at an Iranian translation bureau in London and asked him how my friend's name should be spelled. He told me that a man of that name was well known in Iran and the name was spelled Musa Sadr. He was the leader of a Shiite faction but had been kidnapped a few years ago and had not been heard of since. I can only hope that Musa Sadr is a common name in Iran.

By the time the young Musa Sadr arrived from Persia to join the school, Stone House School had moved to a new home, a large house like a boarding house right on Broadstairs front and near the bandstand. A huge noticeboard on the front of the house proclaimed it to be BRADSTOWE COLLEGE (Bradstowe was the ancient name of Broadstairs). It was a more convenient building for a small boarding and day school, with a brick annexe at the back housing a couple of classrooms, but Chas and I were only there for a short while before our parents moved us on to greater things.

So the few marvellous sand-and-sandals years were beginning to come to an end; it had been a period of steady change and improvement for small boys.

One magnificent advance in our living standards was the arrival in our lives of the Mars bar. Before the launch of this rich and superb orchestration of chocolate, soft toffee and creamy whip, sweets were more basic. Chocolate usually came in a thin rectangle, like a thickish credit card.

Uncle William's Toffee was offered in many flavours (my favourite was banana) and was not wrapped in chew-sized pieces but came in a 6 by 4 by ½-inch slab which the shopkeeper held in the palm of his hand and smote with a hammer. He picked up the shattered shards of toffee from the floor, wiped them on his pullover, weighed them on worn brass scales and handed them over in a screw of paper. The first fragment you popped into your mouth was usually the biggest piece, triangular with sharp points almost piercing your cheeks.

When you tried to talk to somebody you sprayed them with a fine jet of toffee juice.

Liquorice was a favourite, sometimes called Spanish. It came in all manner of shapes including bootlaces, pipes, All-Sorts, and batons, and when stamped into the shape of document seals was known as Pontefract cakes. Although the blackness of liquorice stained small faces and clothes, on the whole parents did not mind children chewing the stuff as, unknown to the children, it was a mild but effective laxative.

Boiled sweets, be they acid drops tasting of car batteries or pear drops tasting of nail-varnish remover, came loose in a jar, but they seldom stayed loose very long as they tended to co-agulate into a hard mass which the shopkeeper had to hack viciously with an ice pick (sweetshops were much more labour-intensive in those days). The result was that, to our delight, most sweetshops had a jar filled with clumps of broken boiled sweets which they sold off cheaply.

Another favourite, i.e. inexpensive, chew which has now virtually disappeared was the tiger nut. This fibrous morsel could be described as resembling an owl pellet dropped by a constipated bird which had been feeding solely on the insides of horsehair mattresses and the tufts on top of coconuts, with perhaps a beakful of haircord carpet for pud. You chewed and chewed your tiger nut but it yielded little flavour and did not diminish as the hours went by. I cannot say I miss it.

The chap in the park who sold tiger nuts from a tricycle also sold inexpensive nougat with peanuts in it like gravel, candy twist (a rock-hard spiral of translucent boiled sweet tasting of cloves and therefore associated in the young mind with toothache), and sparkling Fanta, another cheap treat in those days, which came in many flavours and in bright colours not to be found in nature. The chap dispensed this stuff by filling a mug with water, adding concentrated Fanta in the flavour of your choice and tickling it up into bubbles with a huge cylinder of some sort of gas.

Another item which has all but disappeared from present-day young people's balanced diet is sherbet. This sweet fizzing powder used to come in two forms, the sherbet fountain – a graspable cylinder of yellow cardboard with a liquorice tube sticking out of the top; sherbet was sucked up the tube and when it hit saliva, fizzed and tickled the tongue. The other form was the sherbet dab, a triangular paper packet of sherbet with a toffee-based mini-lollipop sticking out of one corner. The technique was to take out the lollipop, lick it until it was tacky and then dab it back in the sherbet and swiftly convey the toffee-flavoured dab to the mouth whilst still fizzing. Delicious.

When we first went to Broadstairs neither Chas nor I had been in a motor car; we did not even know anybody who owned one. The streets were busy with horse-drawn carts, errand boys delivering groceries on bikes which had huge baskets on top of the small front wheel, and horse-drawn milk floats from which the milkman ladled milk into your jug from a churn.

In dairies the produce was also 'loose'. Cream stood on the counter in a wide brown bowl, guarded from air attack by a squadron of wasps. Butter was a huge yellow lump on a marble slab. A half-pound block was shaped up by the shopkeeper by hacking off a suitably sized piece and patting and slapping it very loudly into a rectangle with two grooved paddles. This was the job we all wanted to do when we grew up.

The first motor car Chas and I actually touched belonged to the girlfriend of our nice Uncle Alex. Uncle Alex was only a few years older than Chas and me but he was a very good cricketer and altogether a bit of a goer. It was unnerving for him when cutting a dash on the sands at Broadstairs in his pearl-grey flannel bags and cricket blazer, chatting up a likely lass, suddenly to be addressed by two largish lads as 'Uncle'. He had a threatening word with us.

Alex's permanent girlfriend was Tilly, an archetypal flapper, lean, bony and fascinating, with a tulip haircut and Clara Bow lips. She was an unconventional girl who was, rather surprisingly, a good long-distance swimmer. But unpredictable. She eventually married Uncle Alex's best friend.

Tilly's father was a successful Ramsgate greengrocer, and for her twenty-first birthday he gave her a new Austin Seven Ruby saloon car. This was the late 1920s. Chas and I were not only allowed to run our hands along the Austin Seven's beautiful flanks, but for five wonderful minutes sweet Tilly let us sit in it. The colour scheme was chocolate brown and beige and a little silver vase was mounted on a windscreen pillar with a dead flower in it. There was a ring which the driver pulled steadily and a roller blind rolled upwards over the rear window, shielding the driver from the glare of headlights from the car behind.

During the last of our years in Broadstairs there were noticeably more private cars on the road than there had been when we arrived, and horse-drawn delivery carts had begun to give way to square, sit-up-and-beg vans and lorries like the Foden, with its exterior gate-change gears and solid tyres perforated with big horizontal holes to give the hard rubber some illusion of springiness.

Happily, our Sunday mornings were still occasionally enlivened by a distant cry of 'Hottttttt Rollllls!' and either Chas or I was deputed to dress swiftly and track down the Hot Roll Man by following his shout. The baker carried the fresh warm rolls on a tray covered by a cloth.

When you are very young anything is possible and your personal limitations, if any, have yet to make themselves known. One of the evil effects of growing older is to become progressively aware of the activities in life which you are simply not equipped ever to be any good at.

During my early days at Broadstairs I realized that becoming an architect was not on as a career. What happened was that Mackintosh, the toffee-makers, decided to promote their new wrapped toffees by a series of sandcastle competitions at holiday resorts round the coast. There were glittering money prizes to be won; a whole £1 note for the winner, 10s. and 5s. for the runners-up.

I worked hard on my castle; it had a moat and turrets, a castellated keep and a cardboard drawbridge. I had most intelligently carted damp malleable sand from the edge of the sea, but I had forgotten the sun. By eleven o'clock my entry, bone dry, was crumbling away at the edges. Then as the judging party began its tour of inspection I stepped back to see how far they had got and trod on my castle. And that was that, though some good did come from it: every competitor was given a small scarlet pail of about twelve Mackintosh toffees, by then warm and soft from the sun and most welcome as a mid-morning snack.

In those early days I trod the boards for the first time. Broadstairs' popular beach entertainment for many years was Uncle Mack's Minstrels, a wondrously politically incorrect alfresco concert party which performed on a white wooden stage on the sands. The cast, dressed in spangly romper suits and black mortarboards, sweated behind a faceful of burned cork in the last flutterings of the tradition of 'nigger minstrel' shows. Uncle Mack's Minstrels was an innocent display of what is now looked upon as being offensively racist (among my books I have a collection of classic jokes and sketches taken from those original nineteenth-century minstrel shows entitled, if you please, *Niggerosities*).

Every Wednesday morning Uncle Mack conducted a talent competition for young hopefuls; the winner got 5*s*. At the time there was a play doing the rounds of the repertory companies called *White Cargo*, which then became a popular film. It was a throbbing story of sex in the jungle, a bit like the work of Somerset Maugham. A young British planter is tempted by the ravishing, dusky beauty Tondelayo into joining her in a spot of 'mammypalava' (we all knew what that meant), but she catches a social disease or is poisoned or something and at the end staggers off into the jungle, clearly not feeling at all well, leaving our hero to smile devilishly at the audience and declaim (splendid curtain line), 'If she lives – she lives with ME!'

I decided that I would sing the audience the theme song from the film version of *White Cargo*, accompanied by Uncle Mack on his banjo.

I have a snapshot of myself at the time of what turned out to be my tragic stage début. I was short of two front teeth and the pockets of my short trousers were bulging with such boyhood necessities as a tobacco tin full of worms gathered from the foreshore for use as bait, some pebbles for skimming through the waves, a bottle of iodine in case I cut myself, some useful string and an orange.

Now the song was a steamy, very sexy ballad, written by, of all people, Noel Gay, who wrote 'Me and My Girl', 'Let's

43

Have a Tiddley at the Milk Bar', 'Run Rabbit Run', and about a thousand other popular hits, and it described the singer's longing for more mammypalava with the seductive Tondelayo. With an introductory twang from Uncle Mack's banjo I launched into song.

Sadly, it was not my audience. I had hardly piped out the first few lines when the punters became restive. I think perhaps I put a bit too much passion into it because well before I had got to 'nights of madness' Uncle Mack had taken me by the elbow and propelled me firmly off-stage, murmuring, 'Have another go when you're a bit older, sonny.'

It was a pity because I needed the five-bob prize. I had developed an interest in photography. This was a new thing for families, following a brilliant breakthrough by the Kodak company in making cameras cheap enough for everybody to own and simple enough for anybody to use. Instead of a camera being like an expensive piece of laboratory equipment, all shiny mahogany and brass, the Kodak Box Brownie was made of what seemed to be dimpled black cardboard. It had a tiny reflex viewfinder, which you had to shield from the light with a hand otherwise you could not see anything, and when you pressed the lever to take a photograph a large safety pin moved across the lens opening, followed reluctantly by a sheet of metal with a hole in it. And that is all there was to it.

The film was an eight-exposure strip of celluloid backed by paper and wound on a spool. After taking a snap you turned the Brownie upside down, peered into a little window at the back and wound on for the next snap, being guided by a pointing hand, dots and the number of the next exposure.

I have no idea how much the Brownie cost because Dad got it by saving up cigarette coupons. Tobacconists' shelves were stocked with different names then. Craven A was still going strong with the new cork tip (originally paper printed to look like cork) but there were lots of other popular brands, now rarely seen, such as the cheapest of them all and a great favourite during the First World War, Woodbines, sold five at a time in a flat, green, open paper packet. When we did *A Midsummer Night's Dream* at school, a titter was enjoyed by all during Puck's big speech: 'I know a bank whereon the wild thyme blows' when he got to 'luscious woodbine'.

There was also the modestly priced Turf, Park Drive and Black Cat to choose from, and at the upper end of the market De Reske, Du Maurier and Passing Cloud. This last brand, quite expensive, came in a pink packet with a picture on it of a toff puffing out smoke with a dreamy look, like a deb's delight at a party enjoying a modern-day exotic substance. The cigarettes were oval, as though somebody had sat on the packet.

Black Cat was one of the earliest brands to issue gift coupons to be collected and exchanged for items from a catalogue. Dad was not a heavy smoker so heaven knows how long it took him to puff through enough Black Cat fags to provide us with a Kodak Box Brownie, but he managed it.

I became deeply interested in photography, but there was not enough spare money for the parents to waste on films and processing so I had to be more or less self-financing, hence going in for competitions with cash prizes. The chemicals needed were quite cheap and I taught myself developing and printing, developing my films in a cupboard, see-sawing the film in darkness through a soup plate of developer and then through another of hypo. I adapted an old picture frame to make contact prints.

A good source of money for photography was programme-selling at the annual Broadstairs Water Sports. This was an exciting event in itself. Narrow boardwalks were run out into the bay for the swimming-race contestants to dive from, and there were dinghy races and water-polo matches while a regimental band played marches and 'Gems from *The Merry Widow*'. The high spot of the day was a sea battle between boatloads of white-clad bakers and boatloads of black-clad chimney sweeps. For ammunition the bakers hurled paper bags of flour at the black sweeps and the sweeps hurled paper bags of soot at the white-clad bakers. It ended up as a tremendously satisfying mess, with all the whitened sweeps and blackened bakers swimming around in the water trying to scrape themselves clean enough for their wives to allow them into the house when they got home.

An ambitious young programme-seller, remorselessly aggressive and prepared to trudge all day up and down the esplanade and the sands accosting holiday makers, could earn himself a cool 2 or 3s. commission.

Life for Chas and me was soon to change radically and the good days of slopping about on the sands most of the time and acquiring the minimum of learning were about to change. The parents had decided that we were old enough to go to a real school and they managed to have us accepted for Chatham House School, Ramsgate.

About that time I went through a strange rite-of-passage experience, perhaps preparing me for the rather more earnest existence I was due to face in a more grown-up world.

My love for my mother had never been obsessive; it was the normal warm trust, respect and love of son for mother and vice versa, and I had the same kind of relationship with Dad. But Mother did stand in a slightly different light in that, unlike Dad, who used to be away for long periods, Mother had always been there, a permanent source of comfort and safety in a world often difficult to understand.

Then, lying in bed one night, it occurred to me that Mother would *not* always be there. One day she would die and I would never see her again. This was much too enormous a concept for my tiny split-pea brain to cope with calmly and I simply gave way to inconsolable misery, sobbing into the pillow far into the night, with Chas eventually having to come in and say, 'Oh, for God's sake, shut up!'

But I could not shut up. Night after night for about two weeks, as I lay in bed, the dread black thought crept back that one day Mother would not be there; it was like a medieval nightmare crouching over me. I just did not know what to do but to howl as quietly as possible and hope that sleep would soon bring oblivion.

Mother chose a good moment and gave me a gentle talking-to, explaining that I was quite right about her having to leave us all one day (she actually lived way into her late seventies), but that was how it all worked and I must learn to accept death as a fact that none of us could do much about.

Suddenly, a few days later, as if the sun had emerged from behind a cloud, everything became all right again and life returned to being warm and secure, dread evaporated and my strange emotional and irrational experience was over; it never returned.

For Chas and me life entered a new phase and we cycled off to Chatham House every morning with a packed lunch which we ate from its greaseproof paper in company with lots of other boys in the school dining hall, which smelled of the previous day's in-house meals.

Chatham House was, at last, a real school with properly qualified teachers and opportunities to act and write things and play cricket and rugby and make music; a senior pupil when we were there was a boy from nearby Dumpton Gap, a very good organist named Edward Heath; I understand he later went into politics.

My good friend Uncle Alex had been there and had played cricket for the school. Chatham House was and remains an excellent grammar school by any standards.

But then, a year afterwards, our lives suddenly changed yet again and the Muirs moved away from the sands and the sea for ever and went to live in London.

It was a happy move for Dad. A firm of machinery manufacturers named Belliss and Morcom Ltd, which made turbines and reciprocating engines, had equipped an engine room for a firm named Caribonum which made high-grade typewriter ribbons, carbon paper, and Field's ink. The factory was in a somewhat far-flung London suburb, Leyton, E10. The installation was giving trouble which proved difficult to fix and somebody at Belliss and Morcom remembered Dad, who had worked successfully with their equipment when he was a marine engineer in New Zealand. They traced Dad to Thanet and recommended him for the job of looking after Caribonum's generating machinery.

I went up to London with Dad for his interview. We sailed on the paddle steamer *Royal Sovereign*. A fine way to go. The ship was somehow proud and broad, and the thunder and splashing of the paddles was both exciting and comforting. Dad took me down to the engine room where steam hissed and shiny things went in and out and it was, I remember, very hot.

Dad fixed the trouble with Caribonum's engine, was offered the permanent job of Caribonum's deputy factory engineer

47

and, of course, took it. So quite suddenly it was farewell to swimming in sea water tasting of petrol, and Chatham House School, and lying on the beach with friends listening to a portable gramophone with the Rexine peeling off the lid and the gramophone needle ploughing sand out of the record's groove as the Tiger Ragamuffins, Ivor Moreton and Dave Kaye, played 'Tiger Rag' at hectic speed on two pianos. And the almost erotic luxury of being pink and hot from lying in the sun all day, and then at night sliding between cool, crisp sheets with a new story from the *Robin Hood Library* (4*d*.).

Could life in London possibly match such delights?

Chapter 3

GROWING UP

Number 28 Church Road, Leyton, E10, was the first house my parents ever owned; they paid for it very slowly over many years. It was in a short terrace of similarly low-priced, fairly basic homes in Church Road built just after the First World War, each with a useful strip of back garden and a useless patch of front garden.

Dad immediately planted grass seed on the near half of the back garden to give us a lawn, erected a rustic trellis screen with climbing roses and packed the far half of the garden with veg.

With Dad in a real job and the kitchen garden flourishing, food was now good and plentiful. It always had been for Chas and me, but during the bleaker years I think the parents exercised a little secret parental hold-back.

Two regular meals I remember with great affection from those early Leyton days: in summer we had huge platefuls of Dad's lettuce dressed with vinegar and sugar, and in winter we had a little joint of lamb or beef on Sundays, the surplus of which was curried by Mother on Mondays.

It was not the curry or the meat which Chas and I enjoyed so much as the copious spoonfuls of Sharwood's Green Label mango chutney which it was our joy to spread over it. But on one traumatic Monday, Mother found that she had run out of the delicious sweet chutney. Chas and I were desolated and stared in dismay at our unchutneyed curried lamb. To us it was like being asked to eat 'sour pork' without the 'sweet and', or Heinz baked beans not in tomato sauce but in hot water. Mother rose magnificently to the problem and graced our curry with liberal spoonfuls of Allen and Hanbury's cod-liver oil and malt. We found it delicious.

The Borough of Leyton once had one foot in Epping Forest and the other in London, but as the years passed the forest withdrew and the London suburbs crept outwards, engulfing Leyton and its neighbours. But when we moved to Leyton in the early 1930s there was still a blacksmith in the High Street with his forge in a white, wooden clapboard smithy, and near us in Grange Park Road lived and worked the Childs, a family of glass-blowers, and at the top of the road in the High Street was a tiny factory which made church organs.

Church Road is a kind of wriggly hypotenuse running from Leyton High Street down to Lea Bridge Road. The purpose-built Caribonum factory lay down a side road off Church Road, about a mile away from us and well within walking distance.

Chas and I were immediately enrolled at Leyton County High School for Boys. The rather longish title was to differentiate the school from its sister establishment, the Leyton County High School for Girls. They were not all that difficult to differentiate as the girls' school was full of girls and was not in Leyton at all but in Leytonstone.

To get to school Chas and I only had to walk about 100 yards up the road to the High Street and catch a tram. Tram tickets were sold at the school at a specially subsidized cheap rate. Of course, being sent off to school on a Monday morning bearing cash to buy the week's tickets was a terrible temptation, and most of us dipped into our tram money for sweets and had to walk to school in the latter part of the week. It was about a mile and a half from us to Essex Road and we developed a kind of shambling jog to avoid being late.

One tiny urban pleasure which partly compensated us for the loss of beach life was the antisocial manner in which we got off the tram, which satisfyingly infuriated the tram driver.

On the floor by the driver's foot was a thing like an iron mushroom. This was connected by a lever to a clapper, so that when the driver stepped on the iron mushroom, the clapper hit a huge iron gong under the floorboards and gave a very audible warning of the tram's approach. A dozen or so of us LCHS lads used to travel to school every morning on the upper deck of the tram. When we arrived at our stop we all streamed down the staircase and jumped the last three stairs, landing heavily one by one on the iron mushroom. The clangour was ear-splitting.

Leyton County High turned out to be an extraordinarily good school. In rank it was not even a grammar school – our nearest local grammar school was Sir George Monoux School (pronounced locally as 'Sir George Monarchs') in nearby Walthamstow – but a county high, a grade of secondary school which provided an almost free education; I think my parents had to find £11 a term (harder to find then than it sounds now). The syllabus was amazingly extensive: French was compulsory and another language had to be taken as well, usually either Latin or modern Spanish or German. There were classes in woodwork and metalwork, there were tennis courts and football and cricket pitches to play on, a dramatic society which performed plays in the school hall, musical appreciation classes, a school orchestra and a gymnastic team so proficient that it made an annual performance tour of Denmark.

A third of the sixth form was expected to win a scholarship to Oxford or Cambridge, and did, and over the years the school notched up an impressive list of distinguished old boys, including John Lill, the classical pianist; Arnold Diamond, smooth villain in many a film and telly play; Levy, a sixth-former (can't remember his first name) who achieved fame in the RAF for being acclaimed the most successful hitch-hiker of the war, reputed to have thumbed his way during one leave to, through and back home again from Canada; John Dankworth, saxophonist and jazzman; Sir Derek Jacobi, actor; and perhaps the best-known face of all, my contemporary at LCHS, the actor John Hewer, who has been on our small screens for many years as the white-haired and curly champion of the fish finger, Captain Birds Eye.

The headmaster of LCHS, Dr Couch, was an awesome figure to us, capped and gowned and ascetic-looking, nephew of the great literary authority 'Q', Sir Arthur Quiller-Couch.

Teachers taught in their gowns, adding their degree hoods at formal events. Wearing gowns in class should not have mattered but it did. We mocked the teachers but we also respected most of them; the academic dress gave them a touch of remoteness and helped them to achieve a natural authority in the classroom.

My attempt to become part of the great gymnastic tradition of the school ended in a little pain, a lot of humiliation and a realization that as well as having no future as a castle architect working with sand, I also had no future as an acrobat. The shame came on me quite early in a gym class conducted by the school PT instructor, a short, stocky, appallingly healthy Scot who busied around the gym in squeaky plimsolls.

The exercise was a forward somersault. My instructions were to sprint down the gym gathering speed, leap onto the spring-board and shoot into the air, curl up into a ball and bring both my fists down sharply so that I would spin forward and land lightly on my feet on the mat.

What could be simpler?

Other boys went before me and spun forward in the air with natural grace and dexterity, but they had the short, chunky build of PT instructors, with calf muscles like grapefruit. I had been short and chunky, rather unpleasantly so, for quite a bit of my childhood, but I was now aged eleven and had elongated. I was taller than anybody else in my year and very narrow, about 14 inches at the widest part which was my feet, and I seemed to have no calf muscles at all; my legs were narrow pink cylinders from hip to ankle, the line only broken by bony knees.

My turn came. I pounded forward confidently, my feet mak-ing booming noises on the wooden floor of the gym, leaped onto the springboard and hurtled athletically up into the air. That was when I realized that the physical agility game was not for me. Almost fainting with the excitement of flying up towards the roof, I forgot to curl up into a ball. Instead I rose into the air rigid, slowly turned over like a caber tossed at the Braemar Highland Games and landed on my head. I toppled forward on the mat, stiff as a plank and momentarily unaware of where, or who, I was.

The mat was padded to save the necks of unco-ordinated parcels of skin and bone like me, so the result was a brief headache but no blood ('Pity it wasn't cement,' muttered the PT instructor, rather bitterly I thought), and I was given a chit saying, 'Excused all PT classes. Extra Hygiene instead.'

I had greater success in more sedentary areas of effort. During my first year I wrote a one-act play, *Almost a Crime*, which was directed by Collins of the sixth form and performed in the school hall on Parents' Day. I wrote a kind of gossip column for each issue of the school magazine under the pseudonym 'Nuncio' (which I hardly need to remind readers is Italian for 'the Pope's special messenger'), I joined the Dramatic Society and played, in a quite outstandingly hammy performance, the Persian poet Suleiman in *The Poetasters of Ispahan*, but good came of it because I had made a splendidly long and wispy beard out of grey crêpe hair which reached down to the waist and was so impressive that Mr Lewis the English master appointed me the school's official make-up artist (Collins of the sixth form, a tall, thin, funny chap, was good on Mr Lewis, whom we all liked. 'What a fine literary figure,' Collins would say in awed tones as Mr Lewis strode into view down the corridor. 'The Byronic limp, the Shelley-like toss of the head, the Shakespearean semi-baldness . . .').

Woodwork classes were an option which I jumped at. I had just learned how to cut mortise and tenon joints (I still can if given enough time, say about ten times as long as it took me then) when the metalwork master started a class in jewellery-making and I rushed to join. For the rest of my time at LCHS I spent happy hours every week in metalwork class making a pair of silver cuff links.

I must have made about fifteen pairs during that time, or more accurately one pair fifteen times. Cutting the cuff links from sheet silver, engraving them with the letters 'F' and 'M', melting black enamel into the letters and making the chain from silver wire wrapped round a knitting needle were all no problems to an unathletic lad with patience. The snag with the whole process became apparent when the time came to solder the bits together. The method was to warm up the silver with a mouth-operated methylated-spirit blowpipe until the proper temperature had been reached, and then touch the two bits to be joined with a bit of silver solder. Theoretically the solder would then melt, run and join the bits of silver together. Now for the snag. Silver solder melted at about half a degree lower than the silver itself so if – or rather, when – I blew through the blowpipe too strongly, the whole damn cuff link melted into a blob of silver and I had to start again from the beginning.

I did eventually complete a pair of cuff links and wore them proudly in the great outside world when I left school, but silver is soft and after only a few weeks the links of the chain wore through and both cuff links fell to pieces.

Perhaps I should have persevered with forward somersaults.

School life was busy and enjoyable, but then so was life outside. I found that the world was full of new interests, the problem was to sort them out and ration time and energy to fit in as many as possible. I became fascinated with the various escapements of watches. I couldn't afford to buy watches, of course, but I could look at them in the High Street pawnshops and occasionally persuade 'uncle' to open up the back of a couple.

I bought, very cheaply, an odd length of brown velveteen which had been salvaged from a fire and made myself a smoking jacket (I did not smoke). I had not realized what an extraordinarily difficult thing it was to attempt. I found a book on tailoring in Leyton Public Library, doggedly read it up and then had a go. Luckily mother had an ancient Singer hand-turn sewing machine with flying cherubs all over it, which was a great help. The finished jacket was wondrously ill-fitting and quite awful, of course, but that was not the point; I had made it.

On the other hand, although I tried very hard, I failed to build a typewriter, which I had planned to assemble from a collection of items including a rolling pin, a John Bull rubber printing set and the wire from a number of straightened-out coat-hangers.

When I was about twelve I took up bell-ringing at our parish church down the road. This was mainly to bring a little diversity to Sundays as Chas and I were shooed out of the house and sent to morning service, afternoon Sunday school and evening service. Bell-ringing was agreeably dangerous for a young person as the bells were extremely heavy and if you pulled one off balance and held on to the rope too long it could whisk you off your feet and crash your skull against the belfry roof.

But there was the annual and wonderful bell-ringers meat tea. This was arranged by our team leader (ringmaster?), Mr Hughes, a printer by trade. We went on a brief tour of several country parish churches as guests of their bell-ringers, rang a few 'changes' on their bells for friendly then sat down with them in a village pub to enjoy the traditional bell-ringers' meat tea of ham and salad and mustard pickles.

The high spot of our campanology year was New Year's Eve. We climbed up the belfry ladder and tied heavy leather muffles to the bell clappers. Just before midnight, we rang a few minutes of softly sounding 'changes' and three minutes before midnight climbed up again into the belfry, whipped off the muffles and scrambled back down in time to welcome in the new year with the brilliant sound of a clear, loud, un-muffled peal.

Photography had to be fitted into this busy schedule. I was by then interested in making movies as well as taking stills, so money had become a grievous problem. There was the usual routine embezzlement of tram-ticket money. Actually, it had now become bus-ticket money as the trams had been super-seded by privatized bus services. Our favourite buses were painted brown and had on their sides, in gold lettering, *PRO BONO PUBLICO*. Besides dipping into bus-ticket money I had my pocket money (3*d*. a week), and occasional half-crown tips from relations, but there was a massive shortfall which I decided I could best meet in two ways: one by buying small items and selling them at a profit, and the other by inventing and making the equipment I could not afford.

There were a number of junk shops as well as pawnshops strung along the High Street and I rapidly became Leyton's small-time Arthur Daley, wheeling and dealing vigorously. An early coup was to buy a rusting birdcage for 2*s*. 6*d*. at one end of the High Street, buff it up a bit and sell it for £1 at the other end.

After a series of complicated transactions worthy of a tall thin Medici, I had amassed a working capital of about £5 and I bought an ancient 9.5mm cine-camera from a pawnshop for

£2. It was almost a museum piece, hand-operated (two turns of the handle a second), but by an extraordinary piece of luck I found a rusty motor attachment for it in a photography shop which cost only £1 10s. I also found a cheap and tinny hand-operated 9.5mm projector, broken but repairable, which cost me 10s. I fitted it with an electric motor from a broken-backed Hoover which a dealer let me have for nothing.

To process the 30-foot reels of 9.5mm film, 'reversal' stock which did not need printing, I built a winding drum and tank from plywood and bits and pieces. I fitted the drum with glass rods with elastic bands round them at intervals to keep the wound-on film from sliding about and sticking to itself.

The tank worked rather well until disaster struck. I did the processing in the evening on our kitchen dresser which Dad had covered with a sheet of marble rescued from the council dump. Now the last chemical to be used in developing the film was acid, which dissolved the metallic silver and 'reversed' the image from negative to positive. That evening, working in pitch-darkness, I poured the acid wide of the mark and it sloshed onto the marble table top.

As every child left alone in a school chemistry lab learns, with the possible exception of dropping a pellet of phosphorus into the chemistry master's cup of tea, there is little in science which produces quite so dramatic an effect as pouring acid on marble. The marble hisses, it smokes, it bubbles, it gives off chemical fumes, it produces what is known in the trade as 'vigorous chemical action'. Which is a fair description of what the accident produced in my mother. I had to switch on the kitchen light, which fogged the film, and then swiftly rinse the marble with a bucket of water from the sink, which soaked everywhere. When Mother came in and saw the mess I had made of her kitchen her ring finger went to work again and, big lad that I was, I endured what the French delicately describe as *un mauvais quart d'heure*.

For some odd reason, I had up until then thought that making people laugh and writing prose for them to read were two different pursuits. I was writing busily all the time for the school magazine and for English classes and so on, and a fair bit of it was fiction, but my short stories, perhaps all stories written by boys in their pre-teens, owed more to O. Henry than P. G. Wodehouse; they tended to be deeply dramatic and rely for effect on a surprise ending. The sort of thing was a moody piece about an athlete contemplating losing his record for the 100-yard dash (oh, innocent sporting term) the following day, ending with the revelation that the athlete was actually a felon in the condemned cell.

But I came to my senses one autumn in, I think, 1934, when I nearly died. I had a low-down pain which niggled. We thought it might be just a strained innard from hauling on the church bell-ropes, but it persisted and got worse and it became clear that it was something nasty. One afternoon, with suitable dramatic effect, the skies clouded over and the earth went dark and the ambulance came. I had acute appendicitis and was whisked away to Whipps Cross Hospital, where it emerged that we had left it a bit late and the thing had burst and peritonitis had set in. I was in there for months. Recovery was slow and lacked charm, involving a piece of hosepipe inserted in the operation scar for drainage, and prevented by a huge safety pin through the top of it from dropping down (where to?). I wrote the whole experience up for the school magazine. It was my first attempt at a funny piece and I realized then, for the first time, how much comedy feeds on serious matters. And times were becoming serious. I was now aged fourteen and getting anxious about my future.

Our geography master at school was a small, plump, Pickwickian figure named Mr Cohen, who used to goad us all to work harder by staring pityingly at us through his thick spectacles and exclaiming, 'You'll all end up twopenny-ha'penny clerks, twopenny-ha'penny clerks.' Mr Cohen was not to know that the future was going to be even bleaker than that for pen-pushers because the rise of computers would mean no jobs even for twopenny-ha'penny clerks.

I enjoyed classes and at LCHS it was OK to do a bit of work, you were not sneered at or biffed by your classmates and I had no particular worries at facing the big exam the following year: Matric. But I had no clear idea of how to go about carving a career from then on.

Unless we were sons of military men or of doctors, in which

57

case we knew from childhood that we would either follow our father's profession or be seen dead rather than follow our father's profession, very few of us had the faintest idea of what we wanted to do.

In county high schools the thinking was less in terms of a career as of simply getting some sort of a job with the hope that the job would develop into a career. All I ever *wanted* to do was be a writer and amuse people, but in my situation that was about as feckless an ambition as wanting to become Pope Frank I. I had never in my life knowingly met a professional writer or publisher or impresario or agent or comic. How to begin?

I made a start one school open day by finagling a meeting with the editor of the local paper – I think he was a governor of the school – and asking him how I could become a journalist. He said he would consider taking me on as an apprentice if I would come and see him once I had my Matric exam results.

Was I on my way? No, I was not.

Our family world suddenly changed completely and tragically. Dad died.

He died in a manner which was very Dad. He was at home in bed with the flu when somebody arrived by bike from Caribonum, breathless, with the news that the boiler had developed a fault and had to be shut down, and the factory now had no power. Could he advise? Being Dad, he got up, struggled into clothes, made his way to the factory through the cold air and climbed into the warm boiler to locate the problem. Back home he developed pneumonia and a week later he died.

Chas and I had to leave school immediately to bring in some money and to do this we had to find jobs without having any exam qualifications to flourish. Chas was aged sixteen and a bit and I was fourteen and a half.

The outlook was grim but Caribonum was helpful. It was a family company founded by a Yorkshireman, C. F. Clark, who ran it according to modern American business methods, but with a strong Yorkshire paternalism. Mr Clark was stocky, with an underslung Habsburg jaw; he was getting on in years but still played cricket on Saturday afternoons at the company's sports ground in Walthamstow and awarded a cream flannel shirt to any employee who bowled him out. Good bowlers dreaded hitting C.F.'s stumps as the shirts were expensive but very thick and tickly to wear.

Once a year we were all invited to C.F.'s house in the country where he held a kind of open day. We were greeted in the Great Hall by church music coming from a huge pipe organ played by C.F. himself, bent over the keys in a scene later to become familiar in Hammer horror films starring Vincent Price.

C.F. sent somebody down to help Mother sort out arrangements for the funeral and business matters, gave her a small pension and found jobs for Chas and me in Caribonum.

So I went to work in a carbon-paper factory, which sounds about as Dickensian as you can get, but was actually interesting and enjoyable. Most evenings I spent Mother-sitting. This suited both Chas and me as Chas, who could immediately play any musical instrument by ear and could draw very well, was altogether a more gregarious and socially welcome person, and I could nip swiftly to and from home and the public library. During the next few years I took out plays and ploughed through most of the middle-of-the-road playwrights, now little read or produced, like John Van Druten and Edward Knoblock (who?), and I read a great number of novels. My taste in humour developed from the *Just William* stories in *The Happy Mag* (a thick magazine seemingly printed on blotting paper) to Dornford Yates's *Berry* stories, to P. G. Wodehouse . . .

Mother would not go out and took to listening to the radio for hours every evening; the regular broadcasters became her friends and she could recognize a voice instantly, even if only heard once and months before. Another unlikely gift Mother had was a natural ability to spell. I only had to sing out a word and Mother would spell it correctly, although her education had been so brief that she had almost certainly never met the word before nor knew its derivation.

Leytonstone Public Library had a small theatre attached to it used by a flourishing play-reading society which read a play (aloud) every Thursday evening to a loyal and appreciative audience of OAPs and vagrants sheltering from the weather. I joined the society and much enjoyed myself, but there was an inherent problem in reading a play rather than learning it by heart, a problem never solved by me, which was how to play either a passionate love scene or a fight to the death whilst reading from a book held in the left hand.

I provoked much merriment when playing love scenes as for some reason all amateur actresses seemed to be short in stature and I was then well over 6 feet, which meant that I either had to woo the beloved by sagging down at the knees like a chimpanzee enjoying his cup of tea, or by leaning forward with my behind stuck out at an acute angle.

I wrote, I think, five one-act plays in all for the society to perform. Shrewdly, love scenes and fights did not occur in any of them, so that the producer could cast me in the lead if she was so disposed.

Sadly, or from another point of view mercifully, none of these plays has survived.

Chapter 4

THE WAR (PART ONE)

Caribonum again behaved generously in Dad's memory when war loomed. The inevitability of conflict in Europe was brought home to us by *Daily Express* headlines stating authoritatively THERE WILL BE NO WAR.

In 1939 I was aged nineteen. To fill in my time profitably before joining up, the company took me off checking invoices in the general office, put me through their training course for salesmen and sent me out on the road with a bag of samples, a Homburg hat and a card index of customers on my territory, which was mainly a length of the Commercial Road in East London. The point was that the job of salesman carried with it much more money, no less than £4 10s. a week plus commission.

The training course was interesting. It taught the sales force to wear a clean white shirt, scrub its fingernails, display an expression of happy confidence at all times and to say nothing in the sales pitch which the 'prospect' – the potential victim – could answer with a 'no', like, 'Can I interest you in a new sort of carbon paper?'

I was hopeless at it, but no matter. Customers knew that very soon it would be virtually impossible to buy any stationery at all, and coaxing office managers into ordering an extra typewriter ribbon or box of carbon paper was about as difficult as persuading a spaniel to accept an extra chocolate drop.

One of my customers decided to befriend me. She was a Miss Cohen, a very large genial lady who ran a somewhat unconventional business from under a railway arch; she bought second-hand uniforms of no further use to the post office and exported them to India.

The business thrived (I gathered that the red piping round the jacket and down the trouser seams was much esteemed) and when I was part of England's might, kindly Miss Cohen sent me comfort parcels – socks and chocolate and Penguin paperbacks – every month for two or three years.

With a teenager's deep concern for personal comfort rather than for the war needs of the nation, I opted for service in the RAF rather than the Army or the Navy, because it seemed to me that in the RAF I would get to sit down more. Propaganda films and newsreels showed that the Army went in for a great deal of marching up and down carrying heavy rifles and haversacks, and my father, who was a professional sailor, was sick every time he went to sea, and as no doubt he had passed on to me some of the relevant chromosomes, I thought it would be wise to avoid a life aboard ship. Also, although a flying job was the objective, there was such a long wait for a training course that a 'trade' had to be taken up first, and the RAF, alone of the services, wanted photographers.

The first few months of service life in uniform, squarebashing, learning how to drill and to march and to do without privacy and swallow the basic service philosophy of 'if it moves salute it, if it doesn't move, paint it' was an educational experience, and not all of it was unpleasant; only parts of it were.

For instance, ritual humiliations. During square-bashing training we slept on three tough little square mattresses known as 'biscuits' on folding iron bedsteads. In charge of our hut was a chunky and dismal physical training corporal who had his own little room at the end of the hut. When the post was delivered in the morning we had to line up in front of this oaf, and if he called out our name we had to raise a hand. He would then toss our envelope into the air so that it fluttered under a bed and had to be grovelled for on hands and knees.

I had a problem from time to time with service language. I had never in my life heard such a concentration of profanity and obscenity. About my fourth day in uniform our drill sergeant disliked some manoeuvre our squad had messed up and shouted at us in fury, 'Jesus Christ Al-f***ing-mighty!' My blood froze. But eventually one got used to it.

There was, too, a communication problem, which was not a class matter (I was educated in E10 not Eton) but simply a difficulty in understanding what was required of me when the pronunciation was homely regional rather than standard English.

One morning we were all paraded to tidy up the bits of greenery and garden round the huts for a visit from some bigwig, and a sergeant with a sheet of paper was singing out the duties we had each been allocated.

'Willis!'

'Sarge.'

'Paper picking-up, you. Right?'

'Sarge.'

'Challis!'

'Not on parade, Sarge. Had to report sick.'

'Got no business reporting sick when the grass 'as got to be tidied for the air commodore. Doesn't 'e know there's a bleedin' war on?'

The sergeant, a regular, sighed at the pathetic standard of conscripts he was supposed to train into magnificent fighting machines.

'Muir!'

'Sarge.'

'Do the edges. Right?'

'Right.'

But it was not right at all. As I made for the tool store I realized that I didn't know whether I was supposed to trim the edges of the grass, or cut the hedges? 'Edges or (h)edges? I could hardly go back and ask the Sarge whether he meant an aitch to be present.

Willis J. was in the tool store signing for a sack, hemp, waste paper for the putting into, and I asked him whether he thought Sarge meant the hedges or the edges, and Willis J. said, 'You got cloff ears? 'E said, "Do the *Adj's*." That's the flower bed in front of the adjutant's office with the rope round it painted white. You repaint the rope. Gottit, berk?'

The service mind revealed more of its individuality when I was posted to RAF Farnborough to take my photography course.

The teaching was conducted by four almost identical, late-middle-aged instructors with very short, brushed-down hair. They wore those long beige overall coats associated with carpet warehousemen. All four instructors were civilians, retired regular sergeants from various RAF photography sections. Their method of instruction was by means of monologues committed to memory (I think probably with some difficulty). The method bore oddly little relation to teaching, but then RAF photography bore little resemblance to civvy photography. Aesthetics played no part. The cameras, which were bolted into the aircraft, looked more like large domestic mincing machines than cameras: grey metal castings with a heavy hood protecting the lens. The film inside was 5 inches wide and provided the photo reconnaissance intelligence officers with a series of 5 x 5 inch prints of the territory flown over.

'On removing your camera from the appropriate aircraft once it's landed and the engine has been discontinued,' the instructor would recite in a rapid, expressionless baritone, 'you will hold the camera firmly against your chest or up your tunic and proceed rapidly with it to the photography section darkroom, taking care whilst *en route* not to wallop the camera against nothing solid or fall over thus causing damage to Air Ministry property for which you will be held financially responsible. Once within your darkroom, switch the top light off, the red light on, and holding the camera firmly in your right hand, repeat RIGHT hand, you will activate with your left thumb, repeat LEFT thumb, the sliding button "G" which I described to you where it was yesterday afternoon. For purposes of committing the button to memory, you will find it marked "G" in diagram 804A in your instruction manual, volume four, page two hundred and forty-seven.

'Operating button G will cause the back of the camera to be released from its locked position and thus be openable at will. Insert the fingernail of your right hand into the crack in the side of the back opposite to the hinge and ease the back open. Carefully, repeat CAREFULLY, remove the spool of exposed film with the right hand without, if possible, touching it. Once you have the film in your grasp, don't for Christ's sake drop it in the sink or tread on the bloody thing or the pilot'll have to go back up and fly the sodding sortie again, won'e? Is all that crystal clear?'

At the end of the course we had to undergo an exam called the TTB (Trade Test Board). It was very important to get high marks in this as a brilliant result would earn a posting to a crack squadron.

I failed the test.

My nemesis was the mime sequence. Looking back over the years I even now find it difficult to think of any test quite so pointless, but then I suppose I would think that having failed it.

For this piece of what I still think was archetypical service idiocy, I had to close my eyes and, in broad daylight, mime developing a film in the unit darkroom, each movement of which I had been made to learn by heart and practise endlessly under the piercing if somewhat lunchtime-beer-dampened eye of my instructor.

I thought I worked well in the test. Neatly, rapidly, concentrating on getting all movements in the right order. I finished, as taught, by miming pinning up the film to dry on a line, rather like hanging up a wet bathing costume.

I opened my eyes, returned to my chair and waited while the bunch of visiting examiners conferred like boxing-match judges. I felt confident. In the oral test I had, I thought, got the chemistry answer right: 'At what temperature does a solution of hypo recrystallize and become unstable?' And also, 'Which RAF camera should be used for which particular job?' ('The recording of the effectiveness of a fighter aircraft's machine-gun fire requires the fitting, in the fitting provided in the aircraft's leading edge, port wing, of a loaded cine-camera, model CC/A/804/MK/624.')

'Aircraftsman Muir, rise to a standing position', said the head warehouseman in a sepulchral voice, like an eighteenth-century hanging judge addressing a doomed felon who had been caught nicking a handkerchief. I stood up. 'You done well in the early tests, Muir, but you let yourself, and worse still your instructor, down in the last test by a gross piece of forget-fulness. We have no other alternative but to pronounce you as having failed.'

I was stunned.

'What did I do wrong?'

'It's not what you *did* do, Muir, it's what you *didn't* done,' said the hanging judge. 'What you forgot to perform was to *mime switching off the top light when you entered the darkroom*. As you know well enough, with the top light on, as soon as you opened the back of the camera the entire film would have been fogged and ruined.'

'But . . .' I said, 'it was *mime*! If it had been real I would have *seen* the light was on and switched it off, wouldn't I?'

'That is supposition,' said the judge. 'Cap on, about turn, by the left – quick march!'

So, instead of developing cine-film shot during the Battle of Britain or printing out 5 x 5 inch prints of German cities, I was posted to RAF Warmwell, Dorset, where at the time they had no accommodation for a photography section and I was allocated a chair and table in the armoury, where I spent months watching armourers pouring boiling water down rifle barrels.

To cheer myself up I wrote a three-act farce. It was titled *Bishop's Leap* and was one of those pieces which began with the title and then had to have a story invented to fit the title. The play was so awful that merciful memory has obliterated the details, but I recall that the first act ended with a plump but sporty bishop, for charity, sprinting across the church-hall stage about to perform a back somersault. The curtain descended quickly before the bishop actually rose into the air. The following two acts explained all.

Barrack-room life was quite jolly. There were various traditional japes which we were taught by old hands and they all seemed to contain a streak of cruelty. One game was to argue some nonsensical point with a recruit who knew with absolute certainty that he was right, which he was. It was possible, eventually, to make him break down in frustration and burst into tears.

For instance, one of the group, who was pretending to read a newspaper, would say, 'It says here there's a new breed of killer slug which attacks red cabbage.'

Shouts of scorn.

'Get art of it! There's no such thing as *red* cabbage!'

The victim, a country boy or a lad whose dad grew vegetables, takes the bait.

'Course there's red cabbage. My mum pickles it.'

Howls of laughter.

'Cabbage is green, mate, everyone knows that! How can you have *red* cabbage? You'd believe anything, you would.'

'But I've seen it growing! I've picked it! I've eaten it!'

More corporate mirth.

'Cabbages is *green*! It's a law of nature! You don't have red lettuce, do you? Admit it.'

The victim is now near tears.

'There *is* red cabbage! There *is*!' he shouts and runs to the safety of his bunk.

Another version of the game denied the existence of pit ponies.

'Ponies down a coal mine? How do you get 'em down there – drop 'em down the shaft? And how did they see where they was going – were they issued with torches? If so, how did they sign for them?'

'I tell you they *did* have ponies down pits.'

'Never!' And so on.

Another game, doubly effective when played on a victim with a weak heart, was popular when rumours were rife that the Germans were about to invade the South Coast. A dozen pranksters got up in the middle of the night when the victim was asleep, silently put on their gas masks and gathered round his bed, their black, rubber-clad faces pressed only a few inches from his. One of them would then shake the victim awake, and as he recoiled from the ring of horrible masks surrounding him, everybody shrieked in simulated terror: 'THEY'RE *'ERE*!'

But there were also gentler activities in the social life of RAF Warmwell.

Local Devon ladies had banded together and opened a canteen where, mid-morning, they served the most wonderful doughnuts I have ever eaten. Without slobbering too much over the memory of those perfections, I have to report that they were British, not American doughnuts, in that they did not have a hole in the middle like a deck quoit but were classically spherical, fried to a golden brown and rolled in soft sugar so that the outside was crunchy. They had a gobbit of strawberry jam in their centre (how did they get it in there?) and were served warm.

I was glad to discover that RAF Warmwell had an active dramatic society, run by the entertainments officer who, after the war, became a colleague and a personal friend, Flight Lieutenant Arthur Howard, father of the actor Alan Howard and brother of the famous film actor Leslie (*Gone with the Wind*) Howard.

Arthur was a very funny comic actor in the dithering tradition and he had a beautiful speaking voice. He encouraged me – no, in fact he bullied me – into writing innumerable comedy sketches for the station concert party which was invaluable experience, and he made me act as compère for the concerts, work for which I developed a morbid affection and which proved again to be excellent experience.

In the middle of 1940 I bought my first car from a garage in nearby Dorchester. It was an elderly Triumph saloon, a tad larger than an Austin Seven with a rather chic, fabric-covered roof (with the fabric mostly rotted off) and no dynamo. The asking price was £15, but the garage man let me drive it away for a down payment deposit of £5 in cash.

I learned to drive by simply watching closely for a week or so beforehand how drivers drove – when they pressed the clutch, when they pushed the gear lever – and I felt confident that I had mastered the technique and could drive the car back to Warmwell without bother.

The journey of 6 miles took me over three hours. I did not know about letting the revs drop when changing up so I never got beyond second gear, and getting into second gear was so difficult that most of the time I stayed in first gear and ground noisily and very slowly back to camp.

The garage man prudently retained the logbook in the hope that I would eventually pay the other £10. Without the logbook I could not apply for petrol coupons and so had to rely on help from my flight-mechanic friends to 'liberate' the odd gallon of RAF petrol. This was coloured with green or red dye which stained the carburettor and so gave the game away to the station police, but the fitters had found a way of neutralizing the dye, so finding the small amounts of petrol needed to occasionally take a carload of aircraftsmen to a Dorchester pub or cinema was no problem.

The lack of a dynamo to recharge the battery was more of a problem. We put the battery on to an RAF trickle charger as soon as we returned from a spin, but the car would sometimes lose power alarmingly.

One night we were on our way back from a trip to the cinema in Dorchester, the car bursting with humanity like a passenger train in Calcutta, and had reached the perimeter road of the airfield when the battery began to fail. The car faltered to a stop in the middle of the road and all the lights went out.

We sat there for a while in the pitch-dark, wondering what on earth to do, when we heard the dread sound of an approaching vehicle. When our eyes got used to the darkness we could see that lumbering straight for us was a huge, heavily armoured defence vehicle called an Armadillo which must have weighed at least a couple of tons.

'Lads,' said Corporal Tyzack, quietly and sincerely, 'I think that as trained fighting men we all know how to deal with a crisis like this. Right?'

And they all began to sing with fervour, 'Abide with me, fast falls the eventide . . .'

The Armadillo ground to a halt a few inches away from our radiator and the driver gave us a tow back to camp.

London was being blitzed, but life was comparatively peaceful at RAF Warmwell, Dorset. It was a fighter station and most days we could see the German bombers, very high over us, crossing the Channel and making for targets inland. Our Spitfires and Hurricanes were scrambled immediately, but mostly they took so long climbing to the height of the bombers that by the time they reached the right altitude the German planes had disappeared.

A year or two back, when I was working at Caribonum, I had the chance of bringing a touch of serendipitous pleasure to an old lady on top of a bus. I had been presented with a liqueur chocolate by an aunt who had been given a box of them for her birthday. The chocolate, I remember well, was in the shape of a tiny bottle, and on its label it claimed to contain real green chartreuse. I put it in my pocket, waiting for an occasion momentous enough to celebrate by drinking a tiny chocolate bottle of liqueur.

A few days later I was on the top deck of a bus when two elderly ladies on the seat behind me began discussing, quite loudly, what they had always wanted from life but had never achieved. One said, 'A fur coat – anything but rabbit.' The other said, 'All my life I've thought that luxury was having a liqueur chocolate all to myself. Not just a nibble of somebody else's; not sharing it with the grandchildren or letting my husband suck the booze out of the bottom. All to myself.'

It was an extraordinary situation for me, and irresistible. I reached into my jacket pocket and took out my liqueur chocolate, twisted round and said to the lady behind me, 'Look, I have to get off the bus here and this chocolate will melt if I leave it in my pocket any longer. Please will you have it?' The lady looked at the liqueur chocolate in her hand in utter disbelief and I rushed downstairs and off the bus before she could mutter polite refusals.

I found myself standing on a pavement in Leytonstone with a light drizzle falling when I should have been warm and dry on a bus taking me to Caribonum's branch office in Woodford, but Dame Fate knew what she was doing.

At RAF Warmwell my tiny scrap of impulsive generosity on the bus in Leytonstone found a mirror image and I was the grateful recipient of a much more generous gesture.

The fifth of February 1941 was my twenty-first birthday. What to do to commemorate this deeply important milestone? I decided to drive into Weymouth for a hell-raising night of wild pleasure.

This proved difficult to achieve. For one thing my car, the dynamo-deprived Triumph saloon, became engine-deprived on the way back from watching an interstation footer match when the sump plug unscrewed itself, the oil glugged out and the engine seized up. On 5 February 1941, my engine lay in bits on a hangar floor being worked on by my friends, but I found there was a wartime bus service which ran every three hours from RAF Warmwell to crazy, fun-loving Weymouth. The last bus back left at 8.15 p.m.

Also, I only had £1 to fund my Babylonian evening and at the last moment I was put on fire-picket duty – which meant patrolling the station all night making sure it had not burned to the ground unnoticed by the official fire brigade – and it cost me 10s. to bribe a corporal with girl trouble and concomitant money problems to do my fire-picket duty for me. So I arrived at Weymouth with not a lot of money left for hell-raising.

This was just as well as there was nothing to buy. It was a dark night, the seafront cafés were shut and boarded up, the beach ugly with huge iron anti-tank spikes sticking up from the sand as Weymouth braced itself for invasion. I couldn't even find a cinema which was open. I had a beer at a pub, but this was a cheerless experience so I just walked the deserted streets. I knew how chilly in spirit out-of-season seaside resorts can be from my years in Thanet, but Weymouth in 1941 was a very great deal gloomier than anything I had experienced.

To my great relief I noticed that it was just gone half-past seven, time to make my way to the bus station and the last bus home to Warmwell and the warmth of the familiar.

Opposite the bus station was the possibility of some sort of birthday pleasure to be had: a brightly lit milk bar.

Milk bars were an odd phenomenon of those days. I suppose nowadays they would be denounced by newspaper health correspondents as 'temples of cholesterol' and 'purveyors of mad cow juice', but in the war days they were bright, cheap and cheerful places to sit and enjoy a cheap sandwich and a drink. The drink was always milk, usually in the form of a milk shake, a beaker of chilled milk which was flavoured and then fluffed up by an electric whizzer. Milk bars were everywhere; there were many in London's West End and every resort had plenty of them, so there was clearly a strong demand for that kind of informal café. Why have they virtually disappeared? Did we all go off milk because of the post-war fad for dieting, or was it just that we developed a distaste for the stuff?

I went into the milk bar opposite the bus station in Weymouth and sat on a tall stool at the counter. I was the only customer. There was a plump lady with orange hair behind the bar, clad in the blue and white uniform of the milk-bar chain. She was smoking a cigarette, occasionally tipping the ash into a milk-shake beaker.

'What's up, love?' she said. 'You look like a bloodhound what's trod in something.'

'It's my twenty-first birthday,' I said.

'Christ!' she said. 'You poor bugger! Now, I wonder . . . Hang on a sec . . .' She got off her chair and rummaged for quite a long while in the back of a huge refrigerator, eventually producing a half bottle of champagne, giving me two thirds of it.

'There you are,' she said, handing me my glass. 'It was give me years ago by the deputy area manager who was after my body. Happy birthday, love!'

So I celebrated my twenty-first birthday by drinking champagne with a warm-hearted lady in a milk bar at the royal seaside resort of Weymouth, where in the eighteenth century the middle-aged King George III is said to have caught his first glimpse of the sea ('Is that all it does, Charlotte?').

I was still a cuckoo in the armoury waiting for the photography section to be completed when I was joined by another graduate from the Farnborough course, A/C 1 Bickerstaffe, an important figure in my service career.

Whilst on leave in London, A/C 1 Bickerstaffe was sent a telegram by the Warmwell adjutant ordering him back to Warmwell immediately as he had been posted to Iceland. Bickerstaffe replied by telegram to the adjutant: 'Cannot return. Fell down a bomb hole in the Haymarket and best blue uniform at dry-cleaners.' This does make a kind of service sense as we were forbidden to travel in civilian clothes.

So the next day I was sent to Iceland in place of Bickerstaffe.

The journey from Dorset to Iceland was not enjoyable. The train up to the Scottish embarkation port, Gourock, on the Firth of Clyde, seemed to take about three weeks with its long halts and brief spurts of movement and total lack of lighting and heat. The servicemen packing the carriages lapsed into a kind of hibernation, a temporary moratorium on living.

The midwinter voyage on a troopship across the North

Atlantic was also less than charming, although in spite of my morbid fear of being seasick I was about the only person on board who wasn't. It was a close-run thing though when we were on parade on deck for lifeboat drill and some idiot opened the door from the galley. The smell of boiling cabbage wafted across our nostrils and the entire parade broke ranks and lurched for the rail. I only avoided being sick because all the places at the rail were taken and I was unable to get in.

A sergeant gave us a stern educational talk about the importance of personal hygiene when we disembarked at Reykjavik, which he referred to as 'Reek-JAR-vick' (normal pronunciation, 'Recky-a-vick'). His hilarious lecture was mostly inaudible due to a boisterous wind sweeping across the deck, but I caught his warning, rather Old Testament, that most of us would probably catch VD, so we should report to the medical officer as soon as we sighted a red blotch because there was a new ointment. And we were to avoid spitting. This was meant literally, i.e., to take evasive action when walking busy Reykjavik pavements. According to the sergeant the air contained volcanic dust and Icelanders of both sexes spat copiously and frequently. Oddly, this turned out to be quite true and had been true for well over a century because in *Travels in Iceland*, published in 1812, the scientist Sir George Mackenzie noted, 'The unrestrained evacuation of saliva seems to be a fashion all over Iceland.'

A group of us were posted to a new RAF station being built at Kaldadharnes, a flat area beside the sea about 70 miles up the road from Reykjavik and rumoured, without truth, to be sinking into the sea. We were installed in a new wooden hut with an iron stove in the middle and that was all. Home comforts had to be foraged for, i.e., stolen. My bed was four empty petrol tins supporting a brand-new door with a sign screwed to it reading 'Your Chaplain – Knock And Enter At Any Time'. On this I placed my Lilo, an inflatable canvas and rubber mattress which I had carried all the way from England, and Lilos weighed heavy in those days.

On about the third evening I sat comfortably on the bed darning a sock. When I had finished I thoughtlessly parked the needle by sticking it into the Lilo. Realizing what I had done,

I even more foolishly yanked the needle out. Later, in the middle of the night, my hip grounded on door; the Lilo had deflated. However carefully I searched I never did find the puncture; even when the Lilo was pressed under water the pin-hole was too small to release tell-tale air bubbles, so during the eighteen months I spent in Iceland I had to get up every night at about three in the morning and go dizzy blowing into the Lilo.

The station's runways and hangars were already completed and in use and a section of Royal Engineers was busy putting up the station's living accommodation, NAAFI, admin offices and so on. This was a lengthy process, as during the hours of darkness a third of the new doors and floorboards disappeared. Well we, the established residents, had to have beds to lie on and it was our duty to find wood to burn in our stoves to stop us from freezing to death (we were, after all, Air Ministry property). So by the time a new hut had been erected it had taken three times the material it should have done and taken three times as long to put up. But nobody seemed to be bothered much.

Eventually we managed to make the huts comfortable and warm, which led to inquisitive visits from small furry things. My bedside table was a pair of square empty petrol tins balanced on one another, which brought the top to the same height as my face. One night I brought back a bar of chocolate from the NAAFI, took a bite before going to sleep and left the rest on my table. In the morning I woke to find only half my bar of chocolate left. It had been nibbled all the way round, and according to the size of the fang marks, by a sizeable rat or a small wolf. The chocolate was an inch from my nose.

Photography was not a very vital part of our squadron's activities. The aircraft were mainly Hudsons, chunky, medium-sized reconnaissance planes, and their function was to make painstaking anti-submarine sweeps, depth charges primed, over the northern approaches of the Atlantic.

The squadron had one remarkable and famous coup when a German U-boat, trolling along on the surface for a breath of fresh air, its crew fed up to the teeth with the war and their dangerous and uncomfortable job, surrendered to one of our planes which then, to its annoyance, had to fly patiently round and round the slow U-boat to escort it back to Reykjavik harbour and peaceful captivity for its crew.

As most of our aircrews' time was spent searching for the enemy on the North Atlantic's waves there was not much point in them repeatedly photographing stretches of heaving sea, so although a handsome darkroom cum caravan arrived from England, once again I was underemployed.

Soon after the British had moved into Iceland to stop Germany grabbing it as a U-boat base, a small force of Americans arrived. We helped them land on the quay and carry their stuff to waiting lorries. When they arrived back home in the USA they were given a medal, which is more than we were.

The GIs were different from us in many ways, the most immediately striking being their startlingly clean, white, high-necked vests which peeped above their open-necked shirts. We must have had some sort of laundry arrangements of our own but I cannot remember ever changing my one vest, a greyish, friendly garment which also kept me warm in bed during the Icelandic winter and was useful for blocking out draughts from an ill-fitting window near my bed and for acting as a back-up towel.

As soon as our rich allies had settled in, our ground crews started schemes to separate them from some of their surplus dollars. The lads' most successful swindle was to acquire a chunk of aluminium, machine it into a crude cigarette lighter and sell it reluctantly to a GI as a personal souvenir to take back home to the USA, made from a German Messerschmitt fighter shot down by Uncle during the Battle of Britain. The demand was so brisk that the fitters and riggers laboured far into the night at their workbenches, and suitable lumps of aluminium were like nuggets of gold.

There was a constant flow of jeeps and trucks between Kaldadharnes and Reykjavik and it was easy to cadge a lift. It was a curiously alien journey, about 70 miles through a barren landscape surrounded by glaciers and a variety of different types of volcano, including the great, still occasionally erupting, Hekla. Hot springs were everywhere and the hot water was piped into villages and towns for heating; every village seemed to have nearby a small and rather ugly concrete open-air swimming pool, like a static water tank, steaming away in the cold air, and ranges of naturally heated greenhouses abounded. I read somewhere recently that Iceland was the second largest exporter of bananas. Well, well (if true).

Near at hand, too, was the huge and famous spouting hot spring, the Great Geysir (whence our word 'geyser', as in Ewart's 'Victor' geyser, came). Much of the farmland which the road to Reykjavik passed through was once lava fields and still looked like a moonscape with 10-foot-high broken lava bubbles scattered around.

The farmhouses were shack-like, made with cement and corrugated iron, many with turf propping up the sides and holding down the roof. There were small flocks of huge sheep nosing about for blades of grass, and many grey ponies and a white hen or two. Outside most farmhouses there was a complicated structure of poles and wires from which stockfish hung to dry. Occasionally one glimpsed a small church painted white. There was little vegetation and no trees at all. It was rumoured that Akureyri in the north of the island possessed ten trees with real leaves which anybody could look at and even touch, but we put that down to boasting.

Nightlife at RAF Kaldadharnes tended to be on the quiet side, usually spent lying on our beds talking and reading, only springing into action when an eldritch howl rent the night air as some unlucky lad, weaving his way back to his billet after a couple of pints in the NAAFI, broke through the ice covering a ditch and had to be swiftly hauled out before he froze rigid, which took about two minutes.

Compared with Kaldadharnes, Reykjavik was a combination of Babylon, Las Vegas and Sin City. There was a popular Salvation Army canteen known as the Holy Grocer's, two cafés which sold real cream cakes and two cinemas built some years apart, called, with cool Scandinavian logic, the Old Cinema and the New Cinema. Both of these dream palaces had frequent trouble with their projectors. The audience sat in total darkness except for the scrape and sparking as thirty or forty GIs tried to get their souvenir aluminium cigarette lighters to light.

Taking a taxi out of Reykjavik was a physical experience. The taxis looked as though they had come from some early Hollywood gangster film, battered and bulbous old American Chevies with their gear lever on the steering column. Every time I saw one I expected Edward G. Robinson to be crouched in the back cuddling a Thompson sub-machine-gun.

Reykjavik was then quite a small city, and when a cab reached city limits the concrete road ceased and there was a sudden 8-inch drop onto a dirt road. The local cabbies took the drop at speed and all the passenger suffered was a traumatic bounce and a bang as the car's suspension touched bottom. Returning to Reykjavik was more difficult, but most cabbies kept a few bricks in the boot to help the car climb up the concrete step into town.

I discovered to my delight that in Reykjavik there was a forces radio station. It was actually Iceland's national radio station which – Oh, how British – was hired by our conquering occupying force for quite a large sum of money to broadcast to its own troops for an hour or so every afternoon.

I made contact with the officer who ran it, Major Roberts-Wray, a kind man, and infiltrated myself into his operation as a scriptwriter and occasional broadcaster, in neither of which disciplines I had had any experience at all.

On my first visit to the studios I began my study of the Icelandic language by learning the Icelandic word for 'recording studio', which was written above the door. It is *Rikisutvarpssalur*, and it took a bit of learning. It turned out to be the first of only two Icelandic words I ever did learn during my eighteen months there. The other was the Icelandic for 'journalist', a much better word than ours, *bladamadur*, pronounced 'blather-meister'.

My superiors at Kaldadharnes seemed only too glad to get shot of me. I was allowed to shunt backwards and forwards to Reykjavik more or less whenever the forces radio needed me there. And they had many needs. There were several good readers, including the Navy's flag-lieutenant, to cope with news items and scripted talks, but the station was woefully short of light entertainment. There was an Iceland Forces Orchestra but nobody knew what to do with it apart from getting it to play interminable Glenn Miller numbers at unit dances.

The Americans had a showbiz saying that a beginner starting a showbiz career needed first of all to have 'somewhere to be lousy in', a luxury denied most present-day comedy writers because very high minimum fees mean that radio and TV producers are understandably reluctant to take a chance on an untried talent who costs them almost as much as an award winner.

Iceland Forces Radio was my opportunity to be lousy and I seized it gratefully, being energetically lousy over quite a large spread of programmes. There was acting as compère to the band and giving the concerts a little humour; there was a music programme I invented called *Once Upon a Time* in which I linked the musical numbers the band wanted to play into adult fairy stories of a rambling, shaggy-dog nature, which were read admirably by the flag-lieutenant; there was a piano programme with commentary written and spoken by me called *Ivory Interlude*; there was a music cum comedy sketch show called *Roadhouse* in which the band played being the roadhouse's band and I mainly ad libbed most of the roadhouse's staff and guests; and there were little comic serials inspired by (i.e., stolen from) strip cartoons in the *Daily Mirror*.

I got on very well with the forces orchestra. The musical director was Sapper Edwin Braden, a friendly Northerner who was an unbelievably badly designed human being, ginger hair, a stained and tangled moustache like an old toothbrush used for cleaning eggy spoons and a body shaped like an unpeelable potato. But a fine professional musician, unflappable, right on top of the job, frequently still finishing off an arrangement as the band's coach pulled into an army camp for a concert.

I had so much writing to do that it was easier working at a table in the NAAFI than crouching on my bed, so I plugged away at the funnies with conversation surging round me and the bellowing of complicated orders only heard in NAAFIs, e.g., 'Hey, Mave – cup o' char and a wad (cup of tea and a cake), hussif ('housewife' – i.e., sewing kit in a roll), packet of envelopes and a pork pie. Ta, luv.'

And I much enjoyed visits to the Forces Dance Orchestra in the hut where they lived in Reykjavik. They were quite a distinguished bunch in the dance-music world: besides Edwin Braden there was Cyril Stapleton as lead violin, later to form his own orchestra with great success on the radio. We had two vocalists – essential to dance orchestras at that time – the deservedly popular and famous Denny Dennis, and the equally so Sam Costa.

Denny, real name Dennis Pountain, a quiet, dull man with a beautifully deep and true voice, was supposed to be Britain's answer to Bing Crosby, in much the same way that later, Matt Munro was supposed to be Britain's answer to Frank Sinatra. They were both excellent singers but wrong answers.

Sam Costa, a good jazz singer and a funny man in the show-biz style, always seemed to be sitting on the end of his bed grooming his feet. He took enormous trouble with his toes, clipping the nails, buffing them up with a buffer, massaging them for hours. After the war he was a great success, firstly as the third star of the comedy show *Much-Binding-in-the-Marsh* and later as a disc jockey on BBC Radio 2. Not as a dancer. Interesting, that. Could a job not have been found for Sam's excellent feet on Radio 2?

When I first arrived in Iceland I found that among our superiors in the chain of command were a few quite elderly officers, delightful old boys but long in the tooth, if any. I worked out the reason. They were survivors of the First World War who were keen as mustard to do what they could for the old country in its Second World War, and the authorities had to take notice as the old boys still had about an hour and a half to go before reaching the age when they were too old to be recommissioned and could tactfully be sent out to grass.

The veterans were duly welcomed back into the services, but what to do with them?

The answer was to post them abroad to non-trouble spots, to areas where crises were unlikely to occur and where young station commanders could find odd jobs to keep the old boys busy without them actually clogging up the war effort. The perfect non-trouble spot to post the old warriors was, of course, Iceland, and we had our due share of them.

One of the German pocket battleships, I think it was the *Scharnhorst*, slipped through the net of Allied naval vessels penning it in a fjord and steamed straight for Iceland. What it hoped to do when it got there I have no idea but there was no panic in RAF ranks. The RAF regiment at Kaldadharnes had fifteen rifles and these were coolly issued to airmen to defend the airfield to their last gasp should the battleship be foolhardy enough to attack.

I was broadcasting in Reykjavik at the time, where the Army, which proudly produced a Bofors anti-aircraft gun, was a bit more excited. I was issued with a rifle and ordered to man a sandbagged observation post on the airfield perimeter and shoot on sight any battleship which did not reply satisfactorily to my challenge, 'Who goes there, friend or foe?'

The only good thing which came out of all this was the marvellous view I had that night of the aurora borealis, the northern lights, a breathtaking sight like a Dada-esque firework display in very slow motion.

During this I leaned my rifle against the sandbag wall of the bunker in order to find a hanky and have a blow. Suddenly before me, coming up to the waistband of my tunic, stood a tiny bald figure with a captain's pips on his shoulders. I was young then and nowadays I might judge differently, but at the time he seemed to me to be about 104 years old and frail with it, like a pensionable stick insect.

'Whar's your wifle, airman?' he demanded in a high quavery voice.

'There, sir,' I said, pointing at it.

'Nevah be parted from your wifle, man,' he said. 'Don't you wealize I could overpaar you?'

There was another golden oldie at Kaldadharnes, a wing commander who always wore his old Royal Flying Corps uniform, which he must have cleaned and brushed daily since 1918. He strode about in his ancient jodhpurs, high brown boots and Sam Browne belt with a pistol in the holster. This he rested his right hand upon and occasionally slapped. He looked like Biggles.

The wingco was not Biggles, but according to William Amos in his book *The Originals: Who's Really Who in Fiction*, Biggles was in Iceland at the time. He was the air officer commanding Iceland, Air Commodore Cecil Wigglesworth, by all accounts the man on whom the author Captain W. E. Johns based Biggles.

The wingco painted beautifully sensitive watercolours of the volcanos and glaciers which surrounded us and he gave them away to anybody, of any rank, who wanted one. I think his official function was education officer but he seemed to spend a great deal of his time flying the station Gypsy Moth upside down over the runway.

He died suddenly. His funeral was in the station all-purpose chapel, but he was buried near a forlorn little church about 7 miles away in the middle of an old lava field, now a farm. Considering the transport difficulties of getting there, there was a surprisingly large turnout of volunteers from all ranks to give him a decent send-off.

Another elderly gentleman (laundry officer) promoted me, for quite the wrong reasons. Promotion was most welcome to me, not as a matter of prestige but because the promotion, air-craftsman first class to leading aircraftsman, represented in material terms something like an extra three cream cakes, four pints of NAAFI bitter and six cups of café coffee per week.

It came about because I was doing a broadcast of *Roadhouse* at the *Rikisutvarpssalur* (how the word trips off the tongue) in Reykjavik and I had a lift back to Kaldadharnes in the 15 cwt Commer truck which had been recently instituted as a shuttle service for RAF personnel. It was a dark cold night in March and the roads were gleaming with frozen snow and ice.

About 20 miles out of Reykjavik, in the middle of nowhere, as we in the back were harmonizing an emotional version of 'You Stepped out of a Dream', the Commer, being nursed by the driver slowly round a bend, began to slide sideways towards the edge of the road. It continued to slide side-ways until it reached the edge and slid into a ditch.

This was not high drama, not a Formula One racing car hitting the crash barrier at 232 m.p.h.; the Commer simply came to rest slowly and gently on its side like an elephant succumbing to a tranquilliser dart. None of us was injured, just slightly shocked and not at all happy at being stranded on a very cold night far from home.

I was unanimously voted the honour of walking to the

nearest farmhouse and ringing the station duty officer for help; it was a long walk. Volcanic earth was not fodder-friendly and the farms had to be enormous to support just a few sheep and a cow or two, and the farmhouses were miles apart.

I picked my way across the rock- and lava-strewn land towards a light. Luckily there was a moon and I only fell over about thirty times before arriving at the farmhouse. The farm family were very kind and after I had mimed the Commer sliding over and the need to phone, they led me to the telephone and I rang the duty officer.

'RAF Kaldadharnes,' said an unlovely voice.

'Is that the duty officer?' I asked.

'The duty officer's off-duty. It's Sergeant Meadows 'ere!' said Sergeant Meadows irritably. I knew the horrible sergeant well. He had an inch-high forehead and a personal grudge against Hitler because the war had postponed his retirement and his plans to spend the rest of his life peacefully making his wife's life hell and bullying the children.

'Well, what do you want?' he barked down the phone.

'It's A/C 1 Muir, Sergeant, nine-three-one-one-one-zero' (you never, ever forget your service number). 'I wish to report that the Commer's come to a full stop.'

He put me on a charge.

The charge was 'dumb insolence to a superior', a magnificent example of the service mind at work. How can somebody be accused of dumb insolence because of something he said?

It seemed to me that I should not have much difficulty in getting off the charge when my case came up. I sailed through five years in the RAF and several petty charges without being found guilty by simply listening to the wording of the charge and replying to it rationally. At Warmwell I was put on a charge when an officer could not find me. The charge accused me of being 'absent from my place of duty'. I explained to the 'judge' that as the photography section had yet to be built, I had no place of duty. And got off.

And I once lost my RAF identity card. The charge read, 'Carelessness in losing identity card,' and I argued that the charge as written could not be proved until circumstances of the loss were determined, e.g., it could have been stolen by a master pickpocket, in which case it was not carelessness on my part but a matter of him being better at picking my pocket than I was at preventing my pocket being picked. I got off.

But it was a dangerous game. At any moment word could have gone round the officers' mess that A/C 1 Muir F. 931110 was a smart-arse, a barrack-room lawyer who should be taught a lesson. On the other hand, as far as I was concerned, any gamble was worth a try rather than being given 'jankers' on some feeble charge and having to scrub the guardroom floor at dawn every morning for a month.

A few days later my case came up and the dread Sergeant Meadows marched me smartly into a room to face the duty officer: 'Lef'-right! Lef'-right! Right turn! 'At orf.' Sitting behind the table was a white-haired old gentleman with wings on his uniform breast and an herbaceous border of medal ribbons. He looked at the charge sheet, put on spectacles and had another look, 'Ah,' he said. 'Muir.' He looked at me hopefully. 'Muir?'

'Sir,' I said, adding helpfully, 'nine-three-one-one-one-zero.'

'Hah,' he said. 'Commer truck. Reykjavik, eh? Why? Eh? Duty, what?'

'Sort of semi-duty actually, sir,' I said.

His brows corrugated with thought.

'You. Muir,' he said after quite a pause, 'in Reykjavik for . . . eh?'

'I was broadcasting, sir. On the forces radio programme.'

'Great heavens!' he murmured. He polished his glasses on his tie and stared at me with interest. 'Broadcasting? You mean you . . . talk things and . . . sing music . . . and . . . similar?'

'I try not to sing, sir.'

'But talk? Into a whatchamacallit – microphone? Chat on about this and that . . . and so forth?'

'Yes, sir.'

'Great heavens!' He leaned back in his chair, stunned. It occurred to me that the reason he was so impressed was that he himself was not a talker. A man of action, yes, but he clearly had only a very limited vocabulary at his command, and if

83

everyday expressions like 'pass the marmalade' and 'does this train stop at Tunbridge Wells?' were excluded, he probably got through a normal day on about 120 words.

'Sergeant,' he said. 'What rank he? . . . er . . . broadcasting airman?'

'It says it clearly on the charge sheet in front of you, sir. See, sir? Aircraftsman first class.'

'Have him promoted!'

Sergeant Meadows, his face a mask of venom, marched me smartly out of the room and shortly afterwards I became Leading Aircraftsman Muir F. (931110), and *slightly* richer.

The tour of duty in Iceland was only for one year because cookhouse food was none too nourishing over a long period; fresh vegetables were unobtainable and every meal consisted of a chunk of sheep cooked in a simple and semi-edible fashion, a couple of slices of tinned beetroot and an ascorbic-acid tablet to prevent scurvy. Pudding was usually industrial apple pie and custard substitute. The technique when dining was to queue up for the first course, find a place at a table and eat the sheep and beetroot while they were hot, then turn the tin plate over and collect the pud on the back, thus only having one tin plate to sluice in the communal bucket of tepid water on the way out.

The Icelanders ate a tremendous amount of fish, usually dried in hunks and a challenge to the teeth, or dried whole and a challenge to the nose. W. H. Auden wrote in his *Letters from Iceland*, 'The tougher kind tastes like toe-nails, and the softer kind like the skin off the soles of one's feet'.

I tried eating in a restaurant in Reykjavik but it was not an unqualified treat. Icelanders like their soup sweet and mine turned out to be hot cocoa with grains of uncooked rice floating about in it. The main course was the choice of either dried fish or sheep and beetroot. The pudding, which was a cream cake, and the coffee were both delicious.

I was so involved in enjoyable tours round army camps introducing the forces orchestra and writing and performing in about five series of radio shows that I volunteered to stay in Iceland for a further six months, which I found was possible if your reason was deemed worthy enough, which mine was judged to be.

In between the two tours I returned to England for a short leave and was interviewed about forces broadcasting in Iceland by Alan Keith on a new BBC radio programme called *In Town Tonight*.

In the hospitality room after the show the producer pointed out to me a smallish lean figure in army uniform and a warm British camel-hair overcoat. He was slumped in a chair, tapping his leg rhythmically with a swagger cane. He had a Mediterranean face and complexion, and when he stood up and went over to the sandwich trolley he walked with a rather dramatic limp.

'That's Philip Ridgeway,' explained the producer. 'I rather think he's a captain. He's some kind of a roving army entertainments officer and he's going to Iceland with you; that's why I invited him here.'

The figure limped back clutching about eight sandwiches wrapped in a paper doily.

'Captain Ridgeway?' I said.

'Major,' he said. He sat down, sticking out his gammy leg to make sitting down possible. His trouser leg rode up and a curved dagger in a jewelled sheath fell out of the top of his sock. He picked up the dagger and jiggled it back into place.

'One of our undercover chaps in Cairo gave it to me when I managed to get him out of a spot of bother in a cellar,' he said, quietly. 'I've only had to use it once.'

This was preposterous, B-picture stuff, but I realized that it could *just* be true. The Ridgeways were unconventional: the major's father, also named Philip Ridgeway, was a pioneer radio impresario who as early as 1930 produced a new sort of radio variety show called *The Ridgeway Parade*, which combined cabaret, variety and revue in a highly entertaining mix. He had great success with it in the theatre, too.

Philip Ridgeway, junior (the good major), tried for a while to follow in his father's footsteps but found his chance of making a reasonable living lay in more fringe showbiz activities; he did a bit of acting in his father's shows, but concentrated more on becoming a public relations and publicity man for film companies and a minder for stars at first nights.

'You did *quite* well in your interview, Muir,' he said to me mid-sandwich, 'but from a professional point of view, don't sound so enthusiastic. It's very amateur to show enthusiasm.'

With this dubious advice ringing in my ears we set sail back to the Land of the Midnight Sun.

Back in Iceland I did not see much of the major as his duties lay more with army unit concert parties. But I saw enough.

I have always wanted to declare an Ad Libber's Charter, which would establish that if a good ad lib is only heard by three people then the ad libber is entitled to repeat his ad lib later to a wider audience.

For instance, years ago I was at a local dinner party and the lady next to me said, 'Do you cook, Mr Muir?' I replied, 'No, I'm afraid I don't. I eat a bit but I don't cook at all.' 'You should learn,' she said. 'There are some very easy-to-understand recipes on cards by that man with the nice grey hair who runs restaurants and cooks on television. You know, Robert le Carré.' And I said, 'Oh, yes, didn't he write *The Pie That Came in from the Cold*?' Only that one lady was within earshot and she had never heard of John le Carré.

A choice instance of my credo not working at all occurred years ago during the run of the BBC2 television game show, *Call My Bluff*. Patrick Campbell and I, the team captains, were taken to lunch by a publisher, Geoffrey Strachan of Eyre Methuen, to discuss putting together a book based on the programme (we did it, too, and illustrated it ourselves, revealing to our great surprise that neither of us could draw).

The lunch took place at one of the first of the trendy trattorias, Mario and Franco's in Soho. I ordered something not very Italian but trustworthy like grilled sole and Paddy Campbell ordered quenelles – those bits of fish mucked about with in a frying pan. It was an expensive item on the menu in those days, £15.

When the food was served Paddy saw, sadly, that he was only given four bits of the very expensive mucked-about-with fish.

I said to Geoffrey, 'Well, really! Four quenelles for fifteen quid?' Then imitating Paddy's Irish accent, 'Four quenelles!'

Paddy always said it was the best pun he had ever heard. As he lived in the South of France where quenelles were often on the menu, he tried to appropriate my pun and dazzle his friends, but, alas, life is not as compliant as that. Whenever Paddy entertained in a Nice restaurant he would hopefully order quenelles and they were duly laid in front of him; sometimes there were three quenelles on the plate, frequently there was a more generous helping of five, six, or seven quenelles, but never, ever, was Paddy served four quenelles.

I now lean on the Ad Libber's Charter to support me in retelling an ad lib which I made many years ago. It was only heard at the time by the one person to whom it was said, that delightful, blonde, cheerfully sexy singer, Frances Day.

The plot started a couple of months after I returned to Iceland on my extension six-month tour of duty. I began to feel ill. Most of the day I had a kind of V-shaped ache in the groin. I had a very busy schedule of shows to write and as usual with any sort of illness, my way of coping with the problem intelligently was to ignore it and hope that it would go away. But it did not go away; it got worse.

I eventually reported sick and was immediately sent to the Army hospital at Reykjavik. It seems that I had developed a tubercular infection of a testicle which was growing to the size of a King Edward's potato and would have to come out. The operation had a beautiful name: orchidectomy.

Life in the hospital was rather pleasant. An elderly American GI in the next bed fed me endless Camel cigarettes. A bottle of Guinness was served to us morning and evening to build up our constitutions after living so long on sheep and beetroot, and the surgeon, Major Edwards, was not only efficient but cheerful with it. He told me not to worry or get a complex over the op. It was a tiny op, he assured me, and was like having an ear off: nature had provided a second ear and the body soon adapted to working on only one. I was not too happy about the analogy of my extremely personal operation being like having an ear off but his manner was reassuring.

On the days leading up to the operation the only book I could find to read was James Joyce's *Ulysses*. Not perhaps an ideal choice under the circumstances but there you go.

The op itself was no problem. It only required a local anaesthetic, so I chatted to Major Edwards while he busied himself. While he was at it he also removed a rather volcano-like boil which had suddenly popped up on my neck.

After the operation, drowsy from medication, I was slid into a bed in a ward and, as a new boy, inspected by Matron.

'And what have they been doing to *you*?' she enquired cheerily, reading my clipboard for details.

'Had a boil removed,' I mumbled drowsily.

Matron froze. 'We prefer the word "testicle",' she said.

Major Edwards sat alongside my bed many times over the next few days questioning me to find out how I had become infected. No doubt worried about a possible epidemic.

Eventually he found what was almost certainly the answer. In our hut was a corporal cook in charge of disposing of the considerable mass of waste food collected in bins at the back of the cookhouse. He did a deal with a local Icelandic farmer to exchange bins of pig food for churns of the farmer's fresh milk, which the corporal parked in our hut for us all to dip into, and enjoyably thick and creamy milk it was, too. But the milk was not pasteurized, and I drank a lot of it every day.

QED.

By an extraordinary coincidence, I found many years later that my experience was not unique.

The cast of the BBC radio show, *My Music*, which Denis Norden and I had been in for ever, was invited to record a special edition of the show at the Hong Kong Arts Festival. Also in the show were, of course, Ian Wallace and John Amis. On our free weekend, we were all sitting on a luxury junk belonging to our rich hostess, clutching half litres of gin and tonic, when I found myself talking to Ian in a rambling sort of way about Iceland. And I told him about the tainted milk and the op.

'But this is remarkable!' said Ian. 'I had the same thing! Early part of the war. Stationed in a lonely bit of Dorset farmland. Drank lots of milk more or less straight from the cow. Hospital and the same operation!'

What is more, John Amis reminded us that Sir Malcolm

Sargent also endured the same loss. Could it be an affliction which haunted only the highly musical?

And so to the ad lib which laid for me the ghost of this otherwise not very humorous medical experience.

The year was about 1952. The scene was the stage of the BBC radio's audience studio at Aeolian Hall, New Bond Street. The show we were performing was *The Name's the Same*, a confection in which a panel of grown-up and fairly intelligent people like Denis and me spent an hour or so of our lives, lightly paid, deciding whether the chap standing before us, who played the double bass in a nightclub, was really named Julius Caesar, or if he was bluffing (his name really *was* Julius Caesar).

The guest member of our panel for that show was the lovely Frances Day, then mature and all the more attractive for it.

Before the show, the cast regulars were gathered together in an ante-room waiting for Frances to arrive – we had not met her before – chatting away and sipping our room-temperature white wine from the hospitality trolley. I was standing with one foot up on a chair, expounding away to Denis about something boring when, from behind me, a hand came between my legs and grabbed my vitals. I turned round, considerably shocked, to find Frances Day looking up at me with her cute little pixie smile.

Still holding on: 'Hello!' she said.

But I had my moment after the show.

We are all standing about signing autographs for the contestants ('For Marie Antoinette – all good wishes for the future,') when a little old lady gave me a card to sign. I drew a heart pierced by an arrow and added the words, 'You are ever in my memory: the stranger who blew you a kiss from his Rolls-Royce on St Valentine's Day.' The old lady was thrilled.

Frances said, 'You really are diabolical!'

'Actually,' I said, 'I'm monobolical.'

Chapter 5

THE WAR (PART TWO)

I was to find that RAF Ringway was different, very different, from RAF Kaldadharnes. There was not a volcano in sight nor one smelly fish drying on a clothes line to disturb the neat greenery of the gardens and parks and trees around RAF Ringway, which was and is again now the civil airport, situated on the pleasant Altrincham side of Manchester.

To my surprise I felt quite an emotional twinge leaving Iceland. Thanks to the warm Gulf Stream (every English child is taught at school about the benign influence of the Gulf Stream; even our nice Mr Murphy, geography master/ferry bar steward at Bradstowe College, Broadstairs, managed to get it right), Iceland was not all that icy. Perhaps I was just so much younger then but I do not think of it being unbearably cold, although I do remember standing at the window of the NAAFI drinking a beer on Christmas morning and the froth freezing on my new and already rather revolting moustache.

There really was a midnight sun in the summer, but not every day, only when the weather was right, whereupon we all rushed out with our cameras and photographed each other with a clock tower in the background showing round about twelve o'clock. It could have been midday, of course, but no, it was midnight all right because the shadows were different. The trouble with all that bright sunshine was that sleep became difficult and we began to look forward to winter and a bit of good old relaxing night.

Unhappily, winter with no sunshine at all turned out to be gloomy and progressively dispiriting. The days never became really light, except for a glimmer or two around midday, and it was not relaxing at all but deeply depressing.

I liked the Icelanders. Their blonde girls were often astonishingly beautiful, which helped, and I found that most of the population, as so often happens in a land where living is hard, were noticeably hospitable and friendly. But they were not exactly zany funsters. In his *Letters from Iceland*, W. H. Auden wrote to Christopher Isherwood that he thought that Iceland was the place for enjoyable but brief visits. 'I think that in the long run, the Scandinavian sanity would be too much for you.'

In his book, Auden presented what he claimed were translations of a number of Icelandic sayings including, 'Every man likes the smell of his own farts.' And, 'Pissing in his shoe keeps no man warm for long.' At a poetry reading in London I accused Auden of inventing these, but he insisted that they were genuine, sane, Icelandic proverbs.

There was no prospect of my volunteering for a third term of duty on the island, particularly after having had an operation because wounds healed extremely slowly out there, so I packed my kitbag (almost tearfully) to go home.

I gave my heavy Lilo to a newly arrived airman who was pathetically grateful, not knowing of its need to be given the kiss of life in the middle of the night. I could not get the second-hand portable typewriter I had bought out there into the kitbag, so I made a rope loop and when embarking on the troopship for home wore the typewriter round my neck, balancing the kitbag on my shoulder. Climbing the ship's ladder with that lot made me feel like an Egyptian slave humping a 6-foot cube of stone up the side of a pyramid.

On my last night at Kaldadharnes I found sleep difficult. The sun was shining brightly through the window and my mind was busy remembering. I remembered that before leaving RAF Warmwell I had been rehearsing one of the leading parts in a play which was a great favourite with amateur dramatic societies at that time, *Outward Bound*. It was one of those 'well-made' plays in which a group of assorted characters with heavy problems were closely confined together, in this case on a cruise liner, and eased their problems by thrusting them on to one another. The big twist in *Outward Bound* was that everybody was dead.

I played a decent, stiff-upper-lip sort of chap. All was going well and I was word-perfect in my part when I had this sudden posting to Iceland.

Reykjavik had a theatre and in my first week there I discovered to my astonishment and delight that an Icelandic amateur company was playing *Outward Bound* in Icelandic. I went. It was a weird experience because I knew almost the whole play by heart in English.

The Icelander playing my part of the cool British gent was short and tubby with a Ronald Colman moustache, plus-fours, cricket blazer, clip-on bow tie and a deerstalker hat; he looked like the comic in Butlin's holiday camp 'Family Variety Hour' in Bognor Regis.

And then in my bunk just when I was at last happily nodding off, I sat bolt upright and wide awake again. I had remembered my car. My beloved Triumph saloon! Short of a dynamo and roof fabric but *my first car* and I had left it, forsaken, forgotten in my rush to catch the train to Iceland.

I left the Triumph parked on the grass verge about 100 yards on the Dorchester side of the main gate of RAF Warmwell, and it should still be there. As far as I am concerned anybody who finds the car may keep it, it's just that in the glove compartment there should be a partly consumed packet of Victory-V extra-strong throat pellets – real killers – and my local chemist has never heard of them. The packet may be sent c/o my publisher.

The voyage home from Iceland was without incident and I had great pleasure in finding a post office back in Gourock and sending Mother a telegram: 'FATTED CALF FOR ONE TOMORROW EVENING?'

I hesitated before sending it because I knew Chas was abroad; he had been posted to India, and there still lingered from the First World War the dread of seeing a postman at the front door bearing a buff envelope; it was the War Office's way of notifying that a next of kin had been killed in action or was missing believed dead. But I was glad I did send it because when I arrived home I found that the telegram had given Mother no dreads, just pleasure.

The fatted calf was a piece of cod escorted by parsley, mashed potatoes and fresh beans from the garden, a dinner which was caviar and pâté de fois gras after eighteen months of sheep and beetroot. And not an ascorbic-acid tablet on the premises.

My two weeks leave at home produced some surprises. Unlike Kaldadharnes, Iceland, where life was peaceful and mostly routine, Leyton, London, E10 was in the middle of the war. To observe blackout restrictions was tedious but vital, and to walk outside at night, with searchlights sweeping the sky, lighting up barrage balloons and picking out the high silver slivers which were enemy aircraft, was to walk suddenly into a gloomy, lonely and noisy world. No cheerful lights shone and anti-aircraft guns thumped away all round, and even a quick dash to the postbox on the corner was accompanied by the 'ping' and 'tinkle' of chunks of jagged metal from spent anti-aircraft shells falling about one's ears.

When the sirens began wailing, Mother, like all the wives and families who endured the bombings almost every night, became expert at judging from the throb of the aircraft's engines whether the planes could well pass directly overhead and be a real threat or were moving away.

If the enemy throb was ominous we rapidly trooped out into the garden and down into the air-raid shelter. The shelter was a little triumph of wartime invention, cheap and easy to erect; it looked like an arched hut made from bent corrugated-iron sheets bolted together. Once it was half buried in the garden and the curved roof covered with a foot of earth and planted with potatoes it was protection against almost everything short of a direct hit from a landmine.

These shelters started out as grim little cells of damp darkness but the process of cheering them up soon began. The floor soil was trodden hard, duckboards were laid and bits of old carpets were cut to size and nailed down. Heavy curtains of anything to hand from sacking to moth-eaten velvet were made into draught-excluders for the shelter's entrance. Old deckchairs and benches were brought in, and cushions and some form of lighting. And the shelters could be warmed up quickly with a small paraffin heater if some source of paraffin could be located. Bookshelves were erected and a torch was kept in a cupboard.

No bombs fell alarmingly near during those two weeks, the bombers' main targets being the City and the docks, but for various reasons, such as bad navigation or the need to conserve fuel to get home, the bombers would sometimes empty their bomb bays indiscriminately over a suburb, and one exciting night Church Road, Leyton, E10 experienced the sprinkling upon it of a load of enemy incendiary bombs. These had been horribly successful when used on the City but we were luckier.

I think they must have been seconds. Half of them didn't ignite and were carried off by neighbours as extremely dangerous souvenirs, and many of the bombs ignited but only fizzed and sparkled in a desultory sort of way, like fireworks bought from a damp sweetshop. Some of the bombs did their job well and produced immense heat very quickly, but most of these seemed to land in the middle of the road or in a field, which I believe both sides found could be the problem with incendiaries unless they were scattered over crowded inner cities.

I wistfully hoped that a stray incendiary might land on Laurie's Preserves, the marmalade factory about 100 yards upwind of number 28 – as long as it was empty and fully insured, of course – because when it was boil-up day at Laurie's, the tingly acrid smell of the hot marmalade could penetrate reinforced concrete at a thousand paces.

One well-made incendiary bomb did land on the church roof and ignite but the voluntary services dealt with it promptly. There was a patrol already up there in case of trouble, and while we service personnel on leave were in the street below bumbling into each other in the half light from smouldering privet hedges, the Civil Defence and fire-pickets were rapidly dealing with the incendiary on the church roof with the regulation-issue bucket of water, stirrup pump and small length of garden hose.

The only really tragic moment in the night's excitement came when all of us had at last bored each other rigid with our own experiences ('We were in the shelter and I said to the wife, "Something fallen on my cabbages." She said, "Never!" I said, "I deffnly heard something fall. I'm going to take a look".') We quietly slunk back to our own houses.

A pale, anxious young lad in khaki was waiting for me at the gate of number 28. 'Excuse me bothering you,' he said, 'but have you by any chance seen a rifle? Lee-Enfield, bolt action?

I rested it against a fence and I can't seem to find it . . .'

I could, of course, have overpaared him, but to what end?

On the train up to report to No. 1 PTS, RAF Ringway, kit-bag on rack, I tried to conjecture what the letters No. 1 PTS stood for. Nobody had told me when my posting notice was handed to me in Kaldadharnes. They probably did not know – initials proliferated in the services – but it was where I was bound and I was keen to find out the activity going on there, in which I would be heavily involved for perhaps years.

It was quite a long train journey in wartime from Euston to Manchester and as I dozed, my mind drifted away in search of possible meanings of No. 1 PTS.

No. 1 Paper-Tearing Secretariat? Something to do with spying? The Far East? Don't the Japanese call it 'oregano' or is that growing miniature trees? Anyway, no.

No. 1 Pupil-Teacher Symposium? Could be. Everybody in the services, corporal and above, seemed to spend half their time teaching colleagues how to do something. Perhaps the teachers get together with their pupils in a symposium and learn from the pupils how they think they should be taught? No.

No. 1 Pentecostal Tabernacle and Synagogue. No.

At New Street Station, Manchester, I had to sign for another travel warrant from the Transport Office to get me on to Ringway so I asked the duty travel officer the vital question.

'Parachuting, lad,' he said. 'That's what they do at Ringway: parachuting. Teaching the Army how to jump out of planes and float down to earth as light as a lump of thistledown. Ringway is Number One Parachute Training School for the whole of the British armed forces, so stick your chest out proudly and pray that *you* don't have to jump. Four fifteen p.m., platform three and don't miss it.'

After RAF Warmwell and RAF Kaldadharnes, RAF Ringway was a luxury billet, warm and comfortable and busy; not a new shanty town built on commandeered farmland, but a going concern newly borrowed by the RAF from the civic authorities, with comfortable brick barrack blocks. The NAAFI was on one side of the main road to Altrincham and on the other side the guardroom guarded a number of enormous aircraft hangars, admin buildings and workshops, including – at last – a well-equipped photographic unit. On the opposite side of the airfield stood a factory belonging to Fairey Aviation where Fairey planes were assembled and tested. Never a dull moment on the runways.

Britain was the last of the great powers to go in for dropping troops into action by parachute and it completely changed the established technique of landing. Films of German and Russian (and American) pre-war mass drops showed that the soldiers were trained to land with their feet apart, if possible in a standing position, so that in theory they could then sprint swiftly into battle. The snag to this was that the parachute's direction and velocity of landing in those days was not easily controllable and the parachutists frequently landed more heavily on one leg than the other and it then bent or broke; the number of such minor casualties was formidable.

The British authorities, rather brilliantly, decided that as the RAF was going to have to fly the troops into action it might as well train them how to drop as well, so the British army was taught their parachuting by RAF physical training instructors. The RAF's PTIs' greatest improvement was to change the other nations' method of landing from an attempt to achieve a standing position to curling up with feet and knees together and rolling over, thus avoiding a shock impact. In a short while most other nations switched to our technique.

There was a graver problem. Sometimes the parachute failed to open. The unfortunate trainee fell swiftly to earth, his parachute clinging tightly to itself, a narrow column of white silk instead of a billowing umbrella. This fatal occurrence was known, and dreaded, as a 'Roman candle'.

But miracles do sometimes happen. The late Roland Gant, who was my editor at Heinemann the publishers, spoke perfect French and had a dangerous and secret job operating in occupied France. He told me that one night he had to rendezvous with a British radio operator due to be dropped from a Lysander plane at 1,000 feet onto a secret dropping point in Normandy. The Lysander was on time, its navigation was spot on and all was going well until the agent jumped. Roland, to his horror, saw in the moonlight that the parachute was not opening; it was a Roman candle. The dark figure hanging beneath the white silk streak gathered speed and finally hit the earth with a sickening thud. As Roland ran towards the parachute, the parachutist suddenly rose up and called out, 'That you, Roland? Fuck this for a game of soldiers!'

By a million to one chance the agent had landed in a soft peat bog. He had broken bones but he had survived.

Too many Roman candles occurred during the intensive training courses at No. 1 PTS and the boffins brooded. Tests were made on the possibility of static electricity sticking the silk together and it was decided that more hard information would be helpful, e.g., does the parachutist's manner of exit from the plane have a bearing? Are there rogue parachutes which deploy in the wrong manner? It was decided that the photography section would photograph *all* training drops on Bell and Howell amateur 16mm cine-cameras filming at their maximum speed (producing slow motion) of sixty-four frames per second. Which was when I arrived on the scene.

The aircraft used at the time for training drops was the old Armstrong Whitworth, 'Whitley', a heavy, ponderous bomber which was ideal to jump from as it could stay airborne at low speeds. But where could the camera be mounted?

I was unanimously elected by the photography section to volunteer to be the one to undergo the experiments.

The first bright idea was that I should film drops from the unused bomb bay, so two planks were roped to the bay and I was laid face down on them and strapped in place, pointing forwards, looking downwards, camera in shaking hand. It was dark and nasty in there but terror was to come. The plane took off well enough; noisy and draughty but tolerable. And then . . . and then the doors of the bomb bay slowly opened beneath me and I lay there, hanging from my ropes, with nothing between my face and the surface of the earth. I might well have screamed.

The whole terrifying experience proved to be a waste of time. When we landed it was realized that the aperture in the floor of the aircraft through which the parachutists jumped was aft of my bomb bay, so they all jumped out behind me and there was nobody for me to film.

The boffins' second bright idea was to remove the rear-gunner's turret at the back of the Whitley and for me, clutching the Bell and Howell, to lie on the floor in a prone position where the turret once stood, facing to the rear and taking up a bent posture not unlike a wasp's sting.

The plan was for a colleague to sit on my ankles to prevent me falling out of the plane, and when jumping commenced I was to lean downwards at right-angles, with the camera pointing forwards (into the slipstream, note), and film the squaddies as they emerged from the jumping aperture ahead of me.

There was so much wrong with this plan that I can hardly believe we eventually won the war. For one thing, when I tried bending down and pointing the camera forwards towards the aperture the slipstream took my breath away and almost tore the camera from my grasp. And once bent over, I found that, like doing a forward somersault, rearing back up again required powerful, well-exercised muscles which I did not possess. So I just dangled there like a rag doll over the side of a pram until my colleague managed to pull me up into the aircraft by the back of my flying jacket.

This suggested a method and I lowered myself again into the slipstream. But this time my colleague had looped my long woollen scarf around my neck, hanging on to both ends. A parachutist jumped and my colleague hauled on the scarf and drew me up as the parachutist passed below me and drifted rapidly away behind the aircraft. It was painful on my Adam's apple but I managed to get a reasonably good shot of the parachute deploying.

It was when the film had been developed and we were all gathered round the projector to view it that the asininity of the method became apparent. Firstly, as I was upside down when I began filming, the parachutist apparently came out of the aperture upside down on the screen. As he passed beneath me and my colleague hauled on the scarf, the parachutist appeared to gently turn over and drift rapidly away, the right way up. Worse, the parachutists jumped in a stick of ten at a time and all I had time to get on my film was the first man out. The method was totally impractical for recording mass jumps.

It was our officer i/c photography unit who came up with the solution. This time the *front* gun turret was modified. A wooden camera-mounting was devised, which held the camera pointing backwards below the belly of the Whitley and towards the jumping aperture. The camera was instantly removable so that its spring could be wound up by hand (no electronic gadgetry in those days) and reloaded with film.

My colleagues and I had to lie prone in our turret, forefinger on the camera button, and when we heard through our headphones the despatcher screaming, 'Action stations! – GO!' begin filming. It all worked well. We had to keep careful records so that we could develop any specific drop the boffins called for, and the boffins had a library of thousands of slow-motion picture sequences of deploying parachutes to study.

After a couple of years of this and other lines of research, Roman candles became a satisfactorily rarer phenomenon.

Monitoring every training jump meant a great deal of flying for the five of us in the photographic unit. I recently found my old flying logbook and was reminded that a normal working day started about 0730 and consisted of anything from ten to twenty flights to and from the dropping zone. But the dropping zone was Tatton Park, a large country estate only a few miles away, and an average flight took only fifteen to twenty minutes. I saw in the logbook that by 28 October 1943 I had clocked up 1,000 flights.

The dropping zone had a different atmosphere to the airfield. To have jumped and still be alive, no bones broken, was such an exhilarating experience that Tatton Park, with a good canteen run by local ladies, was a happy place. Not without an occasional problem, of course. I was there on some kind of duty one day and a matronly lady in tweeds grabbed my arm rather painfully in the canteen and drew me to one side. 'I am the volunteer regional organizer, food and comforts,' she said. Her voice dropped to a commanding whisper and she looked away as she spoke. 'It's the chemical lavatories. Would you be good enough to ask your commanding officer to arrange for them to be emptied more frequently. They are, well, let me just say that the chemicals in them are odorous . . . and my volunteer ladies find them offensive to dignity and hygiene and try not to use them, which causes problems . . .' She paused, in a sudden agony of embarrassment at talking so frankly to a peasant, and then recovered. 'Doesn't bother *me*, of course,' she added with a bright smile, 'hunting woman, you know!'

I did not know that ladies who hunted had a more convenient system of plumbing than lesser mortals, but it was an interesting thought.

In those early days parachutists launched themselves into space through a hole cut in the floor of the Whitley aircraft halfway down the fuselage. The hole was lined with a deep wooden collar, of conical shape, about 2 feet deep and about 5 feet wide at the top, narrowing down to about 3 feet.

The trainee wore a quick-release harness with his parachute at the back of it, and he hooked the static line, which tore the parachute pack open automatically when he jumped, on to a cable which ran down the length of the fuselage at shoulder level. When 'Action Stations!' was called he sat down with his legs dangling through the hole, his hands gripping the edge, looking straight ahead. On the command 'GO!' he went. He did this by pushing off smartly with his hands and jerking to attention. This resulted (with a bit of luck) in him dropping cleanly through the centre of the hole, whereupon his static line would pull the cover off his parachute, which would deploy into the slipstream and be blown open.

Jumping through the aperture was in practice a bit trickier than it sounds. If he did not push off hard enough, his parachute pack caught on the edge of the aperture behind him and tipped him forward so he went into the slipstream upside down – not nice. Worse still, if he pushed too hard, his face hit the aperture facing him and he left a couple of his front teeth imbedded in the woodwork. This painful misfortune was quite frequent and was known to the troops with grim jocularity as 'ringing the bell'.

I made my first jump from a barrage balloon and it was an abysmal effort. I was up in a balloon which had a jumping aperture fitted to the floor of its cage for training purposes. All soldiers made their first two descents from a balloon. I finished filming a stick of Polish trainees jumping through the aperture, happily singing (I think Polish troops sang in their sleep), and the sergeant instructor suggested that as I had a parachute on, as required when up in the balloon, it would be easier and quicker for me to jump rather than wait for the balloon to be slowly wound to ground level by winch.

He yelled, 'Action stations!' and I sat gingerly on the edge of the aperture as I had seen the trainees do. He moved me to a less suicidal position and told me not to worry, it was a piece of cake. The opposite side of the aperture looked very close and I thought I saw a tooth in the wood, but it was probably only a knot. On the scream of 'GO!' I went rigid as instructed and dropped, unwounded to my surprise, through the hole.

The descent was not at all what I expected, not that I knew *what* to expect. It is quite a long drop from a balloon before the parachute opens, about 200 feet, because unlike an aircraft drop there is no slipstream to whip the silk quickly into action. There was no feeling of dropping through space, just a very strong, not disagreeable, but wholly novel physical sensation, not unlike beginning to feel the effects of an anaesthetic. After quite a while the chute billowed open somewhere above my head with a loud welcome crackle and it was as though a hand had grabbed my harness and was holding me safely and firmly.

It was a terrific moment. There I was, suspended on a sky hook with nothing but air between my boots and the world. And there was no feeling of descending, instead the earth was very slowly rising up to meet *me*. And then the world rose at an increasingly rapid rate until I thudded quite heavily onto the Tatton Park turf.

I had a colleague down below, chortling, taking photographs of my descent. Oh, dear. My landing looked like a shop-window dummy falling off the back of a lorry.

Some time later the PTS commanding officer decided that it might be a good idea for somebody from the photographic section to go on an official parachuting course. My colleagues (as all my colleagues everywhere seem to have done during my war service) unanimously decided that it was I who should have the honour of breaking a leg or two for the war effort.

The training programme turned out to be forward somer-saulting all over again, slightly glamorized.

We were trained by RAF physical training instructors, mostly sergeants, for whom no praise can be adequate. They were physically impressive, of course, tough and indestructible; one felt that if they jumped out of a plane without a chute they would just bounce twice and stroll to the NAAFI for a pint, but they had humour and character as well, and we trainees clung to their strength and reliability as one used to depend on one's bank manager.

In fact, the instructors did jump without chutes by tradition on Christmas Day, in sticks of ten from upstairs windows of a barrack block onto the rose beds below.

Another Christmas tradition was to have a drunken afternoon swim in the static water tank near the main gate. This was covered with green and slimy algae and was colder than anything I had known in Iceland. As I have a touch of Raynaud's – that thing where your fingers go bloodless in cold weather – I stayed in the water for about a second and a half. Even then I emerged with chattering teeth and my whole body was the bluish-white colour of the French girl's bosom at Broadstairs.

We were split into groups of ten and began with 'synthetic training' in one of the big hangars. On a busy day the hangar was like an Hieronymus Bosch picture sprung to life: the air was rent with great echoing shouts of, 'ACTION STATIONS! – GO!' Figures flew through the air clinging to pulleys and swooping down cables; bodies thudded onto mats as they practised their rolling; they clung to trapezes and jumped down from the top of the hangar to make whirring descents by a frightener called 'the Fan', so called because the speed of descent was (slightly) diminished by a large fan on the end of the drum of cable.

At this time the lumbering old Whitley Mk V warhorses were gradually being replaced by the smart new Douglas DC-3s, 'Dakotas', from America. The great change for the better was that Dakotas had no hole in the floor to be jumped through; the parachutist now hooked his static line onto the wire and ran out of the door.

On their morning drop to work at Tatton Park the instructors had a small competition amongst themselves as to how quickly they could launch ten men out of the door. They found that the best technique was for the man with the longest arms to stand back from the door gripping the sides whilst three or four of the thinnest instructors in his stick squeezed in front of him, holding on to each other. The rest of the stick lined up behind. At the cry of 'GO!', the man with the long arms gave a mighty pull, ejecting the men in front of him and himself, and the rest sprinted down the aisle and hurled themselves almost as one through the door. The point was to determine how to drop a stick of parachutists onto the smallest possible landing area.

Life at RAF Ringway for Leading Aircraftsman Muir 931110 became increasingly busy and rewarding. Besides the flying and the other photographic duties, I wrote a moving story entitled *Return to Sheol* (the title is the only thing I can remember about it), and a play in the Terence Rattigan mode about a young Hudson pilot in Iceland whose radio went wrong on his homeward flight and he completely missed the island. It had a happy ending but I cannot imagine what it was. How on earth did I get him home in one piece?

My ambition to get on an aircrew course came a step nearer. I was summoned to RAF headquarters, Adastral House, a large building at the bottom of Kingsway which later became the offices of the commercial television company Associated Rediffusion. (James Thurber, on his last visit to Europe, thought the name Associated Rediffusion sounded like a complicated nervous disease. On that visit he also said, 'A woman's place is in the wrong,' and when a lady at a reception in Paris gushed that she had read all his books in both English and French and, oddly, preferred them in French, he murmured modestly, 'I guess I do tend to lose a little in the original.')

In the Kingsway building I was interviewed by a board of mature RAF officers and probed as to my zeal and general airworthiness and given a small medical, which seemed all right, and my height was measured with some difficulty, as the arm of the measuring gadget did not go up that far; it stopped at 6 feet 3 inches, and in those days I stood a weedy 6 feet 6 inches. Alas, no longer. A literary stoop and natural shrinkage of the spinal discs have brought about a diminution. It seems that one's discs dry out with age, and there are a lot of them back there. I have now stabilized at a bent 6 feet 4 inches.

My eyes were also tested. Good result, 20/20, but again measured with difficulty as my eyes were, and still are, of course, unusually wide apart. The eye chap was fascinated with how wide apart they were and kept saying, 'My, my,' and checking the measurement with his calipers.

'Does it matter that my eyes are unusually wide apart?' I asked, a bit nettled. 'Is there any significance to it?'

'Well, yes,' he said, 'it's more or less accepted that eyes which, unlike yours, are close together indicate a person who will tend to be a little more cunning and untrustworthy in his dealings than a person with an average eye-separation measurement.'

'I see,' I said, thoughtfully. 'And what do eyes as wide apart as mine indicate?' I asked.

'Er – stupidity,' he said.

I returned to Ringway to await my call to higher things. The call did not come, so for something like three more years I walked about with a curved white flash tucked in the front of my forage cap which indicated to the world that I was potential aircrew waiting to be put on a flying course. By the end of the war the flash was about as white as my beloved old vest, which my mother eventually scraped off me, making me wear a dauntingly white, crisp but unfriendly new one. The new vest was never as warm as the old one, nor as effective in cold weather when worn as a hat.

Then life at Ringway began to warm up. The RAF High Command, with an eye to the future when the tide would turn and our forces would invade Europe, rashly decreed that ground crew tradesmen like photographers should learn to be more generally useful so that they could be called upon to drive heavy-goods vehicles and troop-carrying buses.

And so another terror was added to Ringway's parachuting course. In spite of never having been taught how to drive anything and my experience limited to main-road runs from RAF Warmwell to Dorchester in my Triumph saloon, I was cheerfully added to the list of volunteer auxiliary bus drivers.

My approach to driving a bus full of parachutists back from Tatton Park to Ringway was one of blithe, unwarranted confidence. There was, of course, no period of training because there was nobody trained to do the training, so on my maiden trip I just climbed into the driver's cab, glanced round to see where everything was and kangarooed off.

I found that hauling the bus round corners was hard work and I had to learn that a bus is very long and it is necessary to steer wide round sharp bends because the back wheels tend to cut the corners. Happily, on my first couple of trips the trainee parachutists were Polish and sang so spiritedly after their drop that they did not hear the rear side of the bus side-swiping bushes, trees and the occasional wall.

The troops (and some instructors) put in a petition to the transport officer asking for me to be put on to other duties because, they said, travelling back from Tatton Park in my bus was more terrifying than the jump. So that little bit of fun came to an end.

Another and far more interesting bit of fun soon replaced it. The Air Ministry issued a memo telling squadron commanders that those airmen waiting for a pilot's course should be given as much flying experience as possible.

This move was warmly welcomed by the Ringway pilots because they were mostly ex-bomber types who had survived their tours of duty and were bored to sobs making twenty-minute flights all day like air taxis, and as I seemed to be the only potential aircrew eligible I had a great time. Between them they gave me a complete flying course.

A typical entry in my logbook reads:

24 June 1943. 1500–1705. MENTOR training plane. Dual instruction: Flt. Lt. Hooper. Taking off and landing, flying straight and level, rate 1 turns, climbing, flying on course.

That was straightforward enough, but the following day's log entry read:

25 June 1943. 1520–1630. Whitley. Dual Instruction: WO Blake. Straight and level. Flying on course. Rate 1 turns. Climbing and gliding.

The Whitley was another matter. WO Blake would have flown it on the outward leg and dropped his stick of ten trainees. This could not be left to a learner pilot as it entailed flying the plane as slowly as possible for the parachutists' sake without the plane falling out of the sky, and anyway I had to be up front, face down, filming. After the drop I would get up and race back to the cockpit and take the co-pilot's wheel (there were no co-pilots) and WO Blake would say, 'It's all yours!' and I would bring the empty plane home and, after a bit of experience, even land it. The controls were heavy and responded slowly. Making a three-point landing meant hauling the wheel back as far as it would go at exactly the right moment – it felt as though the wheel was attached to heavy industrial elastic – and the beast would gently subside onto the runway, as though glad of the rest.

The flashiest entry in my logbook was the day I flew what was perhaps the heaviest aircraft then in service, followed by the lightest. The heavy job was a Stirling bomber, full of para-chutists newly arrived at Ringway and being given 'air experience'. This was the most boring of all the Ringway pilot's duties, as all he was required to do was fly the trainees anywhere for an hour, straight and level, and then fly them back. So the pilot was perfectly happy for me to fly the plane up and down the Welsh coast on his behalf while he put his feet up on the instrument panel and wrote to his wife.

On landing that day I then climbed into the station Tiger Moth for some dual-control with WO Curtis. The Moth was so light to handle after the big one that I flung it around a bit at first, but settled down eventually. Unlike the old Whitleys you could land it with a finger and thumb on the control stick. We looped the loop, which was a simple, fun manoeuvre and centrifugal force kept everything in place, but then WO Curtis flew the plane upside down like the nice old wingco did at Kaldadharnes and that was not fun at all. There was no cen-trifugal force and one dangled dangerously upside down from the safety straps while dust, dead spiders and other detritus on the floor of the cockpit dropped down one's trouser leg and lodged in the catchment area of the crutch.

Warrant Officer Curtis, soon Pilot Officer Curtis, gave me as much flying instruction as he could. In return I used to babysit so that he could take his wife to the pictures. He had been a commercial artist before joining up, and together we made a huge wall-newspaper, changing it monthly. It became quite popular. I wrote the text, which was largely made up of limericks and clerihews featuring station 'characters', jokes, spurious official notices like, 'In future all beds must be made up as laid down in standing orders,' and each edition had an episode of a serial parodying some genre of popular literature; our first target was James Hadley Chase's *No Orchids for Miss Blandish*, a cunning and hugely popular mix of soft porn and violence.

Our version, which featured in its plot that pioneer of contraception, Dr Marie Stopes, was entitled *No More Kids for Mrs Blandish*. My typed sheets of text (I still had the portable typewriter) were pasted onto a huge stretch of paper pinned to the NAAFI noticeboard and PO Curtis brought the whole presentation together with some inventive and funny artwork.

And so, in this fashion, the days and months passed. Then a year and then another year. It was known as having a 'soft war', that is to say being warm and fed and still alive.

But there were occasional little hiccups in the steady breathing.

I notice in my logbook that the entry for Christmas Eve, 1942, reads:

Whitley. PO Bruton. Dropped stick of ten, then forced landing. Starboard engine on fire.

And on 24 July 1943:

Whitley. PO Bruton. One stick of ten and then forced landing. Starboard engine cut out.

After taking the jumping course I made a total of eleven jumps. The first two were, as required, from a balloon, but these were now equipped with a door frame to jump through rather than that beastly hole in the floor, and when the despatcher bellowed, 'GO!' in my ear, my reflexes worked well and I shot through the door as though voice-propelled.

I was allowed to make the second jump immediately, a great treat as the euphoria of having survived the first overcame the awful anticipation of the second. The balloon was winched down, I put on a fresh chute, climbed in and we floated back up to 600 feet. 'ACTION STATIONS!' roared the instructor. I stood tall in the doorway gripping the sides of the door frame, the picture of an intrepid and confident parachutist waiting for the 'GO!' to propel him on his way.

It did not come. The instructor decided to play a little sadistic trick which instructors sometimes did to cheer themselves up after a hard day of shouting soldiers out through doors.

'OK, Lofty,' he said in a quiet kindly voice. Lofty was my wartime name. 'No hurry, old lad, just go whenever you feel like it.'

It was awful. I drew back from the doorway, twitching, then moved resolutely forward, then retreated again, and then dithered on the edge. And I realized how much of a parachutist's training was to accustom him to leap automatically on the shout of 'GO!' without any kind of thought process holding things up. I eventually fell out.

When I made my last balloon jump much later I sustained my one and only war wound, but I suspect that it does not count as it was self-inflicted. I forked myself in the behind.

It was a murky November day and I was up in a balloon with a boffin and an instructor, filming some experimental parachutes being hurled out of the balloon attached to rubber dummies which weighed the same as a human being.

A fog came up and we suddenly seemed to be suspended in damp cotton wool. The drop was cancelled and the instructor telephoned the winch-lorry below to find out what it was like down there and the winch-man reported that a breeze had cleared the fog away at ground level. The instructor decided that he and I should jump. Me first. So out into the damp cotton wool I stepped.

Very odd sensation. No feeling of height whatsoever because there was nothing in sight to tell the brain that it was not at ground level. That strange powerful feeling overwhelmed me again, of being weightless, non-human, then the welcome clacking, crackling sound of the chute opening.

It was traditional in the lower echelons of the RAF to carry the personal knife, fork and spoon (the 'irons') in the right hip pocket at all times, so as to be able to cope instantly, anywhere, if somebody offered food. I had my irons in my right hip pocket when I landed backwards, in a rolling movement as taught, and the fork's four prongs stabbed into my bottom, drawing blood. Not enough blood for me to put in for a Purple Heart, or even a morning's sick leave, but for a year or more afterwards my right buttock bore an honourable scar in the form of four dark-blue dots. But to whom could I, with pride, display my war wound?

I made nine other parachute leaps at Ringway, all of them water jumps into the large lake in Tatton Park. The excellent thing about jumping into water was that it was really very difficult to break a leg on landing and quite impossible to stab yourself in the behind. Thus it was the preferred sort of jump to offer elderly visiting brass hats, like General 'Windy' Gale who made many drops into the lake. The visiting party was usually only the brass hat and an aide, so the stick was usually beefed up by the inclusion of Wing Commander Kilkenny, who was the training school's headmaster, any instructors to hand and occasionally, at the last moment if nobody else was available, me ('Busy, Lofty? Wanna water jump? Grab a chute from the packers and see you on the tarmac in a couple of minutes. Hurry!').

Jumping into water was relatively harmless but called for new skills. The parachute harness felt safe and indeed was safe because the wearer sat in a loop of webbing and was held in place by other webbing which clicked into a junction box on his chest. All he had to do to get out of the harness was to thump the quick-release catch on his junction box which released all the retaining straps and left him sitting in the loop.

On a water jump the parachutist had to detach himself from his harness before hitting the water or the silk might settle over his head and drown him. The technique was for the jumper, at about 10 feet up, to bang his quick-release box and so release the lateral straps, then, clinging on like grim death to the harness straps above his head, slip out of the loop in which he was sitting, let the parachute go, and drop the last few feet into the water unencumbered. The parachute would drift along on its own for a little way and then settle into the water, vast and translucent like a huge silken jellyfish. The trick was to judge accurately the moment to let go.

I finished writing another unproducible play, a thin cautionary comedy of a frightened German spy, a conscript, staying in a country house hotel near an RAF bomber airfield and, mid-spying duties, falling in love with his aristocratic landlady. I called the play *The First Casualty* from a good line attributed to an American senator: 'The first casualty of war is truth.' And I wrote a number of humorous monologues about parachuting (in verse, too, of a sort) which the padre and I recited at the drop of a hat and at the top of our voices at boozy PTS end-of-term parties.

Another episode in my war which was a good thing rather than a hiccup was the experience of first love, although I was a bit old for that sort of thing. I was no longer a gangly youth with spots but a grown man in my early twenties with spots, the owner of a small fawn moustache, a Morris open two-seater car with a drop-head hood and a hernia.

The object of my affection was a slim, intelligent, sweet young girl named Joan Young, who helped out as a volunteer in the Ringway canteen run by local ladies. Joan had just finished school and was waiting to go up to university.

For something like a year we had a most enjoyable friend-ship, not meeting very often because it was not possible, but finding much pleasure in each other's company when we did. It was totally innocent, a fun affair but not an *affaire*, and when it reached its natural end we parted as equably as we had met. We never saw each other again but I have always been grateful to Joan for making me consider somebody else's feelings other than my own and for opening my eyes to the richness that a close relationship can bring to day-to-day living.

Before I met Joan I found that I had this hernia, which hardly came as a surprise the way I jumped. The condition manifested itself as a smooth bump which popped out from time to time in the groin area. It could be fingered back to whence it came but would emerge again, particularly during one of the rare occasions when I was being energetic. No pain. As ever, my way of coping was to hope it would go away, which of course it did not. So I went into the RAF hospital to have it darned back into place.

Just before the surgeon came to inspect the damage, I hung a sign over my bed: 'Does my hernia concern ya?' but Matron made me take it down. After the op I had to try to live for a week or two without coughing or laughing, both of which induced sharp pain, but that was about all the suffering involved. On the credit side I was given post-natal contraction exercises by a beautiful, muscular little blonde WAAF sergeant physiotherapist.

After a couple of weeks in hospital I was sent off with two or three others to convalesce in a boarding house in Blackpool. The town was then empty of people and deep in gloom beneath scudding rain clouds; I sent a picture postcard of the trams on Blackpool front to my sergeant physiotherapist and wrote on the back:

> Those blue lagoons
> And tropic moons
> Are nowhere near Blackpool,
> H. de Vere Stackpoole.

One of the surprisingly few rackets operated by the photographic section at Ringway was the developing and printing of the station's snapshots. These were almost always rolls of 120 film. By working in the evening we could give a swifter and cheaper service than Boots the chemist or their rivals Timothy White's, and besides speed and economy our service could offer discretion. In other words, we would discreetly process any naughty pictures which Boots might refuse to print, or, worse still, hand over to the police.

Just such a roll of Kodak 120 film was passed to our sergeant by a pretty WAAF officer. He developed and printed it in secrecy and it turned out to be a series of flashbulb snaps of the pretty WAAF officer and another pretty WAAF officer larking about in the bath. Nothing at all sordid, just two girls giggling and fooling about, but a wartime bath was quite revealing as Ministry regulations allowed a maximum of only 5 inches of bathwater, which wasn't much cover for a couple of bouncy

WAAFs. One snapshot was an echo of that famous School of Fontainebleau painting of the two naked, po-faced aristos, the Duchesse de Villars and Gabrielle d'Estrées, sitting very upright in a bath, one of them holding delicately 'twixt finger and thumb the nearest nipple of the other, as though switching off the bathroom light.

The sergeant quickly printed a couple of sets of prints for the WAAF officers and then spoiled any good name our section might have had for discretion by printing off fifty more sets to sell in the sergeants' mess, and he told A/C 1 Clive Cook to hide the negatives under the darkroom floorboards for use if demand grew for more copies.

Clive came back to the section day room where we were all cleaning cameras and loading film for the morning. He was clutching a box.

Clive said, 'I found these under the floorboards.'

He put the box on the table and opened it. Inside were about thirty or forty glass negatives and their contact prints. They were all portraits of a plumpish girl with no clothes on sitting on our office Windsor chair, her legs immodestly arranged.

The lads whooped and wolf whistled and settled into the traditional services method of looking at rude photographs. The owner or custodian sat in a chair and the others sat on the floor round him. The owner counted the pictures out one by one and counted them back.

We grabbed the pictures eagerly and went, 'COR!' but not for long. The trouble was that nothing happened in the photographs, just a tubby girl slumped in a chair; missing was the usual lean, dark-haired gentleman wearing only shoes, socks and sock-suspenders who usually provided some action. The sergeant's pictures of the same girl became a bit boring after the initial excitement and there were too many of them.

Then somebody said, 'I know her! She's that WAAF who doles out the breakfast porridge! You know – Spotty Dotty!'

'So it is!' somebody else said. 'Well, well. Spotty Dotty! Should be Spotty Botty.'

Horseplay ensued, during which Clive carefully slid the photographs back into their box and took them back to their hiding place under the darkroom floor.

One of the great parental warnings in those days, meant to terrify – and a great favourite with my mother – was, 'Carry on the way you're going and you'll end up in the *News of the World*.' Which is just what happened to our sergeant. A year after I was demobbed, Clive sent me a cutting from the *News of the World*. RAF SERGEANT IN NUDE WAAF PHOTO SCANDAL rang out the headline. It seems that our sergeant had become careless in pursuing his little hobby and had been shopped by the aunt of one of his WAAF sitters. The WAAF was so pleased with her portrait, which from the neck up made her faintly resemble Betty Grable, that she took it home and rather carelessly left it on the sideboard where it was spotted by her aunt. The sergeant was successfully prosecuted. Thus, it could be said, does retribution eventually overtake the ungodly hobbyist.

Over on the far side of Ringway's airfield, almost hidden amongst trees, stood a large Edwardian house. This was where the men and women of Special Operations, the SOE, the saboteurs, wireless operators, regional organizers and so on lived for a few days while they took a brief intensive course in parachuting by night. They were not allowed to come near the NAAFI or the camp cinema or the rest of us. Nobody saw them arrive or train or jump or depart.

In charge of this operation was a Major Edwards (most of the army men I came up against during the war seemed to have been named Major Edwards, e.g., the army surgeon in Reykjavik).

This latest Major Edwards had a profitable sideline in civilian life writing a form of popular song known as the 'novelty foxtrot'. I was told he wrote the hugely successful novelty foxtrot of the Thirties, 'All By Yourself in the Moonlight'. I can still remember the melody but not the words, which is probably just as well.

The unit's second-in-command was Captain Dalton. My connection with the group was acting as their photographer when they needed one, e.g., taking identity photographs for their forged passports. I was lent an album of continental mugshots to study so that I could reproduce the slight differences in lighting, the way the subjects sat, how they arranged their faces (they tended to be more po-faced than the Allies), and so on. And, most impressively, I was given a box of real continental photographic paper to print the mugshots on.

Almost exactly fifty years later, in autumn 1994, I was ambling across the *place* in Monticello, a hill village in Corsica of which more later, when an Englishman and his wife came out of the small hotel and he waved at me and called me by name (actually he called out 'Lofty!'). The Englishman was Captain Dalton of the special agent section on the other side of the airfield at RAF Ringway.

We stood and had a good long natter – long nattering was normal in Monticello; it could take an hour to cross the 50 metres of *place* if you met somebody – and our nattering about those colourful special-agent days at Ringway produced the riveting information that Captain Dalton's son was the actor, Timothy Dalton, who had recently played James Bond, Special Agent 007, on our silver screens. A happy coincidence which rounded off rather neatly my memories of RAF Ringway. Except for just one more happening.

The general atmosphere in the forces at that time was not jolly. It was like a heavy industry awaiting takeover and bracing itself for huge redundancies. The Arnhem drop was over, VE and VJ day had come and gone, and the large number of air-men and back-up ground staff who had been fed (and well fed, on the whole) would soon have to feed themselves, and find themselves a job. Being demobbed, once so eagerly looked forward to, was being viewed with increasing apprehension by many of the younger servicemen now it was about to happen.

One result was the proliferation of little training courses which the authorities set up to help ease the problem. Anybody who had been a teacher in civvy street was asked to arrange a course in any subject he was capable of teaching, or incapable but interested in. There were courses all over the place in everything from whippet management to operatic singing.

At Ringway, where I and everybody else was waiting to be posted or demobbed or something, a course was started in practical geography, which turned out to be map-reading. The instructor was an elderly retired photographic intelligence officer and he was deeply bad news; a real pill, arrogant, sarcastic, humourless and pompous. Most of our section joined his class because it was vaguely to do with photography and got us off a morning parade, but we suffered for it in being humiliated and patronized and demoralized by this dreadful man.

Ironically, he was extremely good at his job. He really could read a map like a newspaper and could pinpoint an aerial photograph more swiftly and accurately than anybody else in the RAF. We knew this because he told us so. Miserably, he was probably right. He offered a £5 note (in those days a huge crisp white document which had to be unfolded) to any of us who could show him an aerial photograph taken within a 10-mile radius of Ringway which he could not identify on an Ordnance Survey map within an hour.

One of our section produced a 5 x 5 inch print of a piece of woodland near Wilmslow and the flight lieutenant had his finger on it on the map in about thirty seconds.

I think it might well have been A/C 1 Clive Cook, later a freelance journalist, who devised a devilish scheme of revenge. Suffice it to say we gave the flight lieutenant a 5 x 5 aerial print to pinpoint. Minute after minute went by as he repeatedly peered from photograph to map and back again. When the class came to an end he grabbed the map and the print and strode out without a word.

News reached us that the flight lieutenant had become obsessed with our challenge, and even during meals in the mess would sit there with a small magnifying glass, trying to match the rivulets and coppices on the photograph with features on the map.

And then I was suddenly posted off to RAF Henlow to spend my last months before being demobbed.

Arriving at a new station is a tedious business as everything is unfamiliar and you don't know who anybody is or where to find them and you have left all your friends behind you so you have nobody to moan to. But I was fortified in spirit during that difficult period by the knowledge that, back at RAF Ringway, the frightful flight lieutenant was trying very hard indeed to plot on an Ordnance Survey map a 5 x 5 photographic enlargement of a square inch of Spotty Dotty's pudenda.

Chapter 6

'HEIGH-HO! HEIGH-HO! IT'S OFF
TO WORK WE GO'

The beginning of my career as a professional writer was a heady moment at RAF Henlow when I first received money for a script instead of a pat on the back and a spam fritter in the NAAFI.

The year was 1945; the war was over and demobilization was the only thing that seemed to matter; there was little serious parachuting photography going on at Henlow and that work was done by two experts. One was a small hypochondriacal sergeant – when he had to drive me to RAF Farnborough in his own car he brought along gauntlets for us both to wear, cough sweets to suck, a rug to go over our knees, and he had cut and fitted domestic patterned carpet to prevent killer draughts from rising through the floor and giving our legs bronchitis.

His colleague was a vast, elderly, white-maned and duffle-coated ex-army man named Major Court-Treatt. The major, brother-in-law of the great W. O. Bentley who designed the early classic Bentley cars, had returned to Britain from being a cinematographer in Hollywood to do his bit for the war effort and seemed happy to stand for hours on a Henlow runway in ferocious weather which would have carried off the delicate sergeant, patiently operating a highly technical 35mm Newman-Sinclair cine-camera on a tripod.

As once again there was little official photography work for me to do, I looked about to see what was going on in the way of station entertainment. I did not have to look far. One of the first people I bumped into at Henlow was my old entertainments mentor from RAF Warmwell, Flight Lieutenant Arthur

Howard. Arthur had been posted from Warmwell to Cairo, where he said he had found a much more interesting young protégé than me to help on his way, a young airman who was determined to become a straight actor. Arthur said that he was a very promising young actor indeed. At this point the hairy hand of coincidence touched us.

Arthur said, 'His name's Richard Gale.'

He was my cousin.

Richard did become a professional actor and a good one, but later, when he was married and had every hope of a decent career ahead of him, he was taken ill and died appallingly young.

Arthur was determined to put on a sophisticated revue at RAF Henlow, I think mainly because he had a close friend, Derek Waterlow, who wrote brilliantly clever and tuneful revue songs.

This immediately post-war era saw the rise of the 'intimate' or 'little' revues; they provided the kind of charming musical numbers and 'camp' humour which the public seemed to enjoy after years of more basic entertainment.

The big success in London at that time was Alan Melville's witty revue *Sweet and Low* with Hermione Gingold, followed in due course by *Sweeter and Lower* and *Sweetest and Lowest*. I saw *Sweet and Low* and, inspired, wrote Miss Gingold a deftly grotesque monologue. Brimming with quiet confidence, I sent it to Miss Gingold. She sent it back.

I toiled and produced the book of the revue which Arthur so wanted. I was quite pleased with one sketch, a proposal of marriage that might have been written by August Strindberg, Beatrix Potter and Noel Coward. I played the part of the chap in the three playlets and the girl was played – beautifully – by our best actress at Henlow, LACW Gabrielle Hamilton.

The camp's verdict on the revue was that it was not at all that bad but, on the whole, not much good. One trouble was that our amateur actors, including me, were just not up to that kind of delicate playing, moreover most of the sketches were much too flimsy for the taste of our service audiences, which was still for more boisterous comedy.

Flight Lieutenant Arthur Howard departed to civvy street to

resume his acting career, ENSA shows came and went, and then another impresario set about producing the sort of show that Henlow audiences really wanted. His name was A/C Dave Aylott, a large, gentle man who, pre-call-up, had been a make-up artist at MGM Film Studios, Elstree. After demob, Dave started a firm called Eyelure, which made and marketed false eyelashes with great success.

Dave's closest friend and aide at Henlow was an airman named Charlie, who used an unlikely chat-up routine on his partners at NAAFI dances. As they waltzed dreamily to 'Who's Taking You Home Tonight?' Charlie would murmur to the girl that he was now fully recovered from an early bout of VD which had left him impotent. Charlie's conquests were a Henlow legend.

Dave's idea for the new show was breathtakingly ambitious; he wanted to build an authentic old time music hall auditorium inside one of the empty hangars, serving beer throughout the performance and a cold supper in the interval (supper to be included in the price of admission, which was 1s. 6d.), with a proper stage and scenery, flanked by boxes filled with Victorian roisterers.

And Dave Aylott succeeded. One key to success was that hundreds of ex-civilians waiting to be demobbed and with nothing much to do had in their midst useful talents and experience which Dave could put to work. For instance, in charge of all aspects of scenery was Corporal Johnny Russell, a month or two short of returning to his old civvy job of being one of Jack Hylton's production directors. Dave's house manager was A/C Ben Arbeid, whose ambition was to be a film producer, which he later became. Warrant Officer Parsons assembled and rapidly trained a full-sized pit orchestra. The dances were arranged by an excellent comic in the Danny Kaye mould, who had a splendid bass-baritone singing voice. He also had huge feet but was, oddly, an excellent dancer. He was LAC Alfred Marks ('Alfredo' in the programme). I sorted out the songs and put together the continuity and Dave gave me a thump on the back and bought me a spam fritter in the NAAFI. Best of all, Dave's connection with Elstree film studios resulted in them lending us lorryloads of props, plaster pillars and other assorted scenery.

Four or five of us took turns at the table to be chairman. This was necessary because controlling a hangar full of happy, yelling, beer-primed airmen and women played havoc with the vocal cords, and I was also singing some of the songs on stage (I was the Great Gus Herbert).

I recently found the menu for the cold supper served during the interval. For 1s. 6d. the punter not only enjoyed the show but also: 'Assorted Cold Meats. Sliced Beetroot' (was I never to escape it?) 'Vegetable mayonnaise. Cold Baked Beans. Bridge Rolls – Biscuits and Cheese, French Cakes and Pastries. Sausage Rolls – Minerals 6d. Best Beer 1s.'

No wonder we ran for two weeks (an enormous run for a camp show) and were packed out every night.

The show's success attracted some enjoyable publicity. Terry Ashwood came down and filmed Alfred Marks doing his 'Alfredo' act for showing in cinemas as an item in *Pathé Pictorial*, culminating in a colour spread and story in the weekly magazine *Illustrated*. The story was written by a young journalist soon to be snapped up by the BBC as a cricket commentator, Brian Johnston.

Encouraged by all this, I read in an evening paper that an agency for hopeful radio comedy writers had been set up by Ted Kavanagh, a pear-shaped New Zealander who was the founding father of professional British scriptwriting. He wrote the great wartime radio comedy *ITMA* and became as famous and respected as the show's star, Tommy Handley.

Ted gave the calling of scriptwriter some prestige and dignity. Before Ted Kavanagh, scriptwriting was a somewhat nondescript occupation and comedy writers were often a touch furtive. Ted Ray told me that when he was playing the London Palladium, a small cabby in a raincoat used to sidle into his dressing room regularly with foolscap pages of jokes, most of which were topical, witty and thoroughly usable. Ted accepted them and then had the greatest difficulty in getting the writer to accept any sort of realistic payment. Eventually the cabby accepted 5s. per foolscap page; less than a shilling a joke.

I sent some samples of sketches and bits to Ted Kavanagh Associates and Ted replied in person accepting me as a client of the agency and giving me my first job, to write a six-minute radio script for a clarinet player who wanted to be a comic (in those days almost everybody seemed to want to give up what they did well and be a comic). I worked hard on the clarinet player's script and sent it in.

A few days later a letter arrived from Ted Kavanagh saying that the clarinet player had changed his mind about being a comic and had been persuaded by his wife to join his father-in-law as a French polisher. Enclosed was a cheque for £20 in payment, which I later learned was Ted's own money.

Pre-Ted Kavanagh and *ITMA*, and indeed for some time after, scriptwriters simply did not exist in the public mind. A year or so later I was driving home after watching a radio show, *Monday Night at Eight*, for which I had written a routine for Jimmy Edwards. During rehearsal Jimmy played a funny piece on the trombone and Geraldo, the great band leader, said words to Jimmy which etched themselves on my memory:

'Jim,' he said (nobody called Jimmy 'Jim' in those days except Geraldo), 'Jim, you're playing much more betterer.'

I was driving home after the show when I was gonged by a police car (I was driving at about 31 m.p.h.). I apologized to the officers for my dangerous turn of speed and explained that I was driving home with my mind rather occupied with how well the script I had written had worked on the air.

The two police officers were stunned. 'What do you mean – script?' one said. 'Don't they make it up as they go along?'

To avoid them turning ugly and arresting me, I said I would send them tickets to a performance of *Monday Night at Eight* so that they could see for themselves. They turned up on the night, unmistakable in their huge boots and identical mackintoshes, and afterwards, having seen the performers reading everything off their scripts, were a little like two elderly children who had discovered that there was no Father Christmas but were not going to show their bitter disillusionment.

The first time I worked for the BBC was in 1947, as a performer on television rather than as a writer. I was demobbed by then and had collected my chalk-striped grey flannel suit – not all that bad a fit – a pork-pie hat made of stiffish cardboard and a gratuity of £40. All were most welcome.

The television job was compèring a revue celebrating the BBC's twenty-fifth anniversary. It starred Claude Hulbert and, according to the front of the script, a leading comedian from the Players Theatre, Olive Dunn. 'Olive' turned out to be a misprint of 'Clive'.

Before the war, the BBC led the world in providing a public television service, but the war put a stop to it. The corporation was keen to get the pieces together and open up a TV service again, which it did in 1946 with magazine programmes, much music, lots of news and one or two variety shows.

The receiving sets in use were like huge veneered filing cabinets with a little screen in front the size of a birthday card. It was a limited service because it could only be satisfactorily received in the London area. A television executive told me that in the first few months television was only received by about 200 wireless dealers and, inexplicably, the late Queen Mary.

The studios were at Alexandra Palace in North London, a huge building in a large public park which had never quite worked successfully in any activity it had been put to. But BBC TV now had a centre and the transmission masts worked well because of the park's high location.

Not that the BBC's bit of Ally Pally was all that suitable for conversion to studios. The rooms were too small and a drama production which would normally have required a large studio had to be split between two small studios. It was quite usual to be ambling peaceably along the corridor towards the bar and suddenly have to squash flat against the wall as a fully armed centurion and his cohort belted out of Studio 1 and clattered past, jangling and sweating, to their next scene in Studio 2.

It was relatively easy in those days to get some kind of booking on BBC TV if you had anything at all to offer. The BBC's system of auditioning was comprehensive and generous, and almost anybody demobbed from the services who had done some troop shows could get a chance to show the BBC what they were worth. Most of these hopefuls were more extrovert than gifted and soon dropped out of show business, but some are happily still with us – the golden oldies of broadcast comedy.

Television auditions were managed by the splendid Mary Cook and took place in rooms off the Tottenham Court Road above the Theosophical Society. Mary Cook not only coped with new talent when it applied to the BBC but also looked for it, in that she provided a supply of volunteer singers and comedians for a services canteen in the old Café de Paris nightclub. Her brilliant method of attracting talent for her shows was to supply performers with an enormous tray of marvellous free sandwiches; gourmet delights unobtainable elsewhere such as lettuce and shrimp paste or blue cheese and banana. The attraction of Mary Cook's sandwiches should not be underestimated in any serious social history of this period of television.

Most of my colleagues were like me, hopeful writers, or performers or writer/performers, without a spare twopence between us, constantly bumping into each other in our search for eateries where food was just a little bit cheaper. For instance, word went round that sandwiches in The Black and White Milk Bar in Leicester Square were a halfpenny cheaper than elsewhere because they were spread with cream cheese instead of butter, and all BBC canteens were cheap and good if we could avoid being thrown out – we had no real right to be in them in the first place.

Mary Cook offered us not only endless and delicious sandwiches and the experience of performing at the Café de Paris, but if we were any good the chance of a BBC TV audition above the Theosophical Society.

I had my audition. I traced the gifted Gabrielle Hamilton; she joined me, and for our audition piece we played my showy, three-part 'Engagement' sketch from the RAF Henlow revue.

They booked Gabrielle.

But all was not lost. The BBC's twenty-fifth anniversary revue came up, and as it seemed to its TV producer to be the sort of show I could probably cope with, and I was cheap, I was offered the job. Then followed an offer to compère a Saturday afternoon telly series set up to display the talents of the best of the new performers sieved out by Mary Cook's auditions. The series was called *New to You*.

Among the young stars-to-be I introduced on *New to You*,

making their first television appearance, were Norman Wisdom (achingly funny; fifty years ago his falls were, naturally, that bit crisper and more startling) and Ian Carmichael, who did a delightful song and dance à la Jack Buchanan in full white tie and tails.

The enjoyable thing about working on television in those days was that it was very intimate and nervy. A satisfactory method of recording programmes was not to be invented for many more years, and until then TV was gloriously 'live' and dangerous. But not frightening. When a camera broke down, a frequent occurrence, viewers were immediately on your side. I used to chat to them and say things like, 'You're no doubt wondering why Ian Carmichael has just disappeared in his best clothes. It's because we are experiencing one of those famous BBC events known as a "technical hitch" and you are very privileged to be in the middle of one. Mr Carmichael will be back again very soon unless you see two men turn up in white coats and attack the camera with screwdrivers. This means that its boiler has gone out or something and we're in trouble.'

Two men frequently did turn up and take off the top of the camera. This meant a long delay, so I would advise viewers to put the kettle on and my place in front of the one still-functioning camera would be taken by a tank of goldfish wheeled in on a trolley.

I did find danger in another aspect of early post-war television: the make-up. Before the war it had been hideous and unnatural, greens and greys because of the odd colour sensitivities of the early cameras, but by the time I joined the colours were fairly normal, just rather unnaturally bright, like the make-up of the soubrette in an end-of-pier concert party: pink face, scarlet lipstick in a cupid's bow shape, blue eyeshadow, carmine dots at the corners of the eyes (what on earth were they for?).

One Saturday, after presenting *New to You*, I was due to go to a party with friends in the beautifully named old Essex town, Theydon Bois – pronounced 'Theydon Boys'.

It was one of those shows when cameras fused one after the other and the goldfish cavorted heroically and everything ran very late. So when I was finally allowed to go I didn't waste time taking off my make-up but rushed down to my open sports car and roared off. At Ilford I realized I was lost, so I cruised up to a policeman and stopped the car.

'What can I do for you, sir?' he said amiably.

'I'm looking for Theydon Bois,' I said.

The officer gazed at me steadily for a moment and then said, 'Well, you won't find any round here, ducky.'

The finale of my first fine flourish as a pioneer telly performer came soon after the conclusion of the run of *New to You*. The show's producer was the veteran Bill Ward, one of the world's first ever television producers, who asked me if I could think hard and come up with some sort of original solo act which I could perform in a show he was lining up. I told him, with that mindless confidence of the young which is so infuriating to the no longer young, that it would present no problem.

I then forgot about it because my mind was busy on other important tasks like devising a style and writing the trial script for a semi-known, nightclub band leader who wanted to be a comic, and doing something about the exhaust system of my car, which had fallen off at Dalston Junction.

I came to with a jerk when a letter arrived from Bill asking me whether I had any special production requirements as the show was three days away. I rang back and said I hadn't and that I was a bit tired from rehearsing my act but was eagerly looking forward to the show.

After about ten minutes of deep thought I went on a tour of the junk and bric-a-brac shops along Leyton High Street and bought odd-looking, incomplete and broken pieces of pottery, china statues and vases, in fact any lump of something which did not clearly look like anything specific. I also bought a porcelain paperknife in the shape of an Indian army cutlass, and an ancient lace doily, partially torn.

My plan for the act was to display my rubbish to viewers as exceedingly rare and ancient artefacts of enormous value. Staring unblinkingly at the camera as lecturers did in those days, I would talk about the museum treasures and hold them up to view, and then as I fumbled about I would drop them on the floor or knock them over and eventually destroy the whole tableful. As it was obviously an act impossible to rehearse, I put all my rare bits into a carrier bag ready for the show and went to the pictures.

I thought up what I was going to say on the way to Ally Pally in the BBC's free green minibus service from Broadcasting House and formulated the significance of my items. For instance: the old and torn Victorian cake doily was a religious Tibetan prayer shawl crocheted by nuns from the softest wool tweaked by priests from the armpits of young albino goats found only in the Himalayan village of Pawa. They were exceedingly rare. The tall thin vinegar bottle (cracked, from a boarding-house cruet) was an Aztec tear vase used by Incas to collect their weepings after losing a religious battle. The tears inside the vase (Stephen's blue-black ink) traditionally went dark with age, and the present fluid was believed by British Museum carbon-dating experts to be about 1,204 years old.

The idea of the act was that I would begin by expatiating first on the history of the doily/prayer shawl and its rarity and value. I would then put it down carefully, without looking, on the table. Then I would start talking about the vinegar bottle/tear vase, and, in reaching for it, accidentally knock it over. As the ink flowed over the table I would grope around, still talking straight to camera, pick up the priceless Tibetan prayer shawl and mop up the blue-black ink with it, finally dropping the soiled fabric onto the floor like a spent Kleenex. And so on. I would end with just the porcelain paperknife and a large blue china vase which once held stem ginger (rare Transylvanian burial urn). Then came the really difficult bit. Without taking my eyes off the camera lens I had to position the paperknife so that it was balanced on the near edge of the desk, half on the desk and half off it. Then on the far end of the paperknife I had to casually position the ginger jar/burial urn.

'. . . and so', I would say, 'my time is up. I only hope that I have not only given you some pleasure, but that I have struck a BLOW – for the cultures of the past.'

On the word 'BLOW' I would bring my fist down heavily in a gesture. It would strike the protruding end of the paperknife, and the vase resting on its other end would shoot high into the air, disappear over the top of the scenery and be heard smashing to bits against the studio wall.

And it all happened beautifully on the live broadcast. At the end the table was bare and bits of broken crockery and glass were everywhere. I still think that on screen the act *sort* of worked.

One of the good things about people who work in television is that when you have done something which was a bit of a disaster, they do not rub salt in. They do not come up and say, 'Did you really think that was going to be funny?' They do not say anything. They just try not to meet your eye.

I negotiated the dangerous corridor to the bar without being trodden on, but when I reached the bar, which was busy after the show, I knew how well the sketch had gone down because nobody at all spoke to me, or even looked my way.

I suddenly felt my elbow gripped. 'Well done!' It was the nice Bill Ward, speaking quietly. 'Bit ahead of its time, that's all.'

Something like twenty years later, Bill Ward was setting up a BBC TV commemorative show at Lime Grove Studios and he asked me to perform my lecture on antiquarian artefacts once more. Understandably excited by this, I stocked up with another carrier bag of assorted broken rubbish from along the Shepherd's Bush Road and devised colourful provenances for them.

The lecture went off without a hitch. The china bits broke on cue and at the end the vase went sailing up and over the scenery like a kamikaze owl. As I was picking up my shards after the show, nice Bill Ward came down to the floor. He gripped my elbow. 'Still a great sketch, Frank. Lovely. Well done!' he said, and looked away. 'A little ahead of its time, that's all.'

With a wisdom beyond my years, I realized that my chances were slim of earning enough money from performing comedy on television to live comfortably and buy a younger car with treads on the tyres, and I made the decision to concentrate on being a radio writer. Not that I was one yet, but I had at least had a tiny whiff of that side of the game.

My first professional experience of writing radio comedy to suit an established comedian happened at RAF Henlow when I went to an ENSA concert starring a conjuror turned comedian named Peter Waring.

It was said that ENSA stood for 'Every Night Something Awful', but ENSA shows were put on with professional entertainers and actors and many were excellent. I think that (sometimes) it was a demi-semi-affectionate jibe, rather as the NAAFI was described as 'where you can eat dirt cheap'.

I was attracted by Peter Waring's style of humour, which was cool, deft and witty, quite different from the robust material of the usual stand-up comic of those (and these) days. Waring was one of the new 'class' acts, a slim, good-looking thirty-something, with the shiny, slightly wavy black hair then much admired, a good dinner jacket and a cork-tipped cigarette, which he held a little awkwardly because of a badly wounded right arm.

ENSA's programme notes explained that Peter Waring's real name was Commander Peter Roderick-Mainwaring DSO RN, and that he had been invalided out of the Navy after an enemy shell had smashed his right arm in a naval action on the Murmansk convoy run. As it happened, Peter Waring was in need of a scriptwriter. He was getting some radio work and each broadcast needed something like eight minutes of new material.

Most music-hall comedians began by writing their own scripts, or more usually remembering, pinching and adapting jokes from other comedians. When starting out in the game this one act would do them for a long while in the music halls, or, like Peter Waring when I first met him, performing mainly on a live circuit of hunt balls, company dinners and deb dances. Radio was another matter. Every performance needed a fresh script, and as this effort was beyond the range of most comics, the need for professional comedy scriptwriters came into focus.

I found Peter Waring's style fairly easy to pick up. I wrote a sample radio script for him which he liked and accepted thankfully. He was reluctant to part with any money for it to a uniformed airman, but I now had the Ted Kavanagh Associates agency to collect my fee, and so at last I lost my writing virginity, as it were, and became a money-earning pro.

Radio immediately after the war was a growth industry for comedians and writers. The Forces Programme – later called the Light Programme and now, I suppose, the cheerful end of Radio 4 – was stiff with variety shows such as *Music Hall*, *Workers' Playtime*, *Calling All Forces*, *Variety Bandbox* and *Garrison Theatre*, which used not only a star comic but also one or more newcomers who were given shorter spots earlier in the show. So short sometimes that the Australian comedian Bill Kerr, who later joined the Tony Hancock team in *Hancock's Half-Hour* and then went home and became a fine character actor in Australian films, began his radio act by announcing lugubriously, 'I've only got four minutes . . .'

One of the happiest of the smaller shows was a confection named *Caribbean Carnival*, a joy to all writers and performers as almost nobody heard it so the material could be used again elsewhere. The show was produced in the best of the BBC's audience studios, the Paris Cinema, in front of a mostly silent audience of Caribbeans and OAPs, but Edmundo Ros and his band played cheerfully and singers sang calypsos in between the comedy acts and the show had a happy air.

It seems that the programme was beamed solely to the Caribbean and so could not be heard distinctly by any other far-flung listeners. Moreover, according to legend, the broadcasts did not even arrive in the Caribbean, the signal weakened on its way like the light from a torch growing dimmer, and it finally expired completely just west of the Azores.

There was a lot of BBC radio work to be had in those days but not a lot of money. Unlike the present day, writing for radio in the 1940s provided bread and butter and occasionally jam, but not cake.

The usual fee offered to a new comic for a six- or eight-minute spot was £10 and he almost certainly had to buy a script which would have cost him his £10. So how did the economics work?

The answer lay in song. In those days it was the custom for a comic to end his act by singing the verse of a popular song of the day such as, perhaps, 'All By Yourself in the Moonlight' or 'Ever So Goosey'.

Some old time music-hall double-acts found this new discipline difficult to adjust to; it did not fit comfortably into the way they had worked all their lives. A comic often did not learn his stage act in a word-perfect way nor read his script for radio as written, but left it to his straight man to prompt him along, which gave the performance a more impromptu feeling.

Radio producers met the problem by flashing a green light to the comical duo when it was time for them to end their patter and go into their finishing song. So post-war listeners became used to comedy acts finishing like this:

STRAIGHT MAN:	You were telling me about your mother-in-law.
COMIC:	What about her?
STRAIGHT MAN:	Isn't she fat?
COMIC:	Fat?
STRAIGHT MAN:	Yes, fat.
COMIC:	(*light shining*) Did I ever tell you about my fat mother-in-law?
STRAIGHT MAN:	(*amazed*) You've got a fat mother-in-law?
COMIC:	My mother-in-law, she's that fat — when she sits on a bar stool it's like batter spreading.

(*possibly some laughter*)

STRAIGHT MAN:	How's your dog?
COMIC:	'E's a funny dog is my dog. Do you know 'e doesn't eat meat?
STRAIGHT MAN:	Your dog doesn't eat meat! Why doesn't your dog eat meat?
COMIC:	I don't give 'im any!

(*perhaps a little more laughter*)

COMIC:	'Ere, I'll tell you another funny thing about my dog, he can play 'Star Spangled Banner' on the piano-accordion. All you do is give 'im a kick in the . . .
	(*a green light starts flashing urgently*)

STRAIGHT MAN:	(*ruthlessly cutting in*) Well, it's certainly a funny old world we live in, but as a wise man once said . . .
	(*a note is struck on the piano and both sing romantically, in creditable harmony*):
	Red sails in the sunset,
	Way out on the sea,
	Oh, bring back my loved one,
	Home safely to me . . .

Music publishers, most of the smaller ones located in Denmark Street, London's Tin Pan Alley, encouraged comics to sing the song they were currently trying to make into a hit by employing song-pluggers. These were personable young men whose job was to persuade the BBC producer of the show to feature the song, or to pay the comic to sing it.

A typical successful song-plugger was young Bill Cotton, partner with Johnny Johnson of a small music publishing firm in Denmark Street. Young Bill was called 'Young' to differentiate him from his father, the veteran band leader (and racing motorist) Billy Cotton.

Young Bill was good at plugging songs because he was gregarious, cheerful and an irrepressible teller of stories and so was welcome as a ray of sunshine in most of the dark offices of the BBC Variety Department at Aeolian Hall, New Bond Street. Bill's style was to play the record and if the producer was not impressed, say something like, 'Yes, it *is* a bit of a bugger, isn't it? Never mind, I'll drop in tomorrow morning with a ballad. You'll like it.'

Young Bill moved onwards and upwards to become a television producer, then BBC TV's Head of Variety and eventually Managing Director of BBC Television. A nice man and very good company.

So the comic had his original BBC fee of £10 and now had another £10 from the song-plugger, 'plug money', to buy himself a script. And in those days a young writer like me with few financial responsibilities could exist on writing two or three such scripts a week.

The hope of a writer was then to make himself so indispensable to his up-and-coming comic that if and when his comic was given his own series by the BBC, he would want his own writer to write it. Which is what I had well in mind when, lately retired from the complicated new world of television, I discovered that Peter Waring, my first, indeed only client for my scripts so far, was now doing his conjuring/comic act at the Windmill Theatre.

Peter gave me an enthusiastic welcome in his dressing room, not because he had missed me personally but because he was beginning to get a diaryful of guest appearances on radio and was in desperate need of a writer who was familiar with his style and was available and cheap.

I think that, inexperienced though I was, I was able to help Peter Waring quite a bit during the following year. In those days, scriptwriters thought of themselves as comedian's labourers. They tended to be writers who had little they wanted to say but were skilful in how to say things, and their concern was to build up those aspects of comedy for which their lad had some talent and to obscure his deficiencies.

I managed to wean Waring off the bits of conjuring in his stage act, which were really only a kind of crutch for use when the laughs were not coming. The trouble was it was not real conjuring, just the operating of simple tricks bought from the joke shop that used to be on the corner of Old Compton Street and Wardour Street in Soho. His main illusions were the egg-in-the-bag trick (a china egg and a black velvet bag covered with invisible pockets) and the magic cube (a boring box which the magician looked through at the audience to show it was empty and then from it produced a series of tatty cardboard dice).

He liked to conclude with a comical monologue, which was no problem, but then he would sign off with a benediction to the audience which I loathed but to which he was attached. He would smile his charming sexy smile, hold up his wounded hand over the audience like an army bishop and say, 'Good night, good luck (and then quietly and with deeply bogus sincerity) – *God bless.*'

After a few months of being a guest comic on other people's

programmes, his fresh, upper-classy style grew in the affection of post-war listeners and Peter Waring suddenly became a hot property. The BBC offered him his own comedy radio series, and he asked me to write it.

So I worried out of the typewriter (the same old rattler) the trial programme for what is now known as a situation comedy, which I called *Heigh-Ho!*, with the subtitle *It's Off to Work We Go*. The idea was topical: a demobbed naval commander (Peter Waring) tries to get a job, not helped much by his uncle (Kenneth Horne) or his girlfriend (Charmian Innes). The series was to be produced by a youngish Scot, Charles Maxwell, who had come to the BBC from working across the Channel with Roy Plomley as a producer and announcer for the pioneer commercial radio station, Radio Luxembourg.

Each programme of the six would find our hero applying for, and failing to get, a different kind of job. And in the middle of the show Charmian Innes would sing a relevant original song (lyric by me – delivered to the composer by Tuesday morning at the latest, please).

The trial programme went on, light laughter occurred, and the show, with the three stars working well, showed enough promise for the BBC to commission a series of six. This was pleasant and gratifying. I had spent the dry run crouched at the back of the auditorium, panicking at the way things were happening so quickly.

From the riches I had earned during my late television career I had saved nearly £100 and I had lashed out and bought an open Singer Sports car of some age for £35. It was a bit slow for a sports car and tended to come apart. On rounding Trafalgar Square at a steady but exhilarating 15 m.p.h. one day the gear lever came away in my hand. Happily it was nine o'clock in the morning and there was hardly any traffic (ah, memories) and I was able to cruise safely to the side of the road and stop. I managed to fiddle the gear lever back into its hole and keep it there until I found a garage.

Like most old bangers of the period, the door catches had come adrift and driver and passenger were prevented from being pitched out onto the road on sharp corners by ordinary domestic brass bolts screwed to the doors. There was sometimes a bonus to this arrangement. When giving a lift to a girlfriend it was clearly one's duty to ensure her safety by reaching across her to check that the bolt on her door was safely home . . .

My old banger had now become a necessity because I was busy at all sorts of hours and I could just make my petrol ration last if I drove maddeningly slowly to and from the BBC in Bond Street, Peter Waring's place and 28 Church Road.

Peter Waring's house, which he rented, was a tiny mews cottage buried in the hinterland of West Kensington. He was looked after by Bill, a very un-Jeeves-like driver-cum-dresser-cum-drinks-pourer.

When I was in conference with Peter in the morning it was quite usual for a prettyish girl in a dressing gown to wander in from the shower, eyes still puffy from the previous night's vigorous pleasures, squeaking in a voice you could engrave glass with, 'Will you get Tom or whatever his name is to drive me to the station, Peter darling, I must get back to Cirencester before two o'clock or Mummy'll kill me.'

These *Country Life* one-night stands of his had expensive tastes, as indeed did he; he was always short of money and was amazed how little I (and my mother) could live on.

One day he said he was in a bit of trouble and could I lend him a few quid. I told him that I had £70 in the world and he was welcome to borrow £35 of it. He said it was only for a couple of weeks and he would return it with interest.

I found the first two or three scripts of *Heigh-Ho!* fairly easy to write and the songs not difficult, but then it all became progressively harder and daunting, I think because I was inexperienced and working alone. Being in a partnership halves the fees but it also halves the worries.

The day of the first transmission arrived. Rehearsals had gone well and Kenneth and Charmian were delightful to work with. Kenneth Horne was doing the show in between seasons of the hugely successful *Much-Binding-in-the-Marsh*. He was also the sales director of Triplex Glass. Kenneth was an immensely likeable man, the kindly old uncle, the decent officer, and he and Richard Murdoch brought to broadcast comedy an intelligent charm and insouciance which has never been equalled since; perhaps not even wanted nowadays.

They usually met and worked on the *Much-Binding* scripts over lunch in the RAC Club in Pall Mall, which was near Kenneth's Triplex office in St James's Street. Kenneth and Dickie would tiptoe respectfully into the vast morning room past snoozing members towards the magazines and reading matter arranged on a table. It was then Kenneth's pleasure to sprint past Dickie towards the table with a cheerful yell of, 'Bags I the *Port of London Authority Quarterly*!'

One of the standard devices used by comedy writers is the social introduction made funny by wordplay with names, for instance one which Denis Norden and I wrote for an early *Take It From Here*: a lackey announcing guests began with 'Sir Filthy and Lady Lucre!' One of my favourites from Dickie and Ken's *Much-Binding* was 'Mr and Mrs Sam Wanamaker Junior!'

Dickie Murdoch told me of a time when the two of them were trying to think up new announcements on their way to performing in a Sunday concert. They were deep in thought when Kenneth suddenly said, 'How about "Mr and Mrs Tittybelt and their son Chas?"'

Heigh-Ho! was broadcast from one of the minor studios rented by the BBC, formerly newsreel cinemas which showed only non-stop news and short cartoon films, highly popular with children on holiday and parents too early for trains. Our studio was the Monseigneur Cinema, one of two or three which the BBC leased in Oxford Street.

During the rehearsal in the Monseigneur on the afternoon of the first *Heigh-Ho!* broadcast, our producer Charles Maxwell was called to the phone. We waited for him and when he rejoined us a few minutes later he seemed a bit distracted. We decided that it was probably some small domestic problem and thought it best to carry on as normal.

That evening the performance went well. The show got its laughs and the audience seemed to like it, as did the critics in the next morning's papers. We all took it for granted that the BBC would want a second series and planned accordingly. But there were to be no more radio shows starring Peter Waring, or even with Peter Waring as a guest.

Charles Maxwell later told us the extraordinary truth. The

phone call he had received which interrupted rehearsals of the first *Heigh-Ho!* was from Pat Hilliard, then Head of the BBC Variety Department. He told Charles to go ahead with producing the six programmes of *Heigh-Ho!* because they were contracted, audience tickets had been issued and so on, but there were to be no more. Peter Waring was not to be employed again by the BBC.

It seems that Commander Peter Roderick-Mainwaring DSO RN had never existed. He was bogus, an identity which Peter Waring, in reality not a comedian but a small-time conman, had invented for himself. The Navy would never have recruited Waring because of his injured arm, which was not caused by an enemy shell but by a burn resulting from Waring leaning against a hot steam pipe on a pre-war cross-Channel ferry.

A few years previously Waring had worked as a clerk in a BBC office and had absconded with the cash box. In true BBC tradition he was not prosecuted in a splash of unwelcome publicity but discreetly sacked.

When awkward questions about his family arose he would quietly explain that his distinguished father, the admiral, and his dear mother, the pianist, had been killed in a car accident in Greece.

At the end of his radio series Peter Waring disappeared completely from public view, eventually surfacing at Blackpool months later in prison. Newspapers reported that he had been arrested on a charge of fraud.

He hanged himself in his cell.

My lasting memory of that charming, lightly talented, doomed petty crook who played such a part in my early career was him borrowing that £35 from me, half of all the money I had in the world, and promising to return it in a few weeks with interest.

Two weeks later he handed me back £50.

Chapter 7

TAKE IT FROM HERE,
Don't go away when you can
TAKE IT FROM HERE,
Why don't you stay and maybe
Join in the fun, now the show has begun.
Half an hour of laughter beckons,
Every minute packed with seconds . . .

After Peter Waring's second sacking by the BBC and miserable end, I returned to freelancing and found that useful small writing jobs were forthcoming from BBC producers I had worked with, especially Charles Maxwell. And through many visits to Peter Waring at the Windmill I was judged to be harmless by the Windmill Theatre's short but fierce ('They Shall Not Pass') stage-door keeper, and he allowed me to have a coffee in the canteen with the new comedians starting their careers at the theatre, one of whom I hoped would have a style which needed my sort of writing.

The Windmill was an extraordinary part of the theatrical scene; more than just another nude show, it grew in stature during the war to become a semi-cherished London institution.

The performances were continuous as in a cinema, five shows a day, featuring brand-new comedians, a small resident ballet, a singer or two and, of course, the famous nudes. Indeed, as far as the general (male) public was concerned the Windmill meant nudes and not much else, certainly the comics had a tough time trying to hold the audience's attention between the fleshly *scenae*.

It was the only theatre in London to keep open throughout the war and its proud slogan, 'We never closed', was immediately modified by wags to 'We never clothed'.

When I squeezed past the girls on the narrow staircase up to the canteen, they mostly wore bullet-proof tartan dressing gowns and hair curlers. The legend – put about by the management? – was that the nudes were really prim, middle-class girls, many of them daughters of the clergy, but I never met any of those. The girls I knew were much like any group of busy working girls, though prettier than most, and had the normally complicated private lives of pretty girls.

One luscious dancer was the resident nymphomaniac (if there is such a thing as a nympho she certainly *was* one) who was obsessed with the leading male dancer, and when he leaped on stage she would swoon with lust and slump to the floor, which was dramatically unhelpful and physically quite dangerous for the other dancers teetering about the tiny stage on their points. Sadly, no sexual liaison between her and her loved one was feasible, but many Windmill girls, in the Gaiety Theatre tradition, married admirers.

The Windmill was owned and run by a small neat man smoking a cigar, Vivien van Damm, known affectionately but unfortunately as V.D. He was tremendously important to hopeful comics and writers because his policy was to audition pretty well everybody who applied and then give any new and unknown talent he discovered a chance on his stage.

In Piccadilly one day I met a disconsolate Alfred Marks ('Alfredo' of the Henlow Music Hall). He was demobbed and could find no opening at all in show business so was going to try his luck in America. It was extremely difficult to get any kind of permit to work in America so a number of what seemed to me to be tricky deals had to be arranged through friends to acquire the papers. I begged Alfred, whom I knew, liked and admired as a performer, to have one last go over here and apply for an audition at the Windmill.

He went for an audition, V.D. booked him, and Alfred stayed as resident comedian at the Windmill for twenty months. This was the beginning of his fine career in theatre, television and radio.

Besides Alfred Marks, performers who began their career playing some kind of part in Windmill productions included Kenneth More (song and dance man), Bruce Forsyth, Jimmy Edwards, Michael Bentine (part of a double act, 'Sherwood and Forest'), Michael Howard, John Tilly, Peter Sellers, Eric Barker, Harry Secombe, Arthur English, and many others too humorous to mention.

All were only too happy to begin at the Windmill where they were lightly paid but, as Jimmy Edwards put it, were able to scratch a bare . . . living. The productions were not variety shows but complete revues in miniature called *Revuedeville*, devised and produced by V.D. and his team of a resident composer, lyric-writer, costume designer and choreographer. A new *Revuedeville* was staged every few months.

The Lord Chamberlain's Office ruled, surprisingly, that the girls could be completely naked so long as they did not move. So the high spots of the show for the punters, in fact the whole reason for the punters buying tickets in the first place, were the three or four production numbers based on themes like classic paintings brought to life, or vaguely religious medieval groupings, in practice any theme which could include a rigid nude pretending to be part of a stained-glass window, or a Greek slave standing in an alcove balancing a vase of paper lilies on her shoulder.

Rather sweetly, although modesty would seem inappropriate to the work, the girls (unlike Spotty Dotty) had a code of prudery. Although they had permission from the Lord Chamberlain to display their all in static attitudes, they were unkeen to expose to the punters their most private part. So when a girl had to assume a new pose, her colleagues would observe her in rehearsal from all parts of the small auditorium, stalls to balcony, to reassure her that her stance of one leg forward and knee bent, or whatever, did the trick and she was, as the girls called it, 'safe'.

When one performance finished, the lights came on and there was vigorous movement in the auditorium as those patrons who had seen enough, perhaps three performances, filed out and the queue outside surged in. Some of the regulars stayed behind to watch another performance and as they were scattered all over the auditorium, they pushed forward eagerly to occupy newly emptied, better-situated seats, preferably in the front row.

There are lines which can encapsulate a person or an event in a few words. I was once told a story, allegedly true, which demonstrates the point.

It seems that Ethel Merman, the strong-voiced and hugely successful American musical comedy star, retired to California where her pleasure was to take her best friend, a largish lady, to all the opening nights of comedians and singers in the cabarets of Los Angeles and around.

Miss Merman was a popular and recognizable star and when fans came to her table to pay their respects, her routine was to say to them all, 'Hi, sit down and have a drink.' One such admirer was a filthy-rich elderly Texan, with the big hat and thin tie and bits of silver all over him. He sat down and had a drink, in the course of which Miss Merman spotted, with interest, his cuff links, which were miniature pistols. 'They work,' he said, 'try one.'

He proffered his wrist. Miss Merman carefully took hold of one of the tiny pistols and pulled the trigger. There was a sharp 'crack', a little smoke and Miss Merman's best friend let out a loud yelp and clutched her large bosom. The wad of the blank cartridge had struck her painfully.

Miss Merman, who thought it was a live round, let out a shriek of anguish which, taking into account Miss Merman's formidable vocal chords, might well have put a wobble on all the roulette wheels within a square mile, and howled what is perhaps the definitive line expressing middle-aged Californian culture of the 1960s: 'Shit – I've just shot my best friend in the tit with a cuff link!'

The Windmill line is a lot less colourful but might in its own way indicate something about class and British nudity.

During the hurly-burly of audiences changing over at the Windmill, a slide came up on the screen reading: 'GENTLEMEN ARE REQUESTED NOT TO CLAMBER OVER THE SEATS.'

It's the word 'gentlemen' that does it.

In spite of the work insecurity, they were happy days for me. I drove home to Leyton every night, a fair old way in the

Singer Sports, tooting when I passed 28 Church Road to let my mother know that I was nearly home. She was always in bed by then but never went to sleep until I was back. I parked the car in the forecourt of a garage in the High Street.

Caribonum had always said that they would have a job for me when I was demobbed and I did some agonizing over whether I owed it to my mother to go back there and give her some financial security, but my mother would have none of it. I knew she deeply distrusted the entertainment world of which she knew nothing (I knew very little more), but she insisted that I had a go at what I wanted to do and if it came unstuck – well, I could try something else.

I had several fledgling writer and writer/performer colleagues similarly brimming with the same hopes and the same cheerful camouflaging of worries and we all got along well. I was never aware of any deep jealousies or bitter rivalries between any of us. Our main hang-out was Daddy Allen's Club, a modest, first-floor drinking club and restaurant above a shop in Great Windmill Street. It was a prime position because it overlooked Archer Street and the stage door of the Windmill.

Archer Street was the headquarters of the Musicians' Union and the street itself was a market place for instrumentalists look-ing for gigs. The way it worked was that orchestras had one member who was known as the 'fixer'. The fixer's function was to hire musicians when his orchestra needed them to augment the regulars, or to act as substitutes. He would know most of the lads chatting in the middle of the road and would pass among them offering, perhaps, 'Ted, guitar doubling trumpet? Bar mitzvah, Bournemouth, Thursday evening?' Or, 'Trombone? Pit orchestra at the Finsbury Park Empire. Charity concert, Sunday? Anybody?'

The club's proprietor, Daddy (or Papa) Allen, spoke with a thick nobbly foreign accent, perhaps Hungarian, but his pretty daughter had married an absurdly handsome RAF Spitfire pilot who helped serve in the bar when on leave and the family was becoming more British every day.

The club had a licence to serve drinks all afternoon, plus Jenny Bell, a plump and pretty young restaurant waitress with what Terry-Thomas described as 'knockers like vintage Bentley headlamps'. Those delights, together with roast lamb and two veg at 1s. 9d., were an irresistible combination to growing lads.

One could tell when somebody in the club was working at the theatre by a movement of the wrist known as the 'Windmill Twitch'. With five shows a day and several appearances in each show, a performer never had more than a few minutes completely free all day and was forever twitching his wrist over to check the time on his watch.

There was a sad illusionist whose task of frantically stuffing his feather flowers back into slits in his dinner jacket and folding his silk flags-of-all-nations and ramming them into pouches in his shirt took so long that he had only *just* finished when it was time for him to go back on stage and pull them all out again. He eventually suffered a comeover and, reluctantly, gave up the glitter and tinsel of show business.

Spike Milligan was an *habitué*. At the time he was playing the guitar and trumpet in a funny lugubrious musical act called the Bill Hall Trio. Spike found the showbiz at Daddy Allen's (and the delightful waitress) happily stimulating after surviving unpleasant war experiences in Italy and fourteen days in the army prison, Preston Barracks in Brighton, for not treating his rifle with enough love and respect. Even in those days Spike fizzed with original comedy ideas. In Daddy Allen's bar one wet afternoon, Spike said, 'We're in an audience in a theatre, full house, staring at the curtain. Fanfare. The curtain slowly rises. On the other side is another audience staring at *us*!'

Cripplingly expensive set to build just for one laugh, but no matter, plenty more ideas where that one came from.

And there was Terry-Thomas, escapee from the meat trade at Smithfield market and working as a singing impressionist at the Prince of Wales Theatre. In his act, set in a BBC studio, he played a DJ who has mislaid his records and in desperation has to sing them all himself.

Terry stood with me for almost the whole of one afternoon in the bar of Daddy Allen's clutching his half pint of bitter, at blood heat like everybody else's after being frugally nursed for two or three hours, and said to me with deep sincerity,

'I can create *anything* to the sound of Mexican music.'

And then, very shortly afterwards, a new young comic began work at the Windmill. He was a stout figure with a handlebar moustache and an educated voice. He came on stage lugging an empty beer crate in one hand and a large euphonium case in the other. He wore crumpled sponge-bag trousers with bicycle clips, morning coat, winged collar and gold pince-nez specs. He put down the beer crate and sat on it. Opening the huge euphonium case he took from it a small penny whistle and played a sprightly tune. He then said, 'Encore,' pushed the mouthpiece up a nostril and played the tune again. Then he tucked the penny whistle away in his top pocket and announced, 'The second encore has been banned.'

He was 'Professor' Jimmy Edwards. At our first meeting in the Windmill canteen, I realized that he was in need of a writer, and his seedy schoolmaster act on radio with its fake erudition was the sort of stuff I would enjoy writing. It was a key cup of coffee in both our lives. I became Jimmy's scriptwriter.

Jimmy began to get more radio guest spots. Pretending to be a schoolmaster taking a class was a useful formula and one with which the audience could immediately identify – they had all been to school and been shouted at. It was relatively easy stuff to write because the built-in setting meant that about a tenth of the script was more or less written.

For instance, Jimmy would begin with some vigorous schoolmasterly commonplaces like, 'All right, pay attention! Sit up straight! Don't fidget! That boy – you're chewing in class. Spit it out. NOT IN THE HAIR OF THE BOY IN FRONT OF YOU! Write out a thousand times, "I am a mindless pain in the sphincter and spotty with it." Now let's get on. Those of you able to read might have seen in the newspapers that the prime minister . . .'And then on to the topical jokes with the useful saver that if a joke flopped, Jimmy could cover up by bellowing, 'WAKE UP AT THE BACK THERE!'

Meanwhile, Charles Maxwell was about to produce the final series of a wartime show entitled *Navy Mixture*, so called because it was aimed at the Royal Navy. This targeting of a particular service seems a mite odd now but it made more sense during the war when a show like *Navy Mixture* would include items of specific interest to its own particular service. By the last years of the war the services each had their own series: the RAF had Dickie Murdoch's and Kenneth Horne's *Much-Binding-in-the-Marsh*, the Army had Charlie Chester's bright and breezy *Stand Easy*, the Merchant Navy had *Shipmates Ashore*, presented by Doris Hare, with lots of messages from sailors' families, and civilians had *ITMA*.

Then Dame Fate stepped in and set Jimmy Edwards on the road to a successful career, and, in a smaller way, me too.

Charles Maxwell decided to cast the last series of good old *Navy Mixture* with some new talent. He had already found a girl presenter, a singing and comedy girl freshly arrived from Australia, Joy Nichols, and he now needed a new funny man as resident comedian.

The previous series of *Navy Mixture* had been written by Eddie Maguire, a pleasant and helpful writer who was planning to take things easier and lead a country life. Through the producer's grapevine, Charles heard that there was a new comic at the Windmill, Jimmy Edwards, who seemed to have good potential for radio and should be looked at, so Charles asked Eddie to go and see Jimmy at work and report back.

It was at this point that Dame Fate started playing her tricks. She arranged for Eddie Maguire to shoot himself metaphorically in both feet (not that Eddie minded, he wanted to retire anyway).

The first shot Eddie misfired was when he went to the Windmill, sat through the comic's act and then reported to Charles that the act was no good. But he had watched the wrong comic.

The second shot, in the other foot, was his report on the comic he *had* seen. He told Charles that the act involved a razor and lots of lather, demonstrating how different men shaved differently, and ended with a bit of singing. Eddie found the act messy and the comedian not interesting. It was Harry Secombe.

So after due consideration – and things did get their due and proper consideration from Charles – he contracted Joy and Jimmy for the final series of *Navy Mixture*, and as he knew my work from *Heigh-Ho!* and I was now writing Jimmy's material, he contracted me to write the scripts.

So for a few months I was earning regularly what seemed to me a huge sum of money. The *Navy Mixture* script paid something like £35 a week. This sounds a skinny sum, but I recently rang the Bank of England information service and the good man there told me that the equivalent of £1 in 1946 is now £19.95p. So my £35 was equal to a present-day £694.75p per week.

The series was easy work, taking about three days writing a week; a fairly straight but chirpy continuity for Joy, a comic solo routine for Jimmy and some sort of sketch for the two of them. The show also had musical items, plus a bit of singing from Joy or a close-harmony group, and a guest comic.

The most successful guest comedian we had was a newly arrived, middle-aged Australian named Dick Bentley. On stage Dick did the popular stand-up act of playing a few bars of music rather badly on his violin and then stopping to tell a joke, but his radio routines were another matter; topical, self-deprecatory, crisp and witty.

Navy Mixture finished its long and honourable life and I was out of work again. But not for long. Ted Kavanagh Associates arranged for me to co-write with an experienced old hand of the game, Dick Pepper, a new and eventually long-running radio series for the American comedian Vic Oliver. It was given the dreadful title of *Oliver's Twists*.

Vic Oliver was (not that it did him much good) Winston Churchill's son-in-law. He had a mid-European-cum-American accent and in retrospect I do not think that I was a good choice as a supplier of comic material suitable for Mr Oliver. Most of my stuff seemed too English and local in allusion for him to understand, and he was clearly more comfortable with simpler comicalities. When he had read through my contribution for the first script of the show he laid it down for quite a while, rubbed his eyes and then explained patiently the kind of material which he preferred. As an example he told me a sure-fire gag which for years had never failed to cause audiences throughout the world to fall about with helpless laughter.

His humdinger went, 'When I sang in the church choir,

The older lad, who looks like a Swedish goalkeeper, is my brother Chas. I am the one clutching an unidentifiable lump of knitted wool and looking up expectantly for food, which I clearly do not need.

All mothers are beautiful and ours most certainly was.

Our happy family in the sunshine. This was taken at Fern Bank, Broadstairs, just before Dad went up to Selby in Yorkshire to find work. The result was a well-paid job but also, unfortunately, double pneumonia.

Dad. Unflappable. Totally reliable. I think the portraits of both Dad and Mother date from the First World War.

Leyton County High School's talent-free production of *The Poetasters of Ispahan*. Playing Suleiman, the poetaster clutching the scroll, was my first disastrous taste of the thrills of ham acting, from which I have never escaped. Note that to my left is the long beard that I teased out from crêpe hair and which greatly impressed Mr Lewis, our English master.

One of my weekly letters to Dad in Yorkshire when he was lying in bed steaming with pneumonia. This one told of our school sports and must be one of the few fervent descriptions of a potato race to be found in English literature.

Litte
89 RAM
Broa
hen
E.

Dear mother and dad

you can se
that this letter is all over the p
because I am writing it in b
Today the half-holiday, there
sports there were first of all a p
race, there were six caps likes this
in that posture you will see si
and then you see six lines of po

the six you see six
if had to rams to th
so and put it in the
then go and get the s
potato and put it in the ca
so on when we hade firedr

Do not be misled. This is not a small rodent in the RAF Photography Section, it is me. No.1 Parachute Training School, Ringway, Manchester, c. 1945.

Ringway. 'It'll be a bit cold filming on top of the van, but as long as you don't forget to take a ladder...'

The best part of parachuting: packing up the chute after surviving.

1947. A slim Jimmy Edwards posing with Joy Nichols for a *Radio Times* picture promoting a new series of *Navy Mixture* (radio, of course). *BBC* ©

I can't remember much about this except that it was a production still from a little film I co-starred in, in about 1947, entitled *The Clouded Crystal Ball*. Don't know what happened to the film; had I won an Oscar I think I would have remembered.

A study of two fine 1950s haircuts (and suits). The full ashtray hits the eye, but Den used to take only a couple of small puffs and then mash the rest of his cigarette into extinction. He must have been quite rich in those days. *BBC* ©

Another jolly little pic to herald a new series of *Take It From Here*. Time has elapsed; it is 1954, Joy has left and June Whitfield is now in the company. *BBC* ©

A party in a café in Old Cannes to celebrate the wedding of one of Polly's French cousins. I seem to be entertaining the company with a wildly feeble impression of Charles Boyer.

A rare picture of Polly looking dangerous, taken during the war when she was in the WRNS and being used as a model. *Basil Shackleton.*

1949. On honeymoon in the South of France.

Very newly-wed (2 mins).

Polly loathes this photograph. Might have been better if the lighting had not made me appear to be wearing a Thai gent's evening skirt, but it does show what the British used to wear in the 1950s when seeking tempestuous fun on a sultry Mediterranean night.

Back room Boys

by

A cartoon from the cover of the Australian radio magazine *The Broadcaster*. Denis is the one who looks like a political spin doctor and I am the bent head waiter.

Another exciting picture from the Australian magazine advertising our radio series.

Take It From Here takes to the stage. Did rather well. *Mander and Mitchenson Theatre Collection.*

The Cleopatra sketch from *Take It From Us* at the Adelphi (in those days all stage revues and comic films seemed to include a Cleopatra sketch). Jimmy Edwards and Joy Nichols are working strongly. *Mander and Mitchenson Theatre Collection.*

1953. For some reason (public clamour?) somebody decided to take a photograph of the Muirs and Nordens back from Australia.

Jamie and I pretending we love gardening. Actually, now that Jamie has his own garden he has broken ranks and become a bit of an enthusiast. Well, you do your best, but eventually they go their own way...

At the flat in Addison Road just after I had half drowned Jamie in the rubber bath.
Tom Blau/Camera Press

Outside Anners with two large poodles, Polly and an exciting new fast car.
There seems little more to be said. *Cyril Baker*

Polly and I posing on a canal hire craft just before we had our own *Samanda*
built. They were, in the main, great holidays on the 'cut': vigorous yet restful,
exciting yet peaceful (and dry land was only about 4 feet away).
Bernard Alfieri

two hundred people changed their religion.'

I was hardly either prospering or advancing my career during those Vic Oliver years – about two years of jollity-writing in all – but I was surviving. And much brighter prospects were beginning to build up back at the BBC Variety Department, Aeolian Hall, New Bond Street. The last series of *Navy Mixture* had produced surprisingly good figures and Charles Maxwell was pressing his bosses to let him produce some sort of new comedy series starring the successful newcomers who had done so well in *Navy Mixture*, Joy Nichols, Jimmy Edwards and Dick Bentley.

Charles was given the go-ahead, and as I had written Joy and Jimmy's material and Dick's very good guest appearances were written by the Kavanagh office's staff writer, Denis Norden, Charles took Denis and me to lunch at an expensive Italian restaurant in Jermyn Street and asked us if we would try to knock out some sort of a show between us.

Denis worked in a large room in the Kavanagh offices in Waterloo Place, Lower Regent Street, just down the road from Jermyn Street, so we trailed down there after lunch for a get-together talk. Denis proved to be almost as tall as me but two years younger and better dressed; I recall a modish 'drape shape' suit and a sharp hairstyle reminiscent of Tyrone Power in *Lloyds of London*.

It was rather a gloomy meeting. Both of us already had un-interesting but time-consuming writing commitments – I had *Oliver's Twists* and Denis had a number of Kavanagh's comedian clients to keep funny – so we decided we had better write this new show for Charles in the evenings. Denis was married to Avril and had a baby son, Nicky, so the sensible solution was to work in his flat, which was just to the north of Regent's Park, and Avril would most kindly feed me supper along with her family.

The show was given a starting date in 1947 and Denis and I got down to the problems of setting up the show. We were not certain of Joy Nichol's potential so we went to see her per-forming at the Finsbury Park Empire. With her brother George she did a good old-fashioned, song-and-dance double-act.

We thought, beforehand, it might be a good thing to book

George to do the odd-voice parts, but it turned out to be rather a bad idea. Brother George was deeply into mystic beliefs and at one point in the evening said to us rather alarmingly, 'I could destroy myself with a single thought.' Brother George went home to Australia shortly afterwards and disappeared from show business and from view. Perhaps he thought his thought.

My memory is a bit hazy on what we actually turned out for those early *Take It From Here* programmes but the series certainly went through structural changes as soon as we got to understand our cast's great capabilities and grew a little more confident ourselves.

I do remember that the setting for the first shows was something to do with being a commercial radio station and that Maurice Denham played a character named Major Network (this he denies!). And Clarence Wright, who was in *ITMA* and was an original Ovaltiney on Radio Luxembourg, sang 'Transatlantic Lullaby' in a high tenor voice with a gentle, built-in bleat.

The first series limped to its finish to modest listening figures, and there it would all have ended had Charles Maxwell not had faith in all of us and argued with the Head of Variety Department, Michael Standing, that we should have another chance. Which, thank God, he gave us.

In the months before the next series went on air, Denis and I found the odd-voice character man we needed working in a revue (written by Eric Maschwitz) at the Playhouse Theatre, the brilliant Wallas Eaton. And we listened closely to American comedy shows transmitted on the American Forces Network in Europe. We had a lot to learn from American radio comedy in those days, such as Fred Allen's brilliant use of odd but real characters popping in, and fresh satirical techniques from Henry Morgan.

The second series of *Take It From Here* was quite a different set-up. We dropped the commercial radio idea and arranged the show in three parts. The brief opening spot featured Joy, Dick and Jimmy being themselves and swapping topical banter. Then a current popular song from Johnny Johnson's close-harmony group The Keynotes (originally and improbably named The Harmony Heralds), then the middle spot which we called the 'gimmick', which consisted of 'idea' sketches which our cast played brilliantly.

The 'ideas' ranged from *Hamlet* played as a pantomime, the London Passenger Transport Board Operatic Society's version of Gilbert and Sullivan ('Don't cuss the poor old bus, swearing at the drivers, wanting change for fivers. Up the LPTB, it's quicker to get out and walk'), to the operatic weather forecast ('Taking the temperature with a thermometer, Fahrenheit, Centigrade, where's the barometer? Check the velocities, what a dead loss it is, mucking about on the ministry roof. The mercury's sunk to the figure o. Figure o? Figure o, Figure o, *Feeeeger* o!').

After the 'gimmick' came a song from Joy, or perhaps Dick, sometimes a duet, then the last spot, which was a longish parody of a genre of film or play or book. This last part was something of a small breakthrough in radio comedy because as far as we knew it was the first time in a prime-time series that the listener was credited with having been to school, taken a newspaper and read a few books.

Radio was advancing rapidly on all fronts from the mid-Forties on, finding its own voice in drama, pioneering a style of documentary programme which only radio could produce, and *TIFH* (as our programme soon became known) made its small contribution by attempting a humour different from end-of-pier, music-hall material ('when I sang in the church choir . . .'), and presenting instead parodies of films and literature.

Our approach was to take a well-known book or a period of history or a type of popular film, sort out in our minds what the subject immediately suggested, the clichés in fact, and work up the jokes accordingly.

For instance, we wrote an episode set in Roman Britain, a period remembered from school by most people for having dead straight roads, which were built by Romans with strange names that sounded like Anonymous, Lascivious or Titus Anewticus, and Roman numerals which looked more like letters of the alphabet than numbers. We had our Roman platoon being drilled by the centurion:

CENTURION:	'Roman soldiers, by the left, *numbah!*'
1ST SOLDIER:	'I.'
2ND SOLDIER:	'I, I.'
3RD SOLDIER:	'I, I, I.'
4TH SOLDIER:	'I, V.'
5TH SOLDIER:	'V.'

John Watt, who was a notable early Head of BBC Variety Department (heads rolled rather frequently then due to retirements), said that the Roman soldiers numbering off was the first new joke he had heard on the air since the war.

Dick Vosburgh, the American writer of comedy and musicals who settled in England with his family, to our enrichment, always referred to *TIFH* as 'The Source'. Certainly some of the wheezes in those early shows seem to have passed into common use, which is a pleasing thought. For instance, we parodied the fashion for films and books about North Country factory owners facing industrial action and called our parody *Trouble at t' Mill*, a title which lives on.

Most radio humour is by its nature ephemeral and it is rewarding to find that quite a few effective lines from *Take It From Here* have been preserved on film and are still quoted. This happened because a close friend and colleague of ours, Talbot 'Tolly' Rothwell, was signed up by Peter Rogers and Ralph Thomas to write the *Carry On* films, which were very much like a cinema version of our radio parodies of popular literary genres in *TIFH*.

Tolly ran out of time and asked us for help, so Denis and I dug out those of our early *TIFH* scripts which ended with a film or book parody and passed them to Tolly to borrow from.

The pleasure which Denis and I have of seeing our early quips and fancies preserved on film is tempered by the irony that it is an old *TIFH* line which is quoted as the archetypal *Carry On* line: Dick Bentley as Caesar, attacked by Brutus and Co., cries, 'Oh, infamy! Infamy! They've all got it in for me!'

At the end of the series Michael Standing summoned us into his office and made a statement which Jimmy Edwards later said was one of the high spots of his whole life. 'I am very happy to tell you', said Michael, 'that we have a hit on our hands.'

And so *Take It From Here* settled into its eleven-year run. Denis and I worked to a routine: the show was first transmitted live, and then, with a workable recording machine at last available, recorded on Sundays. On Monday morning we started on the next week's script. We never in eleven years had a spare script standing by.

We began by writing the last spot, the dramatic or literary parody. We would settle on a subject, inspect it from all angles, discuss what must inevitably be included in some form, think up an opening and then start getting it on paper, discussing each line as we went. Denis did the actual transcription because his rapid writing was more legible than mine, but it was not a grievous chore; even on a smoothly productive day only three or four pages were produced.

The next day we tackled the 'gimmick' spot. This could be time-consuming. For instance, one of our techniques was writing what we called 'mathematical dramas'. A typical example would be three Noel Cowardish playlets performed by our three stars which were so unfunny that Jimmy (say) would suggest that they interleave the three playlets into one. This produced a totally different (hopefully funnier) play.

The last item to be written was the brief opening sequence, usually quips exchanged by the stars as themselves, e.g., (as a general election loomed):

JIMMY EDWARDS: I am considering entering politics and being the Grand Old Man of the Conservative Party.
DICK BENTLEY: Watch it, Jimmy. Politics is a dirty business.
JIMMY EDWARDS: Then I'll be the Dirty Old Man of the Conservative Party.

It was a punishing regime for Denis and me. One night when I was driving back from Denis's flat at midnight in my Singer Sports along the deserted Essex Road I fell asleep at the wheel. I woke up to see a lamp-post approaching me at speed. The lamp-post either dodged out of the way or I managed to swerve, but no impact occurred, and after a rest and some deep breathing I cautiously drove home with the windows open.

Then, breakthrough. Denis and I managed to slough off our other commitments and from then on put in a full working day together on *Take It From Here*, no evenings, on either side of Denis's desk at the Kavanagh offices.

For the next few years our lives were lived to the same pattern; meet and write all week, have Saturday off, do the show on Sunday, start the next week's script on Monday. On Sundays, show days, we met just after lunch at the Paris Cinema, Lower Regent Street, and chatted for a while. Dick would be very funny about his Pekinese dog, Yulu, which he seemed to spend most of his week taking for walkies in Regent's Park.

Dick was always fascinated by Jimmy's extraordinary honesty; Jimmy seemed to be incapable of telling even the whitest of lies. When asked how his week had gone playing variety in Glasgow he would say to Dick, 'I think they actually *hated* me.'

Joy Nichols became romantically involved with a baritone cowboy in the London production of *Oklahoma*, a quiet American (when not singing) named Wally Peterson, and with matrimony in view Joy had a gynaecological examination which resulted in bits of her having to be adjusted. One Sunday afternoon's whole pre-show chat was taken up by Joy describing to us in candid detail exactly what had to be rearranged within her and how it had been done. Wallas Eaton – who never married – was beginning to turn green when Dick said to Joy with deep sympathy, 'You poor thing. And my Yulu's got diarrhoea . . .'

At the end of that series Joy resigned from the cast to wed her Wally and go back to the States with him to become, she hoped, a star of Broadway musicals. When she came to say goodbye she gave us little presents.

Joy settled in New York with Wally, had a daughter, Roberta, but the marriage was uneasy, perhaps because she never did get anywhere in American show business. Eventually she drifted back to England, but could only get small parts. Just before she died she was working behind the counter of a Mothercare shop. Wally was with her at the end.

Replacing Joy in the show presented difficulties because Joy really was very good at comedy as well as being a useful singer. We had to replace her with two girls, a singer and a comedy actress.

For our singer we were lucky to sign up Alma Cogan, a large, happy girl who was beginning to make her mark with records and international cabaret appearances (in wondrous 'gowns') and her swinging, chuckly style of singing was just right for a comedy show.

We auditioned many girls for the actress job and had pretty well settled on Prunella Scales, whose readings were excellent, when we heard one last girl, a singer/actress from the chorus of *South Pacific* named June Whitfield. And so June joined the show as our actress. Her range of voices, even then, was extraordinary. She did a particularly wonderful 'debby' screech and was also a very good mimic.

With our two excellent additions to the cast, *TIFH* began to collect awards. The first prize we won as a comedy show was a life-size silver microphone from the *Daily Mail*; each of us was also given a tiny silver replica about an inch and a half tall, too small to mount on a stand and too big to make into a cuff link, but encouraging to have.

Then in 1950 the show hit a kind of jackpot when a new voice was heard in the land: 'OOOOOOoooooooooooo, Ron!'

Eth and the Glum family began as a one-off sketch in the 'gimmick' segment of *TIFH*. At that time BBC Radio was having success with a warm-hearted series about nice families such as the Huggetts in *Meet the Huggetts*, which featured the formidably lovable team of Jack Warner, Kathleen Harrison and a very young Petula Clark. As an antidote we invented a repugnant family.

In the original sketch Alma Cogan played Ma Glum as a grumpy matriarchal figure permanently sunk in an armchair by the fire, and Ron and Eth had yet to emerge in their true relationship. Pa Glum was always the same, the pioneer male chauvinist pig, years before Andy Capp made his appearance.

That first sketch went so well that Denis and I realized we were on to something. We changed things round and made Eth a plain girl whose only hope of getting married was to stand up to Pa Glum's dreadfulnesses and hang on like grim death to her fiancé, the terminally dim Ron. For example:

ETH: Oh, Ron, nobody's perfect!

RON: *You* are, Eth.

ETH: (*purring with pleasure*) I'm not, Ron! I have faults like everybody else. Tell me one.

RON: You haven't got any faults, Eth.

ETH: Of course I have, Ron! Come on, there must be *something* you don't like about me. Something tiny.

RON: No, Eth.

ETH: Some little thing . . . ?

RON: Well, there is *something*.

ETH: (*roguishly*) Come on, then – out with it!

RON: You're a bit ugly.

We realized that the state of being engaged had not been overused and had interesting comedy potential. In the 1950s it was still an unnatural state of suspended animation, a social arrangement not found in nature which had its own rules of semi-permissive behaviour. To the boy it was like driving with one foot on the accelerator and the other on the brake.

We banished Ma Glum from the room and only heard her from afar shouting and screaming incoherently as something awful happened, usually caused by her husband.

For example, there is a loud thumping and banging and a scream from Ma Glum followed by incoherent wailing (Alma was very good at this):

PA GLUM: (*sighs*) I dunno – that woman! I ask her to do a simple task like getting the garden roller down from the loft . . .

We evolved a formula. Each Glum episode began with Ron and Eth on the sofa. June did her wonderful Eth voice and began, 'OOOoooooooh, Ron!' and Dick Bentley – after a pause and he was a master of pauses – said in Ron's extra-ordinary flat Australian accent (Australian!):

RON: Yes, Eth?

And Eth would start the plot rolling, saying something like:

ETH: I do think you should try again to get a job,
              Ron. It is four years since you last tried. And
              when we marry I want to feel secure.
RON: (*uncomprehending, repeats dully*) Secure.
ETH: Yes, Ron, secure. You do know what 'secure'
              means, beloved?
RON: Of course I do, Eth. It's that metal spike that
              keeps the Sunday joint from unwinding.
ETH: No, beloved, that's 'skewer'. 'Secure' means
              having money coming in regularly . . .

Ron was a randy lad and Eth was definitely not at all in
favour of that sort of thing. Halfway through her argument to
persuade Ron to get a job, Ron would suddenly say:

RON: Give us a kiss, Eth!
ETH: Don't, Ron! Ron, get off! You know how
              this skirt seats . . .

As they grappled Pa Glum would burst in, see them struggling and say something like:

PA GLUM: 'Ello, 'ello, 'ello! All-in wrestling? Break clean!

And then he would explain why he had rushed in:

PA GLUM: Ron, run upstairs and fetch me your mother's
              toothbrush – I've got my new suede shoes on
              and I've trodden in something.

Or:

PA GLUM: Ron, have you seen the *Radio Times*? – the
              boiler's gone out.

The expanding success of *TIFH* brought Denis and me to the notice of other producers and we now had no problem finding work to fill in the six months of the year when *TIFH* was not on the air. One interesting new sideline was rewriting scenes in comedy films, particularly for the Norman Wisdom pictures. The producer would find that a scene was not working and would ring us and ask if we could sort it out ('by tomorrow').

In one Wisdom film the producer, Hugh Stewart, urgently needed a big comic catastrophe, full of as much physical action as possible. We set to and in an hour had mapped out and phoned through to Hugh Stewart a sequence set in a theatre in which a symphony orchestra was giving a concert. It was a huge orchestra and it was seated on a revolving stage. When the scenery had been built and they were about to shoot the scene, Den and I went down to the studios to watch.

For reasons of plot – Wisdom was probably trying to escape from villains – we had our star frantically crashing about backstage amongst the switches and levers which controlled the stage effects. So the symphony orchestra, which doggedly played on throughout, began to revolve. Then all the lights went out. The lights came on to reveal that it was raining heavily on stage. The orchestra revolved faster and faster. The rain stopped and thick snow began to fall. Dry-ice mist spread. Cannon, as in the 1812 Overture, boomed. The scene ended in what might be described as orchestrated chaos.

'To think,' said Den to me, thoughtfully, 'that fifty-thousand-pound charade took us just an hour to write.' And we crept away.

It was an era of rather colourful radio producers. One, Vernon Harris, was successfully writing feature films on the side (one of them was *Three Men in a Boat*, which starred David Tomlinson, Jimmy Edwards and Laurence Harvey). We met Vernon in the lift as he came down from a high-level Variety Department meeting and he was ashen-faced. 'They've given me a *programme!*' he muttered desperately. 'This is going to seriously interfere with my work.'

The Assistant Head of Variety was an ex-Indian army officer, a really delightful man named (Major) Mike Meehan. At that time the still very Reith-minded BBC management had just issued to all its Variety producers a book of guidelines to what was broadcastable and what was subversive filth. This was the famous *Green Book*. It warned against such evils as saying that BC stood for 'Before Crosby', and cold weather meant 'winter drawers on'.

Mike Meehan went into hospital with a respiratory problem and to cheer him up Denis and I wrote to him asking if, in light of the *Green Book*'s guidelines, he would kindly OK the enclosed script.

The script began: ' "C-C-C-Christ!" said the king to the one-legged nigger.'

It took us half a morning's work, but in this splendidly politically-incorrect sentence we managed to get five infringements of the *Green Book*'s dicta into eight words.

One of the most unconventional producers was Pat Dixon, pushing retirement age and a rebel by nature, apt to turn up to departmental meetings carrying an American Civil War Confederate flag. Over the years we wrote several series for Pat, including *Listen My Children*, *Third Division*, which was the first comedy series for the BBC's new arts network, the Third Programme, and a number of hour-long monthly revues. Pat was always happy to try out new talent and the young comedians he booked for these shows were cheap to hire at the time but would cost a fortune a few years later, e.g., Benny Hill, Peter Sellers, Michael Bentine, Harry Secombe . . .

An interesting innovative series started by Pat Dixon, which Denis and I helped him push into shape, was *In All Directions*, starring Peter Ustinov and Peter Jones. In this the two Peters were supposedly wandering about London trying to find their way to somewhere called Copthorne Avenue. On the way they asked various people how to get there, thus setting up a number of character conversations and sketches. It was an innovative show because nothing was written down. They improvised the dialogue and Pat recorded the items in takes, as with a film.

Another bright but none too successful idea of Pat Dixon's was to send Denis and me to Paris with a new invention, a portable tape recorder. Ours was called (I think) a Soundmirror, and was a large heavy mahogany box with two tape spools which whizzed round, controlled by a kind of sturdy gear lever. Pat's idea was to call the programme *Ça c'est Paris* and Denis and I would go behind the scenes at the fashionable Parisien *haute couture* salon of Pierre Balmain and discuss this and that with the models changing in their dressing rooms. We were nothing loath. It seemed to us to be an excellent idea, in fact, quite the best that had been put to us for years.

Pat set it up in the summer months when *TIFH* was off, put in for the tape recorder and in due course BBC Accounts paid us, as was usual, an advance on our fee.

Pat Dixon had organized matters so that we would linger around the supermodels' dressing rooms with our tape recorder in mid-July. In fact 14 to 16 July. The truth then dawned on somebody that this was the great French holiday, the *quatorze juillet*, and everything would be shut, especially the fashion houses. Paris would be empty.

Pat had to cancel the whole enterprise.

Then Den and I received a memo from the BBC Accounts Department asking us to repay the advance they had given us. Den and I considered this request most carefully and then sent a letter back to BBC Accounts saying, 'Thank you for your memo requesting the repayment of the advance we received for the *Ça c'est Paris* project. We regret that we have no machinery for returning money.' The BBC Accounts Department was perfectly happy with this.

The great Peter Sellers was then an unknown at the Windmill doing an act which consisted mainly of a very long story about various dodgy street-market characters with funny voices selling each other a tin of sardines. The pay-off was that the man who ended up with the tin opened it and the sardines had gone mouldy. He protested to the chap who sold it to him who pointed out that the sardines were for buying and selling, not eating. This story, in various versions, has since become an urban myth but it may always have been one.

Den and I wrote a spot each week for Peter in *Third Division*; he played all the street traders in what we called *Sellers' Market*.

We also used his extraordinary gift for character voices in sketches, one of which was a parody of those Fitzpatrick Traveltalks which seemed to be a part of every cinema programme in those days ('. . . and as the sun sinks slowly in the west we bid farewell to Bali, Isle of Enchantment . . .'). We called our version *Bal-ham, Gateway to the South*.

Peter was very quickly taken famous and was persuaded by George Martin (who later produced the Beatles' records) to record a comedy LP. Peter asked us if he could include three of our sketches which he had enjoyed performing: the mad headmaster of a progressive school talking to a timid potential parent, an interview with a moronic pop star and his gaoler/manager ('Come back here! I've told you repeatedly, where the carpet starts, you stop!'), and *Bal-ham, Gateway to the South*.

Some forty years on, in 1990, a group of Balham businessmen known as the Triangle Action Group, bent on making the centre of Balham an even more attractive place to shop, decided that as *Bal-ham, Gateway to the South* had more or less put Balham on the map for the tourist trade, they should erect a statue to its begetter, the famous Peter Sellers.

The *Evening Standard* got to hear of this and it made a good story, which Denis and I read with some alarm. Sellers was not the begetter, he was the actor who performed it, and there is often an assumption (rather dangerous to writers) that somebody as famous as Sellers wrote his own material and owned it. We had recently had an altercation with the late Peter's American lawyer, who had graciously handed out permission to a book publisher to include the script of *Bal-ham* in a book, on the quite baseless assumption that the copyright belonged to Peter's estate.

So Den and I, anxious to affirm our copyright in this curiously long-lived and quite famous piece for which we have considerable affection, wrote a letter to the *Standard*, which they published. The letter read:

Further to your article (Balham calls for a statue, 15 February 1990), while we are all for putting up a statue to Peter Sellers, we may be able to save the good burghers of Balham a bit of money.

It wasn't Sellers who dubbed their fair suburb *Gateway to the South*. The sketch was one of several we wrote for him in a Fifties radio series called *Third Division*, some of which he included on his album. However, this does not mean that the Triangle Action Group must now involve itself in the expense of putting up *two* statues.

For a trifling sum, we would be prepared to go along to the new shopping centre and stand there personally.

Frank Muir and Denis Norden

After forty years the LP is still selling, gently but steadily.

Again for Pat Dixon, Denis and I wrote a new sort of relaxed, early morning radio series starring a recently arrived Canadian named Bernard Braden and his wife Barbara Kelly. We called this show *Breakfast with Braden*. Braden was a brilliant broadcaster and the show achieved a kind of cult status. We followed the original series with a late-night version, *Bedtime with Braden*, and then *Between Times with Braden*.

The various Braden series were major series which meant that they went out in the autumn and winter when *Take It From Here* was also on, so our working week in the winter was busy.

We now had an office in the maid's quarters at the top of a building on the corner of Regent Street and Conduit Street. On Thursdays we would stroll down to Maddox Street, have a snack-bar lunch and then cross New Bond Street to Charles's office in Aeolian Hall and read him the *Take It From Here* script we had just finished (Denis would read it, it was after all in his own writing, and I would 'laugh it up a little' as American writers say). Then we would spend Thursday afternoon doing such rewriting as Charles called for. He called for quite a bit from time to time which we tended to resent. Later we worked for a producer in television who never queried anything and treated our scripts as Holy Writ. We felt lost and insecure.

On Fridays we wrote the Braden show. We only had a day to write this, so we evolved techniques like interrupting pieces of comedy rather than having to give them an ending. A typical example in a Braden show went:

BERNIE:	So to this week's recipe, which is for oxtail soup. Bring a saucepan of water to the boil. Get an ox and back it slowly towards . . .
BENNY LEE:	(*breathless*) Sorry I'm late, Mr Braden. I'll sing my song faster to catch up . . .

One Thursday, after lunching as usual at the snack bar, Denis and I strolled over to Aeolian Hall only to find, to our dismay, that neither of us had the script. We rushed back to the snack bar but it was not there. In something of a state we went back to our eyrie in Conduit Street wondering what the hell to do, whether we should try to remember the entire script and type it out, or what? About an hour later a man telephoned us from his office in a factory in Surrey. He had found our script in his briefcase and had kindly put it on a passenger train back to London.

It seems that Denis had parked the script on the shelf under the plastic tabletop and the man sitting opposite us had also parked *his* papers there, and he scooped first. On leaving he had slid all the papers on the shelf into his briefcase.

An agitated Charles rang. 'It's gone four o'clock! *Where's the script?*'

Denis said, 'It's in a small umbrella factory just outside Reading.'

It was at about this time that we experienced our first important newspaper interview. We were taken to lunch at the Connaught Hotel and interviewed in depth by two of the most powerful feminine journalists of the day, Anne Edwards and Drusilla Beyfus, then of the *Sunday Express*. The lunch was delicious, ending with sliced bananas poached in red wine.

The ladies wanted to know everything about us and wrote away briskly in their notebooks: how we each started, how we met, the sort of comedy we enjoyed, the comedians we did not enjoy, early mistakes, ambitions – it was about four o'clock in the afternoon when we staggered back to the office, exhausted and a little hoarse, but glowing with satisfaction that we had at last been recognized as worth interviewing by a national newspaper.

On Sunday morning we both dashed out and bought a

Sunday Express. Yes, there was the column, and there, at the end, was the interview with us. It read, in its entirety:

> Pudding of the Week. Lunching at the Connaught with writers Frank Muir and Denis Norden, we finished off the meal with a delicious new entry on the menu – sliced bananas poached in red wine.

With work now coming in from all directions and the prospect of ending in a debtor's cell receding, I thought that now was the time for me to move my life forward a large notch.

I decided to get married.

But to whom?

Chapter 8

THE PLIGHTING OF TROTHS

I first saw Polly McIrvine in the BBC canteen at Aeolian Hall. I was queueing right behind her, clutching my tray as we reached the coffee urn, my face about 6 inches above her blond hair (naturally blond, I noted, rather unromantically, as if it mattered). She had on her tray beans on toast and an apple.

I was immediately attracted, surprisingly strongly, not by Polly's good looks but by her voice. An attractive speaking voice seems to me to be being bred out of the British, which is a pity. It is not at all a matter of accent or not dropping aitches but of timbre, of a musical sound, which is still occasionally present in the voices of older folk but rarely in the young, and never in the voices of present-day presenters of children's television programmes, on whom children model themselves.

It was summertime and Polly was wearing a cotton dress with wide horizontal stripes of bright blue alternating with white, like an old-fashioned milk jug. I watched her every move beadily from a safe distance as she ate her beans and apple, and then I followed her into the lift at Aeolian Hall – the biggest and slowest lift in the Western hemisphere, built to elevate grand pianos to what was once a concert hall on the first floor – and trailed behind her stealthily along the third-floor corridor, flitting from one doorway to another like an inept private eye, eventually seeing her disappear into the Bookings Department, the office which issued all our contracts (which were in lovely guineas in those days).

Polly was hardly a BBC career girl. Labour was directed then, and unless a girl could get a job with a corporation like the BBC, which was deemed a public necessity, she could theoretically end up down the mines or weighing fish on Grimsby docks. Polly, newly demobbed from the WRNS, was fortunate in getting an extremely dull job at the BBC typing contracts for the Variety Department's bookings manager (and Gilbert and Sullivan enthusiast) Pat Newman.

A couple of days later I made my first move, and a shrewd gambit it was, too. *TIFH* was by then a much-talked-about new hit and tickets to see the show going out live from the Paris Cinema were much in demand. Those of us connected with the show were allowed a small ration of tickets.

A few days later I watched Polly's office door for quite a while before I decided the coast was clear, then I knocked gently and went in. There was the milk-jug dress sitting at a typewriter. She looked up.

I cleared my throat a couple of times and went suavely into the speech I had rehearsed for an hour or two. 'Er – I wondered – er,' I said, putting the *TIFH* ticket on her desk in front of her, 'whether you – if you haven't actually got anything better to do, of course, which you probably have, and why shouldn't you? – Whether you – er – would like to come to this?'

She picked up the card and read it. I felt wholly confident because offering a *TIFH* ticket to a keen listener was like offering a cup-final ticket to a football fanatic.

'What's *Take It From Here*?' she asked, curiously.

My heart sank. It was clear that if my prey had never heard of *Take It From Here*, my trump card was worthless. In the long reaches of that night I realized that it was stupid to expect an attractive girl to spend her evenings glued to the wireless.

'I'm so sorry,' she said, 'but I've arranged to spend that evening with a girlfriend.'

'Bring her along!' I blurted. 'I'll book a table for dinner at the Screenwriters' Club.' This was a splendid private restaurant and bar in Deanery Street at the back of the Dorchester Hotel, set up by the screenwriter Guy Morgan and others. The club bore about as much resemblance to Daddy Allen's Club as the Dorchester did to the Union Jack Sailors' Mission, but much of the overheard conversation at the Screenwriters' was just as unlikely. At lunch there one Saturday I heard one mink-clad lady discussing a famous violinist with another mink-clad lady. She was saying, 'Then they moved to New York, I remember that. But what became of *her*?'

'She was murdered.'

'No, the *other* one, his second wife?'

I remember little of my first date with Polly, which is perhaps all for the best because I heard many years later that when I dropped the girls off at the block of flats where they both lived, Polly's friend said to her, 'He seems awfully keen. Are you interested?' And Polly said, 'Good God, no!'

But I persevered. This was not wholly due to love at first sight, although there was a lot of that, but it was also due to my ignorance of the practice of wooing. I simply did not know the rules of the game and did not recognize the codes which Polly was probably issuing – she had plenty of casual boyfriends – to warn me not to nurse more serious ambitions. So I blundered on.

Brother Chas would have played it like the game it usually was. He would have known the rules and the codes because he had always had stacks of girlfriends and was much experienced in complicated flirtations. My few experiences always seemed to consist of taking a liking to a girl because of her nose or something and then going off her bit by bit as I got to know her. Naturally I expected this diminution of ardour to happen with Polly, but it did not. Polly was not just a pretty voice; the more I got to know her the more I found to admire and like, and then love. It began to get serious my end.

With more money coming in I was able to part-exchange the Singer Sports for a drop-head Frazer-Nash BMW. This sounds grand but it was actually a very old car; the hood leaked, there was so little pressure in the cylinders that I could crank the engine holding the starting handle between finger and thumb, and it had been rebored so many times that the garage said that there was no more metal left for another rebore. On the bright side, it had real door handles and looked quite sporty on a dry day.

With a bit of research I managed to establish Polly's hours of work, so when she emerged from Aeolian Hall at about six she would find me parked outside, elbow nonchalantly stuck out of the car window. I would exclaim, surprised, 'Hello again! Look, I'm going west, can I give you a lift home?' and I would rush round and fling open the passenger door.

My journey home to Leyton was actually to the east but what matter? I was beginning to establish a bridgehead in Polly's awareness.

The recurring coincidence of finding me parked outside when it was time for her to go home lasted a month or two and then we progressed to occasionally going to films and events together and we began to draw closer.

One chilly Saturday we drove down for a day's excursion to Brighton and Hove. On Hove front we ran into Ted Kavanagh. I was alarmed because Ted was strongly Roman Catholic, as was Polly (Ted was a member of the Knights of St Columba), and I did not want him to think that Polly and I had nipped away for a dirty weekend, so I introduced Polly carefully.

Ted took a photograph of us on my camera and I sent Polly an enlargement on which I wrote:

> Don't laugh at my jokes too much,
> People will say we're in Hove.

At the end of one of my lifts home, Polly invited me upstairs to her flat (her mother was out), pinned me down safely to the sofa with two or three heavy family photograph albums and I learned about her background. About the same time that my grandfather sailed for New Zealand, Polly's grandfather left Aberdeen University with his degree, swiftly married, and in 1856 sailed with his bride, a cradle and a huge mahogany dining-room table to the island of Mauritius in the Indian Ocean, a journey which took six months by auxiliary sail. There he began his work as the island's first Presbyterian minister.

Their son, Polly's father, was born in Mauritius, became a businessman in the capital, Port Louis, exporting and importing. When on leave in France in 1914 (because of the slow travel they had terrific leaves in those days; usually a whole year every three or four years) he married a French girl from the north of France. They just managed to escape from France and get back to Mauritius before the Great War overwhelmed Europe.

Polly was born in Mauritius and managed to survive the high infant-mortality rate of the sub-tropics. An elder brother, Brian, and an elder sister, Isabelle, known to all as 'Pigeon', also survived. Brian became an actor and Pidge became a nun at the IBVM convent and girls' school at Ascot, later Reverend Mother for a couple of tours of duty.

This background was somewhat different from mine and I am eternally grateful that my ignorance of courtship practices meant that I did not realize that my determination to marry Polly was an almost hopeless dream. So on with it I went. As far as I was concerned I had found the girl I wanted to grow old with and that was that. The example of my own parents had shown me what a good thing marriage was and I was not going to be put off by theoretical problems.

I told my mother that I wanted to marry a girl I had met at the BBC and that she came from Mauritius. 'Oh, dear!' said my mother, not even knowing where Mauritius was but fearful of complications. 'She's a natural blonde,' I went on. 'Huh!' said my mother.

One evening I took Polly down to 28 Church Road to meet my mother, and it must have been an ordeal for both of them. Polly and *her* widowed mother lived in North End House, a block of large modern flats with flowers in the vestibule, a lift operated by an attendant and the flats had a short corridor of small rooms off the kitchen to house the staff (not that there were any after the First World War). Twenty-eight Church Road was not quite like that. Polly was marvellous, but when I saw her home on the tube she was unusually quiet and thoughtful.

My mother, typically, changed her tune completely after meeting Polly and from then on sided with Polly against me for the rest of her life. 'Have you asked Polly what *she* wants to do? No, you just go your way without giving her a thought . . .' Or, 'What does Polly think about it? You might give her *some* consideration . . .' Or, 'How Polly puts up with your selfish behaviour . . .'

To smarten myself up, a long-overdue move, I bought a cheap off-the-peg tweed jacket from Austin Reed which, by a miracle, happened to fit. My mother commented, with that kind of affectionate injustice which one never forgets, 'Spending more money? Oh, well, easy come, easy go.'

Easy come!

My campaign moved forward a notch when Polly disclosed that she and her mother were going to France to visit a French aunt and various relations.

'But that's marvellous!' I exclaimed, starting back in surprise at the good news. 'I have to go to Paris to see a man. Let's arrange to meet!'

How much Polly realized that she was being wooed with a string of blatantly fake coincidences has never emerged. She probably enjoyed the whole charade.

Polly and her mother were going first to Vouvray, the town of wine caves, and then on to Paris to stay at a Dominican convent with one of Maman's nun sisters, Tante Isa. It was arranged that when I had booked into a hotel in Paris I would send a telegram to Polly in Vouvray with my hotel's phone number and Polly would phone me when she and her mother arrived back in Paris.

I had never been to France before and spoke only schoolboy French. It was an extremely tedious business shipping the car over, with great wads of forms. No fancy drive-on ferries; at Newhaven the car was hoisted off the quay by a crane and lowered roughly into the forward hold of the small cargo ship.

The drive to Paris was fascinating and exciting. Many of the roads were still cobbled and had a terrific camber so that the car heeled over at an alarming angle when close to the kerb, almost hitting its head on roadside trees. I stopped for petrol at one of the strange, very French kerbside petrol pumps which had huge glass vases on their tops. When I ordered my precious litres – special cheap coupons for tourists – a crone in rusty black, bent with age and arthritis, painfully worked a handle to and fro and petrol rose into one of the glass vases. When enough had been pumped, she pulled a lever and the petrol golloped down the hose into the car's tank.

I hadn't the faintest idea where to stay in Paris, but I

happened upon a tiny square up in Montmartre which seemed to consist entirely of small hotels and I booked in for the night at a safe bet, the Hôtel d'Angleterre. There was a very sweet and helpful African receptionist who sorted out my passport and the various personal details then officially required and I went to bed. In the morning a very pleasant African girl brought me coffee and a croissant. I went downstairs and in the hallway was a coachload of friendly Africans queueing to book in. I realized that for my one-night stay I had chosen a hotel entirely manned by, and catering for, Africans.

I drove along the almost deserted Champs Elysées and parked the car at the kerb. The morning was warm and sunny and I sat at a pavement table at the elegant café, Fouquet's, and enjoyed that French civilized pleasure of a glass of chilled white wine at eleven in the morning (it was actually champagne but sipping champagne mid-morning sounds too dissolute to admit to).

I had an urgent problem. Polly and her mother were due to leave Vouvray at any moment for the Paris convent and I had promised to send a telegram to Polly telling her in which hotel I was staying, but I now had no hotel. I looked about me for help.

The pavement tables were almost deserted, but a few tables away sat a pleasant-looking Frenchman, a bit older than me. He smiled, stroked his tie and then pointed at me. I was wearing a striped RAF tie. I went over to his table to get some advice on hotels. He was drinking a glass of white wine (non-bubbly) and invited me to join him. In excellent English he asked what I did in the RAF and parachuting at RAF Ringway came up. An extraordinary coincidence emerged.

My French friend had also been at Ringway. He had been recruited into the SOE and had been sent to learn night parachuting at the course for agents at Ringway run by Major Edwards and Captain Dalton.

He told me stories of his spy days, of walking into a café full of Germans just after being dropped into Normandy and inadvertently pulling out of his jacket pocket with his handkerchief a packet of twenty Players cigarettes, which clattered to the floor. He passed the cigarettes round to the

German soldiers as souvenirs liberated from a captured British colonel.

I managed to interrupt my friend's sparkling stream of reminiscences long enough to ask him to recommend a modest hotel for me for a couple of nights. No problem. The address he gave me was about a quarter of a mile away, just down from the Arc de Triomphe. Hôtel les Acacias, rue des Acacias.

Seeing me into the car with his chatter back on full flow, I learned that he lived in a flat near the Louvre and was back at his old trade of designing nightclub decors. He said that he had several old SOE friends and resistance colleagues whom he would invite that evening to a party at his flat to meet me and celebrate whatever any of us could think of to celebrate.

Exhausted already by his nervous energy and relentless charm, I drove round to the Hôtel les Acacias which was exactly right. Small, family-run, cleanish, cheapish. Polly and I used it many times later and we were treated as regulars.

On one visit we coincided with an international rugger match, France versus Wales, and a batch of Welsh fans had booked into the hotel. Wales won and that night the Welsh fans sang in triumph, emotionally and very loudly. They seemed to be set to sing all night. About three in the morning Madame, in dressing gown and hairnet, knocked on our door and asked me whether we would be kind enough to do something to diminish the noise coming from room 2-10 (by then the boyos were treating the whole arrondissement to 'Land of My Fathers', fortissimo and *con amore*). I knocked on the door of room 2-10, not that they could have heard me above the din they were making, and went in. There were extraordinarily few of them making all that noise and they were not all that drunk, just dog-tired and in a kind of ecstasy of patriotic pleasure at their team's victory.

'Lads! Lads!' I shouted. 'You must stop this singing, you're keeping the whole hotel awake! Next thing is, they'll call the police and then you'll be locked up in the Bastille, and once you are in the Bastille *you'll never be heard of again!*'

This got through. Three or four of them mumbled apologetically and quietly trailed back to their own rooms, leaving just their host lying on his bed. He looked up at us and said, in a gentle Welsh tone of infinite sadness, a line which is now part of our family's private language: 'There's no 'arm in being 'appy.'

On another of our visits to Paris and the Hôtel les Acacias a further family code expression was born. The hotel did not serve food other than a continental breakfast (with croissants never older than an hour away from the local baker's oven, where they were baked in small batches all day), but there was a little café/restaurant just along the road and there was a small underground garage where we could leave the car.

One morning we went to collect the car and found that a customer with his thoughts on a higher plane had left his large Citroën car at the foot of the ramp, blocking it off, and had gone away with the keys. The garage owner, a small plump man in blue overalls, was in a paroxysm of rage, jumping up and down and flailing his arms. He stopped eventually, breathing heavily, banged his hand down on the car's bonnet and delivered judgement: '*Cet homme, il est véritablement LE ROI des cons!*' This, abbreviated to '*il est véritablement . . .!*' has proved a useful code message between Polly and me ever since.

I settled in at the hotel, sent a telegram to Polly at Vouvray giving the hotel's name, address and phone number, unpacked – which took about forty seconds – wandered round Paris a bit, had a rest on the bed and drove to my French friend's flat for his party of ex-resistance men.

The evening, which went into the early hours, produced a great deal of storytelling and bellows of laughter and champagne. It was a gay party (I think probably in both senses) and when I woke up in the late morning I was in a huge and very chic bedroom wearing putty-coloured silk pyjamas. I dressed with great speed and rushed back to the hotel.

I was too late. Polly had already telephoned, twice, and madame had reported, no doubt with relish, that I had been out all night. No, monsieur did not say where he was going, or with whom. And I had still not returned . . .

I begged madame to ring the convent's number for me immediately.

The line was engaged.

Standing there in the hotel's tiny foyer I started to sweat at the delay. It wasn't a question of explaining what I was doing out all night, I just suddenly had this strange deep longing to *see* Polly.

In Paris, of all places, I should have been able to make considerable progress towards wedded bliss, but I seemed to be making a porridge of the whole thing.

I then realized how much I disliked the courting process. I have never been very competitive and for months I lived with the constant fear that any moment I might lose Polly to somebody she liked better – when we first met there were several eligible young men circling in the background. And losing Polly was simply too disastrous a possibility to even contemplate.

This way of thinking was of course insulting to Polly, seemingly treating her as a pawn in a game and taking little account of her own wishes, but I was feeling very jumpy and scared as I paced the tiny lobby.

Then madame got through to the convent. Polly and her mother were out shopping. I left a message with the duty nun that unless I heard from Polly that it was inconvenient, I would collect her from the convent after Mass the following morning – a Sunday – give a toot on the car horn to announce that I had arrived and then whisk her off to coffee and lunch *chez* Fouquet's and in the afternoon a drive along the river to St Cloud.

Tante Isa's convent was in the suburb of Asnières, not too far away, and the roads next morning were almost empty of traffic, so I arrived comfortably early. I felt a quiet confidence that this was going to be a good day.

As I drew up in the car I tooted a modest toot on the horn to announce my arrival.

The horn stuck.

It is quite extraordinary how deafening a noise an elderly Frazer-Nash BMW's horn can make on a quiet Sunday morning in a narrow French street outside the high wall of a convent. I prayed that Mass had finished. I was also interested to note a scientific phenomenon which I might designate 'The Muir Effect'. This states: the longer a stuck horn blares, the louder it becomes.

Then Polly emerged from the convent's front door and jumped in beside me. Conversation was impossible, so I put the car into gear and, with the horn still blaring as though warning the citizenry of an invasion, drove off.

Just along the road the horn unstuck as mysteriously as it had stuck and the blissful diminution of noise made speech possible. Polly looked terrific and at last here I was, sitting close to her, and we were *talking*. It was a good feeling. I explained what had happened, apologized like steam and did what I could towards what would nowadays be called damage limitation. I think I was slightly forgiven.

The rest of the day went (fairly) well. At Fouquet's a gypsy lady with a huge flat basket of cut flowers went on a semi-begging tour of the pavement tables, dragging a dirty, large-eyed little girl behind her. I bought a spray of red roses which I formally presented to Polly, meeting her eye and giving her a deeply significant look.

In the European language of flowers, the gesture of presenting Polly with red roses represented a floral declaration of my love. But Polly grew up in Mauritius. Years later Polly told me that when I dropped her back at the convent that evening she gave my roses to the Reverend Mother, who liked flowers.

'But you must not give me your roses!' protested the Reverend Mother. 'Do you not know what it means when a young man gives you red roses?'

'Well, actually, no I don't!' said Polly cheerfully.

Back in England, autumn set in and a new series of *Take It From Here* was scheduled, and Denis and I had to begin thinking about what we were going to do with the show. New ideas had to be found, old characters replaced.

The preparation of the first show of a run of *Take It From Here* was nerve-racking. The problem was that although we got down to it and produced the first script a week before the show, the *Radio Times* had to have information about it for their publicity three weeks ahead, so we fed them generalizations along the lines of, 'Jimmy Edwards is as outrageous as ever and Dick Bentley is as cool and calm as ever. Watch out for fun with the Glums,' and more of such waffle.

The awful part came when the *Radio Times* was published ten days before the show. There was – probably on the cover – a photograph of our stars looking comical and an article inside welcoming the series back, which would include new problems for the Glum family, Jimmy being as outrageous as ever, etc. And not a word of it was yet written.

Polly and I were by now going almost everywhere together and one day I blurted out a desperately unromantic half proposal which was more like a declaration of intent to merge – with conditions. I said that I would very much like to marry her but we would have to wait until next summer because of *Take It From Here*.

As the weather worsened and moved into winter, the sun came out figuratively for Polly and me when we admitted being in love with each other. I then met many of Polly's family friends, mainly ex-pat Mauritians who had retired to England, French families who traditionally ran the sugar estates and Brits who ran almost everything else – it was still a British colony then. We made plans to get engaged at Christmas; in those days an engagement was like a mini-marriage in the social pattern, an important formal step.

In the run-up to Christmas we wandered through Burlington Arcade and chose the engagement ring, which Polly had to hide away in a drawer until the engagement was announced. This pre-engagement period sounds very un-romantic and non-Barbara Cartland, with no blurted proposal coming as a total surprise to the lady, or the sudden whipping out of an engagement ring from a little box and the ring fitting perfectly, but for us it was a magical period when we planned our immediate future and exchanged long-range hopes.

Next I had to formally declare my intentions to Polly's mother. This turned out to be trickier than I imagined.

I liked Anna McIrvine very much. I think I always puzzled her a little by my deeply English way of not being very serious and using irony a lot, but she called me her *géant* and we always got on extremely well. My problem was that the time I had arranged for our formal meeting was not well chosen.

It was on her return from a drinks party given by an ex-Mauritian friend for fellow ex-Mauritians. I suppose Maman, as

I now called her, had enjoyed one glass of sherry – no more. She asked me into her room, sat at her dressing table and had a good look at herself in the mirror. 'Do you like my hat?' she asked, pushing it about a bit as ladies do with hats.

The elegant phrases I had prepared, like, 'requesting the honour of your daughter's hand . . .' and, 'would make me, and I hope Polly, very happy if you . . .' withered on the lips. I was in deep trouble. I knew nothing about hats and I did not much like Maman's. In fact, I thought it was not a good hat at all; it seemed to me to be a bit too dark and formal.

I later learned the tradition of hat maintenance which French ladies practised earlier in the century. One good hat was bought of strong and classic structure and then, as the years passed, was retrimmed in the current fashion by those ladies – pretty well all ladies then – who were nifty with a needle. So I was being asked to pass judgement not only on Maman's taste in hats but also on her colour-sense and needlecraft. In a panic it occurred to me that the coward's way out would be to lie and praise the hat warmly.

What to do?

I praised the hat, of course.

I explained to Maman that the work I did gave almost no financial security but it was going very well at the moment, Denis and I had a hit show and there was every chance of work coming in steadily for the next year or so. I regretted my lack of capital – I would bring to the marriage about £80 in cash and a second-hand freezer (actually a flip-flop ice-cream container bought from a sweetshop), but Denis and I were winning some sort of a reputation, which was how the system worked, and there was money due to us from repeats and royalties, and by the summer I should have saved quite a bit towards a flat.

'But supposing,' said Maman, twitching her hat and looking at it in the mirror, and innocently asking the question which puts the fear of God into every writer, 'supposing one day you can't think of anything to write?'

That stopped me in my tracks. I had no idea how I would then support Polly. What were the chances of Denis and me drying up? Did it happen frequently to comedy writers? I did eventually stifle the panic and that Christmas Eve, in a small room off Maman's kitchen, I proposed to Polly – on one knee and rather emotional about it, too, I am glad to remember – and I was accepted.

We went out to a nightclub to celebrate. It was about eight o'clock in the evening, too early for the night people, so Polly and I were almost the only clubbers, but Edmundo Ros and his band played for us, and when we told him what we were celebrating he arranged for the waiter to pour us wine from somebody else's bottle (I did not know that customers then had to bring their own wine and leave their bottles in a storeroom, with a pencil line on the label showing how much they had drunk. The pencil mark was, of course, easily repositioned lower down by a bent waiter).

The following six months were rather blissful. Except when the bliss almost turned to fury when, in a burst of foolhardiness, I decided to teach Polly to drive. I do not think I have done anything quite as silly before or since.

'Gently,' I would say soothingly, 'let the clutch out now . . . MIND THAT BUS ON THE LEFT!'

'DON'T SHOUT AT ME!'

'Brake! BRAKE!' . . . and so on, both our nervous systems in tatters.

Common sense prevailed in time to save our marriage and Polly went to a professional driving instructor ('Ease out into the main road now, Miss McIrvine. Keep creeping. That's good, keep creeping . . .')

Polly booked our wedding for 16 July 1949, at the Church of the Holy Redeemer, Cheyne Row, Chelsea. The priest was Father de Zulueta, a well-known name in Catholic circles. Ours was a 'mixed' marriage, Polly being RC and I being ostensibly C of E, but really a lapsed agnostic – my doubts were beginning to waver – and I had to agree that our children, if any, would be brought up as Roman Catholics, which I was happy to do. I also had to attend a course of instruction from Father de Zulueta on the beliefs and practices of Catholicism.

My instruction took place on Thursday afternoons after work, in Father's small, book-crammed study in Cheyne Row. As it was a little chill the gas fire purred away, raising the temperature to about 95 degrees Fahrenheit and consuming most of the oxygen in the room.

Father was a good deal older than me and it was the end of his day's work as well as the end of mine. I only hope that he was the one to nod off first, and nod on again (as it were) last. I cannot honestly remember one item from my course of instruction.

I hired my thick otiose wedding suit from Moss Bros. It was the London season and I was amid impatient queues of honking and braying young men (a line of Oscar Wilde's sprang to mind which, given a little tweak, became, 'The unbearable in full pursuit of the unwearable').

Polly had prudently chosen a high lacy head-dress which, with high heels, enabled the photographer to get both our faces into the same picture.

Before the day I had a small panic about Polly's passport – we were planning to spend our honeymoon in Cannes. The drill was for the bride's passport to be sent to the authorities to be altered to her new married status. It was then lodged with the vicar or priest who handed it over to the bride after the ceremony. Just before the day I checked with Father de Zulueta.

'Ah,' he said. 'Yes. Polly's passport. Yes, I have it. The complication is I have to go to Cambridge tomorrow and I just might not be back in time for the wedding. But have no worry. I have an old friend standing by to marry you should I not be back in time. I have told him about Polly's passport which I have left for him on the mantelshelf in my study – no, it's not there, I put it for safety in the bottom – no, top drawer of my desk. But I shifted it. I thought I might forget it there, so I rather think it's on the hallstand, or did I hide it amongst my books? You will like my old friend, but I should warn you, I'm afraid he tends to be a little vague.'

We found a flat. It was in Addison Road, West Kensington, and was the top floor of a largish house which had been bombed. The building was being repaired and converted into flats with a government grant by a Mr Waite, a small builder in a bowler hat whose first burst of free enterprise this was, and he was finding it a strain. Mr Waite may have been a dab hand with a putty knife, but setting up a business was another matter. He seemed to have no capital at all; several times he borrowed money from me to pay the weekly wages of his two workers, and when Polly and I sought him out on some decorating point we would sometimes find him leaning against a wall quietly sobbing.

Father de Zulueta managed to get back from Cambridge in time to marry us and bore such a startling resemblance to our eccentric and maverick producer Pat Dixon that the large BBC contingent in the congregation burbled and snorted throughout with suppressed laughter.

We had a spot of thunder and lightning and rain at one point, but as an omen on our future it was hopelessly wrong. Then the sun came out and we all went down to the Embankment for the reception at the painter and wit James Abbot McNeill Whistler's house in Cheyne Row. There were speeches in the book-lined drawing room (Ted Kavanagh expressed his pleasure at speaking in the middle of Whistler's gag library) and then Polly and I rushed back to Maman's flat, changed and started out in the car, hood down, for the Royal Albion Hotel, Brighton, and on the next day to the Newhaven ferry and our Riviera honeymoon.

Immediately becalmed at the traffic lights into North End Road, an elderly neighbour came over to the car and said to Polly, 'Hello! And what have you been doing recently – anything interesting?'

Exchange control was very tight and we could only take out £45 each for our month in the South of France. Various schemes were tried by others to defeat regulations, the only effective one being to borrow francs from a Frenchman over there who was coming to England and pay him back here in sterling. A well-off friend of ours, Johnny Johnson, the music publisher and leader of The Keynotes singing group, tried to smuggle out a wad of £5 notes stuffed into his shoes, but the weather was very hot and when he arrived at Villefranche he found that each shoe contained a rigid papier mâché inner sole.

Pol and I had decided that the best way to have a relaxed honeymoon was to make it the best holiday possible.

We had a dodgy start. Polly's girlfriend, the one who came

to dinner with us on our first date, knew the South of France well and kindly booked us into a cheap, clean room along the road, past old Cannes. The weather was very hot so she sensibly booked us twin beds. For our honeymoon! Twin beds!

There are times when being sensible is so utterly senseless. Of course we clambered into one bed, which was very French, short and narrow. For night nourishment we had brought with us a bottle of Cointreau that a wedding guest had given us and which Polly had on her bedside table. Five minutes later we saw an army of ants marching in Indian file up from the garden, across the tiny balcony, through the French windows, along the floor, up the table leg, and then each having his (or her? – one doesn't often hear about female ants but they must exist or there would not be any ants at all) share of the sweet orange liqueur lurking round the cork of the bottle, and then they had their long march back home, quite a bit of it clambering over the backs of incoming millions of their relations.

This was the beginning of our honeymoon and to make as much room as possible for my bride, I eased well over on my side of the single bed until I was half out of it. To stop myself thudding to the ground, I put my arm down on the floor to act as a prop and went to sleep. When the sun woke us quite late the next morning, my arm had stiffened, locked and was devoid of feeling. When I got up it hung down rigidly at my side like an oar. It gradually came round, of course, and by lunchtime it tingled but was back in service as an arm.

It was a good month. We spent most of our time on the beach on a hired mattress beneath a hired parasol. These mattresses, the beach leaseholder's main income, were only about 4 inches apart and it took a long time to teeter between the mattresses to have a swim. The bit of leasehold beach we favoured was called Les Flots Bleu, kept by a most pleasant late-middle-aged, white-haired couple, Monsieur et Madame Barrioz, whose obligatory bikinis were pathetically inadequate to control their rolls of sun-burned, late-middle-aged body.

Swimming was taught by their resident *Professeur de Natation*, Monsieur Maurice, a handsome young blond hunk, but nice, and good at teaching swimming. My demonstration of the

British trudgeon stroke came as a profound culture shock to him.

For food we went each morning to the market, *en route* to the beach, and bought two or three slices of cold veal, a pocketful of *salade Macédoine* and a length of bread. A treat was a brace of bananas and a little tub of sour cream. An excellent invention of Polly's was the in-car picnic, which could be eaten whilst driving along. This was a baguette of bread with a slab of chocolate broken into strips and stuffed down the middle of the bread.

In the hot evenings we would sit at a seafront pavement table at Chez Felix, a popular and rather chic café on the Croisette, and we found that we could make a shared *orange pressée* last a whole evening. It's a wonder the Café Felix did not take legal proceedings.

And then our lovely month was over. On the way back up France to the ferry the Frazer-Nash BMW stopped going. It was on a long straight road in the middle of a forest. I struggled with the carburettor, hitting it with a shoe and swearing professionally, when by an extraordinary piece of luck two slightly shifty-looking men appeared on bicycles with sacks on their handlebars. The sacks moved. It emerged that the men were car mechanics from a nearby Citroën factory who were moonlighting for a day's sport in the woods with their ferret. In a moment they had got the car going and we were smoothly on our way again. But not for long. A terrible grinding noise started up from a rear wheel. With the confidence of the lightly knowledgeable I diagnosed that a ball-bearing had cracked and was breaking up.

It was a horrible noise. My diagnosis was correct but there was nothing whatever we could do about it except pray that the bearing held up and got us home. And so the young marrieds, Mr and Mrs Muir, too broke to stop at a café and eat, feeding each other bites from a baguette with chocolate stuffed down its middle, both of us bronzed from the sun and very, very happy, drove slowly up France to the Dieppe ferry, the off-side rear wheel scrunching and crunching like a coffee grinder.

I will now state, hand on heart, that most important of all the many good and happy things which happened to me as a growing lad, the years that I have been married to Polly, getting on for fifty of them, as compared with those early empty years when I was *not* married to Polly, have been, to borrow Geraldo's masterly phrase, much, *much* more betterer.

Chapter 9

THE FITFUL FIFTIES

Australia.
The arrival (late) of a son, Jamie.
A real home at last: Anners, Thorpe.
And . . . 'We made a sudden Sally.'
     (see Tennyson's 'The Brook')

My marriage to Polly in 1949 made such a happy curtain, act 2, for the 1940s that it would have been helpful to this chronicle if I could have picked up the momentum with a bright crisp assessment, excitingly labelled, of the predominant mood of the 1950s. But no mood seemed to predominate, so I have called the decade 'fitful', which at least reflects its unsettled nature as far as we were concerned.

Polly and I were not yet in our flat in Addison Road, although Mr Waite, the tearful builder, seemed to have accidentally completed his conversion work and had sold the building as an investment to the owner of an Indian restaurant in Kensington High Street. The restaurateur and his family took up residence in the ground floor flat.

We were short of furniture so Maman, with heroic indulgence, allowed me to construct a rectangular oak footstool in her kitchen. Now there was a mother-in-law to cherish.

It was a horrific job, sawing 2-inch-square sections of oak lengthwise on her kitchen lino without a workbench or a vice, and fitting in stout, bought-in bow-legs which seem to have been designed for supporting Dutch hotel wardrobes. Polly made a tapestry cover for it, then a second, and she is, as I write, needling away at a third. Tapestry does not wear out, it just shrinks and becomes too grubby to live with, like old husbands.

We eventually moved into the Addison Road flat and immediately acquired a dog, the first of a great many dogs (and latterly cats). She was a huge beige standard poodle with a wonderful nature and we named her Pastis, after – call us sentimental if you will – that cloudy drink which, in the South of France with the Mediterranean sun shining on it, tastes like a romantic blend of oil of aniseed and torpedo fluid.

Although Polly had taken a domestic science course at St Mary's, Ascot, was an excellent cook and dietician and was familiar with all those vital modern kitchen skills which are taught at finishing schools such as 'nurturing your stockpot' and 'keeping your teak sink fresh and hygienic', she naturally wanted to extend her horizons and so joined a brief, two-day course in European cuisine run by an ample Hungarian lady named Madame de Biro from her own kitchen in Phillimore Gardens.

Polly spent the first day learning to make *apfelstrudel*, which she then tried out at home. This involved plonking a lump of short dough on the kitchen table, rolling it out into a huge circle and then shuffling slowly round and round the table, pulling gently at the dough's skirt for four or five hours.

The pastry was delicious, of course, so Polly immediately had a go at another delicacy, which proved to be even more desperately labour-intensive: Maids of Honour – elegant, subtle tartlets of cream cheese made by hand from curds and whey, lightly flavoured with freshly ground almonds and encased in the product of another afternoon's trudge round the kitchen table, incredibly light and airy puff pastry.

It was the sort of laborious task which had it been prescribed for the punishment of Victorian burglars would have been instantly denounced by the Howard League for Penal Reform, but Polly completed her batch of tiny *bonnes bouches*, twenty-four of them in all, and beautiful they were to see and smell.

That evening Jimmy Edwards called in for a quick whisky on his way home and Pol put the plate of Maids of Honour at his side. Jimmy took a bite and started talking. An hour later, after much laughter and so on, Jimmy left. The plate was empty.

Jimmy had eaten all Polly's Maids of Honour *without even*

noticing what he was eating. But our marriage survived, and if it could survive that it could survive anything, which indeed it has.

As far as work was concerned, the 1950s began interestingly. *TIFH* was making a breakthrough overseas, particularly in Commonwealth countries and especially – having Dick and Joy in the cast – on the ABC in Australia. And from Australia came a newspaper report on *Take It From Here* which was, quite simply, as gratifying, appreciative and encouraging a piece as we could ever have hoped to read:

Australia Can 'Take It . . .'

Every Sunday night there occurs in Australia one of the strangest phenomena in the whole bizarre history of show business. A BBC radio show called *Take It From Here* goes on the air and all Australia stops to listen. What's so phenomenal about that? Just the fact that *TIFH* runs head on against every important dogma in the textbooks of variety entertainment.

Any Australian producer or entrepreneur will tell you, without qualification, what is needed to make a variety show click here. It must have Australian significance, it must have Australian gags, delivered in the Australian idiom. It must be topical, but above all else it must not be too clever. These are the inflexible axioms.

But *TIFH* has lost all its topicality months before the transcriptions arrive here; the gags, so far from being local, are invariably aimed exclusively at British audiences, and are quite often so subtle, so casually thrown away that only a tiny minority of our audiences can possibly appreciate them. Yet everywhere on Monday morning, in all our coastal capitals from Perth to Brisbane, you will hear people asking, 'Did you hear *Take It From Here* last night?' and then they will start exchanging the wisecracks that made them chuckle.

Whether they realize it or not, Muir and Norden emancipated the radio listener when they hatched *TIFH*. They defied the ancient shibboleth of the trade that you must blunt your wit to suit the mentality of the dullest member of the audience. They worked on the brave new concept that audiences have minds; they gave their listeners credit for some small smatterings of intelligence, and listeners appreciated the compliment.

How could an all-scripted, slick, sophisticated half-hour recorded overseas hope to win the approval of a people whose sense of humour was believed to be stubbornly wedded to the banana skin and the custard pie. It couldn't, of course, but it did. Gags that were topical in Britain six months before, and which should have been quite incomprehensible to us, brought gales of laughter, *TIFH* gag lines slipped easily into everyday conversation, and the throwaway technique, allegedly poison ivy to us, tickled us as we had never been tickled before.

By the end of the last series we had reached a stage where the *TIFH* half-hour was taboo for phone calls and visits. It just didn't, and doesn't, make sense, but some-how, without benefit of claques, or cheerleaders, or prizes, this British show, produced I suspect without even a thought for overseas audiences, has firmly planted itself on the Australian hearth and in the Australian heart.

. . . *Take It From Here* has taken.

Kirwan Ward

If much, or any, of that was true reporting, then it was not perhaps surprising that when in 1951 the Australian Broadcasting Commission decided to celebrate its jubilee, they invited Dick Bentley, now through *TIFH* a big star in radio, to return home to broadcast a special series of ten half-hour comedy programmes. They hoped it would be written in Australia by Denis and me.

This was not a wholly welcome idea as I was not at all keen on leaving my bride on her own for three months and Denis and Avril were equally unkeen to leave their four-year-old son Nick and his baby sister Maggie, so we tried to get out of the trip by asking for a large fee, expenses, a rented flat each and our wives and Nick to be with us. To our dismay our terms were accepted and we had to go.

The flight from Heathrow to Sydney took five days. The plane was a BOAC Super Constellation, a large airliner shaped like a banana. We landed in Rome at midday and all piled into a coach clutching a packed lunch in a cardboard box (like the Institute of Directors at their Albert Hall AGM) and were conducted on a tour of the Holy City by a sweet Italian girl student ('Roma was-a beelt on seven eels'). In the afternoon we flew on to Cairo where we disemplaned again and spent the night in Shephard's Hotel.

We began to get to know some of the other passengers. In the seats behind us was a pair of prep-school boys on their way home, unaccompanied, to holiday with their army parents in Sydney. The taller of the two looked after his younger brother's welfare in exemplary fashion. When exchange control asked us if we had any sterling currency to declare, the senior brother's voice piped up fearlessly, 'Please, sir, yes, sir! I have two pounds fifteen shillings and my younger brother Robin has three and tuppence.'

Next to the boys sat Mrs Macnamara, a broad elderly Irish lady not enjoying her first taste of flying. Her fare had been paid by her son and daughter-in-law, who had emigrated, so that she could see her grandchildren in Melbourne.

It was a long way from Dublin to Melbourne and as we flew eastwards, Mrs Macnamara suffered more and more from the heat. All her belongings seemed to be crammed into a huge string bag which she wedged on the empty seat between herself and the boys, but every time we disembarked to refuel or eat or sleep, Mrs Macnamara's ankles grew thicker and her string bag grew thinner.

We asked Mrs Macnamara whether she had enjoyed her night in Cairo.

'No, I didn't enjoy it, I didn't, no,' she said. 'What with the heat, and the flies, and the soft-walking natives.'

Next day on to Calcutta, where we changed aircrews. This was an alarming experience, as while we were pretending to enjoy our lunch in the airport restaurant, we watched a happy crew of mechanics in dhotis sitting on top of one of our plane's engines, laughing and chattering and banging vaguely at the engine with spanners.

As we were called to board the plane for its long next leg to Singapore over the shark-infested Timor Sea, the captain and crew stood up and the captain called out to us, rather pointedly I thought, 'Good luck!'

We had to sleep in flight that night, which was comfortable enough, though an electric storm with lightning was unnecessarily Wagnerian.

Our overnight stay the next day at Raffles Hotel, Singapore (in an annex at the back), was memorable on two scores. Polly had bought me one of the new nylon shirts for travelling. The good thing about a nylon shirt was, of course, that it dried quickly in the hotel room after being washed. The bad thing was that in Singapore it dried *too* quickly. I washed it in our bedroom basin, wrung it out and by the time I had hung it up in the wardrobe to dry, it had dried and become a wrinkled crumpled mess like a used face tissue. I tried again and sprinted across with the damp shirt to the wardrobe, but on arrival it was again bone-dry and unwearably twisted.

The second Singapore memory was having drinks in the famous Raffles Long Bar with a friendly bear of an Australian who was the editor of a Brisbane newspaper and a most generous host. When he at last called for the bill he told the waiter to charge it to room 141.

When the waiter departed I asked, 'Are you sure there *is* a room one-four-one?' 'Never failed me yet, mate!' he said.

We took off the next morning for the last leg of the journey, refuelled in sub-tropical Darwin and then flew on, flying south to lob down at last, on our fifth day, in Sydney, New South Wales.

The two schoolboys behind us were ecstatic at glimpsing their parents waiting on the tarmac, he in his rather grand uniform and she waving emotionally at every plane which taxied anywhere near her.

Mrs Macnamara was still not enjoying herself much. She had mislaid her huge straw hat in Asia and had spent the last leg of the journey fanning herself vigorously with BOAC's instruction card on how to put on your life jacket when the plane fell into the sea. Her string bag was worryingly empty.

Denis and I reported to the ABC the next afternoon (tired

from the journey but jet lag had yet to be invented), meeting the British ex-actor who was going to produce our show, and Harry Pringle, Head of Variety programmes, who showed us round the offices of ABC in Pitt Street. Just before six o'clock, when all the grog shops and pubs had to close for the day, Harry took us downstairs for a quick drink down in the 'hotel' next door. Keen drinkers were standing about on the pavement knocking back schooners of lager as quickly as they could get them refilled at the bar.

A lean leathery character, looking like a sheep shearer, staggered out carrying a glass in each hand and sipping carefully at them in turn so that he wouldn't spill too much. Harry introduced his colleague, who was wearing a flat pork-pie hat with a wide brim. He was having some difficulty with his balance.

Harry said, 'I'd like you to meet a colleague of mine, ABC's Federal Director of Education.'

The ABC was Australia's leading promoter of classical music, mounting concerts and arranging visits from important international soloists. Tickets could be bought by the public at the counter in ABC's Pitt Street offices.

It seems that the ABC once arranged a tour for the pianist Solomon and the ABC's chief, Charles Moses, went to the airport as usual to welcome the great man personally. They met in the VIP lounge. The famous pianist took the ABC chief's hand and bowed slightly.

'Solomon,' he said.

'Moses,' said the ABC's chief, bowing back.

'I do not think that is very funny,' said the great pianist.

Charles Moses was then in late middle age but still relentlessly athletic. He was shortish but barrel-chested and devoted to tree-felling.

Chopping up fallen trees into two lengths was an Aussie competitive sport. The feller stood on the tree bole sideways, swung his axe and whacked a wedge out of the side of the tree between his feet. He then leaped into the air, spun round 90 degrees and whacked a wedge out of the other side of the tree. He repeated this as swiftly as possible until the job was done or he went dizzy and severed a foot. It took quite a few whacks to bisect a thick gum tree.

One Sunday Charles and his wife kindly drove the two Muirs and the two and a half Nordens up into the Blue Mountains for a purist barbecue lunch. Purist because Mr Moses was not one of those urban softies who used firelighters to get the show going, or used already prepared logs, or charcoal, or indeed a barbecue machine itself. He preferred to practise survival techniques.

Mr Moses felled a medium-sized gum tree, axed it to pieces in minutes and arranged the logs and twigs in a hollow in the ground. Then, eschewing the effete use of matches, he spun a twig between his palms until, much, much later, a wisp of smoke arose. We were now about two hours into the afternoon and a light drizzle was falling.

Denis, with a display of woodsmanship which made me proud of him, whispered to me to lure Charles and his wife away towards the panoramic view of Sydney. When we were out of sight, Denis dipped Avril's handkerchief into the car's petrol tank and urged it under the bonfire with a twig. We heard a 'whoosh!' and when we returned from contemplating the rooftops of Sydney there was a huge cloud of smoke billowing up from the damp boskage and in the middle a tiny flame flickered, like the pilot light of the ancient Ewart's 'Victor' geyser at the Derby Arms Hotel.

It was not exactly a gourmet lunch which we eventually sat down to eat in the rain, but the partially burned and partially raw chops were redeemed by plenty of powerful Aussie red wine and a warm feeling that we were being pioneers. Which indeed we were. It was the first barbecue in which we Pommies had ever participated, in fact it was the first barbecue we five had ever *seen*. Meat rationing was still going strong in England and you could not barbecue 'a book and a half of mince'.

The ABC had found Polly and me a small pleasant flat in Pott's Point, which was the property of the gay son of the owner of one of Australia's hamburger chains. It was well furnished except, perhaps, for a tad too many portraits on the walls of heavily muscled, Bambi-eyed young men.

The Nordens were just round the corner in a comfortable flat in Elizabeth Bay. Unfortunately their daughter Maggie was too young to be taken on such a long trip, a sensible decision which she resented at the time, and, now that she is more mature and wiser, still does.

It was in Sydney that we first heard real local radio, neighbourhood stuff. The first radio commercial we caught was an announcement between records of popular music (as distinct from 'pop') that 'Dexters Caff on the corner of Market Place has just got in a delivery of that chocolate cake of theirs, so you'd better get round there right away – I warn you, mates, it'll all be gone by five o'clock!'

The Sydney of forty years ago has changed so much that it is almost unrecognizable now, except for the bridge, the harbour and Bondi beach. It was always an energetic, busy sort of city, but now it has become (which large capital city hasn't?) more international than national. Back in 1951 it seemed more Australian and friendlier. Sydney had just two expensive restaurants and it was a tiny adventure for a visitor to cross over to the North Shore; they had huge ticks there, we were told proudly, which could kill a dog.

We noted with pleasure the tiny differences in English usage, like a placard for an evening paper we saw when we arrived which read, 'OLD MAN BASHED IN PARK'.

As soon as the weather came good the working population tended to drift off to the beach for a swim. Even waiters were known to disappear mid-meal. The effect of this was that 'refos' (refugees from Europe) who continued to trundle their sewing machines in back rooms making handbags when the sun shone were gradually taking over the retail trades.

It was early spring and although the sun was hot the water was too cold for us to cavort happily in the briny and be flattened by huge unpredictable Pacific waves ('dumpers'), but while Den and I were writing, Polly and Avril and small Nicky sat happily on the beach, and the sand was excellent for construction work (Nick is now an architect).

We had left an England still in the grip of restrictions; items such as meat, sweets and clothing were still rationed, and it was a joy for us to be able to buy as much meat as we wanted. But Australia also had its problems; there were odd little strikes and some strange items were in short supply: potatoes, for instance.

Hotels and restaurants coped with this by serving well-boiled rice pressed into shape by an ice-cream scoop, so that it looked like mashed potato. And there was a shortage of beer. Beer!

Australia was still a beer-drinking society then (changing to enjoying its own wine in recent years) and one result of this beer shortage tragedy was that the champagne bucket on restaurant tables held ice and, nestling amidst the ice cubes, a bottle of Fosters lager.

With 'Time gentlemen please!' being shouted at six o'clock in the evening and the sun still hot overhead it is hardly surprising that a small web of illegal drinking places sprang up, known as 'sly grog joints', where you could drink on into the night. Denis and I were deeply impressed by these because we were brought up on early Hollywood films when Prohibition was very much a subject for drama, and here it was in reality, life imitating art.

The door of a sly grog joint had an iron grille protecting a sliding panel, so that the owner of the face which appeared on the sly grog side could not be dragged through the hatch by a thirst-crazed non-member of the club. I actually had to say to the face through the grille, 'Rupe Dumbrell sent us,' before bolts were withdrawn and we were allowed in.

Rupe, really Rupert (almost all given names were shortened in Australia, e.g., 'Ian' became 'Ee'), arranged the music for our programme; he was Canadian, cool and a very amusing talker. His father was an archbishop.

Another relic of old Australia which was still around was the illegal gambling game of Two-Up. In this, a couple of punters bet on whether two coins spun into the air would both come down heads or tails (I think that was what it was about). There was a neutral third party who spun the coins. This he did on hearing the punters utter the great old Australian cry, 'Come in, spinner!' It does not sound all that exciting a game but it was.

A more sophisticated and much cheaper method of acquiring grog than in a sly grog joint was demonstrated by the producer of our programme, a very British ex-actor who had emigrated from England when the going became tough and was making himself less than popular in Australian circles by coming out with observations like, 'How I miss my little flat in Half Moon Street and Morny soap.'

Before the run of our show, which we called Gently, Bentley, this man kindly invited Dick and the cast, plus Denis and me, to a Sunday lunchtime bottle party. 'Bring a bottle of anything, whisky, champagne, even wine would do.'

On arrival everybody dutifully handed over their bottle which soon formed a colourful collection on the sideboard. When we had all gathered, our host disappeared for a moment to check, he said, how the cooking was proceeding. He returned a few minutes later haggard of face, biting his lip and clearly bearing bad news.

'Dreadfully sorry, loves,' he said, 'I'm afraid lunch is off. The lady wife . . . the dreaded migraine has struck again . . . poor old dear will be in a darkened room for hours, in agony. If you hurry you should be able to get some lunch in a pub downtown.' We found ourselves being hustled out of the front door. 'Don't bother about your bottles; you can leave them where they are . . .'

Gently, Bentley took to the airwaves at 7.15 p.m., 31 August 1951, for ten weeks, and on the whole did its job well. In those days radio acting fees were low and Australian radio actors had to cram a lot of shows in per week to make a decent living, so we found our supporting cast extremely swift in finding the right voices for their characters and bringing the characters to life.

The show had good reviews, Dick Bentley and his wife Peta enjoyed a paid working holiday – they travelled from England comfortably by sea – and due to forethought on our part in taking with us some spare unused ideas from TIFH and Breakfast with Braden, the Muirs and the Nordens too managed to have an enjoyable three months semi-holiday.

A lack of stress was important as Pol and I were beginning to worry about not producing a baby and we had hoped that our three months of serious meat-eating might have helped our chances. A few days before our flight home Polly needed to rest all day, feet up, and this was not at all easy to arrange in our schedule. But fate leaped to our aid. The key day turned out to be Yom Kippur, a day on which Denis was then unkeen to work, so we took the day off and Polly rested.

As Australia is about as far as you can fly before you start fly-ing back home again, it costs no more to make the round trip, so we all came home via Fiji, Hawaii, San Francisco and New York. The flight across the Pacific was memorable for its comfort. It was a night flight and in a few minutes the cabin staff converted the whole plane into sleepers; seats became bunks and an upper row of bunks hinged down from the ceiling. Each bunk had curtains to draw for privacy and everybody changed into pyjamas, climbed between sheets and had a good night's kip. A wonderful way to travel.

Polly found that she was indeed pregnant – good old Yom Kippur – and as we only had a short stop of a day or so in New York we rushed to Macy's to buy American nappies – designer nappies compared with austerity British equivalents. In the Expectant Family-Maker's department the sales assistant, a plump white-coated American Mom-figure, helped Polly care-fully across the carpet.

'And how far are you into your pregnancy?' the Mom-figure asked discreetly, letting Polly sink slowly into a chair.

'About four days,' said Polly.

The pregnancy held firm and when we arrived back at Addison Road there was a lot to do. Polly wanted to have her baby at home and she was recommended a splendid female gynaecologist, Dr Mary Adams, who in her turn recommended a monthly nurse, Sister Toft – the late dear Tofty.

The baby arrived on Saturday 4 July at 19 Addison Road, West Kensington (top flat).

I had been banished to the drawing room, to my great relief as I would have keeled over at the first sign of anything, and I would now be able to watch Drobny play in the Wimbledon men's final on television. But it was not to be. As Drobny pottered onto the court clutching his five or six tennis rackets, Dr Adams shot in.

'Have you got the phone number of the blood bank?'

'Er – no,' I muttered, switching off the telly, 'I'll look it up in the directory.'

Dr Adams shot back to the action.

I found the directory and began feverishly searching.

Dr Adams shot in again.

'Hot-water bottles!' she said. 'Quickly! As many as you can find!' And away she went again.

I stumbled around and found one hot-water bottle, which seemed a bit inadequate, so I ran downstairs to see if I could borrow more from the flats below. Nobody was in. I rushed back upstairs, almost knocking Dr Adams over in the corridor.

'Don't bother about the hot-water bottles,' she said, 'or the blood bank,' and she went back into the bedroom.

I slumped down in front of the telly and switched on, nerves jangling. 'Play!' said the umpire. Drobny bounced the ball five or six times, threw it high in the air and was about to wallop it when I heard the thin, not unhappy, first cry of a new baby.

He was 10 pounds 2 ounces, quite an achievement for small lean Polly. He had to be helped out with those pastry tong things, which gave him blue bruises here and there and a black eye which, combined with some dark, greasy-looking hair, made our son and heir look like a heavy-weight boxer who had just lost his title after fifteen gruelling rounds.

We wanted to christen him Jamie, but as this seemed in those days an obscure and slightly pretentious name, we decided to call him Peter James and leave it to him to choose which name he preferred when he reached the age of reason. At school he asked to be called Peter and then mysteriously changed into Jamie on his twenty-second birthday.

Once I almost drowned the infant Peter James. I was bathing him in a rubber portable bath arrangement, supporting his neck in my left hand in the correct Norland Nanny manner when the lad turned over, rolled off my hand and disappeared under the soapy water. However, no lasting harm was done (I think). I fished about in the water for a while and retrieved him; he was a bit green and blowing bubbles but seemed otherwise intact. I was not much help to Polly, not that fathers were expected to be all that helpful in those days; Denis and I were working rather hard.

I was reminded just how busy Denis and I were in the mid-1950s when Denis recently found his working diary for 1950-something-or-other and rang me in awe at the amount of work, meetings and interviews which we got through in a working day. And this was in the summer when *TIFH* was not on air. But then we were both semi-young, just into our early thirties (except Denis who was still clinging on to his late twenties) – a sketch which then would have taken us an hour to write would take us about six weeks now.

A typical entry in Den's diary was July 1955, 'Lunch with Jack Waller. Savoy Grill. 12.45.'

Jack Waller was a successful theatrical impresario who had just produced a smash-hit farce, *Sailor Beware* by Philip King, starring Peggy Mount in her first appearance in a West End play. We presumed, rightly as it turned out, that Mr Waller was hoping that Den and I had a couple of brilliant farces in the middle drawer of our desk waiting to be produced. He soon realized that we did not have anything in our middle drawer except some indigestion tablets (we tended to have hot bacon sandwiches for lunch when pressed for time) and lots of bits of paper covered with once urgent, but now meaningless notes.

Jack Waller was a small, neat, quite old man, and as soon as he realized that we had no play to offer him, nor time to write him one, he relaxed and was rivetingly interesting about his early life in show business. He had begun at the end of the last century as a musician in a minstrel troupe and he composed music for many of his own later productions. He was an actor and a music-hall performer before becoming a 'producing manager' and organizing extensive tours of plays and musicals in what were then known as the British Dominions.

His stories of touring small towns in the hinterland of South Africa – the 'dorps' – before the First World War were notable for the colourful excuses given to him by local theatre managers for the small audiences which had turned up at their theatres. Such as: 'You picked the wrong time, Jack. Everybody stays behind locked doors when the elephants are in must.'

(*OED*: *MUST* / *n*. A male elephant on heat and in a state of dangerous frenzy.)

Another theatre manager: 'Trouble is, Jack, we had a troupe of Swiss handbell ringers here only a month ago. This town is over-entertained.'

I was never very good at working lunches. A bit like

President Ford of the USA who was accused by a political enemy of not being able to chew gum and fart at the same time, I have always found difficulty in simultaneously chatting and eating.

Denis's diary revealed that when Kenneth Horne and Richard Murdoch's radio show *Much-Binding-in-the-Marsh* was at its peak, the highly successful British film-maker, Sydney Box, invited Denis and me to lunch at his Lime Grove studios to discuss the possibility of us writing a film version of *Much-Binding*. It was all rather splendid. The dining room, just along the corridor from the front door, was handsomely panelled and the long table was brilliant with linen, silver and glass.

We were joined for lunch by the studio's producers and directors, some of whom we knew, and I was for once talking wittily to Sydney Box whilst helping myself to Brussels sprouts from a dish held by a waitress when a quiet fell and I noticed that I was being looked at.

Whilst talking wittily to Sydney Box I had inadvertently helped myself to all the Brussels sprouts. With mantling cheeks I spooned them back.

A few evenings after the Lime Grove embarrassment, I was with Polly at the Caprice restaurant and we were sitting just a table away from Sydney and Betty Box. We had ordered steak, asparagus and peas. My steak was on the tough side and I was sawing away at it when Mr Box gave a friendly wave. Put off my rhythm, my knife slipped and I sprayed both Sydney and Betty Box with a machine-gun-like burst of hot peas.

Denis and I never did work for Sydney Box. Nor did he eat near me again, come to think of it.

Many years later my unhappy knack of doing something silly whilst trying to eat and think at the same time surfaced again one lunchtime (like chickenpox, the virus never dies; it just lies dormant for ages and then reactivates).

This time I was Head of Entertainment for London Weekend Television and I had unwisely agreed to have an important working lunch in the Park Lane Hotel Grill with Yorkshire Television's Head of Comedy. It was unwise because I was breaking in a new little dental bridge.

My big mistake was to begin with prawn cocktail, which

was half a dozen violently pink prawns with reproachful eyes lying on a bed of strips of lettuce in a wineglass, the whole lightly sprinkled with an 'exotic sauce', actually a mixture of bottled mayonnaise and tomato ketchup (£8.50 – not including tip). I was talking vehemently when I noticed that my companion was watching my mouth with a kind of fascinated horror.

Looking downwards as far as I was able, I could see that I seemed to have grown a new tongue, much longer than the old one, and narrower and bright green. Whenever I began talking, it shot out and fluttered like a yacht burgee in a good racing wind at Cowes, and as it fluttered it made a kind of low buzzing sound.

I sucked it back in several times, but it blew out again whenever I tried to keep our important conversation going. What had clearly happened was that one end of a strip of lettuce had become trapped beneath my unfamiliar bridgework. The low buzz I was making was attracting considerable attention from the other eaters, as was the fluttering length of lettuce, and swift action was called for.

I hissed sharply. The green strip blew out and trembled in the wind, 'zzzzzz'. I reached up, grabbed it and gave it a discreet pull. My two new teeth in their bright metal setting shot out and dropped into the butter.

Much-Binding-in-the-Marsh cropped up once more when Dickie Murdoch was commissioned by *Lilliput* magazine to write some short stories based on the radio series. Once the contract was signed, Dickie went off the whole idea; he did not enjoy writing prose and he asked me to ghost write the stories for him, which I was quite happy to do, reckoning it would be useful experience, my first bursting into print since my parish magazine serial about the Chinese airmen. Dickie then lived in Staines, just by the river, and I went down there one evening to discuss payment.

Absolutely typical of Dickie – a charming and delightful man – was that he could not bear to talk money face to face, so he waited until it was dark, drew the curtains, switched off the lights and we discussed my fee in pitch-darkness.

Denis and I were beginning to do quite a bit of writing for

stage revues, mainly sketches for George and Alfred Black and Jack Hylton summer shows. One of the first of these jobs was to write a revue for Jack Hylton starring Jimmy, Dick and Joy. It went on at the Piccadilly Theatre and was called, inevitably, *Take It From Us*.

Jimmy by then had become a very strong theatre performer, and his schoolmaster act — which Denis and I helped put together for him — was successful and reliable. For theatre purposes we had given him much more visual comedy. He strode on stage in gown and mortarboard, swishing his cane and glowering at the audience as though they were a difficult class, and went straight to a tall stand-up desk which had two handbells on its top. He took one of these off and rang it vigorously, shouting, 'Quiet, everywhere! Fags out! Pay attention!' He put the handbell back and pulled at the handle of the other bell. It was a beer pump. He pumped a few strokes then lifted the desk lid and produced a frothing half pint of bitter. 'Cheers!' he said.

He glanced out of the window and noticed somebody. 'It's our dear matron!' he explained to the audience. 'She's going to watch the cricket match sitting on her shooting stick.' He smiled benignly and looked out of the window again. Shock, horror!

'Matron! *No!*' he yelled out of the window, then mimed turning the shooting stick round the other way.

George and Alfred Black booked Jimmy for many of their Blackpool summer seasons and before the first of these shows Denis and I went up there to see the theatre and generally get the feel of Blackpool. We were wandering along the Golden Mile one afternoon when we idly wandered into one of the sideshows: it was the World's Fattest Lady. She was probably not in fact the world's fattest lady — in Russia there is usually somebody fatter or hairier or older than anybody else — but she was a vast enough person, slumped in a strong chair in the corner of a small room. There was nobody else in the room. The gentleman who had taken our half-crowns had nipped along to the pub.

It was difficult to know where to look. It seemed rude to stare at her rolls of fat, yet those were her contribution to public pleasure.

''Ow do,' she said in a friendly way, after an agonizing ten minutes or so of silence. 'It's took warm again, 'ant it?'

That was a tricky remark to reply to. 'I suppose you feel it more than most of us . . .' would have been insensitive. Den said, 'Yes, the chap on the radio said it's set in for a couple of days,' a long pause, 'which brings us to next Friday.'

'Good Lord!' I said. 'Does it?' I examined my watch. 'Then it's time we got going.'

We went.

Jimmy was now well established as a top-of-the-bill comic. He had bought a 2,000-acre farm in Fletching, Sussex, which was run by his brother Alan, and he kept his own hunters and polo ponies. He loved playing polo but there was not a lot of it happening on a Sunday in Blackpool, and Windsor Great Park, Cirencester and most polo grounds were an awkwardly long way away from Blackpool for Jimmy to get a game in on his one day off, so he bought himself a plane. It was a little Cessna which he flew carefully and safely, very Bomber Command, straight and level and no showing off.

I went on a few trips with him and occasionally he let me have a go at the controls which was exhilarating. Flying a plane is a bit like riding a bike (only more expensive); once you have done it you never forget how to do it, and a plane is a little like a boat – slow to react, no brakes.

He kept his little plane at Blackpool's Squires Gate airport, from which field modest airlines with small planes such as the de Havilland Dragon, which had about ten seats, flew holiday-makers to the Isle of Man.

These small airlines had to be careful with money, and when a pilot left to better himself they tried to find a replacement who would fit the other man's uniform (like dance orchestras in those days which wore expensive uniforms and whose trade papers carried small ads such as, 'Violinist doubling sax wanted urgently for prestigious Manchester nightclub; 48-inch chest.'

Jimmy told me of a legendary character at Blackpool Airport, an Irish pilot who had newly joined the airline and was too big to fit into his predecessor's official kit so had to wear his own clothes.

One summer morning, in a checked shirt and shorts, he

joined a planeload of sunseekers off to the Isle of Man for their holidays and sat himself down in a seat at the back of the air-craft. After a few minutes waiting he muttered very loudly, 'If the pilot doesn't turn up in two minutes, begorra, I'll fly the thing meself!'

Two minutes later, he cried, 'Time's up!' strode down the aisle, squeezed through the narrow doorway into the pilot's compartment and flew the planeload of petrified passengers to a perfect landing at Douglas, IOM.

There is a PS.

Jimmy Edwards told this jape to a group of us after lunch at the Savile Club, and the Scottish novelist Eric Linklater suddenly said, 'But I know him; he's a legend in the Highlands. A friend of mine was on an Islander plane well on the way to the Outer Hebrides and on automatic pilot when the pilot's door opened and the pilot, our large Irishman, backed out slowly, unwinding a ball of string as he went. He stopped at a frail old lady, gave her the string to hold and said, "I've got to take a wee-wee at the back there, me lovely. The plane's nice and steady at the moment, but if her nose starts to drop just give the string a steady strong pull. Will ye do that for me?"'

Jimmy eventually gave up his plane because it was noisy, bouncy in boisterous weather and it was slow. The decision came one summer evening when he was flying back to Blackpool after playing an afternoon's polo in Windsor Park, and the headwind was so strong that quite small cars on the Great North Road beneath him were going north much faster than he was.

One of the best things about Jimmy was that he was ex-cellent company. He loved amusing people, not by telling jokes (which are frequently little nuggets of malice) but with humour, recounting gently amusing things he had heard people say and which he wanted to share.

He was one of those rare comics who could say uncon-ventionally provocative things without raising hackles. Playing polo once against the Duke of Edinburgh's team and being ridden off the ball by the duke, Jimmy cried out, 'Stay close to me, sir, and you'll get your face in the newspapers!' (perhaps a small royal hackle might have lifted a little).

And during the warm-up before a recording of *Take It From Here*, Jimmy would indicate his huge tummy and explain to the audience, 'It's only puppy fat. I had a puppy for lunch.'

How many comics could get away with that without being lynched?

Many of our Sunday-afternoon get-togethers in the Paris Cinema before recording *TIFH* were lit by Jimmy's reminiscences of his week in the country. Like when he held a rough shoot over the farm with some friends in the hope of a pheasant or two and they accidentally shot one of the beaters. He had been banging about the undergrowth with his stick and had put up some pheasants, but the birds had flown low and the guns had winged the beater.

Jimmy rushed forward to see what damage had been done to the wounded man, who lay writhing face down on the ground.

'It's all right, sir,' groaned the beater, 'only shot me in the arse. I were born lucky.'

And a truly memorable occasion one winter when Jimmy, newly engaged, arranged a small, very rough shoot in a water-logged wood on the farm.

His fiancée, Valerie, sporting an engagement ring with enormous diamonds glinting in the cold sunshine, thought she would make herself useful by joining the beaters, so off she sloshed through the mud. A little while later we heard her give a shriek. Then she shouted, 'Jimmy! I'm in deep mud and sinking! Quick, help me!'

Jimmy shouted back, 'Listen very carefully. Take off your engagement ring and THROW IT AS HARD AS YOU POSSIBLY CAN IN THIS DIRECTION!'

From 1950 to 1955, Jack Hylton starred Jimmy in a series of revues and variety shows at the Adelphi Theatre, London, for which Denis and I wrote Jimmy's material, Jimmy's co-stars ranged from Tony Hancock to Vera Lynn. Vera was off one week and Hylton replaced her with a new, young, strong-voiced singer he had found in Cardiff; it was Shirley Bassey.

Jack Hylton was an impresario of the old order, an ex-highly successful band leader, shrewd, dictatorial, coarse-textured, given to eating fish and chips in the back of his Rolls followed by a pound or so of grapes, the skins and pips of which he spat in the direction of an ashtray. But with all that he was a remark-ably good judge of popular taste.

The Crazy Gang were just back from a tour of the Far East and Jack Hylton, anxious to get a new show together for them, asked Denis and me to write them some sketches and pieces. This we did and read them over to the assembled Gang at a planning meeting.

An interesting point emerged. The Crazy Gang shows were essentially ribald, smutty in the good old English music-hall tradition, so we had worked touches of this kind of colour into the scripts. The Gang was shocked. And so, at this response, were we. The group of funny old men who ten minutes before had been gleefully showing us the porno souvenirs they had brought back from the Far East – playing cards with explicit nudes on the back, handkerchiefs with a little border of crude drawings of couplings, rude matchboxes – were taking offence at the harmless saucy lines we had written for them.

'I couldn't say *that*!' said Nervo (or Knox), vigorously scratching out the offending line with a ballpoint pen which revealed a naked lady when turned upside down.

Back at the office Den and I tried to work out their curiously paradoxical attitude and light eventually dawned.

'I think', said Den, 'the problem is that they feel a bit insulted when given smutty lines, as though we think their comedy is built on that kind of humour . . .'

'Which it is,' I said.

'Which it is,' Den agreed. 'But *they* have to put in the smut themselves.'

Which is what eventually happened. The Gang started out not using our pieces in the new show, but then they worked them in, and Denis and I were interested to see that the pieces were now rich in little smutty jokes which were not of our making.

Months later Jack Hylton asked us to call in at his office.

'I haven't paid you enough for those bits you wrote for the Gang,' he said.

Not paid enough? Was this the great Jack Hylton, notably careful with money, speaking? Denis and I looked at each other fearfully. Were we somehow being manipulated? Was it a trap?

He gestured towards the safe on the wall and his general manager, the genial and gifted Hughie Charles (he co-wrote Vera Lynn's 'We'll Meet Again' and many more wartime songs of cheer and encouragement), drew out a packet of banknotes. Mr Hylton took two bunches and gave them to us. 'A hundred each,' he said. 'Unless . . .' he said, raising his eyebrows, 'unless you'd rather have equity shares in the new Rediffusion Television Company?'

Associated Rediffusion had just won their commercial TV licence and Hylton was in the thick of it, promoting profitable ideas and acting as Rediffusion's Head of Variety.

Denis and I, clutching our lovely banknotes, exchanged glances. Green we may have been in money matters, but we knew instinctively when taking a risk would almost certainly be financial suicide.

'We'll take the money!' we said, smiling quietly to show that we knew better than to be palmed off with a few dodgy shares.

Some forty years later, Denis had lunch with the late Lord Willis, plain Ted as he was back in 1951, a very successful TV writer – *Dixon of Dock Green*, *Taxi!* – who had just been signed up by Hylton to provide ideas for new light-drama series for Rediffusion. Ted had been made the same offer as us and had chosen the shares.

Den told Ted about our canny decision to take the cash. Ted did a sum on the tablecloth. 'If you, like me, had taken the shares,' he said, peering at his sums, 'they would now be worth about fifty thousand pounds to each of you.'

As the 1950s progressed, Denis and I wrote all manner of shows, *TIFH* in the winter and then other radio shows in the summer break; and there were the usual requirements of summer-season sketches, and Adelphi shows for George and Alfred Black from 1950 to 1955, and comedy film scenes to rewrite.

At home on the top floor of 19 Addison Road, Polly was finding that a small flat three floors up was not the perfect place to bring up a large child. It meant leaving the pram – a large-wheeled gondola in those days – by the front door and carrying the heavy lad up the three flights of stairs.

The nearest stretch of healthy air and greenery was Kensington Gardens, which was quite a long trudge with a big pram and a big baby and a big dog, so we decided to find a house with a bit of a garden which was within our somewhat slender means.

It took a year.

Jamie was still young enough to need close attention, so it was mainly my job on Saturday afternoons to work through the estate agents' lists, driving briskly from 'small family house of character, would respond to improvement' (ex-railway worker's cottage with dry rot in Ruislip) to 'modern chalet-style architectural gem, divided for convenience, close to quiet railway line' (semi-detached bungalow near Woking with tremendously busy railway line to Waterloo running past the bottom of the garden).

It was a depressing exercise. Finally, just to reassure ourselves that there was somewhere in the world a house in which we would like to live, we upped the top amount we were prepared to pay from £4,000 to £6,000. From Harrods, of all people, came details of what they called 'a small manor house' (which it never was; it had always been a farmhouse) in the quiet village of Thorpe, which lies in the middle of Staines, Egham, Virginia Water and Chertsey. The ancient, listed, Grade II house belonged to a lady who had just got divorced, and to get rid of her unhappy home quickly she had whitewashed the beautiful old red-brick exterior, and this could not be economically removed.

The house, named Anners (originally Gorings Farm), lay in 2½ acres of farmer's uncared-for, overgrown land with about fifty scabrous apple trees, lots of ancient wooden outbuildings about to fall down and a coach house/garage. A dirty grey horse peacefully grazed on the rough meadow grass which should have been the lawn, and a neighbour's rusty car was permanently parked in the driveway.

I peered through the kitchen window. An ancient ATCO lawnmower was standing in the shallow sink and the stone floor was a-swim with silverfish. Further inspection revealed that many windows were broken and the lead had been stolen from the roof.

We had found our dream home.

I drove Maman down and excitedly showed her round, and then Polly was able to get away from Addison Road domesticity for an afternoon. It was agreed all round, albeit reluctantly, that Anners had capability.

The price asked was too high for us, but the unhappy lady was open to a lower offer to get rid of the place and we bought it for £4,500. Oddly, for a house which had seen much unhappiness, it has always been a most happy home for us, seeming to exude calm and friendliness from its bricks.

As the house had been derelict for a couple of years there was quite a bit of repairing and decorating to be done. We hired a small local builder to do it. Wallpaper and glossy paint and Wilton carpeting were beyond our means – we had hardly any means at all after buying the house – so we began life at Anners with the walls painted with faintly tinted distemper (which we bought wholesale from a friend of a friend) and art felt floor covering. Art – short for 'artificial' not 'artistic' – had curious non-qualities. Unlike real carpet it did not recuperate. When the huge poodle peed on the blue-grey felt, which she did hourly being an urban dog and distrustful of grass, the large stain grew darker and then settled down to become a bright orange-yellow. Nothing at all could be done about this. And where one turned on one's heel, as at the foot of the stairs, a large hole immediately began to wear through the felt. Nothing could be done about that, either.

I had one rather bright idea. To put on a shelf next to the bed in our guest bedroom a selection of the sort of reading matter which would discourage guests from making their stay with us a long one (Benjamin Franklin wrote in *Poor Richard's Almanack for 1735*, 'Fish and visitors smell in three days').

The title of some of these (they are all genuine books) should have had the average visitor backing the car out before breakfast on day two:

Teach Yourself Practical Concreting (A. E. Peatfield)
Hiawatha, Rendered into Latin (F. W. Newman)
Hull Celebrities from 1640–1858 (W. A. Gunnell)

The Poetry and Philosophy of Sewage Utilisation (E. D. Girdlestone)
Little Elsie's Book of Bible Animals (1879)
Effective Punting (James Pembroke)

And lastly – slightly worrying?

Hindustani Self-Taught by the Natural Method (E. Marlborough)

The bright idea did not work because the books were old and curious and rather fun to leaf through.

Two and a half acres of garden – actually 'rough meadow' would be more accurate – was something of a nightmare to me with only Saturdays to do anything about it, but sheer delight for Polly whose priorities I believe to have been (1) flowers and any other kind of beautiful or useful bits of nature, (2) our poodle, or any other make of dog, cat, or small furry mammal, (3) me.

Polly was the horticulturist, I was the labourer. I bought a huge and ancient lawnmower, a Dennis as used to trim Lord's Cricket Ground before a Test. It weighed about a ton and seemed to have been lightly converted from a First World War tank. I also bought a petrol-driven Allen scythe. With these I set about subduing the vast stretches of nettles, cow-parsley and rough tufts of grass, and I hacked down, Charles Moses fashion, dozens of spindly, half-dead fruit trees. I tackled the bumps and dips in the ground by mixing together a small mountain of peat, top-soil and a bit of sand and, helped by friends, spread and pushed it about all over the grass with the back of a wooden rake. The treatment worked rather well.

In February 1953, on a bright and clear day with the sun shining, we moved into Anners, and we are still there, and what is more we have almost got the place straight.

The sun continued to shine on us in that following year, and in December 1954, Polly had our second child. This was not a home *accouchement*, for which I was profoundly grateful. After the previous little problems with producing Jamie, Dr Mary Adams thought it wiser for Polly to go into a nursing home this time and arranged a bed in a clinic in Queen's Gate, London. I remember little about that establishment except that in those more innocent days Polly's staff nurse went about her healing duties with a cigarette permanently on the go, an inch of ash trembling on the end.

The night the baby was expected, I was due at a dinner at Claridges for show-business folk thrown by Sir Bernard and Lady Docker, the entertainingly flamboyant, wealthy, ageing couple who were the great standbys of 1950s tabloid newspaper tut-tutting headlines. I was not allowed to stay at the nursing home and wait for the baby, I was sent off to Claridges. Dr Adams and Tofty wanted a full report of the dinner, who was there, what we ate, what Lady Docker was wearing . . .

The next morning I was allowed into Polly's room. She lay in bed cuddling her daughter. My first sight of Sally was not of a battered and bruised baby like poor old Jamie had been, but of a daughter who was neat, totally feminine and, well, perfect.

'We'll have a marquee on the lawn for her wedding!' I cried out to Polly in a kind of wild surge of happiness.

Chapter 10

A WIND OF CHANGE WHISTLES
THROUGH THE AERIALS

I happen to be a shower person, believing that having a shower is not only much quicker than taking a bath but is more hygienic. Swishing life's detritus away with running water must be better than scrubbing it off, together with the skin's natural protective oils, with a chemical cake of rancid grease boiled up with caustic soda, and then wallowing in the unholy mixture. We all agree with John Wesley that 'cleanliness is, indeed, next to godliness', but he was talking about clothes.

Anners did not have a shower so we had to install one. It is an ancient house and the header tank in the loft is only about 18 inches above the shower-head, so one was not exactly clubbed to the bottom of the bath by the force of water. He who took a shower (women usually prefer baths) was required to stand patiently beneath a misty trickle which dropped like the gentle rain from heaven upon the earth beneath, until we could afford to put in a small electric pump.

All this domestic detail, as you must have instantly twigged, is a mood-setting prelude to the night of 15 December 1955 when Jimmy Edwards, Alma Cogan and I, with Polly looking after us, took part in the cabaret at the Christmas Staff Ball held in the Waterloo Chamber, Windsor Castle, in the presence of the royal family.

An invitation to entertain at the castle was, of course, an honour, and was arranged by a kind of royal talent-procurer general. For many years this was Peter Brough, an elegant amiable man whose day job was manufacturing shirts, but who was a ventriloquist at night. His dummy was a schoolboy character named Archie Andrews. I always thought that, technically, Peter was not a very good ventriloquist, his lips moved almost as much as Archie's, but his routines with the boy, and he in person, had considerable charm.

Perhaps due to the success in MGM films of the brilliant American ventriloquist Edgar Bergen with his dummy Charlie McCarthy, interest in vents ran oddly high for a while in Britain and Peter Brough and Archie were given their own series on radio, *Educating Archie*. Peter was Britain's first radio ventriloquist starring in his own series. A strange turn of events really; not only did he not have to bother about moving his lips on radio, but strictly speaking he did not even need to have a dummy. *Educating Archie* was well produced by, amongst others, Eric Spear, who later wrote the signature tune for *Coronation Street* and retired to a Channel Island. *Educating Archie* became hugely popular and ran from 1950 to 1960, winning two National Radio Awards for Best Comedy Show.

The set-up was that Peter Brough tried to have Archie educated at home by a succession of tutors. These were played by comedy actors and comics just beginning to make a name for themselves. The show helped them all to prosper. Hattie Jacques was in the Brough household and Julie Andrews played Archie's young girlfriend. The actors who played tutor to Archie included James Robertson Justice, Bernard Miles and Warren Mitchell; and among the up-and-coming comedians who took a turn were Max Bygraves ('I've arrived, and to prove it I'm 'ere!'), Dick Emery, Tony Hancock, Bruce Forsyth, Sid James, Alfred Marks and Harry Secombe.

Peter Brough was an excellent choice to put together entertainment for the Queen. Not only did he know pretty well everybody in the business, but he was personable, discreet, and perhaps most importantly, was not an agent or impresario and therefore had no axe to grind in selecting performers. I cannot think that he ever had much difficulty in assembling the entertainers he wanted. I wonder if anybody who was free on the date ever turned down an invitation to play to the royal family and their guests?

We accepted the invitation happily enough, and Jimmy and Alma changed at Anners and stayed overnight as we are only twenty minutes from Windsor Castle.

The huge and noble Waterloo Chamber was full. For the

cabaret, there was a row of gilt chairs in front for the royals and everybody else sat on the floor. Alma sang and bubbled with happy laughter, and Jimmy and I exchanged some topical patter which I had knocked up for the occasion (at one point, after a royal joke, I said, 'I didn't write that line, ma'am, it was written by a man called Les Majesty.' The Queen looked worried and Prince Philip leaned across to her and explained).

Then Jimmy and I launched into the operatic weather forecast, *TIFH*'s attempt to make opera more popular by combining it with the very popular radio weather forecast. The opening item was sung to 'Libiamo', the rousing drinking song from Act I of Verdi's *La Traviata*:

> South Cones,
> Have been hoisted in areas Tyne,
> Dogger Bank, Hebrides and Thames,
> Dover Straits and Portland Bight.
> The wind's
> Veering north to the Firth of the Forth,
> But it's bright,
> Nearly every night,
> Round the Isle of Wight . . .

After the cabaret, dancing was resumed and I found myself partnering Her Majesty the Queen in the Palais Glide.

Oldies will remember that the Palais Glide was a novelty dance, highly popular in the Fifties at boozy works outings and holiday camp gala nights. It required the participants to put their arms across each other's shoulders and form a line, rather like that Zorba dance with which waiters in Greek restaurants tended to spoil one's moussaka. We all then pointed a hoof and tapped the floor this way and that in the manner of a dressage horse, did little runs forwards and then backwards and, I seem to remember, stamped energetically.

Dancing, like making sandcastles and somersaulting forwards, is yet another natural gift which I lack. I am exhausted by a slow foxtrot after a minute and a half and I cannot waltz because my feet keep kicking each other, and anyway I go dizzy.

After half a lap of the Palais Glide I said breathlessly to Her Majesty, 'Can we please sit down now, ma'am? I'm a bit exhausted . . .'

Her Majesty's answer was entirely feminine, even wifely: 'No, you can't,' said Her Majesty. 'Come on, you can keep going a bit longer.'

Afterwards, when we lined up and were presented to the royals by Peter Brough, the Queen Mother said to Polly, and this is the point of this rather tortuous anecdote, 'Does he think up funny things in the bath?'

To which my little wife, my loyal helpmeet, said to the Queen Mother, 'It's all I can do to get him *into* a bath.'

During the next year, 1956, Den and I took on something quite new to us. Tony Shryane, radio producer at BBC Birmingham, and Edward J. Mason, writer, were principal begetters of the long-running daily radio serial *The Archers*. They decided that for a change of pace they would devise and produce a new kind of not-very-academic literary quiz. It was to be produced as a Midland Regional programme recorded in hospitals and town halls in the region, but the pilot programme was to be recorded at 6 p.m. in London at the Aeolian Hall studio, Bond Street, just down the road from our office in Conduit Street.

One of the wordsmiths invited to take part in the pilot was the dramatist and journalist, Lionel Hale, a man of lively wit. It was Lionel who christened the Brendan Behan kind of aggressively Irish play, 'the sod-em and begorra school of drama'. He married A. P. Herbert's daughter Crystal, who had parted from her husband, the poet John Pudney. Soon afterwards the newly-weds turned up at Covent Garden Opera's annual fancy dress ball with Crystal dressed as the Bartered Bride.

Lionel was notoriously late for appointments but compensated for the trouble this caused by brilliantly inventive excuses.

The cast for Tony's literary quiz had been called for 5 p.m., but there was no sign of Lionel until five thirty, when he telephoned the studio and apologized for not being there. He explained that he had accidently bitten a piece out of the tumbler in which his gin and tonic reposed and a tiny sliver of glass had lodged between two of his front teeth; he had to go immediately to casualty at Bart's Hospital to have it removed.

There was also a problem with the other chap. I cannot remember quite what the problem was (or who the other chap was), but having problems with the cast of trial recordings was not unknown as they were paid a specially modest recording fee which was just about enough to cover their bus fare to the studio.

At about 6 p.m. on the evening of the trial recording, while Denis and I were trying to finish a script, Tony Shryane rang and pleaded with us to drop everything and race down to Aeolian Hall, a couple of hundred yards away, and sit in for his two missing contestants.

We explained to Tony that our workload was hideous and the last thing we wanted was to add to it by having to perform in a weekly radio show, that our few remaining free evenings were precious, etc., etc. Tony assured us that there was no obligation for us to be in the show should 'the powers' want a series, it was just to help him out of an emergency; the invited audience was already queueing outside, etc., etc.

We galloped down to Aeolian Hall and did the show. As we were not going to be in the series should there be one, we touched the whole thing lightly, fooling about with the answers and not treating literature, especially poetry, with the kind of po-faced reverence which nourished the attitude that it was élitist and irrelevant. Instead, Tony and Edward J. encouraged us to indulge in what Robert Frost called 'perhapsing around'.

In the last round of questions, Denis and I were given a quotation which we had to identify and then explain how and when it first came to be used. My quotation was, 'Let not poor Nelly starve,' and Den's was, 'Dead! . . . and never called me mother.' As the first was too easy and the second too difficult as to names and dates, we invented answers. (1) 'Let not poor Nelly starve' was first said by the chef at the Savoy when, late at night and short of puddings, he poured bits of this and that over a peach, hastily christened it Peach Melba and sent a waiter out with it to Dame Nelly Melba who was famished after her concert. (2) 'Dead! . . . and never called me mother' was first said by a lad reeling out of a vandalized phone box after failing to telephone his parents.

The audience liked the show to an agreeable extent.

I would say that the definition of a good radio or television producer is somebody who manipulates you into *happily* doing something which you had no intention whatever of doing in the first place. Tony was a very good producer. In spite of his promises not to involve us if the trial recording went into a series, and in spite of our firm resolve not to be trapped, a week or so later Den and I were happily signing our contracts for the first series of *My Word!* It ran for thirty-four years.

As time went by, the explanations given by Denis and me to explain the origin of our given quotations grew longer and more elaborate and the puns at the end, apart from giving pleasure to listeners who had guessed what the puns would be before we got to them, became less important and more desperate. Also, flexible quotations which lent themselves to our treatment were becoming increasingly difficult to find. For some reason proverbs proved the best source, but as the years sped by Edward J. Mason was running out of them.

Tony Shryane also had his problems with our stories. The early ones were not really stories, just one or two sentences – as above – which talked the listener into the pun, but after a year or two the stories, lengthened to around about six minutes each, were complicated and appallingly difficult to ad lib. Tony's problem was that if one of us failed to get our story to work there was no show. Reluctantly, he asked Denis and me to find our own quotations and to do some groundwork on the stories so that the show was safe for transmission and the evening would not be a total waste of BBC money. He also altered the chairman's dialogue from, 'I will now give Denis and Frank the lines on which they will base their stories,' to, 'Here are the two lines which have been given to Frank and Denis . . .' No listener seems to have noticed the change.

Our weekly chore of finding a well-known line to pun upon and dreaming up a fitting story to be ad libbed on the air was a nightmare which we lived with all those years. Keen listeners kindly sent us quotations to base stories upon but, strangely, they rarely worked. We must have received only about a dozen usable suggestions during all those years.

One of the few good ones sent to me was the notion that a story might well be based on a twist of the title of James Hilton's novel, *Good-bye Mr Chips*. My helpful friend explained that the idea came to him when he was driving home with his wife from a holiday in France. They bought pork pies in a pub in Dover, and near Maidstone pulled into a lay-by for a snack lunch.

'Did you enjoy it?' his wife asked, back in the car.

He said, 'Good pie, missed the chips.'

I think the problem which faced listeners wanting to be helpful is that puns are tricky things, not as easy as they might look with which to beguile an audience. For some reason the British public loves to boo and hiss puns and moan and groan at them, which is a bit dispiriting. But then many puns are intellectually clever without being at all funny, e.g., the following very clever American triple pun:

A rich Texan has four grown-up lads who live in Argentina and breed cattle for the Chicago beef market. He calls their ranch *FOCUS*, because it's where the sons – raise – meat.

I do not think that any of our *My Word!* puns achieved quite that height of arid perfection; ours tended to be shaggier and, I hope, jollier, as demonstrated by a couple of examples.

Geoffrey Strachan of Methuen Books persuaded us to put the stories into book form. He published five slim volumes and then an omnibus edition of all five volumes called *The Utterly Ultimate* My Word! *Collection*, whence I give you the following samples, chosen more or less at random and mercifully abbreviated:

DENIS: 'The least said, soonest mended.'
                        Charles Dickens, *Pickwick Papers*

            Denis's story told of a lady who rented a house
            which had a sauna under the stairs in which

the previous tenant had accidentally locked himself and steamed to death. The lady insisted, as a condition of the lease, that the sauna was made safe before her family moved in. Then followed a romp in the sauna between the son of the new occupant and an Italian girl (both unclad, of course), who wilfully got themselves locked in and . . . Well, anyway, the girl's Sicilian parents were all for revenge, blaming the unsafe sauna for their daughter having to marry an Englishman, but the new lady of the house insisted that they had no case against her. As she pointed out: '*The lease said sauna's mended.*'

FRANK: 'There's many a slip 'twixt the cup and the lip.'

Proverb

In my story it emerged that *Déjeuner sur l'herbe* was painted by Edouard Manet in the Bois de Boulogne in a remote glade between a carp pond and a heap of rocks known as Lover's Leap. When exhibited, the painting was hissed and booed for being decadent. Poor Manet, bitterly disappointed, went into hiding. His friends searched Paris afraid that he had committed suicide, then Mr Rory Bremner (an English Impressionist) suggested that they look at the spot where Manet painted his picture. And indeed, there in the Bois was a figure lying in the long grass, clutching an empty wine bottle and snoring. '*Voilà!*' cried Mr Bremner (in perfect French): '*There's Manet, asleep, 'twixt the carp and the leap.*'

I was told recently that the novelist J. G. Ballard much enjoyed the *My Word!* stories, and after hearing a story of mine in which, for purposes of the plot, I extolled the virtues of living in beautiful Shepperton, Surrey (Thorpe is about 5 miles away) – I described Shepperton as 'the Malibu of the Thames Valley' – he was moved by this warm recommendation and drove over in his car, liked what he saw and bought a house there, in which he still lives.

Could this be true? I do hope so.

Recordings of many BBC radio programmes, mainly classical music and drama and some comedy, were sold to other countries by a department known as the BBC Transcription Service, a valuable contribution to keeping the rest of the world aware that Britain was still a force in broadcasting and doing some things rather well, the sort of things which other nations had given up attempting.

After *My Word!* had been on the air for a year or two, the department announced in its international sales brochure that *My Word!* was the most popular radio programme in the world.

We thought this was going it a bit so we got on to the Transcription Service. They were unabashed, pointing out that the BBC was the only worldwide exporter of radio programmes and *My Word!* was its most popular export, bought by over thirty-five countries including Chile, Germany and Russia. 'QED,' they said. 'Well, well,' we said.

One thing which Denis and I learned, and appreciated, during those early years of *My Word!* was how much the success of the show depended on the inconspicuous skill of the man who compiled it, Edward J. Mason. He had a gift for the common touch which is rare in areas like literary quizzes. He worked within the general awareness of listeners who had been to school; most of his poetic questions were to do with poems in Palgrave's *Golden Treasury*, most quotations were semi-familiar and in most books of quotations. We reckoned that 80 per cent of listeners felt that, given a bit of time for thought, they could answer almost 80 per cent of the questions.

Then in 1967, Tony Shryane struck again. He decided to set up a sister show to *My Word!*, hoping that Denis and I would join the team and bring a similar attitude of unapologetic semi-ignorance to the subject of music.

Tony had signed up the completely professional Steve Race, jazz pianist, accompanist, author, composer, to set the questions

and be question master, and he had begun casting the contestants by signing up the bass and broadcaster, David (Bill)
Franklin, and the Glyndebourne bass-baritone and splendid
raconteur, Ian ('Mud, Mud, Glorious Mud') Wallace. Would
Denis and I consider . . .?

Of course, it was out of the question. *My Word!* was a big
success and fun to be in, apart from those damned stories hanging over our heads all week, and now Tony was proposing that
Denis and I enter another tunnel, because the new show was
to end with all four of us singing a song in turn. This meant
that every week Den and I would have to find a song each and
learn it, all in the midst of much writing work.

'Sorry, Tony,' we said. 'It just simply is not *possible*! Many
thanks for thinking of us and all that, but it's not on, and anyway we don't know anything *about* music!'

'That's all right,' he said, 'don't worry. No pressure will be
applied. If you can't do it, that's that! When Steve has finished
the first script in a couple of weeks' time, I'll drop in and show
it to you for interest's sake.'

'Yes, of course,' we said, relieved that Tony was not going
to give us a big sales pitch or appeal to our better natures, if any.
It was a grave error of judgement on our part.

Tony came and talked gently and reassuringly about the
show, and a week or so later Denis and I happily signed our
contracts for the first series of *My Music*. It ran for twenty-four
years.

My partner in the show, Bill Franklin, died, and in came the
splendid John Amis, music journalist, broadcaster, critic and
administrator; a large, colourful personality whose striking
manner of dressing made him seem not so much clothed as
upholstered. John brought to the show a plethora of excellent
anecdotes (musicians seem to have even more stories than
actors) which he told in an admirably crisp style. He also sang
in a high tenor voice, which the rest of us did not dare to
attempt for fear of injury, and he whistled beautifully.

Ian Wallace, Glyndebourne bass-baritone, actor in musicals
and famed impersonator of a singing hippopotamus, is a
pleasure to be with on any show, or even just to be in a room
with. So many times during the series Ian embarked on what

seemed to be a rambling anecdote, not leading anywhere in particular, only to bring it suddenly to a totally unexpected and hilarious finish. The only thing wrong with the man is that he is far funnier than a singer has any right to be. It is simply not fair.

It was only when Denis and I took part in *My Music* that we realized we could not sing. It had not occurred to us before because it had not arisen. We were writers not vocalists, our job was to sit down and write, not to belt out a chorus of 'Burlington Bertie', but as our singing was part of the programme, and we were being lightly paid for it, we had to ignore our humiliation and sing.

One of Denis's problems was that his voice drifted mid-song from one key to another, as though it was hoping to find a key which would produce a more bearable sound. In the old *Twenty Questions* terminology, I would describe Den's voice as an unreliable, domestic baritone with vegetable connections.

Den overcame his disability by searching out and singing obscure (and funny) Victorian comic songs which could be half sung, half croaked in the manner of Rex Harrison in *My Fair Lady*. A particular favourite with listeners, which he was repeatedly requested to reprise, was the romantic ballad (meant to be sung by a woman): 'He Was More Like a Friend than a Husband to Me'.

John Amis pointed out to me recently that Denis's singing had improved enormously over the years. But why? Had he been going in for clandestine singing lessons? Herbal tablets? Meditation? It was a riddle inside an enigma.

My own trouble was not being able to stay on a note without sliding off it. This is quite different from not being able to keep in key. I could put a fair amount of fervour or pathos into a performance, I could do a number con brio to order, as long as I was not required to hang on to a note for longer than half a second; after that my voice developed a vibrato and went wandering.

My solution to the problem was to avoid all songs which had to be properly sung and to choose those with a meaningful lyric which I could concentrate on delivering with poignance, as though it were an item in a rather noisy poetry reading.

The ignorance of classical music which Denis and I brought to the programme was mitigated by two circumstances. Whereas questions on *My Word!* were general and could have been asked of any of us, Steve Race tailored his questions to the four of us individually so that we could show up to best advantage. John Amis would be asked about, say, orchestral history and music-makers' eccentric behaviour and Ian might be asked questions about experiences in opera, Denis was asked about music in films and stage musicals, on which he was sound, and I might be given questions about musical history, which I had written about. Also, Denis and I were saved from humiliation when Steve hopefully gave us the odd question about classical music (we knew the piece so well but what was its *name?*) because we both had chaps beside us who knew *everything* about classical music, and they either scribbled the answer swiftly and slid it across the desk to us, or whispered it. Denis made no attempt to hide this help. 'Just a mo,' he would say to Steve, 'I've got a spirit message coming in from the right.'

A typical Denis ad lib came when Ian described a small crisis during a performance of Mozart's *Don Giovanni* at Glyndebourne. Apparently the producer had altered a sequence but had forgotten to tell Ian, who was singing away in the graveyard scene.

'Suddenly,' said Ian, 'I saw that behind the commendatore's statue the stage manager was crouching. "Psssst!" hissed the figure urgently, "Psssst!"'

'And were you?' asked Denis.

The influence of the two radio shows abroad was extra-ordinary. When Kenneth Adam took over as Head of BBC Television he went first on the customary tour of the BBC's overseas offices. On his very first day back at Television Centre he nipped into our office to tell us of an experience he had had whilst *en route* to Australia.

It seems he stayed overnight in a hotel in Fiji. Early in the morning he was wakened by a cheerful Fijian, about 9 feet tall, holding a cup of tea. As he carefully positioned the saucer on the bedside table, the Fijian, smiling happily with all his thirty-two magnificent teeth, said, 'And how is your dear Queen and the noble Duke of Edinburgh, sir?'

'Very well, both of them, as far as I know, thank you,' Kenneth managed to mumble, struggling to sit up.

'And how are dear Mr Muir and Mr Norden of *My Word!*?'

Kenneth said that it was such an extraordinary thing to hear under those circumstances that he had to tell us as soon as he arrived home.

'Well, our billing was about right,' said Denis to me.

And much more recently, in the early 1990s, I was at the Author of the Year party given by Hatchards the bookshop. The guest of honour was the bestselling American writer Kitty Kelley, whose highly successful approach to her work is to write steamingly frank biographies of famous people such as Frank Sinatra and Nancy Reagan.

Miss Kelley was late. Eventually she arrived, a little iron butterfly in powder blue, almost hidden midst a posse of her publisher's publicity staff, like a serial adulteress being hustled into court to protect her from enraged wives.

A few minutes later one of Miss Kelley's young publicity persons came over to me and said, 'Would you like to meet Miss Kelley?'

'No, not much,' I said, after some thought. 'Well, she lives in a different sort of world to mine.'

'But she wants to meet *you*,' he said.

So, intrigued (to say the least), I allowed myself to be steered across to the corner where wee Miss Kelley was holding court. I was introduced and she immediately grabbed my hand in both of hers and pressed it to her bosom.

'This is wonderful!' she cried. 'Nobody told me *you* would be here!'

It was, as far as I was concerned, inexplicable behaviour. Then it all became a little clearer.

'That voice!' she cried. 'As a schoolgirl back home in Washington I used to listen to you under the bedclothes. And now I'm actually talking to you!' She really was genuinely moved, even a little moist-eyed. 'Frank, I want you to know I grew up listening to *My Music*.'

She asked for a signed copy of my book and off she went clutching it happily. I was happy, too.

Both *My Word!* and *My Music* produced much correspondence, some of it testimony to a wavering standard in the teaching of English in our schools. For instance, the beginning of school holidays always seemed to produce a little rush of notelets reading something like:

You are a great fan of mine and my sister, please would you send her and I a singed photo.

Then there were the hopelessly demanding letters which would take about a week to answer properly:

I have for many years been an admirer of yours and Mr Nordern's scripts and it is my earnest wish, also, to become a successful BBC comedy writer. Will you please tell me how you managed to get in? How do I set about writing comedy? Is it any different from homework? What books have you read? Who have you met? Have you got an animal? – I have got, until she died last week of a complaint, a gerbil. What's your family like? . . .

Another favourite went something like:

As you can deduce from the address at the top of this letter, my husband Ralph and I have emigrated from Herne Bay and are now happily ensconced in Toronto, Canada. Imagine our pure pleasure when we turned on the radio last Sunday morning and heard you and your friend (sorry, I cannot remember his name) in *My Music*. The series was about five years old, but at the end of it your friend sang a comic love song about a cockney boy and girl. Will you please send me a copy of the music and the words. Also will you please tell me who first sang it and where? Trusting this will not prove a bother, Kindest regards . . .

The worst ones read something like:

I enclose the first draft of my novel. I wish you to read the book carefully and tell me frankly whether I have the touch of comic genius which my friends and my aunt assure me that I am in possession of. I should explain that the novel is set in the gas showroom of a town in Durham where I live, and the humour arises naturally from the variety of local people who drop in to order a fitted kitchen or a gas poker. The hero is Matt who wants to be a poet but stutters (which I do a little). Please return the manuscript to me with your *constructive* comments by Thursday.

But there are the other kinds of letter. I have a slim file of these, labelled '*Belles Lettres*'.

There is an early one from a lady who was driving down the M1 with *My Music* on her car radio when she heard me wrestling with my song at the end, that old sad Irving Berlin song, 'What'll I Do?'. It seems that I had put into my singing some of the passionate emotion which had lain dormant since my erotic rendition of 'Tondelayo' in Uncle Mack's kiddies' competition on Broadstairs sands those many years ago. The lady was so moved to tears that she had to stop the car and have a little sob.

After reading her letter I rang Tony Shryane. 'What did I *do* with the song?' I asked. 'What was it about the way I sang it which made the lady burst into tears?'

Tony could not remember. 'Perhaps she's a music lover,' he said.

Appreciative letters did not exactly choke the letter box; they came in thinly and slowly rather than thick and fast, but one did float in from time to time.

Another I kept was from a lady, Mrs Brendan McCluskey of nearby Staines, who was expecting her third child, which she was warned might turn up early. She already had two girls and was hoping for a boy. By accident she turned on a radio programme which had Alfred Marks and me in it, called *Frank Muir Goes Into . . . parties*, and laughed so much that she went into labour. The baby turned out to be another girl, so Mrs McCluskey named her Francesca.

My favourite unsolicited testimonial was a postcard from a lady explaining that her best friend was a nun in Rome. Her friend was ill in hospital, so to cheer her up she had sent her a copy of my book, *The Frank Muir Book: An Irreverent Companion to Social History*. A little while later the nun wrote back thanking her friend for the present. She said she was enjoying the book so much that she had given it up for Lent.

Radio comedy matured in the first ten years of peacetime radio, and by the early 1950s the older formats like *ITMA* and Charlie Chester's *Stand Easy*, which depended on techniques inherited from the variety theatre such as quick-fire entrances and exits and rapid little topical jokes enacted in funny voices, were giving way to character comedy, as in the superb *Hancock's Half-Hour*, written by Ray Galton and Alan Simpson, and for many listeners rising above them all was *The Goon Show* – noisy, irreverent, cunningly smutty, brilliantly inventive and dotty.

The show's original title was *Crazy People*, and the pilot script was written by Spike Milligan, Michael Bentine and a new writer full of odd ideas named Larry Stephens, who was working as a kind of assistant to Spike. This post did not carry a salary because Spike had no money. He also had nowhere to live. But he met Harry Secombe's half agent, Jimmy Grafton (who shared the other half of Harry with another agent), and Jimmy Grafton owned a family pub in Westminster, the Grafton Arms. He also wrote comedy. Thus the ambitious and gifted little group suddenly had somewhere to meet and write, and Spike had an attic to sleep in.

The producers of *Crazy People* were Pat Dixon and the very young and wildly enthusiastic Dennis Main Wilson. In 1952 the first programme was made. It was not quite right, so back to the drawing board (i.e., pub) they all went, changes were made and the first series of the programme, now produced solely by Dennis Main Wilson, went out on the air with a range of eccentric characters who lasted throughout *The Goon Show*'s long life. These included the cheerful, heroic idiot, Neddy Seagoon; Moriarty the perpetual villain; Major Bloodnok; Spike's simpleton character Eccles, whose voice, perhaps unconsciously, echoed Disney's cartoon dog Goofy, etc. These inventions, plus bizarre plots and lots of explosions and vigorous sound effects, dismayed, delighted, worried, puzzled and intrigued listeners according to taste. The style came as a breath of stimulating air to broadcast comedy and probably had a greater influence on later generations of writers and performers than any radio comedy programme has ever had.

My only criticism of *The Goon Show* is that the cartoon-like comic voices were dangerously easy to imitate. Indeed, throughout the Fifties and Sixties, breaking into a comical Goon voice in the course of ordinary conversation (to the amusement only of the breaker-inner) was practised by a great many citizens who should have known better, including, alas, Prince Charles.

Although by the 1950s radio had developed its own techniques and was a genuine art form, in that it had an important limitation – there was nothing to look at – it was about to be replaced as the public's favourite mass entertainment by a gadget called television.

I think a tiny tragedy of the twentieth century, very tiny indeed when compared to the big ones, but nevertheless in its own world a tragedy, was that just when radio had matured, found its own techniques and knew what it could do better than film or the theatre, it was suddenly overwhelmed by television.

Television is a technical miracle, but it is, unlike radio, fundamentally a gadget. It is not as precise to work with as film; you cannot iron a shirt or read a newspaper while it is on and still enjoy it as you can with a radio programme; it engages the eyes but rarely the imagination; it does not have the interplay between actor and audience which distinguishes theatre; it is the only medium in which the performers rehearse for hours beforehand, sometimes all day, and then perform the show itself dog-tired; and it presents a number of new hazards to the writer. Radio is a medium of the imagination and the writer can write, 'Over to the doge's masked ball in Venice,' and you are there. The writer in radio speaks straight into the ear of the listener.

Television had grown slowly but steadily in the years since those dear pre-war Ally Pally days when, according to the BBC's distinguished Head of Audience Research, Robert Silvey, the TV service was able to invite its entire audience to tea in one studio. What a splendidly British thing to have even *thought* of doing.

In the very earliest of the pioneering days in television, problems arose which had to be solved by *ad hoc* ingenuity, there being no precedents to help. Such as what to do when the delectable Joan Miller, introducing *Picture Page*, could not hear the floor manager giving her a cue because of the loud introductory music, and could not see him because of the set she was sitting in. The problem was solved, as usual, by the engineers. They devised a gadget like a small electric cattle probe which they wired up to Miss Miller's ankle, so that when her beautiful 1938 vowels were needed for an introduction, the producer only had to press a button and Miss Miller received a short sharp electric shock to prompt her into action.

Early television sets were expensive and, perhaps as a defensive measure, were widely regarded by the public as being a bit 'common' ('We don't have television in our house. What civilized person wants to sit and watch footer or a concert party of an evening?'). Then in the early 1950s the public attitude to television changed and it began to become a symbol of social affluence, of having 'got on'. It was rumoured that many homes displayed a TV aerial on their roof to impress neighbours but had no TV set below. It became normal to see a crowd gathered round a television dealer's shop window in the high street, peering in and blocking the pavement as they enjoyed a free gawp at a display of screens transmitting something exciting like Wimbledon tennis or a unicyclist in a variety show.

All the screens showed the same black-and-white picture because at that time there was no colour and only one channel: BBC. ITV did not set up shop until 1955 and BBC2 even later.

Then in 1953 came the big event which accelerated the rate of sale of new sets from a trickle to an avalanche: the televising of the Coronation.

Almost everybody in the country wanted to see the pomp

and majesty of the Coronation on television, and almost all seemed to manage it. Owners of television sets found themselves immensely popular in their neighbourhood, and on the big day their front rooms were crammed with neighbours sitting all over the furniture, on kitchen chairs they had brought with them, or the floor, anywhere so long as they could wallow all day in the joy of watching a great ceremony which but for television they would never have even glimpsed. And television hire firms did great business.

With more television sets being sold every year, the BBC's income from TV licences went up steadily and they could afford to pay high fees for virtuoso musicians and could attract big-name American performers to star in more complicated and expensive variety productions.

Comedy shows had always been a large and successful part of the BBC's radio schedules and as television grew and many of the younger BBC producers moved across from radio, they naturally continued this tradition and from, say, 1952 to 1955, the last of the comfortable BBC's monopoly years, when every viewer who was watching was watching your show, there was a natural drift of top-of-the-bill comics and their writers from the quiet backwater of radio to the expanding excitements of telly.

The first serious go at television which Denis and I had came in 1956 when we wrote a sketch show for Dick Bentley which we called *And So to Bentley*. It went out from Lime Grove studios which BBC Television then occupied. Lime Grove was, of course, the scene of my toe-curling Brussels sprout affair, the first of the two gaffes I committed within shooting range of Sydney Box.

Dick's chief support was Peter Sellers and each programme ran for forty-five minutes every other week. The fees in those days hold a kind of melancholy interest in these days of huge payouts. Our fee was a guinea a minute, plus a little bit more because there were two of us, which came to £105 between us, once a fortnight.

It was not a bad show. Dick was fine. Self-deprecating, the kind of understated performance he gave in *TIFH*, which made many sensitive listeners prefer him to the more boisterous

Jimmy Edwards. Sellers was, of course, excellent. And that was the problem. Dick became painfully aware that he, nominally the star, was overwhelmed on screen by the charismatic brilliance of the versatile Sellers.

And So to Bentley did not go into a second series, but Denis and I had learned a great deal about the problems and possibilities of working in television, and it was clear that the time had come for us to take the plunge. In a way this was a realistic decision as we had had a good innings with *TIFH* – eleven years – and now there was a temptation to ease the pressure by living off our fat a little, to rewrite past episodes of the Glums and pretend to ourselves that they were new, or improved, and to tart up old sketches.

We decided it really was time to call it a day and we wrote a letter to the Head of Radio Variety explaining that we thought, with great regret, that the time had come for us to stop writing *TIFH* and to move across into television, beginning with a series for Jimmy Edwards.

The BBC Radio Variety Department's reaction was of dismay. *TIFH* was still pulling in good listener figures and a bit of prestige, and for the bosses, not being writers, that was the main (if not only) consideration. We held firm. They asked us whether they could continue *TIFH* with other writers (the copyright of a show was held by us, the writers; we legally owned the show, the BBC only paid us a fee to broadcast it). We agreed to this and a new series of *TIFH* was written by two established comedy writers.

It was astonishingly naive of us not to have asked for a copyright fee, after all it was our show, but it simply did not occur to us. It might have been an expensive blunder had *TIFH* run on for another ten years, but under its new writers the show just managed to complete the one series.

The question of what Jimmy Edwards' television series would be about was simple enough to answer; he would revert to his original comic character of a venal, boozy, devious and incompetent headmaster of a small, tatty public school. We invented a name for his school which sounded vaguely unreliable – Chiselbury – and we called the series *Whack-O!*

We began casting and found a very good Taplow (the

schoolboy character who outmanoeuvres the headmaster at every clash), and we amassed a useful team of masters. We were particularly happy with having Edwin Apps to play Mr Halliwell, who was young, upper-middle-class, kind to the boys, loyal and incorruptible. The headmaster *loathed* him.

Jimmy had to have an assistant master, and I remembered Flight Lieutenant Arthur Howard whose speciality in comedy was being dithery and dim. Denis agreed that we might give him a go, so we wrote to him explaining that we had no idea how big the part would be, but if it did not matter to whom the headmaster talked, it would be to Mr Pettigrew, the assistant master (it turned out to be a bit of a life-saver for Arthur. He was doing quite well in small cameo parts in films, e.g., *Passport to Pimlico*, but jobs in television were scarce) and dear Arthur joined the team. So excellent was Arthur as downtrodden, bullied Mr Pettigrew that he very quickly became Jimmy's co-star in a kind of Laurel and Hardy relationship.

During one memorable episode, Mr Pettigrew hurt his head due to machinations of the plot and it was wreathed in bandages. The headmaster kept thumping Mr Pettigrew on his sore head to emphasize points, until at one point he bent over his desk to reach something and poor, in-pain Mr Pettigrew broke. He hauled off and delivered a terrific kick to the headmaster's backside. The headmaster lay sprawled across the desk for quite a long time, immobile, while Mr Pettigrew writhed in silent agony. Finally Jimmy rose slowly and faced Mr Pettigrew. 'I wish I was dead!' sobbed Mr Pettigrew. The headmaster said, quietly, 'That can be arranged.'

It was an enjoyable series to write (when it went well). One of the lines I remember fondly was during the early moments of a programme when Jimmy looked out of his study window, outwards and upwards, reacted dramatically to something he saw, said, 'What's that object somebody's hung on the chapel spire?' produced an air rifle, took careful aim and fired. There was a 'ping' followed by the sound of breaking china. Jimmy said to the audience, 'Funny, that. During the war it was the Jerry that shot *me* down!' (Quite true. The plane Jimmy was flying home after towing a glider to Arnhem was shot down by a German fighter plane.)

In another programme there was an inspection of the school account books by a Ministry of Education auditor:

AUDITOR: Can you explain this entry, Headmaster? 'Owed to turf accountant . . .'?

HEADMASTER: Alas, we had to have the first eleven cricket pitch returfed.

AUDITOR: But the entry goes on: 'For my losses on the Oaks, £80.00.' Is the Oaks not a horserace, Headmaster?

HEADMASTER: I don't listen to gossip, sir, I am a man of the Arts. The entry refers to my selling two of our oak trees to a furniture manufacturer who refused to pay up as the trees were riddled with the dread Hungarian gunge beetle.

The auditor is now getting exasperated in face of the headmaster's slippery, confident and clearly bogus answers.

AUDITOR: (*Hotly*) But this entry really does need some explaining, Headmaster. Here it is in black and white, d'you see? 'For Prize-Giving Day. 50 crates.' FIFTY CRATES! You provided *alcohol* at your school's *prize-giving*?

HEADMASTER: No, no, no, no! It was a book prize. I do apologize for Mr Pettigrew's handwriting; grammar-school boy, you know. It's so difficult to get educated staff these days. That's not '50 crates' – it's 'Socrates'.

Another facet of the headmaster's petty conman virtuosity was the smarmy persona he adopted when visiting the Great House where lived the Lady of the Manor, a bit of a battleaxe who happened to be chairman of the school governors. He was usually trying to impress her with his charm and erudition in order to wheedle money out of her or to avoid gaol.

HEADMASTER:	(*Closely examining an oil painting on her drawing-room wall*) Exquisite, milady! Quite exquisite! All hand-coloured, I'll warrant?
MILADY:	(*Acidly*) It's a Constable.
HEADMASTER:	Really? (*He peers closely at the picture*) In plain clothes, I see . . .

Whack-O! was produced and directed by Douglas (Dougie) Moodie, an epicene, very experienced Scot who at one period was directing two programmes a week, *Dixon Of Dock Green* and *Whack-O!*, an impressive feat of organization when each thirty-minute show normally had a whole week of rehearsal to itself.

Dougie had an acid tongue. He loved the stars of his shows but was a bit hard on small-part players. From his seat up in the control box he would shout down the microphone to his floor manager in the studio things like, 'Tell that oily-haired idiot with a face like Colonel Nasser to get out of the bloody way. I need to see the clock!'

It was customary for the writers to turn up and watch the last outside rehearsal, which was usually conducted in a hired drill hall or ice-cold function room, to check that all was well with their beautiful dialogue before the cast went into the studio the next day, endured a camera rehearsal and then went on and did the show.

When Den and I turned up at the last outside rehearsals of *Whack-O!* we were greeted each time with a loud screech from Dougie: 'Attention everybody – Gilbert and Sullivan have arrived!' Another time it would be: 'Quiet everywhere – Gog and Magog are here!'

Whack-O! was broadcast from a theatre, the Shepherd's Bush Empire. Some time later Denis and I wrote a one-off musical show for Jimmy Edwards (*The Sound of Jim*) to be performed in the theatre. One sketch required a flock of pigeons suddenly to descend over the symphony orchestra which, conducted by Jimmy, was playing a well-loved bird number ('Oh, for the wings, for the wings, of a dooooove') and cause chaos. The producer booked a troupe of performing pigeons for whom this kind of sketch was child's play, and it all went beautifully, the pigeons duly flapped about over the musicians' heads and were comically, if not very wittily, incontinent. Their trainer had brought them down to Shepherd's Bush from Wales by train in baskets, an expensive operation.

When the show was over and everybody was packing up we found the Welsh bird-trainer in high spirits. He had remembered from early days in variety that the Shepherd's Bush Empire's ceiling had a retractable dome and had persuaded the manager to open it up. The bird-trainer then ran up and down the aisles shouting, 'Wow-wow! Off you go! Go on! Home!' and clapping his hands very loudly. The pigeons were puzzled for a while and then realized that there was open air and freedom above them, and in a huge clattering flock they flew up, up and away into the night sky.

'That'll save me a few quid in fares back to Wales!' chortled the trainer.

He spotted at once that we had no idea what he was up to. 'They're homing pigeons,' he explained patiently.

Mounting a farce like *Whack-O!*, which required a realistic production, was not easy on a theatre stage. About the only good thing which came from it was that on the other side of the Goldhawk Road was an excellent little Italian restaurant and bar owned by N. Oddi. It was known to us, naturally, as Noddy's.

Dougie's directing method, an unusual one, was to rehearse his cameras and his actors very carefully so that when the show started there was no need for him to shout at everybody from the control box; his job was done and the cameras and cast knew exactly where to be and what to do.

So while the audience was shuffling into the auditorium, Dougie went with us across the road to Noddy's and enjoyed a medicinal gin and tonic or four. Back in the control box, he would settle himself comfortably into his chair and, now pleasantly relaxed (i.e., lightly befuddled), would quietly enjoy watching his programme.

But at one show, when Denis and I were in the control box, things went wrong. One of the four cameras went down and then there were three.

The cameramen knew all their moves and shots when there were four of them, but with one camera missing their working pattern for the whole show was destroyed. And the show – live, of course – had started. A nasty moment.

Dougie sat up straight and talked to his cameramen quite calmly through his microphone. 'Well, gentlemen,' he said, 'it's fun night! Camera One, could you creep round the table and get me a medium shot of Pettigrew? Meanwhile, Three, see if you can get closer to Jimmy – we're coming to you when Jimmy does the telephone business . . .'

It was a quite extraordinary demonstration of television professionalism. Dougie shook off the effect of his gin and tonics as a spaniel shakes off raindrops, and, ad libbing the shots, talked his camera crews through half an hour of a busy and complicated farce.

As the credits rolled and 'The End' came up, he slumped back in his chair for a moment and then sat up straight again, thrust an elegant hand through the handles of his female vision-mixer's tall, thin, raffia handbag, looked round the control box and said brightly, 'More burgundy anybody?'

Chapter 11

AND A NIGHTINGALE SANG
IN TELEVISION CENTRE

The 1960s were years of sudden change for Denis and me with our careers wandering off in unexpected directions.

One evening in 1960 itself, we were at a party in Shepperton given by Bernard Braden and his wife Barbara Kelly at their home, when the Assistant Head of Light Entertainment Group, Tom Sloan, who enjoyed a social glass, fell over and broke a small occasional table. The next morning Tom invited Denis and me to join the BBC Television Light Entertainment Department as advisors and consultants on comedy.

It is not easy, even at this remove when the dust has settled, to spot the connection between Tom splintering a small table and his offer to us next morning of a four-year contract to advise and be available to producers for consultation in matters of comedy. Had the heavy fumes of French table wine (red) lingered on and caused Tom to be visited by demons?

Of course Den and I signed up at once. Although to begin with our office would be a portable cabin on the back of a lorry in the car park, the grand Television Centre building was nearly completed, and in those days to be a consultant was a sinecure. Nowadays 'I'm a consultant' usually means 'I have just been made redundant and am hoping to go it alone', but then it meant that as soon as Television Centre had been completed, we would sit in a pleasant BBC office, with a secretary and a telly, and the canteen and the BBC club bar only a stroll away. And we could get on with our writing work in comfort in the confident knowledge that our privacy would not be disturbed, because any producer of comedy worth his salt would rather be cast naked into a vat of hissing vipers than admit that he needed to take advice on how to do his job from Denis and me.

And this, in the main, proved to be true. Eventually we moved to the fourth floor of Television Centre, read every script submitted and reported on them, meticulously attended departmental meetings and were consulted quite frequently by our two bosses in the Light Entertainment Group, although these informal meetings took place in the bar or in the lift and were more like an exchange of light chat about the department's output than serious professional discussions. For example Tom had a bee in his bonnet: 'Isn't it time we killed off *Dixon of Dock Green*? Jack Warner is a bit old for a police sergeant; he can hardly walk.'

Our advice was: 'No. The fact that he hobbles doesn't matter; unrealistic though Sergeant Dixon and the series may be, it's part of many viewers' lives now. When you kill off the series you'll kill off some old viewers as well.' The series continued with excellent figures for several more years until Jack Warner died, aged eighty.

I find it difficult to recollect any splendid coups we achieved during our four happy years in office. (There must have been *some*. One little one?) But I do recollect very clearly one rather colourful near miss we had.

It was in the 1950s and Denis and I were sent to the USA by the BBC to persuade Jack Benny to come to England and present a big Saturday night television show. In those days weekend television was dominated by 'spectaculars', expensive and long variety shows often starring a big Hollywood name, and Denis and I had to watch shows and tour the agencies. (When we were in the William Morris Agency's offices in New York, Mel Brooks drifted in and we were introduced as the BBC's experts on comedy. He looked at us in awe. 'You mean, you *know*?' he said.)

The daily expenses allowed by the BBC were enough to keep us lightly fed and watered but left little over for fun items, and we were delighted when the BBC office in the Rockefeller Center arranged for us to appear on the big chat show of that era, *The Jack Paar Show*, which would pay us an expense fee of $100 apiece, enough to buy presents to take home to our dear ones.

Just before we were due to fly across to the West Coast to

tempt Jack Benny to England we were visited at the Algonquin Hotel by a thin blond man with several twitches going at once, whose name was Rick Something-or-other. He said he was one of Jack Paar's talent co-ordinators, which was not very illuminating. It emerged that his job was to interview Jack Paar's potential victims (Mr Paar was famous for the playfully brutal treatment of his guests when he felt like it), find out what subject the guests intended to chat about on the show, so that Mr Paar, armed with pre-information and a team of writers, could outsmart them, and generally put the guests at their ease. Mr Paar's talent co-ordinator bit his nails.

'Anecdotes! Anecdotes!' he suddenly screamed, like a man bitten by a viper calling urgently for antidotes. 'Stories! Go, go, go!'

His ballpoint was poised above a nasty yellow notepad.

Of course our minds immediately went totally blank.

'Needs thought,' mumbled Denis. 'Can't – just like that.'

'Dunno any,' I mumbled after another horribly long silence.

Rick sighed. 'We got trouble,' he said, sadly. 'It's *Jack*.'

We noticed that everybody in the Paar organization spoke their employer's name in a special tone of terrified reverence.

'*Jack* wants for you to tell anecdotes, right? You don't tell *Jack* an anecdote when he wants for you to tell him an anecdote and you know what he'll do? He'll intrude in the middle of while you're talking and say to camera, "OK, let's take a break here and watch a commercial!" The audience will love your evident discomfiture and shout out, "You tell the limeys, Jack! That's our Jack!" You'll be socially hugh-millated and professionally hugh-millated, and if you're lucky enough to get a table at Sardi's it'll be the one next to the kitchen door.'

Rick clicked his ballpoint shut in a telling gesture. Den and I could see our precious $100 disappearing like mist in sunshine.

'The point is, Rick,' said Denis, rescuing the situation, 'in our long years as Britain's top comedy writers, artistes and entrepreneurs we have amassed a wealth of anecdotes concerning our friends, the superstars of British show business, but we don't just want to blurt them out, willy-nilly. We want to talk them over between ourselves and select for Jack only the cream.'

Rick was visibly impressed by this codswallop.

'I like it!' he said. 'I like it! Good thinking, Dallas.'

'Denis,' said Denis.

'Denis,' he said. 'Right. Now, you're both flying to the coast tomorrow to meet up with Mr Benny, right? Be away ten days, right? OK, that leaves four days before *The Jack Paar Show* recording, so as soon as you get back to New York you call me, right?'

He gave us his card and left for wherever talent co-ordinators go when they have finished co-ordinating for the day.

I raised an eyebrow at Den.

'We'll make up some lies on the plane,' he said.

Los Angeles was different. Jack Benny was kind, gentle and funny. He took us to lunch at The Brown Derby, the famous old Hollywood restaurant shaped like a bowler hat, and we sat quite near, only about fifteen tables away, say 40 yards, from Barbara Stanwyck. The following day he took us to his agent's office, a white colonial mansion set in lawns and full of English antique furniture, and we sat watching kinescopes of his recent television shows. At the end he rubbed his face and said, 'Don't I work *slow*!'

Sadly, we could not persuade him to come to England. He was getting on in years and his main interest was mounting charity shows with symphony orchestras. He made a lot of money for good causes by introducing the music, performing little comedy spots in between orchestral items and playing his violin with cunning incompetence. He seemed to us a very nice man.

Denis and I, making the best use of our time before returning to New York, *The Jack Paar Show* and temporary affluence (or hugh-millation), met comedy writers who showed us round their studios and looked after us, and we talked to Carl Reiner, the writer and producer, and generally enjoyed that warm and generous hospitality from our fellow writers which is so much an American tradition.

Stephen Potter called it the American Creative Welcome. He pointed out that in England, when the phone rings, the wife hisses, 'Who is it?' and the husband wraps his hand round the mouthpiece and whispers, 'Those Americans who were so helpful in Corfu when I got that tummy-bug – they're over here for a few days and want to meet up with us!' And the wife says, 'Oh, dear!' and rifles through her diary and says, 'You could ask them to lunch on Thursday week – no, it's one of my coffee mornings – how about three weeks on Tuesday? I could get in some cold meat and knock up a salad.' Whereas when you arrive in New York and telephone friends you get the Creative Welcome. 'Great!' they say instantly. 'Come over right away and we'll have a drink and then send out for some Mexican food!'

But Stephen Potter did also note that when you departed you departed alone: your American friends were busy Creatively Welcoming somebody else.

The BBC office in New York had booked us into the Chateau Marmont Hotel on Sunset Boulevard, Hollywood, a once grand but by then somewhat passé hotel where the great and boozy writers like Hemingway and Scott Fitzgerald once holed up when they were tempted to Hollywood to earn big bucks writing screenplays to order (P. G. Wodehouse, who was one himself except for the boozing, called those lonely, unhappy but rich souls 'the Castaways').

Our ten days sped past swiftly, meeting and talking most usefully on professional matters, and suddenly there were only a couple of days left. The writers urged us to stay on a while as they had organized a day trip by plane to Las Vegas, enough time for a swift look at the gambling palaces, a few goes on the fruit machines and lots of laughter, but we could not linger because we had committed ourselves to appearing on *The Jack Paar Show*.

Then, on our last night in Hollywood, glamour! Excitement! Superstars of Tinseltown all around us!

An old friend and colleague, the writer Michael Pertwee, had worked in Hollywood for years and one of his close, poker-playing friends was the lyricist Ira Gershwin, George Gershwin's elder brother. Michael had written to Ira Gershwin to tell him we were coming over and the good man rang us on our last day, explained that he had just got back from Saratoga and asked us over to his place immediately for an after-dinner drink.

The Gershwin home was long, low and cool; lots of white walls and modern paintings and sculpture. Ira was plumpish, short and white-haired. He took us down to the cellar, which had been converted into a kind of shrine to his brother. There was the old and battered-looking upright piano on which George had picked out 'Rhapsody in Blue', some of George's paintings – he was an enthusiastic, gently gifted Sunday painter – and various bits of memory-jogging memorabilia of George Gershwin's music.

Back upstairs, Ira poured drinks, lit a massive cigar, and we sat at our ease round a white marble table in the centre of which stood a huge Swedish goldfish bowl, shaped like a giant wineglass, not filled with the usual collection of 'My-God-was-that-where-I-was-last-night?' nightclub book-matches but with, oh dear, what seemed to be packets of every known brand of American cigarette.

Now this was the 1950s, when it was a smoker's world and Denis and I innocently puffed away as compulsively as every-body else doing nervy work. But that evening we had both run out of cigarettes. As Ira Gershwin's house was on Sunset Boulevard, as was our hotel, we allowed five minutes to drive there plus five minutes to buy cigarettes *en route*.

Our fatal error was not to realize that American boulevards can go on a bit. The Gershwin residence was indeed on Sunset Boulevard but about 12 miles up it. We had to drive at great speed to get there without being disgracefully late and there was no question of wasting time looking for a shop selling cigarettes.

So there Denis and I sat with the man commonly regarded as the most literate and brilliant lyricist of our century ('Embraceable You', 'I Got Plenty of Nothin' ', 'Let's Call the Whole Thing Off', 'Love Walked Right In', 'Long Ago and Far Away', 'Someone to Watch Over Me', 'They Can't Take That Away from Me', 'S'Wonderful', and hundreds more), letting the conversation flag as, desperate for a drag, we gazed beady-eyed at the cornucopia of fags within reach but un-attainable.

Other factors contributed to the lengthening bouts of awkward silence. Denis and I can claim a small number of extremely minor social graces: we tend to be punctual and leave the washbasin as we would wish to find it and we are both very tall, but that's about it. As for the important social graces, well, to begin with neither of us has any small talk.

Ira Gershwin did his best, but he was now taking life very easily and his main interests were playing poker and betting on horses, neither of which sciences Denis and I knew anything whatever about. And after a while we realized that Mr Gershwin was skilfully concealing the fact that he was rather deaf. As my voice is soft and plummy and Denis's is not much crisper, our host had probably not clearly heard a word either of us had said the whole evening. It was awesome. Faced with two inaudible strangers staring fixedly at a Swedish goldfish bowl full of packets of cigarettes, like a pair of tall thin fortune-tellers whose crystal ball had gone wrong, Ira Gershwin carried on being an impeccable host.

I managed to sneak a peek at my watch. It was nearly ten o'clock, not really late but late enough if we had to catch an early plane to New York, which we did not have to do as our plane left at midday.

'Well,' I said, rising, 'you've been extremely kind, Mr Gershwin, but we have to leave you in peace now because we have a plane to . . .'

But Mr Gershwin had not heard me so I sat down again.

'Do you know the work of the playwright Lillian Hellman?' he asked suddenly.

'*The Children's Hour*,' said Denis, '*The Little Foxes*, *Watch on the Rhine* . . .?'

'Lillian's upstairs,' said Ira Gershwin. 'She had some dental work done this afternoon and is having a little rest. Said she'd come and join us.'

Lillian Hellman!

An hour passed very, very slowly. Miss Hellman's dental treatment seemed to have proved more exhausting than had been expected. She did not come down.

'Moss Hart,' said Mr Gershwin some time later.

Denis woke up. 'MOSS HART!' he said.

'Said he'd drop by this evening. I'd like you to meet him.'

'Moss Hart!' said Denis again, sort of breathing the name.

'*You Can't Take It with You, The Man Who Came to Dinner, Lady in the Dark* . . .?'

Another hour or so dragged by. Moss Hart did not appear. He had probably forgotten or been kidnapped by aliens or something, but it was now after midnight and Denis and I could not, in all decency, keep this elderly gentleman from his bed any longer. His usual bedtime on non-poker evenings was probably around 8.30 p.m.

'I'm so sorry it's been such a dull evening for you,' Mr Gershwin said. 'It would have been so good if you'd met up with Lillian and Moss.'

The cheerful sound of dance music penetrated the night air.

'The noise is coming from Rosemary Clooney's place next door,' said Ira Gershwin apologetically. 'She's throwing a party there for Frank Sinatra. Hey! Would you like to meet Frank?'

'Couldn't possibly intrude . . . private party . . .' we mumbled, hearts thudding.

'Nyah!' said Mr Gershwin, 'Rosie's really nice and Frankie likes writers. Well, he likes writers who like *him*. I'll ring Rosie, she'll be glad to have you over.'

He heaved himself out of his chair, went over to the phone and dialled.

I looked at Den and Den looked at me.

Mr Gershwin held the phone to his ear and waited. I waited, Den waited, we waited all three.

Eventually, after quite a long time, he carefully replaced the phone in its cradle. 'Waddya know!' he said, chuckling. 'They're having such fun nobody can hear the phone ringing!'

Den and I chuckled with him for a moment or two to keep him company and then drove in silence back to the Chateau Marmont.

When we arrived back in New York and telephoned our talent co-ordinator ('Hi, Rick! We're back!'), we found that while we had been rubbing shoulders with 'our friends the stars' in sunny California, Rick had been fired from *The Jack Paar Show*. And in the American tradition this meant he'd had to relinquish his key to the talent co-ordinators' washroom and his numbered space in the company car park, return to the commissariat the unconsumed portion of his Waldorf Salad and

– most important for us – feed into the office shredder the contracts of all the talents he had been personally co-ordinating. Including ours.

So we flew home to England without our lovely dollars. I did manage to scrape together enough dollars and cents and things to present my schoolgirl daughter Sally with a startlingly scarlet, very American plastic sou'wester from Saks Fifth Avenue. Sal has it still. Amazing how long a hat will last if you don't wear it.

On the positive side, back in England we were at once able to rush to the aid of Eric Sykes during rehearsals of the first show of his splendid and long-running series, *Sykes And* . . . in which Hattie Jacques played Eric's twin sister. I think 'rush to the aid' was the important part of our help here. Eric later said that to him the sight of us charging in through the door of the rehearsal room was like the arrival of the US Seventh Cavalry. It was quite a minor blockage he had with his scene and Eric was easy to help; all one did was suggest a line and Eric immediately thought of a better one; it was just a matter of stimulating his own creativity into action.

Our contract allowed us to take a respite from advising and consulting when a new series of *Whack-O!* was due to be written. When that happened we pinned a card on our door saying 'IN PURDAH' and all the members of Light Entertainment scrupulously left us to get on with our writing undisturbed, unconsulted, advice unsought.

With one exception.

Our Head of Light Entertainment Group (Television) was Eric Maschwitz, author of a great many successful plays, revues (including *New Faces* and *Between Ourselves*), musicals (*Good Night, Vienna*; *Balalaika*; *Zip Goes a Million*; *Carissima, Song of Norway*), Hollywood musical films, and just a handful of songs which our generation cherished as icons of romantic wistful love, of elegance and charm: 'Room 504', 'A Nightingale Sang in Berkeley Square', and best of all, 'These Foolish Things'.

Denis always used to say that if he had written 'These Foolish Things' he would have instantly retired on the grounds that no man should be expected to contribute anything more to the public stock of harmless pleasure.

The lyric had an awkward rhyming scheme because 'things' is difficult to rhyme interestingly, but a contestant in an early *New Statesman* competition for parodies of 'These Foolish Things', even though he borrowed 'clings' from Eric, deserves an honourable mention:

> The smell of cooking close to Earl's Court Station,
> Your rabbit curry and then – eructation.
> Oh, how your vol-au-vent clings,
> These foolish things,
> Remind me of you . . .

In purdah Denis and I produced our scripts sitting either side of a desk with our feet on it. We would talk out each line and commit it to paper when it seemed about right.

Eric Maschwitz would occasionally join us. He would just walk into the room and sit down without speaking, clearly escaping from some managerial ennui. He would put his feet up on the desk with ours and sit in happy silence for a while, no jacket, bright crimson braces like streaks of blood on his shirt, nervously pushing his thin hair aside. He was tall, pale and bony. Not bony like a kipper, but like a normal skeleton which has not been given quite enough flesh to cover it comfortably. Then he would reminisce.

Those were most enjoyable interludes for Den and me because Eric was perhaps the last of the great romantics.

'I had a mistress in those days who was a ballet dancer with the Vienna Opera.' (Mistress! Vienna! Ballet dancer with the opera!) 'On one occasion I flew over to Vienna and had a wholly delightful weekend. On the Monday morning, a shade hung-over, I was in a taxi on the way to the airport when I glanced out of the back window and saw that we were being closely followed by a large Alsatian dog pedalling a bicycle with a pipe in his mouth.

'This was unnerving and I almost gave up champagne and the Vienna *corps de ballet* there and then, but the bicycle passed us at a traffic light and I saw that it was actually being pedalled by a small Viennese man in a cap, hidden from our view by his huge Alsatian dog which he had sat in the basket on the handlebars. I am happy to say that I have no idea how the dog came to be smoking a pipe. Some mysteries should never be explained, should they?'

On another occasion, in through the door he strolled, pulled up a chair and arranged his feet comfortably on our desk (now rather crowded with feet and pages of the script we were trying to work on). Scrape, scrape, scrape sideways of hair, then: 'I had this idea for a book, a compilation, which I would call *My Most Memorable Sexual Encounter*.' (The last two words are, of course, a euphemism of the single word which Eric used.)

Eric went on, 'My own contribution would be set during the war when I was in Intelligence and doing a course of something furtive at Woburn Abbey. I was spending most evenings steadily trying to seduce a Wren officer, a delightful creature with promisingly wicked eyes. Eventually, on a beautiful evening after dinner, I took her for a walk in the grounds. Trees and long grass and moonlight. We lay down and I undressed her. With her black silk stockings and white thighs it was like peeling a nut. We were in the middle of pleasure when the ground began to shake.

' "Is the earth moving for you?" she whispered.

' "Yes. But it really *is* moving!" I said. "It feels like a charging bison!"

'Which is what it was. We had strayed into the zoo area of Woburn Park and several tons of angry bison was thundering on its way to deal with us.

'This was coitus interruptus on an operatic scale. My Wren lady and I semi-dressed in haste and scrambled to safety clutching bits of clothing, all passion spent and never, of course – it never can be – rekindled.'

Another day, with rain pelting down outside, Eric dropped in to tell us about a wartime experience of rain in Regent Street. It was nearly midnight on a warm summer's evening and he, like the few people around at that time, was wearing light clothes. Suddenly down came torrential rain. Eric found shelter in the portico of Aquascutum Ltd. A pretty girl scampered in, an evening paper held over her head to protect her hair and make-up. Eric made way for her so that she could be at the back of the alcove in the dry while he kept watch on

Regent Street for a cab. The pretty girl thanked Eric in a Scottish accent for moving and he immediately began to wonder whether a romantic interlude might not be on with this sweet little thing.

A taxi eventually came along with its light on and Eric shot out into the rain waving his arms. The taxi stopped for him. Eric ran back into the alcove and said to the girl, 'Come on, I've got a taxi. Where can I take you?'

'I canna leave here, thank you, kind sir,' said the girl.

'Why on earth not?' said Eric.

She said, 'I'm a wee whore.'

At the regular Light Entertainment Group meetings Eric was terrific value and a fine raiser of morale; he called his eighteen or so producers and their retinues 'my ragged army' and was funny as well as critical in his rundown of the group's activities. As far as we knew he was managing the department extremely well.

Another endearing aspect of Eric as an administrator was that he invented nicknames for many of us. Rather shrill and noisy guitar-playing groups from South America were popular visiting acts at that time and Eric's name for Denis and me was 'Los Layabouts', Dennis Main Wilson was 'Dr Sinister' and Graeme Muir (no relation), a smooth, grey-haired producer of middle-class sitcoms, was 'our resident gynaecologist'.

When considering Eric Maschwitz's achievements in the musical theatre and in Hollywood, and the romantic songs he wrote, it is easy to think of him as a brilliant freelance wit who had drifted into the BBC by accident after the war, but in fact he was an old BBC pro. He had a youthful spell in magazine editing after university and then joined the BBC way back in 1926 (when I was aged six). He edited the *Radio Times* from 1927 to 1933, was a director of radio variety from 1933 to 1937, and after a wartime career in Intelligence and as the architect of forces broadcasting, returned to the bosom of the BBC in 1958 as Head of Light Entertainment (Television).

BBC's Light Entertainment was unique in having a Head who, if he wanted a musical show and couldn't find one he liked, was perfectly capable of writing one himself. Which actually happened while we were there. It was for the August bank holiday. Eric wanted the bank holiday Monday evening's viewing to be built round a happy, very English musical comedy but no suitable script could be found, so Eric sat down with his flat little portable typewriter and tapped one out. It was a musical play which told of a village squire (played by Jimmy Edwards, who led the singing of the champagne finale, 'Fizz, Fizz, Fizz'), and the plots and machinations which resulted in the village, for the first time in its history, winning the annual cricket match against the wealthy neighbouring village's team of weekenders from London.

Eric Maschwitz's assistant, Tom Sloan, was neither a writer nor a producer but a good professional manager. Tom was a rather military figure who had been in the Royal Artillery during the war and had volunteered to become a glider pilot, one of the most dangerous jobs of the war.

The change in management method when Eric left to go on to other things and Tom became Head of Light Entertainment was dramatic. At the first departmental meeting Tom welcomed us all and then said, 'This department has a lot of work to do and we are all professionals so you can forget any "ragged army" nonsense.'

Tom Sloan was keen on things which he felt were due to him like 'discipline' and 'loyalty', but he was professionally adroit at winning money for his Light Entertainment Group from the controllers. He was strict on producers keeping to their budgets and he tried hard to maintain the old Reithean strictures on free thought and language. Like a company chairman who in his career will move smoothly from one company to another and control the destinies of, say, an airline, followed by the manufacture of pills, and then the running of the Royal Ballet, Tom's real interest lay not in the product but in the management of it.

Eric Maschwitz, on the other hand, loved romantic music and wit and fun and he was much more than the Head of Light Entertainment Group, he was its leader. But then Eric had written 'These Foolish Things'.

Arranging *Whack-O!* for live production in the Shepherd's Bush Empire presented some severe strictures which were no doubt good for our souls, as most things troublesome are claimed to be. There were usually some six to eight scenes in the half-hour show and the programme was performed non-stop on a theatre stage which was a much smaller area than a studio floor.

Dougie Moodie's method was to have a black curtain hung to divide the stage into two halves. Each half had a black front curtain to close it off from the audience's view so as not to distract them when a scene was being changed. The most used scene, the headmaster's study, permanently occupied the left-hand half of the stage, and while a scene was being played in it the right-hand half would be closed off by the curtain and the stage staff would rapidly, and as quietly as possible, set the furniture and props for the next scene. Backstage visitors of a religious disposition would occasionally be discomposed by seeing a large sign reading, 'Have You Got Soft Soles?'

Our responsibility was to write the scenes in Jimmy's study so that they lasted long enough for the scene-shifters to change the other half of the stage; to quote one actual requirement, 'From Lower Fourth's dormitory to a table in the Savoy Grill.'

A live production also raised problems for the actors, such as the peril of eating peanuts. It was quite usual to have a party scene where the actors enjoyed nibbling a salted peanut or two; the problem was that a nut does not disappear entirely when eaten as does a Smartie or a potato crisp. True, the peanuts are ground by the molars into tiny fragments, most of which are harmlessly swallowed down, but a few of them lurk in the dark caverns between the teeth and work their way out later and demand to be chewed smaller. Or worse still, tiny fragments drop down onto a tonsil and demand to be removed, which can only be done by the actor making short high barking coughs.

We first hit the problem when, ignorant of the Peanut Peril, we wrote a scene depicting a staff party in the headmaster's study. Jimmy poured tiny glasses of British sherry for the staff, then went to a globe of the world, opened a hatch in it and pulled out a bottle of whisky.

'There's always something new out of Africa!' he said and poured himself half a tumblerful. 'Cheers!'

Salted peanuts were passed round, thrown up and caught in

the teeth and hurled about. Jimmy tossed a handful into his mouth and munched.

A caption card came up on the screen announcing, 'TWO WEEKS LATER'.

We then cut to the other half of the stage to show the drawing room of a noble prospective parent, Lord Portly. The butler ushered in the headmaster who bowed in a grovelly manner.

'Good morning, oh Lord. How gracious of you to grant me a few moments or two of your time to discuss how your elder son – the one with the ginger hair – did in his entrance exam to Chiselbury. By a happy provenance he scraped in. With marks of ninety-nine out of a possible hundred.'

Jimmy unknowingly chewed vagrant fragments of peanut throughout this speech, every now and then putting a hand-kerchief to his mouth and giving the high-pitched, throat-clearing bark.

Jimmy was rarely fazed by things going wrong during a live transmission, even peanut fragments on the epiglottis. It was often a chance for him to ad lib, such as in the scene of a later programme when the local tax inspector went through the school accounts, tut-tutting, until he came across something deeply suspicious. He put his spectacles down on the desk and rubbed his eyes in a tired manner before resuming his inspection. In the script it said:

> (*While the inspector is rubbing his eyes and cannot see what is going on, Jimmy picks up the whole telephone, reaches across the desk and bangs the telephone down on the inspector's spectacles, breaking the lenses. He picks up the specs, hands the ruins to the now half-blind inspector and says:*)

HEADMASTER: I'm so sorry, I seem to have accidentally dented your spectacles.

On the live performance Jimmy picked up the phone and gave the specs a good thump, but nothing happened to them, so he gave them another thump. Nothing. A couple more thumps. The spectacles showed no sign of injury. The audience was now beginning to appreciate Jimmy's predicament and enjoying it. Mortarboard and gown now askew, tie twisted, clearly sweating, Jimmy thumped the specs all over the desk and finally, exasperated, raised the phone set up in both hands and brought it down with a tremendous bang onto the specs. He picked them up. At last they were twisted and bent and the plastic lenses were broken.

The audience burst into a round of applause.

HEADMASTER: (*Holding out the little mass of twisted wire and bits of plastic to the inspector.*) I'm so sorry, I seem to have accidentally dented your spectacles.

It was a good moment.

Whack-O!, starring Jimmy and Arthur Howard, became an established success, and in 1960 a feature film was made of it called *Bottoms Up*, written up from our scripts by our good friend Michael Pertwee. It was a modest success, but nevertheless a success. *Bottoms Up* can still occasionally be seen on afternoon television when the channel is in need of a filler.

But the film marked a sudden and sad crisis. Arthur Howard was arrested for 'cottaging', the slang word used to describe anonymous homosexual encounters, usually with 'rough trade', in a public convenience.

After a week on remand in Brixton Prison, Arthur came up before the magistrates. Denis and I offered to speak on his behalf and to stand security for his future good behaviour.

The solemn process of the law was not helped by Denis and me trying to enter the small witness box side by side and getting jammed. We broke free to muffled tittering.

The clerk of the court spoke up, 'Are you able to stand surety of one hundred pounds each for the accused's good behaviour over the next six months?'

The court rang with our sincere and confident cries of, 'Oh, yes! And only too happy to, your worships!'

The clerk of the court continued, 'And are you able to stand surety for one hundred pounds each *when all your debts are paid*?'

Our confident cries were replaced by an embarrassed hush.

'Er – yes, sir,' we eventually mumbled. Arthur was fined £50 and put on surety for good behaviour for six months.

Polly and I insisted on Arthur coming down to Anners to convalesce for a week or two and this was a success.

Sally, not yet at boarding school, was entranced by Arthur's ineptitude with his breakfast egg. An adult unable to cope with a boiled egg! Arthur mishit his egg with his spoon, and yolk and white of egg besmirched the tablecloth in huge spots and streaks. We were all astonished at how much egg there was in an egg; it was a lively topic of conversation for weeks.

Arthur's particular homosexual inclination had no connection whatsoever with corrupting young boys, but nevertheless the BBC thought that he could not continue to work in a television series featuring a young cast. So Arthur had to go, and *Whack-O!* had to come to an end.

Jimmy was furious and unforgiving. His successful show had been abruptly ended by what he saw as Arthur's selfish and stupid behaviour.

The ultimate irony was that two decades later, when Jimmy was spending part of each year in Australia, his young male friend of that time revealed to an English tabloid newspaper (for a hefty sum of money) that he was Jimmy's lover and Jimmy was, and always had been, homosexual. Jimmy said at the time, 'I did not "come out", I was booted through the door.'

And so Pol and I offered another colleague and old friend a refuge with us, but in Jimmy's case it was not necessary. He was rehearsing for a pantomime and Arthur Askey and the rest of the cast were understanding and reassuring.

Jimmy's real pleasures were riding to hounds and playing polo, and he was afraid that his county friends would be deeply reactionary and would no longer even speak to him. But to his great relief he was wrong; his horsey friends were superbly uninterested in his private life. And to the general public, too, the startling revelation that Jimmy Edwards was homosexual passed almost unnoticed. People couldn't believe, or didn't want to believe, that Pa Glum was gay.

Arthur Howard talked to Polly and me about his week on remand in Brixton Prison. His colleagues awaiting trial were mostly thieves and case-hardened, grievous-bodily-harm regulars – Arthur's closest friend for the week had been accused of stabbing his girlfriend in the cheek with a pair of scissors – but they quickly recognized that Arthur was not a threat but a kindly gent in an unfamiliar situation which was only too familiar to them. They protected him, easing his way through the ugly prison regime with such kindnesses as making sure that he had first shave with the morning's communal razor blade while it was still sharp.

Every morning Arthur scoured the newspapers with us for reports on how his new friends had fared when they came up in court. Breakfast would be punctuated by sudden cries from Arthur of, 'Oh, no! They've given Rocky the Horror three months! Just for hitting a Manchester United fan with a fire extinguisher.' Or, 'Oh good! Mick's case was dismissed. He accidentally set fire to his son's school while wiring up the staffroom tea urn. I think he was guilty, but he was very good to me so I'm glad he got away with it.'

A treasury of anecdotes illustrating Arthur's inability to cope with ordinary life could have been compiled.

One weekend he brought his wife, the actress Jean Compton, and their infant son Alan, down to us at Thorpe for Sunday lunch. Arthur was buzzing along happily in their little Morris when halfway up Egham Hill the steering wheel came off in his hands. He turned round in his seat and waved the wheel at Jean, crying, 'Jean, look, the steering wheel's come off!'

'Well, put it back *on*!' said Jean. Which he promptly did.

Next day, when he had the steering wheel checked at a garage, an awed mechanic revealed to him that on that particular model of car the steering wheel was not on a spline but, like an interchangeable camera lens, could only be fitted back in one position. Arthur and his family had avoided crashing by a 1 in 365 chance.

In London one evening, Arthur was walking a little ahead of Jean along Jermyn Street when a lady of the night stepped out of a doorway and murmured enticingly to Arthur, 'Hello, darling!'

Arthur, with his usual impeccable good manners, raised his hat in case she was a family friend he hadn't recognized and said with his warm smile and beautiful voice, '*Hello*! How lovely to see you again . . . !'

Jean accelerated and grabbed his arm: 'Oh, come on, you fool!'

Then Arthur's brief good fortune began to leak away. Jean died and Arthur no longer had his beloved minder to stop him tripping over so many of life's broken paving stones.

Arthur's personal problem seems to have been that he was the least successful duckling of a highly successful brood of achievers. His parents were European refugees originally named Steiner (later Stainer). His elder brother Leslie became a matinée idol of the stage, then an actor and director in films, famously playing Ashley in *Gone with the Wind*.

As Arthur grew up, his mother constantly prodded him to be more like Leslie. 'Why don't you smoke a pipe like Leslie? It's manly.' 'Why don't you read more? Leslie always has a book in his hand.' The consequence of all this, of course, was that Arthur never smoked a pipe and hardly ever read a book.

His sister Dorice Stainer had a successful dancing academy in Ascot and taught dancing at local schools, and his other sister Irene Howard was the casting director for MGM films in England.

Jean also had distinguished relations. Her uncle was the novelist Compton Mackenzie – she was his favourite niece – and her aunt was the actress Fay Compton. Moreover, Arthur's son Alan and his nephew Ronald ('Wink') were both leading actors.

One day Arthur explained to Polly and me what to him was the point of cottaging. At a smart dinner party, where everybody there was more talented and had achieved more in the theatre than he could ever have hoped to do, he would make an excuse, slip away and do his cottaging. And when he returned to the party, he was 'somebody' for an hour or two. He had a secret. He knew something they did not know.

It does seem a pity that life was not just a little kinder to dear harmless Arthur; he was kindness itself.

★ ★ ★

After the demise of *Whack-O!* Denis and I wrote quite a few series for BBC TV during the late Fifties and early Sixties, including an adaptation of Henry Cecil's book, *Brothers-in-Law*, which did for barristers what Richard Gordon's *Doctor in the House* had done for medics.

I had been impressed by a young actor, Richard Briers, whom I had seen a year or so previously in Lionel Hale's stage play *Guilt and Gingerbread*. Denis agreed he was right and we persuaded Richard Briers to play the young barrister hero. This was, I think, his first starring role on TV.

We had another fortunate piece of casting when one episode required our pupil barrister to settle into digs and come to terms with an awkward landlady. The landlady turned out to be difficult to cast, and then Denis remembered a remarkable performance he had seen in Joan Littlewood's musical, *Fings Ain't Wot They Used To Be*. The actress had never worked in television and was terrified of it; Denis had to spend many hours persuading her that she would be right for the part and there was nothing for her to be afraid of. She eventually agreed and so began the brilliant television career of Yootha Joyce.

Henry Cecil was our co-writer on the series and vetted our stuff for legal plausibility as well as contributing story ideas and dialogue. Henry was a County Court judge (His Honour Judge Henry Cecil Leon), but he also wrote light amusing novels and plays based on crimes and courts. His sense of character was almost non-existent. Most of his cast seemed to have been cut out of living cardboard and they all spoke in the same kind of amusing, exact, witty way in which Henry himself spoke (except for an occasional 'blimey' when the character was a burglar). But as with Agatha Christie, none of this mattered. His plots were ingenious, absorbing and, above all, amusing, the stories rattled along and the books were enjoyed by a large readership.

He used to come to see us at Television Centre after his day in court, driving himself in a no-longer-young Jaguar car and Denis and I would rush him to the BBC club bar where he would enjoy two large, bone-dry Martinis. He told us, 'I'm one of those lucky people. My body tells me when I have had enough.'

Denis whispered to me, 'He slumps to the floor.'

But Henry did nothing unseemly; he was a very good husband, an unpredictable judge (which always disturbs barristers and keeps them on their toes) and a keen writer. And Henry had another rare gift: a genius for hospitality. He loved entertaining and would go to immense pains to make every occasion, from a dinner party to a sandwich, a memorable pleasure.

He invited Polly to sit as his guest on the bench of his court to hear a case (which is apparently a quite acceptable practice) and later invited us both to the first night of one of his plays, *Alibi for a Judge* (Henry wrote an earlier play, *Settled Out of Court*, in collaboration with the Californian/Armenian writer of impetuous, impressionistic prose, William Saroyan; a sobering thought). Our evening began with a drink and smoked salmon sandwiches in Henry's chambers, then on to his play at the Savoy Theatre. Champagne was provided by Henry in the interval, and after the play Polly and I strolled across to the Savoy Hotel for a late supper with the Cecils. A lovely way to spend an evening.

Denis and I found we had a taste for writing about the law (Henry thought we would have made excellent solicitors but dodgy judges) so we followed *Brothers-in-Law* with a new series we devised to tell legal stories from the point of view of the judge. We called the series *Mr Justice Duncannon*.

The idea was partly inspired by the actor we wanted to play our judge, Andrew Cruickshank. Andrew had played a judge for us previously and he was tremendously effective; the beetling brows, the craggy features, the Scots accent, the teasing humour. Henry Cecil was our legal adviser. The series was more light drama than sitcom, but won respectable figures and did its job.

After some 'how-about?' and 'what-if?' sessions, Denis and I settled on writing a new series of seven entirely different programmes, single comic plays really, starring Jimmy Edwards and similar to the parody dramas which were the popular last section of *Take It From Here*. We called the new series *The Seven Faces of Jim*.

Each show had its own subtitle, e.g., *The Face of Power*. That one had Jim as a ruthless Victorian manufacturer of gas mantles with a troublesome labour force (shop steward Ronnie Barker) and a beautiful daughter (June Whitfield). Just when Jim emerged triumphantly as the King of Gas Mantles, some young engineer developed a form of street lighting based on something called electricity . . .

Another of the shows was a topical story based on the first appearance on our streets of minicabs. The story was a parody of aspects of the film *A Matter of Life and Death*, treating minicabs as RAF planes.

Jimmy played the grizzled old wing commander who, now demobbed, had one battered minicab driven by a David Nivenish Richard Briers. June played the girl despatcher on the microphone who was in love with Richard Briers (as in the film). There was thick fog (as in the film) and Briers was talked safely home by June (as in the film). Her directions over the microphone were so accurate in bringing him safely home that, exactly on time, the minicab crashed through the brick wall of the minicab office and came to rest a few inches from June (not in the film).

The Screenwriters' Guild of Great Britain decided that year to institute an annual ball and present its own professional awards for film and television writing. Denis and I won the first of these. It was a heavy bronze plaque (each), inscribed:

'SEVEN FACES OF JIM'
THE BEST WORK IN BRITISH TELEVISION
LIGHT ENTERTAINMENT SERIES
1961

We wrote another series for Jimmy Edwards called *Six More Faces of Jim* which was gratifyingly successful with viewers (though was not brilliant enough for the Screenwriters' Guild to give us another bronze plaque), and then our four years at the BBC were up and we went back to working in our eyrie high above Conduit Street.

We devised and wrote several sitcom series, including *The Big Noise*, starring Bob Monkhouse as a brash disc jockey, but we found a restlessness setting in. We had been writing together now for seventeen years – writing *everything* together – and our joint product was not a Muir and Norden script so much as a Muirandnorden script, with predictable qualities and weaknesses. There was a good enough demand for the product, but we were getting on a bit as far as comedy writers were concerned – comedy writers were supposed to last ten years – and we had begun to wonder whether there was still an untapped Denis Norden style, or Frank Muir style, which had been muffled by the success of the Muirandnorden magimix.

For one thing Denis, who was interested in all aspects of the cinema, really wanted to write films, which I did not. Making films was a bit too much of a committee operation for me, I wanted to write books.

The fates were kind and we moved relatively smoothly into our solo careers. Denis, through Michael Pertwee, with whom he collaborated on a number of films, met and got on well with an independent American comedy writer turned film producer, Mel Frank. A number of successful films resulted, which Den co-wrote, and he later wrote an original screenplay which was filmed. It was called *The Best House In London*.

When my family was away on holiday I spent a weekend with Johnny Johnson, ex-music publisher and leader of The Keynotes singing group (and sometime wearer in the South of France of papier mâché inner soles made of £5 notes: see chapter nine). Johnny's old music publishing partner, young Bill Cotton, was there. Young Bill, after producing many musical programmes for TV, including his father's, had become a rising figure in the BBC staff hierarchy and was now Assistant Head of Light Entertainment, Tom Sloan's number two.

During the weekend I told young Bill that Den and I were going to have a try at finding out whether we had anything worthwhile left to contribute individually, and Den was now happily into films.

A week later Tom Sloan asked for a meeting. It seemed that the Light Entertainment Group at Television Centre needed a bit of reorganizing because the Assistant Head of Light Entertainment, young Bill Cotton, was a tower of strength where pop music and variety programmes were concerned – and there were a lot of them about at that time (musical shows starring Yana, Ruby Murray, Alma Cogan, Petula Clark, and also *The Black and White Minstrel Show, Wakey Wakey!* etc., etc.) – but Bill was less experienced where words were concerned and was overworked. The Head of Television, Kenneth Adam, had proposed that the job of Assistant Head of Light Entertainment should be split in two, and that young Bill should be Assistant Head (Variety) and a new post, Assistant Head (Comedy), should be created. And as young Bill had said that I was available, I should be offered the new job.

I happily accepted; it was the answer to many immediate problems. A devious three-year contract was then haggled over which resulted in my remaining a freelance but 'devoting as much time as was necessary' to do the job (in reality twenty-five hours a day). By this means I could continue doing *My Word!* and *My Music* with Denis for BBC radio, plus the odd commercial.

My first day at Television Centre. The new office smells I would soon get used to; the strangeness of the details of a new environment, e.g., the little slip pasted above the light switch in the loo reading 'PLEASE SWITCH OFF WHEN NOT IN USE'. (?)

I enjoyed the rather tremulous excitement of arriving to take up the first real job I had ever had. I was aged forty-six. But I had no experience whatever of managing anything, not even a car boot sale, and I did not know anybody's name, or far worse, the initials of their jobs on which the whole infrastructure of BBC communications was based, as David Attenborough discovered when he became Controller of the second channel and his wife Jane was greeted at a BBC reception by a keen young man saying, 'How nice that you could come, Mrs C-BBC2.'

I was AHLEG(C)TEL, a slight abbreviation of Assistant Head of Light Entertainment Group (Comedy) Television, which I never used if it was humanly possible not to. It seemed sensible to find an assistant who did know the BBC codes and how the corporation managerial machine actually functioned and let him get on with it, and I had just such a man as my unit manager, an ex-cameraman named Bob Gilbraith who was totally competent at organizing everything.

Penny Sparshott, the secretary Denis and I so prized during

our period as advisers (Penny had grown too tall to remain a ballet dancer and was not only beautiful but beautifully competent), had left the BBC. I had to search for a secretary and found the splendid Helen Morton, who proved very good at organizing me. Helen was a talented girl and could well have been a producer, but she sang in the Philharmonia choir, which was very important to her, so at that time she needed as near to a nine-to-five job as she could find.

I had a Script Department along the corridor to read submitted scripts and report to me, write their own shows and generally advise. It occurred to me that they did much the same job that Den and I had once done. This Script Department consisted of two fine and good writers who became my close friends: John Law, a small neat Scot, who was more valuable a co-writer to Michael Bentine than has been acknowledged; he died tragically young. His colleague was the great (in all senses, a barrage balloon in size) Richard Waring.

Richard, brother of the actor Derek Waring and brother-in-law of Dorothy Tutin, really wanted to open his own restaurant and cook all day, or do conjuring tricks, or collect very tatty horror films involving things rising out of swamps, but instead became the writer who, as much as anybody, made middle-class comedy work on television. Previously, most sitcoms featured comically stupid working-class characters or comically stupid aristos, but Waring made ordinary, educated, middle-class people funny in a number of highly successful series, particularly with *Marriage Lines* (starring Richard Briers and Prunella Scales), a bitter-sweet comedy of a young married couple whose relationship was not going all that well (as in Richard Waring's own marriage).

One morning he found himself sharing the lift with Tom Sloan. To break the silence, Richard blurted out, 'John Law and I have been making anagrams of all our names. In the seventeenth century it was used as a kind of character analysis. An anagram of a person's name was supposed to indicate what sort of person he was . . .'

Tom turned and looked at him steadily. Richard wilted but knew that having started he had to finish.

'You came out "Nola Smot",' he said.

My status in the BBC was that of medium-rare management, entitled to park on the gravel forecourt of Television Centre (an important privilege) and to attend the Wednesday morning programme review meeting when all the heads and assistant heads met and rubbished each other's shows.

I could never treat the meetings very seriously and tended to pass remarks. Such as when they were building an extension to Television Centre and our meeting was punctuated by sundry loud and rhythmic bangs. I said to Kenneth Adam, 'Sir, as the knocking outside the meeting is now louder than the knocking *inside* the meeting, should we not adjourn?'

Peter Dimmock, then Head of Sport, made a point of sitting at the bottom of the long table and while others were talking and arguing would conspicuously busy himself sorting papers from a briefcase and signing things, the image of an efficient executive to whom every second was precious. One Wednesday morning when the meeting had guests from abroad I could not find a seat. Eventually I found a spare chair and Peter shifted his briefcase and papers and made way for me to sit beside him at the bottom of the table. When a point on light entertainment arose, the chairman, Kenneth Adam, peered round the table looking for me. 'Is Frank here?' he said.

I piped up, 'Yes, sir, Peter Dimmock has kindly allowed me to sit in his office.'

We were all given copies of the current *Radio Times* to ponder upon. In one meeting I was glancing idly through my copy when I noticed the subtitle of a gardening programme. 'Excuse me, sir,' I said with youthful eagerness to our chairman, who was half listening to a boring argument about studio lighting, '*Radio Times*, sir. Wednesday, seven forty-five p.m., sir. *Gardener's World*. The title of one of the items would make an excellent, sensitive "Wednesday play" about a young couple's tragic inability to fit into the social system: *Tomatoes in a Cold Greenhouse*.'

I was allotted a large office previously occupied by Tom Sloan, who moved a couple of doors along the corridor to a suite of offices in which he could house his staff. I rearranged my furniture and signed for a small coffee table with some comfortable chairs round it so that I could sit and talk to writers and producers on the same level rather than have them stand at my desk.

On my very first day a very important matter of privilege and seniority arose. Tom was Head of Light Entertainment Group and I was only Assistant Head. The head of a group was entitled to a wall-to-wall carpet, an assistant head was not, and my office still had Tom's wall-to-wall carpet.

On my third day in Television Centre, two men in long brown coats came into my office and cut a foot off the carpet.

Chapter 12

'DREST IN A LITTLE BRIEF AUTHORITY'

The loneliness of command proved to be non-existent once I had settled in at Television Centre. I often longed for a bit of it.

My door was usually open into the next room, which housed Bob Gilbraith and helpers, and Helen, when they were not in my office chatting, and Tom (Nola) Sloan was through a door on the other side. Tom rarely came in, but when he was having an important meeting with a comedian and wild laughter rang out, I rather enjoyed knocking, putting my head round the door and muttering things like, 'Could you keep the noise down please, some of us here are trying to get some sleep.' And hardly a day passed of my three happy years there when the diary was not liberally sprinkled with meetings, many of them with agents hoping to sell a client. I tried to see them all. However hopeless their mission, it seemed to me that as they had to make a forty-five minute journey out to Shepherd's Bush and then back again, they were entitled to thirty minutes of AHLEG(C)TEL's time.

In the BBC it was customary for the producer of a comedy show also to be its director so that he was solely responsible for the whole thing; it was his baby (in ITV the responsibilities were separated, I think because producers and directors were represented by different unions). So when a BBC producer of comedy ran into a problem he brought his baby to me.

Jimmy Gilbert was a most able producer, who later ran the department and then moved from the BBC to ITV (most of the good producers, Jimmy Gilbert, Duncan Wood, Graeme Muir, Michael Mills, John Howard Davies, etc., eventually ended up at ITV because retirement from the BBC was compulsory at sixty and they could then prolong their careers a few more years by joining one of the commercial stations). Jimmy rang me and said that he had a problem. He was producing an enjoyable series featuring two old men who argued with each other and yet needed each other; it was called *The Walrus and the Carpenter*. Jimmy's problem was that one of his old actors, well-known for enjoying a nip or two, was now taking a nip or two too many and it was beginning to show. Could sir have a quiet admonitory word with the actor?

There was a civilized system whereby a head of department could have a working lunch in his office. An impressive trolley was wheeled in with a range of bottles and glasses, food such as cold salmon mayonnaise was laid out and there was coffee in a thermos. But there was an uncivilized aspect to it: the head's guests at lunch could only be artistes or writers or agents; BBC personnel could not be invited. So I had to fumble my way through my meeting with the actor without Jimmy Gilbert.

I did my best. I appealed to the actor's professionalism; the bad effect he was having on the rest of the cast, etc. No threats, no cajoling. I felt quietly confident that with a bit of luck he would go easier on the sauce from now on after our meeting. When he left to go back to rehearsals he thanked me and shook my hand vigorously.

An hour later, Jimmy Gilbert phoned from the outside rehearsal rooms. 'What on earth did you say to him?' asked Jimmy.

'I just tried to give him confidence to overcome his little problem,' I said modestly. 'Why?'

Jimmy said, 'I stopped on the way back to get petrol and he was out of the car in a flash and into a pub. We're supposed to be rehearsing and I can't get him out of the saloon bar.'

When I first sat at my imposing desk I explored it and found it quite empty except for one lower drawer which contained a small, neatly folded white napkin and a tiny sliver of soap. What were they there for? They seemed a trifle sinister, perhaps to be used in some obscure BBC religious rite. To give thanks when *Songs of Praise* got a better viewing figure than ITV's *Stars on Sunday*? An unlikely event as *Stars on Sunday* had such spiritual and aesthetic delights as plump pink Jesse Yates –

Paula's daddy – playing viewers' request hymns on a small electric organ, a huge choir dressed as nuns with glamorous make-up, and celebrities reading the lesson in a scarlet leather wing chair by the side of a (gas) log fire, flanked by rows of eighteenth-century books hired from Books By The Yard.

We seniors had our own dining room with our own waitresses, one of them very Welsh. Huw Wheldon, then Controller of Programmes, used to stride in with vigour and order his lunch in fluent Welsh, which we all thought a bit much, but very Huw. One always hoped to find Young Bill Cotton – AHLEG(V)TEL – having lunch there because he, like Huw, was full of good talk and was a most welcome sight when other production heads were too occupied elsewhere; one could fall amongst administrators.

Gents' suiting in the senior dining room was sombre as in a gentlemen's club, particularly that worn by the administrators. These were decent, amusing fellows who tended to sit together, a little non-riot of dark-grey suits, domestically knitted grey woollen socks and very large black shoes. *Very* large black shoes. There has never been a recorded case of a BBC administrator blowing over in a high wind.

I was acceptable to begin with because my workaday suit was an austere dark green, a tweed fabric seemingly woven from mature spinach. But I tended to do a little light carpentry and house painting in it and not wear a raincoat during showers, so the suit developed a pong. While it was at the dry-cleaner's I made do with dark-grey flannel trousers and a sombre sports jacket with an almost invisible check. On my first entry into the senior dining room wearing this muted ensemble I was greeted by one of the admin group with, 'Hello, Muir, going racing?'

For the first few months I did not have to grub about from scratch to find a whole new schedule of comedy shows, my job to begin with was more to take over and extend the programmes which Bill Cotton had initiated and which were doing well. The comedy series which I think Bill was most proud of having helped to start was Peter Cook and Dudley Moore's *Not Only . . . But Also*.

Peter and Dudley's method of working was strongly

reminiscent of the old radio show *In All Directions* with Peter Ustinov and Peter Jones. Both Peter Cook and Peter Ustinov were bottomless wells of comedy invention, preferably expressed ad lib, and Peter Jones and Dudley Moore made them excellent partners, both far more than 'foils' or 'straight men'.

I went over to Paris where Peter Ustinov was editing a film, and persuaded him to do an *In All Directions* on television with Peter Jones. There was no scenery or costumes. In one sketch Ustinov played a fat American speed cop. He asked the props department for an armchair fitted with good castors, and in the sketch it became his motorbike. He propelled it about the stage with his legs making motorbike and siren noises, and then went into a marvellous accent, brow-beating the unfortunate Peter Jones, an English tourist he had caught speeding.

The final sketch in the radio series was always some swindle attempted by the two Peters playing Morry and Dud, tatty 1950s spivs (the last line of the sketch always ended with Ustinov whispering hoarsely to Jones, 'Morry?' 'Yes, Dud?' 'Run for it!').

The early Sixties was, of course, the period when a break-through was made in the language and subject matter considered acceptable in BBC TV. This relaxing of strictures was greeted with delight by progressive liberal minds and with horror by 'Disgusted of Tunbridge Wells' (who was, incidentally, an off-stage character in *Take It From Here*, played by Wallas Eaton).

Those citizens who hankered after the old values were organized into a group by Mrs Mary Whitehouse, an ex-teacher who believed that the BBC rules of censorship as laid down in the *Green Book* all those years previously should be treated as Holy Writ and strictly adhered to. Mrs Whitehouse's reason for nipping at the heels of the BBC seems to have been her belief that the BBC, under its progressively minded director-general Hugh Greene, was to blame for failing to hold back progress and not sticking to Sir John Reith's bleak, granite-like, 1920s-style morality (e.g., no variety programmes or dance music to be broadcast on Sundays).

She thought, overdoing her zeal perhaps, that Hugh

Carleton Greene, by supporting such important innovative shows as *That Was The Week That Was* was 'the man who, above all, was responsible for the moral collapse which characterized the Sixties and Seventies.'

Hugh Greene's way of coping with Mrs Whitehouse's attempted censorship of not only BBC programmes, but also contemporary books and plays in general, was to keep her at arm's length, not recognizing her officially nor replying to her publicly.

I had a slight but much more amicable brush with the DG (oh, those BBC initials) early on in my BBC contract.

After a holiday abroad I returned to find a general election about to happen and the television schedules polluted with party political broadcasts. Incensed by these (and I take a bit of incensing) I wrote a letter to *The Times*, which they printed. I wrote:

Sir, when I was at school and we were coming up to the end-of-term exams I wrote a letter to my headmaster (in brown ink for some reason, which angered him) and gave it as my view that if the purpose of an exam was to test how much information and wisdom had penetrated our natural defences, then swotting to pass the exam was a form of cheating. The Head did not feel able to fall in with this theory, but I believe there is truth in it. By the same reasoning I believe that we should vote for a political party on its proven record not on wild promises for the future made in party political broadcasts which the party has a snowflake's chance in hell of fulfilling. Thus party political broadcasts are quite clearly only another form of cheating.

What I did not know, as I had just returned from abroad, was that a few days earlier the DG had written a keynote letter to the papers saying how important party political broadcasts on television were to the political health of our democracy. What I also did not know, or had forgotten, was that BBC employees were strictly forbidden to write letters to newspapers expressing their personal views on television and political matters.

A memo emerged from the DG's office in Broadcasting House. The memo was kindly, mainly curious how I could ignore such an important rule as the one preventing staff from blabbing to the press. But the memo then descended from one management office to another, the file growing more threatening and larger as it went like a snowball rolling downhill. Eventually it landed with a thud on Huw Wheldon's desk. Huw passed the huge file on to me with a scribbled note attached saying:

You have an unusual contract but it states quite clearly that you will obey staff rules and regulations as laid down in the *Staff Handbook*, a copy of which you were given on joining. Full explanation, please. Immediately. (Or when you are not too busy.)

I replied:

Dear Huw,
I am so sorry to have wasted so many important people's time and I would certainly not have written to *The Times* had I known that it was forbidden so to do. The trouble is I did not read the *Staff Handbook* thoroughly and commit it to memory as I should have done. In fact, I thought the rather slim booklet was my electric blanket guarantee and I filed it away at home under Domestic Items.

But I do think that you should get Mrs Mary Whitehouse to ban party political broadcasts. To this end could you not persuade the political parties to record their promises in the nude?

And that was the last I heard of the matter.
As I began to assemble my schedule of new comedy shows I realized that I had responsibilities which I needed to clarify in my own mind. Pondering over it all in bed, usually at about four o'clock in the morning, half-awake with an Afghan hound puppy fast asleep across my Adam's apple, I tried to focus what thoughts I had.

It seemed to me that a paternalistic attitude was inescapable considering the enormous influence of television, particularly on children. Commercial television's policy was not to give the public what was good for it, which was how the BBC's Reithean attitude of responsibility was regarded, but to give the public what it wanted. Yes, fine, were we in a free-for-all squabble for maximum audiences where diminution of standards was the quickest and cheapest way to popularity, but the BBC was a public service and was not then – and should not be – part of a brawl for audience figures.

The picture was complicated. There was, and still is, the problem of politicians who are incensed because although they vote the BBC its licence fee, they are not allowed to go on the air whenever they feel like it and use the BBC as a personal political loud hailer. And both major parties have always been convinced that the BBC is hopelessly biased politically and infested with activists from the other side.

The complication arose because the Beeb was committed to quality programming and political impartiality, yet winning the exact percentage of the viewing audience was most important. In the Sixties and Seventies, if the BBC's share of the audience rose much above 50 per cent there were howls of rage from ITV companies claiming they had to earn their money from advertisers while the BBC was subsidized by public licence money, which they thought was unfair. On the other hand, if the BBC's audience share of viewers dropped much below 50 per cent there were howls of rage in the House of Commons that MPs were voting public money to a television service which hardly anybody watched.

One of the Comedy Department's responsibilities was to top up the viewing figures so that the BBC could not only have its required quota of viewers, but could also mount quality pro-grammes of minority appeal (which ironically often turned out to be hugely popular successes, e.g., show jumping; *Animal, Vegetable, Mineral?*; snooker; sheep-dog trials; angling).

It seemed to me that a provider of public service television programmes *had* to be paternalistic, and a helpful analogy was to think of programmes as food. If you were to feed your children only with what they wanted to eat, most would want baked beans at every meal. Nothing wrong with baked beans, of course, great taste and full of unattractive-sounding but apparently healthful stuff like fibre – but every meal?

Parents gradually introduce a child to other foods so that the child's tastes are developed and food becomes healthier and a more interesting part of life than being just pabulum.

So perhaps with television. There will always be a need for a few uncomplicated, 'baked beans' series, and I had the very popular *Meet the Wife*, starring wonderful Thora Hird and the excellent Freddie Frinton.

Freddie made a very good stage drunk and his classic music-hall sketch was *Dinner for One* in which he played James, butler to milady, whose husband and friends had expired years earlier. The sketch was an annual celebration party and his one line was, 'Same as last year, milady?' And she would say, 'Yes, James.' Then the butler would plod round the table pouring out glasses of wine for the toasts and then, as there was nobody there to drink the toasts, drink them all himself. Eventually, hardly able to stand, he said, 'Same as last year, milady?' Milady said, 'Yes, James,' and went sedately up the staircase. The butler took hold of a candelabra and staggered up the staircase after her.

Ever since, that sketch has been transmitted on TV every New Year's Eve, as a kind of tradition, all over Europe.

Thora and Freddie's *Meet the Wife* was a most valuable series for me, cheap to produce, with few sets and highly professional writers and cast; it ran for years. The only faint hint of a problem was when Thora, playing a working-class wife, became fed up with wearing plain dowdy clothes every week, so gradually added brighter, more chic items and a smarter hairstyle, until the north country working-class wife she was portraying began to look like a rich divorcée from Las Vegas.

But in my output I was also keen to have several rather more sophisticated popular shows, such as *The Rag Trade*, starring Peter Jones, Miriam Karlin, Sheila Hancock and Reg Varney in a series of stories about a small dressmaking factory and the nonstop problems the owner had with the tiny group of girls who were his work-force. This series was notable for several reasons; it was remade locally by the Scandinavians, the

Belgians and the Portuguese. In 1988 the *Listener*, not beating about the bush, called it, 'The most popular TV series of all time.'

It was the first show written for television by the highly reliable team of Ronnie Wolfe and Ronnie Chesney, who later wrote *Meet the Wife*, and was a pre-*Dad's Army* example of how to get laughs from character rather than from jokes, and how to conserve your assets during a long run. For example, one of the sewing-machine operators at Fenner's Fashions was played by Esma Cannon, tiny, wispy, fluttery, white-haired and funny. When Esma had a line she stopped the show, but instead of leaning on this bonus and giving Esma so much to do that her comic twittering became predictable and eventually boring, the two Ronnies used her sparingly, perhaps only two or three times in each half-hour, so she continued to delight for years.

But perhaps the most remarkable success story of *The Rag Trade* is that after some thirty years it is due to be shown on post-apartheid black South African television, and a translated version has become the hit sitcom on Swedish television. *The Rag Trade* may be dead but long live – in Oslo, Belgium and Portugal – *Fredricksons Fabrics*, *Freddytex* and *Trapos and Compania*.

Among the main courses on my menu I had the near-genius in writing and performance of Galton and Simpson's *Hancock's Half-Hour*, the gentle humour of Harry Worth in *Here's Harry*, and I had Michael Bentine's brilliantly inventive *It's a Square World*, until Mike decided that he wanted more money; not so much a jump in his personal fee as more money for exterior filming and special effects, which were expensive. So I had to let him go to commercial telly, which I hated doing as he was an old colleague. Sadly, it was the time when changing from the BBC to ITV just did not seem to work in comedy. Michael's series on ITV was as brilliant as ever but the figures were not good, and he only did one series before changing direction and working with ingenious electronic puppets on children's television.

Kenneth Williams once said that the most valuable quality a performer could possess was confidence. Tony Hancock's self-confidence ran out at the height of his career. He began to worry that the success of his show was due to Sid James rather than himself, so he dropped Sid from the show. The ensuing, almost one-man shows (e.g., *The Blood Donor*), reassured Tony that he did not need Sid James.

He then worried that the quality of the scripts was the winning ingredient rather than his comedy talents, so he moved from the BBC to ITV, without Galton and Simpson. But he *did* need Galton and Simpson. Without Ray and Alan's complete understanding of his talents, talents which they had developed over the years, the magic seemed to go out of his work and his career went into a slow, sad, terminal decline.

With my Script Department, that haven of help and laughter a few doors away containing John Law and Richard Waring, we reactivated a valuable BBC series of single programmes designed to try out new ideas from established writers and to find new writers, *Comedy Playhouse*. We spread a wide net and the results were excellent (an early find was *Meet the Wife*).

In 1966 a trial script was submitted by John Wraith, a writer unknown to us. The story had a most unusual setting and a neat, clever O. Henry-style surprise ending. The story concerned the thirteenth-century cathedral dedicated to the Blessed Ogg. The cathedral of St Oggs had a crumbling spire which needed repairing, and the bishop discovered that a rich medievalist had willed a large sum of money to the cathedral if a charming old ceremony was revived. In this ancient ritual the bishop was required on Midsummer's Day to ride round the diocese on a white horse and present a pair of white stockings to twenty virgins.

The script's title was *All Gas and Gaiters* and I bought it. We cast William Mervyn as the bishop and Derek Nimmo played the bishop's chaplain, the Revd Mervyn Noote, a charming, naïve young bungler. Robertson Hare ('O, calamity!') played the ancient archdeacon. The thorn in the bishop's side was the dean, played with due severity by John Barron.

Most of the half-hour script was taken up with the unworldly trio bumbling round in search of local virgins. Finding virgins in the permissive Sixties proved a tricky problem. To begin with, it was difficult for three clergymen to bring up the subject at all: 'Excuse me, Miss Hackett, but are you by any chance still a virgin?' would not do.

The three returned at dusk, defeated, with just one virgin out of the required twenty in the bag, and her shy claim was a little at variance with her nickname in the village pub of Dead Cert Deirdre.

There was a professional precision in the way that John Wraith sorted out the plot in the last four words of the stage direction at the very end of the play:

> (*A motor hooter sounds loudly outside. The bishop and his crest-fallen colleagues idly glance out of the window and then react at what they see. In the courtyard below a motor coach has drawn up and its full load of sightseers are alighting. They are novice nuns.*)

The show was transmitted in the next series of *Comedy Playhouse* and was a success, so I was able to commission a full series, which gave me great pleasure.

Even more pleasure came when I found that 'John Wraith' was a pseudonym adopted by a pair of actors who had become personal friends, Edwin Apps, who played Mr Halliwell in *Whack-O!*, and his wife, the actress Pauline Devaney. It was entirely characteristic of them both that they went to the bother of submitting their first script under a pseudonym so as not to take unfair advantage of a friendship. *All Gas and Gaiters*, written by Edwin and Pauline, ran for five years.

My luck continued with Ray Galton and Alan Simpson putting in a script for *Comedy Playhouse*, a tragicomic, rather Pinteresque story about a trapped relationship between an uncouth, elderly scrap-dealer and his equally uncouth but ambitious son, played, of course, by Wilfrid Brambell and Harry H. Corbett. The show was *Steptoe and Son* and it became one of the most successful comedy series ever broadcast by the BBC.

The caviare end of my menu was enhanced when one morning Alan Bennett's agent turned up and offered me a half-hour comedy script written by Alan. It was marvellous. Not a sitcom but a kind of social revue with wry comments on life in the Sixties and parodies of television programmes, such as a telly celebration of T. E. Lawrence: 'After the war he was, in a way, a lost soul. He would wander along the Strand in his white robes and a curved jewelled dagger in his belt and say to passers-by, "Who am I? Who *AM* I?" And they would say, "You're Lawrence of Arabia and I claim my five pounds." ' Or there was the Northern playwright climbing interminably up a slag heap and muttering things like, 'It's my foonction to get at the reality of life and expose it as a sham. I'm not interested in celebrating the gaudy flower of life, my aim is to take the pith.'

I asked how long Alan would take to write another five scripts to make a run of six programmes. His agent said, 'He's already written them.'

Another happy programme was our adaptation of some of the Jeeves and Bertie Wooster short stories which we put out as a series entitled *The World of Wooster*. I say 'our adaptation' because I was in the thick of it, although it was most ably produced by perhaps the most literary of the department's producers, Michael Mills, and was adapted by Richard Waring. I acted as executive producer, which I suppose was another title for what my job was anyway.

There were huge problems. I thought it important that our series was not dependent upon funny performances by comical actors or on a jokey script but was essentially Wodehouse, otherwise why bother? The solution was simple. The true comedy voice of Wodehouse lay in his similes and his descriptive paragraphs, so I asked Richard to have Bertie narrate the story, voice over. By this device, this important aspect of Wodehouse's genius would not be lost.

Lines such as, 'Jeeves entered – or perhaps one should say shimmered – into the room . . . tall and dark and impressive. He might have been one of the better class ambassadors or the youngish high priest of some refined and dignified religion.' Or, 'His whole aspect was that of a man who had been unexpectedly struck by lightning.' Or, 'Into the face of the young man who sat on the terrace of the Hôtel Magnifique at Cannes there had crept a look of furtive shame, the shifty hangdog look which announces that an Englishman is about to talk French.' Or, 'the unpleasant, acrid smell of burned poetry'.

The method worked well.

Casting was the next problem. The Bertie Wooster we wanted was Ian Carmichael, a highly skilled professional in this kind of deft light comedy. But Ian was in New York about to open in *Boeing Boeing*, a hugely successful stage comedy which had run for years in every theatre in which it had played. We faced a hopelessly long wait. So we turned our attention to finding our Jeeves. We tried a great number of actors – even Robert Helpmann, the ballet dancer turned actor – until somebody suggested Dennis Price, the ex-leading man who went on to become a really good comedy character actor in Ealing comedies.

What happens with casting is that one asks around the BBC bar about an actor one is thinking of employing and directors and producers rave or put the boot in. The word on poor Dennis Price was that he was unreliable and on the bottle.

But *le bon Dieu* looked after us. We wanted Dennis and he was available, so we met him and thought he was exactly right. He lived in the Channel Islands and his companion, we were told, was a lady who had enjoyed a sex-change operation after having previously been a gentleman. We were looking for an actor with an air of reticence and mystery to play Jeeves, and Dennis had both of those all right, so we booked him. He proved to be entirely reliable professionally and his 'drinking' consisted of enjoying a small bottle of Guinness in the morning and one in the afternoon which he brought to rehearsals clinking gently in a British Airways bag.

And then *le bon Dieu* smiled upon us again.

A few days after booking our Jeeves, and now dangerously near our production date, a telegram arrived from Ian Carmichael in New York saying, '*Boeing Boeing* opened to disastrous notices and is closing on Saturday. Whatever happened to your idea of putting Bertie Wooster on television?'

The World of Wooster proved to be a most satisfactory series, agreeably well-received by viewers and critics.

A few months later I flew to America to show P. G. Wodehouse, in his home in Remsenburg, Long Island, what we had made of a couple of the programmes. 'Plum' did not normally welcome intruders in the morning because he was devoted to a mid-morning soap opera (how comforting that the great are like us in their dependence on a regular fix of junk TV), but his wife Ethel was a fan of *My Word!* and persuaded him to let me come.

I took with me two kinescopes (films made of TV programmes; this was before the days of video recordings), and the BBC New York office hired a 16mm projector and a limo to take me from Manhattan right the way down Long Island to Remsenburg. It was a sunny, very hot summer's day and I enjoyed the journey, mostly spent playing with the car's air-conditioning controls. It was all very different and exciting.

At one point we were going quite fast down the highway when we were overtaken by a funeral cortège, a low Cadillac luxury hearse covered in roped-down flowers, followed by a stream of mourners in fast cars. I commented on their speed. My driver kindly explained, 'The more stiffs they plant per day the more dough they make, right?'

Shortly afterwards we were stopped by real speed cops with huge bellies hanging over their belts and guns in unbuttoned holsters. Stepping out of the air-conditioned car was like walking into a wall of hot damp air, but the cops were pleasant and let us go without shooting us.

The Wodehouse residence at Remsenburg was a large white building set in quite a number of green acres. I could hear the barking of many dogs.

Plum (as he asked to be called) apologized for lunching so early (it was midday), explaining that Beulah, who came in to cook for them daily and stir the dust about on Thursdays, had another job to go on to, and hired help was extremely difficult to come by in Remsenburg. Beulah arrived and departed in a huge Plymouth saloon car.

After lunch Plum and I went out onto the patio and slumped into chairs to enjoy a bit of afternoon sun before I showed him the programmes. I asked him if he was considering visiting England after being away for so many years.

'Would I find Dulwich much changed?' he asked. He had been a schoolboy at Dulwich College which had provided him with the sporting and academic stimulations and friendships which had given him the most carefree years of his life.

I did not answer him immediately because I was in agony. A grossly overweight and over-affectionate boxer dog named Debbie had leaped up and was sitting bolt upright, drooling in my lap.

Debbie was one of a large number of stray dogs, each of them either obese, lacking a limb, foul breathed or in some other way socially challenged, who were enjoying the love and full feeding bowls always available at the Wodehouse home.

Plum, then aged eighty-four, was a very friendly man, talking gently and modestly and smiling with pleasure when I managed to slip in a compliment about his work, and worried that arthritis was making typing difficult and painful. He was, I think, the least political man I had ever met, deeply concerned only with his work, boxing and the English public-school cricket results.

We went inside mid-afternoon and the day seemed hotter than ever. Plum sat in an armchair and looked expectantly at the portable screen I had rigged up. Ethel pushed out a small-ish table for me to work on and I dumped the projector onto it, only to see with horror that it was a very fine old antique table, probably seventeenth century, its top aglow with uncommon marquetry. I hauled the projector off the table and apologized, but Ethel was not at all disturbed and waved me to carry on. It was very hot indoors.

I laced up the projector and switched on. Oh relief! The picture was reasonable though a bit jumpy and the sound was excellent. Plum sat up and watched keenly. Dennis Price and Ian Carmichael were working well and the studio audience was beginning to enjoy the show. About ten minutes later the film jumped out of the gate and the top reel started to pour film all over the carpet.

I switched off, took out my Swiss Army knife (what a good commercial this scene would have made for those knives) and stripped down the projector gate. As usual with much-used projectors, bits of emulsion from the surface of the film had built up on the chromium gate. I unscrewed the gate assembly and attacked the emulsion with the knife blade. It was a tricky job because the emulsion had set as hard as rock and I had to scrape it away without scratching the gate. I was sweating like a racehorse. Plum went to sleep.

Kindly Ethel said, 'There really is no need to show any more. Plum loved it.'

I fiddled the gate back on, reeled in the film from the carpet and switched on again. The projector purred smoothly into action and the sound came on with a huge loud roar of audience laughter, a live audience laughing, not canned re-action.

Plum woke up. 'What's going on?' he asked, sleepily.

'It's an audience laughing at Jeeves and Bertie,' I said.

Plum said, 'What a lovely way to wake up!'

I showed him the second show and then asked him for his comments. He thought that Dennis Price was without doubt the best Jeeves he had ever seen, and that included all the Hollywood versions with such actors as Eric Blore and Arthur Treacher ('They pulled faces all the time. Awful.').

He thought Ian Carmichael was excellent, although too old for the part (Bertie was about twenty-four and was almost always played by older leading actors in their late thirties or older). And he praised Michael Mills's production. I asked Plum whether he could write all this on a note that I could take back to the BBC, which he did. When I arrived back at the Algonquin Hotel that evening I cabled the words of the note to Tom Sloan, and when I was back at Television Centre I had the note framed and presented it to Michael Mills. I hated parting with it but it was only fair that it should go to Michael.

Flushed with our praise from the great man for our *World of Wooster*, Michael Mills and I decided to have a go at introducing to television Plum's stories about Clarence, the Ninth Earl of Emsworth, the charming, dotty old earl whose passion in life was fattening his prize-winning pig, the Empress of Blandings. His sister Constance was bossy but needed to be to keep the earl more or less socially acceptable. The earl's resident enemy was the dour Scottish gardener, McAllister, who browbeat the kindly earl over important matters like the moss growing on the gravel paths, which the earl liked but McAllister wanted to grub up.

I thought Ralph Richardson would be perfect as Lord

Emsworth. This was a rather ambitious thought – Ralph Richardson in a telly sitcom? – but I knew Ralph well as a fellow member of the Savile Club and we got on, so I could appeal to him personally. Then I had a rather brilliant thought. Ralph's actress wife Mu (Meriel Forbes) would make a splendid Lady Constance.

Perhaps the opportunity for them to work together, a rare occasion, made the difference, but in the teeth of their agent's displeasure, Ralph and Mu agreed to do the series. Michael Mills cast the elderly Scottish character comedian Jack Radcliffe as McAllister. Jack was very good indeed (in a splendidly aggressive ginger wig) and the success of his appearances in the series made a fitting end to his long career.

John Chapman wrote the scripts, adapting six of Plum's short stories; Michael shot the many exteriors in Penshurst Place, Kent; Stanley Holloway played Beach (one of Plum's earliest butlers); Mu played the earl's formidable sister Lady Constance and I, crouched out of sight in a pigsty, played the pig, the Empress of Blandings. I discovered that I am gifted at imitating pigs (and lions, in an emergency). The trick is to snore whilst breathing in and work the mouth into various shapes. After a few seconds it becomes surprisingly painful.

The series, which was called *Blandings Castle*, went out in February 1967.

Ralph was really excellent as Lord Emsworth. In many ways he *was* Lord Emsworth. He needed Mu as Clarence needed his sister Constance. There was the same distaste of formality, the same insights; when Ralph was discussing with our wardrobe lady what clothes he needed to play Clarence, she said, 'An old tweed suit, of course?' Ralph said, 'Oh, yes, but *thin* tweed, I beg you. It should move with the body and do a bit of talking. Working in thick tweed is like walking about in cardboard.'

He worked very hard. He was acting in a play at the time and when there was daytime filming at Penshurst Place he would arrive sitting in the back of a chauffeur-driven Rolls writing out his part on the back of the previous week's script to help him memorize it. And he thought deeply about every aspect of his role and the script.

It was a most satisfactory series, and I was able to write to

Wodehouse and say that the programmes had gone well and I didn't think we had let him down. I enclosed a wad of good notices. He wrote back thanking all and informing me that Debbie the fat boxer dog had clearly missed me and had moped about the house in a marked manner since my departure. In spite of her sorrow she had managed to eat well and had put on another stone or two.

About this time the BBC ordered me off on a two-week residential course on management in a huge country house quite near Benjamin Disraeli's grand pile. Polly kindly drove me there, dropping me off at the front door with my suitcase and bidding me farewell with the words, 'Remember, if you haven't "been", ask Matron to give you something.' Then speeding off down the drive doubled-up with mirth over the steering wheel. To her it was exactly like dropping a small child off at boarding school.

But it wasn't quite as funny for me when I delivered Jamie to his prep school, Avisford, near Bognor.

It was the first time he was going to be separated from Polly, Sally, the dogs and his bedroom, and he was going into an unknown life amongst complete strangers. He didn't speak during the hour and a half drive, and we went together into the school building to be greeted by the headmaster, Michael Jennings. I knew that it was best for Jamie if I were to leave as soon as possible and we had an oddly formal, almost silent parting. He was pale and shaking, but he smiled good-bye and I left.

I drove up a Sussex lane for a couple of miles, found a lay-by and burst into tears. It was his courage which I found so moving. Green of face and trembling with nerves, he gave no indication whatever that he would rather go home. No whingeing. No pleading. He seemed to be reassuring me, 'I'll be all right in a moment, don't worry about me.' I was terrifically proud of him.

As it turned out, the school was just right. He was very happy there, eventually became Head Boy, and the senior son of the headmaster's massive family, Luke Jennings the novelist and journalist, became and has remained Jamie's close friend.

Polly took Sally and her suitcase to her boarding school, but it was a serene occasion which held no horrors for Sally. The school, St Mary's Convent, Ascot, was just 6 miles away. Polly had been to school there as had her sister Pidge, who was still there because she was now the Reverend Mother. Sally, like Jamie, made lasting friendships at her school, and to her amazement and amusement was made Head Girl.

On 'going-out' weekends Sal used to bring a friend or two home to Sunday lunch. One of the little girls' favourite lunches was a complicated, labour-intensive dish which the recipe called Hot American Chicken Salad. One small girl's thank-you letter to Polly began:

Darling, darling Mrs Muir,
Thank you so much for the chicken do-up.

And 'chicken do-up' it has, of course, remained.

Children so often invent better words than the originals and every family must have a collection: e.g., our pair, when very young, referred to waterproofs as 'mackinsops'; and that hot white stuff they ate with beef was 'horse-rubbish'.

A lady in South Africa wrote to me that her son reported to her that in gym that morning they had 'horrors-on-the-bars'.

The actor Eric Chitty revealed that whilst on holiday he went with his granddaughter to find a chemist to make up a prescription. As the nearest chemist was really only a shop which sold tartan sponge bags and smelled of soap they were advised to go to the nearest pharmaceutical chemist, which was quite a long walk across town. They trudged along and when they stopped for a rest, the tired little girl sighed and said, 'Grandpa, it's such a pity we have to find a "far-more-suitable" chemist.'

The BBC management course was well-organized (which was just as well considering its subject). We were a motley crew, a mixture of high-ranking engineers, foreign correspondents, departmental managers, planners and various other members of that shadowy network of functionaries so important to the BBC that one of them, congratulated on his department being housed in a prestigious new building in Shepherd's Bush, was moved to make the now famous remark,

'The BBC doesn't just make programmes, you know.'

As usual in that kind of conference, we were split up into syndicates of about ten assorted members with a chairman, and mornings and afternoons were given to syndicate sessions in which we had to debate solutions to a mixed bag of problems like, 'Where, ideally, would you put the nine o'clock news?' Or, 'Should BBC official vehicles, like radio cars and television equipment lorries, be bought or be hired as required, and if only hired, should drivers be eligible for a sandwich allowance?'

We each had a Toblerone-shaped wooden wedge on the desk in front of us with our name painted on it. Mine read F. H. MUIR. I objected mildly to the conference organizer, making the point that nobody had called me F. H. Muir since I was at school, so it wasn't really my grown-up name. The organizer was apologetic and blamed the engineers who preferred names to be as formal as possible. I had noted years previously that the BBC engineering department was the Rolls-Royce of departments. Their standards were extremely high on all matters of engineering and they held strong views on social matters as well. As Val Gielgud found out. Val, brother of John Gielgud, was a BBC radio drama producer of some distinction. He was wooed into television, took a course in TV production and was given a play to put on.

There were four cameras and when the camera rehearsal began, Val directed his cameras by saying to them, 'Potter, could you move into a medium close-up? Standby for a lens change, Harrison. A little closer, please, Arkwright-Sanderson . . .'

In the control-box the TOM (Technical Operations Manager) leaped to his feet, pulled the switch which cut off contact with the studio and said to Val, 'Sorry, Val, but in engineering we don't address cameramen as though they're gardeners.'

Val explained mildly, 'Actually calling a chap by his surname means you are treating him affectionately as an equal.'

'Dunno about that,' said the TOM. 'I can only say that cameramen should always be addressed by their Christian names.'

'But all four cameramen are named Fred,' said Val.

'Then you address them as Fred One, Fred Two, Fred Three and Fred Four.'

In the evenings we were lectured by such managerial super-stars as Dr Beeching (the Dr Guillotine of British Rail services); General Hackett and, by some accident, the wonderful late Michael Elliott, who talked and enthused so effortlessly about Shakespeare that he could have gone on for ever as far as our syndicate was concerned. But next evening we were back to reality with a gentleman from ICI and a stern warning about letting our corporate structures sag. He had pitiless pie charts showing vertical management theory as against horizontal management theory and how it should all be combined into New Management theory, the supreme importance of rigid budget control over all other production considerations. He was very keen (not visibly very keen – he was, in himself, very dull indeed – but *intellectually* keen) on New Management. It was the New Managers, he said finally, showing for the first time a tiny trace of emotion, who were going to save English commerce. He did not mention what they were going to do to creative television.

We conferees could buy a book of cloakroom tickets after the lectures and exchange them for glasses of beer at a trestle-table. As the first week wore on the queue for warmish beer became like a rugger scrum.

One evening we had an almost inaudible talk from a small, bird-like but famous chartered accountant stressing the absolute necessity of keeping our shows to their budgets, and our last lecturer was the BBC staff doctor who told us how to recog-nize stress in our staff: the body sits slumped, with the head shrunk between the shoulders. At least I think that is what he said. He was difficult to hear as we were all sitting slumped with our heads shrunk between our shoulders.

My skills as a New Manager were put to the test as soon as the course finished and I arrived back at Television Centre, brimming with undigested facts and theories about something I was not much interested in. I was immediately accosted in the BBC Club bar by one of my producers who had a new series to produce from a successful trial programme in *Comedy Playhouse*, and he had a great idea.

'For the opening credits', he said, 'a helicopter shot of Big Ben, then sweep down to the East End, close-up shot of a lit window, mix through to a crane shot and go through the window to see an elderly couple in bed. Mix to live action in studio and start the dialogue. What do you reckon?'

'But you've already overspent your budget and the series hasn't started yet,' I said.

'Bugger the budget,' said the producer.

'How much would a helicopter cost?' I asked.

He said, 'I could do the shot in an hour, which would cost four hundred pounds.'

It was quite a lot of money in those days. I thought hard. We could amortize the money over the six shows in the series, and it *was* a good, in fact very good, idea for the opening credits . . .

'OK,' I said, 'go ahead with the shot.'

'I'm afraid there's a problem,' said the producer, having the decency to look a bit sheepish. 'The four hundred pounds only stretches to a single-rotor chopper, and in that we are only allowed to fly over the Thames, that is, over water. To fly over land we have to have a twin-rotor job.'

'And how much would that cost?' I asked, starting to breathe heavily.

'The twin-rotor chopper comes out at eight hundred and fifty pounds per hour,' he said. Again I thought hard, and swiftly. There was one hope. Michael Peacock had moved from being Controller of BBC2 to being Controller of BBC1, which 'owned' *Comedy Playhouse*, and I suspected that he had a secret contingency fund for this kind of problem. And I had an idea that as a programme man himself, he would be sympathetic.

'OK,' I said to the producer. 'Go ahead with your shot.'

Then came the double whammy.

'Thanks so much,' he said. 'I knew I could count on your support. The fact is I did the shot last Thursday. It didn't work.'

I went to Michael Peacock, told him a tiny bit of the story and he gave me the extra budget money (and a talking-to about the importance of not letting producers get away with wasteful spending).

So, I had come straight from a senior management

conference where I was lectured by money men on the attitudes required of senior management operating in a market economy and I had not benefited at all. Instead I had worked on old-fashioned instinct and instead of firing the producer, obviously the sensible course, I had arranged for him to have more money for his programme. I had managed to drop the mask of being a New Manager before I'd even put it on properly.

But there was another side to the coin. The producer concerned was Dennis Main Wilson. And I knew that Dennis as a producer may have been 20 per cent near-genius and 80 per cent overenthusiastic, but even when he was in his 80 per-cent mode he was totally devoted and loyal to the show he was producing and would fight to the end for it.

And the series which Dennis was producing turned out to be the great *Till Death Us Do Part*, starring Warren Mitchell as the ranting, right-wing, sexist, male chauvinist pig Alf Garnett, and Dandy Nichols as his placid, toffee-chewing, unimpressed wife, Else, referred to by Alf as the 'silly moo'.

It is impossible to overstate the contribution Dennis made to the success of the show, many times way and above the call of duty; Dennis did nothing by halves. In the early days he almost lived with Johnny Speight to help get the *Till Death* scripts out on time, and even wrestled Johnny out of Annabels nightclub in Berkeley Square in the early hours of one morning to make sure that there would be a script for rehearsal later that day.

This was the mid-Sixties and permissiveness was touching everything. Johnny was anxious to reproduce as nearly as possible the tough language which Alf Garnett, a docker, would have used. I pointed out that the oaths and sexual swearing which would have made up half of Alf's true conversation would be far too strong for television; the shock effect would be out of all proportion. So I persuaded Johnny to stick mainly to the word 'bloody', which would be startling and strong enough for most viewers.

This turned out to be so. Viewers were shocked in a mild sort of way, but recognizing the truth in the word being used by the sort of character who used it, they were not all that offended. Some were, of course, and a few sat silently through several episodes totting up the number of 'bloodies' and then writing to the DG (and me) giving the episode's count. It was usually between forty and sixty 'bloodies' per half-hour, but the prize for bloody-spotting went to Mrs Mary Whitehouse, who wrote to complain that in the last show she had watched she had counted seventy-eight.

I was quite prepared to defend this and devised a kind of form letter of justification. But I was afraid that part of the hostility to what should have been an inarguable artistic decision came from the way that an actor was tempted to say the dread word. Actors rarely got the chance to say a (then) strong word like 'bloody' on television and when a part came along with two or three 'bloodies' per page there was a temptation for the actor to enjoy the experience and to separate the word slightly from the rest of the sentence and enunciate it clearly. I suggested to Warren that his 'bloodies' should really be mumbled. Alf would probably not have thought of his 'bloodies' as swearing, just making an aggressive noise to strengthen his argument.

Warren saw the point immediately. He was keen on that sort of thing because he had become interested in method acting, at which he was very good indeed.

During one rehearsal, Warren had embarked on one of Alf's tirades against Arsenal Football Club, the Labour Party, the Asian grocery shop on the corner which was taking the food out of the mouth of the saintly Lord Sainsbury, and so on, when Dandy Nichols, who had been leaning against the wall by the fireplace, straightened up, wandered past Warren and sank into an armchair.

Warren was furious. 'Dandy!' he said. 'What did you move for? Right in the middle of my speech you wander vaguely right across me. You had no motivation for moving, Dandy. None. If you'd looked chilly and had seen a woolly on the chair, then right, we'd have known what was in your noddle. But to just wander across me . . . You were at position A and you moved, all of your own accord, to position B. Why?'

Dandy said, 'I was at position A and I farted, so I moved to position B.'

Till Death Us Do Part ran for nine years and became one of the most profitable comedy shows (in terms of viewing figures and prestige) the BBC had ever transmitted.

They were long and busy days, but from *Comedy Playhouse* came some good programmes and the discovery of good new writers, including two ex-cartoonists – Brian Cooke and Johnnie Mortimer – who only wrote a mildly successful caper about the diplomatic service for me, but went on to write success after success for ITV, retiring young and, I hope, rich.

The best writers I found were John Esmonde and Bob Larbey, who began well and steadily improved.

When Michael Peacock moved to BBC1 and David Attenborough became Controller of BBC2, David asked me to find him a game show which would be right for BBC2.

This was far from easy. Most formats submitted were hyped-up versions of established successes such as *Twenty Questions* or *Wheel of Fortune*. They demanded a set like a bingo hall from hell with a screaming audience, flashing lights and a pretty, lightly-clad girl to manoeuvre the contestants onto their camera mark (a piece of sticky tape on the floor). The suggested compères tended to be not very successful or elderly comics who were now wisely seeking a change of career.

None of these programmes was suitable for BBC2, or for that matter BBC1 (or ITV), so I let it be known amongst the agents that I was interested in looking at kinescopes of available American game shows.

At least the American compères did not look like ex-comics. They looked like ex-human beings. Their uniform was a dark-blue blazer with an enormous badge on the pocket, hair (if any) dyed shoe-polish ginger, and a tremendous number of teeth winking and blinking in the lights. They were jolly men and when they read out a one-liner joke from their idiot board, the audience, anxious to help, yelped like an overexcited posse of American Indians galloping round John Wayne on their ponies.

And then I found what I was hoping to find: an American game which had capability for entertaining British BBC2 viewers.

The show had been adapted from a parlour game and the copyright was now owned by the two great impresarios of American televised game shows, Goodson and Todman. There was no copyright on family games, but there was copyright in the format of a game show which had been adapted for television.

Messrs Goodson and Todman hit upon this happy state of affairs and worked their way steadily through a great number of old parlour games, mostly British, adapting them and then selling licences to produce them to other countries. Early Goodson and Todman adaptations included *Twenty Questions*, *What's My Line?* and *The Name's the Same* (Denis and I served our time as panel members on all of those).

But not all Goodson and Todman shows were hits. They had a go at adapting one old English parlour game called *The Dictionary Game*. It was played by a player selecting an obscure word from the dictionary and giving three definitions of the word, one of which was true and the other two bluffs. The other contestants had to guess which definition was true.

Goodson and Todman's television version was named *Call My Bluff* and was very American in style. The question master was the usual late-middle-aged teenager with his blue blazer and dyed hair, but instead of having professional broadcasters as contestants, ordinary members of the public were invited up from the studio audience. It was all a bit of a shambles, mainly because bluffs from amateurs were so obviously false that it was painfully easy to spot the trues. The show proved not to be to the taste of American viewers and only lasted one season.

I have always found that British viewers appreciate a programme which they suspect is slyly educating them, and it seemed to me that if I could jack up the IQ of the show sharply and use well-known people as contestants, it could well be the programme David Attenborough was stalking.

The alterations I proposed to make were not greeted with much enthusiasm by Goodson and Todman's London agent, Philip Hindin, probably because he was worried that it might loosen his office's grip on the copyright, but it was a case of making the changes we wanted or no deal. Happily Philip preferred to make the deal.

Choosing the words was a vital part of setting up the shows; the word had not only to be obscure but to yield two bluffs which were more plausible than the truth. I booked Peter

Moore as our compiler. Peter was an old friend, Sally's god-father, an occasional contributor of odd original sketches to *Breakfast with Braden* and a lover of words.

As Peter chose a word because it yielded a pair of good bluffs, it made sense for him to make a note of those bluffs for the contestants to develop and put into their own words. So after a camera rehearsal, the teams went off to their captain's dressing room, the words and Peter's cards were delivered by the producer in a sealed envelope, and with their captain's help the contestants worked on Peter's suggested bluffs and plotted their strategy to confound the enemy.

The result of this system was that *Call My Bluff* became easy to play but extremely difficult to win.

We began to find out what kind of guests worked well on the show. Viewers seemed to enjoy seeing faces which were familiar to them for doing something else, like newsreaders and dramatic actors and actresses. Our most reliable contestants were the new breed of *Beyond the Fringe*-style comedy actors who were witty ad libbers, e.g., Peter Cook, Alan Bennett, Jonathan Miller, and witty actresses and writers such as Joanna Lumley, who was so good at the game that we booked her for every series we made.

We learned to be wary of booking comical comics. They tended to keep slipping into their act and trying to inject their personal comedy into the game instead of extracting fun from the game itself. Some of the biggest laughs came when the next word to be defined appeared on the board above our chairman Robert Robinson's noble head and he, with precision, read it out.

Our audiences and viewers took a pride in the eccentricity of the English language and consistently found it hilarious. Hardly surprising when one considers the wonderful words which Peter Moore found buried in the *Oxford English Dictionary*.

Here are some samples of the words hand-picked by Peter, with their true meanings:

BONZE: An impolite but not necessarily offensive Portuguese word for a Japanese clergy-man.

BEARLEAP:	A Tudor housewife's large shopping basket.
POLLYWOG:	Dialect name for a tadpole.
MOLOCKER:	An old, but renovated, top hat.
COMSTOCKER:	An American affronted by nudity.
ABLEWHACKET:	A naval card game not unlike whist played by able seamen, which was called ablewhacket because, when an able seaman lost, he held out his hand and the winner whacked it.
BANDOLINE:	A hairdressing made from quinces.
MERROW:	An Irish mermaid.

Some twenty years later, Mr Goodson of Goodson and Todman was in England staying at the Savoy Hotel when *Call My Bluff* came on the television screen in his suite. He thought it was a wonderful show, rang Young Bill Cotton at Television Centre, who was by then Head of Light Entertainment Group, and asked whether he could buy the American rights. Young Bill, relishing the moment, pointed out to Mr Goodson that Goodson and Todman owned the programme, the BBC merely had a licence to broadcast our version. What had happened was that the American version had lasted for only one season twenty years previously and Mr Goodson had forgotten all about it.

Our first chairman of *Call My Bluff* was Robin Ray. At David Attenborough's command I was captain of one team and Robert Morley was captain of the other.

We used to do two programmes per show day, one live and then one pre-recorded. This was a good thing as it enabled our guests to earn two small fees instead of one (one would hardly have been worth starting the car for).

Most things that could go wrong did so and usually on the show which went out live. Such as when Lord David Cecil suddenly discovered that all his bluff and true cards had disappeared from his desk. Robert Morley, not of lissom build, managed to crawl underneath, and found that Lord David Cecil, in a moment of deep concentration pondering which of the opposition's definitions was true, had absent-mindedly dropped his cards one by one onto the floor. Robert scooped them up and, when the cameras were on my team, rose into view again like a flushed but triumphant porpoise.

Strangely, of all our various contestants, academics, authors, industrialists, journalists, weather forecasters, musicians (André Previn was excellent), it was the actors who were the most nervous.

Jimmy Villiers was a good example of horror descending upon an actor on suddenly realizing that he had to speak without a script. He had only seen *Call My Bluff* a couple of times and was not all that familiar with it.

At the camera rehearsal, Jimmy, a man of ancient lineage, asked in his superb voice (with vowels mown and rolled for 300 years, like the lawns of Magdalen College, Oxford), 'When it's my turn to choose our opponents' true definition, what do I do?'

Robert said, 'You just say a few words dismissing the two definitions you reckon are bluffs and then say why you believe the one you've chosen is true.'

Jimmy looked appalled. Then he stood up – a long way up as he is very tall – and said, 'Sorry, heart, don't ad lib.' And made for his dressing room.

Happily his wife was there and she had a little talk to Jimmy and he agreed to have a go at chatting as required and, of course, he was excellent.

An actor's worry at 'being himself' without even a funny voice or costume to hide behind was exemplified by Donald Pleasance, the villain in hundreds of stage, TV and film productions, even sinister arch-enemy of James Bond. And here was Donald in the *Bluff* studio pleading with our producer to let him wear a moustache. 'Just a *tiny* one would do. *Please?*'

Wearing a moustache, however near-invisible, would have given Donald confidence because he would have acted Donald Pleasance with a small moustache and not had to be his naked self. But on the show he too, as himself, was excellent.

One evening the female guest on my team was a beautiful American actress. Halfway through the show she laughed so much at Arthur Marshall's definition of a word that the retaining brooch on her blouse flew open and a breast popped into view. Happily for her, the cameras were on Arthur Marshall at the time and she was able to restore her modesty so swiftly that the viewing millions had no idea what a delightful crisis they had missed.

After the recording the good lady told me she was driving to Norfolk to spend the rest of the weekend with friends and could she have a quick bath in the tiny bathroom attached to my dressing room? Of course she could. What is more, there was to be no more accidental immodesty. The lady carefully closed the bathroom door, then opened it slightly and pushed out into the dressing room the most aggressive 8 ounces of white miniature poodle I have ever seen. This Guardian of Virtue did a quick warning run at our ankles, nipping those within range, barked like a falsetto, demented Dobermann pinscher and settled comfortably on the carpet by the bathroom door, giving us all a steely stare which clearly said, 'Come on, punks. Make my day.'

Towards the end of my three-year contract with the BBC my working life was beginning to become uncomfortably demanding. *Bluff* took up many evenings, as did recordings of *My Word!* and *My Music* and warming up the audience for the first show of all my new comedy series. When I managed to get home at a reasonable hour there were shows I felt I should watch, and my days were very full with meetings and duties like reading unsolicited scripts. How I wished I could have dealt with them as Disraeli is said to have done. In a fine example of subtle ambiguity he would reply to the would-be author, 'Thank you for sending me your manuscript. I will lose no time in reading it.'

I had realized early on that running a variety department was like flower arranging. You chose and bought your expensive, eye-catching blossoms and your job was to display them in a good setting, jiggling them around so that they showed to best advantage.

But if you were running a sitcom department you were not just flower arranging, but in the nursery business. You had to plant new untried writing talent, nurture it, take care of it and hope it would grow. Good shows, in this country anyway, are originated by writers not by executives. Ideas are sometimes the easiest part and frequently are not the reason for a show's success; it is the other factors, the handling of character, the quality of the dialogue, the originality of the stories, happy accidents of casting, which matter.

Steptoe and Son was not fun and games with a couple of rag-and-bone men, it was a series about a trapped relationship between a father and his son. Ray and Alan could just as well have set the show in a railway station or a postal sorting office, but I have always had a feeling that they set it in a junkyard to muck up their producer, Duncan Wood – writing out the week's list of props must have taken him at least two days a week.

Tom Sloan once proudly told me of a programme idea he had just had. He called it *Circle Line*, and to a non-writer it might have looked promising. In the series, an underground train stopped every week at a different Circle Line station and on the crowded escalator a story began to unfold. One week, perhaps, a tragedy; the next week a funny piece; then a love story, and so on. Each programme could be any kind of drama from any kind of writer and would surely make a colourful series. What did I think of the idea?

Well, not much. I explained to Tom that his idea of using the Circle Line as the continuity between independent half-hour stories amounted to offering a piece of string and saying, 'If you thread a ruby on this piece of string, then perhaps a diamond, then a pearl and so on, you would end up with a valuable necklace.' The faulty reasoning is that if you acquire a fine ruby, and a valuable diamond and a beautiful pearl, and so on, you don't need the piece of string. And until you have the jewels, all you *do* have is a piece of string.

One evening, in the middle of a series of *Call My Bluff*, I arrived home dog-tired and Polly said, 'Aren't you overdoing it? You look a hundred.' And I felt a hundred. But I could not duck out of the next week's show because one of my guests was an old friend, a young American film and TV director, Richard Lester, who was working in England on off-beat TV comedy shows mostly starring Peter Sellers and/or Spike Milligan (Richard later made the Beatles' films and a stack of other big-screen successes). Richard was nervous of being in front of the cameras and I had to coax him into performing,

Early days of *My Word!* Denis with his partner, the journalist Nancy Spain.
BBC ©

Me with the stunning Dilys Powell. *BBC* ©

1959. *Whack-O!* The dreaded third-form classroom at Chiselbury School. A school cap has been found adorning the head of William Shakespeare (a playwright, the headmaster was told to his surprise). The headmaster, cane at the ready, is Professor Jimmy Edwards, Inter-Ph.D. (Tangiers). Next to him stands Mr Pettigrew (played by Arthur Howard), the only member of staff at Chiselbury to have heard of Shakespeare. Mr Pettigrew is, as usual, silent with terror and trembling. *BBC* ©

1962. Richard Briers starring in a thirteen-week adaptation of Henry Cecil's book about young barristers in training, *Brothers-In-Law*. With Richard are his lovely girlfriend, played by the delectable June Barry, and his not-quite-as-lovely but adequately presentable colleague, played by actor and writer Richard Waring. *BBC* ©

1966. Peter Jones and Peter Ustinov playing 'Morry' and 'Dudley', two hopelessly incompetent conmen in the two Peters' extraordinarily original comedy series of 'impromptu conversations with illustrations' entitled *In All Directions*. *BBC ©*

This is me, on the set of *In All Directions*, looking a little like Graham Greene on a bad day in Nice. I am playing, as usual, the mug punter out of shot, who ad libs awkward questions to try to trip up the two Peters. I never did manage it. *BBC ©*

The hit show of television comedy in 1965 was *Not Only ... But Also*, with Peter Cook and Dudley Moore. It was semi-ad libbed and consisted of brilliantly original 'interviews' (an aristocrat who is devoting his life to teaching ravens to fly underwater), sketches full of surprises (John Lennon turned up as a nightclub bouncer), and the rambling, face-to-face conversations of Pete and Dud – now copied by almost every pair of TV comics. *BBC* ©

The writers Ronnie Wolfe and Ronnie Chesney had other long-lasting successes before *On The Buses*, including *The Rag Trade*, starring Peter Jones as the distraught owner of a tiny clothing factory trying to cope with his incompetent foreman (Reg Varney), and a whole swatch of fine character actresses, led by Miriam Karlin as their aggressive shop steward ('Everybody out!'). *BBC* ©

All Gas and Gaiters began in 1967 and ran for five highly successful series. There was something charmingly English and irresistible in the stories set around the ancient cathedral of St Oggs, presided over by the bishop (William Mervyn), his chaplain Noote (Derek Nimmo) and his ancient archdeacon, the last part played by the old but much-loved farceur, Robertson Hare ('O calamity!'). *BBC* ©

Ray Galton and Alan Simpson's *Steptoe and Son* joined *Till Death Us Do Part* as another of the BBC's greatest comedy series. *Steptoe* was much more than a knockabout comedy, it was an almost Pinteresque series about an ageing rag-and-bone man with ambitions (Harry H. Corbett), trapped in a relationship with his possessive, unhygienic father (Wilfred Brambell). The horse was not emotionally involved. *BBC* ©

1965. *The World of Wooster*. Three series of programmes based upon P.G. Wodehouse's Jeeves and Bertie stories, faithfully adapted by Richard Waring and memorably played by Ian Carmichael and Dennis Price (acknowledged by Wodehouse to be the best Jeeves he had ever seen). *BBC* ©

1967. *Blandings Castle*. Sir Ralph Richardson as the dotty old pig-breeding Ninth Earl of Emsworth in a series of six half-hour sitcoms, adapted by John Chapman from the P.G. Wodehouse books. The earl is reading the only book he has read right through in his whole life: *The Care of the Pig*.
BBC ©

Robert Robinson looking benign and happy. The great Paddy Campbell looking a bit fierce, but then he did a lot of that. When he guessed that a word was a bluff and it was revealed as being true, his eyes seemed to move together as close as cuff links and he would rear up in his chair, rigid with indignation, like an ostrich that has sat in something. *BBC ©*

Warren Mitchell as Alf Garnett, holding the floor as usual in one of the greatest sitcoms ever produced by the BBC, Johnny Speight's *Till Death Us Do Part*. *BBC ©*

A still from London Weekend Television's *On The Buses*, starring Reg Varney. Simple comedy, not enjoyed by the critics but a huge hit with the viewers for years – and still running in various languages in Europe. *London Weekend Television*

Moscow. Being shown round our rooms at the Berlin Hotel by the Russian writer and ex-actor, our dear friend Alexei Kapler.

More Moscow. Three chilly Britons and a more robust Russian (Alexei) on the APN Way. Our friend and interpreter Nina Froud is to the left. *Novosti*

A rehearsal at Anners for a thrilling demonstration of army motor-mowing to the whistle at our village fête. The army team of crack mowers, trained to a hair's breadth, are (left to right) Dick Emery, chest thrust out as a sergeant in the ATS; Michael Bentine; Dick Lester in the driving seat; Clive Dunn, and me, trying to look stupid. Oddly enough I found it quite easy.

Another village fête stunt. This year it was a demonstration of *Z-Bikes*, an élite squad formed to combat a bout of daffodil slashing by disgruntled OAPs. The tough, negative-tolerance team consists of (left to right) Graham Stark, Peter Sellers, Bill Kerr, Bruce Lacey, Dick Lester and son, and Clive Dunn. Once again I contrived (without make-up) to look dim.
Sunday Pictorial

Sent up rotten by my Comedy Department at London Weekend Television after what I had hoped was a secret lunch at Buckingham Palace.

The department bending the knee. In the background Tito Burns and Barry Cryer are hovering (unbending). To my right kneels my then secretary, manager, close friend and nanny, Tanya Bruce-Lockhart.

Be it known to all men that on this day, 19th December in this year of Grace 1968, We were most graciously pleased to have our right loyal & trusted servant F. Herbert Muir Earl of Stonebridge for luncheon, & he was delicious.

Witnessed:

[numerous signatures]

ER

The manuscript document which the unit put together and presented to me. I still have it. Of course.

Just after dawn, Dick Lester and a camera crew near Cannes in the South of France, filming me for a Hovis commercial. At one point I asked Dick why he had bothered to bring us all the way over to Cannes. Dick said, 'Would you rather have spent three days paddling round Ramsgate harbour?'

One of my favourite family photographs. Funny how all four of us seem to wear on our heads little tufts plucked from one end or the other of the Afghan hounds' coats. Notice that Sally is cuddling a very, very brave cat indeed.

This is clearly either the School of Naval Architecture's male voice choir trying out a new piano or a BBC publicity picture taken at a recording of *My Music*. Note John Amis's magnificently restrained (for him) striped suit. *BBC ©*

The entire cast of the radio 'anthology' series, *Frank Muir Goes Into...*, consisting of my old friend and colleague from wartime shows at RAF Henlow, Alfred Marks, and me. Besides having a strong and true bass-baritone singing voice, Alfred was terrific at any kind of accent and knew every Jewish joke, story and anecdote in the book. These he told from time to time, prudently and superbly. *BBC ©*

A flotation in the lagoon which laps around the St Géran Hotel, Mauritius (a quite wonderful holiday experience). The photograph was taken by Polly and is a model of what a portrait should be of any husband less pretty than, say, Sean Connery. A simple, minimalist composition featuring only toes, nose, hat and pipe.

Interviewing Groucho Marx at the New York Hilton for the BBC's *Omnibus*. Was the film a success: Up to a point, Lord Copper... *BBC* ©

Inducted as Lord Rector of St Andrews University. Being pulled round the town in an open coach by the rugger club, dressed in the students' traditional scarlet gown, stopping everywhere to make a short speech and receive a little present. My tour of duty at St Andrews were three of the most rewarding and happiest years of my life.

Giving a reading for Oxfam with Sir John Gielgud of extracts from Jan Morris's *The Oxford Book of Oxford*. All the fine actresses whom Michael Meyer and I used to invite to our readings were unavailable, but then we realized that the mass of items assembled by Jan Morris were concerned with Oxford when it was still a Catholic religious community, and women were not in the book!

1981. Polly and I on Granada Television, still happily together after experiencing the toughest known tests of a human relationship. Firstly I tried to teach Polly how to drive, and secondly Polly and I worked together, choosing writers and artists for an anthology of new children's stories called *The Big Dipper*. And without one quarrel! No wonder we're looking a bit smug presenting Granada's programme about the book.

assuring him that as his team captain I would be there to hold his hand.

At the weekend I began to feel awful, tired, miserable and wobbly. By Wednesday, the day of recording, I was clearly not well. As usual, my team had gathered in my dressing room for our conference and I suddenly found breathing difficult. I asked somebody to find the producer and the duty matron and tell them I thought I might be rather ill.

Matron arrived and asked me to take some deep breaths, which I managed. It was like inhaling broken glass.

'You've probably got pleurisy!' said matron cheerfully. 'You'd better go home immediately and get your own doctor to do what he can.'

The producer phoned Polly to get our doctor to stand by at home and arranged for a car to take me home.

And so, on Dick Lester's first personal appearance on BBC2, his team captain on whom he was relying so much, white-faced, whimpering and trying not to breathe, was carried briskly out on a stretcher.

As it was Christmas, Dr Sam thought I should stay at home in bed. 'You can't spend Christmas Day in a teaching hospital,' he said. 'All that jolly fun. They'd kill you.'

I do not recommend pleurisy. Have something else if you can. Pleurisy lacks charm; there is nothing to enjoy and much to endure, but my pleurisy changed next day – Christmas Day – to pneumonia, which was not nearly so nasty. No pain, just both shivering and overheating at the same time, an odd experience. The only really bad moment was when I realized that my father had died at the age that I was then, forty-seven. And of pneumonia, too. But we now had antibiotics.

Polly cooked the turkey, but it was enormous, so she and the children ate what they could and then, whilst I lay in bed upstairs steaming like a Christmas pudding, buried the rest of the cadaver with suitable ceremony in the garden.

I had a few comfortable weeks in University College Hospital getting better. There wasn't a lot to do in my little room, I found it difficult to concentrate on reading or watching television, but I had regular visitors who dropped in for a (mercifully) few minutes on their way home in the evenings.

My most regular visitors were Denis and Ralph Richardson, both of whom lived in North London. It was marvellous to get all the chat and gossip from Den to keep me up to date.

Ralph and Mu had recommended me to a lung specialist who was excellent, so Ralph had a kind of proprietary interest in my progress. He brought me those expensive glossy magazines like *Apollo*, which seemed to consist largely of advertisements from antique shops in Edinburgh offering small occasional tables for £2,000 a leg. And Alan Bennett sent me a postcard which read, 'Be wary of New Zealand nurses. They are so strong that when they tuck your sheets in they break your ankles.'

Then my specialist said that he thought a little champagne would be good for me, so when friends rang asking whether I would like them to bring me grapes, or would I prefer a book? I replied in a wistful croak, 'I am permitted a little champagne . . .'

As I hoped, within days my room was awash with the stuff. The fridge became full of half-bottles, and nurses made a habit of dropping in for a glass when going off-duty. I suddenly became *the* most popular patient on the wing.

I left hospital, white and wobbly, with a ratty little beard which made me look like a cross between Robin Cook the politician and Iago. Polly said it must come off within twenty-four hours. We then went off to Tenerife to convalesce for a few days, the nearest area certain to be warm and sunny as early in the year as February. And beautifully warm and sunny it turned out to be, too.

We have three strong memories of Tenerife. Firstly the beaches, which consisted not of the normal yellow sand but what looked like a mixture of coke and coal dust. The second memory was of our excellent waiter, who was living and breathing for the following week when he would be taking a not inconspicuous part in Tenerife's street carnival. At every meal he would turn over a plate on the table and while he dreamily honed our knives on the rough pottery ring on the bottom of the plate would tell us about the excitements of the annual carnival, which would last three days and which he would spend, as usual, dancing and prancing about, without sleep, dressed in spectacular drag. He showed us a photograph of himself in his costume; he resembled a narrower Hispanic version of Barbara Cartland. He was unmarried.

And then a man in the British consulate's office presented us with two tickets for the local bullfight, apparently a great treat. We went and found the matador to be about eighteen years old and, when lurching at the bull, entirely lacking in the skill to demonstrate the beauty in death so admired by *aficionados* such as Ernest Hemingway and Ken Tynan. The young man severed one of the dead bull's ears with his sword and flung it bleeding onto Polly's lap. Polly, teeth gritted, was congratulated by all around us on being chosen for this charming traditional gesture of honour.

I am squeamish even when in robust health, but I managed to survive the afternoon because, before leaving the hotel, I swallowed the only thing I could find in the sponge bag which looked helpfully medicinal: a couple of air-sickness pills.

The BBC, patient and generous as ever over illness, gave me a driver for my car and let me work half days for a while, half days turning out to be ten o'clock in the morning until five at night. We continued to find good new shows. I persuaded Kingsley Amis to let us set up a television series based on the hero of his novel *Lucky Jim*. We called it *The Further Adventures of Lucky Jim* and it starred Keith Barron, then at the beginning of his television career, and was written by a new team at the beginning of their writing careers, Dick Clement (then a producer in the department) and Ian La Frenais.

One day I was having lunch at the Savile with Kingsley to discuss various production problems when, to my delight, he blew the gaff on Denis Norden.

It seems that Kingsley and Denis were at public school together, the City of London School. Denis was very active politically and was secretary of the Peace Pledge Union and an activist on behalf of the United Nations and all those pre-war peace movements. He was reckoned to have a fine, sensitive, academic brain and Kingsley reckoned that Den would probably end up writing the definitive monograph on a fourteenth-century French poet nobody had ever heard of. What, I ask myself, went right?

I woke up with a jolt one day to realize that my three-year contract with the BBC was almost up. At the same time I realized that I did not really want to stay – not that anybody had asked me to. It had been a marvellously productive period but to stay on would have meant repeating the same thing over again. What should and could have been altered in the way the Comedy Department dealt with writers and comedy ideas had been altered; there was nothing more that I felt needed changing, so another tour of duty would mean merely consolidating, which was not nearly so much fun.

Then one evening Michael Peacock summoned me for a little talk. He asked me whether I knew much about the reallocation of commercial television licences which was about to take place. I knew nothing, of course, so he explained. The word was that Associated Rediffusion, which broadcast to London and the Home Counties, might be replaced by two companies, one to run weekdays and the other to cover weekends. Michael had given in his notice to the BBC and had been invited to be managing director of a consortium which was going to try for London's weekend licence.

There were already two teams being put together. David Frost had promises from a sparkling assembly of talent, including Peter Hall the director and Galton and Simpson, while Aidan Crawley had put together a mix of politically balanced figures and City money-men. The trouble was that neither team had experience of actually producing a television schedule. Michael was trying to combine the two teams by losing a few of those members obviously included for window dressing and taking on board some experienced programme-makers. Would I join him as potential Head of Entertainment?

It was not exactly joining, there was nothing to join, it was more like being given a ticket in a lottery where the prize was a job yet to come into existence. Polly and I decided that there was no harm in accepting a free lottery ticket so I did. I wrote my brief manifesto for the application, laying out my approach to light entertainment production ('to make shows which are not only popular but are also worth making'), and we virtually forgot all about it except that I saw the Head of

BBC TV Personnel and told him I would be leaving when my contract was concluded.

He seemed a bit thunderstruck. '*Leaving*?' he said.

'Well, nobody's asked me to stay,' I pointed out, reasonably.

'We took it for granted!' he said.

It was, I suppose, a compliment.

But there was no time to worry about trifles, there was the urgent question of what I was going to do in a few months' time when my BBC contract was up and I would be out of gainful employment. I had an idea for a book and I began to research for it. I also built a small brick wall which curved round in front of the house. Still does.

Jamie was at school at Ampleforth in Yorkshire, and Polly and I drove up for the annual Exhibition Weekend to watch, glowing, as he collected the Art Prize. On the drive home down the A1 (by now the car was an elderly Alvis) we suddenly heard the announcer say on the car radio, 'And here is the nine o'clock news. It was announced today that Associated Rediffusion has lost its commercial television licence and the new companies taking over in the London area will be, Monday to Friday, ABC Television headed by Howard Thomas, and London Weekend Television headed by Aiden Crawley and David Frost.'

I slowed the car down, slid into a lay-by, and Polly and I tried to work out all the implications of the news.

'What have we done?' we wondered.

Chapter 13

CROSSING THE CHANNEL

When commercial television first came on air it was jocularly referred to as 'Cad's Television', particularly by BBC personnel. There was a pride then in working in public service broadcasting and in the generally high quality of BBC programmes, and a great many employees felt a surge of loyalty to the BBC when a colleague left to do the same job for more money in Cad's Television.

One deeply BBC-minded man was Tom Sloan. Tom was cut to the quick when, in a break from recordings of *Steptoe and Son*, Harry H. Corbett took part in a play for ITV. 'Has he no feelings of loyalty?' cried Tom at what he took to be Harry Corbett's base act of ingratitude. 'After all the BBC's done for him!' Tom did not for a moment consider what Harry Corbett had done for the BBC.

When a BBC staff man or contract star, however well-liked or successful, moved across to ITV, there was no farewell party thrown for him, at least not in our group. To Tom the traitor had put himself beyond the pale and was treated with remote politeness as though he or she had developed a sinister blister on the lip. How Tom would have recoiled from the situation today when the BBC is legally required to buy a proportion of its programmes from independent production companies, many of which have silly names which Tom would have loathed.

A compromise between the old ethical differences of BBC and commercial programme-making was foreseen without optimism many years ago by Donald Baverstock when he was Controller of BBC1. He called the impending merging of creative minds 'a process of cross-sterilization'.

It would be about four months until my new employer, London Weekend Television, had any premises and the BBC did not want me hanging about recruiting their staff (they claimed), so they paid me my four months' money in a lovely lump sum and asked me to clear my desk and leave Television Centre at once.

A sudden four months of paid autumnal holiday was a treat indeed, although unwarranted, I was not planning to poach BBC staff. Several of my producers had come in for a chat to find out the possibilities and ask my advice and I told them to stay put, if only because I had nothing I could offer them. Meanwhile, I enjoyed a bit of gardening at Anners and made Sally a coffee table (which she wanted to be the same size as an opened-out copy of the *Observer*).

One of LWT's directors was Arnold Weinstock, Chairman of GEC, who reads balance sheets with as much pleasure and hope as other people read menus. He lent us some offices in which to start up at GEC's head office in Stanhope Gate, off Park Lane.

At the first meeting in the autumn of 1968, we heads of production departments sat bunched tightly round a huge but still slightly too small mahogany table. There was Jimmy Hill, Head of Sport, who came to us from Coventry City where he was manager; from the BBC came Doreen Stephen to run religious and educational programmes; Joy Whitby, Executive Producer of children's programmes; Humphrey Burton, Head of Music and the Arts. I was called Head of Entertainment, which managed to give the impression that my colleagues' output was for information only. There was so little room round the table that at one point I said frostily to Humphrey Burton, 'Would Drama, Music and the Arts kindly take its elbow out of Entertainment?'

Apart from the BBC Mafia a number of the production staff came from Associated Rediffusion, the London company we replaced, including our Controller of Programmes, Cyril Bennett. And we had a few more from Granada, notably the excellent Derek Granger, our Head of Plays, who later went back to Granada and produced several series of sensitive rural love stories, a genre which might be termed the 'Sex and

Sensibility' school. He titled his series by borrowing a neatly apt Shakespearean bawdy pun, *Country Matters*. Later still, Derek was responsible for producing the monumental, massively successful *Brideshead Revisited*.

I was given a colleague whose responsibility was the tricky specialist job of booking singers and variety performers, then a substantial part of weekend programming. He was Tito Burns, who once had an accordion band but gave that up to become a wily (and funny) agent. Joining us was a case of gamekeeper turning poacher.

LWT took over a new tower block of offices, Station House in Stonebridge Park, close to Wembley studios which was to be our temporary production centre, but whilst work on our open-plan offices was being completed we worked from a clutch of little offices in Old Burlington Street.

We were a hectically busy band of brothers and sisters during those first few months of getting a television station on the air from scratch; I think our state of mind at the time could be fairly described as hopeful, happy and terrified.

There was so much to do so quickly. It was not only having to make bricks without straw, but also seemingly without clay and during a drought. It seemed to me to be impossible to produce a full schedule of sitcoms and variety shows in the few months I had before we went on the air. Where to start? Where to get hold of a few seed potatoes and bulbs to plant and bring on?

It was all very different from life at the dear old BBC where there was terrific back-up. They had everybody's phone number and address so you could get in touch with anybody; there was a newspaper library and music libraries, classical and pop; press cuttings were photocopied and circulated; relevant newspapers and weeklies were available. Legal advice was to be had, there was a car park, canteen, a matron and a club bar.

And in spite of my built-in resistance to being made into a money-obsessed manager when I believed other considerations were more effective in working with gifted people, I must confess that during my three glorious years at the BBC I willy-nilly learned three valuable skills: how to stand at a superior's desk to be reprimanded and read his correspondence upside down; how to write a critical memo which deeply impresses those who get copies but avoids upsetting the recipient; how to yawn at meetings with mouth closed.

In the middle of this sudden wave of nostalgia, my old colleague and friend Michael Mills rang and asked me to meet him for a drink in the Television Centre club bar, the first time I had been invited back since the estrangement. I agreed immediately, but driving there I was suddenly overcome by a strange fear – a sort of daymare – that once inside the building I wouldn't want to come out again. It would be like a return to the warmth and safety of the womb, and I would rush up to the office of the producer of *The Epilogue*, seize him by the lapels and cry, 'Sanctuary, oh, sanctuary! I wish to eschew the hurly-burly of Cad's Television and rest here for ever in the quiet curved corridors of Television Centre, heart of public service broadcasting which I know and love!'

But when I arrived at Television Centre my fears that I would have an emotional comeover turned out to be groundless. The reception desk wouldn't let me in.

Things began to move in Old Burlington Street.

Thanks to *My Word!* and *My Music* being heard all over the world, Denis and I had become used to writers and performers from the Commonwealth, even from America, coming to see us when they landed in England so that we could brief them on what was going on in radio and television, the possibilities of employment and so on.

There was Richard Lester and Dick Vosburgh from the USA, Bernie Braden and Barbara Kelly from Canada, also Eric Nicol from Canada. The same thing happened when Oxbridge graduates came down looking for work. We tried to help on their way such talents as Leslie Bricusse, Frederick Raphael and John Cleese.

Also, because Denis and I had worked in Australia, Antipodean singers, comics, conjurors, musicians, almost anybody wanting to work in radio and television tended to make a beeline for us on landing at Heathrow. One lad who turned up to see me at Old Burlington Street was a young, curly-haired producer, writer and director of good, off-beat comedy whose name was Maurice 'Mocker' Murphy. He was a kind of Ozzy version of Dennis Main Wilson. Maurice was over here to get directing experience in Britain. This ambition was a little tricky to help along as I was still regarded by old-time executives at Television Centre as though I was a disgraced step-uncle who had left the family to embrace Islam, but I wrote to old friends and Mocker was called to a few interviews.

A couple of weeks later Mocker was back. He was offered one or two comedy things to direct but he turned them down. This was rather brave as he and his producer wife Margaret were hoping to stay a year and then have saved enough money to go home via the USA. It seems that he did not like the 'civil service' feel to the BBC which still lingered, and he found that artistic decisions were made too high up the ladder and too remote from the coalface. I warmed to the lad. Unfortunately LWT had absolutely nothing to offer until we moved into our studios in Wembley and began production; I said I would try to do something then.

Meanwhile I had an idea for an Anglo-Russian exchange of comedy plays. It came about when I went to a lecture given by the distinguished Russian screenwriter, Alexei Kapler. Alexei's speech was simultaneously and brilliantly translated by the literary agent and linguist Nina Froud. Via Nina, I asked Alexei whether he would write a comedy play for us. Nina persuaded Alexei that earning a little hard currency could not be bad.

Alexei almost immediately produced the outline of a delightful satirical comedy of modern Moscow. The action was set in one of those tiny ancient wooden houses which still crouch, gently falling apart, at the foot of Moscow's concrete high-rise offices and vast ministerial blocks. It was a semi-detached bungalow, one half occupied by a failed priest (to be played, I hoped, by Ralph Richardson) with nobody attending his services, and the other half housing a failed science master in a local school (Warren Mitchell) whose pupils take no notice of him. The priest fakes icons to earn an extra rouble. He also brews *kvas*, a highly popular, very Russian drink. The priest mixes up his icon-faking chemicals and accidentally spills some into his friend's *kvas* before leaving the beaker out for him on the balcony to enjoy his usual end-of-day swig. When darkness falls, the science master finds he has developed a bright shining halo. It stays until daylight renders it invisible.

I was thinking that Joan Sims would be just right as his girlfriend, and we could have a scene with Joan, flushed with desire, rushing round the room switching out the lights while the science master, fearful of his halo becoming visible, rushes round the room after her switching them on again.

The development of the plot was how the two men could use the halo to their advantage. Scientifically? Like filling the science master's empty lecture theatre with citizens eager enough to pay a large fee to see the dull little science master with a halo? Or should the priest take a swig of the *kvas* and fill his church and become a famous miracle and a television celebrity?

My scheme was to produce Alexei's play for LWT and then produce, in exchange, a television comedy set in London which Alexei would screen in Moscow.

Michael Peacock was in favour of the project and agreed that I should go over to Moscow for a week to meet Alexei, discuss production problems and so on, and sort out a contract with the relevant government agency (this was a very chilly period of the Cold War when you couldn't officially sneeze without permission from a government agency).

Michael allowed me to take a small team of two with me, namely the indispensable Nina Froud, who spoke perfect Russian and had been in Moscow only a few months previously helping one of her authors research his biography of the great Russian bass singer, Chaliapin, and Polly. Polly, having a French mother, was bilingual, English/French, and Alexei, most surprisingly for a successful and popular Soviet public figure and professor of cinema with his own television programme, had come from a bourgeois Jewish family, had been brought up by a French nanny and was bilingual, too, Russian/French.

So on Saturday 3 February off we went to Moscow.

The word was that the temperature there was 18 degrees below zero so I had hired an enormous fur-lined coat and fur hat from Moss Bros (Polly and Nina had their own sheepskin coats). In a photograph taken by BEA of me standing on the aircraft's steps waving, I resembled a nervous yeti.

The flight was calm and pleasant. There were only ten passengers in our huge BEA aircraft, so we paying customers congregated at the back of the plane and the cabin crew lay down and slept or played cards up in empty seats at the front end. They left the drinks trolley next to us and told us to give them a shout when we wanted lunch. It was like having one's own enormous private jet.

Polly had sensibly invested some time in learning the Russian alphabet so she could at least prevent me being arrested for wandering into the Ladies. While Polly was having a session with Nina on pronunciation and I was having a tentative stab at the crossword in my complimentary copy of *The Times*, I was joined by a genial burly man. He was helpful with the crossword because he had finished his before the aircraft's wheels were up.

He was a senior BEA engineer. His job was to be flown to Moscow, supervise the refuelling of the aircraft, then get back in it and be flown home.

'Watch your ears,' he said.

'Not easy,' I said, ever ready with a merry quip.

'Well, you'd better keep an eye on them somehow, frostbite is cumulative,' he said. 'Builds up without you knowing it. A few months ago I was on the wing of an aircraft checking the tank and my fur ear flaps were up. I was bitten. The remedy is rubbing them with brandy, so I called out to the chief steward and he came running with the bottle. I took one look at the label, gave the bottle back to him and said, 'When I need brandy, Adrian, I expect you to bring me Courvoisier VSOP not rotten tourist class Three-Star!'

He honked with laughter all the way back down the aisle.

The seat across the gangway was occupied by three ample ladies. Two of them chattered away happily to each other for the whole flight, and the third, who had a large magnifying glass harnessed to her formidable bosom, worked silently on a piece of *petit point* embroidery which Polly managed to glimpse and told me was a reproduction of a Landseer painting of animals lying in the heather, bleeding.

A steward whispered to us that two of them were titled, but he had no idea which two.

I had a nasty twinge of panic when the aircraft came in to land. Painted on the front of the Terminal building in huge letters was the name of the airport, MOCKBA.

'It's not Moscow!' I hissed to Polly. 'We've been hijacked!'

'Pull yourself together,' said Polly, collecting her hand luggage peaceably, 'Mockba is Russian for Moscow.' One does feel such a fool.

When the aircraft came to a complete stop the three elderly ladies were the first to disembark. Adrian the head steward joined us as we stood watching the ladies picking their unflurried way down the aircraft steps, wincing but not dismayed by the sudden bitterly cold air.

'Aren't they marvellous?' I said to Adrian. 'Makes you proud to be British.'

'Absolutely,' said Adrian. 'Do you know they shifted fifteen mini bottles of gin between them?'

Snow was falling on the parked aircraft, the roofs, the roads. The cold was intense and I quickly put on my Moss Bros fur hat. It was so huge and heavy that I felt I looked like a toffee apple. Milling all around us in the arrivals lounge were fur-hatted, snowed-upon Russians looking for each other, and young soldiers with smooth round Asiatic faces looking lost, like new recruits reporting for duty with a Tartar horde. The air was heavy with spoken Russian which we had never realized was such a musical, beautiful sound.

We felt a long way from home and in a very alien country and this feeling was not dispersed when we were told that the modern, bang-up-to-date, concrete barn of a hotel we had booked into was required by the authorities for some workers' jolly and we had been summarily off-loaded to an old Edwardian establishment (actually rather famous) called the Hotel Berlin.

But Alexei Kapler was waiting for us at the arrivals barrier, which cheered us up. He was fifty-fiveish, lots of grey hair, plumpish and happy to see us.

We piled into his little car, cuddling our luggage, which was too big to go into his boot, and he drove us to Moscow. Most of the way was through miles of silver birch trees, behind which loomed the dark shapes of firs.

We passed a concrete memorial commemorating a famous heroic occasion during the last war when a small unit of Russian soldiers on a farm held up the entire German invasion force for several valuable hours.

Alexei explained with some glee what had happened. It seems the colonel commanding the small garrison manning the farm was a mean-spirited man who suspected the general commanding this stretch of front line of disliking him and wishing to do him down. When the Germans began their invasion and the tanks were rolling, the general sent a radio message to the farm commander telling him that the German army was on its way and ordering him to evacuate the farm and retreat immediately. 'Aha!' thought the idiot colonel. 'I know his little game. It's only a platoon of Germans on a scouting recce. If I retreat he'll arrest me for cowardice and I will be reduced to the ranks, which is what he's always wanted!' So he commanded his tiny garrison to man their mortars, load their rifles, position their machine-guns and repulse the small scouting sortie at all costs.

The German army suddenly found itself being fired upon and the mighty advance was halted and a worried meeting was held at German Brigade Headquarters. Intelligence had assured them that there would be no serious resistance until they were nearer Moscow, but had the Russians outwitted them and was the main Russian army dug in and waiting to annihilate them ahead? It was too risky to chance, so the German invasion halted to consider tactics and the Russians won a valuable day in which to build up their defences. The lucky garrison commander won himself a statue.

We zinged along in Alexei's car which was a little like Alexei, friendly, slightly battered-looking and lots of surprises. The seats were once very comfortable. Alexei kept reaching down to the floor and producing things to show us. He talked away in his excellent French and Polly translated for me when she felt I was being left behind.

Moscow was a dramatic sight. Huge snowflakes were drifting down, but the city's wide main roads were being efficiently cleared; snowploughs and bulldozers were pushing the snow into heaps in the gutter as it fell. Another machine with steel arms embraced the snow and slid it onto conveyor belts which lifted and dropped it into the back of a queue of lorries.

When darkness fell, the snowy roads continued to be cleared all night by a more traditional Soviet system. An army of quite old, fat women, wrapped in rusty quilted black clothes, emerged from somewhere with picks and hacked away at the nobbles of ice on the pavement which a multitude of feet treading on snow at 20 degrees below had produced. In the freezing cold these fragments of ice and the massive snowflakes still falling were shovelled up into wheelbarrows by the women and carted off by them into the darkness. As the authorities were so right to point out, they had no unemployment problem in Moscow.

Alexei took us to the Hotel Berlin and made sure we were properly registered. We liked the hotel immediately. It was a relic of a different world with decor about as baroque as anyone ever got.

As we peered into the gilt, mirror-lined dining room Polly suddenly gripped my arm. 'There's a waiter fishing!' she said. And indeed there was. At the far end of the room there was a small circular pool surrounded by a brass rail. An ancient waiter was leaning on the brass rail dabbing at the water with what seemed to be a large shrimping net. He straightened up and made his way on painful feet to the kitchen with a wriggling trout in his net dripping onto the carpet.

We were given what the lady on reception insisted was the hotel's de-luxe suite. It consisted of a tiny salon, a minute bedroom with twin beds and a bathroom. The loo did not work, or more accurately it never stopped working. But I found it was possible to staunch the flow cleverly, even when seated, by reaching behind into the cistern and punching the ballcock. The manoeuvre might have been even cleverer had it occurred to me to roll up my sleeve first.

Alexei returned later to take us to dinner at the

Screenwriters' Club. Escorting him downstairs we had to pass close by the two black-clad ladies on duty at a desk in a corner of our corridor. They eyed us suspiciously as we passed, making us feel like escapees sneaking out of a government house of correction.

On the way downstairs we also had to squeeze between a lady wearing furs and a picture hat in earnest conversation with a gentleman in striped pyjamas. The hotel foyer was dimly lit. Near the door was a television set which was difficult to see as the uniformed hall porter was sitting right in front of it and about 6 inches from the screen. Reception did not seem to be at all good but occasionally the crackling noises stopped and the screen went into sharp focus, whereupon the hall porter rose, fiddled at the back of the set and mucked the picture up again to his satisfaction.

It was very hot in the foyer and very cold outside. Through the glass door I could see a furry, assassin-like figure on the pavement gesticulating for me to come outside. What did he want? To enroll me as a secret agent? To bum a cigarette? To steal my hat?

Consumed with curiosity, I befurred myself, let down the flaps of my hat and went out into the aching cold. 'Psssst, man!' said the assassin in a slightly American accent, quickly looking over both shoulders to make sure the coast was clear. 'Wanna buy a glass cutter?'

It wasn't even one of those glass cutters which incorporated a chip of diamond, it was the sort with a little rusty wheel, which in my experience was about as efficient a method of cutting glass as scribing it with a knob of butter. I politely declined the offer and nipped back into the warm foyer of the hotel.

It was the fiftieth anniversary of the Red Army and that evening the entire membership of the Moscow Screenwriters' Club seemed, understandably, to be pissed (which a great many Muscovites appeared to be every evening).

While we were waiting for our table we had an odd conversation with a thin merry man who for quite a long time had been trying to light a broken cigarette. He did not seem to be speaking any language recognized by our party. When something amused him, and almost everything did, he dropped down and squatted on his heels, enjoyed his laugh and then reared up again with a cracking of knees to a standing position. Alexei said that in daylight he was a military historian.

We were joined at supper by Alexei Bolokon, a publisher, with his wife and his daughter Natasha, who spoke excellent English which she used almost exclusively to list for us the recent cultural and humanitarian achievements of the USSR.

We had a splendid meal which began with what seemed to be a selection of about fifty hot Russian hors-d'œuvres followed by delicious Georgian chicken – a small chicken hammered flat with a cleaver until it resembles a recently run-over frog.

Alexei's blonde wife Julia was a poet. On the way back to the hotel, Nina told us that during the war Julia had fought in the Army as a private and now washed her hair every night for the sheer pleasure of being able to.

As Polly and I lay in bed, too exhausted to sleep after what might reasonably be termed a busy day, we decided that the smell of a city is the smell at night of its petrol fumes. Moscow petrol smelled of bubblegum.

The following five days in Moscow were so action-packed that they made our day of arrival seem in memory like a day off. I had somehow to make a deal with a government agency appointed 'to look after Professor Kapler's interests', which in reality meant blocking any deal which required Alexei's presence outside Russia in case he had it in mind, which he certainly hadn't, to defect to the West.

Alexei must have been quite a worry to the authorities. He began as an actor in silent films in 1920 and worked for a while in Leningrad with the splendidly named Eccentric Actors' Factory. In 1928 he turned to screenwriting and became a leading writer of film scripts, working with such directors as Eisenstein. Then, whilst working in Moscow, he met and fell in love with Stalin's daughter Svetlana, and she with him. It was a gentle love story of a highly intelligent man of forty and a sensitive schoolgirl and was beautifully described by Svetlana in her book, *Twenty Letters to a Friend*. Alexei is letter sixteen.

The affair had no future, of course. Stalin was strongly anti-Semitic and Alexei was Jewish. Alexei was arrested and sent to exile in a Siberian mining village for five years. He was ordered to stay away from Svetlana and to make no attempt to contact her ever again. When his five years were up he went back to Moscow and immediately telephoned Svetlana, was arrested again and sent 'north' for another five years. And that was that. Svetlana married (her husband was Jewish) and Alexei got on with his career, but the police must have amassed a thick file on Alexei down at the old Lubyanka.

The government press agency with whom I had to make the deal was called APN (Russia's use of acronyms almost equalled the BBC's). Every morning at about ten, Polly, Nina and I briskly stepped out from the hotel to APN's offices, a fair trot up Gorski Prospect (which we renamed the APN Way). At ten thirty every morning we had a brief meeting with APN's senior man, who told us that the Minister of Culture, who had to authorize every detail of our deal, was at a meeting and would we come back at four fifteen? Then, every afternoon at four fifteen we returned, and as I tried to discuss Alexei's fees and role as supervisor of the production the agency man would fidget and then blurt out that the minister had gone home. Would we please come back at ten thirty tomorrow morning?

During our walks to and from APN, we managed to cram in a bit of shopping and sightseeing, not easy as the streets were thronged with the 2 million visitors from other republics of the USSR who were always trudging round Moscow trying to buy a wedding ring. Queues for wedding rings curled out of the jewellers' shops, went round the block and curled back in again. Customers lined up according to the initial of their sur-name, i.e., those whose names began with A–D queued up on Mondays, E–H on Tuesdays, and so on.

Those of the 2 million not queueing for wedding rings seemed to be trudging along the pavement very slowly in front of us.

Restaurants, for which lengthy queueing was the norm, were mostly ethnic. We had lunch in the Sofia, a Bulgarian restaurant. The only part of the meal I can remember is the coffee. Our Bulgarian coffee was exactly like Turkish coffee except that the grounds floated on top.

One day Alexei collected us from our morning disappointment at APN and drove us on a sightseeing tour round the city. It was amazing how Alexei managed to turn up in his car just when we wanted him, and he was hardly idle at the time: as well as setting up a co-production deal on a film to be made in France, he was trying to get a visa for Julia to read her poetry at a Brussels literary festival, he had a daily lecture to give to his students and he had his weekly television show about films.

Alexei's car was not a massive government limousine. It was a small dented saloon of some age, yet every time we stopped and parked Alexei carefully removed the windscreen-wiper blades and locked them away in the glove compartment. 'Is there much petty theft in Moscow?' I asked him.

He grinned. 'Who knows?' he said. 'It's not reported in the newspapers!'

About every mile Alexei shot out of his seat with a stifled Russian oath and hit his head on the roof. The spring in his seat was broken and every so often it ripped through the upholstery and hit dead centre.

On Sunday we stood at the back of a Russian Orthodox church which was crammed full of devout elderly people and equally devout young soldiers. Just inside the door stood a huge battered roll-top desk at which two old ladies sat selling candles, gossiping quite loudly with friends and entering up account books.

We had lunch back at the hotel. As I could not understand the menu, even when Polly translated the words, we stuck to what we knew and lived on bortsch, or smoked salmon and blinis, or caviare, with a flask each of vodka. It was a tough way of life, I grant you, but it was only for a few days so we gritted our teeth and endured it.

Unfortunately, when I was about to demolish a small mountain of Beluga caviare, Alexei spoiled my lunch by announcing that he had arranged for me to give a lecture at three o'clock to English-speaking students on the subject of humour in English literature. It was to take place in the unconvincingly named House of Friendship.

At three o'clock there were sixty or seventy quiet and respectful students of both sexes and many ages sitting on hard chairs with pencils and pads at the ready. Also present was the British Cultural Attaché who asked Polly if she would phone his mother when we got home.

Alexei introduced me in Russian. As I had no idea what he was saying I tried to adopt a look of nonchalant amusement to give the students hope. I gave them about forty minutes of tedium, waving my arms and leaping about to keep them awake, and then it was question time, always a relief to all. The students were only really interested in why I had not made more of Charles Dickens (clearly a Party hero in Russia) and his fight for the betterment of the working classes. To liven things up I pointed out that although Dickens was against nasty employers he was not very interested in put-upon employees, and I challenged the students to name one major serious Dickens character who was an ordinary worker, not a servant or a clerk. I pointed out that Dickens himself began as a working-class lad in a blacking factory, but managed to pull himself out of squalor and become a member of the well-off middle classes, where he intended to remain.

Afterwards I found the lecture and the bickering about Dickens (whom I enjoyed reading but didn't really know much about) had been recorded for playing on Moscow radio that evening. I was then interviewed by a delicate man with beautiful English and a sound recorder the size of a suitcase. During the interview, to be broadcast that evening as a trailer for the lecture, I gave London Weekend Television a terrific build-up, possibly the most useless bit of public relations ever perpetrated.

The interview had just finished and I could see Alexei struggling towards me through the Dickens fans with a restorative mug of vodka when a rather beautiful lean lady in black with her hair scraped back, like a character from a Chekhov play – I had noticed her smiling and nodding all through my lecture – came up very close to me, still smiling and nodding, put her hand gently on my arm and said, 'You should be in the cinema, Mr Myer, you are so *plastique*.'

Well, *I* think it was a compliment.

We were now in the rhythm of life in Moscow which consisted largely of struggling out of boots, fur coat and hat in enormous vestibules, then eating, or talking, or watching something, and then struggling back into boots, fur coat and hat to brave the icy pavements again. The tiny cloakroom lady in APN's vestibule had got used to the weight of my coat and did not attempt to lift it from the counter but slid it along the floor to a vacant hook.

That evening we saw a witty and imaginative production of *Turandot* which had been running for three years. This was the reproduction of a commedia dell'arte version orginally staged in Moscow in 1929. Afterwards, Nina took us to a supper party given in a high-rise flat belonging to a friend of hers, a young painter who restored icons (honourably) for a living. Also present were a cheerful bunch of young actors, actresses, writers, an architect and a huge puppy called Philip Morris. With the exception of Philip Morris, they all spoke fluent English.

Our artist host unfortunately did not believe in possessions so there was no furniture. We dined upon a large framed religious painting laid on trestles and when we sat down on our beer crates the 'table' came up to chin level.

As the Armenian brandy flowed, the beautiful young wives and girlfriends sang sad Russian songs, danced ancient dances of submission before their lords and offered them gherkins. At something of a loss how I could reciprocate for England I finally got up and sang them 'Miner's Dream' with actions.

'You are beautiful,' said a small actor.

I was a little disconcerted by this until Nina whispered to me that in Russian the word 'beautiful' also meant 'red'. Our host kindly opened the door on to the tiny iron balcony, and in seconds the room was agreeably cool and I was no longer at all beautiful.

About midnight we went back to the Hotel Berlin by taxi. The driver was very drunk and at one point, with a couple of loud thumps and the scraping of branches against paintwork, drove us at speed across a landscaped traffic island.

Next day we asked Alexei whether there was much drunkenness in Moscow. He smiled. 'Who knows?' he said. 'It's not reported in the newspapers!'

Finding ourselves with an hour to spare we did a quick run round the Kremlin Museum. Perhaps 'run' is the wrong word. As a sensible rule to preserve the fine old parquet floors, we added our shoes to the other clobber we handed over in the vestibule, put on huge slippers made from old bits of domestic carpet, and shuffled past such glories as the Tsars' collection of Fabergé eggs and King Charles II's golden coach like a very old couple trying to find the bar in a health farm.

And there was the State Circus. Superbly groomed ponies pranced about the red-carpeted ring. The great Russian clown Popov was excellent, but a reminder that continental clowns don't skimp on their time, usually doing a routine that runs for about two hours. Chocolate cake was served in the interval on a piece of beige unperforated loo paper. The queue – there was always a queue in Moscow – was as kind as ever and as soon as they heard us speaking English waved us to the front. All the women looked at Polly's shoes. They weren't knee-high, scarlet, plastic startlers, just decent shoes, but as such envied.

Polly's shoes were envied again when we went to the Bolshoi Theatre to see a performance of *Prince Igor* and joined the crowd strolling along the grand first-floor promenade between acts. We were seated in the third row of the stalls, not in tip-up seats but in separate and very elegant *fauteuils* on a gleaming parquet floor. It was a suitable way to see *Prince Igor*, particularly in the spectacular production we accidentally booked for. There was a cast of hundreds; the chaps continually broke into gruff and emotional song, real horses galloped at speed about the huge stage, and when the Tartars attacked, the outer fortifications burst into real flames (well, they looked real).

The performance was slightly spoiled for us by Natasha, the publisher's lovely Soviet daughter, giving us a loud, politically correct running commentary on the action on-stage. And the principals had rather faint voices. Nina thought the first company was probably on tour and we were seeing the third or fourth company.

Success with Alexei's contract was in sight. I had upped the money which seemed to have helped. We paid our last visit to APN and the manager handed me the signed contract in a glossy blue folder marked 'Fiftieth Anniversary Of The Revolution'. The handover was photographed by an APN staff photographer as though I had won the pools.

Alexei drove us back past the silver birches to the airport and there produced presents from deep down between his car seats; little jars of caviare for me and a huge engraved walrus tusk, a genuine scrimshaw from Siberia, for Polly, which he had brought back as a reminder of his ten-year exile. Polly tried not to take it as it was clearly of great sentimental value. Alexei insisted. 'What is the point of giving a present unless it's something you'd really like to keep for yourself?' he asked.

Alexei, being a professor, was allowed to come onto the tarmac with us to the aircraft. It was suddenly intolerably sad having to say goodbye. His bear-hug crushed my ribs and his face was surprisingly bristly. 'See you in July,' I managed to say, and Polly, Nina and I climbed into the aircraft and sat silent with our thoughts as we took off into the evening sky.

A British Embassy man was immensely impressed on hearing about my deal with APN. He said that to get what you wanted signed in Moscow in five days might be a world record, but not so. Alexei's play never happened. Nina said afterwards that she thought APN never had any intention of letting it happen.

A few weeks before Alexei was due to come over to England to start work with us he telephoned Nina – for some reason he could telephone from his *dacha* without the call being bugged – and told her that if in the near future somebody claimed that he was ill, she must not believe it and worry. On the contrary, he was in very good health.

Sure enough, a few days later the Russian Embassy in London contacted Nina regretting that unfortunately Professor Kapler was ill with a virus infection and all his overseas commitments had to be cancelled.

Polly and I wanted to thank Alexei and assure him that he was still much in our thoughts. We were trying hard to think of something rather more fun that just writing him a letter when we came across an American advertisement for mail-order fruit cakes which they would send anywhere in the world (and probably anywhere in space by now).

What intrigued us was that the bakery was in a city in Texas named Corsicana (probably because of the influence the pioneer democracy of eighteenth-century Corsica had on the thinking behind the founding of American independence; e.g., Thomas Jefferson called his house Monticello), and we knew Alexei would enjoy the thought of getting a large, rich, American fruit cake stuffed with pecan nuts and fruit, all the way from Texas by post. And it worked; the cake arrived in Moscow safely and was much enjoyed. In return, Alexei sent us a portfolio of thirty watercolour prints of costume designs painted by his friend and colleague Sergei Eisenstein, who was a theatrical designer before he became a film director.

It seemed wrong for us to keep the prints hidden away in a file, they were colourful, exuberant and amusing, so we had them framed simply and, via Godfrey Smith's column in *The Sunday Times*, offered to lend them free to any theatre putting on a Russian play who could use them to decorate the foyer. Eventually they toured all the theatres that wanted them, so what should we do with them next? It was the time that the Groucho Club in Soho was opening its doors to media people and we presented the prints to Groucho's on permanent loan. They now hang on the walls of the staircase leading downstairs from the reception desk. At least they can now stimulate and inspire authors and publishers and rock stars as they clamber their way down to the loo.

When Alexei died a year or so later, our 'quality' newspapers gave him fulsome obituaries, but they did not mention that when he was walking in the woods, birds settled on his shoulders.

Shortly after we arrived home, London Weekend Television moved into its high-rise building (it swayed in a strong wind) just off the North Circular Road and near its Wembley studios. Entertainment Department was open-plan, which was a new experience. It meant that I had to hide the (illegal) portable bar-in-a-suitcase given to me by Jimmy Edwards, which I kept to comfort disconsolate visiting writers, and it was peculiarly difficult to tick somebody off in a whisper, but the open-plan design promoted an all-in-the-same-boat feeling which was good.

One afternoon I had just been comforting one of our

secretaries who had run into trouble with her love-life – she had been at a concert of the Deep Purple pop group and, emotionally stirred, had grabbed her companion's arm and breathed, 'I've 'ad all of them, one by one.' Unfortunately her companion was her new, although from that moment on her ex-, boyfriend.

She thanked me for my wise advice (what on earth could I have said to her?) and I replied, 'Any time, Marlene. My door is always open.' And she said, 'You 'aven't *got* a door!'

Happily I had a super secretary to guide me through this comforting old grey-haired-uncle role, a part of the job of being head of a unit about which I had not been warned but rather enjoyed. At our very first LWT get-together meeting at Stanhope Gate, the bottles of fizzy water and the pencils and pads were arranged on the conference table by a most attractive temp named Tanya Bruce-Lockhart. Months later Tanya rang me at home and said, 'LWT begins as a company in September, which is quite soon, and before that I have to find you a secretary. What would you like me to do? Advertise the job, then arrange interviews and board applicants? Or will *I* do?'

So Tanya was my secretary at LWT right from the start. That meant she was the department's unofficial queen bee. Tanya was very keen on keeping up standards and this was the era of tights and very short miniskirts. On occasional mornings, as the girls were bent over their filing cabinets, Tanya's voice would ring out, rattling the open-plan dividing panels, 'Marlene – you've forgotten to put on knickers again!'

Tanya was very bright, too bright really for the job, but she was marvellous at getting me to settle down and do my correspondence, almost without me noticing. The trouble was that her shorthand speed was much speedier than my thinking speed – dictation was a task which was new to me and I loathed it – and on the many occasions when I was struggling for the right thing to say, Tanya would helpfully break the silence with something like, 'Is that a spot coming up on your nose?'

Eventually I managed to have her promoted to Location Finder, a job which needed considerable initiative. From there she worked her way steadily upwards, eventually becoming an important asset to Humphrey Burton's Arts programme, *Aquarius*.

One sympathetic but occasionally awkward character trait which ruled Tanya was a love of animals. The previous year, on holiday in Spain, Tanya had found a dog on the beach which had been deserted and was starving. She fed him, failed to find his owner, christened him Ricky and brought him back to England with her, paying for his six-month quarantine and visiting him almost every day. Ricky was a large dog, vaguely Alsatian, friendly but odd-looking. Every day Tanya brought him to Station House and he lay under her desk dozing happily.

Unfortunately there was a house rule that no dogs were allowed in the building and Tanya was sent a memo by the premises manager reminding her of this rule and asking her not to bring Ricky to the office any more.

Tanya was devastated and told me frankly, 'I'm sorry, but I go where Ricky goes. How can I leave him all on his own in a flat? If he has to stay at home, so will I.'

I knew the manager was not personally anti-Ricky, he had to play to the rules to cover himself. I needed to give him a reason to overlook Ricky and to have an excuse for Ricky's presence in the unlikely event of the dog getting overexcited and biting the property company's chairman on the ear, or being unsociable on his carpet.

I eventually wrote back, 'I am grateful to you for reminding me of the legal position of Miss Bruce-Lockhart's popular pet which spends its day snoozing under her desk in my department. Happily, I am able to assure you that the animal is not affected by your wise house rule of no dogs in the offices because Ricky is not a dog. Miss Bruce-Lockhart rescued him from a Spanish beach under the impression that he was a dog, but an inspection by a zoologist (the famous one on television) has revealed that he is an Andalusian, hornless, short-haired mountain goat, an uncommon breed which is perfectly harmless to humans and carpets . . .'

Ricky stayed. And so did Tanya.

In an LWT programme conference it was decided that LWT's first programme, to go on early Friday evenings, would be a series reflecting the change from weekday programming to a more carefree weekend schedule. The perfect title would have been *The Weekend Starts Here*, but Rediffusion had already used that. It was decided that the series should not be another pop-music show but would go for humour, and its provisional title was *We Have Ways of Making You Laugh*.

To produce the series, I had one of the best producers who came to us from Associated Rediffusion, Humphrey Barclay, who was young, extremely bright and inventive. We decided that we did not want to start the weekend with an anarchic romp, but with a cheerful, unpredictable, bitty sort of show which viewers could join at any point and then leave at any point to put the potatoes on.

We had the producer and the title, we now wanted the presenter. To my horror and delight (emotions which frequently coincide in television), Humphrey Burton argued strongly that I should present the show. I accepted. It was not all that much of an interruption to my work as unit head once Humphrey Barclay had got things organized.

We put together a team of writers and performers, and writer/performers. Ken Cope, the writer, actor (*Randall and Hopkirk (Deceased)*) and restaurateur, wrote and performed a weekly five-minute piece to camera as the manager of a none-too-successful restaurant (foreshadowing Harry Enfield's Stavros?); Dick Vosburgh, superb writer of topical one-liners and well-known beard, sat at the back with a clipboard and the most bulging briefcase in television, writing his odd funny comments and passing them forward; the then almost unknown Eric Idle did some excellent bits and pieces; Terry Gilliam, an American artist and cartoonist, now director of extraordinarily imaginative Hollywood movies (*Brazil*, *The Adventures of Baron Munchhausen*, *Twelve Monkeys*), sat in the studio happily drawing what was going on and the camera zoomed in on his work from time to time; and Barry Cryer, Benny Green and others popped in with pieces.

As well as introducing *We Have Ways of Making You Laugh*, I contributed material, such as thinking up things to say which would enable us, since it was a live show, to bring it down exactly on time. I sometimes needed a long piece of waffle and sometimes a short piece, and thinking up various lengths of waffle enlivened the tedious daily drive to and from Wembley. The items were like (short waffle):

Surrey Constabulary have asked me to broadcast the following message. Yesterday afternoon at approximately 3.10 p.m., a police vehicle backing out of the forecourt of Woking Police Station was hit by a police vehicle back-ing *into* the forecourt. Nobody was hurt but both vehicles were extensively damaged. If any member of the public witnessed the incident – *please* shut up about it.

Another idea I had was for star comedians to do a bit of their original audition routine, or their first stage or radio act. These turned out, as I had hoped, to be bad, but considering how the comedians had grown in stature over the years, very funny.

Max Bygraves was the first. His original act was so brash and feeble that he could hardly get through it without corpsing. Dick Bentley was also very effective. He did the warm-up routine which he had done every week for over ten years to cheer up the studio audience before *Take It From Here*. Most of it purported to be a letter from his mother in Australia giving him the family news. I remember (how could I forget?) such lines as:

Your Great-Aunt Maude called in on Wednesday. What a marvellous old lady she is, ninety-six and not a grey hair on her head. Completely bald.

And:

Your Aunty Cissie came home drunk again on Thursday, bashed over one of the brick gateposts, flattened a flower bed and crashed into the rear wall of the garage. Thank God she wasn't in a car.

The letter always ended:

Must close now as Granny wants the Biro to do her eye-brows.

One Friday evening, 2 August 1968, *We Have Ways of Making You Laugh* made an almost illegible blur on television history as the first programme of the new station LWT. The show went marvellously, the full audience laughing and clapping their appreciation. The series never went so well over its subsequent fourteen weeks' run, but that was not surprising as the first show's audience consisted almost entirely of friends and investors.

Glowing with sweat and pleasure at the end, I was leaning against a camera feeling happily tired when Humphrey Barclay came up and said, 'I have the most rotten news. The show didn't go out.'

I couldn't believe it.

'The unions pulled the plug just before we went on air,' Humphrey said. 'I took the decision to let you do the whole show in case they plugged us back on, but they didn't. The technicians have called an indefinite strike.'

The cameraman beside us, who had much enjoyed doing the show, tore off his headphones and flung them to the ground in fury. I found myself in the ironic position of comforting a union member – 'Now come on, don't take it too badly, we'll do the show again sometime' – whose union had killed our transmission.

The weeks that the unions were out on strike were, in fact, most helpful to me, and I began to build up some potentially interesting shows.

Ronnie Wolfe and Ronnie Chesney offered me a sitcom series they had devised about a small-town bus driver and his family. This the BBC had turned down as they doubted how many laughs the boys could get out of oil leaks on the bus-depot floor. This was about as sensible a criticism as worrying how many laughs Galton and Simpson could get out of two rag-and-bone men and a horse.

The Wolfe and Chesney series was *On the Buses*, with Reg Varney as the cheery bus driver. It was hated by the critics and ended up being one of the longest-running sitcoms ever shown on ITV.

A quite different kind of programme was a smart domestic sitcom series, *Never a Cross Word*, written by Donald Churchill for Paul Daneman and Nyree Dawn Porter. It was our first big success. In the opening programme of the series the part of a shy awkward Welsh student who was their lodger was played brilliantly by the young John Alderton, previously a doctor in *Emergency – Ward 10*.

When I was at the BBC, a young man named Terry Jones was heavily recommended to me as a potential director and I wangled him onto a BBC directors course. The end-of-course exercise required the student to find a suitable sketch, get an actor to perform it for nothing and then shoot it on tape so that his directing skills could be assessed by the tutors.

Terry wrote his own sketch and it was played by his good friend, an unknown would-be actor/writer named Michael Palin. The sketch was very well played and directed and Terry passed his course.

Then, out of the blue, Terry and Michael turned up at LWT with a wild six-part comedy series which they called *The Complete and Utter History of Britain*. Humphrey Barclay would produce. It was a totally original piece of work for which we needed the right unconventional-minded director. I remembered 'Mocker' Murphy, the young Australian, and with a great deal of cunning string-pulling I managed to get him.

There was one episode which gives an idea of Terry's and Michael's approach to history. The commentator said something like:

VOICE-OVER: In those early days, Britain was a rich target for marauders from less fertile lands and was subject to wave after wave of invaders who proved difficult to cope with.

(*Cut to beach. A modern naval officer in gumboots and holding a loud hailer is addressing unseen invaders.*)

NAVAL OFFICER: Right, Jutes, come on in! Finger out, Jutes, haven't got all day! Saxon hordes, hold off until I tell you, then follow the Jutes onto beach four. Sorry, Vikings,

that's all for today! Can you come back
first thing in the morning, say nine thirty
sharp?

Another good thing was a series written by Ken Cope about
an amiable, mischievous old-age pensioner known to everybody as Thingummybob, which was the name of the show.
Stanley Holloway starred as Thingummybob.

The show had great warmth with some good lines (on the
price of an air ticket to Paris: 'If God had meant us to fly he
would have given us the money'). I even managed to get Paul
McCartney to write the signature tune. But the show was
hampered by being forty-five minutes long instead of the
accepted thirty minutes. This was at the request of Tom
Margerison, a senior management figure, though exactly what
he managed I never knew.

Tom was a very agreeable, softly spoken, ready-to-smile
journalist who specialized in scientific matters (at an earlier
stage in his career he had introduced computers to local papers
in Reading and Hemel Hempstead). At the beginning of LWT
he seemed to be principally concerned with convincing me to
make all sitcoms last forty-five minutes (I tried, but they
suffered because writers, in fact everybody, was so used to the
half-hour length that forty-five-minute shows came out as
thirty-minute shows with padding). He also strode about
carrying plans and considering whether our new studios being
built on the South Bank should have glass walkways going
through them so that visitors to Dear Olde London Towne
could watch a television show being recorded.

Another really good script was brought to me. I was the
writers' second choice, but didn't mind when the writers were
John Esmonde and Bob Larbey. It was a series to be proud of,
set in a comprehensive school in a tough area of London. It was
Esmonde and Larbey working well, the pupils were beautifully
delineated and the staff were a recognizably funny lot. The
central character, the young teacher, was slightly awkward and
gauche but fundamentally tough enough for the job, and
remembering the Welsh lodger in the first *Never a Cross Word*,
we cast John Alderton as 'Privet' Hedges.

The BBC had been offered the series and had turned it down because one of the pupils was 'educationally subnormal' and they thought it was wrong to make fun of afflictions. This was a curious lack of confidence in the tact and taste of the writers. In fact the character in question, Dennis, was handled very well. The other members of the class protected him and he became a popular part of the show to viewers. *Please Sir!* had a long, highly successful run, followed by a spin-off, *The Fenn Street Gang*.

Then I managed to persuade an old friend, Richard Gordon, to let me have the TV rights to his *Doctor in the House* books. John Cleese and Graham Chapman – a writer who was also a doctor – wrote the pilot script for the series and several episodes. Another pair of writers on the series were Graeme Garden – also a doctor – and Bill Oddie (both were later Goodies).

A well-balanced, reasonably happy unit of real television people is a formidable machine, capable at a pinch of swinging into action with breathtaking speed and resourcefulness. My unit had all those qualities and they displayed them to me on Thursday 19 December 1968.

At breakfast a few days earlier I had nearly bitten a lump out of my coffee cup when I opened a letter to find it was an invitation to lunch at Buckingham Palace. It seems that the Queen held random 'Thursday lunches' at the palace, so that she and other members of the royal family could meet and chat about this and that to a selected few citizens.

The Queen and the Duke were to be there, as were Prince Charles and Princess Anne. There were eight of humble us, a cross-section, but of what? We consisted of Lord Rothschild, Professor Asa Briggs, Mr Grima the jeweller, Sir Matt Busby, Sir Michael Tippett, Michael Green the editor of the *Daily Telegraph* and Victor Sylvester, who looked odd sitting quietly in a lounge suit rather than standing upright in white tie and tails, undulating and waving a baton.

It was all rather heady and splendid. Excellent food and plenty of conversation. For me, anyway. I was seated next to the Duke of Edinburgh who had a bee in his bonnet about studio audiences at comedy shows (this was before canned laughter), and he would be pleased if I got rid of studio audiences so he could enjoy his comedy unprompted by squeals.

I was stoutly opposing the Duke's point of view (it's always more fun) when the Queen rose to lead us into another room for coffee. We all immediately rose with her and followed her towards the door, the Duke arguing fiercely with me on a good point about studio audiences being so excited at being present at a recording that they were not a natural audience.

I suddenly realized I was in trouble. The Queen had arrived at the door and was waiting for the Duke to catch up with her, but I was with the Duke and he had what he believed to be a killer argument and was only halfway through it and going strong. What should I do? Rudely break off the argument just when the Duke was in full gallop and retire to my proper place at the back in the queue, or go in with him?

I went in with him. So the little procession weaving its way towards coffee was led by the Queen, after whom came the Duke of Edinburgh and Mr Frank Muir (a peasant), and following them came Princess Anne, Prince Charles and the rest of the guests.

The coffee was served by footmen and then the equerries got to work. Like hyper-intelligent sheepdogs they nudged each of us in turn to the Queen's side for a five-minute chat and then detached us, without us really realizing it, to make way for the next guest.

The Queen and the Duke had had a bad press after visiting South America and the Queen asked me whether I believed what I read in the papers. I said that I didn't *believe* what I read, but because it was in the papers it gave the event or whatever a kind of importance. I said that it was rather like advertisements. One didn't *believe* what was claimed for the product, but because it was advertised it put the product into a more prominent category in the mind than other products.

And the Queen said, 'Oh, yes, I see what you mean. If I bought an electric drill I'd buy a Black & Decker.'

I had gone to great lengths to keep this lunch appointment a secret from my colleagues at LWT, so I had booked a hire car to take me to St James's Street to lunch in the fish restaurant there, and redirected the driver to the palace later. There were no mobile phones then, so there could be no leakage from the car of the secret destination.

And yet, I underestimated television folk. When I returned to Station House and stepped out of the lift, I found my whole department on one knee in a mock-humble welcome. Purple crêpe paper made a special carpet to my desk where I was presented with a gold (coloured) sceptre and a crown, heavily bejewelled (wine gums), and a scroll recording the lunch in ancient script on vellum (wrapping-paper). The wording concluded:

> We were most graciously pleased to have our right loyal
> and trusted servant F. HERBERT MUIR for luncheon,
> and he was delicious.

Well, the exact phrase to describe that little welcome home was 'sent up rotten' and I remember being so sent with great happiness.

Everything now in LWT seemed to be going so well. My department had the usual complement of failures, but also some stunning successes, three of the shows ran for years and there were plenty more in the pipeline. Tito's variety bookings for Saturday nights were excellent and we had not yet been eighteen months on the air.

Then the whole thing suddenly fell apart.

On Monday 5 September 1969, the available unit heads in the building, Doreen Stephen, Terry Hughes, Humphrey Burton, Derek Granger and I, were summoned to an urgent meeting at 6 p.m. that evening at our chairman Aidan Crawley's fine home in Chester Row. Mr Crawley informed us that the directors had that morning sacked Michael Peacock. And our new managing director, chosen to turn round the company's fortunes with an iron hand was – we held our breaths – Tom Margerison.

We were dumbfounded.

Dr Tom Margerison! The gentle, solid-state physicist, some-time science correspondent of *The Sunday Times*?

Our first question was of course, what on earth did the board have against Michael Peacock?

Aidan Crawley's answers were lame, vague and somewhat evasive, as all the directors' answers to the question were to be, e.g., 'It was time for a change . . . Peacock did not get on with the board . . . there was a fall off in advertising revenue . . . faulty purchasing of programmes . . .' And the board of directors' trump card: 'The managing director must carry the can for what the board considers to be poor company performance. It is rightly in the board's power to hire and fire its managing director when it feels it necessary.'

Next day we unit heads met and discussed what to do. There was not a lot we could do at that stage except to protest vehemently and try to find out what the directors' panic move was really about. The most likely truth was the complaint that Michael 'did not get on with the board'. One of the board once said to Michael, 'Could we have more swimming programmes on Saturday afternoons? My daughter likes swimming.'

Had Michael been a well-trained, docile managing director who knew his place, he would have said something like, 'What a splendid idea, sir! Why didn't *I* think of that! I'll have a word with Jimmy Hill right away!' And he would have immediately forgotten all about the idea (as would the member of the board). But Michael was not like that; he had no smarm, was totally professional and he brushed off the director's request by pointing out that programme content was the responsibility of the Unit of Sport, thank you.

The board was mainly composed of professional financiers, courteous kindly men who were highly regarded pension-fund managers, building-society executives, a sugar magnate, a merchant banker, knowledgeable chaps in putting millions of pounds of people's savings to work but – whether or not to have more swimming on Saturday afternoon telly they were not in any way equipped to judge.

We met the senior members of the Independent Television Authority (now renamed the Independent Broadcasting Authority). Seeming not to know much about LWT's crisis, or even wanting to know much about it, we found the IBA massively unhelpful. Trying to persuade them into some kind of action was like pushing a finger into a lump of lard. When the finger was pulled out again there was no trace of the finger ever having been in there.

Was our present crisis really how the business world successfully operated? To we programme-makers, who had left good, well-paid jobs with the BBC and Granada for the excitement of starting up something new and ambitious with an ethic, LWT was *our* station.

Many, many BBC comedy series – from *Take It From Here* upwards – began badly with poor figures and a poor press, but were kept going by the BBC's faith in them, and many became successes. When we at LWT went on air some of our programmes disappointed the press, but might well have improved greatly if given the care and time that the BBC gave to nursing new shows. Most commercial television companies shortsightedly did not bother to do this. The accountants regarded new programmes with low initial viewing figures as financial losers to be chopped as quickly as possible.

We, the programme-makers, knew that our names were paraded at the IBA when the application was being submitted and that that was one of the reasons, even perhaps the major reason, why our group won the licence. Financial backing had been organized, a task in the days of 'licences to print money' about as difficult as organizing rabbits to become involved with a lettuce. In effect, the silken rope was lifted and a few privileged City men were permitted to scramble under it and grab a hunk of LWT's equity shares, an almost sure-fire investment.

Unbelievably to me, a total innocent in the business world, once the company was formed, *our* company we thought, it then belonged to the directors, who, it seemed to me, knew as much about running a television company as I knew about copper futures (promotion in the police force?). And they could do what they wished, sack our leader or any of us if the financial return was not swift and to their liking.

There was no contact at all between the board and the creative side of the company; the programme-makers were not represented on the board or even consulted by the board.

In a brilliant *aide-mémoire* written by Humphrey Burton, he summed up our attitude: the company was no longer the company we joined, its objectives were different and were not ours; we had lost all confidence in the board of directors, they had plenty of integrity and were kind to animals and all that, but they had no idea how to run a television company and no sense whatever of show business; it seemed to us that to many board members LWT was regarded as a prestige toy.

What could we do? We persuaded the board to meet us and discuss the crisis, and a sub-committee of directors, headed by the vice-chairman, Lord Campbell, came to Burlington Street.

Lord Campbell told us that in his experience all management was the same. 'You unit heads may think that managing talented producers and performers raises special problems,' he said, 'but I have been in sugar all my life and I can assure you that the management of people in television is precisely the same as the management of sugar workers.'

It was clear that no bridges were going to be built with him, so we tried yet again to find out why these people had chucked Michael.

Lord Campbell thought a bit. Then he turned to me and said, '*You* will know what I mean, Frank, when I say that he "lacks synthetical propensity".'

As it happened I did know what the line meant, but milord seemed so patronizing that I remained silent. If his assumption was that the other unit heads would never have heard of the phrase it was insufferably insulting.

The phrase came from a fairly well-known letter written by the Revd Sydney Smith to his co-founder of the *Edinburgh Review*, Francis Jeffrey. Jeffrey's literary reviews were growing increasingly crabby and vicious and Smith wrote urging him to make his criticism more constructive, and he accused Jeffrey of lacking 'synthetical propensity', i.e., the urge to build up rather than tear down (which is what the phrase means, I think. I must check with a sugar-cane cutter). Anyway, to accuse Michael Peacock of lacking ambition to build up his company and lead it forward would have been ludicrous.

Our group met later and discussed what we could possibly do to retain the old company; the unions met and over-whelmingly voted to retain the *status quo*, but without us getting some official backing from the IBA, which they were not prepared to give, our case was hopeless. So regretfully, and sorrowfully, we handed in our resignations.

The press had a field day. It was huge headline stuff (anything that happens backstage in television always is) and took up most of the front pages of the *Daily Mail* and the *Guardian*.

It was a horrible time. My unit begged me to stay and I had to say, 'You are children asking me not to leave you alone in the dark, but the roof's on fire.'

I found a copy of the prospectus I had written for our company's application for the LWT licence, a brief description of what I hoped the unit would achieve in comedy. I pinned it up on the unit's cardboard wall and wrote underneath:

And we did it.
Grateful thanks to you all.

I had to start thinking about what I was going to do about money. My shares in LWT would almost certainly mature at a huge profit, but I couldn't in all conscience resign on a matter of principle but keep the money. With a pang, I sold the shares back to the company at face value.

Both children were at fee-paying schools, the ancient matchwood farmhouse staircase at Anners was sagging with age and we had rather rashly gone heavily into expensive pine for a new staircase and new interior doors and fireplace. I had also ordered a new car.

When the papers reported that 'The Six' were being implored to stay, Jamie sent me a postcard. It was a reproduction of the colour painting of young Napoleon campaigning in Italy, heroically flourishing a banner in one hand and a pistol in the other. Jamie had superimposed a colour photograph of my face over Napoleon's. It came with the message, 'Don't weaken, Father'.

I talked it over with Polly, who was quite unfussed and insisted that I must do the work I wanted to do, not bust a gut in the wrong job.

The family's unanimous attitude was wonderfully encouraging and made me realize that, although being freelance must always be financially dodgy, real solid security lay in having a family like mine behind me.

I packed up my portable bar, swiped all the paper-clips, rubber bands and Biros in sight (real freelance behaviour), endured tearful farewells, made a statement to the press that I would now seek employment in some capacity which did not involve boards of directors, which seemed to boil down to the Methodist Church or burglary, and went home for ever.

A couple of days later Dr Margerison's secretary rang to ask would I come into Burlington Street, Dr Margerison wished to see me on an important matter.

With some trepidation I made the journey up to London wondering what on earth the new managing director wanted to see me about; the offer of a directorship? A highly paid job as his comedy consultant?

Tom was as gently amiable as ever. 'When the company started up', he said after some pleasant chit-chat about the traffic, 'you were lent a television set so that you could watch LWT programmes at home. May we have the set back, please?'

Months later Polly and I were flying to Paris where I was giving a speech and the deal included first-class air fares. In the departure area I saw one of the LWT directors, David Montagu the banker (now Lord Swaythling) and his very nice wife. David Montagu was clearly furious about something. He kept striding about and telephoning from the BA desk. I said to his wife, 'What's up with David?' She said, 'Oh, there's no room left in first class so he's been put into tourist – and he's a director of British Airways!'

I said, 'Tell him to loiter near the curtain and when we're airborne I'll pass him through a free glass of champagne.'

I spent the first weekend of freedom at home, theoretically researching for the book I was working on, but mostly just staring at the beautiful pine door and the new car (both as yet unpaid for), and doubting miserably whether after five years on the wrong side of a desk I was still employable as a writer.

On Monday morning the phone rang. It was Richard Lester, film director and friend whom I had last seen sitting rigid in my dressing room at *Call My Bluff* as I was carried out past him on a stretcher.

Dick had a feature-film script he was due to shoot for United

Artists, a very good adaptation by the playwright Charles Wood of the first of the *Flashman* novels, but Dick — and United Artists — wanted a funnier treatment.

Dick had read about the walkout at LWT. Would I do a quick rewrite of the script, beginning immediately?

Chapter 14

Harold Ross, founder/editor of the *New Yorker*, told his writers, 'If you can't be funny, be interesting.' So:

AN INTERESTING CHAPTER

Having a film script to work on urgently was the boost I needed when I reverted to being self-unemployed.

Richard Lester was stimulating to work for, laconic and funny. He knew exactly what he wanted and I spent quite a time driving swiftly to and from Twickenham Studios, mercifully only about twenty minutes from home, bearing the rewrite of a rewrite of a rewrite of a scene.

The character of Flashman, the bully boy of *Tom Brown's Schooldays*, later in life to have a highly successful public career in the Army whilst remaining in private a coward, bully and lecher, was the egregious anti-hero of George Macdonald Fraser's series of *Flashman* novels. Flashman seemed to me to be the perfect and timely alternative to James Bond.

Both Dick and I thought that John Alderton would make a terrific Flashman; he was young, tall, good-looking, rode well, was athletic and an excellent comedy actor.

United Artists in Hollywood had, of course, never heard of John, who had worked mainly in British television, so Dick had to shoot a screen test of John, who worked well, especially when the bed he was lying on in the scene collapsed and he ad libbed brilliantly in character. United Artists were quite happy to go along with John, and the script, when finished, was pronounced 'a knock-out' by somebody in far away sunny California.

A slight hitch came with a request from the United Artists' accountants to cut a million dollars from the production costs of the film. This seemed a lot of dollars to me, but Dick said the traditional way to soothe the accountants was to have the script retyped with much narrower margins and less space at the top and bottom, which would impressively reduce the number of pages. We did this and then met for a weekend at Dick's house in France and cut some scenes.

But it was the Alexei Kapler project all over again. Dick had found locations in Spain for the Afghanistan scenes and was on the point of casting when there was a 'palace revolution' at United Artists in Hollywood and the Head of Film Production, a great admirer of Dick's work, was promoted to running the company's chain of supermarkets or whatever and was replaced by the United Artists Head of Production in Britain, who did not like Dick's style at all. So off this executive went to Hollywood where one of his first moves was to cancel the *Flashman* film.

We were paid, of course, and I was not at all dismayed, in fact faintly relieved, because I had no real ambition to be involved in the movie world, I was far more interested in the book world. I think the unfortunate loser was John Alderton. If ever it was a case of the right actor finding the right part and then losing it through no fault of his own it was John. And there was a whole shelf of the superb *Flashman* novels as source material. Ah, well, that's show business. The wrong side of it.

Earlier, when Dick was still directing unconventional, quirky television comedy in England, mainly with Spike Milligan and Peter Sellers, Polly and I saw more of him and Deirdre. It had become traditional that I found 'openers' for the Thorpe village fête, which meant exerting moral blackmail on a star, and also from time to time thinking up a stunt as a surprise item for the fête.

I still had my sit-on Dennis motor-mower, so one year I decorated the huge grass box with military insignia and stencilled on it, 'MAX SPEED 40 M.P.H.' Comical friends decided it was a fair enough way of spending a June Saturday afternoon so 'army motor-mowing to the whistle' was demonstrated by an élite, drilled-to-a-hair squad, consisting of Michael Bentine, Clive Dunn (in a huge moustache and looking 104), Dick Emery (in drag as an ATS sergeant), and Dick Lester (in skid-lid and racing goggles) as the driver. I was dressed as a second lieutenant, so that I could tell them what to do next through a microphone.

An interesting point arose when I – illegally, the mower had not been licensed as a vehicle – drove the mower back home along Village Road, our main road. It was Ascot Gold Cup day and there was a steady stream of Daimlers full of punters being driven back to London. There, taking up a fair bit of the narrow road and having to be passed with care, was a regimental motor-mower being driven by a second lieutenant in the uniform of a Grenadier Guardsman. Nobody gave me a second glance.

That lack of curiosity about people behaving in a peculiar way was echoed later in France; again it concerned Dick Lester. I was taking part in a commercial for Hovis bread directed by Dick. The plot required me to be a cross-Channel swimmer (in a painful, woollen, Edwardian, knee-length costume which shrank a little at every wetting). In the commercial, when my swimming began to flag, a slice of buttered Hovis was fed to me on an oar and, revitalized, I struck out in a rapid crawl for the horizon. The next scene was in the public gardens on the Croisette at Cannes, in the South of France. There is a large fountain there in the middle of a round pond. I had to submerge myself completely in the pond, count to ten and then rise up, dripping, in my now almost obscene striped woollen costume, push up my goggles, look round me with amazement and then stride off in a purposeful English manner towards the town.

As I emerged from the water and looked round I saw that a few feet away from me was an elderly French gardener watering the shrubs with a hose. He glanced up at me. 'Bonjour,' he said. He did not give me a second glance.

The army motor-mowing wheeze was successful, so the following year we tried another. A kind friend lent us an ancient five-seater bicycle, so our demonstration that year was called *Z-Bikes* (which dates it). In the programme it claimed to be a demonstration of how new technology has been called into use by the modern constable to fight crime in our village if and when any should occur.

The five constables were played by Graham Stark, Peter Sellers, Bill Kerr, Bruce Lacey (eccentric artist, prop-maker and actor), Clive Dunn (looking 105) and, because Dick had just acquired a baby and would not be parted from it, Lester & Son. I was the inspector again, so that I could bawl at them and tell them what to do. It went well enough.

There was plenty of work about at this time, and being free-lance once again after the LWT débâcle meant that I could go back into *Call My Bluff*.

This time I was opposite Patrick Campbell, who hated losing and was jauntily smug when he won ('It's only a game, Frank, only a game, lad!'). Paddy was wonderful. His stammer was a bother to him – he was a natural talker – but when he unthinkingly embarked on a word beginning with an 's' and got stuck, he would rear up in his seat like an ostrich which had sat in something, eyes close together like a cuff link, and he would struggle until he had got the word out, banging the desk and muttering to himself, 'Come on! Come ON!'

Margaret Drabble said that Paddy was a great help to all stammerers because he displayed the mechanics of stammering and dared anyone to pity him.

When Paddy died he was replaced by Arthur Marshall, a cuddly old humorous writer and performer of great charm and intelligence. The producer instructed me to work up the same kind of steely animosity that Paddy and I enjoyed. Steely animosity with dear old Arthur? On his first show he lost five nil and was laughing so much that he couldn't say good night to the viewers.

My Word! and *My Music* were soldiering on. I also had a new BBC radio series, a programme which was a comedy anthology on a different subject each week, e.g., *Frank Muir Goes Into . . . Food*. The series, and the subsequent books, owed almost everything to our producer, now novelist Simon Brett. My co-star in the show, in fact he was the rest of the cast, was 'Alfredo', my very old friend from RAF Henlow's old time music hall, the multi-talented Alfred Marks.

A new kind of work which I enjoyed and which grew with the years was after-dinner speaking. The requirement was about thirty minutes of comedy material disguised as a speech. I soon found that I could use the same speech, with minor modifications, for all occasions. The trick was to avoid jokes; the audience might have heard them. My speech was lightly autobiographical and I had worked in a number of funny incidents based on real happenings. Such as the pig routine.

The pig was in all my speeches and it never failed in its long life. I worked it into a speech I made to the American Booksellers Association's annual conference when my first big book was published. It was in Chicago and the pig went wonderfully, so much so that I was invited back to Georgia a year or so later to make a speech at that year's ABA Conference banquet. Naturally I worked up a new speech. The committee was almost in tears afterwards. 'Why didn't you do the *pig*?' 'What happened to the *pig*?' It was a lesson that the familiar, even in comedy, can be more welcome than the new.

I have been telling the pig story for many years. When my son Jamie was still at school a long time ago he said to me, 'You're not *still* doing that old pig routine, are you?' Indeed I was – and was still doing it until quite recently, in all something like twenty-five years.

In case any reader should be fired with the need to know what this seemingly bullet-proof, humdinger of an anecdote story actually is, I will now tell it.

I first came across my pig – a true story – in a letter to a newspaper forty years ago. It was from a woman and I worked it into my speech as a useful example of how men underestimate women in areas where their macho instinct demands that they predominate. As in driving a car. A good man might admit, reluctantly, that his girlfriend or wife was quite a good driver; he might, in a warm moment, tell her that she was as good a driver as he. But how many of us are saintly enough to admit to our womenfolk that they are better, shrewder drivers than we are?

And yet, and yet.

I don't know how well you know St Anne's Hill in Surrey, whose sharp corners and gentle slopes (before the motorway was built) carried the motorist up from Thorpe and down into Chertsey, but I was taking that rural route one morning in my old, fifteenth-hand Lagonda. I was 'think' driving, driving idly well on my side of the road, hoping that a bright idea might alight like a mustard seed on the damp flannel of my brain, when round the corner ahead came a woman driver at speed, in a clapped-out, dented Morris Minor. She missed the wing of my beautiful Lagonda by a centimeter, wound down her window furiously and yelled at me, 'PIG!'

'Women drivers!' I snorted, drove on round the corner and hit a pig.

NB. Anybody using my pig story without saying where they got it from will be hounded through the law courts of Europe.

Working at home was wonderful. I had a study to work in and there was no dismal rush-hour driving. In the morning I just enjoyed a cup of coffee and a read of the papers and strolled to work through the drawing room at about nine thirty.

I am not sure that the arrangement was all that wonderful for Polly. When I started to live at home I was amazed that I knew so little of the busy constructive life she led, which over the years included doing the rounds with a trolley of Red Cross library books at St Peter's Hospital, Chertsey (fully experienced in hill starts and reversing solo through swing-doors), manning the phone as a Samaritan, acting as a dispatcher for the voluntary CARE organization, as well as enjoying classes in graphology and French literature. And now her leaf of lettuce and a yogurt at midday did not seem adequate for a male to share, so a tedious interruption to her busy activities in order to knock up a more substantial meal seemed inevitable.

This unfortunate turn of events was encapsulated in an old saying: 'I married him for better or for worse but not for lunch.'

According to Eric Partridge in his *Dictionary of Slang*, the phrase was popular with Australian wives when their sheep-shearing husbands retired. It was quoted, with less relevance perhaps, by the Duchess of Windsor in her autobiography, *The Heart Has Its Reasons*.

It seems to me that when we grow old, we either cannot be bothered much with food, or meals become the high points of our existence. I am a 'cannot be bothered' man, perhaps because I have a limited sense of taste and smell due to years of taking snuff and also having a colony of polyps resident in my nasal plumbing.

I gave up cigarettes and pipe for snuff quite easily after many years of smoking but snuff-taking brought its own problems. The good side of it was the beauty of snuffboxes themselves, particularly old ones, and the elegant, slightly theatrical routine of tapping the box, taking a pinch, sniffing it up and then lightly dusting the superfluous snuff off the nose with a spotted red handkerchief.

The bad side was that it was a filthy habit. What goes up must come down and the snuff was not absorbed by the nose but just hung in there for a while and then fell out over whatever lay beneath it, such as a clean shirt-front or a plateful of food or Polly being kissed good night. And if the snuffer wore a moustache, as I do, humiliation was inevitable. Snuff is tobacco leaves and stalks roasted until bone dry and brown and then milled into powder. And when the brown powder got into my moustache I could not entirely wash it out, so when I dried my face on a snow-white hotel towel, or snuggled down in bed amongst the sheets, traces were left. I reached the stage of not being able to stay in a hotel twice. I even thought seriously of ringing the offensive beige stains with a felt pen and writing, 'Actually, it's snuff.' But instead I gave it up.

My sense of taste and smell did not return, so Polly and I, for something like the last twenty-five years, have settled for the sort of simple lunches which we both really enjoy. Our favourites are a salad with the boscage wrenched up only minutes earlier from the kitchen garden, or slices from a fresh Hovis loaf toasted and buttered, a chunk of cheddar cheese and a jar of Polly's home-made marmalade.

I drool whilst writing this.

As Jamie and Sal were away at school so much and Pol and I had busy working lives, we relished our holidays. At first we all trailed off to Broadstairs where we had installed my mother in a bungalow, but after swimming in the waters of the Indian ocean at the temperature of warm milk, Polly found the grey and chilly sea and the boisterous bracing breezes of East Kent less than user-friendly.

Our next move was to take to the canals. There is quite a

choice of places to visit as there are about 2,000 miles of 'cuts' and most of them interconnect.

We caused to be built, with the help of a yacht mortgage, *Samanda*, who was 31 feet 6 inches long, the regulation 6 feet 10 inches wide, so that she could be manoeuvred in and out of narrow canal locks, and flat bottomed so that we could navigate almost anywhere where there were a few inches of water.

The five family summer holidays we enjoyed on *Samanda* were physically demanding yet refreshingly peaceful. There were the locks to work, frequently a strenuous job, but canal cruising would be boring without locks, and we glided through the backyards of towns and farms and the heart of the country-side, our metabolisms slowing as life itself slowed to a walking pace.

And we met canalside folk who are our friends still. We had to get a dud dynamo replaced, so we tied up for a few days at The Boat Inn, Gnosall, Staffs, kept by Stan and Ros Marshall. Stan's mother ran the inn when it was an overnight stopping place for working boats, a different kind of function from sell-ing a couple of shandies and a packet of cheese and onion crisps to townsfolk on a hire cruiser. One memorable night old Mrs Marshall heard banging and cursing and found the drunken crew of a narrow-boat trying to push their shire-horse up the narrow staircase to their bedroom.

Stan kept a parrot in a cage in an inner room. When Stan or Ros rapped sharply on the bar, a voice rang out, 'Cum in, ya booger!' When the bird was asked his name he piped up, cheerfully, 'Tommy Tight-Arse!' What with the parrot for conversation and Ros's home-made pickled onions to crunch upon – possibly the best pickled onions in the world – they were great evenings.

What finally drove us away from canal holidays was the un-certainty of the weather. Rain and cold winds did not bother Polly and me all that much, we put on more clothes, and any-way the boat was worked from a centre cockpit which had a moveable roof and side curtains, but it was tough on Jamie and Sal who had nothing much to do except punch each other in their tiny cabin up front.

When the rain was falling drearily and we were chugging

our way through Birmingham, trying to avoid the submerged boughs of trees, the bloated bodies of dogs and sheep, we felt our family holiday was being spent not so much messing about in boats as boating about in mess.

The fates once again smiled upon us. Denis and I were taken briefly rich by appearing in a television commercial for Mackeson's milk stout and I decided to blow the lot on taking the family for a month's summer holiday in a Mediterranean hotel, with a hire car, after which I would cease to be even slightly rich. We chose Corsica as I had been there briefly the year before as the captain's guest on a Royal Navy destroyer (that's the way to travel) and I liked Corsica a lot; a violent but oddly heart-warming history, granite mountains, ancient hill villages, and away from the beaches it is almost uninhabited.

The hotel was on a rock in the port of L'Ile-Rousse on the north-west coast, and from the hotel we had a good view of the medieval villages of Monticello and Santa Reparata which, like most Corsican hill villages, clung a prudent 600 feet or so up the mountainside to give the villagers a head start when the Corsairs and Saracen pirates came raiding.

We were on the beach or in the sea most of the day, but when it began to grow cool in the early evening we took to driving up to Monticello and having a drink in the bar of its small hotel. This had just been converted into a hotel from two or three houses on the square and was owned and run by the Martini family, whose real work up to then had been milking their *troupeau* of sheep to be made into Roquefort cheese.

Polly and I were much taken with the Martini family and Corsica and the little stone village of Monticello, so when the Martinis invited us to the *langouste* lunch celebrating the official opening of their Hôtel A Pastorella, and we found a sign in front of a house across the square reading, '*A VENDRE*', we asked if we could look round. Fatal, of course.

Very few houses in Corsican hill villages stand apart from their neighbours, the general impression is of a congealed bag of boiled sweets. The property for sale was called A Torra ('the tower') and belonged to Pierre Martini and his wife, who had put together some ancient semi-ruins, including the top of a medieval watchtower, to make up a self-contained dwelling.

The entrance on the *place* was by a wrought-iron gate, beyond which were forty high stone steps each of which seemed to grow higher every year.

There was a Parisian family, the Gustins, staying at the same hotel as us down in the port. They were very chic, with a holiday house in St Tropez, and we proudly showed Madame Gustin round A Torra to see whether she agreed with us what wonderful potential it had.

Unfortunately, running water had only just come to the village and A Torra's drain was connected to the main drains at the bottom but open at the top, waiting for a bath or a loo or something to be installed over it. It had a bit of rag stuffed in it to shield us from the smell of the main village sewers. It was not an efficient shield.

Hurrying Mme Gustin through the noxious area we saw her looking disapprovingly at the not-very-even cemented floors which had been painted with cardinal-red paint. 'How much are they asking for this, this . . .?' said Madame Gustin, hanky to nose. We told her. It proved to be almost exactly what we got from selling our canal boat.

'Much too much for Corsica!' cried Madame Gustin, forcefully. 'I could buy a tiny place in St Tropez for that sort of money!'

In reply, Polly opened the far door. Beyond it was a small ancient stone bridge which led to the tower. We walked through. The tower room had black and white tiles and a vaulted ceiling. Then we walked out onto the little balcony and looked down 600 feet to the port of L'Ile-Rousse and the impossibly blue Mediterranean.

'Take it!' said Madame Gustin (in French).

We took A Torra over thirty years ago and have been back every year. Jamie and Sally went there first as schoolchildren and now go as parents. The village has only one shop, a grocery and 'everything' store kept by ample Janine Canava, and the hotel has been added to and improved and is now popular with English tourists with its busy bar and impressive menu. The English are liked as guests as they are grateful for everything, especially the food, unlike the French on holiday from the Continent who tend to count the chips.

There was a fair amount of work to be done every holiday. The tower ceiling was high up and vaulted to make redecorating a stimulating challenge in the middle of a heatwave. It was painted with a very French, very white emulsion paint called Vinyl-Soixante. When this stuff was attacked from the rear by damp seeping through the stone walls, the paint gently buckled, flaked and came away in beige petals so fine that they clung to clothes and skin and refused to be brushed off.

The lady in the house below us was Dutch and was most helpful in our many crises, except that her English, though charming, was rather opaque. She caught us lunging at the ceiling with putty knives lashed to broomsticks.

'Stop!' she cried. 'I haf a stepcase in my cello!'

True enough, she did have a stepcase (stepladder) in her cello (cellar) and she lent it to us, which was a help. But getting rid of the fine flakes of paint from ourselves was quite a problem. Polly took to wearing a paper bag on her head and a strange tent-like garment which she had made to change beneath on the beach. I worked naked, except for a plastic shower hat nicked from a hotel (the only use I have ever found for those little elasticated bonnets).

We have many good memories of those early years in Corsica, such as Sally meeting an English girl on the beach and finding that they were both about to go to the same school; going on a quick tour and finding that we would rather be in Monticello than anywhere else on the island; Jamie having a sword fight down in the *place* with a small Corsican boy who lost his temper and screamed at Jamie, '*Merde! Merde!*' And Jamie replying coldly and loudly, 'Cow-shit, cow-shit.'

And in with all these we have one particular memory to be cherished. It was during that baking-hot June holiday which Polly and I spent scraping the tower ceiling. It was not the scraping we look back on with affection, it was the golden hour in the evening when the sun was still warm. We took glasses of wine out onto the terrace, lay down on our mattresses and, like a couple of old bonded gorillas, groomed each other, intently easing off with chisels the delicate flakes of old Vinyl Soixante still sticking to our salient features.

★   ★   ★

My first close encounter with the book world, in which I was really interested, came when the publisher Geoffrey Strachan of Methuen took Paddy Campbell and me to lunch (which resulted in the quenelles episode reported for posterity in chapter five). The purpose of the lunch was to get us to write a book version of *Call My Bluff*. Geoffrey also asked us to illustrate our definitions, an interesting suggestion as we did not know how to draw. But incompetence had never held either of us back from accepting an offer of gainful employment so we signed on.

It was quite a short book dealing with just one word per page, with three paragraph-long definitions of it illustrated on the opposite page. Paddy stayed with us at Anners for a week while he and I worked on the book. We immediately settled into a steady routine.

We would start work about half-past nine. About eleven, Paddy would get a bit restive and would say, 'If you happen to have a bottle of champagne in the fridge, don't you think a wee glass each would speed the prose? One glass each should be quite enough to do the trick.' So we had just one glass of champagne.

About half-past twelve Paddy would be overcome with the need for a Bloody Mary – just one. Then we had lunch, a piece of fish helped down by a glass or two of Chablis. We worked in the afternoon until about six when Paddy had another Bloody Mary or two, a bath, then we had supper with an accompanying bottle of red, followed by a sprightly evening of conversation from Paddy with the whisky bottle by his elbow.

By the end of the week I was white and shaking and felt that I had donated my liver to literature, but Paddy was serene and cheerful. He did not binge but drank a fairly large amount in a steady but entirely civilized fashion. In all the years I knew him I never saw him even the slightest bit squiffy.

What a week that was. The book did quite well, too.

My work on the 'Big Book' had gone beyond the enjoyable research, and I now had to buckle down and write the thing between all the other briefer commitments, like writing a book about Christmas with (in fact almost wholly by) my son Jamie, who had just got his degree at London University and was, by profession, unemployed. And Polly and I had persuaded some very good writers and illustrators to contribute to a children's anthology of new work we were putting together for Heinemann called *The Big Dipper*.

I called my major project the 'Big Book' because it was a substantial volume, the first original book I had written, rather than one inspired by, or looted from, one of my radio or TV series, and it took me five years to write.

There was at the time, and probably still is, a dining club consisting of very important people; owners of newspapers, advertising tycoons, media millionaires, chaps of that speed, who met regularly for dinner at Claridges. It was just before Christmas and the honorary secretary of the club, a publisher named Timothy Benn, asked me to make the club's pre-Christmas dinner a howling success by honouring them with an after-dinner speech. He spoke like that; he had enormous enthusiasm and gave the impression of a man who got to his office early in the morning, pinned himself to the wall, span round like a Catherine wheel giving off sparks until 6.30 p.m., and then unpinned himself and went home. He was a very nice man.

Claridges! Media tycoons! I worked hard polishing up the old speech, honing every little routine, positioning my pig in exactly the right place, making the whole thing smarter, slicker, suave.

It went very well. Feeling rather pleased with myself, I was making a move to go home when Timothy Benn shot over, beaming with delight, shook my hand vigorously muttering, 'That was wonderful! Great! Superb! Thank you so much!' He drew me to him, went on tiptoes to get near an ear (he is not a tall man), and said, 'Your speech – I hadn't realized that you talk so *simply*.'

I restrained the impulse to maim him.

He went on, 'A *child* could understand your every *word*! Have you ever thought of writing a children's book?'

I had never thought of doing so because I knew it was a highly specialized area of writing of which I knew nothing, but over the following few weeks Timothy Benn was so keen on the idea that my only way of stopping him fizzing with excitement down the phone every hour was to give in and write him one as swiftly as possible.

I always found with my stories on *My Word!* that those based on truth, however faintly, worked better for me than stories which were wholly inventions, and as I had told a great many stories based on the behaviour over the years of our various cats and dogs, I decided to have a go at writing Ernest Benn Ltd a story about our latest problem animal, an Afghan puppy that was the scruffiest of a litter which had arrived a few months earlier in the space under the stairs.

Afghan puppies are not quite what they seem. An adult Afghan is a very handsome dog, like a greyhound in a fun fur. This fun fur is about two sizes too big, so when an Afghan breaks into a run its body travels about 6 inches before the fun fur starts on its way, which results in a beautiful rippling motion of the silken coat.

But Afghan puppies do not look like Afghans until they are the equivalent of teenagers, they are very woolly and their puppy coats collect a great deal of assorted debris. They are almost impossible to train as, affectionate as they are most of the time, they are not afraid of you, nor do they particularly want you to pat them and coo over them, so it is very rare indeed to see an Afghan puppy – or even a senior Afghan – walking in public beside its owner without being on a lead.

A bitch's pleasure is to pee on the lawn and kill huge circles of grass; a male Afghan's aim in life is to jump over the gate and find out what's happening on the far side of the world.

One lady in the village who owned a male Afghan was telephoned one mid-morning: 'Are you the owner of a cream Afghan hound?' asked a voice. 'Yes,' said the lady, 'why?' 'This is the signalman at Sunningdale railway station speaking, madam. Your dog is at this moment preceding the eleven fifteen on the down-line to Guildford.'

I gave my fictional puppy the noble pedigree name of Prince Amir of Kinjan, but because he was so scruffy, everybody on seeing him said, 'What a mess!' so he thought that What-a-Mess was his real name.

Timothy Benn spent many months trying to find the right illustrator. It seemed that illustrators who could draw well rarely had much humour and those with humour could not draw. Then one afternoon Timmy rang and said, 'May I come down and see you?'

He arrived, bursting with excitement. 'I'll say nothing,' he said, and with a flourish opened up a folder of drawings. And there *was* What-a-Mess. Exactly right, smiling engagingly as though he was as beautiful as his mother, his coat a refuge for rose clippings, bits of eggshell, paint, compost and a small duck resident on top of his head. The artist was the wonderful Joe Wright, a gentle giant of a man who drew a vigorous comic line and crammed every picture with inventive detail.

Joe and I produced seventeen *What-a-Mess* books which three times became TV cartoon films, one of them made in Hollywood. The books were translated into fourteen languages and it was interesting to see how the various translators coped with the difficult job of translating the name 'What-a-Mess'. Some examples:

WEST GERMANY:	O-Schreck-lass nach
NETHERLANDS:	Wat-een-Troep
SOUTH AFRICA:	Bollie-Blaps
FRANCE (BRILLIANT):	Okeloreurrr!

I am not equipped to comment on how well the Japanese and Israeli translators managed.

1974 was our silver wedding anniversary and Polly and I decided to celebrate it by spending a whole month on the island of Mauritius, where Polly was born and to which she had never returned since coming to England at the age of twelve.

Mauritius is one of those islands, like Fernando Po, which most Britishers have heard of but few can point to on a map with one confident stab of the forefinger. The island is about the size of our own dear Isle of Wight, lies in the Indian Ocean, a whisker inside the tropic of Capricorn and an inch and a third to the right of Madagascar (ref: *Philips Modern School Atlas*).

The staple crop of Mauritius was sugar and the 8-feet-tall sugar canes seemed to cover the whole island except for some of the main roads and the middle of the airport runway.

343

There were only one or two hotels on the whole island then (the beaches are lined with hotels now). We booked a package tour to the Troux au Biches, a beach hotel of thatched bungalows. It featured a kind of semi-self-service; guests occupied a bungalow with a bedroom and a kitchen, which had a few cooking facilities and a great many cockroaches and ants. There was a shop where food could be bought and taken back to the bungalows and cooked up for lunch (and shared with the bungalow wildlife). The hotel provided a proper dinner in the restaurant but, perhaps to make us Brits feel at home, although we were in the middle of the Indian Ocean, the menu did not offer curries and mangoes and paw paws and fresh pineapples but roast lamb and two veg.

Polly had no relations left on the island and most old family friends had retired to England, but enough were left to feed us some wonderful curries and generally mark our cards. Perhaps worse than the shortage of hotels was an almost total lack of independent restaurants. The answer for having lunch out, we were advised by Polly's old friends, was to make for a Caltex petrol station, most of which had a perfectly good restaurant round the back.

At the beginning we hired a car and whizzed ourselves about the island, but driving inland was a bit overexciting. Villages of sugar-workers had grown up alongside the roads and on hot nights the whole village population, in pitch-black clothes, played cards, gossiped, ate, practised football, took a siesta, repaired the car and meditated, all in the middle of the road.

Other driving hazards included just missing a goat sitting placidly in the middle of the highway from the capital Port Louis steadily eating its way through a newspaper; a large lorry with a happy grinning worker sitting on the tailboard straphanging from the tail of a cow; bullock carts of cut sugar cane suddenly crossing the road ahead at a speed of 0.5 m.p.h., and tiny Honda motorcycles putter-puttering along the road, ridden by small entrepreneurs in large crash helmets, laden with wares for sale such as iron pots and pans, blankets, a guitar, a mattress, and also, usually, a large glass display cabinet roped sideways to the carrier, full of necklaces and earrings on cards.

We found that owing to a hiccup in the economy it was

cheaper to hire one of the cars outside the hotel complete with its owner/driver than rent a self-drive car. But that facility, too, presented the occasional problem.

It was dusk and we were going to have dinner with friends in the small town of Curepipe. We climbed into the taxi/car and the driver asked us very politely if he could stop at his village *en route* to collect something. The something turned out to be a huge torch, and as the sun sank, the necessity for the torch became apparent: when he braked all the car's lights went out. Undismayed, he shone his torch through the windscreen and accelerated out of danger.

What did not help to soothe his increasingly nervous passengers was a large and pretty green and red toy parrot which dangled from the driving mirror. When the direction indicator was operated the parrot's relevant eye lit up and blinded the driver.

It was a wonderful month. We went up to the teak and ebony forest, happened upon a colourful and impressive Hindu Ceremony of Light at the huge lake of Grand Bassin. We walked along the beach when the tropical sunset so swiftly arrived; one moment the sun would be shining, the next moment it would be setting, all pinks and mauves, behind the range of extinct volcanoes; the next moment – darkness.

The return to Mauritius was a little bitter-sweet for Polly; much had changed, inevitably, and did not match her child-hood memories. But it was exciting to go back; there were old friends still there and the island was so beautiful anyway that it made for a superb celebratory holiday.

The second half of the Seventies proved to be a busy demi-decade. I was invited to be President of the Johnson Society, Lichfield, for 1975–1976. There were no time-consuming duties attached, but a presidential address had to be written on an aspect of Samuel Johnson and delivered at the society's annual banquet in the Guildhall at Johnson's home town of Lichfield.

The theme of my paper, 'Samuel Johnson and his Search for the Wild Guffaw', was that letters from his friends showed that Sam Johnson was a much funnier and jollier man than

Boswell's biography allowed him to be, and he had a nice touch of irony (when a silly young man tried to impress Johnson by claiming that he had, alas, lost all his command of the Greek language, Johnson nodded in sympathy and said, 'I believe it happened at the same time, sir, that I lost all my large estate in Yorkshire.' And when Adam Smith overdid his praise of the beauties of Glasgow, Johnson interrupted him with, 'Pray, sir, have you ever seen Brentford?').

But a sense of humour only became a desirable quality in modern times. In Johnson's eighteenth century a gentleman could pee on the lawn, salute a gentleman friend with a kiss, cry in public, but it was vulgar and simply not done to be seen laughing heartily. Swift proudly stated he had only laughed twice in his life, Lord Chesterfield warned his son, 'Frequent laughter is the characteristic of folly and ill-manners,' and Alexander Pope claimed he had never laughed in his life. Plays and books of the time went in for 'sentimental comedy', which was genteel and called not for a healthy guffaw, but for what the poet Robert Southey called 'a silent and transient simper'.

Boswell almost certainly suppressed the playful joking side of Johnson's nature because he knew his hero would be regarded by eighteenth-century society as having a serious character defect.

The audience at the Guildhall listened to me in silent and transient boredom, but the paper was printed in the society's *Transactions* and it was read by members all over the world, provoking some lively letters.

A little earlier, my working life was changed by a lurch in yet another direction: backwards; that is to say back to performing rather than writing. Michael Elliott, the theatre director, was the driving force behind a new theatre-in-the-round being erected inside the great Cotton Hall of the old Manchester Exchange. To raise funds to complete this, his (and my dear and good) friend Michael Meyer had put together a funny but informative anthology of acting and theatrical history entitled *Rogues and Vagabonds*, which was to be given a reading at the Old Vic Theatre, London, in June 1975. They had assembled a terrific cast, Edith Evans, Wendy Hiller, Polly James, Edward Fox, Tom Courtenay, Albert Finney, with Michael Flanders as compère. I was asked to join the team to read some of the comical bits.

At the rehearsal, still an uncured ham as far as theatrical appearances were concerned, I flung myself into my bits and gave them my all. After a few minutes Michael Elliott took me aside out of hearing of the others.

'You're *acting*!' he said. 'I don't advise it.'

'But . . .' I said, 'surely . . .?'

'No, please don't *act*,' he said. 'Get the feel of the character, make yourself familiar with the lines and then just *say* them. The audience will do the rest of the work.'

Wonderful advice to an enthusiastic overactor.

Then a few days before the show was due to go on, Michael Flanders died. I admired his work enormously, I think he was one of our best light lyricists, but I did not know him personally. As the show now had nobody to do the linking, the two Michaels asked me to take it on as well as non-acting my acting bits. I was happy to do the compèring as I enjoyed semi ad libbing appearances.

The Old Vic was full on the night. It turned out to be Edith Evans's last public performance, and what a performance she gave, playing the pioneer feminist Millamant to Edward Fox's Mirabell in the famous my-conditions-for-marriage scene from *The Way of the World*.

In the Green Room where we all gathered before the show, Edith Evans said to Michael Elliott in that wonderful voice, indicating us, 'Are all these people going to be on the stage while I am acting?'

'Yes,' said Michael.

'Oh, dear!' said Edith Evans.

When she and Edward Fox stood up to play their scene, she went forward and explained to the audience, 'The part I am about to play is Millamant, who is very young and very pretty. I am neither of those things.' Then she began the scene and Edith Evans became before our eyes both of those things. Almost as soon as the little, very old lady in her pink, nightdress-like garment stood up, glared at her lover Mirabell and started putting him in his place, she completely changed into a strong-willed, beautiful girl in her twenties. Magic.

Then a BBC arts programme came up with an irresistible offer. They wanted me to go to America and film three one-hour conversations with the last surviving three great American comedians: Groucho Marx, Jack Benny and Bob Hope. The notion was to discuss with them professional matters of comedy and their formative experiences.

The first programme was to explore the comic genius of Groucho Marx. Before flying off into the great blue yonder I phoned Kenneth Tynan who had worked with Groucho. He said that Groucho loved singing and it was a good way to relax him.

The producer and I took Groucho to dinner at Sardi's restaurant to find out his speed of talking, etc., and to establish what rapport we could for the following day's shoot.

Groucho wore a houndstooth-patterned raincoat and a navy-blue beret throughout the meal, in fact every time we met him. We ate soft-shelled crabs (a mistake), and afterwards I jollied Groucho into singing. He gave us his version of Will Fyffe singing 'Roamin in the Gloamin'. He had toured England's music halls with Will Fyffe back in the mists of time.

Then we got on to Gilbert and Sullivan and Groucho really began to enjoy himself. Spurred on by me he gave the diners at Sardi's his fine, stirring and surprisingly loud version of 'A Wandering Minstrel I'. By the time we had demolished between us 'Poor Wandering One' and 'Three Little Maids From School Are We', the other diners were applauding and the drunks were singing along with us.

The BBC had hired a suite at the Hilton for the recording and had booked in a New York camera crew to film the show. Groucho arrived (a tiny figure, still in his raincoat and beret) and we and the crew crammed into the lift. There was a young secretary there, and on the way up Groucho gave his famous leer and said to her, 'I like your tits.' She was horribly embarrassed. The crew went wild with excitement. 'Ain't Grouch the wittiest!?' said a crew member, pummelling my arm. 'Well, no,' I said, 'not on present form he isn't.'

It was a difficult interview. My inexperience as an interviewer – a subtler craft than it looks – didn't help, and Groucho was not at all interested in talking about the Marx Brothers or comedy. At one point he admitted that he would have switched to making raincoats if there were more money in it.

During the interview, moments of real charm did break through and he made one or two very quick and funny ripostes, but on the whole he relied on his one great Groucho trick, which was to take one's breath away (as he did to the girl in the lift) with remarks of numbing effrontery.

He suddenly said to me on camera when I was asking him about the old days of Hollywood, 'Nelson Eddy was a homosexual, did you know that? Everybody thought he was laying Jeanette MacDonald, but he was a homosexual, and she was a lesbian.'

Groucho wore thick spectacles which were also hearing aids. His red-haired girlfriend/manager took him off to the loo when there was a break to load film and gave him one of his pills. He returned with a springier step and was sparkling for a few minutes before gradually slumping again until it was time to load another film into the camera and another pill into Groucho. We ended up with two hours of filmed interview from which the producer just managed to put together an *Omnibus* programme. But only just.

We had left the whole project about ten years too late, the three old boys were too rich and successful. And private. American showbiz stars had their personal stock of oft-used, safe comical anecdotes which their chat-show hosts were expected to trigger off; the great comics didn't want the boat rocked by having to talk seriously about their work.

After the filming, we were walking the frail figure of Groucho through the foyer of the New York Hilton towards the limo when he suddenly stopped. He looked up at me and said in his gentle slow voice, 'Nelson Eddy wasn't a homosexual, and Jeanette wasn't a lesbian. I think they were a little in love with each other. Now what made me say that?'

Well, yes. Quite.

My Big Book was due to be published in 1976 and I had severe title trouble. The book was a social history of six subjects: music, food and drink, education, literature, theatre and art, from the early Greek to modern times, heavily illustrated by quotations from citizens who were alive at the time and did not like what was going on. This, I hoped, made for a lively and informative book which was also funny.

But what to call it? I thought of *Pieces of Hate*, but then discovered that the title had already been used for a collection of theatre reviews by the American critic George Jean Nathan. Eventually, in despair, Roland Gant of Heinemann and I settled on a feeble and embarrassing main title with a subtitle to do the real work, so the book was published as *The Frank Muir Book: An Irreverent Companion to Social History*.

The publication of the book in South Africa, Australia, New Zealand and the USA before it was published in Britain meant a great deal of global dashing about; personal appearances, bookshop signing sessions, literary lunches and radio and TV interviews throughout 1976. Then in the late Seventies and early Eighties I had more books published which meant more tours. As I have done so much of this author-touring game, I consider myself something of an authority on it.

It is at least a differently daunting experience from writing. I met Kingsley Amis on a train once coming from a book signing and he told me he looked upon it with pleasure as a day off without guilt. So if the saying is true (and I hope to heaven it isn't) that everybody has a book in them, then the following notes on how to survive your own tour might prove helpful.

Very few literary lunches are really literary, most are just social. A bookshop chain or local newspaper might set up a series of literary lunches in a town. They do a deal with a local hotel to provide lunch for £15 a head and start selling tickets for £20 a head. There will be a few genuine book buyers, but many of the tickets are taken up for corporate entertaining; the Midland Bank would probably take a table for ten of its good customers, and so on.

The publicity departments of publishers would be contacted for the free entertainment, a ten-minute speech from you and perhaps up to three more authors who also have a book out. After you have made your ten-minute speech – and try to make it friendly, domestic and jolly; the less literary the better – the authors are shown into another room with desks for them to sit at and a pile of their books to dedicate to eager buyers.

You will find that none of the ladies who queue up for your book wants to read it, it's to give to somebody else. 'Will you please make it out to Mavis on her dread fortieth, with warmest regards from Aunty.' There is always one author who has nobody forming a queue and just sits there, fiddling with his Biro in lonely humiliation.

The classic signing-session story is of Monica Dickens in a bookshop in Sydney, Australia. A lady picked up a copy of the book, peered at it and handed it to Monica who opened it, fountain pen poised over the title page.

'May I dedicate it to someone?' Monica asked, as usual.

'Emma Chisset,' said the lady.

'Is Chisset spelled with a double "s"?' asked Monica.

The lady looked puzzled. 'Emmuch *iss* it?'

Light dawned. 'Thirty-two Australian dollars,' said Monica.

No sale for Monica but a story which has become a book-publicity legend.

And there will be a certain amount of signing autograph books to be done. Try and sit down for this with the book resting on a surface so that the signature does not come out like Guy Fawkes's after torture.

The collecting of signatures has always seemed to me to be an odd hobby, a kind of celebrity version of train-spotting. To what use can the collection be put? What happens to all those scrawled names, mostly illegible, which were written standing up with the writing arm being jogged by other collectors, often in pouring rain? Such is fame that after a few years, months even, the legible names attract the comment, 'Who on earth was he?'

A cautionary word. I was once doing a book-signing session in Leeds. The large bookshop had been constructed from three old Georgian houses knocked through, which meant that the shop was actually a warren of tiny rooms. I was stuck up on the third floor with a pile of books and a Biro, and nobody knew I was there.

Every ten minutes or so a girl's voice was heard on a very crackly Tannoy system saying, helpfully, 'Mr Frank Murr is in room (CRACKLE) on the (CRACKLE) floor signing copies of his book *The* (CRACKLE) *Book; an Irreverent Companion to Social* (CRACKLE). Thank yew.'

My loneliness was relieved from time to time by the head of a lost book-lover peering round the door. 'Birthday cards?'

'Ground floor, back of the shop.'

'Cheers.'

Or, 'Occult?'

'Two floors down. Through Gardening and turn right.'

'Cheers.'

Then a lady towing a tartan shopping trolley trundled in, realized there was no through door and trundled out again. There was a pause and then, as in a cartoon film, she slowly backed back into the room, peering at me.

'You're, er, you know, what's-his-name on the telly, aren't you?' she said.

'I have that honour,' I said.

She fumbled in her handbag and produced a ballpoint pen. 'Would you?' she said.

For the first time that morning I joyfully reached for a copy of my book.

'No, no,' she said. 'I can't afford those things, I just come in to see my friend on the till. Just sign a bit of paper for me, luv, that'll do nicely.'

I searched my desk and pockets and my fan searched her handbag, but neither of us had a bit of paper.

She rummaged in her tartan shopping trolley and triumphantly produced a half-pound packet of Anchor butter. 'There you are!' she said. 'Would you make it out to Mrs Potter?'

Nota bene: It is not possible to autograph half a pound of butter with a ballpoint pen, it merely makes a dent in the shape of your name. I suppose that when she arrived home Mrs Potter could have poured molten lead into the dent, cast my signature in hot metal and printed from that, but it would not have done the butter much good.

Denis had an experience in Bond Street which further demonstrated how baffling is the behaviour of autographarazzi. Denis was stopped outside Aeolian Hall by a young woman proffering a shiny autograph album and a pen.

'Would you, for my daughter?' she said (a question which Denis has always enjoyed).

He took the book and the pen, and while he was writing a friendly message the lady chatted away. 'My daughter loves your show,' she said. 'She's very good at guessing which is a bluff and which is true.'

Denis stopped writing.

'You've got the wrong one,' he said. 'You want Frank Muir. I'm Denis Norden.'

The lady went thoughtful for a moment and then said, 'Well, you might as well carry on signing. She can't read yet.'

The most enjoyable time I had on my author tour of *The Frank Muir Book* was when I was driven from one session to another by Heinemann's publicity director, Nigel Hollis, and he and his wife Sarah very soon became close friends.

It was somehow good fun being driven by Nigel up the M6 in belting rain, squeezed between a coach doing 90 m.p.h. marked 'REGAL LUXURY COACHES – Edinburgh to London – £2.40 Return with toilet', and a vehicle marked 'SCHWEINHUNDBLASTEDROTTENTRANSPORT-GEFUNKEN – HAMBURG'. Nigel seemed to know all about the great houses up on the hills and who lived in them and was totally incapable of being boring about anything.

Tragically, Nige died in his mid-forties. He was a modest man ('I was the worst scholar Balliol ever had.') but in fact he was highly intelligent, had an inquisitive and witty mind and I still miss him very much.

My first coast-to-coast author tour in America, without Nige and all on my own, was rather different. The book had been bought by Stein and Day, good, small, literary publishers but, I later learned, having cash-flow problems.

In a brief but moving ceremony at the Gotham Hotel, New York, I was handed a batch of internal airline tickets; an itinerary which listed which cities, hotels, bookshops and radio and TV studios I was to get myself to, and when; a considerably slimmer wad of dollar bills for taxis and dinners (the itinerary did not allow for lunch) and a genial handshake, all from very likeable Sol Stein.

I glanced through page one of the itinerary and then shot down to the bar and had a swift beer. Page one was a list of commitments for the first day of the tour, Milwaukee. It began with a television interview at 6.45 a.m. (not my time of day at all). Then came a dash across town for a radio programme, then a visit to a downtown bookshop, a live television discussion programme (about American politics) from 11.15 a.m. to 12.30 p.m., another radio interview at 1.15 p.m. (in depth, the itinerary said: a lie), an interview with the *Milwaukee Journal's* columnist at 2.15 p.m., signings at three more bookshops and take-off for Minneapolis at 6.55 p.m. I was delighted to note that my first engagement the following morning in Minneapolis was a radio programme at the ludicrously late hour of 7.45 a.m.

In twenty working days I survived seventeen newspaper interviews, twenty-nine radio programmes, twenty television appearances, fourteen bookshop signing sessions and an after-dinner speech to the American Booksellers' Association (as already noted *re* pig story) in Chicago.

Most of the Midwest lunchtime radio and TV hostesses were either important local matrons without a nerve in their body who resembled wealthy prison visitors, or nervous ex-actresses looking like retired hookers who crouched behind their make-up smiling fiercely at nothing in particular. During the whole tour, some of the researchers had read the book but none of the interviewers, with the honourable exception of the lady on *Good-Morning America* back in New York.

The feminine radio interviewers ranged from an incredibly beautiful Norwegian girl in Cincinnati, who was so intelligent and humourless that she treated everything I said as the babblings of a problem child, to a very funny and massive black lady in Chicago who wore a long black dress with *Dallas*-width shoulder pads and a mass of frizzy hair dyed beige. It was during a heatwave and as she floated down the corridor towards me, shimmering in the heat like Omar Sharif approaching on his horse in *Lawrence of Arabia*, she looked like a beautiful pint of draught Guinness. But a great interviewer.

My problem with most of the male radio interviewers was trying to get a word in edgeways. 'May I ask, sir, how you came to write this thoughtful and fascinating book?' 'Well, I have an interest in social history which—' 'Well, how about that! I majored in history and I have always thought . . .' (fourteen minutes).

One man in a small Los Angeles local radio station interviewed me for an hour and a half during which I failed to complete a sentence. When the red light went out to signal the end of the ordeal, he wrung my hand, his eyes damp with emotion, and swore that it was the most gracious interview he had ever conducted (what *do* Americans mean by 'gracious'?).

An all too important element of my author tour was taxi cabs. In New York most cabs were yellow and all were dented. Just before my first visit the cabs had been adapted to make the driver less open to being bopped on the head by a social malcontent. The protective device was a bullet-proof steel mesh which took up much of the space previously occupied by the passenger, so anybody taller than 5 feet (and I am 6 feet something) had to fold up on the back seat in a foetal crouch.

New York cabbies are inquisitive ('You're foreign, ain't ya?' one said to me. 'You French?'), and much time, when not spent curled up, was spent kneeling painfully on the coconut matting talking to the driver through his square of steel mesh. It was like riding around New York in a very expensive mobile confessional.

Perhaps the worst aspect of the tour, but one which I solved rather brilliantly I thought, was the problem of personal laundry. None of the hotels in my itinerary had enough stars to guarantee that a suit would be pressed, or a shirt washed, overnight, so I bought a tiny travelling iron and a packet of detergent and worked out a system.

The problem with washing small clothes in the bedroom was that the plugs in American hotel washbasins were not made of rubber but metal and they did not seat properly, so my suds slid down the drain before I had begun.

My method was as follows. In America, bathroom wastepaper bins were made of white plastic and were watertight. So my routine (which rapidly became an obsession, but an obsession can be a comfort when you are travelling alone) went thus. All internal flights in America seemed to take an hour, so I booked into the hotel usually at about eight in the evening, exhausted and crumpled after a long day's work in the previous town and too tired to eat in the hotel restaurant.

Most American restaurants equated chic with darkness, so

not only did I usually measure my length on the carpet on the way to the bar, which had a step round it which I could not see, but I also could not see the other diners, if any, or the food. Nor could I read the metre-square glossy menu once brandished at me in the gloom by a giant blond Swedish student who said, 'Hi, I'm Carl, your host for the evening,' and disappeared into the darkness never to return. So I always went straight up to my room and rang room service for a club sandwich and a beer. 'Comin' up right away, sir!'

Next thing was to unpack. Not a long job as a suitcase was too bulky and time-wasting to take on a plane, so 'luggage' meant simply an under-the-seat piece of hand baggage and one of those zip-up 'suiters' which crush the suit inside and have a hook sticking out of the top which catches in fellow travellers' pockets when rushing to board the plane.

Found the plastic waste-paper bin in the bathroom and filled it with hot water from the shower. Tipped in a handful of washing powder, knickers and shirt and left them to soak.

Stripped off, with the exception of socks (the shape of the human hand makes it impossible to wash socks properly when they are hand-held). Enjoyed a hot shower, soaping socks thoroughly (which, note, simultaneously cleaned the feet within them). Took the day's used handkerchief and trod it in shower, scrubbed it with nail-brush, rinsed it and plastered it to the wall of the shower using edge of hand as squeegee.

Next morning the handkerchief peeled off the wall IRONED.

Dried self and pummelled knickers and shirt in waste-paper bin until water went grey. Poured off and refilled with clean water. Repeated until water remained transparent and hung garments to dry over shower rail. Plugged tiny travelling iron into bedside point, laid suit out on a towel and gently urged away the concertina creases which had developed behind the elbows and knees. Hung up suit and got into bed.

The entire laundering operation took exactly twenty-four minutes. Six minutes later room service ('Comin' up right away, sir!') arrived with my club sandwich and can of Budweiser.

I dined.

After my solo tour across the USA I made a point of not going abroad without Polly to act as a kind of manager, to make sure I ate enough to keep me from toppling over from nervous exhaustion, and to block last-minute demands for unscheduled speeches and interviews.

As more of my books were published, we made more author tours together, South Africa, Australia and New Zealand, America and Canada, and we had some good moments.

I admired the protective attitude towards his books adopted by a bent-with-age bookseller in Auckland, New Zealand, who had not quite got the hang of the recent fad for author signing sessions. He greeted me with, 'Well, I dunno, mate. You can sit in my shop for an hour if that's what you want to do, but I don't want you defacing my books by scribbling in 'em.'

New Zealand had only two television channels then, per-haps still has, and I recorded a variety-cum-interview show on one of them, only to find that on the evening it went out I was booked to do a 'serious' interview, live, from a university lecture room, which would go out at the same time as the recorded show. So for one glorious hour New Zealand TV viewers had the choice of either watching Muir or switching off and making a pot of tea.

Halfway through the live interview it began to get too serious, i.e., boring, so to cheer myself up I said to the camera, 'If you're fed up with looking at this suit, switch over to the other channel, I'm in a tweed jacket there.'

When the show finished, the programme's executive descended upon me, white with fury. 'We're in competition with the other channel!' he said, 'and what do you do? Tell our viewers to *switch over to the opposition*! It's unbelievable! In all my years . . . !' He was led away.

Back home to Anners at last, and a few weeks later there was more excitement of a different kind. At about midnight a young Scot telephoned. He sounded a little in wine, or more probably in single malt whisky, and he was ringing on behalf of the Kate Kennedy Club of St Andrews University, Fife: would I stand for election as the university's next lord rector?

I asked him whether it was a jokey thing or if there was a job to be done. He assured me that it was not a joke, it was really up to me what I made of the job.

I discussed it seriously with Polly for about thirty seconds and accepted. I was duly elected rector by the students and enjoyed a three-year tour of duty, 1977–1979, which I will always look back on with misty-eyed pleasure.

My installation as rector was the excuse for a number of ritual celebrations. On 27 April 1977 I was met at the entrance of the town, made a member of the student body by being wrapped in a St Andrews scarlet gown (which centuries ago divinity students had to wear so that they could be spotted nipping into brothels), pulled round the town in an open coach by the university rugby club, stopping frequently to be welcomed with presents.

The gifts included an engraved pewter quaich (neither did I. It's a two-handled, Gaelic drinking cup) from the district council; a most useful silver-handled, very sharp paperknife from the Royal and Ancient Golf Club; from a hall of residence came a mobile made from bars of Cadbury's Fruit and Nut (which I had advertised on television for eight years); and from a girl's hall of residence a pink plastic elephant which emitted a charming but very shrill whistle when squeezed. I managed to get everything home eventually and still have most of the items. The pink elephant is a favourite of the grandchildren at bathtime as they can get it to blow vulgar bubbles.

The only formal duty of the rector was, as father of the university, to chair the monthly meetings of the university court, the governing body which has to approve everything before it becomes university practice. The rector was not involved with the educational side of things, this was the responsibility of the senate (which has to report to the court).

As I had never in my life chaired anything, the university court was daunting. I was saved by having next to me at court meetings the university secretary of that time, David Devine (who wrote thrillers in his spare time and was a Good Thing).

'It's getting a bit boring,' I would whisper anxiously to David out of the side of my mouth.

'It's quite an important issue,' he would whisper back, 'give them a few more minutes and then take a vote.' Eventually I acquired confidence, and on a discussion as to what the court should do about a modern statue lent to the university by the Scottish Arts Council, consisting of a number of bent welded railway lines which students fell over lurching back to their residences late at night, I was able to say, cheerfully, 'Right, gentlemen, time for one more philistine joke all round and then we really must get down to a policy.'

The professors and other members of the court were immensely forbearing with their amateur chairman and I never felt any personal animosity. Perhaps this might have been because they were all busy men and hoped not to have to go back to court for another session in the afternoon. During my three years I always managed to bring the meeting to a close by lunchtime.

Flying BA shuttle once a month up to Edinburgh then picking up a hire car and driving to St Andrews for a long weekend in that lovely stone town with its own private weather, promised to be the perfect escape from the headache-inducing research I was doing for my next book. I imagined having quiet meals all by myself, a steak of Tay salmon perhaps at the Old Course Hotel, a stroll round the town, read for an hour or so . . .

The reality of my monthly 'leisure breaks' was a little different from that vision of delight.

The students elected from one of their number an assessor whose job it was to represent the rector in the university and arrange a programme for his monthly visit.

The university had changed its cooking arrangements and had just moved over to having a central kitchen with a professional chef; the food was fast-frozen and had to be skilfully thawed out. The system had yet to settle down and I was usually greeted by my assessor with, 'You're having a quick lunch in a hall of residence which thinks it's being poisoned. Then I've got down a list of eight students who've got problems and want to see you. Dinner with the girls of University Hall who want to watch their rector eating, and you've been invited to a party after dinner to celebrate an engagement (a lot of St Andrews students seemed to marry each other). It'll be a late night but I said you'd stay on and make a speech at the end.'

I was officially installed in office at a ceremony in Younger Hall where I had to make a rectorial address. In the old days this was all the job amounted to. The distinguished personage, elected for having done something notable elsewhere, such as Rudyard Kipling, Earl Haig, Andrew Carnegie, Sir James Barrie, delivered a powerful address, had a couple of whiskies with the vice-chancellor and that was that for another three years.

Barrie took a villa in the South of France for a month or so to compose his address, a magnificent message to youth which was admired and reprinted all over the place. His theme was courage. Typically, my predecessor-but-one, John Cleese, gave a reasoned address on the usefulness of cowardice.

My address was entitled 'Rectorshipdom'. In it I explained that I was the first rector they had ever had with no qualifications whatever, no letters after my name, I did not even pass a driving test as they did not exist when I started driving, no degree, not even an O level, the most I ever hoped for was a crack at the school cert – and she got married the term I arrived (a little joke to help things along).

The rectorial robes, of medieval design, were enormously heavy, and during the banquet that evening I tilted my chair and very nearly somersaulted backwards.

But a pair of students gave me a warm welcome on my first working weekend. Polly, who loved the town, came with me. Just as we were driving slowly past a hall of residence, a window was thrust up, two carroty heads appeared, yelled in unison, 'FRANK THE WANK!' and dropped out of sight, chortling.

John Cleese with his mocking of Barrie's famous address on courage had broken up the old ground and had set out not to be the Establishment figure that had previously been elected. I felt that my contribution during my three years should be to sow a few seeds in John's broken-up ground and find out whether there was a real job for a modern working rector, and quite what the job was.

I quickly realized that what students wanted above all from their rector was availability. They wanted to see him wandering about the town and they wanted to be able to talk to him, be bought a drink and have a moan in the pub with him. So I put the dates of the court meetings in my diary as soon as they became known and tried hard, unsuccessfully of course, not to miss even one. I had to miss six in my three years, but they assured me this was some sort of a record. A bad or a good record never emerged. And I put a permanent advertisement in the student newspaper, *Aien*, giving my home phone number and address for the benefit of students who had a problem which they thought I might be able to help them with. Not a day passed in those three years without at least one letter thudding in postmarked Kirkcaldy, always by second post for some reason.

Problems varied hugely: a geography expedition to Greenland asked me to arrange for them to have some portable food which was a bit of a treat as well as being nourishing, so I persuaded Cadburys to provide a half-pound bar per man per day of their Fruit and Nut.

A girl student from Belfast working for her finals dearly wanted to work in an English bookshop but did not have the time or the money to tour the country for interviews. I spoke to Peter Giddy, manager of Hatchards in Piccadilly, and he took her on sight unseen. She was a success and went on from Hatchards to become a publisher's rep.

There were students uncertain of their sexuality who could have gone to the perfectly competent university's gaysoc, but did not want to be seen going, so wrote to their dear old white-haired rector for help. I usually recommended a visit to the Catholic chaplain and his nun helper who were very good at this kind of advising.

And there was a round robin from a feminine hall of residence pleading for Rector to arrange for them to have soft loo paper. I wrote to the warden of the hall who explained that the soft kind of loo paper was too wasteful as the girls used it in handfuls as face tissues for removing make-up, polishing their specs, cleaning their shoes, et cetera. I didn't see much harm in that, but the warden was adamant, so I got in touch with the customer care officer at Andrex, luckily a woman, and explained the position. She sided with the girls, as I had hoped, and sent them up, as a free gift, a packing-case full of rolls of

Andrex (very soft) loo paper and a huge woolly Andrex toy puppy.

Students wrote wanting advice about finding jobs, and how to get a novel published, and how to make some money reasonably legally, and would I write a speech for the writer to deliver at his aunt's wedding . . .

Then there was the persuading of friends and colleagues to travel up to St Andrews to take part in events with no fee attached. One of the first of these duties was to supply a speaker for a public lecture series which the university wanted to revive. I asked Robert Morley to do it. '*Must* I, dear Frank?'

'Yes, please, Robert,' I said and arranged to meet him at London airport and escort him up.

Although Robert looked like the comfortably plump chairman of a building society, I knew that he actually leaned strongly to the Left and was quite a rebel. He sat on the edge of a table on the stage in Younger Hall and just talked brilliantly. He described being seduced when a young man by a beautiful older woman, of his playwriting days, of Hollywood, and he told his audience that they would learn little worth learning at university, and the sooner they got out into the real world and started living their lives the better. The students cheered him for a long time.

The university held an arts festival every three years and one was being organized when I was elected, so I had to act as a talent procurer for two festivals. For the first of these my friend Michael Meyer dusted off spare copies of his 'entertainment about actors and acting' which he called *Rogues and Vagabonds* and directed and compèred it for the festival. I managed to talk Peter Ustinov and Dame Wendy Hiller into joining us on stage.

Peter was, and is, probably the cleverest actor in the world at performing this kind of fragmented, character acting in many accents and he was on top of his form.

Dame Wendy wore a terrific dress for the performance, colourful and dramatic with a train long enough to be trodden on. Before we went on stage, as I was goggling, Wendy rather apologetically asked me if I would hand her to her chair as the skirt was very full and quite difficult to manoeuvre. She wore the dress because she thought the girls in the audience would want to see her wearing something theatrical and glamorous. And of course, as we learned afterwards, Wendy was absolutely right.

It was a wonderful evening.

Shortly after, Michael and I put on *Rogues and Vagabonds* at the Edinburgh Festival.

So began for me a tiny sub-career as a platform performer (highly enjoyable but unpaid, which is so often the way). Michael compiled two more programmes: *He and She* about love and marriage, and *Fun and Games* about leisure and sporting activities (my favourite quotation, Max Beerbohm on rowing: 'Eight minds with but one single thought – if that'). We did, in all, four Edinburgh Festivals, but many more performances all over the place for theatre charities.

We almost always performed on a Sunday when actors would be free. We met in the afternoon and had a read-through, did the performance (just over an hour) in the evening and then went home. Those who gave up their Sunday to appear with Michael and me over the years included, in addition to those already mentioned, Alan Bates, Judi Dench, Alec McCowen, Dorothy Tutin, Freddie Jones, Polly James, Brian Cox, Miranda Richardson, Edward Fox, Michael York, Stephen Fry, Robert Powell and Paul Eddington.

Searching in my memory for some spicy sleaze, some kiss-and-tell liaison with a famous star which would make these memoirs headline news and earn an expensive serialization in the *News of the World*, I drew a blank for a long while and then remembered: in our many performances of Michael's *He and She*, Dorothy Tutin and I played a scene from Congreve's *The Old Bachelor*. I played Heartwell, the old bachelor, and Dottie played young Sylvia, in the scene where Sylvia seduces the reluctant old man into kissing her. I know I may be branded the rat of Thorpe, but my wife and family will stand by me when I confess that I much enjoyed kissing Dottie. What is more I enjoyed kissing Dottie Tutin a little more every time we played the scene.

For me the most memorable of these platform performances

was a special show about Oxford compiled by Michael from Jan Morris's *Oxford Book of Oxford* and performed in Oxford in aid of Oxfam.

We had great difficulty trying to find an actress who was free on that particular Sunday until I realized that we did not need one. Oxford dons and almost everybody else quoted in Jan's book were celibate in those earlier days and there were no lines for an actress even if we had one. Then came the great *coup*: Michael managed to persuade Sir John Gielgud to join us.

He was wonderful, of course. That voice. His instant grasp of character, or rather the dozens of characters he had to play, which many actors found difficult under the rough-and-ready, instant-theatre conditions of platform readings, and his instinctive sense of comedy. There was one passage which needed livening; we played two rather dotty old dons rubbishing a colleague, but the dialogue was not quite funny enough (a frequent problem in compilations), so I suggested to Sir John that we do that old people's habit of repeating the last half of what the other one has just said while the other one is still mumbling away. We had a lovely meandering sequence, both talking at once and neither listening.

In between the monthly weekends at St Andrews and dealing with the daily letters postmarked Kirkcaldy and the consequent phone calls and meetings, I was able to fit in some work. Besides *My Word!* and *My Music* on radio and *Call My Bluff* on the telly, I was beavering away on my *Oxford Book of Humorous Prose*.

In 1974 an editor of the Oxford University Press, Bruce Phillips, had written to me saying that in their series of Oxford books they had not as yet tackled an *Oxford Book of Humorous Prose* and would I care to take it on.

There are certain difficulties in anthologizing humour, not the least of which is that as soon as you label something funny, readers instantly want to find it unfunny because you are telling them what their sense of humour should be, and everybody's sense of humour is an extremely personal thing not to be tampered with by others.

I wrote the OUP an argument as to how I thought the book should be approached. I suggested it should be subtitled *A*

Conducted Tour and aim at being a representative selection of humour in prose illustrating how it had developed in the 500 years from Caxton to P. G. Wodehouse.

Furthermore, there was a problem in setting the extracts, which would necessarily be torn out of context. I suggested that I introduce each piece by explaining something about the author and how he came to write what he did and why it was found highly amusing at the time (although perhaps not now). So I had a tremendous load of research to get through, which suited me as I could work happily at home and the London Library posted me the books I needed.

There then followed a serene run of years from the late Seventies through to the late Eighties. Home life was even better than usual; our medieval granite tower in Corsica did not need repainting and Jamie had got his degree, spent a while in rescue archaeology wallowing about in Thames mud with a 4-inch trowel helping to uncover a length of Roman river frontage just along from the Mermaid Theatre, and then changed career slightly by going into making television arts programmes, first as a researcher on Humphrey Burton's *Aquarius*, then as a freelance director and producer.

Sally, after working happily at Hatchards, wanted to get away from London, so got herself a job in Kettering with J. L. Carr, the novelist and compiler of county maps which had little to do with geography but a lot to do with odd local characters and happenings and cricket scores. Then she met Joanna Osborne, a PA at Granada Television who wanted a different kind of life. Together the girls bought a second-hand knitting machine (one of those strips of busy little bits of metal which look like a Chinese typewriter) and, without benefit of art-school training, working from Joanna's bedroom, set up as designers and manufacturers of fashion knitwear, available for sale to the discerning public from a barrow in Covent Garden craft market on Thursdays.

And they won. Their breakthrough was their sheep jumper (the V and A has one in their permanent collection of contemporary designs). The jersey showed a flock of white sheep on a red background with one black sheep. The luck came when Lady Di, as she was then, was given one of the jumpers and wore it to Smiths Lawn polo ground in Windsor Park whilst leaning across a Land Rover. The resultant colour picture was so delightful that just about every glossy magazine in the world used it on their cover.

The girls now had a small but well-established fashion jumper business, Muir and Osborne, selling mostly to America, with a posse of freelance knitters working away in their homes.

Then, out of the blue, a trio of glittering prizes came my way.

In 1978, in the middle of my stretch of rectoring, St Andrews decided to make me an honorary Doctor of Laws (LL.D.). Even more pleasing was that the presentation was to be made during term time so that students could be present, which it seems was a rare honour at St Andrews.

Then, in 1982, Kent University decided to honour one of its local sons, me, with the honorary degree of Doctor of Letters (D.Litt.). This took place during the usual graduation ceremony held in the cathedral in front of a full congregation of students, parents and family friends. It was customary for one of those who had obtained their degree the easy way (i.e., honorary) to elect one of their number to make a brief speech from the pulpit. I was elected to do this. I could find no way of including the pig story.

Anyway, when the talk is of theatres notorious for being the graveyard of comedians and somebody says to me, 'It's all right for you, you've never played Glasgow Empire on a wet Tuesday afternoon,' I can say, 'Well, no – but I've played Canterbury Cathedral in the middle of Help The Aged week.'

In 1980, between the two degrees, came the bestowal of a different kind of honour. The beige envelope had a portcullis insignia on the flap and a nice letter inside asking whether I would accept if Downing Street recommended the Queen to appoint me a Commander of the British Empire.

A few minutes later Denis telephoned and said, 'Have you had your letter?'

Denis was quite troubled about accepting the honour because he thought that people in the entertainment industry tended to be overpaid and honours should be otherwise distributed, but eventually he accepted.

Off we went with our families to Buckingham Palace on the great day, Den and I in correct morning suits but hatless: wearing top hats made us both look like stilt-walking undertakers. It was very splendid being driven in our hire car through the palace gates, underneath an archway and into the central courtyard.

A police sergeant instructed our driver, 'Open the boot of your car and wait for the explosive dog.' After a while a constable arrived with an eager dog which leaped about all round the car and in and out of the boot, tail wagging furiously.

We went upstairs as directed to the 'waiting area', a reception room divided up into squares with red silken ropes threaded on stands, like a tremendously chic cattle market. Most of the roped-off areas were fairly full of chalk-faced, middle-aged citizens (like us) shaking with nerves, but Den and I managed to find a square which contained only a handful of potential heart attacks. We stood there shaking away with the others when I saw my old friend Johnnie Johnston, he of our Boxing Day lunches in Windsor Great Park and now in his capacity as comptroller of the Lord Chamberlain's Office, working his way towards us and looking anxious.

It seems that Den and I were in the wrong enclosure. We were in the area reserved for those about to be knighted. Johnnie extricated us and took us away to a room where he rehearsed us in how to bow so that our quite small Queen could get the CBE medal on its ribbon over our heads. It involved bending our heads forward and gazing stolidly at the floor like Chinese bandits awaiting beheading by sword.

In the event we managed it quite smoothly, marching forward when our turn came without banging into each other and bowing together, only to let ourselves down during our brief conversation with the Queen.

'How long have you two worked together?' the Queen asked.

We answered confidently, in unison:

'Twenty-three years,' said Denis.

'Twenty-six years,' said I.

'And is your work mainly for the radio?' asked the Queen.

'A certain area of it is,' I said.

'No,' said Den.

And so on for what seemed like four hours, but was actually about a minute and a half.

The CBE medallion was heavy and colourful and it came with a pink moiré ribbon with a buckle so that the device could be adjusted to dangle just below the knot of the tie. Unfortunately for its proud owners, it should only be worn on very formal occasions with full evening dress.

Again, although the rule book says that honorary degrees are full degrees and should be regarded as such, in practice they are rarely used except in academic circles. Soon after the investiture I had a letter from St Andrews University addressed to Dr Frank Muir, CBE, LL.D., D.Litt. I found our local postman examining the envelope suspiciously, 'This isn't *you*, is it?' he said.

Denis was right in saying to the Queen that his work was no longer mainly in radio. It has been said that power should only be given to people who don't want it, and perhaps it can also be argued that the only people who should be allowed to go on television regularly are those who don't want to. And Den is a good example: he hates being on telly, but he is very good indeed at what he does on it.

I suppose I must have influenced him into performing against his instincts because when we began working together I loved being 'on' and producers wanted to use *us* as a team, not just me.

Denis began work as a trainee manager for the Hyams Brothers, good, old-fashioned showmen who ran a North London supercinema, the Kilburn Empire. Their successful philosophy, which I think had a lasting influence on Denis, was, 'Charge the customer sixpence and then give him ninepenn'orth of entertainment.' Certainly ever since I have known him, Denis has been extraordinarily thorough in everything he has taken on.

When we began to work separately, Den was asked to be the presenter of *Looks Familiar*, a quiz/nostalgia/chat show about earlier television which ran for years, due as much as anything to his painstaking preparation before each show. And then began his extremely successful (and very funny) series of film clips of actors forgetting their lines, walking into the furniture and generally falling down on the job, which has been winning huge audiences for years and on which Den works very hard viewing clips before making his final selection and writing his links. The show was, of course, *It'll Be Alright on the Night*.

Ironically, as Denis appeared more and more on television I appeared less and less, which was a good thing for me because my next book was approaching point of lay and was very time-consuming. I had chosen humorous pieces from over 200 authors and was very busy writing up the commentary when my blissful three years as Rector of St Andrews came, usefully but sadly, to an end.

Usefully because I was astonished at how much more time I suddenly had to work on the book. No more monthly shuttle trips to Scotland, no more letters from students in the second post, no more doing the hundred and one tiny things which the job required. Sadly, because I had so enjoyed it all and hated the thought of not being rector any longer.

I could have returned for several events shortly after leaving but Polly thought that would be a mistake. She insisted, wisely, that I should leave the new rector to settle himself in and keep well away for a while. In fact we did not go back to St Andrews until 1993. The occasion was the graduation ceremony at which honorary degrees were to be conferred.

The vice-chancellor, Professor Struther Arnott, invited Polly and me up to St Andrews for the ceremony to help him give the Dalai Lama a hot meal afterwards. It was a good lunch. His Holiness the Dalai Lama was great company, wide interests, strong sense of humour, so deeply holy that he did not need to constantly demonstrate it. A remarkably impressive and likeable man.

Although study-bound, forefingers stabbing at the word-processor keys most of the day every day, I still went on the occasional exhausting author tour. In 1980 Pol and I went to Australia and New Zealand yet again. It was two or three more weeks of only seeing the insides of taxis and radio studios and bookshops in those lands of natural beauty, but we had a pleasant happening in Sydney one very hot and sunny morning.

We had a free hour – very rare – and were walking past a huge department store in Sydney when we saw a notice saying that Robert Morley, who was on tour with a play, was inside signing copies of his latest book.

Pol and I joined the queue.

I was on my way to a telly interview, so I was wearing my donkey-coloured tropical suit. As we got near to Robert I noticed that he was wearing khaki shorts. When it was our turn to face the author he saw us and said, 'Good God!'

I said, very loudly, 'I am shocked to see that you've gone native, Robert, and abandoned a proper British suit for a beachcomber's tatty shorts.'

Without a pause, Robert replied cheerfully, 'You must remember, Frank dear, the chief scout, Lord Baden-Powell, laid it down that fresh air wafting around the genitals is beneficial to health.'

My next trip abroad was three years later, sadly without Pol, when the Hong Kong Arts Festival, money coming out of its ears, invited the whole *My Music* team, including the producer and the engineer, to Hong Kong to record one (one!) *My Music* programme as part of their festival.

We had quite a colourful landing at Hong Kong's notoriously difficult airport. We dropped down between the skyscrapers, so close to them that we looked through the windows at the flickering blue of the residents' television sets, and then, because of mist over the runway, the BA pilot aborted the landing and gunned the mighty Jumbo up into the sky again as though it was a fighter plane.

'Sorry about that!' he said cheerfully over the speaker system. 'Took a lot of petrol, but no worry, we've got enough for another go. If we still don't make it we'll go across to China and spend the night in Canton.'

But we made it.

It was then the same old grind for a few happy days; corruptingly luxurious hotel, Denis being taken to the races and being advised by his host which horse was going to win (not which horse *might* win, which horse *would* win), a formal dinner with the governor amid a selection of distinguished and extremely rich Hong Kong businessmen. Industry and movie-making in the city in those prosperous days was perhaps epitomized by a grey-haired Hong Kongian at John Amis's table tilting back his chair and calling across to a friend at another table, 'Hey! Thank you for the million!'

Ah, well, saved the cost of a stamp.

And then it was an author tour of the USA. The American novelist and publisher Sol Stein much enjoyed good hotels and took a suite at the Connaught Hotel on business trips to London. When he sent me on my way across America coast-to-coast he warned me sadly that American hotels did not match up to the standard of British hotels (surely not many British hotels match up to the Connaught, either). But Sol was wrong.

By the time I had worked my way across the Midwest (Sol said only the Midwest could read) I arrived exhausted in Los Angeles to find that Stein and Day Inc's publicity girl had booked me into a downtown Hilton for a weekend in the smog. This was not on. I rang the splendid Beverly Hills Hotel and explained all. They found me a room and I moved out of the smog and up into this slightly old-fashioned hotel – all the best British hotels are slightly old-fashioned, too – with its famous Polo Bar and the one swimming pool in California to be seen at, not swimming but lying on a mattress in the sun pretending to read a film script. And the really 'in' thing was to be paged on the poolside telephone, which demonstrated not only that you were still alive but somebody actually wanted to talk to you.

There is an old and rather sweet Hollywood story about a much-liked small-time agent whose ambition it was to be called to the poolside phone whilst sunbathing. He never achieved it, but when he died his many actor friends raised a fund and paid the hotel to have him paged by the pool every morning for a year.

I am happy to put on record that I was paged by the pool.

A day or so before I left England to do the USA tour, I did an urgent rewrite for an old friend and one-time BBC colleague, Patrick Garland (I had managed to get the BBC's Music and Arts Department to let me borrow Patrick to produce and direct the Alan Bennett comedy series, *On the Margin*.

Persuading another department to release one of its producers and then getting the Head of Light Entertainment, Tom Sloan, to accept the borrowing was, I think, an exercise in guile which was probably my greatest achievement in BBC managementship).

Patrick Garland had become Director of the Chichester Festival and was having a little trouble with a Feydeau farce he was putting on starring Rex Harrison. A couple of scene endings needed a tickle up, which I managed to do in time and then drive up to London and read them to Patrick and Rex Harrison before I flew off to the USA and began my coast-to-coast trudge for Sol. And blow me, at the end of the trudge, sitting by the Beverly Hills Hotel pool was Rex Harrison. I had a copy of my book with me, and I asked him if I could take a photograph of him holding it.

'It won't be used in an advertisement, will it?' he asked, warily.

I assured him not and I still have the photograph in the loo at Anners. It is framed with another photograph, so I have pictures of two rather different kinds of friend clutching copies of *The Frank Muir Book*, an elderly Corsican, Dominic Orsini, the first Corsican Polly and I really got to know when he was building a café/restaurant with his own hands on a L'Ile-Rousse beach, and Rex Harrison.

Then, whilst talking to Rex Harrison by the Beverly Hills Hotel pool, I was paged. Paged at the Beverly Hills Hotel pool!

'Mr Muir, please – telephone!' piped the page-boy, carefully picking his way through the mattresses and scripts and expensive jars of suntan cream. 'Telephone for Mr Muir!'

Reality returned and I realized that I had no idea how the pagee was supposed to react when paged.

'What do I do?' I asked Rex, feebly.

'Answer the phone!' he said. 'Don't hurry, it makes you look anxious about your career. The phone is in the far corner there, just stroll over with a light confident smile, waving intimately to one or two recumbent figures on the way.' I think Mr Harrison was enjoying himself.

The call was from Brits working in Hollywood, John Barry,

the film-music composer, and Ian La Frenais, the writer. They had heard me on a local radio interview and invited me to a British lunch the following day, a Saturday.

When I booked into the Beverly Hills Hotel on the Friday afternoon and unpacked, I found that the coast-to-coast slog across the USA in a heatwave had played hell with my pale donkey-coloured tropical-weight suit, so I rang down to reception and asked if there was any hope of getting the thing pressed as I was flying back to New York on Sunday night for a rather important early morning interview on *Good-Morning America!* and I wanted to look cleanish and tidyish.

Reception deeply regretted, but hoped I understood that Juan the valet was off at weekends. I understood. Then half an hour later there was a tap on the door and a burly young man introduced himself as Juan the valet. 'I live in a bungalow in back of the hotel,' he said. 'I ain't planning to go noplace tomorrow. You give me your suit and I'll do what I can.'

The next morning my suit was laid out on the other bed in the room, beautifully sponged and pressed. No question of touting for a big tip, just wanting to help.

My experience of Los Angeles included, suitably, a shoot-out near a radio studio. I wasn't shot myself, but I saw the drama happening, live.

It was the Saturday evening after my lunch with John Barry and Ian La Frenais and I was doing an interview at a radio studio, which like most similar low-cost enterprises in the USA was a breeze-block building in the middle of a cinder car park. Surrounding it was a bungalow development; it also had some bushes in which I saw fireflies for the first time in my life. Very beautiful and exciting.

After the interview I waited in reception for my hire car to arrive and take me back to the hotel. The interviewer had gone home to her children and I sat in silence with an elderly uniformed security guard. The whole evening was getting very boring when suddenly there was the sound of gunshots from the bungalow area followed by flashing lights and shouting. I rushed to the window and saw two beefy policemen hauling a tiny malefactor out of a bungalow window. He was wriggling like an eel and they dropped him a couple of times, but eventually – perhaps he gave up and bowed to the inevitable – they flung him into the back of their police car, one of them, ironically, protecting the malefactor's head carefully with a hand so that his skull would not hit the top of the car doorway.

The elderly radio-station security guard did not react at all, almost certainly because he was too deaf to hear the shots. A minute or two later the entrance door crashed open and a vast fat man, also in a security uniform, staggered in, clutching his arm as though if he released his grip he would spurt blood all over the ceiling. He blurted out in an extraordinarily high voice, 'Hey, Al, did you see that asshole with the gun? Fired at me, the bastard!'

He slowly withdrew his hand from his arm revealing a tiny round Elastoplast on his elbow.

'Must have been a small bullet,' I ventured.

'He missed me!' he squeaked. 'When he started shootin' I flung myself to the ground and scraped my arm on the brick wall.'

Then it was back to England, Anners, radio and TV recordings, after-dinner speeches, voice-overs and head down on the *Oxford Book of Humorous Prose* for a year or two, before any more excursions abroad.

The last of these was in 1989, a two-week long semi-holiday/semi-session of nervy hard work in Tokyo, giving a short series of one-man shows for the Tokyo British Club to raise money to help the Tokyo British School build up a library. Nervy because I did not happen to have a one-man show to give.

I had stumbled through something of the sort in a theatre in Hong Kong. It was at short notice – a kind of thank-you to our hosts – and consisted mainly of my after-dinner speech with every remembered variation, spoken slowly (the pig lasted about twenty minutes). It was reviewed, in a baffled kind of way, in *The South China Morning Post*, which I read on the flight home. The reviewer did not think my piece was all that comical but found it oddly fascinating. He thought it unpredictable and difficult to describe, but then he pulled himself together and finished agreeably by saying that nevertheless he had enjoyed the evening very much.

This is what the Brits stalwartly endured for several performances in the Tokyo British Club's little theatre. The shows were, to my great surprise, rather successful, which was gratifying as I was not a stand-up comic and only agreed to do what I could to make some money for the British School library.

When it was time to go home the club gave Polly and me a rather emotional send-off (known in Australia as 'a farewelling'). The club handed over to the school governors a cheque for £10,000, and the school library was formally started off by the presentation of a copy of *What-a-Mess* autographed by Margaret Thatcher (who happened to be in Tokyo at the time although our eyes never crossed).

Pol and I have strong memories of Tokyo. Arriving at the Capitol Tokyo Hotel, ordering two coffees and finding they were £6 each. Watching from our hotel-room window, high up, when it was going-home time and seeing a million thin black-and-white clerk-ants streaming out of offices and walking briskly to the tube stations. Black and white because they all wore black trousers or skirts and brilliantly white shirts or blouses.

It was an unnervingly hygienic city. Many cyclists wore gauze masks over their mouths, not to avoid breathing in noxious fumes, but because they thought they might have a cold and did not want to spread their germs. Until recently, if you went upstairs in a department store, a girl with a duster went ahead of you polishing the brass handrail.

The city was free of petty crime (although troubled with the usual organized urban heavy crime). You could leave a bicycle or a purse anywhere and it would still be there when you came back to look for it.

Our richest experience was taking the 'bullet' train to the ancient capital Kyoto to catch a glimpse of the old Japan.

We needed briefing by our Brit hosts as all the signs on the railway were, of course, in Japanese. We successfully bought our tickets from a complicated machine by watching what the travellers in front of us did to it. Our tickets gave us our seat numbers and told us that we were in carriage Q, so we did as the Brits instructed and joined the orderly queue on the part of the platform marked out with parallel white lines and labelled Q. Sure enough, bang on time the train hurtled in and hissed to a halt with the doorway of carriage Q exactly opposite us.

The seats were airline-like and comfortable and the train steady and almost silent at speed – which I think approached the 200 m.p.h. mark. Girls in kimonos, bowing a lot, came round pushing trolleys offering bowls of sushi and cups of green tea (extremely nasty tea I gathered from Polly unless you were inexplicably keen on it).

We had worried how we would know when we reached Kyoto, because the train went on further south. Our friends asked, 'When are you supposed to arrive there?' We said, 'Four-seventeen.' 'Right,' said our friends, 'keep an eye on your watch and when it says four-seventeen, walk out onto the Kyoto platform.' Which is what we did. The train, whispering through the air like a guided missile on rails, was on time to the second.

Our hotel was a small but quite famous traditional Japanese inn dating back to 1818, the Hiragiya Ryokan. The receptionist showed us our room, double futon on the floor, paper sliding doors, rice mats and the alcove which once enshrined a samurai's sword and now displayed a scroll and an ikebana flower arrangement. She asked us not to disturb the holy corner which was part of the great Japanese love of tradition, then gave us our electronic remote control which opened and closed the curtains and switched on the heated loo seat in the bathroom.

The maid allocated to us arrived. She was almost exactly half my size, a bit older, and she took a deep dislike to me, eyeing me venomously when serving supper, mainly because I could never leave my shoes pointing in the right direction. It was customary to keep taking your shoes off when wandering from one room to another and going to the loo, and there was a traditional direction they should be left pointing in, which I never managed to grasp.

Our meals were taken in the Japanese style, legs stretched out under the 9-inch-high table, praying not to be seized with a sudden spasm of cramp, lying on the futon with one elbow propped up on a device remarkably like one of those round china stands used in delicatessens to carve ham upon.

Next day we ordered a car to take us to see the Golden Temple. It was beginning to rain heavily. Our Japanese driver spoke very good English because he had been an insurance broker in the City of London and told us we were experiencing the tail-end of a typhoon. The rain got worse; we arrived back at the inn soaked to the skin and Polly had to blow-dry our clothes with her portable hairdryer.

On the way back in the 'bullet' train in even worse rain, the storm clouds parted for a moment and we had a clear sighting of Mount Fujiyama. A quite emotional moment.

A nature note completes our Tokyo memoirs: total number of animals sighted by Polly during our two-week stay; eight dogs, one cat (on a balcony in Kyoto), five cows (seen from our train window) and some sacred bantam chickens pottering about the Shinto Shrine in Tokyo. Not a lot, really. Are pet animals not liked in Japan? Eaten?

It was good to get home again, as ever.

The following year, 1990, my family and friends celebrated my seventieth birthday and *The Oxford Book of Humorous Prose* was published.

A good year. A kind of culmination.

Coda

(A FEW LATE-FLOWERING
PENSÉES)

Apart from increased sales of my books, there was another product of all that dashing across shopping precincts and making speeches at endless literary lunches and dinners and rushing from one interview to another and enduring long-haul flights across the world. It would have been great experience for an ambitious and athletic young author, but it was not all that wise an activity for an old gent in his seventies.

So in 1992 I had a stroke.

The night before it I had a severe headache, most unusual for me, and in the morning I realized that something was not quite right. No pain, but I could not make sense of the morning papers, and when a policeman came to the door I asked him what he wanted. He told me that I had sent for him to advise on burglar alarms, of which I had no recollection at all. Polly sent for the doctor who arranged for me to go immediately into a hospital in Windsor and for me to be seen by Dr Daffyd Thomas, the neurologist.

At the Windsor hospital they inserted me up a torpedo, switched on a huge electro-magnet inside it which whizzed round me at speed for some thirty noisy (and very expensive) minutes and the resultant print of my poor brain was handed to Dr Thomas.

'You've suffered a TIA,' said the good doctor.

'That's Spanish for "aunty", isn't it?' I said (brain still working well. Or rather, normally).

'Well, the bad news', said the doc, 'is that the 'I.A.' stands for an ischaemic attack. The good news is that the 'T' stands for transient. In other words, you've had a stroke which we hope was too brief to do lasting damage.'

Once again, I had been one of life's lucky ones, but nevertheless the TIA changed my life. I am on six varieties of pill, thrown to the back of the throat three times a day at mealtimes, seventeen colourful baby Smarties in total per day. There is one mischievous little red devil, Persantin (six a day), which lurks in a stiff plastic bubble. I have an old friend, hotelier Hugh Neil, who is on the same regime as me, and his one ambition in life is to thumb his day's ration of Persantin out of their bubbles without one of them flying out of the window.

Since the attack I have become nervously apprehensive about almost everything; meeting people, travelling, performing. All these have now become stressful activities and I am only too grateful to myself for having accidentally arranged my affairs so that at this stage of the game I can stay quietly writing in my study, all dashing about done.

A melancholy aspect of giving up making speeches was having to bid farewell to my pig story, which I do now, formally, by quoting the only poem I know describing the sad parting of a man and a pig (I rather think the little anon verse began life in America or Ireland as a recitation):

> One evening in October,
> When I was far from sober,
> And dragging home a load with manly pride,
> My feet began to stutter,
> So I laid down in the gutter,
> And a pig came up and parked right by my side.
> Then I warbled, 'It's fair weather
> When good fellows get together,'
> Till a lady passing by was heard to say:
> 'You can tell a man who boozes
> By the company he chooses!'
> Then the pig got up and slowly walked away.

★

In his book *Letters from Iceland*, W. H. Auden quotes the longest word in the Icelandic language. It might be worth memorizing as it could well come in useful. The word is:

Haestarjettarmalaflutunesmanskiffstofustulkkonutidyralykill.

It means 'a latch key belonging to a girl working in the office of a barrister'.

★

In early American B-pictures they used to indicate that a character was English by making him say, 'Pip-pip, old fruit!' an expression made popular by P. G. Wodehouse, but originally, according to Partridge's *Dictionary of Slang*, 'A hue and cry after a youth in striking bicycling costumery'. Presumably the phrase mocked the youth's little warning hooter and his colourful clothing.

The French (and the Corsicans) keep another archaic phrase alive by still raising their glass to an Englishman in a bar with the salutation '*chin-chin!*'. This was originally an Anglo-Chinese expression of greeting meaning in Chinese, 'please-please'.

The point is that, when in the Far East, it behoves one to exercise caution when using old English colloquialisms.

In Japan, we were told, '*chin-chin*' is slang for 'little boy's penis'.

★

When I was at the BBC working on the Jeeves and Bertie Wooster series, the family had to go off on holiday to Corsica without me for a few days and the producer Michael Mills, who was spending that weekend with his mother in her cottage on the south coast, kindly invited me down with him.

I took with me a small box of hand-made chocolates as a little pressie for Mrs Mills. She was delighted.

She lightly prodded the chocolates in turn. 'I'll give that one to Mrs Potter,' she said. 'Jane would love that one, and this one I think I'll give to Mrs Turner who loves chocolates and never gets them, poor soul. And this one . . .'

'Oh, really, mother!' said Michael. 'Frank gave them to *you*!'

'Yes, he did,' said Mrs Mills, 'but he didn't impose conditions. He gave them to me as a present, so they are now mine to do what I like with. Eat them, deep-freeze them for Christmas, give them away to friends. Surely, enjoy them in any way I choose?'

Polly and I were so struck with this entirely sensible and honest approach to gifts that ever since, when we find that a present we have given has been lost by the recipient, or sold or thrown away, it hasn't bothered us one jot. 'It's the Mrs Mills story!' we say.

★

During the Suez crisis, when petrol rationing was imposed, I bought a motor scooter and rode to London every day on it until it slipped away from under me one rainy evening in Curzon Street and I was helped to my feet by an elderly tart.

Soon after I bought the bike I was in The Red Lion at home when a local village character, Long Charlie Fimbo, said, 'I saw you riding that foreign bike thing o' yours. You look like a swan on a piece of cheese.'

What an extraordinary expression.

★

When Nigel Hollis first worked for William Heinemann the publishers, he lived in Barnes with his wife Sarah and their two boys and cycled to his office in the West End. Quite a few publishers used to cycle in those days, but most of them eventually came adrift from their bikes round Hyde Park Corner and went back to buses and taxis.

The Hollis family lived in a typical London tall thin house, and breakfasted in a smallish kitchen in the semi-basement. The boys were still at school and would occasionally bring a friend home with them for the weekend.

Sarah said that breakfast in the tiny kitchen doing a fry-up for small boys and their guests, particularly in winter when the heating was on as well as the cooker, was like being in Little Hell. Rain poured down outside, condensation streamed down the windows inside and Nigel had to be got off to work in good time so that he did not have to pedal like mad in and out of the King's Road traffic.

Sarah was trying to cope during one such frantic Monday morning breakfast, with the bacon beginning to burn, the toast really burning, the temperature in the kitchen about 150 degrees centigrade, and Nigel, late, searching for a lost bicycle-clip under the table, when Sarah found her skirt being gently tugged by the small boy guest, a judge's son, whom her boys had brought home for the weekend.

'Do excuse me, Mrs Hollis,' he whispered discreetly, 'but you appear to have forgotten the butter-knife.'

MORAL: Never underestimate the British middle classes, even when they are only schoolboys.

★

Never underestimate the British grandchild, either.

I was seized with a wish for my grandchildren to address me as Grandpapa. The word has an elegant ring to it – a hint of Proust? Gigi?

What a hope.

It is the grandchildren themselves who decide the word they will use to summon us.

Abigail Wheatcroft had a sporting go at saying 'grandpapa' but just couldn't make it, so she reduced 'grandpapa', via *Barbar the Elephant*, to 'bummer'. When we are, say, gathering food-stuffs in a Bath supermarket, her little voice will cry out, loud and clear, 'I'm over here, Bummer!'

Her younger brother, Gabriel, who has just discovered the joys of talking, goes at the problem with energy but as yet little finesse. He has heard how his sister addresses me and has sim-plified it to, 'Hey, Bum-Bum!'

★

Denis and I had to finish a script which meant missing lunch. Then in the evening I had to go to the Odeon cinema, Leicester Square, to watch a film in the *Doctor* series which had somebody in it we were thinking of using in a programme, and I missed dinner. Feeling very hungry by then I bought the most substantial nibble I could find on sale in the cinema foyer, a 1-pound box of Meltis New Berry Fruits. Devotees of eating during films will know that these fruits are soft pastilles filled with a sweet fruit-flavoured syrup and rolled in sugar.

During the film I unthinkingly munched my way through the whole top layer, i.e., a full half pound of Meltis New Berry Fruits.

Nothing alarming happened until I was driving home to the village of Thorpe in Surrey and just past the airport I came over peculiar. I slowed down the car to walking pace and concentrated on driving in a straight line. I was clearly in the way of the car behind me which turned out to be a police car.

It suddenly rang its bell; that dreadful, heart-stopping clangour which police cars made in those days, like the fire-alarm gong going off in a Tibetan monastery. I pulled into a lay-by, palpitating.

Oddly enough, I was to pull into that same lay-by some four years later, also after coming over peculiar. On that occasion I was on my way home from one of those odd anniversaries so beloved by the BBC, the nineteenth and a half anniversary of Radio 3 or something. It was at the Guildhall and after dinner the waiters plied the guests with small glasses of neat whisky and neat brandy, which could not easily be differentiated. The evening became suddenly jollier and voices and laughter a touch shriller.

I found myself standing next to the Archbishop of Canterbury, the Right Revd Michael Ramsey, a tremendously imposing figure with a mane of white hair, the only male in the room not clutching one or more small glasses of whisky/brandy. I felt an overwhelming impulse to tell the archbishop a religious joke to help him to lighten up a sermon or two.

'Archbishop, sir,' I said, 'here's a good one for you. There was this epicene young hairdresser who'd never been to a Roman Catholic service, so one Sunday morning he took himself off to the Brompton Oratory and picked an end seat in the pew. As the procession passed down the nave he was alarmed to see a priest swinging a censer from which emerged little puffs of smoke. The hairdresser, feeling he should do something, leaned across as the priest passed close to him and whispered urgently, 'Excuse me mentioning it, madam, but your handbag's on fire.'

The archbishop did not even smile.

On the way home I remembered telling the Archbishop of Canterbury the joke and was so ashamed that I came over peculiar and pulled the car into a lay-by for a little private palpitate.

Remembering that occasion reminded me of an even worse

instance of self-reproach, a real scarlet-cheeked memory. In this one I palpitated in another lay-by, the small car park on the edge of Thorpe Green.

Over the years my family and I enjoyed the most pleasant custom of having lunch on Boxing Day with friends who lived in Windsor Great Park. Fast-forwarding to 1976, I had just had a book published, *The Frank Muir Book: An Irreverent Companion to Social History*, which had climbed to being the number one bestseller the week before Christmas. On that fateful Boxing Day I had given a copy of the book to our hostess, who had most kindly left it prominently on a side table.

Our hosts had over the years invited those members of the royal family who wanted to get away from their young watching telly at the castle to have a before-lunch drink on Boxing Day.

On Boxing Day 1976, Her Majesty the Queen, Prince Philip and quite a few of the rest of the family turned up. I suddenly spotted that the Queen's equerry had picked up my book and was glancing through it, but what is gloriously more, he was LAUGHING. I casually shot over to his side.

'What is that you're reading?' The queen asked the equerry. He saw me. 'Oh, it's a book by – er – Frank Muir here. Be very useful for writing speeches!'

The Queen said to me, smiling, 'Then we should have a copy.'

It was at that point that, nerves strung tight as a bowstring, I cracked. 'Don't you buy one, ma'am,' I croaked. 'I'll send you one. I get a third off.'

It was on the way home that the tattiness of saying such a shabby thing to the pleasant lady, who was not only my monarch, but also one of the richest ladies in the land smote me and I had to pull into the small car park on the edge of Thorpe Green and have a right royal palpitation.

To return to the original Meltis New Berry Fruits-inspired palpitation, I steered into the lay-by with great care and got out of the car. I found standing up difficult so I hung on to the door and the fresh air helped. A police officer swiftly joined me from the squad car, putting on his hat.

'Is this your vehicle, sir?' he said (why do they always say 'vehicle' and never 'car'?). He was not much concerned whether it was mine or not, it was just the police equivalent of saying, 'How do you do.'

'It will be in two years next September,' I said, rather wittily considering the circumstances.

'Had a little drink, have we, sir?' he said.

'No, I haven't,' I said.

'We've been following you for seven-tenths of a mile and your driving appears to be on the unconventional side.'

He leaned forward and sniffed me. This was before breath-alysers. 'It's unusual in this kind of incident, sir,' he said, 'but you smell of oranges.'

I pointed at the box of sweeties on the passenger seat.

'Meltis!' he said. 'May I?' He selected one with care and swiftly crunched it up. 'Blackcurrant!' he said. 'My favourite!'

'I have not been drinking,' I said, 'nor come to that have I been eating. I came over hungry in the cinema and bought these Meltis Fruits. I ate rather a lot of them.'

'That's it!' said the officer, holding the box and gazing at the pastilles longingly.

'Do have another,' I said.

He popped three into his mouth. 'Your stomach experienced a quick intake of an excessive amount of sugar, sir, that's what you done. On an empty stomach you get what medical science calls "the collywobbles". It's a well-known side-effect.'

He probed the box with a stubby forefinger, seeking another blackcurrant.

'*You'll* get the wobbles if you carry on eating those things,' I said.

'No I won't, I've just had me tea,' he said. 'Well, you're in the clear so off you go, sir,' he said, banging the top of the car in dismissal.

I drove on home. My last glimpse of the law in the driving mirror was of him standing by the kerb, clutching my box of Meltis New Berry Fruits and munching steadily.

★

I had collected a plastic bag full of books from Hatchards in Piccadilly and was strolling past Fortnum's when a tiny middle-aged couple, from south-east Asia I would have thought, emerged. They were clearly filthy rich; the lady was elegantly clad in mink (this was some twelve years ago) and diamonds glittered here and there upon her person. She came up to me, smiled delightfully and said, 'You have the most beautiful trousers I have ever seen!'

Now this happened to be welcome news. Polly had recently told me that all the clothes I had ever bought were in a shade of donkey (Polly occasionally comes out with these confidence-shattering observations. When we were driving to a restaurant on my fiftieth birthday, she suddenly said, 'I never realized you had such cruel eyes'), so I asked Doug Haywood, my tailor and an old friend, to construct me a pair of non-donkey-coloured trousers. These he made from a highly coloured, almost phosphorescent tweed in the sort of strong design which used to be called bookmaker's check.

I was a bit worried about them so when the nice lady asked if she could see the trousers in motion, I obligingly prinked up and down Piccadilly, smiling enigmatically like a supermodel and nonchalantly swinging my plastic bag of books.

The lady said, 'Beautiful! Beautiful!' Then when I had come to rest, laid her hand on the left cheek of my behind, cupped it for a moment in the manner of a Far-Eastern housewife estimating the weight of a mango, and gave it a strong and painful pinch. As my eyebrows shot up, she smiled her sweet smile again and said, 'In my country we always give a pinch when we give praise!'

I was intrigued whether my pinch was a widespread piece of folklore practice or a sudden sexual urge, so I wrote a letter to *The Times* describing what had happened and asking what was the significance of the event. The subject obviously appealed to readers because letters in reply were printed for weeks afterwards. What emerged from the printed letters was that it most certainly *was* a widespread practice.

Mrs Audrey Jones of Ealing wrote that it is well known in Jewish domestic circles, and pointed out that for a child to be praised for being artistic and intelligent and beautiful and then to have a cheek painfully pinched was one of the terrors of having a Jewish grandmother; particularly, it seems, if she came from Russia, Poland or Latvia. Mrs Jones described these immigrants as 'the feared matriarchs of Maida Vale'.

On the other hand, Mrs Tomlinson of London NW8 remembered that when she was a girl in Scotland it was customary to give a schoolfriend wearing new clothes a hard pinch on the upper arm 'for luck'.

Mr P. J. Barlow from Argyll thought that I had got off lightly. He pointed out that had I been an Arab or a Spanish gentleman of the old school I would have been honour bound to whip off my trousers there and then and present them to the lady.

The facts of the matter were explained in a letter from Dr Jacqueline Simpson, honorary editor of *Folklore*, who wrote that my alarming experience simply illustrated the misunderstandings which arose when people who did not traditionally believe in the evil eye encountered those who did. It seems the belief is quite common in India, the Near East and primitive bits of Europe. Its core is the notion that if anyone or anything is praised, this will arouse the envy of a malevolent onlooker with magical powers who will 'cast the eye'.

Dr Simpson's letter to *The Times* went on, 'If nothing had been done to counteract the praise, such as bestowing a powerful pinch, Mr Muir's fine trousers would undoubtedly have met with some dire accident – some soup perhaps, or too hot an iron. Maybe even the anatomy within would have withered under the glance of the unknown eye.'

Phew!

I was also sent a *Folklore* magazine which listed some of the counter-charms traditionally employed by peasantry in the Balkans. It seems that Balkan ploughmen, plodding their weary way homeward, on suspecting that there was a malevolent sprite about, protected themselves from the eye by exposing their organ of manhood.

Suddenly a pattern began to emerge. The use of '*chin-chin*' in Japan to describe the infant version of the Balkan ploughman's counter-charm ties in with a European use of the expression. So when a Frenchman (or a Corsican) in a bar raises his glass in your direction and says '*chin-chin!*', do remember that he is actually protecting you against the evil eye with the French verbal equivalent of a quick flash from a Baltic ploughman.

Back in the Eighties I had a letter from the artist, John Bratby ARA, inviting me to sit for him.

It was an odd letter. He emphasized that I would not be asked to buy the portrait, that was not his point in inviting me to sit; it was to be one of a number of portraits he was painting to make up an exhibition for the National Theatre of contemporary figures of fame and influence (you see what I mean by calling it an odd letter). Already on canvas were the faces of many of my friends, including Dilys Powell, John Cleese and Johnny Speight.

I knew Mr Bratby's work. He had a deserved success at Academy exhibitions with vigorous and colourful paintings of backyards seen through the kitchen window, that kind of thing. I had also seen some of the portraits he had already painted for this new exhibition. There was the familiar Bratby vigour and colour and the use of lots of paint, and a thumb here and there, but they seemed to me to be all the same face.

The rather crumpled face belonged to Johnny Speight, the writer. His portrait by Bratby hung on his wall (all my friends seemed to have bought their portraits) and it was an excellent likeness, but if you didn't look like Johnny Speight Mr Bratby's portrait didn't look like you. John Cleese looked like John Cleese doing an impression of Johnny Speight and Dilys Powell looked a little like Johnny Speight's aunt, but not much like Dilys Powell.

I accepted Mr Bratby's invitation because I had never sat for an artist, I wanted to meet him and the whole thing was intriguing.

I sat for only one afternoon at his studio in Greenwich. He stabbed away at the canvas with his brush (and his thumb) and chatted all the while. It was not a conversation because that suggests an interchange of dialogue and Mr Bratby spent the three hours asking lots of questions, but not listening to the answers because he was busy painting. A weird experience, like being interviewed by somebody who was deaf and had forgotten to put in his hearing aid.

As I left for home he again stressed that there was no pressure on me to buy the portrait, but almost as soon as I arrived back, a Polaroid of the portrait arrived with a thank-you note saying that the picture was mine for £400.

Next day I had to lunch at the Savile Club and I mentioned to the chap next to me, an accountant, that I had been painted by John Bratby, who was offering me the picture for £400. The accountant, with investment in mind, said, 'Buy it.'

I passed him the Polaroid.

'Don't buy it,' he said.

The face in the picture did not look much like me because I do not look like Johnny Speight. If anything, I looked in my portrait like the BBC sports presenter Desmond Lynam after he had been run over.

The final word came from our dear 'daily', Rene Hayes. I showed her the Polaroid of the portrait and said that it was mine for £400. What did she think? Mrs Hayes took it to the window, turned it upside down and sideways, held it at arm's length and then made her judgement: 'Seems a lot of money for a photograph.'

★

One evening Polly and I were lolling on the sofa, semi-watching some pretty awful television. I looked up *Radio Times* and there was no escaping to a better channel, all channels were offering pretty awful television.

It occurred to me that in the fifty years that I had been on and in and in front of television it had changed a great deal. It had to, of course, but so much had changed for the worse.

I was only thinking of programme quality. The curious belief by the present BBC that 'management consultancy' is the mystical answer to the difficulty of making better entertainment is understandable; 'management structures' are mainly about measuring things and doing sums and writing memos, which are not difficult tasks and 'management consultancy' is a comfortingly self-perpetuating, inexact science which manages to get itself paid enormous fees (it is altogether a much more sensible career to put a personable, intelligent, totally ungifted son or daughter into than making TV programmes).

The basic problem is that there are now too many TV

stations, and what is more there are a great many more to come soon due to wonderful digital TV (worked by finger?). Miserably, I think it is probably inevitable that, as Kingsley Amis said about education, 'More will mean worse', and the BBC's public service ethos will be abandoned as it chases the chimera of multi-channel digital plenty. There is simply not enought talent to go round. Not only performing and writing talent but creative production and directing talent, and what exists now will have to be spread even more thinly in the years of 'progress' ahead.

The Americans ran into this problem years ago and met it by rationing talent, which is expensive stuff, and making do instead with talent-substitutes; good humour rather than humour, formulaic comedy, the use of young producers and directors trained to work by the book and produce a show which was good or bad but was, more importantly, on time and within its budget. I speak of American television as a whole, not just the excellent comedy shows we import, which are the lilies on the dungheap of an enormous and mostly un-attractive national output.

We see this talent-substitution in operation now in Britain with the rise in importance of the presenter. Alan Titchmarsh, once the ace gardening presence on *Pebble Mill At One* we now see interviewing showbiz folk and presenting this and that all over the place; attractive weather girls, perfectly competent at reading their autocue and making odd but pretty hand gestures, turn up in front of programmes which have nothing to do with the weather. Ex-Radio 1 disc jockeys present jokey game shows, and journalists front everything from chat shows to travel programmes. Perhaps the best example of this use of an unusual presenter to beef up an otherwise not very original programme idea was a long series about the history of painting presented by Sister Wendy, an enthusiastic nun.

Another discovery by TV chiefs was that popular cheap pro-grammes could be made without using any talent at all, by making 'people shows', programmes which did not feature an expensive star but the antics of the general public. This was another American idea, pioneered by the radio broadcaster Alan Funt. Many years ago he devised *Candid Microphone*, a radio show in which a hidden microphone recorded people being hoodwinked into making fools of themselves. The programme then moved over to TV as *Candid Camera*, orginally presented in Britain by Jonathan Routh and later revived using Jeremy Beadle. Jeremy Beadle was also used to present another American idea which exploited the widespread use of home camcorders. This was an even cheaper way of putting on a half-hour programme than *Candid Camera* as the public took the pictures and just sent the tape in to the programme. If their film was used they were paid a small copyright fee.

This was yet another programme idea which fed the viewing public's keen pleasure in watching somebody else being humiliated. The difference with this one was that the humiliations were not brought about by complicated traps devised by the production staff as in *Candid Camera*, but were supposedly real slip-ups which happened during family filming. And slip-ups was what they literally were. In 99 per cent of the 'funny' clips, an adult, or more frequently a toddler, came out through the French windows and fell over. Sometimes the victim reached the shrubbery before falling over, sometimes started to climb the fence before falling over, but eventually, and usually quite swiftly, the victim fell over, sometimes quite painfully.

On 'humiliation' programmes, the victims have to sign a clearance chit approving the transmission of their moment of misery, but this is rarely a problem. As Andy Warhol might have said, soon everybody will be on television for two minutes and a great number of keen viewers would willingly have a leg off on film if it meant that they might appear on the nation's telly.

A grander programme appealing to the same ignoble pleasure in watching others suffer was the BBC's *Auntie's Sporting Bloomers*, presented by Terry Wogan, a brilliant and witty radio broadcaster who shifted to television, but after a few good years curiously faded in appeal, apart from keeping us all awake with his excellent cheeky commentary on the annual *Eurovision Song Contest*.

Auntie's Sporting Bloomers was simply another version of the very good *It'll Be Alright on the Night* and the naff Jeremy

Beadle amateur videos, but this time with blood. Toddlers falling into puddles was no longer enough so rally cars slid into rivers, pole vaulters' long poles snapped beneath them, racing skiers suffered horrendous crashes or ploughed into spectators, young women fell off jumping horses. (Denis told me that on *It'll Be Alright on the Night* he has a rule that if the victim who falls over doesn't get up, they don't use the clip.)

To a regular viewer these personal disasters induced no more than the normal nervous laugh, yet the companies' excuses for screening them were that they were highly comical. 'They're only fun,' was the defence. So the inherent sadism and loss of human dignity had to be presented as hysterically funny entertainment, which brings us to the nub of this rather long moan.

Among the technical innovations which have proved a great help to television, such as machines which record programmes, and the autocue which enables newsreaders (and, of course, presenters) to read prepared pieces whilst looking into the lens, there was another technical device which to my mind has proved the most destructive and dishonest influence ever on television comedy: manipulated laughter.

Laughter added to a show later – a little 'sweetening' as it is known in the trade – was originally done by using a laughter tape. This is still done, but it is not too successful. Firstly, because the sound doesn't ring true. A live audience bursting out laughing is the sound of audible pleasure growing which is not the same sound at all as the volume control being turned up in the middle of a tape of recorded laughter, and live laughter dying away is a quite different sound from recorded laughter being faded out. And all programmes seem to use the same two or three laughter tapes. The most recognizable has a woman horribly close to the recording microphone who has a con-tinuous cackle (do they audition the laughers?), and in the background is a random squeal of uncalled for shrieking, whooping and whistling.

The second problem is that producers and directors do not seem to know how to handle canned laughter. They use the tapes, of course, to paper over the fact that the show is not as funny as it should be, but then they get carried away and dub howls of laughter over any kind of movement on the screen even if there is nothing whatever going on which would prompt such a reaction.

Producers then moved on from the crude taped-laughter system and devised what they believed was a totally justifiable and efficient method of 'sweetening' a show. This was to record the studio audience laughing at something else, perhaps a smutty joke routine from a comedian warming up the audience before the recording, and then mix this laughter into the actual recording at key points.

The next development was to make sure that the audience provided loud enough hysterical laughter, whoops, whistles and so on. This is now done, particularly on give-away, 'yoof' and game shows, by skilful assistants who train the audience for a long time before the actual recording to make the required noises. The audiences (carefully selected by 'researchers') are only too happy to oblige.

One of the small but real pleasures of watching bad television is when an incompetent producer has dubbed on gales of hysterical laughter but has forgotten that the next shot is a reaction shot of the studio audience, and the audience is slumped silently in its seats, half asleep.

*

In winter I suffer, mostly in heroic silence I must point out, from a boring item known to doctors as Raynaud's Disease (or if they are in private practice, Raynaud's Phenomenon), a widespread little bother where the fingers go white and dead when the weather is cold or the sufferer stays in the water too long when swimming. To relieve this harmless but unhelpful and sometimes quite painful infliction I sent off to a mail-order company for a pair of newly invented hand-warming sachets. They turned up the statutory twenty-eight days later. Happily the weather had turned viciously cold, and as I had to go to London to a *Punch* lunch, it was a good moment to road-test my Mycoal Grabber Hand and Pocket Warmers (Odourless, Non-toxic, Dry, Clean and Disposable). They looked exactly like tea bags.

Obeying instructions, I tore them (with some difficulty) out of their stout plastic envelope and massaged them, whereupon by some scientific miracle they swiftly grew comfortingly warm, almost hot. They stayed so all morning, one in each coat pocket, keeping my hands pink and cosy as I shopped in icy London.

At lunchtime the hot tea bags were still going strong. As I passed the entrance to Hamley's the toyshop, I was pulled up by the sight of a vagrant slumped in the doorway. Not a young, *Big Issue*-selling vagrant but an old-fashioned tramp, elderly, covered in many overcoats and bits of plastic. He had a beard like rusty barbed wire and he was filthy.

On an impulse I took out one of my hot Grabber hand-warmers and pressed it into his very cold and grubby hand. 'This might help to warm you up,' I said cheerfully.

'Giss a quid,' he said.

At the *Punch* lunch I was seated next to Lady Olga Maitland, the slim elegant journalist and politician. I showed her my remaining hot tea bag, explained its magical workings and presented it to her. Lady Olga took it with a charming smile and slipped it down her cleavage.

It would be difficult to think of two more diverse resting places for my pair of Mycoal Grabber Hand and Pocket Warmers (Odourless, Non-Toxic, Dry, Clean and Disposable).

*

People often stop me in the street and ask, 'With your white hair and feeble moustache and vague air of wanting to be somewhere else, why have you never been knighted?'

Actually, not all that many people have stopped me and asked that. To be brutally honest *nobody* has stopped me and asked that, but should somebody ever stop me and ask why I am not Sir Frank, I have a full answer. I blotted my copybook with Prince Philip at a fund-raising dinner in the ballroom of an exclusive (a tabloid newspaper adjective meaning expensive) London hotel.

There used to be a story about a high-born epicene young Guards officer who had somehow survived the First World War and was asked what trench warfare on the Somme was really like. He said, 'Oh, my dear, the *noise*! The PEOPLE!'

That is how, now that I work at home, I tend to feel when

I have to go to London. One evening some years ago I arrived home from London tired and tetchy as usual in time to see the nine o'clock news. The lead story was Prince Charles's maiden speech in the House of Lords. The newsreader said, 'Prince Charles began his speech with the quotation, "As Oscar Wilde said, 'If a thing is worth doing, it is worth doing badly!'" (much respectful laughter).'

A good modest introduction to a speech, but unfortunately the line was not written by Oscar Wilde but by G. K. Chesterton. Ascribing it to Wilde suggested it was nothing more than a witty *bon mot*, one of those amusing Wildean inversions such as, 'Work is the curse of the drinking classes.' But coming from G. K. Chesterton meant it was a more thoughtful observation. In Chesterton's work his humour arose from a serious thought, as an oyster was prompted into action by a gritty grain of sand. What Chesterton was saying (in a piece about playing croquet) was that playing a game simply because you enjoyed playing it, perhaps hoping to get better at it in time, is a worthy enough reason for playing it however badly.

In my tetchy mood I lost my cool for a moment, telephoned *The Times* newspaper and left a message for the editor of The Diary column explaining how important I felt it was that the quotation was given its proper author.

Next morning *The Times* made the Prince's speech its front-page story. It began, 'Last night the Prince of Wales began his maiden speech to the House of Lords by saying "As Oscar Wilde said, 'If a thing is worth doing, it is worth doing badly!'" (laughter).'

Then came an asterisk, and at the bottom of the page was its twin asterisk and, in nasty black type, '**Mr Frank Muir pointed out last night that the Prince had opened his speech with a misquotation. The line was not written by Oscar Wilde but by G. K. Chesterton.**'

And then other newspapers began telephoning for follow-up stories . . .

Worse happened. A year or so later I found myself in the Crystal Room of London's 'exclusive' Grosvenor House Hotel having pre-dinner drinkies with the formidable committee who were mounting the evening's ball, which was an early exercise in prising money out of the rich and good for the World Wildlife Fund. I was there to give my after-dinner speech.

Also speaking was the Duke of Edinburgh. I found myself beside the Duke in a quiet corner of the noisy room. He was looking a bit bored, so I felt it incumbent upon me to put him at his ease.

'Oh, sir,' I said, 'I feel I must apologize for correcting the Prince of Wales on the misquotation in his maiden speech to the Lords. But, sir, I felt rather strongly about it. You see, sir, it wasn't a joke, but a philosophy which I happen to agree with. It is the opposite view to the American cult of winner take all. If your child does not come top of the class does that mean that it is a useless human being? No, of course not . . .'

As I warmed to my theme the Duke closed his eyes several times, presumably in order to concentrate on what I was saying, but as I talked on I remembered that both he and Prince Charles had been to stern Gordonstoun school where, it was rumoured, those pupils who did not come among the top three in exams were shot (only a slight wound in a fleshy part of the thigh, I understood, but still . . .). After something like a quarter of an hour I brought my little apology to a close by saying, laughingly, '. . . anyway, sir, I would have thought the blithering idiot who gave Prince Charles the quotation would have had the nous to check it first!'

The Duke looked at me levelly. '*I* gave him the quotation,' he said.

*

If only Polly and I had been less shy in the early days we might have been younger grandparents and not found it all quite so exhausting, but in our seventies we find that racing after a run-away three-year-old in the garden, or bending down and picking up 200 small, vitally important broken toys from the floor at bed-time is getting to be quite an effort. Even lifting Gabriel out of the bath made Polly long for a domestic fork-lift truck on loan from the district nurse.

The senior Wheatcrofts had to go off somewhere and for the first time left Abigail in our care for a whole week.

Afterwards Polly and I booked into a health farm for four days.

*

Omar Khayyám wrote the wistful lines:

*   Alas that Spring should vanish with the rose,
      And youth's sweet, scented manuscript should close.

For those readers who are worried whether they have reached the stage when their spring has disappeared, their aromatic manuscript is completed and they are about to be dead-headed, Denis and I have isolated some foolproof symptoms. You are beginning to be truly old when:

You do not kneel down unless you have first spotted something you can grab to pull yourself up again.

You get into a car by backing your bottom in and then hauling your legs in by hand.

You have given up eating toffees, stewed figs (the seeds), and anything with nuts anywhere near it.

* I remember those lines from the *Rubáiyát* because in the 1930s they were painted on a wall of the Omar Khayyám Café, next to the Royal Hotel in Albion Street, Broadstairs. They might still be there.

*

Before we oldies can enjoy the great pleasure of cuddling and/or tripping over our grandchildren, there is an interesting intermediary stage: our children have to acquire mates. Neither Jamie nor Sal rushed into marriage. Friendships, yes, but total commitment was not undertaken lightly. Sal met Geoffrey at a party and from then on his name seemed to crop up more and more in conversation. She seemed to be seeing him so frequently that we asked her when she was going to arrange for us to meet him. 'Probably never,' Sal said a little loftily, which was a clear pointer that things were getting serious.

In 1990 I had my seventieth birthday and Sal brought Geoffrey to the party and we liked him very much. After the party the two of them went off to Paris and when they arrived back Geoffrey met me at the Garrick Club for a drink and told me that in Paris he had asked Sal to marry him and she had agreed.

Geoffrey and Sal seemed to spend most of 1990 getting married.

They had a civil ceremony at an off-licence (as Denis and I like to call register offices) in Bath, where Geoffrey lived, then later we all trooped over to Siena where Geoffrey's friend, Jasper Guinness, had arranged a church wedding in an ancient Protestant chapel, conducted by an elderly English vicar from Florence who spent much of his time clad in scarlet leathers happily roaring around Chiantishire on a motorbike.

Back to Bath in mid-summer, the wedding breakfast was held; a joyous party. The temperature outside was in the nineties and inside the marquee it was like a vast mixed sauna.

Theoretically, Sally could have brought into the family a nice kind water-diviner or a non-ferrous metal welder, in which case conversation over Christmas dinner might have been a little difficult to maintain on a sprightly note ('Divined anything interesting recently, Ronald?' 'Do tell us again about the trouble you had fusing copper to brass in the cold spell, Sidney').

But Sally augmented our family to the good with the much respected journalist and author, Geoffrey Wheatcroft, columnist, opera correspondent, writer of newspaper 'think pieces', and author of, amongst other books, *The Randlords*, the riveting story of the gold and diamond barons of South Africa and, more recently, *The Controversy of Zion*, about the founding of the Jewish independent state. And if that was not enough, Geoffrey cooks superbly and is father of Abigail and Gabriel.

Jamie, too, did the family proud. A few months after Sal's wedding, he married Caroline Robertson, an extremely attractive girl who had modelled for the painter John Ward ARA, but when we met her was an editor with Penguin Books. She has since taken a degree in paper conservation and works with museums. Jamie and Caroline have added a daughter, Isobel, to our grandchildren's Christmas-present list.

Caroline's father, John, who was with British Steel before taking early retirement so that he could do what he had always wanted to do, become an antique dealer and whizz about the country with bits of Georgian silver, solved for me a difficult problem of relationship.

I am not very good at that cat's cradle game of who is whose ninth cousin twice removed and where step-grandnephews fit in – it seems to be a game exclusively enjoyed by one's wife – and I could not work out what my relationship was to the father of my son's wife.

The problem was resolved when the good man telephoned me soon after Jamie and Caroline's wedding. 'Hello, Frank?' he said. 'It's me, John-in-law.'

★

In Egham High Street, a frail old man stepped carefully out of the door of Mr Mullan the pharmacist. The old man saw me and halted.

'I know you from the telly,' he said. His face went sad. 'I used to like you,' he said.

★

Mr Mullan the pharmacist came to Egham from Belfast and is a fellow parishioner with Polly of the Catholic church. I know him well as I get my pills from him. Mr Mullan's grey-haired, benign, avuncular appearance belies a swift-thinking and occasionally wicked turn of mind.

I had put in to my health centre for a renewal prescription, but it had not arrived when I noticed that I was almost out of Persantin tablets, which I was told were vital to stop me from slumping occasionally to the floor. A friend advised me to go to my friendly pharmacist and borrow a couple of Persantin to keep me vertical pro tem. So off I went to Mr Mullan.

'Mr Mullan,' I said, 'I have been a foolish virgin . . .'

'Boasting again?' he said.

★

Going through this manuscript, that is to say toning down the adjectives and trying to cut out a hundred or so 'very's, I was very struck by how random and wayward the finger of Fate seems to have been in my life, and presumably everybody's. A coherent plan did not seem to have entered into her thinking; she had clearly not been on a planner's course or had a session with the management consultants.

Theoretically one makes one's own decisions, we are free

spirits, but looking back I have been about as much in control of my progress as a plastic duck in a jacuzzi.

The fact is that the major hinges in life are hidden. When I think of the jobs years ago which Denis and I hoped so much to get, and in hindsight can only say – thank *heavens* we lost that job of writing musicals on ice for Harringay Arena, and the deal which fell through of moving to America to write a version for their TV of *Whack-O!*, a comedy about an English public school whose customs and values American viewers were not in the slightest bit familiar with. And how invisible are the tiny hinges which swing us into our really important human relationships and career moves.

Nearly fifty years ago, when Charles Maxwell took Denis and me to lunch at Frank's, the Italian restaurant in Jermyn Street, and suggested that we might get together and have a go at writing a radio series for Jimmy Edwards and Dick Bentley (which turned out to be *Take It From Here*), we were both so busy already with (small) commitments that we could have strolled along to St James's Street, exchanged pleasantries about the meal, then I could have said something like, 'Interesting offer, but, like you, I'm a bit full up at the moment. Shall I give you a ring in a month or so and see how we're placed then?' and turned right at St James's Street to find my parked car and drive home. And Den could have turned left and gone back to his office.

But we didn't; we both went back to Den's office together. From that day on we wrote everything together for nearly twenty years, radio shows, theatre revues for George and Alfred Black, scenes for films, sketches for summer shows, and so on. And when that stopped we performed in *My Word!* and *My Music* together for many years, and then we had our television shows. Nowadays, now that I am taking things a little more calmly, we make do with phoning each other two or three times a week.

These are pleasant phone calls; Den and I exchange physical symptoms, unpick the previous evening's TV and recount to the other some bit of observed idiocy, knowing that the other is probably the only person in the world who will wholly appreciate the story.

We are quite different people, which is probably why the partnership worked so well. Producers bought the product of two minds; it was an additive process not one comedy approach divided (like the fee) into two.

Denis was a revelation to me. His mind is a fascinating mixture of intellectual rigour and showbiz flair. He is a worrier, alarmingly intelligent, a very hard worker, doodler of complicated geometrical patterns when thinking, a reader of everything, hopeless at doing anything complicated with his hands like putting a refill into a ballpoint pen, but with a keen and original mind for comedy and a love of musicals and good 'flicks' (rather than 'cinema').

Perhaps one reason why we never had a row in all those years, apart from both being good at 'rubbing-along' and never having enough nervous energy to spare for squabbling, was that we hardly ever saw each other outside our office. During the day we were with each other longer than we were with our wives, but then, when we had finished for the day, Denis went home to North London and I drove back to Anners, Thorpe. Polly and Avril Norden have an enjoyable lunch together twice a year; Den and I are always faintly worried what they talk about.

A year or so ago Antonia Fraser threw a drinks party in her garden in Camden Hill Square. Afterwards Polly suggested that all four of us might wander across the road to the Pomme d'Amour, a Mauritian restaurant. While we were menu-studying I said to Den, 'I've suddenly realized this is the first time we four have had dinner together since we were in Australia twenty-five years ago.'

Den said, 'I hope you're not thinking of making a habit of it.'

★

I had ordered from Harrods a made-to-measure venetian blind (we had found to our dismay that for quite a few years Polly and I had tottered stark naked up and down the stone stairs of A Torra in Corsica on our way to the shower in full view of anybody walking across the square below).

The department at Harrods was on a lonely floor, and was empty of customers when I arrived to collect my bespoke blind. The only inhabitant was a young assistant. I gave him my chitty for the venetian blind. 'Sorry, but I'll have to keep you waiting for a few minutes,' he said. 'I have to find your blind in the stockroom on the next floor up.'

Left alone amongst shelves of yard-long bolts of curtain material I suddenly realized that this was a wonderful opportunity to fulfil a childhood ambition – to 'flip-flop' a bolt of cloth noisily along the counter and unwind a length of the material as I had seen so many haberdashery shop assistants do in my childhood. I reached behind me, took out a board, over which was wound blue curtain material, and laid it on the counter, noting with pleasure that there was a yard-long brass measure let into the countertop. 'Flip-flop' the bolt of material went as I flipped it over deftly. In my exhilaration I soon flipped it to the end of the counter and had to stop.

I looked up in my moment of glee and saw that there was an elderly lady standing at the customer's side of the counter looking at the curtain material with interest.

'Have you by any happy chance got it in green?' she asked.

'I'll have a look, madam,' I said.

I *had* got it in green.

'Eight and a half yards, please,' she said.

I slid the bolt of cloth off the shelf and onto the counter and flipped it over, flip-flop, flop, flop, flop. I measured 8½ yards against the imbedded ruler and cut the material with a massive pair of scissors I found lying by the till, folded up the cloth and stuffed it into a dark-green plastic bag.

'How much is that?' asked the lady, fumbling with her purse.

I suddenly went chill. Now that money was involved my little romp could easily turn nasty. The assistant could well take the view that I was a thief and call the store detective . . .

And the assistant was suddenly there, standing by the till clutching my venetian blind and watching.

I gulped. 'This lady asked me for eight and a half yards of the green so I sold it to her,' I said defiantly.

'Cheers,' said the assistant.

★

On the matter of the power of hidden hinges as against one's own control over events, it was certainly no cunning stratagem, nor any feeling of destiny which made me decide one day to wander down the stairs and grab a quick lunch at the BBC canteen in Aeolian Hall, where I stood behind that blonde with a lovely voice, a tray of beans on toast and an apple.

That was forty-nine years ago (as I write) and I still stand behind my blonde with the musical voice when we go to buy the birds' peanuts at Lynne's the ironmongers in Virginia Water on Saturday mornings, and Polly and I will soon be enjoying the rigours of our golden wedding anniversary.

Denis and I wrote a joke once in *TIFH* that being in love is only a temporary mania which after marriage changes into something much more lasting – hatred (not a very jolly joke). As far as Pol and I are concerned, being in love certainly developed into something more lasting – love. And love is altogether a much deeper, give-and-take, *affectionate* relationship than being 'in' love.

Polly and I confirm our feelings towards each other every night along with prayers for the rest of the family and Sal's Dalmatian Dotty, and our cat Cinto (named after the tallest mountain in Corsica, such a sensible name for an Abyssinian cat), so should a feminist journalist from a women's page telephone me today and ask me how often I have told my wife that I love her, I will reply (after a quick arpeggio on the calculator to check), roughly 16,822 times. And I spoke the truth every time.

Pol and I are on paper reasonably incompatible, so important an ingredient in a good partnership. Polly seems to me to have rather over-fastidious views about personal hygiene, such as when one has been greasing the motor mower, nature's method of wiping the mess off one's hands quickly is on a guest towel (normally so rarely used) or a drooping bit of the table-cloth. This sort of *ad hoc* solution to a problem is not encouraged by the management.

Polly enjoys eating pasta. To me, with my diminished sense of taste, pasta tends to be like eating bits of blotting-paper. And Polly has always loved the flower garden and the vegetable patch. When I was more spry I used to labour quite a lot in the garden, but it was only labouring. To me flowers and vegetables were a foreign country, I could never remember their names or recognize them. It was all right when the edible bit appeared and I could name it as a cabbage or a stick of rhubarb, but when it was just green foliage I couldn't tell one plant from another.

A really shaming incident occurred when daughter Sal, aged about six, was in bed slowly recovering from flu. Polly had to go out shopping and she asked me to dig her some potatoes. I toured the kitchen garden and could not see any potatoes. I thought they might hang down from a bush like gooseberries, or hang upwards and sideways like corn on the cob, but there were no potatoes to be seen dangling anywhere.

If I failed to dig the potatoes it would lead to tremendous loss of face, harsh words, and a coolth would develop with Pol which might last for weeks. Frantic, I thought hard and came up with the answer. There was somebody in the house who knew a great deal about nature and in a flash could point me in the direction of potatoes. I rushed upstairs, wrapped little flu-stricken Sal in an eiderdown, staggered downstairs with her, and methodically waved her over the kitchen garden, face downwards, like a metal detector. She was coughing a bit, but soon located the row of Murphys and I was saved.

When brother Chas and I were teenagers our granny decided to give us signet rings. I hated the idea of wearing jewellery and so she gave me something else.

It was coming up to our forty-seventh wedding anniversary and Polly asked me if there was something I would like to have as a keepsake, and suddenly I knew exactly what I wanted. I said, 'Please may I have a wedding ring?'

Polly was very surprised. She said, 'Tell me why you suddenly want a wedding ring after all these years and you shall have one.'

'Well, I wanted to be sure first,' I said, the sort of slick half joke inappropriate for a rather emotional moment, but it gave me time to think. Most readers who have reached this far in the book will know exactly how I feel towards Polly.

The weaker the little jokes which I make at home, the more Polly laughs, which is a thoroughly good sign. We do a fair bit of laughing. And Pol is very sensible, and common sense is becoming a much underrated quality. Polly, above all, is kind and good and unselfish and strong, all the things which her Roman Catholicism has encouraged.

I find it quite impossible to visualize what life without Polly would have been like. Finding Polly was like a fifth rib replacement, or 'the other half' we search for to make us complete in the process which Plato called 'the desire and pursuit of the whole'. It was a wonderfully successful process in my case.

I asked for a wedding ring so that I could wear it as a symbol of the happiness my marriage to Pol has brought. Now that I work at home it is so good just to know that Pol is somewhere around, even though invisible, perhaps bending down picking white currants in the fruit cage and swearing gently, or upstairs shortening a skirt for a granddaughter.

The happy thing is to know that Pol is near.

*

Finally (Oh, happy word to read? Only equalled, according to the poet Robert Southey, by churchgoers nodding through the sermon and suddenly hearing the vicar declaiming '. . . in the name of the Father, the Son and the Holy Ghost . . .').

Finally, a word from Dilys Powell.

When the novelist Arnot Robertson died in the early years of *My Word!* her replacement as my partner was the doyenne of British film critics, Dilys Powell.

Our daughter Sally met Dilys when the whole team came to Anners for a quick snack before we all went off to record *My Word!* at our local hospital. Sally was still at school and began writing to Dilys. The correspondence, and the friendship, went on for years (Sal also had other pen-friends – 'pen-pals' does not seem appropriate to describe Sal's list of quite elderly and distinguished correspondents, which included the county court judge His Honour Judge Leon, and the glass engraver and poet Laurence Whistler).

Then we found that Dilys, twice widowed and getting on in years, spent Christmas alone in her house in London, so we invited Dilys down to be our honorary granny.

It was a huge success and Dilys spent Christmas with us for the next nineteen years, latterly quite old and physically slow, but mentally as brisk and stimulating as ever; although she'd had two happy marriages she warned Sal not to jump into it.

'Do not marry unless you cannot possibly live without him,' was her advice (actually her command) to Sal.

Then one weekend after dinner, Dilys was now in her early nineties, I told her about beginning these memoirs. She asked me whether I regretted anything. I said that there were no deep regrets; I had been helped along so often by sudden shafts of good fortune that life, like democracy and walking, had been a constantly interrupted fall forward.

'Just one mild bleat,' I said to Dil. 'Nowadays young comics in their late twenties and early thirties have their own production companies and control their video sales and so on, and several are millionaires. Den and I did a bit of useful pioneering in the beginnings of radio comedy and then of telly comedy, but pioneers don't make that sort of money. It would have been nice for me, still the breadwinner in my late seventies, to have emerged from the struggle just a little bit rich.'

Darling Dil's reaction was extraordinary. She banged the table, eyes blazing. 'What on earth are you talking about! You ARE rich! You're a very rich man! Just look at what you've got. You have Polly as your wife, you have worked happily for years with Denis as partner, and he is now your closest friend, you have two gifted children with good marriages, three delightful grand-children, you've had a most successful career, you have written bestsellers, your voice is recognized all over the world, you have Anners and Corsica . . . you are rich in everything worth having. How DARE you wish you had more!'

Well! That was telling me.

And of course Dilys was right.

★

It seems that few famous last words were actually uttered by the departing, at least not at the time of their departure. I was assured by a courtier who was present at the bedside that King George V did not expire saying, 'Bugger Bognor,' although apparently it accurately reflected his views. Nor, sadly, did the eighteenth-century pioneering traveller and poet Lady Mary Wortley Montagu review her life and pass on with the words, 'It has all been most interesting.' It seems the phrase was

406

invented for her in a biography, *Portrait of Lady Mary Montagu* by Iris Barry. But what a superbly aristocratic attitude! As though life had been a pageant, like the Coventry Mystery Plays, trundled past on carts to amuse her ladyship.

So, what better way for me to end these memoirs than to adapt the splendid Lady Mary Wortley line which I like so much, and, with dear Dilys's comments ringing in my ears, change just one word of it so that my own summing-up reads:

'It has all been most enrichening.'

Envoi

Although he was not at all well when he wrote his autobiography, I think Pa always wanted *A Kentish Lad* to be a manifesto for his kindly view of the world, and nothing was going to stop him writing to the last page.

Sometimes he used to say ruefully, 'If you don't appear on television or the radio people think you're dead.' The letters he received from the first readers of *A Kentish Lad* were confirmation that he could still entertain a wide audience, and he was touched and delighted by their response.

We all spent Christmas together at Anners. Two days of cheerful chaos – Gabriel calling out, 'Bummer, Bummer, I'm not going to tell you what I've just done in your study' (stamped First Class on every piece of paper on his desk). Pa did his best to join in, watching the Spice Girls on television with Abigail and Isobel – he always loved leaning on the back of the sofa and commenting about whatever was on – handing out presents, carving the goose.

From time to time he would slide away into his study. On one occasion I glimpsed him through the half-open door, rereading a passage from this book, his lips moving as he read. There was nothing self-congratulatory about his absorption. He reminded me of a carpenter running his hand over a well-planed surface. His pleasure was in the craft of words.

I rang Frank and Pol on 31 December to wish them happy new year. The conversation turned to the question of a sample that his doctor had asked him to provide. 'I've been given a little tub and an ice-cream shovel. I'm not at all sure what I'm meant to do with it. I suppose I'll have to use my imagination . . .' It was entirely characteristic of him to make a potentially humiliating incident humorous.

He died of heart failure on the morning of 2 January, in his own bed, in no pain or fear.

We placed in his coffin John Carey's review of *A Kentish Lad* from the *Sunday Times*, a letter from a reader and a small bunch of *Iris stylosa* from the garden at Anners.

His funeral took place ten days later on a clear cold day. The Parish Church of St Mary, Thorpe, like a miraculous transformation in a children's story, seemed to get larger and larger as more and more people from all stages of his life squeezed in.

Denis Norden, who'd known Pa for fifty-one years, concluded his moving, funny address with a remark that Samuel Johnson made about a dear departed friend: 'Howmuchsoever I valued him, I now wish I had valued him more.'

Pa was not a great joke teller, but he had a small store that he loved to retell. He treated them like fables, and they illuminated Sal's and my childhood. One was about an Arctic explorer who ran out of food and had to eat his favourite Husky. Staring down at the pile of picked bones, he said sadly, 'Rover would have enjoyed those . . .'

Pa would have enjoyed seeing a detachment of the Surrey constabulary executing a crisp salute as his coffin left the church. He would have enjoyed seeing so many of his friends together, without his having to appear on *This Is Your Life*. He would have enjoyed seeing *A Kentish Lad* reach the top of the non-fiction bestsellers.

He was a wonderful father.

Jamie Muir

Index

420

THE WALPOLE ORANGE
by Frank Muir

'Captivating . . . Muir has a wonderful ear for dialogue, and a wonderful eye for the comic situation'
Daily Express

William Grundwick has a problem. As secretary of the Walpole Club he's duty-bound to arrange whatever function the Events Committee decides is appropriate to celebrate the Club's 250th birthday. It's just that what they have decided upon seems to William almost wholly inappropriate; worse still he's not sure he knows precisely what form such a function should take. And if that isn't bad enough, the whole business is supposed to be a deep secret, so he can't even discuss it with his lovely young wife Milly. Milly has her own problems. Is she going off William? His secretiveness is certainly disturbing. And now the Baroque Trio she runs has lost its viola and continuo player – Catriona has decamped to Los Angeles with a session guitarist called Trev.

Torn between the demands of the Events Committee, Milly, and an accountant in a diaphanous sari, spied on by a treacherous underporter with a hotline to the tabloids and pressurized by the chairperson of the Golden Horn Ladies Belly-Dancing Ensemble, Catford, the harassed William has some appallingly difficult decisions to make.

The Walpole Orange, astonishingly, is Frank Muir's first novel. As one might expect from Britain's leading humorist, it is highly imaginative, wickedly witty and utterly irresistible.

'Utterly Brilliant'
Daisy Waugh, *Evening Standard*

'Fans will recognise his exuberant wit in this light-hearted romp with a P.G. Wodehouse flavour'
Good Book Guide

0 552 14137 2

THE PAST IS MYSELF
by Christabel Bielenberg

'It would be difficult to overpraise this book. Mrs
Bielenberg's experience was unique and her honesty,
intelligence and compassion makes her account of it
moving beyond words'
The Economist

Christabel Bielenberg, a niece of Lord Northcliffe, married
a German lawyer in 1934. She lived through the war in
Germany, as a German citizen, under the horrors of Nazi
rule and Allied bombings. *The Past is Myself* is her story
of that experience, an unforgettable portrait of an evil
time.

'This autobiography is of exceptional distinction and
importance. It deserves recognition as a magnificent
contribution to international understanding and as a
document of how the human spirit can triumph in the
midst of evil and persecution'
The Economist

'Marvellously written'
Observer

'Nothing but superlatives will do for this book. It tells its
story magnificently and every page of its story is worth
telling'
Irish Press

'Intensely moving'
Yorkshire Evening News

0 552 99065 5

THE DVINA REMAINS
A family memoir
by Eugenie Fraser

The House by the Dvina, Eugenie Fraser's highly
acclaimed and bestselling account of her childhood in
Russia, ended with the author's escape to Scotland
immediately after the Revolution.

Now, almost eighty years later, she takes up the story
again in *The Dvina Remains*, describing her first visit to
Russia in half a century. It was to be many more years
before she was given permission to go to Archangel,
though, where she was at last able to make contact with
her surviving relatives and to revisit the haunts of her
childhood.

Since then, the author has returned once more and has
gradually pieced together the story of her family since the
Revolution. It is an intensely moving and often harrowing
story, beautifully told – much of it through the letters of
Eugenie's cousin. He was able to tell her about the final
years of her father, who had been too ill to leave Russia
with his wife and children. The hardships they endured as
White Russians in a Communist country, and which they
survived against all the odds, are evoked with an intensity
which transcends the years.

'Intriguing'
Highland News Group

0 552 14539 4

LOST FOR WORDS
by Deric Longden

'You know, Deric – ten minutes of this rain will do more good in half an hour than a fortnight of ordinary rain would do in a month.'

Deric Longden's mother had a marvellously dotty way with words and a very private brand of logic. She was one of the most amusing and endearing characters in *Diana's Story*, which Deric wrote some years after his wife Diana's death. Deric's mother is the central figure in *Lost for Words*. Here we find her making her devastating way through Marks & Spencer, conversing with her two cats – almost as eccentric as herself – offering her inimitable comments on the fresh developments in Deric's life, and finally enduring the stroke that led eventually to her death. Sad though the ending is, Deric Longden's gift for blending pathos with rich humour once again offers us far more laughter than tears.

'A lovely read'
Good Housekeeping

0 552 13943 2

A SELECTED LIST OF FINE WRITING AVAILABLE FROM CORGI AND BLACK SWAN

99065 5	THE PAST IS MYSELF	*Christabel Bielenberg* £6.99
13741 3	LETTER TO LOUISE	*Pauline Collins* £6.99
13407 4	LET ME MAKE MYSELF PLAIN	*Catherine Cookson* £5.99
13582 8	THE GOD SQUAD	*Paddy Doyle* £6.99
14239 5	MY FEUDAL LORD	*Tehmina Durrani* £5.99
14396 0	ACTS OF FAITH	*Adam Faith* £5.99
13928 9	DAUGHTER OF PERSIA	*Sattareh Farman Farmaian* £6.99
99530 4	H.G.: THE HISTORY OF MR WELLS	*Michael Foot* £7.99
99479 0	PERFUME FROM PROVENCE	*Lady Fortescue* £6.99
14539 4	THE DVINA REMAINS	*Eugenie Fraser* £6.99
14185 2	FINDING PEGGY: A GLASGOW CHILDHOOD	*Meg Henderson* £6.99
14164 X	EMPTY CRADLES	*Margaret Humphreys* £6.99
99680 7	THE IMAGINARY GIRLFRIEND	*John Irving* £5.99
99691 2	DANCING WITH MISTER D: NOTES ON LIFE AND DEATH	*Bert Keizer* £6.99
14474 6	IN BED WITH AN ELEPHANT	*Ludovic Kennedy* £7.99
99637 8	MISS McKIRDY'S DAUGHTERS WILL NOW DANCE THE HIGHLAND FLING	*Barbara Kinghorn* £6.99
13943 2	LOST FOR WORDS	*Deric Longden* £5.99
14544 0	FAMILY LIFE	*Elisabeth Luard* £6.99
13356 0	NOT WITHOUT MY DAUGHTER	*Betty Mahmoody* £5.99
13953 X	SOME OTHER RAINBOW	*John McCarthy & Jill Morrell* £6.99
99562 2	CARL GUSTAV JUNG	*Frank McLynn* £12.99
14276 X	IMMEDIATE ACTION	*Andy McNab* £5.99
14136 4	THE WALPOLE ORANGE	*Frank Muir* £4.99
14288 3	BRIDGE ACROSS MY SORROWS	*Christina Noble* £5.99
99784 6	FIRST LIGHT	*Richard Preston* £6.99
11487 1	LIFE AFTER DEATH	*Neville Randall* £4.99
14275 1	THE AUTOBIOGRAPHY OF A THIEF	*Bruce Reynolds* £5.99
14052 X	LORDS OF THE RIM	*Sterling Seagrave* £6.99
14433 9	INVISIBLE CRYING TREE	*Tom Shannon & Christopher Morgan* £6.99

PLASTIC SURGERY SECRETS

SECOND EDITION

JEFFREY WEINZWEIG, MD, FACS

Chief of Craniofacial Surgery
Director, Craniofacial Anomalies Program
Division of Plastic Surgery
Illinois Masonic Medical Center
Chicago, Illinois

Director
The Chicago Center
for Plastic & Reconstructive Surgery
Chicago, Illinois

MOSBY

ELSEVIER

MOSBY
ELSEVIER

1600 John F. Kennedy Blvd.
Ste 1800
Philadelphia, PA 19103-2899

PLASTIC SURGERY SECRETS, SECOND EDITION

ISBN: 978-0-323-03470-8

Notice

Knowledge and best practice in this field are constantly changing. As new research and experience broaden our knowledge, changes in practice, treatment and drug therapy may become necessary or appropriate. Readers are advised to check the most current information provided (i) on procedures featured or (ii) by the manufacturer of each product to be administered, to verify the recommended dose or formula, the method and duration of administration, and contraindications. It is the responsibility of the practitioner, relying on their own experience and knowledge of the patient, to make diagnoses, to determine dosages and the best treatment for each individual patient, and to take all appropriate safety precautions. To the fullest extent of the law, neither the Publisher nor the Editor assumes any liability for any injury and/or damage to persons or property arising out or related to any use of the material contained in this book.

The Publisher

Library of Congress Cataloging-in-Publication Data
Plastic surgery secrets / [edited by] Jeffrey Weinzweig. – 2nd ed.
 p. ; cm. – (Secrets series)
 Includes bibliographical references and index.
 ISBN 978-0-323-03470-8
 1. Surgery, Plastic–Examinations, questions, etc. I. Weinzweig, Jeffrey,
1963- II. Series: Secrets series.
 [DNLM: 1. Surgery, Plastic–Examination Questions. 2. Reconstructive Surgical Procedures–
Examination Questions. WO 18.2 P715 2010]
 RD118.P5385 2010
 617.9'5076–dc22

2009046360

Acquisitions Editor: Jim Merritt
Developmental Editor: Andrea Vosburgh
Project Manager: Mary Stermel
Design Direction: Steve Stave

Printed in China

Last digit is the print number: 9 8 7 6 5 4 3 2

To my Ashley,
who inspires me to pursue my greatest dreams,
revels in my successes,
and laughs with me as we share the ride.
She motivates me, indulges me, and tolerates me.
She is my muse.

To my little Leo,
Who has changed my entire world.
He is my anchor.

CONTENTS

IV   CRANIOFACIAL SURGERY II — TRAUMATIC

CONTRIBUTORS

Ghada Y. Afifi, MD, FACS
Clinical Assistant Professor, Department of Plastic Surgery, Loma Linda University Medical Center, Loma Linda, California; Attending Physician, Private Practice, Department of Plastic Surgery, Hoag Hospital, Newport Beach, California; Attending Physician, Private Practice, Department of Surgery, Orange Coast Memorial Hospital, Fountain Valley, California; Volunteer Clinical Assistant Professor, Department of Plastic Surgery, University of California at San Diego, San Diego, California

Edward Akelman, MD
Professor/Vice Chairman, Department of Orthopaedics, Brown University; Chief, Division of Hand, Upper Extremity & Microvascular Surgery, Department of Orthopaedics, Rhode Island Hospital, Providence, Rhode Island

Louis C. Argenta, MD
Julius Howell Distinguished Professor of Surgery, Chairman Emeritus, Director of Experimental Surgery, Department of Plastic and Reconstructive Surgery, Wake Forest Medical Center, Winston Salem, North Carolina

Eric Arnaud, MD
Co-Director, Craniofacial Unit, Department of Neurosurgery, Hôpital Necker Enfants Malades, Paris, France

Duffield Ashmead IV, MD
Assistant Clinical Professor, Department of Orthopaedic Surgery, University of Connecticut School of Medicine; Associate Medical Staff, Department of Plastic and Reconstructive Surgery, University of Connecticut Health Center, Farmington, Connecticut; Active Senior Staff, Clinical Assistant Staff, Department of Plastic and Reconstructive Surgery, Hartford Hospital; Attending Surgeon, Co-Director, Division of Hand Surgery, Department of Plastic and Reconstructive Surgery, Connecticut Children's Medical Center, Hartford, Connecticut

Sherrell J. Aston, MD, FACS
Professor of Surgery, Department of Plastic Surgery, New York University School of Medicine; Chairman, Department of Plastic Surgery, Manhattan Eye, Ear & Throat Hospital, New York, New York

Kodi K. Azari, MD, FACS
Assistant Professor of Plastic Surgery and Orthopaedic Surgery, Chief, UPMC Mercy Division of Hand Surgery, Director, Hand Surgery Fellowship, Division of Plastic Surgery, University of Pittsburgh School of Medicine, Pittsburgh, Pennsylvania

Daniel J. Azurin, MD
Staff Surgeon, Department of Plastic Surgery, University Hospital, Tamarac, Florida

Russell Babbitt III, MD
Resident in General Surgery, Department of Surgery, University of Massachusetts Medical School; Resident in General Surgery, Department of Surgery, University of Massachusetts Memorial Health Care, Worcester, Massachusetts

Stephen B. Baker, MD, DDS
Associate Professor, Department of Plastic Surgery, Georgetown University Hospital, Washington, DC; Co-Director, Craniofacial Clinic, Inova Fairfax Hospital for Children, Falls Church, Virginia

Nabil A. Barakat, MD
Private Practice, Hand & Plastic Surgery Associates, Elmhurst, Illinois

Raymond L. Barnhill, MD
Clinical Professor, Department of Pathology, Department of Dermatology, University of Miami Miller School of Medicine, University of Miami Hospitals and Clinics, Miami, Florida

David T. Barrall, MD
Assistant Clinical Professor of Plastic Surgery, Department of Plastic Surgery, Brown University; Chief of Plastic Surgery, Department of Surgery/Plastic Surgery, Miriam Hospital, Providence, Rhode Island

Scott P. Bartlett, MD
Professor of Plastic Surgery, University of Pennsylvania; Peter Randall Endowed Chair in Pediatric Plastic Surgery, Department of Plastic Surgery, Children's Hospital of Philadelphia, Philadelphia, Pennsylvania

Bruce S. Bauer, MD, FACS, FAAP
Director of Pediatric Plastic Surgery, North Shore University Health System; Clinical Professor of Surgery, University of Chicago; Pritzker School of Medicine, Highland Park Hospital, Highland Park, Illinois

Erik M. Bauer, MD
Pediatric Otolaryngologist, Pediatric Ear, Nose, and Throat of Atlanta, PC, Atlanta, Georgia

Stephen P. Beals, MD, FACS, FAAP
Director, Barrow Craniofacial Center, St. Joseph's Hospital and Medical Center, Pheonix, Arizona; Associate Professor of Plastic Surgery, Department of Plastic Surgery, Mayo Medical School, Rochester, Minnesota

Michael L. Bentz, MD, FAAP, FACS
Professor of Surgery, Pediatrics and Neurosurgery, Chairman, Division of Plastic Surgery, Vice Chairman of Clinical Affairs, Department of Surgery, University of Wisconsin, University of Wisconsin Hospital, Madison, Wisconsin

Samuel J. Beran, MD
Chief of Plastic Surgery, White Plains Hospital, White Plains, New York

Richard A. Berger, MD, PhD
Professor of Orthopaedic Surgery and Anatomy, Mayo Clinic, Rochester, Minnesota

Nada Berry, MD
Resident, Department of Surgery, Division of Plastic Surgery, Southern Illinois University School of Medicine, Springfield, Illinois

Walter L. Biffl, MD
Department of Surgery, Denver Health Medical Center, Denver, Colorado

Kirby I. Bland, MD
Fay Fletcher Kerner Professor and Chairman, Department of Surgery, University of Alabama at Birmingham, Birmingham, Alabama

Loren J. Borud, MD
Assistant Professor of Surgery, Department of Surgery, Harvard Medical School; Department of Surgery, Beth Israel Deaconess Medical Center, Boston, Massachusetts

Vincent Boyd, MD
Fellow, Department of Plastic Surgery, Baylor College of Medicine, Texas Children's Hospital

Lynn Breglio, MS, PT, CHT
Clinical Instructor, Department of Physical Therapy, University of Hartford, West Hartford, Connecticut

David J. Bryan, MD, FACS
Associate Professor, Department of Surgery, Tufts University School of Medicine, Boston, Massachusetts; Vice Chairman, Department of Plastic and Reconstructive Surgery, Lahey Clinic, Burlington, Massachusetts; Lecturer, Harvard-MIT Health Sciences and Technology Program, Cambridge, Massachusetts

Steven R. Buchman, MD
Professor of Surgery and Neurosurgery, Department of Plastic Surgery, University of Michigan Medical School; Chief, Pediatric Plastic Surgery, Director, Craniofacial Anomalies Program, Department of Plastic Surgery, University of Michigan, Ann Arbor, Michigan

Harry J. Buncke, MD
Clinical Professor of Surgery, Division of Plastic Surgery, University of California, San Francisco School of Medicine, San Francisco, California; Associate Clinical Professor of Surgery, Stanford University School of Medicine, Stanford, California; Co-Director, Microsurgical Replantation/Transplantation Division, Davies Medical Center, San Francisco, California

Rudolf Buntic, MD
Chief of Microsurgery, California Pacific Medical Center, San Francisco, California; Clinical Instructor in Plastic Surgery, Stanford University, Stanford, California

Renee Burke, MD
Craniofacial Fellow, Department of Plastic Surgery, Miami Children's Hospital, Miami, Florida

Richard I. Burton, MD
Senior Associate Dean for Academic Affairs, University of Rochester School of Medicine and Dentistry; Emeritus Wehle Professor, Emeritus Chair, Department of Orthopaedics, University of Rochester Medical Center, Rochester, New York

Anthony A. Caldamone, MD, MMS, FAAP, FACS
Professor of Surgery (Urology) and Pediatrics, Department of Surgery, Warren Alpert Medical School of Brown University, Rhode Island Hospital; Chief of Pediatric Urology, Department of Pediatric Urology, Hasbro Children's Hospital, Providence, Rhode Island

Ryan P. Calfee, MD
Assistant Professor, Washington University School of Medicine, Department of Orthopedic Surgery, St. Louis, Missouri

Chris A. Campbell, MD
Resident, Department of Plastic Surgery, University of Virginia, Charlottesville, Virginia

Lois Carlson, OTR/L, CHT
Director of Hand Therapy, The Hand Center, Hartford, Connecticut

Stephanie A. Caterson, MD
Instructor of Surgery, Department of Plastic Surgery, Harvard Medical School; Instructor of Surgery, Department of Plastic Surgery, Brigham and Women's Hospital, Boston, Massachusetts

Christi M. Cavaliere, MD
Lecturer, Section of Plastic Surgery, University of Michigan, Ann Arbor, Michigan

Eric I-Yun Chang, MD
Postdoctoral Research Fellow, Department of Plastic Surgery, Stanford University, Stanford, California; Categorical General Surgery Resident, Department of Surgery, University of Medicine and Dentistry of New Jersey, Robert Wood Johnson Medical School, New Brunswick, New Jersey

Joyce C. Chen, MD
Pediatric Plastic Surgery and Craniofacial Surgery Fellow, Staff Surgeon, Department of Surgery, Division of Plastic and Maxillofacial Surgery, Childrens Hospital Los Angeles, University of Southern California; Staff Surgeon, Department of Plastic and Reconstructive Surgery, Cedars Sinai Hospital, Los Angeles, California

Ben J. Childers, MD
Chief of Plastic Surgery, Department of Surgery, Riverside Community Hospital, Riverside, California; Loma Linda University Medical Center, Loma Linda, California

Gloria A. Chin, MD, MS
Chief Resident, Division of Plastic Surgery, University of Illinois College of Medicine, University of Illinois Hospital and Cook County Hospital, Chicago, Illinois

Simon H. Chin, MD
Former Hand Fellow, Department of Orthopedics, University of Washington, Seattle, Washington; Aesthetics Fellow, Department of Plastic Surgery, Manhattan Eye, Ear & Throat Hospital, New York, New York

Niki A. Christopoulos, MD
Fellow, Department of Plastic and Reconstructive Surgery, Rush University Medical Center, Chicago, Illinois

William G. Cioffi, MD, FACS
J. Murray Beardsley Professor and Chairman, Department of Surgery, The Warren Alpert Medical School of Brown University; Surgeon-in-Chief, Department of Surgery, Rhode Island Hospital, Providence, Rhode Island

Brian S. Coan, MD
Care Plastic Surgery, Durham, North Carolina

Marilyn A. Cohen, BA, LSLP
Administrative Director, Regional Cleft Palate-Craniofacial Program, Cooper University Hospital, Camden, New Jersey; Speech Pathology Consultant, Department of Plastic Surgery, The Children's Hospital of Philadelphia, Philadelphia, Pennsylvania

Mimis Cohen, MD, FACS
Professor and Chief, Division of Plastic, Reconstructive, and Cosmetic Surgery, University of Illinois, University of Illinois Medical Center, Chicago, Illinois

Stephen Daane, MD
Chief, Plastic Surgery Division, Oakland Children's Hospital, Oakland, California

David J. David, AC, MD, FRCSE, FRCS, FRACS
Clinical Professor of Craniomaxillofacial Surgery, Department of Medicine, University of Adelaide; Head of Unit, Australian Craniofacial Unit, Women and Children's Hospital; Head of Unit, Australian Craniofacial Unit, Royal Adelaide Hospital, Adelaide, South Australia, Australia

Jorge I. de la Torre, MD
Professor and Program Director, Division of Plastic Surgery, University of Alabama School of Medicine; Chief, Section of Plastic Surgery, University of Alabama Highlands Hospital; Chief, Plastic Surgery Section, Birmingham VA Medical Center; Director, Center for Advanced Surgical Aesthetics, Birmingham, Alabama

Anthony J. DeFranzo, MD
Associate Professor, Department of Plastic and Reconstructive Surgery, Wake Forest University School of Medicine; North Carolina Baptist Hospital, Winston Salem, North Carolina

A. Lee Dellon, MD, PhD
Professor, Department of Plastic Surgery and Neurosurgery, Johns Hopkins University; Department of Plastic Surgery and Neurosurgery, Johns Hopkins Hospital, Union Memorial Hospital, Baltimore, Maryland

Jaimie DeRosa, MD, MS
Clinical Associate Professor, Otolaryngology–Head and Neck Surgery, Temple University, Philadelphia, Pennsylvania; Associate, Otolaryngology–Head and Neck Surgery, Division of Facial Plastic and Reconstructive Surgery, Geisinger Medical Center, Danville, Pennsylvania

Christine A. DiEdwardo, MD, FACS
Plastic and Reconstructive Surgeon, Department of Plastic and Reconstructive Surgery, Lahey Clinic Medical Center, Burlington, Massachusetts

Joseph J. Disa, MD, FACS
Associate Professor of Surgery, Division of Plastic Surgery, Cornell Weill Medical College; Associate Attending Surgeon, Plastic and Reconstructive Surgery Service, Memorial Sloan-Kettering Cancer Center, New York, New York

Sean T. Doherty, MD
Plastic Surgeon, Department of Plastic Surgery, Emerson Hospital; Plastic Surgeon, Boston Plastic Surgical Associates, Concord, Massachusetts

Rudolph F. Dolezal, MD, FACS
Associate Clinical Professor, Department of Surgery, Division of Plastic Surgery, University of Illinois Medical Center at Chicago, Chicago, Illinois; Attending Surgeon, Department of Plastic Surgery, Lutheran General Hospital, Park Ridge, Illinois; Senior Attending Surgeon, Department of Plastic Surgery, Northwest Community Hospital, Arlington Heights, Illinois; Senior Attending Surgeon, Department of Surgery, Holy Family Hospital, Des Plaines, Illinois

Raymond G. Dufresne, Jr., MD
Professor, Department of Dermatology, Brown University School of Medicine; Director, Dermatologic Surgery Division, Department of Dermatology, Rhode Island Hospital, Providence, Rhode Island

Christian Dumontier, MD, PhD
Professor, Orthopedic Department, Institut de la Main; Professor, Orthopedic Department, Hopital saint Antoine, Paris, France

Raymond M. Dunn, MD
Professor of Surgery and Cell Biology, Chief, Division of Plastic Surgery, University of Massachusetts Medical School, University of Massachusetts Memorial Health Care, Worcester, Massachusetts

Lee E. Edstrom, MD
Professor of Surgery, Department of Surgery, Brown University; Chief of Plastic Surgery, Lifespan, Providence, Rhode Island

W.G. Eshbaugh, Jr., MD, FACS
Medical Staff, Department of Plastic Surgery, Gulf Coast Medical Center, Fort Myers, Florida; Medical Staff, Department of Plastic Surgery, Physician's Regional Medical Center, Naples, Florida

Gregory R.D. Evans, MD, FACS
Professor of Surgery, The Center for Biomedical Engineering, Chief, Aesthetic & Plastic Surgery Institute, University of California, Irvine, Orange, California

Jeffrey A. Fearon, MD, FACS, FAAP
Director, The Craniofacial Center, Dallas, Texas

Alvaro A. Figueroa, DDS, MS
Co-Director, Rush Craniofacial Center, Department of Plastic and Reconstructive Surgery, Rush University Medical Center, Chicago, Illinois

Jack Fisher, MD
Associate Clinical Professor, Department of Plastic Surgery, Vanderbilt University, Nashville, Tennessee

R. Jobe Fix, MD
Professor, Department of Surgery, Division of Plastic Surgery, The University of Alabama at Birmingham; Active Staff, Department of Surgery, Division of Plastic Surgery, University of Alabama Hospital; Active Staff, Department of Surgery, Division of Plastic Surgery, The Children's Hospital of Alabama; Medical Staff, Department of Surgery, VA Medical Center, Birmingham, Alabama

James W. Fletcher, MD, FACS
Assistant Professor, Department of Surgery, Department of Orthopedic Surgery, University of Minnesota, Minneapolis, Minnesota; Chief, Hand Service, Department of Plastic and Hand Surgery, Regions Hospital, St. Paul, Minnesota

Robert S. Flowers, MD
Active Staff, Past Chairman, Department of Plastic Surgery, Queen's Medical Center; Active Staff, Kapiolani Medical Center; Professor and Director, Hawaii Postgraduate Fellowship, Program in Plastic and Asian Plastic Surgery, Honolulu, Hawaii

Christopher R. Forrest, MD, MSc, FRCSC, FACS
Professor, Division of Plastic Surgery, University of Toronto; Chief, Department of Plastic Surgery, Medical Director, Centre for Craniofacial Care and Research, Hospital for Sick Children, Toronto, Ontario, Canada

M. Brandon Freeman, MBA, MD, PhD
Aesthetic Fellow, Department of Plastic Surgery, University of Texas–Southwestern, Dallas, Texas

Jack A. Friedland, MD, FACS
Associate Professor, Department of Plastic Surgery, Mayo Medical School, Scottsdale, Arizona; Chief, Department of Plastic Surgery, Children's Rehabilitation Services, State of Arizona, St. Joseph's Hospital and Medical Center, Phoenix, Arizona; Attending Plastic Surgeon, Department of Plastic Surgery, Scottsdale Healthcare Hospitals, Scottsdale, Arizona

Karen E. Frye, MD
Associate Professor of Surgery, Department of Surgery, University of South Alabama; Associate Director, University of South Alabama Regional Burn Center, University of South Alabama Medical Center, Mobile, Alabama

Brian R. Gastman, MD
Assistant Professor, Department of Surgery (Plastic Surgery), Physician and Surgeon, Department of Surgery (Plastic Surgery) and Otolaryngology, University of Maryland, Baltimore, Maryland

Louis A. Gilula, MD, ABR, FACR
Professor of Radiology, Orthopedics, and Plastic and Reconstructive Surgery, Barnes-Jewish Hospital, Mallinckrodt Institute of Radiology, St. Louis, Missouri

Mark H. Gonzales, MD, MEng
Professor and Chairman, Department of Orthopaedic Surgery, University of Illinois at Chicago; Chairman, Department of Orthopaedic Surgery, Stroyer Hospital of Cook County; Adjunct Professor, Department of Mechanical Engineering, University of Illinois at Chicago, Chicago, Illinois

James T. Goodrich, MD, PhD, DSc (Honoris Causa)
Professor of Clinical Neurosurgery, Pediatrics, Plastic and Reconstructive Surgery, Leo Davidoff Department of Neurological Surgery, Albert Einstein College of Medicine; Director, Division of Pediatric Neurosurgery, Department of Neurological Surgery, Montefiore Medical Center, Bronx, New York

Vijay S. Gorantla, MD, PhD
Research Assistant Professor of Surgery, Division of Plastic and Reconstructive Surgery, Administrative Director, Pittsburgh Composite Tissue Allotransplantation Program, University of Pittsburgh Medical Center, Pittsburgh, Pennsylvania

Mark Gorney, MD, FACS
Chief, Department of Plastic Surgery, St. Francis Memorial Hospital, San Francisco, California; Department of Surgery, Stanford University, Stanford, California

Mark S. Granick, MD
Professor of Surgery, Tenured, Department of Surgery (Plastic), New Jersey Medical School, Newark, New Jersey

Arin K. Greene, MD, MMSc
Instructor in Surgery, Department of Plastic Surgery, Children's Hospital Boston, Harvard Medical School, Boston, Massachusetts

Joshua A. Greenwald, MD, FACS
Attending Surgeon, Department of Plastic Surgery, White Plains Hospital Center, White Plains, New York

Joseph S. Gruss, MBBCh, FRCSC
Professor, Department of Surgery, University of Washington; Marlys C. Larson Endowed Chair, Department of Pediatric Craniofacial Surgery, Childrens Hospital and Regional Medical Center, Seattle, Washington

Punita Gupta, MD
Scott Radiological Group, Inc., St. Louis, Missouri

Geoffrey C. Gurtner, MD, FACS
Associate Professor, Department of Surgery, Stanford University, Stanford, California

Mark N. Halikis, MD
Associate Clinical Professor, Department of Orthopaedic Surgery, University of California, Irvine, Orange, California

Geoffrey G. Hallock, MD
Consultant, Division of Plastic Surgery, Sacred Heart Hospital; Consultant, Division of Plastic Surgery, The Lehigh Valley Hospitals, Allentown, Pennsylvania; Consultant, Division of Plastic Surgery, St. Luke's Hospital, Bethlehem, Pennsylvania

Eric G. Halvorson, MD
Assistant Professor, Director of Microsurgery, Division of Plastic and Reconstructive Surgery, The University of North Carolina, Chapel Hill, North Carolina

Dennis C. Hammond, MD
Director, The Center for Breast and Body Contouring, Grand Rapids, Michigan

Rebecca J.B. Hammond, MBA, MHSM
Research Assistant, Stephen P. Beals, MD, PC, Phoenix, Arizona

Albert R. Harris, MD
Fellow, Hand Surgery, Department of Orthopedic Surgery, Mayo Clinic, Rochester, Minnesota

Raymond J. Harshbarger III, MD
Craniofacial & Pediatric Plastic Surgery, Dell Children's Medical Center of Central Texas University Medical Center at Brackenridge, Austin, Texas

Robert J. Havlik, MD
Professor of Surgery, Department of Surgery, Indiana University; Chief of Plastic Surgery, Director of Cleft and Craniofacial Surgery, Riley Hospital for Children, Indianapolis, Indiana

Tad R. Heinz, MD, FACS
Plastic Surgeon, Plastic Surgery Private Practice, Colorado Springs, Colorado

Vincent R. Hentz, MD
Professor, Department of Surgery, Stanford University; Robert A. Chase Center for Hand and Upper Limb Surgery, Stanford Hospital and Clinics, Stanford, California; Chief of Section, Hand Surgery Center, VA Palo Alto Health Care System, Palo Alto, California

Rosemary Hickey, MD
Professor and Program Director, Department of Anesthesiology, University of Texas Health Science Center at San Antonio, San Antonio, Texas

Larry Hollier, Jr., MD
Professor, Department of Plastic Surgery, Baylor College of Medicine; Professor, Department of Plastic Surgery, Texas Children's Hospital, Houston, Texas

Roy W. Hong, MD
Attending Surgeon, Department of Plastic Surgery, Palo Alto Medical Foundation, Palo Alto, California

Erik A. Hoy, MD
Resident, Department of Plastic Surgery, Brown University, Rhode Island Hospital, Providence, Rhode Island

Andrew Hsu, MD
Resident in General Surgery, Department of Surgery, Northwestern University Feinberg School of Medicine, Chicago, Illinois

Jennifer Hunter-Yates, MD
Boston Dermatology and Laser Center, Boston, Massachusetts

Ian T. Jackson, MD, DSc(Hon), FRCS, FACS, FRACS(Hon)
Director, Craniofacial Institute, Providence Hospital, Southfield, Michigan; Program Co-Chair, Plastic Surgery Residency Training Program, Wayne State University/ Detroit Medical Center, Detroit, Michigan

Lisa M. Jacob, MD
Resident, Division of Plastic Surgery, Department of Surgery, New Jersey Medical School–UMDNJ, Newark, New Jersey

Sonu A. Jain, MD
Assistant Professor, Division of Plastic and Reconstructive Surgery, University of Florida College of Medicine, Gainesville, Florida

Raymond V. Janevicius, MD, FACS
Attending Physician, Department of Surgery, Elmhurst Memorial Hospital, Elmhurst, Illinois

Shao Jiang, MD
Assistant Professor, Department of Surgery, Division of Plastic Surgery, University of Pittsburgh Medical Center; Attending Surgeon, Department of Pediatric Plastic and Craniofacial Surgery, Children's Hospital of Pittsburgh, Pittsburgh, Pennsylvania

Jesse B. Jupiter, MD
Hasjorg Wyss/AO Professor, Harvard University School of Medicine; Chief, Hand and Upper Limb Service, Orthopaedic Department, Massachusetts General Hospital, Boston, Massachusetts

Lana Kang, MD
Attending Orthpaedic Surgeon, Department of Orthopaedic Surgery, Division of Hand and Upper Extremity, Hospital for Special Surgery; Assistant Professor and Clinical Instructor, Department of Orthopaedic Surgery, Weill Medical College of Cornell University, New York, New York; Attending Orthopaedic Surgeon, Department of Orthopaedic Surgery, New York Hospital of Queens, Flushing, New York

Girish B. Kapur, MD, MPH
Assistant Professor, Department of Emergency Medicine and Global Public Health, The George Washington University, Washington, DC

Joseph Karamikian, DO
Member of the International Society of Hair Restoration Surgery; Medical Director, The New York Hair Loss Center, New York, New York

Henry K. Kawamoto, Jr., MD, DDS
Clinical Professor, Department of Surgery, Division of Plastic Surgery, University of California, Los Angeles, Los Angeles, California

Carolyn L. Kerrigan, MD, MSc, FRCSC
Professor, Department of Surgery, Dartmouth Medical School, Hanover, New Hampshire; Section Chief, Residency Program Director, Department of Surgery, Section of Plastic Surgery, Dartmouth Hitchcock Medical Center, Lebanon, New Hampshire

Christopher Khorsandi, MD
Private Practice, Henderson, Nevada, Beverly Hills, California

Dana K. Khuthaila, MD, FRCS(C)
Consultant Plastic Surgeon, Department of Surgery, King Faisal Specialist Hospital and Research Center, Riyadh, Saudi Arabia

David C. Kim, MD, FACS
Attending Physician, Department of Orthopaedic Surgery, Fallon Clinic, Worcester, Massachusetts

Jon Kline, MS, ATS, PA-C
Physician Assistant, Department of Orthopedics, West Virginia University; Physician Assistant, Department of Orthopedics, Section of Hand and Upper Extremity, West Virginia University Ruby Memorial Hospital, Morgantown, West Virginia

Cynthia L. Koudela, DDS, MSD
Affiliate Associate Professor, Department of Orthodontics, University of Washington; Orthodontist, Department of Dental Medicine, Seattle Childrens Hospital, Seattle, Washington

Thomas J. Krizek, MD
Adjunct Professor of Religious Studies, Department of Religious Studies, University of South Florida, Tampa, Florida; Adjunct Professor of Sport Business (Ethics), Department of Sport Business, School of Business, Saint Leo University, Saint Leo, Florida

Matthew D. Kwan, MD
Postdoctoral Research Fellow, Department of Surgery, Hagey Laboratory for Pediatric Regenerative Medicine, Stanford University School of Medicine; General Surgery Resident, Department of Surgery, Stanford University Medical Center, Stanford, California

Albert Lam, DMD
Private Practice, San Francisco, California

Howard N. Langstein, MD, FACS
Professor of Surgery, Division of Plastic Surgery, University of Rochester; Chief, Department of Surgery, Division of Plastic Surgery, Strong Memorial Hospital, Rochester, New York

Don LaRossa, MD
Professor of Surgery Emeritus, Department of Surgery, University of Pennsylvania School of Medicine; Senior Surgeon, Department of Surgery, Children's Hospital of Philadelphia, Philadelphia, Pennsylvania

Donald R. Laub, Jr., MS, MD, FACS
Associate Professor, Department of Surgery, University of Vermont College of Medicine; Interim Chief of Plastic Surgery, Department of Surgery, Fletcher Allen Health Care, Burlington, Vermont

Jonathan L. Le, MD
Director, Chrysalis Aesthetic and Reconstructive Surgery, Los Gatos, California

Raphael C. Lee, MD, ScD, DSc(Hon), FACS
Professor of Plastic Surgery, Dermatology, Molecular Medicine, Organismal Biology, and Anatomy (Biomechanics), Director, Center of Research in Cellular Repair, Director, Electrical Trauma Program, Attending Physician, Department of Surgery, University of Chicago Hospitals; Associate Staff, Department of Surgery, La Rabida Children's Hospital, Chicago, Illinois; Associate Staff, Department of Surgery, St. Mary Medical Center, Hobart, Indiana

W.P. Andrew Lee, MD
Professor of Surgery and Orthopaedic Surgery, Chief, Division of Plastic Surgery, University of Pittsburgh School of Medicine, Pittsburgh, Pennsylvania

Dennis E. Lenhart, MD
Resident, Division of Plastic Surgery, University of Illinois College of Medicine, University of Illinois Hospital, Chicago, Illinois

L. Scott Levin, MD, FACS
Paul B. Magnuson Professor of Bone and Joint Surgery, University of Pennsylvania School of Medicine, Chairman, Department of Orthopaedic Surgery, Professor of Plastic Surgery, Hospital of the University of Pennsylvania, Philadelphia, Pennsylvania

David M. Lichtman, MD
Professor and Chairman, Department of Orthopaedic Surgery, University of North Texas Health Science Center; Chairman, Department of Orthopaedic Surgery, John Peter Smith Hospital; Staff, Department of Orthopaedics, Harris Methodist Fort Worth, Fort Worth, Texas

James Lilley, MD
Resident, Department of Orthopedic Surgery, University of California, Irvine, School of Medicine, UCI Medical Center, Orange, California

Kant Y. Lin, MD
Professor, Department of Plastic Surgery, University of Virginia School of Medicine; Chief, Division of Craniofacial Surgery, Department of Plastic Surgery, University of Virginia Hospital, Charlottesville, Virginia

John William Little, MD, FACS
Clinical Professor of Surgery (Plastic), Department of Surgery, Georgetown University School of Medicine, Georgetown University Hospital, Washington, DC

Michael T. Longaker, MD, MBA, FACS
Deane P. and Louise Mitchell Professor, Division of Plastic and Reconstructive Surgery, Department of Surgery, Stanford University Medical Center, Stanford, California

Matthew S. Loos, MD
General Surgery Resident, Department of General Surgery, West Virginia University, Morgantown, West Virginia

Joseph E. Losee, MD, FACS, FAAP
Associate Professor of Surgery, Department of Surgery, Division of Plastic Surgery, University of Pittsburgh School of Medicine; Chief, Division of Pediatric Plastic Surgery, Director, Cleft-Craniofacial Center, Division of Pediatric Plastic Surgery, Children's Hospital of Pittsburgh, Pittsburgh, Pennsylvania

Arnold Luterman, MD, FRCS(C), FACS
Ripps-Meisler Professor of Surgery, Assistant Dean of Graduate Medical Education, Department of Surgery, University of South Alabama; Director, Regional Burn and Wound Center, University of South Alabama Medical Center, Mobile, Alabama

Sheilah A. Lynch, MD
Clinical Instructor, Department of Plastic Surgery, Georgetown University, Washington, DC

Susan E. Mackinnon, MD
Shoenberg Professor and Chief, Division of Plastic and Reconstructive Surgery, Washington University School of Medicine; Barnes-Jewish Hospital, St. Louis, Missouri

Terry R. Maffi, MD, FACS
Adjunct Faculty, Department of Plastic and Reconstructive Surgery, Mayo Clinic, Scottsdale, Arizona; Adjunct Faculty, Department of Plastic and Reconstructive Surgery, Mayo Clinic, Rochester, New York

Eric J. Mahoney, MD
Assistant Professor of Surgery, Department of Surgery, Boston University School of Medicine; Surgeon, Division of Trauma and Surgical Critical Care, Brown Medical Center, Boston, Massachusetts

Ahmed Seif Makki, MD, FRCS
Senior Consultant Plastic Surgeon, Department of Plastic Surgery, Plastic Surgicentre, Doha, Qatar

Jeffrey V. Manchio, MD
Resident, Department of General Surgery, Saint Joseph
Mercy Hospital, Ann Arbor, Michigan; Research Fellow,
Department of Plastic Surgery, Lahey Clinic Medical
Center, Burlington, Massachusetts

Ernest K. Manders, MD
Professor of Surgery, Department of Surgery, Division of
Plastic Surgery, The University of Pittsburgh, The University
of Pittsburgh Medical Center, Pittsburgh, Pennsylvania

Mahesh H. Mankani, MD, FACS
Associate Professor, Department of Surgery, University of
California, San Francisco, San Francisco, California

Paul N. Manson, MD
Professor and Chief, Department of Plastic Surgery, Johns
Hopkins University; Chief of Plastic Surgery, Johns
Hopkins Hospital; Professor of Surgery, University of
Maryland Shock Trauma Center, Baltimore, Maryland

Daniel Marchac, MD
Professeur Associc', Collège Médecine des Hôpitaux de
Paris, Paris, France

Malcolm W. Marks, MD
Chairman and Professor, Department of Plastic and
Reconstructive Surgery, Wake Forest University/Baptist
Medical Center; Department of Plastic and Reconstructive
Surgery, North Carolina Baptist Hospital, Winston-Salem,
North Carolina

William J. Martin, MD
Chairman, Aspen Institute of Plastic and Reconstructive Surgery;
Chairman, Department of Plastic and Reconstructive Surgery,
Aspen Valley Hospital, Aspen, Colorado

Paul A. Martineau, MD, FRCSC
Assistant Professor, Department of Orthopaedic Surgery,
McGill University; Staff Surgeon, Department of
Orthopaedic Surgery, Section of Upper Extremity Surgery,
McGill University Health Center, Montreal, Quebec, Canada

Stephen J. Mathes, MD
Professor of Surgery, Chief, Division of Plastic Surgery,
University of California, San Francisco, School of
Medicine, San Francisco, California

G. Patrick Maxwell, MD
Director, The Institute for Aesthetic and Reconstructive
Surgery, Nashville, Tennessee

Joseph G. McCarthy, MD
Lawrence D. Bell Professor of Plastic Surgery, New York
University School of Medicine; Director, Institute of
Reconstructive Plastic Surgery, New York University
Medical Center, New York, New York

William T. McClellan, MD
Private Practice, Morgantown Plastic Surgery Associates,
Morgantown, West Virginia

Michael P. McConnell, MD
Fellow, Aesthetic and Plastic Surgery Institute, University of
California, Irvine, Orange, California

Robert M. McFarlane, MD, FRCSC
Professor Emeritus, Hand and Upper Limb Centre and
Division of Plastic Surgery, University of Western Ontario
Faculty of Medicine; Consultant, St. Joseph's Health
Centre, London, Ontario, Canada

Mary H. McGrath, MD, MPH, FACS
Professor of Surgery, Staff Surgeon, Department of Surgery,
Division of Plastic Surgery, University of California, San
Francisco; Staff Surgeon, Department of Plastic Surgery,
San Francisco General Hospital; Attending Surgeon,
Department of Plastic Surgery, San Francisco Veterans
Administration Medical Center, San Francisco, California

Leslie T. McQuiston, MD
Assistant Professor of Surgery, Department of Pediatric
Urology, Dartmouth Medical School, Hanover, New
Hampshire; Staff Pediatric Urologist, Surgery/Pediatric
Surgery Section, Dartmouth Hitchcock Medical Center,
Lebanon, New Hampshire

Vineet Mehan, MD
Resident, Department of Plastic Surgery, Brown University,
Providence, Rhode Island

Anjali R. Mehta, MD, MPH
Chief Resident, Department of Otorhinolaryngology–Head and
Neck Surgery, University of Maryland, Baltimore, Maryland

Julie A. Melchior, MD
Assistant Clinical Professor, Department of Orthopaedic
Surgery, University of California, Los Angeles Medical
Center, Los Angeles, California; Partner Physician,
Department of Orthopaedic Surgery, Colorado
Permanente Medical Group, Lafayette, Colorado

Robert M. Menard, MD, FACS
Surgical Director, Pediatric Plastic and Craniofacial Surgery,
Northern California Kaiser Permanente Craniofacial Clinic,
The Permenente Medical Group, Santa Clara, California;
Clinical Associate Professor of Plastic Surgery, Division of
Plastic Surgery, Stanford University School of Medicine,
Stanford, California

Frederick Menick, MD
Associate Clinical Professor, Division of Plastic Surgery,
University of Arizona; Chief Plastic Surgeon, Surgery
Department, St. Joseph's Hospital, Tucson, Arizona

Martin C. Mihm, Jr., MD
Clinical Professor, Department of Pathology and Dermatology,
Harvard Medical School; Pathologist/Associate Dermatologist,
Department of Pathology and Dermatology Services,
Massachusetts General Hospital, Boston, Massachusetts

**D. Ralph Millard, Jr., MD, FACS, Hon. FRCS(Edin),
Hon. FRCS, OD Ja.**
Light-Millard Professor and Chairman Emeritus, Division of
Plastic Surgery, University of Miami School of Medicine,
Jackson Memorial Hospital, Miami Children's Hospital,
Miami, Florida

Fernando Molina, MD
Professor of Plastic and Reconstructive Surgery,
Universidad Nacional Autonoma De Mexico; Professor
of Plastic and Reconstructive Surgery, Head, Division of
Plastic, Aesthetic and Reconstructive Surgery, Hospital
General Dr. Manuel Gea Gonzalez, S.S., Mexico

Fernando Ortiz Monasterio, MD
Professor Emeritus, Faculty of Medicine, Postgraduate
Division, Universidad Nacional Autonoma de Mexico;
Professor of Plastic Surgery, Chairman, Craniofacial Clinic,
Division of Plastic and Reconstructive Surgery, Hospital
General Manuel Gea Gonzalez, Mexico City, Mexico

Louis Morales, Jr., MD
Director, Foundation of Utah; Director, Pediatric Plastic and
Craniofacial Fellowship, Primary Children's Hospital, Salt
Lake City, Utah

Robert J. Morin, MD
Craniofacial Fellow, Department of Plastic Surgery, Miami
Children's Hospital, Miami, Florida

Chaitanya S. Mudgal, MD, MS(Orth), MCh(Orth)
Instructor, Department of Orthopaedic Surgery, Harvard
Medical School; Staff, Department of Orthopaedic
Surgery, Orthopaedic Hand Service, Massachusetts
General Hospital, Boston, Massachusetts

John B. Mulliken, MD
Professor of Surgery, Harvard Medical School; Director,
Craniofacial Center, Department of Plastic Surgery,
Children's Hospital, Boston, Massachusetts

Thomas A. Mustoe, MD, FACS
Professor and Chief, Department of Surgery, Division
of Plastic and Reconstructive Surgery, Northwestern
University Medical School, Chicago, Illinois; Northwestern
Memorial Hospital, Evanston, Illinois

Jeffrey N. Myers, MD, PhD, FACS
Professor and Director of Research, Deputy Chair for
Academic Programs, Department of Head and Neck
Surgery, The University of Texas M.D. Anderson Cancer
Center, Houston, Texas

Maurice Y. Nahabedian, MD, FACS
Associate Professor, Department of Plastic Surgery,
Georgetown University, Washington, DC

Michael W. Neumeister, MD, FACS, FRCS
Professor and Chairman, Director of Hand Fellowship,
Division of Plastic Surgery, Southern Illinois University
School of Medicine, Springfield, Illinois

Mary Lynn Newport, MD
Department of Orthopaedics, University of Connecticut
Health Center–John Dempsey Hospital, Farmington,
Connecticut

Zahid Niazi, MD, FRCSI, FICS, FNYAM
Chairman, Department of Surgery, Attending Plastic
Surgeon, Department of Surgery, Methodist Hospital,
Sacramento, California

Sacha Obaid, MD
Founder, North Texas Plastic Surgery, PLLC, Southlake,
Texas

Suzanne Olbricht, MD
Associate Professor of Dermatology, Harvard Medical
School; Chair, Department of Dermatology, Lahey Clinic,
Burlington, Massachusetts

Osak Omulepu, MD
Private Practice, Fort Lauderdale, Florida

Sonal Pandya, MD
Senior Staff, Department of Plastic and Reconstructive
Surgery, Lahey Clinic, Burlington, Massachusetts

Marcello Pantaloni, MD
Attending Surgeon, Department of Plastic Surgery, University
of Milan, Milan, Italy

Frank A. Papay, MD, FACS, FAAP
Associate Professor of Surgery, Department of Surgery,
Cleveland Clinic Lerner College of Medicine of Case
Western Reserve University; Vice Chairman and Section
Head of Craniomaxillofacial Surgery, Department of
Plastic Surgery, Cleveland Clinic, Cleveland, Ohio

Robert J. Paresi, Jr., MD, MPH
Attending Plastic Surgeon, Department of Plastic Surgery,
Florida Hospital, Orlando, Florida

Amar Patel, MD
Fellow, Department of Orthopedic Surgery, The Warren
Alpert School of Medicine at Brown University; Fellow,
Department of Orthopedic Surgery, Rhode Island Hospital,
Providence, Rhode Island

Jagruti C. Patel, MD, FACS
Chief of Plastic Surgery, Northeast Hospital Corporation,
Beverly, Massachusetts

Wilfred C.G. Peh, MBBS, MD, FRCP, FRCR
Clinical Professor, Yong Loo Lin School of Medicine, National
University of Singapore; Senior Consultant, Department of
Diagnostic Radiology, Alexandra Hospital, Singapore, China

Jane A. Petro, MD, FACS
Professor of Surgery, Department of Surgery, New York
Medical College, Valhalla, New York; Chief Plastic Surgery,
Department of Surgery, Northern Westchester Hospital,
Mt. Kisco, New York; Chief Medical Officer, Department of
Plastic Surgery, American Academy of Cosmetic Surgery
Hospital, Dubai, United Arab Emirates

John W. Polley, MD
Professor, Chairman, Department of Plastic and
Reconstructive Surgery, Rush University Medical Center;
Co-Director, Rush Craniofacial Center–Plastic and
Reconstructive Surgery, Rush University Medical Center,
Chicago, Illinois

Samuel O. Poore, MD, PhD
Resident, Division of Plastic and Reconstructive Surgery,
University of Wisconsin, University of Wisconsin Hospital,
Madison, Wisconsin

Julian J. Pribaz, MD
Professor of Surgery, Harvard Medical School; Plastic Surgeon,
Brigham and Women's Hospital, Boston, Massachusetts

Somayaji Ramamurthy, MD
Professor, Department of Anesthesiology, University of Texas
Health Science Center at San Antonio, San Antonio, Texas

Sai S. Ramasastry, MD, FRCS, FACS
Associate Professor of Plastic Surgery, Department of
Surgery, University of Illinois at Chicago; Attending Plastic
Surgeon, Department of Surgery, University of Illinois at
Chicago Medical Center, Chicago, Illinois

David L. Ramirez, MD
Plastic and Reconstructive Surgeon, Department of
Craniofacial Surgery, Universidad Nacional Autonoma
de Mèxico; Plastic and Reconstructive Surgeon,
Department of Plastic Surgery, Hospital General "Dr.
Manuel Gea Gonzalez", Mexico City, Mexico; Plastic
and Reconstructive Surgeon, Department of Plastic and
Reconstructive Surgery, Hospital StarMèdica, Morelia,
Michoacàn, Mèxico

Oscar M. Ramirez, MD, FACS
Clinical Assistant Professor, Plastic Surgery Division, The Johns Hopkins University, Baltimore, Maryland; Director, Esthetique Internationale, Timonium, Maryland

Peter Randall, MD, FACS
Emeritus Professor of Plastic Surgery, Department of Surgery, University of Pennsylvania School of Medicine; Retired Chief of Plastic Surgery, Department of Surgery, Hospital of the University of Pennsylvania; Retired Chief of Plastic Surgery, Department of Surgery, Children's Hospital of Philadelphia, Philadelphia, Pennsylvania

Peter D. Ray, MD
Assistant Professor of Surgery, Division of Plastic and Reconstructive Surgery, University of Alabama, Birmingham, Alabama

W. Bradford Rockwell, MD
Associate Professor and Chief, Division of Plastic Surgery, University of Utah School of Medicine, Salt Lake City, Utah

Craig M. Rodner, MD
Assistant Professor, Department of Orthopaedics, University of Connecticut Health Center, Farmington, Connecticut

Alan Rosen, MD
Attending Orthopaedic Surgeon, Houston Northwest Medical Center, Houston, Texas

Harvey Rosen, MD, DMD
Clinical Associate Professor of Surgery, Department of Surgery, University of Pennsylvania, Philadelphia, Pennsylvania

Douglas C. Ross, MD, MEd, FRCSC
Associate Professor and Chair, Division of Plastic Surgery, Hand and Upper Limb Centre, Department of Surgery, University of Western Ontario, London, Ontario, Canada

Shai Rozen, MD
Assistant Professor, Department of Plastic Surgery, University of Texas Southwestern Medical Center, Dallas, Texas

Leonard K. Ruby, MD
Professor of Orthopaedic Surgery, Department of Orthopaedic Surgery, Division of Hand Surgery, Tufts University School of Medicine; Chief Emeritus, Division of Hand Surgery, Department of Orthopaedic Surgery, Tufts-New England Medical Center, Boston, Massachusetts

Jaiyoung Ryu, MD
Professor and Chief, Hand & Upper Extremity Service, Department of Orthopaedics, West Virginia University; Attending Hand and Orthopaedic Surgeon, West Virginia University Hospitals, Morgantown, West Virginia

Justin M. Sacks, MD
Assistant Professor, Department of Plastic Surgery, MD Anderson Cancer Center, University of Texas, Houston, Texas

Jhonny Salomon, MD, FACS
Plastic Surgeon, Department of Surgery, Baptist Hospital; Plastic Surgeon, Department of Surgery, South Miami Hospital, Miami, Florida

Kenneth E. Salyer, MD, FACS, FAAP
Adjunct Professor, Department of Orthodontics and Biomedical Sciences, Baylor Dental School, Texas A&M Systems; Chairman of the Board, World Craniofacial Foundation, Dallas, Texas; Consultant, Craniofacial Surgery, Department of Plastic and Reconstructive Surgery, Chang Gung Memorial Hospital, Taipei, Taiwan; Clinical Professor, Department of Plastic and Reconstructive Surgery, Craniofacial Surgery, Hospital Manuel Gea-Gonzalez, Mexico City, Mexico

Sven N. Sandeen, MD
Attending Surgeon, Department of Plastic and Reconstructive Surgery, Northwest Medical Center, Tucson, Arizona

Shawkat Sati, MD
Chief Resident, Department of Plastic and Reconstructive Surgery, Lahey Clinic, Burlington, Massachusetts

Stefan Schneeberger, MD
Director, CTA Program Pittsburgh, Assistant Professor of Surgery, Division of Plastic Surgery, Department of Surgery, University of Pittsburgh Medical Center, Pittsburgh, Pennsylvania; Associate Professor of Surgery, Department of General and Transplant Surgery, Innsbruck Medical University, Innsbruck, Austria

David P. Schnur, MD
Clinical Assistant Professor, Department of Surgery, University of Colorado Health Science Center, Denver, Colorado

Paul L. Schnur, MD
Associate Professor of Plastic Surgery (Retired), Department of Plastic Surgery, Mayo Medical School, Scottsdale, Arizona; Chair (Retired), Division of Plastic Surgery, Mayo Clinic Hospital; Clinical Associate Professor of Surgery, Department of Plastic Surgery, University of Arizona College of Medicine, Phoenix, Arizona

Richard C. Schultz, MD, FACS
Emeritus Professor of Surgery, Department of Surgery, Division of Plastic Surgery, University of Illinois at Chicago, Chicago, Illinois; Senior Surgeon, Department of Surgery, Lutheran General Hospital, Park Ridge, Illinois

David M. Schwartzenfeld, DO
Botsford General Hospital, Department of Family Medicine, Farmington Hills, Michigan; International Society of Hair Restoration Surgery, Geneva, Illinois

Karl A. Schwarz, MD, MSc, FRCSC
Assistant Professor, Division of Plastic Surgery, McGill University Health Center, Montreal, Quebec, Canada

Brooke R. Seckel, MD, FACS
Assistant Professor of Surgery, Department of Plastic Surgery, Harvard Medical School, Boston, Massachusetts; Staff Surgeon, Department of Plastic Surgery, Emerson Hospital, Concord, Massachusetts; Staff Surgeon, Department of Plastic Surgery, Lahey Clinic, Burlington, Massachusetts

John T. Seki, MD, FRCSC, FACS
Chief, Department of Surgery, Division of Plastic Surgery, Orillia Soldiers' Memorial Hospital, Orillia, Ontario, Canada

Alex Senchenkov, MD
Fellow in Microvascular Reconstructive Surgery, Department of Surgery, Division of Plastic Surgery, The University of Pittsburgh, The University of Pittsburgh Medical Center, Pittsburgh, Pennsylvania

Mark Shashikant, MD
Attending Surgeon, Division of Plastic Surgery, Walter Reed Army Medical Center, Washington, D.C.

Dan H. Shell IV, MD
Plastic Surgery Resident, Department of Surgery, University of Alabama at Birmingham, Birmingham, Alabama

Saleh M. Shenaq, MD, FACS
Professor and Chief, Division of Plastic Surgery, Department of Surgery, Baylor College of Medicine; Methodist Hospital; Texas Children's Hospital; St. Luke's Episcopal Hospital; Texas Institute for Rehabilitation and Research, Houston, Texas

Michele A. Shermak, MD
Associate Professor of Plastic Surgery, Department of Surgery, Johns Hopkins School of Medicine; Chief of Plastic Surgery, Department of Surgery, Division of Plastic Surgery, Johns Hopkins Bayview Medical Center, Baltimore, Maryland

Prasanna-Kumar Shivapuja, BDS, MDS(ortho), DDS, MS(ortho)
Diplomate, American Board of Orthodontics; Private Practice, Roseville, Michigan

Maria Siemionow, MD, PhD, DSc
Professor of Surgery, Department of Surgery, Cleveland Clinic Lerner College of Medicine of Case Western Reserve University; Director of Plastic Surgery Research, Head of Microsurgery Training, Department of Plastic Surgery, Cleveland Clinic, Cleveland, Ohio

Davinder J. Singh, MD
Attending Surgeon, Barrow Craniofacial Center, Barrow Neurological Institute; Attending Surgeon, Department of Surgery, Phoenix Children's Hospital, Phoenix, Arizona

Sumner A. Slavin, MD
Associate Clinical Professor of Surgery, Harvard Medical School; Chief, Division of Plastic Surgery, Beth Israel Deaconess Medical Center, Boston, Massachusetts

Eugene M. Smith, Jr., MD, FACS
Private Practice, Atlanta, Georgia

Erhan Sonmez, MD
Research Fellow, Microsurgery Laboratory, Department of Plastic Surgery, Cleveland Clinic, Cleveland, Ohio

Nicholas J. Speziale, MD, FACS
Private Practice, Palos Heights, Illinois

Melvin Spira, MD, DDS
Professor of Surgery, Division of Plastic Surgery, Baylor College of Medicine; Emeritus Surgical Staff, Department of Plastic Surgery, The Methodist Hospital; Emeritus Surgical Staff, Department of Plastic Surgery, Texas Childrens Hospital, Houston, Texas

John L. Spolyar, DDS, MS
Department of Orthodontics, University of Detroit Mercy School of Dentistry, Detroit, Michigan; Department of Surgery, Providence Hospital of Southfield, Southfield, Michigan; Private Practice, Your Smile Orthodontics, PC, Clinton Township, Michigan

David A. Staffenberg, MD, DSc(Hon)
Associate Professor, Clinical Plastic Surgery, Neurological Surgery, and Pediatrics, Department of Surgery, Albert Einstein College of Medicine of Yeshiva University; Chief of Plastic Surgery, Department of Surgery, Montefiore Medical Center; Surgical Director, Center for Craniofacial Disorders, Children's Hospital at Montefiore, Bronx, New York

Samuel Stal, MD
Chief of Service, Department of Plastic Surgery, Texas Children's Hospital; Chief of Division, Plastic Surgery, Department of Surgery, Baylor College of Medicine, Houston, Texas

Eric J. Stelnicki, MD
Associate Professor, Department of Plastic Surgery, Cleveland Clinic Florida, Weston, Florida; Medical Director, Department of Cleft and Craniofacial Surgery, Joe DiMaggio Children's Hospital, Hollywood, Florida; Associate Professor, Department of Dentistry, Nova Southeastern University, Fort Lauderdale, Florida

Mitchell A. Stotland, MD, MS, FRCSC
Associate Professor, Department of Surgery; Department of Pediatrics, Dartmouth Medical School, Hanover, New Hampshire; Associate Professor, Director, Craniofacial Anomalies Clinic, Department of Surgery; Department of Pediatrics, Dartmouth Hitchcock Medical Center, Lebanon, New Hampshire

James W. Strickland, MD
Clinical Professor of Orthopaedic Surgery, Department of Orthopaedic Surgery, Indiana University School of Medicine; Department of Orthopaedic Surgery, St. Vincent Hospital; Department of Orthopaedic Surgery, Clarian Hospital, Indianapolis, Indiana; Instructor, Department of Orthopaedic Surgery, Washington University School of Medicine, St. Louis, Missouri

Brent V. Stromberg, MD, FACS
Attending Plastic Surgeon, Department of Surgery, St. John's Medical Center; Attending Plastic Surgeon, St. Anthony's Medical Center, St. Louis, Missouri

Patrick K. Sullivan, MD
Associate Professor, Department of Plastic Surgery, Brown University School of Medicine; Associate Professor and Plastic Surgeon, Department of Plastic Surgery, Brown University, Women & Infants; Associated Professor and Plastic Surgeon, Department of Plastic Surgery, Rhode Island Hospital, Providence, Rhode Island

Matthew R. Swelstad, MD
Chief Resident, Division of Plastic and Reconstructive Surgery, University of Wisconsin Hospital and Clinics, Madison, Wisconsin

Julio Taleisnik, MD
Clinical Professor, Department of Orthopaedics, University of California, Irvine, Irvine, California; Department of Orthopaedics, St. Joseph Hospital, Orange, California

Peter J. Taub, MD, FACS, FAAP
Associate Professor, Surgery and Pediatrics, Department of Surgery/Plastic Surgery, Mount Sinai Medical Center; Co-Director, Mount Sinai Cleft and Craniofacial Center, Department of Surgery/Plastic Surgery, Kravis Children's Hospital at Mount Sinai, New York, New York; Attending Surgeon, Department of Surgery/Plastic Surgery, Elmhurst Hospital Center, Elmhurst, New York; Attending Surgeon, Department of Surgery/Plastic Surgery, Westchester Medical Center, Valhalla, New York

Oren M. Tepper, MD
House Staff, Institute of Reconstructive Plastic Surgery, New York University Medical Center, New York, New York

Julia K. Terzis, MD, PhD, FACS, FRCS(C)
Professor, Department of Surgery, Division of Plastic and Reconstructive Surgery, Eastern Virginia Medical School, Norfolk, Virginia

Dean M. Toriumi, MD
Professor, Department of Otolaryngology–Head and Neck Surgery, University of Illinois at Chicago, University of Illinois Medical Center, Chicago, Illinois

Bryant A. Toth, MD
Assistant Clinical Professor of Plastic Surgery, Department of Plastic and Reconstructive Surgery, University of California, San Francisco, San Francisco, California

Thomas Trumble, MD
Professor and Chief, Hand and Microvascular Surgery, Department of Orthopaedics and Sports Medicine, University of Washington Medical Center; Professor, Department of Orthopaedics and Sports Medicine, Harborview Medical Center; Professor, Department of Orthopaedics and Sports Medicine, Children's Hospital and Medical Center, Seattle, Washington

Raymond Tse, MD, FRCSC
Clinical Instructor, Division of Plastic Surgery, Department of Surgery, University of British Columbia;Attending Surgeon, Division of Plastic Surgery, Department of Surgery, Vancouver Island Health Authority, Victoria, British Columbia, Canada

Raoul Tubiana, MD
Associate Professor, Department of Orthopaedics, University of Paris; Hopital Cochin; Founder and Past President, Institut de la Main, Paris, France

Joseph Upton III, MD
Associate Clinical Professor of Surgery, Harvard Medical School; Associate Clinical Professor of Surgery, Attending Surgeon, Department of Plastic Surgery, Beth Israel Deaconess Medical Center; Senior Associate Attending Surgeon, Department of Plastic Surgery, Children's Hospital; Senior Surgeon, Department of Plastic Surgery, Shriners Burn Hospital, Boston, Massachusetts

Luis O. Vásconez, MD
Vice Chair, Department of Surgery, Professor and Chief, Division of Plastic Surgery, University of Alabama-Birmingham; Plastic Surgeon in Chief, University of Alabama Hospital and Clinics, Birmingham, Alabama

Nicholas B. Vedder, MD, FACS
Professor of Surgery and Orthopaedics, Chief, Division of Plastic Surgery, Vice Chairman, Department of Surgery, University of Washington, Seattle, Washington

Adam J. Vernadakis, MD
Senior Staff, Department of Plastic Surgery, Lahey Clinic, Burlington, Massachusetts; Major, Westover ARB, United States Air Force Reserve, Chicopee, Massachusetts

Armand D. Versaci, MD
Emeritus Clinical Professor, Department of Plastic Surgery, Brown Medical School; Emeritus Chief, Department of Plastic Surgery, Rhode Island Hospital, Providence, Rhode Island

William F. Wagner, MD
Clinical Instructor, Department of Orthopedic Surgery and Sports Medicine, University of Washington; Hand Surgeon, Seattle Hand Surgery Group, Seattle, Washington

Jennifer L. Walden, MD, FACS
Associate Attending, Program Director, Department of Plastic Surgery, Manhattan Eye, Ear, and Throat Hospital, New York, New York

Derrick C. Wan, MD
Resident, Division of Plastic and Reconstructive Surgery, University of California Los Angeles, Los Angeles, California

Stephen M. Warren, MD
Associate Professor of Surgery (Plastic), Institute of Reconstructive Plastic Surgery, New York University Medical Center, New York, New York

H. Kirk Watson, MD
Clinical Professor, Department of Orthopaedic Surgery, University of Connecticut School of Medicine, Farmington, Connecticut; Senior Staff, Department of Orthopaedic Surgery, Hartford Hospital; Consultant Staff, Department of Orthopaedic Surgery, Connecticut Children's Medical Center; Director, Connecticut Combined Hand Surgery Fellowship, Hartford, Connecticut

Renata V. Weber, MD
Assistant Professor, Department of Plastic and Reconstructive Surgery, Albert Einstein College of Medicine of Yeshiva University; Attending Physician, Department of Plastic and Reconstructive Surgery, Montefiore Medical Center, Bronx, New York

Andrew J. Weiland, MD
Professor of Orthopaedic Surgery, Professor of Plastic Surgery, Weill Cornell Medical College; Attending Orthopaedic Surgeon, Hospital for Special Surgery, New York, New York

Adam B. Weinfeld, MD
Attending Plastic Surgeon, Department of Plastic Surgery, University Medical Center at Brackenridge; Attending Plastic Surgeon, Department of Plastic Surgery, Dell Children's Medical Center of Central Texas, Austin, Texas

Jeffrey Weinzweig, MD, FACS
Chief of Craniofacial Surgery, Director, Craniofacial Anomalies Program, Division of Plastic Surgery, Illinois Masonic Medical Center; Director, The Chicago Center for Plastic & Reconstructive Surgery, Chicago, Illinois

Norman Weinzweig, MD, FACS
Professor, Department of Plastic and Reconstructive Surgery, Rush Univeristy Medical Center, Chicago, Illinois

Arnold-Peter C. Weiss, MD
Professor of Orthopaedics, Assistant Dean of Medicine (Admissions), Alpert Medical School of Brown University, Rhode Island Hospital, Providence, Rhode Island

Linton A. Whitaker, MD
Professor of Surgery (Plastic Surgery), Chief Emeritus, Department of Surgery, The University of Pennsylvania School of Medicine; Senior Surgeon, Department of Plastic Surgery, The Children's Hospital of Philadelphia; Attending Surgeon, Department of Surgery, Hospital of the University of Pennsylvania; Director, Edwin & Fannie Gray Hall Center for Human Appearance, The University of Pennsylvania Health System, Philadelphia, Pennsylvania

Deborah J. White, MD
Attending Physician, Department of Surgery, Scottsdale Healthcare Shea, Scottsdale, Arizona

Lisa Ann Whitty, MD
Plastic Surgery Fellow, Division of Plastic Surgery, Mayo Clinic, Rochester, Minnesota

S. Anthony Wolfe, MD, FACS, FAAP
Chief, Department of Plastic Surgery, Miami Children's Hospital, Miami, Florida

Ronit Wollstein, MD
Assistant Professor of Surgery and Orthopedic Surgery, Department of Surgery, Division of Plastic and Reconstructive Hand Surgery, University of Pittsburgh Medical School, Pittsburgh, Pennsylvania

Albert S. Woo, MD
Assistant Professor, Plastic Surgery, Department of Surgery, Washington University; Assistant Professor, Plastic Surgery, Department of Surgery, Barnes-Jewish Hospital; Assistant Professor, Plastic Surgery, Department of Surgery, Saint Louis Children's Hospital, Saint Louis, Missouri

R. Christie Wray, Jr., MD
Professor and Chief Emeritus, Department of Surgery, Section of Plastic and Reconstructive Surgery, Medical College of Georgia; Professor of Surgery, Surgery Service Line, Section of Plastic Surgery, VA Medical Center and Downtown Division, Augusta, Georgia

Michael J. Yaremchuk, MD, FACS
Clinical Professor of Surgery, Harvard Medical School; Chief of Craniofacial Surgery, Division of Plastic and Reconstructive Surgery, Massachusetts General Hospital, Boston, Massachusetts

Soheil S. Younai, MD, FACS
Staff Surgeon, Department of Surgery, Tarzana Regional Medical Center, Tarzana, California

Jack C. Yu, DMD, MD, MS ED
Milford B. Hatcher Professor and Chief, Section of Plastic Surgery, Department of Surgery, Medical College of Georgia; Chief of Plastic Surgery, Department of Surgery, MCG Health, Inc., Augusta, Georgia

Eser Yuksel, MD
Associate Professor, Department of Plastic Surgery, Baylor College of Medicine; Attending Physician, Department of Plastic Surgery, Methodist Hospital; Attending Physician, Department of Plastic Surgery, St. Luke's Hospital; Adjunct Associate Professor, Department of Bioengineering, Rice University, Houston, Texas

Alarick Yung, MD
Clinical Instructor, Department of Orthopaedics, Tufts University School of Medicine, Tufts New England Medical Center, Boston, Massachusetts

Priya S. Zeikus, MD
Assistant Professor, Department of Dermatology, University of Texas Southwest Medical School, Dallas, Texas

Richard J. Zienowicz, MD, FACS
Associate Professor of Plastic Surgery, Department of Plastic Surgery, Brown University School of Medicine, Rhode Island Hospital, Providence, Rhode Island

ACKNOWLEDGMENTS

The orchestration of almost 300 authors from four continents was no easy task. Producing the second edition of a text that, over the past decade, has become a household name in the lexicon of trainees and practicing plastic surgeons around the world was even less easy. The goal of such an undertaking must be to over-deliver—to exceed expectations. And expectations were quite high for this volume. Compilation of this text demanded attention to innumerable details and warranted a dedicated team committed to producing a book that would surpass the original. I was extremely fortunate to have had just such a team involved in the vast undertaking of producing the second edition of *Plastic Surgery Secrets*.

I am indebted to the scores of renowned specialists from a multitude of disciplines, including plastic surgery, otolaryngology, dermatology, orthopaedic surgery, general surgery, urology, breast surgery, speech pathology, radiology, hand therapy, anesthesiology, and orthodontics, who contributed their expertise and ingenuity to produce the 155 superbly crafted chapters that comprise the second edition of *Plastic Surgery Secrets*. The coordination of communication with an endless stream of these cleverly elusive contributors was only possible due to the natural predatory instincts of my extraordinary administrative assistant, Carolynn Turke. My appreciation transcends words.

Elsevier provided an editorial and production staff with open minds and a willingness to allow digression now and then from convention. I remain forever grateful to Linda Belfus of Hanley & Belfus, who created the *Secrets*® series before merging with Elsevier and who took a chance on me when I pitched the original idea for *Plastic Surgery Secrets* while still a plastic surgery resident in the mid-1990s. I am especially thankful to my developmental editor, Andrea Vosburgh, my production editor, Kate Mannix, my design manager, Steven Stave, and my senior acquisitions editor, Jim Merritt, whose efforts in bringing this project to fruition have been exemplary. I have no doubt they are greatly relieved with its completion and welcome the serenity that has supplanted the deadline-induced hysteria. At least for now.

FOREWORD

One of the proudest traditions of surgery has been the passing of knowledge from one generation to another. This tradition of surgical education has taken many forms and has undergone continued evolution.

In ancient times, undoubtedly, it was based on the oral tradition—the teacher verbally conveying dogma to the student. The written word was also an important component, as witnessed by the writings of Sushruta in 600 B.C., the famous papyri of Egypt, the monastic manuscripts of the Middle Ages, and the dissemination of books, the latter resulting from the discovery of the printing press by Johann Gutenberg in 1440.

The modern age greatly facilitated the dissemination of surgical knowledge. Improvements in travel allowed surgeons to move from country to country, continent to continent in pursuit of new surgical techniques. Individual master surgeons created pilgrimage sites that drew surgeons from around the world to their operating clinics. Some, however, were secretive and others even charged a fee to attend their operative sessions. The discovery of photography permitted the accurate printing of images in books and eventually led to the discovery of the projected slide—hence, Sir Harold Gillis' famous quip that the greatest advance in plastic surgery in his lifetime was "the discovery of the Kodachrome slide." One wonders what his utterance would have been had he lived to use PowerPoint software!

In this century, each advance in telecommunications was followed by another: radio allowed the first simultaneous national and international surgical conferences; motion picture film was exploited by the American College of Surgeons as a means of teaching technical surgery to large numbers of surgeons; television allowed closed circuit meetings, which could be viewed simultaneously around the world by satellite; and the computer provided multimedia capabilities.

Now in the 21st century we have come to realize that the problem is not only the acquisition of surgical knowledge but also the personal processing and integration of an overwhelming mass of data that increase daily on an exponential scale. Yet, surgical teachers are also confronted by new challenges with the development of rigidly constructed national healthcare systems and a decrease in the number of teaching cases that had been the source of most "hands on" surgical teaching. In the United States, work hour regulations have limited the clinical experience of the surgical trainee. As surgical teachers, we must take advantage of modern technology and develop comprehensive virtual surgery training programs, not unlike what the airline industry has done in training pilots before they are allowed to sit in the cockpit of a real aircraft.

Fundamental to this proud tradition of surgical education remains what Dr. Jeffrey Weinzweig has so accurately defined as the Socratic method, a pedagogic technique attributed to the Athenian philosopher. His educational method, called DIALECTIC, is derived from the Greek word meaning to "converse." In the end, this is the soul of surgical education—the surgeon and the student in continuous dialogue not only to pass on surgical knowledge but, equally importantly, to train for the future a new surgeon who will expand on that knowledge.

In the second edition of the immensely popular *Plastic Surgery Secrets,* several hundred leading practitioners of the discipline of plastic surgery have demonstrated the value of the question-and-answer technique in imparting plastic surgery knowledge. However, one must not forget that it is not only the student who benefits from the well-posed question but also the teacher—it is truly an intellectual interchange. And one must also not forget that it is the questions without answers that propel the discipline forward as the questioner becomes determined to find the answers. This is the true beauty of our plastic surgical educational heritage.

"There is only one good, knowledge, and one evil, ignorance."
Socrates c. 470–399 B.C.

Joseph G. McCarthy, MD
Lawrence D. Bell Professor of Plastic Surgery
NYU School of Medicine
New York, New York

AFTERWORD

I confess that although I have written many forewords, this is my first afterword. Dr. Jeffrey Weinzweig has honored me by having asked me to provide this epilogue. He has taken a chance because he does not know what an editor, used to having the last word, might say.

My first comment is that this is a brilliantly conceived and much needed excellent book that admirably fulfills all its objectives and would have pleased even, or especially, Socrates, whom Dr. Weinzweig cited in his preface to the first edition. He could have entitled this *Everything You Wanted to Know about Plastic Surgery but Didn't Know or Were Too Afraid to Ask*.

One might enter into an abstruse argument about what constitutes "plastic surgery secrets." Are they facts, as the contents of this book implies? Pertinent is the observation by Samuel M. Crothers (1857–1927), an American Unitarian Universalist minister and essayist, who lived in Cambridge, Massachusetts (*The Gentle Reader*, 1903): "The trouble with facts is that there are so many of them." Certainly, after the appearance of this second edition, there are now more facts in plastic surgery than there are secrets.

Gertrude Stein might have said but did not: "A secret to be a secret must remain a secret." Advances in medicine and in the care of the patient depend upon scientists and doctors not withholding information, that is, not keeping secrets, except for respecting the confidentiality of the patient.

A major benefit of this electronic age has caused the cliché to come true: "Everything is an open book."

Praise is due to Dr. Weinzweig, the contributors, and the publishers for educating not just medical students and residents, those who might be asked questions on rounds or on exams, but all plastic surgeons, who can always benefit from more knowledge; certainly, their patients will.

I must register an obvious caveat: questions with answers, facts and secrets revealed do not guarantee "successful plastic surgery." An essential determinant is the personality of the patient and the plastic surgeon. One would hope that the plastic surgeon would be ethical, psychologically astute, compassionate, competent, judicious, and always committed to placing the needs of the patient above his or her own, acting according to what is best for the patient and not convenient or remunerative for the plastic surgeon.

Facts, however, are the necessary equipment of a good doctor–surgeon–plastic surgeon. They constitute the basis of knowledge but they are not the same as knowledge, which is not the same as wisdom, nor is it the same as a discerning eye and a responsive soul.

Worn by repetition but valid still is the secret enunciated by the early twentieth century Boston physician, Francis W. Peabody (1881–1927) (*The Care of The Patient,* The Journal of The American Medical Association; Vol 88, March 19,1927): "the secret of the care of the patient is in caring for the patient."

Too frequently omitted is this equally important quote: "The treatment of a disease may be entirely impersonal; the care of a patient must be completely personal."

And that is a fact to remember and a secret to share.

Robert M. Goldwyn, MD
Clinical Professor of Surgery
Harvard Medical School
Boston, Massachusetts

PREFACE TO THE FIRST EDITION

There is no such thing as a stupid question. Socrates knew this more than two thousand years ago when the interrogative (Socratic) method of teaching was born. The success of The Secrets Series® reaffirms the effectiveness of this approach to teaching. The purpose of *Plastic Surgery Secrets* is to serve as a comprehensive guide to a field in which the earliest procedures, including nasal and earlobe reconstruction, were described by Sushruta in 600 BC, while new frontiers pioneered within the last three decades, including craniofacial surgery, microsurgery, and fetal surgery, continue to evolve.

Nearly 200 authors have contributed the 120 chapters that comprise this volume, many of whom have literally defined the area of the specialty about which they have written. They have provided more than 3000 questions that broach virtually every aspect of plastic surgery and stimulate as many. I am indebted to each of them. The vastness of the field of plastic surgery by necessity presents countless opportunities for collaboration in patient management and medical education with colleagues in numerous other specialties. The scope of this volume is intended to cross over to students and practitioners in these allied fields. It is intended to provoke thought and stimulate further inquiry and represents a distillation of the important concepts and pearls that form the foundation of that alluring discipline of medicine known as *plastic surgery*.

Jeffrey Weinzweig, MD, FACS

PREFACE TO THE SECOND EDITION

The illustrious history of the specialty of plastic surgery, which spans two and a half millennia and includes the contributions of Sushruta, Tagliacozzi, Gillies, Buncke, and Tessier, among scores of other luminaries, demonstrates a consistent stream of advances that are seamlessly interwoven with quantum leaps in a way that no other surgical specialty can match. The playground of the plastic surgeon encompasses "*the skin and its contents*," as many of us are apt to proudly quip. The plastic surgeon is widely considered the innovator, the "aesthetic eye," the "surgeon's surgeon," the last link in the reconstructive chain when all other options have been exhausted. With those references come great expectations on the part of the patient and great responsibility on the part of the plastic surgeon.

The first edition of *Plastic Surgery Secrets* hit the shelves of bookstores around the world in 1999. In the decade since, it has become one of the best-selling books of its kind, with worldwide distribution and translations into four languages. It has served as a reliable and quick reference source for thousands of medical students, residents, and practicing plastic surgeons as well as trainees and colleagues in multiple other specialties.

During this period, the field of plastic surgery has made innumerable great strides in diverse directions to better address a myriad of complex clinical problems. These include the innovation of novel disruptive technology to enhance the treatment of complex craniofacial anomalies and problematic wounds, the development of advanced microvascular techniques to further define the boundaries of flap design, and the expansion of concepts set in motion more than a half century ago when Dr. Joseph Murray—a plastic surgeon—performed the first successful kidney transplant, subsequently receiving the Nobel Prize for his lifesaving accomplishment that ushered in the field of organ transplantation.

To address the explosive progress of our specialty over the past decade, the second edition of *Plastic Surgery Secrets* has been expanded to incorporate 35 new chapters dedicated to topics that reflect the growing complexity of our evolving field since the publication of the first edition. Chapters have been dedicated to facial transplantation, conjoined twins, perforator flaps, hand transplantation, principles of VAC, management of vascular disorders and compartment syndrome of the upper extremity, cleft and aesthetic orthognathic surgery, the pediatric hand and wrist, body contouring after massive weight loss, nonsurgical rejuvenation of the aging face, advances in basic science research, as well as multiple aspects of craniofacial distraction osteogenesis, including distraction of the cranium, midface, and mandible, and numerous other salient topics. To explore the legalistic subtleties and complexities of our specialty, chapters have been dedicated to CPT coding strategies, liability issues, and ethics.

Almost 300 authors have participated in the gargantuan task of revising, updating, and expanding the original edition to create one that contains 155 succinctly and cleverly crafted chapters. I am indebted to each of them. The introduction of full color to this volume and the larger dimensions of the text further enhance the book's strength as an educational tool. At the end of the day, the more easily and enjoyably a book serves as a resource, the more frequently it will be used as a reference. It is hoped that the second edition of *Plastic Surgery Secrets* will meet these expectations.

Jeffrey Weinzweig, MD, FACS

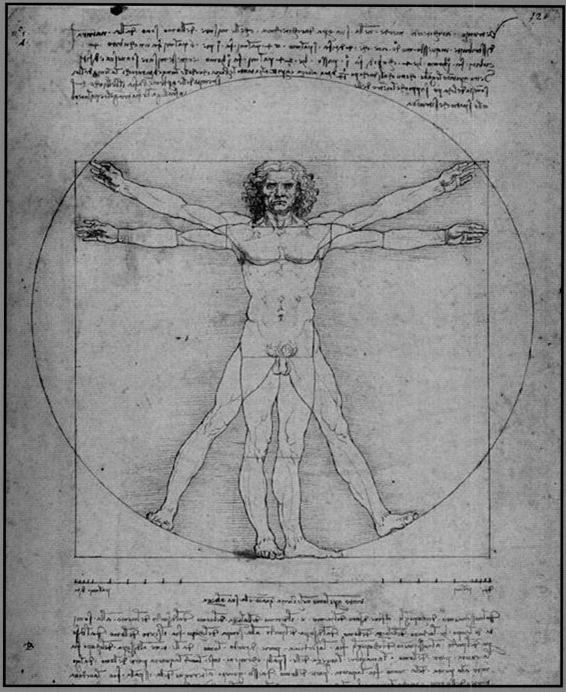

The Human Proportions According to Vitruvius. Leonardo da Vinci, ca. 1492. Pen, ink, and light wash over silverpoint. Galleria dell'Accademia, Venice. © Alinari/Art Resource, New York.

THE PRINCIPLES OF WOUND HEALING

Andrew Hsu, MD, and Thomas A. Mustoe, MD, FACS

1. What events occur during each of the primary phases of wound healing?

Wound healing has three principal phases: inflammatory, proliferative, and remodeling. The **inflammatory phase** begins at the time of injury and lasts for 24 to 48 hours. This phase begins with hemostasis and leads to inflammation. Platelets form the initial thrombus release growth factors that induce the chemotaxis and proliferation of neutrophils and macrophages, which cooperate to remove necrotic tissue, debris, and bacteria from the wound. Macrophages then become the prominent cell of this phase and release various growth factors and cytokines that change the relatively acellular wound into a highly cellular environment. Next, fibroblasts proliferate to become the dominant cell of the **proliferative phase.** They produce collagen, which provides structure to the wound and replaces the fibronectin–fibrin matrix. Angiogenesis of new capillaries occurs to sustain the fibroblast proliferation. Keratinocytes also epithelialize the wound. The **remodeling phase** begins at about 2 to 3 weeks and can last up to 2 years. At this time, collagen synthesis and degradation reach equilibrium. Fibroblasts organize and cross-link the collagen, wound strength gradually increases, wound contraction occurs, and the wound loses its pink or purple color as capillary and fibroblast density decrease. All stages may vary in length because of infection, malnutrition, or other exogenous factors.

2. What roles do platelet-derived growth factor and transforming growth factor beta play in wound healing?

Platelet-derived growth factor (PDGF) is released initially by platelets in the inflammatory phase during the formation of the initial thrombus. It is an important chemoattractant and activator of macrophages, which arrive to orchestrate wound healing. These macrophages then secrete additional growth factors that include more PDGF. These growth factors attract, recruit, and activate additional macrophages.

Transforming growth factor beta (TGF-β) is released by macrophages and platelets. It is a potent chemoattractant and activator of fibroblasts, stimulating them to form collagen. TGF-β is the major growth factor involved in collagen synthesis.

3. What role do macrophages play in wound healing?

Macrophages play a critical role in the inflammatory phase. They help to débride the wound through phagocytosis, but, more importantly, they are the primary source of proinflammatory cytokines and growth factors such as the interleukins (IL-1, IL-6, IL-8), PDGF, TGF-β, epidermal growth factor (EGF), fibroblast growth factor (FGF), vascular endothelial growth factor (VEGF), and insulin-like growth factor (IGF). These humoral factors stimulate the recruitment, activation, and proliferation of additional macrophages, lymphocytes, fibroblasts, and endothelial cells. These cytokines also act in an autocrine fashion to tremendously amplify their expression.

4. Are neutrophils essential for strengthening wounds?

Neutrophils remove necrotic debris and bacteria from the wound initially during the inflammatory phase of wound healing but play no role in strengthening the wound. Unlike macrophages, neutrophils are not a source of growth factors in a healing wound.

5. How does the wound's collagen composition compare between the early and late stages of wound healing?

Type I collagen is the most abundant type of collagen in normal dermis (approximately 80% to 90%). During the early stages of wound healing, fibroblasts actively produce type III collagen, which may account for 30% of the collagen in a healing wound. By week 2, type I collagen again becomes the principal collagen produced by fibroblasts. During remodeling, type III collagen is replaced by type I collagen to restore the normal dermal collagen composition.

6. When does collagen production peak in a healing wound?

Net collagen accumulation peaks after 2 to 3 weeks after injury. Collagen production peaks after 6 weeks but is balanced by collagen degradation. Although no net increase in collagen occurs during remodeling, collagen synthesis and degradation continue at elevated rates for up to 1 year after the initial injury.

7. During remodeling, no net increase in collagen occurs but wound tensile strength increases greatly. Why?

Initial wound healing is notable for production of large amounts of randomly oriented collagen. During remodeling, this collagen becomes cross-linked and replaced with more organized collagen that is better arranged to resist mechanical stress. Like raw wool being woven into strong yarn, the remodeled collagen is compacted into fibers that are many times stronger than random collagen fibrils. However, the final strength of the new collagen never reaches the strength of uninjured collagen.

8. What is the rationale for not allowing patients with hernias to do sit-ups for 6 weeks after a herniorrhaphy?

Wound tensile strength initially is relatively weak. It increases slowly for about 2 weeks and then increases rapidly for 4 weeks in a linear fashion. By 6 weeks after injury, the wound has gained about 50% of its ultimate strength and is strong enough to tolerate moderate forces. In the elderly, it may be prudent to be more patient because gains in tensile strength are slower.

9. A well-healed wound eventually reaches what percentage of prewound strength?

Classic studies by Levenson et al. in 1965, using a rat model, demonstrated that wounds never achieve more than 80% of normal prewound tensile strength.

10. What is the wound healing defect in Ehlers-Danlos syndromes?

Ehlers-Danlos syndromes (EDS) are a heterogeneous group of connective tissue disorders characterized by hypermobile joints, hyperextensible skin, and generalized fragility of connective tissues. They are associated with defects in the synthesis, cross-linking, or structure of collagen that can lead to decreased wound strength and delays in wound healing. Patients are prone to wound dehiscence, which forms broad, thin, shiny scars resembling cigarette paper.

11. What is the mechanism of wound contraction?

Fibroblasts in contracting wounds have increased actin microfilaments and are designated as myofibroblasts. These myofibroblasts orient themselves along lines of tension and pull collagen fibers together. Wound contraction is part of the normal healing process that closes wounds to the external environment. Scar contracture is an abnormal shortening and thickening of a scar that may cause functional (if across a joint) and/or cosmetic deformities.

12. By what three methods can wound healing be achieved?

A wound can heal through **primary intention** in the acute, clean surgical wound. This relatively rapid process involves manual approximation of the wound edges by suture, staples, or adhesive material. In **secondary intention,** a wound is allowed to heal through the physiologic processes of granulation and reepithelialization. This method leads to a relatively slow healing process and is used in chronic wounds that are more likely to be infected. In **tertiary intention,** healing occurs when primary closure is delayed, allowing the wound to granulate for a short period before closure through manual reapproximation or another technique. This method can be used to débride an infected, acute wound before closure. This is also designated *delayed primary closure.*

13. What is contact inhibition and how does it relate to epithelialization?

Contact inhibition is the concept that physical contact halts cell migration. Epithelial cells exhibit contact inhibition. They continue to proliferate and migrate across the surface of a wound until they contact each other, forming a continuous, single-layer sheet.

14. How long should a wound be kept dry after closing a surgical incision?

Well-approximated surgical incisions usually are epithelialized in 24 to 48 hours, forming a fluid barrier. Washing a wound once it is epithelialized to remove dried, crusted blood and exudates can reduce bacterial loads and culture media that could delay wound healing. For example, the benefits of washing and removing dried blood from a facial laceration far outweigh any risks to the wound. However, elderly patients epithelialize slower, so their wounds should be kept dry longer, particularly less well-vascularized areas such as lower extremities. If foreign material such a prosthetic joint is beneath an incision, it may be desirable to keep it dry for much longer to prevent potential contamination of the prosthesis.

15. Why do partial-thickness wounds reepithelialize faster than full-thickness wounds?

Epithelial cells are located not only in the epidermis but also in dermal sweat glands and hair follicles. In partial-thickness wounds, some epithelial islands and these dermal structures are preserved, so epithelial cell migration and proliferation from these remaining dermal appendages, sweat glands, and hair follicles all contribute to faster epithelialization. In full-thickness wounds, the entire dermis is destroyed, so epithelialization can only occur from the outer margins of the wound.

16. You are about to remove an actinic/seborrheic keratosis from a patient's face when he asks if there will be any scarring. How do you respond?

Actinic and seborrheic keratoses are limited to the epidermis. Scarring occurs following injury to the dermis. Injuries to the epidermis can heal without scarring, but if wound closure is delayed or deeper layers are injured, scarring results. Therefore, superficial skin lesions such as actinic/seborrheic keratoses can be removed without scarring if care is taken not to injure the deeper dermis.

17. After giving birth to her first baby, a patient asks if any treatments are available for stretch marks (striae distensae). What causes stretch marks? Are they amenable to treatment?

Stretch marks form when dermal collagen fibers are stretched and disrupted but the epidermis remains intact. The dermis forms a scar that is visible through the translucent epidermis. Because stretch marks are scars in the dermis, treatment involves scar excision or tissue destruction.

18. What techniques can be used to optimize healing of surgical wounds?

Any technique that reduces inflammation, minimizes tissue destruction, clears debris, and promotes a moist environment will optimize healing of surgical wounds. Some specific techniques are to perform meticulous hemostasis, limit the use of electrocautery, handle tissue with atraumatic instruments, achieve early and precise tissue approximation, avoid crush injury, and minimize suture material (foreign bodies) in the wound. Early and frequent cleansing helps to gently débride wounds by clearing surface exudates, bacteria, and debris. Also, evidence indicates that covering immature epithelium with silicone sheeting, paper tape, or other materials that simulate a mature stratum corneum can beneficially modulate the scarring process.

19. Is a wound less likely to spread if it is closed with intradermal polyglactic acid suture (Dexon, Vicryl) versus a nylon suture that is removed in 7 days?

Wounds can spread if closed under tension or if exposed to stretching forces. In the first 3 weeks of wound healing, the strength of a wound is only a small fraction of its eventual strength. Sutures removed or degraded before this time have little effect in preventing wound spreading. Polyglactic acid suture loses strength after 3 weeks, at which time the wound is still relatively weak. These results are similar to removing a nylon suture from the wound in 1 week. Leaving a permanent intradermal suture in place for several months has been shown to decrease spreading, and it is possible that a synthetic suture that retains strength for 6 to 8 weeks may have the same effect.

20. What is the ideal dressing?

In general, the ideal dressing should be simple, inexpensive, highly absorptive, and nonadherent. It should provide a moist environment for healing and should have antibacterial properties. However, wounds are not all the same; therefore, dressings should be selected such that their desirable properties (absorptive, antibacterial, etc.) fit the needs of the particular wound. Hundreds of dressings with various desirable properties are available on the market; however, none of them has been proven superior to gauze.

21. What are the benefits of occlusive dressings?

Occlusive dressings (e.g., polyurethane) maintain moist environments that promote faster reepithelialization than occurs under dry conditions. It has been shown that epithelialization under scabs does not occur as quickly as under moist dressings. When occlusive dressings are used, care should be taken to monitor for infection because the moist environment under the dressing makes an excellent medium for bacterial growth.

22. Which vitamins and minerals affect wound healing?

Vitamin A decreases the inflammation in wounds and may improve wound healing in steroid-dependent patients. Vitamin C is necessary for the hydroxylation of lysine and proline in collagen cross-linking. Essential fatty acids are required for all new cell synthesis. Magnesium and zinc are important cofactors for DNA synthesis, protein synthesis, and cellular proliferation. Copper-based enzymes catalyze the cross-linking of collagen and strengthen the collagen framework. These vitamins and minerals should be supplemented to prevent deficiency states; however, oversupplementation in the adequately nourished patient has not been shown to accelerate wound healing and, instead, may be deleterious.

23. Are there any specific products that help accelerate wound healing?

The Food and Drug Administration (FDA) has approved the use of PDGF for accelerating the healing of clean, well-vascularized, diabetic forefoot ulcers. Apligraf is a synthetic dermis that the FDA has approved for improving the treatment of refractory venous ulcers.

24. What is the wound vacuum-assisted closure, and how does it accelerate wound healing?

The wound vacuum-assisted closure (VAC) is a very useful occlusive dressing that provides a constant negative pressure to the wound bed. This negative pressure reduces tissue edema, removes exudates, lowers the bacterial burden, aids in tissue contraction, and may improve blood supply. This device has allowed many wounds requiring complex reconstruction to heal with simpler options; however, it may be subject to overuse. It has applications for many acute and chronic wounds and has resulted in simpler solutions, such as skin grafts rather than complex flaps for successful wound closure.

25. You are reluctant to débride a decubitus ulcer with necrotic tissue in a chronically ill patient who has multiple medical problems and a coagulopathy. What are the alternatives to surgical débridement?

Several options are available. Topical creams that break down necrotic tissue can be applied to the wound. Commonly used agents include autolytic and enzymatic débridement creams. Autolytic débridement agents work by activating endogenous collagenases within the open wound to remove necrotic tissue. Enzymatic débridement agents are concentrated collagenases that directly digest the nonviable tissue.

26. What is a chronic wound?

Chronic wounds are those that fail to close in 3 months. They fall into three broad categories: diabetic ulcers, pressure ulcers, and ulcers secondary to venous hypertension. With meticulous wound care, most chronic wounds will close without surgical intervention.

27. What factors impair wound healing?

Although many factors influence wound healing in surgical patients, the most important are nutritional deficiencies (albumin <2.5 gm/dL), vitamin deficiencies (unusual), aging, wound infections, hypoxia, edema, steroids, diabetes, and radiation.

28. What effect does radiation have on wound healing?

Radiation damages endothelial cells, capillaries, and arterioles. This results in progressive loss of blood vessel volume and diminishes tissue perfusion in the affected area. Radiated fibroblasts show decreased proliferation and collagen synthesis, leading to diminished deposition of extracellular matrix. Lymphatics are likewise damaged, causing edema and poor clearance of infection in healing tissues.

29. Why does edema impair wound healing?

In normal tissue, each cell is only a few cell diameters away from the nearest capillary and receives oxygen and nutrients by diffusion. Edema impairs wound healing through several mechanisms. First, the additional extracellular water increases diffusion distances, resulting in lower tissue pO_2. Second, chronic edema may result in protein deposition in the extracellular matrix, which can act as a diffusion barrier for growth factors and nutrients, making them less available to cells. Finally, growth factors and nutrients are relatively diluted in the edematous fluid.

30. What factors are responsible for local wound ischemia?

Smoking, radiation, edema, diabetes, atherosclerosis, venous stasis, vasculitis, or prolonged pressure can affect the perfusion and oxygenation of a wound and cause local wound ischemia.

31. Is there a role for hyperbaric oxygen in wound healing?

Recent evidence suggests that oxygen serves not only as a necessary component in aerobic metabolism but as a signaling molecule for growth factor production. Based on the success of a number of retrospective studies, the use of hyperbaric oxygen to increase tissue oxygenation has become widespread, particularly in patients with diabetic foot ulcers. However, large, prospective, randomized trials have not been conducted.

32. What is the definition of wound infection?

It is the product of the entrance, growth, metabolic activities, and resultant pathophysiologic effects of microorganisms in the tissues. A wound with bacterial counts greater than 10^5 organisms per gram of tissue is considered infected and unlikely to heal without further treatment.

33. What causes hypertrophic/keloid scars? What features distinguish them?

Hypertrophic/keloid scars are believed to be due to an excessive inflammatory response during wound healing. Keloids usually extend beyond the boundaries of the original tissue injury and become progressively larger. They act similar to benign tumors and may extend into surrounding tissue. Hypertrophic scars are elevated but do not extend outside the original borders of the wound. Keloids are more common in people with dark complexions. Hypertrophic scarring occurs more often in Asian and African skin. Keloid scarring is transmitted in an autosomal dominant pattern in some patients. Both conditions are remarkable for overproduction of all components of the extracellular matrix, but absolute numbers of fibroblasts are not increased.

34. A patient has two burns on his chest, one of which epithelialized in 1 week, the other in 3 weeks. The second wound now has a hypertrophic scar. Why?

Partial-thickness burns or abrasions that remain open for more than 2 weeks have a high incidence of hypertrophic scarring. Scarring is believed to be secondary to prolonged inflammation and can be minimized by rapidly closing a wound primarily, skin grafting, or other techniques.

35. What treatment options are available for hypertrophic scars?

Pressure garments, topical silicone sheeting, adjunctive use of insoluble steroids, and reexcision may improve hypertrophic scars. In general, simple reexcision and closure is a realistic solution if the cause of the scar was poor wound closure, inadequate support from wound tension, prolonged inflammation from infection, foreign bodies (excess suture), or delayed epithelialization. One should pay particular attention to using permanent sutures to splint the dermis, achieve early wound occlusion, and apply silicone gel sheeting.

36. What treatment options are available for keloid scars?

Proven treatment options include intralesional injection of steroids, radiation therapy, or combination therapy with surgical resection. More recently, interferon has shown some benefits in reducing collagen production and keloid thickness.

37. What effect does aging have on wound healing?

Aged patients have slower wound healing, less scarring, less contraction, decreased tensile strength, decreased epithelialization, delayed cell migration, and decreased collagen synthesis. Aging can be an advantage in performing cosmetic surgery because scarring can be minimized. However, it also can be a disadvantage because wound strength is lower, and a wound may easily be separated if placed under tension.

38. You perform a split-thickness skin graft (12/1000ths of an inch) for burns in a young patient and in an elderly patient, using the same technique and equipment. Several weeks later the young patient is doing well, but the elderly patient has blisters forming on the graft. What may be the cause?

Basal epidermal cells are attached to the underlying dermis by hemidesmosomes. Cells of aged individuals have been shown to be ineffective at forming new hemidesmosomes. Without an adequate dermal base, coverage of the wound by epidermis is unstable and characterized by chronic and recurrent breakdown. Therefore the skin of elderly patients is less tolerant to shearing forces. When shearing occurs, blisters are likely to form.

39. How does the fetal wound differ from the adult wound?

The main difference is that fetal wounds heal with little to no scar formation. Fetal wounds are bathed in amniotic fluid, heal with less inflammation, have increased levels of type III collagen, lack TGF-β, and have a relatively high content of hyaluronic acid.

BIBLIOGRAPHY

Clark AF: The Molecular and Cellular Biology of Wound Repair, 2nd ed. New York, Plenum, 1996.

Fine NA, Mustoe TA: Wound healing. In Mulholland MW, Lillemore KD, Doherty GM, Maier RV (eds): Greenfield's Surgery: Scientific Principles and Practice, 4th ed. Philadelphia, Williams & Wilkins, 2005.

Leibovich SJ, Ross R: The role of the macrophage in wound repair: A study with hydrocortisone and anti-macrophage serum. Am J Pathol 78:71–100, 1975.

Levenson SM, Geever EF, Crowley LV, et al: The healing of rat skin wounds. Ann Surg 161:292–308, 1965.

Madden JW, Peacock EE: Studies on the biology of collagen during wound healing. Rate of collagen synthesis and deposition in cutaneous wounds in the rat. Surgery 64:288–294, 1968.

Mustoe TA: Surgery of scars: Hypertrophic, keloid and aesthetic sequellae. In Teot L, Banwell PE, Ziegler UE (eds): Surgery in Wounds. Berlin, Springer-Verlag, 2004.

Mustoe TA: Wound healing. In Becker JM, Stucchi AF (eds): Essentials of Surgery. Philadelphia, Elsevier, 2006.

Mustoe TA, Cooter R, Gold MH, et al: International clinical guidelines of scar management. Plast Reconstr Surg 110:560–572, 2002.

Robson MC: Wound infection: A failure of wound healing caused by an imbalance of bacteria. Surg Clin North Am 77:637–650, 1997.

Winter GD, Scales JT: Effects of air drying and dressings on the surface of the wound. Nature 197:91–92, 1963.

TECHNIQUES AND GEOMETRY OF WOUND REPAIR

Jeffrey Weinzweig, MD, FACS,
and Norman Weinzweig, MD, FACS

1. What are important considerations in surgical wound closure?

Surgical wound closure is performed in conjunction with biologic events such as fibroplasia, epithelialization, wound contraction, bacterial balance, and host defense mechanisms. All suture materials, including both absorbable and nonabsorbable monofilaments, should be considered as foreign bodies that evoke a tissue inflammatory reaction. This reaction may result in delayed wound healing, infection, or dehiscence. Selection of suture material should be based on the healing properties and requirements of the involved tissue, the biologic and physical properties of the suture material, the location of the wound on the body, and individualized patient considerations.

2. Why is the choice of suture material critical in the early stages of wound healing?

In the early stages of wound healing, the suture is primarily responsible for keeping the wound together. In the first 3 or 4 days after wound repair, the gain in tensile strength is related to the fibrin clot, which fills the wound cavity. Tensile strength is less than 5% of unwounded skin at 1 week, 10% at 2 weeks, 25% at 4 weeks, 40% at 6 weeks, and 80% at 8 to 10 weeks.

3. Which layer of a wound repair contributes the most to wound strength?

The dermal layer. Absorbable sutures placed in the dermis, such as poliglecaprone 25 (Monocryl), polyglactin 910 (Vicryl), polyglycolic acid (Dexon), or polyglyconate (Maxon), provide tensile strength over an extended period prior to suture resorption. Sutures placed in the epidermis, usually 5-0 or 6-0 nylon (depending on location), permit fine alignment of the skin edges only and should be removed within 5 days.

4. What are the basic principles of suturing skin wounds?

Skin edges should be débrided when necessary and always everted and approximated without tension. If simple stitches are not sufficient, horizontal or vertical mattress stitches may be necessary. After tying a knot, the suture appears pear-shaped in cross-section with raised borders. The everted skin edges gradually flatten to produce a level surface. It is important to place the suture so that the wound edges just touch each other. Postoperative edema creates additional tension with potential strangulation of tissue and resultant ischemia that may lead to necrosis.

5. What are the different methods of suturing skin wounds?

Simple interrupted sutures are placed so that the needle enters and exits the tissue at 90°, grasping identical amounts of tissue on each side to permit exact approximation of the wound margins. Of course, this principle applies only when the skin edges line up at exactly the same level. Occasionally, one side of the wound is higher and the other lower. To approximate the edges at the same level, it is necessary to grasp the tissue "high in the high" (closer to the epidermis) and "low in the low" (farther from the epidermis).

Vertical and **horizontal mattress sutures** are especially useful for everting stubborn wound edges. However, horizontal mattress sutures cause more ischemia than either simple interrupted or vertical mattress sutures.

Subcuticular or **intradermal continuous sutures** obviate the need for external skin sutures; thus, they avoid suture marks on the skin and result in the most favorable scar. These sutures should be left in place for 2 to 3 weeks. Prolene is often used because it produces little inflammatory reaction, maintains its tensile strength, and can easily be removed.

Half-buried mattress sutures (McGregor stitch or three-corner stitch) are especially useful for closing a V-shaped wound or approximating skin edges of different textures or thicknesses. This stitch usually prevents necrosis of the tip of the V, which is sometimes seen with simple interrupted sutures. By placing the buried portion of the suture within the dermis of the flap, ischemia and damage to the overlying skin are avoided.

Continuous over-and-over or **running sutures** are most often used for closure of scalp wounds because they can be performed rapidly and are hemostatic. Locking these stitches provides additional hemostasis. Nonlocking running stitches, using fine nylon, can be used in areas such as the face where the wound is uncomplicated and under no tension.

6. What is the role of immobilization in wound healing?

Immobilization of the wound is as important in soft tissue healing as it is in bone healing. By immobilizing the wound, tension across the skin edges is eliminated, yielding a more favorable scar. Immobilization can be achieved by using Steri-Strips, tapes, collodion, or even plaster splinting.

7. How are suture materials classified?

Suture materials are classified as **natural** or **synthetic, absorbable** or **nonabsorbable,** and **braided** or **monofilament.** Further classification takes into consideration the time until absorption occurs, extent of tissue reaction, and tensile strength.

8. What are the differences among the various absorbable suture materials?

Catgut, derived from the submucosal layer of sheep intestine, evokes a moderate acute inflammatory reaction and is hydrolyzed by proteolytic enzymes within 60 days. Tensile strength is rapidly lost within 7 to 10 days. Chromization (chromic catgut suture) slightly prolongs these parameters compared with plain gut. The main indications for use of catgut suture include ligation of superficial vessels and closure of tissues that heal rapidly, such as oral mucosa. Catgut sutures also can be used in situations where one wishes to avoid suture removal, as in small children.

Vicryl and **Dexon** are synthetic materials that behave similarly. They produce minimal tissue reactivity and are completely absorbed within 90 days. Tensile strength is 60% to 75% at 2 weeks and lost at 1 month. Both are useful as intradermal sutures because of their low reactivity, but they should be used judiciously as buried sutures because of their tendency to "spit" with inflammation. Monocryl (a monofilament), on the other hand, can be used comparably as intradermal or buried sutures. Because the braided structure of Vicryl and Dexon may potentiate infection, neither should be used in wounds with potential bacterial contamination.

Polydioxanone (PDS), a synthetic absorbable monofilament, is minimally reactive. Absorption is essentially complete within 6 months, although little occurs before 90 days. Because of this slow absorption, "spitting" is a significant problem. As a monofilament suture, however, PDS is less prone to bacterial seeding. PDS sutures maintain their tensile strength considerably longer: 50% at 4 weeks and 25% at 6 weeks. Absorption is essentially complete at 6 months.

Maxon and **Monocryl** are absorbable monofilament sutures with qualities and advantages similar to those of PDS. However, they retain their tensile strength for only 3 or 4 weeks; absorption of Monocryl is essentially complete between 3 and 4 months.

9. What are the differences among the various nonabsorbable suture materials?

Nonabsorbable monofilament (Ethilon/nylon and Prolene) sutures incite minimal inflammatory reaction, slide well, and can be easily removed, thus providing ideal running intradermal stitches. Prolene appears to maintain its tensile strength longer than nylon, which loses approximately 15% to 20% per year. Nonabsorbable braided materials (Nurolon, Ethibond, and silk) elicit an acute inflammatory reaction that is followed by gradual encapsulation of the suture by fibrous connective tissue.

Staples cause less inflammatory reaction than sutures, have similar strength up to 21 days, and result in a similar final appearance when removed within 1 week postoperatively. Large wounds can be closed faster and more expeditiously with staples, which are useful for procedures such as abdominoplasty, reduction mammaplasty, and skin grafting.

10. What influences the permanent appearance of suture marks?

The key factors influencing scarring due to suture placement are (1) length of time that the skin suture remains in place, (2) tension on the wound edges, (3) region of the body, (4) presence of infection, and (5) tendency for hypertrophic scarring or keloid formation. The most critical factors in avoiding suture marks in the skin are tension-free closure and early removal. Sutures left in place for excessive periods result in severe scarring. Epithelial cells crawl along the path of the suture within the skin, resulting in sinus tract formation; cross-hatching occurs from prolonged compression of the suture on the epidermal surface. Wounds in which sutures are removed within 7 days usually produce a fine linear scar. Wound closure with a running dermal pull-out suture provides the optimal scar without interfering with the development of tensile strength. The finest sutures for any given wound should be used. The timing of removal depends on the region of the body in which the sutures have been placed and ranges from 3 to 5 days in the face to 10 to 14 days in the back and extremities.

11. What are Langer's lines?

Elastic fibers within the dermis maintain the skin in a state of constant tension, as demonstrated by the gaping of wounds created by incising the dermis or by the immediate contraction of skin grafts as they are harvested. In 1861, Langer demonstrated that puncturing the skin of cadavers with a rounded sharp object resulted in elliptical holes produced by the tension of the skin. He stated that human skin was less distensible in the direction of the lines of tension than across them. Shortcomings of Langer's lines are that (1) some tension lines were found to run across natural creases, wrinkles, and flexion lines; (2) they exist in excised skin; and (3) they do not correlate with the direction of dermal collagen fiber orientation. Nonetheless, Langer's lines serve as a useful guide in the planning and design of skin incisions and excisions.

12. What are relaxed skin tension lines?

Relaxed skin tension lines (RSTLs), also known as wrinkle lines, natural skin lines, lines of facial expression, or lines of minimal tension, lie perpendicular to the long axis of the underlying facial muscles. They are accentuated by contraction of the facial muscles, as occurs with smiling, frowning, grimacing, puckering the lips, or closing the eyes tightly. An example is the frontalis muscle, which runs vertically straight up the forehead; RSTLs on the forehead run transversely or perpendicular to the underlying frontalis muscle.

13. What is the optimal scar?

The optimal scar is a fine, flat, concealed linear scar lying within or parallel to a skin wrinkle or natural skin line, contour junction, or RSTL. There should be no contour irregularity, distortion of adjacent anatomic or aesthetic units or landmarks, or pigmentation changes.

14. What causes "stretch" marks?

Significant stretch may result in disruption of the dermis with loss of continuity of the elastic fibers. Once this occurs, elastic recoil and skin tension in the involved area are lost—the result is a stretch mark.

15. Which excisional methods can be used for removal of skin lesions?

Skin lesions can be removed by elliptical, wedge, or circular excisions. Most skin lesions are removed by **simple elliptical excision** with the long axis of the ellipse on, or paralleling, a wrinkle, contour line, or RSTL. The ellipse may be lenticular in shape with angular edges or have rounded edges. Ideally, the long axis should be four times longer than the short axis. **Wedge excisions** are performed primarily for lesions on the free margins of the ears, lips, eyelids, or nostrils. Lip lesions can be excised as either triangular or pentagonal wedges. Pentagonal rather than triangular excision often leads to less contracture and shortening along the longitudinal axis of the incision with a more favorable scar. Closure of **circular defects** can be performed by a purse string suture, a skin graft, or a local flap.

16. What is the purpose of serial excisions?

Large lesions, such as giant nevi, can be removed by serial excisions. This approach takes advantage of the viscoelastic properties of skin and the creep and stress–relaxation phenomenon. It has been especially useful for improvement of male pattern baldness by excision of non–hair-bearing areas of the scalp. However, with the introduction of soft tissue expansion, the technique of serial excision has become less popular.

17. What are the differences among rotation, transposition, and interpolation flaps?

Each of these flaps has a specific pivot point and an arc through which the flap is rotated. The line of greatest tension of the flap is the radius of that arc. The **rotation flap** is a semicircular flap, whereas the **transposition flap** is a rectangular flap, consisting of skin and subcutaneous tissue that rotates about a pivot point into an immediately adjacent defect. The flap donor site can be closed by direct suturing or with a skin graft. A small back-cut from the pivot point along the base of the flap can be made to release a flap that is under too much tension. Because a skin flap rotated about a pivot point becomes shorter in length the farther it is rotated, the transposition flap usually is designed to extend beyond the defect. A sufficient flap design is verified with a cloth template (Fig. 2-1). An **interpolation flap,** although similar in design to the rotation and transposition flaps, is rotated into a nearby but *not* immediately adjacent defect. The pedicle of this flap, therefore, must pass over or under the intervening tissue.

18. What is a bilobed flap?

A bilobed flap is a transposition flap that consists of two flaps often designed at right angles to each other. The primary flap is transposed into the defect, whereas the secondary flap, usually half the diameter of the primary flap, is used to close the donor site (Fig. 2-2).

19. What is a "dog ear"? How can it be eliminated?

In excising a lesion in elliptical fashion, the long axis should be four times the length of the short axis. Dog ears form at the ends of a closed wound when either the ellipse is made too short or one side of the ellipse is longer than the other. Dog ears may flatten over time, but primary correction is best. If the elliptical excision is too short, the ellipse can be lengthened to include the excessive tissue or the redundant tissue excised as two small triangles. If one side of the

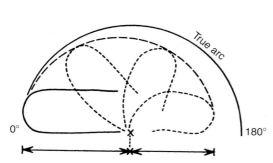

Figure 2-1. A skin flap rotated about a pivot point becomes shorter in effective length the farther it is rotated. Therefore a flap should be designed to extend beyond the defect. (From Place MJ, Herber SC, Hardesty RA: Basic techniques and principles in plastic surgery. In Aston SJ, Beasley RW, Thorne CHM [eds]: Grabb and Smith's Plastic Surgery, 5th ed. Philadelphia, Lippincott-Raven, 1997, p 22, with permission.)

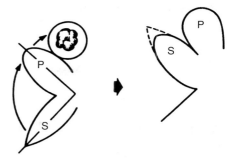

Figure 2-2. Bilobed flap. After excision of the lesion, the primary flap (P) is transposed into the resultant defect. The secondary flap (S) is then transposed to close the donor site defect. (From Place MJ, Herber SC, Hardesty RA: Basic techniques and principles in plastic surgery. In Aston SJ, Beasley RW, Thorne CHM [eds]: Grabb and Smith's Plastic Surgery, 5th ed. Philadelphia, Lippincott-Raven, 1997, p 23, with permission.)

incision is longer than the other, the dog ear can be corrected by making a short right-angle or 45° incision at the end of the ellipse with removal of the redundant tissue.

20. When should scar revision be performed? What are the goals?

Scar revision should be performed once the scar has matured—usually 9 months to 2 years after the original procedure. The goals of scar revision are to reorient the scar, divide it into smaller segments, and make it level with adjacent tissue.

21. What is a Z-plasty?

Referred to by Limberg as "converging triangular flaps," the Z-plasty is a technique in which two triangular flaps are interdigitated without tension, producing a gain in length along the direction of the common limb of the Z (useful in the management of scar contractures) as well as a change in the direction of the common limb of the Z (useful in the management of facial scars).

22. How is a Z-plasty designed?

A Z-plasty consists of a central limb, usually placed along the scar or line of contracture, and two limbs positioned to resemble a Z or reverse Z. The limbs must be equal in length to permit the skin flaps to fit together after transposition. The angles of the Z vary from 30° to 90°. The central limb, oriented along the line of contracture, usually is under considerable tension. After release or division of this contracture, the shape of the parallelogram immediately changes with spontaneous flap transposition and lengthening along the line of the central limb. Lengthening is related to the difference between the long and short axes of the parallelogram formed by the Z. The wider the angles of the triangular flaps, the greater the difference between the long and short diagonals and thus the greater the lengthening. In designing a Z-plasty, sufficient laxity must be available transversely to achieve the appropriate lengthening perpendicular to it. The limbs of the Z-plasty should follow the RSTLs (Fig. 2-3).

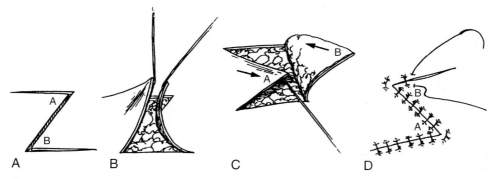

Figure 2-3. Classic Z-plasty using 60° angles. **A, B,** Flap design and elevation. **C, D,** Flap transposition and suture without tension. (From Weinzweig N, Weinzweig J: Basic principles and techniques in plastic surgery. In Cohen M [ed]: Mastery of Plastic and Reconstructive Surgery. Boston, Little, Brown, 1994, p 26, with permission.)

23. Why are angle size and limb length important in performing a Z-plasty?
The angle size determines the percentage increase in length. The original limb length controls the absolute increase in final limb length. As the angle size increases, the degree of lengthening increases. A 30° angle produces a 25% increase in length; a 45° angle, a 50% increase; a 60° angle, a 75% increase; a 75° angle, a 100% increase; and a 90° angle, a 120% increase. Although the length increase values are only theoretical, they provide a good approximation of the actual lengthening. In general, the actual increase in length is slightly less than the theoretical increase.

24. What is the optimal angle for Z-plasty design?
The optimal angle is 60°. Angles significantly less than 60° do not achieve sufficient lengthening, defeating the purpose of the Z-plasty and resulting in flap narrowing and vascular compromise. Angles much greater than 60° produce significant tension in the adjacent tissue, preventing transposition of the flaps.

25. What are the indications for multiple Z-plasties?
A similar degree of lengthening can be produced by a single Z-plasty and multiple Z-plasties, because the total length of the central limbs of multiple Z-plasties can equal the length of the single Z-plasty. Multiple Z-plasties, however, produce less transverse shortening. Lateral tension is reduced and more equally distributed over the entire length of the central limbs. Multiple Z-plasties are useful when insufficient tissue is available for a large single Z-plasty. In addition, multiple Z-plasties of facial scars often produce cosmetically superior results.

26. What is a four-flap Z-plasty?
A four-flap Z-plasty is an effective technique to correct thumb–index web space and axillary contractures. A 90°/90° angle or 120°/120° angle Z-plasty is designed. The two-flap Z-plasty is then converted to a four-flap Z-plasty by bisecting the angles, creating flaps that are 45° or 60°. This technique produces greater lengthening (124%) with less tension on the flaps.

27. What is a double-opposing Z-plasty?
Also known as the combination five-flap Y-V advancement and Z-plasty, the double-opposing Z-plasty is particularly useful for releasing contractures of concave regions of the body, such as the dorsum of the interdigital web spaces and the medial canthal region. The central flap is advanced in Y-V fashion while the flaps of the two Z-plasties on each side of the central flap are transposed (Fig. 2-4).

28. What is a W-plasty?
A W-plasty is another technique for reorienting the direction of a linear scar. Triangles of equal size are outlined on either side of the scar with the tip of the triangle on one side placed at the midpoint of the base of the triangle on the opposite side. At the ends of the scar, the excised triangles should be smaller, with the limbs of the W tapered. The tips of the triangles should be sutured with three-corner stitches to prevent necrosis of the flap tips.

29. What is the main disadvantage of a W-plasty?
A W-plasty does not lengthen a contracted linear scar; a Z-plasty should be used for this purpose. A W-plasty increases rather than decreases tension in the area of the scar because of the necessary sacrifice of tissue and should be used only when there is an abundance of tissue adjacent to the scar.

30. What is the V-Y advancement technique?
The V-Y advancement technique allows forward advancement of a triangular flap (V) without rotation or lateral movement and closure of the resulting defect in a Y fashion. The skin that is actually advanced is on either side of the V (Fig. 2-5).

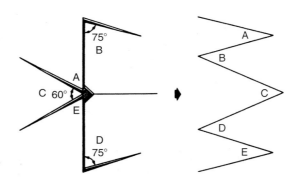

Figure 2-4. Five-flap Y-V advancement and Z-plasty. The central flap (C) is advanced in a Y-V fashion. The flaps of the two Z-plasties on each side of the central flap are transposed. (From Jankauskas S, Cohen IK, Grabb WC: Basic techniques in plastic surgery. In Smith JW, Aston SJ [eds]: Grabb and Smith's Plastic Surgery, 4th ed. Boston, Little, Brown, 1991, p 76, with permission.)

A   B   C

Figure 2-5. V-Y advancement technique. The central V is advanced forward and the defect is closed in a Y configuration. (From Weinzweig N, Weinzweig J: Basic principles and techniques in plastic surgery. In Cohen M [ed]: Mastery of Plastic and Reconstructive Surgery. Boston, Little, Brown, 1994, p 26, with permission.)

31. When is a V-Y advancement flap used?

This technique is extremely useful for lengthening the nasal columella, correcting the whistle deformity of the lip, and closure of selected soft tissue defects. It also can be used in various other skin and mucosal flaps.

32. What is a rhombic flap?

The rhombic flap, originally described by Limberg and often referred to as the Limberg flap, is a combination of rotation and transposition flaps that borrows adjacent loose skin for coverage of a rhombic defect. A rhombus is an equilateral parallelogram with (1) acute angles of 60° and obtuse angles of 120°, (2) long and short diagonals perpendicular to each other, and (3) a short diagonal equal in length to each side of the rhombus. The flap is designed as an extension of the short diagonal opposite either of the two 120° angles of the rhombus. The short diagonal is extended by a distance equal to its length. From this point, a line of equal length is drawn at 60° parallel to either side of the rhombus. Therefore four Limberg flaps are possible for any given rhombic defect (Fig. 2-6).

33. Should lesions be excised to create rhombic defects?

No. Lesions should be excised as circular defects or as necessary to permit adequate excision. A rhombus encompassing the defect and the four possible rhombic flaps can then be drawn. The selected flap is incised and elevated. Wide undermining beneath the base of the flap is necessary to allow the flap to fall into position in the rhombic defect without tension. The initial sutures are placed in the four corners of the defect.

34. What is the Dufourmental flap?

The Dufourmental flap is a variation of the rhombic flap in which the angles differ from the standard 60° and 120° angles in the Limberg flap. Although angles of 30° and 150° usually are used, angles up to 90° are possible. This versatile flap is useful for coverage of a defect in the shape of a rhomboid rather than a rhombus. Although the two terms are often used interchangeably, a rhomboid differs from a rhombus in several important respects: (1) it has acute angles of various degrees, (2) only opposite sides are equal in length, (3) diagonals are not perpendicular, (4) diagonals are not equal in length, and (5) diagonals are not necessarily equal in length to the sides of the parallelogram. Planning is more complex than for the Limberg flap, and it is often easier simply to convert the defect into a rhombus with angles of 60° and 120° (Fig. 2-7).

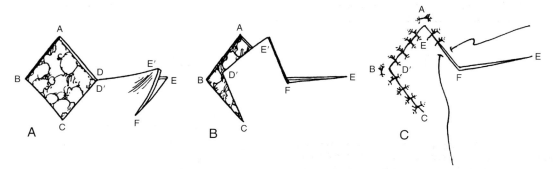

Figure 2-6. Rhombic flap. **A,** Flap design. **B,** Elevation of flap with wide undermining of the base to allow transposition. **C,** Suture of the flap without tension. (From Weinzweig N, Weinzweig J: Basic principles and techniques in plastic surgery. In Cohen M [ed]: Mastery of Plastic and Reconstructive Surgery. Boston, Little, Brown, 1994, p 26, with permission.)

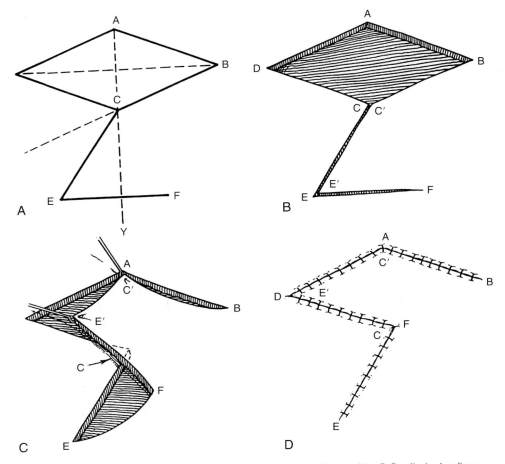

Figure 2-7. The Dufourmental flap. **A, B,** Flap design. **C,** Flap elevation and transposition. **D,** Resultant suture lines. (From Jackson IT: Local Flaps in Head and Neck Reconstruction. St. Louis, Mosby, 1985, p 20, with permission.)

BIBLIOGRAPHY

Borges AF: Elective Incisions and Scar Revision. Boston, Little, Brown, 1973.
Borges AF: Choosing the correct Limberg flap. Plast Reconstr Surg 62:542–545, 1978.
Borges AF: W-plasty. Ann Plast Surg 3:153–159, 1979.
Jackson IT: Local Flaps in Head and Neck Reconstruction. St. Louis, Mosby, 1995.
Limberg AA: The Planning of Local Plastic Surgical Operations. Lexington, MA, Collamore Press, 1984 [translated by SA Wolfe].
McGregor IA: The Z-plasty. Br J Plast Surg 19:82–87, 1966.
McGregor IA: Fundamental Techniques in Plastic Surgery and Their Surgical Applications, 7th ed. Edinburgh, Churchill Livingstone, 1980.
Jankauskas S, Cohen IK, Grabb WC: Basic technique of plastic surgery. In Smith JW, Aston SJ (eds): Grabb and Smith's Plastic Surgery, 4th ed. Boston, Little, Brown and Company, 1991, pp 3–90.
Weinzweig J, Weinzweig N: Plastic surgery techniques. In Guyuron M, Eriksson E, Persing J, et al. (eds): Plastic Surgery. Philadelphia, Elsevier, 2008, pp 1013–1032.
Weinzweig N, Weinzweig J: Basic principles and techniques in plastic surgery. In Cohen M (ed): Mastery of Plastic and Reconstructive Surgery. Boston, Little, Brown, 1994, pp 14–33.

ANESTHESIA FOR PLASTIC SURGERY

CHAPTER 3

Brent V. Stromberg, MD, FACS

1. What is the maximal dose of lidocaine that can be safely used for local anesthesia?

Lidocaine probably is the most commonly used local anesthetic agent. The maximal safe dose is 4 mg/kg. The addition of epinephrine to the anesthetic solution (usually in a 1:100,000 concentration), which slows the absorption of lidocaine due to local vasoconstriction, allows a maximal dose of 7 mg/kg.

Although the above answer has typically been given, some anesthesiologists prefer not to discuss a single maximum dose. Where the block is administered plays a significant role in the amount and rate of absorption and, therefore, the risk of systemic toxicity. For example, the risk of developing systemic toxicity is greater with the same dose of local anesthetic with an intercostal block versus a peripheral nerve block.

2. Which nerves exit the skull through foramina that lie in a sagittal plane?

The supraorbital, infraorbital, and mental nerves exit the skull along a straight line, approximately 2.5 cm from the midline of the face, which includes the pupils of the eye in a midgaze position. The ability to identify these nerves by surface anatomy is crucial to performing successful regional blocks of the face. Aspiration prior to instillation of an anesthetic agent is always advisable to avoid intraarterial injection.

3. How can the forehead and upper eyelid be blocked to permit excision of a large lipoma?

Regional blocks of the supraorbital and supratrochlear nerves provide effective anesthesia of the forehead area. The supraorbital nerve (V_1) emerges from the supraorbital foramen to supply sensation to the upper eyelid, conjunctiva, forehead, and scalp as far posteriorly as the lambdoid suture. The supratrochlear nerve emerges from the medial aspect of the supraorbital rim to supply the medial aspect of the forehead, upper eyelid, skin of the upper nose, and conjunctiva. A supraorbital nerve block is performed by inserting the needle just under the midportion of the eyebrow while palpating the foramen and injecting 2 to 3 mL of 1% lidocaine with epinephrine. A supratrochlear nerve block is performed similarly except that the needle is inserted in the medial portion of the orbital rim just lateral to the root of the nose. Both nerves can be blocked by infiltration along a horizontal line extending 2 cm above the eyebrow from the lateral orbital rim to the midline.

4. Which nerve provides sensation to the lower eyelid and upper lip? How can it be blocked?

The infraorbital nerve (V_2), after emerging from the infraorbital foramen, divides into four branches: the inferior palpebral, external nasal, internal nasal, and superior labial nerves. They supply the lower eyelid and upper lip as well as the lateral portion of the nose and ala, cheek, and mucous membranes lining the cheek and upper lip. Regional block of the infraorbital nerve is performed by first palpating the infraorbital foramen or notch along the infraorbital rim, which should lie below the midline of the pupil with the eye in a straight forward gaze. Instillation of 2 to 5 mL of 1% lidocaine with epinephrine at this site provides excellent regional anesthesia for 60 to 90 minutes.

5. How can the lower lip be anesthetized to permit excision of a basal cell carcinoma?

The mental nerve provides sensation to the lower lip and the submental cutaneous area. This nerve can be blocked transorally or transcutaneously as it exits the mental foramen. It can be palpated just below and posterior to the first premolar tooth 1 cm below the gum line. Intraorally the needle can be inserted into the mucous membrane between the bicuspids at a 45° angle, aimed toward the apex of the root of the second bicuspid, and advanced until bone is contacted. The needle is withdrawn 1 to 2 mm, and 2 to 3 mL of lidocaine is injected. An additional 0.5 to 1.0 mL of lidocaine can be injected once the foramen is located.

6. How can the masseter muscle be relaxed in cases of trismus?

A mandibular nerve (V_3) block can be performed as the nerve exits the foramen ovale by inserting the needle into the retromolar fossa at a point parallel to the mandibular tooth at a 45° angle. The needle is advanced to the posterior wall of the mandible, and the injection is instilled. This block anesthetizes the buccal, auriculotemporal, lingual, inferior alveolar, and mental nerves, providing adequate surgical anesthesia for the lower face, mandible, mandibular teeth to the midline, and anterior two thirds of the tongue for 60 to 90 minutes.

7. How can adequate regional anesthesia of the nose be obtained before performing a rhinoplasty?

Regional anesthesia of the external nose can be obtained by blocking the infratrochlear, infraorbital, nasal palatine, and external nasal nerves. The block is performed by injecting 5 to 10 mL of lidocaine with epinephrine along a line that begins at the nasolabial fold, continues just lateral to the ala and along the base of the nasal sidewall, and finally advances toward the radix on each side of the nose. Regional anesthesia of the internal nose can be obtained by blocking the inferior posterior nasal, nasopalatine, and superior posterior nasal nerves as well as the branches of the ethmoidal nerve. The block is performed by placing small cotton applicators dipped in a solution of 4% cocaine directly on the areas or by packing the nose with plain gauze dipped into the cocaine solution.

8. How can a regional block of the external ear be obtained before performing an otoplasty?

The external ear is supplied by the auriculotemporal nerve anteriorly and by the great auricular and lesser occipital nerves posteriorly. A satisfactory block can be achieved by infiltrating the anesthetic solution (usually 1% lidocaine with epinephrine) around the ear in a ringlike fashion or by using a diamond-shaped pattern that encompasses the ear anteriorly and posteriorly.

9. Just before an augmentation mammoplasty, bilateral intercostal nerve blocks are given with 30 mL of a 1% Xylocaine solution. The patient soon appears agitated and her pulse increases. What is the most likely cause?

Sudden changes in the status of the patient are always a cause for concern. In this situation the most worrisome possibility is a pneumothorax. Intercostal blocks are administered close to the pleura. Even a small increase in the depth of the penetration may result in injury to the lung. However, the most likely cause of the symptoms is lidocaine toxicity. Several areas of the body, including the intercostals areas, have a high degree of vascularity and are known to have a much faster uptake of local anesthetics. The proximity of the intercostal vessels to the point of injection frequently results in a more rapid systemic uptake than expected. One way to avoid this problem when administering a large dose is to fractionate it. Give 5 to 10 mL at a time, shading the lower dose with the longer-acting amide local anesthetics (e.g., bupivacaine). Recognizing the situation early on by consistently asking the patient how he or she is doing is essential. If there is any change in the patient's status during the administration, immediate cessation of the local administration is necessary. A small dose of a benzodiazepine or propofol (if an anesthesia care provider is available) can abort most central nervous system (CNS) reactions.

10. How long should a patient fast before surgery?

The tradition of nothing to eat or drink after midnight the night before seems to have few objective merits. For adults, several studies have shown that solid foods should not be given within 6 hours of surgery but that clear liquids can be given up to 3 hours before surgery. However, some believe that if a large meal has been eaten the night before, 6 hours may not be enough. For infants, reasonable amounts of fluids up to 3 hours before surgery seem safe. Several hours of fasting before surgery does not seem to decrease the amount of gastric contents or to increase the pH of the gastric fluid. It does significantly increase the discomfort of the patient. Prophylaxis against aspiration is of merit in high-risk patients but is not universally beneficial.

11. Why does skeletal muscle contract if stimulated when D-tubocurarine is used as the paralyzing agent in anesthesia?

D-Tubocurarine blocks muscle contraction by acting as a nondepolarizing agent. As such, it blocks nerve transmission at the neuromuscular junction. It does not block direct muscle stimulation by an electrical stimulus such as electrocautery. If complete cessation of muscle contraction is needed, succinylcholine should be used because it depolarizes the muscle and keeps it depolarized.

12. Twenty-four hours after suction-assisted lipectomy of the abdomen and upper thighs, a patient has become confused and somewhat disoriented. She has a petechial rash over the shoulders and anterior chest. Is she possibly allergic to the pain medication?

This presentation is unusual for an allergic reaction to a medication. However, it is a relatively classic presentation for fat embolism. A fat embolism involves the blockage of small vessels by small globules of fat. It is seen most commonly after long bone fractures but also may be seen under other circumstances, such as after liposuction. Two theories address the mechanism. A physiochemical change in the circulating lipids (chylomicrons) may cause them to clump and form microemboli (fat droplets). The second theory states that the trauma from pressure or injury allows small veins to rupture and fat to enter directly through the area of injury. The emboli lodge in small-caliber vascular structures; first the lungs, then the brain and kidneys. Although the cerebral manifestations are often the first noticed (confusion, lethargy, disorientation, delirium, and occasionally coma and stupor), the primary problem results with the lungs. The diagnosis should be made quickly. It depends on prompt recognition of a pattern of pulmonary, cerebral, and cutaneous manifestations. Emboli may appear in retinal vessels. Other abnormalities may include a drop in hemoglobin level and an electrocardiographic (ECG) pattern of myocardial ischemia and right ventricular strain. Lipuria may occur later. Serum lipase elevation occurs in half of patients but may not be evident for several days and reaches its height on day 7 or 8.

Once the diagnosis is made, prompt treatment should include vigorous resuscitative measures, splinting of any fractures, intensive pulmonary care, oxygen, positive and expiratory pressure (positive end-expiratory pressure [PEEP]), intermittent positive pressure breathing, and consideration of digitalization. Corticosteroids usually are recommended (approximately 100 mg every 6 hours). Often low-dose heparin is given to increase lipase activity (25 mg every 6 hours).

13. What are the appropriate preoperative preparations and intraoperative and postoperative considerations for a patient with possible sickle cell disease who is to undergo hand surgery?

Before surgery the patient should be well hydrated. Preoperative transfusions are indicated only if blood loss has been massive or the hematocrit level is below 20% (hemoglobin less than 7 g/100 mL). Patients with sickle cell disease normally tolerate hematocrit levels of 25% to 30%.

During surgery the patient should be well oxygenated. Inspirated oxygen concentrations of 40% to 50% are adequate. Ideally, the patient should be preoxygenated. In addition, the body temperature should be kept normal. Hypothermia may promote sickling. Many sources advise against the use of tourniquets. However, tourniquets have been safely used without evidence of sickling or precipitation of a crisis. If the patient is well hydrated and well oxygenated, tourniquets are safe. Postoperatively the same principles apply.

Sickle cell crisis is treated with bed rest, hydration, oxygenation, analgesics, sodium bicarbonate for acidosis, and possibly transfusions.

14. What are the anesthetic considerations for repair of a trochanteric decubitus ulcer in the lateral position?

During surgery, the position of the patient causes several changes that may be important to the surgeon. In the lateral decubitus position, blood pools in the lower or dependent portion. Pooling may be worsened if the patient also is paraplegic because autonomic regulation of the circulatory system is less effective. In addition, the lateral position limits expansion of the lungs by restricting chest movement. As the dependent lung is compressed, a ventilation/perfusion mismatch occurs, causing increases in physiologic dead space and carbon dioxide retention. Hypoxemia may result. The usual treatment is PEEP.

15. A patient vomits and aspirates during induction of anesthesia. What is the appropriate treatment?

Immediately upon consideration of aspiration the patient should be tilted to a head-down position, which allows residual gastric contents to drain. The mouth and pharyngeal regions should be suctioned, and endotracheal intubation should be performed immediately. Suctioning through the endotracheal tube should precede administration of positive pressure oxygen. After endotracheal suctioning, 100% oxygen should be given. The insertion of a nasogastric tube should be prompt, and the pH of the aspirate should be determined. The specific pH level is 2.5. A pH above 2.5 yields a physiologic response that is not much different from aspiration of water. A pH below 2.5 significantly increases the risk of aspiration pneumonia. A pH below 1.5 involves significant risk of pulmonary damage.

Possibly the earliest sign of significant aspiration is hypoxia. If blood gas analysis shows any element of hypoxia, positive pressure ventilation should be instituted immediately. Adjunctive measures such as antibiotics and steroids have been proposed. Prophylactic antibiotics are not currently recommended. The use of corticosteroids remains controversial.

16. What preoperative instructions should be given to a 10-month-old child before cleft lip repair?

In the past, the policy was avoidance of oral ingestion for 8 hours. However, studies of younger children show that giving clear fluid to infants up to 3 hours before surgery is safe. This principle applies at least through adolescence. Preoperative sedation is possible and sometimes helpful; a typical agent may be Versed 0.5 mg/kg orally or pentobarbital 5 mg/kg. For children younger than 12 months, the problem of separation anxiety is minimal, and sedation probably is unnecessary.

Intraoperatively the use of lidocaine and epinephrine as a local injection is helpful. Large doses of epinephrine are not recommended for patients under halothane anesthesia. With the introduction of sevoflurane, the use of halothane has greatly diminished. Sevoflurane is a much less arrhythmogenic agent than halothane, and its usage with epinephrine is much safer. In addition, the maximal dose of epinephrine, 10 mg/kg, is rarely exceeded because of the small volumes required. Usually, a 1-mL total of injection solution is adequate.

17. What is the critical anesthetic problem in a patient with cleft palate? How is it managed?

Establishment and protection of the airway are the key issues in repair of the cleft palate. During intubation and positioning, frequently with the head and neck hyperextended, maintenance of the airway is crucial, along with meticulous attention to positioning of the endotracheal tube. Postoperative attention should be given to monitoring for airway obstruction, bleeding, and respiration obstruction. Airway obstruction secondary to edema is possible. Significant blood loss may occur with repair of the palate, considering the size of the child. The requirement of blood transfusion is unusual, but blood loss up to 200 mL has been reported. Postoperatively careful attention to airway monitoring and careful suctioning of the pharynx are necessary. Some physicians recommend placement of a traction suture in the tongue in case posterior obstruction due to the tongue occurs. Use of an oral or a nasal airway is contraindicated because of the significant risk of disrupting the surgical repair. Either a lateral or prone position with the patient's head turned to one side and dependent is believed to be optimal. This position is easily achieved by placing a small towel or blanket under the child's hips.

18. A 10-year-old girl is scheduled to undergo a bilateral otoplasty for prominent ears. The parents are concerned because an uncle died during anesthesia several years ago. During the course of anesthesia the patient develops tachycardia, early cyanosis, and some increased rigidity in the muscles. What are the probable diagnosis and appropriate treatment?

Preoperative consideration of possible malignant hyperthermia is necessary. The family history of an anesthetic death is important. Approximately one third of cases of malignant hyperthermia occur in patients who had previous uneventful anesthesia.

Malignant hyperthermia is a clinical syndrome characterized by accelerated metabolism, which usually manifests as tachycardia, cyanosis, sweating, rigidity, blood pressure abnormalities, and an increase in end-tidal CO_2. Only 30% of patients display an increase in temperature. When elevated, temperature commonly rises as high as 42°C to 43°C. The family history frequently is positive for musculoskeletal abnormalities.

If possible, anesthesia should be performed using propofol or occasionally barbiturate sedation and local anesthetics. Both ester and amide local anesthetics are safe. All inhalation anesthetics, except nitrous oxide, are considered unsafe. Curare and phenothiazines are controversial. Most other drugs, including antibiotics, propofol, barbiturates, opiates, antipyretics, and antihistamines, are considered safe.

If malignant hyperthermia is suspected during surgery, all anesthetics should be stopped and 100% oxygen should be administered. The patient should be hyperventilated, good access should be obtained for monitoring of central venous pressure, and an arterial line should be inserted. Dantrolene sodium should be administered at a dose of 2.5 mg/kg. This initial dose may be supplemented with 1-mg boluses to a total of 10 mg/kg. Rapid cooling should be initiated for core temperatures above 40°C. Acidosis and hyperkalemia should be treated (sodium bicarbonate 2 mEq/kg). Arrhythmias usually respond to procainamide (15 mg/kg). Cardiorespiratory support and monitoring should be available.

Postoperatively, coagulopathy, renal failure, hypothermia, pulmonary edema, hyperkalemia, and recurrence are possible. Dantrolene should be given for approximately 3 days after the attacks. In addition, the family and patient should be counseled about the event and its significance.

Questioning the family about the death of the uncle under anesthesia is both appropriate and necessary. If there is a consideration of malignant hyperthermia, then a nontriggering technique should be used to anesthetize the patient. This involves using either propofol or pentothal and a nondepolarizing muscle relaxant (anything but succinylcholine) for the initial induction and intubation. A continuous intravenous technique with nitrous oxide and oxygen should be used for maintenance of anesthesia. A propofol infusion with small amounts of narcotic along with generous local infiltration by the surgeon should suffice for amnesia and analgesia. The key drugs to avoid are succinylcholine and all of the volatile anesthetic agents (this does not include nitrous oxide).

19. Why is sodium bicarbonate sometimes added to local anesthesia?

Local anesthetics are used in a balanced solution between ionized and nonionized forms. The nonionized form goes into the nerve tissue more rapidly. Alkalinization of the solution changes the concentration of the nonionized form and thereby increases the rapidity of onset and effectiveness. Appropriate doses of sodium bicarbonate are 1 mEq per 10 mL of lidocaine and 0.1 mEq per 20 mL of bupivacaine.

20. **A patient with 25% total body surface area burn is taken to the operating room for tangential excision and grafting of burn wounds 2 weeks after injury. During induction of anesthesia, succinylcholine is given as a muscle relaxant. The patient begins to show cardiac irregularities, and the procedure is terminated. What is the probable cause?**

Although the exact mechanism of this response is somewhat unclear, a profound release of potassium from muscle has been well documented in burn patients after administration of succinylcholine. An increased number of muscle receptor sites for acetylcholine has been documented in burn victims. The agonist to acetylcholine, succinylcholine, may be responsible for the massive and sometimes fatal release of this potassium. This response has been documented almost 1.5 years after the burn. For this reason, succinylcholine is not recommended as a muscle relaxant in burn patients for up to 2 years after the injury. Nondepolarizing relaxants, such as D-tubocurarine, pancuronium, atracurium, and vecuronium, are recommended but show a variable response in burn patients. Although these agents are generally considered safe, patients may show variable degrees of resistance. Monitoring with a nerve stimulator is important.

21. **During tangential excision of a 30% full-thickness burn, a patient begins to become hypotensive. What are the most likely causes?**

Burn wound débridement, although relatively straightforward from a surgical point of view, involves complex anesthetic concerns. The patient is metabolically unstable because of the severe injury. Strict attention to fluid and electrolytes is required. A massive amount of fluids can be lost not only through the burn itself but also through the exposure of injured skin and the heating effect of the dry air in the room. Underestimation of fluid loss is common. In addition, the possibility of sensitivity to medications should be considered. In burn patients, one of the most common sensitivities is transfusion reaction. Administration of blood intraoperatively is routine, but a hemolytic-type reaction may occur when incompatible blood is administered. Although rare because of high blood bank standards, this problem still occurs. In awake patients, signs include hypotension, fever, chills, shortness of breath, and pain. However, under general anesthesia the only sign is unexplained hypotension. Documentation of free hemoglobin in the urine is helpful, but response to the hypotension takes precedence.

Treatment consists of cessation of surgery and of all blood products, hydration, vasopressors, and inotropic agents, if necessary. Urine output should be maintained by rapid administration of fluids, and diuretics such as mannitol and loop agents should be considered. Historically, sodium bicarbonate has been proposed. The rationale is that alkalinized urine improves the solubility of the hemoglobin and its breakdown components. The actual value of this strategy has been poorly documented. Another possible cause of hypotension during anesthesia is the overadministration of narcotics and sedatives. The proper anesthetic protocol in a burn patient always consists of careful, slow titration of agents.

22. **What is the maximal amount of bupivacaine (Marcaine) that can be safely added to 50 mL of 0.5% Xylocaine in an intravenous regional anesthetic for the upper extremity to prolong duration of action?**

None. The long action of bupivacaine on skeletal muscle results in significant risk of cardiotoxicity if it is given intravenously. Although there are a few anecdotal reports of its use, intravenous injection is absolutely contraindicated. The only local anesthetic used for intravenous regional anesthesia or Bier block is 0.5% lidocaine.

23. **A 63-year-old man is scheduled to undergo general anesthesia for extensive resection of an oral cancer 4 months after having a myocardial infarction. Should surgery be delayed?**

This is a difficult problem. Multiple studies have consistently shown that perioperative morbidity, reinfarction, and mortality are significantly greater if general anesthesia is used within 6 months of myocardial infarction. The general status of the patient as well as the status of his cardiac disease should be evaluated. If the patient can climb stairs and perform simple exercises without becoming short of breath, demonstrating cardiac arrhythmia, developing chest pain, or having significant symptoms, he may be considered for surgery if medically necessary. On the other hand, the presence of any of the above signs or symptoms is significant. Also important are the expertise of the anesthesiologist in dealing with cardiac patients and the severity and duration of the procedure. Many anesthesiologists in this situation would like to see the results of a preoperative stress test. Although this surgery must be done sooner rather than later, a negative stress test gives some level of comfort, whereas a positive stress test typically would be followed with a cardiac catheterization. If any of these tests was performed post myocardial infarction, repeating them would not be necessary.

24. **When is it usually considered safe to discharge a patient after outpatient surgery under general anesthesia?**

Each facility establishes its own criteria, but they usually include stable blood pressure and pulse, respirations within 20% of preoperative values, alert and oriented mental status, and steady gait with minimal or no assistance. Also important are absence of active bleeding, controllable pain, minimal nausea, and discharge with an appropriate, trustworthy adult. Importantly, a minimal time requirement is not necessary.

25. Does the length of anesthesia increase the risk of complications?

Actual data on this subject are few. What has been shown is that, other factors being similar (type of procedure, blood loss, etc.), a 4- or 5-hour procedure does not seem to have more complications than a 2-hour procedure. Extremely long procedures may have an increased risk. Few plastic surgical procedures last longer than 4 to 6 hours. Surgeries over 8 hours usually are the result of combining multiple procedures. The surgeon may wish to consider serial procedures on separate days. Although at present information is insufficient to rigidly set a standard for the length of surgery, safety should always be first on the list of surgical judgment.

26. If the usual "safe" dose for lidocaine administration is 7 mg/kg, how much can "safely" be given during a suction-assisted lipectomy in tumescent fluid?

In spite of the fact that suction-assisted lipectomy is now the most common plastic surgical procedure performed in the United States, approaching nearly half a million cases annually, the answer is not known! It is true that instillation into the poorly vascularized fat layer delays absorption and thus increases the amount that can be given. However, this absorption continues many hours after termination of the procedure and often increases for nearly 24 hours. In addition, lidocaine is metabolized in the liver. Alternatives in hepatic blood flow or uptake may delay the process of metabolism. The principal lidocaine metabolite, monoethylglycinexylidide, is pharmacologically active and has the potential for antiarrhythmic and convulsant reactions. Drug interactions that delay metabolism are possible.

Thus, although current recommendations are 10 to 50 mg/kg, it seems a prudent surgeon would use the minimum amount that is effective. The surgeon should be aware of the signs and treatment of lidocaine toxicity and should be very aware that these signs may occur hours after termination of the procedure.

27. Are there any dietary supplements that may interact with anesthesia?

The short answer to this is yes. Many dietary supplements have been shown to have an effect on surgery, modifying immunity, bleeding, cardiac response, hepatotoxicity, glycemic response, and some sedation agents. However, there are no supplements that would normally be "allowable" for surgery but not for anesthesia, so the use of supplements (e.g., *Echinacea,* ephedra, ginger, ginseng, hawthorn, kava kava, licorice, St. John's wort, yohimbine) should be avoided. This is only a partial list, and surgeons should recognize that an increasing number of supplements are being found to affect surgery and anesthesia.

28. A patient undergoes outpatient suction-assisted lipectomy of the abdomen and bilateral thighs. A volume of 3500 mL is removed. The patient calls, complaining of significant pain. What are the concerns?

Any unexplained symptom or sign should be a concern for the surgeon. Concerns about vascularity, intraperitoneal perforation, hematoma, and poorly placed dressings, padding, and binders are relevant. Liposuction with removal of relatively small volumes usually is tolerated well. Larger-volume liposuction (generally defined as greater than 3000 mL) usually is painful postoperatively. Strong consideration for overnight observation is recommended for any patient who has undergone treatment of several areas, has aspirated volume greater than 3000 mL, or has any predisposing risk factors or intraoperative concerns.

The real question is monitoring. Complications can arise. Release of local anesthetic/tumescent fluid systemically can cause symptoms such as tinnitus, excitation, dizziness, a metallic taste, and occasionally chest pain and cardiac rhythm problems (bradycardia). Lidocaine is very rapidly metabolized, and treatment of any systemic leakage is rarely required.

BIBLIOGRAPHY

Apfelbaum IL: Current concepts in outpatient anesthesia. Anesthesia Research Society Review Course Lectures, 1989, p 104.
Barash PG, Culien BR, Stoelting RK (eds): Clinical Anesthesia. Philadelphia, Lippincott, 1989.
Eckenoff JE, Vandam LD (eds): Introduction to Anesthesia: The Principles of Safe Practice, 7th ed. Philadelphia, WB Saunders, 1988.
Miller RD (ed): Anesthesia, 3rd ed. New York, Churchill Livingstone, 1990.
Schwartz ST (ed): Principles of Surgery, 5th ed. New York, McGraw-Hill, 1989.
Stromberg BV: Anesthesia. In McCarthy JH (ed): Plastic Surgery. Philadelphia, WB Saunders, 1990.
Vandam LD (ed): To Make the Patient Ready for Anesthesia: Medical Care of the Surgical Patient, 2nd ed. Menlo Park, CA, Addison-Wesley, 1984.
Weinzweig N, Weinzweig J: Basic principles and techniques in plastic surgery. In Cohen M (ed): Mastery of Plastic and Reconstructive Surgery. Boston, Little, Brown, 1994, pp 14–33.
White PF (ed): Outpatient Anesthesia. New York, Churchill Livingstone, 1990.

TISSUE EXPANSION

Alex Senchenkov, MD, and
Ernest K. Manders, MD

CHAPTER 4

1. Is controlled tissue expansion a new concept?

No, it is not. Physiologic tissue expansion occurs in pregnancy and weight loss. The custom of soft tissue expansion of the earlobes, nose, lips, and other body parts has been practiced by primitive tribes for ages. In this century, Dr. Charles G. Neumann of New York was the first to carry out a controlled expansion of periauricular skin using a subcutaneous balloon filled with air. This work was reported in 1956, published in 1957, and then forgotten. Soft tissue expansion entered plastic and reconstructive surgery through the efforts of the late Dr. Chedomir Radovan. Reviewers resisted his idea, and it took 3 years to get his discovery on a national program. His design of a silicone elastomer envelope with a remote self-sealing injection port became the first standard device for tissue expansion. Periodic injections of saline were used to distend the overlying tissues to create flaps for reconstructive surgery.

2. Where does the expanded skin come from?

Austad and Pasyk addressed this question. Both short-term immediate factors and long-term changes yield an increase in dimension. In the short term, pressure forces interstitial fluid out of the tissues and causes microfragmentation of elastic fibers, allowing greater expansion of the skin. Viscoelastic deformation and changes in alignment of collagen, termed "creep," and recruitment of adjacent mobile soft tissue also contribute to the arc of skin over a tissue expansion. Long term, however, it is not just stretching but actual growth of the skin flap that occurs with an increase in the area of skin and the collagen content and ground substance as dimensions increase.

3. What physiologic changes occur in the skin during "creep"?

Baker summarized theses changes as dehydration of tissue, microfragmentation of elastic fibers, increasingly parallel alignment of random collagen fibers, and adjacent tissue migration in the direction of the vector force.

4. What is the body's response to the expander?

A fibrous connective tissue capsule forms around the expander as the tissues react to a foreign body. Expansion elicits angiogenesis with an increase in vascularity, particularly at the junction of the capsule and the expanded tissue. When an expander is removed, the expander capsule rapidly thins. In the cases of breast reconstruction, the tissue expander capsule can be altered, incised, or removed to give the reconstructed breast its optimal shape. It may be advantageous to include the expander capsule in the flap at the time of transfer due to its contribution to the flap blood supply. Due to the excellent vascularity of the capsule, it can be dissected and used as a local or free flap.

5. What happens to the cellular growth and mitotic index of expanded skin?

Stretch-induced cellular growth initiates interaction of several integrated biochemical cascades that include growth factors, cytoskeleton structures, and protein kinases. The mechanical strain triggers deoxyribonucleic acid (DNA) synthesis and cellular proliferation. In tissue culture, 20 to 30 minutes of stretch is enough to initiate a round of DNA synthesis and cellular mitosis. The mitotic rate of skin has been demonstrated to increase with the application of tension. When the expander beneath expanded skin is deflated, the mitotic index falls to a subnormal level. This finding is thought to be consistent with clinical observations of skin contraction with weight loss and flattening of dog ears after surgery.

6. What is the effect of expansion on blood flow in the tissues over the expander?

Laser Doppler flowmetry and transcutaneous oxygen monitoring have documented decreased tissue circulation in response to an increase in pressure in the expander. Over time, this mild ischemia results in augmentation of blood flow in the expanded tissue similar to the changes associated with flap delay. In our studies, the flow in a critical flap was doubled when measured with microsphere perfusion experiments. Expanded skin flaps survive to a length at least equal to that of a delayed flap. Histologic studies have demonstrated a new network of vessels just above the capsule. These vessels involute with time after expander removal.

7. What histologic changes occur with expansion?

Histologic changes of note are thinning of the dermis with eventual collagen realignment and deposition. The epidermis shows definite thickening. Fat may be compressed and, if subjected to high pressure, may atrophy. Thin muscles, such as the frontalis, also may suffer the same injury. Skin appendages are relatively unaffected. The hair follicles are moved apart by large scalp expansions and their telogen phase is shortened. Bone may show resorption at the outer cortical surface. Typically this defect is repaired and a normal contour restored after removal of the expander.

8. Can the expander envelope rupture because of the internal expander pressure?

No. The expander envelope cannot rupture even when the patient lies on the expander. The expander is contained and supported by a tough collagen capsule surrounding the expander. The capsule limits expansion and supports the elastomer envelope when external pressure is placed on the expander mound.

9. What limits the rate of expansion?

The rate of expansion is limited by the relaxation and growth of the tissue overlying the expander. Pain is an important signal and must be avoided at all times. There should be absolutely no pain during the process of expansion. Prior radiation and scar formation may slow expansion or make it impossible. Tissue undergoing expansion must have the capacity for growth. Some tissues elongate more slowly than others and may limit the rate of expansion. Peripheral nerves do not tolerate pressure of more than 40 mm Hg for sustained periods, and if a nerve is located in the expanded flap, or even immediately under an expander, paresthesias may slow the rate of inflation.

10. What expanders are available?

Expanders come in a wide variety of sizes and styles. They may be small, perhaps a few cubic centimeters in size, or designed to hold a liter or more. The devices may be fitted with a remote injection port or a port integrated into the envelopes themselves. The envelopes may be bonded to stiff backers or have no stiff back. The expanders may be round, rectangular, oval, or crescent shaped (the croissant expander). A design with an adjustable base that allows the surgeon to fit the expander to the defect is available. The envelope may be of uniform thickness and compliance or may be constructed to expand differentially or directionally. The envelope may be smooth or textured on its outer surface. Although expanders can be of variable shapes depending on the characteristics of the defect, the width of the expander base ideally should approach at least twice the width of the defect.

11. Does a textured surface on an expander make a difference?

Although some authors suggest that using an expander with a textured surface is beneficial in terms of less patient discomfort and easier expansion, in at least one double-blind prospective study, no benefit was demonstrated. There is evidence that an expander with a textured surface may be less likely to migrate. We have not found a textured surface to be of benefit in the process of expansion. When capsular histology was compared, no differences were observed when one side of a symmetric expander was textured and the other side was smooth.

12. What are the new osmotically active hydrogel expanders?

Self-filling osmotic tissue expanders, which contain osmotically active hydrogel N-vinyl-2-pyrrolidone and modified copolymer methylmethacrylate was developed by Wiese and produced by Osmed in Elman, Germany. With the first-generation osmotically active hydrogel expander that was devised without an investing silicon membrane, a good final result was achieved in 81.5%. The second-generation expander has a silicone membrane with small pores enclosing the osmotic hydrogel. With this membrane controlling expansion speed and accurately defining the final volume, the success rate of expansion was 91%. Once the expander is implanted, the swelling phase usually continues for 6 to 8 weeks. It has been successfully used in delayed breast reconstruction, tubular breast correction, and coverage of defects after excision of tumors, scars, burns, and alopecia.

13. In breast reconstruction after mastectomy, what is the most significant advantage of self-filling osmotic tissue expanders over conventional tissue expanders?

The incidence of infection may be decreased because the technique does not rely on external fillings. The small risk of deflation also is decreased, and any pain of injections is obviated. As with conventional tissue expander breast reconstruction, self-filling osmotic expanders require submuscular placement, 40 to 60 days for filling, and subsequent replacement with a permanent prosthesis in four to six months. Although anatomically shaped osmotic expanders are available, they are prone to rotation with inferior reconstructive results.

14. What are the advantages of the various designs?

Expanders with integrated valves are often used for breast reconstruction. They are especially useful in the head and neck because no dissection of a pocket for the remote port is required. Differential expansion is used in the design of breast reconstruction devices because more tissue is needed at the lower pole of the reconstruction site than in the upper infraclavicular area. The croissant expander is well suited for reconstruction of defects on flat or cylindrical surfaces. The defect is half surrounded by the expander, allowing better geometry of expansion with the largest expansion developed in the line of greatest advance. The newer adjustable base croissant allows the surgeon to fit the expander to the defect so that it will lie flat and be positioned to best prepare the expanded flap needed for reconstruction.

15. What are the options for port placement?

Expander ports can be remote or integrated in the expander. Remote ports can be placed atop the edge of an expander if desired; this technique effectively simulates the convenience of an integrated injection port. External port placement was pioneered by Ian Jackson and offers advantage in pediatric patients. It decreases the amount of intraoperative dissection, shortens operative time, and makes expansions simpler and painless. Complication rates from 5.6% to 17.6% have been described and are believed to be equivalent to the rates associated with standard internal port techniques.

16. How many times can an expander be used?

Many times, but not in North America. The expander devices available in the North American market are extremely well engineered. The U.S. Food and Drug Administration (FDA) has specified that the devices are meant for single use. It is our practice to save expanders after their removal. They are washed and wrapped, then sterilized and sent to surgeons and plastic surgery units in the developing world where they are reused many times.

17. What areas are especially suitable for soft tissue expansion reconstruction?

The scalp and breast are especially well suited to reconstruction using soft tissue expansion. Although many nasal reconstructions do not require expansion, total nasal reconstruction is made straightforward when the forehead is expanded before raising it as a flap. An expanded forehead flap provides complete nasal lining and allows immediate closure of the donor site. The capsule and frontalis in the area turned inward to form the alar rims must be removed to allow a thin, aesthetic reconstruction.

18. Where is it difficult or even inadvisable to use tissue expansion?

Defects of the central face seldom require expansion. The bathtub deformity in the facial fat is an untoward outcome, even if temporary. The hands and feet are seldom rewarding sites for expansion. The neck remains one of the most frustrating sites for expansion. If soft tissue is needed for neck and/or face reconstruction, the best strategy is to expand the supraclavicular skin and turn it up as a large flap. The amount of tissue created by expansion on the neck is almost always overestimated because of the natural concavity under the jaw line. Upward advancements over the jaw line are frequently disappointing in outcome.

19. What are contraindications and relative contraindications to soft tissue expansion?

Contraindications include expansion near a malignancy, under a skin graft, under very tight tissue, near an open leg wound, or in an irradiated field. Relative contraindications include expansion near an open wound (not in the leg), near a hemangioma, under an incision, or in a psychologically incompetent patient.

20. Can tissue expansion be used in reconstruction of soft tissue defects following excision of malignancy?

Non–breast tissue expansion has a limited role in an irradiated field and probably should not be used if preoperative radiation was used or if radiation was used locally in the past and tumor recurred locally. For nonirradiated tumors, tissue expanders can be placed at the time of tumor excision after the margins are known to be free of tumor through a remote incision, and the defect can be covered with a skin graft as the first-stage reconstruction. After healing has been achieved, tissue expansion is performed, followed by expander removal and flap advancement.

In the case of breast reconstruction, expansion is quite effective if the dose of delivered radiation was about 5000 cGy. The tissues are notably stiffer after doses of 5000 to 6000 cGy, and if the dose of radiation exceeded 7000 cGy, tissue expansion is very apt to be unrewarding.

21. What factors should be considered when selecting a patient for tissue expansion?

Not every patient is a suitable candidate for the use of soft tissue expansion as a reconstructive technique. The patient must understand that two operations are required, that the temporary deformity may be inconvenient and hard to disguise, and that it is impossible to say exactly when the expansion will be complete. Patients must understand that the process must be afforded the time required to generate the tissue necessary for reconstruction. Patients who specify that the expansion must be completed over the summer are imposing limitations on the technique and may be disappointed when the actual advancement falls short of the goal. All patients should be counseled that two expansions may be required.

22. Where should the expanders be placed?

Expanders should be placed under tissue that best matches the lost tissue; similar tissue yields the best reconstruction. Normal landmarks must not be distorted. For example, the eyebrow should not be undermined and moved. It is of paramount importance that the surgeon ask, "Where do I want the final scar to lie?" The reconstruction should begin with the goal of imposing a minimum of scars. Vascular territories and patterns of innervation should be preserved whenever possible.

23. Where do you place the incision for a tissue expander insertion?

Where to place the incision for expander insertion is somewhat controversial. Some authorities argue for a remote incision. Some assert that the incision should be oriented radially to the edge of the expander. We believe that the best incision is usually placed at the edge of the defect. The scar in this position will be removed at the time of advancement of the expanded flap. If the defect to be replaced is a nevus, the incision should be placed entirely within the nevus so that the normal skin is not scarred. The reader is reminded of the question, "Where do I want the final scar to lie?" The incision must be made in stable tissue that is expected to heal.

24. What technical failure at the time of insertion will cause an expansion to fail?

The most common reason for the failure of an expansion is the construction of a pocket of inadequate size for the expander that is placed into it. Protrusion of the expander through the incision or projection of envelope through the overlying tissue often results from the surgeon's overestimation of the size of the pocket. The expander must lie flat, and the expander back, if one is present, must not be curled or flexed so that the edge pushes into the line of closure.

25. When do you begin filling an expander? How much saline do you add each time?

It is our practice to begin filling an expander 1 week after surgery if the wound is stable and continue with weekly expansions. The process of filling depends on the pressure in the expander. Prescribing a given volume for injection at regular intervals is not possible. Often the expansion proceeds fairly rapidly and then becomes more difficult with higher ending pressures in the expander and discomfort noted by the patient. At this point the tissues need a rest. You can easily forego a weekly injection or simply inject less saline. On every occasion the safest strategy is to inject until the patient reports that the expansion is just starting to feel tight.

26. When is the patient ready to return to the operating room for advancement?

The patient is ready for advancement when the expanded flap will produce the desired result. If the flap is to be advanced, it must have sufficient dimensions and suitable geometry to cover the defect. The arc over the top of the expander is measured and the width of the expander mass subtracted. The difference is an estimate of the advancement that can be made. The difference should equal or exceed the width of the defect.

For breast reconstruction, the expansion should proceed until the distance in the midmammary line from the clavicle to the inframammary fold on the expanded side equals or exceeds the same distance on the normal, unoperated side. At this point, the overall volume of the reconstructed breast may exceed the target breast volume by 300 to 500 mL. The expander is kept overexpanded for at least 6 to 8 weeks and perhaps longer if the patient can tolerate it. The fluid then is removed until the volume of the expander resembles that of the normal breast or a target volume if contralateral augmentation is desired. The distance from the clavicle to the inframammary fold should be measured again. If the distance has shortened because the pressure on the skin and capsule are reduced by partial deflation of the expander, the fluid should be returned and expansion continued until the partially deflated dimensions of the reconstructed skin envelope equal those of the normal breast or a desired target volume.

27. How long do you keep the expander after the expansion target has been achieved?

In general, 6 to 8 weeks; however, it depends on the location and reconstructive goals. In breast reconstruction, where a pendulous, soft breast needs to be constructed, shrinkage of the previously expanded skin will compromise reconstructive results. For this reason, the longer overexpansion is maintained, the more stable the expanded skin envelope will be. Some experts have kept their patients overexpanded for as long as 1 year. In other areas where retraction of the expanded skin is less critical, 6 weeks usually is acceptable. This period is a balance between the benefit of stability of the expanded skin and the risk of implant infection and patient discomfort.

The alternative to persistent overexpansion as described here is expansion followed by periodic deflation continued until the skin envelope has the desired dimensions after trial deflation, as described in the section above.

28. How do you make the advancement?

The advancement should be simple. The skin is incised with a scalpel, and then an electrocautery blade with a round, not sharp, tip is used to open the subcutaneous tissues and capsule. A needle point usually results in a punctured envelope; avoid using a needle tip. It should not be necessary in most cases—except nasal and ear reconstructions—to excise the capsule formed around the expander. Simply advance the expanded flap and determine that it will replace the defect *before* the defect itself is excised. If the trial advance shows that you come up short, do a subtotal resection of the defect, leave an expander in place, and plan to finish the job on another day.

29. What aftercare is required?
Very little aftercare is required. Patients can shower on the first day after advancement. Drains are managed as usual. Do not rush to touch-up surgery, especially for dog ears, which usually resolve with time, particularly in the scalp.

30. Should families and patients be trusted to do their own expansions at home?
Most certainly. Injection of saline into a tissue expander certainly is less risky than administering insulin. Families can learn to perform home expansion safely and effectively for family members.

31. How can you—or a child's family—measure the intraluminal pressure of an expander during a home inflation?
If using a scalp vein needle with a short length of tubing between the needle and the hub connecting to the syringe, you have a built-in manometer. If the syringe is removed from the hub and the tubing is held extended straight up into the air, the standing height of saline is equivalent to about 20 mm Hg. If the meniscus falls in the tube, the intraluminal expander pressure is less. If the fluid overflows from the hub, the pressure is greater than 20 mm Hg. No tissue is injured if a limit of 20 mm Hg is observed.

32. What touch-up surgery may be required?
The area of the body undergoing surgery determines the size of the final scar. The back usually produces a larger scar than the scalp. Infrequently, dog ears may need to be revised; be patient before attempting revision. Local areas of alopecia from hair follicles in telogen phase often reverse themselves, and hair density returns to normal. Concavities usually disappear, especially the concavities, or bathtub deformities, seen over the skull.

33. What will the future bring in the way of breast reconstruction? Will autogenous tissue reconstruction replace tissue expansion?
As reimbursement for breast reconstruction falls, pressures favoring outpatient reconstruction via soft tissue expansion will mount. It seems likely that the proportion of tissue expansion reconstructions will rise and the number of autogenous tissue reconstructions will fall. Although some have assessed that the costs of the two approaches were almost the same at their institutions, this has not been our experience. We have found the cost of breast reconstruction with tissue expansion has been half the cost of a transverse rectus abdominis muscle (TRAM) flap. Some insurers provide lower reimbursement for bigger procedures to drive doctors toward less cost-intensive alternatives in reconstructive surgery.

34. Is there a role for tissue expansion in treatment of abdominal wall hernias?
The physiologic abdominal wall expansion with pregnancy and weight gain are widely known. Similar effects can be achieved with tissue expansion of the abdominal wall. An original approach with induction of pneumoperitoneum over a period of 6 to 15 days preoperatively starting with 500 mL and continuing to as much as 18,500 mL to achieve preoperative expansion of the abdominal cavity has been used successfully. This allows the return of the abdominal contents into the abdomen and overcomes the "loss of domain" that is problematic in large abdominal hernias. Reports from the Mayo Clinic describe the use of traditional tissue expanders with either subcutaneous or submuscular placement (between the external and internal obliques) with excellent results. Prosthetic mash was required in large abdominal wall defects.

35. What are skin stretching devices?
Various approaches to skin stretching have been proposed. Simple closure of wounds under tension may result in heavy scarring and wound breakdown. Intraoperative maneuvers in addition to undermining and tissue rearrangement include placement of towel clamps and heavy temporary sutures to slowly stretch the tissues. Skin stretching devices ranging from vascular loupes stapled to the skin edges to sophisticated mechanisms have been proposed to exert traction on the edges of the wound over the period from hours to days to achieve wound closure. The wound vacuum-assisted closure (VAC) dressing has been used as an adjunct treatment to decrease tissue edema.

36. What are the common preexpanded flap designs?
The advancement flap is the most commonly used design in tissue expansion reconstruction. Preexpanded transposition and rotational flaps have long-standing track records in meeting reconstructive demands in certain locations. The preexpanding free flap increases the amount of transferred tissue, enhances its blood supply, and lessens donor site morbidity.

37. Where and when do preexpanded transposition flaps play a role?
Bauer and Margulis, based on a review of their experience with 995 expanded flap reconstructions, stress the benefit of modifying expanded flap design from the more traditional advancement flap to transposition or rotational flaps.

They derived the following conclusions. (1) Limiting flap design to expanded advancement flaps alone with an effort to minimize potential scarring restricts the reconstructive capabilities of the added tissue and thus subverts the initial reconstructive goals. (2) In contrast to a direct advancement flap in which all tension is taken directly at the apex of the flap, with appropriate planning, in transposition and rotation flaps tension is taken off the flap apex and distributed more proximally. This design redirects tension lines and minimizes distortion. (3) In the expanded transposition flap, the base of the flap is also expanded skin, which allows the base to advance in addition to the normal transposition of tissues, providing an additional net gain of tissue for reconstruction of larger defects. (4) The price of additional incisions is worth paying to achieve a better final contour of the reconstructed part, decreased risk of anatomic distortion, better position of the scars, and lowered risk of scar contracture. (5) In cases having areas of less complex body contour or sufficient skin for uncomplicated advancement, advancement flaps are obviously an appropriate choice. It is in the other regions (temporal scalp, cheek, neck, proximal or distal trunk) where the expanded transposition flap plays its most powerful role.

Zide and Karp further emphasized the additional gain from single and double back-cut flaps to maximize tissue advancement into the defect following expansion with a rectangular tissue expander.

38. Which patients are the candidates for pretransfer tissue expansion of free flaps?
Three groups of patients may benefit from the use of this technique: those with an absolute or relative lack of local and donor tissues, those with a large defect in the recipient site, and those who might otherwise require multiple consecutive operations. These include burn patients with an absolute lack of tissue and donor site deformities from multiple reconstructions, pediatric patients with relative lack of tissues, patients with large defects, and those with pressure ulcers requiring large flaps who previously underwent multiple operations. Another indication for preexpansion of the free flap is the requirement for a thin flap in an obese person.

39. What are the advantages of reconstruction with preexpanded free flaps?
This reconstructive approach carries the advantages of both tissue expansion and microvascular tissue transfer. Microvascular tissue transfer allows the harvesting of tissues with a good tissue match from a distant donor site. Tissue expansion augments the blood supply of the future free flap. Babovic et al. investigated the effects of tissue expansion on free flaps and found a sevenfold increase in perfusion in the preexpanded flaps that increases their tolerance to secondary ischemia. This phenomenon also permits the surgeon to harvest a larger flap, even beyond the anatomic boundary of the flap's usual blood supply. This can be carried out with decreased morbidity to the donor site because the expansion facilitates direct closure of the donor site that would otherwise require a skin graft. Hallock reported his intriguing work on preexpanded radial forearm free flap transfer that permitted linear closure of the donor site in five of eight patients in his series. Another major advantage of pretransfer tissue expansion is its ability to thin the free flap, which also increases its pliability and elasticity with ever-increasing thickness of the flaps in western patients.

40. Which free flaps have been preexpanded?
Preexpanded fasciocutaneous flaps include groin, lateral arm, radial forearm, scapular, and extended scapular (scapular–parascapular) flaps. Preexpanded musculocutaneous flaps include latissimus dorsi, serratus anterior, pectoralis major, trapezius, rectus, and tensor fascia lata flaps. Tissue expander capsule has also been reported to be used as a free flap.

41. What are the disadvantages of pretransfer tissue expansion of free flaps?
There are three serious disadvantages. First, time is required for tissue expansion of the flap, which usually is transferred as a second-stage reconstructive operation. This period is, in general, 10 to 20 weeks. This is often not an acceptable wait for most oncologic defects and complex wounds. Second, implant complications may necessitate aborting the reconstructive plan. Lastly, the preexpanded free flap procedure is technically more difficult due to the distorted and compromised anatomy of the vascular pedicle and thus requires greater surgical skills.

42. What is the role of intraoperative tissue expansion?
Intraoperative tissue expansion is based on early expansion changes, such as fluid displacement, creep, and mobilization of the adjacent tissue. Stretching followed by relaxation, termed *cyclic loading* or *acute cycled expansion,* as opposed to continuous expansion, is more effective in recruitment of tissue. It has been shown to yield 15% to 20% of the length of the skin flaps. Although skin undermining remains an important technique in closing small defects, intraoperative tissue expansion has been reported to provide lower wound closing tension. Nonetheless, results in the operating room have been largely disappointing despite occasional enthusiastic reports of efficacy, and the technique is now seldom used.

43. What are the complications of tissue expansion?
Potential complications of tissue expansion include pain, infection, seroma, hematoma, skin necrosis, expander extrusion and failure, neuropraxia, insufficient expansion, and adverse psychological reactions. Seldom is the tissue lost; if an exposure or infection occurs, the expander is removed and replaced in 2 or 3 months in most cases. Reported frequency of complications requiring removal of the expander varies widely from 3% to 65%; however, in a survey of over 50,000 tissue expansions, no life-threatening or disfiguring complications occurred.

44. What are some of the inherent advantages of tissue expansion?

Tissue expansion provides tissue for reconstruction that is most like the lost tissue. It is matched in color, texture, and hair-bearing characteristics. The tissue may be sensate. The donor defect is minimal. Usually the contour is superior to that achieved with other techniques. Tissue expansion often can be performed entirely on an outpatient basis under local anesthesia. In preexpanded flaps, new skin is created in addition to increased vascularity of the flap and the expander capsule. It allows more reliable flap transfer with decreased donor site morbidity.

BIBLIOGRAPHY

Acarturk TO, Glaser DP, Newton ED: Reconstruction of difficult wounds with tissue-expanded free flaps. Ann Plast Surg 52:493–499, 2004; discussion 500.

Argenta LC: Controlled tissue expansion in facial reconstruction. In Baker SR, Swanson NA (eds): Local Flaps in Facial Reconstruction. St. Louis, Mosby, 1995, pp 517–544.

Argenta LC: Tissue expansion. In Aston S, Beasley R, Thorne C (eds): Grabb & Smith's Plastic Surgery, 5th ed. Philadelphia, Lippincott-Raven, 1997, pp 91–97.

Argenta LC, Austad ED: Principles and techniques of tissue expansion. In McCarthy JG (ed): Plastic Surgery. Philadelphia, 1990, pp 475–507.

Austad ED: Complications in tissue expansion. Clin Plast Surg 14:549–550, 1987.

Austad ED, Thomas SB, Pasyk KA: Tissue expansion: Dividend or loan? Plast Reconstr Surg 78:63, 1986.

Babovic S, Angel MF, Im MJ, et al: Effects of tissue expansion on secondary ischemic tolerance in experimental free flaps. Ann Plast Surg 34:593–598, 1995.

Baker SR: Fundamentals of expanded tissue. Head Neck 13:327–333, 1991.

Bauer BS, Margulis A: The expanded transposition flap: Shifting paradigms based on experience gained from two decades of pediatric tissue expansion. Plast Reconstr Surg 114:98–106, 2004.

Berge SJ, Wiese KG, von Lindern JJ, et al: Tissue expansion using osmotically active hydrogel systems for direct closure of the donor defect of the radial forearm flap. Plast Reconstr Surg 108:1–5, 2001; discussion 6–7.

Coelho JC, Brenner AS, Freitas AT, et al: Progressive preoperative pneumoperitoneum in the repair of large abdominal hernias. Eur J Surg 159:339–341, 1993.

De Filippo RE, Atala A: Stretch and growth: The molecular and physiologic influences of tissue expansion. Plast Reconstr Surg 109:2450–2462, 2002.

Hallock GG: Refinement of the radial forearm flap donor site using skin expansion. Plast Reconstr Surg 81:21–25, 1988.

Jackson IT, Sharpe DT, Polley J, et al: Use of external reservoirs in tissue expansion. Plast Reconstr Surg 80:266–273, 1987.

Jacobsen WM, Petty PM, Bite U, Johnson CH: Massive abdominal-wall hernia reconstruction with expanded external/internal oblique and transversalis musculofascia. Plast Reconstr Surg 100:326–335, 1997.

Jankauskas J, Cohen IK, Grabb WC: Basic technique of plastic surgery. In Smith JW, Aston SJ (eds): Grabb and Smith's Plastic Surgery, 4th ed. Boston, Little Brown, 1991, pp 67–68.

Johnson PE, Kernahan DA, Bauer BS: Dermal and epidermal response to soft-tissue expansion in the pig. Plast Reconstr Surg 81:390–397, 1988.

Lozano S, Drucker M: Use of tissue expanders with external ports. Ann Plast Surg 44:14–17, 2000.

Maghari A, Forootan KS, Fathi M, Manafi A: Free transfer of expanded parascapular, latissimus dorsi, and expander "capsule" flap for coverage of large lower-extremity soft-tissue defect. Plast Reconstr Surg 106:402–405, 2000.

Manders EK, da Paula P: Repeat tissue expansion. In Grotting JC (ed): Reoperative Aesthetic and Reconstructive Plastic Surgery. St. Louis, Quality Medical Publishing, 1995, pp 137–153.

Manders EK, Schenden MJ, Hetzler PT, et al: Soft tissue expansion: Concepts and complications. Plast Reconstr Surg 74:493–507, 1984.

Maxwell GP: Breast reconstruction following mastectomy and surgical management of the patient with high-risk breast disease. In Smith JW, Aston SJ (eds): Grabb and Smith's Plastic Surgery, 4th ed. Boston, Little Brown, 1991, pp 1203–1247.

Neuman C: The expansion of an area of skin by progressive distention of a subcutaneous balloon. Use of the method for securing skin for subtotal reconstruction of the ear. Plast Reconstr Surg 19:124–130, 1957.

Ninkovic M, Moser-Rumer A, Ninkovic M, et al: Anterior neck reconstruction with pre-expanded free groin and scapular flaps. Plast Reconstr Surg 113:61–68, 2004.

Radovan C: Adjacent flap development using an expandable silastic implant. Presented at the annual meeting of the American Society of Plastic and Reconstructive Surgeons, Boston, 1976.

Radovan C: Tissue expansion in soft-tissue reconstruction. Plast Reconstr Surg 74:482–492, 1984.

Ronert MA, Hofheinz H, Manassa E, et al: The beginning of a new era in tissue expansion: Self-filling osmotic tissue expander—four-year clinical experience. Plast Reconstr Surg 114:1025–1031, 2004.

Sasaki GH: Tissue expansion. In Jurkiewicz MJ, Krizek TJ, Mathes SJ, Aryian S (eds): Plastic Surgery: Principles and Practice. St. Louis, Mosby, 1990, pp 1609–1634.

Shapiro AL, Hochman M, Thomas JR, Branham G: Effects of intraoperative tissue expansion and skin flaps on wound closing tensions. Arch Otolaryngol Head Neck Surg 122:1107–1111, 1996.

Siegert R, Weerda H, Hoffmann S, Mohadjer C: Clinical and experimental evaluation of intermittent intraoperative short-term expansion. Plast Reconstr Surg 92:248–254, 1993.

Tran NV, Petty PM, Bite U, et al: Tissue expansion-assisted closure of massive ventral hernias. J Am Coll Surg 196:484–488, 2003.

Wiese KG, Heinemann DE, Ostermeier D, Peters JH: Biomaterial properties and biocompatibility in cell culture of a novel self-inflating hydrogel tissue expander. J Biomed Mater Res 54:179–188, 2001.

Wilmshurst AD, Sharpe DT: Immediate placement of tissue expanders in the management of large excisional defects on the face. Br J Plast Surg 43:150–153, 1990.

Zide BM, Karp NS: Maximizing gain from rectangular tissue expanders. Plast Reconstr Surg 90:500–504, 1992; discussion 5–6.

ALLOPLASTIC IMPLANTATION

Stephen Daane, MD

1. What are the advantages of alloplastic materials?
- No donor site morbidity from a second surgical site
- Reduced operative time compared with harvesting a graft
- Unlimited supply of alloplastic materials
- Prefabricated implants can be tailored to the individual patient
- Unlike autogenous materials (bone, cartilage, dermis, fat, fascia), there is no scar formation or reabsorption of the implant over time

2. How are biomedical alloplants classified?
Biomedical alloplants are classified as either liquids (injectable silicone, collagen) or solids (metals, polymers, ceramics). The physical form of the implants (solid or mesh, smooth or rough) determines whether the implant is encapsulated as a whole or whether fibrous tissue will penetrate the interstices of the implant. Selection of specific alloplastic implant materials can be advantageous in different clinical situations: vigorous tissue ingrowth into Marlex polypropylene mesh provides a strong, long-lasting repair, whereas fibrous encapsulation of a Hunter rod silicone tendon prosthesis ensures free gliding of a subsequent tendon graft.

3. What are properties of the "ideal" implant?
The "ideal" implant should fulfill certain conditions:

- Biologically compatible
- Nontoxic
- Nonallergenic
- Produces no foreign body inflammatory response
- Mechanically reliable
- Resistant to resorption and deformation
- Nonsupportive of microorganism growth
- Easy to shape, remove, and sterilize
- Radiolucent (does not interfere with computed tomography [CT] or magnetic resonance [MR] scans)

4. What is the goal of alloplastic implantation?
The goal of implantation materials is to simulate a missing part while evoking a minimal reaction from the host. Polymers are the implants most commonly used as bulk space fillers for soft tissue contour restoration, as with nasal, chin, auricular, and breast implants. The biologic response to the polymer group of materials generally consists of a normal inflammatory response, deposition of collagen, and maturation of fibrous connective tissue that completely encapsulates the implant in 4 to 6 weeks. In some instances, a restrictive capsular fibrosis occurs, a biologic response that may be related to myofibroblast activity and may require surgical correction.

The quality of the "tissue envelope" holding the implant must be considered. If the blood supply is marginal (as with irradiated tissues), the chance of extrusion is high. If the implant is placed in a very tight pocket, the chance of bony resorption underneath the implant is high. Principles of placing hard implants include the following: (1) shaping the edges to avoid hard corners, (2) burying the implant as deeply as possible under the skin and subcutaneous tissues, (3) avoiding tension in adjacent tissues or tension against the overlying skin, (4) placing the incision as far as possible from the implant, (5) handling the implant gently, and (6) using the proper stiffness of material (hard implants should never be used for soft tissue replacement).

5. What is the Oppenheimer effect?
In 1948, Oppenheimer reported that metal implants placed in experimental animals could induce tumors. Further experiments showed that the composition of the material was unimportant; maximal tumorigenesis occurred when the material had a smooth, continuous surface. Other characteristics of this phenomenon were a minimum size requirement (0.5 × 0.5 cm in rats) and a minimum time requirement for the implant to remain in situ (6 months in rats). Tumors appeared after a latent period of approximately 300 days.

Rare clinical reports of tumor occurrence adjacent to alloplastic implants in humans is consistent with the Oppenheimer effect, although extensive human clinical experience has never demonstrated a strong association between carcinogenicity and medical alloplants. However, to rule out the oncogenic potential of implants, a follow-up study period of 20 to 50 years would be necessary to match the short latent period of animal tumors.

6. What are bioabsorbable plates and screws?

Experimentation with absorbable polyesters led to the development of poly-L-lactic acid (PLA) and polyglycolic acid (PGA) as resorbable implantable devices. When used alone, poly(L-lactide) forms a strong crystalline lattice that takes months or years to undergo hydrolysis; mixtures of poly(L-lactide) with poly (D,L-lactide) resorb more quickly. PGA implants lose their tensile strength quickly and are resorbed within weeks to months. Pure PGA was first marketed as Dexon suture; Vicryl suture is a mix of 8% PLA and 92% PGA. A chondrocyte-seeded PLA/PGA polymer similar to Vicryl has been used in the "tissue engineering" of cartilage scaffolding. A copolymer of PLA (82%) and PGA (18%) was developed that consistently demonstrated adequate initial strength and complete resorption after 9 to 15 months. This combination was introduced as the LactoSorb craniofacial plate fixation system in 1996. Sculptra is a newly developed PLA product for midfacial soft tissue augmentation due to the wasting caused by protease inhibitors.

The theoretical advantage of absorbable PLA/PGA over titanium hardware in pediatric craniofacial surgery is that the plates do not put the patient at risk for intracranial migration of hardware or growth restriction. Metallic fixation interferes with postoperative radiographic imaging, oncologic follow-up, and evaluation of fracture healing.

7. Which metals are suitable for implantation in plastic surgery?

(1) Stainless steel, (2) Vitallium, and (3) titanium. Their uses include plate and screw fixation sets for craniofacial surgery and hand surgery and as hemoclips, cranial plates, artificial joints, and dental implants.

The term **stainless steel** refers to a large group of iron-chromium-nickel alloys that were first used as biomedical implants in the 1920s. Orthopedic devices of stainless steel were adapted to craniofacial surgery for rigid fixation; however, these implants were found to undergo corrosion with potential for implant failure after several years. Compared with stainless steel, Vitallium and titanium have superior corrosion resistance, partially due to a protective oxide layer that forms on their surface.

Vitallium is a cobalt-chromium-molybdenum alloy introduced in the 1930s. It has a higher resistance to fatigue or fracture than either stainless steel or titanium. Because of its high tensile strength, lower-profile plates that have narrow interconnecting bars between the holes can be implanted.

Titanium was introduced as an implant material in Europe in the 1940s. Unalloyed titanium is much more malleable than stainless steel or Vitallium. Malleability facilitates bending to fit the complex topography of the facial skeleton (e.g., titanium mesh can be useful for orbital floor reconstruction in blowout fractures). Titanium alloy (titanium–aluminum 6%–vanadium 4%) has a tensile strength similar to that of Vitallium. Titanium is the least corrosive of the metals used for implantation and has the least artifact on CT and MR imaging studies.

Biocompatibility of metals depends on whether the metals release ions or particles into the surrounding tissues. In the case of deteriorating stainless steel implants, patients may complain of pain and tenderness around the implant. Skin tests in patients with metallic implants indicate sensitivity to the constituent metals, cobalt, chromium, and nickel; rare allergic reactions have occurred. Detection of metal corrosion products in the hair, blood, and urine are of unknown clinical significance.

8. What is hydroxyapatite?

$Ca_{10}(PO_4)_6(OH)_2$, or hydroxyapatite (HA), is the major inorganic constituent of bone. Corals of the genus *Porites* create a calcium carbonate exoskeleton resembling human bone with an average pore size of 200 µm. Surgical vendors convert the calcium carbonate skeleton into HA through an exchange reaction of the carbonate for phosphate. The resultant ceramic has the porous anatomy of bone with an identical chemical composition. HA is capable of strongly bonding to adjacent bone, and, compared with onlay bone grafts, HA demonstrates excellent maintenance of contour and volume. HA implants elicit no foreign body or inflammatory response.

9. How is HA used in plastic surgery?

HA is available in block form (porous or solid) and as granules. It is used most commonly to augment the contour of the facial skeleton or as a bone graft substitute in orthognathic surgery. Contouring of HA blocks is performed with dental burs. Lag screw fixation is suggested when HA blocks are placed in an onlay manner because osteointegration will not occur if the blocks are mobile.

Experimentally, porous HA blocks and HA granules are rapidly invaded by fibrovascular tissue. Histologic evidence of direct osseous union between implant and bone is seen within 2 to 3 months. HA is "osteoconductive" in that it provides a matrix for deposition of new bone from adjacent living bone. HA is not "osteogenic" because it will not induce bone formation when placed in ectopic sites such as muscle or fat. Long-term radiographic follow-up shows a lack of resorption of HA implants.

HA blocks are brittle but gain rapidly in strength as the implant pores are invaded by fibrovascular tissue. The ultimate compressive strength exceeds the masticatory forces of the jaws. Infection is likely to occur when there is a deficiency of soft tissue coverage.

HA granules may be mixed with Avitene or blood and microfibrillar collagen, then placed into a carefully dissected subperiosteal pocket to produce a desired contour. Granular HA is somewhat more difficult to handle. Although solid HA has a high extrusion rate when used for alveolar ridge augmentation, HA granules have been used successfully for this application, where they become strongly anchored by fibrous tissue.

10. How is synthetic HA used in plastic surgery?

BoneSource is a synthetic HA cement that was first used clinically in 1991 (similar products include Norian and Mimix). When mixed with water and a drying agent (sodium phosphate), BoneSource powder forms a paste that hardens to form a microporous implant within 15 minutes. It is biocompatible, with no inflammatory tissue response. In addition to its ease of application, the infection rate with BoneSource is low.

Although experiments in feline cranial defects and initial anecdotal clinical reports indicated resorption, longer follow-up in humans has shown that HA cement maintains shape and volume over time. The wound bed must be *very* dry at closure. Currently, the approved indication for HA cement is for calvarial defects of up to 25 cm^2, although it is also commonly used for facial skeletal augmentation. Variable bony ingrowth has been reported following the use of HA cement for cranioplasty. Experiments mixing HA cement with protein growth factors to enhance bony ingrowth are ongoing.

11. Which polymer is most often used for facial augmentation? Why?

High-density porous polyethylene (Medpor) is replacing silicone as the most often used material for facial augmentation procedures. Medpor has a void volume of up to 50%. Pore sizes ranging from 100 to 250 μm allow stabilization of the implant through bony and soft tissue ingrowth. The foreign body reaction to Medpor is minimal, with only a thin fibrous capsule and very few giant cells. It has low infection and extrusion rates, with no loss of the implant on long-term follow-up.

Medpor is available in sheets and blocks that can be sculpted at the time of surgery. It also is available as preformed implants available for chin augmentation, malar augmentation, and microtia reconstruction (placed beneath a temporoparietal fascial flap). It is useful for orbital floor blowout fractures and as a columellar strut for cleft rhinoplasty. Medpor implants become adherent to the surrounding bone, whereas silicone implants on the facial skeleton undergo fibrous capsule formation without fixation to bone.

12. What are the physical properties of silicone?

Polydimethylsiloxane (PDMS) or silicone is a repeating chain of –Si–O– units, with methyl groups attached to the silicon atoms. Silicone can simulate different soft tissues as a liquid, gel, or rubber by varying the length and cross-linking of the PDMS chains. Silicone fluids are short, straight chains of PDMS, gels are lightly cross-linked chains of PDMS, and elastomers are longer chains of PDMS that are cross-linked to a greater degree. Amorphous silica particles (30 μm) can be added to increase the tensile strength of silicone rubber.

Silicone is highly biocompatible, nontoxic, nonallergenic, and resistant to biodegradation. The tissue response is limited to a mild foreign body reaction followed by encapsulation. Silicone cannot be rendered porous to improve its incorporation into tissues; instead, a fibrous capsule forms around the implant.

13. What are the disadvantages of using silicone?

Although silicone polymers are considered biologically inert, they may evoke an inflammatory response in humans. Silicone gel particles from breast implants may be engulfed by macrophages to incite a chronic inflammatory reaction. Silicone synovitis occurs after fragmentation of silicone particles from joint replacement prostheses; the foreign body reaction can produce joint space destruction and inflammatory bone resorption. Silicone granulomas are firm, erythematous masses in the skin and subcutaneous tissues due to inflammatory reactions around particles of liquid silicone. Although an immune response to silicone has been demonstrated in laboratory animals (not humans), an association of silicone with "human adjuvant disease" remains unproven.

Disadvantages of using silicone include (1) a propensity of silicone rubbers to tear easily or fail in heavy stress applications (e.g., Swanson finger joint implants), (2) difficulty removing silicone gel from soft tissues in the case of implant failure, (3) bone resorption beneath silicone implants placed subperiosteally for augmentation (e.g., chin), (4) their "smoothness" makes them prone to extrusion when placed superficially (e.g., Silastic placed in the nose or ear), and (5) silicone rubbers are permeable, allowing proteins or lipids to become adsorbed onto the surface of an implant, which may alter its physical properties and lead to failure. Complications related to Silastic orbital floor implants (extrusion, displacement) account for their high removal rate.

Silicone gel is a composition of low-molecular-weight and oligomeric polymethylsiloxane, although there is also a large amount of uncross-linked silicone oil. Silicone gel implants were designed so that a cross-linked silicone rubber shell would contain highly cross-linked silicone gels. However, silicone oils within the gel could diffuse through the elastomer shell (gel bleed), and swelling of the shell by silicone fluid could reduce the mechanical strength of the shell. Silicone gel breast implants were placed under moratorium by the FDA in 1992 because of inadequate safety data. Formation of hard fibrous capsules that could be painful or disfiguring remains a major reason for revision.

As an injectable liquid, silicone once was used for augmentation of facial soft tissues and breast enlargement. However, silicone injections ultimately were affected by gravity, with loss of the augmentation effect after a period of years. Infection and chronic inflammation, migration of the material, and inappropriate usage led to its withdrawal from the market. Topical silicones are successfully used in scar therapy.

14. Are there alternatives to silicone gel for breast implants?

Nonsilicone gel developments include soybean oil, which were used in Europe and the United Kingdom before being withdrawn from the market in 1999. Complications were due to inflammatory and toxic properties of soybean oil released though the silicone shell of the implants. Polyvinylpyrrolidone (PVP) polysaccharide hydrogel is currently under investigation.

15. What is methylmethacrylate used for in plastic surgery?

Methylmethacrylate is a self-curing acrylic resin, used for securing joint components to bone and as a craniofacial bone substitute. Advantages of this inexpensive material include ease of surgical manipulation, density similar to bone, radiolucency, and good long-term tissue tolerance. Methylmethacrylate is available in two forms: a heat-cured, preformed implant or a cold-cured implant that can be molded in the operating room and contoured with burs after hardening. The body's response to methylmethacrylate is minimal, consisting of a typical foreign body reaction that subsides as the implant becomes enveloped by fibrous tissue.

While curing, methylmethacrylate forms an exothermic reaction that can damage tissues. Cardiac arrest due to absorption has been reported during the curing process. The major late problems are infection, extrusion, or mechanical failure due to deterioration of the bone–polymer interface. Risks of infection are decreased by keeping the edge of the implant at least 1 cm away from a skin incision and by avoiding the use of methylmethacrylate under skin grafts or scarred tissues. Cranioplexx is a methylmethacrylate product that is mixed in a sealed pouch, minimizing the odor and exothermic reaction.

Methylmethacrylate is used in orthopedics as a bone cement for joint replacements, in neurosurgery for reconstruction of cranial defects, and in dentistry for dental plates. Often small screws are placed in the skull or facial skeleton to anchor the material. In plastic surgery, gentamicin-impregnated methylmethacrylate beads are used in conjunction with muscle flaps to treat infected long bone fractures. Methylmethacrylate is also used for forehead augmentation and chest wall reconstruction. For difficult reconstructions, implants can be created before an operation based on a moulage or from CT scan data and computer-assisted milling. HTR is a recently available composite of methylmethacrylate that is porous and negatively charged to stimulate bony ingrowth. A meta-analysis of 45 studies using methylmethacrylate for routine cranioplasty revealed an infection rate of 5%.

16. What is cyanoacrylate? How is it used?

Cyanoacrylate ("Superglue") is a strong, biodegradable tissue adhesive that polymerizes upon contact with tissues. It can be used as a hemostatic agent or to "glue" tissues together in a surgical wound. Its binding is not affected by moisture or blood. Cyanoacrylate is widely used in orthopedics for hardware fixation, but it has been of only limited use in plastic surgery for blood vessel anastomoses, wound closure, application of skin grafts, or hemostasis. In strength comparison studies, cyanoacrylate is comparable to plate and screw fixation in the facial skeleton and comparable to suture for wound closure. Cyanoacrylate is easy to handle in the operating room. There is a mild toxicity from the degradation products, formaldehyde and cyanoacetate, which can be detected in the urine.

Dermabond is an FDA-approved cyanoacrylate "topical skin cohesive." In a multicenter trial of more than 800 patients, Dermabond compared favorably with sutures in the emergency repair of lacerations and punctures, general surgical incisions, and facial plastic procedures. Dermabond polymerizes within 1 minute and begins to peel off in 7 to 10 days.

17. Which fluorocarbon polymers are used in plastic surgery?

Fluorocarbon polymers as a group are resistant to chemical degradation and are minimally reactive when placed in the body. Of the fluorocarbon polymers used in plastic surgery, Teflon is limited to vocal cord reconstruction and Proplast was withdrawn from the market in 1990. Only polytetrafluoroethylene (PTFE; Gore-Tex) is in common use today.

Polytetrafluoroethylene (PTFE) consists of non–cross-linked linear polymers of fluorinated carbon units with molecular weights of 6 to 10 million. The carbon–fluorine bonds are highly resistant to degradation. PTFE is inert, nonadhesive, and nonfrictional and elicits virtually no inflammatory response within the body. It is nonallergenic and noncarcinogenic and has no immune reactivity. **Gore-Tex** is a polymer sheet of "expanded" PTFE interconnected by Teflon fibrils, yielding tremendous strength. Pores of up to 30 μm result from the expansion, allowing a small amount of tissue ingrowth. Gore-Tex is useful for vascular reconstruction and soft tissue augmentation. Gore-Tex has been used in the face for correction of wrinkles and has been used for lip, chin, nasal, and forehead augmentation. It is used for ligament repair, chest wall or abdominal wall reconstruction, static suspension of the paralyzed face, and guided tissue regeneration (GTR). Problems with extrusion or migration of Gore-Tex implants are reduced when the implants are properly fixed to the tissues. Infection rates with Gore-Tex implants are very low.

18. What are osseointegrated implants?

Osseointegration is the harmonious coexistence of implant, bone, and soft tissue. Osseointegrated percutaneous implants give the ability to attach a prosthesis to an implant that is anchored to bone but is penetrating the skin or mucosa. In the first stage, a titanium implant is placed into bone and buried underneath the periosteum or soft tissues for 3 months to provide osseointegration. At a second stage, the implant is uncovered and a permanent prosthesis is made for fixation to the implant. The implant must be absolutely stable during the first 3 to 6 months of healing, or connective tissue rather than bone may form at the implant surface. Threaded implants with small pores are more likely to establish initial stability, and titanium is used because the oxide layer that readily forms on the implant's surface is important to the implant's tissue interaction. More recently, HA-coated titanium implants have been used. Success rates greater than 95% have been reported using osseointegrated implants for dental restoration and for prosthetic facial parts on long-term follow-up.

19. What is AlloDerm?

AlloDerm is acellular dermal matrix ("cadaver skin") commonly used in cosmetic procedures such as lip grafting. It is rendered immunologically compatible by chemically removing all immunoreactive components (epidermis, antigenic cell components) while leaving the collagen/elastin structure of skin intact. It has been used in reconstructive surgery to induce granulation tissue over exposed bone and tendon in refractory wounds.

20. Should patients with implants undergo antibiotic prophylaxis?

The potential of an implant material to potentiate infection is an important consideration. For example, experiments have shown that the requirement of 10^6 organisms to produce a pus-forming infection is lowered to just 100 organisms in the presence of a braided silk suture. Although studies have shown a beneficial effect of perioperative antibiotic prophylaxis in patients undergoing implantation with alloplastic materials, usually only patients with prosthetic heart valves or hips receive antibiotics when undergoing dental procedures that can cause a transient bacteremia. It seems possible that breast implants or other materials could serve as a nidus for bacterial colonization, although formal recommendations for antibiotic prophylaxis in these patients have never been made.

BIBLIOGRAPHY

Albrektsson T, Brånemark PI, Jacobsson M, Tjellström A: Present clinical applications of osseointegrated percutaneous implants. Plast Reconstr Surg 79:721–731, 1987.

American Academy of Orthopaedic Surgeons: Metals used in orthopaedic surgery. In: Orthopaedic Knowledge Update I. Chicago, American Academy of Orthopaedic Surgeons, 1984.

Baker S, Weinzweig J, Whitaker L, Bartlett SP: Applications of a new carbonated calcium phosphate bone cement: Early experience in pediatric and adult craniofacial reconstruction. Plast Reconstr Surg 109:1789–1796, 2002.

Constantino PD, Friedman CD: Synthetic bone graft substitutes. Otolaryngol Clin North Am 27:1037–1074, 1994.

Holmes RE: Alloplastic implants. In McCarthy JG (ed): Plastic Surgery. Philadelphia, WB Saunders, 1990, pp 698–731.

Mole B: The use of Gore-Tex implants in aesthetic surgery of the face. Plast Reconstr Surg 90:200–206, 1992.

Montag ME, Morales L, Daane S: Bioabsorbables: Their use in pediatric craniofacial surgery. J Craniofac Surg 8:100–102, 1997.

Oppenheimer BS, Oppenheimer ET, Danishefski I, Stout AP: Carcinogenic effect of metals in rodents. Cancer Res 16:439–441, 1956.

Ousterhout DK: Prosthetic forehead augmentation. In Ousterhout DK (ed): Aesthetic Contouring of the Craniofacial Skeleton. Boston, Little Brown, 1991, pp 199–219.

Scales JT: Discussion on metals and synthetic materials in relation to soft tissues: Tissue's reaction to synthetic materials. Proc R Soc Med 46:647–652, 1953.

Rockell WB, Daane S, Zakhireh M, Carroll KL: Human skin allograft after club foot release. Ann Plast Surg 51:593–597, 2003.

THE PROBLEMATIC WOUND

Thomas J. Krizek, MD

CHAPTER 6

1. What is a problematic wound? What causes it?

The goal of wound healing is to obtain successful closure of the wound with an intact epithelial layer. A wound becomes problematic when it presents unusual difficulty in obtaining such closure. The difficulty may relate to the configuration of the wound in which the technique or mechanics of closure is the main issue. The difficulty also may relate to problems intrinsic to the wound itself. Systemic (e.g., sickle cell anemia, administration of steroids) or local (e.g., bacterial contamination) factors may affect wound healing.

2. What are primary, secondary, and tertiary wound closure?

Closure of wounds in which the edges can be directly approximated is referred to as **first intention** or **primary closure.** The typical example is a surgical wound. Closure with sutures, staples, tape, or other means brings the edges together and maintains approximation while the wound experiences the healing stages of inflammation and early fibroplasia. In certain wounds, such as burn wounds, primary closure cannot be achieved. The surgeon awaits and promotes spontaneous reepithelialization of the wound from viable epithelial elements in the wound itself or from the epithelium at the margin. This approach, called **second intention** or **secondary closure,** is associated with the potential problems created by a wound that remains open: intense and prolonged inflammation, which in turn promotes excessive contraction and excessive fibroplasia. Secondary closure may result in an unsightly scar and, when across a joint, may limit motion due to contracture. One approach to the wound that otherwise would be closed only by secondary means is to close the wound surgically by bringing tissue from elsewhere in the form of a flap or graft. This technique is **third intention** or **tertiary closure.**

3. What systemic problems may make a wound problematic?

Systemic problems may affect the wound directly or indirectly. For example, in patients with Ehlers-Danlos syndrome, a defect in collagen deposition results in less tensile strength and more elasticity. A deficiency in vitamin C (scurvy) makes the hydroxylation of proline to hydroxyproline impossible and causes a collagen cross-linking deficiency. Sickle cell anemia has profound local effects on healing. Chronic administration of steroids interferes with fibroplasia. It is important to recognize how few systemic conditions result in wound closure difficulty. Factors such as malnutrition, anemia, age, and other systemic factors are clinically relevant only at their extremes and only marginally so; the body recognizes wound closure as a biologic priority.

4. What local factors may make a wound problematic?

Far more frequent are local wound problems that render the wound biologically rather than technically problematic. The most common examples include ischemia, pressure, radiation, foreign material/traumatic wounds, and bacterial contamination.

5. What are the guidelines for handling ischemic wounds?

Ischemic wounds must be evaluated for reversible vascular problems (e.g., bypass surgery). Venous wounds also are ischemic, perhaps from functional shunting of blood from the arterial to the venous side of circulation, bypassing the ulcerated area. Some evidence suggests that microvascular free tissue transfer from the arm or scapular area provides venous drainage. Closure with tissue containing valves makes recurrence less severe than closure merely with grafts. Lymphatic disease is particularly difficult because, as in venous wounds, edema is an ongoing problem. Edematous tissue is particularly prone to streptococcal infection, which, when it heals, results in more lymphatic scarring and thus more edema. Unna boots (containing calamine, zinc oxide, and gelatin), elastic support, and prophylaxis against streptococci are of long-term value. Growth factors may soon be commercially available for use in diabetic arterial disease and other wounds. Sickle cell ulcers, when skin grafted, usually recur promptly if the patient is allowed to have a crisis during the healing phase. If the hematocrit is maintained above 35% or so, crisis will not occur, and the grafted skin has a chance to mature and become less easily traumatized.

6. What are the guidelines for handling pressure wounds?

Wounds resulting from unrelieved pressure, usually in patients without sensation (quadriplegics, paraplegics, neuropathics, and patients with chronic debilitating central neurologic problems) are extremely difficult and cannot be successfully managed unless the underlying cause is corrected. Successful wound closure in unselected patients, even with sophisticated muscle flaps, probably is less than 10%. With careful education and limitation of surgery to the most compliant patients, muscle closure of pressure sores is successful in about 75% of cases. Many problematic pressure wounds are best managed by creating a controlled wound, namely, a wound without excessive contamination that can be maintained indefinitely by local wound care. The wound, if not excessively large, is of no danger to the patient; this approach is useful in patients in whom the success of surgery is small. The use of growth factors in compliant patients may result in successful closure of pressure wounds by second intention to a degree formerly thought impossible.

7. How are radiated wounds managed?

Radiation injuries may be acute or chronic. Acute injury, which is seen only in industrial accidents, is rare because the dangers are so well known. Chronic injury may occur from industrial exposure or formerly from therapeutic treatment of acne or other benign conditions. Fortunately the generation of patients so injured has largely passed, and no new patients are being added. Most problematic wounds that we encounter are due to therapeutic radiation for malignancy and fall into the category of subacute injury. The ultimate effect of radiation on the tissue is not necessarily to produce ischemia; in fact, radiated wounds usually are quite well vascularized and bleed easily. Instead, the radiation destroys stem cells necessary for both revascularization and fibroplasia. In many radiation wounds a split-thickness skin graft will close the wound nicely. In others, vascularized tissue in the form of muscular or musculocutaneous flaps or free microvascular flaps gives the wound a new start with tissue that brings its own blood supply and stem cells.

8. What about traumatic wounds?

Sir James Learmonth, surgeon to the Queen of England, provided guidelines on which it is hard to improve. The key to managing such wounds is adequate débridement:

Of the edge of the skin,
take a piece very thin.
The tighter the fascia,
the more you should slash'er.
And muscle much more,
until you see fresh gore,
And the bundles contract,
at the least impact.
Leave intact the bone,
except bits quite alone.

Learmonth emphasized the value of accurate débridement as the single most important factor in preparing the traumatic/contaminated wound for closure. The skin is highly vascular, and excessive removal is unnecessary. Intravenous fluorescein and examination of skin with a Wood's lamp offer accurate delineation of vascular compared with devitalized skin. Foreign bodies must be removed before closure. Wounds should be explored for metallic foreign bodies, such as needles, only if radiographic control is available. The needle in the haystack is easier to find than the needle in the sole of the foot. In addition to accurate débridement and removal of foreign bodies, irrigation is essential. Débridement, irrigation, and bacterial balance are critical to the successful management of the grossly contaminated wound. When these goals are accomplished, our technical virtuosity will be used to close it. But first, **débride** the wound (Fig. 6-1).

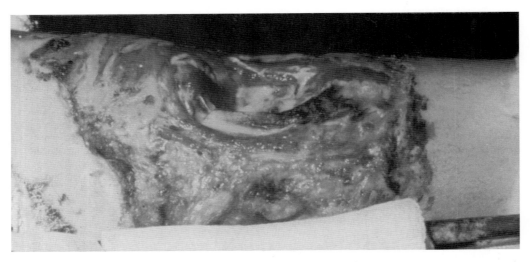

Figure 6-1. Open tibial fracture with contaminated wound. The wound needs to be débrided and irrigated under pressure, and bacterial flora in soft tissue and bone should be determined by quantitative microbiologic techniques. Only when bacterial control can be documented is the technical virtuosity of the reconstructive surgeon used to close the wound.

9. Which irrigation fluid should be used? How much?

Most irrigation is designed to remove particulate matter, which often is difficult to see, and bacteria, which cannot be seen. If you measure particulate matter and bacterial flora in an open wound quantitatively, before and after irrigation, you have an excellent model to study the effect of irrigation. Surface irrigation (e.g., with a bulb syringe) is only marginally effective and then only for surface bacteria. Bacteria lodged in the tissue are not reduced by this technique whether you use 1 L or 20 L. "Dilution is the solution to pollution" only when irrigation is performed with pressure; pressure irrigation with the jet lavage or Systec-like systems at about 70 psi reduces bacteria counts and the amount of particulate matter. Although saline is readily available, Ringer's lactate probably is a better choice. The amount depends on the nature of the wound. Small wounds irrigated in the emergency department with a syringe and fine needle require only a few ounces, whereas large wounds require proportionately more.

10. What about bacterial contamination?

Humans are not germ-free. Our skin is contaminated by bacterial flora that are both transient and resident. Transient flora, which reflect contact with the environment, may be extremely high after contact with heavily contaminated material or relatively low if they are exposed to the air, dry up, and die from lack of nourishment. We remove transient bacteria when we wash our hands before patient contact or before we enter the operating room. Resident flora, which reside in the hair follicles and skin glands, are "normal." A biopsy culture of normal skin identifies about 10^3 microorganisms per gram of skin. Similarly the mucous membrane of the oral cavity and the mucosa of the bowel are colonized. The mere presence of bacteria does not constitute infection. Rather than being free of bacteria, we live in delicate balance with them—a balance that can be identified and measured with great precision.

11. What is quantitative microbiology?

All microbiology laboratories routinely culture urine to determine whether a level of 100,000 (10^5) microorganisms is present. A level less than 10^5 microorganisms indicates contamination, whereas a level more than 10^5 microorganisms indicates invasive infection. For the past 40 years surgical biologists have used the same technology to measure bacterial contamination in the tissue of open wounds. A specimen is obtained, weighed, and converted to liquid on a weight/volume basis and then cultured in the same fashion as urine cultures. The number of microorganisms per gram of tissue is determined. The surface bacteria in a wound are insignificant because they are so easily eliminated. Surface swabs for culture fail to recognize the bacteria in the depths of the wound, which makes the difference.

The rapid slide test provides information about whether the wound has more than 10^5 microorganisms per gram of tissue in less than 30 minutes. It does not identify the exact organisms or their sensitivities, but it is useful in screening contaminated wounds.

12. Does quantitative microbiology make a difference?

Gertrude Stein has been quoted as saying, "A difference, to be a difference, must make a difference." All differences are not necessarily important, but quantitative microbiology *makes* a difference. When fewer than 10^5 microorganisms are present in the tissue, invasive infection will not occur, wounds will close spontaneously, and skin grafts will take with uniform success. When the counts are greater than 10^5 microorganisms per gram of tissue, skin grafts will not take and invasive infection will occur. Streptococci, which are dangerous in *any* quantity, are the exception that proves the rule.

Of interest, 10^8 to 10^9 microorganisms per gram of tissue are necessary to produce clinical evidence of pus; therefore, the difference between what can be seen with the naked eye and the critical level of bacteria is a difference of almost 1000-fold. In a clinical study of random wounds in the emergency department, the number of wounds with more than 10^5 microorganisms per gram was 20%. This is the average infection rate in wounds managed in emergency departments nationwide. When wounds with fewer than 10^5 microorganisms were closed, the infection rate dropped to less than 1%.

The importance of quantitative microbiology in bone also has been demonstrated. When sternal wounds are débrided and closed only when bone cultures show fewer than 10^5 microorganisms per gram, the infection rate for wounds is all but eliminated. Quantitative microbiology adds scientific precision to the measurement of soft tissue contamination and makes wound closure, by any modality, a matter of clinical accuracy rather than guesswork.

13. Should quantitative microbiology be used before closing all wounds?

No. The use of any test in every case, no matter how inexpensive or readily available, is as inappropriate as never using it. Neither approach is biologically sound. Clean surgical wounds and traumatic wounds under clean conditions (e.g., cuts around the home) are most likely free of unusual contamination. Our studies have shown that almost 80% of unselected wounds presenting to the emergency department fall into the clean category. It is the other 20% that cause the infections. Quantitative microbiology is indicated in wounds that are known, by history, to

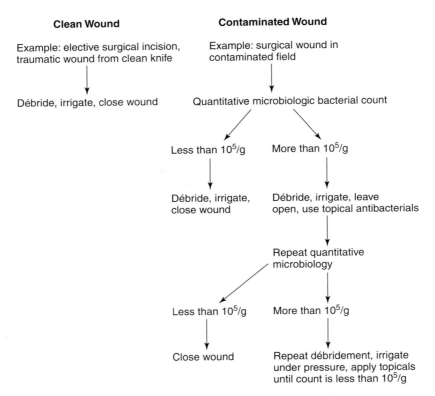

Figure 6-2. Algorithm for managing clean and contaminated wounds.

be contaminated. Human bites involve major bacterial contamination. Most dog bites are "clean" because the dog's mouth has fewer than 10^3 bacteria per gram *unless* the dog has eaten meat in the previous 8 hours. In this case, the counts go as high as 10^7 bacteria per gram. The imaginative surgeon will ask about the dog's eating pattern, recognizing the effect of meat (biscuits and dry food do not raise counts), and discern which wounds will benefit from quantitative counts (Fig. 6-2).

14. What is the value of antibacterial agents in problematic wounds?
Antibacterial agents must be appropriate for the organism most likely to cause the infection and must be given at the proper time, in the proper dose, and by the proper route to be effective.

Time. The proper time to give an antibacterial is *before* the contamination occurs so that an effective level is present in the tissue when bacterial contamination occurs. Most persons do not walk around on antibacterial therapy. In patients with lymphedema or edema of a healing burn, however, long-term prophylaxis against streptococcal infection is appropriate, and a narrow-spectrum agent (penicillin) is indicated. In many elective operations, intravenous administration of an antibacterial as surgery begins is appropriate and should be repeated at intervals if the operation is prolonged. Contaminated traumatic wounds also are appropriately treated with systemic antibacterials if the danger of contamination is high and if the antibacterial can be delivered within the golden period of about 3 hours. Most clean lacerations have minimal contamination, and in large series of patients systemic antibacterials show no advantage. It cannot be emphasized enough that the widespread emerging resistance of microorganisms to most, in some cases even all, antibacterials can largely be traced to the indiscriminate, broad-spectrum use of antibacterials when they are not indicated.

Route. The bloodstream is the finest delivery system yet invented and is to be preferred for all antibacterials unless scientific evidence indicates otherwise. After about 3 to 4 hours, antibacterials in the bloodstream no longer reach the wound. An open wound can be measured by quantitative bacterial culture before and during administration of systemic antibacterials. When systemic administration of the antibacterial at many times the normal dosage has no effect on the bacterial level in the wound, you can conclude only that the route is not appropriate. This, of course, is the scientific and biologic basis for the use of topical antibacterials, which reach the wound and, in fact, reduce the bacterial count. It is logical, therefore, when managing a contaminated wound to use the following steps:

1. Culture the wound by quantitative microbiologic techniques and determine the microorganism that is present, at what level, and which antibacterial is appropriate. If the count is more than 10^5 microorganisms per gram of tissue, it is not safe to close the wound; if fewer than 10^5 microorganisms per gram of tissue are present, close the wound.
2. Use the antibacterial by the proper route until you can demonstrate that the bacterial count has been reduced to a safe level of fewer than 10^5 microorganisms per gram of tissue. Then close the wound. The documented success rate for closure of wounds managed in this fashion is greater than 98%.

15. My laboratory does not perform quantitative microbiology. Please comment.

Hogwash. Every microbiologic laboratory in the United States performs quantitative bacterial cultures on urine on a daily basis. With simple equipment (costing less than $100.00), laboratory workers can weigh, crush, and dilute soft tissue and perform the test in about 30 minutes (rapid slide). They also can give you accurate cultures and sensitivities in 24 hours, as they do with urine samples. They do not perform quantitative analysis because you did not ask them to do so. Hospitals that spend millions of dollars on expensive equipment, such as magnetic resonance imaging (MRI) machines, will gladly perform the test free of charge if you show them that you can prevent even one wound infection or save even one patient a single day in the hospital. There are more resistant surgeons than there are resistant microorganisms.

BIBLIOGRAPHY

Krizek TJ, Gottlieb LJ: Acute suppurative mediastinitis. In Sabiston DC Jr (ed): Textbook of Surgery: The Biologic Basis of Modern Surgical Practice. Philadelphia, WB Saunders, 1997, pp 1929–1933.

Hansen SL, Mathes SJ: Problem wound and principles of closure. In Mathes SJ (ed): Plastic Surgery, 2nd ed. WB Saunders, 2006, pp 901–1030.

Learmonth J, as quoted by Bowen TE: To the soldier medic (editorial). Mil Med 156:638–639, 1991.

Robson MC, Krizek TJ, Heggers JP: Biology of surgical infection. In Ravitch MM, Austen WG, Scott HW, et al (eds): Current Problems in Surgery. Chicago, Year Book, 1973, pp 1–62.

PRINCIPLES AND APPLICATIONS OF VACUUM-ASSISTED CLOSURE (VAC)

Malcolm W. Marks, MD; Louis C. Argenta, MD; and Anthony J. DeFranzo, MD

1. What is vacuum-assisted closure (VAC)?

Vacuum-assisted closure (VAC) is a system that promotes the healing of wounds. VAC is based on the principal that negative pressure applied to the wound will promote an improved environment for wound healing.

The concept of a vacuum was first presented by Evangelista Torriculli in the early seventeenth century. In 1993, Fleischmann described his technique of porous polyvinyl alcohol foam wrapped around suction drains, which was introduced into a wound sealed with a polyurethane drape and attached to a suction apparatus at 600 mm Hg. His description in German presented 15 patients. In 1997, Drs. Louis Argenta and Michael Morykwas presented their experience using the V.A.C. device, which was licensed by Kinetic Concepts of San Antonio, Texas. They presented their experience at Wake Forest University in North Carolina with 175 chronic wounds, 94 subacute wounds, and 31 acute wounds over a 9-year period. In a second paper published at the same time, they presented their animal study experience over the same 9-year period.

2. How is the VAC applied and managed while treating a wound?

VAC requires placement of a sponge material on or into the wound. The sponge is made of reticulated polyurethane ether foam that is cut to fit the wound. An occlusive drape then is placed over the sponge and onto the surrounding skin. An opening is made in the drape, and tubing is fixed to the exposed sponge with an occlusive seal. The suction tube is attached to a collection canister, which is attached to an adjustable vacuum pump (Fig. 7-1).

Foam made of polyvinyl alcohol (white foam) also can be used in VAC. The vacuum pump can be used as continuous or intermittent vacuum using pressures of 75 to 125 mm Hg when using the polyurethane foam and as higher continuous pressures of 125 to 175 mm Hg when using the polyvinyl alcohol foam. The foam dressing is changed every 48 hours. At the time of foam change, other traditional wound healing modalities, such as pulse lavage, can be used. Silver-impregnated foam sponge has been introduced recently to provide a bacteriocidal sponge in patients with colonized wounds.

3. How does the VAC work?

Although clinical and laboratory experience to date has been exhaustive, the exact mechanism explaining why VAC management is so effective in treating wounds is not fully understood. It is evident that suction on the wound results in the following:
1. Removal of interstitial fluid
2. Decrease in bacterial colonization of the wound
3. Increase in wound vascularity

It is also postulated that tissue and cellular deformation creates a steady-state stress on the cell walls, which in turn stimulates growth factor pathways.

4. What have laboratory studies shown?

Morykwas demonstrated in a pig model an increase in blood flow, increased granulation tissue formation, increased bacterial clearance, and increased length of survival in random pattern flaps subjected to negative pressure. He showed an increase in blood flow in both subcutaneous tissue and muscle with a peak blood flow of four times baseline values when 125 mm Hg was applied to the vacuum. The increase in local blood flow declined after 5 to 7 minutes of continuous subatmospheric pressure and finally returned to baseline. With pressures of 400 mm Hg and greater, a fall in blood flow to below that seen in baseline values when applying intermittent subatmospheric pressure was noted (Fig. 7-2). An increase in local blood flow was observed when negative pressure was applied, with a return to baseline when vacuum application was turned off. Wounds treated with VAC were noted to fill with granulation tissue at a significantly increased rate compared with control wounds treated with saline dressing changes. This increase in granulation tissue was noted with continuous suction and was even more significant with intermittent suction.

The V.A.C.™ System

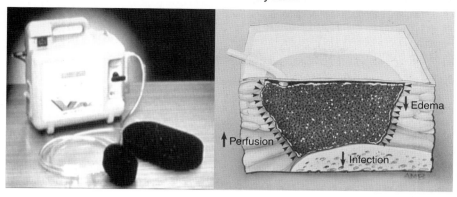

Figure 7-1. The V.A.C. system suction machine and schematic of the sponge filling the dead space of a wound. (From WFUSM Plastic Surgery Collection.)

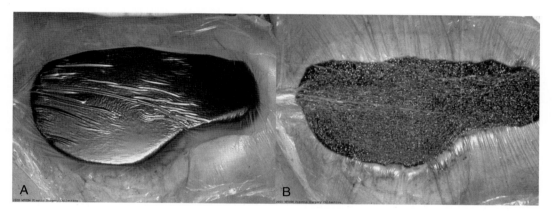

Figure 7-2. A, Foam dressing is cut to fit the wound and the wound sealed with adhesive drape. **B,** When suction is applied the foam dressing collapses into the contours of the wound. (From WFUSM Plastic Surgery Collection.)

Bacterial clearance studies showed a significant drop in organisms per gram of tissue between the fourth and fifth days, with bacterial levels remaining low throughout the duration of VAC treatment. Bacterial levels in the control wounds peaked at day 5 and dropped after a mean of 11 days.

5. What are the indications for use of the VAC?

VAC is indicated in any patient who would benefit from this device, which promotes wound healing. VAC is indicated for chronic open wounds, diabetic ulcers, stasis ulcers, acute and traumatic wounds, and dehisced wounds. It has been shown to be of immense benefit in stabilizing acute skin grafts. It is beneficial in the treatment of venomous bites and extravasation injuries. It is useful in soft tissue decompression in extremities after fasciotomy.

VAC treatment is advantageous compared with traditional dressing changes for a number of reasons. The sponge must be changed every 2 to 3 days compared with traditional dressing, which must be changed daily at a minimum and often two or three times each day. VAC sponges need to be changed only every 2 to 3 days because a closed, moist environment is maintained during the course of vacuum application. The wounds heal more rapidly, resulting in either a more expeditiously healed wound or a shorter time lag between initial injury or débridement and definitive surgical wound closure.

6. What are contraindications to VAC?

The VAC should not be used under several circumstances. It is contraindicated if hemostasis is not adequate. If a wound is bleeding or oozing, the negative pressure may continue removing blood into the collection system. VAC also is not indicated if necrotic or sloughing tissue is present in the wound. The wounds must be surgically débrided prior to application of the sponge, and VAC treatment does not preclude the need for sound surgical principles of adequate débridement and hemostasis. The sponge should not be placed directly over major exposed blood vessels and organs. If vasculature or major organs are exposed, a petroleum-impregnated gauze should be interposed between the vital structure and sponge. If the vital structure is compromised with any question of viability of a vascular wall, VAC treatment probably is not indicated. Instances of exsanguination in situations where the VAC was inappropriately applied to compromised vasculature have been reported. The system should not be used in nonenteric fistulae that are unexplored without knowing what may lie at the base of the fistula.

7. What are the complications of vacuum-assisted therapy?

The skin surrounding the treated wound may develop sensitivity and irritation from the sponge or overlying occlusive drape, yeast infection due to prolonged moisture under or adjacent to the drape may develop, or pressure necrosis of the skin, which is most commonly caused by poorly placed tubing compressed too tightly against the skin, may occur. Hematoma and hemorrhage may occur in wounds with inadequate hemostasis. Wound infection may develop in inadequately débrided wounds. Intermittent débridement, pulse lavage, and standard wound management modalities must be incorporated into the VAC management protocol. Toxic shock when the negative pressure was not maintained has been reported. If the wound fails to respond to VAC management, then other modalities should be instituted. Patients may experience pain. Lowering the suction pressure will often alleviate the pain, but clearly if pain cannot be controlled with analgesia, VAC management may have to be abandoned.

8. What role does the VAC have in the management of chronic nonhealing wounds?

Chronic wounds are those that fail to heal in the orderly phases of inflammation, proliferation, and maturation. Common chronic wounds include pressure ulcers, diabetic ulcers, venous stasis ulcers, vasculitic ulcers, and chronic nonhealing wounds resulting from trauma or dehisced surgical wounds. Systemic reasons such as chronic debilitation, malnourishment, diabetes, and sepsis may be present, but in all cases a local phenomenon inhibits or fails to stimulate the wound healing cascade. The chronic wound develops progressive edema, compromise of perfusion, and protease imbalances. These wounds have elevated levels of proteolytic enzymes and cytokines, which inhibit granulation tissue formation and epithelialization. This unfavorable environment is ideal for bacterial colonization and development of a vicious cycle with inability of the wound to heal.

The fluid that is drawn from the wound by the VAC system is rich in cytokines, acute phase proteins, and proteolytic enzymes, which suggests that inhibiting factors are removed from the wound. As the wound develops increased blood flow resulting from removal of interstitial fluid and a less favorable environment for bacterial proliferation, chronic nonhealing wounds begin to behave more like acute wounds with rapid healing. Wounds that previously were stagnant for weeks, months, and in some instances years usually demonstrate a steady progression to a healed state.

9. What is the role of the VAC in the management of acute wounds?

The VAC provides an ideal wound dressing and can be used either for healing the acute wound or as a bridging and preparatory modality until definitive wound closure is accomplished. The VAC maintains a moist stable wound while minimizing edema formation and maximizing arterial inflow. Prior to application of the VAC the acute wound must be appropriately managed with débridement of nonviable tissues, irrigation, and hemostasis. Because VAC sponges are changed only every 2 to 3 days, patients experience less pain with fewer dressing changes and, in the case of massive wounds where dressings must be changed intraoperatively, operative visits and frequent administrations of anesthesia are minimized.

10. Is the VAC system efficacious in the management of wounds in children?

The VAC device enables earlier coverage with local tissue and skin grafts in children with complex tissue injuries as it does in adult patients. This minimizes the need for microvascular tissue transfers and other local flaps with the attendant donor site scarring and morbidity. Children are more sensitive to the pain and discomfort associated with VAC changes and are more likely to require anesthesia or heavy sedation for VAC changes. Therefore, children are less likely to be good candidates for outpatient VAC. However, the VAC does minimize the need for daily dressing changes and expedites the time from injury to satisfactory wound healing or definitive wound closure.

11. How is the VAC used to treat acute wounds with exposure of bone, tendon, and vital structures?

The VAC is extremely useful for wounds in which bone is exposed, especially when the periosteum is intact. The VAC system promotes granulation tissue, either bridging the time for definitive wound closure or enabling a simpler surgical option such as Integra and a split-thickness skin graft. If healthy tendon is exposed in the wound, a nonadherent dressing beneath the foam may minimize desiccation and trauma to the tendon.

12. How is the VAC used to salvage exposed orthopedic hardware?

If hardware is exposed in the wound, VAC therapy often promotes healthy granulation tissue, enabling secondary wound closure or flap coverage without the need to remove the hardware. Sound surgical principles must be followed, and if loose screws, large plate exposure, or infection is present, hardware must be removed and alternative fixation established.

13. How is the VAC used to manage the open abdominal wound and abdominal compartment syndrome?

If an open abdominal wound is exposed to the fascial level, the VAC system is applied as with any soft tissue wound. If the fascia is open following a fascial dehiscence, care must be taken to avoid injury to the underlying bowel and vital structures.

Exposure of intraabdominal contents will be seen in the abdominal compartment syndrome. Bowel edema due to abdominal trauma from lengthy intraabdominal operations can be significant such that the abdominal wall cannot be closed.

A fenestrated nonstick dressing should be placed over the bowel to act as an interface between bowel and overlying sponges. The VAC will remove intraabdominal fluid, with resolution of bowel edema while aiding skin and fascial approximation. The patient can be returned to the operating room for reexploration as needed. As bowel edema resolves and the defect narrows, the wound will be amenable to secondary closure. If the wound cannot be closed secondarily, for example, following loss of abdominal wall soft tissues in a traumatic injury, usually sufficient granulation tissue will be present on the bowel to enable performance of a temporizing skin graft.

14. What is the role of the VAC in the management of sternal wounds?

Cardiac surgeons have accepted the VAC as an effective method for managing a sternal wound dehiscence. When the vacuum pump draws air from the porous sponge, the sponge collapses, pulling the edges of the sternum toward the midline (Fig. 7-3). This stabilizes the chest wall, minimizing the need for ventilator support in acutely ill patients. Once the wound is adequately débrided, definitive closure of the sternum or defect can be accomplished. Patients with open sternal wounds are at risk for right ventricular rupture as well as leakage of fresh vascular grafts. Care must be taken to interface the heart and overlying sponge with petroleum gauze.

The VAC is efficacious in the management of superficial sternal infections and partial dehiscences. In many instances, appropriate débridement, removal of wires, and VAC management will lead to a healed situation.

15. What is the role of the VAC in extravasation injuries and toxic bites?

We know that the efflux in VAC collecting systems is rich in wound fluids, including cytokines and other wound healing factors. Morykwas showed the efflux to be rich in myoglobin in patients with crush injuries and myoglobinuria. Morykwas also demonstrated that early application of the VAC to a site of doxorubicin injection in a pig model prevented

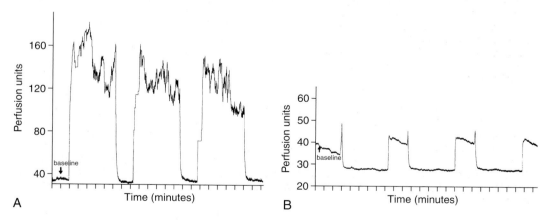

Figure 7-3. A, Recording from laser Doppler needle flow probe placed into subcutaneous tissue at edge of wound. Flow (perfusion units) measured over time (minutes) increased from baseline on cyclical application of 125 mm Hg and returned to baseline during off cycle (5 minutes on, 2 minutes off cycle). **B,** Recording from laser Doppler needle flow probe placed into subcutaneous tissue at edge of wound. Flow (perfusion units) measured over time (minutes) decreased from baseline levels on cyclical application of 400 mm Hg and returned to baseline during off cycle (5 minutes on, 2 minutes off cycle). (Reprinted with permission from Morykwas MJ, Argenta LC, Shelton-Brown EI, McGuirt W: Vacuum-assisted closure: A new method for wound control and treatment: Animal studies and basic foundations. Ann Plast Surg 38:553–562, 1997.)

ulcer formation. It is evident from these experiences that the VAC withdraws fluids from the wound environment. The vacuum system applied to extravasation of toxic medications and venomous bites is an effective means to aspirate toxic materials that remain in the wound environment after débridement. Our group has used this method after extravasation injuries and brown recluse spider bites, with excellent response.

16. How does the VAC benefit patients requiring decompression fasciotomy?

VAC dressings are an ideal way to manage wounds following a decompression fasciotomy. With VAC treatment the edematous muscle and tissue are decompressed rapidly over a period of 2 to 3 days. The interval between fasciotomy and wound closure is lessened. In most instances the fasciotomy wound can be closed secondarily rather than requiring a skin graft for wound coverage, which has been the traditional method for management of fasciotomy wounds treated with daily saline dressing changes.

17. What role can the VAC play in skin grafting?

The VAC is an ideal method with which to stent a skin graft. When the air is withdrawn from the sponge, the firm sponge serves as a stent that holds the graft in place for revascularization. The negative pressure also seems to stimulate more rapid neovascularization, providing a better bed for full-thickness skin grafts, dermal substitutes, and grafts on the diploic layer of bone with little granulation tissue.

18. How is the VAC helpful in managing wounds with artificial dermal substitutes such as Integra?

An advantage of using the VAC in skin grafting is that the sponge conforms to the wound, providing an optimal splint of the underlying skin. This is also true in the case of dermal substitutes such as Integra. Molnar showed both experimentally and clinically that the VAC promotes more rapid vascularization of Integra. Traditionally, Integra is not ready for a secondary skin graft for 2 to 3 weeks, but when managed with the VAC a secondary skin graft can be applied in 1 week or less with 93% skin graft take (Fig. 7-4).

19. How is the VAC used in the management of acute burns?

Morykwas showed in a swine model that the VAC decreases burn wound progression (Figs. 7-5 and 7-6). This is likely due to removal of edema fluid allowing improved blood flow into the burn wound environment. This in turn minimizes tissues in the zone of stasis progressing to the zone of coagulation with resultant tissue necrosis. When applied to hand burns, the VAC results in more rapid reduction of hand edema, allowing improved physical therapy and hand mobility.

20. Can the VAC be placed over a fresh wound closure or fresh flap?

The collapsed VAC sponge does not traumatize a fresh wound closure or a fresh flap. During the first 24 hours after wound closure the wound is not yet sealed, and the VAC is beneficial in drawing serous ooze from between the suture line. It can be applied over a fresh flap and does not result in any compromise to the underlying flap. Indeed, the negative pressure likely enhances blood flow to the distal aspects of the flap.

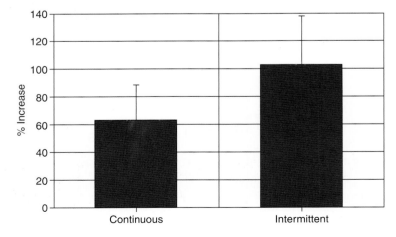

Figure 7-4. Percent increase (mean ± SD) in rate of granulation tissue formation of acute wounds in pigs compared to conventional wet to moist saline gauze dressing changes (control). Both continuous (N = 10) and intermittent (N = 5) application of subatmospheric pressure to the wounds resulted in a significant increase ($P \leq .01$) in the rate of granulation tissue formation. (Reprinted with permission from Morykwas MJ, Argenta LC, Shelton-Brown EI, McGuirt W: Vacuum-assisted closure: A new method for wound control and treatment: Animal studies and basic foundations. Ann Plast Surg 38:553–562, 1997.)

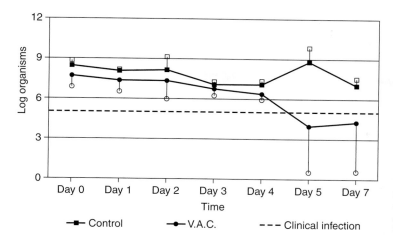

Figure 7-5. Daily quantitative bacterial loads (mean ± SD) (log number of organisms per gram of tissue) of deliberately infected wound tissues. Wounds treated with vacuum-assisted closure (VAC) exhibited a significant decrease in the number of microorganisms after 4 days of treatment (N = 5). (Reprinted with permission from Morykwas MJ, Argenta LC, Shelton-Brown EI, McGuirt W: Vacuum-assisted closure: A new method for wound control and treatment: Animal studies and basic foundations. Ann Plast Surg 38:553–562, 1997.)

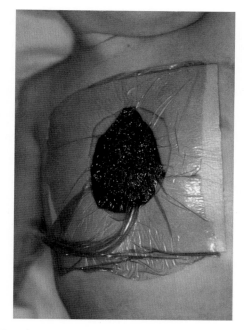

Figure 7-6. Vacuum-assisted closure foam dressing filling a sternal wound. The tubing is attached to the vacuum pump, which is collapsing the foam beneath the occlusive drape. (From WFUSM Plastic Surgery Collection.)

21. Does the VAC require prolonged hospitalization and how is it used in outpatient management?

If the patient's general medical condition lends itself to outpatient care, the patient can be managed with the VAC on an outpatient basis. The Freedom VAC is a small battery-operated vacuum pump that enables the patient to be mobile at home. Nurses who are trained in VAC management only need to visit the home every 2 to 3 days for VAC dressing changes rather than daily or even twice daily for saline dressing changes. This minimizes the need for lengthy hospitalizations of patients who otherwise can be managed at home, with a reduction in the cost of wound management.

22. Is VAC management of a wound cost-effective?

VAC management of a wound has higher costs for the materials, which include the sponges, occlusive drapes, and the vacuum machine, which must be rented per diem. However, because the VAC system promotes more rapid healing, the duration of dressing changes until final wound healing or definitive wound closure is shorter, which more than compensates for the costs of the materials. As physicians, outpatient nurses, and home care specialists become more experienced and adept at managing the VAC, patients are discharged to home VAC treatment, which reduces the need for prolonged inpatient care and these inherent costs.

BIBLIOGRAPHY

Argenta LC, Morykwas MJ: Vacuum-assisted closure: A new method for wound control and treatment: Clinical experience. Ann Plast Surg 38:563–576, 1997.

Banwell P, Teot L: Topical negative pressure (TNP): The evolution of a novel wound therapy. J Wound Care 12:23–26, 2003.

Barker DE, Kaufman HJ, Smith LA, Ciraulo DL, Richart CL, Burns RP: Vacuum pack experience of temporary abdominal closure: A 7-year experience with 112 patients. J Trauma 48:201–206, 2000.

DeFranzo AJ, Argenta LC, Marks MW, et al: The use of vacuum-assisted closure therapy for the treatment of lower extremity wounds with exposed bone. Plast Reconstr Surg 108:1184–1191, 2001.

Fleischmann W, Becker U, Bischoff M, Hoekstra H: Vacuum sealing: Indication technique and results. Eur J Orthop Surg Trauma 5:37–40, 1995.

Joseph E, Hamori CA, Bergman S, et al: A prospective randomized trial of vacuum-assisted closure versus standard therapy of chronic non healing wounds. Wounds 12:60–67, 2000.

Molnar JA, DeFranzo AJ, Hadaegh A, et al: Acceleration of Integra incorporation in complex tissue defects with subatmospheric pressure. Plast Reconstr Surg 113:1339–1346, 2004.

Mooney JF 3rd, Argenta LC, Marks MW, et al: Treatment of soft tissue defects in pediatric patients using V.A.C. system. Clin Orthop Relat Res 376:26–31, 2000.

Morykwas MJ, Argenta LC, Shelton-Brown EI, McGuirt W: Vacuum-assisted closure: A new method for wound control and treatment: Animal studies and basic foundations. Ann Plast Surg 38:553–562, 1997.

Morykwas MJ, David LR, Schneider AM, et al: Use of sub-atmospheric pressure to prevent progression of partial thickness burns in a swine model. J Burn Care Rehabil 20(1 Pt 1):15–21, 1999.

Morykwas MJ, Kennedy AC, Argenta JP, Argenta LC: Use of sub-atmospheric pressure to prevent doxorubicin extravasation ulcers in a swine model. J Surg Oncol 72:14–17, 1999.

Scherer LA, Shiver S, Chang M, et al: The vacuum assisted closure device: A method of securing skin grafts and improving graft survival. Arch Surg 137:8, 930–933, 2002.

Skagen K, Henriksen O: Changes in subcutaneous blood flow during locally applied negative pressure to the skin. Acta Physiol Scand 117:3, 411–414, 1983.

Tang AT, Okri SK, Haw MP: Vacuum-assisted closure to treat deep sternal wound infection following cardiac surgery. J Wound Care 9:229–230, 2000.

THE FETAL WOUND

Jeffrey Weinzweig, MD, FACS; Jeffrey V. Manchio, MD; Christopher Khorsandi, MD;
Eric J. Stelnicki, MD; and Michael T. Longaker, MD, MBA, FACS

CHAPTER 8

1. What is the major phenotypic difference that distinguishes fetal from adult wound healing?

Adult cutaneous wound healing involves the process of scar formation. However, fetal cutaneous wound healing is scarless, appearing more like tissue regeneration than wound repair.

2. How was scarless fetal wound healing discovered?

Scarless fetal wound healing was originally described by Rowlatt in 1979 following his observations of wounds sustained in utero. Later, in the early 1980s, Harrison and his team of pediatric surgeons at the University of California San Francisco made the observation that patients who underwent fetal surgery healed without scar. This second observation sparked the interest of a multitude of scientists around the world and led to a deeper investigation into the process of fetal wound healing.

3. What surgical approaches are used to access the fetus?

The open approach involves performing surgery in a manner very similar to a cesarean section. A hysterotomy is made and the fetus is exposed. At the conclusion of the procedure the fetus is returned to the uterus and the hysterotomy is repaired. The ultimate delivery requires a formal cesarean section. More recently, minimal fetal access surgery, also known as *fetoscopy* or *FETENDO,* has developed into a viable alternative for a number of fetal procedures. Endoscopes as small as 1 mm have been developed to assist in these procedures. Trocars often can be inserted directly through the abdominal wall and uterus percutaneously with ultrasound guidance to assist in locating a safe area of the uterus through which to enter. Depending on the position of the uterus, a minilaparotomy may be needed to access a safe portion of the uterus. Transuteral fetal fixation with fixation sutures is often used to position the fetus in the ideal position within the amniotic cavity.

4. What potential complication is considered the major limiting factor to fetal surgery, and what is done to attempt to prevent it?

Preterm labor is considered the greatest limiting factor when performing fetal surgery. To reduce the likelihood of inducing preterm labor, indomethacin frequently is given to the mother preoperatively. Several inhalational agents may be used to maintain uterine relaxation. Intravenous agents such as nitroglycerine, magnesium, and terbutaline also may help reduce uterine tone. Agents used to achieve uterine relaxation must be balanced against maternal hypotension to avoid decreasing placental perfusion.

5. Does the process of fetal wound healing follow the same patterns as adult wound healing?

No. Adult wound repair is characterized by five stages: hemostasis, inflammation, proliferation, early remodeling, and late remodeling. The first three stages take several weeks to be completed, and the final remodeling stages may last for months to years. In contrast, the scarless fetal wound repair process occurs at an accelerated rate, with restoration of normal tissue architecture within 5 to 7 days after injury. The acute inflammatory stage of healing is absent.

6. Is the ability of the fetus to heal without scar purely a function of being in the womb, bathed by amnionic fluid?

No. Three experiments prove that such is not the case. First, fetal marsupials, which move outside the womb and develop in a maternal pouch, heal without scar. Second, human fetal skin transplanted onto the backs of adult mice with severe combined immunodeficiency regenerates. Neither of these cutaneous tissues is in contact with amnionic fluid during or after the time of wounding, indicating that the process is intrinsic to the fetal cells. Finally, a study in which adult sheep skin was transplanted onto fetal lambs at a point during gestation when scarless repair normally would occur instead healed with scar and fibrosis indistinguishable from adult wound healing.

7. Is there a time limit to the process of fetal cutaneous wound healing?

Yes. The fetus is able to heal its wounds without scar only up to the early third trimester of gestation. After this point, cutaneous wounds develop an increasing amount of scar.

8. Do all fetal cutaneous wounds heal without scar?

No. Excisional wounds greater than 9 mm contract and heal with scar at all gestational ages. However, during the second trimester, excisional wounds less than 9 cm in size will heal scarlessly. From the beginning of the second trimester and onward, the size limit for scarless healing is inversely proportional to gestational age. This period, termed the *transition phase*, continues until the third trimester when the ability to heal scarlessly is completely lost for even the smallest wounds.

9. How do the inflammatory cell mediators differ in fetal and adult wound healing?

The relative number of cells and the functional state of the individual cells differ in fetal wounds. Fewer neutrophils are present during the early fetal wound healing period in comparison to the adult wound, with fetal neutrophils possessing a diminished ability to phagocytize bacteria. Similarly, platelet aggregatory affinity to collagen is lower in the early fetal period, and a developmental ontogeny is evident with a transition to mature platelet aggregatory ability in the third trimester. The function of fetal macrophages has yet to be fully elucidated, but they may demonstrate a similar developmental change that further contributes to the loss of scarless wound healing capability in the third trimester.

10. What effect does inflammation have on the fetal wound?

The induction of inflammation in fetal cutaneous wounds induces adult-like scar formation. Part of the observed effect of inflammation is the increased number of neutrophils and macrophages and the increased collagen deposition in the wound. The same effect is seen regardless of the type of inflammatory stimulus, indicating that inflammatory cells somehow alter the function of the fetal fibroblast and make it respond in a more adult-like manner.

11. How does collagen synthesis differ within the fetal wound?

Fetal collagen synthesis occurs at an accelerated rate with apparently little to no excess deposition. The fetal wound is repaired primarily by the rapid and highly organized deposition of type III collagen. The ratio of type III to type I collagen is 3:1. In contrast, the adult wound type III collagen is laid down early in the healing process but is replaced primarily by type I collagen. At the end of adult wound remodeling, the ratio of type III to type I collagen is 1:3, the opposite of the fetal wound.

12. What are the differences between fetal fibroblasts and adult fibroblasts?

Fetal fibroblasts have been shown to have greater migratory ability. This may be due, in part, to a greater number of hyaluronic acid (HA) receptors on fetal fibroblasts. Fetal fibroblasts synthesize more type III and type IV collagen than do their adult counterparts. Additionally, fetal fibroblasts have no delay in collagen synthesis during the proliferation phase, as is the case in the adult wound.

13. What is the role of the extracellular matrix in fetal wound healing?

Several features of the extracellular matrix (ECM) characterize the fetal wound healing process. First, HA is abundant in the fetal wound, and it is produced 2 weeks longer than in adults. The abundance of HA is thought to aid in fibroblast movement, to promote cellular proliferation, and to inhibit cellular differentiation. Second, fibronectin is deposited faster in fetal wounds (4 hours vs 12 hours in adult wounds), rapidly providing a good scaffolding for epithelial cell migration. Finally, sulfated glycosaminoglycans (GAGs), such as decorin and heparin sulfate, are expressed at low levels in fetal wounds but increase with gestational age. This increase correlates with the development of scar formation after cutaneous wounding. It is thought that GAGs may play a role in the induction of cytodifferentiation.

14. How may HA provide the matrix signal that coordinates healing by regeneration rather than by scarring?

HA is a key structural and functional component of the ECM in instances of rapid tissue proliferation, regeneration, and repair. HA is laid down early in the matrix of both fetal and adult wounds; however, sustained deposition of HA ensues in the fetal wound. Although the mechanism for prolonged HA deposition in fetal wounds remains unclear, the presence of HA–protein complexes in the fetal matrix may provide the signal responsible for promoting healing by regeneration rather than by scarring.

15. Do all fetal tissues heal scarlessly?

No. To date, fetal skin, bone, and palatal mucoperiosteum are the only elements of the mammalian fetus that appear to be able to regenerate after wounding. Studies of tendon, diaphragm, nerve, and gastrointestinal tract have shown scar formation in response to wounding in both fetuses and adults.

16. Do fetal wounds heal differently in congenital models versus surgically created models?

No. Models of dilantin-induced cleft lip in mice and anabasine-induced cleft palate in goats heal in the same manner as analogous surgically created models in both species—scarlessly. However, attributes characteristic of a congenital model, such as inherent facial dysmorphology yielding impaired midfacial growth in the congenital caprine cleft palate model, will not be seen in surgically created models.

17. Does amniotic fluid play a role in wound contraction?

Yes. Both fetal and adult fibroblast contraction are inhibited by human amniotic fluid. This effect progressively decreases with increasing wound size and advancing fetal age.

18. Is the lack of wound contracture in the fetus due to lack of myofibroblasts in the skin?

No. Multiple studies using immunohistochemistry and transmission electron microscopy have demonstrated the presence of myofibroblasts in the fetal wound. However, the mere presence of these cells does not correlate with the ability to form a scar contracture. Studies have demonstrated that, in the fetal wound, myofibroblasts appear earlier after wounding than in the adult wound and, in contrast to adult wounds, disappear completely as healing progresses.

19. Can adult skin placed into a fetal environment heal without scar?

No. Adult skin wounds always heal with scar regardless of their location. Experimental work in a fetal lamb model, in which adult maternal skin was placed as a graft within a fetal cutaneous defect, demonstrated healing by scar formation consistent with typical adult wound healing.

20. How do growth factor profiles differ between fetal and adult wounds?

The fetal wound is characterized by a decrease in the activity of various growth factors, including transforming growth factor beta-1 and beta-2 (TGF-β1 and TGF-β2), platelet-derived growth factor (PDGF), and basic fibroblast growth factor (bFGF), compared with adult wounds. When activated in the fetus, these growth factors are expressed rapidly and for a short time. Experiments have shown that addition of exogenous TGF-β1 and TGF-β2 to the fetal wound induces scar formation, whereas inhibition of TGF-β1 and TGF-β2 through the use of neutralizing antibodies reduces cutaneous scarring in adult rats. This may explain why the presence of growth factor–secreting inflammatory cells in the fetal wound affects fibroblast function such that scar formation results. Another recent observation is that the proportion of growth factor isoforms and not the absolute amount of any single growth factor may alter scar formation. For example, TGF-β3 expression has been noted to be relatively increased in relation to TGF-β1 in the fetal wound, whereas the inverse is true in adult scarring wound: TGF-β1 is increased and TGF-β3 is decreased.

21. What is the role of cyclooxygenase-2 and prostaglandin E$_2$ in fetal wound healing?

The cyclooxygenase-2 (COX-2) pathway and its enzymatic product prostaglandin E$_2$ (PGE$_2$) are known to be critical mediators of the inflammatory response. Studies have demonstrated elevated levels of COX-2 and PGE$_2$ in wounded adult skin compared with normal adult skin. It has been demonstrated that COX-2 expression levels become higher in fetal fibroblasts as gestational age increases. Additionally, fetal wounds created later in gestation have been found to contain higher levels of PGE$_2$. A normally scarless fetal wound healing model has been shown to heal with scar when injected with PGE$_2$. This collection of findings strongly implicates differences in the level of COX-2 expression as a factor in scarless fetal wound healing.

22. How do the levels of the growth factors, interleukins, collagen, ECM modulators, and cell types involved in wound healing differ between fetal and adult wounds?

See Table 8-1.

CONTROVERSIES

23. What regulates the process of fetal wound healing?

Current theories range from growth factor regulation to the coordinated expression of deoxyribonucleic acid (DNA)-binding proteins such as homeobox genes. Whatever the mechanism, it probably involves the process of decreased inflammation and regulation of increased fibroblast and epidermal proliferation.

24. What is the potential advantage of scarless fetal wound healing in the treatment of congenital craniofacial anomalies?

Scarless healing in utero may minimize or prevent facial dysmorphology associated with anomalies such as cleft lip and palate. Maxillary hypoplasia, with resultant midface retrusion and relative prognathism, is often the result of surgically induced scar formation after repair of cleft lip and/or palate. Increased lip pressure after postnatal repair of cleft lip in animals is also associated with progressive midface hypoplasia. Thus, the major advantage of scarless fetal wound healing is unimpaired facial growth without the adverse effect of the lip and/or palate scar.

25. Can scarless healing after in utero repair of cleft lip and palate completely eliminate the facial growth abnormality associated with postnatal, surgically induced scar formation?

Not likely. An intrinsic factor contributes to facial growth impairment in repaired as well as unrepaired congenital clefts. The incidence of this factor is unpredictable and variably expressed. This intrinsic component of facial dysmorphology is unrelated to scar formation and, thus, is largely unaffected by the nature of the healing process. However, the presence of scar may adversely affect the expression of this intrinsic factor, resulting in a greater degree of facial growth impairment.

Table 8-1. Elements Involved in Wound Healing

ELEMENTS	FETAL: ADULT LEVELS
Growth Factors	
TGF-β1	↓
TGF-β2	↓
TGF-β3	↑
PDGF	↓
FGF	↓
VEGF	↑
Interleukins	
IL-6	↓
IL-8	↓
IL-10	↑
Collagen	
Type I	↓
Type III	↑
Type IV	↑
ECM Modulators	
HA	↑
Decorin	↓
Lysyl oxidase	↓
MMP	↓
Fibromodulin	↑
Cells	
Platelets	↓
Neutrophils	↓
Myofibroblasts	↓

ECM, Extracellular matrix; *FGF,* fibroblast growth factor; *HA,* hyaluronic acid; *IL,* interleukin; *MMP,* matrix metalloproteinase; *PDGF,* platelet-derived growth factor; *TGF,* transforming growth factor; *VEGF,* vascular endothelial growth factor.

BIBLIOGRAPHY

Adzick NS, Harrison MR, Glick PL, et al: Comparison of fetal, newborn, and adult wound healing by histologic, enzyme-histochemical, and hydroxyproline determinations. J Pediatr Surg 20:315–319, 1985.

Adzick NS, Lorenz HP: Cells, matrix, growth factors, and the surgeon. The biology of scarless fetal wound repair. Ann Surg 220:10–18, 1994.

Beanes SR, Dang C, Soo C, et al: Downregulation of decorin, a transforming growth factor-beta modulator, is associated with scarless fetal wound healing. J Pediatr Surg 11:1666–1671, 2001.

Cass DL, Bullard KM, Sylvester KG, Yang EY, Longaker MT, Adzick NS: Wound size and gestational age modulate scar formation in fetal wound repair. J Pediatr Surg 32:411–415, 1997.

Cass DL, Sylvester KG, Yang EY, et al: Myofibroblasts association with scar formation and their absence in scarless fetal wound repair. J Pediatr Surg 32:1017–1021, 1997.

Colwell AS, Longaker MT, Lorenz HP: Fetal wound healing. Front Biosci 8:1240–1248, 2003.

Danzer E, Sydorak RM, Harrison MR: Minimal access fetal surgery. Eur J Obstet Gynecol Reprod Biol 108:3–13, 2003.

Ferguson MWJ, Howarth GF: Marsupial models of scarless fetal wound healing. In Adzick NS, Longaker MT (eds): Fetal Wound Healing. New York, Elsevier Scientific Press, 1992, pp 95–124.

Hallock GG: In utero cleft lip repair in A/J mice. Plast Reconstr Surg 75:785–790, 1985.

Harrison MR: Surgically correctable fetal disease. Am J Surg 180:335–342, 2000.

Howarth G, Ferguson MWJ: Marsupial models of scarless fetal wound healing. In Adzick NS, Longaker MT (eds): Fetal Wound Healing. New York, Elsevier Science, 1992, pp 95–124.

Leibovich SJ, Ross R: The role of the macrophage in wound repair: A study with hydrocortisone and antimacrophage serum. Am J Pathol 78:71–100, 1975.

Longaker MT, Adzick NS: The biology of fetal wound healing: A review. Plast Reconstr Surg 87:788–798, 1991.

Longaker MT, Whitby DJ, Ferguson MW, Lorenz HP, Harrison MR, Adzick NS: Adult skin wounds in the fetal environment heal with scar formation. Ann Surg 219:65–72, 1994.

Longaker MT, Burd DA, Gown AM, et al: Midgestational excisional fetal lamb wounds contract in utero. J Pediatr Surg 26:942–947, 1991; discussion, 947–948.

Longaker MT, Whitby DJ, Ferguson MW, Lorenz HP, Harrison MR, Adzick NS: Adult skin wounds in the fetal environment heal with scar formation. Ann Surg 219:65–72, 1994.

Longaker MT, Whitby DJ, Jennings RW, et al: Fetal diaphragmatic wounds heal with scar formation. J Surg Res 50:375–385, 1991.

Lorenz HP, Lin RY, Longaker MT, Whitby DJ, Adzick NS: The fetal fibroblast: The effector cell of scarless fetal skin repair. Plast Reconstr Surg 96:1251–1259, 1995; discussion, 1260–1261.

Lorenz HP, Longaker MT, Perkocha LA, Jennings RW, Harrison MR, Adzick NS: Scarless wound repair: A human fetal skin model. Development 114:253–259, 1994.

Martin P, Nobes C, McCluskey J, Lewis J: Repair of excisional wounds in the embryo. Eye 8:155–160, 1994.

Mast BA, Krummel TM: Acute inflammation in fetal wound healing. In Adzick NS, Longaker MT (eds): Fetal Wound Healing. New York, Elsevier Science, 1992, pp 227–240.

Meuli M, Lorenz HP, Hedrick MH, Sullivan KM, Harrison MR, Adzick NS: Scar formation in the fetal alimentary tract. J Pediatr Surg 30: 392–395, 1995.

Nath RK, LaRegina M, Markham H, Ksander GA, Weeks PM: The expression of transforming growth factor type beta in fetal and adult rabbit skin wounds. J Pediatr Surg 29:416–421, 1994.

Parekh A, Sandulache VC, Lieb AS, Dohar JE, Hebda PA: Differential regulation of free-floating collagen gel contraction by human fetal and adult dermal fibroblasts in response to prostaglandin E2 mediated by an EP2/cAMP-dependent mechanism. Wound Rep Reg 15:390–398, 2007.

Rowlatt U: Intrauterine wound healing in a 20 week human fetus. Virchows Arch A Pathol Anat Histol 381:353–361, 1979.

Shah M, Foreman DM, Ferguson MW: Neutralizing antibody to TGF-β1 and TGF-β2 or exogenous addition of TGF-β3 to cutaneous rat wounds reduces scarring. J Cell Sci 108:985–1002, 1995.

Siebert J, Burd A, McCarthy JG, Weinzweig J, Ehrlich P: Fetal wound healing: A biochemical study of scarless healing. Plast Reconstr Surg 85:495–502, 1990; discussion, 503–504.

Stelnicki EJ, Arbeit J, Cass DL, Saner C, Harrison M, Largman C: Modulation of the human homeobox genes PRX-2 and HOXB13 in scarless fetal wounds. J Invest Dermatol 111:57–63, 1998.

Sullivan WG: In utero cleft lip repair in the mouse with an incision. Plast Reconstr Surg 84:723–730, 1989.

Weinzweig J, Panter KE, Pantaloni M, et al: The fetal cleft palate: I. Characterization of a congenital model, Plast Reconstr Surg 103: 419–428, 1999.

Weinzweig J, Panter KE, Pantaloni M, et al: The fetal cleft palate: II. Scarless healing following in utero repair of a congenital model. Plast Reconstr Surg 104:1356–1364, 1999.

Weinzweig J, Panter KE, Spangenberger A, Harper JS, McRae R, Edstrom LE: The fetal cleft palate: III. A histomorphologic study of palatal development and function following in utero repair of a congenital model, Plast Reconstr Surg 109:2355–2362, 2002.

Weinzweig J, Panter K, Seki J, Pantaloni M, Spangenberger A, Harper J: The fetal cleft palate: IV. Midfacial growth and bony palatal development following in utero and neonatal repair of the congenital caprine model, Plast Reconstr Surg 118:81–94, 2006.

Weinzweig J, Panter K, Patel J, Smith D, Spangenberger A, Freeman MB: The fetal cleft palate: V. Elucidation of the mechanism of palatal clefting in the congenital caprine model. Plast Reconstr Surg 121:1328–1334, 2008.

Wilgus TA, Bergdall VK, Tober KL, et al: The impact of cyclooxygenase-2 mediated inflammation on scarless fetal wound healing. Am J Pathol 165:753–761, 2004.

Yang GP, Lim IJ, Phan T, Lorenz PH, Longaker MT: From scarless fetal wounds to keloids: Molecular studies in wound healing. Wound Rep Reg 11:411–418, 2003.

LIABILITY ISSUES IN PLASTIC SURGERY

Mark Gorney, MD, FACS

1. What makes plastic surgeons such frequent targets for malpractice lawsuits?

It is a combination of factors:

- If your practice is primarily aesthetic surgery, you are not trying to make sick patients well. You are making well patients temporarily "unwell" to make them better, clearly a heavy responsibility.
- The result of our treatment, unlike that of any other physician's, is always in the eye of the beholder; there are no exact parameters.
- Except for psychiatrists, plastic surgeons face a greater variety of hidden patient agendas and psychological barriers affecting the evaluation of the "final product" than any other physician in practice.
- Like it or not, plastic surgeons are physicians not only of flesh and blood but, in a manner of speaking, also of the soul. Our best results can have explosively positive effects and improve the quality of life for the patient, whereas unfavorable results can destroy it, sometimes forever.

2. Can you enumerate those qualities that make one doctor less prone to lawsuit than others?

I can identify at least five:

1. Competence
2. The ability to communicate clearly, which includes careful listening
3. The wisdom to select patients who are appropriate to the procedure they seek and the courage to reject those who are not good candidates
4. The pursuit of valid informed disclosure and accurate documentation in well-kept records
5. An engaging personality

3. Can you expound on what constitutes "competence"?

Three dimensions are important: (1) knowledge and training, (2) natural manual dexterity, and (3) imagination plus flexibility of the brain. Any person who possesses a valid certificate from the American Board of Plastic Surgeons (ABPS) is presumed to have sufficient knowledge and training. Manual dexterity is important for obvious reasons. Imagination and flexibility of the mind, however, gives one a wider range of possibilities and keeps one out of trouble. In other words, if Plan A fails, how quickly can you come up with Plan B? Further, as Luis Vasconez would advise, if Plan A fails, Plan B should not be the same as Plan A.

4. What about "communication"? That covers a lot of ground, doesn't it?

Although many factors enter into the creation of that ephemeral state called "rapport," none is more critical than being able to deliver information clearly and to verify that it has been understood. Remember that you are often talking to a patient who may be maximally distracted by preoperative apprehension or postoperative narcosis. Sometimes communication is impaired by concern or anger at what the patient perceives has happened. It is necessary to maintain a constant demeanor of confident calm and caring, no matter how badly your colon is constricting at the sight of a purple areola. It has been repeatedly noted by your most successful peers that patients who actually feel your touch (within the strictest ethical limitations) will never refer to you later as "cold" or "arrogant." Remember that lawsuits are seldom filed against friends or someone you like.

5. Can you explain the rules of the game in "patient selection"?

A normal temperature and a valid credit card, per se, are totally inadequate criteria for accepting a patient seeking aesthetic surgery. Figure 9-1 gives the breakdown in percentage distribution of all claims at The Doctors Company against plastic and reconstructive surgeons. The pie graph shows the distribution by procedures for the year 2005. Remember that this graphic represents more than 80% of claims of any sort filed against our membership, all deriving from aesthetic operations. All statistics represent only ABPS-certified surgeons. The heavy majority involve surgery of the breast. There is little disagreement between plastic surgeons and psychiatrists that patients exhibiting signs of inappropriate motivation are inevitably poor candidates for aesthetic surgery. Unfortunately for us, these patients seldom walk into the examination room with a label on their lapel. Before you say "yes," take the trouble to investigate whether the problem lies in the anatomic part complained about or inside their head. You must listen "between the lines," read body language, and follow what your gut is telling you. Also *listen* to the comments of the people at the outside desk.

6. Are there any reliable signs by which one can identify potentially problematic patients?
There are three categories of questionable surgical candidates:

1. Anatomic unsuitability
2. Questionable motivation
3. Psychological inadequacy

The first of these should be obvious and need no discussion. No matter how adroit you may be, you cannot make a Dior gown out of sack cloth. The second can be established but needs some probing. Find out why the patient is *really* there. The third is the one that carries the riskiest prospect for the unaware surgeon and one that should be considered carefully *before* deciding whether or not to proceed.

Many years ago we decided to put this into practical application. Although in our discipline there are no Ouija boards, Figure 9-2 shows a chart that I and many other colleagues have found extremely useful. In classifying prospective patients, it helps to contrast the patient's complaint through the surgeon's eyes along the horizontal axis versus the degree of concern, as expressed by the patient, along the vertical axis. Two obvious extremes emerge. The patient with a significant problem but little concern is indicated in the lower right corner, and the patient with a minimal deformity but disproportionate concern is shown in the upper left. You can virtually depend on the probability that the patient on the lower right will regard any degree of improvement with satisfaction, whereas the one in the contralateral upper corner likely will never be satisfied no matter what you do. The reason is simple. This patient probably is manifesting unexpressed, inner turmoil by focusing on a minor imperfection. In its serious manifestation it is called *body dysmorphic syndrome*. He or she is far better served by a psychiatrist's couch than a surgeon's table. Most of your patients will fall along the diagonal axis. The closer they are to the upper left corner, the less you should consider operating. The more they tend to the lower right corner, the likelier you are to emerge with a happy patient. In our office, within the patients' charts a checkered diagram is found on the inside of the back cover of the record with the check mark of my initial impression at first consultation. Then if the patient who is "shopping" calls back, we know immediately whether to make an appointment or find an excuse. Whatever you decide, I strongly urge that you not be swayed by the prospect of a substantial fee or your weak ego. If you err, or an act of God ensues, I can guarantee you that the final price you will eventually pay will be far costlier than forfeited income. Your heaviest cost will be experienced through personal stress-induced consequences you never imagined possible.

7. One hears so much about the importance of "informed consent." What does that mean, and how different is that from plain vanilla consent?
The short answer is that it may be quite simply the difference between winning or losing a malpractice lawsuit if a dispute involves adequate disclosure. A plain consent, the sort they use in hospitals or surgi-centers (and, unfortunately,

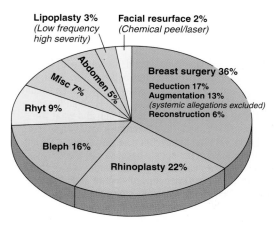

Figure 9-1. Universe of aesthetic claims. *Bleph*, Blepharoplasty; *Rhyt*, rhytidectomy.

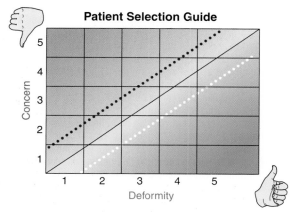

Figure 9-2. Patient selection guide.

by some of our more cavalier colleagues), is invariably a nonspecific, boiler-plate document that seldom refers to the specific procedure to be done. It is an attempt at obtaining sweeping absolution from just about anything and almost never refers to the event in question. It can easily be made irrelevant by plaintiffs' attorneys. Plastic surgeons must adhere to a much more specific and tighter format. You have an "affirmative duty." You are *required* to disclose the most common risks and the appropriate information that applies; not wait until the patient asks. This type of informed consent does not have to include an orgy of mindless disclosure that will scare the patients out of scheduling a desired surgery. However, in medical situations, patients *must* be given sufficient information to make an intelligent decision. The U.S. Supreme Court, long ago, established that it is the patient's prerogative, not the physician's, to decide where his or her best interests lie.

Figure 9-3 shows a typical consent format that will differ for each type of procedure. It is unique in that every item requires the patient's initials next to it. At the bottom, both patient or guardian and doctor sign a confirmation statement. A copy then goes into the office record, a second one with the patient preoperatively to take home, and a third one into the hospital record if needed. In our experience, when this format was used, not a single claim of inadequate disclosure succeeded. Also, it tends to discourage plaintiffs' attorneys from taking such cases. Please understand that no permit is guaranteed to protect you without exception, regardless of how elaborate, but this format comes as close as any.

You can tailor this form according to the way you do the procedure, or you can request copies of The Doctors Company's informed consent form whether or not you are an insured member. Just remember one thing: Information delivered and documented *before* the event is valid consent. Information delivered *after* the fact is a lame excuse.

8. Just how much and what sort of information is needed to fully qualify the consent as "informed"?

The extent of disclosure varies with the condition being treated. In situations in which the contemplated procedure is purely elective, as in aesthetic operations, the range of disclosure may have to expand. It should include a description of the proposed procedure (in layman's terms), reasonable risks, possibility of untoward consequence, possibility of side effects, degree of anticipated discomfort, anticipated range of improvement, time required for complete healing and disappearance of inflammatory effects, degree and length of social disability, and so on according to your own criteria and estimation of the patient's hunger for information. By sharing the uncertainty of clinical practice, this exercise can actually draw the patient and doctor closer together instead of creating two adversaries confronting each other.

9. Can you specify how a surgeon's personality and attitude are factors in malpractice claims?

Certain personal characteristics that are in common among claims-free surgeons help them avoid lawsuits. First, and foremost, is a warm, engaging personality. Obviously, someone who has a sensitive, caring attitude, a cordial demeanor, and a sense of humor will be a less likely target for claims than someone whose demeanor comes across as reserved, distant, and/or arrogant. The ability to communicate well and listen carefully, about which we have already spoken, is an attribute commonly seen in the claims-free surgeon.

10. What can be done to prevent things going from bad to worse?

Once the rapport is damaged, you must put yourself in the patient's head. That patient feels a sense of helplessness and frustration that may quickly convert to uncertainty and then, inevitably, to anger if you do not intervene. "If this is the doctor's fault," the thinking goes, "then the responsibility for fixing it falls on the doctor." Whether or not this perception conflicts with actual facts is another story. This is the time when you should intervene with visible concern, not self-flagellating guilt. Unquestionably, this may clash with your own anxieties and ego loss. You have to put aside your understandable reactions and do what you can to arrest the progress of what will otherwise become a progressive chain of events leading to the lawyer's doorstep. Once misfortune strikes and things begin turning sour, you must do your utmost to make that patient understand what happened, why it happened, and what you plan to do and what you can do to help. Resist the tendency to avoid the patient. To the contrary, insist on seeing him or her regularly. The phone is one of your best friends here. Talk with the family. Get a second opinion. Do not let the patient get billed. Do this, *not* with the aura of being afraid of a claim but openly because you stand by your patients in their uncertainty and anxiety and simply because it is the right thing to do. The conversion catalyst in a crumbling doctor–patient relationship is fear of the unknown. This, plus a few spoonfuls of elixir of abandonment, is the perfect prescription for a call to the lawyer. You can prevent this if you successfully convey to the patient that you understand the dynamics of uncertainty and will join him or her to help to overcome it. If you do that in a timely fashion, you may just have pulled the right lever and it might be the deciding factor as to whether or not that call to the attorney is made.

REDUCTION MAMMOPLASTY
(Breast Reduction)

Breast reduction is usually performed to relieve back, neck, and shoulder pain, and skin irritation that women with large breasts sometimes experience, rather than to enhance the appearance of the breast. The best candidates for this procedure are those who are mature enough to understand and have realistic expectations about the results.

Patient's
Initials

_____ The details of the procedure have been explained to me in terms I understand.

_____ Alternative methods and their benefits and disadvantages have been explained to me.

_____ I understand and accept possible risks and complications include but are not limited to:

- *asymmetry*
- *bleeding*
- *change in nipple and skin sensation*
- *delayed healing*
- *different size than expected*
- *discoloration/swelling*
- *discomfort (pain/sensitivity)*

- *failure to improve symptoms*
- *infection*
- *nipple retraction/poor contour*
- *restricted activity*
- *skin, nipple, flap loss*
- *unsatisfactory results*
- *wound separation*

_____ I understand and accept that there are complications, including the remote risk of death or serious disability, that exist with any surgical procedure.

_____ I understand and accept the risks of blood transfusion(s) that may be necessary.

_____ I understand that tissue cannot heal without scarring and that how one scars is dependent on individual genetic characteristics. The physician will do his/her best to minimize scarring but cannot control its ultimate appearance.

_____ I am aware that smoking during the pre-and postoperative periods could increase chances of complications.

_____ I have informed the doctor of all my known allergies.

_____ I have informed the doctor of all medications I am currently taking, including prescriptions, over-the-counter remedies, herbal therapies and supplements, aspirin, and any other recreational drug or alcohol use.

_____ I have been advised whether I should avoid taking any or all of these medications on the days surrounding the procedure.

_____ I am aware and accept that no guarantees about the results of the procedure have been made.

_____ I have been informed of what to expect postoperatively, including but not limited to: estimated recovery time, anticipated activity level, and the possibility of additional procedures.

_____ I understand that any tissue/specimen removed during the surgery may be sent to pathology for evaluation.

_____ The doctor has answered all of my questions regarding this procedure.

I certify that I have read and understand this treatment agreement and that all blanks were filled in prior to my signature.

I authorize and direct _____, M.D., with associates or assistants of his or her choice, to perform breast reduction mammoplasty on _____.

(patient name)

☐ **right breast**   ☐ **left breast**

continued

3/03
Revised 9/05, 12/05, 1/06

This form is for reference purposes only. It is a general guideline and not a statement of standard of care and should be edited and amended to reflect policy requirements of your practice site(s) and legal requirements of your individual state(s).

Figure 9-3. Informed consent form.

I further authorize the physician(s) and assistants to do any other procedure that in their judgment may be necessary or advisable should unforeseen circumstances arise during the procedure.

_____
Patient or Legal Representative Signature/Date

_____
Relationship to Patient

_____
Print Patient or Legal Representative Name

_____
Witness Signature/Date

I certify that I have explained the nature, purpose, benefits, risks, complications, and alternatives to the proposed procedure to the patient or the patient's legal representative. I have answered all questions fully, and I believe that the _patient/legal representative_ (circle one) fully understands what I have explained.

_____
Physician Signature/Date

_____copy given to patient
initial

_____original placed in chart
initial

3/03
Revised 9/05, 12/05, 1/06

This form is for reference purposes only. It is a general guideline and not a statement of standard of care and should be edited and amended to reflect policy requirements of your practice site(s) and legal requirements of your individual state(s).

Figure 9-3.—cont'd.

11. If you were offering claims avoidance "pearls" to surgeons new to practice, what would they be?

These "pearls" are as follows:

1. If you like to use imaging devices, or if you advertise, be very careful what you promise. You may regret it. You have *no* idea how that enticing image you put on the screen converts into a firm image in the patient's brain. If you can translate the image on the screen into reality 100% of the time you deserve the Nobel prize. Some attorneys are beginning to file lawsuits for breach of warranty when the final result is significantly different from the image that you manipulated on the screen. I strongly recommend you install a running legend in tall red letters across the bottom of your monitor that says something like: WARNING: FOR DISCUSSION ONLY. YOUR RESULTS MAY VARY!

2. Never tell a patient that a procedure is simple. Never minimize the risks.

3. Never "throw in" additional procedures for which you have no specific consent, short of an emergency situation.

4. Always involve the "significant other" or immediate family. They can turn out to be your best allies or your most tenacious detractors, often based on your behavior rather than your result. Go out in your scrubs and talk to them after the procedure. Call the patient the evening of surgery, if he or she is home. You cannot imagine how much that strengthens the rapport.

5. Always provide time for questions. Do not answer in "doctorese." Answer plainly. If there is a language barrier, get an interpreter. Never talk to patients with your hand on the doorknob. Take the time to listen.

6. Encourage patients to make notes after the consultation and to call if they have questions. Give them a copy of the consent form prior to surgery so that they can digest it at home and share it with significant others.

7. Always disclose the identity of all the surgeons in the operating room before the sedation hits. Reassure the patient that you are the responsible surgeon; all the others are there to help because you cannot do it all alone. If feasible, hold the patient's hand so that the last thing he or she sees before medication hits is your confident face smiling down at him or her.

8. There is absolutely no excuse for failing to document your work visually. Take many, many photographs. Ours is a totally graphic specialty. I cannot exaggerate the number of cases won or lost by virtue of photographic evidence. Or lack of it. There is no quicker way of sealing your destiny and causing irreversible harm than by having no visual evidence.

9. Doctors' penmanship is notoriously bad. If yours is in that category, spend the money to have someone type for you. Save yourself a lot of agony by not having your handwritten notation "had no carcinoma" transcribed as "*adenocarcinoma.*"

10. Resist the temptation to be the first kid on the block to try that dazzling new French procedure you saw at the last meeting so that reporters will come banging on your door. Wait until it is proven. Learn the technical procedure from others and *then* do it yourself.

Whether you believe in "karma," or destiny, or luck, is up to you. You are, in fact, exhibiting the temerity to challenge nature by defying the hand that genetic inheritance dealt. That is pretty awesome! However, I have little doubt that it is possible for you to do this for the 30 to 40 years following your emergence from the academic womb without having to look back in sorrow or in anger. That there will be bumps along the way is inevitable; the game is called "life." There are no guarantees, but we can promise you that by apportioning a reasonable segment of your attention on the rules of the game, as we have tried to outline them, there is a pretty good chance you will be able to finish and come out winners.

BIBLIOGRAPHY

Castle DJ, Phillips VA: Disorders of Body Image. Petersfield, UK, Wrightson Biomedical Publishers, 2002.

Goin JM: Rhinoplasty. In: Changing The Body: Psychological Effects of Plastic Surgery, Philadelphia, Williams & Wilkins, 1981.

Gorney M: Choosing patients for aesthetic surgery. Plast Reconstr Surg 88:917–918, 1991.

Gorney M: Claims prevention for the aesthetic surgeon: Preparing for the less-than-perfect outcome. Facial Plast Surg 18:35–42, 2002.

Gorney M: Liability issues in plastic surgery: An insurance perspective. In Mathes S, Hentz V (eds): Plastic Surgery, 2nd ed, Volume I, Philadelphia, WB Saunders, 2006, p 139.

Gorney M: Medical malpractice and plastic surgery: The carrier's point of view. In Goldwyn R, Cohen M (eds): The Unfavorable Result in Plastic Surgery. Philadelphia, Lippincott, Williams & Wilkins, 2001.

Gorney M: Preoperative computerized video imaging. Plast Reconstr Surg 78:268, 1986.

Gorney M: The role of communication in the physician's office. Clin Plast Surg 26:133–141, 1999.

Gorney M: The wheel of misfortune. Clin Plast Surg 26:15–19, 1999.

Gorney M, Knapp T: Lessons in morality and mortality. Plast Reconstr Surg 114:1644–1646, 2004.

Gorney M, Martello J: Patient selection criteria. Clin Plast Surg 26:37–40, 1999.

Gorney M, Martello J: The genesis of plastic surgeon claims. A review of recurring problems. Clin Plast Surg 26:123–131, 1999.

Gorney M, Martello J, Hart L: The medical record. Informing your patients before they consent. Clin Plast Surg 26:57–68, 1999.

CPT CODING STRATEGIES

Raymond V. Janevicius, MD, FACS

1. What is the appropriate CPT coding for the excision of a 10-mm basal cell carcinoma of the cheek with 2-mm margins followed by a layered closure of 3 cm?
A 10-mm lesion excised with 2-mm margins results in an "excised diameter" of 14 mm. An excised diameter is defined as the "greatest clinical diameter of the apparent lesion plus that margin required for complete excision." The lesion diameter (10 mm) plus 2 mm on each side of the lesion is $10 + 2 + 2 = 14$ mm. Use code 11642 for the excision of this malignancy.

The closure is reported in addition to the excision. A layered closure constitutes an intermediate repair, 12052. Thus the entire procedure is reported as follows:

12052   Layer closure of wound of face, ears, eyelids, nose, lips, and/or mucous membranes; 2.6 cm to 5.0 cm
11642-51   Excision malignant lesion including margins, face, ears, eyelids, nose, lips; excised diameter 1.1 to 2.0 cm

2. Three full-thickness ragged lacerations of the face are repaired. Each requires débridement of contused tissues, undermining, and layered closure: 3 cm on the nose, 2 cm on the lip, and 4 cm on the cheek. How is this procedure reported?
13152   Repair, complex, eyelids, nose, ears, and/or lips; 2.6 cm to 7.5 cm
13132-59   Repair, complex, forehead, cheeks, chin, mouth, neck, axillae, genitalia, hands, and/or feet; 2.6 to 7.5 cm

Débridement with undermining and layered closure constitutes a complex repair. Total lengths of repair within the same classification are added together. The nose and lips are grouped together, so the total length of repair in this classification is $3 + 2 = 5$ cm. The cheek is a different anatomic area by CPT definitions and is reported separately, 13132. Modifier "-59" indicates separate, distinct procedures and is appended to the secondary procedure.

3. A 10-cm basal cell carcinoma of the scalp extends into the skull. The lesion is excised with 1-cm margins, and the outer table of the skull is removed. Does the malignant lesion excision code (11646) include the bone resection?
No. The 116XX series appears in the Integumentary Section of the CPT Book and is used to report the excision of soft tissue lesions involving the skin and subcutaneous tissues. This skin lesion excision series (116XX) belies the extent of the procedure described; this soft tissue resection is better described with the "radical resection" code, 21015. This is a soft tissue code and does not include the resection of bone, which is reported with an additional code, 61500.

61500   Craniectomy, with excision of tumor or other bone lesion of skull
21015-51   Radical resection of tumor (e.g., malignant neoplasm), soft tissue of face or scalp

4. How is the removal of an injection port of a permanent expander reported?
The appropriate code is 11971 ("Removal of tissue expander without insertion of prosthesis") with modifier "-52." 11971 includes removal of an expander and its port. Because only the port is removed, use the "reduced services" modifier: 11971-52.

5. Is "division and inset" of the flap included in the cross finger flap code?
No. Division and inset of a flap is not included in the initial flap code, as this is a separate stage of the reconstruction, as is a delay of a flap, for example. Skin grafting of the donor site of a cross finger flap is also separately reported:

15574   Cross finger flap
15240-51   Full-thickness skin graft of donor site

Because this is a planned, staged procedure, append modifier "-58" to the division and inset code, as the second procedure occurs during the 90-day global period of the cross finger flap code:

15620-58   Division and inset cross finger flap.

6. When a transverse rectus abdominis myocutaneous flap is harvested, how is closure of the abdominal fascia with synthetic mesh coded?

The repair of the abdominal wall, with or without mesh, is included in the global transverse rectus abdominis myocutaneous (TRAM) flap codes and is not separately reportable. The three TRAM flap codes, 19367, 19368, and 19369, are global and include the following ("GLOBAL COMPONENTS OF TRAM FLAP CODES"):

- Creation of the breast pocket
- Elevation of the abdominal flap
- Muscle dissection
- Flap transfer
- Fascial closure with or without mesh
- Abdominal closure including umbilicoplasty
- Breast contouring

7. When several skin lesions are removed, why does the insurance company reimburse for only one lesion and disallow the rest?

This occurs if the insurance company does not recognize that multiple lesions are excised. Even though a claim lists multiple procedures with "-51" modifiers as per CPT guidelines, some payers require the use of the "distinct procedural service" modifier "-59" to indicate that separate lesions are excised at the same operative session. Thus the excisions of three facial nevi, each measuring 4 mm, is reported as follows: 11440, 11440-59, 11440-59. Some payers require the use of both modifiers in these situations: 11440, 11440-59-51, 11440-59-51.

8. How many CPT codes are required to report the open reduction internal fixation of a comminuted malar complex fracture with reconstruction of an orbital floor blowout fracture using an implant?

Code 21365 (Open treatment of complicated malar fracture, including zygomatic arch and malar complex) describes the open reduction and internal fixation of a malar complex fracture. This includes exploration of the zygomaticotemporal suture line and the orbital rim, with reduction and fixation of the fractures at these sites. Malar fractures can occur without orbital floor blowout fractures, and code 21365 does not include reconstruction of an orbital blowout fracture, which is separately reported. If an implant is used in the orbital floor, the appropriate code is 21390. Thus, an open reduction internal fixation (ORIF) of a malar complex fracture with reconstruction of a blowout fracture with an implant is reported with two codes: 21365, 21390-51. Some payer software "edit packages" incorrectly overbundle codes 21390 and 21365, so the "distinct procedure" modifier is necessary in such cases: 21365, 21390-59.

9. Is there a code for the "separation of components" technique of abdominal wall reconstruction?

"Separation of components" involves incision of the external oblique muscles and their dissection off the internal oblique muscles laterally. The underlying rectus abdominis, internal oblique, and transversalis muscles are then advanced to the midline to close the abdominal defect. The muscle flap elevation requires preservation of vascular and nerve supply to all the involved muscles and is reported as a muscle flap of the trunk, 15734. When separation of components is performed bilaterally, 15734 is reported twice.

10. Can add-on codes ever be used alone?

By definition, add-on codes are always used with another code and can never be reported alone. The surgical procedures described by add-on codes cannot be performed unless another procedure is also performed. Consider code 15101, "Split thickness autograft, trunk, arms, legs; each additional 100 sq cm." An "*additional* 100 sq cm" of skin cannot be grafted unless 100 sq cm of skin has already been grafted. Thus, 15101 must always be used with 15100 ("Split thickness autograft, trunk, arms, legs; first 100 sq cm"). Add-on codes do not take the "multiple procedure" modifier "-51".

11. When more than one muscle flap is used to close a single defect, should each muscle flap be reported separately?

Yes. Although only one defect may be present, each muscle flap involves a distinct surgical procedure and should be separately reported. CPT guidelines and the "global surgery" concept do not state that one code describes more than one muscle flap. If a total sternectomy is performed for sternal osteomyelitis and the defect closed with bilateral pectoralis major muscle flaps and a right rectus abdominis muscle flap, each flap is reported separately:

15734	Right pectoralis major muscle flap
15734-51	Left pectoralis major muscle flap
15734-51	Right rectus abdominis muscle flap
21630-51	Sternectomy

12. What is considered global in free flap coding?

Global components of an operation are those parts of the procedure that are included in a CPT code and that are not separately coded. Free flap codes include the following ("GLOBAL COMPONENTS OF FREE FLAP CODES"):

- Elevation of the flap
- Isolation of donor flap vessels used for microvascular anastomosis
- Transfer of the flap to the recipient site
- Isolation of recipient vessels used for microvascular anastomosis
- Microvascular anastomosis of one artery
- Microvascular anastomosis of one or two veins
- Inset of flap in recipient site
- Primary closure of the donor site

Reporting any of these components separately would be unbundling.

13. The CPT code for tissue expander placement (11960) reads "Insertion of tissue expander(s) for other than breast, including subsequent expansion." If two expanders are placed in two different areas, should the code be reported only once?

The text "expander(s)" in the CPT book has led to some confusion in interpretation. If one pocket is created and two tissue expanders are placed in the same pocket, 11960 is reported only once. If two separate pockets are created (essentially twice the work of one pocket), then it is appropriate to report 11960 twice. Modifier "-59" should be appended after the second procedure to indicate that two separate distinct procedures are performed: 11960, 11960-59.

14. Medicare does not reimburse for excisions of benign lesions. How does one code these procedures so that Medicare will pay?

Medicare considers the excisions of benign lesions "cosmetic" and not "medically necessary" unless certain strict criteria are met. The excisions, removals, shavings, or destructions of lesions such as nevi, skin tags, inclusion cysts, seborrheic keratoses, and scars are deemed "cosmetic" and will not be covered unless certain specific conditions are met. For these procedures to be covered by Medicare the medical record must document that the lesion bleeds, itches intensely, is painful, has physical evidence of inflammation, or obstructs an orifice. Appropriate ICD-9 codes must be used to substantiate excisions of these lesions.

15. How does one code for repeated skin grafts that are performed during the global postoperative period?

When multiple skin graft procedures are planned, for example, as in the course of burn reconstruction, these are considered "planned" or "staged" procedures. Modifier "-58" should be appended to procedures subsequent to the original procedures so that they will not be disallowed as part of the global surgery package. "-58" is not appended to the procedures performed on the first day. If, for example, a 400 sq cm STSG of the trunk is performed and then 1 week later another area of the trunk is grafted 500 sq cm, the procedures are reported as follows:

First date: 15100, 15101, 15101, 15101
One week later: 15100-58, 15101-58, 15101-58, 15101-58, 15101-58

16. A Dupuytren's contracture requires a fasciectomy of the palm, middle, ring, and small fingers. Y-V flaps are performed to provide extra skin length. How is this coded?

Three codes describe Dupuytren's surgery, and each includes the use of flaps and/or grafts during the reconstruction. 26121 is used to report fasciectomy involving the palm only, with no digital involvement. 26123 describes palmar fasciectomy, including fasciectomy of a single digit. 26125 is an add-on code used to report *each additional digit* operated on after the initial digit. 26125 is always used with code 26123. Thus, in the previous example, the fasciectomy of the palm and the middle finger are reported with code 26123. The fasciectomies of the ring and small fingers are *each* reported with code 26125: 25123, 26125, 26125. Because 26125 is an add-on code, it does not take the "-51" modifier.

17. A pediatrician refers a child to the plastic surgeon with a Salter fracture of the index finger. The plastic surgeon assumes treatment that requires 3 weeks of splinting. Is this considered a consultation?

Not all patients referred by another physician are considered consultations. CPT requirements to report a patient encounter as a "consultation" require three components:

1. A written or verbal request by the referring physician must be documented in the medical record
2. The consulting physician's findings and treatment must be documented in the medical record
3. The consultant's findings must be communicated "by written report" to the referring physician

The consulting physician may initiate diagnostic and/or therapeutic services at the time of the consultation. In the previous example, if the three criteria are met, then the encounter is considered a consultation, even if the plastic surgeon has initiated treatment at the time of consultation.

18. When multiple tendons are repaired in the hand, should each tendon repair be reported separately?

Yes. Each tenorrhaphy CPT code includes the repair of one tendon. Listing each tenorrhaphy is appropriate in reporting multiple tendon repairs. This itemizing of procedures performed is not unbundling, and multiple tendon repairs reported with the same CPT code should not be bundled together by payers. If a wrist laceration transects seven flexor tendons, all of which are repaired, each is listed separately: 25260, 25260-51, 25260-51, 25260-51, 25260-51, 25260-51, 25260-51. Some payers may require use of modifier "-59" rather than "-51" (25260-59). Still others may require both "-51" and "-59" (25260-59-51).

19. A 1-cm basal cell carcinoma below the eyelid margin is excised with 5-mm margins. An inferomedially based rotation flap measuring 5 × 5 cm is used to reconstruct the defect. How is the proper code selected?

This is an adjacent tissue transfer used to reconstruct an eyelid defect, so 14060 or 14061 is used. The adjacent tissue transfer code is selected by the size of the surgical defect, which is defined as the *primary* defect (that from the excision of the lesion) *plus* the *secondary* defect (that created by flap design and elevation). The primary defect measures approximately 3 sq cm. The flap elevation results in a defect measuring 25 sq cm (5 × 5 cm). Total defect is 28 sq cm, so code **14061** (10.1 to 30 sq cm) is selected. Adjacent tissue transfer codes include the excision of the lesion, so this is not separately reported.

20. A sacral decubitus is débrided, including bone débridement, and the defect is reconstructed with bilateral gluteus maximus V-Y flaps. What codes are used?

The 11040–11044 series of débridement codes belies the extent of decubitus ulcer débridements and is inappropriate in reporting this case. The 159XX series of codes is used to report procedures on decubitus ulcers. Because the débridement involves ostectomy, 15937 is the appropriate code. Two separate myocutaneous flaps are performed, and each is reported with a separate code.

15734	Right gluteus maximus myocutaneous flap
15734-51	Left gluteus maximus myocutaneous flap
15937-51	Excision sacral decubitus, including ostectomy

21. If wound edges are undermined and then advanced to close a defect, is this a flap reconstruction?

A flap by definition almost always requires an incision and results in a secondary defect. Undermining does not create a secondary defect, nor does it constitute flap closure. Undermining followed by layered closure constitutes a complex repair. Undermining and a layered closure should be reported as a complex repair (131XX series) and should not be reported as a flap (14XXX series, "adjacent tissue transfer").

22. In a carpal tunnel release, can incision of the fascia proximally be reported separately with 25020?

No. Carpal tunnel release, whether open or endoscopic, includes incising forearm fascia proximally as part of median nerve decompression. This maneuver is included in the global codes for carpal tunnel release (29848, 64721). Code 25020 is used to report decompression of forearm fascia, an extensive procedure performed for compartment syndrome. It is not appropriate to report 25020 in the management of carpal tunnel syndrome.

23. How long has CPT coding been in existence?

The American Medical Association first published CPT in 1966 in a volume containing four-digit codes mostly describing surgical procedures. In 1970 the second edition of CPT was published, using five-digit codes (as today) to describe not only surgical procedures but also diagnostic and therapeutic procedures in medicine and other specialties. In the mid-1980s, the Health Care Financing Administration (HCFA, now CMS [Centers for Medicare and Medicaid Services]) mandated the use of CPT codes for reporting outpatient hospital surgical procedures.

BIBLIOGRAPHY

CPT 2009, Current Procedural Terminology. Chicago, American Medical Association, 2009.
Janevicius RV: CPT Notebook. Arlington Heights, IL, American Society of Plastic Surgeons, 2009.

ETHICS IN PLASTIC SURGERY

CHAPTER 11

Thomas J. Krizek, MD

1. What is ethics?

Ethics is the discipline devoted to the study of the principles and processes of determining right and wrong behavior. Ethics deals with what is good and bad, with moral duty and moral obligation. For plastic surgeons, ethics and its moral duty and obligation deal primarily with our responsibilities to our patients. Additionally, we owe ethical duty and responsibility to our colleagues, to our profession, and to society in general. These duties largely derive from the fact that we are part of the "profession" of medicine.

2. What do you mean by a "profession"?

Professions have a long and enviable history and tradition. They have characteristics and responsibilities that transcend and exceed those of most occupations or "jobs." Professions involve the following characteristics:

1. They have actions that require specialized knowledge or ability.
2. They require long and arduous training and discipline.
3. They are more like a "calling" or vocation.
4. They have internal standards that lead to self-governing.

Plastic surgery is a true "specialty" within the profession of medicine. It is most aptly characterized for its specialized conceptual and scientific body of knowledge and for the artistic and technical facility necessary to practice its art and science. Acquisition of excellence involves long and arduous training and discipline under the guidance and supervision of experienced practitioners and teachers. Plastic surgery is not what we do; rather, it is "who we are." It does not involve a mere series of technical maneuvers, nor does it involve a mere "repertoire" of aesthetic and reconstructive procedures, no matter how great the virtuosity of the practitioner. Finally, it has internal standards that are self-governing, from the Residency Review Committee, which assures the quality of the educational process, to the American Board of Plastic Surgery, which assures the competence and quality of practitioners at both the entry level and ongoing, and the American Society of Plastic Surgeons, which has a major responsibility to society.

Being a "professional" implies far more than merely being paid. Those in religious life or the ministry, those in the military, and those involved in elementary-level education are paid very little but still are professionals. Plastic surgeons who contribute time to residency programs or to missionary or charitable work may receive little if any compensation. In contrast, many activities, both legal and illegal, may be immensely lucrative but may not fulfill the definition of "profession."

The activities of professionals, the "what we do," are called *practices*. The term carries connotations quite different from what might be meant by practicing to ready a team for a big game or to improve one's golf swing.

3. What specifically is meant by a "practice"?

A most influential modern philosopher, Alasdair MacIntyre, described qualities in his definition of practices that seem complex but are illustrative. To him a practice is:

Any coherent and complex form of socially established cooperative human activity through which goods internal to that form of activity are realized in the course of trying to achieve those standards of excellence which are appropriate to, and partially definitive of, that form of activity with the result that human powers to achieve excellence, and human conception of the ends and goods involved systematically extended.

These qualities are important to our understanding the ethics of what our practices involve.

Any coherent and complex form of socially established cooperative activity refers to the fact that we are privileged by society to be allowed to perform this practice, and we, in turn, owe responsibilities to our patients and society for that privilege. It embodies a coherent, albeit complex, approach to patient care that differentiates it from others in the profession of medicine.

…*that produces <u>goods internal</u> to that form of activity* refers to those characteristics that allow us to be fine plastic surgeons. These *internal goods* are qualities that lead to "virtues" such as knowledge, courage, honesty, steadfastness, charity, and practical wisdom, which complement our surgical judgment and skill. These internal goods are the basis for professionalism and moral behavior *and* are distinguished from and challenged by *external goods* such as money, power, and prestige, which, although seductive, do not a better plastic surgeon make.

…*by participants striving to excel by the standards of the activity* means that we as individual plastic surgeons must "internalize" those standards of excellence for which we have been taught to strive and must hold ourselves responsible. The acquisition and maintenance of judgment and technical skills are *internal* to the individual surgeon, and no outside review agency nor monitoring committee can replace our individual responsibilities.

…*that systematically extend the participants' skills and their concepts of the goods and purposes of the activity.* Our specialty attracts persons of intelligence, intuition, three-dimensional skill, and, in some, extraordinary technical or artistic talents that provide immense natural advantages. These talents must be honed in the residency programs but must be the ongoing quest for excellence of practitioners during a lifetime of "practice."

4. What is meant by *"internal goods"* or virtues?

Aristotle described the ultimate human goal to be happiness. Such happiness extends beyond the joy experienced from sex or the pleasure of a good meal to involve a more transcendent and sublime tranquility. Happiness at the personal level and that of the larger society *(polis)* could best be achieved by the acquisition and expression of virtues. These were characterized by the cardinal virtues of prudence, justice, temperance, and fortitude. Even greater than these was *phronesis*, a practical wisdom that would allow one to use these virtues productively. Subsequently, we have added religious virtues such as faith, hope, and charity and practical virtues such as honesty, dependability, constancy, and caring. Caring is a special type of ethics that is likened to the unqualified concern that a mother offers to her infant or the dependable care that military personnel or members of athletic teams offer to each other.

These can be summed up in the word *character*. Casey Stengel, the legendary baseball manager, observed that there were three things that can't be taught: speed, luck, and character. I believe he was wrong on all three. *Speed* can be improved by coaching and training, and *luck* certainly favors those prepared. *Character* is largely learned at a parent's knee but can be solidified, deepened, and finally organized and incorporated into the practice of a profession. All educators from the preschool level to final entry into plastic surgery residencies endeavor to identify those who may be antisocial or otherwise lacking in character or virtue. Despite all efforts, there will be those with character defects who find their way into our specialty. Sadly, no compilations of rules or written "codes of ethics," no matter how comprehensive or detailed, can ever compensate for deficiencies in character, and such persons will exhibit behavior that we recognize as unethical, morally deficient, or illegal.

5. What are the *"external goods"*?

There are *external goods* that tend to detract from these virtues. One example of an external good is *fame*. Although few surgeons truly become famous, there are many examples of how fame influences those in the entertainment industry; movie stars, musicians, rock stars, and some athletes achieve true fame. These persons may possess immense talent that the public recognizes and values but does not necessarily require or involve the virtue expected from physicians, teachers, attorneys, and other professionals. It would seem that such fame detracts from internal goods and virtue and is incompatible with professionalism. We tend to be a bit skeptical of the most famous surgeon or lawyer in town and know that they are not necessarily the best.

Another external good that may detract from professionalism is *power*. Power may take a number of forms. The surgeon's relationship with a patient always represents a discrepancy in power. The surgeon has immense knowledge and skills that the patient lacks. The patient is always dependent on the surgeon to use this knowledge and skill prudently and to not exploit or misuse this power financially or for sexual favor.

Plastic surgeons may also possess power and influence in their hospitals or residency programs. This power should not be misused, for instance, to limit access to facilities or to restrict legitimate opportunities for other professionals. Most in our specialty assume positions of responsibility in training programs or in professional organizations in a spirit of altruism or service. Even so, we know that such power does not necessarily mean that these persons are better surgeons and does not necessarily ensure that their patient care is better.

Finally, *money* is an obvious potential challenge to internal goods and virtue. The richest business persons, the richest entertainers, and certainly the richest surgeons are not necessarily the best nor the most virtuous professionals. All professionals should be compensated appropriately and fairly for their professional services. Plastic surgeons often have control over a scarce resource, often being the only ones in the community who can provide the service. However, an ethical constraint limits charging whatever the market can bear, particularly when the procedure is a medical necessity or emergency.

All surgeons share a potential conflict of interest when a patient is evaluated for a surgical procedure. There is an obvious substantial financial difference between performing and not performing an operation. Immanuel Kant pointed out that persons should always be treated as an "end and not a means." Any operation must be done for the primary benefit of the patient, and considerations of financial reward (even if it is needed to pay the rent) must, ethically, be secondary.

Indications for surgery, particularly in aesthetic procedures, usually are somewhat subjective, as are measurements of the final outcome. Perhaps nowhere, other than in psychiatric practice, are patients more insecure and vulnerable. There are, of course, those patients who are sophisticated and knowledgeable for whom there is no danger of exploitation. For many, however, their goals from surgery often are ill defined and incompletely shaped. The virtuous surgeon will never step beyond the responsibility to provide no more or no less than what can be determined as "best" for the patient.

Only in the last century has there been much question about what was the best treatment for a patient. Intervention, particularly surgical, was fraught with problems and unpredictable results. Physicians did what they thought was best. Two occurrences in the middle of the last century changed medical ethics forever. The first was the invention of respirators that could sustain patients long beyond the time when death otherwise would have naturally occurred. The other was the despicable behavior of physicians during the Holocaust involving experimentation, which cried out for new rules and standards of behavior.

6. What are the "rules" of ethical care?
The four principles of "rules-based" ethical care are as follows:

1. Beneficence: *To do good*
2. Nonmaleficence: *To keep from harm*
3. Autonomy: *To recognize a person's individual integrity*
4. Justice: *To recognize responsibilities to society*

7. This sounds like the Hippocratic Oath!
It certainly does. Some variation of the Hippocratic Oath is still recited at graduation by most medical students. For two millennia the oath has served to articulate the responsibilities of virtuous physicians for all to see. Pertinently, only *beneficence* and *nonmaleficence* are specifically included in the oath. *Beneficence* is recognized as the charge to *do good*. Although good seemed intuitively obvious, modern technology raised issues such as whether sustaining a patient on life support was really "good." Extensive palliative operations and repeated cycles of chemotherapy for cancer may, for many, not be considered a good. People live almost twice as long as a century ago. They bring many different religious, ethnic, and cultural considerations about the goals of any treatment and what is good.

Nonmaleficence is often referred to as *do no harm*. This is incomplete because the term also includes the concept of *keeping a person from harm*, which in many ways is equally important. Technical mistakes as a cause of medical error are rather infrequent. More common are errors in judgment or errors or omissions that place patients in harm's way. Beneficence and nonmaleficence, although still of primary importance, are no longer ethically sufficient, and additions to the Hippocratic Oath have become necessary. These additional rules involve the concepts of autonomy and justice.

8. What is meant by "*autonomy*"?
Autonomy is derived from the Greek word for self-rule or self-determination. The "doctor knows best" paternalism has been replaced by the recognition that persons have individual rights and responsibilities; their decisions about their own bodies must be respected. The concept of autonomy has evolved into the legal and moral standard that all medical intervention must devolve from the *informed consent* of the patient or of the legally defined representative if the patient is unable to give such consent. This concept is more than a legal requirement, it is also an ethical challenge.

Patients must

1. have adequate information about any proposed intervention, including the risks and the implications of nonintervention and alternative therapy;
2. have information, which must be presented in a form that they can understand (e.g., at a minimum, the information must be in the patient's native language); and
3. have the "capacity" to understand and make a decision, that is, they must be old enough, have sufficient mental acuity, and
4. be free from coercion and be able to refuse the treatment.

We have heard these standards mentioned so often that they have become routine, and the process of documenting consent is often delegated to others who assist us in our practices. However, the responsibility extends beyond mere presentation of the information; ethical standards demand that we be sure the patient truly does understand. Aesthetic patients in particular are often so enamored of the possible benefits that they are unable to adequately hear and incorporate the downside of the proposed procedure. The challenge of consent is particularly difficult when the surgeon is involved in residency programs in which the surgeon may not have adequate opportunity to meet with the patient and in a situation where the patient often has no alternative way of gaining access to the treatment. The autonomy of the poor or disadvantaged, particularly in other cultures, is of no less ethical significance.

An additional consideration of autonomy is the responsibility of the surgeon and all of the surgeon's personnel to hold private material in the utmost confidence—*confidentiality*. There are seemingly endless and intrusive demands, usually legitimate, for release of very private information about a patient's condition. The uniform medical record of many hospitals provides access to such information of as many as a hundred people. The private office of a psychiatrist or aesthetic surgeon is one of the last places where such information may have sanctuary, but even this is not absolute. On the other hand, most breaches of confidence are accidental and involve discussion of patients in elevators, lounges, or cocktail parties. Most surgeons are now conscious of the need to gain patient's consent to use pictures or other representations of patient information at professional meetings or in publications.

9. How does *"justice"* apply to these ethical principles?

Justice may take several forms but fundamentally refers to what is owed to others. Perhaps the *golden rule* encapsulates the concept of providing to others that which we would wish for ourselves. Justice involves what is termed *constitutive* justice—the contractual arrangements that we have with others. A patient is responsible for the agreed-on professional fee for services; the surgeon in turn is responsible for providing such goods and services.

Distributive justice is more broadly the responsibility of society to assure the freedoms of life, liberty, and the pursuit of happiness. Our society has chosen to add other rights such as education, housing, adequate access to food, and, pertinently, health care. The degree of health care to which persons are entitled as a right is an ongoing political issue; it is also one of ethics. Persons who have a right to something have the right to possess that object or service, and those who may hold that object or service in turn have a responsibility to honor that right. Society has offered greater access to health care, which has become ever more complex and expensive, and often involves tragic choices of how to distribute scarce resources such as organs for transplantation. In plastic surgery, major craniofacial procedures, severe facial trauma, and major burns may require a level of care that challenges the human resources available and for which compensation is not proportional or even available. Economics has been described as the "rational distribution of scarce resource." As such, it is a true ethical challenge for our society to meet almost insatiable demand for services, almost as a right, in the face of limited resources.

10. How is it determined what is ethical? Who says?

All final determinations about right and wrong become the responsibility of some authority. Our Declaration of Independence states that:

We hold these truths to be self-evident, that all men are created equal, that they are endowed by their Creator with certain inalienable Rights, that among these are Life, Liberty and the pursuit of Happiness.

The Declaration defined the authority as a Creator. For Aristotle the pursuit of happiness rested in individual citizens and together as the *polis*, or citizen-state, which became the authority. At other times the authority has been a king or queen, an emperor, the pope, some other representative of religion, or, in our country, the rule of Law. All are designed to allow persons to live together in some sort of order. What constituted right and wrong was determined by this authority.

In modern times all authority has been questioned, and there is a rather widespread acceptance of the culture of *moral relativism*. Moral relativism implies that human behavior is largely determined by the culture in which one is raised and in which one lives. What would be unacceptable to us may be acceptable in other cultures, and "who are we to tell others what to do?" Despite this relativism, most societies, certainly in Europe and America, consider some behavior to be normatively and absolutely evil. Such actions as genocide, slavery, murder, and rape are evil, no matter what the society or culture in which they occur. They are violations of human dignity and are not acceptable in a peaceful society.

In our multicultural society, we have determined that the final common ethical pathway is the Law. We are a government, not of executives, not of legislators nor even judges, but of Law. To a large extent the law reflects our common ethic and morality. Although unanimity toward individual situations such as the right to life and determinations of death may not be possible, we have established processes whereby disagreements may be resolved peacefully.

11. How does one apply ethical issues to practice?

We apply "ethics" to practice largely as a mirror to our application of ethics in Law in our society. Not everything that is legal is ethical to everyone and not everything that is unethical is illegal, but the overlap is significant. For instance, driving on a deserted country road 10 miles over the posted speed limit may be illegal but probably is not unethical; 10 miles over the speed limit in a school zone is both illegal and unethical. Similarly, having a sexual relationship with an adult patient may not be illegal but usually is unethical.

Ethical process involves several steps, and these steps are equally applicable to whether the surgeon is dealing with a patient, with other professionals, or with society. It applies also to individuals, groups (ethics committees), and society (law). The three steps of ethical process are as follows:

1. Impartiality
2. Discernment
3. Precedent-setting

12. What is the role of "impartiality" in the ethical process?

Those involved in making ethical decisions must be impartial. John Rawls referred to this impartiality as the "veil of ignorance." This did not imply lack of information or blindness to facts but just the opposite, namely, that those deciding must consider the interests of all stakeholders involved in such a decision. An operation on a patient involves others: family, dependents, facilities, and resources. Rawls said we should make our decisions as if we were to unexpectedly find ourselves in the position of one of those stakeholders. Families long since have learned that the way to assure impartial distribution of slices of a pie was to assign the last piece to the one doing the slicing. Because the surgeon has a stake in the decision on whether to operate or not to operate, it is an ethical challenge to be impartial in the decision. The possible conflict is obvious; it is incumbent on the surgeon to attempt impartiality from personal interests. Would another surgeon in similar circumstance make the same decision? Should this patient even undergo surgery? If so, is this really the proper operation for this patient?

13. Is "discernment" an important component of the ethical process?

Absolutely! When making ethical decisions, one does not have to approach every situation as if it had never occurred before. One of my teachers observed that we don't have to begin every patient decision with Hippocrates. Surgical science is based on the reproducibility of phenomena in nature. This use of previous situations or previous cases in ethics is called *casuistry*. It is the desirability of incorporating paradigmatic cases or situations into our deliberations. This is best seen, of course, in the Law in which *Brown v. Board of Education of Topeka*, *Roe v. Wade*, and others are among the most recognized paradigmatic cases.

Plastic surgery provides more individuality than most other surgical disciplines, but not everything that is new is an improvement, and the best standard may not necessarily be the newest. It is the responsibility of the surgeon to remain up to date and to incorporate new approaches and technology into his or her practice. The responsibility to be self-evaluative and self-critical is good practice; it is also good ethics.

14. What is meant by "precedent-setting," and what does that have to do with ethics?

In the Law, not every judicial decision establishes new precedent. Actually, when a court enters a judgment that seems to conflict with similar cases previously decided by others, there is very likely to be judicial review, up to the level of the Supreme Court.

When the Supreme Court rules, it charges all to now follow this new precedent. Kant referred to this as the *categorical imperative*. The categorical imperative challenges us to consider that, should this case or situation fit into a certain category, we have a responsibility, if not an imperative, to act in the same way as we or others have previously acted *and*, were it to arise again, we should again act in the same way. This is a caution against using *subjective* ethical approaches based on intuition or hedonism. *Intuition* would ask us to use hunches or guesses as a substitute of objective ethical standards based on rules or virtue. *Hedonism* is even more subjective and leads to behavior based on feelings, particularly the saw that "if it feels good, do it." We would not be pleased to encounter a judge who wished to establish our guilt or innocence on the basis of a hunch or how he happened to feel about us that day.

15. How do the "three steps of ethical process" apply to providing expert testimony?

There is a temptation to believe that we have insights that may be lacking in others and a surgical truth that only we possess. Such a posture may inappropriately dispose us to judgment about the decisions and performance of others. Before such conclusions are presented in private or public forum, much less in court, it is ethically appropriate that we consider impartiality, discernment, and precedent. Have we impartially considered all the stakeholders and the effect of our decision on them? Are we absolutely sure that we are not influenced by anger, jealousy, or financial considerations? Have we discerned the facts in an objective fashion to the degree that we might conclude that no person could possibly have acted in such fashion other than by criteria of negligence? We have a responsibility to be reflective and to not criticize or testify against another on the basis of our personal feelings or intuition. The criterion should not be whether the action was deviation from "the way I would have done it" but whether it was deviation from science and acceptable practice. Finally, the categorical imperative requires that, should the same situation present again, but this time involving a friend or colleague, we would act in the same fashion.

16. What are the three levels of professional contact?

1. *Surgeon and patient.* We have a responsibility to be impartial with our patients. This does not imply lack of caring or insensitivity; rather, it implies the responsibility to put aside our feelings, hunches, needs, and wants and to impartially determine what is best for the patient. To be reflective means to have at our disposal all relevant scientific information. It demands that surgeons be up to date and not use such intuitive approaches as "it always worked for me" or "I've always done it that way." Finally, if we decide to perform an operation, we should be able to stand back and say that the decision would have been equally appropriate were the patient our spouse or one of our children.

2. *Surgeon and profession.* We are part of a tradition that we are proud to date back to the tile-makers of India, the reconstructive efforts of Tagliacozzi in the sixteenth century, and the modern scientific efforts of those who developed microsurgery, flap transfer, and craniofacial surgery. We are indebted to those who made the scientific contributions as well as to those who, through their political efforts, strove to establish the scientific safety of implant materials. None of us individually deserved to be plastic surgeons nor did we earn the opportunity in isolation. We owe, as the Hippocratic Oath states, a debt and responsibility to those teachers who have gone before us. We have an ethical responsibility to share discoveries and new technology with our colleagues and with those in other specialties who might usefully incorporate such advances for the betterment of their patients. We owe an ethical responsibility not only to colleagues in our specialty but to all those in the profession of medicine.

3. *Surgeon and society.* We live in and among, and not separate from, society. We have a major responsibility toward a society that has provided us the privilege of practicing our profession. A wag once observed that the difference between God and a surgeon is that God does not think he is a surgeon. The ethical responsibilities include such obvious mandates to pay our taxes and obey other laws and statutes. It carries other responsibilities, such as the responsibility to provide appropriate information to insurance companies and government agencies even though it may seem as though the insurance company is large and impersonal and we are only being a bit like Robin Hood if we shade the information so that a patient can receive coverage for an operation.

We must approach all patients with equivalent degrees of respect for human dignity irrespective of race, gender, or ability to pay. No one can ethically mandate a responsibility to society, but virtue would seem to mandate that some return to society is appropriate.

17. What about human experimentation?

The doctors associated with the Nazis demonstrated a staggering level of professional depravity, and most of these physicians had taken the same Hippocratic Oath as most of us did. The Nuremberg Trials and subsequent meetings at Helsinki established international criteria for human experimentation. These emphasized the keystone place of autonomy as an ethical criterion. A patient's capacity to agree to an operation, much less an experimental procedure, remains a complex issue. No matter the level of education, one's ability to understand scientific information is of necessity limited and in a sense incomplete. No patient can possibly achieve anywhere near the degree of understanding that the surgeon possesses. The process of informing is not a mere exchange of information among scientific colleagues but a process of education that remains imperfect at best and dependent on the virtue of the person counseling the patient. Although theoretically desirable, the process can never be totally free from coercion because many patients want to please the doctor and be good patients. Prisoners in particular have been determined to always be in such a conflicted position as to be unsuitable candidates for experiments, so surgical programs using prisons have largely been discontinued. There are serious challenges to assure the ability of patients or participants in studies to refuse without penalty. This has placed immense responsibilities on investigators.

On the other hand, it has not prevented the specialty from being involved in investigation. In particular, two situations are most commonly subjected to ethical scrutiny: (1) aesthetic surgery and (2) use of implant materials.

18. What is the most important ethical challenge to plastic surgeons?

Aesthetic surgery is perhaps the most important and common scientific and ethical challenge to plastic surgeons. Because the same apparent disfigurement, distortion, or merely disagreeable features can have such different meaning to different patients, the ability to establish objective criteria for correcting such problems is a true challenge. Although many studies have been done to interpret the psychological implications of such aesthetic problems, the best that has come from such studies are general patterns of patient concerns. Even more challenging is the problem of determining the actual degree of improvement or satisfaction that an operation accomplishes. The concept of impartiality is particularly true in these circumstances. Every surgeon anticipates and dearly wishes the end result to be happy and pleasing to both surgeon and patient. It makes scientific objectivity very difficult.

The scientific gold standard for clinical evaluation of surgical or other treatment modalities is the randomized double-blind study. In such studies, the patients are randomly distributed among possible treatment groups. After the treatment the evaluation is accomplished by impartial persons not involved in the study and who themselves have no stake in profiting from the results, no matter what the outcome. Particularly with medications, neither the physicians nor the patients are aware of which drug is being administered lest any placebo effect be introduced. Such studies are ethically and scientifically difficult when surgical procedures are involved. "Sham" operations, involving only skin incisions as the control group, are ethically challenging. And yet, in several situations such as ligation of internal mammary operations for angina and some reconstructive procedures on the knee, the sham operation was equally effective.

Sham operations likely will not be acceptable in aesthetic procedures. However, aesthetic patients present a special opportunity for clinical investigation. Many of the procedures are bilateral and symmetrical, and they minimize variables because patients may possibly serve as their own control. A series comparing two approaches to face lifts was conducted in which a different procedure was performed on each side of a single patient; there was no difference between procedures. One of the ongoing issues with aesthetic science is that patients are unique, and it is dauntingly difficult to compare patients even when controlled for sex, age, body habitus, and other variables. There is a scientific truism that a series of anecdotes does not constitute data. There is a certain professional arrogance that suggests controlled clinical studies cannot be done and that the nature of our practice makes it impossible. Although challenging, it is not ethically impossible to conduct such studies. There is no ethical proscription against using the patient as both experiment and control in bilateral procedures. For instance, it was not unethical to perform different face lifts on two sides of the same patient nor, for that matter, would it have been unethical to use two different implants for augmentation. Appropriate scientific and ethical criteria can be met.

1. The procedures being evaluated must be comparable.
2. The patients must be fully informed of risks and benefits.
3. The patients must have full capacity to consent without coercion and must be able to refuse without penalty.

19. Elaborate on these "ethical criteria."

The procedures must be comparable, for example, use comparable variations on approaches to face lift or presumably comparable implants. The data must not be so overwhelming in favor of one or the other approach that no reasonably prudent surgeon would ever perform it. However, few such procedures come to mind.

The patient must be fully informed that two different procedures are to be performed and that there is risk of one side having a better aesthetic result such that subsequent corrective surgery might be required.

The patient must be able to understand and must be able to refuse without penalty. For instance, it would not be appropriate to offer such an approach only to patients who otherwise might not be able to afford a procedure or for whom failure to participate would deprive them of any operation.

Years ago, it was argued that no informed consent was possible and that patients should merely trust their physicians to do whatever they thought was best. This has proven to be incorrect, and such consent is standard. To now suggest that persons cannot be fully informed about investigative procedures is equally implausible. The early planning for surgery for gender reassignment presented challenges that were met, and the discussions regarding issues in facial transplantation are models for preparation for human experimentation.

20. Does the use of implant materials present a special ethical situation for plastic surgeons?

The use of implant materials is common, but not unique, to plastic surgery. Some materials have an anticipated lifetime presence that makes their lasting effects on the body difficult to predict with any degree of scientific certainty. The very difficulty makes the challenge and ethical concern of determining their safety more pertinent.

Silicone Implants. I served as a member of the scientific advisory committee of the Food and Drug Administration during the silicone controversy almost 2 decades ago. Liquid silicone was not (and still is not) approved because of the inadequacy of the scientific data confirming "safety and efficacy."

With regard to breast implants, there is no question that the scientific data were woefully inadequate. Fifteen years have shown that, in fact, acceptable data can be obtained, and gel implants have been released for commercial use. The mandated collection of long-term data is not an irritating bureaucratic imposition but rather application of good science.

The experience with silicone breast implants serves as a lesson and an ongoing challenge to plastic surgeons to be involved in scientifically rigorous evaluation of all new procedures and materials. This ethical challenge is not one restricted to the organized specialty but to each individual surgeon who has the responsibility to be aware of, and use only, what is the best for the patients, even if it means referral to another surgeon. I recall evaluating residency programs years ago that announced, rather defiantly, that "we don't do microsurgery here." Such a statement now would be preposterous, and yet a surgeon who, for whatever reason, does not perform microsurgery and does not refer a patient for a microsurgical procedure, if it is the best approach, is acting unethically.

21. Do international surgery programs that provide care in developing countries have special ethical considerations?

A specific area for consideration is the noble involvement of plastic surgeons in international programs. The world's disadvantaged are richly served by the generosity and dedication of many. It is an ethical imperative that patients so served be approached with the same ethical considerations and standards that would be afforded to patients in our private practice. Such patients possess human dignity, and this dignity is no less in poverty or lack of education. However, the challenges of providing informed consent are immense. The issue of coercion is almost intrinsic to the situation; how could a parent in such circumstances ever refuse? There is a temptation to use such patients to "upgrade" our personal abilities by performing procedures that we would not otherwise perform in our practice. It presents a tempting situation to "innovate" on the grounds that no matter what we do the patient is going to be better off than if we did nothing. There is a temptation to use such situations as a training ground with material for educating residents, a mutually acceptable situation only if the supervision is comparable to what would be afforded in our own institutions back home. Ethical standards are curiously transportable and universal.

22. Where does one find ethical standards for plastic surgery?

The American Society of Plastic Surgeons has a wonderful *Code of Ethics*. It has been observed that professionals who act in a way to promote the internal goods of a practice and thus are acting in a virtuous fashion do not need many additional rules. The *Code*, in fact, has only 11 general principles that charge us to practice scientifically, with constant upgrading of knowledge, for the primary benefit of the patient. It charges us to assure the competence of our colleagues and to assist in safeguarding the public from those who would behave "unethically."

Surgeons should be compensated only for services actually rendered or performed under our direct supervision and should sell or distribute products that we have approved. The sale or distribution of products results in financial reward, and it places responsibility on the surgeon to be assured that such products are safe and effective and that the patient is free from coercion of having to purchase such products as the price of a successful outcome.

23. What are the most common ethical violations?

The most common public violations of ethical standards fall into three categories.

1. *Illegal actions.* Physicians are licensed by society and thus granted the privilege of being a member of the medical profession. This in no way absolves practitioners from their responsibilities to obey the law. Our *Code of Ethics* specifically charges us with carrying out disciplinary actions against surgeons whose licenses have been limited, suspended, or terminated. There are those who have been convicted of murder and other crimes that are not specifically associated with role as physicians. More specifically, there are those who have committed fraud with regard to income tax or dealing with Medicare or other third party carriers.
2. *Sexual misconduct.* The Hippocratic Oath specifically addresses the fact that physicians are in a special relationship with persons who are particularly vulnerable to sexual or other exploitation. Such a differential in power between physician and patient blurs the normal standards for what otherwise would be consensual sexual conduct. A number of variables determine the propriety of a surgeon developing a sexual relationship with a patient. These include the nature of the relationship, the type of procedure, if any, and the time interval involved. For comparison, many psychiatrists would argue that in their specialty, there is no time interval beyond which patients are no longer patients.
3. *The impaired surgeon.* The plastic surgeon is no more protected from age, illness, or addictive disorders than are others in society. A conservative estimate is that more than 10% of all plastic surgeons will be so affected.

24. How does one categorize the "impaired surgeon"?

The "impaired surgeon" falls into one of three categories:

1. *Illness or injury.* Surgeons who have been ill or injured may not be able to practice safely or effectively during recovery. The ethical goal is to assure patient safety; the problems with determining surgeon competence are immensely complicated. Young surgeons in training are closely monitored for several years and then are formally examined by outside agencies. Such a sophisticated process is not readily available to those charged with evaluating the reentry of those who have been temporarily disabled.
2. *Aging surgeon.* Age is not a disability in and of itself. The aging process is, however, accompanied by mental and physical challenges that may compromise a surgeon's ability to practice safely. It is easier to affirm that we have a responsibility to society to assure the competence of our colleagues than to outline how this is to be accomplished. An ethical dilemma is that limiting a colleague's privileges for whatever reason may gain us an economic advantage and, therefore, is always a potentially difficult ethical issue.

3. *Addictive disorders*. The ethical issues pertaining to disorders involving alcohol or other addictive drugs fall into two categories. The first category consists of those surgeons whose addiction has become manifest by dereliction of duty, criminal action while intoxicated or under the influence of drugs, or even actual injury of a patient. Such actions are not acceptable even if the underlying disease can be approached sympathetically. Such action appropriately results in some judicial action that in turn limits the surgeon's ability to practice. This should be addressed by authorities in our states and by the American Society of Plastic Surgeons. Unfortunately, those whose addictive problems have surfaced in the public sphere are the tip of the iceberg and the ones with whom authority can most easily deal. Treatment programs can be mandated, and reentry is monitored by state agencies.

The second, and perhaps most dangerous, category is that large group of surgeons whose addiction has not yet surfaced. Their addiction may or may not yet be recognized and admitted ("denial is not just a river in Egypt"). Their addiction has not resulted in arrests or disciplinary actions. And yet, we know that their addiction will inexorably lead to diminished abilities, impairment, and, if untreated, often personal or public humiliation and tragedy. All states have assistance programs, and surgeons have a moral and ethical responsibility, if not to themselves, then at least to their patients and society, to initiate or help facilitate intervention that can lead to treatment. Addiction is not itself unethical, but the consequences of addiction lead to unethical behavior.

25. What about advertising?

Few professional activities in medicine lend themselves as readily to advertising as aesthetic plastic surgery. Medicine has become a commodity in a number of areas, and the public is bombarded with direct commercials to encourage them to seek pharmacologic help for everything from nasal congestion to erectile dysfunction. The line between patient information and efforts to entice persons to use a product or undergo some form of treatment is not clearly defined. It is a medical reality that few patients actually need aesthetic procedures. Even though our society seems insatiable in seeking such treatment, it is conflicted about whether such treatment should be provided by government or other third party insurers. The very concept of advertising or practice enhancement by commercialization seems unsavory to many, particularly older practitioners.

Although the big principles of ethics require only a few paragraphs in the *Code of Ethics*, addressing the issues of advertising and solicitation requires several pages of fine print. Virtuous physicians acting in a virtuous fashion require only general principles. The closer practitioners and their actions come to the edge of unethical behavior, the more specificity is demanded and the greater are the temptations to mischief. So much of the new technology of improvement in appearance involves applications or injections of materials and other procedures that do not involve traditional surgical expertise. Such technology does not require the degree of surgical judgment or technology as other areas of plastic surgery, and the economic opportunities tend to attract those whose training and expertise are marginal. Access to materials for injection and other skin care products is almost unlimited, and it will be difficult for plastic surgery to claim exclusivity in the use of such substances or techniques.

Immanuel Kant addressed the issue using other terms when he articulated the ethical maxim that persons are to be used as ends and not as a means. The ultimate test of ethical behavior, whether in specific treatment or in efforts to expand or enhance the business aspects of practice, is whether the best interests of the patient are the main consideration.

26. Are there ethical concerns for plastic surgery education?

Until the turn into the twentieth century, medical education was largely entrepreneurial, and there were hundreds of medical schools, some with curricula as long as 1 year. The last century formalized education for the protection of society, and this was voluntarily expanded into graduate medical education. The residency review committees reviewed the training programs, and the American Board of Plastic Surgery assessed the initial and ongoing "quality" of practitioners to the degree that such testing was reflective of ability. Finally, the various state boards of medical quality assured that practitioners met the minimum standards of qualification to practice medicine, including disciplining those who failed moral, legal, or quality standards.

Such "licensure" was *de jure* (force of law) for the states and *de facto* (in fact) for board certification. Such a situation was looked upon by many, particularly on the inside, as maintaining quality in the name of society. Many others, particularly those outside in other specialties, believed that the situation was an effort to restrict trade and legitimate access to patients. A medical license is broadly defined and usually does not restrict scope of practice. Such limitations on scope are largely the function of hospitals and their criteria for privileges. Because aesthetic surgery is largely conducted on an outpatient basis and most skin resurfacing procedures can be office based, organized plastic surgery is no longer in a position to assure quality or claim exclusivity, at least in these areas.

Plastic surgery education has undergone substantial changes as well. Many of the early plastic surgeons possessed a background in oral and maxillofacial surgery. Since World War II, most plastic surgeons have gained entry through general surgery, orthopedic surgery, or otolaryngology, and many training programs were broadly based, providing expertise across a spectrum of the specialty and often involving 7 to 8 years for completion. As the scope of the specialty seems to be contracting, with a preponderance of interest in aesthetic surgery, such broad-based and lengthy programs will become more unattractive and seem less relevant to prospective candidates than dermatology or other disciplines with more focused interests. This will create a major ethical issue for the entire specialty of plastic surgery. Efforts to continue asserting competence and skill in areas such as burns, head and neck surgery, hand surgery, and other more focused areas will be almost impossible, particularly because these areas are more logically the province of the anatomically oriented specialties. Classic and paradigmatic plastic surgery procedures such as repairs of cleft lip and palate have become difficult to teach in residency programs and for surgeons in practice to maintain competence.

A plastic surgery residency program has an ethical responsibility to assure that graduates are, in fact, skilled in all areas claimed to be within the purview of the specialty. More importantly, it is the moral and ethical responsibility of the practicing plastic surgeon to maintain knowledge and technical skills in those areas in which they hold themselves as specialists.

27. Case analysis: A 17-year-old female requests that you implant a tennis ball in the middle of her forehead. What is your response, and what are the ethical issues?
You chuckle of course and dismiss this situation as out of hand. Although the patient may seem competent, her request is bizarre and you promptly discard it. However, with additional information and history provided by the patient, her request no longer seems bizarre, and real issues arise.

The patient is the same 17-year-old female who requested that you implant a tennis ball in the middle of her forehead. She has a 10-year history of epilepsy that is only partially controlled by medication. During seizures she uncontrollably falls forward, repeatedly striking her forehead. She has sustained contusions and hematomas, which have required aspiration. The helmet that she now must wear is unsightly and a social handicap.

Your imagination soars, and it occurs to you that some variation on the tennis ball theme may actually be of benefit and you work with fabricators to fashion a silicone gel padding for her forehead that can easily be inserted. Your ethical intuition also soared as you applied all the virtues and rules to the situation. You approached her with a sense of impartiality, discernment, and a willingness to be precedent-setting. You understood that to *do good* in her circumstance was different from most, and the nonmaleficence or *keeping her from harm* was literal as well as figurative. She is old enough to understand and express her own autonomy. With the involvement and support of her parents, adequate informed consent can be obtained even though such a procedure may never have been done before. You might choose to request consultation from colleagues and even discuss it with the ethics committee of your institution. Because of its unique characteristics you would clear it with your committee on human investigation; it is a form of individual human experimentation in which all stakeholders have been respected. Finally, it is a procedure that, were she your daughter, you would have found it acceptable—the categorical imperative. In the midst of what seemed to be manure, there was a pony.

28. You have said that *"Ethics is like manure!"* What do you mean?
One immersed in a manure pile may dig furiously in the hopes that, because there is so much manure, there must be a pony in there somewhere. More reasonably, one can attack the manure pile and distribute it widely over the field, expecting that rich growth will result. The metaphor applies to ethical dilemmas.

Whereas morality is largely an individual matter of conscience, ethics involves the entire profession, the patients and society in general. When ethical problems arise, they should be shared. Ethics transcends individual disciplines and encompasses religion, philosophy, law, sociology, and anthropology. Profound ethical issues such as stem cell research are national and not merely personal issues. Over the last decades, our societies, our hospitals, and our licensing agencies all have come to incorporate ethics codes, committees, or principles into their decisions. This also applies to individual practitioners who may be faced with ethical dilemmas. Like manure, spreading the problem around and obtaining advice and consultation can resolve many ethical issues before they become ethical problems.

BIBLIOGRAPHY

American Board of Plastic Surgery: Code of Ethics. Philadelphia, American Board of Plastic Surgery, 2003.
American Medical Association: Code of Ethics. Available at www.ama-assn.org. Accessed 2004.
American Society of Plastic Surgeons: Code of Ethics, Arlington Heights, IL, Roster Publication, 2003.
Beauchamp TL, Walters L: Contemporary Issues in Bioethics, 5th ed. Belmont, CA, Wadsworth, 1999.
Bosk C: Forgive and Remember. Chicago, University of Chicago Press, 1979.
Krizek TJ: Ethics in plastic surgery. In Mathes S, Hentz V (eds): Plastic Surgery, 2nd ed, Volume I, Philadelphia, WB Saunders, 2006, pp 93–126.

Krizek TJ: Ethics and philosophy lecture: Surgery…Is it an impairing profession? J Am Coll Surg 194:352–366, 2002.

Krizek TJ: Medical errors: Reporting and punishment. Lancet 356:773, 2000.

Krizek TJ: Substance abuse and the surgical health officer. J Am Coll Surg 181:78, 1995.

Krizek TJ: Surgical error: Ethical issues of adverse events. Arch Surg 135:1359–1366, 2000.

Krizek TJ: Surgical error: Reflections on adverse events. Bull Am Coll Surg 85:18–22, 2000.

Krizek TJ: The impaired surgical resident. Surg Clin North Am 84:1587–1604, 2004.

Loewy EH: Textbook of Healthcare Ethics. New York, Plenum Press, 1996.

MacIntyre A: After Virtue: A Study in Moral Theory, 2nd ed. Notre Dame, IN, University of Notre Dame Press, 1984.

Rawls J: A Theory of Justice. Cambridge, Harvard University Press, 1971.

Sulmasy DP, Ury WA, Ahronheim JC, et al: Publication of papers on assisted suicide and terminal sedation. Ann Intern Med 133:564–566, 2000.

Edelstein Ludwig (trans): The Hippocratic Oath: Text, Translation, and Interpretation. Baltimore, Johns Hopkins Press, 1943.

Lasagna L: The Hippocratic Oath: Modern Version. Boston, Tufts University, 1964.

12 CHAPTER

ADVANCES IN BASIC SCIENCE RESEARCH

Derrick C. Wan, MD; Matthew D. Kwan, MD; Eric I-Yun Chang, MD;
Geoffrey C. Gurtner, MD, FACS; and Michael T. Longaker, MD, MBA, FACS

DISTRACTION OSTEOGENESIS

1. How is distraction osteogenesis used to generate new bone?

Distraction osteogenesis is a powerful form of endogenous tissue engineering that promotes bone formation through the gradual separation of osteogenic fronts. The principles of distraction osteogenesis were first described by Ilizarov, who demonstrated this modality could be consistently applied to long bone reconstruction with acceptable morbidity. Translation to the bones of the craniofacial skeleton first occurred in the mandible. Since that time, this technique has become a standard tool for craniofacial surgeons to achieve both significant midface and mandibular advancement.

2. What are the phases of distraction osteogenesis?

As described by Ilizarov, following the osteotomy or corticotomy, distraction osteogenesis incorporates an early rigid fixation phase, referred to as *latency*, followed by *gradual distraction*. The third and final phase (referred to as *consolidation*) entails stable fixation until radiographic and/or clinical assessment demonstrates the formation of a robust, mineralized bony regenerate.

3. What are common complications associated with craniofacial distraction osteogenesis?

Overall morbidity has been reported to be as high as 35%. Most commonly, soft tissue infection, osteomyelitis, and pin-tract infection have been reported. Loosening of the distraction device has been reported secondary to daily manipulation. Patient discomfort and poor compliance remain salient considerations. Lastly, fibrous nonunion, permanent inferior alveolar nerve injury (mandibular distraction), and relapse of the original condition (typically within the first 6 months following initial distraction) are significant complications.

4. Describe the mechanical forces involved in distraction osteogenesis.

Studies correlating histologic findings with measurements of tensile force have found that the highest rates of bone formation occur during active distraction, with typical strain patterns ranging between 10% and 12.5% across the regenerate. Work with finite element analysis has suggested mesenchymal tissues within the gap experience moderate hydrostatic stress predictive of intramembranous bone formation. In contrast, mild compressive stress has been observed in the periphery, compatible with endochondral bone formation around the periosteal edges. These predictions mirror histologic findings in multiple models of mandibular distraction, with direct intramembranous bone formation within the distraction gap and endochondral bone formation adjacent to osteotomized fronts.

5. Can the period of latency be potentially reduced to shorten the overall course of distraction osteogenesis?

Several studies have raised doubt over the necessity of a latency period. Investigations using ovine and porcine models have demonstrated no differences in mechanical strength, radiographic appearance, or bone density of the regenerate when no latency was used relative to a latency period of 4 or 7 days. Furthermore, retrospective studies have revealed similar results in the clinical setting, suggesting the traditional practice of latency may not be critically important. Thus, reduction and/or elimination of latency may potentially allow for shortening of the total duration of distraction osteogenesis without any detriment to the quality of bony regenerate.

6. How can the period of consolidation be shortened?

The greatest reduction in time to the overall course of distraction osteogenesis may be made by hastening the period of consolidation. Consequently, several studies have specifically evaluated the effects of callus stimulation. Long bone fracture models have already shown that mechanical loading can increase callus bulk, promote fracture healing, and hasten the onset of bony union. Adapting this principle to mandibular distraction, cyclical loading of the regenerate during early consolidation has been found to increase callus size, cortical density, and mineral apposition rate. Alternatively, callus stimulation has also been achieved through pulsed ultrasound in a rabbit model, with analogous proosteogenic effects on the distraction regenerate observed.

7. How may bone morphogenetic proteins improve results of distraction osteogenesis?

Temporospatial histologic and immunohistochemical studies have demonstrated up-regulation in bone morphogenetic proteins (BMPs) 2, 4, and 7 by osteoblasts within the distraction gap. Chondrocytes likewise have been found to increase BMP expression, particularly during the period of consolidation. Based on these findings, several investigations have evaluated the effects of augmenting local BMP levels on the distraction regenerate. Adenoviral-mediated delivery of BMP-2 into the gap during early consolidation has been shown to improve ultimate bone deposition, as assessed by radiographic, histologic, and histomorphometric analyses. Such results suggest BMP-2 to be a potential biologic modality for enhancing clinical distraction outcomes.

8. Which pro-angiogenic cytokines are involved in distraction osteogenesis?

Expression of both vascular endothelial growth factor (VEGF) and fibroblast growth factor-2 (FGF-2) has been found to increase within the regenerate of mice and goats during the period of active mandibular distraction. Quantitative real-time reverse transcriptase polymerase chain reaction (RT-PCR) has demonstrated a fourfold increase in expression of both of these angiogenic factors during bone formation with gradual distraction compared with other models of nonhealing or unsuccessful distraction.

9. How critical is angiogenesis for successful bone formation during distraction osteogenesis?

Studies evaluating the necessity of angiogenesis have found that suppression of new blood vessel formation, through the administration of TNP-470, significantly impairs bone formation during distraction osteogenesis. Platelet/endothelial cell adhesion molecule (PECAM) staining of the distraction gap in mice given TNP-470 revealed an absence of blood vessel formation within the regenerate, suggesting the failure of angiogenesis may have contributed to the failure in osteogenesis observed. These findings support the notion that angiogenesis may be as important as proper mechanical environment for successful distraction.

CRANIOSYNOSTOSIS

10. Mutations in which growth factor receptors have been implicated in several forms of syndromic craniosynostosis?

Of the four known fibroblast growth factor receptors (FGFRs), mutations in three (FGFR-1, FGFR-2, FGFR-3) have been implicated in several forms of syndromic craniosynostosis. Mutations of FGFR-2 are the most common. Most mutations result in missense changes to the linker region between the second and third regions of the immunoglobulin-like domains, resulting in receptor gain of function through constitutive dimerization or enhanced ligand–receptor affinity.

11. What is the role of fibroblast growth factors in cranial suture fusion?

The important role of FGF signaling in regulating cranial suture fusion has been emphasized by the multiple craniosynostosis syndromes found to be caused by gain-of-function mutations in the FGFRs. Significant data from the murine model has specifically highlighted FGF-2 in regulating cranial suture fate. In the murine model, the posterior–frontal (PF) suture fuses postnatally, whereas all other sutures remain patent. Immunohistochemical staining of rat PF and sagittal (SAG) sutures revealed relatively increased immunoreactivity of FGF-2 in the dura mater underlying the PF suture prior to and during the period of active fusion. This suggests that FGF-2 secreted from regional dura mater acts in a paracrine fashion on the overlying suture. The importance of FGF signaling has been further demonstrated by adenoviral-mediated delivery of a dominant negative FGFR-1 construct to the dura mater underlying the PF suture in embryonic rats. Interruption of FGF signaling prevented normal PF suture fusion.

12. What role does Noggin play in the maintenance of suture patency?

Noggin is a known antagonist of the proosteogenic BMP cytokines. In mice, BMPs are found in both fusing sutures and those that remain patent. However, Noggin has been found to be differentially expressed, being found only in sutures that remain patent. These findings suggest that Noggin plays a crucial role in the maintenance of suture patency through suture-specific BMP antagonism.

13. What is BMP-3, and how may this protein affect suture fate?

BMP-3 is a member of the bone morphogenetic protein family. However, unlike other family members, BMP-3 is an antagonist of BMP-2 and BMP-4 signaling. Whereas Noggin directly inhibits BMP ligand–receptor interaction, BMP-3 instead blocks BMP-2 and BMP-4 activity through competition for downstream SMAD signaling intermediates. Microarray analysis of gene expression in rats has demonstrated differential expression of BMP-3 within the cranial sutures. In fusing sutures, BMP-3 has been shown to decrease during the period of active fusion. Contrasting this, BMP-3 has been found to increase in sutures that remain patent during the same time period. Together, these temporospatial expression patterns for BMP-3 imply a role similar to Noggin in the maintenance of suture patency.

14. What is the role of transforming growth factor beta in cranial suture biology?

There are three known isoforms of transforming growth factor beta (TGF-β): TGF-β1, TGF-β2, and TGF-β3. Although no syndromic forms of craniosynostosis have been definitively linked to mutations within the TGF-β signaling pathway, significant data point to its role in the regulation of cranial suture patency. Isoform expression analysis in sutures of patients with craniosynostosis has revealed that TGF-β2 is heavily expressed in fusing sutures. This observation has also been noted in several animal models of suture fusion, implying a potential role for this isoform in facilitating suture closure. In contrast, TGF-β3 has been localized to the osteogenic fronts of patent sutures, suggesting this isoform plays in a role in the maintenance of suture patency.

15. What role does the dura mater play in cranial suture biology?

Significant data suggest that dura mater underlying sutures secretes cytokines that regulate suture patency. Furthermore, investigations with the murine model have suggested regional specification such that the dura mater underlying sutures that fuse expresses multiple proosteogenic cytokines, including FGF-2 and TGF-β2 along with bone-associated extracellular matrix molecules (collagen I, collagen III, osteocalcin). In contrast, minimal FGF-2 expression was observed in the dura mater underlying sutures that remain patent. Finally, studies in the murine model interposing a silicone membrane between the dura mater and overlying suture complex have demonstrated delayed suture fusion.

TISSUE ENGINEERING/REGENERATION

16. What are current techniques used to treat large bone defects, and what are their disadvantages?

Current surgical techniques have used autogenous, allogeneic, and prosthetic materials in various combinations to achieve bone reconstruction. Autogenous bone grafting has generally yielded favorable results; however, this is largely limited by donor-site morbidity and the amount of bone that can be harvested. Allogeneic bone also can be employed, although concerns have arisen regarding infection, immunologic rejection, and graft-versus-host disease. Lastly, alternative synthetic materials have been devised, including metal alloys, glass, plaster of Paris, polymethylmethacrylate, and biodegradable scaffolds. Unfortunately, none of these modalities have yielded favorable results alone, lacking the proper combination of mechanical strength, biocompatibility, and capacity for remodeling.

17. What cellular options exist for cell-based approaches to tissue engineering?

Human embryonic stem cells have been demonstrated to possess the capacity to differentiate along multiple lineages; however, significant political and ethical issues surround the use of these cells, encumbering further investigations. In contrast, postnatal progenitor cells have emerged as an attractive alternative for use in tissue engineering. Most work with these cells has been performed on the mesenchymal stem cell (MSC) fraction residing within the bone marrow. Postnatal progenitor cells have also been identified in the stromal fraction of adipose tissue. These cells possess similar multipotency, with the advantage of ease of harvest and increased cellular yield for the same amount of tissue obtained over those found in bone marrow.

18. Mesenchymal stem cells have the capacity to differentiate into which lineage-specific tissue types?

Investigators have demonstrated that MSCs contribute to the regeneration of a multitude of tissue types in the body, including bone, cartilage, muscle, ligament, tendon, adipose, and stroma. Specific work with bone marrow aspirates have revealed the ability of MSCs to form fat, cartilage, muscle, and bone under appropriate in vitro conditions. Studies on fat-derived MSCs from both humans and mice likewise have shown their capacity to form each of these tissues.

19. What are the three broad types of scaffolds used in bone tissue engineering?

Current scaffolds used can be broadly grouped into three main categories: natural, mineral based, and synthetic polymers. Natural scaffolds, such as collagen and hyaluronic acid, are routinely used as substrates for bone engineering. However, their lack of structural rigidity limits their use to areas with mechanical stability. Mineral-based scaffolds, composed of calcium phosphates in the form of hydroxyapatite and/or beta-tricalcium phosphate, have been used for nearly a century. However, like natural scaffolds, mineral-based scaffolds lack inherent strength for use in reconstruction of sites experiencing mechanical loading. Finally, synthetic polymers, such as polyglycolic acid, polylactic acid, polydioxanone, and polycaprolactone, have recently been developed with increased mechanical strength over natural and mineral-based scaffolds. Although synthetic polymers may be more advantageous in load-bearing regions, they typically lack the osteoinductive properties of these other forms.

20. Neovascularization is the process of new blood vessel formation. How does angiogenesis contribute to new blood vessel growth, and how does it differ from vasculogenesis?

Neovascularization occurs by two distinct processes: angiogenesis and vasculogenesis. Angiogenesis is the proliferation of mature endothelial cells from preexisting blood vessels to form new blood vessels. Vasculogenesis is the formation of new blood vessels in situ from stem cells. In the developing embryo, stem cells proliferate and form blood islands that join and form the capillary network of the yolk sac. Recent evidence has shown that the process of vasculogenesis also can occur in adult life where circulating endothelial progenitor cells contribute to new blood vessel formation in areas of ischemia.

21. Describe the steps involved in the process of angiogenesis.

Ischemic or diseased tissues produce various cytokines that bind to specific receptors on endothelial cells of preexisting blood vessels. These endothelial cells then become stimulated to produce enzymes that dissolve the extracellular matrix of the blood vessels. These resident endothelial cells begin to proliferate and migrate through the newly created pores in the direction of the ischemic or diseased tissue with the help of various cell adhesion molecules and integrins. The endothelial cells eventually form blood vessel tubes that are stabilized with the incorporation of smooth muscle cells and pericytes. Finally, these tubes are connected to form functionally perfused blood vessels.

22. Describe the process of vasculogenesis.

The body produces various cytokines in response to an ischemic insult that mobilizes vascular stem cells from the bone marrow compartment. These stem cells then home to the areas of ischemia, where they egress out of the vasculature to form clusters oriented in the direction of the ischemic gradient. These clusters eventually join into vascular-like cords that become canalized, yielding functional blood vessels.

23. What are the cytokines that stimulate angiogenesis to occur?

At least 20 angiogenic growth factors are known to contribute to this process of new blood vessel growth. Some of the most important of these angiogenic cytokines include FGF, VEGF, and platelet-derived growth factor (PDGF).

24. Are there any cytokines that inhibit angiogenesis?

Currently, more than 300 angiogenic inhibitors are known to decrease new blood vessel growth. Examples are endostatin and various tissue inhibitors of metalloproteinases (TIMPs).

25. Why is the process of angiogenesis important to the field of plastic and reconstructive surgery?

Angiogenesis is the most important determinant to the success of a healing wound. Regardless of whether the wound is a surgical incision from a blepharoplasty, a pressure/decubitus ulcer, or free flap reconstruction, the ability to form new blood vessels will largely dictate whether or not that wound will heal. Recent evidence has demonstrated that diabetic and aged patients exhibit decreased wound healing compared with healthy people due to an impairment in the formation of new blood vessels.

26. How else does the decrease in angiogenesis contribute to disease pathology?

The decreased ability to form new blood vessels contributes to multiple disease processes that are most evident in the elderly and diabetic populations. For example, cardiovascular disease currently is the leading cause of death in the United States. The decrease in angiogenesis is partly responsible for the inability to form collateral vessels in response to ischemia, such as that seen in patients with coronary artery disease, cerebrovascular accidents, peripheral vascular disease, and myocardial infarctions.

27. If a decrease in angiogenesis is associated with a propensity to develop these multiple disease processes, is an increase in angiogenesis always beneficial to the health of the patient?

The process of angiogenesis is extremely complicated and is dictated by the interaction between the angiogenic stimulators and inhibitors. Excessive angiogenesis is also a major contributor to certain illnesses, such as tumor growth and metastasis, psoriasis, and diabetic retinopathy. In addition, excessive angiogenesis is associated with certain vascular malformations such as the development of infantile hemangiomas.

28. What treatment modalities are available to treat these defects in angiogenesis?

Proangiogenic and antiangiogenic therapies currently are at the forefront of intense research, not just in the field of plastic and reconstructive surgery but also in multiple other disciplines such as cardiology and oncology. First, the search for proangiogenic therapies to treat myocardial and limb ischemia has failed to produce any convincingly positive results. However, various angiogenic stimulators, such as becaplermin (Regranex), currently are available for the care of nonhealing wounds. Similarly, the angiogenic inhibitor bevacizumab (Avastin) is the first to receive Food and Drug Administration (FDA) approval for use in combined chemotherapy treatment of patients with metastatic colorectal cancer.

29. What is therapeutic neovascularization?

The concept of therapeutic angiogenesis/vasculogenesis centers on the idea of transplanting vascular stem cells harvested from either the bone marrow or peripheral blood into patients suffering from various ischemic diseases in order to augment new blood vessel growth. Several small preliminary studies have shown a great deal of promise for this treatment modality, but larger, randomized control studies are necessary to corroborate these findings.

BIBLIOGRAPHY

Distraction Osteogenesis

Ashinoff RL, Cetrulo CL Jr, Galiano RD, et al: Bone morphogenic protein-2 gene therapy for mandibular distraction osteogenesis. Ann Plast Surg 52:585–590, 2004; discussion 591.

Campisi P, Hamdy RC, Lauzier D, et al: Expression of bone morphogenetic proteins during mandibular distraction osteogenesis. Plast Reconstr Surg 111:201–208, 2003; discussion 209–210.

De Bastiani G, Aldegheri R, Renzi Brivio L: The treatment of fractures with a dynamic axial fixator. J Bone Joint Surg Br 66:538–545, 1984.

Fang TD, Nacamuli RP, Song HM, et al: Creation and characterization of a mouse model of mandibular distraction osteogenesis. Bone 34:1004–1012, 2004.

Fang TD, Salim A, Xia W, et al: Angiogenesis is required for successful bone induction during distraction osteogenesis. J Bone Miner Re 20:1114–1124, 2005.

Gosain AK: Distraction osteogenesis of the craniofacial skeleton. Plast Reconstr Surg 107:278–280, 2001.

Ilizarov GA, Ledyaev VI: The replacement of long tubular bone defects by lengthening distraction osteotomy of one of the fragments. 1969. Clin Orthop Relat Res 280:7–10, 1992.

Loboa EG, Fang TD, Warren SM, et al: Mechanobiology of mandibular distraction osteogenesis: Experimental analyses with a rat model. Bone 34:336–343, 2004.

McCarthy J: The role of distraction osteogenesis in the reconstruction of the mandible in unilateral craniofacial microsomia. Clin Plast Surg 21:625–631, 1994.

Mofid MM, Inoue N, Atabey A, et al: Callus stimulation in distraction osteogenesis. Plast Reconstr Surg 109:1621–1629, 2002.

Mofid MM, Manson PN, Robertson BC, et al: Craniofacial distraction osteogenesis: A review of 3278 cases. Plast Reconstr Surg 108:1103–1114, 2001; discussion 1115–1117.

Sakurakichi K, Tsuchiya H, Uehara K, et al: Effects of timing of low-intensity pulsed ultrasound on distraction osteogenesis. J Orthop Res 22:395–403, 2004.

Snyder CC, Levine GA, Swanson HM, Browne EZJ: Mandibular lengthening by gradual distraction. Plast Reconstr Surg 51:506–508, 1973.

Tavakoli K, Walsh WR, Bonar F, et al: The role of latency in mandibular osteodistraction. J Craniomaxillofac Surg 26:209–219, 1998.

Troulis MJ, Glowacki J, Perrott DH, Kaban LB: Effects of latency and rate on bone formation in a porcine mandibular distraction model. J Oral Maxillofac Surg 58:507–513, 2000; discussion 514.

Craniosynostosis

Greenwald JA, Mehrara BJ, Spector JA, et al: Biomolecular mechanisms of calvarial bone induction: Immature versus mature dura mater. Plast Reconstr Surg 105:1382–1392, 2000.

Greenwald JA, Mehrara BJ, Spector JA, et al: Immature versus mature dura mater: II. Differential expression of genes important to calvarial reossification. Plast Reconstr Surg 106:630–638, 2000.

Greenwald JA, Mehrara BJ, Spector JA, et al: In vivo modulation of fgf biological activity alters cranial suture fate. Am J Pathol 158:441–452, 2001.

Mehrara BJ, Mackool RJ, McCarthy JG, et al: Immunolocalization of basic fibroblast growth factor and fibroblast growth factor receptor-1 and receptor-2 in rat cranial sutures. Plast Reconstr Surg 102:1805–1817, 1998; discussion 1818–1820.

Nacamuli RP, Fong KD, Lenton KA, et al: Expression and possible mechanisms of regulation of BMP3 in rat cranial sutures. Plast Reconstr Surg 116:1353–1362, 2005.

Opperman LA, Nolen AA, Ogle RC: TGF-beta 1, TGF-beta 2, and TGF-beta 3 exhibit distinct patterns of expression during cranial suture formation and obliteration in vivo and in vitro. J Bone Miner Res 12:301–310, 1997.

Roth DA, Bradley JP, Levine JP, et al: Studies in cranial suture biology: Part II. Role of the dura in cranial suture fusion. Plast Reconstr Surg 97:693–699, 1996.

Roth DA, Gold LI, Han VK, et al: Immunolocalization of transforming growth factor beta 1, beta 2, and beta 3 and insulin-like growth factor I in premature cranial suture fusion. Plast Reconstr Surg 99:300–309, 1997.

Warren SM, Brunet LJ, Harland RM, et al: The BMP antagonist noggin regulates cranial suture fusion. Nature 422:625–629, 2003.

Wilkie AO: Craniosynostosis: Genes and mechanisms. Hum Mol Genet 6:1647–1656, 1997.

Tissue Engineering/Regeneration

Albee FH: Studies in bone growth: Triple cap as a stimulus to osteogenesis. Ann Surg 71:32–36, 1920.

Asahara T, Murohara T, Sullivan A, et al: Isolation of putative progenitor endothelial cells for angiogenesis. Science 275:964–967, 1997.

Bruens ML, Pieterman H, de Wijn JR, Vaandrager JM: Porous polymethylmethacrylate as bone substitute in the craniofacial area. J Craniofac Surg 14:63–68, 2003.

Cowan CM, Shi YY, Aalami OO, et al: Adipose-derived adult stromal cells heal critical-size mouse calvarial defects. Nat Biotechnol 22:560–567, 2004.

Galiano RD, Tepper OM, Pelo CR, et al: Topical vascular endothelial growth factor accelerates diabetic wound healing through increased angiogenesis and by mobilizing and recruiting bone marrow-derived cells. Am J Pathol 164:1935–1947, 2004.

Kim KJ, Li B, Winer J, et al: Inhibition of vascular endothelial growth factor-induced angiogenesis suppresses tumor growth in vivo. Nature 362:841–844, 1993.

Lanza RP, Langer RS, Vacanti J: Principles of tissue engineering, 2nd ed. San Diego, CA, Academic Press, 2000, pp xli, 995.

Losordo DW, Dimmeler S: Therapeutic angiogenesis and vasculogenesis for ischemic disease. Part I: Angiogenic cytokines. Circulation 109:2487–2491, 2004.

Nicholson JW: Glass-ionomers in medicine and dentistry. Proc Inst Mech Eng [H] 212:121–126, 1998.

Nyberg P, Xie L, Kalluri R: Endogenous inhibitors of angiogenesis. Cancer Res 65:3967–3979, 2005.

Pittenger MF, Mackay AM, Beck SC, et al: Multilineage potential of adult human mesenchymal stem cells. Science 284:143–147, 1999.

Prockop DJ: Marrow stromal cells as stem cells for nonhematopoietic tissues. Science 276:71–74, 1997.

Rafii S, Lyden D: Therapeutic stem and progenitor cell transplantation for organ vascularization and regeneration. Nat Med 9:702–712, 2003.

Rah DK: Art of replacing craniofacial bone defects. Yonsei Med J 41:756–765, 2000.

Saadeh PB, Khosla RK, Mehrara BJ, et al: Repair of a critical size defect in the rat mandible using allogenic type I collagen. J Craniofac Surg 12:573–579, 2001.

Saba AA, Freedman BM, Gaffield JW, et al: Topical platelet-derived growth factor enhances wound closure in the absence of wound contraction: An experimental and clinical study. Ann Plast Surg 49:62–66, 2002; discussion 66.

Shenaq SM: Reconstruction of complex cranial and craniofacial defects utilizing iliac crest-internal oblique microsurgical free flap. Microsurgery 9:154–158, 1988.

Takahashi T, Kalka C, Masuda H, et al: Ischemia- and cytokine-induced mobilization of bone marrow-derived endothelial progenitor cells for neovascularization. Nat Med 5:434–438, 1999.

Tepper OM, Capla JM, Galiano RD, et al: Adult vasculogenesis occurs through in situ recruitment, proliferation, and tubulization of circulating bone marrow-derived cells. Blood 105:1068–1077, 2005.

Thomson JA, Itskovitz-Eldor J, Shapiro SS, et al: Embryonic stem cell lines derived from human blastocysts. Science 282:1145–1147, 1998.

Zuk PA, Zhu M, Ashjian P, et al: Human adipose tissue is a source of multipotent stem cells. Mol Biol Cell 13:4279–4295, 2002.

Zuk PA, Zhu M, Mizuno H, et al: Multilineage cells from human adipose tissue: Implications for cell-based therapies. Tissue Eng 7:211–228, 2001.

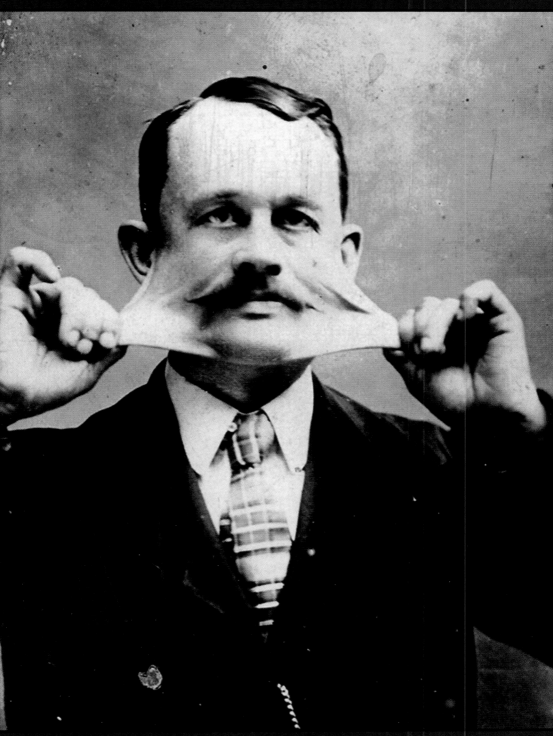

Elastic Skin Man. James Morris, ca. 1890. Albumen print. © 1998 The Wellcome Institute Library,

MALIGNANT MELANOMA

Raymond L. Barnhill, MD, and
Martin C. Mihm, Jr., MD

CHAPTER **13**

1. What are the essential facts about cutaneous melanoma?

Malignant melanoma of the skin is increasingly an important global health problem. The reasons for this are immediately apparent: (1) incidence rates of cutaneous melanoma continue to rise almost inexorably in populations of European origin worldwide; (2) diagnosis of melanoma at an early stage is almost always curable; (3) currently no effective treatment for advanced melanoma is available; (4) a large proportion of melanomas probably can be ascribed to a single (modifiable) risk factor—sun exposure, and (5) whether medical intervention of any kind influences outcome in melanoma has not been established. Major initiatives in recent years have concentrated on education about sun avoidance, the importance of skin awareness and skin examination, and the screening of populations at high risk for melanoma. However, whether any of the latter measures have had any significant influence on mortality from melanoma is unclear.

2. What is the basis for classifying melanoma?

Recent evidence supports the long-standing hypothesis that melanomas have distinct developmental pathways that are related to anatomic site, degree of sun exposure, genetic predisposition, and potentially other factors.

Because almost all melanomas are initially localized to squamous epithelium for some period of time, a classification of melanoma based on the presence or absence and patterns of intraepidermal involvement was described and used for many years. One idea behind such a classification was that particular intraepidermal patterns (also termed *radial* or *horizontal growth phases*) might correlate with differences in etiology and possibly prognosis. Nevertheless, an objective assessment of the classification of melanoma according to intraepidermal pattern or growth phase is that such a classification is artificial in many respects. The reasons for this view are (1) the tremendous morphologic heterogeneity of melanoma; (2) morphologic patterns may correlate with anatomic site; (3) recent data from molecular biologic studies indicate distinct pathways of melanoma development irrespective of type of intraepithelial growth pattern (see Question 3); (4) some intraepithelial components are difficult to recognize as either clearly benign (i.e., a potential precursor such as an atypical nevus) or malignant; (5) the idea that nodular melanomas develop as de novo invasive tumors without any initial intraepithelial melanocytic proliferation is theoretically possible but has not been proved; and (6) after adjustment for Breslow thickness the pattern of the intraepidermal component has no effect on prognosis.

3. What are the major forms of cutaneous melanoma?

Melanoma of intermittently sun-exposed skin. Melanomas in this group, which account for the great majority of melanomas in Caucasians, often (but not always) have an adjacent pagetoid intraepidermal component, a frequent association with *BRAF* mutations and melanocytic nevi (also with *BRAF* mutations), and development in relatively young adults.

Lentigo maligna (solar) melanoma. Melanomas of chronic sun-damaged skin are distinct from other forms of melanoma irrespective of intraepidermal pattern of melanocytic proliferation because of their strong correlation with cumulative sunlight exposure, onset in older persons, uncommon association with melanocytic nevi, and the pattern of genomic aberrations. This group of melanomas seems to have significantly fewer chromosomal aberrations compared with acral and mucosal melanomas, in general an absence of *BRAF* mutations, frequent gains in *CCND1* and regions of chromosome 22, and losses from chromosome 4q.

Acral (and mucosal) melanoma. These melanomas appear distinctive because they develop in relatively or completely sun-protected sites, have infrequent *BRAF* mutations, and show greater numbers of chromosomal aberrations compared with the latter melanomas.

Nodular melanoma. This descriptive term refers to melanomas with no adjacent intraepithelial component and is thought to simply indicate a heterogenous group of melanomas showing rapid tumor progression irrespective of intraepithelial pattern or location.

Continued research is needed to validate differences among the latter variants and to clearly identify avenues for preventive and therapeutic intervention that have real impact on patient suffering and mortality from melanoma. Such substantiation of unique differences among melanomas that provides the basis for meaningful intervention is the only rationale for the continued use of any classification of melanoma. Otherwise there is no real rationale for recording descriptive information in pathology reports, other than information such as Breslow thickness and margins, which has been validated to have a direct bearing on prognosis and patient management.

4. What are the general clinical features of cutaneous melanoma?

In general, cutaneous melanoma affects adult Caucasians most commonly and is rarely observed before puberty. Men and women are equally affected, although some European studies have suggested a higher incidence in females. Patients are most commonly diagnosed with melanoma in the fourth through seventh decades. The most common site is the trunk (back) followed by the upper extremities and head and neck for men, and the lower extremities followed by the back, upper extremities, and head and neck for women. Gross morphologic features of melanoma include size, often >1 cm (range 2 mm to >15 cm); irregular or notched borders; asymmetry; complexity of color including a variable admixture of tan, brown, blue, black, red, pink, gray, and white; and ulceration and bleeding (Fig. 13-1). Early melanomas, especially those involving chronic sun-exposed and acral sites, may be completely flat but with progression usually develop a papular or nodular component (Figs. 13-2 to 13-4). Melanomas lacking pigment (amelanotic melanoma) and those resembling keratoses are particularly difficult to diagnose without a high index of suspicion (Fig. 13-5). Acral melanoma, although accounting for 5% or less of melanomas among Caucasians, is the most frequent form of melanoma among Asians, Africans, and other ethnic groups of color (see Fig. 13-3). However, approximately the same incidence of acral melanoma occurs in all ethnic groups. Subungual melanoma is a distinctive variant of acral melanoma that most often involves the nailbed of the great toe or thumb, where it commonly presents as an ulcerated tumor. However, the initial manifestations may include a longitudinal pigmented band of the nail plate (frequently ≥9 mm in width) or a mass under the nail plate (Fig. 13-6). A useful clinical sign is pigmentation extending from the nail onto the surrounding periungual skin (Hutchinson's sign).

5. What are the general histopathologic features of cutaneous melanoma?

The intraepithelial component. Almost all melanomas begin as a proliferation of melanocytes initially confined to the epidermis (Fig. 13-7). The latter proliferation may develop with or without a detectable melanocytic nevus. Estimates of the frequency of melanomas developing in continuity with a nevus of any kind vary widely; approximately one third of

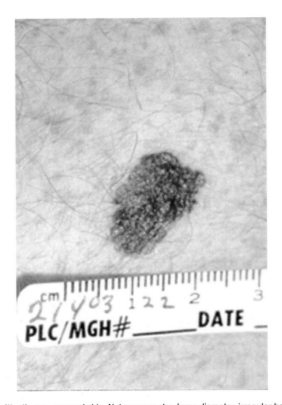

Figure 13-1. Melanoma of intermittently sun-exposed skin. Note asymmetry, large diameter, irregular borders, and complex coloration.

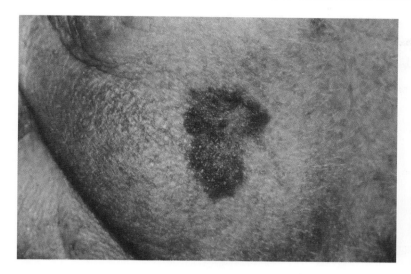

Figure 13-2. Solar melanoma (melanoma of chronically sun-exposed skin). This lesion involves the cheek. The lesion has macular and papular components, asymmetry, large diameter, irregular borders, and complex coloration.

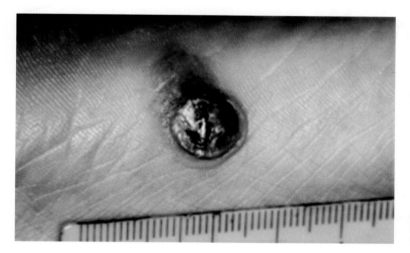

Figure 13-3. Acral melanoma. This lesion demonstrates macular and large nodular components.

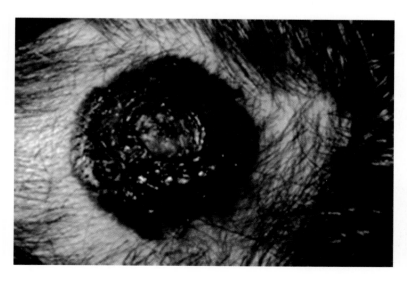

Figure 13-4. "Nodular" melanoma. Melanoma on scalp without demonstrable surround component. Melanomas with this configuration may develop on any anatomic site with or without a clearly identifiable adjacent intraepithelial proliferation of melanoma.

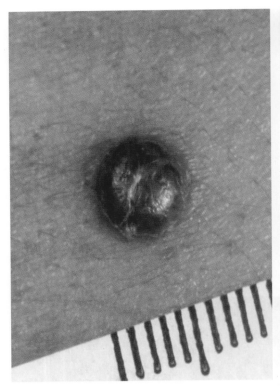

Figure 13-5. Amelanotic "nodular" melanoma. This type of lesion may develop at any location and is indistinguishable from metastatic melanoma.

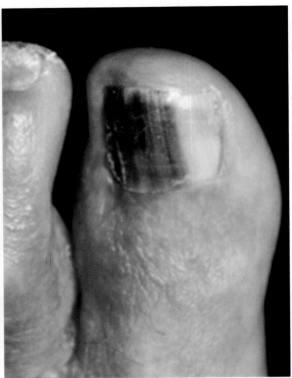

Figure 13-6. Subungual melanoma. Note broad irregularly pigmented band involving nail plate. Pigmentation extends onto periungual skin (Hutchinson's sign).

melanomas have nevus remnants. The duration of this intraepidermal phase ranges from months to many years, during which these proliferative lesions show progressive degrees of architectural and cytologic atypicality.

Increasing cytologic atypia of melanocytes accompanies the aberrant architectural appearance. The melanocytes vary in degree of atypia and the proportion of cells with nuclear atypia. However, atypical melanocytes usually have enlarged nuclei that exhibit variation in nuclear shapes and chromatin patterns, and they may have large nucleoli. Thickening of nuclear membranes and irregular nuclear contours are also characteristic. The cytoplasm of such melanocytes may be abundant with a pink granular quality, may contain granular or finely divided ("dusty") melanin (Figs. 13-7 to 13-9), or may show retraction, resulting in a clear space around the nuclei. Melanocytes with scant

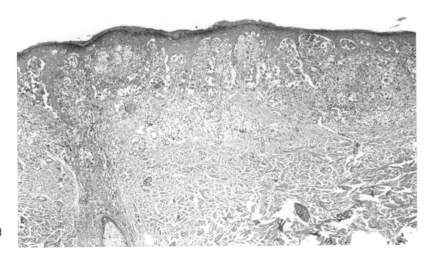

Figure 13-7. Melanoma of intermittently sun-exposed skin (pagetoid melanoma). Scanning magnification shows pagetoid spread of epithelioid melanoma cells.

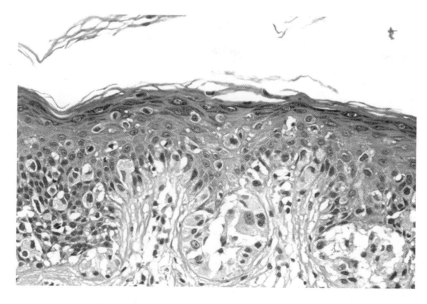

Figure 13-8. Melanoma of intermittently sun-exposed skin (pagetoid melanoma). Higher magnification shows pagetoid pattern and the beginnings of dermal invasion by melanoma cells.

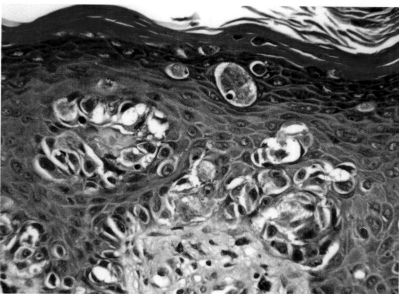

Figure 13-9. Melanoma of intermittently sun-exposed skin (pagetoid melanoma). Pagetoid melanocytosis with large epithelioid melanoma cells.

cytoplasm typically have high nuclear-to-cytoplasmic ratios. Such proliferations have been variously labeled as atypical melanocytic hyperplasia, premalignant melanosis, melanocytic dysplasia, and "pagetoid melanocytic proliferation" as well as melanoma in situ.

Invasive melanoma. After the period of intraepidermal proliferation, there is often invasion of the papillary dermis, primarily as single cells and small aggregates of cells. Microinvasive melanoma is remarkable for a striking host response in the papillary dermis, typically a dense cellular infiltrate of lymphocytes and monocyte/macrophages. Presumably, in consequence of this host reaction, regression, often focal, is common in up to 50% of microinvasive melanomas (see Question 28).

The term *vertical growth phase* (VGP) has been used by some to describe the proliferation of invasive melanoma cells as cohesive aggregates (Fig. 13-10). It has been postulated that the so-called VGP signifies the onset of the metastatic phenotype because it may be indistinguishable from metastatic melanoma. However, melanomas lacking the morphology of the VGP have resulted in metastases.

Melanomas with prominent invasive components may display polypoid morphologies such that more than half (sessile forms) or virtually all (pedunculated forms) of the tumor is above the epidermal surface. Amelanotic variants also may develop in any type of melanoma.

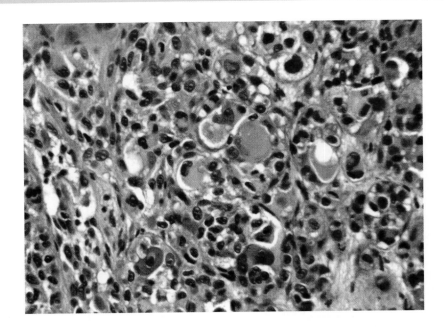

Figure 13-10. Melanoma of intermittently sun-exposed skin (pagetoid melanoma). Invasive component contains epithelioid melanoma cells.

6. What are the clinical and histopathologic features of melanomas of intermittently sun-exposed skin?

CLINICAL FEATURES

- In general onset after puberty, but all ages affected
- Most frequent ages 30 to 70 years
- Caucasians > Africans, Asians
- Women ≥ men
- Most common sites are lower extremities and trunk of women and trunk (back) of men
- Pain, pruritus
- Size often >1 cm (range 2 mm to >15 cm)
- Initially macular, later stages may be papular and nodular
- Asymmetry
- Irregular and often notched borders
- Complexity and variation in color often with admixtures of tan, brown, black, blue, gray, white, red
- May be entirely skin-colored (amelanotic) or black
- Ulceration and bleeding may be present

HISTOPATHOLOGIC FEATURES

ARCHITECTURE

- Asymmetry
- Heterogeneity of lesion
- Large size (>6 mm), but many exceptions
- Poor circumscription of proliferation
- Melanin not uniformly distributed

ORGANIZATIONAL ABNORMALITIES OF INTRAEPIDERMAL COMPONENT

- Pagetoid spread
- Upward migration of melanocytes in random pattern, single cells predominate over nests, cells often reach granular and cornified layers
- Lentiginous melanocytic proliferation
  - Melanocytes reach confluence
  - Nesting of melanocytes (sun-damaged skin)

- Melanocytes not equidistant
- Proliferation of melanocytes along adnexal epithelium
- Nested pattern
  - Variation in size, shape, placement of nests
  - Nests replace large portions of squamous epithelium
  - Diminished cohesiveness of cells in nests
  - Confluence of nests
- Loss of epidermal rete pattern (effacement)
- Mononuclear cell infiltrates, often band-like
- Fibroplasia of papillary dermis
- Regression frequently present

CYTOLOGY

- Nuclear changes
  - Majority of melanocytes uniformly atypical
  - Nuclear enlargement
  - Nuclear pleomorphism (variation in sizes and shapes)
  - Nuclear hyperchromasia with coarse chromatin
  - One or more prominent nucleoli
- Cytoplasmic changes
  - Abundant granular eosinophilic cytoplasm in epithelioid cells
  - Finely divided ("dusty") melanin
  - Variation in size of melanin granules
  - High nuclear-to-cytoplasmic ratios in spindle cells
  - Retraction of cytoplasm
- Mitoses (in dermal component)
- Atypical mitoses
- Necrotic cells

INVASIVE COMPONENT IN DERMIS

ARCHITECTURE

- Tumefactive cellular aggregates
- Pushing, expanding pattern without regard for stroma
- Hypercellularity
- Less host response

CYTOLOGY

- As previously
- Increased nuclear-to-cytoplasmic ratios
- Mitoses in dermal component
- Atypical mitoses
- Necrotic cells

7. **What is the differential diagnosis of melanomas of intermittently sun-exposed skin?**
   - Markedly atypical (dysplastic) nevi
   - Halo nevi
   - Spitz tumors
   - Pigmented spindle cell melanocytic tumors
   - Recurrent/persistent melanocytic nevi
   - Congenital nevi

8. **What are the clinical and histopathologic features of lentigo maligna melanomas?**
   Lentigo maligna is a confusing term because it has been used to describe a histologic spectrum ranging from slightly increased numbers of basilar melanocytes with variable, low-grade cytologic atypia, which is *not* clearly melanoma in situ, to a contiguous and often nested intraepidermal proliferation of highly pleomorphic melanocytic cells, which *is* melanoma in situ. Furthermore, some pathologists consider all lentigo maligna to be melanoma in situ whereas others obviously do not, hence the confusion. Irrespective of terminology used, the pathologist must clearly communicate to the clinician the meaning of the pathologic terms used to describe these lesions.

CLINICAL FEATURES

- Age 60 to 70 years
- Men = women
- Sun-exposed surfaces: cheek (most common), nose, forehead, ears, neck, dorsal surfaces of hands
- 0.2 to 20 cm
- Initial tan macule suggesting a varnish-like stain
- Tan, brown, black macule or patch, black flecks are characteristic (early lesions)
- Pink, gray, white with progression and areas of regression
- Papule or nodule, pigmented or amelanotic (advanced)
- Ulceration, bleeding
- Asymmetry
- Irregular, notched borders

HISTOPATHOLOGIC FEATURES
(FIGS. 13-11 AND 13-12)

- Effacement and thinning of epidermis common
- Prominent solar elastosis

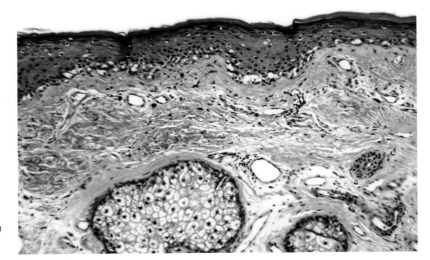

Figure 13-11. Solar melanoma in situ. Note striking basilar proliferation of variably atypical melanocytes in the epidermis.

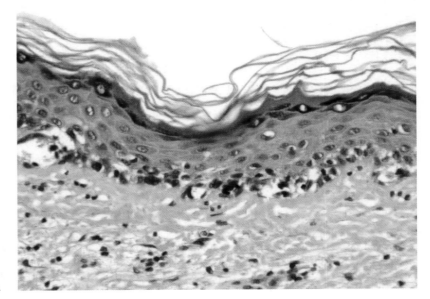

Figure 13-12. Solar lentiginous melanoma. Higher magnification shows atypia of basilar melanocytes.

- Solar intraepidermal melanocytic neoplasia (lentigo maligna)
- Solar intraepidermal melanocytic proliferation (insufficient for melanoma in situ):
  - Lentiginous melanocytic proliferation
  - Pleomorphic melanocytes (variable cytologic atypia)
  - Extension of melanocytic proliferation downward along appendages
  - Usual absence of nesting and pagetoid spread
- Melanoma in situ:
  - Contiguous or near contiguous lentiginous melanocytic proliferation
  - Intraepidermal nesting of melanocytes
  - Pagetoid spread
  - Prominent extension of melanocytic proliferation downward along appendages, often with nesting
  - Significant cytologic atypia
  - Melanocytes somewhat spindled to increasingly epithelioid
- Pigmented spindle cell variant (often on ears):
  - Prominent intraepidermal discohesive nesting of atypical spindle cells
  - Spindle cells often comprise invasive component but polygonal, small cells common
  - Appendage-associated nesting of atypical melanocytes suggests invasion and may be florid (not true invasion)
  - Partial regression relatively common
  - Precursor nevus present ≈3% of cases
  - Desmoplasia, neurotropism, angiotropism common

9. What is the differential diagnosis of lentigo maligna melanoma?

- Solar lentigo
- Solar melanocytic hyperplasia (photoactivation)
  - De novo
  - Occurrence with nevi, fibrous papule, basal cell carcinoma, actinic keratosis, etc.
- Atypical intraepidermal melanocytic proliferation, not otherwise specified
- Solar lentiginous junctional or compound melanocytic nevi with or without atypia (may overlap atypical (dysplastic nevi)
- Pigmented spindle cell tumor
- Pigmented actinic keratosis
- Squamous cell carcinoma, spindle cell type
- Atypical fibroxanthoma
- Cellular neurothekeoma
- Malignant peripheral nerve sheath tumor
- Angiosarcoma
- Kaposi's sarcoma
- Leiomyosarcoma

10. What are the clinical and histopathologic features of acral (and mucosal) melanomas?

CLINICAL FEATURES

- Age 60 to 70 years
- Men = women
- Equal incidence in all racial groups
- Most prevalent form of melanoma in Africans, Asians, Native Americans, other peoples of color
- Glabrous (volar) skin and nail unit
  - Palms, soles, digits 85% of acral melanomas
  - Nail unit 15%
- Feet 90% of cases
  - Soles 68% to 71%
  - Toes 11%
  - Nail units 16% to 20%
  - Palms 4% to 10%
  - Fingers 2%
- 0.3 to 12 cm
  - Often 0.7 cm or larger
  - <0.7 cm with irregular borders, color, or "parallel ridge" pattern on epiluminescence microscopy
- Often jet-black macule early but also tan, brown, gray, blue, pink, white
- Pigmented or amelanotic papule or nodule (advanced) with ulceration, bleeding, eschar
- Irregular borders, notching

HISTOPATHOLOGIC FEATURES
(FIGS. 13-13 TO 13-15)

- Prominent acanthosis with elongated epidermal rete common
- Thickened stratum corneum
- Contiguous or near-contiguous lentiginous melanocytic proliferation in almost all lesions
- Intraepidermal melanocytes appear to lie in lacunae (clear spaces)
- Variable cytologic atypia with minimal atypia in early lesions
- Pagetoid spread (particularly in more advanced lesions)
- Intraepidermal nesting (particularly in more advanced lesions)
- Proliferation of melanocytes downward along eccrine ducts (even into deep dermis and subcutis)
- Pronounced pagetoid spread, large intraepidermal nests, significant numbers of melanocytes in stratum corneum in advanced lesions
- Polygonal to spindled melanocytes often with prominent dendrites
- Nuclear enlargement, hyperchromatism, pleomorphism prominent
- Invasive component:
  - Cohesive nests, sheets of cells, or loosely aggregated files of cells
  - Spindle cells common but also polygonal, small, and highly pleomorphic cells are noted
  - Nevoid and sarcomatoid variants occur
- Desmoplasia, neurotropism, angiotropism common

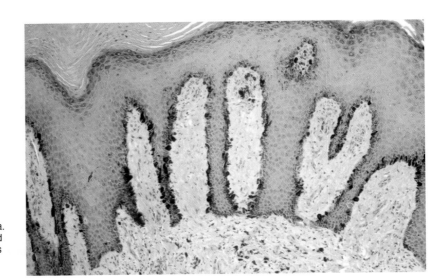

Figure 13-13. Acral melanoma. The epidermis is hyperplastic and exhibits characteristic lentiginous proliferation of pleomorphic melanoma cells.

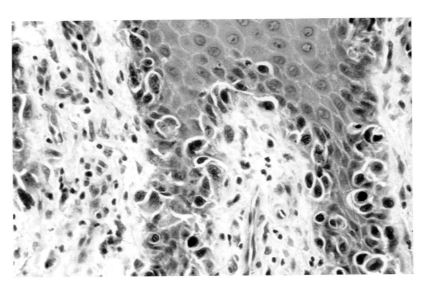

Figure 13-14. Acral melanoma. Higher magnification shows striking pleomorphism of melanoma cells.

Figure 13-15. Acral melanoma. Hyperplastic epidermis exhibits irregular and confluent nesting of melanoma cells.

11. What is the differential diagnosis of acral (and mucosal) melanoma?

- Melanotic macule
- Lentigo
- Atypical intraepidermal melanocytic proliferation, not otherwise specified
- Acral melanocytic nevus with or without atypia (may overlap atypical [dysplastic] nevus)
- Pigmented spindle cell tumor
- Squamous cell carcinoma, spindle cell type
- Atypical fibroxanthoma
- Cellular neurothekeoma
- Malignant peripheral nerve sheath tumor
- Angiosarcoma
- Kaposi's sarcoma
- Leiomyosarcoma

12. What are the clinical and histopathologic features of nodular melanomas?

CLINICAL FEATURES

- Age 30 to 70 years (often 40 to 50, but any age)
- Men = women
- Any site especially trunk dorsal surfaces of hands
- 0.4 to 5 cm
- Often rapid evolution (e.g., 4 months to 2 years)
- Papule or nodule, pigmented or amelanotic (advanced)
  - Often protuberant, polypoid
  - Black, blue-black, pink
- Ulceration, bleeding
- Asymmetry but symmetry may be present
- Often well-defined borders

HISTOPATHOLOGIC FEATURES
(FIG. 13-16)

- Dome-shaped polypoid or sessile tumor often
- May be pedunculated
- Asymmetry
- Epidermis commonly thinned, effaced, ulcerated
- Overlying intraepidermal component may or may not be present and usually does not extend peripherally beyond dermal invasive tumor

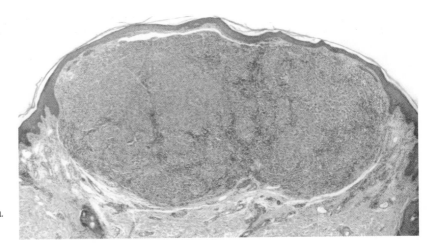

Figure 13-16 "Nodular" melanoma. The tumor has an asymmetrical dome-shaped configuration.

- Pagetoid spread, lentiginous melanocytic proliferation, intraepithelial nesting may be present
- Cohesive aggregate or aggregates of tumor cells fill subjacent dermis, subcutis
- Usually no maturation
- Host response at base and/or tumor-infiltrating lymphocytes common
- Epithelioid cells often compose the invasive component but spindle cells, small cuboidal cells are common and often heterogeneity is present
- Partial regression relatively uncommon
- Precursor nevus present ≈6% of cases

13. What is the differential diagnosis of nodular melanomas?
- Metastatic melanoma
- Spitz tumor
- Pigmented spindle cell tumor
- Atypical halo-like nevus
- Cellular blue nevus with atypia
- Squamous cell carcinoma
- Adnexal carcinomas
- Atypical fibroxanthoma
- Fibrous histiocytoma
- Adult xanthogranuloma
- Lymphoma, particularly large cell anaplastic variants
- Cellular neurothekeoma
- Malignant peripheral nerve sheath tumor
- Capillary hemangioma
- Malignant glomus tumor or with atypia
- Angiosarcoma
- Kaposi's sarcoma
- Leiomyosarcoma

14. What are the most important unusual variants of melanoma?
- Desmoplastic neurotropic melanoma
- Angiotropic melanoma
- Nevoid melanoma
- Small cell melanoma
- Spitzoid melanoma
- Melanoma arising in compound or dermal nevi
- Melanoma originating from or resembling a blue nevus (malignant blue nevus)

15. What are the clinical and histopathologic features of desmoplastic neurotropic melanoma?
These rare variants of melanoma exhibit a continuum of histologic features corresponding to the neuroectodermal origin of the melanocyte. The phenotype of the tumor may include any combination of the following: desmoplasia—fibroblast-like spindle cells usually in fascicles (predominant pattern); neurotropism (perineurial invasion)—invasion of nerve

structures by tumor cells; neural differentiation (both schwannian and perineurial)—formation of nerve-like structures recapitulating perineurium and endoneurium or delicate sheets of spindle cells reminiscent of neurofibroma; and less commonly myofibrocytic or neuroendocrine differentiation, as in Merkel cell carcinoma. Desmoplastic melanoma most frequently arises in association with lentiginous melanomas; however, de novo variants of desmoplastic melanoma also occur.

CLINICAL FEATURES

- Age 60 to 65 years
- Men ≥ women
- Sun-exposed skin, head and neck, but also acral, mucosal sites
- Firm nodule
- Flesh-colored or with pigmented lesion (29% to 43%)
- 1 to 3 cm
- Occasional dysesthesias, nerve palsies

HISTOPATHOLOGIC FEATURES

- Intraepidermal melanocytic proliferation in ≈50% to 75%
- Lentigo maligna melanoma in situ, most common
- Fibrous nodule in dermis and possibly subcutis resembling scar
- Often absence of pigment
- Fascicles of atypical spindle cells
- Atypia varies from minimal (most common) to anaplastic
- Schwannian, perineurial differentiation
- Neurotropism common (perineurial and endoneurial invasion)
- Rare macronodular neurotropic variants occur
- Patchy lymphoid infiltrates common
- Variable myxoid stroma
- Occasional mitoses in dermis (often mitotic rate of 1 to 2 per square millimeter)
- Spindle cells usually vimentin$^+$, S100$^+$ p75 neurotrophin receptor$^+$, HMB45$^-$, Melan A$^-$, tyrosinase$^-$, MITF$^-$

16. What is the differential diagnosis of desmoplastic neurotropic melanoma?

- Sclerosing blue nevi, including variants with hypercellularity
- Desmoplastic (sclerosing) Spitz tumor
- Neurothekeoma, particularly cellular variants
- Malignant peripheral nerve sheath tumors
- Myxoma
- Dermatofibroma
- Dermatofibrosarcoma protuberans
- Atypical fibroxanthoma
- Malignant fibrous histiocytoma
- Scar
- Fibromatosis
- Spindle cell squamous cell carcinoma
- Leiomyosarcoma

17. What are the clinical and histopathologic features of angiotropic melanoma?

The importance of angiotropism as a biologic phenomenon and prognostic factor in localized melanoma and as the likely correlate of *extravascular migratory metastasis* has recently been emphasized. Angiotropism is observed much more frequently than vascular invasion. In a series of 650 consecutive invasive melanomas, the frequency of vascular-to-lymphatic invasion was 1.4%.

CLINICAL FEATURES

- Age 30 to 70 years (often 40 to 50, but any age)
- Men = women
- Any site
- 0.4 to 5 cm

HISTOPATHOLOGIC FEATURES

- Any type of melanoma
- Melanoma cells cuff microvessels in pericytic location
- Often at least level IV
- Increased frequency of neurotropism

18. What are the clinical and histopathologic features of nevoid melanoma?

In very broad terms, the term *nevoid melanoma* could connote any form of melanoma having some resemblance to or mimicking any type of melanocytic nevus. The term is used rather restrictively in this chapter (and by most other authors) to describe melanomas that closely resemble ordinary compound or dermal nevi; the latter lesions generally fall into four groups: (1) those with a raised, dome-shaped or polypoid (nodular nonverrucous) configuration and resemble a predominately dermal nevus, (2) those with a distinctly papillomatous or verrucous surface, (3) those resembling a lentiginous melanocytic nevus arising in sun-exposed skin of older individuals, and (4) those with a predominately or exclusively intraepidermal nested appearance mimicking a junctional or compound nevus.

The concept that melanomas may closely resemble melanocytic nevi probably dates back at least to the introduction of the term *minimal deviation melanoma*. Schmoeckel and colleagues first coined the term "nevoid" melanoma in their description of 33 melanomas with histologic features suggesting a melanocytic nevus. They noted that 15 patients developed metastases and concluded that nevoid melanoma did not seem to have any better prognosis than conventional melanoma. Approximately 70 additional cases have subsequently been reported in the literature.

CLINICAL FEATURES

- Women = men
- All ages, commonly fifth decade
- Occurs anywhere, but trunk and lower extremities most common
- No distinctive features but may have verrucous appearance
- Any size, often relatively small diameter but up to 2 cm or more

HISTOPATHOLOGIC FEATURES

- Striking resemblance to banal compound or dermal nevus at scanning magnification
- Symmetry common
- Well-circumscribed lateral margins
- Pagetoid spread not common
- Often limited intraepidermal component
- Relatively small nevus-like cells, monomorphous appearance
- Some maturation may be present but often incomplete or absent
- Single-cell infiltration at base
- Cytologic atypia
  - Nuclear pleomorphism
  - Angulated nuclei
  - Hyperchromatism
  - Prominent nucleoli may be present
- Mitoses in dermal component, particularly deep
- Infiltration of adnexal structures
- Little or no inflammation

19. What is the differential diagnosis of nevoid melanoma?
- Papillomatous or cellular melanocytic nevi
- Metastatic melanoma

20. What are the clinical and histopathologic features of small cell melanoma?

The term *small cell melanoma* has been introduced into the literature to describe a heterogenous assortment of melanomas from several settings perhaps related only by the common denominator of *small* melanoma cells. This term has been used to refer to (1) rare melanomas developing in children and adolescents on the scalp;

(2) melanomas developing in congenital melanocytic nevi of children and adolescents; (3) melanomas developing in any setting, but particularly in adults, that resemble small round cell malignancies such as Merkel cell carcinoma; (4) melanomas developing in sun-damaged of older individuals in a setting of solar melanocytic neoplasia or atypical lentiginous nevi; and (5) melanomas in adults that have the characteristics of nevoid melanoma, as described above. Because of a considerable overlap of small cell melanomas and nevoid melanomas in adults (see Question 18), the following section discusses only two entities:

1. Exceptionally rare melanomas that mimic high-grade small round cell malignancies
2. Small cell melanomas arising predominately in sun-damaged skin of elderly individuals

CLINICAL FEATURES

HIGH-GRADE SMALL CELL MELANOMA MIMICKING MERKEL CELL CARCINOMA

- Extremely rare
- Adults (any age)
- Any site
- Often 0.4 to 2 cm
- Often amelanotic papule or nodule

SMALL CELL MELANOMA ARISING IN PREDOMINATELY SUN-DAMAGED SKIN

- Age often >50 years (range 18 to 91 years)
- Men > women (2:1)
- Backs of men, legs of women
- Usually >1 cm
- Variegated color
- Often tan, brown, black, gray

HISTOPATHOLOGIC FEATURES

HIGH-GRADE SMALL CELL MELANOMA MIMICKING MERKEL CELL CARCINOMA

- Melanin and intraepidermal involvement may or may not be present
- Often cohesive nests, cords, sheets of small round cells
- Cells with scant cytoplasm
- Round to oval nuclei
- Prominent mitotic rate and necrosis

SMALL CELL MELANOMA ARISING IN PREDOMINATELY SUN-DAMAGED SKIN

- Intraepidermal component often extensive, lentiginous, and nested
- Usually some pagetoid spread
- Elongated epidermal rete ridges common
- Effacement and thinning of epidermis also common
- Small cuboidal melanocytes with scant cytoplasm
- Melanocytes larger that those in nevi
- Nuclear pleomorphism
- Irregular nuclear contours
- Dense chromatin
- Prominent nucleoli
- Dermal nests often large, nodular, cohesive, anastomosing
- Often absence of maturation
- Continued pigment synthesis with depth
- Mitotic figures rare
- Solar elastosis
- Host response with fibroplasia, partial regression common

21. What is the differential diagnosis of small cell melanoma?

HIGH-GRADE SMALL CELL MELANOMA MIMICKING MERKEL CELL CARCINOMA

- Metastatic melanoma
- Primary and metastatic neuroendocrine carcinoma
- Metastatic small cell carcinoma
- Lymphoma
- Other small round cell malignancies

SMALL CELL MELANOMA ARISING IN PREDOMINATELY SUN-DAMAGED SKIN

- Atypical lentiginous nevi of sun-exposed skin

22. What are the clinical and histopathologic features of spitzoid melanoma?

The term *spitzoid melanoma*, if used at all, should be reserved for a melanoma that truly has a striking morphologic resemblance to a Spitz tumor. The term probably best describes a rare group of tumors often developing in young individuals that are only diagnosed as melanoma in retrospect, that is, after the development of metastases and an aggressive course. Given the profound difficulty of distinguishing some Spitz or Spitz-like tumors from melanoma, we discourage the use of term *spitzoid melanoma* because it may result in the indiscriminate labeling of a heterogeneous group of lesions that include benign Spitz tumors, lesions that are biologically indeterminant, conventional melanomas, and a rare controversial group of tumors previously termed *metastasizing Spitz nevus/ tumor*. The latter group of lesions includes some that have given rise to single lymph node metastases without subsequent recurrence of melanoma on long-term follow-up.

We recommend such melanocytic proliferations be categorized, if at all possible, into one of the following groups: (1) Spitz tumor, (2) Spitz-like melanocytic tumor with atypical features (atypical Spitz tumor) and possibly indeterminate biologic potential (describing abnormal features present such as large size, deep involvement, ulceration, lack of maturation, mitotic rate, presence of deep mitoses), and (3) melanoma.

CLINICAL FEATURES

- Women = men
- Any age
- Occurs anywhere
- Any appearance
- Any size, often relatively small diameter but up to 2 cm or more

HISTOPATHOLOGIC FEATURES

- Plaque type, dome-shaped, or polypoid configuration
- Epidermal hyperplasia common
- Striking resemblance to Spitz tumor at scanning magnification
- Asymmetry common
- Size often >1 cm
- Usually enlarged epithelioid to spindled melanocytes
- Diminished or absent maturation
- Mitotic rate >2 to 6 mm^2
- Cytologic atypia
  - Nuclear pleomorphism
  - Angulated nuclei
  - Hyperchromatism
  - Prominent nucleoli may be present
- Mitoses deep

23. What is the differential diagnosis of spitzoid melanoma?
- Atypical Spitz tumor

24. What are the clinical and histopathologic features of melanoma arising in compound or dermal nevi?

CLINICAL FEATURES

- Women = men
- All ages, commonly 40 to 60 years
- Occurs anywhere, but head and neck most common
- Any size, often larger that ordinary nevi
- Often history of recent change or enlargement

HISTOPATHOLOGIC FEATURES

- Often eccentric and/or asymmetrical nodule in melanocytic nevus
- Nodule shows confluence and hypercellularity
- Often abrupt interface with surrounding nevus
- Lack of maturation
- Cytologic atypia
  - Nuclear pleomorphism
  - Angulated nuclei
  - Hyperchromatism
  - Prominent nucleoli may be present
- Mitoses in dermal component >2 to 3/mm^2

25. What is the differential diagnosis of melanoma arising in compound or dermal nevi?
- Cellular nodules (typical or atypical) present in melanocytic nevi

26. What are the clinical and histopathologic features of melanoma originating in or resembling blue nevi (malignant blue nevus)?
Malignant blue nevus is an extremely rare form of melanoma originating from or associated with a preexisting blue nevus and characterized by a dense proliferation of variably pigmented spindle cells without involvement of the epidermis. Approximately 80 cases of malignant blue nevus have been reported.

CLINICAL FEATURES

- Two thirds of patients are men
- All ages (mean age ≈46 years)
- Scalp most common site
- Usually >1 to 2 cm
- Blue-black multinodular appearance

HISTOPATHOLOGIC FEATURES

- Often overtly malignant component juxtaposed to benign usually cellular blue nevus
- Nodule shows confluence and hypercellularity
- Often abrupt interface with surrounding nevus
- Lack of maturation
- Cytologic atypia
  - Nuclear pleomorphism
  - Angulated nuclei
  - Hyperchromatism
  - Prominent nucleoli may be present
- Sarcoma-like presentation without distinct benign and malignant components
  - Hypercellular fascicles or nodules
- Cellular blue nevus-like lesion with additional atypical features
- Mitoses in dermal component >2 to 3/mm^2

27. What is the differential diagnosis of melanoma originating in or resembling blue nevi (malignant blue nevus)?
- Cellular blue nevus and atypical variants
- Metastatic melanoma
- Clear cell sarcoma

28. What is regression in melanoma?

Spontaneous regression refers to the partial or total obliteration of melanoma, presumably by one or more of the following: cytokine-mediated, humoral, or cell-mediated host response. However, regression is poorly understood at present. Regression is seen most often in microinvasive or thin melanoma and is present as focal, partial, and rarely complete regression of the tumor. The changes of regression form a continuum but may be arbitrarily categorized into three stages:

1. *Early (or active).* Zone of papillary dermis and epidermis within a recognizable melanoma, characterized by dense infiltrates of lymphocytes disrupting/replacing nests of melanoma cells within the papillary dermis and possibly the epidermis, as compared with adjoining zones of tumor. Degenerating melanoma cells should be recognizable. No obvious fibrosis.
2. *Intermediate.* Zone of papillary dermis and epidermis within a recognizable melanoma, characterized by reduction (loss) in the amount of tumor (a disruption in the continuity of the tumor) or absence of tumor in papillary dermis and possibly within the epidermis, compared with adjacent zones of tumor, and replaced by varying admixtures of lymphoid cells and increased fibrous tissue (as compared with normal papillary dermis) in this zone. Variable telangiectasia (and new blood vessel formation) and melanophages may be present.
3. *Late.* Zone of papillary dermis and epidermis within a recognizable melanoma, characterized by marked reduction in the amount of tumor compared with adjacent areas of tumor, or absence of tumor in this zone, and replacement and expansion of the papillary dermis in this zone by extensive fibrosis (usually dense fibrous tissue, horizontally disposed) and variable telangiectasia (and new blood vessel formation), melanophages, sparse or no lymphoid infiltrates, and effacement of the epidermis (other than fibrosis, the latter features are frequently present but not essential for recognizing regression).

29. How does melanoma metastasize, and what are the most frequent sites of metastasis?

- Melanoma metastasizes through lymphatic channels, vascular channels, and along the surfaces of vessels (angiotropism)
- Lymph nodes are the most common sites of metastases
- Cutaneous metastases are common and include local satellite, in transit (between primary lesion and regional lymph nodes), and epidermotropic metastases

Melanoma can spread hematogenously, through lymphatic channels, by migration along vascular channels (angiotropism), or by direct local invasion and thus may occur in any site of the body. Metastases are more frequent to lymph nodes, skin, and subcutaneous tissue (nonvisceral sites) than to visceral organs. Lymph nodes are the most common site of metastases, and 60% to 80% of patients with metastatic melanoma develop lymph node metastases. The lymph node groups most commonly involved are ilioinguinal, axillary, intraparotid, and cervical lymph nodes. The metastatic tumor may be clinically apparent (macroscopic metastasis) or detected only by histologic examination (microscopic metastasis).

Nearly half of patients with metastatic melanoma develop skin metastases, which may occur in the area of locoregional lymphatic drainage or at a remote location. Two subtypes of regional cutaneous metastases are arbitrarily distinguished by their distance from the primary melanoma.

Cutaneous satellites are discontinuous tumor cell aggregates that are located in the dermis and/or subcutis within 5 cm of the primary tumor, whereas *in-transit metastases* are located more than 5 cm away from the primary melanoma. The finding of the latter metastases has poor prognostic implications, as the majority of patients with such lesions develop disseminated metastatic disease. Although virtually any organ may be involved, the most common first sites of visceral metastases reported in clinical studies are lung (14% to 20%), liver (14% to 20%), brain (12% to 20%), bone (11% to 17%), and intestine (1% to 7%); first metastases at other sites are very rare (<1%).

30. What are the principal diagnostic problems associated with metastatic melanoma?

- May mimic a wide spectrum of neoplastic lesions
- Amelanotic tumors
- Primary versus metastatic melanoma
- Nodal nevus deposits vs metastatic melanoma in lymph nodes
- Metastatic melanoma with unknown primary
- Melanosis in metastatic melanoma

Several situations may arise in which the diagnosis of metastatic melanoma is not straightforward. The problem may lie in the identification of a metastatic-appearing lesion as melanocytic or in the distinction between a primary and secondary melanoma.

Table 13-1. Primary Cutaneous versus Cutaneous Metastatic Melanoma

	PRIMARY MELANOMA	CUTANEOUS METASTASIS
Location of tumor	Usually both dermis and epidermis	Dermis and/or subcutis
Epidermal involvement (if present)	Usually prominent; pagetoid horizontal and vertical spread commonly present; usually epidermal component extends laterally beyond dermal component	Usually dermal component extends laterally beyond epidermal component; pagetoid spread less common
Size	Nearly always >0.4 cm and usually >1.0 cm	Often small; may be <1.0 cm and occasionally <0.3 cm
Cytology	Usually pleomorphic	Usually monotonous
Reactive fibrosis	May be marked	Usually mild
Vascular invasion	Rarely seen	Angiotropism

Melanoma simulating other neoplasms. Metastatic melanoma may assume a great variety of morphologic appearances and may mimic a number of nonmelanocytic tumors, such as lymphoma, undifferentiated carcinoma, adenocarcinoma, a variety of sarcomas, and many others. The differential diagnosis of amelanotic melanoma is particularly difficult. Often, additional studies are needed, such as melanin stains, immunohistochemistry using a panel of antibodies, and electron microscopy, to identify conclusively a metastatic tumor as melanocytic.

Primary cutaneous versus cutaneous metastatic melanoma (Table 13-1).

31. What are the principal histologic diagnostic criteria for melanoma?
- Size usually >5 to 6 mm
- Asymmetry
- Poor circumscription
- Pagetoid melanocytosis
- Diminished or absent maturation
- Confluence and high cellular density of melanocytes
- Effacement of epidermis
- Dermal mitoses
- Cytologic atypia of melanocytes

The histologic diagnosis of melanoma remains subjective and usually depends on the recognition of a constellation of histologic features, with no single feature being diagnostic of melanoma. Because of the many exceptions to the conventional criteria for melanoma, one must always use as much information as possible and common sense at all times. However, a large percentage of melanomas are diagnosed correctly by a majority of knowledgeable observers. It is also true that a small percentage of melanocytic tumors are histologically challenging and will produce no consensus even among experts (see Question 32).

32. Can all melanocytic lesions be interpreted as benign or malignant?
Not all melanocytic lesions can be classified as benign or malignant. One must make use of all information available to interpret as precisely as possible a difficult melanocytic lesion and to place it into one of three categories: (1) benign, (2) biologically indeterminate, or (3) malignant, for the optimal communication to and management of the patient. A biologically indeterminate lesion is defined as one that has some potential (uncertain) risk for local recurrence and metastasis but cannot be interpreted as malignant using all criteria currently available.

DIAGNOSTIC CATEGORIES

- Benign lesion
- Biologically indeterminate lesion
- Malignant melanoma

33. What are the principal prognostic factors for melanoma?
Over the past 20 to 30 years there has been extensive investigation of prognostic factors in melanoma using large databases and multivariate techniques. In many such studies the most powerful predictors of survival have been thickness of the primary melanoma (measured in millimeters from the granular layer of the epidermis vertically to the greatest depth of tumor invasion) and stage or extent of disease, that is, localized tumor, nodal metastases, distant metastases.

Although a number of studies have described "breakpoints" for tumor thickness and prognosis (e.g., patients with melanomas <0.76 mm have almost 100% 5-year survival), good evidence now indicates that this inverse relationship between thickness and survival is essentially linear. Although thickness is the best prognostic factor available for localized melanoma, occasional melanomas defy this relationship, for example, thin melanomas that metastasize and thick ones that do not. A number of other factors also have been reported to influence outcome in patients with localized melanoma. However, many of these factors largely derive their effect from a correlation with melanoma thickness and generally fail to remain significant after multivariate analysis. Five-year survival for all melanoma patients currently approaches 90%.

Once regional lymph node metastases have developed, 5-year survival drops to the range from 10% to 50% and is largely related to the number and extent of lymph nodes involved. The median survival of patients with distant metastases is approximately 6 months. The factors influencing the time to death are number of metastatic sites, surgical resectability of the metastases, duration of remission, and location of metastases, that is, nonvisceral (skin, subcutaneous tissue, distant lymph nodes) versus visceral sites (lung, liver, brain, bone) (Table 13-2).

34. What should be included in the pathology report for melanoma?

ESSENTIAL INFORMATION

- Diagnosis: Malignant melanoma, in situ or invasive
- Measured depth (in millimeters)
- Presence of histologic ulceration
- Presence of microscopic satellites
- Adequacy of surgical margins

OTHER PROGNOSTIC INFORMATION REPORTED TO BE SIGNIFICANT IN SOME DATABASES

- Mitotic rate (per square millimeter)
- Tumor-infiltrating lymphocytes
- Anatomic level (i.e., I, II, III, IV, V)
- Angiotropism
- Vascular/lymphatic invasion
- Desmoplasia-neurotropism
- Degree of regression, particularly >50% of lesion
- Radial or vertical growth phase
- Histologic subtype

Table 13-2. Prognostic Factors for Localized Melanoma

PROGNOSTIC FACTOR	EFFECT ON PROGNOSIS
Tumor thickness (mm)	Worse with increasing thickness
Level of invasion	Worse with deeper levels
Ulceration	Worse with ulceration
Mitotic rate	Worse with increasing mitotic rate
Tumor-infiltrating lymphocytes (TILs)	Better with TILs
Regression	Unsettled; some studies have shown an adverse outcome whereas other studies have shown no effect or a favorable outcome
Microscopic satellites	Worse prognosis
Angiotropism	Worse prognosis
Vascular/lymphatic invasion	Worse prognosis but rare
Tumor cell type	Better prognosis with spindle cells versus other cell types
Age	Worse prognosis with increasing age
Sex	Women have better prognosis than men
Anatomic site	Extremity lesions have better prognosis than axial lesions (trunk, head, neck, palms, soles)

35. What are current general recommendations for managing melanoma?
- Optimal biopsy for examination of entire lesion if possible
  - Elliptical excision or incision for lesions suspicious for melanoma
- Complete skin and physical examination; scanning of visceral organs if specifically indicated
- Sentinel lymph node (SLN) biopsy may be considered for melanomas >1.0 mm thick
- Surgical margins:
  - Melanomas up to 2 mm to 1 cm
  - Melanomas >2 mm to 2 cm
- Follow-up examinations related to Breslow thickness, stage, etc:
  - Every 3 to 6 months for first 5 years
  - Every 6 to 12 months for the remaining 5 to 10 years

36. What are the current recommendations for biopsy of pigmented lesions suspicious for melanoma?

The optimal method of sampling any pigmented lesion suspicious for melanoma is complete elliptical excision with narrow surgical margins of ≈2 mm. Much has been written about the inappropriate use of shave and even punch biopsy techniques for suspected melanomas. Examination of the entire pigmented lesion allows for the greatest chance of accurate diagnosis and for the measurement of Breslow thickness and the assessment of other prognostic factors. However, particular circumstances such as an excessively large pigmented lesion or a cosmetically or anatomically difficult site may render complete excision unfeasible and thus necessitate partial biopsy, as with a punch or incisional technique.

37. What are the current recommendations for the examination and staging of patients with melanoma?

Patients with newly diagnosed melanoma require a complete cutaneous and physical examination with particular attention to lymphadenopathy, hepatomegaly, and baseline chest radiograph. If the latter examinations fail to detect any evidence of metastatic disease and the patient has no other symptoms or signs, no further laboratory evaluation is indicated. However, patients with melanoma exceeding 1 mm in thickness and with no other evidence of metastatic disease are candidates for SLN biopsy. Selected patients with melanomas measuring <1 mm thick may be considered for SLN biopsy if the primary melanoma is ulcerated, is Clark level IV, or shows extensive regression. Patients with palpable lymphadenopathy and other signs and symptoms require additional evaluation with various scanning techniques and possible lymph node biopsy.

SLN biopsy. The introduction of SLN biopsy has provided the means to examine regional lymph nodes for evidence of metastasis in lieu of a major surgical intervention. If one or more SLNs harbor bona fide deposits of metastatic melanoma (vs. nodal nevi or indeterminate deposits), completion lymphadenectomy then is performed. Although SLN biopsy is currently accepted as a staging procedure, only long-term clinical trials will determine if the procedure has any significant effect on survival of melanoma patients.

38. What are current recommendations for the surgical management of patients with melanoma?

Surgery remains the only effective therapy for melanoma if diagnosed and completely excised at a localized and early stage of development (<1 to 1.5 mm thick). There is currently no effective treatment for advanced melanoma, and only a small percentage of patients survive long term once (even limited) regional metastatic disease has been documented.

Surgical margins for melanoma. The practical and theoretical benefits accruing from excising melanoma with some cuff of normal tissue are (1) greater assurance that the primary melanoma has been removed with truly clear margins and (2) the potential removal of microscopic metastatic foci near the primary melanoma. Although much has been published on the subject of surgical margins for melanoma, no definitive data currently exist on this issue. However, it appears that surgical margins may have no real influence on survival of melanoma patients, and margins probably in excess of 3 cm (and possibly even 1 cm) may provide no benefit to patients. Problems clouding the issue of margins for melanoma are the lack of sufficient knowledge about the initial mechanisms of melanoma metastasis at the primary site, melanoma recurrence versus persistence of the primary melanoma and melanoma metastasis, and other considerations such as field effects. Once the mechanisms of melanoma metastasis are better understood, we will have the information needed to finally address the question of optimal margins.

Current (rather arbitrary) guidelines for surgical management of melanoma are complete excision of the primary lesion with margins of 0.5 cm for melanomas in situ, 1 cm for melanomas ≤2 mm thick, and 2 cm for melanomas ≥2 mm thick. Exceptions to these guidelines clearly exist, for example, wider margins of at least 3 cm probably are indicated for desmoplastic-neurotropic melanoma, and anatomic sites necessitate narrower margins.

39. What are current recommendations for the follow-up of melanoma patients?

Follow-up of melanoma patients is related to stage of disease. Patients with documented distant or visceral metastases require the most vigilant surveillance, followed by individuals with regional lymph node or in transit or satellite metastases, and finally those with localized primary melanomas. The frequency of follow-up examinations is individualized but usually is at least every 3 months initially for regional and distant metastatic disease. Patients with localized primary melanomas >1 to 1.5 mm thick commonly undergo physical examination at 3-month intervals for the first 3 years (period of highest risk for development of metastases), every 6 months thereafter for 2 years, and once annually for an additional 5 years. Patients with low-risk melanomas (<1 mm) are generally followed at 6-month intervals for 3 years and annually thereafter.

BIBLIOGRAPHY

Balch CM, Soong S-J, Murad TM, et al: A multifactorial analysis of melanoma: 111. Prognostic factors in melanoma patients with lymph node metastases (stage II). Ann Surg 193:377–388, 1981.

Balch CM, Soong S-J, Shaw HM, et al: An analysis of prognostic factors in 8500 patients with cutaneous melanoma. In Balch CM, Houghton AN, Milton GW, et al (eds): Cutaneous Melanoma, 2nd ed. Philadelphia, JB Lippincott, 1992, pp 165–187.

Barnhill RL: The Pathology of Melanocytic Nevi and Malignant Melanoma. Boston, Butterworth-Heinemann, 1995.

Barnhill RL, Fine J, Roush GC, Berwick M: Predicting five-year outcome from cutaneous melanoma in a population-based study. Cancer 78:427–432, 1996.

Barnhill RL, Fitzpatrick TB, Fandrey K, et al: The Pigmented Lesion Clinic: A Color Atlas and Synopsis of Benign and Pigmented Lesions. New York, McGraw-Hill, 1995.

Barnhill RL, Lugassy C: Angiotropic malignant melanoma and extravascular migratory metastasis: Description of 36 cases with emphasis on a new mechanism of tumour spread. Pathology 36:485–490, 2004.

Barnhill RL, Mihm MC Jr: The histopathology of cutaneous malignant melanoma. Semin Diagn Pathol 10:47–75, 1993.

Barnhill RL, Mihm MC, Fitzpatrick TB, Sober AJ: Neoplasms: Malignant melanoma. In Fitzpatrick TB, Eisen AZ, Wolff K, et al (eds): Dermatology in General Medicine, Volume I. New York, McGraw-Hill, 1993, pp 1078–1115.

Breslow A: Measurements of tumor thickness. Hum Pathol 9:238–239, 1978.

Breslow A: Tumor thickness in evaluating prognosis of cutaneous melanoma. Ann Surg 187:440, 1978.

Clark WH Jr: A classification of malignant melanoma in man correlated with histogenesis and biologic behavior. In Montagna W, Hu F (eds): Advances in the Biology of the Skin, Volume VIII. New York, Pergamon Press, 1967, pp 621–647.

Clark WH Jr, Elder DE, Guerry D IV, et al: Model predicting survival in Stage I melanoma based on tumor progression. J Natl Cancer Inst 81:1893–1904, 1989.

Clark WH Jr, Elder DE, Van Horn M: The biologic forms of malignant melanoma. Hum Pathol 17:443–450, 1984.

Clark WH Jr, From L, Bernardino EA, Mihm MC: The histogenesis and biologic behavior of primary human malignant melanomas of the skin. Cancer Res 29:705–727, 1969.

Conley J, Lattes R, Orr W: Desmoplastic malignant melanoma (a rare variant of spindle cell melanoma). Cancer 28:914–936, 1971.

Curtin JA, Fridlyand J, Kageshita T, et al: Distinct sets of genomic alterations in melanoma. N Engl J Med 535:2135–2147, 2005.

Elder DE: Metastatic melanoma. In Elder DE, (ed): Pigment Cell, Volume 8. Basel, Karger, 1987, pp 182–204.

Keefe M, MacKie RM: The relationship risk of death from clinical stage I cutaneous melanoma and thickness of primary tumour: No evidence for steps in risk. Br J Cancer 64:598–602, 1991.

Magro CM, Crowson AN, Mihm MC: Unusal variants of malignant melanoma. Mod Pathol 19:S41–S70, 2006.

Mihm MC Jr, Fitzpatrick TB, Brown MM, et al: Early detection of primary cutaneous malignant melanoma. A color atlas. N Engl J Med 289:989–996, 1973.

Miller AJ, Mihm MC: Melanoma. N Engl J Med 355:51–65, 2006.

Schmoeckel C, Castro CE, Braun-Falco O: Nevoid malignant melanoma. Arch Dermatol Res 277:362–369, 1985.

Thomas JM, Newton-Bishop J, A'Hern R, et al: Excision margins in high-risk malignant melanoma. N Engl J Med 350:757–766, 2004.

Vollmer RT: Malignant melanoma: A multivariate analysis of prognostic factors. Pathol Ann 24:383, 1989.

BASAL CELL AND SQUAMOUS CELL CARCINOMA

CHAPTER 14

Girish B. Kapur, MD, MPH; Vincent Boyd, MD; Larry Hollier, Jr., MD; Melvin Spira, MD, DDS; and Samuel Stal, MD

1. Describe the importance of basal cell cancer in the United States.

Skin cancers are the most common of all cancers. Approximately 77% of all skin cancers are basal cell carcinomas (BCCs), 20% are squamous cell carcinomas (SCCs), and 3% are melanomas. There are a few other rare skin cancers. The incidence of skin cancer has been increasing by approximately 4% to 8% per year over the past 40 years, and the incidence of BCC doubled between 1970 and 1986. Much of this is attributed to sun exposure habits and the aging population. Although BCCs rarely cause fatalities, they certainly are important in that they usually occur on the face, are locally invasive, and can potentially cause significant loss of function and scarring. They can be infiltrative, but they rarely metastasize.

2. Are there histologic prognostic indicators in BCC?

No. Degree or variation in atypia is not useful in prognosis for BCC as it is in other cancers. Growth pattern of the lesion is the most important prognostic indicator. Typically, two growth patterns are seen: those that differentiate toward keratin and those that differentiate toward glandular skin elements. These are further subdivided into well-defined and infiltrative feature categories. Well-defined lesions tend to produce collagen and fibroblasts with surrounding reactive stroma. Infiltrative lesions form strands of cells that invade the surrounding stroma.

3. What are treatment choices for superficial basal cell carcinoma?

Superficial basal cell carcinoma (sBCC) is generally a low-risk lesion but often occurs on the face, a high-risk location. Surgical choices for treatment include cryotherapy, curettage, electrodessication, and excision. Pharmaceutical treatments include tazarotene and imiquimod cream. The treatment choice should be made based on the lesion's location, size, and potential to cause harm if it recurs or becomes invasive.

4. Describe features of sBCC.

The sBCCs are frequently misdiagnosed due to their benign appearance. They appear as well-defined, erythematous patches. They are scaly and are found throughout the body, but not often on the face. The patient often describes a scaly patch of skin that has been present for years and has changed little since first being noticed. sBCC usually is solitary, and this is an important diagnostic feature. Close inspection reveals a pearly edge with beading when the skin is placed under tension, and a scaling in the center. The center of the lesion tends to mature with time and forms a scar-like appearance that is atrophic and less erythematous.

5. Describe infiltrative BCC.

Approximately 5% of BCCs are micronodular, and these are typically infiltrative or invasive. The pattern of spread follows the path of least resistance. They can spread quickly along fascial planes and follow nerves to penetrate deeper tissues. If untreated, these lesions can gain momentum and invade firmer tissue such as cartilage and bone.

6. Describe radiation exposure patterns, risk factors, and diagnostic features seen in patients with BCC.

Chronic sun damage is the most common thread in the history of the BCC patient. Diagnostic features include mottling, rhytidosis, telangiectasia, and solar elastosis. Risk factors include fair skin, decreased latitude, male sex, freckles, blue or green eyes, sunburn in childhood, occupational sun exposure, tanning bed use, and Fitzpatrick skin types I and II.

7. Is there a direct correlation between amount of sun exposure in a particular area of skin and incidence of basal cell skin cancer?

Yes. Evidence shows a direct correlation between amount of sun exposure and incidence of basal cell cancer in specific locations on the skin. It is important to note, however, that basal cell cancer does not necessarily occur most commonly in the areas of highest exposure to sunlight, such as the hands.

8. What inherited conditions predispose to cutaneous malignancies?

Xeroderma pigmentosum is an autosomal recessive disorder with an acute sensitivity to sunlight secondary to a defective DNA repair mechanism and results in multiple epitheliomas with subsequent malignant degeneration.

Basal cell nevus syndrome, also known as *Gorlin syndrome,* is an autosomal dominant disorder with three characteristic findings: multiple basal cell nevi on the skin with malignant changes by puberty, jaw cysts, and pitting of the palms and soles. Other associated anomalies include pseudohypertelorism, frontal bossing, syndactyly, and spina bifida.

Albinism manifests as hypopigmentation of the skin, hair, and eyes and increases the risk of SCC and BCC.

Epidermodysplasia verruciformis consists of an autosomal recessive cell-mediated immunity disorder characterized by several subtypes of human papillomavirus that induce numerous polymorphic verrucous lesions with a high propensity for transformation into SCC.

Muir-Torre syndrome is a disorder of multiple internal malignancies, cutaneous sebaceous proliferation, keratoacanthomas, BCC, and SCC.

Porokeratosis is an autosomal dominant disorder of abnormal keratinization with malignant degeneration.

Bazex-Dupre-Christol syndrome is an X-linked disorder characterized by follicular atrophoderma, congenital hypotrichosis, basal cell nevi, and BCC.

9. How is actinic keratosis treated?

Curettage and electrodessication form the foundation for treatment of most lesions. Liquid nitrogen is also an effective modality. More recently 5-fluorouracil (5-FU) in a 1% to 5% concentration (Efudex) has proved effective. Chemical peel and dermabrasion of the skin have been effective but have been replaced largely by 5-FU.

10. What is Bowen's disease?

Bowen's disease is seen in older patients in both sun-exposed and non–sun-exposed areas. It represents an intraepithelial SCC (carcinoma in situ) and may involve the skin or mucous membranes, including mouth, anus, and genitalia. Most of the lesions are solitary, and men are afflicted more often than women. Lesions have a long clinical course, generally years. Clinically the lesion appears as a solitary, rather sharply defined, erythematous, reddish, dull, scaly plaque. Pruritus, superficial crusting, and oozing may be noted. Microscopic examination reveals the stigmata of an intraepidermal SCC with hyperkeratosis, parakeratosis, dyskeratosis, and acanthosis within the epithelial layers. Within the epithelium there is disorder. Cells are keratinized within the prickle cell layer, and hyperchromatic bizarre nuclei and increased cell mitosis are observed. There is no dermal invasion, but a heavy inflammatory infiltrate is frequently noted in the papillary dermis with multinucleated giant cells. Surgical therapy includes either excision or a combination of curettage and electrodessication. The prognosis is excellent with appropriate treatment. However, the prognosis is poor if SCC develops; these lesions are much more aggressive than the SCCs that develop from actinic keratoses.

11. What is Bowen's disease of mucous membranes?

Erythroplasia of Queyrat is often referred to as Bowen's disease of the mucous membranes. It most often affects the glans penis and is seen during the fifth and sixth decades of life, primarily in uncircumcised men. Grossly, erythroplasia consists of solitary or multiple erythematous lesions that are well circumscribed, moist, glistening, and velvety. Microscopically, the lesion resembles Bowen's disease. Erythroplasia is much more likely than Bowen's disease to become invasive and has an increased tendency to metastatic disease.

12. Where is leukoplakia usually found? What is its appearance?

Leukoplakia, literally meaning white patch, is seen primarily on oral, vulvar, or vaginal mucosa. Leukoplakia in the mouth is seen mostly in older men with a history of smoking. Ill-fitting dentures and teeth in poor repair often are associated with this condition. Grossly, the lesions are elevated, sharply defined patchy areas of keratinization, generally lighter in color (white to gray) than the surrounding tissue and of variable thickness. Long-standing or chronic lesions may exhibit a verrucoid appearance. Microscopically, the classic quartet of hyperkeratosis, parakeratosis, keratosis, and acanthosis is seen. Within the epidermal layer, cellular atypia abounds, and an inflammatory infiltrate is seen within the dermis. Of the untreated lesions, 15% to 20% undergo malignant transformation. Evidence of ulceration or underlying induration increases the possibility of cancer. SCCs that develop from premalignant lesions on the mucous membranes are much more malignant than are those associated with actinic keratoses.

13. Where anatomically do most primary BCCs occur?

Approximately 93% occur in the head and neck region; the remaining 7% are found on the trunk and extremities. In the head and neck, BCC is distributed as follows: nose, 25.5%; cheek, 16%; periorbital, 14%; scalp and temple, 11%; ear and periauricular, 11%; forehead, 7.5%; neck, 7%; upper lip, 5%; chin, 2%; and lower lip, 1%.

14. List the different types of BCC.

1. **Nodular ulcerative carcinoma.** Lesions usually are single, occur mostly on the face, and begin as small translucent papules that remain firm and exhibit telangiectasia. They grow slowly and tend to ulcerate, which may result in tissue destruction. They are the most common of the BCCs.

2. **Superficial basal cell carcinoma.** Lesions often occur in multiples, usually on the trunk. They are lightly pigmented, erythematous, scaly, and patch-like. They may resemble eczema or psoriasis.
3. **Sclerosing basal cell carcinoma.** Lesions are yellow-white, morpheaform epitheliomas with ill-defined borders and resemble small patches of scleroderma. They are most frequently associated with recurrent disease. Peripheral growth with central sclerosis and scarring is characteristic.
4. **Pigmented basal cell carcinoma.** Lesions combine the features of the nodular ulcerative type with a deep brownish-black pigmentation.
5. **Trabecular (Merkel cell) carcinoma.** This relatively new entity resembles BCC histologically and may occur as a single tumor in older people. The tumor may be epidermal, dermal, or even subcutaneous in origin, with a microscopic picture of irregularly anastomosing trabeculae and a rosette arrangement of deeply basophilic, uniform tumor cells. The name *Merkel cell* is derived from the fact that the tumor cells contain small granules identical to the neurosecretory granules of the epidermal Merkel cell. Tumors are aggressive and metastasize not only to local nodes but also to viscera and bone. Treatment for cure is difficult but consists of surgery and radiation therapy.
6. **Adnexal carcinoma.** These skin malignancies arise from sebaceous sweat glands. They are relatively uncommon and appear as solitary tumors in older patients. The tumors have no particular distinctive features, grow slowly, tend to recur locally after surgery, and metastasize regionally.

15. What are the microscopic and clinical distinctions among the types of BCC?

The microscopic characteristics of the different clinical types of BCC vary considerably. All cases show proliferation of similar cells, oval in shape with deeply staining nuclei and scant cytoplasm. The tumors are composed of irregular masses of basaloid cells in the dermis, with the outermost cells forming a palisading layer on the periphery. The surrounding stroma frequently exhibits a fibrous reaction. Microscopically, the nodular ulcerative type of basal cell tumor may show differentiation toward adnexal structures; there may be a solid, cystic, adenoid, or keratotic variety. The superficial BCC shows bands of basal cells in the dermis but maintains continuity with the overlying epidermis. This lesion contrasts with sclerosing BCC, which shows clusters and clumps of basal cells in the densely fibrotic stroma without continuity with the overlying epidermis (which, in fact, may be perfectly normal). A blue nevus generally can be differentiated from a deeply pigmented BCC by the character of the overlying epithelium (normal) and duration of the tumor without growth.

16. Which biopsy techniques allow a histologic diagnosis?

Curettage is done under local anesthesia by scraping the tumor with a dermal curette. Tumor cell groups are soft and often can be curetted. Normal underlying dermis or scar tissue is hard and almost impossible to curette. BCC that occurs in a scar or is morpheaform is too difficult to curette. The difference in ability to curette aids in differentiating normal tissue from some BCCs. Shave biopsy of the upper half of the dermis is an excellent way to reveal a recurrent tumor because a wide area can be sampled with minimal deformity. On rare occasions, a tumor is present so deeply that a shave biopsy does not reveal its presence. Rare BCCs present as a subcutaneous recurrence that would be missed by a shave biopsy. In such cases, however, there is a deep-seated nodule, and recurrence is easily recognized by tightly pulling normal or scarred overlying skin. Punch biopsy, 3 or 4 mm in diameter, visualizes only a small area of the suspicious tissue but usually provides a specimen of sufficient size for diagnostic histologic evaluation.

Excisional biopsy is the treatment of choice in dealing with a primary BCC or a pigmented lesion. However, in the context of large tumors (as recurrences often are) and when the location of the actual borders of the tumor are unknown, excisional biopsy is impractical. Deep-wedge biopsy often gives valuable information about the depth below the dermis and extent of infiltration of a recurrent BCC.

17. How is BCC treated?

Most BCCs are treated by curettage and desiccation or by simple excision as a fusiform ellipse and primary closure. Curettage and desiccation are best suited for lesions less than 1 cm in diameter and lesions that are nodular, ulcerative, and exophytic. The technique is not suited for morpheaform BCCs or recurrent disease. When a functional or anatomic deformity may result or when cartilage or bone is involved, other modalities are more effective. Surgical excision provides an immediate pathologic inventory and an index of the adequacy of excision. The lesion can be removed as a fusiform ellipse positioned along the lines of least skin tension with a small perimeter (0.2 to 0.5 cm) of normal tissue. If margins are clear, the defect is undermined and the line of closure is delineated. Excessive tissue (dog ear) is excised, and closure is carried out with the surgeon's preferred technique. Cryotherapy is used for small nodular or ulcerated lesions located over bone or cartilage, on the eyelid, or on the tip of the nose. Liquid nitrogen applied with a cotton-tipped applicator or a spray that freezes the tumor and a 5-mm area of normal tissue for approximately 30 seconds has proved effective.

Immediate edema, exudation, subsequent necrosis, eschar formation, and healing are seen. In recent years, cryotherapy has been increasingly used in the management of skin tumors, but it is associated with local tissue destruction and requires an incisional biopsy for tissue diagnosis before treatment. Radiation therapy with low-penetration X-irradiation to a tumor site in doses of 5000 rads may be useful, particularly around orifices (eyelids, nares, and mouth) or at sites where a scar due to surgical excision may be a difficult problem, as in the deltoid or sternal region. Scars from surgery generally improve with time, whereas scars from radiation therapy worsen. The late changes associated with any type of radiation treatment detract from its use in young and middle-aged patients; however, it can be effective for treating a large tumor in an older person in whom extensive resection is unacceptable or the goal is palliation.

Mohs fresh frozen section technique uses serial tangential excisions and is particularly useful for treatment of sclerosing BCC, especially in dealing with a recurrent lesion, and for large primary tumors with poorly delineated borders or perineural invasion.

18. What are high-risk anatomic areas for BCC recurrence?
High-risk areas for tumor recurrence include the center of the face (periorbital region, eyelids, nasolabial fold, nose–cheek angle), postauricular region, pinna, and forehead. Recurring lesions are most common in young women.

19. What are the clinical signs of recurrence?
1. Scarring with intermittent or nonhealing ulceration
2. Scar that becomes red, scaled, or crusted
3. Enlarging scar with increased telangiectasia in the adjacent area
4. Development of papule or nodule formation within the scar itself
5. Frank tissue destruction

When recurrence of a previously excised BCC is suspected, a biopsy is performed. The clinical types of BCC most likely to recur after excision are infiltrative nodular BCC with a poorly defined border and sclerosing, morpheaform BCC. The outer borders of such tumors often cannot be accurately defined by clinical examination. Mohs micrographic surgery is the mainstay of treatment.

20. SCC arises from which cells?
SCC originates from the keratinizing or malpighian (spindle) cell layer of the epithelium. It is seen primarily in older patients, mostly men. As with BCC, the prime etiologic factor is solar radiation. In addition to radiation, however, chemicals, chronic ulcers (including osteomyelitis), cytotoxic drugs, immunosuppressant drugs, chronic lesions, discoid lupus erythematosus, and hydradenitis suppurativa play a significant role in the development of a relatively small number of SCC skin cancers. Initially the lesion appears smooth, verrucous, papillomatous, or ulcerative and later exhibits induration, inflammation, and ulceration.

21. Describe the two general types of SCC.
The first is a slow-growing variety that is verrucous and exophytic. Although this type may be deeply locally invasive, it is less likely to metastasize. The second general type is more nodular and indurated, with rapid growth and early ulceration combined with local invasiveness and increased metastatic tendency.

22. Where are SCCs anatomically distributed?
Compared with BCC, SCC has a slightly increased incidence on the trunk and extremities. The lesions are distributed as follows: cheeks, 45%; nose, 13%; ear and periauricular areas, 12%; hand, 11%; neck, 10%; anus, 5%; trunk, 2%; and scalp and legs, 1% each.

23. What is the mainstay of treatment for SCC?
Treatment depends on the age of the patient and the size of the lesion. Surgical excision and Mohs micrographic surgery are the mainstays of treatment. Older patients are treated conservatively. The location of the lesion is a factor in choosing the technique. Wound appearance may not matter so much to an older patient.

24. Name factors associated with SCC recurrence.
Degree of cellular differentiation is a significant prognostic indicator, ranging from 7% recurrence for well-differentiated tumors to 28% recurrence for poorly differentiated lesions. Depth of tumor invasion also raises the incidence of recurrence. Perineural invasion usually indicates increased tumor involvement and greater probability of recurrence. The tendency for recurrence of SCC treated by any technique is approximately twice that for the best results of treating BCC.

25. What is the best way to treat recurrent lesions?
A recurrent lesion probably is best treated by excision and skin grafting. Microscopically controlled excision (modified Mohs technique) is a good way to handle difficult and recurrent lesions, specifically in medial canthal and alar areas. Radiation therapy can be used effectively in patients older than 55 years, particularly around the eyelids, nose, and lip.

26. Describe the metastatic potential of SCC.

Approximately 5% to 10% of lesions metastasize. SCCs resulting from Marjolin's ulcer or xeroderma pigmentosum have a much greater tendency to metastasize than do SCCs resulting from sun-induced skin changes. In addition, SCCs of the ears, nostrils, scalp, and extremities are particularly prone to metastasis.

27. What is the significance of perineural and mucoperiosteal invasion?

Perineural, lymphatic, or mucoperiosteal invasion usually indicates advanced disease and worsens the prognosis for local cure and, in cases of SCC, metastasis. The probability of cure when SCC has spread to the mucoperiosteum of the piriform aperture is remote. When such invasion is found, surgical treatment must be aggressive, with wide extirpation the only hope for cure.

28. When should a patient treated for BCC or SCC be clinically reexamined?

The patient should be clinically examined every 6 months for 5 years because approximately 36% of patients who develop BCC develop a second primary BCC within the next 5 years. Diagnosis and treatment of recurring BCC in its early stages result in less morbidity. SCCs have definite metastatic potential, and patients should be reexamined every 3 months for the first several years and followed indefinitely at 6-month intervals.

29. What is an effective technique for periodic self-examination to catch lesions at an early stage?

To perform self-examination, the patient needs a full-length mirror, a hand mirror, and a brightly lit room. The following technique is appropriate:

* Examine the body, front and back, in the mirror, then the right and left sides with arms raised.
* Bend the elbows and look carefully at forearms, back of upper arms, and palms.
* Look at the back of the legs and feet, spaces between the toes and soles.
* Examine the back, neck, and scalp with a hand mirror.
* Check the back and buttocks with a hand mirror.

BIBLIOGRAPHY

Barrett TL, Greenway HT, Massullo V: Treatment of basal cell carcinoma and squamous cell carcinoma with perineural invasion. Adv Dermatol 8:277–304, 1993.
Chao CK, Gerber RM, Perez CA: Reirradiation of recurrent skin cancer of the face. A successful salvage modality. Cancer 75:2351–2355, 1995.
Derrick EK, Smith R, Melcher DH, et al: The use of cytology in the diagnosis of basal cell carcinoma. Br J Dermatol 130:561–563, 1994.
Drake LA, Dinehart SM, Goltz RW, Graham GF: Guidelines of care for Mohs micrographic surgery. J Am Acad Dermatol 33:271–278, 1995.
Fleming ILL, Amonette R, Monaghan T, Fleming MD: Principles of management of basal and squamous cell carcinoma of the skin. Cancer 75:699–704,1995.
Fijan SD, Honigsmann S: Photodynamic therapy of epithelial skin tumours using delta-aminolaevulinic acid and desferrioxamine. Br J Dermatol 133:282–288, 1995.
Gherardini G, Bhatia N, Stal S: Congenital syndromes associated with non-melanoma skin cancer. Clin Plast Surg 24:649–661, 1997.
Ikic D, Padovan I, Pipic N, et al: Interferon reduces recurrences of basal cell and squamous cell cancers. Int J Dermatol 34:58–60, 1995.
Kempf RA: Systemic therapy of skin carcinoma. Cancer Treat Res 78:137–162, 1995.
Kopf AW, Salopek TG, Slade J, et al: Techniques of cutaneous examination for the detection of skin cancer. Cancer 75:684–690, 1995.
Marks R: An overview of skin cancers. Incidence and causation. Cancer 75:607–612, 1995.
Marks R: The epidemiology of non-melanoma skin cancer: Who, why and what can we do about it. J Dermatol 22:853–857, 1995.
Marks R, Motley RJ: Skin cancer. Recognition and treatment. Drugs 50:48–61, 1995.
Multicentre South European Study Helios. I: Skin characteristics and sunburns in basal cell and squamous cell carcinomas of the skin. Br J Cancer 73:1440–1446, 1996.
Multicentre South European Study Helios. II: Different sun exposure patterns in the aetiology of basal cell and squamous cell. Br J Cancer 73:1447–1454, 1996.
Nelson BR, Fader DJ, Gillard F: The role of dermabrasion and chemical peels in the treatment of patients with xeroderma pigmentosum. J Am Acad Dermatol 32:623–626, 1995.
Roberts DJ, Cairnduff F: Photodynamic therapy of primary skin cancer: A review. Br J Plast Surg 48:360–370, 1995.
Stal S, Spira M: Basal and squamous cell carcinoma of the skin. In Aston SJ, Beasley RW, Thome CHM (eds): Grabb and Smith's Plastic Surgery, 5th ed. Philadelphia, Lippincott-Raven, 1997, pp 107–120.

PRINCIPLES OF MOHS SURGERY

Priya S. Zeikus, MD, and
Suzanne Olbricht, MD

1. What is Mohs surgery?

Mohs surgery is a technique used for treatment of difficult skin cancers. The procedure combines the conservative excision of tissue with microscopic examination of the excised tissue and includes innovations in excisional technique, orientation and color coding of specimens, and preparation of tissue as horizontal sections.

2. Who was Frederick Mohs?

Frederick Mohs was a physician at the University of Wisconsin in Madison who developed a staged procedure in 1936 for the treatment of difficult, large, high-risk, recurrent skin cancers. At that time, the procedure was named *chemosurgery* because he applied zinc chloride paste to the cancerous skin to fix the tissue prior to excision. The following day the tissue was excised and examined under the microscope. The process was repeated daily until tumor margins were clear. This procedure was revised in the 1970s by using fresh frozen tissue for microscopic evaluation instead of in vivo fixed tissue, a change that shortened the time between the stages to less than 1 hour and made the procedure much more efficient as well as less toxic to in vivo tissues. Since then, constant revisions in technique and applications have established the technique as an effective way to manage many difficult skin cancers.

3. Are there other names for Mohs surgery?

Yes, other names are sometimes used in the literature, including fresh tissue Mohs surgery, histographic surgery, Mohs micrographic surgery, and Mohs margin controlled surgery. These names reflect the change from the use of the in vivo fixative to the excision of fresh tissue as well as Dr. Mohs' innovations concerning orientation and mapping.

4. What are the basic requirements for Mohs surgery?

1. The tumor must be readily identifiable in stained frozen sections. Its growth pattern should be that of contiguous spread.
2. Because the procedure is performed in an ambulatory setting and patients remain awake during the waiting time for specimen preparation, patients must be cooperative and the environment should be calm and pleasant.
3. The personnel required include a histotechnician who is trained to make horizontal sections and process the specimens accurately. Nursing personnel prepare the patient for surgery, assist with the procedure, and assess the continuing medical condition of the patient. The physician must be able to take appropriate specimens and read pathology slides in horizontal sections.

5. How does Mohs surgery differ from excision with frozen section margin control?

Mohs surgery differs in three ways. First, the specimen is excised as one intact disc with beveled edges. This method of excision is called *saucerization* because of the saucer-like shape of the specimen. A saucer-shaped specimen facilitates orientation and preparation for microscopic evaluation. Excision of multiple pieces distorts orientation, and excision with perpendicular edges does not allow preparation for complete margin evaluation. Second, the processing of specimens is different from that performed by the pathology department. Horizontal sections across the sides and base of the specimen are prepared such that the entire margin from the epidermis to the deepest portion of the specimen can be viewed in one or two slides for specimens up to 2 cm in diameter. Third, the surgeon also reads the slides, allowing him or her to orient any residual tumor to other structures in the skin, such as the plane of sebaceous glands or a prominent blood vessel.

6. Describe the steps involved in a Mohs procedure.

The major steps in performing Mohs surgery are illustrated in Figure 15-1. After ensuring that the patient is medically stable and understands the procedure and gives consent, the Mohs procedure begins with identification of the tumor (see Fig. 15-1A and B). The site is anesthetized. First, the tumor is curetted to grossly appearing normal skin (see Fig. 15-1C) and then a no. 15 blade is used to remove a disc of tissue around and underneath the curetted defect (see Fig. 15-1D). Before complete excision of the disc, while it is still in situ, a small nick or hash mark is made with a blade at one to four sites (usually 12:00 and 3:00, but also often 12:00 and 6:00 or 12:00, 3:00, 9:00, and 6:00) with the nicks extending from the disc into the intact skin, allowing orientation of the specimen (see Fig. 15-1E and F). Electrocautery is used for

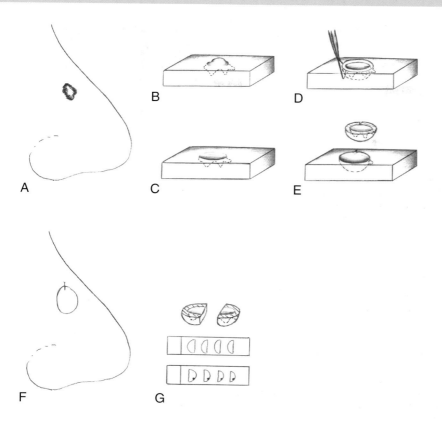

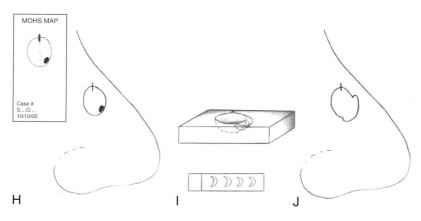

Figure 15-1 A, Basal cell carcinoma on the nose. **B,** Tumor with subepidermal extensions. **C,** Defect after curettage. **D,** Stage I: saucerization. **E,** Tissue removed with a nick in the disc as well as in the defect edge. **F,** Defect with nick for orientation. **G,** Disc cut in half through the nick and inked, laid out horizontally, frozen, sectioned, placed on a slide, and stained. **H,** Map showing residual tumor next to the patient with the margin marked. **I,** Stage II: excision and margin control. **J,** Final defect. (Courtesy of Beatrice Berkes, MD.)

hemostasis, and a bandage is placed. A map of the disc, including the nicks and any pertinent anatomic considerations of the site, is drawn. The disc of tissue is prepared for microscopic evaluation (see Fig. 15-1G). The specimen is cut into two pieces between the nicks and then inked. Both the cutting and the inking are documented on the map. The specimen is turned upside down onto a chuck and pressed into frozen section cutting medium so that the plane of sectioning is horizontal and includes the epidermal margin as well as the sides and deepest portion of the specimen. Once the specimen is adequately frozen in the cryostat, it is cut with a microtome into 12- to 20-micron thick sections that are placed on a labeled slide and stained. The Mohs surgeon reads the slides to identify the sites of residual tumor and marks the corresponding areas on the map.

The map is taken back to the patient who has been reanesthetized (see Fig. 15-1H). Tissue where residual tumor was identified is removed in one piece, and histologic processing is repeated until all margins are clear (see Fig. 15-1I). Stages are counted as excision of a specimen through microscopic evaluation and require 30 to 90 minutes each depending on how thin or thick or fatty the tissue specimen is. When the margins are judged to be completely free of tumor, the final defect can be evaluated (see Fig. 15-1J) and a decision about closure can be made depending on the site, size, and depth of the defect.

7. Why is curettage of the tumor used in Mohs surgery?

Curettage debulks the tumor, which usually is more friable than normal epidermis. It thus assists in defining the tumor margins better than visual inspection alone. In addition, curettage allows for the specimen to be excised in a saucer-like shape, which is essential to be able to process horizontal frozen sections that contain the entire margin. To perform curettage, a dull curette is scraped over the tumor in different directions with moderate pressure, producing fragments of tissue that can be wiped away to reveal a clean solid wound base.

8. In obtaining a Mohs section, at what angle must the scalpel be applied in relation to the skin tissue to facilitate histologic processing?

The lateral edge of the excision must have an angle of 45° to facilitate histologic processing. This technique of beveling the scalpel during excision creates a saucer-shaped disc and allows for a complete horizontal section to be examined microscopically.

9. When obtaining a Mohs section, what size margins around the tumors are taken?

In the first stage of Mohs surgery, a 1- to 2-mm rim of normal tissue is taken around and underneath the curetted defect. If any visible tumor was not curetted, the first excision also includes that tissue. In subsequent stages, the size of the specimen taken around histologically positive margins depends on tumor type and tumor volume and may vary from 1 to 5 mm.

10. How is tissue orientation maintained in Mohs surgery?

Multiple methods are used. Before the disc of tissue is completely removed from the patient, the surgeon makes small nicks or hash marks with a blade along the circumference of the tumor. Generally, for tumors less than 1 cm in diameter, two nicks are made, often at 12:00 and 3:00. More nicks may be made for larger tumors. These nicks are made through the disc of tissue and into the surrounding in situ skin. A map of the specimen with the nicks detailed is drawn and sent to the frozen section laboratory with the specimen. Extra care usually is taken by always placing the specimen on the gauze in the same way (e.g., the fold is 12:00) or by placing a dot of blood at the upper left-hand corner of the gauze (11:00) holding the specimen. For very large tumors, the entire surgical site may be prepared by using a surgical marking pen to create a large grid on the patient. This grid is identified to the laboratory by a detailed map that may even be accompanied by a photographic image. Most importantly, the person processing the specimen in the laboratory marks the map according to the cutting and inking of the specimens. Therefore the physician, when reading the slides, can see the section, the ink, and the residual tumor and mark it accurately on the map. Standardized protocols, rigorous attention to detail, a frozen section laboratory located within the physical space of the Mohs surgery unit, and open communication among personnel facilitate accurate orientation.

11. Which stains are used to stain Mohs sections?

Hematoxylin and eosin usually are used to stain the tissue sections. Dr. Mohs used toluidine blue, which is a rapid stain adequate for identification of basal cell carcinoma and still is sometimes used today. Special stains such as keratin markers may be used to examine tissue when small nests of squamous cell carcinoma (e.g., perineural disease) may be present, but their use slows the process and thus may not be easy for the patient.

12. Why can the defects following Mohs surgery appear much larger than expected based on standard 4-mm margins for nonmelanoma tumors?

The histologic extension of the tumor often is much greater than what is seen clinically, especially for tumors that have sclerosing or infiltrative growth patterns. In addition, once the dermis has been incised, there is no connective tissue holding the wound together and the defect gapes open.

13. Which tumor types are treated by Mohs surgery?

The most common lesions treated by Mohs surgery are basal cell carcinoma and squamous cell carcinoma, the most frequent types of skin cancer. They are ideal for use of Mohs surgery because they are easily seen microscopically, tend to grow in a contiguous fashion, usually are found in anatomically important areas of the head and neck, and often have clinically ill-defined margins. Other less common skin cancers treated by Mohs surgery include dermatofibrosarcoma protuberans, atypical fibroxanthoma, Merkel cell carcinoma, extramammary Paget's disease, eccrine carcinoma, sebaceous carcinoma, leiomyosarcoma, and microcystic adnexal carcinoma. On occasion, nonmalignant tumors that tend to regrow after standard excision and can become troublesome because of their size, site, or potential for malignant transformation are treated with Mohs surgery. Examples of these tumors include granular cell tumor and desmoplastic trichoepithelioma.

14. What are indications for Mohs surgery?

Mohs surgery is indicated particularly for tumors that are (1) recurrent tumors, (2) primary tumors known to have high recurrence rates, and (3) primary lesions for which maximal preservation of tissue is necessary, such as the eyelid, nose, finger, genitalia, and areas around major nerves. Mohs surgical excision should also be considered when excision of the primary lesion will require a flap or graft for closure, because recurrence under the plane of reconstruction can be difficult to diagnose. In addition, for small clinically thin lesions of the scalp, ear, lip, and nose, Mohs surgical excision may allow healing by secondary intention if the tumor is determined histologically to be very superficial, thus saving the patient an extensive reconstructive procedure.

15. Which tumors have the highest recurrence rates?

Primary tumors known to have high recurrence rates include those tumors greater than 2 cm in diameter or tumors that have poorly demarcated margins on visual inspection. In addition, nonmelanoma skin cancers with particular histologic subtypes, including sclerosing and micronodular basal cell carcinomas and moderately to poorly differentiated squamous cell carcinoma, are known to have high recurrence rates after standard excision. Some sites are problematic, such as the ear or the nasofacial sulcus, where wide or deep penetration along fusion planes is common. Tumors already recurrent also have a higher recurrence rate following standard destruction or excision techniques.

16. What are associated tumor recurrence rates with Mohs surgery versus other treatment modalities for nonmelanoma skin cancer?

The recurrence rate for Mohs surgery of basal cell and squamous cell cancers is 1% to 2%. Standard excision for tumors less than 2 cm in diameter with a minimum 4- to 5-mm margin is associated with a 5% to 6% recurrence rate. Electrodessication and curettage is a destructive method for lesions on the trunk and extremities and has recurrence rates from 6% to 10%. This method has higher rates of recurrence if used on the face. Cryosurgery with liquid nitrogen has a recurrence rate of 2% to 6% in skilled hands. Superficial radiotherapy is not recommended for those younger than 60 years and has a reported recurrence rate of 5% to 11%. For tumors already recurrent, the highest cure rates are achieved by Mohs surgery. For previously treated tumors, the 5-year recurrence rate with Mohs surgery is 5.6%, and the recurrence rates associated with non-Mohs modalities to treat recurrent tumors are 19.9%.

17. Why perform Mohs surgery for skin cancers with positive margins after excision?

Skin cancers with positive margins after excision on the face and neck generally recur if not fully excised. With recurrence, they behave more aggressively and may extend under scars and in deeper tissue planes than primary tumors. Because the original excision was meant to be curative, the presence of positive margins probably indicates significant subclinical or histologic spread. Mohs surgery is the easiest and most complete way to identify and remove the subclinical tumor so that it does not recur. Some tumors of the trunk and extremities do not recur even though the margins were reported to be positive by the pathologist. Because recurrence in these sites is unlikely to impinge on functionally or cosmetically important structures, repeat excision without rigorous margin control or observation could be used. However, the clinician must use judgment. If the patient cannot be followed closely for some reason, it would be best to offer the patient Mohs surgery, which is the treatment with the greatest ability to achieve clear margins. Certainly in the case of a nonmelanoma skin cancer with deep margins positive after excision, the standard next step is Mohs surgery. Mohs surgery can be performed almost immediately; however, if the wound is clinically inflamed, histologic inflammation may obscure the tumor. In this instance, Mohs surgery is delayed for 4 to 8 weeks, depending on the tumor type and its suspected aggressiveness.

18. Which tumors should not be treated by Mohs surgery?

Contraindications to Mohs surgery are relative. Although the Mohs procedure can be performed for any histologically identifiable tumor in the cutaneous or soft tissues, sometimes clear margins cannot be obtained. This situation occurs most frequently when the tumor has invaded bone or has extended in the retrobulbar space. It also may occur in tumors with perineural spread. Generally, however, even in these cases, Mohs surgery is helpful in identifying the exact location and method of spread of the residual tumor. For similar reasons, Mohs surgery may not be definitive for tumors with discontiguous growth patterns but may be useful in the overall surgical and adjuvant care of the patient in a multispecialty approach.

19. Can dermatofibrosarcoma protuberans be treated with Mohs surgery?

Dermatofibrosarcoma protuberans is a rare, slow-growing tumor that usually presents on the trunk or extremities. Microscopically, this tumor extends far beyond clinical margins, extending locally into the dermis, subcutaneous, and underlying muscle. Standard treatment had been wide excision often with 2- to 3-cm margins. Because of the subclinical spread of this tumor, standard excision was associated with tumor recurrence at 20% to 41% and distant metastasis. Mohs surgery now is the treatment of choice for this tumor because it is associated with a lower recurrence rate (1%) as well as conservation of normal adjacent tissue.

20. What is the role of Mohs surgery in treating Merkel cell carcinoma?

Merkel cell carcinoma is not a histologically contiguous tumor on presentation. It usually consists of a subepidermal tumor nodule with the leading edge composed of a trabecular infiltrating pattern and small nests of in transit metastases in the adjacent subcutaneous tissues, sometimes located within small lymphatics. Mohs surgery can be helpful in identifying preliminary margins for tumors that impinge on important anatomic structures such as the eyelid but is not the definitive treatment of this tumor. The lowest recurrence rates and highest 5-year survival rates are achieved by using both surgical excision, by either Mohs surgery or standard excision with wide margins, and radiation therapy to the surgical site, surrounding tissue, and draining nodal basin.

21. Can melanoma be treated with Mohs surgery?

The role of treating melanoma by Mohs technique remains controversial. In standard Mohs technique, the frozen preparation of tissue can create freeze artifact, making it difficult to differentiate atypical melanocytes from keratinocytes. Permanent sections, which can be cut thinner, allow a much better definition of atypical melanocytes. In some experienced Mohs surgery units, however, Mohs surgery for melanoma has been performed on a regular basis, resulting in both preservation of normal tissue as well as a low recurrence rate. In many other Mohs units, lentigo maligna and melanomas are excised with a variation of the Mohs technique known as delayed Mohs surgery using formalin-fixed tissue instead of frozen sections.

22. Describe delayed Mohs surgery.

A section of tissue is taken, oriented, and mapped in the same fashion as for the traditional Mohs technique; however, the tissue specimen is then formalin fixed, paraffin embedded, and processed as a permanent section cut tangentially. It is frequently sent to the pathology department for processing; if so, the pathology department must understand how to set up the specimen so the relevant margins can be fully examined. Because this process is longer than the typical frozen section process, the patient is bandaged and sent home, returning after 24 to 48 hours. If the margins are involved with tumor, another specimen is taken and processed by the same procedure. When the margins are judged to be completely clear, a decision about reconstruction can be made.

23. What are the advantages of Mohs surgery over surgical excision?

Because of rigorous and complete histologic examination of all margins of the excision specimen, Mohs surgery can track deep and irregular or unpredictable tumor projections that are not appreciable to the naked eye. This margin control affords higher cure rates and preservation of normal tissue. Because the histologic examination is done on fresh tissue as frozen sections, definitive reconstruction can be done the same day. Reconstruction often is more successful and requires fewer revisions because the margins are known to be clear and yet are as small as possible.

In addition, it is often an advantage that the procedure is accomplished under local anesthesia and in an ambulatory setting. Patients may be fatigued at the end of the procedure but are not ill and have not required any systemic drugs. It is also efficient for the physician because patients can be staggered such that multiple procedures can be performed at the same time. Depending on staffing and space, one physician can perform as many as 8 to 12 procedures in a single day.

24. What are the disadvantages to Mohs surgery?

Although Mohs surgery allows the patient and physician to know the margins are clear in 1 day, the process can take many stages, so the length of the procedure can be troublesome to some patients.

25. What are alternative treatment options for skin tumors not treated by Mohs surgery?

There are many treatment alternatives to Mohs surgery. Many of these options are associated with lower cure rates and higher rates of recurrence and so are best reserved for small primary tumors or tumors on the trunk and extremities. These tumors may be treated with standard excision with or without frozen section margin control, radiation therapy, cryotherapy, electrodessication and curettage, or topical regimens of 5-fluorouracil or imiquimod. Some patients, especially the elderly, ask if treatment of skin cancer is necessary. Basal cell carcinomas continue to grow and will ulcerate and bleed. Squamous cell cancers will continue to grow and may metastasize and cause death. Generally, unless the patient has a terminal illness, it is preferable to definitively treat the skin cancer when it is first diagnosed.

26. What are the economic implications of Mohs surgery?

The total costs of Mohs surgery are comparable to the costs of traditional surgical excision in the office setting and often much lower than surgical excision in an operating room suite or radiation therapy. The costs of standard excision and Mohs surgery include the initial evaluation, skin biopsy, excision, repair, histologic preparation and tissue examination under the microscope, follow-up visits, and the costs of treating projected tumor recurrences. Excision is associated with higher recurrence rates (10% with excision) compared with Mohs surgery (1%), and the costs of treating these recurrent tumors should be accounted into the final cost. Also, with Mohs surgery, as narrow surgical margins are taken around the tumor, defects often are smaller than with adequate surgical excision. Therefore the smaller defects with Mohs surgery permit smaller and more cost-effective repairs.

27. How does one learn Mohs surgery?

Mohs surgical training is optimally obtained in a dedicated 1- to 2-year fellowship after completing a dermatology residency in which the Mohs surgeon has learned clinical and histopathologic diagnosis of skin cancers. Accredited training centers must perform more than 500 cases per year, with a substantial portion of these cases being complex because of site, size, required reconstruction, or tumor type. In addition, these centers characteristically have academic affiliations and regular contact with other specialties, such as plastic surgery, otolaryngology, pathology, and radiation oncology. Training centers may be accredited by either the American College of Mohs Surgery (ACMS) or the Accreditation Council for Graduate Medical Education (ACGME).

28. Is there collaboration between Mohs surgeons and plastic surgeons?

Yes, definitely! Mohs surgeons and plastic surgeons form a natural beneficial alliance in the treatment of difficult skin cancers. Following clearance of tumor by Mohs surgery, the surgical defect can be repaired by the Mohs surgeon or by a plastic surgeon. A plastic surgeon performing the reconstruction can concentrate on the repair because he or she knows the defect is tumor-free. Additionally, in some instances, patients require removal of involved bone, nerve repair, or reconstruction by large complicated flaps necessitating general anesthesia, all of which can be best accomplished by a plastic surgeon. A team approach is the most effective means of taking care of large, difficult tumors.

BIBLIOGRAPHY

Bart R, Schrager D, Kopf AW, et al: Scalpel excision of basal cell carcinomas. Arch Dermatol 114:739–742, 1978.

Bart RS, Kopf AW, Petratos MA: X-ray therapy of skin cancer, evaluation of a standardized method for treating basal cell skin carcinoma. Sixth National Cancer Conference. Philadelphia, JB Lippincott, 1970, pp 559–570.

Bath-Hexatall F, Perkins W: Basal cell carcinoma. In Williams H et al.: Evidence-Based Dermatology, 2nd ed. Malden, MA, BMJ Books, 2008, pp 256–271.

Batra RS, Kelley LC: Predictors of extensive subclinical spread in nonmelanoma skin cancers treated with Mohs micrographic surgery. Arch Dermatol 138:1043–1051, 2002.

Boyd JD, Zitelli JA, Brodland DG, D'Angelo G: Local control of primary Merkel cell carcinoma: Review of 45 cases treated with Mohs micrographic surgery with and without adjuvant radiation. J Am Acad Dermatol 47:885–892, 2002.

Bricca GM, Brodland DG, Ren D, Zitelli JA: Cutaneous head and neck melanoma treated with Mohs micrographic surgery. J Am Acad Dermatol 52:92–100, 2005.

Cook J, Zitelli JA: Mohs micrographic surgery: A cost analysis. J Am Acad Dermatol 39:698–703, 1998.

Cottel WJ, Proper S: Mohs' surgery fresh tissue technique. J Dermatol Surg Oncol 8:576–587, 1982.

Graham FG: Statistical data on malignant tumors in cryosurgery 1982. J Dermatol Oncol Surg 9:238–239, 1983.

Greenway HT, Dobes WL, Goodman MM, et al: Guidelines of care for Mohs micrographic surgery. J Am Acad Dermatol 33:271–278, 1995.

Haycox CL, Odland PB, Olbricht SM, Casey B: Dermatofibrosarcoma protuberans: Growth characteristics based on tumor modeling and a review of cases treated with Mohs micrographic surgery. Ann Plast Surg 38:246–251, 1997.

Holt PJ: Cryotherapy for skin cancer: Results over a 5-year period using liquid nitrogen spray cryosurgery. Br J Dermatol 119:231–240, 1988.

Kopf AW, Bart RS, Shrager D: Curettage-electrodessication in the treatment of basal cell carcinoma. Arch Dermatol 82:197–204, 1960.

Liegeois NJ, Seo SJ, Olbricht S: Squamous cell carcinoma. In Williams H et al: Evidence-Based Dermatology, 2nd ed. Malden, MA, BMJ Books, 2008, pp 248–255.

McKenna JK, Florell SR, Goldman GD, Bowen GM: Lentigo maligna/lentigo maligna melanoma: Current state of diagnosis and treatment. Dermatol Surg 32:493–504, 2006.

Medina-Franco H, Urist MM, Fiveash J, et al: Multimodality treatment of Merkel cell carcinoma: Case series and literature review of 1024 cases. Ann Surg Oncol 8:204–208, 2001.

Mohs FE: Chemosurgery. Microscopically controlled surgery for skin cancer. Springfield, IL, Charles C Thomas, 1978.

Panje WR, Ceiley RI: The influence of embryology of the midface on the spread of epithelial malignancies. Laryngoscope 89:1914–1920, 1979.

Pennington BE, Leffell DJ: Mohs micrographic surgery: Established uses and emerging trends. Oncology 19:1165–1171, 2005.

Rapini R: Comparison of methods of checking surgical margins. J Am Acad Dermatol 23:288–294, 1990.

Rigel DS, Robbins P, Friedman RJ: Predicting recurrence of basal-cell carcinomas treated by microscopically controlled excision: A recurrence index score. J Dermatol Surg Oncol Surg 7:807–810, 1981.

Roenigk RK: Mohs micrographic surgery. Mayo Clin Proc 63:175–183, 1988.

Roses DF, Valensi Q, Latrenta G, Harris MN: Surgical treatment of dermatofibrosarcoma protuberans. Surg Gynecol Obstet 162:449–452, 1986.

Rowe DE, Carroll RJ, Day CL Jr: Mohs surgery is the treatment of choice for recurrent (previously treated) basal cell carcinoma. J Dermatol Surg Oncol 15:424–431, 1989.

Snow SN, Gordon EM, Larson PO et al: Dermatofibrosarcoma protuberans: A report on 29 patients treated by Mohs micrographic surgery with long term follow-up and review of the literature. Cancer 101:28–38, 2004.

HEMANGIOMAS AND VASCULAR MALFORMATIONS

John B. Mulliken, MD

1. **An infant is born with a large vascular lesion. Is it more likely a vascular malformation or a vascular tumor?**

   There is no correct answer to this slippery question, unless you are given more information. A capillary malformation (CM) can be extensive on the trunk or a limb. Lymphatic malformation (LM) and venous malformation (VM) often are large at birth. Arteriovenous malformation (AVM) usually is not seen at birth, although it may manifest as a blush or telangiectasia and often goes undetected. The common infantile hemangioma is barely noticeable at birth and grows rapidly in the neonatal period, but the uncommon congenital hemangioma is large. Kaposiform hemangioendothelioma (KHE) also can be congenital and expansive. Other congenital masses that mimic a vascular tumor or malformation include teratoma and nonvascular tumors, such as infantile fibrosarcoma and infantile myofibroma.

2. **Can hemangioma present as a large tumor at birth?**

   Congenital hemangioma reaches peak of growth at birth, and the lack of postnatal growth is an important characteristic. The two forms are *rapidly involuting congenital hemangioma* (RICH) and *noninvoluting congenital hemangioma* (NICH). Both present as a raised spherical to ovoid tumor, dark red to purple in color, with central telangiectasias, and often a pale rim. Both forms exhibit rapid flow. RICH can cause neonatal congestive heart failure and sometimes thrombocytopenia. Involution of RICH begins at or soon after birth and usually is complete by approximately 16 months. In contrast, NICH grows in proportion to the child, and fast-flow persists. This tumor is often mistaken for an AVM. Discussion is ongoing as to whether these really are hemangiomas because neither tumor stains for GLUT1, a marker of infantile hemangioma. Congenital hemangioma can occur in a child who also has an infantile hemangioma.

3. **Which is more accurate for radiologic diagnosis of a vascular anomaly— ultrasonography or magnetic resonance imaging?**

   Ultrasonography (US) is highly operator dependent. The sonologist not only must be skilled in using the equipment but also must understand the cellular basis and flow characteristics, as well as the clinical features, of a wide variety of vascular anomalies. Magnetic resonance imaging (MRI) is the "gold standard" for study of vascular anomalies. Obtaining the indicated MRI sequences and their interpretation requires a radiologist with specialized knowledge in this field. In general, every MRI study should include contrast enhancement (gadolinium); gradient sequences are needed to visualize fast-flow vessels, and fat-suppression sequences may be useful. There are numerous opportunities for confusion. For example, infantile hemangioma, congenital hemangioma, and AVM all are fast-flow lesions. LM can be difficult to differentiate from VM. Intralesional bleeding in an LM muddles the interpretation of images as that of a pure LM or a lymphaticovenous malformation (LVM).

4. **When is biopsy necessary to differentiate a vascular tumor from a vascular malformation?**

   More than 90% of vascular anomalies can be diagnosed accurately by history and physical examination. Radiologic study (US or MRI) is often indicated to confirm the diagnosis and to determine the extent of the lesion. If there is any equivocation about the diagnosis, biopsy is mandatory. Unfortunately, many pathologists continue to use the word "hemangioma" in a generic sense, applying it to vascular malformations, for example, "cavernous hemangioma," "venous hemangioma," "capillary hemangioma," and "lymphangioma." Even a pathologist familiar with the biologic nomenclature for vascular anomalies can have difficulty giving a name to some rare vascular tumors or recognizing a reactive proliferative process within the channels of a vascular malformation (Table 16-1).

5. **What is Kasabach-Merritt phenomenon?**

   This is a serious thrombocytopenia (typically <5000 platelets/mm^3) that occurs in association with a locally aggressive vascular tumor (KHE) and sometimes with a less aggressive tumor (tufted angioma). KHE is treated initially with a trial of corticosteroid (only 12% effective); thereafter the options are vincristine or interferon alfa.

   If a hematologist is involved, insist that heparin or platelets not be given because these can stimulate growth of the tumor. Unfortunately, in the medical literature, the double eponym Kasabach-Merritt is often misapplied to a localized or

Table 16-1. Biologic Classification of Vascular Anomalies of Infancy and Childhood

TUMORS	MALFORMATIONS
Infantile hemangioma Hemangioendothelioma Angiosarcoma	**Slow-flow** Capillary (CM) Lymphatic (LM) Venous (VM)
	Fast-flow Arterial (AM): Aneurysm, coarctation, ectasia, stenosis Arteriovenous fistula (AVF) Arteriovenous (AVM)

disseminated intravascular coagulopathy that can occur in association with a venous malformation and other disorders. The treatment of these coagulopathies is quite different (see Question 24).

6. Can infantile hemangioma be associated with a malformation?

Yes, there are rare and curious examples, and in these instances the female preponderance is striking. The acronym PHACES denotes such an association in the facial region: **P**osterior fossal malformation; **H**emangioma, often regional; **A**rterial anomalies, agenesis, dilation, and stenosis of intracranial and extracranial vessels; **C**ardiac anomalies, most commonly coarctation; **E**ye anomalies; and **S**ternal cleft and supraumbilical raphe. Midline lumbosacral hemangioma may signal an underlying occult spinal dysraphism. Diagnosis can be ruled out by US in the first 4 to 6 months of life; thereafter MRI is necessary. Extensive "reticular" hemangioma in the lower limb is also associated with urogenital and anorectal anomalies.

7. Can infantile hemangioma cause skeletal overgrowth?

A large hemangioma of the cheek can be associated with minor hypertrophy of the maxilla and zygoma. Parotid hemangioma frequently causes enlargement of the involved ear. There are very rare examples of "reticular" hemangioma of the lower limb associated with minor axial overgrowth. Slow-flow vascular malformations are much more commonly associated with bony elongation, distortion, and deformation. Bony erosion and osteolysis are typical findings with intraosseous LM and with AVM.

8. Which regresses more slowly, "cavernous" hemangioma or "capillary" hemangioma?

This is a deceptive question, because there is no such lesion as "cavernous" hemangioma. The term *hemangioma* usually refers to the common tumor of infancy. There is no difference in rate of regression for a deep (subcutaneous) infantile hemangioma (formerly called "cavernous") versus that for a superficial infantile hemangioma (formerly called "capillary"). Thankfully, the nineteenth-century term "cavernous" hemangioma is slowly disappearing from the literature; more precisely, it refers to VM, whether in skin, hollow or solid viscera (particularly liver), bone, or brain.

9. Are phleboliths seen on plain radiography of infantile hemangioma?

No. Phleboliths (calcified thrombi) are characteristic of VM or LVM. There are rare examples, however, of dystrophic calcification in congenital hemangioma (particularly in the liver) of the rapidly regressing type.

10. You are asked to consult on a baby who has multiple cutaneous vascular lesions. What is your advice?

The infant likely has multiple hemangiomas ("hemangiomatosis"). You should be concerned about the possibility of involvement of the liver, brain, and gastrointestinal tract, in order of frequency. For a patient with more than five cutaneous hemangiomas, order a hepatic US. Intrahepatic tumors can cause cardiac overload, a complication with a high mortality. Also check the hematocrit and stool for occult blood, the result of bleeding hemangiomas in the gastrointestinal tract. Usually the tiny cutaneous lesions involute more quickly than more typically shaped hemangiomas. The visceral lesions often necessitate pharmacologic therapy because of complications; however, they regress as well.

11. An ultrasonographer asks for your advice regarding a vascular lesion on the scalp that has been discovered in a 30-week fetus. What is your opinion?

The most likely diagnosis is fetal hemangioma of the rapidly involuting type (RICH). Other possibilities include infantile fibrosarcoma and KHE. Suggest that the sonologist reexamine the fetus for signs of cardiac overload and repeat US every few weeks. RICH reaches its apogee in growth near term and might even diminish in size and vascularity. If the tumor is large and depending on its location, caesarian section may be indicated.

12. A 1-month-old infant with a rapidly growing hemangioma of the upper eyelid is sent to your clinic. What are your recommendations?

It is well known that infantile hemangioma can distort the upper eyelid, causing obstruction of the visual axis and deprivational amblyopia. Less well appreciated is that even a small hemangioma in the upper eyelid can deform the infantile cornea and cause refractive disturbances, such as astigmatism and anisometropia, which also can result in amblyopia. In contrast, a large hemangioma in the lower eyelid or cheek rarely distorts the cornea, probably because of Bell's phenomenon during sleep.

If a refractive error is present, prompt treatment is mandatory. The normal eye should be patched (even prophylactically) for a few hours per day to encourage use of the affected eye. Intralesional corticosteroid (triamcinolone 2 to 3 mg/kg) is used less frequently (because of the risk of blindness) and only for a well-localized, superficial tumor in the eyelid. Systemic corticosteroid is preferred for a deep or extensive periorbital hemangioma. If astigmatism is over 2 diopters, the risk for amblyopia is high. In an older infant, the response to corticosteroid is less dramatic, and time is critical. If the tumor is well localized, consider partial excision ("debulking") or total resection.

13. You are paged by a pediatric resident in the emergency room and asked to see an 8-month-old baby with a "hemangioma" that is bleeding profusely; the lesion had appeared 2 months earlier. What would be your response, and how would you manage the lesion?

Politely explain that infantile hemangiomas do not appear at 6 months of age. The child likely has a pyogenic granuloma. Notwithstanding the resident's terminologic inaccuracy, see the child and arrange for treatment. Dermatologists usually curette pyogenic granuloma; however, the recurrence rate is 10%. Surgeons prefer excision of the lesion, and the recurrence rate is almost nil.

14. At what age does regression of an infantile hemangioma cease?

The bright red color usually fades by 5 years; however, the tumor will continue to shrink. Regression is complete in 50% of children by age 5 years and in 70% by age 7 years. Some improvement is seen in the remaining children until age 10 to 12 years.

15. What is the role of pulsed-dye laser in the treatment of infantile hemangioma?

Although superficially appealing, there is little, if any, place for laser photocoagulation of hemangioma in the proliferating phase. Pulsed-dye laser (PDL) penetrates no more than 0.75 mm; thus, only the most superficial lesions can be destroyed by heat. PDL does not influence the proliferation of the deep portion of the tumor. There are reports that PDL helps heal ulceration and relieve pain, but these are not controlled studies. Aggressive PDL application can cause ulceration, depigmentation, and scarring.

16. If a problematic facial hemangioma fails to respond after 2 weeks of oral corticosteroid, given at 2 to 3 mg/kg/day, should the dose be increased or should the drug be given intravenously?

Several studies have shown an 85% response rate to 2 to 3 mg/kg/day prednisolone, seen as either slowing of growth and shrinkage or stabilization. No rigorous evidence shows that an unresponsive hemangioma will respond to a higher dose or intravenous administration. If the lesion is a destructive, deforming, obstructing, or endangering hemangioma, consider another agent, such as vincristine or interferon alfa.

17. What are the considerations for removal of a facial hemangioma before the child attends school?

The preschool period is a logical time to consider excision because the facial image forms at approximately 3 years. Furthermore, before this age the child will not remember the operation. The relative guidelines for excision at this time are as follows: (1) a pedunculated lesion will surely leave expanded skin and/or fibrofatty residuum or a lesion with central scarring secondary to ulceration; (2) the scar will be well hidden; or (3) the scar would be the same length and quality if the resection were postponed. Remember, hemangioma is a tissue expander; first consider circular excision and pursestring closure.

18. Which of the following are the features of Sturge-Weber syndrome?: (A) Port-wine stain in V2 distribution; (B) choroidal "angiomatosis"; (C) leptomeningeal vascular anomalies; (D) skeletal and fibrovascular hypertrophy

The correct answers are C and D. CM ("port-wine stain") involving only the V2 neurotome is very unlikely to be associated with Sturge-Weber syndrome. The at-risk distributions are V1; V1 and V2; or V1, V2, and V3. Funduscopic examination and tonometry are essential in the evaluation. Anomalies of the choroidal vasculature are mistakenly called "angiomas"; these are malformed choroidal vessels. Sturge-Weber syndrome patients are at high risk for glaucoma and retinal detachment. The dural vascular anomalies can cause seizures and mental deficiency. Fibrovascular thickening of the involved skin and skeletal overgrowth occur later.

19. Can a CM in the midaxial dorsal line be associated with an underlying structural anomaly?

Any midline capillary stain is a cutaneous red flag that requires investigation. For example, a stain of the scalp can have a central tuft of hair and surrounding alopecia ("hair collar sign") indicating ectopic neural tissue and possible underlying encephalocoele. CM over the cervical or lumbosacral spine can be a clue to occult spinal dysraphism (see Question 7). Thoracic CM can be associated with a metameric spinal AVM (Cobb syndrome).

20. How does flashlamp PDL cause lightening of a CM?

The mechanism is called *selective photothermolysis*. PDL at a wavelength of 595 nm is close to the third (577 nm) absorption spectral peak of oxyhemoglobin. Set pulse duration at 1.5 msec and fluence at 8–12 Joules/cm^2. The absorbed light is released as heat, which damages red cells, perivascular wall, and collagen. Biopsies taken 1 to 2 months later show diminished numbers of ectatic dermal vessels and, thus, a more normal cutaneous hue. With dark skin, PDL treatment can cause damage to melanocytes in the basal epidermis, resulting in hypopigmentation. The overall improvement with PDL is 70% lightening. Results are better in the lateral versus central facial region and are poor in the extremities. Often PDL treatments must be repeated as capillary–venular flow returns.

21. Prenatal ultrasonography reveals a dorsal midline cervicocephalic cystic anomaly. What are the implications?

The so-called "lethal midline cystic lymphatic anomaly" is easily diagnosed by prenatal US as early as 12 to 14 weeks' gestation. The typical finding is a thin-walled, multiseptated cystic mass in the posterior aspect of the fetal head and nuchal region. Often this anomaly is associated with fetal hydrops. Amniocentesis for karyotyping is essential for counseling the parents. More than half of these fetuses will have Turner syndrome (XO) or other aneuploidy, such as trisomy 13, 18, or 21. Terathanasia (spontaneous elimination of a defective embryo) is common. This serious anomaly should not be confused with macrocystic cervical LM.

22. What is the management of an infant born with macrocystic cervical LM?

Often the diagnosis is made prenatally; the airway is the major concern. An EXIT (ex utero intrapartum) procedure may be necessary. If the airway is secure, the next decision is when and how to intervene. Resection has been the first-line approach. Macrocystic LM is easier to dissect than microcystic lesion; however, resection is never complete, and there is a risk of damaging important nerves in the neck. More recently, interventional radiologists have assumed a primary role in this anomaly. OK-432 (killed strain of group A *Streptococcus pyogenes*) is not approved by the Food and Drug Administration (FDA) (and probably never will be). Doxycycline is equally effective as a sclerosant. This antibiotic is known to be antiangiogenic, antilymphangiogenic, and an inhibitor of metalloproteinases, but the mechanism involved in shrinking LM is unknown.

23. What is the treatment of VM?

The answer is sclerotherapy, sclerotherapy, and sclerotherapy. Thereafter resection is considered for correction of contour, size, or scarring. In a few instances resection is the primary treatment, for example, a tiny, well-localized subcutaneous or submucosal lesion, such as in glomuvenous malformation, blue rubber bleb nevus syndrome, or spindle cell hemangioendothelioma. In certain areas in an extremity, operation is preferred over sclerotherapy, for example, if the lesion is well localized to a single muscle group and can be completely excised, or if there is risk of ulceration, nerve damage, or compartment compression.

24. When should clotting be assessed in a patient with a vascular malformation?

A patient with either multiple or large venous malformation (rarely lymphatico-venous malformation) is at risk for localized disseminated intravascular coagulopathy (LIC), defined as the presence of activated clotting and fibrinolytic factors in intralesional blood. Any perturbation (e.g., trauma, sclerotherapy, or an operation) can cause disseminated intravascular coagulopathy (DIC). The coagulopathic patterns are low fibrinogen and elevated prothrombin time, activated partial thromboplastin time, and D-dimer. Unlike Kasabach-Merritt phenomenon, the platelet count is minimally depressed (range 50,000 to 150,000 per cubic millimeter). Coagulopathy is caused by blood stasis within the abnormal channels, which initiates generation of thrombin and local formation of clots. The most effective treatment of LIC or DIC is sclerotherapy to diminish the size of the VM. Heparin is given subcutaneously prior to a procedure (sclerotherapy or resection) is continued for 2 weeks after intervention.

25. Which of the following eponymous vascular disorders are characterized by fast-flow? (A) Bonnet-Dechaume-Blanc (Wyburn-Mason) syndrome; (B) Sturge-Weber syndrome; (C) Klippel-Trenaunay syndrome; (D) Parkes Weber syndrome; (E) Rendu-Osler-Weber syndrome (hereditary hemorrhagic telangiectasia)

The correct answers are A, D, and E. Bonnet-Dechaume-Blanc syndrome is very rare and is comprised of facial staining and intracranial AVM involving the mesencephalon. Sturge-Weber is a slow-flow disorder characterized by facial CM (sometimes on other parts of the body) and capillary–venous anomalies of the leptomeninges.

Table 16-2. Eponymous Vascular Syndromes

Slow-flow
Sturge-Weber: Facial CM, choroidal CM, leptomeningeal CM, VM
Klippel-Trenaunay: CLVM, limb/trunk/pelvis overgrowth
Maffucci: VM, enchondromata

Fast-flow
Rendu-Osler-Weber (HHT): Cutaneomucosal "spider-like" lesions; pulmonary, cerebral, or hepatic AVM
Parkes Weber: CLAVM/CAVM of a limb, often with hypertrophy
Bonnet-Dechaume-Blanc (Wyburn-Mason): AVM involving central face, extracranial/intracranial optic tract

AVM, Arteriovenous malformation; *CAVM*, capillary arteriovenous malformation; *CLAVM*, capillary lymphaticoarteriovenous malformation; *CLVM*, capillary lymphaticovenous malformation; *CM*, capillary malformation; *HHT*, hereditary hemorrhagic telangiectasia; *VM*, venous malformation.

Klippel-Trenaunay syndrome is another slow-flow overgrowth disorder involving abnormal veins and lymphatics, with geographic cutaneous capillary–lymphatic staining (Table 16-2). Parkes Weber syndrome (CLAVM/CAVM) is congenital overgrowth of a limb (more often lower) with fast-flow through multiple, tiny AVFs involving skin and usually the underlying muscle. Hereditary hemorrhagic telangiectasia (HHT) presents as tiny arteriovenous fistulas (AVFs) in the skin and mucous membranes; some patients develop AVMs in the lungs, liver, and brain.

26. What is Maffucci syndrome?

Unfortunately many textbooks characterize Maffucci syndrome as "hemangiomas" in association with enchondromas. The vascular anomalies in this rare disorder are venous in type. The features usually do not manifest until early to middle childhood. Enchondromas of the long bones appear first, presentation with a pathologic fracture is common, and the patient is often diagnosed as having Ollier syndrome. Cutaneous VMs typically appear as dome-like bluish lesions on the limb, typically on the fingers or toes. In time they evolve to become firm, knotty, and verrucous, and they may contain phleboliths. Spindle cell hemangioma often develops in the lesions but is thought to be a reactive lesion rather than a true neoplasm. Patients who have Maffucci syndrome have a predilection to develop various types of malignant tumors.

27. Multiple venous anomalies suggest the possibility of familial transmission (germline mutation). What are the inheritable venous malformations?

The most common are glomuvenous malformations (previously called "familial glomangiomas"). Causative mutations are in the gene *glomulin*, which encodes an intracellular signaling protein. Cutaneomucosal venous malformations are the result of a single amino acid substitution resulting in a gain of function in the gene for *TIE2* (an endothelial receptor for angiopoietin 1 and 2), thought to be responsible for normal recruitment of smooth muscle cells. Another familial venous disorder, well known to neurosurgeons, is cerebral cavernous malformation, caused by mutations in *KRIT, malcavernin*, and *PCD10*. Approximately 12% of these patients have cutaneous and intramuscular VMs. Blue rubber bleb nevus syndrome is the most common vascular anomaly that causes gastrointestinal bleeding. These patients have multiple cutaneous lesions, especially on the palms and plantar surfaces and on the mucosal lesions. Some pedigrees suggest autosomal dominant transmission. The causative gene is unknown.

28. Which are more common, intracranial or extracranial AVMs?

Intracranial AVMs are 20-fold more common than extracranial AVMs.

29. AVM should initially be managed by embolization of the feeding arteries: True or False?

False. The superselective catheter should pass through the feeding arteries into the epicenter (nidus) of the AVM. Proximal embolization of a feeding vessel is just as injurious as proximal ligation, causing collaterals to form with expansion of the AVM. Experienced radiologists agree that "cure" by embolization is unlikely unless the AVM can be completely resected after preoperative interventional preparation. The term *control* is preferred to *cure* by those with experience in managing AVMs.

30. A teenage girl requests a rhinoplasty, but your thorough evaluation reveals a history of epistaxis. What is the differential diagnosis?

Likely diagnoses include (1) hereditary hemorrhagic telangiectasia, (2) prominent vessels in Kiesselbach's triangle, (3) familial bleeding disorder (e.g., von Willebrand's disease), (4) self-mutilation, and (5) cocaine addiction.

BIBLIOGRAPHY

Berenguer B, Mulliken JB, Enjolras O, et al: Rapidly involuting congenital hemangioma: Clinical and histopathologic features. Pediatr Dev Pathol 6:495–510, 2003.

Boon LM, Mulliken JB, Enjolras O, Vikkula M: Glomuvenous malformation ("glomangioma") is a distinct clinicopathologic and genetic entity. Arch Dermatol 140:971–976, 2004.

Brouillard P, Vikkula M: Vascular malformations: Localized defects in vascular morphogenesis. Clin Genet 63:340–351, 2003.

Enjolras O, Mulliken JB, Boon LM, et al: Non-involuting congenital hemangioma: A rare cutaneous vascular anomaly. Plast Reconstr Surg 107:1647–1654, 2001.

Greene AK, Rogers GF, Mulliken JB: Management of parotid hemangioma in 100 children. Plast Reconstr Surg 113:53–60, 2004.

Marler JJ, Fishman SJ, Upton J, et al: Prenatal diagnosis of vascular anomalies. J Pediatr Surg 37:318–326, 2002.

Marler JJ, Mulliken JB: Current management of hemangiomas and vascular malformations. Clin Plast Surg 32:99–116, 2005.

Metry DW, Dowd CF, Barkovich AJ, Frieden IJ: The many faces of PHACE syndrome. J Pediatr 139:117–123, 2001.

Mulliken JB: Vascular anomalies. In Thorne, CHM, Beasley RM, Aston SJ, et al. (eds). Grabb and Smith's Plastic Surgery, 6th ed. Philadelphia, Lippincott Williams & Wilkens 2007, 191–200.

Mulliken JB, Anupindi S, Ezekowitz RAB, Mimh MC Jr: Case records of the Massachusetts General Hospital. Case 13-2004: A newborn girl with a large cutaneous lesion, thrombocytopenia, and anemia. N Eng J Med 350:1764–1775, 2004.

Mulliken JB, Enjolras O: Congenital hemangiomas and infantile hemangioma: Missing links. J Am Acad Dermatol 50:875–882, 2004.

Mulliken JB, Fishman SJ, Burrows PE: Vascular anomalies. Curr Prob Surg 37:517–584, 2000.

Mulliken JB, Rogers GF, Marler JJ: Circular excision of hemangioma and purse-string closure–The smallest possible scar. Plast Reconstr Surg 109:1544–1554, 2002.

KELOIDS AND HYPERTROPHIC SCARS

Stephen Daane, MD, and
Bryant A. Toth, MD

1. What does the term "keloid" mean?

Alibert coined the term *cheloide* in 1806 (from the Greek word meaning crab claw) to describe the lateral expansion of keloid scarring onto surrounding normal tissue. Historically the first mention of keloid treatment is the Smith papyrus from Egypt in 1700 BC. Keloid scars occur with either superficial or deep injuries and are correlated with younger age and darker skin. No animal model can be used for clinical investigation because keloids occur only in humans.

2. What is a keloid made of?

Whereas normal skin contains distinct collagen bundles parallel to the epithelial surface, keloid scars contain collagen that is present in randomly oriented dense sheets. There is an increased proliferation of fibroblasts and an abnormally increased production of collagen up to 20 times that of normal skin and three times that of hypertrophic scars. Keloid fibroblasts overproduce type I collagen; the increased ratio of type I to type III collagen results from differences at both the pretranscriptional and posttranscriptional levels. Most microvessels in keloids are occluded, apparently due to an excess of endothelial cells, supporting the theory that hypoxia is a factor in abnormal scarring.

3. What is a hypertrophic scar?

Clinically, hypertrophic scars remain within the confines of the original wound border, whereas keloids invade adjacent normal skin. Hypertrophic scars generally arise after several weeks, are present for many months, and then regress. Keloids may arise much later after wounding and may enlarge indefinitely.

4. Who gets keloids? Which anatomic areas are commonly involved?

An incidence of keloids between 4.5% and 16% has been reported in a predominately black and Hispanic population and up to 16% in random samplings of black Africans. Although keloids can occur at any age, they are most likely to occur between the ages of 10 and 30 years. The incidence is the same in both sexes. Keloids have been associated genetically with HLA-B14, HLA-B21, HLA-Bw16, HLA-Bw35, HLA-DR5, HLA-DQw3, and blood group A as both autosomal dominant and recessive traits. Keloids commonly occur on the ears, jawline, neck, infraclavicular and sternal areas, shoulders, back, abdomen, and extremities. There have been rare reports of keloids on the face mask area. Keloids usually are firm and raised, but they may be pedunculated.

5. What symptoms are associated with keloids?

Some keloids are tender and some are painful. Some patients complain of pruritus due to an overabundance of histamine-producing mast cells. Left untreated, keloids may continue to take up more "real estate," making their eventual treatment more difficult. Cosmetic concern is the main reason patients seek medical intervention.

6. Why do keloids occur?

Although spontaneous keloid development has been reported, it is generally accepted that all keloids are the result of trauma. Synthesis and remodeling of the extracellular matrix by fibroblasts is thought to be the major determinant of dermal architecture after repair. Hypotheses for keloid formation include wound hypoxia, growth factors, fibroblast proliferation, skin tension, anatomic location, genetic disposition, and alterations in extracellular matrix (increased fibronectin production).

7. What is collagen?

Collagen is the most abundant protein in mammals, constituting one fourth of the total. It forms insoluble fibers that have a high tensile strength. Tropocollagen is the basic structural unit of collagen, with a triple helix of polypeptide chains of approximately 1000 amino acid residues each, measuring 3000 Å long by 15 Å wide. Nearly every third residue is glycine; proline is present to a greater extent along with two other rare amino acids, hydroxyproline and hydroxylysine. Carbohydrate units are covalently attached to hydroxylysine residues. A collagen fiber is a "quarter-staggered" array of tropocollagen molecules, strengthened by cross-links. A defect in hydroxylation of collagen due to absence of vitamin C can lead to scurvy.

Tissue collagenases that break down keloid scars are stimulated by steroid injections. The invasive organism *Clostridium histolyticum* causes spreading gas gangrene by secreting collagenases. Hippocrates observed lathyrism in people who ate ground peas; the beta-aminopropionitrile prevents cross-linking of collagen, reducing its strength.

8. How does wound healing work?

All wounds leave scars; "invisible" skin scarring is only present in amphibians and mammalian fetuses during certain stages of gestation. Wound healing is largely controlled by fibroblasts and has been divided into three phases: inflammatory (3 to 10 days), fibroblastic (10 to 14 days), and maturation. During the proliferative phase of wound healing, procollagen is formed intracellularly by fibroblasts and secreted into the extracellular space. It is transformed to tropocollagen by proteases. Tropocollagen molecules aggregate into immature soluble collagen fibrils that are cross-linked by lysyl oxidase to form mature collagen. The amount of collagen in a healing wound reaches a peak in 3 weeks, but remodeling continues over months to years.

9. What happens if you just excise a keloid?

Simple excision of a keloid stimulates a quick recurrence up to 100% of the time. Intramarginal excision of a keloid also leads to recurrence.

10. What growth factors are involved?

It is accepted that transforming growth factor beta (TGF-β) is altered in abnormal scarring, although why this happens is unclear. Several studies have demonstrated the association of TGF-β with increased collagen and fibronectin synthesis by keloid fibroblasts. Studies have shown that keratinocyte fibroblast in vitro coculture systems can induce the keloid phenotype in normal fibroblasts, suggesting epithelial–mesenchymal interactions.

11. How does silicone gel sheeting work?

Pressure garments and silicone gel sheeting are important therapeutic adjuncts in keloid treatment. Pressure therapy is a long-term treatment, so most patients become less compliant after several months. The mechanism of gel sheeting may be warmth, hydration, or occlusion. Silicone gel itself does not seem to work as well as the sheeting. Nonsilicone gel dressings, such as polyurethane (Curad), also can lead to regression of keloids. The gel sheeting should be worn 23 hours per day for 1 year but may need to be discontinued due to skin breakdown. In published studies, patients show improvement of hypertrophic scars with use of silicone sheeting 80% to 100% of the time; however, silicone sheeting alone is successful in treating keloids only 35% of the time. Silicone gel sheeting generally does not work well on mature keloids.

12. How does pressure work?

Silicone sheeting works better when combined with pressure. Custom garments have been helpful in preventing raised burn scars. Clip-on earrings usually are used after excision of keloids on the lobule or helix of the ear. Pressure is thought to decrease tissue metabolism and increase collagenase activity within the wound. Several other mechanisms suggested in the literature include scar hypoxia, increased hydration, and increased scar temperature. A pressure garment is recommend 23 to 24 hours per day for 1 year; however, effective pressure (25 to 40 mm Hg) cannot be achieved in several important anatomic areas. Massage is recommended in conjunction with any scar reduction regimen. The mechanism of action is not understood.

13. How do triamcinolone injections work?

A mainstay treatment of keloids is triamcinolone (Kenalog) injections, 10 to 40 mg/mL. The corticosteroid inhibits alpha2-macroglobulin, causing elaboration of collagenase and collagen degradation. The interval of treatment is generally every 3 to 6 weeks. Keloid injections are easier and less painful after pretreatment with liquid nitrogen, which makes keloids "softer." Cordran tape (flurandrenolide) applied to a keloid for 12 to 20 hours per day will often cause regression of a keloid and may reduce itching. Patients must be followed for recurrence for a minimum of 2 years. Subcutaneous atrophy, telangiectasias, and pigmentary changes occur in half of patients treated with triamcinolone.

14. What about electron beam radiation therapy?

Electron beam therapy is used immediately after surgical excision in the treatment of difficult keloids. The advantage of low-megavolt electron beam radiation is that the depth of penetration is limited, without appreciable effect on deeper structures. From 1500 to 2000 rads (15 to 20 Gy) is fractionated over 7 days. The primary mechanism of radiation-induced scar control seems to be inhibition of fibroblast proliferation. Radiation typically is not recommended in cancer-prone areas such as breast or thyroid. Reported keloid recurrence rates after excision and electron beam radiation are as low as 25%.

15. What other therapies have been tried?

Other therapies attempted but with poor success include interferon, 5-fluorouracil, imiquimod (Aldara), retinoic acid, clobetasone ointment, tacrolimus, methotrexate, colchicine, zinc, salicylic acid, verapamil, bleomycin, cyclosporine, lathyrogens (beta-aminopropionitrile and D-penicillamine), laser therapy, and ultraviolet light. Other surgical adjuncts include the use of tissue expanders for closure of keloid areas without tension. The pulsed dye laser has been used successfully to treat redness resulting from keloids treated with triamcinolone. Skin grafting can lead to a "keloid wave" at the edges of the grafted lesion and may cause a new keloid to form at the donor site.

16. What is the success rate for treating keloids?

Although the current standard of care is excision followed by intralesional steroid injections or electron beam radiation therapy, keloids are frequently resistant to treatment. Prevention (e.g., avoiding ear piercings) is the first rule in keloid-prone patients. In our series of 95 pediatric keloid patients with Fitzpatrick skin types III to VI treated over the past 6 years with surgery, pressure ear rings, Kenalog, and electron beam radiation, the success rate was <50%. The usual reason for treatment failure was poor patient compliance.

BIBLIOGRAPHY

Al-Attar A, Mess S, Thomassen JM, Kauffman CL, Davison SP: Keloid pathogenesis and treatment. Plast Reconstr Surg 117:286–300, 2006.

Cosman B, Crikelair GF, Ju DMC, Gaulin JC, Lattes R: The surgical treatment of keloids. Plast Reconstr Surg 27:335–355, 1961.

Glori pressure earrings. Padgett Instruments, Kansas City, Missouri.

Ketchum LD, Cohen IK, Masters FW: Hypertrophic scars and keloids—A collective review. Plast Reconstr Surg 53:140–154, 1974.

Lim IJ, Phan TT, Bay BH, et al: Fibroblasts cocultured with keloid keratinocytes: Normal fibroblasts secrete collagen in a keloidlike manner. Am J Physiol Cell Physiol 283:C212–C222, 2002.

Niessen FB, Spauwen PH, Schalkwijk J, Kon M: On the nature of hypertrophic scars and keloids: A review. Plast Reconstr Surg 104:1435–1458, 1999.

Norris JEC: Superficial x-ray therapy in keloid management: A retrospective study of 24 cases and literature review. Plast Reconstr Surg 95:1051–1055, 1995.

Ogawa R, Mitsuhashi K, Hyakusoku H, Miyashita T: Postoperative electron-beam irradiation therapy for keloids and hypertrophic scars: Retrospective study of 147 cases followed for more than 18 months. Plast Reconstr Surg 111:547–553, 2003.

Peled ZM, Chin GS, Liu W, Galliano R, Longaker MT: Response to tissue injury. Clin Plast Surg 27:489–500, 2000.

HAIR TRANSPLANTATION

CHAPTER 18

David M. Schwartzenfeld, DO, and
Joseph Karamikian, DO

1. What is the most common cause of pattern baldness?

Androgenic alopecia (AA) is the scientific name for the genetic predisposition for pattern baldness. AA is the cause of more than 95% of all cases of pattern hair loss, including baldness in men and thinning hair in women. The androgens testosterone and dihydrotestosterone (DHT) are responsible for AA. The enzyme 5-alpha reductase regulates the conversion of testosterone to DHT. Increased levels of DHT, or increased sensitivity to the effects of DHT, leads to miniaturization of the hair follicle, a shortened anagen phase of the hair cycle, and eventual hair loss.

2. What is male pattern baldness?

Patterned hair loss in men is referred to as *male pattern baldness* (MPB). In MPB, the hairs in the frontal, temporal, and vertex regions of the scalp have a genetic sensitivity to the hormone testosterone. The hairs on the sides and back of the scalp do not possess this genetic trait and are not affected. For this reason, hairs removed from the side and back of the scalp (donor hairs) will maintain their genetic predisposition and continue to grow when transplanted to the top of the scalp where hair loss has occurred.

3. List the causes of nonandrogenic alopecia.

The differential diagnosis of nonandrogenic alopecia includes the following:

- *Metabolic disorders:* Iron deficiency anemia, thyroid disease, polycystic ovary syndrome
- *Telogen effluvium:* Prolonged and high fever, acute psychiatric illness
- *Infectious diseases:* Herpes simplex, herpes zoster, kerion, folliculitis decalvans
- *Inflammatory diseases:* Discoid lupus erythematosus, lichen planopilaris (scarring alopecia)
- *Autoimmune disorders:* Alopecia areata
- *Trauma:* Traction alopecia, burns, trichotillomania
- *Medications:* Beta-blockers, angiotensin-converting enzyme (ACE) inhibitors, birth control pills

4. Who is Dr. O'Tar T. Norwood?

Dr. Norwood has been a leader in hair transplant surgery for 30 years and is responsible for many landmark events in the field. He published the first book on hair transplant surgery in 1974 and a second edition in 1984. He is cofounder of the International Society of Hair Restoration Surgery (www.ishrs.org), and he founded, published, and edited the *Hair Transplant Forum International* from 1990 to 1995. The *Forum* was and remains the leading periodical in hair transplant surgery and has led to many of the recent improvements in hair surgery and hair loss.

Dr. Norwood's early research in male pattern baldness produced the Norwood Classification of Male Pattern Baldness. This classification has become the standard throughout the world and is used by everyone discussing and studying male pattern baldness (Fig. 18-1). In September 1998, at the Annual Meeting of the International Society of Hair Restoration Surgery, Dr. Norwood received both the Golden Follicle Award and the Manford Lucas Award. He was the first physician to receive both of these prestigious awards at the same time.

5. Describe the anatomy of a hair follicle and the anatomic importance.

The hair follicle has three major anatomic components: the infundibulum, isthmus, and inferior region. The *infundibulum* is the location from the follicle opening of the skin down to the sebaceous duct. The *isthmus* is the center region. It starts at the sebaceous duct and proceeds inferiorly to the arrector pili muscle. The *inferior region* is located from the arrector pili muscle to the base of the follicle. The base of the follicle is also known as the *hair bulb*. The base of the hair bulb is the dermal papilla, which contains a highly vascularized network, nerves, melanocytes, and matrix cells. The hair bulb and dermal papilla make up the hair root. The anatomic importance of the follicle is that its integrity must be preserved during harvesting and not damaged during insertion. A damaged or transected follicle is not viable for transplantation (Fig. 18-2).

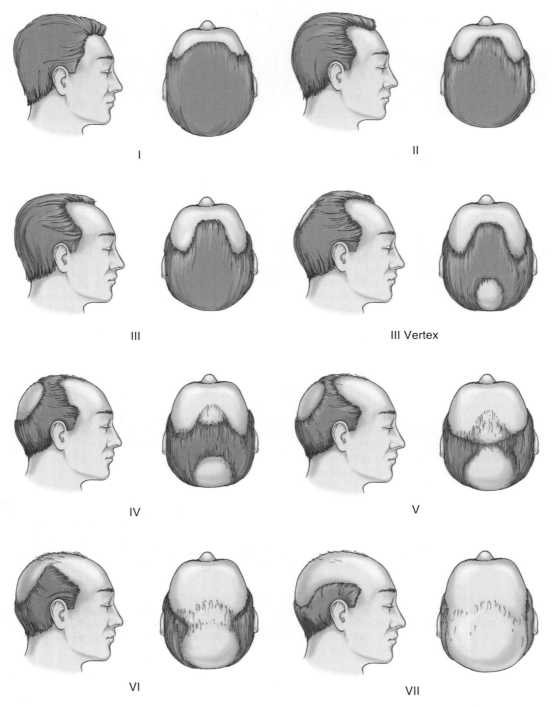

Figure 18-1. Norwood classification of androgenic alopecia. (From Unger MG, Cotterill PC: Hair transplantation. In Achauer BM, Eriksson E, Guyuron B, Coleman JJ, Russell RC, Vander Kolk CA [eds]: Plastic Surgery: Indications, Operations, and Outcomes, Vol 5, Aesthetic Surgery. St. Louis, Mosby, 2000, p 2487. Redrawn from Norwood OT: Male pattern baldness: Classification and incidence. South Med J 68:1359–1365, 1975.)

6. What defines a follicular unit?

A follicular unit (FU) is a discrete anatomic and physiologic entity of one, two, three, or four terminal hairs in their natural distribution. These follicular families can only be seen under a microscope and are meticulously dissected to avoid disrupting their natural pattern in the scalp. The size of a follicular unit is approximately 1 mm. The average follicular unit contains 2.2 hairs.

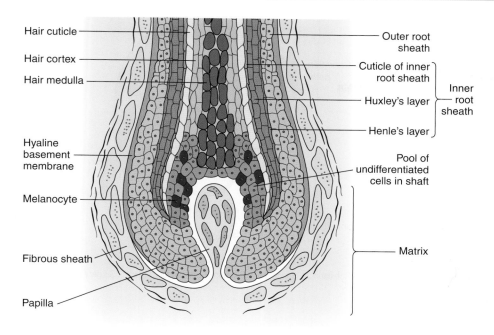

Figure 18-2. Anatomy of a hair follicle. (From Habif T: Clinical Dermatology: A Color Guide to Diagnosis and Therapy, 4th ed. St. Louis, Mosby, 2004.)

7. Describe the factors and important anatomic landmarks when designing a hairline.

The newly designed hairline should be age appropriate and should maintain a natural mature look. To achieve these results, it is important to recognize the following anatomic landmarks: glabella, frontalis muscle, lateral epicanthal line, and temporal points. A general rule of thumb for the new hairline is that it should be four finger breadths, or 7.5 to 9 cm, above the glabella. A hairline should never be designed lower than that to maintain an age-appropriate look. Also, an asymmetric and staggered patterned hairline allows for better cosmetic results to avoid an unnatural pattern.

8. What techniques help to decrease scarring in the donor area?

An optimal scar in the donor area is achieved by paying attention to the scalp's laxity prior to excising the donor strip as well as making an elliptical incision. By keeping the donor strip 1 cm or smaller, there is decreased stretch back, which leads to less scar formation. Some surgeons use the infrared coagulator on the theory that it helps to decrease tension by pulling both sides of the incision closer. Closure of the wound is best accomplished by a low-tension running locking stitch using 3-0 or 4-0 nylon suture. The distance between each stitch should be between 4 and 5 mm. The sutures should be left in place for 10 to 14 days. This approach yields the best cosmetic results with a virtually undetectable scar in 6 months.

9. What are the most widely used harvesting techniques in regard to the donor area?

Three main excision methods are available to remove the donor strip: single-blade, double-bladed, and multi-bladed scalpel. Each technique is operator dependent and offers different results. With all three techniques, the initial scalp incision is parallel to the angle of hair growth. Single- and double-blade scalpels allow the surgeon to excise a single strip of hair with the least amount of transection to the follicles. This is attributed to better visualization and adjustment of the angle as the strip is excised. The multi-bladed approach allows for excision of multiple narrow strips. This is accomplished by use of different-sized spacers between the numerous blades. The main drawback to the multi-bladed technique is less direct visualization of the follicle and therefore a higher transection rate.

10. What is considered the "prime" anatomic location for donor harvesting?

The "prime" or precise anatomic location on the scalp for harvesting the donor strip is at the level of the external occipital protuberance and the superior nuchal line. Making an incision below this level will interfere with underlying muscle motion. Other factors to consider when harvesting include the patient's age, current medical therapies, and concurrent hair loss.

11. What criteria are used for assessing a patient's donor supply?

The criteria are donor site density, scalp laxity, and size of the current donor area. *Donor density* refers to the number of follicular units per square millimeter for a virgin scalp. *Scalp laxity* refers to the mechanics of the scalp to slide and

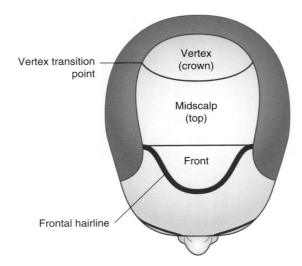

Figure 18-3. Regions of the scalp. (From Robinson JK, Sengelmann RD, Hanke CW, Siegel DM [eds.]. Surgery of the Skin. Philadelphia, Mosby, 2005).

stretch on the galea aponeurotica. A patient with a loose scalp will have a greater density compared to a patient with a tight scalp. Factors that affect the *size of the current donor area* include concurrent medical therapy, patient's age with regard to future hair loss, and present amount of hair loss, that is, does it recede upward from the neck or downward from the crown? In addition, patients must have realistic expectations for the results.

12. What are the most common complications of hair transplant surgery?
The most common complications are postoperative facial edema, folliculitis, wound infection, and wound dehiscence.

13. Define the regions of the scalp.
The frontal region consists of the frontal hair line, the left and right frontotemporal corners back to the midscalp (Fig. 18-3).
The midscalp region is the horizontal area on the top of the head. It extends laterally by the temporoparietal hair-bearing fringes, anteriorly by a line drawn across from one frontotemporal corner to the other, and posteriorly by a curved line that passes through the vertex transition point and leaves a normally shaped vertex area posterior to it.
The vertex is the most posterior portion of the scalp. The vertex transition point divides the midscalp from the vertex (crown). At the vertex transition point the forward direction of the hair changes to a whorl pattern.

14. What are new developments in the treatment of hair loss?
Currently, researchers are working on cloning hair follicles. This would allow a patient to have transplant after transplant without donor depletion and to have an increase in overall hair density. Other new developments include nanotechnology, which may prove to be able to increase medical treatment with minoxidil by efficiently transporting molecules deeper and faster to the hair root.

15. What are the stages of the hair growth cycle?
The hair growth cycle consists of three phases: anagen, catagen, and telogen. *Anagen,* the growth phase, lasts between 3 and 10 years. During this phase, rapid cell division occurs in the hair bulb and dermal papilla. In addition, new hairs begin to protrude from the scalp. *Catagen* is a transitional phase that lasts 2 to 3 weeks. During this phase, cell division stops and the melanocytes stop producing pigment. *Telogen,* the resting phase, lasts 3 to 4 months during which hairs are shed from the scalp.

16. What is the rate of hair growth?
Hair growth occurs at a rate of approximately 1 cm per month.

17. What medical treatments are available for androgenic alopecia?
Finasteride became available in January 1998 and has modified the way physicians treat men with male pattern hair loss. It has proved to be an effective tool that practitioners can now use in the fight against hair loss. The product requires taking a 1-mg pill daily for life. If a patient discontinues finasteride use, the scalp hairs that were saved from

shedding or have regrown will eventually fall out. It works by blocking the formation of DHT (male hormone) and preventing it from binding to and eventually destroying the hair follicle. Specifically, it is an inhibitor of type II 5-alpha reductase. Finasteride was developed to treat baldness in the top, back, and midscalp. It has not been proven to work on recession of the front, temporal area, or hairline. Current data from Merck & Co. (the manufacturer of Propecia) has demonstrated finasteride to be a safe and effective treatment for male pattern hair loss in a long-term clinical trial (5 years). Minoxidil was introduced in the late 1980s for treatment of hair loss in men in women. The mechanism by which minoxidil works is unknown. Minoxidil is available as 2% and 5% topical solution. Minoxidil has been shown to halt hair loss and stimulate new hair growth. Minoxidil works best for early hair loss in small areas. Discontinuation of minoxidil wipes out all the hairs grown and saved through the treatment.

18. What are the most commonly accepted practices for making recipient sites?

The direction of the incision for the recipient site can be sagittal or coronal to the scalp. Many different surgical instruments are available to the surgeon for making recipient sites. Nokor needles (18 gauge) make a 1.8-mm incision for two- to three-hair follicular units. Minde blades, which stands for "minimum depth" knives, come in various sizes and with different types of tips. The theory behind the Minde blade is that it does not affect the major subcutaneous blood vessels, which helps to decrease trauma to the blood supply of the scalp by controlling the depth to 4 mm. Minde blades are produced with either chisel or angle tips. They range in size from 1.3 to 3 mm. Incisions vary from 1.3 mm for a single hair follicular unit to 3 mm for a four- to six-hair follicular unit. Slots and punches vary in size, remove bald tissue, and require larger grafts containing five to eight hairs to be transplanted. Some surgeons make their own blades to match the exact size of the follicles. This is accomplished by using a blade cutter manufactured by Cutting Edge Surgical Equipment. These blades also allow for preservation of the blood supply to the scalp.

19. What are the differences between a micrograft, minigraft, slot graft, and punch graft?

A *micrograft* is a single follicular unit containing one to two hairs. A *minigraft* contains three to six hairs in the form of a follicular unit or two follicular units together (follicular family). A *slot graft* is a larger graft that contains five to eight hairs. A *punch graft* is a large round graft that contains 14 to 30 hairs. It is no longer used since the introduction of follicular unit transplantation.

20. How long does it take to see the full results of a hair transplant?

It can take between 8 and 12 months to see the full results. All scalp hair develops in a growing phase (anagen) and in a resting phase (telogen). Every hair on our head replaces itself every 6 years. The resting phase can be explained as a 3-month hibernation cycle during which the follicle is alive under the skin but no cosmetic hair is produced. After the 3-month dormancy, the follicle once again produces a new cosmetic hair.

21. What is follicular unit extraction?

Follicular unit extraction is a procedure using a small circular punch to harvest follicular units from the donor region. The procedure has advantages and disadvantages. The advantages include a shorter recovery time, no sutures to the donor area (therefore leaving no linear scar), allowing the patient to have a short hair style, and accommodating those who want a small procedure. Disadvantages include a higher transection rate, more time and labor are required, and the amount of grafts harvested in one session is limited to 400 to 600 at a time.

BIBLIOGRAPHY

Barrera A: Hair restoration. Clin Plast Surg 32:163–170, 2005.
Bernstein RM, Rassman WR: Follicular unit transplantation: 2005. Dermatol Clin 23:393–414, 2005.
Haber RS: Pharmacologic management of pattern hair loss. Facial Plast Surg Clin North Am 12:181–189, 2004.
Harris JA: Follicular unit transplantation: Dissecting and planting techniques. Facial Plast Surg Clin North Am 12:225–232, 2004.
Rose PT: The development, anatomy, and physiology of the hair follicle. Hair Transplant Forum Int 9:197–198, 1999.
Shapiro R: Principles and techniques used to create a natural hairline in surgical hair restoration. Facial Plast Surg Clin North Am 12: 201–217, 2004.
Unger WP, Shapiro R: Hair Transplantation, 4th ed. New York, Marcel Dekker, 2004, pp 86–89.

TATTOOS

Jennifer Hunter-Yates, MD, and
Raymond G. Dufresne, Jr., MD

1. What is a tattoo?

A tattoo is a foreign material entered into the dermis by needle or some other trauma that results in a visible, indelible mark in the skin.

2. How do the types of tattoos differ?

The depth and amount of material vary with the type of tattoo and have an effect on the choice of removal technique. Professional tattoos from a tattoo parlor usually are placed superficially in the dermis at a rather uniform layer. As a result, the material is fairly accessible to most removal techniques. However, the amount of dye deposited into the skin may be significant. Homemade tattoos (usually with India ink) have a varied depth (1 to 3 mm), but usually a smaller amount of ink is present. Traumatic tattoos from abrasions tend to be superficial. Traumatic tattoos from penetrating injuries usually have a deeper component. Historically, newer and professional tattoos were believed to be easier to remove. However, with the advent of Q-switched lasers, older and homemade tattoos seem to respond the best.

3. What is the history of tattoos?

The story of tattoos begins with the desire to decorate the human body in an expression of individuality. Tattoos certainly existed in ancient Egypt, as evidenced by mummies dating from the second millennium BC. The Polynesians were known for very extensive tattooing and thus started the seagoing tradition of tattoos. Today, tattoos are prevalent in Western society, and the practice of tattooing is seen in both genders, most races, and all socioeconomic groups.

4. Why do people get tattoos?

Tattoos have been placed for decoration (personal satisfaction, attention-seeking behavior, identification with groups such as Hell's Angels, gangs, or armed forces), identification (prisoners, Nazi concentration camp survivors), and personal proclamations, including love. Tattoos may be used for cosmetic purposes, such as for eyeliner and for eyebrow definition. Tattoos are also used medically for marking radiation ports and for nipple reconstruction. Lastly, tattoos may result from trauma. The most common example is an automobile accident in which road debris enters the skin.

5. Are cosmetic and professional tattoos safe?

Overall, the answer is yes. The dyes are generally selected to have little reaction (i.e., to be inert). Rarely, however, a patient becomes sensitized to a tattoo. For example, the red pigment from cinnabar is a well-described sensitizer. In addition, allergic reactions to blue (cobalt), green (chromium), and yellow (cadmium) dyes have been described. Usually, the reaction is delayed hypersensitivity, but more serious anaphylactic reactions may occur. Delayed hypersensitivity presents as a granulomatous and/or itchy dermatitis-like reaction in the area of a certain dye. At times, the reaction is photoallergic in nature.

Infectious disease transmission is a more serious concern. Hepatitis has been associated with tattoos for decades, and the fear of acquired immunodeficiency syndrome (AIDS) has raised concern about tattooing in the public health sector. Some states ban tattooing, others regulate and license tattooing, and still others have no oversight at all.

6. Have weird reactions been reported in tattoos?

Of course. Anything arising in a tattoo, including skin cancers, becomes a case report; examples include melanoma, basal cell carcinoma, squamous cell carcinoma, keratoacanthoma, and sarcoidosis. Diseases that show koebnerization, such as psoriasis, keloids, discoid lupus, lichen planus, and Darier's disease, have been reported arising within a tattoo. Rarely, systemic immune responses, such as erythema multiforme and scleroderma, occur in association with tattoos. A host of infections, including as leprosy, *Treponema pallidum*, papillomavirus, molluscum contagiosum, and *Mycobacterium tuberculosis*, have been reported in association with tattoos. Reactions of the metal pigments within tattoo dyes may occur during a magnetic resonance imaging scan.

7. Why do individuals want tattoo removal?

Just as people get tattoos for varied reasons, they seek removal due to many different stimuli. For example, if a man is currently married to "Jill," he (and she) may wish for him to remove his tattoo that states "I Love Sally 4ever." Former gang members may wish to remove gang-identifying tattoos. In addition, tattoos are permanent, visible markings that sometimes are misperceived by others, and they may convey an unwanted image or at times limit employment opportunities. It has been reported that more than 50% of individuals with tattoos regret being tattooed and seek removal (Box 19-1).

8. How does motivation affect outcome of removal?

Motivation certainly affects the patient's perception of outcome. In some circumstances, such as the "I Love Sally 4ever" example in Question 7, CO_2 laser removal or excision resulting in a minor scar may be quite acceptable to the patient who is simply anxious to have quick removal. However, when a scar is not acceptable, removal with a Q-switched laser may be the better option. Tattoo removal with a Q-switched laser may require many treatments at substantial cost, and patients must be motivated to expend the energy (and cash) often required to pursue removal. Patients with tattoos from trauma or radiation markers may have psychological problems that the physician must consider and address.

9. Why not simply cut out the tattoo?

There is nothing wrong with cutting out a tattoo. This method of removal is fast, direct, and may be cost-effective. In some circumstances, cutting out the tattoo is the most prudent treatment and, in cases of allergy, the least risky. Simple punch excisions can be used for small traumatic tattoos. For larger tattoos, serial excisions, flaps, tissue expansion, or excision with application of a skin graft may be required. In considering excision, remember that most tattoos occur in sites that tend to heal with problem scars, such as the torso and extremities.

10. What happened to the CO_2 laser?

The CO_2 laser, built on the success of other destructive processes and the current love affair with new high-tech approaches to any problem, was a popular option before Q-switched lasers were developed. CO_2 laser removal was a favored approach due to the bloodless field, ability to view the tattoo particles, and high patient approval. In comparison with other destructive methods, the CO_2 laser vaporizes the tattoo, generally removing it in one session. Larger tattoos are removed in smaller sections ($10 \, cm^2$) to avoid contraction scars on the extremities.

In the first step, the laser vaporizes or blisters off the epidermis, and the tattoo becomes brighter with the loss of the skin cells. The laser is then used to vaporize into the dermis to remove the bulk of the tattoo material. Not all of the material needs to be removed because some of the tattoo is leached out during the healing phase. Some surgeons use the CO_2 laser like dermabrasion to remove the epidermis and then combine it with other destructive techniques, such as salabrasion or tannic acid. Urea (50% ointment) has also been used as an adjunct to superficial laser abrasion.

The wound is allowed to heal by second intention, usually with some type of occlusive dressing (e.g., petrolatum gauze, Vigilon [C.R. Bard, Covington, GA]). Because of the risk of hypertrophic scars, some surgeons use potent topical steroids as soon as reepithelialization occurs. In any case, intervention with intralesional steroids (e.g., 5 to 20 mg/dL triamcinolone) may still be needed. Although the outcomes are sometimes quite good, CO_2 laser removal makes sense only if the patient would be happy with a scar rather than the tattoo and prefers a single treatment session.

Box 19-1. Options for Tattoo Removal

Deep Destruction
CO_2 laser
Infrared coagulator

Superficial Destruction
Chemical peeling
Dermabrasion
Salabrasion
Electrocautery
Argon/KTP lasers
Cryosurgery
Dermaplaning
Q-switched lasers

Inflammatory Methods
Tannic acid
Oxalic acid
Urea

Surgical Methods
Excision, including serial excision
Punch excision
Excision with grafting
Flap
Tissue expansion

Other
Overtattooing

KTP, Potassium titanyl phosphate.

11. What about salabrasion?

If the epidermis is removed and the superficial dermis is invaded in some manner, some of the dyes will leach out of the dermis and may disseminate during the inflammatory process. Salabrasion was classically done with table salt, abrading the skin and leaving salt on the wound for several minutes. Longer periods, up to 4 hours or more, result in more pigment removal but also more scarring. The longer the salt is present, the greater the injury.

12. How does tannic acid work?

Tannic acid or oxalic acid has been used after epidermal abrasion to induce an inflammatory reaction and subsequent leaching of pigment. Tannic acid has been used alone in an overtattooing method without dermabrasion.

13. Can dermabrasion be used alone?

Yes. In this approach, the epidermis and superficial dermis are abraded mechanically. As with CO_2 laser removal, the tattoo brightens with loss of the epidermis. An occlusive dressing is placed and removed daily; the leaching of dye is noted. The wound can then be abraded with gauze (Fig. 19-1). This approach allows more time for the material to leach out of the dermis. If the response is partial, the procedure can be repeated. The depth of destruction is kept superficial; thus, scarring can be minimized. However, scarring, dyschromia, and partial response are significant problems.

14. If dermabrasion works, what about chemical peeling?

Because a chemical peel with trichloroacetic acid (or even phenol) causes epidermal loss and some dermal injury, it may be effective on tattoos. Except for a few reports, including a large Scottish study, chemical peeling has not been widely used.

15. What about dermaplaning?

In addition to the CO_2 laser and dermabrasion, a dermatome can be used to remove the epidermis and upper dermis. This technique has been reported in a small number of cases. It makes sense that any technique of superficial destruction or removal will work in the same manner.

16. Any other thoughts on nonselective destruction?

Light electrocautery can be used in small tattoos, and the infrared coagulator is effective in removing the material in tattoos. The argon laser has been used, but scarring and residual pigmentation often result. As always, the ratio of tissue damage to extent of material removed is the heart of the matter. The Q-switched lasers changed this ratio (and require less skill).

17. What are Q-switched lasers?

Presently, three Q-switched lasers are commonly available: ruby (694 nm), Nd:YAG (1064 nm, double-frequency Nd:YAG at 532 nm), and alexandrite (760 nm). These lasers operate by giving off short pulses (nanoseconds) that disrupt the tattoo material and cause minimal damage to adjacent dermis and epidermis (i.e., they demonstrate selective photothermolysis). Q-switched lasers can disrupt the intracellular pigment selectively, alter the pigment, and allow the redistribution and elimination of pigment because the duration of the laser is so short and the energy so high that the pigment is heated and disrupted before the adjacent dermis is injured.

18. Do all Q-switched lasers work for every tattoo?

Not exactly. The wavelength must be matched to the color pigment, and multiple wavelengths are needed to treat different colors. All Q-switched lasers work well with black and India ink, but the Nd:YAG (1064 nm) and alexandrite lasers have the best results for these colors. The ruby laser is the most effective laser for green tattoos but will not

Figure 19-1. **A,** Multicolored tattoo. **B,** Tattoo immediately after superficial dermabrasion. Note brightening of the tattoo after epidermis removal. **C,** Tattoo pigment on gauze 24 hours after dermabrasion. (Courtesy of Dr. Louis Fragola.)

remove red. The double-frequency Nd:YAG is effective for red but not green colors, and it may be effective for some oranges, yellows, and purples. The alexandrite appears to be effective for blue, black, red, and green but does less well with orange and yellow.

19. Any tips for using Q-switched lasers?

- We routinely use a clear polyurethane or Vigilon-like material over the tattoo to keep the splatter, which moves too quickly for an evacuator, off our faces and out of the air. A cool sheet of Vigilon is soothing and in theory may reduce epidermal damage.
- With treatment, whitening of the epidermis gives you a sense of the endpoint. Heavy bleeding points suggest an overaggressive approach.
- Competitive absorption in a heavily pigmented patient limits effectiveness but can still be used. As expected, the less tanned the patient's skin, the better.
- Do not rush. A period of a few months between treatments is not a problem and, in fact, may be beneficial.

20. Does tattoo removal with a Q-switched laser hurt?

Yes. As with any procedure, the level of discomfort is patient dependent. Use of local anesthesia is recommended to improve patient comfort. Anesthesia can be obtained with topical agents (e.g., EMLA [topical lidocaine and procaine; AstraZeneca Pharmaceuticals LP, Wilmington, DE] or LMX [topical lidocaine; Ferndale Laboratories, Ferndale, MI]) applied for approximately 1 hour prior to treatment or with local injection of various anesthetic agents (e.g., lidocaine 1%).

21. What kind of complications may occur with the Q-switched laser?

In comparison with other techniques, scarring occurs in a small number of cases and usually responds to time and intralesional steroids. Scarring decreases as the time between treatments is lengthened from 2 weeks to 6 to 8 weeks. Most patients have temporary hypopigmentation (Fig. 19-2). However, a white depigmentation may be permanent. Rarely, a tattoo changes color with treatment; light or natural tones turning black with treatment is a well-described phenomenon. This phenomenon occurs when reddish-brown ferric oxide (Fe_2O_3) is reduced via laser energy to ferrous oxide (FeO), which is black. Use of a Q-switched laser in a patient with an allergic reaction is dangerous because the dyes are broken up and freed from macrophages, allowing potential worsening of the reaction. In this situation, excision or possibly the CO_2 laser is a better choice for removal. However, unmet expectations probably are the most common problem.

22. So the worst problem is that it may not work?

Exactly. Even with the right laser, the number of treatments and the final outcome (i.e., how much is removed) cannot be predicted. Imagine the patient's frustration with only partial response of his or her tattoo after 10 treatments.

23. Are some tattoos easier to remove than others using the Q-switched lasers?

The easiest to remove are clearly the amateur lesions, which most commonly use a small amount of India ink. The most difficult are bright, new, multicolored tattoos. Tattoos overlying other tattoos are hard and unpredictable. Old tattoos respond better than new tattoos.

24. What about traumatic tattoos?

In most tattoos, foreign material is introduced on purpose, but material may be entered into the skin by trauma, such as road grit from an automobile accident, powder from a blast, or pencil graphite from rushed movements. The best approach is prevention in the acute phase, trying to remove as much material as possible immediately after the incident. Careful cleaning of the wound, including the use of brushes, should be performed. Use of an occlusive dressing may allow additional material to leach out, much like a therapeutic dermabrasion.

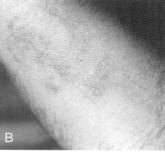

Figure 19-2. A, Old, partially faded professional tattoo after two treatments with the Q-switched YAG. Note slight hypertrophic scar at the strings of the gloves. **B,** Response to four additional laser treatments, with good improvement in tattoo disappearance and resolution of the scar without treatment. Note slight hypopigmentation in the treated area.

25. Once you have a traumatic tattoo, are the choices for removal the same as for a decorative tattoo?

Exactly. The choices are excision, spot dermabrasion, laser abrasion, or Q-switched lasers. The depth and materials vary from case to case, and one needs to be creative in treating the tattoo. In addition, patients may have an underlying scar that becomes more apparent after the pigment is gone. Remember to consider the psychological effects of the trauma when evaluating patient expectations.

26. Does the tattoo have a role in plastic surgery?

The use of medical tattooing procedures is underappreciated. In the past, tattoos were used to hide scars or blend in discolorations, such as port-wine stains. Cosmetic tattooing has been used to camouflage skin grafts and in vermilion enhancement. The use of tattooing in port-wine stains has been replaced with better treatments, and tattoos are more commonly used in circumstances such as permanent eyeliner, eyebrows, postmastectomy periareolar reconstruction, and covering areas of vitiligo. Low-cost units for this purpose (e.g., the Penmark enhancer) are readily available. The loss of pigment in vitiligo can be stressful and quite obvious, especially in a darkly pigmented patient. By using a unit such as the Penmark enhancer with a multineedle brush, wide areas can be covered. This technique is most helpful in localized areas, such as the hand, that respond poorly to psoralens and ultraviolet A (PUVA) therapy and are difficult to cover effectively with concealers.

Cosmetic tattooing can be used to enhance existing eyelids (blepharopigmentation) or eyebrows or to mimic hair for patients with traumatic hair loss or alopecia areata. Ferrous oxide is the most common pigment used, and it appears to have a great safety profile with few allergic reactions. Cosmetic tattooing can be used to create the illusion of an areola and nipple after breast surgery when a formal reconstruction is not desired or possible. It has the advantage of a low invasive approach, and the appearance can be excellent.

Retattooing (i.e., covering a prior tattoo) can be helpful by hiding the offending portion. Examples include tattooing clothes on a nude figure or hiding the name of a loved one (e.g., "Sally") from the past (Box 19-2).

Box 19-2. Medical Uses of Tattooing

Color Blending and Pigment Replacement
Port-wine stains
Skin grafts
Vermilion (coloration of flaps)
Scars/burns
Vitiligo

Miscellaneous
Radiation ports

Mimicking of Lost Structures
Hair loss (eyebrows, eyelids)
Postmastectomy nipple reconstruction

Cosmetic Enhancement
Eyebrows, eyelids
Vermilion

BIBLIOGRAPHY

Adrian RM, Griffin L: Laser tattoo removal. Clin Plast Surg 27:181–192, 2000.
Guyuron B, Vaughan C: Medical grade tattooing to camouflage pigmentation. Plast Reconstr Surg 95:575–579, 1995.
Jacob CI: Tattoo-associated dermatoses: A case report and review of the literature. Dermatol Surg 28:962–965, 2002.
Kuperman-Beade M, Levine V, Ashinoff R: Laser removal of tattoos. Am J Clin Dermatol 2:21–25, 2001.
Mazza JF, Rager C: Advances in cosmetic micropigmentation. Plast Reconstr Surg 79:186–191, 1987.
Piggot TA, Norris RW: Treatment of tattoos with trichloroacetic acid: Experience with 670 patients. Br J Past Surg 41:112–117, 1988.
Sperry K: Tattoos and tattooing, part I: History and methodology. Am J Forensic Med Pathol 12:313–319, 1991.
Zelickson BD, Mehregan DA, Zarrin AA, et al: Clinical, histologic, and ultrastructural evaluation of tattoos treated with three laser systems. Lasers Surg Med 15:364–372, 1994.

CRANIOFACIAL SURGERY I—CONGENITAL

Head 1. Joan Miró, 1974. Acrylic and oil on canvas. © 2008 Successio Miró/Artists' Rights Society (ARS), New York/ADAGP, Paris.

PRINCIPLES OF CRANIOFACIAL SURGERY

Daniel Marchac, MD, and
Eric Arnaud, MD

CHAPTER 20

1. What is the specialty of craniofacial surgery?

Craniofacial surgery is plastic surgery of the cephalic extremity, including the skull, the face, and, in particular, the orbit. Paul Tessier, the pioneer of craniofacial surgery, defined the field as *orbitocentric*. It involves the cephalic skeleton as well as surrounding soft tissues.

2. What three types of pathology can be treated by the craniofacial surgeon?

Congenital anomalies, defects after tumor ablation, and posttraumatic deformities (Table 20-1). Congenital conditions should be treated early in infancy to optimize final results. Reconstruction of resultant defects after tumor ablation and trauma often requires the input of the craniofacial surgeon for both pediatric and adult patients.

3. What are the goals of craniofacial surgery in patients with craniosynostosis or faciocraniosynostosis?

The goals of surgery include correction of the dysmorphogenesis and prevention of functional impairment, such as mental retardation and visual disturbances.

4. What is the incidence of craniosynostosis?

Based on European statistics, the incidence of common craniosynostosis averages 1:2200 live births. Conversely, a rare faciocraniosynostosis, such as Apert's syndrome, is likely to appear in 1:150,000 live births. Although some cases of craniosynostosis clearly are familial, most are sporadic.

5. What is the pathogenesis of craniosynostosis?

Premature fusion of the sutural system of a growing skull is the common mechanism of craniosynostosis. The result is a cessation of calvarial growth perpendicular to the affected suture. The classic law of Virchow predicts compensatory calvarial growth in a direction *parallel* to the affected suture.

6. How is craniosynostosis classified?

Classification is based on the affected suture and its associated morphologic deformity (Table 20-2 and Fig. 20-1).

Table 20-1. Types of Craniofacial Pathology

CONGENITAL ANOMALIES	POSTTRAUMATIC DEFORMITIES	DEFECTS AFTER TUMOR ABLATION
Craniosynostosis and faciocraniosynostosis	Frontoorbitonasoethmoidal fractures	All tumors of the anterior base of the skull
Facial clefts and related hypertelorism	Le Fort fractures (especially Le Fort III fractures)	Fibrous dysplasia
Hemifacial microsomia		
Craniofacial syndromes		

Table 20-2. Classification of Craniosynostosis

MORPHOLOGIC DEFORMITY	AFFECTED SUTURE
Trigonocephaly	Metopic suture
Scaphocephaly	Sagittal suture
Plagiocephaly	Unilateral coronal suture
Brachycephaly	Bilateral coronal sutures
Oxycephaly	Sagittal and both coronal sutures

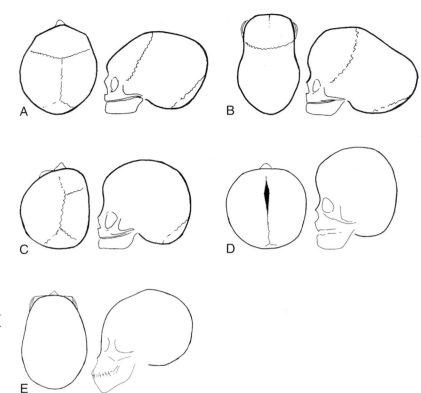

Figure 20-1. Types of craniosynostosis. **A,** Trigonocephaly. **B,** Scaphocephaly. **C,** Plagiocephaly. **D,** Brachycephaly. **E,** Oxycephaly. (From Marchac D, Renier D: Craniofacial Surgery for Craniosynostosis. Boston, Little, Brown, 1982, with permission.)

7. What is the main feature of faciocraniosynostosis compared with craniosynostosis?
In addition to the skull deformities, the facial involvement in pure craniosynostosis is limited to the forehead and orbital regions (hypotelorism or hypertelorism). In addition, faciocraniosynostosis is associated with midface hypoplasia characterized by centrofacial retrusion with a class III intermaxillary relation (malocclusion).

8. Are all craniosynostoses or faciocraniosynostoses present at birth?
No. Although most craniosynostoses are congenital and present at birth as a result of a fetal sutural problem, genuine oxycephaly and Crouzon's disease are delayed conditions, often appearing after 3 or 4 years of age. Because the synostoses appear later, the shape of the skull is different and the functional consequences, such as increased intracranial pressure (ICP) or visual impairment, more insidious. Increased ICP is present in at least 60% of cases of oxycephaly or Crouzon's disease.

9. What is the main functional risk of craniosynostosis?
The main functional risk is increased ICP, the consequences of which are visual loss and brain impairment.

10. In acrocephalosyndactyly (such as Apert's syndrome), which factors may be associated with a better mental outcome?
Cranial remodeling (anterior and posterior) before 1 year of age and a good psychosocial environment are associated with a more favorable mental outcome.

11. Describe the preoperative evaluation of the craniofacial patient.
- Analysis of the morphologic abnormality
- Evaluation of functional risks
- Detection of associated malformations (e.g., cerebral, cardiac)
- Classification of any existing syndrome
- Preparation for surgery

12. Which imaging studies are necessary before surgery?
Standard radiographs of the cephalic skeleton and a computed tomographic (CT) scan are essential before surgery. A magnetic resonance imaging (MRI) scan is indicated in cases of trigonocephaly because of the higher risk for brain abnormalities and in all syndromic patients.

13. **What are the principles of frontoorbital remodeling in craniosynostosis?**
The forehead has two components: the supraorbital bar (or bandeau) and the forehead convexity. After being mobilized separately, these components are joined by resorbable or nonresorbable fixation. Reconstructive goals are tailored to the particular type of synostosis:

- Symmetric advancement in brachycephaly
- Asymmetric advancement in plagiocephaly
- Anterior rotation and Z-plasty in oxycephaly
- Widening in trigonocephaly

14. **Compare the growth of the brain and skull in the first 2 years of life.**
The size of the brain doubles in the first year of life. The anterior base of the skull has reached 70% of its adult size by 2 years of age, whereas the cranial capacity has expanded fourfold since birth.

15. **What is the main factor responsible for frontal sinus growth after frontocranial remodeling?**
The degree of frontoorbital advancement has a significant effect on postoperative sinus growth. The degree of frontal sinus pneumatization correlates inversely with the amount of supraorbital bar advancement.

16. **What complications are associated with craniofacial surgery? How can they be prevented?**
Craniofacial surgery combines the disciplines of plastic surgery and neurosurgery. The complications of craniofacial procedures are mainly neurosurgical and necessitate postoperative management in specialized intensive care units. The perioperative mortality rate remains approximately 1%, depending on the types of procedures performed. The main complications include bleeding, coma, blindness, meningitis, intracranial hematoma, and hydrocephalus. Additional morbidity may result from rhinorrhea, osteitis, and resorption of bone flaps. The incidence of these complications can be reduced by appropriate preoperative planning and an experienced surgical team.

17. **Can surgery improve the mental outcome of craniosynostotic patients?**
Based on comprehensive studies of each type of pathology with comparisons between unoperated and operated patients as well as correlations between preoperative and postoperative status, surgery has never been shown to improve the mental outcome. However, surgery is preventive of mental deterioration if performed before patients are 1 year of age.

18. **What is the most common type of craniosynostosis?**
Sagittal synostosis (scaphocephaly) is by far the most common type of craniosynostosis, affecting 40% to 50% of all cases. Metopic synostosis has became the second most frequent, with a recent increase in incidence (10% to 15%) with no clear explanation.

19. **Is blood transfusion frequently required in craniofacial surgery?**
With open techniques in young infants, the rate of transfusion reaches 99%. The use of minimally invasive techniques with endoscopic assistance might reduce this rate, but further complete evaluation of the results will conclude if the morphologic results are as good.

20. **What is the mortality rate in craniofacial surgery?**
The recent report of a benchmarking questionnaire in the International Society of Craniofacial Surgery (ISCFS), including 23 craniofacial centers, indicated a range of mortality between 0% to 2%. Based on our experience with more than 2500 operated cases, the mortality rate of all pathologies included in our series was 0.8%. Extremely severe conditions, such as cloverleaf skull in Pfeiffer syndrome, represented a major part.

21. **Is distraction always osteogenic?**
Based on the extraordinary remodeling demonstrated on the mandible by McCarthy and Molina, distraction has been applied to every part of the cephalic skeleton. Some areas of the skull demonstrate decreased ability to reossify, probably due to lesser vascularization. These areas include the zygomatic arch, and the skull after 3 years of age.

22. **What is the current safe strategy for treatment of faciocraniosynostosis?**
A two-stage strategy including early frontoorbital advancement and subsequent Le Fort III advancement is the current recommendation.

23. Is frontofacial monobloc advancement a safe procedure?

The classic frontofacial monobloc advancement (FFMA), proposed by Ortiz-Monasterio in 1978, is a risky procedure with high percentages of osteitis and meningitis. With distraction, FFMA is less risky, with a 6% rate of infection in our last series. It is a powerful tool that allows correction of extreme exorbitism as well as respiratory impairment caused by facial retrusion.

24. Is it possible to correct an abnormally shaped skull in an adult who has not undergone surgery in childhood for craniosynostosis?

Occasionally, a limited approach, such as use of an appositional implant, can be sufficient. Most of the time, however, frontofacial remodeling is necessary and is accompanied by the risks associated with an intracranial approach. The presence of the frontal sinuses and the fact that remodeling of an adult skull is more difficult can complicate the surgical procedures required. Nevertheless, after careful evaluation and fully informing the patient, these operations can be undertaken in carefully selected cases.

BIBLIOGRAPHY

Arnaud E, Marchac D, Renier D: The treatment of craniosynostosis: Indications and techniques. Neurochirurgie 52(2–3 Pt 2):264–291, 2006.

Arnaud E, Meneses P, Lajeunie E, et al: Postoperative mental and morphological outcome for nonsyndromic brachycephaly. Plast Reconstr Surg 110:6–12, 2002; discussion 13.

Marchac D (ed): Proceedings of the Sixth International Congress of the International Society of Craniofacial Surgery. Bologna, Monduzzi Editore, 1996.

Marchac D: Radical forehead remodeling for craniostenosis. Plast Reconstr Surg 61:823–835, 1978.

Marchac D, Arnaud E: Midface surgery from Jessier to distraction. Childs Nerv Syst 15:681–694, 1999.

Marchac D, Renier D: Craniofacial Surgery for Craniosynostosis. Boston, Little, Brown, 1982.

Marchac D, Renier D, Arnaud E: Evaluation of the effect of early mobilization of the supraorbital bar on the frontal sinus and frontal growth. Plast Reconstr Surg 95:802–811, 1995.

Marchac D, Renier D, Arnaud E: Unoperated craniosynostosis patients: Correction in adulthood. Plast Reconstr Surg 122:1827, 2008.

Marchac D, Renier D, Broumand S: Timing of treatment for craniosynostosis and fasciosynostosis: A 20-year experience. Br J Plast Surg 47:211–222, 1994.

Mathijssen I, Arnaud E, Marchac D, et al: Respiratory outcome of mid-face advancement with distraction: A comparison between Le Fort III and frontofacial monobloc. J Craniofac Surg 17:880–882, 2006.

Ortiz Monasterio F, Fuente del Campo A, Carillo A: Advancement of the orbits and midface in one piece, combined with frontal repositioning, for the correction of Crouzon deformity. Plast Reconstr Surg 61:507–516, 1978.

Renier D, Lajeunie E, Arnaud E, Marchac D: Management of craniosynostoses. Childs Nerv Syst 16:645–658, 2000.

Tessier P: Relationship of craniostenoses to craniofacial dysostoses, and to faciostenoses: A study with therapeutic implications. Plast Reconstr Surg 48:224–237, 1971.

Tessier P, Kawamoto H, Matthews D, et al: Autogenous bone grafts and bone substitutes—tools and techniques: I. A 20,000-case experience in maxillofacial and craniofacial surgery. Plast Reconstr Surg 116(5 Suppl):6S–24S, 2005.

CRANIOFACIAL EMBRYOLOGY

Oren M. Tepper, MD, and
Stephen M. Warren, MD

CHAPTER **21**

FACIAL PROMINENCES/BRANCHIAL ARCHES

1. The face originates from how many prominences? What are they?

The face is initially made up of five prominences: a *central frontonasal prominence, paired maxillary prominences*, and *paired mandibular prominences*. These initial primordial structures appear during the fourth week of development and surround the primitive mouth, or *stomodeum*, which is initially sealed off from the primitive gut by the oropharyngeal membrane (Fig. 21-1). The frontonasal prominence is a central process that resides at the cranial boundary of the stomodeum and is formed from mesenchyme ventral to the forebrain. The maxillary and mandibular prominences form the superolateral and inferior boundaries of the stomodeum, respectively, and are produced by neural crest cells that migrate from the branchial arches.

2. Which branchial arches give rise to the five facial prominences?

The branchial arch system begins to form in the fourth week and consists of six paired arches that decrease in size from cranial to caudal. Each branchial arch consists of four essential tissue components (cartilage, aortic arch artery, nerve, muscle) that serve as building blocks for the face, neck, and oropharynx. The paired maxillary and mandibular prominences are derivatives of the first branchial arch. The frontonasal prominence, however, is not a derivative of the branchial arch system. (Of note, because the term *branchial arch* is traditionally used to describe the embryonic arch system of fish and amphibians, some authors prefer the term *pharyngeal arch*.)

MAXILLARY PROMINENCE

3. What structures do the maxillary prominences give rise to?

The maxillary prominence gives rise to the upper jaw, lip (lateral to the philtral column), orbital floor, and inferior portion of the lateral nasal wall. Rapid growth of the maxillary prominences, along with medial nasal processes, during weeks 4 to 8 leads to a shift of the frontonasal process away from the stomodeum. The medial nasal processes fuse and give rise to the intermaxillary segment, which ultimately becomes the philtrum of the lip, the premaxilla, and the primary palate. The fusion plane of the medial nasal process and the maxillary process is often referred to as the *nasal fin*. Those portions of lateral nasal wall that are not derivatives of the maxillary prominence are formed from the lateral nasal prominences (i.e., lateral cartilage, lateral crus of the alar cartilage) (Fig. 21-2).

4. What structures give rise to the nasolacrimal duct?

The nasolacrimal duct forms from a space that lies between the maxillary prominence and the lateral nasal process, termed *nasolacrimal groove* (or *naso-optic furrow*). The ectoderm layer from the nasolacrimal groove forms an epithelial cord that subsequently undergoes canalization after birth. The resultant nasolacrimal duct extends from the developing conjunctival sac to the nasal cavity. Of note, failure of fusion between the lateral nasal process and the maxillary prominence results in an oblique facial cleft (Tessier no. 3 cleft).

MANDIBULAR PROMINENCE

5. What structures contribute to formation of the lower jaw?

The lower jaw is formed from the bilateral mandibular prominences, which are derivatives of the first branchial arch. During the fourth week, these prominences are formed by proliferation of neural crest cells that migrate into the arch. As these structures enlarge, they merge at the midline to form the lower point of the jaw (see Fig. 21-2).

6. By what type of ossification does the lower jaw form?

The lower jaw is formed primarily by intramembranous ossification. During early development, a cartilaginous rod forms along the lower jaw, which is derived from the neural crest of the first pharyngeal arch. This cartilaginous structure of the first branchial arch (termed *Meckel's cartilage*) regresses, thereby enabling the symphysis and the ramus to form by membranous ossification. Meckel's cartilage remains in the mandibular condyles, which form by endochondral ossification.

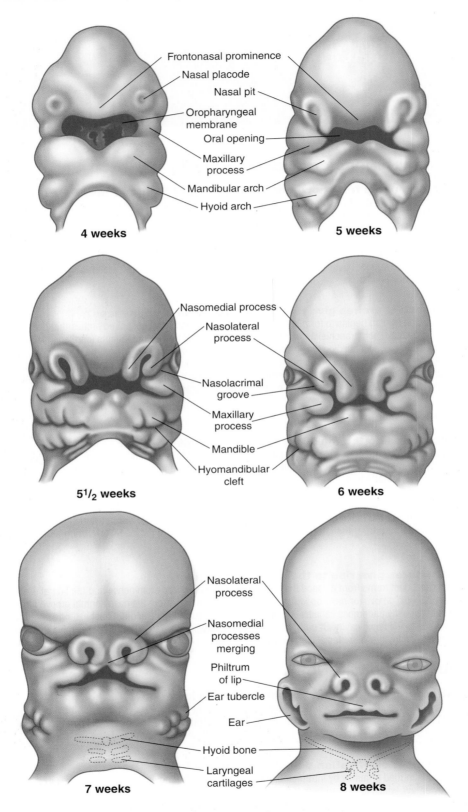

Figure 21-1. Embryology of the facial prominences. (From Carlson BM: Human Embryology and Developmental Biology, 3rd ed. Philadelphia, Mosby, 2004.)

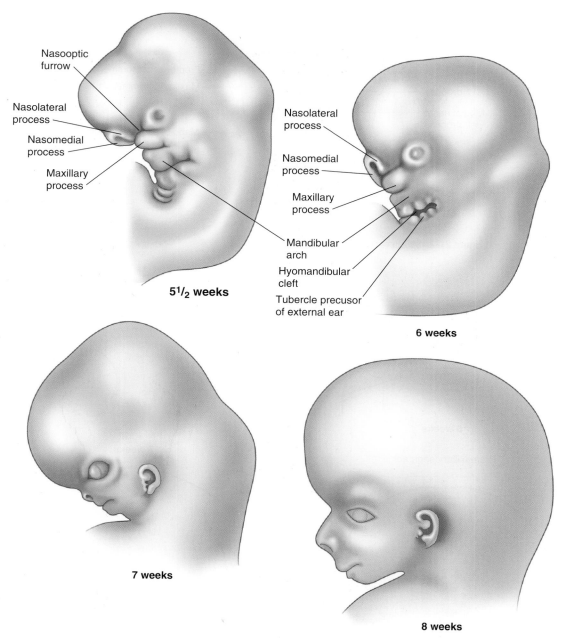

Nasooptic furrow

Nasolateral process

Nasomedial process

Maxillary process

5½ weeks

Nasolateral process

Nasomedial process

Maxillary process

Mandibular arch

Hyomandibular cleft

Tubercle precusor of external ear

6 weeks

7 weeks

8 weeks

Figure 21-1. cont'd.

7. Does the mandible form before, during, or after development of the mandibular branch of the trigeminal nerve?

The first structure that develops in the primordium of the lower jaw is the mandibular branch of the trigeminal nerve. At 6 weeks, a mandibular ossification center arises adjacent to the neurovascular bundle. Ossification spreads around the inferior alveolar nerve with the persistence of a mandibular canal, foramen, and mental foramen. It is believed that the presence of the nerve may lead to release of neurotrophic factors that promote osteogenesis.

PALATAL FUSION

8. What four structures contribute to the formation of the palate?

Palate formation occurs from weeks 6 to 10 and involves four primary structures: the median palatine process, a pair of lateral palatine processes (palatal shelves), and the nasal septum (Fig. 21-3). The median palatine process forms the

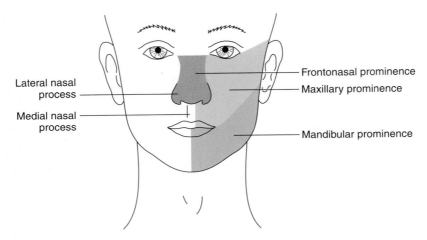

Figure 21-2. Structures arising from the facial prominences.

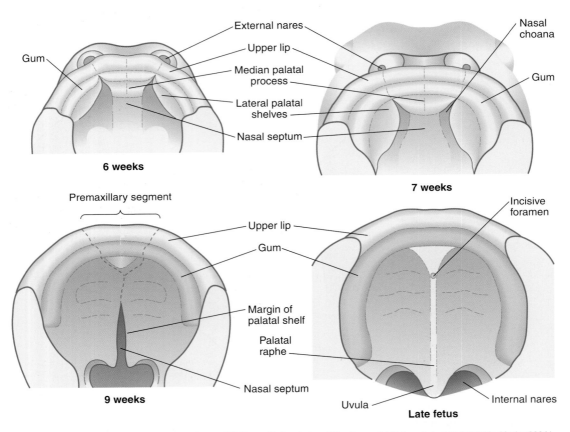

Figure 21-3. Embryology of the palate. (From Carlson BM: Human Embryology and Developmental Biology, 3rd ed. Philadelphia, Mosby, 2004.)

primary palate, which is often referred to as the premaxillary component of the maxilla. This structure ultimately houses the four upper incisors. The *secondary palate* is formed by the lateral palatine processes, which begin to fuse during the seventh week. Lastly, the nasal septum joins the fused palatal shelves to complete the formation of the secondary palate.

9. Are the terms *hard* and *soft palate* synonymous with *primary* and *secondary palate*?
The distinction between *hard* and *soft palate* is different from that of the *primary* and *secondary palate*. As noted in Question 8, the primary palate is formed from the median palatine process, whereas the secondary palate is formed by

fusion of the lateral palatine processes. Anatomically, the incisive foramen marks this division point where the primary palate fuses with the two palatal shelves. During development, ossification occurs in the primary palate as well as the anterior portion of the secondary palate, which together give rise to the hard palate. The posterior portion of the secondary palate does not undergo ossification and therefore remains as the soft palate.

10. What is the mechanism underlying the formation of cleft palate?

Cleft palate results from incomplete or absent fusion of the lateral palatine processes, medial palatine process, or nasal septum. During the eighth week of gestation, the lateral palatine processes undergo a significant change in their orientation from a vertical to horizontal plane. Although the exact mechanism of this transition is not understood, the phenomenon is thought to be a critical step in initiating the fusion of the palatal shelves. The medial edges of the palatal shelves undergo programmed cell death and allow for coalescence, while the oral and nasal surfaces of the shelves remain intact. In adults, a palatine raphe can often be identified in the soft palate and indicates the fusion of the lateral palatine processes. Clinically, a palatal cleft may be complete (involving the entire palatal length) or incomplete. Because the palate fuses from anterior to posterior, an incomplete cleft will extend posterior, not anterior, to the last point of fusion.

11. What is a submucous cleft?

A submucous cleft is a phenotypic variant that results from failed midline palatal fusion. This clinical condition is characterized by the triad of a *bifid uvula, notched posterior hard palate*, and *muscular diastasis of the velum (zona pellucida)*. The exact incidence of submucous cleft is not known but has been estimated to be approximately 1:1200 to 1:6000. The majority of patients with submucous clefts are asymptomatic and do not require operative intervention. However, up to 15% of these patients may exhibit velopharyngeal insufficiency associated with diminished palatal length, mobility, and easy fatigability.

12. What is the etiology of cleft palate in Pierre Robin sequence?

Pierre Robin sequence is characterized by *micrognathia* (undersized jaw), *glossoptosis* (retracted/displaced tongue producing respiratory symptomatology), and *cleft palate*. It is thought that in these micrognathic patients, a relatively prominent tongue leads to mechanical interference of the lateral palatine processes during the time frame of palatal fusion. Therefore cleft palate may result from a delay in the transition of the palatine shelves from a vertical to horizontal orientation.

LIP FUSION

13. What is the most common mechanism underlying cleft lip?

The most common mechanism of cleft lip is failure of fusion between the maxillary prominence and medial nasal processes on the affected side. This can range from small notches in the vermillion to extension through the nostril and maxilla. Failure of the mesenchyme to merge results in a persistent labial groove, which may completely divide the lip into medial and lateral parts (i.e., complete cleft lip). Cleft lips may also have a small bridge of tissue along the nasal sill, controversially known as *Simonart's band*. Bilateral cleft lips form when the maxillary prominence fails to fuse with the merged medial nasal processes.

14. Is the incidence of cleft palate higher in males or females? What about cleft lip?

The incidence of cleft palate is higher in females. This observation may be related to the timing of palatal shelve fusion, which occurs about 1 week later in females than in males, thereby prolonging the susceptibility to cleft formation. Cleft lip occurs more frequently in males, but the etiopathogenesis of this observation is unknown.

15. Are cleft lips more common than cleft palates?

An isolated cleft lip is less common than an isolated cleft palate (21% of cleft patients vs 33%, respectively). However, the most common presentation in cleft patients is a combined cleft lip and palate (46%).

CRANIOFACIAL CLEFTS

16. What is the most common classification system of craniofacial clefts?

The Tessier classification system is the most commonly used method for categorizing craniofacial clefts. The Tessier classification system relates soft tissue to skeletal landmarks and divides the face into an upper portion (cranial clefts) and a lower portion (facial clefts) based on the orbits. Facial clefts are numbered 0 through 7, and cranial clefts are numbered 8 through 14. The system is devised so that the facial component of the cleft and the cranial component always add up to 14 (e.g., 14:0, 13:1, 4:10).

17. Which craniofacial cleft results from failed fusion of the mandibular and maxillary prominences at the lateral commissure?

Lateral facial clefts, producing macrostomia, result from failure of the maxillary and mandibular prominences to fuse at the lateral commissure. This is classified by the Tessier system as a no. 7 facial cleft (temporozygomatic facial cleft).

The Tessier no. 7 cleft is often seen with craniofacial microsomia and Treacher Collins syndrome and can range from mild broadening of the oral commissure to a complete fissure extending toward a microtic ear. In extremely rare cases, the maxillary and mandibular prominences merge completely, resulting in a closed mouth *(astomia)*.

18. What are the midline clefts in the Tessier system, and how do they form?
Cranial clefts of the midline are classified as Tessier no. 14 clefts and include hypotelorism as well as holoprosencephalic disorders (cyclopia, ethmocephaly, cebocephaly). *Facial* clefts of the midline are classified as Tessier no. 0 clefts and represent incomplete fusion of the two medial nasal processes. This rare anomaly may be referred to as median cleft lip but may also be associated with varying degrees of nasal bifidity. If the mandibular prominences fail to fuse in the midline, central defects of the chin and lower lip result (Tessier no. 30 cleft). Soft tissue deformities in this cleft may include notching of the lower lip and a bifid (or even absent) tongue. Skeletal involvement typically includes a cleft between the central incisors down towards the mandibular symphysis.

FRONTONASAL DEVELOPMENT

19. What structures give rise to the nasal cavity?
The medial and lateral nasal prominences give rise to nasal sacs, which initially are separated from the oral cavity by an oronasal membrane. At the end of the sixth week, the oronasal membrane begins to rupture, creating foramina between the nasal and oral cavities. A temporary epithelial plug exists along the nasal cavity but disappears at 13 to 15 weeks in order to allow communication between oral and nasal cavities (primitive choanae). The primitive choanae initially lies posterior to the primary palate, but after development of the secondary palate it is located between the nasal cavity and pharynx. Other important developmental processes occurring during this time include formation of the turbinates (superior, middle, inferior) from the lateral nasal walls and differentiation of epithelial cells into olfactory neurons.

20. Do paranasal sinuses form during fetal or postnatal development?
The paranasal sinuses consist of four pairs of structures: the *maxillary, sphenoidal, frontal,* and *ethmoidal sinuses.* Two of these sinuses appear during fetal life; the other two appear after birth. The first of these structures to form are the maxillary sinuses during the third month of gestation, followed by the ethmoid sinuses during the fifth month of gestation. The sphenoid sinuses, which represent extensions of the ethmoid sinuses into the sphenoid bone, appear during the fifth month of postnatal life. The development of the frontal sinus does not begin until 2 years of age and is not evident radiographically until age 6 years.

CRANIAL SUTURE DEVELOPMENT/FUSION

21. What is the distinction between neurocranium and viscerocranium?
The *neurocranium* represents the structures that surround the brain, versus *viscerocranium* (or splanchnocranium), which surrounds the oral cavity, pharynx, and upper respiratory system and represents the skeleton of the face.

22. By what type of ossification does the neurocranium form during development?
Neurocranium is made up of the calvaria (skull) and cranial base. The cranial base begins as a cartilaginous precursor (chondrocranium) and undergoes endochondral ossification to form the cranial floor, which consists of occipital, sphenoid, and temporal bones. The calvaria surrounding the sides and top of the brain (cranial vault) forms by intramembranous ossification.

23. Will calvarial intramembranous bone formation occur in the absence of an underlying brain?
Ossification of intramembranous calvarial bones is dependent on the presence of an underlying brain. In cases of anencephaly (absence of brain), calvarial bones do not form.

24. What is the clinical significance of cranial sutures during fetal and adult life?
During fetal development, flexible membranous junctions, called *sutures*, develop between the calvarial bone plates. These membranous junctions allow the skull to undergo deformational changes. During birth, molding of the cranium occurs to allow adaptation to the pelvic cavity and is characterized by flattening of the frontal bones, widening of the occipital bones, and overriding of the parietal bones. After birth, the shape of the calvaria returns to normal within in a few days, but the cranial sutures remain open to accommodate subsequent enlargement of the underlying brain. Calvarial growth is most rapid during the first 2 years of postnatal life, during which time the greatest increase in the size of the brain occurs. Premature fusion of one or more cranial sutures *(craniosynostosis)* results in characteristic calvarial dysmorphology. Impaired cranial growth can result in elevated intracranial pressure.

25. What is posterior deformational plagiocephaly, and how does it occur?

The literal translation of *plagiocephaly* is "oblique head," derived from the Greek words *plagio* (meaning oblique) and *cephaly* (meaning head). Plagiocephaly that results from extrinsic forces (rather than craniosynostosis) is referred to as *deformational plagiocephaly*. Many believe that deformational plagiocephaly results from repeated pressure to the same area of the head, such as occurs with positioning of the infant during sleep. Posterior deformational plagiocephaly can be diagnosed based on history (when a change was noted), clinical examination (i.e., occiput flattening), and radiographs (patent sutures). Interestingly, the NYU group reported an increase in the incidence of posterior deformational plagiocephaly that was associated with the 1992 "back to sleep campaign" by the American Academy of Pediatrics (positioning the infant on the back or side).

26. Do the neurocranium and facial skull maintain a similar proportion during development?

During fetal growth, there is a predominance of neurocranium development relative to the face, approximately 8:1. This trend continues during early childhood, during which the cranial vault grows rapidly to accommodate the developing brain. At birth, the skull has achieved 25% of its ultimate size. It subsequently increases to 75% size at 2 years and to near-complete size by age 10 years.

27. Does the relative thickness of calvarial bone change following birth?

Calvarial bones are extremely thin at birth and during infancy. Given the thin calvaria of infants and young children and the lack of a diploic space, a split-calvarial bone graft cannot be harvested. At 3 years of age, only 20% of children have a diploic space. Clinically, surgeons may wait for a calvarial thickness of 6.0 mm prior to splitting the bone. However, this may not occur until approximately age 9 years, even in the thickest portion of the calvaria (the parietal bone, posterior to the coronal suture).

EYE

28. What structures give rise to the eye?

Bilateral lens placodes at the lateral aspect of the frontonasal prominence give rise to the eye. The underlying optic stalk, which ultimately becomes the optic nerve, drives the differentiation of the lens placodes into the lenses. Between weeks 5 and 9, the eyes migrate medially into their normal position. In neonates, an intercanthal distance of 16 mm is considered normal.

BIBLIOGRAPHY

Carlson BM: Human Embryology and Developmental Biology. Mosby, 1999, pp 286–319.

Garcia Velasco M, Ysunza A, Hernandez X, Marquez C: Diagnosis and treatment of submucous cleft palate: A review of 108 cases. Cleft Palate J 25:171–173, 1988.

Gosain AK, Nacamuli R: Embryology of the head and neck. In Thorne CH, Beasley RW, Aston SJ, et al, (eds): Grabb and Smith's Plastic Surgery, 6th ed. Lippincott Williams & Wilkins, 2007, pp 179–190.

Koenig WJ, Donovan JM, Pensler JM: Cranial bone grafting in children. Plast Reconstr Surg 95:1–4, 1995.

Moore KH, Persaud TVN: The Developing Human. WB Saunders, 2003, pp 202–240.

Pensler J, McCarthy JG: The calvarial donor site: An anatomic study in cadavers. Plast Reconstr Surg 75:648–651, 1985.

Sperber GH: Craniofacial Embryology. Wright PSG, 1981, pp 79–86.

Turk AE, McCarthy JG, Throne CH, Wisoff JH: The "back to sleep campaign" and deformational plagiocephaly: Is there cause for concern? J Craniofac Surg 7:12–18, 1996.

Weatherley-White RCA, Sakura CY, Brenner LD, et al: Submucous cleft palate. Its incidence, natural history, and indications for treatment. Plast Reconstr Surg 49:297–304, 1972.

22 CHAPTER

CLEFT LIP

D. Ralph Millard, Jr., MD, FACS, Hon. FRCS (Edin), Hon. FRCS, OD Ja.

1. What is the cause of a cleft of the lip and palate?

Before the first trimester of pregnancy, the five facial elements—frontonasal, two lateral maxillary, and two mandibular segments—fuse by mesenchymal migration to create the face and jaws. When, for whatever reason, these fusions are interrupted, a cleft (or clefts) results.

2. What is the cause of clefting in a specific case?

The cause in specific cases is not known, but genetics, viral infection, lack of certain vitamins, and other factors during the first trimester of pregnancy may be involved.

3. What is the anatomy of a cleft?

A cleft is not just a division through the lip and palate; it is distortion of the anatomy that may involve the lip, nose, septum, vomer, alveolar segments, levator palati muscles, and other structures.

UNILATERAL CLEFTS

4. What is the key factor involved in the treatment of a unilateral cleft?

Correction of asymmetry.

5. Summarize the evolution of unilateral cleft surgery.

For patients with a unilateral cleft lip, early surgeons merely freshened the edges of the lip cleft and approximated them with sutures. Later attempts were made to lengthen the lip on the cleft side with local flaps.

6. What is the Mirault-Blair-Brown method of lip repair?

The lip length on the cleft side is increased by a triangular flap taken from the cleft side. The Cupid's bow is destroyed.

7. What is the Hagedorn-Le Mesurier method?

A rectangular flap from the cleft side is inset into a releasing incision on the noncleft side to create an artificial Cupid's bow.

8. What is the Tennison-Randall method?

A Z-plasty of the cleft lip edges that positions the Cupid's bow but at the expense of an unnatural lip scar across the philtrum column and partial flattening of the philtrum dimple.

9. What is the rotation-advancement method?

The distorted anatomy of the unilateral cleft of the lip is corrected by a rotation incision that releases lip tissue, including the Cupid's bow, downward into normal symmetric position with the opposite side and advances the lateral lip element into the rotation gap to maintain rotation and complete the lip reconstruction. The advancement action assists the correction of the flaring ala, and the C-flap aids in unilateral columella lengthening. The scar of lip union is in the line of a natural philtrum column position, and whatever philtrum dimple is present is preserved as such (Figs. 22-1 and 22-2).

10. What are the most common mistakes made in the rotation-advancement method?

- Inadequate rotation due to failure to cut back on the rotation incision.
- Inadequate use of the lateral advancement flap by failure to pare the cleft edge sufficiently.
- Failure to use the C-flap to reduce the cutback gap in the upper lip and to lengthen the columella on the cleft side.
- Vertical lengthening of the entire lip by extending the cutback across the normal philtrum column.
- Too much reduction of nostril size in incomplete clefts.

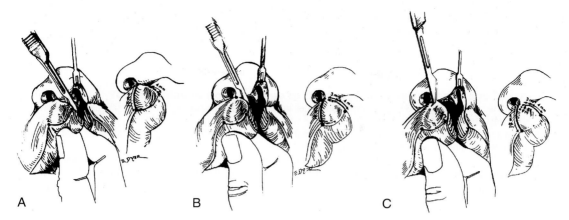

Figure 22-1. Millard rotation-advancement unilateral cleft lip repair. **A,** Points *1, 2,* and *3* mark the residual Cupid's bow on the mucocutaneous junction. The rotation incision pares the edges of the cleft from point *3* to the base of the columella. This distance usually measures 4 to 5 mm compared with 10 mm on the normal (noncleft) side. **B,** The rotation incision hugs the columella and is carried two thirds of the way across the base of the columella to gain an additional 3 mm. Flap C, attached to the columella, is released from the lip. **C,** The backcut is placed in the lip at 90°, running medial and parallel to the normal philtrum column. When carried through the skin, muscle, and mucosa, this incision releases another 3 mm. This maneuver achieves the total of 10 mm required to match the normal side and places the Cupid's bow in balanced position. (From Millard DR Jr: Cleft lip. In McCarthy JG [ed]: Plastic Surgery. Philadelphia, WB Saunders, 1990, p 2637, with permission.)

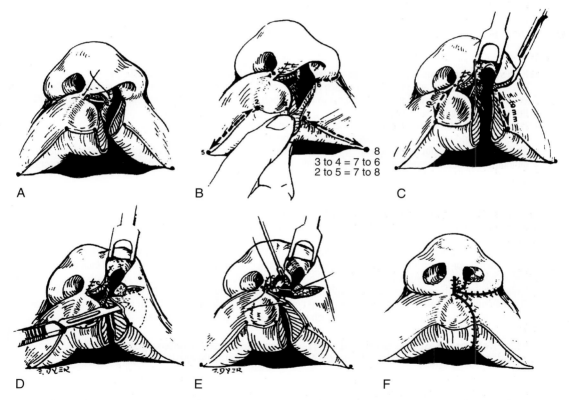

Figure 22-2. Millard rotation-advancement unilateral cleft lip repair. **A,** Flap C is transposed into the backcut and sutured to add length to the columella. **B,** The highest point of the lateral lip is marked at point *6,* where a tranverse incision will free the lip from the flared alar base. Because the pared edge of the advancement flap must match the rotation incision *(3* to *4)* point *7* is marked along the free edge so that *6* to *7* = *3* to *4.* The same distance from the height of Cupid's bow to the commissure on the normal side *(2* to *5)* should be marked on the cleft lip element. With the lateral lip under the tension necessary to close the lip, there is more running room from point *8* for positioning point *7* so that *2* to *5* = *7* to *8.* **C,** Flap C has been sutured into the backcut. The alar base is released from the lip. The height of the lateral lip (10 mm) equals the rotation of 10 mm, thus matching the bow peak-to-columella base of 10 mm on the noncleft side. **D,** The bunched muscle of the lateral lip element is freed generously from the skin and mucosa so that with muscle approximation across the cleft there is no residual muscle bulge. The tip of the alar base is denuded of epithelium. **E,** The denuded tip of the alar base is sutured to the septum near the anterior nasal spine to cinch the alar flare. The key suture first picks up the muscle in the tip of the advancement flap and then crosses into the backcut of the rotation. **F,** After the alar cinch suture and the key lip suture have been tied, the tissues are in correct position and require only three-layer closure of the mucosa, muscle, and skin. (From Millard DR Jr: Cleft lip. In McCarthy JG [ed]: Plastic Surgery. Philadelphia, WB Saunders, 1990, p 2638, with permission.)

11. What are the recent advances in unilateral cleft lip surgery?

Presurgical orthodontics using the Latham appliance to align the alveolar segments carefully so that the cleft of the alveolus and anterior hard palate can be closed with a gingivoperiosteoplasty. Bone grows into this area, negating the need for secondary bone grafting. This alveolar construction presents a symmetric platform on which definitive lip and nose construction can be accomplished much sooner.

12. At what age are the various stages of lip construction accomplished?

- When the patient weighs 10 lb, the Latham appliance is inserted, and the parents turn the screw daily until the segments are in alignment.
- When segments are in alignment and 2 to 3 mm apart (after 2 to 4 weeks), the appliance is removed. Two to three days later the gingivoperiosteoplasty and lip adhesion are performed.
- At 6 to 7 months of age the rotation-advancement of the lip is carried out; the nasal correction is done at the same time.
- At 18 months the remaining cleft of the hard and soft palate is closed with the von Langenbeck method or in some cases a Wardill-Kilner V-Y or unilateral V-Y method, depending on the defect. Minor lip and nose deformities can be improved at this time.

13. Why is the lip adhesion used?

Before the development of presurgical orthodontics, lip adhesion served as a crude orthodontic molding action. After alignment of the alveolar segments and closure of the alveolar cleft, the lip adhesion provides a gentle dressing with the least tension during healing. It also turns a wide complete cleft into an easier-to-correct incomplete cleft.

14. What are the key deformities in the unilateral cleft lip nose? How are they corrected?

- A unilateral short columella is lengthened with a C-flap.
- Deviation and distortion of the septum are corrected during presurgical orthodontics.
- Dislocation and slumping of the alar cartilage are corrected by dissecting the medial two thirds of the alar cartilage and then constructing the medial crus with sutures to the normal side.
- Flaring of the alar base is corrected with the alar cinch procedure.

15. Why is the rotation-advancement lip operation the method of choice?

- The actions of rotation and advancement place normal tissues into normal positions, creating a symmetric Cupid's bow.
- Rotation and advancement position the scar of union along the philtrum column line and preserve the integrity of the philtrum dimple.
- The actions of rotation and advancement aid in the nasal correction.
- A well-executed rotation-advancement is capable of producing an aesthetic result.
- When the method is not done correctly, it is still possible to achieve a satisfactory secondary result without great difficulty. The rotation-advancement method avoids the interlocking of little flaps that are impossible to unscramble.

BILATERAL CLEFTS

16. What are the specific deformities in a bilateral cleft?

- In the complete bilateral cleft the premaxillary vomer segment has not fused with the lateral maxillary segments so that the premaxillary vomer segment grows forward unimpeded to jut far ahead of the lateral segments.
- There is a shortage of skin tissue in the vertical length of the frontonasal component as measured from the nasal tip to the inferior border of the prolabium, particularly in the columella. This shortage is due to lack of stretch during normal embryogenesis.
- Patients have no important muscle in the prolabium, no philtrum columns or dimple, and no Cupid's bow.
- The alae are spread wide; the alar cartilages are dislocated from their mates in the tip and slump along the alae; and the columella is short to nonexistent, which causes the nasal tip to be depressed.

17. What one aspect of the bilateral cleft is sometimes an advantage?

Symmetric bilateral clefts at least have symmetry. Asymmetric bilateral clefts vary in their symmetry.

18. Summarize the evolution of bilateral cleft surgery.

- To ease bilateral cleft lip closure, early surgeons amputated the premaxilla, which produced an oral cripple.
- Early surgery by Brophy used a circumferential wire to encircle the three maxillary elements and crunch them together to facilitate cleft lip closure. This technique affected normal maxillary growth, a problem discovered and criticized by Pruzansky. Berkowtiz, a student of Pruzansky, still harbors fear of early surgery.
- Closure of the lip over the premaxillary prominence caused ventroflexion of the septum.
- Modern alignment of these segments is designed to ease the premaxilla back into the arch, much like sliding a drawer. Many surgeons use presurgical orthodontics to align the maxillary segments. Georgiade and Latham devised a method of retracting the premaxilla. Latham later refined the method with two-pin and chain traction on the projecting premaxilla, along with bilateral spreading of the collapsed lateral maxillary segments, to achieve a reasonable atraumatic alignment of the arch.

19. How is maxillary alignment maintained?
A bilateral gingivoperiosteoplasty creates a mucoperiosteal tunnel across each side of the cleft as the alveolar clefts and the floor of the nose are closed. This technique allows bone to grow across the cleft and prevents the need for later secondary bone grafting.

20. What is the major risk of early alveolar construction?
In a few cases some retrusion of the premaxilla has been noted.

21. Can this risk be avoided?
As experience with this orthopedic approach increases, the premaxillary retrusion can be prevented, reduced, and certainly corrected, often with mere orthodontic treatment.

22. What are the advantages of early orthodontic manipulation and gingivoperiosteoplasty of the alveolar cleft?
- Obliteration of fistulas.
- Creation of a bony bridge across the cleft that later will accept teeth and prevents the need for secondary bone grafting.
- Construction of a stable symmetric platform that enables earlier definitive correction of the lip and nose. This technique enables the surgeon to correct the deformity by 4 years, before the age of memory.

23. How are the soft tissues treated in bilateral clefts?
- Some methods focus entirely on joining the lateral lip elements to the prolabium with no concern for the nose (Manchester).
- Some methods treat both lip and nose.

24. What is the key to correction of the nose?
- Some surgeons acknowledge that the columella is short and requires skin lengthening (Carter, Cronin).
- Some surgeons have devised methods to achieve columella length from above (Mulliken, Trott, Mohan).

25. What is the best method of action?
- In patients in whom some columella is present and in persons of races that require minimal columella length, it may be possible to get by without introducing new skin.
- Approximately 50 years ago, Gensoul took a V-Y flap from the center of the prolabium to lengthen the columella, but this technique made three vertical scars in the lip.
- In patients with little or no columella, a forked flap taken from excessive prolabium skin and scar will provide the extra skin to release the depressed nasal tip.

26. How is the forked flap used?
- The forked flap can be used as a secondary procedure to narrow a wide prolabium, to revise bilateral lip scars, and to construct a columella.
- The flap can be taken from the prolabium after 1 to 2 years of stretching and banked in whisker position under the alae before it is advanced into the columella. This advancement is best done at approximately 4 years of age. At this time the alar cartilages can be freed and joined to each other in the tip to reconstruct the medial crura. The alar bases can be cinched for final correction of the bilateral nasal deformity.

27. How is the lip of a bilateral cleft closed?
At the time of gingivoperiosteoplasty, the lip adhesion involves approximating the sides of the freshened prolabium to the lateral lip elements. The lateral lip elements are freshened by the turndown of mucocutaneous flaps from their sides. The lateral mucocutaneous flaps are used to overlap the turndown of inferior prolabium vermilion. This technique provides several bonuses. The unnatural prolabium vermilion is turned out of view, and a natural-looking Cupid's bow is created that helps to camouflage the bilateral deformity (Fig. 22-3).

At the time of palate closure at 18 months the prolabium usually has stretched enough to spare easily a forked flap that is banked in the whisker position beneath the alae. At the time of advancement of the banked forked flap from whisker position at 4 years, the nasal tip is released, the alar cartilages are freed and sutured to reconstruct the medial crura, and the columella is lengthened.

28. What is important to the future treatment of clefts?
Genetic engineering probably will have more impact in preventing the deformity than in utero surgery in correcting the deformity.

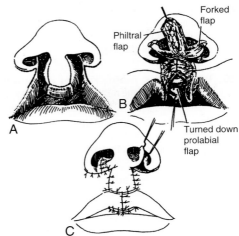

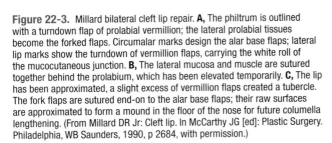

Figure 22-3. Millard bilateral cleft lip repair. **A,** The philtrum is outlined with a turndown flap of prolabial vermillion; the lateral prolabial tissues become the forked flaps. Circumalar marks design the alar base flaps; lateral lip marks show the turndown of vermillion flaps, carrying the white roll of the mucocutaneous junction. **B,** The lateral mucosa and muscle are sutured together behind the prolabium, which has been elevated temporarily. **C,** The lip has been approximated, a slight excess of vermillion flaps created a tubercle. The fork flaps are sutured end-on to the alar base flaps; their raw surfaces are approximated to form a mound in the floor of the nose for future columella lengthening. (From Millard DR Jr: Cleft lip. In McCarthy JG [ed]: Plastic Surgery. Philadelphia, WB Saunders, 1990, p 2684, with permission.)

BIBLIOGRAPHY

Unilateral Clefts

Blair VP, Brown JB: Mirault operation for single harelip. Surg Gynecol Obstet 51:81, 1930.

Brown JB, McDowell F: Small triangular flap operation for the primary repair of single cleft lips. Plast Reconst Surg 5:392, 1950.

Hagedorn W: Die Operation der Hasenscharte mit Zickzachnaht. Zentralbl Chir 19:281, 1892.

Kilner TP: Cleft lip and palate repair. St. Thomas Hosp Rep 2:127, 1937.

Langenbeck B von: Die uranoplastik mittelst Abloesung des mucoesperiostalen Gaumeneuberzuges. Arch Clin Chir 2:205–287, 1861 [also Plast Reconstr Surg 49:326–330, 1972.]

Latham RA: Orthopedic advancement of the cleft maxillary segment. A preliminary report. Cleft Palate J 17:277–282, 1980.

LeMesurier AB: Method of cutting and suturing lip in complete unilateral cleft lip. Plast Reconstr Surg 4:1, 1949.

Millard DR Jr: A primary camouflage of the unilateral harelook. Transactions of the First International Congress of Plastic Sugery, Stockholm. Baltimore, Williams & Wilkins, 1957, pp 160–166.

Millard DR Jr: A Rhinoplasty Tetralogy. Boston, Little, Brown, 1996.

Millard DR Jr: Cleft Craft. Boston, Little, Brown, 1976.

Millard DR Jr: Combining the von Langenbeck and the Wardill-Kilner operations in certain clefts of the palate. Cleft Palate Craniofacial J 29:85–86, 1992.

Millard DR Jr: Earlier correction of the unilateral cleft lip nose. Plast Reconstr Surg 70:64–73, 1982.

Millard DR Jr: Embryonic rationale for the primary correction of classical congenital clefts of the lip and palate. Hunterian Lecture delivered during the meeting of the British Association of Plastic Surgeons held at Oxford on July 7, 1994. Ann R Coll Surg 76:150–160, 1994.

Millard DR Jr, Latham RA: Improved primary surgical and dental treatment of clefts. Plast Reconstr Surg 86:856–871, 1990.

Mirault G: Deux lettres sur operation du bec-de-lievre considere dans ses divers etats de simplicite et de complication. J Chir (Paris) 2:257, 1844; 3:5, 1845.

Randall P: A triangular flap operation for the primary repair of unilateral clefts of the lip. Plast Reconstr Surg 23:331, 1959.

Tennison CW: The repair of the unilateral cleft lip by the stencil method. Plast Reconstr Surg 9:115–120, 1952.

Wardill WBM: Cleft palate. Br J Surg 16:127–148, 1928.

Bilateral Clefts

Brophy TW: The radical cure of congenital cleft palate. Dent Cosmos 41:882, 1899.

Carter WW: The correction of nasal deformities by mechanical replacement and the transplantation of bone. N Y State J Med 14:517–523,1914.

Cronin TD: Lengthening the columella by the use of skin from the nasal floors and alae. Plast Reconstr Surg 21:417, 1958.

Gensoul JJ: Reduction of a thickened columna and advancing the point of the nose. J Hebd Med Chir Pratique 12:29, 1833.

Georgiade NG, Latham RA: Maxillary arch alignment in bilateral cleft lip and palate repair using the pinned coaxial screw appliance. Plast Reconstr Surg 56:52–60, 1975.

Manchester WM: The repair of double cleft lip as part of an integrated program. Plast Reconstr Surg 45:207–216, 1970.

Millard DR Jr: Adaptation of the rotation-advancement principle in bilateral cleft lip. In Wallace AB (ed): Transactions of the Second International Congress of Plastic Surgery, London, 1959. Edinburgh, Churchill-Livingstone, 1960.

Millard DR Jr: A primary compromise for bilateral cleft lip. Surg Gynecol Obstet 111:557–563, 1960.

Millard DR Jr: Columella lengthening by a forked flap. Plast Reconstr Surg 22:454–457, 1958.

Millard DR Jr, Berkowitz S, Latham RA, Wolfe SA: A discussion on pre-surgical orthodontics in patients with clefts. Cleft Palate J 25: 403–412, 1988.

Millard DR Jr, Latham RA: Improved primary surgical and dental treatment of clefts. Plast Reconstr Surg 86:856–871, 1990.

Mulliken JB: Bilateral complete cleft lip and nasal deformity: An anthropometric analysis of staged to synchronous repair. Plast Reconstr Surg 96:9–23, 1995.

Pruzansky S: Factors determining arch form in cleft lip and palate. Am J Orthod 41:827–851, 1955.

Trott JA, Mohan N: A preliminary report on one-stage open tip rhinoplasty at the time of lip repair in bilateral cleft lip and palate. The Alor Setar experience. Br J Plast Surg 46:215–222, 1993.

CLEFT PALATE

CHAPTER 23

Don LaRossa, MD; Peter Randall, MD, FACS;
Marilyn A. Cohen, BA, LSLP; and Ghada Y. Afifi, MD, FACS

1. What is a cleft palate?

It is a failure of the two halves of the roof of the mouth, or palatal shelves, to join in the midline and fuse. The cleft may involve the soft palate or both soft and hard palates.

2. Explain the terms *primary* and *secondary* palate, and *prepalatal* and *palatal* structures.

The *incisive foramen*, which is located behind the incisor teeth, is the site where the lateral maxillary bones meet the midline premaxilla. A cleft lip usually involves structures anterior to the incisive foramen, such as the alveolus, lip, and nasal tip cartilages, as well as the floor of the nose. These structures usually are referred to as the structures of the *primary* palate or *prepalatal* structures. They may be cleft unilaterally or bilaterally.

The structures posterior to the incisive foramen, including the hard palate, soft palate, and uvula, usually are referred to as the *secondary* palate or *palatal* structures. Thus the incisive foramen separates the primary (prepalatal) and secondary (palatal) structures.

3. What is the premaxilla?

The premaxilla is the alveolar segment of the maxilla that includes the nasal spine and four incisor teeth. It is located centrally and anterior to the incisive foramen.

4. When is a cleft palate associated with a cleft lip? What is the overall incidence?

The most frequent combination is a unilateral cleft of the lip and palate, which is seen more often in boys than girls, predominantly on the left side. The hereditary incidence is fairly high. The next most frequent cleft—of the palate alone—is seen more frequently in girls; the hereditary incidence is fairly low. In whites, the incidence is approximately 1.4:1000 live births; in blacks, it is approximately 0.43:1000; and in Asians, it may be as high as 3.2:1000. The most common cleft is a cleft uvula, or bifid uvula, which has an incidence of approximately 2%. Most cases are asymptomatic; however, when it is associated with a submucosal cleft of the palate, as many as 20% of patients may have some degree of velopharyngeal incompetence.

5. How can clefts be classified?

Clefts can be described as complete (i.e., penetrating all the way through the structures) or incomplete. Prepalatal clefts or clefts of the primary palate also should be described as unilateral (right or left) or bilateral; they may be described even further as involving one third, two thirds, or three thirds (complete) of the vertical height of the lip. Similarly, palatal clefts may be described as involving one third, two thirds, or three thirds of the soft palate and one third, two thirds, or three thirds of the hard palate, extending up to the incisive foramen.

A *submucosal cleft palate* is not an overt cleft. The levator muscle fibers fail to fuse completely in the midline, often leading to velopharyngeal incompetence. A thin area, called a *zona pellucida*, is often seen centrally at the site at which the muscle is lacking. A notch often can be palpated at the posterior edge of the hard palate, which normally has a palpable prominence or posterior nasal spine. Patients often have a bifid uvula, which may be a simple bilobed uvula or a completely split uvula.

A *bifid uvula*, seen in 2% of the normal American population, may be associated with palatal incompetence; patients should be followed for possible speech problems. A congenital absence of the muscularis uvulae also may occur with or without a bifid uvula and is often associated with palatal incompetence (Fig. 23-1).

6. What is the etiology of cleft palate?

Cleft palate is believed to be a multifactorial defect; a cleft can be caused in many different ways. A high incidence of clefts in some families suggest a genetic etiology. Clefts may be associated with syndromes such as Stickler syndrome, fetal alcohol syndrome, velocardiofacial and DiGeorge syndromes (22q11.2 deletion), Van der Woude syndrome, ectodermal

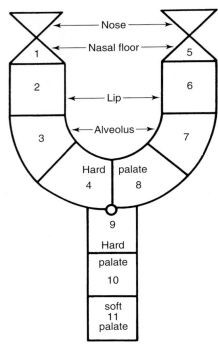

Figure 23-1. Millard's modification of Kernahan's and Elsahy's striped Y classification for cleft lip and palate. The *small circle* indicates the incisive foramen. The *triangles* indicate the nasal tip and nasal floor. (From Randall P: Cleft palate. In Smith JW, Aston SJ [eds]: Grabb and Smith's Plastic Surgery, 4th ed. Boston, Little, Brown, 1991, p 291, with permission.)

dysplasias, and trisomies. Experimentally, clefts have been induced by a number of agents, including alcohol, insulin, tretinoin, corticosteroids, anticonvulsants, phenobarbital, carbon monoxide, salicylates, oxygen deficiency, arabasine, and possibly smoking. Other factors probably exist. In any one case, identifying a single cause usually is difficult.

7. How does a primary or prepalatal cleft form?
Primary clefts result from a lack of mesenchymal development. The mesenchymal islands—one central and two lateral—normally develop and fuse. Lack of development of one of the three islands results in an unstable condition with ectoderm of the skin in contact with ectoderm of the oral mucosa; complete or incomplete breakdown occurs at this point.

8. Why are left-sided secondary or palatal clefts more common than right-sided clefts?
In the 7-week-old embyro, the two palatal shelves lie almost vertically. Normally, the neck straightens from its flexed position, the tongue drops posteriorly, and the shelves rotate superiorly to the horizontal position; they fuse from anterior to posterior to form the intact palate by 12 weeks. In rodents, the right palatal shelf reaches the horizontal position before the left one, leaving the left side susceptible to developmental interruption for a greater period than the right side. This may account for the greater incidence of left-sided clefts.

9. What is Simonart's band?
A cleft of the primary palate is often bridged by a band of lip tissue—Simonart's band. Some regard this band of tissue as the result of a healing process after breakdown of the lip elements. Others propose that Simonart's band may result from partial formation of the epithelial wall.

10. Which muscles are the most important for achieving velopharyngeal closure?
The levator palatini muscles pull the middle third of the soft palate superiorly and posteriorly to produce firm contact with the posterior pharyngeal wall at about the level of the adenoidal pad (Fig. 23-2).

11. Do any other muscles contribute to velopharyngeal closure?
Absolutely. The paired palatopharyngeus muscles pull the soft palate posteriorly; the muscularis uvulae cause the uvula to thicken centrally with contraction, and the superior pharyngeal constrictor muscles move the lateral pharyngeal walls medially or the posterior pharyngeal wall anteriorly with contraction.

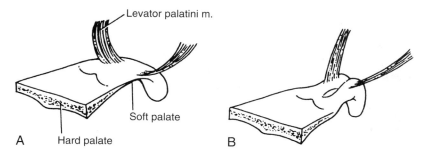

Figure 23-2. The levator muscles pull approximately 45° superiorly and posteriorly. **A,** At rest. **B,** After contraction. (From Randall P, LaRossa D: Cleft palate. In McCarthy JG [ed]: Plastic Surgery. Philadelphia, WB Saunders, 1990, p 2727, with permission.)

12. What is the most important anatomic abnormality seen with a cleft palate?

Disorientation of the levator palatini muscles, which normally join in the midline with a transverse orientation and insert into the palatal aponeurosis at approximately the middle third of the soft palate. In the case of a cleft, the muscles are much more longitudinally oriented and insert into the posterior edge of the palatal bone and along the bony cleft (Fig. 23-3).

13. What is an intravelar veloplasty?

Kriens first emphasized the abnormal orientation of the levator palatini muscles and the need to detach them from their abnormal insertion and reorient them in a transverse direction. Suturing the muscles in an overlapping fashion rather than end to end produces a tighter levator sling.

14. What is Passavant's ridge?

During gagging, the forceful contraction of both the levator palatini muscles and the superior pharyngeal constrictors may produce a bulge or ridge on the posterior pharynx above the arch of the atlas—Passavant's ridge. This ridge also may be associated with velopharyngeal incompetence as a compensatory mechanism to assist with velopharyngeal closure.

15. How can a mother know if her child has a cleft palate?

Before modern ultrasonography, the cleft probably was first identified by the obstetrician or pediatrician. The mother may or may not directly observe the cleft; instead, her only clues may be the child's poor-to-absent ability to build suction along with regurgitation of milk into the nose. Under the right conditions, some clefts of the palate may be detected prenatally by ultrasound even before 18 weeks' gestation. Many clefts involving the lip are diagnosed by this method.

16. How should a mother feed a child with a cleft palate if the child cannot suck?

Most children born with a cleft demonstrate normal sucking motions, but the mother should know that the prime difficulty is inability to build up adequate suction. Usually the ability to swallow is not impaired. The child should be held in a head-up position at about 45° and usually can be bottle-fed with a preemie nipple that has additional cross-cuts in the end. A plastic bottle that can be squeezed or a bulb syringe with a nipple can deliver too much milk and cause choking. The baby can be expected to swallow more air and to need more burping, but with good delivery of milk a long time should not be required for each feeding. Regurgitation through the nose may be expected because of the deficiency of the palatal midline tissues.

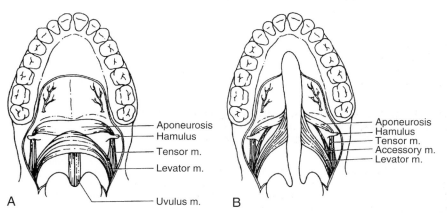

Figure 23-3. Musculature of the soft palate. **A,** Normal musculature. The levator muscles are oriented transversely and insert in the palatine aponeurosis in the midportion of the soft palate. **B,** Cleft musculature. The levator muscles are oriented more longitudinally and insert on the posterior edge of the palatal bone and along the bony cleft edges. (From Randall P, LaRossa D: Cleft palate. In McCarthy JG [ed]: Plastic Surgery. Philadelphia, WB Saunders, 1990, p 2726 and 2730, with permission.)

17. Who should evaluate a newborn with a cleft palate?

Ideally, a newborn with a cleft should be seen by the surgeon who ultimately will repair the cleft so that he or she can discuss the entire spectrum of care with the parents. Introduction to key people on the cleft palate team is advisable so that parents can identify the respective roles of each; hence early intervention is facilitated. Instructions for adequate feeding and airway protection are most important. Introduction to parental support groups is helpful.

18. What disciplines should be available on a cleft palate team?

The team should include a pediatrician, a surgeon experienced in cleft management, a speech pathologist, a pediatric otolaryngologist, a well-versed orthodontist, a pediatric dentist, and an audiologist. The team also should have access to a geneticist, a prosthodontist, an ophthalmologist, a clinical psychologist and/or psychiatrist, a physical anthropologist, a social worker, and a nurse experienced in cleft problems.

19. What are the major sequelae of an unrepaired cleft palate?

Initially, the main problems are an inability to build up suction and nasal regurgitation. The patient usually has poor eustachian tube function, which may lead to fluid in the middle ear space, and is prone to recurrent otitis media. Breathing may be a major problem, particularly if the chin is short and the tongue falls backward, causing inspiratory obstruction as in Pierre Robin sequence. Speech may be significantly affected in the unrepaired or repaired incompetent palate, including hypernasality with vowel sounds and distortion of the pressure consonants. With involvement of the alveolar ridge, the adjacent teeth usually are angled into the cleft and may be malformed or absent. Dental caries and severe malocclusion may be present or develop.

20. At what age should the palate be surgically repaired?

Most authorities concur that repair is best performed by 12 months of age. Some data indicate a slight improvement with closure at 3 to 6 months of age, although other reports show no additional benefit. Most agree that closure should be complete before 18 months of age.

21. What is the benefit of earlier closure?

The greatest benefit is better speech. Even with babbling, a child is learning to articulate. If speech develops before closure of the palate is complete, the child usually has difficulty in building up pressure for the production of sounds such as P and T. He or she will have even more trouble controlling sustained pressure for the production of sounds such as S and SH. As a result, the child may develop speech in which these sounds are missing or distorted. Alternatively, the child may develop what is called *compensatory articulation*, such as the glottal stop and pharyngeal fricative.

22. What is the von Langenbeck operation?

Described in 1859, the von Langenbeck operation remains a reliable method of cleft palate repair. It involves elevation of large mucoperiosteal flaps from the hard palate with midline approximation of the cleft margins of both hard and soft palates with long, relaxing incisions laterally. The levator muscles are completely detached from their abnormal bony insertion, and the soft palate musculature is repaired in the midline. A palatal lengthening procedure is not included in this operation (Fig. 23-4).

23. What is the Furlow double-opposing Z-plasty technique?

This procedure consists of two Z-plasties of the soft palate, one on the oral mucosa and the other in the reverse orientation on the nasal mucosa. The levator muscle on one side is included in the posteriorly based *oral* mucosal Z-plasty, whereas the levator muscle from the opposite side is included in the posteriorly based *nasal* mucosal Z-plasty flap (Fig. 23-5). The hard palate cleft is closed using a vomer flap (see Question 25). This procedure reorients the malpositioned levator muscles, permits overlap of the muscles, and produces some degree of palatal lengthening.

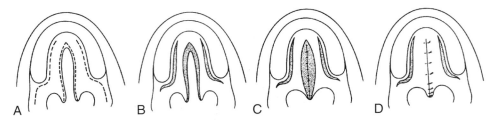

Figure 23-4. The von Langenbeck operation. **A,** Flap design. **B,** The lateral relaxing incisions are made, and the mucoperiosteal flaps are elevated. **C,** The nasal mucosa is closed and the muscles sutured together after detachment from their insertions. **D,** The oral closure. (From Randall P, LaRossa D: Cleft palate. In McCarthy JG [ed]: Plastic Surgery. Philadelphia, WB Saunders, 1990, p 2743, with permission.)

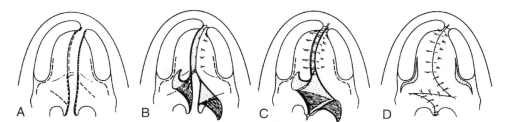

Figure 23-5. The Furlow double Z-plasty operation. **A,** Flap design. **B,** Oral and ansal mucosal Z-plasty flaps are elevated. **C,** The nasal mucosal closure. **D,** The oral mucosal closure. The soft palate has been lengthened and the levator muscles properly oriented. (From Randall P, LaRossa D: Cleft palate. In McCarthy JG [ed]: Plastic Surgery. Philadelphia, WB Saunders, 1990, p 2740, with permission.)

24. What is the Wardill-Kilner-Veau operation?

The Wardill-Kilner-Veau operation is a V-Y advancement of the mucoperiosteum of the hard palate, designed specifically to lengthen the palate in the anteroposterior plane at the time of primary palatoplasty. As a result of the V-Y lengthening, bare membranous bone is left exposed in the area from which the flaps were advanced. These areas granulate and epithelialize within 2 to 3 weeks but remain areas of fibrous scar and may contribute to subsequent maxillary growth disturbances (Fig. 23-6).

25. What is a vomer flap?

Hard palate closure can be performed by elevating a wide superiorly based flap of nasal mucosa from the vomer. With bilateral clefts, vomer flaps can be obtained from each side of the vomer. This technique prevents the need for elevating large mucoperiosteal flaps from the hard palate and the potential risk of resultant maxillary growth disturbances.

26. Is there an alternative to surgical repair?

In rare instances in which the patient has a medical condition that makes surgery or general anesthesia too risky, a dental prosthesis is a possible alternative. Older children (age 15 years and older) in developing countries, for example, can be managed with a prosthesis if dental services are available.

27. What is velopharyngeal incompetence? How soon after surgery should a child be evaluated for velopharyngeal incompetence?

Velopharyngeal incompetence (VPI) is the inability of the soft palate to make contact with the posterior pharyngeal wall (i.e., velopharyngeal closure) during speech, resulting in air escape through the nose and hypernasality. Evaluation of palatal function is an ongoing process that should begin as speech development occurs and continue through puberty. Usually, incompetence can be diagnosed by 4 or 5 years of age and occasionally earlier.

28. Who should decide to operate on an incompetent palate?

This decision usually is made by a competent speech pathologist in conjunction with the surgeon. Even though the trained ear probably is the most accurate way to assess incompetence, if surgery is contemplated, dynamic assessment of palatal function usually is advisable. Assessment can be done through multiplane videofluoroscopy or nasoendoscopic examination. Additional studies of pressure flow or objective nasal resonance measurement also may be helpful.

29. What can be done about residual speech problems after cleft palate repair?

A number of approaches can be used. With minor incompetence or inconsistent incompetence, speech therapy alone may succeed in improving speech. More often, a secondary operation is necessary, such as a posterior pharyngeal flap or sphincter pharyngoplasty. With minimal incompetence, a palatal lengthening operation or a procedure to advance the posterior pharyngeal wall may be advised. Some cases can be managed with a prosthesis that simply lifts the palate into a more competent position to permit velopharyngeal closure or obturates the defect.

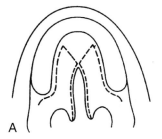
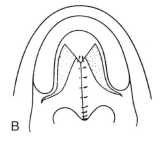

Figure 23-6. The Wardill-Kilner-Veau operation. **A,** Flap design. **B,** V-Y lengthening leaves an exposed bare area of bone after closure. (From Randall P, LaRossa D: Cleft palate. In McCarthy JG [ed]: Plastic Surgery. Philadelphia, WB Saunders, 1990, p 2744, with permission.)

30. Why do children with palatal clefts have ear problems?

The levator veli palatini and tensor veli palatini muscles insert to some extent on the eustachian tube. Both probably are responsible for competence of the tube in preventing reflux from the nasopharynx into the eustachian tube as well as for opening the tube to equalize pressure in the middle ear. With impaired ability to equalize middle ear pressure, infants with clefts usually have fluid in the middle ear space, and the fluid soon becomes thick and viscous. Untreated, this condition leads to an increase in the incidence and severity of otitis media. Treatment consists of myringotomies, evacuation of the fluid, and insertion of indwelling ventilating tubes as well as vigilance for otitis media. Palate repair seems to reduce ear problems, but children whose ear problems have been neglected frequently have a high incidence of permanent hearing loss.

31. What is the likelihood of a cleft in another child from the same parents?

The likelihood depends on a number of factors, but generally, if there is no known teratogen or first-degree relative with a cleft, the likelihood in the Caucasian population is approximately 0.14%. If a first- or second-degree relative has a cleft, the likelihood increases to approximately 5%; if two first- or second-degree relatives have a cleft, the likelihood increases to 15% to 25%.

32. Is there a way to decrease the incidence of clefts?

Other than avoiding exposure to known teratogens, the answer is not clear. Folic acid taken during pregnancy has been shown to decrease the incidence of spina bifida, and some believe that it also decreases the incidence of clefts. However, this theory has not been generally accepted and remains an area of investigation.

BIBLIOGRAPHY

American Cleft Palate–Craniofacial Association: Parameters for evaluation and treatment of patients with cleft lip-palate or other craniofacial anomalies. In Phillips BJ, Warren DW (eds): The Cleft Palate and Craniofacial Team. Chapel Hill, NC, American Cleft Palate Association, 1993.

Bartlett SP, Yu J: Congenital disorders. In Ruberg RL, Smith DJ (eds): Plastic Surgery. St. Louis, Mosby, 1994, pp 271–277.

Berkowitz S: Team Management in Cleft Lip and Palate. San Diego, CA, Singular Publishing Group, 1996.

Burdi AR: Epidemiology, etiology, and pathogenesis of cleft lip and cleft palate. Cleft Palate J 14:262–269, 1977.

David DJ, Bagnall AD: Velopharyngeal incompetence. In McCarthy JG (ed): Plastic Surgery. Philadelphia, WB Saunders, 1990, pp 2903–2921.

Johnson MC: Embryology of the head and neck. In McCarthy JG (ed): Plastic Surgery. Philadelphia, WB Saunders, 1990, pp 2451–2495.

Johnson MC, Bronsky PT, Millicorsky G: Embryogenesis of cleft lip and palate. In McCarthy JG (ed): Plastic Surgery. Philadelphia, WB Saunders, 1990, pp 2515–2552.

Kernahan DA: The striped Y-A symbolic classification for cleft lip and palate. Plast Reconstr Surg 47:469–470, 1971.

McCarthy JG, Cutting C, Hogan VM: Introduction to facial clefts. In McCarthy JG (ed):Plastic Surgery. Philadelphia, WB Saunders, pp 2437–2450.

McWilliams BJ, Randall P, LaRossa D, et al: Speech characteristics associated with the Furlow palatoplasty as compared with other surgical techniques. Plast Reconstr Surg 98:610–619, 1996.

Millard DR: Wide and/or short cleft palate. Plast Reconstr Surg 29:41–57, 1962.

Millard DR: Classification. In Millard DR (ed): Cleft Craft. Boston, Little, Brown, 1977, p 52.

Randall P, LaRosa D: Cleft palate. In McCarthy JG (ed): Plastic Surgery. Philadelphia, WB Saunders, 1990, pp 2723–2752.

Randall P, LaRossa D, Fakhraee SM, Cohen MA: Cleft palate closure at three to seven months of age: A preliminary report. Plast Reconstr Surg 71:624–628, 1983.

Sando WC, Jurkiewicz MI: Cleft palate. In Jurkiewicz MJ, Krizek TJ, Mathes SJ, Ariyan S (eds): Plastic Surgery: Principles and Practices. St. Louis, Mosby, 1990, pp 81–97.

Shaw WC, Asher-McDade C, Brattström V, et al: A six-center international study of treatment outcome in patients with clefts of the lip and palate: Part 1. Principles and study design. Cleft Palate Craniofac J 29:393–397, 1992.

Mølsted K, Asher-McDade C, Brattström V, et al: A six-center international study of treatment outcome in patients with clefts of the lip and palate: Part 2. Craniofacial form and soft tissue profile. Cleft Palate Craniofac J 29:398–404, 1992.

Mars M, Asher-McDade C, Brattström V, et al: A six-center international study of treatment outcome in patients with clefts of the lip and palate: Part 3. Dental arch relationships. Cleft Palate Craniofac J 29:405–408, 1992.

Asher-McDade C, Brattström V, Dahl E, et al: A six-center international study of treatment outcome in patients with clefts of the lip and palate: Part 4. Assessment of nasolabial appearance. Cleft Palate Craniofac J 29:409–412, 1992.

Shaw WC, Dahl E, Asher-McDade C, et al: A six-center international study of treatment outcome in patients with clefts of the lip and palate: Part 5. General discussion and conclusions. Cleft Palate Craniofac J 29:413–418, 1992.

CHAPTER 24

CORRECTION OF SECONDARY CLEFT LIP AND PALATE DEFORMITIES

Robert M. Menard, MD, FACS, and
David J. David, AC, MD, FRCSE, FRCS, FRACS

1. In a newborn infant with cleft lip and palate, what are the number and the timing of surgical procedures that can be anticipated?

Primary unilateral or bilateral cleft lip repair is generally performed at 3 months of age. In infants with wide complete clefts, some authors advocate that lip adhesion be performed first to help narrow the width of the alveolar cleft(s) if nasoalveolar molding or Latham appliances are not available. If close approximation of the alveolar segments is present, gingivoperiosteoplasty can be performed at the time of primary lip repair. Some authors eschew any surgical manipulation of the cleft lip, gingival elements, or periosteum other than the primary lip repair.

The best chance for normal speech and growth results when cleft palate closure is performed between 6 and 12 months of age, with most authorities believing that closure should be complete before 18 months of age. Because of abnormal eustachian tube anatomy in cleft palate patients, serous otitis media is almost universally present, and close ear, nose, and throat (ENT) follow-up and pressure equalization tube placements are routine. Lip/nose revision may be indicated at 5 to 7 years of age based on the aesthetics of the primary lip repair, and velopharyngeal surgery may be needed based on the assessment of the speech pathologist and nasopharyngoscopic examination.

Following orthodontic evaluation and care, alveolar cleft bone grafting is routinely performed between 6 and 9 years of age. Orthognathic surgery to correct skeletal malocclusion and midface deficiencies may be necessary at the completion of facial growth, after which definitive cleft lip septorhinoplasty may be performed. As such, under the best of circumstances, a minimum of three surgeries (lip repair, palate repair, and alveolar cleft bone grafting) can be anticipated. In a series of 67 patients, Cohen et al. reported an average of 6.12 operations per patient for unilateral cleft lip and palate and 8.04 operations per patient for bilateral cleft lip and palate.

Sequence of Cleft Lip and Palate Repair

1. Cleft lip repair at 3 months
2. Cleft palate repair at 10 to 18 months
3. Lip revision/secondary palate surgery as needed
4. Alveolar cleft bone grafting at 6 to 9 years of age
5. Orthognathic surgery and definitive cleft lip septorhinoplasty at completion of growth

2. What are the etiologies of residual lip deformities following primary cleft lip repair?

Vermilion–White Roll Junction Deformities: At the white roll–vermilion border, notching or peaking of the vermilion can occur secondary to scar contracture or due to inadequate rotation of the philtral unit. Inaccurate alignment of the medial and lateral white roll can also result in a mismatch at this level. In bilateral cleft lip repairs, preservation of the prolabial and lateral element white rolls can result in the "triple line" effect of the prolabial white roll, scar, and lateral white roll underneath.

Cupid's Bow/Philtral Unit Deformities: In unilateral repairs, incomplete rotation of the philtral unit with the rotation-advancement repair (i.e., Millard repair) is the primary cause of Cupid's bow deformities, resulting in the short lip deformity. Short lip can also result from significant contracture of the upper lip scar. Long lips are more frequently seen with the now outdated Tennison or Z-plasty lip repairs. In a rotation-advancement repair, excess curvature of the rotation incision will result in a philtral unit that is too rounded, and too little curvature will appear abnormal and result in a short lip. In bilateral cleft lip repair, generally performed between 3 and 6 months of age, designing the philtral unit wider than 4 to 6 mm will result in a wide lip deformity as the philtral skin stretches over time.

Tight Lip: This is most often seen in bilateral clefts or wide unilateral cleft lips not treated with presurgical orthopedics, in which the orbicularis oris and skin elements are brought together under significant tension. It is also seen with poor surgical planning, in which excessive lateral or medial lip skin, vermilion, and mucosa may have been discarded due to misidentification of the medial and lateral element high points.

Vermilion Deficiency: In unilateral repairs, incomplete release and advancement of the mucosa and vermilion, facilitated by gingivobuccal sulcus incisions, can result in a notch or "whistling deformity" at the junction of the medial and lateral element vermilion. In bilateral repairs, preservation of the prolabial vermilion will result in the whistling deformity, which can also be seen when the lateral element vermilion is placed under excess tension when advanced beneath the prolabial skin.

Mucosal Deficiencies: This is most often seen in bilateral deformities, when the prolabial vermilion, always deficient, is used to recreate the upper lip sulcus. It can also be seen in wide unilateral clefts and is often a result of poor planning or technique.

3. When and how should deformities of the vermilion–white roll junction be addressed?

Mild scar contracture within the first 6 months of a primary cleft lip repair is not uncommon. Scar maturation and relaxation should resolve any vermilion–white roll junction deformities in a properly performed repair. When performed by an experienced cleft surgeon, the scars and asymmetries will vary over the first few years following cleft lip repair. No revisions should be considered until prior to the start of school at 5 years of age. For vermilion–white roll junction asymmetry less than 2 mm, a diamond-shaped excision and realignment can be performed. Z-plasty revisions should be avoided because they place scars on the lip that do not fall along anatomic landmarks. For discrepancies in the vermilion–white roll junction greater than 3 mm, the asymmetry is the result of inadequate philtral rotation during primary unilateral cleft repair. Such repairs should be taken down and repeat rotation and advancement performed with adequate philtral rotation and proper muscle reapproximation and resuturing.

4. What treatment options are available for midline vermilion deficiencies?

Mild vermilion deformities can be addressed with a dermofat graft placed under the vermilion, harvested from an iliac crest donor site scar (if present), or by autogenous fat grafting as described by Coleman. More severe deformities where scarring prevents expansion of the vermilion where it is most needed and compromises revascularization of a dermofat or fat graft need to be addressed with a midline vermilion-only Abbe flap for vermilion deficiencies. A conventional midline Abbe flap, reconstructing the entire philtral unit with lower lip midline skin and vermilion, is most often used in bilateral cleft lip deformities when both the vermilion and philtral skin are deficient.

5. When should secondary cleft septorhinoplasty be performed?

The timing of cleft septorhinoplasty is subject to multiple differences of opinion. In our opinion, primary rhinoplasty techniques performed at the time of lip closure should not include dissection involving the septum because significant nasal and maxillary growth disturbances can be seen with septal disruption prior to the completion of facial growth. Anderl and others advocate anterior septal work at the time of primary lip repair. Primary rhinoplasty, which repositions the cleft side lower lateral cartilage into proper anatomic location, can be performed with limited dissection, thereby minimizing the effects of scar on the growing alar cartilages. As mentioned in Question 1, definitive secondary cleft septorhinoplasty should be performed (1) at the completion of facial growth and (2) following all necessary alveolar cleft bone grafting, orthodontia, and orthognathic surgeries to reposition the maxilla. The sliding flap cheilorhinoplasty, as described by Vissarionov (1989) and modified by Wang and Madorsky (1999), allows for equalization of the dome tip points, improved nostril symmetry, and replacement and reconstruction of the deficient vestibular skin on the cleft side.

Secondary Palatal Procedures

1. Furlow palatoplasty
2. Sphincter pharyngoplasty
3. Pharyngeal flap
4. Posterior wall implant

6. What are the etiologies of palatal dysfunction following primary cleft palate repair?

Palatal Fistulae: The reported recurrence rate of palatal fistulae following primary repair ranges between 6.8% and 37%. Palatal fistulae can develop secondary to

- Mechanical forces such as fingers or hard objects placed in the mouth in the early postoperative period. Some surgeons advocate arm restraints in the early postoperative period to help prevent objects being placed in the mouth by infants and toddlers.
- Excess tension from incomplete mobilization of the palatal mucosa resulting in devascularization and wound dehiscence.
- Infection resulting in wound dehiscence.
- Resorption of excess suture material.

Velopharyngeal Insufficiency: Incomplete closure of the soft palate against the posterior nasopharyngeal wall following primary palatoplasty can occur secondary to

- A congenitally short palate despite an adequate cleft palate closure.
- Excessive scarring in the velum following palatal repair.
- Improper reapproximation of the soft palate musculature at the time of primary repair.
- A large, deep nasopharynx as seen in velocardiofacial syndrome.
- Cleft palate repair in which there is a significant postadenoidectomy defect.
- Cleft palate in association with neurologic dysfunction.

7. What techniques are available for assessing velopharyngeal insufficiency?

Both direct and indirect techniques are available. Direct techniques, involving visualization of the nasopharynx and velopharyngeal closure, include nasopharyngoscopy and multiview videofluoroscopy. Indirect techniques, which qualitatively or quantitatively describe the sequelae of velopharyngeal insufficiency, include voice and resonance assessments by speech language pathologists and nasometer evaluation to assess the ratio of oral to nasal airflow (Figs. 24-1, 24-2, and 24-3).

8. What patterns of velopharyngeal closure are commonly seen in cleft palate patients with velopharyngeal insufficiency? What is the treatment of each?

Four patterns are most commonly seen with nasopharyngoscopy in cleft palate patients with velopharyngeal insufficiency (Figs. 24-4 through 24-9):

1. *Active velar elevation with little lateral pharyngeal and posterior pharyngeal wall movement*, in which the soft palate fails to reach the posterior pharyngeal wall, resulting in a long, slit-like gap from lateral pharyngeal wall to lateral pharyngeal wall. These patients are best treated with a sphincter pharyngoplasty such as a modified Hynes pharyngoplasty, where bilateral palatopharyngeus/posterior tonsillar pillar flaps are transposed horizontally to a transverse incision made at the junction of the posterior pharyngeal mucosa and adenoid tissue, at the level of the atlas.
2. *Active lateral pharyngeal wall movement to the midline with little to no velar or posterior pharyngeal wall movement*, resulting in vertically oriented slit-like insufficiency. These patients are best treated with a superiorly based pharyngeal flap, with the width tailored to the size of the transverse defect.
3. *Active contribution to velar closure from the velum and lateral pharyngeal walls*, with the lateral walls squeezing around the midline of the velum, resulting in a small midline gap. This occurs secondary to deficient midline muscle bulk in the velum. These patients benefit from Furlow palatoplasty for improving muscle reapproximation in the velum and lengthening the palate to help obturate the midline defect, performed alone or in combination with a small superiorly based pharyngeal flap that can be placed at the time of Furlow palate revision.

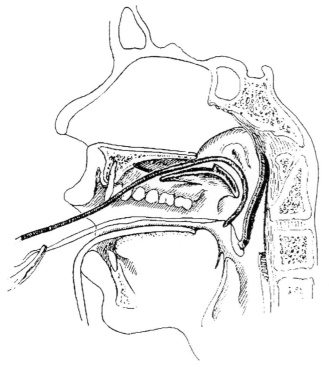

Figure 24-1. Pushback pharyngeal flap elevation and inset. Following elevation of the superiorly based pharyngeal flap and elevation of the hard palate mucosa with division of the soft palate aponeurosis, a Robinson catheter is passed through the junction of the palatal bone and soft palate and sutured to the tip of the pharyngeal flap. (From Jobe R: The pharyngeal flap-pushback procedure. Oper Tech Plast Reconstr Surg 2:245–249, 1995.)

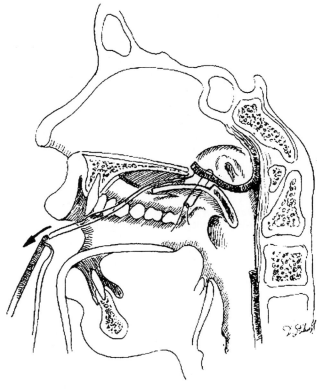

Figure 24-2. Pushback pharyngeal flap elevation and inset. The Robinson catheter, sutured to the tip of the pharyngeal flap, is removed, elevating the flap onto the dorsal surface of the hard palate mucosa, and is sutured in place with a through-and-through suture. (From Jobe R: The pharyngeal flap-pushback procedure. Oper Tech Plast Reconstr Surg 2:245–249, 1995.)

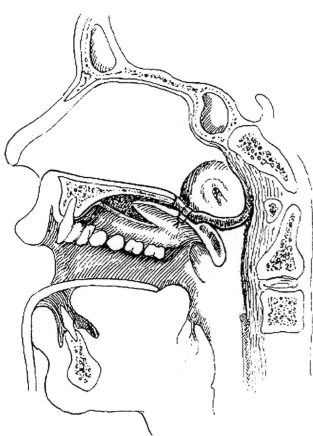

Figure 24-3. Pushback pharyngeal flap elevation and inset. Final result, with pharyngeal flap inset into the pushback defect between the back of the hard palate and front of the soft palate; this achieves effective lengthening of the palate and obturation of the central gap without tethering the soft palate. (From Jobe R: The pharyngeal flap-pushback procedure. Oper Tech Plast Reconstr Surg 2:245–249, 1995.)

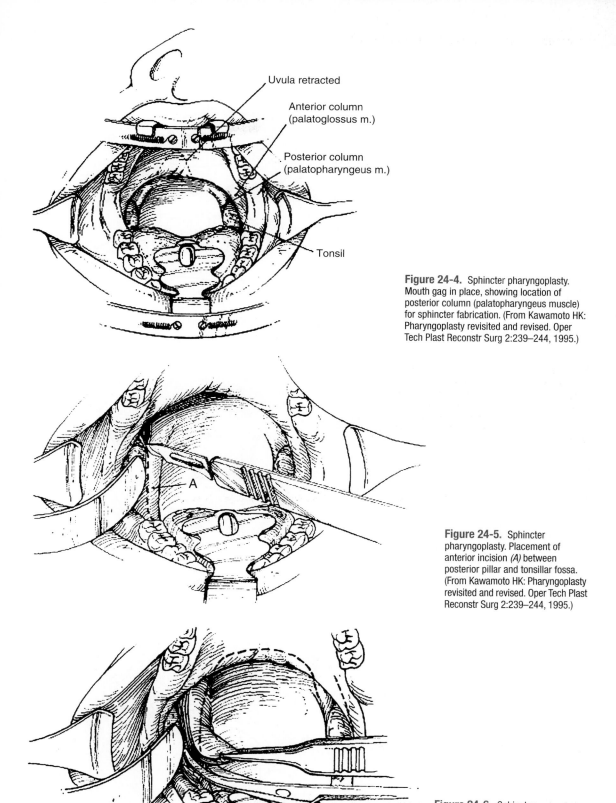

Uvula retracted

Anterior column
(palatoglossus m.)

Posterior column
(palatopharyngeus m.)

Tonsil

Figure 24-4. Sphincter pharyngoplasty. Mouth gag in place, showing location of posterior column (palatopharyngeus muscle) for sphincter fabrication. (From Kawamoto HK: Pharyngoplasty revisited and revised. Oper Tech Plast Reconstr Surg 2:239–244, 1995.)

A

Figure 24-5. Sphincter pharyngoplasty. Placement of anterior incision *(A)* between posterior pillar and tonsillar fossa. (From Kawamoto HK: Pharyngoplasty revisited and revised. Oper Tech Plast Reconstr Surg 2:239–244, 1995.)

Figure 24-6. Sphincter pharyngoplasty. The superiorly based palatopharyngeus flap is separated from the lateral pharyngeal wall using right-angle scissors. (From Kawamoto HK: Pharyngoplasty revisited and revised. Oper Tech Plast Reconstr Surg 2:239–244, 1995.)

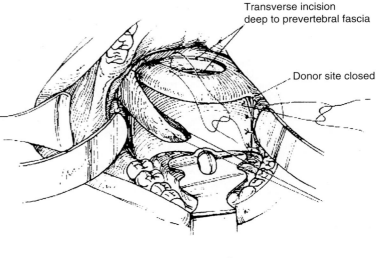

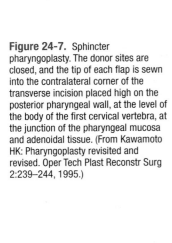

Figure 24-7. Sphincter pharyngoplasty. The donor sites are closed, and the tip of each flap is sewn into the contralateral corner of the transverse incision placed high on the posterior pharyngeal wall, at the level of the body of the first cervical vertebra, at the junction of the pharyngeal mucosa and adenoidal tissue. (From Kawamoto HK: Pharyngoplasty revisited and revised. Oper Tech Plast Reconstr Surg 2:239–244, 1995.)

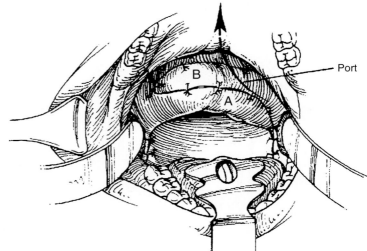

Figure 24-8. Sphincter pharyngoplasty. Intraoral view following completion of flap inset. **A,** Right palatopharyngeus flap. **B,** Left palatopharyngeus flap. *Arrow,* Direction of nasopharyngeal port. (From Kawamoto HK: Pharyngoplasty revisited and revised. Oper Tech Plast Reconstr Surg 2:239–244, 1995.)

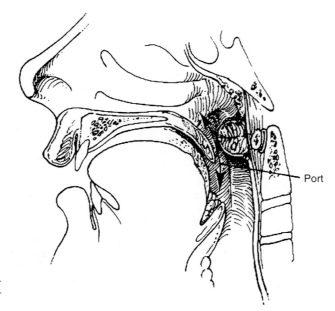

Figure 24-9. Sphincter pharyngoplasty. Cross-sectional view of midline of posterior pharyngeal wall. The palatopharyngeus flaps not only narrow the transverse opening but also result in an effective transverse mound that assists in obturation during speech. (From Kawamoto HK: Pharyngoplasty revisited and revised. Oper Tech Plast Reconstr Surg 2:239–244, 1995.)

4. *Poor velar and lateral pharyngeal wall movement*, resulting in both lateral and anteroposterior insufficiency (i.e., a gap that is both wide and long). These patients may benefit nonsurgically from a speech bulb, a prosthesis designed to elevate the soft palate for obturating the posterior defect, or surgically from a pharyngeal flap pushback procedure, in which a wide superiorly based pharyngeal flap is performed in conjunction with a palatal pushback procedure. The insertion of the soft palate is freed from the posterior palatal bone after the hard palate is taken down, and the pharyngeal flap is inserted superior to the hard palate mucosa, obturating the posterior defect and lengthening the palate.

9. What procedures are available for closure of palatal fistulae?

Palatal fistula closure can be achieved by total elevation of the palatal gingivoperiosteum starting at the dental sulcus, excision of the fistula margins, and watertight closure of the nasal and palatal mucosa by means of the transoral approach. Intrapalatal rotation or transposition flaps further devascularize the already fistula-compromised palate and should be avoided. Local flaps that have been described include tongue flaps as well as the facial artery myomucosal (FAMM) flap, which is useful in larger fistulae. Microvascular soft tissue transfer (radial forearm flap) has been described and in most cases should be reserved for fistulae recalcitrant to prosthetic or other closure techniques.

10. What special considerations must be observed in patients with velocardiofacial syndrome?

Children with velocardiofacial syndrome (VCFS), also known as Shprintzen syndrome, DiGeorge syndrome, or conotruncal anomaly unusual face syndrome, have a defect in chromosome 22q11, which can result in a myriad of findings including cleft palate, submucous cleft palate, velopharyngeal insufficiency, and medially displaced internal carotid arteries (ICAs). Correction of velopharyngeal insufficiency has focused on proper muscle repair in those affected with both cleft soft palate and submucous cleft palate in addition to pharyngeal procedures such as the sphincter pharyngoplasty and pharyngeal flap. Given the possibility of medially displaced ICAs that may be at risk with pharyngoplasty surgeries, some authors have advocated preoperative magnetic resonance angiography (MRA) to assess the course of the ICA. Sommerlad et al. reported 43 consecutive VCFS patients, only one of whom had preoperative MRA, who underwent sphincter pharyngoplasty without complications, and emphasize the importance of palpating the pharyngeal walls once the patient is positioned for surgery.

11. What is the purpose of alveolar cleft bone grafting? When is it performed and what donor site bone is preferred?

The purpose of alveolar cleft bone grafting (ACBG) is to (1) stabilize the maxillary segments, (2) provide bony support for the teeth adjacent to the cleft, (3) give bony support to the cleft alar base, and (4) allow for movement of the cuspid into the lateral incisor position. Because the lateral incisor erupts at approximately 7 years of age and the canine erupts at approximately 11 years of age, bone grafting is ideally performed after eruption of the lateral incisor but before eruption of the canine. In a survey of 240 American Cleft Palate–Craniofacial Association teams, 93% performed secondary ACBG, with 78% performing the ACBG between 6 and 9 years of age, during the transitional dentition stage. Eighty-three percent of centers reported using iliac crest as the preferred cancellous bone donor site, with calvarial bone, rib, and tibial bone listed as alternate donor sites. Should ACBG not be performed prior to the eruption of the canine, it can be performed (1) prior to any planned Le Fort I osteotomies and (2) as a preprosthetic measure in patients who may need osseointegrated implants.

Bibliography

Anderl H: Unilateral cleft lip nose. Plast Reconstr Surg 79:661–662, 1987.

Bajaj AK, Wongworawat AA, Punjabi A: Management of alveolar clefts. J Craniofac Surg 14:840–846, 2003.

Becker DB, Grames LM, Pilgram T, et al: The effect of timing of surgery for velopharyngeal dysfunction on speech. J Craniofac Surg 15:804–809, 2004.

Clark JM, Skoner JM, Wang TD: Repair of the unilateral cleft lip/nose deformity. Facial Plast Surg 19:29–39, 2003.

Cohen SR, Corrigan M, Wilmot J, Trotman CA: Cumulative operative procedures in patients aged 14 years and older with unilateral or bilateral cleft lip and palate. Plast Reconstr Surg 96:267–271, 1995.

Coleman SR: Facial recontouring with lipostructure. Clin Plast Surg 24:347–367, 1997.

David DJ, Anderson PJ, Schnitt DE, et al: From birth to maturity: A group of patients who have completed their protocol management. Part II. Isolated cleft palate. Plast Reconstr Surg 117:515–526, 2006.

David DJ, Bagnall AD: Velopharyngeal incompetence. In McCarthy JG (ed): Plastic Surgery, Vol. 4. Philadelphia, WB Saunders, 1990, pp 2903–2921.

Denny AD, Amm CA: Surgical technique for the correction of postpalatoplasty fistulae of the hard palate. Plast Reconstr Surg 115: 383–387, 2005.

Jobe R: The combined pharyngeal flap and palate pushback procedure: Improvements in technique. Br J Plast Surg 26:384–386, 1973.

Kawamoto HK: Pharyngoplasty revisited and revised. Oper Tech Plast Reconstr Surg 2:239–244, 1995.

LaRossa D, Jackson OH, Kirschner RE, et al: The Children's Hospital of Philadelphia modification of the Furlow double-opposing z-palatoplasty: Long-term speech and growth results. Clin Plast Surg 31:243–249, 2004.

Lo LJ, Kane AA, Chen YR: Simultaneous reconstruction of the secondary bilateral cleft lip and nasal deformity: Abbe flap revisited. Plast Reconstr Surg 112:1219–1227, 2003.

Losken A, Williams JK, Burstein FD, et al: An outcome evaluation of sphincter pharyngoplasty for the management of velopharyngeal insufficiency. Plast Reconstr Surg 112:1755–1761, 2003.

Mackay D, Mazahari M, Graham WP, et al: Incidence of operative procedures on cleft lip and palate patients. Ann Plast Surg 42:445–448, 1999.

Mehendale FV, Birch MJ, Birkett L, et al: Surgical management of velopharyngeal incompetence in velocardiofacial syndrome. Cleft Palate Craniofac J 41:124–135, 2004.

Mehendale FV, Sommerlad BC: Surgical significance of abnormal carotid arteries in velocardiofacial syndrome in 43 consecutive Hynes pharyngoplasties. Cleft Palate Craniofac J 41:368–374, 2004.

Murthy AS, Lehman JA: Evaluation of alveolar cleft bone grafting: A survey of ACPA teams. Cleft Palate Craniofac J 42:99–101, 2005.

Peat BG, Albery EH, Jones K, Pigott RW: Tailoring velopharyngeal surgery: The influence of etiology and type of operation. Plast Reconstr Surg 93:948–953, 1994.

Robinson PJ, Lodge S, Jones BM, Walker CC, Grant HR: The effect of palate repair on otitis media with effusion. Plast Reconstr Surg 89:640–645, 1992.

Schnitt DE, Agir H, David DJ: From birth to maturity: A group of patients who have completed their protocol management. Part I. Unilateral cleft lip and palate. Plast Reconstr Surg 113:805–817, 2004.

Seagle MB, Mazaheri MK, Dixon-Wood VL, Williams WN: Evaluation and treatment of velopharyngeal insufficiency: The University of Florida experience. Ann Plast Surg 48:464–470, 2002.

Shprintzen RJ, Golding-Kushner KJ: Evaluation of velopharyngeal insufficiency. Otolaryngol Clin North Am 22:519–536, 1989.

Stal S, Hollier L: Correction of secondary lip deformities. Plast Reconstr Surg 109:1672–1681, 2002.

Vissarionov VA: Correction of the nasal tip deformity following repair of unilateral clefts of the upper lip. Plast Reconstr Surg 83:341–347, 1989.

Wang TD, Madorsky SJ: Secondary rhinoplasty in nasal deformity associated with the unilateral cleft lip. Arch Facial Plast Surg 1:40–45, 1999.

DENTAL BASICS

Albert Lam, DMD, and
Cynthia L. Koudela, DDS, MSD

CHAPTER 25

1. How are teeth identified?

The most common notation system for permanent teeth is the Universal System. The maxillary teeth are numbered 1 through 16, starting with the upper right third molar (no. 1) and proceeding to the upper left third molar (no. 16). The mandibular teeth are numbered 17 through 32, starting with the lower left third molar (no. 17) and preceding to the lower right third molar (no. 32). Thus, the maxillary left central incisor is no. 9.

Right $\dfrac{1 \quad 2 \quad 3 \quad 4 \quad 5 \quad 6 \quad 7 \quad 8 \ | \ 9 \ 10 \ 11 \ 12 \ 13 \ 14 \ 15 \ 16}{32 \ 31 \ 30 \ 29 \ 28 \ 27 \ 26 \ 25 \ | \ 24 \ 23 \ 22 \ 21 \ 20 \ 19 \ 18 \ 17}$ Left

The 20 deciduous or primary teeth are noted in the same manner, using letters A through T. The upper right second primary molar is A, and, proceeding around the arches, the lower right second primary molar is T.

Right $\dfrac{A \ B \ C \ D \ E \ | \ F \ G \ H \ I \ J}{T \ S \ R \ Q \ P \ | \ O \ N \ M \ L \ K}$ Left

The Palmer Notation System, used mostly by American orthodontists, numbers the teeth 1 to 8 in each quadrant, starting with the central incisor (no. 1) and proceeding to the third molar (no. 8). Each quadrant is indicated by a specific bracket around the number (⌋, ⌊, ⌐, ⌐). Thus, the maxillary left central incisor is ⌊1.

Right $\dfrac{8 \ 7 \ 6 \ 5 \ 4 \ 3 \ 2 \ 1 \ | \ 1 \ 2 \ 3 \ 4 \ 5 \ 6 \ 7 \ 8}{8 \ 7 \ 6 \ 5 \ 4 \ 3 \ 2 \ 1 \ | \ 1 \ 2 \ 3 \ 4 \ 5 \ 6 \ 7 \ 8}$ Left

A two-digit system introduced in 1970 by the Federation Dentaire Internationale (FDI) has been adopted by the International Standards Organization (ISO). The ISO/FDI system identifies each of the 32 permanent teeth with a two-digit number. The first digit identifies the quadrant (1 to 4), and the second digit identifies the tooth type (1 to 8). Thus, the maxillary left central incisor is 21 (pronounced "two-one").

Right $\dfrac{18 \ 17 \ 16 \ 15 \ 14 \ 13 \ 12 \ 11 \ | \ 21 \ 22 \ 23 \ 24 \ 25 \ 26 \ 27 \ 28}{48 \ 47 \ 46 \ 45 \ 44 \ 43 \ 42 \ 41 \ | \ 31 \ 32 \ 33 \ 34 \ 35 \ 36 \ 37 \ 38}$ Left

The 20 deciduous or primary teeth are represented in similar fashion: quadrant (5 to 8) and tooth type (1 to 5). Thus, the primary maxillary left central incisor is 61 (pronounced "six-one").

Right $\dfrac{55 \ 54 \ 53 \ 52 \ 51 \ | \ 61 \ 62 \ 63 \ 64 \ 65}{85 \ 84 \ 83 \ 82 \ 81 \ | \ 71 \ 72 \ 73 \ 74 \ 75}$ Left

2. How are the surfaces of the teeth described?

The surfaces of the teeth that face the central incisors (toward the midline) are the *mesial* surfaces. Those that face away from the midline (toward the mandibular condyles) are the *distal* surfaces. The *labial* and *buccal* surfaces of teeth indicate areas that face either the lip or the cheek, respectively. The palatal and lingual surfaces of teeth indicate areas that face either the palate or the tongue, respectively. The functioning surfaces of the molar and premolar crowns are called the *occlusal* surfaces and for the canines and incisors are called the *incisal* edges.

3. What is the Angle classification?

The Angle classification of malocclusion, developed in 1890 by Edward Angle, is based on the position of the upper first molar. In class I occlusion, the mesiobuccal cusp of the maxillary first molar occludes in the mesiobuccal groove of the mandibular first molar, producing a normal anteroposterior relationship. In class II malocclusion, the lower first molar is distal to the ideal class I position, usually a half to one full cusp distance. Angle divided class II malocclusion into two divisions. In class II, division 1, the upper anterior teeth are flared forward. In class II, division 2, the anterior teeth of both the maxilla and mandible are retruded with a deep overbite. In class III malocclusion, the lower first molar is mesial to the ideal class I position, usually a half to one full cusp distance. The lower incisors may be edge to edge or labial to the upper incisors, producing an anterior crossbite or underbite. Angle's classification of malocclusion provides a description only of the anteroposterior tooth relationship (Fig. 25-1).

4. Describe the anatomy of a tooth

A tooth consists of a *crown,* the portion one sees in the oral cavity, and a *root,* which is attached to the bony walls of the alveolar socket by periodontal membrane fibers. The crown is covered by enamel, and the root is covered by cementum. Their junction is called the *cervical line.* Beneath the enamel and cementum is the dentin, which makes up the bulk of the tooth. In the center of the crown is the pulp chamber, which continues as the pulp canal in the root. The pulp tissue furnishes the nerve and blood supply to the tooth through the apical foramen (Fig. 25-2).

5. What are the names of the teeth?

The 32 permanent teeth are divided into four quadrants. Starting at the midline, each quadrant has a central incisor, lateral incisor, canine (cuspid), first premolar (bicuspid), second premolar (bicuspid), and first molar, second molar, and third molar. The 20 deciduous or primary teeth are divided into four quadrants. Starting at the midline, each quadrant has a central incisor, lateral incisor, canine, first molar, and second molar (Fig. 25-3).

6. What is the nerve supply to the teeth?

The only nerve supply to the mandibular teeth is the inferior alveolar branch of the mandibular division of the trigeminal nerve. The maxillary teeth are supplied by the maxillary division of the trigeminal nerve, which divides into the posterior superior alveolar branch from the pterygopalatine portion and the middle and anterior superior alveolar branches from the infraorbital nerve. The three superior alveolar branches form a plexus that directly supplies the maxillary teeth.

7. What are natal and neonatal teeth?

Natal teeth are found in the oral cavity at birth. Neonatal teeth erupt during the first month of life. They are most common in the mandibular anterior region and usually are shells of enamel without roots. Neonatal teeth are commonly seen in cleft palates, often in eruption cysts.

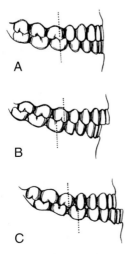

Figure 25-1. Angle classification of occlusion. **A,** Class I, normal occlusion. **B,** Class II, malocclusion. **C,** Class III, malocclusion. (From Manson P: Facial fractures. In Aston SJ, Beasley RW, Thorne CHM [eds]: Grabb and Smith's Plastic Surgery, 5th ed. Lippincott-Raven, Philadelphia, 1997, p 386, with permission.)

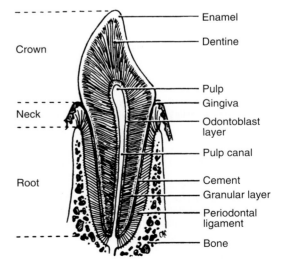

Figure 25-2. Anatomy of a normal tooth. (From Manson P: Facial fractures. In Aston SJ, Beasley RW, Thorne CHM [eds]: Grabb and Smith's Plastic Surgery, 5th ed. Lippincott-Raven, Philadelphia, 1997, p 387, with permission.)

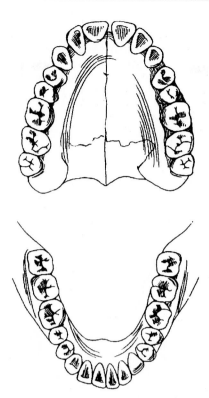

Figure 25-3. Normal adult dental arches contain 32 teeth, 16 in each arch. There are 3 molars, 2 bicuspids, 1 cuspid, and 2 incisors on each half of both maxillary and mandibular dental arches. (From Manson P: Facial fractures. In Aston SJ, Beasley RW, Thorne CHM [eds]: Grabb and Smith's Plastic Surgery, 5th ed. Lippincott-Raven, Philadelphia, 1997, p 386, with permission.)

8. What is a supernumerary tooth?

A supernumerary tooth is an extra tooth in excess of normal dentition. It is more common in permanent dentition, occurs more often in males, and may or may not erupt. They are most frequently found in the maxilla. A supernumerary tooth located between the maxillary central incisors is called a *mesiodens.* Syndromes associated with supernumerary teeth (hyperdontia) are Apert, cleidocranial dysplasia, Crouzon, Curtius, Down, Ehlers-Danlos, Gardner, and Sturge-Weber.

9. What is the most common congenitally missing tooth, and what are the syndromes associated with developmentally missing teeth?

The most common missing tooth is the third molar, followed by the mandibular second premolar, maxillary lateral incisor, and maxillary second premolar. Agenesis of numerous teeth (oligodontia) or failure of all of the teeth to develop (anodontia) is often associated with ectodermal dysplasia and oral-facial-digital syndrome. Syndromes associated with developmental absent teeth (hypodontia) are Crouzon, Down, ectodermal dysplasia, cleft lip, cleft palate, Ehlers-Danlos, Goldenhar, Gorlin, Hurler, Sturge-Weber, and Turner.

10. What is the difference between overbite, overjet, and anterior openbite?

Overbite is the amount of vertical overlap measured between the upper and lower incisal edges when the teeth are in occlusion. *Overjet* is the horizontal overlap measured from the labial surface of the lower incisor to the labial surface of the upper incisor, parallel to the occlusal plane, when the teeth are in occlusion (Fig. 25-4). *Anterior openbite* is a negative overbite in which the upper and lower incisors do not overlap.

11. What is a posterior dental crossbite?

A posterior crossbite is an abnormality in the buccolingual relationships of the teeth. In neutral occlusion, the buccal cusps of the upper teeth overlap those of the lower teeth. A *buccal crossbite* results from tilting of the maxillary teeth toward the cheek. A *lingual crossbite* results from lingual displacement (toward the tongue) of the upper teeth in relation to the lower teeth. The buccal cusps of the upper teeth no longer overlap those of the lower teeth (Fig. 25-5).

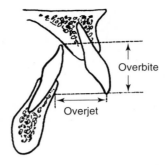

Figure 25-4. Relationship of the incisal edges. Overbite is the vertical overlap and overjet is the horizontal overlap of the incisal edges. (From McCarthy JB, Kawamoto HK, Grayson BH, et al: Surgery of the jaws. In McCarthy JG [ed]: Plastic Surgery. Philadelphia, WB Saunders, 1990, p 1194, with permission.)

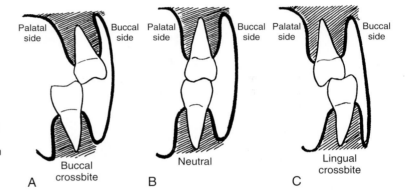

Figure 25-5. Buccolingual relationship of the teeth. **A,** Buccal crossbite. **B,** Neutral (centric) occlusion. **C,** Lingual crossbite. (From McCarthy JB, Kawamoto HK, Grayson BH, et al: Surgery of the jaws. In McCarthy JG [ed]: Plastic Surgery. Philadelphia, WB Saunders, 1990, p 1194, with permission.)

12. What is an anterior dental crossbite?

In an anterior dental crossbite, the maxillary anterior teeth are behind the mandibular anterior teeth when the teeth are in occlusion. This may be caused by a class III malocclusion or by missing teeth on the maxillary arch.

13. What is the occlusal plane?

When teeth erupt to meet each other, they form the occlusal plane. The anteroposterior curve of the occlusal plane is called the *curve of Spee*. An occlusal curve also exists in the transverse plane, called the *curve of Wilson*. The teeth are not positioned straight up and down in the mouth but align along a spherical, three-dimensional curve.

14. What is the difference between centric relation and centric occlusion?

Centric relation is a position determined by maximal contraction of the muscles of the jaw. It is considered a stable, reproducible position that relates bone to bone through the temporomandibular joint. It does not depend on interdigitation of the teeth. *Centric occlusion* is a position determined by the way the teeth fit best together with the greatest amount of interdigitation. It is related to tooth occlusion and not muscle or bone. Wear facets or abraded surfaces of teeth are a function of centric occlusion.

15. Describe the most common injuries involving the teeth

Concussion: Injury to the tooth that may result in hemorrhage and edema of the ligament surrounding the root of the tooth, but the tooth remains firm in its socket. Dentist will treat by occlusal adjustment of the tooth with recommendation of soft diet.

Subluxation: Loosening of the involved tooth without displacement. Dentist will treat by occlusal adjustment of the tooth with recommendation of soft diet.

Intrusion: Tooth is displaced apically into the alveolar process. If root formation is incomplete, treat by allowing the tooth to reerupt over several months. If root formation is complete, then the tooth should be repositioned orthodontically. Tooth must be closely monitored by dentist because pulpal necrosis is frequent.

Extrusion: Tooth is partially displaced out of the socket. Treat by manually repositioning tooth into socket, and dentist should splint in position for 2 to 3 weeks. A dental radiographic examination should be performed after 2 to 3 weeks.

Lateral Luxation: Tooth is displaced horizontally with fracture of the alveolar bone. Treat by gentle repositioning of tooth into socket followed by dental splinting for 3 weeks. A dental radiographic examination should be performed after 2 to 3 weeks.

Avulsion: Total displacement of the tooth out of the socket. Ideal treatment is immediate reimplantation. The tooth should not be handled by the root. Rinse the tooth in saline and flush the socket with saline. Replant the tooth, and splint in place with semirigid splint for 1 week. Place the patient on antibiotic therapy (e.g., penicillin VK, 1 g loading dose followed by 500 mg four times per day for 4 days). Alternative is to place in mouth under tongue, place in milk, or place in saline and have a dentist reimplant tooth within 30 minutes. Follow-up dental radiographic examination should be performed at 3 and 6 weeks, and at 3 and 6 months.

16. When do the primary teeth erupt?

The primary teeth begin to erupt at approximately age 6 months in the following order:

- Central incisors, 6 to 7 months
- Lateral incisors, 7 to 9 months
- First primary molars, 12 to 14 months
- Canines, 16 to 18 months
- Second primary molars, 20 to 24 months

Approximately four teeth erupt every 4 months in the primary dentition. The eruption sequences of the maxillary and mandibular teeth are approximately the same.

17. When do the permanent teeth erupt?

The mandibular permanent teeth tend to erupt before the maxillary permanent teeth. The first permanent tooth to erupt is the first molar at approximately age 6 years. It erupts distal to the primary second molar. The remaining permanent teeth erupt in the following order:

- Mandibular central incisors, 6 years
- Mandibular lateral incisors, 7 years
- Maxillary central incisors, 7 years
- Maxillary lateral incisors, 8 years
- First premolars, 10 years
- Mandibular canines, 10 years
- Second premolars, 11 years
- Maxillary canines, 11 years
- Second molars, 12 years
- Third molars, 17 years

The permanent incisors, canines, and premolars are called *succedaneous teeth* because they replace (succeed) the primary teeth.

18. What is a mamelon?

A mamelon is a rounded protuberance found on the incisal edges of newly erupted incisor teeth. Each tooth has three mamelons. They are soon worn down through normal attrition. Mamelons will remain if the teeth are malaligned and there is no opposing incisal contact, as in an openbite.

19. Describe the embryology of teeth

As early as 28 days in utero, odontogenic epithelium is recognized on the mandibular and maxillary processes. This tissue proliferates and forms the dental laminae from which tooth buds develop. Each tooth goes through a series of stages as cells differentiate and proliferate. Odontoblasts give rise to dentin, a process called *dentinogenesis,* and ameloblasts form enamel, a process called *amelogenesis.* As enamel and dentin are deposited, the crown is formed from the cusp tips to the cervical region. After enamel formation is nearly completed, root development begins.

Knowledge of tooth embryology is helpful in understanding oral pathology. Ameloblastoma, for example, is an aggressive odontogenic tumor that is thought to form from ameloblasts that do not differentiate to the stage of enamel formation.

20. What is the process of dental decay?

The earliest clinically recognizable stage of dental decay is a white-spot lesion, which results from oral bacteria (mainly *Streptococcus mutans*) that proliferate in the presence of fermentable carbohydrates and form acids that cause tooth demineralization. At this point the surface of enamel is still intact, and the lesion is reversible. Once the decay process goes through the enamel and reaches the dentin, it spreads laterally and quickly inflames the pulp tissue. Pulp tissue is not capable of healing. Severe pain usually is present by this time, and a periapical abscess may form in the surrounding bone. Dental decay may be difficult to see clinically. Dental radiographs show a decayed area of a tooth as more radiolucent than the unaffected area.

21. What are the muscles of mastication?

The masticatory muscles concerned with mandibular movement include the masseter, medial pterygoid, lateral pterygoid, and temporalis muscles. These muscles are paired.

22. How do the muscles of mastication move the mandible?

The lateral pterygoid is divided into two heads. The superior head is active during jaw-closing movement; the inferior head is active during jaw-opening and protrusion movement. The masseter muscle is the most powerful muscle of mastication; it elevates the mandible and assists in protrusion. The medial pterygoid muscle, like the masseter, elevates the mandible and is active during protrusion. It also helps in lateral positioning of the jaw. The temporalis muscle is divided into two parts. It is the principal positioner of the mandible during closing. The posterior part retrudes the mandible; the anterior part is active in clenching.

23. What are the average measurements of mandibular movement in an adult?

The maximal mandibular opening is 50 to 60 mm as measured from the incisal edges of the anterior teeth. A person should be able to open the equivalent width of three fingers. The maximal lateral movement is 10 to 12 mm, approximately the width of the maxillary central incisor. The maximal protrusive range is 8 to 11 mm. The retrusive range is 1 to 3 mm. Retrusive movement is the discrepancy between centric occlusion and centric relation. Age, size, and skeletal morphology of the individual must be taken into consideration in evaluating these measurements.

24. What is a dental implant?

A dental implant is an artificial tooth root replacement. There are several types, but the most widely used is the osseointegrated implant based on the premise that a titanium implant can be successfully integrated into bone when osteoblasts attach to the surface of the titanium. This integration can take between 3 and 6 months. A porcelain or ceramic crown can then be attached to the implant as a single tooth replacement. A variation on the implant procedure is the implant-supported bridge or implant-supported denture to replace more than one missing tooth. The success rate of an osseointegrated implant prosthesis is greater than 90%.

25. What is Invisalign?

Invisalign is an orthodontic appliance system that straightens teeth without using traditional metal braces. Instead, Invisalign uses a series of clear, removable custom-made aligners that gradually and sequentially move teeth to their desired positions. The main advantage to the treatment is esthetic; the aligners are transparent. In addition, the aligners are relatively comfortable to wear and do not interfere with speech. However, there are limitations to its use, as more complex orthodontic cases are better and more efficiently treated with conventional braces.

26. What is periodontitis?

Periodontitis is an infection of the tissues supporting the teeth that results in loss of bone around the teeth. It is diagnosed by dental radiographs and clinical examination. Depending on the specific type and severity, periodontitis can be treated by deep dental cleanings, surgical intervention, and/or antibiotics.

27. What drugs may cause gingival hyperplasia (overgrowth of gingival tissue)?

Phenytoin, cyclosporine, and nifedipine may cause hyperplasia of gingival tissue.

28. What is endodontics?

Endodontics is a specialty of dentistry that deals with the tooth pulp and tissues surrounding the root of a tooth. When the pulp becomes inflamed and is unable to repair itself, endodontic treatment is required, which in most cases is a procedure called *root canal therapy*. Root canal therapy involves the removal of the irreversibly inflamed or necrotic pulp tissue. After the pulp is removed, the canals are cleaned, shaped, filled, and sealed. Most teeth that have had a root canal will need to be restored with a crown.

BIBLIOGRAPHY

Andreasen JO, Andreasen FM: Essentials of Traumatic Injuries to the Teeth. Copenhagen, Munksgaard, 1990.
Ash MM: Wheeler's Dental Anatomy, Physiology and Occlusion, 7th ed. Philadelphia, WB Saunders, 1993.
Avery JK (ed): Oral Development and Histology. Baltimore, Williams & Wilkins, 1987.
Mathes SJ (ed): Plastic Surgery, 2nd ed. Philadelphia, WB Saunders, 2006.
Neville BW, Damm DD, Allen CM, Bouquot JE: Oral and maxillofacial pathology, 2nd ed. Philadelphia, WB Saunders, 2002.
Peck S, Peck L: Tooth numbering progress. Angle Orthod 66:83–84, 1996.
Ranly DM: A Synopsis of Craniofacial Growth, 2nd ed. Norwalk, CT, Appleton & Lange, 1988.
Thaller SR, Montgomery WW (eds): Guide to Dental Problems for Physicians and Surgeons. Baltimore, Williams & Wilkins, 1988.

ORTHODONTICS FOR ORAL CLEFT CRANIOFACIAL DISORDERS

CHAPTER 26

John L. Spolyar, DDS, MS

PASSIVE PROSTHETICS (NEONATAL PERIOD)

1. What is a passive infant oral prosthesis?

An infant oral prosthesis is a passive device much like a denture without teeth that covers and follows the anatomic outline of the hard palate and its defect. To maintain position and to resist displacement, the margins of the prosthesis usually extend over the lateral alveolar segments and may extend into and over the lateral surfaces of the nasal cavity and vomer. The prosthesis is routinely made from polymerized methylmethacrylate (acrylic) (Fig. 26-1).

2. What does the prosthesis do?

A palatal prosthesis divides the oral and nasal cavities into functional spaces while providing a tactile reference for the tongue. Function is then segregated with the nose for airway and the oral cavity for feeding and proper tongue posturing. This segregation aids feeding and breathing and facilitates proper physiologic resting posture for the tongue with tip forward.

3. Does a prosthesis affect growth?

After surgical lip repair in cases of complete unilateral cleft lip/palate (UCLP) and bilateral cleft lip/palate (BCLP), medial displacement of the cleft segments is inevitable. A passive prosthesis, especially with proper nasal extension, prevents medial relocation of the cleft segments and provides normalized maxillary displacement growth in width achievement. Preventing medial collapse and promoting maxillary transverse growth have positive effects and serve to optimize oral volume, nasal respiration, dentoalveolar segment alignment, facial development, and overall anatomic balance. Perhaps the best potential growth and facial skeletal development are achieved by integrating passive prosthesis stabilization with rehabilitation protocols.

4. When is the prosthesis worn?

A prosthesis is best used as early as possible in the neonate's life—perhaps before the initial repair to facilitate feeding. If provided in coordination with the initial repair, a prosthesis is best left in place for 1 to 2 weeks before daily removal for cleaning. The appliance is best used on a full-time basis until a few weeks before palatoplasty, when it is used only during feeding. Appliance cleaning more frequent than daily may be indicated during upper respiratory tract infections that obstruct the nasal port because of mucus drainage.

5. How long does it take before a prosthesis is outgrown?

Facial growth occurs most in the vertical plane and least in the transverse plane. The prosthesis must be adjusted approximately every 6 weeks to reduce retentive undercuts and to broaden alveolar contacts. Generally, once the weight of the infant doubles, effective appliance retention is lost, and the appliance is no longer useful.

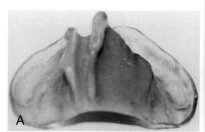
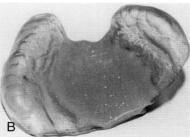

Figure 26-1. Passive infant oral prosthesis. **A,** Prosthesis on anatomic side shows nasal extension for retention. **B,** Oral side of prosthesis.

6. Does extension of the prosthesis over the alveolar structures restrict normal development of the lateral dental segments?

The "pressure" of alveolar remodeling growth easily exceeds the passive resistance of the appliance. With appliance adjustments over the alveolar extensions, normal development should proceed without restriction.

PRESURGICAL ORTHOPEDIC CORRECTION (NEONATAL PERIOD)

7. What is presurgical orthopedic correction?

Presurgical orthopedic correction (POC) is a procedure used to correct an anatomically abnormal bony relationship before any primary reconstructive surgery is performed.

8. How does POC apply to oral cleft patients?

In neonates with complete BCLP and UCLP, cleft maxillary components are distorted and abnormally positioned. The overlying soft tissue mirrors the skeletal deformity and gives the recognizable pattern of deformity in UCLP and BCLP. The objectives of POC are to reposition displaced basal segments and to realign soft tissue margins of like kind before corrective surgery is performed.

9. What problems attend oral cleft treatment without POC?

- Lip closure alone does not reposition the maxilla and premaxilla in BCLP or pull the cleft maxillary segment forward in UCLP well enough for closure of the cleft.
- Lip repair alone does not reposition the maxilla forward in BCLP to provide a full midface or pull the cleft maxillary segment forward in UCLP to balance the malar and alar bases or reduce the stigmatizing "crooked face."
- A protruded premaxilla at the base of the columella makes columellar lengthening and nasal tip correction impossible until the patient reaches adolescence.
- Persistent fistulas and residual clefts in the alveolus require the difficult surgery of bone grafting when the patient is between 6 and 8 years old.

10. What are the benefits of POC?

- A better platform is produced for the lip and nose as well as for the alveolus.
- Primary surgical closure can be performed without tension.
- A more precise method controls the cleft components without dependence on simple closure of the lip over the deformity to mold the distorted parts.
- Dissection of mucoperiosteum at the edge of the cleft facilitates a two-layer closure without tension.
- Alveolar integrity is established to facilitate dental development.
- Closure of the hard and soft palate is facilitated.
- An intact primary palate is achieved at an early age.
- Gingivoperiosteoplasty can be done with or without primary bone grafting.
- A normal maxillary arch without fistulas is achieved with early secondary palate closure. Early "fork-flap" columellar surgery is possible in BCLP and may produce a good nose and lip.
- An intact oral cavity without fistulation is routinely established well within the first year of life with a clearly improved possibility for intelligible speech to follow.

11. What are the various techniques used in POC?

The techniques are best grouped by type of device retention as either passive or fixed (pinned).

12. What techniques use passive retention?

In the 1950s, McNeil and Burston used a passive oral prosthesis and external facial or head straps to effect segment repositioning and remodeling. Also, Nordin uses a T-shaped traction device applied to the nostril on the normal side in UCLP cases. The design tactic is to use extraoral transverse traction to correct the midfacial asymmetry and to minimize the posterior retraction forces on the developing maxilla.

Another technique reported by Figueroa for BCLP used a passive oropalatal prosthesis as an anchor, and a latex rubber retraction strip looped over the prolabium to reposition the maxilla and premaxilla.

13. How effective are passive techniques?

The results are variable in regard to achieving treatment objectives. All of these early techniques share the following disadvantages:

- Inconsistency and difficulty with patient compliance
- Incomplete control of directional mechanics best directed at the orthopedic deformity

- Unpredictable and partial achievement of treatment objectives
- Extended treatment time
- Labor intensive
- More expensive than non-POC treatment protocols

The techniques have the following advantages:

- Less invasive than pinning techniques, which require general anesthesia for placement
- Less expensive than pinning techniques

14. What techniques use pinned retention?
- In 1957, Hagerty first reported the use of pins to retain an expandable stainless steel bar in cleft palate treatment.
- In 1965, Hagerty et al. reported the use of an expandable acrylic palatal prosthesis with intraosseous pinning for anchorage.
- Contemporary techniques were reported during the 1970s and 1980s by Georgiade and Latham. BCLP was treated with a coaxial mechanism that expanded the maxillary base and repositioned the premaxilla at the same time. Latham et al. reported on the design and use of this extraorally activated expansion device that applied elastic traction to the premaxilla.
- In 1980, Latham reported the treatment of UCLP with a device for orthopedic advancement of the cleft maxillary segment. It was much like the maxillary base device used today.

15. How effective are pinned techniques?
Results are highly consistent in achieving treatment objectives with the attending benefits and advantages described above. The disadvantages include the following:

- Device placement requires a hospital operating room (OR).
- Pinned techniques are more expensive than passive retention POC.

16. How is POC used in UCLP and BCLP treatment?
- Soon after birth an impression is obtained, and the maxillary POC device is fabricated on a stone model.
- OR placement of the device is coordinated with myringotomy and pressure-equalizing tube procedures.
- The maxillary base device is retained by four channel-locking pins, two on each side, which pass through the acrylic base material into the palate for intraosseous fixation.
- For cases of BCLP, a staple is placed through the bony septal structure of the premaxilla to connect respositioning chains.

17. How does the UCLP device produce orthopedic correction?
- Once the device is in place, a drive screw is activated a half turn (0.25-mm displacement), and activation is continued once or twice a day by the parent at home (Fig. 26-2).
- The patient is observed on a regular basis. Activation continues until, by design, no further turning of the screw is possible. The segments should be well aligned with 1 to 3 mm of space (defect) between the nearly abutting segments.

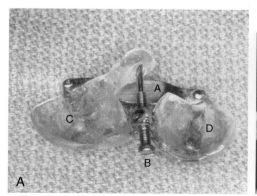
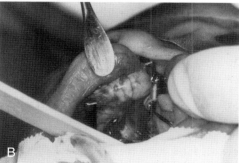

Figure 26-2. Unilateral cleft lip/palate presurgical orthopedic correction device. **A,** Viewed from its anatomic side. A coplanar double hinge *(A)* allows rotation and translation of the greater segment (GS) and lesser segment (LS) to one another. Turning screw *(B)* against GS *(C)* pulls LS *(D)* forward. The principal action is LS advancement with outward rotation and GS advancement with inward rotation. **B,** With device in place, the drive screw lies adjacent to the cleft segment and is easily accessed at the front of the cleft defect.

18. How long does it take before a patient with UCLP is ready for reconstructive surgery?
- Screw activation takes from 3 to 6 weeks to complete, depending on the size of the cleft, rate of activation, and amount of correction designed into the device (up to 14 mm).
- A resting period of 2 to 3 weeks allows dissipation of any residual load (strain) that builds up after applying the active force (stress).
- If the device is applied by age 4 weeks, the first reconstructive surgery can be done at age 3 months.

19. How does the BCLP device produce orthopedic correction?
- Once the device is in place, as the case demands, an expansion screw can be activated one-quarter turn (0.25-mm expansion at the anterior cleft segment) at a time. As instructed, activation once or twice a day by the parent at home or, perhaps better, one full revolution by the physician during weekly follow-up well achieves proper lateral segment placement (Fig. 26-3).
- The elastic chain tension is checked for possible adjustment on a weekly basis. The pressure should not exceed 2 ounces per side. Excessive force causes undue septal staple translation without orthopedic effect and possible failure.
- The patient is observed on a regular basis until the case is fully corrected with proper maxilla–premaxilla segment alignment and 0 to 2 mm of space at each cleft defect.

20. How long does it take before a patient with BCLP is ready for reconstructive surgery?
- Elastic chain repositioning takes from 4 to 7 weeks to complete, depending on amount of premaxillary protrusion, size of premaxilla, age of patient, and rate of activation.
- A resting period of 2 to 3 weeks allows dissipation of any residual load to reduce rebound.
- If the device is applied by age 4 weeks, the first reconstructive surgery can be done at age 3 to 4 months.

21. What are the significant treatment effects in BCLP?
The single most important response is forward maxillary repositioning to achieve premaxillary–maxillary alignment. The premaxilla shows less orthopedic adjustment and the vomer the least. This response is apparently age dependent.

22. What is the incidence of postalveolar cleft palate fistulation in patients treated with and without POC?
Cleft palate fistulation (CPF) is reported in 20% to 25% of patients treated without POC. The incidence may be as high as 50% in one-stage neonatal protocols. CPF was reported to be less than 8% in UCLP and BCLP treated with POC.

23. Do pinned POC devices stimulate maxillary growth?
Yes, in BCLP treatment. Maxillary forward translation in BCLP is about twice normal during the active phase of treatment.

24. Does pinned POC treatment adversely affect maxillary growth?
No.

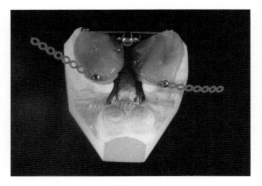

Figure 26-3. Bilateral cleft lip/palate pinned presurgical orthopedic correction base device can be expanded, enabling lateral segment placement to fit the premaxilla. The expansion screw at the drive box is activated from the front of the mouth. The device also acts as a base appliance for maxillary protraction in response to the coupling force for premaxillary retraction. Bilateral elastic chains attached to the premaxilla pass around a roller (not shown) under the drive box and then proceed forward and laterally to hook onto buttons for tensioning at the head of each segment.

ORTHODONTIC MANAGEMENT

PRIMARY DENTITION (AGE 3 TO 6 YEARS)

25. What is the primary dentition?

The first teeth to erupt, also known as *milk teeth* and *baby teeth*. Because the primary dentition is completely replaced by the adult dentition, *deciduous dentition* is a proper designation. Most children complete their primary dentition by the age of 2.5 to 3.0 years.

26. Why is orthodontic treatment important at this age?

Treatment positively influences postural and vegetative functions, occlusal function, facial growth, speech, eustachian tube and middle ear effusion, and reconstructive efforts.

27. What is achieved with orthodontic treatment?

Early treatment offers an opportunity for greater ease and efficacy of orthopedic procedures to increase space and optimize conditions for eruption and root formation; to attain proper occlusion; to increase oronasal volume; and to change the maxillary facial platform.

28. What physical signs are most important?

- Severe dental crossbites, both bilateral and anterior occlusal
- Very narrow maxillary dental arch
- Anterior (incisal) openbite
- Shallow or narrow palate
- Shifting of the bite, usually to one side, causing functional or postural mandibular asymmetry (functional shifts)
- Other important related problems are encumbered speech, oral respiration with noisy sleeping pattern, bad oral habits (thumb [digit] sucking, tongue thrusting, bruxism, severe attrition), and recurrent otitis media.

29. What procedures are undertaken at this age?

Principally, orthopedic with transverse maxillary distraction (expansion) and anterior respositioning (protraction).

30. What kinds of devices are used for maxillary expansion?

Expansion devices are either removable or fixed. *Removable* devices use a slow continuous expansion rate of 2 mm/month until completed. *Fixed* devices, either attached by stainless steel bands or directly bonded to posterior segment teeth, may use rapid continuous expansion at a rate of 0.5 mm/day or less to completion of expansion (Fig. 26-4).

31. How long of a rest period is needed after expansion?

A bonded fixed device is used with expansion over a 2-week period in a regimen of 4 to 5 mm segments followed by a 4- to 6-week period of rest. This sequence is repeated until expansion is completed. Accumulation of residual load during rapid expansion is dissipated during the rest periods. Research has shown that residual load accumulating during rapid palatal expansion completely dissipates in 5 to 7 weeks, depending on patient age. Many orthodontists prefer a 3-month rest period after rapid palatal expansion. Such long periods of rest are unnecessary after slow expansion.

32. How much expansion is necessary?

The amount of appliance expansion varies from as little as 7 mm to as much as 20 mm with use of two devices. In certain cases expansion beyond that necessary for occlusal balance may be desirable to increase nasal airway volume.

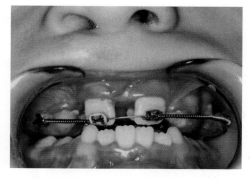

Figure 26-4. Intraoral view of rapid palatal expansion device directly bonded to the dentition with simultaneous orthodontic treatment for incisor alignment and decompensation for anterior crossbite correction. Note the separation of central incisors, a rare event in complete oral cleft patients, well after alveolar bone graft.

33. When was maxillary expansion first used?

No one knows, but it was first reported in the literature in 1859 for the correction of constricted maxillary dental arches over a period of 2 weeks.

34. What other use do expansion devices have?

A fixed expansion device or retained removable device is a handle to the maxilla. This handle of opportunity is realized in maxillary protraction for correction of maxillary midfacial deficiency and anterior dental crossbite (Fig. 26-5).

35. During primary dentition, when is the best time for maxillary protraction?

The best time is determined by the eruption of the permanent central incisors, which secure the repositioned maxilla with a proper bite. This translates to a dental age of at least 5 years to begin protraction treatment, which continues for 12 months. In general, the best time is before age 7 years.

MIXED DENTITION (AGE 7 TO 11 YEARS)

36. What is mixed dentition?

The period when both primary and permanent teeth are present in the mouth. It is referred to as the "ugly duckling stage" and represents a period of marvelous complexity in dental arrangements and numbers. At inception (before incisors erupt) there is a total of 48 teeth; this number is reduced to 28 over a period of approximately 5 years.

37. What are the succedaneous or successional teeth?

The incisors, cuspids, and bicuspids occupy a place in the arch once held by a primary tooth.

38. What are the accessional teeth?

All teeth that erupt posterior to the primary teeth (e.g., first, second, third molars).

39. What is achieved by orthodontic treatment of mixed dentition?

During this period there is, perhaps, one last opportunity for segment alignment of the maxillary components, dental alignment, and space definition at sites of agenic teeth (almost always lateral incisors). In a nutshell, it is a most important opportunity to define maxillary dental arch perimeter.

40. What treatment procedures are used?

- Maxillary expansion and protraction
- Preparatory extractions
- Orthodontic treatment
- Tooth straightening

Preparatory extractions often include supernumerary teeth (teeth not present in a normal dentition and, in oral cleft patients, associated with cleft margins by the alveolar defect). Supernumerary teeth are commonly ectopic. If multiple, the additional supernumerary teeth usually are unerupted (impacted) and elevated within the anterior maxillary cleft segment. Orthodontic treatment is used to remove incisor irregularities, to create space for the agenic lateral incisor(s) and prospective graft sites, and to define buccal segment dental arch length. The decision to extract permanent teeth to reduce excessive dental crowding is often made during this period.

41. Why is this period critical for the alveolar bone graft?

With the canine root 25% to 50% formed, success rates for grafting are high during this age range.

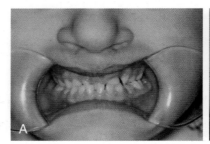 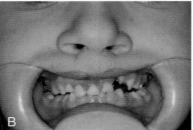

Figure 26-5. **A,** Intraoral view before maxillary protraction. **B,** Same view after maxillary protraction.

42. Why is it important to graft the alveolar defect when the canine root is less than 50% formed?

Canine teeth may erupt and migrate through the bone graft. With root formation beyond 50%, teeth begin eruptive bodily relocation in excess of root lengthening, and the cuspid may penetrate from its intraosseous crypt into the void of the alveolar defect.

ADOLESCENT AND ADULT DENTITION (AGE 12 TO 17 YEARS AND BEYOND)

43. What is adolescent dentition?

The first 6 years after onset of full eruption of succedaneous teeth during the period of accelerated adolescent growth in stature and facial development.

44. What orthodontic appliances are used during this period?

Occasionally, maxillary expansion may be indicated for a second time or, less often, primarily. Rigidly bonded or banded jackscrew appliances are most effective, but often spring wire-type expansion devices attached to two molars may be used successfully for buccal segment dental expansion. However, the principal procedures are carried out with comprehensive orthodontic appliances and complete bracing of all clinically erupted permanent teeth. This technique gives virtual control over the six possible bodily movements in space for each tooth.

CONTROVERSY

45. Is alveolar bone grafting a definitive procedure?

Bone grafting is not a definitive procedure even when it is entirely successful. The first graft may not compensate for vagaries of cleft type and individual variation, and results may be impossible to predict. A fuller alveolus for an osseointegrated implant or multiunit fixed prosthesis or elevation at the ala base is often a legitimate indication for a second graft during adolescence and adulthood.

FACIAL GROWTH IN ORAL CLEFT PATIENTS

46. Is craniofacial morphology of parents related to susceptibility for oral cleft in offspring?

Yes. Good evidence from cephalometric studies in parents of children with cleft lip (CL) and/or cleft palate (CP) supports this hypothesis. In the *lateral view*, all such parents have significantly shorter upper facial height compared with lower facial height. A larger cranial base saddle angle was found in parents of children with CLP and CP. In the *frontal view*, all parents had a significantly narrower head (skull) width (HW) and smaller cephalic index. There were also greater ratios of HW to interorbital, interzygomaticofrontal suture, nasal, bizygomatic, and alar width. Parents of children with CLP also showed asymmetries in the nasal alveolar shelf. In summary, shorter height and greater width in the upper face characterize all parent types.

47. How is the craniofacial status of adult patients with isolated unilateral cleft lip/alveolus surgically treated in childhood different from that of normal samples?

Facial height is greater than in controls, and the maxilla–mandibular relationship demonstrates a flat facial angle. Patients with unilateral cleft lip/alveolus (UCLA) have a balanced retrognathic–apertognathic profile. With the least severe deformity, UCLA craniofacial status is closer to the normal population than to the remaining oral cleft population.

48. How is the craniofacial status of adult patients with isolated UCLP surgically treated in childhood different from that of normal samples?

Facial height tends to be larger than in controls. The facial angle demonstrates a retrusive configuration with midfacial deficiency. The maxillofacial abnormality is explained by the severity of the deformity of patients with UCLP, manifest as a long-face, backward-divergent, and midfacial-deficient profile. Mandibular deformity is independent of severity of UCLP deformity.

49. How is the craniofacial status of adult patients with isolated BCLP surgically treated in childhood different from that of normal samples?

A similar deformity pattern to UCLP is found in BCLP with bimaxillary dentofacial retrusion, clockwise facial rotation, lower facial height enlargement, and retrocheilia (reduced upper lip thickness).

50. How is the craniofacial status of infants with isolated CP different from that of the CLA sample?

The structures that are shorter in infants with CP compared with CLA (an acceptable normal standard) are maxillary length, posterior maxillary height, mandibular length in both corpus and ramus, nasopharyngeal depth and height, and anterior cranial base length. Larger structures are mandibular angle (gonial), palatal plane angle, and open facial rotation. In summary, infants with CP represent a different population from infants with isolated clefts of primary palate.

51. How is the craniofacial status of adult patients with isolated CP treated and untreated in childhood different from that of normal samples?

Whether or not surgically treated in childhood, the craniofacial status is about the same in adults with CP. The maxilla is shorter in length and retruded in position. The mandible is more posterior and retrognathic and smaller, with an increased plane angle; it is like the mandible found in patients with complete oral cleft and primary cleft palate. The facial angle, however, is not unlike that of controls. Differences are also found among the different types of CP. Patients with clefts of only the soft palate have the least affected maxilla but the most retrognathic profile. Patients with soft and partial hard palate cleft have the most retruded maxilla. Cases with soft and complete hard palate cleft have the best overall facial balance, nearly normal mandibular form, and profiles that are not retrognathic.

52. How does a pharyngeal flap affect facial development?

Done rather early in life, a pharyngeal flap contributes mechanical, functional, and tissue factors affecting facial growth. The flap causes a greater reduction in forward maxillary growth than what ordinarily occurs. The maxillary vertical dimension is unaffected. A greater facial opening rotation maintains facial balance. In general, restraint, scar, and increased nasal impedance to airflow disturb maxillary growth.

BIBLIOGRAPHY

Bishara SE: Cephalometric evaluation of facial growth in operated and non-operated individuals with isolated clefts of the palate. Cleft Palate J 10:239–246, 1973.

Bishara SE, Krause CJ, Olin WH, et al: Facial and dental relationships of individuals with unoperated clefts of the lip and/or palate. Cleft Palate J 13:238–252, 1976.

Bishara SE, Staley RM: Maxillary expansion: Clinical implications. Am J Orthod Dentofacial Orthop 91:3–14, 1987.

Blechschmidt E: Principles of biodynamic differentiation. In Bosma JF(ed): Development of the Basicranium. Bethesda, MD, U.S. Department of Health, Education, and Welfare, 1976, pp 54–80.

Burston WR: The early treatment of cleft palate conditions. Dent Pract 9:41, 1958.

Dahl E, Kreiborg S, Jensen BL, Fogh-Andersen P: Comparison of craniofacial morphology in infants with incomplete cleft lip and infants with isolated cleft palate. Cleft Palate J 19:258–266, 1982.

El Deeb M, Messer LB, Lehnert MW, et al: Canine eruption into grafted bone in maxillary alveolar cleft defects. Cleft Palate J 19:9–16, 1982.

Farkas LG, Lindsay WK: Morphology of the adult face after repair of isolated cleft palate in childhood. Cleft Palate J 9:132–142, 1972.

Figueroa AA, Reisberg DJ, Polley JW, Cohen M: Intraoral-appliance modification to retract the premaxilla in patients with bilateral cleft lip. Cleft Palate J 33(6):497–500, 1996.

Hayashi I, Sakuda M, Takimoto K, Miyazaki T: Craniofacial growth in complete unilateral cleft lip and palate: A roentgenocephalometric study. Cleft Palate J 13:215–237, 1976.

Isaacson RJ, Wood JL, Ingram AH: Forces produced by rapid maxillary expansion. Angle Orthod 34:256–270, 1964.

McNeil CK: Orthodontic procedures in the treatment of congenital cleft palate. Dent Rec 70:126–132, 1950.

Moyers RE: Handbook of Orthodontics, 2nd ed. Chicago, Year Book, 1963.

Nakasima A, Ichinose M: Characteristics of craniofacial structures of parents of children with cleft lip and/or palate. Am J Orthod 84:140–146, 1983.

Nordin K-E: Treatment of primary total cleft palate deformity. Preoperative orthopedic correction of the displaced components of the upper jaw in infants followed by bone grafting to the alveolar process clefts. Trans Europ Orthod Soc 333–339, 1957.

Rosenstein SW: Early maxillary orthopaedics and appliance fabrication. In Kernahan DA, Rosenstein SW (ed): Cleft Lip and Palate: A System of Management. Baltimore, Williams & Wilkins, 1990, pp 120–127.

Rune B, Jacobsson S, Sarnas KV, Selvik G: A roentgens stereophotogrammetric study of implant stability and movement of segments in the maxilla of infants with cleft lip and palate. Cleft Palate J 16:267–278, 1979.

Smahel Z: Craniofacial morphology in adults with bilateral complete cleft lip and palate. Cleft Palate J 21:159–169, 1984.

Smahel Z, Brejcha M: Difference in craniofacial morphology between complete and incomplete unilateral cleft lip and palate in adults. Cleft Palate J 20:113–127, 1983.

Spolyar JL: The design, fabrication, and use of a full-coverage bonded rapid maxillary expansion appliance. Am J Orthod 86:136–145, 1984.

Spolyar JL: Growth comparison of cases with and without presurgical or orthopaedic correction. Proceedings of the 9th Annual Cleft Lip and Palate Symposium. Atlanta, Scottish Rite Children's Medical Center, 1996, pp 339–340.

Spolyar JL, Jackson IT, Phillips RJL, et al: The Latham technique: Contemporary presurgical orthopedics for the complete oral cleft technique and preliminary evaluation—A bone marker study. Perspect Plast Surg 6:179–210, 1992.

Subtelny JD, Nieto RP: A longitudinal study of maxillary growth following pharyngeal-flap surgery. Cleft Palate J 15:118–131, 1978.

Tindland RS: Skeletal response to maxillary protraction in patients with cleft lip and palate before age 10 years. Cleft Palate Craniofac J 31:295–308, 1994.

Tindland RS, Rygh P, Boe OE: Intercanine widening and sagittal effect of maxillary transverse expansion in patients with cleft lip and palate during the deciduous and mixed dentitions. Cleft Palate Craniofac J 30:195–207, 1993.

Tindland RS, Rygh P, Boe OE: Orthopedic protraction of the upper jaw in cleft lip and palate patients during the deciduous and mixed dentition periods in comparison with normal growth and development. Cleft Palate Craniofacial J30:182–194, 1993.

Zilberman Y: Observations on the dentition and face in clefts of the alveolar process. Cleft Palate J 10:230–238, 1973.

CEPHALOMETRICS

Prasanna-Kumar Shivapuja, BDS, MDS(ortho), DDS, MS(ortho), and John L. Spolyar, DDS, MS

CHAPTER 27

1. What is cephalometrics?

Cephalometrics is the science of measurement of the skull, which began in the early eighteenth century. After the introduction of X radiation, measurements were made on standardized radiographs. The technique of radiographic cephalometrics was introduced by Hofrath in Germany and Brodbent in the United States in 1934. The initial purpose was to research the growth and development of skeletal structures and to establish a quantitative method for obtaining descriptive information about dentofacial patterns.

2. How is cephalometric analysis performed?

It is performed by acquiring a standardized lateral view of the skull (Figs. 27-1, 27-2, and 27-3). A tracing is made of the skull film, and measurement is taken between points and planes constructed from anatomic landmarks.

3. How is a standard cephalogram obtained?

There are two specific requirements for obtaining a true standardized lateral head film. The distance from the x-ray source to the object should be 60 inches. The distance from the object to the film should be 6 inches. The central beam is directed through the center of the ear rods to strike the x-ray film at right angles. To limit parallax distortion due to shifting, the head should be stabilized with a head holder called a *cephalostat*. When these constants are maintained, a standardized lateral cephalogram is obtained with 10% magnification of the head. The lateral cephalogram must be made with the mandible in a centric position and lips relaxed (see Fig. 27-1).

4. Why is a cephalostat used?

The cephalostat provides a means to standardize image and magnification distortions of the cephalograph with standard positioning of the x-ray source from the subject.

5. How do you trace a cephalogram?

Tracing is done on a 0.003-inch acetate paper with a 0.05-mm lead pencil. The side closest to the film is traced. In tracing the mandibular structures, the superior part of the body and distal part of the ramus should be traced (the side closest to the film). Whenever there is a double image, the contours of the image can be traced by bisecting the two images. Figure 27-4 shows the representative landmarks that need to be traced.

6. What are the requirements for a landmark?

- The landmarks should be easily seen on a radiograph, uniform in outline, and easily reproducible.
- Lines and planes should have significant relationship to the vectors of growth of specific areas.
- Landmarks should permit valid quantitative measurements of lines and angle projected from them.
- Measure points and measurements should have significant relationship to the information sought.
- Measurements should be amendable to statistical analysis.

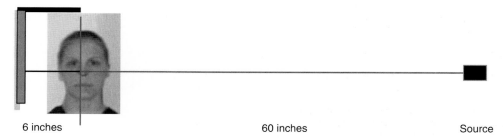

6 inches   60 inches   Source

Figure 27-1. Technique of cephalometrics.
- Distance from source to midsagittal plane of object = 60 inches
- Distance from object to film = 6 inches
- Magnification ratio = 1:10
- Central ray should pass through external auditory meatus perpendicular to the film cassette

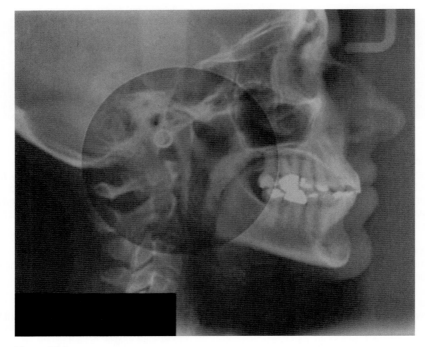

Figure 27-2. Lateral cephalogram.

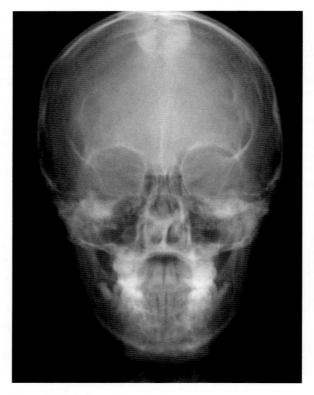

Figure 27-3. Posteroanterior cephalogram.

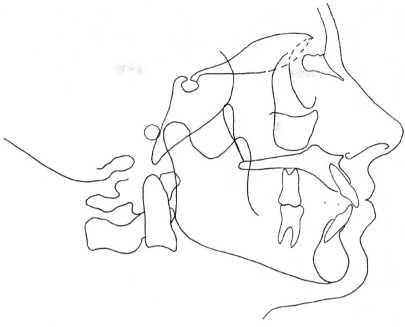

Figure 27-4. Cephalogram tracing.

7. What are the most commonly used landmarks?

The most commonly used landmarks are shown in Figure 27-5:

1. Nasion (N): Anteriormost point on the frontonasal suture
2. Basion (Ba): Lowermost point on the anterior point of the foramen magnum
3. Articulare (Ar): Point of the cranial base and the posterior border of the mandibular ramus
4. Porion (Po): Midpoint of the upper contour of the external auditory canal
5. Sella (S): Center of the sella turcica
6. Pterygomaxillary fissure (PTM): Point on the base of the fissure where the anterior and posterior walls meet
7. Orbitale (Or): Lowest point on the inferior margin of the bony orbit
8. Anterior nasal spine (ANS): Tip of the anterior nasal spine (sometimes modified as the point on the upper or lower contour of the spine where it is 3 mm thick)

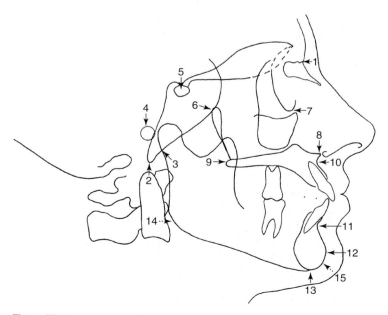

Figure 27-5. Commonly used landmarks.

9. Posterior nasal spine (PNS)
10. Point A (A): Innermost point on the contour of the premaxilla between the anterior nasal spine and incisor tooth
11. Point B (B): Innermost point on the contour of the mandible between the incisor and the bony chin
12. Pogonion (Pog): Anteriormost point on the contour of the bony chin
13. Menton (Me): Most inferior point on the mandibular symphysis
14. Gonion (Go): Point on the angle of the mandible obtained by bisecting the angle formed by intersection of a tangent drawn to the lower and posterior borders of the ramus
15. Gnathion (Gn): Constructed point located between the pogonion and menton

8. What is a cephalometric plane?

A plane by definition connects three or more points. A line by definition connects two or more points. These two terms are often used synonymously. The commonly used planes are as follows (Fig. 27-6):

Cranial Base Planes
1. Basion-nasion (Ba-N)
2. Sella-nasion (S-N)
3. Frankfort horizontal plane (Po-Or)

Maxillary Planes
1. Palatal plane: Constructed by joining the anterior nasal spine to the posterior nasal spine
2. Occlusal plane: Plane extending between the mesial cusp of the maxillary molar through the point that bisects the overbite
3. Nasion–point A
4. Long axis of mandibular incisor

Mandibular Planes
1. Mandibular plane: Line drawn tangent to the lower border of the mandible and passing through the menton
2. Nasion–point B
3. Nasion–pogonion facial axis plane
4. Long axis of mandibular incisor

9. What are the components of cephalometric analysis?
- Skeletal analysis
- Soft-tissue profile analysis
- Dental analysis

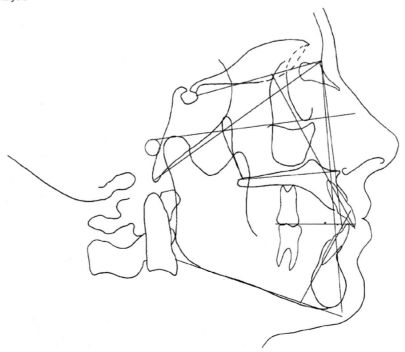

Figure 27-6. Cephalometric planes.

Table 27-1. Normal Values for Commonly Used Measurements

MEASUREMENT	MEAN VALUE (CAUCASIAN)	MEAN VALUE (AFRICAN-AMERICAN)
SNA	82	85
SNB	80	81
ANB	2	4
U1-NA	22	23
	4 mm	7 mm
L1-NB	25	34
	4 mm	10 mm
U1-L1	131	111
L1-MP	90	—
FMA	25	25
Facial axis	0–2	—

FMA, Frankfort-mandibular plane angle; *L1-MP*, mandibular incisor-mandibular plane; *L1-NB*, mandibular incisor-nasion to A-point plane; *U1-NA*, maxillary incisor-nasion to B-point plane.

10. What is the purpose of skeletal analysis?

The main purpose is to classify facial types and to establish the relative anteroposterior relation of the basal arches to the cranial base and to themselves (Table 27-1). Angle SNA indicates the anteroposterior positioning of the maxilla in reference to the cranial base. The normal angle for a Caucasian is 82°. An angle that exceeds 82° indicates maxillary protrusion, and an angle less than 82° indicates maxillary retrusion. Angle SNB indicates the anteroposterior relation of the mandible in reference to the cranial base. The mean is 80°. Basal arch analysis indicates the relation between the maxilla and mandible (ANB angle). The normal value is 2°.

Another method involves first correcting the length of the cranial base sella-nasion. In adult females the length is 77 mm, and in adult males the length is 83 mm. From this corrected position of nasion, draw a perpendicular to the Frankfort plane. Maxillary reference point A should lie on the plane, and, chin projection (Holdaway ratio) being normal, pogonion should be on the plane in adult males and should be 2 mm behind the plane in adult females. If point A is ahead of the plane, it indicates horizontal maxillary excess. If point A is behind this plane, it indicates horizontal maxillary deficiency. Similarly, if pogonion is ahead of this plane, it indicates mandibular excess. If it is behind this plane in adult males and is more than 2 mm behind in adult females, it indicates mandibular deficiency. (Value for sella-nasion plane reconstructed to the correct length and angulation obtained from the University of Michigan Growth Center standards.)

An important factor in skeletal analysis is the vertical relation of the maxilla and mandible to the cranial base. The first measurement is to relate the anterior maxilla, done by evaluating tooth exposure on the lateral cephalogram (with lips relaxed) and frontal facial picture. Both should show tooth exposure of approximately 2 mm. The second group of measurements is the palatal plane. It should be parallel to the Frankfort plane. The occlusal plane angle should be 7°, and the mandibular plane angle should be 25° to the Frankfort plane.

The third measurement is the posterior facial height. The posterior cranial base (S–Ar) and ramus height (Ar–constructed gonion Go) should be a ratio of 3:4. If the ramus height ratio is less than 3:4, it indicates a short posterior face height. A ratio greater than 3:4 indicates an excessive posterior facial height. A short posterior face height should be evaluated in connection with the mandibular plane angle and is suggestive of a condylar problem and, therefore, a more difficult case to treat. An increased posterior face height usually suggests a distracted condyle due to a functional shift and indicates the need for a splint. The fourth of these measurements is the ratio of the total facial height (measured from nasion to menton). If this value is considered to be 100%, the upper part of the face (nasion to anterior nasal spine) should be 45% and the lower part (anterior nasal spine to menton) should be 55%, although men tend to be slightly longer in the lower third of the face.

11. What does the dental analysis indicate?

It indicates anteroposterior positioning of the teeth in relation to their basal bones. The long axis of the maxillary incisor should be angled at 104° to the cranial base. The long axis of the mandibular incisor should be angled at 90° to the mandibular plane.

12. What does the profile analysis assess?

Profile analysis permits appraisal of the soft tissue that covers the skeletal facial profile. Remember that the soft tissue profile is related to facial skeletal dimensions, tonicity of the soft tissue, and habitual posture of the face in the head in space. An easy way to evaluate the profile is to relate the face to Ricketts' aesthetic plane (the line extending from the soft tissue nose tip to the soft tissue chin). The upper lip should lie 2 mm behind the plane; the lower lip should lie on the plane.

The nasolabial angle is formed at the base of the nose by a line drawn parallel to the base of the nose and a tangent drawn to the upper lip. It is also an important factor in establishing the anteroposterior position of the maxilla. The nasolabial angle should be 102° in both men and women, with a standard deviation of 8°. An acute nasolabial angle may be a reflection of maxillary dentoalveolar protrusion. To rule out the influence of the nose on this angle, the upper lip should be evaluated in relation to the vertical orientation of the face. The tangent drawn to the upper lip should be 8° in men and 14° in women, with the nasion perpendicular. An obtuse nasolabial angle or a decreased cant of the upper lip is an indication of a retrusive maxilla.

13. What is the Holdaway ratio?
The Holdaway ratio, which is used to evaluate chin retrusion or prominence, is an orthodontic method that relates the prominence of the mandibular incisor to the NB and the pogonion to the NB line. For an ideal Holdaway ratio, the lower incisor and the pogonion should be the same distance from the NB line. The ratio is depicted as 1:1. Per cephalometric standards, the lower incisor should be 4 mm in front of the NB line; therefore the chin also should be 4 mm in front of the NB line. It is important that the surgeon not advance the chin beyond the confines of the mandibular incisor teeth.

14. What are the applications of cephalometrics?
- Diagnosis
- Growth prediction
- Visual treatment objective
- Surgical treatment objective (STO)

15. How is the STO carried out?
The STO is carried out on a lateral cephalogram taken in centric position with the lips relaxed. A frontal facial picture with the lips relaxed and a picture with a wide smile on are also helpful in deciding the vertical positioning of the maxilla.

16. How do you evaluate the effect of treatment?
It can be evaluated by the process called *superimposition*. There are three basic types:

- *Overall superimposition* is usually done by superimposing the anterior cranial base on the de Caster plane. After age 7 years, the sphenoethmoidal synchondrosis is fused, after which the anterior cranial basis is a stable structure that can be used for superimposition. This form of superimposition indicates the overall change in the maxilla and mandible in reference to the cranial base.
- *Maxillary superimposition* is done by superimposing the anterior nasal spine on the palatal plane (ANS–PNS). It reveals the dental changes in the maxilla.
- *Mandibular superimposition* is done by superimposing on the lingual aspect of the symphysis parallel to the lower border of the mandible or mandibular plane. It indicates the changes in the mandibular dentition due to the treatment.

17. Have there been any recent advancements in cephalometrics?
Yes. There are three major advancements:

- Digital imaging
- Computerized cephalometrics
- Cone beam computed tomographic (CT) scan

18. What is digital imaging?
In digital imaging, a static or dynamic sensor is used to capture the image instead of a silver halide film.

19. What are the advantages of digital imaging?
- Digital imaging allows the possibility of digital archiving.
- The image can be digitally enhanced for better landmark identification.

20. What are the disadvantages of digital imaging?
- Distortion, especially if a dynamic sensor is used for scanning.
- Standardization ruler must be used. If not, magnification/constriction cannot be accounted for.

21. What is computerized cephalometrics?
Computerized cephalometrics is a process of using a scanned lateral cephalometric radiograph or digital radiograph and a computer to make a tracing that, in turn, is used to make measurements and superimposition (Figs. 27-7 and 27-8). The image can also be used to create multiple simulated treatments (STO) without destroying the initial image.

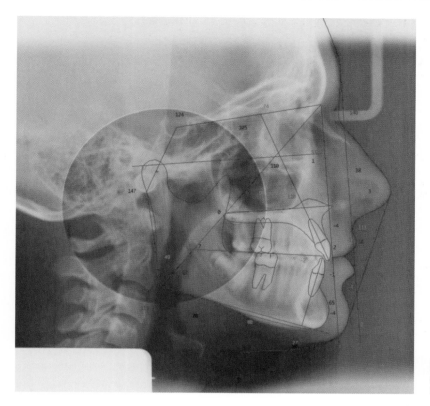

Figure 27-7. Radiograph with computer-generated tracing and measurements superimposed.

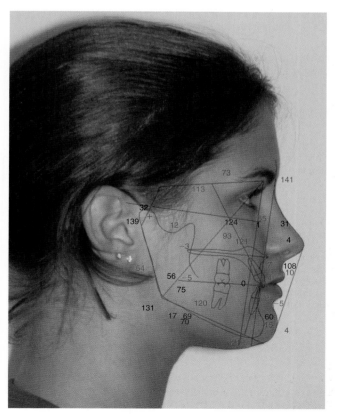

Figure 27-8. Tracing superimposed over lateral facial photograph.

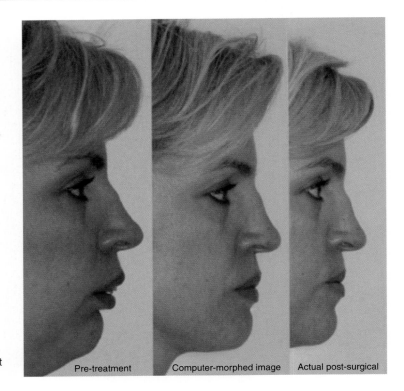

Pre-treatment   Computer-morphed image   Actual post-surgical

Figure 27-9. Comparison of pretreatment morphing and actual postsurgical result.

22. What is the advantage of computerized cephalometrics?

One of the greatest advantages is the ability to superimpose the tracing over a picture and manipulate the facial picture to match the changes made on the radiographic tracing. This procedure is called *morphing* (Fig. 27-9).

23. What are the disadvantages of morphing a picture?

Morphing can be performed only on the lateral profile, and the accuracy of morphing still is questionable.

24. What is cone beam CT?

Cone beam CT is an in-office CT scan that provides a three-dimensional image of the facial complex. This is the future of imaging in the field of orthodontics.

Cephalometrics is a valuable tool in the diagnosis and treatment planning of orthodontic and surgical cases, but it must be used only as an adjunct to clinical diagnosis. After all, we treat patients and faces, not x-rays.

BIBLIOGRAPHY

Grayson B, Cutting Bookstein FL, et al: The three-dimensional cephalogram: Theory, technique and clinical applications. Am J Orthod Dentofacial Orthop 94:327–337, 1988.

Profitt WR, Thomas PM, Camilla-Tulloch JF: Contemporary Orthodontics. St. Louis, Mosby, 1986.

Riolo ML, Moyers RE, McNamara AJ, et al: An Atlas of Craniofacial Growth: Cephalometric Standards from the University Growth Study. Ann Arbor, MI., Center for Human Growth and Development, University of Michigan, 1979.

Salzman JA: Practice of Orthodontics, Vols. 1 and 2. Philadelphia, Lippincott-Raven, 1966.

Spolyar JL: Design, evaluation, and use of a portable cephalometric cephalostat: The Porta-Stat (an x-ray sub-system). Spec Care Dent March-April 1988, pp 64–70.

PRINCIPLES OF ORTHOGNATHIC SURGERY

Mitchell A. Stotland, MD, MS, FRCSC, and
Henry K. Kawamoto, Jr., MD, DDS

CHAPTER 28

1. What is the Angle classification?

The universally accepted system for describing dental occlusion was developed by the orthodontist Edward Angle. The Angle classification regards the upper first molar as its point of reference and describes the anterior–posterior (mesial–distal) relationship between the maxillary and mandibular arches (Fig. 28-1).

In *class I occlusion (neutroclusion)*, the mesiobuccal cusp of the maxillary first molar articulates within the buccal groove of the lower first molar.

In *class II malocclusion*, the lower arch is in a distal or posterior position relative to the maxillary arch. Thus, the mesiobuccal cusp of the maxillary first molar articulates with the distal portion of the mandibular second bicuspid and the mesial cusp of the first molar. Class II occlusion is subclassified into divisions 1 and 2, in which the anterior teeth are flared labially or palatally, respectively.

In *class III malocclusion*, the mandibular dentition is positioned mesially in relation to the maxillary dentition. Thus the mesiobuccal cusp of the first upper molar intercuspates with the distobuccal groove of the lower first molar.

2. What do the terms *centric occlusion* and *centric relation* mean?

Centric occlusion refers to a position of maximal, bilateral, balanced contact between the cusps of the maxillary and mandibular arches.

Centric relation is the most retruded, unstrained position of the mandibular condyle within the temporomandibular joint (TMJ), that is, within the glenoid fossa. Ideally, in centric occlusion the condyle sits anatomically within the glenoid bilaterally, reflecting simultaneous centric occlusion and centric relation. A number of problems, however, can result in asymmetric, premature dental contact upon closure with an unbalanced slide into occlusion that distracts the condyle and destroys its unstrained position. With prolonged loss of centric relation the distracting forces may lead to muscular, soft tissue, and bony pathologic changes in and around the TMJ. In repositioning the maxillary and/or the mandibular arches, it is critical not to overlook the concept of centric relation while focusing primarily on achieving centric occlusion. When repositioning the jaws, therefore, the orthognathic surgeon must make certain that the condyle is properly seated within the TMJ before initiating rigid bony fixation.

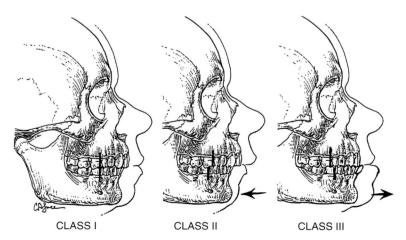

CLASS I   CLASS II   CLASS III

Figure 28-1. Angle classification of dental occlusion. (From McCarthy JG, Kawamoto HK Jr, Grayson BH, et al: Surgery of the jaws. In McCarthy JG [ed]: Plastic Surgery. Philadelphia, WB Saunders, 1990, p 1193, with permission.)

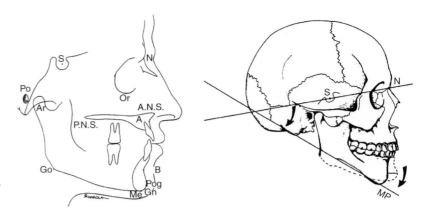

Figure 28-2. Cephalometric relationships. (**Left**, from Ferraro JW: Cephalometry and cephalometric analysis. In Ferraro JW [ed]: Fundamentals of Maxillofacial Surgery. New York, Springer-Verlag, 1997, p 236; **Right**, from McCarthy JG, Kawamoto HK Jr, Grayson BH, et al: Surgery of the jaws. In McCarthy JG [ed]: Plastic Surgery. Philadelphia, WB Saunders, 1990, p 1196, with permission.)

3. What do the cephalometric relationships SNA, SNB, and mandibular plane angle signify?

Cephalometry is a scientific measure of the dimensions of the head. Based on a standardized technique, a lateral radiogram (cephalogram) is obtained and used for analysis of facial proportions. Some of the more commonly used landmarks include the following (Fig. 28-2):

- *Sella (S):* Center of the pituitary fossa
- *Nasion (N):* Most anterior point at the nasofrontal junction
- *A (A):* Deepest midpoint on the maxillary alveolar process between the anterior nasal spine and the alveolar ridge
- *B (B):* Deepest midpoint on the mandibular alveolar process between the crest of the ridge and the most anterior point along the contour of the symphysis (pogonion [Pog])
- *SNA:* Angle that relates the maxilla to the cranial base (mean: 82° ± 3°)
- *SNB:* Angle that relates the mandible to the cranial base (mean: 80° ± 3°)
- The *mandibular plane angle* relates the posterior facial height to the anterior facial height. It is derived from the angle between the Frankfort horizontal plane and the mandibular plane. The mean mandibular plane angle is 21° ± 3° and is more obtuse in patients with an anterior-open bite and/or micrognathia or retrognathia. Patients with a deep bite and/or the short face syndrome tend to have a more acute mandibular plane angle.
- The *Frankfort horizontal plane* is formed by the line joining the point located at the most superior extent of the external auditory meatus (porion [Po]) with the lowest point on the inferior bony border of the left orbital cavity (orbitale [Or]).
- The *mandibular plane* is formed by the line joining the most inferoposterior point at the mandibular angle (gonion [Go]) with the lowest point on the contour of the mandibular symphysis (menton [Me]).

4. What is the normal amount of incisor show with the lips in repose and during smiling?

With the lips in repose, 2 to 3 mm of upper central incisor exposure is considered attractive. Up to 4 to 6 mm of show may be attractive in women as long as mentalis strain (manifested by chin dimpling) is not needed to achieve lip competence. With smiling, the full length of the upper incisors ideally should be visible with little or no evidence of gum exposure.

5. Describe the classic vertical proportions of the face in profile.

The proportions derived from the so-called *classic canons* are used only as a point of reference (Fig. 28-3). Variation is the norm. What is considered "ideal" proportion has changed somewhat over the centuries and certainly differs with race and culture. It is often useful to evaluate the face in terms of vertically equal thirds. The hairline (trichion) to supraorbital rims represents the upper third; supraorbital rim to subnasale is the middle third; and subnasale to menton is the lower third. The lower third is often further subdivided: subnasale to stomion represents the upper third and stomion to menton the lower two thirds of the facial lower third. The upper lip in profile usually sits at the level of the lower lip or slightly anterior. The labiomental groove is approximately 4 mm deep in women and 6 mm deep in men. Changes in lip position, labiomental groove depth, and vertical dimension of the facial thirds can be key indicators of facial disproportion that may be corrected by orthognathic surgery.

6. What is the value of a surgical splint in an orthognathic procedure? How are splints made?

Precise control of three-dimensional movements is necessary for surgically repositioning tooth-bearing segments of bone. This principle is critical in the achievement of a balanced, stable, and aesthetically pleasing bimaxillary relationship. However, after mobilizing an osteotomy segment, exact control of three-dimensionality can be difficult. Surgical splints are used to guide the movements of the osteotomized segments before performing rigid fixation. Preoperatively one obtains dental impressions of both jaws. From these impressions stone models of the upper

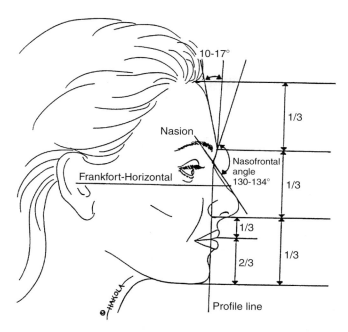

Figure 28-3. Vertical proportions of the face in profile. (From Guyuron B, Cohen SR: Facial evaluation for orthognathic surgery. In Ferraro JW [ed]: Fundamentals of Maxillofacial Surgery. New York, Springer-Verlag, 1997, p 227, with permission.)

and lower dental arches are prepared. It is also necessary to acquire an occlusal registration from the patient (e.g., a wax bite). The models then are mounted together in their occlusal relationship onto an articulator. Based on a cephalometric and facial profile evaluation, the exact movements required at surgery are determined and performed on the stone models in a mock procedure. Then, with the model arches resting together in their final position of maximal intercuspation, a thin wafer of acrylic is allowed to harden along the occlusal surfaces. This represents the guiding splint that is used at the time of surgery to help determine bony repositioning.

7. What is the rationale behind orthodontic preparation prior to orthognathic surgery?
The objective of presurgical orthodontics is to align the teeth properly over basal bone (i.e., maxilla and mandible) and to coordinate the two arches so that they fit together ideally at the time of surgical mobilization. Dental models are serially obtained during the period of orthodontia to determine precisely the dental movements that will result in a stable, class I occlusal relationship after surgery. In many patients dental compensations develop in response to long-standing skeletal deformity (e.g., flared lower incisors in class II cases, retroclined lower incisors in class III cases). Such compensations usually need to be corrected preoperatively to allow maximal postoperative dental intercuspation. This orthodontic correction results in a temporary, preoperative worsening of the deformity but ultimately leads to a more stable postoperative outcome.

8. What are the most common osteotomies used to perform mandibular repositioning?
(1) Vertical and oblique ramus osteotomy, (2) inverted L osteotomy, and (3) sagittal split osteotomy. All three techniques can be used to perform a mandibular setback procedure for the treatment of mandibular prognathism. The sagittal split osteotomy is generally the procedure of choice for mandibular advancement in the treatment of micrognathia.

9. Classify chin deformities.
A chin deformity may exist independently of an overall maxillary or mandibular deformity. A patient exhibiting class I occlusion and otherwise pleasing facial proportions may suffer aesthetically from an abnormally proportioned chin. Therefore osseous genioplasties may be performed alone or in conjunction with orthognathic procedures to improve facial harmony. A useful classification breaks down chin deformities into seven categories. Appreciation of the exact nature of the chin deformity helps to determine the specific method of skeletal or soft tissue correction required.

- *Macrogenia:* Horizontal, vertical, or combination bony excess
- *Microgenia:* Horizontal, vertical, or combination bony deficiency
- *Combined microgenia and macrogenia:* Combination deformity; excess and deficiency in different planes
- *Asymmetric chin*
- *Pseudomacrogenia:* Normal bony volume with excessive soft tissue
- *Pseudomicrogenia:* Normal bony volume with retrogenia secondary to excessive maxillary growth and associated mandibular clockwise autorotation
- *Witch's chin deformity:* Secondary to a soft tissue ptosis

10. What is the long face syndrome? Suggest a basic surgical approach.

This appearance is associated with vertical maxillary excess. Physical findings may include excessive lower-third facial height, narrowed alar base, obtuse nasolabial angle, anterior-open bite with associated mentalis strain or lip incompetence, excessive gingival show and upper incisor display in repose and with smiling, and retrognathia associated with a backward autorotation of the mandible (clockwise rotation and obtuse mandibular plane angle, as seen on the lateral cephalogram). After prior orthodontic preparation, surgical treatment typically includes a Le Fort I osteotomy with maxillary impaction. A baseline class II malocclusion may not be corrected by a combination of maxillary impaction and mandibular autorotation. Correction of occlusion is achieved either by incorporating a posterior movement of the maxilla or by adding a mandibular advancement to the maxillary impaction. If a true microgenia exists (i.e., separate from the retrogenia caused by backward mandibular rotation), an osseous genioplasty may be added to achieve desired facial harmony. Decisions are based on an overall assessment of the patient's facial profile and balance.

11. What is the short face syndrome? Suggest a basic surgical approach.

This appearance is associated with vertical maxillary deficiency. Physical findings may include decreased lower-third facial height, lack of incisor show with an edentulous appearance, widened alar bases, acute nasolabial angle, deep bite with excessively protruding chin, and an acute mandibular plane angle. Surgical treatment includes a Le Fort I osteotomy with downfracture. The procedure often necessitates an interposition bone graft to enhance stability and to prevent relapse. Often a horizontal maxillary advancement is also needed. A downward and/or backward movement of the chin is frequently required to address residual lower-third facial deficiency or chin protrusion.

12. Describe the vascular supply of the mobilized Le Fort I maxillary segment.

(1) The descending palatine artery (which divides into greater and lesser palatine vessels), (2) posterior superior alveolar artery, (3) infraorbital artery, (4) ascending palatine branch of the facial artery, which arises directly from the external carotid artery, and (5) palatine branch of the ascending pharyngeal artery, a branch of the external carotid artery. *Note:* The descending palatine, posterior superior alveolar, and infraorbital arteries arise from the internal maxillary artery.

The posterior superior alveolar and infraorbital arteries perfuse the maxillary buccal alveolus, periodontium, and teeth. The other vessels listed above, which provide palatal contribution, supply the majority of blood to the mobilized Le Fort I maxillary segment. In fact, anatomic studies indicate that the descending palatine artery is commonly sacrificed during Le Fort I pterygopalatine disjunction. As as result, the major vascular supply of the mobilized Le Fort segment relies on the ascending palatine branch of the facial artery and the palatine branch of the ascending pharygeal artery.

13. What are the risks of nerve injury during orthognathic surgery?

Sagittal Split Mandibular Osteotomy:

- Neurosensory disturbance of the inferior alveolar nerve occurs in the vast majority of cases immediately after sagittal split osteotomy. However, long-term deficits (not all of which are symptomatic) occur in 10% to 15% of patients younger than 40 years.
- Lingual nerve sensory disturbances are not common. Immediate postoperative tongue paresthesia secondary to lingual nerve injury probably occurs in less than 10% of patients. Long-term deficit occurs in less than 1%.
- Facial paralysis or paresis secondary to facial nerve injury is extremely rare and typically is associated with mandibular setback procedures. Facial nerve disturbances associated with sagittal split osteotomies have resolved spontaneously in all reported cases.
- Vertical ramus mandibular osteotomy involves an extremely low incidence of injury to either the inferior alveolar or the lingual nerves. With an intraoral approach to this procedure, facial nerve injury is also uncommon.

Genioplasty:

- Long-term dysfunction of the distal inferior alveolar nerve (mental nerve) should occur in less than 5% of cases.

Le Fort I Osteotomy:

- Temporary sensory disturbance resulting from traction injury to the infraorbital nerve and to the greater palatine neurovascular bundle is common immediately after Le Fort I osteotomy. Fortunately, these changes almost always resolve spontaneously over the ensuing weeks or months.
- During downfracture of the maxillary segment the nasopalatine nerve is necessarily severed. This results in a sensory loss to the region of the premaxillary palatal mucosa that typically is self-limited or nonsymptomatic.

14. What is the normal range of vertical mandibular opening in adults? Describe the normal motion of the TMJ.

The average interincisal opening is 40 to 50 mm. The first 20 to 25 mm of opening is provided by a hinge action of the TMJ. The remaining 15 to 20 mm of opening occurs through an anteroinferior translation of the condyle along the articular eminence. Vertical mandibular opening of 10 to 24 mm is severely limiting. An opening of 25 to 35 mm is functional but is not ideal. Excessive mandibular opening may be associated with laxity of the TMJ capsule and may result in joint subluxation or dislocation.

CONTROVERSIES

15. Does orthognathic surgery improve TMJ symptoms?

The relationship between TMJ dysfunction and malocclusion has been a subject of long-standing debate. Some patients with skeletal malocclusion habitually assume a convenient bite, sliding the mandible out of a centric relation position to approximate more closely a neutral class I dental relationship. With time, the associated strain on the TMJ may lead to symptomatic pathologic changes. By attempting to achieve simultaneous correction of both skeletal and dental occlusion (i.e., combining centric relation with centric occlusion), orthognathic surgery may relieve some of the abnormal forces applied to the joint. Overall, however, although it may prove beneficial in any given case, clinical reports are conflicting and do not suggest that orthognathic surgery reliably leads to an improvement in TMJ symptoms, probably because of the complex nature of TMJ disease in general.

16. What is progressive condylar resorption? What is its cause? How is it treated?

Condylar resorption occurs in adults and results in progressive retrusion of the mandible (high-angle mandibular deficiency). Progressive condylar resorption (PCR) occurs mainly in young females. The multiple theories about its cause include condylar avascular necrosis, increased TMJ estrogen responsiveness, and joint loading. Although some consider PCR to be a one-time event without recurrence, clinical reports have demonstrated multiple episodes of condylar resorption separated by intervals of quiescence. With respect to orthognathic surgery, TMJ loading after mandibular advancement may lead to postoperative PCR and clinical relapse. Opinion differs as to the treatment of PCR after orthognathic surgery. The application of maxillomandibular fixation is advocated by some to rest the condyles before allowing them to adapt gradually to the increased stress following mandibular advancement. Others believe that early and active TMJ function is indicated to promote optimal pericondylar blood flow and nutrition. Results of reoperation for relapse secondary to PCR have been disappointing, with evidence of renewed flare-ups of condylar resorption leading to further clinical relapse.

BIBLIOGRAPHY

Crawford JG, Stoelinga PJ, Blijdorp PA, et al: Stability after reoperation for progressive condylar resorption after orthognathic surgery: Report of seven cases. J Oral Maxillofac Surg 52:460–466, 1994.

Ferraro JW(ed): Fundamentals of Maxillofacial Surgery. New York, Springer-Verlag, 1997.

Frydman WL: Nerve injuries. Oral Maxillofac Surg Clin N Am 9:207–218, 1997.

Guyuron B, Michelow BJ, Willis L: A practical classification of chin deformities. Aesthetic Plast Surg 19:257–264, 1995.

McCarthy JG, Kawamoto HK Jr, Grayson BH, et al: Surgery of the jaws. In McCarthy JG (ed): Plastic Surgery. Philadelphia, WB Saunders, 1990, p 1187.

Onizawa K, Schmelzeisen R, Vogt S: Alteration of temporo-mandibular joint symptoms after orthognathic surgery: Comparison with healthy volunteers. J Oral Maxillofac Surg 53:117–121, 1995; discussion, 122–123.

Siebert JW, Angrigiani C, McCarthy JG, Longaker MT: Blood supply of the Lefort I maxillary segment: An anatomic study. Plast Reconstr Surg 100:843–851, 1997.

CLEFT ORTHOGNATHIC SURGERY

29 CHAPTER

Fernando Ortiz Monasterio, MD, and
David L. Ramirez, MD

1. What are the maxillomandibular abnormalities in cleft lip and palate patients?
In unoperated patients several changes have been described:

- Misaligned dentoalveolar arch
- Dentoalveolar bone gaps
- Bone and tooth loss
- Transverse maxillary collapse
- Vertical and sagittal maxillary hypoplasia
- Class III malocclusion with pseudoprognathism in the cleft side or protruding premaxilla in bilateral cases
- Deviation of nasal spine, resulting in nasal asymmetry

2. Do surgical procedures on the lip and palate contribute to these abnormalities?
Yes, lip surgery produces transverse forces that collapse the maxillary segments. Palatal surgery may have significant influence on the growth of the midface. Surgical scar tissue is known to interfere with growth. Early mucoperiosteal closure without subsequent orthodontics contributes to maxillary collapse. The volume of the oral cavity is decreased and the mandible projects anteriorly, resulting in true prognathism.

3. What can we do to prevent these abnormalities?
- Limit soft tissue dissection to minimize scar formation during the initial surgery
- Early orthodontics to expand maxillary segments
- Alveolar bone grafting to provide support for canine eruption and remodeling of the maxillary arch

4. How often is orthognathic surgery needed in cleft patients?
Ross reported that in approximately 25% of adults with a repaired unilateral cleft lip and palate, orthognathic surgery is necessary to achieve an adequate functional relationship of the jaws and teeth; this evidently is also true for bilateral clefts. Although they are a good reference to have, the cephalometric criteria used by Ross underestimated the actual number of adolescents who would benefit from orthognathic surgery. Facial aesthetics should be considered in addition to skeletal measurements.

5. Is orthognathic surgery avoidable in cleft patients?
All clefts are different. The main difference is the tissue deficiency. Orthognathic surgery may be avoided in many patients with refined surgical technique and optimal orthodontic care. In spite of good management during infancy and childhood, a subgroup of patients in adolescence manifest some of the abnormalities listed in Question 1. Patients who present for secondary care after receiving inadequate early treatment very commonly demonstrate the skeletal deformities that warrant orthognathic surgery.

6. What are the most frequent orthognathic procedures performed in cleft patients?
Besides bone grafting, which should be done at approximately 8.5 years of age, the most common orthognathic procedure performed is Le Fort I type osteotomy to achieve maxillary advancement and elongation, followed by two-jaw surgery, segmental mandibular osteotomies, sliding genioplasty, and, in rare cases, segmental maxillary osteotomies.

7. How does one prepare a cleft patient for orthognathic surgery?
To achieve optimal results following orthognathic surgery, it is necessary to complete the orthodontic preparatory work placing the maxillary segments in the best possible position, depending on the severity of the malformation. At the time of orthognathic surgery, it is mandatory to have a stable dental occlusion. For this reason, orthodontic treatment is planned to achieve that ideal occlusion at the time of surgery. This requires careful cephalometric analysis and performance of accurate model surgery. An occlusal splint should be prepared preoperatively to be used as a reference during the operation. It should be anticipated that the scar tissue, fistulas, and other soft tissue problems frequently found in secondary cases will limit the extent of maxillary mobilization.

8. What is the optimal timing to perform orthognathic surgery in cleft patients?
The maxillary or jaw deformity must be corrected when the permanent dentition is fully erupted, the teeth have been orthodontically aligned, and maxillomandibular growth is complete. Usually this is at 14 to 16 years in females and 16 to 18 years in males. Corticotomies associated with osteogenesis distraction can be safely performed at an earlier age.

9. What are the goals when performing a maxillary osteotomy?
- To achieve a class I dental occlusion whenever possible
- To obtain a normal facial convexity, eliminating the flattening of the middle third of the face
- To advance the nasal spine to provide support to the nasal tip
- To elongate the vertical dimension of the middle third of the face

10. What is the basic technique for a Le Fort I maxillary osteotomy?
See Fig. 29-1:

- "Gullwing" incision in the vestibular mucosa slightly above the sulcus
- Subperiosteal undermining of the anterior and lateral aspect of the maxilla to the pterygomaxillary junction
- Subperiosteal undermining of the lower half of the nasal cavity
- Horizontal or slightly oblique osteotomy
- Osteotomy of the pterygomaxillary junction
- Downfracture and mobilization of the maxilla
- Maxillomandibular fixation (MMF) and rigid fixation with miniplates and screws
- Removal of MMF and wound closure

11. Is the Le Fort I maxillary osteotomy technique performed differently in cleft patients?
Yes. The cleft usually manifests an alveolar bone gap that may produce unstable maxillary segments, a "two-piece maxilla" in the unilateral cleft, and a "three-piece maxilla" in the bilateral cleft. In these cases, an additional transversely oriented miniplate is used to realign and stabilize these separated segments. Posnick described a modified Le Fort I osteotomy in cleft patients in which the alveolar bone gap is closed by medial rotation of the lateral maxillary arch segments. This can be performed in unilateral or bilateral cases with good results (Figs. 29-2 and 29-3).

12. What is the main indication for two-jaw surgery?
Simultaneous maxillary advancement and mandibular retropositioning are indicated when major maxillomandibular discrepancy (>10 mm) is present. Although considerable maxillary advancement can be achieved in normal individuals, in cleft patients the advance is limited by maxillary scars produced by the original palatoplasty, and mandibular osteotomies are necessary to obtain good dental occlusion (Fig. 29-4).

13. How do you select the optimal technique for mandibular osteotomies?
If good occlusion can be achieved at the molar level by maxillary advancement, a segmental mandibular osteotomy is indicated. In this technique only the canines and incisors are mobilized posteriorly. Retropositioning this segment

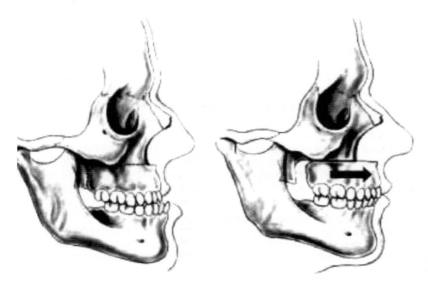

Figure 29-1. Le Fort I type osteotomy (maxillary advancement).

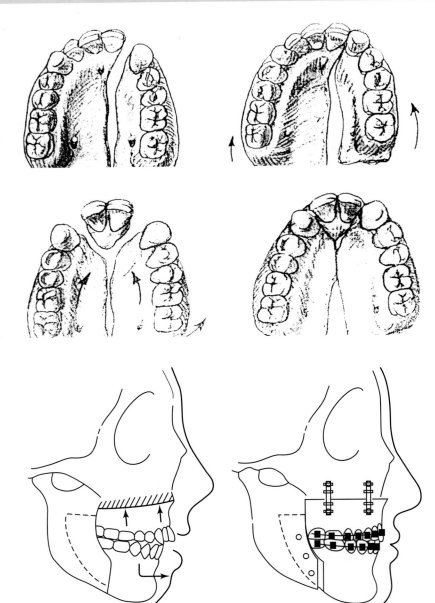

Figure 29-2. Unilateral maxillary medial rotation of the lateral cleft side (modified Le Fort I osteotomy).

Figure 29-3. Bilateral maxillary medial rotation of the lateral cleft side (modified Le Fort I osteotomy).

Figure 29-4. Two-jaw surgery. Le Fort I osteotomy and bilateral sagittal split mandibular osteotomy are shown.

results in an improvement of the facial profile with a normal labiomental groove. More severe discrepancies require retropositioning of the whole mandibular body by performing a bilateral sagittal split osteotomy. It is important to perform screw fixation of the split mandibular segments to eliminate the need for postoperative MMF.

14. What is the aesthetic effect of mandibular retropositioning? Is it enough?

Mandibular prognathism usually is associated with anterior displacement of the mandibular alveolar ridge, produced by the pressure of the tongue. This is manifested in the profile view by the absence of the labiomental groove. This is not corrected by mandibular retropositioning, and a sliding osseous genioplasty may be necessary to obtain a harmonious result.

15. What is the indication for a maxillary segmental osteotomy?

When the lateral incisor is missing and there is a gap in the alveolar bone, it is sometimes convenient to medially rotate the lesser segment so that the canine occupies the position of the lateral incisor. This may be done as an independent procedure or during a Le Fort I osteotomy, mobilizing the two segments independently resulting in advancement and rotation of the lesser segment.

16. Is velopharyngeal closure affected by a Le Fort I maxillary advancement?

In general, speech is not affected by maxillary advancement. Some studies suggest performing speech evaluation and nasopharyngeal endoscopy preoperatively in patients with borderline or established velopharyngeal insufficiency (VPI). These patients are at high risk for increased VPI after the advancement. Simultaneous or secondary pharyngoplasty should be considered in this group of patients.

17. Is the presence of a pharyngeal flap a limiting factor when performing a maxillary advancement?

No, a pharyngeal flap is not a limiting factor when performing a maxillary advancement. The pedicle of the flap is often found in a low position producing caudal tension. In this group of patients the pedicle should be reinserted in a higher position during the same procedure.

18. Are the results of orthognathic surgery in cleft patients permanent?

Minor to moderate relapse is observed after maxillary advancement despite adequate technique. This is related to soft tissue retraction and is more common in patients with scarred soft tissues. Segmental and sagittal split osteotomies maintain the benefit of the initial result without relapse.

19. What are the complications of orthognathic surgery in cleft patients?

Intraoperative bleeding requiring blood transfusion may occur in some cases. Dental malocclusion is observed as a result of inadequate preoperative preparation, and relapse of maxillary advancement is not uncommon. Incomplete union of bony segments may occur, especially following major maxillary advancement.

20. How do you treat relapse of a maxillary advancement?

The procedure should be repeated after 6 months. Distraction osteogenesis can be used to elongate the soft tissues and prevent further relapse. Once the desired advancement has been obtained by the distraction process, rigid fixation with miniplates and screws can be performed.

BIBLIOGRAPHY

Phillips JH, Klaiman P, Delorey R, MacDonald DB: Predictors of velopharyngeal insufficiency in cleft palate orthognathic surgery. Plast Reconstr Surg 115:681–686, 2005.

Posnick JC: Cleft orthognathic surgery. In Achauer BM: Plastic Surgery. Indications, Operations and Outcomes, Vol. 2. Philadelphia, Mosby, 2000, pp 851–867.

Posnick JC, Ricalde P: Cleft-orthognathic surgery. Clin Plast Surg 31:315–330, 2004.

Posnick JC, Tompson B: Modification of the maxillary LeFort I osteotomy in cleft-orthognathic surgery: The unilateral cleft lip and palate deformity. J Oral Maxillofac Surg 50:666–675, 1992; discussion 675–676.

Posnick JC, Tompson B: Modification of the maxillary LeFort I osteotomy in cleft-orthognathic surgery: The bilateral cleft lip and palate deformity. J Oral Maxillofac Surg 51:2–11, 1993.

Ross RB: Treatment variables affecting facial growth in complete unilateral cleft lip and palate: 7. An overview of treatment and facial growth. Cleft Palate J 24:17, 1987.

Shetye PR: Facial growth of adults with unoperated clefts. Clin Plast Surg 31:361–371, 2004.

Wolford LM: Effects of orthognathic surgery on nasal form and function in the cleft patient. Cleft Palate Craniofac Surg 29:546–555, 1992.

CRANIOSYNOSTOSIS

Jeffrey Weinzweig, MD, FACS, and
Linton A. Whitaker, MD

1. What is craniosynostosis? Who first described it?
Craniosynostosis designates premature fusion of one or more sutures in either the cranial vault or the cranial base. Although the term *craniosynostosis* was first used by Otto in 1830 to describe the entity of premature suture fusion, Hippocrates provided the first description of this anomaly in 100 BC. He noted the variable appearance of calvarial deformities and correlated it with the pattern of cranial suture involvement.

2. What structure is currently believed to be the primary site of abnormality responsible for craniosynostosis?
The cranial suture. Three theories of the pathogenesis of craniosynostosis are proposed:

- The suture is the primary site of abnormality, resulting in secondary cranial base deformities.
- The cranial base is the primary site of abnormality, resulting in secondary cranial deformities.
- The defect is in the mesenchymal blastema of both the cranial base and the cranial sutures.

The first theory is the most widely accepted. Cultured sagittal suture synostotic cells demonstrate higher alkaline phosphatase levels, thought to be related to osteoblastic cell activity. In addition, the doubling time is longer for synostotic cells than for both normal suture and bone, suggesting a potential cellular mechanism for growth deficiency.

3. What structure is critical to suture patency?
The dura mater. The influence of the dura mater on the overlying cranial suture is integrally involved in determining the biology of the overlying suture. Studies have suggested that the dura mater exerts its influence on cranial sutures either by transmitting biomechanical tensional forces via fibrous tracts or by providing growth factors (e.g., fibroblast growth factors) and extracellular matrix components in a paracrine fashion. Osteoprogenitor cells within the dura mater may synthesize locally acting osteogenic-inhibiting factors that regulate suture patency and fusion.

Levine et al. demonstrated that the location of the dura mater–suture complex is important in determining either suture patency or closure in the rat posterior frontal suture model. Normal closure of the suture overlying the posterior frontal dura mater demonstrates that the dura mater itself, or forces derived in specific cranial locations, determines the overlying suture biology. Craniosynostosis likely results from abnormalities in the equilibrium between proliferation and differentiation of the osteoprogenitor cells of the cranial sutures from disturbances in signaling, tissue interactions, or a combination of these elements. Thus, the fate of the fusing and patent suture is thought to be directed by signals given from the dura mater to the overlying suture, as opposed to being intrinsic to the suture itself.

4. How are cranial bones formed?
- *Intramembranous ossification* begins at the end of the second month of gestation. A center of osteogenesis develops directly in vascularized mesenchyme. Expansion of the ossification center proceeds radially via appositional growth. Initially cancellous bone forms, but as trabeculae thicken and the bone becomes less porous, it becomes compact bone. Eventually each intramembranous cranial bone has enlarged to the point at which it articulates with an adjacent bone via a syndesmosis or suture. Growth then proceeds at the sutures. Until approximately 8 years of age, the intramembranous cranial bones are single plates of compact bone. After this time, they become two plates of compact bone, separated by marrow and cancellous bone, or diploë.
- *Endochondral ossification* is the method by which the majority of the bones of the cranial base form. This method of ossification is more complex and proceeds by the replacement of preexisting cartilaginous models. Endochondral ossification is also the mode of ossification for the axial and appendicular skeleton. Cranial base articulations differ from those of the vault in that they are synchondroses—bones connected by cartilage instead of syndesmoses.

5. What are the two regions of the skull?
- The *viscerocranium* or *splanchnocranium* is the facial skeleton.
- The *neurocranium* houses the brain. The neurocranium consists of the vault, which forms its roof and walls, and the cranial base, which forms its floor.

6. What is the primary stimulus for growth at the cranial suture?
Growth at the suture area is a secondary, compensatory, and mechanically obligatory event following the primary growth of the enclosed brain and ocular globes. The bones of the calvaria are displaced outward by the enlarging brain. Each bone of the domed skull roof responds to the expansion of the brain by depositing new bone at the contact edges of the sutures.

7. At what age are brain volume and cranial capacity approximately 50% that of the adult?
At 6 months of age. Brain volume in the normal child almost triples within the first year of life. By 2 years, the cranial capacity is four times that at birth. For this rapid brain growth to proceed normally, the open cranial vault and base sutures must spread during phases of rapid growth. Craniosynostosis thus presents an obstacle to normal cranial vault growth.

8. In which direction does cranial growth occur with relation to a synostotic suture? What is Virchow's law?
In 1851, Virchow noted a cessation of growth in a direction perpendicular to that of the affected suture. As a result, growth proceeds (with or without overcompensation) in a direction *parallel* to the affected suture. This is Virchow's law.

9. What is the incidence of craniosynostosis?
Craniosynostosis is a relatively common congenital defect affecting approximately 1:2000 to 1:2500 live births worldwide. Most cases of nonsyndromic, single-suture synostosis are sporadic, whereas syndromic cases usually are inherited in an autosomal dominant or recessive pattern with variable penetrance, depending on the syndrome.

10. What is syndromic craniosynostosis? How common is it?
Craniosynostosis usually occurs as an isolated condition but also can manifest in association with a syndrome as part of a constellation of congenital abnormalities. The coronal suture is most commonly involved in these cases, as in Crouzon and Apert syndromes. More than 100 craniosynostosis syndromes have been described and attributed to specific mutations. Syndromic synostosis accounts for only 6% of all cases of craniosynostosis (approximately 2:100,000 live births).

11. Are growth factors involved in syndromic craniosynostosis?
Absolutely. Studies have demonstrated that mutations in fibroblast growth factor receptors (FGFRs) are associated with syndromic forms of craniosynostosis. Warren et al. demonstrated that noggin, an antagonist of bone morphogenetic proteins (BMPs), is expressed postnatally in the suture mesenchyme of patent, but not fusing, cranial sutures, and that noggin expression is suppressed by fibroblast growth factor-2 (FGF-2) and syndromic FGFR signaling. Because noggin misexpression prevents cranial suture fusion in vitro and in vivo, the authors suggest that syndromic FGFR-mediated craniosynostoses may be the result of inappropriate down-regulation of noggin expression.

Genetic and immunohistochemical investigations have demonstrated the importance of growth factors, including the FGFRs and the transforming growth factor beta (TGF-β) proteins, in the processes of both normal and premature cranial suture fusion. Jackson-Weiss, Crouzon, Apert, and Pfeiffer syndromes all are autosomal dominant conditions and have been linked with several different mutations in FGFR-2, which is a member of the tyrosine kinase superfamily and maps to areas on chromosome 10. A less severe form of Pfeiffer syndrome has been mapped to a region on chromosome 8, which is consistent with a mutation in the gene coding for FGFR-1. Thus, FGFRs are integrally linked with craniofacial abnormalities.

12. What is "functional" synostosis?
"Functional" synostosis is observed when cranial sutures do not appear synostotic radiographically but behave functionally as if they are fused (Fig. 30-1). A small segment of "suture bridging" that serves to fuse the suture in a limited region, but is not observed radiographically, is one explanation of this phenomenon.

13. What is the incidence of increased intracranial pressure with single-suture and multiple-suture involvement?
Using an epidural sensor device to monitor 121 patients with craniosynostosis, Marchac and Renier documented intracranial hypertension (intracranial pressure [ICP] >15 mm Hg) in 42% of patients with involvement of multiple sutures and in 13% of patients with only single-suture involvement. A progressive reduction of ICP over time was noted in patients who underwent cranial vault remodeling.

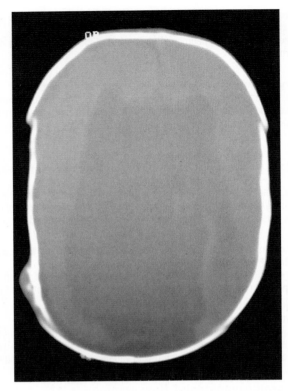

Figure 30-1. "Functional" synostosis. Involved sutures do not appear synostotic radiographically but behave functionally as if they are fused. A small segment of "suture bridging" that serves to fuse the suture in a limited region but is not observed radiographically is one explanation of this phenomenon.

14. What is the pathognomonic ophthalmologic sign of increased ICP?
Papilledema.

15. What does "thumb printing" or a "copper-beaten" appearance indicate?
Both terms describe the classic radiographic evidence of increased ICP on skull films. Imagine the craterlike surface of a golf ball or the irregular surface of hammer-beaten copper. Transfer those images to the inner surface of the cranium (Fig. 30-2) and voilà—thumb printing!

16. What is the most common isolated, nonsyndromic, single-suture synostosis?
Sagittal synostosis. It produces scaphocephaly, which is characterized by a narrow, elongated cranial vault and reduced bitemporal dimension (the basic "toaster head"). In terms of morphologic phenotypes, sagittal synostosis is seen in 40% to 55% of nonsyndromic cases. Coronal synostosis is the second most common (20% to 25%), followed by metopic synostosis (5% to 15%); lambdoid synostosis is rare (0% to 5%). More than one suture is affected in 5% to 15% of cases.

17. Which type of craniosynostosis is most often associated with hypotelorism?
Metopic synostosis. In addition to the more common finding of a palpable, midline forehead ridge, this type of craniosynostosis is associated with a decreased distance between the bony orbits (hypotelorism).

18. When does the metopic suture normally fuse?
Only the metopic suture normally fuses during early childhood. All other cranial sutures normally fuse much later in life, generally in the fourth and fifth decades, with complete fusion rarely occurring before the age of 30 years. In an attempt to define the normal temporal sequence of metopic suture fusion, Weinzweig et al. analyzed computed tomographic (CT) scans of 76 trauma patients, ranging in age from 10 days to 18 months, which provided normative craniofacial data to which similar data obtained from the preoperative CT scans of 30 patients who had undergone surgical treatment for metopic synostosis were compared. Weinzweig's study established that the metopic suture normally fuses between 6 and 8 months of age. In addition, evidence of partial suture fusion was present as early as 3 months of age. Therefore, a fused suture on CT scan *after* 6 months of age is *not* by itself diagnostic of metopic synostosis. Fusion of the metopic suture was found to be a progressive process initiated at the nasion and completed at the anterior fontanelle, in a manner analogous to a zipper closing, during this time interval.

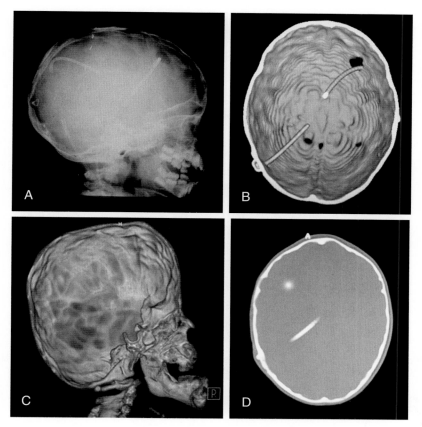

Figure 30-2. Radiographic indicators of increased intracranial pressure. A "copper-beaten" appearance or "thumb printing" is shown by plain radiograph **(A)** as well as axial **(B)** and sagittal **(C)** views of three-dimensional computed tomographic (CT) scans following placement of multiple shunts. Scalloping of the inner calvarial table is appreciated on standard axial CT scan **(D)**.

19. What is a "metopic notch"?

Although an endocranial ridge is not commonly seen in patients with metopic synostosis, an endocranial notch can be observed on axial CT images and is virtually diagnostic of premature suture fusion. Weinzweig termed this radiographic finding the *metopic notch,* a morphologic abnormality that is seen in 93% of synostotic patients. A metopic notch is not seen in *any* nonsynostotic patients and therefore can be used to diagnose metopic synostosis even *after* the period of physiologic suture closure. This notch represents the anatomic site of attachment of the falx, a dural reflection off the crista galli with basicranial origins, and suggests a role for the cranial base in metopic suture fusion (Fig. 30-3).

20. What is a "metopic groove"?

Whereas a *metopic notch* describes the endocranial finding on axial CT images in patients with metopic synostosis, a corresponding three-dimensional groove is found on the endocranial surface of the actual skull that extends from the nasion to the anterior fontanelle in these patients. Weinzweig termed this clinical finding the *metopic groove,* an anatomic abnormality that can reliably be found in patients with metopic synostosis (Fig. 30-4).

21. What are the different types of nonsyndromic isolated craniosynostoses?

See Table 30-1.

22. To which multiple-suture synostoses do the terms "tower skull," "pointed head," and "cloverleaf skull" refer?

Acrocephaly and turricephaly ("tower skull") designate a type of untreated brachycephaly with an excess of skull height and vertical elongation of the forehead. There may be multiple-suture involvement in addition to bicoronal synostosis.

Oxycephaly ("pointed head") is characterized by a retroverted forehead, tilted posteroinferiorly on a plane with the nasal dorsum. The forehead usually is reduced in the horizontal dimension with elevation in the region of the anterior fontanelle. There may be multiple-suture involvement in addition to bicoronal synostosis.

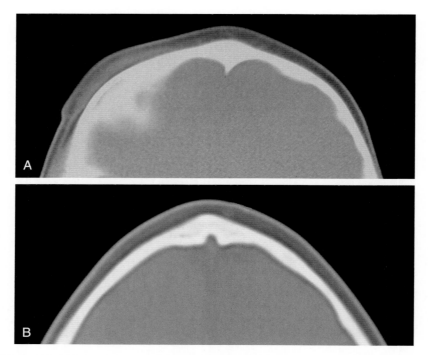

Figure 30-3. Metopic notch. Axial computed tomographic images show the endocranial bony spur associated with normal metopic suture fusion **(A)** and the "Ω" (omega)-shaped metopic notch **(B).** Moderate ectocranial ridging is also appreciated in this patient.

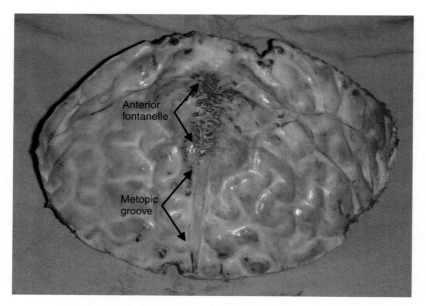

Figure 30-4. Metopic groove. Intraoperative evaluation of the inner table of the anterior cranial vault of a previously untreated 9-year-old child with metopic and bicoronal synostosis and Crouzon syndrome demonstrates a *metopic groove.* Although Crouzon syndrome is commonly associated with bicoronal synostosis, this child had both a metopic notch and a metopic groove, pathognomonic findings consistent with metopic synostosis. The metopic groove typically extends from the nasion to the anterior fontanelle. Note the severe depressions of the inner table of the skull indicating increased intracranial pressure in this older child. Such findings are described as thumb printing, scalloping, or a copper-beaten appearance on radiographs.

Table 30-1. Types of Nonsyndromic Isolated Craniosynostoses

HEAD SHAPE ABNORMALITY	AFFECTED SUTURES
Scaphocephaly	Sagittal
Frontal plagiocephaly	Unilateral coronal
Occipital plagiocephaly	Unilateral lambdoid
Frontal brachycephaly	Bilateral coronal
Occipital brachycephaly	Bilateral lambdoid
Trigonocephaly	Metopic

The Kleeblattschädel anomaly is characterized by a trilobed "cloverleaf skull" with bitemporal and vertex bulging. The spectrum of suture synostosis is broad; newborns with the deformity may show no evidence of sutural synostosis.

23. What characteristics differentiate Crouzon syndrome from Apert syndrome?

Crouzon and Apert syndromes both are characterized by craniosynostosis and a froglike facies secondary to exorbitism, telecanthus, and midface hypoplasia, all of which tend to be more severe in Apert syndrome. A number of additional features distinguish the two anomalies (Table 30-2).

24. Name three syndromes associated with hand anomalies.

- *Apert syndrome* (acrocephalosyndactyly) is transmitted by an autosomal dominant mode of inheritance. It is characterized by craniosynostosis, exorbitism, midface hypoplasia, and symmetric syndactyly of the hands and feet. Although Tessier noted multiple additional characteristics of patients with Apert syndrome, syndactyly essentially differentiates it from Crouzon's syndrome.
- *Pfeiffer syndrome* is autosomal dominant in transmission. It is characterized by craniosynostosis, exorbitism, midface hypoplasia, and spoonlike thumbs and great toes.
- *Carpenter syndrome* is autosomal recessive in transmission. It is characterized by craniosynostosis, polysyndactyly of the feet, and short hands with variable soft tissue syndactyly.

25. What is secondary craniosynostosis?

Any pathologic condition that interferes with the normal development of the cranial bones may cause a compensatory synostosis of the cranial sutures and secondary craniosynostosis. An abnormally high incidence of craniosynostosis has been seen in patients with hematologic disorders, malformations (microcephaly or encephalocele), metabolic disorders (hyperthyroidism, vitamin D–resistant rickets, mucopolysaccharidosis), and other disorders, such as Hurler syndrome and achondroplasia, that affect generalized skeletal development.

26. What is "slit ventricle syndrome"?

Slit ventricle syndrome occurs as a complication in 1% to 5% of patients after shunting procedures for hydrocephalus during infancy and was first described in the 1960s. These patients usually have had a shunt in place for years with overdrainage of cerebrospinal fluid resulting in very small ventricles. Slit ventricle syndrome is recognized as a triad of chronic, intermittent headaches accompanying findings of a slowly refilling shunt reservoir on physical examination and "slit" ventricles on radiographic evaluation. Additional radiographic findings include a "copper-beaten" appearance or "thumb printing" and scalloping of the inner calvarial table (Fig. 30-5). Excessive intracranial decompression may result in cranial vault collapse with secondary craniosynostosis. With continued brain growth within the now-restricted cranium, increased ICP recurs with potentially devastating consequences.

Table 30-2. Distinguishing Characteristics of Crouzon Syndrome and Apert Syndrome

CHARACTERISTIC	CROUZON SYNDROME	APERT SYNDROME
Affected sutures	Coronal (most common), sagittal, lambdoid	Coronal (usually)
Calvarial deformity	Brachycephaly, scaphocephaly, trigonocephaly, oxycephaly	Brachycephaly, turricephaly
Hand anomalies	None	Symmetric syndactyly of the hands and feet
Ocular findings	Nystagmus, strabismus, optic nerve atrophy	Ptosis, antimongoloid slant of palpebral fissure
Development	Normal	Retardation common

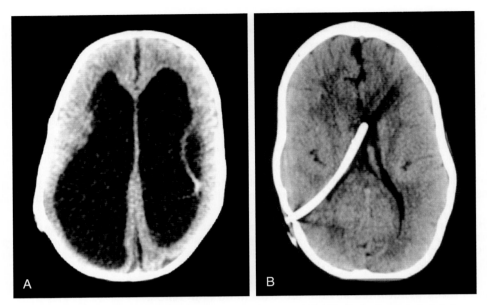

Figure 30-5. Slit ventricle syndrome. Management of congenital hydrocephalus **(A)** with shunt placement results in ventricular collapse (slitlike ventricles) **(B).**

27. What is "postshunt craniosynostosis"? What causes it?

Following excessive intracranial decompression and ventricular collapse, cranial vault collapse ensues with resultant secondary or *postshunt* craniosynostosis. Craniosynostosis, which may involve multiple sutures or a single suture, results due to an unidentified signal that is conveyed to the cranial sutures secondary to this intracranial decompression, which erroneously indicates completed brain growth and provides the stimulus for suture fusion (Fig. 30-6).

Although the signals for sutural synostosis are more complex than cessation of brain growth and are potentially related to the *overdrainage* or *intracranial decompression* phenomenon associated with shunting, they remain poorly understood. As the brain continues to grow within the now-restricted cranium, increased ICP recurs. Patients' symptoms are similar to those seen with shunt malformation; the most common complaints are repetitive or cyclical headaches and nausea and vomiting, correlating with increased ICP. Further shunting produces additional overdrainage, which exacerbates the ventricular collapse, thus creating a progressive cycle (Fig. 30-7).

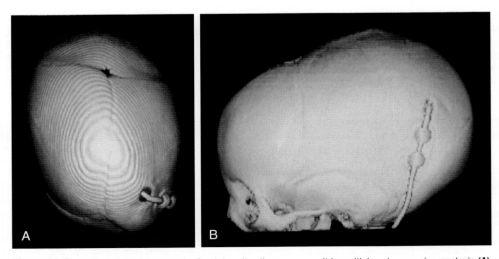

Figure 30-6. Postshunt craniosynostosis. Cranial vault collapse can result in multiple suture craniosynostosis **(A)** or isolated sagittal synostosis **(B).**

Post-Shunt Craniosynostosis: Sequence of Events

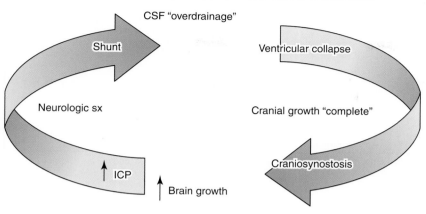

Figure 30-7. Postshunt craniosynostosis: Sequence of events. *CSF,* Cerebrospinal fluid; *ICP,* intracranial pressure.

28. How is postshunt craniosynostosis treated?

Management of this complex problem is complicated. Initial conservative treatment includes observation and medical therapy, including antimigraine treatment. With failure of conservative therapy, surgical intervention is warranted. Various surgical approaches have been described, including upgrading the existing shunt valve, adding a siphon-resistant component, or changing to a flow control valve for low-pressure symptoms. High-pressure symptoms pose a more difficult problem, and treatment has included shunt revision as well as cranial expansion and subtemporal decompression. Technical considerations have included dilating the ventricular system with subsequent reinsertion of a catheter, using endoscopy, fluoroscopy, or stereotaxis during revision, as well as performing a third ventriculostomy. In addition, morcellation of the posterior cranium or subtemporal craniectomy are used to expand or vent the skull to relieve the episodic increases in ICP.

Weinzweig et al. reviewed a series of patients who had undergone cranial vault expansion for management of postshunt craniosynostosis and slit ventricle syndrome refractory to other treatment modalities. The most frequent symptom of shunt malfunction was chronic headaches. Seizures, papilledema, bradycardia, and blindness occurred less commonly. Patients in this series demonstrated pancraniosynostosis, multiple sutural fusion, isolated sagittal synostosis, or "functional" synostosis with narrowed, overlapping sutures that were not actually fused. The majority of patients underwent bilateral frontoorbital advancement with frontotemporoparietal expansion; one patient underwent only posterior vault expansion. Improvement in cranial vault shape was achieved in all of the patients as well as improvement of neurologic symptoms in 75% of the patients. Thus cranial vault expansion is a useful approach in the management of the restricted cranium associated with slit ventricle syndrome and postshunt craniosynostosis.

29. How does one differentiate between deformational and synostotic plagiocephaly? Which is more common?

Synostotic frontal plagiocephaly, secondary to unilateral coronal synostosis, is an uncommon disorder that occurs in 1:10,000 live births. It is approximately 2% as common as deformational plagiocephaly, although the true incidence of deformational plagiocephaly is unknown. Isolated unilateral lambdoidal synostosis is an extremely rare cause of synostotic occipital plagiocephaly, accounting for only 0.8% to 1.3% of all syndromic and nonsyndromic cases.

Deformational frontal plagiocephaly may result in an ipsilateral narrow palpebral fissure and lower eyebrow, inferiorly positioned ipsilateral ear, and no angulation of the nasal root. Each of these findings may or may not be observed in each case depending on the severity of the plagiocephaly and whether or not only the mid and upper frontal bone is involved with or without involvement of the supraorbital rim and orbit. Deviation of the chin toward the involved side and inferior positioning of the ear occur infrequently. From the vertex ("bird's eye") view, the deformational plagiocephalic cranium appears as though it has been compressed from forehead to opposite occiput ("parallelogrammic head"). The cheek and ear are retruded on the same side as the flattened forehead, with bossing of the ipsilateral posterior parietal bone and contrecoup flattening of the opposite occipitoparietal region.

Synostotic frontal plagiocephaly results in an ipsilateral widened palpebral fissure, superiorly and posteriorly displaced supraorbital rim and eyebrow, higher ipsilateral ear, and deviation of the nasal root toward the flattened side. The chin sometimes points to the contralateral side. The anterior fontanelle, if open, is displaced toward the normal side. Sutural ridging is inconsistently found in coronal synostosis; its absence does not exclude the diagnosis (Table 30-3).

Table 30-3. Deformational versus Synostotic Plagiocephaly

ANATOMIC FEATURE	SYNOSTOTIC	DEFORMATIONAL
Ipsilateral supraorbital rim	High	± Posterior*
Ipsilateral eyebrow position	High	Normal
Ipsilateral ear	Anterior and high	Posterior
Ipsilateral cheek	± Posterior†	± Posterior
Nasal root	Ipsilateral deviation	Midline
Ipsilateral palpebral fissure	Wide	± Narrow and high
Anterior fontanelle deviation	Contralateral	None

*Depends on whether or not the pressure on the frontal region is confined to the upper area, lower area, or both.
†This finding is related more to hypoplasia than malpositioning.

30. Once the diagnosis of deformational plagiocephaly is made in a 2-month-old infant with a pronounced posterior head shape abnormality, what is the appropriate management?

The parents should be advised to have the infant sleep prone or on his/her side to avoid applying further pressure to the flattened spot. If some degree of improvement is not appreciated within a few months, a molding helmet should be fabricated and worn 23 hours each day until normal cranial shape has been restored. Close follow-up every 2 to 3 months is warranted. It is generally believed that little improvement in plagiocephaly will occur with the use of a helmet beyond 12 months of age, although some improvement is sometimes seen until 18 months of age.

31. What is the harlequin deformity?

The harlequin deformity is the characteristic radiographic finding in patients with synostotic frontal plagiocephaly. It describes the abnormal shape of the orbit due to ipsilateral superior displacement of the lesser wing of the sphenoid, creating an elongated oval, medial to lateral.

32. What is torticollis?

Torticollis, which literally means "twisted neck," results from shortening of the sternocleidomastoid muscle. It is characterized by a tilting of the head toward the affected side; the chin points up and toward the opposite side. The shoulder is higher on the affected side, and the external ear is sometimes more prominent on the affected side. When the condition persists beyond a few weeks in infancy, an asymmetry develops in which the face and skull on the affected side appear smaller.

33. Is there an association between deformational plagiocephaly and torticollis?

Definitely. True torticollis—in which the head tilts toward the abnormal side—is present in 64% of children with deformational plagiocephaly. Ocular torticollis, in which the child attempts to correct for strabismus-induced diplopia by tilting the head toward the normal side, is present in approximately 50% of children with synostotic plagiocephaly.

34. What are the two goals of surgery for patients with craniosynostosis?

- Decompression of the intracranial space (to reduce ICP, prevent visual problems, and permit normal mental development)
- Achievement of satisfactory craniofacial form

35. What is the ideal timing for correction of craniosynostosis?

The thickness of the calvarial bone between 6 and 12 months of age usually is adequate to permit reconstructive osteotomies yet is soft enough to facilitate remodeling. Reconstructions performed in children earlier than 6 months of age have a greater likelihood of requiring subsequent procedures, including frontoorbital readvancement, whereas in children older than 1 year, bone gaps do not close in a predictable fashion.

36. When can defects of the skull be expected to spontaneously heal? How does this affect reconstructive plans?

Paige et al. evaluated the ability of the immature skull to spontaneously heal large bony defects created after frontoorbital advancement and anterior cranial vault reconstruction (FOAR) had been performed. They found that children who closed a bony defect following FOAR were significantly younger than were children who had a persistent bony defect. Thus healing of bony defects after FOAR is related to the child's age at the initial operation, with a mean age for defect closure of less than 12 months. The authors noted that between 9 and 11 months of age, a change occurs that results in an increasingly lower probability of bony defect closure. Therefore all other factors being equal, initial FOAR ideally should take place before this occurs (i.e., within the first year of life).

37. Which reconstructive procedures are performed before 1 year of age? Which are performed after 1 year of age?

Frontal bone advancement with or without strip craniectomies, cranial vault remodeling, and shunt surgery for hydrocephalus are performed within the first year of life. Late procedures include Le Fort III advancement with or without concomitant frontal bone advancement (usually at 3 to 4 years of age), monobloc advancement, and jaw surgery (usually in early adolescence), which may include a Le Fort I osteotomy and genioplasty.

38. Is a strip craniectomy sufficient treatment for sagittal synostosis?

Possibly, depending on the severity of the cranial vault deformity. Sagittal or parasagittal strip craniectomy have been used successfully in many cases of isolated sagittal synostosis. Most cases of sagittal synostosis, however, require cranial vault remodeling, with removal of the affected suture and performance of frontal, parietal, and occipital "barrel-stave" osteotomies.

39. Is the treatment strategy for sagittal synostosis different in older children?

Definitely. Reconstruction of the scaphocephalic skull that results from sagittal synostosis is an age-dependent approach. The vast majority of such patients are surgically treated within the first year of life.

However, in a small percentage of patients with sagittal synostosis, diagnosis of a skull shape abnormality is delayed, as a result of either the subtleness of the scaphocephalic deformity or the lack of familiarity with the anomaly by the primary pediatrician. Despite the fact that all of these patients have the same diagnosis, they present with a myriad of anatomic deformities, including varying degrees of frontal bossing and occipital shelving. Delayed presentation because of a failure to appreciate the craniosynostotic abnormality often results in a more severe cranial vault deformity, with frontoorbital involvement in almost half of these patients.

Significant frontal bossing with involvement of the supraorbital bandeau and prominent occipital shelving will necessitate a total vault reconstruction with transverse frontoorbital expansion and resetting of the supraorbital bar inclination to prevent temporal indentations and ensure a smooth transition of the supraorbital bandeau and frontal bone. The decision to perform this extensive procedure in one stage *(considerably more risk)* or two will depend on several factors, including patient age and additional medical problems that might preclude such an undertaking. Similarly, mild to moderate frontal bossing in the absence of occipital shelving may require only an anterior two-thirds vault reconstruction. Proper tailoring of the reconstructive procedure to address each anatomic abnormality should permit the management of all cases of sagittal synostosis, regardless of the extent of deformity.

40. How is metopic synostosis corrected?

Except in the mildest cases of trigonocephaly, supraorbital and frontal remodeling usually is necessary. Despite the fact that metopic synostosis is an uncommon form of craniosynostosis, with an incidence of less than 10% of all cases of craniosynostosis, the resultant deformity is readily recognized due to the prominent frontal keel, narrow forehead, and occasional hypotelorism. Removal of the deformed supraorbital bar and flattening of the nasion angle, using a midline osteotomy, facilitates correction with a frontoorbital advancement.

With more severe cases of metopic synostosis, in which hypotelorism is present, a nasofrontal osteotomy is performed before attachment of the supraorbital bar to the inferior midfacial segment. The frontonasal junction is separated with an osteotome, and a bone graft is inserted. This procedure immediately increases the intercanthal distance and partially corrects the hypotelorism. However, a nasofrontal osteotomy also increases the risk of distortion of nasal growth so unless the hypotelorism is extreme, it is probably better to leave it as is because some degree of spontaneous improvement occurs following treatment of metopic synostosis.

41. What is the appropriate treatment of an infant with bilateral coronal synostosis and a moderate degree of exorbitism? Is this approach useful in an infant with syndromic synostosis (Crouzon or Apert syndrome)?

The Tessier type of frontal bone advancement is advocated for the infant with bilateral coronal synostosis and a moderate degree of exorbitism as well as the infant with syndromic synostosis. The osteotomies are made across the nasofrontal junction, across the roof of the orbit, and along the lateral orbital walls. Osteotomy extensions are made into the temporal fossa to provide a tongue-in-groove arrangement that obviates the need for bone grafts for fixation purposes. Advancement of the frontal bandeau (supraorbital bar) more than 20 mm can be performed in this manner, with significant expansion of orbital volume. The frontal bone flap is then wired or plated to the advanced supraorbital bar. Closure of the scalp after significant frontal bone advancement can be facilitated by the temporary use of large stay sutures or by scoring of the galea.

42. How does treatment of unilateral coronal synostosis (plagiocephaly) differ from treatment of bilateral coronal synostosis (brachycephaly)?

Early approaches to the treatment of plagiocephaly included simple coronal strip craniectomies and extended strip craniectomies with removal of the involved suture, but these procedures do not reliably produce upper craniofacial symmetry.

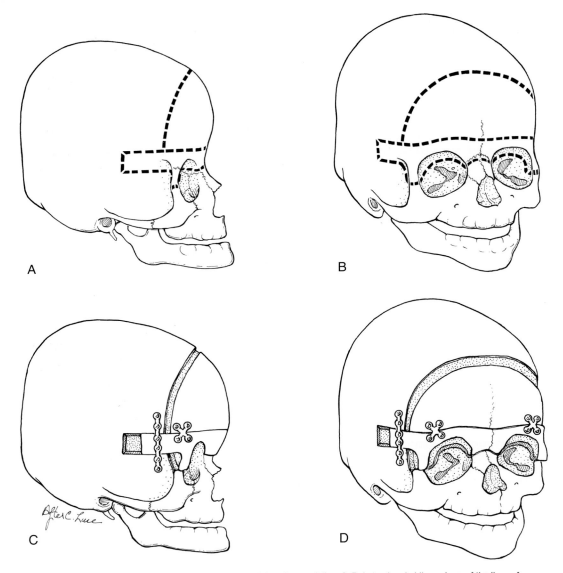

Figure 30-8. Bilateral frontoorbital advancement and cranial vault remodeling. **A, B,** Lateral and oblique views of the lines of osteotomy. **C, D,** Lateral and oblique views after advancement of the frontoorbital segment and repositioning of the frontal bone flap. Resorbable plates and screws are used for fixation. The position of the tenon denotes the amount of skeletal advancement that was achieved. (From McCarthy JG, Hollier LH: Reconstruction: Craniosynostosis. In: Mathes S [ed]: Plastic Surgery, 2nd ed. Philadelphia, WB Saunders, 2006, p 473.)

Although plagiocephaly is a unilateral malformation, some surgeons prefer to perform bilateral forehead remodeling along with removal and modification of a single supraorbital bandeau extending across both orbits. In selected cases, this technique permits simultaneous restoration of forehead symmetry as well as correction of the anteroposterior position and superoinferior discrepancy of the supraorbital rims. Plagiocephaly reconstruction is very similar to brachycephaly correction in that, in some cases, a bilateral approach may be optimal; however, orbital symmetry presents a greater problem in the case of plagiocephaly, requiring anteroinferior and slight medial translocation of the affected supraorbital rim.

Our approach to the treatment of unicoronal synostosis is a tailored one. In many cases of unicoronal synostosis, an excellent result can be obtained from a unilateral approach in which the supraorbital bandeau on the affected side is osteotomized and advanced. This osteotomy usually extends just past the midline to encompass the entire extent of the bony deformity. Advancement of the contralateral bandeau often is not necessary. The anterior cranial vault is contoured to accommodate both sides of the supraorbital bar and yield a seamless reconstruction (Fig. 30-8).

43. What is a Le Fort III advancement osteotomy?

A Le Fort III advancement osteotomy is performed for the purpose of advancing the midface in the patient with severe midfacial retrusion. The bony framework of the nose is divided at the nasofrontal junction. The osteotomy line is continued backward across the medial wall of the orbit on each side, then downward to the floor of the orbit. A narrow osteotome is used to section the delicate lamina papyracea of the ethmoid, which forms the portion of the medial wall posterior to the lacrimal bone. A transverse cut is made across the orbital floor and joins the inferior orbital fissure to the lower end of the medial wall osteotomy.

The lateral orbital wall is sectioned transversely in the region of the frontozygomatic suture line or above it. The orbital contents are retracted medially, and the lateral orbital wall is divided at its junction with the cranium. The zygomatic arch is similarly sectioned. The lateral orbital wall osteotomy is continued inferiorly and posteriorly through the pterygomaxillary fissure. Once the osteotomies have been performed, the midfacial skeleton can be loosened with the

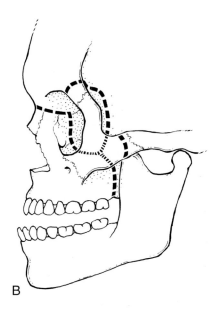

B

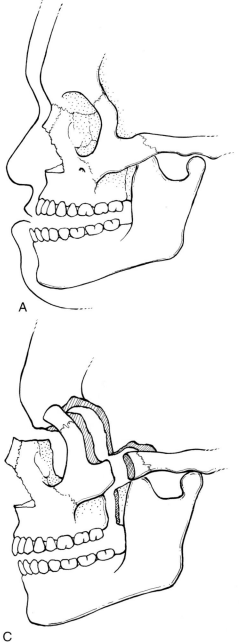

A

C

Figure 30-9. Subcranial Le Fort III osteotomy. **A,** Lateral view showing the pathologic process. Note the midface hypoplasia, anterior crossbite, and anterior open bite. **B,** The lines of osteotomy: across the nasofrontal junction, through the medial orbital wall, floor of the orbit, full thickness of the lateral orbital wall, zygomatic arch and retromaxillary area, and pterygomaxillary junction. **C,** Mobilization of the osteotomized segment and the resulting skeletal defects. (From McCarthy JG, Hollier LH: Reconstruction: Craniosynostosis. In: Mathes S [ed]: Plastic Surgery, 2nd ed., Philadelphia, Saunders, 2006, p 478.)

Rowe disimpacting forceps. Bone grafts are placed in the defects of the nasofrontal junction, and, occasionally, the lateral orbital wall and pterygomaxillary fissure. After intermaxillary fixation, interosseous wires or miniplate fixation is used to stabilize the nasofrontal, zygomaticofrontal, and zygomaticotemporal osteotomies (Fig. 30-9).

44. When should a Le Fort III advancement osteotomy be performed with a simultaneous Le Fort I osteotomy or frontal bone advancement?

The combination of Le Fort III and Le Fort I osteotomies permits differential advancement of the midface and maxillary segments. This approach is indicated for patients in whom the deformity is restricted to the upper aspects of the midface (exorbitism and maxillary hypoplasia) and in whom dental occlusal relationships are within acceptable range. Le Fort I osteotomy is performed superior to the apices of the teeth and below the infraorbital nerve. It is continued medially and superiorly to terminate at the upper margin of the piriform aperture. The osteotomy continues laterally to join the pterygomaxillary fissure. This procedure is indicated only rarely, as instability of the bony segments can easily occur if the Le Fort I and III components are separated, in which case you would be left with only a portion of the orbits (Fig. 30-10).

The combination of Le Fort III and frontal bone advancement osteotomies permits simultaneous advancement of the midface as well as the frontal bone. This approach is preferred in patients with brachycephaly and midfacial retrusion. Once the frontal bone flap is removed, the supraorbital osteotomy is extended horizontally to the region of the temporal fossa and continued in stepwise fashion inferiorly toward the base of the skull. The step design of this osteotomy permits bony contact after advancement of the frontal bandeau. The osteotomy is continued in a horizontal fashion through the lateral orbital wall and roof posteriorly. The procedure is completed by performing the Le Fort III osteotomy. This combination permits simultaneous advancement of the frontal bone, part of the roof, and lateral wall of the orbits. In essence, this combination of osteotomies constitutes the equivalent of a monobloc advancement.

CONTROVERSIES

45. What is a monobloc advancement? Is it safe?

Thirty years ago, Ortiz-Monasterio popularized a method of increasing orbital volume for the correction of severe exorbitism by the simultaneous advancement of the forehead, orbits, and midface. The lines of osteotomy for the monobloc advancement are similar to those for the combined Le Fort III/frontal bone advancement except that the nasofrontal junction and frontozygomatic suture are not osteotomized. Inclusion of the orbits with this advancement results in a considerable expansion of orbital volume (Fig. 30-11).

Although this procedure is advocated by a number of highly experienced surgeons, including Tessier, the increased risk of infection and associated cerebrospinal fluid leak remains a significant concern. This risk is due to the communication created between the nasal and intracranial cavities by the osteotomy design. Despite the use of pericranial flaps to separate these cavities, the increased risk associated with their potential persistent communication remains.

46. Is there a role for alloplastic bone substitutes during craniosynostosis reconstruction?

Over the past decade, a multitude of biomaterials, typically pastes and cements composed of calcium phosphate, have been promoted as "bone substitutes" for osseous augmentation and reconstruction of the craniofacial skeleton with expectations that these compounds would provide a structural lattice during the remodeling phases of healing and would be fully replaced by host bone over time. Others have promoted carbonated calcium phosphate compounds that crystallize in situ to more closely resemble the mineral phase of bone, thus offering the potential for enhanced bioresorption and osteoconductivity without restriction of craniofacial growth. Reports of fistula formation, infection, cement microfragmentation, and other complications following the use of these biomaterials discourage their use by some. Proper use of these biomaterials, including avoiding sinuses, using limited amounts of material, and avoiding contact with the dura, can minimize or eliminate the incidence of the aforementioned complications.

The precise age at which such bone substitutes can be safely used in the growing calvarium remains controversial. Of those surgeons who include such substitutes in their surgical armamentarium, the majority resort to their use more commonly during secondary cranioplasty procedures for the correction of residual cranial defects following primary craniosynostosis reconstruction several years earlier, rather than during the initial procedure.

47. Is there a role for the endoscopic approach to craniosynostosis reconstruction?

The role of endoscopic-assisted strip craniectomies/suturectomies combined with postoperative skull molding helmets for correction of various forms of craniosynostosis is currently one of the most controversial topics in craniofacial surgery. The essential features of treating craniosynostosis are (1) release of the fused suture and (2) remodeling of the cranial vault deformities. Limited surgical approaches rely on the potential of the expanding brain to correct the skull deformity following release of the skull restriction at the fused suture and guidance provided by a molding helmet.

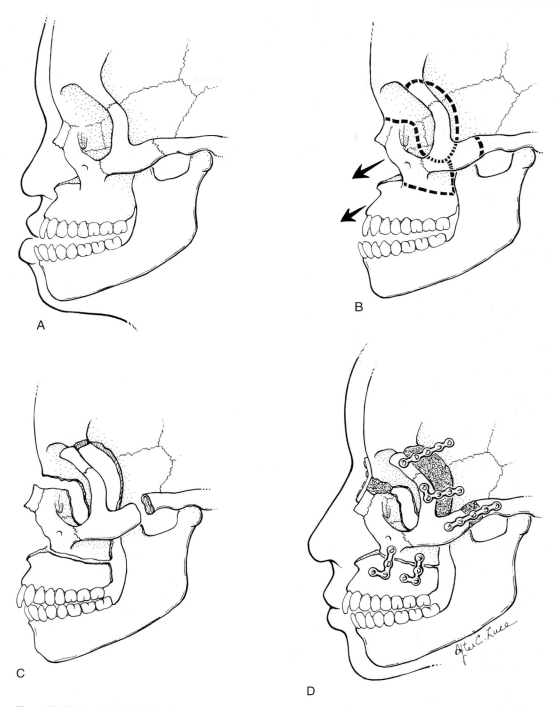

Figure 30-10. Combined Le Fort III–Le Fort I osteotomy. **A,** Lateral view of the preoperative deformity showing that the hypoplasia in the orbital–maxillary area is different from that at the maxillary occlusal plane. **B,** Lines of osteotomy. *Arrows* designate the direction of movement of the skeletal segments. **C,** View after mobilization of the osteotomized segments. **D,** Appearance after placement of interposition bone grafts and the establishment of rigid skeletal fixation. (From McCarthy JG, Hollier LH: Reconstruction: Craniosynostosis. In: Mathes S [ed]: Plastic Surgery, 2nd ed. Philadelphia, WB Saunders, 2006, p 484.)

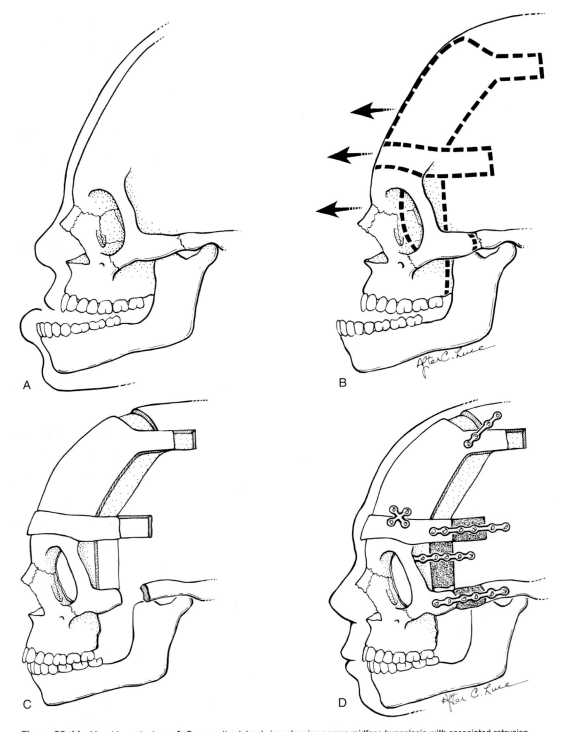

Figure 30-11. Monobloc osteotomy. **A,** Preoperative lateral view showing severe midface hypoplasia with associated retrusion of the supraorbital rim and frontal bone. There is also an anterior crossbite. **B,** Lines of osteotomy. Note the projected vectors of advancement. **C,** Lateral view after mobilization of the monobloc, supraorbital, and frontal bone segments. Note the resulting skeletal defects. **D,** Lateral view showing interposition bone grafts with the establishment of rigid skeletal fixation with plates and screws. (From McCarthy JG, Hollier LH: Reconstruction: Craniosynostosis. In: Mathes S [ed]: Plastic Surgery, 2nd ed. Philadelphia, WB Saunders, 2006, pp 487–488.)

As endoscopic procedures, once limited to strip craniectomies, have been expanded to be more comprehensive, they continue to have a reduced ability to stop bleeding from remote bleeding points. Thus, although good results have been obtained using the endoscopic approach and the advantages of this technique have been reported to include decreased operative time, decreased need for intraoperative transfusions, and earlier hospital discharge, they must be balanced with reports of dural tears, pseudomeningoceles, and life-threatening injuries of the sagittal sinus.

BIBLIOGRAPHY

Baker S, Weinzweig J, Whitaker L, Bartlett SP: Applications of a new carbonated calcium phosphate bone cement: Early experience in pediatric and adult craniofacial reconstruction. Plast Reconstr Surg 109:1789–1796, 2002.

Barone CM, Jimenez DF: Endoscopic craniectomy for early correction of craniosynostosis. Plast Reconstr Surg 104:1965–1973, 1999; discussion 1974–1975.

Barone CM, Jimenez DF: Endoscopic approach to coronal craniosynostosis. Clin Plast Surg 31:415–422, 2004.

Bartlett SP, Whitaker LA, Marchac D: The operative treatment of isolated craniofacial dysostosis (plagiocephaly): A comparison of the unilateral and bilateral techniques. Plast Reconstr Surg 85:667–683, 1990.

Bresnick SC, Schendel SA: Crouzon's disease correlates with low fibroblastic growth factor receptor activity in stenosed cranial sutures. J Craniofac Surg 6:245–248, 1995.

Bruneteau RJ, Mulliken JB: Frontal plagiocephaly: Synostotic, compensational or deformational. Plast Reconstr Surg 89:21–31, 1992.

Cohen MM Jr: Epidemiology of craniosynostosis. In Cohen MM Jr, MacLean RE (eds): Craniosynostosis, 2nd ed. New York, Oxford University Press, 2000, pp 112–118.

Eppley BL, Sandove AM: Surgical correction of metopic suture synostosis. Clin Plast Surg 21:555–562, 1994.

Jimenez DF, Barone CM: Early treatment of anterior calvarial craniosynostosis using endoscopic-assisted minimally invasive techniques. Childs Nerv Syst 23:1411–1419, 2007.

Kirschner RE, Karmacharya J, Ong G, et al: Repair of the immature craniofacial skeleton with a calcium phosphate cement: quantitative assessment of craniofacial growth. Ann Plast Surg 49:33–38, 2002.

Levine JP, Bradley JP, Roth DA, McCarthy JG, Longaker MT: Studies in cranial suture biology: Regional dura mater determines overlying suture biology. Plast Reconstr Surg 101:1441–1447, 1998.

Marchac D: Radical forehead remodeling for craniostenosis. Plast Reconstr Surg 61:823–835, 1978.

Marchac D, Renier D: Craniofacial Surgery for Craniosynostosis. Boston, Little, Brown, 1982.

McCarthy JG, Hollier LH: Reconstruction: Craniosynostosis. In Mathes SJ (ed): Plastic Surgery, Vol. 4, 2nd ed. Philadelphia, WB Saunders/Elsevier, 2006, pp 465–493.

Ocampo RV, Persing JA: Sagittal synostosis. Clin Plast Surg 21:563–574, 1994.

Ortiz-Monasterio F, Fuente Dell Campo A, Carrillo A: Advancement of the orbits and the midface in one piece, combined with frontal repositioning, for the correction of Crouzon's deformities. Plast Reconstr Surg 61:507–516, 1978.

Ortiz-Monasterio F, Fuente Dell Campo A: Refinements on the bloc orbitofacial advancement. In Caronni EP (ed): Craniofacial Surgery. Boston, Little, Brown, 1985, pp 263–274.

Paige KT, Vega SJ, Kelly CP, et al: Age-dependent closure of bony defects after frontal orbital advancement. Plast Reconstr Surg 118:977–984, 2006.

Posnick JC: The craniofacial dysostosis syndromes: Current reconstructive strategies. Clin Plast Surg 21:585–598, 1994.

Roth DA, Longaker MT, McCarthy JG, et al: Studies in cranial suture biology: Part I. Increased immunoreactivity for TGF-beta isoforms (beta 1, beta 2, and beta 3) during rat cranial suture fusion. J Bone Miner Res 12:311–321, 1997.

Roth DA, Bradley JP, Levine JP, McMullen HF, McCarthy JG, Longaker MT: Studies in cranial suture biology: Part II. Role of the dura in cranial suture fusion. Plast Reconstr Surg 97:693–699, 1996.

Roth DA, Gold LI, Han VK, et al: Immunolocalization of transforming growth factor beta 1, beta 2, and beta 3 and insulin-like growth factor I in premature cranial suture fusion. Plast Reconstr Surg 99:300–309, 1997; discussion 310–316.

Selber JC, Brooks C, Kurichi JE, Temmen T, Sonnad SS, Whitaker LA: Long-term results following fronto-orbital reconstruction in non-syndromic unicoronal synostosis. Plast Reconstr Surg 121:251e–260e, 2008.

Slater BJ, Lenton KA, Kwan MD, Gupta DM, Wan DC, Longaker MT: Cranial sutures: A brief review. Plast Reconstr Surg 121:170e–1788e, 2008.

Spector JA, Greenwald JA, Warren SM, et al: Dura mater biology: autocrine and paracrine effects of fibroblast growth factor 2. Plast Reconstr Surg 109:645–654, 2002.

Tessier P: Relationship of craniostenoses to craniofacial dysostoses, and to faciostenoses: A study with therapeutic implications. Plast Reconstr Surg 48:224–237, 1971.

Tessier P: The definitive plastic surgical treatment of the severe facial deformities of craniofacial dysostoses, Crouzon's and Apert's disease. Plast Reconstr Surg 48:419–442, 1971.

Warren SM, Brunet LJ, Harland RM, Economides AN, Longaker MT: The BMP antagonist noggin regulates cranial suture fusion. Nature 422:625–629, 2003.

Warren SM, Greenwald JA, Nacamuli RP, et al: Regional dura mater differentially regulates osteoblast gene expression. J Craniofac Surg 14:363–370, 2003.

Weinzweig J, Baker S, Bartlett S, Whitaker LA: Delayed cranial vault reconstruction for sagittal synostosis in older children. Plast Reconstr Surg 110:397–408, 2002.

Weinzweig J, Kirschner R, Farley A, Bartlett SP, Hunter J, Whitaker LA: Metopic synostosis: Defining the temporal sequence of normal suture fusion and differentiating it from synostosis on the basis of computed tomography images. Plast Reconstr Surg 112:1211–1218, 2003.

Weinzweig J, Bartlett SP, Chen JC, et al: Cranial vault expansion in the management of postshunt craniosynostosis and slit ventricle syndrome. Plast Reconstr Surg 122:1171–1180, 2008.

CHAPTER 31

PRINCIPLES OF DISTRACTION OSTEOGENESIS

Stephen M. Warren, MD; Sacha Obaid, MD; and
Joseph G. McCarthy, MD

1. What is distraction osteogenesis?

Distraction osteogenesis is the generation of viable bone by the gradual separation of osteotomized bone segments. The force and tension applied to the separated bone ends signals the body to form new bone in the gap between the bony edges. In so doing, a bone can be lengthened over time to treat skeletal deficiencies.

2. How long has the concept of skeletal molding been in use?

The concept of skeletal molding has been practiced by various cultures for thousands of years. A study of Neanderthal skulls (45,000 BC) may represent the first demonstration of cranial molding. The ancient Egyptians favored an elongated skull and pointed chin, such as those of Nefertiti. The ancient Greeks applied a mold to an infant's head shortly after birth to give it a shape symbolic of aristocracy. The practice of head molding by application of a headdress or bandeau continued in the middle ages in France, where conical head shapes were believed to be a sign of aristocracy. The Chinook tribes in North America, also known as the *Flathead Indians* of the Pacific Northwest, placed infants in a cradle board that compressed the occiput and forehead between two pieces of wood to create a tall, posteriorly inclined forehead and a flat occiput.

3. Who performed the first distraction?

Codvilla, in 1905, reported performing an osteotomy of the femur and then applying external traction to lengthen the lower extremity. Abbot, in 1927, published a similar report. The biologic principles were insufficiently studied, and the devices were poorly designed, causing the technique to be fraught with complications.

Ilizarov, a Russian orthopedic surgeon, noted new bone generation in response to the mistaken distraction of two ends of a fractured bone by a device that was intended to compress the two fractured ends. He studied this observation in the laboratory and performed distraction on canine tibias. Eventually, he applied the technique to humans with lower extremity skeletal deficiency.

McCarthy and his team at New York University first applied the techniques of distraction osteogenesis to the membranous bones of the craniofacial skeleton in a series of canine mandible studies. McCarthy eventually introduced clinical craniofacial distraction in 1989 with the first successful distraction of the human mandible.

4. What are the phases of distraction?

Distraction occurs in three phases. The first, or *latency phase*, occurs just after the performance of the osteotomy/corticotomy and application of the distraction device. During the latency phase, time is provided for reparative callus formation in the distraction zone. The latency period can last from 1 to 7 days depending on the age of the patient and the site of distraction. Following the latency period, gradual distraction forces are applied during the *activation phase* to separate the edges of the bone segments and elongate the intersegmentary callus under tension, leading to new bone formation. At the end of activation, the distracted bone is maintained in fixation to allow for consolidation of the newly formed bone—the *consolidation phase*, which typically lasts for 8 weeks.

5. What are the four zones of tissue generation in the intercalary gap?

Four zones of tissue formation are found in the intercalary gap between the two ends of osteotomized bone. The first zone is a fibrous *central zone* with longitudinally oriented fibrous bundles. Adjacent to this is a *transition zone* that features osteoid formation along the collagen bundles in the distraction gap. The third zone is the *remodeling zone*, where osteoclasts work to remodel the newly formed bone. Finally, the fourth zone is a *zone of mature bone* (Fig. 31-1).

6. What are the three types of distraction?

The three types of distraction are *unifocal*, *bifocal*, and *trifocal*. In *unifocal distraction*, a single osteotomy is made and distraction forces are applied by a device attached by screws on either side of the osteotomy. *Bifocal distraction* can be used when trying to close an existing gap between two ends of a bone. An osteotomy is made near the border on one side of the bony defect to create an island of bone called a *transport segment*. Three sets

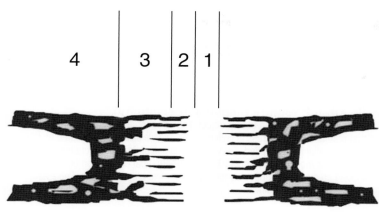

4   3   2   1

1: Fibrous central zone
2: Transition zone
3: Remodeling zone
4: Mature bone zone

Figure 31-1. Four distinct zones of tissue formation in the newly generated bone during distraction osteogenesis. (From Karp NS, McCarthy JG, Schreiber JS, et al: Membranous bone lengthening: A serial histological study. Ann Plast Surg 29:2–7, 1992.)

of pins are placed: two on either side of the osteotomy (i.e., in one end of the bone and in the transport segment) and another on the other side of the defect. Distraction forces then are applied, separating the transport segment of bone from its original location and advancing it across the bony defect. New bone is generated behind the advancing transport segment. Finally, *trifocal distraction* is similar to bifocal distraction except that osteotomies are created on both ends of a bone with a bony gap. Thus two transport segments are created, which are advanced toward each other to close the defect (Fig. 31-2).

7. Can distraction be performed without an osteotomy?

Distraction can be performed without an osteotomy; this is called *transutural distraction*. Orthodontic maxillary arch expansion using a device placed across the palatine suture is one example. Distraction osteogenesis is also seen in nature as the rapidly enlarging brain of an infant separates the individual cranial bones, leading to deposition of new bone at the cranial sutures.

8. What is distraction histogenesis?

The term *distraction histogenesis* emphasizes not only the generation of new bone with distraction but also the lengthening and generation of additional soft tissues. The associated skin, muscle, nerves, and vascular tissues lengthen in concert with the lengthened bone. Distraction histogenesis accounts for the decreased force needed to lengthen bone and the subsequent decreased relapse rate when a bone is lengthened by distraction, as opposed to that following surgical advancement.

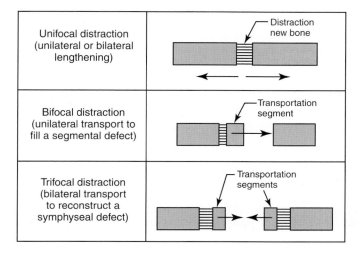

Unifocal distraction (unilateral or bilateral lengthening)	Distraction new bone
Bifocal distraction (unilateral transport to fill a segmental defect)	Transportation segment
Trifocal distraction (bilateral transport to reconstruct a symphyseal defect)	Transportation segments

Figure 31-2. Three different types of distraction: Unifocal, bifocal, and trifocal. (From McCarthy JG: Distraction of the Craniofacial Skeleton. New York, Springer-Verlag, 1999.)

9. What is "molding of the generate"?

During the phases of activation and early consolidation, the newly generated bone can be molded to create the shape desired by the surgeon, irrespective of the location of the original osteotomy made in the bone and the vector of distraction. In a canine model, mandibles distracted to create an anterior openbite of 30° could have the openbite closed by applying a constant molding force to the generate bone. Guiding dental elastics and/or angulation of distraction devices can mold the distracted human mandible to create a more acceptable dental occlusion.

10. What is tensile stress? Tensile strain? Young's modulus of elasticity?

The application of force to an elastic object causes deformation of that object. The effect of applied force is referred to as *stress*. The resulting deformation that results from the stress is called *strain*. *Tensile stress* is calculated as the force divided by the cross-sectional area across which it is applied. *Tensile strain* is calculated as the change in length of an object divided by the original length. *Young's modulus of elasticity* is the mathematical description of an object or substance's tendency to be deformed along an axis when opposing forces are applied along that axis. The *elastic modulus* is defined as the ratio of tensile stress to tensile strain.

It is believed that mechanical stress applied to the healing fracture signals the body to produce new bone and directs the bone to be formed along the fracture gap. In addition, tensile strain determines when the body is capable of forming bone. For example, at an activation rate of 1 mm/day and an osteotomy defect of 1 mm, the strain is 100% on the first day of activation. By activation day 10, when the fracture gap is 10 mm, the tensile strain has decreased to 10%. Bone cannot tolerate more than 1% to 2% tensile strain. For this reason, bone formation is not seen in the distraction zone until approximately 4 weeks of activation.

11. What is the range of nominal strain in the mandibular distraction gap?

Because the area on which the tensile stress changes with time, the concept of nominal strain is important. Nominal strain in turn is the strain calculated with respect to the original length of the bone prior to beginning distraction osteogenesis. The nominal strain in the distracted rat mandible is 10% to 12.5% during the activation phase.

12. What is mechanical transduction? What are the mechanicobiologic principles thought to guide mesenchymal tissue differentiation?

Mechanical transduction is the process by which mechanical signals stimulate and direct tissue differentiation. In studies of the mechanobiology of skeletal regeneration, it was found that cyclic hydrostatic pressure can lead to cartilage formation. Similarly, high tensile strain leads to fibrous tissue formation, and a combination of hydrostatic pressure and tensile strain leads to fibrocartilage formation. If the vascular supply is adequate, low hydrostatic stress and tensile strain can signal the direct formation of bone. If mild hydrostatic tension is applied as well, the rate of bone formation can be accelerated.

13. What is the theoretical mechanism for new bone formation?

Shortly after the bone is divided, there is hematoma formation and migration of inflammatory cells into the fracture gap. The zone of injury is relatively hypoxic, causing an angiogenic response with up-regulation of vascular endothelial growth factor, which stimulates the migration of primitive mesenchymal cells and the synthesis of collagen I matrix. Angiogenesis is a precursor to osteogenic activity, and canine distraction models have shown blood flow increased up to 10 times that of controls. The increase in blood flow peaked at 2 weeks postoperatively. Elevated blood flow two to three times control values was observed for as long as 17 weeks postoperatively.

As the distraction device is activated, there is a marked increase in transforming growth factor beta-1 (TGF-β1), which induces collagen deposition and the formation of noncollagen extracellular matrix proteins. Tapered cells, similar in morphology to fibroblasts, and new blood vessels are organized in a longitudinal fashion along the distraction vector. Approximately 14 days after activation of the device, osteoid synthesis and mineralization become apparent. Three weeks after activation, calcification of the linear oriented collagen bundles occurs in response to the up-regulation of osteocalcin. This is followed by the appearance of osteoblasts along the collagen bundles and the formation of bony spicules that extend from the edges of the osteotomy toward the central portion of the distraction zone. Progressive calcification of the generate bone occurs, and the bony defect is closed. The newly formed bone continues to remodel with the appearance of osteoclasts and the generation of lamellar bone with marrow elements of adequate volume.

14. What are the molecular signals that play a role in distraction osteogenesis?

A marked increase in TGF-β1 is seen 3 days after the creation of the fracture. TGF-β1 plays a regulatory role in the induction of collagen deposition and the formation of noncollagen extracellular matrix proteins, which are involved in the mineralization and remodeling of bones. TGF-β1 activates vascular endothelial growth factor (VEGF) and fibroblast growth factor-2 (FGF-2). TGF-β1 also plays a regulatory role in osteoblast migration, differentiation, and bone remodeling.

The bone morphogenetic proteins (BMPs) are growth factors belonging to the TGF-β superfamily of proteins. During the first 4 days after fracture formation, BMP-2 and BMP-4 are markedly up-regulated. During the activation phase, BMP-2, BMP-4, and BMP-7 remain up-regulated. The elevated levels of BMPs continue well into the consolidation phase.

Insulin-like growth factor-1 (IGF-1) is a skeletal growth factor that is elevated during early activation.

FGF-2 stimulates osteoblast proliferation and enhances bone formation. In addition, FGF-2 augments the expression of TGF-β1 and its myriad pro-osteogenic effects. FGF-2 is elevated during distraction osteogenesis.

Osteocalcin is initially decreased in the latency phase but is increased in the activation phase. Osteocalcin helps to control mineralization and bone remodeling. The rigidity and hardness of bone are attributable to mineralization of the extracellular matrix.

VEGF, which is up-regulated 5 to 7 days after osteotomy, is an angiogenic cytokine that regulates the budding and growth of new vessels from existing vascular structures. This is critical in establishing blood flow to the initially hypoxic area at the fracture gap.

15. What are the two basic types of distraction devices?

Internal devices are almost entirely buried beneath the soft tissues except for a small activation arm that exits the skin and is accessible for turning. External devices are placed almost entirely outside the skin with the exception of multiple pins that pass through the skin and into the bone.

16. What are the advantages of distraction osteogenesis compared with traditional surgical movements of the craniofacial skeleton?

Distraction osteogenesis has many advantages compared with conventional surgical movements. It is a simpler, often less invasive, operative procedure with reduced need for blood transfusion and with lower morbidity, especially with regard to infection and reduced operative time and hospitalization. Because distraction osteogenesis is less invasive, it can be performed at a younger age. Because the bone must be exposed only at the site of the osteotomy, less subperiosteal elevation is required, which in turn prevents devitalization of the bone. The avoidance of bone grafts with distraction prevents the associated morbidity of a distant operative site and the potential complications that may occur to the bone graft, including resorption, nonvascularization, and infection. Another advantage of distraction is that the soft tissues are gradually lengthened, causing new soft tissue formation in addition to bone generation, a process called *distraction histogenesis*. The formation of new soft tissue causes the soft tissue to exert less pressure on the lengthened bone, thus contributing to a lower relapse rate compared with bone advanced by conventional craniofacial surgical techniques.

17. What are the disadvantages of craniofacial distraction?

Distraction osteogenesis does have some disadvantages compared with conventional surgical movements of the craniofacial skeleton. The most obvious is that distraction osteogenesis represents a prolonged therapy, typically lasting at least 3 months and requiring multiple clinical visits and close postoperative follow-up. Often external distraction devices need to be placed. They are visible and may cause scarring. Finally, because the optimal occlusion is not always obtained at the time of the initial operation with distraction, the generate bone often must be molded using elastics or device manipulation to achieve the optimal occlusion.

18. Are there age limits on distraction?

There are no age limits as to when distraction can be performed, provided the patient is physiologically capable of undergoing the operation. Successful distraction of neonates younger than 1 month can be performed to prevent tracheostomy in patients with micrognathia and associated upper airway obstruction. Despite a documented decrease in osteogenesis with advancing age, this is not a contraindication to distraction as clinical and experimental studies have shown successful long bone and mandibular distraction in older subjects.

19. Can irradiated bone be distracted?

In 1994, Gantous et al. demonstrated in the canine mandible that irradiated bone could be distracted. Since that demonstration, successful distraction of irradiated human mandibles has been reported.

20. Can craniofacial distraction treat obstructive sleep apnea?

Bilateral mandibular distraction can be used to advance not only the mandibular arch but also the base of the tongue and the hyoid bone. The mandible and soft tissue advancement increases airway volume and flow. The airway improvement may allow for successful decannulation of patients with severe obstructive sleep apnea who are tracheostomy dependant secondary to mandibular deficiency.

21. When would you perform mandibular distraction?

Mandibular distraction can be used to treat deficiencies resulting from congenital hypoplasia of the mandible (with or without associated obstructive sleep apnea), posttraumatic defects, and defects resulting from oncologic resection.

In patients younger than 2 years, mandibular distraction should not be performed unless airway compromise is present. Between ages 2 and 6 years, mandibular distraction can be considered for patients with all ranges of mandibular deficiencies, except those with mild Pruzansky type I mandibles and a horizontal occlusal plane. These patients should be treated by orthodontic therapy and preparation for eventual skeletal surgery at the completion of craniofacial growth. From age 6 years to adolescence, during the period of mixed dentition, orthodontic therapy should be used to promote the growth of the affected dentoalveolus and to aid in the proper eruption of the permanent teeth. Mandibular distraction should not be performed in this age group unless the patient has obstructive sleep apnea or has severely dysmorphic facies. Mandibular distraction in the teenage years should be postponed until skeletal maturity, which is approximately age 16 years in girls and age 17 years in males, unless there is severe mandibular deficiency secondary to relapse or skeletal malocclusion.

22. When would you perform alveolar ridge distraction?

Distraction osteogenesis can be used to augment a hypoplastic dentoalveolar segment secondary to congenital deficiency, trauma, absent dentition, or oncologic resection. The hypoplastic alveolar ridge of the mandible can be augmented to allow for sufficient bony volume to hold osseointegrated dental implants. Small alveolar deficiencies that may arise from alveolar clefts can be closed using horizontal and vertical lengthening of the adjacent alveolus. This technique can correct malocclusions and obviate the need for more invasive surgical procedures. These procedures should be performed after eruption of the permanent dentition.

23. When would you perform maxillary distraction?

Cleall et al. in 1965 were the first to successfully perform orthodontic expansion of the midpalatal suture using juvenile rhesus monkeys. This concept has been adapted clinically by orthodontists who use rapid palatal expanders to expand horizontally deficient maxillary palates.

Distraction can also be used to treat maxillary deficiency in the anteroposterior dimension, causing Angle class III malocclusion with anterior crossbite. This is often the result of unilateral or bilateral cleft lip and palate or craniofacial microsomia. These patients are treated by a Le Fort I osteotomy/corticotomy followed by application of a distraction device. Le Fort I maxillary distraction typically is reserved for patients who are in the period of mixed dentition or skeletal maturity.

24. When would you perform midface distraction?

The entire midface can be advanced using a subcranial Le Fort III osteotomy and distraction osteogenesis (Fig. 31-3). The procedure typically is performed in patients with syndromic craniofacial synostosis and exorbitism, malocclusion, sleep apnea, midface retrusion, and severe dysmorphism. Patients with orbitofacial clefts also may benefit from midface distraction. Unless there is severe upper airway obstruction from midface hypoplasia, midface distraction should not be performed until approximately 3.5 years of age to ensure that there is adequate bony stock to perform the procedure successfully.

25. When would you perform frontoparietal (monobloc) distraction?

Frontoparietal or monobloc distraction advances not only the midface but also the orbits and frontal bones. It should be reserved for patients who have, in addition to midface hypoplasia, severe exorbitism or increased intracranial pressure requiring expansion of the cranial vault (Fig. 31-4).

26. What are the critical factors for successful distraction?

There are many critical factors for successful distraction. The device must be rigidly fixated to prevent motion at the distraction site to avoid fibrous nonunion. There must be sufficient bone stock to create an osteotomy and to secure the device with pins and screws. The distraction device must be activated at a rate that is slow enough to prevent disruption of the callus at the osteotomy site and development of fibrous nonunion and yet rapid enough to prevent consolidation of the bone prior to completion of activation. In addition, there must be adequate blood supply to the bone and the surrounding soft tissue to allow for distraction histogenesis. Precise preoperative planning is essential to determine the optimal vector of distraction, the site of osteotomy, and the amount of advancement needed. When distraction is performed in the growing child, it is essential to overcorrect the deformity because the hypoplastic bone that is being distracted often will not grow commensurately with the surrounding bones. Finally, it is essential to work closely with an orthodontist in treatment planning and molding of the generate to ensure optimal occlusion at the completion of distraction. In the case of unilateral distraction of the mandible, postoperative orthodontic therapy and bite blocks are used to allow hypereruption of the maxillary dentoalveolus and prevent relapse of the advanced bone.

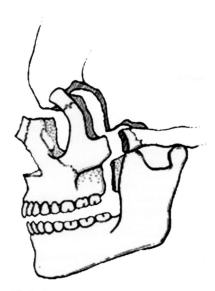

Figure 31-3. Classic Le Fort III osteotomy separates the midface from the cranium and allows the midface to be distracted forward. (From McCarthy JG, Galiano R, Boutros S: Current Therapy in Plastic Surgery. Philadelphia, WB Saunders, 2006.)

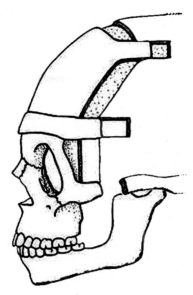

Figure 31-4. Monobloc distraction advances the frontal bones and the supraorbital rim in addition to the midface. (From Mathes S [ed]: Plastic Surgery, 2nd ed. Philadelphia, WB Saunders, 2006.)

27. What is the optimal latency?

The optimal latency usually is 5 to 7 days. Shorter latency periods have been shown to be associated with decreased callus volumes with subsequent inadequate osteogenesis. Longer latency periods have been shown to cause premature consolidation of the bone.

28. What is the optimal activation rate of distraction osteogenesis?

Distraction osteogenesis can occur at rates ranging from 0.5 to 2 mm/day. The optimal rate is 1 mm/day. Accelerated rates (1.5 to 2 mm) are reserved for the neonate or infant patient.

29. How do you determine when the activation phase is complete?

Activation should continue until the deformity being treated is corrected. However, it is important to overcorrect the deformity in the growing child because the hypoplastic bone that is being distracted usually will not grow commensurately with the surrounding bones. For this reason, in the growing child undergoing *unilateral* mandibular distraction, the endpoint of activation is movement of the chin to the contralateral side with lowering of the ipsilateral oral commissure, the inferior border of the mandible, and the occlusal plane to a level below that of the contralateral side. In *bilateral* mandibular distraction of the growing child, activation should proceed until a slight anterior crossbite is produced. Finally, in midface and maxillary distraction of the skeletally immature, activation should continue until a class II malocclusion or overjet is produced.

30. What is the optimal length of consolidation? How do you determine when consolidation is complete?

The optimal length of consolidation is 8 weeks. In patients sufficiently cooperative to have radiographs, the latter should show mineralization of the generate bone, a finding that consolidation is complete.

31. How does distraction fail?

Distraction can fail in at least four ways: ischemic fibrogenesis, cystic degeneration, fibrocartilage nonunion, and late buckling, bending, or fracture of the regenerate bone. Ischemic fibrogenesis occurs as a result of excessively rapid activation or inadequate local blood supply during distraction. Fibrous tissue forms across the distraction gap, and there is no bone column formation. Cystic degeneration occurs when there is blockage of venous outflow from the system. Large vascular channels form within the distraction gap and are filled with a lymph-like fluid. If external fixation is unstable, microfractures occur with hemorrhage and cartilage interposition in the distraction gap causing fibrocartilage nonunion. If the distraction device is removed prematurely, buckling or bending of the generate bone will occur.

32. What are the most common complications following distraction osteogenesis?

The most common complications following distraction osteogenesis are pin-tract soft tissue infections, pin dislodgement, and device failure. Other complications include premature consolidation, hypertrophic scarring, neurapraxia, dentigerous cyst formation, and parotid fistula.

BIBLIOGRAPHY

Aronson J: Experimental and clinical experience with distraction osteogenesis. Cleft Palate Craniofac J 31:473–481, 1994.

Bouletreau PJ, Warren SM, Longaker MT: The molecular biology of distraction osteogenesis. J Craniomaxillofac Surg 30:1–11, 2002.

Denny AD, Talisman R, Hanson PR, Recinos RF: Mandibular distraction osteogenesis in very young patients to correct airway obstruction. Plast Reconstr Surg 108:302–311, 2001.

Gantous A, Phillips JH, Catton P, Holmberg D: Distraction osteogenesis in the irradiated canine mandible. Plast Reconstr Surg 93:164–168, 1994.

Ilizarov GA: Clinical application of the tension-stress effect for limb lengthening. Clin Orthop Relat Res 250:8–26, 1990.

Karp NS, Thorne CH, McCarthy JG, Sissons HA: Bone lengthening in the craniofacial skeleton. Ann Plast Surg 24:231–237, 1990.

Loboa EG, Fang TD, Warren SM, et al: Mechanobiology of mandibular distraction osteogenesis: Experimental analyses with a rat model. Bone 34:336–343, 2004.

McCarthy J: Principles of craniofacial distraction. In Thorne CH, Beasley RW, Aston SJ, Bartlett SP, Gurtner GC, Spear SL (eds): Grabb and Smith's Plastic Surgery, 6th ed. Philadelphia, Lippincott Williams & Wilkins, 2006, pp 96–102.

McCarthy JG, Katzen JT, Hopper R, Grayson BH: The first decade of mandibular distraction: Lessons we have learned. Plast Reconstr Surg 110:1704–1713, 2002.

McCarthy JG, Stelnicki EJ, Mehrara BJ, Longaker MT: Distraction osteogenesis of the craniofacial skeleton. Plast Reconstr Surg 107:1812–1827, 2001.

McCarthy JG, Schreiber J, Karp N, Thorne CH, Grayson BH: Lengthening the human mandible by gradual distraction. Plast Reconstr Surg 89:1–8, 1992.

McCarthy JG, Stelnicki EJ, Grayson BH: Distraction osteogenesis of the mandible: A ten-year experience. Semin Orthod 5:3–8, 1999.

McCarthy JG, Hopper RA, Hollier LH Jr, Peltomaki T, Katzen T, Grayson BH: Molding of the regenerate in mandibular distraction: Clinical experience. Plast Reconstr Surg 112:1239–1246, 2003.

Shetye PR, Grayson BH, Mackool RJ, McCarthy JG: Lon-term stability and growth following unilateral mandibular distraction in growing children with craniofacial microsomia. Plast Reconstr Surg 118:985–995, 2006.

Tubbs RS, Salter EG, Oakes WJ: Artificial deformation of the human skull: A review. Clin Anat 19:372–377, 2006.

Williams JK, Maull D, Grayson BH, Longaker MT, McCarthy JG: Early decannulation with bilateral mandibular distraction for tracheostomy-dependent patients. Plast Reconstr Surg 103:48–57, 1999.

DISTRACTION OSTEOGENESIS OF THE MANDIBLE

Sacha Obaid, MD; Stephen M. Warren, MD; and Joseph G. McCarthy, MD

CHAPTER 32

1. What are the causes of a hypoplastic mandible?

Mandibular hypoplasia or deficiency may result from congenital or acquired processes. Among these, congenital mandibular hypoplasia is the most common, and craniofacial microsomia is the most common congenital cause with an incidence between 1:3500 and 1:6500. Other causes of congenital hypoplasia of the mandible include Pierre Robin sequence, Treacher Collins syndrome, and Nager syndrome. Acquired problems secondary to trauma, tumor, or infection may also cause mandibular hypoplasia.

2. What is Pierre Robin sequence?

Pierre Robin sequence is the triad of micrognathia, glossoptosis, and a U-shaped cleft palate. It is believed that the micrognathia leads to posterior and superior positioning of the tongue that does not allow the palatal shelves to fuse. The terminology has now been changed to Robin sequence because other theories, including a primary growth deficiency causing the mandibular hypoplasia and the cleft palate or a causally heterogeneous relationship between the two, have been expressed. We suggest that Robin sequence is really a tetrad that includes sleep apnea as well.

3. What is craniofacial microsomia?

Craniofacial microsomia is the second most common congenital anomaly of the head and neck after cleft lip and palate. Craniofacial microsomia affects both the skeletal and soft tissues derived from the first and second branchial arches. The pathognomonic finding in craniofacial microsomia is underdevelopment of the ramus and condyle of the mandible that may be unilateral or, less commonly, bilateral. Other components of the craniofacial skeleton may also be involved. The maxilla is deficient in all dimensions on the affected side with an associated upward occlusal cant. The zygoma, orbit, and frontotemporal bones can also be affected in shape and volume. Soft tissue deficiencies include thin skin with a bluish hue and diminished subcutaneous fat. A spectrum of associated ear deformities ranges from a residual lobule to an ear of normal shape with all components present but reduced in size. Facial nerve function, especially of the marginal mandibular branch, may be diminished or absent. The muscles of mastication, including the masseter, pterygoids, and temporalis, may be hypoplastic.

4. What are the differences in the mandibles in patients with Robin sequence and those with craniofacial microsomia?

The classic deformity of the mandible in patients with craniofacial microsomia is a unilateral deficiency of the ramus and the condyle. Craniofacial microsoma occurs bilaterally less commonly. Children with Robin sequence typically have bilateral mandibular hypoplasia, which tends to be most pronounced in the body of the mandible.

5. What is the Pruzansky classification of mandibular deformities?

Pruzansky described a three-class system for defining mandibular deficiency; Mulliken and Kaban subsequently modified the classification system. A Pruzansky type I mandible features hypoplasia of the ramus and the condyle, but the overall morphology of the mandible is normal. The type IIA mandible has a reduction in the volume of the body, ramus, and condyle, but the vertical orientation of the ramus is normal because the temporomandibular joint (TMJ) is preserved. In a type IIB mandible, there is a lingual inclination of the ramus in the vertical dimension in addition to the reduction in volume of the body, ramus, and condyle. The lingual inclination of the short ramus causes the condyle to be situated medial to glenoid fossa, an anatomic variation that in turn causes a restricting hinge-like function of the joint. In the type III mandible, the ramus is reduced to a thin lamina or bone or is completely absent; there is no evidence of a TMJ (Fig. 32-1).

6. What are the indications for mandibular distraction?

The indications for mandibular distraction are both functional and aesthetic. Functional indications for mandibular distraction include lengthening the hypoplastic mandible to relieve tongue-based airway obstruction/sleep apnea. Mandibular distraction also can be performed to treat TMJ ankylosis, skeletal defects resulting from trauma, tumor resections, or other pathology. The technique is also applied for augmentation of the hypoplastic or edentulous mandibular dentoalveolus. Mandibular distraction can be used in patients with severe facial dysmorphisms and hypoplasia of the mandible in the absence of functional problems.

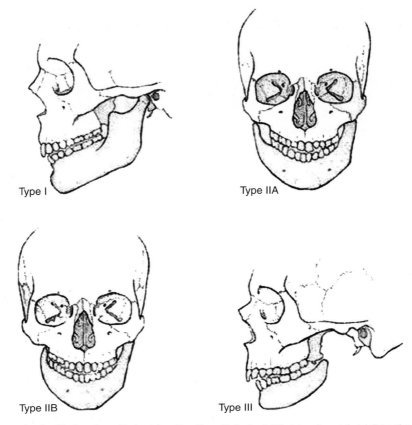

Figure 32-1. Pruzansky classification of mandibular deformities. (From McCarthy J: Principles of craniofacial distraction. In Thorne CH, Beasley RW, Aston SJ, Bartlett SP, Gurtner GC, Spear SL [eds]: Grabb and Smith's Plastic Surgery, 6th ed. Philadelphia, Lippincott Williams & Wilkins, 2006, pp 96–102.)

7. Can mandibular distraction treat obstructive sleep apnea? Can mandibular distraction prevent tracheostomy or allow for removal of an existing tracheostomy?
It has been demonstrated that bilateral mandibular distraction in neonates and infants can be used to advance not only the mandibular arch but also the base of the tongue and the hyoid bone. This leads to an increase in airway volume in tracheostomy-dependent patients who suffer from upper airway obstruction secondary to mandibular deficiency.

8. How do you assess the mandibular deformity preoperatively?
The mandibular deformity is assessed by combination of physical examination and radiographic studies. Pertinent history includes assessment for signs of obstructive sleep apnea, as well as evidence of problems with nutritional status, oral intake, oral excursion, and occlusion. Physical examination should include assessment of the thickness and quality of the facial soft tissues and the oral commissure and the position/contour of the chin, the inferior border of the mandible, and the ear. Intraoral examination should assess the occlusion, presence or absence of crossbites, occlusal plane/cant, amount of mandibular excursion, and interincisal opening. Finally, motor and sensory function should be documented. Sleep apnea studies should be done to assess for the presence of obstructive sleep apnea. Bronchoscopy and endoscopy can determine if obstructive sleep apnea is secondary to a posterior tongue-based obstruction (which would be alleviated by mandibular distraction) or secondary to other obstructive causes such as hyperplastic tonsils/adenoids or tracheomalacia.

9. What is the preoperative workup for a patient undergoing mandibular distraction?
The workup for a patient undergoing mandibular distraction includes facial photographs, a three-dimensional (3D) computed tomographic (CT) scan, lateral and posteroanterior cephalograms, and a panoramic radiograph (Panorex). The cephalograms and Panorex allow for assessment and documentation of the deformity and the location of unerupted tooth buds. The 3D CT scan demonstrates the skeletal pathology in detail and serves as a baseline study for postdistraction documentation of the increase in bony volume and change in mandibular morphology. Dental study models should also be obtained. The study models provide not only a 3D record of the preexisting occlusion but also allow for the construction of orthodontic splints, which are invaluable in maintaining the mandibular height resulting from the distraction. The splint can be gradually modified postoperatively to guide hypereruption of the affected maxillary dentoalveolus, allowing for closure of the openbite.

10. Which areas of the mandible can be distracted?

Any area of the mandible can be distracted. In congenital cases, the mandibular body and ramus are commonly distracted.

11. How do you decide when to distract the neonate or infant with mandibular deficiency and respiratory insufficiency or sleep apnea?

The decision to perform distraction on the neonate with mandibular deficiency is made on the basis of demonstrating tongue-based airway obstruction that is causing respiratory insufficiency so severe as to otherwise necessitate tracheostomy. The diagnosis is established by evaluating weight gain, oral intake, oxygen saturation, CT scans, direct laryngoscopy, flexible fiberoptic bronchoscopy, and sleep studies. Other potential causes of respiratory insufficiency must be ruled out prior to performing distraction.

12. What are the options when a Pruzansky III mandible is present? What if the tooth follicle is in the way?

The Pruzansky II and III mandible represents a significant challenge because the ramus usually is so hypoplastic as to be inadequate for pin placement and osteotomy. There are two options in this situation. The first is to curette a tooth follicle and allow an interval for bony regeneration before performing distraction. An alternative, especially in the Pruzansky II mandible, is to perform iliac or rib bone graft reconstruction of the ramus followed at a later date by distraction of the neomandible.

13. What are the vectors of distraction?

The vector of distraction is based on the long axis of the distraction device. In the mandible, there are three types of distraction vectors: horizontal, oblique, and vertical. The vectors are relative to the maxillary occlusal plane. A horizontal vector is 0° to 30°, an oblique vector is 30° to 45°, and a vertical vector is greater than 45°. The trajectory of the distracted mandible can be predicted based on the vector of distraction. The horizontal vector is preferred in the patient with predominantly a deficiency of the mandibular body as in the Robin sequence. The vertical vector usually is used in the craniofacial microsomia or Treacher Collins patient with hypoplasia of the ramus (Fig. 32-2).

14. How do you choose from among an extraoral, intraoral, or semi-buried approach?

An extraoral approach can be used to place an external distraction device, which consists of four transcutaneous pins that are placed in the bone, two on each side of the osteotomy. The technique is simple and the device can be easily monitored, a distinct advantage in the young patient who is uncooperative in terms of obtaining serial radiographs. The disadvantage of this approach is the scarring caused by the incision and the subsequent path of the transcutaneous distraction pins (Fig. 32-3).

An intraoral or buried device has the advantage of fewer cutaneous scars, but the device requires a much larger piece of bone to support the multiple plates and screws used to secure the device. The semi-buried device is similar to the buried device except that the activation arm is brought out through the skin (Figs. 32-4 and 32-5).

15. What is the utility of a multiplanar device?

The initial mandibular distractions were performed using a unidirectional distraction device. Follow-up of these patients has shown a change in device vector during and after active distraction, a finding that can be attributed to the effects of the muscles of mastication on the newly formed regenerate. A multiplanar distraction device was designed to allow more control in achieving vertical elongation of the ramus, horizontal elongation of the body, recreation of the mandibular angle with closure of the anterior openbite, and transverse widening or increase in the bigonial distance. A curvilinear or J device can be used to distract the mandible along an anteroinferior trajectory, closely mimicking the natural growth process of the mandible.

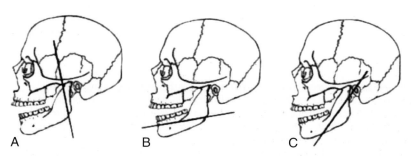

A   B   C

Figure 32-2. Vectors of distraction. **A,** Vertical. **B,** Horizontal. **C,** Oblique. (From McCarthy JH, Grayson BH: Craniofacial microsomia. In Mathes S, Hentz V [eds.]: Plastic Surgery, Vol.4, 2nd ed. Philadelphia, WB Saunders, 2006, pp 119–134.)

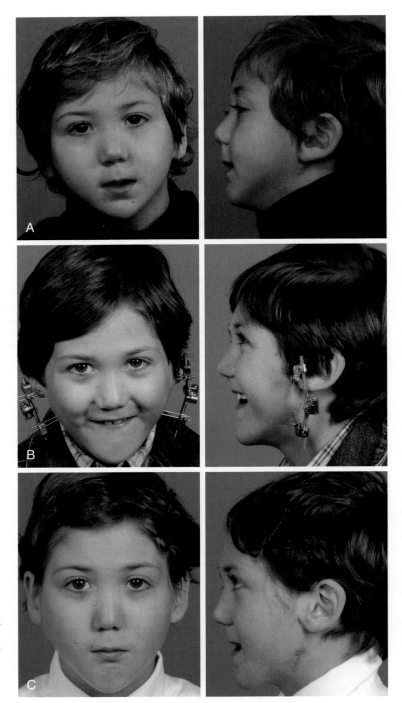

Figure 32-3. A, The patient is a 4-year-old boy with bilateral micrognathia and obstructive sleep apnea. **B,** The patient was treated with bilateral external mandible distraction. **C,** The patient had improved menton projection, retroglossal airspace, and resolution of obstructive sleep apnea.

16. When is transport distraction helpful for mandibular deformities?

There are two types of transport distraction. In trifocal distraction, an osteotomy is made on both ends of the bony defect. Each end is distracted until the two distracted segments join each other in the center of the intercalary gap. Thus, trifocal transport distraction is especially useful for reconstruction of intercalary mandibular defects arising from tumor, trauma, or other pathology. Bifocal transport distraction has been shown to be useful for reconstruction of TMJ ankylosis. The ankylosed mandibular condyle is resected (in a technique known as *gap arthroplasty*), and bifocal transport distraction is used to reconstruct the condyle defect. The fibrocartilaginous zone that is generated at the end of the transport segment functions as a pseudocondyle for the TMJ.

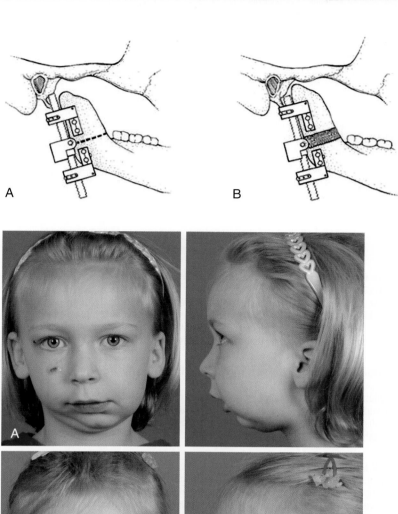

Figure 32-4. Application of internal mandibular distraction devices. **A,** Osteotomy is marked with a *dotted line*. **B,** Distraction is performed.

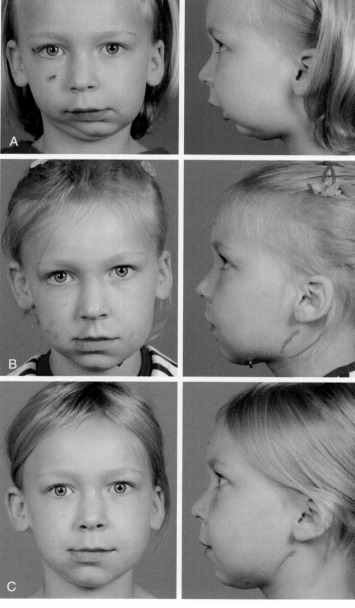

Figure 32-5. A, The patient is a 3-year-old girl with left craniofacial microsomia. **B,** The patient was treated with left semi-buried mandible distraction osteogenesis. Note the activation arm below the jawline. **C,** The patient had improved menton projection, leveling of the left commissure, and mandibular occlusal plane. Note the over correction of the chin and oral commissure.

17. Does skeletal elongation with distraction osteogenesis have an impact on the associated soft tissue?

Not only is new bone generated with distraction, but lengthening and generation of additional soft tissues occur. Skin, muscle, nerves, and vascular tissues increase in concert with the lengthened bone. Termed *distraction histogenesis*, the process accounts for the decreased soft tissue force opposing the advanced bone and the subsequent decreased relapse rate when a bone is lengthened by distraction, as opposed to traditional surgical advancement.

18. Which incisions can be used?

An intraoral incision or a modified Risdon incision can be used to perform distraction on the mandible. An *intraoral* incision is made over the oblique line of the mandible, and the buccal surface of the mandible is exposed in a subperiosteal plane. The modified *submandibular* (Risdon) incision is made in the relaxed skin tension lines of the submandibular fold. After the platysma muscle is incised, care is taken to preserve the marginal mandibular nerve. The masseter muscle is sharply dissected off the buccal aspect of the mandible, exposing the mandible in a subperiosteal plane.

19. What orthodontic measures can be practiced during activation and consolidation to achieve the optimal occlusion?

During the activation and consolidation phases, the generate bone can be molded and shaped by using guiding elastics to help establish the optimal occlusion. In unilateral mandibular distraction, an intraoral splint or bite plate can be used to maintain a posterior openbite during the distraction process. The openbite can be closed orthodontically by encouraging descent of the maxillary dentoalveolus by serial reduction of the bite plate.

20. How is the progress of mandibular distraction monitored clinically and radiographically?

The progress of mandibular distraction is monitored clinically by evaluating the relative relationships of the anterior maxillary and mandibular occlusal surfaces and the position or level of the occlusal plane, oral commissure, and chin point as well as the changes in the distraction device. These same criteria are used to evaluate the effectiveness of mandibular distraction radiographically on the cephalograms.

21. What are the endpoints of unilateral distraction?

In unilateral distraction, the treatment endpoint is movement of the chin to the contralateral side with lowering of the ipsilateral oral commissure, the inferior border of the mandible, and the occlusal plane to a level below that of the contralateral or less affected side. Overcorrection is essential in the growing child because distraction does not alter the inherent genetic growth program of the mandible. As a result, the hypoplastic side that is distracted will not grow as fast or as well as the unaffected side. In a study of long-term growth following unilateral mandibular distraction in growing children with craniofacial microsomia, McCarthy and his team found that the unaffected ramus grew 1.15 mm/year and the affected ramus grew 0.87 mm/year.

22. What are the endpoints of bilateral distraction?

In bilateral mandibular distraction, the endpoint is achievement of an anterior crossbite. As in the case of unilateral distraction, it is important to overcorrect the distracted hypoplastic mandible because it will likely not grow as well as the relatively unaffected maxilla.

23. When do you remove the distraction device?

Prior to removing the distraction device, a minimum of 8 weeks should elapse after cessation of activation for the newly generated bone to consolidate. In patients who are sufficiently old to comply, radiographs can be obtained to assess for evidence of bone mineralization at the distraction site.

24. What are the most common complications following mandibular distraction? How are they treated?

The most common complications following mandibular distraction are pin-tract soft tissue infections and device problems. Other less common complications include pin dislodgement, hypertrophic scars, tooth injury, dentigerous cysts, temporary neuropraxia of the marginal mandibular nerve, temporary parotid fistulas, and premature consolidation. Pin-tract soft tissue infections usually are successfully managed with oral antibiotics. Pin dislodgement or device problems are treated with replacement of the pins and device. Hypertrophic scars can be treated with steroids or scar revision. Distraction failure secondary to inadequate bone volume can be treated with waiting for further growth of the mandible before reattempting distraction or bone grafting followed by distraction. Dentigerous cysts secondary to distraction across a tooth follicle should be treated with resection of the cyst with or without bone grafting of the site. Temporary neuropraxia of the marginal mandibular nerve is managed conservatively. Parotid fistulas usually resolve spontaneously. Finally, in patients with premature consolidation, repeat distraction may be necessary to correct the deformity.

25. Is the distracted mandible stable? Does the distracted mandible grow?

The distracted mandible is stable over the long term. Study of 1-, 5-, and 10-year follow-ups of distracted mandibles showed a decrease in total mandibular length of the distracted mandible of only approximately 6% over the first year. After the first year, the distracted mandible did not decrease in height and showed some evidence of growth. The same study showed that the distracted mandible demonstrates significant and consistent growth over 5 and 10 years, albeit at a lower rate than normal.

26. Does mandibular distraction affect the TMJs?

Study of the TMJs in unilateral mandibular distraction has shown transient posterior condylar flattening on the ipsilateral side of distraction and posterosuperior flattening on the contralateral side. Biopsy of the joints revealed subchondral degeneration followed by repair and remodeling, which ultimately lead to correction of the condylar flattening. In general, condyle/TMJ morphology improves after mandibular distraction.

BIBLIOGRAPHY

Denny AD: Distraction osteogenesis in Pierre Robin neonates with airway obstruction. Clin Plast Surg 31:221–229, 2004.

Denny AD, Talisman R, Hanson PR, Recinos RF: Mandibular distraction osteogenesis in very young patients to correct airway obstruction. Plast Reconstr Surg 108:302–311, 2001.

McCarthy JG: Principles of craniofacial distraction. In Thorne CH, Beasley RW, Aston SJ, Bartlett SP, Gurtner GC, Spear SL (eds): Grabb and Smith's Plastic Surgery, 6th ed. Philadelphia, Lippincott Williams & Wilkins, 2006, pp 96–102.

McCarthy JG GB: Craniofacial microsomia. In McCarthy JG, Galiano RD, Boutros SG (eds): Current Therapy in Plastic Surgery. Philadelphia, WB Saunders/Elsevier, 2006, pp 506–517.

McCarthy JG, RA, Grayson BH: Craniofacial microsomia. In Mathes S, Hentz V (eds): Plastic Surgery, Vol. 4, 2nd ed. Philadelphia, WB Saunders/Elsevier, 2006, pp 119–134.

McCarthy JG: Distraction of the Craniofacial Skeleton. New York, Springer; 1999.

McCarthy JG, Williams JK, Grayson BH, Crombie JS: Controlled multiplanar distraction of the mandible: Device development and clinical application. J Craniofac Surg 9:322–329, 1998.

McCarthy JG, Stelnicki EJ, Grayson BH: Distraction osteogenesis of the mandible: A ten-year experience. Semin Orthod 5:3–8, 1999.

McCarthy JG: Craniofacial microsomia. A primary or secondary surgical treatment program. Clin Plast Surg 24:459–474, 1997.

McCarthy JG, Katzen JT, Hopper R, Grayson BH: The first decade of mandibular distraction: Lessons we have learned. Plast Reconstr Surg 110:1704–1713, 2002.

McCormick SU, McCarthy JG, Grayson BH, Staffenberg D, McCormick SA: Effect of mandibular distraction on the temporomandibular joint: Part 1, canine study. J Craniofac Surg 6:358–363, 1995.

McCormick SU, Grayson BH, McCarthy JG, Staffenberg D: Effect of mandibular distraction on the temporomandibular joint: Part 2, clinical study. J Craniofac Surg 6:364–367, 1995.

Mulliken JB, Kaban LB: Analysis and treatment of hemifacial microsomia in childhood. Clin Plast Surg 14:91–100, 1987.

Shetye PR, Grayson BH, Mackool RJ, McCarthy JG: Long-term stability and growth following unilateral mandibular distraction in growing children with craniofacial microsomia. Plast Reconstr Surg 118:985–995, 2006.

Stucki-McCormick SU: Reconstruction of the mandibular condyle using transport distraction osteogenesis. J Craniofac Surg 8:48–52, 1997.

DISTRACTION OSTEOGENESIS
OF THE MIDFACE

Robert J. Paresi, Jr., MD, MPH; William J. Martin, MD; Niki A. Christopoulos, MD;
Alvaro A. Figueroa, DDS, MS; and John W. Polley, MD

1. What is distraction osteogenesis?

Distraction osteogenesis is the process of generating new bone between two bone segments in response to the application of gradual stress across that bone gap. The technique requires the creation of an osteotomy followed by the application of a mechanical distractor to separate the bone segments at a controlled rate. This process is based on the principle that tension stimulates histogenesis and does not require the use of a bone graft or rigid fixation of the bone segments. Recently, it has been applied to the mandible, maxilla, cranium, and dentition.

2. Which patients are potential candidates for maxillary distraction osteogenesis?

- Cleft or syndromal patients, including cases associated with Crouzon syndrome and Apert syndrome
- Severe maxillary hypoplasia (vertical, horizontal, and transverse planes) with class III malocclusion
- Patients requiring horizontal maxillary advancement of 10 mm or more
- Patients with normal mandibular morphology and position associated with maxillary hypoplasia
- Patients with severe palatal and pharyngeal scarring
- Patients with airway obstruction and sleep apnea

3. What are some physical deformities and functional deficits exhibited by patients with severe maxillary hypoplasia?

- Dish face or concave facial profile due to midface hypoplasia
- Class III malocclusion, which can result in compromised mastication
- Speech abnormalities
- Nasopharyngeal airway constriction

4. How does rigid external distraction work?

In rigid external distraction, first a custom-made intraoral orthodontic splint is fabricated by the orthodontist. This acts as the link between the maxillary skeleton and the distraction apparatus (Fig. 33-1). The splint is cemented to the first permanent molars or second primary molars and is further secured at the time of surgery with circumdental stainless steel surgical wire. Patients undergo a high complete Le Fort I osteotomy below the level of the infraorbital foramina, including pterygomaxillary and septal disjunction. The halo portion of the distraction device is then placed immediately after closure of the intraoral incision, and the intraoral splint and halo are connected to one another to initiate distraction after a latency period of 3 to 7 days (Fig. 33-2).

5. Is autogenous or alloplastic bone grafting or internal skeletal fixation used with the rigid external distraction device?

No.

6. Why is internal fixation and autogenous bone grafting not needed?

With the rigid external distraction device one can very gradually and precisely reposition a severely hypoplastic maxilla to the exact horizontal and vertical planes desired. Distraction osteogenesis creates new autogenous bone during this process, allowing for correction of the entire maxillary skeletal and soft tissue discrepancy.

7. What is the latency period for midface distraction?

The period after the osteotomy and before distraction is known as the *latency period.* The length of the latency period is between 3 and 7 days.

8. What is the activation period?

The latency period is followed by the *activation period.* This is the period of active distraction. The activation period typically lasts 12 to 15 days, but the duration is determined clinically by the severity of midface deficiency and anterior crossbite. The patients are followed weekly during the activation period until satisfactory and stable skeletal and occlusal changes are achieved.

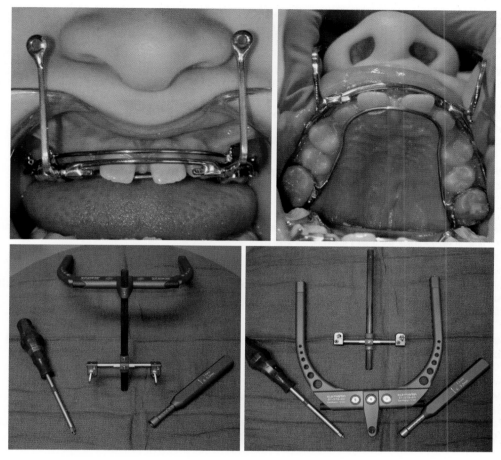

Figure 33-1. Intraoral splint and rigid external distractor.

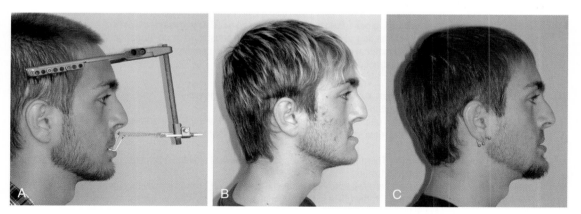

Figure 33-2. A, Distraction in progress. **B,** Before distraction. **C,** After distraction.

9. What is the period of rigid retention?

After the period of active distraction, a *period of rigid retention* is undertaken. During this period, the distraction device is kept in place without any advancement. The purpose of this period is to allow the maxillary position to achieve clinical stability through bone mineralization and consolidation.

10. How is the distraction vector determined?

The distraction vector, or direction of applied stress, is determined by the cephalometric analysis and physical examination of the clinical condition.

11. What is the rate of distraction during the activation period?

Distraction is performed by the patient or caregiver at home at a rate of 1 mm/day.

12. What are the postoperative instructions for patients after the osteotomies and placement of the distraction device?

Routine oral hygiene and unrestricted soft diet are started 24 hours postoperatively after surgery.

13. What is the mean horizontal maxillary advancement in patients treated with a traditional Le Fort I advancement?

Between 4 and 7 mm.

14. What is the long term relapse in horizontal maxillary advancement in patients treated with a traditional Le Fort I advancement?

Between 25% and 50%.

15. What is the complication rate of traditional Le Fort I maxillary advancement in cleft patients?

25% or greater.

16. What is the mean horizontal maxillary advancement in patients undergoing rigid external distraction?

10 mm or greater.

17. What is the mean horizontal relapse in patients undergoing rigid external distraction?

Patients who have undergone maxillary distraction continue to be stable up to 9 years after surgery, with no clinically significant relapse.

18. What is the complication rate in cleft patients undergoing rigid external distraction?

Less than 1%.

19. Where is the area of most bone formation after maxillary distraction?

Both bone samples and follow-up imaging studies have demonstrated substantial bone formation in the pterygomaxillary region after rigid external distraction. Bone samples have demonstrated well-ossified dense lamellar bone that provides stability after distraction.

20. What are some advantages of rigid distraction osteogenesis?

- No limitation of age at which patients can be treated.
- Surgery is less extensive and can be performed on either an outpatient or a 23-hour admission basis.
- Operative times are significantly reduced with very low morbidity compared with the traditional Le Fort I maxillary advancement.
- Only an osteotomy is performed. There is no need to reposition individual skeletal fragments or to use bone grafting, intermaxillary fixation, or internal fixation.
- Allows treatment of patients who are refractory to traditional cleft Le Fort I maxillary advancement.
- The halo device is easily removed in the office setting without even local anesthesia, except for very young patients who may require mild sedation.

21. Are all surgeons currently using distraction osteogenesis to advance the maxilla in cleft patients?

Most craniofacial and maxillofacial surgeons now routinely use distraction to treat patients with moderate to severe maxillary hypoplasia secondary to clefts. Few experienced clinicians do not recognize distraction as a valuable addition to the surgical techniques available to treat this challenging group of patients.

BIBLIOGRAPHY

Figueroa AA, Polley JW, Friede H, Ko EW: Long-term skeletal stability after maxillary advancement with distraction osteogenesis using a rigid external distraction device in cleft maxillary deformities. Plast Reconstr Surg 114:1382–1392, 2004.

Kramer FJ, Baethge C, Swennen G, et al: Intra- and perioperative complications of the LeFort I osteotomy: A prospective evaluation of 1000 patients. J Craniofac Surg 15:971–977, 2004.

Molina F, Monasterio FO, de la Paz Aguilar M, Barrera J: Maxillary distraction: Aesthetic and functional benefits in cleft lip-palate and prognathic patients during mixed dentition. Plast Reconstr Surg 101:951–963, 1998.

Polley JW, Figueroa AA: Rigid external distraction: Its application in cleft maxillary deformities. In Berkowitz S (ed): Cleft Lip and Palate, 2nd ed. Heidelberg, Germany, Springer, 2005, pp 519–531.

Polley JW, Figueroa AA, Theodorou SJV: Maxillary distraction osteogenesis. Oper Tech Otolaryngol Head Neck Surg 13:12–16, 2002.

CHAPTER 34

DISTRACTION OSTEOGENESIS OF THE CRANIUM

Fernando Molina, MD, and
David L. Ramírez, MD

1. Briefly describe the history of craniofacial distraction osteogenesis.

Ilizarov, in the 1950s, pioneered the idea of distraction osteogenesis (DOG) of the long bones in the orthopedic literature, and his concepts form the foundation of distraction in the craniofacial skeleton. Snyder, in 1973, reported mandibular lengthening in a canine model using an extraoral device. McCarthy, in 1992, first applied this technique in humans, lengthening the mandible with bicortical osteotomies. Later, Molina introduced the intraoral–subperiosteal approach, the importance of distraction vectors, and the concept of bilateral–bidirectional distraction for micrognathia. Currently, a variety of techniques are being evaluated, including orbital distraction for the treatment of microorbitism, cranial vault distraction to treat craniosynostosis, and midface distraction to improve midface biomechanics.

2. Is special equipment required to perform DOG?

In addition to standard craniofacial instrumentation, a distraction device is required. The device is applied at both sides of the osteotomy, oriented along the desired vector, and gradually activated to elongate the bone. The vector, or the direction in which the bone is elongated, can be single or multiple. Different devices have been used: L shape, anchored, double anchored, internal, external, and rigid external. In 1998, Lauritzen designed a spring-loaded device for the distraction of fused cranial sutures (Fig. 34-1). Each device has its advantages and disadvantages.

3. Describe the technique for cranial DOG.

Because new bone formation is the goal of DOG, osteotomies/corticotomies must preserve vascularity. The surgeon has to perform a "clean osteotomy," that is, one with no greenstick fracturing or ragged edges that might create instability or prevent smooth bone regeneration. Subsequently, the device is fixed to the bone with plates, screws, or pins. In some cases, the tip of the device has a hook that anchors to the bone edge. Once bony fixation has been achieved, the system is activated to assess bone mobility intraoperatively. Incisions are closed, and the postoperative distraction protocol begins at the surgeon's discretion.

4. What are the DOG periods?

Latency is a period from 5 to 7 days after surgery when many surgeons allow bony callus formation without distracting the bone. Thereafter, elongation of the callus, or the *distraction* period, starts. Distraction usually proceeds at a rate of 0.5 to 2 mm/day until the desired bone lengthening has been achieved, usually in 3 to 4 weeks. Then, the *consolidation* period begins, which is the period when callus becomes mineralized bone. This may last from 6 to 12 weeks; every case must be evaluated individually. The last step is removal of the device. Some new devices, including spring-mediated DOG, do not require a latency period because the mechanical forces within the spring begin working as soon as they are placed. Thus distraction begins immediately, which works well in some locations, such as the cranial vault, but not in others, such as the midface. Immediate distraction of the midface results in the generation of fibrous tissue instead of bone and thus is prone to relapse and growth disturbances.

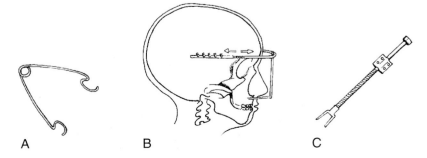

Figure 34-1. Distraction devices.
A, Metallic spring. **B,** Rigid external distraction in a Le Fort III osteotomy.
C, Submerged "Molina design."

A   B   C

5. Is there an "ideal" distraction device?

There is no single "ideal" distraction device. The "ideal" device must be selected for each individual case based on the deformity being treated, the age of the patient, and the bone to be distracted. Children younger than 2 years old have softer frontoorbital bone union, and mechanical forces must be tailored to the bone stock. Design, size, and strength of the device are important too. Various materials have been used (titanium, stainless steel, absorbable plastics), and various locations for the device have been tested (submerged, internal, external).

6. What is the distraction vector? Why is it important?

The distraction vector represents the orientation of the mechanical forces and thus the direction in which the bone is to be elongated. A proper distraction vector guides new bone regeneration in the desired (and preoperatively planned) manner. It is oriented perpendicular to the osteotomy/corticotomy line so as to maximize new bone formation. This is especially important in the midface where soft tissue resistance is difficult to overcome and often leads to relapse with conventional osteotomies. Frequently, a well-planned distraction vector is the key to a return to normal anatomy and function (Fig. 34-2).

7. What craniofacial disorders have been successfully treated with DOG techniques?

Nonsyndromic craniosynostosis: Metopic (trigonocephaly) and sagittal (scaphocephaly) sutures have been successfully treated with conventional and spring-mediated distraction. Recently, a Japanese group reported correction of lambdoid synostosis (posterior plagiocephaly) but with limited results. In unilateral coronal (anterior plagiocephaly) and bilateral coronal (brachycephaly) synostoses, a complete correction of the frontal bone, orbit, and malar prominence has been reported with simultaneous soft tissue expansion to produce facial symmetry (Fig. 34-3).

Syndromic craniosynostosis: The combined cranial vault, cranial base, and facial effects of syndromic craniosynostosis lend themselves to correction with DOG. DOG can be used to correct the frontal bone, orbits, and midface simultaneously. Crouzon, Apert, Pfeiffer, Saethre-Chotzen, and Klatteschaddel syndromes have all been reconstructed with DOG. In addition to improved aesthetics, as in the nonsyndromic group, DOG has functional benefits such as improved respiration, improved globe protection, improved speech, and sometimes improved ocular movements.

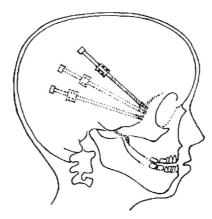

Figure 34-2. Distraction vectors of midface advancement. A horizontal vector will produce anteroposterior displacement of the maxilla. A more oblique vector will produce a simultaneous vertical midface elongation.

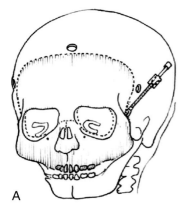

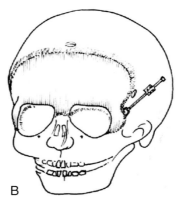

Figure 34-3. Distraction craniofacial osteotomies. **A,** "True monobloc" distraction. The frontal bone, orbits, zygoma, and maxilla are included in a single piece. **B,** Frontorbital advancement. The tip of the device reaches the superolateral aspect of the orbital rim.

A

B

8. What are the advantages of cranial vault distraction?

DOG has major advantages over traditional methods of rigid fixation with bone grafts: the quality of the regenerated bone, the reduction in long-term relapse of the advanced segments, and the simultaneous elongation of soft tissues that accompanies distraction of the bone creating a more pleasing aesthetic result. Furthermore, DOG permits bony advancement without the need for bone grafts in the cranial vault, orbital walls, and pterygomaxillary junction and avoids large "dead spaces" that result from ambitious advancements, thus minimizing surgical time, donor site morbidity, and neuroinfection. The absence of acute bony disjunction decreases blood loss and postoperative pain. Cranial bone is not stripped of all its blood supply, so it is not likely to resorb. Lack of bony resorption translates into fewer secondary deformities and fewer secondary corrective procedures.

9. What are the disadvantages of cranial vault distraction?

DOG can be difficult to tolerate when external distraction devices are used because the patient must wear a large, unseemly device for several months, making socialization difficult. The distraction phase can be painful, as overcoming soft tissue (especially skin) resistance requires force sufficient to cause pain. Pain also may result from premature consolidation of the bone or device penetration of the cranial vault. Furthermore, DOG requires a high degree of patient and family compliance, and not all families have the organizational skills to successfully complete DOG. Like all new surgical procedures, cranial DOG has a learning curve, and surgeons who are not familiar with the techniques may experience complications early in their experience that color their view of it. Without long-term results, those surgeons fail to see the long-term benefits of DOG.

10. What is the optimal timing for cranial vault DOG?

Optimal timing for DOG of the cranium must be determined on a case-by-case basis. That said, we have developed a treatment protocol for DOG based on years of experience. Generally, we operate on nonsyndromic craniosynostosis between 6 and 18 months of age. Syndromic craniosynostosis patients require cranial vault remodeling between 12 and 24 months of age, and most need some form of midface advancement between the ages of 5 and 7 years. Because the cranial bone is more elastic in children younger than 2 years, we perform DOG cranial vault remodeling before the second birthday. The reason to wait until the ages of 5 to 7 before performing DOG of the midface is to allow time for the cranial base to mature before disrupting it with an osteotomy. That said, we perform early midface distraction in cases of intracranial hypertension, globe exposure, and respiratory compromise due to midface retrusion.

11. Describe spring-mediated craniofacial distraction.

Spring-mediated craniofacial distraction is a technique whereby a spring-loaded device is affixed to both sides of a cranial suture or osteotomy. The inherent mechanical forces within the spring produce a continuous force that spreads the bony segments with subsequent bone elongation and cranial reshaping. Multiple springs are required along the suture being distracted, and it is possible to distract along multiple vectors simultaneously. Two drawbacks of springs are that their lack of control and the bony resorption occurring immediately beneath the springs as a result of the pressure they apply.

12. What craniofacial disorders can be corrected with spring-mediated distraction?

The distraction technique is best suited to treatment of sagittal synostosis to expand temporal bones and metopic synostosis to expand the frontal bone laterally. It also has been used in cases of unilateral and bilateral coronal synostosis and in some mild cases of multiple suture synostosis. Importantly, the best results with spring-mediated distraction occur when performed early in life (Fig. 34-4).

13. What are important factors to take into account for spring-mediated distraction?

Important factors to take into account for spring-mediated distraction are the physical properties of the spring itself, the length of the legs of the spring, and the number of coils composing the spring. The power of the spring is dictated by the composition of the steel alloy used in making the spring, the thickness of the spring, and the number of coils composing the spring. The length of the legs determines how far the device can distract.

Optimal results are obtained when springs are placed at 3 to 4 months of age. There is no latency phase with springs; the distraction phase lasts for 3 to 4 months, and the spring is maintained until all bone gaps have remineralized. Usually, the spring is removed at 2 years of age.

14. What is combined distraction–compression cranial vault remodeling?

Combined distraction–compression cranial vault remodeling is a technique whereby a given bone segment is expanded using DOG while another segment is compressed to diminish it. Often, the distraction is perpendicular to the

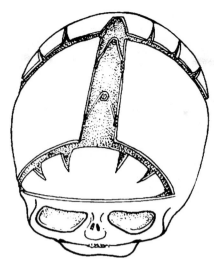

Figure 34-4. A pair of springs is inserted along the suturectomy for scaphocephaly correction. The spring forces will gradually expand the cranial vault during a period of 2 to 3 months. Simultaneously, a custom-made helmet is used to compress the posterio-anterior dimension of the cranial vault. The springs are left in place until the patient is 2 years of age.

compression. This technique is used in the treatment of scaphocephaly to expand the temporal area while compressing the frontal and occipital regions. Frequently, this technique is used with endoscopic assistance, enabling the surgeon to remodel the cranium without large incisions in the scalp.

15. What are the complications of cranial vault DOG?
Complications of cranial vault DOG can be divided into intraoperative, distraction, and long-term complications. Intraoperative complications include cerebrospinal fluid (CSF) fistulas, hematoma (epidural, subdural, subcutaneous), infection, and nerve injury. Distraction complications include dislocation or exposure of the device, fibrous union of the bone, premature consolidation, and misalignment of the distraction vector. Long-term complications consist of hypertrophic scarring from external distracters, bony relapse, and bony resorption.

16. What is the frequency of complications in cranial DOG?
A few large series reviewed complication rates in cranial DOG. Early series reported high rates of pin-track infections, bony relapses, and CSF fistulas. These reports reduced the number of surgeons interested in the technique. In reviewing our results over the past 6 years, we noted very low complication rates in 51 cases. Our most common complication was device failure/dislocation, which occurred 17% of the time. Our infection rate was 1.7%, and our bony relapse rate (defined as relapse requiring an additional operation) was 3.4%. We observed no nerve injuries, CSF fistulas, premature consolidation, fibrous union, or hypertrophic scarring at the pin sites.

17. What special considerations are needed when performing DOG for Apert syndrome?
Many patients with Apert syndrome have a large anterior fontanelle and some degree of hypertelorism. Their frontal bones are thin and their supraorbital rims are fragile. Because of these factors, long-term bony deformities occur more often in cranial DOG in these patients than in patients with other craniosynostosis syndromes. Also, cranial DOG cannot treat the hypertelorism associated with Apert syndrome.

18. What is the future direction for cranial DOG?
The advantages of cranial DOG are making it a more widely practiced art, and its future looks bright. DOG represents the first example of tissue engineering in reconstructive surgery. To improve the quality of engineered tissue, surgeons are investigating ways to manipulate the bony callus to shorten treatment time, produce more normal bony anatomy, and minimize morbidity. To this end, devices have been impregnated with growth factors, various distraction rates have been tried, and less invasive approaches have been attempted. Many surgeons have experimented with resorbable distraction devices that are controlled by an external magnet, eliminating the need for device removal. DOG lends itself to computer-assisted operative planning and computer-assisted intraoperative imaging. All of these innovations will likely play a role in the future of cranial DOG.

BIBLIOGRAPHY

Komuro Y, Yanai A, Hayashi A, et al: Cranial reshaping employing distraction and contraction in the treatment of sagittal synostosis. Br J Plast Surg 58:196–201, 2005.

Komuro Y, Yanai A, Hayashi A, et al: Treatment of unilateral lambdoid synostosis with cranial distraction. J Craniofac Surg 15:609–613, 2004.

Lauritzen C, Sugawara Y, Kocabalkan O, Olsson R: Spring mediated dynamic craniofacial reshaping. Case report. Scand J Plast Reconstr Hand Surg 32:331–338, 1998.

Matsumoto K, Nakanishi H, Seike T, et al: Application of the distraction technique to scaphocephaly. J Craniofac Surg 11:172–176, 2000.

McCarthy JG, Schreiberg J, Karp N, et al: Lengthening the human mandible with gradual distraction. Plast Reconstr Surg 89:1–8, 1992.

Molina F: Distraction osteogenesis: Remodeling the hypoplastic mandible. In Achauer BM (ed): Plastic Surgery: Indications, Operations and Outcomes, Vol. 2. St. Louis, Mosby, 2000, pp 673–682.

Molina F: From midface distraction to the "true monoblock." Clin Plastic Surg 31:463–479, 2004.

Raposo DOG, Amaral CM, Di DOGmizo G, et.al: Gradual bone distraction in craniosynostosis. Scand J Plast Reconstr Hand Surg 31:25–27, 1997.

Yonehara Y, Hirabayashi S, Sugawara Y, et al: Complications associated with gradual cranial vault distraction osteogenesis for the treatment of craniofacial synostosis. J Craniofac Surg 14:526–528, 2003.

ORBITAL HYPERTELORISM

CHAPTER 35

Matthew R. Swelstad, MD, and
Louis Morales, Jr., MD

1. What is orbital hypertelorism?
Orbital hypertelorism (OHT) refers to an increase in interorbital distance (IOD). It is a finding on physical examination, not a syndrome.

2. How do you measure IOD?
IOD is defined as the distance between the medial walls of the orbit at the dacryon. The dacryon is the union of the lacrimal, frontal, and maxillary bones.

3. What is the significance of pseudohypertelorism?
Pseudohypertelorism is caused by lateral displacement of the medial canthal tendons, not by an increase in the IOD. It is easy to mistake pseudohypertelorism for OHT if you are not careful.

4. Why is interpupillary distance not used to measure OHT?
Many patients with OHT have esotropia or exotropia, making interpupillary distance unreliable.

5. Describe the changes that occur in IOD with age.
IOD is approximately 16 mm at birth. By 12 years of age, the IOD is approximately 25 mm. In adult males the IOD continues to increase until skeletal maturation is complete. The average IOD for adult females is 25 mm and for adult males is 28 mm.

6. Describe the two classifications of OHT.
Tessier divided OHT into three types based on IOD: type I (30 to 34 mm), type II (35 to 39 mm), and type III (≥40 mm). The Munro classification system is based on the anatomy of the medial orbital wall. In type A, the medial orbital walls are parallel. The medial orbital wall width is greatest anteriorly in type B, in the middle in type C, and posteriorly in type D (Fig. 35-1).

7. What causes OHT?
Remember, OHT is a finding on physical examination, not a syndrome. The cause of each case needs to be examined individually. Patients with Apert or Crouzon syndrome may have cranial base disturbances. Mass effect from sincipital encephaloceles, dermoid cysts, and tumors may lead to OHT. Facial clefts and early ossification of the lesser wings of the sphenoid also have been suggested.

8. What is an encephalocele?
Encephalocele is herniation of intracranial contents through a cranial defect. If the herniated material includes cerebrospinal fluid and the meninges, then it is a meningocele. Herniation of meninges and brain parenchyma is a meningoencephalocele.

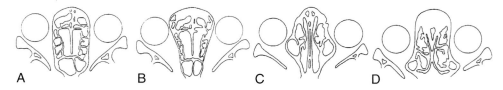

Figure 35-1. Munro classification of orbital hypertelorism. **A,** Parallel medial orbital walls. **B,** Ballooning out of anterior inferorbital tissue. **C,** Ballooning out of central portion of medial wall. **D,** Widening of posterior ethmoid cells. (From Munro IR, Das SK: Improving results in orbital hypertelorism correction. Ann Plast Surg 2:499–507, 1979, with permission.)

9. Describe the various types of encephaloceles.

Encephaloceles are classified by location and include sincipital (also known as *frontal* or *frontoethmoidal*), parietal, basal, and occipital. Sincipital encephaloceles are located between the bregma and the anterior ethmoid bone. Sincipital encephaloceles are further divided by the direction of the herniated contents (nasofrontal, nasoethmoidal, nasoorbital). Sincipital encephaloceles occur more commonly in people from Southeast Asia and Nigeria and rarely among people of European descent.

10. How does the level of the cribriform plate compare between people with OHT and those with a normal IOD?

The cribriform plate normally is 10 mm below the orbital roof. In OHT, it may be as low as 20 mm below the orbital roof.

11. How is OHT surgically managed?

Three fundamental approaches have been accepted to surgically correct OHT: combined intracranial/extracranial approach, subcranial approach, and facial bipartition.

12. What are "box osteotomies" of the orbit?

"Box osteotomies" refer to the combined intracranial/extracranial approach with circumferential ("box") orbital osteotomies. Ethmoidal air cells and paramedian sections of the anterior cranial vault are resected with preservation of the cribriform plate and the associated mucosa. Once mobilized, the orbital segments should medialize with minimal effort.

13. A "U-shaped" osteotomy is performed with which type of OHT reconstruction?

A "U-shaped" osteotomy is performed with the subcranial approach. It involves an osteotomy through the medial wall, lateral wall, and orbital floor. It is used in less severe forms of OHT when the cribriform plate has not prolapsed inferiorly.

14. What is a facial bipartition?

Facial bipartition mobilizes the orbit and midface in one piece. It generally is used in patients with OHT and transverse constriction of the maxillary dental arch. This procedure simultaneously narrows the IOD, expands the transverse width of the maxillary dental arch, and levels the maxillary occlusal plane (Fig. 35-2).

15. What steps must be taken to preserve olfactory function during surgical correction of OHT?

Olfactory function depends on avoidance of injury to the cribriform plate and preservation of superior turbinate mucosa. The olfactory nerve penetrates the cribriform plate and terminates within this mucosa.

16. What effect does the intraorbital/intranasal exoneration have on future growth of the midface?

This is controversial. McCarthy reports normal development of the midface after OHT reconstruction in pediatric patients. However, Mulliken and others demonstrated an adverse effect on anterior facial growth in young children who underwent OHT correction. Ortiz Monasterio reported no significant growth disturbances following facial bipartition.

17. After correction of OHT, what is done with the excess interorbital skin?

Medial translocation of the orbits results in excess skin over the nasal dorsum. This excess skin may be excised at the time of OHT correction or allowed to contract over time to avoid a midline nasal scar. Nasal dorsum augmentation with a cantilevered bone graft helps to improve the nasal dorsum profile and fill the nasal soft tissue envelope. Excess nasal skin also creates medial epicanthal folds, which may require surgical repair.

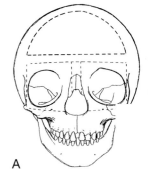
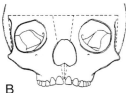
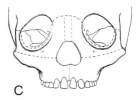

Figure 35-2. Surgical correction of orbital hypertelorism. **A,** Intracranial/extracranial approach. **B,** Facial bipartition. **C,** Subcranial approach. (From Dufresne CR: Complex Craniofacial Problems. New York, Churchill Livingstone, 1992, with permission.)

A   B   C

18. Why is proper management of the medial canthal tendon important in OHT repair?

Failure to secure the medial canthus with transnasal wires results in canthal drift and pseudohypertelorism. This gives the false impression of OHT relapse.

19. What is the role of the lateral orbital wall in OHT repair?

Lateral orbital wall translocation most closely approximates globe movement. Medial translocation of the dacryon is not as reliable for predicting the effects on medial movement of the globe.

20. What are the key steps to keep in mind during surgical planning for OHT correction?

- Remember the average IOD is 25 mm in females and 28 mm in males.
- Check the level of the cribriform plate prior to surgery.
- Preserve continuity of the nasal mucosa to the cribriform plate to minimize loss of smell.
- Choose the surgical procedure that best suits the patient's anatomy (facial bipartition, U-shaped osteotomies, or box osteotomies).
- Discuss postsurgical redundant nasal skin with family and the options for correction.

21. What are the most common complications following OHT repair?

The most common problems can be remembered with the mnemonic "PREST IN" (Pseudohypertelorism, Relapse from inadequate exoneration of interorbital contents, Enophthalmos, Strabismus, Temporal hollowing, Infection, Nasolacrimal dysfunction).

22. What is Cohen craniosynostosis syndrome?

Cohen craniosynostosis syndrome is also known as *craniofrontonasal dysplasia*. Patients are more commonly female and have coronal synostosis, frizzy or curly hair, and frontonasal dysplasia.

BIBLIOGRAPHY

Cohen MM, Richieri-Costa A, Guion-Almeida ML, Saavedra D: Hypertelorism: Interorbital growth, measurements, and pathogenetic considerations. Int J Oral Maxillofac Surg 24:387–395, 1995.

David DJ, Simpson DA: Frontoethmoidal meningoencephalocele. Clin Plast Surg 14:83–89, 1987.

Daw JL, Morales, Jr. L: Orbital hypertelorism. In Weinzweig J (ed): Plastic Surgery Secrets. Philadelphia, Hanley and Belfus, 1999, pp 94–96.

Dufresne CR: Orbital hypertelorism. In Dufresne CR, Carson BS, Zinreich SJ (eds): Complex Craniofacial Problems. New York, Churchill Livingstone, 1992, pp 227–249.

McCarthy JG, Thorne CHM, Wood-Smith D: Principles of craniofacial surgery: Orbital hypertelorism. In McCarthy JG (ed): Plastic Surgery. Philadelphia, WB Saunders, 1990, pp 2982–3002.

Mulliken JB, Kaban LB, Evans CA, et al: Facial skeletal changes following hypertelorism correction. Plast Reconstr Surg 77:7–16, 1986.

Munro IR, Das SK: Improving results in orbital hypertelorism correction. Ann Plast Surg 2:499–508, 1979.

Orr DJ, Slaney S, Ashworth GJ, Poole MD: Craniofrontonasal dysplasia. Br J Plast Surg 50:153–161, 1997.

Ortiz-Monasterio F, Molina F: Orbital hypertelorism. Clin Plast Surg 21:599–612, 1994.

Ortiz Monasterio F, Molina F, Sigler A, et al: Maxillary growth in children after early facial bipartition. J Craniofac Surg 7:440–448, 1996.

Panchal J, Kim YO, Stelnicki E, et al: Quantitative assessment of osseous, ocular, and periocular changes after hypertelorism surgery. Plast Reconstr Surg 104:16–28, 1999.

Simpson DA, David DJ, White J: Cephaloceles: Treatment, outcome, and antenatal diagnosis. Neurosurgery 15:14–20, 1984.

Tessier P, Tulasne JF: Stability in correction of hyperorbitism and Treacher Collins syndromes. Clin Plast Surg 16:195–199, 1989.

van der Meulen JCH, Vaadrager JN: Surgery related to the correction of hypertelorism. Plast Reconstr Surg 71:6–17, 1983.

CRANIOFACIAL SYNDROMES

Shai Rozen, MD, and
Kenneth E. Salyer, MD, FACS, FAAP

1. What is a syndrome? What are craniofacial syndromes?

The term *syndrome* derives from Greek and literally means "run together." In medicine the term *syndrome* is the association of several clinically recognizable features, signs, or symptoms resulting from multiple malformations occurring during fetal development. In genetics a syndrome represents multiple malformations occurring in embryonically noncontiguous areas.

Currently, the classification of craniofacial syndromes is still most commonly based on morphologic craniofacial characteristics and occasional associated extracranial anomalies. It may help the reader to distinguish craniofacial syndromes in which the pathology is early fusion of cranial vault and base sutures with associated facial features from syndromes in which the main pathology is in the facial region without premature suture closure.

Despite our attempts to clearly delineate and define craniofacial syndromes, there often is overlap in presentations and etiologies with only one additional feature differentiating between syndromes. With future advancements in genetics and molecular biology we may find that certain syndromes we consider separate entities are in actuality identical in etiology but represent a different scale of severity (expression) of the same syndrome.

2. What is the difference between malformation, deformation, and disruption?

Most congenital anomalies can be divided into three types: *malformation, deformation,* and *disruption.*

Malformation is the most common process causing craniofacial anomalies. It is considered a morphologic defect in an organ area of the body caused by abnormal intrinsic development.

Deformation is a process that may be caused by extrinsic forces of lesser amplitude than those causing disruption. An example is a clubfoot thought to be caused by intrauterine compression secondary to oligohydramnios. Another example is a cleft palate in a patient with Pierre Robin sequence in whom, in utero due to limited extension of the head and jaw, the tongue does not drop in the oral cavity, thus interfering with migration of the palatal shelves from a vertical position to a horizontal position, creating a cleft.

Disruption is a breakdown of the original fetal developmental process secondary to severe external forces, as seen in severe facial clefts secondary to amniotic bands.

3. What is craniosynostosis? Do all patients with craniosynostosis have syndromes?

The cranial sutures together with cranial fontanelles separate the skull bones and offer mobility and overlapping, enabling the head to squeeze through a tight birth canal and later allow expansion of the skull with brain growth. Early closure of a single or any combination of multiple sutures is termed *craniosynostosis.* In general, single suture synostosis is nonsyndromic whereas multiple suture synostosis is associated with syndromes. The overall relative prevalence of craniosynostosis is 1:2500, with syndromic craniosynostosis accounting for only 10% to 20% of these cases.

4. How does cranial growth occur, and what are the theories regarding the etiology of sutural synostosis?

Skeletal growth is dependent on both intrinsic and extrinsic forces. Craniofacial growth occurs through two basic mechanisms. First, most initial growth occurs at growth centers by expansion at sutures, especially the neurocranium. Second, bone remodeling occurs through deposition on the outer surface of the bone and resorption on the inner surface, which occurs in the neurocranium but more so in the facial region. The exact etiology of suture synostosis is unclear and probably is multifactorial. Certain theories state that the main pathology is within the suture and/or adjacent bone biology (primary craniosynostosis). Others believe it is secondary to abnormal growth of surrounding structures, for example, the brain (secondary craniosynostosis).

5. How is cranial growth affected by suture synostoses?

Virchow was the first to note abnormal cranial growth patterns associated with early sutural synostosis and stated that growth occurs parallel to the affected suture and is restricted perpendicular to the suture. This classic theory, however, does not explain growth patterns of complex deformations extending to the cranial base, orbit, and other cranial regions. Delashaw formulated four rules that try to explain growth patterns seen in complex deformations:

- Cranial bones connected by a fused suture act as a single bone plate with restricted growth.
- Increased bone deposition occurs at perimeter sutures away from the synostotic bone plate, causing abnormal and asymmetric growth.
- Enhanced bone deposition occurs at the open sutures at the edges of the synostosed suture, as seen in frontal bossing from the normal contiguous, contralateral coronal suture.
- Greater compensatory growth is seen in adjacent sutures than in perimeter sutures.

6. Which sutures are most commonly involved in craniofacial syndromes?

All sutures may be involved in craniofacial syndromes, but the majority of the cases show bilateral coronal synostosis causing brachycephaly (increased width to anteroposterior ratio). This condition is often found associated, in variable degrees, with other types of sutural synostosis.

7. Why do most patients with syndromic craniosynostosis have some level of midface hypoplasia (midface underdevelopment)?

Premature fusion of the cranial base has been postulated to occur in patients with syndromic craniosynostosis. Experimental studies performed in rabbits showed premature synostosis of the cranial base alone may account for many dysmorphic features seen in craniofacial syndromes. This is one potential explanation for dysmorphic facial features, including midface hypoplasia, in patients with syndromic craniosynostosis. Synostotic extension into the basilar coronal hemi-ring is also seen in some patients with unilateral coronal synostosis but has not been associated with increased cranial base angulation.

8. Which type of suture synostosis relates to which morphologic appearance?

- Premature fusion of the sagittal suture: Scaphocephaly
- Premature fusion of one coronal suture: Anterior plagiocephaly
- Premature fusion of bilateral coronal sutures: Brachycephaly
- Premature fusion of one lambdoid suture: Posterior plagiocephaly
- Premature fusion of the metopic suture: Trigonocephaly

9. List some common craniofacial syndromes and their distinguishing features, frequency, mode of inheritance, and associated genetic abnormalities.

See Table 36-1.

10. What is acrocephalosyndactyly?

From the Greek *akros*—extreme/extremity, *kephalo*—head, and *sundaktulos*—fused fingers/toes. Also known as *acrodysplasia*. *Acrocephalosyndactyly* is simply another term to describe syndromes that include premature fusion of cranial sutures and abnormalities of the limbs, mainly syndactyly (fusion of fingers/toes), with different levels of complexity. See Table 36-1 for correlation between the name of the syndrome and its acrocephalosyndactyly classification.

11. What are the goals in the treatment of patients with craniofacial syndromes, and what procedures are commonly used?

The basis of any problem solving in plastic surgery should address two fundamentals: *form* and *function*.

FORM

No medical treatment exists for craniosynostosis. As discussed in Questions 5 and 7, synostosis of both the cranial vault and cranial base causes abnormal growth of the calvarium and midface. Initially, surgeries involving strip craniectomies (cutting out the fused suture) failed to produce long-lasting results. Only with the development of techniques involving resection of sutures and extensive remodeling of the calvarium have we seen longer lasting results.

Nearly all syndromic patients have some extent of bilateral coronal craniosynostosis involving the base of the skull as well. They suffer from frontoorbital recession, often shallow orbits with short anterior cranial fossa, which contributes to the development of proptosis in these patients. Frontoorbital advancement may correct these abnormalities (Fig. 36-1).

Table 36-1. Common Craniofacial Syndromes

NAME OF SYNDROME	RELATIVELY UNIQUE FEATURES OTHER THAN CRANIOSYNOSTOSIS	FREQUENCY	MODE OF INHERITANCE
Apert (acrocephalosyndactyly type I)	Severe brachycephaly, moderate hypertelorism, turricephaly, midface hypoplasia often causing airway obstruction, high-arched palate, 30% cleft palate, parrot beak deformity of nose, acne vulgaris, complex syndactyly of fingers and toes, lower than average IQ	1:160,000	AD One of two FGFR-2 mutations
Crouzon (acrocephalosyndactyly type II)	Most common craniofacial dysostosis, higher potential for increased intracranial pressure, high potential for optic nerve compression, no limb involvement	1:10,000	AD Multiple possible mutations in FGFR-2
Saethre-Chotzen (acrocephalosyndactyly type III)	Craniosynostosis not obligatory, bicoronal if present, low-set frontal hairline, upper lid ptosis, facial asymmetry, brachydactyly, usually partial simple syndactyly	1:25,000–50,000	AD Mutation in TWIST gene
Pfeiffer (acrocephalosyndactyly type V)	Broad thumbs and great toes, conductive hearing loss Type I: Mild form, bilateral coronal synostosis, normal intelligence, mild proptosis Type II: Most severe, cloverleaf skull, severe proptosis, hydrocephalus, midface deficiency Type III: Type II without cloverleaf skull, neurologic compromise, limited life span	1:100,000	AD FGFR-1 and FGFR-2
Carpenter	Tower-shaped skull, short neck, preaxial polydactyly, syndactyly, mild to moderate mental deficiency although may be normal, often associated with cloverleaf skull (pansynostosis), cardiovascular anomalies in up to one third of patients	Very rare	AR

AD, Autosomal dominant; *AR*, autosomal recessive; *FGFR*, fibroblast growth factor receptor.

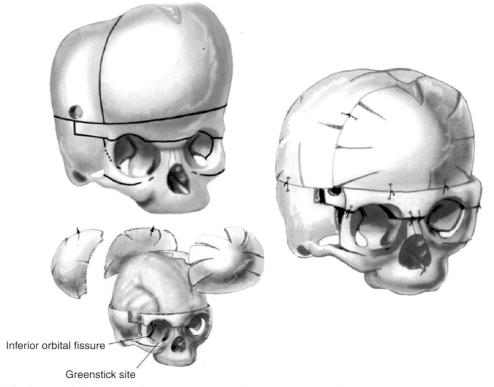

Inferior orbital fissure

Greenstick site

Figure 36-1. Patients with syndromic craniosynostosis usually have involvement of the coronal sutures bilaterally associated with short anterior cranial fossa, frontoorbital recession, and shallow orbits. Frontoorbital advancement attempts to restore frontoorbital relations and correct the proptosis.

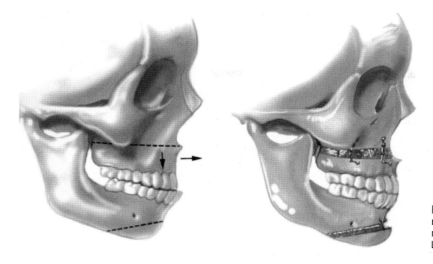

Figure 36-2. Syndromic patients most commonly have Angle class III malocclusion, which is treated by a Le Fort I advancement.

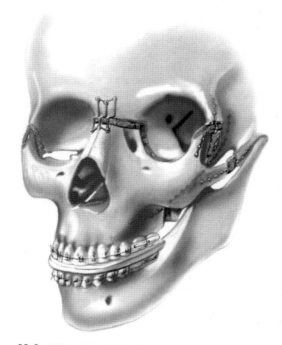

Figure 36-3. Midface hypoplasia is often treated with Le Fort III advancement.

Patients with involvement of other suture fusions will have associated shape abnormalities (see Question 8) requiring other procedures, such as posterior remodeling for patients with posterior plagiocephaly secondary to lambdoid suture synostosis or additional midvault remodeling in patients with involvement of the sagittal suture.

Patients with midface hypoplasia and malocclusion, most commonly Angle class III, will need appropriate Le Fort osteotomies (Figs. 36-2 and 36-3).

FUNCTION

Intracranial Hypertension: Single suture nonsyndromic craniosynostosis is less commonly associated with increased intracranial pressure (ICP). When more than one suture is involved, as seen in syndromic patients, the risk of increased ICP is amplified. This may produce brain dysfunction and visual compromise. Also, syndromic patients reportedly have a 10% to 42% increased risk for hydrocephalus causing elevated pressures. In these patients ventriculoperitoneal shunting usually is indicated rather than cranial expansion.

Progressive Exophthalmos Threatening the Eyes: Syndromic patients often suffer from shallow orbits, often caused by short anterior cranial fossa, orbital floor, and lateral orbital walls secondary to vault and cranial base synostosis. Increased exophthalmos may cause exposure keratopathy and corneal ulceration and may even lead to blindness.

Progressive Maxillary Hypoplasia Causing Breathing Problems: Midface hypoplasia is often seen in patients with syndromic craniosynostosis. It rarely causes acute life-threatening respiratory problems (although these have been reported needing urgent midface distraction) but may cause chronic breathing difficulties more commonly seen during sleep and often associated with increased risk of pulmonary infections, cor pulmonale, neurologic dysfunction, and brain damage. Most of these patients will require midface advancement.

12. What is normal ICP, and are craniofacial syndromes always associated with increased ICP?

Normal ICP is 15 mm Hg or 150 to 200 mm H_2O. Values up to 8 mm Hg are considered normal in the first few months of life. Cerebral blood flow is dependent on ICP. Cerebral perfusion pressure can be thought of as the difference between systemic blood pressure and ICP. For this reason ICP must be maintained at a steady state. Not all syndromic patients have increased ICP, but different series show pressures above 15 mm Hg in up to 40% of patients with multiple suture synostosis who remain untreated. Patients with Pfeifer or Carpenter syndrome who have a higher percentage of pansynostotic cloverleaf skulls and patients with Crouzon syndrome who have a higher incidence of increased ICP and optic neuropathy require diligent attention and early decompression.

13. Are craniofacial syndromes associated with mental retardation or learning deficiencies?

The answer is not clear. Causes of low scores on current IQ tests or low learning disability scores may be affected by multiple factors, including environmental factors, and may not always be inherent to the syndrome. Also, many of these patients undergo operations early in life, and the natural history of unoperated patients is hard to define. Shprintzen reported various complex craniofacial disorders that may be associated with a higher incidence of mental retardation or neurolinguistic deficits, including but not limited to syndromes as Apert, velocardiofacial, Opitz, Carpenter, Noonan, and others. Some conditions, such as frontonasal dysplasia or Crouzon syndrome, may have completely normal values unless increased ICP develops secondary to craniosynostosis, causing brain damage.

14. Which craniosynostosis syndromes involve the limbs? Is there a difference in the magnitude of limb involvement?

Apert syndrome has the most severe involvement of the limbs, seen as complex and complicated forms of syndactyly involving the index, middle, and ring fingers. Patients with Saethre-Chotzen syndrome have brachydactyly, patients with Pfeiffer syndrome have large broad great toes and thumbs, and patients with Carpenter syndrome tend to have short hands and polysyndactyly of the feet. Patients with Crouzon syndrome have no limb abnormalities.

15. Name a few facial syndromes and their main characteristics.

See Table 36-2.

16. In patients with velocardiofacial syndrome, what presurgical consideration is important prior to treatment of velopharyngeal insufficiency?

When considering a pharyngeal flap for treatment of velopharyngeal insufficiency in patients with velocardiofacial syndrome, the surgeon must verify the location of the carotid arteries, which are abnormally medially displaced in these patients.

17. Is Pierre Robin syndrome truly a syndrome?

No. Better understanding of the etiology of the findings of cleft palate, micrognathia, and glossoptosis has changed the terminology from syndrome to *sequence.* The cause of this triad is a sequence of events occurring in utero. Early in gestation the palatal shelves are oriented vertically and separated by the tongue. Normally, as the head extends and the mandible grows the tongue drops, allowing palatal shelve apposition in the horizontal plane. In these patients the fetal head does not extend sufficiently and mandibular growth is retarded. This causes the tongue to disrupt closure of the palate, thus creating a U-shaped cleft palate. Some studies claim that a specific syndrome was noted in 25% of these patients, with an additional 35% having multiple anomalies but without an identifiable syndrome. Depending on the degree of severity and expertise of the treating surgeon, treatment may include merely positioning in a prone position, lip tongue adhesion, mandibular distraction osteogenesis, or tracheostomy.

18. Can craniofacial anomalies be treated anywhere? What is the importance of a multidisciplinary team?

The importance of a multidisciplinary team is paramount to the successful treatment of patients with craniofacial syndromes. These teams should include plastic surgeons, neurosurgeons, otolaryngologists, orthodontists, oral surgeons, speech pathologists, developmental specialists, psychologists, and geneticists. Not only is a team

Table 36-2. Facial Syndromes

NAME OF SYNDROME	RELATIVELY UNIQUE FEATURES	FREQUENCY	MODE OF TRANSFERENCE
Treacher Collins (mandibulofacial dysostosis, Fransceschetti-Zwahlen-Klein syndrome)	Bilateral facial deformity, anomalies of the first branchial arch, groove, and pouch, absence of inferolateral orbital wall and medial zygoma, caudal rotation of maxilla, clockwise rotation of mandible, downward slant of palpebral fissure, lower lid coloboma, parrot beak nasal deformity, 35% cleft palate, 15% macrostomia, internal and external ear abnormalities	1:50,000	AD Variable expressivity
Nager syndrome (split hand deformity, mandibulofacial dysostosis)	Similar to Treacher Collins with hypoplastic or absent thumbs, radius and ulna fusion, radial and metacarpal hypoplasia or aplasia, more severe mandibular hypoplasia, higher incidence of cleft palate, lower incidence of coloboma	Rare	Mostly sporadic AD but also AR reported
Hemifacial microsomia (heterogenous group including oculoauriculovertebral syndrome, craniofacial microsomia, first and second branchial arch syndrome)	Second most common facial deformity after cleft lip and palate, 3:2 male>female, right face>left face, soft tissue, bone, cranial nerve VII may be involved, severe microtia, variations include cleft lip and palate, additional cranial nerve involvement	1:3500–5600	Sporadic, various chromosomal abnormalities reported, possible in utero vascular disruption
Goldenhar syndrome (oculoauriculovertebral syndrome)	Variant of hemifacial microsomia with additional epibulbar dermoids and vertebral anomalies		
Velocardiofacial syndrome	Possible cleft palate, vertical maxillary excess, malar flattening, mandibular retrusion, small ears, ventricular septal defect, tetralogy of Fallot, right-sided aortic arch, highly associated with learning disability	1:4000 births 5%–8% of patients with cleft palate	AD chromosome 22q abnormality, diagnosis confirmed by fluorescent in situ hybridization
Van der Woude syndrome	Most common syndrome associated with cleft lip and palate, bilateral paramedian lower lip pits at dry and wet vermilion junction	1:35,000–100,000 1% to 2% of patients with facial clefts	AD Variable expressivity

AD, Autosomal dominant.

approach necessary, but also understanding the importance of continuity of care is vital. The relationships developed with these patients are critical because the treatment plans of these patients rarely include just one surgery but rather a sequence in which the patients are treated in a stepwise fashion, with one surgery forming the foundation for the next.

BIBLIOGRAPHY

Cohen MM: Sutural biology and the correlates of craniosynostosis. Am J Med Genet 47:581–616, 1993.

Delashaw JB, Persing JA, Jane JA: Cranial deformation in craniosynostosis. A new explanation. Neurosurg Clin N Am 2:611–620, 1991.

Goodrich JT: Skull base growth in craniosynostosis. Childs Nerv Syst 21:871–879, 2005.

Goodrich JJ, Hall CD: Craniofacial Anomalies: Growth and Development from a Surgical Perspective. New York, Thieme Medical Publishers,1995.

Mathes S (ed): Plastic Surgery. Philadelphia, WB Saunders, 2006.

Moss ML: The functional matrix hypothesis revisited. The genomic thesis. Am J Orthod Dentofacial Orthop 112:338–342, 1997.

Rogers GF, Mulliken JB: Involvement of the basilar coronal ring in unilateral synostosis. Plast Reconstr Surg 115:1887–1893, 2005.

Rosenberg P, Arlis HR, Haworth RD: The role of the cranial base in facial growth: Experimental craniofacial synostosis in the rabbit. Plast Reconstr Surg 99:1396–1407, 1997.

Salyer KE: Salyer and Bardach's Atlas of Craniofacial & Cleft Surgery. Vol. 1: Craniofacial Surgery. Philadelphia, Lippincott-Raven, 1999.

CRANIOFACIAL CLEFTS

Jeffrey Weinzweig, MD, FACS

1. When does the embryologic development of the face take place?

Embryogenesis of the face takes place between the fourth and eighth weeks of gestation, during which the crown–rump length (CRL) of the fetus enlarges from 3.5 to 28 mm.

2. When does the most rapid phase of facial development occur?

The most dramatic changes in facial development occur in the extraordinarily brief period between 17 and 27 mm CRL (seventh and eighth weeks of gestation). In embryos with a 17-mm CRL the facial processes have fused, marking the end of the transformation phase.

3. Morphogenesis of the craniofacial skeleton begins with the formation of which bone?

The sphenoid body and its extensions. Morphogenesis continues with the formation of the middle and anterior cranial fossae and a reduction of the interorbital distance. Evolution proceeds with the union of the two nasal halves and the development of the nasomaxillary complex, which expands forward, downward, and laterally. In embryos with a 27-mm CRL the skeleton is completed with a lengthening of the mandibular ramus, which adapts itself to the formation of the nasomaxillary complex.

4. Why do craniofacial clefts occur?

Embryogenesis of the craniofacial region is extremely complex. Significant demands are placed on the coordination of cell separation, migration, and interaction during a brief 4-week period. The proper amount of tissue must be present at an exact moment in the correct three-dimensional relationship for normal craniofacial development to occur. Any mishap in this intricate program can lead to disastrous consequences. Evidence from animal and clinical studies supports a multifactorial etiology. Factors such as infection with influenza A_2 virus, infestation with toxoplasmosis protozoan, maternal metabolic disorders, and exposure to teratogenic compounds, including anticonvulsants, antimetabolic and alkylating agents, steroids, and tranquilizers, are believed to play a role in the etiopathogenesis of craniofacial clefts.

5. What are the two leading theories of facial cleft formation?

1. *"Classic Theory": Failure of Fusion.* This classic theory, proposed by Dursy (1869) and His (1892), contends that the central region of the face is the site of union of the free ends of the facial processes. The face takes form as the various processes fuse. After epithelial contact is established by these processes, penetration by the mesoderm completes the fusion. Disruption of this sequence results in cleft formation.
2. *"Modern Theory": Mesodermal Migration and Penetration.* This theory, proposed by Pohlman (1910) and Veau and Politzer (1936), contends that separate processes are not found in the central portion of the face; therefore free ends of the facial processes do not exist. Instead, the central portion of the face is composed of a continuous sheet of a bilamellar membrane of ectoderm known as the *primary plate,* which is demarcated by epithelial seams that delineate the principal "processes." Into this double layer of ectoderm, referred to as the *epithelial wall,* mesenchyme migrates and penetrates to smooth out the seams. The lower face and neck are formed by a series of branchial arches that consist of a thin sheet of mesoderm lying between the ectoderm and endoderm. The craniofacial mesoderm is augmented by neuroectoderm brought in by the migrating neural crest cells, from which the craniofacial skeleton is believed to be principally derived. If penetration by the neuroectoderm does not occur, the unsupported epithelial wall breaks down to form a facial cleft. The severity of the cleft is inversely proportional to the degree of penetration by the neuroectoderm. If penetration fails altogether, a complete cleft is formed as the epithelial wall dehisces. Partial penetration results in the development of an incomplete cleft.

6. What is the incidence of craniofacial clefts?

The exact incidence of craniofacial clefts is unknown because cases are rare and series tend to be small. However, extraction of cases of rare facial clefts from larger series of common clefts of the lip and palate provides a comparative incidence of 9.5 to 34 rare facial clefts per 1000 common clefts. Common clefts of the lip and palate occur with an overall incidence of approximately 1.5 per 1000 live births, so the extrapolated incidence of rare facial clefts is approximately 1.4 to 5.1 per 100,000 live births.

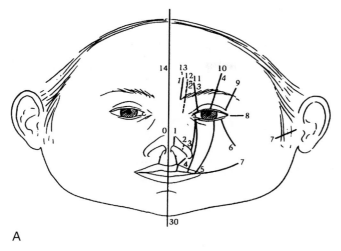

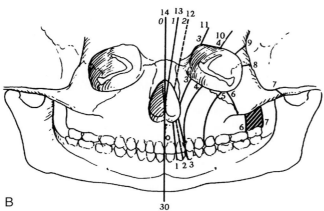

Figure 37-1. Tessier classification of craniofacial clefts. **A,** Path of various clefts on the face. **B,** Location of the clefts on the facial skeleton. (Courtesy Dr. Paul Tessier.)

7. Who was the first to recognize the three-dimensional complexity of craniofacial clefts?
Dr. Paul Tessier, who stated that "a fissure of the soft tissues corresponds as a general rule with a cleft of the bony structures."

8. How is the Tessier classification of craniofacial clefts structured?
The orbit, nose, and mouth are key landmarks through which craniofacial clefts follow constant axes. The clefts are numbered from 0 to 14, with the lower numbers (0 to 7) representing the facial clefts and the higher numbers (8 to 14) representing their cranial extensions. When a malformation crosses both hemispheres, a craniofacial cleft is produced that generally follows a set "time zone." Examples of these combinations include no. 0-14, 1-13, 2-12, 3-11, and 4-10 clefts (Fig. 37-1).

9. Can a patient have more than one type of craniofacial cleft? What are the rules?
The only rule, apart from craniofacial clefts following the constant "time zone" axes defined by Tessier, is that there are no rules. Multiple craniofacial clefts may occur, and often do, in any combination, unilaterally or bilaterally, in the same patient, creating an infinite spectrum of anomalous possibilities and reconstructive challenges for which Tessier marveled, "No two clefts are alike."

10. What is internasal dysplasia? To which Tessier cleft does this term apply?
Internasal dysplasia is a developmental arrest in the groove separating the two nasal halves before union has occurred. This anomaly is known as the *Tessier no. 0 cleft.* Depending on the time of developmental arrest, a wide spectrum of anomalies is seen. In less severe cases, the anomaly is characterized by bifidity of the columella, nasal tip, dorsum, and distal part of the cartilaginous septum. Occasionally, a median cleft of the lip, a median notch in the Cupid's bow, or a duplication of the labial frenulum is found. In more severe cases, the nasal halves are widely separated and orbital hypertelorism is present (Fig. 37-2A). The premaxilla may be bifid, and the maxilla may demonstrate a keel-shaped deformity in which the incisors are rotated upward in each half of the alveolar processes. A medial cleft of the palate may extend upward to the cribriform plate. The wider the cleft, the greater the interorbital distance, the shorter the nose, and the more arched the maxillary vault. At the other extreme, the nose may be totally absent or represented by a proboscis. In such cases the median bony defect extends into the ethmoids to produce orbital hypotelorism or cyclopia (Fig. 37-2B). The associated brain malformation usually limits the life span to infancy.

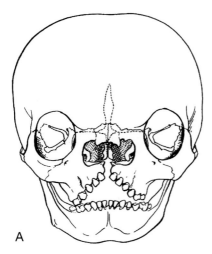
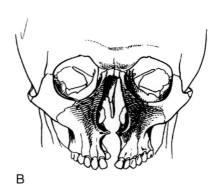

Figure 37-2. No. 0 cleft. **A,** The osseous cleft passes between the central incisors, resulting in broadening of the nasal framework and orbital hypertelorism. **B,** Portions of the premaxilla and nasal septum are absent, and the supporting structures of the nose are hypoplastic with resultant orbital hypertelorism. (Courtesy Dr. Paul Tessier.)

11. Which craniofacial clefts begin at Cupid's bow?

Tessier no. 1, 2, and 3 clefts begin at Cupid's bow. In addition, no. 4 and 5 clefts and, rarely, no. 6 clefts may involve Cupid's bow. Therefore all common cleft lips must be evaluated closely for additional structural anomalies.

12. What is nasoschizis? To which clefts does this term refer?

Nasoschizis is related to clefts of the lateral aspect of the nose. These clefts are commonly referred to as Tessier no. 1 or 2 clefts (Fig. 37-3). The no. 1 cleft begins at Cupid's bow. The common cleft of the lip is an example of this malformation. The spectrum of these anomalies ranges from a small notch in the alar rim to a wide defect involving one or both nasal halves. Clefting of the alveolar arch between the central and lateral incisors is commonly seen. The piriform aperture is violated lateral to the anterior nasal spine. The no. 2 cleft also begins in Cupid's bow and crosses the alveolus in the region of the lateral incisor. The piriform aperture is divided at its base, and the nasal septum is intact but deviated by the maxillary distortion.

13. What is an oronasoocular cleft?

Also referred to as an *oblique facial cleft,* the oronasoocular cleft is a no. 3 cleft that begins at Cupid's bow, undermines the base of the nasal ala, and continues cephalad into the lower eyelid (Fig. 37-4A). This is the first of the Tessier clefts to involve the orbit directly. The osseous component of the cleft passes through the alveolus between the lateral incisor and canine (Fig. 37-4B). The cleft continues cephalad through the piriform aperture and the frontal process of the maxilla and terminates in the lacrimal groove. The underlying nasolacrimal system is disrupted, producing an obstructed nasolacrimal duct and a sac that is prone to recurrent infections. The lower canaliculus is malformed and irreparable. This cleft is seen more commonly than the no. 1 and 2 clefts.

Figure 37-3. **A,** No. 1 cleft. The osseous location of this malformation is paramedian with compensatory lateral displacement of the orbit on the noncleft side. **B,** No. 2 cleft. Clefting of the alveolar arch occurs in the region of the lateral incisor. The piriform aperture is involved at its base as the cleft passes through the broadened frontal process of the maxilla to produce orbital hypertelorism. (Courtesy Dr. Paul Tessier.)

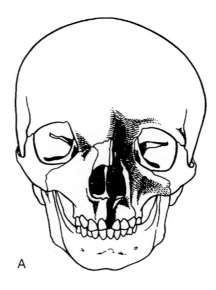
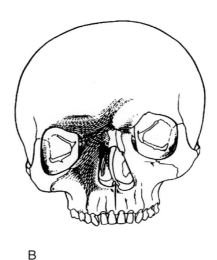

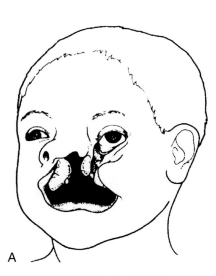
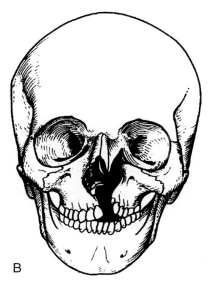

A   B

Figure 37-4. No. 3 cleft. **A,** This cleft begins at Cupid's bow, undermines the base of the nasal ala, and continues cephalad into the lower eyelid, where a coloboma is found medial to the punctum. **B,** The no. 3 cleft is the first cleft to involve the orbit directly. The osseous component of the cleft passes through the alveolus between the lateral incisor and canine, then continues cephalad through the piriform aperture and the frontal process of the maxilla to terminate in the lacrimal groove. (From Stratoudakin AC: An outline of craniofacial anomalies and principles of their correction. In Georgiade GS, Georgiade NG, Riefkol R, Barwick WJ [eds]: Textbook of Plastic, Maxillofacial and Reconstructive Surgery, 2nd ed. Baltimore, Williams & Wilkins, 1992, p 343, with permission.)

14. What are colobomas? Where are they found in relation to the punctum in the no. 3 cleft?

Colobomas, which are notches (clefts) of the eyelid of varying degrees, involve the lower eyelid and are found medial to the punctum.

15. Why is the no. 4 cleft also called meloschisis?

First described by von Kulmus in Latin in 1732, the no. 4 cleft represents a departure of the deformity from the median facial structures. The cleft moves onto the cheek and, therefore, is also referred to as *meloschisis.* This orooccular or oculofacial cleft begins lateral to the Cupid's bow and philtrum. It passes lateral to the nasal ala, which is largely uninvolved, and onto the cheek. The cleft terminates in the lower eyelid, medial to the punctum (Fig. 37-5A). The

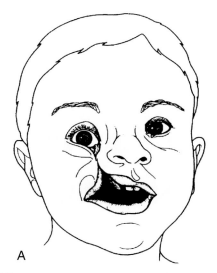
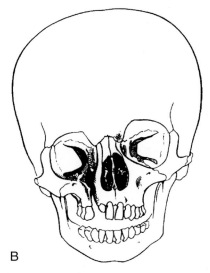

A   B

Figure 37-5. No. 4 cleft. **A,** This oculofacial cleft begins lateral to Cupid's bow and philtrum. It passes lateral to the nasal ala and onto the cheek, then terminates in the lower eyelid, medial to the punctum. (From Stratoudakin AC: An outline of craniofacial anomalies and principles of their correction. In Georgiade GS, Georgiade NG, Riefkol R, Barwick WJ [eds]: Textbook of Plastic, Maxillofacial and Reconstructive Surgery, 2nd ed. Baltimore, Williams & Wilkins, 1992, p 343, with permission.) **B,** The cleft passes between the infraorbital foramen and the piriform aperture. The orbit, maxillary sinus, and oral cavity are united by the cleft. (Courtesy Dr. Paul Tessier.)

osseous component of the cleft starts between the lateral incisor and canine. The piriform aperture, nasolacrimal canal, and lacrimal sac are spared as the cleft courses medial to the infraorbital foramen to terminate in the medial aspect of the inferior orbital rim and floor (Fig. 37-5B).

16. Which of the oblique facial clefts may permit orbital content prolapse into the maxillary sinus?

Prolapse of orbital contents into the maxilla occurs most commonly with no. 4 clefts and to a lesser degree with no. 5 clefts. The no. 5 cleft is rare; it originates in the lip just medial to the oral commissure. This cleft courses cephalad across the lateral portion of the cheek (meloschisis) into the area of the medial and lateral thirds of the lower eyelid (Fig. 37-6A). The vertical distance between the mouth and lower eyelid is decreased, and the upper lip and lower lid are drawn toward each other. The eye may be microphthalmic. The alveolar portion of the cleft is found posterior to the canine in the premolar region. The cleft then passes lateral to the infraorbital foramen and enters the orbit through the middle third of the orbital rim and floor (Fig. 37-6B). The orbital contents may prolapse through the gap into the maxillary sinus.

17. Which cleft represents an incomplete form of the Treacher Collins anomaly?

The no. 6 cleft. A coloboma of the lateral third of the eyelid marks the cephalic end of the cleft as it descends lateral to the oral commissure toward the angle of the mandible. The palpebral fissures have an antimongoloid slant. The bony cleft passes through the zygomaticomaxillary suture and involves the lateral third of the infraorbital rim. The zygoma is present but hypoplastic.

18. Which is the least rare of the craniofacial clefts? With which more familiar anomaly is it associated?

The no. 7 cleft, the least rare of the craniofacial clefts, is more commonly referred to as *hemifacial microsomia.* Additional descriptive terms include first and second branchial arch syndrome, otomandibular dysostosis, craniofacial microsomia, intrauterine facial necrosis, oromandibuloauricular syndrome, and lateral facial clefts. The incidence of this malformation is between 1:3000 and 1:5642 births.

Clinical expression is highly variable. A skin tag may represent the "forme fruste" or microform of the malformation. A severe no. 7 cleft begins as a macrostomia at the oral commissure and continues as a furrow across the cheek toward a microtic ear. The fifth and seventh cranial nerves and the muscles that they supply also may be involved. The osseous component of the no. 7 cleft is centered in the region of the zygomaticotemporal suture with hypoplasia of the zygoma and temporal bone. The zygomatic arch is disrupted and represented by proximal and distal stumps; varying degrees of mandibular deficiency, including complete absence of the ramus, are seen on the affected side.

19. When was hemifacial microsomia first described?

The earliest description of the malformation is the cuneiform inscriptions on the teratologic tables written by the Chaldeans of Mesopotamia about 2000 BC.

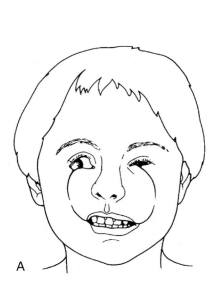
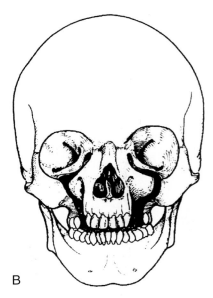

Figure 37-6. No. 5 cleft (bilateral). **A,** This cleft begins just medial to the oral commissure and courses cephalad across the lateral cheek into the area of the medial and lateral thirds of the lower eyelid. **B,** The bony cleft begins posterior to the canine, then passes lateral to the infraorbital foramen and enters the orbit through the middle third of the orbital rim and floor. (From Stratoudakin AC: An outline of craniofacial anomalies and principles of their correction. In Georgiade GS, Georgiade NG, Riefkol R, Barwick WJ [eds]: Textbook of Plastic, Maxillofacial and Reconstructive Surgery, 2nd ed. Baltimore, Williams & Wilkins, 1992, p 343, with permission.)

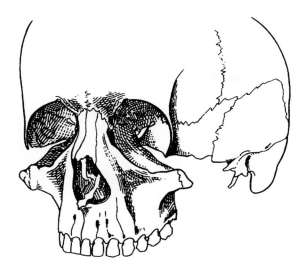

Figure 37-7. Nos. 6, 7, and 8 clefts (bilateral). These three clefts are responsible for the absence of the zygoma in this malformation, the hallmark of the complete form of Treacher Collins syndrome. (Courtesy Dr. Paul Tessier.)

20. What syndrome is closely related to hemifacial microsomia but has the additional features of epibulbar ocular dermoids and vertebral anomalies?

Goldenhar syndrome. However, less than 5% of hemifacial microsomia cases actually demonstrate the findings that distinguish them as Goldenhar syndrome, so many do not recognize this as a distinct entity.

21. Which craniofacial cleft is often occupied by a dermatocele?

The no. 8 cleft. The bony component of this cleft is centered at the frontozygomatic suture. It begins at the lateral commissure of the palpebral fissure and extends into the temporal region.

22. The bilateral combination of no. 6, 7, and 8 clefts represents the complete form of which syndrome? (Hint: The zygomas are absent.)

Treacher Collins syndrome. The three clefts involve the maxillozygomatic, temporozygomatic, and frontozygomatic sutures and are responsible for the absence of the zygoma in this malformation, the hallmark of the complete form of Treacher Collins syndrome (Fig. 37-7). The no. 6 cleft is responsible for the coloboma of the lower eyelid. The no. 7 cleft is responsible for the absence of the zygomatic arch. The no. 8 cleft completes the malformation by contributing to the absence of the lateral orbital rim.

23. Which is the rarest of the craniofacial clefts and the first to involve the superior hemisphere of the orbit?

The no. 9 cleft, which is found in the superolateral angle of the orbit and affects the underlying superior orbital rim and orbital roof. The eyelid is divided in its lateral third, as is the eyebrow, because the cleft extends into the temporal hairline.

24. Which cleft is the cranial extension of the no. 4 facial cleft and is often occupied by a frontoorbital encephalocele?

The no. 10 cleft, which traverses the middle third of the orbit, upper eyelid, and eyebrow. The osseous component of the cleft involves the midportion of the superior orbital rim, the adjacent orbital roof, and the frontal bones. A frontoorbital encephalocele frequently displaces the entire orbit in an inferior and lateral direction to produce orbital hypertelorism (Fig. 37-8).

25. Which cleft is usually found in combination with the no. 3 cleft? When is it associated with orbital hypertelorism?

The no. 11 cleft is the cranial extension of the no. 3 facial cleft and has not been reported as an isolated deformity. The cleft traverses the medial third of the upper eyelid and eyebrow as it courses into the frontal hairline. The osseous cleft may pass lateral to the ethmoid bone to create a cleft in the medial third of the superior orbital rim. Alternatively, the cleft may course through the ethmoidal labyrinth, in which case orbital hypertelorism is produced.

26. Why is orbital hypertelorism usually associated with the no. 12 cleft?

The no. 12 cleft, which is the cranial extension of the no. 2 facial cleft, disrupts the eyebrow just lateral to the medial border. The bony cleft passes through the frontal process of the maxilla or between this structure and the nasal bone. The ethmoidal labyrinth is increased in its transverse dimension to account for the associated hypertelorism.

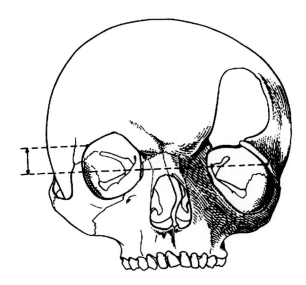

Figure 37-8. No. 10 cleft. The osseous cleft involves the midportion of the superior orbital rim, adjacent orbital roof, and frontal bones. A frontoorbital encephalocele frequently displaces the entire orbit infralaterally to produce orbital hypertelorism. (Courtesy Dr. Paul Tessier.)

27. Which cleft is associated with transverse widening of the cribriform plate?

The hallmark of the no. 13 cleft, which is the cranial extension of the no. 1 facial cleft, is widening of the olfactory groove with concomitant transverse widening of the cribriform plate. The cleft lies medial to the eyebrow, which usually is displaced inferiorly. Orbital hypertelorism is a constant finding with the cleft traversing the nasal bone, ethmoidal labyrinth, and olfactory groove.

28. "The face predicts the brain." Explain

Because of the intimate association of the frontonasal prominence with the development of the forebrain, the severity of centrally located craniofacial malformations appears to parallel that of forebrain defects. Therefore, the extent of facial deformity provides a clue to the severity of the developmental arrest of the forebrain.

29. In addition to the no. 0 cleft, which other cleft is associated with both hypotelorism and hypertelorism?

The no. 14 cleft, which is the cranial extension of the no. 0 facial cleft, may result from structural agenesis or tissue overabundance. When the cleft is secondary to agenesis, orbital hypotelorism is usually seen. The holoprosencephalic malformations, in which embryologic division of the prosencephaly into two parts is disrupted, fall into this group of anomalies. When frontonasal dysplasia (medial cleft face syndrome) or a frontonasal encephalocele occurs, orbital hypertelorism is seen (Fig. 37-9). The basic fault in embryogenesis lies in the malformation of the nasal capsule. The developing forebrain thus remains in its low-lying position. As a result of morphokinetic arrest of the normal medial movement of the eyes, the orbits remain in their widespread fetal position. In such cases, the crista galli may be widened, duplicated, or absent, and the cribriform plate may be caudally displaced as much as 20 mm.

30. Which structures must be considered in the reconstruction of a craniofacial cleft?

Reestablishment of facial integrity in patients with median or paramedian clefts involves all disrupted structures—the skeleton, facial muscles, and skin. Reconstruction is based on the following principles:

- Reconstruction of the skeleton is accomplished by removal of abnormal elements, transposition of skeletal components, and use of bone grafts.
- Reinsertion of the facial muscles is achieved by transposition and fixation of dystopic remnants. An intact muscular layer serves to establish and maintain form, to animate the face, and to stimulate growth.
- Restoration of the skin is performed by transposition of local flaps. The cutaneous layer provides protection for the underlying structures and preserves facial contour by its attachment to the skeleton.

31. What is a no. 30 cleft?

Median clefts of the lower lip and mandible represent the caudal extension of the no. 0 cleft. The cleft of the lower lip may be limited to the soft tissue and present, in its most minor form, as a lip notch. More frequently, however, the cleft extends into the bony mandibular symphysis. As the severity of the malformation increases, the neck structures, hyoid bone, and even sternum are progressively involved. This group of deformities is classified as no. 30 clefts. *(Take a closer look at Fig. 37-1.)*

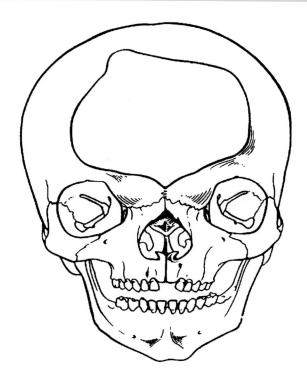

Figure 37-9. No. 14 cleft. When this cleft is associated with a frontonasal encephalocele, orbital hypertelorism is seen. (From Tessier P: Anatomical classification of facial, craniofacial and latero-facial clefts. J Maxillofac Surg 4:69, 1976, with permission.)

CONTROVERSY

32. What other congenital anomalies have been associated with craniofacial clefts?

Amniotic band syndrome, a rare disorder in which bands of mesoderm emanate from the chorionic side of the amnion and insert on the fetal body, can generate a broad spectrum of severe, disfiguring malformations. It usually occurs sporadically; the incidence is approximately 1:15,000 live births. The pathologic cause of both rare craniofacial clefts and congenital limb ring constrictions remains controversial. Despite the rarity of these two conditions, in a series of 85 patients with rare craniofacial clefts, Coady et al. demonstrated that 22 (26%) patients had concomitant congenital limb anomalies. Eleven of these patients (13% of the entire group) demonstrated evidence of limb ring constrictions, an incidence much greater than that of the general population. This study confirmed an association between rare craniofacial clefts and limb ring constrictions, suggesting the two conditions may result from a common etiology.

33. Are the location and complexity of craniofacial clefts affected in patients with concomitant limb ring constrictions?

Definitely. Coady et al. showed that the group of patients with limb ring constrictions had a significantly greater complexity of craniofacial clefting than did the non–limb ring constriction group *(4.27 clefts per patient vs 2.3 clefts per patient)*. The distribution of craniofacial cleft locations in patients with limb ring constrictions was found to differ significantly from those with other or no limb anomalies. The clefts in cases in which limb ring constrictions coexist are largely restricted to the paramedian axes: 2-12, 3-11, and 4-12.

34. What about an association between rare craniofacial clefts and craniosynostosis?

No definite association has been established between rare craniofacial clefts and craniosynostosis. However, sporadic cases have been reported, such as one by MacKinnon and David in which unicoronal synostosis and an oblique facial cleft occurred in the same patient. A rare event, indeed.

BIBLIOGRAPHY

Bradley JP, Kawamoto H: Craniofacial clefts and hypertelorbitism. In Thorne CH, Beasley RW, Aston SJ, et al (eds): Grabb & Smith's Plastic Surgery, 6th ed. Philadelphia, Lippincott Williams & Wilkins, 2007, pp 268–280.

Coady MS, Moore MH, Wallis K: Amniotic band syndrome: the association between rare facial clefts and limb ring constrictions. Plast Reconstr Surg 101:640–649, 1998.

David DJ: Reconstruction: Facial clefts. In Mathes SJ (ed): Plastic Surgery, Vo. 4, 2nd ed. Philadelphia, WB Saunders, pp 381–464.

David DJ, Moore MH, Cooter RD: Tessier clefts revisited with a third dimension. Cleft Palate J 26:163–184, 1989; discussion 184–185.

DeMoore MH, Trott JA, David DJ: Soft tissue expansion in the management of the rare craniofacial clefts. Br J Plast Surg 45:155–159, 1992.

Kawamoto HK Jr: The kaleidoscopic world of rare craniofacial clefts: Order out of chaos [Tessier classification]. Clin Plast Surg 3:529–572, 1976.

Kawamoto HK Jr: Rare craniofacial clefts. In McCarthy JG (ed): Plastic Surgery. Philadelphia, WB Saunders, 1990, pp 2922–2973.

MacKinnon CA, David DJ: Oblique facial clefting associated with unicoronal synostosis. J Craniofac Surg 12:227–231, 2001.

Marchac D, Renier D: Craniofacial Surgery for Craniosynostosis. Boston, Little, Brown, 1982.

McCarthy JG, Cutting CB, Hogan VM: Introduction to facial clefts. In McCarthy JG (ed): Plastic Surgery. Philadelphia, WB Saunders, 1990, pp 2437–2450.

Moore MH, Trott JA, David DJ: Soft tissue expansion in the management of the rare craniofacial clefts. Br J Plast Surg 45:155–159, 1992.

Muraskas JK, McDonnell JF, Chudik RJ, et al: Amniotic band syndrome with significant orofacial clefts and disruptions and distortions of craniofacial structures. J Pediatr Surg 38:635–638, 2003.

Myer W, Zeman W, Palmer CA: The face predicts the brain: Diagnostic significance of median facial anomalies for holoprosencephaly. Pediatrics 34:256–263, 1964.

Sigler MO, Stein J, Zuker R: A rare craniofacial cleft: Numbers 7, 2, and 3 clefts accompanied by a single median lip pit. Cleft Palate Craniofac J 41:327–331, 2004.

Stelnicki EJ, Hoffman W, Foster R, et al: The in utero repair of Tessier number 7 lateral facial clefts created by amniotic band-like compression. J Craniofac Surg 9:557–562, 1998; discussion 563.

Stelnicki EJ, Hoffman WY, Vanderwall K, et al: A new in utero model for lateral facial clefts. J Craniofac Surg 8:460–465, 1997.

Stratoudakis AC: An outline of craniofacial anomalies and principles of their correction. In Georgiade GS, Georgiade NG, Riefkohl R, Barwick WJ (eds): Textbook of Plastic, Maxillofacial and Reconstructive Surgery, 2nd ed. Baltimore, Williams & Wilkins, 1992, pp 333–362.

Taub PJ, Bradley JP, Setoguchi Y, et al: Typical facial clefting and constriction band anomalies: An unusual association in three unrelated patients. Am J Med Genet A 120:256–260, 2003.

Tessier P: Anatomical classification of facial, cranio-facial, and latero-facial clefts. J Maxillofac Surg 4:69–92, 1976.

Tessier P: Colobomas: Vertical and oblique complete facial clefts. Panminerva Med 11:95–101, 1969.

Tessier P: Fente orbito-faciales verticales et obliques (colobomas) completes et frustes. Ann Chir Plast 14:301–311, 1969.

Turkaslan T, Ozcan H, Genc B, Ozsoy Z: Combined intraoral and nasal approach to Tessier No. 0 cleft with bifid nose. Ann Plast Surg 54:207–210, 2005.

Van der Meulen JC: Oblique facial clefts: Pathology, etiology and reconstruction. Plast Reconstr Surg 71:6–19, 1983.

Van der Meulen JC: The classification and management of facial clefts. In Cohen M (ed): Mastery of Plastic and Reconstructive Surgery. Boston, Little, Brown, 1994, pp 486–498.

Van der Meulen JC, Mazzola R, Vermey-Keers C, et al: A morphogenetic classification of craniofacial malformations. Plast Reconstr Surg 71:560–572, 1983.

CRANIOFACIAL MICROSOMIA

*Chris A. Campbell, MD; Jack C. Yu, DMD, MD, MS ED; and
Kant Y. Lin, MD*

CHAPTER 38

1. What is craniofacial microsomia and how frequently does it occur?

First described by Gorlin in 1963, craniofacial microsomia is a spectrum of morphogenetic anomalies involving the cranial skeleton, soft tissue, and neuromuscular structures derived from the first and second branchial arches. It is the second most common congenital facial anomaly after cleft lip and palate, with an incidence of 1:5600 live births. The anomaly is unilateral in 80% of cases. The male-to-female ratio is 3:2, and the anomaly has a 3:2 preference for the right side.

2. Does craniofacial microsomia and hemifacial microsomia represent the same entity?

Yes, as do the first and second branchial arch syndrome, oculoauriculovertebral sequence, otomandibular dysostosis, and lateral facial dysplasia. The variety of names reflects the wide spectrum of clinical deformities included in this category.

3. What are the current theories of the pathogenesis of craniofacial microsomia?

Current theories include stapedial artery hematoma during the fourth to eight weeks of gestation, and failure of neural crest cell development and migration.

4. Are any genetic or familial factors believed to play a role in craniofacial microsomia?

Most cases are sporadic, although both autosomal dominant and recessive patterns have been reported with association with chromosomes 8, 22q, and 14q. Some cases have been associated with maternal diabetes and second-trimester bleeding. The recurrence rate in first-degree relatives is estimated to be 3%.

5. Describe the typical clinical appearance of a patient with craniofacial microsomia.

Hypoplasia of the mandibular ramus, which usually is accompanied by hypoplasia of the zygoma, maxilla, and temporal bone, causes flattening of the lateral part of the face. In unilateral cases, the nose and chin are deviated to the affected side and the occlusal plane is tilted upward on the affected side. Varying forms of microtia and soft tissue hypoplasia contribute to facial asymmetry.

6. What is Goldenhar syndrome?

Also referred to as *oculoauriculovertebral sequence,* Goldenhar syndrome is a variant of hemifacial microsomia characterized by unilateral craniofacial abnormalities including epibulbar dermoids, preauricular skin tags, and spinal anomalies. A greater incidence of cleft lip and palate has been reported with Goldenhar syndrome relative to other syndromes.

7. What is the role of prenatal ultrasound in diagnosing conditions affecting development of the first and second branchial arches?

Cases of both craniofacial microsomia and Goldenhar syndrome have been diagnosed prenatally, thus allowing for early parental counseling and subsequent genetic testing. Microphthalmia, ear anomalies, epibulbar dermoids, and facial clefts all have been identified by prenatal ultrasound.

8. What diagnostic tests, in addition to physical examination, are useful tools in the assessment of patients with craniofacial microsomia?

Panoramic views (Panorex), anteroposterior, lateral, and basal cephalometry, computed tomographic (CT) temporal bone scan, and audiology all are useful tools in the assessment of patients with craniofacial microsomia.

9. Are clinical ear findings of craniofacial microsomia associated with hearing loss?

Although children with craniofacial microsomia have a higher incidence of hearing abnormalities compared with the general population, neither the degree of auricular hypoplasia nor malposition is associated with audiology results.

10. Classify the mandibular malformations associated with craniofacial microsomia.

The Pruzansky classification is often used to define mandibular deficiency. In type I, all components of the mandible are present but hypoplastic to varying degrees. The temporomandibular joint is present, but the cartilage and joint space are reduced. In type IIA, the condylar process is cone shaped and forms an articulation that allows hinge but not translatory movement. In type IIB, no condylar process articulates with the temporal bone, but a coronoid process of varying size is present. In type III, the entire mandibular ramus is absent.

11. What classification systems have been used in an attempt to encompass the range of abnormalities found in craniofacial microsomia?

The SAT classification system allows classification of **s**keletal, **a**uricular, and soft **t**issue deformities (Fig. 38-1). The OMENS-plus classification system describes involvement of **o**rbit, **m**andible, **e**ar, facial **n**erve, and **s**oft tissue structures, plus extracranial abnormalities (Table 38-1).

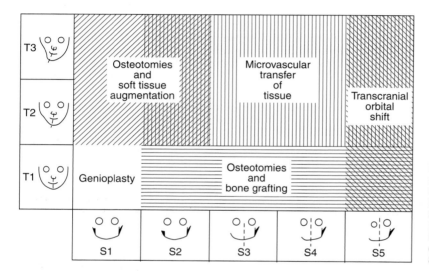

Figure 38-1. SAT classification of craniofacial microsomia in which abnormalities are categorized based on involvement of skeletal, auricular, and soft tissue. (From David DJ, Mahatumarat C, Cooter RD: Hemifacial microsomia: A multisystem classification. Plast Reconstr Surg 80:525–535, 1987.)

Table 38-1. OMENS-Plus Classification

O	0	Normal orbit
	1	Abnormal size
	2	Abnormal position
	3	Abnormal size and position
M	0	Normal mandible
	1	Hypoplastic mandibular ramus
	2	Hypoplastic and malformed mandibular ramus
	3	Absence of ramus, glenoid fossa
E	0	Normal ear
	1	Auricular hypoplasia
	2	Absence of external auditory canal
	3	Absent auricle and malpositioned lobe
N	0	Normal facial nerve
	1	Upper facial nerve involvement
	2	Lower facial nerve involvement
	3	All branches affected
S	0	No soft tissue abnormality
	1–3	Minimal, moderate, severe soft tissue/muscle deficiency
Plus		Extracraniofacial abnormalities

OMENS-plus, **O**rbit, **m**andible, **e**ar, facial **n**erve, and **s**oft tissue structures, plus extracranial abnormalities.

12. What orthodontic treatment is used in patients with craniofacial microsomia?

For mild cases, an intraoral functional appliance is constructed to hold the affected mandible in a lowered, forward position and may improve the osseous and soft tissue architecture during the time period when the child is growing. It has little negative effect. It is also used in the presurgical phase of treatment and may be particularly beneficial in patients with type I deformities. It is also used in the postoperative period to prevent relapse of the mandibular deformity and to stimulate growth of the maxilla.

13. What are the goals of surgical treatment in craniofacial microsomia?

The goals are construction and reshaping of the craniofacial skeleton, augmentation of soft tissue, and treatment of associated conditions such as auricular malformation and facial paralysis. Functional considerations include temporomandibular joint articulation and subjective and objective occlusion.

14. What surgical methods are available to reconstruct the mandibular ramus and increase the size of the mandible?

In type I and II malformations in which the mandibular ramus is present, bony length can be increased by distraction osteogenesis in younger children or by sagittal split mandibular osteotomies or bone grafts (as interpositional or onlay) in patients with a mature cranial skeleton. In type III malformations, the mandibular ramus and condyle need to be constructed with costochondral and/or iliac bone grafts.

15. What new surgical treatments are being used for type III mandibular deformities?

Microvascular techniques including second metatarsophalangeal joint transfer has been described to provide two epiphyseal plates for continued growth on the affected side and a functioning articulation to approximate the temporomandibular joint.

16. What structure is subject to anatomic variation in patients with craniofacial microsomia and is of special concern during mandibular surgery?

The position of the inferior alveolar nerve is extremely variable in patients with craniofacial microsomia, especially types IIB and III, making identification of this structure paramount before proceeding with osteotomies.

17. What are the indications for maxillary operation?

After construction of the mandibular ramus, abnormalities such as maxillary rotation, openbite, contralateral maxillary excess, and maxillary narrowing should be addressed. If maxillary leveling cannot be achieved with orthodontics alone, a Le Fort I osteotomy is indicated.

18. What are the goals of mandibular distraction?

The three goals of mandibular distraction are (1) to lengthen the mandibular ramus and body, (2) to reduce the gonial angle, and (3) to increase the intergonial distance.

19. How do you know when mandibular distraction is adequate?

When the distance between the lateral canthus and lateral commissure of the mouth on the affected side is the same as that on the unaffected side and when the mandibular occlusal midline is overcorrected by 3 to 4 mm, mandibular distraction is considered adequate.

20. What surgical methods are used for treatment of deformities of the nose and chin after completion of bony reconstruction?

If septal deviation persists after maxillary reconstruction, septal reconstruction and inferior turbinectomy may be required. The chin often is deviated toward the side of the defect in a retruded, inferior position often requiring an asymmetric, jumping, sliding osseous genioplasty.

21. What is the sequence of reconstructive surgery in children with craniofacial microsomia?

The sequence of reconstructive procedures includes correction of macrostomia in the first few months of life, excision of preauricular skin tags within the first year, mandibular distraction at age 2 years, costochondral grafts if needed, ear reconstruction and zygomaticoorbital complex reconstruction at 6 to 7 years, followed by soft tissue augmentation in adolescence.

22. What are the methods of soft tissue deficiency treatment?

Treatment of soft tissue deficiency includes autologous fat injections or dermal fat grafts for mild contour irregularities, pedicled or free muscle flaps for muscle atrophy, and microvascular free tissue transfer for large volume deficiencies. The parascapular flap is the preferred free muscle flap. The serratus anterior flap would atrophy over time, and the superficial temporal fascial flap would not provide the necessary volume.

23. What is the most common postoperative complication after sagittal split osteotomy?

Paresthesia of the lower lip is the most common immediate postoperative finding after a bilateral sagittal split osteotomy. It is generally bilateral and is due to neurapraxia resulting from stretch and compression of the inferior alveolar nerve as the mandible is mobilized and fixed into its new position. Studies have shown that the incidence of this finding ranges from 85% to 97% in the immediate postoperative period. The older the patient, the more protracted the sensory deficit.

24. In patients with craniofacial microsomia, which cranial nerve is most frequently involved?

The facial nerve is the most commonly involved cranial nerve, occurring in 10% to 45% of patients.

25. How does distraction osteogenesis differ from sagittal split osteotomy for treatment of mandibular hypoplasia?

After sagittal split osteotomy, the bone fragments are rigidly fixed and in touch with each other, whereas in distraction osteogenesis, the bony fragments do not touch each other, and fragments are not rigidly fixed to each other.

Sagittal split osteotomy of the ramus produces two overlapping bony fragments in the retromolar region. A sagittal complete osteotomy is performed lateral and parallel to the course of the mandibular nerve, leaving the nerve in the medial and distal fragment. This distal fragment is then advanced anteriorly, and osteotomy segments are rigidly fixed with screws.

In distraction osteogenesis, circumferential cortical osteotomies are performed on the mandible, leaving the mandibular nerve untouched in the cancellous part. A distraction device is then fixed on either side of the osteotomy, and daily distractions are performed starting on postoperative day 2 to 5 at a rate of 1 mm/day to stimulate bone growth between fragments.

26. In a sagittal split osteotomy of the mandible, the neurovascular bundle should remain in which of the following segments of the mandible?

The mandibular branch of the trigeminal nerve (V3) enters the mandible at the lingual foramen at the proximal and medial aspect, travels through the mandibular canal distally and laterally, and emerges through the mental foramen, which is located at the level of the second premolar halfway between the superior and inferior borders of the mandible. It innervates the lip and teeth. During mandibular sagittal split osteotomy, the neurovascular bundle must remain in the distal segment of the mandible to maintain innervation of the lip and teeth.

27. What is the optimal daily rate of distraction?

Distraction at a rate of 1 mm/day has been shown to be optimal in most situations. In infants the osteogenic potential is higher and distraction can be done at a rate of 2 mm/day, but this high rate is associated with delayed ossification. Rates of 0.5 mm daily or less are associated with an increased risk for premature consolidation.

BIBLIOGRAPHY

Junt JA, Hobar PC: Common craniofacial anomalies: The facial dysostoses. Plast Reconstr Surg 110:1714–1725, 2002.

Martinelli P, Maroutti GM, Agangi A, et al: Prenatal diagnosis of hemifacial microsomia and ipsilateral cerebellar hypoplasia in a fetus with oculoauriculovertebral spectrum. Ultrasound Obstet Gynecol 24:199–201, 2004.

McCarthy JG, Katzen JT, Hopper R, et al: The first decade of mandibular distraction: Lessons we have learned. Plast Reconstr Surg 110:1704–1713, 2002.

Ousterhout DK, Vargervik K: Hemifacial microsomia. In Cohen M (ed): Mastery of Plastic and Reconstructive Surgery. Boston, Little Brown, 1994, pp 536–547.

Poon CH, Meara JG, Heggie AC: Hemifacial microsomia: Use of the OMENS-Plus classification at the Royal Children's Hospital of Melbourne. Plast Reconstr Surg 111:1011–1018, 2003.

Vargervik K: Mandibular malformations: Growth characteristics and management in hemifacial microsomia and Nager syndrome. Acta Odontol Scand 56:331–338, 1998.

Vargervik K, Hoffman W, Kaban LB: Comprehensive surgical and orthodontic management of hemifacial microsomia. In Turvey TA, Vig KWL, Fonesca RJ (eds): Facial Clefts and Craniosynostosis. Philadelphia, WB Saunders, 1996.

Vilkki SK, Hukki J, Nietosvaara Y: Microvascular temporomandibular joint and manidibular ramus reconstruction in hemifacial microsomia. J Craniofac Surg 13:809–815, 2002.

Wan J, Meara JG, Kovanlikaya A: Clinical, radiological, and audiological relationships in hemifacial microsomia. Ann Plast Surg 51:161–166, 2003.

Werler MM, Sheehan, JE, Hayes C, et al: Demographic and reproductive factors associated with hemifacial microsomia. Cleft Pal Craniofac J 41:494–550, 2004.

SKULL BASE SURGERY

CHAPTER 39

Stephen P. Beals, MD, FACS, FAAP, and
Rebecca J.B. Hammond, MBA, MHSM

1. What are the anatomic divisions of the cranial base?

Anterior Cranial Fossa: Formed *anterolaterally* by the frontal bone, *inferiorly* by the orbital plates and the anterior portion of the body of the sphenoid, *medially* by the cribriform plate of the ethmoid bone, and *posteriorly* by the lesser wings of the sphenoid bone.

Middle Cranial Fossa: Formed *anteriorly* by the posterior margins of the lesser wings of the sphenoid bone, the anterior clinoid processes, and the ridge forming the anterior margin of the chiasmatic groove; *laterally* by the temporal squamae, the parietal bones, and the greater wings of the sphenoid; and *posteriorly* by the petrous portion of the temporal bone and dorsum sellae.

Posterior Cranial Fossa: Formed *anteriorly* by the dorsum sellae and the clivus of the sphenoid, *inferiorly* by the basal part of the occipital bone, *anterolaterally* by the petrous and mastoid portions of the temporal bone and the mastoid angles of the parietal bones, and *posteriorly* by the occipital bone.

2. List the foramina found in each segment of the cranial base and their contents.
See Table 39-1.

3. What tumors (malignant and benign) are commonly found in the cranial base?
- *Malignant Extracranial Tumors:* Squamous cell carcinoma, adenoid cystic carcinoma, rhabdomyosarcoma, hemangiopericytoma, esthesioneuroblastoma, malignant schwannoma
- *Malignant Intracranial Tumors:* Esthesioneuroblastoma, malignant schwannoma
- *Malignant Primary Basicranial Tumors:* Chondrosarcoma, osteogenic sarcoma, metastatic disease

Table 39-1. Foramina and Contents in Each Segment of the Cranial Base

FORAMEN	CONTENTS
Anterior Cranial Fossa	
Foramen cecum	Vein from nasal cavity to superior sagittal sinus
Anterior ethmoidal foramen	Anterior ethmoidal vessels and nasociliary nerve
Posterior ethmoidal foramen	Posterior ethmoidal vessels and nerve
Foramina for olfactory nerves	Olfactory nerves
Middle Cranial Fossa	
Optic foramen	Optic nerve
Superior orbital fissure	Cranial nerves III, IV, VI, V1
Foramen rotundum	Cranial nerve V2
Foramen ovale	Cranial nerve V3
Foramen spinosum	Middle meningeal artery
Anastomotic foramen	Branch from middle meningeal artery to lacrimal artery
Emissary foramen	Vein from cavernous sinus to pterygoid plexus
Innominate canal	Lesser petrosal nerve to otic ganglion
Foramen lacerum	Small nerve of pterygoid canal and small meningeal branch from ascending pharyngeal artery
Posterior Cranial Fossa	
Jugular foramen	Inferior petrosal sinus, lateral sinus, meningeal branches from occipital and ascending pharyngeal arteries, glossopharyngeal nerve, pneumogastric nerve, spinal accessory nerve
Foramen magnum	Medulla oblongata and its membranes, spinal accessory nerves, vertebral arteries, anterior and posterior arteries, occipitoaxial ligaments
Internal auditory meatus	Facial nerve, auditory nerve and artery
Anterior condyloid foramina	Cranial nerve XII and meningeal branch from ascending pharyngeal artery

- *Benign Extracranial Tumors:* Inverted papilloma, angiofibroma, salivary gland pleomorphic adenoma, paraganglioma, mucocele, cholesteatoma
- *Benign Intracranial Tumors:* Pituitary adenoma, craniopharyngioma, meningioma, schwannoma, ossifying fibroma
- *Benign Primary Basicranial Tumors:* Fibrous dysplasia, osteoma, osteoblastoma, chordoma, congenital dermoid

4. What are the common clinical findings associated with tumors of the skull base?

History and physical examination provide valuable information about the location and extent of a tumor. Presenting signs and symptoms may be vague and varied, depending on the type, size, and location of the tumor in the skull base. A skull base tumor may even remain silent until it has grown to a compromising size when symptoms then become evident. Signs of benign tumors are usually due to compression of adjacent tissues, causing in the orbital region, for instance, proptosis, diplopia, epiphora, and conjunctival exposure. Symptoms of malignant tumors, which are invasive, are often headaches, focal seizures, and loss of cranial nerve function (i.e., blindness, anosmia, diplopia, ptosis, altered facial sensation and/or animation, altered speech and/or swallowing, tinnitus and/or hearing loss).

5. How has the development of transfacial approaches to the cranial base enabled more successful skull base surgery?

Access to the midline skull base has always been difficult because of the complex anatomy of the vital structures. Transfacial approaches, developed over the past 2 decades, offer safe avenues of skull base exposure, often allowing single-stage resection, which shortens operating time and reduces morbidity (Fig. 39-1). The simultaneous advancement of medical technology in neurosurgery, radiographic techniques, anesthesia, and intraoperative and postoperative monitoring has further aided in the success of transfacial techniques.

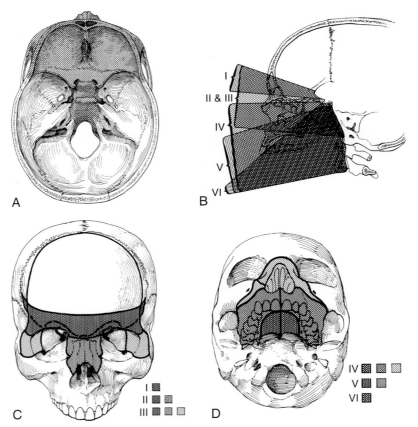

Figure 39-1. A, Scope of tumor sites in the anterior skull base and clivus that can be exposed by transfacial routes. **B,** Summation of the six different levels of approach demonstrating that the anatomic site of the tumors and direction of growth determine the level of transfacial exposure. The overlapping exposure shared by these approaches allows flexibility in choosing the best angle of surgical approach. **C,** The upper three approaches (levels I, II, III) are derived from the supraorbital bar. **D,** The lower three approaches (levels IV, V, VI) provide exposure through the maxilla. Variations of each of these approaches have been developed over time to customize the osteotomy further to the location and size of the tumor. The approaches are lateralized or centralized, and maxillectomies are added. (Reprinted with permission of the Barrow Neurological Institute, Phoenix, AZ.)

6. What are the advantages of transfacial approaches?
- Separation of facial units with minimal traumatic displacement due to the embryonic fusion of the facial units in the midline or in the paramedian region
- Viability of displaced facial units because the primary blood supply has a lateral-to-medial direction of flow
- Relative ease of surgical access to the central skull base due to the multiple hollow anatomic spaces of the midface
- Greater tolerance to postoperative swelling with displacement of facial units as opposed to similar displacement of the contents of the neurocranium
- Ability to reconstruct the facial units and maintain functional as well as aesthetic goals

7. What are the disadvantages of transfacial approaches?
- Contamination of the surgical wound with oropharyngeal bacterial flora
- Occasional need for facial incisions and subsequent scar development
- Emotional consideration for the patient related to surgical facial disassembly
- Potential need for tracheostomy or endotracheal intubation postoperatively

8. Why is the team approach important in conducting cranial base surgery?
A multidisciplinary team approach is essential. A team allows for the best care by combining the experience of a variety of specialists and by promoting good communication and coordination of the treatment plan and projected outcomes. The integral specialties are neurosurgery, head and neck surgery, plastic surgery, and neurotology. Specialists in the field of endovascular radiology, radiation oncology, chemotherapy, ophthalmology, neurology, and neurorehabilitation also make critical contributions to the skull base team.

9. What diagnostic tests are most commonly used in the diagnosis of skull base tumors?
- *Computed tomographic (CT) scan with contrast* provides information about bony involvement. Displacement of bone is generally seen with benign tumors, whereas malignant lesions show invasion and lysis.
- *Magnetic resonance imaging (MRI) with T1- and T2-weighted images* provides details about soft tissue and extent of tumor margins.
- *Positron emission tomography (PET)-CT* provides three-dimensional information about tumor location and viability of surgical removal.
- *Angiography* provides information about tumor vascularity and involvement of the carotid artery and/or other critical vascular structures.
- *Nasoendoscopy* provides information about tumor presence in the nasal and paranasal regions.

10. What is the role of tumor biopsy in diagnosing lesions of the skull base?
A direct biopsy is desirable before the final treatment plan for accessible tumors is determined. For inaccessible lesions, it is sometimes feasible to use CT-guided fine-needle aspiration to obtain a biopsy sample before surgery. When a specimen cannot be obtained preoperatively, a frozen section biopsy is taken during surgery before full exposure of the tumor.

11. How do you prepare a patient for cranial base surgery?
- Complete history and physical examination along with informed consent
- Clinical photographs
- Cephalometric x-rays, dental models, and splint fabrication if occlusion will be interrupted
- Routine laboratory tests and type and crossmatch for 4 to 6 units of blood
- Cryoprecipitate, in anticipation of use in fibrin glue
- CT scan or MRI on the way to surgery for immune serum globulin wand referencing
- Prophylactic antibiotics given in meningicidal doses
- Arrangements for psychological or family support

12. What transfacial surgical approach is used to access tumors of the anterior cranial fossa and tumors that extend into the superior orbital region?
The transfrontal approach, level I is performed through a bicoronal scalp incision. The radix and upper orbits are exposed, and the temporalis muscles are reflected so that a bicoronal craniotomy can be done. The incision must be posterior enough to provide an adequate frontogaleal flap. The dura is then dissected from the exposed anterior cranial fossa and cribriform plate. This procedure is facilitated by removal of the supraorbital bar. Watertight reconstruction, maintaining separation between the nasopharynx and cranial fossa, is achieved with local flaps, cranial autografts, and fibrin glue where indicated (Fig. 39-2A–C).

13. What are the variations of the transfrontal approach, and what are indications for their use?
The transfrontal approach, level I can be customized centrally or unilaterally based on tumor location with the centralized transfrontal osteotomy and the unilaterial transfrontal osteotomy (Fig. 39-2D and E).

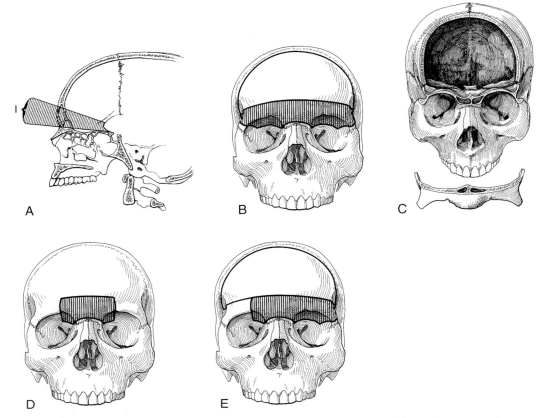

Figure 39-2. A, Level I transfrontal exposure for anterior cranial fossa and cribriform lesions. **B, C,** Level I exposure requires osteotomy of the supraorbital bar. Central **(D)** and unilateral **(E)** transfrontal osteotomies customize the approach based on tumor site. (Reprinted with permission of the Barrow Neurological Institute, Phoenix, AZ.)

14. What transfacial surgical approach is used to expose the anterior cranial fossa, nasopharynx, clivus, orbit, and tumors that grow anteriorly?

The transfrontal nasal approach, level II is performed through a bicoronal incision. The radix, nasal bones, and nasal process of the maxilla are exposed, and the periorbita are stripped by reflecting the flap anteriorly. The medial canthal ligaments are taken down, the upper lateral cartilages are detached from the nasal bones, and the nasolacrimal ducts are exposed and preserved. A bifrontal craniotomy is performed, and dural dissection is completed. The supraorbital bar and nasal orbital complex are osteotomized and removed. After tumor resection, the frontal nasal fragment is affixed in its anatomic position with rigid fixation. The upper lateral cartilages are reattached to the nasal bones, and the medial canthal ligaments are repaired by transnasal wiring. Skull base reconstruction is achieved with local flaps and cranial autografts as needed (Fig. 39-3A–C).

15. What are the variations of the transfrontal nasal approach and indications for their use?

The transfrontal nasal approach, level II can be customized with cribriform plate osteotomy, central transfrontal nasal osteotomy (with or without cribriform plate osteotomy), and unilateral tranfrontal nasal osteotomy based on the tumor site (Fig. 39-3D and E).

16. What transfacial surgical approach is used for resection of large anterior cranial fossa or nasopharyngeal lesions and clival lesions with anterior extension?

The transfrontal nasal-orbital approach, level III is done with dissection identical to that used in the level II approach. The osteotomy includes the lateral orbital walls from the level of the infraorbital fissure as part of the supraorbital fragment. Most of the superior orbital roof also can be included in the fragment to facilitate lateral retraction of the globes and greater midline exposure (Fig. 39-4A and B).

17. What are the variations of the transfrontal nasal-orbital approach and indications for their use?

The transfrontal nasal-orbital approach, level III can be customized with cribriform plate osteotomy, unilateral transfrontal nasal-orbital osteotomy (with or without cribriform plate osteotomy), and orbitozygomatic osteotomy based on the tumor site (Fig. 39-4C–F).

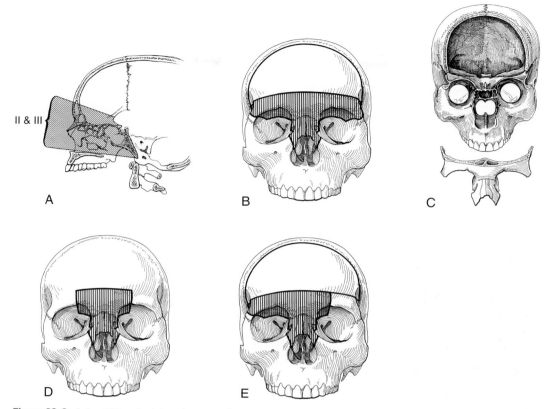

Figure 39-3. A, Level II transfrontal nasal exposure for anterior approach to the anterior cranial fossa and clivus. **B, C,** Level II exposure requires removal of the frontonasal unit. Level II approach with **(D)** cribriform plate osteotomy, central transfrontal nasal osteotomy (with or without cribriform plate osteotomy) and **(E)** unilateral transfrontal nasal osteotomy customize the approach based on tumor site. (Reprinted with permission of the Barrow Neurological Institute, Phoenix, AZ.)

18. What transfacial surgical approach is used for wide exposure of the entire midline skull base region and large nasopharyngeal and clival lesions that extend in all four directions?

The transnasomaxillary approach, level IV is done through a modified Weber-Ferguson incision, which is directed across the radix and along the opposite subciliary margin of the lower lid. After exposing the skeletal components, a Le Fort II osteotomy is performed. The osteotomy crosses just medial to the infraorbital foramen and nasolacrimal duct where the nasal fragment is divided into two fragments. It is done at the nasal process of the maxilla on one side and at the midline of the palate. The nasolacrimal duct often can be preserved if caution is used not to retract the nasal fragment excessively. The nasal soft tissue complex remains intact and is retracted with the fragment. This approach now is rarely used to avoid facial incision whenever possible. Instead, a combination of level III and level V approaches is used (Fig. 39-5A–D).

19. What are the variations of the transnasomaxillary approach and indications for their use?

The transnasomaxillary approach, level IV can be customized to include nasal osteotomy and medial maxillectomy (Fig. 39-5E and F).

20. What transfacial surgical approach is used for small clival lesions with superior, posterior, and inferior extensions, and small to moderate nasopharyngeal lesions?

The transmaxillary approach, level V is performed through an intraoral approach in which an upper buccal sulcus incision is made. The anterior maxilla is prepared for a Le Fort I osteotomy, and, if a midline palatal split is required, the soft palate is incised to one side of the uvula. The Le Fort I osteotomy is then performed and split through the midline. A watertight reconstruction of the skull base is performed at closure (Fig. 39-6A and B).

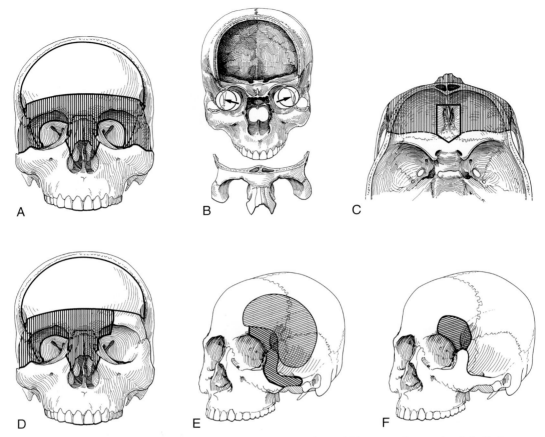

Figure 39-4. A, Level III transfrontal nasal-orbital exposure for larger anterior cranial fossa, nasopharyngeal, and clival lesions. **B,** This approach is similar to level II, except that it provides a wider exposure by allowing lateral retraction of the globes. Level III exposure requires inclusion of the lateral orbital walls on the frontonasal fragment. Level III approach with **(C)** cribriform plate osteotomy, **(D)** unilateral transfrontal nasal-orbital osteotomy (with or without cribriform plate osteotomy), **(E)** full orbitozygomatic osteotomy, and **(F)** mini orbitozygomatic osteotomy customize the approach based on the tumor site. (Reprinted with permission of the Barrow Neurological Institute, Phoenix, AZ.)

21. What are the variations of the transmaxillary approach, and what are the indications for their use?

The transmaxillary approach, level V can be customized to include a two-piece Le Fort I osteotomy. The two maxillary fragments then can be rotated laterally to expose the clivus. If greater exposure is needed, the pterygoid plates can be included on the fragments (Fig. 39-6C and D).

22. What transfacial surgical approach is used to expose the lower clival and upper cervical region for resection of small tumors?

The transpalatal technique, level VI is approached through the palate by incising both the nasal floor and oral mucosa. An incision is also made in the upper buccal sulcus, allowing the nasal floor to be approached extramucosally. The soft palate is incised to one side of the uvula and continued around the alveolar margin. The mucoperiostial flaps are elevated, and the bony palate is osteotomized. The septum and nasal groove are separated along the nasal floor, and cuts are made in the lateral nasal wall into the antra with an osteotome. The bony palate is removed, and the soft tissue portions are retracted. For further exposure, the vomer and perpendicular plate of the ethmoid are removed with a rongeur. After tumor resection, the bony palate is secured with rigid fixation, and the soft tissue is repaired (Fig. 39-7A–C).

23. What are the variations of the transpalatal approach and indications for their use?

The transpalatal technique, level VI can be customized to include a transvelar approach (Fig. 39-7D).

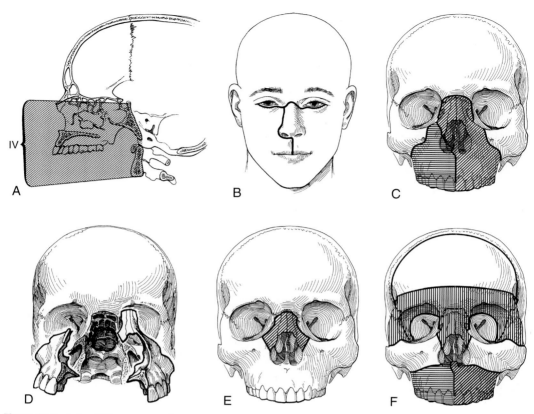

Figure 39-5. A, Level IV transnasomaxillary exposure yields a wide exposure of the entire central skull base from the radix to the cranial cervical junction. A similar degree of exposure usually can be obtained with a combination of level III and level V exposures. **B,** Incisions for the transnasomaxillary approach. Level IV exposure requires a Le Fort II osteotomy **(C)**, then splitting of the maxillary fragment **(D). E,** Level IV approach can be customized to include nasal osteotomy and medial maxillectomy. **F,** Combined level III and V approaches give exposure of entire midline skull base without a facial incision. (Reprinted with permission of the Barrow Neurological Institute, Phoenix, AZ.)

24. What are the important aspects of closure and reconstruction of the cranial base?
- Watertight separation from the nasopharynx with local flaps and cranial autografts
- Fibrin glue to seal suture lines
- Rigid fixation of bone fragments
- Use of an occlusal splint and preregistered plates when osteotomies involve occlusion

25. What are the options for flap reconstruction?
- Local
  - Pericranial Flap: Anteriorly based or laterally based on the temporalis muscle. This long flap extends the entire length of the anterior skull base but is very thin. It is best for the midline area.
  - Temporalis Muscle: Substantial but short muscle flap that usually cannot reach past the midline. It is best for lateral and orbital areas.
  - Frontogaleal Flap: Last resort for secondary reconstruction. It leaves the forehead skin very thin and vulnerable to breakdown and radiation (Fig. 39-8).
- Regional
  - Pectoralis major, latissimus dorsi, and trapezius muscles are useful for lateral skull defects.
- Distant
  - Rectus abdominis free flap is versatile for closure of skull base defects. It can be used as a composite flap with the peritoneum and posterior rectus sheath as a vascularized dural graft. The latissimus dorsi and omentum also have been used to fill dead space and to cover the surface of the skull and upper face. The anterolateral fasciocutaneous thigh flalp is thin and versatile for external coverage. A fascia venous flap is taken with a perforator or muscle cuff. It will reach into the midface and orbital region because of its long pedicle. It can be customized for dura repair by including vastus intermedius muscle (Fig. 39-9).

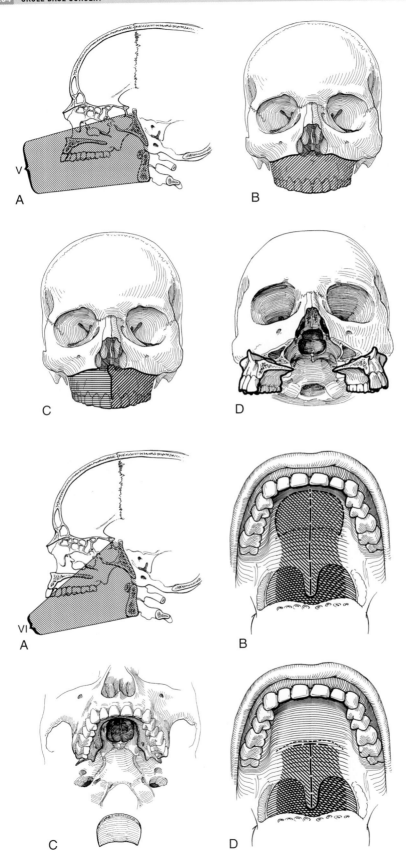

Figure 39-6. A, Level V transmaxillary approach provides exposure of the clivus and nasopharyngeal area. **B,** Level V approach requires a Le Fort I osteotomy and splitting of the palate for further exposure. **C, D,** Level V can be customized to include two-piece Le Fort I osteotomy for further exposure. (Reprinted with permission of the Barrow Neurological Institute, Phoenix, AZ.)

Figure 39-7. A, Level IV transpalatal exposure provides access to the lower clivus and upper cervical spine. **B, C,** Level VI exposure requires removal of the hard palate. **D,** Level VI can be customized to include a transvelar approach. (Reprinted with permission of the Barrow Neurological Institute, Phoenix, AZ.)

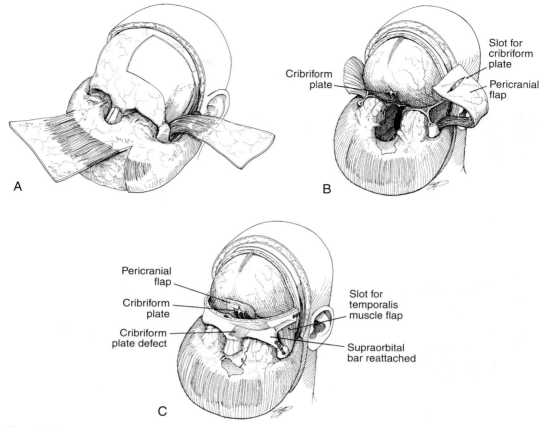

Figure 39-8. **A,** Scalp incisions must be planned and dissected to preserve and maximize the use of the pericranial, temporalis, and frontogaleal flaps. **B,** The osteotomy around the preserved cribriform plate is sealed with a perforated, laterally based pericranial flap. **C,** The cribriform plate is dropped through the flap and wired in place, then sealed with fibrin glue. The flap courses through a lateral defect in this level II transfrontal nasal approach. (Reprinted with permission of the Barrow Neurological Institute, Phoenix, AZ.)

26. What are the indications for use of free flaps in skull base reconstruction?
- Local flap options depleted or too small
- Large defects
- Previous radiation
- Complex wounds requiring multilayer repair

27. What is the postoperative management protocol for a patient who has undergone skull base surgery?
- Intensive care unit monitoring
- Postoperative CT scans or MRIs to evaluate the brain, tumor site, and presence of any dead space and/or intracranial air
- Endotracheal intubation until adequate resolution of swelling to ensure airway protection
- Continuation of prophylactic antibiotics
- Lumbar drain for cerebrospinal fluid CSF management
- Close surveillance for infection, bleeding, and neurologic and/or medical complications
- Arrangements for psychologic or family support

28. What complications may occur after skull base surgery?
- Neurologic complications
- Systemic complications
- Wound infection
- Cerebrospinal fluid leak
- Malocclusion
- Palatal fistula

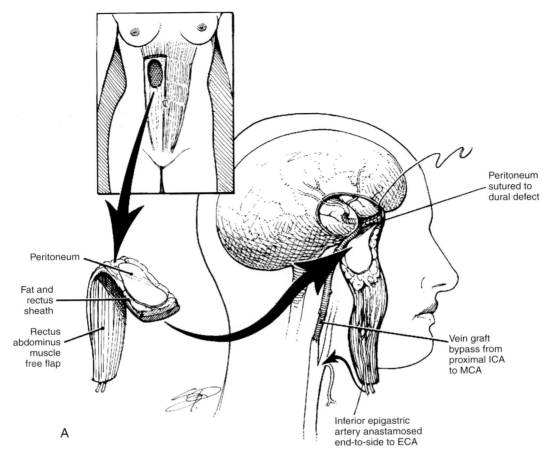

Peritoneum sutured to dural defect

Peritoneum

Fat and rectus sheath

Rectus abdominus muscle free flap

Vein graft bypass from proximal ICA to MCA

Inferior epigastric artery anastamosed end-to-side to ECA

A

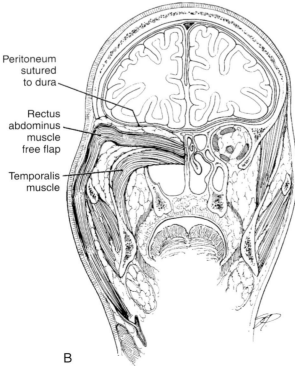

Peritoneum sutured to dura

Rectus abdominus muscle free flap

Temporalis muscle

B

Figure 39-9. **A,** Rectus abdominus free flap is used for a large skull base defect requiring multilayer reconstruction. **B,** Coronal view of flap inset. *ECA,* External carotid artery; *ICA,* internal carotid artery; *MCA,* middle cerebral artery. (Reprinted with permission of the Barrow Neurological Institute, Phoenix, AZ.)

- Speech abnormalities
- Epiphora
- Bleeding
- Flap or graft failure

29. What improvements in survival rates after skull base surgery have been seen over the past 4 decades?

In a 1995 study, O'Mally and Janecka demonstrated an increase in survival rates from 52% at 3 years after surgery and 49% at 5 years after surgery (in the 1960s and 1970s) to 57% to 59% at 3 years after surgery and 49% at 5 years after surgery (in the 1970s and 1980s). A 5-year survival rate of 56% to 70% has been achieved in the 1980s and 1990s. The advances of skull base surgery over the past 40 years have allowed the decline in mortality rates and improved resectability of tumors once thought to be inoperable.

BIBLIOGRAPHY

Anderson JE: Grant's Atlas of Anatomy, 7th ed. Baltimore, Williams & Wilkins, 1978.
Beals SP, Joganic EF: Transfacial approaches to the craniovertebral junction. In Surgery of the Craniovertebral Junction. Dickman CA, Sonntag VLJ, Spetzler RF (eds): New York, Thieme, 1998.
Beals SP, Joganic EF, Hamilton MG, Spetzler RF: Posterior skull base transfacial approaches. Clin Plast Surg 22:491–511, 1995.
Beals SP, Joganic EF, Holcombe TC, Spetzler RF: Secondary skull base surgery. Clin Plast Surg 24:565–581, 1997.
Goss CM: Gray's Anatomy, 28th ed. Philadelphia, Lea & Febiger, 1966.
Janeka IP, Tiedemann K: Skull Base Surgery, Anatomy, Biology and Technology. Philadelphia, Lippincott-Raven, 1997.
O'Malley BWJ, Janeka IP: Evolution of outcomes in cranial base surgery. Semin Surg Oncol 11:221–227, 1995.

CONJOINED TWINS

David A. Staffenberg, MD, DSc (Hon), and
James T. Goodrich, MD, PhD, DSc (Hon)

1. What is the incidence of conjoined twins?

Conjoined twins occur as often as once in every 40,000 births but only once in every 200,000 live births.

2. What are the types of conjoined twins?

- *Craniopagus:* Cranial union only. Simple cases may involve only scalp and calvarium, whereas more complete cases involve scalp, calvarium, dura, venous sinuses, and brain (Fig. 40-1A).
- *Pygopagus:* Posterior union of the buttocks (Fig. 40-1B).
- *Thoracopagus:* Anterior union of the upper portion of the trunk. This form of conjoining is the most common type of conjoined twinning (Fig. 40-1C).
- *Cephalopagus:* Anterior union of the upper half of the body with two faces on opposite sides of a conjoined head (extremely rare); the heart may be involved (Fig. 40-1D).
- *Rachipagus:* Dorsal union of the trunk with fused vertebral columns (Fig. 40-1E).
- *Parapagus* (sometimes called *Diprosopus*): Lateral union of the lower half of the body, extending variable distances upward; heart may be conjoined to varying degrees (Fig. 40-1F).
- *Ischiopagus:* Union of the lower half of the body; heart is not involved, but conjoined spines are not uncommon and increase the difficulty of separation (Fig. 40-1G).
- *Omphalopagus:* Anterior union of the midtrunk (Fig 40-1H).
- *Craniopagus/Thoracopagus Parasiticus Parasitic Twins:* Asymmetrical conjoined twins; one twin is small and less developed. The less developed twin survives only as a parasite upon the other.
- *Fetus-in-fetu:* An imperfect fetus is contained completely within the body of its sibling.

3. What are the relative percentages of each type of conjoined twin?

- Craniopagus: 2%
- Pygopagus: 19%
- Thoracopagus: 35%
- Cephalopagus: Rare
- Rachipagus: Rare
- Parapagus: 5%
- Ischiopagus: 6%
- Omphalopagus: 30%
- Parasitic twins: Rare
- Fetus-in-fetu: Rare

4. What percentage of conjoined twins are the same sex?

One hundred percent. All conjoined twins are identical twins who develop with a single placenta from a single fertilized ovum. Female conjoined twins appear to be about three times more common than male conjoined twins.

5. What are the embryologic issues that lead to the formation of conjoined twins?

Approximately 2 weeks after fertilization, during the primitive streak stage, the embryonic axis incompletely splits. This occurs much later than the split that leads to separate monozygotic twinning. Conjoined twinning occurs exclusively in monoamniotic, monochorionic twins and, with the exception of parasitic conjoined twins, is generally symmetrical and the same parts are always united to the same parts. Although some omphalopagus twins appear to be oriented head to toe, careful examination reveals a twist where they are conjoined.

6. How did conjoined twins become known as "Siamese twins"?

Conjoined twins throughout history have captivated people. They have been worshipped as gods or feared as bad omens, leading them to be abandoned, exiled, or even killed. As time passed, they were viewed as curiosities, and those who survived became sideshow acts, performed in circuses, or even became stage performers. Until the late 1800s conjoined twins were called "monsters." The term *Siamese twins* comes from the twin conjoined brothers Chang and Eng Bunker who were born in Siam, now Thailand. When they first arrived in England to become circus exhibits, they were called "The Siamese Twins."

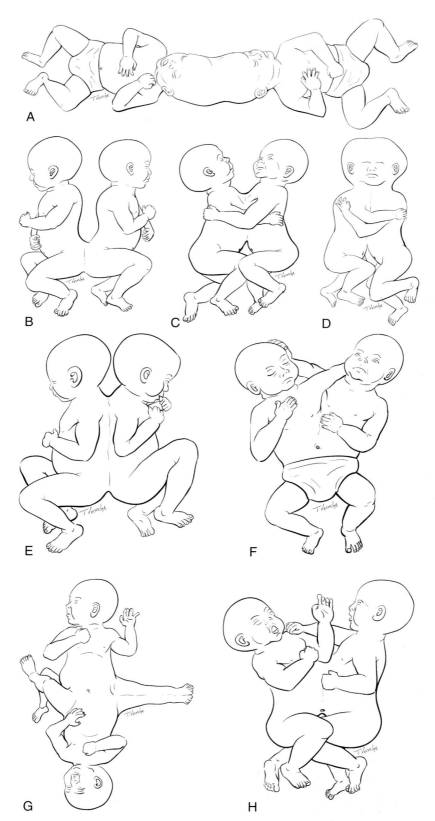

Figure 40-1. **A,** Craniopagus. **B,** Pygopagus. **C,** Thoracopagus. **D,** Cephalopagus. **E,** Rachipagus. **F,** Parapagus. **G,** Ischiopagus tripus. **H,** Omphalopagus. (Copyright © 2006 Medical Modeling LLC. Reproduced with permission.)

7. Who were some of the historically noted conjoined twins?

The Biddenden Maids (1100–1134). Eliza and Mary Chalkhurst were born in England and were known as the Biddenden Maids. When one of the parapagus twins died, the remaining twin is said to have refused an attempt at separation, saying, "As we came together, we will also go together." The twins left 20 acres of land to the poor, and every Easter biscuits decorated with their image are given to visitors of the village.

Lazarus and Joannes Baptista Colloredo (1617–1640s or 1650s). Lazarus and Joannes Baptista Colloredo are an example of parasitic twinning. Joannes grew as a parasitic appendage that grew out of Lazarus's torso. These twins toured Europe as circus performers and become quite wealthy as a result.

Chang and Eng Bunker (1811–1874). Chang and Eng Bunker are the most famous of all conjoined twins. They were born in 1811 in Siam (what is now Vietnam/Thailand). The King initially threatened them with death because they were believed to represent bad omen, but ultimately they were given permission to travel the world. They joined an English touring circus and eventually joined Barnum's Circus. They became quite wealthy as circus performers. Chang and Eng married sisters and had 21 children between the two of them. They each ran separate farms, spending a few days on one farm before moving to the other. Chang died of pneumonia at 63 years of age; Eng refused separation and died hours later.

Millie and Christine McCoy (1851–1912). The "Two-Headed Nightingale" were slaves born in North Carolina. In infancy they were separated from their family and sold. Four years later they were reunited with their mother. These rachipagus twins toured the world as a Vaudeville act, singing, dancing, and playing the piano. Income from their circus performances allowed them to buy the original property on which they were born as slaves. At the age of 61 years, Millie died of tuberculosis, and Christine died hours later.

Simplico and Lucio Godina (1908–1936). These twins from the Philippines were conjoined at the back. They married twin sisters, and the foursome made a living as entertainers. After Lucio died of pneumonia, Simplico was separated but soon died of an infection.

8. What were some of the historical separations?

Although surgeons have always been captivated by the exceptional challenges posed by separation, few have had the opportunity to operate on conjoined twins.

Before the 1950s the indications for separation were as follows:

- A simple conjoining without shared viscera, and the conjoining was remote from the head, heart, or pelvis.
- The children would have to survive the first few months.

The first successful separation (both twins survived) on record was performed in 1689. A ligament 2.5 cm long × 12 cm wide joined the twins. In 1860 a physician separated his conjoined twin daughters, but only one survived. In 1955, Dr. Rowena Spencer separated the Duckworth twins 18 hours after delivery in an effort to save the stronger twin.

In 1952–1953, Dr. Oscar Sugar separated the Brodie boys, who were craniopagus conjoined twins. One of the 14-month-old twins died 34 days after surgery. The second twin survived with a temporary hemiparesis but died at age 11 years due to complications of hydrocephalus.

In 1957, Voris et al. described the long-term survival of a set of 7-month-old craniopagus twin girls with minimal parietal union and a thin sheet of bone across the plane of union. One twin reportedly survived the separation neurologically intact while the other was severely impaired. Twenty-eight years later, the neurologically impaired sister donated a kidney to her twin.

In 2004, we successfully separated a set of craniopagus twins at The Children's Hospital at Montefiore. The junction included the skull, dura, a large venous plexus, and brain. A staged technique over 10 months was designed, which allowed successful separation without cerebrospinal fluid leak, meningitis, or hydrocephalus. While twin A has no post-surgical issues, twin B developed epilepsy and left-side neglect approximately 1.5 years after surgical separation.

Although advances in technology have led to more frequent attempts at separation, the discussion of medical, ethical, religious, and cultural questions continue. Parents of conjoined twins and the physicians caring for them are constantly trying to provide the best care to ensure the long-term well-being for these children.

9. If not separated, why does the surviving twin die soon after the first dies?

The dead twin loses vascular tone, and the surviving twin loses his/her blood volume into the first.

10. What is the plastic surgical technique that has allowed the most reliable separation and reconstruction of conjoined twins?

Tissue expansion has revolutionized conjoined twin separation. Free tissue transfer in infants does not provide enough tissue for coverage. The key to favorable outcome is durable soft tissue coverage of each twin after separation. Each twin will have a deficit of soft tissue across the conjoined plane, and after separation vital structures must be covered with viable tissue. When dura is involved (e.g., in craniopagus twins), this requirement is obvious; if soft tissue coverage is not complete and viable, cerebrospinal fluid leak will lead to meningitis.

Except for simple conjoining, conjoined twins who are to undergo separation surgery usually undergo a preliminary operation to insert tissue expanders. Another possible exception is the separation of parasitic conjoined twins in which the parasitic twin is not sufficiently developed to survive separation. In these cases, flaps using tissue from the parasitic twin can be applied to the "viable twin."

11. Why is ethics concerning the possible separation of conjoined twins a particularly difficult issue?

An ethics committee must consider each case of conjoined twins separately. The decisions that must be made are occasionally complicated by problems involving patient privacy, the treatment of shared organs, and the possibility of one twin dying to save the other. The risk of *not* separating the twins as well as their projected quality of life if they remain conjoined also must be taken into account.

BIBLIOGRAPHY

Aird I: Conjoined twins: Further observations. Br Med J 1:1313–1315, 1959.
Aird I, Hamilton WJ, Wijthoff JPS, LordJM: The surgery of conjoined twins. Proc R Soc Med 47:681–688, 1954.
Cameron DE, Reitz BA, Carson BS, et al: Separation of craniopagus Siamese twins using cardiopulmonary bypass and hypothermic circulatory arrest. J Thorac Cardiovasc Surg 98:961–967, 1989.
Cameron HC: A craniopagus. Lancet 1:284–285, 1928.
Drummond G, Scott P, Mackay D, Lipschitz R: Separation of the Baragwanath craniopagus twins. Br J Plast Surg 44:49–52, 1991.
Gaist G, Piazza G, Galassi E, et al: Craniopagus twins: an unsuccessful separation and a clinical review of the entity. Childs Nerv Syst 3:327–333, 1987.
Goodrich JT, Staffenberg DA: Craniopagus twins: Clinical and surgical management. Childs Nerv Syst 20:618–624, 2004.
Grossman HJ, Sugar O, Greeley PW, Sadove MS: Surgical separation in craniopagus. JAMA 153:201–207, 1953.
Hoyles RM: Surgical separation of conjoined twins. Surg Gynecol Obstet 170: 549–561, 1990.
O'Connell JEA: Craniopagus twins: Surgical anatomy and embryology and their implications. J Neurol Neurosurg Psychiatr 39:1–22, 1976.
O'Neill JA Jr, Holcomb GWIII, Schnaufer L, et al: Surgical experience with 13 conjoined twins. Ann Surg 208:299–312, 1988.
Raffensperger J: A philosophical approach to conjoined twins. Pediatr Surg 12:249–255, 1997.
Roberts TS: Cranial venous abnormalities in craniopagus twins. In Kapp JP, Schmidek HH (eds): The Cerebral Venous System and its Disorders. Orlando, FL, Grune & Stratton, 1984, pp 355–371.
Spencer R: Conjoined twins: Developmental Malformations and Clinical Implications. Baltimore, The Johns Hopkins University Press, 2003, pp 293–311.
Staffenberg DA, Goodrich JT: Separation of craniopagus conjoined twins: An evolution in thought. Clin Plast Surg 32:25–34, 2005.
Todorov AB, Cohen KI, Spilotro V, Landau E: Craniopagus twins. J Neurol Neurosurg Psychiatr 37:1291–1298, 1974.
Voris HC, Slaughter WB, Christian JR, Cayia ER: Successful separation of craniopagus twins. J Neurosurg 14:548–560, 1957.
Winston KR, Rockoff MA, Mulliken JB, et al: Surgical division of craniopagi. Neurosurgery 21:782–791, 1987.
Wolfowitz J, Kerr EM, Levin SE, et al: Separation of craniopagus. S Afr Med J 42:412–424, 1968.
Wong KC, Ohmura A, Roberts TH, et al: Anesthetic management for separation of craniopagus twins. Anesth Analg 59:883–886, 1980.
Wu J, Staffenberg DA, Mulliken JB, Shanske AL: Diprosopus: A unique case and review of the literature. Teratology 66:282–287, 2002.
Zubowicz VN, Ricketts R: Use of skin expanders in separation of conjoined twins. Ann Plast Surg 20:272–276, 1988.

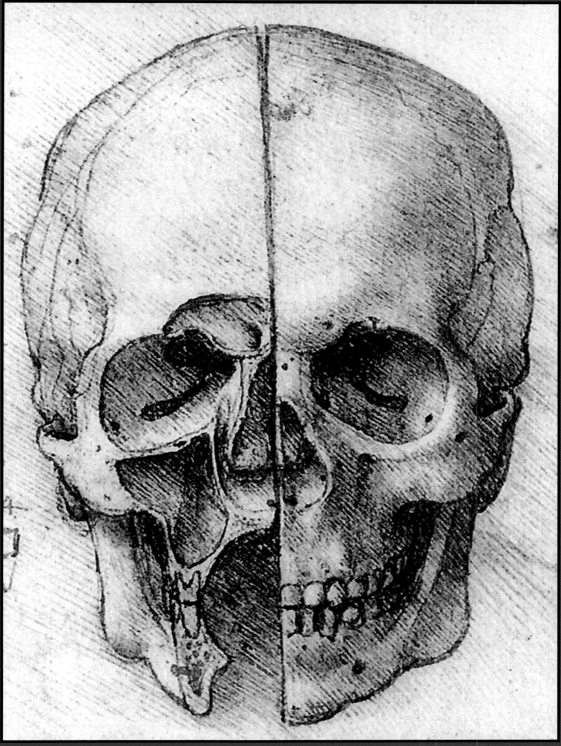

The Skull Sectioned. Leonardo da Vinci, 1489. Pen and ink over traces of black chalk. The Royal Library at Windsor Castle, Windsor. The Royal Collection. © 1998 Her Majesty Queen Elizabeth II.

ASSESSMENT AND MANAGEMENT OF FACIAL INJURIES

Paul N. Manson, MD

CHAPTER 41

1. What are life-threatening facial injuries?

Hemorrhage: Occasionally, profuse hemorrhage results from maxillofacial injuries. Such injuries are either upper Le Fort fractures or nasoethmoidal fractures in which nasal and sinus wall vessels are transected. Usually, hemorrhage is controlled by anterior–posterior nasal packing. A posterior nasal pack acts as an obturator against which the anterior packing can be placed. Failure to control bleeding should prompt repacking. In the case of Le Fort fractures, placement of the patient in intermaxillary fixation often dramatically limits blood loss. If these measures are not successful, hemorrhage may be occurring from the cranial base, where lacerations of the carotid or jugular system are possible with skull-base fractures. Angiography should be performed, and embolization of appropriate bleeding areas may be attempted. If these measures fail, ligation of the external carotid and superficial temporal arteries will limit blood flow in the common area of maxillofacial artery transection (generally the internal maxillary artery and nasal and sinus branches) by up to 90%.

Airway: Airway obstruction is seen with fractures of the nose or upper and lower jaws or with swelling in the floor of the mouth. Either jaw may displace posteriorly to partially obstruct the pharynx.

Aspiration: Aspiration occurs when patients are unable to manage their airway. Fractures of the upper and lower jaw commonly permit aspiration. Neck swelling, pharynx and tongue swelling and obtundation, and floor of mouth swelling disturb swallowing mechanisms.

2. The presence of fat in a periorbital laceration should mandate what examination?

It implies the possibility of a globe-penetrating injury, and the globe should be carefully examined, both externally and funduscopically, for the presence of a laceration. As a baseline, visual acuity should be recorded in every patient with a facial injury, as should the presence of double vision as well. The pupillary reaction is noted.

3. The presence of a Marcus Gunn pupil implies what cranial nerve injury?

Injury to the optic nerve, if partial, may present as a Marcus Gunn pupil. The Marcus Gunn pupil implies paradoxical pupillary dilation when a light is swung between the intact and the injured eyes. Normally, light causes constriction on the side of the injured and normal eyes as the light is swung back and forth between the opposite eye and the eye in question. When the optic nerve is injured, paradoxical dilation rather than constriction occurs. This finding implies a partial lesion of the optic nerve. Optic nerve lesions are first detected by a change in the rapidity of the response of the pupil to light. Thereafter, visual acuity deficits occur, including Marcus Gunn pupil. Any diminished vision should prompt treatment of an optic nerve injury and/or evaluation of the cause, such as retinal detachment, hyphema, or other intraocular problem.

4. The presence of nasal bleeding implies fracture of what craniofacial structure?

Nasal bleeding is a nonspecific event that accompanies many craniofacial fractures. Frontobasal fractures present as nasal bleeding, as do fractures of the frontal sinus. Medial orbital fractures commonly produce ipsilateral epistaxis, as do fractures of the inferior orbit (floor) and zygoma. Bilateral epistaxis is seen in bilateral midface fractures, such as those of the Le Fort type, the nasoethmoidal region, and the nose.

5. Numbness in the infraorbital division of the trigeminal nerve is consistent with what fracture?

It is consistent with a fracture of the floor of the orbit or the zygoma. The absence of numbness should place the diagnosis of these fractures in question. The presence of numbness in an orbital floor fracture is not a prognostic sign that implies the necessity for operative intervention. Numbness following a zygoma fracture, where the zygoma is medially impacted into the infraorbital canal, affects the prognosis of sensory recovery if the fracture displacement is not corrected. Decompression of the infraorbital foramen by fracture reduction is indicated. The infraorbital nerve travels from the posterior margin of the inferior orbital fissure anteriorly and medially across the floor of the orbit.

In the proximal two-thirds of the orbit the nerve is in a groove; in the distal third it is in a canal. The canal exits the maxilla approximately 10 mm below the infraorbital rim parallel to the lateral margin of the cornea in straightforward gaze. A branch of the nerve travels in the anterior wall of the maxilla to reach the anterior incisor and cuspid teeth. Other branches enter the soft tissue to innervate the upper lip, ipsilateral nose, and skin of the medial cheek. Numbness in either of these areas implies damage to the nerve from crushing within fracture sites. Symptoms may be partial or total in each set of branches. Therefore numbness of the teeth and lip implies that the fracture affects one or more branches of the nerve.

6. **The presence of cyanosis, drooling, and hoarseness implies damage to what structures and the necessity for operative intervention in what area?**

Such symptoms indicate impending complete respiratory obstruction. Fractures of the upper and lower jaws, fracture of the larynx, or swelling in the floor of the mouth produce respiratory obstruction. If possible, a tracheostomy should be performed under operative conditions that permit careful identification of the trachea. A tracheostomy should be performed through a horizontal incision in the skin and a vertical incision between the strap muscles, dissecting down to the trachea. A vertical incision is made into the second and third tracheal rings, and a tube can be inserted. In urgent situations, a cricothyroidotomy may be performed between the cricoid and the hyoid cartilages. Cricothyroidotomy is meant to be a rapid, life-saving maneuver and should be converted to a tracheostomy as soon as possible.

7. **Cervical spine fractures accompany what maxillofacial injury?**

Cervical spine fractures commonly accompany maxillofacial soft tissue or bony injuries and are frequently seen on frontal impact and mandibular fractures. An association with mandibular fractures has been both confirmed and denied in separate studies. Several studies have shown a slight association of mandibular fractures with upper cervical spine fractures. Generally the upper and lower cervical areas are the most difficult to image radiologically; if they cannot be cleared, the patient must be treated as if he or she has a cervical spine fracture until the injury is excluded. The presence of a cervical spine fracture may dictate that standard approaches to facial injuries must be converted to alternative approaches that do not require rotation or extension of the neck.

8. **Which maxillofacial fractures are more difficult to localize in computed tomographic scans?**

The presence of a nondisplaced fracture (classically of the ramus of the mandible) is one of the most difficult to identify in computed tomographic (CT) scans. Axial and coronal imaging with appropriate bone windows is preferred. Soft tissue windows often miss nondisplaced maxillofacial fractures. Proper imaging, proper slice thickness, and combining physical examination findings with CT scan data help to prevent "missed" injuries. The orbital floor fracture is missed in axial CTs. The frontobasilar fracture is also missed on axial CT scans.

9. **Panorex examination of the mandible is likely to miss fractures in what mandibular region?**

The Panorex radiograph is a flat view taken by a movable x-ray tube that displays the entire mandible as a flat structure. The examination generally requires patient cooperation. Some overlap and blurring usually is seen in the symphysis–parasymphysis region, so nondisplaced fractures in this area are frequently missed. The combination of Panorex examination and CT scan detects almost all mandibular fractures.

10. **Split palate and alveolar fractures have what symptoms in contrast with a Le Fort fracture?**

Fractures of that palate and alveolus generally present with mucosal and palatal lacerations. These are not the usual symptoms of Le Fort fractures and imply damage to the dental alveolar structures. Both Le Fort fractures and palatal alveolar fractures present with nasal bleeding and may present with numbness in the teeth. Alveolar fractures and fractures of the palate allow lateral mobility of the maxillary dentition (displacement of one side versus the other). Le Fort fractures have a mobile maxilla, but the segments of the dental arch are not mobile. Segments of the arch in palate fractures often are or can be displaced laterally and are mobile, whereas the Le Fort fracture displays mobility at the Le Fort I, II, or III level. In Le Fort fractures, the maxillary dental arch moves as a one-piece unit. The presence of a palatal alveolar fracture demands additional reduction techniques and/or splinting in combination with techniques used to stabilize Le Fort fractures.

11. **Which nasoethmoidal fractures do not display telecanthus?**

Nasoethmoidal orbital fractures that are "greenstick" or incomplete at the junction of the internal angular process of the frontal bone with the frontal process of the maxilla usually are rotated posteriorly and medially at the inferior orbital rim and piriform aperture (type I). Therefore they tend to tense the medial canthal attachment and lengthen the palpebral fissure. A "bowstringing" effect on the palpebral fissure is created, along with an ipsilateral depression along the side of the nose and the inferior orbital rim. The presence of a complete fracture at the internal angular process of the frontal bone allows attachment of the medial canthal ligament to the frontal process of the maxilla to move laterally, which produces the classic telecanthus seen in complete nasoethmoidal orbital fractures.

12. Cerebrospinal fluid fistulas can be detected by what examinations?

Cerebrospinal fluid fistulas are detected by suspicion. If nasal drainage is examined, the presence of a double ring on absorption of the nasal drainage on a paper towel implies that the blood is separate from another component. The blood ring is internal and the lighter blood ring in external, implying the presence of another substance (cerebrospinal fluid). Cerebrospinal fluid contains glucose, whereas nasal mucous or drainage does not. The location of a cerebrospinal fluid fistula is often suspected on a carefully performed CT scan. Alternatively, dye or radiographically active material can be placed in the spinal fluid with a lumbar puncture and collected in the nose to identify the presence of cerebrospinal fluid with a lumbar puncture and to identify the presence of cerebrospinal fluid rhinorrhea. Dyes also can be imaged as they pass through the site of the fistula.

13. Subcondylar fractures of the mandible generally present with what occlusal disturbance?

Subcondylar fractures of the mandible usually present with a contralateral openbite in the anterior dentition and premature contact on the ipsilateral side. The ramus is shortened by the fracture on the affected side; therefore a premature contact in the molar dentition on the injured side opens the bite on the contralateral anterior dentition.

14. Untreated Le Fort II and III fractures generally present with what changes in facial structure and occlusion?

Untreated fractures of the Le Fort variety generally present with bilateral eyelid ecchymosis, bilateral infraorbital nerve numbness, bilateral nasal bleeding, and dramatic facial swelling. A malocclusion is present. Generally the maxilla has dropped inferiorly in its posterior aspect, creating premature contact in the posterior dentition and an anterior openbite. The maxillary dental arch usually is rotated. The facial features are flattened and elongated, producing the so-called donkey facies of maxillary and zygomatic retrusion, nasal retrusion, and increased length of the middle third of the facial region.

15. Incomplete or greenstick Le Fort fractures present with what symptoms and are characteristically found at what level?

Incomplete Le Fort fractures present with minimal signs of facial injury. Often they masquerade as an isolated zygomatic fracture. Incomplete fractures are more common in upper (Le Fort II and Le Fort III) fractures. Maxillary mobility is normally the hallmark of a Le Fort fracture; however, it is absent in incomplete injuries. Displacements usually are slight, so the malocclusion can be ascribed to swelling and easily missed. The fracture is also easily missed in radiographs because there is no displacement between fragments and the CT scans do not image undisplaced fractures with clarity. Therefore the diagnosis must be suspected in any patient with minor malocclusion and periorbital bruising. The injury usually is treated satisfactorily by the application of arch bars and traction elastics for a short (3-week) period. Missing the fracture generally requires a maxillary Le Fort I osteotomy as an elective corrective procedure.

16. The presence of an anterior cranial fossa fracture is suspected by what clinical signs?

Generally, fractures of the anterior cranial fossa are not only easily missed on radiographs (they generally require carefully taken CT scans), but they may be missed on physical examinations. The presence of a forehead bruise or laceration is common. The patient may demonstrate a "spectacle" hematoma, a hematoma in the upper lid confined to the distribution of the orbital septum. Therefore the bruise abruptly stops where the orbital septum attaches to the superior orbital rim and produces a classic hematoma of the upper eyelid. Such hematomas are diagnostic of a fracture within the superior orbit; therefore it is an anterior cranial fossa fracture. Disturbances of olfaction and a cerebrospinal fluid leak also may accompany these injuries. The most common cerebral symptom is a slight disturbance of memory or consciousness. Even brief periods of unconsciousness imply brain contusion.

17. What is the difference between enophthalmos and ocular dystopia?

Fractures of the lower two-thirds of the orbit commonly produce changes in eye position by expansion of the orbit. Fractures of the superior portion of the orbit generally are displaced inward and downward and cause the globe to be driven forward and downward by orbital volume constriction. Fractures of the inferior portion of the orbit may either constrict or expand the orbital cavity. Constriction is most commonly produced by a medially displaced zygoma fracture, which may cause exophthalmos of the globe. In fractures of the zygoma, orbital floor, or medial orbit that expand the volume of the orbit, the globe is displaced posteriorly and medially. The posterior displacement of the globe is termed *enophthalmos*. Generally, an increase of 1 cc in orbital volume is required for each millimeter displacement of the globe. Inferior globe displacement is called *ocular dystopia*. Displacement is permitted by expansion of the floor, the medial orbital wall, and, in cases of the zygoma, the inferior orbital rim.

18. How are injuries of the parotid duct detected?

Parotid duct injuries should be suspected on the basis of physical examination. Lacerations in the vicinity of the duct (which travels on a line between the ear canal and the base of the nose and exits into the mouth opposite the second maxillary bicuspid–first molar area) are suspect for parotid duct injury. Because the buccal branch of the facial nerve and the parotid duct run close to each other, injury to either structure alone is less common than is injury to both. Therefore lacerations that present with buccal branch facial nerve weakness should raise suspicion for parotid duct injuries. The duct can be cannulated with an Angiocath intraorally. If saline is flushed into the duct, the appearance of saline in the wound is diagnostic of a duct or anterior glanular laceration. Such injuries benefit from operative exploration and repair of the duct. Repair is conducted over a fine "stent" catheter with nonabsorbable sutures.

19. Blunt craniofacial injuries accompanied by facial nerve palsy are generally due to fracture of what bone structure?

Fractures of the temporal bone are common skull-base fractures. They may be longitudinal or transverse. Steroids administered at a high dose rate and decompression are considered for certain injuries. The prognosis varies with the site of fracture.

20. Subluxation of the condylar head anterior to the glenoid fossa produces what symptom?

It produces an openbite and inability to close the mouth. The mandible is "locked" open. The joint usually is anesthetized to relax the muscles, then finger pressure is delivered downward to the posterior maxillary dentition to ease the condylar head back into the fossa. Limited mouth opening is prescribed. Occasionally, surgical intervention is necessary to prevent recurrent dislocations.

21. Transection of the lacrimal system is suggested by what physical signs?

It usually is heralded by a laceration in the vicinity of the medial canthus. The lacrimal punctum may be dilated and saline squirted through the punctum into the system. Appearance of saline in the wound is diagnostic of a canalicular laceration. Both upper and lower canalicular lacerations should be repaired. Tubes are placed into the nose, through the lacerated canaliculus to splint the repair. Damage to the lacrimal system commonly accompanies Le Fort III and nasoethmoidal fractures. However, such damage usually produces compromise or obstruction of the lacrimal system within the nasal lacrimal duct. Repair and repositioning of the fracture fragments often permit adequate function of the system. Repair of a chronically obstructed nasal lacrimal duct is accomplished with a dacryocystorhinostomy.

22. Facial lacerations rarely require débridement because the blood supply is good and the tissue will usually heal. True or false?

Most facial lacerations benefit from débridement. The facial blood supply is excellent, and often contused bits of tissue will heal but with increased scarring. Therefore the zone of contusion should be excised, if permitted by flexibility and availability of soft tissue, to prevent distortion. Excision should not be performed in the upper and lower eyelid areas because the eyelids may not be able to close completely over the globe. In general, excision also should not be performed in eyelid or eyelid margin lacerations, nostril rim lacerations, or lacerations of the lip margins or ear because distortion may be noticeable. In other areas, resection of the contused skin allows conversion to a primary surgically created wound with more predictable healing and generally improved appearance. A layered repair of the facial soft tissue, including the fat mimetic system and the skin dermal and epidermal components, should be performed.

23. Three-dimensional CT scans are indicated in what kind of fracture evaluation?

Three-dimensional CT scans are helpful for an overall picture of the fracture and are most useful for comparing symmetry between the sides or displacement of the zygoma or mandible. They are not as useful in the orbit because they are not sensitive to orbital wall displacement. The combination of axial and coronal CT scans with both bone and soft tissue windows provides the most accurate facial injury assessment.

24. What potentially lethal facial fracture emergency is commonly overlooked?

Aspiration often accompanies fractures of the upper and lower jaws. It is easily missed and accounts for pulmonary complications that may have severe consequences. It is prevented by recognition, patient positioning, and intubation.

25. What disastrous complications result from instrumentation or unrecognized fractures of the anterior cranial fossa?

Disastrous complications may occur if nasal instrumentation procedures are performed carelessly in unrecognized fractures of the anterior cranial fossa. Fractures of the anterior cranial fossa produce a bony discontinuity that allows penetration of nasogastric tubes, nasal fracture reduction instruments, and nasal packing into the anterior cranial fossa. One must be aware of the usual location of the cribriform plate, and instruments must be angled away from this region specifically. Both instruments and nasogastric tubes have been inadvertently introduced into the anterior cranial fossa with disastrous consequences.

26. Numbness of the lower lip usually accompanies what type of mandibular fracture?

The inferior alveolar nerve enters the mandible in the upper ramus and travels through the angle region and the body of the mandible until it reaches the mental foramen opposite the first bicuspid tooth. It then exits the jaw and travels in the soft tissue. Therefore fractures of the angle and body region may produce numbness by displacement of fragments impinging on and/or transecting the nerve. The presence of numbness should prompt a thorough examination for mandibular fracture. Generally, such fractures are accompanied by malocclusion and bleeding from a tooth socket.

27. Acutely, orbital floor fractures present with what symptoms? What criteria should be used to establish the need for operative reduction?

Orbital fractures generally present with numbness in the distribution of the infraorbital nerve, double vision, periorbital and subconjunctival hematoma, and perhaps a visual acuity deficit. The visual acuity deficit is not specific to the orbital fracture but implies damage to the globe or the optic nerve. Generally, orbital fractures present with exophthalmus due to swelling. Exophthalmus is present within 1 to 3 weeks if the orbital cavity is significantly enlarged and appears as the swelling resolves. Orbital volume enlargement of more than 5% to 10% justifies open reduction. Generally, orbital fractures are accompanied by diplopia when the patient looks upward or downward. Diplopia in downgaze is quite disabling and most commonly is due to muscular contusion. Diplopia due to interference with the excursion of the extraocular muscle system, either by entrapment of fat that is tethered to the muscles by fine ligaments or, less commonly, by entrapment of the muscle itself, should be treated with operative intervention. Diplopia due to muscle contusion usually improves significantly without operative intervention.

28. A young boy is watching a football game in a grandstand when he is pushed forward and falls several rows, breaking his nose. He is bleeding profusely from his nose, says he blacked out for a brief period, and has pain when he turns his head side to side. What is the most important examination to do first?

The first examination should be flexion/extension views of the neck. Injuries to the face present a geographic injury to the head and neck region. The patient actually was briefly unconscious, justifying a CT scan of the head. He also was complaining of neck pain. Flexion/extension views should be performed to rule out a cervical spine fracture, and these are the most important because now he is conscious. A directed physical examination is also important. These head and neck examinations exclude more life-threatening injuries and take priority over simple nasal bone assessment.

29. In secondary facial reconstruction, is one most likely to have difficulty with bone repositioning, soft tissue repositioning, or retained plates?

Facial injuries involve both bone and soft tissue. The soft tissue heals with a pattern of internal scarring that sometimes is difficult to reduce or oppose. Although the bone can be more easily repositioned, the soft tissue is thick, inflexible, and less conforming. The bone injury is classically more reversible than is the soft tissue injury.

30. Following bone grafting, what "take" of a bone graft is generally expected?

Generally, 30% to 70%. Bone graft take depends on the host bed, the donor site of the bone graft, and fixation. Rib grafts have the least persistence, probably due to their open structure, which is less compact than bone grafts of the iliac or calvarial region. Calvarial bone grafts have the densest structure and so are resorbed less following bone graft transfer. Depending on these factors the "take" of a bone graft is generally 30% to 70% and conceptually can be improved by rigid fixation of the bone graft. Rarely, complete take or complete absorption of a bone graft is seen.

31. What is the most frequent reason for failure of alloplastic cranioplasty in the skull?

Alloplastic cranioplasty generally fails because of poor skin cover with secondary exposure or, most commonly, performance next to damaged sinuses with secondary infection. Conceptually, the sinus should be eliminated or obliterated with bone graft prior to cranioplasty. All intranasal or middle ear disease should be eliminated prior to the cranioplasty. Any thin areas in skin cover should be remedied prior to the performance of a cranioplasty.

32. What is the best material for frontal sinus obliteration?

Bone. Obliteration of a sinus cavity with bone is based on the ability to revascularize a portion of the grafted material, forming a vascularized seal between the nose and the intracranial cavity or frontal sinus. Therefore material that can be revascularized (rather than alloplastic material) is conceptually the best material to use in this situation. Alloplastic materials, including methylmethacrylate, porous polyethylene, and plaster of Paris, exposed to the nasal cavity have a high incidence of secondary infection.

33. Osteomyelitis is common after frontal sinus repair. True or false?

False. Approximately 10% of frontal sinus repairs are complicated by infection, which can be either low grade or more troublesome. Osteitis is infection in devascularized bone and is by far the most common bone infection. Osteomyelitis is infection in living bone and is unusual after frontal sinus infection, as is the complication of meningitis.

34. Supraorbital fractures usually displace the eye in which direction?

Supraorbital bone fractures are generally displaced downward and backward, which displaces the globe *forward and downward.* In reconstruction one must be careful to reconstruct the "double curve" of the orbital roof, which connects to the supraorbital rim. This allows space for the globe to sit comfortably in the orbit. Occasionally a supraorbital fracture will be displaced severely enough that the globe is displaced forward to such an extent that the lids cannot close. In this situation, the lids must be sutured shut over the globe to protect it, or an acute open reduction should be performed.

35. In many nasoethmoidal fractures, the medial canthal ligament may be left attached to what structure during reduction?

The frontal process of the maxilla. In many nasoethmoidal fractures in which the medial canthal ligament is not avulsed from the bone (which includes the majority of fractures) or transected by a laceration, the bone forming the frontal process of the maxilla to which the medial canthal ligament is attached can be used as a single soft tissue–bone unit in reconstruction. This bone piece can be repositioned, which simultaneously repositions the canthal ligament. Bone fixation without detaching the ligament saves an important and more difficult step in reconstruction, which is reconstructive of the canthal ligament separately.

36. A Stranc plane II nasal fracture would be expected to require what type of reconstruction?

Stranc plane II nasal fractures are displaced posteriorly and typically require *dorsal augmentation.* There is overlapping of the septal fragments, depression of the bone, and cartilaginous support of the nose posteriorly decreasing the height of the nose. When the loss of height is sufficient, regaining this height by any open reduction maneuver is difficult. Therefore dorsal and caudal bone and cartilage grafting may be required. If nasal packing is used for support, the support either is insufficient or disappears with removal of the nasal packing. The skin contracts, shortening the skin envelope and making secondary volume augmentation of the nosed skeleton more challenging. Therefore the best treatment is immediate correction by augmentation of the skeletal volume of the nose, both dorsally and caudally.

37. The majority of zygomatic fractures require what type of surgical approach?

The majority of zygomatic fractures require a *limited open reduction.* Approximately 20% of zygomatic fractures are so minimally displaced that perception of significant deformity is difficult. Therefore these zygomatic fractures do not need a reduction. Approximately 10% of zygomatic fractures are so comminuted or posteriorly displaced that they benefit from a coronal incision to expose the posterior attachments of the zygoma and the zygomatic arch. The *majority* of zygomatic fractures can be managed by anterior approaches alone, which include an approach to the zygomaticofrontal suture, the inferior orbital rim and the internal orbit, and the gingivobuccal sulcus. Many zygomatic fractures in this group can be approached with a gingivobuccal sulcus approach alone, simply reducing the medial displacement of the zygoma. Placing an endoscope in the maxillary sinus, one can then ballot the globe and visualize any area of floor dehiscence and determine whether this is significant enough to have an open reduction through one of the lower eyelid incisions. Fractures that are not displaced at the zygomaticofrontal suture do not require an approach at this area. Commonly, zygomatic fractures benefit from a limited open reduction with anterior approaches alone in the sequence described.

38. In a patient with 6 mm of enophthalmos, 20/20 vision, and diplopia looking upward, will correction of the enophthalmos correct the diplopia?

Not likely. Enophthalmos with double vision implies an injury that displaces the globe and impairs movement of the extraocular muscle system. Commonly the diplopia is due to scarring in the extraocular muscles and less commonly to displacement of the globe itself. Following repositioning of the eye, the double vision can be the same, worse, or better. The double vision tends to be better or worse in approximately 10% of cases, respectively. The average patient will not experience a significant change in double vision following repositioning of the globe. Therefore globe repositioning should be accomplished first because it may change the adjustment necessary for extraoccular muscle correction.

39. A Le Fort fracture doesn't exist if the maxilla is not mobile. True or false?

False. The majority of Le Fort fractures are diagnosed by mobility of the maxilla. However, the maxilla may not be mobile under two conditions: the impacted fracture and the "greenstick" or incomplete fracture where the fracture is immobile because it is not complete. The majority of greenstick fractures are high (Le Fort II or III) with a small displacement—a fraction of a cusp. Impacted fractures are driven and wedged into adjacent bones, and they must be operatively released or completed in order to accomplish osteotomy for reduction. Malocclusion is the only symptom common to all Le Fort fractures because mobility sometimes cannot be detected.

40. Rigid fixation of a Le Fort fracture allows the patient to return to a regular diet following the operation. The rigid fixation makes it unnecessary to observe the occlusion. True or false?

False. Rigid fixation provides important stability to maxillary and mandibular fractures. However, depending on the comminution of the fracture and its extent, midface fractures can even "drift" following the application of rigid fixation. Therefore one should observe the occlusion in patients released from intermaxillary fixation on at least a weekly basis to detect any malposition by confirmation of correct occlusion. Also, many fracture reductions, such as open reduction of subcondylar fractures, are not stable to a regular diet and require a soft diet until healing has occurred.

41. How should split palate fractures be treated?

Fractures of the palatal vault and alveolus of the maxilla render more common maxillary fractures less stable and occur in approximately 10% of patient with maxillary fractures. They often require treatment by an orthodontist after healing to achieve a fine adjustment of the occlusion. Although classically treated with a splint, now they are stabilized by rigid fixation in the palatal vault and at the piriform aperture in combination with intermaxillary fixation. Because they provide a reduction that keys the occlusion, they should be stabilized first before application of intermaxillary fixation. Although classically treated with a splint, now large-fragment palatoalveolar fractures are more easily treated by open reduction and internal fixation.

42. In a subcondylar mandibular fracture that has healed following closed reduction with a shortened ramus height but has good condylar motion, how should a premature contact in the molar dentition and an anterior openbite be managed?

A condylar fracture that has healed following closed reduction with a minimal early posterior molar contact and a contralateral anterior openbite can be managed by occlusal grinding of the ipsilateral posterior maxillary teeth. A dental splint would be of no use in the secondary rehabilitation of this injury. If the condylar motion is good, the best procedure for restoring good occlusion would be a sagittal splint osteotomy lengthening the ramus while avoiding any secondary injury to the area of the joint. If the joint motion is not good or an ankylosis is present, a costochondral graft can be used to restore the ramus height and improve limited motion of the joint.

43. What is the optimal treatment of a comminuted parasymphysis fracture?

In comminuted fractures of the symphysis and parasymphysis region, the geniohyoid muscles often displace some of the inferior border fragments posteriorly. These should be retrieved and restored to provide good bony volume. Generally, the smaller fragments are attached to the larger fragments, and then the larger fragments are spanned with a plate that is long and strong enough to hold the angles inward and reform the mandibular arch. As the intermaxillary fixation is tightened, the lateral portions of the mandible tilt lingually, producing an "open bite" in the occlusion of the medial cusps of the molar dentition. The angles flare laterally. The reduction can be improved by placing pressure on the angles inward at the time when plate and screw fixation is applied to the anterior mandible. When the labial cortex of the mandible just begins to gap, the reduction of the lingual cortex is correct. A longer plate with the strength to hold the angles in is necessary. There is no place for discarding loose bone fragments. Even if a laceration is present, one can seldom extend it enough to provide enough exposure intraorally to place a longer plate on these fractures.

44. In a close-range, self-inflicted shotgun wound of the central midface and mandible, what is the most appropriate approach to managing the resultant complex injuries?

Immediate stabilization of existing bone and soft tissue in anatomic position is the critical first step in approaching such injuries. In avulsive gunshot or shotgun wounds, the areas of soft tissue and bone loss and the areas of soft tissue and bone injury should separately be identified. In the area of soft tissue injury and bone injury, an acute open reduction stabilizing the existing bone is performed as it would be for classic facial injuries. In the area of soft tissue loss, bone gaps should be stabilized to length by rigid fixation. The existing soft tissue is closed as much as possible. The patient then is returned to the operating room every 48 hours for "serial second look" procedures to address any hematoma or further evolution of devitalized tissue. Once no further soft tissue loss is seen, reconstruction of the soft tissue defect and the bone defect can be accomplished. A composite flap and/or separate bone and soft tissue reconstruction are required for definitive treatment.

Stabilizing the bone volume to length prevents soft tissue contracture. Closing the soft tissue is an important step in keeping the soft tissue to length following loss of underlying bone. One of the most important defects to correct is lining, especially in the mandibular or midface areas where bone cannot be expected to survive if significant amounts of it are exposed to sinus cavities or the intraoral area.

BIBLIOGRAPHY

Clark N, Manson P: Complication in maxillofacial trauma.In Maull KI, Rodriguez A, Wiles CE III (eds): Complications in Trauma and Critical Care. Philadelphia, WB Saunders, 1996, PP 239–269.

David DJ, Simpson DA: Craniomaxillofacial Trauma. New York, Churchill Livingstone, 1995.

Dufresne C, Manson P: Pediatric facial injuries. In Mathes S (ed): Plastic Surgery, 2nd ed. New York, Elsevier, 2006, pp 381–463.

Fonseca R, Walker R: Oral and Maxillofacial Trauma. Philadelphia, WB Saunders, 1991.

Manson P: Facial fractures.In Mathes S (ed): Plastic Surgery, 2nd ed. New York, Elsevier, 2006, pp 77–381.

Manson P, Vander Kolk C, Dufresne C: Facial trauma. In Oldham K, Columbani P, Foglia R (eds): Surgery of Infants and Children. Philadelphia, Lippincott Williams & Wilkins, 2005, pp 395–413.

Manson PN: Facial fractures. In Aston SJ, Beasley RW, Thorne CHM (eds): Grabb and Smith's Plastic Surgery, 5th ed. Philadelphia, Lippincott-Raven, 1997, pp 383–412.

Manson PN: Midface fractures. In Georgiade N Riefhohl R, Barwick W (eds): Plastic, Maxillofacial and Reconstructive Surgery, 2nd ed. Baltimore, Williams & Wilkins, 1992, pp 409–433.

Manson PN: Reoperative facial fracture repair. In Grotting J (ed): Reoperative Aesthetic & Reconstructive Plastic Surgery. St. Louis, Quality Medical Publishing, 2006, pp 903–1013.

Mueller RV: Facial trauma: Soft tissue injuries. In Mathes S (ed): Plastic Surgery, 2nd ed. New York, Elsevier, 2006, pp 1–45.

Rowe NL, LI Williams:Rowe & Williams' Maxillofacial Injuries. Edinburgh, Churchill Livingstone, 1994.

Wolf A, Baker SA: Facial Fractures. New York, Thieme Medical Publishers, 1993.

RADIOLOGIC EXAMINATION OF THE CRANIOFACIAL SKELETON

Jeffrey A. Fearon, MD, FACS, FAAP

1. When should x-rays be obtained for patients with suspected nasal fractures?

For patients who have sustained nasal trauma, emergency room physicians routinely order plain x-rays. Lateral films are most helpful at showing dorsal fractures, and anteroposterior (AP) views are best at revealing displacement of the nasal pyramid and deviation of the perpendicular plate of the ethmoid. As the force of injury increases, computed tomographic (CT) scan evaluation becomes more important for assessing associated fractures, especially when nasoorbitoethmoidal fractures are suspected. However, in terms of clinical decision-making, most isolated nasal fractures do not require any x-rays. The decision to reduce, or repair, any nasal fracture is based on clinical examination. If there is no change in appearance and there are no septal hematomas or posttraumatic deviation, then no treatment is necessary. If the nasal appearance has been significantly changed by a traumatic event resulting in significant displacement, then treatment is indicated.

2. What is the best way to evaluate the orbit for potential fractures?

Blunt trauma to the orbit can produce fractures of the roof, walls, or floor, which are not clinically evident. The most sensitive tool in the diagnosis of orbital fractures is the CT scan. Axial CT cuts are helpful in diagnosing medial and lateral orbital fractures, coronal CT cuts are best for evaluating orbital roof and floor fractures, and sagittal CT reconstructions can be helpful in assessing muscular entrapment of the inferior rectus (Fig. 42-1).

3. Is there a role for plain x-rays in facial trauma?

Plain x-rays are often obtained in the evaluation of facial trauma; however, the CT scan provides the greatest sensitivity for assessing fractures. One of the few indications for obtaining plain x-rays in trauma is to determine the presence and location of foreign bodies. Otherwise, plain films offer little in comparison with CT scans, aside from the reduced costs and radiation exposure.

4. What is the best way to diagnose single sutural craniosynostosis?

The diagnosis of craniosynostosis can be made on plain x-rays by looking for sclerosis along a suture or by obvious absence of the suture. With fusion of one or both coronal sutures, subsequent inhibited growth of the superior lateral orbital rim and sphenoid wing produces the "harlequin orbital deformity." However, plain x-rays are not always reliable, and false positives can occur. For this reason, CT scans are considered the radiologic examination of choice. Many centers also rely on three-dimensional reconstructions (Fig. 42-2).

Of all the various CT views, maximum intensity projection (MIP) reconstructions are most accurate at assessing sutural patency. However, most craniofacial surgeons can accurately diagnose single sutural synostosis solely on the basis of a clinical examination, with reported accuracy of 98% (Fig. 42-3).

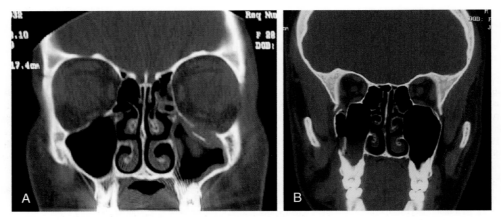

Figure 42-1. Orbital floor blowout fracture seen on coronal computed tomographic images. **A,** Left orbital floor fracture with soft tissue herniation. **B,** Right orbital floor fracture with a trapdoor deformity.

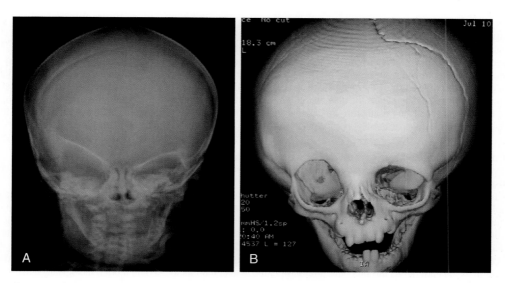

Figure 42-2. "Harlequin orbital deformity," diagnostic of right unicoronal synostosis, seen on plain film **(A)** and three-dimensional computed tomographic scan **(B)**.

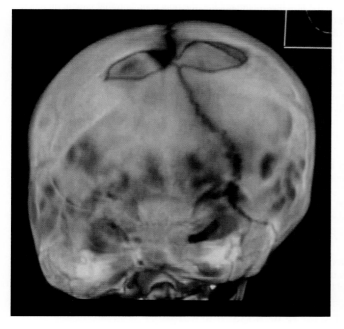

Figure 42-3. Unilambdoidal synostosis appreciated using maximum intensity projection computed tomographic reconstruction.

5. What is the best examination to evaluate a child with positional plagiocephaly?

The diagnosis of positional plagiocephaly almost always can be made on physical examination. Children with posterior positional plagiocephaly present with a parallelogram deformity, with the ear and sometimes the forehead shifted forward on the affected side. In contrast, infants with a lambdoid synostosis present on the affected side with a shorter AP skull length, a low mastoid bulge, and a lower posterior skull height. Often, plain x-rays taken to assess positional plagiocephaly may result in false positives, secondary to the frequent presence of perilambdoid sclerosis. Unlike the sclerosis seen in conjunction with craniosynostosis, the sclerosis seen with positional plagiocephaly may be the result of an indented or overlapped open suture, which can also produce the appearance of sclerosis. Therefore for patients in whom the diagnosis of positional plagiocephaly is not clinically certain, a CT scan should be ordered.

6. What is the best way to determine ideal cranial bone graft harvest sites?

The ideal locations for harvesting cranial bone grafts usually are the parietal bones, especially the posterior regions. The best way to assess the thickness of the diploic space is evaluation of the coronal sections of a CT scan.

7. In determining increased intracranial pressure, how reliable is a copper-beaten skull appearance, or Lückenschädel?

Increased intracranial pressure cannot be assessed radiologically. The presence of a copper-beaten skull is not necessarily indicative of raised intracranial pressure. Neuroradiologists use a number of subtle signs in assessing increased pressure, but many of these signs require comparison films. For example, any decrease in the size of the lateral and/or third ventricles may indicate raised pressure. Also, loss of extra-axial cerebrospinal fluid may indicate increased pressure. Sometimes the diameter of the optic nerves increase with raised pressure. Thinning or scalloping of the skull may indicate raised pressure, but this finding is not diagnostic. Other more subtle signs may include the development of cerebellar tonsillar herniation and a raised ridge of bone around an open fontanelle.

8. For infants and children with one of the craniofacial dysostoses (e.g., Apert syndrome, Crouzon syndrome, Pfeiffer syndrome), what radiologic studies need to be performed?

A number of reasons are often cited for obtaining a CT scan in infants born with craniofacial dysostoses: to diagnose sutural fusion, assess the patency of the nasal passages, and evaluate the brain parenchyma. Of course, the primary reason for ordering any study is to determine the best treatment course. Yet, most often, treatment is not at all affected by these preliminary studies. For example, it is possible for experienced craniofacial surgeons to accurately diagnose sutural fusion based on physical examination, and for patients in whom the diagnosis is in question, it is best to delay the CT scan until just prior to considering surgical intervention. This may be helpful because some sutural fusions are not as obvious right after birth and can take months to become more radiologically distinct. The patency of the nasal passages may be affected in the craniofacial dysostoses. Although it can be debated that the nares never require targeted operative intervention, even surgeons who attempt to surgically open the nares will agree that it is best to wait until the child is older. In my experience, treating the congenitally narrowed nasal passages never *significantly* alters the airway. In the first few months of life, the only condition that cannot be easily diagnosed clinically is hydrocephalus. However, because the ventricles are enlarged in the craniofacial dysostoses, pediatric neurosurgeons must rely on other criteria to determine the need for shunting (e.g., sudden increase in the percentile ranking of head circumference). Ultrasound has been shown to be an effective screening tool for hydrocephalus, especially during the perinatal period. With growth, especially for children with Crouzon and Pfeiffer syndromes, it is important to monitor children for the development of acquired cerebellar tonsillar herniation. These Chiari malformations are best diagnosed by magnetic resonance imaging (MRI) scan. At our center in Dallas, children with craniofacial dysostosis (e.g., Apert syndrome, Crouzon syndrome, Pfeiffer syndrome) as well as many of the complex craniosynostoses undergo yearly MRI evaluations. Serial MRI scans also can provide information that may suggest the presence of elevated intracranial pressure, such as reduced extra-axial fluid, reduction in ventricular size, along with the development of a Chiari malformation.

9. Are there any risks of performing a CT scan in infants and small children?

Based on a number of studies, which have sought to ascertain the risks of tumor induction and cognitive delays following ionizing radiation associated with CT scans in children, the National Cancer Institute (NCI) has recommended that guidelines for scanning be used in children, based on size and weight parameters. The NCI also has recommended that the region scanned be limited to the smallest necessary area, the lowest resolution scans needed for diagnosis be used, and other imaging modalities be considered.

10. Aside from CT scans, are there any other ways to assess sutural patency?

There have been a few reports of assessing sutural patency by ultrasound. The sensitivity and specificity of this modality have yet to be determined, and the accuracy of the technique appears to be highly dependent on operator experience.

11. What studies need to be obtained prior to orthognathic surgery?

AP and lateral cephalograms provide useful information for orthognathic surgical planning. The lateral cephalogram is used to establish the forward projection of the nasion, subnasale, and gonion, which establishes the relationship of different horizontal facial levels to the skull base. Dental relationships can be visualized on the lateral cephalogram, revealing the tilt of the occlusal plane. The AP cephalogram helps to establish the relationship of the horizontal occlusal plane to the skull base, which is especially important in treating hemifacial microsomia (HFM). In HFM, the horizontal occlusal plane is higher on the affected side, secondary to an ipsilateral vertical maxillary hypoplasia. Measurements of this discrepancy in vertical heights can be determined on the AP cephalogram. On the x-ray film, a horizontal line is established at the level of the orbital roofs, and a second line is drawn across the floor of the nose, which parallels the horizontal occlusal plane. Two vertical measurements are then taken laterally over the right and left molars, which are used to calculate the discrepancy in heights between the affected and the unaffected sides. Once the vertical difference has been determined, one can predict the needed lengthening of the affected side (and/or shortening on the unaffected side) to achieve a horizontal occlusion and a balanced facial appearance. Although cephalograms are taken with standardized equipment and magnification, intrinsic errors are introduced with these views, which diminishes their accuracy somewhat.

12. Is it necessary to obtain an x-ray prior to performing a genioplasty?

Some surgeons order a Panorex of the mandible prior to performing a sliding genioplasty. This is done to visualize the position of the bony canal through which the inferior alveolar nerves travels, in relation to the inferior margin of the mandible. This canal may course inferior to the mental foramen. Knowledge of the anatomic variations of this canal eliminates the need for a Panorex. The lateral cephalogram allows the surgeon to calculate the vector and amount of movement of the chin relative to standardized values. However, most experienced surgeons are able to develop a surgical plan based solely on the physical examination.

BIBLIOGRAPHY

Fearon JA: Hemifacial microsomia. In VanderKolk CA (ed): Plastic Surgery: Indications, Operations, and Outcomes, Vol II. St. Louis, Mosby, 2000, pp 911–912.

Fearon JA, Singh DJ, Beals SP, Yu JC: The diagnosis and treatment of single sutural synostoses: Are CT scans necessary? Plast Reconstr Surg 2007;120:1327–1331.

Fearon JA, Swift DM, Bruce DA: New methods for the evaluation and treatment of craniofacial dysostosis-associated cerebellar tonsillar herniation. Plast Reconstr Surg 108:1855–1861, 2001.

Huang MH, Gruss JK, Clarren SK, et al: The differential diagnosis of posterior plagiocephaly: True lambdoid synostosis versus positional molding. Plast Reconstr Surg 98:765–774, 1996.

National Cancer Institute: Radiation Risks and Pediatric Computed Tomography (CT): A Guide for Health Care Providers. Available at: www.cancer.gov/cancertopics/causes/radiation-risks-pediatric-ct. July 17, 2009.

Potter JK, Muzaffar AR, Ellis E, et al: Aesthetic management of the nasal component of naso-orbital ethmoid fractures. Plast Reconstr Surg 117:10e–18e, 2006.

Tuite GF, Evanson J, Chong WK, et al: The beaten copper cranium: A correlation between intracranial pressure, cranial radiographs, and computed tomographic scans in children with craniosynostosis. Neurosurgery 39:691–699, 1996.

PEDIATRIC FACIAL FRACTURES

Joseph E. Losee, MD, FACS, FAAP; Shao Jiang, MD; and Richard C. Schultz, MD, FACS

1. What is the most common type of pediatric facial fracture?

Many studies report that mandible fractures are the most common pediatric facial fracture. These are followed by nasal fractures, zygoma fractures, orbital fractures, and skull fractures. Midface fractures are rare because of the lack of maxillary sinus development, the immaturity of bone with an increased cancellous to cortical bone ration, and the presence of tooth buds in the maxilla, which cushion the impact. However, the studies likely are flawed secondary to bias in gathering and reporting the data.

2. What are the growth patterns of the pediatric craniofacial skeleton?

- *Facial dimension*
  - Newborn: 40% adult
  - 4 years: 70% adult
  - 5 years: 80% adult
  - 17 years: 95% adult
- *Orbit:* Adult size at 6 to 8 years of age
- *Maxilla:* Adult size at 12 years of age
- *Mandible*
  - Boys: Adult size at 17 to 19 years of age
  - Girls: Adult size at 16 to 18 years of age

3. Where are the growth centers of the pediatric craniofacial skeleton?

- *Cranium:* Cranial sutures
- *Upper face:* Orbits
- *Midface:* Sphenoethmoidonasal region, vomeropremaxillary region, pterygopalatomaxillary region
- *Lower face:* Mandibular condyles

4. What is the sequence of frontal and maxillary sinus pneumatization?

- *Frontal sinus:* Starts at 6 years and completed at 20 years of age
- *Maxillary sinus:* Starts at 5 years and completed at 18 years of age

5. What is the epidemiology of pediatric facial fractures?

Before age 6 years, facial fractures are rare due to the usual protective environment in which children live. The incidence increases between the ages of 6 and 12 years due to independent play and sports. Mechanisms of injury of pediatric facial fractures include motor vehicle accidents (50%–70%), falls (10%–20%), sports (5%–15%), and physical violence (1%–5%).

6. What are the common pediatric facial fracture patterns?

Unlike adults, Le Fort fracture patterns are rare in the pediatric population. Rather, oblique craniofacial fracture patterns are more common (Fig. 43-1). Fractures typically run obliquely across the frontal bone, radiating into the cranial base, and across the orbit onto the maxilla. Mandibular involvement is less common. This pattern is due to the lack of developed facial buttresses.

7. What are the advantages and disadvantages of open versus closed treatment of pediatric facial fractures?

Although open reduction internal fixation (ORIF) is avoided whenever possible in young children, the advantages of open treatment include better reduction and more stable internal fixation. However, the disadvantages of ORIF include periosteal dissection that may lead to growth disturbances. The advantages of closed treatment include less periosteal stripping and scarring that may have less growth disturbances; however, the disadvantages to closed treatment include the possible need for external fixation, such as maxillomandibular fixation, in a pediatric population.

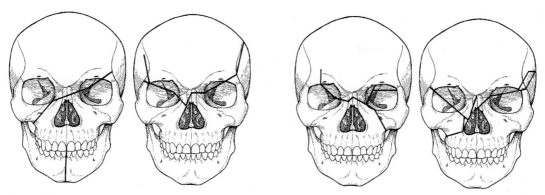

Figure 43-1. Pediatric oblique craniofacial fracture patterns. (From Bartlet S: Pediatric facial fracture patterns. In Bentz M [ed]: Pediatric Plastic Surgery. Stamford, CT, Appleton & Lange, 1998, p 474, with permission.)

8. Should absorbable or metallic fixation be used when treating pediatric facial fractures?

Although metallic fixation materials have proven to be stable and easy to use, their effects on the growing pediatric facial skeleton can be detrimental. Metallic fixation usually should be removed after adequate healing in the growing craniofacial skeleton. Absorbable plating systems often are more challenging to use and have a greater profile. Although commonly used in the upper face and skull, they have not completely been proven to provide rigid fixation in mandible fractures. However, there is no need for secondary removal.

9. How do you diagnose pediatric facial fractures?

A high index of suspicion must be maintained when examining a pediatric patient with multiorgan trauma. Obtaining an adequate history, complaint, or physical examination often is not possible. A physical examination must be performed, even if the examination is performed under anesthesia. In addition, formal ophthalmologic, neurosurgical, and radiographic evaluations often are warranted.

10. What radiographic studies should be obtained in pediatric patients with facial fractures?

The single most informative radiographic study in pediatric patients suspected of having facial fractures is the fine-cut facial computed tomographic scan with three-dimensional reconstructions whenever possible. Plain films have limited value in the diagnosis of pediatric facial fractures because they routinely underdiagnose pediatric facial fractures. Panorex film can be useful in diagnosing dental and jaw anomalies in patients old enough to cooperate for the examination.

11. How common are pediatric frontal sinus fractures?

Pediatric frontal sinus fractures are uncommon due to the lack of aeration of the sinus. Most forehead fractures in children are skull fractures and should be managed as such (Fig. 43-2).

12. What is a "growing skull fracture"?

Growing skull fractures are skull and skull base/orbital fractures that are associated with a defect in the dura. When these fractures are present, the pulsations of the brain actually push the fractures further apart, resulting in an enlarging and nonhealing fracture. In the growing child, fractures of the skull, skull base, and orbital roof should be followed carefully for complete healing. When a growing skull fracture is diagnosed, a transcranial procedure with repair of the herniated intracranial contents and bony reconstruction is required (Fig. 43-3).

13. What are the principles of treating pediatric orbital fractures?

The goal of treating pediatric orbital fractures is to prevent diplopia and appearance-related deformities (enophthalmos, orbital dystopia). In the absence of acute enophthalmos, orbital dystopia, and reportable diplopia, a conservative approach is taken despite the size of the bony defect. Unlike adults, rather large bony defects in children will remain asymptomatic and require no surgical intervention. Close follow-up is important to ensure that healing is complete and detrimental findings do not occur over time.

14. How do you treat pediatric nasal fractures?

In the pediatric population, early attempts should be made to reduce nasal fractures in a closed fashion. This may be followed by 10 to 14 days of external splinting. For younger children, this is most easily accomplished in the operating room rather than in the emergency department. Despite the adult literature citing a high frequency of revision surgery

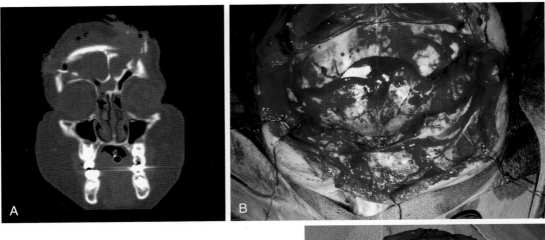

Figure 43-2. **A,** Coronal computed tomographic scan of forehead trauma and frontal bone fracture. **B,** Intraoperative image of comminuted frontal bone fracture. **C,** Intraoperative image of the reconstructed frontal skull, reassembled with absorbable plates and screws.

Figure 43-3. **A,** Posttraumatic axial computed tomographic (CT) scan of left frontal bone and superior orbital fracture. **B,** Axial CT scan of left frontal bone and superior orbital growing skull fracture, several months after injury.

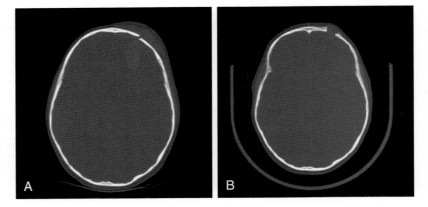

following closed reduction of nasal fractures, it should be attempted in the pediatric population. This is because major reconstructive nasal surgery often is deferred until growth is complete around puberty, and the correction obtained with closed reduction often is beneficial.

15. How do you treat pediatric mandible fractures?

Most pediatric mandible fractures can be treated with closed reduction and a short course of external fixation by mandibulomaxillary fixation. Open treatment of pediatric mandible fractures is problematic because of the need for periosteal stripping, the injury to developing tooth follicles with internal fixation, and the need for secondary removal of metallic hardware. When condyle head and neck fractures are found in association with other mandibular fractures, the other fractures can be treated with ORIF, so condylar head fractures can be managed with range-of-motion physical therapy.

16. What are some issues surrounding maxillomandibular fixation in pediatric patients?

Although use of arch bars is possible in most children with teeth, arch bars in those with primary dentition can be difficult and may risk tooth extraction. Circummandibular wiring with piriform rim drop wires can be exceedingly helpful in providing stable postoperative fixation for the child requiring maxillomandibular fixation (Fig. 43-4). Maxillomandibular fixation is needed for a shorter duration in pediatric facial fractures because these fractures routinely heal in a fraction of the time required for adult fractures to heal. For some minimally displaced or nondisplaced mandibular fractures, jaw immobilization with a C-collar or Barton-type bandage may be adequate.

17. What pediatric facial fracture is considered a true surgical emergency?

The pediatric orbital floor trapdoor fracture, with entrapped extraocular muscle, is considered a true surgical emergency. All pediatric patients with orbital fractures ideally should be evaluated by an ophthalmologist, and when entrapment of muscle is diagnosed by physical examination and CT scan (Fig. 43-5), the child should be immediately brought to the operating room for release of the muscle and bony reconstruction when necessary. This is necessary because the extraocular muscles are acutely sensitive to hypoxia, and permanent diplopia resulting from ischemic injury is possible.

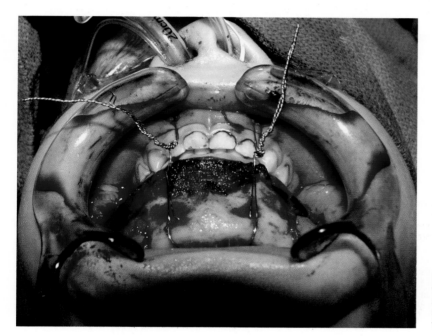

Figure 43-4. Intermaxillary fixation achieved with piriform suspension drop wires and mandibular wires placed through the inferior border.

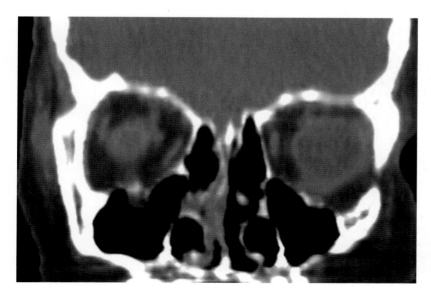

Figure 43-5. Coronal computed tomographic scan of right-sided orbital trapdoor fracture with entrapped inferior rectus muscle.

18. **What is the concern for associated injuries in patients with pediatric craniofacial fractures?**

Studies have shown that children with facial fractures suffer from significant associated injuries at a much greater incidence than adults. For this reason, CT scans of the head (and often chest and abdomen) are required, and a complete evaluation by pediatric trained emergency personnel must be performed.

19. **What are the effects of pediatric facial fractures on facial growth?**

Craniofacial growth in children following facial fractures is unpredictable. The disturbances of growth most likely occur from several factors, including injury to craniofacial growth centers, the fracture itself, open approaches to treatment, or treatment with internal fixation.

20. **What is the follow-up for pediatric facial fracture patients?**

Follow-up for the pediatric facial fracture patient ideally should extend beyond the acute phase of treatment and until skeletal growth is complete. Once adequate healing has been assured, a minimum of annual visits to the surgeon is ideal. Optimal assessment includes annual craniofacial examinations, complete photography, cephalograms, Panorex films, and assessment by a craniofacial orthodontist and ophthalmologist. This evaluation serves to document any growth disturbances. Those who participate in the care of pediatric facial fracture patients should track patient growth and development until skeletal maturity has been reached.

BIBLIOGRAPHY

Amaratunga NA de S: Mandibular fractures in children—A study of clinical aspects, treatment needs, and complications. J Oral Maxillofac Surg 46:637–640, 1988.

Bartlett SP, Delozier JB: Controversies in the management of pediatric facial fractures. Clin Plast Surg 19:245–258, 1992.

Carroll MJ, Hill CM, Mason DA: Facial fractures in children. Br Dent J 163:23–26, 1987.

Dufresne CR, Manson PN: Pediatric facial injuries. In Mathes SJ (ed): Plastic Surgery, Vol 3. Philadelphia, Elsevier, 2006, pp 381–462.

Enlow DH: Handbook of Facial Growth, 2nd ed. Philadelphia, WB Saunders, 1982.

Gupta Sk, Reddy NM, Khosla VK, et al: Growing skull fractures: A clinical study of 41 patients. Acta Neurochir (Wien) 139:928–932, 1997.

Koltai PJ, Wood GW: Three dimensional CT reconstruction for the evaluation and surgical planning of facial fractures. Otolaryngol Head Neck Surg 95:10–15, 1986.

Manson PH, Hoopes HE, Su CT: Structural pillars of the facial skeleton: An approach to the management of LeFort fractures. Plast Reconstr Surg 66:54–61, 1980.

Moore MH, David DJ, Cooter RD: Oblique craniofacial fractures in children. J Craniofac Surg 1:4–7, 1990.

Posnick JC, Wells M, Pron GE: Pediatric facial fractures: Evolving patterns of treatment. J Oral Maxillofac Surg 51:836–844, 1993.

Reedy BK, Bartlett SP: Pediatric facial fractures. In Bentz ML (ed): Pediatric Plastic Surgery. Stamford, CT, Appleton & Lange, 1998, pp 463–486.

Schultz RC (ed): Facial Injuries, 3rd ed. Chicago, Year Book Medical Publishers, 1988.

Singh DJ, Bartlett SP: Pediatric craniofacial fractures: Long-term consequences. Clin Plast Surg 31:499–518, 2004.

Sticker M, Raphael B, Van der Meulen J, Mazzola R: Craniofacial development and growth. In Stickler M, Van der Meulen R, Raphael B, Mazzola R (eds): Craniofacial Malformations. New York, Churchill Livingstone, 1990, pp 61–85.

Yaremchuk MJ, Fiala TGS, Barker F, et al: The effects of rigid fixation on craniofacial growth in rhesus monkeys. Plast Reconstr Surg 93:1–10, 1994.

FRACTURES OF THE FRONTAL SINUS

CHAPTER 44

M. Brandon Freeman, MBA, MD, PhD, and
Raymond J. Harshbarger III, MD

1. What are the most common causes of frontal sinus injury?
The great majority of injuries (60%–80%) result from automobile accidents. Assaults run a distant second (approximately 20%–30%), and the rest are due to falls from a height.

2. How common are fractures of the lower frontal bone compared with other facial bones?
Although fractures occur at the sutures between the frontal and zygomatic bones in the malar complex fracture, fractures of the lower frontal bone are much less common (5%–15% of all maxillofacial injuries). This portion of the frontal bone represents the anterior table of the frontal sinus and is extremely thick. The forces required to fracture this bone are two to three times greater than the forces needed to fracture the zygoma, maxilla, or mandible. Such fractures typically occur with a direct blow to the glabella region or supraorbital rims. Most glabellar fractures involve the frontal sinuses.

3. Is frontal sinus injury typically associated with other maxillofacial injuries?
Yes. Because of the great energy required to fracture this portion of the frontal bone, other significant maxillofacial injuries are the rule, not the exception. Frontal sinus fractures are most frequently associated with nasoorbitoethmoidal fractures.

4. Is frontal sinus injury typically associated with other bodily injuries?
Yes. In one large series of patients who suffered frontal sinus injury, approximately 75% had other bodily injuries, 50% presented in shock, and 25% died within the first 2 weeks of presentation to the hospital.

5. Who is at a much higher risk for involvement of the frontal sinuses in craniofacial fractures: children or adults?
Adults. The frontal sinus starts as merely an ethmoidal anlage at birth and begins pneumatic expansion at age 7 years; development is complete by 18 to 20 years. The remnants of this embryonic connection between sinuses are the nasofrontal ducts, a bilateral structure that drains the frontal sinus from its posteromedial aspect, through the ethmoidal air cells and out to the nasal cavity, usually at the middle meatus (below the middle turbinate).

Thus, before pneumatization, children are not susceptible to frontal sinus fractures. However, although rare, underpneumatized pediatric frontal sinus fractures are more commonly associated with major intracranial injury (55%–65%) because force is more efficiently transferred to the cranial base and internal structures.

6. What are the initial signs of frontal sinus fracture?
Any blow to the forehead causing lacerations, contusions, or hematoma heralds a possible injury of the frontal sinus. Such findings associated with cerebrospinal rhinorrhea or palpable bony depression of the brow evoke strong suspicion of frontal sinus involvement. (*Caution:* A visible or palpable depression is not always appreciated in the initial days after injury because of swelling or hematoma.) Supraorbital anesthesia, subconjunctival hematoma, and subcutaneous air crepitus are other associated findings. A great majority of people presenting with frontal sinus fractures have associated eye injuries. Initial signs of fracture may range from minimal to none; complications may develop years later due to lack of treatment.

7. What radiographic modality best detects and delineates the presence and extent of frontal sinus fractures?
Historically, plain radiographs detected large and often displaced fractures, but small defects commonly went undetected. The Waters view of the skull shows a well-developed frontal sinus with its scalloped superior border but does not demonstrate significant detail. Consequently, computed tomographic (CT) scan has become the standard for evaluation of craniofacial trauma and is most sensitive in determining frontal sinus fractures. Small, minimally displaced

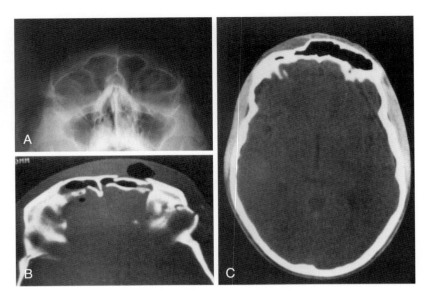

Figure 44-1. A, Waters view plain radiograph of the skull showing a normal, well-developed frontal sinus. **B,** Computed tomographic (CT) scan of the head showing a displaced fracture of the anterior table of the frontal sinus. **C,** CT scan of the head showing displaced fracture of both anterior and posterior tables of the frontal sinus. Note the small pneumocephaly behind the posterior table of the right frontal sinus. (From Rohrich RJ, Hollier LH: Management of frontal sinus fractures: Changing concepts. Clin Plast Surg 19:219–232, 1992, with permission.)

fractures of the floor, septum, or anterior or posterior tables are easily seen (Fig. 44-1). Unfortunately, direct visualization of the ducts and assessment of possible injury to the ducts are inconsistent, even with high-resolution and three-dimensional reformatted CT imaging.

8. What are the anatomic boundaries of the frontal sinus?

The frontal sinus typically is a bilateral, air-filled cavity that is triangular in cross-section. A thick anterior table provides the contour of the glabella, brow, and lower forehead. A thin posterior table separates the air space from the frontal lobes in the anterior cranial fossa. The floor of the sinus overlies the ethmoidal air cells anteromedially and the orbits posterolaterally. The extent of the lateral and superior margins is variable. The supraorbital rims demarcate the lower anterior border.

9. What are the foramina of Breschet?

These foramina are sites of intracranial venous drainage with mucosal invaginations that can serve as a route of intracranial infection or mucocele formation.

10. What complications are associated with frontal sinus fractures? What causes them?

Most of the complications associated with frontal sinus injury are secondary to obstruction of the nasofrontal duct, entrapment of mucosa in the fracture lines, or dural tears (Fig. 44-2). Early complications include epistaxis, cerebrospinal fluid leakage, meningitis, and intracranial hematomas. Complications occurring within weeks are sinusitis, mucoceles, and meningitis. Later complications (up to many years) include osteomyelitis, mucopyoceles, intracranial abscesses, and orbital abscesses.

11. What is the function of the frontal sinuses?

Although the function of the paranasal sinuses is conjectural, it is certain that the frontal sinuses serve as a mechanical barrier to protect the brain. The frontal sinuses are air-filled compressible cavities that absorb impact energy that otherwise would be imparted to brain parenchyma. The paranasal sinuses are lined with columnar epithelium replete with cilia and mucus-secreting glands that drain through the nasofrontal ducts and are in continuity with the upper respiratory tract.

12. Are frontal sinus fractures a surgical emergency?

Fractures of the frontal sinuses are not a surgical emergency unless other associated ophthalmologic or neurologic injuries require emergent surgery. Patients with suspected frontal sinus fracture should be placed on a broad-spectrum intravenous antibiotic as soon as possible to prevent early infectious sequelae.

13. How can frontal sinus fractures be classified?

Isolated posterior table fractures are rare. Involvement of anterior and posterior tables invariably leads to frontonasal duct injury, as do concomitant nasoethmoidal complex and medial orbital rim fracture patterns (Fig. 44-3).

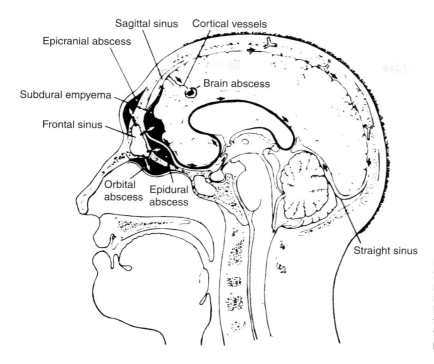

Figure 44-2. Midsagittal section through the frontal sinus depicting possible routes for spread of infection. (From Mohr RM, Nelson LR: Frontal sinus ablation for frontal osteomyelitis. Laryngoscope 92:1006–1015, 1982, with permission.)

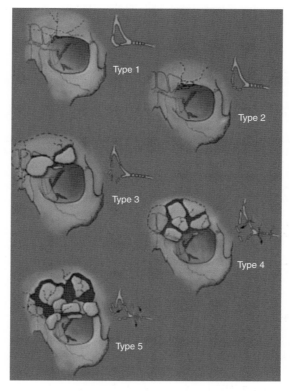

Figure 44-3. Frontal sinus fracture classification. (From Manolidis S: Frontal sinus injuries: Associated injuries and surgical management of 93 patients. J Oral Maxillofac Surg 62:882–891, 2004; reprinted with permission.)

CONTROVERSIES

14. What are the indications for surgery?

The status of the anterior and posterior tables and the nasofrontal ducts dictates the need for surgery. Nondisplaced anterior table fractures can be safely observed. Displaced anterior table fractures may cause an overlying contour deformity and require surgical reconstruction. The indications for management of minimally or nondisplaced posterior table fractures remain controversial. Most clinical studies and animal models show that such fractures can be observed if there is no cerebrospinal fluid leak or suspicion of nasofrontal duct injury. Displaced posterior table fractures greater than one wall thick merit surgical exploration and reduction. Suspicion of nasofrontal duct involvement also dictates the need for exploration.

15. What are the surgical approaches to exploration and repair of frontal sinus fractures?

Although exploration can be done in a preexisting wound or local incision, a coronal incision offers the greatest access to the whole frontal sinus as well as the ethmoidal, orbital, and intracranial regions and is the least conspicuous incision. Exploration and reduction of anterior table fractures alone usually can be performed through an osteoplastic bone flap, which is created by unroofing the remaining anterior table while keeping it in continuity with its periosteum for complete access to the sinus. Posterior table fractures that are significantly displaced in the presence of cerebrospinal fluid rhinorrhea require a frontal craniotomy performed in conjunction with a neurosurgical team to assess and repair dural or parenchymal injuries.

16. How does frontonasal duct injury impact the surgical treatment?

The diagnosis of frontonasal duct injury necessitates sinus obliteration. Sinus mucosa is removed and curettage performed to remove fragments from fracture lines and the foramina of Breschet. The duct is plugged, and the sinus is obliterated with autogenous fat, muscle, cartilage, bone, pericranium, alloplastic materials or allowed to undergo spontaneous osteoneogenesis. Complete and stable obliteration provides separation of the nasal cavity and anterior cranial fossa, thus preventing ascending infection or retrograde mucosal growth.

17. What are the indications for cranialization?

Cranialization involves removal of the entire posterior wall of the frontal sinus and separation of the intracranial contents from the aerodigestive tract using a galeal frontalis flap allowing frontal lobe expansion. Severely comminuted posterior wall fractures with duct injury or CSF leaks and dural tears are indications for cranialization. Nondisplaced fractures with CSF leak can be observed for up to 10 days, but failed resolution warrants exploration.

BIBLIOGRAPHY

Disa JD, Robertson BC, Metzinger SE, Manson PN: Transverse glabellar flap for obliteration/isolation of the nasofrontal duct from the anterior cranial base. Ann Plast Surg 36:453–457, 1996.
Emanuela C, Giovanni R, D'Andrea G, Delfini R: Management of the entered frontal sinus. Neurosurg Rev 27:286–288, 2004.
Hoffman HT, Krause CJ: Traumatic injuries to the frontal sinus. In Fonseca RJ, Walker RV (eds): Oral and Maxillofacial Trauma. Philadelphia, WB Saunders, 1991, pp 576–599.
Ioannides C, Freihofer HP, Friens J: Fractures of the frontal sinus: A rationale of treatment. Br J Plast Surg 46:208–214, 1993.
Rohrich RJ, Hollier LH: Management of frontal sinus fractures: Changing concepts. Clin Plast Surg 19:219–232, 1992.
Rohrich RJ, Mickel TJ: Frontal sinus obliteration: In search of the ideal autogenous material. Plast Reconstr Surg 95:580–585, 1995.
Whatley WS, Allison DW, Chandra RK, et al: Frontal sinus fractures in children. Laryngoscope 115:1741–1745, 2005.
Wolfe SA, Johnson P: Frontal sinus injuries: Primary care and management of late complications. Plast Reconstr Surg 82:781–789, 1988.
Yavuzer R, Sari A, Kelly CP, et al: Management of frontal sinus fractures. Plast Reconstr Surg 115:79e–93d, 2005.

FRACTURES OF THE NOSE

Davinder J. Singh, MD; Dennis E. Lenhart, MD; and Rudolph F. Dolezal, MD, FACS

CHAPTER 45

1. The nose is composed of which five bones?
See Fig. 45-1.

1. *Maxilla:* Frontal process of the maxilla
2. *Frontal bone:* Nasal process of the frontal bone
3. *Nasal bones*
4. *Vomer:* Contributes to the septum
5. *Ethmoid:* Perpendicular plate of the ethmoid contributes to the septum

2. What are the cartilaginous structures of the nose?
The cartilaginous framework of the nose consists of the nasal septal cartilage, the paired upper lateral and lower lateral cartilages, and the accessory nasal cartilages. The upper lateral cartilages are fused along the dorsal border of the septum to the midline and laterally to the bony margin of the maxillary processes (Fig. 45-2).

3. Which structures contribute to the internal nasal valve?
The upper lateral cartilages form an angle of 10° to 15° with the anterior septal edge. This valve functions to maintain a patent nasal airway during respiration. Collapse of this anatomic valve will contribute to nasal airway obstruction.

4. Numbness of the nasal tip after trauma results from injury to which nerve?
The external branch of the anterior ethmoidal nerve emerges between the nasal bone and the upper lateral nasal cartilage and supplies sensation to the skin of the lower dorsum and nasal tip after. The innervation of the nose consists of the following:

Trigeminal Nerve (Cranial Nerve V)

- V1 (ophthalmic division)
  - Infratrochlear nerve: Skin of bridge and upper lateral area
  - Anterior ethmoidal nerve to internal and external nasal branches

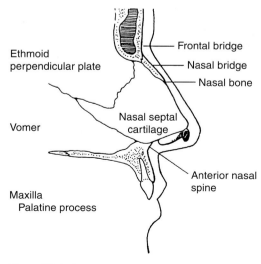

Figure 45-1. Structural anatomy of the nose—bones.

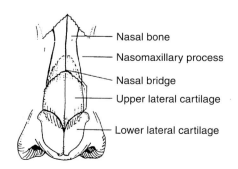

Figure 45-2. Structural anatomy of the nose—cartilaginous structures.

- V2 (maxillary division)
  - Infraorbital nerve: Skin of lower lateral half
  - Nasopalatine nerve: Nasal septum and anterior hard palate

5. Where do nasal bones most commonly fracture?

Fractures typically occur in the distal nasal bones. The bony skeletal framework is composed of the paired nasal bones and the ascending frontal processes of the maxilla. The joined nasal bones are thick cephalomedially but are extremely thin as they extend inferolaterally. The proximal bones are resistant to fracture, whereas the distal bones are most susceptible to fracture from direct frontal blows. Only high-velocity or severe force injuries cause the proximal bones to fracture.

6. What is the role of radiographs in the diagnosis and treatment of nasal fractures?

Standard facial radiographs may not clearly demonstrate nasal fractures but are taken frequently in the emergency department setting. They serve as a physical record of a nasal fracture if visualized, but they do not replace the clinical findings or determine if surgical correction is necessary. Computed tomographic scans clearly image the nasal bony and cartilaginous structure and typically are done to determine the presence of any concomitant facial fractures. For isolated nasal trauma, a thorough physical examination will indicate if surgical intervention is necessary.

7. What is the rhinion, and what is its role in nasal fractures?

The rhinion is the junction of the bony and cartilaginous nasal framework. The pyramidal structure of the nose consists of two nasal passages separated by the septum in the midline. The upper third of the nose is supported by the nasal bones, whereas the lower third of the nose is supported by the septum and paired lateral cartilages. The proximal portions of the upper lateral cartilages are overlapped by the caudal portion of the nasal bones, whereas the distal portions of the upper lateral cartilages lie under the cephalic border of the lower lateral cartilages. The septum is responsible for the major portion of the dorsal support. Fractures at the rhinion may dislocate the upper lateral cartilage attachment under paired nasal bones, creating a saddle deformity of the dorsum.

8. A patient with severe nasal trauma resulting in comminution of the entire bony skeleton underwent repair 4 days after injury. He now complains of epiphora. What has caused this?

Obstruction of the nasolacrimal system results in epiphora (excessive teasing). The nasolacrimal sac is housed adjacent to the nasal bones, and drainage occurs into the inferior meatus. Severe nasal fractures can result in disruption of the drainage system.

9. How is the medial interorbital distance affected by nasal fractures?

Severe nasal trauma resulting in comminution of the nasal bones may also involve the lacrimal bones, resulting in displacement of bone fragments to which the medial canthal ligaments are attached. This displacement in addition to loss of dorsal support of the nose manifests as *traumatic telecanthus.*

10. Why is it critical to perform an intranasal examination for patients with nasal trauma?

The extent of septal injury must be determined. A septal hematoma must be diagnosed and treated urgently. A septal hematoma occurs when blood is trapped between the mucoperichondrium following nasal trauma with damage to the cartilaginous septum. Left untreated, the hematoma may fibrose to form a thickened area of septum and obstruct the nasal airway. If the hematoma results in excessive pressure on the cartilage, necrosis of the septum may occur and create a septal perforation. If a significant portion of the septum is destroyed, the support of the cartilaginous dorsum is reduced and typically results in a saddle deformity. Fractures of the septum should be reduced acutely to prevent late deformity.

11. How are septal hematomas treated acutely?

An incision along the base or most inferior portion of the hematoma allows dependent drainage and will prevent refilling of the space. Bilateral hematomas can be treated with bilateral incisions of the mucoperichondrium as long as the septal cartilage is left intact. After drainage, nasal packing and antibiotics are recommended.

12. What is the incidence of septal fracture in simple nasal bone fractures?

The incidence of septal fractures in simple nasal bone fractures is 96%. Mucosal tearing is commonly associated with septal fracture and should heighten suspicion for such injury.

13. What is the management of nasal fractures?

A septal hematoma and any nasal lacerations should be treated urgently. In the absence of these conditions, treatment may be delayed for 3 to 5 days until severe nasal swelling resolves. Once the edema has resolved, the fractures of the bone and cartilage should be treated under anesthesia (general or intravenous sedation). A closed reduction of the nasal bone and septal fractures should be conducted. If the cartilaginous septum is displaced off the nasal spine, it must be repositioned and fixated with suture. After reduction of the fractures, internal and external nasal splints should be used. Internal splints must be placed underneath the nasal bones so that the bone fragments are sandwiched between the external and internal splints. Antibiotics are administered while the internal splint is in place for approximately 5 days. The external splint should be maintained for 7 to 10 days.

14. What is the treatment of severely comminuted nasal fractures?

Severely comminuted nasal fractures usually can be reduced primarily and supported with intranasal packing and externally applied splints. Some severely comminuted fractures may require open reduction and bone grafting to restore nasal dorsal projection. Authors have described techniques whereby an open reduction is performed through intercartilaginous incisions with intranasal Kirschner wire splinting as fixation, thus preventing extensive periosteal dissection and exposure.

15. What is the ideal timing of closed reduction in adult and pediatric patients?

Nasal fractures in adults should be reduced within the first 2 weeks following trauma. Fractures in pediatric patients (younger than 12 years) should be treated within the first week due to the more rapid healing of facial bones.

16. What are the indications for septoplasty at the time of closed reduction?

The septum is important in determining the position of the nasal bones and the appearance of the external nose. If septal injury is not identified and corrected, the reduction of the nasal bones may be inadequate and may result in airway obstruction and secondary aesthetic deformities. Indications for septoplasty are as follows:

- Inability to obtain reasonable alignment by closed method
  - Dislocation of the caudal septum from the vomerine groove usually does not reduce with repositioning of the bony nasal pyramid. Manipulative reduction may be attempted; if it is unsuccessful, open reduction (septoplasty) should be performed. The procedure may involve repositioning the caudal septum or removing a small strip of cartilage along the inferior border.
  - Septal fractures may be severely displaced and irreducible. Local or limited submucosal resection of the area of septal overlap releases the locked septal displacement and provides better alignment, appearance, and function of the nose.
- Patients with a preinjury history of nasal airway obstruction
- Septal deformity due to undetected or late treatment of a septal hematoma

17. Can a septoplasty be performed in the pediatric patient as either early or late treatment of nasal septal fractures?

In general, surgical intervention beyond closed reduction of the septum is deferred until the child has completed growth because of the potential for growth disturbance produced by disruption of the septum and anterior nasal spine.

18. What is the cause of the saddle nose deformity?

Saddle deformities result from loss of support of the nasal dorsum. They usually are composite injuries that involve both bone and cartilage, allowing the nasal bones and upper lateral cartilages to drop into the piriform aperture. Such injuries include telescoping septal fractures and fractures at the rhinion that dislocate the upper lateral cartilage attachments. Untreated septal hematomas may result in saddle deformity by causing necrosis of the septum and subsequent loss of dorsal support.

19. What is the incidence of posttraumatic nasal deformity?

The incidence of postreduction nasal deformities requiring subsequent rhinoplasty or septorhinoplasty ranges from 14% to 50%.

20. What are late complications of nasal fractures?

- Nasal airway obstruction may develop from septal hematomas, malunited fractures, or scar contractures. Septal hematomas may organize and fibrose, calcify, or chondrify, forming a thickened portion of the nasal septum that obstructs the airway. Malunited fractures of the piriform margin and scar contracture of the vestibular lining also may result in obstruction.
- Saddle deformity due to shortening and collapse may develop.
- Dorsal hump due to periosteal reaction to hematoma may develop.
- Nasal deviation due to malunion may develop.
- Synechiae may form between the septum and turbinates in areas where soft tissue lacerations occur and tissues are in contact.
- Osteitis associated with compound fractures or infected hematomas may develop.
- Epistaxis may develop.
- Headaches may develop.

21. When is secondary treatment of nasal fractures indicated?

It is indicated for patients with either functional or cosmetic problems. Even with adequate reduction, late deformity may still occur, and patients should be warned. Late deformities may include a dorsal prominence or deviation, loss of dorsal height, septal deviation, and nasal airway obstruction. Most authors recommend early closed reduction followed by late correction of residual cosmetic deformities or functional problems with formal rhinoplasty.

BIBLIOGRAPHY

Clayton M, Lesser T: The role of radiography in the management of nasal fractures. J Laryngol Otol 100:797–801, 1986.

Fernandes SV: Nasal fractures: The taming of the shrewd. Laryngoscope 114:587–592, 2004.

Hollinshead WH: Anatomy for Surgeons, 3rd ed. New York, Harper and Row, 1982.

Mayell MJ: Nasal fractures. Their occurrence, management, and some late results. J R Coll Surg Edinb 18:31–36, 1973.

Molina F: Surgical anatomy. In Ortiz-Monasterio F (ed): Rhinoplasty. Philadelphia, WB Saunders, 1994, pp 9–18.

Murray JAM, Maran AGD: The treatment of nasal injuries by manipulation. J Laryngol Otol 94:1405–1410, 1980.

Pollock RA: Nasal trauma: Pathomechanics and surgical management of acute injuries. Clin Plast Surg 19:133–147, 1992.

Rhee SC, Kim YK, Cha JH, et al: Septal fracture in simple nasal bone fracture. Plast Reconstr Surg 113:45–52, 2004.

Rohrich RJ, Adams WP: Nasal fracture management: Minimizing secondary nasal deformities. Plast Reconstr Surg 106:266–273, 2000.

Waldron J, Mitchell DB, Ford G: Reduction of fractured nasal bones; local versus general anesthesia. Clin Otolaryngol Allied Sci 14(4): 357–359, 1989.

White FW: Submucous resection of the nasal septum in children. Arch Otolaryngol 11:415–425, 1930.

Yabe T, Ozawa T, Sakamoto M, Ishii M: Pre- and postoperative x-ray and computed tomography evaluation in acute nasal fracture. Ann Plast Surg 53:547–553, 2004.

CHAPTER 46

FRACTURES OF THE ORBIT

Jeffrey Weinzweig, MD, FACS; Peter J. Taub, MD, FACS, FAAP; and Scott P. Bartlett, MD

ANATOMY

1. The orbit is composed of how many bones?

Seven. The zygoma, the sphenoid (lesser and greater wings), the frontal, the ethmoid, the lacrimal, the palatine, and the maxillary bones articulate to form each orbit. The paired structures are separated in the midline by the nasal bones and paranasal sinuses (Fig. 46-1).

2. The orbital rims are composed of which bones?

- *Superiorly:* Supraorbital rim is formed mainly by the frontal bone.
- *Inferiorly:* Infraorbital rim is formed by the zygoma laterally and the maxilla medially.
- *Medially:* Nasal spine of the frontal bone and the frontal process of the maxilla constitute the anteromedial orbital wall.
- *Laterally:* Frontal process of the zygoma and the zygomatic process of the frontal bone constitute the lateral orbital rim.

3. The orbital walls are composed of which bones?

The *roof* is composed mainly of the orbital plate of the frontal bone. Posteriorly it receives a minor contribution from the lesser wing of the sphenoid.

The *orbital floor* is composed of the orbital plate of the maxilla, the zygomatic bone anterolaterally, and the orbital process of the palatine bone posteriorly. The orbital floor is equivalent to the roof of the maxillary sinus.

The *lateral wall* is formed primarily by the orbital surface of the zygomatic bone and the greater wing of the sphenoid bone. The sphenoid portion of the lateral wall is separated from the roof by the superior orbital fissure and from the floor by the inferior orbital fissure.

The *medial wall* is quadrangular in shape and composed of four bones: (1) ethmoid bone centrally; (2) frontal bone superoanteriorly; (3) lacrimal bone inferoanteriorly; and (4) sphenoid bone posteriorly. The medial wall is quite thin; the ethmoidal portion has been termed the *lamina papyracea* (paperlike), which is the largest component of the medial wall.

4. Which is the only bone that exists entirely within the orbital confines?

The lacrimal bone.

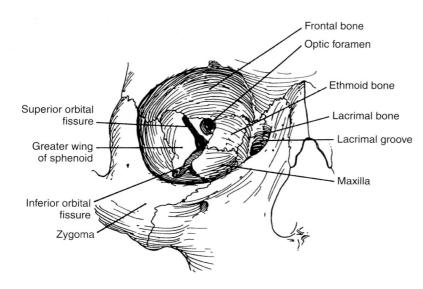

Figure 46-1. Anatomy of the orbit. (From Whitaker LA, Bartlett SP: Craniofacial anomalies. In Jurkiewicz MJ, Krizek TJ, Mathes SJ, Ariyan S [eds]: Plastic Surgery: Principles and Practice. St. Louis, Mosby, 1990, p. 104, with permission.)

5. What is the relationship between the anterior cranial fossa and the orbit?

The orbits are situated immediately below the floor of the anterior cranial fossa, the lateral portion of which is formed by the roof of the orbits. The medial portion of the anterior cranial fossa is formed by the roof of each ethmoid sinus laterally and by the cribriform plate medially.

6. Which nerve traverses the floor of the orbit?

The infraorbital nerve. The infraorbital groove courses forward from the inferior orbital fissure. Anteriorly, the groove becomes a canal within the maxilla, finally forming the infraorbital foramen on the anterior surface of the maxilla. The groove and canal transmit the infraorbital nerve and artery.

7. The orbit is best described by which geometric shape?

Each orbit is conical or pyramidally shaped, but neither term is completely accurate. The widest diameter of the orbit is located just behind the orbital rim approximately 1.5 cm within the orbital cavity. From this point posteriorly, the orbit narrows dramatically in its middle and posterior thirds. The orbital rim is an elliptically shaped structure, whereas the orbit immediately behind the rim is more circular in configuration. The floor of the orbit has no sharp demarcation with the medial wall but proceeds into the wall by tilting upward in its medial aspect at a 45° angle. The medial wall has a quadrangular rather than a triangular configuration.

8. Through which bone do all neurovascular structures pass into the orbit?

The sphenoid bone. All nerves, arteries, and veins entering the orbit pass through this bone.

9. How deep is the orbit?

Orbital depth measured to the optic strut (the bone between the optic foramen and superior orbital fissure) varies from 45 to 55 mm. At the entrance, orbital height measures approximately 35 mm and orbital width approximately 40 mm.

10. Where is the optic foramen located? What about the optic canal?

The *optic foramen* is situated medial to the superior orbital fissure within the substance of the lesser wing of the sphenoid. It is found at the junction of the lateral and medial walls of the orbit in its most posterior aspect. It is close to the posterior portion of the ethmoid sinus, not at the true apex of the orbit. The posterior ethmoidal vessels are found within 5 mm of the optic nerve. The optic nerve usually is located 40 to 45 mm behind the infraorbital rim.

The *optic canal* is 4 to 10 mm in length. The optic nerve and ophthalmic artery pass through the optic canal from an intracranial to an intraorbital position. The canal is formed medially by the body of the sphenoid and laterally by the lesser wing. The bony optic canal forms a tight sheath around the optic nerve. Fractures with swelling predispose to vascular compression of the nerve in the canal.

11. Where is the superior orbital fissure located? Which structures pass through it?

The superior orbital fissure is a 22-mm cleft that runs lateral, anterior, and superior from the apex of the orbit. This fissure, which separates the greater and lesser wings of the sphenoid and lies between the optic foramen and the foramen rotundum, provides passage to the three motor nerves to the extraocular muscles of the orbit: oculomotor nerve (CN III), trochlear nerve (CN IV), and abducens nerve (CN VI). The ophthalmic division of the trigeminal nerve (CN V1) also enters the orbit through this fissure.

12. Nothing passes through the inferior orbital fissure. True or false?

False. The inferior orbital fissure, which separates the greater sphenoid wing portion of the lateral wall from the floor, permits passage of the (1) maxillary division of the trigeminal nerve (CN V2) and its branches (including the infraorbital nerve), (2) infraorbital artery, (3) branches of the sphenopalatine ganglion, and (4) branches of the inferior ophthalmic vein to the pterygoid plexus.

13. What is Tenon's capsule?

Tenon's capsule is a fascial structure that subdivides the orbital cavity into two halves: an anterior (or precapsular) segment and a posterior (or retrocapsular) segment. The ocular globe occupies only the anterior half of the orbital cavity. The posterior half of the orbital cavity is filled with fat, muscles, vessels, and nerves that supply the ocular globe and extraocular muscles and provide sensation to the soft tissue surrounding the orbit.

14. What is the annulus of Zinn?

The annulus of Zinn, or common tendinous ring, is the fibrous thickening of the periosteum from which the recti muscles originate.

15. What are the functions of the extraocular muscles?

- Lateral rectus muscle: Abduction
- Medial rectus muscle: Adduction
- Inferior rectus muscle: Depression, adduction, and extorsion (i.e., the superior pole of globe moves laterally)
- Superior rectus muscle: Elevation, adduction, and intorsion (i.e., the superior pole of the globe moves medially)
- Superior oblique muscle: Depression, abduction, and intorsion
- Inferior oblique muscle: Elevation, abduction, and extorsion

16. Why is the medial canthal tendon so important?

The medial canthal tendon is a complex of fascial support mechanisms that includes anterior, posterior, and vertical components. They insert in the frontal process of the maxilla (the medial orbital margin) from the anterior lacrimal crest to the nasal bone. The orbicularis oculi muscle originates from the medial canthal tendon. In addition, branches of the canthal tendon divide to extend through the upper and lower eyelids and to attach to the medial margin of the tarsal plates. Release of this tendon, as with fractures of the medial orbital wall, may result in telecanthus (increase in distance between medial canthi, which may create the illusion of hypertelorism when bilateral).

17. Distinguish between intraconal and extraconal fat. Which is important for globe support?

The orbital fat can be divided into anterior and posterior portions. The anterior, extraocular fat is largely *extraconal* (exists outside the muscle cone). Posteriorly, only fine fascial communications separate the extraconal from the intraconal fat compartments. *Intraconal* fat constitutes three fourths of the fat in the posterior orbit and may be displaced outside the muscle cone, contributing to a loss of globe support from loss of soft tissue volume. The fat on the anterior portion of the orbital floor is extraconal and does not contribute to globe support.

PATHOLOGY

18. What is the most common orbital fracture?

Zygomaticoorbital or malar complex fractures are the most common. Moderately displaced zygomatic injuries are frequently associated with fractures of the lateral orbital wall with comminution of the orbital floor and infraorbital rim (Figs. 46-2 and 46-3).

19. What is the most common site of an isolated intraorbital fracture?

The most frequent intraorbital fracture involves the orbital floor just medial to the infraorbital canal and usually is confined to the medial portion of the floor and the lower portion of the medial orbital wall. Depressed fractures involving this portion of the orbit may allow the orbital soft tissue to be displaced into the maxillary and ethmoid sinuses, effectively increasing orbital volume (Fig. 46-4).

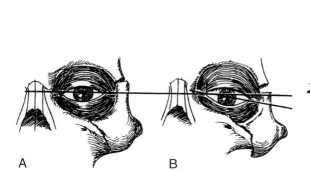

A   B

Figure 46-2. Fractures of the zygoma. **A,** Nondisplaced. Lateral canthus maintains normal position. **B,** Displacement of the zygoma and orbital floor. Downward displacement of the globe and lateral canthus results. (From McCarthy JG [ed]: Plastic Surgery. Philadelphia, W.B. Saunders, 1990, p 995, with permission.)

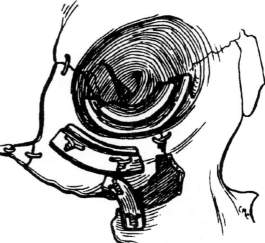

Figure 46-3. Zygomatic fractures may require orbital floor reconstruction, depending on the extent of the fracture. (From Smith JW, Aston SJ [eds]: Grabb and Smith's Plastic Surgery, 4th ed. Boston, Little, Brown, 1991, p 364, with permission.)

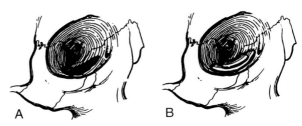

Figure 46-4. A, Orbital blowout fracture. **B,** Orbital floor reconstruction with bone graft. (From Smith JW, Aston SJ [eds]: Grabb and Smith's Plastic Surgery, 4th ed. Boston, Little, Brown, 1991, p 371, with permission.)

20. What is a "blowout" fracture? What is the responsible mechanism?

A blowout fracture is caused by a traumatic force applied to the orbital rim or globe and usually results in a sudden increase in intraorbital pressure. The incompressible intraorbital contents are displaced posteriorly, and the traumatic force is transmitted to the thin orbital floor and medial orbital wall, which are the first to fracture. The mechanism usually involves direct force transfer from the orbital rim to the orbital floor and medial wall, resulting in buckling and fracture. Force transfer through the globe occurs less frequently; otherwise, global injuries would accompany orbital fractures more often. Intraorbital contents often herniate through the fractured site and may become incarcerated by the edges of the fracture or by a "trapdoor" displacement of a segment of thin orbital bone (Fig. 46-5).

21. What is the difference between pure and impure blowout fractures?

Pure blowout fractures involve the thin areas of the orbital floor, medial wall, and lateral wall. The orbital rim, however, remains intact. *Impure blowout fractures* are associated with fracture of the adjacent facial bones. The thick orbital rim is also fractured; its backward displacement causes comminution of the orbital floor. Transmission of the traumatic force to the orbital contents produces a superimposed blowout fracture.

22. What key findings should be sought on physical examination in a patient with a suspected orbital fracture?

A five-point ocular assessment has been proposed to evaluate patients with periorbital trauma. The five key items are (1) visual acuity, (2) pupillary function prior to any dilation, (3) examination of the anterior chamber for blood or fluid, (4) examination of the posterior segment with a funduscope, and (5) ocular motility. This examination should be repeated during the course of treatment and should accompany a formal evaluation by the ophthalmologist.

23. What physical findings suggest an orbital fracture?

Periorbital edema, ecchymosis, and subconjunctival hemorrhage are seen with most orbital fractures. Fractures of the anterior orbit are characterized by palpable bony step-offs at the inferior and lateral orbital rims and sensory nerve disturbances in the cheek and upper gingiva and teeth. Fractures of the middle orbit may lead to changes in the position of the globe, oculomotor dysfunction, and diplopia, whereas fractures of the posterior orbit may present with visual and oculomotor disturbances.

Figure 46-5. A, Mechanism of blowout fracture from displacement of the globe itself into the orbital walls. The globe is displaced posteriorly, striking the orbital walls and forcing them outward, causing a "punched out" fracture the size of the globe. **B,** "Force transmission" fracture of orbital floor. (Copyright © AO Foundation, used with permission.)

Globe-to-wall

Buckling

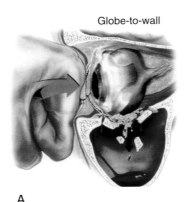

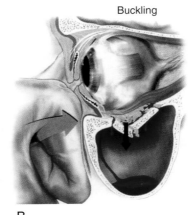

A   B

24. Hypoesthesia or anesthesia in the distribution of which nerve is seen in 90% to 95% of orbital floor fractures?
The infraorbital nerve.

25. How can entrapment of orbital contents be diagnosed?
Entrapment is diagnosed by noting inability of the eyeball to rotate through its normal range of motion. Entrapment of the inferior rectus muscle would be noted as an inability of the globe to roll in a vertical plane. On observation, the patient may not be able to look upward with the affected eye. In the comatose patient (or following administration of topical anesthetic into the inferior fornix in an awake patient), insertion of a rectus muscle onto the ocular globe approximately 7 mm from the limbus may be gently grasped with a forceps. The globe is then rotated in all four directions and any restriction noted. The inferior rectus muscle usually is used, although the superior, medial, or lateral recti muscles may be used as well.

26. What is a Marcus Gunn pupil?
With lesions involving the retina or optic nerve back to the chiasm, a light directed into in the unaffected eye produces normal constriction of the pupils of both eyes (consensual response). However, a light directed into in the affected eye produces a paradoxical dilation rather than constriction of the affected pupil. This afferent pupillary defect is referred to as a *Marcus Gunn pupil.* Such lesions, as well as globe rupture, lens dislocation, and vitreous hemorrhage, are uncommon but may accompany orbital fractures and underscore the need for an ophthalmologic evaluation in all cases of orbital fractures upon presentation.

27. What is the superior orbital fissure syndrome?
Fractures involving the superior orbital fissure produce a combination of cranial nerve palsies known as the *superior orbital fissure syndrome.* The syndrome consists of ptosis of the eyelid, proptosis of the globe, paralysis of cranial nerves III, IV, and VI, and anesthesia in the distribution of the first (ophthalmic) division of the trigeminal nerve (CN V1). Sensory disturbances of the forehead, upper eyelid, conjunctiva, cornea, and sclera are seen.

28. What is the orbital apex syndrome?
If blindness occurs in combination with superior orbital fissure syndrome, the condition is referred to as the *orbital apex syndrome.*

29. What is the best radiographic study for diagnosis of an orbital fracture?
Computed tomographic (CT) scan. Axial scans at 3-mm intervals demonstrate abnormalities of the medial and lateral walls and identify fractures of the nasoethmoidal region. Coronal scans, obtained by direct or reformatted images, demonstrate fractures of the orbital floor, roof, and interorbital space. In the absence of a CT scan, a Waters view is often sufficient to diagnose an orbital floor fracture. It allows visualization of blood in the maxillary sinus as well as orbital floor depression and herniation of orbital contents. Other findings may include disruption of the medial wall and separation of the zygomaticofrontal (ZF) suture.

30. What are the goals of surgical treatment of orbital fractures?
The goals of surgical treatment are (1) reduction/release of any herniated or entrapped orbital contents and (2) restoration of normal orbital architecture. Intraorbital soft tissue contents must be freed from any fracture sites. Range of motion of the ocular globe after freeing of the orbital soft tissue should be confirmed by an intraoperative forced duction test. This test should be performed before the entrapped tissue is released, after release, and again after insertion of any material used to reconstruct the orbital floor.

31. What are the principles of orbital fracture management?
The principles of orbital fracture management are (1) stabilization and reconstruction of the orbital ring (medial orbital, lateral orbital, supraorbital, and infraorbital rims); (2) reconstruction of orbital floor defects; (3) repair and redraping of orbital soft tissue, including the medial and lateral canthal tendons; and (4) careful postoperative evaluation for changes in comfort, vision, or other adverse sequelae. Sufficient exposure of all fracture sites is necessary to permit adequate reduction and fixation of all fracture fragments. Fixation usually is achieved with the application of microplates or miniplates and screws across the site of the fracture. These usually measure 1.0 to 1.5 mm in width. Bone grafts may or may not be required. The integrity of the orbital floor is restored with either a bone graft or an alloplastic implant. The purpose of orbital floor reconstruction is to reestablish the size of the orbital cavity. Occasionally, a depressed segment of orbital floor can be retrieved and, if of sufficient size and appropriate configuration, rotated 90° to provide coverage of the floor defect. Any material used for floor reconstruction should be anchored to prevent displacement or extrusion of the material. Medial and/or lateral canthopexies are performed, when necessary, to restore proper suspension of the orbital globe.

32. What materials are used to reconstruct the orbital floor?
- *Autogenous bone grafts* (split calvarial, iliac, or split rib) (see Figs. 46-2 to 46-4)
- *Allogenic bone grafts* (radiated cadaveric tibia)
- *Inorganic alloplastic materials* (e.g., Medpor, Silastic, Vitallium, stainless steel, Teflon, Supramid, or titanium implants)

33. What are the most frequent sequelae of inadequately treated fractures of the orbital floor?
Diplopia and enophthalmos.

34. What is the principal mechanism responsible for posttraumatic enophthalmos?
Displacement of a relatively constant volume of orbital soft tissue into an enlarged bony orbital volume. Fat atrophy does not appear to play an etiopathogenic role. Enophthalmos in excess of 5 mm results in a noticeable deformity. Correction of enophthalmos involves correction of orbital cavity size and restoration of the shape of its walls to their original configuration.

35. What is diplopia? Is it always an indication for surgery?
Diplopia means double vision and is *rarely* an indication for surgery. It usually is transient and, if present only at the extremes of gaze rather than within a functional field of vision, is not a critical symptom. It is commonly attributed to hematoma or edema that causes muscular imbalance by elevating the ocular globe or to injury of the extraocular musculature and temporary effects on the oculorotary mechanism.

36. What are the major surgical indications for orbital fracture repair?
Muscle entrapment and increased orbital volume. Entrapment, which is confirmed by a forced duction test and CT scan demonstrating soft tissue incarceration, warrants early exploration. Increased orbital volume secondary to significant fractures that have an area greater than 2 cm^2 of displaced orbital wall may result in globe displacement (enophthalmos and globe dystopia) and necessitates fracture repair. Enophthalmos secondary to a floor defect is managed with a lower lid or transconjunctival incision. Enophthalmos secondary to expansion of the medial wall can be approached from the floor if the enlargement is in the lower half of the medial orbital wall. Otherwise, a coronal incision is warranted. Enophthalmos secondary to lateral wall involvement usually requires a coronal incision.

37. What complications are associated with fractures of the orbital roof?
Fractures of the orbital roof usually involve the supraorbital ridge, frontal bone, and frontal sinus and frequently reduce orbital volume. Globe displacement occurs in an inferolateral direction and may result in proptosis. The trochlea of the superior oblique muscle is often damaged because of its proximity to the surface of the roof, resulting in transitory diplopia. CN VI may be traumatized with orbital roof fractures, resulting in paralysis of the lateral rectus muscle and limitation of ocular abduction. Additional complications include dural tears, anterior cranial base injuries, cerebrospinal fluid leaks, cerebral herniation, and pulsatile exophthalmos.

38. Which fracture may result in an antimongoloid slant of the palpebral fissure? Why?
Inferoposterior displacement of a malar complex or zygoma fracture causes an antimongoloid slant. This slant results from the inferior displacement of the lateral canthal tendon, which moves with the fractured lateral orbital wall.

39. What incisions are used to approach the orbit?
There are multiple approaches to the orbit, and one or a combination is required for operative reduction and rigid fixation.

The orbital floor can be approached through one of three standard incisions:
- A *subciliary incision* begins approximately 2 to 3 mm below the lash line and extends from the punctum to 8 to 10 mm lateral to the lateral canthus. This incision is made through the skin, and the dissection is continued to the inferior edge of the tarsus. A skin-muscle flap is then raised from the tarsus. The septum orbitale is followed below the tarsus until the rim of the orbit is reached. An incision is made through the periosteum on the anterior aspect of the orbital rim to avoid damaging the septum, which inserts on the anterolateral portion of the orbit at the recess of Eisler. The periosteum is elevated from the rim and orbital floor. This approach allows easy access to the lateral and medial walls and floor of the orbit (Fig. 46-6).
- A *transjugal incision* is performed within the lid crease, 4 to 5 mm below the ciliary margin and tarsal plate. This incision avoids many of the problems associated with the subciliary incision.
- A *transconjunctival incision,* advocated by Tessier for correction of craniofacial anomalies and by Converse for posttraumatic deformities, is made through the conjunctiva, capsulopalpebral fascia (lid retractors), and onto periosteum to the orbital rim, traversing either anterior posterior to the orbital septum. The transconjunctival approach avoids an external scar and minimizes the risk of postoperative ectropion. Additional exposure may be gained by performing a lateral canthotomy (Fig. 46-7).

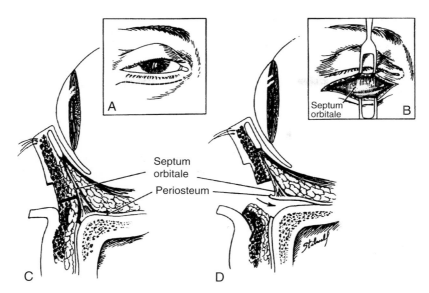

Figure 46-6. Subciliary eyelid incision. **A,** Incision design. **B,** Exposure of the septum orbitale. **C,** Sagittal section demonstrating the skin incision extended through the orbicularis oculi muscle and the path of dissection over the septum orbitale to the orbital rim. **D,** Periosteum of the orbit (periorbita) is elevated from the orbital floor. (From Converse JM, Cole JG, Smith B: Late treatment of blowout fractures of the floor of the orbit. A case report. Plast Reconstr Surg 28:183, 1961, with permission.)

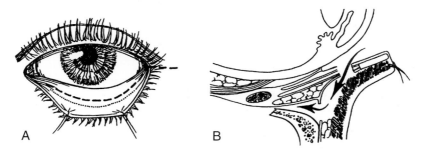

Figure 46-7. Transconjunctival incision combined with lateral canthotomy. **A,** Incision design. **B,** Sagittal section demonstrating the incision through the conjunctiva, capsulopalpebral fascia, and periosteum to the orbital rim. The preseptal approach is used to prevent herniation of periorbital fat into the operative field. (From Manson PN, Markowitz BL: Fractures of the orbit and nasoethmoidal bones. In Cohen M [ed]: Mastery of Plastic and Reconstructive Surgery. Boston, Little, Brown, 1994, p 1147, with permission.)

Exposure to the orbit may be enhanced by several additional approaches:

- A *lateral brow incision* provides exposure of the frontozygomatic suture and part of the lateral wall and roof of the orbit.
- A *transcaruncular incision* is used for isolated fractures of the medial wall of the orbit. Similarly, a medial canthal incision may be used to provide excellent exposure of the medial canthus, medial wall of the orbit, and nasal bones. It usually is made in a curvilinear fashion to improve cosmesis.
- A *gingivobuccal incision* provides excellent exposure of the inferior orbital rim, maxilla, and zygoma.
- Finally, much of the orbit may be approached through a *coronal incision*. Popularized by Tessier, it provides wide access to the orbits, nose, and zygomas as well as the cranium. It is the preferred incision for extensive surgery, especially when the orbital roof must be visualized and the orbital contents must be mobilized 360°.

40. Which incision has the greatest propensity for complications such as scleral show or ectropion?
The subciliary incision. Scleral show and ectropion are frequent sequelae after lower lid surgery due to lid retraction. Many of these conditions improve with time, but permanent scarring within the lower eyelid may result in permanent deformity that requires release of scar tissue and even grafting.

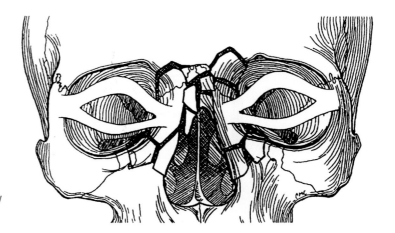

Figure 46-8. Bilateral comminuted nasoethmoidal-orbital fractures. Note displacement of the medial orbital wall fragments containing the attachment of the medial canthal tendons. (From Manson PN, Markowitz BL: Fractures of the orbit and nasoethmoidal bones. In Cohen M [ed]: Mastery of Plastic and Reconstructive Surgery. Boston, Little, Brown, 1994, p 1150, with permission.)

41. Is the Caldwell-Luc approach to the orbital floor a wise one?

Absolutely not. A Caldwell-Luc approach to the orbital floor through an opening in the anterior wall of the maxillary sinus is *not* recommended for reduction of orbital floor fracture. This transmaxillary approach is potentially dangerous because it is a blind approach. Complete reduction of herniated orbital contents is therefore not ensured, and thorough exploration of the orbital floor is not possible.

42. What is an NOE fracture?

Medial orbital wall fractures often accompany orbital floor fractures and sometimes are an undiagnosed cause of residual postoperative enophthalmos. More severe medial orbital wall fractures usually involve the nasoethmoidal structures and thus are referred to as nasoethmoidal–orbital or nasoorbitoethmoidal fractures, or simply *NOE fractures* (Fig. 46-8).

43. What classic clinical findings are associated with an NOE fracture?

Telecanthus and a saddle nose deformity. NOE fractures consist of injury to one or both frontal processes of the maxilla and nose. The frontal process of the maxilla contains the attachment of the medial canthal ligament. If the medial orbital rim and its canthal attachment are dislocated, the result is telecanthus, which is an increase in the distance between the medial canthi (intercanthal distance). In contrast to orbital hypertelorism, the orbit itself is not displaced laterally. The pseudohyperteloric appearance of the orbits is accentuated by the flattening and widening of the bony dorsum of the nose. As a result, the eyes appear far apart. The most reliable clinical sign of an NOE fracture is movement of the frontal process of the maxilla on direct finger pressure over the medial canthal ligament.

44. How can the intercanthal distance be preserved after an NOE fracture?

The most important step in the management of an NOE fracture is performance of a transnasal canthopexy. The segment of bone to which the medial canthal tendon is attached is mobilized so that drill holes can be placed behind the canthal ligament for transnasal wires. Two parallel holes are placed in the most superior and posterior aspects of the bone fragment, above and posterior to the lacrimal fossa. Interosseous wires are used to link the medial orbital rim with the frontal bone, nasal bones, and inferior orbital rim. The bone fragments attached to the medial canthal ligament are reduced and secured to the surrounding bone by interosseous wires. Two 26-gauge wires are passed through the canthal ligament fragment from one frontal process to the other and tightened. This procedure preserves the intercanthal distance and corrects the telecanthus.

45. What is the surgical approach to treatment of an NOE fracture?

Three incisions—coronal, subciliary or mid-lid, and maxillary gingivobuccal sulcus—are usually necessary to expose adequately the nasoethmoidal–orbital region. NOE fractures are complex and require specific reduction and fixation techniques based on the pattern and comminution of the fracture. A combination of interfragmentary wiring and plate and screw fixation is necessary to reconstruct the medial orbital wall, inferior orbital rim, nasofrontal junction, nasomaxillary buttress, and nasal bones. Despite interfragmentary wiring, the nasal dorsum almost always requires augmentation with a cantilever bone graft.

BIBLIOGRAPHY

Gossman MD, Roberts DM, Barr CC: Ophthalmologic aspects of orbital injury: A comprehensive diagnostic and management approach. Clin Plast Surg 19:71–85. 1992.

Gruss JS: Naso-ethmoid-orbital fractures: Classification and role of primary bone grafting. Plast Reconstr Surg 75:303–317, 1985.

Jackson IT: Classification and treatment of orbito-zygomatic and orbito-ethmoid fractures: The place of bone grafting and plate fixation. Clin Plast Surg 16:77–91, 1989.

Kawamoto HK: Late post-traumatic enophthalmos: A correctable deformity? Plast Reconstr Surg 69:423–432, 1992.

Manson PN: Facial fractures. In Aston SJ. Beasley RW, Thorne CHM (eds): Grabb and Smith's Plastic Surgery, 5th ed. Philadelphia, Lippincott-Raven, 1997, pp 383–412.

Manson PN: Facial fractures. In Mathes S (ed): Plastic Surgery, Vol 3, 2nd ed. New York, Elsevier, 2006, pp 77–380.

Manson PN, Iliff N: Management of blow out fractures of the orbital floor. II. Early repair for selected injuries. Surg Ophthalmol 35: 280–292, 1991.

Markowitz B, Manson P, Sargent L, et al: Management of the medial canthal ligament in nasoethmoidal orbital fractures. Plast Reconstr Surg 87:843–853, 1991.

McCarthy JG, Jelks GW, Valauri AJ, et al: The orbit and zygoma. In McCarthy JG (ed): Plastic Surgery. Philadelphia, WB Saunders, 1990, pp 1574–1670.

Taub PJ, Kawamoto HK. Orbital injuries. In Thaller SR, McDonald WS (ed): Facial Trauma. New York, Marcel Dekker, 2004, pp 235–260.

Whitaker L, Yaremchuk M: Secondary reconstruction of post-traumatic orbital deformities. Ann Plast Surg 25:440–449, 1990.

Yaremchuk M: Changing concepts in the management of secondary orbital deformities. Clin Plast Surg 19:113–124, 1992.

Zide BM, Jelks GW: Surgical Anatomy of the Orbit. New York, Raven Press, 1985.

FRACTURES OF THE ZYGOMA

Albert S. Woo, MD, and
Joseph S. Gruss, MBBCh, FRCSC

1. Describe the anatomy of the zygoma.

The zygoma is a pyramidal bone of the midface. Its anterior convexity gives prominence to the malar eminence of the cheek, and its posterior concavity helps to form the temporal fossa. The zygoma forms the superolateral and superoanterior portions of the maxillary sinus. It articulates with the frontal, temporal, maxillary, and sphenoid bones (Fig. 47-1). Superolaterally, the frontal process of the zygoma articulates with the zygomatic process of the frontal bone and forms the lateral orbital wall along with its intraorbital articulation with the sphenoid bone. The temporal process of the zygoma posterolaterally articulates with the zygomatic process of the temporal bone to create the zygomatic arch, which links the base of the skull with the zygomatic body. The broad articulation of the zygoma inferiorly and medially with the maxilla forms the zygomaticomaxillary (ZM) buttress, the major buttressing structure between the midface and the cranium, as well as the infraorbital rim and lateral part of the orbital floor.

2. What different terms have been used to describe fractures of the zygoma?

Zygomaticomaxillary complex/compound (ZMC), zygomatic, orbitozygomatic (OZM), malar complex, trimalar, tetrapod (quadrapod), and tripod fracture are among the terms used by clinicians to describe the fracture pattern involving the zygoma. The term *zygomaticomaxillary complex fracture* is among the more popular terms used to describe this fracture pattern. The term *tripod fracture* is a misnomer because these fractures consist of four components (see Question 4).

3. What is the pattern of the typical zygoma fracture?

Because of natural points of structural weakness in the area of the zygoma, a reproducible pattern of zygomatic complex fractures frequently occurs. Typically, the fracture line travels through the zygomaticofrontal (ZF) region and into the orbit at the zygomaticosphenoidal suture to the inferior orbital fissure. Anterior to the fissure, the fracture involves only the maxilla, where it traverses the orbital floor and infraorbital rim, goes through the infraorbital foramen, and continues inferiorly through the ZM buttress. Posterior to the buttress, yet still in continuity, the lateral wall of the maxillary sinus is fractured. In addition, the zygomatic arch is fractured at its weakest point, approximately 1.5 cm posterior to the zygomaticotemporal suture, in the zygomatic process of the temporal bone (Fig. 47-2). This typical fracture pattern is commonly encountered, but great variety exists depending on factors such as the direction and magnitude of the force, the density of the adjacent bones, and the amount of soft tissue covering the zygoma. Most displaced zygomatic fractures are depressed and rotated laterally. In other circumstances, only isolated arch fractures may occur.

4. Why is the commonly used term *tripod fracture* a misnomer for zygomatic complex fractures?

The term *tripod fracture* has been used to consolidate the typical fracture pattern of the zygomatic complex into a concise description that reflects the configuration of the complex as it relates to adjacent bones. However, it wrongly implies that only three legs, or processes, are involved. In reality, the usual zygomatic complex fracture involves *four* major processes: ZF suture, infraorbital rim, ZM buttress, and zygomatic arch. In addition, the zygomaticosphenoid suture is often referred to as a fifth point of articulation.

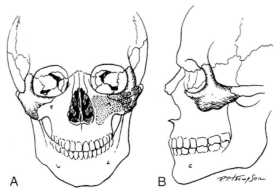

Figure 47-1. Zygoma and its articulating bones. **A,** The zygoma articulates with the frontal, sphenoid, maxillary, and temporal bones. The *dots* show the portion of the zygoma and the maxilla occupied by the maxillary sinus. **B,** Lateral view of the zygoma. (From Manson PN: Facial injuries. In McCarthy JG [ed]: Plastic Surgery. Philadelphia, WB Saunders, 1990, p 992, with permission.)

A   B

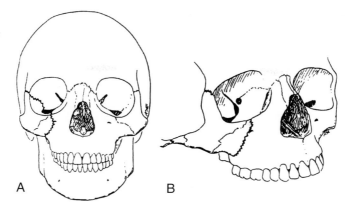

Figure 47-2. Common fracture pattern in zygomaticomaxillary complex/compound injury. **A,** Frontal view of skull showing fracture medial to zygomaticomaxillary suture and along zygomaticosphenoid suture within orbit. **B,** Oblique frontal view of skull showing fractures through frontozygomatic suture and posterior to zygomaticotemporal suture. (From Ellis E III: Fractures of the zygomatic complex and arch. In Fonseca RJ, Walker RV [eds]: Oral and Maxillofacial Trauma. Philadelphia, WB Saunders, 1991, p 573.)

5. Which muscles attach to the zygoma?

The masseter, temporalis, and zygomaticus muscles all hold attachments to the zygoma. The masseter muscle originates along the inferior aspect of the body and temporal process of the zygoma. This exerts a downward force on the zygoma and can pull an unstable ZMC fracture inferiorly. The temporalis fascia attaches along the superior aspect of the arch and posterior body.

6. What are the signs and symptoms of zygomatic fractures?

- Pain
- Periorbital ecchymosis and edema
- Flattening of the malar prominence and widening of transverse facial width
- Palpable bony step-off at the ZF suture, infraorbital rim, and/or ZM buttress
- Subconjunctival ecchymosis
- Diplopia
- Enophthalmos (often a late finding)
- Asymmetric pupillary levels
- Upward gaze lag secondary to entrapment of the orbital contents, including the inferior rectus muscle
- Infraorbital nerve sensory disturbance
- Trismus
- Unilateral epistaxis due to tearing of the ipsilateral maxillary sinus mucosa
- Subcutaneous emphysema
- Gingival buccal sulcus ecchymosis or hematoma
- Antimongoloid slant of the lateral palpebral fissure due to downward displacement of the attachment of the lateral palpebral ligament on Whitnall's tubercle of the zygoma
- Orbital dystopia from downward displacement of Lockwood's ligament
- Lower lid retraction from downward displacement of the orbital septum

7. What is the mechanism of trismus caused by fracture of the zygoma?

Trismus is characterized by a limitation of mouth opening and is present in approximately one third of all ZMC fractures. This can be explained by the fact that the coronoid process of the mandible is closely associated anatomically with the zygoma. Displaced fractures of the body or arch of the zygoma may impinge on the coronoid process, thereby interfering with its movement (Fig. 47-3). Trismus may be secondary to edema or muscle spasm of the temporalis or masseter muscles.

8. Which diagnostic images provide the most information in evaluating and formulating a treatment plan for zygomatic fractures?

Computed tomographic (CT) scan shows in detail the location of the fractures, displacement of the bones, and status of the soft tissues. Axial views are best to evaluate the medial/lateral orbital walls and zygomatic arch, whereas coronal views are necessary to determine the extent of orbital floor involvement. With the latest advent of high-resolution CT scanners, three-dimensional reconstructions can be performed as an additional aid in diagnosis and operative planning. Posteroanterior oblique (Waters) and submental vertex ("jug handle") plain radiographs are the most useful plain films for evaluating these fractures, but CT scan is currently the diagnostic imaging tool preferred by most surgeons.

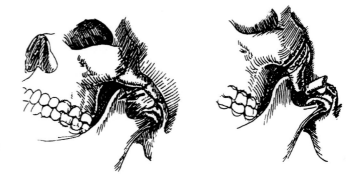

Figure 47-3. Fracture of the zygomatic arch with medial displacement against the coronoid process of the mandible, limiting mandibular motion. (From Manson PN: Facial injuries. In McCarthy JG [ed]: Plastic Surgery. Philadelphia, WB Saunders, 1990, p 993, with permission.)

9. **How many points must be evaluated by a surgeon when evaluating a fracture of the zygoma?**

Five: ZF suture, infraorbital rim, ZM buttress, zygomatic arch, and lateral orbital wall (Fig. 47-4). Surgical intervention should be based on both clinical and radiographic findings. Fractures that display significant displacement and/or instability at these points require operative intervention to correct immediate problems or to prevent long-term sequelae such as facial dysmorphism, enophthalmos, and orbital dystopia. The long-term sequelae are much more difficult to correct once fracture healing is complete. Fractures managed nonoperatively should be monitored with close follow-up with the surgeon. Patients should remain on a soft diet, and the malar eminence should be protected for 4-6 weeks, especially during sleep. This can be managed with protective devices, such as an AlumaFoam splint.

10. **What are the surgical principles for reconstruction of zygomatic fractures?**
   - Early operative anatomic reduction
   - Wide exposure of fracture segments
   - Rigid internal fixation
   - Primary bone grafting of significant skeletal defects

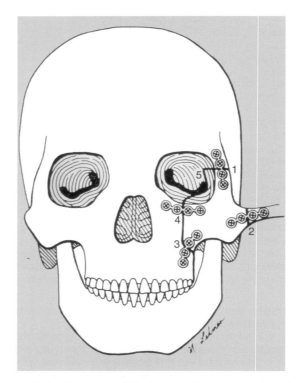

Figure 47-4. Schematic diagram showing the five points at which a fracture of the zygoma may be evaluated: **(1)** zygomaticofrontal suture, **(2)** zygomatic arch, **(3)** zygomaticomaxillary buttress, **(4)** infraorbital rim, and, most importantly **(5)** lateral orbital wall (zygomaticosphenoid suture). Of these, the lateral orbital wall is most useful when assessing whether the zygomatic complex is appropriately reduced. Rigid plate fixation at each of the first four points also is shown.

11. When is the optimal time to operate on zygomatic fractures?

There are important points to keep in mind in deciding when to operate on zygomatic fractures. Zygomatic fractures are not emergencies, and any associated life-threatening injuries must be addressed first. Initially, soft tissue edema makes open reduction more difficult and may compromise the final result. However, delay in intervention beyond the time for soft tissue fibrosis and fracture healing to occur (3 to 4 weeks) makes simple repositioning of the bones difficult. Ideally, open reduction should be performed on an otherwise uninjured patient before the onset of edema. In reality, this rarely occurs. Waiting several days for edema to resolve and, in the case of multiple trauma, for the patient to stabilize does not compromise the surgical outcome and often results in better surgical results. Most surgeons prefer to operate on facial fractures within 14 days after injury.

12. Name the four points at which the zygoma can be fixated.

The ZF suture, infraorbital rim, ZM buttress, and zygomatic arch. The gold standard of fracture repair and reduction consists of fracture alignment at three points. Therefore, of the four major processes described, at least three must be anatomically corrected under direct visualization to ensure anatomic reduction of the entire complex. Most frequently, these are the ZF suture, inferior orbital rim, and ZM buttress. Integrity of the orbital floor also must be ascertained. Alignment at only two points can allow for significant rotational malalignment at the other fracture site (Fig. 47-5). Frequently, these three points are fixated with plates. Nevertheless, this topic remains controversial because methods of one- and two-plate fixation have also shown acceptable results.

13. Which anatomic structure is most useful when assessing whether the zygomatic complex is appropriately reduced?

The lateral orbital wall. This structure is a broad, relatively flat interface between the greater wing of the sphenoid and the zygoma. It is easily visualized by medial dissection into the orbit when obtaining access to the ZF suture. The benefits of the lateral orbital wall are twofold. (1) It is least likely to be comminuted during fracture. (2) The lateral orbit is also the most sensitive index of both the degree of displacement and the rotation of the orbitozygomatic complex. Visualization from inside the orbit allows for anatomic reduction of the sphenoid wing to the orbital portion of the zygoma. Accurate alignment of this interface is essential because it permits simultaneous reduction of the fracture in all planes.

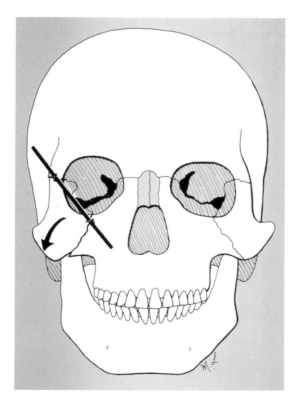

Figure 47-5. In displaced, unstable fractures of the zygoma, two-point fixation at the zygomaticofrontal suture and the infraorbital rim may still allow for rotation around these two points in the axis shown. As the masseter muscle contracts, it can pull the entire complex in a downward direction, causing residual depression of the zygomatic complex. The possibility of this occurring is increased by comminution or bone loss at the zygomaticomaxillary buttress. (From Gruss JS, Phillips JH: Rigid fixation of zygomatic fractures. In Yaremchuk MJ, Gruss JS, Manson PN [eds]: Rigid Fixation of the Craniomaxillofacial Skeleton. Boston, Butterworth-Heinemann, 1992, p 267.)

14. How are isolated, displaced zygomatic arch fractures treated?

Zygomatic arch fractures often displace medially. One popular approach to elevate a medially displaced zygomatic arch fracture is that described by Gillies. Others prefer access via the gingivobuccal sulcus, sometimes referred to as a *reverse* Gillies approach or a Keen approach. Many surgeons believe that these fractures, once reduced, are stable because of the support of the underlying edematous temporalis muscle and require no fixation as long as no pressure is exerted to the ipsilateral face postoperatively.

15. Describe the temporal (Gillies) approach to the zygomatic arch.

A small incision is initially made in the temporal scalp approximately 2.5 cm anterior and 2.5 cm superior to the helix of the ear, avoiding injury to the branches of the superficial temporal artery. Dissection is carried down through skin, subcutaneous tissue, and superficial and deep temporal fascia. The plane between the deep layer of the deep temporal fascia and the underlying temporalis muscle is bluntly developed with an elevator down to the zygomatic arch. The surgeon can then elevate the depressed fracture segments.

16. Name the three standard approaches to the infraorbital rim and orbital floor.

The subciliary or lower blepharoplasty incision, the subtarsal or mid-lid incision, and the transconjunctival incision (Fig. 47-6). Among these, the subciliary incision has fallen increasingly out of favor for fracture reduction due to an increased risk for ectropion compared with the other approaches.

17. What are the common approaches to the lateral orbital rim?

The lateral brow incision, lateral extension of the upper eyelid blepharoplasty incision, and the coronal incision. Of the first two, the lateral extension of the blepharoplasty incision is favored because an incision in the skin of the eyelid tends to leave a less noticeable scar than in the brow. The coronal approach is utilized when other injuries are present, requiring access to the frontal bone or skull. A lateral extension of the subciliary incision has also been utilized for this purpose, although access is less direct through this approach.

18. How is access obtained for manipulation and reduction of the ZM buttress?

Through an upper buccal sulcus incision, access is gained to the entire anterior and lateral surface of the maxilla. Through this incision, the ZM buttress as well as the nasomaxillary buttress can be easily visualized. A rigid instrument is passed into this space to elevate and reduce the zygoma as well as to rigidly fixate the ZM buttress. Plating at this site maintains strong support against the downward pull of the muscles of mastication.

19. What are the advantages of the coronal incision for reduction of zygomatic fractures?

The coronal incision provides excellent exposure to the orbit, zygomatic body, and zygomatic arch while keeping the scar hidden in the hairline. It is most useful in complex injuries of the midface in which the zygomatic arch is comminuted, outwardly displaced, and/or telescoped. When a combination of fractures exists, the arch cannot be easily popped into position and must be reduced and plated via this approach.

20. Describe the approach to the zygomatic arch from a coronal incision.

A zigzag "stealth incision" (a term coined by Ian Munro) is frequently made to allow for a less obvious scar when establishing coronal access. The temporoparietal fascia overlying the temporalis muscle is frequently elevated with the coronal flap. Careful dissection is made down to the outer layer of the deep temporal fascia, avoiding injury to the frontal branch of the facial nerve, which travels within the superficial layer of the deep temporal fascia. Blunt dissection then is carried just superior to the zygomatic arch. Several centimeters above the arch, the deep temporal fascia splits to envelop the temporal fat pad, which is situated on the superior border of the zygomatic arch. The deep temporal fascia above the arch is incised obliquely to obtain full access to this structure. Dissection is not made directly over the arch because the periosteum and overlying fascial areas are very adherent, with the frontal branch embedded between these two layers (Fig. 47-7).

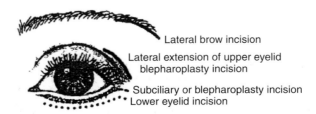

Figure 47-6. Common incisions to approach the zygoma. (From Ellis E III: Fractures of the zygomatic complex and arch. In Fonseca RJ, Walker RV, Betts NJ, et al [eds]: Oral and Maxillofacial Trauma, 3rd ed. St. Louis, Elsevier, 2005.)

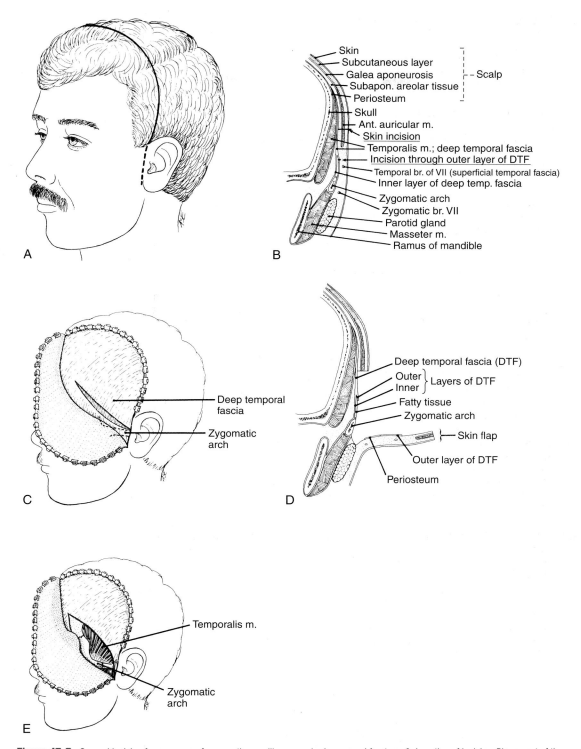

Figure 47-7. Coronal incision for exposure of zygomaticomaxillary complex/compound fracture. **A,** Location of incision. Placement of the incision should be well behind the hairline. **B,** Anatomic layers of scalp and temporal area. **C,** Dissection of the flap anteriorly just above the deep temporal fascia. **D,** Anatomic layer of dissection with a second incision through the outer later of the deep temporal fascia into the temporal fat pad just above the zygomatic arch. The temporal branch of the facial nerve travels within the superficial layer of the deep temporal fascia and is thereby protected from injury with this deeper approach. **E,** Subperiosteal dissection of the lateral orbit and zygomatic arch. (From Ellis E III: Fractures of the zygomatic complex and arch. In Fonseca RJ, Walker RV, Betts NJ, et al [eds]: Oral and Maxillofacial Trauma, 3rd ed. St. Louis, Elsevier, 2005, p 602.)

21. Summarize the commonly used incisions for surgical exposure.

To the ZF suture:
- Lateral brow
- Lateral limb of upper blepharoplasty incision
- Coronal (allows additional access to the zygomatic arch)

To the infraorbital rim:
- Transconjunctival (± lateral canthotomy)
- Subtarsal/mid-lid
- Subciliary (increased risk of ectropion)

To the ZM buttress:
- Gingival buccal sulcus

22. A patient appears to have an increase in facial width after complex facial injuries requiring plating of the zygomatic arch. What went wrong?

Remember that the zygomatic arch is not truly an arch at all. This structure (which connects the skull base to the midface) curves as an arch anteriorly and posteriorly but remains flat at its midportion. A common error is to reconstruct this as a true arch, thereby creating an appearance of excess facial width.

23. What is the dreaded OIF?

Surgical management of facial fractures involves open reduction internal fixation (ORIF). An open internal fixation (OIF) describes a situation in which a surgeon has fixated fracture segments without adequate reduction into anatomic position; hence, OIF *without* reduction. It is also the sound most surgeons make when seeing the postoperative result.

24. What is the most feared complication after surgical treatment of the zygoma fractures?

Albeit rare, blindness may result from direct damage to the optic nerve due to displacement of a bony fragment or fracture of the optic canal, edema that causes compression of the nerve, or retrobulbar hematoma. Preoperative ophthalmologic assessment of both eyes is imperative. Preexisting blindness in the contralateral, uninvolved eye has been considered by some as a relative contraindication to treatment because surgical reduction complicated by blindness in the eye on the involved side would be absolutely devastating to the patient (and surgeon).

25. How is malunion of the zygoma treated?

When minor deformity is present without orbital involvement or when comminution precludes repositioning of the zygoma en bloc, placement of subperiosteal implants may be used to restore normal malar contour. When more pronounced deformity exists along with functional deficits, zygomatic osteotomy to re-create the fracture followed by bony repositioning, fixation, and possible bone grafting is the best surgical option.

26. What are the common late sequelae of inadequate fracture reduction?

Inadequate reduction of the zygoma can result in increased width of the midface, decreased projection of the malar eminence, and enophthalmos. The zygoma is frequently displaced posteriorly and laterally, which translates into lateral displacement of the zygomatic arch. Enophthalmos can result from the associated fracture of the orbital floor, which effectively increases the volume of the orbit, allowing the eye to sink posteriorly.

27. A patient demonstrates facial asymmetry and an inferiorly displaced malar mound on the affected side despite anatomic reduction of a zygoma fracture. What was forgotten?

One consequence of wide undermining of the midface during surgical repair of facial fractures is destruction of soft tissue attachments to bone, including the zygomatic ligament. Therefore the soft tissue of the cheek must be resuspended to the zygoma. Without doing so, facial asymmetry can result, with "sagging" of the face ipsilaterally.

28. During reconstruction of a comminuted ZMC fracture, three-point fixation was established and the soft tissues were resuspended. However, the patient continues to have facial asymmetry. What fracture could have been missed?

A unilateral NOE fracture may have been present in this patient. In this situation, the medial portion of the infraorbital rim may be displaced laterally. If this malpositioning remains unnoticed, the ZMC will be laterally malpositioned. The face will continue to appear wide, and orbital volume may also be increased. Therefore, the medial orbital wall must be closely evaluated on CT preoperatively. When found, the NOE component must be anatomically reduced in addition to the ZMC.

BIBLIOGRAPHY

Betts NJ, Barber HD, Powers MP (eds): Oral and Maxillofacial Trauma, 3rd ed. St. Louis, Elsevier, 2005, pp 569–642.

Ellis E III: Fractures of the zygomatic complex and arch. In Fonseca RJ, Walker RV (eds): Oral and Maxillofacial Trauma. Philadelphia, WB Saunders, 1991, pp 435–514.

Feinstein FR, Krizek TJ: Fractures of the zygoma and zygomatic arch. In Foster CA, Sherman JE (eds): Surgery of Facial Bone Fractures. New York, Churchill Livingstone, 1987, p 136.

Gruss JS: Advances in craniofacial fracture repair. Scand J Plast Reconstr Hand Surg Suppl 27:67–81, 1995.

Gruss JS: Internal fixation in facial fractures: Specific anatomic aspects. In: Marsh JL (ed): Current Therapy in Plastic and Reconstructive Surgery: Head and Neck. Philadelphia, BC Decker, 1989, pp 113–117.

Gruss JS, Van Wyck L, Phillips JH, Antonyshyn O: The importance of the zygomatic arch in complex midfacial fracture repair and correction of posttraumatic orbitozygomatic deformities. Plast Reconstr Surg 85:878–890, 1990.

Manson PN: Facial fractures. In: Mathes SJ (ed): Plastic Surgery, 2nd ed. Philadelphia, WB Saunders, 2006, pp 77–380.

Manson PN: Reoperative facial fracture repair. In Grotting, JC (ed): Reoperative Aesthetic and Reconstructive Plastic Surgery, Vol 1. St. Louis, Quality Medical Publishing, 1995, pp 677–759.

Phillips JH, Gruss JS, Wells MD, Chollet A: Periosteal suspension of the lower eyelid and cheek following subciliary exposure of facial fractures. Plast Reconstr Surg 88:145–148, 1991.

FRACTURES OF THE MAXILLA

Robert J. Morin, MD; Renee Burke, MD; and
S. Anthony Wolfe, MD, FACS, FAAP

1. What are the buttresses of the maxilla?
The main vertical buttresses of the maxilla, which absorb the majority of forces, are the paired nasomaxillary, zygomaticomaxillary, and pterygomaxillary buttresses. Another structurally important component, the vomer, connects the posterior maxilla to the cranial base. Horizontal maxillary support is provided by the orbital rims and palate.

2. At what age does the maxillary sinus become mature?
The floor of the maxillary sinus remains above the level of the floor of the nose up to the age of 8 years. Eruption of the permanent maxillary dentition determines the inferior growth of the maxillary floor. Growth of the maxillary sinus, therefore, is not complete until the age of 12 to 16 years.

3. Who was Le Fort? What are Le Fort fractures?
At the end of the 1800s the French surgeon René Le Fort's interest in midfacial fracture patterns led him to perform a series of experiments on cadaver heads. These experiments consisted of dropping the heads from roof tops onto a paved courtyard or striking them with a piano leg. He determined three basic fault lines along which the face fractured. In his initial description, the highest facial fracture was referred to as no. 1 and the lowest as no. 3.

In current parlance, the Le Fort I fracture refers to the horizontal transmaxillary fracture that goes through the maxilla at about the level of the piriform rim. The Le Fort II fracture involves the nasofrontal junction, the nasal processes of the maxilla, and the medial aspect of the inferior orbital rim. In addition, it crosses the anterior maxilla and extends back to and through the pterygoid plates. The Le Fort III fracture is a craniofacial dysjunction. It results in a separation at the frontozygomatic suture, nasofrontal junction, medial orbital wall, orbital floor, and zygomatic arch. The lower maxilla is intact in a pure Le Fort III fracture (Fig. 48-1).

Clinically, Le Fort fractures are often not simply one type and greater than 60% have associated frontal and mandibular fractures.

4. What is the difference between a Le Fort fracture and a Le Fort osteotomy?
In a Le Fort fracture, the fracture line usually extends through the pterygoid plates. In an osteotomy, one attempts to preserve the pterygoid plates by precise separation through the pterygomaxillary junction.

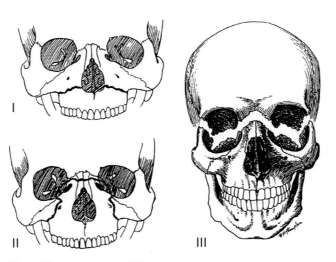

Figure 48-1. Le Fort I, II, and III fractures.

5. How do you clinically diagnose a midface fracture?

The most critical part of a lower midface trauma exam is the evaluation of a patient's occlusion. In an awake patient, the sensation of malocclusion is a fairly sensitive diagnostic modality. Mobility of the maxilla with the head stabilized is another sign of a significant Le Fort fracture. Palpating the midface for bony step-offs, especially in the vicinity of the orbital rims, is important as well. Decreased sensation in the distribution of the infraorbital nerve is a sign of an upper midface or orbital floor fracture. Inspection of the oral and nasal mucosa is important to rule out palatal fractures and nasal septal hematomas respectively. Evaluation of the eye is incredibly important and should be performed by an ophthalmologist as well if injury to the globe is suspected. Subconjunctival hemorrhage is almost pathognomonic for a ZMC fracture. Acute enopthalmos and signs of extraocular muscle entrapment are strongly suggestive of an operative orbital floor fracture. Finally, evaluation of the facial width and malar projection will help diagnose zygomatic arch and zygomaticomaxillary complex fractures.

6. What is the characteristic deformity associated with an untreated Le Fort I fracture?

Midface retrusion and elongation with an anterior openbite.

7. What if loose teeth are associated with a maxillary fracture?

Teeth maintained by even a small blood supply can potentially survive. The outlook depends on both the condition of the tooth and the quality of the surrounding alveolar bone. The teeth should be placed carefully in occlusion and splinted not only with arch bars but also with an interocclusal splint to immobilize the teeth as carefully as possible. The patient should receive antibiotics, maintain oral hygiene, and be referred to a dentist as soon as possible.

8. What should one do with a tooth that has been completely pulled out of its socket?

The tooth should be placed in either sterile saline or, if that is not available, milk. If replaced promptly (<30 minutes) into the socket, a certain number of teeth will survive but will require subsequent root canal.

9. What imaging test should be obtained in patients with a suspected maxillary fracture?

A high resolution computed tomographic (CT) scan with either 1.5- or 3-mm cuts should be performed on all patients with significant facial trauma. Ideally, this should be performed at the time of the initial head CT during the trauma evaluation. Radiographic evaluation should include all structures from the inferior border of the mandible to the superior aspect of the frontal sinus. The scan should be reformatted to obtain coronal, sagittal and three-dimensional views. A panorex may also be obtained to evaluate the mandible and teeth in their entirety.

10. What are the goals of panfacial fracture management?

The most critical goals of panfacial fracture management include the restoration of proper occlusion, the reconstruction of the facial support system, and the preservation of function. Achieving the best aesthetic result possible is extremely important as well.

Once a diagnosis is established and it is determined that surgical intervention is indicated, several vital surgical concepts should be followed. Early one-stage operative repair with wide subperiosteal exposure through well planned incisions should be performed. Precise anatomic reduction must be achieved prior to rigid fixation. Osteotomies may be performed to help restore correct anatomic alignment when appropriate. Immediate autologous bone grafting should be performed if necessary. Finally, resuspension and definitive closure of the soft tissue is vital to the proper management of these injuries.

11. What incisions are necessary for adequate fracture exposure?

The type of incision used is determined by the location of the fracture. A coronal incision provides the most extensive exposure of the frontal sinus, NOE complex, orbits, and zygoma. This is the incision of choice for large pan-facial fractures.

The orbital floor and inferior orbital rim can be approached through a transconjunctival, subciliary, or lower eyelid incision (5-7 mm below the ciliary margin). Subciliary incisions are associated with the highest incidence of lower eyelid ectropion and have been increasingly replaced by the lower eyelid incision, which carries the lowest risk of ectropion while providing the best exposure.

Fractures in the zygomaticofrontal region can be accessed through a lower eyelid or lateral brow/upper blepharoplasty incision. Isolated, depressed fractures of the zygomatic arch can be approached through a Gilles, or temporal hairline, incision. A coronal incision, however, is necessary when wide exposure of the arch is required.

The zygomaticomaxillary and nasomaxillary buttresses, in addition to the pyriform rim, are easily approached through a superior gingivobuccal sulcus incision.

12. **What would you do if you were operating on a patient with a displaced, impacted Le Fort I fracture that could not be reduced? Why is it important to reduce it?**

Initially, mobilization of the maxilla can be attempted with Rowe forceps. If the maxilla does not easily reduce, proceed with a Le Fort I osteotomy. If the maxilla is not reduced before placing the jaws in maxillomandibular fixation, the mandibular condyles may become unseated from the glenoid fossa. This would result in malocclusion. In addition, incomplete reduction of an impacted fracture would result in a decrease in maxillary height.

13. **What is the order of fixation of multiple fractures of the mandible, maxilla, and orbit?**

Fixation of pan-facial fractures often begins with making a dental model to assist with obtaining proper intraoperative occlusion. Once in the operating room, begin with a coronal incision for adequate exposure of all fractures. We prefer to work from the top down. Begin with the orbits and zygoma, using the zygomaticosphenoid suture and the lateral orbital wall to assess the reduction. This reestablishes the anteroposterior projection of the face and correctly orients the zygomaticomaxillary complex. Bone grafting of the orbital floor fracture can be performed once the ZMC is rigidly fixed. Next, the vertical height of the face can be assessed. If both condyles are fractured they must be reconstructed. The teeth are then brought into proper occlusion, using a preformed splint if available, and secured via maxillomandibular fixation. Any further mandibular fractures are reconstructed at this time. Once the AP projection and vertical height of the face are reestablished and the patient is in proper occlusion, the maxillary buttresses are stabilized with rigid fixation and bone grafts if needed. The patient is then taken out of MMF and proper occlusion is reassessed. Finally, the nasal bones are assessed and any reductions or bone grafts to the nose can be performed last.

14. **When should bone grafts be used in the treatment of maxillary fractures?**

Primary bone grafting should be performed when there is insufficient bone to repair any of the major buttresses of the maxilla, with the exception of the pterygomaxillary buttress. In addition, bone grafts should be used to replace bone in the anterior maxillary wall to support the overlying soft tissue. If repair of an orbital floor fracture is indicated, primary bone grafting should be performed in this location as well.

15. **What are the indications for exploration and repair of orbital floor fractures?**

The decision to explore and repair orbital floors in the setting of facial trauma is made based on both imaging studies and clinical exam. Clinically, patients with evidence of acute enopthalmos or restricted globe range of motion secondary to extraocular muscle entrapment have indications for operative intervention. Radiographic evidence of a significant fracture as demonstrated by a defect greater than 2 cm on CT scan is an indication to operate as well. Finally, the orbital floor should be explored if surgical repair is indicated in the treatment of any other midfacial fracture and exposure to the floor is already provided.

16. **What material should be used for reconstruction of internal defects in the orbital cavity, such as the medial orbital wall and orbital floor?**

Many substances are available for use in orbital reconstruction. The best material, however, is still the patient's own bone. Autogenous bone can be harvested quickly and easily by a well trained plastic surgeon. Bone can be contoured to fit any defect and it is associated with the lowest rate of long-term complications, including infection and extrusion. Other materials, including titanium mesh and Medpor, can be used; however, late prosthetic infection and extrusion will remain a possibility for the remainder of the patient's life.

17. **What is the preferred donor site for bone grafts for the orbit and maxilla?**

The bone grafts most commonly used for facial reconstruction include split calvarial, iliac crest, and rib. Each site provides adequate bone with minimal morbidity when harvested properly. Calvarial bone is used most frequently. It should be harvested from the non-dominant parietal area. The surgeon should avoid bone overlying the sagittal sinus, in the relatively thin temporal area and along the coronal suture.

18. **When is intermaxillary fixation properly required after a maxillary fracture?**

If an isolated maxillary fracture is repaired properly with rigid internal fixation, resulting in stable occlusion at the end of the operation, the patient should not require intermaxillary fixation. If, however, the maxilla is severely comminuted and the mandible is involved as well, a course of intermaxillary fixation may be indicated.

19. **When miniplates and screws are used to obtain rigid internal fixation for maxillary and orbital fractures, should they be removed later?**

In general, it is not necessary to subject a patient to a second operation to remove hardware. This is especially true if a low profile plating system was used. If, however, hardware is bothersome to a patient due to palpability or visibility, then removal is not unreasonable provided sufficient time for fracture healing has occurred. Biodegradable plates may be useful in pediatric craniofacial surgery since permanent fixation in the setting of facial growth is not ideal.

20. What is the cause of permanent diplopia after orbitozygomatic fractures?

Initial transient diplopia is present in a significant percentage of patients due to the edema associated with facial trauma. Permanent diplopia, however, may be caused by mechanical globe restriction that results from entrapment and/or injury to the inferior oblique or inferior rectus muscle, Lockwood's ligament, Tenon's capsule, or the periorbital fat. Nonrestrictive causes of diplopia include injury to extraocular muscles, neural injury or an increase in orbital volume secondary to a displaced orbital floor.

21. What are the causes of late enophthalmos?

Late enophthalmos is the result of an increase in orbital volume causing the globe to be recessed within the orbit. This most commonly occurs after the initial edema from a facial trauma resolves in the setting of a significant orbital floor fracture. Other causes of increased orbital volume include orbital fat necrosis and extraocular muscle atrophy.

22. What is the treatment of progressive loss of vision after blunt facial trauma?

Visual loss in the setting of facial trauma should be evaluated immediately by an ophthalmologist. Interventions to prevent progression of visual loss vary based on the etiology but include high doses of steroids and surgical decompression.

23. What are the contraindications to immediate treatment of panfacial fractures?

Operative treatment of pan-facial fractures should be delayed in the setting of an unstable patient. Trauma patients should undergo an advanced trauma life support (ATLS) protocol evaluation and be cleared by a neurosurgeon, trauma surgeon, and ophthalmologist if indicated prior to performing any facial bone repair. Life- and vision-threatening injuries must obviously be treated first.

BIBLIOGRAPHY

Anderson RL, Panje WR, Gross CE: Optic nerve blindness following blunt forehead trauma. Ophthalmology 89:445–455, 1982.
Andreasen JO: Luxation injuries. In Andresen JO (ed): Traumatic Injuries of the Teeth. Philadelphia, WB Saunders, 1981, pp 151–202.
Barkley TL: Some aspects of the treatment of traumatic diplopia. Br J Plast Surg 16:214–220, 1963.
Cole P, Boyd V, Banerji S, Hollier L: Comprehensive management of orbital fractures. Plast Reconstr Surg 120(Suppl 2):57S, 2007.
Dutresne CR, Manson PN: Pediatric facial trauma. In McCarthy JG (ed): Plastic Surgery. WB Saunders, Philadelphia, 1990, pp 1142–1187.
Forrest CR, Antonyshyn OM: Acute management of complex midface fractures. Oper Tech Plast Reconstr Surg 5:188–200, 1998.
Kawanoto HK Jr: Late posttraumatic enophthalmos: A correctable deformity? Plast Reconstr Surg 69:423–432, 1982.
Kelly P, Hopper R, Gruss J: Evaluation and treatment of zygomatic fractures. Plast Reconstr Surg 120(Suppl 2):5S, 2007.
Le Fort R: Etude experimentale sur les fractures de la machoire superieure. Rev Chir Paris 23:208, 360, 479, 1901.
Manson P: Facial injuries. In McCarthy JG: Plastic Surgery. Philadelphia, WB Saunders, 1990, pp 867–1141.
Manson PN, Calrk N, et al: Subunit principles in midface fractures: The importance of sagittal buttress, soft-tissue reduction, and sequencing treatment of segmental fractures. Plast Reconstr Surg 103:1287–1307, 1999.
Manson PN, Su CT, Hoopes JE: Structural pillars of the facial skeleton. Plast Reconstr Surg 66:54–62, 1980.
Nguyen PN, Sullivan P: Advances in the management of orbital fractures. Clin Plast Surg 19:87–98, 1992.
Rowe LD, Miller E, Brandt-Zawadski M: Computed tomography in maxillofacial trauma. Laryngoscope 91:745–757, 1981.
Rowe NL, Killey HC: Fractures of the Facial Skeleton, 2nd ed. Baltimore, Williams & Wilkins, 1968.
Sargent L: Nasoethmoid orbital fractures: Diagnosis and treatement. Plast Reconstr Surg 120(Suppl 2):16S, 2007.
Tessier P, Kawamoto H, Matthews D, et al: Autogenous bone grafts and bone substitutes—tools and techniques. I. A 20,000 case experience in maxillofacial and craniofacial surgery. Plast Reconstr Surg. 116(Suppl): 6S, 2005.
Tessier P, Woillez M, Rougier J, et al: Maxillomalar fractures. In Wolfe SA (trans): Plastic Surgery of the Orbit and Eyelids. Chicago, Year Book, 1981, pp 42–57.
Wolfe SA: Treatment of post-traumatic orbital deformities. Clin Plast Surg 15:225–238, 1988.
Wolfe SA, Baker S: Facial Fractures. New York, Theme, 1993.
Wolfe SA, Berkowitz S: Autogenous bone grafts versus alloplastic material. In: Plastic Surgery of the Facial Skeleton. Boston, Little, Brown, 1989, pp 25–38.
Wolfe SA, Berkowitz S: Maxilla. In: Plastic Surgery of the Facial Skeleton. Boston, Little, Brown, 1989, pp 227–290.

FRACTURES OF THE MANDIBLE

49 CHAPTER

Robert J. Paresi, Jr, MD, MPH; William J. Martin, MD;
Alvaro A. Figueroa, DDS, MS; and John W. Polley, MD

1. What is the anatomy of the mandible?
The mandible is the largest and strongest of the facial bones. It consists of a basal bone and three processes. The basal bone extends from the symphysis at the chin to the lateral condyles on each side. In addition, it contains a horizontal portion, the body, and two perpendicular portions, the rami, which join the body at nearly right angles. The processes include the alveolar process, to which the teeth are attached; the coronoid process, to which the temporalis is attached; and the angle, to which the masseter and medial pterygoid muscles attach. The temporomandibular joint (TMJ) is a hinge joint to which the transverse head of the lateral pterygoid muscle attaches (Fig. 49-1).

2. What are the five *P*s of mandible fractures?
1. *Panorex:* Panoramic roentgenography produces a survey of the tooth-bearing portions of the maxilla and mandible. This information can be used to evaluate the fracture sites, position of the fragments, and postoperative healing. (Computed tomographic [CT] imaging of the mandible has largely replaced Panorex at many institutions.)
2. *Penicillin:* Drug of choice to combat the constant percolation of oral microorganisms. This, coupled with the continuous disruption of vascular ingrowth and osteolysis, is the most common and predictable source of fracture infection. The microorganisms most often encountered in the oral cavity are streptococci and *Bacteroides* sp.
3. *Peridex:* Peridex is an oral rinse containing 0.12% chlorhexidine gluconate. Approximately 30% of the antimicrobial active ingredient is retained after rinsing. The retained drug is then slowly released in oral fluids.
4. *Preoperative Workup:* The physician who first examines a patient with a mandibular injury should examine all of the soft tissues thoroughly, evaluate the current status of dental hygiene, examine the teeth for evidence of trauma (chipped, mobile, displaced), evaluate the mandible for discontinuity with a bimanual examination, and look for ecchymosis in the floor of the mouth. Deviations in mandibular movements and malocclusion are the sine qua non of mandible fractures.
5. *Postoperative Instructions:* Emphasize vigorous oral hygiene, oral antibiotics, mechanical soft diet, and the importance of follow-up examinations.

3. List the clinical signs that may be associated with mandibular fractures.
- Changes in occlusion
- Changes in mandibular excursions: Limited opening, deviation
- Step in occlusion
- Ecchymosis of the floor of the mouth, mucosa, or skin
- Soft tissue bleeding
- Soft tissue swelling
- Palpable fracture line
- Crepitation on manual palpation
- Sensory disturbances
- Trismus
- TMJ disorders

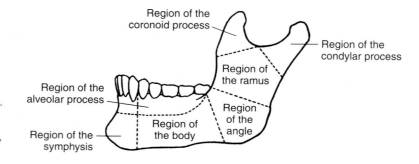

Figure 49-1. Regions of the mandible. (From Manson PN: Facial injuries. In McCarthy JG [ed]: Plastic Surgery. Philadelphia, WB Saunders, 1990, p 931, with permission.)

4. **Why does ecchymosis occur in the floor of the mouth in mandible fractures?**
   Bleeding caused by the fracture is trapped by the fanlike attachment of the mylohyoid musculature to the mandible. This condition presents clinically as ecchymosis in the floor of the mouth.

5. **What percentage of mandibular fractures are multiple?**
   More than 50% of mandible fractures are multiple. For this reason, if one fracture is noted along the jaw, the patient should be examined closely for evidence of additional fractures. Radiographic films must be scrutinized carefully for discrete fracture lines.

6. **What percentage of patients with mandibular fractures present with concomitant cervical spine injuries?**
   Associated injuries are present in 43% of all patients with mandibular fracture, most of whom were involved in vehicular accidents. Cervical spine fractures were found in 11% of this group of patients. It is imperative to rule out cervical spine injury, especially in patients who are intoxicated or unconscious. Posteroanterior and lateral films should be reviewed with the radiologist before treatment is initiated.

7. **Describe the biomechanical response of the mandible to trauma.**
   The two principal components involved in fractures of the mandible are the dynamic factor (blow) and static factor (jaw). The most common causes are altercations (47.5%) and automobile accidents (27.3%). The location, intensity, duration, and direction of the traumatizing force, with respect to the physical properties of the mandible, influence its biomechanical response. The condylar region of the mandible has the smallest cross-sectional area and the least ability to bend of any region of the mandible. Force applied to the chin shows a high frequency of condylar neck fractures (72%). A severe force can push the condylar fragments out of the glenoid fossa. Body and angle fractures usually result from direct impact over these regions and are more often unilateral. Angle fractures are often associated with a parasymphyseal fracture on the contralateral side. The dynamic factor is characterized by the intensity of the blow, its duration, and its direction. Whereas a light blow may cause a greenstick fracture, a heavy blow may cause a compound, comminuted fracture. The direction of the force largely determines the location of the fracture.

8. **What is the concept of favorable and unfavorable fractures?**
   A fracture is classified as *favorable* when the direction of the line of the fracture does not allow independent muscular distractions. An *unfavorable* fracture occurs when the line of fracture permits the fragments to separate. The four muscles of mastication are the temporalis, masseter, and medial and lateral pterygoids. These muscles exert their forces on the mandibular fragments after fracture, leading to malocclusion. At the mandibular angle, the posterior fragment is elevated and drawn forward by the action of the medial pterygoid and masseter muscles. The unfavorable oblique fracture is caused when the line of fracture runs from anterosuperior to posteroinferior. However, if the inferior border fracture occurs further anteriorly and the line of fracture extends in a distal direction toward the ridge, a favorable fracture is seen. The angle of the anteroinferior portion locks the posterior fragment mechanically to withstand upward muscular pull. Most angle fractures are horizontally unfavorable fractures. Medial displacement may be considered in a similar fashion. Oblique fracture lines can form a large buccal cortical fragment that prevents medial displacement. A bird's eye view reveals that a vertically unfavorable fracture line extends from a posterolateral point to an anteromedial point. No obstruction counters the action of the lateral pterygoid and mylohyoid muscles, and the posterior fragment is shifted medially. The forces of the lateral pterygoid muscle frequently result in anterior and medial displacement of the condyle in the presence of a subcondylar fracture. A vertically favorable fracture extends from an anterolateral to a posteromedial point (Fig. 49-2).

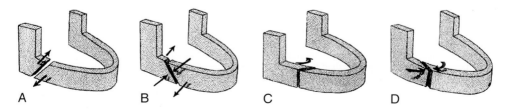

A   B   C   D

Figure 49-2. Favorable versus unfavorable fractures. **A,** Horizontally unfavorable fractures extend downward and posteriorly. **B,** Horizontally favorable fractures extend downward and forward. **C,** Vertically unfavorable fractures extend forward and medially. **D,** Vertically favorable fractures extend from the lateral surface of the mandible posteriorly and medially. *Arrows* indicate the direction of muscle pull. With unfavorable fractures, the direction and bevel of the fracture line do not resist displacement by muscular action. With favorable fractures, the bevel and fracture line resist displacement and oppose muscular action. Fractures beveled in this direction tend to impact the fractured bone ends. (From Manson PN: Facial injuries. In McCarthy JG [ed]: Plastic Surgery. Philadelphia, WB Saunders, 1990, p 940, with permission.)

9. How is the interocclusal distance measured?

The interocclusal distance is measured as the distance between the incisal edges of the maxillary and mandibular central incisors at the midline. Normal interocclusal distance is approximately 3 to 4.5 mm.

10. Why is Angle classification of malocclusion so important?

Edward Angle, who presented his classification of dental malocclusion in 1898, recognized that facial balance was ideal when the midfacial position was in a harmonious relationship to the mandible. Angle noted that the most pleasing facial profile occurred when the supraorbital ridge, subnasal area, lower lip, and chin fall on a straight line. The engraving made by Angle illustrated how the normal occlusal relationships between the maxilla and mandible resulted in this profile.

11. How is malocclusion classified?

Normal occlusion occurs when the mesiobuccal cusp of the upper first molar is received in the buccal groove of the lower first molar (Angle class I occlusion). An Angle class II malocclusion exists when the lower molars are displaced distally so that the mesiobuccal developmental groove fits under the distal cusp of the upper first molar or even further back, giving the profile of the classic retrognathic appearance. The Angle class III malocclusion is characterized by mandibular prognathism. The lower dental arch is carried forward so that the mesiobuccal developmental groove of the lower molar may be under the upper second bicuspid or even the first.

12. Does mixed dentition play a role in mandible fractures?

The mixed dentition stage is the age at which both deciduous and secondary teeth have erupted in the oral cavity. With children, fractures of the mandible are complicated by the presence of mixed dentition with teeth in various stages of eruption; thus the malocclusion cannot be easily evaluated. It should be emphasized that developing tooth buds may react in many unfavorable ways after disturbance. Roentgenograms may be misleading when undisplaced fractures are covered by developing tooth buds. Primary teeth lend themselves to wiring procedures for stabilization; however, only a few teeth may be present for attachment of fixation.

13. How do pediatric mandibular fractures differ from adult mandibular fractures?

Mandibular fractures are far less common in children than in adults. Greenstick fractures of the mandible, particularly in the condylar region, are relatively common in children. The increased ossification capability of the juvenile periosteum allows faster healing and distinguishes it from the adult mandible. As a result, many mandible fractures in children can be treated with immobilization for a short period. Direct osteosynthesis is reserved for displaced fractures. Problems with osteosynthesis in children include the need to avoid damage to developing tooth buds.

14. What is intermaxillary fixation?

Intermaxillary fixation (IMF) refers to an era when the mandible was known as the inferior maxilla. Current terminology includes maxillomandibular fixation (MMF), IMF, and interdental fixation (which is used in the Current Procedural Terminology coding system). IMF is obtained by applying wires or elastic bands between the upper and lower jaws to which suitable anchoring devices can be attached. Arch bars are a common method for obtaining IMF. The application of IMF screws is another commonly used method.

15. What is the basic sequence of treatment in mandibular fractures?

1. Establishment of dental occlusion
2. Exposure of fracture site
3. Reduction of fracture—closed or open
4. Rigid internal fixation, if needed

16. What is the spherical sliding principle in rigid osteosynthesis of mandible fractures?

Dynamic and eccentric compression plates create interfragmental pressure by the *spherical sliding principle*. The practical application of this principle is based on clinical and experimental evidence that bone fragments immobilized with interfragmental pressure greater than the forces tending to displace the fragments will mend by primary bone healing without callus formation. In the technique of rigid fixation with a compression plate, the vertical movement of the screw is changed to a horizontal compression force vector as the screw head follows the incline of the screw hole. Thus the fragments are reapproximated with interfragmental pressure as the screw head is tightened.

17. What are the concepts of "zone of compression" and "zone of tension" in the treatment of mandible fractures with internal fixation?

The mandible is subjected to forces created by the muscles of mastication and reaction forces applied to the TMJs and the teeth. These forces create zones of stress within the mandibular fragments after fracture. The zones of stress can be classified as either compressive or tensile. In the *zone of compression*, the forces on the fracture site are such that the fragments are brought together. In the *zone of tension*, the forces on the fracture site are such that the fragments are pulled apart. Using the straight cantilever model, stresses on the upper border of the mandible are tensile whereas stresses on the lower border of the mandible are compressive. To avoid the separation of fracture fragments at the zone of tension, frequently located at the alveolar border, placement of a tension band is necessary. This can take the form of arch bars, dental splints, or osteosynthesis plates. Compression plates then can be placed on the inferior border of the mandible corresponding to the zone of compression. More recent three-dimensional models have demonstrated that the biomechanical forces on the mandible are more accurately demonstrated with a suspended beam model rather than the cantilever model.

18. What is the incidence of fractures in the different areas of the adult mandible?
- Angle: 31%
- Condyle: 18%
- Molar region: 15%
- Mental region: 14%
- Symphysis: 8%
- Cuspid: 7%
- Ramus: 6%
- Coronoid process: 1%

19. What complications are associated with repair of mandibular fractures?
Infection, malocclusion, tooth injury, delayed union, nonunion (pseudoarthrosis), osteomyelitis, inferior alveolar, and facial nerve injury. Of these, infection is one of the most problematic; it is the most frequent complication and is an important cause of nonunion.

20. What risk factors increase the possibility of infection with mandibular fractures?
Infected mandibular fractures are encountered in patients who sustain facial trauma and fail to seek immediate treatment. Mucosal tears and fractures extending through the periodontal ligament produce contamination of the fracture by oral flora. Therefore fractures that occur through the tooth-bearing area should be regarded as contaminated. Soft tissue injury also has been shown to be a key factor in infection rates. Bony sequestra, devitalized teeth, and hematoma also contribute to infection. Movement at the fracture site due to loose, mobile hardware, such as a loose screw in an otherwise stable plate, may cause infection in the presence of bacterial contamination. Poor oral hygiene is a major key to infection.

21. What role does dentition play in mandibular fractures?
The body of the mandible (molar, mental, cuspid regions) is involved frequently in mandible fractures (36%) because of the lines of trajectory that pass along the longitudinal axis of the teeth. Several factors influence the location of mandible fractures, including site, force, direction of impact, and presence of impacted teeth. When a force is distributed to the mandible, the mandible fractures at its weakest point. The weakest points are at the angle of the mandible (third molar) and the canine region (tooth length 26 mm).

22. What treatments are ideal for symphyseal and parasymphyseal fractures?
Wire osteosynthesis alone may not provide rotational stability; thus symphyseal and parasymphyseal fractures should be treated with compression plates. In addition, the bilateral posterior and lateral pull exerted by the mylohyoid and digastric muscles contributes to displacement of the fragments. Once MMF is obtained, the incision in the mucosa is made deep into the labial–alveolar sulcus, taking care to leave sufficient attached gingival mucosa to enable closure without tension. The mandible is degloved, taking the utmost care not to injure the mental nerve. The bone fragments are then reduced with bone forceps and secured, if necessary. Next a compression plate is contoured to the mandible, and two screws are placed on each side of the bony plate to ensure compression and stability.

23. What techniques are used for fractures of the condyles?
Condylar process fractures are common (18%) and are classified by fracture level, anatomic displacement, and position of the condyle. Generally, they are treated by MMF alone. Immobilization usually ranges from 2 to 4 weeks for isolated fractures. Duration depends on type of dentition, level of the condylar fracture, degree of dislocation of the condylar head, and presence of other fractures. Condylar fractures differ from mandibular body fractures in that MMF is of shorter duration to prevent pathologic changes in the TMJ. MMF may not be needed for unilateral condylar fractures in edentulous patients because small occlusal discrepancies can be corrected on renewal of the dentures.

24. What muscle is primarily responsible for condylar displacement in patients with a subcondylar fracture?
The lateral pterygoid is the only muscle that inserts directly on the neck of the mandibular condyle. The forces of this muscle frequently result in anterior and medial displacement of the condyle in the presence of a subcondylar fracture.

25. What are the indications for open reduction internal fixation of condylar fractures?

- Displacement into the middle cranial fossa
- Presence of foreign body thought to require removal (gunshot pellets)
- Inability to obtain preinjury occlusion by closed reduction or awake manipulation
- Extracapsular lateral displacement of the condylar fragment
- Severe angulation of the condyle
- Condyle outside the glenoid fossa

26. How do you repair edentulous mandible fractures?

Occlusion cannot be achieved because of the lack of teeth for fixation and alveolar ridge atrophy. If wearable dentures are present, the mandible may be effectively fixed by the application of circumdental wires. Splints or fabricated acrylic saddles may ensure reduction and stabilization. Edentulous mandibular fractures may be good candidates for open procedures. Advantages include direct visualization, excellent stability of the fixed segments, early return of masticatory function, and stimulation of osteogenesis by the use of compressive forces. Open procedures also reduce the incidence of injury to the inferior alveolar nerve, located at the superior border of the atrophic mandible. Conservative periosteal stripping is paramount. Two-plate internal fixation is advisable. Lag screws also can be used for edentulous fractures. Generally, they are best suited for fractures of the symphyseal region, where both the buccal and lingual cortices can be engaged.

27. Before the application of MMF, how do you establish a patient's pretraumatic occlusion?

Occlusal wear facets occur because of the constant action of the tooth cusps rubbing across one another. Occlusal wear patterns on the teeth should be noted because they relate to the normal movement of the mandible. By lining up the coinciding wear facets of the interdigitating maxillary and mandibular teeth for MMF, the surgeon can estimate the patient's normal occlusion.

28. What are the indications for removal of teeth involved in fracture lines in the mandible?

- Severe loosening of the tooth with chronic periodontal disease
- Fracture of the root of the tooth
- Extensive periodontal injury and broken alveolar walls
- Displacement of teeth from their alveolar socket.

BIBLIOGRAPHY

Anderson T, Alpert B: Experience with rigid fixation of mandibular fractures and immediate function. J Oral Maxillofac Surg 50:555–560, 1992.
Angle EH: Treatment of Malocclusion of the Teeth and Fractures of the Maxillae: Angle's System. Philadelphia, SS White Dental Manufacturing, 1898.
Angle EH: Treatment of Malocclusion of the Teeth: Angle's System, 7th ed. Philadelphia, SS White Dental Manufacturing, 1907.
Bertz JE: Maxillofacial injuries. Clin Symp 33:1–32, 1981.
Buchbinder B: Treatment of fractures of the edentulous mandible. 1943 to 1993: A review of the literature. J Oral Maxillofac Surg 51:1174–1180, 1993.
Calloway DM, Anton MA, Jacobs JS: Changing concepts and controversies in the management of mandibular fractures. Clin Plast Surg 19:67–68, 1992.
DuBrul EL: Sicher's Oral Anatomy, 7th ed. St. Louis, Mosby, 1980.
Ellis E, Walker LR: Treatment of mandibular angle fractures using one noncompression miniplate. J Oral Maxillofac Surg 54:864–871, 1996.
Fernandez JA, Mathog RH: Open treatment of mandible fractures with biphase technique. Arch Otolaryngol Head Neck Surg 113:262–266, 1987.
Fridrich KL, Pena-Velasco G, Olson RAJ: Changing trends with mandibular fractures: A review of 1,067 cases. J Oral Maxillofac Surg 50:586–589, 1992.
Gateno J: Basic principles in the treatment of mandibular fractures. In Stewart MG (ed): Head, Face, and Neck Trauma: Comprehensive Management. New York, Thieme, 2005, pp 83–116.
Gerald N, D'Innocenzo R: Modified technique for adapting a mandibular angle superior border plate. J Oral Maxillofac Surg 53:220–221, 1995.
Greenberg SA, Jacobs JS, Bessette RW: Temporomandibular joint dysfunction: Evaluation and treatment. Clin Plast Surg 16:707–724, 1989.
Howard P, Wolfe SA: Fractures of the mandible. Ann Plast Surg 17:391–407, 1986.
Johansson B, Krekmanov L, Shomsson M: Miniplate osteosynthesis of infected mandibular fractures. J Craniomaxillofac Surg 16:22–27, 1988.
Kerr NW: Some observations on infection in maxillo-facial fractures. Br J Oral Surg 4:132–136, 1966.
Koury M, Ellis III E: Rigid internal fixation for the treatment of infected mandibular fractures. J Oral Maxillofac Surg 50:434–443, 1992.
Kruger GO (ed): Textbook of Oral and Maxillofacial Surgery, 5th ed. St. Louis, Mosby, 1979.
Manson PN: Facial injuries. In McCarthy JG (ed): Plastic Surgery. Philadelphia, WB Saunders, 1990, pp 1032–1059.
McDonald RE, Avery DR: Dentistry for the Child and Adolescent, 3rd ed. St. Louis, Mosby, 1978.
Oikarinen KS: Clinical management of injuries to the maxilla, mandible, and alveolus. Dent Clin North Am 39:113–130, 1995.
Reynolds FC, Zaepfel F: Management of chronic osteomyelitis secondary to compound fractures. J Bone Joint Surg 30A:331–338, 1948.
Rittmann WW, Perren SM: Cortical Bone Healing After Internal Fixation and Infection. New York, Springer Verlag, 1974.

Strelzow VV, Strelzow AG: Osteosynthesis of mandible fractures in the angle region. Arch Otolaryngol 109:403–406, 1983.

Tevepaugh DB, Dodson TB: Are mandibular third molars a risk factor for angle fractures? A retrospective cohort study. J Oral Maxillofac Surg 53:646–649, 1995.

Theriot BA, Van Sickels JE, Triplett RG, Nishioka GJ: Intraosseous wire fixation versus rigid osseous fixation of mandible fractures: A preliminary report. J Oral Maxillofac Surg 45:577–582, 1987.

Weinberg S: Surgical correction of facial fractures. Dent Clin North Am 26:631–658, 1982.

50 CHAPTER

MANAGEMENT OF PANFACIAL FRACTURES

Steven R. Buchman, MD, and
Christi M. Cavaliere, MD

1. What is a panfacial fracture?

A panfacial fracture involves injury to the facial skeleton with fractures located in the upper, middle, and lower face. The upper face is made up of the frontal bone, including the frontal sinus. Fractures of the midface are located between the zygomaticofrontal suture and the maxillary occlusal plane, including fractures of the orbits, zygomatic bones, nasoorbitoethmoidal complex, and maxilla. Injury to the lower face consists of fractures of the mandible.

2. Describe the mechanisms of injury necessary to produce panfacial fractures.

High-energy injuries, such as motor vehicle crashes, falls from a significant height, aggressive interpersonal violence, and other blunt forces, result in panfacial fractures. A gunshot wound produces an extreme form of panfacial fracture. Because of the energy necessary to produce a panfacial fracture, extensive comminution, soft tissue damage or loss, globe injury, brain injury, carotid injury, and other life-threatening conditions may result.

3. What are the main support structures in the facial skeleton, and how do they relate to panfacial fractures?

The craniofacial skeleton contains vertical and horizontal buttresses that provide structural support and resistance to external deforming forces. Vertical support includes the zygomaticomaxillary, pterygomaxillary, and nasofrontal buttresses. Horizontal buttresses include the frontal bar, infraorbital rims, zygomatic arches, and basal portion of the mandible. The relative lack of sagittal support in the central midface makes this region particularly prone to comminuted fractures with collapse and loss of projection.

Fracture of a single buttress makes realignment of the craniofacial skeleton fairly straightforward because the remaining intact buttresses maintain facial height, width, and projection. However, the patient with panfacial fractures typically presents with multiple comminuted fractures of the buttresses; therefore, little frame of reference exists for reconstruction in any dimension. Severe comminution or loss of bone may preclude reduction and fixation of a buttress with plates and screws alone. Grafting with cortical bone from the calvarium or rib may be necessary and should be considered during preoperative planning.

4. Discuss the types of imaging studies available for the diagnosis and treatment of panfacial fractures.

Plain Radiographs: A facial series including at least four views of the skull previously was considered the standard of care for maxillofacial imaging. Today, plain radiographs of the skull have limited utility in the management of panfacial fractures but may be useful as a screening modality in patients with minor maxillofacial injuries. In the patient with panfacial fractures, plain radiographs may aid in defining the spatial relationship of fracture fragments, the degree of comminution, and the location of foreign bodies. A mandibular series also may be of benefit, often complementing other imaging studies.

A Panorex is extremely valuable in the diagnosis and treatment of mandible fractures. To obtain a Panorex, the patient must be able to sit upright, so the study may be unavailable in the setting of potential spine injury or other serious injuries.

Computed Tomographic Scan: With improvements in imaging techniques, maxillofacial computed tomographic (CT) scanning has become the standard of care for significant facial trauma. Advantages of CT scanning include detailed visualization of the brain along with osseous and soft tissue structures of the craniofacial region. Image format can include axial, coronal, and sagittal views to define anatomic structure in great detail. Three-dimensional reformatting may be useful for complex deformities and in planning reconstructive procedures. Coronal images are quite valuable and provide detailed views of the mandibular condyles and orbital floors as well as the extraocular muscles and globes, which are not as well defined with other imaging techniques. Of note, the axial portion of the scan usually contains the images with the highest resolution. Coronal images can be obtained directly during the scan or they can be digitally reformatted from the axial data. Reformatted images often have a grainy quality due to lower resolution, making the scan less sensitive for the detection of subtle abnormalities. Coronal imaging may require positioning the patient with the neck extended and therefore may not be possible in the setting of a potential cervical spine injury. With the patient on a backboard, tilting the board may facilitate adequate positioning to obtain formal coronal CT images. Even with high-resolution CT scanning, some fractures may be difficult to detect, including fractures of the pterygoid plates, certain portions of the mandible, and nondisplaced fractures. Imaging studies always remain an adjunct to physical examination.

Magnetic Resonance Imaging: Magnetic resonance imaging (MRI) may provide further detailed imaging of cerebral parenchymal or vascular lesions, but its role in the setting of acute trauma is limited. MRI scanning is costly, and the scan itself takes a longer period of time to obtain than a CT. MRI typically is not as useful as CT scanning for evaluation of bony structures. For workup of potential vascular injury, angiography remains the standard of care.

5. What is the optimal timing for repair of panfacial fractures?

Whenever possible, facial fractures are optimally treated within the first few days after injury. Severe facial trauma often occurs in the setting of other life-threatening injuries that must be addressed first. Definitive intervention may be delayed for up to 2 weeks but is not generally advisable because early soft tissue scarring and callus formation make adequate reduction more challenging. Over time, the facial soft tissue envelope contracts and becomes less pliable. The skin and soft tissues then are more difficult to redrape over the reconstructed facial skeleton, potentially compromising the ability to achieve an excellent or even an adequate result.

6. Explain the preoperative planning necessary for successful treatment of panfacial fractures.

Treatment of panfacial fractures requires thorough preoperative planning. Fractures must be identified and assessed for displacement, comminution, and bone loss. Careful physical examination is necessary to determine whether a mildly displaced fracture is causing functional or aesthetic deformation. A maxillofacial CT scan along with a Panorex are often the only necessary imaging studies. For extremely severe injuries, three-dimensional images may demonstrate loss of projection, segmental bone loss, and bony distortion more clearly than two-dimensional images. The potential need for bone grafting should be assessed preoperatively and discussed with the patient. Soft tissue coverage may be problematic with severe crush injury or gunshot wounds. Options for flap coverage should be reviewed before proceeding to the operating room. Fractures of the maxilla and mandible can make establishment of baseline occlusion difficult; therefore dental impressions and splints made preoperatively may save valuable time. If intraoperative dental impressions or splints may be necessary, additional assistance should be recruited ahead of time and the impressions taken early during the case. Preoperative evaluation by other consulting services, including ophthalmology, neurosurgery, prosthodontics, dentistry, and general surgery, may reduce the need for intraoperative consultation and allow for performance of additional complementary procedures in a combined fashion.

7. What soft tissue considerations are necessary in the management of panfacial fractures?

Panfacial fractures result from high-energy injuries; therefore, the possibility of significant soft tissue damage or tissue loss is much greater than with lower-energy, isolated facial fractures. In the acute setting, determining whether an area of soft tissue is viable can be difficult. An initial washout followed by formal operative débridement in 24 to 48 hours allows the soft tissue adequate time to declare viability. The soft tissue must be thoroughly inspected and any clearly nonviable tissue removed, including scalp, facial skin, and mucosa. In the event of severe tissue crush or extensive contamination, serial débridement may be necessary. Primary closure of skin defects is desirable whenever feasible without distortion. Local flaps typically are the next best option because they allow tissue to be replaced with nearby tissue of similar thickness, color, and texture. Regional and distant flaps or microvascular free tissue transfer occasionally are necessary for optimal reconstruction. Mucosal areas or raw intraoral surfaces will granulate and heal by secondary intention and may not require further intervention. The facial soft tissue envelope rapidly contracts if the underlying bone volume decreases, so definitive reconstruction should be pursued early to allow optimal soft tissue redraping.

8. What sequence is used in the surgical approach to panfacial fractures?

Several sequences of fracture repair have been described, including top to bottom, bottom to top, lateral to medial, etc. Regardless of sequence, repair begins with exposure of the fracture sites and débridement of any nonviable bone or soft tissue. Clean bone fragments can be saved and used for bone grafting later in the procedure. Areas of stable bone should be determined because they will be used as the starting point for reduction and fixation of unstable bone.

One of the most useful sequences for severe injuries includes beginning with restoration of the maxillary and mandibular arches. With severe disruption of the arches, dental impressions are taken and models prepared. The models then are cut and used to re-create the occlusal relationship. Palatal and/or lingual splints can be created and placed to guide fracture reduction and maxillomandibular fixation. Gunning splints are prepared for the edentulous patient. Mandible fractures then are plated, including body, angle, ramus, and subcondylar fractures. The upper face is addressed next. Skull fractures are treated, followed by treatment of frontal sinus fractures. Upper facial width is addressed through reduction and fixation of the nasoorbitoethmoidal complex. Orbital exploration may reveal fractures of the orbital floor or medial wall. Repair continues with reconstruction of the zygomatic complex, which is necessary for restoration of facial width. Bone grafts are placed in areas of missing bone or areas requiring additional rigid

Table 50-1. Incisions for Rigid Fixation in the Craniofacial Skeleton

INCISION	STRUCTURES EXPOSED
Coronal	Frontal, nasoethmoidal, upper three fourths of orbit, nasal root, zygomatic arch, cranial bone for harvest
Upper lid	Frontozygomatic suture, lateral orbital rim
Transconjunctival with lateral canthotomy Subciliary Subtarsal/mid-lid	Inferior orbital rim, orbital floor
Maxillary gingivobuccal sulcus	Maxilla, midfacial buttresses
Mandibular gingivobuccal sulcus	Anterior mandible, may visualize up to sigmoid notch
Preauricular/retromandibular	Ascending ramus, mandibular condyle
Existing laceration	Direct access to underlying structures

support. Finally, midface reconstruction is carried out with anatomic reduction of the remainder of the midface, including restoration of buttress support. The maxilla is positioned and aligned at first with the reconstructed mandibular arch and placed in maxillomandibular fixation. Appropriate repositioning of a free-floating reconstructed maxilla is performed by autorotating the maxillomandibular complex to the correct midfacial height.

9. **List the types of incisions that provide access for rigid fixation in the craniofacial skeleton.**
   See Table 50-1.

10. **What types of fixation are available for treatment of maxillofacial fractures?**
    Rigid fixation with biocompatible plates and screws evolved from earlier fixation methods including interosseous wiring. Wiring does not prevent rotation of bone fragments; therefore, satisfactory reduction and fixation often are difficult to achieve. Current plating systems include metal alloys (e.g., titanium alloys and Vitallium) that are strong but remain sufficiently malleable to allow bending of the plates to conform to bony contour. For maxillary fractures, plates typically are 0.7 to 1 mm thick and are used with 2-mm diameter screws. Lower-profile plates are available for areas of the facial skeleton with thin skin, such as the nasal dorsum. Fixation of mandibular fractures can be achieved with plates 1.25 to 3.2 mm thick and 2.3- to 2.7-mm diameter screws. Mandibular reconstruction plates can be used to span segmental defects or areas of severe comminution. A reconstruction plate stabilizes the mandible and helps prevent collapse of the soft tissue envelope. Absorbable plates and screws have limited application in the management of panfacial fractures. External fixation can be used to stabilize fractures, primarily in the setting of severe contamination or following removal of infected hardware.

11. **Describe the types of splints that may be useful in the management of panfacial fractures.**
    Splints may provide additional support following bone and soft tissue repair. *Occlusal splints* are used for alignment of the maxillary and/or mandibular arches. *Nasal trumpets* can be used to maintain patency of the nasal airway in the setting of soft tissue injury and repair. *External nasal splints* give added protection following reduction of nasal fractures. A *prosthesis* can be fabricated to act as a spacer, especially in the setting of bone loss. For example, a self-inflicted gunshot wound to the face frequently produces loss of a portion of the maxilla and midface not readily amenable to free bone grafting. A prosthetic spacer can be placed to prevent contraction of the soft tissue and to maintain facial height, allowing more definitive reconstruction in the future. Such future reconstruction may include free flaps, permanent prosthesis, and osteointegrated implants.

12. **What long-term deformities are potential undesirable outcomes of panfacial fractures?**
    Following severe injury and reconstruction of the facial skeleton, long-term deformity may result from incorrect diagnosis, inadequate fracture exposure or reduction, lack of rigid fracture stabilization and buttress reconstruction, and contraction of the soft tissue envelope. Unsatisfactory results typically include increased facial width due to flattening of the zygomatic complexes, widening of the nasoorbitoethmoidal region, and lateral migration of the mandibular angles. Decreased facial height and loss of projection may reciprocally occur, resulting in a "dish face" deformity. A long face-type deformity may occur with maxillary fractures complicated by downward migration of the maxilla. If the fracture is inadequately reduced, the face may take on an elongated appearance.

13. **What functional problems may persist even after satisfactory treatment of panfacial fractures?**
    Long-term functional problems frequently occur even after treatment of facial fractures. Problems include diplopia or other visual disturbances, enophthalmos, ectropion, abnormal breathing due to disruption of the nasal or oral airway, malocclusion, temporomandibular joint dysfunction, difficulties with mastication, and impaired speech.

14. Discuss the role of tracheotomy in the management of patients with panfacial fractures.

The patient with panfacial fractures frequently sustains multisystem injury and may undergo tracheotomy due to inability to protect the airway or anticipated need for prolonged mechanical ventilation. In this subset of patients, the decision to perform a tracheotomy often is independent of the patient's facial fractures. Airway management in patients with panfacial fractures depends on the severity of the fractures and the ability to obtain satisfactory rigid fixation. If a patient does not need maxillomandibular fixation to establish occlusion, an oral airway may be sufficient. For edentulous patients, maxillomandibular fixation with Gunning splints or dentures can be performed with a space cut out of the central denture or splint. The space can accommodate an oral airway, so tracheotomy may not be necessary. An oral airway cannot be used in fully dentate patients requiring maxillomandibular fixation. Nasal intubation may be an option; however, the nasal airway will make a coronal approach more difficult and is often a necessary approach for panfacial fracture management. Severe midfacial injuries, including nasal and nasoorbitoethmoidal fractures, are difficult to address with a nasal airway in place. Management of severe panfacial fractures usually involves tracheotomy for intraoperative airway management as well as postoperative airway protection.

BIBLIOGRAPHY

Farinas CA, Diaz-Daza O, Diaz-Marchan PJ: Diagnostic imaging in head and neck trauma. In Stewart MG (ed): Head, Face, and Neck Trauma Comprehensive Management. New York, Thieme, 2005, pp 9–15.

Girotto JA, MacKenzie E, Fowler C, et al: Long-term physical impairment and functional outcomes after complex facial fractures. Plast Reconstr Surg 108:312–327, 2001.

Manson PN, Hoopes JE, Su CT: Structural pillars of the facial skeleton: An approach to the management of Le Fort fractures. Plast Reconstr Surg 66:54–62, 1980.

Marchena JM, Johnson JV: Le Fort and palatal fractures. In Stewart MG (ed): Head, Face, and Neck Trauma Comprehensive Management. New York, Thieme, 2005, pp 77–85.

Markowitz BL, Manson PN: Panfacial fractures: Organization and treatment. Clin Plast Surg 16:105–114, 1989.

McGraw-Wall B: Sequencing in facial fracture repair. In Stewart MG (ed): Head, Face, and Neck Trauma Comprehensive Management. New York, Thieme, 2005, pp 142–149.

Wolfe SA, Baker S: Operative techniques in plastic surgery. In Goin JM (ed): Facial Fractures. New York, Thieme, 1993.

1. What is enophthalmos?

Enophthalmos can be defined as a retrodisplacement of the globe within the bony confines of the eye socket. It is characterized by increased depth and hollowing of the supratarsal fold, decreased anterior projection of the globe, shortening of the horizontal dimension of the palpebral fissure, pseudoptosis of the upper lid, and a decrease in the canthal angles. Enophthalmos becomes clinically obvious if the anterior globe projection is less than 12 mm or differs from the opposite side by 3 mm or more as measured by a Hertel exophthalmometer. The Hertel exophthalmometer uses the lateral orbital rim as a reference point. As such, if enophthalmos is associated with a displaced and healed orbitozygomatic complex (OZC) fracture, this method of assessment may not be valid due to the malposition of the lateral orbital wall.

2. How does posttraumatic enophthalmos occur?

The major cause of posttraumatic enophthalmos is a volumetric enlargement of the bony orbit. The factors that contribute to the development of posttraumatic enophthalmos are as follows:

- Escape of orbital fat
- Retention of the globe in a recessed position due to entrapment
- Fat necrosis
- Scar contraction
- Changes in the connective tissue septal support network
- Enlarged bony orbital volume
- Change in shape of the orbital contents from a conical to a spherical shape

Several studies have focused on the amount of orbital volume expansion resulting from displacement of fracture fragments. An isolated floor displacement of 7 mm resulted in a volume increase of 12%. A 7-mm displacement of the lateral wall resulted in a volume increase of 16%. A similar 7-mm displacement of the medial wall caused a 20% volume increase. Orbital roof defects with a rim fracture increased orbital volume by 38%. The volume differences doubled when the fracture was associated with a corresponding rim fracture.

The main cause for the development of posttraumatic enophthalmos is bony orbital expansion. Failure to restore the normal orbital volume either by not recognizing all the ledges of the defect or by inadequate surgical reconstruction results in the majority of cases of posttraumatic postsurgical enophthalmos. Specifically, failure to identify the posterior bony ledge or to recognize defects in the posterior inferomedial aspects of the orbit is the most common surgical mistake.

Another theoretical cause of enophthalmos include fat atrophy. Although this may occur in some cases of orbital fractures, several studies have demonstrated that fat atrophy is significant in only 10% of cases. Neurogenic theories of enophthalmos in which fat atrophy occurs secondary to sympathetic nerve disruption have been suggested but have no clinical relevance. Malposition of orbital fat from an intraconal position to a dislocated extraconal position has been postulated to produce loss of globe support and may contribute to enophthalmos.

Other soft tissue causes include dislocation of the trochlea and of the trochlea and the superior oblique muscle resulting in the globe being pulled back into the orbit. Long-standing entrapment of the inferior rectus muscle in an orbital floor blowout or trapdoor fracture may have the same effect. Scar contracture of the postbulbar soft tissue with disruption of the delicate orbital ligaments and fascial bands that support the globe may pull the globe backward.

3. What is the treatment of posttraumatic enophthalmos?

Restoration of normal orbital volume is the key to returning the globe to its normal position. Assessment includes a computed tomographic (CT) scan to determine the nature of the volume increase and to distinguish between defects of the orbital floor or medial wall with tissue herniation and an increase in orbital volume due to a displaced OZC fracture.

If the OZC is malpositioned, osteotomy and anatomic repositioning of the displaced OZC segment are necessary to restore normal orbital perimeters, followed by reconstruction of any floor or wall defects using alloplastic or autogenous materials. In the case of an isolated floor or medial wall missed fracture, replacement of intraorbital contents by surgical release and reconstruction of wall/floor defects is the preferred management for long-standing enophthalmos. This problem is difficult to solve surgically because of scar tissue and retraction of the supporting ligaments of the globe; it may require two or, in rare cases, more procedures. Often circumferential subperiosteal dissection may be required to mobilize the soft tissue contents of the orbit. Overcorrection of globe position by a few millimeters is recommended.

Multiple authors have commented on the difficulty of correcting established enophthalmos, with an average of at least two operations necessary to reestablish globe position. This underlies the importance of early primary and definitive repair in orbital fracture cases.

4. Does correction of established enophthalmos improve diplopia?

Posttraumatic diplopia may be classified depending on field of view affected (primary gaze vs secondary gaze) and may have a complex etiology. Extraorbital intracranial causes should be ruled out. Intraorbital nerve damage to the cranial nerves III, IV, and VI may be due to apical fractures, superior orbital fissure, or orbital apex syndrome. Direct damage to the extraocular muscles in the form of laceration, contusion, disruption of attachment, scarring, or compartment syndrome may occur. Finally, prolapse or incarceration of the periorbital tissue, delicate connective tissue support system, or rarely involving the extraocular muscle (in trapdoor fractures in children) may occur.

This is a difficult question to answer because of the lack of consensus on the matter. However, from the patients' point of view it is an important question to address because relief from diplopia may be the prime reason why patients consider surgical reconstruction.

A review of the literature reveals that in five studies examining the effects of late surgical reconstruction of orbital fractures, after correction of enophthalmos, between 50% (8/16) and 90% (10/11) of patients with preoperative diplopia had complete postoperative resolution of diplopia. However, in one study by Hammer and Prein, although 5 of 9 patients who underwent operation for late enophthalmos had improvement, no patients had complete resolution of preoperative diplopia. It is also important to recognize that worsening of preoperative diplopia was documented in 35% (6/21) of patients in a study of enophthalmos correction by Iliff.

The presentation of enophthalmos with diplopia should be investigated with CT orbital imaging and preoperative ophthalmologic assessment including visual fields. It is generally recommended that orbital reconstruction be the first step toward the resolution of diplopia, except in cases of mild (<3 mm) enophthalmos or diplopia in secondary fields of gaze. Following bony orbital reconstruction, residual symptoms of diplopia can be managed simply by prism or extraocular muscle surgery. Reassuring the patient that enophthalmos correction is a guarantee of diplopia resolution is not recommended.

5. What is telecanthus?

Telecanthus is a palpebral anomaly that can be defined as an increased distance between the medial canthi. It may be unilateral or bilateral. Isolated telecanthus is rare. It may be seen as a finding in blepharophimosis syndrome, canthus inversus, or Waardenburg syndrome in association with epicanthal folds and overlapping of the caruncles. Telecanthus is produced by an abnormal insertion or length of the medial canthal tendons. The distance between the inner canthi can be determined by the "rule of fifths," in which the face is divided sagittally into five equal parts between the two helices. Each of the fifths should be equivalent to the width of one eye (Fig. 51-1).

Telecanthus should be differentiated from hypertelorism (hypertelorbitism), which is an increased distance between the bony orbits taken at the region of the dacryon (lacrimal crest) and an associated increase in interpupillary distance. Tessier distinguished among varying severities of hypertelorism as first degree (30–34 mm interorbital distance [IOD]), second degree (35–40 mm IOD), and third degree (>40 mm IOD). Some believe that a distinction should be made between orbital hypertelorism in which there is true lateral displacement of the entire orbit and interorbital hypertelorism in which the distance between the medial walls is increased but there is no divergence of the orbital axes and lateral orbital walls (Fig. 51-2).

Traumatic telecanthus is the result of facial injuries due to either the medial canthal tendon being lacerated or avulsed from its bony attachments around the lacrimal crest or displacement of the nasoorbital component following a nasoorbitoethmoidal (NOE) fracture (Fig. 51-3). The medial canthus may be displaced as much as 30% of the normal palpebral width, and normal interpupillary distance may be maintained.

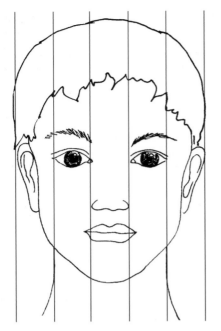

Figure 51-1. Image of a face divided vertically into equal fifths.

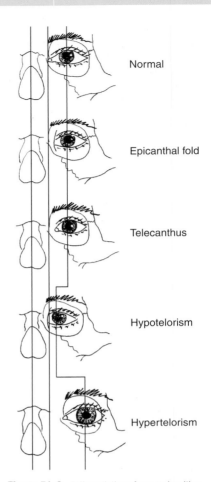

Normal

Epicanthal fold

Telecanthus

Hypotelorism

Hypertelorism

Figure 51-2. Differentiation of eye malposition.

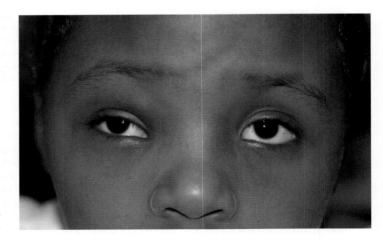

Figure 51-3. Right-sided telecanthus in a 4-year-old girl after a right nasoorbitoethmoidal fracture.

6. What are the features of the secondary deformity from an untreated NOE fracture?

The NOE complex forms the central portion of the midface region. Fractures of this area usually are high velocity, and the incidence of concomitant injuries such as brain contusion is high. The hallmark of a NOE fracture involves the region of the medial canthal insertion into the region of the lacrimal crest and has been classified on the basis of the size of bone fragment attached to the medial canthus. The fracture pattern involves the medial orbital wall, nasal bone complex, and medial orbital rim, and often is associated with a frontal sinus fracture.

The secondary deformity following an untreated NOE fracture manifests according to the severity of the original injury. Enophthalmos is present as the result of a medial orbital wall fracture with increased severity depending on the degree of displacement of the orbital rim. An element of vertical globe dystopia may be present. Telecanthus occurs as the result of splaying of the nasal bone component and lateral displacement of the medial canthal tendon. Blunting and scarring of the medial canthal region is seen as well as loss of the normal contours of the nasoorbital valley, which may be unilateral or bilateral. There is flattening and widening of the nasal dorsum, an acute nasofrontal angle in association with cephalic rotation of the nasal tip and an increase in the columellar labial angle. This occurs as a result of loss of support along the nasal base and telescoping superiorly and may be compounded by severe septal comminution with loss of mid-third nasal support. Furthermore, lacrimal drainage problems may occur with epiphora and/or mucocele. Anosmia may be present as the result of cribriform plate fractures and damage to the olfactory nerve.

7. How do you treat the secondary deformities of a NOE fracture?

Treatment aims in the management of the secondary deformities of a NOE fracture are directed at restoring globe position to normal, restoration of normal intercanthal distance, and reconstruction of the nasal dorsum. The key in approaching this problem is careful clinical examination and preoperative imaging with axial, coronal, and three-dimensional CT scans allowing identification of the extent of the fracture pattern.

Restoration of normal globe position and correction of enophthalmos associated with a NOE fracture involves identifying defects involving the medial orbital wall, replacing herniated periorbital soft tissue within the orbital confines, and reconstructing the defects with alloplast or allograft. Displacement of the medial orbital rim may require a segmental osteotomy for repositioning. Correction of telecanthus is dependent on the fracture pattern, as segmental osteotomy with preservation of canthal attachments and restoration of anatomic alignment will restore normal intercanthal distances in the event of a type I NOE fracture. With significant comminution of the medial rim, the medial canthal tendon may have to be detached from the small bony fragments and a transnasal canthopexy performed using either a small titanium bone anchor or a transnasal wire. Restoration of normal canthal position may be difficult because of poor bone stock along the medial wall. An effort must be made to place the medial canthal ligament posterior to the lacrimal crest and avoid a tendency to place the ligament too far anteriorly. Postoperative relapse of telecanthus may be avoided by the judicious use of percutaneous lead plates for a period of time. Finally, a cantilever bone graft can be used to reconstruct the nasal dorsum and restore the frontal–nasal angle. Narrowing of the nasal base can be accomplished by lateral wall nasal osteotomies.

8. Following treatment of a NOE or medial orbital fracture, what happens to the lacrimal drainage system?

The nasolacrimal drainage system is intimately associated with the medial orbital wall and is located in the lacrimal fossa. It is protected by the medial canthal ligament. Studies have demonstrated that even in severe NOE injuries, the nasolacrimal system injury is less common than expected. In one study of 46 patients with severe NOE fractures, only 17.4% eventually required dacryocystorhinostomy for nasolacrimal duct obstruction. Postoperative epiphora was more commonly due to eyelid malposition than nasolacrimal duct obstruction. Obstruction usually occurs in the bony nasolacrimal canal, and open reduction internal fixation in anatomic position of the bony fragments may reduce the incidence of obstruction. Obvious lacerations of the nasolacrimal duct and sac identified at the time of bony repair should be managed with repair and intubation, but prophylactic intubation is not necessary.

9. What is a growing skull fracture?

Growing skull fractures or craniocerebral erosions are rare sequelae of cranial fractures in which progressively growing cranial defects follow lacerations involving the dura mater. Growing skull fractures occur nearly exclusively in young children. The incidence of growing skull fractures ranges from less than 0.05% to 1.6%. They present as a cystic, nontender swelling with an underlying palpable bony defect. Falling is the most common cause of skull fracture. They may develop in any region in which there is a fracture with underlying dural injury, but most occur in the parietal regions. Rare cases of pulsatile exophthalmos following the development of an orbital growing skull fracture have been described. In most cases, the extent of the dural defect is greater than that of the bony defect.

Growing skull fractures should be suspected in children younger than 3 years with a palpable mass. Diagnosis is demonstrated by CT or magnetic resonance imaging (MRI), which shows a bony defect and underlying brain herniation (Fig. 51-4). Treatment principles involve duraplasty with/without cranioplasty depending on the age of the child. Rarely, cerebrospinal fluid (CSF) shunting is required.

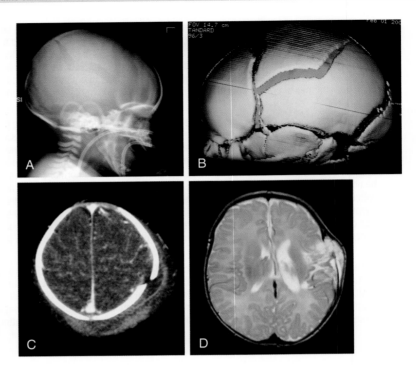

Figure 51-4. Plain x-ray **(A)**, computed tomography **(B)**, and magnetic resonance images **(C, D)** of a growing skull fracture in a 3-month-old infant with herniation of brain through the left parietal fracture site.

10. Discuss the pathophysiology of the posttraumatic temporal contour deformity.

Temporal contour deformity is defined as a concavity or depression in the temporal region located superior to the zygomatic arch and immediately posterior to the lateral orbital rim. It usually is iatrogenic in origin. The site of the contour deformity gives some clue as to its etiology. A defect along the line of origin of the temporalis muscle may occur from an overzealous approach to the temporal fossa after a craniotomy for bleeding where the temporalis muscle is divided or denervated along the incision line. Failure to resuspend the temporalis muscle from its origin along the superior temporal line or its attachment to the lateral orbital rim may lead to a dehiscence and inferior displacement of the muscle.

The deformity can present as a consequence of extended coronal flap elevation for exposure of the lateral craniofacial skeleton and zygomatic arch. It is imperative to protect the superficial temporal fat pad during dissection to the zygomatic arch. This can be accomplished by staying on the superficial surface of the deep temporal fascia until the zygomatic arch is identified and incising directly through the fascia overlying the arch or alternatively incising the fascia 1 cm above the arch and continuing the plane of dissection above the fat pad. MRI studies have demonstrated that the etiology of temporal contour deformity after extended coronal flap elevation is related to a decrease in volume due to injury-induced atrophy and/or inferior displacement or prolapse of superficial fat pad.

Treatment involves alloplastic augmentation of the defect, usually in a submuscular plane. Attempts at resuspending a dehisced temporalis muscle are unsatisfactory due to muscle shortening and lack of fixation of the muscle free margin.

11. What are the possible long-term complications following a frontal sinus fracture?

Frontal sinus fractures are classified anatomically (anterior wall, posterior wall, and floor/drainage system) and by the degree of displacement. Approximately one third of fractures involve the anterior table alone, and 60% involve the posterior table and floor. Dural tears are present in 40% of frontal sinus fractures. However, in 10% of individuals, the frontal sinus develops unilaterally, in 5% it is a rudimentary structure, and in 4% it is absent. Long-term complications can be defined by the area of involvement.

Nondisplaced anterior and posterior wall fractures usually heal without event. Contour deficiencies and flattening of the forehead will occur after displacement of the anterior table fragments by more than 3 mm. Sensory changes due to supratrochlear and supraorbital nerve involvement usually are transient and resolve within months.

Displaced posterior table fractures are more likely to be associated with significant intracranial injury and an increased risk of CSF fistulae, meningitis, extradural or intradural abscess, intracranial abscess, frontal bone osteitis, and osteomyelitis as a result of dural tears and contamination from the paranasal sinuses.

Involvement of the drainage system of the frontal sinus may result in blockage of the nasofrontal system. The nasofrontal duct is highly variable, and in up to 85% of the population a true duct is absent and the frontal sinus drains into the middle meatus through a large ostium. Any injury to the frontal sinus mucosa may result in a mucocele, but this usually occurs after blockage of the drainage system (see Question 12).

12. What is a frontal sinus mucocele?

A mucocele is a retention cyst composed of an enclosed collection of mucus that usually results from inadequate sinus drainage. A mucocele of the frontal sinus traditionally develops after an obstruction of the nasofrontal drainage system, which is involved in more than one third to half of patients with frontal sinus fractures. The frontal sinus is lined with respiratory epithelium with a ciliated membrane and mucus-secreting glands. The cilia beat in the direction of the nasofrontal drainage system. Blockage of the drainage system prevents normal drainage of mucus and predisposes to the development of obstructive epithelium-lined cysts called *mucoceles*. Mucoceles may develop when islands of epithelium become trapped in the fracture lines and continue to grow. Growth of a mucocele results in local bony destruction through the production of bone-resorbing factors such as prostaglandin E_2 and collagenase. When mucoceles become infected, osteitis, osteomyelitis, intracranial abscess, and meningitis may ensue, in part due to venous drainage of the frontal sinus mucosa through the foramina of Breschet to the dural veins. Common infecting agents include group B α-hemolytic streptococcus, *Haemophilus influenzae*, *Staphylococcus*, and *Bacteroides*. Mucoceles typically develop an average of 7.5 years after frontal sinus trauma. Traditional techniques of mucocele management consisting of frontal sinus obliteration have been supplanted with endoscopic drainage maneuvers.

13. Classify posttraumatic cranial vault defects.

Posttraumatic defects of the cranial vault can simply be classified by location (anatomic bone, hair bearing vs non–hair bearing), depth (full thickness vs partial thickness), and soft tissue coverage (simple vs complex). Relevant factors include age of patient, cognitive state, etiology of defect (post decompressive craniotomy, postinfectious), stability of soft tissue cover, and proximity to paranasal sinuses.

14. Describe the management of posttraumatic cranial vault defects

The indications for surgical reconstruction of posttraumatic cranial vault defects include neuroprotection, aesthetic, psychosocial (social isolation secondary to wearing protective helmet), and neurologic (headaches secondary to bony defect). Cranioplasty techniques have been described extending back to prehistoric times. Cranioplasty techniques can be categorized by the material used into autograft, allograft, or alloplast.

The principles of cranioplasty are to provide bony continuity, neuroprotection, and restoration of normal contour. Autogenous options include split skull cranioplasty and rib grafts. The iliac crest lacks sufficient bone stock for most cranioplasty cases. Calvarial bone offers a better biomechanical advantage than does rib, with lower rates of resorption, ease of fixation, and less donor site morbidity. Autogenous techniques are prone to contour irregularities due to unpredictable rates of resorption, which may have significant aesthetic implications in non–hair-bearing areas of reconstruction. Autogenous reconstruction is preferable when the cranial defect is in close proximity to the paranasal sinuses due to improved tolerance to infection over alloplasts.

Alloplastic techniques have the advantage of no donor site morbidity and maintenance of volume at the expense of increased risk of infection and implant failure. Almost any named alloplast has been used at one time as a cranioplasty material. Calcium phosphate cement and hydroxyapatite bone pastes briefly were popular due to ease of use and ability to contour but have been associated with long-term failure rates up to 50% with fragmentation, sinus tract formation, and low-grade inflammatory responses. Polymethylmethacrylate has been used for decades and recently has been developed for use in custom-made computer-designed CT-based implants. High-density polyethylene implants and custom-made titanium implants are also excellent alloplast options.

Allograft materials are available but suffer from unpredictable rates of resorption and poor biomechanical advantage.

15. What is the pathophysiology of cheek ptosis following open reduction internal fixation of orbital and midfacial fractures?

Although exposure of fractures of the OZC and midface at a subperiosteal level is necessary to allow anatomic reduction and internal fixation, the combination of a lower eyelid approach and upper buccal sulcus incision will result in release of the periosteum and the overlying medial facial musculature. These soft tissues will drift inferiorly, but posttraumatic and postsurgical edema may mask the descent of the soft tissue until several months later. The key to prevention is careful soft tissue management during exposure with identification and suture marking of the periosteal margins to allow for precise soft tissue resuspension using series of nonabsorbable periosteal sutures to the lateral orbital and inferior orbital rims after completion of fracture fixation. It is important to reattach the lateral canthus, which may have been detached during exposure. Established soft tissue ptosis of the cheek may be difficult to correct due to cicatricial contracture. Principles of repair involve wide undermining and nonabsorbable suture suspension to the zygomatic arch, lateral orbital rim, and inferior orbital rim.

16. What are the late features of an untreated healed OZC fracture?

The typical features of a displaced healed OZC fracture consist of flattening of the zygomatic high point as a result of posterior displacement partly due to the mechanism of injury and in part due to masseter pull. Increased transverse facial width may be present due to outward bowing of the zygomatic arch. Enophthalmos and lateral canthal dystopia with inferior displacement may be evident.

17. How do you treat a healed displaced OZC fracture?

The management of a healed displaced OZC fracture is dependent on the presence or absence of enophthalmos. With significant (>3 mm) retrodisplacement of the globe, restoration of normal facial balance requires a segmental osteotomy of the OZC with anatomic restoration of the bony segments and reapproximation of the normal orbital volume. Exposure can be achieved through an upper buccal incision to access the anterior maxilla, inferior orbital rim, and lateral maxillary (zygomaticomaxillary) buttress. The frontozygomatic and lateral orbital wall region can be approached through a modified upper blepharoplasty incision. Alternatively, a coronal approach sometimes is necessary to safely osteotomize the displaced OZC. Anatomic restoration of the OZC is judged by alignment along the lateral orbital wall at the junction of the greater wing of the sphenoid and the zygoma. Once the perimeter of the orbit has been restored, reconstruction of the orbital walls with autogenous bone graft or alloplast (titanium mesh, polyethylene implants) is performed. Usually, as the lateral canthus has been detached during the surgical exposure, a lateral canthoplasty is performed through drill holes along the lateral orbital margin. Overcorrection of the lateral canthal position is achieved by insertion above the position of Whitnall's tubercle, which is found along the lateral orbital wall 10 mm below the frontozygomatic suture and 2 to 4 mm interior to the rim. Finally, soft tissue suspension of the cheek tissue should be performed.

When no enophthalmos is evident, restoration of cheek projection can also be achieved through the use of alloplast augmentation of the zygomatic prominence.

18. In an untreated Le Fort I midface fracture, what are the biomechanical forces on the maxilla, and what type of facial deformity may exist?

Failure to diagnose and manage a Le Fort I fracture may result in elongation ("equine facies") or flattening ("dishpan facies") of the midface due to maxillary displacement. This displacement is due to the force of trauma with collapse of the maxillary buttresses, but dorsal and caudal pull by the medial pterygoid muscles may produce an anterior openbite and a tendency to class III malocclusion with vertical elongation. Maxillary support is dependent on the integrity of the vertical and transverse bony buttresses. Comminution of these buttresses predisposes to a greater degree of displacement. The absence of maxillary dentition may weaken bone stock, resulting in posterior retrusion and vertical collapse making secondary dental rehabilitation difficult.

19. What are the long-term risks of titanium fixation used in facial fracture management?

Titanium miniplates have been used in the three-dimensional fixation of facial bone fragments for more than 3 decades. As a biomaterial, it is considered to be biocompatible, inert, and nonferromagnetic. Titanium is recognized as a biologically compatible material with osseointegrative properties and has elemental characteristics equivalent to calcium. It has a characteristic surface oxide layer that helps form a thin proteoglycan layer over the implant that helps its ability to osseointegrate with bone. Titanium is safe for patients undergoing CT and MRI, with minimal artifact.

There is no evidence that titanium is degraded over time, and it appears to be well tolerated by the body. Allergic reactions and hypersensitivity are rare. Complications directly related to titanium plates are unusual. Stress shielding with plate-induced porosity may occur in the mandible and may lead to localized osteoporosis. Removal of implants may be problematic due to bony overgrowth.

Removal of fixation plates after trauma has been reported in the literature occurring in up to 26% of cases. The usual reason for removal is loose fixation with associated inflammatory response. The most common cause of loosening is related to technical error, such as inadequate irrigation at the time of drilling resulting in ring sequestra of devitalized bone with implant loosening or improper drilling technique with eccentric orientation of the drill bit resulting in an oval hole. Miniplate-related cold sensitivity is a common complaint in northern climates. Nonspecific posttraumatic pain is a common complaint following open reduction internal fixation of facial fractures but rarely is relieved by plate removal. Proximity of stainless steel wires to titanium may result in generation of a galvanic current creating pain.

Transcranial implant migration of titanium plates has been well documented in infants following cranioorbital reshaping secondary to the cycle of bony deposition and resorption that is necessary for skull growth (Fig. 51-5). However, in general, the proximity of titanium fixation to the dura or brain is not believed to be a realistic health concern, but reoperation may be technically demanding with increased risk of dural tear and/or brain injury. Use of bioresorbable fixation in the management of pediatric facial fracture repair has eliminated this hazard.

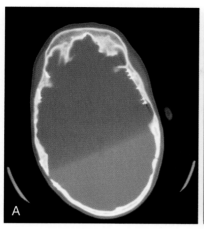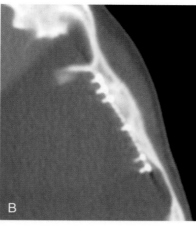

Figure 51-5. Transcranial migration of titanium miniplates used for cranial bone fixation in a 2-year-old child. Note proximity of plates to dura and brain.

20. What is a saddle nose deformity, and why is it called that?

Frontal trauma to the nose will cause a depression of the nasal bridge due to fracture and comminution of the lateral walls with a posterior collapse of the dorsum and often is associated with comminution of the septum. This produces a characteristic flattened and widened nasal dorsum. However, a saddle nose deformity usually refers to the loss of mid-third dorsal support of the nose occurring as the result of septal collapse. In a true saddle nose deformity, maintenance of upper third projection is provided by the bony nasal pyramid. In the lower third of the nose, tip projection is maintained to some degree by the medial crura of the lower lateral cartilage. However, as the upper lateral cartilages collapse inward, loss of cephalic support causes the nasal tip to rotate superiorly, with some loss of tip projection and an increase in the columellar–labial angle with increased nostril show.

Septal collapse may occur following multiple episodes of repetitive trauma (e.g., boxing), septal hematoma with necrosis of the cartilage, or infection. Other causes (nontraumatic) include collagen vascular diseases and postsurgical and recreational drug use (e.g., cocaine).

The term *saddle nose* may originate from the drooping seen along the back of an old saddle-worn horse. Surgical treatment of a posttraumatic saddle nose deformity involves dorsal augmentation using allograft (calvarium, rib) as an onlay.

21. What is a posttraumatic carotid cavernous sinus fistula?

A posttraumatic carotid cavernous sinus fistula (CCF) is a pathologic connection between the internal carotid artery and the venous channels that make up the cavernous sinus. They occur in 1% of patients with facial fractures and result from a tear in the wall of the internal carotid artery. CCF can be classified as high flow versus low flow and direct versus indirect using angiography. A direct CCF has a direct communication between the internal carotid artery and the cavernous sinus. Posttraumatic CCF nearly always are direct high-flow lesions and occur due to either a partial or a complete transection of the internal carotid artery or one of its intracavernous branches. Connective tissue diseases, arteriosclerotic vascular disease, pregnancy, and other diseases that cause vessel wall fragility also may predispose to nontraumatic spontaneous CCF.

The cavernous sinus consists of bilateral dural venous structures adjacent to the sella turcica and consist of slow flowing multiple communicating venous sinusoids. The circular nature of blood flow through the sinus accounts for variations in the presentation of CCF such that patients may manifest unilateral, contralateral, or bilateral signs and symptoms. The internal carotid artery enters the skull base, courses through the petrosal canal, and enters into the cavernous sinus. The intracavernous segment of the internal carotid artery runs parallel and medial to cranial nerves III, IV, V, and VI and then exits under the clinoid process. At its point of exit, the internal carotid artery is strongly tethered by the dura. A sudden shearing force at this spot may disrupt the internal carotid artery.

22. What are the clinical findings of CCF?

The clinical findings of CCF are the result of venous hypertension of the venous channels of the cavernous sinus and the orbit and may present in a delayed manner up to years after the injury. Symptoms also may be in part related to arterial steal with ischemic changes to the orbital structures. Patients may complain of swollen, red, painful eye(s), exposure keratitis; loud bruit; diplopia; retroorbital headaches; and progressive visual loss. Examination may demonstrate pulsatile exophthalmos, conjunctival edema, injected sclera, chemosis, periorbital edema, ophthalmoplegia, and bruit over the orbital region. Funduscopic examination may show dilated retinal veins, retinal hemorrhage, papilledema, and optic atrophy. Compression of cranial nerves III, IV, or VI may result in extraocular muscle dysfunction. Venous hypertension may result in glaucoma and subsequent visual loss. Life-threatening epistaxis, progressive visual loss, intracerebral hemorrhage, facial disfigurement, and annoying bruits may occur as the result of CCF.

Radiologic investigation with CT may show evidence of basilar skull fractures, dilated cavernous sinus, and/or engorged superior ophthalmic vein using contrast. Magnetic resonance angiography is superior for showing reversal of flow within the cavernous sinus and superior ophthalmic vein. However, the best way to establish a diagnosis is with a four-vessel cerebral angiogram.

Treatment is indicated as soon as the diagnosis is established. Although 5% of high-flow CCFs may close spontaneously, treatment has evolved from surgical to endovascular techniques with intraarterial occlusion using various embolization maneuvers.

23. How common is mandibular nonunion? How is it categorized?

Nonunion following mandibular fractures is a rare event. In one series, seven cases in 853 patients were identified, for an incidence of 0.8%. Mandibular nonunion has been defined as a failure of a fracture to unite after a period of at least 4 months. Diagnosis is based on clinical and radiologic assessment.

Mandibular nonunion can be categorized as aseptic or infected, vascular or avascular, and contact or defect types of nonunion. The reactive vascular nonunion is the most common type of fracture healing disturbance and is the result of movement at the fracture site. Mechanical motion results in increased vascularity, resorption, and rounding or occasionally hypertrophy of the bone ends that looks like an "elephant's foot" on x-ray. The most common cause is related to technical error in the application of open reduction internal fixation techniques with failure of fixation. Improper plate size and length, failure to place adequate numbers of screws on each side of the fracture, screws in the fracture line, and failure to stabilize comminuted segments all predispose to loosening of fixation and biomechanical movement at the fracture site.

Edentulous mandibles that are severely atrophic and osteoporotic may develop a nonreactive avascular nonunion. Open reduction internal fixation with periosteal stripping in an edentulous mandible with a vertical height of 10 mm or less is at much greater risk for avascular nonunion.

In the event of an infected nonunion, neither bone healing nor resolution of the infection can occur without stabilization of the fracture. Infected nonunions present with swelling, redness, and often a draining fistula arising from sequestered infected devitalized bone, loose hardware, or retained devitalized teeth.

24. What is the treatment of mandibular nonunion?

Identification of risk factors is key to effective management of mandibular nonunion. Risk factors include the presence of infection, bony sequestra, retained devitalized or fractured teeth, loose fixation hardware, mandibular defects, edentulous mandible, malposition with malocclusion, and any systemic factors that may contribute, such as substance abuse (alcohol, drugs), illness (diabetes), poor dental hygiene, and medications (immunosuppressants, antiinflammatories).

Imaging of the mandible can be performed with Panorex or CT to determine the extent of the problem. However, the mainstay of treatment of mandibular nonunion is surgical. The basic principles consist of incision and drainage, fistulectomy, anatomic reduction by restoration of premorbid occlusal relationships, wide exposure, débridement of devitalized bone, removal of loose fixation hardware, and establishment of rigid fixation using appropriate means of stable osteosynthesis. External fixation devices are unnecessary. It is well recognized that stable fixation can be left in situ in the face of infection, and, provided there is no biomechanical instability, the infection will resolve despite the presence of foreign material. Mechanical immobilization of bone fragments by compression will promote healing and consolidation.

In most cases, the expanded sclerotic ends of the bone are quite vascular, and resorption along the margins has occurred as a result of biologic response to mechanical movement at the fracture site. This response occurs in a manner to reduce stress on new blood vessels by increasing the interfragmentary distance and widening the cross-sectional surface area of the interposed connective tissue. Therefore stabilization of the bone will promote union. Bone gaps are managed by thicker, stronger reconstruction plates designed to bridge bone gaps. Primary bone grafting of these defects is not routinely performed but is best managed secondarily after resolution of infection and settling of the soft tissue response between 3 to 6 months.

BIBLIOGRAPHY

de Djientcheu VP, Njamnshi AK, Ongolo-Zogo P, et al: Growing skull fractures. Childs Nerv Syst 11:1–5, 2006.

Ersahin Y, Gulmen V, Palali I, Mutluer S: Growing skull fractures (craniocerebral erosion). Neurosurg Rev 23:139–144, 2000.

Gruss JS, Hurwitz JJ, Nik NA, et al: The pattern and incidence of nasolacrimal injury in naso-orbital-ethmoid fractures: The role of delayed assessment and dacryocystorhinostomy. Br J Plast Surg 38:116–121, 1985.

Hammer B, Prein J: Correction of post-traumatic orbital deformities: Operative techniques and review of 26 patients. J Craniomaxillofac Surg 23:81–90, 1995.

Iliff NT: The ophthalmic implications of the correction of late enophthalmos. Trans Am Ophthalmol Soc 89:477–548, 1991.

Jimenez D, Bernard C: Posttraumatic carotid cavernous sinus fistulae. In Holck DEE, Ng JD (eds): Evaluation and Treatment of Orbital Fractures. Philadelphia, Elsevier Saunders, 2006, pp 341–350.

Kim S, Matic DB: The anatomy of temporal hollowing: The superficial temporal fat pad. J Craniofac Surg 16:760–763, 2005.

Lacey M, Antonyshyn O, MacGregor JH: Temporal contour deformity after coronal flap elevation: An anatomical study. J Craniofac Surg 5:223–227, 1994.

Manson PN, Clifford CM, Su CT, et al: Mechanisms of global support and posttraumatic enophthalmos: I. The anatomy of the ligament sling and its relation to intramuscular cone orbital fat. Plast Reconstr Surg. 77:193–202, 1986.

Manson PN, Grivas A, Rosenbaum A, et al: Studies on enophthalmos: II. The measurement of orbital injuries and their treatment by quantitative computed tomography. Plast Reconstr Surg. 77:203–214, 1986.

Phillips JH, Gruss JS, Wells MD, Chollet A: Periosteal suspension of the lower eyelid and cheek following subciliary exposure of facial fractures. Plast Reconstr Surg 88:145–148, 1991.

Schmoker R: Management of infected fractures and non-unions of the mandible. In Yaremchuk MJ, Gruss JS, Manson PN (eds): Rigid Fixation of the Craniomaxillofacial Skeleton. Toronto, Butterworth-Heinemann, 1992, pp 233–244.

Zachariades N, Papvassilou D: Traumatic carotid-cavernous sinus fistula. Craniomaxillofacial Surgery 16:385–388, 1988.

RECONSTRUCTION OF COMPLEX CRANIOFACIAL DEFECTS

Ian T. Jackson, MD, DSC (Hon), FRCS, FACS, FRACS (Hon)

1. What are the causes of complex craniofacial defects?
- Acute trauma
- Old trauma
- Congenital deformity
- Post tumor resection

2. What is the most debilitating aspect of posttraumatic deformity?
Double vision (diplopia) undoubtedly is the worst. It significantly limits the ability to drive and to perform one's occupation, and it is difficult to correct.

3. How is diplopia evaluated?
(1) Computed tomographic (CT) scan, (2) three-dimensional CT scan, and (3) ophthalmology consultation. The scans will clearly show the extent of orbital trauma and why the orbit is deformed. This may be due to medial orbital wall or floor expansion fracture of one or both structures. A lateral wall and inferior rim fracture with lateral displacement also expands the orbit considerably. Escape of fat through a floor blowout is another cause. Frequently a degree of enophthalmos is associated.

4. What is the best approach to the orbit in such a situation?
A coronal flap is ideal for the majority of cases. In localized floor fractures, a lower lid transconjunctival approach is satisfactory for exposure. Some surgeons prefer to use a mid-lid incision for access to the orbital floor.

5. What is the treatment of isolated orbital floor fracture with enophthalmos?
After radiologic assessment, the fracture is approached through a transconjunctival incision with elevation of the orbital contents at the subperiosteal plane. Complete exposure of the floor beyond the fracture site is essential. The defect is covered with a thin cranial bone graft, a polyethylene implant (e.g., Medpor), thick silicone sheet, or any other material that can overlap the undisplaced floor edges and is stiff enough to contain the orbital fat.

6. What is the treatment of a displaced lateral wall fragment causing enophthalmos?
After radiologic assessment, the fracture is exposed through a coronal flap. The orbital contents are elevated at a subperiosteal level, and the fracture is exposed and reduced. It is plated or wired in position. If a bony defect is present, a cranial bone graft is inserted. This fracture usually is easy to reposition and stabilize. Long-term problems, either cosmetic or functional, are rare. Alloplastic sheeting can also be used. It should be thick enough to contain the orbital contents. The position of the lateral canthus should be inspected and proper attachment confirmed.

7. What is the treatment of an acute, complex lateral inferior rim and floor fracture with severe displacement and significant comminuted bony injury?
After radiologic assessment and accurate diagnosis, the fracture is approached through a coronal incision with as much elevation of the temporalis muscle as required. The orbital contents then are freed up completely. Placement of wire fixation on the rim, both laterally and inferiorly, often is useful because the rim is not palpable through the skin. A cranial bone graft is harvested and used to reconstruct the floor of the orbit, if required. Fixation usually is not necessary. To reconstruct the lateral wall defect, a plate can be used to span the defect, secured on the temporal bone and the lateral orbital rim. A cranial bone graft of the correct dimensions is placed on the medial aspect of the plate, and a screw is used to fix it in place. Any displacement of the lateral canthal ligament is accurately wired in position to the inner aspect of the lateral orbital rim.

8. Discuss the management of an established posttraumatic deformity of the orbitozygomatic complex with enophthalmos
Assessment is by CT scan; a three-dimensional scan is helpful in complex cases. The approach is by coronal flap with anterior elevation of the temporalis muscle to expose the lateral aspect of the lateral orbital wall.

The floor and walls of the orbit are exposed widely, again, subperiosteally. If there is displacement of the orbitozygomatic complex, osteotomies are made at the frontoorbital region, lateral orbital wall, floor, and inferior rim of the orbit. The orbitozygomatic complex is mobilized and stabilized with plates and screws; wires also can be used. The floor of the orbit is reconstructed as necessary with a cranial bone graft, as are the lateral and medial walls as required. For any remaining enophthalmos, bone grafts or soft Gore-Tex can be placed posteriorly to advance the globe.

9. What is the best method of performing a medial canthopexy?

The traditional method of transnasal wiring is mechanically unsound because the bone on the contralateral medial orbit is thin and will give way when twisting is tight. The correct method is to drill from the contralateral nasofrontal region where the bone is thick and pass the wire from there and back. When the wire is tightened there is no danger of breaking this bone, no matter how tight the wire is made.

10. What are the causes of posttraumatic enophthalmos with and without vertical displacement of the globe?

Posttraumatic enophthalmos can result from any fracture that enlarges the orbital volume. Lateral and sometimes inferior displacement of the orbitozygomatic complex may be present. Isolated floor or medial orbital wall fractures with displacement can enlarge the orbit significantly. What is necessary for inferior displacement of the globe is injury to the periorbitum in addition to the bony injury, but this is the usual situation. An intact periorbita will hold the eye in place, but this occurrence is very rare. Vertical displacement of the globe may occur in extensive floor injuries of the blowout type. Most frequently these injuries are also associated with fracture and displacement of the orbitozygomatic complex.

11. Discuss the treatment of posttraumatic frontal bone deformity without cerebrospinal fluid leak

Exposure is by a coronal incision with elevation of a bicoronal flap at the subperiosteal level. Many substances are available for correcting contour irregularities. Initially the hydroxyapatite compounds were believed to be the answer to this problem. Unfortunately, many of these compounds have been associated with complications. The best approach is use of what has been a complication-free reconstruction. The area is marked out, multiple drill holes are made, and corresponding small screws are placed, leaving the screw heads and part of the screw shafts exposed. Methylmethacrylate cement containing antibiotics is placed to reconstruct the area. Once the cement is solid it can be contoured. The results of this technique have been satisfactory and, as yet, free of complications. Small full-thickness defects can be filled with several layers of Surgicel and the described technique performed, but the screws are placed into the *edges* of the defect. In all cases, ice-cold saline is sprayed on the methylmethacrylate. Contouring can be carried out as required.

Another technique is to harvest full-thickness cranial bone, split it, and place it into the defect. It is stabilized with miniplates and screws, which can be metal or resorbable.

12. What is the best method for reconstruction of the flat nose of either congenital or posttraumatic origin?

Although many materials are available (e.g., silicone), they are associated with problems that occur sooner or later. The best material is cranial bone, which can be taken as split thickness or full thickness. The latter is preferred because harvest with a contouring drill is safer than harvesting split-thickness bone with an osteotome. The approach for insertion of the graft is by a vertical incision in the glabellar area. Extensive dissection is performed to the nasal tip. Subperiosteal dissection is performed in the glabellar area. This should be sufficient to expose the glabellar and nasal bridge area. Using a contouring burr, a reception area sufficient to receive the graft is cut out. The distal edge is contoured so that it will act as a fulcrum. A hole is drilled in the proximal end of the bone graft, which then is inserted. A single screw is used to secure the graft in place. As the screw is tightened, the distal part of the graft elevates the tip of the nose to the required degree. This produces a stable and predictable result. Follow-up over the past 15 years has revealed no significant resorption. Usually a plaster cast is applied to prevent lateral displacement of the tip. The only necessary precaution is to avoid excessive elevation of the tip, which may cause the bone graft to erode the skin.

The alternative techniques that were used previously (e.g., alloplastic materials and cartilage grafts) were associated with significant complications of infection, exposure, and displacement. To date, the described method has been free of complications. The glabellar incision usually heals very well because it lies in an ideal natural crease.

13. What foreign materials are useful in head and neck reconstruction and why?

Methylmethacrylate has remained the most useful material, especially when it is impregnated with antibiotics. The only complications noted have been related to exposure, which, with good clinical judgment, is extremely rare. Fixation is virtually essential. Several small screws projecting from the surface supply secure fixation. Metal mesh is useful but also must be fixed securely with screws. Any material that is not rigidly fixed appears to have a tendency to develop local fluid collections that frequently are associated with infection. Any mesh that is not fixed can loosen and extrude. In addition, the mesh may contain surface irregularities.

Nonfixed materials and hydroxyapatite compounds are not recommended because they have been associated with complications.

14. Discuss the types of cranial bone grafts available for skull defect reconstruction.
Bone Dust: This is collected with a slow-speed hole-boring craniotome. Constant moistening and cooling are provided by cold water irrigation. After the dust is collected it can be used for full- or partial-thickness defects. With full-thickness defects, a layer of Surgicel is placed directly on the dura. The bone dust is applied using the volume to completely or slightly overfill the defect. Another layer of Surgicel stabilizes the external surface. With partial-thickness defects, the dust is placed into the area and Surgicel is applied on top. The amount and quality of bone produced vary, but children usually have the best results. Bone dust can be used as an adjunct material as well, as in cases where it is used to smooth off a split rib reconstruction.

Partial-Thickness Cranial Bone Graft: After the skull is exposed the amount of bone required is drawn out with a sterilized lead pencil. Using a contouring burr, the bone is cut around and the external table is removed lateral to these cuts. Careful use of the osteotome and the mallet will allow removal of even large portions of intact bone. If there is concern about the amount of cortical bone required, an alternative method, which probably is safer for harvest of large grafts and for those with little or no experience in these areas, is to request the neurosurgeon, if available, to take the graft. Splitting the cranial bone is not always easy. The saw can cut only so far, even with long blades, and use of long, fine straight or curved osteotomes may be necessary to complete the split.

Vascularized Bone Graft: Two methods of transferring vascularized cranial bone grafts can be used. One method of transfer is on a vascular axis, such as the temporal vessels; the other method of transfer is on the galea. In both cases, it is best to leave the galea undisturbed because it has the most reliable blood supply. Large segments of full-thickness cranium can be transferred using this technique. The largest case has consisted of the ascending ramus and body of the mandible, which were reconstructed with a full-thickness cranial bone transfer: the temporal area for the ascending ramus and the full frontal area for the body. The contralateral ramus was intact. Osseointegration of the reconstructed mandible was possible at a later date.

15. What are the most useful materials for skull reconstruction?
- *Cranial Bone:* Used as split thickness, full thickness, or dust
- *Foreign Materials:* Methylmethacrylate, hydroxyapatite, metal plates

CRANIAL BONE

Small amounts of split bone can be harvested by cutting around the bone with a contouring burr and removing the cortical bone laterally. This leaves the remaining cortical bone like an island, which can be harvested with an osteotome. Alternatively, full-thickness skull can be harvested with a drill or osteotome and split. The cranial defect can be filled with bone dust collected during the harvesting or by the unused split cranium. Cranial bone dust harvesting is discussed in Question 14.

FOREIGN MATERIALS

Hydroxyapatite: Our experience with hydroxyapatite has been disappointing. In some cases, some kind of reaction appeared to have caused loss of skin. This reaction has been reported by other craniofacial surgeons. We no longer use this material.

Metal Mesh: Thick mesh is difficult to use, and thinner plates can have fixation problems and occasionally erode through the scalp. Custom-made implants are very expensive.

Methylmethacrylate: This is our choice of material. The impregnation of antibiotics into the methylmethacrylate has been useful, and we have yet to observe a complication. Like any foreign material, it must be securely stabilized. To achieve this, multiple small plates and screws are placed to increase adhesion and prevent shearing. In full-thickness defects, several layers of Surgicel are placed over the dura. Good stabilization is achieved by placing pins transversely on the edges of the defect, and methylmethacrylate is used to reconstruct the defect. As yet, no complications have been observed with this technique.

16. What is the treatment of a fracture of the zygomatic arch?

This is usually a tripartite fracture. It can be elevated with a malar elevator, but often it is unstable and a coronal approach may be necessary to expose the fracture and to place a plate on the lateral surface. The plate can be contoured to produce the correct arch shape. It is also possible to produce a good result by wiring the segments with a large-gauge wire.

17. What is the treatment of an orbitozygomatic fracture?

The fracture can be elevated using a malar elevator introduced through the temporal area under the temporal fascia. The fracture is elevated and may remain in place. It may relapse, but it can be stabilized by an incision over the lateral wall, and through this the lateral fracture is stabilized. Through a lower lid transconjunctival incision the infraorbital rim is stabilized with wire. Plates and screws can also be used.

18. What is the treatment of an orbital floor blowout fracture when isolated? In conjunction with an orbitozygomatic fracture?

For an isolated orbital floor blowout fracture, a transconjunctival incision in the lower lid fornix allows exposure to the infraorbital rim. The periosteum of the floor is elevated, and a polyethylene implant (e.g., Medpor) or other material (e.g., silicone sheet) can be used to reconstruct the floor. It must cover the floor defect completely. A mid-lid incision and cranial bone can also be used.

When an orbital floor fracture is encountered in conjunction with an orbitozygomatic fracture, it probably is best to use a coronal flap to stabilize the lateral orbital wall and to expose the orbital wall and floor fracture. Some surgeons use an extended upper blepharoplasty incision to expose the lateral orbital wall. It may be necessary to explore the infraorbital rim with a transconjunctival or mid-lid incision for rim stabilization and floor reconstruction.

19. Describe the treatment of a severely displaced maxillary fracture in conjunction with a nasoorbitoethmoidal fracture and a mandibular fracture.

The approach to the maxillary fracture should be via a coronal flap with exposure of the nose as well as the medial and lateral orbital walls. The floors of the orbits should also be explored through this approach. The maxilla is mobilized, the fractures are reduced, and plates and screws are applied to the lateral orbital rims and possibly the nasal bridge. If the nose is comminuted, a split cranial bone graft is used to recreate the nasal support system. This is fixed to the glabellar area with a screw.

The patient is placed in intermaxillary fixation, and the mandibular fractures are reduced. Through a lower buccal sulcus incision they can be stabilized with plates and screws. If the occlusion is satisfactory, the intermaxillary fixation is then released.

20. What is the sequence of treating a displaced three-level (skull, maxilla, mandible) fracture with a cerebrospinal fluid leak?

Look for a cerebrospinal fluid leak and a dural tear; if found, repair them. Replace and stabilize the skull fracture, then the maxillary fracture and finally the mandibular fracture.

21. A patient presents with a full-thickness frontal bone defect following tumor resection. The skin cover is satisfactory. What is your next step in this patient's reconstruction?

The area should be explored through a coronal incision and the defect exposed. A pattern of the defect is traced using sterile glove paper.

If the defect is small, the pattern can be redrawn further posteriorly on the skull. This area of bone is harvested as a split-thickness graft as described. Bone wax is used to control any bone bleeding. Drill holes are made around the defect with the brain protected. Corresponding holes are made in the bone graft, and it is wired securely in position.

22. A large full-thickness scalp defect results after tumor resection or trauma, with a skull defect that requires reconstruction. How can this best be managed?

The area is exposed using a scalp flap, and a pattern is made of the bony defect using sterile glove paper. This pattern is placed on another part of the skull and traced. If the skull defect is of significant size such that harvest of a split skull graft is not possible, the neurosurgeon can cut it with a craniotome. If this is not possible, a contouring burr can be used to cut through the cranium all around and the full-thickness graft harvested. The graft is split with an osteotome, and one portion is used to close the original defect and the other to close the donor site. These grafts are wired or plated in position. Bone dust is placed around the edges, and Surgicel is placed over the dust. A scalp flap, either rotation or transposition, is used to close the scalp defect, and a split-thickness graft is placed on the residual donor site area.

23. Discuss methods of filling small, medium, and large full-thickness bone defects

- *Small Defects:* These can be covered with bone chips or bone dust. Surgicel is used to stabilize them. Saline is sprayed on.
- *Medium Defects:* These can be reconstructed in a similar way, or split skull can be harvested and stabilized with wires or miniplates.
- *Large Defects:* Full-thickness skull of a similar size is harvested, split, and stabilized in position with plates or wires.

If there are any problems with harvesting bone, many defects can be reconstructed with bone dust and Surgicel placed on the dura. This can also be applied to deformities on the external surface of the cranium.

24. How should a defect of the cribriform plate area after tumor excision with direct opening into the nasal cavity be reconstructed?

Exposure should be obtained with a coronal flap and frontal craniotomy. If necessary, the area should be débrided. A central galeal frontalis flap of sufficient dimensions is elevated, with the base inferiorly oriented. Drill holes are made around the defect in the anterior cranial fossa. The galeal frontalis flap, which is vascularized from its inferior base, is placed over the defect. It is stabilized in position using the drill holes and sutures. Because it overlaps the defect when the frontal lobes come forward, the intracranial/extracranial connection is sealed off. The exposure craniotomy is replaced, and the scalp is closed.

25. What is the best reconstruction for an established posttraumatic flat nose?

The ideal reconstruction is to harvest a cranial bone graft with the desired shape (straight or curved, full thickness or partial thickness) using a contouring burr. This graft is taken from an area of the skull with an appropriate curvature. A vertical incision is made on the frontoglabellar region, the periosteum is elevated, and a pocket is created down to the nasal tip using scissors. A small area is cut from the bone in the glabellar area, again using the contouring burr. Distally, a ledge is left to act as a fulcrum. A hole is made in the bone graft, and a countersink is produced with the contouring burr. The graft is shaped to take off sharp edges and to make the tip area wider and without sharp points. The shaped graft is inserted right to the tip of the nose. A screw is placed in the hole, and it is inserted and tightened until the tip of the nose is cantilevered into its correct position. Ischemia of the nasal tip should be avoided. The glabellar incision is closed in layers. The graft is firmly fixed. A small plaster cast may or may not be used.

BIBLIOGRAPHY

El-Mazar H, Jackson IT, Degner D, et al: The efficacy of Gore-Tex versus hydroxyapatite and bone graft in reconstruction of orbital floor defects. Eur J Plast Surg 25:362–368, 2003.

Hussain K, Wijetunge DB, Grubnic S, Jackson IT: A comprehensive analysis of craniofacial trauma. Trauma 46:34–47, 1994.

Ilankovan B, Jackson IT: Experience in the use of calvarial bone grafts in orbital reconstruction. Br J Oral Maxillofac Surg 30:92–96, 1992.

Jackson IT: The wide world of craniofacial surgery. J Oral Maxillofac Surg 41:103–110, 1983.

Jackson IT, Adham MN, Marsh WR: Use of the galeal frontalis myofascial flap in craniofacial surgery. Plast Reconstr Surg 77:905–910, 1986.

Jackson IT, Helden G, Marx R: Skull bone grafts in maxillofacial and craniofacial surgery. J Oral Maxillofac Surg 44:949–955, 1986.

Jackson IT, Pellett C, Smith JM: The skull as a bone graft donor site. Ann Plast Surg 11:527–532, 1983.

Jackson IT, Smith J, Mixter RC: Nasal bone grafting using split skull grafts. Ann Plast Surg 11:533–540, 1983.

Jackson IT, Somers PC, Kjar JG: The use of Champy miniplates for osteosynthesis in craniofacial deformities and trauma. Plast Reconstr Surg 77:729–736, 1986.

Kelly CP, Cohen AJ, Yavuzer R, et al: Cranial bone grafting for orbital reconstruction: Is it still the best? J Craniofac Surg 16:181–185, 2005.

Lo AKM, Jackson IT, Ross JH, Dickson CB: Severe orbital floor fractures: Repair with a titanium implant. Eur J Plast Surg 15:35–40, 1992.

HEAD AND NECK RECONSTRUCTION

Woman Dressing Her Hair. Pablo Picasso, 1940. Oil on Canvas. The Museum of Modern Art, New York.
© 2008 Estate of Pablo Picasso/Artists' Rights Society (ARS), New York.

HEAD AND NECK EMBRYOLOGY AND ANATOMY

Mark S. Granick, MD, and
Lisa M. Jacob, MD

CHAPTER 53

1. What is a branchial arch?

Paired branchial arches form in the head and neck region of the developing embryo during the fourth week of gestation. They are derived from migrating neural crest cells and consist of ectoderm, mesoderm, and endoderm. The arches are complemented by invaginating branchial grooves and evaginating branchial pouches. These masses of tissue form the building blocks for the later development of nerve, muscle, and skeletal structures.

2. Describe the derivatives of the branchial arches and pouches.

See Table 53-1.

3. A 12-year-old boy has a draining sinus at the anterior upper one-third border of the sternocleidomastoid muscle. What is the likely source?

A branchial cleft cyst. Between the branchial arches are branchial clefts or grooves that are lined with surface ectoderm. The first cleft becomes the external auditory canal. The second, third, and fourth clefts usually are obliterated by the sixth week of gestation. Failure to obliterate or duplication of these structures may result in fistulas, sinus tracts, or cysts. Such anomalies can be found along the anterior border of the sternocleidomastoid muscle at any point from the external auditory canal to the clavicle. The second branchial cleft anomaly is most common.

4. How would you treat this patient?

The tract must be excised under general anesthesia with a thorough understanding of the involved anatomy. For second branchial cleft cysts, the external component is found at the junction of the middle and lower thirds of the anterior

Table 53-1. Derivatives of the Branchial Arches and Pouches

ARCH	MUSCLES	BONE/ CARTILAGE	LIGAMENTS	POUCH	NERVE
First	• Muscles of mastication • Mylohyoid • Anterior belly of digastric • Tensor tympani • Tensor palatini	• Meckel's cartilage • Malleus • Incus	• Anterior ligament of malleus • Spheno-mandibular ligament	• External auditory canal • Tympanic membrane	• Trigeminal
Second	• Muscles of facial expression • Stylohyoid • Posterior belly of digastric • Stapedius	• Hyoid bone • Lesser horn • Upper body • Stapes • Styloid process	• Stylohyoid ligament	• Palatine tonsil crypts	• Facial
Third	• Stylopharyngeus	• Hyoid bone • Greater horn • Lower body		• Thymus • Inferior parathyroid	• Glossopha-ryngeal
Fourth	• Muscles of soft palate • Muscles of pharynx • Muscles of larynx	• Thyroid cartilage • Cricoid cartilage • Arytenoid cartilage		• Thyroid C-cells • Superior parathyroid	• Vagus
Fifth	• Obliterated				
Sixth	• Sternocleido-mastoid • Trapezius				• Spinal accessory

border of the sternocleidomastoid muscle. The tract passes over the glossopharyngeal nerve and between the external and internal carotid arteries en route to the tonsillar fossa. Third branchial cleft anomalies, although rare, present in the same region as the second, but they course beneath the internal carotid. First branchial cleft cysts are less common but must be considered when excising masses above the hyoid bone because their course may involve branches of the facial nerve. The surgeon must be aware of the anatomy of these vital structures to avoid injury. Preoperative patient counseling and planning are essential.

5. **A 6-month-old infant has had a mass of the nasal root since birth. On physical examination, the mass measures 1.5 cm, it is firm, noncompressible, and nonpulsatile, and it does not transilluminate or change with Valsalva maneuver. What is the most likely diagnosis?**
Congenital midline nasal masses include nasal dermoids, nasal gliomas, and encephaloceles. Although rare, these disorders are clinically important because of their potential for connection to the central nervous system. The findings in this case are consistent with a glioma, which presents as a red or bluish lump at or along the nasomaxillary suture, or intranasally. Gliomas are characteristically firm and noncompressible, do not increase in size with crying, and do not transilluminate. The overlying skin may have telangiectasias. They can be associated with a widened nose or with hypertelorism. Abnormal closure of the fonticulus frontalis can lead to an ectopic rest of glial tissue being left extracranially. Bony defects, intracranial connections, and cerebrospinal fluid leakage are rare. Histology shows astrocytic neuroglial cells and fibrous and vascular connective tissue that is covered with skin or nasal mucosa.

Nasal dermoid sinus cysts are the most common of the congenital midline nasal masses. They can occur as an isolated cyst or with a sinus tract opening to the skin. Typically they are firm, noncompressible, nonpulsatile lesions that do not transilluminate and may be lobulated. They can present as a midline nasal pit, fistula, or infected mass. They usually terminate in a single subcutaneous tract, which sometimes has hair at the opening. They are derived from ectoderm and mesoderm, are lined with squamous epithelium, and contain specialized adnexal structures such as hair follicles, pilosebaceous glands, and smooth muscle. Connection with the central nervous system has been variably reported to occur from 4% to 45%. Suspicion of intracranial involvement should remain high, and preoperative computed tomography (CT) or magnetic resonance imaging (MRI) is recommended.

Encephaloceles involve herniation of cranial tissue through a skull defect. They can be classified as meningoceles (containing meninges only), meningoencephaloceles (containing meninges and brain), or meningoencephalocystoceles (containing meninges, brain, and part of the ventricular system). Encephaloceles are soft, bluish, compressible, pulsatile masses that are located at the nasal root and transilluminate. They typically enlarge with crying and Valsalva maneuver. A characteristic sign is the *Furstenberg test,* which is enlargement with compression of the internal jugular veins. They also can cause hypertelorism. The embryologic origin is failure of the fonticulus frontalis to close properly, which leads to herniation of intracranial contents with a connection to the subarachnoid space. This connection with the central nervous system and the possibility of containing brain tissue make encephalocele an important entity to rule out when a midline nasal mass is found.

6. **A young boy presents with a small mass in the midline of the neck below the hyoid bone. The mass has been present since birth. What is this finding consistent with?**
A thyroglossal duct cyst. These cysts arise from remnant tissue left during embryonic descent of the thyroid tissue from the base of the tongue to its pretracheal position by the eighth week of gestation. This "thyroglossal duct" usually disappears. However, duct remnants may be present as sinuses or cysts anywhere along the migration pathway. Thyroglossal duct cysts usually are in midline at the level of the thyroid membrane, inferior to the hyoid bone. They usually are identified by the second decade. Symptoms may include infection and rupture, which should be treated with antibiotics if they occur. Definitive treatment includes complete excision, including the entire duct remnant, which may pass through the hyoid bone and requires resection of the bone (known as the Sistrunk procedure).

7. **Are any preoperative tests important?**
The mass may represent the patient's only thyroid tissue. Therefore it is necessary to demonstrate normal functioning thyroid tissue by thyroid scans and thyroid function tests.

8. **From which embryologic structure does the external auditory meatus develop?**
During the sixth week of development, the external ear develops from six mesenchymal swellings or hillocks that surround the first branchial cleft. The first three hillocks arise from the first branchial arch (mandibular arch), and the second three hillocks develop from the second branchial arch (hyoid arch). The hillocks of the first arch form the tragus, helix, and cymba concha. The hillocks of the second arch become the antitragus, antihelix, and concha. The first branchial cleft lengthens to form the external auditory meatus (Fig. 53-1).

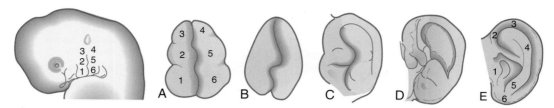

Figure 53-1. Stages in the development of the external ear. Components *1* to *3* are derived from the mandibular arch. Components *4* to *6* are derived from the hyoid arch. (From Carlson BM: Human Embryology and Developmental Biology, 4th ed. Philadelphia, Mosby, 2009.)

9. Describe the function of the facial nerve.

The facial nerve (CN VII) is a mixed motor and sensory nerve. The motor root *(facial nerve proper)* of the facial nerve supplies the muscles of facial expression, muscles of the scalp and auricle, the buccinator, platysma, stapedius, stylohyoid muscles, and posterior belly of the digastric muscle. The sensory root *(nervus intermedius)* supplies taste fibers to the anterior two thirds of the tongue via the chorda tympani nerve and to the soft palate via the palatine and greater petrosal nerves. The sensory root also supplies parasympathetic secretomotor innervation to the submandibular, sublingual, and lacrimal glands, and to the nasal and palatine mucosae.

10. Define the surface anatomy of the facial nerve.

The facial nerve enters the internal auditory meatus, passes through the petrous part of the temporal bone, and exits the skull through the stylomastoid foramen. The nerve then enters the parotid gland and breaks up into its five terminal branches: temporal, zygomatic, buccal, mandibular, and cervical. The temporal branch can be found along Pitanguy's line, which runs from 0.5 cm below the tragus to 1.5 cm above the lateral eyebrow. The facial nerve becomes more superficial as it courses medially but remains consistently deep to the superficial musculoaponeurotic system (SMAS). The muscles of facial expression are innervated on their deep surfaces, except for levator anguli oris, mentalis, and buccinator muscles, which run deep to the plane of the nerve and are innervated on their superficial surfaces (Fig. 53-2).

11. A patient presents with a deep facial laceration in the emergency department. Clear fluid is draining from the wound. What structure was most likely damaged?

The parotid gland or duct. The parotid (Stensen's) duct emerges from deep within the parotid gland and travels from the anteromedial border of the gland to the anterior border of the masseter muscle. From that point it dives and courses

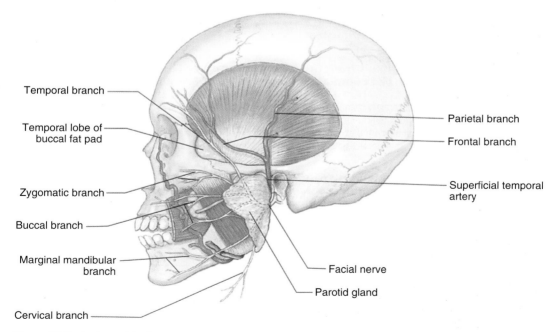

Figure 53-2. Anatomy of the facial nerve. (From Baker TJ, Gordon HL, Stuzin JM: Surgical Rejuvenation of the Face, 2nd ed. St Louis, Mosby-Year Book, 1996, p 167.)

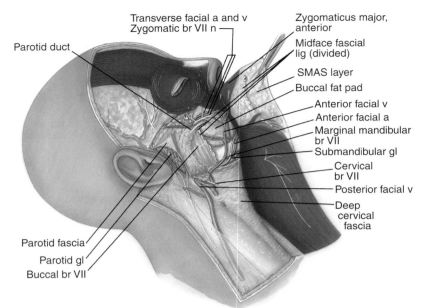

Figure 53-3. Anatomy of the parotid gland and duct. *SMAS,* Superficial musculoaponeurotic system. (From Owsley JQ Jr: Aesthetic Facial Surgery. Philadelphia, WB Saunders, 1994, p 20.)

below the zygomatic arch to enter the buccal space, inserting into the buccinator and then entering the oral cavity through a papilla opposite the upper second molar. The duct is approximately 7 cm long and generally follows a line drawn from the tragus to the middle of the upper lip. A vertical line drawn from the lateral canthus approximates the intraoral path. The parotid duct travels adjacent to the buccal branch of the facial nerve and the transverse facial artery, which also are at risk for injuries causing damage to the parotid duct (Fig. 53-3).

12. How do you diagnose and treat this injury?
Successful treatment depends on prompt recognition and appropriate intervention. To diagnose a parotid duct injury in the emergency department, cannulate the intraoral parotid duct papilla with a small Silastic tube and observe if the tube is visible in the wound. If any doubt remains, a small amount of saline can be injected through the tube and observed for flow through the wound. The mainstay of operative treatment includes repair of the duct over a stent, ligation of the duct, or fistulization of the duct into the oral cavity. Delay in diagnosis and treatment may lead to parotid fistula and sialocele formation.

13. You receive another consult from the emergency room. The patient has a superficial laceration to the neck but complains of numbness of the earlobe. What is the cause?
The great auricular nerve is a sensory branch from the cervical plexus that crosses the anterior border of the sternocleidomastoid muscle to supply sensation to the skin inferior to the external auditory meatus. It can be found consistently at a point 6.5 cm below the external auditory canal. It is a superficial structure that can be injured during facelift, parotid, carotid, and other neck dissections, leaving a bothersome numbness to the inferior ear.

14. A 50-year-old man has gustatory sweating and flushing of the right cheek after undergoing superficial parotidectomy for removal of a parotid tumor. What is the most likely cause of his current symptoms?
The patient has Frey syndrome. The first description of a unilateral gustatory hyperhidrosis was provided as early as 1757 by the French surgeon M. Duphenix and in 1847 by Baillarger. In 1923 Frey correlated the unusual physiologic phenomena and applied the descriptive term "auriculotemporal syndrome." The syndrome is characterized by warmth and sweating in the malar region of the face upon eating, thinking, or talking about foods that produce a strong salivary stimulus. It may follow damage to the parotid region by trauma, mumps, purulent infection, or parotidectomy. It is thought to be caused by the development of anastomoses between parasympathetic fibers from the otic ganglion, which are carried by the auriculotemporal nerve, and the sympathetic fibers in the sweat glands that lie within the vascular plexus of the skin. Fibers from both systems are cholinergic and mediated by acetylcholine. Treatment involves intracutaneous injection of botulinum toxin, which relieves symptoms by blocking neurotransmission of acetylcholine. Operative management includes direct excision of involved skin and interposition of autologous tissue. Acellular dermal matrix allografts have been used recently for interposition grafting with some success. Botulinum toxin provides relief for 4 to 6 months and needs to be repeated. Operative interventions have poor long-term success.

15. A 45-year-old woman develops left shoulder pain and weakness after undergoing a left neck lymph node biopsy. What is her diagnosis?

The patient has an iatrogenic spinal accessory nerve palsy. During dissections of the posterior triangle of the neck, the spinal root may be damaged. The spinal accessory nerve is a motor nerve consisting of spinal and cranial nerve (CN XI) roots, which join to form a trunk and exit through the jugular foramen to enter the anterior and posterior triangles of the neck. After exiting the foramen, the spinal root separates and passes posteriorly and inferiorly to supply the sternocleidomastoid muscle. It then traverses the posterior cervical triangle superficial to the deep fascia to supply the trapezius muscle approximately 5 cm superior to the clavicle. If the spinal root is damaged, paralysis of the superior part of the trapezius occurs. This results in inferior and lateral rotation of the scapula and drooping of the shoulder. If the nerve is transected, the sternocleidomastoid muscle is also affected. The patient experiences weakness in turning the head to the opposite side.

16. A 20-year-old man has suffered a full-thickness injury to the scalp and is bleeding profusely. What are the layers and blood supply of the scalp?

There are five layers of the *SCALP:* Skin, sub-cutaneous tissue, aponeurosis, loose areolar tissue, and pericranium. The vascular supply to the scalp comprises five paired arteries: (1) supraorbital, (2) supratrochlear, (3) superficial temporal, (4) occipital, and (5) posterior auricular arteries. The supraorbital and supratrochlear are branches of the internal carotid artery. The superficial temporal, occipital, and posterior auricular are branches of the external carotid artery.

17. Your patient has a neoplastic lesion of the posterior third of the tongue and is experiencing ear pain. Describe the phenomenon of referred pain.

The ear is innervated by multiple nerves, including the trigeminal, facial, glossopharyngeal, vagus, and posterior nerve roots of C2 and C3. The phenomenon of referred otalgia occurs from pathology arising in *other* branches of these nerves that result in ear pain (Table 53-2).

18. List the layers of the eyelid.

Anterior Lamella

- Skin
- Subcutaneous tissue
- Orbicularis oculi muscle

Posterior Lamella

- Submuscular areolar tissue
- Orbital septum
- Preaponeurotic fat pad
- Levator aponeurosis (upper eyelid)
- Muller's muscle (upper eyelid)
- Capsulopalpebral fascia (lower eyelid)
- Tarsal plate
- Conjunctiva

Table 53-2. Referred Pain

NERVE	STIMULUS FOR REFERRED PAIN
Trigeminal nerve via auriculotemporal nerve	Malocclusion, impacted molars of lower jaw, dental abscess, TMJ disease, sinusitis
Facial nerve via nervus intermedius of Wrisberg, chorda tympani, greater superficial petrosal nerve	Herpes zoster of geniculate ganglion, lesions of nasal cavity, sphenoid sinus, posterior ethmoid sinus, mobile tongue
Glossopharyngeal nerve via Jacobson's nerve	Neoplastic lesions of the tonsil, posterior third of tongue, vallecula, pyriform sinus, hypopharynx, post-tonsillectomy pain
Vagus nerve via Arnold's nerve	Neoplastic lesions of the larynx and tracheobronchial tree
Posterior roots C2 and C3	Cervical disc lesions, osteoarthritis

TMJ, Temporomandibular joint.

19. Which palatal muscle acts to close off the nasopharynx from the oropharynx?

There are five muscles of the soft palate. The *palatopharyngeus muscle* forms the palatopharyngeal arch. It attaches superiorly to the hard palate and palatine aponeurosis and inferiorly to the lateral wall of the pharynx. Its function is to tense the soft palate and pull the pharyngeal walls superiorly, anteriorly, and medially during swallowing, effectively closing off the nasopharynx from the oropharynx. The *palatoglossus muscle* functions to close off the oral cavity from the oropharynx by elevating the posterior tongue and drawing the soft palate inferiorly. It attaches superiorly to the palatine aponeurosis and inferiorly to the side of the tongue. The *levator veli palatini muscle* attaches superiorly to the cartilage of the auditory canal and the petrous part of the temporal bone. It extends anteriorly and inferiorly to attach to the palatine aponeurosis. It functions to elevate the palate, drawing it superiorly and posteriorly during swallowing and yawning. It works in conjunction with the tensor veli palatini. The *tensor veli palatini muscle* attaches superiorly to the medial pterygoid plate, spine of the sphenoid, and cartilage of the auditory tube and extends to the palatine aponeurosis. During swallowing, it tenses the soft palate by using the hamulus as a pulley. It also pulls the auditory canal open to equalize air pressure between the middle ear and pharynx. The *musculus uvulae* is a delicate slip of muscle that attaches to the posterior nasal spine and palatine aponeurosis and inserts into the mucosa of the uvula. It shortens the uvula and pulls it superiorly, assisting in the closing of the nasopharynx during swallowing.

20. Describe the nasolacrimal drainage system.

Tears move from lateral to medial on the eye and are collected by the upper and lower puncta, which can be found 5 to 7 mm lateral to the canthal angle. They travel in the canaliculi 2 mm vertically, then 8 mm horizontally, to the common canaliculus, which drains into the lacrimal sac. The nasolacrimal duct then transports the tears through the ethmoid bone to exit into the nose below the inferior nasal concha.

21. What other structures empty into the nasal cavity?

The nasal concha or turbinates (inferior, middle, and superior) are found on the lateral walls of the nasal cavity. They divide the lateral nasal walls into the inferior, middle, superior, and supreme meati. The frontal, maxillary, anterior ethmoid, and middle ethmoid sinuses drain into the middle meatus. The posterior ethmoid cells drain into the superior meatus. The sphenoid sinus drains into the supreme meatus, also known as the sphenoethmoidal recess.

22. After downfracture of the maxilla during a Le Fort I osteotomy, profuse bleeding is seen. What vessel is most likely responsible?

The descending palatine artery is a branch of the third portion of the maxillary artery. It descends vertically through the perpendicular portion of the palatine bone. Injury of this vessel during Le Fort I osteotomy is not uncommon.

23. You plan a radial forearm free flap to reconstruct a floor of mouth defect for squamous cell carcinoma (SCCA). During dissection of the external carotid artery you note that the superior thyroid artery was damaged in the lymph node dissection of the neck. Which vessel will you use for your anastomosis?

The external carotid artery begins at the bifurcation of the common carotid at the level of the superior border of the thyroid cartilage. It runs superiorly and posteriorly between the neck of the mandible and the lobule of the auricle. It gives off six branches before it divides into two terminating braches. They are in ascending order: superior thyroid, ascending pharyngeal, lingual, facial, occipital, and posterior auricular. The two terminating branches are the maxillary and superficial temporal arteries. Occasionally, the lingual and facial arteries arise as a common trunk. Of the six branches, the superior thyroid, the lingual, and the facial arise anteriorly and are of adequate caliber for anastomosis.

24. What major congenital syndromes are associated with first and second branchial arch abnormalities?

Treacher-Collins (Mandibular Dysostosis): Autosomal dominant disorder with variable penetrance and expression. Linked to the gene sequence 5q31.3. Involves bilateral hypoplasia of the zygoma, maxilla, mandible, and adnexal structures. Presents with downward slanting of the palpebral fissures, absences of eyelashes, colobomas of lower eyelids, auricular defects, and Tessier clefts 6, 7, and 8.

Nager Syndrome (Acrofacial Dysostosis): Autosomal recessive disorder that involves bilateral hypoplasia of the orbits, maxilla, zygoma, mandible, and soft palate. Presents with cleft palate, auricular defects, preaxial defects of the extremities, and mental retardation.

Microtia: Involves abnormal development of the first and second branchial arches during weeks 4 to 12 of gestation. Ear structures affected include the auricle, external auditory canal, tympanic membrane, and ossicles. The structures derived from the otic capsule, including the inner ear, internal auditory meatus, and vestibular surface of the stapes, are normal. Infants may have conductive hearing loss but normal neurosensory hearing.

Table 53-3. Developmental Embryologic Clefts

CLEFT TYPE	EMBRYOLOGIC ORIGIN
Median cleft lip	Medial nasal prominences fail to fuse with each other
Unilateral cleft lip	Medial nasal prominence fails to fuse with maxillary prominence
Oblique facial cleft	Lateral nasal prominence fails to fuse with maxillary prominence
Cleft chin	Mandibular prominences fail to fuse to each other
Cleft of oral commissure	Maxillary and mandibular prominences fail to fuse together

Goldenhar Syndrome (Oculoauriculovertebral Dysplasia): Involves hypoplasia of the hard and soft tissues of the first and second branchial arches. Infants present with microtia, epibulbar dermoids, vertebral anomalies, rib anomalies, and unilateral frontal bossing.

25. Developmental embryologic clefts result as a failure of fusion between adjacent structures. Describe the processes responsible for the major facial clefts.
See Table 53-3.

26. What are the foramina of the 12 cranial nerves?
See Table 53-4.

27. What is the motor function of the trigeminal nerve?
In addition to serving as the sensory cutaneous nerve of the anterior and lateral face, the mandibular division of the trigeminal nerve (CN V3) is the motor nerve for the muscles of mastication. This group of four muscles acts directly on the mandible and traditionally includes the masseter, temporalis, and medial and lateral pterygoid muscles. Accessory muscles, referred to as *suprahyoid muscles* because of their position superior to the hyoid bone, include the mylohyoid, digastric, and geniohyoid and are also innervated by the trigeminal nerve.

28. Describe the action of the muscles of mastication on the mandible.
Contraction of the masseter, temporalis, and medial pterygoid results in elevation of the mandible, whereas contraction of the lateral pterygoid and suprahyoid muscles results in mandibular depression. Lateral and medial pterygoid contraction also results in mandibular protrusion. Mandibular retraction results from contraction of the suprahyoids and posterior portion of the temporalis.

Table 53-4. Foramina of Cranial Nerves

CRANIAL NERVE	FORAMEN
Olfactory (CN I)	Cribriform
Optic (CN II)	Optic foramen
Oculomotor (CN III)	Superior orbital fissure
Trochlear (CN IV)	Superior orbital fissure
Trigeminal (CN V1)	Superior orbital fissure
Trigeminal (CN V2)	Foramen rotundum/inferior orbital fissure
Trigeminal (CN V3)	Foramen ovale
Abducens (CN VI)	Superior orbital fissure
Facial (CN VII)	Stylomastoid foramen
Vestibulocochlear (CN VIII)	Internal acoustic meatus
Glossopharyngeal (CN IX)	Jugular foramen
Vagus (CN X)	Jugular foramen
Spinal accessory (CN XI)	Jugular foramen
Hypoglossal (CN XII)	Hypoglossal canal

BIBLIOGRAPHY

Bartlett SP, Lin KY, Grossman R, et al: The surgical management of orbitofacial dermoids in the pediatric patient. Plast Reconstr Surg 91:1208–1215, 1993.

Johnston MC: Embryology of the head and neck. In McCarthy JG (ed): Plastic Surgery, Vol 4. Philadelphia, WB Saunders, 1990, pp 2451–2495.

Kaplan GC, Granick MS, Rhee ST: Pediatric neck masses. In Bentz RM, Bauer BS, Zucker PS (eds): Pediatric Plastic Surgery, St. Louis, Quality Medical Publishing, 2008, pp 967–1000.

Langman J: Medical Embryology. Baltimore, Williams & Wilkins, 1981.

Moore KL: The branchial apparatus and the head and neck. In Moore KL (ed): The Developing Human, 4th ed. Philadelphia, WB Saunders, 1988, p 170.

Netter FH: Atlas of Human Anatomy. Summit, NJ, Ciba-Geigy Corp., 1991.

Pensler JM, Ivescu AS, Ciletti SJ, et al: Craniofacial gliomas. Plast Reconstr Surg 98:27–30, 1996.

Pitanguy I, Silveria-Ramos A: The frontal branch of the facial nerve: The importance of its variation in face-lifting. Plast Reconstr Surg 38:352–356, 1966.

Ricciardelli E, Persing JA: Plastic surgery of the head and neck (anatomy/physiology/embryology). In Ruberg RL, Smith DJ (eds): Plastic Surgery: A Core Curriculum, Vol 4. St. Louis, Mosby, 1994, pp 251–270.

Schwember G, Rodriguez A: Anatomic dissection of the extraparotid portion of the facial nerve. Plast Reconstr Surg 81:183–188, 1988.

Sood R, Coleman JJ: Scalp and calvarial reconstruction. In Coleman JJ (ed): Plastic Surgery—Indications, Operations, and Outcomes, Vol 3, St. Louis, Mosby, 2000, pp 1519–1539.

Zide BM, Jelks GW: Surgical Anatomy of the Orbit. New York, Raven Press, 1985.

HEAD AND NECK CANCER

Brian R. Gastman, MD; Anjali R. Mehta, MD, MPH; and
Jeffrey N. Myers, MD, PhD, FACS

CHAPTER 54

1. **A patient returns 6 years after having a resection of a T1 squamous cell carcinoma of the floor of mouth with a biopsy-proven cancer in close proximity to the lesion. Does this represent a persistence or recurrence of the disease process?**

   Neither. This is a not uncommon scenario representing a *second primary,* which is defined as a tumor that presents itself more than 5 years after diagnosis and treatment of the first primary tumor with a disease-free interval. After approximately 3 years, less than 10% of head and neck squamous cell carcinomas have recurred. In fact, more than half of recurrences occur within 1 year. If the disease is evident within the first year, then many surgeons consider this a *persistence* of disease.

2. **What is field cancerization?**

   Described in 1953 by Slaughter, *field cancerization* represents changes by environmental factor, genetic factors, or both that make the mucosal lining of the upper aerodigestive tract abnormally susceptible to development of both premalignant and malignant lesions. This phenomenon is one of the reasons why panendoscopy (laryngoscopy, bronchoscopy, esophagoscopy) is performed as part of the initial evaluation for a head and neck tumor and why frequent follow-up is paramount.

3. **What are the relative contraindications to resecting a head and neck cancer?**
   - *Involvement of the prevertebral fascia:* The lymphatics in this area travel inferiorly well into the thorax. In addition, if the lesion abuts or invades the periosteum of the spine, resection of the bony spine is required. However, this has not been shown to improve survival and could lead to significant morbidities.
   - *Involvement of the carotid artery:* Usually 270° of tumor surrounding the carotid on computed tomographic (CT) scan makes invasion into the vessel a high probability.
   - *Skull base involvement:* Particularly at the level of the nasopharynx.
   - *Bilateral jugular vein involvement:* This is a relative contraindication because resection of both veins can lead to significant cerebral edema and even blindness.

4. **What is the appropriate evaluation of a lateral neck mass present in an adult for at least 3 weeks?**

   The differential diagnosis of a neck mass in an adult includes neoplastic or inflammatory disease, congenital anomalies, and other miscellaneous conditions. The likelihood of malignancy is increased in a patient with a history of tobacco or alcohol abuse, age greater than 40 years, chronic hoarseness, weight loss, persistent dysphagia, odynophagia, or otalgia, or a history of malignancy of the skin or mucosal surfaces of the head and neck.

   Diagnostic evaluation of a neck mass begins with a complete history and examination of the head and neck. After identification of a primary lesion, an imaging study of the head and neck (magnetic resonance imaging [MRI] or CT) usually is indicated to evaluate the extent of disease and to guide treatment planning. When a primary lesion is not found on examination, fine-needle aspiration (FNA) biopsy of the neck mass is indicated. If FNA biopsy demonstrates a benign lesion, treatment is tailored to the type and extent of disease. If malignancy is identified, positron emission tomography (or PET CT) can be helpful in searching for the occult primary lesion. Examination under anesthesia and endoscopy also are indicated. Directed biopsies of the nasopharynx, tonsil, tongue base, and pyriform sinus may be performed if the primary lesion remains occult. When FNA is nondiagnostic or equivocal for malignancy, open biopsy is performed concurrently.

5. **What is the classification of lymph node regions in the neck?**

   Devised at Memorial Sloan-Kettering Cancer Center, level I contains the submental and submandibular triangles. Level I is further subdivided into Ia and Ib, representing the submental and submandibular triangles respectively. Levels II to IV include lymph nodes along the internal jugular vein and nodes found within the fibroadipose tissue medial to the sternocleidomastoid muscle. Level II corresponds to the upper third and includes the upper jugular, jugulodigastric, and upper posterior cervical nodes. Nodes anterior to the spinal accessory nerve are said to be in level IIa. Nodes posterior are considered to be in level IIb. Levels III and IV are divided at the point where the omohyoid crosses the internal jugular vein. Level V includes those nodes in the posterior triangle of the neck (from the posterior border of the sternocleidomastoid muscle to the anterior border of the trapezius muscle). Level VI includes the pretracheal and paratracheal lymph nodes (Fig. 54-1).

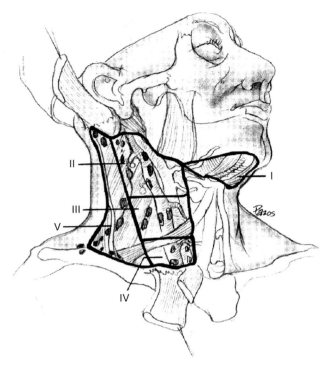

Figure 54-1. Lymph node regions in the neck. (From Bailey BJ: Head and Neck Surgery: Otolaryngology, 3rd ed. Philadelphia, Lippincott Williams & Wilkins, 2001, p 1348.)

6. **What are the differences among radical, modified radical, and selective neck dissections?**

   Radical neck dissection, or cervical lymphadenectomy, consists of cervical dissection with removal of the sternocleidomastoid muscle, omohyoid muscle, internal jugular vein, spinal accessory nerve, cervical plexus nerves, submandibular salivary gland, tail of parotid gland, and all intervening lymphoareolar tissue containing lymph nodes (described as nodal levels I through V). The principal indication for radical neck dissection is surgical management of bulky (N2 or greater) cervical nodal metastasis. However, given the evolution of neck dissection to more function-sparing yet oncologically sound operations, this procedure is not used that often in contemporary practice. Furthermore, the radical neck dissection is not indicated in the absence of palpable cervical metastasis (Fig. 54-2).

   Modified radical neck dissection removes all of the same lymph node groups as the radical neck dissection but spares at least one of the nonlymphatic structures removed with the radical neck dissection such as the sternocleidomastoid, accessory nerve, or internal jugular vein (Fig. 54-3).

   Selective neck dissection removes the cervical lymph nodes considered to be at high risk for metastasis from a given primary site. Selective neck dissections are generally performed on an elective basis. Rather than use specific names for a particular neck dissection, it has become standard practice to call the neck dissection performed according to the levels of the neck dissected and the nonlymphatic structures resected. Thus a modified radical neck dissection type I should be called a selective neck dissection of levels I through V with resection of the sternocleidomastoid muscle and the internal jugular vein.

7. **What are the principal indications for adjuvant postoperative external beam radiation therapy for patients with squamous cell carcinoma of the head and neck?**

   Adjuvant radiation therapy is indicated in cases of close or positive surgical margins, extracapsular extension of nodal disease, perineural or perivascular invasion, multiple positive nodes, high risk of occult disease in an undissected neck, invasion of bone or cartilage, and subglottic extension of laryngeal carcinoma. In these circumstances, postoperative radiation therapy improves locoregional control rates and survival compared with surgery alone.

8. **What are the most common benign and malignant tumors of the nose and paranasal sinuses?**

   The most common benign tumors are osteomas, followed by hemangiomas and papillomas. Of the malignant variety, squamous cell carcinoma accounts for approximately 70% of tumors, followed by adenocarcinoma (10% to 15%) and adenoid cystic carcinoma (5% to 10%).

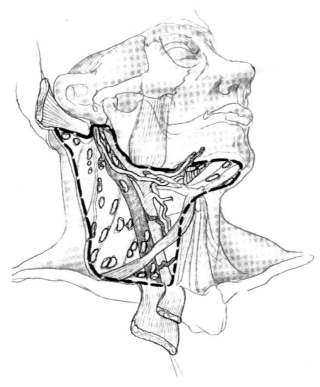

Figure 54-2. Radical neck dissection. (From Bailey BJ: Head and Neck Surgery: Otolaryngology, 3rd ed. Philadelphia, Lippincott Williams & Wilkins, 2001, p 1351.)

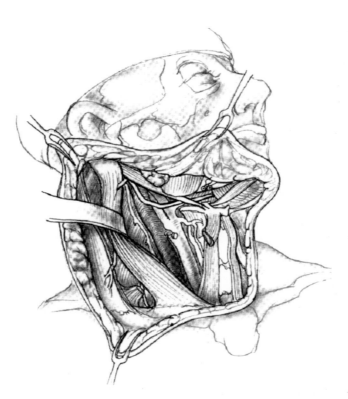

Figure 54-3. Modified radical neck dissection with preservation of the spinal accessory nerve. (From Bailey BJ: Head and Neck Surgery: Otolaryngology, 3rd ed. Philadelphia, Lippincott Williams & Wilkins, 2001, p 1348.)

9. Where do nasal and sinus tumors originate?

The maxillary sinus is the most common site (55% to 60%), followed by the nasal cavity (30% to 40%) and ethmoid sinus (9%).

10. Describe the lymphatic drainage of the oral tongue.

The oral tongue (or anterior two thirds of the tongue) has an extensive array of lymphatics that drain to the cervical nodes. The superior cervical (level II) lymph nodes are the most common site of cervical metastasis from oral tongue cancers. Lymph nodes in levels I and III are also at high risk for metastasis from early tongue cancer.

11. What is the role of elective neck dissection in the management of patients with early (stages I and II) squamous cell carcinoma of the oral tongue?

Elective supraomohyoid neck dissection (zones I to III) usually is recommended for patients with stage I and II oral tongue cancers. Patients with T1N0M0 and T2N0M0 oral tongue cancers have a substantial risk (30% and 50%, respectively) of occult metastatic disease in the neck. If elective dissection of levels I to IV of the neck identifies occult nodal metastasis in two or more lymph nodes or extracapsular nodal extension of disease, adjuvant radiation may be warranted (Table 54-1).

12. What is the role of elective radiation therapy in oral tongue cancer?

Elective radiation therapy can be an effective option for treatment of the N0 neck for patients with squamous cell carcinoma of the oral tongue. No studies comparing elective radiation therapy with elective neck dissection have clearly demonstrated the benefit of one treatment modality over the other. Regardless of the choice of treatment, the prevailing opinion favors elective treatment of the N0 neck for patients with invasive squamous cell carcinoma of the oral tongue because of the high likelihood of occult metastases.

Table 54-1. AJCC Tumor Staging for Oral Cavity Cancers

Primary Tumor (T)

TX	Primary tumor cannot be assessed
T0	No evidence of primary tumor
Tis	Carcinoma in situ
T1	Tumor 2 cm or less in greatest dimension
T2	Tumor more than 2 cm but not more than 4 cm in greatest dimension
T3	Tumor more than 4 cm in greatest dimension
T4a	Moderately advanced local disease*

(Lip) Tumor invades through cortical bone, inferior alveolar nerve, floor of mouth, or skin of face, that is, chin or nose
(Oral cavity) Tumor invades adjacent structures only (e.g., through cortical bone 'mandible or maxilla] into deep [extrinsic] muscle of tongue [genioglossus, hyoglossus, palatoglossus, and styloglossus], maxillary sinus, skin of face)
T4b   Very advanced local disease. Tumor invades masticator space, pterygoid plates, or skull base and/or encases internal carotid artery

Regional Lymph Nodes (N)

NX	Regional lymph nodes cannot be assessed
N0	No regional lymph node metastasis
N1	Metastasis in a single ipsilateral lymph node, 3 cm or less in greatest dimension
N2	Metastasis in a single ipsilateral lymph node more than 3 cm but not more than 6 cm in greatest dimension; or in multiple ipsilateral lymph nodes, none more than 6 cm in greatest dimension; or in bilateral or contralateral lymph nodes, none more than 6 cm in greatest dimension
N2a	Metastasis in a single ipsilateral node more than 3 cm but not more than 6 cm in greatest dimension
N2b	Metastasis in multiple ipsilateral lymph nodes, none more than 6 cm in greatest dimension
N2c	Metastasis in bilateral or contralateral lymph nodes, none more than 6 cm in greatest dimension
N3	Metastasis in a lymph node more than 6 cm in greatest dimension

Distant Metastasis (M)

M0	No distant metastasis
M1	Distant metastasis

Anatomoc Stage/Prognostic Groups

Stage 0	Tis	N0	M0
Stage I	T1	N0	M0
Stage II	T2	N0	M0
Stage III	T3	N0	M0
	T1	N1	M0
	T2	N1	M0
	T3	N1	M0
Stage IVA	T4a	N0	M0
	T4a	N1	M0
	T1	N2	M0
	T2	N2	M0
	T3	N2	M0
	T4a	N2	M0
Stage IVB	Any T	N3	M0
	T4b	Any N	M0
Stage IVC	Any T	Any N	M1

*Note: Superficial erosion alone of bone/tooth socket by gingival primary is not sufficient to classify a tumor as T4.
From Edge SB, Byrd Dr, Compton CC, Fritz AG, et al. (eds): AJCC Cancer Staging Manual, Seventh Edition. New York, Springer-Verlag, 2009. Used with the permission of the American Joint Committee on Cancer (AJCC), Chicago, Illinois.

13. **What methods are available for assessing mandibular bony invasion with carcinomas of the oral cavity?**

Determination of the presence and extent of mandibular invasion is critical in formation of a treatment plan for the patient with oral cavity cancer, particularly floor of mouth neoplasms. Various imaging studies are available for assessment of mandibular bone invasion, including plain films, orthopantography, PET, PET/CT, CT, and MRI. CT (especially with the aid of the dental CT software program DentaScan) remains the most sensitive imaging study for assessing the integrity of the mandibular cortical bone. MRI is advantageous when evaluating for marrow space and/or nerve involvement.

14. **What surgical techniques are appropriate for management of oral cavity cancers that are adjacent to or invade the mandible?**

Segmental mandibulectomy is indicated when carcinoma invades the mandible. *Mandibular-sparing techniques* involving marginal (or rim) resections are appropriate when the tumor invades the periosteum and/or minimally erodes cortical bone. This technique involves resecting a portion of the lingual cortex as part of the surgical margin. This can be indicated when adequate margins would be difficult to obtain with soft tissue resection alone. If direct invasion of the mandible is identified during the course of marginal mandibulectomy, the procedure should be converted into segmental mandibulectomy (bicortical bone resection).

15. **What are the subsites of the oropharynx?**

Tonsils, tongue base, soft palate, and pharyngeal wall. Note the hard palate is part of the oral cavity.

16. **What is the role of surgery versus radiation in the treatment of early (T1 and T2) squamous cell carcinomas of the oropharynx?**

Early cancers of the oropharynx are stage I and stage II lesions. Such lesions are not commonly diagnosed because patients often are asymptomatic. In a significant number of cases, a neck mass is the first presenting symptom. The presence of a neck mass increases the disease stage to at least stage III.

Surgery or radiation therapy provides effective control of early oropharyngeal cancers. Because of the possibility of tissue preservation and diminished morbidity after radiation, many patients and physicians choose radiation therapy as the initial treatment of early oropharyngeal cancers. However, complications of radiation (e.g., significant fibrosis of the oropharynx) have been reported. Furthermore, if surgery is needed for salvage or in a recurrence situation, the postoperative complication rate is higher if the patient was previously radiated and is worse if the patient had received both chemotherapy and radiation.

17. **How is the oropharynx accessed surgically?**

The oropharynx is accessed transorally via a pharyngotomy or a transmandibular approach. The transoral approach is appropriate for T1 cancers of the anterior tonsillar pillar, soft palate, and superior pharyngeal wall. Limited exposure to the lateral pharyngeal wall and inferior tongue base can be achieved with lateral and/or transhyoid pharyngotomy. Larger tumors and tumors of the tongue base typically require broader exposure. Mandibulotomy with mandibular swing offers excellent exposure for access to larger tumors of the oropharynx and parapharyngeal space.

18. **What are the major differences in clinical behavior between cancers of the glottic and supraglottic larynx?**

The *glottic larynx* includes the true vocal cords, anterior commissure, and posterior commissure. The anterior commissure, vocal ligament, thyroglottic ligament, and conus elasticus are the principal anatomic structures that surround the glottic larynx and act as barriers to the spread of malignancy. The glottis is poorly supplied with blood and lymphatic vessels. Accordingly, the risk of cervical metastasis with cancers confined to the glottis is less than 10%.

The *supraglottic larynx* is composed of the epiglottis, preepiglottic space, aryepiglottic folds, ventricular bands (false cords), and arytenoids. The supraglottic larynx is richly supplied with blood and lymphatic vessels. Unlike glottic cancer, early cervical nodal metastasis is much more likely because of the extensive supraglottic lymphatic network. The overall cervical metastasis rates for T1 and T2 squamous cell carcinomas of the supraglottis are approximately 25% and 70%, respectively. Behavioral patterns of early glottic and supraglottic cancers often allow function-sparing treatment. T1 and T2 glottic cancers usually are treated with conservation surgery, such as laser excision of the lesion, cordectomy, or radiation therapy. Because of the high risk for cervical metastasis, consideration should be given to elective treatment of bilateral cervical lymph nodes in all cases of supraglottic squamous cell carcinoma.

19. **What is the role of a larynx preservation strategy using radiotherapy with or without chemotherapy in advanced laryngeal cancers?**

Total laryngectomy was the accepted standard form of treatment for most patients with advanced laryngeal cancer for many years. More recently, however, chemotherapy used in combination with radiation therapy has increased the efficacy of preserving the larynx and providing local regional control and survival rates comparable with those of surgery and adjuvant radiotherapy. This approach to laryngeal conservation gained support after the study performed by the Department of Veterans Affairs Laryngeal Cancer Study Group clearly demonstrated that a population of patients with advanced laryngeal cancer could be cured without laryngectomy. Large randomized studies that have followed this landmark study have shown that this approach is effective for many T3 lesions but only selected T4 lesions. Larger T4 lesions still are most effectively managed surgically with adjuvant radiation. These studies have shown that in addition to providing local-regional control, the added benefit of chemotherapy is a decrease in development of distant metastases. Nevertheless, for individual patients, predicting whether speech and swallowing function will be better with a surgical or an organ-sparing approach is difficult. In this regard, many partial laryngectomies are available, such as supracricoid, supraglottic, hemi, and others that can be performed either open or transorally with a laser, which can provide excellent functional and oncologic results.

20. What methods are currently available for speech rehabilitation in patients who undergo total laryngectomy?

Return of speech function is one of the most important determinants of quality of life after total laryngectomy (the other being swallowing). The three general methods of speech restoration after total laryngectomy are tracheoesophageal puncture (TEP) speech, esophageal speech, and use of a mechanical artificial larynx. Of the three, TEP speech has emerged as the favored method.

TEP speech requires surgical creation of a small fistula between the esophagus and trachea. The fistula is created with TEP at the time of laryngectomy (even in the setting of a flap for pharyngeal reconstruction) or as a secondary procedure. A prosthesis consisting of a one-way valve is placed into the fistula, usually at the time of laryngectomy. To produce sound, the tracheostoma is occluded on exhalation, forcing air into the pharyngoesophageal segment. As in esophageal speech, vibration of the pharyngeal and esophageal walls creates sound. Injection of air via TEP is much easier than with the esophageal speech method. Successful vocalization occurs in up to 95% of patients who have primary or secondary TEP.

21. What is the role of laser surgery in the treatment of early laryngeal cancer?

Early glottic disease encompasses lesions ranging from carcinoma in situ to T2 lesions with normal cord mobility. Traditionally, treatment of these lesions would be either radiation therapy or partial laryngectomy. With the advent of microsurgical techniques and the coupling of the carbon dioxide laser to the microscope, endolaryngeal techniques for resection of early glottic tumors have become a new but widely accepted modality of treatment. In most cases, tracheostomy is not required and hospitalization is minimal. Small case series comparing cure rates among laser resection, radiation therapy, and open procedures show similar outcomes. Even larger tumors recently have been successfully treated in this manner.

22. Name the most common benign and malignant tumors of the parotid gland.

Pleomorphic adenoma is the most common tumor of the parotid gland overall. Warthin's tumor is the second most common tumor of the parotid gland and the most common bilateral tumor. It is an interesting tumor in that it has significant amount of mitochondria, which accounts for its high uptake in technetium-99 scanning. Although there is a small chance of malignant transformation with pleomorphic adenoma, there is no such relationship with a Warthin's tumor. Oncocytoma is another benign tumor of the parotid gland that is rich in mitochondria and has a similar pattern of uptake with technetium-99 scanning.

Eighty percent of parotid tumors are benign; thus the other 20% are malignant. The three most common tumors of the parotid gland in order are mucoepidermoid carcinoma, adenoid cystic carcinoma, and acinic cell carcinoma. Adenoid cystic carcinoma is especially virulent, with significant neurotropism and a propensity to metastasize to the lung. Other carcinomas that are seen in the parotid gland are squamous cell carcinoma, although usually from a skin metastasis, and lymphoma, which has a high association with Sjögren's disease. In children the most common benign lesion is a hemangioma, and the most common malignant lesion is a rhabdomyosarcoma.

23. What is the biopsy technique for a lesion of the parotid gland?

In the case of a parotid lesion, any "typical" lesion that is nonfixed, has normal facial nerve function, or is long-standing in nature should be evaluated further. Imaging is rarely needed unless something unusual exists with the lesion (e.g., patient has a history of skin cancer or Sjögren's disease). The biopsy for a parotid lesion is a *superficial parotidectomy with facial nerve preservation.* Enucleation puts the patient at risk for a local recurrence and injury to the facial nerve.

24. What are the major indications for facial nerve sacrifice during surgery for parotid gland neoplasms?

The only indications for sacrifice of all or portions of the facial nerve during parotid gland surgery for neoplasm are direct nerve invasion and inability to remove the tumor without nerve sacrifice. Histologic diagnosis (e.g., adenoid cystic carcinoma, which has a propensity for perineural invasion) and proximity of tumor to nerve without direct invasion are not appropriate indications for facial nerve resection.

25. What is the appropriate initial management of patients with a thyroid nodule?
Initial evaluation of a thyroid nodule should determine which patients will benefit from a surgical procedure and which patients require medical management before or in lieu of surgery. The first appropriate diagnostic step is determination of the serum level of thyroid-stimulating hormone (TSH). If the patient is determined to be hyperthyroid, a radionuclide scan is indicated to distinguish a hyperfunctioning nodule from a cold nodule. Identification of a hyperfunctioning nodule negates the need for further evaluation because the risk of malignancy is extremely low.

Most patients with a thyroid nodule have a normal serum TSH level. FNA biopsy of the nodule is indicated in such patients. All patients who have identifiable malignancy on FNA should be considered candidates for surgical resection of thyroid malignancy. However, only approximately 5% of patients have lesions identified as malignant or suspicious for malignancy. The vast majority (at least 60%) have benign solitary nodules that can be treated initially with thyroid suppression therapy.

26. What are the major prognostic factors that predict clinical outcomes for patients with differentiated thyroid (papillary and follicular) cancers?
Various classification and staging schemes attempt to predict outcomes for patients with differentiated thyroid cancers. Important prognostic factors are sex, age at diagnosis, tumor size, histologic grade, extrathyroidal extension, unifocal versus multifocal disease, cervical nodal metastasis, and distant metastasis.

27. What is the appropriate surgical margin for resection of cutaneous melanomas in the head and neck region?
Recommendations for surgical resection margins for melanoma are based on tumor thickness. For in situ lesions, a 0.5-cm margin of surrounding skin and into the underlying subcutaneous tissue should be resected. For lesions 1 to 2 mm deep, a margin of 1 cm is required, and lesions 2 to 4 mm thick should be resected with a 2-cm margin. Any lesion thicker than 4 mm should have margin greater than 2 mm.

A principal problem with head and neck melanomas is that a 2-cm circumferential margin often is not possible without inflicting major cosmetic or functional deformity. As a general rule, the wide excision is carried to the anatomic margin of the cosmetic or functional unit. If narrower margins (1 cm) are used for lesions 1.5 mm or greater in depth, perineural invasion and/or ulceration adjuvant radiotherapy can provide local-regional control in 85% to 90% of patients. However, radiobiology of melanoma is different from that of other tumors; therefore it is given in five 6-Gy fractions given over a 2.5-week period.

28. What is the role of elective neck dissection in the management of melanomas of the head and neck?
The value of elective neck dissection for all patients with cutaneous melanoma of the head and neck is uncertain in terms of promoting improved survival. The most significant benefit of elective dissection currently appears to be identification of patients with occult metastatic disease.

Given the results of the Eastern Cooperative Oncology Group trials of adjuvant interferon alfa-2b, identification of occult nodal disease and subsequent treatment with adjuvant interferon should provide survival benefit. Other methods for identification of occult cervical metastasis, such as lymphoscintigraphy and sentinel node biopsy, may prove to be more cost-effective means of identifying patients who will benefit from postoperative adjuvant treatment.

29. What are the indications for a selective neck dissection versus modified radical neck dissection in patients with squamous cell carcinoma? What if the tumor is papillary thyroid cancer or melanoma?
In general, the selective neck dissection has been reserved for patients with no palpable cervical lymphadenopathy, that is, the N0 neck. A prospective, multicenter study conducted in Brazil demonstrated no survival benefit of performing a modified radical neck dissection in patients without palpable neck disease. In such patients a selective neck dissection is appropriate, thus sparing the patient the morbidity associated with a modified radical neck dissection. More recent studies show that in the case of oral cavity cancer, a selective neck dissection also may be feasible in the case of N1 and N2a disease, with control rates as high as 94% reported in one series.

In non–squamous cell carcinomas of the head and neck (e.g., thyroid or melanoma), a modified radical neck dissection is the current treatment of N1 disease. This includes levels II to V and, in the case of thyroid cancer, the central compartment of paratracheal nodes (level VI). The location of the primary lesion in the case of melanoma or nonmelanoma skin cancers dictates the necessity of dissecting the parotid gland, the postauricular nodes, and/or suboccipital nodes in addition to levels I to V of the neck.

BIBLIOGRAPHY

Amdur RJ, Parsons JT, Mendenhall WM, et al: Postoperative irradiation for squamous cell carcinoma of the head and neck: An analysis of treatment and complications. Int J Radiat Oncol Biol Phys 16:26–36, 1989.

Balch CM, Soong SJ, Bartolucci AA, et al: Efficacy of an elective regional lymph node dissection of 1 to 4 mm thick melanomas for patients 60 years of age and younger. Ann Surg 224:255–263, 1996.

Bonnen MD, Ballo MT, Myers JN, et al: Elective radiotherapy provides regional control for patients with cutaneous melanoma of the head and neck. Cancer 100:383–389, 2004.

Brazilian Head and Neck Cancer Study Group: Results of a prospective trial on elective modified radical classical versus supraomohyoid neck dissection in the management of oral squamous carcinoma. Am J Surg 176:422–427, 1998.

Callender DL, Sherman SI, Gagel RF, et al: Cancer of the thyroid. In Myers EN, Suen JY (eds): Cancer of the Head and Neck, 3rd ed. Philadelphia, WB Saunders, 1996, pp 485–515.

Callender DL, Weber RS: Modified neck dissection. In Shockley WW, Pillsbury HC (eds): The Neck: Diagnosis and Surgery. St. Louis, Mosby, 1994, pp 413–430.

Department of Veterans Affairs Laryngeal Cancer Study Group: Induction chemotherapy plus radiation compared with surgery plus radiation in patients with advanced laryngeal cancer. N Engl J Med 324:1685–1690, 1991.

Kowalski LP, Carvalho AL: Feasibility of supraomohyoid neck dissection in N1 and N2a oral cancer patients. Head Neck 24:921–924, 2002.

Myers EN, Gastman BR: Neck dissection: An operation in evolution. Arch Otolaryngol Head Neck Surg 120:14–25, 2003.

Peretti G, Nicolai P, Redaelli De Zinis LO, et al: Endoscopic CO_2 laser excision for Tis, T1, and T2 glottic carcinomas: Cure rate and prognostic factors. Otolaryngol Head Neck Surg 123:124–131, 2000.

CHAPTER 55

LOCAL FLAPS OF THE HEAD AND NECK

Michael P. McConnell, MD, and
Gregory R.D. Evans, MD, FACS

GENERAL PRINCIPLES

1   What are the advantages of using local flaps in the head and neck?
- Local flaps have similar skin color and texture for the site of the defect.
- Donor sites frequently can be closed directly.
- Partial or complete loss of skin grafts can leave color mismatch to native skin.
- Use of local flaps is associated with less scar contracture.

2. Full-thickness defects up to what width can be repaired with composite grafts?
From 1 to 1.5 cm. In practicality, the color and texture mismatch precludes the use of grafts. One should make every attempt to use local tissue, when available, for reconstruction. Good candidate sites for composite graft reconstruction include the nasal ala and the ear. Good donor sites for composite graft harvest include the concha and helical root of the ear.

3. What are the major problems with the use of local flaps?
Local flaps of the head and neck require planning and experience. Flaps should be the same size and thickness of the defect; otherwise, problems will develop. Flaps that are designed too small for the defect can lead to trapdoor deformities. The use of local flaps is more difficult in children because of their relative lack of skin laxity. Preservation of local anatomic landmarks such as the temporal hairline and eyebrows is imperative.

4. In the planning of local flaps, what are the two main vasoelastic biomechanical properties of the skin of which the surgeon must be aware?
- *Stress relaxation* occurs when a constant load is applied to the skin, causing it to stretch. With time the load required to maintain the skin in its stretched position decreases.
- *Creep* occurs when a sudden load is applied to the skin and is kept constant. The amount of extension increases with the passage of time.

5. Where should incision lines for local flaps and donor areas be placed?
Lines of minimal relaxed tension. The skin tension is at right angles to these lines.

6. In the design of a rotational flap the defect should be excised in what shape?
A triangle with the base as the shortest side.

7. In a rotation flap, where is the line of greatest tension?
The line of greatest tension extends from the pivot point of the flap to where the edge of the defect nearest to where the flap previously lay (Fig. 55-1).

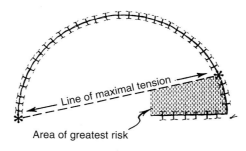

Figure 55-1. Rotation flap. (From Jackson IT: Local Flaps in Head and Neck Reconstruction. St. Louis, Mosby, 1985, p 10.)

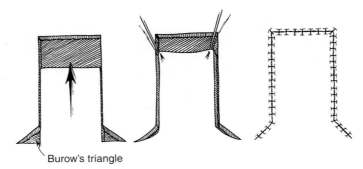

Figure 55-2. Burow's triangles. (From Jackson IT: Local Flaps in Head and Neck Reconstruction. St. Louis, Mosby, 1985, p 13.)

8. In an advancement flap, what is excessive skin at the base called?
Burow's triangles, which are excised lateral to the flap base (Fig. 55-2).

9. How many potential flaps can be designed from each rhomboid defect?
Four (Fig. 55-3).

10. What are the common angels of the rhomboid defect created for flap closure?
60° and 120°.

11. Large circular defects can be converted into a hexagon to facilitate closure. How many rhomboid flaps are available for closure of this defect?
Six (Fig. 55-4).

12. How many rhomboid flaps are most commonly used for closure of a hexagonal defect?
Three.

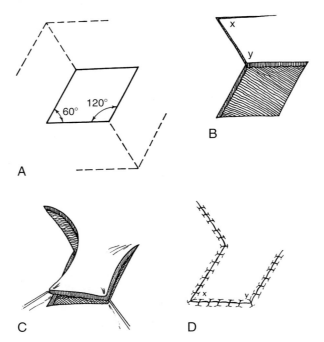

Figure 55-3. Rhomboid (Limberg) flap. **A,** Four potential flaps can be designed from each rhomboid defect. **B,** As with Z-plasty, flap elevation should extend slightly beyond the base of the flap. **C, D,** The angles of the flap are secured with three-point sutures, and the donor site is closed directly. (From Jackson IT: Local Flaps in Head and Neck Reconstruction. St. Louis, Mosby, 1985, p 17.)

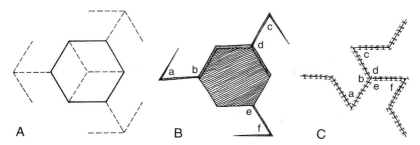

Figure 55-4. Triple rhomboid. A hexagon can be converted into three rhomboids. Rhomboid flaps can be planned on the 120° angle; thus six potential flaps are available. Three of these flaps are used for closure of the defect. (From Jackson IT: Local Flaps in Head and Neck Reconstruction. St. Louis, Mosby, 1985, p 19.)

13. What are the angles used for a Dufourmental flap?
30° and 150°. This flap adheres to similar principles as the rhomboid flap but is based on 30° and 150° angles instead of 60° and 120°. This allows closure with less tension than the traditional rhomboid flap.

14. What are the major indications for performing a Z-plasty?
- Adjusting contours through tissue reorientation.
- Realigning scars within lines of minimal tension.
- Lengthening linear scar contractures.
- Dispersing linear scars for cosmetic adjustment.

15. In the design of a Z-plasty, what angles yield what percent gain in length?
See Table 55-1. The 60° Z-plasty is most commonly used because it adds considerable length while minimizing the closure tension.

16. What is the major indication for a W-plasty?
Scar revision.

17. What are the causes for local flap failure in the head and neck include?
- Small flap design to fill a large defect
- Hematoma
- Damaged blood supply *(technical error)*
- Making the flap extend outside the blood supply *(design fault)*
- Suturing the wound under tension and failing to use a back-cut

18. Describe the fallacy of the length-to-width ratio in designing skin flaps in the head and neck.
The fallacy is that by widening the base of a flap you can improve the perfusion length of the flap by incorporating a greater number of vessels at the base. In the past, flaps were designed by this length-to-width ratio so that a wider base was needed to transfer a longer flap. These wider flaps may incorporate more vessels; however, the vessels all have the same perfusion pressure, and necrosis still occurs at the distance where the perfusion pressure falls below the closing pressure of a capillary bed. The survivability of the distal portion of a flap depends on the physical properties of the vessels supplying the flap and their perfusion pressures.

Comment: All of the flaps discussed can be used for defects in the head and neck.

Table 55-1. Z-Plasty Design	
Z-PLASTY	**THEORETIC GAIN**
30°	25%
45°	50%
60°	75%
75°	100%
90°	120%

FOREHEAD

19. Much of the forehead can be anesthetized by infiltration of local agents around which nerves?
The supraorbital nerves. These nerves are located at the junction of the central and medial thirds of the supraorbital rim and are from cranial nerve (CN) V.

20. The key concept in forehead reconstruction is a firm knowledge of which structures?
Fixed aesthetic structures, such as the eyebrows and hairline.

21. Which area of the forehead has thinner and more pliable skin?
The glabella region.

22. What is the motor supply to the forehead musculature?
The frontal branch of the facial nerve (CN VII), which travels along a line from 0.5 cm below the tragus to 1.5 cm above the lateral end of the eyebrow. The frontal branch of the facial nerve lies within the temporoparietal fascia superior to the zygomatic arch. This facial nerve branch is located in a deep plane in the facial area and becomes more superficial as it crosses the zygomatic arch into the temporal region. Operative procedures that involve exposure of the zygomatic arch for reconstruction or subperiosteal exposure of the facial skeleton should be performed through dissection deep to the temporoparietal fascia to prevent injury.

23. Where are the lines of minimal tension in the forehead?
Transverse in the forehead and vertical in the glabella region. Scars placed on the diagonal are least satisfactory.

24. To avoid pin cushioning, how should incisions be placed?
Vertically oriented through the skin.

25. What are the four aesthetic units of the forehead?
- Main forehead
- Supra eyebrow
- Temporal
- Glabella

26. Which technique allows additional rotational length for flaps on the forehead and scalp?
Galeal scoring with intervals of 0.5 to 1 cm.

27. When scalp mobility and galeal scoring are not sufficient, which technique allows for closure of difficult defects?
Bilateral rotational flaps. The defect is triangulated and bilateral scalp flaps are elevated. The forehead is denervated; however, because bilateral flaps are elevated, symmetry is maintained. Problems may arise if the lateral incisions are carried too posterior to interfere with the blood supply.

28. How is supra eyebrow reconstruction best achieved?
With island flaps based on the superficial temporal artery.

29. How is the eyebrow best reconstructed?
Micrografts (hair follicle transplantation).

30. Because of the limited amount of forehead skin, epidermolysis can occur. How should it be treated?
Conservatively. Bony exposure may require removal of the outer cortex and permitting the wound to granulate or skin grafting of the defect. Alternatively, another local flap may be required; however, most defects heal remarkably well by secondary intention.

LIPS

31. What are the major functional muscles of the lips and cheeks?
The orbicularis oris is a complex sphincter that functions in conjunction with the muscles of facial expression. Its deep and oblique fibers are positioned in and about the vermilion and function as a sphincter to approximate the lips to the alveolar arch. The superficial elements receive decussating fibers from the buccinator and function to purse and

protrude the lips. A major muscle of the cheek is the buccinator, which originates from the alveolar process of the maxilla, mandible, and pterygomandibular raphe and inserts at the corners of the mouth deep to the other muscles of facial expression. The buccinator fibers from above become continuous with the orbicularis of the lower lip and those from below merge with the orbicularis fibers of the upper lip. On the superficial surface of the buccinator are the buccopharyngeal fascia and the buccal flap pad. In the region of the third molar, the muscle is pierced by the parotid duct. The action of the buccinator is cheek compression, which serves to assist other muscles in mastication. The principal elevator of the upper lip is the levator labii superioris. The zygomaticus major draws the lip up and back while the risorius and buccinator clear the gingival sulci. Depression and lip retraction are mainly controlled by the platysma, depressor labii inferioris, and depressor anguli oris.

32. What are the reconstructive goals of the lip?
- Complete skin coverage
- Reestablish the vermilion
- Adequate stomal diameter
- Reestablishment of sensation
- Oral sphincter competence

33. Anesthetic blockade of the lower lip can be accomplished by infiltration of anesthesia at the mental nerve foramen located beneath the apex of which mandibular tooth?
The mental nerve foramen can be found beneath the apex of the second bicuspid tooth. This nerve supplies sensory innervation to the skin and mucous membranes of the lower lip as well as the skin of the anterior mandible and chin.

34. During surgical resection and reconstruction, the vermilion–skin junction should be crossed at what angle?
90°. The vermilion–skin junction should be tattooed with methylene blue and a 25-gauge needle prior to surgical resection. This prevents the loss of the white roll with the application of anesthetic combined with epinephrine. Discrepancies in alignment as little as 1 mm may be noticeable.

35. In the staircase or stepladder technique for lip reconstruction, what is the measure of the horizontal component of the step excisions?
The step technique allows closure of defects of up to two thirds of the lower lip. This type of flap retains relatively good sensation, muscle continuity, and function and can be adjusted for lateral defects. The horizontal component of the step excisions measure half the width of the defect; thus usually two to four steps are required. The vertical dimension of each step is 8 to 10 mm (Fig. 55-5).

36. What are the indications for an Abbe flap?
The Abbe flap is a highly useful flap that can be used for moderate-sized defects of the upper and lower lips. Indications for the flap include a moderate-sized defect of the lower lip that is off center but spares the commissure, a defect of the philtrum of the upper lip, and restoration of symmetry to an overly small lower lip as part of a staged reconstruction. The flap should be positioned so that the width of the vermilion of the donor site matches the lip segment being replaced. The flap is designed with the width half of the defect so that tissue deficiency will be shared equally between the upper and lower lip. If a discrete aesthetic unit is being replaced, the exact corresponding size of the flap should be outlined. Division of the flap occurs at 2 to 3 weeks (Fig. 55-6).

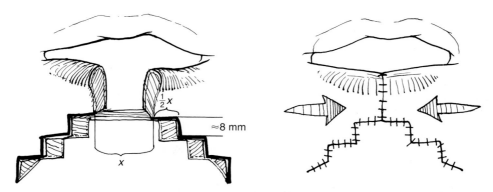

Figure 55-5. Staircase of stepladder method introduced by Johanson et al. in 1974 can be used for both central and lateral defects. Although function and sensation may be preserved, the incisions usually are obvious. (From Zide BM: Deformities of the lips and cheeks. In McCarthy JG [ed]: Plastic Surgery. Philadelphia, WB Saunders, 1990, p 2009.)

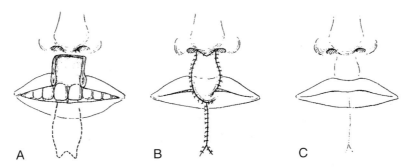

Figure 55-6. A, Central upper lip full-thickness defect, with design of shield-shaped flap (Abbe flap) from lower lip based on inferior labial artery. **B,** Transposition of central Abbe flap, with donor site inferior edge descending to labial mental sulcus. **C,** Maturation of wound: End result. (From Lesavoy MA: Lip deformities and their reconstruction. In Lesavoy MA [ed]: Reconstruction of the Head and Neck. Baltimore, Williams & Wilkins, 1981, p 95.)

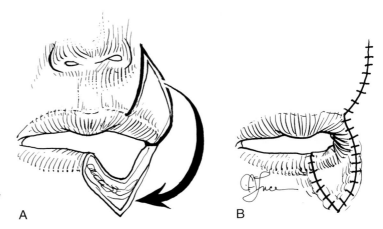

Figure 55-7. A, B, Estlander flap. Although this flap provides closure for lower lip defects, it produces a rounded commissure that may require secondary revision. (From Zide BM: Deformities of the lips and cheeks. In McCarthy JG [ed]: Plastic Surgery. Philadelphia, WB Saunders, 1990, p 2009.)

37. How are defects of the commissure addressed?

The Estlander flap is most useful in medium-sized lateral defects of the upper or lower lip that includes the commissure. Its dissection is similar to the Abbe flap, but because it does not have to preserve an intact commissure it can be performed in one stage. As with the Abbe flap, the Estlander flap is designed to include approximately half of the defect. Secondary revisions of the commissure may be required (Fig. 55-7).

38. Which flap restores lip continuity with preservation of the motor and sensory function?

The Karapandzic flap, a modification of the Gilles fan flap, maintains the neurovascular pedicle in the soft tissue while rotating and restoring sphincter continuity. For this reason it tends to provide better functional results (Fig. 55-8).

39. The Bernard operation advances full-thickness local flaps with concomitant triangular excisions to allow proper mobilization. What does the Webster modification of the Bernard-Burow cheiloplasty include?

- Excision of skin and subcutaneous tissue only in Burow's triangles to maintain innervated muscle-bearing flaps
- Location of the triangular excisions farther laterally in the nasolabial fold instead of next to the commissure
- Paramental Burow's triangles to ease inferior advancement of the cheek tissue (Fig. 55-9)

40. What are the options for restoration of the hair-bearing skin for lip reconstruction?

The nasolabial flap can be used for hair-bearing reconstruction of the upper lip. However, full-thickness flaps destroy innervation to the upper lip. The temporal island scalp flap also can be used for hair restoration. Additionally, micrograft hair follicle transplantation can be used.

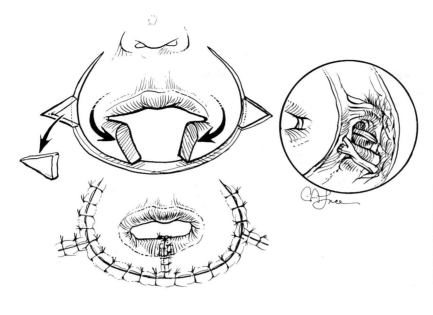

Figure 55-8. Karapandzic technique produces a functioning sphincter and can be used bilaterally. Central defects of up to 80% can be reconstructed. (From Zide BM: Deformities of the lips and cheeks. In McCarthy JG [ed]: Plastic Surgery. Philadelphia, WB Saunders, 1990, p 2009.)

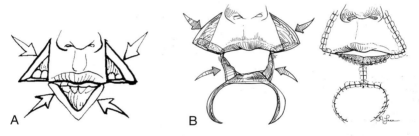

Figure 55-9. **A,** Original Bernard operation used for full-thickness triangular incisions. **B,** Webster modification provided major technical advances. Mucosal flaps *(stippled)* were used for vermilion reconstruction. The nasolabial excisions became partial thickness. Schuchardt flaps facilitated cheek advancement. (From Zide BM: Deformities of the lips and cheeks. In McCarthy JG [ed]: Plastic Surgery. Philadelphia, WB Saunders, 1990, p 2009.)

41. In commissure reconstruction, restoration of what structure is critical?
Restoration of the orbicularis oris sphincter mechanism is critical for oral competence. This can be performed by approximation of this muscle with suture.

CHEEK

42. What are the aesthetic units of the cheek?
The aesthetic units of the face are composed of topographic zones of the cheek. These zones include the suborbital, preauricular, and buccomandibular zones.

43. The cheek can be anesthetized by infiltration of local agents around what nerves?
The *infraorbital nerve* is located at the junction of the central and medial thirds of the infraorbital rim at a point 0.5 to 1 cm below the rim. The *mental nerve* exits from the foramen 1 to 1.5 cm above the lower rim in the region of the canine premolar teeth. It lies in the vertical plane along with the supraorbital and infraorbital nerve. The *mandibular nerve* supplies an area extending to the tragus but not incorporating the ear and stopping short of the inferior border of the mandible. The lower cheek and neck are supplied by the *anterior cutaneous nerves* and the *great auricular nerve*.

44. What is the motor nerve supply to the muscles of the cheek?
CN VII to the superficial muscles and CN V to the masseter.

45. Reconstruction over the malar eminence may impinge upon what important structures?

The lower lid and canthal areas. Flap design should be performed to place the minimal amount of tension within this area. Prevention of lower lid ectropion can be performed by securing the advancing flap to the periosteum of the zygoma thus preventing pull on the lower lid.

46. Small defects of the cheek area are best reconstructed with what type of flaps?

Defects that are not amenable to primary closure frequently are suited for small local flaps. The laxity and vasculature of the facial skin enable the closure of defects that may not be acceptable in other body locations. The Limberg (rhomboid) local transposition and rotational flaps offer well-vascularized tissue for wound closure. In addition, use of these flaps over the malar eminence may prevent an ectropion due to skin graft contracture. The nasolabial flap provides well-padded vascularized tissue. The bulky nature of the flap and the requirement of further revisions of the dog ears may preclude the use of this flap for some patients.

47. Defects approaching 4 × 6 cm are best reconstructed with what type of flap?

The cervicofacial flap describes a reconstructive method that requires extensive cervical cheek, retroauricular, and chin undermining for flap advancement. The flap can be extended onto the chest if necessary. The rotation of the flap is in a superomedial direction, and a superior dissection lateral to the eye must be performed to prevent possible ectropion as the flap is advanced. In smokers, that flap should not be raised in the subcutaneous plane alone. Dissection into the mucosa can allow closure of intraoral and through-and-through defects with this flap.

48. Describe the submental mycocutaneous flap and blood supply. What regions of the face/neck can be reconstructed with this flap?

The submental mycocutaneous flap provides an option for reconstruction of defects in the lower, central, and portions of the inferior aspect of the upper third of the face. Defects up to 10 × 6 cm can be covered with this flap, offering contour, color match, and tissue texture that are suitable for facial reconstruction. The flap is raised below the level of the platysma and incorporates the submental artery and vein (branches of the facial artery and vein).

49. What are the advantages of a cervicopectoral flap?

The medially based cervicopectoral flap offers many advantages. First, it is vascularized by anterior thoracic perforators off the internal mammary artery. Second, when the flap is delayed it may replace the entire aesthetic unit of the cheek. The flap is elevated deep to the platysma muscle and anterior pectoral fascia.

HEAD AND NECK

50. What are the optimal characteristics of a technique required for head and neck reconstruction?

Reliability is the most important factor in any type of oncologic reconstruction. Patients requiring head and neck reconstruction usually have advanced disease, with either a limited survival or the need for adjuvant therapy. A failed reconstruction that prolongs hospitalization time and increases cost does not improve quality of life. Furthermore, prolonged reconstruction is time taken away from family and/or additional adjuvant therapy. A reliable reconstructive technique reduces temporal demands. This attribute must be kept in mind when choosing a reconstructive method.

Expediency must be considered for any reconstructive technique. In most cases a one-stage reconstruction should be used. Patients seldom benefit from multistage procedures that will take several months to complete, delaying adjuvant therapy and interfering with valuable family time.

Function and cosmesis are other important considerations during the planning of any type of reconstruction. Whether restoration of contour is possible depends on the defect size, the location, and the structures involved. The type and grade of the tumor as well as the psychological makeup of the patient determine the reconstructive method that will provide the best function and contour.

51. How are defects of the head and neck classified?

Three categories of head and neck defects have been identified by Hanna. The type of defect must be defined prior to choosing a reconstructive modality.

- *Class A: Defects Requiring Mandatory Cover.* Class A defects include exposed brain and/or dura, ocular structures, great vessels of the neck, upper mediastinum and lungs, and/or bone (cranium and facial bones). Coverage of these structures is critical for wound healing and survival.

- *Class B: Defects Yielding Significant Functional Deficit.* Class B defects include those involving the mucosa and soft tissue of the oral cavity, mandible, lips and cheeks, and/or facial nerve. Reconstruction of these structures is not critical for survival; however, marked functional deficits occur without adequate reconstruction.
- *Class C: Defects Yielding Significant Aesthetic Deficits.* Class C defects involve specialized structures such as the nose, ears, eyes, hair-bearing areas, and/or external skin contours. Although loss of these structures can result in significant loss of cosmesis and quality of life, the timing of reconstruction is less important than with class A and B defects. Temporized wound coverage with simpler reconstructive methods can be used. Definitive reconstruction can be postponed until adjuvant therapy has been completed.

52. Which flap, based on the superficial temporal vessels, can cover large external or intraoral defects?

The forehead flap can include half to two thirds of the forehead and traditionally was used for intraoral reconstruction with a two-stage procedure. The original flap did not include the contralateral forehead tissue; however, the entire forehead can be included with the dissection. Significant donor site morbidity and use of microsurgical reconstruction preclude the use of this flap except for a few indications.

53. The blood supply of the sternocleidomastoid myocutaneous flap is derived from what three sources?

- Occipital artery in the proximal third
- Superior thyroid artery in the middle third
- Branch from the thyrocervical trunk in the distal third

The main limitation of this flap is its variable blood supply and limited arc of rotation. It has been called the most tenuous of all the musculocutaneous flaps used for head and neck reconstruction.

54. Based on the transverse cervical artery, which flap can be elevated in a lateral or descending direction?

The trapezius myocutaneous flap can be designed in several directions. The lateral trapezius flap provides thin, pliable skin over the proximal deltoid area. The origin of the superficial branch of the artery and venous drainage hampers the elevation of this flap. The lower trapezius myocutaneous flap is based on the deep branch of the transverse cervical artery and is innervated by the posterior branch of the spinal accessory nerve. The flap frequently is limited by its arc of rotation, and the donor site over the acromioclavicular joint is subject to high operative morbidity.

55. Which versatile flap is based on the pectoral branch of the thoracoacromial artery?

The pectoralis myocutaneous flap is based on the thoracoacromial artery (pectoral branch), which exits the subclavian artery at the midportion of the clavicle and courses medial to the insertion of the pectoralis minor tendon. The flap can be designed with a skin paddle centered over the lower portion of the muscle, which can be placed intraorally if necessary. The flap has been described as being raised as high as the orbits; however, in practicality it is difficult to secure the closure without significant downward pull on the muscle. The flap can be modified with an extended random skin component or with two separate skin paddles, which can be divided. A rib can be harvested with the flap for bony reconstruction. Higher elevation of the flap can be performed with division of the clavicle.

56. What is the dominant blood supply of the latissimus dorsi muscle?

The dominant blood supply is the thoracodorsal branch of the subscapular artery. The flap is elevated and skeletonized on its vascular pedicle. The muscle is detached from its insertion on the humerus and transferred by tunneling or curving it around to the head and neck defect. The main attributes of the latissimus dorsi are its large size, wide excursion, and low donor site morbidity. The arc of rotation for head and neck defects is difficult and frequently precludes the use of this flap.

BIBLIOGRAPHY

Abulafia AJ, Edilberto L, Fernanda V: Reconstruction of the lower lip and chin with local flaps. Plast Reconstr Surg 97:847–849, 1996.
Ariyan S: One-stage reconstruction for defects of the mouth using a sternomastoid myocutaneous flap. Plast Reconstr Surg 63:618–625, 1979
Ariyan S: The pectoralis major myocutaneous flap. A versatile flap for reconstruction in the head and neck. Plast Reconstr Surg 63:73–81, 1979.
Baker SR, Swanson HA: Local Flaps in Facial Reconstruction. St. Louis, Mosby, 1995.
Bernard C: Cancer de la levre inferieure opere par un procede nouveau. Bull Mem Soc Chir Paris 3:357, 1853.
Crow ML, Crow FJ: Resurfacing large cheek defects with rotation flaps form the neck. Plast Reconstr Surg 58:196–200, 1976.
Dyer PV, Irvine GH: Cervicopectoral rotation flap. Br J Plast Surg 47:68–69, 1994.
Edmond JA, Padilla JF: Preexpansion galeal scoring. Plast Reconstr Surg 93:1087–1089, 1994.
Gandelman M, Epstein JS: Hair transplantation to the eyebrow, eyelashes, and other parts of the body. Facial Plast Surg Clin North Am 12:253–261, 2004.

Goding GS, Hom DB: Skin flap physiology. In Baker SR, Swanson NA (eds): Local Flaps in Facial Reconstruction, St. Louis, Mosby, 1995, pp 15–30.

Gonzalez-Ulloa M, Stevens E: Reconstruction of the nose and forehead by means of regional aesthetic units. Br J Plast Surg 13:305–309, 1961.

Hudson DA: Some thoughts on choosing a Z-plasty: The Z made simple. Plast Reconstr Surg 106:665–671, 2000.

Isenberg JS: Trapezius island myocutaneous flap. Plast Reconstr Surg 107:285–286, 2001.

Jackson IT: Local Flaps in Head and Neck Reconstruction. St. Louis, Mosby, 2002.

Juri J, Juri C: Cheek reconstruction with advancement-rotation flaps. Clin Plast Surg 8:223–226,1981.

Karapandzic M: Reconstruction of lip defects by local arterial flaps. Br J Plast Surg 27:93–97, 1974.

Kolhe PS, Leonard AG: Reconstruction of the vermilion after "lip-shave." Br J Plast Surg 41:68–73, 1988.

Kuttenberger JJ, Hardt N: Results of a modified staircase technique for reconstruction of the lower lip. J Craniomaxillofac Surg 25:239–244, 1997.

McConnell MP, Evans GRD: Advances in reconstructive/plastic surgery in head and neck cancer. In Harrington KJ (ed): Head and Neck Cancer: Biology, Diagnosis and Management. New York, Oxford University Press, 2001.

Netter FH: Atlas of Human Anatomy, 3rd ed. Teterboro, NJ, Icon Learning Systems, 2002.

Pistre V, Pelissier P, Martin D, et al: Ten years of experience with the submental flap. Plast Reconstr Surg 108:1576–1581, 2001.

Ridenour BD, Larrabee WF: Biomechanics of skin flaps. In Baker SR, Swanson NA (eds): Local Flaps in Facial Reconstruction. St. Louis, Mosby, 1995, pp 31–38.

Rodgers BJ, Williams EF, Hove CR: W-plasty and geometric broken line closure. Facial Plast Surg 17:239–244, 2001.

Rohrich RJ, Zbar RI: A simplified algorithm for the use of Z-plasty. Plast Reconstr Surg 103:1512–1517, 1999.

Tobin GR, O'Daniel TG: Lip reconstruction with motor and sensory innervated composite flaps. Clin Plast Surg 17:623–632, 1990.

Tollefson TT, Murakami CS, Kriet JD: Cheek repair. Otolaryngol Clin North Am 34:627–646, 2001.

Webster RC, Coffey RJ, Kelleher RE: Total and partial reconstruction on the lower lip with innervated muscle-bearing flaps. Plast Reconstr Surg 25:360–371, 1960.

Zide BM, Swift R: How to block and tackle the face. Plast Reconstr Surg 101:840–851, 1998.

CHAPTER 56

FOREHEAD RECONSTRUCTION

Mahesh H. Mankani, MD, FACS, and
Stephen J. Mathes, MD

1. How is the forehead histologically similar to, and different from, the scalp?

Like the scalp, the forehead is composed of five tissue layers, including (from superficial to deep) the skin, subcutaneous tissue, epicranius aponeurosis or muscle, loose areolar tissue, and pericranium. In contrast to the scalp, the forehead is thin and has superficially situated hair follicles.

2. What is the vascular supply of the scalp?

The bilateral supratrochlear and supraorbital arteries, terminal branches of the internal carotid arteries, traverse foramina of the same names to enter the forehead just superior to the eyebrows (Fig. 56-1). They cross the plane of the frontalis muscle to lay in the subcutaneous tissues of the anterior forehead, where they freely anastomose with each other. These interconnections allow for the rich variety of forehead flaps. The anterior branch of the superficial temporal artery, which is a terminal branch of the external carotid artery, begins approximately 2 cm superior to the zygomatic arch, courses anteriorly at the level of the anterior temporal hairline, and retains anastomotic connections with the supraorbital and supratrochlear arteries.

3. What is the innervation of the scalp?

Motor innervation of the muscles of the forehead, the frontalis, procerus, and corrugators is via the frontal branch of cranial nerve (CN) VII (Fig. 56-2). The nerve exits the superficial lobe of the parotid gland to cross the zygomatic arch at its middle third. The nerve lies along the superficial surface of the arch within the temporoparietal or superficial temporal fascia. From here it enters the frontalis muscle above the orbital rim. The nerve lies inferior and parallel to the anterior branch of the superficial temporal artery. Its course can be described by a line extending from the anterior border of the lobule of the ear to a point just lateral to the lateral border of the eyebrow. As a result, reconstruction of the forehead in a plane superficial to the frontalis muscles or superficial temporal fascia should spare the frontal branch of CN VII.

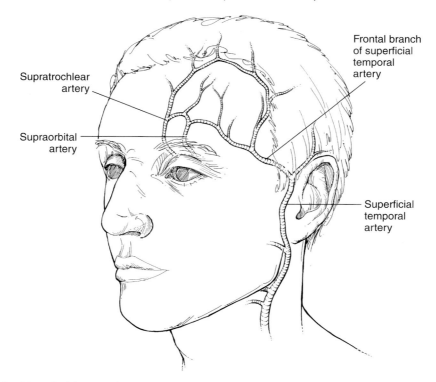

Figure 56-1. Arterial supply of the scalp. (From Mankani MH, Mathes SJ: Forehead reconstruction. In Mathes SJ [ed]: Plastic Surgery, 2nd ed. Philadelphia, WB Saunders, 2006, pp 699–734.)

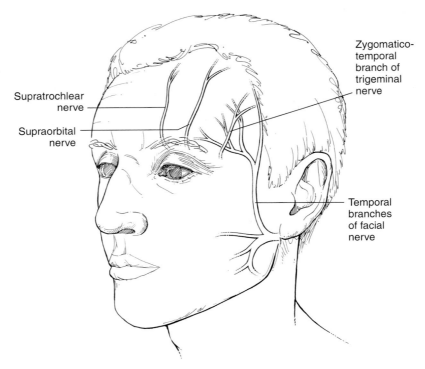

Figure 56-2. Innervation of the scalp. (From Mankani MH, Mathes SJ: Forehead reconstruction. In Mathes SJ [ed]: Plastic Surgery, 2nd ed. Philadelphia, WB Saunders, 2006, p 702.)

Sensation of the forehead arises from the bilateral supraorbital and supratrochlear nerves, each a terminal branch of the ophthalmic division of CN V. Sensation of the pretemporal region arises from the zygomaticotemporal nerve, a branch of the maxillary division of CN V.

4. What are the risks of closing forehead defects via direct approximation of the wound margins?

Direct approximation occasionally necessitates extensive mobilization of the surrounding tissues, which can result in lateral displacement or focal elevation of the eyebrows, disruption of the anterior hairline, or elevation of the upper eyelids resulting in exposure of the ocular globe.

5. Describe the principles inherent to closing large forehead defects.

When defects are large enough to encompass more than half of the forehead, reconstruction of the entire forehead as a single aesthetic unit should be considered. Such en bloc reconstructions can extend from the superior border of the eyebrows to the anterior hairline. Should the defect include a portion of one of the eyebrows, consideration should be given to preserving the fully intact eyebrow while reconstructing the eyebrow already partially or completely lost.

6. What reconstructive options are available in the forehead? What are their relative advantages and their limitations?

The options available for forehead reconstruction are typical of those used elsewhere in the body and include direct wound approximation, closure by secondary intention, skin grafting, local flap, distant flap, skin expansion, microvascular composite tissue transplantation, and flap prefabrication (Table 56-1). The optimum reconstructive option depends on the defect location and size, the patient's clinical condition, and the patient's specific desires and expectations.

7. What types of forehead wounds are optimal for direct closure?

Direct closure is most appropriate for elliptical defects that are transversely oriented in the anterior portion of the forehead, parallel to lines of relaxation. The resultant scar will parallel or even lay within a natural wrinkle, and the natural laxity of the skin may preclude the need for undermining to achieve a tension-free closure. The transverse dimension of the defect can be as long as the full width of the forehead; however, the wound must have a limited vertical height.

Table 56-1. Forehead Reconstructive Options

	ADVANTAGES	LIMITATIONS	APPROPRIATE DEFECT SIZE AND SHAPE	BONE VIABILITY AT WOUND BASE	CONTOUR QUALITY	TISSUE PLIABILITY	TISSUE STABILITY	APPEARANCE
Direct wound edge approximation	Rapid operative time One stage procedure Absence of additional scars	Difficult for wounds close to the anterior hairline or eyebrows	For elliptical transverse defects with a limited vertical height	Can cover bone denuded of periosteum	Excellent	Pliability increases with time	Excellent	Excellent
Closure by secondary intention	Non-operative No additional scarring	Long healing time Possible distortion of surrounding structures	3–4mm punch biopsy wounds Medial forehead flap donor sites	Necessitates viable bone at base	Adequate	Poor to adequate	Adequate	Adequate Skin is occasionally thin and shiny
Skin grafting	Minimizes distortion of surrounding structures High likelihood of success Rapid operative time	Donor site scar, usually at supraclavicular fossa	Small, partial thickness defects, <2 cm diameter	Necessitates viable bone and periosteum at base. May first necessitate transfer of a periosteal flap to support the graft	May become depressed over time	Adequate	Adequate	Poor to adequate Over time, skin appears shiny and depressed.
Local flap	Rapid operative time One stage procedure	Flap donor site scar	5mm to 3cm in size	Can cover bone denuded of periosteum	Excellent	Excellent	Excellent	Very good
Distant flaps	Entire forehead can be reconstructed without use of microvascular composite tissue transplantation	Significant donor defect	Entire forehead can be reconstructed as a unit	Can cover bone denuded of periosteum	Adequate Can be bulky	Excellent	Excellent	Very good
Skin expansion	Uses adjacent forehead skin, minimizing additional donor defects Excellent appearance.	Staged procedures Transient deformity during expansion Risk of expander loss or infection.	Subtotal forehead defects	Can cover bone denuded of periosteum	Very good	Excellent	Excellent	Excellent
Microvascular composite tissue transplantation	Single stage reconstruction for entire forehead Can provide a functional reconstruction.	Complex procedure Long operative time Risk of flap loss.	Total forehead defects	Can cover bone denuded of periosteum	Adequate Can be bulky	Excellent	Excellent	Very good
Flap prefabrication	Can theoretically provide for the creation of complex flaps incorporating novel combinations of tissue elements	Complex staged procedures	Total forehead defects	Can cover bone denuded of periosteum	Adequate Can be bulky	Excellent	Excellent	Very good

(From Mankani MH, Matnes SJ: Forehead reconstruction. In Mathes SJ [ed]: Plastic Surgery, 2nd ed. Philadelphia, WB Saunders, 2006.)

8. What are the advantages and disadvantages of direct closure?

Advantages of this technique include the relative rapidity of the closure, the ability to complete it in one stage, and the absence of additional scars in the forehead. It can be used to close full-thickness defects, including those extending to the cranium. Among its disadvantages are its inappropriateness for wounds that are long in the transverse dimension and for some unilateral wounds adjacent to the eyebrows because it may distort eyebrow position.

9. What are the advantages and disadvantages of closure by secondary intention?

Closure by secondary intention is of limited utility in forehead reconstruction. It is most appropriate for very small lesions, such as 3- to 4-mm punch biopsy wounds. Additionally, it is useful for those patients with a large defect who are unable to tolerate a larger operative procedure. It is commonly used for closure of the median forehead flap donor site where direct closure is not possible.

10. What is the "Crane principle"?

The Crane principle can be used to resurface bare bone (Fig. 56-3). The Crane principle involves placing a flap on a poorly vascularized wound for a short period of time and then returning it to its location while leaving behind a layer of vascularized tissue at the recipient site on which a skin graft can be placed. For instance, a scalp flap can be elevated just deep to the galea and transferred to the forehead. Three weeks later, at the second stage, the flap is elevated in the subcutaneous plane and returned to its scalp donor site, leaving galea and subcutaneous tissue at the forehead. The forehead wound now can be covered with a split-thickness skin graft from a supraclavicular site. The advantages include minimal donor site morbidity, creation of a smooth pliable bed in the forehead, and adequate color match using supraclavicular skin. However, the technique has the disadvantage of requiring two operative stages.

11. What are the advantages and disadvantages of using local flaps in the forehead?

Because they come from adjacent forehead skin, local flaps provide excellent color and texture match. Proper patient and flap selection can minimize donor site morbidity and scarring. These operations are limited in scope and can be completed using local anesthesia. They are most appropriate for wounds of limited size, from 5 mm to 3 cm in diameter, although the Worthen flap can cover more sizable defects by rotation of adjacent forehead tissue (Fig. 56-4).

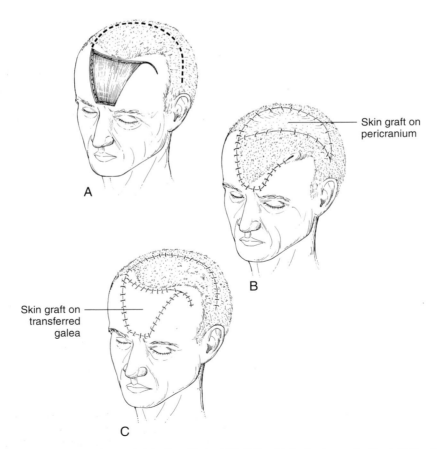

Figure 56-3. A–C, Flap based on the Crane principle. (From Mankani MH, Mathes SJ: Forehead reconstruction. In Mathes SJ [ed]: Plastic Surgery, 2nd ed. Philadelphia, WB Saunders, 2006, p 709.)

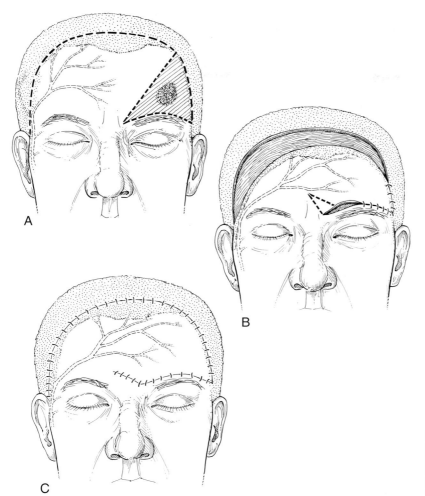

Figure 56-4. **A–C,** Worthen flap. (From Mankani MH, Mathes SJ: Forehead reconstruction. In Mathes SJ [ed]: Plastic Surgery, 2nd ed. Philadelphia, WB Saunders, 2006, p 709.)

12. Which local flaps are appropriate for the forehead?

Random local flaps appropriate to the forehead include the rhomboid, dual rhomboid, banner, and bilobed flaps. Among pedicled flaps, the bilateral temporal artery V-Y fasciocutaneous advancement flaps are appropriate for closing medial forehead defects and can cover the full width of the brow if necessary. Pedicled flaps based on the bilateral supratrochlear and supraorbital vessels can be advanced to close lateral forehead wounds. Shutter flaps using lateral forehead tissue can be used to close central defects (see Fig. 56-5).

13. How are shutter flaps used in the forehead?

Shutter flaps can be based superiorly or inferiorly (Fig. 56-5). Inferiorly based flaps, perfused by the supraorbital vessels, are appropriate for midline defects. The limits of the flap are the anterior and pretemporal hairline; the flaps should be incised outside the hair-bearing scalp to preclude hairline distortion. The dissection of the flaps should extend just deep to the dermis, but not into the frontalis muscle fascia, to minimize danger to the frontal branch of the facial nerve. The flaps can be transposed to the midline and secured with fine nonabsorbable suture. The donor site can be closed directly if temporal scalp can be elevated and mobilized anteriorly. Alternatively, the donor site can be closed with a skin graft, which subsequently can be serially excised.

14. What are the advantages of skin expansion during forehead reconstruction?

Expanded skin can have a color, texture, and thickness similar to the skin that it is replacing. Use of skin expansion can minimize scars in the donor site. In addition, expanded flaps are more resistant to infection than random cutaneous flaps. Unfortunately, expander use necessitates a two-stage reconstruction, and the patient must bear a transitory deformity from the expanders during the expansion phase.

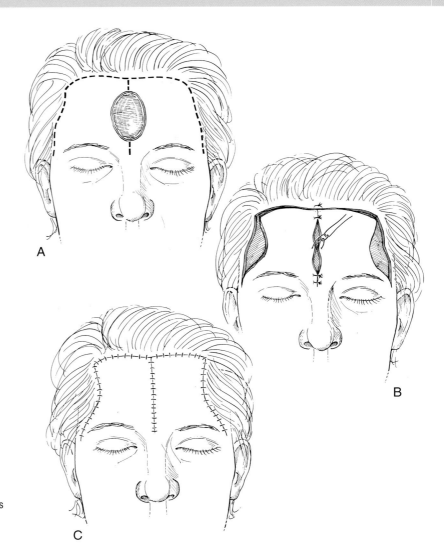

Figure 56-5. A–C, Shutter flap. (From Mankani MH, Mathes SJ: Forehead reconstruction. In Mathes SJ [ed]: Plastic Surgery, 2nd ed. Philadelphia, WB Saunders, 2006, p 711.)

15. What are the optimum locations for skin expander placement for forehead reconstruction?

Central forehead defects can be closed by expanding normal forehead skin on either side. Alternatively, a unilateral suprabrow wound can be closed by expanding the contralateral forehead. Likewise, a pedicled supratrochlear flap can be preexpanded before transfer to a contralateral defect.

16. Describe a distant flap that can be used to reconstruct the forehead.

Few distant non–hair-bearing flaps will reach the forehead. The vertical pedicled trapezius musculocutaneous flap, perfused by the descending branch of the transverse cervical artery and vein, is one such flap.

17. What are the advantages and disadvantages of reconstruction using microvascular composite tissue transplants?

These flaps can reconstruct defects as large as the entire forehead in a single stage, and they can provide functional reconstruction of the frontalis muscle. Unfortunately, such flaps are associated with long operative times and a defined risk of flap loss. Although the tissue pliability, stability, and appearance are good, these flaps can be excessively bulky.

18. What flaps serve as appropriate sources for microvascular composite tissue transplants to the forehead?

Optimal flaps include the latissimus dorsi musculocutaneous flap, radial forearm fasciocutaneous flap, groin fasciocutaneous flap, and lateral arm fasciocutaneous flap. The superficial inferior epigastric artery (SIEA) fasciocutaneous flap is preferred over the groin fasciocutaneous flap because the SIEA flap offers a longer and more consistent vascular pedicle.

19. Describe a flap that can confer function to the forehead.

Functional reconstruction of the frontalis muscle using a free, thinned gracilis musculocutaneous flap has succeeded in conferring eyebrow motion. Consistent with other functional muscle transplantations, it is critical to place the transplanted muscle under appropriate tension at the time of placement.

20. What characteristics are unique to eyebrows among hair-bearing areas?

Eyebrow hair is notable for its thinness and complicated pattern of direction and for the acute angle between hair shaft and skin. Each of the hairs is of small diameter, has a short length, and grows slowly.

21. Describe the orientation of hair within the eyebrows.

Hairs in the medial and lower eyebrow grow in a superolateral direction, whereas those in the lateral and upper regions grow in an inferolateral direction (Fig. 56-6).

22. What are the options for total eyebrow reconstruction?

The options for total eyebrow reconstruction center on three categories of repair: hair plug transplants, hair strip grafts, and pedicled scalp flaps. Each method has its own indications and advantages.

23. What are the advantages and disadvantages of hair plug transplants?

Hair plug transplantation is a low-morbidity procedure. It is most appropriate where healthy recipient bed is available to accept the grafts. The scalp is a good donor site because of the readily available hair and the ease in camouflaging the harvest; however, the hair usually is far from ideal given its far greater thickness and faster growth rate than that needed for the eyebrow. Hair plugs can be placed at the desired acute angle relative to the skin. Multiple procedures often are required to create a sufficiently normal hair density. Additionally, patients must periodically trim the fast growing transplant hairs to maintain length parity with the contralateral normal eyebrow.

24. When are hair strip grafts useful for eyebrow reconstruction?

Free composite grafts of hair-bearing skin, also referred to as hair strip grafts, deliver hair more quickly to the reconstruction site than do hair plug transplants. Like hair plug transplants, they require a healthy, minimally scarred bed. As with hair plugs, the scalp is the most common donor site, but the hairs and follicles are uniformly oriented but often overly dense. Survival of these grafts is less certain than that of hair plugs because of the larger volume of tissue transferred. Survival can be optimized by removal of residual galea aponeurosis and as much fat as possible while still leaving the follicles intact. Nonetheless, multiple procedures still may be necessary to achieve a complete eyebrow.

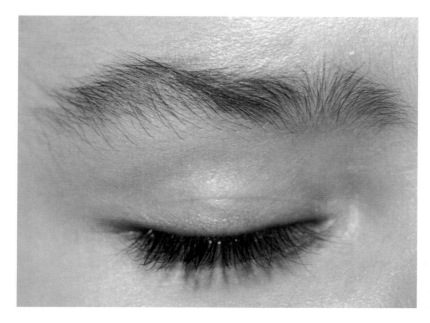

Figure 56-6. Eyebrow hair follicle direction is specific to its location on the eyebrow, as seen in this 10-month-old boy. (From Mankani MH, Mathes SJ: Forehead reconstruction. In Mathes SJ [ed]: Plastic Surgery, 2nd ed. Philadelphia, WB Saunders, 2006, p 727.)

25. What technique should be used to reconstruct the complete eyebrow when the recipient bed is inhospitable to a graft?

Pedicled scalp flaps provide a safe alternative to free grafts. Care should be taken when designing these flaps so that the hairs will grow in the same direction as the intended eyebrow hairs. Inattention to this detail can lead to a hairbrush-appearing eyebrow. In male patients, the scalp donor site should be away from expected areas of male pattern baldness because any tendency toward alopecia will travel with the flap. The postauricular temporoparietal region, perfused by a branch of the superficial temporal artery, is a popular donor site for these reasons.

BIBLIOGRAPHY

Barker DE, Dedrick DK, Burney RE, et al: Resistance of rapidly expanded random skin flaps to bacterial invasion. J Trauma 27:1061–1065, 1987.

Di Giuseppe A, Di Benedetto G, Stanizzi A, et al: Skin expansion versus free forearm flap in forehead reconstruction. Microsurgery 17: 248–253, 1996.

Dzubow LM: Basal-cell carcinoma of the eyebrow region. J Dermatol Surg Oncol 10:609–614, 1984.

Earley MJ, Green MF, Milling MA: A critical appraisal of the use of free flaps in primary reconstruction of combined scalp and calvarial cancer defects. Br J Plast Surg 43:283–289, 1990.

Eufinger H, Wehmoller M, Scholz M, et al: Reconstruction of an extreme frontal and frontobasal defect by microvascular tissue transfer and a prefabricated titanium implant. Plast Reconstr Surg 104:198–203, 1999.

Fan J, Yang P: Versatility of expanded forehead flaps for facial reconstruction. Case report. Scand J Plast Reconstr Surg Hand Surg 31: 357–363, 1997.

Goldman GD: Eyebrow transplantation. Dermatol Surg 27:352–354, 2001.

Gruber S, Papp C, Maurer H: Case report. Reconstruction of damaged forehead with bilateral fasciocutaneous temporal V-Y-advancement island flaps. Br J Plast Surg 52:74–75, 1999.

Hamilton R, Royster HP: Reconstruction of extensive forehead defects. Plast Reconstr Surg 47:421–424, 1971.

Iwahira Y, Maruyama Y: Expanded unilateral forehead flap (sail flap) for coverage of opposite forehead defect. Plast Reconstr Surg 92: 1052–1056, 1993.

Jackson IT: Local Flaps in Head and Neck Reconstruction. St. Louis, CV Mosby, 1985.

Juri J: Eyebrow reconstruction. Plast Reconstr Surg 107:1225–1228, 2001.

Kasai K, Ogawa Y: Partial eyebrow reconstruction using subcutaneous pedicle flaps to preserve the natural hair direction. Ann Plast Surg 24:117–125, 1990.

Levine NS, Sahl WJ, Stewart JB: The "shutter flap" for large defects of the forehead. Ann Plast Surg 36:425–427, 1996.

Mathes SJ, Nahai F: Reconstructive Surgery: Principles, Anatomy, and Techniques. Edinburgh, Churchill Livingstone, 1997.

Millard DR: The crane principle for the transport of subcutaneous tissue. Plast Reconstr Surg 43:451–462, 1969.

Okada E, Maruyama Y: A simple method for forehead unit reconstruction. Plast Reconstr Surg 106:111–114, 2000.

Sasaki K, Nozaki M, Nada Y, Yamaki T: Functional reconstruction of forehead with microneurovascular transfer of attenuated and broadened gracilis muscle. Br J Plast Surg 51:313–316, 1998.

Stuzin JM, Wagstrom L, Kawamoto HK, Wolfe SA: Anatomy of the frontal branch of the facial nerve: The significance of the temporal fat pad. Plast Reconstr Surg 83:265–271, 1989.

Sutton AE, Quatela VC: Bilobed flap reconstruction of the temporal forehead. Arch Otolaryngol Head Neck Surg 118:978–982, 1992; discussion 983–984.

Weinzweig N, Davies B, Polley JW: Microsurgical forehead reconstruction: An aesthetic approach. Plast Reconstr Surg 95:647–651, 1995.

Worthen EF: Repair of forehead defects by rotation of local flaps. Plast Reconstr Surg 57:204–206, 1976.

Yenidunya MO: Axial pattern bilobed flap for the reconstruction of the midline forehead defects. Plast Reconstr Surg 103:737, 1999.

Ziccardi VB, Lalikos JF, Sotereanos GC, Patterson GT: Composite scalp strip graft for eyebrow reconstruction: Case report. J Oral Maxillofac Surg 51:93–96, 1993.

CHAPTER 57

NASAL RECONSTRUCTION

Roy W. Hong, MD, and
Frederick Menick, MD

1. What are the nasal subunits? Are they important in reconstruction?

The nose can be divided into nine topographic subunits composed of the dorsum, tip, columella, and paired sidewalls, alae, and soft triangles (Fig. 57-1). Each subunit has a characteristic skin quality, unit outline, and three-dimensional contour. The normal nose is reestablished only if each of these characteristics is restored. More than obtaining a healed wound, the subunits that describe the nose visually must be restored.

2. What are the principles of subunit reconstruction? How are they applied?

If a defect is to be repaired and the nose looks normal, the characteristics of each subunit must be reestablished. The surgeon must recreate the unit, not just fill the defect. If a defect encompasses more than 50% of a subunit, it is useful to discard adjacent normal tissue about the defect so that the skin of the entire subunit is replaced, not just the missing skin of the defect. This approach positions border scars in the expected shadows or reflections of subunit borders and ensures a uniform skin quality to the unit. A patch-like effect is avoided. Also, when an entire convex unit is resurfaced with a flap, the inevitable trapdoor contraction that occurs in the underlying scar bed acts to recreate the expected convex contour of the entire subunit. This technique avoids the pincushion effect, which may occur when a small flap is placed within a defect that includes only part of a unit. Missing tissues also must be replaced exactly, bringing neither too much nor too little to the wound. If excessive or too little tissue is placed within a defect, the adjacent landmarks and outline will be distorted outward or inward. Similarly, flaps and grafts should be fashioned with a template designed from the contralateral subunit or the ideal so that the outline and quantity of replaced tissue are exact. Contour is the most important determinant of normal. Judicious subcutaneous sculpturing and the use of primary bone and cartilage grafts to create a nasal framework must be used primarily to prevent soft tissue collapse and late soft tissue contraction.

3. Is the quality of nasal skin uniform over its surface?

Skin quality (color, texture, and thickness) differs from one region of the nose to the other. The skin of the nasal dorsum and sidewalls is thin, smooth, and pliable. The skin of the tip and alar subunits is thick, stiff, and pitted with sebaceous glands (Fig. 57-2). These regional differences in skin quality suggest different methods of reconstruction based on the location of the defect and method of wound closure. Skin grafts, because of the temporary ischemia associated with revascularization, always appear thin and shiny after transfer. They frequently become hypopigmented or hyperpigmented. Thus a full-thickness skin graft can be expected to blend well in the smooth-skinned zones of the dorsum or sidewalls. The lax skin of these subunits also lends itself to the use of a local single-lobed flap. In contrast, a thin, shiny skin graft will appear as a patch if placed within the normally thick, pitted skin of the tip or ala. A local or regional flap that will maintain its skin quality is a better choice for tip or alar resurfacing.

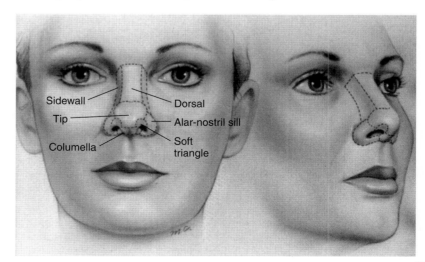

Figure 57-1. Nasal subunits. (From Burget GC, Menick FJ: Aesthetic Reconstruction of the Nose. St. Louis, Mosby, 1994, with permission.)

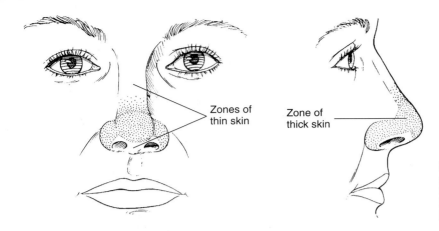

Figure 57-2. Zones of nasal skin quality. (From Burget GC, Menick FJ: Aesthetic Reconstruction of the Nose. St. Louis, Mosby, 1994, with permission.)

4. How should a nasal defect be analyzed? What are the reconstructive implications?

The nose is covered by skin that matches the face in color and texture, supported by a bone and cartilage framework, and lined by thin vascular stratified epithelium and mucosa. The tissue loss from each layer must be identified and replaced with similar material. Lining material must be thin enough to prevent a bulky obstruction of the airway, pliable enough to conform to the desired framework contour, and vascular enough to nourish overlying cartilage or bone grafts. The shape and internal framework of the reconstructed nose must be provided by cartilage or bone grafts. These supporting materials should be placed primarily to prevent soft tissue collapse and late contracture due to scarring associated with wound healing. Finally, covering skin that matches the face in color and texture must be provided.

Just as a surgeon analyzes the anatomic loss, he or she also must examine the aesthetic loss. The wound may be healed but the visual appearance of the nose not restored if the characteristics of the nasal unit and each of its subunits are not reestablished. Each visual subunit must be analyzed and its character restored by using appropriate tissues and lining techniques that recreate the expected visual subunit appearance.

5. What are the advantages and disadvantages of potential donor sites for skin grafting in nasal reconstruction?

For superficial defects with a vascularized bed, full-thickness skin grafts can be used to resurface defects of the upper two thirds of the nose in the zone of smooth skin but usually are an inappropriate choice for defects within the thicker sebaceous skin of the tip or alae. Preauricular skin provides an ideal match. Grafts of 2 to 2.5 cm can be harvested from the hairless skin anterior to the ear in both males and females. The donor site is closed primarily. Postauricular skin is also of value but may appear red postoperatively. Supraclavicular skin is available to resurface the entire nose if necessary, although the color match is less satisfactory. Supraclavicular skin usually has a brownish hue once it has healed in place. Split-thickness skin grafts are used only as temporary wound dressings and are infrequently used in nasal reconstruction.

6. What is the role of composite grafts?

The most common donor site for a composite graft is the root of the auricular helix. A skin sandwich containing thin ear cartilage positioned between two layers of skin is available. Adjacent preauricular skin also can be harvested in continuity with the root of the helix and the donor site closed primarily. Composite grafts must be placed on a well-vascularized bed. The size of the graft should be limited to 1.5 cm or less to enhance survival. Postoperative cooling with cold saline compresses may be helpful. Composite grafts are used for full-thickness defects of the alar rim and may provide a relatively simple one-stage reconstruction. In the long term, they usually appear thin and shiny and do not blend perfectly. Nevertheless, composite grafts are a useful option, especially for defects of the alar margin.

7. How are local flaps used in nasal reconstruction?

For small nasal defects, local flaps are an excellent option. Various flaps can be used for defects in the thin, mobile skin of the upper nose. All of them redistribute the relative excess of lax skin within the sidewall and dorsum to cover the defect while allowing primary closure of the donor site. Fortunately, most incisions on the nose heal with good scars. A local flap can be used if the defect is less than 1.5 cm in diameter and if cartilage grafts are not needed. There is not enough excessive nasal skin to redistribute over the nose to cover larger defects, and the tension created by wound closure will collapse a delicate cartilage framework. A forehead or nasolabial flap is required for defects greater than 1.5 cm or those requiring reconstruction of a cartilage framework.

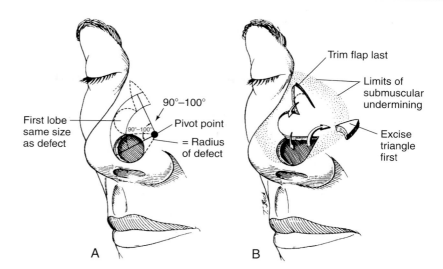

90°–100°

First lobe
same size
as defect

90°–100°

Pivot point

= Radius
of defect

Trim flap last

Limits of
submuscular
undermining

Excise
triangle
first

Figure 57-3. Geometric bilobed flap. (From Burget GC, Menick FJ: Aesthetic Reconstruction of the Nose. St. Louis, Mosby, 1994, with permission.)

A

B

8. What are the advantages of a bilobed flap? Where is it most useful?

The thick sebaceous and adherent skin of the tip and ala does not lend itself to the use of a local flap as easily as the upper nasal two thirds. The bilobed flap (as modified by Zitelli) is an excellent option for nasal tip and alar defects, however. It redistributes excessive tissue from the upper nose to the tip and alae by transferring skin as a bilobed flap. Limiting the rotation of each lobe to less than 50°, performing a primary excision of the dog ear, and wide undermining of the submuscular plane just above the perichondrium and periosteum aid in its success. Resurfacing the tip and alae with a classic single-lobed flap is difficult. The pedicle blood supply to a single-lobed flap is in jeopardy at the time of dog-ear excision, and the rotation of this stiff tissue through 90° of rotation is difficult (Fig. 57-3).

9. How is the nasolabial flap used in nasal reconstruction? What is its blood supply?

The use of cheek tissue was popularized by French and German surgeons in the 1800s. The blood supply of a modern flap is based on the perforators from the facial and angular arteries that pass through the underlying levator labii and zygomatic muscles to the skin. The flap design is positioned just lateral to the nasolabial fold; on closure, the scar lies exactly within the nasolabial crease. Its proximal base is positioned over the rich subcutaneous blood supply that enters from its deep aspect. The distal tip of the flap, situated at or just distal to the oral commissure, can be elevated with just a few millimeters of subcutaneous tissue and then rotated on its thick subcutaneous superior pedicle to cover the alar subunit. Three weeks later, the flap pedicle is divided and the alar base inset completed. Nasolabial tissue is an ideal replacement for the alae. However, the amount of available tissue is limited, and attempts at extending the pedicle to reach the tip or dorsum are risky because of an unreliable blood supply.

A nasolabial flap also can be folded on itself to provide both cover and lining for a full-thickness defect. However, the blood supply is put at risk by folding, primary cartilage grafts are difficult to position, and the result usually appears bulky and thick. Excessive skin from the nasolabial fold can be transferred in one stage as an extension of a random cheek flap. However, a second revision usually is required to recreate the normal alar crease, and it is almost impossible to create a truly aesthetic alar base inset when such a nasolabial flap design is used to rebuild a defect that includes the nasal sill and alar base (Fig. 57-4).

10. What do you know about the history of nasal reconstruction?

In 600 BC, Sushruta described the reconstruction of the nose with forehead and cheek flaps in the *Hindu Book of Revelation.* In the late sixteenth century, Tagliacozzi, an Italian, published a treatise on the use of the pedicle arm flap. The forehead flap was first used in the Western world by Joseph Carpue in England, who had read accounts of the Indian forehead flap in a 1795 issue of *Gentleman's Magazine.* He published two case reports in 1816. In this century, Gillies, Converse, and Millard have pioneered developments.

11. How can forehead tissue be transferred?

Lateral forehead skin can be transferred on the unilateral superficial temporal artery (New's sickle flap) or the contralateral superficial temporal artery (Converse's scalping flap). Both relatively extensive procedures use a hairy scalp pedicle to transfer forehead skin to the nose. The traditional median forehead flap takes central forehead skin based on both right and left supraorbital vascular arcades. However, because of the profuse blood supply to the forehead, midline forehead tissue can be transferred as a paramedian flap based on a unilateral supratrochlear pedicle. Enough skin is available to resurface an entire nose.

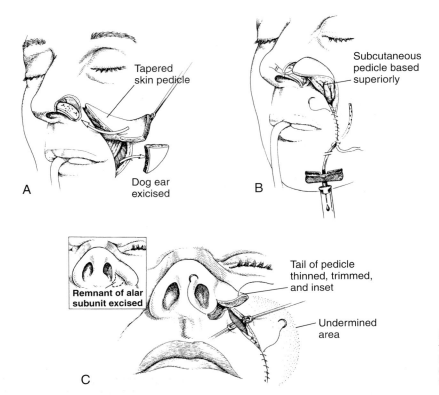

A

Tapered
skin pedicle

Dog ear
exicised

B

Subcutaneous
pedicle based
superiorly

C

Remnant of alar
subunit excised

Tail of pedicle
thinned, trimmed,
and inset

Undermined
area

Figure 57-4. Subunit nasolabial
two-stage flap. (From Burget GC,
Menick FJ: Aesthetic Reconstruction
of the Nose. St. Louis, Mosby, 1994,
with permission.)

12. Describe the blood supply to the paramedian forehead flap.

The blood supply of the central forehead enters vertically from below the supraorbital rim and ascends vertically just above the periosteum. The rich arcade of vessels arising from the supraorbital, supratrochlear, infratrochlear, and dorsal and angular branches of the facial artery pass superiorly from deep to superficial. Above the mid forehead and toward the hairline, the axial vessels lie in the subcutaneous tissue just deep to the dermis. It is safe to elevate the distal 1 to 2 cm of a paramedian forehead flap with skin and a thin layer of subcutaneous tissue. More inferiorly, the flap should be elevated deep to the frontalis muscle, just above the periosteum, to protect the blood supply. The forehead flap itself should be designed vertically to include the vertical axial blood supply.

13. Is there enough skin to make a nose from the midline forehead? Is the reach too short? How wide should the pedicle be? Should I delay the procedure for safety?

Enough skin to resurface an entire nose can be easily transferred with a paramedian forehead flap (Fig. 57-5). The flap can be designed on either the right or left supratrochlear vessel. Either can be used for midline defects, but the reach of the flap is easier when it is based on the same side as a lateral defect. A template of the required missing forehead skin should be placed at the hairline and designed with a 1.5-cm pedicle above the supratrochlear vessels. The narrow pedicle allows easy rotation without undue tension. If the arc of rotation is short, an additional 1.5 cm can be added by extending the flap tip into hair-bearing scalp. If the patient is a healthy nonsmoker, the distal flap can be thinned to the subcutaneous tissue layer and hair follicles destroyed by excision and light coagulation. An additional 1.5 cm can be obtained by extending the flap pedicle base below the supraorbital rim towards the canthus, snipping fibrous bands under magnification but maintaining vessels intact. The flap should be designed vertically to maintain its axial blood supply. When so designed, the flap does not require delay and has sufficient length to reach all nasal defects, including the columella. Curving the flap eccentrically across the forehead destroys its axial nature and puts the distal flap in jeopardy. There are few indications for flap delay. The resulting scarring and stiffness only make later transfer more difficult.

14. How and why are primary bone and cartilage grafts used in nasal reconstruction?

A nose looks like a nose because of its shape. It is the underlying bone and skeletal framework that provides support, nasal projection, and airway patency and recreates a subtle contour that defines the normalcy of each nasal subunit. Cover and lining alone are inadequate.

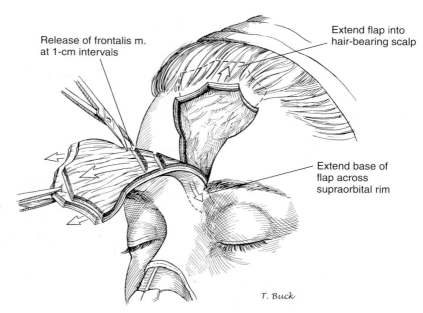

Release of frontalis m.
at 1-cm intervals

Extend flap into
hair-bearing scalp

Extend base of
flap across
supraorbital rim

T. Buck

Figure 57-5. Three ways to gain length for a paramedian forehead flap: (1) extend the flap into the hair-bearing scalp and depilate the flap; (2) extend the flap 1.5 cm over the orbital rim, lifting the eyebrow with the flap, if necessary; and (3) score only the frontalis muscle at 1-cm intervals, allowing the flap to expand up to 1.5 cm longitudinally. (From Mathes S [ed]: Plastic Surgery, 2nd ed. Philadelphia, WB Saunders, 2006.)

15. When and how should bone or cartilage grafts be used?

The soft tissues of cover and lining will collapse without support and be fixed into a shapeless mass by scar. Once scar contraction has occurred, it is difficult to reexpand soft tissues. Thus bone and cartilage grafts should be placed primarily before wound healing is completed. Cartilage grafts depend on lining for vascularity, and lining and covering skin depend on primary cartilage grafts for support and contour. If missing, a support framework for the dorsum, sidewalls, alae, columella, and tip must be replaced. Although the ala normally contains no cartilage, a cartilage alar batten should be used when the ala is reconstructed to maintain its support and shape and to fight the upward contraction associated with wound healing.

16. What donor tissues are available for nasal support? What are the advantages and disadvantages of each?

If available, septal cartilage is the first choice for most nasal grafts. It can be harvested much as cartilage is removed in a submucous resection, leaving a strong septal L for central midline nasal support. The concha of the ear also provides excellent material for ala and tip support. Rib cartilage or rib osteochondral grafts are used for large support defects of the dorsum. Cranial bone grafts also can be used but have a higher rate of reabsorption. Remember that a nasal framework provides support, braces the soft tissue against myofibroblast contraction, and imparts, when seen through a thin covering skin, a nasal shape. Thus every nose must have a dorsal buttress, sidewall brace, alar cartilage reconstructions, and a columellar strut support. Although the normal ala contains no cartilage, an alar batten placed along the alar rim provides its shape and support. Although the importance of support has been stressed in this century, only recently has the importance of a precise, complete skeletal framework been emphasized. Limiting nasal support to a cantilever bone graft or rib L strut does not provide the requirements for long-term success.

17. Is tissue expansion helpful?

Advocates of tissue expansion have used it before nasal reconstruction to increase the available tissue and to assist in primary closure of the forehead. In fact, tissue expansion is rarely necessary. Enough skin can be transferred on an ipsilateral paramedian forehead flap pedicle to resurface the entire nose. Because the pedicle is narrow, closure of the inferior forehead defect is easy. Any defect that remains and cannot be closed primarily is high in the forehead under the hairline. Simply dressed with petrolatum gauze, it will heal by secondary intention and autoexpansion of the forehead. It is unnecessary to skin-graft the forehead defect or to use preliminary tissue expansion. In fact, the capsule that forms around the tissue expander may diminish the pliability of the forehead flap or the quality of the overlying skin. Predicting the degree of tissue retraction that follows expansion and the late effects of skin shrinkage is difficult. Tissue expansion favors the donor site at the expense of the nose. As a central facial defect, the nose always takes priority. The forehead is a forgiving donor site and is of lesser aesthetic importance. Although rarely required, tissue expansion may be used secondarily after nasal reconstruction to improve the donor site.

18. Practically speaking, what is the most important anatomic layer in nasal reconstruction?

Replacement of missing lining tissue is the most difficult challenge in nasal reconstruction and frequently determines the final outcome. Lining must be vascular enough to nourish primary cartilage grafts, supple enough to conform to the appropriate nasal shape, and thin enough so that the airway is not obstructed. Poor results of nasal reconstruction often can be traced to initial provision of insufficient or poorly vascularized lining tissue.

19. What are the options for nasal lining?

The importance of nasal lining has been emphasized since the work of Gillies in World War I. Traditionally, nasal lining has been supplied with turnover hinge flaps of adjacent intact covering skin, folding of a forehead flap upon itself to supply both cover and lining, or skin grafting the forehead flap at a preliminary operation as it lies in the forehead before transfer. All of these methods have the disadvantage of providing poorly vascularized lining and make the placement of primary cartilage grafts difficult.

In most circumstances, residual intranasal lining is the first choice for reconstruction because of its vascularity, availability, and pliability. Fortunately for surgeons, the septum is perfused by the septal branch of the superior labial artery, which permits elevation and lateral transfer of the septal mucous membrane on a 1.2-cm pedicle based in the soft tissue at the nasal spine. The entire septum can be rotated out of the piriform aperture as a sandwich of cartilage between the right and left septal mucosa when based on both superior labial arteries. The facial artery and its angular branches also supply numerous branches to the soft tissues of the lateral nose and alar base.

Frequently, when part of the ala is missing, residual vestibular skin remains intact above the defect. In such circumstances, a bipedicle flap of residual vestibular skin can be incised in the area of the intercartilaginous line and advanced inferiorly to the desired alar rim level. The defect above can be filled with a full-thickness skin graft, raw surface outward, or by an ipsilateral septal mucosal flap based on the ipsilateral superior labial artery. For larger defects, mucoperichondrial flaps based on septal and anterior ethmoid vessels provide significant amounts of highly vascularized thin and supple tissue. The entire septum also can be used as a composite chondromucosal flap to provide both lining and cartilage support (Fig. 57-6).

20. Is there a role for microsurgery in nasal lining reconstruction?

Absolutely. Walton et al. reported their promising experience using free tissue transfer for reconstruction of total or subtotal nasal lining, including the nasal floor, columella, and vestibule. The majority of cases have used the radial forearm free flap, although successful nasal lining reconstruction also has been achieved using the free first dorsal metacarpal artery flap. Use of microsurgical free tissue transfer allows reconstruction of complex three-dimensional anatomy without violating adjacent soft tissues of the face.

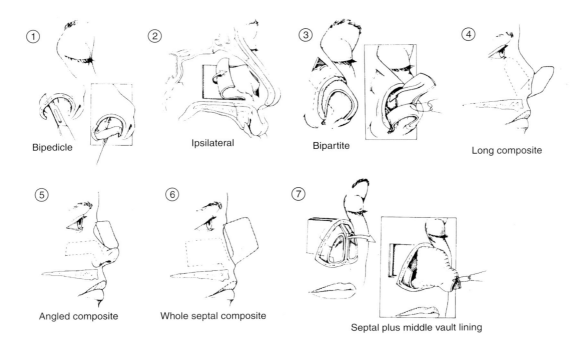

Figure 57-6. Variations of the septal intranasal lining flaps. (From Burget GC, Menick FJ: Aesthetic Reconstruction of the Nose. St. Louis, Mosby, 1994, with permission.)

21. What are the most frequent mistakes in nasal reconstruction?

- Not visualizing the desired aesthetic result before surgery
- Not planning each step in three dimensions and imagining the outcome of a reconstruction for the specific location and method of transfer
- Not taking the time or requisite skill to fabricate your goal.

BIBLIOGRAPHY

Barton FE Jr: Aesthetic aspects of nasal reconstruction. Clin Plast Surg 15:155–166, 1988.
Beahm EK, Walton RL, Burget GC: Free first dorsal metacarpal artery flap for nasal lining. Microsurgery 25:551–555, 2005.
Burget GC, Menick FJ: Nasal reconstruction: Seeking a fourth dimension. Plast Reconstr Surg 78:145–157, 1986.
Burget GC, Menick FJ: Nasal support and lining: The marriage of beauty and blood supply. Plast Reconstr Surg 84:189–202, 1989.
Burget GC, Menick FJ: Subunit principle in nasal reconstruction. Plast Reconstr Surg 76:239–247, 1985.
Burget GC, Walton RL: Optimal use of microvascular free flaps, cartilage grafts, and a paramedian forehead flap for aesthetic reconstruction of the nose and adjacent facial units. Plast Reconstr Surg 120(5):1117–1207, 2007.
Converse JM: Reconstruction of the nose by the scalping flap technique. Surg Clin North Am 39:335–365, 1959.
McCarthy JG, Lorenc PZ, Cutting C, et al: The median forehead flap revisited: The blood supply. Plast Reconstr Surg 76:866–869, 1985.
Menick FJ: A new modified method for nasal lining: The Menick technique for folded lining. J Surg Oncol 94:509–514, 2006.
Menick F: Artistry in facial surgery: Aesthetic perceptions and the subunit principle. In Furnas D (ed): Clinics in Plastic Surgery, Vol 14. Philadelphia, WB Saunders, 1987.
Menick FJ: Nasal reconstruction: Forehead flap. Plast Reconstr Surg 113:100E–111E, 2004.
Menick FJ: A 10-year experience in nasal reconstruction with the three-stage forehead flap. Plast Reconstr Surg 109:1839–1855, 2002.
Menick FJ: Triple-flap technique for reconstruction of large nasal defects. Arch Facial Plast Surg 3:22–23, 2001.
Millard DR: Reconstructive rhinoplasty for the lower two-thirds of the nose. Plast Reconstr Surg 57:722–728, 1976.
Walton RL, Burget GC, Beahm EK: Microsurgical reconstruction of the nasal lining. Plast Reconstr Surg 115:1813–1829, 2005.
Zitelli JA: The bilobed flap for nasal reconstruction. Arch Dermatol 125:957, 1989.

EYELID RECONSTRUCTION

Daniel J. Azurin, MD, and
Armand D. Versaci, MD

1. What are the components of the posterior lamella of the upper lid?

Each eyelid is a bilamellar structure divided by the orbital septum. The anterior lamella of the upper lid is composed of the skin and the orbicularis oculi muscle. The posterior lamella of the upper lid is composed of the tarsus, levator aponeurosis, Müller's muscle, and conjunctiva. The levator aponeurosis is unique to the upper lid and is analogous to the capsulopalpebral fascia of the lower lid. The anterior lamella of the lower lid is composed of the skin and orbicularis oculi muscle. The posterior lamella of the lower lid is composed of the tarsus, capsulopalpebral fascia, and conjunctiva. The orbital septum is a fascial membrane of variable thickness that resists the spread of infection, hemorrhage, and inflammation (Fig. 58-1).

2. Describe the anatomy, innervation, and function of the orbicularis oculi muscle.

The orbicularis oculi muscle, which is innervated by the facial nerve, is responsible for lid closure. It is subdivided into the pretarsal, preseptal, and orbital muscles. The orbicularis oculi is continuous with the superficial musculoaponeurotic system (SMAS) in the upper face as is the platysma in the lower face. The lacrimal pump mechanism is intimately associated with the orbicularis muscle. Contraction of the pretarsal muscle shortens and closes the canaliculi, whereas the preseptal muscle pulls on the lacrimal diaphragm, resulting in a negative pressure within the lacrimal sac. Upon relaxation, tears are driven into the nasolacrimal duct.

3. What is the vertical dimension of the upper and lower tarsus?

The tarsal plates form the structural framework of the eyelids. The vertical height of the upper tarsus is approximately 10 mm. The vertical height of the lower lid ranges from 3.8 to 4.5 mm.

4. How is levator palpebrae superioris function measured?

The levator muscle, a striated muscle innervated by the third cranial nerve, is responsible for raising the lid. The muscle originates from the superior/posterior orbit (lesser wing of the sphenoid) and broadens into the levator aponeurosis, which in turn inserts onto the tarsus. The levator aponeurosis extends laterally and medially into the horns, each of which attaches to the lateral retinaculum and posterior lacrimal crest, respectively. The lateral horn divides the orbital and palpebral lobes of the lacrimal gland. Levator function is measured by the distance (in millimeters) that the upper lid margin travels from downward gaze to upward gaze with the brow immobilized.

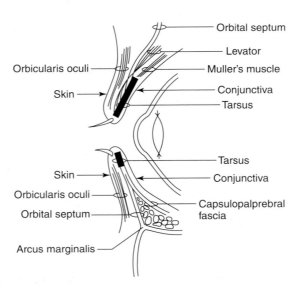

Figure 58-1. Anterior and posterior lamellae of the eyelids.

5. **What pathologic condition is caused by paralysis or laceration of Müller's muscle?**

Müller's muscle is a smooth muscle with sympathetic innervation. It is located in the posterior lamella of the upper lid and has intimate attachments to the levator muscle and the tarsus. It originates from the posterior aspect of the levator muscle and inserts onto the superior border of the tarsus. Müller's muscle provides tone for the upper lid, and injury to this muscle may result in ptosis (2 to 3 mm).

6. **What structures must be transected to explore the orbital floor through a transconjunctival approach?**

The transconjunctival approach is an exposure technique through the posterior lamella of the lower lid, beginning with an incision through the conjunctiva. This incision is followed by transection of the capsulopalpebral fascia. At this point, the approach can be either retroseptal or preseptal to reach the orbital floor, which then is explored in a subperiosteal plane. In a standard blepharoplasty, once the capsulopalpebral fascia is transected, the inferior compartments of orbital fat are directly accessible. In exploring the orbital floor, a lateral canthotomy is added for greater exposure. The capsulopalpebral fascia arises from condensations of the investing layers of the inferior rectus and inferior oblique muscles and inserts onto the inferior border of the tarsus. The capsulopalpebral fascia, which is unique to the lower lid, is involved with the coordinated downward movement of the lower lid during downward gaze. It is somewhat analogous to the levator aponeurosis of the upper lid. The orbital septum, orbicularis muscle, and skin are anterior to the capsulopalpebral fascia. Because the anterior lamella is not transgressed, the transconjunctival approach minimizes the problems of lower eyelid retraction, which are significantly more common after the cutaneous approach. The arcus marginalis is the periosteal attachment of the orbital septum to the bony orbital margin.

7. **What structures contribute to the lateral retinaculum?**

The lateral retinaculum or lateral canthus is a complex integration of a number of structures. It is composed of Lockwood's ligament (inferior suspensory ligament), the lateral extension or horn of the levator aponeurosis, the continuations of the pretarsal and preseptal muscles, and the check ligament of the lateral rectus muscle. This confluence of structures attaches to the lateral orbital wall at Whitnall's tubercle. Whitnall's tubercle is located within the lateral rim of the orbit below the frontozygomatic suture on the frontal process of the zygoma. Therefore inferiorly displaced zygoma fractures pull the lateral canthus inferiorly, resulting in downward slant of the palpebral fissure. Whitnall's ligament is a check ligament of the levator muscle that limits its excursion and is not a part of the lateral retinaculum.

8. **Where does the medial canthus insert?**

The medial canthal tendon is a complex structure that attaches onto the medial aspect of the orbit in a tripartite manner. The insertion points include the anterior lacrimal crest and a portion of the nasal bone, the posterior lacrimal crest, and a less well-defined point around the nasofrontal suture. The medial canthal tendon is intimately associated with the lacrimal pump mechanism. The lacrimal sac lies between the anterior and posterior insertions of the medial canthal tendon. Because the anterior attachment extends medially onto the nasal bones, reattachment of this portion to the anterior lacrimal crest may result in an impression of telecanthus.

9. **Which extraocular muscle originates from the anterior orbit?**

The inferior oblique muscle is the only extraocular muscle that originates from the anterior orbit. It also separates the medial and central fat compartments of the lower lid. The anatomic position of the inferior oblique muscle makes it prone to injury during blepharoplasty. All of the other extraocular muscles originate from the annulus of Zinn near the apex of the orbit.

10. **What defines the supratarsal fold?**

The supratarsal fold corresponds to dermal attachments of the levator aponeurosis. Above these attachments, the overhanging skin creates a fold. The supratarsal fold is approximately 10 mm above the eyelid margin and is often absent in people of Asian descent. The position of the supratarsal fold is important in the evaluation of patients with eyelid ptosis. A high-positioned supratarsal fold may suggest a levator defect.

11. **The fascial framework of the orbit is composed of what structures?**

The fascial framework of the orbit is a connective tissue network that not only provides support to the globe, but also allows coordinated movements among all the orbital contents so that the eye and its associated structures can move in concert. This framework consists of the bulbar fascia or Tenon's capsule, the investing fascial layers of the extraocular muscles, the intermuscular septa, and the check ligaments (condensations of fascia from the medial rectus and lateral rectus, which serve as anchors to the periorbita). Lockwood's ligament is formed by the intermuscular septum between the inferior oblique and the inferior rectus muscle.

12. **What are the most common malignant tumors of the eyelids? What is the most common location for a malignant tumor of the eyelids?**

Basal cell carcinoma is by far the most common malignant tumor of the eyelids, followed by squamous cell carcinoma and sebaceous carcinoma. For well-demarcated, nonsclerosing basal cell carcinomas less than 2 cm in diameter, a 1- to 2-mm grossly free margin will be histologically free of tumor in 94% to 95% of cases. With recurrent or more aggressive tumors, it is necessary to resect larger margins, and it is often wise to delay reconstruction until permanent pathologic specimens are examined. Sebaceous carcinoma of the eyelid is uncommon and difficult to diagnose, and it carries a poor prognosis. The lower lid is the most common site for occurrence.

13. Which region of the eyelid is most likely to have a recurrent or an advanced tumor?

Tumors of the medial canthal region are more likely to be advanced and have a higher chance of recurrence. Medial canthal complexity and location make reconstruction difficult. Tumors of this region often are recognized late and often are inadequately resected.

14. What factors predict postoperative dry eye syndrome?

Orbital and periorbital morphology along with abnormal ocular histories have been shown to be better predictors of postoperative dry eye complications than Schirmer's test. Morphologic abnormalities include proptosis, exophthalmos, lax lower lids, scleral show, and maxillary hypoplasia. Abnormal histories include problems such as allergic conjunctivitis and corneal ulceration. Schirmer's test is an objective measure of the lacrimal secretory capacity. Schirmer's test I measures both basic and reflex secretion by the amount of wetting that occurs on a 5 × 35-mm filter paper placed on the lower conjunctiva for 5 minutes. Less than 10 mm of wetting is considered abnormal. Schirmer's test II is similar to the first test, except that a local anesthetic is dropped into the eye to block reflex secretions.

15. What are the basic principles of eyelid reconstruction?

The eyelid is a dynamic, complex, and delicate structure, which performs indispensable functions related to the eye, serves as a source of beauty, and is not easily duplicated by noneyelid tissues. A clear understanding of the anatomy and functional aspects of the orbital regions is paramount for the success of eyelid reconstruction. The basic principles of eyelid reconstruction include maintenance of the integrity of the upper lid, replacement of deficient tissue with like tissue when possible, maintenance of eye mobility, establishment of an aesthetic balance, and provision of a protective lining, stable skin covering, and internal lid support.

16. A 38-year-old woman with a malignant tumor fixed to the upper tarsus undergoes a full-thickness resection. The resultant defect measures 30% of the horizontal dimension of the lid. What is the most appropriate reconstructive option?

Once a tumor involves the eyelid margin, a full-thickness excision is required, whereas the same tumor that does not involve the lid margin may require only a partial-thickness excision that can be closed directly or with a skin graft. Numerous methods exist for upper eyelid reconstruction. The horizontal dimension of the defect is an important consideration in selecting a reconstructive method, as are the basic principles outlined in Question 15. Generally, for an upper lid defect that is less than 25% of the horizontal length of the lid, the defect can be closed with direct approximation. In elderly patients with lid laxity, defects slightly greater than 25% can be closed by direct approximation. For defects greater than 25% of the horizontal dimension that cannot be closed by direct approximation, reconstruction usually consists of selective lateral cantholysis of the superior crus of the lateral canthal tendon with medial transposition of the lid. The combination of a local skin flap may be necessary. Larger upper lid defects up to 60% of the horizontal dimension require lid switch procedures that borrow like tissues from the lower lid, which are based on the marginal palpebral artery. Lid switch flaps can be designed 25% narrower than the defect width; however, the pedicle should be designed 5 to 6 mm in vertical dimension to avoid injury to the marginal artery. Defects that are 60% to 100% of the horizontal dimension typically are reconstructed with either a Cutler-Beard flap or a Mustardé total lid flap. The Cutler-Beard flap is a full-thickness lower lid advancement flap that is advanced under the intact lower lid margin (bridge) and then set into the upper lid defect. The Mustardé total lid flap closes the upper lid defect with a lateral canthotomy and a full-thickness lid switch flap using as much of the lower lid as needed. This procedure is followed by reconstruction of the lower lid donor defect with a composite graft and cheek advancement flap. Both are two-stage procedures. Other local flaps, such as the nasolabial or glabellar flap, combined with mucosal or composite grafts when needed, are sometimes used for lid and periorbital reconstruction (Fig. 58-2).

17. How much vertical height of upper tarsus is used in the design of a tarsoconjunctival flap for lower lid reconstruction?

As with upper eyelid reconstruction, numerous methods are used to reconstruct the lower lid. Significant differences, however, exist between upper and lower eyelid reconstruction. Because the upper lid is far more dynamic than the lower lid and is essential for corneal protection, lower lid reconstructions generally do not borrow like tissues from the upper lid; rather, reconstructions usually borrow tissues from other sources, such as the cheek. However, lid-sharing techniques for lower lid reconstruction can be highly successful. The Hugh's tarsoconjunctival flap is a well-accepted example. The Hugh's tarsoconjunctival flap is a staged advancement flap using the posterior lamella of the upper lid to reconstruct a lower lid defect. A horizontal incision is made through the posterior lamella of the upper lid, marking the advancing edge of the flap. The incision is made approximately 5 mm away from the lid margin. Approximately 4 to 5 mm of inferior upper lid tarsus needs to be preserved to maintain upper lid support and lid margin stability.

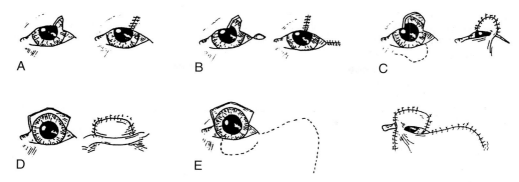

Figure 58-2. Reconstruction of the upper eyelid. **A,** Direct approximation. **B,** Selective lateral cantholysis and medial transposition of the lid. **C,** Lid switch flap. **D,** Cutler-Beard flap. **E,** Mustardé total lid flap.

The flap includes conjunctiva, tarsus, levator aponeurosis, and Müller's muscle. After the flap is advanced and properly inset layer for layer into the defect, a full-thickness skin graft is secured onto the flap for coverage. Flap division usually is performed 6 to 8 weeks after the first stage.

For lower lid defects that extend up to 25% of the horizontal dimension of the lid, direct approximation, layer for layer, usually is possible. Defects of 25% to 60% of the horizontal dimension usually are reconstructed with a selective cantholysis and medial transposition of the lid with or without a local skin flap. Defects of 75% to 100% of the horizontal dimension require either a Hugh's tarsoconjunctival flap (two stages) or a Mustardé cheek flap (one stage) with composite grafting for lid support and lining. The tarsoconjunctival flap is best suited for defects that have a vertical dimension of 4 to 5 mm. Marginal defects of either the upper or the lower lid can be reconstructed with a bipedicle skin/muscle Tripier flap in conjunction with a composite graft, such as a septal chondromucosal graft (Fig. 58-3).

18. Is lower lid ectropion a common complication after a Cutler-Beard flap reconstruction?

No. Upper lid retraction may occur after the division of a Hugh's tarsoconjunctival flap secondary to scar formation and foreshortened Müller's muscle fibers in the donor bed. During the design and execution of the Cutler-Beard flap, care must be taken to avoid injury to the marginal artery of the lower lid. The marginal artery courses parallel to the lid margin approximately 3 to 4 mm from the edge. The inset-advanced Cutler-Beard flap usually is left in place for 6 to 8 weeks. Any unused portion is returned to the lower lid after division. Because of significant elongation in the flap, lower lid ectropion is not a typical complication. The Mustardé cheek advancement flap may cause lower lid ectropion secondary to flap retraction and gravitational forces. Notching at the area of marginal reapproximation is a common problem.

19. Is the contralateral eyelid a preferred site for skin graft harvest?

An optimal area for skin graft harvest in terms of color and texture is the contralateral eyelid; however, the amount of skin is limited. The following sites are preferred areas for skin graft harvest: retroauricular, preauricular, and supraclavicular. The infraclavicular region yields a graft with poor color match.

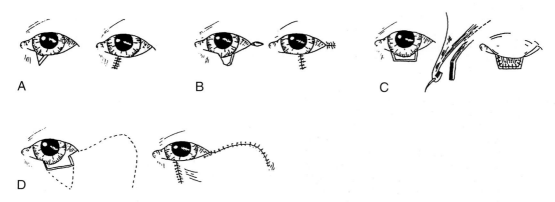

Figure 58-3. Reconstruction of the lower eyelid. **A,** Direct approximation. **B,** Selective lateral cantholysis and medial transposition of the lid. **C,** Hugh's tarsoconjunctival flap. **D,** Mustardé cheek flap with composite graft.

20. Describe the evaluation of lid ptosis.

Ptosis of the upper lid can be classified as congenital, neurogenic, myogenic, aponeurotic, or mechanical. The underlying cause, degree of ptosis, amount of levator function, position of the globe, presence of a Bell's phenomenon, and position and contour of the upper lid fold are important in the evaluation of the ptotic lid. The degree of lid laxity, or the result of a "snap-back" test, is not a critical factor; however, lid tone is important. The Tensilon test is useful in the diagnosis of ocular myasthenia. Topical phenylephrine is useful in evaluating Horner syndrome, a neurologic form of ptosis.

21. For most patients with lid ptosis, what is the most important factor in determining which operation to perform?

The most important factor in selecting the optimal surgical approach for patients with lid ptosis is the measure of levator function. The normal lid covers 1 to 2 mm of the upper limbus of the cornea. Levator function (excursion) is measured by the distance (in millimeters) that the upper lid margin travels from downward gaze to upward gaze with the brow immobilized. Although many ptosis repair techniques exist, four are most frequently used: Fasanella-Servat operation, aponeurosis surgery, levator resection, and brow suspension.

22. What is the underlying cause of congenital ptosis?

Congenital ptosis is present at birth and involves an isolated dystrophy of the levator muscle.

23. A patient who has lid ptosis secondary to an attenuated levator aponeurosis, 4 mm of ptosis, and a levator function of 8 mm is best treated by which ptosis procedure?

Levator function is classified as good (>10 mm), fair (4 to 10 mm), or poor (<4 mm). The degree of ptosis is classified as mild (1 to 2 mm), moderate (3 to 4 mm), or severe (>4 mm). In general, the Fasanella-Servat operation is optimal in patients with good levator function and mild ptosis. Aponeurosis surgery is most appropriate for patients with good levator function and moderate ptosis. Levator resection is used when the levator function is fair and the degree of ptosis is moderate. Brow or frontalis suspension techniques are used in patients with poor levator function and severe ptosis. Suspension procedures are mostly applied to treat severe congenital ptosis. The Fasanella-Servat operation involves a conjunctival, tarsal, and Müller's muscle resection. Aponeurosis surgery involves direct repair or advancement of the levator aponeurosis. Levator resection surgery involves resection of the levator aponeurosis. Brow or frontalis suspension entails suspending the lid margin to the frontalis muscle. The Neo-Synephrine test helps to determine if the Fasanella-Servat operation will yield a satisfactory result. If 10% Neo-Synephrine drops do not elevate the lid significantly, the Fasanella-Servat operation probably will result in undercorrection.

24. Match the following

1. Ectropion	A. Abnormal skin fold that may cause inversion of the eyelid
2. Epicanthus	B. Frequently caused by chemical burns
3. Blepharophimosis	C. Associated with ptosis of the upper lids
4. Entropion	D. Fold of skin overhanging the medial canthus
5. Epiblepharon	E. Ocular irritation secondary to turned-in lashes
6. Trichiasis	F. May involve significant lid retraction leading to exposure keratinization
7. Symblepharon	G. May be caused by horizontal laxity

Ectropion is an eversion of the eyelid margin, often first producing scleral show. It may lead to serious oculopathies, such as exposure keratinization.

Epicanthus is an overhanging skin fold that partially hides the medial canthus. Congenital epicanthus most frequently occurs in Asians.

Blepharophimosis is a congenital malformation associated with ptosis and epicanthal folds, telecanthus, and shortening of the horizontal fissure of the lids.

Entropion is the inversion of the eyelid. Horizontal lid laxity may lead to involutional entropion. This malposition of the lid often causes corneal irritation from friction elicited by turned-in lashes.

Epiblepharon is an abnormal skin fold that folds over the skin margin, usually resulting in the inversion of the eyelid margin.

Trichiasis refers specifically to eyelashes that are turned against the globe, with the lid remaining in its normal position.

Symblepharon is a cicatricial fusion between the globe and the inner surface of the eyelid. It usually occurs as a complication of a chemical burn.

Answers: 1 F, 2 D, 3 C, 4 G, 5 A, 6 E, 7 B.

25. What factors contribute to entropion?

Congenital entropion may result from an abnormal tarsal plate. Involutional entropion usually is the result of horizontal lid laxity or an overriding preseptal muscle. Cicatricial entropion occurs secondary to shortening of the posterior lamella. Facial paralysis, particularly of the orbicularis oculi muscle, results in a paralytic ectropion.

26. What factors contribute to ectropion?

Congenital ectropion usually is caused by a deficiency of eyelid skin. Involutional or senile ectropion is most often a result of laxity of the tarsus, canthal structures, and lid retractors. Cicatricial ectropion is a relative deficiency of skin and muscle from various causes, ranging from retraction and contraction (of the anterior lamella) to excessive removal of skin during blepharoplasty. Paralytic ectropion is a complication of facial nerve palsy. Repair of ectropion depends on the underlying pathology. Enophthalmos from periorbital fat atrophy decreases posterior lid support and leads to involutional entropion.

27. How does the Asian eyelid differ from the Occidental eyelid?

The Asian eyelid differs from the Occidental eyelid by the common presence of epicanthal folds and lack of a supratarsal fold. The supratarsal fold is defined by dermal attachments of the levator aponeurosis, which is lacking in the Asian eyelid. Often retroorbicularis fat is also increased. Furthermore, the preaponeurotic fat may extend lower in the Asian eyelid secondary to a lower insertion of the orbital septum to the levator aponeurosis.

28. Describe tear secretion and the composition of tear film.

Tear secretion is either basic or reflexive. The precorneal tear film is composed of three layers. The innermost layer is the mucin layer, composed mainly of polysaccharides secreted by the conjunctival goblet cells. This layer stabilizes the tear film, provides lubrication, and prevents desiccation. The intermediate layer is the aqueous layer, which accounts for 90% of the tear film and is composed of an aqueous (98% water) solution secreted by the accessory and main lacrimal glands. The most superficial layer is mainly composed of lipids secreted by the meibomian, Zeis, and Moll glands. This layer also stabilizes the tear film and minimizes evaporation. The tear film break-up test measures the amount of time required for discontinuities or "holes" to form in the tear film when the eye is not allowed to blink. A time of less than 10 seconds is considered abnormal.

29. What are the indications for performing dacryocystorhinostomy?

Dacryocystorhinostomy (DCR) is a surgical technique that opens the lacrimal sac directly into the nasal cavity. DCR is most commonly performed on patients with lacrimal obstruction distal to the common canaliculus, including patients with paralysis of the pump mechanism. DCR may be used to treat chronic dacryocystitis. For obstruction of the common canaliculus, a canaliculodacryocystorhinostomy is performed. If both upper and lower canaliculi are obliterated, a conjunctivodacryocystorhinostomy is performed.

30. During the reduction of an avulsed medial canthal tendon, injury to the nasolacrimal duct is suspected. What is the appropriate course of action?

The initial management of traumatic telecanthus and nasoethmoidal fractures does not include exploration of the nasolacrimal duct. In this situation, delayed obstruction is not common and would be treated by DCR. Unnecessary initial exploration may cause trauma to the lacrimal drainage system.

31. After selective cantholysis and medial transposition of the lid for reconstruction of a moderate upper lid defect, a patient complains of severe pain, photophobia, blurred vision, epiphora, and a foreign body sensation on the eye. Extraocular movements are intact, and funduscopic examination appears normal. Does the initial appropriate management include releasing all the incisions and administering mannitol?

Retrobulbar hematoma is a serious complication after eyelid surgery and may lead to blindness. Sudden-onset pain, proptosis, and conjunctival edema indicate the likelihood of a retrobulbar hemorrhage. The patient also may have limited extraocular movements, periorbital ecchymosis, and firmness to the eye. Immediate intervention is necessary, including opening all wounds and pharmacologically decompressing the orbit, as by administration of mannitol. An emergent ophthalmologic consultation should be obtained. The patient's complaints, however, are consistent with a corneal injury. After application of a topical anesthetic, the eye should be irrigated and examined. Fluorescein dye, which is dropped onto the corneal surface and then illuminated with a Wood's lamp, readily confirms the diagnosis of corneal abrasion. The patient is then treated with a topical antibiotic. A topical short-acting cycloplegic can be applied if ciliary spasm is significant; however, local anesthetics should not be continued (or ever prescribed for the patient) because they delay reepithelialization, mask complications, and decrease the protective sensibility of the eye. Although the vast majority of corneal abrasions heal rapidly within 1 to 3 days without complication, the possibility of superinfection and recurrent epithelial erosions must be kept in mind.

BIBLIOGRAPHY

Boutros S, Zide B: Cheek and eyelid reconstruction: The resurrection of the angle rotation flap. Plast Reconstr Surg 116:1425–1430, 2005.
Carraway JH: Levator advancement technique for eyelid ptosis. Plast Reconstr Surg 77:395–403, 1986.
Jelks GW, Glat PM, Jelks EB, Longaker MT: Medial canthal reconstruction using a medially based upper eyelid myocutaneous flap. Plast Reconstr Surg 110:1636–1643, 2002.
Jelks GW, Jelks EB: Prevention of ectropion in reconstruction of facial defects. Clin Plast Surg 28:297–302, 2001.

Jelks GW, Jelks EB: Reconstruction of the eyelids. In Cohen M (ed): Mastery of Plastic and Reconstructive Surgery. Boston, Little, Brown, 1994, pp 864–882.

Jelks GW, Smith BC: Reconstruction of the eyelids and associated structures. In McCarthy JG (ed): Plastic Surgery. Philadelphia, WB Saunders, 1990, pp 1671–1784.

McKinney P: The value of tear breakup and Schirmer's test in preoperative blepharoplasty evaluation. Plast Reconstr Surg 84:572–576, 1989.

Newman MI, Spinelli HM: Reconstruction of the eyelids, correction of ptosis, and canthoplasty. In Thorne CH, Beasley RW, Aston SJ, et al. (eds): Grabb & Smith's Plastic Surgery, 6th ed. Philadelphia, Lippincott Williams & Wilkins, 2007, pp 397–416.

Peist K: Malignant lesions of the eyelids. J Dermatol Surg Oncol 18:1056–1059, 1992.

Siegel R: Essential anatomy for contemporary upper lid blepharoplasty. Clin Plast Surg 20:209–212, 1993.

Siegel R: Involutional entropion: A simple and stable repair. Plast Reconstr Surg 82:42–46, 1988.

Weinstein G: Lower eyelid reconstruction with tarsal flaps and grafts. Plast Reconstr Surg 18:991–992, 1988.

Zarem B: Minimizing deformity in lower blepharoplasty. The transconjunctival approach. Clin Plast Surg 20:317–321, 1993.

Zide B: Surgical Anatomy of the Orbit. New York, Raven Press, 1985, pp 47–50.

CHAPTER 59

EAR RECONSTRUCTION

Bruce S. Bauer, MD, FACS, FAAP and
Erik M. Bauer, MD

1. What are the normal size, position, protrusion, and axis of the ear?

The normal adult ear height is between 5.5 and 6.5 cm. The width varies from 66% of the height in children to 55% of the height in adults. Eighty-five percent of ear development occurs by age 3 years, and full development occurs between the ages of 6 to 15 years. For children 4 years of age, a subnormal ear height (i.e., <2 SD) is below 4.5 cm. General guidelines are as follows:

- The ear should lie one ear length posterior to the lateral orbital rim.
- The lateral protrusion of the helix from the scalp is between 1.5 and 2.0 cm.
- The mean inclination of the ear from the vertical is 20° posterior.

2. Using Figure 59-1, name the landmarks of the external ear.

A. Helical rim	E. Concha	I. Cymbum concha	M. Cavum concha
B. Superior crus	F. Tail of helix	J. Root of helix	N. Intertragal notch
C. Scapha	G. Triangular fossa	K. External auditory meatus	O. Antitragus
D. Antihelix	H. Inferior crus	L. Tragus	P. Lobule

3. What is the vascular supply of the ear?

ARTERIAL SUPPLY

- Superficial temporal artery: Supplies lateral surface of auricle
- Posterior auricular artery: Branch of external carotid artery; dominant blood supply to posterior surface of ear, lobule, and retroauricular skin in 93% of cases
- Occipital artery: Minor contribution; dominant blood supply to posterior ear in only 7% of cases

VENOUS OUTFLOW

- Posterior auricular veins: Drain into external jugular vein
- Superficial temporal and retromandibular veins: Drain anterior auricle

4. Can an amputated ear be replanted?

Yes. An amputated ear can be replanted by microanastomosis of the posterior auricular artery (diameter 0.6 to 2.0 mm) and a posterior auricular vein (diameter 0.8 to 2.5 mm) to donor vessels, provided these vessels can be identified.

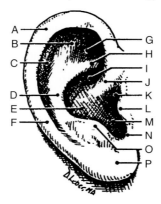

Figure 59-1. Landmarks of the external ear (From Leber DC: Ear reconstruction. In Georgiade GS, Georgiade NG, Riefkol R, Barwick WJ [eds]: Textbook of Plastic, Maxillofacial and Reconstructive Surgery, 2nd ed. Baltimore, Williams & Wilkins, 1992, p 494, with permission.)

5. **Describe the nerve supply of the auricle. Why can a patient with an oropharyngeal carcinoma present with ear pain?**
   - *Great Auricular Nerve (C2, C3):* Sensation to lower half of lateral surface of the ear and lower portion of the cranial surface of the ear
   - *Auriculotemporal Nerve (Branch of V3):* Sensation to superolateral surface of ear and anterior and superior surface of external auditory canal
   - *Lesser Occipital Nerve:* Sensation to superior cranial surface of ear
   - *Arnold's Nerve (Auricular Branch of Vagus Nerve):* Sensation to concha and posterior auditory canal; patients with cancers of the oropharynx (tonsil, base of tongue, soft palate) may complain of ear pain referred via the branches of the vagus nerve that innervate both the oropharynx and concha

6. **What is the embryologic origin of the external ear? Why is this knowledge significant in treating malignant tumors of the external ear?**
   During embryologic development, the auricle arises from the first (mandibular) and second (hyoid) branchial arches. Three anterior hillocks of the first branchial arch from the tragus, helical crus, and superior helix. Three posterior hillocks of the second branchial arch form the antihelix, antitragus, and lobule. The first branchial groove forms the external auditory meatus.

   Cutaneous carcinomas of the external ear may spread via lymphatic channels that follow embryologic development. Cancers of the tragus, helical crus, and superior helix drain into the parotid nodes. Cancers of the antihelix, antitragus, and lobule drain into the mastoid nodes. Cancers of the concha and meatus may drain into the parotid and mastoid nodes. Clinicians must be alert to these drainage patterns making diagnoses and prescribing treatment.

7. **What is the incidence and etiology of microtia?**
   Microtia (hypoplastic deformity of the auricle) occurs 1:6000–8000 births. Male-to-female ratio is 2:1, and right-to-left-to-bilateral ratio is 5:3:1.

   Microtia is thought to be a component of first and second branchial arch syndrome (hemifacial microsomia) with varying degrees of hypoplasia of the bony and soft tissues of the involved half of the face. The proposed mechanism is thought to be obliteration of the stapedial artery during early embryonic life. Agents implicated have included viruses (rubella), drugs (thalidomide), and multifactorial inheritance.

8. **What factors enter into the timing of microtia reconstruction?**
   Optimal reconstruction requires costal cartilage of sufficient size and shape to carve the key framework details and maintain the strength to display these details through the overlying skin envelop. Although some surgeons begin the reconstruction as early as 6 or 7 years of age, better results can be obtained at age 9 to 10 years or later. Clearly the potential psychological issues of the child dealing with his or her deformity must be balanced against the benefits of delaying the surgery for a few more years. Being one who has gradually made the transition of reconstruction at the lower end of that spectrum to one who feels strongly that the surgery is better delayed, I (BB) believe the majority of children deal with the delay of the reconstruction without ill effects. It must be made clear to the parents that the best chance for an ideal reconstruction is the first attempt, even if this means putting the surgery off for a few years. Patients should be reminded that once the reconstruction is completed, the child will have the remainder of his/her life to benefit from the improved outcome.

9. **In what cases and at what time is middle ear surgery indicated?**
   Complete deafness is rare in microtia because the inner ear, or neurosensory apparatus, is normal. Children have normal speech and adapt well without middle ear surgery. Middle ear surgery is generally reserved for bilateral microtia patients and is done after auricular reconstruction. In selected cases middle ear reconstruction can be performed in patients with unilateral microtia but should be planned following completion of the external reconstruction to avoid further complicating these procedures.

10. **What are the basic steps in microtia reconstruction?**
    - Cartilage framework construction
    - Dissection of auricular vestige and placement of framework
    - Lobule transposition
    - Tragal construction and conchal excavation
    - Helical rim elevation

    The sequence of procedures and what is accomplished in each stage varies depending on the technique chosen by the operating surgeon, but it is agreed that the cartilage framework should be placed in the first stage to make maximal use of the unscarred bed of the vestige. Opinions also vary on whether the lobule should be rotated in the first or second stage. Current techniques demonstrate a significant benefit of lobule rotation at the time of cartilage graft placement. Nagata demonstrated that the tragus can be reconstructed as part of the initial framework rather than at a separate stage. Following other techniques, the lobule rotation, tragal construction, and elevation of the helical rim are performed in either the second or third stage of reconstruction (Figs. 59-2 and 59-3).

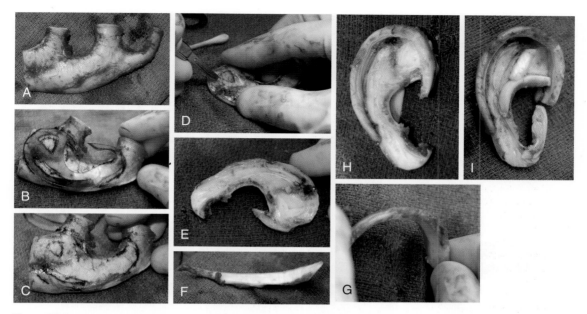

Figure 59-2. First stage reconstruction. **A,** The costal cartilage graft is harvested from either contralateral or ipsilateral 6th–8th cartilages depending on the surgeon's preference. **B–E,** The framework is constructed from a base block of the 6th and 7th cartilages, which can be carved to show as much of the highlights of the lower helical rim, antihelix, and crura as the graft thickness will allow. **F–H,** The helical rim is carved from the 8th costal cartilage and is mounted on the base block, which is further elevated in height with a segment of graft mounted under the base block mimicking the posterior conchal wall, and additional highlights are created with grafts sutured onto the antihelix. **I,** The graft is completed with addition of the tragal portion of the framework.

11. Which costal cartilages are harvested for construction of the framework in microtia reconstruction?

A cartilage framework is constructed from varying portions of the sixth to ninth costal cartilages depending on the technique selected. Authors vary on whether to use ipsilateral or contralateral cartilages, basing their decision on how the cartilage segments are most easily spliced. Opinions also differ on whether to retain perichondrium on the graft or to leave it behind in the donor area. Although maintaining some perichondrium on the graft helps to maintain long-term graft integrity, some believe that maintaining at least the visceral perichondrium in the donor site may minimize the risk of subsequent donor site deformity.

12. What options are available if the skin envelope is insufficient?

On some occasions insufficient skin is available to cover the cartilage framework. These circumstances arise as a result of associated facial deformity (hemifacial microsomia, Goldenhar syndrome, Treacher Collins syndrome) in which the auricular vestige is malpositioned and the hairline is low lying or in cases of excessive scarring surrounding the vestige (from trauma or prior unsuccessful surgery).

Tissue expansion has been used in selected ear reconstruction cases, but the associated risk of expander complications, such as exposure, are significantly higher in this region than in other areas, and expansion is generally not recommended. This is particularly the case in the treatment of significant facial scarring around the vestige or in the remaining ear segment following trauma.

The most readily available tissue for reconstruction in these cases is the temporoparietal fascial flap (TPFF) or occasionally its extension into the postauricular area. This flap usually is based on the superficial temporal artery but is best raised on both superficial temporal and postauricular vessels for total auricular reconstruction. In cases of severe tissue loss and deep scarring, use of the contralateral TPFF by microvascular transfer may be necessary. In most cases of fascial coverage of the framework the fascia is covered with a split-thickness skin graft. We prefer a 0.016-inch thick graft from the scalp. This donor site is totally hidden as the hair regrows, and the color match of the graft is excellent.

13. Discuss some of the complications of ear reconstruction. How would you remedy them?

- *Rib Donor Site Problems:* Pneumothorax, atelectasis. When recognized intraoperatively, aspirate the pneumothorax with a red rubber catheter and repair the pleural rent during positive pressure ventilation. Incentive spirometry and pulmonary toilet are indicated for atelectasis.

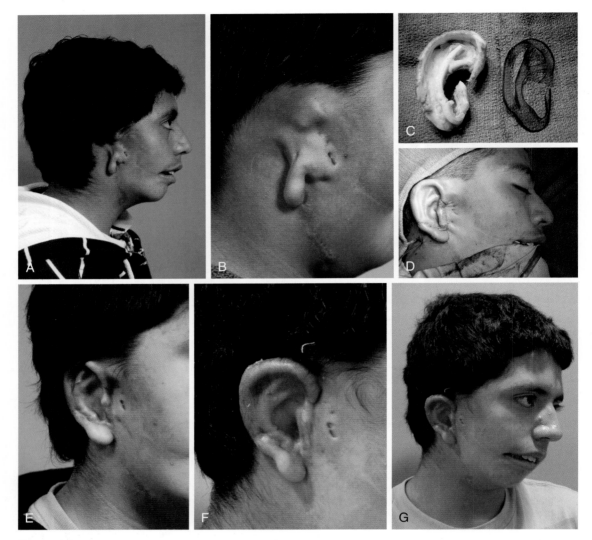

Figure 59-3. Total ear reconstruction. **A-D,** The pre-op deformity is shown in this 14-year-old male with a moderately dystopic auricular vestige with significant skeletal and soft tissue hypoplasia. The lobule is rotated in the first stage, and the soft tissues handled similar to Nagata's technique, with a subcutaneous pedicle maintained into the upper flap as the lobule is freed to allow its safe rotation and splicing. **E,** The result is seen 4 months following first stage reconstruction with excellent cartilage detail, but the helical rim has not yet been elevated. **F, G,** The result is shown 5 months after elevation of the helical rim and split thickness scalp graft to the post-auricular sulcus. In this case, the additional banked cartilage graft was not needed for further projection.

- *Ischemia or Necrosis of the Skin Envelope with Graft Exposure:* Graft exposure mandates aggressive care, either antibiotic ointment for very small areas of exposure or coverage with well-vascularized tissue. Failure to gain coverage may result in either partial or complete framework loss. Primary closure can be attempted after trimming the end of the exposed cartilage, but rarely is the adjacent skin healthy enough to allow advancement and closure. Coverage with a narrow TPFF or postauricular fascial flap and skin graft often is safer and provides better vascularization of the underlying cartilage.
- *Ischemia of Transposed Earlobe:* If performed during the first stage, lobule transposition requires leaving the adequate subdermal pedicle attached to the lobule in the location of the intertragal notch. Leaving the transposition for a second stage may be safer in experienced hands.
- *Hematoma and Seroma:* Ensure complete hemostasis and always place a suction drain in the pocket.
- *Resorption of Framework/Failed Reconstruction:* Avoid cartilage exposure; if it occurs treat it aggressively. Leave the perichondrium on the graft that is in contact with the skin. Failed reconstruction usually requires starting anew.
- *Flaws in Planning:* Poor ear position, poorly designed framework.

14. Faced with a patient with a traumatic avulsion of the ear, you are unable to identify any uninjured vessel to perform an anastomosis. What should be done with the avulsed part?

The optimal treatment of cases where replantation with anastomosis of a healthy vessel is not possible still is controversial. Anecdotal cases have described salvage of an entire ear by replantation without microvascular anastomosis, but this approach cannot be relied on and typically results in total or near-total loss of the avulsed segment. In the past it was suggested that the skin be carefully dissected from the amputated part and the cartilage buried beneath the skin in the abdominal area or retroauricular area to be later retrieved and used as the framework for subsequent reconstruction. Unfortunately, in almost all cases, this approach results in deformation and loss of the cartilage substance with a nonuseable graft of cartilage being retrieved from the banking site. Selected single cases in which the denuded cartilage was covered with either a regional fascial flap or a distant flap with subsequent microvascular transfer have been reported. In the majority of these cases the final result of the reconstruction had poor definition.

Brent and other authors, including us, agree that a far superior result can be obtained in experienced hands with débridement and preservation of the remaining ear segment with subsequent formal staged reconstruction with cartilage framework, TPFF, and skin graft coverage. Unless the operating surgeon has experience with more complex alternative fascial flap coverage techniques, the use of the fascia acutely for coverage of the replanted cartilage will significantly complicate further reconstruction when an unacceptable outcome results.

15. What principles of treatment are observed for a burned ear? How are segmental defects reconstructed?

- Reconstruction begins with preservation of viable tissue, not with early surgical intervention.
- Exposed, nonviable cartilage will not heal, and surgical débridement and reconstruction need to be performed.
- Excision of dry, nonsuppurative eschar should be condemned. Sulfamylon cream is the most effected topical antibacterial because of its eschar penetration.
- Segmental cartilage resection of tragus, antitragus, inferior crus, and midportion of the antihelix does not alter the overall appearance of the ear. Local skin flap advancement or skin graft may be all that is needed.
- Segmental loss of helix can be reconstructed with a local chondrocutaneous advancement (Antia) flap, wedge excision and closure, contralateral conchal cartilage graft with local skin flap, or composite grafts (if defect <1 cm).
- Sulfamylon rather than Silvadene is the preferable topical antibiotic for treatment because of its superior cartilage penetration.
- Major loss of ear cartilage and soft tissue requires reconstruction with costal cartilage framework, TPFF, and split-thickness skin graft.

16. What are the three most common cancers of the auricle?

Squamous cell carcinoma (50% to 60%), basal cell carcinoma (30% to 40%), and melanoma (2% to 6%). Approximately 12% of head and neck squamous cell carcinomas and basal cell carcinomas occur on the periauricular areas. Invasion of the perichondrium necessitates excision of the underlying cartilage.

17. List the main causes of auricular chondritis. What is usually the causative organism in infectious cases?

Infectious chondritis of the auricle is induced by auricular injury, which may be secondary to burns, surgical manipulation of the auricle (e.g., conchal cartilage graft harvest), or cosmetic piercing of the ear cartilage. *Pseudomonas aeruginosa* is responsible in 95% of these cases. If there is no preceding injury, consider relapsing polychondritis, an autoimmune disorder that affects auricular cartilage in 90% of cases; nasal, laryngotracheobronchial, and peripheral joint cartilage may be involved as well.

18. What is the typical clinical presentation of post piercing suppurative chondritis of the auricle? How is it treated acutely?

Patients typically present within the first week after piercing with dull pain of the auricle that progresses over hours to severe edema, erythema, warmth, and exquisite tenderness, often with frank abscess formation. There is effacement of the postauricular sulcus and concomitant protrusion of the auricle. The superior helical rim at the piercing site is involved first, followed by the scapha and adjacent antihelix and, if untreated, the remainder of the pinna.

Acute treatment should consist of incision and drainage of the suppurative pocket via a scaphal incision parallel to the helix, followed by admission for intravenous antipseudomonal antibiotics. Sulfamylon dressings are applied to the ear and changed every 8 hours. Conservative débridement of clearly necrotic cartilage is indicated early.

19. Describe the appearance of a mature post chondritis deformity. What are the considerations in timing of reconstruction?

The deformity involves loss of structural support of the upper third of the auricle, including the superior helical rim, scapha, and superior antihelix, with resulting malacia and notching of the cartilage contour. The skin and soft tissue envelope often are scarred from the infection and drainage incisions but typically are intact and capable of supporting a reconstructive framework. Reconstruction should be deferred until all signs of acute inflammation are eliminated, all remaining cartilage is viable, and no evidence of recurrence is seen over a 6- to 9-month observation period.

20. How should the reconstruction of a post chondritis auricular deformity be performed?
Structural support should be obtained from a contralateral conchal cartilage graft modeled on the normal ear, with costal cartilage reserved for the most extensive cases of cartilage loss. The local skin/soft tissue envelope, preserved by careful dissection from the damaged cartilage, usually is sufficient for coverage of the new framework. If the skin is injured beyond salvage, soft tissue coverage can be accomplished using an ipsilateral TPFF with a full-thickness skin graft from the contralateral postauricular sulcus. Xeroform gauze and a head wrap are applied, and postoperative oral antibiotics are continued for 1 week.

CONTROVERSY

21. What alternative materials have been advocated for use as a framework in microtia reconstruction? What are the pros and cons of these materials?
In an effort to avoid the use of autogenous cartilage and potential risks associated with its harvest, Reinish has advocated the use of a porous polyethylene framework. Although many have found as great a risk of extrusion with this material as with earlier silicone frameworks, the combination of its inertness and porous quality are stated to be better for tissue anchorage than early Silastic implants. With total fascial coverage Reinish states that extrusion of the implant can be avoided. However, the few advocates of this method tend to overstate the risks of harvesting autogenous cartilage and underestimate the frequency that many surgeons have seen with implant exposure. Although Reinish reports high numbers of cases done over many years, he presents statistics that are drawn from a very small sample of this large series. Whether the results will be stable throughout the child's life remains to be seen. Until then autogenous reconstruction regardless of the surgeon's preference of staging and framework construction remains the gold standard.

BIBLIOGRAPHY

Allison GR: Anatomy of the auricle. Clin Plast Surg 17:209–212, 1990.
Bauer BS: The role of tissue expansion in reconstruction of the ear. Clin Plast Surg 17:319–325, 1990.
Bauer BS: Aesthetic ear surgery. In Marchac D, Granek MS, Solomon MP, et al. (eds): Male Aesthetic Surgery. Boston, Butterworth-Heinemann, 1996, pp 255–286.
Brent B: Reconstruction of the auricle. In McCarthy JG (ed): Plastic Surgery. Philadelphia, WB Saunders, 190, pp 2094–2152.
Brent B, Byrd HS: Secondary ear reconstruction with cartilage grafts covered by axial, rand, and free flaps of temporoparietal fascia. Plast Reconstr Surg 72:141–151, 1983.
Eriksson E, Vogt PM: Ear reconstruction. Clin Plast Surg 19:637–643, 1992.
Furnas DW: Complications of surgery of the external ear. Clin Plast Surg 17:305–318, 1990.
Margulis A, Bauer BS, Alizadeh K: Ear reconstruction after auricular chondritis secondary to ear piercing. Plast Reconstr Surg 111:891–897, 2003.
Menick FJ: Reconstruction of the ear after tumor excision. Clin Plast Surg 17:405–415, 1990.
Reinish J: Ear Reconstruction Panel, American Society of Plastic Surgeons, Annual Meeting, San Francisco, October, 2006.
Rosenthal JS: The thermally injured ear: A systemic approach to reconstruction. Clin Plast Surg 19:645–661, 1992.
Thomson HG, Winslow J: Microtia reconstruction: Does the cartilage framework grow? Plast Reconstr Surg 84:908–915, 1989.
Tolleth H: A hierarchy of values in the design and construction of the ear. Clin Plast Surg 17:193–207, 1990.

LIP RECONSTRUCTION

John T. Seki, MD, FRCSC, FACS

CHAPTER 60

1. What are the key anatomic features of the lip?

The key landmarks include the vermilion border, commissure, tubercle, philtral columns, and Cupid's bow (Fig. 60-1).

2. What is the significance of the vermilion border?

The vermilion border, also known as the *white roll* or the *mucocutaneous line*, is the transition zone between the mucosa of the lip and the skin. In the surgical repair of this structure, anatomic alignment is critical, as even a 1-mm discrepancy is noticeable at a conversational distance.

3. What is Cupid's bow?

Cupid's bow is the central portion of the upper mucocutaneous line at the base of the philtral columns. Defects of Cupid's bow may be covered by a mustache in males. In females, however, absence of this landmark leads to a flattened appearance of the upper lip.

4. What is the primary function of the lips?

The main function of the lips is to provide oral competence. This function is controlled by the orbicularis oris muscle. Its muscle fibers originate at an area of mingling of various muscle bundles lateral to the commissure (known as the modiolus), cross the lip at the midline, and insert at the opposite philtral column.

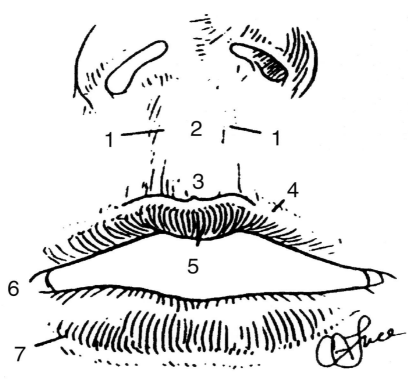

Figure 60-1. Topographic anatomy of the lips. *1*, Philtral columns. *2*, Philtral groove or dimple. *3*, Cupid's bow. *4*, White roll upper lip. *5*, Tubercle. *6*, Commissure. *7*, Vermilion. (From Zide BM: Deformities of the lips and cheeks. In McCarthy JG [ed]: Plastic Surgery. Philadelphia, WB Saunders, 1990, p 2009.)

5. What are the muscles of the upper and lower lips?

The orbicularis oris produces an oral sphincter integral to facial expression and oral competence. The levator labii superioris, zygomaticus major, and levator anguli oris elevate the upper lip. The depressor labii inferioris (quadratus) and depressor anguli oris (triangularis) are the depressors of the lower lip and angle of the mouth. The mentalis muscle elevates the central portion of the lower lip.

6. What is the motor and sensory innervation of the upper and lower lips?

The buccal and zygomatic branches of the facial nerve supply motor innervation to the upper lip. The marginal mandibular branch of the facial nerve supplies motor innervation to the lower lip. Sensory innervation of the upper lip is provided by the infraorbital branch of the trigeminal nerve, whereas the mental nerve supplies the lower lip.

7. Discuss the vascular anatomy of the lips.

The facial artery emerges bilaterally between the mandible and anterior border of the masseter muscle and divides at the commissure to form the superior labial artery, which supplies the upper lip, and the inferior labial artery, which supplies the lower lip. Venous drainage occurs mainly via branches of the facial vein.

8. Are the inferior labial arteries always bilateral and constant?

No. Cadaveric anatomic studies show that the vascular distribution, the anatomic location, and the caliber of the inferior labial arteries are variable, and Doppler evaluation should be performed before attempting axial flap or microsurgical reconstruction.

9. Discuss the lymphatic drainage of the lips.

Lymphatic drainage of the upper lip and lateral third of the lower lip is facilitated by the submandibular lymph nodes. The central third of the lower lip drains into the submental lymph nodes bilaterally.

10. How is an infraorbital nerve block performed?

The infraorbital foramen is 4 to 7 mm inferior to the infraorbital rim in the axis of the pupil. Transcutaneous injection with local anesthetic is performed just lateral to the nasal alar base. Intraoral or transmucosal technique requires needle insertion superior to the canine eminence.

11. How is a mental nerve block performed?

To locate the mental nerve, roll the lower lip outward and stretch the mucosa. The mental nerve should be visible at the canine root, lateral to the canine sulcus. Avoid injection of anesthetic into the mental foramen.

12. Is the mental nerve block sufficient for anesthesia of the chin?

No. To block the region below the labiomental fold, an inferior alveolar nerve block should be performed at the medial border of the mandibular ramus intraorally.

13. Can the lip be locally infiltrated with an anesthetic agent?

Yes. The advantage of local anesthesia with the addition of epinephrine is hemostasis. However, the increased volume can distort the anatomy, especially at the vermilion border. It is imperative to mark the edges of the mucocutaneous junction with ink before infiltration of local anesthetic.

14. What are the principles of lip reconstruction?

- Maintain oral sphincter competence
- Restore anatomic landmarks
- Provide adequate stomal opening for speech and eating
- Preserve sensation
- Restore aesthetic appearance

15. How should lesions near the vermilion border be managed?

Lesions near the vermilion border should be excised in a vertical ellipse. If the lesion is oriented horizontally, excision can be performed transversely. The mucocutaneous line should be avoided, if possible. If the lesion crosses the vermilion, the incision must cross the mucocutaneous line at a 90° angle. In all planned excisions that cross the vermilion, dye should be used to mark the junction before infiltration of local anesthetic.

16. Should sutures be placed directly on the mucocutaneous junction to align the vermilion border?

No. Erythema may develop at the suture line secondary to inflammation and distort the mucocutaneous line. Sutures can be placed immediately above and below the vermilion border for proper alignment.

17. How much tissue loss still permits a satisfactory primary closure of the lips?
Up to 25% of the lip can be excised without subsequent functional or aesthetic defect. In elderly patients, the length may be increased to one third because of tissue laxity.

18. How should full-thickness lip lacerations be repaired, and what suture material can be used?
The buccal mucosa can be repaired with 4-0 or 5-0 chromic suture, either interrupted or running. The muscles must be well aligned and reapproximated to preserve proper oral sphincter function; 4-0 Monocryl or Vicryl may be used. The dermal layer can be closed with 5-0 Monocryl or Vicryl, and the skin with either running or interrupted 6-0 nylon. Nylon can be used at the dry portion of the lip mucosa.

19. What is the distribution of lip cancers of the oral region?
Carcinomas of the lips represent 25% to 30% of all cancers of the oral regions.

20. Why is the lower lip a more common site for tumors than the upper lip?
The lower lip receives more direct actinic radiation (i.e., sun exposure), making it the site of 95% of all lip cancers.

21. What is the most common cancer of the lip?
Squamous cell carcinoma (SCC) is the most common neoplasm of the lip, with a high male predominance. Risk factors include fair skin, working outdoors with excessive sun exposure, smoking, and receiving immunosuppressive agents following transplantation.

22. Which benign lesion closely resembles SCC? How is it distinguished?
Keratoacanthoma (KA) may have a clinical appearance very similar to that of SCC. It also often is difficult to differentiate the two histologically. A rapid growth phase occurs more commonly with KA than with SCC, often allowing one to distinguish the two lesions. Seventy-five percent of KAs are located in the head and neck region; 10% are located equally on the upper and lower lips.

23. What is the biology of SCC?
The three morphologic types of SCC are exophytic (most common), ulcerative, and verrucous (rarely occurs on lips). The ulcerative type is generally more invasive and has a higher histologic grade than does the exophytic type. Potential for regional metastasis is directly proportionate to the size and duration of the lesion and inversely proportionate to the degree of differentiation prior to treatment. Distant metastases are unusual. Local recurrence rate doubles if the primary lesion is located at the oral commissure. Less than 2% of all lip cancers involve the commissure. In general, upper lip cancers grow more rapidly and have a higher metastatic rate and a lower 5-year survival.

24. What are the key considerations in lip reconstruction?
The size of the oral aperture is important to provide adequate access for oral hygiene, dental repair, and denture insertion or removal. Sensation should be carefully preserved because a decrease may lead to impaired ability to retain liquids in the oral cavity. Preservation of neurovascular supply during flap mobilization, proper anatomic alignment, and restoration of function and cosmesis are critical. Revisions after initial flap reconstruction may be necessary.

25. What is an important and common complication of lip reconstruction?
Reduction of the size of the oral stoma is a common problem after reconstruction.

26. Why is the lower lip a more suitable donor for reconstruction than is the upper lip?
The lower lip has no distinguishing features such as the Cupid's bow, philtrum, or tubercle. It may sustain greater tissue loss and can donate tissue for upper lip reconstruction.

27. Do V wedge resections provide adequate margins for SCCs of the lower lip?
No. V excisions are suboptimal because tumors tend to spread downward or laterally. Furthermore, the apex of the excision that crosses the labiomental fold may promote hypertrophic scars. The W excision, or the modified flared W-plasty, allows a wider resection and avoids crossing the labiomental fold (Fig. 60-2).

28. What options are available for repair of localized mucosal and vermilion defects?
Notch or saddle deformities of the lower lip involving the vermilion can be managed by excision and Z-plasty reconstruction (Fig. 60-3). Other options include the V-Y mucomuscular advancement flap and the lateral mucomuscular advancement flap (Fig. 60-4).

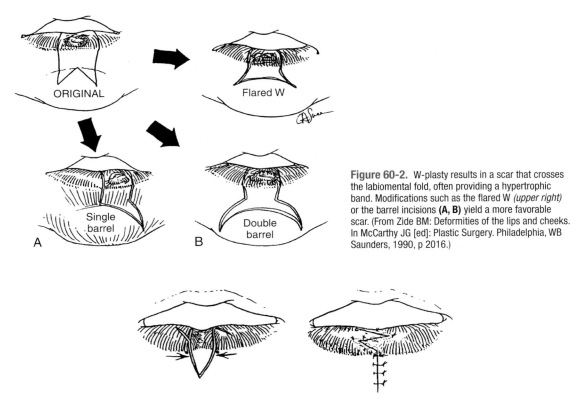

Figure 60-2. W-plasty results in a scar that crosses the labiomental fold, often providing a hypertrophic band. Modifications such as the flared W *(upper right)* or the barrel incisions **(A, B)** yield a more favorable scar. (From Zide BM: Deformities of the lips and cheeks. In McCarthy JG [ed]: Plastic Surgery. Philadelphia, WB Saunders, 1990, p 2016.)

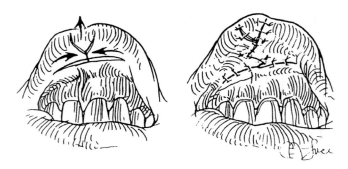

Figure 60-3. Significant notch deformities may require excision and Z-plasty to prevent further retraction. (From Zide BM: Deformities of the lips and cheeks. In McCarthy JG [ed]: Plastic Surgery. Philadelphia, WB Saunders, 1990, p 2015.)

Figure 60-4. V-Y mucomuscular advancement flap can be used for a midline whistle deformity of deficiency of the tubercle. (From Zide BM: Deformities of the lips and cheeks. In McCarthy JG [ed]: Plastic Surgery. Philadelphia, WB Saunders, 1990, p 2028.)

29. What is a lip shave operation, and how do you reconstruct the resultant defect?

This procedure is also known as a *total vermilionectomy*. The vermilion is resected from the junction of the wet and dry lip to the mucocutaneous line. It usually is indicated for extensive actinic cheilitis or leukoplakia. Defects involving the entire vermilion can be reconstructed with a mucosal advancement flap. For defects less than one third of the lower vermilion, an axial musculovermilion advancement flap can be used (Figs. 60-5 and 60-6).

30. How do you reconstruct the oral commissure?

Major indications for oral commissure reconstruction include congenital macrostomia, postsurgical and/or posttraumatic scar, and electrical burns. In congenital cases, this may be associated with other craniofacial clefts; thus auditory testing is essential. Reconstruction usually is performed at 18 months of age. The midsagittal plane of the face is identified,

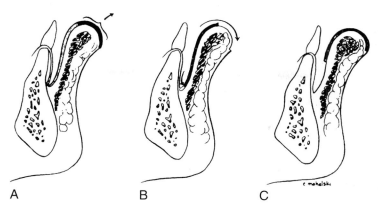

Figure 60-5. Vermilion reconstruction with buccal mucosa. **A,** Resection of the affected vermilion. **B,** Buccal sulcus relaxing incision and undermining of the anterior portion of the mucosal flap in a plane just deep to the minor salivary glands. **C,** Advancement of the mucosal flap. Buccal sulcus incision is allowed to heal secondarily. (From Behmand RA, Rees RS: Reconstructive lip surgery. In Achauer BM, Eriksson E, Guyuron B, et al. [eds]: Plastic Surgery Indications, Operations, and Outcomes. St. Louis, Mosby, 2000, pp 1197.)

Figure 60-6. Axial musculovermilion advancement flap. **A,** The flap is elevated deep to the labial artery. The position of the labial artery can be identified at the time of the resection of the lesion. **B,** Forward advancement of the flap permits primary closure of the defect. (From Behmand RA, Rees RS: Reconstructive lip surgery. In Achauer BM, Eriksson E, Guyuron B, et al. [eds]: Plastic Surgery Indications, Operations, and Outcomes. St. Louis, Mosby, 2000, pp 1198.)

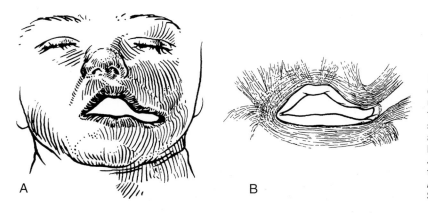

Figure 60-7. A, Topographic view of a lateral cleft. **B,** Schema of the underlying muscle pathology. Note the discontinuity of the orbicularis sphincter with tapering of the upper and lower bundles. The cleft lies between the latter. (From McCarthy JG: Oral commissure repair technique. In Brent B [ed]: The Artistry of Reconstructive Surgery. St. Louis, CV Mosby, 1987, pp 268–270.)

and the distance between the philtral column and the unaffected commissure is measured. Incisions are made at the junction of the atrophic vermilion and the skin to create turnover flaps for recreating mucosa. The upper and lower muscle bundles are overlapped and sutured to complete the orbicularis ring. A Z-plasty is incorporated into the skin closure (Figs. 60-7 to 60-12).

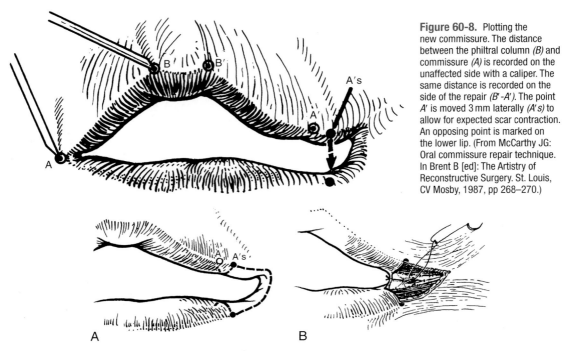

Figure 60-8. Plotting the new commissure. The distance between the philtral column *(B)* and commissure *(A)* is recorded on the unaffected side with a caliper. The same distance is recorded on the side of the repair *(B'-A')*. The point *A'* is moved 3 mm laterally *(A's)* to allow for expected scar contraction. An opposing point is marked on the lower lip. (From McCarthy JG: Oral commissure repair technique. In Brent B [ed]: The Artistry of Reconstructive Surgery. St. Louis, CV Mosby, 1987, pp 268–270.)

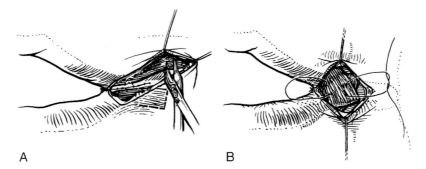

Figure 60-9. Mucosal lining in commissuroplasty. **A,** The incision lines outlined for the turnover vermilion flaps. **B,** Elevation and approximation of the vermilion flaps provide oral closure. (From McCarthy JG: Oral commissure repair technique. In Brent B [ed]: The Artistry of Reconstructive Surgery. St. Louis, CV Mosby, 1987, pp 268–270.)

Figure 60-10. Reconstitution of the orbicularis muscle ring. **A,** Skeletonization and transection of the upper and lower orbicularis muscle flaps. *Dashed lines* designate the division of the lower muscle bundle. **B,** The upper muscle bundle is plicated over the lower one to simulate the normal overhang of the upper lip. (From McCarthy JG: Oral commissure repair technique. In Brent B [ed]: The Artistry of Reconstructive Surgery. St. Louis, CV Mosby, 1987, pp 268–270.)

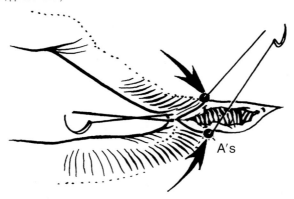

Figure 60-11. The commissure is established by a suture at point *A's.* (From McCarthy JG: Oral commissure repair technique. In Brent B [ed]: The Artistry of Reconstructive Surgery. St. Louis, CV Mosby, 1987, pp 268–270.)

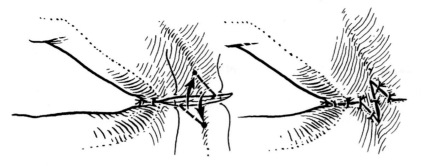

Figure 60-12. Cutaneous coverage is achieved by interdigitating Z-plasty flaps. The latter are designed so that the scar's resulting central limb falls in the nasolabial fold. (From McCarthy JG: Oral commissure repair technique. In Brent B [ed]: The Artistry of Reconstructive Surgery. St. Louis, CV Mosby, 1987, pp 268–270.)

31. Describe the flaps commonly used for lip reconstruction.

The following are full-thickness, musculomucocutaneous flaps:

- *Abbe Flap:* V-shaped lower lip flap based on the inferior labial artery and designed opposite the area of defect for the central upper lip region. The flap is raised, transposed 180°, and inset. The donor site is closed directly. Second-stage division of the pedicle and final inset take place 14 days later (Fig. 60-13, *A*).
- *Estlander Flap:* Triangular flap based on the superior labial artery and designed for reconstruction of the lateral lower lip defects involving the commissure. The flap is transposed 180° from the upper lip to the lower lip. This procedure results in a smaller oral stoma and indistinct commissure, which may require further revision (Fig. 60-13, *B*).
- *Gillies Fan Flap:* Fan-shaped rotational advancement flap based on the superior labial artery and designed for large defects involving greater than 50% of the lower lip. The flap is made lateral to the defect around the nasolabial fold with a 1-cm back-cut. This procedure also may reduce the oral aperture (Fig. 60-13, *C*).
- *McGregor Flap:* Rectangular-shaped flap modified from the Gillies fan flap and based on the superior labial artery. This flap is rotated around the commissure without altering the size of the oral stoma. The width of the flap equals the vertical height of the defect, whereas the length of the flap equals the width of the defect plus the width of the flap. A mucosal advancement flap is required to reconstruct the lip mucosa (Fig. 60-13, *D*).

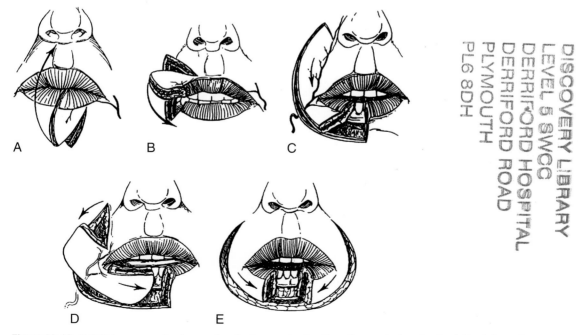

Figure 60-13. Full-thickness musculocutaneous flaps for lip reconstruction. These flaps can be based on the right or left superior or inferior labial arteries and are useful for lip and oral sphincter reconstruction. **A,** Abbe flap arc to central upper lip. **B,** Estlander flap arc to oral commissure and lower lip. **C,** Gillies fan flap to central upper lip. **D,** McGregor flap arc to central lower lip. **E,** Karapandzic flap arc to central lower lip. (From Mathes SJ, Nahai F: Orbicularis oris flap. In Mathes SJ, Nahai F [eds]: Reconstructive Surgery: Principles, Anatomy, and Technique. New York, Churchill Livingstone, 1997, pp 301–320.)

- *Karapandzic Flap:* Rotational neurovascular advancement flap designed for upper or lower lip defects or both simultaneously. Semicircular incisions are performed from the edge of the skin defect toward the nasal ala bilaterally. The facial nerve branches and the branches of the superior and inferior labial arteries must be preserved (Fig. 60-13, *E*).

BIBLIOGRAPHY

Batsakis JG: Squamous cell carcinomas of the oral cavity and the oropharynx. In Batsakis JG (ed): Tumors of the Head and Neck: Clinical and Pathological Considerations, 2nd ed. Baltimore, Williams & Wilkins, 1979, pp 149–152.

Behmand RA, Rees RS: Reconstructive lip surgery. In Achauer BM, Eriksson E, Guyuron B, Coleman JJ, Russell RC, Vander Kolk CA (eds): Plastic Surgery, Indications, Operations and Outcomes. St. Louis, Mosby, 2000, pp 1193–1209.

Edizer M, Magden O, Tayfur V, et al: Arterial anatomy of the lower lip: A cadaveric study. Plast Reconstr Surg 111:2176–2181, 2003.

Fonseca RJ, Walker RV (eds): Oral and Maxillofacial Trauma. Philadelphia, WB Saunders, 1991.

Godek CP, Weinzweig J, Bartlett SP: Lip reconstruction following Moh's surgery: The role for composite resection and primary closure. Plast Reconstr Surg 106:798–804, 2000.

Hollinshead WH, Rosse C (eds): Textbook of Anatomy, 4th ed. New York, Harper & Row, 1985.

Mathes SJ, Nahai F (eds): Orbicularis oris flap. In Mathes SJ, Nahai F (eds): Reconstructive Surgery: Principles, Anatomy, and Technique. New York, Churchill Livingstone, 1997, pp 301–320.

McCarthy JG: Oral commissure repair. In Brent B (ed): The Artistry of Reconstructive Surgery, Selected Classic Case Studies. St. Louis, Mosby, 1987, pp 267–284.

Netter FH: Atlas of Human Anatomy. Summit, NJ, Ciba-Geigy Corporation, 1989.

O'Daniel TG: Lip reconstruction. In Marsh JL (ed): Decision Making in Plastic Surgery. St. Louis, Mosby, 1993, pp 134–135.

Strauch B, Vasconez LO, Hall-Findlay EJ (eds): Grabb's Encyclopedia of Flaps. Boston, Little, Brown and Company, 1990, pp 635–713.

Zide BM: Deformities of the lips and cheek. In McCarthy JG (ed): Plastic Surgery. Philadelphia, WB Saunders, 1990, pp 2009–2037.

Zide B, Swift R: How to block and tackle the face. Plast Reconstr Surg 101:840–851, 1998.

CHAPTER 61

RECONSTRUCTION OF THE ORAL CAVITY

Eser Yuksel, MD; Sven N. Sandeen, MD; Adam B. Weinfeld, MD;
Saleh M. Shenaq, MD, FACS; and Howard N. Langstein, MD, FACS

1. What are the borders and contents of the oral cavity?

The oral cavity extends from the vermilion of the lips to the junction of the hard and soft palates superiorly and to the line of the circumvallate papillae of the tongue inferiorly. It contains the lips, buccal mucosa, alveolar ridges, retromolar triangle, floor of the mouth, hard palate, and anterior two thirds of the tongue (Figs. 61-1 and 61-2).

2. What are the borders and contents of the floor of the mouth?

The floor of the mouth is a horseshoe-shaped area formed by reflections of mucous membrane from the mandibular alveolus to the ventral surface of the tongue. The posterior limit of the floor of the mouth is the anterior tonsillar pillar. Minor salivary glands are visible as small submucosal bulges on either side of the lingual frenulum. The paired sublingual glands are seen as larger bulges emerging from under the tongue more posteriorly. Each sublingual gland has multiple excretory ducts, most of which open separately into the floor of the mouth along an elevation of mucous membrane called the *sublingual fold*. Others join with the ipsilateral submandibular duct (Wharton duct), and the ducts exit together at the sublingual papilla that sits adjacent to the lingual frenulum near its base (Fig. 61-3).

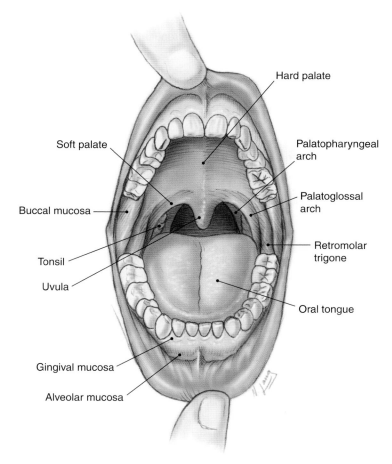

Figure 61-1. Oral cavity (intraoral view). (From Mathes S [ed]: Plastic Surgery, 2nd ed. Philadelphia, WB Saunders, 2006.)

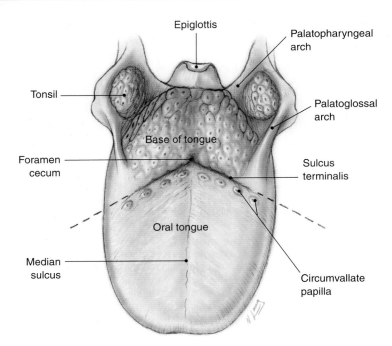

Figure 61-2. Tongue. (From Mathes S [ed]: Plastic Surgery, 2nd ed. Philadelphia, WB Saunders, 2006.)

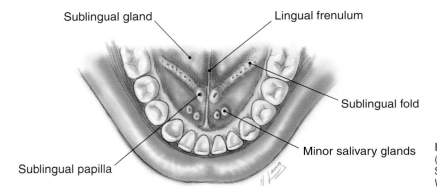

Figure 61-3. Floor of the mouth. (From Mathes S [ed]: Plastic Surgery, 2nd ed. Philadelphia, WB Saunders, 2006.)

3. Which risk factors are associated with oral cancer?

Tobacco products are the most significant risk factor; heavy alcohol consumption is the second. Of patients diagnosed with oral cancer, 75% are tobacco users. Concomitant tobacco and alcohol use has a synergistic effect and increases the risk of oral cancer by a factor of 15. Noncessation of smoking after diagnosis of a primary tumor increases the risk of developing a second primary tumor, increases the rate of recurrence, and decreases the response to radiotherapy.

Age is a relative risk factor, with the majority of patients older than 40 years. The male-to-female ratio is 2:1, as is the occurrence in blacks versus whites. White patients have a 5-year survival rate of 55% compared with only 33% for blacks.

Ultraviolet exposure is a risk factor for lip cancer. Poor oral hygiene, exposure to human papillomavirus-16 or human papillomavirus-18, syphilis, Plummer-Wilson syndrome, chronic candidiasis, and chronic exposure to toxic irritants are additional risk factors for oral cancer.

4. What are the benign and premalignant lesions of the oral cavity?

Benign lesions of the oral cavity include sialocele formation due to the obstruction of minor salivary glands, sialolithiasis, pleomorphic adenoma, necrotizing sialometaplasia of the hard palate, dermoid cysts of the floor of the mouth, granular cell myoblastoma, hemangioma and lymphoma, mucosal polyps, fibroma, median rhomboid glossitis, aphthous ulcers, and tuberculous granulomas. *Premalignant lesions* of the oral cavity include leukoplakia and erythroplakia; they are bright white or bright red in color, respectively. Histologic examination of these premalignant lesions reveals existing dysplasia or consequent malignant transformation.

5. What is the distribution of oral cavity cancers by location and histologic types?
Malignant tumors of the oral cavity account for approximately 30% of all head and neck cancers. The tongue is the most common site for oral cavity cancers, accounting for 22% to 30% of all cases. The floor of the mouth is the second most common site of malignancy. Squamous cell carcinoma represents more than 90% of oral cancers. Adenocarcinomas are second in frequency. Subtypes of squamous cell carcinomas are differentiated, undifferentiated (transitional, spindle cell), adenoid squamous, and verrucous carcinoma. Verrucous carcinoma has a tendency to grow more radially than vertically.

6. How can you predict the outcome and formulate a treatment of intraoral carcinoma?
Tumor size and thickness and presence of cervical nodal involvement are major determinants of outcome; however, immunohistologic quantification of tumor angiogenesis may help to predict the aggressiveness of the tumor. Tumor-node-metastasis (TNM) classification is still the basis for formulating treatment (Table 61-1). Surgery remains the main treatment modality, although extended procedures cause functional problems with swallowing and speech. Reconstructive procedures are designed to minimize functional and aesthetic problems. Despite its acute morbidity (mucositis, odynophagia, swelling) and long-term morbidity (loss of taste perception, dry mouth, tissue necrosis), radiotherapy often is used as an adjuvant therapy in advanced cases and as primary treatment in lesions T2 or smaller.

7. What are the objectives of oropharyngeal reconstruction?
The objectives are to maintain oral continuity, facilitate swallowing, prevent aspiration, preserve satisfactory speech, and provide primary wound healing in one stage. These functional restorations require adequate tongue mobility and oral sealing.

8. Squamous cell carcinoma of the tongue is most frequently located at the base. True or false?
False. Three fourths of all tongue cancers are located in the anterior mobile portion. Forty percent of all tongue cancers have nodal involvement, and 20% of all cases demonstrate bilateral nodal involvement. Elective node dissection is recommended for tumors thicker than 10 mm. Tumors of the posterior third of the tongue are less well differentiated, and 75% of cases have nodal involvement at the time of diagnosis.

9. A tumor located in the floor of the mouth will preferentially metastasize to which lymph nodes?
Tumors in the floor of the mouth, lower lip, and anterior cheek mucosa will preferentially metastasize to level I (submandibular) lymph nodes. Tumors from the posterior tongue, tonsil, posterior gingival, and retromolar triangle will metastasize to level II (upper jugular) lymph nodes.

10. Describe the goals and methods for reconstruction of tongue defects.
Restoration of tongue mobility, bulk, and sensation are the three primary goals of tongue reconstruction. The reconstruction is tailored to the size of the resection. T1 lesions treated with wedge excision and 1- to 2-cm margins may be closed primarily, skin grafted, or reconstructed with local flaps. Partial or hemiglossectomies may need to be reconstructed with local flaps or with free fasciocutaneous flaps (e.g., radial forearm or anterolateral thigh flap). Subtotal to total glossectomy cases will require free muscle or myocutaneous flaps for restoration of bulk.

11. How are palatal defects reconstructed?
Palatal island flaps, temporalis muscle flaps, lingual flaps, or fasciocutaneous free flaps serve well for reconstruction of palatal defects. Extensive composite defects caused by maxillectomy may require free muscle and/or bone composite flap transfers.

Table 61-1. TNM Classification

TUMOR	NODE	METASTASIS	STAGING	
T1: <2.0 cm	N1: <3.0 cm	M0: No metastasis	Stage I	T1N0M0
T2: 2.1–4.0 cm	N2: 3.1–6.0 cm	M1: + Metastasis	Stage II	T2N0M0
T3: >4.1 cm	N3: >6.1 cm		Stage III	T3N0,1M0
T4: Invasive			Stage IVa	T4N0,1M0
				Any T, N2M0
			Stage IVb	Any T, N3M0
			Stage IVc	Any T, any N, M1

12. What is the reconstructive strategy for floor of mouth defects?

Selection of a proper method is based on the quantity of tissue removed, tongue mobility, and radiotherapy. Primary closure or skin grafting is adequate for defects of limited size. Skin grafts also can reconstruct larger floor of mouth (FOM) defects without restricting tongue mobility. Removal of the mylohyoid complex necessitates regional or free flap reconstruction. Reconstruction of the lingual nerve can be accomplished with innervated free flap transfers. Muscle flaps are used in larger-volume defects to prevent the pooling of saliva and food in this region. Composite defects that include bone require vascularized bone transfers in addition to volume and surface reconstruction.

13. Buccal mucosa defects should not be left to heal by secondary intention. True or false?

False. Small defects can be closed primarily or allowed to heal by secondary intention. Reconstruction of larger defects with skin or mucosal grafts is rapid and reliable. Temporalis muscle or fascia flaps, with or without skin grafts, can be used for thicker or less vascularized defects. Other regional flaps may be used for volume and surface reconstruction. For through-and-through cheek defects, cervical rotation advancement flaps (prior radiotherapy or neck dissection should be ruled out) or free fasciocutaneous flaps can be used.

14. Periosteum is always a physiologic barrier for bone involvement in alveolar ridge malignancies. True or false?

False. In cases of previous radiotherapy, the periosteum loses its ability to serve as a barrier for local invasion because irradiation alters the structural integrity of periosteum. This factor should be considered during surgical planning. Stage I and II malignancies can be treated with resection of the primary tumor with a marginal mandibulectomy and local flap coverage. Advanced cases require en bloc resection of a full-thickness mandibular segment and treatment of the affected neck. Mandibular reconstruction modalities are applied for reconstruction in such cases (osteocutaneous free flaps).

15. List the reconstructive options for oral malignancies.

In general, small defects can be reconstructed with local flaps. Larger defects (or those bound to receive radiation) will require a more substantial pedicled flap or a free flap.

Alternatives for surface and volume reconstruction of intraoral defects include the following:

Basic Approaches	Cervical rotation-advancement flaps
Secondary healing	Sternocleidomastoid muscle flaps
Primary closure	Latissimus dorsi muscle flaps
Grafts	Pectoralis major muscle flaps
	Trapezius flaps
Split-thickness skin graft	**Free Flaps**
Full-thickness skin graft	Radial forearm flaps
Local Flaps	Fibula flaps
Mucosal flaps	Anterolateral thigh flaps
Lingual flaps	Lateral arm flaps
Palatal flaps	Ulnar flaps
Regional Flaps	Scapular flaps
	Iliac crest flaps
Platysma flap	Rectus abdominis muscle flaps
Nasolabial flaps	Groin flaps
Temporalis muscle and fascia flaps	Dorsalis pedis flaps
Forehead flaps	Jejunum flaps
Posterior auricular flaps	Gastroomental flaps

16. Are free tissue transfers always the preferred reconstructive method?

Not necessarily. The reconstructive technique is tailored to the size and composition of the defect, the specific functional requirements, and whether or not the patient will receive postoperative radiation. For smaller defects, local flaps are sufficient and offer less morbidity. However, for larger resections (which may include a bony defect), the longer operative time and increased morbidity of a free flap may be justified, especially if the reconstruction will be radiated.

17. What are the reconstructive options for a composite defect that includes a missing bony segment?

This type of defect (which often occurs in a patient who eventually will be radiated) requires a vascularized bone graft, and this effectively limits the options to free tissue transfers. The fibula is the most frequently used flap because it has a favorable donor site, a relatively lengthy pedicle, and adequate bone length for contouring. Other options include iliac crest, rib, scapula, and the radial forearm flap with an included segment of the radius.

18. **What are the advantages and disadvantages of free flap applications in oral reconstruction?**

Advantages	Disadvantages
Superior wound healing	Require microsurgical skill
Better functional and aesthetic outcome	Longer operation time (risk of anesthesia in
Higher quality of life	debilitated and older patients)
Shorter hospitalization	
Use of neurotized flaps	
One-stage, immediate reconstruction	
Suitable for simultaneous two-team approach	
Ability to restore composite defects	
Fewer complications in irradiated patients	

19. **Which arteries and veins in the head and neck region are preferred as recipient vessels for microvascular anastomoses?**

Branches of the ipsilateral external carotid system are suitable for arterial anastomoses, including the superior thyroid artery, lingual artery, facial artery, and superficial temporal artery. In irradiated or operated cases, contralateral neck vessels or the ipsilateral common carotid artery may be selected. For veins, tributaries of the superficial and deep jugular system are convenient.

20. **Describe the elevation of the platysma flap and outline the indications for intraoral reconstruction.**

This flap is based on the submental branch of the facial artery and raised on a subcutaneous superior muscle pedicle. The skin island is designed on a transverse axis distally. The pedicle area is supported by anastomoses with both labial arteries, the superior thyroid artery and superior labial artery. Because a motor branch of the facial nerve and sensory branches innervate the musculocutaneous unit, this flap can be used to give motor function to the lip and to provide sensation to the reconstructed area. It can be transposed 180° to reconstruct defects of the tongue and FOM. Previous irradiation to the neck area is the main contraindication for use of this flap.

21. **What are the limitations of the temporalis muscle and fascia flaps for oral reconstruction?**

The temporal muscle flap is based on the deep temporal vessels, whereas the temporal fascial flap is based on the superficial temporal vessels. Either can easily be transposed to the buccal region, palate, and lateral portions of FOM. The length of the pedicle precludes its use for the tongue and central portion of FOM. Flaps can be lined with skin grafts; however, adaptation and epithelialization of the raw surface of the flaps are satisfactory even with secondary healing. Muscle is included in the flap when bulk is needed. The main problems after flap transfer are temporal depression (in temporal muscle flap cases) and limitations of the oral aperture.

22. **Can the posterior auricular flap be used for tongue reconstruction?**

Yes. The posterior auricular flap can be transferred as an island or as a free flap based on the posterior auricular vessels for oral cavity reconstruction. Dissection of this flap is a difficult and time-consuming procedure, and the area of the skin island is limited. Complications due to the extensive dissection and close proximity to the facial nerve have been reported. However, the less visible donor site scar and the pliability of the transferred skin place this flap among the alternatives for intraoral reconstruction when simultaneous neck dissection is carried out.

23. **Explain the extension arc of nasolabial musculocutaneous flaps.**

Inferiorly based nasolabial flaps can be transferred transbuccally to reconstruct buccal defects and FOM defects of 2.5 cm × 7.0 cm. It is essential not to include hair-bearing skin in the flap. Unlike the subcutaneous pedicle flaps, the muscle-incorporated flaps (nasalis, levator superioris, zygomaticus muscles) can be transposed for distances greater than 2 cm and undergo minimal contraction.

24. **Classify the lingual flaps.**

Dorsal lingual flaps. These flaps must not cross the median raphe. They are elevated at 8-mm thickness to include mucosa, submucosa, and superficial musculature. Posteriorly based dorsal tongue flaps can be used to reconstruct moderate defects of the retromolar triangle. Anteriorly based dorsal tongue flaps offer greater mobility and can be used to repair anterior cheek and commissure defects. Transverse dorsal tongue flaps can be used in bipedicle fashion to reconstruct FOM defects when the tongue is extra long.

Flaps from the Lingual Tip. Perimeter flaps and dorsoventrally based flaps may be raised.

Ventral Surface Flaps. These flaps can be used for FOM defects; however, the donor area must be skin-grafted to avoid limitation in tongue mobility.

25. What is the role of palatal flaps in oral reconstruction?

Total palatal mucoperiosteal tissue (up to 24 cm²) can be raised on a single greater palatine artery. This flap can be transposed to cover neighboring defects of the buccal mucosa, retromolar triangle, tonsillar region, and soft palate. The donor area is left to granulate. The palatal mucosa is not pliable, and caution must be taken to avoid pedicle torsion. As with other local flaps, previous irradiation to the oral cavity precludes the use of palatal flaps.

26. What are the drawbacks of the forehead flap?

The major drawback is that this is a pedicled flap that requires at least one additional operation to divide its pedicle. Before pedicle division, the tubed pedicle is conspicuous and unaesthetic. The donor site ultimately heals remarkably well if portions are left to close secondarily but likely will heal unaesthetically if skin-grafted.

27. When should the latissimus dorsi muscle and musculocutaneous flaps be used?

The latissimus dorsi muscle or musculocutaneous flaps can be used to cover extensive defects of the oral cavity, especially when volume reconstruction is needed and/or recipient bed conditions are poor. When both internal and external linings are required, this flap can be used with one side grafted or with separate skin islands.

28. What are the limitations of the pectoralis major muscle and musculocutaneous flaps?

- Donor site scar is not aesthetic (unacceptable in female patients).
- Pedicle produces bulk in the subcutaneous tunnel.
- Hair-bearing skin is a disadvantage for intraoral reconstruction.
- Too much bulk may cause problems in tongue and FOM reconstruction.
- Dissection is carried out over a large area.
- The close proximity to the recipient site prevents a simultaneous two-team approach.

29. Can the sternocleidomastoid musculocutaneous flap be raised over an inferior pedicle?

Yes. The skin island can be outlined over the inframastoid area and the flap based on an inferior blood supply; however, it usually requires sacrifice of the eleventh nerve. The sternocleidomastoid has three blood supplies (superior, middle, and inferior); the flap is more frequently raised on the superior pedicle with a distally placed skin island over the supraclavicular area. In functional neck dissection cases, this flap can be used for intraoral reconstruction.

30. Describe the variants of the trapezius muscle and musculocutaneous flaps for intraoral reconstruction.

The trapezius musculocutaneous flap can be elevated along the descending portion of the transverse cervical artery with a vertical skin island or in a transverse direction, mobilizing the upper portion of the muscle on the transverse cervical artery. The flap is elevated only with the portion of the muscle necessary to incorporate the pedicle area and provide a base with the skin paddle.

31. What is the first-line choice in free flap reconstruction for tongue and FOM defects?

The radial forearm fasciocutaneous flap.

32. What are the advantages of the radial forearm flap for intraoral reconstruction?

- Thin pliable skin is suitable for intraoral lining.
- Distant donor area enables a two-team approach.
- Reliable and constant pedicle and internal vascular architecture provide satisfactory flap circulation; pedicle is of adequate length for almost all applications.
- Incorporation of cutaneous nerves serves to restore sensation to the reconstructed area.
- Lack of bulkiness avoids limitation of tongue mobility for tongue and FOM reconstruction.
- Versatility of the skin island–pedicle alignment facilitates comfortable anastomoses.
- Brachioradialis muscle can be included with the flap when additional bulk is needed.
- A partial-thickness segment of radius can be harvested within the flap for bone and soft tissue reconstruction.

33. What are the advantages and disadvantages of the jejunum free flap for intraoral reconstruction?

Advantages: It is best for correction or prevention of xerostomia in irradiated patients. It retains secretory ability. Use of bowel components to provide coverage and bulk as well as lining is possible. Jejunal reconstruction of tongue and FOM defects allows full range of motion of the tongue. The vascular pedicle is reliable and suitable for microsurgical anastomoses. The flap can be harvested endoscopically. Reconstruction is a one-stage procedure.

Disadvantages: The intraabdominal procedure carries the associated donor site risks. Hypersecretion and extreme mobility of the flap lining are other drawbacks.

34. Describe the vascular anatomy and harvest of the jejunum flap.

An arcade formed by branches of the superior mesenteric artery supplies the jejunum. Each branch (usually larger than 1.5 mm in diameter) can support a segment of jejunum up to 24 cm long. Usually a segment of proximal jejunum (within the first 2 feet) is used for reconstruction.

After the ligament of Treitz is identified through a left upper quadrant transverse incision, a suitable proximal segment is located. The vascular pedicle is dissected toward its superior mesenteric origin. All other anastomosing vessels are tied off, leaving the pedicle as the only blood supply to the flap. Next, the proximal and distal ends of the jejunal segment are divided, usually with a stapling device. Once the viability of the flap is assessed, the vascular pedicle is divided close to its origin, and the flap is transferred. The tubular flap can be converted to a flat flap by opening it through its antimesenteric border longitudinally. Bowel continuity in the donor site is reestablished.

35. Evaluate the lateral arm flap for tongue reconstruction.

The lateral arm flap provides soft, supple, mobile, innervated tissue of 12 cm × 18 cm for tongue and FOM reconstruction. It receives its blood supply from the radial collateral artery (1.2 mm in diameter). The lateral brachial cutaneous nerve can be transferred within the flap to reconstruct the lingual nerve. This flap possesses similar advantages to the radial forearm flap; however, the pedicle is shorter, the diameter of the vessels is smaller, the course of the vascular pedicle may vary, and the pedicle enters the middle of the flap under most harvest circumstances. The donor site for the lateral arm flap is more forgiving than is the radial forearm flap because it does not have the potential for tendon exposure.

36. What is the role of the laser in oral cavity cancer?

Transoral laser resection of oral cavity carcinomas is widely used in the absence of nodal involvement. The surface is left to granulate, and satisfactory epithelialization is observed. Low morbidity and successful control of the disease have supported the use of laser resection in combination with staged neck dissection in advanced cases when mandibular or deep visceral involvement is ruled out.

BIBLIOGRAPHY

Ariyan S: Cancer of the upper aerodigestive system. In McCarthy JG (ed): Plastic Surgery. Philadelphia, WB Saunders, 1990, pp 3412–3477.

Bakamjian VY: Lingual flaps in reconstructive surgery for oral and perioral cancer. In McCarthy JG (ed): Plastic Surgery. Philadelphia, WB Saunders, 1990, pp 3478–3496.

Eckel HE, Volling P, Zorowka P, Thumfart W: Transoral laser resection with staged discontinuous neck dissection for oral cavity and oropharynx squamous cell carcinoma. Laryngoscope 105:53–60, 1995.

Hagan WE: Nasolabial musculocutaneous flap in reconstruction of oral defects. Laryngoscope 96:840–845, 1986.

Lenert JJ, Evans GRD: Oral cavity reconstruction. In Mathes SJ (ed): Plastic Surgery, 2nd ed. Philadelphia, Elsevier, 2006, pp 917–956.

Leonard AG, Kolhe PS: The posterior auricular flap: Intra-oral reconstruction. Br J Plast Surg 40:570–581, 1987.

Panje WR: Immediate reconstruction of the oral cavity. In Thawley SE, Panje WR (eds): Comprehensive Management of Head and Neck Tumors. Philadelphia, WB Saunders, 1987.

Panje WR: Oral cavity and oropharyngeal reconstruction. In Cummings CW (ed): Otolaryngology—Head and Neck Surgery. St. Louis, Mosby, 1992.

Papadopoulos ON, Gamatsi IE: Platysma myocutaneous flap for intraoral and surface reconstruction. Ann Plast Surg 31:15–18, 1993.

Wells MD, Edwards AL, Luce EA: Intraoral reconstructive techniques. Clin Plast Surg 22:91–108, 1995.

MANDIBLE RECONSTRUCTION

Norman Weinzweig, MD, FACS, and Jeffrey Weinzweig, MD, FACS

1. Who was Andy Gump?

Caricaturized in the 1930s, Andy Gump was a real-life person with head and neck cancer who had an unreconstructed resection of the anterior mandible. A statue in his memory stands in Lake Geneva, Wisconsin.

2. Describe the functional deficits associated with the Andy Gump deformity.

The Andy Gump deformity results from loss of height, width, and projection of the lower third of the face due to resection of the anterior mandibular arch with anterior and medial deviation of the lateral mandibular segments by the residual mylohyoid muscles and superior displacement by the medial pterygoid, masseter, and temporalis muscles. Loss of the anterior mandible results in impairment of oral competence, speech, deglutition (swallowing), and mastication. Loss of support for the hypomandibular complex contributes to aspiration, dysphagia, oral incompetence, and difficulty with mastication.

3. What functional deficits are associated with lateral mandibulectomy?

Loss of continuity in the lateral and posterior segments is far less severe than with central defects. Lateral mandibulectomy defects result in cheek contour deformity with deviation of the symphysis from the midline when the mouth is open. Upward and lateral displacement of the mandibular remnants results from uninhibited pull of the opposite intact muscles of mastication and scar contracture on the resected side. This displacement creates difficulty with bimaxillary relationships and occlusion.

4. What are the main goals and considerations in mandibular reconstruction?
- Primary wound healing
- Early functional oral rehabilitation
- Restoration of aesthetics
- Restoration of the patient's body image

5. What are the advantages of immediate mandibular reconstruction?

Immediate reconstruction provides the best opportunity to achieve optimal aesthetic and functional outcome after loss of the mandible. Delayed reconstruction, on the other hand, is associated with deformity and functional deficits as the resected ends of the mandible become tethered by soft tissue scarring, fibrosis, and contracture and often cannot be fully corrected.

6. How do you manage a patient with a shotgun wound to the face?
- Airway, breathing, circulation: ABCs of resuscitation
- Tracheostomy: Often necessary to secure an airway
- Serial débridements of devitalized soft tissue and bone
- Temporary stabilization of the mandibular fragments with rigid plate(s) or external fixation
- Definitive composite reconstruction when the patient's overall status permits

7. What are conventional techniques for mandibular reconstruction?
- Free bone grafts
- Alloplastic materials (metallic implants, metal or Dacron trays packed with cancellous bone)
- Freeze-dried, autoclaved, or irradiated bone allografts
- Pedicled flaps

These techniques have poor or, at best, unpredictable results due to variability of the traumatized, irradiated, or avascular recipient beds. Reconstructions often require multiple-stage procedures with long hospitalizations; patients often succumb before completion of the reconstruction.

8. What are the indications for a no-bone reconstruction?
- Poor surgical candidates
- Short life expectancy
- Edentulous patients with only small posterior mandibulectomy defects

9. What is the role of nonvascularized bone grafts?
- Limited to small lateral defects (<5 cm) in patients with excellent soft tissue coverage who have not received and will not receive radiation
- Condylar reconstruction in children

10. What are the advantages of reconstruction plates, with or without soft tissue reconstruction?
- Ease of application
- Rigid fixation
- Lack of donor site morbidity
- Reduced operative time
- Condylar replacement
- Reconstruction of extensive bony defects in elderly and infirm patients

Best indicated in patients with poor prognosis, lateral defects, and good soft tissue coverage who have not received and will not receive radiation.

11. What are the disadvantages of reconstruction plates, with or without soft tissue reconstruction?
- Lack of long-term reliability
- Stress on mandibular fragments may cause screw loosening, plate fatigue, and fracture
- Inadequate soft tissue coverage or radiated tissues result in plate extrusion in many anterior reconstructions
- No bone stock for osseointegrated dental implants

12. What are the advantages of the radial forearm osteocutaneous flap?
- Up to 14 cm of straight unicortical bone
- Multiple osteotomies may create an anterior mandible or hemimandible
- Thin, pliable, abundant, relatively hairless skin
- Excellent intraoral lining; conforms well to sulci and prevents tethering of tongue
- Can be split into separate skin paddles for intraoral mucosal lining and external skin coverage
- Flexibility in three-dimensional orientation of bone and skin paddle(s)
- Possible reinnervation by coaptation of lateral or medial antebrachial cutaneous nerves with lingual, mental, or great auricular nerves may facilitate oral rehabilitation
- Long pedicle, large-caliber vessels, dual venous drainage

13. What are the disadvantages of the radial forearm osteocutaneous flap?
- Donor radius fracture
- Skin graft loss with tendon exposure
- Displeasing appearance of donor site
- Prolonged extremity immobilization
- Osseointegration *not* possible

14. What are the major reasons for donor radius fracture?
- Harvesting an excessive amount of bone
- Perpendicular osteotomies with cross-cutting of the radius, which further weakens it
- Inadequate length of postoperative immobilization of arm
- Failure to prevent pronation and supination by application of a long-arm cast

15. How can donor radius fracture be prevented?
The radial forearm osteocutaneous flap has received a bad reputation because of donor radius fracture. This complication can be prevented by avoiding the problems cited above as well as by a modification of the standard technique in which the radius is harvested as a keel-shaped segment of bone. Early series reported incidences of fracture ranging from 10% to 67%. However, two series by Weinzweig et al. and Swanson et al. demonstrated a combined fracture incidence of only 2.9% (1/34). The solitary fracture perhaps was preventable.

16. What are the advantages of the iliac crest osteocutaneous flap?
- Up to 14 cm of thick corticocancellous bone
- Natural bone curvature (its unique shape resembles a hemimandible)
- Best bone stock for osseointegration

17. What are the disadvantages of the iliac crest osteocutaneous flap?
- Soft tissue too bulky for intraoral lining unless glossectomy is performed
- Poor tissue for intraoral, chin, and submental contour
- Least degree of three-dimensional flexibility of skin and bone
- Skin reliability is unpredictable
- Delayed ambulation and gait disturbances
- Contour deformity at donor site, especially when a large amount of bone is harvested
- Abdominal wall weakness or herniation
- Injury to lateral femoral cutaneous nerve

Modifications include use of the internal oblique muscle and skin graft for intraoral lining and split inner cortex bone harvest.

18. What are the advantages of the scapular osteocutaneous flap?
- Up to 14 cm of straight lateral scapular bone
- Independently vascularized bone and skin paddle(s)
- Greatest three-dimensional flexibility
- Good external skin coverage
- Osseointegration possible
- Minimal donor site morbidity

19. What are the disadvantages of the scapular osteocutaneous flap?
- Bulky soft tissue for intraoral lining
- Osteotomies can devascularize bone segments
- Two-team approach not facilitated
- Seroma formation

20. What are the advantages of the fibular osteocutaneous flap?
- Up to 25 cm of straight bicortical bone, by far the largest amount of bone
- Multiple osteotomies
- Osseointegration possible
- Minimal donor site morbidity

21. What are the disadvantages of the fibular osteocutaneous flap?
- Unreliability of skin paddle (no longer a problem)
- Limited amount of skin available
- Objectionable appearance of skin-grafted donor site
- Delayed ambulation
- Neurapraxia

22. Compare the common vascularized composite tissue transfers and donor sites for oromandibular reconstruction.
See Tables 62-1 and 62-2.

23. Provide algorithms for microvascular mandibular reconstruction.
See Figures 62-1 and 62-2.

24. Is there a role for sequential free flaps?
Sequential or simultaneous free flaps combine the best qualities of bone and soft tissue of the individual flaps; however, they prolong operative time, add complexity to the case, and increase donor morbidity. Their role, if any, is limited to extensive bone and soft tissue defects not satisfactorily reconstructed by a single flap.

25. What is the role of dental rehabilitation by osseointegration?
Dental rehabilitation by osseointegration achieves the ideal end-goal in mandibular reconstruction, maximizing aesthetic and functional outcome. Unfortunately, few patients are candidates for osseointegration, and even fewer actually

Table 62-1. Comparison of Common Vascularized Composite Tissue Transfers for Oromandibular Reconstruction

| DONOR SITE | BONE | | SOFT TISSUE | | | | |
	LENGTH (CM)	QUALITY	QUALITY	RELIABILITY	HARVEST	MORBIDITY	PEDICLE
Fibula	25	Excellent	Skin/muscle, excellent, potentially sensate	Good	A, B	Minimal	Peroneal artery, up to 15 cm
Scapula	14	Good	Skin/muscle, good, not sensate	Excellent	D	Moderate	Subscapular artery, up to 10 cm
Iliac crest	14	Excellent	Skin/muscle, fair, not sensate	Good	A, C	Moderate to severe	Deep circumflex iliac artery, 5–6 cm
Radial forearm	10	Poor	Skin, excellent, potentially sensate	Excellent	A, B	Moderate to severe	Radial artery, up to 15 cm

A, Two-team approach; *B*, easy; *C*, intermediate; *D*, more difficult.

Table 62-2. Comparison of Free Flap Donor Sites for Mandible Reconstruction

| DONOR SITE | TISSUE CHARACTERISTICS | | | DONOR SITE CHARACTERISTICS | |
	BONE	SKIN	PEDICLE	LOCATION	MORBIDITY
Fibula	A	C	B	A	A
Ilium	B	D	D	B	C
Scapula	C	B	C	D	B
Radius	D	A	A	C	D

A, Excellent; *B*, good; *C*, fair; *D*, poor.

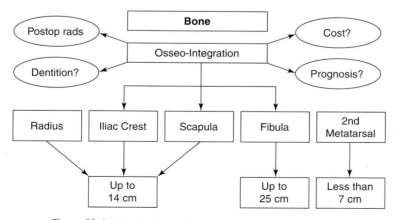

Figure 62-1. Algorithm for mandibular reconstruction: Bone component.

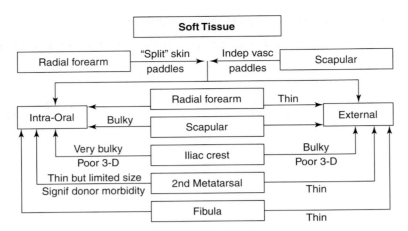

Figure 62-2. Algorithm for mandibular reconstruction: Soft tissue component.

undergo the procedure. Justifying this approach is difficult; it requires several stages over 6 to 9 months in patients with advanced intraoral malignancies who have poor prognoses (approximately 50% of such patients die within 1.5 to 2 years). Moreover, many patients were edentulous or had poor dentition before tumor ablation. In addition, the significant cost associated with this procedure may not be covered by many insurance companies. Finally, the fate of osseointegrated implants in the face of postoperative radiation is uncertain.

26. What are important considerations in reconstruction (or construction) of the pediatric mandible?
The pediatric mandible is dynamic, constantly changing with growth and development. Reconstructive options are based on the higher osteogenic potential, the tremendous capacity of the temporomandibular joint (TMJ) for remodeling, and the implicit requirement for growth. The mandibular body and parasymphysis are filled with developing tooth buds. One must consider not only the three-dimensional problems of aesthetics and occlusion but also the fourth dimension of time. Techniques include conventional bone and cartilage grafting, orthognathic surgery, distraction osteogenesis, and microvascular free tissue transfer, alone or in combination. Because of these factors, the diversity of reconstructive options in pediatric cases is greater than in adult cases.

27. Name three primary indications for mandibular reconstruction in the child.
- *Posttraumatic:* Management of significant fractures with bone loss and treatment of their sequelae of growth disturbances and TMJ ankylosis
- *Congenital:* Hypoplasia associated with oculoauricular vertebral syndrome, including hemifacial microsomia and craniofacial microsomia
- *Tumor:* After resection of facial tumors or radiation therapy for orbitofacial tumors

BIBLIOGRAPHY

Coleman JJ III: Mandible reconstruction. Oper Tech Plast Reconstr Surg 3:213–302, 1996.
Cordeiro PG, Disa JJ, Hidalgo DA, Hu QY: Reconstruction of the mandible with osseous free flaps: A 10-year experience with 150 consecutive patients. Plast Reconstr Surg 104:1314–1320, 1999.
Disa JJ, Hidalgo DA, Cordeiro PG, et al: Evaluation of bone height in osseous free flap mandible reconstruction: An indirect measure of bone mass. Plast Reconstr Surg 103:1371–1377, 1999.
Hidalgo DA: Aesthetic improvements in free-flap mandible reconstruction. Plast Reconstr Surg 88:574–585, 1991.
Hidalgo DA: Fibula free flap: A new method of mandibular reconstruction. Plast Reconstr Surg 84:71–79, 1989.
Hidalgo DA, Pusic AL: Free-flap mandibular reconstruction: A 10-year follow-up study. Plast Reconstr Surg 110:438–449, 2002.
Millard DR, Maisels DO, Batstone JHF: Immediate repair of radical resection of the anterior arch of the lower jaw. Plast Reconstr Surg 37:153–161, 1967.
Shenaq SM, Klebuc MJA: The iliac crest microsurgical free flap in mandibular reconstruction. Clin Plast Surg 21:37–44, 1994.
Shusterman MA, Reece GP, Kroll SS, et al: Use of the AO plate for immediate mandibular reconstruction in cancer patients. Plast Reconstr Surg 88:588–593, 1991.
Shusterman MA, Reece GP, Miller MJ, et al: The osteocutaneous free fibula flap: Is the skin paddle reliable? Plast Reconstr Surg 90:787–793, 1992.
Soutar DS, Widdowson WP: Immediate reconstruction of the mandible using a vascularized segment of radius. Head Neck Surg 8:232–246, 1986.
Steckler RM, Edgerton MT, Gogol W: Andy Gump. Am J Surg 138:545–547, 1974.

Swanson E, Boyd JB, Manktelow RT: The radial forearm flap: Reconstructive applications and donor-site defects in 35 consecutive patients. Plast Reconstr Surg 85:258–266, 1990.

Swartz MM, Banis JC, Newton E: The osteocutaneous scapular flap for mandibular and maxillary reconstruction. Plast Reconstr Surg 77:530–545, 1986.

Taylor GI: Reconstruction of the mandible with free iliac bone grafts. Ann Plast Surg 9:361–376, 1986.

Weinzweig N, Jones NF, Shestak KC, et al: Oromandibular reconstruction using a keel-shaped modification of the radial forearm osteocutaneous flap. Ann Plast Surg 33:359–369, 1994.

Weinzweig N, Weinzweig J: Current concepts in mandibular reconstruction by microsurgical free flaps. Surg Technol Int VI:338–346, 1997.

Wells MD, Luce EA, Edwards AL, et al: Sequentially linked free flaps in head and neck reconstruction. Clin Plast Surg 21:59–67, 1994.

SCALP RECONSTRUCTION

Shawkat Sati, MD; Ahmed Seif Makki, MD, FRCS; Mark Shashikant, MD; and Sai S. Ramasastry, MD, FRCS, FACS

1. What are the common causes of scalp defects?

Scalp defects may result from trauma, tumor excision, or tissue necrosis due to burns or radiation therapy.

2. What are the five anatomic layers of the scalp?

- **S** = **S**kin. Scalp skin is considered the thickest skin in the body and can be used as a donor site for split-thickness skin grafts.
- **C** = **S**ub**c**utaneous tissue, which contains hair follicles and sweat and sebaceous glands, blood vessels, lymphatics, and nerves.
- **A** = **A**poneurosis (galea aponeurotica or epicranium), which connects the frontalis muscle with the occipitalis muscle. Laterally the galea becomes the temporoparietal fascia (superficial temporal fascia).
- **L** = **L**oose connective tissue, which allows the scalp to be mobile on the cranium. It also creates a point of separation during traumatic scalp injuries and is the site where abscesses tend to occur after scalp closures.
- **P** = **P**ericranium, which invests the skull bone by Sharpey fibers.

Scalp avulsion injuries occur at the level of the loose areolar tissue. The scalp is defined as the anatomic area overlying the skull between the superior orbital rims anteriorly and the superior nuchal line posteriorly (Fig. 63-1).

3. What is the arterial supply of the scalp?

The scalp is endowed with an extensive circulatory network. Anteriorly, it is supplied by the supraorbital and supratrochlear arteries, which are end vessels of the ophthalmic artery arising from the internal carotid. Laterally, it is supplied by the superficial temporal artery (which divides into the frontal and parietal arteries), a branch of the external carotid, supplying the temporal, parietal, and frontal regions. Posteriorly, it is supplied by two lateral and two medial branches of the occipital artery, a branch of the external carotid. The postauricular artery, also a branch of the external carotid, supplies the posterolateral scalp. The pericranium is supplied by the middle meningeal artery and the intracranial circulation to the calvarial bone.

4. What is the sensory nerve supply of the scalp?

Sensory nerves lie in the superficial fascia: supratrochlear nerve (V1), supraorbital nerve (V1), zygomaticotemporal nerve (V2), auriculotemporal nerve (V3), greater occipital nerve (dorsal rami of C2), and occipital nerve (C3 from cervical plexus).

5. How many fascial layers can be found in the temporoparietal region of the scalp? Describe the relationship of the frontal branch of the facial nerve to these fascial layers.

There are four distinct fascial layers in the temporoparietal region. The most superfical fascial layer is the *temporoparietal fascia* or *superficial temporal fascia*, a lateral extension of the galea that is difficult to dissect from the overlying skin. Deep to the superficial temporal fascia is the *subgaleal fascia*, a layer that is well developed and easily dissected. The subgaleal fascia contains the superficial temporal artery and the frontal branch of the facial nerve. Beneath the subgaleal fascia lies the *superficial temporal fat pad*. Under the temporal fat pad lies the *deep temporal fascia*.

6. Describe the course of the deep temporal fascia.

The deep temporal fascia is a thick fascial layer overlying the temporalis muscle. Superiorly, it fuses with the pericranium. Inferiorly, at the level of the superior orbital margin, it splits into two layers. The superficial layer attaches to the lateral border of the zygomatic arch; the deep layer fuses with the medial aspect of the arch. There is a small amount of fat between these layers. Dissection in this layer allows reflection of the coronal flap without injury to the frontal branch of the facial nerve as it passes over the zygomatic arch (Fig. 63-2).

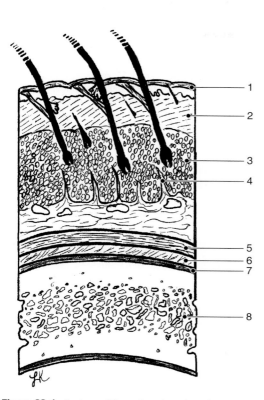

Figure 63-1. Anatomy of the scalp and cranium: *1*, Epidermis; *2*, dermis; *3*, subcutaneous fat; *4*, fibrous septa; *5*, galea aponeurotica; *6*, subgaleal tissue; *7*, pericranium; *8*, calvaria. (From Mathes S [ed]: Plastic Surgery, 2nd ed., Philadelphia, Saunders, 2006.)

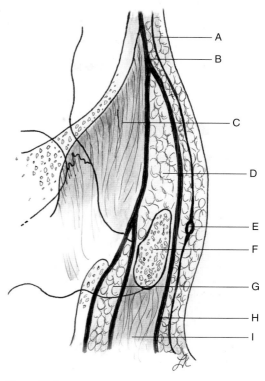

Figure 63-2. Cross-section of the temporal region at the level of the zygomatic arch showing the relationship of the frontal branch of the facial nerve to superficial and deep temporal fascia. *A*, Temporoparietal fascia; *B*, deep temporal fascia splitting at the line of fusion; *C*, superficial temporal fat pad; *D*, temporalis muscle; *E*, frontal branch of the facial nerve; *F*, zygomatic arch; *G*, deep temporal fat pad from the buccal fat; *H*, parotid-masseteric fascia; *I*, masseter muscle. (From Mathes S [ed]: Plastic Surgery, 2nd ed., Philadelphia, Saunders, 2006.)

7. What factors affect the selection of a scalp reconstruction method?

- Replace like tissue with like tissue. The scalp should be reconstructed with hair-bearing skin whenever possible.
- Wound repair depends on location, size, and depth of the wound.
- Careful preoperative and intraoperative planning.
- Wounds without tissue loss, no matter how long after injury, can be closed by direct approximation.
- Overzealous débridement is unnecessary because the robust circulation often allows salvage of the tissues.
- In large defects, skin grafting, scalp flaps, and non–scalp flap transfer from a regional or distant site come into play.

8. What are the principles of the management of acute scalp wounds?

- The goal is to obtain a healed wound while preventing desiccation, infection, and bone necrosis.
- Wounds with vascularized tissue covering the bone, such as the pericranium, can be covered by skin grafts.
- Keep the tissues moist in every acute situation.
- If all layers are absent and the calvarial bone is exposed, immediate coverage must be provided by either local flaps or distant flaps.
- If the tissue defect also involves the bone, vascularized soft tissue coverage must be provided. Bone can be replaced at the same time or at a later date.

9. What are Hatchet, Worthen, and Orticochea flaps?

A Hatchet flap is a V-Y advancement flap, in which bilateral triangles are raised on subcutaneous pedicles and skin pedicles are rotated medially. A Worthen flap is a rotational flap of the entire forehead elevated below the frontalis muscle. It allows coverage of massive defects, although distortion of the eyebrows and hairline may result. Orticochea flaps, or "banana peel flaps," were originally described as four large flaps based on named vessels, allowing coverage of defects involving 30% of the scalp. Orticochea modified the technique to rely on three flaps, two based off the superficial temporal vessels.

10. Describe the anatomy and uses of the temporalis myofascial flap.

The temporalis myofascial flap is composed of the temporalis muscle and the deep temporal fascia. It is primarily supplied by the deep temporal artery, which is a branch of the external carotid. It runs posterior and medial to the mandibular ramus and inserts into the medial and inferior margin of the temporalis. It is used in patients with chronic derangement of the temporomandibular joint who have continued dysfunction despite conservative treatment. It is used to reconstruct the articular disc. The superficial temporal artery is *not* part of this flap.

11. What is aplasia cutis congenita?

Aplasia cutis congenita is a congenital disorder of unknown etiology characterized by a scalp defect most commonly in the midline of the vertex. It may be associated with a skull defect and/or exposure of the dura or the brain. Most defects are less than 2 cm, and spontaneous resolution frequently occurs. Treatment consists of dressing changes and is aimed at prevention of infection. For larger defects and/or exposed dura, complex reconstruction is required.

Patients may exhibit chromosomal disorders and familial inheritance. It can be associated with hydrocephalus, myelomeningocele, and cleft lip and palate. Twenty-five percent of patients have more than one affected area.

12. What are the indications and advantages of using a skin graft for coverage of scalp wounds?

A skin graft is an option for partial-thickness wounds. The recipient bed must be well vascularized and free of infection. Split-thickness skin grafts provide a simple, fast, and economic way to obtain reliable wound healing. Grafts are not commonly meshed for cosmetic purposes and to provide greater shearing resistance. In some situations, the calvarial bone can be drilled on the outer cortex of the bone and decorticated to allow granulated tissue growth to facilitate skin graft take.

13. Can a skin graft be used to cover decorticated outer table skull?

Yes. Two to three days after decortication of the outer table of the skull, a skin graft remains an option in special circumstances. This method provides an epithelial cover for the skull. The procedure is most useful as a temporary measure before definitive scalp reconstruction (e.g., by tissue expansion).

14. How do you manage scalp wounds after radiation therapy or tumor resection?

The presence of multiple scalp incisions makes the use of scalp tissues somewhat problematic. Previous radiation therapy complicates the situation because of its deleterious effect on local tissue blood supply. When it is important to protect the bone or underlying brain tissue, you must provide soft tissue coverage with an independent and robust blood supply. This task often requires transfer of a regional flap or the microvascular transfer of a free flap.

15. Do periosteal flaps have any role in scalp reconstruction?

When bone is exposed, skin graft coverage may not be possible. Local pericranial flaps may be used in such cases for bone coverage, thus providing the vascularized bed necessary for skin graft take.

16. What is the major indication for use of regional or distant flaps for scalp reconstruction?

Large defects involving greater than 30% of the scalp that must be closed acutely and cannot be reconstructed with a skin graft or local flap. This situation is seen most commonly after full-thickness excision of a scalp tumor.

17. What are the indications for the use of free flaps for scalp reconstruction?

Free tissue transfer should be reserved for patients for whom reconstruction by conventional pedicle flap is not feasible. Free flaps are becoming increasingly used in the acute coverage of large defects after burns, radiation, and, occasionally, full-thickness excision of large tumors. In most cases, however, a carefully planned local transposition or rotation flap may be equally effective.

18. What are the advantages of free flaps?

Microvascular free tissue transfer allows one-stage coverage of large defects with exposed bone or underlying brain tissue.

19. What are the most commonly used free flaps for scalp reconstruction?

- Omental flaps
- Latissimus dorsi muscle flaps followed by split-thickness skin grafts
- Radial forearm flaps

20. What makes a radial forearm flap an ideal free flap for the scalp?

The radial forearm flap is a versatile flap for the reconstructive surgeon because of its thinness, durable skin quality, aesthetic match, and relative ease of dissection. It provides a reliable single-stage method to cover difficult scalp defects when other local methods are unsuitable. One of the drawbacks is its relatively small size. Preexpansion of the radial forearm flap can be used to cover a large scalp defect. In addition, the radial forearm flap is relatively non–hair bearing.

21. What are the disadvantages of free flaps for scalp reconstruction?

The flaps often are bulky and do not provide hair-bearing tissue for reconstruction. Technical difficulties and donor site problems associated with microsurgical tissue transfer are other drawbacks.

22. What are the available options for reconstruction of scalp bony defects?

- Cranial bone graft, which is available in the same operative field
- Split rib graft
- Cancellous bone graft from a distant bone site
- Alloplastic materials, such as methyl methacrylate

23. What is the role of tissue expansion in scalp reconstruction?

Tissue expansion has become the preferred method of secondary scalp reconstruction. It offers the reconstructive surgeon a better option than the conventional methods of skin grafts or transfer of non–hair-bearing, regional, or microvascular flaps for reconstruction of large defects that cannot be repaired with adjacent hair-bearing flaps. Reconstruction of large scalp defects depends on the ability to cover them with hair-bearing tissue. When the area of alopecia is large, the normal scalp is not sufficient to cover the defect resulting from excision of alopecia. Using tissue expansion techniques, large wounds (up to 50% of the scalp can be reconstructed) can be totally resurfaced while normal hair growth is maintained. Expansion should be continued until the expanded flap is approximately 20% larger than the size of the defect.

24. What is the major drawback of tissue expanders?

The main disadvantage of tissue expansion is the long duration of treatment (2 to 3 months), the need for two or more operations, and the visual deformity of the expanded site. Complication rates are 6% to 25%. Hair thinning is a concern when hair density decreases by 50%.

25. What is the main concern in the use of scalp tissue expansion in children?

There is a risk of skull deformation after a prolonged period of expansion. Little is known about the long-term effects on the skull and the ability of the skull to remodel after removal of the expander. The skull will return to normal by 2 to 18 months. The inner table is not affected by the tissue expanders.

26. What are the potential complications of scalp tissue expansion?

Infection, exposure of the expander, extrusion, device failure, and skin necrosis from overzealous expansion.

27. What are the advantages of an expanded free scalp flap?

Expansion of a large free scalp flap before transfer allows direct closure of the flap donor site, thereby avoiding the need for a skin graft or local flap to close the donor site.

28. What is the role of scalp replantation?

Scalp replantation is the treatment of choice in complete or near-complete scalp avulsions. The plane of avulsion is in the loose areolar tissue. Microvascular anastomosis should be outside the zone of injury. Up to 18 hours of cold ischemia is tolerated; arterial anastomosis should be done first if warm ischemia time is more than 10 hours.

29. Is there a role for biomaterials in scalp reconstruction?

Recently, bioengineered dermal matrix (Integra) has been used as a dermal regeneration matrix for large full-thickness scalp defects in both oncologic and burn applications. It offers the advantage of avoiding free tissue transfer, may yield better outcomes when exposed to post-operative radiation, and following micrograft hair transplantation has the potential for a better aesthetic match than the normal scalp.

BIBLIOGRAPHY

Alpert BS, Buncke HJ, Mathes SJ: Surgical treatment of the totally avulsed scalp. Clin Plast Surg 9:145–159, 1982.
Argenta LC, Watanabe MJ, Grabb WC: The use of tissue expansion in head and neck reconstruction. Ann Plast Surg 11:31–37, 1983.
Arnold PG, Rangarathnam CS: Multiple-flap scalp reconstruction: Orticochea revisited. Plast Reconstr Surg 69:605–613, 1982.
Hallock GG: Cutaneous coverage for the difficult scalp wound. Contemp Surg 38:22, 1991, pp 22–32.

Jackson IT, Sharpe DT, Polley J, Costanzo C, Rosenberg L: Use of external reservoirs in tissue expansion. Plast Reconstr Surg 80:266–273, 1987.

Komorowska-Timek E, Gabriel A, Bennett DC, et al: Artificial dermis as an alternative for coverage of complex scalp defects following excision of malignant tumors. Plast Reconstr Surg 115(4):1010–1017, 2005.

Orticochea M: Four-flap scalp reconstruction technique. Br J Plast Surg 20:159–171, 1967.

Orticochea M: New three-flap reconstruction technique. Br J Plast Surg 24:184–188, 1971.

Shestak KC, Ramasastry SS: Reconstruction of defects of the scalp and skull. In Cohen M (ed): Mastery of Plastic and Reconstructive Surgery. Boston, Little, Brown, 1994, pp 830–841.

Spector JA, Glat PM: Hair-bearing scalp reconstruction using a dermal regeneration template and micrograft hair transplantation. Ann Plast Surg 59(1):63–66, 2007.

Tolhurst DE, Carstens MH, Greco RJ, Hurwitz DJ: The surgical anatomy of the scalp. Plast Reconstr Surg 87:603–612, 1991.

Wells MD: Scalp reconstruction. In Mathes SJ (ed): Plastic Surgery, Vol 3, 2nd ed. Volume 3. Philadelphia, WB Saunders, 2006, pp 607–632.

Yeong EK, Huang HF, Chen YB, Chen MT: The use of artificial dermis for reconstruction of full thickness scalp burn involving the calvaria. Burns 32(3):375–379, 2006.

SURGICAL ANATOMY OF THE FACIAL NERVE

Soheil S. Younai, MD, FACS, and
Brooke R. Seckel, MD, FACS

1. From which foramen does the main trunk of the facial nerve exit the skull, and what type of fibers does it contain?

The main trunk of the facial nerve leaves the skull from the stylomastoid foramen, and at this point it contains only motor and sensory fibers; its parasympathetic fibers leave the cranial fossa along with other cranial nerves.

2. How do you locate the main trunk of the facial nerve during a parotidectomy?

As the facial nerve trunk travels from the stylomastoid foramen to the parotid body, it passes anterior to the posterior belly of the digastric muscle, lateral to styloid process and the external carotid artery, and posterior to the facial vein. At the beginning of a parotidectomy, start by mobilizing the tail of the parotid superiorly and retracting the anterior border of the sternocleidomastoid laterally to identify the posterior belly of the digastric muscle. Follow this muscle superiorly toward its insertion at the mastoid tip. After bluntly separating the parotid from its attachment to the cartilage of the external auditory canal, the tragal pointer comes into view. The facial nerve trunk lies approximately 1 cm deep and slightly anteroinferior to the tragal pointer.

3. "Great nerves travel together." How does this apply to the relationship of the facial nerve to other cranial nerves?

1. Facial nerve accompanies the acoustic nerve (CN VIII) as they leave the cranial fossa via the internal acoustic meatus.
2. Facial nerve's parasympathetic fibers travel with the trigeminal nerve (CN V).
    A. V1: Lacrimal nerve to lacrimal gland
    B. V2: Pterygopalatine nerve to nasal and palatal glands
    C. V3: Lingual nerve via chorda tympani to taste buds of anterior two thirds of the tongue, and submandibular and sublingual glands
3. Facial nerve's sensory fibers travel with the auricular branch of the vagus nerve (CN X) to provide sensation to the external auditory meatus.

4. Does the facial nerve innervate the posterior or the anterior belly of the digastric muscle?

The facial nerve innervates the posterior belly of the digastric muscle; the trigeminal nerve innervates its anterior belly.

5. What muscle does the facial nerve innervate in the middle ear, and what does it do?

The facial nerve innervates the stapedius muscle, which dampens loud noise.

6. Which brachial cleft arch does the facial nerve arise from? Which brachial cleft arch does the trigeminal nerve arise from?

The first brachial cleft arch gives rise to the trigeminal nerve; the second arch gives rise to the facial nerve.

7. What are the major branches of the facial nerve before and after it enters the parotid?

The facial nerve trunk has six major branches: temporal, zygomatic, buccal, mandibular, cervical, and auricular. The auricular branch comes off before the facial nerve turns into the parotid body. It innervates the superior auricular, posterior auricular, and occipitalis muscles, as well as providing sensation to the area behind the ear lobe. Within the parotid, the facial nerve divides into two main divisions, the temporofacial and the cervicofacial, which further divide into the temporal, zygomatic, buccal, mandibular, and cervical branches.

8. What is the relationship of the facial nerve to the superficial musculoaponeurotic system?

As the facial nerve branches leave the parotid body they are covered by a very thin layer of parotideomasseteric fascia. The superficial musculoaponeurotic system (SMAS) is located superficial to this layer.

9. What is Bell's palsy?

Bell's palsy is paralysis of the facial nerve. It was first described by Charles Bell in 1814 after he noted the features of facial paralysis in a laboratory monkey with a transected facial nerve. More than 75 different etiologic factors for Bell's palsy have been identified, including (1) congenital (Möbius syndrome), (2) traumatic (iatrogenic laceration, fractures, gunshot wound), (3) neoplastic (tumor of parotid, central nervous system, head, neck), (4) neurologic (cerebral vascular accident, degenerative), (5) infectious (bacterial, viral), (6) metabolic, and (7) idiopathic. The specific findings in facial paralysis depend on the level of the lesion, which are summarized in Table 64-1.

10. Do the facial muscles of expression receive their innervation along their superficial or deep surface?

It depends. Facial muscles such as the mentalis, levator angularis superioris, and buccinator are located deep within the facial soft tissue. Because these muscles lie deep to the plane of the facial nerve, they receive their innervation along their superficial surfaces and may be damaged during rhytidectomy if the dissection is carried out superficially. On the other hand, all other facial muscles of expression are located superficial to the plane of the facial nerve and thus receive their innervation along their deep or posterior surfaces. For example, the platysma, orbicularis oculi, and zygomaticus major and minor are situated superficial to the level of the facial nerve; therefore during rhytidectomy the dissection should be performed superficial to the surface of these muscles to avoid their denervation.

11. What is the course of the frontal branch of the facial nerve?

The frontal branch of the facial nerve travels approximately along a line from 0.5 cm below the tragus to 1.5 cm above the lateral end of the eyebrow.

12. What is the relationship of the frontal branch of the facial nerve to the SMAS and temporoparietal fascia?

Temporoparietal fascia is the extension of the SMAS superior to the zygomatic arch. Inferior to the zygomatic arch the frontal branch of the facial nerve travels deep to the SMAS. As it crosses over the zygomatic arch it becomes very superficial. At this point it is sandwiched between the periosteum (extension of the deep temporal fascia) and the temporoparietal fascia (extension of the SMAS). Superior to the zygomatic arch, the frontal branch of the facial nerve travels within or on the undersurface of the temporoparietal fascia and superficial to the superficial layer of the deep temporal fascia.

Table 64-1. Findings in Facial Paralysis

LEVEL OF INJURY	PARALYSIS	SIGNS/SYMPTOMS	TEST
Extracranial	Muscles of facial expression	Inability to close eyes Lower lid laxity/ectropion Eyebrow ptosis Asymmetric facial animation Oral sphincter incompetence/drooling	Facial movement Electrodiagnostic tests
Tympanomastoid	Chorda tympani:		
	A. Taste fibers	A. Loss of taste in anterior two thirds of tongue	Bitter taste test
	B. Parasympathetic innervation to sublingual and submandibular glands	B. Dry mouth	Salivary test
	Stapedius muscle	Hyperacoustic sounds	Stapedial reflex
Geniculate ganglion/greater petrosal nerve	Lacrimal nerve Parasympathetic to nasal and palatal secretory glands	Dry eye Dry nose	Schirmer test
Internal	CN VII + CN VIII	+ Loss of hearing	Audiology
Auditory canal		+ Loss of balance	Electronystagmogram
Central nervous system	Supranuclear Nuclear Infranuclear/ cerebellopontine angle	All of the above (unilateral upper motor neuron lesion does not affect muscle function of forehead or eyes)	Central neurologic examination

CN, Cranial nerve.
From Seckel BR: Facial Danger Zones: Avoiding Nerve Injury in Facial Plastic Surgery. St. Louis, Quality Medical Publishing, 1994.

13. What are the "facial danger zones"?

They are defined areas in the face and neck that correspond to the location of the important nerves. A surgeon must know their exact locations to avoid injuring them during rhytidectomy (Figs. 64-1 and 64-2, and Table 64-2).

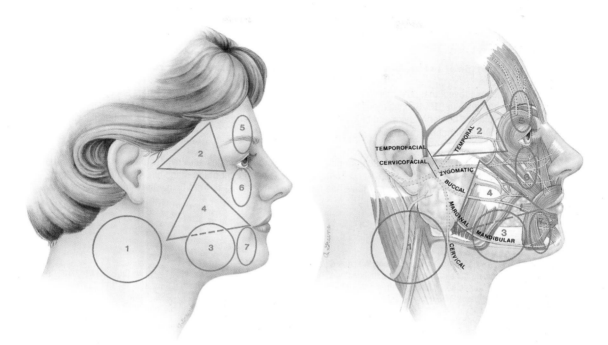

Figure 64-1. External topographic outlines of the seven facial danger zones. (From Seckel BR: Facial Danger Zones: Avoiding Nerve Injury in Facial Plastic Surgery. St. Louis, Quality Medical Publishing, 1994.)

Figure 64-2. Underlying nerves running through each facial danger zone after the skin and superficial musculoaponeurotic system layer have been removed. (From Seckel BR: Facial Danger Zones: Avoiding Nerve Injury in Facial Plastic Surgery. St. Louis, Quality Medical Publishing, 1994.)

Table 64-2. Facial Danger Zones

FACIAL DANGER ZONES	MIDPOINT LOCATION	NERVE	RELATIONSHIP TO SMAS	SIGN OF INJURY
1	6.5 cm below the external auditory canal	Great auricular nerve	Beneath	Numbness of inferior two thirds of ear
2	Below a line drawn from 0.5 cm below tragus to 2.0 cm above lateral eyebrow	Temporal branch of facial nerve	Within	Paralysis of forehead
3	Midmandible 2.0 cm posterior to oral commissure	Marginal mandibular branch of facial nerve	Beneath	Paralysis of lower lip
4	Anterior to parotid gland and posterior to zygomaticus major muscle	Zygomatic and buccal branch of facial nerve	Beneath	Paralysis of upper lip
5	Superior orbital rim above midpupil	Supraorbital and supratrochlear nerves	Beneath	Numbness of forehead, upper eyelid, nasal dorsum
6	1.0 cm below inferior orbital rim below midpupil	Infraorbital nerve	Beneath	Numbness of side of upper nose, cheek, upper lip
7	Midmandible below second premolar	Mental nerve	Beneath	Numbness of half of the lower lip

From Seckel BR: Facial Danger Zones: Avoiding Nerve Injury in Facial Plastic Surgery. St. Louis, Quality Medical Publishing, 1994.

14. What is the incidence of facial nerve injury during a standard rhytidectomy? Which nerve is damaged most often? What are the chances for recovery?

The incidence of facial nerve paralysis after rhytidectomy in a series of more than 6500 reported cases was approximately 0.7%, of which only 0.1% were permanent. The most frequently injured branches were the temporal and the marginal mandibular. Most patients recovered within 6 months.

CONTROVERSY

15. Does the marginal mandibular branch of the facial nerve really run at the margin of the mandible?

Cadaver dissections reveal that posterior to the facial artery the marginal mandibular nerve runs above the inferior border of the mandible in 81% of specimens. In the other 19%, it runs in an arc, the lowest point of which is 1 cm or less below the inferior border of the mandible. Anterior to the facial artery, all of the branches of mandibular rami are above the inferior border of the mandible.

On the contrary, clinical observations made during hundreds of parotidectomies and rhytidectomies showed that the mandibular branch *always* runs between 1 and 2 cm below the lower border of the mandible. In some individuals with lax and atrophic tissues, the branches have been noted to be located 3 to 4 cm below the inferior border of the mandible.

BIBLIOGRAPHY

Anderson JE (ed): Grant's Atlas of Anatomy. Baltimore, Williams & Wilkins, 1983, pp 7:16–7:18.
Baker DC, Conley J: Avoiding facial nerve injuries in rhytidectomy: Anatomical variations and pitfalls. Plast Reconstr Surg 64:781–795, 1979.
Hussey AJ, O'Sullivan ST: Auricularis inferior: Another pointer to the facial nerve. J Plast Reconstr Aesthet Surg 60:336–337, 2007.
May M: Facial paralysis: Differential diagnosis and indications for surgical therapy. Clin Plast Surg 6:277–282, 1979.
Miehlke A: Surgery of the salivary glands and the extratemporal portion of the facial nerve. In Naumann HH (ed): Head and Neck Surgery: Indications, Techniques, Pitfalls. Philadelphia, W. Saunders, 1980, pp 421–440.
Pansky B: The facial (VII) nerve. In: Review of Gross Anatomy. New York, Macmillan, 1984, pp 32–35.
Saylam C, Ucerler H, Orhan M, Uckan A, Ozek C: Localization of the marginal mandibular branch of the facial nerve. J Craniofac Surg 18: 137–142, 2007.
Seckel BR: Facial Danger Zones: Avoiding Nerve Injury in Facial Plastic Surgery. St. Louis, Quality Medical Publishing, 1994.
Stuzin JM, Wagstrom L, Kawamoto HK, Wolfe SA: Anatomy of the frontal branch of the facial nerve: The significance of temporal fat pad. Plast Reconstr Surg 83:265–271, 1989.
Zuker RM, Manktelow RT, Hussain F: Facial paralysis. In Mathes SJ (ed): Plastic Surgery, Vol 3, 2nd ed. Philadelphia, WB Saunders, 2006, pp 883–916.

REANIMATION OF THE PARALYZED FACE

CHAPTER 65

Julia K. Terzis, MD, PhD, FACS, FRCS(C)

1. Describe the embryogenesis of the facial nerve.

The main pattern of the facial nerve's anatomic path and relationships is established during the first trimester of prenatal life. At the end of the third week of gestation when the entire embryo is 3 mm long, a cluster of neural crest cells appears just cranial to the auditory placode. This grouping of cells is called the *facioacoustic primordium*, or crest.

At the fifth week of gestation, the facial motor nucleus can be identified. The geniculate ganglion becomes well defined by the seventh week of gestation. The course of the intratemporal segment of the facial nerve and its branches forms before that of the extratemporal portion.

The first branch of the intratemporal portion of the facial nerve to develop is the chorda tympani nerve. In the extratemporal segment, the posterior auricular branch and the branch to the digastric are recognizable in the 6-week embryo.

The facial nerve is not fully developed until 4 years after birth.

2. What is the primary function of the facial nerve?

The primary function of the facial nerve (cranial nerve [CN] VII) is to express voluntary movement of the muscles in the face and expression of involuntary emotions. The frequency and intensity of facial expressions may vary, but all of us understand the meaning of these expressions. Such expressions include happiness, joy, fear, anger, scorn, disapproval, and many others. We use these expressions to communicate our emotional needs.

3. Where is the motor nucleus of the facial nerve located?

The cell bodies of the motor fibers of the facial nerve are located in a cluster of cells in the brainstem. On each side of our face, each facial nerve innervates 23 facial muscles. The exact topography of cells within the facial motor nucleus has not been clearly delineated. In addition to the muscles of facial expression, the facial nerve innervates the stapedius muscle in the middle ear, the platysma muscle in the neck, the stylohyoid muscle, and the posterior belly of the digastric muscle.

4. Which side of the brain controls voluntary facial expression?

The system responsible for voluntary expressions is the left hemisphere of the brain only. Signals are sent to the right motor nucleus; at the same time, signals cross the corpus callosum to the right hemisphere. Thus symmetric facial expressions can be generated.

5. How does an upper motor neuron lesion present?

The muscles of the upper face are innervated by motor neurons that receive bilateral projections from the motor cortex, whereas the motor neurons that innervate the muscles of the lower face receive projections only from the contralateral motor cortex. Therefore upper motor neuron lesions present with an ipsilateral lower facial paralysis only, whereas upper facial function is preserved.

6. What is the neural pathway of spontaneous facial expressions?

Unlike voluntary facial expressions that are triggered by the left hemisphere only, spontaneous facial expressions are managed by both hemispheres. Usually these signals do not originate from the motor cortex but from other regions of the forebrain (e.g., amygdala and hypothalamus), and after they make a connection at the brainstem reticular formation, signals finally reach the right and left motor nuclei of the facial nerves. Thus a patient with a lesion in the motor cortex will be unable to move the facial musculature of the lower face. However, the same patient can generate symmetric involuntary facial animation when laughing, frowning, or when in distress because the requisite pathways are not affected by the cortical lesion.

7. **What is "synkinesis," and what causes these abnormal movements?**

There are two "sphincter" systems in the face: the upper and lower sphincters. All other mimic muscles correspond to one or the other sphincter, and each of these two systems is innervated independently. Thus innervation of the upper half of the face (forehead and eye) is distinct from innervation of the lower half of the face (cheek and mouth).

Following damage to the facial nerve, aberrant regeneration leads to loss of the functional autonomy of each system, leading to *synkinesis* and mass movements. Such secondary defects are always present after injury and misdirected reinnervation.

Normally, a natural balance exists between "constrictor" and "dilator" muscles. When one contracts, the other relaxes. This mutual antagonism is lost following injury and aberrant regeneration. This leads to "cross-wiring," with both sets of muscles contracting at the same time, resulting in ineffective and weakened movements of each set of muscles. The term *autoparalytic syndrome* has been used to describe this phenomenon, which translates to paradoxical innervation of antagonistic muscles.

8. **How does an intratemporal lesion of the facial nerve differ in presentation from an extratemporal lesion?**

An extratemporal lesion will only have motor sequelae without any sensory deficits. In contrast, an intratemporal lesion may involve (1) the superficial petrosal branch, which innervates the lacrimal glands; (2) the nerve to the stapedius, which helps dampen loud noises; and (3) the chorda tympani nerve, which provides innervation to the anterior two thirds of the tongue.

9. **How can you differentiate an intratemporal from an extratemporal lesion of the facial nerve?**

- *Schirmer test* assesses lacrimation of the normal and paralyzed sides. A 25% decrease in tear production is abnormal.
- *Stapedius reflex test* measures the ability of the stapedius to dampen loud sounds.
- *Electrogustometry test* measures the sensation of the anterior two thirds of the tongue by using galvanic current.

10. **When obtaining the history from a patient with facial paralysis, what are the key questions you should ask?**

The onset of the paralysis is the most important aspect of the history that will give clues to the cause of the patient's facial paralysis. If the onset is acute, then the paralysis may be due to infection, trauma, medication, or vascular causes. Slow onset is most indicative of tumor. Other important questions are the presence of hyperacuity, dizziness, and changes in tearing, taste, and hearing.

11. **What should you look for on physical examination?**

Encourage the patient to talk about his/her condition, and carefully observe the patient's face while he/she is talking. Also observe the patient while he/she is at rest and while he/she is laughing, smiling, or drinking. Focus special attention on whether the patient has a blink reflex, whether the blink reflex is symmetrical, or whether the patient stares at the observer and blinks only from one eye. Movements of the commissure of the mouth, nasolabial fold, and forehead and the ability to depress or elevate the lips are important for assessing symmetry. Ask the patient to close the eyes tightly, puff the cheeks, wrinkle his/her nose, smile both broadly and lightly, and show his/her teeth. Downward movement of the lower lips indicates depressor and platysma function. Note any synkinesis, "twitching," mass movements, "crocodile" tears, or epiphora.

Carefully assess the overall psychological status of the patient. Try to identify whether the patient's expectations are realistic and whether he/she listens to your assessment, to the surgical strategy you have proposed, and to the answers you have given to the questions the patient has raised.

12. **What other documentation is necessary in the office setting?**

Prior to embarking on any type of surgical treatment, it is mandatory that all observations of the patient's animation be documented. A protocol should be established that involves accurate audiovisual documentation, including videos of the patient raising his/her brows, frowning, wrinkling the nose, exhibiting soft and strong eye closure, smiling with and without teeth showing, and depressing the lower lip. A 4-minute video strip of the patient blinking should be recorded, as well as a recording of the patient's face during involuntary animation. The latter can be accomplished by having the patient watch a "funny" show in front of the TV while the camera is videotaping the patient's face. Thus voluntary and involuntary expressions can be recorded. Similar documentation should take place after facial reanimation surgery during the patient's follow-up visits.

The videos and still photography are important components of the patient's presentation preoperatively and after every stage of reconstruction.

13. **How long after injury to the facial nerve can some function be restored with microsurgery?**

The timing of surgery is critical. If immediate repair of the damaged facial nerve is possible, it should be done. The repair should be done under the operating microscope. Immediate repair prevents scar and neuroma formation and allows easier identification of the injured nerve ends. It also allows intraoperative stimulation of the distal branches, which leads to better fascicle alignment and improved results.

If reconstruction is delayed because of the patient's condition, a period of up to 6 weeks will still allow optimal results. After this time, the quality of the results deteriorates because of retraction of the severed ends, thickening of the muscle membrane, proximal neuroma formation, and proliferation of scar tissue. In general, for a complete lesion, the optimal time for repair is within 3 months. If the lesion is partial, however, adequate results may be obtained even after 2 years.

14. Once the diagnosis is made, how do you establish a strategy of reconstruction?

The strategy of reconstruction is determined by the extent and level of the injury. If both proximal and distal stumps are available, direct repair is recommended. If only the proximal stump is available, attempts should be made to neurotize the facial muscles directly with nerve grafts. If only the distal nerve stump of a facial nerve branch is available, ipsilateral nerve transfers from other motor donors or cross-facial nerve grafting (CFNG) should be considered. If the main facial nerve is extensively damaged, other available ipsilateral donors may have to be used, such as the hypoglossal nerve, spinal accessory nerve, or trigeminal nerve, usually in combination with CFNG.

The key to establishing a strategy of reconstruction is the condition of the facial musculature. If electrophysiologic testing determines that the facial muscles are present but denervated (i.e., needle electromyograms [EMGs] show fibrillation potentials), then the patient only needs provision of a motor nerve for reinnervation of the target to take place. If needle EMGs show partial denervation of the muscle, in the face of weak movement in the patient's face, then the strategy should be to provide additional motor nerve without downgrading existing movement. An inability of needle EMGs to pick up any signals denotes total atrophy of the mimic muscles. In this case, in addition to provision of a motor nerve, muscle substitution should be used.

These strategies are determined by the age and condition of the patient, his/her ability to withstand several stages of reconstruction, whether the patient will be compliant with postoperative rehabilitation, and the demands and expectations of the patient.

15. Which branch of the facial nerve is most commonly injured during a routine facelift?

The mandibular branch is the most commonly injured because it courses inferior to the parotid just beneath the superficial masseter fascia superiorly and along the lower border of the mandible. Usually it is injured during removal of fat from the submental and submandibular areas.

16. What preoperative tests are mandatory in facial paralysis work? Why?

Plain radiographs of the skull usually demonstrate lesions such as meningiomas and outline any bony invasion that may be present. Bilateral temporal bone polytomography or computed tomographic (CT) scans help to visualize the right and left facial nerve canals and are important tests in differentiating developmental absence of the facial nerve from acquired lesions. Coronal-cut CT scan helps to demonstrate transverse skull fractures, and longitudinal views demonstrate temporal damage. EMG helps assess which muscles are partially or totally denervated and defines which targets need to be reinnervated or substituted.

17. What are the advantages and disadvantages of ipsilateral nerve grafting?

Ipsilateral nerve grafting is the treatment of choice for lesions of isolated branches of the facial nerve. It gives faster, stronger regeneration in a shorter time. However, ipsilateral nerve grafting to the main trunk of the facial nerve is invariably followed by severe mass action and synkinesis. A "smarter" strategy is to innervate the upper face (eye sphincter) with the ipsilateral facial nerve and to restore animation to the lower face using CFNGs from the contralateral side.

18. What is CFNG?

CFNG is a technique that borrows motor axons from the normal facial nerve and delivers them via interposition nerve grafts to the contralateral paralyzed side. CFNG allows the possibility of synchronized, coordinated movements as well as the possibility of self-expression. Although it can be done as a one-stage or two-stage procedure, most surgeons prefer the two-stage approach. The advantage of the two-stage approach is that the distal stump of the CFNGs can be assessed histologically at the second stage before coaptation with the branches of the facial nerve on the injured side.

19. What are the advantages and disadvantages of CFNG?

CFNG is a physiologic approach that, if done properly, gives satisfactory reinnervation to the damaged contralateral facial nerve. Disadvantages include invasion of the normal facial nerve, donor deficits from the harvesting of the nerve grafts, need for interposition nerve grafts with two coaptation sites, and long interval for target connectivity. CFNG is considered a relatively weak motor donor and thus provides the best results if used in the first 3 months after onset of facial paralysis.

20. In the CFNG procedure, how do you determine when the regenerating facial nerve motor fibers have crossed the face?

Clinical examination is used to assess the nerve grafts postoperatively. After consulting the intraoperative drawings, Tinel's sign is elicited. Tinel's sign is observed when the paralyzed side is percussed and the patient feels tingling in the appropriate site on the normal face. The degree of tingling sensation usually corresponds to the effectiveness of regeneration of the particular nerve graft. In addition, conduction velocities can be obtained noninvasively and are a useful and objective means to evaluate each CFNG individually.

21. Describe the postoperative management after a completed CFNG procedure.

The most important factor in postoperative care is protection of the coaptation sites of the CFNG. A splint is placed around the patient's head, limiting the patient's ability to open the mouth. Manipulation of the area in which the repairs are located should be limited. Antiemetics are given because a sudden episode of projectile vomiting will invariably disconnect the repair. Talking should be limited. In 6 weeks, ultrasound and massage should be instituted in the cheek to soften the area and to decrease scar formation around the nerve repairs. Intensive slow-pulse stimulation of the denervated muscles prevents atrophy while the facial motor fibers are regenerating. After the second stage, a certain degree of facial muscle reinnervation takes place. The same postoperative precautions are taken, and slow-pulse stimulation again is recommended at 6 weeks along with ultrasound, intensive physical therapy, and facial exercises. Physical therapy includes training the patient to use both sides of the face in a symmetrical, coordinated fashion and to use each side of the face independently. Biofeedback is a useful tool that facilitates the reeducation process.

22. When are crossover procedures considered? Why?

In irreversible damage to the facial nerve, other ipsilateral motor nerves are considered as donors of motor fibers, including the hypoglossal, spinal accessory, and trigeminal nerves. The downside to these donors is that resulting facial movement is not coordinated with the normal side.

23. What is the "babysitter" principle?

The *babysitter principle* uses ipsilateral cranial nerve to send strong motor fibers quickly to the denervated facial muscles. This technique can stop the denervation clock and maintain the bulk of the facial muscle while the first stage of CFNG is done. Donors include the hypoglossal, trigeminal, or spinal accessory nerve. Only 30% to 40% of the donor nerve is used. Thus morbidity associated with these transfers is minimal. At the second stage, the distal ends of the CFNG are coapted to the peripheral branches of the involved facial nerve (Fig. 65-1). The coaptation with the babysitter is not severed at this time; instead, it is kept to give additional motor fibers to the affected facial musculature. The babysitter serves only to preserve bulk to the facial muscles; the CFNG functions as the pacemaker that enables coordinated animation.

24. What are the indications for free muscle transfer in facial paralysis?

If the denervation time (time after injury) is excessively long, the facial muscles invariably atrophy. In such cases, free muscle transfers are required. Preoperative needle EMGs demonstrate the degree of denervation of the facial musculature. If there is no hope of adequate reinnervation by ipsilateral or contralateral neurotization procedures, foreign muscle in the form of a free vascularized muscle transplant is indicated (Fig. 65-2).

Figure 65-1. Twenty-eight-year-old female patient who presented with a right facial paralysis secondary to a high-velocity motorcycle accident. She was an unhelmeted passenger when the motorcycle hit a truck head-on. She suffered multiple facial bone fractures as well as a right temporal bone fracture. She was treated 6 months postinjury with a "babysitter" procedure, which consisted of end-to-side coaptation of the right facial nerve to the ipsilateral hypoglossal nerve. At the same time, three CFNGs were placed. Ten months later, she had secondary microcoaptations of the CFNGs to eye, smile, and depressor branches of the right facial nerve. The patient is seen here six months after her second stage of reconstruction.

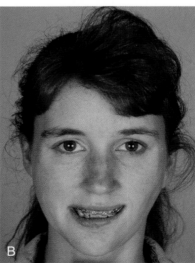

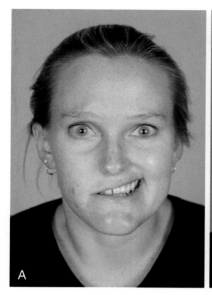

Figure 65-2. Patient is a 21-year-old female with a history of idiopathic right facial paralysis since the age of 12 years. She was treated with CFNG × 4. A year later, a free gracilis muscle was transferred to the right cheek for smile restoration. The patient is seen here a year following revisions.

25. What criteria determine the choice of foreign donor muscles?

The choice of muscle depends on the dynamic requirements of the nonparalyzed side. The selected muscle should provide a range of excursion that corresponds to the opposite normal side. The origin and insertion must appropriately fit the line of excursion intended to be restored. Muscle transplantation can be done to correct mild asymmetry or complete paralysis of the nasolabial fold and angle of the mouth. The free muscle must have a reliable neurovascular pedicle and be dispensable, easily contoured, and capable of generating sufficient force to provide the needed symmetry to the face. The most commonly used muscles for smile restoration are the gracilis and pectoralis minor.

26. What are the advantages and disadvantages of the gracilis free muscle transfer (Fig. 65-3)?

ADVANTAGES

- A predictable, long, and constant neurovascular pedicle makes the gracilis a very dependable transfer.
- Harvesting of the gracilis is relatively easy because of easy reach: thus trimming, debulking, and contouring can be accomplished prior to dividing the pedicle and harvesting the muscle.
- After transfer and upon reinnervation, the muscle can generate sufficient force to obtain the desired excursion.

Figure 65-3. Patient is a 4-year-old female who presented with developmental facial paralysis. She was treated with three cross-facial nerve grafts (CFNG × 3). A year later, a free gracilis muscle was transferred to her left face for smile restoration. The patient is shown here 9 months later and before any revisional surgery.

DISADVANTAGES

- The gracilis is bulky and too long for facial reanimation purposes and always requires sculpturing to fit the face.
- The debulking process, if extensive, may cause injury to the endplates and may result in a successful transfer that cannot generate adequate force.
- The gracilis has only one direction of pull: thus it is best used for restoring certain types of smile, especially retraction and some elevation of the modiolus.

27. What are the advantages and disadvantages of the pectoralis minor muscle transfer?

ADVANTAGES

- Donor site morbidity is minimal.
- The muscle has ideal form and shape for the face.
- The muscle can yield adequate excursion in the needed direction of pull.
- If the hilus of the muscle is placed over the zygomatic arch, its slips of origin can be separated and fashioned to substitute not only for the zygomaticus major muscle but also for the elevators of the upper lip as well as the retractors of the commissure. Thus a multidirectional pull can be achieved. Dual innervation is the most important advantage. The upper third is innervated by a branch of the lateral pectoral nerve, whereas the lower two thirds are innervated from the medial pectoral nerve. Dual innervation allows independent movements of the upper and lower parts of the muscle. This advantage can be used to address the separate needs of animation of the eye and the mouth or of animation of the commissure and the upper lip.

DISADVANTAGES

- The position of the muscle is deep; thus harvesting is difficult for the inexperienced.
- Debulking the muscle is difficult; thus it has to be debulked during ischemia time, which may have functional repercussions.
- Because the neurovascular pedicle is short, you need to carry the recipient vessels on the posterior surface of the muscle to accomplish the anastomoses.
- The pectoralis muscle has a variable dominant vascular supply. The lateral thoracic artery is the main artery in most cases, but a contributing branch from the thoracoacromial trunk occasionally shares codominance, making the muscle nontransferable because of the small size of both vessels.
- The muscle cannot be used in adults with highly developed upper torsos as it is too bulky. In contrast, it is ideal for children with unilateral developmental facial paralysis.

28. What are the advantages and disadvantages of local muscle transfers?
The masseter and temporalis muscles are the local muscle transfers used most often. They offer more expedient return of function (within weeks) and are easier to perform than free muscle transfers. The main disadvantage is that their function is not synchronized with the function of the contralateral face.

29. What are the prerequisite criteria for the diagnosis of Möbius syndrome?
Möbius syndrome is a developmental disorder characterized by bilateral facial paralysis. This condition usually involves the sixth and seventh cranial nerves. It also may involve the third, fifth, ninth, and twelfth cranial nerves. Limb abnormalities occur in 25% of cases, and the pectoral muscles are abnormal in 15% of cases. Occasionally, the paralysis is unilateral, but such patients still have contralateral involvement of the cranial nerves.

30. What are the reconstructive goals in a child with Möbius syndrome?
The reconstructive goals are to provide symmetrical and functioning nasolabial folds that may mimic a smile. Reconstruction is done in stages. The first stage focuses on bringing motor donors to one side of the face by using the ipsilateral partial spinal accessory nerve and/or branches of the trigeminal nerve with or without interposition nerve grafts. The second stage involves provision of muscle targets in the form of a free muscle transplant. These procedures are repeated for the contralateral face with the goal of producing symmetric results. The contralateral facial nerve and ipsilateral hypoglossal nerve usually cannot be used because they are often absent or abnormal.

More recently, children with Möbius syndrome have been treated with free muscle transfer with end-to-side coaptation of the obturator nerve (in the case of gracilis) with the masseteric nerve. In some centers, the entire masseteric nerve is sacrificed to achieve an end-to-end coaptation. This is not recommended because it further downgrades the ability of the child to chew, speak, and manipulate a bolus of food.

31. Discuss current microsurgical approaches for the paralyzed eye sphincter.

When reconstructing the eye, the surgeon should determine if the upper lid, lower lid, or both need to be corrected. If a lower lid ectropion exists, the lower lid needs support. Support can be provided through a minitendon transfer to the lower lid. The usual donor is the palmaris longus tendon. To restore animation to the upper lid, a gold weight may be considered. The weight allows gravity to close the eye when the levator is relaxed. The gold weight is indicated in patients who may be noncompliant, who have modest expectations, or who are not amenable to frequent visits for adjustments. If the patient is cooperative, is concerned about aesthesis, and has residual but not normal blink reflex, an eyespring is the treatment of choice. Eyesprings can be tedious to place and invariably need adjustment. The results are superior to that of gold weights both aesthetically and functionally. Local and free muscle transplantation in combination with CFNG can replace the missing eye sphincter and provide coordinated and dynamic eye closure, but the procedure should be left in the hands of an experienced surgeon.

32. What are the surgical options for correction of unilateral lower lip palsy?

Unilateral lower lip paralysis is a challenging problem. If direct coaptation of the damaged mandibular nerve is not an option, other donors must be found. A small segment of the hypoglossal nerve can be coapted directly to the damaged distal mandibular nerve. If neural microsurgery is not indicated because of the longevity of the palsy, muscle transfer may be necessary. The most commonly used muscles are the platysma and the digastric, which are transferred to help with depression of the lower lip.

33. What are the indications for use of digastric versus platysma muscle in lower lip reanimation?

Because the platysma is innervated by the facial nerve, it gives coordinated depressor function when used for reanimation of the lower lip. When the ipsilateral platysma is absent or paralyzed, the digastric muscle may be transferred in combination with a CFNG.

34. What outcomes can be obtained with free muscle transfer for long-lasting facial paralysis?

According to a review by the senior author of 100 cases of free muscle transplants for facial paralysis, 94% of patients had improved results postoperatively. Eighty percent were rated moderate or better by an independent panel of four judges that included one doctor, one medical student, one photographer, and one journalist.

Other results showed the following:

- Women received higher scores and had a slightly earlier onset of muscle function than men.
- Younger patients had earlier onset of muscle function than did older patients.
- Patients with developmental facial paralysis did better than did patients with posttraumatic or infectious causes.
- Pectoralis minor transplants recovered function more quickly than did gracilis transplants.
- Intraoperative ischemia time did not correlate with onset of muscle function as long as the ischemia time was kept below 3 hours.

BIBLIOGRAPHY

Hamilton SGL, Terzis JK, Carraway JT: Surgical anatomy of the facial musculature and muscle transplantation. In Terzis JK (ed): Microreconstruction of Nerve Injuries. Philadelphia, WB Saunders, 1987, pp 571–586.

Lee KK, Terzis JK: Management of acute extratemporal facial nerve palsy. In Terzis J (ed): Microreconstruction of Nerve Injuries. Philadelphia, WB Saunders, 1987, pp 587–600.

Lee KK, Terzis JK: Reanimation of the eye sphincter. In Portmann M (ed): Facial Nerve. New York: Masson Publishing, 1985, pp 119–131.

Liberson WT, Terzis JK: Some novel techniques of clinical electrophysiology applied to the management of brachial plexus palsy. Electromyogr Clin Neurophysiol 67:371–383, 1987.

Manktelow RT: Free muscle transplantation for facial paralysis. In Terzis JK (ed): Microreconstruction of Nerve Injuries. Philadelphia, WB Saunders, 1987, pp 607–615.

Terzis JK, Tzafetta K: Facial reanimation. In Guyuron B, Eriksson E, Persing JA (eds): Plastic Surgery: Indications and Practice, vol. 1. Philadelphia: Saunders, pp 907–926.

Terzis JK, Tzafetta K: The "babysitter" procedure: Minihypoglossal to facial nerve transfer and cross-facial nerve grafting. Plast Reconstr Surg 123(3):865–876, 2009.

Terzis JK: Pectoralis minor: A unique muscle for correction of facial palsy. Plast Reconstr Surg 5:767–776, 1989.

Terzis JK, Bruno W: Outcomes with eye reanimation microsurgery. Facial Plast Surg 18:101–112, 2002.

Terzis JK, Kalantarian B: Microsurgical strategies in 74 patients for restoration of dynamic depressor muscle mechanism: A neglected target in facial reanimation. Plast Reconstr Surg 105:1917–1931, 2000.

Terzis JK, Noah ME: Analysis of 100 cases of free-muscle transplantation for facial paralysis. Plast Reconstr Surg 99:1905–1921, 1997.

Terzis JK, Noah EM: Dynamic restoration in Möbius and Möbius-like patients. Plast Reconstr Surg 3:40–55, 2003.

Terzis JK, Noah EM: Möbius and Möbius-like patients: Etiology, diagnosis and treatment options. Clin Plast Surg 29:497–514, 2002.

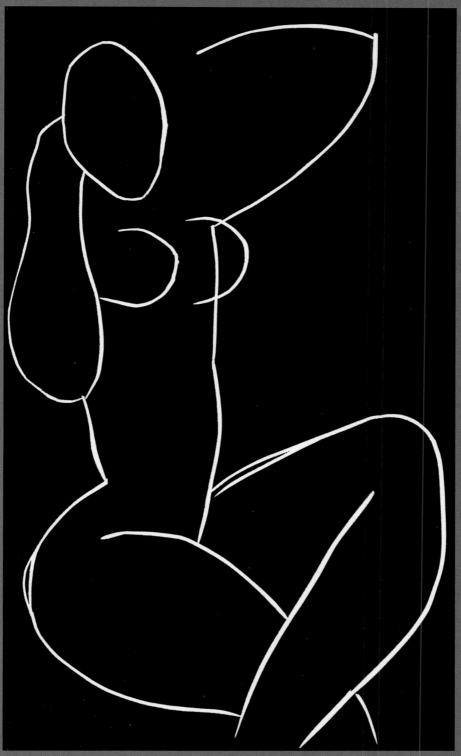

Seated Nude, Legs Crossed, II. Henri Matisse, 1941-1942. Linogravure.
© 2009 Succession H. Matisse/Artists' Rights Society (ARS), New York.

AUGMENTATION MAMMAPLASTY

CHAPTER 66

Dennis C. Hammond, MD, and
Dana K. Khuthaila, MD, FRCS(C)

1. What is augmentation mammaplasty?

Augmentation mammaplasty is an aesthetic procedure designed to increase the volume of the breast. Along with the increase in breast size, other surgical goals include improvements in breast shape, symmetry, and nipple position. The procedure is accomplished by making an incision, surgically creating a space or "pocket" under the breast, and then inserting an appropriately sized breast implant.

2. Who was the first to perform this procedure?

The first breast augmentation was performed in 1890 using paraffin injections. In 1920, this technique was abandoned in favor of fat transplants. Fatty tissue was surgically removed from the abdomen and buttocks and transferred into the breasts. In the 1950s, polyvinyl "sacs" were frequently used to achieve fuller, more projected breasts. The earliest known implant was attempted by Vincenz Czerny, who used a woman's own adipose tissue from a lipoma on her back, which he transferred to a submammary position.

The modern age of augmentation mammaplasty began with Thomas Cronin and Frank Gerow, two Houston, Texas, plastic surgeons, who developed the first silicone gel-filled breast prosthesis with the Dow Corning Corporation in 1961. The first woman was implanted in 1962.

3. What are the indications for breast augmentation?

Women choose to undergo breast augmentation because they are naturally small-busted, have developed excessive volume loss with pregnancy or weight loss, develop breast sagging, have an asymmetry in breast size or shape, or simply want to enhance their existing breast contour.

4. Does the preoperative shape of the breast affect the results obtained by augmentation mammaplasty?

The width, cleavage, projection, and size of the breast can be manipulated by the dimensions of the pocket and the shape of the implant. Ptosis of up to 2 to 3 cm can be corrected with a subglandular or subpectoral placement of the implant or by lowering the inframammary fold with submuscular placement of the implant. Deformities of the breast may require use of implants of different sizes with or without the addition of mastopexy.

5. Is there an age limit to breast augmentation?

There is no age restriction per se for any patient wishing to undergo breast augmentation. Ideally, the procedure should be performed only on a patient who has had a stable breast size after initial breast development for at least 1 year. Eighteen years is considered an appropriate lower age limit for breast augmentation because most women will be fully developed by this time. The emotional maturity of the patient must be considered when deciding the appropriate time to perform such an intensely personal procedure, and it is advisable to perform the operation only on those younger women who have realistic expectations and a stable support system from family and friends.

6. Who performs breast augmentation procedures?

Although many different types of "cosmetic" surgeons offer breast augmentation services, it is highly advisable to seek out a board-eligible or board-certified plastic surgeon to perform the procedure. Such surgeons are specifically trained in the various techniques required to successfully perform the procedure and provide the very best aesthetic results with the fewest complications.

7. What type of anesthesia is required?

Although some surgeons attempt to perform breast augmentation under local anesthesia, with or without complementary intravenous sedation, generally speaking the procedure is done under general anesthesia. Typically the surgery is performed at an outpatient surgical center because an overnight stay in a hospital setting is not required.

8. Should prophylactic antibiotics be used?

The incidence of infection in augmentation mammaplasty is 2.2%. Because the implant is a foreign body, infection can be a catastrophic event requiring its removal. The most commonly isolated organism is *Staphylococcus epidermidis*. Some studies have reported other organisms, such as atypical mycobacteria and fungi, as a cause of local infection. There is no consensus regarding the use of antibiotic prophylaxis in breast surgery. The variation in practice regarding antibiotic prophylaxis in breast surgery reflects the lack of reliable evidence for its efficacy. Some surgeons use antibiotics such as soaking the implant in Bacitracin solution. The decision to continue with postoperative antibiotics for 24 hours or longer depends on the surgeon's preference. Thus, in addition to an adequate skin preparation, 1 g of cephalothin should be administered intravenously prior to the skin incision. Postoperatively the patient should be given cephalexin 500 mg po qid for 5 to 7 days.

9. How do you choose the size of the breast implant?

Choosing implant size is one of the most difficult decisions to make when planning a breast augmentation. Many factors must be taken into consideration, including the preoperative size of the breast, the elasticity of the skin, the base diameter of the breast, and the desire of the patient. The surgeon must have a clear understanding of what the patient perceives her ultimate size result will be to prevent postoperative disappointment on the part of the patient, which can lead to reoperation for size change.

10. What incisions are used for augmentation mammaplasty?

Several different incision sites can be used to provide access to the breast, allowing appropriate dissection of the surgical pocket and easy placement of the breast implant. Three incisions are most often used for augmentation mammaplasty. The *periareolar incision* is a semicircular incision at the border of the nipple–areolar complex. The *inframammary incision* is located at the inframammary fold; it does not extend medially beyond the medial border of the nipple-areolar complex. The *axillary incision* is located in the hair-bearing region of the axilla.

Placing the incision in the inframammary fold or at the inferior junction of the areola with inferior breast skin affords direct visualization of the pocket with the aid of a lighted retractor during dissection and easy placement of either silicone or saline breast implants, which are either round or anatomically shaped. Alternatively, a more remote incision site in the axilla can afford adequate access to the breast while keeping the scar hidden under the arm. Some surgeons use an endoscope with this approach to still allow direct visualization when the pocket is dissected. In this way bleeding is best controlled and the dimensions of the pocket are accurate. Use of silicone implants with this approach is somewhat more difficult, and properly positioning anatomically shaped silicone implants is difficult. The periumbilical approach *(periumbilical incision)* keeps the scar completely off the breast but requires blunt dissection of the pocket, which risks hematoma formation and inaccurate pocket dissection. Furthermore, only saline implants can be used with this approach.

There are other, less commonly used incisions to access the breast, including the transareolar, transumbilical (TUBA), and transabdominoplasty approaches.

11. Where is the implant placed in augmentation mammaplasty?

The implant may be *subglandular, submuscular*, or *subpectoral*. The subglandular placement is below the breast tissue and above the muscular fascia. The submuscular placement is above the chest wall and below portions of the pectoralis major and minor, serratus anterior, rectus abdominis, and external oblique muscles. The subpectoral placement is above the chest wall and below the pectoralis major muscle superiorly and in the subglandular, subfascial, or subcutaneous plane inferiorly.

The standard pocket into which an implant is placed is partially under the pectoralis major muscle such that the upper portion of the implant is under the muscle and the lower portion of the implant is in contact with the overlying breast. Alternatively, to avoid distortion of the breast contour when the pectoralis major muscle is contracted, the subglandular approach can be used where the pocket is created entirely on top of the pectoralis major muscle. If this approach is used, the patient must have an adequate amount of soft tissue about the breast so that the implant does not show through in an unaesthetic fashion.

12. What is the "dual-plane" technique?

The "dual-plane" technique refers to a variable release of the breast from the lower edge of the pectoralis major muscle to avoid unattractive tethering of the lower pole of the breast when an implant is placed in the partial subpectoral position.

13. What types of breast implants are available?

Breast implants are constructed by manufacturing a pliable silicone elastomer shell that is filled with either silicone or saline. Some specialty implants combine both types of fillers. Implants can have a smooth external surface, or they can have a rough texture added in an attempt to reduce the rate of capsular contracture and limit postoperative implant migration. Finally, implants can have either a round configuration or a more anatomic teardrop shape. Essentially any combination of these variables is or has been available.

14. What are the advantages of anatomic implants?

Anatomic teardrop-shaped implants are advantageous in small-busted women who have minimal breast tissue to cover the implant. The anatomic shape contributes to an improved postoperative breast contour in these patients. These implants are better reserved for primary surgery on the breast to allow the pocket to appropriately fit the implant to minimize the possibility of postoperative implant rotation.

15. Are silicone gel-filled implants currently available for augmentation mammaplasty?

Before April 1992, silicone gel-filled implants were the most common implants used for augmentation. Subsequently, the Food and Drug Administration (FDA) ruled that silicone gel-filled implants could be used only for breast reconstruction after cancer ablation surgery and replacement of silicone gel-filled implants in previously augmented patients. In 2006, almost 15 years later, the FDA lifted the ban on the use of silicone implants, which once again are available for augmentation as well as reconstruction.

16. What postoperative care is required after augmentation mammaplasty?

Postoperatively many surgeons use displacement exercises to help keep the implant space open, which results in the implant maintaining a soft feel. When anatomically shaped implants are used, it is best to avoid these exercises because pressure on the implant could cause the implant to rotate. Postoperative support garments are worn to provide comfort and help reduce swelling.

17. What are the potential complications?

IMMEDIATE COMPLICATIONS

- Hematoma
- Seroma
- Wound dehiscence
- Infection

LATE COMPLICATIONS

- Capsular contracture
- Implant rupture
- Asymmetry
- Visible skin wrinkles
- Palpable implant folds
- Scarring
- Shape problems
- Nipple sensation alteration
- Late infection
- Silicone granuloma

18. What is capsular contracture?

Capsular contracture refers to the development of an acellular collagenous sheath (scar tissue) surrounding the implant. This scar layer forms around every foreign device placed in the body, including breast implants. For reasons that remain unclear, in some patients this scar layer becomes reactive and contracts, resulting in a tight, distorted appearance of the breast. The rate of capsular contracture varies among the various types of implants used, but generally capsular contracture occurs in approximately 5% to 10% of patients.

19. What is the classification of capsular contracture?

Capsular contracture was classified by Baker in 1975 as follows:

- Grade I: Soft
- Grade II: Minimal contracture; implant palpable but not visible
- Grade III: Moderate contracture; implant palpable and visible
- Grade IV: Severe contracture; hard, painful breast, with distortion

We have modified this classification system to better distinguish between the degree of contracture and any associated symptoms:

- Grade I: Pocket surface area greater than surface area of implant, that is no contracture; breast is as soft as implant will allow

Table 66-1. Capsular Contracture Treatment

CAPSULAR CONTRACTURE	TREATMENT
Grade I	None
Grade IIA	Pavabid, breast massage
Grade IIB	Pavabid, breast massage
Grade IIIA	Pavabid, breast massage, or surgery
Grade IIIB, IV	Surgery (capsulotomy or capsulectomy)

- Grade IIA: Pocket surface area slightly smaller than implant surface area resulting in mild firmness to feel of the implant but no implant distortion and no pain
- Grade IIB: Same as IIA but with pain
- Grade IIIA: Pocket surface area moderately smaller than implant surface area resulting in mild firmness to feel of the implant with visible implant distortion and no pain
- Grade IIIB: Same as IIIA but with pain
- Grade IVA: Pocket maximally contracted, breast visibly distorted and firm, no pain
- Grade IVB: Same as IVA but with pain

20. How is capsular contracture treated?

Typically early contracture can be improved with aggressive displacement exercises. It is our practice to add a smooth muscle relaxant (Pavabid 150 mg po bid for 3 months; Pavabid is an oral formulation of Papaverine) to aid in the effect. For more severe or mature contractures, surgical release of the scar is required. Most commonly this procedure involves complete removal of the scar in the form of a capsulectomy (Table 66-1).

21. Is there a risk of rupture of the breast implant?

All manufactured devices have a finite life expectancy. Patients should be counseled that the risk of failure of the implant depends on the physical properties of the device and the time elapsed since implantation. The risk is cumulative and is speculated to be approximately 2% per year.

22. How do you diagnose implant rupture?

Implant rupture is diagnosed either clinically or radiologically. A saline implant will deflate, resulting in an obvious loss of fullness. However, rupture of a silicone gel-filled implant is less obvious because the escaping gel usually is contained in the surgical pocket by the capsule. Rupture is suspected if a change in the character of the device, such as a change in the softness, texture, or shape of the implant, is noted. Magnetic resonance imaging (MRI) is the best diagnostic tool for detecting rupture.

23. How is implant rupture treated?

Once the rupture has been confirmed, the implant has to be removed and replaced with an intact implant.

24. Can you breastfeed after undergoing breast augmentation?

Women are more likely to be able to breastfeed after breast augmentation if an inframammary fold, axillary, or periumbilical incision has been used. The periareolar approach can be associated with lactation insufficiency. Breastfeeding after a silicone gel breast augmentation is generally considered to be safe and poses no health risk to the baby.

25. Is sensation to the nipple and areola affected after breast augmentation?

Sensation to the nipple and areola can be either diminished or completely lost after a patient undergoes breast augmentation. It is important for patients to be made aware of this potential complication, particularly when intact sensation in and around the nipple and areola is an important part of the patients' sexual health.

26. Is there an increased risk for breast cancer in patients undergoing breast augmentation?

The incidence of breast cancer among women who have undergone breast augmentation is the same as that among the general population. It is generally accepted that breast augmentation does not in any way increase the risk for developing breast cancer.

27. How can you screen for breast cancer in a patient with breast implants?

Mammography, physician examination, and breast self-examination still are the screening modalities of choice for patients who have undergone breast augmentation. It is important to notify the mammographer about the presence of a breast implant when the patient is having a mammogram because special techniques or additional views of the breast may be required to adequately evaluate the breast for suspicious lesions. In difficult situations, ultrasound evaluation can supplement the information provided by mammograms. More recently MRI evaluation has also been recommended.

28. Are silicone gel-filled implants safe?

Thirty-one studies from four countries encompassing a cohort of more than 500,000 women failed to find a statistical relationship between any known or newly recognized disease and silicone. For this reason, it is generally accepted by both the scientific and medical communities that silicone does not cause any type of systemic disease.

29. Is breast augmentation covered by insurance?

Breast augmentation for purely aesthetic reasons is not covered by insurance and is considered a cosmetic procedure.

BIBLIOGRAPHY

Brody G: Lactation after augmentation mammoplasty. Obstet Gynecol 87:1063–1064, 1996.

Brown SL, Pennello G, Berg WA, Soo MS, Middleton MS: Silicone gel breast implant rupture, extracapsular silicone, and health status in a population of women. J Rheumatol 28:996–1003, 2001.

Bryant H, Brasher P: Breast implants and breast cancer—Reanalysis of a linkage study. N Engl J Med 332:1535–1539, 1995.

Czerny V. Plastischer brasatz der brusthus durob ein lipoma. Zentralbl Chir 27:72, 1895.

Cronin T, Gerow F: Augmentation mammaplasty: A new "natural feel" prosthesis. In Broadbent TR (ed): Transactions of the Third International Congress of Plastic and Reconstructive Surgery. Amsterdam, Excerpta Medica Foundation, 1963, pp 41–49.

Deapen DM, Pike MC, Casagrande JT, Brody GS: The relationship between breast cancer and augmentation mammaplasty: An epidemiologic study. Plast Reconstr Surg 77:361–368, 1986.

Eklund GW: Diagnostic breast imaging in plastic surgery of the breast. In Noone RB (ed): Plastic and Reconstructive Surgery of the Breast. Philadelphia, BC Decker; 1993, pp 48–69.

Gabriel SE, O'Fallon WM, Kurlan LT, Beard CM, Woods JE, Melton LJ: Risk of connective–tissue diseases and other disorders after breast implantation. N Engl J Med 330:1697–1702, 1994.

Henriksen TF, Fryzek JP, Holmich LR, et al: Surgical intervention and capsular contracture after breast augmentation: A prospective study of risk factors. Ann Plast Surg 54:343–351, 2005.

Hurst NM: Lactation after augmentation mammoplasty. Obstet Gynecol 87:30–34, 1996.

Little G, Baker J: Results of closed compression capsulotomy for treatment of contracted breast implant capsules. Plast Reconstr Surg 65:30–33, 1985.

Pittet B, Montandon D, Pittet D: Infection in breast implants. Lancet Infect Dis 5:94–106, 2005.

Spear SL, Carter ME, Ganz JC: The correction of capsular contracture by conversion to "dual-plane" positioning: Technique and outcomes. Plast Reconstr Surg 112:456–466, 2003.

CHAPTER 67

REDUCTION MAMMAPLASTY

Deborah J. White, MD, and
G. Patrick Maxwell, MD

1. What is the blood supply to the breast?

The primary blood supply to the breast comes from the following:

- Perforating branches of the internal mammary artery (60%)
- Branches from the axillary artery (mostly the lateral thoracic artery, but also pectoral branches and the highest thoracic artery)
- Lateral branches from the third, fourth, and fifth posterior intercostal arteries

Rich anastomoses between these arteries allow survival of the breast with varying breast reduction techniques, as long as sufficient vessels remain (Fig. 67-1).

2. What is the nerve supply to the breast? To the nipple?

The sensory innervation is from the following:

- Supraclavicular nerves from the third and fourth branches of the cervical plexus
- Anterior cutaneous branches from intercostal nerves 2 to 6
- Anterior branches of the lateral cutaneous nerves 3 to 6; lateral cutaneous branch of T4 is believed to be the primary innervation to the nipple (Fig. 67-2)

3. Why do pedicles other than the inferior ones seem to have as much sensation postoperatively?

There appears to be enough innervation from the other branches so that no clinical difference is detectible postoperatively between superior pedicle and inferior pedicle techniques, despite the fact that anatomic studies have demonstrated more branches to the inferior pedicles.

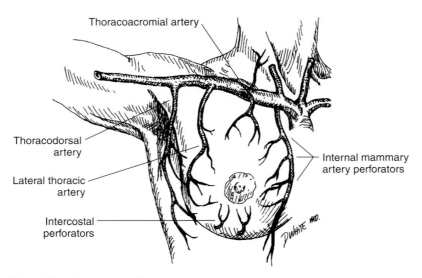

Figure 67-1. Blood supply to the breast.

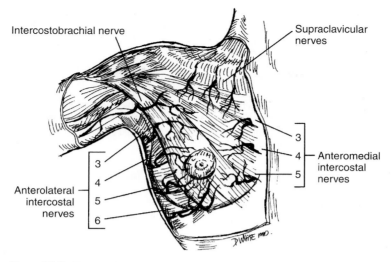

Figure 67-2. Nerve supply to the breast.

4. What are the most popular techniques used for breast reduction in the United States?

Surveys of board-certified plastic surgeons taken in 1998 and 2002 showed that 74% and 75%, respectively, preferred the inferior pedicle/Wise pattern techniques—not much change! Fifty-six percent of the respondents in 2002 used *only* this technique. Compare this with a German study showing that 53% of their surgeons preferred the short scar technique in 2001, with the number of surgeons increasing to 66% in 2003 (Fig. 67-3).

5. What are the advantages and disadvantages of the vertical reduction technique?

ADVANTAGES

- Can elevate the inframammary fold (IMF) on the chest and avoid fixation of the base of the breast at the inframammary fold because of pedicle location.
- Allows inferior glandular excision, where the excess is often located.
- Can narrow the base of the breast and give better projection.

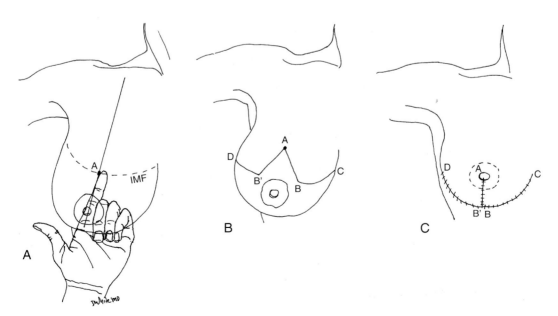

Figure 67-3. Inferior pedicle technique. IMF, inframammary fold.

- Faster procedure with less blood loss.
- Patients are "less disappointed by scars" and feel they have "better aesthetic results."

DISADVANTAGES

- Better for small/medium reductions than for extremely large reductions.
- Steeper learning curve. You don't see the final shape at the time of surgery, so the technique requires some experience. (Although, in actuality, you don't have the final shape in the inverted T incision either! The areola-to-inframammary fold distance is made shorter than desired in anticipation of stretching out.)
- Requires better quality of skin to allow redraping because the technique depends on glandular reshaping rather than reshaping of the envelope for the final shape.

6. What are the advantages and disadvantages of the inferior pedicle reduction technique?

ADVANTAGES

- Can be used on a large range of reductions, including very large reductions.
- More predictable.
- Relatively easy to learn and teach.
- Fewer revisions needed.
- Overall patient satisfaction is statistically equal for vertical versus Wise pattern reduction.
- Better for patients with poor skin quality because redraping is not as important.
- Usually has good preservation of nipple sensation and lactation potential.

DISADVANTAGES

- Produces very large scars that not uncommonly can become hypertrophic (especially the inframammary scars).
- Has a tendency to produce a wide, flat breast and to "bottom out" with time, leaving superior pole hollowness and nipples that point up.

7. What are some other methods of breast reduction, and what are the advantages and disadvantages of each?

Reduction by Liposuction Alone (Controversial): In patients with minimal to moderate breast hypertrophy, satisfactory breast shape and nipple location, good skin tone, and fatty breasts, this can be an appealing alternative. Only small scars are produced and the skin can retract, resulting in decreased sternal notch-to-nipple distances. It is almost impossible to predict preoperatively what percentage of the breast is fat, but older patients tend to have more fat than do younger patients. Many plastic surgeons believe that fat should neither be suctioned from nor added to breast tissue because of oncologic concerns. Dr. Madeleine Lejour reported a study examining the material removed from breasts using traditional suction-assisted lipectomy (SAL). No glandular tissue was found on pathologic examination. Others disagree and recommend that liposuction specimens be sent for examination. Postoperative mammographic changes can typically be distinguished from malignancies by experienced radiologists.

Careful application of this technique in women whose complaints are based on breast weight and not ptosis is crucial. One study of 117 patients showed that 80% were "very satisfied" or "completely satisfied," and 87% would do it again. The unhappy patients did not achieve the amount of reduction desired. The glandular component of the breast can limit the effectiveness of liposuction alone.

Reduction Using Ultrasound-Assisted Liposuction (Even More Controversial): Ultrasound-assisted liposuction (UAL) can remove fat from even more dense breast tissue, but studies with the aspirate have not yet been done. Studies from the gynecologic and neurologic literature have shown that tumor histology can be performed on ultrasonic aspirate with great accuracy. The concern over the use of UAL is the lack of data on the long-term effects of ultrasonic energy on the breasts and the fear of litigation.

Short Scar Techniques: Marchac and Chiari, in particular, have reported excellent results, with reduction of the scar in the inframammary fold along with attractive breast shapes.

Vertical Techniques: Popularized by Lejour, these techniques have been gaining in popularity because of the reduced number of scars and the attractive and long-lasting breast shape. The biggest drawbacks to these techniques are the steep learning curve and an unappealing immediate postoperative appearance that can take over a month to resolve. Dr. Hall-Findlay has developed a simplified version of these techniques that has gained popularity as the Lejour technique has declined in favor in the United States.

Periareolar Techniques: These techniques accomplish breast reduction and reshaping via an incision around the areola alone. Common problems with periareolar surgery have been a flattening of the breast shape with loss of nipple/ areolar projection and widening of the scars and the areolas. Benelli's "round block" technique in which a permanent pursestring suture is placed may help prevent the scar and areolar spread. Góes of Brazil has obtained good projection and shape with the use of a Vicryl/polyester mesh between the gland and the skin; however, use of this material would be difficult for medicolegal reasons in the United States.

8. Why are the short scar techniques not popular in the United States?
Some cited concerns are (1) fear of the superior pedicle, (2) fear of complications, (3) fear of litigation, (4) reluctance to leave the operating room without the final breast shape, and (5) steep learning curve.

9. What are the primary differences between Dr. Lejour's vertical reduction technique and Dr. Hall-Findlay's modified technique?
- Hall-Findlay uses a medial (or lateral) dermoglandular pedicle versus a superior dermal pedicle that can be difficult to inset.
- Hall-Findlay uses no undermining of skin.
- Hall-Findlay rarely uses liposuction, whereas Lejour uses it routinely.
- Hall-Findlay does not suture the breast to the pectoralis fascia (Fig. 67-4).

10. What technique(s) generates the most litigation?
Short scar techniques, especially those that involve a pursestring suture.

11. What are common indications for breast reduction?
Physical complaints include shoulder grooving; neck, back, and shoulder pain; mastodynia; maceration and infection of the inframammary regions; neurologic sequelae secondary to neck problems (e.g., ulnar nerve impingement); and difficulty finding clothing that fits and is attractive. Respiratory complaints are not associated with mammary hypertrophy.

Psychological complaints include embarrassment, feelings of physical unattractiveness, self-consciousness, unwillingness to exercise, and loss of sexual appeal and femininity.

12. Do studies support the efficacy of breast reduction for symptomatic patients?
Several studies, many of them prospective in nature, now confirm results such as decreased pain, improved posture, improved quality of life, high patient satisfaction, and decreased disability. As to determining the amount of tissue that must be removed to be considered "medically necessary," some studies reinforce the conclusion that the patients' symptomatic complaints represent the logical threshold for authorizing surgery rather than breast weight per se.

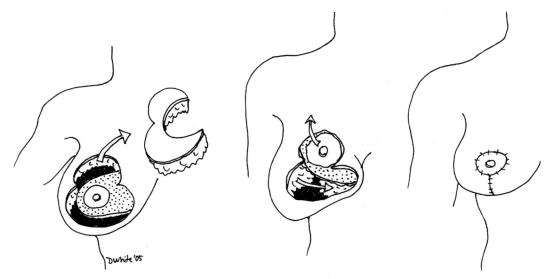

Figure 67-4. Hall-Findlay vertical reduction.

Pain relief, postural changes, and musculoskeletal strength are not strictly correlated with the amount of breast tissue removed. Therefore it is believed that women who are willing to undergo breast reduction surgery are suffering significantly, and most obtain relief after surgery.

13. At what age should breast reduction be performed?
Ideally, you should wait for the patient to achieve full breast maturation, which is generally several years after onset of menstruation. However, if the oversized breasts interfere with the patient's activities and self-esteem, the procedure can be performed earlier. The patient and her family must understand that the procedure may need to be repeated if the breasts continue to grow. They also must understand the extent of scarring and the potential for loss of sensation and loss of the ability to lactate.

14. Is lactation possible after breast reduction?
Yes, depending on the technique used. However, many women who have never had breast surgery can't breastfeed, so you can't guarantee it. Obviously, those procedures that leave the underlying gland attached to the nipple (e.g., inferior and central pedicle techniques) are much more likely to be successful at preserving the ability to breastfeed. One study showed 100% of the women who became pregnant after inferior pedicle reductions lactated, although 65% of the women didn't breastfeed for various personal reasons.

15. How has the postoperative hospital stay changed over the last 10 years?
The stay has changed from over a week with the patient's arms secured to prevent movement a couple of decades ago, to overnight or outpatient status. The patient is allowed to cautiously use her arms almost immediately.

16. Is autologous blood donation recommended?
Not anymore. The use of electrocautery, careful hemostasis, and epinephrine-containing solutions has made the loss of large amounts of blood a rare event.

17. Are drains necessary?
Many surgeons still use drains for several days (until the drainage decreases to a certain level), others remove them the next morning, and others do not use them at all.

18. Are patients satisfied with their results?
This procedure has excellent long-term patient satisfaction, despite the scars. In most series, more than 95% of patients would have the surgery again and would recommend it to others. They are more comfortable buying clothes and exercising, and they feel better about their self-images. The majority of patients report a postoperative decrease in physical symptoms.

19. When are free nipple grafts recommended?
This technique is usually reserved for patients with massive gigantomastia. The procedure tends to produce inferior nipple projection and sensation and destroys lactation potential, but it is very quick. Elderly patients (with no need for lactation) and patients with medical problems/poor health have traditionally been candidates. Patients with gigantomastia have a greater risk of nipple/areolar necrosis (and necrosis of the distal pedicle) with pedicle techniques and are believed to be candidates. Many believe that a better breast shape can be obtained with the free nipple graft technique. Poor nipple/areolar perfusion intraoperatively that is unresponsive to other measures is an indication for conversion to a free nipple graft.

20. What is the incidence of occult breast cancer in reduction specimens?
Different studies have reported an incidence ranging from 0.06% to 0.4%. Some of the studies predate screening mammograms. It is *extremely* important to carefully record from where breast tissue is removed. It is a disaster to receive a report of an occult malignancy and to not know from which breast it came!

21. What are the most common complications of reduction mammaplasty?
- Asymmetry
- Not enough tissue removed
- Too much tissue removed
- Poor shape
- Poor scarring
- Delayed healing at base of the inverted T incision
- Change in nipple/areolar sensation
- Infection

- Partial/total loss of nipple
- Skin loss/necrosis
- Fat necrosis

22. Do nipple grafts regain sensation? Erectile capacity?

Yes, nipple grafts regain sensation to varying degrees (even transverse rectus abdominis myocutaneous flaps can regain some sensation). Erectile capacity is sometimes regained, particularly if the graft is thick and contains smooth muscle tissue.

23. How can nipple viability be determined intraoperatively?

Pale-skinned women with light nipple color usually can be evaluated visually, looking for a healthy pink color, and by assessment of capillary refill. White or dark nipple color is indicative of poor blood supply and venous congestion, respectively. Seeing if the cut edges bleed or poking a large-gauge needle into the tissue and looking for bright red blood also can help.

Dark-skinned women can present more of a challenge, and visual inspection can be supplemented with fluorescein and/or laser Doppler evaluation. Laser Doppler perfusion values that are consistently 1 to 2 mL/min per 100 g indicate marginal perfusion and should be followed closely. Values less than 1 mL/min per 100 g are considered to indicate low perfusion and need to be addressed.

24. What do you do if the nipples look compromised?

Try releasing some incisions and checking to see if the pedicle is kinked. If the pedicle is not twisted and releasing some incisions revives the nipples, the closure may be too tight. In some cases this can be remedied by removing more breast tissue either by an open technique or by liposuction. If no maneuvers improve the dire condition of the nipple or if Doppler readings remain less than 1.0 mL/min per 100 g, you can consider conversion to free nipple grafts. Successful leech use in the postoperative period has been reported.

25. What do you do with those lateral dog ears?

The inverted T incision often leaves large lateral dog ears, especially in heavy women with large breasts that may appear to continue back to the scapula. Large incisions in this area can be very disappointing, especially to the young patient who wishes to wear a bikini. Standard methods of eliminating dog ears at wound ends can be used along with attempts to work the excess skin medially. Liposuction of this dog ear often is beneficial but may be difficult because of the fibrous nature of the lateral chest. In these cases UAL can be extremely efficacious *(controversial)*.

26. What about medial dog ears?

The inverted T incision can often leave dog ears here, too, on very large, wide breasts. You generally try to work the excess tissue medially. However, if this is impossible, in certain cases it is acceptable to extend the incisions across the midline and connect them. Again, liposuction (SAL or UAL) can be useful, bearing in mind the increased propensity for sternal wounds to become hypertrophic.

CONTROVERSY

27. Are the patients' chances of developing breast cancer affected by breast reduction?

Perhaps. Recent studies suggest that patients with large breasts are at an increased risk for breast cancer and that breast reduction may decrease the risk (relative risk 0.2 to 0.7 compared with controls). This may be due to the removal of potential foci of breast cancer. Some studies show a correlation between decreasing amount of risk and increasing amounts of tissue removed; others showed decreasing risk in women older than 40 years at the time of surgery or women with a positive family history. Another explanation is that women with large breasts tend to have a high body mass index (BMI). Increased BMIs are associated with more fatty tissue and elevated peripheral estrogen production. This is associated with an increased breast cancer risk in postmenopausal women.

BIBLIOGRAPHY

Benelli L: A new periareolar mammaplasty: The "round block" technique. Aesthetic Plast Surg 14:93–100, 1990.

Boice JD, Jr, Persson I, Brinton LA, et al: Breast cancer following breast reduction surgery in Sweden. Plast Reconstr Surg 106:755–762, 2000.

Brinton LA, Malone KE, Coates RJ, et al: Breast enlargement and reduction: Results from a breast cancer case-control study. Plast Reconstr Surg 97:269–275, 1996.

Chao JD, Memmel HC, Redding JF, et al: Reduction mammaplasty is a functional operation, improving quality of life in symptomatic women: A prospective, single-center breast reduction outcome study. Plast Reconstr Surg 110:1644–1652, 2002.

Chiari A, Jr: The L short-scar mammaplasty: A new approach. Plast Reconstr Surg 90:233–246, 1992.

Cruz-Korchin N, Korchin L: Vertical versus Wise pattern breast reduction: Patient satisfaction, revision rates, and complications. Plast Reconstr Surg 112:1579–1581, 2003.

Cunningham BL: Discussion: Reduction mammaplasty is a functional operation, improving quality of life in symptomatic women: A prospective, single-center breast reduction outcome study. Plast Reconstr Surg 110:1653–1654, 2002.

Dupont WD, Page DL: Breast cancer risk associated with proliferative disease, age at first birth, and a family history of breast cancer. Am J Epidemiol 125:769–779, 1987.

Góes JCS: Periareolar mammaplasty: Double skin technique. Rev Soc Bras Cir Plast 4:55–63, 1989.

Goldwyn RM: Outcome study in liposuction breast reduction. Plast Reconstr Surg 114:55–60, 2004.

Goldwyn RM: Pulmonary function and bilateral reduction mammaplasty. Plast Reconstr Surg 53:84, 1974.

Gross MP, Apesos J: The use of leeches for treatment of venous congestion of the nipple following breast surgery. Aesthet Plast Surg 16: 343–348, 1992.

Hall-Findlay EJ: A simplified vertical reduction mammaplasty: Shortening the learning curve. Plast Reconstr Surg 104:748–759, 1999.

Hamdi M, Greuse M, De Mey, et al: A prospective quantitative comparison of breast sensation of superior and inferior pedicle mammaplasty. Br J Plast Surg 54:39–42, 2001.

Hamdi M: Breast sensation after superior pedicle versus inferior pedicle mammaplasty: Anatomic and histological evaluation. Br J Plast Surg 54:43–46, 2001.

Harris L, Morris SF, Freiberg A: Is breast feeding possible after reduction mammaplasty? Plast Reconstr Surg 89:836–839, 1992.

Hidalgo DA, Elliot LF, Palumbo S, et al: Current trends in breast reduction. Plast Reconstr Surg 104:806–815, 1999.

Kenkel JM, Rohrich RJ, Adams WP: Current trends in breast reduction. Plast Reconstr Surg 104:817–818, 1999.

Kerrigan CL, Collins ED, Striplin D, et al: The health burden of breast hypertrophy. Plast Reconstr Surg 108:1591–1599, 2001.

Lejour M: Vertical Mammaplasty and Liposuction. St. Louis, Quality Medical Publishing, 1994.

Marchac D, de Olarte G: Reduction mammaplasty and correction of ptosis with a short inframammary scar. Plast Reconstr Surg 69:45–55, 1982.

Maxwell GP, White DJ: Breast reduction with ultrasound-assisted liposuction. Oper Tech Plast Reconstr Surg 3:207–212, 1996.

McCulley SJ, Hudson DA: Short-scar breast reduction: Why all the fuss? Plast Reconstr Surg 107:965–969, 2001.

Morimoto T, Komaki K, Mori T, et al: Juvenile gigantomastia: Report of a case. Surg Today 23:260–264, 1993.

Nahai F: Discussion: Current preferences for breast reduction techniques: A survey of board-certified plastic surgeons 2002. Plast Reconstr Surg 114:1734–1736, 2004.

Orgill DP, Iglehart, JD, Gelman R: Breast reduction surgery and breast cancer risk: Does reduction mammaplasty have a role in primary prevention strategies for women at a high risk of breast cancer? Plast Reconstr Surg 113:2111–2112, 2004.

Rohrich RJ, Gosman AA, Brown SA, et al: Current preferences for breast reduction techniques: A survey of board-certified plastic surgeons 2002. Plast Reconstr Surg 114:1724–1733, 2004.

Roth AC, Zook EG, Brown R, et al: Nipple-areolar perfusion and reduction mammaplasty: Correlation of laser Doppler readings with surgical complications. Plast Reconstr Surg 97:381–386, 1996.

Snyderman RK, Lizardo JG: Statistical study of malignancies found before, during, or after routine breast plastic operations. Plast Reconstr Surg 25:253–256, 1960.

Tarone RE, Lipworth L, Young VL, et al: Breast reduction surgery and breast cancer risk: Does reduction mammaplasty have a role in primary prevention strategies for women at high risk of breast cancer? Plast Reconstr Surg 113:2104–2110, 2004.

Toledo LS, Matsudo PKR: Mammoplasty using liposuction and the periareolar incision. Aesthet Plast Surg 13:9–13, 1989.

MASTOPEXY

Daniel J. Azurin, MD; Jack Fisher, MD; and G. Patrick Maxwell, MD

CHAPTER **68**

1. What defines an aesthetically pleasing breast?

Opinions about what defines the ideal breast vary greatly among different societies and subcultures. The average or normal breast may not coincide with an aesthetically pleasing breast. Furthermore, patients occasionally request that you surgically alter their breast into a form that may be both unnatural and aesthetically unpleasing. However, certain criteria define the aesthetically pleasing breast. Variables of particular importance are position, contour, symmetry, size, and proportion of both the breast mound and nipple–areolar complex. Tactile aspects are as significant as visual ones, including softness, mobility, and sensibility.

2. Describe the form and dimensions of the normal breast.

The breast is best situated on the anterolateral chest wall, with the majority of its mass or fullness located in the inferior hemisphere. The lines of contour should converge smoothly on the nipple–areolar complex, which serves as the focal point of the breast. The inferior hemisphere should have a full convexity spanning from the areola to the inframammary fold (a distance of approximately 5 to 6 cm from the inferior areolar edge to the inframammary fold), whereas the superior hemisphere should possess less volume and have only a subtle, sloping convexity on the lateral view (spanning a distance of approximately 19 to 21 cm from the sternal notch to the nipple). A small amount of ptosis is natural and pleasing. The nipple–areolar complex projects slightly from the underlying breast mound on an inclined plane. It represents the point of maximal projection of the breast and is located slightly inferior and lateral (to the midclavicular line) on the breast mound. As breast volume increases, the nipple–areolar complex moves more inferiorly and laterally. The diameter of the areola should be approximately 35 to 45 mm, depending on the overall size of the breast. The size of the breast should be in proportion to the patient's chest, torso, hips, and buttocks. Full cleavage, which is desired by many patients, in reality results only from external forces, such as a brassiere. Attempts to create such full cleavage require unacceptable compromise to other aesthetic factors of the breast. Despite the fact that true symmetry between both breasts is rare, symmetry is extremely important for a good aesthetic outcome. Preoperative asymmetries must be studied and made known to the patient, because often symmetry can be only approached at best; in some cases, preexisting asymmetries are even more evident after surgery.

3. Describe the developmental phases of the breast

The breast originates from the ectoderm. The milk line and subsequently the milk ridge are formed at approximately the fifth week of intrauterine life. Prior to involution, the milk ridge gives rise to the ectodermal milk hill. Incomplete involution of the milk ridge results in supernumerary nipples and accessory breast tissue. The milk hill vascularizes and forms the mammary structures. After birth, with the withdrawal of maternal steroids and the decline of fetal prolactin, the mammary tissues are not altered again until adolescence. Under multiple hormonal influences, the breast begins to grow and differentiate. During adolescent development there is usually no breast ptosis. Development continues until the woman's maximal height is attained, typically at the age of 16 years. From this point the breast matures as the parenchyma and nipple–areolar complex gravitate inferiorly and laterally, with continued superior hemisphere (upper pole) flattening and settling of the breast fullness into the inferior hemisphere. At menopause, the breast undergoes significant glandular involution and a decrease in vascularity. Glandular tissue is reduced and fat content is increased. Thus the youthful appearing breast is full and uplifted, whereas the aging breast is flattened and ptotic. Breast ptosis, a relentless process, is a sign of aging.

4. What are the supporting structures of the breast?

The skin envelope and fascial attachments (Cooper's ligaments) are the major supporting structures of the breast. The thickness and quality of the skin brassiere greatly contribute to the support of the breast and, thus, to breast shape. The quality of skin is affected by aging, hormonal influences (cyclic engorgement), and physical forces, such as gravity and expansible factors (weight gain, pregnancy, prosthetic expansion). Thin skin with loss of elasticity will not support the weight of the breast, resulting in ptosis. Striae, found typically in the supraareolar and periareolar areas, are the result of tears in the dermis and represent thin, inelastic skin. Skin of poor quality may lead to less than optimal aesthetic results and earlier recurrence of ptosis. Suspensory ligaments of Cooper are connective tissue attachments that run from the deep fascia underlying the breast through the parenchyma and attach to the overlying dermis. Cooper's ligaments provide parenchymal support. As with skin, loss of elasticity or attenuation of these ligaments results in ptosis.

5. What are the characteristics of a ptotic or sagging breast?

The ptotic breast is characterized by the inferolateral descent of both the glandular breast and the nipple–areolar complex. In the early stages of ptosis, the nipple–areolar complex and gland descend at the same rate. More advanced stages of breast ptosis are marked by a nipple–areolar complex descent out of proportion to the glandular descent. Thus the nipple–areolar complex assumes a dependent position on the lower pole convexity of the breast rather than the youthful position at the point of maximal projection higher on the breast mound. As the breast parenchyma moves downward, the upper hemisphere or pole of the breast becomes flatter, with loss of significant breast volume. Attentuation of both the skin and Cooper's ligaments results in redundant, loose, inelastic skin with striae. In addition, the breast has considerable increased mobility on the chest wall. The tendency toward increased fat content after lactational or menopausal glandular involution results in a breast that is less firm.

6. What factors contribute to breast ptosis?

Although hypertrophic breasts certainly exhibit ptosis, breast ptosis usually is associated with the combination of volume loss and compromise of the skin brassiere. Loss of breast volume commonly results from significant weight loss, postpartum atrophy, or postmenopausal involution. Gravity exerts a continual ptotic pull on the breast, elongating Cooper's ligaments and stretching the skin. Heavy mammary prostheses contribute to ptosis. The quality of the skin is influenced by a number of factors, such as aging. Simple cyclic or lactational engorgement, weight gain, and expandable prosthetic devices may stretch the skin detrimentally. Thin, inelastic skin creates an ineffective natural brassiere.

7. Describe the classification system for grading breast ptosis.

The classification system set forth by Regnault is perhaps the most useful. This system and similar modifications focus on the position of the nipple–areolar complex relative to the inframammary fold and breast mound. The patient should be in an upright standing position. *First-degree* or *minor ptosis* is defined as location of the nipple–areolar complex at or slightly above the inframammary fold and above the lower hemispheric convexity of the breast. *Second-degree* or *moderate ptosis* is defined by descent of the nipple–areolar complex to a position below the inframammary fold, but it is situated on the anterior projection of the breast mound. *Third-degree* or *major ptosis* is defined by a nipple–areolar complex that is not only below the inframammary fold but also on the dependent position of the inferior convexity of the breast mound. In severe forms of third-degree ptosis, the nipple points directly downward. In *pseudoptosis*, the nipple–areolar complex remains above the inframammary fold, the breast mound descends below the inframammary fold, and other characteristics of breast ptosis are present, such as glandular hypoplasia. *Glandular ptosis* refers to an otherwise normal breast (with the nipple–areolar complex at or above the inframammary fold) except that the breast mound or glandular portion has descended below the inframammary fold. The degree of breast ptosis is an extremely important consideration in choosing an operative technique for correction.

8. What are the goals of mastopexy?

Mastopexy is a surgical procedure that attempts to reverse the normal progression of breast ptosis, thus restoring the breast to a more youthful form. Some breasts never enjoy a full, nonptotic appearance, even in youth. Important in the management of breast ptosis are not only the particular abnormalities of the patient's breast but also her desires and expectations. The goals of mastopexy are to reposition the nipple–areolar complex, to reposition the breast mound and optimize its contour and volume, to remove redundant skin and tighten the skin brassiere, and to provide support for the breast in a lasting manner. Mastopexy techniques, which have paralleled the evolution of breast reduction techniques, are also used to treat congenital deformities (e.g., tubular breasts), correct asymmetries (congenital or acquired), and optimize the aesthetic outcome after explantation of augmented breasts.

9. Are the effects of mastopexy permanent?

No. As soon as the mastopexy procedure is completed, ptotic forces, such as aging and gravity, resume their relentless attack on the breast.

10. What are the major drawbacks to mastopexy?

Compared with other aesthetic breast procedures, mastopexy is particularly challenging and full of compromise:

- Mastopexy requires that incisions be made directly on the breast. Depending on the degree of ptosis and mastopexy technique, the scars may be quite extensive. The patient must be willing to accept the extent of scars as a tradeoff for a more youthful and aesthetically pleasing breast.
- The effects of surgery are only temporary (even though the scars are permanent).
- The medium for surgical manipulation most often includes thin, inelastic skin of poor quality and involuted breast parenchyma with attenuated internal support and frequently decreased vascularity.
- The inherent upper pole flatness of the ptotic breast cannot be addressed by simple mastopexy alone; correction typically requires an implant.
- Although mastopexy delivers a more uplifted breast, the necessary repositioning and redraping of the breast makes the breast appear smaller.
- In addition to nonspecific problems such as tissue loss, hematoma, seroma, and infection, loss or alteration of sensibility is always a possibility.

11. What are the advantages and disadvantages of implants after mastopexy?

The addition of an implant can enhance size and contour. Of interest, an implant also increases the longevity of the uplifting effects of mastopexy and often reduces the length of incisions needed to perform an adequate mastopexy. However, the skin envelope of a ptotic breast may not be able to handle adequately the weight and possible expansibility of an implant. Furthermore, the addition of an implant brings with it the associated complications and risks of breast prostheses. A tightened breast without an implant also loses some projection.

12. How are scars tolerated on the breast?

Because scars probably are the greatest drawback to aesthetic breast surgery, there is a constant effort to minimize the length of incisions and to place incisions in hidden areas. Decreasing incision length, however, may limit the ability to achieve the optimal aesthetic result. Although periareolar and intraareolar incisions are located on the most prominent and focused position of the breast, the resultant scars are the most predictable and best tolerated. Areolar scars are less likely to become hypertrophic than are inframammary scars. Areolar scars still may be subject to significant widening if placed on tension. In addition, intraareolar scars are unpigmented; therefore they may be readily apparent on a darkly pigmented areola. A median inferior longitudinal (vertical) scar is generally well tolerated on the breast compared with the inframammary horizontal scar. Scars on the thorax typically are unpredictable and often unsightly, especially scars that approach or encompass the sternal region, such as an overextended medial limb of an inframammary incision. All attempts should be made to keep incisions off the superior hemisphere of the breast and the medial lower quadrant because these areas often are not covered by clothing.

13. What are the blood supply and innervation to the breast?

Familiarity with breast anatomy is paramount to achieving optimal results, preserving sensibility, and avoiding complications, especially in reoperative surgery. The three main routes of arterial blood supply to the breast are the internal mammary artery, lateral thoracic artery, and intercostal arteries. The dominant supply originates from the internal mammary artery (approximately 60%), a branch of the subclavian artery. The internal mammary artery gives off perforating vessels that enter the breast approximately 2 cm lateral to the sternal edge. The nipple–areolar complex depends on the underlying breast parenchyma and an enhanced subdermal plexus for its blood supply. This dermal blood supply is fed chiefly by the lateral thoracic artery with significant contributions from anastomosing internal mammary vessels. Postmenopausal (often ptotic) breasts have decreased blood flow. Smoking, diabetes, and atherosclerosis contribute to decreased blood flow. In reoperative surgery, every attempt must be made to establish the precise nature of previous operations. Cutting across a previous flap carries the risk of vascular compromise. Innervation to the nipple–areolar complex is primarily from the fourth anterolateral intercostal nerve, which travels lateral to medial beneath to deep fascia before coursing upward through the breast parenchyma to innervate the nipple and areola. The third and fifth anterolateral intercostals (along with their medial counterparts) also contribute to the overlapping innervation of the nipple–areolar complex. In evaluating the breast parenchyma from the pectoralis, care must be taken not to dissect too far laterally because of the risk of nipple denervation.

14. What are the pertinent anatomic features in planning a mastopexy procedure?

All of the following anatomic features must be examined before undertaking a mastopexy: degree of ptosis and nipple–areolar position; breast volume; distribution of breast volume; breast contour; length, position, and definition of the inframammary fold; lower pole constriction; quality of the skin; fascial attachments (breast mobility); lateral breast/chest folds; and symmetry. Of these features, the degree of breast ptosis predominantly dictates which form of mastopexy is best suited to achieve the optimal aesthetic goals.

15. What are the various surgical options available for treatment of breast ptosis?

The "breast lift" is perhaps the most difficult aesthetic breast procedure. The fact that the breast needs to be lifted means that the tissues with which the surgeon will be working are of poor quality. Furthermore, the myriad of techniques that exist for correction of breast ptosis demonstrate the large variation in degrees of breast ptosis and underscore the fact that no one technique is ideal. Treatment must be individualized. In general, surgical options for mastopexy are characterized by the manner or pattern in which redundant skin and breast tissue is removed or tightened. Typically, the addition of a breast implant to the mastopexy procedure enhances the result significantly. The purpose of the implant is not so much about making the breast larger but more about adding fullness to the upper pole of the breast. Lifting the breast alone will not add any volume to the upper pole of the breast. The augmentation mastopexy is inherently difficult to perform because the augmentation and the lift have opposing goals. The augmentation enlarges and stretches the breast and maintains a downward vector. The lift tightens the breast and maintains an upward vector. If an implant is used, the breast should be augmented before the final nipple–areolar complex position is defined because augmentation decreases the amount of ptosis and thus changes the optimal position of the nipple–areolar complex. Attempting to correct true breast ptosis with an implant alone requires the use of large-volume implants that may be aesthetically unpleasing and do not adequately address the ptosis. In addition, without the necessary skin tightening, the native ptotic breast may hang over the less mobile and higher positioned breast implant. This postoperative contour deformity, termed a "double bubble," is not easily corrected.

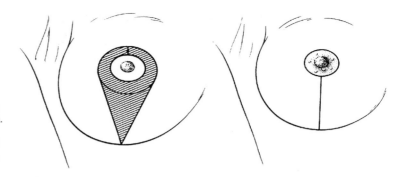

Figure 68-1. For minor ptosis, the circumareolar excision with a vertical ellipse tightens the skin and lifts the nipple without the need for an inframammary incision. This incision can be shortened because the vertical component is used primarily to close the defect from the transposed nipple–areola. It also tends to shorten with postoperative scar contraction. (From Bostwick J: Aesthetic and Reconstructive Breast Surgery. St. Louis, Mosby, 1983, p 234.)

Typically, the degree of ptosis, along with nipple position and magnitude of breast atrophy, will determine the choice of surgical technique. The nipple–areolar complex can be moved and the breast tightened by circumareolar skin excisions. For greater degrees of breast ptosis with more skin redundancy, in which the nipple–areolar complex must be moved a farther distance, a vertical excision component is added. As the degrees of ptosis increase, a horizontal excision component (placed at the most inferior point of the vertical excision) is often added, ultimately resulting in a full inverted T incision. Also, excision of inferior pole breast tissue and fat is often indicated to minimize both the tension on the vertical limb of the excision and the likelihood of postsurgical "bottoming out" of the breast. Hence the typical surgical options for ptosis correction are augmentation only, circumareolar mastopexy, circumareolar excision with a vertical excision component, and circumvertical excision with a short or full inverted T excisional component. Each of these procedures can be performed with or without an implant and/or excision of lower pole breast tissue (Figs. 68-1 and 68-2).

16. What is a Benelli mastopexy?

A donut mastopexy refers merely to a concentric skin excision around the areola; the outer dermal circumference is reapproximated to the areola. A Benelli mastopexy refers to a method of pursestringing the outer dermal circumference with a strong nonresorbable suture. This maneuver eliminates the tension placed on the areola by a donut mastopexy. The addition of the pursestring or "round block" overcomes many of the inherent problems of previous forms of concentric mastopexies, thus expanding their indications and optimizing their results. A Benelli mastopexy, in the strictest sense, includes a remodeling of the breast parenchyma by pexying the retroglandular surface to underlying periosteum at the aponeurotic prepectoral level in a crisscross fashion.

17. What is tailor-tacking?

Tailor-tacking allows the surgeon to view the result before making any incisions. Proposed areas of resection or deepithelialization are simply invaginated and the outer edges are tacked together, usually with staples, to simulate a resection with edge-to-edge closure. When the desired result is achieved, the outer edges are marked, the tacks are released, and all areas within the marks are identified for removal. This method is particularly useful for determining the correct position for the nipple–areolar complex.

18. What is meant by a constricted breast or inferior-pole hyperplasia?

In a constricted breast the inframammary fold is tight and elevated. Because of a deficiency of lower pole skin and breast tissue, the distance between the lower edge of the areola and the inframammary fold is short. As a result, the upper pole rotates over the high, tight inframammary fold. The appearance suggests constriction and ptosis. The ptosis is not related to an inferiorly descended nipple–areolar complex but rather to a higher inframammary fold and inferior breast hypoplasia. Correction includes releasing and lowering the fold, along with radial releases inferiorly and expansion inferiorly. Severe constriction is represented by the tubular breast.

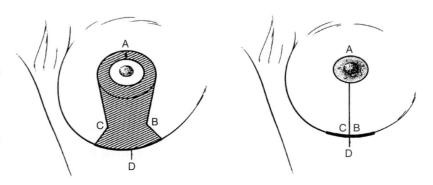

Figure 68-2. For moderate ptosis, the circumareolar excision with a vertical and short horizontal ellipse produces a short inframammary scar and tightens the breast while shortening the inframammary distance. (Modified from Bostwick J: Aesthetic and Reconstructive Breast Surgery. St. Louis, Mosby, 1983, p 235.)

19. What are the common complications of mastopexy?

Complications common to mastopexy are recurrent ptosis, nipple–areolar complex asymmetry, breast asymmetries, upper pole flattening, poor scarring, and nipple–areolar necrosis. Most complications are the result of poor planning. Nipple–areolar complexes that are malpositioned superiorly are particularly troublesome because it usually is necessary to place scars on the superior hemisphere to lower the nipple–areolar complex.

BIBLIOGRAPHY

Benelli L: A new periareolar mammaplasty: The "round block" technique. Aesthet Plast Surg 14:93–100, 1990.

Bostwick J: Aesthetic and Reconstructive Breast Surgery. St. Louis, Quality Medical Publishing, 1990.

Brink RR: Evaluating breast parenchymal maldistribution with regard to mastopexy and augmentation mammaplasty. Plast Reconstr Surg 86:715–721, 1990.

Dinner M, Artz J, Fogelietti M: Application and modification of the circular skin excision and pursestring procedures. Aesthet Plast Surg 17:301–309, 1993.

Erol OO, Spira M: A mastopexy technique for mild to moderate ptosis. Plast Reconstr Surg 65:603–609, 1980.

Gasperoni C, Salgarello M, Gargani G: Experience and technical refinements in the "donut" mastopexy with augmentation mammaplasty. Aesthet Plast Surg 12:111–114, 1988.

Georgiade N, Georgiade G, Riefkohl R: Aesthetic Surgery of the Breast. Philadelphia, WB Saunders, 1990.

Georgiade G, Riefkohl R, Levin LS: Plastic, Maxillofacial, and Reconstructive Sugery, 3rd ed. Baltimore, Williams & Wilkins, 1997.

Grotting J: Reoperative Aesthetic and Reconstructive Surgery. St. Louis, Quality Medical Publishing, 1995.

Gruber R, Jones H: The "donut" mastopexy: Indications and complications. Plast Reconstr Surg 65:34–38, 1980.

Lejour M: Vertical mammoplasty and liposuction of the breast. Plast Reconstr Surg 94:100–114, 1994.

Netscher D, Sharma S, Thornby J, et al: Aesthetic outcome of breast implant removal in 85 consecutive patients. Plast Reconstr Surg 100:206–219, 1997.

Puckett C, Meyer V, Reinisch J: Crescent mastopexy and augmentation. Plast Reconstr Surg 75:533–539, 1985.

Regnault P, Daniel R: Aesthetic Plastic Surgery. Boston, Little, Brown, 1984.

Regnault P, Daniel R, Tirkantis B: The minus-plus mastopexy. Clin Plast Surg 15:595–599, 1988.

Ship A, Weiss P, Engler A: Dual-pedicle dermoparenchymal mastopexy. Plast Reconstr Surg 83:282–289, 1989.

Westreich M: Anthropomorphic breast measurement: Protocol and results in 50 women with aesthetically perfect breasts. Plast Reconstr Surg 100:468–479, 1997.

Whidden P: The tailor-tack mastopexy. Plast Reconstr Surg 62:347–354, 1978.

DISEASES OF THE BREAST

Kirby I. Bland, MD, and
Peter D. Ray, MD

1. What are the incidence, risk probability, and mortality for female breast cancer? Does radiation increase survival?

In 2004, it was estimated that 215,000 new cases of invasive breast cancer would be diagnosed and that 40,010 women would die of the disease. The incidence of breast cancer depends on whether a woman is in an average risk group or an increased risk group. Women at average risk have a 10% to 14% chance of having breast cancer by age 90 years.

2. Which factors are known to increase the risk of breast cancer? What factors are known to decrease the risk of breast cancer?

The strongest risk factor for the development of breast cancer is age. Race plays a role in risk as well, with whites having a higher risk than other racial groups. Breast cancer risk also is increased by nulliparity, high levels of combined exogenous estrogen and progestin, hyperplasia or proliferative pathology on previous breast biopsy, prior breast cancer on the contralateral side, greater breast tissue density, physical inactivity, and prior radiation exposure. Breast cancer risk is reduced by young age at first live birth. Oral contraceptive use is not associated with increased risk of breast cancer.

3. Can breast cancer be inherited? What is the increased risk if a woman carries BRCA1, BRCA2, or both?

From 5% to 10% of female breast cancers occur in women with genetic risk factors. In families with susceptibility to both breast and ovarian cancer, mutations in *BRCA* genes are present in nearly 100% of these patients. Mutations in *BRCA* genes are responsible for nearly half of familial breast cancers. Estimated lifetime risk of breast cancer is 85% for mutations of *BRCA1* and *BRCA2* genes. The vast majority of breast cancers occur in women with no family history of the disease.

4. What is ductal carcinoma in situ? Is it a precancerous state? What is the risk of invasive cancer? What is the treatment? What about lobular carcinoma in situ?

Ductal carcinoma in situ (DCIS) is a precursor of invasive cancer. The risk for developing invasive cancer is considered to range from 30% to 50% over 10 years. The gold standard treatment is total mastectomy. Because of the success in using conservation therapy for invasive cancer, this treatment is being applied to DCIS. The National Surgical Adjuvant Breast and Bowel Project-17 (NSABP-17) is examining lumpectomy versus lumpectomy and radiation therapy. Early data reveal a significant decrease in event-free survival and invasive cancer with radiation therapy. However, there is no change in overall survival and distant disease.

Lobular carcinoma in situ (LCIS) is a marker rather than a precursor for invasive cancer. It carries a 10% to 37% risk of breast cancer, with most incidences occurring more than 15 years later. Fifty to sixty-five percent of the invasive cancers are not lobular but ductal in origin and can occur in either or both breasts. If operative intervention is chosen, anything less than total mastectomy is inappropriate because the disease process is multicentric and often bilateral.

5. When should a woman begin mammographic screening? Are there exceptions? Has routine mammography reduced mortality?

The American Cancer Society recommends annual mammography for women beginning at age 40 years. If a woman has had thoracic radiation, she should undergo mammography 8 to 10 years following radiation or at age 40 years, whichever is earliest. Women with known BRCA1 and/or BRCA2 mutations should begin screening mammography at age 25 years. It is clear that screening mammography does reduce mortality, with some Swedish trials showing a reduction of up to 44%.

6. What features make a mammographic lesion suspicious for malignancy? Do all lesions require biopsy?

Suspicious lesions consist of fine microcalcifications and/or density lesions such as masses, architectural distortions, and asymmetries. Microcalcifications that are fine, branching, clustered, pleomorphic, and numerous are most suspicious. Masses that are stellate and irregular also are most suspicious. The combination of such masses with microcalcifications gives the highest yield for malignancy. Any suspicious lesions should be biopsied with needle localization or stereotactic core needle biopsy if available. Lesions deemed less suspicious by the surgeon and radiologist may be followed closely by mammography.

7. **Is there a role for fine-needle aspiration for palpable breast masses? Is there a role for mammography?**
Yes. Fine-needle aspiration (FNA) is an inexpensive, quick, and easy technique to differentiate solid from cystic masses with low morbidity. If nonbloody fluid is obtained and the mass disappears, the patient can be followed closely by physical examination and mammography. If the fluid is bloody or the mass persists or recurs after two aspirations, the patient should undergo open biopsy. The fluid should also be sent for cytologic evaluation. If no fluid is found, the mass is assumed to be solid, and the patient should undergo outpatient open biopsy. If the cytology specimen is positive, the patient may undergo a one-step procedure that includes open biopsy and frozen section confirmation prior to conservation therapy or mastectomy. However, a two-step approach is preferred.

Mammography should be obtained in all women over 30 years of age with a palpable breast mass. The combination of physical examination, mammography, and FNA yields a diagnostic accuracy approaching 100%.

8. **What is the diagnostic accuracy of physical examination, mammography, and FNA combined?**
100%.

9. **What are the borders of the axilla?**
   - *Anterior Wall:* Pectoralis major, subclavius, and pectoralis minor muscles and clavipectoral fascia
   - *Posterior Wall:* Subscapularis, latissimus dorsi, and teres major muscles
   - *Medial Wall:* Upper four or five ribs and the intercostal spaces covered by the serratus anterior muscle
   - *Lateral Wall:* Coracobrachialis and biceps muscles

10. **Which nerves can be identified during an axillary lymph node dissection? What is their role?**
The *intercostobrachial nerve* supplies sensory innervation to the upper medial aspect of the arm and is preserved if possible.

The *long thoracic nerve* (respiratory nerve of Bell) originates from roots C5, C6, and C7 of the brachial plexus and provides motor stimulation to the serratus anterior muscle. It usually can be found adjacent to the lateral thoracic artery's origin and runs along the serratus anterior. Transection results in a "winged scapula."

The *thoracodorsal nerve* originates from the posterior cord of the brachial plexus and usually can be found posterior to the origin of the subscapular vessels. It provides motor innervation to the latissimus dorsi muscle and should be preserved unless it is encased in tumor. Minimal morbidity is associated with its transection compared with that of the long thoracic nerve. However, for myocutaneous flaps that use the latissimus dorsi muscle, the thoracodorsal neurovascular bundle must be spared to ensure flap function, form, and viability.

The *medial pectoral nerve* supplies motor innervation to the pectoralis major muscle, and 40% of the time it wraps around the lateral border of the pectoralis minor muscle. This nerve should be spared.

11. **What features on presentation suggest a hereditary breast cancer?**
Early onset (age <40 years), ovarian cancer combined with a family history of ovarian or breast cancer, breast and ovarian cancer in the same woman, bilateral breast cancer, male patient with breast cancer.

12. **How does tamoxifen work? Who benefits? How much?**
Tamoxifen is a selective estrogen receptor modulator (SERM). It blocks the estrogen receptors on breast tissue. Women who are at high risk greatly benefit from tamoxifen therapy. It can reduce by half the chance of developing breast cancer over 5 years in high-risk women (age >60 years, history of LCIS, or predicted risk of 1.6% by the Gail model). It also is more beneficial in women who have estrogen receptor–positive tumors.

13. **What is the STAR trial?**
STAR is the Study of Tamoxifen and Raloxifene. Raloxifene acts similar to tamoxifen, but it is not approved by the Food and Drug Administration (FDA) for chemoprevention of breast cancer as of 2005. Raloxifene has already been deemed safe by the FDA for use in reducing bone density loss in women, so it is a reasonable medication for examining chemoprevention effects on breast cancer as well.

14. **What are the current controversies surrounding chemotherapy benefit in female patients with breast cancer?**
   Optimal chemotherapy regimen, number of chemotherapy cycles, timing of adjuvant chemotherapy, sequencing of adjuvant radiotherapy and chemotherapy, and duration of hormonal therapy.

15. **What are the most common areas of recurrence?**
   Locally, breast cancer recurs in the breast and regional lymph nodes. Distant metastases can affect almost any site. The most common are lung, liver, bone, and, less commonly, gastrointestinal tract, adrenals, brain, and soft tissues.

16. **What is trastuzumab?**
   Trastuzumab is a recombinant deoxyribonucleic acid (DNA)-derived humanized monoclonal antibody that selectively binds to the extracellular domain of HER2. It was approved by the FDA for metastatic breast cancer therapy in 1998.

17. **What is the American Joint Committee on Cancer (AJCC) 5-year survival rate for breast cancer?**
   In patients diagnosed with breast cancer between 1995 and 1998, the stage-by-stage survival is stage 0, 100%; stage I, 100%; stage IIA, 92%; stage IIB, 81%; stage IIIA, 67%; stage IIIB, 54%; and stage IV, 20%.

18. **What is the most common solid breast mass in women younger than 30 years? Does this lesion have malignant potential?**
   The most common solid breast mass in this age group is a fibroadenoma, a benign tumor composed of both stromal and epithelial elements. Women may be managed with FNA and observation or excisional biopsy, depending on the patient's age.

19. **What are the most common organisms cultured from nipple discharge in a woman with a breast abscess? What is the treatment?**
   Staphylococcus aureus and streptococci. Most abscesses are subareolar and occur within the first few days of breastfeeding. Treatment is conservative and combines broad-spectrum antibiotics, warm soaks, and a mechanical breast pump. More serious infections may require intravenous antibiotics and incision and drainage. The incisions should be small and circumareolar for optimal cosmesis.

20. **A woman presents with diffuse, bilateral breast pain associated with her menstrual cycle. Palpation reveals multiple nodular irregularities. What is the disorder? Is it premalignant?**
   Fibrocystic disorder. It is not a premalignant state unless it is associated with atypia. Thirty percent of fibrocystic change is proliferative with cellular atypia. If a dominant mass is present, it should be aspirated and treated like any other suspicious cyst or mass.

21. **What is Her2? Why is it important?**
   Her2, also known as c-erbB-2 or HER2/neu, is a tyrosine kinase epidermal growth factor receptor. It regulates cell growth, and when overexpressed it increases growth and reproduction of cells. It is associated with shorter survival, higher recurrence, and poorer response to both chemotherapy and hormone-based therapies.

22. **What is *p53*? Why is it important?**
   p53 is the first mutant gene found in tumors, in 1979. It is transcribed into a nuclear protein that has a role in DNA repair and orderly cell death (apoptosis). When functioning correctly it inhibits proliferation and angiogenesis. Patients with high levels of abnormal p53 have poorer overall outcomes and lower disease-free survival rates. Regional radiation therapy increases survival in breast cancer cases with *p53* mutations compared to the wild type.

23. **Besides BRCA1 and BRCA2, name three other autosomal dominant syndromes that carry an increased risk of breast cancer.**
   Li-Fraumeni syndrome, Cowden disease, and Peutz-Jeghers syndrome.

24. **What is atypical hyperplasia? Does it increase the risk of breast cancer?**
   Atypical hyperplasia is a histologic entity that increases risk of breast cancer if found on biopsy. The two types of atypical hyperplasia are lobular and ductal. Atypical ductal hyperplasia increases risk by fourfold to fivefold. Atypical lobular hyperplasia increases risk by fourfold to 10-fold.

25. What is the Gail model? What are its limitations?

The Gail model is a breast cancer risk assessment tool developed in 1989 based on data from the Breast Cancer Detection Demonstration Project. It is used to estimate a woman's 5-year and lifetime risk of invasive breast cancer.

The Gail model can underestimate the contribution of family history because it includes only first-degree relatives, it does not include paternal history, and it does not capture ovarian malignancy (a potential genetic marker for increased risk in *BRCA* gene carriers).

26. What is chemoprevention?

Chemoprevention is the use of medications to lower the risk of breast cancer.

BIBLIOGRAPHY

American Cancer Society: How is breast cancer staged? Retrieved November 30, 2005. Available from: http://www.cancer.org.

Chung MA, Bland KI: Neoplasms of the breast. In Bland KI, Daly JM, Karakousis CP (eds): Surgical Oncology Contemporary Principles and Practice. New York, McGraw-Hill, 2001.

Fisher B, Constantino JP, Wickerham DL, et al: Tamoxifen for prevention of breast cancer: Report of the National Surgical Adjuvant Breast and Bowel Project P-1 Study. JNCI 90:1371–1388,1998.

FORCE: Facing our risk of cancer empowered. Chemoprevention and breast cancer. Retrieved November 11, 2005. Available from: http://www.facingourrisk.org/risk_management/chemoprevention_breast_cancer.html.

Jemal A, Tiwari RC, Murray T: Cancer statistics. CA Cancer J Clin 54:8–29, 2004.

Korde LA, Calzone KA, Zujewski J: Assessing breast cancer risk. Postgrad Med 116:6–8, 2004.

Sunpaweravong S, Sunpaweravong P: Recent developments in critical genes in the molecular biology of breast cancer. Asian J Surg 28:71–75, 2005.

BREAST RECONSTRUCTION

Maurice Y. Nahabedian, MD, FACS

1. What are the options for breast reconstruction following mastectomy?

At present, a breast can be reconstructed by two methods: *implants* and *autologous tissue*. Factors associated with implant reconstruction include timing, method of reconstruction, and filler material. The reconstruction can be performed immediately at the time of mastectomy or on a delayed basis, it can be performed in one or two stages, and it can include implants filled with saline or silicone gel. The principal methods of breast reconstruction using autologous tissue include the latissimus dorsi musculocutaneous flap, the transverse rectus abdominis musculocutaneous (TRAM) flap, and the various perforator flaps. Perforator flaps are the most recent advance; they tend to minimize donor site morbidity by preserving the muscles.

2. What are the indications for prophylactic mastectomy, and why is the incidence increasing?

The preventative reasons for prophylactic mastectomy include a history of breast cancer, a family history of breast cancer, positive genetic testing, and alleviating the fear of developing breast cancer. These reasons along with the fact that current techniques of breast reconstruction are so effective have prompted many women to opt for prophylactic mastectomy. The options for breast reconstruction are unchanged and include one- and two-stage implant reconstruction and the use of autologous tissue.

3. Why do some women have an immediate reconstruction and others a delayed reconstruction?

The primary advantage of immediate reconstruction is that the aesthetic outcome usually is improved because the natural breast contour is preserved. Given that the risk of recurrence is the same for women with and those without reconstruction and that breast reconstruction does not impede the ability to detect a recurrence, the incidence of women seeking immediate reconstruction has increased. Current indications for immediate reconstruction include women with stage I and stage II breast cancer. The indications for delayed reconstruction generally include women with advanced breast cancer who are at significant risk for local recurrence. These include women with inflammatory cancer, ulcerated tumors, and metastatic disease as well as women who are certain to receive postoperative radiation.

4. What are the best methods of surveillance following breast reconstruction in women with a history of breast cancer?

Recommendations for surveillance include careful examination of the cutaneous surface of the breast for nodularity, discoloration, or skin retraction. This is sufficient for the majority of women following immediate or delayed reconstruction. In women with a history of advanced breast cancer (stages III and IV) or in women with deep-seated tumors that approximate the pectoralis major muscle, adjuvant means such as magnetic resonance imaging, ultrasound, or mammography may be necessary.

5. Is there an optimal time to perform breast reconstruction in the setting of radiation therapy?

For the reconstructive surgeon, the beneficial effects of radiation therapy must be weighed against the untoward effects, which include perivascular and soft tissue fibrosis, delayed wound healing, cutaneous pigmentation, and contracture. When radiation is necessary, the usual recommendation is to delay reconstruction for 6 to 12 months following its completion. The combination of radiation and implant reconstruction is associated with a higher incidence of failure; therefore autologous reconstruction is often preferred. Autologous reconstruction tolerates the effects of radiation relatively well, although some shrinkage and fibrosis can occur.

6. What is a TRAM flap?

The TRAM (**T**ransverse **R**ectus **A**bdominis **M**usculocutaneous) flap incorporates skin, fat, and variable amounts of the rectus abdominis muscle from the lower abdomen to reconstruct a breast. The blood supply of the flap can be based on the superior epigastric (pedicle TRAM) or the inferior epigastric (free TRAM) artery and vein. The free TRAM flap is generally indicated for women with increased risk factors, such as elevated body mass index (BMI) and tobacco use.

7. What is the delay procedure, and when should it be used?

The delay procedure is a surgical technique by which the perfusion to the adipocutaneous component of a pedicle TRAM flap can be improved. The operation usually is performed 2 to 3 weeks prior to the scheduled TRAM flap. It involves ligating the inferior epigastric artery and vein as well as incising a portion of the cutaneous surface of the proposed flap outline. The purpose of this procedure is to promote vascular reorganization within the flap such that the principal blood supply is derived from the superior epigastric artery and vein. The benefit of this procedure is that it minimizes the occurrence of fat or partial flap necrosis.

8. What is the importance of supercharging?

Supercharging is the process of performing a microvascular anastomosis of the inferior epigastric artery and vein of a pedicle TRAM to the thoracodorsal artery and vein. This is sometimes necessary following a pedicle TRAM flap that is showing evidence of compromised vascularity, such as venous congestion or arterial insufficiency. The additional arterial and venous flow usually will compensate for the inadequate inflow or outflow of the superior epigastric vessel within the flap.

9. What is a perforator flap, and why is it becoming a popular method of breast reconstruction?

A perforator flap is a flap consisting of skin and subcutaneous tissue that is perfused by an isolated artery and vein that perforates the deep tissues (muscle or fascia). Although a variety of perforator flaps have been described, four are currently used for breast reconstruction: deep inferior epigastric perforator (DIEP), superior gluteal artery perforator (SGAP), inferior gluteal artery perforator (IGAP), and thoracodorsal artery perforator (TAP) flaps. These flaps all are differentiated from their conventional musculocutaneous counterparts in that no muscle is removed with the flap, so donor site morbidity is reduced. The DIEP flap is the most commonly performed perforator flap because the abdomen usually has a mild to moderate amount of lipodystrophy and is generally considered an excellent donor site.

10. Are there functional and aesthetic differences between the TRAM flap and the DIEP flap?

The pros and cons of performing the TRAM flap or the DIEP flap have been highly debated over the past several years. Most studies of the pedicle TRAM flap have demonstrated an incidence of abdominal bulge/hernia between 1% and 20%, fat necrosis from 5% to 10%, and total flap loss from 0% to 2%. Most studies of the free TRAM have demonstrated that the incidence of abdominal bulge/hernia ranges from 1% to 10%, fat necrosis from 5% to 15%, venous congestion from 2% to 5%, and total flap loss from 1% to 5%. Most studies evaluating the DIEP flap have demonstrated that the incidence of abdominal bulge ranges from 1% to 5%, fat necrosis from 5% to 10%, venous congestion from 2% to 10%, and total flap loss from 1% to 5%. Studies also have demonstrated an increase in abdominal strength with increasing muscle preservation as demonstrated by the ability to perform sit-ups and by isokinetic testing. Thus both methods have their associated risks and benefits, and both methods are capable of delivering excellent outcomes.

11. What are the ideal recipient vessels for microvascular breast reconstruction?

The two vascular systems that currently are used are the internal mammary and the thoracodorsal artery and vein. The thoracodorsal vessels are preferred following a modified radical mastectomy. The internal mammary vessels are preferred following skin-sparing mastectomy and for delayed reconstruction. Advantages of the internal mammary include no risk of injury to the intercostobrachial nerve, no associated risk lymphedema, and higher perfusion pressure.

12. How can microvascular complications be minimized?

Microvascular complications following free tissue transfer usually are the result of thrombosis of the artery or vein, external pressure or kinking of the vascular pedicle, and poor vessel mismatch. Studies have demonstrated, however, that the most important factor in preventing thrombosis is meticulous surgical technique; the administration of pharmacologic agents such as heparin or dextran is secondary in importance. Attention to the vascular pedicle during inset will minimize the occurrence of a kink or twist that can compromise circulation. An end-to-end anastomosis is performed in the majority of cases; however, an end-to-side anastomosis may be necessary in the event of caliber mismatch.

13. What are the indications for a latissimus dorsi flap?

The latissimus dorsi flap incorporates skin, fat, and muscle from the posterolateral thorax. Although not generally considered a "first choice" for most plastic surgeons, it is often used as an alternate for patients with certain body types. In general, women who are best suited for a latissimus dorsi flap include women with an elevated BMI and women after previous abdominal operations that violated critical zones. Because the adipocutaneous component of the latissimus dorsi flap usually is less than what is needed, an implant is sometimes necessary to supplement for the volume discrepancy.

14. What are the indications for breast reconstruction with implants?

Breast reconstruction with implants is a first choice for many women. Reasons include rapid recovery, ability to modify breast volume, and avoidance of donor site morbidity. The recovery phase is expedited in terms of decreased hospitalization, decreased pain, and an earlier return to activities of daily living compared with autologous reconstruction. Implant reconstruction can be performed in one or two stages. One-stage reconstruction usually is reserved for women with smaller breasts (A or B cup) or for women who will have a skin-sparing or subcutaneous mastectomy. Two-stage reconstruction is the most common method and is used when the mastectomy skin requires temporary expansion to obtain the desired volume or symmetry. Once the desired volume is obtained, the expander is exchanged for a permanent implant.

15. How does a surgeon decide on the size, shape, texture, and filler material of an implant?

The size of the implant is principally based on the base diameter of the breast, which should correspond to the diameter of the implant. The shape or contour of the implant is selected based on the expectation of the woman and the need to obtain symmetry. In general, a contour profile implant is used to obtain projection and a round implant is used to create ptosis. The surface characteristics of the implant can be smooth or textured. Smooth surface implants will adhere less to the surrounding tissues and will slide within the pocket. Textured implants will adhere to the surrounding skin and are a characteristic of contour profile devices. The filler material for the implant can be either saline or silicone gel. Silicone gel will mimic the natural breast more closely because the material feels much like natural breast tissue.

16. What is the evidence that silicone gel breast implants are safe and effective devices?

Since 1992, the use of silicone gel breast implants has been restricted by the Food and Drug Administration (FDA) based on concerns related to autoimmune and connective tissue disorders. The decision to allow all women to have the right to choose silicone gel implant is controversial and complex. Over the past 15 years, a number of studies have demonstrated that these devices are safe and effective. The Institute of Medicine report of 1999 concluded that these devices do not cause cancer, autoimmune disorders, or connective tissue disease and pose no risk to health. The National Cancer Institute study of 2004 demonstrated no conclusive evidence that breast implants affect the development of connective tissue disease. The Institute of Epidemiology from Denmark demonstrated in 2004 that untreated silicone gel implant rupture is a relatively harmless condition that rarely progresses and rarely gives rise to notable symptoms.

17. What are the reasons for premature removal of an implant or expander?

Reasons for premature removal of implants include, but are not limited to, rupture, capsular contracture, pain, distortion, rippling and wrinkling, infection, delayed healing with or without exposure, and patient dissatisfaction. Patient-related factors that can be associated with these factors and increase the risk of failure include chemotherapy, diabetes, obesity, radiation therapy, and a history of tobacco use. Fortunately, the incidence of implant failure is generally low. It is estimated that approximately 80% to 90% of women will retain their original implant by 5 years. However, it must be emphasized that the incidence of failure will increase the longer an implant is in place.

18. How often are secondary procedures necessary following breast reconstruction?

Secondary procedures include reduction mammaplasty, mastopexy, augmentation, recontouring, and implant exchange. Studies have demonstrated that secondary procedures are more common following reconstruction with implants, performed in 89% of delayed reconstructions and 57% of immediate reconstructions. The incidence is lower with flaps, which are performed in 59% of delayed reconstructions and 18% of immediate reconstructions.

19. What are the options for nipple reconstruction?

The final stage in the process of breast reconstruction is the creation of a nipple–areolar complex. The methods for reconstructing a nipple are varied and include the use of local flaps, contralateral nipple sharing, and grafted skin from remote sites. The most common method is the use of local flaps, which include C-V, skate, star, and bell flaps, to name a few. All are based on the concept of adjacent tissue rearrangement. The areola is created by tattooing the skin around the nipple and usually is performed 3 months later. The major limitation with all of these techniques is that the nipple will flatten by approximately 50%, and sometimes more, in most cases. Current options to improve projection of the nipple include secondary reconstruction as well as augmentation using fat, dermis, cartilage, bone, synthetic materials, and AlloDerm. These methods have been demonstrated to be useful, resulting in final projections of 4 to 5 mm.

20. Is there evidence that quality of life is improved following breast reconstruction?

The diagnosis of breast cancer can have a significant negative impact on the short- and long-term psychological well-being of women, often producing depression, fear, and anxiety. The reasons for performing breast reconstruction are to improve the self-esteem, self-image, and confidence of women following mastectomy. Studies and personal observation have demonstrated that women are generally pleased with the aesthetic outcomes and are able to reintegrate into society sooner than women who have not undergone reconstruction. These benefits have been observed regardless of patient age, method of reconstruction, and timing of reconstruction.

BIBLIOGRAPHY

Allen RJ: Microsurgical breast reconstruction. www.diepflap.com

Blondeel PN, Van Landuyt KHI, Monstrey SJM, et al: The "Gent" consensus on perforator flap terminology: Preliminary definitions. Plast Reconstr Surg 112:1378–1383, 2003.

Brinton LA, Buckley LM, Dvorkina O, et al: Risk of connective tissue disorders among breast implant patients. Am J Epidemiol 160:619–627, 2004.

Disa JJ, Ad-El DD, Cohen SM, Cordeiro PG, Hidalgo DA: The premature removal of tissue expanders in breast reconstruction. Plast Reconstr Surg 104:1662–1665, 1999.

Elliott LF: Options for donor sites for autologous tissue breast reconstruction. Clin Plast Surg 21:177–189, 1994.

Gill PS, Hunt JP, Guerra AB, et al: A 10-year retrospective review of 758 DIEP flaps for breast reconstruction. Plast Reconstr Surg 113:1153–1160, 2004.

Girotto JA, Schreiber J, Nahabedian MY: Breast reconstruction in the elderly: Preserving excellent quality of life. Ann Plast Surg 50:572–578, 2003.

Nahabedian MY: The internal mammary artery and vein as recipient vessels for microvascular breast reconstruction: Are we burning a future bridge? Ann Plast Surg 53:311–316, 2004.

Nahabedian MY: Secondary nipple reconstruction using local flaps and AlloDerm. Plast Reconstr Surg 115:2056–2061, 2005.

Nahabedian MY: Symmetrical breast reconstruction: Analysis of secondary procedures following reconstruction with implants and with autologous tissue. Plast Reconstr Surg 115:257–260, 2005.

Nahabedian MY, Momen B, Galdino G, Manson PN: Breast reconstruction with the free TRAM or DIEP flap: Patient selection, choice of flap, and outcome. Plast Reconstr Surg 110:466–475, 2002.

Nahabedian MY, Momen B, Manson PN: Factors associated with anastomotic failure following microvascular reconstruction of the breast. Plast Reconstr Surg 114:74–82, 2004.

Nahabedian MY, Momen B, Tsangaris T: Breast reconstruction with the muscle sparing (MS-2) free TRAM and the DIEP flap: Is there a difference? Plast Reconstr Surg 115:436–444, 2005.

Spear SL, Carter ME, Schwarz K: Prophylactic mastectomy: Indications, options, and reconstructive alternatives. Plast Reconstr Surg 115:891–909, 2005.

Tebbetts JB: A system for breast implant selection based on patient tissue characteristics and implant-soft tissue dynamics. Plast Reconstr Surg 109:1396–1409, 2002.

NIPPLE–AREOLA RECONSTRUCTION

John William Little, MD, FACS

1. Should nipple–areola reconstruction be an integral part of breast reconstruction or an added option for certain patients?

It should be an integral part of the overall surgical plan for every breast reconstruction. Until a realistic nipple–areola has been added, a breast has not been reconstructed—only a breast mound. One of the key psychological benefits of breast reconstruction is relief from the daily reminder of mastectomy and its mortal implications. The more realistic the reconstruction, the more likely the relief. Nipple–areola reconstruction contributes greatly to such realism. In truth, if the majority of a surgeon's patients do not elect nipple–areola reconstruction, the results of the breast mound reconstruction probably are not very good. A previous study confirms a high correlation between the presence of a nipple–areola and the patient's overall satisfaction with breast reconstruction to a level that is statistically highly significant. In addition, the morbidity for the procedure is negligible.

2. Should nipple–areola reconstruction be performed at a second stage after primary reconstruction of the mound?

Generally, yes, if there is reasonable symmetry between the breasts at the second stage. If significant additional work will be required on the breast mound or on the contralateral breast to improve symmetry at the second stage, the nipple–areola reconstruction should be postponed to a third stage, when proper position can be more precisely determined. In such circumstances the nipple–areola typically is added in an office setting with local anesthesia alone and no additional medication. There is little justification for nipple reconstruction at the time of the initial breast mound reconstruction because exact positioning becomes very difficult. Furthermore, single-stage breast reconstruction creates an unrealistic expectation on the part of the patient and a difficult burden for any surgeon who is critical of the final result.

3. Is banking of the nipple–areola in the groin area an appropriate alternative to reconstruction if the primary cancer is located away from the nipple–areola?

No. Such banking cannot be justified on an oncologic basis in the presence of an invasive cancer. Studies in the Scandinavian literature have revealed breast cancer cells in the areola, not to mention nipple, of specimens in which the primary cancer was a significant distance from the nipple–areola. Furthermore, the cosmetic outcome of such twice-transferred composite grafts is inferior to what can be produced de novo.

4. Do options for nipple reconstruction include composite grafts from the toe or earlobe?

No. Such grafts are woefully inadequate for the purpose of nipple reconstruction. The only grafting source that is effective is a composite graft from the opposite nipple. Although this technique continues to be used by many surgeons, the overall price is a reduced and scarred opposite nipple in a woman who has already suffered the sensory and psychological assault of mastectomy. Assuming that the sharing technique results in two nipples of equal size, the final projection of the nipple pair will be less than half of what could have been achieved if the remaining nipple had been respected and matched by existing techniques.

5. What is the treatment of choice for nipple reconstruction?

Local flap. Virtually any opposite nipple can be matched by a local flap technique with a minimum of morbidity and distortion at the donor site if the proper technique is selected.

6. Is the best way to determine nipple–areola position by measurement from the other side?

Only in part. Such measurements should be made, but they are only the initial step in determining the proper final position. Measurements should be taken of the transverse midsternal line-to-nipple distance as well as the sternal notch-to-nipple distance. Then the appropriate-sized areola should be sketched around the intersection site. The surgeon–scientist then must become surgeon–artist and stand back to observe the overall impact of symmetry. Because of inherent asymmetries in nearly all final results of breast mound reconstruction, the best final position may well fall somewhat off the precise mathematic determination. The final position is an artistic compromise among various factors.

7. Are flap techniques for nipple reconstruction interchangeable and merely a matter of the surgeon's preference?

No. Some are inherently unsound in design and are not sufficiently reliable to be recommended. Others present a strict limitation to the amount of final projection.

8. What type of nipple reconstruction is inherently unreliable?

Reconstruction based on a central subcutaneous pedicle without dermal continuity, such as the quadrapod design. Although such techniques may give impressive results in the operating room and in the immediate postoperative period, long-term projection is unreliable; far too many results suffer late loss of projection.

9. Do the best designs in nipple reconstruction allow closure of the donor site, thus avoiding the need for grafting?

No. Such designs, which include the double opposing flap and the star flap, may be excellent for matching small- or moderate-sized nipples but prove generally inadequate for larger nipples. Donor-site closure limits the amount of possible projection in designs that attempt to match opposite large nipples.

10. Is the skate flap the best design to use for matching an opposite large nipple?

Yes. The technique can be executed with or without a skin graft. However, when large dimensions are required, a skin graft invariably is required. An opposite nipple of virtually any size can be matched using this technique with proper preoperative planning (Fig. 71-1).

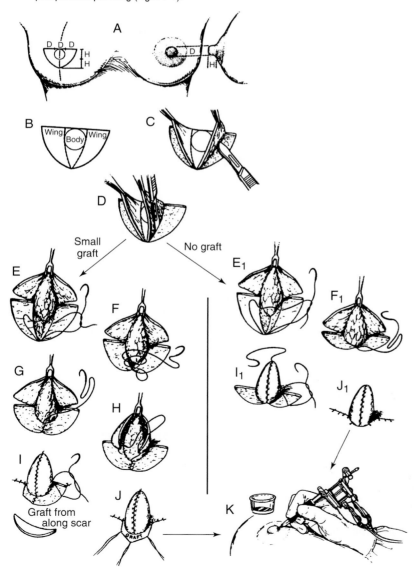

Figure 71-1. Nipple reconstruction using a skate flap. **A–D:** Flap design and elevation. *D*, Nipple diameter; *H*, height of opposite nipple when erect. **E–J:** Donor-site closure with a skin graft. E_1–J_1: Donor site closure without a skin graft. **K:** Nipple–areola tattooing. (From Little JW: Nipple-areolar reconstruction. In Cohen M [ed]: Mastery of Surgery: Plastic and Reconstructive Surgery, Vol 2. Boston, Little, Brown, 1994, p 1345, with permission.)

11. Is there a disadvantage to the use of a skin graft in the final outcome of the nipple–areola?

No, as long as the area of graft falls within the pattern of the final areola. Full-thickness skin grafts placed on an appropriate deep dermal bed are far preferable in the overall outcome of nipple–areola reconstruction than spread scars, which follow primary closure under tension.

12. Can subsequent intradermal tattoo hide spread donor-site scars after nipple reconstruction?

No. Spread scars are poor beds for the receipt of intradermal tattoo pigments and mar the final result. Well-healed full-thickness skin grafts, on the other hand, accept such pigments as well as surrounding native tissues and are not discernible within the pattern of the final areola.

13. What are the other disadvantages to spread scars after primary closure of nipple donor sites?

Final increased surface tension at the site of nipple reconstruction favors late loss of nipple projection for reasons not yet elucidated. Furthermore, tension at the site of nipple reconstruction flattens the aspect of the breast silhouette where maximal convexity is desired. Donor-site closure under tension is wrong-minded. Three strikes—you're out!

14. When using a local flap to reconstruct the missing nipple, should the dimensions of the planned nipple match those of the opposite nipple?

No. The dimensions of the reconstructed nipple should match only the diameter of the opposite nipple. Nipple height should be at least twice that of the opposite stimulated nipple. Partial loss of projection is inherent in any design for nipple reconstruction and must be factored into the final result.

15. Are some nipples too large to match by nipple reconstruction?

No. The skate technique with skin graft can match virtually any nipple size if the appropriate dimensions are used in the preoperative plan. Early in my experience with the skate technique, I documented many late results exceeding 2 and 3 cm of final projection. All of these cases required drastic reduction. A final result in nipple reconstruction that does not match the other side in projection typically represents an error in planning, with an inadequate initial design. Errors in execution or inherent local ischemia at the donor site are far less common causes.

16. Does raising the skate flap with full-thickness wings produce a better overall result?

No, not when a large nipple is being matched and a skin graft is required. Even a small amount of reticular dermis covering the donor site allows closure of the composite defect because of the suture-holding ability of the fibers. Furthermore, the final exposed bed is far more receptive for grafting than is fat.

17. Do the best results in areola reconstruction follow the grafting of skin that later becomes pigmented spontaneously?

No. Although grafting from an opposite areola undergoing reduction remains appropriate as reconstruction in kind, only occasionally is enough skin available to replace completely the missing areola. Furthermore, with the sophisticated techniques of breast mound reconstruction now available, alteration of the opposite breast is much less necessary or desirable than in the past. The transfer of skin that will become pigmented after grafting, such as from the upper inner thigh, allows no control over final coloration and matches the opposite areolar color only by chance. Furthermore, such darkened grafts invariably lose color over time, typically becoming indiscernible from surrounding breast skin within 5 to 10 years after transfer. Finally, the high morbidity rates of donor sites from such grafts cannot be justified.

18. What is the treatment of choice for areola reconstruction?

Tattoo. The only justification for grafting during areola reconstruction is to close the nipple donor site when matching a large opposite nipple. Otherwise, tattoo alone gives the best result in areola reconstruction because it allows accurate matching of both shape and surface area of the opposite areola as well as the best available color match.

19. Are coloration or tattoo techniques at the time of nipple reconstruction helpful?

No. Techniques that tattoo the nipple at the time of nipple reconstruction increase the likelihood of flap failure. Techniques that tattoo before nipple reconstruction miss the point and waste an extra stage. Location for the tattoo remains imprecise, and the opportunity for fine tuning of the ultimate result is forfeited. Finally, techniques that paint pigments beneath grafts, although imaginative, are impractical, both in terms of their unpredictability in final coloration and their reliance on otherwise unnecessary areolar grafting.

20. When is the ideal time for nipple–areola tattoo?

Generally 4 months after nipple reconstruction, when the majority of nipple shrinkage has occurred and final resolution has come to the second-stage balancing procedure. At this point final adjustments to both breast mound and nipple–areola may be carried out with minor surgery, liposuction, and tattoo.

21. Is one of the most important attributes of nipple reconstruction a centric position within the areola?

No. A far more important attribute of nipple–areola reconstruction is symmetry of the areolar color patch compared with the opposite side. If at the time of final tattoo it becomes necessary to shift the areolar pattern from a position that is concentric to the nipple, an eccentric nipple within a symmetric areola is a far better compromise than the alternative.

22. Is the best equipment for nipple–areola tattoo the delicate machinery supplied by manufacturers specializing in medical equipment?

Not necessarily. The most important attribute of tattoo equipment for nipple–areola reconstruction is sufficient torque to imbed pigments in skins of various thicknesses, such as that overlying the latissimus dorsi muscle, as well as sites that may be inherently scarred. These requirements are often very different from the characteristics of machines that imbed pigments in the delicate skin of an eyelid, for example.

23. Does nipple–areola reconstruction require a long learning curve until acceptable results can be achieved?

Not really. In truth, the earliest experiences with intradermal tattoo produce results that are superior to those available by any other means, including the transfer of grafts that later darken at random. On the other hand, matching the hue, tint, and depth of color of an opposite areola is an artistic challenge for even the experienced surgeon–tattooist. Quite naturally, the accumulation of experience aids in achieving such matched results.

24. Should the final color immediately after tattoo match the opposite nipple–areola?

No. It must be significantly darker. Hemosiderin is invariably imbedded with the tattoo earth pigments, producing a dark appearance to the proper immediate result. This initial darkness fades within the first few weeks after tattoo. The final tattoo, in turn, continues to fade slowly over the months and years ahead. Secondary tattoo, however, is especially rapid and straightforward because areolar borders are already determined. The particular patient may require a secondary boost of color, and this possibility should be discussed before the initial tattoo.

BIBLIOGRAPHY

Little JW: Nipple-areolar reconstruction. Adv Plast Reconstr Surg 3:43, 1986.

Little JW: Nipple-areolar reconstruction. In Cohen M (ed): Mastery of Surgery: Plastic and Reconstructive Surgery. Boston, Little, Brown, 1994, pp 1342–1348.

Little JW: Nipple-areolar reconstruction. In Marsh JL (ed): Current Therapy in Plastic Surgery. Philadelphia, BC Decker, 1989, pp 55–60.

Little JW: Nipple-areola reconstruction. In Spear SL, Little JW, Lippman ME, Wood WC (eds): Surgery of the Breast: Principles and Art. Philadelphia, Lippincott-Raven, 1998, pp 661–669.

Little JW: Nipple-areolar reconstruction and correction of inverted nipple. In Noone RB (ed): Plastic and Reconstructive Surgery of the Breast. Philadelphia, BC Decker, 1991, pp 467–480.

Little JW, Spear SL: Nipple-areolar reconstruction. Perspect Plast Surg 2:1, 1988.

Little JW, Spear SL: Nipple-areolar reconstruction and tattoo. In Russell RC (ed): Instructional Courses, Vol 2. St. Louis, Mosby, 1989, pp 199–207.

Spear SL, Convit R, Little JW: Intradermal tattoo as an adjunct to nipple-areolar reconstruction. Plast Reconstr Surg 83:907–911, 1989.

Wellisch DK, Schain WS, Noone RB, Little JW: The psychological contribution of nipple addition in breast reconstruction. Plast Reconstr Surg 80:699–704, 1987.

GYNECOMASTIA

Jonathan L. Le, MD; Nicolas J. Speziale, MD, FACS; and
Mary H. McGrath, MD, MPH, FACS

1. What is gynecomastia?
Gynecomastia is the excessive development of the male breasts.

2. What is the pathophysiology of gynecomastia?
Gynecomastia is caused by excess estrogen action and usually is the result of an increased estrogen-to-androgen ratio.

3. What is the histology in gynecomastia?
Gynecomastia results from variable degrees of ductal proliferation and stromal hyperplasia and can be described as *florid, intermediate*, or *fibrous*. The *florid* pattern shows ductal hyperplasia surrounded by loose cellular connective tissue. The *fibrous* pattern has extensive fibrosis of the stroma with little ductal proliferation. The *intermediate* pattern represents a transition between the florid and the fibrous types, with the fibrous type occurring with greater than 1-year duration of gynecomastia.

4. Classify the etiologies of gynecomastia.
Physiologic, pathologic, and pharmacologic.

5. In what age groups does gynecomastia occur?
Physiologic or idiopathic gynecomastia with no pathologic basis commonly develops in the newborn period, during puberty, and in old age.

6. How common is gynecomastia in each age group?
Palpable breast tissue transiently develops in more than 60% of all newborns due to exposure of transplacental estrogens. During puberty a transient imbalance between estrogen and testosterone leads to a prevalence of 50% to 60%. It usually develops during midpuberty (14 years) and is self-limited, with an average duration of 1 to 2 years. During middle age, approximately 30% to 36% of men develop gynecomastia, with the prevalence gradually increasing to greater than 70% in the seventh decade.

7. How often does gynecomastia occur bilaterally? Is one side more commonly affected?
Gynecomastia occurs bilaterally in approximately 50% to 55% of men. In unilateral gynecomastia, the right side is affected more often than the left side.

8. How does obesity correlate with gynecomastia?
Gynecomastia is increased in generalized obesity as a result of increased conversion of testosterone to estradiol in adipose tissue. In one study more than 80% of those with a body mass index (BMI) >25 had gynecomastia.

9. Are patients with gynecomastia symptomatic?
Most patients are asymptomatic. If symptoms occur, they generally include tenderness, soreness, sensitivity, and general discomfort.

10. What questions are pertinent in taking the history?
- What is the duration of the breast enlargement?
- Does the patient have any breast pain or tenderness?
- Is the patient taking any medications?
- Does the patient have any history of weight gain or loss?
- Does the patient have any history of hepatic disease or hyperthyroidism?
- Has the patient had any changes in sexual function or virilization?

Table 72-1. Laboratory Studies

PREPUBERTAL MALES	PUBERTAL MALES	ADULT MALES	
Estradiol	Estradiol	Estradiol	Thyroid function
LH/FSH	LH/FSH	LH/FSH	Hepatic function
HCG	HCG	HCG	Renal function
Adrenal CT scan	Testosterone	Testosterone	Chest x-ray

If estradiol is increased, check adrenal CT scan to rule out feminizing tumor.
If HCG is increased, check ultrasound of testes to rule out tumor.
If testosterone is low and LH/FSH are elevated, check karyotype for Klinefelter's syndrome.
CT, Computed tomography; *FSH,* follicle-stimulating hormone; *HCG,* human chorionic gonadotrophin; *LH,* luteinizing hormone.

11. What physical findings should be sought?
- *Breast:* If gynecomastia exists, thickened breast tissue should be palpable under the nipple. If a small, hard, eccentrically located mass or skin dimpling is found, suspect carcinoma.
- *Thyroid:* Assess for enlargement and nodularity.
- *Abdomen:* Examine for possible adrenal mass, hepatomegaly, or ascites.
- *Testes:* If testes appear small, consider a chromosome study. If asymmetrical, evaluate for testicular tumor with ultrasound.
- *Overall Degree of Virilization:* Look at body hair, voice, and muscles.

12. What laboratory studies should be obtained?
See Table 72-1.

13. Should routine imaging studies be ordered?
No, unless clinical signs or laboratory results dictate them. Studies may include testicular ultrasound, computed tomographic scan of the adrenals, magnetic resonance imaging of sella turcica, and mammography.

14. What are the most common causes of pathologic gynecomastia?
The most common causes include cirrhosis, malnutrition, hypogonadism, Klinefelter's syndrome, neoplasms, renal disease, hyperthyroidism, and hypothyroidism.

15. Which tumors may lead to gynecomastia?
Testicular tumors (Leydig cell and Sertoli cell tumors, choriocarcinomas), adrenal tumors, pituitary adenomas, and lung carcinomas.

16. Does gynecomastia ever resolve?
- During puberty, gynecomastia often regresses spontaneously within 2 years.
- Withdrawal of the offending medication leads to regression in drug-related cases.
- Gynecomastia of long duration is unlikely to regress spontaneously.

17. What is the differential diagnosis?
Gynecomastia, pseudogynecomastia, breast carcinoma, diabetic mastopathy, lipoma, and leiomyoma.

18. Which drugs may cause gynecomastia?
See Table 72-2.

19. What is pseudogynecomastia?
Pseudogynecomastia is an increase in male breast size that results from fat deposition. There is no hyperplasia of breast tissue, and involvement is bilateral.

20. Is there any relationship between gynecomastia and breast cancer in adult males?
No, except in Klinefelter's syndrome, in which the incidence of mammary carcinoma is 20 to 60 times greater than in men without the chromosomal aberration. Multiple studies have shown no increased incidence of breast cancer in men with gynecomastia.

21. What is the role of medical therapy?
Testosterone can be effective in the treatment of gynecomastia secondary to testicular failure. Tamoxifen has been shown to reduce gynecomastia in middle-aged men. Danazol acts as a gonadotrophin inhibitor, reducing both the pain and extent of gynecomastia.

Table 72-2. Drugs That May Cause Gynecomastia

DRUG CLASS	DRUG
Antiandrogens	Flutamide, finasteride, cyproterone acetate
Antibiotics	Ethionamide, isoniazid, ketoconazole, metronidazole
Antiulcer drugs	Cimetidine, ranitidine, omeprazole
Cancer drugs	Alkylating agents, methotrexate, vincristine, busulfan, imatinib
Cardiovascular drugs	Amiodarone, amlodipine, captopril, digitalis, digitoxin, diltiazem, enalapril, methyldopa, nifedipine, spironolactone, verapamil
Drugs of abuse	Alcohol, amphetamines, heroine, marijuana, methadone
Hormones	Androgens, anabolic steroids, human chorionic gonadotrophin, estrogens, diethylstilbestrol, growth hormones, oral contraceptives
Other drugs	Diazepam, haloperidol, risperidone, theophylline, Lasix, melatonin, phenytoin

22. What is the role of radiation therapy?

Low-dose x-ray and electron irradiation has been used successfully as a prophylactic therapy for prevention of gynecomastia in patients scheduled to receive hormone therapy for prostate cancer. Frequency of gynecomastia was reduced from 67% to 28% with 12- to 15-Gy electrons.

23. What are the indications for surgery?

- Symptomatic patients
- Adolescent males with enlargement persisting for 18 to 24 months
- Gynecomastia of long duration leading to fibrosis
- Patients at risk for carcinoma (e.g., those with Klinefelter's syndrome)

24. Describe the surgical classification of gynecomastia.

- *Grade 1:* Small visible breast enlargement without ptosis
- *Grade 2A:* Moderate breast enlargement without ptosis
- *Grade 2B:* Moderate breast enlargement with grade 1 ptosis
- *Grade 3:* Marked breast enlargement and grade 2 or 3 ptosis

25. Discuss the surgical techniques used for gynecomastia.

- *Mild to moderate gynecomastia* can be treated by either suction-assisted lipectomy (SAL) or ultrasound-assisted liposuction (UAL), or by direct excision through either a semicircular incision along the inferior aspect of the areola or a transverse incision in the apex of the axilla (Fig. 72-1).

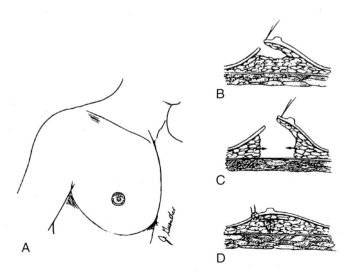

Figure 72-1. A, B, Mastectomy for gynecomastia through a semicircular intraareolar incision. **C, D,** Resection of cone-shaped mass of breast tissue tapering away at periphery with sufficient fat left on pectoral fascia. (From McGrath MH: Gynecomastia. In Jurkiewicz MJ, Krizek TJ, Mathes SJ, Ariyan S [eds]: Plastic Surgery: Principles and Practice. St. Louis, Mosby, 1990, p 1128.)

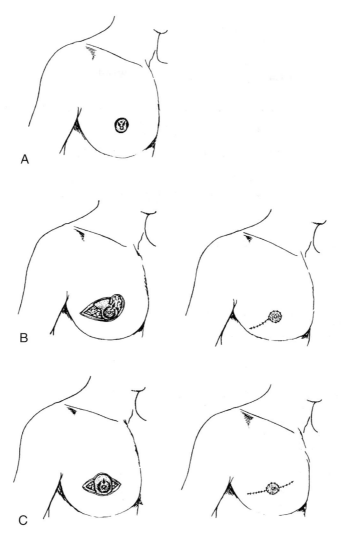

Figure 72-2. Operations for reduction of moderate to large breasts with nipple transposition or reduction and transposition of periareolar skin around stationary nipple. **A,** Superior periareolar incision with skin excision. **B,** Nipple transposition on single dermal pedicle with oblique breast scar. **C,** Nipple transposition on vertical dermal bipedicle with transverse breast scar. (From McGrath MH: Gynecomastia. In Jurkiewicz MJ, Krizek TJ, Mathes SJ, Ariyan S [eds]: Plastic Surgery: Principles and Practice. St. Louis, Mosby, 1990, p 1130.)

- *Moderate to large gynecomastia* requires skin resection and nipple transposition. After the skin is resected, the nipple–areola complex is rotated superiorly and medially based on a single dermal pedicle. Some surgeons elect to perform only SAL or UAL with a delayed skin excision (usually 6 to 9 months) based on skin retraction (Fig. 72-2).
- *Massive gynecomastia* requires en bloc resection of excessive skin and breast tissue. Free nipple grafting can be performed. The final scar is placed within the inframammary crease using a cresenteric transverse incision. The nipple–areola graft is then placed on the dermis overlying the fifth rib (Fig. 72-3).

26. What are the most common complications after surgery?

Hematoma and seroma formation are common secondary to extensive soft tissue dissection through a small incision with a substantial dead space. Good hemostasis and placement of a drain may be helpful. Evacuate any hematomas that may occur. Other less common complications include infection and nipple slough. Late complications include unequal breast size and contour irregularities.

27. Which techniques may prevent unwanted results?

- Be sure to leave an adequate layer of subcutaneous fat over the pectoralis fascia to prevent a concave breast.
- Perform liposuction to produce a smooth contour peripherally.
- Leave a 1-cm-thick layer of tissue beneath the areola to avoid nipple inversion.

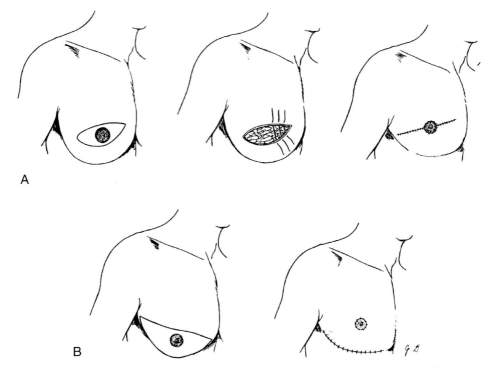

Figure 72-3. Operation for excessively large breasts with radical excision and free transplantation of nipple. **A,** Grafting of nipple onto dermal bed prepared in center of breast scar. **B,** En bloc excision with nipple grafting and inframammary crease scar. (From McGrath MH: Gynecomastia. In Jurkiewicz MJ, Krizek TJ, Mathes SJ, Ariyan S [eds]: Plastic Surgery: Principles and Practice. St. Louis, Mosby, 1990, p 1132.)

BIBLIOGRAPHY

Baraunstein GD: Gynecomastia. N Engl J Med 328:490–495, 1995.

Bembo SA, Carlson HE: Gynecomastia: Its features, and when and how to treat it. Cleve Clin J Med 71:511–517, 2004.

McGrath MH: Gynecomastia. In Jurkiewicz MJ, Krizek T, Mathes SJ, Ariyan S (eds): Plastic Surgery: Principles and Practice. St. Louis, Mosby, 1990, pp 1119–1136.

Rohrich RJ, Ha RY, Kenkel JM, Adams WP: Classification and management of gynecomastia: Defining the role of ultrasound-assisted liposuction. Plast Reconstr Surg 111:909–923, 2003.

Vetto JT: Breast disease in males. In Jatoi I (ed): Manual of Breast Diseases. Philadelphia, Lippincott Williams & Wilkins, 2002, pp 417–430.

Wise GJ, Roorda AK, Kalter R: Male breast disease. J Am Coll Surg 200:255–269, 2005.

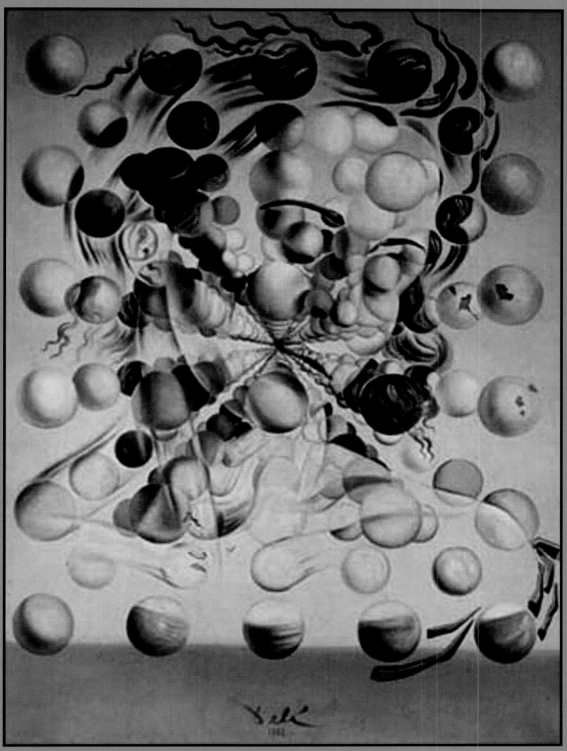

Portrait of Gala in Spheres. Salvador Dali, 1952. Oil on canvas. Private Collection, New York. © 1998 Demart Pro Arte B.V.®, Geneva/Artists' Rights Society (ARS), New York.

EVALUATION OF THE AGING FACE

CHAPTER 73

Jack A. Friedland, MD, FACS, and
Terry R. Maffi, MD, FACS

1. Give examples of trigger events that may cause a person to seek consultation for aesthetic facial rejuvenation.
- Observation of a friend who has undergone facial rejuvenative surgery with good results.
- Self-criticism and realization of signs of aging in the face, eyes, and neck.
- Realization of a need for self-enhancement that may pave the way for career advancement.
- Realization of the need for self-enhancement to keep competitive in the work environment.
- Realization that a social relationship with a younger person would be enhanced by a more youthful appearance.

2. What elements compose the initial aesthetic facial surgery consultation?
- Evaluation and discussion of the patient's desires as well as current and past medical history.
- Thorough physical examination, which is best done with the patient comfortably seated in front of a large mirror with appropriate lighting. In addition, a reversing mirror can be used to demonstrate to the patient his/her actual appearance rather than the image that he/she sees in a standard mirror.
- Consideration of appropriate laboratory and radiographic tests to determine general health status. If a specific medical problem becomes apparent, consultation with the patient's physician should be done.
- Visual examination, including acuity, Schirmer test (if indicated), and visual fields (if indicated).
- Photographic documentation of preoperative status.
- Patient education:
  - Videotapes
  - Instructional brochures
  - Discussion of arrangements for surgery with office staff (patient coordinator, nurse, secretary)

3. What factors contribute to the aged appearance of the face?
- Atrophy and loss of skin tone due to sun damage
- Genetic inheritance
- Chronic smoking of cigarettes
- Chronic abuse of alcohol
- Large gains or losses in weight
- Morphologic changes of the facial bones
- Health-related problems
- Emotional stress
- History of trauma
- Chronic facial muscular contractions
- Environmental damage due to excessive sun exposure and pollution

4. What intrinsic changes of the skin may be seen in the aging face?
- Loss of elasticity
- Keratoses, epitheliomas, other hyperpigmented lesions
- Fine lines and wrinkles
- Decreased amount of subcutaneous adipose tissue due to atrophy
- Abnormal pigmentation
- Environmental damage

5. Outline the chronologic appearance of signs of aging in the face and neck.
- *Decade of the 30s:* Upper eyelid skin becomes redundant; crow's feet form lateral to the canthi.
- *Decade of the 40s:* Nasolabial folds become more prominent; transverse forehead furrows and vertical glabellar frown lines develop.
- *Decade of the 50s:* Rhytids develop in the neck; jawline becomes less distinct; jowls form; tip of nose droops.
- *Decades of the 60s, 70s, and 80s:* Cutaneous and subcutaneous tissues atrophy, contributing to formation of increased wrinkles and sagging of skin (Fig. 73-1).

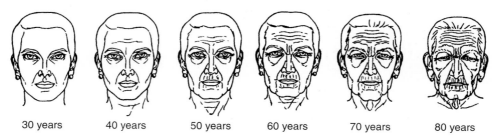

| 30 years | 40 years | 50 years | 60 years | 70 years | 80 years |

Figure 73-1. Changes observed in the external appearance of the aging face. (From Gonzalez-Ulloa M, Flores ES: Senility of the face: Basic study to understand its causes and effects. Plast Reconstr Surg 36:239, 1965, with permission.)

6. What changes in the facial skeleton occur with aging?
- Decreased height of mid and lower portions of face
- Increased prominence of frontal sinus
- Increased prominence of zygomatic arch
- Slight increase in facial width
- Increased prominence of chin
- Increased facial depth

7. Which anatomic structures of the face are vital to know when planning facial rejuvenation surgery?
It is extremely important to know the osteocutaneous and musculocutaneous ligaments that provide support to the soft tissue and skin of the face. It is essential that these be released or modified during facial rejuvenation surgery (i.e., face lift) to achieve optimal results.

8. Which retaining ligaments provide support to the soft tissues and skin of the face over the bony skeleton?
- Zygomatic osteocutaneous ligaments
- Mandibular osteocutaneous ligaments
- Platysma-auricular ligaments
- Anterior platysma-cutaneous ligaments

The most important of these are the zygomatic and mandibular ligaments (Fig. 73-2).

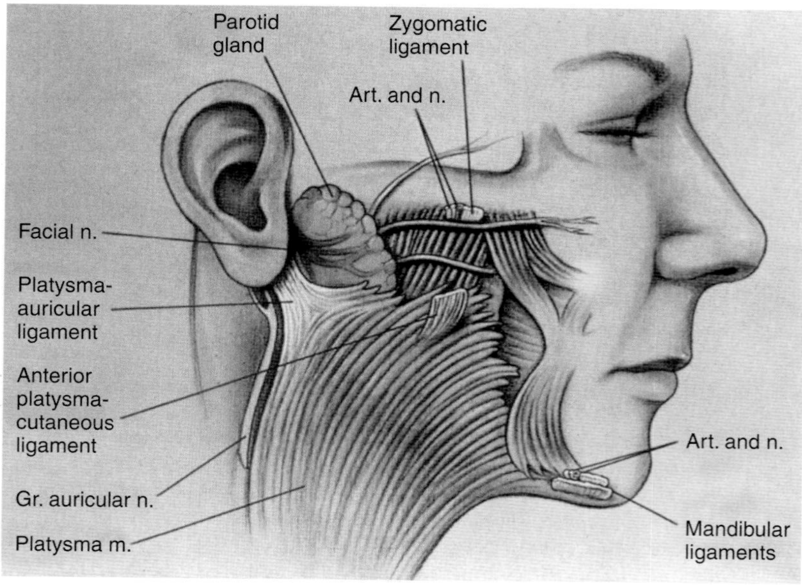

Figure 73-2. Retaining ligaments of the cheek that must be divided for proper skin drapage. Zygomatic ligament (McGregor's patch) and mandibular ligaments tether the skin to the facial skeleton. The platysma-auricular ligament and the anterior cutaneous ligaments are condensations of platysma fascia that extend to the dermis. (From Furnas DW: The retaining ligaments of the cheek. Plast Reconstr Surg 83:11, 1989, with permission.)

9. What signs of facial aging are correctable by aesthetic rejuvenative surgery?

- Sag and laxity of the skin of the cheeks and neck
- Prominence of the nasolabial folds
- Deepening of the nasolabial and perioral commissural creases
- Formation of jowls with laxity and sag of the facial skin over the border of the mandible, causing the jawline to become less distinct
- Formation of rhytids in various areas of the face
- Atrophy of the skin and subcutaneous adipose tissues
- Ptosis of the soft tissues of the anterior aspect of the chin (Fig. 73-3)

10. What signs noted on physical examination of the forehead can be corrected by aesthetic facial rejuvenative surgery?

- Transverse furrows
- Vertical glabellar frown lines
- Ptosis of the brows
- Fullness and hooding of the upper eyelids
- Fullness in the glabellar region
- Transverse creases over the dorsum of the nose in the area of the radix
- Crow's feet

11. What is the normal or ideal position for the female eyebrow?

- The brow is located approximately 1 cm above the superior orbital rim (whereas it lies approximately at the level of the rim in men).
- The medial aspect of the brow is delineated by a vertical line drawn superiorly and perpendicular through the alar base.
- The lateral aspect of the eyebrow is delineated by an oblique line drawn from the lateral aspect of the alar base through the lateral canthus.
- The medial and lateral ends of the brow are at approximately the same horizontal level. The highest portion or apex of the brow is delineated by a vertical line extending superiorly from the lateral aspect of the corneal limbus (Fig. 73-4).

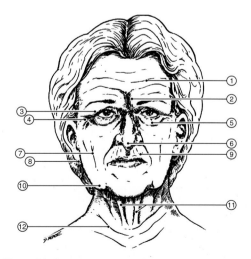

Figure 73-3. Stigmata of the aging face. Common findings include *(1)* ptotic and wrinkled brow, *(2)* glabellar laxity and frown lines, *(3)* ptotic eyebrows, *(4)* periorbital folds and lids, *(5)* redundant lower eyelid skin, *(6)* droopy nasal tip, *(7)* laxity of cheeks, *(8)* ptotic earlobes, *(9)* perioral wrinkling, *(10)* jowls, *(11)* platysmal bands, and *(12)* laxity of cervical skin. The possible combinations are infinite, and each patient must be carefully analyzed to formulate a treatment plan. (From Baker TJ, Gordon HL, Stuzin JM: Surgical Rejuvenation of the Face. St. Louis, Mosby, 1995.)

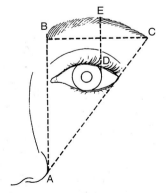

Figure 73-4. Spatial relationships of the ideal female eyebrow. (From Ellenbogen R: Transcoronal eyebrow lift with concomitant upper blepharoplasty. Plast Reconstr Surg 71:490, 1983, with permission.)

12. What signs of aging in eyelids are correctable by aesthetic rejuvenative surgery?
- Increased amount and laxity of skin of the lids
- Increased protrusion of periorbital fat
- Ptosis of the brows, which, along with upper eyelid skin redundancy, causes hooding
- Crow's feet, or rhytids, in the lateral canthal region
- Ptosis of the lacrimal glands
- Formation of xanthelasma
- Hypotonicity and horizontal laxity of the lower lids

13. Is an ophthalmologic consultation required for all patients before undergoing aesthetic rejuvenation of the eyelids?
No, unless the patient is found to have a previously unknown defect in visual acuity or tear production or physical examination reveals an anatomic deformity that may require further ophthalmologic testing or treatment. A baseline vision examination should be performed in your office preoperatively.

14. What signs of aging in external ears can be corrected by aesthetic rejuvenation?
- Increased prominence due to an increase in the conchoscaphoid angle and/or unfurling of the antihelix
- Increased size of the earlobes
- Increased size of pierced earlobe holes due to chronic wearing of heavy earrings

15. What signs of aging of the nose are correctable by aesthetic rejuvenative surgery?
- Drooping nasal tip or decrease in the nasolabial angle
- Thickening of the skin of the nose
- Enlargement and thickening of alar cartilages
- Elongation of the nose
- Widening of the nostrils (Fig. 73-5)

16. What signs of aging in the perioral region can be corrected by surgical rejuvenation?
- Vertical rhytids extending from the vermilion borders of the upper and lower lips
- Increased vertical height of the white portion of the upper lip
- Flattening of the contour of the upper lip
- Thinning and decreased fullness of the vermilion of the upper and lower lips
- Downturning of the lateral oral commissures
- Appearance and deepening of "marionette" lines

17. What signs of aging in the neck can be corrected by aesthetic rejuvenation?
- Wrinkling of the skin
- Formation of vertical bands in the platysma muscle
- Formation of a less acute and more obtuse cervicomental angle (due to laxity of the platysma and/or excessive deposition of subcutaneous and subplatysmal adipose tissue)
- Laxity and sag of the submental and anterior and lateral cervical skin
- Ptosis of the submandibular glands

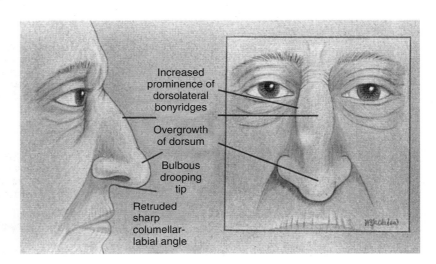

Increased prominence of dorsolateral bonyridges

Overgrowth of dorsum

Bulbous drooping tip

Retruded sharp columellar-labial angle

Figure 73-5. Signs of the aging nose. (From Gruber RP, Peck GC: Rhinoplasty: State of the Art. St. Louis, Mosby, 1993.)

18. Why are preoperative photographs necessary?
- They assist in preoperative planning and patient discussion.
- They are invaluable for reference during surgery.
- They are essential for postoperative counseling and review.
- They provide necessary medicolegal documentation.

19. What visual records are used to document preoperative appearance?
Preoperative photographs are an essential part of the patient's permanent medical record. They serve two purposes. The first is for medicolegal documentation; the second is for documentation of present status to assess postoperative results. Historically, photographs were taken with a 35-mm camera with a high-grade portrait lens (105 mm). However, in the digital age, a digital SLR camera is preferred. Note that many existing lenses will work with digital SLR cameras; however, there is usually a 1.4 or 1.5 "multiplier" effect. The digital photographs can be archived along with the patient's medical record. Several paperless systems that allow attachments to the photographs are available. Computer imaging programs can "morph" photographs in order to help predict postoperative results. Of note, this will also give the patient a "visual imprint," which may otherwise be difficult to achieve.

20. What standard views of the face and neck are taken for photographic documentation?
Anteroposterior, right lateral, right oblique, left lateral, and left oblique.

21. What additional views may be taken to demonstrate deformities?
- Close-up of the eyes to demonstrate fine lines and asymmetry of the lids
- Close-up of the eyes to demonstrate bulging of the periorbital fat in the lower lids
- Smiling profile to demonstrate change in position of the nasal tip
- "Worm's eye" view to demonstrate the basilar orientation of the inferior aspect of the nose and its relationship to the cheeks and lip
- Flexed lateral view to demonstrate laxity and sag of the skin of the lower face and neck
- Posteroanterior view to demonstrate protrusion of the ears from the side of the head (conchoscaphoid angle)
- Close-up of the mouth at rest, smiling, and puckering to demonstrate muscular function, asymmetry, and rhytids

22. Does the consultation for aesthetic facial rejuvenative surgery differ for men and women?
No. However, physical characteristics and psychological considerations may be greatly different and must be explored and adequately discussed.

23. What differences are noted between men and women in evaluating patients for aesthetic facial surgical rejuvenation?
- The position of the eyebrows is different. In women, the brow usually is located above the superior orbital rim, whereas in men it is located at or slightly below the rim.
- Different patterns of hair growth in the scalp. Men tend to have recession of the frontal forehead hairline with loss and thinning of hair much earlier in life than do women.
- The presence of a beard in men causes an increase not only in the thickness of the skin but also in the blood supply due to a richer subdermal plexus.
- Psychologic differences are evident. Active men like to be in control of all aspects of their situation and are less likely to follow postoperative instructions such as restriction of activity and taking medication. Men seem to be less demanding about the results of surgery and usually have more realistic goals.

24. As people age, is it better to "start early" and undergo procedures when signs of facial aging begin or to wait and have "everything done at once"?
As people age, the intrinsic changes in the skin and soft tissue and the changes in the facial skeleton require a corresponding increase in the complexity and number of procedures required to achieve improvement. Signs of facial aging should be addressed when they begin to appear. Early signs may be correctable with injectable products. As time progresses, particular areas, such as the eyes, chin, nose, cheeks, and forehead, can be addressed and treated to improve the patient's overall appearance.

25. What is the best age at which to undergo aesthetic facial rejuvenative surgery?
There is no one best age. The timing of surgery depends on (1) the patient's desires, (2) the patient's general health status, (3) the patient's mental health status, (4) the presence of signs of aging that the plastic surgeon believes can be surgically corrected, and (5) the patient's history of sun exposure and presence of environmental damage to the skin.

26. Is there an age at which the patient is "too old" to undergo facial rejuvenative surgery?
No, as long as the patient's general mental and physical health status are deemed satisfactory.

27. How long do the results of facial rejuvenative surgery last?

The answer depends not only on the general health status of the patient but also on the age at which the procedure is performed. Usually foreheadplasties and eyelidplasties do not need to be repeated, but facialplasties are considered to last for 8 to 10 years.

28. Where can facial rejuvenative surgery be performed?

Facial rejuvenative surgery may be performed in a hospital, in a free-standing ambulatory outpatient surgical facility, or in a physician's office. Any of these options is acceptable as long as the appropriate equipment for performance of the surgery and resuscitation is available. In addition, the necessary trained and certified medical personnel must be available.

29. What type of anesthesia is most appropriate for facial rejuvenative surgery?

The type of anesthesia depends on the procedure, the patient's general health status, and the surgeon's preference. For some procedures, local anesthetics may be sufficient. However, for the great majority of procedures, local anesthetics must be combined with intravenous sedation and analgesics. General anesthesia is used for procedures requiring complete relaxation (e.g., complete relaxation of the abdominal muscles during abdominoplasty).

30. Who may *not* be considered candidates for facial rejuvenative surgery?

- Patients who have difficulty with describing or delineating the changes they desire
- Patients who feel that their deformities are greater than they actually are
- Patients with unrealistic expectations
- Patients with severe mental or physical health problems who are poor surgical risks
- Patients who are addicted to cigarettes, alcohol, and/or drugs
- Patients with nonsupportive family members

31. Who else may not be considered good candidates for aesthetic facial rejuvenative surgery?

- Patients who are overly concerned about minimal defects
- Patients who are too demanding or direct the physician about what to do and how to do it
- Patients who constantly interrupt when explanations are given by the physician
- Patients who have previously undergone surgery by another physician with less than desirable results and are antagonistic and defensive

32. What five rare skin conditions may present as premature aging with or without skin laxity? Is facial aesthetic surgical rejuvenation indicated?

- *Ehlers-Danlos Syndrome:* Rare, genetically transmitted disease of connective tissue characterized by thin, friable, and hyperextensible skin, hypermobile joints, and subcutaneous hemorrhages. It may be associated with posttraumatic bleeding and poor wound healing. It is caused by a genetic defect with inadequate production of the enzyme lysyl oxidase. Rhytidectomy is not indicated.
- *Cutis Laxa:* Degeneration of the elastic fibers in the dermis, associated with chronic obstructive pulmonary disease, pulmonary infections, cor pulmonale, gastrointestinal and genitourinary diverticula, and hernias. The genetic defect is a deficiency of lysyl oxidase. Aesthetic facial rejuvenation is indicated and beneficial as long as the patient's general health status is satisfactory.
- *Progeria:* Rare disorder of unknown etiology, transmitted in an autosomal recessive manner and characterized by growth retardation, craniofacial disproportion, baldness, protruding ears, pinched nose, micrognathia, atherosclerotic heart disease, and shortened life span. Plastic surgery is not indicated.
- *Werner's Syndrome (Adult Progeria):* Rare autosomal recessive disorder that consists of scleroderma-like skin changes, including patchy induration associated with baldness, aged facies, hypo/hyperpigmentation, short stature, high-pitched voice, cataracts, diabetes, muscle atrophy, osteoporosis, various neoplasms, and premature atherosclerosis. Plastic surgery is not indicated because of the presence of diabetic microangiopathy.
- *Pseudoxanthoma Elasticum:* Degenerative disorder of the elastic fibers with premature skin laxity. Aesthetic facial rejuvenative surgery is beneficial.

BIBLIOGRAPHY

Baker TJ, Gordon HL, Stuzin JM: Surgical Rejuvenation of the Face. St. Louis, Mosby, 1995.

Cohen M (ed): Mastery of Plastic and Reconstructive Surgery. Boston, Little, Brown, 1994.

Connell BF: Male face lifts. Aesthet Surg J 22:385, 2002.

Georgiade GS, Georgiade NG, Riefkohl R, Barwick WJ: Textbook of Plastic, Maxillofacial and Reconstructive Surgery. Baltimore, Williams & Wilkins, 1992.

Gruber RP, Peck GC: Rhinoplasty: State of the Art. St. Louis, Mosby, 1993.

Gunter JP, Jackney FL: Clinical assessment and facial analysis. In Gunter JP, Rohrich RJ, Adams WP Jr (eds): Dallas Rhinoplasty: Nasal Surgery by the Masters. St Louis, Quality Medical Publishing, 2002, p 53.

Knize DM: An anatomically-based study of the mechanism of eyebrow ptosis. Plast Reconstr Surg 97:1321–1333, 1996.

Lewis JR (ed): The Art of Aesthetic Plastic Surgery. Boston, Little, Brown, 1989.

Mendelson BC, Muzaffar AR, Adams WP: Surgical anatomy of the midcheek and malar mounds. Plast Reconstr Surg 110:885–896, 2002.

Mos JC, Mendelson BC, Taylor GI: Surgical anatomy of the ligamentous attachments in the temple and periorbital regions. Plast Reconstr Surg 105:1475–1490, 2000.

Marten TJ: Forehead aesthetics and preoperative assessment of the foreheadplasty patient. In Knize D (ed): The Forehead and Temporal Fossa: Anatomy and Technique. Philadelphia, Lippincott Williams & Wilkins, 2001.

Rees TD, LaTrenta GS: Aesthetic Plastic Surgery. Philadelphia, WB Saunders, 1994.

Sigal RK, Poindexter BD, Weston GW, Austin HW: Rejuvenating the aged face. Perspect Plast Surg 14:1, 2000.

Singer DP, Sullivan PK: Submandibular gland I: An anatomic evaluation. Plast Reconstr Surg 112:1150–1154, 2003.

Smith JW, Aston SJ: Grabb and Smith's Plastic Surgery. Boston, Little, Brown, 1991.

FOREHEAD AND BROW LIFT

David P. Schnur, MD, and
Paul L. Schnur, MD

1. Describe the arterial and nerve supply to the forehead.

Understanding the anatomy is necessary for dissection of a forehead flap or endoscopic dissection of the brow. The forehead receives blood from both the internal and external carotid arteries. The frontal branches of the superficial temporal artery arise from the external carotid artery. The supratrochlear and supraorbital arteries arise from the internal carotid artery via the ophthalmic artery. The supraorbital and supratrochlear cutaneous nerves are derived from the ophthalmic division of the trigeminal nerve (cranial nerve V1). The supraorbital nerve exits through the supraorbital foramen to innervate the lateral part of the forehead and the front of the scalp. The supratrochlear nerve exits medial to the supraorbital nerve and supplies the middle portion of the forehead.

2. The supraorbital nerve has a deep and superficial division. Describe the course of each division and the area that it innervates.

The deep division innervates the frontoparietal scalp. It runs from the orbital rim just under the deep galeal plane toward the superior temporal line of the skull. It then runs just medial (0.5 to 1.5 cm) and parallel to the superior temporal line and then takes a medial course to enter the scalp. The superficial division of the nerve courses from the orbital rim over the frontalis muscle to enter the anterior scalp.

3. Describe the anatomy of the frontal nerve.

The frontal nerve is a branch of the facial nerve. It emerges from beneath the parotid gland on a line extending from a point 0.5 cm below the tragus to a point 1.5 cm superior to the lateral position of the eyebrow. The nerve enters the frontalis muscle on a deep surface at a point where the orbicularis oculi intersects the lateral aspect of the frontalis muscle (approximately 1.5 cm above the lateral aspect of the eyebrow).

4. What is the function of the musculi frontalis?

Eyebrow elevation. The musculi frontalis are vertically oriented, paired muscles that blend in the midline. They originate from the epicranial aponeurosis (galea) at the level of the anterior hairline, extended inferiorly to cover most of the forehead, and insert into the dermis of the forehead skin.

5. Which three facial muscles oppose the brow-lifting activity of the musculi frontalis?

Corrugator supercilii, procerus, and orbicularis oculi muscles.

6. Describe the orbital ligament and its significance in brow lifting.

The orbital ligament lies near the junction of the temporal fusion line and the orbital rim. It is a dense fibrous band that connects the superficial temporal fascia to the orbital rim. Because of the anatomic connection between the superficial temporal fascia and the overlying skin, the orbital ligament tethers the lateral eyebrow segment to the bony orbital rim and must be released to achieve an adequate lift.

7. Which muscles of the face are responsible for the deep transverse forehead lines, vertical glabellar creases, and transverse wrinkles at the root of the nose?

Frontalis, corrugator, and procerus muscles, respectively.

8. Describe Ellenbogen's criteria for the ideal eyebrow position and contour.

- The brow begins medially at a vertical line extending through the ipsilateral alar base and ipsilateral medical canthus.
- The brow ends laterally at an oblique line extending through the ipsilateral alar base and lateral canthus.
- The medial and lateral ends of the eyebrow lie at approximately the same horizontal level.
- The apex of the brow lies directly above the lateral limbus of the eye.
- The brow arches above the supraorbital rim in women and lies approximately at the level of the rim in men.

9. Which systematic approach should be used to evaluate the contour of the eyebrow?

The contour of the brow is evaluated in thirds: medial, central, and lateral. If the medial eyebrow is lower than the lateral, the patient looks angry or distressed. In contrast, a lower lateral eyebrow gives the patient a concerned or sad appearance. An excessive medial elevated eyebrow gives the patient a surprised look.

10. What are the indications for a forehead and brow lift?

Primary indications include ptosis of the forehead and eyebrows and fullness of the lateral upper lids. The forehead and brow lift also helps to correct transverse forehead lines, glabellar creases, and transverse folds at the root of the nose.

11. Where is the plane of dissection for the development of the forehead flap?

The flap for a coronal brow lift is elevated in the areolar plane between the galea and the pericranium. The other potential planes of dissection are subcutaneous or subperiosteal.

12. What is the supraciliary eyebrow lift?

It is a procedure that elevates the eyebrow by excision of skin directly above the eyebrow. This relatively simple excision produces dramatic eyebrow elevation but leaves a permanent visible scar, thus limiting its popularity. The procedure is best limited to men with thick eyebrows or women willing to accept a scar that may or may not be covered by makeup.

13. What is a midforehead lift?

This procedure helps to correct deep forehead creases and brow and glabellar ptosis. The incision is placed centrally in a prominent horizontal forehead crease to allow direct interruption of the frontalis muscle and elevation of the eyebrows (with optional excision of the medial muscles). The procedure leaves a visible scar and thus is limited to men with deep forehead creases.

14. What is a bitemporal lift?

This procedure has the advantages of elevating the lateral brow while concealing the paired incisions in the temporal hair. There is no muscle resection. It is primarily indicated for younger patients with lateral orbital hooding.

15. What is a limited incision (lateral) forehead lift?

As described by Dr. David Knize, the limited incision forehead lift selectively corrects the ptosis of the lateral segment of the eyebrow. This technique uses a 4.5- to 5-cm incision placed 1.5 to 2 cm behind the hair line. The medial aspect of the incision is just medial to the superior temporal line and is perpendicular to the tension vector that best corrects the lateral brow ptosis. Dissection is carried inferiorly just above the deep temporal fascia. Subperiostial dissection is extended for 2 cm medial to the zone of fixation, which is the confluence of the superficial and deep temporal fascias and lies just medially to the temporal fusion line. The orbital ligament must also be divided to elevate the lateral brow. Dr. Knize removes a window of deep temporal fascia at the incision to form a cicatricial bond to keep the brow elevated and sutures the superficial fascia of the inferior flap to the superior edge.

16. Before the development of the endoscope, what were the most popular techniques for forehead and brow lift?

The bicoronal and modified anterior hairline forehead lift. In the standard bicoronal lift, the incision in the frontal and temporal regions is placed far enough posteriorly so that after resection of the redundant scalp it remains approximately 5 cm behind the hairline. In the modified anterior hairline lift, the incision follows the hairline in the frontal region and then turns posteriorly in the temporal region for 7 to 9 cm before curving caudally toward the top of the ear.

17. Which factors determine the preference for a standard bicoronal or modified anterior hairline incision?

Patient choice, height of the hairline, and thickness of the hair determine which incision should be used. For patients with a normal anterior hairline and without excessive thinning of the hair, a standard coronal incision is preferred. When the anterior hairline is high, the modified incision is used.

18. What are the potential complications of a forehead and brow lift?

The incidence and severity of complications from a forehead and brow lift are quite low, and virtually all complications are apparent in the early postoperative period. Complications include hematoma, transient loss of sensation (<5% permanent loss), tightness, chronic pain, hair loss, unacceptable scars, irregularities, and skin necrosis.

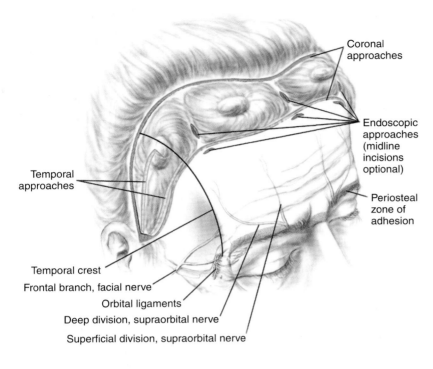

Coronal approaches

Endoscopic approaches (midline incisions optional)

Temporal approaches

Periosteal zone of adhesion

Temporal crest

Frontal branch, facial nerve

Orbital ligaments

Deep division, supraorbital nerve

Superficial division, supraorbital nerve

Figure 74-1. Anatomic considerations in brow and forehead lift: Incision options, ligaments and nerves, and zones of adhesion. (From LaTrenta GS: Surgical approaches to the forehead and brow. In LaTrenta GS: Atlas of Aesthetic Face and Neck Surgery. Philadelphia, Saunders/Elsevier, 2004, p 79.)

19. What are the major operative principles of an endoscopic forehead lift?
- Several small incisions are made within the hairline.
- An extensive subperiosteal dissection is performed to include the orbital rim and the root of the nose.
- Release and resection of the corrugator and procerus muscles.
- Preservation of the supratrochlear and supraorbital neurovascular elements.
- Forehead elevation and fixation with percutaneous microscrews or other techniques allow reattachment to bone at a higher position.

20. What are the advantages of an endoscopic forehead lift?
No scalp resection, less scarring, decreased and less permanent numbness, and less bleeding. This procedure is beneficial for patients with alopecia and permits a comfortable, fast recovery.

21. What are the disadvantages of an endoscopic forehead lift?
New training and instruments are necessary, careful patient selection is essential, deep wrinkles of the forehead and glabellar area are not completely eradicated, and correction of severe eyebrow ptosis is limited.

22. Describe several fixation techniques for the endoscopic brow lift.
These techniques include creating a bone tunnel in the outer skull cortex, Mitek bone anchors (DuPuy Mitek, Inc., Raynham, MA), small screws, fibrin glue, and the Endotine Forehead device (Coapt Systems, Inc., Palo Alto, CA) (Fig. 74-1).

BIBLIOGRAPHY

Berkowitz RL, Jacobs DI, Gorman PJ: Brow fixation with the Endotine Forehead device in endoscopic brow lift. Plast Reconstr Surg 116:1761–1770, 2005.

de la Torre JI, Vasconez LO: Brow lift, endoscopic. Available from: www.emedicine.com/plastic/topic39.htm. Accessed September 4, 2008.

Knize DM: An anatomic based study of the mechanism of brow ptosis. Plast Reconstr Surg 97:1321–1333, 1996.

Knize D: Limited-incision forehead lift for eyebrow elevation to enhance upper blepharoplasty. Plast Reconstr Surg 97:1334–1342, 1996.

LaTrenta GS: Surgical approaches to the forehead and brow. In LaTrenta GS (ed): Atlas of Aesthetic Face & Neck Surgery. Philadelphia, Saunders/Elsevier, 2004, pp 68–116.

Paul MD: The evolution of the brow lift in aesthetic plastic surgery. Plast Reconstr Surg 108:1408–1424, 2001.

Thorne CH, Steinbrech DS: Face lift and brow lift. In McCarthy JG, Galiano, RD, Boutrous, SG (eds): Current Therapy in Plastic Surgery. Philadelphia, Saunders/Elsevier, 2006, pp 273–282.

BLEPHAROPLASTY

Robert S. Flowers, MD, and
Eugene M. Smith, Jr., MD, FACS

CHAPTER 75

1. What is blepharoplasty?

Blepharoplasty comes from two Greek words: *blepharon,* meaning eyelid, and *plastikos,* meaning fit for molding. Blepharoplasty is any procedure that is performed to shape or modify the appearance of the eyelids. It may be performed purely to remove bagginess, fatty protrusions, and lax hanging skin around the eyes or to correct a "lazy" or blepharoptotic eyelid. This last procedure is more often referred to as *blepharoptosis,* or more simply a "ptosis" repair. Blepharoplasty also refers to the creation of lid creases on eyelids that have little or no visible infolding and a similar operation on eyelids with ill-defined or asymmetric folds.

Traditionally, blepharoplasty denotes the removal of skin and perhaps a sliver of muscle from the upper lids, together with protruding or excessive orbital fat. On the lower lid, blepharoplasty suggests an elevation of skin or skin-muscle flaps and removal of skin, muscle, and/or fat, or more recently the removal of a sliver of skin without raising a flap.

2. What is the difference between blepharochalasis and blepharodermatochalasis (dermatochalasis)? Between steatoblepharon and blepharoptosis?

True *blepharochalasis,* a rare inherited disorder that appears in childhood, is characterized by repetitive episodes of eyelid edema that eventually lead to attenuation and/or dehiscence of the levator aponeurosis with resultant ptosis. The periorbital tissues stretch out, and dehiscence of the canthal tendons sometimes occurs. More often blepharochalasis refers to the stretching of the skin of the eyelids associated with aging. A more accurate term for involutional loosening of the eyelid skin is *dermatochalasis.* The puffiness of fat that is either excessive or protruding through a lax septum is *steatoblepharon. Blepharoptosis* is drooping of the upper eyelid. When the eyebrow is ptotic, juxta brow skin, lid fat, together with the eyelid skin, hangs over the margin and may cause the illusion of ptosis when the eyelid occupies a normal position. The proper term for this condition is *pseudoblepharoptosis.*

3. Is blepharoplasty the procedure of choice for brightening and refreshing the eye region?

Since its inception, traditional blepharoplasty has been touted as the procedure to brighten and refresh the eye region. Commonly it fails miserably in this quest. Failure comes from five sources:

1. Misdiagnosis and/or misapplication of the procedure. Operations must address the causative factors responsible for the undesirable condition being treated. The most common cause of upper eyelid bagginess or heaviness is brow descensus, that is, a dropped or partially dropped eyebrow. The procedure of choice for correcting the resulting upper lid bagginess is a brow lift, preferable a forehead lift (coronal or endoscopic), elevating the eyebrows—*not excising the precious irreplaceable eyelid skin. In the same way that we don't operate on knees to correct a hip problem, neither should we operate on upper eyelids to solve a brow problem!* However, *sometimes* an upper eyelid blepharoplasty needs to accompany the brow elevation.
2. A surgeon will often recognize the problem as being the brow but will go ahead and do a blepharoplasty (because the patient requested it and was willing to pay for it). The *wrong* operation produces the *wrong* result and renders the surgeon liable for such misapplication.
3. Failure to recognize and correct the causative or hidden underlying factors in droopy, baggy, or wrinkled lower lids. Atonic lids with attenuated lateral canthal tendons must be tightened (and restored to proper position) to prevent severe scleral show as a result of lower lid blepharoplasty. A well-done canthopexy will often correct the appearance of redundant skin on the lower lid.
4. A misconceptualized design of blepharoplasty from the beginning, having been conceived on a static model rather than the dynamic tissues of the human face, in which everything moves in relationship to everything else (in the static model the eyebrows would not drop as a result of upper lid skin and/or tissue removal).
5. Poor patient selection.

Disclosure: The tear trough implants discussed in this chapter were designed by Robert S. Flowers, MD, and manufactured by Implantech. Currently the implants are marketed by Mentor Corporation. Dr. Flowers receives a small royalty for each pair of implants purchased.
Note: The authors retain the copyright to this chapter, which is used here with their permission.

Only in unusual adults with superb lower lid tonicity is lower lid blepharoplasty indicated *without* an accompanying effective canthopexy and/or lid shortening procedure. In all other patients the effect of lower blepharoplasty is to create vertical dystopia, drop lid posture, increase scleral show, and sadden the patient's appearance. Unfortunately, patients requesting blepharoplasty who satisfy these criteria of superb lid tonicity are few and far between.

4. What is compensated brow ptosis?

In considering the upper face, understanding the concept of compensated brow ptosis is absolutely essential. Most people presenting for blepharoplasty have a resting position of the eyebrow that is far too low for effective and/ or comfortable forward and lateral vision. It is also too low for optimal aesthetics. People remedy this situation by constant contraction of the frontalis muscle whenever the eyes are open. This muscle activation is continuous for 16 to 18 hours per day. Removal and/or invagination of overhanging eyelid tissues from the upper lids partially or totally relaxes the brow-elevating musculature, depending on how much vision-obstructing tissue was removed or displaced. Frontalis muscle activation checks the descent of the eyebrow and lid skin at a point just short of visual interference or weighty discomfort of the lids. Upper blepharoplasty (tissue excision and/or lid invagination in people with compensated brow ptosis) allows the eyebrow to position itself lower in the resting eye-open posture after surgery without visual interference or weighty discomfort, compared with the preoperative position. The usual result is an operated lid with precisely the same amount of overhang as before surgery, leading to a second or even a third redo, with yet more upper lid tissue excision. The result is a postoperative patient who looks older, more tired, and angry as well.

Only in people with an adequately high resting position of the brow in the eye closed–forehead relaxed position and little to no compensated brow ptosis is isolated upper blepharoplasty a procedure of choice for brightening and refreshing the eye region. Blepharoplasty without brow lifting can also be of benefit in people with so much overhang that they can't raise their brows enough to clear their vision. In all other situations the brow lift is either the preferred operation or an essential companion to blepharoplasty.

5. If blepharoplasty is not the procedure of choice, what is?

Coronocanthopexy is the basic foundation for aesthetic repair around the orbital region without deforming the lids, the periorbital aesthetics, or the aperture shape. This is a forehead lift with accompanying canthopexy, at the minimum securing the tendon and associated retinacular tissues into the orbital rim periosteum but preferably into the bone, with a second layer of orbicularis support. This is secured to the bone and temporalis fascia more laterally. Such an operation maintains normal healthy eyelids without sacrificing any of the precious and irreplaceable eyelid tissue. Dropped posture of the lower lids, due to attenuation of the canthal tendon and reduced lid tonicity, is commonly responsible for what appears to be excessive lower lid skin. Canthopexy restores position, tone, and the youthful upward tilt to the eye, whereas blepharoplasty (including transconjunctival fat removal) adds downward cicatricial traction to an already weakened eyelid. This lowers the lid posture and imparts a saddened appearance along with a shortened aperture length. When a secure canthopexy with long-lasting tone restoration accompanies blepharoplasty, whatever tissue is truly excessive can be removed without adversely altering the shape of the eye. Elevation and tightening of the lid also tighten the orbital septum and add restraint to bulging fat. The canthopexy can be extended into a midcheek lift with yet further improvement in outcome.

The key effect of a frontal lift is to check the brow against precipitous descent after blepharoplasty, which makes the eye look older, more tired, and angry (due to the relaxed frontalis ceasing its pull against the corrugator activity). When the eyebrow is properly positioned, the eye appearance morphs into a youthful version of the same patient. Coronocanthopexy often eliminates the need to resect lid skin. If redundant or excessive skin remains when the brow is examined preoperatively (positioning it at its estimated post browlift posture), a simple excision of skin (with or without a tiny sliver of orbicularis) just above the supratarsal crease suffices to create the desired correction. With the lateral brow properly positioned, extending the lid excisions beyond the edge of the orbital rim rarely is necessary. If excessive upper lid skin is obvious with the brow manually raised to its estimated postoperative position, such a conservative excision can then accompany the forehead lift.

6. What is the youngest age at which a patient should consider blepharoplasty?

A functional blepharoplasty is indicated sometimes within the first few weeks of life if the upper eyelids block the infant's vision, as in severe cases of congenital blepharoptosis. If one or both eyelids block the child's vision, normal visual pathways may not develop, leading to irreversible visual loss in one or both eyes. This phenomenon is called *amblyopia*. In epiblepharon, an anomaly common in young Asian children, the lower lid eyelashes are in contact with the cornea. Surgery may be required to correct this deformity. Cosmetic blepharoplasty also may be considered in children and young teenagers of Asian ancestry with heavily pseudoblepharoptotic lids, where lid folds need to be created. In general, it is preferable to wait until a person is old enough to cooperate under local anesthesia with intravenous sedation.

7. Is the preaponeurotic fat continuous with the deeper orbital fat?

Yes. The preaponeurotic fat is an important landmark during blepharoplasty and blepharoptosis surgery. It is often the first fat encountered in making an incision through the orbicularis muscle and orbital septum, but beware. In some people, especially those with sunken-in upper lids, the sling, composed of septum connecting caudally with the aponeurosis, fuses higher than expected. In these people no fat buffer zone will be encountered to help identify the vulnerable lid

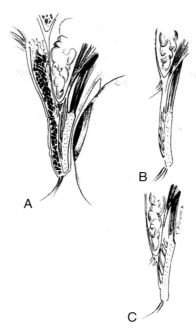

Figure 75-1. Upper eyelid anatomy. **A,** Note fusion of the levator aponeurosis and orbital septum to form the septoaponeurotic vehicle that serves as a ball-bearing mechanism for eyelid opening and closure. Sympathetically innervated Müller's muscle inserts into the superior tarsus. **B, C,** The septum and aponeurosis may fuse at variable levels in the eyelid. In Caucasians the attachment usually is higher, whereas in Asians it usually is more inferior.

opening structures. Often excessive bits of this preaponeurotic fat beg for removal during upper blepharoplasty. In the upper lid it is the *lateral* fat that is contained within this septo-aponeurotic *sling*. The *white* or *medial* fat compartment is medial to this upwardly directed sling. It is because the aponeurosis of the levator muscle is located immediately posterior to this orbital fat that it is called *preaponeurotic fat*. All of it is in continuity with the deeper orbital fat (Fig. 75-1).

8. **Is it important to remove most of the fat from the lateral or central-lateral upper eyelid during blepharoplasty?**
   No. The contrary is true. The central-lateral fat, together with its sheath, provides a "ball-bearing" mechanism for the septoaponeurotic vehicle, which serves an important function during eyelid opening and closure. Excessive or aggressive removal of central fat may produce scarring capable of interfering with lid opening and result in blepharoptosis or lagophthalmos. Most people have a deep, hollowed-out area between the medial and lateral (central-lateral) compartments in the upper orbit. Loss of fat worsens this deformity and creates excessively deep-set upper lids or a superior sulcus deformity.

9. **What structure is often mistaken for fat in the upper eyelid?**
   The lacrimal gland. Look for its grayish coloration and texture differences. Its lobular character is more compact than fat. Be careful when removing fat from the lateral portion of the upper lid. Injury to the lacrimal gland may result in dryness of the eyes and the possible need for permanent use of artificial tears and lubricating ointments. If the gland is abnormally large, it is far better to tuck the gland beneath the orbital rim with one or more sutures, anchoring its capsule to the deep periosteum, than to resect the gland itself. Know that the septoaponeurotic sling descends lower laterally, making it easier to enter at this location. However, many Caucasians and some Asians have high fusion points of the septum and aponeurosis, allowing an unwary surgeon's dissection to transect the aponeurosis and enter into Müller's muscle and conjunctiva without first encountering lateral fat.

10. **Does removal of the palpebral lobe of the lacrimal gland have any deleterious consequences? What about the orbital lobe?**
    Removal of either the palpebral or orbital lobe of the lacrimal gland may adversely affect tear secretion. The lacrimal gland is divided into the palpebral and orbital portions by the lateral horn of the levator aponeurosis. The ducts for secretion of tears travel from the orbital lobe through portions of the palpebral lobe to reach the superior lateral fornix. Therefore cutting into or removing the palpebral lobe may decrease tearing by severing ducts and interrupting the passage of tears. Injury or removal of the orbital lobe of the lacrimal gland may adversely affect the secretion of tears by eliminating secretomotor innervation to both the orbital and palpebral lobes. Resist the temptation to resect parts of the gland.

11. What is a retrobulbar hemorrhage? What are the common causes and possible consequences?

A retrobulbar hemorrhage is bleeding that occurs posterior to the orbital septum or globe in sufficient quantity to exert pressure on the globe. It may result from trauma, orbital surgery, and especially the removal of fat during blepharoplasty. It also occurs as a result of injection of anesthetic in the retroseptal space and of frontal (brow) lifting with violation of the orbital septum during dissection, allowing scalp bleeding to enter the orbit. Orbital hemorrhage is much more common in hypertensive patients, in normotensive patients with intraoperative elevation of blood pressure, and in patients who use aspirin or other medications with anticoagulant properties. The risk of retrobulbar hemorrhage can be minimized by controlling pain and blood pressure preoperatively and intraoperatively, by precisely cauterizing all fat "mesentery" and vessels before transecting them (preferably by forceps coagulation rather than Colorado needle coagulation), and by using blunt-tip needles for deep orbital anesthesia. Except in severe exophthalmos, all significant retrobulbar hemorrhage usually causes visible protrusion of the globe.

Too much pressure on the globe may lead to irreversible loss of vision. The intraocular pressure at first remains within the normal range but may increase rapidly if the cause goes untreated. Normal intraocular pressure is 10 to 22 mm Hg. Pressures of 30 to 40 mm Hg should sound an alarm and motivate the surgical team to control contributing factors immediately. Intraocular pressure greater than 40 mm Hg represents real risk of visual compromise and demands immediate treatment. Intraocular pressures approaching diastolic levels put the eye in imminent danger of vein occlusion or retinal or nerve infarction, causing severe or total loss of vision. We strongly recommend that surgeons performing blepharoplasty and other orbital surgery have tonometry devices available during surgery.

12. How is a retrobulbar hemorrhage treated?

Treatment requires prompt recognition followed by measures to decrease pressure on the globe. Prompt control of pain and blood pressure elevation are often the most pressing needs, with application of light intermittent pressure on the orbit until these factors are controlled. A blunt instrument placed into the orbit through an existing incision may allow some blood to drain. Maximal exposure and illumination are essential in attempting to identify and cauterize the offending vessel, which often cannot be located. Lateral cantholysis may be necessary to allow the orbital tissues and eyelids to bulge forward to decrease the orbital pressure transmitted to the globe. Some physicians recommend the immediate use of mannitol or acetazolamide (Diamox) to lower the intraocular pressure.

Immediately after recognizing the condition, during or after a blepharoplasty or blepharoptosis surgery, reopen the incision and orbital septum, and drain the orbit with a blunt instrument. Monitor progress by taking tonometry readings. Another technique involves using a hemostat to create an opening in the orbital floor to decompress the orbit emergently. This technique is rarely indicated unless all other maneuvers fail. Anterior chamber decompression is not indicated.

13. What are the advantages and disadvantages of a transconjunctival blepharoplasty?

Transconjunctival incisions are useful lower eyelid surgical approaches when only fat (steatoblepharon) removal or orbital septum tightening with little or no removal of skin (minimal dermatochalasis) is required. Resultant scarring still exerts downward traction on the lower lid, although typically less than with skin or skin-muscle flap approaches. The incisions are within the lower conjunctival sac, going through the lower lid retractors to gain access to the lower eyelid fat. One clear advantage is the absence of visible external incisions, but conjunctival hemorrhage is commonly greater and hinders cosmetic concealment. Disadvantages include occasional difficulty in locating the proper tissue planes to identify the fat in respective compartments; inability to reduce lower eyelid skin; inability to tighten lower eyelid laxity, which usually is present; increased risk of injury to the inferior oblique muscle by inexperienced probing; and postoperative downward lid traction that can be both profound and surprising. Also, when the fatty bulge is eliminated, excessive skin will cause visible redundancy.

14. What effect does blepharoplasty or tissue removal from the upper eyelid have on the position of the eyebrows?

Most people requesting upper eyelid surgery have significant compensated eyebrow ptosis, that is, they must contract the frontalis muscle to effect comfortable, unobstructed forward and lateral vision. A clue to this condition may be transverse forehead creasing or corrugation, but young people and other individuals with lots of subcutaneous padding may telescope the skin when the frontalis muscle contracts and show no transverse wrinkling. In all people with *compensated* brow ptosis, the brow posture drops after upper blepharoplasty. Patients themselves often fail to see it because they automatically and subconsciously raise their brows and tilt their head backward when looking in a mirror, when facing a camera, or when under careful scrutiny. Therefore, all patients require a careful preoperative evaluation that compares the eye-closed, head vertical, and nontilted brow in a relaxed resting *(uncompensated)* position with the corresponding eye-open *compensated* elevated brow position. Full relaxation of the brow usually is best achieved with the eyes closed. The position of the eyebrows with the eyes closed and the forehead relaxed is the position toward which the eyebrows will drop after an upper lid blepharoplasty when no concurrent procedure is performed to secure proper eyebrow position, thereby preventing significant brow descensus.

15. Does lower lid skin or skin-muscle resection change the shape of the eye? If so, how?

Resection of even a small or conservative amount of lower eyelid skin in the presence of a lax lower lid will result in aesthetically unpleasing results. Skin resection in the setting of lower eyelid laxity results in a rounded lower eyelid with increased scleral show (especially laterally), directly mirroring the triangular section of skin typically removed.

This altered shape of the lower eyelid gives the patient a sadder and more tired appearance. Significant corneal and conjunctival exposure with characteristic symptoms typically accompanies lower eyelid retraction with vertical dystopia. True ectropion may occur if laxity of the lower eyelids is not addressed before or during lower eyelid blepharoplasty by some meaningful canthopexy procedure. The best approach is a secure two-layer canthopexy, even better when combined with a midcheek lift (referred to as optimaplasty or Mag 5). Good canthopexies allow more lower lid tissue resection, especially when combined with midcheek lifting, but remember that few periosteal canthopexies have long-lasting results. Significantly undercorrect skin excess when canthopexy support is limited to the periosteum.

16. What are the most common causes of postoperative eyelid ptosis?

The most common cause of postoperative ptosis is undiagnosed preoperative ptosis. Ptosis (blepharoptosis) describes a drooping of the upper eyelid. In a patient undergoing cosmetic or functional blepharoplasty, the type of ptosis most commonly encountered is due to brow ptosis, usually asymmetrically. The weight of the brow on the lower side results in ptosis, or a greater ptosis than on the less ptotic brow side. The more blepharoptotic upper eyelid usually is on the same side as the lower eyebrow. Half of these ptotic lids correct with effective brow elevation. This can be demonstrated manually preoperatively. After traditional blepharoplasty the preexisting ptosis usually is exaggerated during the first 4 to 8 weeks postoperatively. This is because edema adds weight to the lid, which exaggerates the ptosis. The next most commonly encountered ptosis is due to dehiscence of the levator aponeurosis. Another common, but operative, cause of ptosis is accidental separation of the levator aponeurosis when the orbicularis is lifted and resected. Other causes include cicatricial restriction of lid opening and closing, usually as a result of previous surgeries; excessive tissue dissection via an upper lid incision, such as corrugator muscle removal; excessive tissue removal (especially fat); hemorrhage within the surgical field; and/or inflammation.

17. How is blepharoptosis categorized?

Congenital ptosis is present at the time of birth, whereas *acquired ptosis* occurs after birth. These broad categories can be divided into additional types based on the specific etiology. Various terms describing both congenital and acquired varieties include dysmyogenic, myogenic, neurogenic, involutional (or senile), aponeurotic, traumatic, cicatricial, mechanical, and structural. Many of these descriptive classifications overlap; a disease process may fit under more than one category.

Myogenic (dysmyogenic) blepharoptosis, the most common congenital type, results from dysgenesis or faulty development of the levator muscle. Much of the striated muscle is replaced with fibrous tissue and sometimes fat, resulting in limited contractile ability and capacity to relax. A child with congenital myogenic ptosis may have unilateral or bilateral involvement with decreased ability to open and close the eyes. Examples of acquired myogenic ptosis include muscular diseases, such as muscular dystrophy, oculopharyngeal dystrophy, or chronic progressive external ophthalmoplegia (CPEO), and orbital trauma with muscle injury.

Neurogenic blepharoptosis results from faulty innervation of the upper lid retractors. Ptosis is profound with complete interruption of innervation to the levator muscle (through the superior division of the oculomotor nerve) and subtle with interruption of the sympathetic innervation to the superior tarsal (Müller's) muscle. One example of congenital or acquired neurogenic ptosis is Horner's syndrome with sympathetic disruption, resulting in miosis, anhidrosis of the skin, and mild blepharoptosis.

Mechanical or *traumatic blepharoptosis* may result from any condition that interferes with the levator muscle or its innervation.

18. What is the treatment of postsurgical lagophthalmos?

Postsurgical lagophthalmos (inability to close the eyelids completely or to cover the globe adequately on caudal gaze) is common. It often is temporary but may be permanent. Far too much skin is commonly resected with upper blepharoplasty; as a result, the patient may have skin deficiency with a temporary or permanent lagophthalmos. Usually inherent mechanisms protect against it by dropping the brow dramatically. Brow elevation surgery rarely, if ever, results in skin deficiency unless the patient had previous (typically excessive) lid skin resection(s). Local anesthesia and swelling contribute to ptosis in the immediate postoperative period by blocking the orbicularis oculi more than the levator muscle. Postoperative edema of the upper lids during the first weeks after surgery commonly interferes with normal eyelid excursion as well as with blinking and may aggravate drying of the eye. We prefer to give all patients artificial tears and/or lubricating eye ointment for routine surgical aftercare. In general, 30 mm of upper lid skin is required for a normally functioning lid with a normally positioned brow; less than this amount often requires life-long use of artificial tears, lubricants, and other measures to prevent drying. (Measure from bottom of midbrow hair to eyelash margin with the eyelid under gentle stretch.)

19. What forms the supratarsal fold?

The upper eyelid supratarsal fold is also referred to as the *upper eyelid* or *supratarsal crease*. *Supratarsal* implies that the fold or crease is above the superior border of the tarsus, but this is not always the case, particularly in Asians. The crease is formed by insertions of fibrous extensions of the levator aponeurosis into the muscle and/or skin. It is beneficial to reestablish or preserve these connections during blepharoplasty so that the incision is appropriately hidden within the lid crease. It is pertinent, and of interest, that the lid always creases at a line marking the caudal extent of where the sling created by the aponeurosis and septum descends into the lid. Even with no fibrous connections into the skin, a lid fold would be created by the rotary motion of this sling, which surrounds the ball-bearing–like orbital fat. If the crease is not being recreated, you should always preserve the existing supratarsal crease, even when it seems exceptionally indistinct. Make the caudal margin of any skin excision approximately 1 mm above the supratarsal crease.

20. What is the double eyelid operation often requested by Asians or people of Asian ancestry?

Most people of East Asian ancestry, including those from China, Japan, Korea, and Southeast Asia, have a visible crease on the eyelid, at least during the first 2 or 3 decades of life. In many people they are quite well formed. In others the lid folds begin to be visible only on the central to lateral part of the eyelid. Because this fold (or crease) divides the lid into two sections (i.e., the part above and the part below the crease), the eyelids are referred to as *double.* An eyelid with no visible crease is referred to as *single.* These terms are uniformly used by most persons of East Asian ancestry. Often one eyelid is *double* and the other is *single,* or one lid fold is simply much more clearly defined than the other. Most people have an understandable desire for symmetry. The many different methods of lid fold creation fall into two groups: the *closed* or *suture technique* and the *open technique.* The senior author (R.S. Flowers) has often used a combination of the two when a conservative lid fold was desired with minimal postoperative swelling and morbidity.

In the *closed technique,* three or four tiny incisions are made at the desired level of fold creation on the external lid to allow the knot of suture to disappear into the substance of the lid, with a suture closing the skin overlying it. There are many variations to this technique. The sutures secure the lid skin to the aponeurosis (Fig. 75-2).

In the *open technique,* an incision is made across the lid. Skin and/or muscle is excised, after which the pretarsal skin flap is attached to the tarsus, the aponeurosis, or both. If the pretarsal skin height is made small, it can be attached to the conjoint tendon or the pretarsal extension of the aponeurosis. Clearing off the tarsus and tarsal attachment makes it more secure (Fig. 75-3).

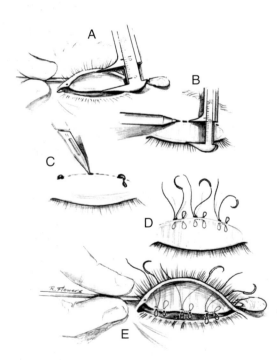

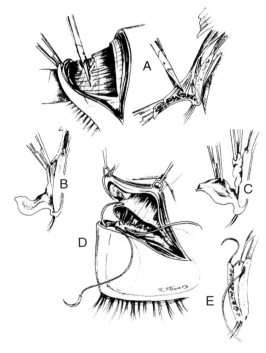

Figure 75-2. Upper eyelid crease fixation using the closed or suture technique. **A,** The vertical height of the tarsus is measured. **B,** The superior edge of the tarsus is marked on the skin. **C,** Several small incisions are made along the marked line. **D, E,** Full-thickness nonabsorbable sutures are passed through the eyelid to create eyelid crease fixation at the superior edge of the tarsus. (From Flowers RS: Upper blepharoplasty by eyelid invagination: Anchor blepharoplasty. Clin Plast Surg 20:193–207, 1993, with permission.)

Figure 75-3. Open technique of upper eyelid crease fixation. **A,** The orbital septum is opened, and the pretarsal extension of the aponeurosis is dissected free from the pretarsal orbicularis. **B, C,** Pretarsal portions of the eyelid are debulked if needed. **D, E,** The inferior cut edge of the aponeurosis is secured to the edge of the pretarsal skin and the superior anterior tarsus using absorbable buried sutures. (From Flowers RS: Upper blepharoplasty by eyelid invagination: Anchor blepharoplasty. Clin Plast Surg 20:193–207, 1993, with permission.)

In the *combination technique,* skin, with or without a sliver of muscle, is removed just above the level of suture creation of the lid fold. The lid sutures are placed through the open portion of the lid, and no additional small incisions are necessary on the lid. The sutures pull the pretarsal tissue to the tarsus and secure it there.

A conservative *medial epicanthoplasty* is helpful in achieving a long aperture and avoiding the appearance of esotropia and/or telecanthus. It also assists in creating a lid crease that originates outside or just above the remaining small epicanthus and looks maximally normal.

21. Where is the peripheral arterial arcade of the eyelid located?

The peripheral arterial arcade is located superior to the tarsus between the levator aponeurosis and Müller's muscle. Many of these little arteries are within the substance of Müller's muscle where it inserts into the tarsus. Great care must be taken when placing sutures into the cephalad margins of the tarsus to avoid these vessels. Puncture leads to hemorrhage into Müller's muscle, which occasionally causes lid ptosis that may persist for 2 or 3 months after surgery.

An arcade is also located in the lower eyelid between the inferior tarsal muscle and lower eyelid retractors. These peripheral arcades anastomose with the marginal arcades, which are located near the lid margins of both upper and lower eyelids. The marginal and peripheral arterial arcades serve as points of anastomosis between the internal and external carotid systems. These arcades receive contributions from the angular artery, which is a branch of the facial artery from the external carotid system, and from the terminal portions of the orbital artery, which arises from the internal carotid system.

22. When is a coronal lift contraindicated?

- When simulated brow elevation feminizes the eye in men.
- When one or more previous blepharoplasties have excised too much skin from the upper eyelids. Further brow elevation will result in lagophthalmos.
- When manual elevation of the brows preoperatively reveals lid retraction with eye opening, with exposure of the upper limbus. In such cases a frontal lift should be performed only with sufficient lower lid–canthal elevation to effect lid closure of the forehead "lift" limited to corrugator resection and lateral pull. If the lagophthalmus exists with lid skin resection, then a levator-lengthening procedure is in order.
- When a deep and unattractive hollowed-out upper lid is exposed or made worse by manual brow elevation, which simulates the result of a surgical frontal lift.
- When short or small eyelid apertures (measured horizontally, medial to lateral) are present. This is particularly relevant in men. However, the ptotic brow and lid overhang commonly disguises the apertures shortness. This is much less undesirable in women who can "lengthen" their eyes with makeup.

23. When is it appropriate to resect frontalis muscle?

Rarely, if ever. Sometimes a combination of both blepharoplasty and frontal lift is required to eliminate transverse forehead wrinkling, especially when brow ptosis is profound and dermatochalasis or pseudoblepharoptosis of the eyelid is advanced. Often, blepharoplasty (upper) alone or coronal lift alone (or endoscopic) causes the transverse creases to disappear.

24. Why does the medial brow commonly drop after blepharoplasty and/or elevation of the lateral brow?

The frontalis muscle inserts more effectively and consistently into the medial brow than into the lateral brow. When most people raise their eyebrows, the medial end elevates more than the lateral brow does. The need to clear up the residual lateral tissue overhang drives the frontalis contraction, causing overcorrection of the medial brow to adequately clear the lateral upper lid and/or juxtabrow tissue overhang. When lateral overhang is cleared by either blepharoplasty or lateral brow elevation (via direct excision or frontal lift), the medial brow will always drop. The cause is frontalis muscle relaxation, and it is almost always beneficial to the brow component of facial aesthetics. A negative aspect is that frontalis relaxation eliminates antagonistic pull against the corrugator, resulting in corrugator frown exaggeration.

25. How do you plan a medial epicanthoplasty?

Prominent epicanthal folds are common in many people, particularly Asians. These little canopies covering the medial apertures are best corrected with a small W-shaped incision, with the wide part of the W facing laterally and the small part facing medially. The middle point of the W should be level with and point directly to the medial canthus. Placing the central point of the W 0.5 mm lateral to the desired medial extent of the aperture. After completion of the design, excision of small skin triangles from the wings of the W follows, often joined centrally by a 1- to 2-mm connecting bridge. Closure is with interrupted 6–0 monofilament sutures on a tapered needle rather than a cutting one. This is an excellent technique for removing small or large epicanthal folds, which are common to all races. We believe that the most effective approach to epicanthal folds is the Flowers modification of the Uchida "split V-W" epicanthoplasty (Fig. 75-4).

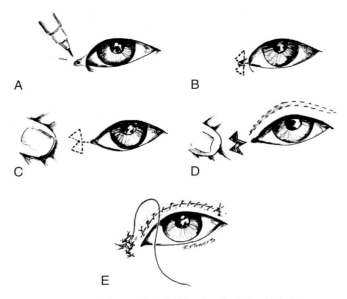

Figure 75-4. Medial epicanthoplasty. Flowers' modification of the Uchida epicanthoplasty, which often accompanies the anchor procedure in patients of Asian ancestry. **A,** The central point of the W is marked 0.5 to 1 mm lateral to the desired medial exposure of the inner canthus. **B,** The W is drawn, varying in size with the prominence of the epicanthal fold. **C,** The two triangles are excised, often with a 1- to 3-mm skin bridge between them. **D,** The V is split down toward the medial canthus. **E,** The angles formed are sutured into the wing of the W with seven tiny sutures. Note that the upper arm of the W stays well above the medial extension of the lid fold incision to avoid a deforming band of contracture and a medial lid fold that is too high. Sometimes muscle and fibrous tissues contribute to the epicanthal fold and require transection before closure. The triangular flaps sometimes must be further shortened. (From Flowers RS: Upper blepharoplasty by eyelid invagination: Anchor blepharoplasty. Clin Plast Surg 20:193–207, 1993, with permission.)

26. How do you avoid lash or lid eversion and areas of lid retraction associated with invagination or "double eyelid" blepharoplasty?

First of all, understand that a prominent globe predisposes toward lash eversion and lid retraction. In performing an invagination blepharoplasty, the surgeon must take care not to attach the pretarsal skin segment under excessive tension when anchoring it to the tarsus and/or aponeurosis. Tension on the pretarsal skin causes the eyelashes to evert or turn upward, giving an abnormal "surprised" appearance whether the procedure is done in Asians or Caucasians. Tension on the pretarsal skin can be adjusted by changing the level at which the skin is anchored on the tarsus (the tarsal attachment of the pretarsal skin "checks" against lash eversion). Careful measurements of the height of the tarsus and the amount of skin for resection during blepharoplasty should be part of the preoperative assessment. To avoid retraction, make sure that the septum is opened with scissors angled slightly cephalad, leaving a small tuft of septum attached to the aponeurosis to lengthen it if necessary. Another way to lengthen the aponeurosis is by making diagonal fingers in the aponeurosis, rotating them downward. This can lengthen the aponeurosis up to 4 mm. In most normal adults a minimum of 30 mm of skin between the eyebrow and eyelashes should remain to allow attractive lid contour and normal function. With the brow in its relaxed position, the amount of excessive skin overhang obscuring the pretarsal lid multiplied by two gives an approximation of how much skin needs to be removed. From 1.5 to 2 mm should be added to that pretarsal measurement to allow for the tightly stretched skin and its "U turn" heading back up to the attachment point of invagination.

27. Are wedge resections and tarsal strip canthopexies recommended procedures for tightening the lower lid?

Various techniques are available for tightening the lower lid. Traditional wedge resections shorten the aperture but fail to correct the downward migration of muscle requiring tightening for gaping ectropions, and markedly lax and elongated lower lids. Always combine wedge resections with a well-done canthopexy to restore canthal position. The tarsal strip procedure, if done properly on carefully selected patients in these groups, can prove extremely helpful. Our preferred technique for tightening the lower lid in the vast majority of patients is a canthopexy anchoring the tendon–lateral retinacular complex of the lower eyelid into the bone, just inside the lateral orbital rim. Anchoring the retinaculum into bone results in a highly effective tightening and lateral canthal lift and positional restoration. It provides permanent and secure lateral canthopexy with superb results, which still are intact and competent 20 or more years later. Wedge resections fail to correct the commonly dropped tilt of the intercanthal axis lid while shortening the lid aperture. They also commonly result in small and "beady" eyes that are difficult, if not impossible, to correct.

28. What are the pros and cons of the endoscopic forehead lift?

The main advantage of the endoscopic forehead lift is less total scar length on the scalp, which may be of particular benefit for men or even women with various balding patterns. Another advantage is a potential for less bleeding because fewer scalp vessels are cut in the process. Usually only three to five incisions measuring 1.5 to 2.0 cm are made within the hairline for endoscopic techniques.

The disadvantages of the endoscopic forehead lift are numerous. Maximal removal of the corrugator muscles, one of the most important aspects of forehead lifting, is difficult and exceptionally time-consuming endoscopically. Because of the difficulty in identifying tissue planes, the risk of injury to important motor and sensory nerves increases. The major drawback is the repertoire of important tasks that are extremely difficult, if not impossible, endoscopically. The list includes canthopexies, especially those into the bone with its commonly accompanying second layer muscle canthopexy, as well as orbital rim, root of the nose, and glabellar ostectomies. Periosteal flaps and other anchoring devices that help secure the eyebrow into its most optimal position (especially with asymmetrically ptotic brows) generally require open approaches. The endoscopic approach also does not enjoy the advantage of the coronal incision's easy access for inserting and/or straightening nasal dorsum grafts or implants. Finally, the blind subperiosteal dissection of the endoscopic approach often leads to transection of aberrant or anomalous supraorbital and supratrochlear nerves and encourages central brow elevation and overcorrection.

An open technique allows thorough visualization of the corrugator, depressor supercilii, and procerus muscles for their modification. It also allows access to the periosteum and supraorbital cranium above the orbital rim for a whole host of other surgical possibilities, including orbital expansion, and the most secure and long-lasting canthopexy possible.

29. Are transblepharoplasty methods of corrugator muscle resection and brow elevation effective for eliminating deformity? How do they compare with other techniques?

Transblepharoplasty approaches may improve the deformity but do not compare with the effectiveness of a direct maximal excision, especially with the aid of good surgical loupes. When removal of the corrugator muscle is incomplete, other methods can be used to decrease the corrugator frown, such as repeated injections with botulinum toxin, injections of various "fillers," cutting the motor nerve to the corrugator, or placement of alloplastic implants. However, these methods compensate for an operation that failed to achieve its goal. The route to the corrugator muscles through a blepharoplasty incision not only is lengthy and somewhat tedious, but it also predisposes to deep scarring and lid deformity, such as cicatricial ptosis and/or lagophthalmos, in a significant number of patients. Precise transblepharoplasty corrugator removal is extremely difficult without causing injury to important nerves. Accurate identification of the supratrochlear nerve and its isolation from the corrugator muscle before muscle excision become quite difficult, as does the delicate removal of corrugator fibers as they weave their way anterior to the supraorbital nerve branches. Such a maneuver is easy through the open approaches.

Transblepharoplasty approaches to the orbital rim and frontal area for brow suspension offer some help but prove inadequate for the quality of repair needed. In our opinion, they are poor substitutes for open and complete removal of the corrugator muscle.

30. When is a direct excision of lower eyelid skin indicated?

Direct excision of lower eyelid skin is indicated for patients who have *true* excess rather than merely a dropped lid posture with *pseudoexcess.* Extreme care must be taken so that skin removal does not result in a pulling down or rounding of the lower eyelids. This problem always occurs *unless an effective lid support procedure or canthopexy (canthal tightening) is also performed.* Counsel all patients about the impossibility of completely removing the wrinkles of the lower eyelid, especially during smiling. Sometimes a type of resurfacing, with either laser modalities or chemical peel, may be a preferred treatment, but these too are lid skin shortening procedures, just as are skin excisions. These "resurfacing" procedures as well as most all skin excisions must be accompanied by some effective form of canthopexy if deformity is to be prevented. An advantage of resurfacing is the uniform skin shortening, which contrasts with the almost inevitable triangular-shaped surgical excision. Skin can be removed independently or as a portion of a skin-muscle flap, depending on the surgical procedure. Our preference is a short skin flap leaving a small amount of pretarsal orbicularis beneath the subciliary incision. Below that increase the flap thickness to include orbicularis. If there is no arcus marginalis and subperiosteal midcheek release, then proceed with a generous orbicularis muscle elevation in the lateral, malar, and subcanthal area. Then perform a two-layer canthal support and tightening of tendon, followed by orbicularis. Our preference is to leave the orbicularis and septum attached to each other, going deeper in the lid (deep to the orbital septum) and releasing the *arcus marginalis* at the orbital rim, continuing the dissection subperiosteally, and doing a generous malar release that divides the periosteum distally and facilitates a superb midcheek lift. A two-layer canthal tightening procedure (tendon and retinacular tissue as one layer and orbicularis as the other) follows. We usually attach the malar tuft to a small drill hole in the orbital rim with an absorbable 3–0 Vicryl suture. The orbicularis support is enhanced and broadened by several laterally placed Vicryl sutures attaching lateral orbicularis to deep temporal fascia. This has an amazing effect of eliminating the crease at the lid–cheek crease junction and diminishing the prominence of tear trough deformities. With limited undermining there usually is no need to remove more than several millimeters of lower eyelid skin.

31. What is the best method to rid a patient of the deep grooves commonly present near the junction of the eyelid and cheek skin?

Deep grooves near the junction of the eyelid and cheek are either *tear trough deformities* or *nasojugal grooves.* With tear trough deformity, the problem is primarily a bone defect. The nasojugal groove represents the muscular deficiency between the orbicularis oculi muscle and the angular head of the levator labii superioris (levator labii superioris alaeque nasi). Another contributing factor is the often tight adherence of muscle and orbital septum to the orbital rim and the arcus marginalis.

Different techniques have been used through the years. Loeb, Flowers, Hamra, and others have described techniques in which pedicles of orbital fat are mobilized into these areas. Free fat can be transplanted (or injected) as another method. The use of tissue fillers is yet another approach. The Flowers tear trough implant is the best option when a palpating finger clearly discerns and defines a suborbital malar bony defect. In such instances, an eyelet cut within the implant accommodates passage of the infraorbital nerve. The implant fits nicely into the defect, allowing a nasal attachment to the inferior orbital rim periosteum. Small holes throughout the implant allow tissue ingrowth and fixation. Implants can be inserted through subciliary, transconjunctival, intraoral, or direct incisions. The transconjunctival incision is best reserved for patients without prominent supraorbital ridges. Free grafts commonly leave irregularities, and fat injections leave palpable and often unacceptable visible protuberances. The same is the case for a host of other tissue fillers, most of which are temporary. Among this myriad of possibilities, our preference is injectable calcium hydroxylapatite (Radiesse), built up in rows of filler "cylinders" around the infraorbital nerve.

32. How do you permanently secure the brow into its desired (elevated) position?

Many techniques have been used. Surgeons involved in endoscopic brow lifting sometimes use screws, plates, or permanent sutures to anchor the brow until adequate healing and fibrosis are able to secure the brow in its new position. Similar techniques can be used with open large flap procedures, but fixation hardware is less frequently required. With the open procedures, markedly improved fixation is produced by removing the superficial temporal fascia (subgaleal tissue) in the parietotemporal area. This method allows better adhesion of the forehead flap to the skull. Remember that it is easy to overcorrect the medial brow and difficult to adequately correct the lateral brow. For these reasons, periosteal flaps occasionally are used with developmentally low, and especially asymmetrically low, eyebrows. In patients with asymmetry, the flap usually is restricted to the lower side (which usually is the right). This secures the brow into the desired elevated position. The superiorly based periosteal flaps are inserted into a beveled incision, made within the eyebrow hairs at the junction of the medial and lateral thirds of the eyebrows. The 2-mm-wide flap is taken just at the border of the temporalis fascia. This technique limits the caudal descent of the lateral brow, but the brow still can be raised by frontalis animation. This technique is far better than methods that fix the brow in place without allowing movement.

33. What is Whitnall's ligament?

It is a condensation of the sheath overlying the anterior superior part of the levator muscle. Medially, it arises from connective tissue of the frontal bone posterior to the trochlea. Laterally, it attaches to the capsule of the orbital lobe of the lacrimal gland and to the frontal bone portion of the lateral orbital wall approximately 10 mm above the lateral orbital tubercle. This structure is the point at which the direction of pull of the levator muscle changes from a horizontal to a vertical direction. It serves to limit the elevation of the eyelid with check ligaments. During blepharoptosis procedures, do not suture Whitnall's ligament to the tarsus or other eyelid structures because this may result in a permanent lagophthalmos or inability to close the eyes. The superior transverse ligament was first described by Whitnall in 1910.

34. What is Lockwood's ligament?

It is a hammock-like system with contributions from the inner muscular septae, retinaculum, Tenon's capsule, and lower eyelid retractors. Posteriorly, Lockwood's ligament arises from fibrous attachments from the inferior side of the inferior rectus muscle and continues anteriorly as the capsular palpebral fascia and lower eyelid retractors. This suspensory system has medial and lateral horns that extend into the retinacula. The medial retinaculum, in turn, attaches to the posterior lacrimal crest, and the lateral retinaculum attaches to the lateral orbital tubercle of Whitnall. The suspensory system of the globe was initially described by Lockwood in 1886. This suspensory system is tightened, the sagging globe is lifted, and the upper orbital hollowness is reduced by two-layer canthopexies secured into bone.

35. In patients with eyeliner and eyebrow tattoos, where should the blepharoplasty incisions be placed?

If a person wants the eyeliner tattoos on the lower lid removed or reduced, a subciliary incision superior to, or within, the tattoos allows their eradication, or reduction, provided the tattoos are not within the eyelash "line," sufficient lower lid skin is present, and the lid is properly supported with canthopexies. Do not forget these supporting maneuvers. Tattoos on the gray line or surrounding the lashes cannot be removed without sacrificing eyelashes. If a person wants to preserve the tattoos, make the lid incision at the caudal margin of the tattooed eyeliner or just within it (to "spiff up" the "bleed" of pigment into surrounding areas.) The scar helps prevent the eventual, or continued, "bleed" into adjacent tissues.

Often, eyebrows have been tattooed to make up for deficient, nonexistent, or excessively caudal positioning. Rarely is it desirable to excise skin cephalad to these tattoos, nor is it feasible to perform other types of frontal lifts because they all will further elevate the tattooed brow. When there is excessive skin on the upper lid of the sort that normally would be corrected by a brow positioning procedure, the optimal solution often is a direct excision of brow tissue bordering the tattooed eyebrow. In this way the illusion of the brow remains in the optimal position, and special irreplaceable, thin eyelid skin that functions far better on the eyelid than thick, unwieldy brow or juxtabrow skin remains.

36. Which cranial nerve innervates the lacrimal pump that drains the tears?

The seventh cranial nerve innervates the orbicularis oculi muscle. The deep heads of the medial pretarsal and preseptal orbicularis contract and exert traction on the fascia immediately lateral to the lacrimal sac, known as the *lacrimal diaphragm*. This traction during contraction of the orbicularis creates a relatively negative pressure within the lacrimal sac that draws tears through the puncta and canaliculi into the lacrimal sac. Relaxation of the orbicularis oculi allows the lacrimal sac to collapse, and the tears traverse the nasolacrimal duct to the nose.

37. What is the difference in the terms "canthopexy" and "canthoplasty" as applied to tightening procedures on the lower eyelids?

For most patients the goal is not *to alter* so much as *to recapture* the shape and contour of the eyes they had in their youth. For others with natural or developmental transverse or reversed (antimongoloid) intercanthal axis tilts, the goal *is* indeed *to raise* the canthal insertion. One operation achieves the desired end result for both conditions, whether degenerative or congenital. The same operation also offers superb correction of iatrogenic and posttraumatic deformities. One name can efficiently describe that flexible procedure and eliminate the confusion between *−pexy* and *−plasty,* which hinges on a positional change of 1 to several millimeters in drill hole and/or suture position. Whether in actuality or illusion, because the eye *appears lifted* (with restoration of youthfulness and pleasing aesthetics), the choice and most logical descriptive term seems to be *canthopexy!*

38. During blepharoplasty, where is the "white" fat?

The medial or nasal upper eyelid fat usually has a color that is paler (white or yellow-white) than other fat of the eyelids and orbit. The lateral fat of the upper eyelid has a deeper yellow color. The medial fat pad of the upper lid may move anteriorly more prominently than do the other fat pads, resulting in a large bulge of the upper medial eyelid just inferior to the trochlea of the upper medial orbit. Often there is a hollowed-out defect in the area between the white medial fat compartment and the lateral "yellow" fat compartment, where the nasal portion of the septoaponeurotic sling housing the fat migrates superiorly. The medial lower eyelid fat is likewise pale in color.

BIBLIOGRAPHY

Flowers R: Asian blepharoplasty. Aesthet Surg J 22:558–568, 2002.
Flowers RS: Canthopexy as a routine blepharoplasty component. Clin Plast Surg 20:351–365, 1993.
Flowers R: Correcting suborbital malar hypoplasia and related boney deficiencies. Aesthet Surg J 341–355, 2006.
Flowers RS: Cosmetic blepharoplasty—State of the art. Adv Plast Reconstr Surg 8:31–67, 1992.
Flowers RS: Optimal procedure in secondary blepharoplasty. Clin Plast Surg 20:225–237, 1993.
Flowers RS: Periorbital aesthetic surgery for men. Clin Plast Surg 18:689–729, 1991.
Flowers RS: Tear trough implants for correction of tear trough deformity. Clin Plast Surg 20:403–415, 1993.
Flowers RS: The biomechanics of brow and frontalis function and its effect on blepharoplasty. Clin Plast Surg 20:225–268, 1993
Flowers RS: Upper blepharoplasty by eyelid invagination: Anchor blepharoplasty. Clin Plast Surg 20:193–207, 1993.
Flowers R, DuVal C: Blepharoplasty and aesthetic periorbital surgery. In Aston S, Beasley R, Thorne C (eds): Grabb and Smith's Plastic Surgery. Philadelphia, Lippincott-Raven, 1997, pp 627–650.
Flowers R, Nassif J: Aesthetic periorbital surgery. In Mathes S (ed): Plastic Surgery, 2nd ed. Philadelphia, Saunders/Elsevier, 2006, pp II:77–126.
Smith EM, Dryden RM: Eyelids: Anatomy, ectropion, entropion, blepharoptosis, blepharoplasty and abnormalities. In Chern KC, Wright KW (eds): Review of Ophthalmology: A Question and Answer Book. Baltimore, Williams & Wilkins, 1997, pp 199–204.

THE NASOLABIAL FOLD

Jeffrey Weinzweig, MD, FACS; Marcello Pantaloni, MD; Erik A. Hoy, MD; Jhonny Salomon, MD, FACS; and Patrick K. Sullivan, MD

1. What are the nasolabial crease, nasolabial fold, and malar fat pad?

The nasolabial crease (NLC), or sulcus, is the facial line between the upper lip and cheek, extending from the alae nasi to the lip commissure. The crease may extend superiorly to the side of the nose and inferiorly below the commissure. The nasolabial fold (NLF) is the bulging fat pad and skin lateral to the NLC. The malar fat pad is the triangular fat pad with its base along the NLC and, in young people, its apex along the body of the zygoma. It lies over the zygomaticus major muscle, levator labii superioris muscle, and orbital portion of the orbicularis oculi muscle.

2. What are marionette lines?

Bilateral inferior extensions of the NLC below the commissure resemble the vertical lines on the lower face of a ventriloquist's dummy and thus are referred to as *marionette lines*.

3. What is one of the more noticeable aesthetic changes between a young adult and the same person 30 years later?

Deepening of the NLC and accentuation of the fold with concomitant inferior, lateral, and anterior displacement of the cheek mass and the tissue lateral to the fold occur with aging. The inferior migration of the cheek mass leaves a noticeable hollow in the infraorbital area.

4. What is the anatomy of the NLF area?

In the superficial layer the subcutaneous tissue from the adjacent cheek area crosses the NLF in the upper lip, where it changes to a dense, thin fascial–fatty layer closely attached to the skin and to the superficial portion of the orbicularis oris muscle. Beneath the subcutaneous tissue the superficial musculoaponeurotic system (SMAS) extends across the NLF and merges with the superficial portion of the orbicularis oris muscle of the upper lip. The deep layer of the orbicularis oris muscle merges with the superficial layer at the NLF, together with the SMAS.

5. What are mimetic muscles? What is the relationship between the SMAS and the mimetic musculature near the NLF?

The mimetic musculature is composed of individual muscles that receive their innervation from the facial nerve and are responsible for facial movement. The mimetic muscles and superficial facial fascia (SMAS) function as a single anatomic unit in producing movement of the facial skin. The SMAS is intimately associated with the mimetic muscles. Muscle contracture is translated into movement of overlying facial skin through the vertical fibrous septa extending from the SMAS into the dermis. Anatomically the SMAS divides into superficial and deep fascial leaves and invests or surrounds the superficially lying mimetic muscles (platysma, orbicularis oculi, zygomaticus major and minor, and risorius). The investiture of the mimetic muscles by the SMAS forms a single functional anatomic layer with muscle and fascia working in continuity to produce movement of facial skin.

6. What is the anatomic and clinical difference between the tissue medial and lateral to the NLC?

The tissue medial to the crease has subcutaneous muscle attachments that protect against the effect of gravity. Lateral to the crease the muscle does not insert into the skin and thus remains without deep support. For this reason, the lateral tissue descends at a quicker rate than does the medial tissue.

7. What are the retaining ligaments of the face?

Facial skin is supported in normal anatomic position by retaining ligaments that run from deep, fixed facial structures to the overlying dermis. The two types of retaining ligaments are (1) true osteocutaneous ligaments, which are a series of fibrous bands that run from periosteum to dermis (e.g., zygomatic and mandibular ligaments); and (2) supporting ligaments formed by a coalescence between the superficial and deep facial fascias in certain regions of the face (e.g., parotidocutaneous and masseteric cutaneous ligaments) (Fig. 76-1).

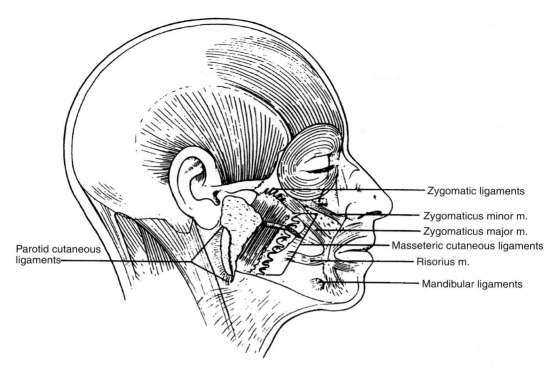

Figure 76-1. Facial soft tissue is supported in normal anatomic location by a series of retaining ligaments. The zygomatic and mandibular ligaments are examples of osteocutaneous ligaments that originate from periosteum and insert directly into dermis. The masseteric and parotid cutaneous ligaments are formed as condensations between the superficial and deep facial fascias. Rather than originating from periosteum, these ligaments originate from relatively fixed facial structures such as the parotid gland and the anterior border of the masseter muscle. Attenuation of support from these retaining ligaments is responsible for many of the stigmata seen in the aging face, including deepening of the nasolabial crease and increased prominence of the nasolabial fold. (From Stuzin JM, Baker TJ, Gordon HL: The relationship of the superficial and deep facial fascia: Relevance to rhytidectomy and aging. Plast Reconstr Surg 89:441–449, 1992, with permission.)

8. Which of the retaining ligaments suspend the malar fat pad?
The zygomatic ligaments, which are a series of fibrous septa that originate from the periosteum of the malar region. They begin where the zygomatic arch joins the body of the zygoma and continue over the malar eminence. A particularly stout ligament originates along the most medial portion of the zygoma near the zygomaticomaxillary suture. The fibers composing the zygomatic ligament extend through the malar fat pad (McGregor's patch) and attach to the dermis of the malar skin to suspend the fat pad over the underlying zygomatic eminence.

9. Does any other anatomic structure contribute to supporting the malar fat pad?
The maxillary eminence. Patients with a greater anterior slope of the maxilla have increased support of the cheek tissue and less prominent NLF.

10. What is the cause of a prominent NLF?
Aging is associated with attenuation of the zygomatic retaining ligaments. Because of ligamentous laxity, the malar soft tissue migrates downward along the direction of the zygomaticus major muscle, bulging against the NLC. The skin lateral to the crease stretches and becomes redundant, forming a prominent NLF.

11. What are the sequential migration vectors of the cheek mass?
Initially, the migration vectors are inferior and parallel to the contraction of the mimetic muscles and perpendicular to the NLC. When inferior movement is restrained by the dermal–fascial attachments of the NLC, the tissue slides laterally and anteriorly over the crease with accentuation of the NLF.

12. What is the role of midface muscle in a prominent NLF?
The mimetic muscle contraction transmits a shearing force on the fascial attachments between the SMAS and overlying subcutaneous tissue and skin. The malar fat pad migrates downward and forward, producing a prominent NLF. Accentuated contraction of the levator muscle, as seen with smiling, pulls cephalically and deepens the NLC with further bulging of the ptotic fat pad.

13. What is the effect of facial nerve paralysis on NLF appearance?
Facial nerve paralysis results in less prominence of the fold because the tissue medial to the crease no longer has underlying support and descends in a similar fashion to the lateral tissue.

14. What can you inject or insert in the NLC to improve its appearance?
Both autologous tissue and synthetic material may be used. Fat and various synthetic materials can be injected in the NLC. Silicone injections are *not* appropriate. Hyaluronic acid substances have been well tolerated beneath the NLC. They resorb with time.

15. When should fat injection of the NLC be considered?
Fat injections of the NLC are used frequently. This technique is especially appropriate in patients who are having other facial rejuvenation procedures at the same time. The best candidates for fat injections are younger patients, but older patients may benefit as well.

16. When performing fat grafting, how much fat should be injected?
Fat grafting is the long-term injectable par excellence. It is readily available, it does not require pretesting, and the result is very natural. The fat usually is suctioned from the abdomen and medial and lateral thighs using special fat-harvesting cannulas and injected into the NLC. Some surgeons overfill by approximately 30% because they believe that 30% will resorb in the few weeks following. Complications such as hardness or infection are rare.

17. What short-term injectable agents are available to treat the NLC?
Many products now are available for temporary treatment of the NLC. These products last an average of 3 to 6 months. They include the collagen agents (Zyderm 1, Zyderm 2, Zyplast), which last 3 to 4 months and require pretesting. CosmoDerm and CosmoPlast last approximately 4 months and do not require pretesting because they are cadaver derived. The newer products on the market are the hyaluronic acid derivatives (Hyaloform and Hyaloform Plus, Restylane, Juvéderm, Perlane). These hyaluronic acid derivatives last 4 to 7 months and do not require pretesting.

18. What are the two most commonly used longer lasting agents for the treatment of the NLC?
Sculptra and Radiesse are two longer-lasting injectable agents that remain over a year and close to 2 years. Granuloma formation requiring excision may be a problem with these agents.

19. Who is the best candidate for direct crease excision?
Direct crease excision is rarely, if ever, indicated because it leaves a permanent scar. Fillers and lifting are more appropriate treatments of deep creases.

20. What can you offer a patient with thick skin and slight fold prominence who prefers a minimally invasive procedure?
Fat injection or a dermal–fat graft can be used. The fat is obtained from the deep plane of the lower abdomen and injected beneath the crease after the fibrous bands between dermis and muscle are released. With this technique some overcorrection can be considered, but the result is not always predictable because of the variable survival of the injected fat cells.

Dermal–fat or SMAS grafts may be considered.

21. How can the malar fat pad be repositioned?
Elevation of the skin-subcutaneous flap or the SMAS flap can reposition the malar fat pad.

22. How extensive need the SMAS dissection be to elevate the malar fat pad to its original position and decrease NLF prominence?
The SMAS dissection usually should reach the malar region. The zygomatic and masseteric ligaments are released incrementally as well as the ligaments medial to the zygomaticus minor muscle. The division of these restraints allows greater mobility of the malar portion of the SMAS and the NLF. The malar fat pad, along with the SMAS, is repositioned over the zygomatic eminence, perpendicular to the NLC and parallel to the zygomaticus major muscle. The amount of undermining varies for each patient as the surgeon follows the mobilization and the effect on the patient's face.

23. With the extended SMAS dissection, what step should be performed at the level of the zygomaticus major muscle to maximize resuspension of the malar fat pad?
Because of the tethering effect of the retaining ligaments in the area of the zygomaticus major muscle, this release to which the SMAS is closely attached is effective. Traction exerted on the skin and fat superior and lateral to the NLC is transmitted to the NLC after release of these zygomatic-retaining ligaments. This tethering effect is otherwise maximal at the bony origin of the zygomaticus major muscle.

24. What change do you expect in the NLF with superior and lateral SMAS pulling without releasing the SMAS from the zygomaticus major muscle?

The pulling of the SMAS shortens the mimetic muscles between the modiolus and their bony origin. The overlying soft tissue moves for a smaller distance than does the muscle. The pull is transmitted from the SMAS to the orbicularis oris muscle medial to the crease. The medial tissue moves superiorly and laterally for a greater extent than does the lateral tissue, which is attached less strongly to the underlying structures. The consequences of these dynamic changes are deepening of the NLC and accentuation of the NLF. A similar situation can be seen during smiling. The actions of the zygomaticus major muscle and deep orbicularis oris muscle transmit a similar pulling to the medial tissue via the joining structure, the SMAS.

25. In the malar fat pad suspension technique, the fat pad vector is the skin flap. Describe this approach.

The skin-subcutaneous flap incorporates the malar fat pad, which needs to be completely dissected from the underlying retaining ligaments. The platysma-SMAS flap is elevated as needed. A fixation suture is sewn from the apex of the fat pad to the superficial fascia of the malar eminence or deep temporal fascia. The suture is placed along a line perpendicular to the NLC approximately 2 cm above and 1 cm in front of the ear until the pad is maximally elevated.

26. When the malar fat pad is based within a skin flap vector, what is the direction and the amount of fat pad lifting needed to correct the NLF?

The direction of the lifting is superolateral and roughly perpendicular to the crease. With mild laxity the fat pad can be repositioned and adequately supported by the cheek flap alone. With more severe laxity a wider and stronger repositioning is needed, necessitating a suspension technique.

27. What is the role of suction-assisted lipectomy in corrective surgery of the NLF?

After raising the SMAS for the extent required to obtain repositioning of the ptotic malar pad, any residual fullness of the NLF area can be sculpted under direct vision using a 2-mm liposuction cannula.

28. What is the role of the subperiosteal approach in corrective surgery of the NLF?

The subperiosteal approach allows detachment of the central third of the face at the subperiosteal level. After SMAS and subcutaneous dissection, superior and lateral pulling allows transmission of the forces to the full thickness of the NLC and NLF areas that are completely freed from the underlying bone. Movement of the tissue to a higher and more lateral position results in flattening of the NLF.

29. What is the recommended amount of undermining below the fat pad to address the NLF?

The amount of undermining varies for each patient but can be extensive. For mild midface laxity and mildly prominent NLF, some believe the undermining should extend beyond the malar eminence over the inferolateral orbicularis oculi muscle to the origin of the zygomaticus major muscle. For more severe midface laxity and migration of the fat pad, some surgeons believe the entire fat pad should be undermined to the level of the NLC.

30. Describe the anatomy of the subcutaneous fat deposits in the face. How do these deposits affect the appearance of the NLF and the aging face?

Pessa and Rohrich identified 17 compartmental subcutaneous deposits of fat in the face. Accordingly, the face does not age uniformly. In youth, the transition between these compartments is largely imperceptible. However, with aging, some compartments undergo apparent loss of volume while others may expand or deform. The differential expansion or volume loss in these compartments may lead to altered facial contour. This includes the deepened NLC and the accentuated NLF, both of which result in a prematurely aged appearance.

31. What adjunct can be offered to the patient who requests treatment of the NLCs that is both minimally invasive and reversible?

The efficacy of Botox in addressing rhytides in the upper third of the face is well documented. The effects of Botox can be used to minimize rhytides in the lower third and NLC as well, by targeting the mimetic muscles that are responsible for their formation. However, this often provides suboptimal treatment of the deep NLC. This is due to the fact that the NLC–NLF complex is the combined result of cutaneous, muscular, and osseous factors.

32. Which muscles of the face are most responsible for the smiling mechanism? Which is most responsible for forming the medial NLC?

In a study of the dynamic forces of the mimetic muscles, the elements of the smiling mechanism were isolated. The zygomaticus muscles generate the vectored forces responsible for the majority of smile formation. Conversely, the tension forces most responsible for the formation of the medial NLC are generated by the paired levator labii superioris alaeque nasi muscles. Therefore these muscles are a target for Botox injection or surgical resection to improve the appearance of the NLC. Interestingly, the normally occurring anatomic variants of facial muscle insertions into the skin and soft tissues are responsible for the presence or absence of dimpling in this area when smiling. The formation of a "dimple" on smiling is the result of aberrant mimetic muscle fibers fusing to more superficial layers of the face, including the skin.

33. Which of the following approaches to rhytidectomy best addresses the NLF: Lateral SMAS-ectomy, conventional SMAS, extended SMAS, or composite rhytidectomy?

In a prospective review, patients undergoing these various approaches to facial rejuvenation were evaluated. The study has received much criticism. It is believed that each surgeon must decide what works best in his/her hands. The extended SMAS with emphasis on facial augmentation and anatomic reduction of fat deposits has proved helpful. Various methods also have been used to address submandibular gland ptosis (Fig. 75-2).

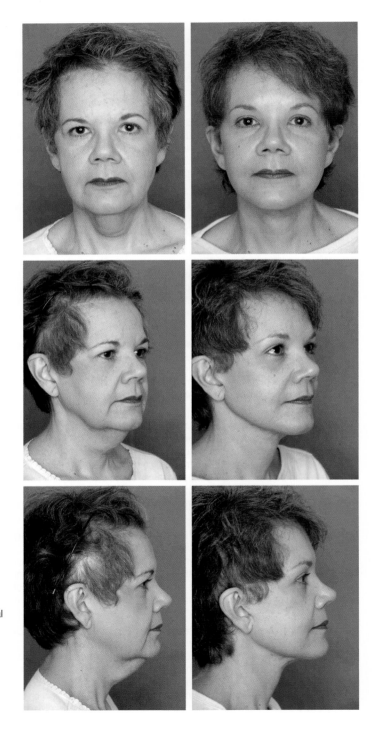

Figure 76-2. Preoperative **(left)** and postoperative **(right)** photographs of a patient who underwent endoscopic forehead rejuvenation, upper blepharoplasty, rhytidectomy, and neck rejuvenation. Correction of the prominent nasolabial folds and jowls helped to provide a more youthful postoperative appearance of the lower third of the face. (From Sullivan PK, Salomon JA, Woo AS, Freeman MB: The importance of the retaining ligamentous attachments of the forehead for selective eyebrow reshaping and forehead rejuvenation. Plast Reconstr Surg 117:95–104, 2006, with permission.)

BIBLIOGRAPHY

Barton FE Jr: Rhytidectomy and the nasolabial fold. Plast Reconstr Surg 90:601–607, 1992.

Barton FE Jr: The SMAS and the nasolabial fold. Plast Reconstr Surg 89:1054–1057, 1992.

Barton FE Jr, Gyimesi IM: Anatomy of the nasolabial fold. Plast Reconstr Surg 100:1276–1280, 1997.

Furnas DW: The retaining ligaments of the cheek. Plast Reconstr Surg 83:11–16, 1989.

Furnas DW: Strategies for nasolabial levitation. Clin Plast Surg 22:265–278, 1995.

Guyuron B: The armamentarium to battle the recalcitrant nasolabial fold. Clin Plast Surg 22:253–264, 1995.

Ivy EJ, Lorenc ZP, Aston SJ: Is there a difference? A prospective study comparing lateral and standard SMAS facelifts with extended SMAS and composite rhytidectomies. Plast Reconstr Surg 101:1135–1143, 1996.

Kane MA: The effect of botulinum toxin injections on the nasolabial fold. Plast Reconstr Surg 112(5 Suppl):66S–72S, 2003.

Owsley JQ: Elevation of the malar fat pad superficial to the orbicularis oculi muscle for correction of prominent nasolabial folds. Clin Plast Surg 22:279–293, 1995.

Owsley JQ, Roberts CL: Some anatomical observations on midface aging and long-term results of surgical treatment. Plast Reconstr Surg 121:258–268, 2008.

Pessa J: Independent effect of various facial mimetic muscles on the nasolabial fold. Presented at the 25th Annual Meeting of the American Society for Aesthetic Plastic Surgery, Los Angeles, California, May 1992.

Rohrich RJ, Pessa JE: The fat compartments of the face: Anatomy and clinical implications for cosmetic surgery. Plast Reconstr Surg 119:2219–2227, 2007.

Rubin LR, Mishriki Y, Lee G: Anatomy of the nasolabial fold: The keystone of the smiling mechanism. Plast Reconstr Surg 83:1–10, 1989.

Singer DP, Sullivan PK: Submandibular gland I: An anatomic evaluation and surgical approach to submandibular gland resection for facial rejuvenation. Plast Reconstr Surg 112:1150–1154, 2003.

Stuzin JM, Baker TJ, Gordon HL: The relationship of the superficial and deep facial fascias: Relevance to rhytidectomy and aging. Plast Reconstr Surg 89:441–449, 1992.

Sullivan PK, Salomon JA, Woo AS, Freeman MB: The importance of the retaining ligamentous attachments of the forehead for selective eyebrow reshaping and forehead rejuvenation. Plast Reconstr Surg 117:95–104, 2006.

Sullivan PK, Freeman MB, Schmidt S: Contouring the aging neck with submandibular gland suspension. Aesthet Surg J 26:465–471, 2006.

Yousif NJ, Mendelson BC: Anatomy of the midface. Clin Plast Surg 22:227–240, 1995.

Zufferey J: Anatomic variations of the nasolabial fold. Plast Reconstr Surg 89:225–231, 1992.

1. What are the different types of face lift procedures?

There are four basic types of face lift surgeries:

1. Skin only
2. Skin and superficial musculoaponeurotic system (SMAS)-platysma
3. Skin and SMAS-platysma and midface suspension
4. Deep plane and/or a combination of 1, 2, and 3

2. Describe the various face lift techniques used and give an example of a good candidate for each.

- *Skin Undermining and Redraping Only:* This technique does not involve any manipulation of the SMAS. It is useful in the patient with a very thinned face who may be undergoing secondary or tertiary rhytidectomy.
- *SMAS Plication:* This technique involves suturing the edges of the SMAS together without excision or incision into the tissue. Plication pulls on unreleased facial fascia (still bound by the retaining ligaments), so obtaining proper vectors of elevation and long-lasting fixation may be problematic. A good candidate for this technique is a patient with a thin face and thin facial fascia from whom you do not want to excise any more soft tissue. Secondary and tertiary face lift patients usually are good candidates for this procedure (Fig. 77-1).
- *Skoog Rhytidectomy:* This early face lift procedure involved elevation of the skin and SMAS as a single unit, which then was advanced posteriorly onto the cheek and neck. The SMAS was used to transmit a stronger and more lasting suspensory pull on the facial tissues. Skoog's method had a major impact on facial aesthetic surgery for its identification of the SMAS as a discrete layer that could be used to augment skin suspension. This procedure is suited for someone with cervical laxity without much nasolabial fold ptosis or midface descent.
- *Lateral SMASectomy:* Described by D.C. Baker, lateral SMASectomy involves excision of a strip of SMAS along the anterior border of the parotid (from just above the angle of the mandible to the malar prominence). It is performed at the interface of the superficial fascia fixed by the retaining ligaments and more mobile anterior superficial facial fascia. Upon closure, this brings the mobile SMAS up to the junction of the fixed SMAS, producing a durable elevation of both superficial fascia and facial fat. This technique is applicable to patients with a wide variety of anatomic problems, is reproducible, and is safe (Fig. 77-2).
- *SMAS Flap:* With this technique, the skin is elevated first, then the SMAS is elevated as a separate flap. Many surgeons have popularized and used this technique, and it is ideal in many patients with the classic signs of facial aging, especially those with a substantially thick SMAS, and in primary rhytidectomy patients (Fig. 77-3).
- *Extended SMAS Flap:* Mendelson advocates an extended SMAS dissection that continues beyond the zygomatic ligament, identifies the zygomaticus major, and releases the SMAS from that muscle. The key to satisfactory correction of the nasolabial fold is complete release of the SMAS from the zygoma and zygomaticus major. The SMAS then is sutured to the periosteum of the zygoma. Stuzin has also advocated extending the SMAS dissection over the zygomaticus major to adequately release the SMAS, set appropriate tension on the nasolabial fold, and superiorly reposition the jowl and cheek fat. These techniques rely on the anatomic fact that mimetic muscles are innervated from their deep surfaces except for the three that are deeper in location and innervated on their superficial surface (mentalis, depressor anguli oris, and buccinator). To obtain mobility of the superficial fascia in the extended SMAS dissection, mobilization of the SMAS peripheral to the retaining ligaments with complete dissection of the SMAS from the underlying parotid gland and from the superior aspect of the masseteric ligaments is done. The ideal patient for this procedure has prominent nasolabial folds and jowls, but the procedure can be used on a variety of patients.
- *Deep Plane Rhytidectomy:* In the deeper plane techniques the fat overlying the zygomaticus muscles is elevated in the face lift flap and the platysma is left attached to the skin flap. This procedure is generally indicated for the patient with midface descent and ptosis. This technique was popularized by Hamra.
- *Composite Rhytidectomy:* Variations of this procedure have been described by Hamra, Barton, and Aston. The platysma, malar fat, and orbicularis are elevated in the face lift flap. Barton describes releasing the investing fascia and moving the plane of dissection superficial to the SMAS at the level of the belly of the zygomaticus major muscle so that the anterior cheek skin is placed under enough tension to stretch out or efface the nasolabial fold. See Question 5 for the senior author's technique.

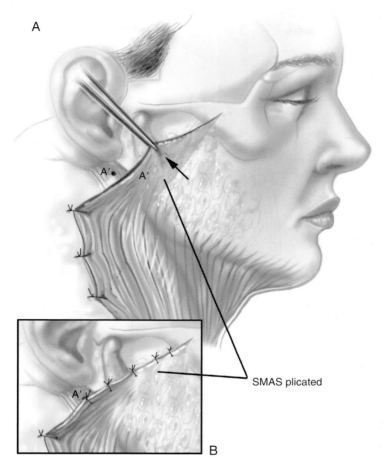

Figure 77-1. Superficial musculoaponeurotic system (SMAS) plication technique in rhytidectomy. (Illustration by Bill Winn, 2001.)

3. What are the retaining ligaments of the face?

Facial skin is supported in normal anatomic position by retaining ligaments that run from deep, fixed facial structures to the overlying dermis. The two types of retaining ligaments are (l) true osteocutaneous ligaments, which are a series of fibrous bands that run from periosteum to dermis (e.g., zygomatic and mandibular ligaments), and (2) supporting ligaments formed by a coalescence between the superficial and deep facial fascias in certain regions of the face (e.g., parotidocutaneous masseteric cutaneous ligaments) (see Fig. 76-1).

4. When does a patient need a deep-plane lift of the midface?

When there is ptosis of the midface (the region medial from the lateral canthi of the lids to the corners of the mouth). Ptosis may include significant nasolabial and nasojugal creases, marionette down lines, and sagging of the malar tissues below the infraorbital rim.

5. How can the malar fat pad be repositioned?

Elevation and tightening of the skin-subcutaneous flap or the SMAS flap can reposition the malar fat pad. The senior author prefers elevating the fat pad as it is attached to the skin flap in the finger-assisted malar elevation (FAME) procedure. With index finger pulp surface down, under the orbicularis oculi muscle, pressure is exerted down and inferomedially across the malar prominence. The finger glides under the orbicularis oculi muscle laterally and the malar fat pad medially, which separate rather easily from the fascia overlying the preperiosteal fat. The entire malar fat pad is undermined with the index finger to near the nasal alar attachment. The index finger is turned over with the pulp surface up to permit leverage for complete mobilization of the malar fat pad. Bimanual palpation with one index finger in the

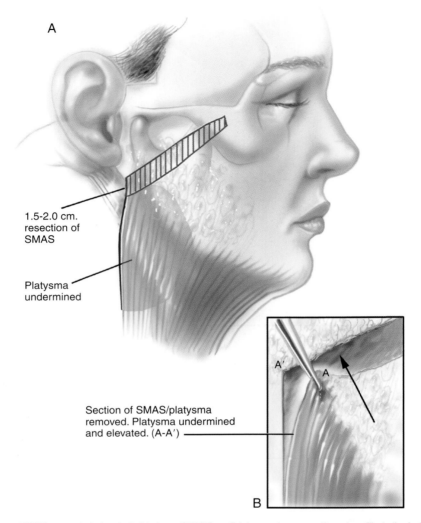

Figure 77-2. Lateral SMASectomy technique in rhytidectomy. *SMAS,* Superficial musculoaponeurotic system. (Illustration by Bill Winn, 2001.)

"deep plane" helps evaluate malar fat pad thickness and mobilization. At this point the levels of dissection have been established: (1) subcutaneous, and (2) submalar fat pad and orbicularis oculi (in the deep plane and a composite flap). Redraping of the composite flap in a cephaloposterior direction with emphasis on the vertical vector will reposition the malar fat pad to its earlier location over the malar prominence.

6. What are some of the common tell-tale signs of face lift surgery?

Visible scars (from poorly planned incisions and closure under tension)
- Overlifting of temporal hairline
- Stepped occipital hairline
- Distorted tragi and distorted auditory meatuses that are no longer shielded by appropriate tragal positions (caused by excessive cheek flap tension and a retrotragal incision)
- Distorted earlobes (from an error in skin flap vector dynamics, tension under closure from excessive skin resection, incision placement)
- Windswept look of the cheek and neck skin due to incorrect lift vectors (usually too cephalically oriented)
- Lack of balance in the lift of the face and neck (e.g., patient with tightened smooth cheeks but deformities such as ptotic, wrinkled brow/forehead region, senile chin ("witch's chin") deformity, or persistent platysmal cords)

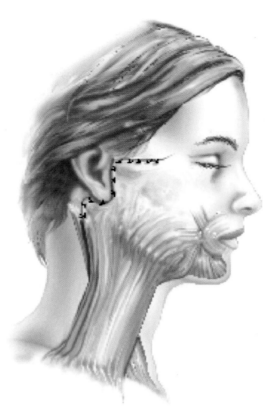

Figure 77-3. Superficial musculoaponeurotic system flap fixation in rhytidectomy. (Illustration by Bill Winn, 2001.)

7. What are the acceptable locations for the preauricular incision, and what are the indications for each?

The *pretragal incision* is a good choice (1) if the tragus is protruding and there is a moderately deep preauricular rhytid, (2) in older patients, (3) in male patients, and (4) for smokers or other patients who may have impaired cutaneous circulation. Incisions following the contours of the helix, tragus, and lobule normally result in nearly imperceptible scars.

Indications for a *retrotragal incision* are (1) small, flat, nonprotruding tragi, (2) youthful female patients without a pronounced pretragal rhytid, and (3) nonsmokers. The retrotragal incision provides an imperceptible incisional scar line as well. However, if closed under tension, this incision may cause deformity or obliteration of the tragal contour and may distort the tragal shielding of the auditory meatus, causing the appearance of an outwardly protruding tragus. These deformities are overt signs of face lift surgery (Fig. 77-4).

8. How does a surgeon avoid creating a "step" or surgical distortion of the occipital hairline?

This can be done by minimizing the tension of the closure of postauricular skin flap to the scalp and placing the incisions so that excised skin will alter the hairline only minimally, if at all. Markings are made around the lobule and ear ending at the level of the helical root postauricularly. This is extended in a wavy line into the hair-bearing scalp approximately 4 cm. The appropriate amounts of scalp and postauricular flap skin are removed by excising the superior flap edge to match the wavy, undulating line within the scalp from the posterior apex of the incision into the hairline. Care is taken to spread out the tension posteriorly, as well as superiorly, to prevent a "draping" effect. A preplanned inferior Burrow's triangle incision can be placed in the posterior edge of the flap to achieve this goal.

9. What is a "witch's chin" deformity?

A witch's chin deformity results from ptosis of the integumentary and muscular tissues of the mentum as a consequence of aging. However, it also may occur for other reasons, such as chin implant surgery or sliding genioplasty surgery by the intraoral approach, when the attachments of the lip and chin musculature (specifically, the mentalis) are cut across or stripped away from the mandible by periosteal elevation. Subsequently, the chin sags below the mental protuberance, and the platysmal and subcutaneous fat may become lax and ptotic. Jowls may appear, and a geniomandibular sulcus or concavity occurs below and lateral to the sagging chin.

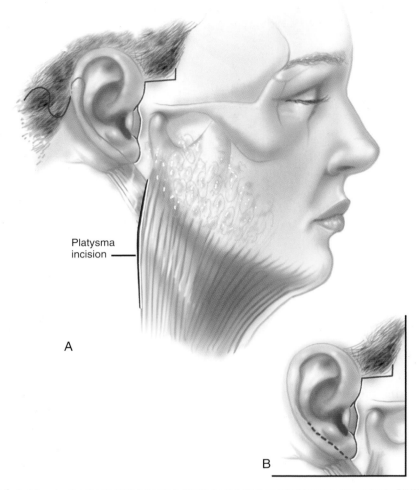

Figure 77-4. Incision planning for standard full scar rhytidectomy and short scar rhytidectomy. (Illustration by Bill Winn, 2001.)

10. How can jowls be corrected?

After the SMAS flap lift and/or midface deep-plane lift is completed, it is convenient to liposuction the ovoid mass of subcutaneous tissue, mostly fat, that may overhang the mandibular margin. A small suction cannula (1.5- to 2.4-mm diameter) can be inserted through the incision just under the earlobe into the jowl. The ovoid mass is suctioned, taking care to confine the suction first to the jowl and, as necessary, very carefully to the submandibular area to define the mandibular margin and contour the regions adjacent to the previous lipectomy of the submental area.

11. What factors can lead to hematoma formation after face lift surgery?

- Postoperative pain, which causes anxiety and hypertension with subsequent bleeding. After general anesthesia, this sequence may begin in the operating room.
- Nausea and vomiting, through the physical motion of the act of vomiting and from sudden blood pressure fluctuations.
- Ingestion of aspirin or other anticoagulant medications before or immediately after surgery.
- Postoperative increase in blood pressure, or rebound hypertension, from medications given preoperatively and intraoperatively to lower the blood pressure.

12. What is the treatment of an expanding hematoma?

For small blood collections recognized early, the treatment is suction–aspiration with a soft suction cannula, which can be done at the bedside. Saline irrigation mixed with 1% lidocaine with epinephrine is performed after fluid removal, and manual pressure is applied for several minutes after hematoma removal. A new compression dressing is wrapped in place, and the patient is observed for recurrence. If a large expanding hematoma has formed, the patient should be taken to the controlled environment of an operating room for evacuation and location and control of any actively bleeding points. Preoperatively, an intravenous line should be placed and fluid resuscitation started because the patient's blood pressure may precipitously drop upon induction of anesthesia and quick evacuation of a large amount of blood. The incisions are again repaired, and a new face lift dressing is applied for 24 hours. In this instance the patient should be observed in a hospital setting.

13. What is the incidence of hematoma formation requiring evacuation after rhytidectomy?

From 3% to 5%. Hematoma formation is the most frequent complication following rhytidectomy. Hematomas can vary from large collections of blood that compromise the skin flap and require surgical evacuation to very small collections that subside on their own. Most clinically significant expanding hematomas occur within the first 10 to 12 hours after surgery and are usually noticed in the recovery room. Signs and symptoms include unilateral pain, unilateral facial fullness, and unilateral excessive periorbital ecchymosis. The reported incidence of major hematoma formation requiring evacuation following rhytidectomy varies from 0.9% to 8%, with the largest series (a review of 7700 cases) reporting an incidence of 7%. The reported incidence in men is 7% to 8%, and the reported incidence in women is 3% to 4%. Control of expanding hematomas is performed in the operating room under general anesthesia. Small hematomas (2 to 20 mL) generally do not become apparent until postoperative edema has subsided. These hematomas occur in 10% to 15% of patients and, if visible, can be aspirated 10 to 12 days after surgery as they begin to liquefy. Most will subside on their own within several months but may result in overlying skin contour irregularity. An association has been suggested between hematoma formation and either an immediate postoperative increase in blood pressure or rebound hypertension. There is no known correlation between intraoperative bleeding and subsequent hematoma formation. Substances known to cause bleeding problems, such as aspirin and other nonsteroidal antiinflammatory drugs, large doses of vitamin E, and dipyridamole, should not be taken for 2 weeks prior to surgery.

14. Five days after an SMAS face lift a 50-year-old woman has a ballotable fluid collection of approximately 8 mL in the right preauricular area over the angle of the mandible. Needle evacuation shows a yellowish pink fluid. What is the differential diagnosis?

Seroma, salivary fluid from parotid leak, and hematoma.

15. Two days later the fluid has reaccumulated. What is the likely diagnosis?

The most likely diagnosis is a salivary fluid collection due to parotid leak. Significant accumulations may drain through the incision as a parotid fistula. The cause of these problems is injury to the gland during dissection, and techniques that elevate the SMAS are more likely to violate the parenchyma of the gland. The diagnosis is made by assessing the fluid amylase level, which would be high in this case. Treatment at this point would be insertion of a small drain from a postauricular location over the area until the defect seals itself and the drainage diminishes. A bland diet may help to decrease drainage as well.

16. What may be the cause of persistent lower cheek fullness in a patient who has undergone a face lift?

Ptosis of the buccal fat pad. The buccal fat pad lines the masticatory space and allows smooth muscle gliding during mastication. It is composed of four parts: the body of the fat pad, the buccal segment, the pterygoid portion, and the temporal portion. The body of the fat pad lies along the upper portion of the maxilla and is visualized through an upper buccal sulcus incision. The buccal segment covers the buccinator muscle and provides fullness to the cheek. The pterygoid portion lies between the medial and lateral pterygoid muscles, separating them from the mandibular ramus. The temporal portion lies deep to the zygomatic arch, separating it from the temporalis muscle during mastication.

17. Which nerve is the most commonly injured during a rhytidectomy?

The great auricular nerve. Nerve injury, specifically motor nerve injury, is one of the most severe potential complications of rhytidectomy. Fortunately, most nerve injuries noted after rhytidectomy are limited to the sensory nerves. The lower portion of the ear, the preauricular skin, and the cheeks are always transiently hypesthetic following rhytidectomy because of the interruption of small sensory nerves intraoperatively. The most common nerve injury during rhytidectomy, occurring at a rate of 3% to 5%, involves the great auricular nerve. Such injury occurs when the dissection penetrates deep to the sternocleidomastoid fascia over the middle portion of the muscle where the nerve crosses the muscle belly approximately 6. 5 cm below the caudal edge of the external auditory canal. Injury to the great auricular nerve can be avoided during a sub-SMAS–platysma dissection by incising the deep layer just anterior to the sternocleidomastoid muscle (Fig. 77-5).

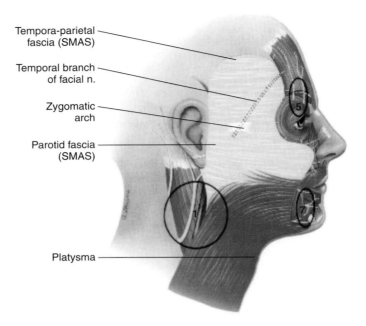

Tempora-parietal fascia (SMAS)

Temporal branch of facial n.

Zygomatic arch

Parotid fascia (SMAS)

Platysma

Figure 77-5. Anatomy of the great auricular nerve. (From Seckel BR: Facial Danger Zones: Avoiding Nerve Injury in Facial Plastic Surgery. St. Louis, Quality Medical Publishing, 1994, with permission.)

18. **If you recognize injury to the great auricular nerve at surgery, what should you do?**
   Repair it with fine sutures and cover the repair with the platysmal portion of the deep tissue flap.

19. **What symptoms may occur after surgery if the great auricular nerve is injured?**
   - Numbness in the inferior portions of the ear and ear lobule
   - Painful, neuralgic sensations in the sternocleidomastoid and ear area
   - Painful neuroma at the site of injury

20. **What is the motor innervation of the platysma muscle, and what role does it play in facial animation?**
   The cervical branch of the facial nerve innervates most of the body of the muscle, and the marginal mandibular branch of the facial nerve innervates the upper anterior portion. The platysma muscle functions synchronously with the depressor anguli oris and the depressor labii inferioris to move the lip and corner of the mouth down.

21. **Which of the following branches of the facial nerve lies superficial to the deep facial fascia?**
   The temporal or frontal branch. The facial nerve traverses the superficial surface of the masseter muscle and lies deep to the deep facial fascia. The buccal, cervical, marginal mandibular, and zygomatic branches penetrate the deep facial fascia and innervate the overlying mimetic muscles. The temporal branch of the facial nerve crosses the zygomatic arch and travels along the deep surface of the temporoparietal fascia. This branch lies in a more superficial position in the temporal region. It then penetrates the temporoparietal fascia to innervate the frontalis muscle along its deep surface. Knowledge of the anatomy of the temporal branch is essential in performing rhytidectomy as well as temporal and/or endoscopic brow lifts (Fig. 77-6).

22. **What is the topographical course of the frontal branch of the facial nerve?**
   The frontal branch of the facial nerve travels approximately along a line from 0.5 cm below the tragus to 1.5 cm above the lateral end of the eyebrow (Fig. 77-7).

23. **Four weeks after undergoing an extended SMAS rhytidectomy, a 57-year-old woman has persistence of dense hemiparesis over the distribution of the right marginal mandibular nerve. The problem was first noted immediately after surgery. Which of the following is the most appropriate next step in management?**
   Observation. During rhytidectomy, the major nerve that is most frequently injured is the great auricular. The motor nerves that are most frequently injured are the buccal nerves. Because crossover and arborization occurs between the branches of the buccal nerves, this injury may go unnoticed by the surgeon. A more significant motor nerve injury is that of the temporal and/or marginal mandibular nerves. Obvious signs of injury to the marginal mandibular nerve include an asymmetrical

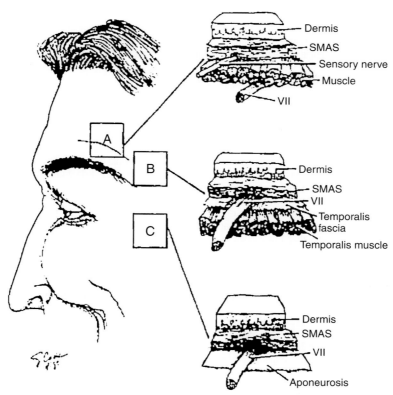

Figure 77-6. Frontal branch anatomy in relation to the superficial musculoaponeurotic system (SMAS). (From Liebman EP, Webster RC, Berger AS, DellaVecchia M: The frontalis nerve in the temporal brow lift. Arch Otolaryngol 108:232–235, 1982, with permission.)

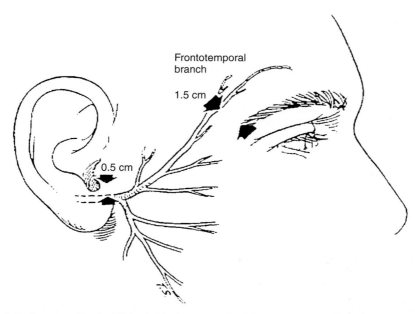

Figure 77-7. Predicting the course of the frontal branch of the facial nerve. *SMAS,* Superficial musculoaponeurotic system. (From Pitanguy I, Silveira Ramos A: The frontal branch of the facial nerve: The importance of its variations in face lifting. Plast Reconstr Surg 38:352–356, 1966, with permission.)

"full-denture" smile and the inability to depress, pull laterally, and evert the vermilion of the ipsilateral lower lip. This injury can be caused by trauma due to electrocautery, a suture inadvertently encircling the nerve or, most likely, neurapraxia from stretching. A less likely cause is complete accidental transection of the nerve, usually as it exits the tail of the parotid or where it descends below the angle of the mandible with the patient's head turned laterally with the neck extended.

Immediate postoperative weakness of the marginal mandibular nerve noted in the recovery room may be the result of infiltration of local anesthetic and should resolve within several hours as the drug is metabolized. A more persistent paresis lasting 24 hours to a few weeks may occur from nerve trauma during blunt dissection, injection of anesthetic solution into the nerve, edema within the nerve sheath, or electrocautery trauma. If a facial nerve branch is noted to be transected during a surgical procedure, immediate meticulous microsurgical repair should be performed. In most cases, however, motor nerve injury is not recognized during surgery, and the surgeon and patient are placed in the difficult position of waiting for return of function. Conservative management is warranted for the first 6 months because spontaneous resolution with complete return of function is likely in up to 80% of patients. Close follow-up and physiotherapy to increase the use of platysma as a lip depressor may be helpful to minimize facial asymmetry. After 6 months, it is advisable for the physician to discuss the deformity with the patient and outline further treatment options. Management options include baseline electromyography after 6 months with a repeat test in 1 month. Injection of botulinum toxin in the unaffected side can be used to decrease obvious facial asymmetry and decrease activity of overactive compensatory muscles. Correction of the deformity can be considered after 1 or 2 years when reinnervation of the facial muscles is less likely.

24. A 62-year-old woman who underwent subcutaneous rhytidectomy with SMAS plication 1 week ago notices that the left side of her upper lip does not elevate when she attempts to smile. The most likely cause is injury to which of the following nerve branches?
The buccal branch. The patient's inability to elevate her upper lip is most likely caused by injury to the branch of the buccal nerve that innervates the levator labii superioris muscle. The buccal nerve branches, which lie superficial to the parotid fascia, are positioned beneath the SMAS as they cross the masseter muscle and can be easily injured during dissection of the SMAS. Most deficits resulting from buccal nerve injury improve spontaneously over time because of the cross-innervation that occurs in this region. Injury to the cervical branch causes weakening of the platysma, resulting in an asymmetric smile. Injury to the frontal branch manifests as eyebrow ptosis or inability to raise the eyebrow. Because this branch is likely to be terminal, the deficit often is permanent. Injury to the zygomatic branch, which is rare, leads to a decrease in facial animation in the area overlying the zygomaticus major and minor muscles.

25. In the aging face, which procedure is most likely to worsen the prominence of the nasolabial fold?
Preauricular tightening of the SMAS. The appearance of the nasolabial fold remains a significant obstacle to adequate restoration of the aging face. Without actually correcting the anatomic problem, several techniques have been described to blunt the transition between the fatty cheek and the lip. Both dermis and autologous fat grafts as well as newer soft tissue injectables such as Restylane and Radiesse have been used to fill the area. Dermis and fat grafts give modest results and require a donor site. Most soft tissue fillers give only temporary correction. Direct excision of the fold has been described but requires use of an external incision that results in visible scarring. The SMAS attaches medially to the orbicularis oris. Attempting to tighten the SMAS in the preauricular region will displace this orbicularis laterally, actually deepening the nasolabial fold. When the SMAS is freed from its medial and inferior attachments and rotated to include the malar fat pad, improvement in the depth of the nasolabial fold may be seen.

26. A 58-year-old man with prominent nasolabial folds undergoes rhytidectomy. Sub-SMAS dissection is performed to the level of the nasolabial folds. What is the most likely result?
Denervation of the zygomaticus major muscle. The sub-SMAS dissection beyond the lateral border of the zygomaticus major muscle is not a safe plane for anatomic dissection. Although the zygomatic facial nerve branches course deep to the SMAS muscle layer, the nerve fibers become more superficial to innervate the muscles on their deep surface. Any dissection in the sub-SMAS plane, whether a standard dissection of the SMAS as a separate layer or as a composite rhytidectomy, requires the surgeon to change planes at the zygomaticus major muscle. Further dissection in the sub-SMAS plane beyond the zygomaticus major will denervate this muscle by injuring its nerve branch as it turns superficially to innervate the muscle.

27. A 60-year-old woman requests rhytidectomy. She has smoked two packs of cigarettes daily for 20 years. What postoperative complication would most likely occur?
Skin slough. The most likely complication of rhytidectomy in a patient who smokes is the development of skin slough. Smoking is associated with increased flap loss because it decreases oxygen to the skin in two ways: (1) decreased blood flow due to nicotine-induced vasoconstriction and (2) carbon monoxide–induced tissue hypoxia due to hemoglobin in the red blood cells preferentially binding carbon monoxide over oxygen (and thereby forming carboxyhemoglobin). A study examining the effects of smoking in patients undergoing rhytidectomy found a 7.5% incidence of skin slough. Another study showed a 19% incidence of skin slough. Abstinence from smoking for 2 weeks has been shown to decrease the incidence of skin slough. During rhytidectomy, limiting undermining of the skin flaps to 2 to 3 cm preserves circulation and decreases the incidence of skin slough.

28. After undergoing an uncomplicated primary rhytidectomy, a 59-year-old woman has early onset of ischemia and subsequent full-thickness skin slough of a 3 × 5-cm area anterior to the left earlobe. What is the most appropriate first step in management?
Local wound care and healing by secondary intention. Appropriate initial management of this patient with skin slough following rhytidectomy should be conservative with local care and healing by secondary intention and reepithelialization. During this stressful time for both patient and surgeon, frequent physician–patient contact is critical. The wound should be kept moist and clean, with monitoring for the development of secondary infection. Many small skin sloughs heal spontaneously within several weeks and may not require any secondary scar revisions. Larger wounds can also be allowed to heal, with scar revisions performed as necessary only after a minimum of 1 year has passed. Débridement and skin grafting are not appropriate alternatives to obtain wound closure because they would produce quilt-like mismatches of texture and color. Tension is a key factor in producing slough, so delayed primary closure by readvancement of the cervicofacial flap will only compound the problem, which likely led to the complication in the first place.

29. Prominence of the nasolabial folds in the aged patient results primarily from loss of support in which of the retaining ligaments?
The zygomatic ligament. This ligament suspends the soft tissue in the malar region over the zygomatic eminence. In older patients, ptosis of the malar soft tissue caused by loss of support from the zygomatic ligaments occurs adjacent to the nasolabial fold, resulting in prominence of this fold. Rhytidectomy procedures may improve the appearance of the nasolabial fold by lifting the malar pad and reattaching it over the zygomatic eminence. The mandibular ligaments arise from the periosteum through the facial soft tissue and insert into the dermis. They provide support to the facial soft tissue over the mandible. The masseteric and parotid-cutaneous ligaments are formed between the superficial and deep facial fascia. They provide support to the soft tissue over the masseter muscle and parotid glands. Loss of support from the masseteric ligaments will result in prominent facial jowls.

30. Which vessel is the dominant blood supply to the preauricular skin that is undermined during rhytidectomy?
The transverse facial artery. The traverse facial artery provides the dominant vascular supply to the preauricular skin and is undermined during rhytidectomy. Its perforator is positioned approximately 3 cm lateral and inferior to the lateral canthus. Collateral circulation is minimal. Knowledge of this region prior to surgery is particularly crucial because inadvertent transection can result in the development of preauricular skin necrosis. In patients who smoke or have other factors that may compromise their blood supply, this vessel can be located and preserved.

31. Why is rhytidectomy more difficult to perform in men than in women?
Several factors frequently make rhytidectomy procedures more difficult to perform in men than in women. In general, facial skin is thicker in men, which may obscure postoperative results. Men are more likely to develop hematomas due to increased vascularity in the beard area. Because men often have thinner, shorter hair or baldness, the surgical incisions need to be placed more carefully in areas where they can be disguised. In addition, performing a retrotragal incision can result in posterior displacement of the beard. This problem can be addressed by depilation of the skin or positioning of the incision between the hair-bearing area of the cheek and preauricular area, which typically is alopecic. One advantage that men undergoing rhytidectomy have is the position of their sideburns. Because the beard covers the cheek below the jawline, cephalad displacement of the sideburns following rhytidectomy is not as much of a concern because the hair can be shaved at any level to determine sideburn position. In contrast, cephalad displacement of sideburns in women will result in an unnatural appearance.

32. A 58-year-old woman is scheduled to undergo full-face rhytidectomy followed by phenol chemical peeling for facial rejuvenation. For the most appropriate management of this patient, what is the minimum number of months after the rhytidectomy procedure that you should delay the chemical peel?
Three months. This allows sufficient time for the undermined skin to heal. Performing full-face chemical peeling at the time of rhytidectomy is not recommended because full-thickness skin loss may result. In addition, skin flap lower lid blepharoplasty and chemical peeling of the eyelids should not be performed simultaneously. Regional perioral peeling can be performed at the time of rhytidectomy without complications in certain surgical candidates due to the absence of undermining in this area.

33. Who is the ideal patient for a short scar rhytidectomy?
A patient who does not have much neck laxity.

34. What technical maneuvers are often necessary when performing a short scar rhytidectomy?
A primarily vertical vector of SMAS lift and the possible need for an anterior temporal hairline incision.

35. What are the potential complications of submandibular gland excision for neck contouring in rhytidectomy?

Expanding hematoma, marginal mandibular (VII), hypoglossal (XII), and lingual nerve injury, dry mouth, salivary fistula, neck irregularities or depressions, and a cadaveric or hollowed-out appearance of the neck.

36. What are the criteria for a youthful neck as described by Ellenbogen and Karlin?

Distinct inferior mandibular border, subhyoid depression, visible thyroid cartilage bulge, visible anterior sternocleidomastoid border, cervicomental angle of 105° to 120°, and submental–sternomastoid angle of 90°.

37. When is suction lipectomy of the neck indicated for improvement of cervicomental contour?

The primary indication for performing suction lipectomy of the neck is the presence of excess supraplatysmal fat as determined by physical examination and pinch testing. The supraplatysmal fat can be suctioned through small stab incisions in the submental and retroauricular areas. Patients younger than age 30 years will often experience excellent results following suction lipectomy because of better skin elasticity, which diminishes with age. These patients are more likely to have contraction of the skin following a decreased fat volume after surgery. As a result, cervical suction lipectomy is frequently performed as a single procedure with good success in patients aged 20 to 40 years.

Vertical skin wrinkling is not a favorable indicator for performing suction lipectomy. Patients with vertical skin wrinkling have decreased skin elasticity and therefore will have suboptimal results following cervical suction lipectomy.

38. A 65-year-old woman desires facial rejuvenation and has an obtuse cervicomental angle, noticeable fat pads in the anterior neck, and vertical, diverging subcutaneous bands within loose redundant skin in the neck that are present in repose. What is the most appropriate management in conjunction with a face lift?

Lipectomy of preplatysmal cervical fat and anterior platysmaplasty. Correction of anterior banding of the platysma muscle at rest as well as localized anterior neck fat is best accomplished with lipectomy of preplatysmal fat performed with anterior platysmal plication. A small submental incision is made, and the fatty neck deposits can be excised directly or removed via open suction lipectomy. Midline plication then can be performed to tighten the platysma muscle with excision of a wedge of muscle below the level of the thyroid cartilage for improved contour (Fig. 77-8).

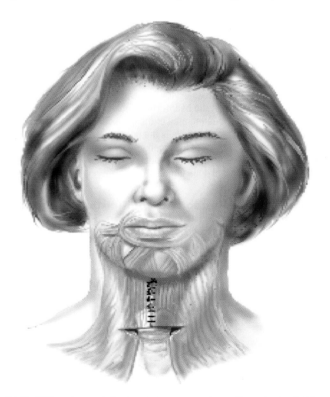

Figure 77-8. Midline platysmal plication during platysmaplasty. (Illustration by Bill Winn, 2001.)

BIBLIOGRAPHY

Aston SJ: Platysma-SMAS cervicofacial rhytidoplasty. Clin Plast Surg 10:507–520, 1983.

Aston SJ, Thorne CH: Aesthetic surgery of the aging face. In Smith JW, Aston SJ (eds): Grabb and Smith's Plastic Surgery. Boston, Little, Brown and Co., 1991, p 627.

Baker DC: Complications of cervicofacial rhytidectomy. Clin Plast Surg 10:543–562, 1983.

Baker DC: Face lift with submandibular gland and digastric muscle resection: Radical neck rhytidectomy. Aesthet Surg J 26:85–91, 2006.

Baker DC: Minimal incision rhytidectomy (short scar face lift) with lateral SMASectomy: Evolution and application. Aesth Surg J 21:14–26, 2001.

Baker TJ, Stuzin JM: Chemical peeling and dermabrasion. In McCarthy JG (ed): Plastic Surgery, Vol 2. Philadelphia, WB Saunders, 1990, pp 748–786.

Barton FE Jr: Rhytidectomy and the nasolabial fold. Plast Reconstr Surg 90:601–607, 1992.

Barton FE Jr: The aging face: Rhytidectomy and adjunctive procedures. Sel Read Plast Surg 9:22, 2001.

Ellenbogen R, Karlin JV: Visual criteria for success in restoring the youthful neck. Plast Reconstr Surg 66:826–837, 1980.

Hamra ST: The deep plane rhytidectomy. Plast Reconstr Surg 86:53–61, 1990.

Mendelson BC: Extended sub-SMAS dissection and cheek elevation. Clin Plast Surg 22:325–339, 1995.

Mitz V, Peyronie M: The superficial musculo-aponeurotic system (SMAS) in the parotid and cheek area. Plast Reconstr Surg 58:80–88, 1976.

Rees TD, Barone CM, Valauri FA, et al: Hematomas requiring surgical evacuation following face lift surgery. Plast Reconstr Surg 93:1185–1190, 1994.

Rees T, LaTrenta G: Aesthetic Plastic Surgery, Vol 2, 2nd ed. Philadelphia, WB Saunders, 1994, p 683.

Rees TD, Liverett DM, Guy CL: Effects of cigarette smoking on skin flap survival in the face lift patient. Plast Reconstr Surg 73:911–915, 1984.

Skoog T: Plastic Surgery. New Methods and Refinements. Philadelphia, WB Saunders, 1975.

Stuzin JM, Baker TJ, Baker TM: Extended SMAS dissection as an approach to midface rejuvenation. Clin Plast Surg 22:295–311, 1995.

Stuzin JM, Baker TJ, Gordon HL: The relationship of the superficial and deep facial fascias: Relevance to rhytidectomy and aging. Plast Reconstr Surg 89:441–449, 1992.

Stuzin JM, Wagstrom L, Kawamoto HK Jr, et al: Anatomy of the frontal branch of the facial nerve: The significance of the temporal fat pad. Plast Reconstr Surg 83:265–271, 1989.

Stuzin JM, Wagstrom L, Kawamoto HK, et al: The anatomy and clinical applications of the buccal fat pad. Plast Reconstr Surg 85:29–37, 1990.

RHINOPLASTY

Jaimie DeRosa, MD, MS, and
Dean M. Toriumi, MD

1. **The proximal, middle, and distal thirds of the nose are associated with what underlying anatomic structures?**
   - Proximal third: Nasal bones
   - Middle third: Upper lateral cartilages
   - Distal third: Lower lateral cartilages

2. **List the nasal subunits.**
   There are nine nasal subunits.
   - 3 unpaired: dorsum, tip, columella
   - 3 paired: sidewalls, soft tissue triangles, alae

3. **How are the nasal bones, upper lateral cartilages, and lower lateral cartilages situated in relation to each other?**
   The upper lateral cartilages lie deep to *both* the nasal bones and the lower lateral cartilages.

4. **What are the major tip support mechanisms?**
   There are three major tip support mechanisms.
   - Length and strength of lower lateral cartilages
   - Attachment of cephalic margin of lateral crura with caudal margin of upper lateral crura
   - Attachment of medial crura to caudal septum

5. **What are the minor tip support mechanisms?**
   There are six minor tip support mechanisms.
   - Interdomal ligament between lower lateral cartilages
   - Sesamoid complex
   - Soft tissue skin envelope and its attachment to lower lateral cartilage
   - Anterior nasal spine
   - Cartilaginous septal dorsum
   - Membranous septum

6. **How is the nasal length defined?**
   It is the distance from the nasofrontal angle to the tip-defining point.

7. **What is the scroll?**
   It is the area of the cephalic margin of the lateral crus that overlies the upper lateral cartilage.

8. **What is the keystone area?**
   It is the area where the upper lateral cartilages overlap with the nasal bones.

9. **What is the "ideal" nasolabial angle in a male? In a female?**
   - Male: 90° to 105°
   - Female: 95° to 110°

10. **What are the surgical approaches for rhinoplasty?**
    There are several ways to perform rhinoplasty. The two main approaches are *external* (open) and *endonasal* (closed). Endonasal approaches to rhinoplasty can be further subcategorized into delivery and nondelivery methods. Nondelivery approaches include cartilage-splitting and retrograde techniques (Fig. 78-1). The method used should be based on the patient's problem, the goals for surgery, and the surgeon's skill in a given technique.

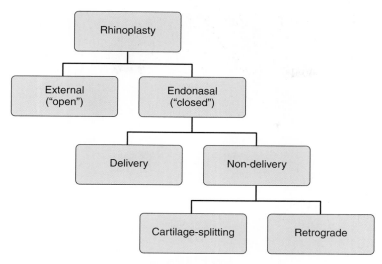

Figure 78-1. Surgical approaches for rhinoplasty.

11. How is tip projection determined?

Nasal tip projection is defined as the distance from the alar crease to the tip-defining point.

12. Name three ways to determine nasal tip projection.

- Crumley method ("3-4-5 triangle"): Projection to height to length = 3:4:5
- Goode method: Projection to length = 0.55:0.6
- Simons method: Projection = Length of the upper lip

13. What is the brow-tip aesthetic line?

It is a line drawn from the medial aspect of the brow, along the side of the nose to the nasal tip formed from the contrasts and transitions between these subunits. Ideally, the lines should be mirror images of each other, creating slight width at the nasal bony vault, narrowing at the middle vault, and then width at the nasal tip. The line drawn has a subtle hourglass configuration (Fig. 78-2).

14. Which structures make up the internal nasal valve, and what should its angle be?

The internal nasal valve angle is made up of the dorsal nasal septum, the caudal margin of the upper lateral cartilages, and the floor of the nose. (If the inferior turbinate is large, it also may contribute to the valve.) This angle should be at least 15°. The internal nasal valve is the main site of airway resistance during inspiration. Decrease in this angle due to high septal deviation or inferomedial collapse of the upper lateral cartilage (as can be seen after rhinoplasty) can significantly impair nasal breathing.

15. What is the blood supply to the nasal tip?

The lateral nasal artery, off the angular and/or facial artery, is the main blood supply to the nasal tip (Fig. 78-3).

16. Where is the nasal starting point for rhinoplasty in a Caucasian patient? Is it different for an Asian patient?

The starting point is at the level of the upper eyelid crease in the Caucasian patient. In the Asian patient, the nasal starting point is lower, at the midpupillary level.

17. When performing septoplasty, how much cartilage should be left intact?

At least a 1.5-cm dorsal and caudal septal L-shaped strut should be left intact after septoplasty. This strut helps to support the nasal framework and reduces the risk of postoperative saddling (Fig. 78-4).

18. What are the three main sources for grafting in rhinoplasty?

The main material used in grafting for rhinoplasty is autologous cartilage. The primary sources of the cartilage are the nasal septum, auricular concha, and costal cartilage.

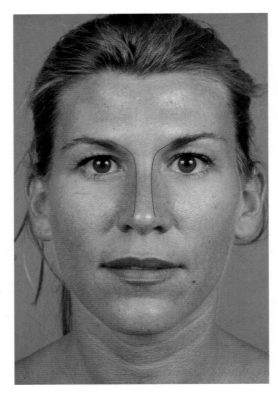

Figure 78-2. Brow-tip aesthetic line runs from the medial brow, along the nasal dorsum and middle vault to the nasal tip. This line should be unbroken and regular in contour.

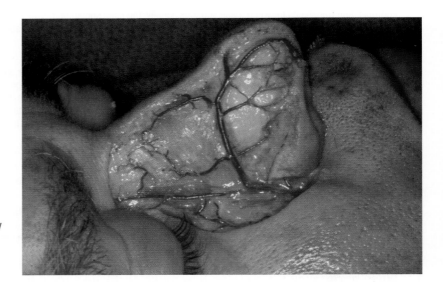

Figure 78-3. Lateral nasal artery in a fresh cadaver injected with red dyed methylmethacrylate. The lateral nasal artery comes off the angular or facial artery.

19. **What grafting technique(s) can the surgeon use to open/widen the internal nasal valve?**

Spreader grafts, placed between the upper lateral cartilages and the dorsal septum, can be used to open the internal nasal valve.

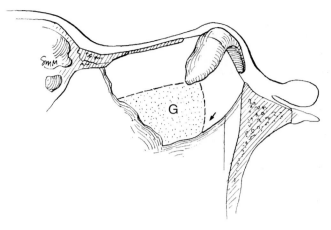

Figure 78-4. When performing septoplasty, an intact L-shaped strut of cartilage should be left intact to avoid saddling. The strut should measure at least 1.5 cm to keep adequate dorsal and caudal support. Additional cartilage can be left intact along the maxillary crest and at the connection to the perpendicular plate of the ethmoid bone to maximize support. (From Toriumi DM, Johnson CM: Open structure rhinoplasty: Featured technical points and long-term follow-up. Facial Plast Surg Clin North Am 1:93–113, 2005.)

20. Which structures make up the external nasal valve? How can external valve collapse be corrected?

The columella, alar rim, and nasal floor compose the external nasal valve. Alar rim grafts, placed at the caudal margin of the marginal incision, can be used to support and stabilize a narrowed or weak external nasal valve.

21. What is a common cause of postoperative supraalar pinching, and how can it be corrected?

Supraalar pinching is a characteristic of poor lateral wall support. It may occur after excessive resection of the lower lateral cartilages, or it may be seen in patients with inherently weak cartilages.

Alar batten grafts can be used to correct preexisting external valve compromise, lateral wall collapse, and/or supraalar pinching. These grafts also can be placed prophylactically to reduce the risk of postoperative supraalar pinching and lateral wall collapse. An alar batten graft is placed into a precise pocket at the point of maximal lateral wall collapse or supraalar pinching (Fig. 78-5).

22. What techniques are available surgically to stabilize the base of the nose?

Postoperative loss of tip projection is a feared complication after rhinoplasty. By stabilizing the base of the nose, this risk is reduced substantially. Three grafting methods and one suturing method can be used to achieve nasal base stability.

- Columellar strut graft
- Caudal extension graft
- Extended columellar strut graft
- Suturing the medial crura onto the caudal septum

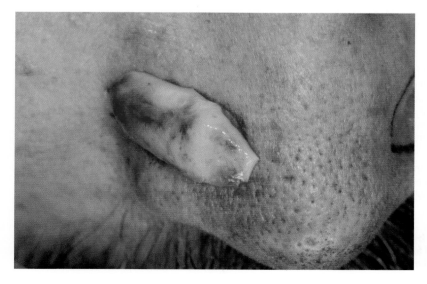

Figure 78-5. Alar batten graft placed along the nasal sidewall at the point of maximal lateral wall collapse.

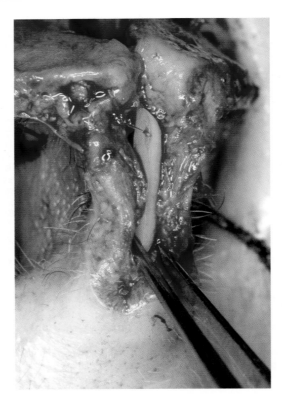

Figure 78-6. Columellar strut is placed between the medial crura and sutured into position.

23. What are the indications for each method of nasal base stabilization, and how is each performed?

A columellar strut graft can be used when the alar–columellar relationship is appropriate and the tip does not require major structural changes. This graft will help to improve tip support without significantly changing tip projection. The columellar strut graft is carved so that it is rectangular and then it is placed between the medial crura, leaving soft tissue between it and the nasal spine (Fig. 78-6).

The caudal extension graft is a versatile graft that can be used to correct a variety of problems, depending on the way the graft is carved. Because the graft must be strong and stable over the long term, either septal or costal cartilage is preferred over auricular cartilage. In the patient with a rotated nasal tip and/or foreshortened nose in whom counterrotation is desired, the graft can be made longer superiorly (Fig. 78-7, *A*). On the other hand, when a patient has an acute nasolabial angle or a retracted columella, the graft is fashioned so that the inferior edge is longer (Fig. 78-7, *B*). In patients who have poor tip support but adequate projection and alar/columellar relationship, the caudal extension graft can be made so that it is rectangular in shape and placed to overlap with the caudal septum.

An extended columellar strut graft is indicated in patients with severely deficient tip support, retracted columella, ptotic tip, excessive scar tissue, deficient premaxilla, and/or heavy thick skin. These problems may be encountered in patients with congenital deficiencies (e.g., Binder's syndrome and cleft lip nasal deformity) or in those who have undergone previous rhinoplasty with excessive resection of the caudal septum. This graft typically is made from costal cartilage because it needs to be very strong to correct the presenting deformity. The graft is carved so that it is flared at the base, with a notch that can integrate with the nasal spine (Fig. 78-8).

The medial crural setback can be used in patients with a hanging columella or tension tip because, in these patients, the caudal septum tends to be too long. After dissecting between the medial crura and raising bilateral mucoperichondrial flaps off of the septum, the medial crura are positioned back onto the caudal septum and sutured in place (Fig. 78-9).

24. What action should be taken in a patient with an infected nasal allograft?

As in most cases of infected foreign materials, an infected nasal allograft must be removed and the patient started on broad-spectrum antibiotics until culture-specific antibiotic therapy can begin.

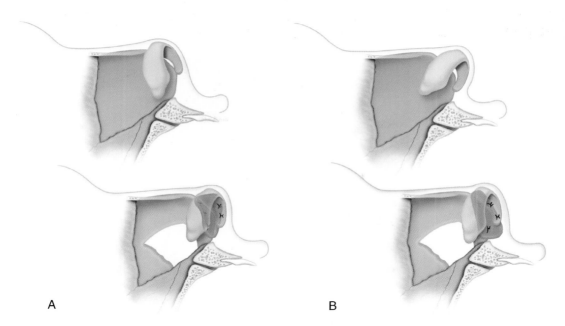

Figure 78-7. **A,** Caudal extension graft. For the overrotated nose the graft should be longer along the superior margin. **B,** Caudal extension graft. For the ptotic nasal tip the graft should be longer along the inferior margin. (From Toriumi DM: Structure approach to rhinoplasty. Facial Plast Surg Clin North Am 13:93–113, 2005.)

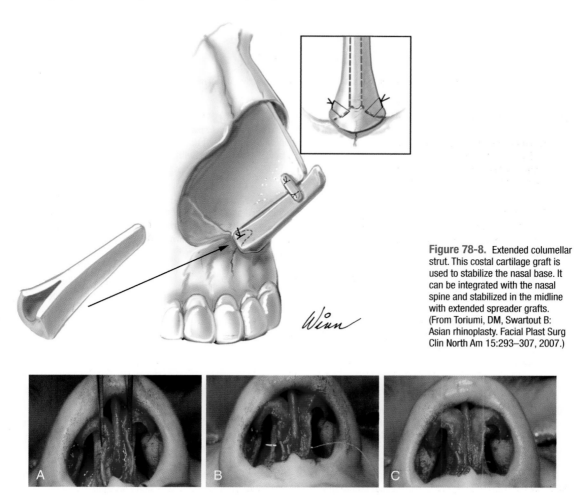

Figure 78-8. Extended columellar strut. This costal cartilage graft is used to stabilize the nasal base. It can be integrated with the nasal spine and stabilized in the midline with extended spreader grafts. (From Toriumi, DM, Swartout B: Asian rhinoplasty. Facial Plast Surg Clin North Am 15:293–307, 2007.)

Figure 78-9. Setback of the medial crura on a midline overly long caudal septum. **A,** Medial crura are dissected to allow repositioning. **B,** Suture is used to secure the medial crura to an overly long caudal septum. **C,** Medial crura are sutured into position.

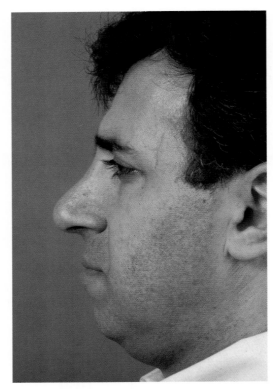

Figure 78-10. Patient with pollybeak deformity due to thick skin and postoperative loss of nasal tip projection. The skin envelope is too large for the underlying structure.

25. What is a saddle nose deformity, and what are its causes?

A saddle nose deformity refers to loss in dorsal height. It can be due to loss of underlying septal support (e.g., subtotal septal perforation) or collapse of the height of the middle vault. Dorsal grafting, with septal or costal cartilage, typically is required for correction.

26. What is a pollybeak deformity and what are its causes?

A pollybeak deformity refers to supratip fullness or convexity in relation to the rest of the nose, especially the nasal tip. This can be due to problems such as postoperative loss of tip projection, excessive resection of the cartilaginous framework with thick skin that does not redrape well, or underprojected nasal tip/low radix in comparison to high supratip region (Fig. 78-10).

27. What is an "inverted V" deformity?

An inverted V deformity refers to loss of support where the upper lateral cartilages meet the nasal bones. Collapse of the upper lateral cartilages creates a shadow and accentuates the caudal margin of the nasal bones, giving the appearance of an inverted V (Fig. 78-11).

28. What is a stairstep deformity? How can it be prevented?

A stairstep deformity refers to a prominent ledge of nasal bone after in-fracture of the narrowed nasal bone. It can be avoided by keeping the osteotomy low on the maxilla.

29. What is cephalic positioning of the lateral crura?

The lateral crura normally angle off of midline at an approximately 45° angle (Fig. 78-12, *A*). When the lateral crura are cephalically positioned, they can angle off of midline at an angle of less than 30° and can even parallel the middle nasal vault. There are differing degrees of cephalic positioning, but many patients present with a parenthesis deformity or a bulbous-appearing tip (Figs. 78-12, *B* and *C*). These patients typically lack lateral wall support and will require lateral wall grafting (alar batten grafts) or repositioning of the cephalically positioned lateral crura into a more caudal location (Fig. 78-12, *D*). To reposition the lateral crura, they can be dissected from the vestibular skin and supported with lateral crural strut grafts (Fig. 78-12, *E*). The lateral crura then can be placed into caudally positioned pockets (Fig. 78-12, *F*). This will create a more normal nasal tip shape (Fig. 78-13).

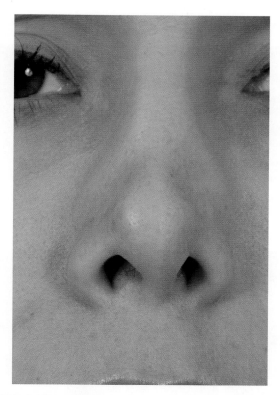

Figure 78-11. Inverted V deformity due to inferomedial collapse of the upper lateral cartilages and wide nasal bones.

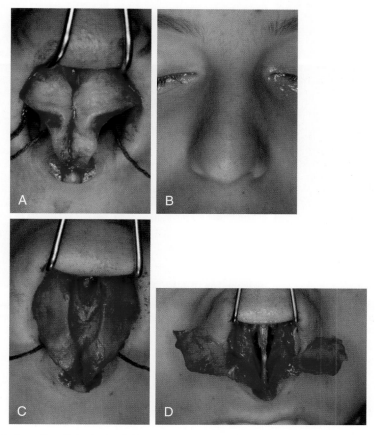

Figure 78-12. Cephalically positioned lateral crura. **A,** Normal positioned lateral crura. **B,** Bulbous round nasal tip shape. **C,** Corresponding cephalically positioned lateral crura. **D,** Lateral crura dissected from vestibular skin.

Continued

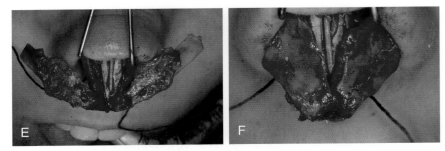

Figure 78-12. cont'd, E, Lateral crural strut grafts applied to undersurface of lateral crura. **F,** Lateral crura repositioned into caudal pockets.

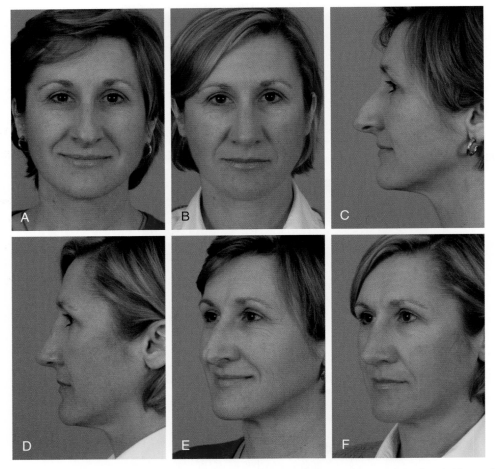

Figure 78-13. Patient with cephalically positioned lateral crura and overprojected nasal tip. Lateral crura were dissected from vestibular skin, supported with lateral crural strut grafts, and then repositioned into caudally positioned pockets. **A, C, E, G,** Preoperative views. **B, D, F, H,** One-year postoperative views.

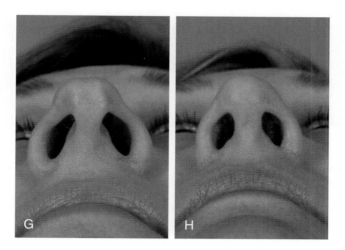

Figure 78-13. cont'd

BIBLIOGRAPHY

Gunter JP, Rohrich RJ, Adams WP (eds): Dallas Rhinoplasty: Nasal Surgery by the Masters. St. Louis, Quality Medical Publishers, 2002.

Hanasono MM, Kridel RWH, Pastorek NJ, Glasgold MJ, Koch RJ: Correction of the soft tissue pollybeak using triamcinolone injection. Arch Facial Plast Surg 4:26–30, 2002.

Kim DW, Toriumi DM: Management of posttraumatic nasal deformities: The crooked nose and the saddle nose. Facial Plast Surg Clin North Am 12:111–132, 2004.

Peck GC Jr, Peck GC: Rhinoplasty. In Weinzweig J (ed): Plastic Surgery Secrets. Philadelphia, Elsevier, 1999.

Porter J, Toriumi DM: Surgical techniques for management of the crooked nose. Aesthet Plast Surg 26(Suppl 1):18, 2002.

Quetela VC, Slupchynskyj OS: Surgery of the nasal tip. In Papel I (ed): Facial Plastic and Reconstructive Surgery. New York, Thieme Medical Publishers, 1998.

Toriumi DM: Structure approach in rhinoplasty. Facial Plast Surg Clin North Am 13:93–113, 2005.

Toriumi DM, Swartout B: Asian rhinoplasty. Facial Plast Surg Clin North Am 15:293–307, 2007.

Toriumi DM, Josen J, Weinberger M, Tardy ME Jr: Use of alar batten grafts for correction of nasal valve collapse. Arch Otolaryngol Head Neck Surg 123:802–808, 1997.

Toriumi DM: Management of the middle nasal vault in rhinoplasty. Op Tech Plast Reconstr Surg 2:16–30, 1995.

Toriumi DM, Mueller RA, Grosch T, Bhattacharyya TK, Larrabee WF Jr: Vascular anatomy of the nose and the external rhinoplasty approach. Arch Otolaryngol Head Neck Surg 122:24–34, 1996.

OTOPLASTY

Jeffrey Weinzweig, MD, FACS

1. What is a prominent ear?

A prominent ear, also commonly referred to as a *lop ear, cup ear,* or *Dumbo ear,* protrudes excessively from the temporal surface of the head. The normal external ear forms an angle of approximately 21° to 25° with the temporal scalp. A more obtuse angle (>25°) may cause the ears to appear overly prominent on frontal or posterior view.

2. What are the pathologic characteristics of the prominent ear deformity?

The three major pathologic characteristics of the prominent ear deformity are (1) a poorly defined or absent antihelical fold, (2) conchal excess (>1.5 cm deep), and (3) a conchoscaphal angle greater than 90°. Each of these characteristics may exist in varying degrees. Thus the excessive depth of the concha may be evenly distributed or may affect the upper pole (cymbum) more than the lower pole (cavum). Similarly, the entire antihelical fold may be underdeveloped or just a specific part, such as the superior crus or inferior crus (Fig. 79-1).

3. What are the embryologic origins of the ear?

The mandibular (first) branchial arch and the hyoid (second) branchial arch each contributes three hillocks of approximately equal size to the formation of the ear. Ultimately, the hyoid arch contributes 85% to the formation of the ear, including the helix, scapha, antihelix, concha, antitragus, and lobule. The mandibular arch contributes the tragus and helical crus only.

4. When does antihelical folding begin in utero?

The ear begins to protrude from the developing face by the third to fourth month of gestation, at which time antihelical folding commences. Incomplete folding of the antihelix results in a conchoscaphal angle greater than 90°, producing the prominent ear deformity.

5. By what age has the ear attained 85% of adult size? When should otoplasty be performed?

Three years. Therefore otoplasty is ideally performed in the interval between age 3 years and the commencement of school so that the child can avoid the psychological trauma of ridicule by classmates.

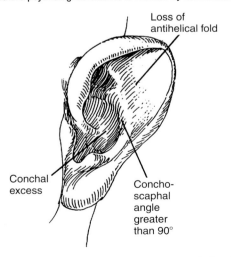

Figure 79-1. Components of the prominent ear deformity: (1) poorly defined or absent antihelical fold, (2) conchoscaphal angle greater than 90°, and (3) conchal excess. (From LaTrenta GS: Otoplasty. In Rees TD, LaTrenta GS [eds]: Aesthetic Plastic Surgery, 2nd ed. Philadelphia, WB Saunders, 1994, pp 891–924.)

6. **What is the nerve and vascular supply to the ear?**
   The auriculotemporal nerve (V3) provides sensibility to the tragus and crus of the helix only. The great auricular nerve (a branch of the cervical plexus) provides sensibility to the lobule, antitragus, antihelix, scapha, external acoustic meatus, postauricular sulcus, helix, and concha. The external acoustic meatus receives additional sensory supply via auricular branches of the vagal and glossopharyngeal nerves. The vascular supply to the external ear is via the posterior auricular and superficial temporal arteries, both terminal branches of the external carotid artery.

7. **What are the normal proportions of the ear?**
   The ear's width is typically 50% to 60% of its length, with an average width of 3 to 4.5 cm and average length of 5.5 to 7 cm. Viewed from the front, the ear extends from the brow superiorly to the base of the columella inferiorly. Laterally, the ear should lie a single ear-length behind the lateral orbital rim.

8. **How is ear protrusion defined?**
   Protrusion of the ear is defined in terms of both distance and angle. The distance from the scalp to the anterior edge of the helix ranges from 1.5 to 2 cm. The cephaloauricular angle is a mean of 25° in men and 21° in women.

9. **What is the average distance of each third of the ear from the head?**
   The helical rim measures approximately 10% of the vertical height of the ear (7 mm) and protrudes to 10 to 12 mm at the helical apex (upper third), 16 to 18 mm at the midpoint (middle third), and 20 to 22 mm at the lobule (lower third).

10. **What is the normal incline of the ear?**
    The normal ear inclines posteriorly approximately 20° off the vertical, which is slightly less steep than the plane of the nasal dorsum.

11. **Should the helix be visible from the frontal view?**
    Yes. From the frontal view, the helix of both ears should be visible beyond the antihelix.

12. **What are the anatomic goals of otoplasty?**
    The anatomic goals are threefold: (1) production of a well-defined antihelical fold, (2) conchal reduction, and (3) conchoscaphal angle of 90°. Of course, the extent to which each of these goals is pursued depends on the severity of the specific characteristics of the deformity. In addition, several general guidelines are applicable:
    - The position of the two ears with respect to the temporal surface of the head should match within 3 mm at any specific point.
    - Protrusion of the upper third of the ear must be completely corrected. Mild protrusion of the lower two thirds may be acceptable if the upper third is fully corrected.
    - The postauricular sulcus should not be significantly decreased or distorted.
    - The helix should have a smooth and regular contour.
    - The ears should not be placed too close to the head.

13. **Who performed the first otoplasty?**
    Although Dieffenbach usually is credited for having performed the first correction of a prominent ear in 1845, his technique was used for correction of a posttraumatic deformity. The earliest elective otoplasty for prominent ear deformity was reported by Ely in 1881. Dieffenbach's procedure consisted of postauricular skin excision and conchomastoidal suture fixation. Ely's procedure included these techniques as well as conchal strip excision.

14. **Can skin excision alone correct the prominent ear deformity?**
    No. Although skin excision is virtually always performed during otoplasty, it is done to avoid skin redundancy in the postauricular sulcus rather than to maintain the setback position of the ear. Although some beneficial effect on ear position may initially be attributed to skin excision, over time the elasticity of the skin inevitably results in recurrence of the prominent ear deformity. Even Dieffenbach knew this 150 years ago and included conchomastoidal sutures in his technique (see Question 18).

15. **What important concept did Luckett contribute to the principles of otoplasty?**
    In 1910 Luckett introduced the concept of restoration of the antihelical fold for correction of the prominent ear deformity. He used a cartilage-breaking technique that consisted of excising a strip of medial skin and cartilage along the entire vertical length of the antihelical fold. In some cases a sharp edge was created along the antihelical fold, which Luckett attempted to correct with several horizontal mattress sutures.

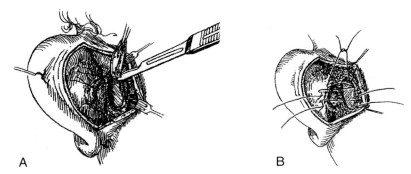

Figure 79-2. Conchomastoidal sutures. **A,** Resection of postauricular soft tissue. **B,** Several permanent mattress sutures secure the conchal cartilage to the mastoid fascia. (From LaTrenta GS: Otoplasty. In Rees TD, LaTrenta GS [eds]: Aesthetic Plastic Surgery, 2nd ed. Philadelphia, WB Saunders, 1994, pp 891–924.)

16. What is Gibson's principle?
Gibson's principle states that cartilage spontaneously bends or warps away from the scored surface by "release of interlocked stresses." A number of cartilage-weakening techniques (e.g., incision, abrasion, scoring) take advantage of this principle to recreate the antihelical fold by interrupting the anterior surface of the auricular cartilage.

17. What is the Stenstrom technique?
Through a small postauricular incision, an otoabrader is used to rasp the anterior surface of the antihelix to recreate the antihelical fold. Stenstrom and Heftner were the first to apply the Gibson principle in otoplasty. Cartilage scoring also can be achieved with a 2-mm anterior skin incision along the inside edge of the helix. After cartilage weakening, five or six radially oriented Mustardé sutures (4-0 clear nylon) are placed.

18. What is the purpose of conchomastoidal sutures?
Conchomastoidal sutures are simple or mattress sutures that penetrate the full thickness of the cartilage of the posterior conchal wall and the fascia/periosteum of the mastoid process. These sutures anchor the posterior wall of the concha to the mastoid prominence, reducing conchal projection and decreasing the depth of the postauricular sulcus. Before placing these sutures, it is helpful to resect a portion of the soft tissue (muscles and ligaments) in the postauricular sulcus. This resection permits closer approximation of the conchal cartilage to the mastoid fascia/periosteum and facilitates the conchal reduction (Fig. 79-2).

19. Is there another way to reduce conchal projection?
Conchal cartilage excision. Through an anterior incision, a full-thickness crescent of excessive cartilage can be excised from the prominent conchal rim to reduce its height. Alternatively, a posterior incision can be used to excise a strip of cartilage from the deepest part of the conchal cup.

20. What is the purpose of Mustardé sutures?
Mustardé sutures, also referred to as *conchoscaphal sutures,* are used to create the antihelical fold. These permanent mattress sutures are placed posteriorly through the full thickness of the scaphal and conchal cartilage on either side of the antihelix. As the sutures are tied, the antihelical fold is created. The cartilage surfaces are approximated only far enough to produce an aesthetic fold. The cartilage surfaces usually do not meet; instead, the sutures span the gap between them. Placement of these sutures usually is facilitated by first making several pairs of ink marks on the concha and outer aspect of the antihelix while pressing medially on the helix. These pairs of marks outline the position of the mattress sutures to be used in the repair. A 25-gauge needle dipped in ink is used to transfer the ink marks through the postauricular skin and tattoo the underlying cartilage. The cartilage can be directly tattooed if the postauricular skin excision has already been performed. The sutures (usually 4-0 clear nylon) are placed as described and tied simultaneously (Fig. 79-3).

21. How is a prominent lobule corrected?
Prominence of the lobule, or lower third of the ear, is corrected by a modified fishtail excision extending from the posterior surface of the lobule to the mastoid skin (Fig. 79-4).

22. Correction of which third of the ear is most important?
The upper third. Although a minor degree of remaining protrusion of the middle or lower third may be acceptable if the top is completely corrected, the reverse is not true.

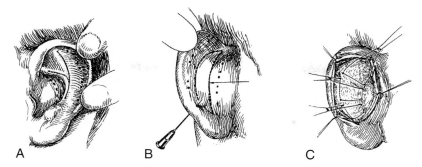

Figure 79-3. Mustardé (scaphoconchal) sutures. **A,** Several pairs of ink marks are made on the scapha and concha on either side of the antihelix. **B,** Markings are transferred to the postauricular skin and cartilage with 25-gauge needles dipped in ink. **C,** After postauricular skin excision down to cartilage, several permanent sutures are placed in the full thickness of the scaphal and conchal cartilage, piercing the perichondrium of the anterior cartilage. The sutures are tied simultaneously. (From LaTrenta GS: Otoplasty. In Rees TD, LaTrenta GS [eds]: Aesthetic Plastic Surgery, 2nd ed. Philadelphia, WB Saunders, 1994, pp 891–924.)

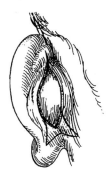

Figure 79-4. Correction of prominent lobules. A modified fishtail excision is performed in the postauricular sulcus. (From LaTrenta GS: Otoplasty. In Rees TD, LaTrenta GS [eds]: Aesthetic Plastic Surgery, 2nd ed. Philadelphia, WB Saunders, 1994, pp 891–924.)

23. What is a "telephone ear" deformity?

Inadequate correction of a projecting antitragus and lobule may result in a secondary telephone ear deformity in which the upper and lower thirds of the ear appear relatively prominent with respect to a properly corrected middle third. The ear resembles a telephone receiver.

24. What is the difference between cartilage-*molding* and cartilage-*breaking* techniques?

Cartilage-molding techniques, such as those of Mustardé and Furnas, take advantage of the soft, pliable characteristics of cartilage, especially in children. Such techniques use Mustardé conchoscaphal mattress sutures to maintain the new antihelical fold without excising any cartilage. Scoring of the anterior surface of the antihelix is performed as needed.

Cartilage-breaking techniques, such as those of Converse and Wood-Smith, are especially useful for the stiffer cartilage of adults. These techniques use full-thickness incisions or breaks through the cartilage to permit tubing of the antihelix, which then is stabilized with several sutures. The amount of conchal excess is estimated by pressing inward on the newly folded antihelix, and an elliptical conchal strip is excised. The edges of the newly folded antihelix and freshly contoured conchal rim are approximated with several permanent 4-0 mattress sutures. Care is taken not to evert the edges of the cartilage because eversion may cause secondary sharp ridging, the main complication of cartilage-breaking techniques.

25. What is the most common late deformity after otoplasty?

Residual deformity, which usually is identified within 6 months of surgery, may present a problem in as many as 10% to 24% of patients after otoplasty (according to review of several series). Such problems may result from sharp ridges and irregular contours along the antihelical fold (more common with cartilage-breaking techniques), sinus tracts secondary to the presence of permanent sutures, overcorrection with any cartilage-weakening technique, and secondary telephone deformity. Despite the potential for residual deformity, in most series fewer than 10% of patients require subsequent otoplasty revision.

26. What is the most likely cause of sudden onset of pain after otoplasty?

Hematoma. Sudden-onset, persistent, or unilateral pain should raise the index of suspicion for hematoma and warrants immediate dressing removal and evaluation. Evacuation of a clot after suture removal often is easily accomplished and should be followed by reapplication of a head dressing with mild compression.

27. Which organisms usually are responsible for cellulitis after otoplasty?

Staphylococci or streptococci usually are the culprits, although *Pseudomonas* spp occasionally is responsible. Intravenous antibiotics are often indicated. Topical mafenide acetate (Sulfamylon) cream often is useful in preventing further spread of the infection and chondritis. Infections must be controlled immediately because long-term sequelae may include the development of residual deformity.

28. Can chondritis occur after otoplasty?

Although rare, chondritis may occur after inadequate treatment of postoperative infection. Chondritis is a surgical infection requiring immediate exploration, débridement of necrotic cartilage, and soft tissue coverage to prevent severe cartilage destruction and resultant deformity.

29. When can prominent ears be treated nonoperatively?

Within the first 72 hours of the neonatal period, the cartilage elasticity is affected by high levels of circulating maternal estrogens, resulting in unusual malleability of the auricular cartilage that permits nonoperative treatment of several congenital ear anomalies, including prominent ear deformity. After 72 hours, these hormonal levels drop and the cartilage becomes stiffer. Splinting materials for nonoperative management of congenital ear deformities include Steri-Strips, rubber-coated electrical wire, and lead-free solder covered by a polyethylene suction catheter. Splinting of the prominent ear to the mastoid surface for 1 to 2 months often corrects the deformity.

30. Which is the best technique for correction of the prominent ear deformity?

Each patient requires individual assessment to determine which technique(s) is best suited to meet the specific needs of the deformity. Not every prominent ear warrants conchal excision, conchoscaphal (Mustardé) sutures, conchomastoidal sutures, or abrasion of the anterior surface of the antihelix. Most, however, require some combination of these techniques to achieve the desired goals of otoplasty. Most otoplasty procedures (e.g., Mustardé technique) include a maneuver to recreate the antihelical fold (see Fig. 79-3).

31. Describe patient management after otoplasty.

A dressing of mineral oil–soaked cotton and fluffed gauze is applied under a light cotton wrap. This dressing is removed within the first few postoperative days, sooner if signs or symptoms of infection or hematoma are present. The sutures are removed after 7 to 10 days, and the patient is instructed to sleep wearing an elastic ski band over the ears for 2 to 3 weeks after surgery.

CONTROVERSY

32. Should postauricular skin excision always be performed during otoplasty?

Not necessarily. Much has been written about various approaches to postauricular skin excision during otoplasty. Some advocate centering the excision over the postauricular sulcus; the excision thus includes skin from the posterior surface of the ear as well as the mastoid region. Others prefer to bring the excision within several millimeters of the postauricular sulcus without actually crossing it or including mastoid skin. Still others contend that skin preservation is necessary to compensate for excessive skin contraction that may obliterate the posterior sulcus or pull the midhelix into a hidden position on frontal view, creating a telephone ear deformity. Therefore, excision of postauricular skin is based on the surgeon's experience and preference.

BIBLIOGRAPHY

Bauer BS: Nonoperative treatment of congenital deformities of the ear. Oper Tech Plast Reconstr Surg 4:104–108, 1997.

Elliot RA: Complications in treatment of prominent ears. Clin Plast Surg 5:479–490, 1978.

Ely ET: An operation for prominent auricles. Arch Otolaryngol 10:97, 1881 [reprinted in Plast Reconstr Surg 42:582–583, 1968].

Furnas DW: Correction of prominent ears by conchal mastoid sutures. Plast Reconstr Surg 42:189–193, 1968.

Furnas DW: Otoplasty. In Aston SJ, Beasley RW, Throne CHM (eds): Grabb and Smith's Plastic Surgery, 5th ed. Philadelphia, Lippincott-Raven, 1997, pp 431–438.

LaTrenta GS: Otoplasty. In Rees TD, LaTrenta GS (eds): Aesthetic Plastic Surgery, 2nd ed. Philadelphia, WB Saunders, 1994, pp 891–924.

Luckett WH: A new operation for prominent ears based on the anatomy of the deformity. Surg Gynecol Obstet 10:635, 1910 [reprinted in Plast Reconstr Surg 43:83–89, 1969].

Mustardé JC: The correction of prominent ears using simple mattress suture. Br J Plast Surg 16:170–176, 1963.

Stal S, Klebuc M, Spira M: An algorithm for otoplasty. Oper Tech Plast Reconstr Surg 4:88–103, 1997.

Stenstrom SJ: A "natural" technique for correction of congenitally prominent ears. Plast Reconstr Surg 32:509–518, 1963.

Stenstrom SJ, Heftner J: The Stenstrom otoplasty. Clin Plast Surg 5:465–470, 1978.

Tanzer RC: An analysis of ear reconstruction. Plast Reconstr Surg 31:16–30, 1963.

Tolleth H: Artistic anatomy, dimensions and proportions of the external ear. Clin Plast Surg 5:337–350, 1978.

Weinzweig N, Chen L, Sullivan WG: Recurrence following correction of prominent ears: A histomorphologic study in a rabbit model. Ann Plast Surg 33:371–376, 1994.

ABDOMINOPLASTY

Christine A. DiEdwardo, MD, FACS; Stephanie A. Caterson, MD; and
David T. Barrall, MD

1. What is the blood supply of the anterior abdominal wall?

The anterior abdominal wall has superior, inferior, and lateral vascular supplies. The superior epigastric artery and the musculophrenic artery, both branches of the internal mammary, feed the upper half of the abdominal wall. The inferior blood supply consists of the inferior and superficial epigastrics medially as well as the deep and superficial circumflex iliac arteries laterally. The skin and subcutaneous tissue derive their blood supply from the medial rectus perforators as well as laterally from the intercostals and lumbar segmental arcades.

Vascular zones related to abdominoplasty can be separated into superior medial (zone I), inferior medial (zone II), and lateral (zone III) areas. Zone II and most of zone I (depending on the extent of the dissection) are devascularized in an abdominoplasty. As a result, the abdominal wall flap is vascularized primarily by the intercostals and lumbar arcades of zone III (Fig. 80-1).

2. What are the layers of the anterior abdominal wall?

The layers of the anterior abdominal wall vary according to the location on the wall. The basic layers of the lateral abdomen from superficial to deep are (1) skin, (2) Camper's fascia, (3) Scarpa's fascia, (4) external oblique, (5) internal oblique, (6) transversalis fascia, and (7) peritoneum. The arcuate line, which is found below the umbilicus in the midabdomen, demarcates a change in the thickness of the anterior and posterior rectus sheath. Above the arcuate line (Fig. 80-2), the external oblique fascia and half of the internal oblique fascia give rise to the anterior rectus sheath. The other half of the internal oblique fascia combines with the transversalis fascia to form the posterior rectus sheath. Below

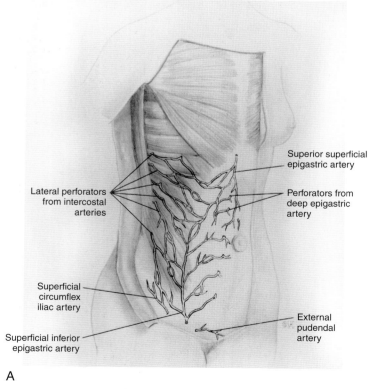

Superior superficial
epigastric artery

Perforators from
deep epigastric
artery

Lateral perforators
from intercostal
arteries

Superficial
circumflex
iliac artery

External
pudendal
artery

Superficial inferior
epigastric artery

A

Figure 80-1. Superficial **(A)**

Continued

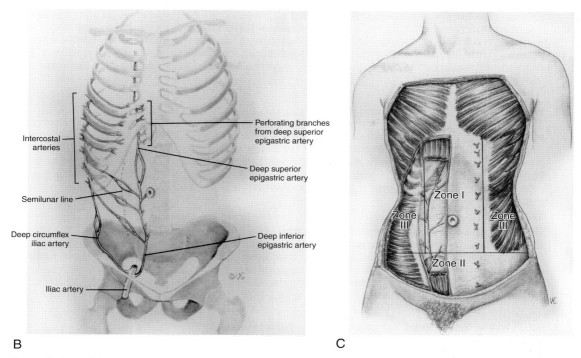

Figure 80-1. cont'd, and deep **(B)** vasculature supply to the anterior abdominal wall. (From Pitman GH [ed]: Liposuction and Aesthetic Surgery. St. Louis, Quality Medical Publishing, 1993, with permission.) **C,** Vascular zones of the anterior abdominal wall. (From Matarasso A: Abdominoplasty. Clin Plast Surg 16:289–303, 1989, with permission.)

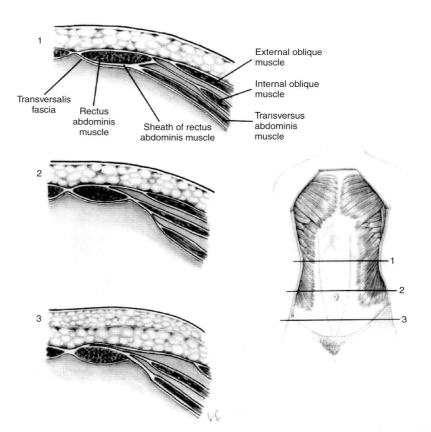

Figure 80-2. Cross-sectional anatomy of the fascial system of the anterior abdominal wall at three different levels. (From Pitman GH [ed]: Liposuction and Aesthetic Surgery. St. Louis, Quality Medical Publishing, 1993, with permission.)

the arcuate line, the internal oblique fascia contributes all of its fibers to the anterior sheath, and the transversalis alone forms the posterior sheath. This may result in a relatively weaker fascial segment below the arcuate line that is more susceptible to laxity. Overlying and closely adherent to the anterior rectus and external oblique fascia is the innominate fascia, or fascia of Gallaudet, which covers a plexus of small arteries and veins. Undermining of the abdominal wall flap in an abdominoplasty should proceed above this layer to preserve the delicate vasculature and reduce the incidence of postoperative seroma formation.

3. What is the superficial fascial system?

The superficial fascial system (SFS) is made up of a horizontal, loose connective tissue layer and its investing vertical and oblique septa. The distinct compartmentalization of the SFS defines the adipose layers of the anterior abdominal wall. The layer of adipose tissue superficial to Scarpa's fascia in the anterior abdominal wall is usually of uniform thickness with a compact septal framework, whereas the deep layer is highly compartmentalized with a globular septal framework. The deep adipose layer is primarily responsible for distinct contouring of the abdomen. In a male or android pattern, this fatty layer is in the upper abdomen and flanks; in the female or gynoid pattern, the fatty layer is in the lower abdomen, hips, and thighs.

4. What are the basic elements of abdominal contour abnormalities?

Most patients seek abdominoplasty because they wish to correct a contour abnormality. The abnormality is often a complex composite of multiple basic problems. Four fundamental areas of concern should direct the plastic surgeon in correction of the abnormality: (1) to evaluate the degree of skin redundancy and flaccidity, (2) to assess the degree of excessive adipose tissue and its location, (3) to evaluate muscle diastasis and aponeurotic laxity, and (4) to assess undesirable scars or striae and their location. These four basic elements direct the surgical approach for optimal correction of anatomic problems.

5. What is the basic surgical approach to abdominoplasty?

One of the most important steps in the abdominoplasty procedure begins before the surgery with supine and upright marking of the patient's abdomen. Skin laxity is assessed, and the area of proposed resection is marked. Regnault's open-W incision is the most widely used and modified of the abdominoplasty incisions (Fig. 80-3). Some advocate angling the lateral incision toward the anterior superior iliac crest to maximize blood supply in the abdominal flap and avoid dog ears during closure. The abdominal skin flap is elevated off the rectus sheath from pubis to xyphoid with preservation of the umbilical stalk and circumferential excision from the skin flap. The musculoaponeurotic fascia is plicated in the midline, and the lower aspect of the skin flap is resected. The umbilicus is placed at the intersection of a line connecting the highest point of the iliac crests with a line bisecting the abdomen from the sternum to pubis, and the new superior margin of the skin flap is sutured to the original inferior margin. Liposuction can be performed concomitantly (with caution) to remove excess fat from the flanks and hips.

6. What is a fleur-de-lis abdominoplasty?

Fleur-de-lis describes the shape of the incision in this inverted T-type abdominoplasty. It is useful in patients with a significant amount of medial obesity or when a large pannus must be excised. The procedure begins with a traditional W-type or Regnault low transverse incision, which is used in conjunction with a vertical wedge component that may be taken as high as the xyphoid as well as inferiorly over the mons pubis, if necessary. This method resects medial tissue and draws the new medial margins into the midline.

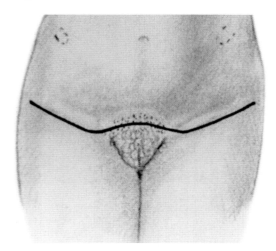

Figure 80-3. Low transverse or W-type incision. (From Pitman GH [ed]: Liposuction and Aesthetic Surgery. St. Louis, Quality Medical Publishing, 1993, with permission.)

7. What are the indications for the so-called miniabdominoplasty?

The miniabdominoplasty uses a shortened low transverse incision and is used primarily in patients with infraumbilical skin and fat excess. The same techniques of skin flap undermining, occasionally with the aid of endoscopic equipment, are used as in a standard abdominoplasty. However, the umbilicus is often left in continuity and simply retracted inferiorly after resection of the redundant skin in the superior flap. The rectus sheath and external oblique fascia are then plicated, usually in the midline and laterally.

8. What are the contraindications for abdominoplasty?

General contraindications to abdominoplasty include previous surgical procedures of the abdominal area resulting in interruption of regional blood supply to the abdominal wall (e.g., previous open cholecystectomy); comorbid medical conditions such as hematologic, thromboembolic, cardiovascular, or metabolic disorders; obesity; and desire for future pregnancy. Patients who have diabetes or who smoke have an increased risk for complications. As with any elective cosmetic procedure, unrealistic patient expectations should be weighed heavily in determining an appropriate operative candidate.

9. What is the difference between an abdominoplasty and a panniculectomy?

An abdominal pannus is an apron of skin and fat that hangs down from the abdomen, sometimes covering the anterior thighs, hips, and knees. A large pannus can interfere with activities of daily life. Skin infections and rashes are common complaints in patients with a substantial pannus. A panniculectomy is performed to relieve these symptoms. During a panniculectomy, the excess skin and fat are removed. Plication of the abdominal wall fascia is not performed. An abdominoplasty is a cosmetic procedure, usually involving fascial plication.

10. Can liposuction alone be used to rejuvenate the abdomen?

Yes. In patients who have good skin tone and isolated lipodystrophy, liposuction with no surgical resection can be the best choice. Usually these patients are younger, have good skin tone, and have minimal musculofascial laxity or diastasis.

11. What is the role of liposuction in abdominoplasty?

The extent of liposuction used in abdominoplasty varies greatly, depending on the desired result and amount of tissue to be resected. Suction-assisted lipectomy (SAL) and abdominoplasty are complementary modalities in body contouring and, in general, are used inversely, depending on the severity of the contour abnormality.

Typically, liposuction has its greatest role in procedures requiring minimal tissue excision and minimal musculofascial repair; however, it is often used in large abdominoplasties to tailor areas such as the flanks. SAL of the upper and lateral abdomen (zones II and III in Fig. 80-1) should be used with caution because it may jeopardize blood supply to the abdominal flap.

Matarasso described "safe" zones for liposuction in combination with abdominoplasty on the basis of blood supply to the abdominal wall (Fig. 80-4). According to Matarasso the unrestricted safe areas are lateral and superior, but the central medial flap must be suctioned with caution. The surgeon should preserve flap thickness and avoid defatting between Scarpa's fascia and the skin. Safe liposuction must strike a balance between the extent of undermining and tension on the wound closure. Matarasso also proposed a risk factor index for patient selection (Table 80-1).

12. Can musculofascial laxity of the abdominal wall be repaired?

Yes. Musculofascial repair is indicated in patients with musculofascial laxity (Table 80-2). Quite often females will have laxity of the rectus fascia with associated rectus diastasis after multiple pregnancies. The anterior aponeurosis of the abdominal wall is the frame on which the cutaneous flaps are draped, and a significant amount of trunk contouring can be achieved at this level. Plication of the anterior rectus sheath to tighten the musculofascial layer can be performed several ways. Most surgeons vertically plicate the anterior rectus fascia in the midline. Additional lateral horizontal plication sutures can be placed to further contour the abdominal wall. Permanent suture material should be used for the plication.

13. Where and how should umbilicus be placed?

The umbilicus usually lies in the midline at the level of the superior iliac spines. From an anatomic standpoint, these landmarks are used to replace it within the superior skin flap. Multiple techniques have been described, with the basic desired aesthetic result being a small, vertically oriented umbilicus with superior hooding. Freeman and Weimer recommend defatting the umbilical stalk to less then 1.5 cm in diameter and insetting it to a reverse omega incision in the superior skin flap. The reverse omega incision is reported to add hooding to the superior aspect of the umbilicus. The vertical midline of the skin flap is slightly defatted above and below the new umbilicus site to recreate the vertical raphe. The umbilical stalk is then affixed to the skin flap with sutures that both approximate the skin edges and capture the deep fascial margin. This technique not only strengthens the closure but also helps to create the invagination of the umbilicus (Fig. 80-5).

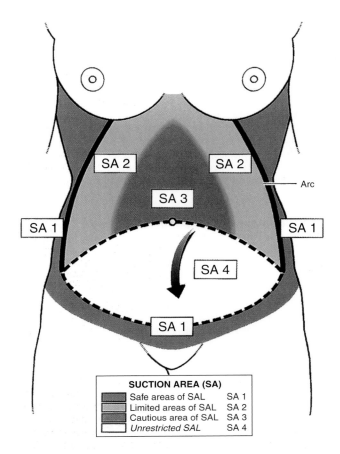

Figure 80-4. Anatomic regions for suction lipectomy in abdominoplasty. Suction areas are SA 1 (safe), SA 2 (limited), SA 3 (cautious), and SA 4 (unrestricted).

Table 80-1. Risk Factor Index	
Class I (low risk)*	Age Volume of suction-assisted lipectomy Concomitant procedures Intraabdominal surgery†
Class II (moderate risk)	Suction-assisted lipectomy location, extent, sites Obesity T closure scars
Class III (high risk)	Deep vein thrombosis risks Smoking exposure Comorbid medical conditions Multiple risk factors

Note: The risk factor index system is used to establish a patient profile and determine the feasibility of combined surgery.
*These factors lengthen the procedure, which increases the possibility of deep vein thrombosis.
†Subject of conflicting reports.

Table 80-2. Abdominoplasty Classification System				
CATEGORY	SKIN	FAT	MUSCULOFASCIAL SYSTEM	TREATMENT
Type I	Minimal laxity	Variable	Minimal flaccidity	Suction-assisted lipectomy
Type II	Mild laxity	Variable	Mild lower abdominal flaccidity	Miniabdominoplasty
Type III	Moderate laxity	Variable	Moderate lower and/or upper abdominal flaccidity	Modified abdominoplasty
Type IV	Severe laxity	Variable	Significant lower and/or upper abdominal flaccidity	Standard abdominoplasty with suction lipectomy

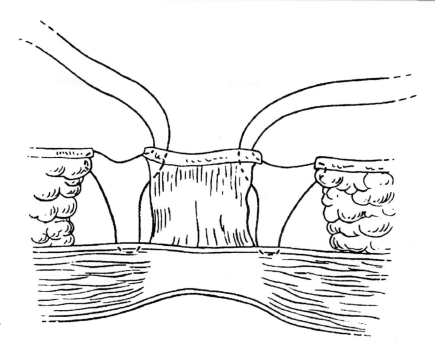

Figure 80-5. Suturing technique for affixing the umbilicus to the superior skin flap and anterior rectus fascia. (From Pitman GH [ed]: Liposuction and Aesthetic Surgery. St. Louis, Quality Medical Publishing, 1993, with permission.)

14. What are the complications of abdominoplasty? How can they be minimized?

Wound infection, seroma, hematoma, minor skin edge necrosis, and minor skin edge dehiscence occur in approximately 12% of all abdominoplasties and are responsible for greater than 98% of all complications reported. Major skin necrosis requiring reoperation, deep vein thrombosis, and pulmonary embolism are significantly more serious complications; however, they occur less commonly. Careful patient selection, surgical planning, and deep vein thrombosis prophylaxis are important factors in minimizing complications. Some surgeons believe that progressive tension sutures used during closure may reduce local complications.

BIBLIOGRAPHY

Beran SJ, Rohrich RJ: Body contouring (overview). Select Read Plast Surg 8:38, 1999.
Castanares S, Goethel JA: Abdominoplasty lipectomy: A modification in technique. Plast Reconstr Surg 7:378, 1967.
Craig SB, Faller MS, Puckett CL: In search of the ideal female umbilicus. Plast Reconstr Surg 105:389–392, 2000.
Dellin AL: Fleur-de-lis abdominoplasty. Aesthet Plast Surg 9:27–32, 1985.
Dubou R, Ousterhout DK: Placement of the umbilicus in an abdominoplasty. Plast Reconstr Surg 61:291–293, 1978.
Freeman BS Weiner DR: Abdominoplasty with special attention to construction of the umbilicus: Technique and complications. Aesthet Plast Surg 2:65, 1978.
Grazer FM, Goldwyn RM: Abdominoplasty assessed by survey with emphasis on complications. Plast Reconstr Surg 59:513–517, 1977.
Hansel JM, Lehman JA Jr, Tantri MP, et al: An outcomes analysis and satisfaction survey of 199 consecutive abdominoplasties. Ann Plast Surg 46:357–363, 2001.
Huger WE Jr: The anatomic rationale for abdominal lipectomy. Am Surg 45:612–617, 1979.
Lewis TS: Midabdominoplasty. Aesthet Plast Surg 3:195, 1979.
Markman B, Barton FE: Anatomy of the subcutaneous tissue of the trunk and lower extremity. Plast Reconstr Surg 80:248–254, 1987.
Matarasso A: Abdominoplasty. Clin Plast Surg 16:289–303, 1989.
Matarasso A: Liposuction as an adjunct to a full abdominoplasty. Plast Reconstr Surg 95:829–836, 1995.
Pitanguy I: Abdominal lipectomy. Clin Plast Surg 2:401–410, 1975.
Pitman GH (ed): Liposuction and Aesthetic Surgery. St. Louis, Quality Medical Publishing, 1993.
Pollack H, Pollack T: Progressive tension sutures: A technique to reduce local complications in abdominoplasty. Plast Reconstr Surg 105:2583–2586, 2000.
Psillikas JM: Plastic surgery of the abdomen with improvement in the body contour, physiopathology and treatment of the aponeurotic musculature. Clin Plast Surg 11:465–477, 1984.
Regnault P: Abdominal dermolipectomies. Clin Plast Surg 2:411–429, 1975.
Regnault P: Abdominoplasty by the W technique. Plast Reconstr Surg 55:265–274, 1975.
Van Uchelen JH, Kon M, Werker PMN: The long-term durability of placation of the anterior rectus sheath assessed by ultrasonography. Plast Reconstr Surg 107:1578–1584, 2001.
Wilkinson TS: Limited abdominoplasty techniques applied to complete abdominal repair. Aesthet Plast Surg 18:49, 1994.

BODY CONTOURING

Samuel J. Beran, MD, and
Joshua A. Greenwald, MD, FACS

1. What is the anatomic distribution of fat in men and women?

Men and women generally accumulate fat in distinct and predictable patterns, which are genetically and hormonally related. The distribution in men is primarily around the abdomen and torso (android pattern). Women accumulate fat around the hips and thighs (gynoid pattern).

2. Are there differences in the layers of fat?

The subcutaneous fat in the trunk is composed of two layers, superficial and deep. The superficial layer is dense and compact, with multiple fibrous septa. The deep layer is more loose and areolar with few septa. The deep layers are principally located around the umbilical, paralumbar, gluteal, and medial thigh regions.

3. How is cellulite formed?

The fat present in cellulite is no different from ordinary subcutaneous fat. The distinct appearance of cellulite is due to the architecture of the superficial fat in these areas. The presence of dense vertical septa separates the fat into pockets. As the fat hypertrophies or the skin relaxes with age, the septa act as anchor points to the skin. This results in the classic accordion appearance of cellulite.

4. If fat is removed, will it come back?

Fat cells are produced by the body during three different periods: in utero, early childhood, and early adolescence. In general, after reaching maturity, the total number of fat cells in the body will not increase. Fat cells that are removed through liposuction or other techniques will not be replaced by other fat cells. However, the remaining cells may hypertrophy, and the total fat mass in the area may increase. The one exception is morbid obesity, in which the fat cells may become hyperplastic and multiply.

5. What is liposuction?

Liposuction, also known as *lipoplasty* or *liposculpture,* is the surgical removal of adipose tissue through the use of small metal cannulas.

6. Who originally developed liposuction? When did it become accepted?

Dujarrier is generally accredited with the first use of liposuction in 1921. He attempted to remove fatty deposits from around the knees of a ballerina but perforated the femoral artery, resulting in an amputation. This set back liposuction for several years. The modern development of liposuction can be traced to such surgeons as Schrudde, Fisher, Meyer, and Illouz in the 1970s and 1980s.

7. What are the indications for liposuction?

Liposuction works best for treating localized fat deposits that do not respond to traditional diet and exercise. The treated areas will retain the new contour unless the patient has large weight gains. Liposuction is not a treatment of obesity. Patients who have significant medical problems, who have poor skin tone or inelasticity, or who are taking anticoagulants should not undergo liposuction.

8. What is the difference between ultrasound-assisted liposuction and traditional liposuction?

Traditional liposuction removes fat cells through the mechanical avulsion of fat. Ultrasound-assisted liposuction (UAL) uses an ultrasound generator and handpiece to produce ultrasound energy to destroy fat cells in vivo through a process known as *cavitation.* The emulsified fat is removed through a hollow channel in the cannula using standard suction.

9. What is wetting solution? Why do we use it?

Wetting solution is the delivery of subcutaneous infiltration into the subcutaneous fat before the use of liposuction. It was pioneered by Illouz in the 1970s and later adapted by many surgeons, most notably Klein, who developed the tumescent technique. The use of wetting solution has two advantages: an anesthetic effect secondary to the use of lidocaine and a hemostatic effect due to the use of epinephrine (Table 81-1).

Table 81-1. Liposuction Techniques

TECHNIQUE	INFILTRATE	ESTIMATE OF BLOOD LOSS (% OF VOLUME)
Dry	No infiltrate	20–45
Wet	200–300 cc per area	4–30
Superwet	1 cc infiltrate per 1 cc aspirate	1
Tumescent	Infiltrate to skin turgor 2–3 cc infiltrate per 1 cc aspirate	1

10. What are the compositions of the more common wetting solutions?

The two most commonly used wetting solutions for liposuction are the Klein tumescent solution and the Hunstad solution. The Klein formula combines 1 L of saline with 50 mL of 1% lidocaine, 1 mL of 1:1000 epinephrine, and 2.5 mL of 8.4% sodium bicarbonate. The bicarbonate is added to augment the potency of the lidocaine and decrease the discomfort of the injection. The Hunstad formula uses lactated Ringer's solution with the same lidocaine and epinephrine solution as in the Klein formula. Because lactated Ringer's solution has bicarbonate, there is no need to add bicarbonate. The final lidocaine concentration of both solutions is 0.048%, and the epinephrine is slightly more dilute than 1:1,000,000.

11. How are intravenous fluids managed during liposuction?

Maintenance fluids are replaced throughout the duration of the procedure. For each milliliter of lipoaspirate greater than 5 L, an additional 0.25 cc of crystalloid is administered. As with any procedure, the overall health of the patient and the patient's cardiovascular status must be accounted for.

12. What are the recommended aspirate volumes for outpatient liposuction?

Routine inpatient postoperative observation in an accredited facility for patients undergoing aspiration greater than 5 L have resulted in lower complication rates.

13. What is a maximal safe dose of lidocaine when administered as a wetting solution?

With tumescent infiltration into the subcutaneous tissues, 35 mg/kg is considered the maximal safe dose. For an 80-kg patient, this corresponds to 2800 mg of lidocaine. Thus, if 5 L of tumescent fluid is infused into an 80-kg patient (500 mg of lidocaine per liter of tumescent), a total of 2500 mg of lidocaine is infiltrated, which is below the maximal safe dose.

14. Should you be concerned about lidocaine toxicity during the procedure?

Lidocaine toxicity is not a major concern during the procedure unless there is inadvertent intravascular injection of tumescent solution. Maximal lidocaine concentration in the blood peaks 8 to 16 hours from initiation of infiltration. Several studies have documented that administration of tumescent solution up to 35 mg/kg of lidocaine does not result in toxic blood levels of lidocaine (blood concentration >5 mcg/mL).

15. If you are planning a large-volume liposuction (>5 L), how should the infiltrate be modified?

The surgeon should be well aware of the maximal safe dose of lidocaine as indicated in Question 13. If this level is being approached, infusing tumescent solution without lidocaine will provide the desired hemostatic effect without administration of additional lidocaine. Warming of all infiltration fluids and use of a Foley catheter should be routinely used in this subset of patients.

16. What are the most common sequelae of liposuction?

The difference between sequelae and complications is what the doctor tells the patient: the patient *will* have the sequelae after the procedure but *may* have the complications. The most common sequelae include contour irregularities, paresthesias, edema, ecchymosis, and discoloration, which occur routinely in almost all patients who undergo liposuction. However, they resolve spontaneously or with minimal treatment such as massage.

17. What are the most common complications of liposuction?

The most common complications of liposuction include significant blood loss, fluid shifts, asymmetries, and contour deformities. The possible complications of skin loss, skin burns, and seroma formation are seen more frequently with UAL than with traditional liposuction.

18. Is it safe to perform liposuction with abdominoplasty?

It is safe to perform liposuction in some areas of the trunk in conjunction with abdominoplasty. These areas include the flanks and anterolateral abdominal wall; however, the central abdomen should not be treated because skin or flap loss may occur.

19. What is the recommended treatment of gynecomastia?

Currently, UAL is an excellent modality for treatment of gynecomastia. It removes the dense fibrous fat of the male breast and contours the area around the central core. Occasionally, resection of the small fibrotic remainder may be needed.

20. Does the excessive skin need to be resected after removal of fat via liposuction?

In general, even despite large amounts of removed fat, skin has good elasticity and will conform to the new underlying volume. However, in patients with inelastic skin or in elderly patients, the skin may not redrape and skin resection may be needed.

21. How do you determine whether a patient will benefit from abdominoplasty versus liposuction?

The first determinant is the status of the abdominal wall musculature. During examination it is critical to check for the presence of a lax abdominal wall. Diastasis or wall laxity cannot be treated by liposuction. Second, if the patient has inelastic skin or severe skin excess, the skin may not redrape, so excisional techniques are more appropriate.

22. What is the treatment of arm ptosis and lipodystrophy?

There are two approaches. In mild to moderate cases, liposuction, either traditional or ultrasound assisted, may be effective. If the deformity is moderate to severe or the patient has inelastic skin, direct excision (brachioplasty) can be performed.

23. Where should the final scar in a formal brachioplasty lie?

The scar should lie slightly posterior to the bicipital groove.

24. How do you prevent complications from a medial thigh lift?

The most common complications from a medial thigh lift are wide scars, vulvar distortion, and relapse. They may be prevented by anchoring the thigh flap to the deep layer of the superficial perineal fascia (Colles' fascia).

25. What is autologous fat transplantation?

In this process, fat is harvested from one area of the patient and transplanted to another. Examples include removal of abdominal fat for procedures such as lip augmentation, repair of postliposuction deformities, and facial sculpturing. The survival rate of transplanted fat cells is controversial. In general, if the fat is treated gingerly, rinsed, and centrifuged, the survival rate is 25% to 50%.

26. What are Autologen and Alloderm?

Autologen is autologous processed dermis. Alloderm is processed cadaver dermis. Both products can be used for augmentation of the lip, contour deformities, and the nasolabial fold. Although no large long-term studies have analyzed survival rates of the dermis, several reports show no resorption after 1 year.

27. Does the use of Autologen and Alloderm involve any risk?

The significant risks with use of Autologen are infection and resorption. Alloderm is treated by a number of techniques to eliminate viable viral and/or cell structures.

CONTROVERSIES

28. Will UAL replace traditional liposuction?

Although initially greeted as the replacement for traditional liposuction, the clinical applications of UAL now are more apparent. UAL appears to be more effective than traditional liposuction in fibrous tissue such as the buttocks, gynecomastia, and secondary liposuction. There may be increased skin shrinkage with the use of UAL. However, UAL will not replace traditional liposuction. Instead, it extends the use of liposuction in body contouring.

29. Is fat transplantation the best way to perform lip augmentation or minor contouring procedures where augmentation is required?

The use of fat transplantation is somewhat controversial. Although some surgeons believe that 50% or more of grafts will survive, many believe that the survival rates are too variable and unpredictable for safe use. Alternatives include biologic products such as autogenous dermis, processed cadaver dermis, porcine or bovine collagen, and synthetic products such as Gore-Tex.

30. Does tumescent liposuction have an advantage over other techniques?

Liposuction performed without the use of subcutaneous infiltration has a much higher rate of blood loss than does liposuction performed with wetting solutions. However, the exact dosage of subcutaneous infiltration required to provide the beneficial effects has not been thoroughly studied. The risk of true tumescent infiltration is fluid overload.

31. Are there cures for cellulite?

At present a number of modalities are purported either to ameliorate or to cure cellulite. However, no definitive studies show clear results in reducing or eliminating cellulite. Techniques that have been reported to be effective include ultrasound liposuction, Endermologie, massage techniques, and application of creams. None of these has proved to be fruitful.

BIBLIOGRAPHY

Dillerud E: Suction lipoplasty: A report on complications, undesired results, and patient satisfaction based on 3511 procedures. Plast Reconstr Surg 88:239–246, 1991.

Guerrerosantos J: Analogous fat grafting for body contouring. Clin Plast Surg 23:619–632, 1996.

Kenkel JM, Lipschitz AH, Shepherd G, et al: Pharmacokinetics and safety of lidocaine and monoethylglycinexylidide in liposuction: A microdialysis study. Plast Reconstr Surg 114:516–524, 2004; discussion 525–526.

Klein JA: Tumescent technique for local anesthesia improves safety in large-volume liposuction. Plast Reconstr Surg 92:1085–1098, 1993.

Lockwood TE: Fascial anchoring technique in medial thigh lifts. Plast Reconstr Surg 82:299–304, 1988.

Markman B, Barton FE Jr: Anatomy of the subcutaneous tissue of the trunk and lower extremity. Plast Reconstr Surg 80:248–254, 1987.

Rohrich RJ, Beran SJ, Fodor PB: The role of subcutaneous infiltration in suction-assisted lipoplasty: A review. Plast Reconstr Surg 99:514–519, 1997.

Rohrich RJ, Leedy JE, Swamy R, et al: Fluid resuscitation in liposuction: A retrospective review of 89 consecutive patients. Plast Reconstr Surg 117:431–435, 2006.

Strauch B, Greenspun D, Levine J, et al: A technique of brachioplasty. Plast Reconstr Surg 113:1044–1048, 2004; discussion 1049.

Zocchi M: Clinical aspects of ultrasonic liposculpture. Perspect Plast Surg 7:153, 1993.

BODY CONTOURING AFTER MASSIVE WEIGHT LOSS

Michele A. Shermak, MD; Sonal Pandya, MD; and Sean T. Doherty, MD

1. What is the incidence of morbid obesity in the United States?

Obesity is a worldwide epidemic and continues to grow at an alarming rate in the United States (U.S.). The number of annual deaths attributed to obesity in the U.S. is estimated to be 112,000. Approximately 65% of adults in the U.S. are overweight, 60 million are obese, and nine million are severely obese. The clinical definition of obesity is a body mass index (BMI) ≥30. Obesity is a progressive disease. It is a major health concern with significant economic implications, costing the U.S. medical system more than $70 billion per year. A constellation of medical problems known as *metabolic syndrome* is associated with morbid obesity, including hypertension, dyslipidemia, type 2 diabetes, coronary artery disease, stroke, gallbladder disease, osteoarthritis, obstructive sleep apnea, and cancers such as breast and colon cancer.

2. What is the BMI, and how is it determined?

BMI is a ratio of weight to height. It is the most commonly used method for determining a patient's weight status and is calculated as follows:

$$BMI = Weight\ (in\ kilograms)/Height\ (in\ meters^2)$$

BMI of 30 to 35 is classified as obesity, 35 to 40 defines severe obesity, 40 to 50 defines morbid obesity, and ≥50 defines "super obesity." Higher BMI is associated with greater health risks and greater risk for complications from surgery, such as wound healing problems, infection, seroma, and venous thromboembolism (VTE).

BMI is not a direct measure of body "fatness" or health as it is calculated from an individual's weight, which includes both muscle and fat. In this way, highly trained athletes may have a high BMI but not have a high percentage of body fat.

3. What are the surgical options available for patients with morbid obesity?

Bariatric surgery is the only effective therapy for successful maintenance of weight loss in morbidly obese patients. The two major categories of surgery are restrictive operations and malabsorptive operations. Restrictive operations include vertical banded gastroplasty, gastric banding (lap band), and gastric bypass. Malabsorptive operations include biliopancreatic diversion, duodenal switch, and distal gastric bypass. In the U.S., gastric bypass composes 80% of obesity procedures, lap band approximately 5% to 10% (more common in Europe and Australia), and duodenal switch approximately 5% to 10% of bariatric surgery cases.

In 2004, more than 144,000 Americans had bariatric surgery, representing a 40% increase over 2003 and 100% over 2002 (Fig. 82-1). There is significant improvement of the concomitant medical problems associated with obesity in patients who have lost weight.

4. What is the impact of this on the field of plastic surgery?

Massive weight loss leads to skin redundancy and laxity, resulting in rashes, skin breakdown, hygiene problems, pain within the skin, and exacerbation of back and joint pain. Some patients are limited in achieving further weight loss by impedance of skin redundancy. Aesthetically, the excess skin can negatively impact body image to the point where some patients express that they wished they never lost the weight. Excess skin can affect the face and neck, chest, abdomen, and upper and lower back and thighs.

More patients are exploring options for body contouring, which has developed into a specialty in its own right. The latest statistics from the American Society for Aesthetic Plastic Surgery show that massive weight loss body contouring procedures increased at a rate of 38% for lower body lift and 61% for brachioplasty in 2003 to 2004.

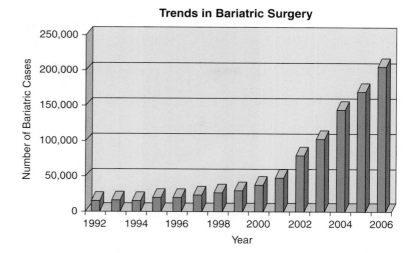

Figure 82-1. Number of bariatric surgeries performed in the United States by year.

5. Why is body contouring in massive weight loss patients a greater challenge?

From the medical, psychological, and cosmetic viewpoint, the postbariatric patient population presents a unique and growing challenge to the plastic surgeon. These patients present a very different profile from those who have not been obese. Their deformities are more severe, with more excess skin, poor tone, and greater degree of laxity. Due to the global weight loss and hence the global laxity of skin, traditional body contouring techniques often are insufficient to correct these deformities. Multiple procedures may be required, surgeries are time consuming, and blood loss can be substantial. Patients often have medical comorbidities, previous surgical scars, and nutritional deficiencies. Some massive weight loss patients still are obese, which puts them at greater risk for complications after surgery (Fig. 82-2).

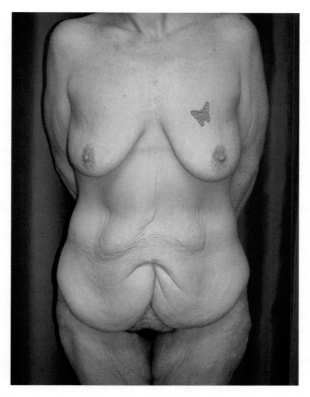

Figure 82-2. Standard presentation of massive weight loss patient, including skin with poor tone and laxity and upper midline scar.

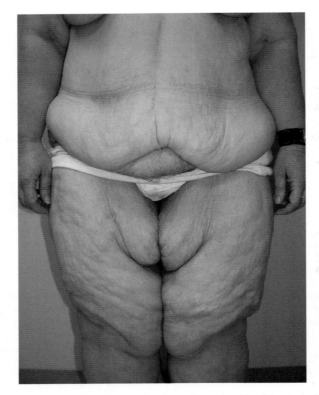

Figure 82-3. In body regions with significant lipodystrophy requiring liposuction and excision, it is safer to stage the procedures, performing liposuction of thick subcutaneous tissue in a first stage followed by excision at a second stage. Maximal and stable weight loss must be ensured prior to undertaking these procedures.

6. What is the ideal time interval to initiate body contouring surgery?

Bariatric surgery patients typically achieve stable weight loss in 12 to 18 months, but some patients present in as few as 6 months for panniculectomy due to interference from overhanging skin.

7. What is the role of liposuction in morbidly obese patients?

Rarely is liposuction the only procedure that a patient with massive weight loss would need for body contouring. Liposuction can be used to assist in contouring or in release of tissues to allow better lift. For example, liposuction of the outer thigh can help in lower body lift by improving contour and allowing release to afford better lift. It is risky to combine liposuction with excision of a body region such as the thigh or arm. It is safer to stage liposuction and excision if liposuction is needed to improve contour, performing liposuction of thick subcutaneous tissue in the first stage followed by excision as the second stage (Fig. 82-3).

8. What are some of the considerations of breast surgery in massive weight loss patients?

Breast deformity in massive weight loss patients is greater and more technically challenging than in non–massive weight loss patients. The breast tends to have a deflated, flat appearance, with excess skin laxity, significant ptosis, and often a prominent axillary roll or fatty roll that continues into the back.

Approaches to shaping and contouring the breast include mastopexy alone or in combination with implant augmentation, saline or silicone. Mastopexy with an inverted T incision extending into the axilla and possibly all the way into the back will treat "bat wings." The lateral tissue can be used for autologous augmentation of the central breast mound. Vertical mastopexy can be considered if ptotic tissue is limited to the anterior chest.

Augmentation mastopexy can be performed as a single or a staged procedure. Staging surgery affords less risk of wound healing problems and allows better predictability of outcome due to the fact that sagging may occur after mastopexy, particularly in this population. Mastopexy would be performed first, followed by second-stage augmentation (Fig. 82-4).

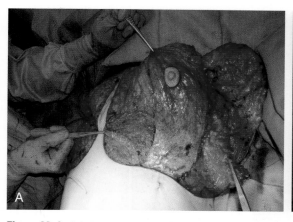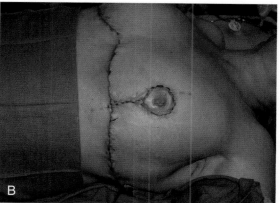

Figure 82-4. A, Lateral and medial breast tissue that would otherwise be discarded in standard mastopexy can be rotated to supplement the central breast mound. **B,** On the table result, with skin closed.

9. How is gynecomastia in the male treated after massive weight loss?

Gynecomastia presentation in this population spans a broad spectrum, ranging from patients who require only some liposuction to patients who require a full upper body lift from front to back. In patients with minimal ptosis who do not desire a perceptible scar, liposuction may work. In patients with a large amount of excess skin and breast tissue, a Wise pattern approach with mastectomy and nipple grafting is recommended. Rather than mastectomy and nipple grafting, others may recommend liposuction and nipple transposition with an inverted T scar or with just a horizontal scar (Fig. 82-5).

10. Describe some techniques used for brachioplasty after massive weight loss.

- *Short Scar Brachioplasty:* Treats mild skin excess of the proximal arm, with scar limited to the axillary fold. This approach has limited application and conservative results.
- *Traditional Brachioplasty:* Treats severe skin excess with scar from axilla to elbow. Discussion of scar placement and appearance prior to surgery is of paramount importance because these scars are visible and may remain hypertrophic for a prolonged period.
- *Extended Brachioplasty:* Traditional scar extended to below the axilla along the lateral chest to treat skin excess (i.e., "bat wing deformity"). Placing a Z-plasty within the axilla will help protect against contracture and limited range that may result in a scar traversing straight across the axilla (Fig. 82-6).

11. Explain the different terminologies used for contouring procedures of the abdomen and the lower body.

- *Standard Abdominoplasty:* Removal of excess abdominal skin with undermining and plication of the abdominal wall.
- *Extended Abdominoplasty:* Removal of the roll of loose skin and fat that wraps around the waistline or the love handle. Results in longer scars.
- *Anchor (Fleur-de-Lis) Abdominoplasty:* Removal of a vertical strip of tissue resulting in a midline vertical scar, with tightening of the horizontal vector as well.

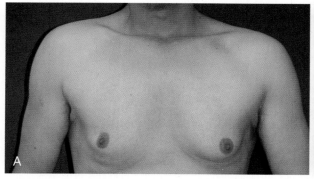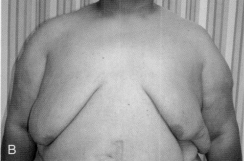

Figure 82-5. A, Minimal gynecomastia post massive weight loss, which can be treated with liposuction alone to flatten the chest. **B,** More marked gynecomastia with chest ptosis and skin redundancy extending around the back, requiring upper body lift.

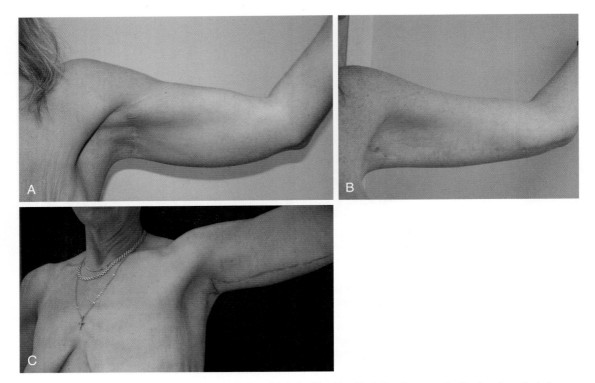

Figure 82-6. A, Short scar brachioplasty limits scar to the axilla. **B,** Traditional brachioplasty with scars extending from the axilla to the elbow in a T. **C,** Extended brachioplasty scar to address lateral chest, using Z-plasty across the axilla.

- *High Lateral Tension Abdominoplasty:* Lateral tension at the outer margins of the scar, popularized by Ted Lockwood, MD.
- *Reverse Abdominoplasty:* Contouring of the upper abdomen using an incision placed in the inframammary crease, often performed at a separate stage from traditional abdominoplasty (Fig. 82-7).
- *Panniculectomy:* Removal of the abdominal panniculus, a large apron of skin and fat that overhangs the pubis. Not as extensive as abdominoplasty and does not involve undermining, translocation of the umbilicus, or plication of the fascia. Tends to be applicable to high-risk or morbidly obese patients.
- *Belt (Circumferential) Lipectomy:* Removal of tissue from the abdomen circumferential to the back.
- *Lower Body Lift:* Belt lipectomy that treats the lower truncal subunit and may include the inner thighs.

12. What is a lower body lift? An upper body lift?

A lower body lift comprises abdominoplasty and lower back lift, also known as *circumferential torsoplasty*. In patients who may benefit, autologous subcutaneous fat and dermis based on the gluteal arteries may provide buttock augmentation in combination with the back lift. Thigh lift may be attached to this procedure. Lower body lift helps address the abdomen, pubis, back, and inner and outer thighs, improving adjacent body regions above and below the resection.

An upper body lift comprises mastopexy in women and mastectomy for gynecomastia in men, combined with excision of upper back skin. Some include brachioplasty within the category of upper body lift.

13. What are some considerations in markings for a lower body lift?

Markings must be performed in the preoperative area with the patient standing. For back lift, the upper marks follow the buttock subunit and are guided by the patient's desire for a particular scar location. A pinch test is used to assess tissue laxity and to determine the inferior incision, which should be in the form of an S, removing more lateral tissue than central tissue. Incision placement should not be so low as to connect to the gluteal cleft, which could result in unsightly lengthening of the cleft. Anterior markings must address ptosis of the mons. The incision for the mons usually is 5 to 7 cm above the introitus. The lateral anterior markings are made after lifting up the anterior lateral thigh skin toward the iliac spine. Pulling upward and inward these markings are connected with the posterior markings. In general, scars should lie posteriorly above the gluteal cleft, laterally at the iliac crest, above the inguinal ligament in the groin, and approximately 5 to 7 cm above the introitus.

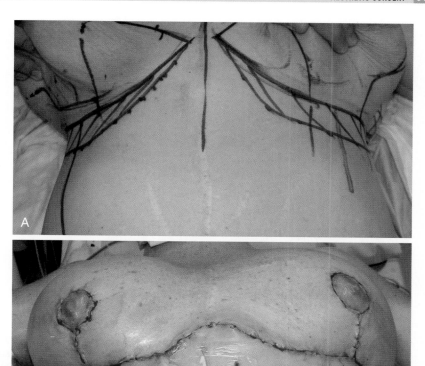

Figure 82-7. **A,** Reverse abdominoplasty markings. Excision into the inframammary fold provides better access to upper abdominal skin redundancy. **B,** Upper abdominal approach is incorporated into a mastopexy.

14. **What are positioning options for lower body lift? What precautions need to be taken with this positioning?**

    Positioning options include prone/supine and lateral decubitus/supine. Pressure on the head and neck must be avoided. Undue pressure around the eyes can cause blindness. Neck position must be neutral to avoid kinking of the carotid and vertebral arteries, which may cause stroke. Axilla and elbows should be kept at 90° without extension to avoid stretching of the nerves. Pressure on the joints must be avoided because any compression of the nerves could lead to long-term disability.

15. **What are the surgical options for inner thigh lift?**

    Thigh lift incisions may be limited to the anteromedial thigh as advocated by Ted Lockwood or may be extended down the inner thigh to the knee, analogous to traditional brachioplasty. For the anteromedial thigh approach no more than a 7-cm resection of skin is recommended, and suspension to Colles' fascia/pubic periosteum is critical to avoid downward scar migration. Extending the anteromedial incision into the gluteal crease posteriorly, more skin may be removed. The benefit of this approach is limitation of the scar to the groin crease; however, the drawback is that only skin in the upper third to half of the thigh is tightened. Performing thigh lift with extension to the knee allows better skin tightening along the entire thigh to the knee in exchange for a longer, visible scar. Care must be taken with keeping a superficial plane of excision to avoid injury to venous and lymphatic structures. This approach is also best performed on an operative bed that allows separation of the legs (Fig. 82-8).

16. **What are some common risks of body contouring surgery after massive weight loss?**

    Common risks include seroma formation, wound healing problems, infection, scarring, bleeding, and VTE. Problems specific to these surgeries include the possibility of asymmetry and relapsing skin laxity due to poor skin tone. Patients may need revisions due to difficulty in ensuring a taut result with poor skin quality that may result from malnutrition. Reducing the complexity of surgery and staging surgery in patients with medical comorbidities or BMI >30 can help reduce risk and optimize outcomes.

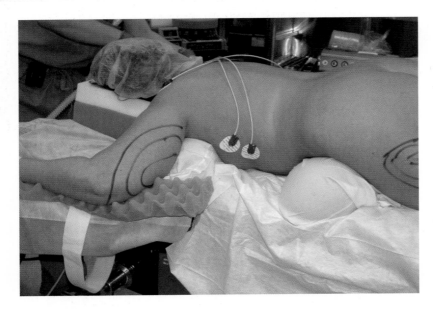

Figure 82-8. Prone positioning precautions include neck in neutral position and axilla and elbow at 90°. Facial prone pillow protects the face and eyes from pressure, as does eggcrate padding for all other pressure points including the joints.

17. What measures can surgeons take to reduce the risk of VTE?
Conservative prophylactic measures against VTE include intraoperative knee flexion; support hose and sequential compression devices until ambulation; and heparin or low-molecular-weight heparin subcutaneous in prophylactic doses. Patients with prior VTE or high BMI require a Greenfield filter, either temporary or permanent, and must be considered for therapeutic anticoagulation after surgery.

BIBLIOGRAPHY

Aly AS (ed): Body Contouring Surgery after Massive Weight Loss. St. Louis, Quality Medical Publishing, 2005.
Aly AS, Cram AE, Chao M, Pang J, Mckeon M: Belt lipectomy for circumferential truncal excess: The University of Iowa experience. Plast Reconstr Surg 111:398–413, 2003.
Aly AS, Cram AE, Heddens C: Truncal body contouring surgery in the massive weight loss patient. Clin Plast Surg 31:611–624, 2004.
Hurwitz DJ, Rubin JP, Risin M, Sajjadian A, Sereika S: Correcting the saddlebag deformity in the massive weight loss patient. Plast Reconstr Surg 114:1313–1325, 2004.
Kenkel JM (ed): Body contouring surgery after massive weight loss. Plast Reconstr Surg 117:1S–86S, 2006.
Lockwood TE: Maximizing aesthetics in lateral-tension abdominoplasty and body lifts. Clin Plast Surg 31:523–537, 2004.
Manahan M, Shermak MA: Massive panniculectomy after massive weight loss. Plast Reconstr Surg 117:2191–2197, 2006.
Nemerofsky RB, Oliak DA, Capella JF: Body lift: An account of 200 consecutive cases in the massive weight loss patient. Plast Reconstr Surg 117:414–430, 2006.
Rubin JP: Mastopexy after massive weight loss: Dermal suspension and total parenchymal reshaping. Aesthet Surg 26: 214–222, 2006.
Sebastian JL, Capella JF, Rubin JP: Body Contouring Surgery after Massive Weight Loss. Omaha, NE, Addicus Books, 2006.
Shermak M, Shoo B, Deune EG: Prone positioning precautions in plastic surgery. Plast Reconstr Surg 117:1584–1588, 2006.
Steinbrook R: Surgery for severe obesity. N Engl J Med 350:1075–1079, 2004.
Taylor J, Shermak MA: Body contouring following massive weight loss. Obes Surg 14:1080–1085, 2004.
Young VL, Watson ME: The need for venous thromboembolism (VTE) prophylaxis in plastic surgery. Aesthet Surg 26:157–175, 2006.

CHEMICAL PEELING AND DERMABRASION

Sheilah A. Lynch, MD, and
Karl A. Schwarz, MD, MSc, FRCSC

1. What is chemical peeling?

Chemical peeling, also called *chemexfoliation, chemosurgery,* or *dermapeeling,* is the application of one or more exfoliating agents to the skin, resulting in destruction of portions of the epidermis and/or dermis with subsequent regeneration of new epidermal and dermal tissues. The various agents used can be categorized according to the depth of wounding that they produce. Superficial or light peeling involves wounding to the papillary dermis; wounding to the upper reticular dermis is considered medium-depth peeling; and deep-depth peeling is to the midreticular dermis (Box 83-1).

2. What are the indications for chemical peeling?

Chemical peeling can be used for photoaging, including actinic keratoses, solar elastosis, solar lentigines, and rhytids; pigmentary disturbances, including melasma, postinflammatory pigmentary changes, and other pigmentary dyschromias; superficial scarring; acne vulgaris (except ice pick acne, which is best treated with excision); rosacea; and milia.

3. What agents are most commonly used for chemical peeling? What are the typical concentrations?

Phenol and trichloroacetic acid (TCA) are most commonly used. Several formulas that include phenol as the main peeling agent have been developed. The Baker formula for phenol is as follows:

- 3 mL USP phenol (C61-150H) (88%)
- 2 mL tap water
- 8 drops liquid soap (Septisol)
- 3 drops Croton oil

Phenol, a keratocoagulant, denatures and coagulates the surface keratin. Croton oil is a skin irritant that enhances the action of phenol. Soap acts as a surfactant to enhance penetration. Water is a diluent that slows down keratocoagulation and enhances absorption. TCA strength can be varied depending on the depth desired:

Box 83-1. Chemical Peeling Wounding Spectrum*

Superficial Wounding (to Stratum Granulosum-Papillary Dermis)
Very light: TCA, 10%–20% (TCA, superficial), resorcinol, Jessner's solution, salicylic acid, solid CO_2, alpha-hydroxy acids, tretinoin
Light: TCA, 35%, unoccluded, single or multiple frost

Medium-Depth Wounding (to Upper Reticular Dermis)
Combination CO_2 + TCA, 35%–50%, unoccluded, single or multiple frost
Combination Jessner's solution + TCA, unoccluded, single or multiple frost
Combination glycolic acid 70% + TCA 35%
TCA, 50%, unoccluded (TCA, deep), single frost
Full-strength phenol, 88%, unoccluded
Pyruvic acid

Deep-Depth Wounding (to Midreticular Dermis)
Baker's phenol, unoccluded
Baker's phenol, occluded

*Depth depends on prepeel skin defatting preparation, wounding agent strength or amount applied, and skin thickness or location. Clinical reepithelialization may depend on skin location and the character of the dermal pathology, which may determine the degree of inflammatory response evoked.
TCA, Trichloroacetic acid.
From Brody HJ: Chemical Peeling. St. Louis, Mosby, 1992, p 21.

- Light peeling: 10% to 25%
- Intermediate peeling: 26% to 50%
- Deep peeling: 51% to 75%

The major advantage of TCA is its versatility. The depth of peeling can be individualized for a particular patient's needs, skin type, and underlying pathology. Several TCA-based, "designer peels" have surfaced over the last several years. For instance, the Obagi Blue Peel system is TCA based. (The milder Obagi Nu-Derm system is based on phytic acid.) The most common complication of TCA peels is hyperpigmentation.

4. What does Jessner's solution contain?

Jessner's solution contains the following:

- Ethanol
- Lactic acid
- Resorcinol
- Salicylic acid

5. How do you choose a particular peeling agent to suit your patient's skin type?

Fitzpatrick has classified skin into six types based on color and response to sunlight (Table 83-1). Types I to III are ideal for peeling of all varieties, but the line of demarcation between peeled and unpeeled skin is most prominent in actinically damaged type I skin with marked neck poikiloderma. Red-haired, freckled people should forgo the treatment. Type IV skin can be peeled with all peeling agents. If the patient has an eye color other than brown, however, the likelihood of postinflammatory pigmentation is reported to be less. Types V and VI also can be peeled with all peeling agents, but the risk of unwanted pigmentation is greater. Test spots should be performed at the hairline in patients who are at greatest risk (types V and VI), but this test does not guarantee that the remainder of the face will respond identically.

6. Is pretreatment necessary before chemical peeling?

Yes. For patients undergoing TCA peels, tretinoin (Retin-A) and 4% hydroquinone should be used for 4 to 6 weeks before treatment. Tretinoin decreases the thickness of the stratum corneum, thereby increasing the permeability of the epidermis to chemical peeling. Hydroquinone suppresses melanocyte activity and helps to prevent the tendency toward postpeel hyperpigmentation. For patients who cannot tolerate tretinoin, glycolic acid facial creams, used for 4 to 6 weeks before peeling, have yielded comparable results. Glycolic acid works by decreasing keratinocyte cohesion, leading to desquamation.

7. Is taping necessary during chemical peeling?

The use of occlusive adhesive-type tape after phenol-based solutions has been applied as standard procedure. The results are definitely more profound and last longer when tape is used. If a lesser degree of depth of peeling is desired, the peel can be performed without tape, using petroleum jelly as the occlusive barrier. In contrast, tape occlusion with TCA does not increase penetration.

8. Can peeling be done simultaneously with surgery?

Peeling solution should not be applied to any areas that have been undermined during a surgical face lift. The only areas that can be considered for peeling are those areas around the mouth that have not been surgically altered. Simultaneous disruption of the blood supply by undermining and the chemical burn produced by the application of the phenol solution are likely to produce irreversible skin changes, perhaps even skin necrosis.

Table 83-1. Fitzpatrick Classification of Sun-Reactive Skin Types		
SKIN TYPE	**COLOR**	**REACTION TO FIRST SUMMER EXPOSURE**
I	White	Always burns, never tans
II	White	Usually burns, tans with difficulty
III	White	Sometimes mild burns, tans average
IV	Moderate brown	Rarely burns, tans with ease
V	Dark brown*	Very rarely burns, tans very easily
VI	Black	Never burns, tans very easily

*Asian, Indian, Oriental, Hispanic, or light African descent, for example.
Data from Brody HJ: Chemical Peeling. St. Louis, Mosby, 1992, p 36.

9. Which should be done first: facial surgery or facial peeling?

If both procedures are planned, surgery should be performed first and the peeling performed at least 3 months later. If the peeling is done first, somewhat more time must elapse before the surgery can be safely performed because of the slower healing after peeling. The choice as to which procedure to perform first depends on whether the sagging of the face or the lines of the face are the primary concern of the patient.

10. What complications may be encountered after peeling?

Postoperative changes can be classified into two categories.

Category 1 consists of sequelae that are expected as procedural side effects and resolve completely. Examples include pigmentary changes, prolonged erythema (<3 months), colloid milia, pustulocystic acne, reactivation of latent facial herpes simplex virus infection, and superficial bacterial infection.

Category 2 consists of sequelae that are characteristic of the individual agent, occur regardless of patient setting, may be secondary to poor postoperative care, and are considered true complications. True complications include pigmentary changes, prolonged erythema (>3 months), hypertrophic scarring, atrophy, and systemic effects such as hepatic, renal, or cardiac abnormalities associated with phenol.

Skin depigmentation may occur, and patient selection is important. Patients with multiple freckles and other sun-induced blotches, as commonly seen in people with red hair, should forgo the treatment. Special care should be taken to stop the peel just under the jawline to hide the line of demarcation and to feather, or blend, the edge. Milia, which are small, superficial epidermal inclusion cysts, may occur during the first 6 to 8 weeks after treatment. In most instances they resolve with vigorous washing and/or scrubbing. Persistent cysts need to be punctured and evacuated.

11. What peeling solution may cause cardiac arrhythmias when it is applied too rapidly to too large an area?

Electrocardiographic (ECG) changes, premature atrial or ventricular contractions, bigeminy, and trigeminy may occur in patients who absorb large amounts of phenol through the skin. To prevent such problems, patients should be well hydrated and under cardiac monitoring, and treatment of large areas at one time should be avoided. Beware of patients with renal insufficiency because phenol is cleared by the kidney. TCA is not cardiotoxic. Cardiac arrhythmias have not been reported following TCA use.

12. Regeneration of the epidermis and upper dermis occurs via dermal appendages. What previous procedures or medications affect the concentration of dermal appendages and consequently regeneration?

Laser procedures for hair removal and electrolysis leave the tissue with a reduced number of appendages and therefore a limited regenerative capacity. Accutane (isotretinoin), used for treatment of acne vulgaris, inhibits sebaceous gland function. Accutane presents a transient risk for reepithelialization problems, and patients should not undergo peeling or dermabrasion while taking this medication or for at least 12 months after termination of its use.

13. What histologic changes do chemical peels cause in the skin?

Chemical peels lead to an increase in dermal thickness, elastic tissue, and fibroblast density within the skin. There is a decrease in nonlamellar collagen, with the new collagen laid down in a lamellar pattern.

14. Discuss the Glogau classification for photoaging and how treatment strategy changes for each group.

The Glogau classification of photoaging divides patients into four groups based on the degree of actinic keratoses, wrinkling, and acne scarring and the amount of makeup worn by the patient (Table 83-2). This classification helps to assess the degree of sun damage in patients with and those without a history of acne scarring and to make treatment decisions.

15. What are alpha-hydroxy acids?

Alpha-hydroxy acids (AHAs), a group of nontoxic organic acids found in natural foods, have been incorporated into a variety of creams, lotions, and cleansers for general use. They include glycolic, lactic, malic, tartaric, and citric acids. The clinical applications of AHAs have expanded to include their use as alternative chemical peeling agents generally used to treat fine wrinkling, areas of dryness, uneven pigmentation, and acne. They can provide patients who can't spare the time to recover from deeper peels with smoother, brighter looking skin. A series of peels may be necessary. Glycolic acid is currently the most commonly used AHA. It is frequently applied as a series of peels separated by 1 to 4 weeks in a 50% to 70% nonneutralized concentration. TCA peels usually have a longer interval between applications.

Table 83-2. Glogau Classification of Photoaging Groups

Group I—Mild (Usually Age 28–35 Years) No keratoses Little wrinkling	No acne scarring Little or no makeup
Group II—Moderate (Usually Age 35–50 Years) Early actinic keratoses—subtle skin yellowing Early wrinkling—parallel smile lines	Mild acne scarring Little makeup
Group III—Advanced (Usually Age 50–65 Years) Actinic keratoses—obvious skin yellowing with telangiectasia Wrinkling—present at rest	Moderate acne scarring Wears makeup always
Group IV—Severe (Usually Age 65–75 Years) Actinic keratoses and skin cancer have occurred Wrinkling—much cutis laxa of actinic, gravitational, and dynamic origin	Severe acne scarring Wears makeup that does not cover but cakes on

From Brody HJ: Chemical Peeling. St. Louis, Mosby, 1992, p 38.

16. How do glycolic acid peels compare with standard chemical peels?

Many of the risks and complications associated with the other peeling agents are minimized with the use of glycolic acid. Virtually every patient is a candidate for glycolic acid peels, including Asians, African Americans, Hispanics, and others with deeply pigmented skin. In addition, almost every part of the body can be peeled, including the back, chest, arms, and legs.

17. Can the different peeling agents be used in combination?

Yes, different peeling agents can be used simultaneously. In fact, many of today's popular peels are made up of a combination of agents. Typical combinations include TCA and another agent. Some examples include Jessner's + 35% TCA (Monheit); 70% glycolic acid + 35% TCA (Coleman, Futrell); and solid CO_2 followed by 35% TCA (Brody). Single-agent, 50% TCA peels for medium-depth wounding have fallen out of favor because of the high risk of scarring and pigmentary changes. It has been replaced with combination peels that include 35% TCA. These combination peels have been found to be as effective as 50% TCA alone but have fewer risks. Many new, popular, and well-marketed superficial peels contain multiple chemexfoliants as well.

Because of its strength, phenol is generally not combined with other peeling agents, although it often is mixed with differing amounts of Septisol or glycerin (liquid soap), croton oil, olive oil, and water, all of which can be altered to affect the depth of the peel. Popular formulas have been developed by Baker-Gordon, Venner-Kellson, Hetter, and Stone.

18. What is dermabrasion?

Dermabrasion is the surgical process by which the skin is resurfaced by planing or sanding, usually by means of a rapidly rotating abrasive tool such as a wire brush, diamond fraise, or serrated wheel. This process removes the epidermis and superficial dermis as treatment of a variety of dermatologic conditions.

19. What are the indications for dermabrasion?

Dermabrasion can be used to treat a variety of scars, including traumatic, acne, and surgical scars as well as superficial lentigos, actinic keratoses, both decorative and traumatic dermal tattoos, and, most commonly, fine facial wrinkling, particularly in the perioral region.

20. How do you know how deep to dermabrade?

The depth of dermabrasion is determined by the surgeon during the treatment itself. The goal is to reach the level of the superficial reticular dermis. With dermabrasion of the epidermal layer, you encounter essentially no bleeding and a smooth surface. Once at the superficial papillary dermis, sparse, punctate bleeding is seen. The endpoint is reached when you encounter confluent bleeding with a coarse background; this is the level of the superficial reticular dermis.

21. How long after dermabrasion does reepithelialization occur?

Reepithelialization typically occurs within 7 to 10 days.

22. Compare the effects of dermabrasion in the perioral area with the effects of phenol.

Because dermabrasion is a mechanical process, the depth of peel is more controllable; thus healing is faster, with less discomfort. Erythema following dermabrasion resolves faster than that seen with phenol. For patients with dark complexions, dermabrasion has less of a bleaching effect than does phenol.

23. Should patients undergoing chemical peel or dermabrasion of the perioral area receive acyclovir prophylaxis?

Yes. For patients with a history of herpes simplex the use of prophylactic acyclovir (Zovirax) is warranted. Adequate prophylactic doses of acyclovir have not been clearly established by a randomized, controlled study. Data suggest that 800 mg po TID for 5 days clinically minimizes postoperative herpes simplex virus infection rates and reduces the severity and duration of illness in patients who become infected. Valacyclovir (Valtrex) can be conveniently administered as 500 mg po BID for 5 days.

24. What is dermasanding?

Dermasanding is the use of silicone/carbide sandpaper (found at your local hardware store) to abrade the patient's skin. It can be used immediately after medium-depth chemical peels, when further resurfacing is needed. Examples include deeper wrinkles (on the lips, temple, and forehead), acne scars, thick epidermal lesions (seborrheic keratoses, cutaneous horns, actinic keratoses), and for blending.

25. What is microdermabrasion?

Microdermabrasion is an office-based mechanical resurfacing technique in which a pump generates a high-pressure stream of aluminium oxide or salt crystals that pass through a handpiece. The handpiece is passed over the patient's skin (slower and multiple passes or increased pressure against the skin leads to more aggressive abrasion) and a vacuum removes the crystals and exfoliated skin. It can be used on the face, neck, chest, and hands. The endpoint of treatment is erythema, which resolves within a few hours of treatment. Other "crystal-free" techniques use a wand embedded with diamond chips. The skin is pulled to the wand by a vacuum system, and the skin is abraded as the wand passes over it. Wands with different-size diamond chips are available, and the vacuum pressure is adjustable, leading to a controlled and predictable abrasion of the superficial skin. It can be used safely around the eyes without the risk for corneal abrasion by errant crystals seen with standard dermabrasion.

26. What are the indications for microdermabrasion?

Indications for microdermabrasion include patients with superficial skin conditions, such as early photoaging, fine lines, and superficial scarring.

27. Compare the effects of microdermabrasion with those of dermabrasion and chemical peeling.

Microdermabrasion causes a superficial exfoliation involving *only* the epidermis. It is not effective for deep wrinkles, scars, or ice-pick acne because these lesions extend into the dermis. Pigmentary problems, such as melasma or postinflammatory hyperpigmentation, also arise from the dermis and therefore are unaffected by microdermabrasion. Patients with skin problems involving the dermis are best treated with dermabrasion or chemical peeling. The advantage of microdermabrasion is the very little down time, no need for anesthesia, and virtually no risk of scarring (only temporary erythema). However, the superficial nature of the exfoliation limits its effectiveness in deeper skin conditions. Microdermabrasion often requires multiple treatments over several weeks to be effective.

28. What histologic skin changes does microdermabrasion cause?

Microdermabrasion causes an increase in epidermal and dermal thickness as well as an increase in organized collagen within the dermis.

BIBLIOGRAPHY

Baker TJ, Gordon HL, Stuzin JM: Surgical Rejuvenation of the Face, 2nd ed. St. Louis, Mosby, 1996.
Baker TJ, Stuzin JM: Chemical peeling and dermabrasion. In McCarthy JG (ed): Plastic Surgery. Philadelphia, WB Saunders, 1990, pp 748–786.
Brody HJ: Chemical Peeling. St. Louis, Mosby, 1992.
Coimbra M, Rohrich R, Chao J, Brown S: A prospective controlled assessment of microdermabrasion for damaged skin and fine rhytides. Plast Reconstr Surg 113:1438–1443, 2004.
Fitzpatrick TB: The validity and practicality of sun-reactive skin types I through VI. Arch Dermatol 124:869–871, 1988.
Glogau RG: Chemical Peel Symposium. American Academy of Dermatology, Atlanta, Georgia, December 4, 1990.
Gross BG: Cardiac arrhythmias during phenol face peeling. Plast Reconstr Surg 73:590–594, 1984.
Murad H, Shamban AT, Premo PS: The use of glycolic acid as a peeling agent. Dermatol Clin 13:285–286, 1995.
Perkins SW, Sklarew EC: Prevention of facial herpetic infections after chemical peel and dermabrasion: New treatment strategies in the prophylaxis of patients undergoing procedures of the perioral area. Plast Reconstr Surg 98:428–429, 1996.
Resnik SS, Resnick BI: Complications of chemical peeling. Dermatol Clin 13:309–311, 1995.
Rubin MG: Chemical Peels. Philadelphia, Elsevier/Saunders, 2006.
Stuzin JM, Baker TJ, Gordon HL: Treatment of photoaging: Facial chemical peeling (phenol and trichloro acetic acid) and dermabrasion. Clin Plast Surg 20:9–25, 1993.
Swinehart JM: Test spots in dermabrasion and chemical peeling. J Surg Oncol 16:557–563, 1990.
Truppman ES, Ellenby JD: Major electrocardiographic changes during chemical face peeling. Plast Reconstr Surg 63:44–48, 1979.
Whitaker E, Yarborough JM: Microdermabrasion. Available at:http://emedicine.medscape.com/article/843957-overview. Retrieved September 20, 2009.

AESTHETIC LASER SURGERY

William T. McClellan, MD, and
Brooke R. Seckel, MD, FACS

1. What does the acronym LASER mean?

*L*ight *a*mplification by *s*timulated *e*mission of *r*adiation. The laser was first theorized by Albert Einstein in 1917. However, the technology was not developed until 1960, 43 years following Einstein's mathematical theories.

2. What was the predecessor of the laser?

The maser (*m*icrowave *a*mplification by *s*timulated *e*mission of *r*adiation). The maser was born from the early radar systems from World War II and developed independently by Charles Townes and Nilolai Basov. However, the maser could not sustain the energy level possible for utilizing light emission, and the research faded.

3. Who invented the laser?

Theodore Maiman is credited with producing the first laser, a ruby laser, in 1960.

4. What is the visible spectrum of light?

Wavelength from 385 to 785 nm on the electromagnetic spectrum.

5. How is laser light different from other forms of light?

Laser light is different from ordinary light (e.g., flashlight) in that it is much more organized, being monochromatic, collimated, and coherent. All light from a laser is monochromatic because it originates from a common source and exhibits the same wavelength or color. Additionally, the laser light travels in a nondivergent, parallel fashion called a *collimated beam*. Laser light is coherent in that it travels synchronously (space and time) in parallel for a great distance.

6. What is power density and fluence?

Power density is the units of energy delivered to the tissue and is measured in watts per square centimeter (W/cm^2). *Fluence* is the power density delivered over a specific period of time and is measured in joules per square centimeter (J/cm^2).

7. Define pulse width, wavelength, and spot size. What do these have in common?

All of these qualities of a laser affect the penetration of the laser into the skin. *Pulse width* is the duration of exposure of the tissue to the laser. The longer the pulse width of an ablative laser, the deeper the ablation. *Wavelength* is the distance between the peaks of the wave and is specific to the lased medium. The longer the wavelength the deeper, the penetration into the skin. *Spot size* is the area over which the focused laser is distributed and is reported in square centimeters (cm^2). The larger the spot size, the greater the penetration because of less scatter of the beam.

8. How does the laser interact with the skin?

Laser light can be reflected, transmitted, or absorbed. The specific targets or chromophores absorb the laser light and convert it into thermal energy, creating the desired clinical effect.

9. What is selective photothermolysis and thermal relaxation time? Why are these concepts important in aesthetic laser surgery?

Selective photothermolysis is a concept that was introduced by Anderson in 1983 and is the selective heating of a chromophore that absorbs a specific wavelength of laser light. The selective heating destroys the cells containing the laser target without damaging surrounding cells, which do not contain the specific target of the laser. This is possible if the thermal relaxation time is longer than the duration of the laser pulse.

Thermal relaxation time is the time needed for the target tissue to cool by 50% of its peak temperature following laser pulse exposure. In other words, when you heat a cell and it cools quicker than the delivered pulse, the energy spills to surrounding cells and causes unwanted collateral damage. A longer thermal relaxation time decreases the chance of collateral damage.

10. What is the difference between an ablative and a nonablative laser?

An *ablative laser* causes epidermal vaporization to create its intended effect of collagen remodeling within the dermis. Carbon dioxide and erbium:yttrium-aluminum-garnet (YAG) are two examples of ablative lasers.

A *nonablative laser* selectively injures the dermis but protects the epidermis by cooling during treatment. A nonablative laser emits a coherent beam, like ablative lasers, in wavelengths from 1320 to 1550 nm. Although the thermally injured dermis produces neocollagen, the aesthetic results and predictability are generally less than with ablative lasers.

11. What are the wavelengths of lasers commonly used in plastic surgery?

- 585 nm: Pulsed dye
- 694 nm: Q-switched ruby
- 755 nm: Alexandrite
- 1064/532 nm: Q-switched neodymium (Nd):YAG
- 2940 nm: Erbium
- 10,600 nm: Carbon dioxide

12. What is the laser of choice for a port-wine stain?

The 585-nm pulsed-dye laser specifically targets oxyhemoglobin and is the laser of choice for this particular lesion.

13. What is the mechanism of action of the Q-switched Nd:YAG laser?

The laser causes selective fragmentation of the intracellular targeted pigments, which then are cleared by phagocytosis.

14. What does Q switched mean, and why is it important?

The "quality" (Q) switch allows the skin to be exposed to the laser for 20 to 50 nanoseconds. This short exposure time enables delivery of very high energy with a short pulse duration well below the thermal relaxation time minimizing collateral tissue damage.

15. What is the Fitzpatrick classification, and why is it important in laser surgery?

Pigmentary changes following resurfacing is one of the most common complications after resurfacing in all Fitzgerald classes; however, it is more common in the darker skin types, Fitzpatrick types IV to VI (Table 84-1).

16. How is the carbon dioxide laser used in aesthetic surgery?

The CO_2 laser selectively targets intracellular water in the near-infrared region at 10,600 nm. The laser heats its target instantaneously to greater than 100°C causing vaporization of the target cell and denaturation of extracellular proteins. This ablative laser removes the entire epidermis and partial layers of the dermis, depending on the energy delivered. Heat-induced collagen shrinking produced by the laser results in smoother skin and ablation of unwanted fine rhytids.

Carbon dioxide resurfacing for facial rhytids has not been matched by other laser technology; however, the pigmentary changes, erythema, edema, and other complications create significant down time for the patient. These deficiencies have driven the development of alternative resurfacing modalities.

A new CO_2 resurfacing modality called the CO_2 Lyte ActiveFX peel has been introduced that obviates many of the deficiencies of traditional CO_2 laser resurfacing. The new modified scanning device, called the computerized pattern generator (CPG), places the scanned laser pattern in a randomized pattern with individual skip areas, different from previous scanning patterns in which individual CO_2 beams were placed adjacent to each other. As a result, with

Table 84-1. Fitzpatrick Classification		
TYPE	SKIN COLOR	REACTION TO FIRST YEARLY SUN EXPOSURE
I	Very white or freckled	Always burns, never tans
II	White	Usually burns, tans with difficulty
III	White to olive	Sometimes burns, usually tans
IV	Brown	Rarely burns, tans with ease
V	Dark brown	Very rarely burns, tans very easily
VI	Black	Never burns

randomization of individual treatment zones and intermixed nontreated areas, thermal injury is reduced significantly. Recovery time is 3 to 5 days, and no erythema occurs after the 3- to 5-day recovery. Power of the laser is also reduced so that a 70-micron, fractionated skin injury is produced, allowing adjacent untreated skin to speed healing. Unlike the case with use of the Fraxel laser, microablation is produced, so physical removal of photodamaged superficial epidermis occurs as well as thermally induced collagen remodeling. Impressive wrinkle removal and skin tightening is seen after one to two treatments under topical anesthesia.

17. What is the erbium:YAG laser?

The erbium:YAG laser is a 2940-nm ablative laser that targets intracellular water like the CO_2 laser does; however, its affinity for intracellular water is 10 times greater than that of carbon dioxide laser. This greater affinity allows for a cleaner target cell ablation with less thermal collateral cell damage. Collagen shrinking is reduced with the erbium, resulting in decreased effect on rhytids. Yet the erythema and complications are greatly diminished compared with the CO_2 laser due to the decreased collateral thermal necrosis.

The zone of thermal necrosis can be modified from 20-micron to 200-micron ablation based on the pulse width chosen. Even with variable pulse widths the side-effect profile and recovery period are still more favorable than with CO_2 resurfacing.

Care must be taken with the erbium laser because the cellular char that is present after CO_2 resurfacing is not present with the erbium. The char layer can limit the depth of further dermal ablation due to the decreased water content in this layer. However, the erbium laser affinity for water is so great and the ablation so clean that deeper ablation is possible without the visible warning provided by the CO_2 laser.

18. A patient comes to your office 3 to 6 days after a 120-micron erbium laser facial resurfacing with a perioral, malodorous, pruritic, yellow crusting. The skin has a "beefy red" appearance. What is your diagnosis and treatment?

The diagnosis is a postoperative fungal infection, most commonly *Candida*. It should be treated with oral Diflucan 100 mg twice daily for 7 days. Frequent postoperative visits are recommended to verify resolution and provide patient reassurances.

19. What is a fractional photothermolysis?

First reported in 2005, the theory of fractional photothermolysis is use of a specifically designed nonablative laser array, targeting intracellular water, to create collimated dermal injury at varying depths between 0 to 550 microns. The columns of thermal damage created were elliptical in shape and 10 to 150 microns in diameter. These small areas of thermally injured dermis, termed *microscopic treatment zones,* are surrounded by uninjured dermal columns 125 to 500 microns away.

The unaffected stratum corneum serves as a biologic dressing, and the treatment columns heal at 24 hours. Some believe that the failure of nonablative treatments to provide significant exfoliation is a limitation in the attempt to remove wrinkles and photodamaged epidermis, holding to the belief that epidermal surface irregularity is an important component of the wrinkle that must be removed for effective wrinkle reduction The Food and Drug Administration (FDA) has approved the Fraxel laser for treatment of pigmented lesions, melasma, skin resurfacing, and fine rhytids. The best clinical results have been seen in patients with melasma and fine acne scarring. To date, wrinkle removal has been disappointing. Prolonged postinflammatory hyperpigmentation is common in skin types IV to VI.

20. How do lasers remove hair?

The laser selectively targets the melanin in the hair bulb, destroying the hair follicle at the root.

21. Will laser hair removal remove all hair in one treatment?

No. Hair must be in the anagen (growth phase) for the laser to be effective. At any given time only approximately 85% of hair is in the anagen phase; the remaining 15% is in the telogen (resting) phase and is unaffected by the laser. Typically three to 10 treatments spaced 4 to 6 weeks apart are necessary.

22. Why is laser hair removal most successful in the winter?

Optimal response to hair removal is seen in Fitzpatrick skin types I to III due to the greater melanin concentration in the hair bulb compared to the surrounding skin. In patients who tan during the summer, the increased melanin concentration in the surrounding skin decreases the ability to selectively destroy the hair follicle. Therefore winter treatment of Fitzpatrick I to III skin types may result in greater selective hair removal with diminished collateral damage.

23. What is intense pulsed light?

Intense pulsed light (IPL) differs from laser light in that it is a polychromatic, noncoherent light covering a broad spectrum from 510 to 1200 nm. It is used in the treatment of sun damage, telangiectasias, and rosacea and in hair reduction. It is considered a nonablative laser and typically takes four to six treatments to achieve optimal therapeutic effects. The most common side effect is redness, which usually lasts fewer than 4 days. Because of the large treatment spot size (2 to 3 cm²), advanced cooling methods, rapidity of treatment, and minimal collateral tissue injury (thus minimal down time), IPL has become the preferred treatment of rosacea, facial telangiectasias, and pigment on the face, chest, and hands. Whole face, chest, and hand treatments for the pigmentary and vascular photoaging changes on the face and chest are very effective with minimal down time and are called *photofacial treatments*. Results can be significantly enhanced by application of the photosensitizer Levulan.

24. What perioperative precautions should be taken in a patient who is to undergo laser resurfacing and has a history of oral herpes infection?

All patients should receive Valtrex 500 mg twice daily beginning 1 day before laser treatment and for 7 days posttreatment. An active herpes infection is an absolute contraindication to facial laser resurfacing.

25. What happens when patients are pretreated with botulinum toxin prior to laser resurfacing?

These modalities of nonoperative facial rejuvenation are often used in concert. The literature suggests that chemodenervation with botulinum toxin type A for 1 week prior to laser resurfacing on movement-associated rhytids may improve results. However, the inflammatory phase following resurfacing may hasten receptor recovery from the chemodenervated areas. Botox maintenance after resurfacing is recommended for optimal results.

26. What medication can be applied before laser surgery to improve pain?

EMLA cream is an emulsion of the amide esters lidocaine 2.5% and prilocaine 2.5% in a 1:1 ratio. These mixtures provide analgesia to the epidermis and dermis. Duration of application and total surface area applied affect the systemic absorption of the drugs. EMLA should be placed under an occlusive dressing for approximately 1 hour to achieve adequate effect and should persist for 1 to 2 hours after removal.

For adults undergoing a facial procedure, the typical dose is 2 g applied over 10 cm² for 1 to 2 hours. The maximum recommended dose is 20 g applied over 200 cm² for a duration of 4 hours.

Complications of EMLA application can range from local erythema, blistering, and itching to anaphylactic reactions. Systemic signs include seizures, respiratory depression, and cardiac arrest.

27. What are the contraindications to facial laser resurfacing?

The following are considered relative or absolute contraindications to facial laser resurfacing: active oral herpes infection or other facial infection, recent Accutane use, history of abnormal scarring, active smoker, excessive lower lid laxity, collagen disorders, or unrealistic patient expectations.

28. How long before reepithelialization occurs after facial resurfacing?

Following resurfacing with either the CO_2 or erbium:YAG laser, the epidermis is largely or completely removed, and, in some instances, the papillary dermis is removed. On average, reepithelialization following CO_2 laser is 8.5 days and after erbium:YAG resurfacing is only 5.5 days.

29. What are the side effects and complications following laser resurfacing?

Erythema following CO_2 laser is most intense in the first month following resurfacing and can last up to 6 months. Erythema following erbium:YAG usually dissipates after the first 7 to 10 days. Makeup can be used to cover erythematic after 1 week.

Edema is common during the first 4 days following resurfacing and can be effectively controlled with head elevation and ice packs. Pruritus is another common sequela that can be treated with corticosteroids and antihistamines.

Acne flares are commonly caused by the occlusive dressings or ointments applied after the procedure. Patients with a significant history of severe acne are at higher risk for developing an acne flare following resurfacing. Treatment is conservative, and acne usually resolves once the ointment or dressing is discontinued.

30. What are common topical treatments recommended or prescribed prior to resurfacing?

All patients should use sunscreen at least 4 to 6 weeks prior to resurfacing and continue using sunscreen for at least 6 weeks postoperative. Exposure to ultraviolet light increases stimulation of melanocytes and increases the chance of pigmentary changes following laser resurfacing. Limiting sun exposure and use of sunscreen can decrease the chance of hyperpigmentation and extend the results of laser resurfacing.

Some physicians pretreat patients with Retin-A and hydroquinone to reduce pigmentary alterations following laser treatment. Hydroquinone causes reversible depigmentation of the skin by inhibiting melanocyte metabolic activity. It should not be used during pregnancy. Retin-A or tretinoin is a retinoid that promotes exfoliation of the skin and neocollagen formation.

31. Facial resurfacing should be avoided in patients taking what medication?

Accutane or isotretinoin destroys the adnexal structures, which are necessary to provide the epithelial cells for reepithelialization of the skin. Laser resurfacing should not be performed within 1 year of Accutane use.

32. What postoperative dressing is available following laser resurfacing?

The two basic treatment modalities are the *open* technique and the *closed* technique. Each has potential benefits and drawbacks, and many surgeons now incorporate a combined modality in an attempt to capture the benefits of both techniques.

The *open* technique is generally more commonly used because it is simple, is inexpensive, and has decreased chance of postoperative infection. The first 3 to 4 days of this treatment involves continuous application of soaking with wet sponges dipped in a solution of 3 tablespoons of white vinegar per cup of distilled water. Laser wounds produce prodigious amounts of exudates, and the patient is instructed to wipe away the exudates every hour with a sponge. If crusts form during the first few days the chance of yeast or bacterial infection is greater. The wounds must be kept pink, clean, and free of exudates. Three to four times a day, a very fine layer of a healing ointment such as Aquaphor, Gentle Healing Ointment, BioBalm, or plain petroleum can be applied for comfort, especially when the patient begins to feel skin tightening. Additionally, frequent application of ice gauze or ice packs is necessary to reduce edema. The advantages of this technique are decreased rate of infection and the relative ease of monitoring the wound. However, the disadvantage is that the postoperative pain can be more intense with the open technique. This technique has become more popular with the increased use of the erbium:YAG laser, which inherently is associated with less pain and fewer infections than the CO_2 laser.

The *closed* technique uses semiocclusive biosynthetic dressings such as Biobrane and Flexan for approximately 5 days postoperative. These dressings are applied immediately postoperative and generally remain in place until they are removed. This technique has the advantage of decreased pain and minimal patient responsibility, and it may speed reepithelialization. The disadvantages are its expense, the inability to monitor the wound, and the higher incidence of infection. *Staphylococcus aureus, Pseudomonas aeruginosa,* and *Candida* are the most common pathogens isolated.

33. What are the safety issues related to the laser plume?

Thermal destruction of tissue creates a smoke plume that may contain toxic gases such as benzene, formaldehyde, and hydrogen cyanide. Additionally, cellular materials and viruses can be transported in the plume.

During any laser procedure, a laser protective mask (0.1 micron) should be used to prevent inhalation of particulate matter. Additionally, smoke evacuators should be used and maintained near the origin of the plume. Use of a high-efficiency particulate air (HEPA) filter is recommended to trap gases and particulate matter.

34. What precautions should be taken in the operating room where a laser procedure is being performed?

A sign should be displayed at all entrances indicating a laser procedure is in progress. Protective eyewear should be kept on the door in case entry by other personnel is required. Eye injury is the most common reported laser accident, representing almost 70% of injuries. Laser-specific eyewear with appropriate wavelength and optical density should be worn by all health care workers.

Fire is a dreaded but real entity and should be taken seriously by the operative team. Preventative measures include moist sponges, wet towels, laser-safe endotracheal tubing, and careful inventory of flammable or combustible agents.

35. Summarize the types of lasers commonly used in plastic surgery.

See Table 84-2.

Table 84-2. Lasers in Plastic Surgery

LASER	WAVELENGTH (nm)	TARGET/MECHANISM	USES/BENEFITS	DRAWBACKS
Pulsed dye	595	Oxyhemoglobin Red, yellow, orange pigments/ selective fragmentation and phagocytosis	Port-wine stains Vascular lesions Scars	Can be painful Posttreatment bruising Multiple treatments necessary for effect
Q-switched ruby	694	Melanin—rupture of cells Black, blue, violet pigments/ selective fragmentation and phagocytosis	Very effective on dark pigments Nevus of Ota Road rash Hair reduction Minimal collateral thermal injury	Not effective on red or yellow pigments May cause breaks in the skin
Q-switched Nd:YAG (neodymium:yttrium- aluminum-garnet)	532 + 1064	Red, brown, orange pigments/ selective fragmentation and phagocytosis	Wider spectrum of uses Pigmented lesions Hair reduction Superior red pigment removal (532)	Not effective on darker pigments
Alexandrite	755	Melanin Green and black pigments	Tattoos Hair reduction	Not effective on red pigments
Intense pulsed light (IPL)	510–1200		Sun damage (pigmented lesions) Telangiectasias Rosacea Hair reduction Simple and easy to use, no sedation necessary Nonablative, minimal complications	Nonselective Multiple treatments necessary for effect
Erbium	2940	Water	Skin resurfacing One pass yields 10–30 μm of ablation Affinity for H_2O is 10× that of CO_2 laser Minimal collateral damage	No visual endpoint to ablation No limit to ablative depth Less collagen remodeling Ablative
Carbon dioxide (CO_2)	10,600	Water	Skin resurfacing One pass yields 150–200 μm of ablation Immediate collagen tightening Increased neocollagen formation Visual color change highlights endpoint Dermis devoid of H_2O prevents further ablation	Increased collateral tissue damage Increased pigmentary alterations Increased postoperative erythema Ablative Sedation required

BIBLIOGRAPHY

Achauer B: Lasers in plastic surgery: Current practice. Plast Reconstr Surg 99:1442–1450, 1997.

Alam M, Pantanowitz L, Harton A, Arndt K, Dover J: A prospective trial of fungal colonization after laser resurfacing of the face: Correlation between culture positivity and symptoms of pruritus. Dermatol Surg 29:255–260, 2003.

Alster T: Prevention and treatment of side effects and complications of cutaneous laser resurfacing. Plast Reconstr Surg 109:308–316, 2002.

Anderson R: Selective photothermolysis: Precise microsurgery by selective absorption of pulsed irradiation. Science 220:524–527, 1983.

Avram D, Goldman M: The safety and effectiveness of single pass erbium:YAG laser in the treatment of mild to moderate photodamage. Dermatol Surg 30:1073–1076, 2004.

Batra R, Ort R, Jacob C, Hobbs L, Arndt K, Dover J: Evaluation of a silicone occlusive dressing after laser skin resurfacing. Arch Dermatol 137:1317–1321, 2001.

Christian M: Microresurfacing using the variable pulse erbium:YAG laser: A comparison of the 0.5 and 4 ms pulse durations. Dermatol Surg 29:605–611, 2003.

Coates J: Basic physics of erbium laser resurfacing. J Cutan Laser Ther 1:71–75, 1999.

Fitzpatrick T: The validity and practicality of sun reactive skin types I through VI. Arch Dermatol 124:869–871, 1988.

Fodor L, Peled I, Rissin Y, et al: Using intense pulsed light for cosmetic purposes: Our experience. Plast Reconstr Surg 113:1789–1795, 2004.

Geronemus R: Fractional photothermolysis: Current and future applications. Laser Surg Med 38:169–176, 2006.

Goldman M, Roberts T, Skover G, Lettieri J, Fitzpatrick R: Optimizing wound healing in the face after laser abrasion. J Am Acad Dermatol 46:399–407, 2002.

Greene D, Egbert B, Utley D, Kock R: In vivo model of histologic changes after treatment with the superpulsed CO_2 laser, erbium:YAG, and blended lasers: A 4 to 6 month prospective histologic and clinical study. Lasers Surg Med 27:362–372, 2000.

Ha R, Burns J, Hoopman J, Burns A: Lasers in plastic surgery. Sel Read Plast Surg 9, 2003.

Jasim M: Achieving superior results resurfacing results with the erbium:YAG laser. Arch Facial Plast Surg. 4(4):262–266, 2002.

Khatri K, Machado A, Magro C, Davenport S. Laser peel: Facial rejuvenation with a surperficial erbium: Yag laser treatment. J Cutan Laser Ther 2(3):185–189, 2000.

Maiman TH: Stimulated optical radiation in ruby. Nature, 187 4736, pp. 493–494, 1960.

Manstein D, Herron G, Sink R: Fractional photothermolysis: A new concept for cutaneous remodeling using microscopic patterns of thermal injury. Laser Surg Med 34:426–438, 2004.

Papadavid E, Katsambas A: Lasers for facial rejuvenation: a review. Int J Dermatol. 42(6):480–487, 2003.

Seckel B, Younai S, Wang K: Skin tightening effects of the ultrapulse CO_2 laser. Plas Reconstr surg 102:872–877, 1998.

Tanzi E, Alster T: Side effects and complications of variable pulsed erbium: yttrium-aluminum-garnet laser skin resurfacing: Extended experience with 50 patients. Plast Reconstr Surg 114(4):1524–9, 2003.

Weinstein C: Postoperative laser care. Clin Plast Surg 27(2):251–62, 2000.

Zimbler M, Holds J, Kokoska M, Glaser D, Prendiville S, Hollenbeak C, Thomas J: Effect of botulinum toxin pretreatment on laser resurfacing results: A prospective, randomized, blinded trial. Arch Facial Plast Surg 3(3):165–169, 2001.

ENDOSCOPIC SURGERY

Oscar M. Ramirez, MD, FACS, and
W.G. Eshbaugh, Jr., MD, FACS

CHAPTER 85

1. Who is credited with the birth of modern endoscopy?

Bozzini, in 1807, first used an apparatus to illuminate internal body cavities and redirect the light to his eye. He was censured by the Medical Faculty of Vienna for "undue curiosity" after reporting the use of his device to inspect the inside of a woman's urethra.

2. What technologic advances enabled the rapid proliferation of endoscopic techniques in surgery?

- *Creating an Optical Cavity:* Techniques such as insufflating the abdominal cavity with nonflammable gas (e.g., CO_2), filling synovial spaces with saline, and use of specialized retractors and sleeves for soft tissue endoscopy allow enlargement of the workspace for endoscopic procedures.
- *Electrocoagulation:* The earlier uses of high-frequency currents produced destructive temperatures and were hazardous with insufflated oxygen in closed body cavities. The modern use of monopolar and bipolar electrocautery with nonflammable gases allows hemostasis with much lower temperatures.
- *Light Source:* With the advent of fiberoptics and "cold light" (heat shield placed around the bulb) consisting of an incandescent tungsten element in iodine, halogen, or xenon vapor, abundant light with minimal heat can be transmitted to the surgical cavity.
- *Imaging:* Coherent bundling of glass fibers, the Hopkins rod-lens system scope, solid-state chip sensor video cameras, of which the charged coupled device (CCD; Fig. 85-1) is the most common, and high-resolution video monitors allow mainstream use of endoscopy in surgery.

3. What is the Hopkins rod endoscope?

Named for the British physicist who introduced it, the Hopkins rod greatly improved the optics of endoscopy by using a glass rod with interspersed air spaces rather than the traditional tube of air with interspersed glass lenses (Fig. 85-2).

4. How is endoscopic surgery different in plastic surgery compared with other specialties?

Most endoscopic procedures in other specialties are performed in naturally occurring, readily accessible body cavities, such as the abdominal, thoracic, synovial, and sinus cavities, or in hollow organs, such as the gastrointestinal tract and urinary bladder. In plastic surgery, most endoscopic procedures are performed in surgically created soft tissue planes, which required the development of specialized instrumentation. Lack of natural cavities and incompatibility with existing instrumentation are the main reasons why endoscopic techniques for plastic surgery were developed much later than in other specialties.

5. Which procedures in plastic surgery are commonly performed endoscopically?

The endoscopic forehead, or brow, lift has gained widespread popularity. It has been shown to be safe and effective over time. Endoscopic techniques for harvesting of certain flaps (muscle, jejunum, and omentum), removal of benign

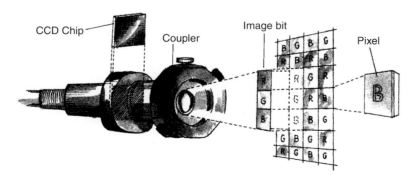

Figure 85-1. Charged coupled device (CCD).

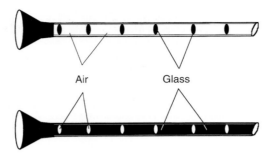

Figure 85-2. Hopkins rod endoscope *(bottom)* compared with the traditional glass rod endoscope *(top)*.

subcutaneous tumors, carpal tunnel release, placement of tissue expanders, and rejuvenation of the face and neck have become common. Breast procedures for augmentation, implant inspection, gynecomastia correction, mammary hypertrophy, and ptosis are performed endoscopically in select patients.

Less commonly performed procedures include reduction and fixation of facial fractures, tendon and nerve harvesting, and strip craniectomies and limited cranial vault expansion for craniosynostosis.

6. What are the advantages and disadvantages of endoscopic transaxillary breast augmentation?

The advantages of using the endoscope for transaxillary breast augmentation are optimum visualization of the dissection pocket, which allows more precise implant placement, and identification of the medial branches of the intercostal nerves, which better preserves skin sensation. Avoidance of scars on the breast is the main advantage of the blunt or endoscopic transaxillary procedure. Disadvantages include possible injury to the sensory nerves of the arm and forearm, transient axillary bands, and difficulty with revisions due to the distant access point.

7. Which muscles are responsible for forehead animation?

The frontalis, corrugator supercilii, depressor supercilii, procerus, and orbicularis oculi. Over time, repeated contractions of these muscles lead to prominent wrinkle lines perpendicular to the axis of the muscle. Transverse forehead creases are associated with activity of the frontalis, glabellar frown lines with the orbicularis, corrugator supercilii, and depressor supercilii, and horizontal creases at the root of the nose with the procerus.

8. The locations of which nerves are important during an endoscopic forehead lift?

The *frontal (or temporal) branch of the facial nerve* is a motor nerve that innervates the frontalis and portions of the orbicularis oculi, corrugator supercilii, and procerus muscles. It traverses the superficial fat pad above the superficial temporal fascia toward the lateral brow.

The *supraorbital* and *supratrochlear nerves* are sensory branches of the ophthalmic division of the trigeminal nerve. The supraorbital nerve exits the superior orbit adjacent to the periosteum, travels superiorly penetrating the frontalis muscle, and continues at the subcutaneous level to provide sensory innervation to the forehead and scalp. The supratrochlear nerve exits the orbit medial to the supraorbital nerve and courses through the glabellar muscles to its subcutaneous location in the scalp.

9. What are the important components of an endoscopic forehead lift?

Although there are numerous variations in technique, a few principles are fairly constant.
* *Dissection:* Optical cavity is created with specialized instrumentation in the subgaleal or subperiosteal plane.
* *Soft Tissue Modification:* Brow depressor muscles in the glabellar region are wholly or partially resected, and the periosteum is released near or just above the supraorbital rim (Fig. 85-3).
* *Fixation:* Numerous techniques using both absorbable and permanent sutures, screws, and similar devices are used for both bony and soft tissue fixation of the mobilized brow.

10. Who is the ideal candidate for endoscopic facial rejuvenation?

The ideal candidate is one in whom soft tissue repositioning is desired without the need for skin excision. As with the forehead lift, in cases with severe dermatochalasia requiring excision of excess skin, the open approach is indicated. With minimal to moderate dermatochalasia, endoscopic soft tissue repositioning is often complemented with dermal planing or a tightening procedure such as laser resurfacing, chemical peeling, or dermabrasion.

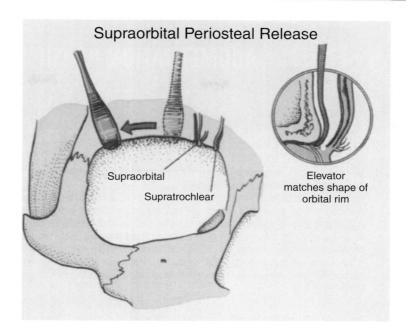

Figure 85-3. Release of the periosteum using specialized instruments.

11. What are the advantages and disadvantages of endoscopic surgery versus the traditional or open approach?

Advantages: When there is no excess skin to excise, endoscopic techniques allow for small, remote incisions with magnification and illumination of the operative field. Patients often have a quicker recovery with less morbidity than with open techniques. Teaching is enhanced with the use of multiple high-resolution monitors that allow many to view the procedure simultaneously.

Disadvantages: Equipment costs and a learning curve are associated with developing proficient skills in endoscopic procedures. Critics cite the loss of stereoscopic viewing and tactile sensory information with endoscopic surgery.

BIBLIOGRAPHY

Baker TJ, Gordon HL, Stuzin JM: Surgical Rejuvenation of the Face. St. Louis, Mosby, 1996, pp 531–541.
Core GB: 10-year experience with endoscopic breast augmentation: P67. Plast Reconstr Surg 116(Suppl):205–207, 2005.
Gardner PM: Endoscopic Breast Augmentation. McCullough Aesthetic Surgery Symposium. Birmingham, Alabama, May 1998.
Isse NG: Endoscopic facial rejuvenation and remodeling. In Greer SE, Benhaim P, Lorenz HP, Chang J, Hedrick MH (eds): Handbook of Plastic Surgery. New York, Marcel Dekker, 2004.
Potter JK, Janis JE, Clark CP III: Blepharoplasty and browlift. Select Read Plast Surg 10, 2005.
Price CI: Equipment and instrumentation. In Ramirez OM, Daniel RK (eds): Endoscopic Plastic Surgery. New York, Springer-Verlag, 1996, pp 10–15.
Ramirez OM, Eshbaugh WG: Endoscopic surgery. In Weinzweig J (ed): Plastic Surgery Secrets. Philadelphia, Hanley & Belfus, 1999, pp 329–331.
Rosenberg PH, Cooperman A: A chronology of endoscopic surgery and development of modern techniques and instrumentation. In Ramirez OM, Daniel RK (eds): Endoscopic Plastic Surgery. New York, Springer-Verlag, 1996, pp 3–15.
Young RV, Bindrup TR: Transaxillary submuscular breast augmentation and subcutaneous fibrous bands. Plast Reconstr Surg 99:257, 1997.

AUGMENTATION OF THE FACIAL SKELETON

Michael J. Yaremchuk, MD, FACS

1. Why is most augmentation of the facial skeleton done with alloplastic implants instead of autogenous bone?

Unlike alloplastic materials, autogenous bone has the potential to be revascularized and then assimilated into the facial skeleton. In time, it could be biologically indistinguishable from the adjacent native skeleton. These attributes make it ideal and the only material available to reliably reconstruct segmental load-bearing defects of the facial skeleton. However, when used as an onlay graft to augment the contours of the facial skeleton, revascularization provides access for osteoclastic activity, graft resorption, and hence unreliable augmentation. Use of autogenous bone also requires a donor site, which may be unsightly or painful. Finally, use of autogenous bone as an implant material is more time consuming and therefore more expensive. Alloplastic implants do not change their shape with time and do not require a donor site.

2. How does an implant's surface characteristics affect the host's response to the implant?

The host responds to an alloplastic implant by forming a fibrous capsule around the implant. This is the body's way of isolating the implant from the host. The implant's surface characteristics impact the nature of this process. Smooth implants (e.g., solid silicone) result in the formation of thick, smooth-walled capsules. Porous implants (e.g., polytetrafluoroethylene [Gore-Tex], porous polyethylene [Medpor]) allow varying degrees of soft tissue ingrowth, which results in a less dense capsule.

Animal studies have demonstrated that implant pore sizes greater than 100 microns encourage tissue ingrowth. Pore sizes less than 100 microns limit tissue ingrowth, whereas materials with large pore sizes (>300 microns) have drawbacks associated with material breakdown. Clinical observation has shown that porous implants, as a result of fibrous tissue ingrowth, have less tendency to erode underlying bone, to migrate due to soft tissue mechanical forces, and, perhaps, to be less susceptible to infection when challenged with inoculums of bacteria.

3. What alloplastic implant materials are most commonly used to augment the facial skeleton?

- Silicone rubber, polytetrafluoroethylene
- Porous polyethylene (Medpor, Porex, Fairborn, GA)
- Polymethylmethacrylate (polyhydroxyethyl methacrylate HTR [hard tissue replacement], Walter Lorenz Surgical, Inc., Jacksonville, FL)

Silicone rubber is the material most commonly used. Silicone has the following advantages: it can be sterilized by steam or irradiation, it can be carved with either scissors or a scalpel, and it can be stabilized with a screw or a suture. Because it is smooth, it can be removed quite easily. Disadvantages include the tendency to cause resorption of bone underlying it, the potential to migrate if not fixed, and the potential for its fibrous capsule to be visible when placed under a thin soft tissue cover.

Polytetrafluoroethylene has a nonadherent surface that is very flexible. Implants are available for both subdermal and subperiosteal placement. Preformed implants are made with a pore size between 10 and 30 microns, which allows for some soft tissue ingrowth. However, it is smooth enough to be maneuvered easily through soft tissues. This material can be fixed to underlying structures with sutures or screws.

Medpor is firmer than polytetrafluoroethylene and has a porosity between 125 and 250 microns, which allows more extensive fibrous tissue ingrowth than does polytetrafluoroethylene. The advantages of porous polyethylene include its tendency to allow extensive soft tissue ingrowth, thereby lessening its tendency to migrate and to erode underlying bone. Its firm consistency allows it to be easily fixed with screws and contoured with a scalpel or power equipment without fragmenting. However, its porosity causes soft tissue to adhere to it, making placement more difficult and requiring larger pockets to be made than with smoother implants. The soft tissue ingrowth also makes implant removal more difficult than with smooth surface implants. HTR is porous, allowing some tissue ingrowth, but is inflexible.

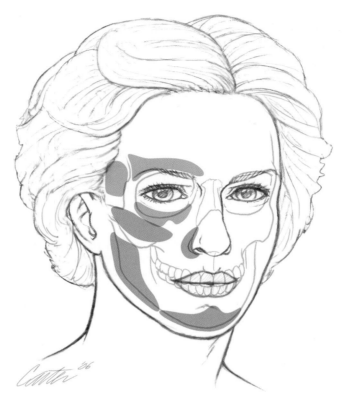

Figure 86-1. Areas of the facial skeleton augmented with alloplastic implants.

4. What areas of the face are most often augmented with implants?

The chin and cheekbones are the most common sites for alloplastic skeletal augmentation. Chin implants are the most frequently used alloplastic implants in facial aesthetic surgery. Malar implants are the second most frequently used alloplastic implant. Implants are available to augment all areas of the facial skeleton, including the orbital rims, the pyriform aperture, and the mandible (Fig. 86-1).

5. What surgical approaches are used for placement of malar implants?

Malar implants are placed through both extraoral and intraoral approaches. Extraoral approaches may use eyelid, preauricular, or transcoronal incisions. Eyelid approaches are used by some when malar augmentation is combined with lower lid blepharoplasty. This approach allows excellent visualization of the zygoma and precise implant placement. However, lid malposition is not an uncommon sequela due to lid scarring and implant-induced capsular contracture. The preauricular approach can be used when malar augmentation is combined with a face lift. Transcoronal placement of malar implants can be used when malar augmentation is combined with forehead lift or subperiosteal face lift.

The intraoral approach is preferred by most surgeons. Although this approach risks bacterial contamination of the implant by organisms from the mouth, infection rates are low. Advantages of the intraoral approach include excellent visualization, ease and rapidity of placement, and no visible scar.

6. What is the most common complication after placement of a malar implant?

Malposition is the most common complication after malar implant surgery. This may result from inadequate exposure of the area to be augmented or failure to immobilize the implant. Sensory changes due to impingement of the implant on the infraorbital nerve are not uncommon.

7. What are the advantages of wide subperiosteal exposure of the skeletal area to be augmented?

Alloplastic implants used to augment the contours of the facial skeleton are placed in the subperiosteal plane. Wide subperiosteal exposure of the area to be augmented has several advantages. It allows accurate identification of the area to be augmented; of important adjacent structures, such as the infraorbital nerve, thereby preventing their iatrogenic damage; and of landmarks for orientation and, hence, symmetric implant positioning. Wide exposure also allows easy access for immobilization of the implant by sutures or screws. The resultant soft tissue mobilization allows tension-free closure of the access incision. Implants placed in large subperiosteal pockets must be immobilized to prevent their postoperative movement.

This technique differs significantly from the traditional approach in which dissection of only the area to be augmented was advocated. The resultant small pocket was intended to prevent postoperative implant migration. A limited dissection is possible for placement of smooth surfaced implants but is not possible for placement of porous implants to which soft tissues tend to adhere (e.g., Velcro), making placement difficult.

8. Why should I consider fixing an implant to the skeleton with a screw?

Screw fixation of the implant to the skeleton provides both practical and theoretical advantages. Screw fixation prevents movement of the implant, which adds precision as well as early and late predictability to the result. Theoretically, elimination of implant motion should hasten fibrous incorporation while minimizing capsule formation and underlying bone resorption. By applying the implant to the skeleton, screw fixation eliminates any gaps between the implant and the recipient bed. Gaps are potential sites for hematoma or seroma accumulation. Gaps also result in an effective increase in augmentation. For example, a 2-mm gap between the posterior surface of a 5–mm implant would produce an augmentation equivalent to a 7-mm implant whose posterior surface was applied directly to the anterior surface of the skeleton. Screw immobilization of the implant allows in-place contouring of the implant at the recipient site. This final adjustment can be performed with a scalpel, rasp, or high-speed burr, depending on the material properties of the implant.

9. What is considered an ideal chin projection relative to the lips?

Suggested ideal relationships between the chin and the lips based on normative cephalometric data by different authors are in consensus that the chin shoulder should rest slightly posterior to the lower lip and the lower lip posterior to the upper lip.

10. How does the inclination of the labiomental angle impact chin augmentation?

The inclination of the labiomental angle must be evaluated when considering an increase in the sagittal projection of the chin. There is a considerable variability in this inclination. In general, the inclination is more acute in men ($113° \pm 21°$) than it is in women ($121° \pm 14°$). When the angle is already acute, chin augmentation will make it more acute, thereby deepening the labiomental angle. Such deepening usually is dysesthetic. In certain patients with retrognathia the upper central incisors abut on the lower lip, thrusting it forward and creating a deep sulcus. These patients are better served with repositioning of the entire mandible by sagittal split osteotomy.

11. What is the soft tissue response to augmentation of the chin?

Objective analyses showed that the soft tissue to hard tissue changes in patients undergoing alloplastic augmentation of the chin averaged between 77.7% and 90%. Variations in the soft tissue response would be anticipated because of the variability in the thickness of the chin soft tissue envelope. The thicker the overlying soft tissue envelope, the less its surface response to the underlying skeletal augmentation. The thickness in the soft tissue envelope overlying the chin varies within the individual and between individuals for any given area, and it usually is thicker in males than in females.

12. What muscle is most frequently injured during chin implant surgery?

The mentalis is the most frequently damaged muscle during chin surgery, usually associated with the intraoral approach for implant placement. The mentalis muscle is an elevator of the central lower lip. It arises from the mandible at the level of the root of the lower lateral incisor and therefore defines the inferior limits of the sulcus intraorally. It fans inferiorly as a truncated cone whose base inserts on the skin and therefore dimples the skin when elevating and protruding the lower lip. If it is divided and improperly reapproximated or stripped from its origin and allowed to descend to a more inferior position, the result is inferior malposition of the lower lip with increased lower incisor show and deepening of the sulcus as well as inferior displacement of the chin pad. Use of a submental approach usually avoids injury to the mentalis muscle.

13. How would you treat a patient who complains that the silicone chin implant placed several years ago is too large and asymmetric?

Revision surgery requires implant removal and replacement with an appropriately sized, shaped, and positioned implant. An advancement sliding genioplasty is an alternative approach to limit capsule-related soft tissue distortion. Removal of a smooth surfaced implant often reveals a distorted soft tissue envelope. The distortion will worsen with time due to ongoing soft tissue contraction forces. This distortion can be lessened if the soft tissue envelope is redraped over another implant or advanced skeletal segment.

14. Can fat grafts substitute for alloplastic implants to augment the facial skeleton?

Because the ultimate expression of skeletal or soft tissue structure is reflected on the skin's surface, some surgeons have used this as a justification for the equivalence and interchangeability of soft and hard tissue augmentation. For example, malar skeletal implants are used to restore cheek fullness, whereas fat grafts are used to create malar prominence. Up to a millimeter or so, the visual effect of either augmentation modality may be equivalent depending on the thickness of the overlying soft tissue envelope. However, beyond a minimal augmentation, the visual effects of these modalities are markedly different. This is easily conceptualized when envisioning large augmentations. A large implant placed on the malar bone will make the cheek project more, making the face appear more defined, angular, and, therefore, thinner and more skeletal. Implanting fat into the cheeks will also make the cheek project more; however, the face will appear increasingly round and, therefore, less defined and less angular.

15. A patient has a large nose and weak chin. In what order should rhinoplasty and chin augmentation with an implant be performed?

Facial balance and harmony are important concepts in aesthetic surgery. Underdeveloped areas may exaggerate other areas of disproportion (e.g., a small chin makes the nose appear larger). Bringing this area of underdevelopment to normal dimensions with an implant changes the balance of the face and makes the nose appear smaller. For this reason, chin augmentation should be performed *before* rhinoplasty. After chin augmentation, less extensive nasal reduction is required to create facial balance and harmony.

16. What are common complications after placement of alloplastic facial implants?

The most common complications are implant malposition and sensory nerve disturbance. Hematoma, infection, extrusion, and facial muscle weakness occur less commonly. Most complications are related to postoperative hematoma that causes wound healing problems and infection. The incidence of infection, extrusion, or hematoma has been found to be less than 1% in several series.

BIBLIOGRAPHY

Rubin JP, Yaremchuk MJ: Complications and toxicities of implantable biomaterials used in facial reconstructive and aesthetic surgery: A comprehensive review of the literature. Plast Reconstr Surg 100:1336–1353, 1997.
Terino EO: Alloplastic facial contouring by zonal principles of skeletal anatomy. Clin Plast Surg 19:487–510, 1992.
Wilkinson TS: Complications in aesthetic malar augmentation. Plast Reconstr Surg 71:643–649, 1983.
Yaremchuk MJ: Infraorbital rim augmentation. Plast Reconstr Surg 107:1585–1592, 2001.
Yaremchuk MJ: Mandibular augmentation. Plast Reconstr Surg 106:697–706, 2000.
Yaremchuk MJ: Facial skeletal reconstruction using porous polyethylene implants. Plast Reconstr Surg 111:1818–1827, 2003.
Yaremchuk MJ: Improving aesthetic outcomes after alloplastic chin augmentation. Plast Reconstr Surg 112:1422–1432, 2003.
Yaremchuk MJ: Making concave faces convex. Aesthetic Plast Surg 29:141–148, 2005.
Yaremchuk MJ: Atlas of Facial Implants. Philadelphia, Elsevier-Saunders, Philadelphia, 2006.
Zide BM, Pfeifer TM, Longaker MT: Chin surgery: I. Augmentation—The allures and the alerts. Plast Reconstr Surg 104:1843–1853, 1999.

87 CHAPTER

AESTHETIC ORTHOGNATHIC SURGERY

Stephen B. Baker, MD, DDS, and
Harvey Rosen, MD, DMD

1. What is orthognathic surgery?

Orthognathic surgery is the term used to describe surgical movement of the tooth-bearing segments of the jaws as well as the maxilla and mandible. It can be used to correct problems related to developmental anomalies, posttraumatic deformities, and sleep apnea. The goal of orthognathic surgery is to establish ideal dental occlusion with the jaws in a position that optimizes facial aesthetics.

2. What is dental compensation?

The term *dental compensation* is used to describe the tendency of teeth to tilt in a direction that minimizes the dental malocclusion. For example, in a patient with an overbite (class II malocclusion), the upper incisors will retrocline while the lower incisors will procline. The opposite occurs in a patient who has dental compensation for an underbite (class III malocclusion). Thus dental compensation will mask the true degree of skeletal discrepancy. Typically, the true skeletal discrepancy is worse than what appears on intraoral examination due to dental compensation.

3. Why is it important to discuss orthodontic camouflage versus surgical treatment prior to initiating orthodontic therapy?

In an attempt to correct an overbite with orthodontics alone, an orthodontist will retrocline the upper incisors in an attempt to normalize overjet. This will reduce upper lip support, which will make the nose look more prominent. Many patients who had moderate to severe class II malocclusions corrected with orthodontics alone present for rhinoplasty, complaining of an overprojecting and large nose. In actuality, the nasal dimensions often are normal. It is the jaw relationship that requires correction. It is important to meet with patients before they decide whether to proceed with surgical or nonsurgical orthodontic correction. If the patient elects surgical treatment, the teeth are moved in the opposite direction rather than if nonsurgical orthodontic correction was selected. Therefore it is imperative for this consultation to take place prior to initiation of treatment.

4. What is orthodontic decompensation?

Prior to orthognathic surgery, the orthodontist will *decompensate* the occlusion by removing the degree of dental compensation produced by the skeletal discrepancy. Preoperative orthodontic decompensation allows the surgeon to take advantage of the maximal amount of skeletal advancement possible.

5. What is the ideal vertical position of the maxilla?

The vertical position of the maxilla is determined by the amount of the incisors that is visible with the lips in repose. A man should show at least 2 to 3 mm, whereas as much as 5 to 6 mm is considered attractive in a woman. If the patient shows the correct degree of incisor in repose but shows excessive gingiva in full smile, the maxilla must not be impacted. The correct degree of incisor in repose is more important than is visible gingiva in full smile. It is undesirable to bury the incisors in repose just to reduce the degree of gingiva in a full smile. If the patient exhibits a long lower face with proper incisal show, the chin may be reduced to reestablish the aesthetic height of the lower facial third (Fig. 87-1).

6. How does the clinician determine the anteroposterior position of the jaws?

The profile evaluation focuses on the projection of the upper and lower jaws relative to fixed structures such as the forehead, orbits, and malar regions. The clinician usually can determine whether the deformity is due to the maxilla, mandible, or both just by looking at the patient. The details of the millimeter movements are determined on the cephalometric tracings (Fig. 87-2).

7. What is skeletal expansion and why is it important?

Movements that result in a net skeletal expansion (anterior or inferior repositioning of the jaws) will attenuate the creases and folds, whereas skeletal contraction (posterior or superior movements of the jaws) will accentuate these problems. A prematurely aged appearance is an unfavorable result from jaw movements that result in net skeletal contraction. It is important that the surgeon develop a treatment plan that will expand or maintain the preoperative

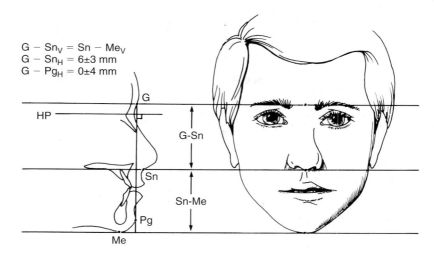

$$G - Sn_V = Sn - Me_V$$
$$G - Sn_H = 6\pm3 \text{ mm}$$
$$G - Pg_H = 0\pm4 \text{ mm}$$

Figure 87-1. Soft tissue cephalometric measurements. *Left,* Vertical perpendicular dropped from glabella *(G),* the horizontal distance from which is measured at the subnasale *(Sn)* and pogonion *(Pg).* Normal values are 6 ± 3 mm and 0 ± 4 mm, respectively. *Right,* Normal vertical facial proportions: Glabella to subnasale is equal to subnasale to menton *(Me).* (From Rosen H: Aesthetic Perspectives in Jaw Surgery. New York, Springer-Verlag, 1999.)

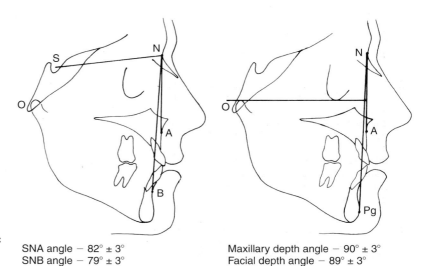

SNA angle — 82° ± 3°
SNB angle — 79° ± 3°

Maxillary depth angle — 90° ± 3°
Facial depth angle — 89° ± 3°

Figure 87-2. Skeletal cephalometric measurements describing sagittal positions of the jaws. *Left,* SNA and SNB measurements relate the maxilla and the mandible to the cranial base. Normal values are 82° ± 4° and 79° ± 3°, respectively. *Right,* Maxillary depth and facial depth angles relate the maxilla and the mandible to the Frankfort horizontal. Normal values are 90° ± 3° and 89° ± 3°, respectively. (From Rosen H: Aesthetic Perspectives in Jaw Surgery. New York, Springer-Verlag, 1999.)

volume of the face. If a superior or posterior (contraction) movement of one of the jaws is planned, an attempt should be made to neutralize the skeletal contraction with an advancement or inferior movement of the other jaw or the chin. It is important to avoid a net contraction of the facial skeleton because this may result in a prematurely aged appearance.

8. How is a lateral cephalometric radiograph obtained?

A lateral cephalometric radiograph is performed under reproducible conditions so that serial images can be compared. This film usually is done at the orthodontist's office using a cephalostat, an apparatus specifically designed to maintain consistent head position. The surgeon must be able to visualize bony as well as soft tissue features on the image to facilitate tracing of all landmarks. A piece of transparent acetate tracing paper is secured with tape over the radiograph and the following landmarks are traced: sella, inferior orbital rim, nasion, frontal bone, nasal bones, maxilla, maxillary first molar and central incisor, external auditory meatus, condylar head and mandible, and mandibular first molar and incisor. The soft tissue of the forehead, nose, lips, and chin also are traced. Once the normal structures are traced, several planes and angles are determined (see Chapter 27, Questions 2 and 21).

9. What is the difference between an absolute and relative crossbite?

Dental casts allow the clinician to distinguish between absolute and relative transverse maxillary deficiency. Absolute transverse maxillary deficiency presents as a posterior crossbite with the jaws in a class I relationship. A relative maxillary transverse deficiency is commonly seen in a patient with a class III malocclusion. A posterior crossbite is observed in this type of patient, leading the surgeon to suspect inadequate maxillary width. However, as the maxilla is advanced or the mandible retruded, the crossbite is eliminated. Articulation of the casts into a class I occlusion allows the surgeon to easily distinguish between relative and absolute maxillary constriction.

10. Is facial disproportion ever acceptable in facial aesthetics?

It has been shown that skeletal expansion is aesthetically pleasing even if facial disproportion is necessary to achieve the expansion. Fashion models often exhibit slight degrees of facial disproportion and are considered beautiful. The aesthetic benefits the patient receives by expanding the facial envelope frequently justify the small degree of disproportion necessary to achieve them. Even in young adolescent patients who do not show signs of aging, one must not ignore these principles. A successful surgeon will incorporate these principles into the treatment plan of every patient so that as the patient ages, the signs of aging will be minimized and a youthful appearance will be maintained as long as possible.

11. Why is a final splint necessary?

The occlusion desired may not be the same as maximum intercuspal position. The splint is useful in maintaining the occlusion in the desired location when it does not correspond to maximal intercuspal position. It is easy for the orthodontist to close a posterior openbite, but it is very difficult to close an anterior openbite with orthodontics alone. At the end of the case it is important to have the anterior teeth and the canines in a class I relationship without an openbite. If the desired occlusion is the same as that produced when the models are placed into maximal intercuspal position, a final splint is not necessary.

12. What is the least stable movement?

The least stable movement is transverse expansion of the maxilla. Stable movements include mandibular advancement and superior positioning of the maxilla. Movements with intermediate stability include maxillary impaction combined with mandibular advancement, maxillary advancement combined with mandibular setback, and correction of mandibular asymmetry. The unstable movements include posterior positioning of the mandible and inferior positioning of the maxilla.

13. What are the causes of malocclusion after skeletal fixation?

Improper positioning of the jaws is noted by poor occlusion or an obvious unaesthetic result. If this complication results from improper condyle position during fixation or improper indexing of the splint, fixation must be removed and reapplied. It is wise to verify splint fit prior to surgery. Meticulous treatment planning prior to surgery minimizes splint-related problems.

14. How is lip length affected by closure of the circumvestibular incision?

A linear closure of a circumvestibular incision will shorten lip length and cause thinning of the lip. According to Rosen, the lip shortens by 20% to 50% of the amount of vertical maxillary reduction. The best way to minimize this shortening is to do a V-Y closure at the midline of the incision. A skin hook can be placed at the midline and used to pull the incision up while the vertical limb of the V-Y closure is performed. This limb typically is approximately 1 to 1.5 cm but can be modified in specific indications (Fig. 87-3).

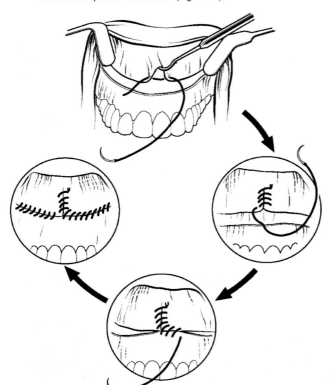

Figure 87-3. V-Y closure at the anteriormost portion of the maxillary buccal incision minimizes lip shortening. A skin hook is placed in the mucosa superior to the incision at the midline. The vertical limb is closed for 1 cm with a running suture. Each lateral incision is closed with a continuous locking 4-0 chromic suture. (From Booth PW, Schendel S, Hausamen JE [eds]: Maxillofacial Surgery, Vol 2, 2nd ed. New York, Churchill Livingstone, 2006.)

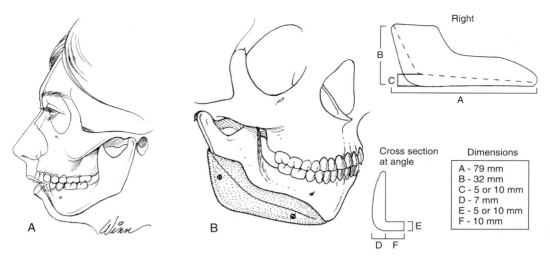

Right

B
C
A

Cross section
at angle

Dimensions

A - 79 mm	
B - 32 mm	
C - 5 or 10 mm	
D - 7 mm	
E - 5 or 10 mm	
F - 10 mm	

A   B   D F   E

Figure 87-4. A, Soft tissue contour and skeletal configuration of patient with mandibular deficiency and class II malocclusion. **B,** Configuration and dimensions of mandibular body implant used to augment the deficient mandible. Because it extends beyond the posterior border of the ramus and inferior edge of the ramus and body, it closes the mandibular angle and lessens the plane of the mandibular border. Screw fixation guarantees position and ensures application of implant to skeleton. (From Yaremchuk MJ: Mandibular augmentation. Plast Reconstr Surg 106:697, 2000.)

15. What is the role of alloplastic augmentation in orthognathic surgery?

Alloplastic augmentation can be a useful tool in achieving aesthetic augmentation with minimal morbidity and recovery in a patient who may benefit from the skeletal augmentation but has no occlusal problems that require an osteotomy. Mandibular angle implants will enhance mandibular definition and soft tissue support in the patient with short rami and a steep mandibular plane. In facial rejuvenation patients, this skeletal augmentation can greatly enhance the aesthetic result and provide much better soft tissue support than can be achieved with soft tissue repositioning alone. Piriform and malar implants can provide soft tissue support that enhances facial aesthetics as well as in patients who have a class I occlusion but suffer from lack of adequate midfacial skeletal projection (Figs. 87-4 and 87-5).

16. When should the nose be addressed in the orthognathic patient?

Because Le Fort I osteotomy will alter the dimensions of the nose, definitive rhinoplasty should be deferred until after the patient recovers from the maxillary osteotomy. The Le Fort procedure requires dissection and release of tissues from the anterior nasal spine. The effects of these maneuvers will cause nasal tip rotation. Even in isolated mandibular osteotomies, the surgeon must remember that nasal intubation is required to place the patient in maxillomandibular fixation prior to application of rigid fixation. If rhinoplasty is to be performed at this time, the patient must be reintubated orally after the mandibular procedure is completed. It is acceptable to perform rhinoplasty in conjunction with mandibular osteotomies, but we recommend doing rhinoplasties at least 6 months after maxillary procedures.

17. What nasal changes are seen after orthognathic surgery?

If the maxilla is moved anteriorly, the nasal tip moves anterior and the dorsum may appear too low for the new position of the nasal tip. If the maxilla is moved posteriorly, the nasal tip will decrease its projection and the dorsum of the nose may appear too high relative to the new position of the nasal tip. The nasal length may decrease with maxillary movement and the nasolabial angle will increase. Maxillary osteotomies will result in increased alar width.

18. How can alar widening be reduced in maxillary surgery?

The alar cinch is a procedure that places a suture from an intraoral incision that takes a bite from each transversalis nasi muscle and pulls them together to normalize ideal alar width. Weir excisions also can be useful in restoring ideal alar aesthetics after maxillary osteotomies (Fig. 87-6).

19. What are the soft tissue changes in the upper lip that occur after Le Fort I osteotomy?

The upper lip will thin approximately 2 mm from its preoperative thickness after a Le Fort I sulcus incision has been closed. Flattening of the lip also occurs, and downturning of the lateral commissures can be seen. It is important to counsel patients about these changes prior to surgery. Fat grafting or Restylane may be useful in restoring lip volume. These soft tissue fillers also are useful for nonsurgical modification of incisal show if postoperative modifications are necessary.

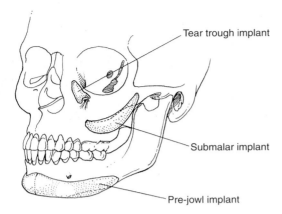

Figure 87-5. Three implants used primarily to fill out involutional soft tissue deficiencies that occur with aging. Depicted are the tear trough, the submalar implant, and the prejowl implant. (From Mathes S [ed]: Plastic Surgery, 2nd ed. Philadelphia, Saunders, 2006.)

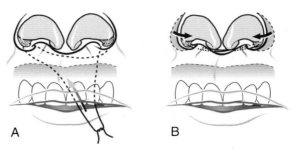

Figure 87-6. Alar cinch stitch is designed to prevent alar widening after Le Fort I osteotomy and allow the surgeon to control the width of the nose. 2-0 Prolene suture is used to grasp the transversalis nasi muscle on each side of the nose. The suture is tightened to the point that normal alar width is restored. (From Booth PW, Schendel S, Hausamen JE [eds]: Maxillofacial Surgery, Vol 2, 2nd ed. New York, Churchill Livingstone, 2006.)

20. What is the role of genioplasty in orthognathic surgery?

A genioplasty is commonly required in orthognathic surgery to optimize chin position after the jaws have been moved into the desired location. When the mandible is moved either anteriorly or posteriorly the chin will move with the mandible. If the final position of the chin is not ideal, it should be moved into the optimal location based on the anticipated facial changes that will occur from the orthognathic procedure. These anticipated postoperative facial changes and the new desired position of the chin are based on the postoperative cephalometric tracings that are performed as part of the treatment planning phase of the procedure.

21. What is the role of fat grafting?

Autogenous fat grafting can be a useful adjunct procedure in the adult orthognathic patient. Many patients desire cosmetic as well as functional improvements, and fat grafting is a relatively benign method for augmenting any remaining deficiencies in the soft tissue envelope after skeletal expansion. Fat can be easily harvested using either Coleman or Tulip syringes and injected into the desired areas to fill depressions that can persist in the nasolabial crease, paramandibular, or piriform regions. As our understanding of adipocyte biology as well as the effects on the adipocytes from harvesting, processing, and injection improves, fat grafting will be used more commonly to achieve an optimal aesthetic result for the orthognathic surgical patient.

BIBLIOGRAPHY

Coleman SR: Structural fat grafts: The ideal filler. Clin Plast Surg 28:111–119, 2001.

O'Ryan F, Schendel S: Nasal anatomy and maxillary surgery. II Unfavorable nasolabial esthetics following the Le Fort I osteotomy. Int J Orthodon Orthognath Surg 4:75–84, 1989.

Proffit WR, Sarver DM: Treatment planning: Optimizing benefit to the patient. In Proffit WR, White RP, Sarver DM (eds): Contemporary Treatment of Dentofacial Deformity. Mosby, St. Louis, 2003, pp 213–223.

Proffit WR, Turvey TA, Phillips C: Orthognathic surgery: A hierarchy of stability. Int J Adult Orthod Orthogn Surg 11:191–204, 1996.

Rosen H: Aesthetics in facial skeletal surgery. Perspect Plast Surg 6:1, 1993.

Rosen HM: Facial skeletal expansion: Treatment strategies and rationale. Plast Reconstr Surg 89:798–808, 1992.

Rosen HM: Lip-nasal esthetics following Le Fort I osteotomy. Plast Reconstr Surg 81:171–182, 1988.

Stella JP, Streater MR, Epker BN, Sinn DP: Predictability of upper lip soft tissue changes with maxillary advancement. J Oral Maxillofac Surg 47:697–703, 1989.

Stuzin J: Restoring facial shape in facelifting: The role of skeletal support in facial analysis and midface soft-tissue repositioning. Plast Reconstr Surg 119:362–376, 2007.

Terino EO: Facial contouring with alloplastic implants. Facial Plast Surg Clin North Am 7:85–103, 1997.

GENIOPLASTY

Stephen B. Baker, MD, DDS

CHAPTER 88

1. What is a genioplasty?
Genioplasty is an operation on the chin that uses either an osteotomy or an implant to change the position of the chin.

2. How do you determine the relationship of the nose to the chin?
The ratio of nasal projection to nasal length should be 2:3. Assuming nasal projection and nasal length are correct, the aesthetic balance between the nose and chin can be clinically assessed. If the chin appears too far anterior or posterior to the nose, the occlusion should be evaluated. Orthognathic surgery can be done to correct skeletal malocclusions. If the patient does not desire orthognathic surgery or if the occlusal discrepancies are minimal, a genioplasty can be performed to minimize the chin deformity.

3. What factors determine sagittal projection of the chin?
The lower lip and the nose play an important role in chin aesthetics. Several tools can be used to assess chin projection. If nasal length is ideal, a line can be dropped from the middorsum of the nose inferior and tangential to the upper lip. According to Byrd, the chin should be approximately 3 mm posterior to this line. Another method is to drop a line inferior and perpendicular to Frankfurt horizontal that is tangential to the lower lip. The chin should be just posterior to this line in females and at, or slightly anterior to, this line in males. A final analysis is Riedel's line. This line connects the most prominent points of the upper and lower lips. The most prominent point of the chin should be the third point on this line. These references are general guidelines. Each patient's particular facial shape, skeletal form, and soft tissue characteristics should be taken into account. For instance, in a patient with a mandibular retrognathia whose occlusion has been compensated, it would be inadvisable to move the chin as far forward to the ideal position because of adverse changes in the labiomental crease. An undercorrection in this case may give an improvement that is more aesthetically pleasing than moving the chin into the "ideal" position.

4. What is the relationship of the soft tissue to hard tissue when the chin is moved?
The response of the soft tissue to a genioplasty is better than is the soft tissue response to an implant. Because the mentalis attaches the skin to the bone of the anterior chin, the skin will move in a 1:1 relationship with the bone in a genioplasty. When an implant is used, the soft tissue to implant response is 0.8:1. This is a useful guide when doing prediction tracings of the anticipated chin position and its relationship to the nose.

5. What factors determine the vertical position of the chin?
The vertical height of the face can be divided into thirds. The trichion to the glabella is the upper third, the glabella to subnasale is the middle third, and subnasale to menton is the lower third. The vertical height of the chin should be set so that the lower third of the face is approximately equal to the upper and middle thirds. Another factor that affects the aesthetics of the vertical height of the chin is the depth of the labiomental crease. The crease should not exhibit effacement nor should it be deep. Moving the chin forward or superior will deepen the crease. Moving the chin inferiorly or posteriorly will efface the crease. These anticipated changes should be taken into account when developing a treatment plan to change the vertical height of the chin. In an advancement genioplasty, the surgeon must be careful to ensure that the osteotomy is parallel to Frankfurt horizontal. If the osteotomy is angled superiorly from anterior to posterior, the chin will become elongated as it is advanced (see Pharaoh deformity, Question 12).

6. What factors determine the transverse position of the chin?
The clinical evaluation often reveals whether the midline discrepancy is due to osseous tissue, soft tissue, or a combination of both. When examining the facial midline, it is useful to mark several points (glabella, nose, dental midlines, vermillion, chin) to see if all are congruent. Occasionally, these points are not aligned, and the surgeon needs to point this out to the patient preoperatively to explain the limitations of surgery. Ideally, the center of the chin is congruent with the mandibular skeletal and dental midlines. If the chin is not centered, a simple centering genioplasty is indicated. If the chin as well as the mandibular midline is not centered, a mandibular osteotomy is necessary to correct the asymmetry. Occasionally, the mandible and the chin both require independent movements to achieve the best result. When the chin is moved, a 1:1 ratio of bone to soft tissue movement is anticipated when planning the final position.

7. What imaging is necessary prior to osseous genioplasty?

A panoramic radiograph (Panorex) should be obtained prior to performing an osseous genioplasty to rule out the presence of periapical or other bony pathology. This image helps differentiate any osseous component of chin asymmetry from that related to soft tissue. Important diagnostic information regarding the deformity also can be assessed, such as asymmetry, vertical height, proximity of tooth roots to proposed osteotomy, and location of the mental foramen. A lateral cephalometric radiograph is helpful for predicting the degree of movement required to obtain the desired result.

8. How does the concept of skeletal expansion apply to the chin?

Moving the chin anteriorly or superiorly deepens the labiomental crease. In contrast, inferior or posterior movements soften the labiomental crease. In the patient with a normal crease, an anterior movement will create a deep crease. This effect can be negated by moving the chin inferiorly if the patient's facial shape can tolerate the change. Otherwise, it is advisable to reduce the degree of anterior advancement. If a patient with an effaced crease requires an inferior movement, the surgeon should also move the chin forward, if possible, to normalize the crease. Frequently, compromises are required, and it is up to the surgeon to plan the ideal movements based on each patient's preoperative facial dimensions.

9. When is an osseous genioplasty preferable to a chin implant?

A chin implant is only capable of increasing chin projection. A chin implant cannot change the vertical dimension of the chin nor can it correct transverse asymmetry. An osseous genioplasty is the only method for manipulating the chin in all three dimensions. Additionally, an osseous genioplasty will advance the genial tubercles and thus the suprahyoid musculature. This advancement produces an improvement in the neck–chin contour that is not as pronounced as the neck tightening seen with implants.

10. What are the advantages of alloplastic chin augmentation?

An implant can add volume to the lateral mandible, which can increase lower facial width; often this is useful in patients with small pointed chins. There is less risk to the mental nerve with the submental incision and dissection used to place a chin implant. If the patient does not like the implant, it can be removed. However, if the implant is removed, a slight soft tissue droop due to compromise of the attachment of the mentalis to the bone may be noted.

11. Where should the incision be placed for a chin implant?

A submental incision is the best choice for inserting a chin implant. This reduces the chance of the implant migrating in a superior direction. Because the mentalis is not violated, the risk of witch's chin deformity is reduced. This incision is easy to make under local anesthesia with or without sedation, making insertion of a chin implant an easy procedure to perform in the office.

12. What potential adverse aesthetic effects are associated with advancement genioplasty? What is a Pharaoh deformity?

When an osseous genioplasty is advanced more than 5 to 6 mm, a notch can occur at the junction of the segments. Typically, this resolves as the bone resorbs, but if it persists beyond 6 months, a bone graft or implant can be placed to minimize the notch and smooth the mandibular contour in this region. An overadvanced chin also can cause excessive deepening of the labiomental crease, creating a prematurely aged appearance. The labiomental crease should never be more than 4 mm in women and no more than 6 mm in men. Additionally, excessive vertical elongation can occur as the chin is advanced. This can elongate the lower facial third and create a very unaesthetic appearance, especially in a patient who exhibits a long lower face preoperatively. This elongation leads to a "Pharaoh deformity," which is an elongated narrow chin (Fig. 88-1).

13. What potential adverse esthetic effects are associated with setback genioplasty?

Only an osseous genioplasty can be done to reduce the projection of the chin. You must be careful not to posteriorly position the chin excessively because of the potential to create soft tissue redundancy in the submental region. Also, as the symphysis of the chin is posteriorly positioned, a boxy appearance can be created as the facial shape becomes more square and loses the ideal oval shape. For these reasons, posterior movements of the chin should not be more than 3 to 4 mm in most cases. Patients should be warned preoperatively that they will have a palpable step where the edge of the posteriorly placed chin is wider than the mandible. Typically this irregularity resolves over several months as the bone resorbs, but if this step-off is noted to be excessive at the time of genioplasty, it can be reduced with the burr at the time of surgery.

14. How much subperiosteal dissection is recommended to perform an osseous genioplasty?

As little subperiosteal reflection as possible is done to visualize the mental nerves and apply fixation. Limiting the dissection will minimize chin ptosis (witch's chin) and maintain a 1:1 ratio of osseous to soft tissue during the movements. Retractors are used to visualize the nerve and retract it away from the saw during the osteotomy.

Figure 88-1. The Pharaoh deformity.

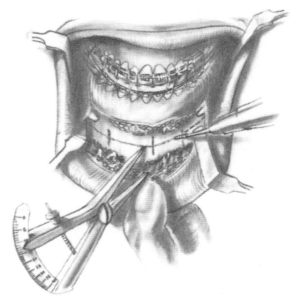

Figure 88-2. Calipers are used to make measurements and verify chin position. Vertical drill lines are used to maintain orientation after the chin has been osteotomized. (From Bell WH [ed]: Modern Practice in Orthognathic and Reconstructive Surgery, Vol 3. Philadelphia, WB Saunders, 1992, p 2448.)

15. Where are the osteotomy cuts made?

The cuts should be made 5 mm below the mental foramen and should extend posteriorly to the molar region. This posterior extension keeps the osteotomy transition under the thicker soft tissues of the mandibular angle. The posterior extension also minimizes the hourglass deformity, which can occur when the cuts are made too far anteriorly (Fig. 88-2).

16. What are the various types of genioplasties?

- *Sliding Genioplasty:* This osteotomy is performed as a single cut through the chin at least 5 mm inferior to the apices of the mandibular teeth. It allows the chin segment to be moved anteriorly or posteriorly while maintaining contact between the two bone segments. Prefabricated chin plates can be used to easily secure the segments when in the desired position (Fig. 88-3).
- *Jumping Genioplasty:* The jumping genioplasty is performed by making an osteotomy cut through the inferior mandible and then bringing the segment forward and superior so that the posterior edge of the chin segment rests against the anterior portion of the inferior mandible.
- *Reduction Genioplasty:* This is done when the vertical height of the chin is excessive and the maxillary vertical position is normal. Two parallel cuts are made, with the distance between the cuts corresponding to the degree of vertical reduction desired. It is useful to make the inferior osteotomy cut first so that the second cut is still on stable bone as opposed to making the second cut on a mobile chin segment (Fig. 88-4).
- *Double Step Genioplasty:* This osteotomy is indicated in cases of severe deficiency. A double cut is made (inferior portion first). The upper osteotomized portion is advanced and secured to the intact mandible. The inferior segment is moved anteriorly and secured to the middle segment while maintaining bony overlap at each area of advancement (Fig. 88-5).
- *Vertical Elongating Genioplasty:* The osteotomy is performed, and a bone graft or piece of block hydroxyapatite is placed interpositionally to maintain the gap between the segments as the lower portion of the chin is inferiorly displaced (Fig. 88-6).
- *Widening Genioplasty:* A narrow chin can be widened by doing a horizontal osteotomy cut and then dividing the inferior portion of the chin at the midline with a vertical osteotomy. The inferior pieces can be widened using a bone graft or block hydroxyapatite as a midline spacer for stability.

17. What are the potential complications of an osseous genioplasty?

Potential complications of an osseous genioplasty include asymmetry, wound dehiscence, overadvancement or underadvancement, chin ptosis, and lip paresthesia. Despite the multitude of potential complications, their frequency is rare (<5%).

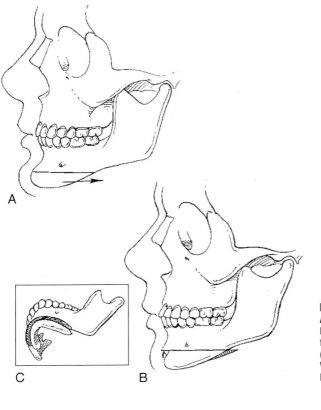

A

C   B

Figure 88-3. Horizontal osteotomy with setback.
A, Sliding genioplasty osteotomy requires special attention laterally at the inferior border **(B, C)** to ensure a smooth transition between the mobilized segment and mandible. (From Fonseca RJ [ed]: Oral and Maxillofacial Surgery, Vol 2, Orthognathic Surgery, Betts NJ, Turvey TA [eds]. Philadelphia, WB Saunders, 2000, p 409.)

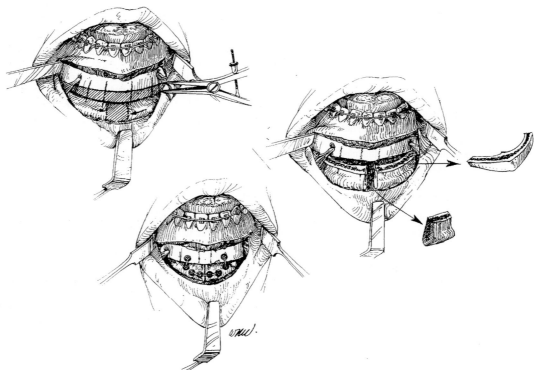

Figure 88-4. Reduction genioplasty. Narrowing of the inferior chin can be achieved by removing a central block of bone and moving the lateral segments to the midline. Rigid fixation is used to maintain the position of the segments. (From Bell WH [ed]: Modern Practice in Orthognathic and Reconstructive Surgery, Vol 3, Philadelphia, WB Saunders, 1992, p 2470.)

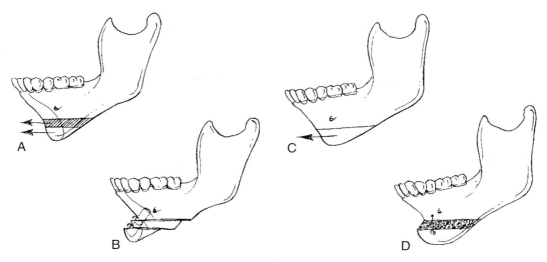

Figure 88-5. Double sliding genioplasty. **A,** This osteotomy can be used in cases of severe deficiency. **B–D,** Often, it is necessary to provide grafts over the step defects to ensure a predictable contour. (From Fonseca RJ [ed]: Oral and Maxillofacial Surgery, Vol 2, Orthognathic Surgery, Betts NJ, Turvey TA [eds]. Philadelphia, WB Saunders, 2000, p 410.)

Figure 88-6. Wedge vertical reduction osteotomy. This osteotomy allows for **(A)** anteroposterior repositioning in addition to **(B)** vertical shortening. (From Fonseca RJ [ed]: Oral and Maxillofacial Surgery, Vol 2, Orthognathic Surgery, Betts NJ, Turvey TA [eds]. Philadelphia, WB Saunders, 2000, p 410.)

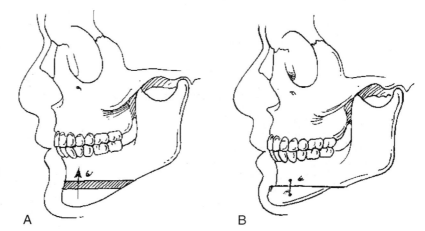

18. What are the potential complications of a chin implant?

The potential complications of chin implantation include selection of the wrong size or shape implant, infection, extrusion, malposition, capsular contracture, and chin ptosis. For chin implantation, the risk of a complication is low but is slightly higher than that of osseous genioplasty.

19. What is a witch's chin deformity?

The "witch's chin deformity" results from a transection of the mentalis muscle that is not properly reapproximated. It is characterized by a clockwise rotation of the soft tissue in the chin causing it to droop over the osseous menton. At closure of the intraoral incision, the mentalis should be closed with several interrupted resorbable sutures to prevent this. Care must be taken to prevent dimpling of the skin that results from excessively deep bites (Fig. 88-7).

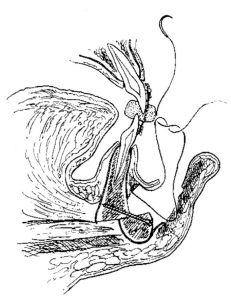

Figure 88-7. Mentalis is reapproximated with 2-0 monocryl as the chin is closed. This maintains proper position of the lower lip and reduces the chance of developing a witch's chin. (From Bell WH [ed]: Modern Practice in Orthognathic and Reconstructive Surgery, Vol 3. Philadelphia, WB Saunders, 1992, p 2451.)

BIBLIOGRAPHY

Bell WH (ed): Modern Practice in Orthognathic and Reconstructive Surgery. Philadelphia, WB Saunders, 1992, pp 2431–2488.
Byrd HS, Burt J: Dimensional approach to rhinoplasty: perfecting the aesthetic balance between the nose and chin. In Gunter JP, Rohrich RJ, Adams WP (eds): Dallas Rhinoplasty: Nasal Surgery by the Masters. St. Louis, Quality Medical Publishing, 2002, 117–131.
Fonseca RJ (ed): Oral and Maxillofacial Surgery. Philadelphia, WB Saunders, 2000.
Riedel RA: An analysis of dentofacial relationships. Am J Orthod 43:103, 1957.
Guyuron B: Genioplasty. In Goldwyn RM, Cohen M (eds): The Unfavorable Result in Plastic Surgery: Avoidance and Treatment, 3rd ed. Philadelphia, Lippincott Williams & Wilkins, 2001, pp 1036–1042.
Rosen HM: Aesthetic refinements in genioplasty: The role of the labiomental fold. Plast Reconstr Surg 88:760–767, 1991.
Rosen HM: Aesthetic guidelines in genioplasty: The role of facial disproportion. Plast Reconstr Surg 95:463–469, 1995.
Rosen HM: Aesthetic Perspectives in Jaw Surgery. New York, Springer Verlag, 1997, pp 247–272.

CHAPTER 89

NON-SURGICAL REJUVENATION OF THE AGING FACE

William T. McClellan, MD, and
Brooke R. Seckel, MD, FACS

1. According to the American Society of Aesthetic Plastic Surgeons, how many nonsurgical cosmetic procedures were performed in the United States in 2005?

In 2005, more than nine million nonsurgical cosmetic procedures were performed in the United States. This number drastically contrasts with the two million surgical procedures performed in the same year.

The top four nonsurgical procedures in 2005 were Botox (3.3 million), laser hair removal (1.6 million), hyaluronic acid injection (1.2 million), and microdermabrasion (1 million).

As direct consumer marketing and external pressure from non–plastic surgeons increases, mastery of nonoperative techniques will be paramount to success.

2. What are the clinical and histopathologic manifestations of photodamage to the skin?

Photodamage to the skin is characterized by repeated exposure to the ultraviolet radiation from sunlight, which causes cumulative damage. This damage can be seen clinically with increased roughness of the skin, fine wrinkles, pigment discrepancies, and lentigines. Microscopically the skin will demonstrate alterations in the dermal extracellular matrix with disorganized and degraded collagen.

3. What is tretinoin, and how can it be used for facial rejuvenation?

Tretinoin is a vitamin A derivative that has been used for many years and has proved to be quite safe and effective for reduction of dyschromia and fine wrinkles. Histologically this can be confirmed after 6 months of use by increased epidermal thickening, increased granular layer thickness, decreased melanin content, and stratum corneum compaction.

4. What is the dosing, application, and safe duration of use of tretinoin?

Tretinoin is dispensed in an emollient cream at strengths of 0.01%, 0.025%, and 0.5%. The 0.5% cream is the most commonly used and can be applied once daily on the facial skin following exfoliation. Multiple studies with follow-up of 4 years have shown no adverse long-term effects of tretinoin use.

5. What are the side effects, complications, or warnings about tretinoin you should tell your patients?

The most common side effects that occur with tretinoin use are erythema, burning sensation, and skin irritation. All of these side effects are more common following the initiation of therapy and usually subside after a few weeks. Typically they can be alleviated with moisturizer application. It is important for the patient to avoid excessive sun exposure because of increased susceptibility to sunburn and further irritation. Encourage the use of sunscreens that contain moisturizer for patients who are exposed to the outdoors while using tretinoin.

Because tretinoin use during pregnancy has not been studied, female patients should cease tretinoin use if pregnant. Tretinoin has been shown to cause delayed bone development in animal studies.

6. What is ascorbic acid, and how is it used for facial rejuvenation?

L-Ascorbic acid, also known as vitamin C, has been shown to regulate collagen production and stimulate procollagen synthesis. Topical 5% vitamin C cream has been shown to clinically and topographically improve fine facial wrinkles and dyschromia when applied daily over 6 months.

7. What is Botox?

Botulinum toxin type A is a purified toxin produced from the fermentation of the Hall strain of the bacteria *Clostridium botulinum*.

8. How does Botox work?

Botox chemically denervates muscle by irreversibly binding to the SNAP-25 protein, which prevents release of acetylcholine from motor or sympathetic nerve terminals. There is reduction in motor activity and partial muscle atrophy that is slowly reversed by reinnervation of muscle and development of extrajunctional acetylcholine receptors.

9. How was the Botox unit calculated?

One unit of Botox is the median intraperitoneal lethal dose (LD_{50}) in mice. Each vial contains 100 units of Botox, 0.5 mg of human albumin, and 0.9 mg of saline that is vacuum dried without a preservative.

10. How is Botox reconstituted?

Botox comes vacuum dried in a vial containing 100 units. Each vial should be reconstituted with 2.5 mL of 0.9% nonpreserved saline for a final concentration of 4 units per 0.1 mL. Some data suggest that preserved saline actually decreases pain experienced by the patient on injection. The Botox Consensus Group states that preserved saline is preferable to nonpreserved saline as a dilutant for Botox based on the improved patient comfort during injection reported by Alam.

11. How long can Botox be used after it has been reconstituted, and how should it be stored?

The prescribing information states that Botox should be used within 4 hours of reconstitution. However, according to the Botox Consensus Group, Botox can be stored safely at 4°C for up to 6 weeks prior to use. Prior to reconstitution, Botox can be stored at 2°C to 8°C for up to 24 months.

12. What are the contraindications to Botox use?

There are many contraindications to use of this medication for cosmetic purposes in patients. A thorough history of prior medical conditions, medications, and allergic reactions should be undertaken before Botox is administered.

Botox should not be used in a patient who is pregnant or lactating. Additionally, any patient with a neuromuscular disorder, such as myasthenia gravis or amyotrophic lateral sclerosis, should not receive Botox because even low doses might cause a neuromuscular crisis. Aminoglycoside antibiotics have the potential to interfere with the metabolism of Botox and may prolong the half-life of the drug. Patients using warfarin or other anticoagulants should not receive Botox.

13. What is the most common side effect and complication of Botox injection?

The most common side effect of Botox is mild headache following injection. However, data suggest that this may be due to the injection itself and not necessarily the Botox.

The most common reported complication following Botox injection is hematoma at the site of injection. Patients should be counseled to discontinue aspirin and other antiplatelet drugs prior to injection. Coumadin (warfarin) anticoagulation is a contraindication to Botox injection because of possible drug interactions and high risk for hematoma.

14. What type of syringe and anesthetic can be used for Botox injection?

A 1-cc tuberculin or insulin syringe with a small-bore needle (e.g., 30 or 32 gauge) is optimal for injection.

Topical anesthetic such as EMLA cream, injectable anesthetic such as lidocaine, or a simple ice pack all can be used to improve patient comfort during injection.

15. What are the postinjection instructions to the patient?

The patient should not massage the injected area, should limit laborious activity, and should avoid bending over for 24 hours to prevent unwanted diffusion of the product. Additionally, patients may be instructed to contract the injected area for approximately 2 hours, which may speed uptake. Ice to the injection area will help reduce local bruising and edema.

16. What is the glabellar complex, and what are the recommended Botox dosages to treat this area?

The glabellar complex is composed of the corrugator supercilii, procerus, and depressor supercilii (medial orbicularis oculi) muscles. These muscles function to adduct and depress the brow, resulting in a vertically oriented wrinkle.

Five to seven injection sites are recommended in a V formation along the medial brows. The median dose for this area reported in the literature is 20 units (range 10 to 80 units) divided across the glabellar complex.

17. A new physician asks you to teach a medical student how to inject Botox into the crow's feet of a patient. What pearls would you give the student to optimize the outcome of the injection technique? What are the dosage and the injection pattern of the lateral orbit?

- Appropriate lighting and loupe magnification can help identify small periorbital veins that can lead to postinjection hematoma or bruising. Ice compress following injection may lessen bruising.
- A positive snap test may identify a patient with potential for postinjection ectropion.
- Start with low doses of Botox and stay at least 1 cm lateral to the orbital rim to avoid ptosis.
- Ask the patient to animate the area while you are injecting. This will help guide the injections into specific muscular targets. Remember to keep the injection superficial in the deep dermis or superficial subdermis and to keep the needle angled away from the orbit.

Typically women require 8 to 12 units per side and men 12 to 16 units per side divided among four vertically oriented injection sites.

18. A patient calls your office 24 hours after Botox injection and states that she wants her money back because she sees no effect from the treatment. What do you tell her? How long do you tell her the effects will last?

Explain to the patient that the onset of action is not for 2 to 3 days after injection and the peak effect usually is not seen for 2 to 3 weeks. The effects are variable; however, they generally last 3 to 4 months.

19. What is hyaluronic acid?

It is a glycosaminoglycan that consists of regularly repeating nonsulfated disaccharide units of glucuronic acid and *N*-acetylglucosamine. It is essentially a component of the extracellular matrix. It is quite hydrophilic, and the water that surrounds it is able to occupy a larger volume relative to its mass. It is biocompatible and lacks immunogenicity, making it a good dermal filler. No skin testing is required prior to injection, giving it a significant advantage over bovine collagen fillers (Table 89-1).

20. What are four commonly used Food and Drug Administration–approved hyaluronic acid formulas available in the United States?

Restylane, Captique, Hylaform, and Hylaform Plus are four Food and Drug Administration (FDA)–approved hyaluronic acid fillers used in the United States. They all are approved for mid to deep dermal implantation for correction of facial wrinkles and folds. Restylane is made from bacterial (streptococcus) fermentation, cross-linked with 1,4-butanediol diglycidyl ether, with a hyaluronic acid concentration of 20 mg/mL and a particle size of 400 microns. It remains the most popular in use.

21. Why is periorbital injection of soft tissue fillers problematic?

The anatomy of the periorbital region is complex and the area difficult to augment because the skin is very thin and will easily show contour irregularities, color discrepancies, and inflammation from poorly placed filler. In addition, patients may be at higher risk for visible bruising from the procedure and for the remote severe complication of vision loss.

22. In which layer is periorbital tissue filler placed?

If the filler is placed too shallow, then surface and color irregularities may be seen; therefore a suborbicularis plane is optimal. Using a 30-gauge needle, a fan-shaped area can be injected with 0.3 to 1cc of Restylane to augment periorbital hollows. Periorbital injection of filler should be performed only by those very experienced with the subtle technical aspects of precise filler deposition.

23. What are technical considerations for filler injection?

There are many subtle technical considerations to allow for optimal placement of fillers throughout the face. It is preferable to use ice and EMLA cream instead of local anesthetic, which may distort the intended injection anatomy secondary to volume displacement.

A steady, gentle pressure should be applied to the plunger of the syringe so that a constant and symmetric flow of filler is ejected as you withdraw the needle. Variable pressure and speed of withdrawal can alter the amount of product deposited under the superficial defect, creating a visible lump.

Pattern of filler deposition is important in creating a three-dimensional construct augmenting the desired area. The most common methods for developing this pattern construct are fanning, linear threading, and serial puncture. It is important to pick a surface reference point on which to build the pattern. Deposition of filler in an unintended overlapping nature may produce unwanted augmentation.

24. Can Restylane be used in conjunction with other cosmetic procedures?

Yes. According to the Restylane Consensus Group, based on current data it is safe to use Restylane in conjunction with surgery (e.g., facelift) as well as energy-based treatments (e.g., Thermage, laser resurfacing). However, it is recommended to perform the energy treatment prior to placement of Restylane so as not to displace or disrupt the substance.

Table 89-1. Types of Filler

FILLER	COMPOSITION	INJECTION SITE	LONGEVITY	SKIN TEST
Bovine Collagen				
Zyderm I	3.5% BC	Perioral wrinkles	2–4 months	Yes
Zyderm II	6.5% BC	Coarse rhytids	2–4 months	Yes
Zyplast	3.5% BC + glutaraldehyde cross-links	Coarse rhytids	6–8 months	Yes
Artecoll	3.5% BC + polymethylmethacrylate microspheres	Glabella, nasolabial, perioral, deeper defects	Years	Yes
Endoplast 50	BC + solubilized elastin peptides	Coarse rhytids	12 months	Yes
Human Collagen				
Isolagen	Cultured human fibroblasts from patient	Moderate wrinkles	4–6 months	No
Alloderm	Cadaveric collagen in sheet form	Deep wrinkles/lip augmentation/ nasolabial fold	9–12 months	No
Cymetra	Cadaveric collagen micronized/gel	Moderate to deep wrinkles/lip augmentation	3–6 months	No
CosmoDerm	Purified HC	Periorbital wrinkles	2–4 months	No
CosmoPlast	Purified HC cross-linked with glutaraldehyde	Periorbital wrinkles	3–6 months	No
Hyaluronic Acid (Avian Derived)				
Hylaform	HA (nongender chicken combs) divinyl sulfone X links	Moderate to severe wrinkles	3–4 months	No
Hylaform Plus	HA (nongender chicken combs) divinyl sulfone X links	Moderate to severe wrinkles	4 months	No
Hyaluronic Acid (Bacteria Derived)				
Restylane	HA *(Streptococcus)* 1,4-butanediol diglycidyl ether X links	Moderate wrinkles, lip volume	6–8 months	No
Restylane Perlane	HA *(Streptococcus)*	Deeper wrinkles, lips	6–8 months	No
Restylane Touch	HA *(Streptococcus)*	Fine lines around eyes/mouth	6–8 months	No
Restylane SubQ	HA *(Streptococcus)*	Deepest wrinkles/ facial augmentation/ HIV lipodystrophy	9–12 months	No
Captique	HA divinyl sulfone X links	Moderate to severe facial wrinkles	5–6 months	No
Juvéderm	HA *(Streptococcus equi)* 1,4-butanediol diglycidyl ether X links	Fine to deep wrinkles	6–9 months	No
Other				
Radiesse	Calcium hydroxylapatite + carboxymethylcellulose + glycerin	Moderate to deep wrinkles	1–2 years	No
Sculptra	Poly-L-lactic acid	Deep wrinkles/facial lipoatrophy	1–2 years	

BC, Bovine collagen, *HA,* hyaluronic acid, *HC,* human collagen.

25. **Shortly after Restylane is injected into the nasolabial fold of a 36-year-old healthy woman, her right ala turns blue. Twenty-four hours later a small, painful ulcer develops. What has happened, and how can it be prevented?**
    The product was injected intraarterially, likely into the dorsal nasal artery. Intracerebral embolization is theoretically possible given the possible anastomosis between the angular artery and the dorsal nasal artery. Intraarterial injection of bovine collagen has been reported to occur at a rate of 0.09%.

    Simple aspiration before injection of fillers reduces the chance of intraarterial injection and potential complications.

26. A palpable and visible lump of recently injected hyaluronic acid has been identified by one of your patients. What is one chemical that you could use to alleviate the problem?

Hyaluronidase has been used successfully in a number of cases as a management avenue for filler placement aberrations. Data concerning its further utilization are eminent, but until the data are reported, one remedy is gentle massage over the lump, which can help to distribute the uneven placement.

27. What is the Tyndall effect, and how is it important in filler placement?

The Tyndall effect is the way in which light is reflected by the subcutaneous substances it encounters. Physicists refer to the effect as Raleigh scattering, named after Sir Walter Raleigh who showed that the amount of light scattered is inversely proportional to the fourth power of wavelength for sufficiently small particles. Particles of approximately 400 microns in the skin tend to reflect blue light while allowing other light to pass. This effect is demonstrated in the blue color of veins that lie under the skin and carry red blood. If fillers are placed too superficially in the skin, then a Tyndall effect may create a noticeable blue discoloration.

28. What is a percutaneous suture meloplication?

Contour threads, Aptos sutures, and Isse facelift sutures are permanent monofilament sutures with mechanically created barbs used to elevate and tighten soft tissues of the face. These sutures are FDA approved for use in the brow, midface, and neck. They are placed percutaneously and are anchored to the temporal fascia along various vectors that elevate skin in the desired direction.

29. Who are ideal candidates for barbed suture placement?

Those with mild to moderate laxity, moderately deep nasolabial folds or jowl formation, limited skin wrinkling, and thicker subcutaneous skin who do not want surgical correction.

30. What are the long-term effects and complications associated with barbed suture lifting of the face?

Currently no data document the long-term efficacy of suture lifting of the face; however, many practitioners state effects can last up to 1 year. One report suggests that up to 20% of patients will not have a noticeable difference 1 year after the procedure. Reported complications include thread disruption, hemorrhage, skin dimpling, asymmetry, visible threads, and difficult suture removal due to the fibrous shell surrounding the suture.

31. What is microdermabrasion, and how is it used in facial rejuvenation?

Microdermabrasion has become one of the more common instruments of facial rejuvenation used in the plastic surgeon's practice. It is a device in which inert crystals, typically aluminum oxide crystals, are projected against the skin at high velocity and then vacuumed away in a closed circuit. These crystals are chosen for their hardness and serve to mechanically ablate approximately 8 microns of the epithelium. Dermal matrix remodeling is induced by up-regulation of epidermal signal transduction pathways induced by the microdermabrasion.

32. What influences the degree of tissue ablation achieved during microdermabrasion?

The particle flow rate and amount of vacuum pressure affect the number of particles impacting the skin. In addition, the angle of particle impaction and the number of wand passes over the skin are important in determining the extent of ablation.

33. What are the histologic changes following microdermabrasion?

On average the thickness of the epidermis can increase by 20 microns and the dermis by 30 microns after six treatments. Rete pegs flatten and become more widely spaced throughout the epidermis. A greater amount of activity occurs in the dermis, with increased quantity and organization of collagen bundles, increased elastin content, and increased myofibroblast migration.

34. What is the frequency of microdermabrasion treatments, and what do you tell your patients to expect?

The typical treatment regimen consists of four passes of the handpiece, once weekly for 5 to 6 weeks. Patients typically have facial erythema and mild edema for 2 to 3 days.

BIBLIOGRAPHY

Alam M, Dover J, Arndt K: Pain associated with injection of botulinum A exotoxin reconstituted using isotonic sodium chloride with and without preservative: A double blind, randomized controlled trial. Arch Dermatol 138:510–514, 2002.

Bellman B: Complication following suspected intra-arterial injection of Restylane. Aesthet Surg 26:304–305, 2006.

Botox Cosmetic Purified Neurotoxin Complex. Package Insert. Allergan Inc., Irvine, California.

Carruthers J, Fagien S, Matarasso S: Consensus recommendations on the use of botulinum toxin type A in facial aesthetics. Plast Reconstr Surg 114(Suppl):1S–22S, 2004.

Delorenzi C: Barbed sutures: Rationale and technique. Aesthet Surg 26:223–229, 2006.

Freedman B, Pedraza E, Waddell S: The epidermal and dermal changes associated with microdermabrasion. Dermatol Surg 27: 1031–1033. 2001.

Goldberg R: Nonsurgical filling of periorbital hollows. Aesthet Surg 26:69–71, 2006.

Hirsh R, Narurkor V, Carruthers J: Management of injected hyaluronic acid induced Tyndall effects. Lasers Surg Med 38:202–204, 2006.

Humbert P, Haftek M, Creeidi P, et al: Topical ascorbic acid on photoaged skin. Clinical, topographical and ultrastructural evaluation: Double blind study verses placebo. Exp Dermatol 12:237–244, 2003.

Isse N, Lee S: Barbed polypropylene sutures for midface elevation. Arch Facial Plast Surg 7:55–61, 2005.

Karimipour D, Kand S, Johnson T, et al: Microdermabrasion with and without aluminum oxide crystal abrasion: A comparative molecular analysis of dermal remodeling. J Am Acad Dermatol 54:405–410, 2006.

Kwan S, Bergfeld W, Gottlieb AB, et al: Long-term efficacy and safety of tretinoin emollient cream 0.05% in the treatment of photodamaged facial skin: A two year, randomized, placebo-controlled trial. Am J Clin Dermatol 6:245–253, 2005.

Lambros V: The use of hyaluronidase to reverse the effects of hyaluronic acid fillers. Plast Reconst Surg 114:277, 2004.

Matarasso S, Carruthers J, Jewell M: Consensus recommendations for soft tissue augmentation with non-animal stabilized hyaluronic acid. Plast Reconstr Surg 117(Suppl):3S–43S, 2006.

Schanz S, Schippert W, Ulmer A: Arterial embolization caused by injection of hyaluronic acid. Br J Dermatol 148:379, 2003.

Seckel B: Save Your Face, 2nd ed. Concord, MA, Peach Publications, 2006.

Wollina U, Konrad H: Managing adverse events associated with botulinum toxin type A. A focus on cosmetic procedures. Am J Clin Dermatol 6:141–150, 2005.

TRUNK AND LOWER EXTREMITY

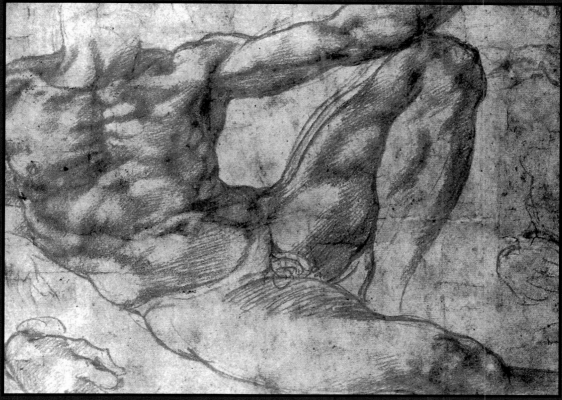

Sketch of Adam [For the *Creation of Adam* in the Sistine Chapel]. Michelangelo, 1511. Red chalk. The British Museum, London. © The Trustees of the British Museum. All rights reserved.

CHEST WALL RECONSTRUCTION

CHAPTER 90

Jeffrey Weinzweig, MD, FACS

1. When do the skeletal components of the chest wall form embryologically?

The ribs, costal cartilages, and sternum form during the sixth week of gestation. The primitive sternum arises from two lateral mesenchymal bands that fuse by the ninth week of gestation. During this period the thoracic ribs, costal cartilages, and intervening musculature develop independently of the sternum. By the ninth week, the ribs have matured and cartilages 1 to 7 have joined the sternum. Cartilages 8 to 10 are incorporated shortly afterward. Congenital chest wall anomalies arise from developmental disturbances during this period.

2. What are the muscular layers of the chest wall?

Between the overlying skin and underlying rib cage are a number of muscles that can be divided into two main groups: *inspiratory* and *expiratory* muscles. The inspiratory muscles serve as elevators of the superior aperture of the rib cage and assist with expanding the chest volume. They include the sternocleidomastoid and scalene muscles, which insert onto the clavicle and the first and second ribs. Major resections of the upper sternum and ribs result in a partial collapse of the ribs inferiorly and a measurable functional loss in ventilation. The expiratory muscles attach to the much larger inferior aperture of the rib cage and constrict the skeletal structure downward, forcing the abdominal contents upward against the diaphragm to assist with expiration, coughing, and sneezing. They include the rectus abdominis, internal oblique, and external oblique muscles (Fig. 90-1). Muscles attached to the clavicle, scapula, and humerus, such as the pectoralis major, trapezius, and latissimus dorsi, are primarily involved in movement of the shoulder and arm.

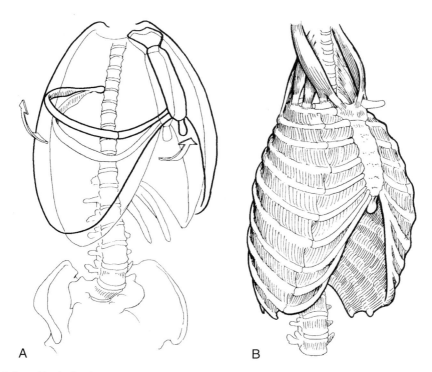

A   B

Figure 90-1. **A,** Forced inspiration depends on the "bucket-handle" motion of the ribs and the "pump-handle" motion of the sternum. This energy-consuming effort is mediated through the accessory muscles of respiration and occurs when metabolic demand outstrips ventilatory capabilities at rest. Excessive removal of the chest wall in the wrong patient can activate this response and lead to exhaustion. **B,** The accessory muscles of inspiration include the sternocleidomastoids, the scalene muscles, the external intercostals, and the parasternal intercartilaginous muscles. These activate the bucket-handle and pump-handle mechanisms. (From Seyfer A, Graeber G, Wind G [eds]: Atlas of Chest Wall Reconstruction. Rockville, MD, Aspen Publications, 1986, p 28.)

3. What are the functions of the chest wall?

The chest wall has both structural and functional roles:

- It provides a bony shell for protection of vital visceral organs, including the heart, lungs, liver, spleen, pancreas, and kidneys.
- It provides a flexible frame for respiratory movements.
- Muscular components actively contribute to inspiration and expiration.
- Chest wall muscles attached to the clavicle, scapula, and humerus contribute to movement of the shoulder and arm.
- Overall expansion of the rib cage is crucial to creating negative pressure necessary for lung expansion during inspiration; loss of rigid support over a large area of the rib cage results in an inward motion of the chest wall—paradoxical movement.

4. What are the most common indications for chest wall reconstruction?

Defects of the chest wall requiring reconstruction most often result from (1) trauma, (2) tumor resection, (3) infection, (4) radiation ulcers, and (5) congenital defects. These defects may be superficial, involving only the soft tissue of the chest wall, or complex, involving the skeletal framework, thoracic cavity, or mediastinum.

5. What are the principles of chest wall reconstruction?

- Adequate débridement and resection of all tumor, osteoradionecrotic tissue, or infection
- Obliteration of intrathoracic dead space
- Skeletal stabilization if more than four ribs or greater than 5 cm of chest wall is resected en bloc
- Adequate soft tissue coverage
- Aesthetic consideration

6. What type of tissue is most often used for reconstruction?

Muscle and musculocutaneous flaps are the tissues of choice for chest wall reconstruction. Local skin flaps, regional pedicle flaps, and thoracoabdominal tube flaps were used until the popularization of muscle and musculocutaneous flaps in the mid 1970s. The pectoralis major, latissimus dorsi, serratus anterior, and rectus abdominis muscles are most frequently used.

7. What are the indications for free tissue transfer?

Free tissue transfer for chest wall reconstruction is performed infrequently. It is reserved for cases in which regional flaps are unavailable or have already been used. Microvascular anastomoses can be performed using the thoracodorsal, subscapular, or internal mammary arteries as recipient vessels.

8. What options are available for skeletal stabilization?

Stabilization of the sternum for defects encompassing more than four contiguous rib segments is necessary for restoration of normal protective and respiratory function of the chest wall. Various materials can be used in this capacity, including autogenous tissue (rib grafts, fascia, large muscle flaps), synthetic compounds (Teflon, Prolene mesh, Gore-Tex), and composite mesh (Marlex–methylmethacrylate composite). Muscle flaps can also stabilize large chest wall defects without resulting in flail segments, especially in the radiated chest wall, in which local tissues have stiffened secondary to chronic inflammation from radiation exposure.

9. What is the incidence of median sternotomy infection?

Median sternotomy infection occurs in 0.4% to 5.0% of cardiac procedures.

10. What is the significance of sternal wound infections?

Postcardiotomy sternal wound infection is a life-threatening complication. Mortality rates range from 5% to 50%. Infection may extend into the mediastinum, affecting prosthetic valves, bypass grafts, and suture lines.

11. Should serial débridement be performed after sternal wound dehiscence?

Not necessarily. Nahai et al. reported a series of 211 consecutive cases of sternal wound coverage. The pectoralis major muscle flap was used in 56% and the rectus abdominis muscle in 38%. Single-stage débridement with muscle flap coverage immediately on diagnosis of sternal dehiscence was successful in 95% of cases.

12. Is there a correlation between use of the internal mammary artery for bypass grafting and the incidence of sternal wound infections?

Yes. Perforators of the internal mammary artery (IMA) are the main blood supply to the sternum. Therefore use of the IMA for bypass grafting may compromise the vascular supply of the sternum, delaying wound healing and increasing the risk of infection. Cosgrove et al. demonstrated no sternal wound complications in patients in whom saphenous vein grafts were used for bypass, a 0.3% incidence in patients in whom unilateral IMA grafts were used, and a 2.4% incidence in patients in whom bilateral IMA grafts were used.

13. How are sternotomy wound infections classified?

Pairolero classified infected sternotomy wounds into three types:

Type I infected sternotomy wounds occur in the first 1 to 3 days postoperatively and consist of serosanguinous drainage with negative wound cultures without cellulitis, costochondritis, or osteomyelitis. Wounds require reexploration, minimal débridement, and rewiring of the sternum.

Type II infected sternotomy wounds occur in the first 2 to 3 weeks postoperatively and consist of purulent mediastinitis with positive wound cultures, cellulitis, costochondritis, and osteomyelitis.

Type III infected sternotomy wounds present months to years after cardiac procedures. Draining sinus tracts result from chronic costochondritis and osteomyelitis. Type II and type III wounds require thorough débridement and reconstruction.

14. How are median sternotomy wounds reconstructed?

Because of its location on the chest wall, its size, and its arc of rotation, the pectoralis major muscle is the flap of choice for reconstruction of median sternotomy wounds (Fig. 90-2). This muscle originates on the clavicle, sternum, six upper ribs, and aponeurosis of the external oblique muscle and occupies the anterior chest wall. It inserts on the intertubercular sulcus of the humerus, forming the anterior wall and fold of the axilla. The pectoralis major muscle is a type V muscle supplied by the thoracoacromial artery, its dominant pedicle, and segmental perforators from the IMA.

The muscle is harvested through the sternotomy wound. Wide undermining at the level of the pectoralis fascia is performed, and the muscle is detached from the ribs and sternum. Dissection proceeds laterally after identification of the thoracoacromial pedicle on the undersurface of the muscle, and the humeral attachment is divided. The muscle is dissected from the clavicle and advanced medially to cover the defect. Coverage of large defects with exposed heart and great vessels can often be accomplished with bilateral pectoralis major muscle flaps.

15. How can the pectoralis major muscle be used as a "turnover" flap?

The pectoralis major muscle can be based medially on the perforating branches of the IMA if it is intact. After the anterior surface of the muscle is exposed, dissection of the muscle from the chest wall is performed from lateral to

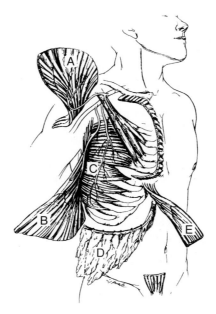

Figure 90-2. Pedicle flap donor sites for chest wall reconstruction: *(A)* Pectoralis major muscle flap, *(B)* latissimus dorsi muscle flap, *(C)* serratus anterior muscle flap, *(D)* greater omentum flap, *(E)* rectus abdominis muscle flap. (From Cohen M: Reconstruction of the chest wall. In Cohen M [ed]: Mastery of Plastic and Reconstructive Surgery. Boston, Little, Brown, 1994, p 1250, with permission.)

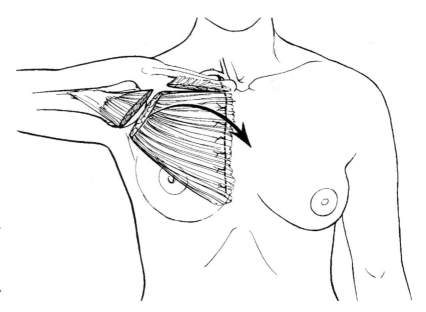

Figure 90-3. Pectoralis major turnover flap. The pectoralis major turnover flap is based on the minor segmental pedicles and is used predominantly for coverage of the sternum and mediastinum. This modified flap will preserve the anterior axillary fold. Arc to sternum and anterior mediastinum. (From Mathes SJ, Nahai F: Reconstructive Surgery: Principles, Anatomy, and Technique. New York, Churchill Livingstone, 1997, pp 450–453.)

medial to avoid injury to the IMA perforators. The thoracoacromial pedicle is identified and ligated, and dissection is continued up to 2 to 3 cm lateral to the midline—again, to protect the perforators (Fig. 90-3). The muscular attachment to the humerus is divided, and the muscle is turned over like a page in a book to cover the defect. When possible, preservation of a partial attachment of the superior portion of the muscle to the humerus provides a better aesthetic result by preserving the anterior axillary fold.

16. When is the rectus abdominis muscle used?
The rectus abdominis muscle can be used to supplement a pectoralis major muscle flap when additional bulk is needed or when the pectoralis major muscle is not available. Based superiorly on the deep superior epigastric artery, a terminal branch of the IMA, this type III muscle can be turned on itself to fill a defect of the chest wall or mediastinum. The rectus abdominis muscle is harvested through a midline or paramedian skin incision. The anterior rectus sheath is incised, and the muscle is divided at the necessary level inferiorly and elevated from the posterior rectus sheath in a caudad to cephalad fashion. The muscle is mobilized on its superior pedicle and transposed into the defect.

17. Can the rectus abdominis muscle be used when the ipsilateral IMA has been harvested for bypass grafting?
Yes. The rectus muscle can be harvested based on the eighth intercostal vessel. However, the distal third of the rectus muscle often has tenuous vascularity.

18. What role does the greater omentum play?
Weinzweig and Yetman reported the largest series of omental transposition flaps for coverage of infected sternal wounds. In their series of 25 patients, the greater omentum, either alone or in combination with muscle flaps, provided reliable coverage after radical sternectomy for deep infections, including osteomyelitis, chronic chondritis, and mediastinitis, as well as for extensive and lower third sternal wounds (Fig. 90-4). Ninety-five percent of wounds ultimately healed without intraabdominal problems or chest wall instability.

19. What is a sternal cleft?
Sternal clefts, described as early as 1772 by Sandifort, are rare deformities in which a grotesque depression in the middle of the chest may reveal the pulsating heart through the overlying skin. Interruption of sternal fusion may result in these impressive anomalies. A superior sternal cleft occurs secondary to a deficiency in cephalad fusion; a distal sternal cleft results from a premature cessation of fusion.

20. Which congenital anomalies are associated with developmental abnormalities of the ribs?
Developmental abnormalities of the ribs may result in supernumerary ribs or hypoplasia of the costal cartilages, which may be associated with Poland's syndrome. Anomalous rib development also may result in pectus excavatum and pectus carinatum.

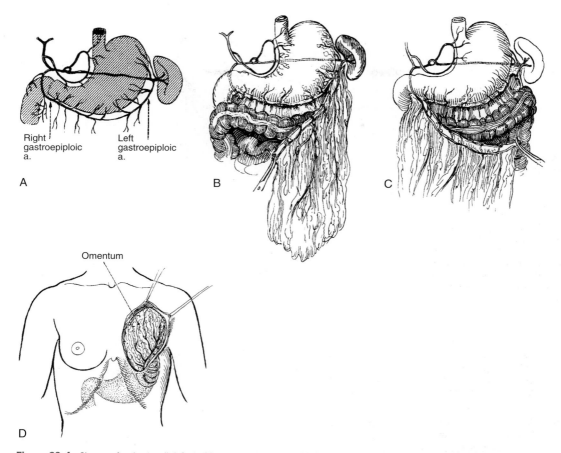

Figure 90-4. Closure of a chest wall defect with greater omentum. **A,** Main arterial supply of the greater omentum. **B, C,** The greater omentum can be pedicled on the right or left gastroepiploic arery, depending on the site of the defect to be closed. The omental flap is freed from the stomach at the muscularis layer to maintain the integrity of the vascular gastroepiploic arch. **D,** The greater omentum is transferred to the thoracic defect through the superior portion of the abdominal wall incision or through a separate stab wound. A subcutaneous tunnel can be used to pass the omentum to the defect. (After Dupont C, Menard Y: Transposition of the greater omentum for reconstruction of the chest wall. Plast Reconstr Surg 49:263–267, 1972.)

21. Which congenital chest wall anomaly is associated with ipsilateral hand deformities?
Poland's syndrome.

22. What is Poland's syndrome?
Described by Alfred Poland in 1841, this congenital anomaly is characterized by partial or complete absence of the pectoralis major muscle and hypoplastic or absent adjacent musculoskeletal components. The deformity consists of a number of unilateral findings, including partial agenesis of the ribs and sternum, brachysyndactyly, mammary aplasia, and absence of the latissimus dorsi, serratus anterior, and pectoralis major muscles in the severe form. In the mildest form of Poland's syndrome, mild hypoplasia of the breast and lateral nipple displacement may be the only findings.

23. Do the reconstructive goals differ in females and males with Poland's syndrome?
Yes. Although the goal in both cases is restoration of a natural contour to the anterior chest wall, reconstruction of a symmetric breast mound, a normal-appearing nipple–areolar complex, and subclavicular fullness are necessary in female patients. In both male and female patients, the best aesthetic result usually is accomplished by a latissimus dorsi muscle transfer to the anterior chest wall. In women, simultaneous insertion of a submuscular mammary prosthesis usually is performed. Depending on the severity of the anomaly, a muscle flap may be performed without the need for a mammary implant. Similarly, reconstruction of mild forms of the syndrome may require use of a prosthesis alone.

24. What is pectus excavatum?
Pectus (chest) deformities occur as commonly as 1:300 live births. Pectus excavatum (funnel chest) is the most common chest wall deformity. The depression of the anterior chest wall usually begins at the sternal angle (angle of

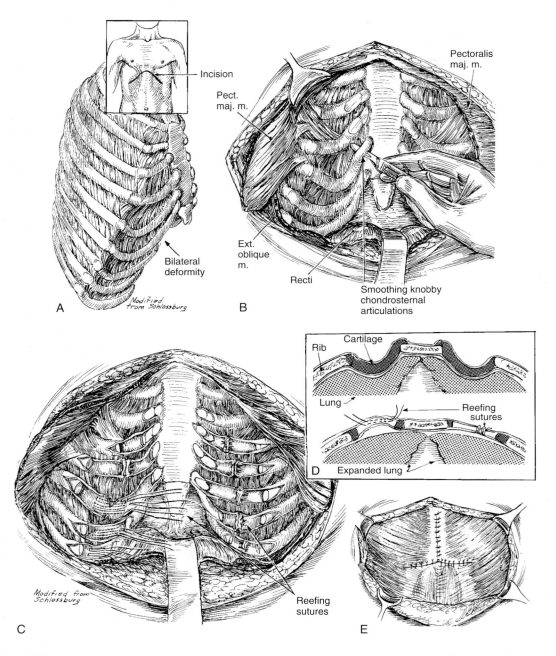

A

Incision

Bilateral deformity

Modified from Schlossburg

B

Pectoralis maj. m.

Pect. maj. m.

Ext. oblique m.

Recti

Smoothing knobby chondrosternal articulations

C

Modified from Schlossburg

Reefing sutures

D

Rib

Cartilage

Lung

Reefing sutures

Expanded lung

E

Figure 90-5 Ravitch technique for correction of chondrogladiolar type of pectus carinatum. **A, B,** Transverse curvilinear incision is used to elevate flaps down to and including the pectoralis muscles. The rectus muscle attachments are divided. Cartilaginous irregularities and knobby projections of the chondrosternal articulations are sharply smoothed out. **C, D,** The posteriorly curved, deformed cartilage is resected subperichondrially. The redundant perichondrium is tightened by mattress silk reefing sutures so that the new cartilage will grow in a straight line from the ribs to the sternum. **E,** Pectoralis muscles and recti are reattached to the sternum. (After Ravitch MM: General Thoracic Surgery. Philadelphia, Lea & Febiger, 1972.)

Louis) and reaches its deepest point at the level of the xiphoid. The concave deformity occasionally is so severe that the sternum contacts the vertebral bodies or passes to one side of the vertebral bodies into the paravertebral gutter, accounting for the associated cardiopulmonary and physiologic abnormalities. This anomaly is believed to result from overgrowth of the costal cartilages, which forces the sternum posteriorly in the case of pectus excavatum and anteriorly in the case of pectus carinatum (see Question 26).

25. How is pectus excavatum treated?

The *Ravitch technique* for reconstruction involves elevation of perichondrial flaps and resection of the involved costal cartilages (usually four or five on each side) with preservation of the costochondral junction when possible. The xiphoid process is divided to permit elevation of the sternum. A posterior transverse osteotomy of the sternum is performed superiorly, and the sternum is fractured forward. A bone wedge is used to stabilize the sternum at the osteotomy site posteriorly. An anterior transverse osteotomy is performed inferiorly and stabilized with a bone wedge anteriorly. The sternum is stabilized with wires to adjacent ribs and bilateral pectoralis flaps are sutured to the sternum in the midline.

The *sternum turnover procedure* involves transection of the ribs and intercostal muscles bilaterally at the costal arches along the margin of the deformity. The sternum is transected above the level of the deformity, removed en bloc, and turned over. The convex side is flattened by wedge resections and trimmed to fit the chest wall defect. The sternum is sutured in place with wires, and each costal cartilage or rib is sutured with heavy silk.

26. What is pectus carinatum? How is it related to pectus excavatum?

Pectus carinatum (pigeon breast) is a protrusion deformity of the anterior chest wall and is considered the opposite of the pectus excavatum deformity. This condition occurs much less commonly than the excavatum anomaly. Surgical reconstruction for pectus carinatum is similar to that used to correct pectus excavatum. In both cases, the *Ravitch technique* can be used. The abnormal costal cartilages are resected through a subperichondrial approach, and the sternum is repositioned to restore the anterior chest wall contour. A substernal metallic strut is used to support the repositioned sternum. Wires are used to secure the strut to the sternum and surrounding ribs (Fig. 90-5).

BIBLIOGRAPHY

Arnold PG, Pairolero PC: Chest wall reconstruction: Experience with 100 consecutive patients. Ann Surg 199:725–732, 1984.
Arnold PG, Pairolero PC: Surgical management of the radiated chest wall. Plast Reconstr Surg 77:605–612, 1986.
Boyd A: Tumors of the chest wall. In Hood RM (ed): Surgical Diseases of the Pleura and Chest Wall. Philadelphia, WB Saunders, 1986.
Carberry DM, Ballantyne LWR: Omental pedicle graft in closure of large anterior chest wall defects. N Y State J Med 75:1705, 1975.
Cohen M: Reconstruction of the chest wall. In Cohen M (ed): Mastery of Plastic and Reconstructive Surgery. Boston, Little, Brown, 1994, pp 1248–1267.
Hester TR, Bostwick J: Poland's syndrome: Correction with latissimus muscle transposition. Plast Reconstr Surg 69:226–233, 1982.
Hugo NE, Sultan MR, Ascherman JA, et al: Single-stage management of 74 consecutive cases of sternal wound complications with pectoralis major myocutaneous advancement flaps. Plast Reconstr Surg 93:1433–1441, 1994.
Jurkiewicz MJ, Arnold PG: The omentum: An account of its use in reconstruction of the chest wall. Ann Surg 185:548–554, 1977.
Knoetgen J, Johnson CH, Arnold PG: Reconstruction of the chest. In: Mathes, SJ (ed): Plastic Surgery, 2nd ed. Philadelphia, Elsevier, 2006, pp 411–439.
Nahai F, Rand RP, Hester TR, et al: Primary treatment of the infected sternotomy wound with muscle flaps: A review of 211 consecutive cases. Plast Reconstr Surg 84:434–441, 1989.
Pairolero PC, Arnold PG: Management of infected median sternotomy wounds. Ann Thoracic Surg 42:1–2, 1986.
Poland A: Deficiency of the pectoralis muscle. Guy's Hosp Rep 6:191, 1841.
Ravitch MM: Congenital Deformities of the Chest Wall and Their Operative Correction. Philadelphia, WB Saunders, 1977.
Roth DA: Thoracic and abdominal wall reconstruction. In Aston SJ, Beasley RW, Thorne CHM (eds): Grabb and Smith's Plastic Surgery, 5th ed. Philadelphia, Lippincott-Raven, 1997, pp 1023–1029.
Seyfer A: Congenital anomalies of the chest wall. In Cohen M (ed): Mastery of Plastic and Reconstructive Surgery. Boston, Little, Brown, 1994, pp 1233–1239.
Shaw WW, Aston SJ, Zide BM: Reconstruction of the trunk. In McCarthy JG (ed): Plastic Surgery. Philadelphia, WB Saunders, 1990, pp 3675–3796.
Weinzweig N, Yetman R: Transposition of the greater omentum for recalcitrant sternotomy wound infections. Ann Plast Surg 34:471–477, 1995.

91 CHAPTER

ABDOMINAL WALL RECONSTRUCTION

Dan H. Shell IV, MD; Luis O. Vásconez, MD; Jorge I. de la Torre, MD;
Gloria Chin, MD, MS; and Norman Weinzweig, MD, FACS

1. What is the functional role of the abdominal wall?

The abdominal wall consists of vertically, obliquely, and transversely oriented muscles that play a key role in posture maintenance, standing, walking, bending, and lifting. The abdominal wall muscles also protect the abdominal viscera and increase intraabdominal pressure to aid in coughing, vomiting, defecation, micturition, and parturition. The muscles also serve an important role in respiration.

2. What are the layers of the abdominal wall?

- Skin
- Superficial fascia: Superficial fatty layer, Camper's fascia, Scarpa's fascia
- Muscles and their aponeuroses: External oblique, internal oblique, transversus abdominis, rectus abdominis, and pyramidalis
- Properitoneal fat
- Peritoneum

3. What are the origins and insertions of the abdominal wall muscles?

The *external oblique muscle* is the most superficial and largest of the three muscles in the lateral aspect of the abdominal wall. It arises from the lower eight ribs and interdigitates with the serratus anterior and latissimus dorsi muscles. It inserts on the anterior half of the iliac crest; inferiorly its aponeurosis forms the inguinal ligament (Poupart's ligament), which extends from the anterosuperior iliac spine to the pubic spine. Its fascicles are directed in a superolateral to inferomedial direction. Its aponeurosis passes anterior to the rectus abdominis muscle.

The *internal oblique muscle* lies beneath the external oblique and its fibers course in an opposite direction. Originates from lumbodorsal fascia, anterior two thirds of iliac crest, and lateral two thirds of the inguinal ligament. The lower fibers join those of the transverses abdominis muscle to form the conjoined tendon, which inserts on the pubic crest and spine and on the iliopectineal line. The superior fibers insert as a broad aponeurosis into the linea alba and cartilages of the seventh to ninth ribs. Its aponeurosis splits above the arcuate line to envelope the rectus abdominis. Below the arcuate line it passes anterior to the rectus abdominis.

The *transversus abdominis muscle* is located deep to the internal oblique muscle. It is the deepest and smallest of the muscles of the lateral abdominal wall. It originates from the lower six ribs, lumbodorsal fascia, anterior two thirds of the iliac crest, and lateral third of the inguinal ligament. It inserts on the linea alba and contributes to the conjoined tendon that inserts on the pubic spine and iliopectineal line.

The *rectus abdominis muscle* is a longitudinal muscle located in the medial aspect of the abdominal wall. It arises from the front of the symphysis and pubic crest and inserts on the xiphoid process and cartilages of the fifth through seventh ribs.

The *pyramidalis muscle* is present in 80% to 90% of patients. It is a small triangular muscle that lies superficial to the rectus muscle. It arises from the front of the pubis and inserts on the linea alba halfway between the symphysis and umbilicus.

4. What are the functions of the abdominal wall muscles?

The rectus muscles flex the body anteriorly and are important in climbing into and out of bed. The external and internal oblique muscles are important in rotating the upper body against the lower body. Trunk rotation results from the joint contraction of one external oblique and the contralateral internal oblique. The vertical component of the oblique musculature can substitute for the rectus muscles if they are absent.

5. What fascial layer lines the entire abdominal wall?

The transversalis fascia is an internal investing fascia that lines the entire abdominal wall. It exists on the deep surface of the transversus abdominis fascia and is continuous from side to side deep to the linea alba. It extends into the thigh to form the femoral sheath. In the inguinal canal it forms the internal spermatic fascia. Internal to this layer is the peritoneum.

6. What is the arterial supply to the abdominal wall?

- *Superior Epigastric Artery:* Terminal branch of the internal mammary artery that supplies the upper central abdominal skin through the upper rectus muscle
- *Thoracic and Lumbar Intercostal Arteries:* Travel between the external and internal oblique muscles with direct lateral skin perforators
- *Deep Inferior Epigastric Artery:* Branch of the external iliac artery that enters the lower rectus muscle and supplies it and the accompanying vertical or transverse skin paddle
- *Deep Circumflex Iliac Artery:* Branch of the external iliac artery supplying the inner aspect of the ileum and skin over the iliac crest
- *Superficial Inferior Epigastric Artery:* Branch of the femoral artery that supplies the skin and subcutaneous tissue over the lower abdomen
- *Superficial Circumflex Iliac Artery:* Branch of the femoral artery that supplies the skin and subcutaneous tissue over the anterosuperior iliac spine
- *Superficial External Pudendal Artery:* Branch of the femoral artery that supplies the skin and subcutaneous tissue over the pubis

7. Describe the three vascular zones of the abdominal wall.

The midabdomen is supplied by the deep epigastric arcade *(zone I),* the lower abdomen by the external iliac artery *(zone II),* and the lateral abdomen by the intercostal, subcostal, and lumbar arteries *(zone III;* Fig. 91-1). After an abdominoplasty, the majority of the abdominal wall skin is supplied by intercostal lumbar perforating arteries of zone III.

8. What are the venous and lymphatic drainages of the abdominal wall?

The venous drainage parallels the arterial supply to the abdominal wall. The upper abdomen is drained by the superior epigastric, intercostal, and axillary veins. The lower abdomen is drained by the superficial inferior epigastric, superficial circumflex iliac, and deep inferior epigastric veins.

The lymphatic drainage is divided by the umbilicus. Above the umbilicus, the superficial and deep lymphatics drain into the ipsilateral axillary and internal mammary lymph nodes, respectively.

Below the umbilicus, superficial and deep lymphatics flow into the ipsilateral inguinal and deep iliac lymph nodes, respectively.

9. What is the motor and sensory innervation to the abdominal wall?

The nerve supply to the abdominal wall is predominantly from intercostal nerves. A neurovascular plane exists between the internal oblique and transversus abdominis muscles. Through this plane pass the nerves as well as intercostal blood vessels that supply the abdominal wall. The main trunks of the anterior cutaneous rami nerves are found in this neurovascular plane as they pass anteriorly to provide sensation to the overlying skin. There is slight overlap of the sensory dermatomes. Motor innervation of the abdominal obliques and transversalis muscles are from the lower thoracic and lumbar dorsal rami. Motor innervation to the rectus abdominis is from the fifth through twelfth intercostal nerves. The ilioinguinal and iliohypogastric nerves pass between the internal oblique and transversus abdominis muscles as they extend from the lateral costal margin to the pubic region. Although they do not supply innervation to

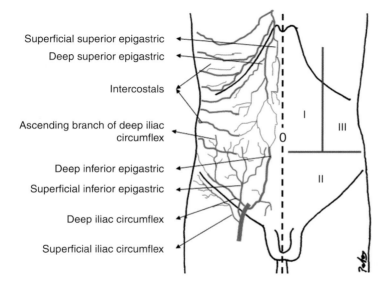

Superficial superior epigastric

Deep superior epigastric

Intercostals

Ascending branch of deep iliac circumflex

Deep inferior epigastric

Superficial inferior epigastric

Deep iliac circumflex

Superficial iliac circumflex

Figure 91-1. Vascular zones of the abdominal wall. *Zone I,* deep epigastric arcade; *zone II,* external iliac branches; *zone III,* intercostal, subcostal, and lumbar arteries. (Courtesy Patricio Andrades, MD, Clinical and Research Fellow, Division of Plastic Surgery and Transplant Immunology, Division of Plastic Surgery, University of Alabama at Birmingham, Birmingham, Alabama.)

the abdomen, their course can be disrupted with dissection in the lateral abdomen. Loss of function results in sensory defects in the medial thigh and groin.

10. Describe the mechanism by which an adynamic abdominal wall contributes to lumbosacral pain.

Patients with an adynamic segment of the abdominal wall as a result of ventral hernia or adynamic reconstruction and those with a decreased efficiency of the abdominal wall musculature from diastasis are prone to development of lumbodorsal back pain. The internal oblique–transversus abdominis complex fuses to the anterior and middle layers of the lumbodorsal fascia. Gracovetsky et al. demonstrated that contraction of these muscles tightens the lumbodorsal fascia, adding ligamentous support to the fixed spine and reducing the need for back muscle action with a resultant increase in lumbosacral disc pressure. When an adynamic or "stretched out" segment exists, the internal oblique and transversus abdominis are not stretched to physiologic length. This laxity prevents maximum force generation with contraction and weakens support by means of the lumbodorsal fascia. Toranto et al. demonstrated complete relief of back pain in 24 of 25 patients treated with wide rectus placation.

11. What are the most frequent causes of abdominal wall defects?
- Postoperative incisional hernia
- Posttraumatic planned ventral hernia
- Blast injury
- Tumor resection
- Massive infection (necrotizing fasciitis)
- Radiation therapy
- Congenital defects (gastroschisis, omphalocele)

12. What are important considerations in the evaluation of abdominal wall defects?
- *Absolute versus Relative Loss of Domain:* Is there an actual or absolute loss of abdominal wall tissue that may need to be replaced with local or distant flaps or is the defect a result of fascial dehiscence with widening from the unopposed lateral contractions of the oblique musculature.
- *Underlying Disease Process:* Acute or chronic wound? Reconstruction can proceed either immediately as in the case of tumor ablation or radiation, or in delayed fashion as in the case of infection or trauma with contamination and/or visceral edema.
- *Wound Stability:* Has the necrotic tissue and/or infected tissue been removed from the wound?
- *Gastrointestinal Fistula*
- *Location of the Defect*

13. What studies aid in the evaluation of abdominal wall defects?

Computed tomographic scans and magnetic resonance imaging studies may be helpful in evaluating the extent of tumor invasion and the integrity of potential muscle or musculocutaneous flaps to be used in reconstruction. The vascular status of these flaps can be determined by color flow duplex Doppler study that combines Doppler ultrasound and B-mode ultrasound to produce images of blood vessels and their surroundings. A fistulogram or intestinal contrast study may be needed to evaluate for the presence of gastrointestinal fistulas.

14. How are acquired abdominal wall defects managed?

Acute Traumatic Wounds: Temporizing measures such as a wound vacuum-assisted closure (VAC), Vicryl mesh, x-ray cassette cover, vacuum pack, and Velcro mesh (Whitman patch) provide coverage while the acute problems are addressed. Varying rates of secondary fascial closure have been reported, but no randomized, comparative data support one method of temporary closure over another.

Infection:

- Infection limited to the skin and subcutaneous tissue, including abscesses and synergistic infections, requires drainage and wide débridement with preservation of the underlying muscle and fascia.
- Infection of the abdominal wall fascia, such as necrotizing fasciitis, requires wide débridement of the involved fascia and overlying infected skin and subcutaneous tissue.
- Clostridial myonecrosis involves all layers of the abdominal wall and requires full-thickness resection.

Tumor Resection: Primary tumors of the abdominal wall include desmoid tumors, sarcomas, and their malignant variants. There also may be primary skin malignancies, malignant degeneration of chronic scars, fistulas, and radiation injury. Secondary tumors result from extensions of carcinomas of the colon, bladder, gallbladder, and other visceral malignancies. The primary goal of treatment is definitive resection. Once the wound margins are free of tumor, definitive reconstruction can be performed.

Radiation Wounds: These wounds involve an area of skin prone to ulceration or infection that does not heal. Treatment is wide resection and examination of the specimen for recurrence. Once the wound margins are tumor free, definitive reconstruction can be performed while the wound is temporarily covered with dressings or mesh.

Postoperative Defects: Abdominal wall defects after surgery include incisional hernias, parastomal hernias, planned ventral hernias after trauma, and those resulting from mesh-related complications. Definitive reconstruction is performed when the initial problem and associated complications are resolved.

15. What are the reconstructive options?
- *Prosthetic Materials:* Used for abdominal wall support
- *Skin Grafts:* Most often used in cases of massive abdominal trauma. When the wound is stable, they can be removed by dermabrasion or excision. The hernia is repaired with mesh and/or rectus advancement techniques.
- *Local Flaps:* Skin and subcutaneous flaps can be based laterally on the intercostal vessels, on perforators from the deep circumflex iliac artery, or on axial vessels from the superficial circumflex iliac, superior epigastric, or superficial external pudendal arteries. The external oblique can be used as a medially based musculofascial turnover flap or a laterally based musculocutaneous flap. The rectus muscle, based on either the superior epigastric or the deep inferior epigastric vessels, can be used as a muscle or musculocutaneous flap.
- *Regional Flaps:* The tensor fascia lata and the rectus femoris muscles are most commonly used. The gracilis muscle is more limited in its application. It originates from the inferior pubic symphysis and inserts as a tendon on the upper medial tibia. The major pedicle is a branch of the profunda femoris artery located 8 to 10 cm from the adductor tubercle; one or two minor pedicles are located distally from the superficial femoral artery. It can be used as a muscle or musculocutaneous flap that reaches to the inguinal and perineal regions. The skin paddle is often unreliable.
- *Distant Flaps:* These flaps include the omentum, extended latissimus dorsi musculofascial flap, and free flaps. Free tissue transfer may be necessary when the defect is large and no adequate local or regional flaps are available.

16. What is the "components separation" technique? What size defect can be closed using this technique?
A significant contribution to the repair of incisional hernias was the description by Ramirez et al. of the *components separation* technique. The evolution of the components separation technique is based on early descriptions by Vasconez et al. of transverse rectus abdominis myocutaneous (TRAM) closure that involves separation of external and internal oblique musculature and release of the posterior rectus sheath. Ramirez et al. noted that the abdominal wall is formed by overlapping muscle layers that may be separated while preserving their innervation and blood supply, specifically, elevation of the external oblique off of the internal oblique while maintaining the neurovascular supply to the rectus, which travels in segmental fashion between the internal oblique and transversus abdominis. The rectus can then be released from the posterior rectus sheath. Once this is accomplished, medial advancement of a compound flap of rectus muscle and attached internal oblique–transversus abdominis complex. Unilateral advancement of 5 cm in the epigastric region, 10 cm at the umbilicus, and 3 cm in the suprapubic region were described.

The efficacy of this particular technique and modifications of the anatomic principles described by it have been substantiated in multiple series. Fabian et al. described a modification involving division of the internal oblique component of the anterior rectus sheath, which allowed for unilateral advancement of 8 to 10 cm in the epigastric area, 10 to 15 cm in the midabdomen, and 6 to 8 cm in the suprapubic region.

A lower hernia recurrence rate, avoidance of prosthetic material, restoration of dynamic abdominal wall function, and improvement in back pain and postural abnormalities have been cited in the literature. Wound-related complications have been problematic with this technique and are related to the wide undermining required. Studies have demonstrated a reduction in wound-related complications with the preservation of periumbilical perforators (Figs. 91-2 and 91-3).

17. Describe the concept of staged abdominal reconstruction.
When an abdominal wound is unstable as a result of contamination or if primary fascial approximation is not possible due to visceral edema, then temporary abdominal closure with a wound VAC, vacuum pack, or absorbable Vicryl mesh is indicated. Failure to perform secondary fascial approximation in a timely fashion is an indication for staged abdominal reconstruction. Fabian et al. described a technique that is divided into three stages. In stage I, Vicryl mesh is applied for visceral coverage. If fascial approximation is not able to be obtained by 2 weeks, the mesh is removed and a split-thickness skin graft (STSG) is placed over the viscera (stage II). Six to twelve months later the skin graft is removed, and definitive reconstruction is performed using a modification of the component separation technique (stage III). They found the risk of fistula formation correlated with the duration of mesh, with a statistically significant increase in risk after 18 days. They also found that delay in definitive reconstruction beyond 1 year leads to loss of abdominal domain and difficulty obtaining a tension-free repair.

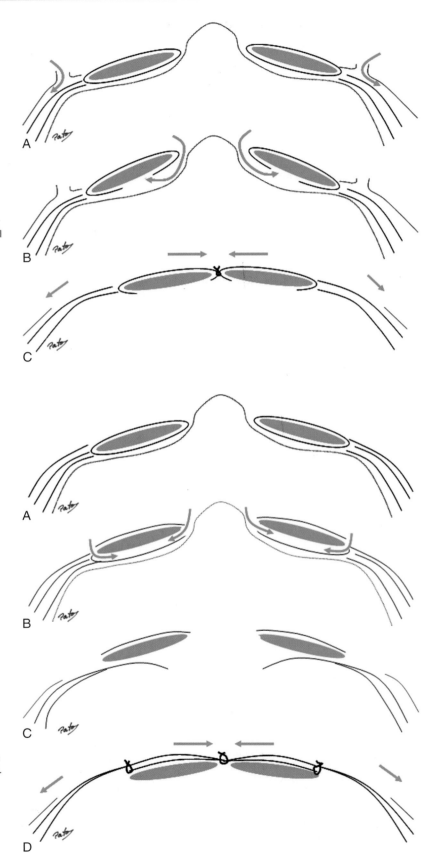

Figure 91-2. Component separation technique. **A,** External oblique release with separation of external oblique and internal oblique in an avascular plane. **B,** Incision and release of the posterior rectus sheath. **C,** Midline myofascial approximation of compound flaps composed of rectus abdominis with attached internal oblique/transverses abdominis. (Courtesy Patricio Andrades, MD, Clinical and Research Fellow, Division of Plastic Surgery and Transplant Immunology, Division of Plastic Surgery, University of Alabama at Birmingham, Birmingham, Alabama.)

Figure 91-3. Fabian modification of component separation technique. (Courtesy Patricio Andrades, MD, Clinical and Research Fellow, Division of Plastic Surgery and Transplant Immunology, Division of Plastic Surgery, University of Alabama at Birmingham, Birmingham, Alabama.)

18. **What is the incidence of incisional hernia formation after laparotomy? What are commonly associated risk factors?**

More than two million laparotomies are performed annually in the United States, with a reported 2% to 11% incidence of incisional hernia formation. It is the most common complication after laparotomy by 2:1 over bowel obstruction and is the most common indication for reoperation by 3:1 over adhesive small bowel obstruction. In a review of 1000 midline laparotomies by Condon et al., no single factor was associated with the development of incisional hernia on univariate analysis. On multivariate analysis, the combination of reopening and reclosure of previous incisions combined with wound infection influenced the development of incisional hernia.

Postoperative wound infection has been found in other studies to be associated with the development of incisional hernias. Obesity, aneurysmal disease, smoking, male gender, chronic obstructive pulmonary disease, malnourishment, malignancy, corticosteroid dependency, and prostatism are other risk factors reported in the literature.

19. **What suture material and technique are associated with the lowest rate of incisional hernia formation?**

A meta-analysis of randomized trials comparing suture material and technique found that abdominal fascial closure with nonabsorbable, monofilament suture in continuous fashion had a significantly lower incisional hernia rate. In work that has been reinforced by others, Jenkins et al. found that a suture length to wound length ratio of 4:1 was optimal for fascial closure. To use this length of suture, bites should encompass 1 cm of tissue at 1-cm intervals with attention to simply approximate the fascia. They also found nonabsorbable suture used in continuous fashion to be the material and technique of choice.

20. **What is the natural history of incisional hernia formation?**

The presence of an incisional hernia is an indication for repair. The linea alba serves as the midline anchor for the aponeurotic insertions of the rectus sheath and oblique musculature. Disruption results in gradual enlargement of the hernia defect due to the unopposed lateral contractions of the oblique musculature. As the defect widens, task-dependent functions of the abdominal wall musculature are interfered with and significant physiologic derangements occur.

21. **What are the primary goals in abdominal hernia repair?**

DiBello et al. defined several goals that the surgeon should accomplish when repairing abdominal wall hernias: Prevention of visceral eventration
- Incorporation of the remaining abdominal wall in the repair
- Provision of dynamic muscular support
- Restoration of abdominal wall continuity in a tension-free manner

The application of these principles with an emphasis on restoration of midline myofascial continuity has led to a reduction in hernia recurrence rates and improved functional and cosmetic outcomes in abdominal wall reconstruction.

22. **What are the criteria for use of synthetic mesh?**

Prosthetic material is used for structural support of the abdominal wall in a stable wound or as a temporizing measure in an open acute or infected wound. Mesh should meet certain criteria prior to its use. Mesh should be resistant to mechanical stress; it should be strong, durable, and of significant tensile strength so that it will not fragment with usage. It should be chemically inert; it should not be modified by tissue fluids or induce an inflammatory response. It should be capable of host tissue incorporation. Mesh should be tolerant to infection and capable of being reentered in the presence of infection or in the need for further exploratory surgery. Mesh should be easy to handle and capable of being fabricated into a desired shape.

23. **How has the application of mesh affected the surgical approach and outcomes in abdominal hernia repair?**

Use of synthetic mesh in the repair of incisional hernias increased from 34% in 1987 to 65% in 1999. The American Hernia Society has declared that the use of mesh now represents the standard of care in incisional hernia repair. A multicenter, prospective randomized trial by Luijendijk et al. comparing mesh and primary suture repair of incisional hernias 6 cm in greatest dimension found a 46% recurrence rate in the suture repair group compared with 23% in the mesh repair group at 3-year follow-up. A long-term 10-year follow-up of this study by Burger et al. revealed a cumulative recurrence rate of 63% for the primary suture repair group compared with 32% for the mesh repair group. An expert panel meeting on incisional herniorrhaphy concluded that primary suture repair should be used only for small hernias, less than 5 cm in greatest dimension, and if the repair is oriented horizontally with nonresorbable, monofilament suture with a suture to wound length ratio of 4:1.

24. Describe the experience with prosthetic materials.

The two most commonly used prosthetic materials are polypropylene and expanded polytetrafluoroethylene (ePTFE). Polypropylene was first introduced in the 1950s by Usher. The large pore size of polypropylene mesh allows for macrophage and neutrophil infiltration providing for greater resistance to infection. Its porosity allows for better fibrovascular ingrowth and a reduced incidence of seroma formation.

Expanded polytetrafluoroethylene (Gore-Tex, W.L. Gore and Associates, Flagstaff, Arizona) has a microporous structure that minimizes cellular infiltration and tissue incorporation. Studies have shown ePTFE prosthesis to be equivalent to polypropylene in terms of suture retention strength. As a result of its flexibility, conforming nature, and minimal tissue ingrowth, ePTFE can be placed directly on bowel. The disadvantages are related to its microporous structure. The material is virtually impenetrable, preventing host tissue ingrowth and leading to seroma formation. Once infected, ePTFE requires explantation. The micropores range from 3 to 41 microns in size, which are large enough for bacteria (1 micron) but too small for macrophages (>50 microns).

In an effort to reduce mesh-related complications and more closely duplicate abdominal wall physiology, research has focused on the development of composite materials that combine absorbable and nonabsorbable or barrier materials. Well-designed comparative studies with long-term follow-up are needed.

25. What is the clinical course of prosthetic materials capable of incorporation?

Within 18 to 24 hours, a fibrous exudate seals the viscera from the mesh. At 5 to 10 days, there is ingrowth of granulation tissue into the interstices of the mesh. At 14 to 21 days, the granulation tissue is ready for skin grafting or flap coverage. Fabian et al. demonstrated a statistically significant reduction in enteroatmospheric fistula formation with skin grafting of open abdominal wounds prior to 18 days after mesh placement.

26. Describe the technique for prosthetic material placement during abdominal wall reconstruction.

Several methods of securing the mesh to the fascia have been described; the most common are mesh onlay, mesh inlay, retrorectus placement, and intraperitoneal underlay. The retrorectus technique popularized by Rives and Stoppa and the intraperitoneal underlay technique have become popular and are associated with the lowest recurrence rates. Recurrence after mesh repair is rarely due to an intrinsic failure in the prosthetic material. Failure to identify healthy fascia and technical error in securing the mesh to the fascia commonly lead to recurrence at the mesh–fascia interface.

Retrorectus and intraperitoneal underlay techniques involve placement of the mesh beneath the abdominal wall. When possible, omentum should be interposed between the mesh and the viscera. It is generally recommended to place the mesh with at least 4 cm of contact between the mesh and the fascia. This allows for a distribution of pressure over a wider area (Pascal's principle), and the pressure-induced apposition promotes fibrous ingrowth at the mesh–fascial interface. It has also been experimentally demonstrated that polypropylene (Prolene) may shrink up to 30% after implantation. By placing the mesh beneath the abdominal wall, the repair is bolstered by the anterior abdominal wall, providing for a more secure and physiologic repair. Recurrence rates of less than 5% have been reported with these techniques (Fig. 91-4).

27. What are the advantages and disadvantages of using bioprosthetics in abdominal wall reconstruction?

Concern regarding mesh-related complications, such as infection, extrusion, abdominal wall stiffness, pain, and fistula formation, has led to the search for more biocompatible prosthetic materials. Advances in tissue engineering technology have led to the development of biomaterials derived from human and animal tissues. Materials such as human acellular dermis (AlloDerm, LifeCell, Branchburg, New Jersey), porcine acellular dermis (Permacol Tissue Science Laboratories, Covington, Georgia), and porcine small intestinal submucosa (Surgisis, Cook Surgical Incorporated, Bloomington, Indiana) are the most commonly used biomaterials. These materials consist of an acellular collagen matrix that promotes host tissue remodeling while maintaining mechanical integrity. They differ in that they heal by a regenerative process rather than by scar tissue formation. They have demonstrated resistance to infection, biocompatibility, tolerance to cutaneous exposure, and mechanical stability when used in incisional hernia repair. Disadvantages are their high cost and the lack of long-term follow-up studies validating their use.

28. What is gas gangrene of the abdominal wall? How do you differentiate it from anaerobic clostridial cellulitis?

Gas gangrene, or clostridial myonecrosis, is a rare but highly lethal postoperative complication that requires early recognition and prompt surgical débridement of all involved layers of the abdominal wall. Clinical signs include wound swelling, tenderness, drainage, discoloration that changes from pink to magenta within a few hours, and usually a small amount of crepitation. The patient is toxic out of proportion to the temperature elevation, with signs of tachycardia and hypotension. The wound culture is polymicrobial with at least one species of *Clostridium,* usually *C. oedematiens* or

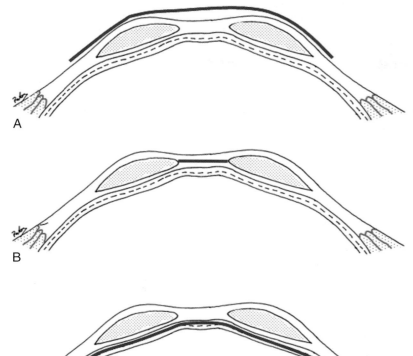

Figure 91-4. Mesh positions.
A, Onlay technique. **B,** Inlay technique.
C, Retrorectus underlay technique.
(Courtesy Patricio Andrades, MD,
Clinical and Research Fellow, Division
of Plastic Surgery and Transplant
Immunology, Division of Plastic
Surgery, University of Alabama at
Birmingham, Birmingham, Alabama.)

C. septicum. The most important exotoxin is lecithinase. The main difference between anaerobic clostridial cellulitis and clostridial myonecrosis is the relationship of gas to the signs of toxicity; a small amount of gas with severe toxicity usually represents clostridial myonecrosis.

29. What are the most important congenital defects of the abdominal wall?
Omphalocele and gastroschisis.

30. What is an omphalocele? What causes it?
An omphalocele is a developmental anomaly of the abdominal wall that occurs in 1: 3200 to 1:10,000 live births, often in association with sternal or diaphragmatic abnormalities, heart defects, or extrophy of the bladder. Large defects, often associated with syndromes, have a high mortality rate. An omphalocele results from failure of the four folds of the abdominal wall (endoderm, ectoderm, inner splanchnic, outer somatic mesoderm) to fuse at the umbilical ring. The sac (yolk sac) of amnion and chorion that covers the eviscerated mass commonly contains the liver and midgut. The defect develops during the extracolemic phase, between the sixth and twelfth weeks of intrauterine life, when the entire midgut passes out of the abdomen and into the yolk sac. After a period of linear growth, the bowel rotates 270° counterclockwise around the superior mesenteric vascular axis before returning to the abdomen. Defects range from those limited to the umbilicus to those extending from the xiphoid to the pubis. The umbilical cord attachment is most often at the apex of the sac.

31. What is gastroschisis?
A gastroschisis is a full-thickness defect of the abdominal wall that occurs lateral to the umbilical ring (usually to the right) with the umbilical cord attached at the normal position. A variable amount of intestine and occasionally parts of other abdominal organs are herniated outside the abdominal wall with no covering membrane or sac. It likely is the result of an abdominal wall ischemic event. Most of the morbidity is the result of in utero bowel injury.

32. Besides the physical findings of the abdominal wall, what characteristics do patients with gastroschisis have in common?
Nonrotation of the bowel, abnormally short midgut, and small peritoneal cavity.

33. How does gastroschisis differ from omphalocele?

A gastroschisis differs from an omphalocele in that it lacks a covering sac, and it is rare to see liver or other organs in the defect. The intestines usually are thickened, matted, and shortened because of prolonged contact with the amniotic fluid. Umbilical cord insertion is normal. The abdominal wall defect is lateral to the umbilicus, usually on the right side where the umbilical vein has resorbed, leaving it structurally weaker. The long-term outcome in gastroschisis is mainly related to the degree of associated intestinal injury, whereas the long-term outcome in omphalocele is primarily related to the severity of associated anomalies.

34. What is the treatment of patients with gastroschisis or omphalocele?

Primary closure, if it does not produce dangerously high intraabdominal pressure. Otherwise, staged procedures are indicated. Silon (Silastic-coated Dacron), polyethylene, or Teflon sheets are sutured to the edges of the fascial defect, and the viscera are gradually returned into the abdomen as the abdominal wall becomes more compliant and the cavity enlarges. If necessary, local or regional flaps are used.

35. What is "prune belly" syndrome?

Prune belly syndrome, also known as *triad syndrome* or *Eagle-Barrett syndrome,* consists of a triad of anomalies found almost exclusively in newborn boys: (1) absent or hypoplastic abdominal wall musculature, (2) bilateral cryptorchidism, and (3) dilation of the urinary tract. On physical examination, the muscular deficiency may be limited to one area, ranging from complete absence of muscle to the presence of all muscles as thin but recognizable structures. Complete absence of lower rectus muscles is most common. The abdomen appears as wrinkled or flabby, much like a prune, because of the weakened abdominal wall. As the child grows, the body contour resembles a pear or pot belly more than a prune. Children are often subject to respiratory complications due to impaired diaphragmatic motion and scoliosis due to the absence of the abdominal support mechanism. Reports describe the use of tensor fascia lata and rectus femoris muscle flaps to strengthen the abdominal wall.

36. What are the options for lower abdominal wall reconstruction?

- Tensor fascia lata musculofascial flap
- Rectus femoris musculofascial flap
- External oblique muscle and aponeurosis
- Inferiorly based rectus abdominis flap with or without anterior rectus sheath and overlying skin paddle
- Groin flap

37. What are the options for upper abdominal wall reconstruction?

- Superiorly based rectus with or without rectus sheath and overlying skin paddle
- External oblique muscle and aponeurosis
- Thoracoepigastric flap
- Extended latissimus dorsi musculofascial flap with pregluteal and lumbosacral fascia; also can be used for large or ipsilateral abdominal defects; for added length and mobility the latissimus muscle can be detached from its humeral insertion

38. What is commonly described as the "flap of choice" for abdominal wall reconstruction?

The tensor fascia lata is an ideal reconstructive option for abdominal wall defects. A dense, strong sheet of vascularized fascia and overlying skin can be transferred as a single unit in a single stage with minimal donor deficit. It is useful in irradiated and contaminated fields. Protective sensation can be maintained by inclusion of the lateral femoral cutaneous nerve (T12), and voluntary control is provided by the descending branch of the superior gluteal nerve. Flaps wider than 8 cm usually require skin grafting of the donor site; narrower flaps can be closed primarily. There is a tremendous disparity between the small size of the tensor muscle, originating from the greater trochanter, and the surrounding tensor fascia lata flap. The cutaneous paddle is reliable to approximately 5 to 8 cm above the knee; the distal portion is essentially a random pattern flap supplied largely by cutaneous perforators from the vastus lateralis muscle. The dominant pedicle, the lateral femoral circumflex femoral vessels arising from the profunda femoris, pierces the medial aspect of the flap 8 to 10 cm below the anterosuperior iliac spine. The arc of rotation allows the tip of the flap to reach the ipsilateral lower chest wall and xiphoid, especially in the thin patient. The flap can be used to resurface the entire suprapubic region, lower abdominal quadrants, or ipsilateral abdomen.

39. What is the role of the rectus femoris in abdominal wall reconstruction?

The rectus femoris is an excellent flap for reconstruction of the ipsilateral or lower abdominal wall. For extensive defects, a larger cutaneous paddle can be incorporated with the adjacent fascia lata in the musculocutaneous flap. The tip of the flap reaches a point midway between the umbilicus and the xiphoid. The flap is supplied by the lateral femoral circumflex vessels. It also can cover the entire suprapubic region and extend to the contralateral anterosuperior iliac spine. After transposition, the vastus lateralis and vastus medialis are approximated to prevent a functional deficit resulting in loss of the terminal 15° of knee extension.

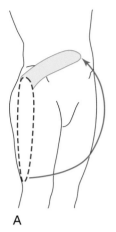 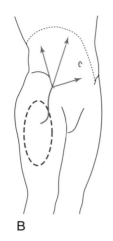 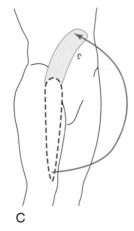

A   B   C

Figure 91-5. Flaps used in abdominal wall reconstruction. **A,** Tensor fascia lata. **B,** Anterior lateral thigh. **C,** Rectus femoris. (Courtesy Patricio Andrades, MD, Clinical and Research Fellow, Division of Plastic Surgery and Transplant Immunology, Division of Plastic Surgery, University of Alabama at Birmingham, Birmingham, Alabama.)

40. What is the "mutton chop" flap?

Described by Dibbell et al., the mutton chop flap or extended rectus femoris myocutaneous flap allows for reconstruction of large full-thickness abdominal wall defects, including the epigastrium, without prosthetic material (Fig. 91-5).

41. What is the role of the omentum in abdominal wall reconstruction?

The omentum, a double layer of fused peritoneum arising from the greater curvature of the stomach, is supplied by the right and left gastroepiploic arteries. This flap can cover the entire abdominal wall and perineal areas. It can be used with mesh and provides a good bed for a skin graft.

42. What is the role of tissue expansion in abdominal wall reconstruction?

Tissue expansion is a reconstructive option that has been used in congenital abdominal wall defects for extensive soft tissue defects. Expanders can be placed between the external oblique and internal oblique muscles to create an enlarged external oblique musculocutaneous flap and to allow greater mobilization with rectus advancement techniques.

43. What is the incidence of herniation following TRAM flaps?

Kroll et al. reported using mesh in 21.4% of free TRAM flaps and in 45% of conventional TRAM flaps. The incidence of lower abdominal wall laxity following conventional TRAM flaps ranged from 0.2% to 16% and was lower in free TRAM flaps (1.0% to 5.0%). There was no difference in abdominal wall strength, based on ability to perform sit-ups, in patients who had a pedicled or free TRAM flap in age-matched controls.

BIBLIOGRAPHY

Bleichrodt RP, Simmermacher RKJ, van der Lei B: Expanded polytetrafluoroethylene patch versus polypropylene mesh for the repair of contaminated defects of the abdominal wall. Surg Gynecol Obstet 176:18–23,1993.

Bostwick J, Hill HL, Nahai F: Repairs in the lower abdomen, groin, and perineum with myocutaneous flaps or omentum. Plast Reconstr Surg 63:186–194, 1978.

Boyd WC: Use of Marlex mesh in acute loss of the abdominal wall due to infection. Surg Gynecol Obstet 144:251, 1977.

Brown GL, Richardson JD, Malangoni MA: Comparison of prosthetic materials for abdominal wall reconstruction in the presence of contamination and infection. Ann Plast Surg 13:705–711, 1984.

Burger JW, Luijendijk RW, Hop WC, Halm JA., et al: Long term follow up of a randomized controlled trial of suture versus mesh repair of incisional hernia. Ann Surg 240:578–583, 2004.

Byrd HS, Hobar PC: Abdominal wall expansion in congenital defects. Plast Reconstr Surg 84:347–352, 1989.

Caix M, Outrequin G, Descottes B: Muscles of the abdominal wall: a new functional approach with anatoclinical deductions. Anat Clin 6:101–108, 1984.

Carlson MA, Ludwig KA, Condon RE: Ventral hernia and other complications of 1,000 midline laparotomies. South Med J 88:450–453, 1995.

Caulfield WH, Curtsinger L, Powell G, et al: Donor leg morbidity after pedicled rectus femoris muscle flap transfer for abdominal wall and pelvic reconstruction. Ann Plast Surg 32:377–382, 1994.

De Troyer A: Mechanical role of the abdominal wall muscles in relation to posture. Respir Physiol 53:341–353, 1983.

Dibbell DG Jr, Mixter RC, Dibbell DG Sr: Abdominal wall reconstruction (the "mutton chop" flap). Plast Reconstr Surg 87:60–65, 1991.

DiBello Jr JN, Moore Jr JH: Sliding myofascial flap of rectus abdominis for the closure of recurrent ventral hernias. Plast Reconstr Surg 98:464–469, 1996.

Fabian TC, Croce MA, Pritchard FE: Planned ventral hernia: Staged management for acute abdominal wall defects. Ann Surg 219: 643–650, 1994.

Gracovetsky S, Farfan HF, Helleur C: The abdominal mechanism. Spine 10:317, 1985.

Hodgson NC, Malthaner RA, Østbye T: The search for the ideal method of fascial closure: A meta-analysis. Ann Surg 231:436–442, 2000.

Hui K, Lineweaver W: Abdominal wall reconstruction. Adv Plast Reconstr Surg 14:213–244, 1997.

Jenkins TP: The burst abdominal wound: A mechanical approach. Br J Surg 63:873–876, 1976.

Jernigan TW, Fabian TC, Croce MA, et al: Staged management of giant abdominal wall defects: acute and long term results. Ann Surg 238:349–355, 2003.

Klein MD, Hertzler JH: Congenital defects of the abdominal wall. Surg Gynecol Obstet 152:805–808, 1981.

Kroll SS, Marchi M: Comparison of strategies for preventing abdominal wall weakness after TRAM flap breast reconstruction. Plast Reconstr Surg 89:1045–1051, 1992.

Livingston DH, Sharma PK, Glantz AI: Tissue expanders for abdominal wall reconstruction following severe trauma: Technical note and case reports. J Trauma 32:82–86,1992.

Luijendijk RW, Hop WC, van den Tol MP, et al: A comparison of suture and mesh repair for incisional hernia. N Engl J Med 343:392–398, 2000.

Parkas S, Ramakrishman K: A myocutaneous island flap in the treatment of a chronic radionecrotic ulcer of the abdominal wall. Br J Plast Surg 33:138–139, 1980.

Peled IJ, Kaplan HY, Herson M, et al: Tensor fascia lata musculocutaneous flap for abdominal wall reconstruction. Ann Plast Surg 11: 141–143, 1983.

Ramirez OM, Ruas E, Dellon AL: "Components separation" method for closure of abdominal wall defects: An anatomic and clinical study. Plast Reconstr Surg 86:519–526, 1990.

Shaw WW, Aston SJ, Zide BM: Reconstruction of the trunk. In McCarthy JG (ed): Plastic Surgery. Philadelphia, WB Saunders, 1990, pp 3755–3796.

Stoppa RE: Treatment of complicated groin and incisional hernias. World J Surg 13:545–554, 1989.

Suominen S, Asko-Seljavaara S, von Smitten K, et al: Sequelae of abdominal wall after pedicled or free TRAM flap surgery. Ann Plast Surg 36:629–636, 1996.

Taylor GI, Watterson PA, Zelt RG: The vascular anatomy of the anterior abdominal wall: The basis for flap design. Perspect Plast Surg 5:1–30, 1991.

Toranto RI: The relief of back pain with the WARP abdominoplasty: A preliminary report. Plast Reconstr Surg 85:545–555, 1990.

Voyles CR, Richardson JD, Bland KI, et al: Emergency abdominal reconstruction with polypropylene mesh: Short term benefits versus long term complications. Ann Surg 194:219, 1981.

RECONSTRUCTION OF THE POSTERIOR TRUNK

CHAPTER 92

Eric G. Halvorson, MD, and
Joseph J. Disa, MD, FACS

1. What are the most common reconstructive problems of the posterior trunk?
Defects following oncologic resection, spinal pressure sores, radiation necrosis wounds, infections following spinal surgery (with or without hardware), traumatic wounds, and spina bifida.

2. What types of flaps can be used for coverage of posterior trunk defects?
Advancement, rotation, island, unipedicled, bipedicled, turnover, reverse turnover, and/or free flaps. Skin grafts should be used only for non–weight-bearing areas; they usually leave a contour deformity. Free tissue transfer is rarely necessary because of the availability of local muscle flaps.

3. Describe the principles of wound management prior to reconstructive surgery of the posterior trunk.
Basic wound management principles should be followed. Necrotic or infected tissue should be débrided, on a repeated basis if necessary, until a clean wound base of viable tissue is achieved. Antibiotic-impregnated beads can be used between operative débridements, a practice popular among orthopedic surgeons, especially when hardware is exposed. Also commonly used is negative-pressure wound therapy, which promotes granulation with fewer dressing changes.

4. Which factors impact the surgeon's choice of flap when approaching a posterior trunk defect?
Depth of the Wound: Superficial wounds are treated by advancement or rotation of local muscle or musculocutaneous flaps with or without local cutaneous advancement flaps. Deep wounds are treated with rotation or turnover of paraspinal muscle flaps, with overlying coverage as described for superficial wounds. Alternatively, two regional muscle units can be used, such as a combination of trapezius and latissimus dorsi muscle flaps.

Width of the Wound: Every effort should be made to deliver well-vascularized tissue with enough bulk to obliterate all dead space. The latissimus dorsi muscle supplies most bulk, whereas the paraspinal muscles are more appropriate for smaller wounds. The trapezius muscle provides medium bulk.

Pedicle Location: The flap pedicle ideally should be outside the zone of injury, whether due to trauma, resection, or radiation therapy. Flap planning should consider the possibility that certain pedicles may be unavailable, the most important being those derived from the subscapular system (Fig. 92-1). Prior radiation may preclude the use of reverse turnover flaps, which rely on secondary segmental paravertebral perforators, depending on the extent of local radiation effect.

5. What are the functional goals of posterior trunk reconstruction?
Maintenance of neural continuity, control of cerebrospinal fluid leakage, spinal skeletal stability, integrity of the chest wall, obliteration of dead space, control of infection, and coverage of hardware.

6. In what ways do defects of the posterior trunk differ from those of the anterior chest wall?
Bony stability is less critical because the scapula and layered muscles usually provide adequate support for the respiratory function of the thoracic cage. In addition, more muscles are available for transfer and wound coverage.

ANATOMY OF POSTERIOR TRUNK FLAPS

7. How are the scapular and parascapular flaps designed? Which vascular axis supplies these flaps?
The circumflex scapular artery, a branch of the subscapular artery, divides into a transverse branch, which supplies the scapular flap, and a descending branch, which supplies the parascapular flap (see Fig. 92-1). Both of these are

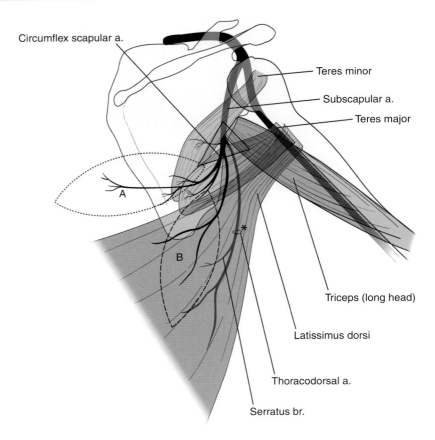

Figure 92-1. The circumflex scapular artery emerges from the triangular space *(shaded red)*, between teres major, teres minor, and the long head of triceps. Transverse and descending branches supply the scapular *(A)* and parascapular *(B)* flaps. The thoracodorsal artery arises from the subscapular artery deep to the triangular space and supplies the latissimus dorsi. The preferred recipient site for microvascular anastomosis is proximal to the serratus branch *(asterisk)*, which can supply the latissimus dorsi with retrograde blood flow via intercostals. (Copyright MSKCC 2006.)

fasciocutaneous flaps, with arcs of rotation that allow coverage of defects of the superolateral posterior trunk, shoulder, axilla, and lateral chest wall. The scapular flap is oriented horizontally from the triangular space to a point midway between the medial border of the scapula and the spine. The parascapular flap is oriented vertically, from the triangular space to a point midway between the tip of the scapula and the iliac crest. A variant of the parascapular flap is the inframammary extended circumflex scapular (IMECS) flap, in which the axis of the flap is rotated anteriorly, across the lateral chest and into the inframammary fold. Based on radial branches of the descending branch of the circumflex scapular artery, the donor scar of this flap is less noticeable.

8. Define the triangular space.
The circumflex scapular artery and venae comitans exit through the triangular space to supply the fasciocutaneous flaps described above. This space is palpable approximately 2 cm above the posterior axillary crease. It is bordered superiorly by the teres minor, inferiorly by the teres major, and laterally by the long head of the triceps (see Fig. 92-1). As the circumflex scapular artery is a branch of the subscapular artery, dissecting proximally in the triangular space can increase flap pedicle length and diameter.

9. Describe the functional anatomy of the trapezius muscle.
The trapezius is a flat, triangular muscle with a broad-based origin (Table 92-1 and Fig. 92-2). The upper third of the muscle is supplied by branches of the occipital artery, the middle third by the superficial branch of the transverse cervical artery (also called the superficial cervical artery), and the lower third by the descending or deep branch of the transverse cervical artery (also called the dorsal scapular artery) and secondary segmental intercostal perforators. Minimal functional deficit results from harvest of the lower trapezius muscle below the scapular spine.

10. Describe the functional anatomy of the latissimus dorsi muscle.
The latissimus dorsi is also a flat, triangular muscle, but it is larger than the trapezius muscle (see Table 92-1 and Fig. 92-2). Loss of function generally does not result in significant morbidity. The latissimus dorsi has a Mathes-Nahai type V blood supply, with a dominant pedicle (thoracodorsal branch of the subscapular artery) and secondary segmental pedicles (posterior intercostal and lumbar artery perforators). The most reliable skin territory lies over the proximal two thirds of the muscle. In most patients the pedicle divides into an upper branch, which courses medially and horizontally,

Table 92-1. Functional Anatomy of Common Muscle Flaps of the Posterior Trunk

FLAP	ORIGIN	INSERTION	FUNCTION	NERVE	ARTERY
Trapezius	C/T vertebrae	Scapula, clavicle	Shoulder elevation	Cranial nerve XI	Occipital, TCA (SCA, DSA)
Latissimus dorsi	L/S vertebrae, SI crest	Humerus	Adduction, extension, internal rotation	Thoracodorsal	TDA
Gluteus maximus	Ilium, sacrum, coccyx	Greater trochanter, TFL	Extension, lateral rotation	Inferior gluteal	Superior and inferior gluteal

C/T, Cervical and thoracic; *DSA*, dorsal scapular artery; *L/S*, lumbar and sacral; *SCA*, superficial cervical artery; *SI*, sacroiliac; *TCA*, transverse cervical artery; *TDA*, thoracodorsal artery; *TFL*, tensor fascia lata.

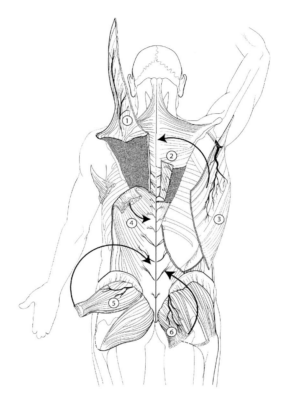

Figure 92-2. Posterior trunk flap options: *(1)* Trapezius flap, *(2)* distal trapezius reverse turnover flap, *(3)* latissimus dorsi flap, *(4)* reverse turnover latissimus dorsi flap, *(5)* superior gluteal flap, *(6)* inferior gluteal flap. (Copyright MSKCC 2006.)

and a lateral branch, which courses laterally and inferiorly. Harvest of a portion of the latissimus dorsi is possible based on one of these branches. Previous surgery in the axilla, which may have caused interruption of the thoracodorsal artery, does not necessarily preclude use of the latissimus dorsi, as retrograde profusion is possible via the serratus branch of the thoracodorsal artery.

11. Can the latissimus dorsi musculocutaneous flap design be modified into a perforator flap? How?

With the thoracodorsal artery perforator (TDAP) flap, the latissimus dorsi muscle is preserved and its anterolateral skin territory harvested based on a single musculocutaneous perforator. Although significant donor site morbidity is not seen following latissimus dorsi muscle transfer, this design limits flap bulk and donor site contour deformity. Most perforators exit the muscle along the course of the descending branch of the thoracodorsal artery or curve around the anterior border of the muscle; therefore dissection usually is begun anteroinferiorly. The lateral edge of the muscle is identified, and dissection proceeds posterosuperiorly in the suprafascial plane. Once a suitable perforator is chosen, it is dissected by splitting the muscle and is harvested with the thoracodorsal pedicle. Care should be taken to preserve the thoracodorsal motor nerve. A pedicled TDAP flap requires a larger split in the muscle to pass the flap through. A vertically designed flap can reach the elbow, neck, shoulder, axilla, and upper back. The horizontal flap usually is used for partial breast reconstruction.

12. What is the relevant anatomy when transferring paraspinal muscle flaps?

Narrow deep "gutters" of paraspinal musculature border the thoracic, lumbar, and sacral spine. These muscles have segmental blood supply, derived from dorsal branches of the aorta, and have a limited arc of rotation. Bilateral turnover flaps are useful for small, deep wounds, or as a deep layer when other muscles are transferred for superficial coverage. Flap elevation is achieved by incising the paravertebral fascia approximately 2 to 3 cm from the spinous processes along the length of the muscle, after which the lateral edge of muscle is mobilized. The medial cut edges of bilateral paravertebral fasciae are then sutured together in the midline.

13. Describe the functional anatomy of the gluteus maximus muscle.

This thick, parallelogram-shaped muscle has a Mathes-Nahai type III blood supply with two dominant pedicles (superior and inferior gluteal arteries; see Table 92-1 and Fig. 92-2). Harvest of the entire muscle results in significant functional deficit; however, the superior or inferior half can be harvested based on either the superior or inferior gluteal artery, respectively, with preservation of function. In cases of sacral radiation necrosis, this muscle can be used safely because the pedicles are deep and 5 cm lateral to the sacral origin of the muscle.

14. Can the gluteus maximus muscle flap design be modified into a perforator flap? How?

The gluteus maximus can be harvested as a perforator flap by dissecting the largest cutaneous perforator of either the superior gluteal artery perforator (SGAP) or inferior gluteal artery perforator (IGAP) through the muscle until adequate pedicle length and/or diameter are obtained. The flap can then be harvested for free tissue transfer or rotated for local coverage. The SGAP flap is a good choice for sacral wound coverage because it provides good bulk with little donor site morbidity. It can be rotated 90° to 180° without flap compromise.

15. Name some less commonly used flaps for posterior trunk reconstruction.

The omentum can be transferred, based on the right or left gastroepiploic artery, for coverage of lumbar defects. After dividing its attachments to the transverse colon, either the left or right gastroepiploic artery is ligated (depending on defect location), attachments to the greater curvature of the stomach are divided, and thus the arc of rotation is greatly lengthened. A tunnel is created through the retroperitoneum and lumbar fascia, and the flap is transferred and covered with bilateral cutaneous advancement flaps.

The intercostal muscle flap, based on any posterior intercostal artery (and its lateral cutaneous branch when a musculocutaneous flap is required), can be rotated to all thirds of the posterior trunk for coverage of small defects. The lateral cutaneous branches are variable in location, flap dissection is difficult with risk of pedicle injury, and the muscle is small, making this flap of limited utility.

REGIONAL APPROACH TO POSTERIOR TRUNK DEFECTS

16. How should the posterior trunk be approached when considering reconstructive options?

Conceptually, the posterior trunk should be divided into upper, middle, and lower thirds. The cervical spine and sacrum are considered separately, as defects of the former are rare, and defects of the latter are considered in the context of pressure sore management. Defects of the shoulder, axilla, and lateral chest wall also are considered separately. In principle, the regional approach is like that used for lower extremity wounds. Each third has specific muscle flap options that are best suited for coverage of that part of the posterior trunk (see Fig. 92-2). All flaps described here can be transferred as muscle flaps or musculocutaneous flaps. In the latter, primary closure of the donor site may require the use of skin grafts depending on the patient's body habitus, skin laxity, and flap size requirements.

17. Outline the regional approach to posterior trunk reconstruction.

- *Deep Wounds:* (1) Paraspinal turnover and superficial muscle flaps or (2) two superficial flaps (e.g., trapezius and latissimus dorsi)
- *Cervical Spine:* Lower trapezius flaps
- *Upper Thoracic:* (1) Lower trapezius (including reverse turnover) and/or (2) latissimus dorsi flaps
- *Midthoracic:* (1) Latissimus dorsi (including reverse turnover) and/or (2) lower trapezius flaps
- *Lower Thoracic:* Latissimus dorsi (including reverse turnover) flapsw
- *Lumbosacral:* Latissimus dorsi (including reverse turnover), gluteus maximus (including SGAP), omentum, latissimus dorsi, or trapezius flaps with vein extension

18. What are the options for coverage of cervical defects?

The lower trapezius flap, based on the descending or deep branch of the transverse cervical artery (also called the dorsal scapular artery), can be rotated, turned over, or transferred as an island flap for coverage of the posterior cervical spine. This flap can be used reliably for coverage of the dura, spinal hardware, or exposed hardware even in the setting of prior radiation.

19. Which flaps should be considered for coverage of upper thoracic defects?

The trapezius flap, as described in Question 18, is best for smaller wounds. The lower trapezius muscle can be considered a Mathes-Nahai type V muscle with a dominant pedicle (dorsal scapular artery) and secondary segmental pedicles (posterior intercostal perforators). Thus for upper thoracic defects, it can also be transferred as a "reverse turnover" flap based on secondary segmental vessels, much like the latissimus dorsi and pectoralis major reverse turnover flaps.

The latissimus dorsi flap, based on the thoracodorsal artery, also can be rotated, turned over, or transferred as an island flap for medium-size defects. Large or deep defects may require a combination of trapezius, latissimus dorsi, and/or paraspinal muscle flaps.

20. Name the flaps available for coverage of midthoracic defects.

The lower trapezius flap works well for smaller wounds and the latissimus dorsi for larger wounds. In this area, the latissimus dorsi can be transferred as a reverse turnover flap based on secondary segmental posterior intercostal and/or lumbar artery perforators. Large, deep wounds may require the addition of paraspinal muscle flaps or a combination of trapezius and latissimus dorsi flaps.

21. Describe flap options for lower thoracic and lumbosacral defects.

The latissimus dorsi can be rotated or advanced with or without a thoracolumbar fasciocutaneous extension. Because this cutaneous territory has a random blood supply, it should be used only in patients with optimal vascular profiles. It also can be used as a reverse turnover flap. Gluteus maximus muscle or musculocutaneous flaps, based on the superior gluteal artery, can be advanced alone or as a latissimus dorsi/gluteus maximus composite flap. This composite flap is ideal for coverage of meningomyelocele defects (see Question 24). More recently, the S-GAP flap, which preserves the gluteus maximus muscle but requires intramuscular perforator dissection, has been described (see Question 14). Use of the omentum, as described in Question 15, is also possible.

22. Are free flaps ever necessary for posterior trunk reconstruction? What are the options?

When local muscles are not available because of extensive trauma or resection or when flap pedicles are compromised by radiation, trauma, or scarring from previous surgery, free tissue transfer is appropriate. The dorsal branch of the fourth lumbar artery is a useful recipient vessel and is found between the third and fourth lumbar vertebrae at the lateral border of the sacrospinalis muscle. It has a diameter of 1.3 mm. Other recipient vessels include the superior gluteal and intercostal vessels.

Virtually any free flap could be used if appropriate for a given defect, and the reader is referred to Mathes and Nahai's classic text *Reconstructive Surgery* for detailed descriptions of most free flaps available and an excellent discussion of options for posterior trunk free flap reconstruction.

The latissimus dorsi and lower trapezius muscle flap pedicles can be extended with vein grafts to increase the arc of rotation for coverage of more distant sites such as the thoracolumbar spine and sacrum. These muscles can also be used as free flaps.

SPINA BIFIDA

23. Name the four types of spina bifida.

- *Meningocele:* Cystic herniation of intact meninges, neurologically intact
- *Meningomyelocele:* Cystic herniation of meninges and neural tissue, motor and sensory deficit; *most common form*
- *Syringomyelocele:* Similar to meningomyelocele, with dilated central cord canal; *rare*
- *Myelocele:* Exposed neural elements without meningeal/cutaneous coverage, high fatality; *rare*

24. Which flaps can be used for coverage of spina bifida defects?

Wide undermining and mobilization of large bilateral cutaneous advancement flaps is successful in most cases. Lateral relaxing incisions may be required for larger defects, creating bipedicled flaps that necessitate skin grafting of the resultant lateral defects. Composite muscle or musculocutaneous latissimus dorsi and gluteus maximus flaps can be used as described in Question 21.

BIBLIOGRAPHY

Disa JJ, Smith AW, Bilsky MH: Management of radiated reoperative wounds of the cervicothoracic spine: The role of the trapezius turnover flap. Ann Plast Surg 47:394–397, 2001.

Mathes SJ, Nahai F: Reconstructive Surgery. New York, Churchill Livingstone, 1997.

Ramasastry SS, Schlechter B, Cohen M: Reconstruction of posterior trunk defects. Clin Plast Surg 22:167–185, 1995.

Roche NA, Van Lunduyt K, Blondeel PN, et al: The use of pedicled perforator flaps for reconstruction of lumbosacral defects. Ann Plast Surg 45:7–14, 2000.

Siebert JW, Longaker MT, Angrigiani C: The inframammary extended circumflex scapular flap: An aesthetic improvement of the parascapular flap. Plast Reconstr Surg 99:70–77, 1997.

Van Landuyt K, Hamdi M: Thoracodorsal artery perforator flap. In Blondeel PN, Morris SF, Hallock GG, Neligan PC (eds): Perforator Flaps. St. Louis, Quality Medical Publishing, 2006, pp 441–459.

1. How does a plastic surgeon become involved in lower extremity reconstruction?

Many vascular, surgical, oncologic, and orthopedic wounds benefit from plastic surgical consultation and intervention because of large soft tissue defects and/or combined vascularized bone graft and soft tissue requirements.

2. What types of pathology may require lower extremity reconstruction?

Open fractures of the distal tibia, chronic wounds of the distal third of the leg, unstable scars, defects from sarcoma resections, diabetic ulcers, radiation wounds, osteomyelitis of the tibia, and wounds resulting from ischemia of the lower extremity often require reconstruction.

3. What are common coverage methods for the thigh?

- Local rotation or advancement flaps of the thigh muscles, with or without skin grafts, in particular, the gracilis, vastus lateralis, and tensor fascia lata (TFL) flaps.
- Fasciocutaneous flaps such as the medial thigh, lateral posterior thigh, anterior lateral thigh, or rectus femoris fasciocutaneous flap.
- More distant flaps such as the rectus abdominis based on the deep inferior epigastric artery and vein.

4. What are the alternatives and considerations for soft tissue coverage of the knee?

Muscle flaps, fasciocutaneous flaps, and free tissue transfer are useful for knee coverage. The gastrocnemius muscle flap is readily available for knee coverage; however, it does not reliably cross the midline to the contralateral aspect of the knee or to the superior aspect of the knee. The distally based vastus lateralis has been described; however, partial necrosis is a frequent occurrence. The saphenous fasciocutaneous flap as described by Walton and Bunkis is useful if available. For extensive defects covering the entire surface of the knee, free tissue transfer of a large fasciocutaneous flap or muscle flap is the most reliable. A microdissected wraparound deep inferior epigastric perforator (DIEP) flap can be considered.

5. What is appropriate soft tissue coverage for the proximal tibia?

Local muscle flaps include the medial gastrocnemius and lateral gastrocnemius, which usually is shorter than the medial gastrocnemius. Fasciocutaneous flaps include the saphenous flap, a distally based medial or lateral fasciocutaneous flap, or a combination of a gastrocnemius flap with a proximally or distally based fasciocutaneous flap. Free flaps are indicated when the local soft tissue injury contraindicates the use of local muscle or fasciocutaneous flaps and the area is extensive.

6. What are appropriate choices of soft tissue coverage of the mid-tibial region?

For small defects a turnover flap of the anterior tibialis muscle may be useful. However, most defects are larger and may require the soleus muscle, which is readily available and transposes well over this area. Fasciocutaneous flaps from the lateral or medial leg, based distally or proximally, are useful. Of course, free flaps are appropriate when local soft tissue coverage is not available or the defect is extensive.

7. What local coverage is available for ankle or distal tibial exposure?

Small defects of the ankle less than 4 cm^2 can be covered by the extensor brevis muscle flap, slightly larger defects by the lateral supramalleolar flap, and somewhat larger defects by the dorsalis pedis fasciocutaneous flap. These flaps require a blood supply not compromised by the injury. The distally based soleus flap has been used but has a high incidence of partial necrosis. Distally based fasciocutaneous flaps (based laterally or medially), including the sural neurocutaneous flap, can be safely used, with demonstration of comparable perforators at the respective base of the flap.

8. What factors increase the complication rate for sural flaps?

The sural flap has become a workhorse for coverage of the ankle and foot. However, comorbidities of diabetes mellitus, arteriosclerosis, venous insufficiency, and vasculitis as well as a tight subcutaneous tunnel and underlying osteomyelitis may increase the risk of sural flap failure.

9. What are common coverage methods for wounds of the foot?

The sural artery flap and lateral supramalleolar flap may be of benefit for small; or moderate-size wounds of the ankle and proximal foot. Other local flaps include the instep flap based on the medial branch of the plantar artery, V-Y advancement flaps, toe fillet flaps, and local fasciocutaneous flaps are helpful for coverage of small- to moderate-size wounds. Extensive wounds and global injury to the foot and ankle area may indicate free flap coverage. Several small muscle flaps such as the flexor hallucis and abductor hallucis brevis are available but rarely are of practical use given the frequent global injury to the foot and ankle area.

10. Why are the wounds of the distal leg so problematic for coverage?

The distal portion of the leg has poor skin elasticity, frequent severe edema, and osseous structures that lie in the subcutaneous tissue and are quite vulnerable. Such wounds also have a high rate of osteomyelitis, which often results in amputation. The distal third of the leg has significant tendinous structures that take skin grafts poorly. Finally, the foot and ankle require good flap durability because they are so frequently exposed to friction and shear by walking and footwear.

11. What are the indications for free tissue transfer to cover the distal lower extremity?

Indications for free tissue transfer include large or circumferential defects exposing fractures, open joints, or the Achilles tendon; incisions or soft tissue trauma that compromises the lateral or medial fasciocutaneous areas; and compromise of the distal arterial flow, which may prevent the use of lateral supramalleolar or dorsalis pedis flaps.

12. List absolute indications for flap coverage of the lower extremity.

Exposed bypass grafts, open fractures, and tendon and nerve exposure.

13. What are the six angiosomes of the foot and ankle region?

- Three branches of the posterior tibial artery:
  - Medial, calcaneal artery—Heel
  - Medial plantar artery—Instep
  - Lateral plantar artery—Lateral plantar and plantar forefoot
- Two branches of the perineal artery:
  - Anterior perforating artery—Anterior lateral ankle
  - Lateral calcaneal branch—Plantar and lateral heel
- Anterior tibial artery—Dorsum of the foot

14. What is the significance of the angiosome territories?

Knowledge of the angiosomes and the associated choke vessels is used to provide optimal blood supply to skin flaps, amputations, and incisions.

15. What are special considerations for plantar foot coverage?

Probably the foremost problem in coverage of the plantar foot is the ability of the transferred tissue to tolerate the shear forces involved in walking. Interface problems between the native plantar glabrous skin and the transferred skin are common. Durability, the need to cover fusion or any other osseous work, and the lack of sensation in the transferred tissue also are important. Any insensate tissue transferred is at significant risk for breakdown.

16. What is the most appropriate source of free tissue transfer for coverage of extensive plantar foot defects?

The jury is still out. May et al. presented convincing evidence for the use of muscle flaps with skin grafts; however, fasciocutaneous flaps have been used as effectively. Probably the most important criteria are (1) a familiar flap with an adequate pedicle length of sufficient caliber, (2) a flap that is well tailored to the defect and not excessively thick, (3) muscle flaps to cover deep or irregular defects, and (4) skin flaps for resurfacing superficial degloving tissue defects. Abnormally high pressure points in the plantar surface lead to recurrent breakdowns after reconstruction. Bony abnormalities should be corrected. The patient should be educated about meticulous foot care, and orthotics should be provided.

17. How can abnormal weight-bearing in the neuropathic foot be corrected?

Bone spurs and joint dislocation can and must be corrected. For ulceration of the fifth metatarsal head, resection through the metatarsal neck is recommended. The first metatarsal head is débrided only if it is involved in the ulcer base. More commonly the medial or lateral sesamoid bone needs to be removed in the base of the first metatarsal head ulcer. For the second, third, and fourth metatarsal heads, a metatarsal neck osteotomy should be performed. Midfoot bony prominences may require judicious resection around the areas of the metatarsal bases, cuneiform, or navicular bones. Limited midfoot fusions should be considered. Orthotics may be useful to shift weight away from a particular pressure point.

18. What advantage does the VAC device provide for lower extremity wounds?

It removes fluid, promotes soft tissue healing and provides coverage of limited areas of bone and hardware. It is a superior temporary coverage until definitive closure is accomplished, providing there is no necrotic bone or soft tissue or purulence.

19. Are there any contraindications for the vacuum-assisted closure device in the lower extremity?

A vacuum-assisted closure (VAC) device will not clear up grossly purulent wounds nor will it débride necrotic soft tissue or bone. The VAC device should not be counted on to granulate over extensive bone or hardware exposure or an extensive fracture line.

20. What are the muscle groups and major nerves and arteries of each of the four compartments of the lower leg?

The *anterior compartment,* bounded by the tibia, interosseous membrane, and anterior intermuscular septum, contains the extensor muscles of the foot and ankle with the tibialis anterior, extensor hallucis longus, and extensor digitorum longus muscles. The major artery is the anterior tibial artery, and the deep peroneal nerve courses along with the artery.

The *lateral compartment* is bounded by the anterior intermuscular septum, fibula, and posterior intermuscular septum. The muscles in this compartment are the peroneus longus, peroneus brevis, and peroneus tertius muscles. There is no major artery in the lateral compartment; however, the superficial peroneal nerve runs within it.

The *superficial posterior compartment* is bounded by the deep surface of the soleus muscle and the plantaris tendon. It contains the soleus and gastrocnemius muscles.

The *deep posterior compartment* is bounded by the tibia, interosseus membrane, and fibula. The muscle groups contained within it are the tibialis posterior, flexor digitorum longus, and flexor hallucis longus muscles. This compartment contains the posterior tibial artery, which courses medially between the flexor digitorum longus and soleus muscles, and the peroneal artery, which courses slightly more laterally between the tibialis posterior and flexor hallucis longus muscles. The major nerve in the deep posterior compartment is the posterior tibial nerve.

21. Why should we invest significant resources to salvage an ulcerated diabetic limb when the patient can just as well have a below-knee amputation and prosthesis?

The incidence of a second amputation in the contralateral limb approaches 50% within 2 years of the initial amputation. Therefore within 2 years you may expect a diabetic to have either bilateral below-knee amputations or a combination of below-knee and above-knee amputations, either of which sentences the patient to a wheelchair.

22. What is tarsal tunnel syndrome? What are its clinical findings? How is it treated?

Tarsal tunnel syndrome results from compressing the posterior tibial nerve within a fibroosseous canal that has for its roof the flexor retinaculum. The classic history includes pain that usually is burning and localized in the plantar aspect of the foot but may radiate up the medial side of the calf. The symptoms are increased by activity and are diminished by rest or rubbing the foot. Night symptoms may occur. A positive Tinel's sign may be elicited along the medial or lateral plantar nerve. Sensation to pinprick may be decreased. The diagnosis may be confirmed by nerve conduction velocity studies with prolonged terminal latency to the abductor hallucis or abductor digiti quinti muscle and abnormal potentials with fibrillations. Vascular insufficiency should be absent. When accurately diagnosed, tarsal tunnel syndrome can be treated with release of the fibroosseous tunnel by lysing the flexor retinaculum.

23. What is compartment syndrome?

In compartment syndrome, muscle and nerve viability is threatened by increased tissue pressure within a fixed, fascially bounded compartment in the body over a prolonged period. There are four compartments in the leg: anterior, lateral, deep posterior, and superficial posterior. The increased pressure results from postischemia reperfusion or direct crush to the limb, as in a tibial fracture. An open wound in the leg does not indicate released or decompressed compartments. Most authors agree that an increase from the normal tissue pressure of 2 to 7 mm Hg to 30 mm Hg is concerning and that an increase to 35 to 40 mm Hg is an absolute indication for treatment. A more accurate measurement is differential pressure (diastolic pressure minus compartment pressure); a differential pressure less than 30 mm Hg is an absolute indication for treatment. Failure to treat creates a vicious cycle of increasing compartment pressures due to lymphatic and venous obstruction without arterial obstruction. The results are neuropraxia, muscle necrosis, and, finally, axonotmesis and limb ischemia. The tissue injury becomes irreversible in hours with resultant nerve and muscle loss.

24. Is pulselessness a reliable sign of compartment syndrome?

Pulselessness is only seen upon very late progression of compartment syndrome. More reliable signs are paresthesias, pain with passive stretch of the muscle, inappropriately severe pain, and paralysis.

25. How is compartment syndrome recognized and treated?

Awareness and early intervention are the keys to treatment. In borderline cases, tingling and increased pain in the limb associated with pain on passive extension of the involved muscle compartment can be treated by major limb elevation and intravenous mannitol. Tissue compartments can be measured by a needle catheter technique. Obvious severe compartment syndrome or expected severe compartment pressure elevation from reperfusion or crush mandates surgical compartment release as an emergency. The urgency cannot be overemphasized.

26. How are the foot sensory nerves evaluated?

Light touch can be used to evaluate the domains of the foot listed in Table 93-1.

27. What are indications for primary amputation in patients with tibial level injury?

The major indication is severe combined injury to bone, skin, joint, nerve, and vessels such that long-term limb survival and function are unlikely. The disruption of sciatic or posterior tibial nerve function may be the most important element because meaningful recovery in these patients, even after repair, is poor. Consequences include an insensate plantar surface and almost certain recurrent ulceration, infection, and osteomyelitis. A tradeoff must be made with prosthetics that allow high-level function. Other indications include severe infections or contamination, multilevel severe injury, and absent pedal pulses. Scoring systems such as the Gustilo fracture score (Table 93-2) and the Mangled Extremity Severity Score (MESS) help in decision making. Amputation should be considered seriously in any patient with a limb score greater than 7. The parameters for MESS are outlined in Table 93-3.

28. What are the contraindications to salvage of a Gustilo IIIC injury of the lower extremity?

Preexisting severe medical illnesses, severed limb, tibial loss greater than 8 cm, ischemic time greater than 6 hours, and severance of the posterior tibial nerve in adults.

29. What are the indications for lower extremity replantation?

For several reasons, lower extremity replantation is not uniformly practiced. The most important limitation is the inability to restore neurologic function to the lower extremity. In addition, prosthetic legs are relatively well accepted and widely used, although they have their disadvantages. The loss of a leg is frequently associated with other severe injuries. The provision of a marginally functional replanted lower extremity may create a greater liability with respect to long-term rehabilitation, pain, time lost from employment, and associated risk of replantation surgery.

Table 93-1. Foot Sensory Nerves	
NERVE	**DOMAIN**
Sural nerve	Lateral midfoot
Posterior tibial nerve	Heel/plantar midfoot
Deep peroneal nerve	First web space
Superficial peroneal	Dorsal distal foot
Saphenous nerve	Medial ankle

Table 93-2. Gustilo Scoring for Open Fractures	
Gustilo II	Moderate soft tissue injury and stripping
Gustilo IIIA	High energy, adequate soft tissue despite laceration or undermining
Gustilo IIIB	Extensive soft tissue injury and periosteal stripping, usually gross contamination
Gustilo IIIC	Gustilo B with limb ischemia

From Gustilo RB, Mendoza RM, Williams DN: Problems in the management of type III (severe) open fractures: A new classification of type III open fractures. J Trauma 24:742, 1987, with permission.

Table 93-3. Mangled Extremity Severity Score (MESS)

Skeletal soft tissue injury	Low energy	1
	Medium energy (open fractures)	2
	High energy (military gunshot wound)	3
	Very high energy (gross contamination)	4
Limb ischemia (double score for ischemia >6 hr)	Near-normal	1
	Pulseless, decreased capillary refill	2
	Cool, insensate, paralyzed	3
Shock	Systolic blood pressure always >90 mm Hg	0
	Transient hypotension	1
	Persistent hypotension	2
Age (yr)	<30	0
	30–50	1
	>50	2

From Johansen K, Daines M, Howey T, et al: Objective criteria accurately predict amputation following lower extremity trauma. J Trauma 30:568–573, 1990, with permission.

Replantation in a child is expected to have improved neurologic function. Replantation should be considered only when the amputation is a single-level, clean transection without crush or avulsion injury and warm ischemia time is less than 6 hours.

30. What are absolute contraindications for lower extremity replantation?
Poor baseline health, multilevel injury to a joint that results in immobility of the knee or ankle, warm ischemic time greater than 6 hours, and older age.

31. Are there any other considerations for the use of an amputated part?
You should not discard any tissue until you consider its possible use in reconstruction of the injured patient. Certainly nerve grafts, skin grafts, and bone grafts can be borrowed from the amputated part to reconstruct other injured extremities. Muscle flaps or foot fillet flaps can be used to cover below-knee amputation stumps that otherwise would need conversion to an above-knee stump.

32. In planning flap coverage of the lower extremity, what considerations are involved for concomitant or future bone reconstruction?
- Shortening of the limb length to decrease the need for intercalary bone graft or flap coverage
- Subsequent bone grafting that may require a posterior lateral approach or reelevation of the soft tissue flap
- Placement of a methylmethacrylate antibiotic-impregnated spacer followed by subsequent bone grafting
- Ilizarov bone transport
- Immediate nonvascularized or vascularized bone graft

33. Can bone transport (Ilizarov technique) be done across or through a free flap?
Yes. The rate of bone transport with movement of wires through a flap at 1 mm/day has not been shown to be detrimental to overlying soft tissue coverage, including free flaps.

34. Why may free flaps fail in the leg?
Failure is rare in fresh wounds, which have a flap patency rate of approximately 95% or greater and an infection rate of 1.5%. However, the infection rate is much increased in more chronic wounds (longer than 5 days). The flap survival rate in a chronic wound may be as low as 80% with significant take-back rates. The increased complication and failure rates in more chronic wounds is due to a combination of factors, including contamination, infection, and damaged lymphatics and veins. Significant tissue edema, perivascular fibrosis, and valvular incompetence may contribute to this difficulty. Godina demonstrated good evidence for the benefits of achieving soft tissue wound coverage within 5 days after open fracture. This approach minimizes infection and maximizes flap survival.

35. How do you determine the zone of injury when preparing recipient vessels?
The zone of injury would be expected to be larger with high energy injuries. However, local signs during the dissections will help to determine the zone of injury. These signs are intimal petechiae, vessel wall fibrosis, and poor quality of bleeding from the recipient vessels.

36. Provide an appropriate algorithm for primary operative care of lower extremity trauma.
See Figure 93-1.

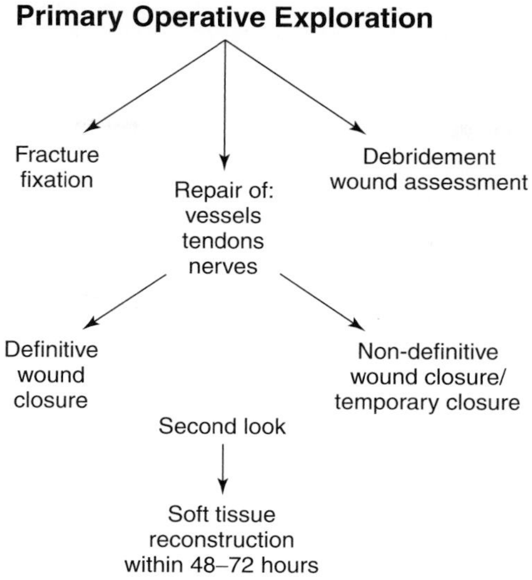

Primary Operative Exploration

Figure 93-1. Algorithm for primary operative care of lower extremity trauma.

37. **Is a muscle or a fasciocutaneous flap better for open fracture treatment?**
Mathes et al. cite better healing and adherence in an infected wound with a muscle flap. Overall, however, the best choice still is unclear. Muscle seems to conform better to regular cavities and to adhere or fibrose better than does a fasciocutaneous flap. Fasciocutaneous flaps, however, seem to suit most wounds well and to heal equally well; they also can be transferred as a sensate flap and are much thinner and cosmetically superior. The fasciocutaneous flap has the additional advantage of providing easier reoperations, if necessary, such as for an ankle fusion, bone graft, or nail removal.

BIBLIOGRAPHY

Anthony JP, Mathes SJ, Alpert BS: The muscle flap in the treatment of chronic lower extremity osteomyelitis: Results in patients over 5 years after treatment. Plast Reconstr Surg 88:311–318, 1991.

Arnez ZM: Immediate reconstruction of the lower extremity—An update. Clin Plast Surg 18:449–457, 1991.

Attinger CE, Evans KK, Bulan E, et al: Angiosomes of the foot and ankle and clinical implications for limb salvage: Reconstruction, incisions, and revascularization. Plast Reconstr Surg 117(7 Suppl):261S–293S, 2006.

Baumeister SPS, Spierer R, Berdmann D, et al: A realistic complication analysis of 70 sural artery flaps in a multi morbid patient group. Plast Reconstr Surg 112:129–140.

Bosse MJ, McCarthy ML, Jones AL, et al., and the Lower extremity Assessment Project (Leap) Study Group: The insensate foot following severe lower extremity trauma: An indication for amputation? J Bone Joint Surg 87:2601–2608, 2005.

DeFranzo AJ, Argenta LC, Marks MW et al: The use of vacuum-assisted closure therapy for the treatment of lower-extremity wounds with exposed bones. Plast Reconstr Surg 108:1184–1191, 2001.

Fix RJ, Vasconez LO (eds): Reconstruction of the Lower Extremity. Clin Plast Surg Philadelphia, WB Saunders, 1991.

Fix RJ, Vasconez LO: Fasciocutaneous flaps in reconstruction of the lower extremity. Clin Plast Surg 18:571–582, 1991.

Godina M: Early microsurgical reconstruction of complex trauma of extremities. Plast Reconstr Surg 78:285–292, 1986.

Gustilo RB, Mendoza RM, Williams DN: Problems in the management of type III (severe) open fractures: A new classification of type III open fractures. J Trauma 24:742–746, 1987.

Johansen K, Daines M, Howey T, et al: Objective criteria accurately predict amputation following lower extremity trauma. J Trauma 30:568–573, 1990.

Mann RA: Tarsal tunnel syndrome. Orthop Clin North Am 5:109–115, 1974.

Masquelet AC, Romana MC, Wolf G: Skin island flaps supplied by the axis of the sensitive superficial nerves: Anatomic study and clinical experience in the leg. Plast Reconstr Surg 89:1115–1121, 1992.

May JW Jr, Rohrich RJ: Foot reconstruction using free microvascular muscle flaps with skin grafts. Clin Plast Surg 13:681–689, 1986.

Walton RL, Bunkis J: The posterior calf fasciocutaneous free flap. Plast Reconstr Surg 74:76–85, 1984.

LEG ULCERS

Norman Weinzweig, MD, FACS; Russell Babbitt III, MD; and Raymond M. Dunn, MD

1. What are the most common chronic wounds seen in our population?

Leg ulcers. They may result in cellulitis, osteomyelitis, gangrene, amputation, and even death. Leg ulcers know no social bounds, crippling all patients, including those in their prime working years, with extraordinary morbidity and costs to society.

2. How often is ulceration the precursor to amputation?

Ulceration is the most common precursor to amputation (84% of cases).

3. What is the differential diagnosis of leg ulcers?

The differential diagnosis of lower extremity ulcers is extensive. Included are many common (and some uncommon) causes; however, the listing in Box 94-1 is by no means complete.

Box 94-1. Differential Diagnosis for Lower Extremity Ulceration

Vascular Disease
Arteriosclerosis obliterans
Thromboangiitis obliterans
Hypertension
Livedo reticularis
Venous
    Chronic venous insufficiency
    Deep vein thrombosis

Lymphatic
Elephantiasis nostra (lymphedema)

Vasculitis
Lupus erythematosus
Rheumatoid arthritis
Periarteritis nodosa
Allergic vasculitis

Metabolic Disease
Diabetes mellitus
Necrobiosis lipoidica diabeticorum
Pyoderma gangrenosum
Porphyria cutanea tarda
Gout

Hematologic Disease
Sickle cell anemia
Thalassemia
Hypercoagulable states
Deficiency of:
    Antithrombin III
    Protein C
    Protein S
Polycythemia vera
Leukemia

Drugs
Halogens
Ergotism
Methotrexate

Burns
Thermal
Electrical
Chemical

Infectious Disease
Bacterial
Fungal (coccidiomycosis, blastomycosis, histoplasmosis, sporotrichosis)
Tuberculosis
Syphilis

Tumors
Squamous cell carcinoma (Marjolin's ulcer)
Basal cell carcinoma
Kaposi's sarcoma
Lymphoma (mycosis fungoides)

Insect Bites
Brown recluse spider
Sandfly

Other
Trauma
Radiation
Frostbite
Weber-Christian disease
Lichen planus
Trophic ulcers
Factitial (self-induced)

Box 94-2. Evaluation of the Patient with Lower Extremity Ulcers

History
Ulcer specific
  Onset
  Location
  Size
  Depth
  Drainage
  Infection
Previous treatment
  Surgical
  Nonsurgical
Ambulatory status
Vascular status
  Claudication
  Rest pain
Shoe wear
Past medical history
  Tobacco use
  Diabetes mellitus
  Injury
  Deep vein thrombosis
  Chronic venous insufficiency
  Collagen vascular disease
  Sickle cell anemia

Physical Examination
Atrophic changes
Skin temperature
Sensation/neurologic status
Complete vascular examination
Ankle–brachial indexes
Limb or foot deformity

Diagnostic Studies
Blood tests
  Culture and sensitivity
  Complete blood count
  Hemoglobin A^{1C}
  Erythrocyte sedimentation rate
Radiologic examination
  Plain radiographs
  Computed tomographic scan
  Magnetic resonance imaging/angiography
  Bone scan
Noninvasive arterial/venous studies
  Pulse-volume recording
  Photoplethysmography
Bone biopsy
Formal angiographic evaluation
Rheumatologic workup if systemic or autoimmune illness is suspected

4. **How do you evaluate a patient who presents with leg ulcers?**
The elements of a thorough history, physical examination, and diagnostic workup for leg ulcer patients are outlined in Box 94-2.

5. **What are the goals of leg ulcer treatment?**
  - Healing of ulcer within a reasonable period
  - Return to ambulation as soon as possible
  - Institution of long-term preventative measures against recurrence
  - Ensuring patient tolerance and compliance with the treatment regimen

6. **What is the most common cause of leg ulceration?**
Ambulatory venous hypertension is responsible for the overwhelming majority of leg ulcers, accounting for 70% to 90% of all cases. Twenty-seven percent of the adult population has lower extremity venous abnormalities, 2% to 5% have clinical manifestations of superficial or deep venous insufficiency, and 1.5% (more than a half-million people in the United States) have frank ulceration. Up to 10% of patients with ulcers have concomitant arterial occlusive disease.

7. **What is venous hypertension?**
Venous hypertension occurs when the blood pressure inside the veins, which is normally 15 mm Hg in a resting supine position, is elevated to a pathologic level over a prolonged period.

8. **What causes venous hypertension?**
Venous hypertension is caused by incompetent valves in the veins of the legs. The most common cause of abnormally functioning valves is a history of blood clots in the legs (thrombophlebitis) and the breakdown of the clots, which damages the delicate valves, particularly their ability to sustain the column of blood from the foot to the heart.

9. **How do you diagnose venous hypertension?**
In the past the gold standard for evaluation was the venogram, an invasive test. Venograms are rarely performed today. Many noninvasive tests can evaluate the anatomy and function of the veins of the leg. The most common and widely used test is duplex ultrasound, which in experienced hands can assess the anatomy as well as the function of veins. Photoplethysmography and air plethysmography are noninvasive tests that attempt to measure how quickly blood flows backward or refills the leg when the blood moves from the supine to the upright position. They are general measures of valvular incompetence and venous hypertension.

10. Name the major veins of the leg.

The major veins of the leg accompany the major arteries: the anterior tibial, posterior tibial, and peroneal veins. These are the deep veins of the leg, or the deep venous system. The greater and lesser saphenous veins make up the superficial system of veins.

11. Describe the anatomy of the veins of the leg.

The deep veins of the leg are paired and travel with the named artery; they are called *venae comitantes*. The deep veins surround the artery and are connected to each other by small crossing branches, much like the rungs on a ladder. The superficial veins do not travel specifically with significant arteries and are not paired. Both the deep and superficial veins have valves that direct the flow of blood toward the heart and communicate between connecting perforating veins. When the valves of these veins do not function properly, a host of abnormalities may develop in the local area, the most significant of which is an open wound or venous ulcer.

12. What are perforating veins?

Perforating veins connect the superficial and deep systems of venous drainage of the leg. Perforating veins run predominantly between the greater saphenous and posterior tibial veins but are found to a lesser extent throughout the leg between the superficial and deep systems. The perforators on the medial leg (posterior tibial) generally contribute to leg ulceration in this area when they are incompetent or their valves do not work.

13. What is the difference between "primary" and "secondary" chronic venous disorders?

Primary chronic venous insufficiency encompasses all chronic venous disorders that are not associated with an identifiable etiology to explain the dysfunction. Primary disorders are thought to result from structural and biochemical abnormalities of the vein wall.

Secondary chronic venous disorders, also called *postthrombotic syndrome,* are those that follow an episode (or episodes) of acute deep vein thrombosis. The morphologic changes that occur within the lumen of the vein due to recanalization lead to venous hypertension and reflux. Currently, the best means to avoid secondary chronic venous disorders hinges on early and aggressive treatment of proximal deep vein thrombosis.

14. What are varicose veins?

Varicose veins are dilated, tortuous veins of the superficial system (subcutaneous).

15. What is a varicose ulcer?

Patients with varicose veins who have normal deep veins may develop leg ulceration with prolonged lack of treatment. In such a case, surgical removal of the incompetent superficial veins (ligation and stripping of varicose veins) is effective treatment of the leg ulceration, which then should respond well to conservative care or simple skin grafting.

16. What are the etiology and pathogenesis of venous ulcers?

The etiology and pathophysiology of venous ulcers are not completely understood. Current concepts include the loss of venous valvular competence in the deep and/or superficial venous systems, leading to venous hypertension. Prolonged venous hypertension promotes the extravasation of protein-rich edema fluid and red blood cells into the subcutaneous tissues of the lower leg. A pericapillary fibrin cuff functions as a diffusion barrier to oxygen, cytokine, and nutrient exchange at a cellular level. In addition, inflammation caused by chronic red blood cell extravasation (hemosiderin deposition) and leukocyte trapping in the tissue bed leads to the densely scarred, fibrotic, hyperpigmented skin and subcutaneous tissue changes known as *lipodermatosclerosis* ("brawny edema"). Lipodermatosclerotic tissue is poorly vascularized, is easily traumatized, and is prone to slow, poor wound healing with frequent ulcer recurrence.

17. Describe the role of inflammation in the development and perpetuation of chronic venous ulcers.

Traditionally, hypoxia was believed to be a primary factor in the development of venous ulceration due to a diffusion barrier created by the pericapillary fibrin cuffs found in chronic venous insufficiency. It has since been shown that hypoxia does not exist to the degree expected, and in many cases the tissue may not be hypoxic at all. Investigations into the biochemical and molecular characteristics of chronic venous disease suggest that local inflammation, as a direct result of deranged venous flow, plays a critical role in the development and propagation of lipodermatosclerosis and venous ulceration. Evidence suggests that increased venous pressure, turbulent blood flow, and altered shear stresses within the veins lead to leukocyte activation and subsequent inflammation, with release of cytokines, growth factors, and abnormal collagen deposition in the most superficial tissues. It has also been shown that the fibrin cuff contains many extracellular matrix components, suggesting that these cuffs represent fibrosis rather than simple deposits of fibrin. Based on this information, it has been further suggested that these structures might actually trap growth factors, thereby slowing wound healing by preventing normal influx of mediators into the tissue bed.

18. **Where are venous ulcers located?**

Venous ulcers are generally located in the so-called *gaiter region* of the leg, which is between the medial and lateral malleoli and gastrocnemius musculotendinous junction. It is thought that perforating veins may transmit excessive pressure to the subcutaneous tissue with contraction of the calf muscle, predisposing to tissue damage. Ulcers also may be located on the foot, between the toes, and on the posterior calf, but these sites are unusual and should encourage consideration of other diagnostic possibilities.

19. **Describe conservative management of venous ulcers.**

Conservative management of leg ulcers consists of elastic compression to reduce edema, prolonged bed rest with leg elevation, Unna boot application, local wound care with frequent dressing changes, and hygiene. This approach requires a lifestyle change that often is impractical. None of these modalities corrects the underlying pathophysiology.

20. **What is an Unna boot?**

Compression bandaging with materials impregnated with various paste substances such as calamine and zinc oxide, wrapped from the toes to the upper calf, including coverage of an open ulcer, was promulgated by Unna in the late nineteenth century for the treatment of venous ulcers. Any paste bandaging of venous leg ulcers or even dry compression bandaging has come to be known as an Unna boot.

21. **How does an Unna boot work?**

The value of compression bandaging in the treatment of venous ulceration has been recognized since it was used by Celsus. Various supportive dressing regimens have been developed and promulgated over the centuries. Compression has been shown to enhance fibrinolysis, reducing the pathologic deposition of fibrin in abnormal legs. No clear evidence indicates that the addition of emollients to treat the open wound and surrounding leg skin in patients with lipodermatosclerosis provides greater clinical benefit than compression alone.

22. **Describe the surgical management of venous ulcers.**

Traditional surgical approaches include skin grafting, varicose vein stripping, subfascial perforator ligation, valvuloplasty, and vein segment transposition and transplantation. Skin grafting is associated with poor long-term results and recurrence rates of up to 43%. Vein stripping usually deals with isolated superficial valvular insufficiency, which rarely causes ulceration. Perforator ligation is associated with frequent wound complications (2% to 44%) and high recurrence rates (6% to 55%). Valvuloplasty has demonstrated good results in cases of primary valvular incompetence. Valve transposition and transplantation have demonstrated poor results in cases of postthrombotic recanalization. Although these surgical approaches may improve the regional venous hemodynamics of the lower leg, none addresses the irreversibly scarred lipodermatosclerotic bed.

23. **What is a Linton flap?**

It is generally believed that perforating veins between the posterior tibial (deep) and saphenous veins (superficial) contribute to venous leg ulceration. In 1938, Linton described an operation to divide the perforating veins in the hope that it would prevent the occurrence of ulceration. Since that time, the ligation of perforating veins has commonly borne the eponym Linton flap. The operation consists of an incision parallel and 2 cm posterior to the medial tibial border from the medial malleolus to midcalf prominence (gastrocnemius bulge). The deep muscle fascia is divided, and all perforating veins are ligated. Currently, this operation is performed endoscopically whenever technically feasible to avoid wound-healing complications associated with the original open operation.

24. **Who should get a skin graft for a venous leg ulcer?**

Patients who have venous leg ulcers should undergo diagnostic evaluation to confirm the status of competence of the deep veins (see Question 8). Superficial venous insufficiency with ulceration (approximately 10% of patients with ulcers) can generally be treated successfully by skin grafting (and removing pathologic superficial and communicating veins). Elderly patients who do not respond to conservative treatment of ulcers may be candidates for skin grafts.

25. **What are the goals for long-term cure of recalcitrant venous ulcers?**

Restoration of normal venous hemodynamics at the level of and in the region of the venous ulcer, and complete removal of the ulcer and all surrounding lipodermatosclerotic skin and subcutaneous tissue.

26. **What is the role of free tissue transfer in the management of venous ulcers?**

Dunn et al. and Weinzweig and Schuler reported their experience with the use of fasciocutaneous and muscle free flaps, respectively, in the treatment of recalcitrant venous ulcers. Both groups found that free tissue transfer provides a long-term cure by replacing the diseased lipodermatosclerotic tissue bed with healthy tissue containing multiple, competent microvenous valves and a normal microcirculation, thereby improving regional hemodynamics. In addition, the transfer can be accomplished in one reconstructive procedure with excellent results. Both groups reported no recurrence of venous ulceration within the flaps. In a few cases, failing to excise all of the liposclerotic tissue led to breakdown and slow healing of the flaps at the margins. Each of these cases eventually healed with conservative measures.

27. Who should get a free flap for a venous leg ulcer?

Patients with deep venous insufficiency, localized recurrent ulceration, and liposclerotic (scarred) tissue benefit from a subfascial excision of the ulcer and scarred tissue and reconstruction with a tissue replacement microvascular flap.

28. What kind of free flap is best for a venous ulcer?

Multiple tissue types have been used successfully to reconstruct leg ulcer defects, including fasciocutaneous flaps, muscle flaps with skin grafts, and omental flaps with skin grafts. Flap selection is commonly based on available donor sites as well as the size and extent of the ulcer defect that is expected after excision.

29. What intrinsic role does the flap tissue play in treatment of venous ulcers?

Fasciocutaneous and muscle free flaps contain multiple valves in their venous systems. These valves may provide the limited flap area with some long-term protection from reulceration, essentially "curing" the chronic condition in the proper surgical candidate. Aharinejad et al. and Taylor et al. have done excellent anatomic studies of the microvenous valvular anatomy of the human dorsal thoracic fascia and various muscle flaps, respectively.

30. How does one approach the patient with mixed arterial and venous ulcers?

Identification of patients with mixed venous and arterial disease and ulceration is of critical importance, as many therapies aimed at treating venous ulcers can have catastrophic effects, such as critical ischemia with limb loss, when arterial diseases is also present. Arterial disease may coexist with venous ulceration in up to 20% of patients, mandating careful consideration and investigation before instituting a treatment regimen. In patients with moderate arterial disease, use of modified compression therapy with decreased pressure has been suggested; however, in patients with severe arterial occlusive disease, the first priority should be revascularization and restoration of arterial inflow. Humphreys et al. reported a series of 2011 ulcerated legs in which 1416 had venous reflux. Among these, 193 also had moderate arterial disease (ankle–brachial index [ABI] >0.5 to 0.85) and 31 had severe arterial disease (ABI <0.5). Patients who had moderate disease were treated with a modified compression stocking regimen (30 mm Hg at the ankle instead of 40 mm Hg), whereas those with severe disease were referred for angiography and potential revascularization prior to instituting any therapy aimed at treating the ulcers.

31. What is the CEAP classification?

The CEAP (clinical-etiology-anatomy-pathophysiology) system was developed by the American Venous Forum in 1994 (revised in 2004) with the goal of providing a comprehensive and objective way to classify chronic venous disease and standardize reporting in the literature.

32. How is the CEAP classification used?

Clinical stage is described by indicating the clinical manifestation of the disease followed by the subscript A (asymptomatic) or S (symptomatic). Etiology is broken down based upon the underlying cause as congenital, primary, secondary, or unknown. Anatomic location of the disease specifies whether it involves the superficial, deep, or perforating veins of the leg. The pathophysiology category further stratifies the disease by denoting the presence or absence of reflux or obstruction within the involved veins. The specific classifications are listed in Box 94-3.

For example, $C_{4b,s}$, E_p, $A_{s,p}$, P_r describes a symptomatic patient who has lipodermatosclerosis or atrophie blanche of primary origin involving superficial and perforating veins in which reflux has been confirmed. An advanced version of this classification also specifies the veins in which the pathology has been identified, with specific numbers corresponding to venous segments of the lower extremity.

33. What are the relationships among ulceration, diabetes, arterial occlusive disease, and amputation?

- 50% to 70% of leg amputations are secondary to diabetes.
- 28% of these amputations fail to heal, resulting in a higher level of amputation.
- 50% of patients undergo amputation of the contralateral leg within 2 to 5 years.
- 5-year survival rate after amputation is 40%.
- Personal, emotional, and socioeconomic consequences are enormous.

Box 94-3. CEAP Classification

Clinical Classification

C_0: No visible or palpable signs of venous disease
C_1: Telangiectases or reticular veins
C_2: Varicose veins
C_3: Edema
C_{4a}: Pigmentation or eczema
C_{4b}: Lipodermatosclerosis or atrophie blanche
C_5: Healed venous ulcer
C_6: Active venous ulcer
S: Symptomatic, including ache, pain, tightness, skin irritation, heaviness, muscle cramps, and other complaints attributable to venous dysfunction
A: Asymptomatic

Etiologic Classification

E_c: Congenital
E_p: Primary
E_s: Secondary (postthrombotic)
E_n: No venous cause identified

Anatomic Classification

A_s: Superficial veins
A_p: Perforator veins
A_d: Deep veins
A_n: No venous location identified

Pathophysiologic Classification

Basic CEAP
P_r: Reflux
P_o: Obstruction
$P_{r,o}$: Reflux and obstruction
P_n: No venous pathophysiology identifiable

CEAP, Clinical-etiology-anatomy-pathophysiology.
Adapted from Eklof B, Rutherford RB, Bergan JJ, et al: Revision of the CEAP classification of chronic venous disease. J Vasc Surg 40:1248–1252, 2004.

34. What is the etiopathogenesis of diabetic foot ulcers?

Diabetic foot ulcers arise primarily from neuropathy (altered proprioception, touch, or pain sensation), vascular disease (with associated ischemia), or both, often complicated by infection. Contributing factors include limited joint mobility, callus formation, high foot pressures, and increasing susceptibility to ulceration.

The neuropathic foot (poor sensation, good circulation) is characteristically healthy, well nourished, and hair bearing, with good dorsalis pedis and posterior tibial pulses and a high arch. Thick callus formation occurs on pressure points of the soles or toes. Bruising of the subcutaneous tissue and extravasation of blood beneath the calluses leave a rich culture media for local bacteria. The bacteria spread beneath the callus to the underlying joint capsule and metatarsal head, eventually resulting in osteomyelitis.

The ischemic foot (poor circulation, acute sensation), on the other hand, is dry, atrophic, scaly, hairless, and undernourished. It is cool to the touch with diminished or absent pulses. Infected areas often are painful to touch or pressure. Ulcers often have full-thickness skin necrosis in the center with a surrounding rim of erythema. Seldom is osteomyelitis or a true abscess found with pus located behind the necrotic tissue. Ischemia makes any lesion a serious condition that may quickly become a limb- or life-threatening problem.

35. Discuss two common misconceptions about diabetic foot infections.

- *Small Vessel Disease:* Arteriolar occlusive disease may cause ischemic lesions in the presence of normal pulses.
- *Endothelial Proliferation in Small Vessels:* Thickening of capillary basement membrane but not narrowing or occlusion.

An uncontrolled study by Goldenberg in 1959 indicated that amputation specimens from diabetics showed an increased incidence of arteriolar occlusion due to proliferation of endothelium and deposition of periodic acid–Schiff (PAS)–positive material. In 1984 this misconception was repudiated by LoGerfo and Coffman in a prospective controlled study of amputation specimens from diabetics and nondiabetics, and a similar prospective study using a sophisticated arterial casting technique failed to confirm Goldenberg's theory. No small artery or arteriolar occlusive lesion is associated with diabetes.

36. What is the fate of the contralateral foot in diabetics?

According to the classic study by Kucan and Robson of 45 patients followed for a minimum of 3 years, 22 (49%) patients developed a severe infection of the contralateral foot within 18 months. Fifteen (68%) of these patients required some type of amputation of the contralateral foot (3 toe, 2 ray, 4 transmetatarsal, 6 below knee). Fourteen of the patients (64%) with severe infections of both feet maintained bipedal ambulation.

37. What is the diabetic Charcot foot?

In 1868, Jean-Martin Charcot first described the neuropathic joint changes associated with tabes dorsalis, believing them to be a secondary effect of the neurologic deficit related to tertiary syphilis. In 1936, Jordan first described neuropathic arthropathy in diabetics, and in 1947 the Joslin Clinic published the first series of cases. Today diabetes is the most common cause of Charcot joints, which occur in 1:680 diabetic feet. Charcot neuroarthropathy of the foot is one of the most devastating consequences of diabetes, occurring in patients with an average duration of diabetes of 12 to 18 years; 18% of cases are bilateral. The radiographic findings are characterized by a severely destructive form of degenerative arthritis with simultaneous bone destruction, joint destruction, subluxation or dislocation, and fragmentation in addition to hypertrophic periosteal reaction.

Neuropathic arthropathy is a relatively painless, progressive, and degenerative arthropathy of single or multiple joints caused by the underlying neurologic deficits. The most frequent sites of involvement include the tarsometatarsal joints (60%), metatarsophalangeal joints (61%), and ankle joint (9%). On examination, the foot is grossly deformed with a typical rocker bottom subluxation of the midtarsal region or subluxations of the metatarsophalangeal joints and a high arch with cocked-up toes. The foot is erythematous, warm to the touch, and anhidrotic. The exact mechanism is unknown; however, it is hypothesized that hyperemia from autonomic neuropathy results in ligament laxity and osteolysis. With continued microtrauma due to sensory neuropathy, the bone and joint surfaces are destroyed. Loss of normal protective mechanisms subjects joints to extreme ranges of motion, resulting in capsular and ligamentous stretching, joint laxity with eventual dislocation, fracture, and bone and joint destruction. This process occurs in the presence of bounding pulses and elevated ABIs. The hyperemia or increased blood supply promotes resorption of the normal bone, creating a vicious cycle.

38. Describe the status of the arterial system in diabetics.

Not all diabetics have poor circulation. Moreover, many diabetics have absent femoral, popliteal, or pedal pulses yet do not manifest foot problems. This finding suggests that ischemia usually is only one component of the problem. The pathology of atherosclerosis for diabetic and nondiabetic patients is similar, but there are several distinguishing characteristics. Diabetics have a predilection for macrovascular occlusive disease involving the tibial/peroneal vessels between the knee and the foot, as evidenced by the fact that 40% of diabetics presenting with limb-threatening ischemia have a palpable popliteal pulse. The presence of a pulse does not mean that circulation is adequate. No occlusive small vessel disease of the diabetic foot precludes successful revascularization. Occlusive microvascular disease of the foot does not exist (see Question 35). Revascularization can restore tissue perfusion to the ischemic diabetic foot. Diabetics also have a diminished ability to develop collateral circulation. Calcification involving the intimal plaque and media (medial calcinosis or Monckeberg's sclerosis) frequently involves arteries at all levels but often spares the foot vessels. Medial calcinosis often gives erroneous ABIs and other noninvasive testing results. The classic indications for surgical intervention include incapacitating claudication, rest pain, and threatened limb loss (ulceration or gangrene).

39. Describe considerations in the surgical management of diabetic patients with a leg or foot ulcer.

- General medical condition
- Ambulatory status
- Peripheral circulation
- Compliance
- Local wound status

In addition, you must consider whether amputation is more favorable than revascularization and reconstructive procedures.

40. Describe the management of plantar forefoot ulcers.

Difficult wounds involving the plantar forefoot typically are located over the metatarsal heads. Ulceration often exposes bone and tendon and usually is managed by digital amputations. Forefoot ulcers often require toe fillet, ray, or transmetatarsal amputations. Metatarsal head resections reduce the amount of bone in this area, often allowing the wound to be closed primarily. With respect to the metatarsal head, conservative débridement is performed for the great toe, dorsal free-floating osteotomies for the second through fourth toes, and complete excision for the fifth toe. Soft tissue coverage can be obtained by plantar V-Y advancement flaps, island neurovascular toe flaps or toe fillet flap, and distally based muscle flaps. Free tissue transfer is sometimes necessary to salvage nonhealing transmetatarsal amputation stumps.

41. Describe the management of plantar midfoot ulcers.

Most difficult wounds in the plantar midfoot are associated with Charcot's disease. Fracture dislocations result in significant architectural changes, collapse of the arch, and alteration of the normal weight-bearing surface. Management often involves extensive resection of the ulcer, including scar tissue, bursal tissue, and underlying bony prominence. The wound is closed by filling its depths with a local muscle flap and a rotation advancement fasciocutaneous flap from the instep based on the medial plantar vessels. The muscle usually is the flexor digitorum brevis or abductor digiti minimi, depending on the location of the ulcer. More extensive defects arc managed by free tissue transfers.

42. Describe the management of hindfoot (heel) ulcers.

Hindfoot ulcers often require wide local osseus débridement, especially of the calcaneus. Such ulcers involve defects on the plantar and posterior aspect of the heel. For the plantar aspect, techniques include local rotation or advancement heel-pad tissue flaps, instep island pedicle flaps, turnover muscle flaps, and free tissue transfer. For the posterior heel, where the Achilles tendon is often exposed, skin grafts or local flaps (V-Y advancement, local rotation, distally based vascularized pedicle flaps) usually suffice. Often the posterior tibial artery is occluded, and free tissue transfer may be necessary with anastomosis to the dorsalis pedis vessels or in situ distal bypass graft. Well-vascularized coverage generally cannot be achieved by local arterialized flaps, such as the lateral calcaneal, dorsalis pedis, and fasciocutaneous instep island flaps. Free tissue transfer usually is required.

43. How are multiple tarsal and metatarsal ulcers managed?

Such ulcers often interfere with ambulation, and below-knee amputation usually is indicated.

44. What methods are used to prevent foot ulcers?

- Proper footwear: The most attractive shoes are not necessarily the best fitting
- Proper hygiene: Wash feet every day with mild soap and dry thoroughly, especially between toes
- Application of moisture cream everywhere except between toes
- Avoidance of self ("bathroom") surgery
- Avoidance of foot soaking
- Avoidance of heat, heating pads, and sleeping next to the stove or radiator
- Regular physician visits to control blood glucose, weight, and blood pressure
- Avoidance of smoking
- Daily exercise
- Periodic neurologic and vascular examinations

45. What is the bacteriology of lower extremity infections?

Most foot infections (70% to 80%) severe enough to require hospitalization are polymicrobial (two to six microorganisms), including gram-positive and gram-negative aerobic (and facultative) organisms as well as anaerobic isolates in 30% to 80% of cases. *Staphylococcus aureus* is recovered in one third to half of cases. *Enterococci* are seen in 25% to 30% of patients, almost always as mixed microbial flora. Among gram-negative organisms are *Proteus* species, *Escherichia coli*, and a variety of *Enterobacteriaceae. Pseudomonas aeruginosa* is less common but is important because organisms may be resistant to antimicrobials effective against other gram-negative bacilli. Anaerobic species include gram-positive cocci *(Peptococci, Peptostreptococci),* bacilli *(Clostridium* species), and gram-negative bacteria *(Bacteroides* species).

46. What are the basic rules for treating any lower extremity infection?

- Absolute bed rest
- Administration of appropriate antibiotics
- Regulation of diabetes
- Adequate drainage
- Adequate wound culture
- Appropriate wound care

47. What is the role of the vascular surgeon and plastic surgeon in salvage of the diabetic foot?

The limb salvage rates in diabetics with difficult foot wounds have increased significantly because of the close collaboration of plastic surgeons and vascular surgeons. This collaboration is largely due to a better understanding of the blood supply in the foot, which allows a wider arsenal of foot flaps as well as more successful revascularization. The recent role of free tissue transfer, which facilitates the closure of wounds of any size in any location, is especially important. The goal is stable wound coverage and bipedal ambulation.

48. Describe the rehabilitation team for the diabetic foot.
- Podiatrist for patient education, preventive maintenance, orthotics, and special shoes
- Physical therapist for return to normal activity, gait training to prepare for a prosthesis, and prophylactic exercises to maintain body tone
- Nutritionist for advice on diet needs
- Surgeon to ensure proper wound healing and proper prosthetics
- Endocrinologist to make the final decision about diabetes management

49. Describe the nature of sickle cell ulcers.
Sickle cell ulcers occur in patients with homozygous sickle cell disease (0.5% to 3% of the black population in North America). Disabling ulcerations develop in 25.7% to 73.6% of patients. Ulcerations of the lower extremities are chronic, recurrent, excruciatingly painful, and disabling. They occur in areas of marginal vascularity where minor abrasions become foci of inflammation, which in turn cause decreased local oxygen tension, sickling of red cells, increased blood viscosity, and thrombosis with consequent ischemia, tissue breakdown, and further inflammation. This vicious cycle, initiated spontaneously or by relatively insignificant trauma, results in the replacement of normal tissue by scar tissue, a permanent *locus minor resistentiae*.

50. What role does skin grafting play in the management of sickle cell ulcers?
Unfortunately, skin grafting is not an answer to this frustrating clinical problem. Skin grafting does not alter the underlying pathophysiology or increase the blood supply to the involved region. Despite adequate wound care, exchange transfusion to lower the percentage of hemoglobin S, and skin grafting, as many as 97.4% of ulcers recur at the same site within 2 years. An average hospital stay of 55 days is required to treat each ulceration.

51. What other reconstructive options are available for patients with homozygous sickle cell disease?
A paucity of fasciocutaneous, muscle, or musculocutaneous flaps are reliable, well vascularized, and locoregional. Free tissue transfer is the reconstructive procedure of choice for defects of the lower third of the leg. However, the key question is whether the obligate period of ischemia inherent in free tissue transfer inevitably dooms a flap to failure.

52. What is the role of free tissue transfer for limb salvage in patients with homozygous sickle cell disease?
Weinzw eig et al. reported a series of successful free flaps in patients with homozygous sickle cell disease. Special perioperative measures were taken to optimize the chances of a successful outcome. The obligate period of ischemia did not inevitably doom the flap to failure. Perioperative measures include the following: Exchange transfusion to lower hemoglobin S to below 30%
- Maintenance of hematocrit at 31% to 35%
- Intraoperative flap washout and perfusion with warm heparinized saline–dextran solution
- Administration of dextran and aspirin intraoperatively and postoperatively
- Prophylactic topical and systemic antipseudomonal antibiotics
- Supplemental oxygen
- Warm ambient room temperature

53. Is there any evidence to support vacuum-assisted closure in the treatment of chronic leg ulcers?
Yes. A prospective, randomized controlled trial by Vuerstaek et al. followed 60 patients with chronic leg ulcers who were assigned to receive either vacuum-assisted closure (VAC) dressing or conventional compressive therapy. In the VAC group, median time to complete wound closure was 29 days compared with 45 days in the control group ($P = .0001$). A secondary end point in this study was the amount of time to prepare the wound bed for skin grafting, defined as 100% coverage of the wound bed with granulation tissue. The authors found that, using VAC therapy, the median time to wound bed preparation was 7 days compared with 17 days in the control group ($P = .005$). There also was a significant difference in median percentage of successful skin grafts and total nursing time consumption between the two groups (longer in the control arm). However, there was no significant difference between the groups with respect to ulcer recurrence at 1 year.

Bibliography

Aharinejad S, Dunn RM, Fudem GM, et al: The microvenous valvular anatomy of the human dorsal thoracic fascia. Plast Reconstr Surg 99:1–9,1997.

Banis JC Jr, Richardson D, Den JW Jr, Acland RD: Microsurgical adjuncts in salvage of the ischemic and diabetic lower extremity. Clin Plast Surg 19:881–893, 1992.

Bergan JJ, Schmid-Schonbein GW, Smith PD, et al: Chronic venous disease. N Engl J Med 355:488–498, 2006.

Bergan JJ, Yao JST: Venous Disorders. Philadelphia, WB Saunders, 1991.

Chen WYJ, Rogers AA: Recent insights into the causes of chronic leg ulceration in venous diseases and implications on other types of chronic wounds. Wound Repair Regen 87:529–535, 1991.

Chowdary RP, Celani VJ, Goodreau JJ, et al: Free tissue transfers for limb salvage utilizing in situ saphenous vein bypass conduit as the inflow. Plast Reconstr Surg 87:529–535, 1991.

Cikrit DF, Nichols WK, Silver D: Surgical management of refractory venous stasis ulceration. J Vasc Surg 7:473–477, 1988.

Colen LB: Limb salvage in the patient with severe peripheral vascular disease: The role of microsurgical free-tissue transfer. Plast Reconstr Surg 79:389–395, 1987.

Dunn RM, Fudem GM, Walton RL, et al: Free flap valvular transplantation for refractory venous ulceration. J Vasc Surg 19:525–531, 1994.

Eklof B, Rutherford RB, Bergan JJ, et al: for the American Venous Forum International Ad Hoc Committee for Revision of the CEAP Classification. Revision of the CEAP classification for chronic venous disorders: Consensus statement. J Vasc Surg 40:1248–1252, 2004.

Goldenberg S, Alex M, Joshi RA, Blumenthal HT: Nonatheromatous peripheral vascular disease of the lower extremity in diabetes mellitus. Diabetes 8:261, 1959.

Hume M: Venous ulcers, the vascular surgeon, and the Medicare budget. J Vasc Surg 16:671–673, 1992.

Humphreys ML, Stewart AHR, Gohel MS, Taylor M, Whyman MR, Poskitt KR: Management of mixed arterial and venous leg ulcers. Br J Surg 94:1104–1107, 2007.

Kistner RL, Eklof B, Masuda EM: Diagnosis of chronic venous disease of the lower extremities: The "CEAP" classification. Mayo Clin Proc 71:338–345, 1996.

Kozak GP, Campbell DR, Frykberg RG, Habershaw GM: Management of Diabetic Foot Problems, 2nd ed. Philadelphia, WB Saunders, 1995.

Kucan JO, Robson MC: Diabetic foot infections: Fate of the contralateral foot. Plast Reconstr Surg 77:439–441, 1986.

Lai C-S, Lin S-D, Yand CC, et al: Limb salvage of infected diabetic foot ulcers with microsurgical free tissue transfer. Ann Plast Surg 26:212–220, 1991.

LoGerfo FW, Coffman JD: Vascular and microvascular disease of the foot in diabetes. N Engl J Med 311:1615–1619, 1984.

Meissner MH, Eklof B, Coleridge Smith P, et al: Secondary chronic venous disorders. J Vasc Surg 46:S68–S83, 2007.

Meissner MH, Gloviczki P, Bergan JJ, et al: Primary chronic venous disorders. J Vasc Surg 46:S54–S67, 2007.

O'Donnell TF: Chronic venous insufficiency: An overview of epidemiology, classification, and anatomic considerations. Semin Vasc Surg 1:60–65, 1988.

Pascarella L, Schonbein GW, Bergan JJ: Microcirculation and venous ulcers: A review. Ann Vasc Surg 19:921–927, 2005.

Serletti JM, Deuber MA, Guidera PM, et al: Atherosclerosis of the lower extremity and free-tissue reconstruction for limb salvage. Plast Reconstr Surg 96:1136–1144, 1995.

Serletti JM, Hurwitz SR, Jones JA, et al: Extension of limb salvage by combined vascular reconstruction and adjunctive free-tissue transfer. J Vasc Surg 18:972–978, 1993.

Shestak KC, Fitz DG, Newton ED, Swartz WM: Expanding the horizons of severe peripheral vascular disease using microsurgical techniques. Plast Reconstr Surg 85:406–411, 1990.

Vuerstaek JDD, Vainas T, Wuite J, Nelemans P, Neumann MHA, Veraart JCJM: State-of-the-art treatment of chronic leg ulcers: A randomized controlled trial comparing vacuum-assisted closure (V.A.C.) with modern wound dressings. J Vasc Surg 44:1029–1037, 2006.

Weinzweig N, Schuler J, Marschall M, Koshy M: Lower limb salvage by microvascular free-tissue transfer in patients with homozygous sickle cell disease. Plast Reconstr Surg 96:1154–1161, 1995.

Weinzweig N, Schuler J: Free tissue transfer in treatment of the recalcitrant chronic venous ulcer. Ann Plast Surg 38:611–619,1997.

95 CHAPTER

PRESSURE SORES

Mimis Cohen, MD, FACS, and
Sai S. Ramasastry, MD, FRCS, FACS

1. What is the pathophysiology of pressure ulcers?

Tissue pressures higher than the pressure of the microcirculation (32 mm Hg) cause ischemia. If the ischemic period is long enough or repeated frequently, the eventual outcome is tissue necrosis. Thus the prime mechanism of pressure ulceration is cellular ischemia.

2. What are the Braden scale and the Norton scale?

These scales and their modifications are validated risk assessment tools to identify patients at high risk for developing pressure ulcers. The Braden scale has been evaluated in diverse sites such as medical/surgical units, intensive care units, and nursing homes. The Norton scale has been tested with elderly patients in hospital settings.

3. What are the primary risk factors for developing pressure ulcers in chair-bound people or people with impaired ability to reposition?

- Immobility
- Incontinence
- Nutritional factors such as inadequate dietary intake and impaired nutritional status
- Altered levels of consciousness.

4. Which areas of the body are more prone to pressure ulcerations?

All areas around bony prominences are at risk. Most pressure ulcers occur on the ischial tuberosity (28%), trochanter (19%), and sacrum (17%). Heel ulcers have the highest incidence (9%) outside of the pelvic area.

5. What is the staging system for pressure sores?

See Table 95-1.

6. In patients with spinal cord injury, what is the pathophysiology of lower extremity spasms?

Spasticity develops because spinal reflex arcs are separated from the controlling influences of higher centers in the nervous system. Incoming fibers from muscle spindles end directly on motor cells as the afferent arm of myotatic or stretch reflexes; activation of such reflexes causes the muscle to contract.

7. How do you manage spasticity in paraplegic patients?

Spasticity can be managed pharmacologically and surgically. The most commonly used drugs include diazepam 10 to 40 mg/day and baclofen 40 to 80 mg/day. For spasticity refractory to medications, intrathecal phenol or alcohol is recommended. Neurosurgical alleviation with cordotomy or rhizotomy is indicated for severe cases not responsive to medical care.

Table 95-1. Pressure Sore Staging System

Stage I	Nonblanchable erythema of intact skin (heralding lesion of skin ulceration).
Stage II	Partial-thickness skin loss involving epidermis or dermis. The ulcer is superficial and presents clinically as an abrasion, blister, or shallow crater.
Stage III	Full-thickness skin loss involving damage to or necrosis of subcutaneous tissue that may extend down to, but not through, underlying fascia. The sore presents clinically as a deep crater with or without undermining of adjacent tissue.
Stage IV	Full-thickness skin loss with extensive destruction, tissue necrosis, or damage in muscle, bone, or supporting structures (e.g., tendon or joint capsule).

From U.S. Department of Health and Human Services: Pressure Ulcers in Adults: Prediction and Prevention. Clinical Practice Guideline No. 3, Publication 97-0047, 1992.

8. **What is the best modality for evaluation of pelvic osteomyelitis in patients with pressure sores?**
The best modality is bone biopsy, which should not be done through the ulcer but rather through healthy skin. Several biopsies from various areas of the pelvis are necessary when generalized pelvic osteomyelitis is suspected.

9. **What other tests are helpful in establishing the diagnosis of pelvic osteomyelitis?**
Several laboratory and imaging tests can be used, including erythrocyte sedimentation rate, white cell count, plain radiographs, computed tomography, and magnetic resonance imaging. Combined results of plain radiographs, white cell count, and erythrocyte sedimentation rate may have sensitivity as high as 89%.

10. **What is the treatment for pelvic osteomyelitis?**
Patients with established pelvic osteomyelitis need to be treated for 6 to 8 weeks with appropriate intravenous antibiotics. Repeat bone biopsies may be necessary to confirm successful treatment prior to extensive reconstructive procedures.

11. **How does vacuum-assisted closure assist in pressure sore care?**
   - Removes excess interstitial or third space fluid, decreases capillary afterload, and promotes better capillary circulation and inflow
   - Decreases bacterial colonization
   - Increases vascularity and granulation tissue formation
   - Reduces size of wound; in some instances complete closure can be achieved
   - Assists in management of underlying osteomyelitis

12. **How does the collection of third-space fluid interfere with wound healing?**
   - It mechanically compromises the microvasculature and lymphatic system.
   - Increases capillary and venous afterload, thus impeding the delivery of oxygen and nutrients.
   - Inhibitory factors and toxins are accumulated around the wound. These factors suppress the proliferation of keratinocytes, fibroblasts, and vascular endothelial cells.

13. **List the surgical steps for pressure sore closure.**
   - Drainage of all collections
   - Wide débridement of all devitalized and scarred soft tissue
   - Excision of the pseudobursa
   - Ostectomy of all involved bone
   - Careful hemostasis and suction drainage
   - Obliteration of all residual dead space with well-vascularized tissue (muscle, musculocutaneous, fasciocutaneous flaps)
   - Closure without tension

14. **What is the blood supply to the gluteus maximus muscle?**
The superior and inferior gluteal arteries (branches of the internal iliac) supply the superior and inferior portions of the muscle. The piriform muscle is interposed between the superior and inferior pedicles. Both pedicles cross from medial to lateral and enter the undersurface of the muscle.

15. **What are the various designs for the gluteus maximus musculocutaneous flap?**
The gluteus maximus flap can cover sacral and ischial pressure sores. For coverage of sacral pressure sores, the gluteus maximus flap usually is used as a sliding musculocutaneous flap, as a V-Y musculocutaneous advancement flap, or as a rotation flap. For coverage of an ischial pressure sore, the most common method is to detach the muscle laterally from the greater trochanter and rotate it medially to cover the ischium. With the V-Y advancement, the muscle can be detached completely from the greater trochanter. In nonparalyzed patients, the central portion of the iliotibial tract and the muscle should be left attached to the trochanter to preserve function of the muscle.

16. **What is the innervation of the gluteus maximus muscle? Can the gluteus maximus flap be used in nonparaplegic patients without functional deficit?**
The gluteus maximus receives innervation from the superior and inferior gluteal nerves. The inferior gluteal nerve is more dominant; it is the strongest external rotator and extensor of the hip. As long as the inferior gluteal nerve is left intact and the muscle is not completely detached from the iliotibial tract and the greater trochanter, function can be preserved in ambulatory patients.

17. **What are the advantages of the gluteal perforator flap versus the classic gluteus maximus design?**
   - Provides freedom in design and minimal donor site morbidity
   - Can be used in ambulatory patients

- Preserving the muscle provides the opportunity for repair of subsequent sores in paraplegic patients
- Can provide coverage for sacral, ischial, and trochanteric defects
- Can be used for defects in perineal and lumbosacral regions
- Minimal blood loss during dissection
- Various flaps can be concomitantly elevated from one donor site

18. **Which are the most significant anatomical considerations for the gluteal perforator flap?**
   - There are 20 to 25 perforators penetrating the gluteus maximus muscle.
   - The length of these vessels varies between 3 and 8 cm, with diameters ranging from 1 to 1.5 cm.
   - Large-caliber perforators are found in the parasacral and central portion of the gluteus maximus muscle.
   - According to Koshima, use of even one perforator can be sufficient for flap perfusion.

19. **Which are the most significant technical considerations for the gluteal perforator flap?**
   - Localization of the perforators around the sacrum is performed using a Doppler.
   - Flaps can be planned close to the defect and shaped as an island rectangular, elliptical, or triangular. Dimensions could vary according to the defect and can extend beyond the borders of the gluteus maximus muscle.
   - Flap dissection from the underlying muscle should proceed from the distal border of the flap to the proximal.
   - Major perforators are preserved and skeletonized by blunt dissection. If additional pedicle length is necessary, dissection of the vessels continues into the muscle.
   - Three to five perforators usually are preserved.
   - After inset of the flap, donor site is closed primarily.

20. **What is the blood supply to the gracilis musculocutaneous flap?**
   The dominant blood supply is the medial circumflex femoral artery, a branch of the profunda femoris. The pedicle courses from medial to lateral. It enters the undersurface of the muscle 10 to 12 cm inferior to the pubic tubercle.

21. **What is the blood supply of the lumbosacral back flap? What are its applications?**
   The lumbosacral or transverse back flap is based on the contralateral lumbar perforators, usually L1-L5. The flap covers a medium-size pressure sore of the sacral area. It includes only skin and subcutaneous tissue and does not provide adequate bulk. The lumbosacral flap is a secondary option for sacral pressure sores when other primary options are not available. The donor site needs to be skin grafted.

22. **What is the blood supply to the vastus lateralis muscle?**
   The descending branch for the lateral circumflex femoral artery, a branch of the profunda femoris. The vessel courses from medial to lateral. After emerging from beneath the rectus femoris muscle, it enters the anterior proximal belly of the vastus lateralis muscle approximately 10 cm inferior to the anterosuperior iliac spine.

23. **What is the blood supply to the rectus femoris muscle?**
   The blood supply of the rectus femoris muscle is derived from branches of the lateral circumflex femoral artery. The vessel courses from medial to lateral. Two to three branches enter the undersurface of the muscle at the proximal third.

24. **What is the blood supply to the gluteal thigh flap?**
   The blood supply to the gluteal thigh flap is the descending branch of the inferior gluteal artery. The surface landmark for flap design is the midpoint between the greater trochanter and the ischial tuberosity proximally. Distally, the flap can extend to the medial femoral condyle and the posterior border of the tensor fascia lata.

25. **What is the blood supply to the tensor fascia lata flap?**
   The blood supply to the tensor fascia lata flap is derived from a terminal branch of the lateral circumflex femoral artery from the profunda femoris artery, which supplies blood to the small tensor fascia lata muscle. The entire lateral thigh skin is vascularized by perforating arteries from this vessel.

26. **Describe the surgical anatomy and applications of the posteromedial thigh fasciocutaneous flap.**
   - There are approximately 60 musculocutaneous perforators from the gracilis and the adductor magnus perfusing the area of the posteromedial thigh.
   - The main perforator, a branch of the medial circumflex artery, perforates the deep fascia from the adductor magnus at a mean vertical distance of 8 cm (range 6 to 10 cm) from the pubic tubercle.
   - This flap is located in the vicinity of the ischial area. It is simple to raise, and its use causes no donor site morbidity.

27. Which flap can be used to cover perineal pressure sores?

In patients with an intact lower extremity, the gracilis muscle/musculocutaneous flap can be used. In patients with an urethrocutaneous fistula, the urethra should be reconstructed first over a stent, with a full-thickness skin graft tube. A gracilis muscle flap can then provide surface coverage. If the lower extremity is not present, the perineal defect can be covered with an inferiorly based rectus abdominis flap based on the deep inferior epigastric pedicle.

28. When is a total thigh flap recommended?

The total thigh flap should not be considered the optimal choice for management of primary sores. It is recommended for recurrent multiple pressure ulcers around the pelvis and perineum. Before reconstruction, coexisting pelvic osteomyelitis must be managed. A urethral fistula, if present in the perineum, should be repaired, or urine should be diverted before final reconstruction.

29. What measures does a successful total thigh flap include?

- Extensive débridement of all devitalized soft tissue and bone
- Careful planning of surgical incisions to maximize soft tissue use from the thigh and leg
- Amputation of leg at appropriate level (if extensive defect is present, you can extend the thigh leg flap almost to the level of the malleoli)
- Meticulous hemostasis and placement of multiple suction drains
- Obliteration of all residual spaces and a tension-free closure

30. Which are the indications and technical consideration for use of the rectus abdominis musculocutaneous flap in patients with pressure sores?

- Multiple and recalcitrant trochanteric and ischial pressure sores
- Alternative technique for closure and reconstruction to hip disarticulation and total thigh flap or to a free flap
- Extension of the overlying skin island at a minimum to the costal margin is necessary to provide coverage in the ischial area
- Ipsilateral, but contralateral flap designs also can be used when needed
- Division of the inguinal ligament provides for a relative increase in the flaps arc of rotation
- No clinical deficit secondary to sacrifice of the rectus muscle should be anticipated

31. What are the advantages of close collaboration between the plastic surgery and rehabilitation medicine services in the treatment of pressure sores?

- Decreased number of recurrences or new sores in the same patient
- Better patient education aids rehabilitation efforts
- Education of patients and their immediate families about skin care, pressure release cyclical maneuvers
- Close inspection of satisfactory conditions for wheelchairs and pressure-related devices
- Assistance with community reintegration

BIBLIOGRAPHY

Argenta LC, Morykwas MJ: Vacuum-assisted closure: A new method for wound control and treatment, Ann Plast Surg 38:536–576, 1997.

Braden BJ: Clinical utility of Braden Scale for predicting sure sore risks. Decubitus 2:44–46, 50–51, 1989.

Cannon BC, Cannon JP: Management of pressure ulcers. Am J Health System Pharm 61:1985–2005, 2004.

Colen SR: Pressure sores. In McCarthy JC (ed): Plastic Surgery, Vol 6. Philadelphia, WB Saunders, 1990, pp 3797–3838.

Coskunfirat OK, Ozgentas HE: Gluteal perforator flaps for coverage of pressure sores at various locations. Plast Reconstr Surg 113:2012–2017, 2004.

Kierney PC, Engrav L, Isik FF, Esselman PC, Cardenas DD, Rand RP: Results of 268 pressure sores in 158 patients managed jointly by the plastic surgery and rehabilitation medicine. Plast Reconstr Surg 102:765–772, 1998.

Lewis VL, Bailey H, Pulawski G, et al: The diagnosis of osteomyelitis in patients with pressure sores. Plast Reconstr Surg 81:229–232, 1988.

Lyder CH: Pressure ulcer prevention and management. JAMA 289:223–226, 2003.

Mancoll JS, Phillips LG: Pressure sores. In Achauer BM, Eriksson E, Guyron B, Colleman JJ III, Russel RC, Vander Kolk CA (eds): Plastic Surgery: Indications, Operations, Outcomes, Vol 1. St Louis, Mosby, 2000, pp 447–462.

Marschall MA, Dolezal RF, Cohen M: Pressure sores. Probl Gen Surg 6:687–698, 1989.

Marschall MA, Cohen M: Pressure sores. In Cohen M (ed): Mastery of Plastic and Reconstructive Surgery, Vol 2. Boston, Little, Brown, 1994, pp 1371–1386.

Mathes SJ, Nahai F: Clinical Applications for Muscle and Musculocutaneous Flaps. St. Louis, Mosby, 1982.

Mathes SJ, Nahai F: Reconstructive Surgery Principles: Anatomy and Techniques. Vol 1, pp 499–535, Vol 2, pp 1173–1206, 1271–1306. New York, Churchill Livingstone-Quality Medical Publishing, 1997.

McGraw JB, Arnold PG: Atlas of Muscle and Musculocutaneous Flaps. Norfolk, VA, Hampton Press, 1986.

Norton D: Calculating the risk reflections on the Norton Scale. Decubitus 2:24–31, 1989 [published erratum appears in Decubitus 2:10, 1989].

Roger J, Pickrell K, Georgiades N, et al: Total thigh flap for extensive decubitus ulcer. Plast Reconstr Surg 44:108–118, 1969.

U.S. Department of Health and Human Services: Pressure Ulcers in Adults: Prediction and Prevention. Clinical Practice Guideline No. 3, Publication 97-147, 1992.

LYMPHEDEMA

Arin K. Greene, MD, MMSc; Loren J. Borud, MD; and
Sumner A. Slavin, MD

1. What are lymphatics?

Endothelial-lined channels, derived from the outpouchings of veins, that travel with the venous system. Unlike blood vessels, lymphatics have a poorly defined basement membrane and large intercellular gaps that facilitate the diffusion of large proteins and lipids into the lumen.

2. Describe the anatomy of the lymphatic system.

The lymphatic system is part of the circulatory system. It consists of lymphatics that connect lymph nodes as well as aggregations of lymphoid tissue in the walls of the alimentary canal, tonsils, spleen, and thymus. Circulating lymphocytes are produced in these tissues, including myeloid aggregations in the red bone marrow. Lymphatics transporting lymph (L. *lympha*, clear water) toward a lymph node are called *afferent* lymphatics, whereas lymphatics leaving a lymph node are termed *efferent* vessels.

Like the venous system, the extremities contain both superficial and deep lymphatics. Lymphatics in the superficial dermis do not contain valves and drain into valved subdermal and subcutaneous lymphatics. The deep system is located below the muscular fascia and contains valves. The superficial and deep systems are connected at regional lymph nodes. The thoracic duct drains the majority of the body (lower extremities, left trunk, left upper extremity). The thoracic duct originates from the cisterna chyli (which drains the intestinal and aortic lymphatic trunks) at the level of L4 and empties into the left subclavian vein. The right lymphatic duct drains the right head and neck, right upper extremity, and right thorax into the right subclavian vein.

3. Are lymphatics present throughout the body?

No. Lymphatics are not found in the bone marrow, cartilage, cornea, central nervous system, intralobar liver, muscle, or tendon.

4. What are the functions of the lymphatic system?

- *Transportation of Fluid and Proteins from the Interstitial Space to the Vascular System.* Approximately 50% to 100% of circulating plasma proteins (20 L/day) leaves the bloodstream and is recycled. Ninety percent of fluid and protein is returned to the vascular system by venous capillaries. The remaining 10% of high-molecular-weight proteins and osmotically associated water are either reduced in size by macrophages to reenter venous capillaries or are returned to the circulation via lymphatics. Lymphatic flow is propelled by adjacent muscle contractions, venous pulsations, variations in intraabdominal and intrathoracic pressure, as well as valves that ensure unidirectional flow.
- *Transportation of Triglycerides and Chylomicrons in the Intestines.* Small lymphatic capillaries, the lacteals, drain the intestine and contain high fat content. The content of these lymphatics, termed *chyle* (Greek *chylos,* juice), is returned to the bloodstream by the thoracic duct.
- *Defense Mechanism Through the Clearance and Presentation of Foreign Material to the Immune System.* As lymph passes through nodes, particulate matter and microorganisms drained from an area are filtered and ingested by phagocytes and macrophages, preventing their entry into the bloodstream. In addition, when foreign proteins are drained by lymphatics, antibodies are produced as initial contact is made between the antigen and lymphocytes in the lymph node.

5. What is lymphedema?

Lymphedema is the accumulation of protein-rich fluid in the interstitial space due to lymphatic dysfunction. Lymphatic flow must be reduced by 80% before interstitial fluid begins to accumulate as compensatory mechanisms such as increased macrophage activity and spontaneous lymphovenous anastomoses are exhausted. Dysfunction can be due to hypoplastic (83%) or hyperplastic (17%) lymphatics. Elevated concentrations of interstitial protein cause inflammation and fibrosis, leading to a cycle of further damage to lymphatics, worsening inflammation, and an enlarged extremity. Chronic lymphedema leads to deposition of fat and fibrous tissue.

6. Does lymphedema affect the superficial, deep, or both areas of the extremity?

Lymphedema involves only the superficial tissues, as lymphatics are not present in the muscle of the deep extremity compartments. In addition, increased intralymphatic pressure leads to valvular incompetence and backflow into the dermal plexus. The deep lymphatic system is more resistant to backflow because the lymphatics are adjacent to contracting muscle and are enveloped in tight fascia.

7. Classify lymphedema.

See Table 96-1.

8. Describe the epidemiology of lymphedema.

Lymphedema may affect as many as 140 to 250 million people throughout the world. Lymphedema usually involves the lower extremity (90%), upper extremity (10%), or genitalia (<1%). However, lymphedema can occur almost anywhere in the body, including the face, trunk, and breast. The most common cause of lymphedema in developing countries is infection due to the parasite *Wuchereria bancrofti* (filariasis), which can cause "elephantitis." Treatment includes diethylcarbamazine, nonsteroidal antiinflammatory drugs (NSAIDs), and antihistamines. In the developed world, iatrogenic injury from the treatment of breast cancer is the most common inciting event. Lymphedema occurs in at least 8% of women after mastectomy, with as many as 38% developing lymphedema after axillary lymph node dissection and radiation. Nine percent of patients suffer bilateral lymphedema, and 40% of patients have progressive size of the extremity, although proximal extension occurs in only 7% of patients after the first year. Primary lymphedema affects women twice as often as men, usually involves the lower extremity, and is familial in 15% of patients. The most common type of primary lymphedema, lymphedema praecox, has a prevalence of approximately 1:100,000.

9. What is the differential diagnosis of lymphedema?

Other conditions that may cause increased limb size include venous stasis disease and lipedema. A swollen limb may be caused by systemic conditions that lead to fluid overload, such as cardiac and renal failure. In addition, disorders that result in low levels of intravascular proteins, such as nephrotic syndrome, hepatic failure, and malnutrition, will cause fluid accumulation in the extremity.

10. How do you diagnose lymphedema?

Approximately 90% of patients can be diagnosed by history and physical examination (Table 96-2). Patients may report a history of mastectomy and radiation, travel to a developing country, or trauma or surgery in the axilla or groin area. On physical examination, lymphedema is nonpitting, affects the feet and hands, usually is not painful, has minimal pigment change, rarely ulcerates, typically is unilateral, and has a fluid protein content of 1 to 5 g/dL. In addition, patients with lymphedema have a positive Stemmer sign, which is the inability to grasp the base of the second toe or finger due to thickening and fibrosis of the subcutaneous tissue.

In contrast, venous stasis disease typically has pitting edema, pain, pigment changes, ulceration, and fluid protein content less than 1 g/dL. Lipedema usually is bilateral and does not involve the distal extremity. Patients with lipedema also have a negative Stemmer sign because lipedema does not affect the hands or feet. Systemic causes of fluid accumulation in the extremities usually are bilateral and respond to diuretics and elevation.

Table 96-1. Classification of Lymphedema

PRIMARY (IDIOPATHIC)		SECONDARY (DUE TO INCITING EVENT)	
TYPE	CHARACTERISTICS	TYPE	EXAMPLES
Congenital (15%)	Present at birth Milroy's disease (inherited)	Infection	Parasite *Wuchereria bancrofti* Infections involving groin, axilla
Praecox (75%)	Between age 1 and 35 years Usually occurs at puberty Meigs' disease (inherited)	Iatrogenic	Division of lymphatics Excision of lymph nodes Radiation therapy
Tarda (10%)	Late onset after age 35 years	Trauma	Blunt Penetrating

		Systemic disorders	Autoimmune diseases
			Benign growths (external
			   compression)
			Malignancy (intralymphatic,
			   external compression)
			Metastasis to lymph nodes

Table 96-2. Differentiating Lymphedema from Other Causes of Swollen Extremity

	LYMPHEDEMA	VENOUS STASIS DISEASE	LIPEDEMA	SYSTEMIC DISEASE (CARDIAC, RENAL, HEPATIC FAILURE)
History and Physical Examination				
Foot/hand affected	+	+	−	+
Bilateral	−	−	+	+
Pain	−	+	−	±
Pigment change	−	+	−	±
Pitting edema	−	+	−	+
Responds to diuretics	−	+	−	+
Stemmer sign	+	+	−	+
Ulceration	−	+	−	±
Laboratory and Radiographic Investigation				
Fluid concentration >1 g/dL	+	−	−	−
Increased skin thickness (CT/MRI)	+	−	−	−
Large muscle compartment (CT/MRI)	−	+	−	−
Delayed flow on lymphoscintigram	+	−	−	−

CT, Computed tomography; *MRI,* magnetic resonance imaging.

11. **How do you measure the severity of lymphedema and follow treatment response?**
    Limb circumference should be measured every 5 cm during the initial consultation and at each visit to determine the severity of disease and the response to treatment. A 10% difference in limb circumference between the diseased and noninvolved extremity is mild disease, a 20% difference is moderate disease, and greater than 30% difference in limb circumference is severe lymphedema.

12. **What is the best imaging modality to confirm the diagnosis of lymphedema?**
    Lymphoscintigraphy has replaced lymphangiography as the gold standard for confirming the diagnosis of lymphedema. Lymphoscintigraphy is less invasive, more accurate, and does not risk allergic reaction to contrast dye or exacerbation of lymphedema. Lymphoscintigraphy has a sensitivity of 97% and a specificity of 100%. The test requires injection of technetium Tc99m-labeled antimony sulfur or albumin into the first or second interdigital web space of the affected extremity.

    Lymphangiogram may be indicated to determine the location of an anatomic occlusion for preoperative planning of a bypass procedure. However, injection of contrast dye into lymphatics worsens the disease; 32% of patients will have an increase in leg volume and 19% will develop lymphangitis. Computed tomographic scan can differentiate between lymphedema and venous stasis because lymphedema usually has a honeycomb appearance. In addition, lymphedema shows increased skin thickness with normal subfascial muscle compartments. Venous stasis disease, in contrast, has normal skin thickness and an increased size of the muscular compartment. Lipedema shows normal skin and muscular compartment thickness with an enlarged subcutaneous space.

13. **What are the complications of lymphedema?**
    Psychosocial morbidity is the most common sequela of lymphedema. Infection is the next most frequent problem. Because of lymphatic stasis and the subsequent destruction of the lymph node cortex, patients with lymphedema are prone to cellulitis following minor trauma. Patients with lower extremity lymphedema are 71 times more likely to develop cellulitis than are nonlymphedematous patients. Twenty-nine percent of patients with lymphedema will have had at least one infection during the previous year, leading to hospitalization in one fourth of cases. Other complications of lymphedema include diminished extremity function and epidermal lymph leak (lymphorrhea).

    Lymphangiosarcoma has an incidence of 0.5% in patients with lymphedema but may be as high as 10% in patients with severe lymphedema lasting for more than 10 years. Average survival is 19 months due to early metastasis. Because lymphangiosarcoma is resistant to chemotherapy and radiation, treatment is amputation. Lymphangiosarcoma in a lymphedematous upper extremity after mastectomy is termed *Stewart-Treves syndrome*.

14. How do you manage cellulitis in a lymphedematous extremity?

Cellulitis in an extremity with lymphedema may spread rapidly, causing sepsis and even death. Oral antibiotics should be started immediately, with a low threshold for admitting the patient for intravenous therapy. Patients must be educated about the prevention of local trauma as well as the maintenance of good skin hygiene. Prophylactic antibiotics reduce the incidence of cellulitis and are given to patients who have more than three episodes of cellulitis per year. Multiple episodes of infection are an indication for surgical intervention.

15. What is the first-line treatment of symptomatic lymphedema?

Lymphedema should be treated initially with elevation and skin hygiene to prevent epidermal breakdown, lymphorrhea, fungal growth, and bacterial entry. Low pH, water-based lotions are used for skin care. Next, compression in the form of multilayer bandaging, custom-made elastic stockings, massage, or pneumatic pumps may be used. Pressure has been shown to reduce limb volume in a randomized, prospective manner. Specifically, compression bandaging and massage reduce volume by 26%, and pneumatic pumps decrease limb size by as much as 69%. Controlled compression therapy (CCT) using sequentially tighter custom-fit garments reduces edema by 47% after 1 year compared with a 15% volume reduction using a nonfitted sleeve without adjustments. Complex lymphedema therapy (CLT), which includes manual lymph drainage, compression bandaging, and physical therapy, can reduce limb volume by 80%, possibly by recruiting collateral lymphatics.

16. How does pressure reduce limb volume?

Because pneumatic compression does not improve lymph transport by lymphoscintigraphy, pressure may reduce volume by increasing transport of lymph fluid (without protein) or by decreasing capillary filtration and thus the formation of lymph. Alternatively, compression may injure the lymphatic wall, opening junctions that facilitate fluid entry into the lymphatics. Another hypothesis is that a reduction of interstitial pressure allows collapsed lymphatics to become functional, which may explain why elevation improves lymphedema.

17. What are the indications for surgical treatment of lymphedema?

Patients with significant loss of function, recurrent infections, or severe psychological morbidity, despite conservative therapy, are candidates for surgical intervention.

18. Describe the surgical treatment options for lymphedema.

Surgical management may either reestablish lymphatic connections (physiologic procedures) or remove tissue (excisional procedures). Physiologic procedures have had little success, so excisional procedures are most commonly performed. Excising subcutaneous tissue and skin reduces lymph production while the subsequent increase in skin tension favors lymphatic return. Staged subcutaneous resection has been the most commonly performed procedure for lymphedema. Brorson has popularized the use of suction-assisted lipectomy for treatment of upper extremity lymphedema.

19. List the types of physiologic procedures that have been described for the treatment of lymphedema.

- *Lymphangioplasty:* Silk threads or other alloplastic materials have been used to act as a wick for improved lymph flow or to stimulate regenerating lymphatics. This technique has been complicated by infection and given poor results.
- *Flap Transposition*
  - *Thompson Procedure:* An attempt to reestablish a connection between the superficial and deep lymphatics by burying a dermal flap into the muscle compartment. Success of the procedure is likely due to the large subcutaneous excisional component because reestablishment of lymphatic communications has not been proven. This technique has a high complication rate.
  - *Omentum:* Potentially efficacious for scrotal lymphedema but poor long-term results without evidence of lymphatic connections for extremity lymphedema. There is a risk of significant donor site complications.
  - *Pedicled Flaps:* After myocutaneous pedicled flap transfer in animal models, lymphatics are reestablished across the obstructed site and prevent lymphedema. However, this modality has had poor results in humans. The pedicled transposition flap with the greatest chance for success is an axial flap with normal lymphatics at the base of the flap as close as possible to the regional node basin.
  - *Free-Tissue Transfer:* Although lymphatics are reestablished between the transferred tissue and the recipient site in humans, this modality has not been used to treat lymphedema.
- *Microsurgical Anastomosis:* Attempts to bypass a lymphatic obstruction or nonfunctioning lymphatics in patients with hyperplastic lymphedema. Because lymphatics have higher pressures than veins, lymph drains into veins.
  - *Lymph Node–Venous Anastomosis:* Must have normal nodes (not possible after node dissection). Patency 0% at 3 months due to obliteration by scar tissue ingrowth.
  - *Lymphaticovenous Anastomosis:* Best results if treated early in the disease, with at least three anastomoses, and combined with an excisional procedure. The patency rate is 66% after 12 weeks. Improvement is obtained in 42% of patients with lymphaticovenous anastomosis only and in 60% of patients when combined with an excisional procedure after 4 years of follow up. For patients who improve, the average volume reduction is 44%.

- *Lymphatic Grafting:* For upper extremity lymphedema, two to three lymphatic trunks and afferent branches have been harvested from the upper medial thigh and used to bypass the axilla from the distal arm to the proximal neck. In the lower extremity, lymphatics have been harvested from the normal limb, keeping their afferent connection to the inguinal nodes and pedicled across the groin to the lymphedematous limb. After 3 years some patients had an 80% reduction in limb volume. Complications included lymphedema in the donor extremity.

20. List the types of excisional procedures that have been described.

- *Charles Operation:* Excision of skin, subcutaneous tissue, and fascia with skin grafting of muscle. Although this procedure has a very low recurrence rate, the cosmetic appearance of the extremity often is worse than that of the limb with lymphedema. The complication rate is high, and complications include ulceration, oozing, and contracture.
- *Staged Subcutaneous Excision:* The most commonly performed surgical procedure for lymphedema. Subcutaneous tissue is excised maintaining skin flaps. It requires two stages: a medial resection followed by a lateral resection 3 months later. Long-term improvement is seen in 79% of patients with lower extremity lymphedema. Less favorable results have been obtained treating upper extremity lymphedema.
- *Suction-Assisted Lipectomy:* Liposuction has recently become the favored surgical intervention for upper extremity lymphedema. Using modern liposuction techniques, Brorson has prospectively maintained 106% volume reduction when combined with postoperative compression for greater than 4 years of follow-up compared with 47% volume reduction in patients treated with controlled compression therapy alone. This modality is better suited for early disease before fibrosis prohibits suctioning. Suction-assisted lipectomy reduces the annual risk of cellulitis from 41% to 10%.

21. What are the benefits of suction-assisted lipectomy compared with staged subcutaneous excision?

Subcutaneous excision requires multiple stages, is technically challenging, and requires long hospital stays. In addition, subcutaneous excision is associated with a 10% wound complication rate, sensory nerve injury, and extensive cutaneous scarring. In contrast, liposuction is minimally invasive, can be performed in one stage, and requires shorter hospital, operative, and recovery time. Furthermore, suction assisted lipectomy for upper extremity lymphedema is more efficacious for long-term volume reduction.

22. Is suction-assisted lipectomy effective for treatment of lower extremity lymphedema?

Yes. Although reports by O'Brien et al., Sando et al., and Louton et al. during the 1980s showed disappointing results, these authors did not perform circumferential suctioning, infuse tumescent solution, or use modern cannulas. Using current liposuction techniques, similar to those used by Brorson for treatment of upper extremity lymphedema, we have maintained 75% volume reduction of lower extremity lymphedema after more than 2 years of follow-up. Specifically, we use tumescence, power-assisted cannulas, circumferential suctioning, and postoperative compression.

23. What is the mechanism of liposuction edema reduction?

Subcutaneous fat contributes to the pathogenesis of lymphedema. First, lipids from interrupted lymph are consumed by adipocytes, leading to fat hypertrophy, thickened subcutaneous tissue, chronic swelling, and ultimately fibrosis. Second, because liposuction does not improve impaired lymph transport, its effect appears to be due to the removal of hypertrophied subcutaneous adipose tissue. In addition to removing pathologic adipose tissue, liposuction may slow the recurrence of lymphedema and protect against recurrent cellulitis, as liposuction has been shown to improve cutaneous blood flow. Interestingly, liposuction does not harm or improve the impaired lymph transport based on postoperative lymphoscintigraphy.

24. Is circumferential suctioning of the extremity safe?

Yes. Brorson has extensive experience with circumferential upper extremity liposuction without skin devascularization. In fact, cutaneous blood flow increases after suction-assisted lipectomy. Using tumescence and directing the cannula parallel to the extremity increase safety and reduce the risk of further lymphatic injury in extremity liposuction.

CONTROVERSIES

25. Is blood pressure monitoring contraindicated in a lymphedematous extremity?

No. In the patient with bilateral upper extremity lymphedema or in whom an unaffected extremity may not be monitored due to bandages, anomalies, or infection, it is safe to obtain blood pressure measurements from the lymphedematous extremity. Bilateral upper extremity lymphedema is increasing as more women are undergoing bilateral mastectomy due to a greater prevalence of BRCA testing. The use of a blood pressure cuff should not be harmful to a limb with lymphedema because pressure is used to treat the disease. The mainstay of therapy for symptomatic lymphedema is compression in the form of multilayer bandaging, massage, custom-made elastic stockings, and pneumatic pumps. Custom compression garments exert a pressure of 40 mm Hg, whereas graduated compression garments transmit pressures up to 80 mm Hg. Higher pressures are exhibited by pneumatic pumps that emit a force of 150 mm Hg. Not only has the long-term application of compression garments and pneumatic pumps been shown to be safe, but they also reduce extremity volume and the incidence of infection. If hours of pneumatic pump use and months of continuous pressure garments are not harmful to the lymphedematous limb, then sporadic blood pressure readings should not cause injury either. In fact, the pressure applied by the blood pressure cuff may potentially improve lymph drainage proximal to the site of application. However, as with any diseased extremity, manipulation of a lymphedematous limb should be avoided when possible. If no alternative site for blood pressure monitoring exists, the extremity with lymphedema can be used safely.

26. Does venipuncture increase the risk of infection in the lymphedematous limb?

No. The major risk of cannulating a vein in an extremity with lymphedema is infection because lymphedematous limbs are prone to cellulitis following minor trauma. However, evidence suggests that *sterile* penetration of the skin in a lymphedematous extremity does not cause infection. First, no reports of cellulitis from venipuncture in a lymphedematous extremity exist in the literature. Second, lymphangiogram, which requires a sterile cutdown to lymphatics in a lymphedematous extremity, has been associated with one case of infection in three studies of more than 32,200 lymphangiograms. Third, cellulitis after lymphoscintigraphy, which requires the sterile injection of radiolabeled colloid into the interdigital web space of an affected extremity, has not been reported in studies of 573 cases. Finally, sterile surgical incisions do not increase the risk of wound infections in the lymphedematous extremity. Wound infection after suction-assisted lipectomy, with up to thirty 3-mm stab incisions, has not been described. In addition, after staged subcutaneous excision, despite long incisions, the incidence of infection in the extremity is significantly reduced. It is possible that surgical volume reduction reduces the risk of infection by improving skin circulation, removing colonized tissue, or decreasing proteinaceous fluid. Although venipuncture is safe in the lymphedematous extremity, venipuncture should be attempted in the unaffected extremity when possible.

BIBLIOGRAPHY

Brorson H: Liposuction gives complete reduction of chronic large arm lymphedema after breast cancer. Acta Oncol 39:407–420, 2000.

Brorson H, Svensson H: Liposuction combined with controlled compression therapy reduces arm lymphedema more effectively than controlled compression therapy alone. Plast Reconstr Surg 102:1058–1067, 1998.

Brorson H, Svensson H: Skin blood flow of the lymphedematous arm before and after liposuction. Lymphology 30:165–172, 1997.

Brorson H, Svensson H, Norrgren K, et al: Liposuction reduces arm lymphedema without significantly altering the already impaired lymph transport. Lymphology 31:156–172, 1998.

Glovicki P, Calcagno D, Schirger A, et al: Noninvasive evaluation of the swollen extremity: Experiences with 190 lymphoscintigraphic examinations. J Vasc Surg 9:683–689, 1989.

Greene AK, Borud L, Slavin SA: Blood pressure monitoring and venipuncture in the lymphedematous extremity. Plast Reconstr Surg 116:2058–2059, 2005.

Greene AK, Slavin SA, Borud L: Treatment of lower extremity lymphedema with suction-assisted lipectomy. Plast Reconstr Surg 118:118e–121e, 2006.

Louton RB, Terranova WA: The use of suction curettage as adjunct to the management of lymphedema. Ann Plast Surg 22:354–357, 1989.

Miller TA, Wyatt LE, Rudkin GH: Staged skin and subcutaneous excision for lymphedema: A favorable report of long-term results. Plast Reconstr Surg 102:1486–1498, 1999.

O'Brien B, Khazanchi RK, Vumar PA, et al: Liposuction in the treatment of lymphoedema; a preliminary report. Br J Plast Surg 42:530–533, 1989.

O'Brien BM, Mellow CG, Khazanchi RK, et al: Long-term results after microlymphaticovenous anastomoses for the treatment of obstructive lymphedema. Plast Reconstr Surg 60:562–572, 1990.

Sando WC, Nahai F: Suction lipectomy in the management of limb lymphedema. Clin Plast Surg 16:369–373, 1989.

Slavin SA, Upton J, Kaplan WD, et al: An investigation of lymphatic function following free-tissue transfer. Plast Reconstr Surg 99:730–741, 1997.

Slavin SA, Van den Abbeele AD, Losken A, et al: Return of lymphatic function after flap transfer for acute lymphedema. Ann Surg 229:421–427, 1999.

Szuba A, Achalu R, Rockson SG: Decongestive lymphatic therapy for patients with breast carcinoma associated lymphedema. A randomized, prospective study of an adjunctive intermittent pneumatic compression. Cancer 95:2260–2267, 2002.

RECONSTRUCTION OF THE GENITALIA

Leslie T. McQuiston, MD, and
Anthony A. Caldamone, MD, MMS, FAAP, FACS

1. Describe the anatomy of the penis, including the fascial layers.

The anatomy of the penis begins with three erectile bodies: two corpora cavernosa and the corpus spongiosum, which surrounds the urethra. The corpora cavernosa, which contain the majority of erectile tissue, are surrounded by the tunica albuginea. The neurovascular bundle, containing the deep dorsal vein, dorsal artery, and paired dorsal nerves, lies between the tunica albuginea and Buck's fascia, which surrounds all three corpora, followed by dartos fascia and skin (Fig. 97-1).

2. Name the origin and branches of the common penile artery.

The common penile artery is a branch of the internal pudendal artery. Its branches are the bulbourethral artery, dorsal artery, and cavernosal artery. The branches of the dorsal artery include the circumflex branches, which contribute to the blood supply of the urethra, and the terminal branches, which supply the glans.

3. What is the role of testosterone in genital development?

The enlargement of the genital tubercle and subsequent elongation of the phallus and developing urethra depend on the presence of testosterone. After conversion to dihydrotestosterone by the 5-alpha reductase enzyme testosterone is responsible for virilization of the external genitalia.

4. Describe the common features of hypospadias.
- Dystopic urethral meatus in a ventral position on the penis, scrotum, or perineum
- Urethral plate distal to the dystopic meatus
- Dorsally hooded foreskin (97% to 98%)
- Ventral chordee (more than 50% of cases)

5. Where is the most common location of the meatus in hypospadias? The least common?
- Anterior meatus (glanular, subcoronal, distal penile shaft): 65%
- Posterior meatus (posterior penile shaft, penoscrotal, scrotal, perineal): 20%
- Medial meatus (midshaft): 15%

6. What are the goals and components of hypospadias repair?
- Straightening of the penile shaft (orthoplasty)
- Creation of an adequate caliber urethra (urethroplasty)
- Repositioning of the urethral meatus to the tip of the penis and creation of a symmetrical glans (meatoplasty and glanuloplasty)
- Achieving a good cosmetic result (skin coverage and scrotoplasty) with normalization of voiding and erection

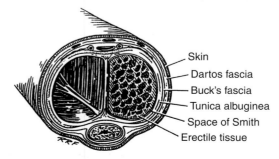

Skin
Dartos fascia
Buck's fascia
Tunica albuginea
Space of Smith
Erectile tissue

Figure 97-1. Transverse section of the penis at the junction of its middle and distal thirds. The septum is correctly illustrated as strands that interweave with the tunica albuginea both ventrally and dorsally. (From Jordan GH, Schlossberg SM, Devine CE: Surgery of the penis and urethra. In Walsh PC, Retik AB, Vaughn ED, Wein AJ [eds]: Campbell's Urology, 7th ed. Philadelphia, WB Saunders, 1998.)

7. Describe the distribution of the dorsal nerves to the penis. Why is it important to consider in surgical techniques for the correction of congenital penile curvature?

In 1997, Baskin et al. presented neuroanatomic studies of the human fetal penis. They demonstrated that the branches of the dorsal nerve extend from the 11 o'clock and 1 o'clock positions to the 5 o'clock and 7 o'clock positions on the corpora cavernosa. In dorsal plication techniques for correction of congenital penile curvature, or chordee, the plication should be performed at the 12 o'clock position. In this area, the tunica albuginea is the strongest and potential nerve injury, which could affect later sexual function, can be avoided.

8. What are the causes of chordee?

Congenital Causes	Acquired Causes
Fibrosis of the corpus spongiosum	Peyronie's disease
Skin tethering to the corpus spongiosum	Periurethral fibrosis associated with stricture disease
Deficiency of Buck's fascia or corpora cavernosa	
Hypoplastic urethra	
Differential corporal growth	

9. What are the two most common complications of a hypospadias repair?

Urethrocutaneous fistula and urethral stricture complicate approximately 10% to 15% of all hypospadias repairs.

10. Should you look for other congenital anomalies in a patient with hypospadias?

The most common anomalies associated with hypospadias are cryptorchidism and inguinal hernia; the incidence of each is approximately 9%. Anomalies of the upper urinary tract are infrequent unless other organ system anomalies, such as myelomeningocele or imperforate anus, are present. Routine screening of the upper urinary tract is not indicated in patients with isolated hypospadias or with hypospadias associated with undescended testes or inguinal hernia.

11. What are the classic features of the exstrophy/epispadias complex?
- Divergent rectus with exposed bladder plate
- Low umbilicus
- Widening of the symphysis pubis
- Anteriorly displaced anus
- Short penis with divergent corpora, dorsal chordee, and dorsally displaced meatus (epispadias)
- Short urethra
- Short vagina with stenotic anteriorly displaced orifice
- Bifid clitoris and divergent labia, mons pubis, and clitoris

12. How does exstrophy occur?

Exstrophy results from failure of the cloacal membrane to rupture, which prevents medial mesenchymal ingrowth. Therefore proper development of the lower abdominal wall is impeded.

13. What are the goals of extrophy reconstruction?
- Abdominal wall closure
- Bladder closure with adequate capacity
- Achievement of urinary continence
- Preservation of renal function
- Functional and cosmetic genital reconstruction

14. What is the most common cause of ambiguous genitalia? What is the most common enzyme abnormality?

Congenital adrenal hyperplasia is the most common cause of ambiguous genitalia; deficiency of 21-hydroxylase is the most common enzyme abnormality.

15. List the categories of ambiguous genitalia.
- *Female Pseudohermaphroditism.* Affected children have a 46XX chromosomal pattern and ovaries. Congenital adrenal hyperplasia is the most common diagnosis.
- *Male Pseudohermaphroditism.* Affected children have a 46XY karyotype and testicular tissue. Defects in androgen synthesis, response to androgens, and failure of müllerian regression are among the many causes of incomplete virilization.
- *True Hermaphrodite.* The most common karyotype in affected children is 46XX, but the 46XY or mosaic karyotype is also found. Both ovarian and testicular tissues are present.

- *Mixed Gonadal Dysgenesis.* Most affected children have a 46XY/45XO karyotype with a testis on one side and a dysgenetic or streak gonad on the other. The internal structures are variable.
- *Pure Gonadal Dysgenesis.* Affected children may have a 45XO, 46XX, or 46XY karyotype. They usually do not present with ambiguous genitalia but rather with delayed puberty in adolescence or adulthood. Bilateral streak gonads and müllerian ductal structures are present. Because of high malignant potential, early bilateral gonadectomy is recommended for patients with 46XY karyotype.

16. What considerations contribute to gender assignment?
A multidisciplinary approach is paramount to successful diagnosis, management, counseling, and gender assignment. Functional anatomic potential, including consideration of phallus size, plays a major role in gender assignment. Less consideration is given to potential fertility and karyotype.

17. What are the anatomic divisions of the urethra?
- The *posterior urethra* is the portion proximal to the bulb and includes the prostatic and membranous urethra.
- The *anterior urethra* lies distal to entry into the bulb and includes the bulbar, penile, or pendulous urethra and fossa navicularis. The anterior urethra is contained within the corpus spongiosum.

18. Name three causes of urethral stricture disease.
- Trauma or crush injury
- Instrumentation such as Foley catheterization or cystourethroscopy
- Infection (most likely gonorrhea)

19. What studies are involved in the preoperative evaluation of urethral stricture?
As always, you must begin with a history and physical examination. The presence of a stricture is suggested by voiding symptoms such as decreased force of stream, urinary frequency, nocturia, and dysuria. Physical examination may reveal the inability to pass a catheter. Urinalysis and culture should be performed to rule out infection. The stricture must be characterized radiographically using a retrograde urethrogram, voiding cystourethrogram, or both. Ultrasound helps to characterize the length, depth, and density of the stricture. Urethroscopy provides information about the elasticity of the stricture.

20. What tissues are available for reconstruction of the urethra?
- Preputial, penile shaft, or scrotal skin
- Free graft of buccal or bladder mucosa
- Free graft of extragenital skin
- Tunica vaginalis pedicle flap
- Mucosa of the tongue (lingual mucosal graft, LMG)

21. Who was Peyronie?
François de la Peyronie was a French barber surgeon who commanded the surgical corps for King Louis XIV. Although descriptions of similar penile deformities can be found in ancient Roman literature, Peyronie described the disease that bears his name in a patient who "had rosary beads of scar tissue causing an upward curvature of the penis during erection."

22. What is the cause of Peyronie's disease? What is the most commonly associated physical finding other than penile curvature?
The exact cause of Peyronie's disease is elusive. The most commonly held belief is that the plaque is the end result of an inflammatory response to trauma to the erect penis. Beta-blocking agents also have been associated with the development of plaques. Dupuytren's contracture occurs in approximately 10% to 30% of patients with Peyronie's disease.

23. If a patient presents with significant penile curvature, what are the important considerations for recommending treatment?
The goal of treatment in Peyronie's disease is to preserve or restore sexual function. Important considerations in the treatment include concomitant erectile dysfunction, penile pain, duration and stability of curvature, and patient satisfaction with sexual function. Treatment should begin with vitamin E until the plaque has matured or the degree of curvature is stable.

24. What materials or tissues have been used in plaque incision or excision and grafting?

Dermis	Dacron	Dura
Tunica vaginalis	Dexon	Vein
Modified human fascia lata	Dorsal lamina of rectus sheath	Buccal mucosa

25. What additional procedure should be considered in patients with erectile dysfunction and Peyronie's disease?

In patients with erectile dysfunction in addition to penile curvature, placement of a penile prosthesis at the time of repair of the curvature should be considered. Placement of a prosthesis in patients without erectile dysfunction is controversial.

26. After exploration to determine the extent of the injury, how should you manage a degloving injury to the penis?

Currently, most degloving injuries to the penis and scrotum are managed with immediate reconstruction using split-thickness skin grafting. A sheet graft is used on the penis, and a meshed graft reproduces a rugated appearance on the scrotum. Another option is to bury the penis in a subcutaneous abdominal pouch and the testes in thigh pouches for delayed reconstruction.

27. What is Fournier's gangrene?

Fournier's gangrene is a rapidly progressive, fulminating infection of the perineum and genital area caused by multiple organisms, including aerobic and anaerobic bacteria. The most common predisposing factor is diabetes mellitus; however, local trauma, paraphimosis, perianal or perirectal infections, periurethral extravasation of urine due to instrumentation, and stricture disease are other risk factors. The disease most commonly presents as a cellulitis with prominent pain and marked systemic toxicity. Crepitus is an early finding. Recognition of a potential case of Fournier's gangrene is critically important due to the rapid progress of the disease, with a mortality rate of approximately 20%. Broad-spectrum antimicrobial therapy, intravenous hydration, and wide surgical débridement are essential in the early management. Urinary and fecal diversion may be necessary. Because the blood supply to the testes arises from the spermatic cord, the testes usually are spared and orchiectomy is not required. Thigh pouches may be created for coverage of the testes. Serial débridement and later reconstruction with skin grafting and myocutaneous flaps may be necessary.

28. What is the most common technique for penile reconstruction and phallic construction?

In the past, phallic reconstruction was performed using tubed abdominal flaps in multistage procedures. Chang and Hwang popularized the use of radial forearm flaps in 1984. Although the technique has undergone many modifications since its original description, use of the forearm flap remains the standard. Penile rigidity is achieved by use of an external device or an implanted prosthesis. Prosthesis implantation is delayed at least 1 year from reconstruction to ensure urethral patency and durability as well as viability of the forearm flap.

29. What are the options for construction of a vagina?

- Bowel (sigmoid colon most commonly)
- Flaps (pudendal–thigh flap)
- Split-thickness skin graft or full-thickness skin graft (with or without tissue expanders)

BIBLIOGRAPHY

Baskin LS, Yee YT, Cunha GA: Neuroanatomical ontogeny of the human fetal penis. Br J Urol 79:628–640, 1997.

Brant WO, Bella AJ, Garcia MM, Tantiwongse K, Lue TF: Surgical atlas. Correction of Peyronie's disease: Plaque incision and grafting. Br J Urol 97:1353–1360, 2006.

Chang TS, Hwang WY: Forearm flap in one-stage reconstruction of the penis. Plast Reconstr Surg 74:251–258, 1984.

Devine CJ, Horton CE: Surgical treatment of Peyronie's disease with a dermal graft. J Urol 43:697–701, 1974.

Donahoe PK, Schnitzer JJ, Pieretti R: Ambiguous genitalia. In Grosfeld JL, Fonkalsrud EW, O'Neill JA, Caldamone AA, Coran AG (eds): Pediatric Surgery, 6th ed. Philadelphia, Mosby, 2006, pp 1911–1934.

Dunsmuir WD, Kirby RS: Francois de LaPeyronie (1678–1747): The man and the disease he described. Br J Urol 78:613–622, 1996.

Flynn BJ, Webster GD: Urethral stricture and disruption. In Graham SD (ed): Glenn's Urologic Surgery, 6th ed. Philadelphia, Lippincott Williams & Wilkins, 2004, pp 394–407.

Grady RW, Carr MC, Mitchell ME: Complete primary closure of bladder exstrophy. Epispadias and bladder exstrophy repair. Urol Clin North Am 26:95–109, 1999.

Hensle TW, Shabsign A, Shabsign R, Reiley EA, Meyer-Bahlburg HF: Sexual function following bowel vaginoplasty. J Urol 175:2283–2286, 2006.

Jordan GH, Schlossberg SM: Surgery of the penis and urethra. In Wein AJ, Kavoussi LR, Novick AC, Partin AW, Peters CA (eds): Campbell-Walsh Urology, Vol. 1, 9th ed. Philadelphia, WB Saunders, 2002.

Jordan GH, Virasoro R, Eltahawy EA: Reconstruction and management of posterior urethral straddle injuries of the urethra. Urol Clin North Am 33:97–109, 2007, pp 1023–1097.

Keating MA, Rich MA: Hypospadiology. Atl Urol Clin North Am 12:65–104, 2004.

MacLellan DL, Diamond DA: Recent advances in external genitalia. Pediatr Clin North Am 53:449–464, 2006.

Selvaggi G, Ceulemans P, De Cuypere G, et al: Gender identity disorder: general overview and surgical treatment for vaginoplasty in male-to-female transsexuals. Plast Reconstr Surg 116:135e–145e, 2005.

Fire! Norman Rockwell, 1931. *The Saturday Evening Post*, Cover, 28 March 1931. Printed by permission of the Norman Rockwell Family Agency. Copyright © 1960 Norman Rockwell Family Entities.

THERMAL BURNS

Karen E. Frye, MD, and
Arnold Luterman, MD, FRCS(C), FACS

CHAPTER 98

1. List three functions of the skin that are lost when thermal injury occurs. What are the consequences?
- Skin, *the largest organ of the body,* is a *barrier to heat loss.* In the case of an acute burn, care must be taken to keep the patient warm and avoid hypothermia.
- Skin is a *barrier to evaporative losses.* Free water losses frequently need replacement in patients with major burn injury.
- Skin is a *barrier to microbial invasion.* Thus the burn patient is highly susceptible to infection.

2. What is the incidence of burn injury in the United States?
In the United States, 500,000 burn injuries requiring medical attention occur annually. Approximately 40,000 of these require hospitalization; 2500 of these have major burns involving at least 30% of their total body surface area (TBSA).

3. What are the criteria for referring a patient to a specialized burn center?
- Inhalation injury
- Burn size >10% TBSA in any patient
- Any full-thickness burn
- Burn wound involvement of the face, hands, feet, perineum, genitalia, or major joints
- Associated trauma
- Comorbid states
- Special social situations (e.g., child abuse)
- Electrical burns, including lightning injury
- Chemical burns
- Burned children in hospitals without qualified personnel or equipment for the care of children

4. What are the immediate concerns about the airway of patients with a thermal injury?
The airway must be assessed immediately. If the patient has suffered a burn to the upper airway, intubation is necessary to prevent upper airway obstruction due to edema. The airway is assessed most accurately by nasopharyngoscopy. If the examination is performed immediately after injury (0 to 4 hours) and the result is normal, it may need to be repeated 4 to 6 hours later. Edema may not manifest until 6 to 8 hours after injury. Edema should reach a maximum by 24 hours after injury.

5. What three factors suggest an inhalation injury?
History of the fire occurring in an enclosed space, production of carbonaceous sputum, and elevated carboxyhemoglobin (COHG) level (>10%). If all three factors are present, it is highly likely that the patient has suffered an inhalation injury.

6. What diagnostic measures can be used to confirm inhalation injury?
Fiberoptic bronchoscopy can be performed at the bedside. Examination of the lower airway may reveal deposition of carbonaceous particles as well as mucosal edema. If the examination is done soon after injury or if the patient has not been adequately resuscitated, edema may not be evident. Regardless of the findings on bronchoscopy, clinical management of the inhalation injury initially is based on adequate oxygenation and ventilation. A xenon ventilation–perfusion lung scan is the most definitive study for diagnosis of inhalation injury, but it is time consuming and requires transport of the patient to the radiology department.

7. What are the concerns in transporting a burn victim from a community hospital to a specialized burn center?
The airway must be adequate. If there is any question that the airway may obstruct, the patient should be intubated, preferably via the endotracheal route. Fluid resuscitation should be in progress using the Parkland formula. Two large-bore IVs should be placed. The patient must be kept warm. Avoid wet dressings, which tend to make the patient hypothermic. The simplest strategy is to wrap the patient in a dry, sterile sheet.

8. **How is inhalation injury managed acutely?**

An adequate airway must be secured. The patient must be adequately ventilated and oxygenated. Mechanical ventilation may be required; 100% oxygen should be administered to enhance the offloading of carbon monoxide from hemoglobin. The half-life of carbon monoxide on room air is 4 to 5 hours; on 100% oxygen it is reduced to approximately 45 minutes. The patient should be maintained on 100% oxygen until the COHG level is <10%. The patient's mental status must be assessed and monitored. If the patient's mental status improves initially but subsequently deteriorates, hyperbaric oxygenation treatments may be indicated.

9. **When are prophylactic antibiotics and/or steroids indicated for inhalation injury?**

Never. Prophylactic antibiotics for an inhalation injury do not prevent postinhalation pulmonary infectious complications; they only select resistant organisms. Once a pulmonary infection develops, it is more difficult to treat. Steroids should not be used in inhalation injury. They are of no benefit and increase mortality threefold.

10. **Describe the resuscitation of thermally injured patients.**

Burn wounds involving greater than 20% TBSA typically mount a systemic inflammatory response with resultant capillary leak. Fluid requirements are estimated initially with *the Parkland formula:*

Fluids required for the first 24 hours = (4 cc) × (Patient's weight in kilograms) × (%TBSA burned)

Half of the fluid is given over the first 8 hours after injury. The second half is given over the remaining 16 hours. The Parkland formula is only an estimate. Some patients require more than the predicted amount of fluid, and some patients require less. The patient must be continually monitored by repeatedly evaluating heart rate, blood pressure, urine output, and acid–base status. Fluids need to be adjusted accordingly.

11. **Describe the initial resuscitation of a child with burn injuries.**

Fluid requirements in children are estimated with the Parkland formula, as in adults. In addition, because of a larger body surface area-to-weight ratio, pediatric patients require additional maintenance fluids, usually administered as D5 ½NS. In addition to the fluid volume, some carbohydrate is provided with the D5 ½NS. Because glycogen stores are minimal in young children, hypoglycemia is a potential problem unless exogenous carbohydrate is provided.

12. **How is the size of the burn estimated?**

The most accurate method is the Berkow diagram (Table 98-1), which allows for differences in various age groups. The rule of nines is a simpler method but less accurate:

Head and neck = 9% TBSA	Posterior torso = 18% TBSA
Each upper extremity = 9% TBSA	Anterior torso = 18% TBSA
Each lower extremity = 18% TBSA	Perineum = 1% TBSA

For small or scattered burns, a helpful rule is that the area of the patient's open hand (palm and extended fingers) is approximately 1% TBSA.

13. **How is the depth of the wound classified?**

Historically, wound depth has been classified as first, second, or third degree. A first-degree wound involves only the epidermis. The classic example is sunburn. A second-degree wound involves the epidermis and dermis but does not extend through the dermis. Second-degree wounds are further classified as superficial partial or superficial dermal and deep partial or deep dermal depending on the depth of the wound. Superficial partial-thickness wounds appear pink and moist and usually heal spontaneously within 3 weeks. Deep partial-thickness wounds look dry and pale, sometimes having a mottled appearance. These wounds usually take longer than 3 weeks to close spontaneously. A third-degree burn is a full-thickness injury that involves the entire epidermis and dermis. The pathognomonic finding on physical examination is thrombosed vessels. A fourth-degree burn extends deep to the bone.

14. **Describe the management of burn wounds involving the extremities.**

Any limb with a burn wound requires elevation acutely to minimize edema formation. If wounds are circumferential or nearly circumferential, pulses need to be assessed hourly. Doppler ultrasound may be required for accurate assessment, as palpation of pulses is difficult in the edematous limb. In the upper extremity, the palmar arch pulse, radial pulse, and ulnar pulse should be evaluated. In the lower extremity, the dorsal pedal and posterior tibial pulses should be

Table 98-1. Berkow Diagram to Estimate Burn Size (%) Based on Area of Burn in an Isolated Body Part*

BODY PART	0–1 YR	1–4 YR	5–9 YR	10–14 YR	15–18 YR	ADULT
Head	19	17	13	11	9	7
Neck	2	2	2	2	2	2
Anterior trunk	13	13	13	13	13	13
Posterior trunk	13	13	13	13	13	13
Right buttock	2.5	2.5	2.5	2.5	2.5	2.5
Left buttock	2.5	2.5	2.5	2.5	2.5	2.5
Genitalia	1	1	1	1	1	1
Right upper arm	4	4	4	4	4	4
Left upper arm	4	4	4	4	4	4
Right lower arm	3	3	3	3	3	3
Left lower arm	3	3	3	3	3	3
Right hand	2.5	2.5	2.5	2.5	2.5	2.5
Left hand	2.5	2.5	2.5	2.5	2.5	2.5
Right thigh	5.5	6.5	8	8.5	9	9.5
Left thigh	5.5	6.5	8	8.5	9	9.5
Right leg	5	5	5.5	6	6.5	7
Left leg	5	5	5.5	6	6.5	7
Right foot	3.5	3.5	3.5	3.5	3.5	3.5
Left foot	3.5	3.5	3.5	3.5	3.5	3.5

*Estimates are made, recorded, and then summed to gain an accurate estimate of the body surface area burned.
From Townsend CM, Beauchamp RD, Evers BM, Mattox KL (eds): Sabiston Textbook of Surgery: The Biological Basis of Modern Surgical Practice, 18th ed. Philadelphia, Saunders, 2008.

checked. If a pulse previously detectable by Doppler examination is lost, escharotomies must be performed. The obvious exception is the patient who is not adequately resuscitated, as manifested by decreased blood pressure, inadequate urine output, and poor perfusion in an uninvolved limb.

15. Why is pain control important in burn patients?

Pain causes a rise in heart rate, blood pressure, and metabolic rate. With adequate pain control, the patient is less hypermetabolic, and heart rate and blood pressure are better controlled. Inadequate pain control also results in an increased incidence of posttraumatic stress disorder during recovery and rehabilitation. The rate of nurse burnout is also decreased when nursing staff is allowed to adequately control patients' pain.

16. What is burn wound anemia?

A patient with a significant thermal injury frequently manifests anemia until the wounds are closed. Anemia results from the shortened half-life of red blood cells in burn patients (40 days vs normal half-life of 120 days).

17. What are the various options available for managing the partial-thickness burn wound?

Initially a topical antimicrobial is used for most partial-thickness wounds. Various agents are available, including povidone-iodine ointment, silver sulfadiazine cream, silver nitrate solution, mupirocin ointment, Polysporin ointment and powder, and mafenide acetate cream and solution (5%). Mafenide acetate is the only agent that penetrates eschar. It is a carbonic anhydrase inhibitor and, when used in the cream form over a larger surface area, can cause a metabolic acidosis. Its use in the cream form is also associated with significant pain. The 5% solution rarely has these side effects.

Enzymatic agents are useful in expediting the débridement of partial-thickness wounds. Presently, the only available débriding agent is collagenase. When use of collagenase was compared with silver sulfadiazine, earlier débridement to a clean dermis occurred with collagenase. Furthermore, with earlier débridement to a clean dermis, reepithelialization occurred faster.

Once a clean wound bed has been achieved (i.e., no necrotic tissue and no bacteria), a barrier dressing can be applied. Options include allograft (cadaver skin), xenograft (pigskin), Biobrane, and Transcyte. Allograft provides for good vascularization of the wound bed. A major disadvantage to its use is cost. Recent concerns exist concerning possible transmission of viral infections. Xenograft is less expensive. It is a reasonable option in the superficial partial-thickness wound. Biobrane, one of the older synthetic barrier dressings, is a bilaminar material with an outer layer composed of silicone and nylon fabric and an inner layer of collagen. Transcyte is Biobrane with the addition of neonatal fibroblasts. Silver-containing barrier dressings have become available. A variety of materials that contain silver, such as Acticoat, Aquacel Ag, and Silveron, provides the clinician more options for treatment of clean open wounds. The perfect temporary wound dressing has not been found, and new products are continually marketed.

18. What is meant by tangential excision and fascial excision?

Tangential excision is a technique used to remove the burn eschar. Basically, the eschar is removed tangentially in layers until all of the necrotic tissue has been excised and a viable wound bed is present.

Fascial excision removes the skin and entire subcutaneous layer down to the fascia. Usually it is reserved for very deep burn wounds or burn wounds in elderly patients.

19. How and when is a skin graft done?

The first step in grafting a burn wound involves preparation of the recipient site with tangential or fascial excision of the eschar. Once a viable bed is present, a split-thickness graft is harvested from a donor site. The skin graft usually is secured to the recipient site with sutures, staples, or fibrin sealant. This procedure, referred to as *excision and grafting,* is indicated for any deep partial- or full-thickness burn wound and should be performed at the earliest convenient time once the patient has been adequately resuscitated and is stable from a hemodynamic and respiratory standpoint. Indeterminate wounds should be observed initially. Once it becomes evident that spontaneous closure will take longer than 3 weeks, excision and grafting should be performed. Wound closure should be accomplished by day 21 after the burn to avoid contracture and scarring and thereby offer optimal functional and cosmetic results.

20. What are the reasons for graft failure?

- Inadequate vascular perfusion
- Infection
- Accumulation of fluid under the graft
- Residual eschar (necrotic tissue) on the graft bed
- Mechanical shear forces

21. What is a meshed graft versus a sheet graft?

In a meshed graft, perforation holes are created to prevent accumulation of fluid or blood under the graft. Depending on the size of the mesh, a skin graft can be stretched to cover an area significantly larger than the original donor site. Because sheet grafts have no holes, the risk of hematoma formation or fluid accumulation under the graft is increased. Sheet grafts are preferred from a cosmetic and functional standpoint.

22. What is Integra artificial skin? When should it be used?

Integra artificial skin is a matrix of glycosaminoglycan and collagen. It provides a scaffold whereby the body's fibroblasts can lay down collagen in an organized fashion. Thus, a neodermis is formed rather than scar tissue. A sheet of Silastic covers the artificial skin, providing barrier function. The burn wound must be excised early. The artificial skin is laid in place and secured with staples. A neodermis is allowed to form, then the Silastic is removed and a thin skin graft (6/1000 inches) is used to close the wound. With such a thin graft, little dermis is transferred. Thus donor sites can be used numerous times. The indications for artificial skin are large burn injuries and the need to limit the size of the donor site (e.g., in patients with an associated inhalation injury or geriatric patients). Integra artificial skin is also used for burn scar reconstruction.

23. How are thermal injuries to the perineum and genitalia managed?

Good local wound care is the mainstay for wounds of the perineum and genitalia. Because this area has an excellent blood supply, most wounds heal spontaneously. Excision and grafting to the perineum and/or genitalia are technically difficult. For these reasons, wounds of the perineum and genitalia usually should not be managed with early excision and grafting. If after 3 to 4 weeks a red granulating wound results, skin grafting can be performed. Catheterization is not indicated for burns of the perineum or genitalia unless it is needed to monitor fluid status.

24. Describe the management of foot burns.

Foot burns are the most common burns to fail attempted outpatient management. The foot is often in a dependent position, thus contributing to post burn edema. The persistent edema provides an environment in which cellulites can easily develop. Early elevation is mandatory for any foot burn. The skin of the foot has fewer skin appendages, so wounds on the foot are often slow to heal. Because the foot is a functional part of the body, an expedient closure with a skin graft is often indicated to minimize scaring and optimize function.

25. How is wound healing affected by the aging process?

As a person ages, the dermis atrophies. Burn injury depth often is deep partial- or full-thickness in the elderly. Furthermore, fewer skin appendages are present in the skin of geriatric patients. Thus spontaneous reepithelialization of a middermal or deep dermal wound is slow. If wounds are located on the feet or legs, an element of peripheral vascular disease may contribute to delayed healing.

26. Why is nutrition important in the burn patient, and how are nutritional requirements determined?

Severe burn injury results in an increased metabolic rate and oxygen consumption. Weight loss is directly proportional to the size of the burn injury. Inadequate supply of protein and kilocalories leads to decreased immunocompetence and abnormal wound healing. Caloric requirements can be estimated using the *Curreri formula,* which recommends a daily amount of *25 kcal/kg plus 40 kcal/% of TBSA burned.* Protein requirements can be met with 1 to 2 g/kg/day. Nutritional status should be monitored at least twice weekly with a serum prealbumin. Nitrogen balance studies are difficult to interpret in the burn patient secondary to nitrogen losses from the wounds.

BIBLIOGRAPHY

American Burn Association: www.ameriburn.org/resources_factsheet.php.Accessed July 2009.

Baxter CR: Fluid volume and electrolyte changes in the early post-burn period. Clin Plast Surg 1:693–703, 1974.

Curreri PW: Nutritional support of burn patients. World J Surg 2:215–222, 1978.

Gallagher JJ, Wolf SE, Herndon DN: Burns. In Townsend CM, Beauchamp RD, Evers BM, Mattox KL (eds): Sabiston Textbook of Surgery: The Biological Basis of Modern Surgical Practice, 18th ed. 2008, pp. 559–585.

Guidelines for the Operation of Burn Centers (pp. 79–86), Resources for Optimal Care of the Injured Patient2006, Committee on Trauma, American College of Surgeons.

Hansbrough JF, Achauer B, Dawson J, et al: Wound healing in partial-thickness burn wounds treated with collagenase ointment versus silver sulfadiazine cream. J Burn Care Rehabil 16:241–247, 1994.

Herndon DN (ed): Total Burn Care, 3rd ed. Philadelphia, Elsevier Saunders, 2007.

Moylan JA, Alexander LG Jr: Diagnosis and treatment of inhalation injury. World J Surg 2:185–191,1978.

CHAPTER 99

ELECTRICAL INJURIES

Mahesh H. Mankani, MD, FACS, and
Raphael C. Lee MD, ScD, DSc(Hon), FACS

1. What is an electrical injury?

Lee and Astumian have defined electrical injury as tissue injury resulting from exposure to supraphysiologic electric currents or forces.

2. How common are electrical injuries in the United States?

Deaths from electrical exposure typically occur in 0.5:100,000 population per year in the United States. In 1994, 84 deaths due to lightning strikes and 561 deaths due to electrical exposures not related to lightning occurred in the United States.

3. What are the mechanisms for electrical injury?

Tissue damage pathomechanics in electrical injury are complex. However, three mechanisms dominate:
1. Current-generated heating with resulting thermal burn,
2. Direct electrical forces puncture of cell membranes (electroporation), and
3. Direct electric force denaturation of cell membrane protein.

Passage of electrical current through a solid body results in conversion of electric energy to heat, a phenomenon termed *joule heating*. The heat production (Q) is proportional to the square of the current (I), the tissue resistance (R), and the time of contact (t):

$$Q \propto I^2Rt$$

The direct effects of the electric forces on the cell membrane can lead to the creation of large pores, a process referred to as *electroporation*. These pores can lead to ion leakage, the escape of metabolites, and a pathologic membrane permeability to macromolecules as large as deoxyribonucleic acid (DNA). Electric forces can also lead to the denaturation of membrane proteins.

4. Why is the term "electrical burn" imprecise?

The use of the term "burn" implies that the mechanism for tissue injury is entirely thermal in origin. However, electrical injuries arise from both thermal and nonthermal mechanisms.

5. To what does the term "entrance and exit points" refer?

This somewhat archaic term arises from the concept of a direct current traveling from a site of higher potential (voltage) to a site of lower potential, with the intervening human body serving as a conductor. The portion of the patient in contact with the higher voltage is considered the "entrance" site, whereas the site of lower potential is the "exit" site. Alternating current (AC) is characterized by a reversal of the direction of current flow with each half cycle of the frequency of the power source. Therefore in most circumstances each anatomic contact point is both an entrance and exit point.

6. What is the voltage of typical wall outlets in the home?

Wall outlets in American homes are characterize by AC of 60 Hz (cycles per second) and a line-to-line voltage of 110 V or 120 volts for general use. In addition, most homes have a line-to-line voltage to 240 V for high-power appliances.

7. Describe how to calculate the current that a victim might be exposed to during an electrical injury.

The current that is involved in an accident must be calculated, using the known voltage from the outlet and estimating the resistance offered by the body, the contact, and the ground. These parameters are often not known because of the various types of clothing and protective gear often used. The resistance offered by the tissues of the human body, excluding resistance at the interface between the skin and the voltage source, is approximately 500 to 1000 ohms between the two hands, between the two feet, or between a hand and a foot. Thus the maximum current that an individual could experience while grounding their home electrical outlet is:

$$I = V/R,$$

or

$$I = 120 \text{ V}/500 \text{ ohms} = 0.24 \text{ A}$$

We expect the actual current that the individual experiences to be much less because of the additional resistance between the skin and the contacts.

8. What is the minimum voltage necessary for soft tissue injury?

The type of current, its frequency, and its magnitude determine the body's response to the injury. For an individual to experience ventricular fibrillation following contact with a voltage source, for instance, the magnitude of AC necessary is measurably less than that required from a direct current source. Likewise, a 1-kHz source will require a higher current than a 60-Hz source to produce ventricular fibrillation.

A 60-Hz current, which is typical of wall outlets, with a magnitude of 0.5 mA will produce a startle response. Current greater than 10 mA through the forearm may not allow the victim to release his/her grip on the contact. This is referred to as the *let-go threshold* and likely is due to electrical stimulation of the dominant forearm flexors. Exposure to a current of 50 mA for more than 2 seconds can induce ventricular fibrillation, whereas 1 A can induce immediate fibrillation or asystole as well as lysis of skeletal muscle and nerve lysis. The effect on the heart depends on the anatomic path of current flow.

9. Describe the common modes of exposure to damaging electric fields.

Victims experience electrical injury when electrical contact is established with an electric power source. Arcs and flames are good electrical conductors and often mediate the contact under high-voltage conditions. Thermal and thermoacoustic blast injury from the heat from the electric arc also may cause injury.

Electrical contact with the voltage source contributes to joule heating, electroporation, and protein denaturation.

Thermal injury from an electric flash commonly occurs when the victim is in proximity to an electrical arc. The temperature of an electrical arc can approach 25,000°C. Heat from the arc can cause a blast injury or thermal injury. The patient may describe being some distance from the site of the electrical disturbance. On examination, the patient may not have identifiable contact points. Instead, the patient may have partial- to full-thickness thermal burns similar in character to other nonelectrical burns.

Secondary injuries from the electrical exposure include falls from elevated high-tension wires and tetanic contractions from the current leading to cervical or long bone fractures.

10. How are electrical injuries classified?

Clinicians divide electrical injuries into high- and low-voltage injuries based on the voltage at the point of contact. High-voltage electrical injuries arise from contact with sources greater than 1000 V; low-voltage electrical injuries arise from contact with voltages less than 1000 V. This definition has significance in that, at high voltage, the contacts typically are arc mediated, which means that the victim is very unlikely to hold on to the electrified contact.

The clinical classification of high- and low-tension injuries is distinct from an electrical utility industry classification scheme for power lines. Clinically, high-voltage shock differs from low-voltage shock in that arc-mediated electrical current flow can precede mechanical contact under high-voltage conditions. The voltages delivered by three-phase power lines are categorized as low, medium, high, extra-high, and ultra-high. Low voltages are less than 600 V, medium voltages range from 2400 V to 69 kV, high voltages range between 115 kV and 230 kV, extra-high voltages range from 345 kV to 765 kV, and ultra-high voltages are greater than 1.1 MV. The most common injuries involving utility lines involve medium-range voltages because of the prevalence of these voltages among transmission lines. Using this scheme, note that a medium line voltage may cause a high-voltage injury.

11. What additional portions of the history, as they relate to the electrical exposure, must be explored?

Determine the type of contact and the length of time that the patient had contact with the voltage source. Determine whether the patient experienced mechanical contact with the current source, made electrical contact with an arc, or suffered flash burns. If the patient had direct contact with the voltage source, identify those portions of the patient's anatomy that were involved and the duration of the contact.

12. What laboratory studies are appropriate at the time of admission?

Blood gases and serum electrolytes, particularly potassium concentration, are important to measure immediately to guide therapy. If high serum potassium and acidosis suggest extensive muscle necrosis, surgical débridement likely will be needed as soon as feasible. Serum creatinine and creatine phosphokinase (CPK) elevation also suggest massive tissue destruction. Urine myoglobin content is more qualitative.

13. What are the findings of compartment syndromes in the extremities, and when is treatment appropriate?

In victims of electrical shock, the usual symptoms and signs of compartment syndromes cannot be relied on because sensory and motor nerve injury resulting from the electrical shock are the hallmark of muscle and nerve ischemia. Palpation of the injured compartment for tenseness also is unreliable because few have enough personal experience. Arterial pulses usually are intact. When suspected, the diagnosis must be confirmed by directly measuring the compartment pressure.

Recommendations vary with regard to the appropriate compartment pressure at which to perform a fasciotomy. Whitesides advocates performing the fasciotomy when the compartment pressure rises to within 10 to 30 mm Hg of the patient's diastolic pressure. Matsen, however, recommends performing a fasciotomy when the compartment pressure exceeds 45 mm Hg.

14. What is the role of magnetic resonance imaging in the identification of compromised, electrically injured tissue?

Magnetic resonance imaging with new open architecture magnetics provides rapid and detailed information regarding the anatomic sites and severity of injury. Also, the technetium-99 pyrophosphate and similar radionucleotide scans distinguish between uninjured and injured muscle following electrical injury with high specificity and sensitivity. However, in major electrical trauma, the radionucleotide scans require too much time to provide information to aid clinical surgical interventions and have not been found to reduce hospital stay or decrease the number of operative procedures.

15. How are fluid requirements calculated in electrical injury resuscitation?

Maintenance of an appropriate intravascular volume can be challenging in major electrical injuries. A high degree of tissue destruction may not be reflected by a limited, discrete cutaneous burn. Rather, the adequacy of resuscitation must be confirmed by noting adequate renal perfusion.

When mannitol is used to enhance diuresis in the face of myoglobinuria, urine output cannot be used as a reliable indicator of renal perfusion. In such situations, the central venous pressure (CVP) or the pulmonary capillary wedge pressure (PCWP) should be monitored with an intravenous catheter.

16. What is the significance of myoglobinuria?

Myoglobinuria in the face of electrical injury is indicative of rhabdomyolysis and, if left untreated, is associated with intratubular deposition of pigments, leading to acute renal failure. It also should raise concern for development of muscle compartment syndrome.

17. How are hemoglobinuria and myoglobinuria diagnosed and treated?

The urine will characteristically become dark red or burgundy colored. The patient should undergo a forced diuresis, and the patient's urine should be alkalized to maintain the solubility of the pigments. This can best be accomplished by adding sodium bicarbonate 88 to 132 mEq of per liter of intravenous (IV) infusate. Urine output can be maintained through the administration of mannitol 25 to 37.5 g IV or furosemide 40 mg IV.

18. In the midst of a lightning storm, describe the safest location to avoid lightning injuries.

Victims of lightning strikes either are struck directly by the lightning or receive the side flash. The side flash is a discharge from the primary target through the air or ground to another object. A victim standing beneath a tree during a thunderstorm could receive a side flash via the tree.

The safest place to stay during a lightning storm is in a protected shelter with grounded metal fixtures, such as plumbing, which will provide a safe path for the lightning to reach ground. Alternatively, remaining in a closed automobile is safe because the individual cannot easily serve as a conduit to ground. However, standing next to the automobile again leaves a person vulnerable to side flash.

19. Can victims of electrical injury develop delayed neurologic sequelae?

Yes. In a study of 90 patients suffering from electrical trauma, 11 patients developed late neurologic symptoms, including muscle weakness, sensory deficit, paresthesias, and new pain complaints. Other series add credence to these observations.

20. What advice would you give the parents of a child with an electrical injury of the oral commissure?

Electrical burns of the oral commissure in children typically arise when children bite down on a live household electrical cord. Tissue loss ranges from superficial ulceration to full-thickness losses of the lips and cheek. In the second and third weeks after the injury, sloughing of devitalized tissue can be accompanied by bleeding from the labial artery. Parents can control this hemorrhage through finger compression of the commissure. They should be advised of this possibility at the time of the injury.

21. What are the ocular manifestations of electrical injury, and what is the most common of these?

Ocular manifestations of electrical injury can occur whether the contact sites are above or below the neck. The most common ocular injury is cataract formation, occurring in up to 5% of electrical injury patients. Cataracts can occur in low-, medium-, and high-voltage injuries. Contact points close to the eye can result in lens opacities in as early as a few hours. More distal contact points can be associated with a slower onset of cataract formation.

Other ocular manifestations of electrical injury include iritis, uveitis, formation of macular cysts, and macular degeneration. Electrical injury can result in abnormalities of ocular motility, conjunctival changes, corneal thinning or perforation, atrophy of the iris, optic neuritis or atrophy, retinal vascular occlusion or coagulative necrosis, and choroidal rupture or atrophy.

22. Describe neuropsychological changes following electrical injury.

In a controlled, age and demographics-matched comparison of 29 electrically injured electricians with 29 healthy controls, the electrically injured group performed more poorly on neuropsychological measures of attentional interference, mental processing speed, current Full Scale IQ, and motor skills, suggesting that cognitive changes can occur in patients as a result of electrical injury.

BIBLIOGRAPHY

Baxter CR: Present concepts in the management of major electrical injury. Surg Clin North Am 50:1401–1418, 1970.

Bernstein T: Electrical injury: Electrical engineer's perspective and an historical review. Ann N Y Acad Sci 720:1–10, 1994.

Bradley W, Salam-Adams M: Acute and subacute myopathic paralysis. In Petersdorf R, Adams R, Braunwald E, et al. (eds): Harrison's Principles of Internal Medicine. New York, McGraw-Hill Book Company, 1983, pp 2184–2187.

Council NS: Accident Facts. National Safety Council, 1997.

Dalziel C: Electric shock hazard. IEEE Spectrum 9:41–50, 1972.

DeFranzo A: Injuries from physical and chemical agents. In Georgiade G, Georgiade N, Riefkohl R, Barwick W (eds): Textbook of Plastic, Maxillofacial, and Reconstructive Surgery, Vol 1. Baltimore, Williams & Wilkins, 1992, pp 253–268.

Donelan MB: Reconstruction of electrical burns of the oral commissure with a ventral tongue flap. Plast Reconstr Surg 95:1155–1164, 1995.

Fontanarosa PB: Electrical shock and lightning strike. Ann Emerg Med 22(2 Pt 2):378–387, 1993.

Grube BJ, Heimbach DM, Engrav LH, Copass MK: Neurologic consequences of electrical burns. J Trauma 30:254–258, 1990.

Hammond J, Ward CG: The use of technetium-99 pyrophosphate scanning in management of high voltage electrical injuries. Am Surg 60:886–888, 1994.

Hunt JL, Sato RM, Baxter CR: Acute electric burns. Current diagnostic and therapeutic approaches to management. Arch Surg 115:434–438, 1980.

Lee R: Injury by electrical forces: Pathophysiology, manifestations, and therapy. Curr Probl Surgery 34:677–765, 1997.

Lee RC, Astumian RD: The physicochemical basis for thermal and non-thermal "burn" injuries. Burns 22:509–519, 1996.

Matsen FA 3rd, Winquist RA, Krugmire RB Jr: Diagnosis and management of compartmental syndromes. J Bone Joint Surg Am 62:286–291, 1980.

Miller BK, Goldstein MH, Monshizadeh R, Tabandeh H, Bhatti MT: Ocular manifestations of electrical injury: A case report and review of the literature. CLAO J 28:224–227, 2002.

Pliskin NH, Ammar AN, Fink JW, Hill SK, Malina AC, et al: Neuropsychological changes following electrical injury. J Int Neuropsychol Soc 12:17–23, 2006.

Robson M, Smith D: Thermal injuries. In Jurkiewicz M, Krizek T, Mathes S, Ariyan S (eds): Plastic Surgery, Principles and Practice, Vol 2. St. Louis, CV Mosby, 1990, pp 1392–1397.

Rowland S: Fasciotomy: The treatment of compartment syndrome. In Green D (ed): Operative Hand Surgery, Vol 1. New York, Churchill Livingstone, 1993, pp 661–694.

Schwab S: Renal diseases. In Orland M, Saltman R (eds): Manual of Medical Therapeutics. Boston, Little, Brown and Company, 1986, pp 177–195.

Tsong TY: Electroporation of cell membranes. Biophys J 60:297–306, 1991.

Whitesides T, Hirada H, Morimoto K: Compartment syndromes and the role of fasciotomy, its parameters and techniques. AAOS Instructional Course Lectures, Vol 26. St. Louis, CV Mosby, 1977, pp 179–196.

CHEMICAL INJURIES

Osak Omulepu, MD, and
David J. Bryan, MD, FACS

1. **Why is the management of chemical injuries important?**
   Although only 3% of all burns are due to chemical exposure, approximately 30% of burn deaths are due to chemical injuries. More than 25,000 substances can cause chemical injuries.

2. **What common items are associated with chemical injuries?**
   Most injuries are caused by either sulfuric acids or alkalis, which can be found in common household chemicals, in agriculture, in industry, and in war. Toilet bowl cleaners may contain sulfuric acid. Drain cleaners and paint thinners contain lye. Deodorizers, sanitizers, and disinfectants contain phenols. Self-inflating automotive airbags contain sodium azide. When ignited, sodium azide breaks down to sodium hydroxide, which can cause burns to the hands and face. Although rarely seen in civilian hospitals, agents used in armed conflicts, such as white phosphorous, are associated with chemical injuries. In some countries acid is used as a form of punishment or revenge.

3. **Which substances can cause more tissue destruction: Acids or alkalis?**
   Alkalis. Alkali burns have an insidious course. They initially appear benign but can progress to full-thickness injuries if left untreated. Alkali burns cause saponification of fat cells and liquefaction necrosis. Unattached alkali molecules then are free to penetrate deeper into the wound, causing more tissue destruction and severe pain.

   Acid burns produce immediate tissue destruction. Acids hydrolyze proteins soon after contact, causing coagulation necrosis and forming a tough, leathery eschar. This eschar limits further spread of the agent. Acids can also generate heat, causing a mixed chemical and thermal injury.

4. **What are some systemic effects associated with chemical injuries?**
   The patient with chemical burns should be carefully monitored to detect signs of systemic effect. Central nervous system (CNS) depression and cardiopulmonary collapse frequently accompany phenol toxicity. Renal failure (dichromate toxicity), hepatic necrosis (chromic, formic, picric, and phosphorus exposure), and metabolic complications, including hypocalcemia (hydrofluoric acid burns) and methemoglobinia (sodium and potassium nitrate exposure), are some of the systemic effects of chemical injuries.

5. **What are the criteria for hospital admission of patients with chemical burns?**
   - High-risk patients (concurrent illnesses)
   - Burns of hand, foot, face, eye, perineum
   - Burns of greater than 15% of total body surface
   - Deep burns (deep second- or third-degree burns)
   - Burns with substances that have systemic toxicity

6. **How do you acutely treat a chemical burn victim?**
   The management of chemical burns should always start with the ABCs. However, unlike other burn patients, immediate wound care takes priority in patients with chemical injuries. In a chemical burn, the burning process will stop only when the chemical substance is inactivated and removed from the area, or it exhausts its capacity to cause tissue destruction. In managing chemical burns, you must stop the burning process by removing the chemical to prevent further tissue injury. Remove *all* contaminated clothing, brush away any dry particles, and in most instances rinse the area with large amounts of *room-temperature water*. Irrigation is the mainstay of therapy for most chemical burns and should be performed with low pressure and high volumes. Patient resuscitation should occur concurrently.

7. **How long should you irrigate a chemical burn wound?**
   Chemicals can continue to damage the skin long after first contact, so irrigation should continue for a minimum of 30 minutes. One to two hours of continuous irrigation is recommended. A toxicologist should be contacted immediately.

Specific antidotes are available for some chemical agents. Neutralizing agents have no advantage over water and may even worsen the injury. Time may be wasted searching for the neutralizing agent, and the heat of reaction between the chemical and the neutralizing agent may cause a mixed thermal and chemical injury.

8. What are common pitfalls in treating chemical injuries?

Common pitfalls in the treatment of patients with chemical injuries, in addition to the failure to remove all contaminated clothing and a delay in water lavage, include inadequate lavage and inaccurate assessment of tissue injury. Skin damaged by contact with strong acids has a tanned appearance and a smooth texture. If these areas are mistaken for a suntan rather than the full-thickness injury that they are, fluid requirements may be underestimated. As with thermal burns, inadequate resuscitation may extend tissue damage from second to third degree. In the case of strong alkali injuries, irrigation should be extended for a longer period of time.

9. What is the difference between thermal and chemical burns?

A thermal injury is a momentary event, whereas a chemical injury is continuous. Unlike thermal burns, chemical burns cause tissue necrosis and may have serious systemic effects. *Alkalis cause liquefaction necrosis and acids cause coagulation necrosis.* The severity of chemical injuries is directly proportional to the length of time that the substance remains on the skin. Burning pain indicates chemical still is in contact with the skin (Table 100-1).

Table 100-1. Chemical Agents

AGENT	COMMON USE	CHARACTERISTICS	AGENT TO REMOVE OR DILUTE	SYSTEMIC EFFECTS
Oxidizing Agents				
Chromic acid	Metal cleaning	Ulcerates, blisters	Water lavage	
Potassium permanganate	Bleach, deodorizer, disinfectant	Thick, brownish purple eschar	Water lavage, egg white solution	
Sodium hypochlorite	Bleach, deodorizer, disinfectant	Local irritation, inflammation	Water lavage, milk, egg white solution, paste, starch	
Corrosive Agents				
Phenol	Deodorant, sanitizer, plastics, dyes, fertilizers, explosives, disinfectants	Soft white eschar, brown stain when eschar removed, mild to no pain	Copious water lavage, polyethylene glycol solution, vegetable oil	Minor exposure: Tachycardia, arrhythmias Significant exposure: Cardiopulmonary depression, hypothermia
White phosphorous	Explosives, poisons, insecticides, fertilizers	Necrotic with yellowish color, garlic odor, glow in dark, pain	Lavage with 1% copper sulfate, cover with water or castor oil	Nephrotoxic, hepatic necrosis
Sodium metal, lye, KOH, NaOH, NH$_4$OH, LiOH, Ba$_2$(OH)$_3$, Ca(OH)$_3$	Cleaning agent (washing powder, drain cleaner, paint remover), cement	Soft, gelatinous, brown eschar	Sodium metal: Oil immersion Lye: Water lavage	
Metabolic Competitors/Inhibitors				
Oxalic acid	Industrial	Chalky white ulcers	Large-volume calcium salts, copious water lavage, intravenous calcium	Hypocalcemia
Hydrofluoric acid	Industrial	Painful, deep ulcerations	Water lavage, subcutaneous calcium, subcutaneous magnesium sulfate	Hypocalcemia hypomagnesemia

10. Describe the nature and appearance of acid burns

Acid burns are generally quite painful. Their appearance may range from erythematous, as in a superficial injury, to a yellow-gray or black eschar with a leather-like appearance in deeper burns.

- Sulfuric acid: Green-black to dark brown eschar
- Nitric acid: Yellow eschar and tissue staining
- Hydrochloric acid: Yellow-brown eschar and tissue staining
- Trichloroacetic acid: Whitish, soft tissue slough

11. What is hydrofluoric acid?

Hydrofluoric acid is a highly corrosive, inorganic acid of elemental fluorine that is used in the production of plastics, semiconductors, pottery glazing, and rust removal and is a component of aluminum brighteners. Hydrofluoric acid injury is an occupational hazard for petroleum refinery workers and for those engaged in the cleaning of air conditioning equipment. It has been widely used since the discovery in the late seventeenth century of its ability to dissolve silica. Contact with hydrofluoric acid typically is initially pain-free, with subsequent localized pallor. This pallor progresses to penetrating tissue necrosis and severe tissue pain.

12. Why are hydrofluoric acid burns so severe?

The hydrogen ion causes a typical caustic injury common to all acid burns. However, it is the extremely reactive fluoride ion that is responsible for the severe systemic effects of a hydrofluoric acid burn. By combining themselves with other cations, such as calcium or magnesium, the reactive fluoride ions are inactivated. These cations will be leached from the patient's intracellular and extracellular stores, a process that can produce life-threatening hypocalcemia and bony decalcification. This process can continue for hours or days if left untreated and have severe biochemical consequences. A patient with hydrofluoric acid burns presents in excruciating pain, with erythema, edema, and bullae.

13. What is the first sign of hypocalcemia after a hydrofluoric acid burn?

The first sign of hypocalcemia is profound bradycardia, which usually occurs within 30 to 45 minutes after exposure. The dysrhythmia may respond to high doses of intravenous (IV) calcium and surgical excision of the burn wound.

14. What are the signs of acute systemic fluoride toxicity?

Hypocalcemia, hypomagnesemia, hypotension, bradycardia, ventricular fibrillation (often intractable), respiratory depression, pulmonary edema, seizures, CNS depression, carpopedal spasm, tetany, and coagulation disorders (rare).

15. How do you treat a hydrofluoric acid burn?

All clothing and shoes must be removed. While resuscitating the patient, begin treatment with immediate 30-minute water lavage of the affected areas. All bullae and vesicles should be aspirated to remove fluoride-containing fluid. Fingernails should be clipped to ensure removal of acid trapped underneath them. The fluoride ions should be inactivated with topical calcium gluconate (or magnesium oxide or calcium chloride) massaged into the skin. Unrelenting pain is an indication for injection of a 10% calcium gluconate solution into the burn, to further bind the fluorine ion. Multiple injections of 0.1 or 0.2 mL are given through a 30-gauge needle without anesthesia. This deposits calcium directly into the tissues and eventually provides pain relief. Recurrence of pain is an indication for reinspection and reinjection.

Very severe injuries may require intraarterial calcium infusion. Treatment is continued until the patient is free from pain for 4 hours. Local excision with skin grafting may be necessary for definitive pain control and removal of damaged tissue.

16. What substances account for the majority of alkali burns?

Sodium hydroxide and cement. Sodium hydroxide, a strong alkaline corrosive, can be found in clogged drain products, oven cleaners, and paint removers. Alkali burns can also result from calcium oxide contained in lime, cement, and fertilizer. Alkalis are the most common chemicals found in homes. These substances are less soluble in water and take longer to clear with water irrigation.

17. What type of alkali injuries merit special attention?

Alkali burns of the eye produce some of the most severe injuries encountered in medicine. When a strong alkali contacts the eye, the epithelium is destroyed and allows the alkali access into the cornea. This produces immediate opacification of the cornea and coagulation of scleral and corneal proteins. The pH of the anterior chamber rises within 2 to 3 minutes, damaging the iris, lens, and ciliary body. This can lead to an irreversible blindness within 3 minutes of exposure. Irrigation is the mainstay of treatment. Eyelid spasm may be decreased by use of tetracaine or other ophthalmologic anesthetic solutions.

18. **How does cement cause a chemical burn?**
Cement generates an exothermic reaction when mixed with water. Interestingly, sweat is sufficient to initiate this reaction. Hydrated calcium oxide (the main ingredient in cement) becomes calcium hydroxide, a strong alkali. This burn was first described in a patient who developed burns after kneeling in premixed cement.

19. **What is a boot-cuff burn injury?**
Boot-cuff burn injuries are caused by wet cement collecting inside the shoes, burning the ankles or knees. These injuries result from kneeling in wet cement without protection. As a result, most injuries occur in the setting of "do-it-yourself" home projects. Typically the victim does not know that a burn has occurred because it is often under clothing and painless. The resulting burn often is serious because the material is allowed to remain in contact with the skin for prolonged periods.

20. **What chemical burns should *never* be treated with water irrigation?**
Elemental sodium, potassium, and lithium burns. Sodium, potassium, and, to a lesser extent, lithium will spontaneously ignite when in contact with water, including water vapor in the air or on the skin. When these metals combine with water, hydroxides are formed, which are among the strongest alkalis known and are capable of causing severe caustic burns. Using water to irrigate these burns will only intensify the combustion.

21. **How do you treat these burning metals?**
To extinguish these burning metals, oxygen and water must be removed from the area. A fire extinguisher or sand can be used to smother the fire. After the fire is extinguished, the area should be covered with mineral oil. Small metal pieces should be removed. Dispose of particles by placing them in alcohol. Embedded pieces must be removed surgically. Following débridement and confirmation that all pieces have been removed, the area can be irrigated with water.

22. **How are tar and grease best removed?**
Immediate treatment consists of cooling the hot adherent material with cold water. Tar and grease are derived from petroleum and coal hydrocarbons. Therefore petroleum-based products such as Bacitracin and Neosporin ointment are ideal for tar and grease emulsification and removal.

23. **What chemical burn has the characteristic smell of garlic?**
White phosphorous.

24. **What is white phosphorous?**
Phosphorous is an incendiary agent used in a variety of military munitions. Burns are seen mainly in military personnel but may be encountered in persons in contact with fireworks and fertilizer and in insecticide and rodenticide manufacturers. Phosphorous is a waxy, translucent solid that spontaneously ignites on contact with air. It usually is preserved in water.

25. **How do you treat a white phosphorous burn?**
Immediate treatment involves removing all of the victim's clothing, irrigating the area with water, and removing any easily identifiable particles. The burns should be covered in water-soaked dressings and kept continually wet to prevent ignition of retained particles.

Irrigation with copper sulfate in a 0.5% solution results in the formation cupric phosphide, a blue-gray material that coats the retained phosphorus particles. This facilitates identification of particles for removal and impedes ignition. Another way to identify particles of white phosphorus is to shine ultraviolet light on a burn in a darkened operating room. The phosphorous particles glow. Following removal, phosphorus particles should always be placed under water, lest they ignite and cause a fire.

26. **What metabolic and systemic complications are associated with white phosphorous burns?**
Hypocalcemia, hyperphosphatemia, hepatotoxicity, renal toxicity, and electrocardiographic abnormalities (prolonged QT interval, bradycardia, nonspecific ST-T wave changes).

27. **What chemical injury is treated with polyethylene glycol (antifreeze)?**
Phenol.

28. **What is phenol?**
Phenol (carbolic acid) is an aromatic acid alcohol that is a highly reactive and corrosive contact poison. Phenols denature and precipitate cellular proteins and have been used as bactericidal agents, chemical bases for plastics and organic polymers, and cosmetic skin peels. In the form of creosote, it is used as a wood preservative. Lister first used phenols as antiseptics in 1867.

Table 100-2. Treatment Measures for Specific Chemical Burns

Irrigation with water	Acetic acid, ammonium hydroxide, barium hydroxide, calcium hydroxide, cantharides (Spanish fly), chromic acid, cresylic acid, dichromate salts, dimethyl sulfoxide (DMSO), formic acid, gasoline, hydrofluoric acid, lyes and alkalis, phenol, picric acid, potassium hydroxide, potassium permanganate, sodium hydroxide, sodium hypochlorite, sulfosalicylic acid, tannic acid, trichloroacetic acid, tungstic acid
Calcium salts irrigation and/or injection	Hydrofluoric acid
Cover burn with oil	Sodium metal, lithium metal, mustard gas
Cover burn with water	Phosphorous metal

Special measures for certain chemicals:
Sodium and lithium metals: Pieces must be excised.
Hydrofluoric acid: Calcium gluconate injection.
Phenol: Polyethylene glycol wipe.
White phosphorous: Copper sulfate irrigation.
Alkyl mercury agents: Débride and remove blister fluid.

29. How quickly can systemic phenol toxicity manifest itself?

Within 30 minutes of skin contact, loss of consciousness can occur. Phenol is rapidly absorbed through skin surfaces; phenol vapors are easily absorbed by the lungs in either liquid or vapor form. The most common manifestation of systemic phenol poisoning is profound central nervous system depression, accompanied by coma, hypothermia, intravascular hemolysis, loss of vasomotor tone, hypotension, shock, pulmonary edema, and respiratory arrest and death.

30. How do you treat phenol injuries?

After treating phenol injuries with an initial water lavage, these wounds should be washed with a lipophilic solvent, such as polyethylene glycol. Isopropyl alcohol, glycerol, Tween 80, and vegetable oil are also effective in removing phenols. Phenol is only slightly soluble in water (Table 100-2).

31. What chemical injury is often accompanied with frostbite?

Anhydrous ammonia. Anhydrous ammonia is used extensively as an agricultural fertilizer and in the manufacturing of nylon, rayon, and explosives. Anhydrous ammonia is stored at approximately −28 °F, so exposure to this substance can cause both frostbite and a chemical injury.

BIBLIOGRAPHY

Corazza M, Trincone S, Virgili A: Effects of airbag deployment: lesions, epidemiology, and management. Am J Clin Dermatol 5: 295–300, 2004.
Erdmann D, Hussman J, Kucan JO: Treatment of a severe alkali burn. Burns 22:141–146, 1996.
Hatzifotis M, Williams A, Muller M, et al: Hydrofluoric acid burns. Burns 30:156–159, 2004.
Herbert K, Lawrence JC: Chemical burns. Burns 15:381–384, 1989.
MacKinnon MA: Hydrofluoric acid burns. Dermatol Clin 6:67–74, 1988.
Moran KD, O'Reilly T, Munster AM: Chemical burns: A ten-year experience. Am J Surg 53:652–653, 1987.
Mozingo DW, Smith AA, McManus WF, et al: Chemical burns. J Trauma 28:642–647, 1988.
Murray J: Cold, chemical, and irradiation injuries. In McCarthy JG (ed): Plastic Surgery. Philadelphia, WB Saunders, 1990, pp 5431–5451.
Sawhney CP, Kaushish R: Acid and alkali burns: Considerations in management. Burns 15:132–134, 1989.
Spoo J, Elsner P: Cement burns: A review 1960–2000. Contact Derm 45:68–71, 2001.
Wolf SE, Herndon DN: Burns and radiation injuries. In Moore EE, Feliciano DV, Mattox KL: Trauma, 5th ed. New York, McGraw-Hill, 2004, pp 1081–1097.
www.burnsurgery.com, 2000. Accessed September 2009.

FROSTBITE

Jagruti C. Patel, MD, FACS, and
James W. Fletcher, MD, FACS

CHAPTER 101

1. What are the three common types of cold injury?
Tissue-freezing injury (frostbite), non–tissue-freezing injury (trenchfoot, chilblain, or pernio), and hypothermia.

2. What is frostbite?
Frostbite occurs when the temperature falls to 28°F (−2°C) and tissue freezes, resulting in formation of intracellular ice crystals and microvascular occlusion.

3. What is chilblain (pernio)?
Chilblain refers to skin exposed to chronic high humidity and low temperature without tissue freezing. The core body temperature remains normal. Mountain climbers typically are affected.

4. What is trenchfoot?
Trenchfoot develops when the extremities are exposed to a damp environment over long periods at temperatures of 32°F to 50°F (1°C to 10°C). Heat is lost because the extremity is wet, and vascular flow is poor because of vasoconstriction.

5. What are the symptoms of trenchfoot?
Trenchfoot is characterized by numbness, tingling, pain, and itching. The skin initially is red and edematous, then gradually takes on a gray-blue discoloration. After a few days the foot becomes hyperemic. Within 3 to 6 weeks the symptoms resolve, but the extremity still may be sensitive to cold.

6. What is cold urticaria?
Cold urticaria is a syndrome consisting of urticaria and angioedema due to exposure to cold temperatures (seen especially with aquatic activities). Anaphylaxis may occur, depending on the severity of the disease. The two types of urticaria are familial and acquired. History and a cold stimulation test confirm the diagnosis.

7. What predisposing risk factors contribute to frostbite?
- Substance abuse (30% to 50%), especially alcohol
- Psychiatric illness (10% to 20%)
- Environmental factors (lack of appropriate clothing and weather conditions)
- Peripheral vascular disease (decreased flow)
- Age (elderly and very young)
- Race (African Americans are at greater risk than are whites)
- Medications (e.g., aminophylline, caffeine, fiorinal, ergot alkaloids)

8. How is frostbite classified?
See Table 101-1.

9. What is the pathophysiology of frostbite?
Tissue damage may result from direct cellular damage or the secondary effects of microvascular thrombosis and subsequent ischemia. The recognized changes during freezing are (1) extracellular ice formation, (2) intracellular ice formation, (3) cell dehydration and crenation, (4) abnormal electrolyte concentrations due to above, and (5) perturbations in lipid–protein complexes. With rewarming, ice crystals melt and injured endothelium promotes edema. Epidermal blisters form, and free radical formation continues the insult. Elaboration of inflammatory mediators, prostaglandins, and thromboxanes induces vasoconstriction and platelet aggregation, which worsen ischemia (Fig. 101-1).

Table 101-1. Classification of Frostbite

DEGREE OF INJURY	CLINICAL FEATURES	OUTCOME
First degree	White/yellow plaque, hyperemia, edema Causalgia and pain may indicate nerve damage	Tissue loss and necrosis are rare
Second degree	Blisters contain clear or milky fluid Erythema and edema are common	Characteristic recovery without tissue loss
Third degree	Deep, full-thickness skin necrosis	Tissue loss is common
Fourth degree	Cyanosis, gangrene, necrosis	Underlying muscles and bone are affected

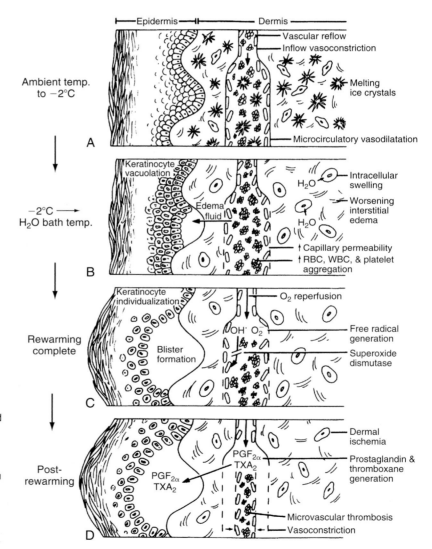

Figure 101-1. Pathophysiology of frostbite. **A,** As rewarming begins, ice crystals melt. **B,** Injured endothelium promotes edema. **C,** Epidermal blisters and free radicals form. **D,** Inflammatory mediators induce vasocontriction and platelet aggregation. (Redrawn from Heggers JP, Robson MC, Manavalen K, et al: Experimental and clinical observations on frostbite. Ann Emerg Med 16:1056–1062, 1987.)

10. What vascular changes occur with frostbite?

The vascular endothelium is particularly susceptible. Seventy-two hours after freezing and thawing, the endothelium may be completely obliterated and replaced by fibrin deposition. Investigators also have observed electron microscopic evidence of perivascular fluid extravasation and endothelial swelling and lysis.

11. What immunogenic factors play a role in frostbite?

Neutrophil–endothelial cell adhesion mediated by integrins (CD11a/CD18) and selectins (L, P, and E) plays a germane role in modulating cellular dysfunction in frostbite as well as other disorders of interest to the plastic surgeon (ischemia/reperfusion, hemorrhagic shock, allograft rejection). Factors elaborated from pathways set in motion by the recruited immunocompetent cells, such as thromboxane B_2 and prostaglandins E_2 and $F_{2\alpha}$, have been isolated from frostbite blisters. Evidence suggests that blockade of the inflammatory cascades may influence outcome.

12. How is frostbite treated?

Rapid rewarming is the cornerstone in the acute management of frostbite. Immersion in water heated to 104°F to 108°F (40°C to 42°C) is the standard of care for all degrees of frostbite. This tight range of temperatures should be strictly followed because the benefit to frozen tissues at lower temperatures is reduced and burn injury may occur at higher temperatures. Parenteral analgesia should be administered as needed for pain. Massage of the area is contraindicated because it may exacerbate the injury. After rapid rewarming the standard protocol to prevent progressive tissue/dermal ischemia includes the following:

- Débride clear blisters.
- Leave hemorrhagic blisters intact, but aspirate if infected.
- Elevate affected areas to decrease edema.
- Apply topical thromboxane inhibitor (aloe vera [Dermide]) to injured areas.
- Give systemic antiprostaglandin agent (e.g., aspirin, ibuprofen).
- Give tetanus toxoid prophylaxis when appropriate.
- Whirlpool treatments to decrease the incidence of infection and early mobilization with passive manipulation of injured extremities are advocated when appropriate.

13. What is the role of surgery in the treatment of frostbite?

Reconstruction has no role in the acute phase of frostbite. Attempts to débride aggressively in the early phase of frostbite or amputation may compromise viable tissue. The only indication for early operative intervention is amelioration of a constricting eschar or drainage of a subeschar infection that has not responded topical antimicrobials. If tissue injury progresses to gangrene, amputation and/or coverage may be required. Surgery should be delayed until the area is thoroughly demarcated.

14. What is the role of hyperbaric oxygen in the treatment of frostbite?

A number of clinical cases have documented the therapeutic benefit of using hyperbaric oxygen (HBO) therapy for treatment of mild to deep frostbite. One such case used HBO therapy in an 11-year-old boy with third-degree frostbite on four fingers of one hand and two fingers on the other hand. The protocol used required daily HBO treatments for 14 days at a depth of 2.4 atm for a total dive time of 90 minutes (alternating 100% oxygen with air breathing), resulting in complete reversal of the frostbite. Twenty-eight months after the initial injury the patient reported fully regained sensibilty and no pain.

15. What other diagnostic modalities are used in determining the extent of frostbite?

Radioisotope vascular and bone imaging, angiography, thermography, and digital plethysmography have been used to assist in making earlier determinations of tissue viability.

16. Is any adjuvant therapy useful in the treatment of frostbite?

- Use of an intermediate alpha-blocker has been advocated as pharmacologic sympathectomy to relieve arteriospasm. Tolazoline HCl and injected reserpine begin to block sympathetic vascular effects in 3 to 24 hours; their effects may last for 2 to 4 weeks.
- Nifedipine in doses of 20 to 60 mg has been advocated for chilblain to prevent new lesions and to clear present lesions through vasodilatory effects.
- Free radical scavengers such as dimethyl sulfide, vitamin C, and vitamin E may have potential in treating the reperfusion component of injury. Thrombolytics such as low-molecular-weight dextran, heparin, urokinase, and streptokinase have shown promise in experimental models but require further clinical trials to determine whether they are beneficial.

17. What are the late sequelae of frostbite?

Arthritis is common after frostbite. Pain, hyperasthesias, and cold sensitivity are more infrequent and are seen with more severe cases. Hyperhydrosis and pigment changes may occur. Of interest to the hand surgeon is the occurrence of epiphyseal insult in children and subsequent growth deformities.

BIBLIOGRAPHY

Blair JR, Schatzki R, Orr ND: Sequelae to cold injury in one hundred patients: Followup study four years after occurrence of cold injury. JAMA 163:1203–1208, 1957.

Britt DL, Dascombe WH, Rodriguez A: New horizons in management of hypothermia and frostbite injury. Surg Clin North Am 71: 345–370, 1991.

Brown FE, Spiegel PK, Boyle WE Jr: Digital deformity An effect of frostbite in children. Pediatrics 71:955–959, 1983.

Demling RH: Cold injury. In Demling RH (ed): Thermal Injury. New York, Scientific American, 1995.

Korthuis RJ, Anderson DC, Granger DN: Role of neutrophil-endothelial cell adhesion in inflammatory disorders. J Crit Care 9:47–71, 1994.

McCauley RL, Heggers JP, Robson MC: Frostbite: Methods to minimize tissue loss. Postgrad Med 88:67–77, 1990.

McCauley RL, Hing DN, Robson MC, Heggers JP: Frostbite injuries: A rational approach based on the pathophysiology. J Trauma 23: 143–147, 1983.

Porter JM, Wesche DH, Rosch J, Baur GM: Intra-arterial sympathetic blockage n the treatment of clinical frostbite. Am J Surg 132:625–630, 1976.

Rustin M, Newton JA, Smith NP, Down PM: The treatment of chilblains with nifedipine. Br J Dermatol 120:267–275, 1989.

Urschal JD: Frostbite: Predisposing factors and predictors of poor outcome. J Trauma 30:340–342, 1990.

Von Heimberg, Noah EM, Sieckmann UP, Pallua N: Hyperbaric oxygen treatment in deep frostbite of both hands in a boy. Burns 27:404–408, 2001.

METABOLISM AND NUTRITION

Eric J. Mahoney, MD; Walter L. Biffl, MD; and
William G. Cioffi, MD, FACS

1. What are the daily requirements of carbohydrates, lipids, and proteins?
Generally, the amount of carbohydrates should not exceed 5 to 7 mg/kg/min. The lipid requirement is approximately 2.5 g/kg/day and should be no more that 30% of the daily caloric requirement. Protein requirements vary based on the clinical situation: normal patients require 0.8 to 1.0 g/kg/day, highly stressed patients may require 1.5 to 2.0 g/kg/day, and renal failure patients should receive only 0.5 g/kg/day. Overall, the ratio of nonprotein to protein calories should be between 100:1 to 120:1.

2. What methods are used to determine a patient's daily caloric requirement?
The most accurate method is indirect calorimetry, which uses the measured oxygen consumption (VO_2) and carbon dioxide production (VCO_2) to determine the measured resting energy expenditure (MREE):

$$MREE = (3.9 \times VO_2) + (1.1 \times VCO_2) \times 60 \times 1/\text{Body surface area}$$

More commonly, the *Harris-Benedict equation* is used to estimate the basal energy expenditure (BEE). This is then multiplied by an arbitrary factor based on the degree of stress: for uncomplicated postoperative patient, × 1.05; cancer cachexia, × 1.1 to 1.4; severe peritonitis, × 1.25; multiple trauma, × 1.5; and severe burns, × 1.8.

$$BEE \text{ (females)} = 655 + (9.6 \times \text{weight in kilograms}) + (1.8 \times \text{height in centimeters}) - (4.7 \times \text{Age in years})$$

$$BEE \text{ (males)} = 66 + (13.7 \times \text{weight in kilograms}) + (5 \times \text{height in centimeters}) - (6.8 \times \text{Age in years})$$

3. How is protein synthesis hormonally regulated?
Hormones such as growth hormone, insulin, and testosterone are anabolic and lead to increased protein synthesis. Antagonistically, glucocorticoids lead to protein catabolism peripherally (but increased hepatic protein synthesis).

4. How does stress or injury alter metabolism?
Stress or injury activates a neurohormonal cascade that is able to alter metabolism and better respond to the stressors. Classically, this is described as occurring in two phases: an *ebb phase* and a *flow phase.* The ebb phase occurs acutely within hours and is characterized by decreased energy expenditure and hyperglycemia. This is followed by the flow phase, during which the individual is hypermetabolic and demonstrates active lipolysis, protein catabolism, and a net negative nitrogen balance. This net negative nitrogen balance is refractory to attempts to correct it through enteral or parenteral nutrition, and it can last from days to weeks.

5. What is the effect of stress or injury on blood sugar levels?
Stress or injury leads to the release of large amounts of epinephrine and glucagon. These hormones suppress insulin and activate an enzyme called *phosphorylase,* which leads to glycogenolysis in the liver and ultimately to higher blood glucose levels.

6. What is gluconeogenesis?
Gluconeogenesis is the process by which glucose is synthesized from protein (amino acids) and glycerol. This is stimulated by hypoglycemia as well as by the hormone cortisol, especially in times of stress.

7. What is the effect of insulin therapy in critically ill patients?
The use of insulin to maintain blood glucose levels less than 110 mg/dL has been shown to decrease intensive care unit mortality, overall in-hospital mortality, bloodstream infections, acute renal failure, critical-illness polyneuropathy, the number of red cell transfusions, and the requirement for prolonged mechanical ventilation.

8. **List several host factors that can impair wound healing.**

Factors that can impair wound healing include malnutrition, obesity, disorders of collagen synthesis, renal insufficiency, diabetes mellitus, chemotherapy, and corticosteroid use.

9. **What is the effect of protein malnutrition on wound healing?**

Protein malnutrition leading to hypoalbuminemia is associated with increased wound complications and delayed wound healing. This was further illustrated in animal studies in which researchers found that animals with protein deficiencies had decreased bursting strength at colonic anastomoses.

10. **How is a malnourished patient identified?**

Current methods of identifying malnourished patients include objective measures such as physical examination, recent weight loss, measurement of serum protein levels, anthropometric measurements (e.g., triceps skin fold), anergy testing, grip strength testing, and the use of nutritional indices such as the Nutrition Risk Index and the Subjective Global Assessment.

11. **Which are the best indicators of overall nutritional status?**

A complete history and physical examination.

12. **What are signs of malnutrition that can be identified on physical examination?**

Physical signs of malnutrition include hair loss, bitemporal muscle wasting, conjunctival pallor, xerosis, glossitis, bleeding of gums or mucosa, poor dentition, thyromegaly, edema, poor wound healing, hepatomegaly, ascites, and deltoid and quadriceps muscle wasting.

13. **Which serum proteins are used to assess a patient's nutritional status?**

Serum albumin, transferrin, prealbumin, and retinol-binding protein. Given its short half-life of 2 days, the prealbumin level is the most accurate in assessing acute nutritional deficiencies. Albumin, with a half-life of 21 days, is a better index of chronic malnutrition.

14. **Which comorbid conditions can lead to decreased levels of nutritional indexes irrespective of a patient's nutritional state?**

Albumin levels may be decreased in patients with congestive heart failure, cirrhosis, renal failure, burns, and overhydration. Similarly, prealbumin levels are decreased in patients with cirrhosis, hepatitis, and inflammatory states.

15. **Describe several adverse consequences of malnutrition in a surgical patient**

Malnutrition increases a patient's susceptibility to infection. This is due to impaired production and activation of complement, impaired bacterial opsonization, and impaired function of inflammatory cells. Malnutrition also leads to poor wound healing and increased incidence of decubitus ulcers.

16. **How soon after surgery or trauma should exogenous nutritional supplementation be initiated?**

Exogenous nutritional supplementation, whether enteral or parenteral, should be initiated in severely malnourished patients only after proper volume resuscitation and hemodynamic stability have been established. Risks of premature enteral feedings include gastrointestinal intolerance and intestinal ischemia. In burn patients, enteral feedings should be started as soon as feasible because a delay increases the incidence of gastroparesis. In patients with severe traumatic brain injuries, however, gastrointestinal motility can be impaired for up to 2 weeks after injury, and these patients are better suited for total parenteral nutrition. Total parenteral nutrition can be started immediately after resuscitation has been completed in most malnourished patients.

17. **What deleterious effects have been attributed to total parenteral nutrition versus enteral nutrition?**

Parenteral feedings have been shown to decrease intestinal immunoglobulin A levels and to increase gut permeability and bacterial translocation to mesenteric lymph nodes, implying a breakdown in gastrointestinal mucosal integrity. Overall, parenteral nutrition is associated with a higher incidence of septic complications compared with enteral nutrition.

18. **What is immunonutrition?**

Immunonutrition involves the administration of supernormal amounts of certain nutrients to gain a potential pharmacologic effect from those nutrients.

19. Name several proposed immunonutrients and their theorized modes of action.

Proposed immunonutrients include omega-3 fatty acids, arginine, ribonucleic acid (RNA), and glutamine. Omega-3 fatty acids suppress proinflammatory cytokine production. Arginine enhances T-lymphocyte number and function and stimulates growth hormone production. RNA improves T-lymphocyte function. Glutamine improves gut barrier function.

20. What benefits have been identified using immunonutrition?

A reduced rate of infection and wound complications was seen in surgical patients with upper gastrointestinal cancer who received enteral nutrition with arginine, RNA, and omega-3 fatty acids. Overall, a lower rate of infections and a reduced intensive care unit and hospital length of stay were found in patients given immunonutrition. However, no mortality benefit was seen, and whether these benefits can be translated to other surgical patients has yet been determined.

21. What effects does the oxygen tension have on wound healing?

Low oxygen tensions are believed to cause poor wound healing and inhibit wound closure. Supernormal oxygen tensions, on the other hand, created within hyperbaric chambers, have been used to improve healing in chronic wounds in patients with peripheral vascular disease or profound anemia.

22. What is the hypermetabolic response to burn injury?

The hypermetabolic response to burn injury is characterized by increases in cardiac output, minute ventilation, and core body temperature and a decrease in nitrogen balance. The magnitude of response is directly proportional to burn wound size. In patients with burns greater than 50% of total body surface area (TBSA), the metabolic rate can reach 1.5 to 2 times the predicted resting energy expenditure.

23. What are the responsible mediators?

Catecholamines are the primary mediators of the hypermetabolic response, and their excretion correlates well with burn size and increased metabolic rate.

24. How can the hypermetabolic response to burns be blunted?

During the burn hypermetabolism, heat production is increased and core body temperature is elevated. Cooler ambient temperatures will cause catecholamine release and an increased metabolic rate. Maintaining a high ambient temperature to keep the core body temperature at approximately 100°F prevents additional energy expenditure. In children with burns, beta-adrenergic blockade has been shown to reduce the hypermetabolic response; its effect in adults has not been clearly defined.

25. When does the metabolic rate return to normal?

Once wounds are closed after excision and grafting, the metabolic rate begins to return to baseline. Normal baseline metabolism, however, will not be reached until the wound remodeling is complete, which may take 1 to 2 years.

26. Describe burn wound resuscitation.

Judicious but adequate fluid resuscitation is vital in the treatment of patients with burns. Several mathematical formulas have been developed, including the following:
- Parkland: 4 cc/kg/% body surface area burn
- Brooke: 2 cc/kg/% body surface area burn

In both formulas, the fluid is given as lactated Ringer's solution, with half of the calculated amount given during the first 8 hours after the burn occurred and the other half given over the following 16 hours (with hourly adjustments based on urine output). In patients with burns greater than 30% TBSA, intravenous albumin should be started as follows:
- 30% to 50% TBSA: 0.3 cc/kg/%TBSA/24 hours
- 50% to 70% TBSA: 0.4 cc/kg/%TBSA/24 hours
- >70% TBSA: 0.5 cc/kg/%TBSA/24 hours

27. What effect does insulin therapy have on the immune response to burn?

In children with burns, exogenous insulin therapy has been shown to decrease levels of proinflammatory cytokines, increase levels of antiinflammatory cytokines, and decrease levels of acute-phase reactants.

28. What effect does oxandrolone have on the immune response to burn?

The anabolic steroid oxandrolone has been shown to reduce the level of acute-phase reactants and to improve albumin levels early after burns. Long-term use of oxandrolone has been shown to improve lean body mass, bone mineral content, and bone mineral density.

BIBLIOGRAPHY

Albina JE: Nutrition and wound healing. J Parent Enter Nutr 18:367–376, 1994.

Carlson DE, Cioffi WG, Mason AD, et al: Resting energy expenditure in patients with thermal injury. Surg Gynecol Obstet 174: 270–276, 1992.

Cone JB: What's new in general surgery: Burns and metabolism. J Am Coll Surg 200:607–615, 2005.

Grimble RF: Immunonutrition. Curr Opin Gastroenterol 21:216–222, 2005.

Jacobs DG, Jacobs DO, Kudsk KA, et al: Practice management guidelines for nutritional support of the trauma patient. J Trauma 57: 660–679, 2004.

Li W, Dasgeb G, Phillips T, Li Y, et al: Wound-healing perspectives. Dermatol Clin 23:181–192, 2005.

Martindale RG, Cresci GA, Leibach FH: Nutrition and metabolism. In O'Leary JP: The Physiologic Basis of Surgery, 3rd ed. Philadelphia, Lippincott Williams & Wilkins, 2002.

Roth RN, Weiss LD: Hyperbaric oxygen and wound healing. Clin Dermatol 12:141–156, 1994.

Van der Berghe G, Wouters P, Weekers F, et al: Intensive insulin therapy in critically ill patients. N Engl J Med 345:1359–1367, 2001.

BURN RECONSTRUCTION

Jane A. Petro, MD, FACS, and
Zahid Niazi, MD, FRCSI, FICS, FNYAM

CHAPTER 103

1. What are the general principles of burn rehabilitation?

- Adequate treatment in the acute injury phase includes the prevention of infection; prompt débridement and wound closure; preservation of mobility, strength, and endurance; maintenance of independence in self care; control of edema; and education of the patient, patient's family, and patient's peers about burn recovery
- Preparation of the patient for a return to a preburn level of function, if possible, as soon as the acute burn care is completed
- Prevention of contracture through exercise, splinting, and physical and occupational therapy
- Early intervention and treatment of burn scars, contractures, and disability
- Psychological support

These activities begin at the time of admission and continue throughout the hospitalization and subsequent recovery.

2. Is a burn scar unique?

Burn scars can be readily recognized and have a very different appearance (Fig. 103-1). A burn scar differs from other types of scars as a result of the extent of surface area injured and a variable healing process due to the differing recovery potential of superficial or deep burn injuries. Very superficial burns are confined to epidermal layers, which can nearly regenerate, leaving minimal or no disfiguring marks. Deeper burns, resulting from injury to both the dermis and the epidermis, are characterized by a healing process that takes 2 weeks or more. As the injury level deepens, fewer ductal rests of epithelium survive, impairing reepithelialization. This prolongs the inflammatory phase of healing,

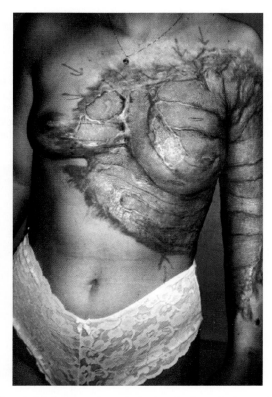

Figure 103-1. Characteristic burn scar, demonstrating hypertrophy, contracture, and a ropy appearance.

increases proliferation of fibroblasts and myofibroblasts, and results in increasingly profound scar deformity. If substantial dermis survives, pigment formation may be fairly normal, and contracture will be minimal. As more dermis is lost, changes may include loss of hair growth, absent or irregular pigmentation, shiny smooth appearance to the skin, inability to sweat, and inability to produce sebaceous oils that normally lubricate the skin. The resulting healed scar from this type of deep dermal injury may become hypertrophic, with a ropy, reddened, irregular texture, and cause intense itching and burning. These hypertrophic scars can be avoided or reduced with aggressive burn care, early use of compression garments, steroid injections into the forming scar, and use of silicone compression sheets.

3. What is the primary goal of burn rehabilitation?

The primary goal is to return the person to his/her preburn level of function. This goal is complicated by the nature of the injury, which can be devastating physically as well as emotionally, and by the fact that burns occur more frequently among disadvantaged populations, the elderly, the very young, individuals from lower socioeconomic status, or as a result of drug, alcohol, and tobacco use. The overall goals of burn rehabilitation change over time as the patient progresses from the acute to the final stages of hospitalization and discharge. Maintenance of function, including strength, range of motion, and ability to perform tasks of daily living, reduction in edema, scar management, and splinting, are among the priorities of the rehabilitation team.

4. Why do burn scars contract?

Burn scars contract secondary to a prolonged healing process, delayed reepithelialization, injuries across the flexor surfaces of joints, or prolonged positioning in a flexed, "fetal" position. The role of the myofibroblast is significant in this process. Massive collagen deposition, uncontrolled collagen cross-linking, and prolonged neoangioplasia are among the wound healing complications that are features of contracture. Contracture can result from the burn scar itself or from joint capsule contracture. Contracture is the hallmark of burn care that fails as a result of suboptimal care, severe injury, or patient noncooperation (Fig. 103-2).

5. How do you prevent burn scar formation?

Early débridement, early skin grafting, good nutrition, and an absence of infection all promote healing but cannot, when the injury is severe, eliminate scarring. Only prevention of burns can prevent burn scars. Reduction of burn scar edema through massage, compression, and physical activity is critical in reducing long-term scar formation. The need for secondary burn scar surgeries has been greatly reduced in recent years through the aggressive use of early débridement and grafting, compression garments, and silicone sheet inserts to provide surface compression on the healed burn wound. Although the mechanism of action is unknown, use of compression and silicone sheeting has resulted in a significant decrease in hypertrophic scar formation, better appearance, and improved functional recovery following serious burn injury.

6. How do you prevent burn scar contracture?

Burn injuries across joint surfaces, muscle wasting, or direct muscle injury, prolonged "fetal positioning" in response to pain, and failure to initiate early physical therapy can result in contracture. The most common cause of contracture previously was the result of permitting the burn to heal spontaneously, a process that might have taken months. During that time, myofibroblast proliferation, in the open granulating wound, promoted contracture across the wound surface, one of the mechanisms of "natural" wound healing. Only with the completion of reepithelialization, which is a slow

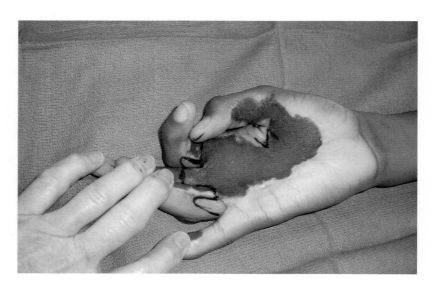

Figure 103-2. Burn scar contracture can severely limit motion and cause significant tissue distortion.

process across a large surface area, would myofibroblast activity cease. As a result of this process a healed burn might result in grotesque deformities. Early wound closure has nearly eliminated this problem in areas where modern burn care is available.

7. What are the best ways to treat burn scar contracture?

The best treatment is to prevent it, which is the goal of modern burn care. Once established, burn contractures can be treated with serial splinting, release of contracting bands with Z-plasties, incision and skin grafting or excision and resurfacing with skin grafts or flaps, local rotation flaps, use of tissue expanders, or with free flap reconstruction (Figs. 103-3, 103-4, and 103-5). Choices are based on the duration of the contracture, joint or surface areas involved, cosmetic considerations, and functional rehabilitation concerns. If possible the patient should be a major decision maker in selecting the reconstruction plan. If the patient is incompetent, surgical goals should be structured toward function, appearance, and the abilities of the individual.

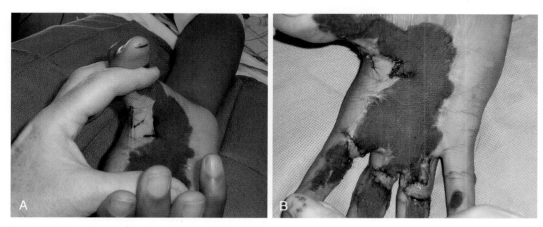

Figure 103-3. Burn scar release with Z-plasty and ulnar-based flag flaps.

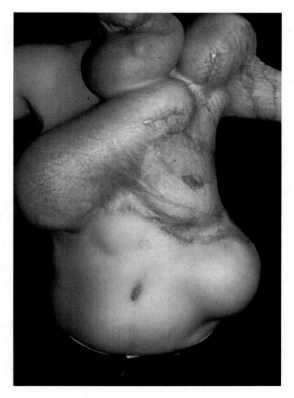

Figure 103-4. Use of tissue expanders to increase surface area of unburned skin, creating flaps for reconstruction.

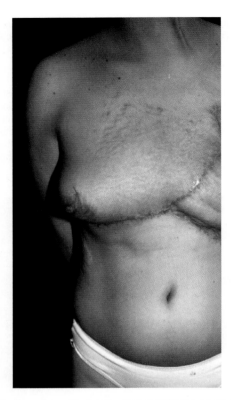

Figure 103-5. Reconstructed chest wall, after excision of burn scars, removal of tissue expanders, and advancement flap reconstruction. (Courtesy Dr. Nelson Piccolo, Pronto Socoro para Quemaduras, Goiania, Goias, Brazil.)

8. What does burn rehabilitation include, and when does it begin?

Physical and occupational therapy; psychological or psychiatric counseling as needed; reconstructive surgery if needed; use of compression garments, splints, or casts; massage of burn scars; social work with family, school, or occupational guidance; medical management of pain, itching, sleep disturbances, or depression if they occur; and any other services required by the medical, psychological, or social situation of the patient. They begin the day the patient is first seen for burn care. A plan should include attention to rehabilitation as part of the total burn care planning process. This may simply include plans to return to work or school but may involve occupational therapy, physical therapy, splinting, and range-of-motion exercises.

9. What are the differences between scald, flame, and electrical injuries in terms of the care needed after the injury heals?

Scald burns classically involve only the skin, although they may involve deeper tissues when the skin is thin, as in the dorsum of the hand or face. Flame burns, if contacted only briefly, may be superficial but will, with contact or if clothing burns, involve the full thickness of the skin and may even affect deeper subcutaneous tissues. Depending on how the burn occurred, inhalation injury must also be considered. Electrical burns, when there are entry and exit points, conduct along bone, nerve, and deep tissue plans. In addition to charred superficial structures, serious internal injuries may be present. Each of these injuries requires unique care plans and different approaches to rehabilitation. When débridement of the burn includes amputation, deep muscle resection, and extensive tissue removal or if neurologic injury has occurred, the rehabilitation process is considerably more complicated. Care plans may include long-range goals such as free flap reconstructions, joint replacement, manufacture of custom-made splints, prostheses, and other unusual requirements.

10. What are compression dressings and how are they used? What are compression garments?

Compression dressings are pressure dressings that can be provided by Ace wrap-type bandages, elastic custom-made garments, tubular gauze-type bandages, and elastic wraps such as Coban or even plaster casts, if immobilization or serial stretching is required. The classic compression garments originally were made by the Jobst Company. Many manufacturers now produce these devices. For large surface areas of burn scar, custom-made compression garments, with silicone sheet inserts over particular scars, are used. These may need to be refabricated frequently for growing children. They are used for at least 6 months for maximum efficacy in adults and for 18 to 24 months in children. They may be required for more months, or years, if the scar remains thickened and red. A simple means of determining whether the garment is still needed is to discontinue its use for a few days. If the scar is still active, redness and itching will intensify, indicating that the garment will still be beneficial.

11. How do compression garments work?

Compression provides multiple therapies to the healing burn scar. Compression has the following characteristics:
- Protects the fragile skin from shearing and other trauma
- Reduces itching
- Reduces burn scar edema
- Stretches the skin, reducing contracture bands
- Can be used to keep moisturizers in contact with the skin
- Reduces dependent pain in lower extremity wounds
- Eliminates need for bulkier dressings
- Appears to reduce burn scar hypertrophy and neoangioplasia when started early in the healing process

The exact mechanism of action is poorly understood but is believed to be partially the result of relative hypoxia in the burn scar. Pressure has been shown to improve the alignment of collagen fibers in the scar on histologic evaluation. The application of pressure ranging from 20 to 30 mm Hg is recommended for use in burn scar treatment. Garments providing less compression are not efficacious.

12. What is the role of silicone?

Silicone in sheets or as a gel has been shown to improve hypertrophic scars. Pressure may help when the surface is broad but is not an essential component of its function. Several theories have been proposed, indicating that (1) silicone oils may be beneficial, (2) surface temperature increases that occur under the sheet may play some role, (3) retained moisture under the silicone is important, or (4) silicone increases oxygen tension in the wound, improving wound healing. If wound healing is normal, silicone is not necessary, but when the scar forming has a hypertrophic or keloid appearance, treatment with silicone appears to be beneficial.

13. Who developed the use of compression?

The first reference in medical literature to the use of compression therapy was by Ambrose Pare, the father of modern wound healing, in 1678. Dr. Sally Abston, at the Shrine Children's Burn Center in Galveston, Texas, popularized the use of compression garments to reduce burn scar formation in the United States in the 1970s.

14. Is there any advantage to early burn wound surgical intervention?

If the burn is superficial, no surgical intervention is required because the wound heals spontaneously. The earlier a burn wound is healed, the less scarring will be apparent. The development by Janzekovic in Eastern Europe in the 1960s of tangential burn wound excision and skin grafting provided a powerful rationale for modern burn care. When the injury involves the deeper dermis, early excision and grafting, subsequently popularized by Dr. John Burke and colleagues at Massachusetts General Hospital in the early 1970s, speeds healing and produces a better functional and cosmetic appearance of the healed wound. Newer techniques, including the use of skin substitutes, permit closure of even massive wounds and appear to result in better quality of scar tissue. Further advantages of early closure include shortened hospital stay, reduced contracture rates, and fewer requirements for long-term reconstruction.

15. Which anatomic sites should take precedence in burn reconstruction, even in the earliest phases of burn care?

Hands and face.

16. When was the first recorded treatment of a burn? What was the recommended treatment plan?

Circumstantial evidence indicates that Neanderthal man in Iraq valued herbs as early as 60,000 BC. In the first recorded record of burn care, the Ebers Papyrus 482 (dated 1500 BC) dictates a burn regimen as follows:
- Day 1: Black mud
- Day 2: Dung of calf mixed with yeast
- Day 3: Dried acacia resin mixed with barley paste, cooked colocynth, and oil
- Day 4: Paste of beeswax, fat, and boiled papyrus with beans
- Day 5: Mixture of colocynth, red ochre, leaves, and copper fragments

Of interest, the burned limbs were supported in copper splints, demonstrating that even then physicians were aware of contractures and tried to prevent them.

17. What are the most common complaints that burn survivors have?
- Wound-related complications include appearance, itching, burning, and pain in the burn wound and donor sites.
- Functional complaints may be related to the areas burned, with attendant limitations in the use of burned hands or feet, or lost strength and an inability to return to preburn activities.
- Psychological complaints include depression, sleeplessness, anxiety, posttraumatic stress disorder, impotence, loss of joy, and changes in family, work, or school dynamics.
- Physiologic complaints are related to inability to tolerate sun exposure, inability to sweat, dryness of burn scars caused by loss of sebaceous gland function, and toxicity related to burn treatment, such as deafness or reduced renal function from antibiotic use, pulmonary insufficiency from inhalation injury, and changes in appetite.

18. What are the delayed wound complications associated with burn injury?
- Pigment changes in the skin, either darker or lighter
- Texture changes in the burn and donor sites
- Scar contractures resulting in physical deformities
- Aesthetic concerns for changes in appearance
- Heterotopic calcification

19. What is heterotopic calcification?

Heterotopic calcification is bone formation in the soft tissues, most frequently found at the elbow following upper extremity burn injury. Bone forms in the soft tissues around the joint, in the triceps insertion, causing loss of range of motion. This may resolve spontaneously, or it may require surgical resection. Care must be taken to protect the ulnar nerve when this procedure is done. Early treatment with indomethacin or naproxen may be beneficial. Medical management of established heterotopic bone formation has been tried with etidronate, which must be administered for several months. This is an uncommon burn problem but is seen more frequently following spinal cord injury.

20. What are the most common burn contracture deformities and how may they be prevented or minimized?
- *Neck.* This occurs with burns of the head and neck area but also can occur in patients who are intubated and on a ventilator. It is prevented by avoiding placing a pillow under the head and using neck splints and traction.
- *Axilla.* This occurs more frequently when the area is burned. It is prevented by abduction splints, range of motion, and proper use of pillows with the arms extended.
- *Elbow.* This occurs with burns in the area. It is prevented by early excision and grafting, splinting, and early diagnosis and intervention if heterotopic bone formation develops. Splinting the elbow in extension is important in critical care of the burn patient. This may be alternated with flexion splints, or with use of continuous passive motion, to maintain range of motion.
- *Flexion Deformity of the Hands.* This can occur in the absence of burn injury and is treated with functional splinting during acute burn care, when the patient is unconscious. Burn scar deformities of the hand commonly are of the type called "claw hand." This develops as a contracting scar that pulls the metacarpophalangeal joints into hyperextension, flexing the interphalangeal joints, adducting the thumb, ulnarly rotating the fifth digit, and flattening the longitudinal and transverse arches of the hand. If the scar is unopposed, thickening and contracture of the joint capsules and ligaments, subluxation, and shortening and/or adhesions of the tendons may result.
- *Equinus Deformity of the Ankle and Foot.* The ankle is flexed to the plantar surface and the foot is in a varus position, a deformity that can occur in any patient unable to move. Splinting the foot from toe to calf in a neutral position is important in maintaining foot orientation.
- *Flexion Deformities of the Hips and Knees.*

The most commonly seen contractures involve the hand, followed by the neck. Hip and knee contractures are often seen in children.

21. What is microstomia?

Microstomia is a contracture of the mouth, particularly at the oral commissure, caused by perioral facial burns. The most common of these burns results from electrical burns sustained when a child chews on an electrical cord or extension cord plug. Deep burns of the face caused by ingesting lye may also cause this deformity. The tissue loss from this injury may lead to cosmetic and functional impairment, oral dysfunction with eating, impaired oral hygiene, dental care, facial expression, and speech. Devices to treat microstomia are commercially available, or they can be fabricated with standard dental and orthodontic materials. Surgical reconstruction requires the use of an appropriate splint postoperatively. Patient compliance is often a limiting factor in success.

22. How do neck contractures affect function, and how are they treated?

Scarring and contracture of the neck region may severely limit function, causing alterations in normal posture, make intubation for surgery difficult, make driving unsafe, and contribute to secondary deformities of the face, including lips and lower eyelids. Scarring that descends onto the chest may affect shoulder motion and cause contracture of the breast with upward displacement of the nipple–areolar complex. The neck is the second most common site of burn scar contracture. Reconstruction in this area depends on the severity of scarring and the extent of involvement. Excision of the scar and regrafting with a split-thickness skin graft requires long-term care to prevent recurrence. Splitting the scar and grafting the defect also are acceptable. When grafts are used, splinting will be required to prevent recurrence. Use of free flaps, such as the radial forearm free flap, often referred to as the "Chinese flap," provides thin supple vascularized tissue for neck coverage, as first described by Guofan in 1978.

23. How long after surgery for burn scar reconstruction is it possible to begin scar management?

Compression garments can be started 1 week after the postoperative dressing is removed. For scar remodeling of the superior chest, anterior shoulders, and pectoral region, flexible inserts of a Silastic elastomer and/or prosthetic foam are used to distribute the pressure of the compression jacket. Silicone gel also can be used under the splint and/or garment. The average time for wearing the splint or garment is approximately 1 year. Use can be discontinued when the graft is flat and no longer hyperemic.

24. What are the appropriate grafts for burned hand reconstruction (Fig. 103-6)?

- Palmar burns need to be released by Z-plasty, or either thick split-thickness or full-thickness skin grafts, or flaps, if available. A reverse radial forearm flap, ulnar- or radial-based digital flag type flaps, groin flaps, or abdominal pedicle flaps all have been advocated and their use depends on availability.
- Dorsal burn scars, when extensive, can be treated by complete scar excision and regrafting, followed by long-term splinting and compression gloves.
- Interdigital webbing can be treated as syndactyly. It requires splinting and compression in the postoperative period as well.
- Many burn deformities of the hand may involve joint capsule contracture or adhesive tendonitis. When present, they must also be released if full range is to be regained.

25. What underlying pathology results in an intrinsic minus hand in the recently burned upper extremity, and how should it be treated?

Compartment syndrome of the deep muscles of the hand causes the intrinsic minus deformity. This is best treated by prevention, performing escharotomies of the hand when needed in the immediate postburn period. When established, treatment is accomplished by making radial incisions between the metacarpals on the dorsum of the hand, dissecting down to the muscle compartments and releasing them.

26. What are escharotomies, and what do they do?

Escharotomy simply means opening the eschar. Circumferential burns, generally deep second or third degree in nature, whether of the extremities or of the trunk, can cause compression of the underlying soft tissues as burn edema develops beneath an unyielding eschar. Ischemia of the underlying tissues and as well as of the distal tissue will result in increased tissue damage. Failure to identify and treat this constriction creates a compartment syndrome that

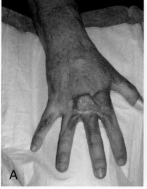 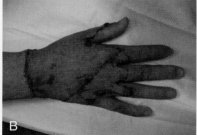 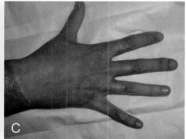

A   B   C

Figure 103-6. Hypertrophic burn scars of the hand can be significantly improved by excising the existing scar to subcutaneous fat and regrafting the surface with thick split-thickness skin grafts. Full flexion and extension were maintained by aggressive hand therapy throughout the care of this patient's hand.

contributes to further injury. Longitudinal incisions through the burned skin laterally and medially in the extremities, or from the axilla to the groin on the trunk, will release the tissue. Fasciotomies may also be required and should be considered especially in patients with electrical burns or very deep thermal injuries. Escharotomy should be considered in all cases of circumferential burns. Decreased Doppler pulses are the most reliable physiologic clinical measurements used to indicate the need for this procedure. Escharotomy is most effective if it is performed prior to the onset of lactic acidosis. Compartment pressure measurements are not necessary and may be misleading.

27. What are the clinical signs of ischemia in a circumferentially burned extremity?

Alert patients may report numbness and tingling. In sedated or unconscious patients, the earliest signs are Doppler findings of diminished or absent digital pulses. In the unburned finger, pulse oximetry may be useful.

28. When does the need for an escharotomy first appear?

During the first 48 hours after burn injury, during the resuscitation process. As burn edema accumulates during that time period, even incompletely circumferential burn injuries may require surgical release. One of the theoretical advantages of hypertonic resuscitation is a reduced need for escharotomy. The risks of escharotomy far outweigh the complications that can arise when it is deferred, if needed.

29. Spill scalds of the chest are common in toddlers. What are the long-term consequences?

In girls, restrictive scarring of the anterior chest will cause breast maldevelopment at the time of puberty. This may result in micromastia, asymmetry, or a "unibreast" appearance, depending on the extent and areas involved. Release of contracting scars will permit normal breast evolution. Such release can be accomplished with skin grafts, tissue expanders, or flaps. Nipple–areola reconstruction may be needed if burns are deep.

30. What is burn alopecia, and how is it treated?

Burn alopecia is baldness caused by burn injury (Fig. 103-7). Burns of the scalp are treated by débridement and skin grafting. The hair follicles extend beneath scalp skin, and hair may regrow after such treatment. If it does not, the resulting baldness is called *burn scar alopecia*. It is treated by excision of the burn scar and flap reconstruction using adjacent hair-bearing scalp. If hair-bearing scalp tissue is limited, tissue expansion can markedly increase the available normal scalp tissue. Up to 50% of the scalp can be reconstructed by this method. Hair follicle grafting into burn scar is notoriously unreliable.

31. What are the long-term consequences of burn scars 20 years or more after a burn injury?

The most serious long-term burn scar problem is burn scar carcinoma, also called *Marjolin's ulcer*. Cases occurring as soon as 3 years after burn healing is complete and as many as 60 years after have been reported. Not every patient will develop malignancy. The mean age of onset is 50 years, and the mean latency at onset is 31 years after injury. The most common malignancy is squamous cell carcinoma (71%), but basal cell carcinoma (12%) and melanoma (6%) have

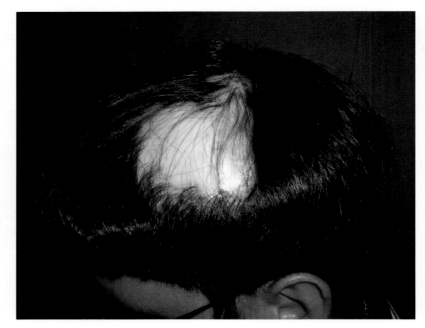

Figure 103-7. Burn scar alopecia, another condition for which tissue expansion can be useful, permitting resurfacing of up to 50% of the scalp.

been reported. Sarcomas (5%) and rare or combination mixed tumors (6%) also have been reported. Burn scar tumors, especially squamous cell carcinoma, can be highly aggressive, and extended radical resections are recommended. Local recurrence has been reported in 16% of cases and regional node metastasis in 22%. The reported mortality rate is 21%. Any open wound in a burn scar should be biopsied if it does not heal with proper care. The usefulness of sentinel node assessment has not been confirmed, as significant disruption of lymphatics in burn scar has been noted.

Subcutaneous heterotopic calcification can occur many years after burn injury and cause painful, hard masses. Excision of these benign processes can be difficult because the burn scarred skin lacks elasticity and wound closure by direct approximation may not be possible.

32. What are the long-term consequences of lightning injuries?

There are many long-term sequelae of lightning strikes in humans:
- Neuropathy
- Chronic pain syndromes
- Transverse spinal myelitis or spinal artery syndrome
- Ischemic damage from vasospasm (anywhere in the body)
- Myocardial insufficiency secondary to infarction
- Deafness or blindness
- Hepatic or renal insufficiency
- Sleep disorders
- Psychomotor instability
- Personality changes
- Posttraumatic stress disorder

CONTROVERSIES

33. What is the best indicator of quality in burn care?

Survival statistics, once the hallmark of care, have improved to the extent that they can no longer be considered the sine qua non of burn management. Forty years ago, a 30% total body burn represented the LD_{50} of a burn injury. Today, that LD_{50} has increased to nearly 90% for certain burns, especially those involving children, in the absence of associated complications such as inhalation injury, fractures, or other trauma or illness. Long-term outcome measures such as quality of life, exercise tolerance, and return to preburn activity levels are more sensitive measures of competent care.

34. What is the role of engineered skin substitutes in burn wound management?

Cultured epithelium, with or without dermal structures, is indicated for very large burn wounds when donor area is limited. The cost of these therapies and their role in smaller burns and in burn reconstruction are still being evaluated. Reported advantages, which include better scar appearance, fewer contractures, and reconstitution of skin organelles, are not completely accepted. The first cultured epithelial grafts were used in burn care in 1981.

Dermal structure using either cultured dermal elements or cadaveric nonviable substrate can be added to the burn wound as part of wound preparation following excision of full-thickness injury, but the cost and long-term benefits are still considered experimental despite widespread usage in the United States.

BIBLIOGRAPHY

Burke JF, Bondoc CC, Quinby WC: Primary burn excision and immediate grafting, a method shortening illness. J Trauma 14:389–396, 1974.
Cone J: What's new in general surgery, burns and metabolism. J Am Col Surg 200:607–615, 2005.
Edriss AS, Mestak, J: Management of keloid and hypertrophic scars. Ann Burns Fire Disasters 18: 202–210, 2005.
Gatewood MO, Zane RD: Lightning injury. Emerg Med Clin North Am 22:369–403, 2004.
Grossman JAI: Burns of the upper extremity. Hand Clin 6:163–354, 1990.
Hunt JL, Purdue GF, Pownell RH, Rohrich RJ: Burns: Acute burns, burn surgery, and postburn reconstruction. Sel Read Plast Surg 8:1–37, 1997.
Janzekovic Z: A new concept in the early excision and immediate grafting of burns. J Trauma 10:1103–1108, 1970.
Kwal-Vern A, Criswell BK: Burn scar neoplasms: A literature review and statistical analysis. Burns 31:403–413, 2005.
Musgrave MA: The effect of silicone gel sheets on perfusion of hypertrophic burn scars. J Burn Care Rehabil 23:208–214, 2002.
O'Connor NE, Mulliken JB, et al: Grafting of burns with cultured epithelium prepared from autologous epithelial cells. Lancet 1:75–78, 1981.
Pereira C: Outcome measures in burn care. Is mortality dead? Burns 30:761–771, 2004.
Scarborough J: On medications for burns in classical antiquity. Clin Plast Surg 10:603–611, 1983.
Sheridan RI, Tompkins RG: What's new in burns and metabolism. J Am Coll Surg 198:243–264, 2004.
Van Loey NE: Psychopathology and psychological problems in patients with burn scars: Epidemiology and management. Am J Clin Dermatol 4:245–272, 2003.

TISSUE TRANSPLANTATION

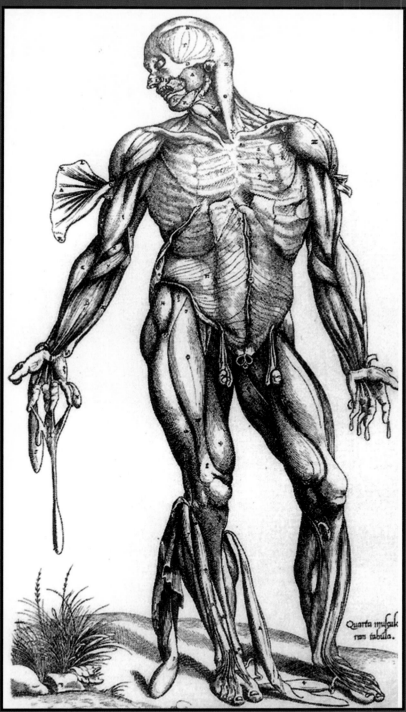

Fourth Muscle Plate. Jan Stefan van Calcar, 1543. Woodcut. From Andreas Vesalius, *De humani corporis fabrica* [Venice, 1543]. © 1998 The Wellcome Institute Library, London.

PRINCIPLES OF SKIN GRAFTS

CHAPTER 104

Joyce C. Chen, MD, and
Sonu A. Jain, MD

1. Who performed the first skin graft?

The technique of skin harvesting and transplantation initially was described approximately 2500 to 3000 years ago by the Hindu Tilemaker Caste. In the technique, skin grafting was used to reconstruct noses that were amputated as a means of judicial punishment. Reverdin is credited with the first skin transfer in 1870. Initial skin grafts were either very thin or full-thickness grafts. Ollier first described his use of the split-thickness graft in 1872; Wolfe described his use of the full-thickness graft in 1875.

2. What are the different types of skin grafts?

Skin grafts are classified as either split-thickness skin graft (STSG) or full-thickness skin graft (FTSG). STSG can be subclassified as thin (0.006 to 0.012 inches), intermediate (0.012 to 0.018 inches), or thick (0.018 to 0.024 inches). STSG consists of the entire epidermis with a portion of the dermis, whereas FTSG includes the entire thickness of the skin, both epidermis and dermis.

Skin grafts also are classified by their donor site as *autograft,* self; *homograft,* same species; *isograft,* homograft between genetically identical people; *allograft,* homograft between genetically different people; and *heterograft/xenograft,* different species.

3. What are the advantages and disadvantages of STSG versus FTSG?

See Table 104-1.

4. Which epithelial appendages are present in the skin?

Cells of the developing epidermis invade the dermis in the third month of gestation to form intradermal epithelial structures: hair follicles, sebaceous glands, and sweat glands. Only FTSGs contain these appendages and therefore are capable of sweating, oil secretion, and hair growth.

5. How do hair follicles and sebaceous glands affect skin grafts?

In transplanted skin, the growth of hair in an area that should be hairless can be a problem. Hairs grow in a slanted, not vertical, direction. When hair is being transplanted, incisions should be made obliquely following this direction. Soon after the fourth postgraft day, when original hair shafts are shed, the original hair follicles begin to produce new hair. Fine hair is present by the fourteenth postgraft day.

Sebaceous glands, as appendages of hair follicles, are largest and are most densely located in skin of the forehead, nose, and cheeks. They secrete oily sebum, which lubricates the hair, keeps the skin supple, and protects it against friction. Thinner STSGs do not contain functional sebaceous glands and usually appear dry and brittle after take.

Table 104-1. Advantages and Disadvantages of STSG and FTSG

	ADVANTAGES	DISADVANTAGES
STSG	Graft takes more favorably Uniform thickness of graft Donor site heals quickly Reuse of donor site in 1–2 months	Considerable contracture Abnormal pigmentation Increased susceptibility to trauma
FTSG	Less contracture Color/texture match more similar to normal skin Potential for growth	Requires well-vascularized bed Donor site must be closed/covered

FTSG, Full-thickness skin graft; *STSG,* split-thickness skin graft.
From Hierner R, Degreef H, Vranckx JJ, et al: Skin grafting and wound healing: The "dermato-plastic team approach." Clin Dermatol 23:343–352, 2005.

6. **How do sweat glands affect skin grafts?**

Apocrine sweat glands are concentrated in the axillae and groin. They become active at puberty, secrete continuously, and produce an odor due to bacterial decomposition. *Eccrine sweat glands* are found throughout the body except at mucocutaneous junctions and the nail beds. There are two types of eccrine glands: those located in the palms of the hand and soles of the feet and those located on the remainder of the body surface; the former respond to emotional and mental stress whereas the latter function in temperature regulation.

The sweat pattern of a skin graft follows that of its recipient site because sweat gland function is directed by sympathetic nerve fibers within the graft bed. Skin grafts initially lack the lubrication provided by the sweat glands because they are temporarily deinnervated. Therefore, lubricant creams should be applied to the graft until the glands are reinnervated.

7. **What happens to the epidermis in the postgraft period?**

STSGs show significant mitotic activity in the epidermis by the third postgraft day, in contrast to FTSGs, in which mitotic activity is reduced. The graft "scales off," and the epithelium doubles in thickness in the first 4 days. This is due to swelling of the nuclei and cytoplasm of the epithelial cells, epithelial cell migration toward the graft surface, and accelerated mitosis of follicular and glandular cells. Between days 4 and 8, rapid turnover of cells leads up to a sevenfold increase in epithelium thickness. Not until approximately the end of the fourth week after grafting is the epidermal thickness back to normal.

8. **Describe the cellular and fibrous components of the dermis in skin grafts.**

The source of fibroblasts in a skin graft is debated. They may be derived from mononuclear cells in the blood or from local perivascular mesenchymal cells. However, it is understood that fibroblasts in a healing skin graft do not come from indigenous fibrocytes.

In the first 3 days after grafting, the fibrocyte population decreases. After day 3, fibroblast-like cells appear in the graft and increase in number and enzymatic activity greater than in normal skin by the seventh and eighth days. Fibroblast levels return to normal in the following few weeks.

The source of collagen in skin grafts is also debated. Some have shown that the collagen persists for 40 days after grafting. Others have shown that collagen undergoes significant turnover. The peak concentration of collagen or rate of replacement occurs in the first 14 to 21 days after grafting. By the end of the sixth week, all of the old dermal collagen is replaced. Collagen turnover in skin grafts is three to four times faster than it is in unwounded skin. Elastin fibers, also part of the fibrous component, provide skin resilience. Elastin has a high turnover rate with continued degeneration through the third week until new fibers start growing at 4 to 6 weeks postgraft.

9. **What is the function of the extracellular matrix?**

The extracellular matrix (ECM) of skin is composed of proteins of both fibroblast and keratinocyte origin. These proteins are involved in directing keratinocyte behavior and keratinocyte–fibroblast communication. The ECM regulates cell-to-cell interaction and cellular behavior, particularly with regard to cell proliferation, differentiation, migration, and attachment.

10. **Describe the healing process of a skin graft.**

The skin graft is immediately white on removal from the donor site. Over the next few days a pink hue develops, and good capillary refill is elicited. By the sixth postgraft day, lymphatic drainage becomes established through the connection of the host and graft lymph channels. As a result, the graft rapidly loses fluid weight until its original pregraft level is reached by the ninth postgraft day. Collagen replacement begins by the seventh day and is nearly complete by the sixth week after grafting. By the fourteenth to twenty-first days, the graft surface, which originally was depressed, becomes level with the surrounding skin. A large number of polymorphonuclear cells and monocytes remain in the dermis for several weeks. Vascularization and remodeling may take many months and result in numerous newly formed vessels with greater arborization than the vessels of normal skin.

11. **How does a skin graft take?**

Skin graft take occurs in three phases:
1. The *serum imbibition (plasmatic circulation) phase* occurs during the first 48 hours and allows the graft to survive the immediate postgraft period before circulation is established. Plasma exudate from host bed capillaries provides the serum (not plasma), which nourishes the graft.
2. The *revascularization phase* occurs after 48 hours through the growth of blood vessels into the graft from the host bed *(neovascularization)* and the anastomosis between graft and host vessels *(inosculation).* The former serves as the primary method of revascularization.

3. The *organization phase* begins within hours of graft placement. A fibrin clot forms an interface between the graft and host bed, initially causing adherence and later, by postgraft day 7, is infiltrated by fibroblasts. By postgraft day 9, the graft is firmly secured to the host bed with its vascular supply.

12. What are the most common causes of autologous skin graft failure?

The most common cause of autologous skin graft failure is *hematoma.* The blood clot inhibits direct contact of the graft with the endothelial buds of the host bed preventing revascularization. Fluid beneath the graft bed *(seroma)* may also cause graft failure. A light pressure dressing minimizes the risk of fluid accumulation.

The second most common cause of graft loss is *infection,* which can be prevented by carefully preparing the wound bed. Other causes of failure include poor vascularity of the graft bed and movement of the placed graft. Care must be taken to immobilize the grafted area. Also, properties of the skin graft itself can determine its survival, that is, grafts from a highly vascularized donor site heal better than those from a less vascular site.

Another common cause of graft loss is *shear.* Proper immobilization of a skin graft, using splints, tie-over bolster dressings, or the vacuum-assisted closure (VAC) device, depending on the type of graft and recipient site, are paramount to preventing graft shear and loss.

13. What sensory changes occur as a skin graft becomes reinnervated?

Sensation is regained as the graft is reinnervated. Initially, skin grafts are hyperalgesic and then slowly regain normal sensation. Sensory recovery begins at approximately 4 to 5 weeks and usually is completed by 12 to 24 months. Pain returns first, with light touch and temperature returning afterward. Patients need to be warned of thermal insensitivity to prevent injury.

14. What are the choices for donor sites?

STSG can be taken from any area of the body. Factors to consider with regard to a donor site include donor skin characteristics (color, texture, and thickness), amount of skin required, convenience, and scar visibility. STSG for the face should be harvested from the supraclavicular area or scalp. For larger areas, STSG can be taken from the anterolateral thigh or abdomen. STSG for the extremity and trunk are harvested from the abdomen, upper thighs, or buttocks.

FTSGs usually are harvested where the skin is thin: upper eyelids, preauricular and postauricular area, melolabial area, or supraclavicular area for the face. Other donor sites used for FTSG include the hairless groin, flexor crease of the wrist, and elbow crease.

15. What is a dermatome?

A dermatome is a cutting instrument used for harvesting STSGs. It provides a skin graft of consistently uniform thickness. Air-powered (Brown or Zimmer) or electric-powered (Padget) dermatomes usually are used. The width and thickness of the graft can be adjusted on the dermatome. Harvested graft thickness can be judged by the type of bleeding at the donor site. Superficial grafts leave many small punctate bleeding points, whereas deep grafts leave fewer bleeding points that bleed more.

16. What is meshing? When are meshed grafts used?

Meshing is the process of cutting slits into a sheet graft and expanding it prior to placement. Meshed STSGs are used primarily when insufficient donor skin is available, a highly convoluted area needs coverage, and/or the recipient bed is less than optimal. Mesh grafts are contraindicated for coverage of a joint or for the back of the hand because of significant contracture during healing. Graft meshing usually is performed in 1:1.5 or 1:2 ratios.

17. What are the advantages and disadvantages of meshing?

ADVANTAGES

- Covers larger area while minimizing area harvested
- Contours and adapts easily to fit an irregular bed
- Allows drainage of fluid, reducing the formation of seromas and hematomas
- Increases the edges for reepithelialization

DISADVANTAGES

- Heals by secondary intention between meshed interstices, potentially leading to wound contracture
- Results in unaesthetic cobblestone, uneven appearance of graft

Box 104-1. Primary versus Secondary Contraction

Primary Contraction
- *Definition:* Immediate recoil of the graft as it is harvested due to the elastin in dermis
- FTSG contracts more (loses 40% of original area)
- STSG contracts less (loses 10% of original area)

Secondary Contraction
- *Definition:* Wound contraction occurring over 6 to 18 months due to myofibroblast activity
- FTSG contracts less (myofibroblast population decreased by speeding up its life cycle)
- STSG contracts more (depends on amount of dermis, i.e., less contraction with more dermis)

FTSG, Full-thickness skin graft; *STSG,* split-thickness skin graft.
From Place MJ, Herber SC, Hardesty RA: Basic techniques and principles. In Aston SJ, Beasley RW, Thorne CHM (eds): Grabb and Smith's Plastic Surgery, 5th ed. Philadelphia, Lippincott Raven, 1997, pp 17–19.

18. What methods of graft expansion are available besides meshing?
- *Pinch grafts* are produced by breaking up a graft of skin into small pieces to increase the edge area; they are effective in treating small- and medium-size venous ulcers, pressure sores, radiodermatitis, and small burns.
- In *relay transplantation* a graft is cut into 3- to 6-mm strips, which are laid down 5 to 10 mm apart. After 5 to 7 days when the epithelial growth is apparent, the original strips are removed and transplanted, leaving the epithelial explants in place. This process can be repeated up to four times.
- *Meek (1958) island sandwich grafts* involve use of a specialized dermatome and prefolded gauzes to expand squares from small pieces of split-thickness skin graft. The ratio of expansion is reportedly 1:9 (vs 1:4 with Zimmer Dermatome II). This method is useful for coverage of granulating wounds that have poor grafting conditions.

19. Compare primary and secondary contraction.
See Box 104-1.

20. What factors in the wound bed promote skin graft take?
- *Blood Supply.* Skin graft survival depends on blood supply from the wound bed. Graftable beds with adequate blood supply include periosteum, perichondrium, and paratenon, as well as débrided cortical bone with granulation tissue proliferation. Poor grafting surfaces with inadequate blood supply include exposed bone, cartilage, and tendon. Chronic granulation tissue should be débrided down to red, beefy, more vascular, healthier tissue before grafting.
- *Absence of Infection.* The bed must be free of pus and necrotic tissue. The bacterial load should be less than 10^5 organisms per gram of tissue. Higher bacterial loads need to be treated with local wound care and antibiotics.

21. What is the optimal dressing for a skin graft?
In most cases, a bolster or tie-over dressing is the best dressing for a skin graft and is usually left in place for 4 to 5 days. It improves the survival rate by promoting adherence of the graft to the wound to allow imbibition, minimize shearing, and prevent hematoma and seroma formation. For an extremity skin graft, this technique involves a circumferential compression dressing, often with a splint to immobilize an adjacent joint.

More recently, the wound VAC has been used to provide subatmospheric pressure dressings over the skin graft. It is especially useful for large, irregular wounds that would otherwise be difficult to bolster.

22. How can skin graft pigmentation mismatch be minimized? When does hyperpigmentation or hypopigmentation occur?
Pigmentation changes as a graft heals, depending on the area from which it was harvested. FTSGs maintain the best pigment match and thus are preferred in highly exposed areas such as the face. The skin of the face and neck above the clavicle provides the best color match for grafting facial areas.

Hyperpigmentation occurs regardless of the donor site. STSGs often develop darker pigmentation than do FTSG grafts from the same site. Also, grafts harvested from the thigh, buttocks, and abdomen become darker as they heal. Sunshine is thought to play a role in permanent graft hyperpigmentation and should be avoided for 6 months after grafting. Hyperpigmented grafts are best treated by dermabrasion; the best results are achieved when dermabrasion is done after the graft becomes reinnervated.

In contrast, skin grafts to the palm lighten, resulting in *hypopigmentation*.

23. What types of dressings are used for donor sites?
See Table 104-2.

Table 104-2. Types of Dressings

	OPEN	SEMIOPEN	SEMIOCCLUSIVE	OCCLUSIVE
Advantages	Cheapest	Allows egress of fluid and bacteria Xeroform: Infection-free, inexpensive, reepithelializes in 10 days Biobrane: Comfortable for patient	Impermeable to bacteria and liquid but permeable to moisture Promotes faster and less painful healing	Does not adhere to the bed, so no pain or skin irritation Enhances the rate of epithelialization and collagen synthesis Reduces bacterial count by increasing the acidity of the exudates
Disadvantages	Prolonged healing time, increased pain	Biobrane: Expensive, donor site infections	Requires frequent drainage of fluid collecting under dressing	Impermeable to oxygen
Examples		Biobrane, fine mesh gauzes impregnated with scarlet red, Vaseline, calcium alginate, Xeroform	Op-Site, Tegaderm	DuoDerm

From Kelton P: Skin grafts. Select Read Plast Surg 9:1–26, 1999.

24. How many times can a split-thickness graft be harvested from the same site?
A single donor site can be harvested multiple times. The epithelium always regenerates but the dermis does not. Thus the number of harvests is dependent on the dermis thickness.

25. What is dermal overgrafting?
In dermal overgrafting, a surface epithelium is replaced with an STSG after the epithelium is removed by dermabrasion or sharp dissection. Overgrafting preserves subcutaneous tissues and is a relatively simple procedure, and the tissue consequences of graft failure are minimal. Indications for overgrafting are hypertrophic scars, hyperpigmented skin grafts, large pigmented nevi, radiation damage, and tattoos.

26. Compare allografts and xenografts.
See Table 104-3.

27. What other effective temporary biologic dressings exist as a bridge to autografting in patients with extensive burns (total body surface area >50%)?
Human amniotic membrane is one option that can be used as a temporary dressing. It is composed of an inner membrane (amnion) and an outer membrane (chorion). These membranes have a mesenchymal surface in addition to their epithelial (amnion) and decidual (chorion) surfaces. They have been effectively used as temporary dressings for leg ulcers and for contaminated or infected raw surfaces (e.g., burns, pilonidal cyst sinuses), and as coverage of donor sites. Recent use of freeze-dried, gamma-sterilized amniotic membrane has prevented the problem of bacterial and viral contamination from donors.

Table 104-3. Allografts versus Xenografts

	ALLOGRAFT	XENOGRAFT
Indications	Effective temporary biologic dressings. Useful when total body surface area >50% resulting in insufficient autograft donor sites.	Effective temporary biologic dressing. Useful when total body surface area >50% resulting in insufficient autograft donor sites.
Advantages	Becomes vascularized.	Low cost, availability, easy storage, easy sterilization.
Disadvantages	Rejected 10 days or later if immunosuppressed. Should be changed every 2–3 days to avoid rejection. Risk of human immunodeficiency virus transmission.	Rejected quickly and does not become vascularized. Can induce significant inflammatory response resulting in delayed healing.

From Kelton P: Skin grafts. Select Read Plast Surg 9:1–26, 1999.

Parental allografts intermingled with the child's autograft are another option. The parental skin persists for a longer time without rejection even in the absence of deliberate immunosuppression. Although the cellular elements of the parental skin do not survive, the parental dermis contributes to the final skin. Other benefits include psychological benefits to the parent, who feels that he/she is contributing to the child's care, and elimination of the risk of human immunodeficiency virus transmission with other allografts.

28. What is tissue-cultured skin?

Tissue-cultured skin is composed of human epidermal cells grown in vitro that is stable for grafting. Whole skin is enzymatically digested with trypsin to produce a single-cell suspension of keratinocytes that are then grown on a monolayer of lethally radiated mouse fibroblasts in a culture flask. Keratinocyte autografts or allografts are used in the treatment of burns or other extensive skin wounds. From a section of skin the size of a postage stamp, 1 m^2 sheet of keratinocytes can be cultured in 3 to 6 weeks.

A disadvantage of cultured skin is the presence of hyperkeratosis for relatively long periods. It is postulated that the newly formed epidermis remains in a hyperproliferative state due to the absence of a modulating dermal factor. A major disadvantage is the potential risk of malignancy due to the presence of mitogens as keratinocytes are cultured, leading to spontaneous transformation. Other hindering factors to the use of cultured keratinocytes are their high expense, fragility, sensitivity to infection, and time length to cultivate, during which the patient's condition may deteriorate.

29. What are unilaminar and bilaminar skin substitutes?

Skin substitutes act as artificial skin and are designed to be left in place for a long period, unlike temporary dressings. They have unilaminar or bilaminar membranes and are composed of synthetic and/or biologic materials. Unilaminar membranes include hydrogels, hydrocolloid dressings, and vapor-permeable membranes. They provide no mechanical protection but effectively débride the wound, decrease bacterial count, and stimulate granulation tissue growth. Bilaminar skin substitutes include completely synthetic, biologically inert materials, autologous tissue, and collagen-synthetic composite materials. Apligraf (Organogenis, Canton, Massachusetts), a bioengineered bilayer skin equivalent composed neonatal fibroblasts and keratinocytes, also functions as an effective skin substitute.

30. What are the applications of fibrin glue in skin grafting?

Fibrin glue prepared from fibrinogen concentrates is useful as a biologic adhesive. Its hemostatic properties help to reduce blood loss and to secure the graft in place. This results in decreased hematoma formation and decreased graft motion, both of which enhance graft survival. Another benefit is the antibacterial action of fibrin glue. In a clot of fibrin glue, bacterial growth has been found to be slower than in a physiologic clot. Fibrin glue, whether derived from an autologous, single donor, or multidonor source, does not interfere with the healing process. Autologous preparation techniques eliminate the small but present danger of disease transmission with multidonor preparations.

31. What is a free dermal-fat graft?

A free dermal-fat graft (FDFG) provides a lasting and effective source of implant material for repair of soft tissue contour defects and is often used in the reconstruction of defects of the face. When implanting an FDFG, overcorrection of approximately 30% to 40% is necessary to compensate for graft shrinkage. One of the risks is epithelial cyst formation, which can be minimized with adequate deepithelialization of the FDFG.

32. What is the role of skin grafting in the treatment of vitiligo?

Stable vitiligo that is refractory to conventional treatment can be effectively treated with a very thin split-thickness graft followed by psoralen and ultraviolet A (PUVA) treatment. However, the success rate depends on the site of the lesion. The forehead yields the most favorable results, whereas the lip, nose, neck, and bony prominences are difficult to treat in this manner.

BIBLIOGRAPHY

Andreassi A, Bilenchi R, Biagioli M, et al: Classification and pathophysiology of skin grafts. Clin Dermatol 23:332–337, 2005.
Bennett RG: Anatomy and physiology of the skin. In Papel ID (ed): Facial Plastic and Reconstructive Surgery, 2nd ed. New York, Thieme, 2002, pp 3–14.
Currie LJ, Sharpe JR, Martin R: The use of fibrin glue in skin grafts and tissue-engineered skin replacements: A review. Plast Reconstr Surg 108:1713–1726, 2001.
Fisher JC: Skin grafting. In Georgiade GS, Riefkohl R, Levin LS (eds): Georgiade Plastic, Maxillofacial and Reconstructive Surgery, 3rd ed. Baltimore, Williams & Williams, 1997, pp 13–18.

Grande DJ, Mezebish DS: Skin grafting. Available from: www.emedicine.com/derm/topic867.htm. Accessed April 2006.

Kelton P: Skin grafts. Select Read Plast Surg 9:1–26, 1999.

Kreis RW, Mackie DP, Hermans RR, et al: Expansion techniques for skin grafts. Comparison between mesh and Meek island (sandwich) grafts. Burns 20(Suppl 1):S39–S42, 1994.

Njoo MD, Westerhof W, Bos JD, et al: A systematic review of autologous transplantation methods in vitiligo. Arch Dermatol 134: 1543–1549, 1998.

Place MJ, Herber SC, Hardesty RA: Basic techniques and principles. In Aston SJ, Beasley RW, Thorne CHM (eds): Grabb and Smith's Plastic Surgery, 5th ed. Philadelphia, Lippincott Raven, 1997, pp 17–19.

Rudolph R, Ballantyne DL: Skin grafts. In McCarthy JG (ed): Plastic Surgery. Philadelphia, WB Saunders, 1990, pp 221–274.

Shen JT, Falanga V: Innovative therapies in wound healing. J Cutan Med Surg 7:217–224, 2003.

Triana RJ, Murakami CS, Larrabee WF: Skin grafts and local flaps. In Papel ID (ed): Facial Plastic and Reconstructive Surgery, 2nd ed. New York, Thieme, 2002, pp 38–54.

Venturi ML, Attinger CE, Mesbahi AN, et al: Mechanisms and clinical applications of the vacuum-assisted closure (VAC) device: A review. Am J Clin Dermatol 6:185–194, 2005.

PRINCIPLES OF SKIN FLAP SURGERY

Mitchell A. Stotland, MD, MS, FRCSC, and
Carolyn L. Kerrigan, MD, MSc, FRCSC

1. How do main distributing arteries reach the cutaneous circulation of a flap?

Arteries that perfuse a surgical flap pass into the skin component in one of two fundamental ways:

- *Musculocutaneous arteries* travel perpendicularly through underlying muscle bellies into the overlying cutaneous circulation of the skin. They are most prevalent in the supply of skin covering the broad, flat muscles of the torso (e.g., latissimus dorsi, rectus abdominis).
- *Septocutaneous arteries,* which arise originally from either segmental or musculocutaneous vessels, pass directly within intermuscular fascial septae to supply the overlying skin. This arrangement is most common between the longer, thinner muscles of the extremities (e.g., radial forearm flap, dorsalis pedis flap).

2. What are the three main characteristics of skin-containing flaps?

Composition, blood supply, and method of movement.

3. Classify skin-containing flaps in terms of their composition.

Based on which tissues are contained within a flap, they can be described as cutaneous, fasciocutaneous, myocutaneous, osseocutaneous, or innervated (sensate) cutaneous.

4. Classify skin-containing flaps in terms of their blood supply (Fig. 105-1).

The blood supply of a flap originates from either a musculocutaneous or a septocutaneous artery. The flap is then designed so that the skin is nourished via randomly or axially oriented feeder vessels.

1. Musculocutaneous Artery as Main Source

- *Random Flaps:* Supplied by one or more musculocutaneous perforating arteries that penetrate the overlying cutaneous circulation specifically at the flap's anatomic base. Their incorporation into the flap base occurs on a random basis.
- *Axial Flaps:* Supplied by a named musculocutaneous vessel that is axially oriented within the underlying muscle. By including the muscle in the flap, the overlying skin is supplied by a series of musculocutaneous perforating arteries that exit the muscle and penetrate the overlying cutaneous circulation at multiple

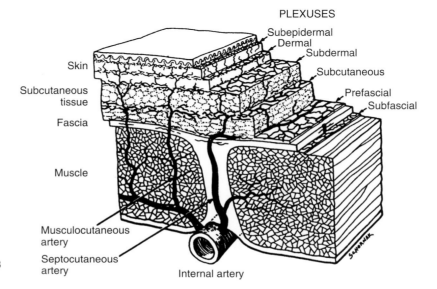

Figure 105-1. Cutaneous microcirculation. (From McCarthy JG: Plastic Surgery. Philadelphia, WB Saunders, 1990, p 282.)

points along the course of the flap's axis. With this configuration, the vascular pedicle (i.e., the main musculocutaneous artery) is said to be cantilevered far beyond the flap's anatomic base, providing greater length and reliability.

2. Septocutaneous Artery as Main Source
   - *Random Flaps:* Supplied by one or more branches off the septocutaneous system that penetrate the overlying cutaneous circulation specifically at the flap's anatomic base. Their inclusion in the flap base occurs by random selection.
   - *Axial Flaps:* Supplied by a named septocutaneous vessel that runs longitudinally along the axis of the flap. The vessel may be located deep and incorporated into the flap via a fascial/septal attachment that provides segmental perforators (e.g., radial artery in the forearm flap), or it may be located in a more superficial position free of a fascial association (e.g., superficial circumflex iliac artery in the groin flap).

5. Classify skin-containing flaps in terms of their method of movement (Fig. 105-2).
Flap transfer is commonly described in the following ways:
- *Local Transfer:* Advancement, pivot (rotation), and interpolation (transposition)
- *Distant Transfer:* Direct, tubed, and microvascular

6. Classify the following flaps according to their three major characteristics.
See Table 105-1.

7. In what year did plastic surgeons successfully introduce free tissue transfer as a reconstructive option? What type of procedure was performed?
In 1973 a new era of reconstructive plastic surgery was inaugurated with the publication of a series of reports describing the use of island skin flaps from the abdomen and groin region. These flaps were based variably on the superficial inferior epigastric or superficial circumflex iliac arteries. The initial reports described the use of these flaps for coverage of posttraumatic soft tissue defects of the lower extremity. A subsequent period of widespread experimental and anatomic investigation soon led to an explosion of donor site options and flap compositions for use by the reconstructive surgeon.

8. What is an angiosome? What is its significance in flap design?
Analogous to a sensory dermatome, which is an area of skin innervated by a named sensory nerve, an *angiosome* is a composite block of tissue supplied by the same source artery. The source artery (i.e., a segmental or distributing artery) supplies the skin and underlying structures within the given three-dimensional block of tissue. The entire skin surface of the body is perfused by a multitude of angiosome units. Adjacent angiosomes are linked by intervening reduced-caliber vessels referred to as *choke vessels.* In principle, a flap can support one angiosome supplied in a random cutaneous fashion. Moreover, an axial-pattern flap can carry with it an additional angiosome of tissue that is perfused via an

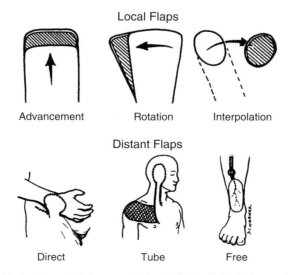

Figure 105-2. Classification of skin flaps by method of movement. (From McCarthy JG: Plastic Surgery. Philadelphia, WB Saunders, 1990, p 277.)

Table 105-1. Classification of Flaps by Composition, Blood Supply, and Movement

FLAP	COMPOSITION	BLOOD SUPPLY	MOVEMENT
Limberg flap	Cutaneous	Musculocutaneous artery (random)	Local pivot
Abbe flap	Myocutaneous	Musculocutaneous artery (axial: labial artery)	Distant direct
Groin flap	Cutaneous	Septocutaneous artery (axial: superficial circumflex iliac artery)	Distant direct, tubed, or microvascular
Radial forearm flap	Fasciocutaneous	Septocutaneous artery (axial: radial artery)	Local interpolation or distant microvascular
Cross-finger flap	Cutaneous	Septocutaneous artery (random)	Distant direct
Forehead flap	Myocutaneous	Musculocutaneous artery (axial: supratrochlear with or without supraorbital artery)	Distant direct or local interpolation
TRAM flap	Myocutaneous	Musculocutaneous artery (axial: superior and/or inferior epigastric artery)	Local interpolation or distant microvascular

TRAM, Transverse rectus abdominis myocutaneous.

intervening choke vessel in a random cutaneous fashion (beyond the domain of the main flap pedicle). Examples include (1) a Bakamjian deltopectoral flap designed with a lateral, random cutaneous extension existing beyond the domain of the medially based intercostal perforating vessels and (2) a transverse rectus abdominis myocutaneous (TRAM) flap incorporating cutaneous extensions lateral to the perforators arising through the underlying rectus abdominis muscle (zones 3 and 4).

9. **What is the "delay procedure"? What is the "delay phenomenon"?**
   The *delay procedure* is a preliminary surgical intervention wherein a portion of the vascular supply to a flap is divided before the definitive elevation and transfer of the flap. The resulting benefit, termed the *delay phenomenon,* is extension of the longitudinal reach of a flap's vascular pedicle, creating a greater flap area due to the survival of a more extended random cutaneous component distally. The mechanism of this phenomenon is somewhat controversial. Explanations include sympathectomy-induced enhancement in vascularity, longitudinal vascular reorientation, vascular enlargement, improved tissue tolerance to hypoxia (metabolic adaptation), and dilation of choke vessels between vascular territories, allowing capture of adjacent angiosomes.

10. **What does the term *critical ischemia time* mean?**
    Critical ischemia time (CIT) refers to the maximal period of ischemia that a given tissue can withstand and still remain viable after resumption of vascular flow. You can look at the CIT_{50} value, which is the ischemia time that results in flap necrosis in 50% of cases (analogous to the median lethal dose [LD_{50}] of a pharmacologic agent). Critical ischemia is a temperature- and tissue-dependent parameter. Skin grafts can tolerate up to 3 weeks of complete ischemia when stored at 3°C to 4°C. Clinical reports have described the survival of human free flaps and amputated human digits after more than 24 hours of ischemia when they were preserved at hypothermic conditions. Experimental studies in a normothermic skin flap model have shown a CIT_{50} of 9 hours. Muscle, because of its metabolic requirements, is relatively more sensitive than skin to the stress of ischemia. Other metabolically demanding organs (e.g., brain, heart, kidney) are even more vulnerable to the stress of hypoxia and energy depletion, as reflected by much shorter CIT_{50} values.

11. **What is primary versus secondary ischemia?**
    In microsurgery, the term *primary ischemia* refers to the obligatory interval between pedicle division at the donor site and removal of the vascular clamps after microanastomosis at the recipient site. *Secondary ischemia* occurs postoperatively when the flap pedicle is compromised by either extrinsic or anastomotic obstruction.

12. **What does the term *ischemia–reperfusion injury* mean?**
    Ischemia–reperfusion injury refers to the finding that postischemic reestablishment of vascular perfusion may result in tissue damage above and beyond that directly resulting from the ischemia itself. The distinction between ischemic injury and reperfusion injury has been characterized as *cellular death of attrition* versus *cellular death by bombardment*. Ischemia results in a death of attrition through processes such as oxygen deprivation, adenosine triphosphate/energy depletion, calcium depletion, and cell membrane dysfunction. Reperfusion results in death by bombardment through processes such as neutrophil respiratory burst with free radical formation; up-regulation of cell adhesion molecules, which results in neutrophil diapedesis and degranulation; and leukocyte, platelet, and endothelial cell release of peptide and lipid proinflammatory mediators. Therefore the experimental and clinical approaches to improving flap survival must consider the implications of both ischemia and reperfusion.

13. What mechanisms may lead to the failure of a pedicled flap? A free flap?

Tissue loss after the transfer of a *pedicled flap* typically results from distal necrosis. In such a situation, the flap is designed too large for its inherent vascular supply, and an associated random cutaneous component exists beyond the flap's zone of perfusion. Alternatively, mechanical trauma, a compressive dressing, or an adjacent hematoma may compromise the flap pedicle and result in more extensive tissue loss. A *free flap,* in contrast, has classically been described as exhibiting an all-or-none survival pattern. In reality, segmental free flap loss is occasionally seen in distal flap zones that represent random extensions of the axially supplied flap (e.g., zones 3 and 4 in a free TRAM flap). Occurring more commonly than extrinsic mechanical compromise of the pedicle, intraluminal problems arising directly at the level of the microsurgical anastomosis may lead to vascular thrombosis and complete flap loss.

14. How can you optimize the viability of a pedicled flap?

With the use of pedicled flaps, segmental loss usually is due to distal necrosis. In contrast to the early, vigilant surveillance of free flaps, which allows salvage of anastomotic complications by emergent reexploration, there is little need for use of sophisticated techniques to monitor pedicled flap viability. Rather, proper flap design based on an adequate knowledge of relevant anatomy and published clinical experience are critical to the prevention of distal flap necrosis. Avoidance of (1) extrinsic pedicle compression, (2) undue tension upon wound closure, and (3) excessive flap dependency, with attendant venous congestion, are essential principles. The delay procedure, based on the rationale provided, also can be used to improve flap viability or to extend flap area. Intravital dyes (e.g., fluorescein) occasionally are used to help determine the zone of perfusion in a pedicled flap. The management of distal flap necrosis typically is conservative or expectant, involving conventional wound care and possible secondary, delayed revision. Clinical observation alone is generally sufficient to identify the rare instance in which a correctable, mechanical disturbance results in impending, total pedicled flap failure.

15. What methods are used to monitor the viability of a free flap that contains a cutaneous component?

More than 20 years after the clinical introduction of microsurgical free tissue transfer, monitoring of free flap viability remains controversial. However, all experts agree that flap monitoring is crucial in the early postoperative period because of the possibility of total free flap failure secondary to microanastomotic thrombosis. Early flap reexploration rates, depending on the series, may be upward of 15%, although ultimate free flap success typically is achieved in 95% of cases. These figures clearly indicate a significant chance for free flap salvage if secondary ischemia is promptly detected before the onset of the no-reflow phenomenon.

In general, viability is easier to evaluate in skin-containing free flaps than in flaps containing only muscle, bone, or viscera. Clinical observation of skin color, capillary refill, or postpuncture dermal bleeding is a simple and valuable method of flap assessment. A multitude of more sophisticated methods have been used, including intravenous fluorescein (either conventional bolus technique or low-dose sequential dermatofluorometry), surface Doppler monitoring, temperature probes, laser Doppler flowmetry, tissue pH readings, pulse oximetry, and direct tissue oxygen measurement (via transcutaneous or implantable PO_2 electrodes). Depending on the particular setting, strong arguments can be made on behalf of some or all of these techniques. Yet in experienced hands, clinical observation of *skin-containing* free flaps remains the most useful and reliable monitoring technique.

BIBLIOGRAPHY

Daniel RK, Kerrigan CL: Principles and physiology of skin flap surgery. In McCarthy JG (ed): Plastic Surgery. Philadelphia, WB Saunders, 1990, p 275.
Daniel RK, Taylor GI: Distant transfer of an island flap by microvascular anastomoses. Plast Reconstr Surg 52:111–117, 1973.
Jones NF: Intraoperative and postoperative monitoring of microsurgical free tissue transfers. Clin Plast Surg 19:783–797, 1992.
Kerrigan CL, Stotland MA: Ischemia reperfusion injury: A review. Microsurgery 14:165–175, 1993.
Khouri RK: Avoiding free flap failure. Clin Plast Surg 19:773–781, 1992.
O'Brien BM, Macleod AM, Hayhurst W, Morrison WA: Successful transfer of a large island flap from the groin to the foot by microvascular anastomoses. Plast Reconstr Surg 52:271–278, 1973.
Picard-Ami LA, Thomson JG, Kerrigan CL: Critical ischemia times and survival patterns of experimental pig flaps. Plast Reconstr Surg 86:739–743, 1990.
Stotland MA, Kerrigan CL: Discussion on "Ischemia reperfusion injury in myocutaneous flaps: Role of leukocytes and leukotrienes" by Kirschner RE, Fyfe BS, Hoffman LA, Chiao JC, Davis JM, and Fantini GA. Plast Reconstr Surg 99:1494–1495, 1997.

1. What exactly is a fasciocutaneous flap?

According to Tolhurst, any vascularized flap that contains fascia for the intent to augment the overall vascularity is a fasciocutaneous flap. Lamberty disagrees with such a simplistic viewpoint, arguing that a "true" fascial flap must include a specific known "septocutaneous" perforator that discretely supplies the fascia. A broader and very reasonable definition by Nahai states that fasciocutaneous flaps are skin flaps made more reliable by inclusion of the deep fascia, a maneuver that usually ensures preservation of circulation to the skin by whatever means.

BASIC ANATOMY

2. Describe the vascular contributions to the "fascial plexus."

The fascial plexus is not a discrete structure per se but represents a confluence of multiple, adjacent vascular networks and their branches that have emanated from the perforators of the deep fascia or "fascial feeders." Intercommunications among these networks exist at the subfascial, fascial, suprafascial, subcutaneous, and subdermal levels.

3. Where are "fascial feeders" found?

These are branches of the source vessels to a given angiosome that do not perforate the deep fascia. Instead, they terminate within the subfascial plexus.

4. What are the six patterns of perforators of the deep fascia that can each supply a distinct type of fasciocutaneous flap?

See Fig. 106-1.

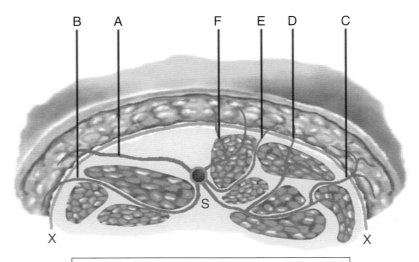

Figure 106-1. Pathways of the various known cutaneous perforators that pierce the deep fascia to supply the fascial plexus. *S,* Source vessel; *X,* deep fascia. (Modified with permission from Hallock GG: Direct and indirect perforator flaps: The history and the controversy. Plast Reconstr Surg 111:855–866, 2003.)

A = Direct cutaneous
B = Direct septocutaneous
C = Direct cutaneous branch of muscular vessel
D = Perforating cutaneous branch of muscular vessel
E = Septocutaneous perforator
F = Musculocutaneous perforator

5. **Are direct septocutaneous vessels and septocutaneous perforators actually different?**

   Indeed they are. Both traverse an intermuscular septum, but direct septocutaneous vessels are of relatively large caliber and can nourish the fascial plexus of a large cutaneous territory alone, for example, the circumflex scapular vessels whose cutaneous branch supplies almost the entire dorsal thoracic fascia. Septocutaneous perforators are diminutive and tend to be found as a sequential and close-knit array of branches from the same source vessel, for example, those found nourishing the radial forearm flap.

6. **The dorsal thoracic fascia is synonymous with the territory of what fasciocutaneous flaps?**

   The dorsal thoracic fascia is equivalent to the upper back fascia. It can almost in toto be supplied by the cutaneous branch of the circumflex scapular vessels, which historically has been used to base the scapular and parascapular flaps and their variants. Of course, there are other contributions, such as from intercostal and musculocutaneous perforators.

7. **Is a "muscle" perforator flap just a type of fasciocutaneous flap?**

   This is an extremely controversial point, yet a "muscle" perforator flap relies on the large perforating musculocutaneous branches of the source pedicle to a muscle. These are identical to the "perforating cutaneous branches of a muscular vessel" according to Nakajima et al., and the latter are the basis of one of their types of fasciocutaneous flaps.

8. **Simplify the stratification of the types of deep fascial perforators as being either "direct" or "indirect" perforators.**

   The system of nomenclature for skin flaps has become incredibly chaotic due to use of terms such as "axial flaps," "random flaps," and "septocutaneous flaps." This can be simplified by considering that all perforators contributing to the fascial plexus do so either directly or indirectly. Using the terms introduced by Nakajima et al., *direct* perforators (e.g., axial, septocutaneous, or direct cutaneous branch of a muscular vessel) course from the source vessel of the given angiosome to the skin without first supplying any other deep structure. *Indirect* perforators (e.g., musculocutaneous perforators) first pass through some intermediary structure before reaching the subdermal plexus. The corresponding flaps would then be either *direct* or *indirect* fasciocutaneous flaps.

9. **What role does the deep fascia have in most fasciocutaneous flaps?**

   Although the deep fascia does have an intrinsic microcirculation, for all practical purposes it is avascular. Its real value, when included as part of a fasciocutaneous flap, may be to prevent inadvertent injury to the suprafascial portion of the fascial plexus, thereby increasing the reliability of the flap.

10. **Can a fasciocutaneous flap be neither fascial nor cutaneous?**

    Because the deep fascia itself adds little to the overall circulation to a fasciocutaneous flap, it can be excluded totally as long as the vasculature within the overlying tissues is kept intact. Typically, this maneuver still will allow survival of what then would be a non-fascia fasciocutaneous flap. The skin is an end organ relying on the subdermal plexus fed by the fascial perforators, and it too is superfluous because it does not contribute to vascularization of the fascial plexus per se but is, in fact, a parasite. Thus it also could be excluded without affecting the viability of the rest of the fasciocutaneous flap.

11. **Describe the composition of the subcutaneous flap and the adipofascial flap.**

    If both the skin and deep fascia are excluded from a fasciocutaneous flap, what is left is a *subcutaneous flap*. Similarly, retention of the deep fascia without the skin component creates an *adipofascial flap*. Because the major portion of the fascial plexus usually is found within the subcutaneous tissues, both can be most simply considered just variations of fasciocutaneous flaps that differ only in their composition.

12. **Define the three subtypes of fasciocutaneous flaps using either the Cormack-Lamberty or Nahai-Mathes schema.**

    These two major classification schemas categorize fasciocutaneous flaps into three subdivisions according to the pathway of origin of their fascial perforators (Fig. 106-2).
    - Cormack-Lamberty Subtypes
      - Type A: Multiple perforators (without any known discrete origin; may be a combination of direct or indirect [more likely] perforators)
      - Type B: Solitary perforator (single perforator, usually direct)
      - Type C: Segmental perforators (multiple, arising periodically from the same underlying source vessel, usually direct)

Cormack & Lamberty

Type A: Multiple   Type B: Solitary   Type C: Segmental

Nahai & Mathes

Figure 106-2. Two major classification schemas for fascia flaps stratified according to the origin of their fascial perforators. (Courtesy Carol Varma, Multimedia Communication Manager, The Lehigh Valley Hospital, Allentown, Pennsylvania.)

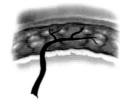

Type A: Direct Cutaneous   Type B: Septocutaneous   Type C: Musculocutaneous

- Nahai-Mathes Subtypes
  - Type A: Direct cutaneous perforator (similar to the older term "axial")
  - Type B: Septocutaneous perforator (courses directly along an intercompartmental or intermuscular septum)
  - Type C: Musculocutaneous perforator (indirect)

13. In what body regions do direct fascial perforators predominate when compared with musculocutaneous perforators?

Because most direct perforators of the deep fascia arise within intercompartmental or intermuscular septa, they are more prevalent wherever long, slender muscles are found, such as in the extremities. In contrast, musculocutaneous perforators are more numerous over the broad, flatter muscles associated with the trunk, where muscular septa are few and far apart.

BASIC PHYSIOLOGY

14. Explain how the axis determines the proper orientation for designing a fasciocutaneous flap.

The predominant direction of blood flow within a given fascial plexus determines its axis. For the most part, the vector summation of the contributions to the fascial plexus by all perforators is longitudinal in the extremities and somewhat oblique or horizontal in the torso. The design of a fasciocutaneous flap oriented along this axis or direction of flow will maximize its potential length by best capturing adjacent perforator territories.

15. How can the maximum potential length of a fasciocutaneous flap be estimated?

Safe limits for the design of a fasciocutaneous flap have been determined only by trial and error, for example, a length-to-width ratio of 2:1 for the lower extremity (compared with 1:1 for random flaps). There can be no set rules because deep fascia perforators are so frequently anomalous in caliber and location not only among individuals but also in opposite sides of the same individual.

16. What is the point of rotation of a fasciocutaneous flap?

Applicable to local flaps, this corresponds to the site where the flap is tethered by its vascular pedicle.

17. What is the arc of rotation of a fasciocutaneous flap?

The distance from the point of rotation to the most distant safe length of the given flap determines the range of coverage or arc of rotation through which a local fasciocutaneous flap can be transposed. Whereas the expected range in flap size for a given body region has been learned through the experience of other surgeons, the maximal arc of rotation really remains conjectural at this time.

18. **Who is Pontén, and what are his "superflaps"?**

Bengt Pontén of Sweden is generally credited for reintroducing the concept of the fasciocutaneous flap. He observed that undelayed cutaneous flaps from the lower leg, if oriented along a longitudinal axis with retention of the deep fascia, had extraordinary viability up to even a 3:1 length-to-width ratio. Historically, only 1:1 flaps (without fascia) previously had been considered safe in this region. His flaps were proximally based and sensate, with no discrete perforator ever identified (i.e., Cormack-Lamberty type A). Some authorities consider these "superflaps" to be identical to the neurocutaneous flaps of the lower extremity, which also have a unique robustness; and in both cases may be more than just a coincidence.

19. **Define a distal-based fasciocutaneous flap. Why is it more dependable than its muscle flap counterpart?**

For muscle flaps, distal-based implies that the vascular pedicle chosen to sustain the muscle enters that border of the flap either farthest away from the heart or its dominant vascular supply, which by definition would be a minor or secondary blood supply. Usually for distal-based fasciocutaneous flaps, the pedicle is found at that boundary farthest from the heart. They are more dependable because flow in the fascial plexus typically is multidirectional, which would be equivalent if the chosen distal fascial perforator had characteristics comparable to the proximal perforator. It is the quantity of flow via the chosen perforator (usually proportional to caliber) rather than the pedicle orientation per se that determines the extent of viability of a fasciocutaneous flap.

20. **State the primary advantage of a distal-based fasciocutaneous flap.**

Proximal skin territories known to be reliable can be transposed on a distal pedicle for potential coverage of acral defects. This is especially valuable in the extremities where otherwise a free flap might be the only acceptable alternative. In this regard, the distal-based sural flap has become a workhorse flap. The skin of the calf, relying on a distal perforator of the peroneal artery, can be transferred to cover the foot and ankle, primarily in lieu of a microsurgical tissue transfer.

21. **Are distal-based fasciocutaneous flaps and retrograde flow-flaps the same entity?**

Sometimes they can be. Retrograde-flow flaps usually are distal-based flaps where both arterial inflow to and venous outflow from a more proximal skin territory is in a reverse direction from the normal. A good example is the distal-based radial forearm flap where the radial artery is perfused in a reverse fashion from the ulnar artery via an intact superficial palmer arch. However, a distal perforator sustaining a distal-based flap, if appropriately designed, still could maintain an orthograde pattern of flow. This is true, for example, if the radial recurrent artery is chosen to supply a distal-based lateral arm flap. Suffice it to say that a distal-based flap may be the same as, but is not necessarily synonymous with, a retrograde-flow flap. Furthermore, reverse flow does not necessarily mean retrograde flow.

22. **How does venous regurgitation occur in a retrograde flow flap?**

Normally, the reversal of venous outflow is obstructed by valves. Two hypotheses currently explain the clinical observation of venous regurgitation in retrograde-flow flaps despite the presence of valves:

- *Bypass Theory:* Alternative anatomic structures for venous flow circumvent the valves.
- *Incompetent Valve Theory:* Some intrinsic or extrinsic physiologic factors overcome the normal function of the valve, rendering it nonfunctional.

The next time you dissect a major limb artery, carefully check the two venae comitantes and note the numerous communicating branches that cross over the artery to reach each other. Usually just a mere nuisance that hinders dissection of that artery, these branches may be an important avenue for circumventing the valves in that segment of veins (Box 106-1).

23. **How is Allen's test relevant to the Chinese flap?**

Because the radial forearm flap initially was developed by the Chinese, it is sometimes referred to as the "Chinese flap." If the radial artery is included with the flap, the ulnar artery must maintain sufficient collateral circulation to the hand. Compression of both arteries at the wrist followed by release of only the ulnar artery must demonstrate complete hand perfusion (i.e., a negative Allen's test). Otherwise, sacrifice of the radial artery with this flap would be contraindicated.

24. **What is the superficial ulnar artery trap?**

The superficial ulnar artery trap is an excellent example of the potentially disastrous complications that plague the fasciocutaneous system of flaps due to the frequency of anatomic anomalies. Normally, the ulnar artery lies deep within the medial intermuscular septum of the forearm. However, in approximately 9% of individuals it lies superficial to the deep fascia. Thus the unsuspected inclusion of all suprafascial structures within a radial forearm flap would totally devascularize the hand!

Box 106-1. Mechanisms that Allow Reversal of Venous Outflow in Retrograde Perfused Fasciocutaneous Flaps

A. Bypass via Alternative Venous Pathways
  1. Macrovenous (involving the venae comitantes)
     a. Interconnecting communicating branches between comitantes
     b. Collateral branches that go proximal and distal to the valve to rejoin the same comitans
  2. Microvenous (avalvular veins accompanying the venae arteriosae)
  3. Avalvular vein segments
B. Valve Incompetency
  1. Intrinsic (alternations in valve structure)
     a. Structural anomalies preventing cusp contact
     b. Intrinsic smooth muscle contractions
  2. Extrinsic
     a. Intraluminal factors
        I. Excessive luminal distension
        II. Overcome by increased proximal/distal pressure gradient
     b. Extraluminal factors: External pressures opening the valve

APPLIED ANATOMY

25. Why has the radial forearm flap fallen into disrepute in some quarters of the world?

Although the flap itself has numerous attractive attributes, donor site morbidity potentially can be disastrous. This includes hand ischemia, dysesthesias, dysfunction from tendon adhesions, osteomyelitis, and a nonesthetic appearance if a skin graft was used. Other cutaneous flaps now can offer the same advantages without the risks.

26. What is the Becker flap?

The territory of the Becker flap (named after the noted anatomist) corresponds to the dorsal ulnar border of the forearm. Becker described a fairly constant dorsal branch of the ulnar artery that supplies this region. Because the point where it pierces the deep fascia is only a few centimeters proximal to the pisiform, it can be used as a distal-based island flap (with orthograde perfusion) to take the proximal ulnar forearm skin for provision of coverage of the hand without sacrificing the ulnar artery itself.

27. Why has the groin flap fallen into disfavor?

Although a cutaneous flap from the groin still can be useful as a pedicled or free flap, the dissection can be hampered by the high frequency of vascular anomalies. The groin flap is a notorious example of a not so uncommon and major problem with using fasciocutaneous flaps as a group. The lateral groin is nourished medially by both the superficial circumflex iliac artery (SCIA) and superficial inferior epigastric artery (SIEA) and laterally by contributions from the deep circumflex iliac artery. A reciprocal relationship in the size or variation even in the presence of these vessels is the norm. In 48% of cases, the SIEA and SCIA share an origin from the common femoral artery. They may be inversely related or equal in diameter, or one may be altogether missing.

28. The importance of the triangular space of the thorax is because what direct fascial perforator emanates through it?

The largest branch of the subscapular artery usually is the circumflex scapular, which in turn passes through the triangular space to give off a cutaneous perforator to the dorsal thoracic fascia. This in turn terminates in branches that radiate like the spokes of a wheel to supply many named upper back fasciocutaneous flaps, such as the ascending scapular (ascending branch), scapular (transverse branch), parascapular (descending branch), and inframammary extended circumflex scapular flap (unnamed branch).

29. Name the muscles that define the boundaries of the triangular space.

The teres minor superiorly, the teres major inferiorly, and the long head of the triceps muscle laterally form a potential triangular shaped opening located just superior to the posterior axilla (Fig. 106-3).

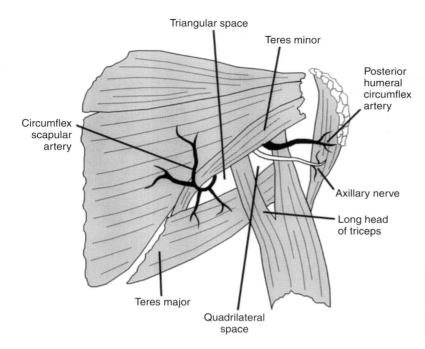

Triangular space

Teres minor

Posterior humeral circumflex artery

Circumflex scapular artery

Axillary nerve

Long head of triceps

Teres major

Quadrilateral space

Figure 106-3. Boundaries of the triangular and quadrilateral spaces. (Courtesy Carol Varma, Multimedia Communication Manager, The Lehigh Valley Hospital, Allentown, Pennsylvania.)

30. What important structures pass through the quadrilateral space to form the neurovascular pedicle for a sensate upper arm fasciocutaneous flap?
The posterior circumflex humeral (PCH) vessels and axillary nerve traverse the quadrilateral space. A cutaneous branch of the PCH and the lateral brachial cutaneous nerve from the axillary nerve supply the deltoid flap, which is a potentially sensate flap from the upper outer arm.

31. Name the structures that define the boundaries of the quadrilateral space.
The medial side of the quadrilateral space is formed by the long head of the triceps, the inferior side by the teres major, and superior border by the teres minor muscle. The humerus defines the lateral border (see Fig. 106-3).

32. Perhaps the most notorious liability of the fasciocutaneous flap is the risk of morbidity at the donor site, especially if a skin graft has been required for closure. Describe at least three ways in which this specific risk can be minimized.
Any variants of the fasciocutaneous flap that exclude the cutaneous component (e.g., subcutaneous, fascial, or adipofascial flap) leave behind the original skin with its intact subdermal plexus. This can be used to close the donor site directly. In patients with enough local skin redundancy, primary closure may also be possible even with a fasciocutaneous flap if the desired flap is small or if pretransfer or posttransfer tissue expansion has been performed. Finally, certain geometric designs of local flaps can be used with the intent not just to close the defect but also to provide simultaneous donor site closure, such as a V-Y advancement or bilobed fasciocutaneous flap.

33. Name some advantages of fasciocutaneous flaps when compared with muscle flaps.
Probably the most valuable asset is that no functioning muscle is expended. Fasciocutaneous flaps are readily accessible because they are near the skin surface. As a corollary, deep underlying neurovascular structures can be avoided and risk of their injury minimized. If a cutaneous nerve can be incorporated into the flap design, true sensate flaps are possible (Table 106-1).

34. Identify the source vessel and type of perforator in these 10 commonly used fascia flaps.
See Table 106-2 and Fig. 106-4.

Table 106-1. Attributes and Liabilities of Fasciocutaneous versus Muscle Flaps

	FASCIOCUTANEOUS FLAPS	MUSCLE FLAPS
Accessibility	+	−
Anatomic anomalies	−	+
Availability	+	−
Composite flaps	=	=
Use in infected or irradiated wound	±	+
Donor site morbidity	−	+
Dynamic transfer	−	+
Expendable	+	−
Malleability	−	+
Microsurgical tissue transfer	=	=
Reliability	=	=
Sensate	+	−
Size	+	±
Thinness	−	+

+, Asset; −, detriment; =, no significant difference; ±, variable.

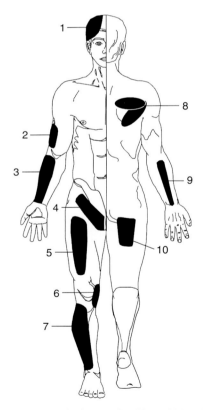

Figure 106-4. Donor sites of 10 commonly used fascia flaps. (Courtesy Carol Varma, Multimedia Communication Manager, The Lehigh Valley Hospital, Allentown, Pennsylvania.)

Table 106-2. Source Vessel and Flap Subtype Perforator

FASCIA FLAP	SOURCE VESSEL	SUBTYPE PERFORATOR
1. Temporoparietal	Superficial temporal	Axial (direct)
2. Lateral arm	Posterior radial collateral	Septocutaneous (direct)
3. Radial forearm	Radial	Septocutaneous (direct)
4. Groin	Superficial circumflex iliac or inferior epigastric	Axial (direct)
5. Anterolateral thigh	Lateral circumflex femoral descending branch or perforating branch of muscular vessel	Septocutaneous (direct) Musculocutaneous (indirect)
6. Saphenous	Descending geniculate	Septocutaneous (direct)
7. Peroneal	Peroneal or perforating branch of muscular vessel	Septocutaneous (direct) Musculocutaneous (indirect)
8. Dorsal thoracic	Circumflex scapular	Septocutaneous (direct)
9. Posterior interosseous	Posterior interosseous	Septocutaneous (direct)
10. Gluteal thigh	Inferior gluteal descending branch	Septocutaneous (direct)

BIBLIOGRAPHY

Becker C, Gilbert A: The ulnar flap: Description and applications. Eur J Plast Surg 11:79–82, 1988.

Chuang DCC, Colony LH, Chen HC, Wei FC: Groin flap design and versatility. Plast Reconstr Surg 84:100–107, 1989.

Cormack GC, Lamberty BGH: A classification of fasciocutaneous flaps according to their patterns of vascularization. Br J Plast Surg 37:80–87, 1984.

Cormack GC, Lamberty BGH: The Fasciocutaneous System of Vessels: The Arterial Anatomy of Skin Flaps, 2nd ed. Edinburgh, Churchill Livingston, 1994, pp 105–129.

del Pinal F, Taylor GI: The deep venous system and reverse flow flaps. Br J Plast Surg 46:652–664, 1993.

Devansh D: Superficial ulnar artery trap. Plast Reconstr Surg 97:420–426, 1996.

Donski PK, Fodgestam I: Distally based fasciocutaneous flap from the sural region. A preliminary report. Scand J Plast Reconstr Surg 17:191–196, 1983.

Hahn SM, Kim NH, Yang IH: Deltoid sensory flap. J Reconstr Microsurg 6:21–28, 1990.

Hallock GG: Clinical scrutiny of the de facto superiority of proximally versus distally based fasciocutaneous flaps. Plast Reconstr Surg 100:1428–1433, 1997.

Hallock GG: Direct and indirect perforator flaps: The history and the controversy. Plast Reconstr Surg 111:855–866, 2003.

Jones BM, O'Brien CJ: Acute ischaemia of the hand resulting from elevation of a radial forearm flap. Br J Plast Surg 38:396–397, 1985.

Kim PS, Gottlieb JR, Harris GH, Nagle DJ, Lewis VL: The dorsal thoracic fascia: Anatomic significance with clinical applications in reconstructive microsurgery. Plast Reconstr Surg 79:72–80, 1987.

Lin SD, Lai CS, Chiu CC: Venous drainage in the reverse forearm flap. Plast Reconstr Surg 74:508–512, 1984.

Mathes SJ, Nahai F: The reconstructive triangle: A paradigm for surgical decision making. In: Reconstructive Surgery: Principles, Anatomy, & Technique, Churchill Livingstone, New York, 1997, pp 9–36.

Nahai F: Surgical indications for fasciocutaneous flaps (invited comment). Ann Plast Surg 13:502–503, 1984.

Nakajima H, Fujino T, Adachi S: A new concept of vascular supply to the skin and classification of skin flaps according to their vascularization. Ann Plast Surg 16:1–17, 1986.

Nakajima H, Minabe T, Imanishi N: Three-dimensional analysis and classification of arteries in the skin and subcutaneous adipofascial tissue by computer graphics imaging. Plast Reconstr Surg 102:748–760, 1998.

Niranjan NS, Price RD, Govilkar P: Fascial feeder and perforator-based V-Y advancement flaps in the reconstruction of lower limb defects. Br J Plast Surg 53:679–689, 2000.

Ohsaki M, Maruyama Y: Anatomical investigations of the cutaneous branches of the circumflex scapular artery and their communications. Br J Plast Surg 46:160–163, 1993.

Ozkan O, Coskunfirat OK, Dikici MD, Ozgentas HE: A rare and serious complication of the radial forearm flap donor site: Osteomyelitis of the radius. J Reconstr Microsurg 21:293–296, 2005.

Pontén B: The fasciocutaneous flap: Its use in soft tissue defects of the lower leg. Br J Plast Surg 34:215–220, 1981.

Richardson D, Fisher SE, Vaughan ED, Brown JS: Radial forearm flap donor-site complications and morbidity: A prospective study. Plast Reconstr Surg 99:109–115, 1997.

Timmons MJ, Missotten FEM, Poole MD, Davies DM: Complications of radial forearm flap donor sites. Br J Plast Surg 39:176–178, 1986.

Tolhurst DEL: Fasciocutaneous flaps and their use in reconstructive surgery. Perspect Plast Surg 4:129–145, 1990.

Touam C, Rostoucher P, Bhatia A, Oberlin C: Comparative study of two series of distally-based fasciocutaneous flaps for coverage of the lower one-fourth of the leg, the ankle, and the foot. Plast Reconstr Surg 107:383–392, 2001.

Wei FC, Jain V, Celik N, Chen HC, Chuang DCC, Lin CH: Have we found an ideal soft-tissue flap? An experience with 672 anterolateral thigh flaps. Plast Reconstr Surg 109:2219–2226, 2002.

Wei FC, Jain V, Suominen S, Chen HC: Confusion among perforator flaps: What is a true perforator flap? Plast Reconstr Surg 107:874–876, 2001.

PRINCIPLES OF MUSCLE AND MUSCULOCUTANEOUS FLAPS

Chapter 107

Geoffrey G. Hallock, MD

BASIC ANATOMY

1. Why can a muscle be used as a flap?

Any organ that contains a discrete, intrinsic arteriovenous network can be used as a vascularized tissue transfer, and muscle is no exception. Of course, other factors must be considered, and, especially with muscles, sacrifice of any function must be acceptable.

2. Where do the vascular pedicles enter a muscle?

The motor nerve(s) of a muscle is(are) always accompanied by an arteriovenous system or vascular pedicle, which typically is the major source of circulation to that muscle. Virtually every muscle has multiple other vascular pedicles that are *not* associated with the means of innervation. These are often found near the site of muscle origin or insertion and may represent an important source of collateral circulation. The latter are highly variable in their location or even presence, usually overlooked in most anatomy textbooks, and frequently insignificant from a surgical standpoint.

3. Differentiate the terms "dominant," "minor," and "segmental" in reference to the vascular pedicle of a muscle.

The *dominant* pedicle to a muscle usually can independently sustain virtually the entire muscle. A *minor* pedicle, even if a reasonable caliber, will maintain only a lesser portion of a given muscle. Previously, the dominant pedicle of a muscle that has other minor pedicle(s) was termed the "major" pedicle, an important distinction as occasionally the portion of a muscle supplied by the minor pedicle becomes precarious when only the major pedicle is left intact. Many muscles have multiple, unrelated sources of blood supply that each nourishes only a small segment of that muscle, hence termed *segmental* pedicles.

4. What is the importance of a "secondary segmental" vascular pedicle?

In addition to a dominant pedicle, some muscles have a supplemental source of vascularization via an array of segmental pedicles. Although each independently supplies only a distinct segment of the muscle, if retained as a group they often can sustain the entire muscle if the dominant pedicle were ligated. The point of rotation of the flap then can be altered to create a "reverse" muscle flap, but orthograde flow persists through this "secondary" source.

5. Classify muscle flaps according to their source of vascular supply.

The classic schema of Mathes and Nahai has subdivided muscles into five basic groups arranged according to their principal means of blood supply (Fig. 107-1):

- *Type I:* Single pedicle
- *Type II:* Dominant pedicle(s), with minor pedicle(s)
- *Type III:* Dual dominant pedicles
- *Type IV:* Segmental pedicles
- *Type V:* Dominant pedicle, with secondary segmental pedicles

6. If based on vascular pedicle type only, which muscles would be the *most* and which the *least* versatile for use as a flap?

Large muscles that have a single, dominant pedicle that will entirely sustain it (type I) are the most useful. Although an immediately adjacent portion of muscle may survive if captured by its neighbor's segmental vascular pedicle, usually the combination still will represent only a relatively small fraction of the whole muscle that could be expected to remain viable, especially if the majority of segmental pedicles had to be divided during elevation of the flap. Predictably, therefore, muscles with segmental pedicles (type IV) have the most limited role.

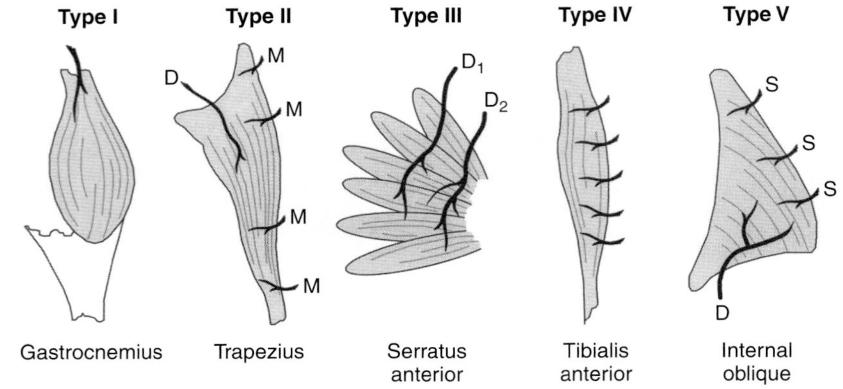

Figure 107-1. Classification of muscle flaps according to their vascular supply. *D,* Dominant; M, minor; S, secondary segmental. (Courtesy Carol Varma, Multimedia Communication Manager, The Lehigh Valley Hospital, Allentown, Pennsylvania.)

Type I	Type II	Type III	Type IV	Type V
Gastrocnemius	Trapezius	Serratus anterior	Tibialis anterior	Internal oblique

7. **Classify muscle flaps according to their mode of innervation.**

Taylor developed an alternative schema to stratify muscles according to the increasing complexity of their innervation and concomitant diminished suitability for use as a dynamic muscle transfer (Fig. 107-2):

- *Type I:* Single, unbranched nerve that enters muscle
- *Type II:* Single nerve, branches just prior to entering muscle
- *Type III:* Multiple branches from the same nerve trunk
- *Type IV:* Multiple branches from different nerve trunks

8. **Identify the most common vascular pattern for muscles.**

Most muscles belong to the type II group. During their clinical dissection, even type I and type III muscles can be observed to often have so-called anomalous collateral branches (usually minor) that probably evolved as a safety factor to compensate for the potential loss of the dominant pedicle. By a strict definition, these types should also be type II muscles.

BASIC PHYSIOLOGY

9. **According to their vascular pattern, which muscle types would be the *most* or the *least* reliable as a flap?**

Reliability refers to the predictable maintenance of viability of a flap. Viability is directly related to preservation of the circulation to the required dimensions of the chosen flap. Thus those muscles with a recognized dominant pedicle alone serving the majority of a flap would be the most reliable (i.e., types I, III, and V). Sometimes the territory of a minor pedicle is poorly captured by the dominant pedicle in a type II muscle, so these may be somewhat less reliable. Due to their segmental perfusion, type IV muscles allow potential use of only small flaps that have limited applications.

10. **Define the standard arc of rotation of a muscle flap.**

If used as a local flap, the range or extent of reach of the muscle when transposed about its point of rotation, which usually corresponds to the point of entry of its vascular pedicle, is the standard or usual arc of rotation.

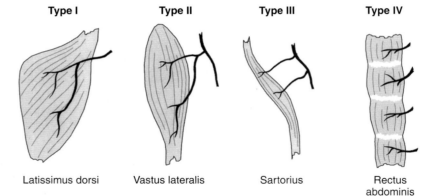

Figure 107-2. Classification of muscle flaps according to their mode of innervation. (Courtesy Carol Varma, Multimedia Communication Manager, The Lehigh Valley Hospital, Allentown, Pennsylvania.)

Type I	Type II	Type III	Type IV
Latissimus dorsi	Vastus lateralis	Sartorius	Rectus abdominis

11. In contrast, what is the arc of rotation of a "reverse" muscle flap?

If muscle circulation is based on secondary pedicles instead of the dominant pedicle and because the former often are distal to the standard point of rotation, a so-called distal-based flap can be elevated to permit more distal coverage. The movement of the flap is in a reverse direction from the norm. This should not be confused with a "reverse flow" flap, such as a latissimus dorsi muscle perfused retrograde via the serratus branch of the thoracodorsal artery. In the latter case, the range would be slightly less than the standard arc of rotation, as the point of rotation will remain virtually unchanged.

12. Explain the concept of function preservation when using a muscle flap.

If some portion of that muscle chosen as the flap is left intact at its insertion and origin with retention of innervation, some function will be preserved after the rest of the muscle has been transferred. This can be achieved by splitting the muscle into distinct segments, each otherwise served by a different dominant pedicle (e.g., hemi-soleus flap) or by individual secondary segmental pedicles (e.g., reverse latissimus dorsi muscle flap). As an alternative, the muscle can be divided at the bifurcation of a major branch of the dominant pedicle with an intramuscular dissection to maintain a distinctly separate circulation to all different parts of the muscle as desired.

13. How are the arterial territories linked within a muscle that has multiple vascular pedicles?

Connections between regions within a given muscle otherwise supplied by a distinct vascular pedicle are via small caliber so-called "choke" vessels that provide bidirectional flow. The best known example of the importance of this concept is the pedicled lower transverse rectus abdominis myocutaneous (TRAM) flap where the superior epigastric pedicle captures the territory of the deep inferior epigastric system via choke anastomoses at the watershed level just above the umbilicus.

14. What is the relationship of veins to the corresponding arteries found in muscles?

Fortunately, venous territories assume a "mirror image" paralleling the arterial pattern in muscles. The venous outflow typically is directed toward the major arterial pedicle in the given arterial territory.

15. How are venous territories linked together within a given muscle?

In a manner similar to arterial territories in a given muscle that are linked by bidirectional "choke" arteries, venous flow from one territory to another occurs through "oscillating" veins that are devoid of valves. For example, a superior-pedicled lower TRAM flap, which normally would have venous outflow directed toward the dominant pedicle in the groin, instead has outflow that proceeds in a reverse direction cephalad across the "oscillating" veins to enter into the superior epigastric system.

MUSCULOCUTANEOUS FLAP
PHYSIOLOGY

16. How do myocutaneous flaps differ from musculocutaneous flaps?

These terms are used interchangeably. Both are composite flaps where the overlying skin, fat, and fascia are intimately connected to the muscle.

17. Describe how the skin paddle of a musculocutaneous flap normally obtains its blood supply.

The source vessel to a muscle occasionally gives off direct branches to the skin before it enters the muscle. More commonly, however, within the muscle branches spin off that perforate the deep fascia with the primary intent to anastomose within the subdermal plexus and in turn nourish the skin. In addition to these perforating muscular branches, ultimately the source vessel terminates as smaller musculocutaneous branches that provide a lesser contribution.

18. Why is the muscle considered only a passive carrier of the skin in a composite musculocutaneous flap?

The muscle itself can be completely isolated from the source pedicle and its musculocutaneous branches without jeopardizing skin perfusion. The intramuscular dissection necessary to separate the cutaneous circulation from the muscle is the basic premise of the approach to "muscle" perforator flaps. Retention of the muscle is no longer mandatory to ensure survival of the cutaneous component, so its inclusion serves only a totally passive role primarily to avoid the need for any tedious intramuscular dissection of the vascular tree, which thereby simplifies flap harvest.

19. Can any skin configuration overlying a muscle be expected to survive as a musculocutaneous flap?

If a proposed cutaneous flap solely nourished by musculocutaneous perforators is expected to survive, it is imperative that they be included during flap elevation. Unfortunately, musculocutaneous perforators are randomly distributed, may be sparse in number, and often are widely dispersed throughout a muscle. Even if known perforators are included in a given flap design, if the flap is based distally or far from the dominant pedicle (especially if opposite a series of "choke" arteries or oscillating veins), even if arterial supply is adequate, venous outflow could be obstructed by valves leading to necrosis secondary to venous congestion.

20. Are there nonoperative modalities to assist the preoperative identification of musculocutaneous perforators to ensure their inclusion?

The best noninvasive method other than CI angiography is color duplex ultrasound. It has a high sensitivity for identifying musculocutaneous perforators, which allows creation of a map of their location unique to each patient. Unfortunately, it has a low specificity as only a small area can be visualized at a given time. A handheld audible Doppler is more accessible for bedside use for rapid perforator identification. Sometimes its sensitivity is too high, as background noise may reflect underlying source vessels or diminutive perforators that may later prove to be inadequate.

21. List several methods to maximize viability of the skin paddle of a musculocutaneous flap.

- Precisely identify the location of musculocutaneous perforators preoperatively.
- Maximize inclusion of as many musculocutaneous perforators as possible:
  - Design the skin paddle over the vascular hilum where the source vessel usually enters the muscle, as its cutaneous branches usually emanate in clusters nearby.
  - The skin portion should be as broad as possible; avoid narrow and/or small skin islands.
  - Bevel the subcutaneous tissues away from the skin edges over as wide an area overlying the muscle as possible.
- Avoid distal skin paddles.
  - Most major musculocutaneous perforators have their origin proximally near the point of entry of the source vessel into the muscle.
  - If distal to the intersection of several territories within a given muscle, valves can potentially obstruct outflow causing venous congestion and the demise of the flap.
- Consider a "delay" maneuver.

22. It has been postulated that the "delay" of a musculocutaneous flap is best achieved by the alteration of its venous physiology by what mechanism?

The intent of "delay" of any flap is to increase its likelihood of survival. Whether achieved by surgical or medical maneuvers, one theory is that afterward the venous valves in the affected territory become regurgitant. For example, division of the deep inferior epigastric vessels 2 weeks prior to elevation of a superior-pedicled lower TRAM flap may ensure greater skin paddle survival. Venograms have shown that the direction of venous outflow is redirected away from the groin unencumbered because the venous valves have become incompetent.

23. Does neovascularization occur more rapidly in a muscle or musculocutaneous flap to allow pedicle independence?

Neovascularization or the process of ingrowth of a new vasculature from the recipient site is highly variable and dependent on the quality of the recipient bed and tissues at its perimeter. If either is marginal, neovascularization cannot be guaranteed and the flap may permanently remain pedicle dependent. Because neovascularization at the skin level occurs more rapidly due to the ubiquity of small vessels in the dermal and subdermal plexuses, a musculocutaneous flap would become pedicle independent more quickly, all else being equal.

APPLIED ANATOMY

24. What are the advantages of muscle flaps when compared with cutaneous flaps?

- Less bulky, greater malleability, more readily conformed to multidimensional wounds
- Immunologic superiority for wounds compromised by infection or irradiation, perhaps due to superior blood flow rates
- Well-defined vascular anatomy with fewer anomalies, which simplifies intraoperative harvest and decision making
- Allow a dynamic, functioning tissue transfer (Table 107-1)

25. Although never a concern with cutaneous flaps, what is the greatest liability if using a muscle flap?

Even if function preservation techniques are used, the selection of a muscle flap always sacrifices function to some degree. The chosen muscle preferably should be expendable; if not, it perhaps would not be the best flap option.

26. Why are muscle flaps infrequently used for coverage in the upper extremity?

The greatest liability of muscle flaps is the risk of sacrifice of function, and this is a major concern in the upper extremity where there is little redundancy of agonists and antagonists. Especially for the injured hand, preservation of *any* residual function assumes paramount importance, so use of local muscles as flaps is often contraindicated.

Table 107-1. Attributes and Liabilities of Muscle versus Cutaneous Flaps

	CUTANEOUS FLAPS	MUSCLE FLAPS
Accessibility	+	−
Anatomic anomalies	−	+
Availability	+	−
Composite flaps	=	=
Use in infected or irradiated wound	±	+
Donor site morbidity	−	+
Dynamic transfer	−	+
Expendable	+	−
Malleability	−	+
Microsurgical tissue transfer	=	=
Reliability	=	=
Sensate	+	−
Size	+	±
Thinness	−	+

+, Asset; −, detriment; =, no significant difference; ±, variable.

27. **Name the two "workhorse" muscle flaps of the leg and state their corresponding range.**
    The medial and lateral heads of the gastrocnemius muscles can individually cover the knee and upper third of the leg. The soleus muscle is the muscle flap of choice for the middle third and sometimes even for the upper part of the distal third. More distal leg and foot defects are amenable to microsurgical tissue transfers or distal-based cutaneous flaps.

28. **Which of the two heads of the gastrocnemius muscle has the longer reach?**
    Look at any bare calf, with the foot in plantar flexion! The medial head is several centimeters longer, terminating in a more distal insertion into the triceps surae. In addition, the lateral head during transfer must first pass around the head of the fibula, with care taken to protect the common peroneal nerve, prior to reaching a proximal leg defect.

29. **What two important structures help to demarcate the two heads of the gastrocnemius muscles?**
    Just proximal to their insertion at the triceps surae, the two heads of the gastrocnemius muscle usually decussate together and require sharp dissection for their separation. A branch of the lesser saphenous vein and the median sural cutaneous nerve typically pass in the midline between these two muscle heads and are important landmarks to distinguish this point of separation while ensuring their preservation.

30. **The internal oblique muscle has what in common with the pectoralis major and latissimus dorsi muscles?**
    All are type V muscles on the basis of their blood supply. The dominant pedicle to the internal oblique muscle is the ascending branch of the deep circumflex iliac artery, with secondary segmental pedicles arising from the thoracic and lumbar arteries.

31. **Describe two ways the pectoralis major muscle can be transposed to cover sternal defects.**
    The standard arc of rotation of the pectoralis major muscle is about its dominant thoracoacromial pedicle, which enters its undersurface just medial to the pectoralis minor muscle. The costal, sternal, and sometimes clavicular origins must then be taken down to allow medial transposition over the sternum. Similar coverage is possible with a reverse muscle flap based on its secondary segmental pedicles, which are branches of the internal mammary artery. This requires that the segment of muscle be divided from its insertion, but the origin may be left intact.

32. **From the schematic (see Fig. 107-3), name the source vessel(s) and corresponding muscle type based on blood supply of these 10 commonly used muscle flaps.**
    See Table 107-2.

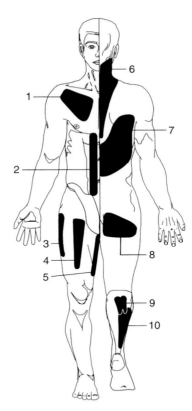

Figure 107-3. Donor sites of 10 commonly used muscle flaps. (Courtesy Carol Varma, Multimedia Communication Manager, The Lehigh Valley Hospital, Allentown, Pennsylvania.)

Table 107-2. Source Vessel(s) and Corresponding Muscle Type

MUSCLE FLAP	SOURCE VESSEL	MATHES-NAHAI TYPE
1. Pectoralis major	Thoracoacromial, internal mammary	V
2. Rectus abdominis	Superior and deep inferior epigastric	III
3. Tensor fascia lata	Lateral circumflex femoral (ascending branch)	I
4. Rectus femoris	Lateral circumflex femoral (descending branch)	II
5. Gracilis	Medial circumflex femoral	II
6. Trapezius	Transverse cervical	II
7. Latissimus dorsi	Thoracodorsal, lumbar, posterior intercostal	V
8. Gluteus maximus	Superior and inferior gluteal	III
9. Gastrocnemius	Medial or lateral sural	I
10. Soleus	Popliteal, posterior tibial, peroneal	II

BIBLIOGRAPHY

Bostwick J, Scheflan M, Nahai F, Jurkiewicz MJ: The "reverse" latissimus dorsi muscle and musculocutaneous flap: Anatomical and clinical considerations. Plast Reconstr Surg 65:395–399, 1980.

del Pinal F, Taylor GI: The deep venous system and reverse flow flaps. Br J Plast Surg 46:652–664, 1993.

Dhar SC, Taylor GI: The delay phenomenon: The story unfolds. Plast Reconstr Surg 104:2079–2091, 1999.

Fisher J, Bostwick J, Powell RW: Latissimus dorsi blood supply after thoracodorsal vessel division: The serratus collateral. Plast Reconstr Surg 72:502–509, 1983.

Gosain A, Chang N, Mathes S: A study of the relationship between blood flow and bacterial inoculation in musculocutaneous and fasciocutaneous flaps. Plast Reconstr Surg 86:1152–1162, 1990.

Hallock GG: Getting the most from the soleus muscle. Ann Plast Surg 36:139–146, 1996.

Hallock GG: The utility of both muscle and fascia flaps in severe upper extremity trauma. J Trauma 53:61–65, 2002.

Hallock GG: Doppler sonography and color duplex imaging for planning a perforator flap. Clin Plast Surg 30:347–357, 2003.

Mathes SJ, Nahai F: Classification of the vascular anatomy of muscles: Experimental and clinical correlation. Plast Reconstr Surg 67: 177–187, 1981.

Mathes SJ, Nahai F: Clinical Applications for Muscle and Musculocutaneous Flaps. St. Louis, CV Mosby, 1982, pp 27–29.

Mathes SJ, Nahai F: Reconstructive Surgery: Principles, Anatomy, and Technique. New York, Churchill Livingstone, 1997.

Mathes SJ, Nahai F: Muscle flap transposition with function preservation: Technical and clinical considerations. Plast Reconstr Surg 66: 242–249, 1980.

McCraw JB, Arnold PG: McCraw and Arnold's Atlas of Muscle and Musculocutaneous Flaps. Norfolk, VA, Hampton Press Publishing, 1986.

Millican PG, Poole MD: Peripheral neovascularization of muscle and musculocutaneous flaps. Br J Plast Surg 38:369–374, 1985.

Moon HK, Taylor GI: The vascular anatomy of rectus abdominis musculocutaneous flaps based on the deep superior epigastric system. Plast Reconstr Surg 82:815–829, 1988.

Nahai F, Morales L, Bone DK, Bostwick J: Pectoralis major muscle turnover flaps for closure of the infected sternotomy wound with preservation of form and function. Plast Reconstr Surg 70:471–474, 1982.

Nakajima H, Fujino T, Adachi S: A new concept of vascular supply to the skin and classification of skin flaps according to their vascularization. Ann Plast Surg 16:1–17, 1986.

Paletta CE, Huang DB: Intrathoracic application of the reverse latissimus dorsi muscle flap. Ann Plast Surg 43:227–231, 1999.

Sano K, Hallock GG, Rice DC: The relative importance of the deep and superficial vascular systems for delay of the transverse rectus abdominis musculocutaneous flap as demonstrated in a rat model. Plast Reconstr Surg 109:1052–1057, 2002.

Taylor GI, Caddy CM, Watterson PA, Crock JG: The venous territories (venosomes) of the human body: Experimental study and clinical implications. Plast Reconstr Surg 86:185–213, 1990.

Taylor GI, Gianoutsos MP, Morris SF: The neurovascular territories of the skin and muscles: Anatomic study and clinical implications. Plast Reconstr Surg 94:1–36, 1994.

Taylor GI, Palmer JH: The vascular territories (angiosomes) of the body: Experimental study and clinical applications. Br J Plast Surg 40: 113–141, 1987.

Tobin GR, Schusterman M, Peterson GH, Nichols G, Bland KI: The intramuscular neurovascular anatomy of the latissimus dorsi muscle: The basis for splitting the flap. Plast Reconstr Surg 67:637–641, 1981.

Wei FC, Jain V, Suominen S, Chen HC: Confusion among perforator flaps: What is a true perforator flap? Plast Reconstr Surg 107; 874–876, 2001.

PRINCIPLES OF PERFORATOR FLAPS

Geoffrey G. Hallock, MD

BASIC ANATOMY

1. Define "perforator."

The word "perforator" is derived from the Latin *per* (through) and *forare* (to pierce or bore). Any blood vessel that passes through a defined fenestration in the deep fascia should be considered a "perforator" of the deep fascia, regardless of the origin of that perforator.

2. How do *direct* and *indirect* "perforators" differ?

All perforators arising from the underlying source vessel to a given angiosome contribute to the latter's "fascial plexus" either directly or indirectly. Using the terms for specific types of deep fascia perforators introduced by Nakajima et al., *direct* perforators (e.g., axial, septocutaneous, direct cutaneous branch of a muscular vessel) course from the source vessel to the skin without first supplying any other deep structure. *Indirect* perforators (e.g., musculocutaneous perforators) first will have passed via some intermediary structure (e.g., muscle) before ultimately reaching the subdermal plexus (Fig. 108-1).

3. Where is the "fascial plexus"?

The "fascial plexus" is not a discrete structure per se but represents the confluence of multiple, adjacent vascular networks and their branches that have typically emanated from any of the deep fascia "perforators," whether *direct* or *indirect* perforators. Intercommunications between these networks exist at the subfascial, fascial, suprafascial, subcutaneous, and subdermal levels.

4. What is a "mother" vessel?

The "mother" vessel refers to the source vessel to a given angiosome, from which the perforator takes its origin.

5. What is a "perforator flap"?

Tissue receiving its vascular supply via any "perforator" of the deep fascia is considered a "perforator flap." Because this could be by "direct" or "indirect" perforators, the corresponding flaps then would be either *direct* or *indirect* "perforator flaps." (Further emphasis on direct perforator flaps can be found in Chapter 106.)

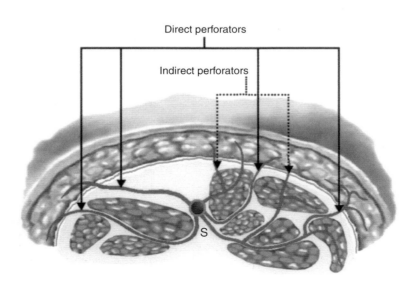

Figure 108-1. Direct and indirect perforators of the deep fascia arising from the underlying source vessel *(S)*. (Modified with permission from Hallock GG: Direct and indirect perforator flaps: The history and the controversy. Plast Reconstr Surg 111:855–866, 2003.)

Table 108-1. Attributes and Liabilities of Perforator versus Muscle Flaps

	PERFORATOR FLAPS	MUSCLE FLAPS
Accessibility	+	−
Anatomic anomalies	−	+
Availability	+	−
Composite flaps	±	+
Use in infected or irradiated wound	±	+
Donor site morbidity	−	+
Dynamic transfer	−	+
Expendable	+	−
Malleability	−	+
Microsurgical tissue transfer	=	=
Reliability	=	=
Sensate	+	−
Size	+	±
Thinness	±	+

+, Asset; −, detriment; =, no significant difference; ±, variable.

6. What is a "true" perforator flap?

According to Wei et al., only muscle perforator flaps are "true" perforator flaps. Only a "true" muscle perforator flap requires an intramuscular dissection of the perforator. This is considered an important point to distinguish the technical differences (and difficulties) encountered in the raising of such flaps in comparison to other forms of fasciocutaneous flaps. The muscle is also always excluded so that function is preserved (Table 108-1).

7. Could muscle perforator flaps be considered a form of fasciocutaneous flap?

Unequivocally yes! A muscle perforator flap relies on large perforating musculocutaneous branches from the source pedicle to a muscle. These are identical to the "perforating cutaneous branches of a muscular vessel," which, according to Nakajima et al., represent one type of deep fascia perforator and is the basis of one of their corresponding types of fasciocutaneous flaps. However, this remains an extremely controversial point.

8. Name different types of *indirect* perforator flaps.

Remember that indirect perforators first have passed along or through some intermediary structure before reaching the subdermal plexus. Musculocutaneous perforators obviously pass through muscle on their way to the deep fascia, so muscle perforator flaps are *indirect* perforator flaps and at the present time represent the most common clinical application of this genre.

The cutaneous sensitive nerves often pierce the deep fascia along with their accompanying circulation that has secondary cutaneous branches. Thus neurocutaneous flaps are another form of *indirect* perforator flap. A good example is the distal-based sural neuroadipofascial flap that today is commonly used for lower leg defects in lieu of free-tissue transfers. The medial cutaneous branch of the sural nerve is an intrinsic part of this flap. It pierces the deep fascia at the level of the triceps surae, often accompanied by the median sural artery. Sometimes the nerve can be excluded from this flap, but the lesser saphenous vein must then be retained. It too pierces the deep fascia more proximally with its own accompanying vascular system, so venous flaps may represent yet another form of *indirect* perforator flap. Niranjan has also shown the existence of periosteal and peritendinous *indirect* perforator flaps.

9. Must all perforator flaps be cutaneous flaps?

As long as the requisite perforator and its corresponding fascial plexus are maintained within the flap, the cutaneous component can be eliminated. As an adiposal or adipofascial flap, this will simplify direct donor site closure, sometimes important to eliminate the need for a skin graft.

10. Does the deep fascia have to be included with a perforator flap?

On the contrary, the deep fascia is not essential and typically is excluded from a perforator flap, an especially valuable maneuver for tension-free closure obviating the need for reinforcement of a deep inferior epigastric artery perforator (DIEAP) flap donor site. However, it can be included as a composite flap if vascularized fascia is needed at the recipient site. In addition, sometimes inclusion of the deep fascia simplifies the initial identification of the perforators at a subfascial plane.

11. In what body regions do musculocutaneous perforators practical for muscle perforator flaps predominate compared with direct perforators of the deep fascia?

Because most direct perforators of the deep fascia arise along intercompartmental or intermuscular septa, they are more prevalent wherever long, slender muscles are found, as in the extremities. In contrast, musculocutaneous perforators are more numerous over the broad, flatter muscles associated with the trunk, where muscular septa are few and far apart. However, many important musculocutaneous perforators can also be found piercing other larger muscles, especially of the lower extremity.

12. Describe the course of the perforator veins.

Perforator veins usually accompany the perforator arteries at the site of penetration through the deep fascia. However, within the subcutaneous tissues they often diverge from the arteries and have an unpredictable course. Sometimes outflow from the perforator veins proceeds to nearby superficial veins rather than to the deep venous system.

13. List some methods that allow preoperative identification of perforators.

Color duplex ultrasound is highly sensitive not only for identifying the site of a perforator but also for providing qualitative information such as caliber and flow characteristics. Unfortunately, it is time consuming. Multidetector-row helical computed tomograph angiography is a more rapid method. The most pragmatic method universally available, although not as precise, is use of the ubiquitous handheld audible Doppler to survey the given territory. This method also allows intraoperative localization, which may be necessary.

14. While thinning perforator flaps, Kimura found what three different branching patterns of musculocutaneous perforators through the subcutaneous tissues in their course to the subdermal plexus?

Type 1 perforators pass almost directly from the deep fascia to the subdermal plexus without branching. Type 2 perforators branch in the adipose tissue just before reaching the subdermal plexus, with the branches then running parallel to the flap surface. In type 3 perforators, branches follow the deep fascia for an indeterminate distance before eventually proceeding into the subcutaneous tissues (Fig. 108-2).

15. Do different donor sites have predictable suprafascial branching patterns of perforators?

An axiom in perforator flaps is that anatomic anomalies are the norm, and nothing is routine. Nevertheless, Kimura found that the lateral circumflex femoral artery-tensor fascia lata (LCFA-*tfl*) and DIEA perforator flaps consistently displayed a type II pattern (see Fig. 108-2), branching just before reaching the superficial adipose layer. The LCFA-vastus lateralis (LCFA-*vl,* as known as the anterolateral thigh) perforator flap often had early branching or a type 3 pattern.

BASIC PHYSIOLOGY

16. When exploring the potential vessels for a perforator flap, what is the smallest size that should be chosen?

A good rule of thumb is to choose an artery that has an external diameter ≥0.5 mm or if pulsations are readily visible. This is not to say that smaller perforators cannot be chosen, but the dissection then becomes increasingly more difficult.

Type 1

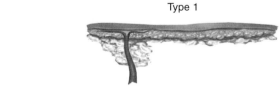

Type 2   Type 3

Figure 108-2. Three types of branching patterns in the suprafascial course of musculocutaneous perforators. (Courtesy Carol Varma, Multimedia Communication Manager, The Lehigh Valley Hospital, Allentown, Pennsylvania.)

17. Although a single perforator could sustain an entire flap, state some good reasons to include more.

Twisting of a single perforator >360° could go unrecognized and be disastrous because flow would be totally obstructed. This occurrence is grossly more obvious if at least two perforators are included. Inadvertent injury (it happens!) to a single perforator would likewise be disastrous. More perforators, especially if spread far apart, should logically also sustain a longer flap more safely.

18. How can the potential territory of a perforator flap be estimated?

Safe limits for the design of perforator flaps have been determined only by clinical trial and error. Deep fascia perforators are frequently anomalous in caliber and location not only among individuals but also in opposite sides of the same individual, so an exact preoperative prediction of safe flap boundaries remains impossible. Ongoing injection studies of discrete perforators can only provide estimates, as again the anatomy of each individual is different and the dynamic territory for each perforator cannot be known beforehand.

19. What is the point of rotation of a perforator flap?

Especially applicable when used as a local flap, this corresponds to the site where the flap is tethered by its vascular pedicle.

20. Describe the arc of rotation of a local perforator flap.

The distance from the point of rotation to the most distant safe length of the given flap will determine the range of coverage or arc of rotation through which a local perforator flap can be transposed.

21. How can the arc of rotation of a local perforator flap be increased?

Further dissection of the requisite perforator back to its origin from its "mother" vessel or even more dissection of the source vessel itself is the only way after the flap has been elevated. The flap initially can be designed eccentrically or more distally in relation to the required perforator, rather than centered about it, to increase reach. Either maneuver can be used to increase the pedicle length if used as a free flap.

22. How can venous congestion in a perforator flap be aborted?

Because the course of the perforator veins often is anomalous, whenever possible a subcutaneous vein should be preserved while harvesting a perforator flap. This is especially true if large superficial veins are encountered during flap elevation, as a reciprocal relationship often exists with the deep system. The superficial vein then can be used to "supercharge" the venous outflow. In addition, other large perforator veins should be identified as divided and set aside to allow the same possibility of "supercharging" them later, particularly if the superficial veins are inadequate.

23. Is the immediate thinning of a perforator flap hazardous?

The arbitrary removal of fat from the bottom surface of a perforator flap, even while intentionally leaving fat around the perforator itself, could potentially interfere with maximum viability. The exact course of perforators in the subcutaneous tissues can be variable. Also, venous outflow could depend on maintaining an intact superficial system that could thereby be disrupted.

MUSCLE PERFORATOR FLAPS

24. Describe the nomenclature for muscle perforator flaps.

Systems for nomenclature have been based on the name of the source vessel to the flap, its anatomic region of origin, and/or the muscle traversed. A universal system has yet to be adopted.
- *Gent Consensus:* Listed by source vessel name or anatomic region if "mother" vessel supplies multiple muscles
- *Korean System:* Muscle traversed [add (MCp) for musculocutaneous perforator to distinguish from direct or septocutaneous perforators]
- *Canadian Schema:* Source artery + suffix AP (for "artery perforator") [add initials of muscle if more than one supplied by that artery or (-s) if perforator found to be septocutaneous].
- *American Proposal:* Source artery$_{MUSCLE\ TRAVERSED}$ [named by source artery only if perforator found to be septocutaneous]

25. Based on the aforementioned four nomenclature systems for muscle perforator flaps, label a flap from the anterolateral thigh if based on a lateral circumflex femoral (LCF) perforator of the vastus lateralis muscle.
- *Gent Consensus:* Anterolateral thigh perforator flap (lateral circumflex femoral source pedicle supplies multiple other muscles, e.g., rectus femoris, tensor fascia lata)
- *Korean System:* Vastus lateralis perforator flap (MCp)

- *Canadian Schema:* LCFAP-*vl* flap.
- *American Proposal:* LCF~VASTUS LATERALIS~

26. Based on the aforementioned four nomenclature systems for muscle perforator flaps, label a flap if based on a superior epigastric (SE) perforator of the rectus abdominis muscle.
- *Gent Consensus:* SEP flap
- *Korean System:* Rectus abdominis perforator flap (MCp)
- *Canadian Schema:* SEAP flap
- *American Proposal:* SE~RECTUS ABDOMINIS~

27. Does a muscle perforator flap capture the same territory as its corresponding musculocutaneous flap?
It would seem intuitively obvious that if only a single or a few musculocutaneous perforators were kept with a perforator flap, flow would be less than to the same cutaneous territory where all perforators had been kept with a musculocutaneous flap. Indeed, using laser Doppler flowmetry in a rat perforator flap model, flow was shown to be less. Interestingly, total surface area viability nevertheless proved not to be different!

28. List the source vessels for the muscle perforator flaps identified here by the corresponding muscle (Fig. 108-3):

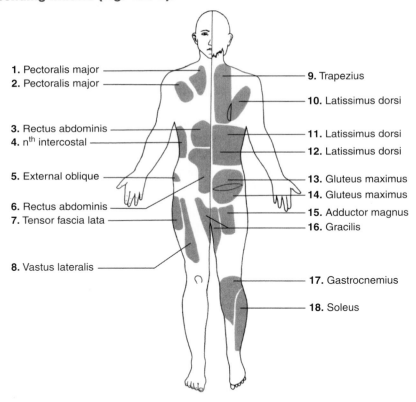

1. Pectoralis major
2. Pectoralis major
3. Rectus abdominis
4. nth intercostal
5. External oblique
6. Rectus abdominis
7. Tensor fascia lata
8. Vastus lateralis
9. Trapezius
10. Latissimus dorsi
11. Latissimus dorsi
12. Latissimus dorsi
13. Gluteus maximus
14. Gluteus maximus
15. Adductor magnus
16. Gracilis
17. Gastrocnemius
18. Soleus

Figure 108-3. Territories of muscle perforator flaps. (Courtesy Carol Varma, Multimedia Communication Manager, The Lehigh Valley Hospital, Allentown, Pennsylvania.)

- Internal mammary
- Thoracoacromial
- Superior epigastric
- nth intercostal
- Deep circumflex iliac
- Deep inferior epigastric
- Lateral circumflex femoral–ascending branch
- Lateral circumflex femoral–descending branch
- Transverse cervical or dorsal scapular
- Thoracodorsal
- nth intercostal
- Lumbar
- Superior gluteal
- Inferior gluteal
- Adductor branch of profundus femoris
- Medial circumflex femoral
- Sural
- Peroneal

NONMUSCLE PERFORATOR FLAPS

29. Explain the basis of circulation to a neurocutaneous flap.
The cutaneous sensitive nerves have both an intrinsic and an extrinsic neurocutaneous blood supply. The intrinsic supply, well known as the vaso nervorum, is maintained throughout the course of the nerve. It has multiple interconnections with the extrinsic system that arise either directly from a regional source vessel or secondarily from the surrounding fascial plexus. The latter forms "choke" and sometimes true anastomosis between networks of adjacent deep fascia perforators. Both not only supply the given cutaneous nerve, which is its primary intent, but also periodically are the origin of branches to the skin.

30. What is the axis of a neurocutaneous flap?
Because the paraneural vascular plexus follows the course of the nerve via either "choke" or true anastomoses, the predominant direction of blood flow or axis of a neurocutaneous flap will follow the path of the nerve itself.

31. Why were Pontén's so-called "superflaps" so robust?
Pontén's proximal-based and sensate fasciocutaneous flaps raised from the lower extremity, which he called "superflaps," probably included the local cutaneous sensitive nerves. In reality, these probably were neurocutaneous flaps. As we know, any cutaneous flap oriented along the course of the sensitive nerve by definition has an axis with the same orientation that ensures maximizing blood flow to that flap and in turn greater survival length.

32. What landmarks can be used to ensure the appropriate orientation of a neurocutaneous flap in the extremities?
The major superficial venous channels in the extremities serve a dominant role as the means for outflow from the paraneural vascular plexus and thus tend to parallel the cutaneous sensory nerves. The sural flap (usually containing the lesser saphenous vein and medial sural cutaneous nerve) and cephalic flap (cephalic vein and lateral antebrachial cutaneous nerve) are two examples in which inclusion of the anatomically obvious vein will almost automatically allow incorporation of the nerve and usually its vascular plexus within the flap.

SUPERMICROSURGERY

33. Define "supermicrosurgery."
A term coined by Koshima, supermicrosurgery is any microsurgery on structures 0.5 to 0.8 mm in diameter.

34. What is Koshima's perforator-based flap?
Usually free-tissue transfers, in these flaps only the perforator is retained with the vascular pedicle. The "mother" vessel is not included. Because only the perforator is needed, dissection can stop at the fascial level. Microanastomoses are then made to the perforators alone, often truly requiring the skills of a "supermicrosurgeon."

35. Describe how to design a "free-style" local or free flap.
If a satisfactory, discrete perforator can be identified anywhere in the body, a flap can be designed about it. The constraints of using only described territories can be disregarded, allowing the choice of donor site to be determined by selection of the best possible available tissues as needed to match color, contour, texture, etc., at the recipient site.

36. How does "microdissection" more safely allow reduction of the thickness of a perforator flap?
In this technique developed by Kimura, an operating microscope is used, essentially for careful separation of the superficial and deep adipose tissue layers from each other. The deep adipose tissue is teased away from the perforator starting at the level of the deep fascia. This dissection continues up to the superficial adipose layer, creating a void about the intact perforator and its branches. Flap elevation is then completed at the superficial adipose level proceeding away from the requisite perforator (Fig. 108-4).

37. What is a "subdermal vascular network" flap?
This is an ultrathin cutaneous flap with both the superficial and deep adipose layers removed, except carefully where retained about nutritive perforators. Both direct and indirect perforators have been used to supply this flap, often with disparate pedicles used for supercharging as necessary.

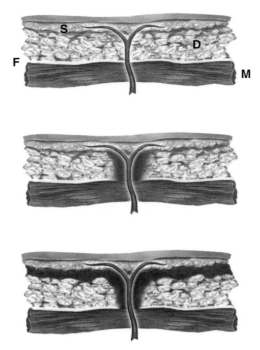

Figure 108-4. Technique of microdissection. **Top,** Initial course of perforator. *D,* Deep adipose layer; *F,* deep fascia; *M,* muscle; *S,* superficial adipose layer. **Center,** Removal of deep adipose tissue begins around the perforator starting at the level of the deep fascia to create a hole extending to the superficial adipose layer. **Bottom,** Completion of elevation of the cutaneous flap peripheral to the perforator, staying just beneath the superficial adipose layer. (Courtesy Carol Varma, Multimedia Communication Manager, The Lehigh Valley Hospital, Allentown, Pennsylvania.)

BIBLIOGRAPHY

Alkureishi LWT, Shaw-Dunn J, Ross GH: Effects of thinning the anterolateral thigh flap on the blood supply to the skin. Br J Plast Surg 56:401–408, 2003.

Blondeel PN, van Landuyt KHI, Monstrey SJM, et al: The "Gent" consensus on perforator flap terminology: Preliminary definitions. Plast Reconstr Surg 112:1378–1383, 2003.

Blondeel PN, Arnstein M, Verstraete K, Depuydt K, van Landuyt KH, Monstrey SJ: Venous congestion and blood flow in free transverse rectus abdominis myocutaneous and deep inferior epigastric perforator flaps. Plast Reconstr Surg 106:1295–1299, 2000.

El-Mrakby HH, Milner RH: The vascular anatomy of the lower anterior abdominal wall: A microdissection study on the deep inferior epigastric vessels and the perforator branches. Plast Reconstr Surg 109:539–543, 2002.

Geddes CR, Morris SF, Neligan PC: Perforator flaps: Evolution, classification, and applications. Ann Plast Surg 50:90–99, 2003.

Hallock GG: Muscle perforator flaps: The name game. Ann Plast Surg 51:630–632, 2003.

Hallock GG: Doppler Sonography and color duplex imaging for planning a perforator flap. Clin Plast Surg 30:347–357, 2003.

Hallock GG: The superior epigastric RECTUS ABDOMINIS muscle perforator flap. Ann Plast Surg 55:430–432, 2005.

Hallock GG, Rice DC: Comparison of TRAM and DIEP flap physiology in a rat model. Plast Reconstr Surg 114:1179–1184, 2004.

Hallock GG: Direct and indirect perforator flaps: The history and the controversy. Plast Reconstr Surg 111:855–866, 2003.

Kim JT: New nomenclature concept of perforator flap. Br J Plast Surg 58:431–440, 2005.

Hyakusoku H, Gao JH, Pennington DG, Aoki R, Murakami M, Ogawa R: The microvascular augmented subdermal vascular network (ma-SVN) flap: Its variations and recent development in using intercostal perforators. Br J Plast Surg 55:402–411, 2002.

Kimura N, Satoh K, Hsaka Y: Microdissected thin perforator flaps: 46 cases. Plast Reconstr Surg 112:1875–1885, 2003.

Kimura N, Satoh K, Hasumi T, Ostuka T: Clinical application of the free thin anterolateral thigh flap in 31 consecutive patients. Plast Reconstr Surg 108:1197–1208, 2001.

Koshima I, Moriguchi T, Fukuda H, Yoshikawa Y, Soeda S: Free, thinned, paraumbilical perforator-based flaps. J Reconstr Microsurg 7:313–316, 1991.

Koshima I, Inagawa K, Urushibata K, Moriguchi T: Paraumbilical perforator flap without deep inferior epigastric vessels. Plast Reconstr Surg 102:1052–1057, 1998.

Koshima I, Nanba Y, Takahasi Y, Tsukino A, Kishimoto K: Future of supramicrosurgery as it relates to breast reconstruction: Free paraumbilical perforator adiposal flap. Semin Plast Surg 16:93–99, 2002.

Kroll SS: Venous congestion and blood flow in free transverse rectus abdominis myocutaneous and deep inferior epigastric perforator flaps. Plast Reconstr Surg 106:1295–1299, 2000.

Kuo YR, Juo MH, Chou WC, Liu YT, Lutz BS, Jeng SF: One-stage reconstruction of soft tissue and Achilles tendon defects using a composite free anterolateral thigh flap with vascularized fascia lata: Clinical experience and functional assessment. Ann Plast Surg 50:149–155, 2003.

Masquelet AC, Romana MC, Wolf G: Skin island flaps supplied by the vascular axis of the sensitive superficial nerves: Anatomic study and clinical experience in the leg. Plast Reconstr Surg 89:1115–1121, 1992.

Nakajima H, Fujino T, Adachi S: A new concept of vascular supply to the skin and classification of skin flaps according to their vascularization. Ann Plast Surg 16:1–17, 1986.

Nakajima H, Imanishi N, Fukuzumi S, Minabe T, Aiso S, Fujino T: Accompanying arteries of the cutaneous veins and cutaneous nerves in the extremities: Anatomical study and a concept of the venoadipofascial and/or neuroadipofascial pedicled fasciocutaneous flap. Plast Reconstr Surg 102:779–791, 1998.

Niranjan NS, Price RD, Govilkar P: Fascial feeder and perforator-based V-Y advancement flaps in the reconstruction of lower limb defects. Br J Plast Surg 53:679–689, 2000.

Nojima K, Brown SA, Acikel C, et al: Defining vascular supply and territory of thinned perforator flaps: Part I, anterolateral thigh perforator flap. Plast Reconstr Surg 116:182–193, 2005.

Pontén B: The fasciocutaneous flap: Its use in soft tissue defects of the lower leg. Br J Plast Surg 34:215–220, 1981.

Taylor GI: The "Gent" consensus on perforator flap terminology: Preliminary definitions (discussion). Plast Reconstr Surg 112: 1384–1387, 2003.

Villafane O, Gahankari D, Webster M: Superficial inferior epigastric vein (SIEV) "lifeboat" for DIEP/TRAM flaps. Br J Plast Surg 52:599, 1999.

Wei FC, Jain V, Suominen S, Chen HC: Confusion among perforator flaps: What is a true perforator flap? Plast Reconstr Surg 107;874–876, 2001.

Wei FC, Mardini S: Free-style free flaps. Plast Reconstr Surg 114:910–916, 2004.

Wei FC, Celik N, Jeng SF: Application of "simplified nomenclature for compound flaps" to the anterolateral thigh flap. Plast Reconstr Surg 115:1051–1055, 2005.

PRINCIPLES OF MICROVASCULAR FREE TISSUE TRANSFER

Rudolf Buntic, MD, and
Harry J. Buncke, MD

1. What is a microvascular free tissue transfer?

A microvascular free tissue transfer (also known as a *microvascular transplant* or *free flap*) involves transplanting expendable donor tissue from one part of the body to another. The tissue must be able to survive on a single pedicled blood supply with an artery and draining vein. With microsurgical techniques the transplanted part is reanastomosed to recipient site vessels to reestablish blood flow. It is essentially an autotransplant.

2. What are the indications for a microvascular free tissue transfer?

Microsurgical transplants have multiple indications, often to reconstruct complex wounds where complex tissue loss has occurred. Common indications include reconstruction after tumor ablation, reconstruction of congenital defects, reconstruction of chronic wounds, and reconstruction after trauma.

3. What are the success rates of microsurgically transplanted tissues?

Tissue survival rates in microvascular free flaps were approximately 80% in the 1970s and now have improved to over 95%. Survival rates of 98% to 100% for some transplants is common.

4. Which donor tissue should be chosen?

The choice of donor site in microsurgery requires multiple considerations and planning. Size of the donor tissue, type of wound, pedicle length, location of wound, and donor deformity all play a role in selecting the appropriate flap. The size of the donor tissue must adequately cover a wound. Different types of wounds require different donor tissues. Wounds on the hand may require pliable tissues, with tendon or even bone needed to complete the reconstruction. For instance, loss of the thumb is best reconstructed by a toe, whereas wounds that are irregular with significant dead space may best be closed with a muscle and skin graft. The donor tissue must have a pedicle length that can reach appropriate vessels in the recipient area. Long vascular pedicles may be required if appropriate recipient vessels are not near the wound. The donor deformity also needs to be considered to minimize scarring and potential loss of function.

5. Who should perform microsurgery?

Microsurgical procedures should be performed under the direction of a skilled microsurgeon. Meticulous technique and experience play the greatest role in success. Fine handling and dissecting of small blood vessels should be learned in the laboratory while clinical operative responsibility is gradually increased.

6. What role do anticoagulants play in microsurgery?

The role of routine postoperative anticoagulation in microsurgery has not been determined precisely. In elective microvascular transplants there are no definite indications for anticoagulation. Surgeon preference plays a role in the choices made. Anticoagulation is believed by some to reduce the chance of postoperative thrombotic complications at the anastomosis site. However, anticoagulation can increase the chance of hematoma at both the donor and the recipient site, and, in rare circumstances, anaphylaxis complicating the use of dextran has been reported. If postoperative clotting becomes evident requiring reexploration, anticoagulation usually is indicated if the flap is salvaged. The most common pharmacologic agents used in routine postoperative care are aspirin and dextran. Intravenous heparin is generally used when difficulty such as postoperative thrombosis is encountered.

A survey of 73 centers in 22 countries revealed equal success rates for transplants performed with and those without anticoagulation.

7. What is the no-reflow phenomenon?

Failure to reperfuse an ischemic organ after reestablishing blood supply is known as the *no-reflow phenomenon.* The mechanism is believed to be related to endothelial injury, platelet aggregation, and leakage of intravascular fluid. The severity of this effect is correlated with ischemia time.

8. What methods can be used to minimize ischemia?

Generally, muscle does not tolerate warm ischemia well for more than 2 hours. Skin and fasciocutaneous flaps can tolerate longer ischemia times, from 4 to 6 hours. Meticulous planning is the most important factor to minimize the effects of ischemia because planning decreases ischemia time. All structures in the recipient site should be ready for the flap when the pedicle is divided so that no time is wasted after blood flow to the donor tissue has stopped.

Cooling increases the tolerance of tissue to ischemia. Some surgeons cool the transplant on the operative field with cold wraps and ice. Pharmacologic manipulation of donor tissue has been investigated in the laboratory to prevent formation of free radicals and tissue destruction on reperfusion. Ischemia preconditioning with cyclical clamping and reperfusion of tissues has shown laboratory success. These methods are not yet routinely used clinically.

9. Which is more successful, end-to-end or end-to-side arterial anastomosis?

Both end-to-end and end-to-side anastomoses in appropriately selected cases have similar patency rates in most studies. End-to-side anastomosis may be advantageous where there is significant vessel size discrepancy or where only one artery is available and required for downstream flow.

10. From where do you obtain vein grafts?

You can use the saphenous vein by harvesting starting anterior to the medial malleolus and following it superiorly, or you can use the dorsum of the foot if you need small vessels. You also can use the volar forearm for small vessels. If your flap or harvest field has an extra vein, sometimes you can use that as well. Off-the-shelf grafts are not recommended given the abundance of autologous local sources. Vein grafts can be performed to the arterial or venous system. Remember that a vein graft needs to be reversed when used as inflow to the arterial system because of the valves in veins, whereas it is not reversed when used to graft a vein.

11. What benefit do coupled anastomoses have?

The microvascular coupler is a ring device that allows repair of vessels without hand sewing. Coupled (stapled) anastomoses appear to have patency rates similar to those of hand-sewn anastomoses when used in the appropriate cases. Often, stapled anastomoses can be performed more quickly that those sewn by hand. Staples tend to be easier to use on veins rather than on arteries because of the thinner, more pliable walls in veins. This makes veins simpler to evert around the configuration of the coupler. Vessel size must be precisely matched, and vessel mobilization requirements can be greater to use the device.

12. How can you tell if a flap is failing?

Clinical evaluation of free flaps postoperatively is crucial to prevent flap loss. Often it can be difficult to tell if a flap has a circulatory problem. Flap failure can be divided into arterial insufficiency and venous insufficiency. If there is an arterial circulatory problem the flap usually will look pale and lack capillary refill. Muscle flaps can be particularly difficult to judge; color change with loss of a beefy red appearance is most common. If venous clot is the cause of flap failure, the flap generally becomes congested and bluish in color. Capillary refill is brisk. Sometimes poking a flap with an 18-gauge needle (away from the pedicle site) can help you judge flap circulation. If there is no bleeding, the problem is inflow. If there is rapid exit of dark red blood, venous congestion likely is the problem.

13. What factors lead to free flap failure?

Failure in microsurgery is most often due to technical factors and poor planning. Technical factors are multiple and too numerous to list, but a few examples illustrate their importance. If sutures are tied too loosely, media can be exposed and result in clot. If sutures are tied too tightly on small delicate vessels, they can tear all layers of a vascular repair and distort the intimal surface, resulting in clot. Too many sutures can lead to increased subendothelial exposure and clot formation.

Other factors leading to flap failure include anastomosis in the zone of injury (poor planning), excessive tension (poor planning), external compression on the pedicle, hematoma formation (which causes compression on the pedicle), and vessel spasm. Twisting in the arterial or venous pedicle will lead to clotting where the twist migrates to a fixed branch.

14. How long before new endothelium covers the anastomosis site?

After a microvascular repair is performed, a pseudointima forms within the first 5 days of healing. By 1 to 2 weeks after repair, new endothelium covers the anastomosis. At the time of repair, platelet deposition occurs where intima has been lost or injured. Platelets begin to disappear over the course of 1 to 3 days and pseudointima appears. Platelet deposition does not lead to fibrin deposition and thrombosis unless intimal damage is more severe and media is exposed more extensively. Significant damage to vessel walls can result from imprecise and traumatic technique. Traumatic suturing with excessive needle puncture and forceful pull-through of needles without following their natural curvature can damage endothelium.

15. What are some methods to relieve spasm?

Topical lidocaine can be used to relieve spasm. The safe topical dose in microsurgery has not established. Topical papaverine dilates small vessels with a strong local effect. Adventitia can be mechanically stripped, resulting in dilation of blood vessels and relief of spasm. Hydrostatic dilation can be used, usually in vein grafts where heparinized saline can be squirted into the vessel under pressure to relieve spasm. Epidural, spinal, or stellate ganglion blocks can interrupt the sympathetic fibers near the spinal cord and inhibit sympathetically mediated spasm.

16. What is the order of vessel repair in a free flap? Artery or vein first?

Usually intraoperative anatomic factors come into play. If repair of the artery first will result in poor exposure of the veins, then venous repair should be done first. The reverse is also true.

17. Should both arterial and venous repairs be completed before clamps are removed and flow is reestablished?

Some surgeons prefer to perform both arterial and venous repairs before removing the clamps and reestablishing blood flow. Others prefer to repair the artery, release the arterial clamp, and then clamp the vein of the flap before repairing it. The advantage of the latter is that inflow is reestablished sooner and ischemia time is minimized. Filling of the vein after this maneuver also helps to judge the excision of redundant vein (a redundant tortuous vein can lead to thrombosis). Some argue that blood stagnates in the flap and leads to sluggish arterial flow and a higher chance of clot. Usually the flap bleeds through its open edges, however, and flow continues when the vein is clamped. The advantage of repairing both artery and vein before removing the clamp is that blood in the field is minimized and blood does not stagnate in the flap.

18. Does smoking increase the risk of free flap failure?

Numerous studies have shown that wound healing is impaired in smokers. Flap failure does not appear to be increased significantly in smokers; however, wound healing complications at the recipient site appear to be more frequent.

19. Name several options for skin/fasciocutaneous flap reconstruction.

There are more than 40 donor areas from which to choose free flaps, and multiple combinations of flaps are possible. You should consult an atlas of microvascular surgery for a more complete armamentarium. Following is a partial list of the more popular flaps:

- *Transverse rectus abdominis myocutaneous (TRAM) flap:* Most common flap used for microvascular breast reconstruction; based on deep inferior epigastric vessels
- *Radial forearm:* Based on radial artery
- *Scapular, parascapular:* Based on circumflex scapular vessel
- *Dorsalis pedis:* Based on first dorsal metatarsal artery and dorsalis pedis
- *Lateral arm:* Posterior radial collateral artery
- *Groin flap:* Less popular now but was one of the originals, based on superficial circumflex iliac artery
- *Superficial inferior epigastric artery (SIEA) flap*
- *Bilateral inferior epigastric artery flap (BIEF):* Based on bilateral superficial inferior epigastric arteries
- *Deltoid flap:* Based on posterior circumflex humeral artery
- *Transverse upper gracilis (TUG) flap*

20. Name several free muscle flaps. Which muscles can be transplanted as functional muscles?

- *Rectus:* Based on deep inferior epigastric vessels
- *Latissimus:* Based on subscapular-thoracodorsal vessels
- *Serratus:* Based on subscapular-thoracodorsal vessels
- *Gracilis:* Branch to gracilis off medial femoral circumflex artery
- *Extensor brevis:* Branch to extensor brevis off dorsalis pedis artery

The latissimus, serratus, and gracilis muscles are most commonly used as functional transplants, that is, the nerve is repaired and they are used as a motor. The rectus and extensor brevis could be used functionally as well, but this practice is less common.

21. Name several perforator flaps.

- *Deep inferior epigastric artery perforator (DIEP) flap*
- *Periumbilical perforator (PUP) flap*
- *Anterolateral thigh flap:* Can be a perforator or a septal flap
- *Thoracodorsal artery perforator (TAP) flap*
- *Superior gluteal artery perforator (SGAP) flap*
- *Medial plantar artery perforator flap*

22. Name several osseous flaps.

- *Great toe:* Based on first dorsal metatarsal artery
- *Second toe:* Based on first dorsal metatarsal artery
- *Rib:* Tough dissection, based on intercostal neurovascular pedicle
- *Fibula:* Used most often in mandible reconstruction, based on peroneal vessels
- *Radial forearm:* Based on radial vessels
- *Iliac crest:* Based on deep circumflex iliac system
- *Scapula:* Based on circumflex scapular vessels
- *Calvarium:* Based on superficial temporal artery
- *Lateral arm:* Based on posterior collateral radial artery
- *Second metatarsal:* Based on first dorsal metatarsal

23. Are there any other types of free flaps?

- *Fascial Flaps*
  - Temperoparietal fascia
  - Dorsal thoracic fascia
  - Radial forearm fascia
  - Virtually any skin flap can be turned into a fascial flap
- *Small Bowel Flaps*
  - Jejunum and ileum can be transplanted for esophageal or intraoral reconstruction
  - Large bowel can be transplanted as a free flap
  - *Omentum:* First human free flap. Main disadvantage of omentum is requirement for laparotomy.
  - *Free-Style Flaps:* Based on perforators to fat and skin, these flaps can be small and harvested via the perforator to a larger source artery and vein. A PUP flap is a type of free-style flap that is also a perforator flap.

24. What are chimeric flaps?

A *chimeric flap* is composed of more than one flap each on its own pedicle but with both on a common source pedicle. With a single pedicle supplying more than one flap, only one pair of microsurgical inflow and outflow recipient vessels is needed. For example, the serratus muscle and the latissimus muscle can be harvested together on the common subscapular pedicle to make a serratus-latissimus chimeric flap. Many chimeric flap combinations can be created.

Examples of chimeric flaps include the following:

- Serratus-latissimus-scapular-scapula bone as a four component flap
- Anterolateral thigh and rectus femoris muscle
- Anterolateral thigh flap split into two skin and fat paddles on two different perforators both connected to the lateral femoral circumflex system
- A myriad of combinations can be developed

25. Which free flaps are used for facial reanimation?

Gracilis and serratus flaps are most commonly used for reconstruction in facial paralysis. They provide a good vascular pedicle with a suitable single nerve. There is also enough excursion to reconstruct a smile. Their main disadvantage is bulk. The latissimus can also be split into two separate muscle units.

CONTROVERSIES

26. Do you need a microscope to perform a free tissue transfer?

Many surgeons believe the comfort and magnification achieved with a microscope make microsurgical repair with a microscope superior to that performed with loupe magnification. Some authors argue that loupe magnification is cost effective and portable and results in success rates comparable to those reported with use of the microscope. Loupe magnification up to 6× is available; microscope magnification ranges from 6× to 40×.

27. Name two composite tissue allotransplants.

The human hand and parts of the face both have been transferred as free flaps from donors to nonidentical twin recipients. These microsurgical free flaps require immunosuppression and are very controversial because they require the recipient to take life-long immunosuppressants, which can be toxic and produce severe side effects, including induction of tumors and diabetes. The journal *Plastic and Reconstructive Surgery* used to have the title *Transplantation* appended onto it, but that was dropped 3 decades ago. Interestingly, plastic surgeons are returning to transplantation, and this will be a very exciting area for the field in the future. Right now it is likely the most controversial area.

BIBLIOGRAPHY

Buncke HJ (ed): Microsurgery: Transplantation-Replantation. An Atlas Text. Philadelphia, Lea & Febiger, 1991.

Buncke HJ, Lowenberg DW, Quatra F, Buncke GM, Buntic RF, Brooks D: Composite tissue allografting (CTA). Surg Technol Int 11:292–302, 2003.

Khouri RK: Avoiding free flap failure. Clin Plast Surg 19:773–781, 1992.

Reus WF, Colen LB, Straker DJ: Tobacco smoking and complications in elective microsurgery. Plast Reconstr Surg 89:490–494, 1992.

Shenaq SM, Klebuc JA, Vargo D: Free tissue transfer with the aid of loupe magnification: Experience with 251 procedures. Plast Reconstr Surg 95:261–269, 1995.

Zhang F, Pang Y, Buntic R, Jones M, Cai Z, Buncke HJ, Lineaweaver WC: Effect of sequence, timing of vascular anastomosis, and clamp removal on survival of microsurgical flaps. J Reconstr Microsurg 18:697–702, 2002.

FREE FLAP DONOR SITES

Mahesh H. Mankani, MD, FACS, and
Julian J. Pribaz, MD

CHAPTER 110

1. What is a composite free flap?
A composite free flap, like a composite graft, is derived from two or more germ layers and contains at least two layers of tissue.

2. What is the quadrangle space? Which structures traverse it?
The space is bounded by the teres minor muscle above, the teres major muscle below, the long head of the triceps muscle medially, and the humerus laterally. It is traversed by the posterior circumflex humeral vessels, which perfuse the deltoid free flap.

3. What is the triangular space? Which structures traverse it?
The triangular space lies medial to the quadrangle space and is bounded laterally by the long head of the triceps muscle, the teres minor muscle above, and the teres major muscle below. It is traversed by the circumflex scapular vessels, which perfuse the scapular free flap.

4. Describe the Mathes and Nahai classification of muscle circulation and list examples of muscles used for free transfers from each group.
- *Type I:* One vascular pedicle
- *Type II:* One dominant pedicle and minor pedicles
- *Type III:* Two dominant pedicles
- *Type IV:* Segmental vascular pedicles
- *Type V:* One dominant and secondary vascular pedicles

Type I
- Tensor fascia latae is perfused solely by the transverse branch of the lateral femoral circumflex artery.
- The extensor digitorum brevis is perfused by a branch of the dorsalis pedis artery.

Type II
- The gracilis muscle is perfused by a major pedicle that is a terminal branch of the medial femoral circumflex artery. One to two minor pedicles from the superficial femoral artery enter the muscle distally.
- The soleus muscle is perfused by branches directly from the popliteal vessels. The distal 4 to 5 cm of muscle is perfused by segmental perforating vessels from the posterior tibial artery.

Type III
- The rectus abdominis is perfused by two dominant pedicles, the superior arising from the superior epigastric artery and the inferior arising from the deep inferior epigastric artery.
- The serratus anterior is perfused by the lateral thoracic artery superiorly and the thoracodorsal artery inferiorly.

Type IV
- No type IV muscles are appropriate for free transfers.

Type V
- The latissimus dorsi is perfused predominantly by the thoracodorsal artery. The muscle also receives a segmental blood supply medially by branches of the intercostal and lumbar arteries.
- The pectoralis major receives its major blood supply from the thoracoacromial artery. It is also perfused by the lateral thoracic artery, the internal mammary artery, and the intercostal artery.
- The pectoralis minor is predominantly perfused by the lateral thoracic artery. A direct branch of the axillary artery and the pectoral branch of the thoracoacromial artery provide secondary vascularization.

5. **What are the advantages and disadvantages of including a skin paddle with a muscle flap?**

Inclusion of the skin paddle in a muscle flap transfer, or transfer of a myocutaneous flap, has two major advantages. The skin island can serve as a method for monitoring the health of the flap, and the quality of the skin often is superior to that of a skin graft placed on the muscle. On the other hand, inclusion of the skin paddle may make the flap excessively bulky, an issue of concern in obese patients and in recipient sites of limited depth.

6. **Which muscles are suitable for facial reanimation because of their size and segmental innervation?**

These muscles include the gracilis and the pectoralis minor. The gracilis is innervated by a single motor nerve with multiple fascicles to different portions of the muscle. The pectoralis minor muscle is innervated by both the medial and lateral pectoral nerves.

7. **Name a reliable donor muscle for coverage of large defects.**

The latissimus dorsi muscle provides the largest available transfer, with a size of $25 \times 35 \, cm^2$.

8. **Name four muscles that are appropriate for functional free transfers.**
   - Latissimus dorsi
   - Pectoralis minor
   - Serratus anterior
   - Gracilis muscles

9. **What are the uses and advantages of the gracilis flap?**

The gracilis muscle is thin, strap-shaped muscle with a consistent pedicle, straightforward harvest, and option for inclusion of a cutaneous component. Its loss is associated with minimal morbidity. The donor site can be closed primarily with a reasonable appearance. Inclusion of the anterior branch of the obturator nerve provides functionality. The flap can be used for facial reanimation.

10. **Which portions of the serratus anterior muscle can be safely harvested without risk of inducing winging of the scapula?**

To avoid winging of the scapula, the middle and lower four to five digitations of the muscle should be used.

11. **What sensory deficit may result from injudicious harvest of the lateral gastrocnemius muscle?**

The common peroneal nerve lies superficial to the lateral head of the gastrocnemius muscle. Traction on the nerve during dissection of the muscle impairs the deep and superficial peroneal nerves. Patients can experience a paresis of the dorsiflexor and eversion muscles of the foot and numbness along the dorsum of the foot and in the first web space.

12. **Describe one of the primary uses of the pectoralis minor flap.**

Because of the muscle's shape, small size, flatness, and dual nerve supply, the muscle is suited for facial reanimation. Additionally, removal of the muscle is not associated with disability or with a significant scar.

13. **List 10 sensate cutaneous flaps and their innervation.**

More Commonly Used Flaps
   - Lateral arm flap, innervated by the posterior brachial cutaneous nerve
   - Radial forearm flap, innervated by the medial and lateral antebrachial cutaneous nerves
   - Dorsalis pedis flap, innervated by the deep branch of peroneal nerve in the first web space and by the superficial peroneal nerve over the remainder of the flap.

Less Commonly Used Flaps
   - Transverse cervical artery flap, innervated by the supraclavicular nerves
   - Deltoid flap, innervated by a cutaneous branch of the axillary nerve
   - Gluteal thigh flap, innervated by the posterior cutaneous nerve of the thigh
   - Medial thigh flap, innervated by the medial femoral cutaneous nerve
   - Lateral thigh flap, innervated by the lateral femoral cutaneous nerve
   - Saphenous flap, innervated by the medial femoral cutaneous and saphenous nerves
   - Posterior calf flap, innervated by the medial or posterior cutaneous nerves of the thigh and by the sural nerve

14. What are the advantages of the anterolateral thigh free flap?

The anterolateral thigh free flap is a septofasciocutaneous or musculocutaneous flap perfused by the descending branch of the lateral femoral circumflex artery. Advantages of the flap include its long vascular pedicle, its capacity to perform as a flow-through flap, the option for keeping the flap sensate, the flap's ease of harvest, the option for simultaneous donor and recipient site dissections, and the flap's minimal donor site morbidity.

15. What are the advantages of using the medial forearm flap in reconstruction of the face or hand?

This is a thin, supple, hairless, and sensate septofasciocutaneous flap that is innervated by the medial cutaneous nerve of the forearm.

16. Under what circumstances can donor site appearance be improved in use of the cutaneous lateral arm flap?

Although the size of the flap can reach 14×20 cm, harvest of a flap this large will require closure of the donor site with a skin graft. If the width of the flap is reduced to 6 cm, the donor site can be closed primarily.

17. What are the limitations of one of the earliest free flaps, the groin flap?

The groin flap suffers from variations in its vasculature, a small-caliber pedicle, a short pedicle length, and a difficult harvest.

18. What are the two most commonly used vascularized free bone flaps? What are their advantages and disadvantages?

The vascularized fibula flap and the vascularized iliac crest flap are the two most commonly used free bone flaps.

The free fibular flap has several distinct advantages, including a length approaching 26 cm, a thick cortex giving the bone profound structural strength, and minimal donor site morbidity. The flap suffers from a short pedicle and from the necessary sacrifice of the peroneal artery. This latter disadvantage is of particular importance in patients with lower extremity arterial insufficiency.

The free iliac crest flap has a long pedicle, a curvature appropriate for mandibular reconstruction, and the possibility for inclusion of overlying muscle and skin with minimal morbidity. However, the mass of transferable bone is limited, the patient is left with a profound contour deformity, and abdominal herniation is a documented morbid consequence of the harvest.

19. With which pedicles can the iliac crest osteocutaneous flap be harvested?

The available pedicles include the superficial circumflex iliac artery (SCIA), the deep circumflex iliac artery (DCIA), and the dorsal branch of the fourth lumbar artery. The deep branch of the superior gluteal artery typically can provide an osseous flap but is not amenable to creation of an osteocutaneous flap.

20. What morbidity is associated with harvest of the vascularized free iliac crest bone flap?

Abdominal herniation is a significant risk.

21. What are the advantages of using the great toe for thumb reconstruction?

Patient grip strength is greater with use of the great toe than with use of the second toe. It involves transfer of two phalanges and a large nail, similar to the thumb. However, use of the great toe impairs the appearance of the foot much more than does use of the second toe.

22. What is the most commonly used free fascial flap? What are its advantages and disadvantages?

The free temporoparietal fascial (TPF) flap is the most commonly used free fascial flap. The TPF flap, like other fascial flaps, offers thin, nonbulky, supple, and highly vascularized tissue. The flap has been draped over denuded cartilage and has been used to restore a gliding surface for tendon reconstruction in the hand. Particular advantages of the temporoparietal fascia flap include a size of up to 14×17 cm, an inconspicuous donor site scar, the option for simultaneous donor and recipient site dissections, and the capacity for inclusion of bone from the outer table of the calvarium. Unfortunately, dissection of the flap is tedious, and the harvest is associated with alopecia.

23. Is patient positioning important when considering an appropriate donor site?
Very important. Some flaps, such as the gracilis muscle, are considered extremely versatile because recipient site preparation and flap harvest can be completed simultaneously. Other flaps, such as the latissimus dorsi muscle, often require patient repositioning between dissection of an anterior recipient site and flap harvest, a factor that must be taken into consideration when selecting a donor site during reconstruction planning.

24. What methods are used for closing donor site defects following flap harvest?
Donor sites can be closed directly or skin grafted. Skin grafting can use either split-thickness or full-thickness skin. Whereas a split-thickness skin graft can offer more rapid healing, a full-thickness skin graft offers greater stability and durability once healing has occurred.

BIBLIOGRAPHY

Banis J, Abul-Hassan H: Cutaneous free flaps. In Georgiade G, Georgiade N, Riefkohl R, Barwick W (eds): Textbook of Plastic, Maxillofacial, and Reconstructive Surgery, 2nd ed. Baltimore, Williams & Wilkins, 1992, pp 977–1008.

Levin L, Pederson W, Barwick W: Free muscle and myocutaneous flaps. In Georgiade G, Georgiade N, Riefkohl R, Barwick W (eds): Textbook of Plastic, Maxillofacial, and Reconstructive Surgery, 2nd ed. Baltimore, Williams & Wilkins, 1992, pp 1009–1020.

Manktelow RT, Zuker RM, McKee NH: Functioning free muscle transplantation. J Hand Surg [Am] 9A:32–39, 1984.

Mathes SJ, Vasconez LO: Myocutaneous free-flap transfer. Anatomical and experimental considerations. Plast Reconstr Surg 62:162–166, 1978.

Mathes SJ, Nahai F: Classification of the vascular anatomy of muscles: Experimental and clinical correlation. Plast Reconstr Surg 67: 177–187, 1981.

McCraw J, Arnold P: McGraw and Arnold's Atlas of Muscle and Musculocutaneous Flaps. Norfolk, VA, Hampton Press Publishing, 1986.

Moore K: Clinically Oriented Anatomy, 3rd ed. Baltimore, Williams & Wilkins, 1992.

Musgrave R, Lehman J: Composite grafts. In Georgiade G, Georgiade N, Riefkohl R, Barwick W (eds): Textbook of Plastic, Maxillofacial, and Reconstructive Surgery, 2nd ed. Baltimore, Williams & Wilkins, 1992, pp 47–51.

Nunley J, Barwick W: Free vascularized bone grafts and osteocutaneous flaps. In Georgiade G, Georgiade N, Riefkohl R, Barwick W (eds): Textbook of Plastic, Maxillofacial, and Reconstructive Surgery, 2nd ed. Baltimore, Williams & Wilkins, 1992, pp 1021–1032.

Pribaz JJ, Orgill DP, Epstein MD, Sampson CE, Hergrueter CA: Anterolateral thigh free flap. Ann Plast Surg 34:585–592, 1995.

Robinson DW: Microsurgical transfer of the dorsalis pedis neurovascular island flap. Br J Plast Surg 29:209–213, 1976.

Strauch B, Yu H: Atlas of Microvascular Surgery. New York, Thieme Medical Publishers, 1993.

Terzis JK: Pectoralis minor: A unique muscle for correction of facial palsy. Plast Reconstr Surg 83:767–776, 1989.

Whitney TM, Buncke HJ, Alpert BS, Buncke GM, Lineaweaver WC: The serratus anterior free-muscle flap: Experience with 100 consecutive cases. Plast Reconstr Surg 86:481–490, 1990; discussion 491.

LEECHES

CHAPTER 111

Stephen Daane, MD

1. What are leeches? Sneeches?

Leeches are worms of the Annelid phylum that feed on blood extracted from a host. Based on the practice of leeching in the middle ages, the word "leech" is derived from the English word "laece," meaning physician. Leeches were used extensively in nineteenth-century European medicine for bloodletting, a practice believed to cure virtually any ailment. Consumption of leeches reached a peak in the 1830s, when tens of millions were used annually in France, England, Germany, and the United States.

Sneeches live on beaches and were created by Dr. Seuss. They have nothing to do with plastic surgery.

2. How long have leeches been used in medicine?

The first known use of leeches dates to 3500 years ago in Egypt, where a tomb painting depicts the application of leeches by a barber-surgeon. Detailed documentation of leeching also dates to 3300 years ago in India. In the West, leeches were first used for medicinal bloodletting 2200 years ago by Nicander of Colophon, Greece.

3. How long have leeches been used in plastic surgery?

The modern use of leeches in flap surgery began in 1960 with a report of 70% complete salvage and 30% partial salvage in 20 threatened flaps treated with leeches. They were used in hand surgery in 1981, with a report of 60% survival of 10 artery-only digital replantations treated with leeches. This was a marked improvement over the survival of artery-only replants treated by systemic anticoagulation alone.

Current survival estimates for threatened replanted digits treated with leeches are 60% to 70%; salvage estimates for threatened pedicle flaps treated with leeches also are 60% to 70%. *Hirudo medicinalis,* the leech endemic to Southeast Asia and Europe, is the most commonly used species.

4. What are the indications for using leeches?

Venous congestion is a recognized complication of digital replantation that may lead to a sequence of edema, capillary and arterial slowing, venous and arterial thrombosis, flap ischemia, and, finally, necrosis. Leeches are not a panacea for poor flap design or technical problems with vascular anastomoses, but they are indicated as an adjunct for salvage.

Leeches have been used successfully to decongest replanted parts, including completely avulsed ears and digits and partially avulsed segments of the lip, penis, nose, and scalp. They also have been used on threatened digits in purpura fulminans, ear and periorbital hematomas, and traumatically degloved tissues, and in the salvage of nipple necrosis in breast reduction procedures.

5. What are the signs of arterial occlusion versus venous occlusion?

Signs of venous congestion include cyanotic skin color, cool temperature, rapid capillary refill, increased tissue turgor, and rapid dark bleeding in response to a pinprick. Doppler imaging should be the first tool used postoperatively to document arterial circulation because leeches will not be helpful in cases of insufficient arterial inflow. Venous congested tissues may be salvaged if arterial blood flow is maintained until new venous ingrowth occurs. Venous competence usually is restored by postoperative day 4 or 5 for replanted digits and by postoperative day 6 to 10 for free flaps (Table 111-1).

In the absence of overt signs of threatened tissue loss, early detection of complications is aided with temperature monitoring, fluorescein dye injection, or laser Doppler flowmetry, although distinguishing between arterial or venous occlusion with any of these modalities is difficult.

6. How do leeches work?

The leech front sucker conceals cartilaginous cutting plates that make a 2-mm incision. In 30 minutes a single hirudo leech can ingest up to 10 times its body weight or 5 to 15 cc of blood. However, the primary therapeutic benefit is

Table 111-1. Arterial Occlusion versus Venous Occlusion

	ARTERIAL OCCLUSION	VENOUS OCCLUSION
Color	Pale	Blue-purple
Tissue turgor	Decreased	Increased, engorged and tense
Capillary refill	Slow, absent	Brisk, instantaneous
Temperature	Low	Low

derived from an anticoagulant hirudin, which is injected from the leech salivary glands. The effect of the anticoagulant may last several hours after the leech detaches, permitting the wound to ooze up to 50 cc of blood.

Hirudin is a polypeptide that inhibits the thrombin-catalyzed conversion of fibrinogen to fibrin. Hirudin also blocks platelet aggregation in response to thrombin and may inhibit factor X. Because factor II (thrombin) is believed to be the final common pathway in all causes of thrombosis, hirudin is regarded as the most potent natural anticoagulant known. Hirudin has two advantages over heparin: (1) it does not require antithrombin III to inactivate thrombin, and (2) it is not bound by heparin-neutralizing platelet factor 4. Clinical trials are in progress to compare the efficacy of heparin and recombinant hirudin in preventing acute coronary closure after angioplasty, in the treatment of unstable angina, and in prophylaxis of deep vein thrombosis (DVT).

Other pharmacologic agents within leech saliva include (1) a local anesthetic; (2) hyaluronidase, a spreading factor; and (3) a histamine-like vasodilator that increases regional blood flow.

7. What are the possible complications of using leeches? What precautions are necessary?
The main complications in using leeches are infection and blood loss. *H. medicinalis* relies on a symbiotic relationship with *Aeromonas hydrophila* within its gut. *A. hydrophila* is a gram-negative rod that causes infection at rates varying from 0% to 20% within 1 to 10 days after leech use. Some authors recommend an empiric aminoglycoside or third-generation cephalosporin. Leeches are not natural carriers of viruses, but they can transmit hepatitis B to humans if infected. Universal precautions (handling leeches with gloves and a forceps) must be followed.

A potential result of prolonged leech therapy is a significant drop in hematocrit. Transfusions are often required because of systemic anticoagulation and continuous oozing from leech bites, which may contraindicate leech therapy for Jehovah's Witnesses.

8. How are leeches administered?
The skin is cleansed and isolated with an Op-Site dressing or saline-soaked sponge. The leech's head (narrow end) is directed to the area needing treatment. A leech can be induced to feed by keeping it in a beaker held over the attachment site or by pricking the feeding site with a needle to produce a drop of blood. It is important to protect the area of the anastomosis with a gauze. Observe the leech frequently until it drops off the patient (usually in 30 minutes). If bleeding stops after the leech is removed, wiping the leech-bite area with a heparin-soaked gauze pledget may promote rebleeding.

Leech rejection is failure of the leech to attach rapidly to a replanted part, poor sucking, or consumption of less than a full meal. These findings have been suggested as poor prognosticators of tissue survival because of arterial insufficiency despite a favorable tissue color.

Dispose of leeches by placing them in a container of alcohol and discarding the container with infectious waste. Leeches can never be reused.

9. How many leeches should you use?
The desired venous outflow of a flap or replanted digit is tailored to the needs of the specific patient by adjusting the number and frequency of leeches applied. In some published reports, leeches were used on venous congested parts as infrequently as 1 leech per day or as frequently as one leech six times per day for a duration of 5 to 10 days.

When the wound does not continue to bleed after leech application, fresh leeches can be reapplied to a digit or flap as frequently as every 30 minutes.

10. Where do you get leeches in the middle of the night?

Because venous congestion may arise suddenly in the immediate postoperative period, an immediately available supply of at least five to 10 leeches is desirable. In the United States, hirudo leeches are available from two vendors on the East Coast who advertise prominently in plastic surgery journals. However, even under the best circumstances, obtaining leeches may take 12 to 14 hours. Tissue bleeding caused by abrasion of the nailbed of the replanted digit with heparin-soaked sponges every hour usually maintains tissue viability until leeches are available. Telephone calls to the pharmacies of neighboring hospitals may yield an available supply of "loaner" leeches.

Leeches vary in price but are approximately $12 each. In comparison with the costs of an operation and postoperative intensive care unit monitoring, leeches are one of the least expensive parts of a patient's hospitalization. The expense usually is covered as a medication by insurance companies.

Bibliography

Daane S, Zamora S, Rockwell WB: Clinical use of leeches in reconstructive surgery. Am J Orthop 25:528–532, 1997.
Dabb RW, Malone JM, Leverett LC: The use of medicinal leeches in the salvage of flaps with venous congestion. Ann Plast Surg 29:250–256, 1992.
Kraemer BA: Use of leeches in plastic and reconstructive surgery: A review. J Reconstr Microsurg 4:381–386, 1988.
Lineaveaver WC, Hill MK, Buncke GM, et al: Aeromonas hydrophila infections following use of medicinal leeches in replantation and flap surgery. Ann Plast Surg 29:238–244, 1992.
Smoot CE, Ruiz-Inchaustegui JA, Roth AC: Mechanical leech therapy to relieve venous congestion. J Reconstr Microsurg 11:51–55, 1995.
Wells MD, Manktelow RT, Boyd JB, et al: The medicinal leech: An old treatment revisited. Microsurgery 14:183–186, 1993.

Maria Siemionow, MD, PhD, DSc; Erhan Sonmez, MD; and Frank A. Papay, MD, FACS, FAAP

1. What are the functions of the face?

The human face has intrinsic aesthetic and functional importance. It plays a central role in the perception of identity and self and represents the most identifiable aspect of an individual's physical being. It is paramount to multiple functional needs, such as eye protection, oral competence, speech, and emotional communication. The face's expressive function carries with it additional social, symbolic, and psychological importance. Its role in a person's identity, communication, and sense of being cannot be overstated.

2. What are the established techniques for repairing the human face?

Established techniques for repairing the human face can be categorized as those using autologous tissues and those producing repair by allotransplantation. Conventional techniques use autologous local cutaneous tissue flaps and free flap autografts, which allow the transfer of more complex components such as skin, bone, and muscle. Local flaps, such as bilobed, nasolabial, and forehead skin flaps, often produce good results in selective cases with small defects. However, coverage of complex defects such as central facial tissue defects usually requires free transfer of autologous tissues such as fibular or forearm flaps. Despite many revision procedures for shaping the flap, the functional and aesthetic results of reconstruction usually remain poor. For such major and complex tissue defects, allotransplantation offers a unique and preeminent advantage by restoring "like with like."

3. Can you estimate the size of the skin needed to cover an entire face, scalp, front of neck, and ears?

Approximately 1200 cm^2 of skin is needed to cover the entire hair-bearing scalp, front of neck, and ears. This is one of the reasons for the aesthetic failure of conventional skin reconstruction of the face with autologous tissues.

4. What types of face allotransplantations have been defined thus far?

Two types of face allotransplantations have been defined.

Partial Face: On November 27, 2005, a team of French surgeons led by Devauchelle and Dubernard transplanted a triangular allograft consisting of a distal nose, lips, and chin to a 38-year-old female recipient in Amiens, France. The world's first partial face allograft, entailing skin, mucosa, fat, and some muscle, was used to restore a defect resulting from a disfiguring dog bite. The 5-hour transplant operation included revascularization via the facial arteries and veins bilaterally.

Complete Face/Scalp: Full facial transplantation has become the newest and most debatable composite tissue allotransplantation topic in recent years. To date, successful facial/scalp allotransplantation has been limited to animal and cadaveric studies. At present there is an established full facial/scalp allograft cadaver model. In this model a composite facial/scalp flap was based bilaterally on the external carotid arteries serving as the arterial pedicles, on the external jugular and facial veins serving as the venous pedicles, and the supraorbital, infraorbital, mental, and great auricular nerves included in the facial flaps.

The full facial/scalp allograft model in rats is established and includes a bilateral external ear component. The cutaneous/subcutaneous flap is elevated via subplatysmal dissection and then divided based on its vascular pedicle of the common carotid arteries and external jugular veins. Siemionow has shown in rats that acceptance of facial allografts can be drastically increased (up to 100% at 200 days posttransplant) when modifying the arterial anastomoses to include only a unilateral common carotid artery anastomosis.

5. Name the current surgical and technical protocols of face allotransplantation?

Currently, there are two primary models in place. The "*Partial Face Transplantation Model*" (France) focuses on central facial transplantation: the nose, lips, and chin are transplanted. The "*Full Face Transplantation Model*" (Cleveland Clinic, Cleveland, Ohio) focuses on reconstruction for full facial burn traumas (and craniofacial reconstruction patients). In addition, the French have advocated surgical candidates who have not undertaken prior extensive reconstructive attempts, whereas Cleveland Clinic advocates restricting the surgery to patients who have failed prior treatments.

6. What are the goals of performing a face allotransplantation procedure?

Although it is not classified as a life-essential transplant, face allotransplantation is certainly a reconstructive procedure. It is a procedure performed in patients with severe facial deformities to accomplish two primary goals: (1) to provide a less disfigured facial appearance to facilitate a more normal social interaction, and (2) to reestablish basic facial function, such as blinking, mouth closure, and facial expression.

7. Which vessels are used for vascularization of the face allotransplant?

Vascularization of the entire facial flap would rely on the terminal branches of the external carotid artery, superficial temporal artery, and internal maxillary artery for the upper third and the deep structures of the face and on the facial artery for the central and lower parts of the face. The ophthalmic artery, a collateral branch of the internal carotid artery, contributes to vascularization of the periorbital area. Venous drainage of the face relies on the external, internal, and anterior jugular veins, which drain the superficial temporal, facial, and inferior labial and chin veins, respectively. Thus transplantation of the whole face would involve all of these vascular systems, which should be dissected proximal enough to ensure vascularization of the entire facial flap and to enable anastomosis to the recipient's counterparts.

8. Which nerves should be included in a facial/scalp allotransplant?

Three branches of the trigeminal nerve should be included in a facial/scalp allotransplant as sensory nerves:

- *Supraorbital Nerve:* Supplies the skin and conjunctiva covering the upper eyelid, and the skin over the forehead and anterior scalp.
- *Infraorbital Nerve:* Supplies the skin of the lower eyelid, possibly the conjunctiva and the skin over the maxilla.
- *Mental Nerve:* Supplies the skin of the lower lip and chin.

Four branches of the facial nerve should be included in a facial/scalp allotransplant as motor nerves:

- *Temporal Branch:* Supplies the muscles around eyebrow and ear.
- *Zygomatic Branch:* Supplies the periorbital muscles.
- *Buccal Branch:* Supplies the perioral muscles.
- *Mandibular Branch:* Supplies the perioral muscles.

9. Organ transplantations are commonly performed all over the world. Is there any difference between these transplantations and face transplantation?

Unlike other commonly transplanted organs, such as the heart or liver, musculocutaneous grafts such as facial structures are histologically heterogeneous and contain tissue components that express different degrees of antigenicity (e.g., skin, glands). Like organ transplantations, face allotransplantation technique mandates substantial lifelong immunosuppression to prevent rejection, and failure of the regimen chosen could prove devastating, with possible loss of the transplanted face at any time. However, there is an ethical debate on the face transplantation issue because of the requirement for lifelong immunosuppression for a nonvital organ.

10. The face allograft includes diverse tissues such as skin, muscle, tendon, nerve, bone, and vessels. Which of these tissues express the highest antigenicity?

Skin has the highest antigenicity of all the tissues in composite tissue transplantation, followed by muscle, bone, nerve, tendon, and vessels.

11. What is the current immunosuppressive protocol used in the face allotransplantation?

The induction immunosuppressive protocol includes antithymocyte globulin, tacrolimus, mycophenolate mofetil, and prednisone. Infusion of donor bone marrow cells can be performed to promote graft acceptance. The maintenance treatment includes tacrolimus, mycophenolate mofetil, and prednisone, the doses of which can be temporarily adjusted during periods of rejection.

12. What methods are used to evaluate the signs of face allograft rejection?

Patients should be checked regularly for signs of rejection. Allografted skin (face and sentinel skin graft) and oral mucosa of the patients are regularly examined clinically; punch biopsies are taken at various time intervals. Biopsies are obtained whenever clinical findings of rejection are present.

13. What are the earliest clinical signs of rejection seen in face allotransplantation?

Long-term face allograft survival depends on adequate immunosuppression. Signs of rejection should be investigated, especially in the first 6 months postoperatively. The earliest signs of rejection would be visible on the skin surface and would present as erythema, rash, and pinpoint swelling. Diffuse erythema and edema are the earliest signs of rejection visible on the mucosa.

14. Describe the types of rejection of allograft transplants.

Rejection of allotransplants occurs in three basic forms:

- *Hyperacute/Accelerated Rejection:* This type of rejection occurs rapidly following reperfusion of the graft within minutes to hours and is mediated by antibodies that are present in the recipient's circulation before transplant. Because it is irreversible, this type of rejection must be avoided by thorough screening of transplant candidate serum for preformed antibodies and avoidance of the corresponding antigen in donors.
- *Acute Rejection:* This type of rejection occurs within days to months following transplant. To date, 100% of all composite tissue allotransplantation recipients have experienced at least one rejection episode. Although antibody-mediated, or humoral, rejection is common, acute rejection most often is mediated by T cells as evidenced by the absence of acute rejection in research animals that are T-cell deficient. Most acute rejection episodes occur in the first 3 to 6 months following transplant, and most of them are successfully reversed with treatment.
- *Chronic Rejection:* It is the third major form of allotransplant rejection and seen later than acute rejection. The characteristic lesions of chronic rejection involve fibrosis and atrophy of the graft parenchyma with progressive arteriopathy within the engrafted vasculature.

15. What are the major causes of sensitization of the recipient facilitating the hyperacute/accelerated rejection?

These events include exposure to transfusions, pregnancy, deceased donor tissue transplants, infections, and immunizations. Patients are instructed to inform the transplant coordinator of any potentially sensitizing events that occur while they await transplant.

16. What is the treatment of choice when signs of rejection are present?

If signs of rejection are present, skin biopsies should be performed to evaluate the stage of rejection, immunosuppression should be increased specifically with high doses of steroids, and topical tacrolimus and steroids should be used on the skin surface.

17. What is the treatment of choice in acute rejection, if the initial treatment fails?

In cases where the initial treatment fails to resolve the rejection, patients usually will be treated with an antilymphocyte antibody preparation such as an anti-CD3 monoclonal antibody or polyclonal antithymocyte preparation.

18. What is the treatment of choice for chronic rejection?

The immunosuppressive protocols currently in use are essentially ineffective at slowing or reversing the process of chronic rejection. Rapamycin and mycophenolate mofetil have demonstrated some efficacy in the treatment of chronic rejection.

19. What is the estimated risk of acute and chronic face allotransplant rejection?

It is estimated that the rate of acute rejection is high as 10% for the first year, and the risk of loss of graft function (resulting from scarring from chronic rejection) is estimated to be 30% to 50% over a period of 2 to 5 years. However, recent results of the first partial face allograft transplant show over 1-year survival without rejection, and results of the first hand allograft transplant show over 8-year survival once the patients maintain lifelong immunosuppression.

20. What are the long-term side effects of the immunosuppressants used in facial allotransplantation?

Long-term side effects of the immunosuppressants fall into three categories:

- *Opportunistic Infections:* Cutaneous, fungal, and tinea infections; cytomegalovirus and herpes virus recurrences
- *Metabolic Disorders:* Diabetes, Cushing's syndrome
- *Malignancies:* Basal cell and squamous cell carcinomas; Epstein-Barr virus B-cell lymphoproliferative disorders

These side effects are a major limiting factor in tissue allotransplantation for correcting physical or functional disabilities.

21. What factors influence the success rate of a face allotransplantation?

Although control of the immune response to an allograft dominates the focus for extending graft survival, many other factors that influence the success rate have been defined. These factors include human leukocyte antigen (HLA) matching between donor and recipient; ischemia time; time and temperature of organ preservation; age of the donor; race of the recipient; and cause of donor death.

22. What would be the fate of the patient if the face allograft is lost?

The patient would require additional reconstructive procedures, but the loss would not be life threatening. The potential for graft rejection means that candidates must have appropriate tissue sites for regrafting. If the graft is rejected, immunosuppression would be discontinued, eliminating its risks. Candidates for this procedure would have undergone multiple reconstructive procedures previously, so their ability to weigh the burden of further procedures would be expected.

23. What are the pretransplant assessments of candidates for facial allotransplantation?

Candidates for facial allotransplantation should undergo rigorous pretransplant assessment, which includes psychiatric, psychosocial, and bioethical evaluations. The patients offered this innovative procedure should be fully informed of the risks and reasonable benefits that can be expected from participation in this trial. They and their families should receive counseling about the risks and challenges of being the first patients to undergo a procedure that has drawn so much media and public attention. Potential candidates for facial resurfacing by facial skin allograft transplantation should undergo a thorough screening process by a team of multidisciplinary specialists under an Institutional Review Board-approved protocol as suggested by the Royal College of Surgeons and National Consultative Committee.

24. What should be included in the informed consent for candidates for facial allotransplantation?

A thorough informed consent needs to be developed and given to the potential allotransplantation patient and his/her family. Such consent should include discussion of the probability of surgical failure and/or transplant rejection, and it should clearly discuss the lifelong risks associated with an immunosuppressive regimen. The patient should be informed about the origin of the graft coming from the human donor and about the facial tissue that will be transplanted. Precisely what will be harvested and transplanted, and how the harvesting and transplantation will be conducted, require clarification. Finally, patients should be informed that a separate informed consent is obtained from the donor and the donor's family.

25. What are the next steps in the recovery of the patient who has undergone facial allotransplantation surgery?

Recovery from the surgical procedure(s) is only the initial step in recovery for the composite tissue allotransplantation patient. Long-term immunotherapy for transplant patients has been discussed. Additional therapy includes rehabilitation training, which consists of static and dynamic facial exercises, mainly focusing on restoration of lip suspension, mouth occlusion, and facial expression training. Psychological support for acceptance of the new face is mandatory.

BIBLIOGRAPHY

Agich GJ, Siemionow M: Until they have faces: The ethics of facial allograft transplantation. J Med Ethics 31:707–709, 2005.

Agich GJ, Siemionow M: Facing the ethical questions in facial transplantation. Am J Bioeth 4:25–27, 2004.

American Society of Plastic Surgeons: Position of the Society for Reconstructive Microsurgery on Facial Transplantation. Arlington Heights, IL, American Society of Plastic Surgeons, 2006.

Comité Consultatif National d'Ethique pour les sciences de la vie et de la santé: L'allotransplantation de tissu composite (ATC) au niveau de la face (Greffe totale ou partielle d'un visage). Report Opinion 82. Paris, Comité consultatif national d'éthique pour les sciences de la vie et de la santé, 2004.

Devauchelle B, Badet L, Lengele B, et al: First human face allograft: Early report. Lancet 368:203–209, 2006.

The first facial transplant. Lancet 366:1984, 2005.

Garcia R, Pinheiro-Machado PG, Felipe CR, et al: Conversion from azathioprine to mycophenolate mofetil followed by calcineurin inhibitor minimization or elimination in patients with chronic allograft dysfunction. Transplant Proc 38:2872–2878, 2006.

Gordon CR, Nazzal J, Lozano-Calderan SA, et al: From experimental rat hindlimb to clinical face composite tissue allotransplantation: Historical background and current status. Microsurgery 26:566–572, 2006.

Hettiaratchy S, Melendy E, Randolph MA, et al: Tolerance to composite tissue allografts across a major histocompatibility barrier in miniature swine. Transplantation 77:514–521, 2004.

Kanitakis J, Badet L, Petruzzo P, et al: Clinicopathologic monitoring of the skin and oral mucosa of the first human face allograft: Report on the first eight months. Transplantation 82:1610–1615, 2006.

Lantieri LA: Face transplantation: The view from Paris, France. South Med J 99:421–423, 2006.

Petit F, Paraskevas A, Minns AB, Lee WP, Lantieri LA: Face transplantation: Where do we stand? Plast Reconstr Surg 113:1429–1433, 2004.

Pidwell DJ, Burns C: The immunology of composite tissue transplantation. Clin Plast Surg 34:303–317, 2007.

Rohrich RJ, Longaker MT, Cunningham B: On the ethics of composite tissue allotransplantation (facial transplantation). Plast Reconstr Surg 117:2071–2073, 2006.

Rumsey N: Psychological aspects of face transplantation: Read the small print carefully. Am J Bioethics 4:22, 2004.

Siemionow M, Unal S, Agaoglu G, Sari A: A cadaver study in preparation for facial allograft transplantation in humans: Part I. What are alternative sources for total facial defect coverage. Plast Reconstr Surg 117:864–875, 2006.

Siemionow M, Agaoglu G, Unal S: A cadaver study in preparation for facial allograft transplantation in humans: Part II. Mock facial transplantation. Plast Reconstr Surg 117:876–878, 2006.

Siemionow M, Papay F, Kulahci Y, et al: Coronal-posterior approach for face/scalp flap harvesting in preparation for face transplantation. J Reconstr Microsurg 22:399–405, 2006.

Steinmuller D: The enigma of skin allograft rejection. Transplant Rev 12:42, 1998.

Unal S, Agaoglu G, Zins J, Siemionow M: New surgical approach in facial transplantation extends survival of allograft recipients. Ann Plast Surg 55:297–303, 2005.

Warnke PH: Repair of a human face by allotransplantation. Lancet 368:181–183, 2006.

Working Party on Facial Transplantation of the Royal College of Surgeons of England: Facial Transplantation: Working Party Report. London, UK, Royal College of Surgeons of England, 2003.

PRINCIPLES OF HAND TRANSPLANTATION

Vijay S. Gorantla, MD, PhD; Stefan Schneeberger, MD; and
W.P. Andrew Lee, MD

CHAPTER **113**

1. What is the first comprehensive account of upper extremity transplantation?

Dr. R.H. Hall reported the first detailed description of cadaveric upper limb transplantation in 1944. His protocol discusses the operative technique (vascular anastomoses, osteosynthesis), importance of organ preservation, and complications (including thrombosis and infection) while stressing the need for an experienced team in a well-equipped hospital.

2. Who performed the first hand transplantation under immunosuppression?

In February 1964, at the Clinica Guayaquil in Ecuador, Dr. Roberto Gilbert Elizalde performed a right forearm transplant on a 28-year-old sailor with a blast injury. The donor was a 43-year-old laborer who had died of massive gastrointestinal bleeding in a local hospital. Recipient immunosuppression (primitive by current standards) included total body irradiation, prednisone, and azathioprine. The graft rejected within 21 days, leading to amputation.

3. Which team performed the second hand transplant in history?

A French team, led by Dr. Jean Michel Dubernard, performed the operation in Lyon, France, in September 1998. The patient, 48-year-old Clint Hallam, lost his right hand in a circular saw accident in 1984 while in incarceration for fraud in New Zealand.

4. How many hand transplants have been performed around the world?

At the time of this publication, 53 hands have been transplanted in 38 patients between 1998 and 2009 (Table 113-1). Of these, 39 transplants were performed in 27 recipients in the United States and Europe. In addition, 14 hands were transplanted onto 11 patients in China. See figure 113-2 for updated data on page 736.

5. The longest surviving hand transplant belongs to which patient?

At over 8 years (104 months), the first American patient has the longest surviving transplant.

6. What is the overall graft and patient survival in recipients on immunosuppressive therapy?

To this day, no mortality has been reported, and no hands have been lost in patients who took immunosuppressive drugs. Thus the short- and intermediate-term graft and patient survival is 100%.

7. Explain the terms "induction" therapy and "maintenance" therapy.

Induction therapy refers to intraoperative or perioperative treatment with very potent drugs/antibodies to "switch off" the immune response temporarily (for weeks to months) after transplantation. The goal of induction is to reduce the chance of early acute rejection. *Maintenance* therapy refers to ongoing treatment of the recipient to reduce the risk of graft loss secondary to acute rejection. Maintenance immunosuppression can involve either combination therapy or monotherapy. Combination therapy uses drugs with different mechanisms of action or molecular targets. Lowering of individual drug dosage is possible while maintaining efficacy and limiting overall risk of side effects. Although reducing maintenance immunosuppression to monotherapy has been successful in some organ transplants, it has not yet been possible in hand transplants. Induction and maintenance agents used in hand transplants are listed in Table 113-2.

8. If the "ideal" immunosuppressive drug was available, how would you describe it?

The ideal drug must be selective and specific in action, should synergize optimally with other drugs that are part of the regimen, must be free of toxic adverse reactions, should be easy to administer, and, importantly, should be inexpensive. No such drug exists today.

Table 113-1. Combined American and European Experience with Hand Transplantation

DATE	LOCATION	TRANSPLANT	SEX
09/1998	Lyon, France	Unilateral	Male
01/1999	Louisville, USA	Unilateral	Male
01/2000	Lyon, France	Bilateral	Male
03/2000	Innsbruck, Austria	Bilateral	Male
10/2000	Milan, Italy	Unilateral	Male
02/2001	Louisville, USA	Unilateral	Male
10/2001	Milan, Italy	Unilateral	Male
06/2002	Brussels, Belgium	Unilateral	Male
11/2002	Milan, Italy	Unilateral	Male
02/2003	Innsbruck, Austria	Bilateral	Male
05/2003	Lyon, France	Bilateral	Male
02/2006	Wroclaw, Poland	Unilateral	Male
06/2006	Innsbruck, Austria	Bilateral	Male
11/2006	Louisville, USA	Unilateral	Male
11/2006	Valencia, Spain	Bilateral	Female
02/2007	Lyon, France	Bilateral	Female
11/2007	Valencia, Spain	Bilateral	Male
01/2008	Wroclaw, Poland	Unilateral	Male
06/2008	Louisville, USA	Unilateral	Male
07/2008	Munich, Germany	Bilateral arm	Male
11/2008	Louisville, USA	Unilateral	Male
03/2009	Pittsburgh, USA	Unilateral	Male
03/2009	Paris, France	Bilateral + face	Male
05/2009	Pittsburgh, USA	Bilateral	Male
07/2009	Lyon, France	Bilateral	Male
07/2009	Innsbruck, Austria	Unilateral	Male
09/2009	Wroclaw, Poland	Unilateral arm	Male

9. Define the term "acute" rejection. How is it classified or scored?

Acute rejection is the recipient immune response to the foreign graft chiefly mediated by mature host T cells that occurs within days to months after transplant. T cells undergo activation after interaction with donor antigen-presenting cells, clonally expand and proliferate into cytotoxic and helper T cells, mediate production of antibodies and cytokines by B cells, and finally cause cell death, edema, and graft loss if left untreated. An established scoring system proposed by Schneeberger et al. is based on the distribution of T-lymphocytic infiltrate, necrosis of keratinocytes, and dermal/epidermal changes. The infiltrate is first localized around the dermal vessels (grade I) and then, as acute rejection progresses, spreads to the area between the dermis and epidermis and/or adnexal structures such as hair follicles or sebaceous glands (grade II). When acute rejection is not detected or treated at this "moderate" stage, it evolves into a more "severe" phase with necrosis of single keratinocytes and focal separation of the dermis and epidermis (grade III). With further progression, acute rejection ultimately results in "irreversible" necrosis and loss of epidermis and compromises graft viability (grade IV).

10. Explain the importance of the human leukocyte antigen transplant rejection.

Human leukocyte antigen (HLA) antigens are unique to each person, are coded by genes on chromosome 6, namely, HLA-A and B (class I) and HLA-DR and DQ (class II), and are important in identification of self from non-self. Class I molecules are found on all nucleated cells, whereas Class II molecules are restricted to B cells, macrophages, and antigen-presenting cells. In hand transplants the most potent antigen-presenting cell is the Langerhans cell in the skin. After transplantation, peptide fragments of donor HLA molecules are captured and displayed by these cells in the recipient. Once these peptides are deemed foreign, a cascade of immune events results in infiltration of the graft by T cells, B cells, and macrophages, culminating in acute rejection.

Table 113-2. Immunosuppression in Hand Transplantation

DRUG/AGENT	CATEGORY	DESCRIPTION	MECHANISM OF ACTION	ADVERSE EFFECTS/TOXICITY
Antithymocyte globulin	Induction	Polyclonal IgG from horses or rabbits immunized with human thymocytes	Binds to surface of T cells, depleting them from both circulating and lymphoid compartments	Anaphylaxis, serum sickness, cytokine release syndrome (fever, chills, flushing, hypotension), thrombocytopenia, leukopenia, phlebitis, nephritis
OKT3 (muromonab-CD3)	Induction	Mouse monoclonal antibody against human CD3 glycoprotein associated with the T-cell receptor	Binds to CD3 component of T-cell receptor. Leads to activation and cytokine release followed by depletion of T cells	Severe cytokine release syndrome, hypotension, encephalopathy, nephropathy, pulmonary edema, central nervous system effects, thrombosis leading to graft failure
Basiliximab	Induction	Chimeric monoclonal antibody against IL-2 receptor alpha chain (CD25)	Binds and blocks the CD25 antigen on activated T cells. Inhibits IL-2 activation of T cells and depletes T cells	Side effects very uncommon. Rarely hypersensitivity reactions. Two doses needed for effect
Alemtuzumab (campath 1H)	Induction	Humanized monoclonal antibody against CD52 antigen on B cells, T cells, monocytes, macrophages, natural killer cells	Globally binds to all CD52-bearing cells causing cell lysis and profound and prolonged depletion	Mild variant of cytokine release syndrome, neutropenia, anemia, pancytopenia, autoimmune thrombocytopenia, thyroid disease
Methylprednisolone	Induction	Endogenous corticosteroid analog	Form steroid receptor complexes at subcellular level that bind to DNA and affect gene expression and protein synthesis that suppress cytokine transduction and production	Hypertension, diabetes, weight gain, osteoporosis, peptic ulceration, gastrointestinal bleeding, opportunistic infections, avascular necrosis, cataracts, poor wound healing among a myriad range of side effects
Tacrolimus		Macrolide antibiotic derived from *Streptomyces tsukubaensis*. Is 100 times more potent than cyclosporine	Binds to immunophilin ligands within T cells (FKBP-12, -12, -25, -52). Binding to FKBP-12 suppresses T cell activation via calcineurin inhibition	Similar risk profile as cyclosporine but less severity. Hypertension, hypercholesterolemia, skin changes, hirsutism. Higher risk of posttransplant diabetes and neurologic toxicity
Mycophenolate mofetil	Maintenance	Ester of mycophenolic acid that is a reversible noncompetitive inhibitor of IMPDH	Blocks IMPDH enzyme that is critical to purine synthesis in T and B cells. Selectively blocks T-cell proliferation and B-cell synthesis of antibody	Gastrointestinal symptoms (diarrhea, esophagitis, gastritis), neutropenia, mild anemia, leukopenia, opportunistic infections
Sirolimus (rapamycin)	Maintenance	Macrolide antibiotic derived from *Streptomyces hygroscopicus*	Binds to FKBP-12 like tacrolimus but does not inhibit calcineurin. Affects G1 phase of cell cycle acting on a separate cell target called target of rapamycin (TOR), thereby inhibiting T-cell proliferation	Hypercholesteremia, delayed wound healing, lymphoceles, pneumonitis, interstitial lung disease, thrombocytopenia. Can cause increased toxicity of other calcineurin inhibitors
Prednisone	Maintenance	See Methylprednisolone		

FKBP-12, FK binding protein-12; *Ig*, immunoglobulin; *IL-2*, interleukin-2; *IMPDH*, inosine monophosphate dehydrogenase enzyme.

11. Why is prior "sensitization" of recipients to donor HLA antigens a problem in hand transplantation?

In certain circumstances such as pregnancy, repeated blood transfusions, implantable devices, and prior transplantation, people can encounter HLA molecules from "foreign" donors. This could "sensitize" them and stimulate production of anti-HLA antibodies. If such a person is chosen as a recipient for hand transplant, these circulating antibodies can result in increased risk of acute rejection and decreased overall graft survival.

12. How is presence of anti-HLA antibodies measured, and what is their significance?

Recipient serum is tested for reactivity against a pool of lymphocytes from control donors with known HLA markers. The amount of reactivity is graded as a percentage called the *panel reactive antibody* (PRA), and correlates with a recipient's risk of positive reactivity with donors from the normal population who may serve as potential donors of the hand. A person's PRA can range anywhere from 0% to 99%. To put it simply, the "percent" PRA represents the percent of the U.S. population that the anti-human antibody in the recipient blood is reactive against. For example, if the recipient has a PRA of 25%, then the antibodies in his/her blood would bind to the tissue types of 25% of the people in the population. The higher the PRA, the greater the chances of a waitlisted recipient to reject a prospective donor graft. Plasmapheresis and immunoadsorption are two methods for lowering circulating HLA antibodies and consequently PRA levels.

13. Describe the phenomenon of "chronic" rejection.

Chronic rejection (CR) is an immune phenomenon characterized by vasculopathy (intimal hyperplasia, perivasculitis obliterative endarteritis of graft vessels), fibrosis, and atrophy of graft with progressive loss of function that culminates in graft loss. The pathogenesis of CR is poorly defined. The vasculopathy may reflect injury of blood vessels by antibody and/or cell-mediated mechanisms that leads to chronic ischemia. The fibrosis may be mediated by a low-grade, persistent delayed-type hypersensitivity response in which activated macrophages secrete mesenchymal cell growth factors such as transforming growth factor beta (TGF-β). Emerging data from experimental limb transplant models indicate that the risk of CR is exacerbated by increased acute rejection episodes, that macrophages play an important role in CR and that vasculopathy occurs later in the process.

14. What are some immunologic and nonimmunologic factors that play a role in the etiopathogenesis of CR?

Based on insights gained in solid organ transplants, some of the immunologic factors implicated in CR include the frequency, severity, and time of onset of acute rejection; greater HLA mismatch; recipient PRA status; racial mismatch between donor and recipient (e.g., Caucasian donor into non-Caucasian recipient); sex mismatching (male donor to female recipient); and cytomegalovirus (CMV) sero-mismatch (CMV[positive] donor to CMV[negative] recipient). Nonimmunologic factors implicated in CR include older donor age, donor atherosclerosis, cadaver donor, prolonged cold ischemia, and conventional risk factors for atherosclerosis in the recipient (e.g., hypertension, diabetes, hyperlipidemia, obesity).

15. Have any hand transplants been lost to rejection?

Confirmed (published/presented) reports indicate that two hands have been amputated electively due to acute rejection (the first French patient and the first Chinese patient, both unilateral). In the rest of the American and European experience, there have been no reports of CR. It has been reported that most patients in China could not afford medications after the first year and that some transplants were lost to follow-up. Thus many more patients could have succumbed to acute rejection due to lack of medications. The question of whether any of these patients suffered from CR remains to be confirmed. The fourth hand transplant recipient in the United States, underwent amputation of his unilateral transplant 9 months after surgery due to graft ischemia. The underlying pathogenesis has been hypothesized to be CR but remains to be conclusively confirmed.

16. How is the term "chimerism" defined? What is the difference between microchimerism and macrochimerism?

Chimerism is defined as the harmonious coexistence of hematopoietic cells derived from a genetically disparate donor in the recipient. *Microchimerism* occurs due to migration of "passenger" leukocytes after transplantation of solid organs and cellular allografts. Donor cells persist at low levels ($\leq$1 donor cell per 10^4 or 10^5 recipient cells), frequently detectable by molecular techniques such as polymerase chain reaction (PCR) assay. *Macrochimerism* usually occurs when donor bone marrow transplantation is performed in a host that is conditioned by antibodies or irradiation. In macrochimerism, donor cells are detectable by flow cytometry at levels of 1% to 100%. In small and large animal models, microchimerism and macrochimerism have been shown to induce "tolerance" to allografts. Tolerance is graft acceptance without the need for extraneous immunosuppression. However, confirming the association of chimerism with tolerance is clinically difficult. Rejection can occur in the presence of microchimerism or macrochimerism, and persisting chimerism does not necessarily correlate with clinical tolerance or the ability to wean from or reduce immunosuppressive drugs. Conversely, indefinite solid organ transplant survival has been reported in patients who have been weaned completely off immunosuppression despite the absence of chimerism.

17. Have any hand transplant recipients thus far shown evidence of chimerism? What about graft-versus-host disease?

Transient microchimerism has been reported in a few cases, but sustained presence of donor-derived cells has not been confirmed. Graft-versus-host disease (GVHD) is a condition mediated by mature donor T cells that attack the recipient who usually is immunosuppressed or immunocompromised. In bone marrow transplants, recipients are conditioned (myeloablated) with radiation or cytotoxic chemotherapy. In such a situation, GVHD can be lethal. In hand transplants, the radius and ulna contain bone marrow that could potentially cause GVHD depending on how the recipient is treated with drugs/depleting antibodies. However, no GVHD has been observed in any patient.

18. List the specific criteria that are used to select donors and recipients for hand transplantation.

As of today, there are no standard/established criteria for selection of donors/recipients in hand transplantation. The following criteria are broad guidelines and must be adapted according to institutional goals and regulations. Important donor requirements are family consent for limb donation, stable donor (does not require excessive vasopressors to maintain blood pressure), age between 18 to 55 years, limb matched for size with recipient, same blood type as recipient, negative cross-match, and, importantly, accurate matching of gender, skin tone, and race. Recipients may be male or female and of any race, color, or ethnicity. Amputation may be recent (acute injury) or remote (patient may have undergone rehabilitation with prostheses). Important requirements are age between 18 and 65 years (recipients younger than 18 years are excluded due to issues of informed consent and the potentially increased risk of lymphoproliferative disorder), no serious coexisting medical (coronary artery disease, diabetes) or psychosocial problems (including alcoholism, drug abuse), no history of malignancy (for 10 years) or human immunodeficiency virus (at transplant), negative cross-match with donor, negative pregnancy test in female recipient of child-bearing potential, and consent to use reliable contraception for at least 1 year following transplantation.

19. What is the International Registry of Hand and Composite Tissue Transplantation?

The International Registry of Hand and Composite Tissue Transplantation (IRHCTT) (www.handregistry.com) was established in 2002 to serve as an up-to-date collection of scientific data contributed by individual centers performing hand or composite tissue transplants. Insights gained from data sharing between centers could help teams to modify treatment strategies and improve allograft outcomes.

20. Describe the effects of tacrolimus on nerve regeneration.

Tacrolimus has been shown to promote nerve regeneration (by its effects on neuroimmunophilin ligands such as FKBP-52, hsp-90, and p23) in animal models after nerve injury (crush/transection). Such an effect has not yet been confirmed in human hand transplant recipients taking this drug.

21. In the United States, retrieval of donor organs/tissues is managed and controlled by OPOs. What does this acronym refer to?

"OPO" refers to organ procurement organization. There are approximately 60 of these nonprofit agencies in the United States. OPOs approach families to seek donation, evaluate potential donors for suitability, and coordinate recovery, preservation, and transportation of organs/tissues.

22. Describe the phenomenon of "brain plasticity" that has been observed after hand transplantation.

Following amputation, the areas of the premotor cortex that represent the lost structures (on the homunculus) are reassigned to areas controlling the residual components of the limb. However, after a hand transplant (as confirmed by functional magnetic resonance imaging [fMRI]), these areas of the brain can reestablish their original functions, and the signals from the new hand go back to the cortical regions that controlled the original hand. Such neural reintegration of the transplanted limb into the premotor cortex is called "cortical reorganization" or "plasticity" of the brain.

23. How is hand transplantation different from replantation? What distinguishes it from solid organ transplants?

The differences are listed in Tables 113-3 and 113-4.

24. Briefly describe the salient aspects of functional rehabilitation and assessment after hand transplantation.

Hand transplant rehabilitation is similar to that after replantation. Early mobilization (within 24 to 48 hours) is important to reduce edema and stiffness. A dynamic crane extension outrigger splint that mimics intrinsic function of the hand

Table 113-3. Hand Transplantation versus Hand Replantation

	HAND TRANSPLANTATION	HAND REPLANTATION
Surgery	Planned and performed electively	Emergency surgery
Donor tissues	Intact	Missing, avulsed, crushed, or contaminated
Modification of donor graft	Tailored to match specific requirements	Limited by type of injury
Recipient site	May be scarred with muscle contracture and reduced tendon excursion	Missing, avulsed, crushed, or contaminated
Warm ischemia time	Minutes	Minutes to hours
Immunosuppression	Long-term antirejection drugs needed	Not necessary

From Weinzweig N, Weinzweig J: The Mutilated Hand. Philadelphia, Mosby, 2005.

Table 113-4. Hand Transplantation versus Organ Transplantation

	HAND TRANSPLANTATION	ORGAN TRANSPLANTATION
Visual monitoring of rejection	Possible	Not possible
Biopsy from site of ongoing rejection	Possible	Not always possible
Topical drug therapy	Possible	Not possible
Rejection episodes affect rate of functional return	No	Yes
Functional return after transplantation	Delayed (motor and sensory return)	Immediate (physiologic function)
Premotor cortical reorganization after transplantation	Yes	Not applicable
Nonimmunosuppressive role of tacrolimus	Nerve regeneration may be improved	None
Posttransplant donor microchimerism	Not been reported	Reported
Graft-versus-host disease	Not been reported in any cases to date (despite bone marrow in limb)	Reported to occur (small bowel and liver transplants)
Human leukocyte antigen matching	Difficult due to small donor pool, effects of human leukocyte antigen mismatch on long-term graft survival unknown	Facilitated by larger donor pool, inverse correlation between human leukocyte antigen mismatch and graft survival
Exit strategy in event of complications	Stop immunosuppression and amputation (less morbidity and mortality)	Retransplantation (greater morbidity and mortality)

From Weinzweig N, Weinzweig J: The Mutilated Hand. Philadelphia, Mosby, 2005.

(Fig. 113-1) can be used to prevent an intrinsic-minus hand/clawing. Promoting early protective active motion and blocking metacarpophalangeal joint extension help achieve a hand with an intrinsic-plus posture and coordinated grasping. Different tests/instruments/scoring systems have been used by teams to assess sensory and motor return after transplantation. To ensure easy comparison of data among programs, the IRHCTT has proposed a classification called the Hand Transplant Score System (HTSS) to measure function. The HTSS measures six parameters that score for a total of 100 points: appearance 15 points; sensation 20 points; motor function 20 points; psychosocial outcome 15 points; activities of daily living and profession 15 points; and patient satisfaction and quality of life 15 points. Outcomes are graded as poor (0 to 30 points), fair (31 to 60 points), good (61 to 80 points), and excellent (81 to 100 points).

25. **What are the important ethical considerations in undertaking hand transplantation?**
Some of the key ethical considerations involve the following: (1) stringent compliance with human studies regulations and institutional review board approval; (2) thorough informed consent of recipients clarifying risks and benefits; (3) selection of appropriate recipients and donors (including thorough psychiatric screening of recipients to determine suitability for participation, personality organization, and compliance ability); and (4) scholarship, transparency/scientific accuracy, and data sharing. For teams wishing to attempt hand transplantation, it is important to (1) ensure open display and public awareness for this innovative surgery and (2) evaluate the field strength (skill and experience of the team) and ethical climate of the institution to determine suitability to perform the procedure.

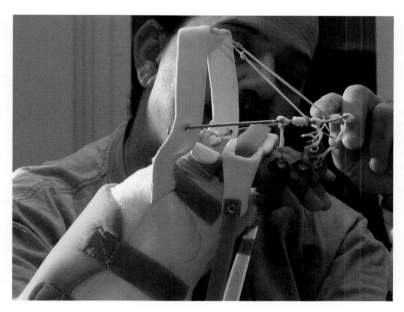

Figure 113-1. Crane outrigger splint.

26. Can you elucidate the psychiatric evaluations that are necessary during recipient screening or follow-up?

A thorough psychiatric workup is critical to recipient selection and plays an equally important role in the follow-up of patients. Psychosocial testing assesses (1) coping/adjustment to hand loss; (2) emotional and cognitive preparedness for transplant; (3) motivation for hand transplant (including history of prosthetic use); (4) anticipated comfort with a cadaver hand; (5) level of realistic expectations regarding posttransplant outcomes; (6) body image adaptation; (7) personality organization and risk of regression; and (8) social support system, family structure, financial situation, and history of medication compliance/substance abuse.

27. What complications have been noted in hand transplant recipients to date?

Surgical complications that were successfully treated included localized skin necrosis, arterial thrombosis, and formation of multiple arteriovenous fistulas. Immunosuppressive drug-related side effects included opportunistic infections (cytomegalovirus reactivation, *Clostridium difficile* enteritis, *Herpes simplex* blisters, cutaneous mycosis, and staphylococcal osteomyelitis), metabolic complications (diabetes mellitus, increased creatinine values, Cushing's syndrome, bilateral avascular necrosis of hips). Most of these complications were treatable. No malignancies or life-threatening conditions have been reported.

28. What is one very special consideration in hand transplantation that may have implications on recipient identity?

Apart from its ethical and psychological implications, hand transplantation brings with it significant social and identity issues. The problem of dual fingerprints is unique to patients undergoing hand transplantation. It raises special concerns for de-identifying donor information and potential infringement of donor privacy as it necessitates criminal background checks (felony, child abuse, etc.) on the donor. Hand transplant teams must inform the appropriate security and intelligence agencies to update the requisite databases with the new fingerprint status of recipients to avoid potential security/identity problems following surgery.

29. How can hand transplantation become a widespread clinically acceptable reconstructive option for upper extremity limb loss?

Early trials with hand transplantation have confirmed the technical feasibility of this procedure and provided key insights into acute rejection and the problems associated with long-term immunosuppression and CR. Widespread application of this procedure is possible only if these risks are reduced. Research into safe and efficacious immunomodulatory protocols that allow minimization or weaning of drug treatment and strategies to diagnose and prevent CR are crucial steps in achieving this goal.

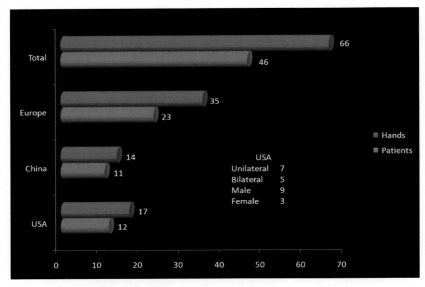

Figure 113-2. Data from hand transplants performed around the world.

BIBLIOGRAPHY

Anonymous: Historic cadaver-to-man hand transplant. Med World News 5:60, 1964.

Giraux P, Sirigu A, Schneider F, Dubernard JM: Cortical reorganization in motor cortex after graft of both hands. Nat Neurosci 4:691–692, 2001.

Gorantla VS, Barker JH, Jones JW Jr, Prabhune K, Maldonado C, Granger DK: Immunosuppressive agents in transplantation: Mechanisms of action and current anti-rejection strategies. Microsurgery 20:420–429, 2000.

Granger DK, Briedenbach WC, Pidwell DJ, Jones JW, Baxter-Lowe LA, Kaufman CL: Lack of donor hyporesponsiveness and donor chimerism after clinical transplantation of the hand. Transplantation 74:1624–1630, 2004.

Hall RH: Whole upper extremity transplant for human being: General plans of procedure and operative technique. Ann Surg 120:12, 1944.

Jones JW, Gruber SA, Barker JH, et al: Successful hand transplantation. One-year follow-up. Louisville Hand Transplant Team. N Engl J Med 343:468, 2000.

Klapheke MM, Marcell C, Taliaferro G, Creamer B: Psychiatric assessment of candidates for hand transplantation. Microsurgery 20: 453–457, 2000.

Lanzetta M, Petruzzo P, Dubernard JM, et al: Second report (1998–2006) of the International Registry of Hand and Composite Tissue Transplantation. Transplant Immunol 18:1–6, 2007.

Monaco AP: Chimerism in organ transplantation: Conflicting experiments and clinical observations. Transplantation 75(9 Suppl):13S–16S, 2003.

Scheker LR, Chesher SP, Netscher DT, Julliard KN, O'Neill WL: Functional results of dynamic splinting after transmetacarpal, wrist, and distal forearm replantation. J Hand Surg [Br] 20:584–590, 1995.

Schneeberger S, Kreczy A, Brandacher G, Steurer W, Margreiter R: Steroid- and ATG-resistant rejection after double forearm transplantation responds to Campath-1H. Am J Transplant 4:1372–1374, 2004.

Tobin GR, Breidenbach WC, Klapheke MM, Bentley FR, Pidwell DJ, Simmons PD: Ethical considerations in the early composite tissue allograft experience: A review of the Louisville Ethics Program. Transplant Proc 37:1392–1395, 2005.

THE HAND AND UPPER EXTREMITY

The Hand of God. Auguste Rodin, 1897–1989. Marble. Museé Rodin, Paris. © 1998 Museé Rodin.

ANATOMY OF THE HAND

Lee E. Edstrom, MD

CHAPTER 114

1. What is the thickest skin in the hand?

The palmar skin has the thickest epidermis due to the stratum corneum, but the dermis is just as thick on the dorsum as the palm.

2. Why are most significant hand burns on the dorsum?

The thick stratum corneum protects the palmar dermis. In addition, the dorsal skin tends to be directed toward the flames in a burn situation. If the fist is closed, the palmar skin is further protected.

3. Why can we get away with single layer closure in the palm?

The thick stratum corneum hides the ingrowth of epithelium down the suture into the dermis, so sutures can be left in place for over a week without leaving stitch marks.

4. Does the thick stratum corneum affect the technique of skin closure in any other way?

The thick stratum corneum exaggerates the problems caused by skin edge overlap; thus mattress stitches often are preferred to ensure skin edge eversion.

5. How is the palmar skin so firmly fixed in place?

The palmar fascia is a unique structure, fixed proximally and distally, from side to side, and to the underlying metacarpals by its vertical fibers. The palmar skin is closely attached to the palmar fascia by a tight network of its own vertical fibers. Hence, edema cannot collect as easily on the palmar side of the hand.

6. Name the three planes of the palmar fascia.

The palmar fascia is aligned in longitudinal, vertical, and transverse components.

7. Which of the three palmar fascia planes is never involved in Dupuytren's disease?

The transverse fibers, located over the metacarpophalangeal joints, are never involved in Dupuytren's disease.

8. Does the palmar fascia extend into the fingers?

Yes. The longitudinal fibers of the palmar fascia extend into the fingers and in the web spaces; the natatory ligaments are part of the palmar fascia. In the proximal and middle phalanges, however, Cleland's (dorsal) and Grayson's (volar) ligaments are the stabilizing structures. On the sides of the fingers, dorsal and palmar to the neurovascular bundles, they are attached to the phalanges along the ridge giving rise to the fibroosseous tunnel. In the distal phalanx, vertical fibers are attached directly to the underlying distal phalanx and form a honeycomb series of compartments, similar to that in the palm between the skin and palmar fascia (Fig. 114-1).

9. What is the "assembly line"?

The volar lateral ridges of the proximal phalanx, in which nestle the flexor tendons and which give attachment to the fibroosseous tunnel, the oblique retinacular ligament, and Grayson's and Cleland's ligaments, are the so-called "assembly lines."

10. What are the "checkrein ligaments"?

In flexion contracture of the proximal interphalangeal (PIP) joint, the proximal sliding volar plate becomes attached to the firm assembly line structures by fibrous adhesions called the "checkrein ligaments," which prevent the volar plate from sliding back distally.

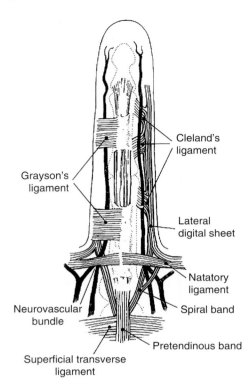

Grayson's ligament

Cleland's ligament

Lateral digital sheet

Natatory ligament

Spiral band

Neurovascular bundle

Pretendinous band

Superficial transverse ligament

Figure 114-1. The digital fascia—continuation of the palmar fascia into the fingers—helps anchor the axial plane skin. It consists primarily of Grayson's ligaments and Cleland's ligaments, palmar and dorsal to the neurovascular bundles, respectively. (From Chang J, Valero-Ceuvas F, Hentz VR, Chase RA: Anatomy and biomechanics of the hand. In Mathes SJ, Hentz VR [eds]: Plastic Surgery, 2nd ed., Vol VII, The Hand and Upper Limb, Part 1. Philadelphia, Elsevier, 2006, p 17.)

11. Name two unique types of infection on the palmar side of the hand that are due to the firm fixation of the skin to underlying structures.

A *collar-button abscess* in the palm starts as a tiny infection between the palmar skin and the palmar fascia. It then erodes through the palmar fascia into the underlying loose space, forming a dumbbell- or collar button-shaped abscess, which may be inadequately drained if the anatomy is not appreciated.

A *felon* in the distal phalanx starts in the same way as the collar-button abscess, but it is inhibited from side to side spread by the tight network of vertical fibers attaching the skin to the distal phalanx. Spread occurs by erosion through the walls formed by the vertical fibers, adding to the abscess compartment by compartment.

12. Name another closed compartment in the hand in which bacterial infections can develop.

The synovial sheaths within the fibroosseous tunnels of each finger are relatively closed systems that can contain closed space infections that can expand and spread quickly ("purulent tenosynovitis").

13. What are the other closed spaces associated with infections?

The thenar and midpalmar bursae and the radial and ulnar bursae all are potential spaces in which infection can develop.

14. How can these compartments communicate with each other with the spread of an infection?

The synovial sheaths of the ulnar fingers communicate with the ulnar bursa, and the sheaths of the index finger and thumb communicate with the radial bursa and can communicate in the midpalmar and thenar spaces (bursae), respectively.

15. Can the ulnar- and radial-sided synovial systems communicate?

Each is capable of draining into the space over the pronator quadratus *(Parona's space)*, producing a pan-palmar infection called a "horseshoe abscess."

16. How does the unique anatomy of the fingertip shape the development of a paronychia?

A paronychia is an infection of the nail fold. It seldom exists without the presence of a nail, which is first a foreign-body irritant and then the roof of the abscess.

17. Can a felon spread around the distal phalanx and become a paronychia? Can a paronychia spread around the nail plate into the palmar pulp and become a felon?

Both events are highly unlikely because of the anatomy of the fingertip. The paronychia spreads around the nail plate and may lift the entire nail plate off the bed but ultimately drains dorsally. The felon spreads on the palmar side, ultimately breaking through the skin. It may spread proximally into the soft tissue of the middle phalanx—or even into the bone and distal interphalangeal (DIP) joint—but not dorsally to the nail fold.

18. Which tissues contribute to growth of the nail plate?

The entire nail bed, including the overlying eponychial fold, contributes material to the developing and growing nail. The proximal nail bed *(germinal matrix)* forms the early developing nail, the overlying fold contributes the smooth surface, and the distal bed *(sterile matrix)* continues to add bulk so that the nail plate does not become too thin from wear.

19. What is the lunula?

The white arc just distal to the eponychium, called the *lunula,* is a result of persistence of nuclei in the cells of the germinal matrix as they flow distally, creating the nail. As the nuclei disintegrate distal to the lunula, the nail becomes transparent.

20. What is the safe position for splinting the hand?

It is useful to think of joints as having certain positions that tend to produce stiffness and other positions that can be maintained for long periods without developing stiffness. The metacarpophalangeal (MP) and interphalangeal (IP) joints are good examples of this concept. The MP joints recover well from flexion, and the IP joints recover well from extension. When splinting the hand, the MP joints should be placed in flexion (70° to 90°), and the IP joints should be maintained in extension. The thumb should be abducted and the wrist maintained in mild extension. This is the position from which it is easiest to regain mobility of the joints after prolonged immobilization.

21. Why is flexion the safe position for the MP joint?

The MP joint is characterized by variable tightness of the collateral ligaments, depending on the position of the joint, because of the unique shape of the metacarpal head and the origin of the collateral ligaments dorsal to the axis of rotation of the joint. The head is ovoid in the sagittal plane (creating a *cam effect*) and possesses a palmar flare in the transverse plane, which requires the collateral ligaments to span a greater distance in flexion than extension. Therefore the collateral ligaments are stretched tight in flexion but are lax in extension. Because ligaments tend to shorten when maintained in a lax position, prolonged extension leads to shortening of the collateral ligaments, rendering them unable to accommodate the joint in flexion and thus producing an extension contracture (Fig. 114-2).

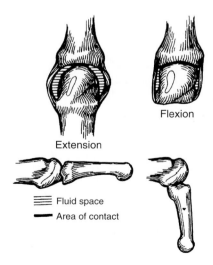

Flexion

Extension

≡ Fluid space
— Area of contact

Figure 114-2. Anatomy of the metacarpophalangeal joint. In extension the collateral ligaments are loose; the joint is relatively unstable and the ligaments are at risk for shortening. In flexion the collateral ligaments are tight secondary to a cam effect; the joint is stable and the ligaments are protected. (From Watson HK, Weinzweig J: Stiff joints. In Green DP [ed]: Operative Hand Surgery, 4th ed. New York, Churchill Livingstone, 1999.)

22. If flexion is the safe position for the MP joint, what do you do if you have to splint the joint in extension, as for extensor tendon repairs or palmar fascia excision for Dupuytren's disease?

The MP joints can tolerate a few weeks of extension, especially in younger patients without widespread injury. Older patients can tolerate up to 4 weeks of extension following isolated injuries or surgical procedures (e.g., extensor tendon repair) but only 2 or 2.5 weeks following extensive Dupuytren's surgery. For burn injuries with extensive edema, MP joints should be protected and maintained in flexion from the beginning.

23. Why is extension the safe position for the IP joints?

The collateral ligaments of the IP joints tend to have the same tightness in flexion and extension and thus are not as important in consideration of safe splinting. Two other points are important instead: (1) the extensor mechanism in the region of the PIP joint and (2) the volar plates. The volar plate overlies the cartilaginous surface of the phalangeal condyles in extension but in flexion slides proximal to the condyles, where it readily becomes adherent to the filmy soft tissue between the tendon sheath and periosteum. Maintenance of this position produces a flexion contracture. The other consideration is that the extensor mechanism is highly stable in extension but is under stress in flexion. This problem is particularly significant when the PIP joint is injured, as in a burn injury. Inflammation may cause attenuation of the delicate extensor mechanism, resulting in disruption of the transverse retinacular ligaments when the joint is stressed in flexion. The lateral bands then slip volarly, creating a boutonnière deformity.

24. The IP joint can be thought of as a box, with the articular surfaces of the phalanges forming the proximal and distal ends. What forms the other sides?

The volar plate forms the bottom and the collateral ligaments the sides. The collateral ligaments extend from their points of origin into a broad, fan-shaped insertion into the phalanx distally and the sides of the volar plate volarly. The volar portion of the collateral ligament is referred to as the *accessory collateral ligament*. The top or lid of the box is formed by the extensor mechanism, which contributes little to the structural stability of the joint (Fig. 114-3).

25. Which is the most mobile carpometacarpal joint?

The carpometacarpal (CMC) joint of the thumb is a saddle joint with motion in three axes, giving the thumb unique mobility.

26. Which are the least mobile CMC joints?

The second and third metacarpals are bound firmly to the trapezoid and capitate, forming a stable structure known as the "fixed unit of the hand." Thus the second and third CMC joints are the least mobile.

27. What is the last muscle innervated by the ulnar nerve as it courses through the palm?

The first dorsal interosseus is the last muscle to receive motor fibers from the ulnar nerve after it passes through the adductor of the thumb, which is next to last.

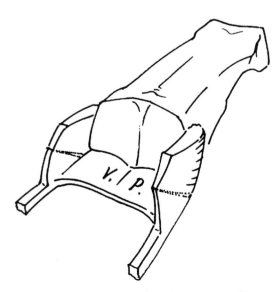

Figure 114-3. Anatomy of the interphalangeal joint. The three-dimensional ligament–box complex provides strength with minimal bulk. At least two sides of this box must be disrupted for displacement of the joint to occur. (From Dray GJ, Eaton RG: Dislocations and ligament injuries in the digits. In Green DP [ed]: Operative Hand Surgery, 3rd ed. New York, Churchill Livingstone, 1993, p 768.)

28. What major peripheral nerve is responsible for extension of the thumb IP joint?

The *median nerve* innervates the radial side of the thenar eminence, which is responsible for MP joint flexion and IP joint extension from the radial side. The *ulnar nerve* innervates the adductor pollicis and ulnar head of the short flexor, which is responsible for the same actions from the ulnar side. The *radial nerve* innervates the extensor pollicis longus (EPL), which is responsible for central IP joint extension. Thus all three major peripheral nerves contribute to extension of the thumb IP joint.

29. How can you test for function of the EPL?

The EPL has the unique function of lifting the thumb dorsal to the plane of the palm. Ask the patient to place the palm on the table and lift up the thumb.

30. There is much crossover of sensory innervation in the hand. Where do the median, ulnar, and radial sensory nerves supply sensibility with the least chance of crossover from neighboring territories?

The median nerve is alone on the index tip, the ulnar nerve on the little finger tip, and the radial nerve over the dorsal surface of the first web space.

31. Where is the one place on the hand where all three sensory nerves may be expected to provide maximal crossover innervation?

On the dorsal surface of the middle phalanx of the ring finger, the digital nerves from median and ulnar nerves course dorsally, whereas the radial nerve sensory branch courses distally, along with the ulnar nerve dorsal sensory branch on the ulnar side.

32. What three vascular arches provide anastomotic connections between the radial and ulnar blood supplies?

The superficial palmar arch courses palmar to the flexor tendons, gives off the digital vessels, and is a direct continuation of the ulnar artery. The deep palmar arch, which is deep (dorsal) to the flexor tendons, gives off the volar metacarpal arteries and is a direct continuation of the radial artery after the takeoff of the princeps pollicis. The dorsal carpal arch travels dorsally over the proximal carpal row, linking the radial and ulnar systems dorsally and giving off the dorsal metacarpal arteries.

33. Despite proper tourniquet application, the wound begins to bleed during repair of a spaghetti wrist. Why?

Blood is shunted down to the hand via nutrient vessels in the humerus. This process may take an hour or even longer. The ascending branch of the humeral circumflex artery enters the bone in the bicipital groove, perfuses the bone through the medullary cavity with connections to the periosteal vessels, and may exit inferiorly at the elbow. Control under these circumstances may be obtained by wrapping an Esmarch or Ace bandage around the elbow at moderate pressure.

34. How can you test the integrity of the vascular anastomotic connections between the two sides of the hand?

Allen's test is performed by occluding both radial and ulnar arteries at the wrist, emptying the hand of blood by repeatedly making a fist, and releasing one of the arteries. The hand should fill with blood immediately, with no significant delay on the side still occluded.

35. What are the boundaries of the carpal tunnel?

The transverse carpal ligament (TCL), in addition to providing a pulley mechanism for the flexor tendons, spans the volar aspect of the proximal palm to form the roof of the carpal tunnel. The TCL courses from the scaphoid tubercle and the crest of the trapezium on the radial side to the pisiform and hamate on the ulnar side.

36. How many structures traverse the carpal tunnel?

Ten. Nine flexor tendons (four flexor digitorum superficialis [FDS] tendons, four flexor digitorum profundus [FDP] tendons, flexor pollicis longus [FPL]) and the median nerve pass through the carpal tunnel.

37. What are the boundaries of Guyon's canal?

The TCL forms the floor, the volar carpal ligament (VCL) the roof, and the pisiform the ulnar wall of the canal of Guyon.

38. Is the primary blood supply of the scaphoid distal or proximal?

The distal pole of the scaphoid is supplied independently by dorsal and palmar branches of the radial artery, leaving the proximal pole deficient and susceptible to devascularization with trauma.

39. What are the six dorsal extensor compartments of the wrist?

The six well-defined tunnels through which the extrinsic extensor tendons pass are numbered from radial to ulnar. The first compartment contains the abductor pollicis longus (APL) and extensor pollicis brevis (EPB) and is located on the surface of the radial styloid. Both the APL and EPB may contain several slips; tenosynovitis in this compartment is known as de Quervain's disease. The second compartment contains the two radial extensors of the wrist (extensor carpi radialis longus [ECRL], extensor carpi radialis brevis [ECRB]), which course through the floor of the anatomic snuffbox on the way to their insertions on the bases of the second and third metacarpals, respectively. Lister's tubercle separates the second compartment from the third compartment, which contains the EPL. The fourth compartment contains the tendons of the extensor digiti communis (EDC) and the extensor indicis proprius (EIP), whereas the fifth compartment contains the extensor digiti quinti (EDQ). The sixth dorsal compartment is located on the head of the ulna and contains the extensor carpi ulnaris (ECU) (Fig. 114-4).

40. Which extrinsic tendons insert into carpal bones?

Except for the flexor carpi ulnaris on the pisiform, there are no extrinsic tendinous insertions into the carpal bones.

41. When is the ECU not primarily an extensor of the wrist?

The sixth dorsal compartment is fixed on the ulnar head. When the radius pivots around the ulnar head in pronation and supination, the ECU assumes different positions relative to the wrist. In full pronation it is ulnar to the wrist and thus primarily an ulnar deviator.

42. Name the four insertions of the extrinsic extensor tendon.

The extrinsic extensor tendon inserts into (1) the base of the proximal phalanx, (2) the base of the middle phalanx, (3) the base of the distal phalanx (via the slips to the lateral bands; see Question 59), and (4) the transverse metacarpal ligament and volar plate.

43. How do you identify the proprius tendons of the index and little fingers?

The proprius tendons (extensor digiti minimi [EDM], EIP) usually lie on the ulnar side of the communis tendon (EDC) and allow independent extension of the little and index fingers, respectively. However, significant variability of the extensor tendons to the index and little fingers, including radial EIP and EDM tendons and supernumerary tendons, has been reported in up to 19% of specimens in anatomic studies.

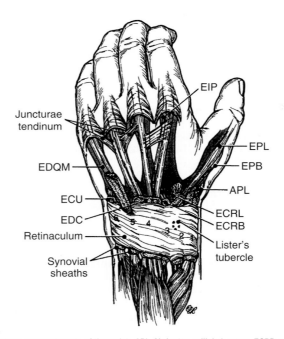

Figure 114-4. The six dorsal extensor compartments of the wrist. *APL,* Abductor pollicis longus; *ECRB,* extensor carpi radialis brevis; *ECRL,* extensor carpi radialis longus; *ECU,* extensor carpi ulnaris; *EDC,* extensor digiti communis; *EDQM,* extensor digiti quinti minimi; *EIP,* extensor indicis proprius; *EPB,* extensor pollicis brevis; *EPL,* extensor pollicis longus. (From Doyle JR: Extensor tendons: Acute injuries. In Green DP [ed]: Operative Hand Surgery, 3rd ed. New York, Churchill Livingstone, 1993, p 1927.)

44. What is the anatomic snuffbox?

It is the hollow on the radial side of the wrist bordered by the contents of the first dorsal compartment on the palmar side, the EPL dorsally, the radial styloid proximally, and the base of the thumb metacarpal distally. The radial artery courses through the snuffbox on its way to the dorsal first web space; in the depths of the snuffbox is the scaphoid. Injury to the scaphoid produces tenderness in the snuffbox.

45. What is the retinacular system of the extensor mechanism?

The retinacular system of the extensor mechanism stabilizes the components of the extensor mechanism. The sagittal bands stabilize the central tendon over the metacarpal head; the transverse retinacular ligaments stabilize the lateral bands and central slip over the PIP joint region; and the triangular ligament stabilizes the lateral bands over the middle phalanx (Fig. 114-5).

46. How do the lumbricals assist in IP joint extension?

The lumbricals originate on the radial side of the FDP tendons. As they contract they simultaneously extend the IP joints by directly pulling on the lateral band and pulling the FDP distally, relaxing the flexion antagonist to extension.

47. What is the primary flexor of the MP joint?

The intrinsic muscle tendons course volar to the MP joint axis of rotation and are the primary flexors of the MP joint.

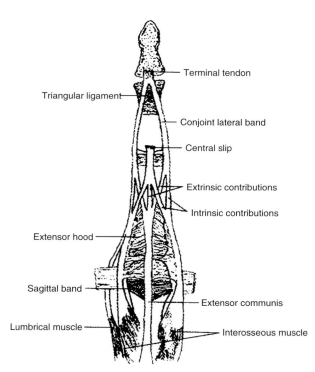

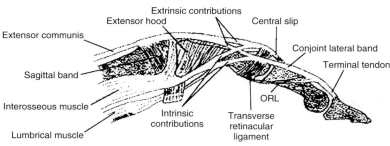

Figure 114-5. The complex retinacular anatomy of the extensor mechanism in the finger. *ORL,* Oblique retinacular ligament. (From Rizio L, Belsky MR: Finger deformities in rheumatoid arthritis. Hand Clin 12:531–540, 1996.)

48. What is the primary extender of the MP joint?

The extrinsic system extends the MP joint.

49. Which extends the IP joint: the extrinsic system or the intrinsic system?

The intrinsic system extends the IP joint when the MP joint is in hyperextension. The extrinsic system extends the IP joint when the MP joint is in flexion.

50. When the intrinsic muscles are paralyzed, how is the finger affected?

Because the primary flexor of the MP joint is lost, the MP joints tend to develop a posture of hyperextension—the position from which the paralyzed intrinsics are needed to extend the IP joints (see Question 47). Thus the IP joints fall into flexion, especially with intact profundus tendons, producing the claw deformity.

51. Which interosseous muscles are innervated by the median nerve?

An easy way to remember the answer is the mnemonic *LOAF: L* for the two radial *l*umbricals, *O* for *o*pponens pollicis, *A* for *a*bductor pollicis brevis, and *F* for the superficial head of the *f*lexor pollicis brevis (FPB). The rest of the intrinsic muscles are innervated by the ulnar nerve. The radial side of the thenar eminence is innervated by the median nerve and the ulnar side by the ulnar nerve (adductor pollicis and deep or ulnar head of the FPB).

52. Which of the interosseous muscles abduct the fingers? Which adduct them?

The four dorsal interossei, which arise from the adjacent surfaces of the shafts of the first, second, third, and fourth metacarpals and insert on the proximal phalanges of the index, middle, and ring fingers, abduct the digits from the midline of the hand. The three volar interossei, which arise from the second, fourth, and fifth metacarpals and insert on the respective proximal phalanges, adduct the digits toward the midline. The tendons from these muscles lie volar to the axis of MP motion but dorsal to the transverse metacarpal ligament (TMCL).

53. What does the oblique retinacular ligament do?

The oblique retinacular ligament (ORL) controls and coordinates flexion and extension between the IP joints. It courses beneath the PIP joint and over the DIP joint. As the DIP begins to flex, the ORL tightens, delivering flexor tone to the PIP joint. When the PIP begins to extend, the ORL tightens, delivering extensor tone to the DIP joint. Thus it ensures smooth, modulated, coordinated flexion and extension to the IP joints. It has been called the "cerebellum" of the finger.

54. What happens to the ORL in a boutonnière deformity?

With the PIP joint in flexion and the DIP joint in extension (the boutonnière position), the ORL is lax. Therefore the ORL shortens (as do all ligaments in a lax position) and helps to maintain the deformity.

55. How, then, can the DIP joint be flexed while maintaining extension of the PIP joint, which would have to stretch the ORL?

The ORL is a very subtle, light structure that stretches and deforms somewhat to allow this type of finger motion.

56. What is the smallest extrinsic flexor tendon?

The FDS to the little finger not only is the smallest tendon but also is frequently nonfunctional or even missing. Its consistently small size helps to identify the individual cut ends in the spaghetti wrist.

57. Which interosseous muscles have insertions into the bases of the proximal phalanges?

The first, second, and fourth dorsal interosseus muscles have bony insertions from their superficial bellies/medial tendons.

58. Where else do the interosseous muscles insert?

All of the interosseous muscles have deep bellies/lateral tendons, which travel superficial to the sagittal bands into the aponeurotic expansion as transverse (dorsally across the proximal phalanges) and oblique fibers (parallel to the lateral bands).

59. Which individual structures are maintained in dorsal position by the transverse retinacular ligament of Landsmeer?

Seven tendons are held in place in the region of the PIP joint: the central slip of the extrinsic extensor, the two lateral bands, the two slips from the central slip to the lateral band, and the two slips from the lateral bands to the central slip.

60. Which are the most important pulleys in the fibroosseous tunnel?

The finger flexor unit functions well if the A2 and the A4 pulleys are preserved. Both are needed to prevent tendon bowstringing. The A2 pulley is located at the proximal portion of the proximal phalanx ("proximal proximal"). The A4 pulley is located at the middle portion of the middle phalanx ("middle middle").

61. Why do the profundus tendons usually not retract into the palm after transection in the fingers?

The profundus tendons are tethered by the lumbricals in the palm and by their adjacent profundus tendons, with which they have a common muscle belly. In addition, they may not have avulsed their vincula and thus still may be attached to either the DIP or PIP volar plates.

62. Why can you not pull a superficialis tendon out through a palmar incision if you release it from its insertions in the middle phalanx?

The superficialis tendon does not simply divide when the profundus passes superficial to it; it reconstitutes itself beneath the profundus (chiasm of Camper) before dividing finally to its two insertions. This structure prevents the superficialis from being pulled out because it completely encircles the profundus tendon.

63. How is the long vinculum of the profundus tendon related to the short vinculum of the superficialis?

The vincula are folds of mesotenon carrying blood supply to both tendons. Normally, each of the profundus and superficialis tendons has a short vinculum (breve) and a long vinculum (longum). The vinculum longum of the profundus tendon traverses the vinculum breve of the superficialis tendon.

64. Where in the tendon is the longitudinal intrinsic blood supply?

It is concentrated in the dorsal (deep) aspect of the tendon, where the vincula enter.

65. How are the flexor tendons arranged in the carpal tunnel?

The profundus tendons lie side by side on its floor. The FPL is the radialmost member of this group. The superficialis tendons lie on the profundus tendons arranged two by two; the middle and ring finger tendons (third and fourth) are superficial; the index and small finger tendons (second and fifth) lie between them and the profundus row. Remember, 34 (third and fourth) is higher (more superficial) than 25 (second and fifth) (Fig. 114-6).

66. How often is the palmaris longus tendon absent?

Approximately 15% of patients do not have a palmaris longus tendon.

67. What is the second most useful tendon for grafting in the hand?

If the palmaris longus tendon is absent, if a longer tendon is necessary, or if additional tendons are needed, the plantaris tendons are excellent sources of graft material.

68. If the two primary tendon graft donors are missing, what is still available?

The extensors of the toes can be used as graft material if necessary

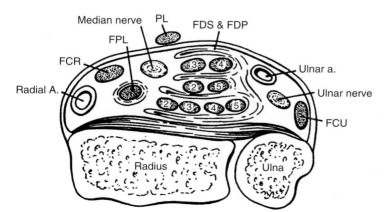

Figure 114-6. Cross-section through the carpal tunnel. *FCR,* Flexor carpi radialis; *FCU,* flexor carpi ulnaris; *FDP,* flexor digitorum profundus; *FDS,* flexor digitorum superficialis; *FPL,* flexor pollicis longus; *PL,* palmaris longus. (From Ariyan S: The Hand Book. New York, McGraw-Hill, 1989, p 10, with permission.)

BIBLIOGRAPHY

Ariyan S: The Hand Book. New York, McGraw-Hill, 1989.

Chang J, Valero-Ceuvas F, Hentz VR, Chase RA: Anatomy and biomechanics of the hand. In: Mathes SJ, Hentz VR (eds): Plastic Surgery, 2nd ed., Vol VII, The Hand and Upper Limb, Part 1. Philadelphia, Elsevier, 2006, pp 15–43.

Gelberman RH, Menon J: The vascularity of the scaphoid bone. J Hand Surg Am 5:508–513, 1980.

Green DP: Operative Hand Surgery, 3rd ed. New York, Churchill Livingstone, 1993.

Landsmeer JMF: The anatomy of the dorsal aponeurosis of the human finger and its functional significance. Anat Rec 104:31–44, 1941.

Landsmeer JMF: The coordination of finger-joint motions. J Bone Joint Surg 45A:1654–1662, 1963.

Lister G: The Hand: Diagnosis and Indications. New York, Churchill Livingstone, 1984.

Netter FH: Atlas of Human Anatomy. Summit, NJ, CIBA-Geigy Corporation, 1990.

Warfel JH: The Extremities: Muscles and Motor Points. Philadelphia, Lea & Febiger, 1993.

PHYSICAL EXAMINATION OF THE HAND

Christian Dumontier, MD, PhD, and
Raoul Tubiana, MD

CHAPTER 115

1. **It takes 2 months for a complete nail plate to grow. True or false?**

   False. Nail plate growth is highly variable among individuals and may be modified by numerous factors. However, it takes approximately 6 months for a complete nail plate to grow. At 2 months after avulsion, the nail plate is visible only at the level of the proximal nail fold.

2. **Is it useful to have a proximal nail fold?**

   Kligman's experiences have shown that the nail matrix is responsible for almost all production of the nail plate but is unable to control its shape. The proximodistal growth of the nail plate is, in part, controlled by the proximal nail fold, which limits the growth in height and forces the nail plate to grow distally. The proximal nail fold is also useful to protect the nail plate, which, at this level of the finger, is thin, fragile, and poorly adherent to the matrix.

3. **What is the Hutchinson's sign? What does it mean?**

   Hutchinson's sign is a dark discoloration of the nail plate and the proximal or distal nail fold. It is highly suggestive of a subungual melanoma.

4. **What is the function of nails?**

   Early medical descriptions state that nails were made for scratching, especially of the small animals that live on our body. Science has since shown that this is not their only function. Nails contribute to thermoregulation because of their richness in neurovascular glomi. Their main function is to serve as a counterpressure for the pulp that enhances discrimination. Patients without nails are unable to button their shirt. Nails also serve to pick up small objects and protect against trauma. Finally, nails have a cosmetic function. Because nails are so useful, maybe you should stop biting them before exams.

5. **What is the best test to appreciate the functional sensibility of the hand?**

   Many sensory tests have been described, but most of them are useful only to appreciate central or medullar neurologic lesions. To pick up and hold small objects correctly, the hand must be able to discriminate and to recognize various forms or textures. The best way to appreciate the functional sensibility of the hand is to test its discrimination.

6. **How can you appreciate the sensory discrimination of a finger pulp?**

   By using the two-point discrimination test described by Weber. The points of calipers are held against the skin at different distances from each other. The test determines the minimal distance at which the patient can distinguish whether one or two points are in contact with the skin. The patient must be comfortable, and the examiner must avoid pushing against the calipers with his/her fingers, thereby artificially increasing the pressure. The higher the pressure, the wider the area of skin that is deformed and stimulated. One or two points are touched in a random sequence along a longitudinal axis in the center of the finger tip. The American Society for Surgery of the Hand recommends seven correct answers out of 10 for two-point discrimination.

7. **What is the normal value for the two-point discrimination test at the pulp of the finger?**

   Values vary according to fingers and individuals. In most patients, normal values vary between 2 and 3 mm at the pulp of the finger. In patients employed in heavy labor, normal values are closer to 5 or 6 mm. In patients with congenital or acquired blindness, it may be as low as 1 to 2 mm.

8. **Why do patients with a low ulnar nerve palsy often have permanent abduction of the small finger? What is the name of this deformity?**

   This acquired deformity is known as Wartenberg's sign. Blacker et al. showed that the extensor digiti minimi tendon has two bundles. The radialmost tendon passes over the center of the axis of abduction–adduction of the metacarpophalangeal (MP) joint or slightly radial to it. The ulnar tendon, which is the thicker of the two, passes ulnar to

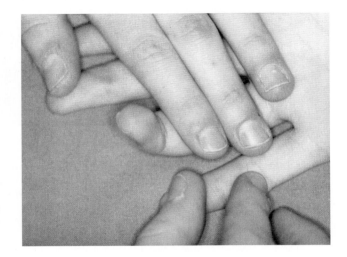

Figure 115-1. The flexor digitorum profundus (FDP) tendon allows flexion of the distal phalanx onto the middle phalanx. To test the FDP tendon, immobilize the proximal interphalangeal joint in complete extension and ask the patient to flex the distal phalanx.

the axis in most patients and gains a firm attachment to the tendon of the abductor digiti quinti. By means of these slips, the extensor digiti minimi has acquired a bony attachment to the tubercle of the proximal phalanx. The extensor digiti minimi thus has the potential to abduct the little finger through this indirect insertion.

9. How do you test the flexor digitorum profundus tendons?
Tendons of the flexor digitorum profundus (FDP) insert on the volar aspect of the distal phalanx of the fingers. The FDP tendon is the only tendon that allows flexion of the distal phalanx onto the middle phalanx. To test this tendon, the examiner should immobilize the proximal interphalangeal (PIP) joint in complete extension and ask the patient to flex the distal phalanx. In patients with limited strength or mobility, it is easier to appreciate even a small amount of motion if you place the wrist and MP joint in complete extension (Fig. 115-1).

10. How do you test the flexor digitorum superficialis tendons of the fingers?
Tendons of the flexor digitorum superficialis (FDS) insert on the volar aspect of the middle phalanx and flex the middle phalanx on the proximal phalanx. However, to examine the FDS tendon, it is mandatory to block the action of the FDP tendon, which is also able to flex the PIP joint after flexing the distal interphalangeal (DIP) joint. To block the FDP, the tendons of which arise from a common muscle belly, you need only to block the DIP joint of two or three fingers in extension. In doing so, you prevent the action of the FDP on the finger you wish to test. You obtain only flexion of the middle phalanx on the proximal phalanx without flexion of the DIP joint. During flexion of the PIP joint, the extensor mechanism glides distally. Patients are unable to control the motion of the distal phalanx from this position. This phenomenon, known as the "floating" distal phalanx, does not always hold true for the index finger, in which the FDP muscle belly is often independent of the three ulnar fingers (Fig. 115-2).

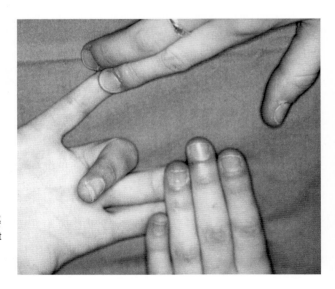

Figure 115-2. When the patient is asked to flex the finger, you obtain flexion only in the proximal interphalangeal joint if the flexor digitorum profundus tendon is blocked. The patient is unable to control the motion of the distal phalanx in this position. This phenomenon is known as the "floating" distal phalanx.

11. If I try to test the FDS of the little finger as described in Question 10, why does the patient flex only the MP joint and not the PIP joint?

- Approximately 15% of people do not have an FDS tendon for the little finger.
- Another group of people (also approximately 15%) has a tendon that is not functional.
- Some people have an FDS tendon for the little finger that is functional but highly adherent to the FDS tendon of the ring finger, which is maintained in extension. If you allow the PIP joint of the ring finger to flex, the patient will flex the PIP joint of the little finger. MP joint flexion of the little finger is provided by the flexor digiti quinti and the abductor digiti minimi.

12. How can you determine whether there is an FDS in the index finger if the FDP of the index is independent?

There is only one test to determine whether the FDS of the index finger is present. Ask the patient to hold a sheet of paper between the pulp of the thumb and index. The examiner pulls on the paper while the patient tries to resist. Because flexion strength is provided by the FDS, in a normal finger the digit will be slightly flexed at the PIP joint and extended at the DIP joint as in a "pseudo-boutonnière" deformity. In a patient without an FDS tendon, the DIP joint will flex to resist the traction and the PIP joint will stay in extension in a "pseudomallet" deformity.

13. In patients with rheumatoid arthritis who are unable to extend the ulnar three digits, what are the possible diagnoses?

- Rupture of the extensor tendons must be suspected. Extensor tendons usually rupture after attrition on a dorsally subluxated ulnar head. In such cases, if you ask patients to extend the fingers, you will see no bowstringing of the extensor tendons beneath the skin.
- In patients with ulnar deviation of the fingers, extensor tendons may dislocate in the intermetacarpal valleys. In such cases, if the MP joints are not stiff, passive extension of the fingers will allow patients to maintain the extension.
- The rarest cause is compression of the posterior interosseous nerve at the elbow. Usually in such cases, extension is weak but still possible, and wrist flexion will draw the fingers into extension as a result of the tenodesis effect.

14. How can you determine that the extensor pollicis longus tendon is intact and functional?

The extensor pollicis longus (EPL) tendon inserts on the dorsum of the distal phalanx of the thumb and is responsible for active extension of the distal phalanx. In most patients, its rupture leads to a flexion deformity of the IP joint and inability to extend the distal phalanx actively. However, extension of the intrinsic muscles of the thumb and adhesions between the EPL tendon and the extensor pollicis brevis (EPB) tendon give some patients the ability to achieve complete active extension of the IP joint even if the EPL tendon is ruptured. To be sure that the EPL tendon is intact, ask the patient to place his/her hand flat on a table. Then ask the patient to raise the thumb off the table (retropulsion). The EPL muscle is the only muscle responsible for this movement. You can also see and palpate the bowstringing of the tendon beneath the skin. Rupture of the EPL tendon was first described in drum players of the Prussian army, but you will probably see it more often in patients with Colles' fractures.

15. If flexion of the MP joint is limited, how can you determine whether the extensor tendons are adherent at the dorsum of the hand or at the wrist level?

By using the tenodesis effect. As most tendons cross several joints, it is possible to contract or relax them by changing the position of these joints. In the case of adhesion at the wrist level, wrist extension adds some flexion at the MP joint, whereas MP joint flexion does not change if the adhesion is located on the dorsum of the hand. This test is valid only if there is no ligamentous retraction at the MP joint.

16. What is Allen's test? How do you perform it?

Allen's test evaluates the patency of the radial and ulnar arteries at the level of the wrist. The patient is asked to raise and clench his/her hand to exsanguinate the cutaneous vascular bed. The examiner compresses the radial artery in the radial groove and the ulnar artery in Guyon's canal. The patient opens the hand without hyperextending the fingers. The palm appears pallid. The examiner releases one compressed artery and notes the time required for the palm to recover its normal color. The maneuver is repeated to evaluate the other artery.

17. How do you determine a rotational deformity of the finger: in flexion or in extension?

In flexion. The only way to determine a rotational deformity is to ask the patient to flex his/her fingers. Because of the orientation of the MP and PIP joints, all of the fingers converge in flexion toward the scaphoid tubercle. Thus even a minor rotational deformity that may not be apparent in extension becomes obvious (Fig. 115-3).

18. Why is DIP joint flexion more important when the PIP joint is flexed than when the PIP joint is extended?

This clinical test is called the Haines-Zancolli test (Fig. 115-4). Limited flexion of the DIP joint, when the PIP joint is maintained in extension, is due to the retaining action of the oblique retinacular (Landsmeer's) ligament. Landsmeer's

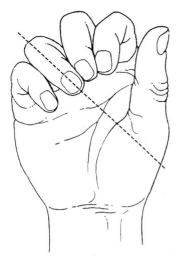

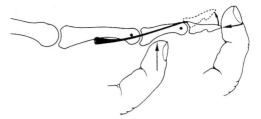

Figure 115-4. The Haines-Zancolli test is considered positive if flexion of the distal phalanx is not possible when the middle phalanx is maintained in extension; it is possible only if the middle phalanx is flexed. A positive test is the result of contraction of the oblique retinacular ligament. (From Tubiana R: The Hand, Vol. III. Philadelphia, WB Saunders, 1988.)

Figure 115-3. In the case of rotational deformity (fracture, malunion), flexion of a finger causes overlapping of one finger upon another in either a radial or an ulnar direction. (From Tubiana R: The Hand, Vol. I. Philadelphia, WB Saunders, 1988.)

ligament inserts on the proximal phalanx and digital sheath, volar to the axis of flexion–extension of the PIP joint. It ends on the extensor tendon, dorsal to the axis of flexion–extension of the DIP joint. As a result, there is more stress on Landsmeer's ligament in extension of the PIP joint than in flexion; thus DIP joint flexion is easier with the PIP joint in flexion than in extension. Landsmeer's ligament coordinates the movement of the IP joints. It is placed under tension by flexion of the DIP joint, which causes simultaneous flexion of the PIP joint. The ligament is also placed under tension by extension of the PIP joint, which in turn causes extension of the DIP joint. Contraction of the oblique retinacular ligament has been described in the boutonnière deformity and Dupuytren's disease.

19. In patients experiencing stiffness with extension of the PIP joint, which clinical test identifies contracture of the interosseous muscles?

The Finochietto-Bunnell test (Fig. 115-5). When the MP joint is in extension, the contracted interosseous muscles impede flexion of the PIP joint because of the traction exerted on the extensors. Flexion of the MP joint relaxes the extensors, and flexion becomes possible at the PIP joints.

20. Which clinical test is specific for de Quervain's tenosynovitis? How is it performed?

Finkelstein's test (Fig. 115-6). De Quervain's tenosynovitis affects the first dorsal extensor compartment as its contents (abductor pollicis longus [APL] and EPB tendons) pass over the radial styloid. Ask the patient to flex the thumb into the

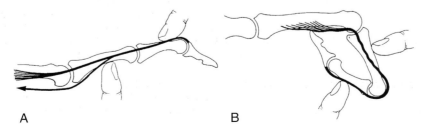

A   B

Figure 115-5. A positive Finochietto-Bunnell test in a swan neck deformity of the finger with intrinsic muscle contracture. When the proximal phalanx is maintained in extension, it is impossible to flex the middle phalanx. In cases of contraction of the intrinsic muscles, flexion of the proximal phalanx allows flexion of the middle phalanx. (From Tubiana R: The Hand, Vol. III. Philadelphia, WB Saunders, 1988.)

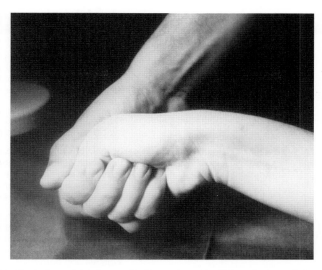

Figure 115-6. Finkelstein's test for de Quervain's tenosynovitis. The test is positive if the patient experiences sharp pain on the radial styloid when you suddenly place the wrist in ulnar deviation.

palm and to maintain it with the other fingers. The wrist is then placed in ulnar deviation, which causes a sharp pain at the radial styloid due to tension on the APL and EPB tendons.

21. Which clinical signs are suggestive of flexor carpi radialis tendinitis?

Flexor carpi radialis (FCR) tendinitis is not a rare disease. As in most cases of tendinitis, pain is the most frequent complaint and is increased by resisted active contraction and passive stretching of the muscle–tendon unit. In FCR tendinitis, pain is localized on the volar aspect of the wrist and frequently radiates to the forearm. Pain is increased by resisted wrist flexion and passive extension of the wrist. Swelling is sometimes present along the tendon of the FCR and must be differentiated from a wrist ganglion. Some patients complain of diffuse pain and paresthesias on the base of the thenar eminence secondary to irritation of the palmar cutaneous branch of the median nerve.

22. If the IP joint of the thumb is flexed, why does the DIP joint of the index finger flex simultaneously?

This anatomic variation, known as Linburg's sign, is present in approximately 30% of people. It is due to adhesions in the carpal tunnel between the flexor pollicis longus and FDP tendons of the index finger. Flexion of the thumb sometimes causes other fingers to flex. This variation usually causes no functional impairment but has been described as a source of problems in some musicians who lack independence of the fingers.

23. In a patient who has sprained an MP joint, how can you diagnose a ligamentous rupture with instability?

To appreciate instability you must apply stress to the collateral ligament in adduction or abduction. However, abduction–adduction laxity of the MP joint in extension is normal because the collateral ligaments are not under tension. If you place the MP joint in complete passive flexion, because of their eccentric insertion and the shape of the metacarpal head, the collateral ligaments will be under tension without laxity in either abduction or adduction in normal patients. Then it is easy to appreciate abnormal laxity in patients with ligamentous ruptures.

24. What are the etiologies of a swan neck deformity of the fingers?

In swan neck deformity, the PIP joint is in extension and the DIP joint in flexion. Swan neck deformity is due to excessive traction by the extensor apparatus inserted on the base of the middle phalanx and is favored by laxity of the PIP joint (Table 115-1).

Table 115-1. Etiologies of Swan Neck Deformity

ORIGIN	CAUSES	EXPLANATION
PIP joint	Volar plate deficiency	Severe sprain of anterior volar plate; sequela of dorsal PIP dislocation; progressive stretching of volar plate due to synovitis, as in rheumatoid arthritis
Anterior structures of the PIP joint	Rupture of FDS tendon	Rupture may be traumatic or secondary to synovitis, as in rheumatoid arthritis
Intrinsic muscle contracture	Primary muscle contracture Secondary muscle contracture	Spasticity, compartment syndrome Volar dislocation of MP joint, as in rheumatoid arthritis; brings intrinsic tendons into position dorsal to axis of MP joints; their force acts to increase forces of extensor apparatus
Extrinsic tendons	Chronic mallet finger Increased tension on extensor apparatus	To extend distal phalanx, patients increase tension on extensor tendon, which results in increased tension on central slip of extensor tendon Wrist flexion deformity, as in rheumatoid arthritis, or destruction of proximal insertion of extensor communis at MP level

FDS, Flexor digitorum superficialis; MP, metacarpophalangeal; PIP, proximal interphalangeal.

BIBLIOGRAPHY

Hunter JM, Schneider LH, Mackin EJ, Callahan AD: Rehabilitation of the Hand, 3rd ed. St. Louis, Mosby, 1990.
Landsmeer JMF: Atlas of Anatomy of the Hand. Edinburgh, Churchill Livingstone, 1976.
Lister G: The Hand: Diagnosis and Indications, 3rd ed. Edinburgh, Churchill Livingstone, 1993.
Tubiana R: The Hand, Vol. III. Philadelphia, WB Saunders, 1988.
Tubiana R, Thomine JM, Mackin E: Examination of the Hand and Wrist. London, Martin Dunitz, 1996.
Zancolli E: Structural and Dynamic Bases of Hand Surgery, 2nd ed. Philadelphia, JP Lippincott, 1979.

RADIOLOGIC EXAMINATION OF THE HAND

Wilfred C. G. Peh, MBBS, MD, FRCP, FRCR, and
Louis A. Gilula, MD, ABR, FACR

CHAPTER 116

1. Who performed the first radiograph of the hand?

Wilhelm Conrad Roentgen, the discoverer of x-rays, performed the first radiograph of the hand in 1895. Roentgen, then Professor at the University of Würzburg in Germany, subsequently was awarded the first Nobel Prize for Physics in recognition of his great discovery. He obtained an image of his wife's hand using a photographic plate. This radiograph is widely accepted as the first radiograph of a human (Fig. 116-1).

2. Name some of the most common causes of diagnostic errors in interpreting radiographs of the hand after trauma.

- Inadequate clinical history and physical examination
- Acceptance of poor-quality radiographs
- Failure to recognize an abnormality that is actually present
- Failure to obtain or insist on an adequate number of proper radiographic projections
- Missing a second significant finding, such as another fracture, dislocation, or foreign body

3. What is Brewerton's view?

A radiographic projection described by D.A. Brewerton in 1967 for demonstrating involvement of the metacarpal heads in rheumatoid arthritis. This projection aims at profiling the second through fifth metacarpophalangeal (MCP) joints with no overlapping of adjacent cortical surfaces. It is sensitive for revealing early erosions due to synovial arthritis and occult fractures of the metacarpal heads that may not be seen on routine views.

4. Why is Rolando's fracture considered a significant injury?

Rolando's fracture is a Y-shaped or comminuted fracture of the metacarpal base of the thumb that involves the carpometacarpal (CMC) joint and usually requires surgical stabilization (Fig. 116-2). Proper alignment may otherwise be difficult to maintain because of the opposing pulls of multiple tendons acting on the thumb.

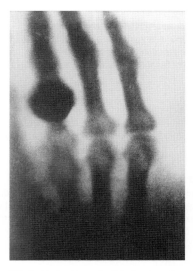

Figure 116-1. First radiograph of the hand, performed in 1895 by Wilhelm Conrad Roentgen (Reproduced with permission of Siemen's Medical Systems, Inc., Iselin, New Jersey.)

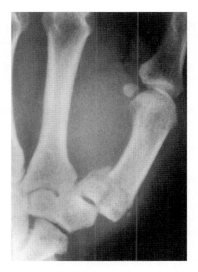

Figure 116-2. A 49-year-old man with Rolando's fracture of the left thumb. The comminuted fracture involves the carpometacarpal joint, and the major shaft fragments are displaced radially. Internal fixation was required for stabilization.

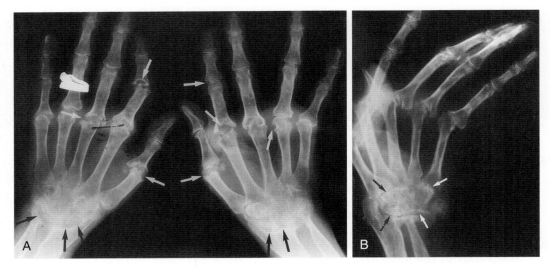

Figure 116-3. A, A 65-year-old woman with rheumatoid arthritis. Erosions *(arrows)* of metacarpophalangeal (MCP) and proximal interphalangeal joints as well as the distal forearm bones are present bilaterally. Note soft tissue swelling around all MCP joints and joint space narrowing at all affected joints. **B,** Advanced rheumatoid arthritis in a 44-year-old woman. Note ulnar deviation at MCP joints of all digits. Bony ankylosis involves the intercarpal bones *(arrows)* and ulnar translation of the carpus is present, other features of rheumatoid arthritis.

5. How are intraarticular fractures of the base of the phalanges classified?
Steele's classification consists of three categories. Type I is a nondisplaced marginal fracture. Type II is a comminuted, impaction fracture. Type III is a displaced intraarticular fracture with subluxation of the fracture fragments.

6. List the radiographic hallmarks of rheumatoid arthritis (Fig. 116-3).

> • Periarticular osteoporosis
> • Periarticular soft tissue
>   swelling
> • Marginal erosions
> • Joint space narrowing
> • Proximal and bilateral symmetrical disease
>   distribution

7. How can the ulnar deviation deformity of rheumatoid arthritis be explained?
The pathogenesis is not fully understood. It appears to be initiated by inflammatory arthritis of the MCP joint with a rise in intraarticular pressure. Destruction of the ligamentous and capsular tissues results in instability of the joint. Another possible contributory factor is instability and ulnar displacement of extensor tendons. Ligamentous laxity of the fourth and fifth CMC joints, resulting in phalangeal volar descent, also may play a role.

8. What is the pattern of involvement of primary osteoarthritis?
Primary osteoarthritis affects the proximal and distal interphalangeal joints of the digits and the CMC joint of the thumbs in a bilateral symmetric fashion. It is found predominantly in the hands of middle-aged and older women. Its major features include bone production and osteophytes around narrowed joints.

9. Which is the most common benign bone tumor of the hand?
Enchondroma. In fact, approximately 50% of enchondromas are found in the hand. Radiographically, the tumor is seen as a well-defined lucent lesion in the diaphysis or metadiaphysis and may have a well-defined sclerotic rim. It is often expansile with a preserved cortex. The endosteal cortex typically is scalloped or has multiple small concavities. The presence of internal chondroid-type calcifications is considered characteristic (Fig. 116-4).

10. Why is the finding of multiple enchondromas significant?
The condition of multiple enchondromas is known as Ollier's disease. When found in combination with soft tissue hemangiomas, the entity is known as Maffucci's syndrome. Radiographically, phleboliths and soft tissue masses may be seen at the sites of hemangiomas. Malignant degeneration of an enchondroma to a chondrosarcoma may occur in up to 25% of patients with Ollier's disease by the age of 40 years. Maffucci's syndrome is associated with an even higher frequency of malignant transformation of enchondromas.

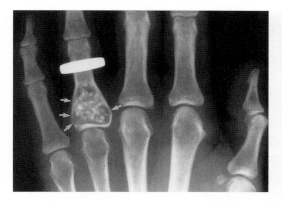

Figure 116-4. Enchondroma of the proximal phalanx of the left ring finger in a 58-year-old woman. The lesion contains typical punctate internal calcifications and expands the bone with preservation of the cortex. Scalloping *(arrows)* involves the endosteal surface of the overlying cortex.

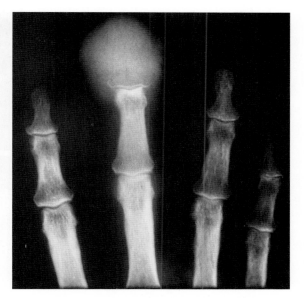

Figure 116-5. Distal phalangeal metastasis in a 67-year-old man. Note bony destruction with associated soft tissue mass, normal mineralization of the adjacent phalanx, and relatively preserved distal interphalangeal joint (or "adjacent interphalangeal joint").

11. Which is the most common malignant bone tumor of the hand?

Metastases. Metastases and myeloma should be considered whenever a lytic lesion is detected in anyone over the age of 40 years, especially if the lesion has ill-defined margins and/or cortical breakthrough. Bronchogenic carcinoma is the most common origin for metastases to the bones of the hand (Fig. 116-5).

12. Besides metastases and enchondromas, what is included in the differential diagnosis of multiple lytic bone lesions in the hand and wrist?

Fibrous dysplasia, eosinophilic granuloma, myeloma, hyperparathyroidism (brown tumor), and infection.

13. What disorder typically produces well-defined erosions with overhanging margins?

Gout. In chronic advanced gout, tophaceous deposits are associated with intraarticular or periarticular erosions. These erosions are well defined, have overhanging edges (that is, the periosteal bone margins extend outside the normal cortical margins), and may have sclerotic margins. Tophi calcification is unusual and may reflect a coexisting abnormality of calcium metabolism.

14. Which disease is characterized by the combination of periarticular soft tissue calcification and subperiosteal bone resorption?

Hyperparathyroidism secondary to renal failure. Subperiosteal resorption is most frequently seen at the radial aspects of the middle phalanges of the hand and is considered a classic finding for hyperparathyroidism. In severe disease, terminal phalangeal resorption also may be present. When the serum calcium–phosphorus ion product is elevated, metastatic calcification may occur within normal tissues, particularly around joints. Chronic renal failure with secondary hyperparathyroidism is the most common cause of metastatic calcification and usually is seen in patients on long-term dialysis. The calcification may decrease or disappear with correction of the metabolic abnormality.

15. List the major causes of a short fourth metacarpal.

Trauma, infarction (e.g., sickle cell anemia), Turner's syndrome, pseudohypoparathyroidism, pseudopseudohypoparathyroidism, idiopathic shortening, and multiple exostoses.

16. What is the best way to image complex regional pain syndrome?

Three-phase bone scintigraphy. All phases should have abnormal increased uptake. The 3-hour delayed images of bone scintiscans have 96% sensitivity and 97% specificity for the diagnosis of complex regional pain syndrome (CRPS; formerly referred to as *reflex sympathetic dystrophy* [RSD]). There is diffuse increased isotope uptake around the radiocarpal, intercarpal, CMC, MCP, and interphalangeal joints (Fig. 116-6). Radiographically, CRPS may manifest as severe osteoporosis and soft tissue swelling.

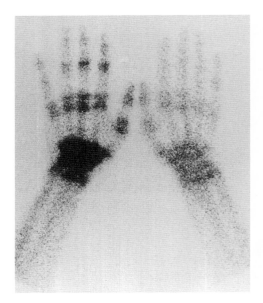

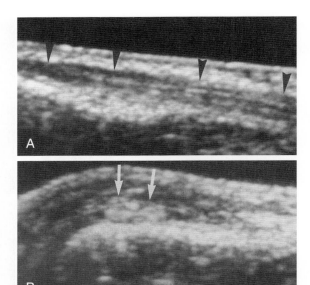

Figure 116-6.　Bone scintiscan (3-hour delay) of a 30-year-old man with reflex sympathetic dystrophy of the left hand. Note diffuse increased isotope uptake at the wrist and proximal finger joints. The first two phases also displayed increased isotope uptake.

Figure 116-7.　Longitudinal ultrasound scans of the finger extensor tendons in two different patients. **A,** Normal tendon in a 64-year-old man has a smooth regular outline *(arrowheads)* with fine linear internal echoes. **B,** Repaired tendon in a 23-year-old man shows an echogenic focus *(arrows)* at the repair site. Range of motion was normal.

17. Does ultrasound have a role in imaging tendons?

Most definitely. By using a high-frequency linear transducer with a stand-off pad, high-resolution images of the tendons can be obtained (Fig. 116-7). The tendons have a general hypoechoic appearance with multiple longitudinal internal fibers. Flexing and extending the finger allow identification and dynamic evaluation of the individual tendons. Indications include tenosynovitis, localized tendinitis, tendon rupture, and functional assessment of repaired tendons.

18. Is magnetic resonance imaging useful in staging soft tissue tumors?

Yes. In fact, magnetic resonance imaging (MRI) currently is the modality of choice for tumor staging because it provides exact information about the location and extent of the tumor and its relationship to the surrounding tissues, particularly the neurovascular structures. This information is important for treatment planning.

Figure 116-8.　**A,** Lipoma of the first web space in a 53-year-old woman. Sagittal T1-weighted magnetic resonance image shows the typical homogeneous high-signal intensity of a well-defined fatty lesion *(arrows).* The lesion signal intensity is similar to that of the subcutaneous and marrow fat. **B,** Acute synovitis and synovial hyperplasia of the left long finger in a 52-year-old woman. Coronal T2-weighted magnetic resonance image shows increased signal of the thickened synovium of the tendon sheath *(arrows).*

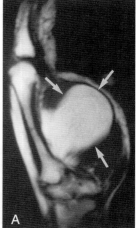

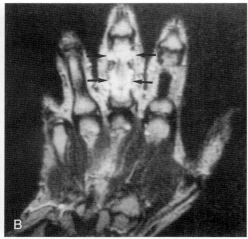

CONTROVERSIES

19. Can MRI provide a specific tissue diagnosis of soft tissue tumors?

Most soft tissue tumors in the hands are benign. From the combination of signal characteristics on different pulse sequences and morphologic appearances, certain benign tumors can be diagnosed with confidence on MRI, including lipoma, giant cell tumor of the tendon sheath, hemangioma, arteriovenous malformation, and ganglion cyst (Fig. 116-8). For benign tumors with atypical appearances or lesions that do not fit into the list given, malignancy cannot be excluded. Plain radiographs should always be evaluated in conjunction with MR images because calcifications, ossification, and cortical abnormalities may be missed on MRI.

20. Does MRI have a role in monitoring the treatment response of inflammatory arthropathies?

Potentially. The role of MRI is evolving. Inflamed synovium can be demonstrated on T2-weighted images. Subtle changes in the synovium, articular cartilage, and bone can be detected before they are apparent radiographically. Use of dynamic gadolinium-DTPA enhancement to identify active pannus appears to be a promising technique. MRI may help in early diagnosis, identify poor prognostic factors, and aid in the monitoring of response to therapy.

BIBLIOGRAPHY

Berquist TH: Hand and wrist. In Berquist TH (ed): MRI of the Musculoskeletal System, 3rd ed. Philadelphia, Lippincott-Raven, 1996, pp 673–734.

Gilula LA, Yin Y (eds): Imaging of the Hand and Wrist. Philadelphia, WB Saunders, 1996.

Helms CA: Fundamentals of Skeletal Radiology, 2nd ed. Philadelphia, WB Saunders, 1995.

Keen HI, Emery P: How should we manage early rheumatoid arthritis? From imaging to intervention. Curr Opin Rheumatol 17:280–285, 2005.

Libson E, Bloom RA, Husband JE, Stoker DJ: Metastatic tumors of the bones of the hands and feet. Skel Radiol 16:387–392, 1987.

Peh WCG, Truong NP, Totty WG, Gilula LA: Magnetic resonance imaging of benign soft tissue masses of the hand and wrist. Clin Radiol 50:519–525, 1995.

Peterfy CG: New developments in imaging in rheumatoid arthritis. Curr Opin Rheumatol 15:288–295, 2003.

Resnick D: Diagnosis of Bone and Joint Disorders. Philadelphia, WB Saunders, 1995.

Resnick D, Pettersson H (eds): Skeletal Radiology. London, Merit Communications, 1992.

Van Holsbeeck M, Introcaso JH (eds): Musculoskeletal Ultrasound. St. Louis, Mosby, 1991.

Winalski CS, Palmer WE, Rosenthal DI, Weissman BN: Magnetic resonance imaging of rheumatoid arthritis. Radiol Clin North Am 34:243–258, 1996.

ANESTHESIA FOR SURGERY OF THE HAND

Rosemary Hickey, MD, and
Somayaji Ramamurthy, MD

ANATOMY AND TECHNIQUES

1. Describe the relevant anatomy for upper extremity brachial plexus blocks.

The brachial plexus is formed by the anterior primary divisions of the fifth to eighth cervical nerves and the first thoracic nerve, with frequent contributions from the fourth cervical and second thoracic nerves (Fig. 117-1). The cervical nerve *roots* reorganize into superior, middle, and inferior brachial plexus *trunks*. The trunks undergo a separation into anterior and posterior *divisions*. As these divisions enter the axilla, they give way to *cords,* now oriented as the lateral, medial, and posterior cords. At the lateral border of the pectoralis minor muscle, the three cords reorganize to give rise to the *peripheral nerves* of the upper extremity. These include the musculocutaneous, median, ulnar, and radial nerves.

2. What is the concept of "plexus anesthesia"?

The concept of "plexus anesthesia" provides a system of single-injection techniques for blocking the brachial plexus. The concept is based on the fact that a fascial envelope, which extends continuously from the intervertebral foramina to the distal axilla, invests the brachial plexus. This fascial sheath may be entered with a single injection of a local anesthetic, and the extent of anesthesia that develops depends on the level of injection and the volume of local anesthetic injected at that level.

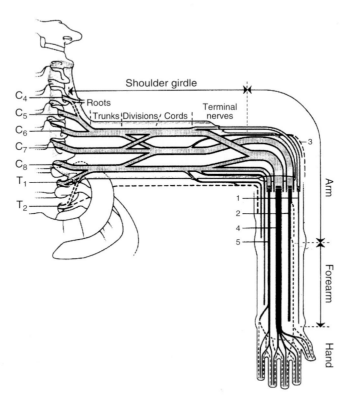

Figure 117-1. Schematic representation of the formation and distribution of the brachial plexus and the level at which the various components leave the sheath. (From Winnie AP: Plexus Anesthesia, Vol 1. Philadelphia, WB Saunders, 1990.)

3. **What parts of the brachial plexus are anesthetized by the interscalene, subclavian perivascular, infraclavicular, and axillary techniques of brachial plexus block?**

The interscalene block anesthetizes the roots, the subclavian perivascular block the trunks, the infraclavicular block the cords, and the axillary technique the terminal nerves of the brachial plexus.

4. **What is the interscalene groove, and how is it located?**

The interscalene groove is the groove located between the anterior and middle scalene muscles. The block needle is inserted in this groove at the level of C6 (which is determined by extending a line laterally from the cricoid cartilage) when performing an interscalene or subclavian perivascular block. To locate this groove, the patient is placed in the supine position with the head turned opposite to the side to be blocked. The patient is instructed to raise his/her head slightly to make the sternocleidomastoid muscle prominent. The anesthesiologist then palpates the posterior border of the sternocleidomastoid muscle and asks the patient to relax. The palpating fingers are rolled laterally across the belly of the sternocleidomastoid muscle until the interscalene groove is located.

5. **Although the block needle enters the interscalene groove for both the interscalene and subclavian perivascular blocks, the needle direction differs for the two blocks. Describe the needle direction for each.**

For the interscalene block, the block needle is inserted in the interscalene groove in a direction that is perpendicular to the skin in every plane, with a slight caudad direction. For the subclavian perivascular block, the block needle is inserted in the interscalene groove in a directly caudad direction.

6. **How is the correct location of the needle in the interscalene or subclavian perivascular space identified?**

Elicitation of a paresthesia in the distribution of the brachial plexus roots (interscalene block) or trunks (subclavian perivascular block) indicates the correct needle position within the brachial plexus fascia. The patient may describe the paresthesia as an electric shock sensation in the arm or hand. A nerve stimulator may also be used to identify correct needle placement. With this technique, the negative terminal of the nerve stimulator is attached to the block needle and the positive electrode is attached to an electrode on the side of the chest opposite to the arm that is being anesthetized. The needle is advanced until a muscle contraction in the arm or hand identifies the part of the brachial plexus being stimulated. The needle is then advanced until the maximal contraction is identified.

7. **Besides the subclavian perivascular and interscalene blocks, what other brachial plexus blocks are performed above the clavicle? Describe how these blocks are performed.**

The classic supraclavicular block and a modification of this block, the so-called "plumb bob" technique, are also performed above the clavicle. In the classic supraclavicular block, the midpoint of the clavicle is identified and the needle is introduced posterior to the subclavian artery in a caudad direction until bone is encountered. The needle is systematically walked anteriorly and posteriorly along the rib until a paresthesia is elicited, indicating that the brachial plexus has been located. In the "plumb bob" technique, the block needle is introduced at the point at which the lateral border of the sternocleidomastoid muscle inserts into the clavicle. It is introduced in a posterior direction (toward the floor in a supine patient), and, if necessary, the needle can be rotated in small steps through an arc of approximately 30° in a more cephalad or caudad direction, following the line of insertion that a plumb bob would generate (Fig. 117-2).

8. **How is an infraclavicular block done?**

The needle is inserted 2 cm below the midpoint of the inferior clavicular border and is advanced laterally. Marking a line between the C6 tubercle and the brachial artery through the midclavicle with the arm abducted is helpful in visualizing the course of the plexus and the needle direction. This block requires a longer needle than with the other techniques because it is introduced in a location more distant from the brachial plexus.

9. **What other techniques of infraclavicular block are described, and how are they performed?**

One approach identifies the midpoint of a line drawn between the jugular notch and the ventral apophysis of the acromion. The needle is introduced beneath the clavicle in a posterior direction. A modification of this technique, known as the *coracoid approach,* uses the coracoid process (located by placing two fingers in the groove between the deltoid and pectoralis major muscles, and gently palpating laterally) as a landmark. In this technique, the needle is inserted 2 cm medial and 2 cm caudad to the coracoid process and is advanced posteriorly.

10. **Describe the axillary technique of brachial plexus block.**

For an axillary block, the patient is placed in the supine position with the arm abducted to 90° and the forearm flexed, with the dorsum of the hand lying on the table next to the patient's head. The axillary artery is palpated and followed proximally until it disappears under the pectoralis major muscle. With the index finger over the pulse, the brachial plexus

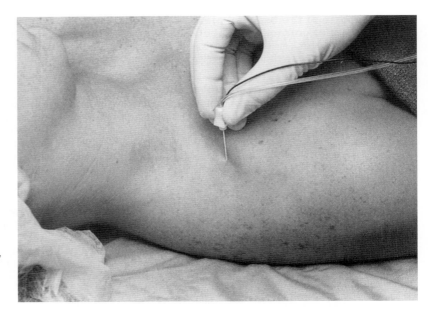

Figure 117-2. Blockade of the brachial plexus via the "plumb bob" supraclavicular technique. (From Mulroy MF, Thompson GE: Supraclavicular approach. In Hahn MB, McQuillan PM, Sheplock GJ [eds]: Regional Anesthesia: An Atlas of Anatomy and Techniques, St. Louis, Mosby, 1996, pp 101–106.)

sheath is penetrated with the block needle and the needle is advanced until one of four endpoints is achieved. (1) A distinctive click is felt as the needle penetrates the brachial plexus sheath, with the short bevel of the block needle contributing to the perception of the click. (2) A paresthesia is elicited in the distribution of the median, radial, or ulnar nerves. (3) Arterial blood is aspirated indicating puncture of the axillary artery. When arterial blood is aspirated, the block needle may be advanced and the injection made behind the artery, or alternatively half of the local anesthetic can be injected behind the artery and half injected after withdrawing the needle to the front of the artery. (4) A nerve stimulator can be used to localize nerves within the axillary sheath. The specific muscle twitch response that is elicited identifies the nerve being stimulated. A contraction of an appropriate muscle group in the hand or forearm at a current of 0.5 A or less indicates proper placement of the block needle within the brachial plexus sheath.

11. Besides a nerve stimulator, what additional tool is being used to facilitate placement of brachial plexus blocks?
Ultrasound is now gaining momentum among many to facilitate placement of brachial plexus blocks. This technique can help identify vascular and neural structures and may make our techniques more predictable.

12. What is the "multiple compartment" concept?
Some authors (Thompson and Rorie) have described the presence of septae extending inward from the brachial plexus sheath, which create multiple compartments around the neurovascular bundle. These septae inhibit the spread of local anesthetic when it is deposited in a single injection technique (as popularized by Winnie). However, other authors have not observed septae or have found them to be thin and incomplete.

13. What is the advantage of using a catheter technique for brachial plexus block, and how is it done?
The insertion of a catheter allows repeated injections of local anesthetic for long surgical procedures. In addition, continuous infusions of analgesic concentrations of local anesthetic may be continued for postoperative pain relief. A blunt tip needle and catheter set (Contiplex) can be used, with identification of a "fascial click" to signify entrance into the brachial plexus sheath. The proper position of the catheter can be tested by injecting 2 to 4 mL of cold (refrigerated, 4°C to 6°C) normal saline through the catheter. This will elicit a short but distinct cold paresthesia into the arm and/or hand, indicating correct position of the catheter. Alternatively, paresthesia or nerve stimulator techniques can be used to identify correct placement of the advancing needle.

CHOICE OF LOCAL ANESTHETIC

14. What determines the choice of local anesthetic for brachial plexus block?
The local anesthetic is chosen based on the desired duration of anesthesia, the necessity of motor block, and any history of local anesthetic allergy. Lidocaine and mepivacaine are useful for outpatient surgical procedures when the desired duration of surgical anesthesia is 2 hours or less. For longer procedures, bupivacaine 0.5% or ropivacaine 0.5% may be used. The addition of epinephrine in a concentration of 1:200,000 is useful in

prolonging the duration of local anesthetic action. It is also useful for early detection of an intravascular injection, which is particularly beneficial in a technique such as the transarterial technique of axillary block, in which the axillary artery is deliberately punctured. Bupivacaine, or the newer local anesthetic ropivacaine, is useful for long procedures (when greater than 4 hours of surgical anesthesia is necessary) or when prolonged postoperative anesthesia is desirable.

15. What is ropivacaine, and what is its advantage over bupivacaine?

Ropivacaine and 5-bupivacaine are the only local anesthetics prepared as the pure *s*-isomer rather than a racemic mixture. Toxicity studies show that ropivacaine is less cardiotoxic than bupivacaine, although ropivacaine still possesses some dysrhythmogenic potential. In a concentration of 0.5%, it is an effective agent for brachial plexus block with an onset and duration similar to bupivacaine. Both are long-acting agents that produce profound sensory and motor block.

16. What is the purpose of "alkalinization" of a local anesthetic?

Alkalinization of local anesthetics has been used to improve onset time and with brachial plexus blocks has produced conflicting results. The principle is that raising the pH increases the percentage of the local anesthetic present in the nonionized free base form. It is this form that crosses the nerve cell membrane to reach the site of action of local anesthetics.

COMPLICATIONS OF BRACHIAL PLEXUS BLOCK

17. What are some potential complications associated with interscalene block?

Some of the main complications of interscalene block include subarachnoid injection, epidural injection, injection into the vertebral artery, pneumothorax, cervical sympathetic block (Horner's syndrome), recurrent laryngeal nerve block (hoarseness), and phrenic nerve block. Complications that may occur with each technique of brachial plexus block include local anesthetic overdose, allergic reaction to the local anesthetic, intravascular injection, hematoma formation, and nerve trauma.

18. What is the mechanism of phrenic nerve block, how can it be diagnosed, and how common is it following interscalene block?

Phrenic nerve block may result from diffusion of local anesthetic cephalad to involve the more proximal cervical roots (C3, C4, and C5) or may be a consequence of an improperly performed block with local anesthetic deposited outside the brachial plexus sheath, anterior to the anterior scalene muscle. Ultrasonography or conventional x-ray technique may diagnose it. One study noted a 100% incidence of ipsilateral hemidiaphragmatic paresis diagnosed by ultrasonography in a group of patients receiving interscalene blocks. Although generally no treatment is required for phrenic nerve block, decreases in pulmonary function (approximately 25% decrease in forced vital capacity and forced expiratory reserve volume at 1 second) do occur. Therefore interscalene blocks should be avoided in patients who cannot tolerate this reduction in pulmonary function, particularly patients in whom the opposite hemidiaphragm is already paralyzed.

19. How is injection into the vertebral artery and epidural or subarachnoid spaces avoided with an interscalene block?

Careful aspiration prior to injection and a slight caudad needle direction lessens the likelihood of inadvertent vertebral artery, epidural, or subarachnoid injection.

20. If the subclavian artery is punctured when performing a subclavian perivascular block, the block needle should be redirected in which direction to locate the brachial plexus trunks?

The needle should be redirected more dorsally because the subclavian artery lies anterior to the trunks of the brachial plexus.

21. How is the risk of pneumothorax minimized when performing a subclavian perivascular block?

The principal cause of this complication is a needle direction that drifts medially toward the cupula of the lung; thus this direction should be avoided.

22. How is a pneumothorax treated if it develops as a complication of interscalene or subclavian perivascular brachial plexus block?

If the pneumothorax is small, the patient can be given oxygen and observed, provided positive pressure ventilation does not have to be initiated for general anesthesia with a failed block. If the pneumothorax is larger than 20%, aspiration through a small-gauge catheter followed by patient observation often is all that is necessary. Rarely, a chest tube is required for reexpansion of the lung.

23. What nerve distribution is frequently missed when an interscalene block is performed?
The ulnar nerve distribution may be difficult to anesthetize with an interscalene block because the block is performed at the level of C6, which is cephalad to the derivation of the ulnar nerve (C8-T1).

24. Name some advantages of axillary block compared with interscalene or subclavian perivascular block.
An axillary block is performed remote from the neck and thorax; thus the site-related complications of blocks carried out above the clavicle are avoided. These include cervical sympathetic block, phrenic nerve block, recurrent laryngeal nerve block, and vertebral, epidural, and subarachnoid injection. The location of the nerves of the brachial plexus is superficial in the axilla, leading to relatively easy identification of anatomic landmarks. One disadvantage of axillary block is that the volume of local anesthetic required is larger than for an interscalene or subclavian perivascular block.

25. What nerves are frequently missed with an axillary block and why?
The musculocutaneous nerve is frequently missed with an axillary block because the musculocutaneous nerve leaves the brachial plexus high in the axilla, which may be proximal to the insertion of the block needle. Thus the local anesthetic may not reach the nerve, particularly if a low-volume technique is used. If block of the musculocutaneous nerve is necessary, a separate injection is made by reinserting the needle superior to the axillary artery and injecting 5 to 8 mL of local anesthetic into the substance of the coracobrachialis muscle. The intercostobrachial nerve is derived from T2, which is not a part of the brachial plexus and must be blocked separately. This nerve is blocked by a subcutaneous skin wheal superficial to the axillary artery pulse, from the anterior to the posterior axillary fold. This injection also blocks the medial brachial cutaneous nerve, which also leaves the brachial plexus high in the axilla. Block of the intercostobrachial and medial brachial cutaneous nerves provides analgesia of the upper, inner aspect of the arm and allows the more comfortable use of a pneumatic tourniquet.

26. If a postoperative nerve deficit develops and you suspect it may have been caused by the anesthetic, what should be done?
A careful neurologic examination should be performed and its results documented. An electromyogram (EMG), if done within 3 weeks of the injury, may be helpful in establishing preexisting pathology if there is evidence of denervation of muscles. The EMG should be repeated 3 weeks after the block and surgery. If a patient had a normal preoperative study or a normal EMG soon after surgery but developed an abnormal EMG 3 weeks after the performance of the block, then the block or surgical procedure (related to the procedure itself or other incident at the time of surgery, such as improper positioning or tourniquet use) may be the cause of the nerve damage.

BLOCKS AROUND THE ELBOW

27. Describe how the ulnar, median, and radial nerves can be blocked around the elbow.
The *ulnar nerve* is blocked behind the medial epicondyle, where it is palpable, using a 1.5-cm, 25-gauge needle and 5 mL of the local anesthetic agent. Avoid impaling the nerve on the bone to prevent damage to the nerve.

The *median nerve* is blocked by introducing a 3.8-cm, 22-gauge short-beveled needle medial to the artery, slightly above the level of a line drawn between the epicondyles. The nerve is identified by paresthesias or by using a nerve stimulator and 5 to 10 mL of local anesthetic is injected.

The *radial nerve* is blocked 3 to 4 cm above the lateral epicondyle, where it is close to the distal humerus, after piercing the lateral intermuscular septum. A 3.8-cm, 22-gauge needle is introduced at this level, and 5 to 10 mL of local anesthetic is injected after the nerve is identified by paresthesias or by use of a nerve stimulator.

WRIST BLOCKS

28. How are wrist blocks performed?
The *median nerve* is blocked by inserting a 1.5-cm, 25-gauge needle between the palmaris longus and the flexor carpi radialis tendons at the level of the ulnar styloid process or the proximal crease of the wrist. In the absence of the palmaris longus, the needle is inserted on the ulnar side of the flexor carpi radialis tendon. After a paresthesia is obtained, 5 mL of local anesthetic is injected, taking care to inject the local anesthetic around the nerve rather than directly within the substance of the nerve.

The *ulnar nerve* is blocked by inserting a 1.5-cm, 25-gauge needle at the level of the proximal crease of the wrist, just radial to the flexor carpi ulnaris tendon, which is made prominent by active flexion of the wrist. After obtaining a paresthesia, 5 mL of local anesthetic is injected, again taking care not to inject directly within the substance of the nerve. The dorsal cutaneous nerve can be blocked by subcutaneous infiltration of approximately 5 mL of local anesthetic beginning at the site where the ulnar nerve was blocked and extending the infiltration to the midpoint of the dorsum of the wrist.

The *superficial branch of the radial nerve* is blocked by a subcutaneous infiltration starting radial to the radial artery and extending around to the midpoint of the dorsum of the wrist, using 5 to 7 mL of local anesthetic.

DIGITAL NERVE BLOCKS

29. Why should a ring block for anesthetizing a digit be avoided?
A circumferential block around the base of the digit can result in compartment syndrome producing gangrene, even if no vasopressor drug has been added to the local anesthetic.

30. How can a digital block be obtained?
A *volar* approach can be used in which a skin wheal is made directly over the flexor tendon just proximal to the distal palmar crease, and 2 to 3 mL of local anesthetic without epinephrine is injected on each side of the flexor tendons where the digital neurovascular bundles are located.

In the *dorsal* approach, which is a less painful method of blocking the digital nerves, the needle is inserted to the side of the extensor tendon, just proximal to the web. A skin wheal is made, and 1 mL of local anesthetic is injected superficial to the extensor hood to block the dorsal nerve. The needle is advanced toward the palm until its tip is palpable beneath the volar skin at the base of the finger, just distal to the web. Another 1 mL of local anesthetic is injected here to block the volar digital nerve. Before the needle is removed, it is redirected across the extensor tendon to the opposite side of the finger, and a small skin wheal is made overlying the other dorsal digital nerve. The needle is then withdrawn and reintroduced into the skin wheal on the opposite side of the finger, and the same technique is repeated. Care should be taken with this technique to use small amounts of local anesthetic to avoid creating a circumferential ring block, which can result in vascular impairment of the digit.

INTRAVENOUS REGIONAL ANESTHESIA (BIER BLOCK)

31. Describe the technique for performing a Bier block.
A dual tourniquet is placed on the upper arm of the side to be blocked. An intravenous line is placed with a 20-gauge plastic cannula and a heparin lock attached. The arm is elevated and exsanguinated with an Esmarch bandage, starting from the fingers all the way up to the tourniquet. The proximal tourniquet is inflated, and the Esmarch bandage is removed. The local anesthetic is slowly injected through the cannula. Lidocaine (3 mg/kg given as 0.5% without preservative) provides anesthesia within 4 to 6 minutes and lasts as long as the tourniquet is inflated. The proximal tourniquet is left inflated for 20 minutes or until the patient notices some discomfort. The distal tourniquet is inflated, and, when its inflation is confirmed, the proximal tourniquet is deflated. Because the distal tourniquet is applied over an anesthetized area, the patient is not likely to experience any discomfort for approximately 40 minutes. At the completion of the surgical procedure, the tourniquet is deflated for 15 seconds, reinflated for 30 seconds, and deflated again, especially if the duration of anesthesia was 20 minutes or less. If the procedure lasts longer than 40 minutes, the tourniquet can be safely deflated without reinflation.

32. What are the advantages of a Bier block?
Technically, the Bier block is very easy to perform and is suitable for outpatient surgery. Bilateral blocks can be done safely. Rapid return of motor function enables the surgeon to evaluate the results of the procedure.

33. List some disadvantages of the Bier block technique.
- *Tourniquet Pain.* Even with use of the double cuff, pain due to the tourniquet limits use of this procedure in operations lasting more than 1 hour.
- *Problems with Tourniquet Release.* When the tourniquet is released, a large bolus of anesthetic enters the systemic circulation. This brief elevation of local anesthetic blood level may produce systemic toxic reactions, including convulsions and cardiac irregularities. The longer the tourniquet remains inflated, the lower the anesthetic blood level. If the cuff is released for 15 seconds, reinflated, and then released again, it will lower the peak blood level and decrease the possibility of systemic reaction. However, if the tourniquet pressure is decreased gradually, when it reaches a pressure below arterial pressure and above venous pressure, local anesthetic enters the circulation producing toxic blood levels.
- *Loss of Anesthesia after Cuff Deflation.* If the surgeon wants to attain hemostasis and then close the wound, there is only 5 to 10 minutes of postdeflation analgesia, which may be inadequate in some procedures.
- *Equipment Problems.* Equipment must be tested and the tourniquet calibrated prior to use. Once the tourniquet is inflated, the local anesthetic is injected only after the absence of the radial pulse is confirmed. If the proximal and distal cuffs are not properly identified and labeled as such, tourniquet pain is likely to be a problem. Constant vigilance is necessary to ensure that the equipment is in working order and to avoid accidental disconnection and deflation of the cuff.

BIBLIOGRAPHY

Brown DL, Cahill DR, Bridenbaugh DL: Supraclavical nerve block: Anatomic analysis of a method to prevent pneumothorax. Anesth Analg 76:530–534, 1993.
Chan VW, Perlas A, Rawson R, Odukoya O: Ultrasound-guided supraclavicular plexus block. Anesth Analg 97:1514–1517, 2003.
Hickey R, Hoffman J, Ramamurthy S: A comparison of ropivacaine 0.5% and bupivacaine 0.5% for brachial plexus block. Anesthesiology 74:639–642, 1991.
Hickey R, Ramamurthy S: The diagnosis of phrenic nerve block on chest x-ray by a double exposure technique. Anesthesiology 70:704–707, 1989.
Quinlan JJ, Oleksey K, Murphy FL: Alkalinization of mepivacaine for axillary block. Anesth Analg 74:371–374, 1992.
Thompson GE, Rorie DK: Functional anatomy of the brachial plexus sheaths. Anesthesiology 59:117–122, 1993.
Urmey WF: Upper extremity blocks. In Brown DL (ed): Regional Anesthesia and Analgesia. Philadelphia, WB Saunders, 1996, pp 254–278.
Urmey WF, McDonald M: Hemidiaphragmatic paresis during interscalene brachial plexus block: Effects on pulmonary function and chest wall mechanics. Anesth Analg 74:352–357, 1992.
Williams SR, Chouinard P, Arcand G, et al: Ultrasound guidance speeds execution and improves the quality of supraclavicular block. Anesth Analg 97:1518–1523, 2003.
Winnie AP: Plexus Anesthesia. Philadelphia, WB Saunders, 1990.
www.nysora.com

CONGENITAL ANOMALIES

Joseph Upton III, MD, and
Benjamin J. Childers, MD

1. **At what age of development does the limb bud appear? When are digital rays evident?**
   Streeter divided human embryonic development into 23 stages. Limb development and differentiation are rapid processes that occur between the third and eighth postovulatory weeks. The limb bud, called Wolff's crest, is well defined at day 30. It is a ventral swelling mesoderm covered by a thick layer of ectoderm, called the *apical ectodermal ridge* (AER). By day 41 digital rays are present, and by day 48 joint interzones are evident histologically. Usually by the time the expectant mother is sure that she is pregnant, most of the upper limb differentiation has been completed.

2. **What does syndactyly mean? Is it the most common congenital anomaly?**
   Syndactyly (Greek: *syn* = together, *dactyly* = finger) is commonly used to describe webbed digits and is the second most common congenital anomaly. The most common are duplications, particularly preaxial or thumb duplications in the Asian population and postaxial or ulnar duplications in African-American and Native-American populations. The incidence of duplications varies according to the population but overall occurs in 3.8:1000 to 12:1000 live births.

3. **What type of correction is best for syndactyly?**
   No one repair is absolutely best. More than 60 methods have been described in the literature, and most use the same basic surgical principles. The surgeon must be comfortable with a few repairs that she/he learns to do well and not experiment with each case.

4. **What are the principles of syndactyly correction?**
   - Use of full-thickness flaps for commissure reconstruction
   - Zigzag incisions on the palmar surface
   - Use of full-thickness skin grafts
   - Equal division of flaps between each partner digit
   - Meticulous, atraumatic technique
   - Adequate postoperative immobilization
   - Staged release of the radial and ulnar sides of a digit; release of both sides during one procedure may compromise the vascular supply to the digit

   When operating on young children, it is important to work under general anesthesia and to use a pneumatic tourniquet and absorbable 6-0 or 5-0 chromic suture material.

5. **What are the most common problems after syndactyly correction?**
   Infection, graft or flap maceration, and graft loss are almost always related to the child's activity and/or inadequate immobilization. Surgeons with children of their own do not hesitate to protect operated limbs in a long arm cast extending well proximal to the elbow flexed at 90°. Single residents without children do not always appreciate the problems that most parents encounter with controlling active young children. Early problems also may occur after children wet their casts or dressings in bathtubs or swimming pools.

   Long-term problems include recurrence of the webbing or "web creep," which is related to scar contracture at the base of the commissure or along the incision lines. Zigzag incisions are intended to reduce this potential contracture. Skin grafts often are hyperpigmented and, if harvested within the hair-bearing escutcheon, may become hirsute during adolescence. Inadequate correction of the first web release may be obtained with tight contractures, which can be widened only with additional soft tissue.

6. **What is the most important web space in the hand?**
   The thumb–index or first web space is unquestionably the most important. Of all techniques described for correction of congenital hand anomalies, release of the first web space is the most significant functionally and aesthetically. In a pure analysis, a "basic hand" has three components: a mobile digit or thumb on the radial side, a first web space, and a post or digit on the opposite side of the hand.

7. What is the best method for surgical release of the first web space?

The surgeon must learn to use one or two methods well. For minimal to moderate contractures, the four-flap Z-plasty provides the greatest release and maintains the best concavity between the thumb and index metaphalangeal (MP) joints. A single Z-plasty and the five-flap Z-plasty, also called the "jumping man," are good alternatives. Many varieties of dorsal rotational flaps from the thumb or index metacarpal regions have been described with the use of skin grafts. These techniques are not preferred because they leave a conspicuous skin graft in a visible position of the hand. These local flaps are indicated in complex problems such as the Apert hand.

For severe contractures, soft tissue is often needed. Free tissue transfers in infants or young children often are cumbersome and technically difficult. Distally based forearm (radial artery or dorsal interosseous artery) fasciocutaneous flaps have been described for children with arthrogryposis, windblown hands, and hypoplastic thumbs with tight contractures and are advised for use by experienced surgeons.

8. What contributes to thumb–index contracture?

Tight skin is the most obvious etiology, but tight investing fascias of the first dorsal interosseous and adductor pollicis muscles almost always are found and must be excised. Often a tight band is present between the two muscles. Occasionally, a tight thumb carpometacarpal (CMC) joint may be found; it usually is suspected on physical examination.

9. How is syndactyly clinically classified?

The level of webbing between digits is *complete* if it extends to the fingertip and *incomplete* with a more proximal termination. A *simple* syndactyly refers to soft tissue connections between adjacent digits, whereas *complex* refers to bone or cartilaginous unions. *Complicated* refers to abnormal duplicated skeletal parts within the interdigital space (Fig. 118-1). The most common pattern is bilateral simple, incomplete syndactyly of the long and ring fingers. Many such patients have a simple syndactyly involving toes 2 and 3 on one or both feet.

10. Do children need more surgery after syndactyly repair?

There is always a chance that contractures will require future correction. The literature cites a secondary operation rate of approximately 10%. The incidence is much higher in complex and complicated cases and in cases with postoperative complications. There is a direct relationship between carefully planned and executed surgery and a low complication rate. Children and adults with central complex polysyndactyly invariably need secondary corrections. This variety is the most difficult to treat.

11. Geneticists and pediatricians use the terms *malformation, deformation*, and *disruption*. What do they mean?

The dysmorphology approach to congenital anomalies divides defects into one of three sequences, which are defined as problems that lead to a cascade of events:

- In a *malformation* sequence, poor formation of tissue within the fetus initiates the chain of defects, which may range from minimal to severe. All gradations of radial dysplasia, ranging from absence of the thenar muscles to complete absence of the radius resulting in the club hand posture, are examples. Occurrence rate is in the 5% range. Radial dysplasias also are associated with malformation in other organ systems, such as the VATER association (vertebral anomalies, anal atresia, tracheoesophageal fistula, renal anomalies, and radial dysplasia) and Holt-Oram syndrome (radial dysplasia and congenital heart disease).
- The *deformation* sequence involves no intrinsic problem with the fetus or embryo; instead, abnormal external mechanical or structural forces cause secondary distortion or deformation. Tethering or constriction of limb parts by anular bands in the constriction ring syndrome is a prime example. The occurrence rate is very low.
- In the *disruption* sequence, the normal fetus or embryo is subjected to tissue breakdown or injury, which may be vascular, infectious, mechanical, or metabolic in origin. The hand deformities associated with maternal ingestion of thalidomide or alcohol are good examples.

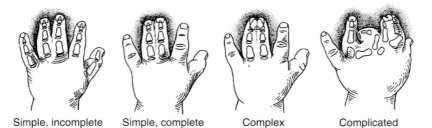

Simple, incomplete   Simple, complete   Complex   Complicated

Figure 118-1. Classification of syndactyly. (From Upton J: Congenital anomalies of the hand and forearm. In McCarthy JG, May J, Littler JW [eds]: Plastic Surgery. Philadelphia, WB Saunders, 1990, p 5280.)

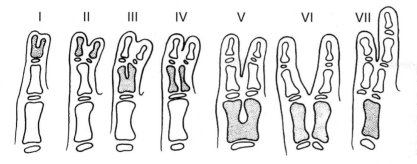

Figure 118-2. Classification of thumb duplications based on the level of duplication. Type VII describes the triphalangeal thumb. (From Upton J: Congenital anomalies. In Jurkiewicz M, Krizek TJ, Mathes SJ, Ariyan S [eds]: Plastic Surgery: Principles and Practice. St. Louis, Mosby, 1990, p 573.)

- Often the patient's problem cannot be explained by a single initiating factor. When the cause of a defect is unknown, the term *malformation* is preferred. Multiple defects are usually referred to as a *malformation syndrome*.

12. What is the relative incidence of congenital hand duplications? How are they clinically classified?

Duplications are the most common anomalies in all large series. They are classified by their position within the hand as preaxial (radial), central, or postaxial (ulnar). In the United States, duplication is most prevalent among African Americans, who have an extremely dominant inheritance pattern with a frequency of 1:300 live births and a predilection for the postaxial border of the hand. In contrast, Caucasians and Asians primarily have preaxial duplication at a rate of 1:3000 live births (see Question 2).

Preaxial thumb duplications are classified into six categories by the level of the duplications. Type II at the interphalangeal (IP) joint and type IV at the MP joint are the most common. The more proximal varieties, type V at the thumb metacarpal level and type VI at the CMC joint level, are uncommon. Additional designations are made if there is an extra phalanx (delta phalanx) or a triphalangeal partner (type VII). Triphalangeal thumbs are unusual and well beyond the experience of most residents (Fig. 118-2).

Central duplications are unusual and account for less than 10% of all duplications; they have no systematic clinical classification system. Because central duplications are often associated with webbing, the term *synpolydactyly* is used.

Postaxial duplications of the fifth ray are divided into three categories. Type I is characterized by a soft tissue nubbin with a skin bridge. Skeletal connections are present in type II, and a complete duplication of the entire ray is seen in type III (Fig. 118-3). Most cases are type I.

13. Is any special workup needed in newborns with a duplication?

In most cases, no. Thumb duplications may have a positive inheritance pattern and are common in Caucasian and Asian populations, whereas fifth finger duplications are extremely common in African-American and Native-American populations. When the opposite is seen, a workup is in order. More than 30 syndromes are associated with postaxial duplications, primarily in non–African-American populations. Conversely, an African American with thumb duplication and negative family history may have a syndrome such as fetal alcohol syndrome. Referral to a geneticist is in order.

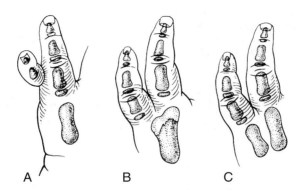

Figure 118-3. Classification of polydactyly (postaxial) demonstrates digits with no skeletal attachment—type I **(A),** skeletal connections—type II **(B),** and complete duplication of the entire ray, including the metacarpal bone—type III **(C).** (From Upton J: Congenital anomalies of the hand and forearm. In McCarthy JG, May J, Littler JW [eds]: Plastic Surgery. Philadelphia, WB Saunders, 1990, p 5345.)

14. How do you treat a newborn in the nursery with a type I floppy nubbin attached to the fifth finger?

Pediatricians like to "tie them off" with a suture. Type I duplications with large skin bridges often do not fall off. Many such children present to the dermatologist 8 years later with a bump at the site of duplication, which is misdiagnosed as a wart. The "wart" does not respond to application of a triple acid ointment or solution. This lump is a cartilaginous remnant or scar. Simple excision and closure with one or two sutures under local anesthesia in the newborn nursery is a more appropriate option.

15. Which side of a thumb duplication should be preserved?

The correct answer depends on which thumb has the better parts. In most patients the radial of the two partners is the more hypoplastic and is ablated. In some more proximal type V and type VI varieties at the metacarpal level, the distal portion of the ulnar partner is transposed on top of the proximal portion of the radial partner.

16. What are the basic principles of thumb duplication correction?

- Create the best possible thumb by using the best parts of each partner.
- Preserve an intact ulnar collateral ligament at the MP joint level.
- Reattach all thenar intrinsic muscles.
- Release a tight thumb index web space (four-flap Z-plasty is most commonly used).
- Preserve as much mobility as possible and preferably have motion in at least two of the three (CMC, MP, IP) joints.

17. What do you tell parents after a thumb duplication correction? Will the thumb be normal?

No. Most large series are incomplete and do not include critical long-term outcomes. What you see initially is what you get later. The reconstructed thumbs usually are smaller and less mobile than the normal side. Thenar muscles, especially the abductor pollicis brevis and flexor pollicis brevis, may be weak. Metacarpophalangeal joint instability or stiffness may occur after a collateral ligament reconstruction. A bulge on the radial side of the metacarpal in a type IV thumb represents a bifid metacarpal head that was not excised. The proximal type V and VI thumbs are never normal postoperatively, do not have normal intrinsic muscles, have short metacarpals, and commonly have inadequate extrinsic extensor and flexor tendon excursion.

18. What are the genetics and incidence of the constriction ring syndrome?

There is no positive inheritance in constriction ring syndrome (CRS). The incidence is less than 10% in large reported series of congenital hand malformations. The cause is related to an in utero deformation in which strands of the inner layer of the chorionic sac detach and wrap around parts of the fetus, usually fingers and toes. There are many examples of monozygotic twins with only one partner affected.

19. What anatomic features distinguish CRS from other congenital anomalies of the upper limb?

The anatomy proximal to the level of deformation or in utero injury is completely normal. For this reason, toe transfers for thumb and digital reconstruction are much more predictable. Unfortunately, many severely affected children have no toes to transfer.

20. What other terms have been used to describe CRS?

Many terms have been used to describe the clinical features seen in CRS.

- *Acrosyndactyly* refers to digits joined together at the tips and creating the appearance of a peak (Greek: *acro* = peak).
- *Anular band* is a ring around a body part; *constriction ring* is the preferred term to describe the same phenomenon.
- *Fenestrated syndactyly* refers to the sinuses at the base of the webbed digits. At the time of ischemic insult caused by the constricting band, separation of the digit via programmed cell death has started. Although the webbing recurs as a result of the distal inflammatory process, the separation may persist and presents as a dorsal-to-palmar epithelial-lined sinus that can be easily probed. The actual level of the sinuses is always distal to the level of the normal commissure.
- *Placental bands* and *amniotic bands* refer to the strands that wrap around body parts. At birth, desiccated strands wrapped around digits represent the loose strands of the chorionic sac that have separated and become entangled around fingers, toes, and other body parts.
- *Congenital amputations* refer to transverse loss of tissue or failure of formation. They are commonly seen in CRS but are not exclusive to it.

This condition has been around for a long time and has been confused in past and recent literature. The term *constriction ring syndrome* has been adopted by the American Society for Surgery of the Hand (ASSH) and the International Federation of Societies for Surgery of the Hand (IFSSH).

21. What is a constriction ring or anular (ring) band?
The constricting ring acts as a tourniquet around the developing digit, toe, or other body part and results in a soft tissue depression beneath the skin. The ring may be superficial or deep, extending into the periosteum. It may extend completely or partially around the circumference of the part. Most digital rings are deep dorsally and extend only partially around the palmar surface. However, this explanation does not account for the frequent association of cleft lip/palate and club feet with CRS. The clefts often are wide lateral clefts that result in a monstrous clinical appearance. It has been postulated that wide bands or aprons of partially separated sac obstruct the fusion of the lateral lip with the prolabial segment.

22. How is CRS treated?
In the past, surgeons performed simple Z-plasties that did nothing more than leave the mark of the infamous cowboy Zorro on operated hands. After excision of the scarred constriction ring, it is necessary to advance flaps of fat and fascial tissue across the depression to correct the contour deformity. Straight-line dorsal incisions are preferred to Z-plasties; they are conveniently placed along the less visible sides of the digit.

23. Why are transverse absences associated with CRS ideal for toe-to-thumb transfers?
CRS is the only congenital anomaly in which the anatomy proximal to the level of complete or partial loss is completely normal. In other conditions, intrinsic and extrinsic muscle and neural and vascular anatomy may be anomalous.

24. What does symphalangism mean? What are the more common clinical presentations?
Symphalangism (Greek: *sym* = together, *phalanx* = bone) refers to phalanges that are fused because of a failure of segmentation or incomplete segmentation with cavitation. More than 15 clinical conditions are associated with these stiff, often short and slender digits. The most important clinical sign is the lack of a flexion crease. There are three general categories of symphalangism:
1. *True symphalangism* demonstrates digits of normal length, positive inheritance, fusion of one or more digits, PIP involvement (common), and long, slender fingers.
2. *Symbrachydactyly* demonstrates all variations of short digits with and without varying degrees of webbing. Formerly many affected hands were classified as atypical cleft hands. DIP and PIP joints are commonly fused.
3. *Syndromic symphalangism* is most commonly seen in the Apert and Poland syndromes. In both the central three rays are most commonly involved. Some degree of digital fusion may be seen in the other acrocephalosyndactyly (ACS) syndromes. In neither of these conditions are the MP joints involved.

25. How is symphalangism treated?
The stiff fingers will always be stiff. Angulation and especially rotation should be corrected early in life without damage to growth centers.

26. In what position should PIP joints be fused?
Index finger, 10°; middle finger, 25° to 30°; ring finger, 40°; and small finger, 45° to 50°.

27. How can IP joints be reconstructed?
Many methods have been tried, but none is satisfactory. Examples include the following:
- Silicone caps and spacers
- Silicone implants with stems into the medullary canals
- Perichondrial resurfacing
- Incision of early cartilage bridges followed by early motion
- Osteointegrated implants (this technique has promise for the future)
- Microvascular second-toe joint transfer

All of these reconstructions have advantages and disadvantages. In children, use of autogenous materials is preferable to avoid the secondary disadvantages of incompatible biomaterials. Perichondrial resurfacing at the MP and PIP levels results in fibrocartilage and stiff joints. Early release and continued motion result in floppy digits that ultimately become stiff. Osteointegrated concepts have not yet been used in children but may have promise. Microvascular defects are labor intensive and biologically make the most sense. The balance of the thin intrinsic and extrinsic extensor mechanism is never maintained.

28. What is the difference between clinodactyly and camptodactyly?
Clinodactyly (Greek: *clino* = deviated, *dactylos* = digit) refers to a digit or thumb that is deviated in a radioulnar or mediolateral direction. An inward (radial) deviation of the fifth digit is most commonly seen and is so often associated with various other types of congenital hand anomalies that it represents "background noise" and gives no specific indication of one condition over another.

Camptodactyly (Greek: *campto* = bent, *dactylos* = digit) refers to a flexion deformity of a digit or thumb in an anteroposterior plane. This deformity also commonly involves the PIP joint of the fifth finger and is seen in two distinct age groups: infants and adolescent girls.

29. What is the main anatomic problem in camptodactyly?

As the digit develops in the fetus or infant or as it continues to grow in the young child and adolescent, the balance of flexion and extension forces at each joint is quite precise. More than 20 abnormal origins and particularly insertions of the intrinsic and extrinsic muscle tendon units within the hand have been described. The most common variations involve abnormal distal insertions of the lumbrical and interosseous muscles within the digits, particularly on the ulnar side of the hand. Tight joint capsules, collateral ligaments, joint contractures, abnormal articulating surfaces, and proliferative fibrous bands (fibrous substrata) within the digit are more likely secondary and are not the primary forces causing camptodactyly.

30. What are the radiologic signs of congenital camptodactyly?

A true lateral radiograph of the digit gives an indication about the duration of congenital camptodactyly. Digits that have been flexed at the PIP joints for longer periods show the following:
- Flattening of the dorsal condylar surface of the proximal phalanx
- Widened base of the middle phalanx
- Flattening of the palmar surface of the condyle
- Indentation within the surface of the middle phalanx
- Narrowed joint space

The most important determining factor in joint formation is motion. A joint that is not moved early in life will not have a rounded condyle and will demonstrate a flat articular surface.

31. What are the indications for joint release in camptodactyly?

Most joint contractures are treated successfully with stretching and splinting. Few require surgical release. Contractures of 15° to 50° usually have favorable outcomes. Adults and adolescents with longstanding contractures greater than 70° of flexion are best treated with arthrodesis. The results of soft tissue releases are inversely proportional to the severity of the contracture. Often initial tight contractures can be improved with conscientious stretching but may need surgery later in childhood to obtain full correction. Surgery may be difficult and must be followed by a strict stretching and night-splinting regimen.

32. What is the differential diagnosis of bilateral flexion deformities of the thumb?

Trigger thumbs due to flexor tenosynovitis are the most common cause. Newborns and infants may demonstrate congenital absence of the extrinsic extensor (extensor pollicis longus), a condition in which the thumb is adducted into the palm (commonly called "clasped thumb"). Congenital camptodactyly does not involve the thumb but should be considered with any flexion deformity of a digit. More generalized musculoskeletal conditions, such as arthrogryposis and Freeman-Sheldon syndrome, also must be considered.

33. When should a trigger thumb be released surgically?

In children younger than 18 months, spontaneous resolution *may* be seen within 6 months. After age 2 years, children with persistent locking develop compensatory hyperextension of the MP joint as the palmar plate is stretched. This hyperextension may not correct itself with growth after the trigger is corrected. No additional surgery is indicated unless functional problems are present. Forget about approaching a young child with a needle for a steroid injection in your office. This method will not work. Percutaneous needle releases have been described in older patients but have little place in the treatment of young children in whom surgical division of the A1 pulley is indicated.

34. What is the worst complication of a trigger release?

The radial digital nerve to the thumb is easily severed with blind cutting in a proximal direction.

35. What conditions should be considered in a child born with gross enlargement of a digit?

Macrodactyly (Greek: *makros* = large, *dactylos* = digit) and gigantism have been used to describe enlarged digits and thumbs. Gigantism is preferred by some because it encompasses enlargement of both soft tissues and skeletal elements. The clinician should consider the following:
- Neurofibromatosis (NF)
- Nerve territory-oriented lipofibromatosis not associated with NF
- Multiple hereditary exostosis

- Proteus syndrome with hyperostotic lesions and overgrowth of phalanges
- Vascular malformations, particularly venous, lymphatic, and mixed venous–lymphatic
- Hemihypertrophy of the limb

These unusual conditions should be referred to a pediatric hand specialist.

36. What is the workup for macrodactyly?

These conditions are rare. Common sense dictates that the clinician obtain radiographs, complete a thorough physical examination, and then hit the books. NF is suspected on clinical examination and has specific criteria. Biopsies are rarely necessary. Genetic analysis is available. Vascular anomalies are distinguished by magnetic resonance imaging (MRI). Bone tumors often require biopsy. Hemihypertrophy is the most difficult and often is a diagnosis by exclusion. In this condition there is a high incidence of adrenal masses, which must be detected by ultrasound. No one other than the pediatric hand specialist has a detailed working knowledge of all of these conditions. It is helpful to contact someone locally or nationally with experience in treatment of each particular condition.

37. What is the difference between hemangioma and vascular malformation?

During the past 10 years knowledge has increased exponentially. Mulliken made the most significant contribution with his classification, which makes a clear-cut distinction between the two on biologic grounds. *Hemangiomas* are vascular birthmarks that appear shortly after birth, undergo a period of rapid growth and proliferation, and spontaneously involute by age 7 to 9 years. The endothelial cells actively proliferate and create new vascular channels during the growth phase. The mechanism for involution is unknown. *Vascular malformations* are biologically quiescent lesions. They result from defective embryogenesis, are present at birth or are recognized shortly after birth, and do not undergo a biphasic growth cycle like hemangiomas. The endothelial cells do not actively proliferate. Malformations are subgrouped according to cell types into capillary, venous, lymphatic, mixed venous–lymphatic, and arterial malformations. Arterial malformations include arteriovenous fistulas with active shunting between the arterial and venous sides of the circulation.

38. Outline the five types of hypoplastic thumbs.

- *Type 1:* Hypoplastic thumb with all joints present; median nerve-innervated intrinsic muscles present but hypoplastic; joints stable; function normal
- *Type 2:* Thumb skeleton more hypoplastic; joints intact with some collateral ligament instability at the MP level; greater hypoplasia of median nerve-innervated intrinsic muscles; first web space often deficient
- *Type 3:* Thumb phalanges present but much smaller; increased collateral ligament instability at the MP level; thenar intrinsic muscles small and weak; ulnar intrinsic muscles hypoplastic; extrinsic muscles hypoplastic; first web space very tight; *type 3A:* Metacarpal intact but small; intact CMC joint; *type 3B:* Metacarpal incomplete; no CMC joint
- *Type 4:* Thumb and all of its components highly deficient; no skeletal connection to the rest of the hand; skin bridge only, constituting a floating thumb or "pouce flottant"
- *Type 5:* Aplasia

39. What are the possible options for reconstruction of type 3B thumbs?

The options are (1) staged osteoplastic reconstruction and (2) excision of the thumb and index pollicization. The second option is preferred by most pediatric hand specialists. Staged reconstruction involves (1) provision of skeletal continuity with a standard bone graft or a microvascular second toe transfer, (2) creation of an adequate web space, and (3) tendon transfers to provide palmar abduction of the first ray as well as MP and IP flexion and extension.

40. What are the long-term functional limitations of a well-performed pollicization procedure?

Such thumbs are never normal. Grip and pinch maneuvers involving the thumb are always deficient. Results fall into two basic groups: (1) complete or partial radius deficiency and (2) normal radius and preoperative range of motion. The second group has predictably better outcomes because extrinsic flexor and extensor muscles as well as intrinsic muscles to the index ray are normal. A stiff index finger preoperatively will become a very stiff thumb.

41. Describe the hand in patients with Apert syndrome.

Apert syndrome (acrocephalosyndactyly) is common only in craniofacial clinics. It occurs in more than 1:45,000 live births. Both hands have enantiomorphic (mirror image) deformities:

- Short radially deviated thumb (radial clinodactyly)
- Deficient first web space
- Complete, complex syndactyly involving the central three rays
- Simple, complete syndactyly between the ring and fifth rays

Three specific types of hand configurations with varying degrees of severity have been described. Additional skeletal anomalies include carpal coalitions, a ring–fifth metacarpal synostosis, symphalangism between the proximal and middle phalanges, and varying degrees of conjoined nails. The hands are subclassified into three separate groups depending on the severity of skeletal coalition.

42. What is Poland syndrome?

In 1849 Alfred Poland, a student dissector in gross anatomy, described a cadaver with chest wall anomalies associated with a hypoplastic webbed hand. The illustration made by a friend did not include the hand, but the head, neck, and thorax were depicted in detail. A century after this description appeared in the Guy's Hospital Reports, Clarkson, the hospital hand surgeon, found the hand that had been preserved in the hospital museum, redescribed the condition, and introduced the term *Poland syndrome*. The hand surgeon's definition includes (1) absence of the sternal head of the pectoralis major muscle (clavicular head usually is present), (2) hypoplastic hand, and (3) brachysyndactyly (short, webbed fingers). We have further described the hand anomalies as affecting primarily the central three rays of the hand. The four variations of severity range from least affected (hypoplastic but present index, long, and ring digits) to a hand with no digits or thumb.

43. How is the chest wall reconstructed in children with Poland syndrome?

Nothing is usually done in children. In adolescents, conspicuous deformities can be reconstructed with correction of the pectus carinatum (pigeon breast) or pectus excavatum (caved-in chest) deformities, followed by a latissimus dorsi muscle transfer to recreate the missing pectoralis major muscle.

44. What is the most persistent request of girls with Poland syndrome?

Girls request breast reconstruction, which is different from a simple augmentation or reconstruction after mastectomy. Expansion and overexpansion must be completed before final implant placement because the integument, including the areola, often is highly deficient. Subpectoral implants are preferred, but this muscle is either deficient or absent. Latissimus transfer with submuscular implants is then performed. It is wise to wait until adulthood before doing a transverse rectus abdominis muscle or free tissue transfer reconstruction.

45. A child is born with impending gangrene of portions of one or both forearms. What condition does the child have? What type of workup is indicated?

This rare and often catastrophic condition, called *cutis aplasia congenita*, probably results from mechanical impingement or pressure on the upper limbs. Usually the forearms are caught between the head or trunk and the pelvic brim. The condition is often associated with multiple births. Mothers often give a history of lack of movement for one or more days before delivery. Routine workup, including blood tests and radiographs, is normal. This condition can be viewed as an in utero Volkmann's contracture.

46. What is Holt-Oram syndrome?

In the late 1950s two pediatricians, working independently in the United States and England, described the association between congenital *hand anomalies* and *congenital heart defects*. The cardiac anomalies vary greatly, but the hand malformations consist primarily of some form of radial dysplasia. If a surgeon has the opportunity to examine a large number of infants with congenital heart defects, he/she will find many cases of minimal radial dysplasias, such as hypoplastic thenar intrinsic muscles. Children with radial club hand or thumb hypoplasia or absence are not difficult to diagnose.

47. What single operation is most beneficial for patients with a congenital hand anomaly?

Release of the first (thumb–index) web space. For mild to moderate deficiencies we prefer the four-flap Z-plasty and for tight, constricted web spaces the distally based radial forearm flap or dorsal interosseous flap. Dorsal sliding flaps are not preferred because of the unsightly, hyperpigmented skin grafts in the donor region. However, they are popular in both orthopedic and plastic surgical literature because of the mobility of the dorsal skin and the technical ease of the procedure.

48. Describe the hand in a child with Freeman-Sheldon syndrome.

The "whistling face" syndrome presents with characteristic hand and facial anomalies. The hands are often narrow with prominent ulnar drift. Incomplete, simple syndactyly and varying degrees of PIP camptodactyly are often present. The first web space usually is tight. The descriptive term "windblown hand" is often applied. Many other musculoskeletal anomalies, such as scoliosis, hip dysplasia, and radial head dislocation, may be present. These children are not retarded mentally.

49. A child presents with a swollen hand and forearm and an associated neck mass diagnosed as a "cystic hygroma." What is the underlying pathophysiology?

Cystic hygroma describes a lymphatic malformation in the head and neck region. The upper limb as well as mediastinum also may be involved. In the hand and forearm the interconnecting lymphatic channels may be much smaller. The size of the limb may be quite large, grotesque on occasion. Besides the symptoms related to bulk and increased weight, many children develop high fevers related to episodic beta-streptococcal infections, which usually originate in the cutaneous vesicles often found in lymphatic lesions. Skeletal enlargement may be present but is not a hallmark of these macrodactylies, which are difficult to treat. Staged aggressive debulking is the treatment of choice once conservative measures and compression garments have failed.

50. What is the difference between a typical and atypical cleft hand?

They are completely different. A *typical cleft* hand has the following characteristics: bilaterality, positive inheritance, foot involvement, V-shaped cleft, and syndactyly (common). A portion or all of the middle ray is commonly missing. It is often called simply a cleft hand. The *atypical cleft* refers to a unilateral anomaly that is nonfamilial and has a U-shaped cleft with no foot involvement. Small nubbins often represent rudimentary digits. This condition often has been called "lobster claw hand." After much discussion at various international meetings, the committees for the study of congenital anomalies of the hand recommend that "atypical cleft hand" be officially classified as symbrachydactyly.

51. Describe the upper limb in a child with severe arthrogryposis multiplex congenita.

Arthrogryposis, a syndrome of unknown etiology, is always present at birth and manifests with persistent joint contractures. It is classified into *myopathic* and *neurogenic* forms. The bottom line is that the muscles do not function. The upper limb appearance is unmistakable. The shoulders are thin and held in adduction and internal rotation. The elbows are extended, and the forearms are usually held in a semiflexed pronated position. Some elbow passive range of motion may be present. In severe cases the wrist is held in flexion and ulnar deviation, and the thumb is tightly adducted into the palm. The digits are flexed and ulnarly deviated at the MP joints. The skin may be atrophied and waxy. Skin dimples dorsally and flexion creases on the palmar surfaces signify mobile joint spaces. The lower extremities are more frequently involved than the upper.

BIBLIOGRAPHY

Dobyns JH, Wood VE, Bayne LG: Congenital. In Green DP (ed): Operative Hand Surgery, Vol 1, 3rd ed. New York, Churchill Livingstone, 1993, pp 251–549.

Flatt AE: The Care of Congenital Hand Anomalies. St. Louis, Quality Medical Publishing, 1994.

Lister G: Congenital. In Lister G (ed): The Hand, 3rd ed. New York, Churchill Livingstone, 1993, pp 459–512.

Mulliken JB, Young AE: Vascular Birthmarks: Hemangiomas and Malformations. Philadelphia, WB Saunders, 1988.

Upton J: Congenital anomalies of the hand and forearm. In McCarthy JG, May J, Littler JW (eds): Plastic Surgery, Vol 8. Philadelphia, WB Saunders, 1990, pp 5213–5398.

THE PEDIATRIC HAND

Samuel O. Poore MD, PhD, and
Michael L. Bentz MD, FAAP, FACS

1. **How are the flexor tendons examined in an uncooperative or unconscious pediatric patient?**

   The flexor tendons can be indirectly examined by visually inspecting the fingers at rest as well as observing the tenodesis effect during passive flexion and extension of the wrist. At rest with the hand in full supination the digits demonstrate an increasing amount of flexion from the index to the small finger that is referred to as the "digital cascade." Any digit that is extended relative to the other fingers and does not conform to the natural cascade suggests a flexor tendon injury. To observe the tenodesis effect the wrist is passively moved from flexion to extension, and when this passive tension at the wrist is transmitted to the flexor tendons the digits are automatically flexed (Table 119-1).

2. **How is sensation evaluated in young children?**

   Two-point discrimination should be evaluated whenever possible. However, in an uncooperative and noncommunicative pediatric patient an accurate two-point examination can be challenging at best. Pinprick is not an ideal method to assess sensitivity in a child; the presence of moisture on the volar fingertips usually is an adequate means of testing sensitivity. In normal fingertips the skin is moist, whereas in denervated fingertips it is dry. The degree of moisture at the fingertip can be directly visualized as small beads of sweat using an ophthalmoscope for magnification (see Table 119-1).

3. **What is the O'Raine test?**

   Placement of normal, innervated digits in warm water (40°C) for 20 minutes, as described by O'Raine, results in wrinkling of the fingertips. Denervated digits do not wrinkle when this test is performed. This maneuver can provide invaluable diagnostic information regarding sensory nerve injury in the uncooperative or unconscious pediatric patient.

4. **Why is a laceration of palmaris longus of special significance?**

   Eighty to ninety percent of children with palmaris longus lacerations also have an associated partial or complete median nerve injury. Therefore when a palmaris longus laceration is present, an associated median nerve injury should be assumed.

5. **What is a Kirner deformity? A pseudoepiphysis? The Pseudo-Terry Thomas sign? What is their significance?**

   All of these are *normal anatomic variants* that can easily be misdiagnosed as fractures or dislocations.

   Kirner Deformity: This is a radial curving of the distal phalanx of the little finger and should be distinguished from trauma by obtaining contralateral comparison radiographs.

Table 119-1. Physical Examination of the Pediatric Hand

EXAMINATION TECHNIQUE	ABNORMAL FINDING	UNDERLYING DIAGNOSIS
With patient's hand in resting position, observe if fingers are flexed or extended relative to one another	Flexed finger Extended finger	Disrupted extensor tendon Disrupted flexor tendon
Passive flexion of the wrist	Lack of tenodesis at proximal interphalangeal or distal interphalangeal joint	Disrupted flexor tendon
Observe for moisture at fingertip (with ophthalmoscope)	Dry fingertip	Disrupted digital nerve
Check two-point discrimination at finger tip (using paper clip)	Patient cannot distinguish points at least 5 mm apart	Neurologic compromise
Check capillary refill at pulp of fingertip	Blanching lasts more than 4 seconds	Microvascular disruption

Pseudoepiphysis: The thumb metacarpal epiphysis occurs at the proximal end of the bone whereas the epiphyses of the finger metacarpals occur at the distal end of the bone. Occasionally the thumb has a second epiphysis that occurs at the distal end of the bone. This pseudoepiphysis must be differentiated from a fracture line, again stressing the importance of obtaining contralateral radiographs. A pseudoepiphysis has also been noted at the proximal end of the second metacarpal.

Pseudo-Terry Thomas Sign: This is the normal distance between the scaphoid and the lunate during hand maturation. Given that the scaphoid ossifies from distal to proximal, a radiologic lucency exists between the scaphoid and the lunate. This area, which is filled with unossified bone and cartilage, can be misdiagnosed as a scapholunate dislocation.

6. Why is an understanding of carpal, metacarpal, and phalangeal ossification patterns essential in diagnosing and treating pediatric hand fractures?

Hand and wrist fractures are relatively uncommon in children and even less common in infants. For carpal, metacarpal, and phalangeal injuries, an understanding of the ossification patterns of these bones is essential to understanding basic fracture patterns and treatment. The carpus of infants is almost entirely cartilaginous and therefore is relatively immune to injury. As the bones ossify the carpus is more vulnerable to both bony and ligamentous injury. The metacarpals and phalanges have distinct growth patterns as well as relatively consistent timing of ossification and closure of epiphyseal growth plates (Fig. 119-1). Unlike other long bones in the body, the small long-bones in the hand have only one ossification center located at either the proximal or distal end of the bone. As ossification occurs and as the bones reach maturation, fractures are more likely to occur. These concepts are important in treatment. Fractures involving the epiphysis (see Salter-Harris classification, Question 8, Figure 119-2) should be given special attention and may require closed or open reduction and fixation for realignment. Failure to do so can result in malunion and ultimately growth abnormality of the effected segment.

7. What is a Seymour fracture?

First described by Seymour in 1966, the "Seymour fracture" is an extraarticular fracture involving the base of the distal phalanx 1 to 2 mm distal to the growth plate. This fracture usually occurs prior to closure of the distal phalangeal growth plate, often accompanied by avulsion of the proximal nail plate. It typically presents as a mallet finger given the anatomic relationship of the flexor and extensor tendons. The extensor tendon inserts on the epiphysis only, whereas the flexor digitorum profundus tendon spans both the epiphysis and metaphysis. Therefore the phalangeal component distal to the fragment is flexed by the flexor digitorum profundus while the epiphyseal fragment remains in extension by the extensor tendon. When avulsion of the proximal nail plate is present, the Seymour fracture should be treated as an open fracture (e.g., irrigated and débrided) to avoid complications associated with infection.

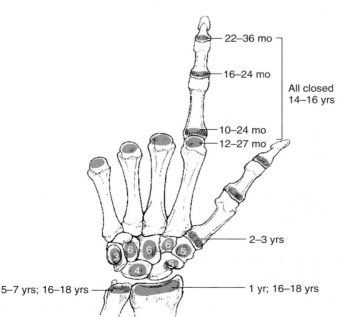

Figure 119-1. Timing of epiphyseal ossification centers and physeal fusion in the developing hand and wrist. As illustrated, the carpus of infants is almost entirely cartilaginous and therefore is relatively immune to injury. The relatively consistent timing of ossification and closure of epiphyseal growth plates has implications for the diagnosis, classification, and treatment of hand injuries. (From Bernard SL, Greco RJ: Pediatric hand trauma. In Pediatric Plastic Surgery. Bentz ML [ed]: Pediatric Plastic Surgery. Stamford, CT, Appleton & Lange, 1998, pp. 827–860, with permission.)

Labels on figure:
22–36 mo
16–24 mo
All closed 14–16 yrs
10–24 mo
12–27 mo
2–3 yrs
5–7 yrs; 16–18 yrs
1 yr; 16–18 yrs

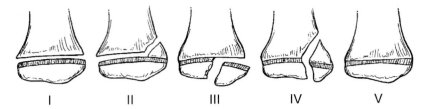

Figure 119-2 Salter-Harris fracture classification. *Type I,* Occurs through the growth plate with separation of the epiphysis from the metaphysic. *Type II,* Fracture through the plate and with a small metaphyseal fragment. *Type III,* Intraarticular fracture of the epiphysis. *Type IV,* Fracture through the epiphyseal plate and metaphysis. *Type V,* Compression fracture confined to the epiphyseal plate. (From Bernard SL, Greco RJ: Pediatric hand trauma. In Bentz ML [ed]: Pediatric Plastic Surgery. Stamford, Connecticut, Appleton & Lange, 1998, pp. 827–860, with permission.)

8. How are long bone fractures of the hand in children described and classified?

Consistent nomenclature should be used to describe all hand fractures. Terminology should include (1) stable versus unstable; (2) open versus closed; (3) dorsal versus volar; (4) rotation; (5) length; and (6) location (e.g., metacarpal neck, epiphysis). Fractures involving the epiphysis should be classified using the universally accepted Salter-Harris classification system (Fig. 119-2).

9. Why are Salter-Harris type III fractures of the middle phalanx rare and Salter-Harris III fractures of proximal phalanx relatively common?

An understanding of capsular anatomy of the metacarpophalangeal (MP) and interphalangeal joints is essential to answering this question. The collateral ligaments of the proximal interphalangeal joint arise from the epiphysis of the proximal phalanx, span the joint, and insert onto the metaphysis of the middle phalanx. Therefore the proximal interphalangeal joint is reinforced in three planes, making fractures through the epiphysis (type III) relatively uncommon. However, the collateral ligaments of the MP joint originate from the metacarpal physis and insert in only two planes on the epiphysis of the proximal phalanx, accounting for why Salter-Harris type III fractures are more common at this site.

10. How are metacarpal base, shaft, neck, and epiphyseal fractures treated?

- *Metacarpal Base:* Both displaced and nondisplaced fractures of the metacarpal base can be reduced in a closed fashion. Reduction is best achieved using long traction on the involved rays and volarly directed pressure on the fractured metacarpal. A splint or cast is applied for 3 to 4 weeks.
- *Metacarpal Shaft:* These fractures are rare in children. Nondisplaced fractures can be treated by closed immobilization for 3 to 4 weeks. Displaced fractures of the metacarpal shaft usually are amenable to closed reduction with close follow-up (2 weeks, first visit) and appropriate radiographs to ensure alignment. For displaced and unstable fractures percutaneous pinning works well. For unstable, spiral, or long oblique fractures, open reduction internal fixation (ORIF) may be required.
- *Metacarpal Neck:* These fractures are best treated with Jahss closed reduction and casting for 3 to 4 weeks. Of note is that the MP joints of children, unlike in adults, can be immobilized in full extension, to allow for better molding of the cast both dorsally and volarly. Stiffness is uncommon, and most children achieve full mobilization 1 to 2 weeks after removal of the cast. One exception are metacarpal neck fractures treated with internal fixation, which are more subject to stiffness from adhesions between tendon and hardware and therefore early mobilization should be advocated.
- *Epiphysis:* These fractures are relatively uncommon. When they do occur most are Salter-Harris II injuries. When the fracture results in a Salter-Harris III, IV, or V fracture, ORIF is often required for realignment and the prevention of growth arrest.

11. How much angulation of the metacarpal neck will be remodeled and therefore should be tolerated in children?

The degree of tolerated angulation varies by finger. Cornwall suggests using the easy to remember sequence of "10, 20, 30, 40": (1) index finger metacarpal, 10°; (2) middle finger metacarpal, 20°; (3) ring finger metacarpal, 30°; (4) small finger metacarpal, 40°.

12. How are phalangeal fractures treated in children?

- *Proximal Phalanx:* Most of these fractures can be treated with reduction and immobilization for 3 weeks. Exceptions that may require ORIF or percutaneous pinning include displaced intraarticular fractures (Salter-Harris III to V), spiral, or oblique fractures particularly associated with a rotational deformity, as well as comminuted midphalangeal fractures (Box 119-1).
- *Middle Phalanx:* Fractures of the base of the middle phalanx usually are Salter-Harris III fractures, and most only require 3 weeks of immobilization. Exceptions include fractures with a displaced volar fragment that may require ORIF if displaced greater than 1 mm.

Box 119-1. Fractures Often Requiring Percutaneous Internal Fixation

- Mallet fractures with subluxed joint or one third of articular surface
- Comminuted middle phalanx fracture
- Comminuted proximal phalanx fracture
- Displaced Salter-Harris III–IV fractures
- Spiral proximal phalanx fractures
- Oblique proximal phalanx fractures
- Metacarpal head fractures
- Multiple metacarpal fractures
- Fracture–dislocation of the fifth metacarpal joint.

Data from Bernard SL, Greco RJ: Pediatric hand trauma. In Bentz ML [ed]: Pediatric Plastic Surgery. Stamford, CT, Appleton & Lange, 1998, pp. 827–860.

- *Distal Phalanx:* Most of these fractures are Salter-Harris I or II fractures that require splinting for 3 weeks. Given the location of these fractures and the mechanisms causing them (e.g., crush), open fractures are common and often require débridement of the crushed segment, repair of the nail bed, and reduction of the distal phalangeal fracture.

13. What is the "extra-octave fracture" and how is it fixed? What is a "cartilaginous cap" fracture?

The *extra-octave fracture* is a Salter-Harris II fracture of the proximal phalanx of the little finger and is the most common fracture of the pediatric hand. The mechanism of injury is forcible abduction of the little finger, and treatment consists of closed reduction and splinting for 3 to 4 weeks. *Cartilaginous cap fractures,* also known as subcapital, subcondylar, and supracondylar fractures, occur through the neck of the proximal and middle phalanges. These fractures, though rare, most likely occur when a digit is trapped in a closing door. These fractures are classified as displaced or undisplaced. Undisplaced cartilaginous cap fractures require splint fixation, although one author reports 90% of displaced cartilaginous cap fractures require ORIF.

14. What is the most common carpal fracture in children, and how does fracture of this bone differ between children and adults?

The scaphoid bone is the most frequently fractured carpal element and most often results from a falling on an outstretched hand. The scaphoid ossifies eccentrically with the distal pole ossifying before the proximal pole, thus accounting for the primary difference between adult and pediatric scaphoid fractures: children most often fracture the distal third (60% to 80% of the time). By early adolescence, fracture patterns resemble that of the adult population.

15. What is the youngest reported case of scaphoid fracture?

The earliest case report of scaphoid fracture occurred in a 4-year-old girl.

16. When should a scaphoid fracture be suspected, and how is it radiologically diagnosed?

The mechanism of injury is important to elucidate while obtaining the history of the injury from the patient or the parents. Fracture of the scaphoid most often occurs from falling on an outstretched and pronated hand. Characteristic physical findings should further the diagnosis and include swelling and tenderness over the scaphoid tuberosity, pain elicited during palpation of the anatomic snuffbox, and pain during axial loading of the first metacarpal. Diagnosis of nondisplaced scaphoid fractures can be vexing, and plain wrist radiographs should include posteroanterior and oblique views as well as a special scaphoid view. This radiograph, consisting of an anteroposterior view with the fingers flexed and the wrist in 25° to 50° of supination, should be specifically ordered to visually enhance the scaphoid.

17. What concomitant injuries are often associated with scaphoid fracture?

Because severe trauma is required to fracture the scaphoid in younger children, due to thick cartilage covering the ossification center and the resultant resilience, the patient must be fully evaluated for associated injuries. These include supracondylar fractures, distal radius fractures, metacarpal fractures, capitate fractures, other carpal fractures and transscaphoid–perilunate dislocation.

18. What is the proper course of action if the clinical suspicion of scaphoid fracture is high and radiographic evidence is low?

These individuals should have their wrist immobilized in a long arm splint, and a repeat clinical and radiologic examination should be performed 1 to 2 weeks from the date of injury. If the pain persists, further imaging should be obtained. The imaging modality of choice is magnetic resonance imaging (MRI), which has largely supplanted other modalities including computed tomographic (CT) scan, bone scanning, and ultrasound.

19. What are the three types of scaphoid fracture?

- *Type I: Pure Chondral Injury.* Usually occurs in children 8 years and younger.
- *Type II: Osteochondral Fracture.* Usually occurs in children 8 to 11 years old.
- *Type III: Ossified Fracture (Adult Variant Fracture).* Usually occurs in children 12 years and older and involves the completely or nearly completely ossified scaphoid

20. What is the blood supply to the scaphoid, and why is this important?

The scaphoid receives majority of its blood supply via dorsal vessels that are branches of the radial artery. The vessels enter the scaphoid via dorsal foramina that run along its dorsal ridge and perfuse the proximal pole in a retrograde fashion. These vessels supply approximately 70% to 80% of the bone including the entire proximal pole. A second blood supply arises from the palmar and superficial palmar branches of the radial artery, entering the scaphoid near its distal tubercle and perfusing approximately 20% to 30% of the bone including the scaphoid tuberosity. Because of this distally based blood supply, fractures to the proximal aspect of the scaphoid (those seen in adolescents and adults) are more likely to develop avascular necrosis.

21. How are scaphoid fractures in children treated, and how is nonunion managed?

For nondisplaced or even minimally displaced fractures, cast immobilization is the gold standard of treatment. Duration of casting varies by fracture type. For avulsion or incomplete fractures, 4 to 6 weeks is appropriate; for transverse fractures, 6 to 8 weeks of immobilization is recommended. The positioning of the hand and arm are as follows. The forearm should be in midsupination and flexed 90°. The wrist should be in slight volar flexion and radial deviation. The thumb should be held in abduction and extension by a thumb spica cast. Scaphoid nonunion requires operative management, including open reduction with a combination of bone grafting, K-wire fixation, or internal fixation.

22. What is the most frequent level of digital amputation in the pediatric population, and what is the youngest age at which replantation is contraindicated?

Amputation through the distal phalanx is the most frequent level of amputation in the pediatric population. Relative to adults the indications for replantation are much broader, and most authors agree that there is no age limit at which replantation is contraindicated.

23. What is the Allen classification of fingertip injuries? Discuss one special consideration of each type (Fig. 119-3).

- *Type I:* Does not include any bony fragment of the distal phalanx. *Special Consideration:* The amputated fragment is often replaced as a composite graft and is not considered a true replantation.
- *Type II:* Amputation through the nail bed, preserving half of the nailbed and sterile matrix. *Special Consideration:* No dorsal vein is available at this level. Venous drainage is most often achieved by controlled bleeding or leeches.
- *Type III:* Contains the nailbed but preserves less than half the nailbed and sterile matrix. *Special Consideration:* Failure of replantation will likely result in a hook nail deformity.
- *Type IV:* Amputation proximal to the nail fold but distal to the insertion of the extensor and flexor tendons of the distal phalanx. *Special Consideration:* Dorsal vein is available for anastomosis to ensure venous drainage of replanted segment.

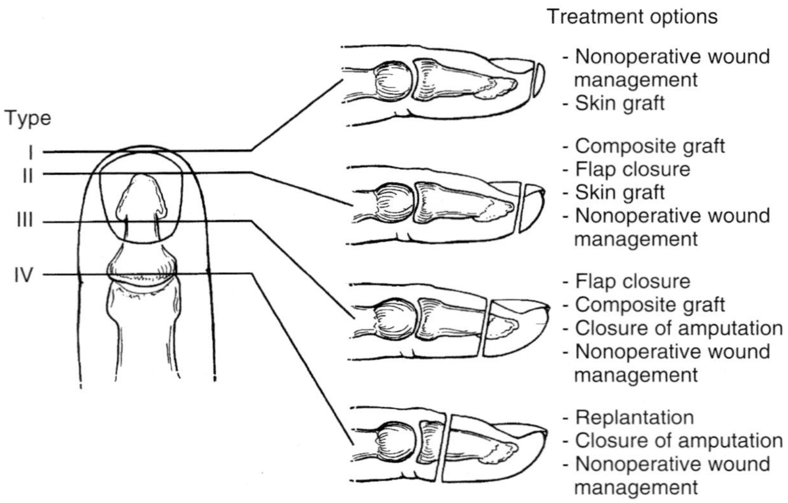

Treatment options

Type I
- Nonoperative wound management
- Skin graft

Type II
- Composite graft
- Flap closure
- Skin graft

Type III
- Nonoperative wound management
- Flap closure
- Composite graft
- Closure of amputation

Type IV
- Nonoperative wound management
- Replantation
- Closure of amputation
- Nonoperative wound management

Figure 119-3. Anatomic landmarks composing the Allen classification of fingertip injuries with associated treatment options. (Modified from Bernard SL, Greco RJ: Pediatric hand trauma. In Bentz ML [ed]: Pediatric Plastic Surgery. Stamford, CT, Appleton & Lange, 1998, pp. 827–860, with permission.)

24. What is the typical order for finger tip replantation in children? Discuss one special consideration for each step.

- *Bony Fixation First. Special Consideration:* Smaller K-wires are typically used, given the size of the amputated fragment. Alternatively a small needle can be placed, minimizing damage to the distal bone segment.
- *Arterial Revascularization Second. Special Consideration:* Given the small size of the segment, there usually is not enough room for double microclamps. Therefore traditional anastomotic techniques must be altered (e.g., back wall first technique).
- *Nerve Repair Third. Special Consideration:* In types I, II, and III, often no neural branch is available for coaptation. Nevertheless, return of true sensation is often achieved.
- *Venous Revascularization Fourth. Special Consideration:* With type II and III injuries, venous reanastomosis is often not possible. Therefore controlled bleeding or the application of leeches is the best method for preventing venous congestion.

25. What is Volkmann's ischemic contracture, what injury is most likely to cause it, and how is it treated?

Volkmann's ischemic contracture is the result of unrecognized or inadequately treated compartment syndrome of the forearm, causing muscle ischemia, necrosis, and ultimately contracture of the hand (see Fig. 119-3). Skeletal trauma is the most likely cause of an acute compartment syndrome of the forearm. Although supracondylar fractures of the humerus are the most likely etiology of compartment syndrome, all patients with humerus and radial/ulnar fractures should be carefully monitored for vascular injury and compartment syndrome. Treatment is difficult and often multifaceted, including excision of fibrous tissue, neurolysis, tenolysis, capsulotomy, nerve grafting, and innervated free tissue transfer.

26. How is an impending compartment syndrome recognized? What are the signs of an acute compartment syndrome?

Signs that are worrisome of an impending compartment syndrome are increasing pain, swelling, tension or tenderness of any compartments, and decreased active movement. The acute signs of a compartment syndrome include extreme and poorly localized pain that increases with passive stretch (extension) of the muscles of the fingers and wrist. When diagnosing compartment syndrome, caution is advised when using the often taught "five Ps": pain, pallor, paralysis, paresthesia, and pulselessness. These are late signs of compartment syndrome, and the key to effective management lies in early recognition.

27. List five major concepts in diagnosing and managing vascular tumors of the hand.

1. Vascular malformations and hemangiomas account for 90% of all vascular tumors in the hand. The remaining 10% include other benign neoplasms (pyogenic granuloma, glomus cell tumor), intermediate neoplasms (benign endothelioma, hemangiopericytoma), and malignant tumors (angiosarcoma, lymphangiosarcoma, Kaposi's sarcoma).
2. Malignant vascular tumors are exceedingly rare but are potentially limb and life threatening and must be included in most differential diagnoses.
3. Differentiating between low-flow and high-flow vascular malformations is essential to treatment. Low-flow lesions are less likely to require treatment. Intervention, if necessary (due to pain, hypertrophy, ulceration, or cosmetic disfigurement), usually involves sclerotherapy, surgical resection, or debulking. High-flow lesions may require embolization, followed by resection.
4. Hemangiomas are well characterized as having a proliferative phase followed by an involution phase. Treatment, when necessary, may include oral steroids, intralesional steroid injection, various types of laser therapy, or, less commonly, excision.
5. Pyogenic granuloma is a common rapidly growing solitary lesion usually resulting from local trauma that occurs on the volar pulp or periungual area of the digit. Complete surgical removal with primary closure is the most reliable method of treatment, although fulguration can be successful.

28. When do pediatric hand burns typically need grafting?

Because of the curious and constantly exploring nature of the pediatric population, small hand burns are common (e.g., fireplaces, curling irons). If these burns do not heal in approximately 2 weeks, grafting should be considered because the risk of significant scarring increases after the 2-week time period. It is often difficult to assess the degree of the burn in the freshly burned hand, so waiting 2 weeks to assess for healing is an appropriate strategy.

29. Which type of graft is most effective for grafting the hand: Split thickness or full thickness?

The principle that should be applied is "the thicker the graft, the less contraction." Therefore for small pediatric hand burns, full-thickness skin grafts should be used. The best location to harvest this skin is from the groin. In larger burns where the availability of donor skin is an issue, as much full-thickness skin as possible should be used in areas prone to contracture (e.g., volar surfaces of the hand).

30. How are hand contractures classified?

- *Grade I:* Contractures have no limitation in range of motion, some symptomatic tightness, and normal architecture.
- *Grade II:* Contractures result in a minor decrease in range of motion and no significant impact on daily living. Normal architecture retained.
- *Grade III:* Contractures are characterized by a noted functional deficit and early changes in normal architecture.
- *Grade IV:* Contractures characterized by loss of hand function with significant distortion of normal hand architecture. Both grade III and IV contractures are further subclassified as type A (flexion contractures), type B (extension contractures), or type C (combination of flexion and extension contractures).

31. What are the basic principles of contracture release in the pediatric hand?

- *Grade IV(B):* Excisional release of scars to restore transverse and longitudinal arches, Kirchner wire fixation with MP joints flexed to approximately 80° and interphalangeal joints at 180° (straight), and resurfacing the dorsum of the hand and fingers with skin grafts or flaps if tendons and joints are exposed.
- *Grade IV (A):* Excisional release and resurfacing with skin grafts or flaps, MP joints kept in extension with Kirchner wires (particularly in young patients), and elevation of the affected part during healing.
- *Interdigital Contractures:* Interdigital contractures (e.g., burn syndactyly) are common and rarely cause functional deficits. However, when the first web space is affected, severe functional deficits can result. These contractures need to be treated surgically. Several methodologies have been described for release of first web space contractures. Although results vary, Z-plasties or local flaps have the lowest rate of recurrence.

BIBLIOGRAPHY

Ablove RH, Moy OJ, Peimer CA: Pediatric hand disease. Diagnosis and treatment. Pediatr Clin North Am 45:1507–1524, 1998.

al-Qattan MM: The cartilaginous cap fracture. Hand Clin 16:535–539, 2000.

Bernard SL, Greco RJ: Pediatric hand trauma. In Bentz ML (ed): Pediatric Plastic Surgery. Stamford, CT, Appleton & Lange, 1998, pp. 827–860.

Buncke GM, Buntic RF, Romeo O: Pediatric mutilating hand injuries. Hand Clin 19:121–131, 2003.

Cook PA, Yu JS, Wiand W, et al: Suspected scaphoid fractures in skeletally immature patients: Application of MRI. J Comput Assist Tomogr 21:511–515, 1997.

Cornwall R: Finger metacarpal fractures and dislocations in children. Hand Clin 22:1–10, 2006.

Elhassan BT, Shin AY: Scaphoid fracture in children. Hand Clin 22:31–41, 2006.

Fleming AN, Smith PJ: Vascular cell tumors of the hand in children. Hand Clin 16:609–624, 2000.

Greenhalgh DG: Management of acute burn injuries of the upper extremity in the pediatric population. Hand Clin 16:175–186, 2000.

Hovius SE, Ultee J: Volkmann's ischemic contracture. Prevention and treatment. Hand Clin 16:647–657, 2000.

Kozin SH: Fractures and dislocations along the pediatric thumb ray. Hand Clin 22:19–29, 2006.

Leclercq C, Korn W: Articular fractures of the fingers in children. Hand Clin 16:523–534, 2000.

Light TR: Carpal injuries in children. Hand Clin 16:513–522, 2000.

McCauley RL: Reconstruction of the pediatric burned hand. Hand Clin 16:249–259, 2000.

Papadonikolakis A, Li Z, Smith BP, et al: Fractures of the phalanges and interphalangeal joints in children. Hand Clin 22:11–18, 2006.

PROBLEMS INVOLVING THE PERIONYCHIUM

CHAPTER 120

Lisa Ann Whitty, MD, and
Duffield Ashmead IV, MD

1. Describe fingernail anatomy and fingernail production.

The fingernail is a plate of flattened cells layered together and adherent to each other. The nailbed is composed of the germinal matrix (intermediate nail), which produces 90% of nail plate volume; the sterile matrix (ventral nail), which contributes additional substance that is largely responsible for nail adherence; and the roof of the nail fold (dorsal nail), which is responsible for the smooth, shiny surface of the nail plate. The sterile matrix is closely associated with the periosteum of the distal phalanx. The germinal matrix is immediately adjacent to the extensor tendon insertion. Distal phalangeal injuries are frequently associated with nail bed disruption (Fig. 120-1).

2. What function does the fingernail serve?

In all likelihood, the fingernail evolved for scratching and self-defense as well as protecting the fingertip. In addition, it serves more delicate functions. By providing counterforce to the finger pulp, it increases the sensitivity of the fingertip; two-point discrimination widens if the nail plate is removed. Nails also assist with picking up fine or thin objects.

3. Describe the surrounding structures and their importance.

The hyponychium, or area immediately under the fingernail at its cut edge, is a keratinous plug that lines the juncture of the overhanging nail plate, the distal margin of sterile matrix, and the fingertip skin. It is heavily populated with lymphocytes and polymorphonuclear leukocytes as a barrier to subungual infection. The perionychium is the skin at the nail margin, folded over its proximal and lateral edges. It is a site of frequent, minor trauma and occasional infection.

4. What is the lunula?

The lunula is the whitish area of the most proximal nail. Attributed to differences in nail adherence and light reflection, it corresponds to the area beyond which cell nuclei within the nail plate have degenerated.

5. What is the blood supply of the nail bed?

The two terminal branches of the volar digital arteries.

6. What is the rate of nail growth?

Complete longitudinal growth takes 70 to 160 days at a rate of approximately 0.1 mm/day.

7. How is growth rate impacted by nailbed injury?

There is a 3-week delay in distal growth of the nail following injury, during which time it thickens proximal to the injury site. Nail growth then is faster than normal for 6 to 8 weeks, followed by less than normal growth for 30 days.

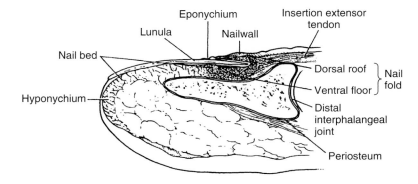

Figure 120-1. Anatomy of the nail bed in sagittal section. (From Zook EG, Brown RB: The perionychium. In Green DP [ed]: Operative Hand Surgery, 3rd ed. New York, Churchill Livingstone, 1993, p 1284.)

8. What is the most common source of nail bed injuries?

Doors, followed by crush between two objects, followed by saw/lawnmower lacerations.

9. Which digit is most commonly injured?

Long finger, followed by ring, index, little, and thumb.

10. Describe several nail changes associated with trauma.

- *Premature nail plate separation* may reflect transverse scarring of the sterile matrix, frequently seen after fingertip crush injuries.
- *Longitudinal splitting* of the nail plate may be due to scar adhesions from the nail roof to the nail floor (synechia).
- *Longitudinal grooving* may reflect disturbances of the nail fold due to adjacent tumors or underlying skeletal change with secondary distortion.
- *Nail spikes or remnants* frequently complicate traumatic fingertip amputations. Residua of germinal or sterile matrix continue to produce small volumes of nail plate, which grow over several months. Ultimately they may prove a source of pain or secondary infection, necessitating excision.
- *Beaking* is a nail deformity caused by inadequate support of the distal sterile matrix. It is usually seen after distal fingertip amputations with loss of phalangeal tuft or healing of distal open wounds by secondary intention. As a result of the process of wound contracture, sterile matrix is drawn volar across the distal tip.

11. What is the significance of a subungual hematoma?

Crush injuries to the fingertip are extremely common. Development of a subungual hematoma invariably reflects nailbed injury with or without an associated fracture of the distal phalanx. Radiographs are almost always indicated. Even small subungual hematomas may be quite painful and should be decompressed. Classic techniques of trepanation include the use of a hot paperclip or battery-powered cautery, although drilling through the nail plate with a large-bore needle is also an option. More significant hematomas (>50%) imply more extensive nailbed injury and should be explored by nail plate removal. In addition to providing complete decompression, nail plate removal allows nailbed repair. Most practitioners advocate the use of fine, absorbable suture (e.g., 6/0 catgut). The nail plate (or a substitute) is then replaced to splint the repair and stent the nail fold to prevent synechiae.

12. What are the different products that may be used as nail substitute/stent following injury?

The purpose of nail substituting/stenting is to prevent the eponychial fold from scarring to the nail bed following the acute injury period.

- Aluminum foil (suture wrapper [senior author's preferred substitute])
- Silicone sheet
- Nonadhesive gauze

13. What is the most appropriate management in the case of delayed presentation of acute injuries to the nailbed?

The nailbed should be explored and accurately reapproximated up to 7 days following the initial injury.

14. Describe several common nail changes that are manifestations of systemic disease.

- *Clubbing.* This exaggerated curvature of the nail plate may be congenital but is classically described in association with pulmonary, bowel, or liver disease.
- *Onycholysis.* Premature separation of the nail plates is seen with thyrotoxicosis and psoriasis. Psoriasis often leads to associated pitting and ridging of the nail plate.
- *Chromonychia.* Changes in nail color may be seen in renal failure. They also may reflect drug effects.

15. What are the usual patterns of infection associated with the fingernail?

- *Acute Paronychia.* Infection (usually staphylococcal) of the nail margin (perionychium) usually responds to direct drainage, marsupialization, or partial nail plate removal.
- *Chronic Paronychia.* Typically seen in patients whose hands are frequently wet (e.g., dishwashers). Maceration appears to lower defenses against local bacterial or fungal colonization. The condition often leads to nail plate deformity and onycholysis. It may respond to local or systemic antibiotics and antifungals with or without limited drainage. Complete nail plate removal is sometimes necessary.
- *Onychomycosis.* Chronic fungal infestation of the perionychium and nail plate may be associated with dramatic discoloration of the nail as well as thickening and onycholysis. Although treatment with systemic antifungals such as griseofulvin has been advocated, simple nail plate removal and use of a topical antifungal as the nail regrows may be equally successful without the risks of systemic drug toxicity.

16. What are the most common benign periungual tumors?

Mucous cysts are small ganglia arising from the distal interphalangeal (DIP) joint, usually in association with a small osteophyte(s). As they encroach on the perionychium either deep or superficial to the germinal matrix, splitting or deep grooving may be seen in the nail plate. Larger cysts are associated with significant attenuation of the overlying skin and occasionally drain spontaneously. Mucous cysts usually are treated by excision, taking care to address the associated osteophyte.

Glomus tumors (tumors of the glomus body) are frequently subungual. Although often extremely small (1 to 2 mm), they are characteristically *painful, exquisitely tender,* and *highly sensitive to cold.* The diagnosis often is empirical. Resection may require transungual exposure or elevation of the nailbed from a lateral approach. These tumors are found in the confined space between the nailbed and distal phalanx or within the soft tissue of the perionychium.

Pyogenic granulomas represent an exuberant excess of granulation tissue in response to relatively minor trauma. They are frequently encountered in the perionychium. Most respond to curettage and chemical or electrical cautery of the base.

17. What is the glomus body?

The glomus body is a specialized arterial venous anastomosis, which regulates blood flow and temperature within the finger tip.

18. What is the differential diagnosis for pigmented subungual lesions?

- *Posttraumatic hemorrhage* is the most common pigmented subungual lesion, although the patient frequently reports no history of injury. These lesions usually "grow out" with the nail plate and can be identified by scoring the overlying plate and observing for several weeks.
- *Benign nevi* occasionally present in a subungual location.
- *Subungual melanoma* is potentially serious and often diagnosed late. The threshold for nail plate removal and incisional biopsy of a suspicious lesion should be low.
- *Hutchinson's sign* is leaching of pigment into the nail fold, perionychium. It is highly suspicious for melanoma. It represents the *radial growth phase of the subungual melanoma.*

19. What are melanonychia striata?

Melanonychia striata are longitudinal pigmented bands of the nail plate, seen more commonly in blacks. Physiologic and pathologic causes are extensive and include pregnancy, trauma, psoriasis, amyloidosis, hyperthyroidism, Addison's disease, Cushing's syndrome, acromegaly, chronic dermatitis, carpal tunnel syndrome, lichen planus, onychomycosis, onychomatricoma, Bowen's disease, myxoid pseudocyst, basal cell carcinoma, fibrous histiocytoma, and verruca vulgaris. Common drugs associated with melanonychia striata are chemotherapeutics, nonsteroidal antiinflammatory drugs, antifungal agents, antiretrovirals, steroids, and antiepileptics. Melanonychia striata typically involve multiple nails. Nail matrix biopsy is warranted in whites, when the melanonychia striata are solitary, are greater than 6 mm with variegated pigmentation, or show proximal widening suggestive of melanoma. Mohs micrographic surgery has been proposed in melanoma presenting as longitudinal melanonychia.

20. What is the current surgical therapy for nail apparatus melanoma?

Nail apparatus melanoma (NAM) has an incidence between 0.7% and 3.5% in whites. In blacks the percentage rises to 20%. The 5-year survival rate is 38% to 61% for stage I and II disease. The most common site is the thumb, followed by the index finger.

The recommended surgical therapy for subungual melanoma varies in the literature. Green recommends a 5-mm margin for in situ disease but amputation at the joint proximal to the nail bed melanoma for invasive melanoma. The World Health Organization (WHO) Melanoma Group's prospective randomized study of primary cutaneous malignant melanoma 2 mm thick or less reported that there was no *significant* difference in survival or recurrence when the biopsy sites were excised with either a 1-cm or a 3-cm margin of skin.

Banfield et al. present the largest retrospective study of 105 patients with NAM from four regional cancer registries in England. Patients with thinner lesions (mean 3.2 mm) treated with local excision had a significantly better 5-year survival of 79% than those with thicker lesions (mean thickness 6.1 mm) treated with amputation, yielding a 41% 5-year survival. This study suggests that the prognosis on NAM is related to the depth of the initial tumor and that local excision is a viable option for treatment.

21. Is there a role for adjuvant therapy in NAM?

The treatment remains essentially surgical. Trials regarding supplemental therapy specifically regarding NAM are lacking. However, studies are under way to evaluate adjuvant therapy for the general management of cutaneous melanoma.

A randomized controlled clinical trial of high-risk resected melanoma patients (T4 or regionally metastatic [N1] melanoma) had an increase in the relapse-free interval and overall survival following adjuvant therapy with interferon alfa-2b.

Treatment of metastatic melanoma includes chemotherapy and immunotherapy. Current agents include interleukin-2, interferon-alpha, cisplatin, vinblastine, dacarbazine, and temozolomide.

BIBLIOGRAPHY

Banfield CC, Redburn JC, Dawber RPR: The incidence and prognosis of nail apparatus melanoma. A retrospective study of 105 patients in four English regions. Br J Dermatol 139:276–279, 1998.

Brodland DG: The treatment of nail apparatus melanoma with Mohs micrographic surgery. Dermatol Surg 27:269–273, 2001.

Fleegler E, Zienowicz RJ: Tumors of the perionychium. Hand Clin 6:113–134, 1990.

Gonzalez Cao M, Malvehy J, Marti R, et al. Biochemotherapy with temozolomide, cisplatin, vinblastine, subcutaneous interlukin-2 and interferon alpha in patients with metastatic melanoma. Melanoma Res 16:59–64, 2006.

Keyser JJ, Littler JW, Eaton RG.: Surgical treatment of infections and lesions. Hand Clin 6:23–36, 1990.

Lateur N, Andre J: Melanonychia: Diagnosis and treatment. Dermatol Ther 15:131–141, 2002.

Sommer N, Neumeister MW: Tumors of the perionychium. Hand Clin 18:673–689, 2002.

Sommer NZ, Brown RE: The perionychium. In Green DP (ed): Green's Operative Hand Surgery, 5th ed. New York, Churchill Livingstone, 2005, pp 389–416.

Spencer JM: Malignant tumors of the nail unit. Dermatol Ther 15:126–130, 2002.

Timmons MJ: Selecting surgery for malignant melanoma. Clin Exp Dermatol 1:115–117, 1997.

Van Beck AL, Kassan MA, Adson MH, Dale V: Management of acute fingernail injuries. Hand Clin 6:23–36, 1990.

Verma S, Quirt I, McCready D, et al: Systematic review of systemic adjuvant therapy for patients at high risk for recurrent melanoma. Cancer 106:1431–1442, 2006.

Zook EG: Anatomy and physiology of the perionychium. Hand Clin 6:1–8, 1990.

Zook EG, Brown RE: The perionychium. In Green DP (ed): Green's Operative Hand Surgery, 3rd ed. New York, Churchill Livingstone, 1993, pp 1283–1314.

FINGERTIP INJURIES

Richard J. Zienowicz, MD, FACS; Albert R. Harris, MD; and Vineet Mehan, MD

CHAPTER 121

1. Which is the most frequently injured finger?

The long (middle) finger. Fingertips are the most frequently injured part of the hand, and the long finger is the most vulnerable because it is the last to be withdrawn from the machine or car door.

2. Where is the greatest quantity of dermal lymphatics in the human body?

The hyponychium. Teleologically it makes sense to protect the parts of the body (fingers and toes) that are in most frequent contact with potential disease-causing organisms.

3. What is the anatomic significant of the lunula?

The lunula represents the transition zone of the proximal germinal matrix and distal sterile matrix of the nail bed. The cells at this point become pyknotic (lose their nuclei).

4. What is the clinical significance of the lunula?

The lunula visibly demarcates the germinal matrix even without the nail plate intact, unless it is heavily contused. If sufficient turgid soft tissue support can be restored (i.e., thick thenar flap), the possibility of preservation of the tip and a reasonable, albeit shorter, nail can be anticipated.

5. What are the goals for reconstruction of fingertip injuries?

- Function
- Appearance
- Shortest time to functional recovery
- Prevention of joint contracture and symptomatic neuromas
- Preservation of length and sensibility

6. What are the reconstructive options?

- Secondary intention
- Skin graft
- Local flap
- Composite graft
- Microvascular replantation

7. Do most injuries involving primarily skin loss from the fingertip heal better with skin grafts?

Usually not. Conservative treatment (healing by secondary intention) has resulted in less hypoesthesia and greater patient satisfaction when compared with skin grafting.

8. Does conservative treatment result in a greater period of unfitness for work?

No. The period of time is not significantly different whether a patient is treated with shortening, skin grafting, or secondary intention.

9. If the nail has been destroyed, why not just shorten the digit to the level of the distal interphalangeal joint?

The profundus tendon attaches to the base of the distal phalanx. Shortening results in profound loss of strength.

10. Describe the lumbrical-plus finger.

The lumbrical-plus finger may arise after amputation of the distal phalanx or unrepaired laceration of the profundus tendon. Loss of its distal insertion allows the profundus tendon to migrate proximally, along with the lumbrical muscle attached to it in zone IV of the palm. When a lumbrical contracts, ordinarily it pulls the profundus tendon in a distal direction and the lateral band in a proximal direction, resulting in extension of the proximal interphalangeal (PIP) and distal interphalangeal (DIP) joints and flexion of the metacarpophalangeal (MP) joint. When flexion is attempted in the lumbrical-plus finger, paradoxical extension occurs as the proximally migrated profundus tendon pulls the lumbrical proximally, forcing the IP joints into extension via the lateral band.

11. Why not preserve the profundus function and pad the stump by suturing it to the extensor tendon?

In most cases, this procedure would result in the quadriga syndrome, which Verdan named after the Roman charioteers who had to control the reins to four horses. Tendon balance is upset by relatively minor changes in length. Verdan described the inability to achieve full composite flexion (i.e., clenched fist) if the profundus tendon of one finger is pulled to greater-than-normal resting length. The effect is simulated by holding the long or ring finger in extension while attempting to make a fist with the others.

12. Which local flap is most suitable for reconstruction of multiple fingertip injuries on the same hand?

The cross-finger flap uses tissue from the dorsum of the middle phalanx but can be designed with equal versatility and reliability from the proximal phalanx or palmar or axial surfaces. This technique allows concurrent repair of three or sometimes even four adjacent fingertip injuries.

13. What vital structure is susceptible to injury during elevation of a thenar flap?

The radial digital sensory nerve to the thumb, which courses along the surface of the flexor pollicis brevis muscle.

14. Some authors have worried about permanent joint contractures after thenar flap use and cautioned against this technique in older patients. Is such concern warranted?

The thenar flap requires 10 to 14 days of immobilization with the PIP joint in flexion. In a review of 150 cases, Melone and Beasley found only six patients who demonstrated stiffness, usually with less than 15° of extension loss. Thirty-one patients were older than 50 years, and only one had persistent stiffness.

15. Neglect of what key technical element in direct closure of a digital amputation typically results in a persistently painful finger?

Failure to resect a sufficient length of each digital nerve to avoid neuroma formation in the prehensile surface area.

16. Anesthesia for fingertip injuries usually is accomplished by digital nerve block. What measures can significantly decrease the pain associated with local injection?

The first step is to choose the dorsal web spaces, where pain and pressure receptor distribution is proportionately far less than in palmar skin. A small-gauge needle (25 gauge or less) disturbs fewer receptors. The pain of injection has been shown to be related primarily to the acidic pH of the injectate (plain lidocaine [Xylocaine] ≈3.3 to 5.5). Addition of sodium bicarbonate (44 mEq/L) to Xylocaine in a 1:9 ratio (i.e., 1 mL bicarbonate to 9 mL Xylocaine) raises the pH to approximately normal tissue range (7.35 to 7.45), lowers pK_a, and results in quicker initiation of the block and shorter duration of action. This procedure can be supplemented with straight local injection and/or bupivacaine to extend the duration of anesthesia. Avoid mixing bicarbonate with bupivacaine (Marcaine) because it will cause milky precipitation. Lastly, a slow injection avoids excessive pressure receptor activation until the anesthetic effect has begun.

17. What is glabrous skin?

Glabrous skin is devoid of pilosebaceous units and generally heals with less scarring. The best location for obtaining glabrous skin for use on hand and fingertip injuries is the ulnar aspect of the hypothenar eminence.

18. Are there any tricks to obtaining a graft of uniform thickness?

The Pitkin technique used to obtain skin grafts from difficult donor sites is ideal for the hypothenar region. Xylocaine with epinephrine is injected subcutaneously to raise a wheal in the shape of the intended graft (drawn with a marking pen). A long blade (Weck or Goulian) is necessary except for small grafts, which can be taken with a no.10 or 20 blade. The best instrument for this area is a Davol dermatome, which looks like an electric toothbrush (Stanley Simon, a general surgeon, designed it in his basement workshop). The Davol dermatome allows harvest of a nearly full-thickness graft that will contract minimally yet leave an inconspicuous donor site.

19. Describe the terminal vascular anatomy of the finger.

The two digital arteries form an anastomotic arch near the terminal insertion of the profundus tendon. The arch then gives off two smaller collateral arteries and one larger (<0.7-mm diameter) artery, all of which remain contiguous distally with the dorsal network of much smaller caliber. Lateroungual veins are too narrow for microsurgical anastomosis. Suitable veins for anastomosis are present on the palmar pulp surface immediately beneath the skin.

20. Do neurovascular island flaps eventually integrate sensorally with their new site after transfer?

In only 20% to 40% of adults but more frequently in children.

21. Aside from local flaps, what other techniques can be used to correct soft tissue losses to the fingertip?

Composite grafts from the toe distal phalanges provide like tissue with minimal donor morbidity and deformity. Distant flaps from the groin, abdomen, chest, and elsewhere are occasionally used, especially when involvement of multiple digits makes local donor sites unusable or impractical. Free tissue transfer of toes, either complete or partial, is an excellent choice for distal phalangeal reconstruction of the thumb because it results in optimal functional and aesthetic restoration.

22. Cold intolerance after fingertip injury is common. When does it resolve?

Probably never. Previous teaching that cold intolerance was a transient phenomenon has been challenged lately by many surgeons' reports of long-standing persistent symptoms that may become more tolerable but nevertheless remain bothersome.

23. How is sensibility affected after advancement flap reconstruction of the fingertip?

The typical V-Y flaps provide near normal (5 to 7 mm) two-point discrimination, whereas the Moberg and other axial refinements of this flap can restore normal sensation (≤5 mm).

24. Flaps are composite tissues intended to replace missing soft tissues (and occasionally muscle, bone, or cartilage) with similar components. Their common denominator, when successful, is patency of arterial inflow and venous outflow. Associate the following flaps with their respective anatomic descriptions:

1. Axial flap 2. Random flap 3. Island flap 4. Pedicle flap

A ( ) Perfusion derived exclusively through the subdermal plexus of vessels.

B ( ) Arteriovenous connection; "leash" of blood vessels supplies flap.

C ( ) Harvested from an area with a known arteriovenous blood supply while remaining connected by skin and subcutaneous tissue to its donor site.

D ( ) In all respects identical to axial pattern flap, but skin and soft tissue attachments are divided, leaving the flap attached only to its dominant blood vessels.

Answers: A (2), B (4), C (1), D (3)

25. Is there a method of systematically describing fingertip injuries?

Yes, the pulp nail bone (PNB) classification system. The PNB classification system is designed to classify fingertip injuries based on damage to pulp, nail, and bone (Table 121-1).

Table 121-1. PNB Classification of Fingertip Injuries

PULP (P)		NAIL (N)		BONE (B)	
No injury	0	No injury	0	No injury	0
Laceration	1	Sterile matrix laceration	1	Tuft fracture	1
Crush	2	Germinal + sterile matrix laceration	2	Comminuted nonarticular fracture	2
Loss: Distal transverse	3	Crush	3	Articular fracture	3
Loss: Palmar oblique partial	4	Proximal nail bed dislocation	4	Displaced basal fracture	4
Loss: Dorsal oblique	5	Loss: Distal third	5	Tip exposure	5
Loss: Lateral	6	Loss: Distal two-thirds	6	Loss: Distal half	6
Loss: Complete	7	Loss: Lateral	7	Loss: Subtotal (intact tendon insertion)	7
		Loss: Complete	8	Loss: Complete	8

Data from Evans DM, Bernardis C: A new classification for fingertip injuries. J Hand Surg 25B:58–60, 2000.

26. Is composite grafting a reliable method for managing fingertip amputations?

Yes. Composite grafting has been shown to be successful in 43% to 80% based on the studies reviewed. The fingertips were replanted without any vascular anastomosis. At least one study reported excellent functional recovery.

27. What factors have the greatest impact on composite graft survival in fingertip injuries?

Smoking is by far the most important factor. Diabetes and a crush mechanism may also have an impact on composite graft survival.

28. Is replantation possible in distal tip amputations?

Yes. Microvascular replantation has become possible and is performed for distal tip amputations at several centers around the world. The practice is somewhat controversial. Several studies showed good outcomes with sensate tips and good cosmetic results. One retrospective study comparing conservative treatment versus replantation showed better functional outcome and patient satisfaction with the replant group. However, the cost, length of stay, and transfusion rates of the replantation group were much higher.

29. Match Figures 121-1 through 121-5 with the following flaps:

A ( ) V-Y advancement flap with unilateral or bilateral applications
B ( ) Heterodigital random pattern flap, optionally providing sensation
C ( ) Axial advancement flap most appropriate for thumb
D ( ) Random-pattern, palmar-based flap with myriad configurations
E ( ) Palmar advancement flap best suited for dorsal oblique amputations

Answers: (Figure number in parenthesis): A (2), B (3), C (1), D (4), E (5)

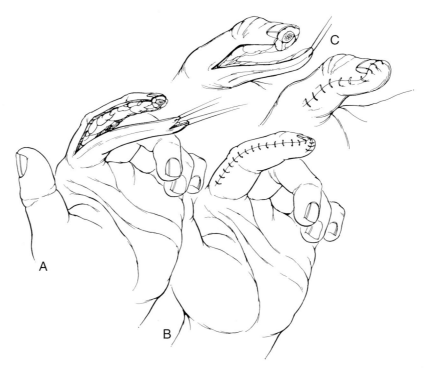

Figure 121-1. Volar advancement flap for coverage of a distal index finger amputation with bone exposed. This technique is more applicable to thumb tip injuries in which less than 1 cm of flap advancement is required for coverage. Injudicious use of this technique in a finger can result in significant complications, including necrosis of the entire flap. (From Jebson PJL, Louis DS: Amputations. In Green DP, Hotchkiss RN, Pederson WC, Wolfe SW [eds]: Green's Operative Hand Surgery, 5th ed. New York, Churchill Livingstone, 2005, p 1944.)

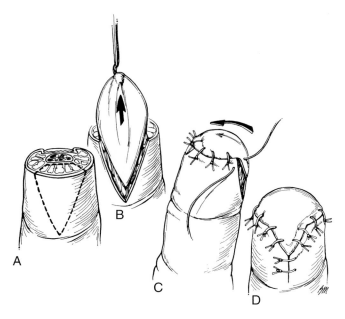

Figure 121-2. Atasoy-Kleinert volar V-Y technique is applicable to distal tip injuries with bone exposed and when the distal injury is either transverse or oblique and sloping in a volar distal-to-dorsal proximal direction. In injuries with more volar pad loss, there is usually insufficient skin for this technique to be used. (From Jebson PJL, Louis DS: Amputations. In Green DP, Hotchkiss RN, Pederson WC, Wolfe SW [eds]: Green's Operative Hand Surgery, 5th ed. New York, Churchill Livingstone, 2005, p 1943.)

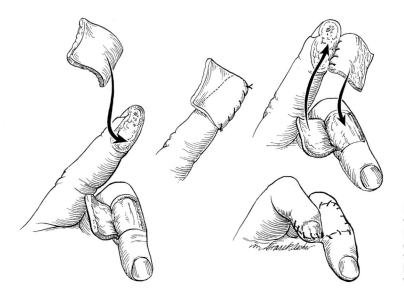

Figure 121-3. Cross-finger flap. The flap is raised from the dorsum of the middle phalanx of the adjacent digit and contoured appropriately to reconstruct the defect. (From the Christine Kleinert Institute for Hand and Microsurgery, Inc., with permission.)

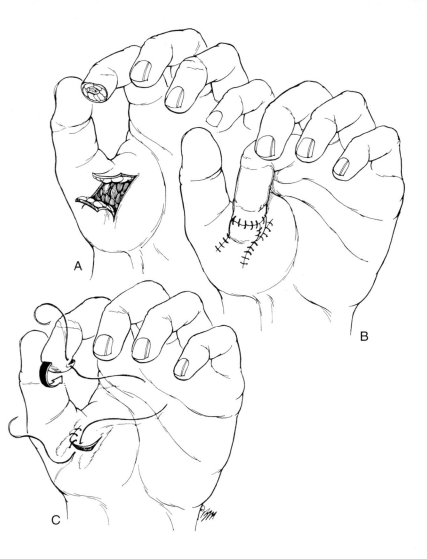

Figure 121-4. Thenar H-flap. (From Jebson PJL, Louis DS: Amputations. In Green DP, Hotchkiss RN, Pederson WC, Wolfe SW [eds]: Green's Operative Hand Surgery, 5th ed. New York, Churchill Livingstone, 2005, p 1947.)

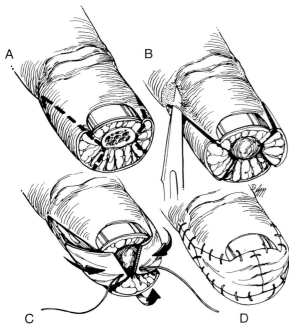

Figure 121-5. Kutler lateral V-Y technique. (From Jebson PJL, Louis DS: Amputations. In Green DP, Hotchkiss RN, Pederson WC, Wolfe SW [eds]: Green's Operative Hand Surgery, 5th ed. New York, Churchill Livingstone, 2005, p 1943.)

BIBLIOGRAPHY

Adani R, Marcoccio I, Tarallo L.: Treatment of fingertip amputations using the Hirase technique. Hand Surg 8:257–264, 2003.

Brown RE, Zook EG, Russell RC: Fingertip reconstruction with flaps and nail bed grafts. J Hand Surg 24:345–351, 1999.

Evans D, Bernardis C: A new classification for fingertip injuries. J Hand Surg 25B:58–60, 2000.

Foucher G, Norris RW: Distal and very distal digital replantations. Br J Plast Surg 45:199–203, 1992.

Heistein JB, Cook PA: Factors affecting composite graft survival in digital tip amputations. Ann Plast Surg 50:299–303, 2003.

Holm A, Zachariae L:Fingertip lesions: An evaluation of conservative treatment vs. free skin grafting.Acta Orthop Scand 45:382–392, 1974.

Lister GD: Skin flaps. In Green DP (ed): Operative Hand Surgery, Vol 2, 3rd ed. New York, Churchill Livingstone, 1993, p 1741.

Melone CP Jr, Beasley RW, Carstens JH Jr: The thenar flap: An analysis of its use in 150 cases. J Hand Surg [Am] 7:291–297, 1982.

Povlsen B, Nylander G, Nylander E: Cold-induced vasospasm after digital replantation does not improve with time. A 12-year prospective study. J Hand Surg [Br] 20:237–239, 1995.

Russell RC, Casas LA: Management of fingertip injuries. Clin Plast Surg 16:405–425, 1989.

Zook EG: Anatomy and physiology of the perionychium. Hand Clin 6:1–7, 1990.

122 METACARPAL AND PHALANGEAL FRACTURES

Norman Weinzweig, MD, FACS, and
Mark H. Gonzalez, MD, MEng

Hand fractures can be complicated by deformity from no treatment, stiffness from overtreatment, and both deformity and stiffness from poor treatment.

A.B. Swanson (1970)

1. Describe the epidemiology of fractures of the metacarpals and phalanges.

Fractures of the metacarpals and phalanges are the most common fractures of the skeletal system, accounting for 10% of all fractures in several large series. They are most common in men in the second and third decades of life. Depending on the patient population, fractures are most likely due to either industrial accidents or personal trauma.

2. What is the distribution of fractures according to location?

The distal phalanx is the most commonly fractured bone in the hand (not even considering nail bed injuries), followed by the metacarpals. The middle phalanx is the least commonly fractured because of its protected position and the higher proportion of cortical to cancellous bone. Metacarpals of the border digits are more exposed and sustain more fractures than the central digits. On the other hand, phalanges of the central digits are longer and sustain more fractures than the border digits. In adults, metacarpal fractures are more common than phalangeal fractures, whereas in children the converse is true. In children, one third of fractures are epiphyseal and 80% Salter II. Fracture stability is seen in three fourths of phalangeal fractures, one third of metacarpal fractures, and two thirds of fractures in children. Approximately 20% of metacarpal and phalangeal fractures are intraarticular.

3. How are fractures classified?

- Bones involved: Distal, middle, or proximal phalanx, metacarpal
- Location within bone: Base, shaft, neck, head
- Pattern: Transverse, spiral, oblique, comminuted
- Displaced or nondisplaced
- Intraarticular or extraarticular
- Closed or open
- Stable or unstable
- Deformity: Angulation, rotation, shortening
- Associated injuries: Skin, tendon, nerve, vessel

4. Describe the initial evaluation of patients with hand fractures.

Crucial to diagnosis and treatment of hand fractures are a thorough history and physical examination. History should include handedness, occupation, avocation, mechanism of injury (e.g., crush injury with compartment syndrome), time since injury ("golden period"), and place of injury (e.g., home, farm, industry). Physical examination often provides the diagnosis and should include local tenderness, swelling, deformity (angulation, rotation, shortening), alignment (all fingertips must point toward the scaphoid), range of motion (active/passive flexion and extension, intrinsics), and neurovascular status.

5. How is rotation of a finger fracture evaluated?

With the fingers partially flexed, the fingernails should form a gentle arc. The digits should point toward the scaphoid without overlap.

6. What type of radiographs should be obtained?

Radiographs should include anteroposterior (AP) and lateral views of the individual digit, oblique views when the fracture is close to or involves a joint, prereduction and postreduction views, and special views as indicated, such as a Brewerton view for clarification of ligament-avulsion injuries of the metacarpal head, a Robert view (true AP of thumb metacarpal with hand in maximal pronation) for the first metacarpal–trapezium joint (Bennett fracture), and a reverse Robert view for the fifth metacarpal–hamate joint.

7. What is the Salter-Harris classification of epiphyseal injuries in children?

Salter-Harris I: Occurs in early childhood when the growth plate is thick with large hypertrophying chondrocytes and a weak zone of provisional calcification. The fracture occurs through the plate itself, with separation of the epiphysis from the metaphysis, usually by a pure shear mechanism. Prognosis is good.

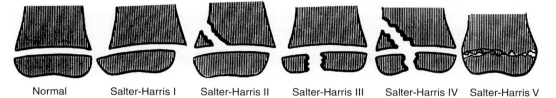

Figure 122-1. Salter-Harris classification of epiphyseal fractures. (From Lister G: The Hand: Diagnosis and Indications, 2nd ed. Edinburgh, Churchill Livingstone, 1984, p 50.)

Salter-Harris II: Usually occurs after age 10 years, through the plate and metaphysis. The epiphysis is separated, and a small fragment of metaphysis is broken off with it. Tension by shear or avulsion with an angular force causes cartilage failure, whereas compression causes metaphyseal failure.

Salter-Harris III: Usually occurs after age 10 years. An intraarticular fracture of the epiphysis occurs secondary to an avulsion force, without involvement of the epiphyseal plate. This type of fracture is associated with a poor prognosis unless accurate reduction is performed.

Salter-Harris IV: Occurs at any age; rare in the hand. Fracture occurs from the articular surface through the epiphysis plate and metaphysis by compression loading of a portion of the articular surface. Prognosis is poor without anatomic alignment.

Salter-Harris V: Occurs at any age; extremely rare in the hand. A compression fracture occurs with damage confined to the epiphyseal plate by severe axial load. The prognosis is poor because of potential growth arrest (Fig. 122-1).

8. What is a Seymour fracture?

A Seymour fracture is an epiphyseal injury of the distal phalanx in children that occurs due to hyperflexion. It is important that these injuries be recognized and treated because they can result in a foreshortened digit with decreased distal interphalangeal (DIP) joint range of motion. This injury usually occurs as an open mallet deformity that is mistaken for a DIP joint dislocation. The terminal tendon is attached to the proximal fragment and the profundus tendon is attached to the distal fragment causing it to flex. This injury is often accompanied by a transverse laceration of the nail matrix with the nail plate malpositioned superficial to the proximal nail fold. Treatment consists of irrigation and débridement, fracture reduction, repair of the nail matrix, and replacement of the nail plate beneath the proximal nail fold to act as a stent. An external splint is used to maintain the distal fragment in extension.

9. Describe the general principles for management of hand fractures.

First and foremost, treat the patient, *not* the radiograph. In general, a force of sufficient magnitude to fracture bone can cause significant injury to enveloping structures such as the intrinsic muscles, tendons, ligaments, and neurovascular structures. In some cases (e.g., roller or crushing injuries), decompression must be performed in a timely fashion.

Most fractures can be treated successfully by nonoperative means. They are functionally stable before or after closed reduction and do well with splintage and early mobilization. The goal is restoration of normal function with the three Rs: reduction, retention, and rehabilitation. After accurate fracture reduction, the hand should be immobilized in the intrinsic-plus or safe position with extremity elevation to minimize edema. Movement of the uninvolved fingers should be permitted to prevent stiffness. An exercise program should be directed toward the specific fracture with early mobilization of the injured finger. Do not forget that the proximal interphalangeal (PIP) joint is the most important joint in the hand.

10. How are stable fractures managed?

Stable fractures can often be treated by buddy taping and/or splinting. Repeat radiographs are performed at 7 to 10 days to check the reduction.

11. What is an unstable fracture?

Unstable fractures cannot be reduced with a closed method or, if reduced, cannot be held in the reduced position without supplemental fixation. Closed or open reduction internal fixation (ORIF) are required to provide stability and allow early mobilization.

12. How are unstable fractures managed?

Initially unstable fractures can be reduced and converted to a stable position by external immobilization (cast, cast with metal outrigger splint, AP plaster splint), closed reduction percutaneous pinning (CRPP), or ORIF.

13. What is the safe position for immobilization of the hand? Why is this important?

The metacarpophalangeal (MCP) joints of the digits are maintained in maximal or near maximal flexion. The head of the MCP is cam shaped, and flexion maintains the collateral ligaments at maximal length. When splinted in extension, the collateral ligaments can shorten, causing a loss of flexion. The interphalangeal (IP) joints of the digits are splinted in near-full extension. Splinting in flexion allows the development of checkrein ligaments, causing volar plate contracture and permanent loss of flexion at the IP joints.

14. Describe the different methods of internal fixation.

See Table 122-1.

15. What is the apex dorsal bending rigidity (Newton-meters) for the different internal fixation techniques in metacarpal fractures?

Dorsal plate and lag screw (0.55), dorsal plate (0.50), and crossed K-wire, K-wire and intraosseous wire, or intraosseous wire (0.07 to 0.08). Although the latter three techniques do not allow true rigid fixation, they do allow bony union and thus fracture treatment.

16. What are the indications for internal fixation?

- Uncontrollable rotation, angulation, or shortening
- Multiple digit fractures that are difficult to control
- Displaced intraarticular fractures involving more than 15% to 20% of the articular surface

Table 122-1. Fracture Stabilization Techniques

	INDICATIONS (FRACTURE TYPES)	ADVANTAGES	DISADVANTAGES
Kirschner pins	Transverse Oblique Spiral	Available and versatile Easy to insert Minimal dissection Percutaneous insertion	Lacks rigidity May loosen May distract the fracture Pin tract infection Requires external support Splint/therapy awkward

Composite wiring	Transverse
	Oblique
	Spiral
		More rigid than
		  Kirschner pins
		Low profile
		Simple and available
			Pin/wire migration
			Secondary removal
			  (sometimes)
			Exposure may be significant

Intramedullary device	Transverse Short oblique	No special equipment Easy to insert No pin protrusion Minimal dissection	Rotational instability Rod migration
Interfragmentary fixation	Long oblique Spiral	Low profile Rigid	Special equipment Little margin for error

Plate and screws	Multiple fractures with soft
	  tissue injury or bone loss
	Markedly displaced shaft
	  fractures (especially
	  border metacarpals)
	Intraarticular and
	  periarticular fractures
	Reconstruction for
	  nonunion and malunion
		Rigid fixation
		Restore/maintain
		  length
			Exacting technique
			Special equipment
			Extensive exposure
			May require removal
			Refracture
			Bulky

External fixation	Restore length for
	  comminution and bone
	  loss
	Soft tissue injury/loss
	Infected nonunion
		Preserves length
		Allows access to bone,
		  soft tissue
		Percutaneous insertion
		Direct manipulation of
		  fracture avoided
			Pin tract infections
			Osteomyelitis
			Overdistraction: Nonunion
			Neurovascular injury
			Fractures through pin holes
			Loosening

From Green DP (ed): Operative Hand Surgery, 3rd ed. New York, Churchill Livingstone, 1984, p 705.

- Fracture–subluxations of the thumb and little finger carpometacarpal joints
- Unstable fractures: Failure of closed manipulation, as in spiral fractures of the proximal phalanx or transverse metacarpal fractures
- Metacarpal head fractures
- Open fractures

17. What are the advantages of K-wire fixation?

- Easiest technically
- Requires minimal dissection
- Universally available
- Much more forgiving than other methods
- Early motion without rigid fixation
- Supplements other methods of fixation
- "Bailout" after failure of more complex techniques

18. What are the disadvantages of K-wire fixation?

- K-wires may loosen
- K-wires may distract fracture fragments
- Lateral bands may be skewered
- Cannot obtain true compression or rigid fixation
- Multiple attempts may convert a simple closed fracture to a comminuted open fracture that is impossible to fixate
- Pin tract infection

19. How soon can motion be started?

For nondisplaced fractures treated in closed fashion, motion can be started within 3 weeks if the fracture is stable. Midshaft proximal phalangeal fractures require 5 to 7 weeks for complete bony healing. Midshaft middle phalangeal fractures require 10 to 14 weeks for complete bony healing of the exceedingly hard cortical portion of the bone (same as scaphoid fractures).

20. How long do fractures requiring open reduction or severely comminuted fractures with disruption of the periosteum take to heal?

Twice as long as simple fractures.

21. Describe the treatment of extraarticular fractures of the distal phalanx.

The distal phalanx is the most commonly fractured bone in the hand. The middle finger and thumb are most frequently involved in fracture. The mechanism of injury usually is a crush injury with significant soft tissue involvement. Comminuted distal phalangeal fractures generally demonstrate twice as many fragments intraoperatively as on radiographs. Anatomic reduction usually is not necessary unless the articular surfaces are involved. Splinting is performed for protection and pain control and discontinued after 3 to 4 weeks. The two more proximal joints are mobilized to prevent stiffness. Epiphyseal plate injuries are treated by closed reduction with hyperextension. Associated nail matrix injuries are treated by drainage of the subungual hematoma, fracture reduction, and nail bed repair with 7-0 chromic suture using loupe magnification.

22. What are the deforming forces in extraarticular fractures of the middle phalanx?

Fragments are displaced by the forces of the central slip, terminal extensor tendon, and flexor digitorum superficialis (FDS) insertion. Fractures proximal to the FDS insertion angulate dorsally, whereas fractures distal to the FDS insertion angulate volarly.

23. What are the deforming forces in extraarticular fractures of the proximal phalanx? How are they treated?

Proximal phalangeal fractures angulate volarly, with the interossei flexing the proximal fragment and the central slip extending the distal portion. Stable, nondisplaced, or impacted middle and proximal phalangeal fractures are treated by temporary protection with a splint followed by dynamic splinting (buddy taping). Closed reduction and immobilization of the forearm, wrist, and injured digit as well as the adjacent digit(s) in a cast, cast with metal outrigger, or gutter splint usually are adequate. Internal fixation may be used. Various traction techniques or external fixation methods are used for markedly comminuted fractures or bone loss. Avoid excessive traction, which may prevent bony union.

24. How are closed diaphyseal fractures of the phalanges treated?

Acceptable angulation of diaphyseal fractures of the proximal and middle phalanges is 10° in any plane. No malrotation can be accepted, and allowable shortening is less than 5 mm. If a fracture is minimally displaced, it may be splinted with the MCP joints in full flexion and the IP joints in near full extension. Active motion should be started in 3 to 4 weeks to avoid stiffness. If the fracture is displaced, closed reduction can be performed. A fracture than cannot be maintained with acceptable displacement in a splint is considered unstable. An unstable fracture can be treated with CRPP (Fig. 122-2) or ORIF.

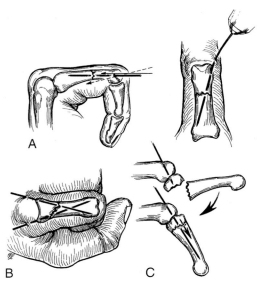

Figure 122-2. Three methods of closed reduction percutaneous pinning of a tranverse phalangeal fracture. **A,** The fracture is reduced, and a Kirschner pin is placed in the proximal phalanx in retrograde fashion. **B,** Alternative method of percutaneous pinning for fractures of the proximal half of the shaft. The pins are driven in anterograde fashion. **C,** Technique for closed reduction percutaneous pin fixation useful for extraarticular fractures near the base of the proximal phalanx in which Kirschner pins cross the MCP joint. (From Green DP [ed]: Operative Hand Surgery, 3rd ed. New York, Churchill Livingstone, 1993, p 732.)

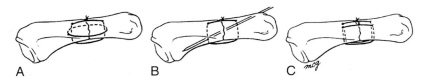

Figure 122-3. Intraosseous wire configuration. **A,** 90-90 wires. **B,** Single loop with supplemental Kirschner pin. **C,** Parallel loops. (From Green DP [ed]: Operative Hand Surgery, 3rd ed. New York, Churchill Livingstone, 1993, p 738.)

Options for internal fixation include intraosseous wiring (Fig. 122-3), compression screws, plates, and intramedullary fixation. Diaphyseal fractures of the distal phalanx can generally be treated with closed reduction and splinting.

25. What are the complications of phalangeal fractures?
- Loss of motion results from tendon adherence at the fracture site and contracture, especially at the PIP joint level. Extensor tenolysis rarely improves active PIP joint extension. With flexor adherence, either excise the FDS or resort to PIP fusion as a salvage procedure for severe flexion contracture.
- Malunion secondary to volar angulation after fractures near the base of the proximal phalanx. Treatment consists of an opening wedge osteotomy and bone graft.
- Malrotation after spiral or oblique proximal and middle phalangeal fractures. Treatment consists of an osteotomy at the metacarpal or phalangeal levels.
- Pin tract infection.
- Nonunion results from bone loss, soft tissue interposition, inadequate immobilization, or distraction at the fracture site. Treatment involves resection of nonviable bone and bone grafting.

26. What is the best view for diagnosing metacarpal head fractures?
Metacarpal head fractures are often difficult to diagnose. Brewerton views should be obtained if a metacarpal head fracture is suspected.

27. How are metacarpal head fractures treated?
- Comminuted or oblique fractures with displacement require ORIF with K-wires or small screws.
- Comminuted fractures limited to the metacarpal head distal to the ligament require early mobilization after protection for several weeks. Displaced fractures proximal to the origin of the ligament may require ORIF.

- Collateral ligament avulsion fractures require ORIF if displaced and/or more than 20% to 30% of the joint surface is involved. Obtain Brewerton views.
- Small osteochondral fracture fragments are generally excised.

28. What are possible complications of metacarpal head fractures?
- Avascular necrosis of the metacarpal head may occur after horizontal fractures.
- Epiphyseal arrest may result in shortening of the metacarpal, usually without functional loss.

29. What is a boxer's fracture?
A boxer's fracture is a metacarpal neck fracture, usually resulting from a direct blow with comminution of the volar cortex and dorsal angulation. Boxer's fracture is a misnomer because most metacarpal neck fractures involve the little and ring fingers, whereas a professional boxer is most likely to injure the middle or index fingers with a more direct central impact of the punch. This results in angulation with the apex dorsal because of the pull of the intrinsic muscles. Malunion results in loss of prominence of the metacarpal head, diminished range of motion, and a palpable metacarpal head in the palm, which causes pain with grip.

30. What is the Jahss maneuver?
The Jahss maneuver is a technique for closed reduction of metacarpal neck fractures. Sixty years ago Jahss recognized that flexing the MCP joint to 90° relaxed the deforming intrinsic muscles and tightened the collateral ligaments, allowing the proximal phalanx to exert upward pressure on the metacarpal head. He applied a cast in two parts, first immobilizing the proximal metacarpal fragment and then flexing the MCP and PIP joints, pushing upward on the flexed PIP joint while applying the second part. The Jahss maneuver remains the best technique for closed reduction of these fractures; however, fingers should never be maintained in the Jahss position (MCP and PIP joints both flexed at 90°). Instead, after reduction the fingers should be held in an intrinsic plus splint (Fig. 122-4).

31. How much angulation can be accepted in metacarpal neck fractures? How are they treated?
The amount of angulation that should be accepted is controversial. Angulation is unacceptable if it involves pseudoclawing of the finger on distal extension. Pseudoclawing is compensatory MCP joint hyperextension and PIP joint flexion on attempted extension of the digit. Up to 40° of angulation can be accepted in the mobile ring and little metacarpals. Closed reduction should be attempted for more than 15° of angulation. No more than 10° to 15° of angulation is acceptable for the index and middle metacarpals. These fractures are often associated with a lack of compensatory carpometacarpal motion. ORIF is required; crossed K-wires or tension band wiring may be used. For less than 15° of angulation, an ulnar gutter splint is applied for 10 to 14 days. For 15° to 40° of angulation, reduce and apply an ulnar gutter splint for 3 weeks. For greater than 40° of angulation, volar comminution, extensor lag, or unacceptable reduction, treat with percutaneous pinning. ORIF usually is not necessary. Angulation exceeding the recommended degrees can lead to a prominent metacarpal head in the palm and painful grasp. Any rotational deformity is unacceptable (Fig. 122-5).

32. How are metacarpal shaft fractures treated?
Transverse fractures usually are caused by direct blows (axial loading). They demonstrate dorsal angulation secondary to the strong volar force exerted by the interosseous muscles. The more proximal the fracture, the less the angulation that can be tolerated. Oblique and spiral fractures result from torsional forces acting on the finger as a lever arm. No rotation is acceptable because as little as 5° of rotation in a metacarpal fracture may cause up to 1.5 cm of digital overlap. Up to

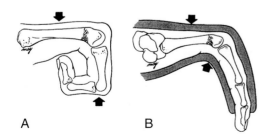

Figure 122-4. Jahss maneuver for reduction of a metacarpal neck fracture. **A,** *Arrows* indicate direction of pressure application for fracture reduction. **B,** After reduction, the fingers are held in an intrinsic-plus position in an ulnar gutter splint with molding as indicated by the *arrows*. (From Green DP [ed]: Operative Hand Surgery, 3rd ed. New York, Churchill Livingstone, 1993, p 701.)

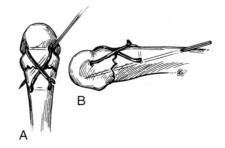

Figure 122-5. Tension band wiring **(A)** and single Kirschner pin fixation **(B)** of a metacarpal neck fracture. (From Green DP [ed]: Operative Hand Surgery, 3rd ed. New York, Churchill Livingstone, 1993, p 703.)

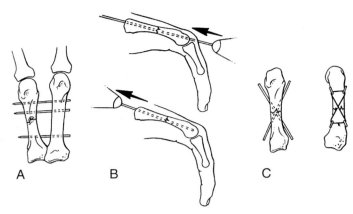

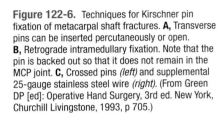

Figure 122-6. Techniques for Kirschner pin fixation of metacarpal shaft fractures. **A,** Transverse pins can be inserted percutaneously or open. **B,** Retrograde intramedullary fixation. Note that the pin is backed out so that it does not remain in the MCP joint. **C,** Crossed pins *(left)* and supplemental 25-gauge stainless steel wire *(right)*. (From Green DP [ed]: Operative Hand Surgery, 3rd ed. New York, Churchill Livingstone, 1993, p 705.)

5 mm of shortening is acceptable. The intermetacarpal ligaments minimize the degree of shortening. Closed reduction and plaster immobilization usually are adequate. Placing a patient in a "clamdigger" or intrinsic plus splint prevents contractures. If closed reduction is unsuccessful, perform an open reduction with percutaneous pinning or another method of internal fixation, such as plating or lag screw compression (Fig. 122-6). Immobility is the chief cause of stiffness.

33. What are the complications of metacarpal fractures?

(1) Malunion causes dorsal angulation, which can disturb intrinsic muscle balance and produce metacarpal head prominence in the palm with pain on grasping. This complication is treated by a volar opening wedge osteotomy and plate fixation. A rotational deformity is corrected by an osteotomy to the metacarpal base. (2) Nonunion is caused by bone loss from a gunshot wound or distraction that prevents bone approximation and healing. (3) Other complications include MCP extension contractures, intrinsic muscle contractures, pin tract infection, tendon adherence, and refracture.

34. What is a Bennett fracture?

A Bennett fracture is an intraarticular fracture–subluxation involving the base of the thumb metacarpal. It results in a vertical or oblique fracture through the volar beak of the metacarpal, exiting the diaphyseal–metaphyseal junction ulnarly. The strong anterior oblique ligament (volar beak ligament) stabilizes the variably sized ulnovolar fragment in anatomic position while the metacarpal fragment subluxates radially, proximally, and dorsally. The major deforming forces are the abductor pollicis longus and adductor pollicis. Supination also occurs.

35. What is the epidemiology of Bennett fractures?

Bennett fractures are 10 times more common in men than in women. Patients usually are in their 30s; the dominant hand is injured in 70% of cases. Most patients sustain an axial blow to the thumb with the metacarpal in some degree of flexion from a fall on an unstretched hand, striking a blow with a clenched fist, falling on a ski slope, or impact of the hand against a dashboard. Concomitant fractures are uncommon; the trapezium is most commonly involved.

36. How are Bennett fractures treated?

Treatment requires anatomic reduction by either CRPP or ORIF and pinning or screw placement (Fig. 122-7). Reduction of the fracture–dislocation is easy, but retention is difficult. Longitudinal traction is applied to the thumb metacarpal, which is radially extended and pronated with direct pressure over the fracture site. The thumb metacarpal is then stabilized by fixing it to the index metacarpal, trapezium, or both, using one or two pins—between the thumb and index metacarpals, thumb metacarpal to trapezium, thumb metacarpal to ulnovolar fragments, or any combination of the above.

37. What is a reverse Bennett fracture?

It is an intraarticular fracture–dislocation involving the base of the little finger metacarpal. It is analogous to a Bennett fracture of the thumb. The deforming forces are the extensor carpi ulnaris and hypothenar muscles. Anatomic reduction of the mobile carpometacarpal (CMC) joint is necessary.

38. What is a Rolando fracture?

A Rolando fracture is an intraarticular fracture of the base of the thumb metacarpal in T, Y, or comminuted form. Treatment consists of closed or open reduction and K-wire pinning. For comminuted fractures, mold in a thumb spica cast for 3 to 4 weeks. A classic two-part Rolando fracture can be reduced and interfragmentary fixation performed with either multiple K-wires or a plate (Fig. 122-8).

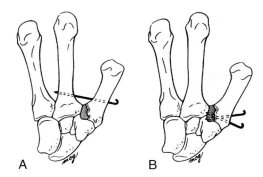

Figure 122-7. Fixation of a Bennett fracture. **A,** Kirschner pin is inserted between the thumb and index metacarpals. **B,** Pins are passed from the metacarpal shaft into the Bennett fragment. (From Green DP [ed]: Operative Hand Surgery, 3rd ed. New York, Churchill Livingstone, 1993, p 749.)

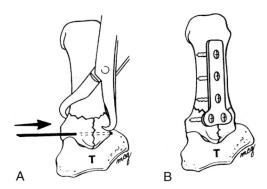

Figure 122-8. Fixation of a Rolando fracture. **A,** Provisional fixation is accomplished with a clamp and Kirschner pin. **B,** Final fixation is accomplished with a T-plate. *T,* Trapezium. (From Green DP [ed]: Operative Hand Surgery, 3rd ed. New York, Churchill Livingstone, 1993, p 751.)

39. What role does the CMC joint of the little finger play?

The CMC joint of the little finger allows 30° of flexion and extension. Rotation allows normal cupping of the palm in grip (opposition). Inadequate reduction results in major residual functional disability with weakness of grip.

40. How are open fractures treated?

All open fractures must be cultured; patients are placed on intravenous antibiotics. Open fractures are converted to clean wounds by thorough irrigation (Hydrojet) and débridement. Fractures caused by gunshot wounds (low velocity) generally sustain minimal damage to tendons and nerves. Formal exploration of the entire bullet tract is not necessary; the entrance and exit wounds are simply cleansed. Skeletal stability is restored either primarily or as soon as possible (as in the case of extensive open injuries with multiple fractures) by simple immobilization, K-wire fixation, external fixation, or immediate bone grafting (in special cases). Severely comminuted fractures extending onto joint surfaces may discourage any form of fixation, and arthrodesis may be necessary. Soft tissue coverage may be necessary before fracture fixation or bone grafting.

41. How are fractures with segmental bone loss treated?

Fractures with segmental bone loss are treated as open fractures. Occasionally, the wound is packed open. Length and stability are maintained by K-wires or external fixation. For definitive reconstruction, the various components of the injury must be addressed. The soft tissue wound often requires flap coverage. Immediate or delayed bone reconstruction is performed with bone grafts. Nerve and tendon reconstruction and vascularized joint transfers may be necessary.

42. What is the "lag screw" technique of interfragmentary compression?

This technique provides rigid fixation and is primarily indicated for long oblique and spiral shaft fractures. It usually is indicated for fractures in which the length of the fracture line is at least twice the diameter of the bone. Lag screw fixation involves passing a screw through a gliding hole in the near fragment (nonthreaded and of wider diameter than the threads of the screw) into a smaller hole in the far fragment (tapped to the same diameter as the screw threads), which then grabs the far cortex. As the screw is tightened (lagged), the threads grip and draw the far fragment towards the near fragment, approximating the fragments and compressing the fracture. Ideally, longitudinal compressive forces are best counteracted by placing the screw 90° to the bone's long axis, and torsional stresses are best resisted by placing the screw 90° to the fracture.

BIBLIOGRAPHY

Green DP, Butler TE: Fractures and dislocations in the hand. In: Rockwood CA, Green DP, Bucholz RW, Heckman JD (eds): Fractures in Adults. Philadelphia, Lippincott-Raven, 1996, pp 607–744.

Seymour N: Juxta-epiphysial fracture of the terminal phalanx of the finger. J Bone Joint Surg Br 48:347–349, 1966.

Stern PS: Fractures of the metacarpals and phalanges. In Green DP (ed): Operative Hand Surgery, 3rd ed. New York, Churchill Livingstone, 1993, pp 695–758.

Swanson TV, Szabo RM, Anderson DD: Open hand fractures: Prognosis and classification. J Hand Surg 16A:101–107, 1991.

Widgerow AD, Edinburg M, Biddulph SL: An analysis of proximal phalangeal fractures. J Hand Surg 12A:134–139, 1987.

Worlock PH, Stower MJ: The incidence and pattern of hand fractures in children. J Hand Surg 11B:198–200, 1986.

Wray RC Jr, Glunk R: Treatment of delayed union, nonunion, and malunion of phalanges of the hand. Ann Plast Surg 22:14–18, 1989.

Yang SS, Gerwin M: Fractures of the hand. In Levine AM (ed): Orthopaedic Knowledge Update: Trauma. Rosemont, IL, American Academy of Orthopaedic Surgeons, 1996, pp 95–109.

JOINT DISLOCATIONS AND LIGAMENT INJURIES

W. Bradford Rockwell, MD, and
R. Christie Wray, Jr., MD

1. Explain the difference between true collateral and accessory collateral ligaments.

The thick collateral ligaments of the phalanges arise from the condyles of the proximal bone and insert on the palmar third of the distal bone and the distal lateral margin of the palmar plate (also called the *volar plate*). The true collateral ligament inserts distally on bone, whereas the accessory collateral ligament inserts distally on the palmar plate.

2. What soft tissue structures provide stability to the proximal interphalangeal joint?

Soft tissue structures that compose a box around the proximal interphalangeal (PIP) joint are the collateral ligaments on either side, palmar plate, and dorsal capsule (Fig. 123-1). The dorsal capsule is very thin and provides minimal stability to the joint. The collateral ligaments on the radial and ulnar sides and the palmar plate are very firm structures. For dislocation to occur, at least two of the three strong structures must be disrupted.

3. How is the functional stability of a joint tested?

The stability is tested through active motion and passive motion. Stability during active motion suggests joint stability although a partial ligament tear may exist. Recurrent displacement with active motion indicates major ligament disruption. The position in which displacement occurs may indicate the site of disruption. Passive motion provides the final assessment of stability. Each collateral ligament as well as the palmar plate is stressed to measure stability.

4. What are the three types of dorsal PIP dislocations?

Joint dislocations are described with respect to the distal bone in relation to the proximal bone. The three dorsal PIP dislocations are (1) subluxation with some articular surface still in contact; (2) dorsal dislocation with no articulating joint surface, indicating avulsion of the palmar plate with major bilateral split of the collateral ligaments; and (3) fracture–dislocation, which may be stable or unstable (Fig. 123-2). Subluxations, dislocations, and stable fracture–dislocations are treated with an extension blocking splint, allowing full active motion except for the last 30° of extension. Unstable fracture dislocations require operative repair.

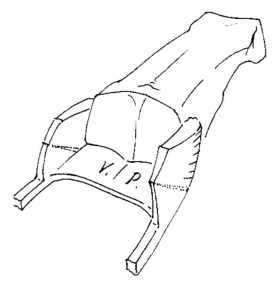

Figure 123-1. Three-dimensional ligament–box complex provides strength with minimum bulk. The collateral ligaments provide stability on the radial and ulnar sides while the volar plate provides stability on the palmar side. At least two sides of this box must be disrupted for displacement of the joint to occur. (From Dray GJ, Eaton RG: Dislocations and ligament injuries in the digits. In Green DP [ed]: Operative Hand Surgery, 2nd ed. New York, Churchill Livingstone, 1988, p 778.)

A   B   C

Figure 123-2. Stable and unstable fracture–dislocations. **A,** The fracture involves less than 40% of the volar base of the middle phalanx and leaves a significant portion of the collateral ligaments still attached. This configuration is stable. **B,** Normal anatomy with collateral ligament insertion into the palmar third of the middle phalanx and volar plate. **C,** This fracture involves more than 40% of the palmar base of the middle phalanx. Little or no collateral ligament remains attached. Congruous reduction is unlikely without these ligaments. This configuration is unstable. (From Dray GJ, Eaton RG: Dislocations and ligament injuries in the digits. In Green DP [ed]: Operative Hand Surgery, 2nd ed. New York, Churchill Livingstone, 1988, p 781.)

5. What is the treatment for chronic PIP dorsal subluxations?
Chronic PIP dorsal subluxations may result from laxity of the PIP palmar plate or an extensor tendon imbalance, usually from a mallet deformity resulting in a swan neck posture. If passive PIP mobilization demonstrates a distal interphalangeal (DIP) extensor lag, treatment is aimed at correcting the extensor mechanism. PIP palmar plate laxity is corrected with either palmar plate reattachment or a joint tenodesis using one slip of the superficialis tendon.

6. What soft tissue injuries may occur with palmar PIP dislocation?
Volar dislocations of the PIP joint are uncommon. A rotatory compressive force results in a unilateral disruption of a collateral ligament and partial avulsion of the volar plate. The involved condyle of the proximal phalanx usually ruptures between the central slip and the ipsilateral lateral band. When the dislocation is straight palmar without a rotatory component, the central slip may rupture. Following reduction, if full active extension is not present, the PIP joint should be immobilized in full extension. Open reduction is necessary only if closed reduction fails.

7. What structure is primarily involved in posttraumatic fibrosis of the PIP joint?
Collateral ligament fibrosis is the inevitable consequence of PIP dislocation. The fusiform swelling of the PIP joint capsule is initially due to hemorrhage and edema. As these resorb, ligamentous fibrosis and inelastic scar develop. To minimize these developments, motion should begin as soon as joint stability is assured. Oral steroids should be considered 4 weeks after dislocation. When significant loss of motion persists despite a good rehabilitation program, surgery should be considered to produce total collateral ligament excision and distal volar plate release.

8. Are dislocations of the finger DIP and thumb interphalangeal joints common?
No. These dislocations are rare and usually dorsal. The majority of these dislocations are reduced closed and immobilized for 10 to 21 days before beginning active motion.

9. With an injury to another part of the hand, what anatomic difference between the metacarpophalangeal (MCP) and PIP joints accounts for MCP joints being immobilized in flexion and PIP joints in extension?
The metacarpal head is characterized by a "cam" effect where the length of the collateral ligament attachment to the articular surface is greater with the joint flexed at least 50° compared with extended. The PIP joint collateral ligament possesses a uniform length in this regard. Splinting metacarpophalangeal (MCP) joints in at least 50° of flexion keeps the collateral ligaments on stretch and will not allow their shortening. PIP joint position does not affect the length of the collateral ligaments. PIP joints are splinted in extension to avoid a flexion contracture.

10. Describe the anatomic structures that contribute to a complex or irreducible MCP joint dislocation.
MCP joint dislocations are most commonly dorsal and involve the index or little finger. The metacarpal head of the index finger is detached from the weak membranous portion of the palmar plate, which may become inserted between the metacarpal head and the base of the proximal phalanx. The lumbrical muscle is stretched around the radial border of the metacarpal head, whereas the flexor tendons are stretched around the ulnar border. The metacarpal head of the little finger is entrapped between the abductor digiti minimi and flexor digiti minimi tendons ulnarly and lumbrical muscle and flexor tendons radially. Axial traction tightens these structures and makes reduction more difficult. MCP joint flexion and axial traction may allow closed reduction.

11. Do digital carpometacarpal dislocations occur?
The ligament configuration of the index and middle carpometacarpal (CMC) joints is very stable, being termed the *fixed unit*. Dislocations of these joints are very uncommon. If dislocations occur at the CMC joints, they most frequently

involve the fifth and then the fourth joints and are dorsal. Frequently, a fifth CMC joint dislocation is accompanied by a fracture, being termed *baby Bennett fracture dislocation*. This may be missed with only a posteroanterior radiograph and requires operative reduction and fixation.

12. What is a gamekeeper's thumb?

Injury to the ulnar collateral ligament (UCL) of the thumb MCP joint is common. Forced radial deviation of the thumb produces the injury, which results in trauma to the dorsal capsule, UCL, and ulnar aspect of the palmar plate. This injury is called a *gamekeeper's thumb* or *skier's thumb*.

13. What is a Stener lesion?

The UCL of the thumb MCP joint has bony attachments deep to the adductor pollicis aponeurosis. In *complete* disruptions of the UCL from the proximal phalanx, the adductor aponeurosis may become interposed between the distal end of the avulsed UCL and its insertion into the base of the proximal phalanx, producing poor healing and persistent ligament laxity on the ulnar side of the joint. The disrupted UCL is displaced superficial to the adductor aponeurosis and, thus, will not heal without operative repair. This displaced end of the UCL is the *Stener lesion*. The adductor aponeurosis is elevated temporarily, allowing repair of the UCL to the proximal phalanx (Fig. 123-3).

14. Is it clinically important to differentiate between partial and complete ruptures of the thumb MCP UCL?

As a general rule, partial ruptures are treated with splint immobilization and complete ruptures require operative repair. Patients with both injuries will have tenderness, ecchymosis, and induration over the UCL. In complete ruptures, radially directed stress will produce at least 30° more instability compared with the contralateral MCP joint. The test should be performed in full extension and in 30° of flexion. Complete ruptures also will not have a definite endpoint to radial stress, whereas partial ruptures will have an endpoint. Median and radial nerve blocks may be necessary to complete an adequate stress test.

15. What soft tissue structure provides the most stability to the thumb CMC joint?

The saddle contour of the articular surfaces of the thumb CMC joint provide inherent intrinsic stability. The capsular thickening composing the volar beak ligament, passing from the trapezium to the volar beak of the thumb metacarpal, is a key structure in maintaining CMC stability.

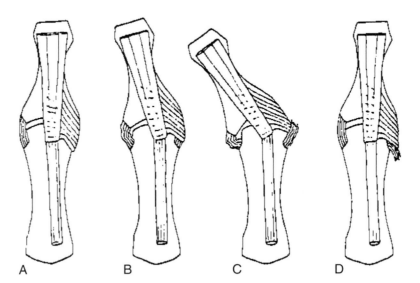

A   B   C   D

Figure 123-3. Displacement of the ulnar collateral ligament of the thumb metacarpophalangeal joint. **A,** Normal anatomy shows the ulnar collateral ligament covered by the adductor aponeurosis. **B,** With slight radial angulation, the proximal margin of the aponeurosis slides distally, leaving a portion of the ligament uncovered. **C,** With significant radial angulation, the ulnar collateral ligament ruptures at its distal insertion. The aponeurosis is displaced distal to the rupture, permitting the ulnar collateral ligament to escape from beneath it. **D,** As the joint is realigned, the proximal edge of the adductor aponeurosis sweeps the free end of the ligament proximally and further away from its insertion. This is the Stener lesion. Unless surgically repaired, the ulnar collateral ligament will not heal properly and will be unstable to lateral stress. (From Dray GJ, Eaton RG: Dislocations and ligament injuries in the digits. In Green DP [ed]: Operative Hand Surgery, 2nd ed. New York, Churchill Livingstone, 1988, p 795.)

16. Does joint subluxation occur at the thumb CMC joint?

The thumb CMC joint is also referred to as the *basal joint*. Joint laxity most commonly occurs in postmenopausal women from laxity of the volar beak ligament. Laxity produces irregular joint wear and basal joint arthritis between the trapezium and metacarpal. The most common form of reconstruction uses the flexor carpi radialis tendon as a soft tissue support for the base of the metacarpal, with the remainder of the tendon interposed in the space created by excision of the trapezium.

17. What is the most common complication following joint or ligament injury?

Ligament injury requires joint immobilization and may require operative repair. Resolution of intraarticular hematoma and swelling leave scar within the joint capsule. Early joint motion will minimize postinjury stiffness, but preference must be given to joint immobilization until adequate ligament stability has developed. Most dislocated joints can be immediately mobilized following reduction.

BIBLIOGRAPHY

Abrahamsson SO, Sollerman C, Lundborg G, Larsson J, Egund N: Diagnosis of displaced ulnar collateral ligament of the metacarpophalangeal joint of the thumb. J Hand Surg 15A:457–460, 1990.

Burnett WR: Rehabilitation techniques for ligament injuries of the hand. Hand Clin 8:803–815, 1992.

Burton RI, Pellegrini VD Jr: Surgical management of basal joint arthritis of the thumb. Part II: Ligament reconstruction with tendon interposition arthroplasty. J Hand Surg 11A:324–332, 1986.

Glickel SZ, Barron OA, Catalano LW III: Dislocations and ligament injuries in the digits. In Green DP, Hotchkiss RN, Pederson WC, Wolfe SW (eds): Operative Hand Surgery. Philadelphia, Elsevier Churchill Livingstone, 2005, pp 343–388.

Henderson JJ, Arafa MAM: Carpometacarpal dislocation: An easily missed diagnosis. J Bone Joint Surg 69B:212–214, 1987.

Liss FE, Green SM: Capsular injuries of the proximal interphalangeal joint. Hand Clin 8:755–768, 1992.

Miller RJ: Dislocations and fracture dislocations of the metacarpophalangeal joint of the thumb. Hand Clin 4:45–65, 1988.

Rosenstadt BE, Glickel SZ, Lane LB, Kaplan SJ: Palmar fracture-dislocations of the proximal interphalangeal joint. J Hand Surg [Am] 23:811–820, 1998.

Schenck RR: Classification of fractures and dislocations of the proximal interphalangeal joint. Hand Clin 10:179–185, 1994.

Zemel NP: Metacarpal joint injuries in fingers. Hand Clin 8:745, 1992.

SMALL JOINT ARTHRODESIS AND ARTHROPLASTY

Lana Kang, MD; Alan Rosen, MD; and
Andrew J. Weiland, MD

SMALL JOINT ARTHRODESIS

1. What are the indications for small joint arthrodesis?

The general indications for arthrodesis of any joint also pertain to the hand. They include the following:

- Pain
- Instability
- Joint destruction
- Deformity resulting from trauma, osteoarthritis, or rheumatoid-type conditions
- Loss of muscle or tendon function across the joint

More specific indications for small joint arthrodesis in the hand include the following:

- Painful posttraumatic arthritis or deformity
- Fixed contractures after burns
- Rheumatoid arthritis (RA)
- Severe infection unresponsive to pharmacologic therapy
- Dupuytren's contracture with fixed deformity
- Nerve palsy leading to instability that impedes function
- Chronic mallet finger deformity unresponsive to conservative treatment
- As a salvage procedure following failed arthroplasty or tendon reconstruction for deformity such as boutonnière or mallet finger

2. Describe the ideal position for fusion of the metacarpophalangeal, proximal interphalangeal, and distal interphalangeal joints of the index, middle, ring, and little fingers.

In general, finger metacarpophalangeal (MP) joints should be cascaded from a radial to an ulnar direction beginning with 25° of flexion in the index finger and adding 5° for each more ulnarly located finger. The proximal interphalangeal (PIP) joints should also be cascaded from a radial to an ulnar direction beginning with 40° of flexion in the index finger and adding 5° for each more ulnarly located finger. The distal interphalangeal (DIP) joints all should be fused in 0° of flexion. In all joints undergoing fusion, there should be no rotation, ulnar deviation, or radial deviation from the normal anatomic position. An exception to this rule is the DIP joint of the index and middle fingers where 5° to 10° of supination may be useful in achieving pulp-to-pulp pinch with the thumb (Fig. 124-1).

3. What is the ideal position for fusion of the MP and IP joints of the thumb?

The MP joint is flexed 5° to 15°, with approximately 10° of pronation to facilitate pulp-to-pulp pinch with the fingers. The IP joint is also fused in slight flexion, anywhere from 0° to 15° (Fig. 124-2).

4. A stiff finger is less cumbersome if it is slightly shorter, right?

This is true only for the index, middle, ring, and little fingers. For the thumb, which is involved in nearly all hand activities, maximal length should be obtained to allow for functions such as pinch and opposition.

5. What general principles must be adhered to so that a successful fusion can be obtained?

Many techniques have been described for fixation of small joint arthrodeses, each with its own proponents and applications. However, no matter what technique is used, several general principles need to be followed:

- Avoid interposition of any soft tissues between bony surfaces.
- Remove all cartilage from the joint surfaces.
- Surface preparation should result in good cancellous to cancellous bone contact.
- The bony surfaces must be held securely together by internal (or, if needed, by external) fixation.
- Regardless of technique, the position of fusion should be as close as possible to the position of function.

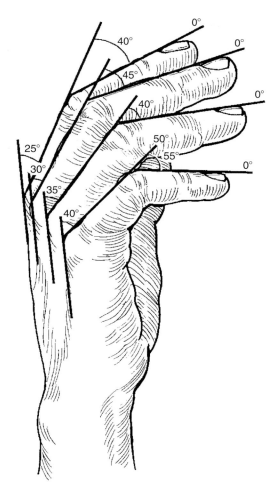

Figure 124-1. Ideal position for small joint arthrodesis of the index, middle, ring, and little fingers. (From Weiland AJ: Small joint arthrodesis. In Green DP, Hotchkiss RN, Pederson WC [eds]: Green's Operative Hand Surgery, 4th ed. New York, Churchill Livingstone, 1999, p 96.)

6. What are the internal fixation techniques available for small joint arthrodesis?

Several techniques are available (Fig. 124-3). Internal fixation techniques include the following:
- Kirschner wires: These can be trimmed at the bone surface and left in situ or be left protruding from the bone so that they can be removed once fusion has set in
- Interosseous wiring
- Tension band wiring
- Screw fixation with cortical, lag, or headless compression screw fixation (e.g., Herbert Whipple Screw [Zimmer, Warsaw, Indiana] or the Mini-Acutrak Screw [Acumed, Beaverton, Oregon])
- Plate fixation
- Bioabsorbable rods and pins: Use of these materials is in its clinical infancy

7. Which internal fixation technique should be used?

No technique is fail-safe. Nonunion and complications do occur, although reported rates are variable and comparably low among the different techniques. The technique that is finally chosen should be based on the size of the bone, the patient, and the surgeon's experience.

8. Discuss the situations when external fixation may be needed for arthrodesis.

External fixation has limited indications and is not generally used for uncomplicated phalangeal and metacarpal joint arthrodesis (Fig. 124-4). Indications for external fixation include the following:
- Open joint injuries with severe bone and articular surface loss
- Septic arthritis or osteomyelitis with joint destruction
- Failed prior arthrodesis by other methods

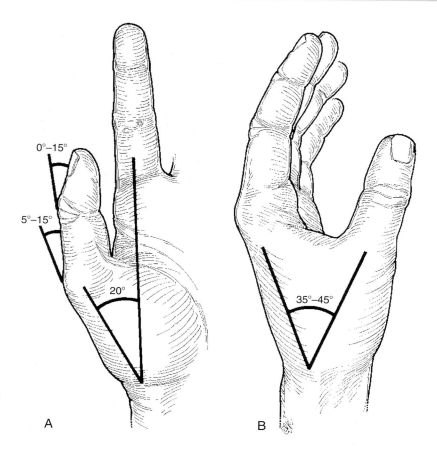

Figure 124-2. Ideal position for thumb joint arthrodesis. (From Weiland AJ: Small joint arthrodesis. In Green DP, Hotchkiss RN, Pederson WC [eds]: Green's Operative Hand Surgery, 4th ed. New York, Churchill Livingstone, 1999, p 97.)

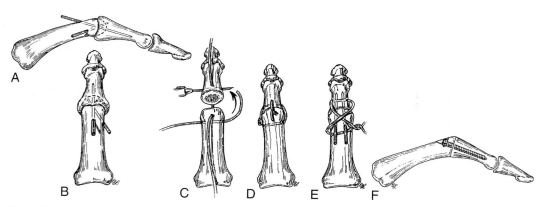

Figure 124-3. Internal fixation techniques available for small joint arthrodesis. **A, B,** Kirschner wiring. **C, D,** Interosseous wiring. **E,** Tension band wiring. **F,** Lag screw fixation. (From Brockman R, Weiland AJ: Small joint arthrodesis. In Green DP [ed]: Operative Hand Surgery, 3rd ed. New York, Churchill Livingstone, 1993, p 104.)

9. Is bone grafting necessary for small joint fusions?

Bone grafts usually are not necessary to obtain successful digital joint arthrodeses. In cases of significant bone loss from trauma, failed arthroplasty, failed prior attempt at arthrodesis, infection, or in the arthritis mutilans form of RA with severe bone loss, bone grafting may be useful.

10. Should all chronic mallet deformities be fused?

No. Studies have shown that even chronic mallet finger deformities may respond to treatment with 8 weeks of DIP joint splinting. Patient preference also should be taken into account. Many patients would rather live with a 10° to

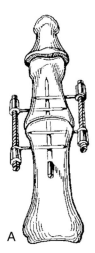

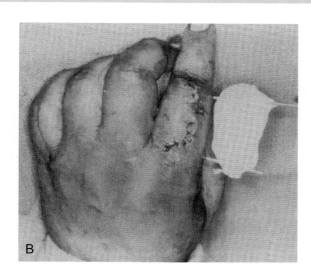

Figure 124-4. External fixation technique. **A,** Double-frame external fixation device. **B,** Bowed Kirschner wires with methylmethacrylate. (From Weiland AJ: Small joint arthrodesis. In Green DP, Hotchkiss RN, Pederson WC [eds]: Green's Operative Hand Surgery, 4th ed. New York, Churchill Livingstone, 1999, pp 1–4.)

A   B

15° extensor lag than undergo surgery to fuse the joint. However, if a significant secondary hyperextension deformity develops at the PIP joint, arthrodesis of the DIP joint may be indicated to preserve PIP joint function.

11. Is small joint arthrodesis ever performed in children with open physes?
Yes. Indications for arthrodesis of digital joints in children with open physes are rare, but it may be indicated in cases involving congenital problems or cerebral palsy.

12. It is impossible to perform a digital fusion in children without interfering with digital growth. True or false?
False. The articular cartilage is carefully shaved off, avoiding damage to the ossification center and the physeal (growth) plate. The prepared articular surfaces are then reduced into the desired position of fusion and held in place with Kirschner wires until fusion has occurred (Fig. 124-5).

13. What are the most common complications encountered with small joint arthrodesis?
Arthrodesis of the small joints can have its share of complications. They include (1) nonunion, (2) malunion, (3) pin tract infection, (4) cold intolerance, (5) skin necrosis, (6) prominent hardware, and (7) vascular insufficiency, seen most often following arthrodesis for a fixed flexion deformity.

14. What are the most important considerations for a successful small joint arthrodesis?
- Indicated for the painful, unstable arthritic joint
- When relief of pain is more desirable than loss of motion

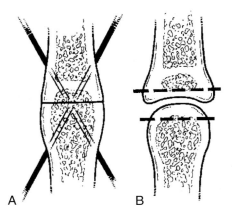

A   B

Figure 124-5. Arthrodesis technique in the presence of open physes. **A,** Articular and subchondral surfaces are removed from both sides of the joint. Note the ossification centers are exposed and preserved. **B,** Coaptation and fixation with K-wires. (From Weiland AJ: Small joint arthrodesis. In Green DP, Hotchkiss RN, Pederson WC [eds]: Green's Operative Hand Surgery, 4th ed. New York, Churchill Livingstone, 1999, p 104.)

- Precise preparation of bone ends
- Solid fixation in an optimal position of function
- Immobilize the fused joint until union is achieved

SMALL JOINT ARTHROPLASTY

15. What should be considered when choosing arthroplasty versus arthrodesis?

Before these procedures in the hand are performed, the condition of adjacent joints must be taken into account. It usually is not recommended to fuse contiguous joints because this will severely limit the range of motion of the affected digit. As a general rule, arthrodesis provides power and stability, whereas arthroplasty provides range of motion. Arthroplasty is more commonly indicated for the more proximal joints (e.g., MP joints of the index, middle, ring, and little fingers), whereas arthrodesis is more commonly performed for the DIP joints. Joints that require stability for specific functions, such as pinch (e.g., index PIP joint and thumb MP joint), are more amenable to fusion.

16. When is arthroplasty in the small joints of the hand indicated?

Arthroplasty is performed for end-stage arthrosis that results in (1) unrelenting pain, (2) deformity, (3) stiffness, and/or (4) dysfunction due to loss of joint surface or joint incongruity.

17. What are some of the underlying conditions for which arthroplasty in the hand are performed?

RA and related collagen diseases such as psoriatic arthritis and systemic lupus erythematosus are some of the most common disease processes that lead to joint destruction requiring arthroplasty. Arthroplasty may also be indicated for osteoarthritis or posttraumatic disease.

18. Arthroplasty in the hand for RA is being performed less frequently. True or false?

True. The course of RA has been remarkably altered by medical management. The arrival of anti–tumor necrosis factor drugs (e.g., Enbrel, Remicade) in combination with earlier disease detection and treatment has virtually halted progression of the disease.

19. What are the contraindications to arthroplasty?

Ongoing infection is an absolute contraindication for any type of implant arthroplasty. Loss of active range of motion across a joint due to damage or paralysis of the flexor or extensor tendons is also a primary contraindication.

20. Name the structures necessary for a stable arthroplasty.

Sufficient bone stock should be present to allow for a stable arthroplasty. In addition, preservation of the capsule and surrounding ligamentous structures is required. Finally, balanced and intact flexor and extensor tendon function is needed to achieve stability. If restoration of joint stability is doubtful, arthrodesis is a better option.

21. Describe the different types of arthroplasty most commonly performed.

Several types of arthroplasty have been described:
- *Resection arthroplasty,* in which the diseased articular surfaces are resected and soft tissue may be interposed between the two bones
- *Silicone elastomer arthroplasty,* in which the distal end of the proximal bone and the proximal end of the distal bone are resected, the phalangeal canals are prepared, and a flexible silicone spacer is interposed between the two (Fig. 124-6)
- *Hemiarthroplasty,* in which only one of the joint surfaces is replaced, usually by a silicone or titanium implant
- *Surface replacement arthroplasty (SRA),* in which bone ends are resected and the phalangeal canals are prepared for placement of a prosthesis that is made up of two articulating components. In addition to the original silicone implants, the new types of SRA prostheses fall into two broad categories: one that is modeled after total hip and knee systems consisting of metal (titanium or cobalt chrome) and ultra-high-molecular-weight polyethylene (UHMWP) that uses cement for fixation (Fig. 124-7); and the other that uses pyrolytic carbon implants having an anatomic design that offers some additional degree of articular stability.

22. What is the average arc of motion after PIP joint arthroplasty?

The average arc of motion attained after surgery is between 40° and 60°. Patients should be informed of this before surgery so that unrealistic expectations are not left unfulfilled. Patients can still benefit from arthroplasty surgery if the arc of motion is redirected into a more functional position or if their postoperative motion becomes pain free.

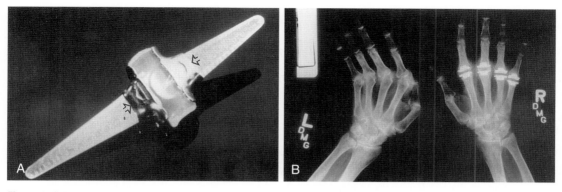

Figure 124-6. Hinged silicone prosthesis with grommets *(arrows).* **A,** Photograph of prosthesis prior to implantation. **B,** Radiograph of implanted prostheses at the metacarpophalangeal joints of the index, middle, ring, and little fingers on the right hand.

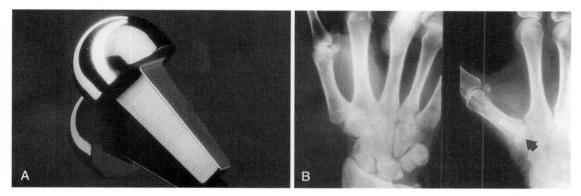

Figure 124-7. Convex condylar titanium implant. **A,** Photograph of prosthesis prior to implantation. **B,** Radiograph of thumb with carpometacarpal arthritis before *(left)* and after *(right)* implantation of the prosthesis *(arrow).*

23. What is perichondral arthroplasty?

This was first described in Europe during the 1970s. Chondral grafts are harvested from the costal cartilages and are sutured over the resurfaced ends of adjacent bones of the affected joint. When only cartilage is used, the procedure fails due to cartilage necrosis. When an osseous base with overlying cartilage is used, satisfactory results have been reported, but only in a small series of patients.

24. Which type of arthroplasty should be performed?

To date, no single implant design far surpasses all others. Silicone elastomer arthroplasty has the longest track record and continues to be the most commonly used. Its ability to provide good pain-free motion is a known quantity, but so is its incidence of complications and reoperation. The new line of cemented and carbon designs may prove to have a lower failure rate, but length of follow-up is relatively short. What may pan out over time is that the level of performance of certain implant designs may be specific to the preexisting disease (e.g., RA vs posttraumatic arthritis).

25. Discuss the common complications encountered with the use of silicone implants.

The most common complications associated with the use of silicone implants are prosthetic fracture, dislocation, and the formation of silicone-induced particulate synovitis with osteolysis and cyst formation. Use of a newer high-performance elastomer and circumferential grommets has reportedly decreased the incidence of fracture in hinged implants. However, high-performance elastomer (especially when used in areas of heavy loading such as the carpus) has also been associated with a higher incidence of silicone-induced particulate synovitis, thus curtailing the indications for its use.

26. What are the early and late complications associated with small joint arthroplasty?

The common complications encountered with small joint arthroplasty are essentially the same as those encountered with arthroplasties in general. Early complications include (1) wound breakdown, (2) infection, (3) prosthetic dislocation, and (4) nerve injury. Late complications include (1) loss of motion, (2) recurrent deformity, (3) prosthetic loosening, and (4) prosthetic fracture.

27. What are the most important considerations for a successful small joint arthroplasty?

- Indicated for painful, stiff, or deformed joint
- Contraindicated when bone stock or soft tissue stability is poor or when infection is ongoing
- Preferred in sedentary patients over heavy laborers
- Anticipate therapy and motion to begin within a few days after surgery
- Advise patients of potential complications

BIBLIOGRAPHY

Beckenbaugh RD, Linscheid RL: Arthroplasty in the hand and wrist. In Green DP (ed): Operative Hand Surgery, 3rd ed. Churchill Livingstone, New York, 1993, pp 143–188.

Gould JS: Arthroplasty of the metacarpophalangeal and interphalangeal joints of the digits and thumb. In Peimer CA (ed): Surgery of the Hand and Upper Extremity. New York, McGraw-Hill, 1996, pp 1677–1689.

Hanel DP: Reconstruction of finger deformities. In: Hand Surgery Update. Rosemont, IL, American Society for Surgery of the Hand, 1996, pp 34–44.

Thompson JS: Small joint arthrodeses. In Peimer CA (ed): Surgery of the Hand and Upper Extremity. New York, McGraw-Hill, 1996, pp 973–997.

Weiland AJ: Small joint arthrodesis and bony defect reconstruction. In McCarthy JG. (ed): Plastic Surgery, Vol 7. The Hand. Philadelphia, WB Saunders, 1990, pp 4671–4694.

Weiland AJ: Small joint arthrodesis. In: Green DP, Hotchkiss RN, Pederson WC (eds): Green's Operative Hand Surgery, 4th ed. New York, Churchill Livingstone, 1999, pp 95–107.

Wright PE: Arthritic hand. In: Crenshaw AH (ed): Campbell's Operative Orthopaedics, Vol 3, 8th ed. St. Louis, Mosby-Year Book, 1992, pp 3301–3339.

FLEXOR TENDON INJURIES

William F. Wagner, MD, and
James W. Strickland, MD

CHAPTER 125

1. Should acute flexor tendon lacerations be repaired primarily?

The concept that tendons can be immediately repaired in zones I and II with the expectation of restoring a favorable amount of tendon excursion has advanced from doubtful theory to general acceptance. Almost all studies have shown superior results compared with flexor tendon grafting. Advantages of primary tendon repair include the fact that the tendon is returned to its normal length, the period of disability necessitated by wound healing and later grafting is reduced, the tendency for joint stiffness is decreased, and the results of secondary lysis, when necessary, should be better.

2. What is the orientation of the flexor digitorum profundus and flexor digitorum superficialis tendons at the level of the proximal phalanx?

Once within the flexor sheath, the flexor digitorum superficialis (FDS) tendon begins to flatten. It then splits and divides around the flexor digitorum profundus (FDP) tendon. The two slips of the FDS tendon reunite deep to the FDP tendon, with half of the fibers decussating and the other half continuing distally on the same side. The reuniting of fibers of the FDS tendon is known as the *chiasm of Camper.* Beyond the chiasm, the FDS tendon splits into radial and ulnar slips, which insert into the middle three fifths of the middle phalanx (Fig. 125-1).

3. Where does the flexor tendon sheath begin and end in the digit? Where are the various pulleys or thickened areas of the flexor sheath located?

In the fingers the flexor sheath arises at the level of the volar plate of the metacarpophalangeal (MCP) joint and ends at the proximal volar base of the distal phalanx. The flexor sheath comprises thickened areas of arcing fibers, referred to as *annular pulleys,* which alternate with thin, flexible areas of crisscrossing fibers called *cruciate pulleys.* The first annular pulley arises from the volar plate of the MCP joint and the second annular pulley from the middle third of the proximal phalanx. The first cruciate pulley extends from the distal end of the second annular pulley to the proximal end of the third annular pulley, which arises primarily from the volar plate of the proximal interphalangeal (PIP) joint. The second cruciate pulley is located between the third and fourth annular pulleys, and the fourth annular pulley arises from the middle portion of the middle phalanx. The third cruciate pulley is located between the fourth and fifth annular pulleys, and the fifth annular pulley arises from the volar plate of the distal interphalangeal (DIP) plate and proximal volar base of the distal phalanx. It is not always possible to identify all of the described pulleys of the flexor sheath (Fig. 125-2).

4. What are the two ways in which flexor tendons receive nutrition?

Vascular injection studies have long shown the significant role of perfusion via small blood vessel networks called *vincula,* which arise from the digital arteries and ultimately connect into an intratendinous vascular network. Other studies have noted that synovial diffusion is the significant nutrient pathway.

5. What two areas of cellular activity contribute to flexor tendon healing?

Tendons heal by a combination of extrinsic and intrinsic cellular activity. The more intrinsic the cellular activity is, the fewer the adhesions. Extrinsic cellular activity primarily relates to peripheral adhesions that are frequently associated

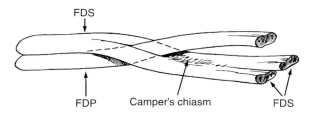

Figure 125-1. Early in the flexor sheath, the flexor digitorum superficialis *(FDS)* tendon divides and passes around the flexor digitorum profundus *(FDP)* tendon. The two portions of the FDS reunite at Camper's chiasm.

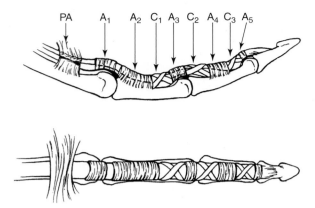

Figure 125-2. Lateral *(top)* and dorsal *(bottom)* views of the finger depict the components of the digital flexor sheath. The sturdy anular pulleys *(A₁, A₂, A₃, A₄, A₅)* are important biomechanically in keeping the tendons closely applied to the phalanges. The thin, pliable cruciate pulleys *(C₁, C₂, C₃)* collapse to allow full digital flexion. A recent addition is the palmar aponeurosis pulley *(PA)*, which adds to the biomechanical efficiency of the sheath system.

with the tendon-healing process. Although these adhesions have been considered an essential source of repair to cells, studies of the intrinsic healing capacity of tendons suggest that adhesions may constitute a nonessential inflammatory response at the site of injury.

6. What is the effect of stress on healing tendons?
If the repaired flexor tendon is not stressed, the healing process may take up to 8 weeks, and repaired tendons have minimal tensile strength throughout the healing process. Stressed tendons heal faster, gain tensile strength faster, and have fewer adhesions and better excursion than do unstressed tendons.

7. During what period are flexor tendons weakest after repair?
Strength usually decreases by 10% to 50% between 5 and 21 days after repair in unstressed tendons. It may not decrease at all in repairs subjected to early application of the appropriate amount of stress.

8. List three factors that may lead to tendon adhesion formation.
Tendon adhesion formation can be precipitated by tendon sheath injury, suture, and immobilization. Of these factors, immobilization has undergone the most extensive experimental and clinical investigation. Based on these studies, early protected mobilization to improve the mechanism by which flexor tendons heal has a sound scientific basis and is the best way of inhibiting adhesion formation. Of course, meticulous surgical technique and the underlying severity of the trauma to the tendon also affect the production of tendon adhesions.

9. What factors contribute to the strength of a repaired flexor tendon laceration?
The strength of a tendon repair is roughly proportional to the number of suture strands that cross the repair site and the caliber of the suture. An epitendinous suture increases strength of the repair as well. Studies have shown that braided polyblend suture (FiberWire, Arthrex, Naples, Florida) has the best biomechanical properties for flexor tendon repair. Increasing the number of suture strands across the repair site increases repair strength but adds to technical difficulty and increases the volume of suture material at the repair site.

10. What causes gapping at the repair site? How does it affect tendon healing?
Gapping may occur as repaired tendons begin to rupture through the suture or knot. Gapping also may occur when locking loops collapse and allow the tendon ends to pull apart. Gapping at the repair site becomes the weakest part of the tendon, unfavorably alters tendon mechanics, and may promote adhesion formation, resulting in decreased tendon excursion.

11. How can the tendency for gapping at the repair site be decreased?
A peripheral epitendinous suture results in an increase in repair strength and a significant reduction in the tendency for gapping at the repair site, particularly if placed 2 mm from the repair site. Improved strength and decreased gapping are maintained with cyclic stress. Horizontal mattress or running locked peripheral epitendinous sutures have been shown to add the greatest strength and resistance to gap formation.

12. What are the most commonly used techniques for flexor tendon repair?
Most techniques involve the use of a core suture consisting of two to eight strands to bridge the repair site. Many times the ends can first be aligned by repairing the dorsal portion of the tendon with a running, locked 6-0 nylon suture.

We currently recommend four-strand cruciate repair using 3-0 FiberWire (Arthrex) or eight-strand cruciate repair using 4-0 FiberLoop (Arthrex). The eight-strand cruciate repair is the same technique as the four-strand repair except that a double "looped" suture is used. The epitendinous suture is then completed around the palmar aspect of the tendon (Fig. 125-3).

13. Describe the zones of flexor tendon injury.

Most hand surgeons use a modification of Verdan's zone system to describe injuries to the flexor tendon system. Zone I flexor tendon injuries occur distal to the insertion of the FDS tendon. Zone II injuries are located from the proximal

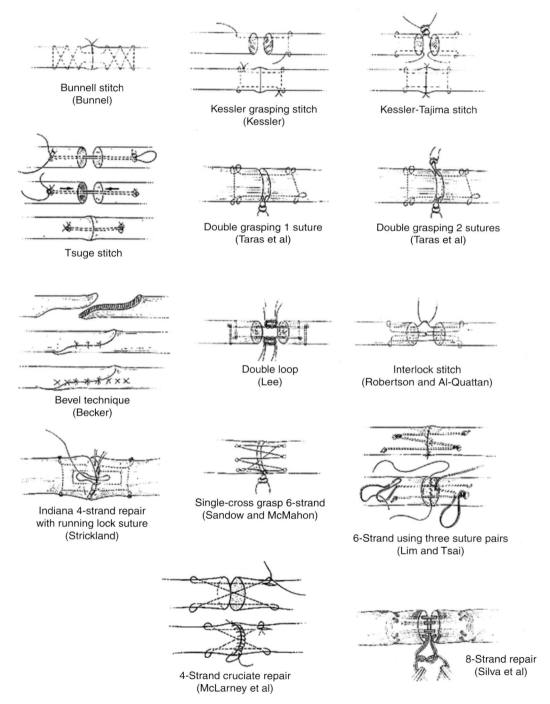

Figure 125-3. Flexor tendon repair techniques. (From Strickland JW: Development of flexor tendon surgery: Twenty-five years of progress. J Hand Surg [Am] 25:214–235, 2000.)

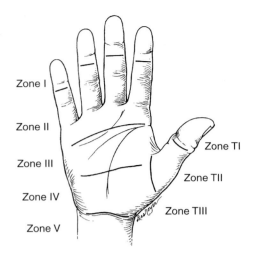

Figure 125-4. Zones of flexor tendon injuries. *T,* Thumb zones.

edge of the fibroosseous flexor tendon canal to the insertion of the FDS. Zone III injuries occur in the area where the lumbricals arise from the FDP tendon in the midpalm. Zone IV injuries occur within the carpal tunnel, and zone V injuries occur proximal to the carpal tunnel in the distal forearm (Fig. 125-4).

14. If the FDS is lacerated in a zone II flexor tendon injury, should it be repaired?

Yes. Decreasing the risk of PIP joint hyperextension, retaining independent motion, and providing a smooth bed for the FDP all are reasons to repair the FDS. A two- or four-strand repair of each slip of the FDS is recommended. If clinical concern exists for too much bulk at the repair site, one strand should be repaired with four strands and the other excised.

15. In zone II flexor tendon laceration repairs, what area of the sheath can be opened for repair? What areas should be preserved?

In opening the intact components of the sheath, every attempt must be made to preserve the A2 and A4 annular components to prevent bowstringing, flexion contracture, and loss of motion. The A3 pulley is of lesser importance, and the A1 and A5 pulleys can be removed in isolation with no detrimental effect. Tendon repairs should be performed in the cruciate synovial sheath windows, which usually can be restored after tendon repair. By acutely flexing the DIP joint and, to some extent, the PIP joint, it is possible to deliver the profundus and superficialis stumps into a cruciate window. If at least 1 cm of the distal tendons can be exposed in this manner, core sutures can be placed in the profundus tendons and two superficial slips without great difficulty. If a lesser length of distal tendon is present in the window, the next most distal cruciate synovial interval must be opened for core suture placement.

16. How do you retrieve a proximal tendon end that has retracted proximally down the tendon sheath?

Many clever tactics have been suggested to facilitate tendon capture and repositioning when the proximal ends have retracted further down the proximal sheath. One of the most commonly used methods is to pass a small catheter from the distal wound into the palm beneath the annular pulleys, where it is sutured to both tendons several centimeters proximal to the A1 pulley. The catheter is then pulled distally and easily delivers the tendon stumps into the distal repair site. A transversely oriented needle secures the tendons for repair, and the connecting suture can be severed in the palm and the catheter withdrawn (Fig. 125-5).

17. When the proximal ends of the lacerated FDS and FDP tendons retract into the palm, how can you correctly orient these tendons when they are brought out more distally into the digit?

When the proximal tendon ends have retracted into the palm, it is extremely important to reestablish the proper anatomic relationship of the FDP and FDS tendons. The FDP must be passed back through the hiatus created by the FDS slips so that it lies palmar to Camper's chiasm and recreates the relative positioning that was present at the level of the tendon laceration. Failure to restore the correct relationship creates an impediment to unrestricted tendon gliding after repair.

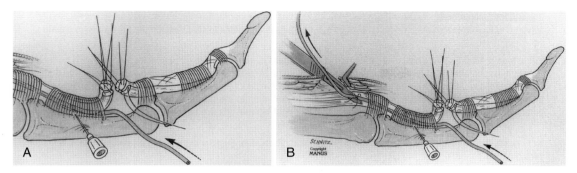

Figure 125-5. Sourmelis and McGrouther's method of retrieving flexor tendons. **A,** A 22-gauge hypodermic needle is passed transversely through the anular sheath to maintain tendon position. **B,** Catheter-tendon suture is cut in palm and withdrawn.

18. How should zone I FDP tendon avulsion injuries be repaired?

If the distal stump is short or nonexistent, the FDP stump can be reattached by first elevating a periosteal flap from the base of the distal phalanx and then drilling an oblique hole beneath the flap to penetrate the dorsal cortex just beneath the proximal fingernail. A double-armed needle with 3-0 sutures is placed in the proximal tendon stump and passed through the bone hole. The sutures are used to pull the tendon beneath the periosteal flap and are tied over a cotton pad/button combination over the nail. If possible, the tendon attachment should be supplemented by sutures through some adjacent sheath or periosteum. Alternatively, two microsuture anchors with 4-0 braided nylon can be used in the distal phalanx with two modified Becker type sutures attached to the radial and ulnar aspects of the tendon. This repair has the advantage of a higher tensile strength that can allow for early active motion.

19. Describe the three main types of avulsion injuries to the profundus tendon insertion.

See Fig. 125-6.

20. How should FDP avulsions in which the diagnosis is delayed for more than several months be treated?

Late untreated patients who are asymptomatic are best left alone. For late instability of the DIP joint, fusion should be considered. A one- or two-stage flexor tendon graft can be performed in carefully selected patients, but the potential risks may outweigh the possible advantages for some patients.

21. Should partial tendon lacerations be repaired?

Most authorities agree that lacerations up to 50% of the cross-sectional area of the tendon are optimally treated without tendon repair and with early mobilization. However, if the tendon laceration is beveled, the risk of entrapment, rupture,

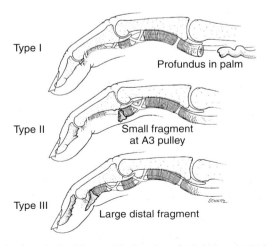

Type I — Profundus in palm

Type II — Small fragment at A3 pulley

Type III — Large distal fragment

Figure 125-6. In type I injuries, the tendon retracts all the way into the palm and is held there by the lumbrical origin. In type II injuries, the tendon retracts to the level of the proximal interphalangeal joint. Type III injuries consist of a large bony fragment that gets caught on the A4 pulley and prevents retraction of the bony fragment beyond the distal portion of the middle phalanx.

and triggering increases significantly. In such situations, the beveled portion of the tendon can be either excised or repaired with simple sutures. The result is a tendon that allows smoother gliding through the fibroosseous sheath.

22. What are the indications for tenolysis after flexor tendon repair?

Tenolysis is indicated after repair whenever the passive range of digital joint flexion significantly exceeds the patient's ability to actively flex at the same joint. All fractures should be healed, and wounds should have reached tissue equilibrium with soft skin and subcutaneous tissues. Reaction around the scars should be minimal. In addition, joint contractures must have been overcome and a normal or near-normal passive range of digital motion achieved.

23. What is the most frequent complication after early postoperative mobilization programs?

A flexion contracture at the PIP or DIP joints may develop after early postoperative mobilization. Prompt recognition of the development of contractures, modification of the motion program to permit greater extension, and judicious use of dynamic splints help to prevent or overcome such deformities before they progress too far.

24. How do ruptures occur after flexor tendon repairs? What is the treatment?

Ruptures occur almost without exception when patients have been doing so well with their rehabilitation program that they use their hands in an extremely strong manner, such as heavy lifting, well before the tendons have sufficient strength to tolerate the extremely high tensile demands of such activity. Rupture of one or both flexor tendon repairs is a significant complication. The preferred treatment is prompt reexploration and repair.

25. Is a four-strand repair augmented by some type of running locked suture strong enough to allow early active motion therapy?

Based on experimental and clinical data regarding the stress applied to digits by various degrees of active flexion, it is believed that light, active digital flexion carried out with the wrist in extension should be relatively safe for flexor tendons repaired with the four-strand technique augmented by a running locked epitendinous suture. This goal can be incorporated into a therapy protocol by allowing light active maintenance of full composite digital flexion once the wrist is brought from flexion to extension. Others have recommended immediate (2 to 3 days postoperatively) active flexion and extension in a splint with the wrist at 30° of extension, the MCP joints flexed to 60°, and both IP joints in extension (Fig. 125-7).

26. When can strengthening exercises be initiated after flexor tendon repair and appropriate early therapy protocols?

Based on multiple studies, it is believed that repaired flexor tendons regain sufficient strength by 8 weeks to initiate strengthening exercises. The exercises are increased in a gradually progressive manner.

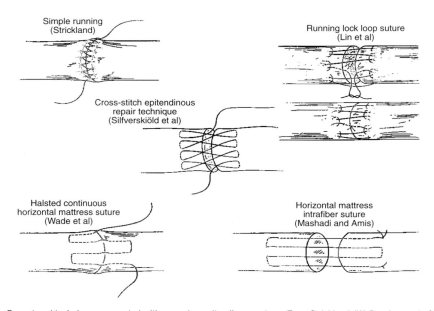

Figure 125-7. Four-strand technique augmented with a running epitendinous suture. (From Strickland JW: Development of flexor tendon surgery: Twenty-five years of progress. J Hand Surg [Am] 25:214–235, 2000.)

27. Outline the appropriate management of acute flexor tendon lacerations.

- Acute flexor tendon lacerations should be repaired primarily.
- A repair technique that involves the use of four to eight strands of suture across the repair site and a running epitendinous suture should be used.
- Preserve the A2 and A4 pulleys to prevent bowstringing, flexion contracture, and loss of motion.
- Light, active digital flexion carried out with the wrist in extension should be relatively safe for flexor tendons repaired with the four-strand technique.
- Tenolysis is indicated after repair whenever the passive range of digital joint flexion significantly exceeds the patient's ability to flex actively at the same joint.

CONTROVERSIES

28. Should the flexor sheath be repaired after repair of the flexor tendon laceration?

- *For:* Repairing the sheath after tendon suture has the theoretical advantages of providing a barrier for adhesion formation, restoring synovial fluid nutrition, and restoring sheath mechanics. Furthermore, repair of the sheath may decrease the coefficient of friction between the pulley and tendon during the first few millimeters of proximal excision when the repaired tendon passes under the edge of the thick annular pulleys.
- *Against:* The sheath often is technically difficult to reestablish, and few valid clinical or experimental data substantiate that it improves the results of flexor tendon repair.

29. Should the epitendinous suture, which is used in repairing acute flexor tendon lacerations, be placed initially or after core sutures are placed?

- *Initially:* (1) Forcible handling of the tendon is minimized, (2) enlargement of the tenorrhaphy is minimized, (3) the sutures may still be buried within the tendon, and (4) the strength of the repair is equivalent to the popular Kessler suture technique.
- *After:* Placement of core sutures initially as part of the flexor tendon repair allows easy retrieval of the tendons from their proximal and distal sites and good approximation of the tendon ends. A running epitendinous suture then can be used to tidy the tendon ends and increase the repair strength.

BIBLIOGRAPHY

Coats RW, Echevarria-Ore JC, Mass DP: Acute flexor tendon repairs in zone II. Hand Clin 21:173–179, 2005.
Lawrence TM, Davis TRC: A biomechanical analysis of suture materials and their influence on a four-strand flexor tendon repair. J Hand Surg [Am] 30:836–841, 2005.
Merrell GA, Wolfe SW, Kacena WJ, et al: The effect of increased peripheral suture purchase on the strength of flexor tendon repairs. J Hand Surg [Am] 28:464–468, 2003.
Murphy BA, Mass DP: Zone I flexor tendon injuries. Hand Clin 21:167–171, 2005.
Strickland JW: Flexor tendon repair. Hand Clin 1:55–68, 1985.
Strickland JW: Results of flexor tendon surgery in zone II. Hand Clin 1:167–179, 1985.
Strickland JW: Opinions and preferences in flexor tendon surgery. Hand Clin 1:187–191, 1985.
Strickland JW: Flexor tendon surgery. Part 1: Anatomy, biomechanics, physiology, healing and adhesions. Orthop Rev 15:632–645, 1986.
Strickland JW: Flexor tendon surgery. Part 2: Flexor tendon repair. Orthop Rev 15:701–721, 1986.
Strickland JW: Flexor tendon surgery—A review Part 1: Primary flexor tendon repair. J Hand Surg 14B:261–272, 1989.
Strickland JW: Flexor tendon surgery—A review. Part 2: Free tendon grafts and tenolysis. J Hand Surg 14B:368–382, 1989.
Strickland JW: Biologic rationale, clinical application, and results of early motion following flexor tendon repair. J Hand Ther 2:71–83, 1989.
Strickland JW: Flexor tendon injuries. Curr Orthop 6:98–110, 1992.
Strickland JW: Flexor tendon repair—Indiana method. Ind Hand Center Newslett 1:1–12, 1996.
Strickland JW: Experimental studies of the structure and function of tendon. Hand Surg Update 1:1–15, 1993.
Strickland JW: Flexor tendon injuries. I: Foundations of treatment. J Am Acad Orthop Surg 3:44–54, 1995.
Strickland JW: Flexon tendon injuries. II: Operative technique. J Am Acad Orthop Surg 3:55–62, 1995.
Strickland JW: Development of flexor tendon surgery: Twenty-five years of progress. J Hand Surg [Am] 25:214–235, 2000.
Strickland JW: The Indiana method of flexor tendon repair. Atlas Hand Clin 1:77–103, 1996.
Strickland JW: Tendon injuries in the upper extremity. In Dee R, Mango E, Hurst LC (eds): Principles of Orthopaedic Practice, 2nd ed. New York, McGraw-Hill, 1997, pp 1173–1187.
Strickland JW: Flexor tendon repair: The Indianapolis method. In Hunter JM, Schneider LH, Mackin EJ (eds): Tendon Surgery in the Hand, St. Louis, Mosby, 1997, pp 353–361.
Strickland JW: Flexor tendon injuries. In Strickland JW (ed): The Hand: Master Techniques in Orthopaedic Surgery. Philadelphia, Lippincott-Raven, 1998, pp 473–490.
Strickland JW, Wagner WF: Recent advances in flexor tendon surgery. Rec Adv Orthop Surg 6:77–101, 1992.
Wagner WF, Carroll C, Strickland JW, et al: A biomechanical comparison of techniques of flexor tendon repair. J Hand Surg 19A:1–5, 1994.

EXTENSOR TENDON INJURIES

Mary Lynn Newport, MD, and
Robert J. Havlik, MD

1. What are the eight zones commonly used to describe extensor tendon injuries?

Zones I, III, V, and VII (the odd zones) overlie the joints of the hand (i.e., distal interphalangeal [DIP], proximal interphalangeal [PIP], metacarpophalangeal [MCP], and carpal joints, respectively). Zones II, IV, VI, and VIII (the even zones) overlie the bones (i.e., middle phalanges, proximal phalanges, metacarpals, and distal radius/ulna, respectively) (Fig. 126-1).

2. The thumb is typically divided into how many extensor zones?

Five. The odd zones (I, III, and IV) overlie the joints (IP, MCP, and carpal joints, respectively), and the even zones (II and IV) overlie the bones (proximal phalanx and metacarpal, respectively) (see Fig. 126-1).

3. Do the extensor digiti minimi and extensor indicis proprius tendons run ulnar or radial to their respective communis tendons?

The extensor digiti minimi (EDM) and extensor indicis proprius (EIP) tendons usually run ulnar to the extensor digitorum communis (EDC) tendon and allow independent extension of the small and index fingers, respectively. However, significant variability of the extensor tendons to the index and small fingers, including radial EIP and EDM tendons and supernumerary tendons, has been reported in up to 19% of specimens in anatomic studies.

4. Unlike the flexor tendons, the extensor tendons pass through discrete compartments at the level of the wrist. What is the orientation of the extensor tendons at the level of the wrist?

The extensor tendons pass through six discrete compartments on the dorsal wrist. The orientation of these tendons can best be remembered by the number series 2-2-1-2-1-1, which describes the number of tendon groups that pass through each of the six dorsal extensor compartments. Two tendon groups pass through the first (extensor pollicis brevis and abductor pollicis longus) and two tendon groups pass through the second dorsal wrist compartment (extensor carpi radialis longus and extensor radialis brevis), whereas only one passes through the third compartment (extensor pollicis longus). The fourth compartment transmits two tendon groups (EDC and EIP), whereas the fifth transmits only the extensor digiti quinti proprius and the sixth transmits only the extensor carpi ulnaris. The orientation of these tendons through the appropriate compartments is essential in tendon reconstruction, and repair (Fig. 126-2).

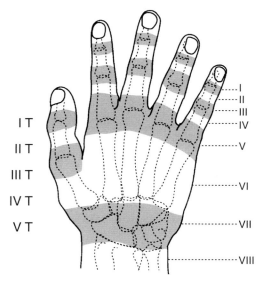

I T
II T
III T
IV T
V T

I
II
III
IV
V
VI
VII
VIII

Figure 126-1. Extensor tendon injury zones.

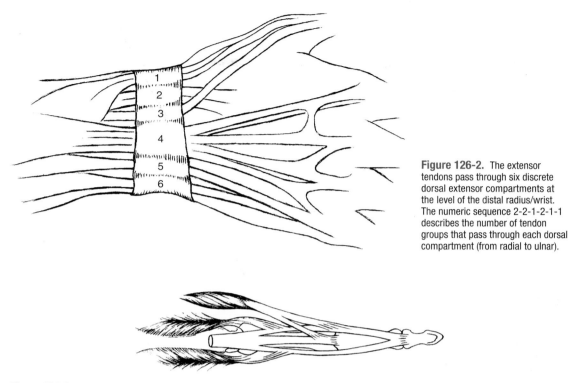

Figure 126-2. The extensor tendons pass through six discrete dorsal extensor compartments at the level of the distal radius/wrist. The numeric sequence 2-2-1-2-1-1 describes the number of tendon groups that pass through each dorsal compartment (from radial to ulnar).

Figure 126-3. The dorsal extensor mechanism, illustrating both extrinsic and intrinsic contributions to the extensor mechanism.

5. Which muscles extend the MCP and IP joints? What is their innervation?

The MCP and PIP joints are extended through the extrinsic EDC (as well as EIP and EDM) tendons supplied by the posterior interosseous nerve branch of the radial nerve. The IP joints are extended by the intrinsic tendons of the interossei and lumbricals supplied by the ulnar nerve. The intrinsics are able to extend the IP joints because they course dorsal to the axis of rotation for these joints (Fig. 126-3).

6. Which finger and which zones are most commonly injured?

The long finger is the most frequently injured (38% of cases), followed by the index (28%), ring (18%), and thumb and small finger (10% each). Zone VI, directly over the metacarpal, is the area frequently injured. (This is also true for the thumb, in which zone IV is the area directly over the metacarpal.)

7. Which general area has the better prognosis after extensor tendon injury: The proximal zone (V through VIII) or the distal zone (I through IV)?

The proximal zones have a significantly better prognosis (65% to 75% good/excellent results) than the distal zones (0% to 40% good/excellent results), probably because the extensor mechanism is simpler more proximally. The extensor tendon covers only one side of bone in the proximal zones, with no intricate connections except the juncturae. The more distal zones have less excursion and cover the phalanx on three sides, thereby increasing the changes of adhesion formation.

8. Following a crush injury to the hand, a man has limited flexion of his fingers. How do you determine whether this is due to intrinsic muscle fibrosis and scarring or due to extensor tendon adherence?

Limited flexion of the fingers after hand injury is a frequent finding. Differentiation of the etiology is essential to guide treatment and effective therapy. The test for *"extrinsic muscle tightness"* is to flex the finger at the PIP joint with the MCP joint in flexion and extension. If the PIP joint is more difficult to flex when the MCP joint is in flexion, the problem is due to extrinsic muscle tightness or possibly even fibrosis/adherence, and the test for extrinsic muscle tightness is positive (Fig. 126-4).

This is because the extensor tendon is draped over the dorsal MCP joint, and the arc of curvature consumes some of the available tendon present in a situation of extrinsic tightness. When the finger is straight at the MCP joint, there is a relative increase in the amount of extensor tendon available, and flexion at the PIP is less restricted and correspondingly "easier."

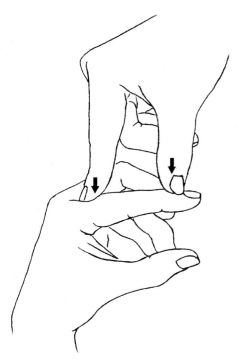

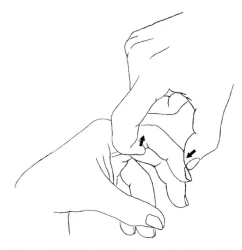

Figure 126-5. Test for "intrinsic muscle tightness." With the metacarpophalangeal joint in extension, the proximal interphalangeal joint is flexed. If there is increased resistance to flexion relative to when the metacarpophalangeal joint is in flexion, the "intrinsic test" is positive, demonstrating intrinsic tendon tightness.

Figure 126-4. Test for "extrinsic muscle tightness." With the metacarpophalangeal joint in flexion, the proximal interphalangeal joint is flexed. If there is increased resistance to flexion relative to when the metacarpophalangeal joint is in extension, the "extrinsic test" is positive, demonstrating extrinsic tendon tightness.

In contrast, the test for *"intrinsic muscle tightness"* is essentially the opposite, with opposite findings. With the MCP joint in extension, the flexion of the PIP joint is more restricted and more difficult, and the test for intrinsic muscle tightness is positive. In contrast, when the MCP joint is in flexion, the PIP joint motion is less restricted and correspondingly "easier" than with the MCP joint in extension. This is caused by the passage of the intrinsic muscle tendons palmar to the center of the arc of MCP joint flexion. As the MCP joint is brought into flexion, the intrinsic tendons course is essentially shorter so that additional tendon length is available to allow flexion of the PIP joint (Fig. 126-5).

9. What are the juncturae tendineae?

Small tendinous bands that course distally from the ring finger EDC to connect with the EDC of the long and small fingers. If an EDC is lacerated in zone VI proximal to the junctura, the pull from adjacent juncturae can extend the affected finger and mask the injury.

10. What is a mallet finger or mallet deformity?

This deformity represents droop of the finger into flexion at the DIP joint with inability to extend the distal phalanx fully, if at all.

11. What causes a mallet deformity?

Almost all are secondary to acute injury of the extensor mechanism, usually from a direct blow to the tip of the finger, forcing it into flexion.

12. What are the different types of mallet fingers?

Type I is a tendinous rupture (with or without a small fleck of bone) from the distal phalanx. Type II is a tendon laceration at or proximal to the DIP joint. Type III is a deep abrasion with loss of extensor substance. Type IV includes a significant fracture of the distal phalanx.

13. How is a mallet finger treated?

Type II (lacerations) should be sutured; some surgeons use a K-wire to hold the joint in extension. Types I and III should be treated with extension splinting consisting of a dorsal or volar AlumaFoam splint or a stack splint. Treatment of type IV injuries is controversial. Most experts agree that if the joint is congruous (not volarly subluxed), treatment should consist of splinting only. If the joint is volarly subluxed, many advocate reduction with percutaneous pinning. Others perform an open reduction with internal fracture fixation.

14. What is the most important consideration in extensor tendon repair: Strength of reconstruction or length of reconstruction?

In the repair of flexor tendons, the critical consideration for tendon repairs is the strength of the repair. This is because the flexor musculotendinous unit has much more power than the extensor musculotendinous unit. In addition, the architecture of the flexor system, with the "free" excursion of the tendons through pulleys, accommodates small to moderate changes in tendon length without difficult or compromise.

Although strength of the repair is always important, the extensor system is a cantilevered system where forces and strength are less important than preservation of the precise lengths of the component tendons. This is particularly true in more distal injuries overlying the dorsal hand and phalanges. The extension of the joints of the digit is contingent upon the precise length relationships of the central slip, the lateral bands, the lateral extensor tendons, and the distal extensor tendon. Unlike the flexor side of the hand, the extensor tendons have discrete insertions and are not "free" to move through a pulley system. A change in length of a given component of the extensor mechanism will lead not only to a deficit in the immediately adjacent joint but also to reciprocal changes in more distal joints. For example, a central slip injury will lead to a flexion deformity at the PIP joint and secondarily create a hyperextension posturing at the DIP joint. At the level of the wrist extensors, changes in extensor length are better tolerated, but not distal to this level.

15. What is a boutonnière deformity?

A boutonnière deformity consists of a flexed position of the PIP joint and hyperextended position of the DIP joint. It is most often found in a chronic inflammatory disorder such as rheumatoid arthritis, but it may occur after an injury in an otherwise normal hand. In chronic deformity, synovitis of the PIP joint produces attenuation or destruction of the central slip insertion on the middle phalanx. The finger adopts a progressively more flexed position as the extensor pull is lost. As the finger slips more into flexion, the lateral bands of the intrinsic mechanism slide volarly, producing an ever greater flexion deformity. As they slide volarly, the tension of the intrinsics to the DIP increases, pulling the DIP joint into progressively more extension.

16. What is an acute boutonnière deformity? What biomechanical process produces it? How is it treated?

The same basic mechanism is present in an acute boutonnière, in which an injury, usually involving forced flexion of the PIP, ruptures the central slip attachment to the middle phalanx. Immediately after an acute injury, the patient usually is still able to extend the PIP joint because the lateral bands have not yet slid volarly. The patient will be tender dorsally and have pain with extension. The injured finger is most comfortable in flexion because the capsule is most capacious in this position. As a consequence, the lateral bands slide volarly, producing deformity at the PIP and DIP joints. This deformity usually is quite noticeable approximately 10 days after injury. Open injuries (e.g., tendon lacerations) are directly repaired, followed by splinting of the PIP joint in full extension for 5 to 6 weeks. Closed injuries (e.g., avulsion) are treated by progressive splinting until extension of the PIP joint is achieved.

17. What is the currently recommended repair technique for extensor tendons?

No repair technique is completely accepted. The modified Bunnell technique has been shown to be the strongest and most biomechanically advantageous in zone VI, whereas the modified Bunnell or modified Kessler technique is best in zone IV.

18. What is the treatment protocol after extensor tendon repair?

No postoperative protocol is universally accepted. Any repair is contingent on other injuries (fractures, skin loss, flexor injury, neurovascular injury). Most surgeons have moved away from static splinting of all joints in extension to protocols that encourage tendon gliding, such as the use static splinting of all joints in extension to protocols that encourage tendon gliding, such as the use of an extensor outrigger with rubber bands, which allows active finger flexion and produces passive finger extension. Newer protocols encourage active finger range of motion under carefully controlled circumstances.

BIBLIOGRAPHY

Browne EZ Jr, Ribik CA: Early dynamic splinting for extensor tendon injuries. J Hand Surg 14 A:72–76, 1989.

Doyle JR: Extensor tendons: Acute injuries. In Green DP, Hotchkiss RN (eds): Operative Hand Surgery, Vol 2, 3rd ed. New York, Churchill Livingstone, 1993, pp 1925–1954.

Gonzalez MH, Gray T, Ortinau E, Weinzweig N: The extensor tendons to the little finger: An anatomic study. J Hand Surg 20A:844–847, 1995.

Gonzalez MH, Weinzweig N, Kay T, Grindel S: Anatomy of the extensor tendons to the little finger. J Hand Surg 21 A:988–991, 1996.

Kleinert HE, Verdan C: Report of the Committee on Tendon Injuries. J Hand Surg 8:794–798, 1983.

Newport ML, Blair WF, Steyers CM Jr: Long-term results of extensor tendon repair. J Hand Surg 15:961–966, 1990.

Newport ML, Pollack GR, Williams CT: Biomechanical characteristics of suture techniques in extensor zone IV. J Hand Surg 20A:650–656, 1995.

Newport MI, Williams CD: Biomechanical characteristics of extensor tendon suture techniques. J Hand Surg 17A:1117–1123, 1992.

TENDON TRANSFERS

Julie A. Melchior, MD; Richard I. Burton, MD; Paul A. Martineau, MD, FRCSC; and Thomas Trumble, MD

1. What is a tendon transfer?

The tendon of a functioning muscle is detached from its insertion and reattached to another tendon or bone, to replace the function of a paralyzed muscle or injured tendon. The transferred tendon remains attached to its parent muscle with an intact neurovascular pedicle.

2. List the general principles of tendon transfers.

- One muscle, one function: If a muscle is asked to perform more than one task, it will only move the joint that has the tightest attachment.
- Full passive range of motion of the joints to be powered.
- Expendable donor.
- Power of the donor muscle should be similar to that of the injured motor unit (brachioradialis and flexor carpi ulnaris are the strongest).
- Amplitude of the donor muscle should be equal to or greater than that of the injured motor unit (finger flexors have the greatest amplitude at 70 mm, wrist flexors and extensors have the least at 33 mm).
- Direction of the transfer (straight line of pull, if possible).
- Location and nature of the pulley, if required (only one pulley ideally).
- Tissue bed into which the tendon is placed ("tissue equilibrium").
- Selected fusion to simplify a polyarticular system (preserve tenodesis access of wrist).

3. How do you select the donor tendons?

- List the functioning muscles.
- List which of the functioning muscles are expendable.
- List hand functions requiring restoration.
- Match the second and third points: Expendable muscles and required functions.
- Staging.
- In phase–out of phase (e.g., finger flexors act in concert with wrist extensors, so transfer of a wrist extensor to restore function of finger flexors is a good transfer).

4. Does a muscle/tendon retain its strength after it is transferred?

No. Typically, the transferred muscle/tendon unit loses one grade of strength, so when choosing donor muscles, bear in mind that it is ideal to start with a full strength (5/5) muscle, as it will at best be 4/5 after transfer.

PERIPHERAL NERVE INJURIES

5. Which deficits in *radial* nerve palsy from a lesion at the midhumeral level require transfers?

- Loss of wrist extension
- Loss of finger extension
- Loss of extension and radial abduction of thumb

6. In a high radial nerve injury associated with a humeral fracture, is exploration of the nerve recommended?

Not in most situations. The results of exploration have not been shown to be any better than observation, except in the following settings:

- Open fracture
- Associated vascular injury
- Loss of radial nerve function after attempted closed reduction

7. List the standard tendon transfers for radial nerve palsy.
- Wrist extension: Pronator teres (PT) to extensor carpi radialis brevis (ECRB) (Fig. 127-1).
- Finger extension: Flexor carpi radialis (FCR) to extensor digitorum communis (EDC) (Starr, Brand) (Fig. 127-2); flexor carpi ulnaris (FCU) to EDC (Jones); flexor digitorum superficialis (FDS) of ring fingers to EDC (modified Boyes, Chuinard) (Fig. 127-3).
- Thumb extension/abduction: Palmaris longus (PL) to rerouted extensor pollicis longus (EPL) (Fig. 127-4); FDS IV (ring) to EPL (and extensor indicis proprius [EIP]) (Boyes, Chuinard).

8. What area is affected by *low median* nerve palsy? What deficits are involved?
Low median nerve injury affects the area distal to the innervation of the flexor pollicis longus (FPL) and flexor digitorum profundus (FDP). The following deficits are involved:

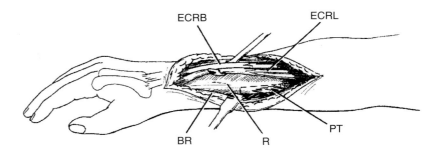

Figure 127-1. Incision along the radial border of the forearm allows for exposure of the pronator teres *(PT)* after the extensor carpi radialis brevis *(ECRB)* and extensor carpi radialis longus *(ECRL)* have been retracted dorsally. The PT is woven into the ECRB to reestablish wrist extension. *BR,* Brachioradialis; *EDC,* extensor digitorum communis; *R,* radius. (From Trumble TE: Principles of Hand Surgery and Therapy. Philadelphia, WB Saunders, 2000. Courtesy Thomas E. Trumble.)

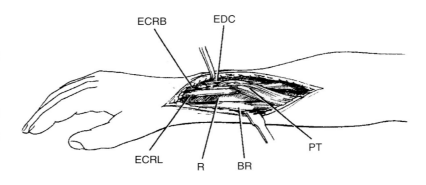

Figure 127-2. The flexor carpi radialis *(FCR)* tendon is transferred dorsally and split into two tails so that it can be attached in a side-to-side fashion to all four of the finger extensor tendons. The extensor digiti minimi to the small finger is used as a recipient tendon in this transfer because the extensor digitorum communis *(EDC)* to the small finger is frequently absent. *ECRB,* Extensor carpi radialis brevis; *ECRL,* extensor carpi radialis longus; *PT,* pronator teres. (From Trumble TE: Principles of Hand Surgery and Therapy. Philadelphia, WB Saunders, 2000. Courtesy Thomas E. Trumble.)

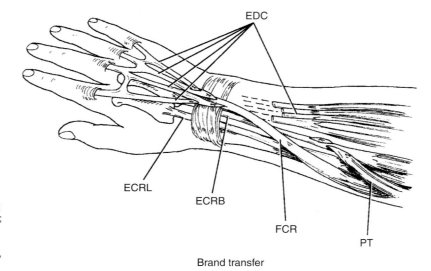

Brand transfer

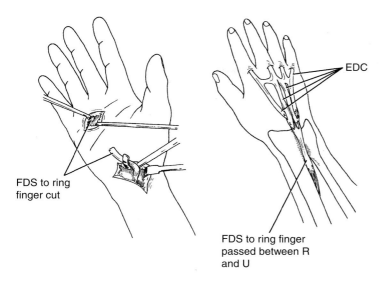

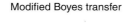

FDS to ring
finger cut

FDS to ring finger
passed between R
and U

EDC

Modified Boyes transfer

Figure 127-3. In the modified version of the Boyes tendon transfer, the ring finger flexor digitorum superficialis *(FDS)* is transferred through the interosseous membrane to the extensor digitorum communis *(EDC)* and extensor digitorum minimi. Alternatively, the FDS can be transferred around the ulnar border of the forearm to the finger extensor tendons. *R,* Radius; *U,* ulna. (From Trumble TE: Principles of Hand Surgery and Therapy. Philadelphia, WB Saunders, 2000. Courtesy Thomas E. Trumble.)

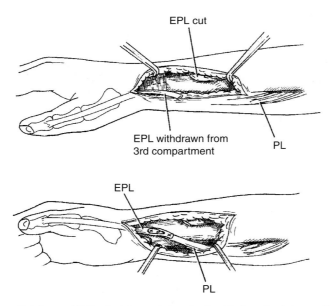

EPL cut

EPL withdrawn from
3rd compartment

PL

EPL

PL

Figure 127-4. The extensor pollicis longus *(EPL)* tendon is transected proximally while the palmaris longus *(PL)* is transected distally. A Pulvertaft weave is performed securing the PL to the EPL to reestablish thumb interphalangeal joint extension. (From Trumble TE: Principles of Hand Surgery and Therapy. Philadelphia, WB Saunders, 2000. Courtesy Thomas E. Trumble.)

- Loss of palmar abduction and pronation of the thumb (opposition)
- Thenar muscles (abductor pollicis brevis [APB], opponens pollicis [OP], variable innervation of flexor pollicis brevis [FPB] from ulnar nerve to both heads of FPB)
- Lumbricals to index and middle fingers
- Critical sensibility to thumb, index, and middle fingers (implications of numbness for function, protection from injury, use of visual feedback after transfers)

9. What movements are necessary for effective thumb opposition?
Palmar abduction and pronation of the metacarpal, with metacarpophalangeal (MCP) joint stability.

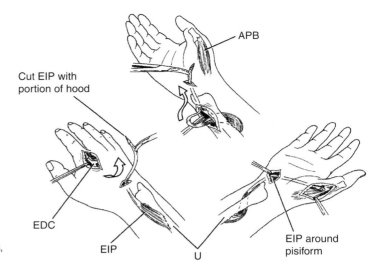

Figure 127-5. Transferring the extensor indicis proprius *(EIP)* around the ulnar border of the forearm to the abductor pollicis brevis *(APB)* provides opposition of the thumb. It is important to remove the EIP tendon elongated by a strip of the extensor hood mechanism to provide adequate length to reach the insertion of the APB. *EDC,* Extensor digitorum communis; *U,* ulna. (From Trumble TE: Principles of Hand Surgery and Therapy. Philadelphia, WB Saunders, 2000. Courtesy Thomas E. Trumble.)

10. List the options for opposition transfers.
- EIP (Burkhalter): Preferred by many because as it does not weaken grip (Fig. 127-5).
- FDS of ring finger through a pulley of FCU (Bunnell, Royle-Thompsen): Divide between A1 and A2 pulleys, not at insertion (Fig. 127-6).
- PL extended by a strip of palmar fascia (Camitz): Preferred in severe carpal tunnel syndrome (CTS), elderly patients; provides primarily palmar abduction, no true opposition (Fig. 127-7).
- Abductor digiti minimi (Huber): Preferred in congenital opposition deficit (Fig. 127-8).
- FDS little (described by Peimer).

11. Where do you insert your opposition transfer?
Single insertion into the APB. Dual insertion no longer believed to be necessary.

12. What are the deficits in a *high median* nerve injury?
- Thumb opposition, critical sensibility
- Loss of flexion at the proximal interphalangeal (PIP) and distal interphalangeal (DIP) joints of the index and middle fingers (FDP and all FDS) (Fig. 127-9)
- Loss of flexion at the thumb interphalangeal (IP) joint (FPL)

13. List the standard tendon transfers for a high median nerve injury.
- Thumb IP joint flexion: Brachioradialis (BR) to FPL
- DIP joint flexion of index and middle fingers: Side-to-side tenorrhaphy of index and middle finger FDP tendons to ring and little finger FDP tendons
- Opposition: EIP to APB

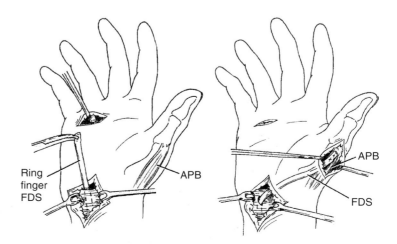

Figure 127-6. Tendon transfer of the flexor digitorum superficialis *(FDS)* of the ring finger to the abductor pollicis brevis *(APB)* reestablishes thumb opposition. (From Trumble TE: Principles of Hand Surgery and Therapy. Philadelphia, WB Saunders, 2000. Courtesy Thomas E. Trumble.)

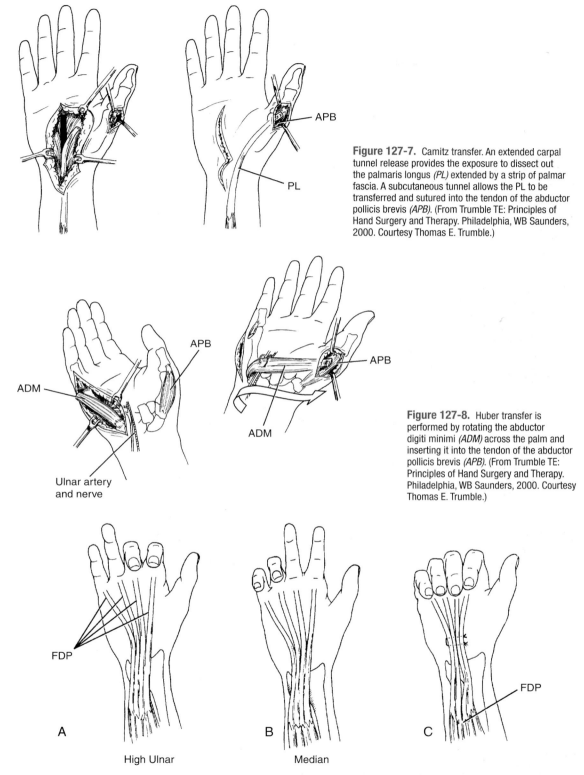

Figure 127-7. Camitz transfer. An extended carpal tunnel release provides the exposure to dissect out the palmaris longus *(PL)* extended by a strip of palmar fascia. A subcutaneous tunnel allows the PL to be transferred and sutured into the tendon of the abductor pollicis brevis *(APB)*. (From Trumble TE: Principles of Hand Surgery and Therapy. Philadelphia, WB Saunders, 2000. Courtesy Thomas E. Trumble.)

Figure 127-8. Huber transfer is performed by rotating the abductor digiti minimi *(ADM)* across the palm and inserting it into the tendon of the abductor pollicis brevis *(APB)*. (From Trumble TE: Principles of Hand Surgery and Therapy. Philadelphia, WB Saunders, 2000. Courtesy Thomas E. Trumble.)

Figure 127-9. **A,** Patient with a high ulnar nerve palsy with paralysis of the flexor digitorum profundus *(FDP)* to the small and ring finger. **B,** Patient with a high median palsy and paralysis of the FDP to the index and middle fingers. **C,** Side-to-side tendon transfer linking all four FDP tendons together to reestablish flexion of the FDP tendons to the fingers affected by the nerve palsy will reconstruct finger flexion for either case. (From Trumble TE: Principles of Hand Surgery and Therapy. Philadelphia, WB Saunders, 2000. Courtesy Thomas E. Trumble.)

14. What are the deficits in a low ulnar nerve palsy?

- "Clawing" (MCP hyperextension, IP joint flexion) of the ring and little fingers due to loss of the interossei (results in loss of independent MCP joint flexion, contributes to loss of grip strength).
- Loss of thumb adduction due to loss of the adductor pollicis (AdP), first dorsal interosseous (DIO), and the FPB, half or all (results in loss of power pinch)
- Loss of index finger abduction due to loss of the first DIO (contributes to loss of power pinch)
- Abducted (ulnarly deviated) little finger (Wartenberg's sign) due to the ulnar deviating force of the extensor digiti quinti (EDQ) unbalanced by the loss of the third volar interosseous

15. What are the transfers for the correction of clawing?

- Static: MCP joint capsulodesis (rarely done alone)
- Dynamic, to provide MCP joint flexion alone: FDS divided, looped through a slit in the A2 pulley, and sutured to itself (Zancolli "lasso") (Fig. 127-10).
- Dynamic, to provide MCP joint flexion and IP joint extension: FDS to radial lateral bands of ring and small fingers (modified Stiles-Bunnell) or to proximal phalanx (Littler) (Fig. 127-11).
- Other dynamic transfers:
  - FCR + BR graft to lateral bands (Riordan)
  - EIP + EDQ to lateral bands through the intermetacarpal spaces (Bunnell-Fowler)

16. Which transfers primarily increase grip strength in the setting of a low ulnar nerve injury?

- ECRB extended by palmaris or plantaris strips dorsally through the intermetacarpal spaces, to the A2 pulleys or radial lateral bands of the middle, ring, and little fingers, plus or minus the index finger (Brand I) (Fig. 127-12).
- Extensor carpi radialis longus (ECRL) extended by fascia lata strips volarly through the carpal canal into the A2 pulleys or the radial lateral bands of the middle, ring, and little fingers, plus or minus the index finger (Brand II).

17. How can you restore thumb adduction?

- ECRB + free tendon graft to AdP (Fig. 127-13)
- FDS of middle or ring finger to AdP (Fig. 127-14)
- BR/ECRL + graft, between the third and fourth metacarpals to AdP (Boyes)

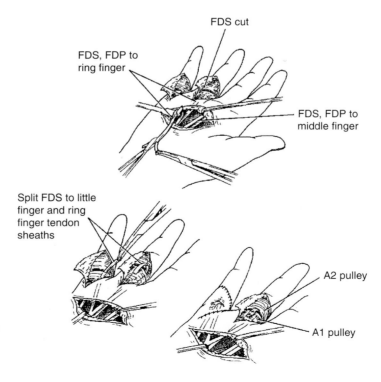

Figure 127-10. Zancolli lasso procedure provides primarily metacarpophalangeal joint flexion by passing slips of the flexor digitorum superficialis tendon around the A1 pulley and suturing them back onto themselves. *FDP,* Flexor digitorum profundus; *FDS,* flexor digitorum superficialis. (From Trumble TE: Principles of Hand Surgery and Therapy. Philadelphia, WB Saunders, 2000. Courtesy Thomas E. Trumble.)

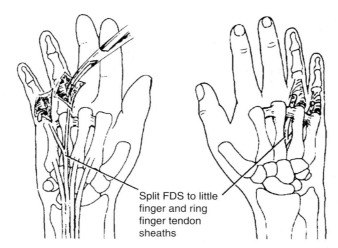

Figure 127-11. Flexor digitorum superficialis *(FDS)* tendon transfer to the lateral bands of the small and ring finger corrects the claw deformity. (From Trumble TE: Principles of Hand Surgery and Therapy. Philadelphia, WB Saunders, 2000. Courtesy Thomas E. Trumble.)

Split FDS to little finger and ring finger tendon sheaths

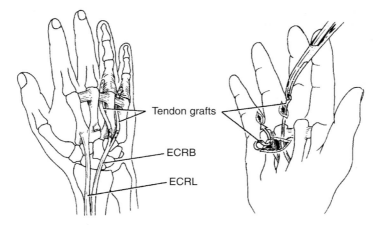

Tendon grafts

ECRB

ECRL

Figure 127-12. Brand tendon transfer to the intrinsics uses a tendon graft that connects the extensor carpi radialis brevis *(ECRB)* tendon to the lateral bands of the small and ring fingers. The ECRB tendon provides enough power for a four-tailed graft and can be used to e-establish intrinsic function to all four digits when combined nerve injuries have produced a complete intrinsic paralysis to the hand. *ECRL,* Extensor carpi radialis longus. (From Trumble TE: Principles of Hand Surgery and Therapy. Philadelphia, WB Saunders, 2000. Courtesy Thomas E. Trumble.)

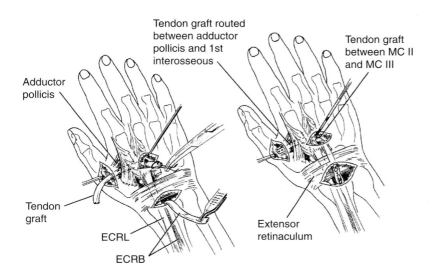

Tendon graft routed between adductor pollicis and 1st interosseous

Tendon graft between MC II and MC III

Adductor pollicis

Tendon graft

ECRL

ECRB

Extensor retinaculum

Figure 127-13. In low ulnar nerve palsy, the extensor carpi radialis brevis *(ECRB)* tendon can be transferred to the adductor pollicis to restore pinch. The tendon graft passes around the second metacarpal, using it as the pulley for the tendon transfer. *ECRL,* Extensor carpi radialis longus; *MC,* metacarpal. (From Trumble TE: Principles of Hand Surgery and Therapy. Philadelphia, WB Saunders, 2000. Courtesy Thomas E. Trumble.)

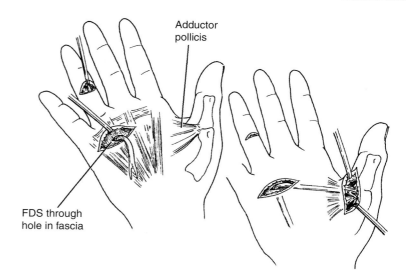

Figure 127-14. Insertion of the flexor digitorum superficialis *(FDS)* tendon and its subcutaneous course to the tendon of the adductor pollicis. (From Trumble TE: Principles of Hand Surgery and Therapy. Philadelphia, WB Saunders, 2000. Courtesy Thomas E. Trumble.)

18. How can you restore index finger abduction?
- Slip of abductor pollicis longus (APL) + palmaris or other free graft to first dorsal interosseous (Neviaser), combined with MCP joint fusion of thumb
- Other options: EIP (Bunnell) or extensor pollicis brevis (EPB) (Bruner) to first dorsal interosseous

19. What is the transfer to correct abduction of the little finger (Wartenberg's sign)?
EDQ to radial collateral ligament of the little finger MCP joint.

20. How might you improve sensibility in a low ulnar nerve injury?
Digital nerve translocation, using a median innervated digital nerve into an ulnar innervated digital nerve in a crucial area, such as the ulnar digital nerve to the small finger.

21. What are the deficits in a *high ulnar* nerve palsy?
- Less clawing of the ring and little fingers (due to loss of the deforming forces of the FDP of the ring and little fingers)
- Loss of DIP joint flexion of ring and little fingers
- Loss of power pinch

22. What are the standard tendon transfers for high ulnar nerve palsy?
- Side-to-side tenorrhaphy of FDP middle to FDP ring and little fingers (see Fig. 127-9).
- Split FDS of middle finger (half to ring, half to small finger radial side of A1 or A2 pulleys) to improve MCP flexion and to help correct Wartenberg's sign
- Conventional tendon transfers for pinch and abducted little finger (ECRB or FDS middle ± graft to AdP; accessory slip of APL + graft to first dorsal interosseous for pinch; FDS ring split volar to MCP joint then to radial lateral bands of ring and little fingers, if required for clawing)

COMBINED NERVE INJURIES

23. In a *low median/ulnar* nerve palsy (the most common combined nerve injury), what are the key deficits?
- Complete loss of palmar and volar digital sensation ("blind hand")
- Volar pulp atrophy
- Intrinsic motor loss

24. What are the recommended tendon transfers for reconstruction?
- Thumb adduction/key pinch: ECRB or ECRL + free graft between third and fourth metacarpals to adductor tubercle of thumb
- Thumb abduction/opposition: EIP around pisiform pulley and through thenar muscle tunnel to APB, or PL to APB, or FDS middle to APB insertion through a pulley of FCU or transverse carpal ligament
- Thumb–index tip pinch: APL slip with free tendon graft to first DIO and arthrodesis of thumb MCP joint
- Power flexion of proximal phalanx and integration of MCP and IP motion (correct clawing): ECRL or BR to all four fingers using four-tailed free tendon graft and insertion into flexor sheath (A2 pulleys) or lateral bands, or FDS ring, split, to A1/A2 pulleys

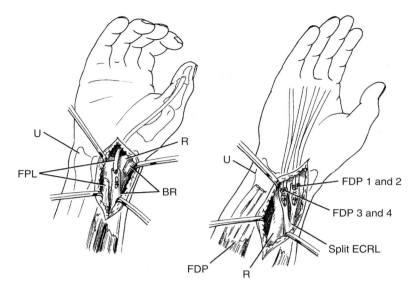

Figure 127-15. In a combined high median and ulnar palsy, flexion to the digits can be reestablished using a transfer of the extensor carpi radialis longus *(ECRL)* to the flexor digitorum profundus *(FDP)*, with the brachioradialis *(BR)* transferred to the flexor pollicis longus *(FPL)*. *R,* Radius; *U,* ulna. (From Trumble TE: Principles of Hand Surgery and Therapy. Philadelphia, WB Saunders, 2000. Courtesy Thomas E. Trumble.)

- Median and ulnar volar sensibility:
  - Neurovascular cutaneous flap from radial-innervated dorsum of hand
  - Superficial radial nerve translocation
  - Cross-finger index-to-thumb fillet flap (superficial radial nerve)

25. What transfers, in addition to those for low median/ulnar nerve palsy, may be useful in a *high median/ulnar* nerve palsy?
- Finger flexion: ECRL to all four tendons of FDP ± tenodesis of DIP joint of middle, ring and little fingers (Fig. 127-15)
- Clawing:
  - Tenodesis of all digits with free tendon graft to dorsal carpal ligament (volar to deep transverse metacarpal ligament) to extensor mechanism (dorsal aponeurosis, lateral bands)
  - Zancolli "lasso" using volar plate as insertion instead of A2 pulley
- Thumb–index (or long) pinch (tip pinch):
  - Thumb MCP arthrodesis
  - APL slip to first DIO
  - EIP or EDQ to APB insertion for opposition
  - Thumb IP flexion: BR to FPL in forearm
- Median and ulnar volar sensibility:
  - Superficial radial innervated fillet flap from index to palm
  - First dorsal metacarpal artery neurovascular island pedicle flap
  - Superficial radial nerve translocation
  - Free vascularized nerve graft

CEREBRAL PALSY

26. List several common hand and upper extremity deformities seen in cerebral palsy that may benefit from tendon transfers.
- Thumb-in-palm deformity (thumb flexed, adducted)
- Thumb MCP flexed, IP hyperextended *or* thumb MCP hyperextended, IP flexed
- Clenched fist
- Wrist flexed, ulnar-deviated
- Forearm pronation
- Elbow flexion

The following factors also should be evaluated:
- Voluntary hand use
- Sensibility/cortical representation
- Fixed joint contractures versus spasticity alone
- Adiadochokinesis (inability to perform rapid alternating movements)
- Intelligence quotient

- Function of opposite upper extremity
- Lower extremities and balance (need for ambulatory aids/wheelchair)
- Need for prolonged postoperative splinting and therapy to prevent recurrence
- Goals (hygiene, cosmesis, function)

It is important to do only one or two transfers at a time; otherwise, you may overcorrect and create the opposite deformity.

27. What procedures are used to correct the thumb-in-palm deformity?
- Imbrication of APL and EPB ± MCP joint arthrodesis, if hypermobile
- Release spastic/contracted intrinsics
- Four-flap Z-plasty of first web space contracture
- EPL rerouting
- FPL abductoplasty (FPL to APB or MCP joint capsule, fusion or tenodesis of thumb IP joint)

28. What transfers help correct the clenched fist?
- Superficialis-to-profundus transfer: Most common
- Flexor/pronator slide (release muscle origins from the medial epicondyle and proximal ulna): Less commonly done today
- FCU or PT or BR to EDC (only after appropriate releases have been done)

29. What soft tissue procedures correct the wrist flexion/ulnar deviation, with or without pronation, seen in cerebral palsy?
- FCU to ECRB (if primary deformity is tight FCU and weak wrist extension); with prolonged splinting, also helps finger contractures
- Extensor carpi ulnaris (ECU) to ECRB (if primary deformity is loss of wrist extension when fingers are flexed)
- PT or BR to ECRB
- PT tenotomy/pronator quadratus release
- Fractional tendon lengthening

30. If the wrist flexion, ulnar deviation, and pronation are due to a fixed bony deformity, what are the treatment options?
- Proximal row carpectomy (preserves some wrist motion)
- Radioulnar arthrodesis (if contracture is severe, but rarely done)
- Wrist (epiphyseal, to preserve growth in a child) arthrodesis (last resort or if sensory loss is profound)
- Tendon transfers may still be needed for soft tissue balancing

31. Elbow flexion contractures are common in cerebral palsy, although they do not often require surgical release. What structures would need to be released?
Biceps, brachialis, brachioradialis, and lacertus fibrosus.

RHEUMATOID ARTHRITIS

32. What is caput ulnae syndrome?
- Dorsal subluxation of the distal ulna, combined with supination of the carpus on the radius
- Loss of MCP joint extension of the small finger due to rupture of the EDQ and EDC_{small}, followed by progressive ruptures of the EDC tendons from ulnar to radial
- Decreased active and passive forearm supination due to the distal radioulnar joint

33. After the EPL, the digital extensor tendons are the most frequently ruptured tendons in rheumatoid patients. They tend to rupture from ulnar (EDQ, $EDC_{small,ring}$) to radial ($EDC_{middle,index}$, EIP). What are the options for transfers if the EPL is intact?
- If only EDQ, EDC_{small} are ruptured: Distal end of EDQ sutured to EDC_{ring}
- If EDQ and $EDC_{small,ring}$ are ruptured: EIP to EDC_{ring}, EDQ
- If EDQ and $EDC_{small,ring,middle}$ are ruptured: EDC_{middle} distal end sutured to EDC_{index} plus EIP to EDC_{ring}, EDQ
- If EIP is also ruptured: FDS_{ring} to EDQ and $EDC_{ring,middle}$
- If all finger extensors are ruptured: FDS_{middle} to $EDC_{index,middle}$ and FDS_{ring} to $EDC_{ring,small}$

34. What are the choices for transfers if the EPL is ruptured?
- EIP to EPL (preferred, if EIP available)
- EDQ (if intact) to EPL
- ECRL to EPL (least preferred)

35. What other disorders are in the differential diagnosis of extensor tendon ruptures in rheumatoid patients?
- Tendon dislocation (due to attenuation of radial shroud fibers)
- MCP joint dislocation (due to joint changes)
- Posterior interosseous nerve palsy

36. Flexor tendon ruptures are also seen in rheumatoid patients. Briefly discuss the major options for transfers.
- If FPL is ruptured (Mannerfelt syndrome): FDS$_{ring}$ to FPL or IP fusion (good choice if IP joint is already arthritic)
- If FDP$_{index}$ and FPL are ruptured: DIP fusion, tenodesis, or transfer FDS$_{index}$ to FDP$_{index}$ plus above transfers for FPL
- If FDS, FDP$_{index}$, and FPL are ruptured: distal FDP$_{index}$ sutured to FDP$_{middle}$ plus above for FPL
- If FDS/P$_{index}$ and FDS/P$_{middle}$ are ruptured: FDS$_{middle,ring}$ to FDP$_{index}$, FDS$_{small}$ to FDP

Note: If swan neck deformities are present, try not to use FDS in transfers because they may worsen the swan neck deformity.

TETRAPLEGIA

37. In tetraplegic patients, elbow extension is important for transfer capabilities and to reach objects from a seated wheelchair position. How can elbow extension be reconstructed with tendon transfers?
- Posterior deltoid to triceps with free tendon graft (Moberg)
- Biceps to triceps (Zancolli)

38. In C6 tetraplegics, the lowest functioning level is C6, and wrist extensors are functional. How can you provide useful grasp (key pinch)?
Thumb IP fusion and release of proximal thumb pulley + tenodesis of FPL to volar surface of radius (Moberg).

39. In C7 tetraplegics with elbow and wrist extension, how can you achieve pinch?
- Divide FDS$_{ring}$ and transfer to APB, then use BR/ECRL to proximal end of FDS$_{ring}$.
- Combine thumb carpometacarpal (CMC) joint fusion with BR to FPL, + EPL tenodesis + split FPL stabilization of IP joint (one-stage reconstruction)
- BR to EDC, EPL + FDS lasso to correct MCP joint hyperextension + thumb MCP volar capsulodesis + thumb CMC fusion (or APL tenodesis) + PT to FPL and ECRL to FDP (House's two-stage reconstruction)

40. List the priorities of reconstruction of function in tetraplegia.
- Elbow extension
- Simple hand mechanics by selected small joint fusions (i.e., thumb)
- Reestablish effective key pinch (rather than opposition)
- Reestablish active finger flexion (with passive tenodesis for digital extension)
- In lower lesions, if active digital flexion and extension are restored, intrinsic function is reestablished by dorsally routed tenodesis

OBSTETRIC BRACHIAL PLEXUS PALSY

41. What are the most common types of brachial plexus injury?
- C5–C6 (upper trunk; Erb-Duchenne palsy)
- C5–T1 (complete plexus)
- C8–T1 (lower trunk; Klumpke palsy) now thought to be very rare

42. What are the most important prognostic indicators in obstetric brachial plexus palsy?
- Recovery of biceps function by 3 to 6 months of age
- Nerve root involvement
- Persistent Horner's sign

43. What are the primary considerations when contemplating primary brachial plexus surgery?
- Identify the lesion, resect the neuroma, sural nerve grafting, intraplexal or extraplexal (if nerve root avulsions) sources or nerve motor donors
- Spinal accessory nerve → suprascapular nerve
- Intercostal nerves
- Phrenic nerve
- Ulnar nerve

44. For a patient with C5–C6 (upper trunk) palsy, what are the primary deficiencies? How might you address them?
- Glenohumeral issues
  - Glenohumeral joint deformities
  - Shoulder weakness of abduction/external rotation (internal rotation and adduction contracture)
  - Scapular winging
  - Glenohumeral arthrodesis
  - L'Episcopo transfer (latissimus dorsi, teres major to posterolateral humeral head with or without anterior capsule and subscapularis release)
- Elbow flexion
  - Bipolar latissimus dorsi pedicled transfer to biceps
  - Functional muscle transfer (free innervated muscle flaps, using musculocutaneous nerve to multiple intercostal nerves, or two stage, with nerve graft to contralateral pectoralis nerve, and 1 year later a free gracilis transfer [Doi et al.])
  - Pectoralis major to biceps (Clark)
  - Triceps to biceps
  - Steindler flexoplasty (transfer origin of flexor/pronator muscles to 5 cm proximal on humerus)
- Elbow flexion contracture
  - Splinting versus surgical release versus humeral osteotomy
- Forearm position
  - May see slight pronation with limited active supination, or supination contracture (total palsy)
  - Biceps rerouting (if good passive pronation) or rotational osteotomy of radius (if fixed in supination, per Al-Qattan, Brunelli)

45. For a patient with C8–T1 (lower trunk) injury, what muscles are deficient? What transfers are useful?
The intrinsics are deficient as well as FCU and FDP$_{ring,small}$.
- Finger flexion: BR to FPL, ECRL to FDP
- Opposition: EIP to APB, ECU + tendon graft through intermetacarpal spaces to lateral bands

TRAUMATIC BRACHIAL PLEXUS PALSY

46. What is the recommended assessment protocol for a traumatic brachial plexus injury?
- Reexamination and electrodiagnostics at 4 to 6 weeks
- Repeat clinical examination at 3 to 4 months
- If no return at that point, consider intervention
- If nerve root avulsions, no reason to wait past 3 months to intervene

47. What options exist for reconstruction/repair of a traumatic brachial plexus injury?
- Neurolysis
- Nerve grafting
- Neurotization (nerve transfer of a functional but less important nerve distally to the motor nerve that innervates a given muscle)
- Free muscle transplantation (gracilis, rectus femoris, contralateral latissimus dorsi)
- Tendon transfers

48. What is the most important function to restore in a traumatic brachial plexus injury?
Elbow flexion.

ARTHRODESES

49. What are the primary purposes for arthrodesis in patients with a nerve palsy, cerebral palsy, or rheumatoid arthritis?
To provide stabilization, to simplify a polyarticular system, and to provide motor power now available for transfer.

50. To facilitate thumb–index tip pinch and to provide proximal thumb abduction stability in combined nerve palsies, cerebral palsy, and quadriplegia, what arthrodeses can be used?
- Thumb MCP joint arthrodesis
- Thumb IP joint arthrodesis
- Index PIP, DIP joint arthrodesis

51. In combined nerve injuries, wrist stability is often a problem. Which arthrodesis is useful?

Radiocarpal arthrodesis, which also makes extensor tendons available for transfer in a combined median/ulnar palsy.

52. If an adducted thumb cannot be stabilized by transfers (as in cerebral palsy, quadriplegia, and combined median/ulnar injury), which bony procedure may be helpful?

Thumb CMC fusion.

53. In an upper trunk brachial plexus palsy, shoulder weakness and/or instability may be seen. What procedure apart from tendon transfer may be useful?

Glenohumeral arthrodesis.

BIBLIOGRAPHY

Al-Qattan MM: Obstetric brachial plexus injuries. J Am Soc Surg Hand 3:41–54, 2003.

American Society for Surgery of the Hand. Available at: www.assh.org. Accessed October 23, 2009.

Brand PW: Tendon transfer reconstructions for radial, ulnar, median and combined paralyses: Principles and techniques. In Brand PW, Hollister A (eds): Clinical Mechanics of the Hand, 2nd ed. St. Louis, Mosby, 1993, pp 208–248.

Burton RI: The arthritic hand. In Evarts CM (ed): Surgery of the Musculoskeletal System. New York, Churchill Livingstone, 1990, pp 1087–1158.

Gerwin, M: Cerebral palsy. In Green DP, Hotchkiss RN, Pederson WC (eds): Operative Hand Surgery, 4th ed. New York, Churchill Livingstone, 1999, pp 259–286.

Green DP, Davis TRC, Omer GE, et al: Nerve reconstruction. In Green DP, Hotchkiss RN, Pederson WC (eds): Operative Hand Surgery, 4th ed. New York, Churchill Livingstone, 1999, pp 1481–1606.

Kozin SH: Tetraplegia. J Am Soc Surg Hand 2:141–152, 2002.

Littler JW: In Converse JM (ed): Reconstructive Plastic Surgery. Philadelphia, WB Saunders, 1977, pp 3103–3151, 3166–3214, 3266–3305.

Littler JW: Tendon transfers and arthrodesis in combined median and ulnar nerve paralysis. J Bone Joint Surg 31A:225–234, 1949.

Moberg EA: Upper limb surgical rehabilitation in tetraplegia. In Evarts CM (ed): Surgery of the Musculoskeletal System. New York, Churchill Livingstone, 1990, pp 915–941.

Ramselaar JM: Tendon Transfers to Restore Opposition of the Thumb. Leiden, HE Stenfert Kroese NV, 1970.

Smith RJ: Tendon Transfers of the Hand and Forearm. Boston, Little, Brown, 1987.

Tomaino MM: Nonobstetric brachial plexus injuries. J Am Soc Surg Hand 1:135–153, 2001.

128 SOFT TISSUE COVERAGE OF THE HAND

Jeffrey Weinzweig, MD, FACS

1. **Which mechanisms of injury to the hand often result in significant soft tissue loss requiring reconstruction?**

   A plethora of destructive culprits awaits the unsuspecting hand. Examples include crush injuries, such as roller or punch press mishaps; frostbite; thermal and electrical injuries; and blast injuries. Soft tissue loss requiring reconstruction also may result from débridement for infection, excision of neoplasms, subcutaneous infiltrations of intravenous solutions, and direct injection of caustic agents.

2. **What injuries present the most difficult challenges for soft tissue coverage?**

   Injuries involving the tactile surface of the hand with disruption of its sensory supply represent the most difficult reconstructive problems. The reconstructive goal must include restoration of sensibility if maximal function is to be achieved.

3. **What are the indications for flap coverage?**

   A skin graft requires a suitable recipient bed, such as muscle, fascia, paratenon, or periosteum. In the absence of structures capable of revascularizing a graft, as in cases of exposed bone without periosteum or exposed tendon without paratenon, a well-vascularized flap is necessary to provide durable soft tissue coverage.

4. **How is a wound prepared for flap coverage?**

   Pulsatile irrigation with several liters of antibiotic solution, débridement of all devitalized tissue, and eradication of infection are mandatory prior to flap coverage. Serial débridement and placement of a string of tobramycin-impregnated beads beneath a Tegaderm pouch (changed after 3 to 5 days) are often useful approaches in the preparation of a contaminated wound.

5. **What is the significance of random and axial flaps?**

   In the early 1970s, Ian McGregor introduced the concept of random and axial flaps, which was a significant breakthrough in the understanding of skin vascularity. Before this time, flap size and design were largely predicated on fortuitous length-to-width ratios on a trial-and-error basis, ranging from 1:1 on the extremities to 5:1 on the face. A random pattern flap "lacks any significant bias in its vascular pattern" and "is subject to the restrictions hitherto generally accepted in flap design," whereas an axial pattern flap "has an anatomically recognized arteriovenous system running along its axis" and, therefore, "is not subject to many of the restrictions that apply to random pattern flaps."

6. **Describe the venous anatomy of the upper extremity.**

   Three venous systems exist in the forearm: the superficial epifascial system, venae comitantes, and perforating veins. The superficial system consists of the cephalic vein, basilic vein, and communicating veins between them. The venae comitantes are paired veins that travel parallel to the radial, ulnar, anterior interosseous, and posterior interosseous arteries deep to the fascia. The perforating veins connect the superficial and deep systems. The superficial system and venae comitantes contain bicuspid valves, preventing retrograde filling. The valves in the communicating system are less constant and usually unicuspid.

7. **How does blood bypass the valves in a retrograde flap?**

   Initially, it was thought that venous flow occurred through the bypassed valves by collateral veins in the superficial and deep systems and by crossover between the venae comitantes, which have valveless communicating branches between certain comitantes valves. However, experimental evidence casts doubt on this process as the only mechanism of retrograde flow. Timmons has postulated that three processes are necessary for reverse flow to occur: (1) increased venous pressure proximal to the valve, (2) disruption of sympathetic tone, and (3) venous filling proximal and distal to the valves.

8. **Can a fasciocutaneous flap be elevated from the dorsal aspect of the forearm?**

   Yes. A large fasciocutaneous flap—the posterior interosseous artery flap—can be elevated from the dorsal aspect of the forearm. This vessel originates from the common interosseous artery in 90% of people and the ulnar artery in 10%

and usually is found 2 cm proximal to the ulnar styloid beneath the extensor indicis proprius. The posterior interosseous artery flap territory has been shown to extend from the level of the wrist to a point 4 cm below the epicondyles, although some contend that the area is limited to the distal and middle thirds of the forearm. It is useful for covering defects of the dorsal and palmar aspects of the hand and the first web space.

9. What is a distant pedicle flap? What are the indications for its use?

Distant pedicle flaps are not based on the involved extremity; donor sites include the chest, abdomen, and groin. Use of such flaps necessitates a delay period (usually 2 to 3 weeks) during which the pedicle flap remains attached to both the recipient and donor sites. The upper extremity is immobilized to prevent flap disruption; stiffness of the hip and upper extremity may occur in older patients as a result. After the delay, the pedicle is divided, the donor site closed, and the flap inset. Use of a distant pedicle flap is indicated when local or regional flaps are either unavailable or insufficient to provide adequate soft tissue coverage or the patient is not a candidate for free tissue transfer.

10. What is the most commonly used distant pedicle flap?

The groin flap.

11. What is the significance of the groin flap?

The groin flap, reported by Ian McGregor and Ian Jackson in 1972, was one of the first axial pattern flaps to be described. It was revolutionary because it allowed greater potential for reconstruction of difficult upper extremity wounds. It is a versatile flap with a reliable vascular supply that is capable of covering large defects of the hand and wrist and provides an excellent tissue bed for subsequent procedures such as tendon reconstruction.

12. How is a groin flap designed?

The groin flap is supplied by the superficial circumflex iliac artery (SCIA), a branch of the femoral artery, and accompanying venae comitantes. The SCIA originates 2 to 3 cm below the midpoint of the inguinal ligament and courses laterally parallel to the inguinal ligament until it reaches the medial border of the sartorius muscle. The flap is designed by drawing a line from the anterior superior iliac spine (ASIS) to the pubic tubercle to mark the course of the inguinal ligament. The femoral artery is palpated 2.5 cm below the ligament at the origin of the SCIA. A line is drawn laterally from this point and parallel to the inguinal ligament to mark the course of the SCIA pedicle. The flap is centered over this line; the dissection is begun laterally and extended medially to the medial border of the sartorius. The fascia over the lateral border of the sartorius is incised and reflected with the flap to ensure inclusion of the pedicle. A flap that is 10 cm wide usually allows tubing when the flap is needed for circumferential coverage of degloved digits. Donor sites up to 12 cm in width can be closed directly (Figs. 128-1 and 128-2).

13. What are the disadvantages of the groin flap?

- Dependent position of the hand during attachment and immobilization causes edema with subsequent joint stiffness
- Difficulty with physical and occupational therapy due to immobilization of the upper extremity
- Patient discomfort
- Two-stage procedure

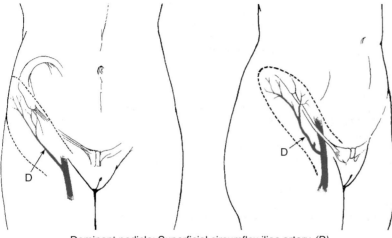

Dominant pedicle: Superficial circumflex iliac artery (D)

Figure 128-1. Groin flap design. (From Mathes S, Nahai F: Reconstructive Surgery: Principles, Anatomy, and Technique, Philadelphia, Churchill Livingstone, 1997, p 1007.)

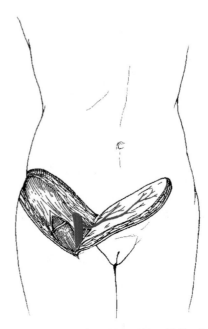

Figure 128-2. Relationship of flap pedicle to groin muscle and fascial layers. (From Mathes S, Nahai F: Reconstructive Surgery: Principles, Anatomy, and Technique, Philadelphia, Churchill Livingstone, 1997, p 1013.)

14. How are anterior chest wall and abdominal wall flaps designed?

Anterior chest wall flaps are designed on the anterolateral chest wall or the infraclavicular region. The blood supply is derived from the intercostal vessels or the thoracoepigastric system and is oriented in a transverse-to-oblique direction toward the midline. Flaps designed on the contralateral chest wall permit easier immobilization of the extremity with the elbow flexed than do flaps on the ipsilateral chest wall.

Flaps elevated from the abdominal wall are called *epigastric flaps* when they are above the umbilicus and *abdominal flaps* when they are below. Epigastric flaps are useful for coverage of large defects of the distal forearm or hand. A superiorly based flap crossing the midline obtains vascular supply from both sides. The forearm is placed in a comfortable position across the lower chest, and the flap is designed as needed. Most abdominal flaps are inferiorly based random flaps in which flap length is restricted to 1.5 times the width. Axial pattern abdominal flaps can be based on the superficial inferior epigastric artery (SIEA), a branch of the SCIA, as described by Shaw and Payne in 1946. These flaps vary in length from 5 to 18 cm and in width from 2 to 7 cm and can be used as tubed flaps with the base of the tube rotated through an arc of 180° to facilitate positioning of the hand. Division and inset of each of these flaps is performed at 2 to 3 weeks; donor site defects are covered with split-thickness skin grafts at the time of flap elevation or division.

15. What is a fillet flap?

A fillet flap is a salvage flap consisting of the vascularized soft tissue of an otherwise mutilated digit. After excision of the phalanges and tendons, the fillet flap can be used for coverage of adjacent soft tissue defects.

16. What are the indications for free tissue transfer?

Various situations preclude the use of local, regional, or distant pedicle flaps. Involvement of the hand and forearm in an injury may eliminate all potential local or regional flap donor sites. Although distant pedicle flaps, such as the groin flap, are useful for coverage of large defects, defects resulting from circumferential injuries are extremely difficult to cover with such a flap. Occasionally, defects involving the volar and dorsal aspects of the hand or more proximal circumferential defects can be covered by a combined groin and epigastric flap. However, free flaps offer far greater versatility and availability of donor sites for coverage of extensive defects. In addition, tailoring of the free flap to suit the reconstructive needs of the wound is easily accomplished because of the diversity of available flaps. Limb elevation, early mobilization, and the ability to cover even extensive circumferential defects are additional advantages to the use of free tissue transfer.

17. Which free flaps are most commonly used?

Numerous flaps are available for free tissue transfer. A flap is selected based on the particular needs of a given wound, including size, geometry, location, and function. Thin, pliable coverage for the dorsum of the hand can be provided by

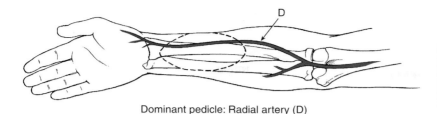

Figure 128-3. Radial forearm flap design. (From Mathes S, Nahai F: Reconstructive Surgery: Principles, Anatomy, and Technique, Philadelphia, Churchill Livingstone, 1997, p 776.)

Dominant pedicle: Radial artery (D)

a temporoparietal fascia, dorsalis pedis, or radial forearm flap. Thicker coverage for a palmar or forearm defect can be provided by a scapular or lateral arm flap. Coverage of an extensive circumferential defect can be provided by a rectus abdominis, serratus anterior, or latissimus dorsi flap.

18. Which flap is commonly used as a regional pedicle flap or free flap?
The radial forearm flap (Fig. 128-3).

19. How can the radial forearm flap be used as a regional pedicle flap?
The radial forearm flap is designed to include the radial artery when raised as a pedicle fasciocutaneous flap. It can be based proximally to cover defects involving the proximal forearm and elbow or distally (reversed) to cover defects involving the distal forearm, wrist, and hand (Fig. 128-4).

20. How is a radial forearm flap elevated?
The course of the radial artery is mapped out with a Doppler and marked on the volar surface of the forearm. The required length of the vascular pedicle is measured, and a template of the soft tissue defect is outlined on the proximal forearm (for a reversed or distally based flap). The flap may include virtually all of the volar forearm skin, if needed (up to 14 cm by 24 cm); the donor site is then skin-grafted.

The radial artery and its two venae comitantes are invested in a layer of deep fascia known as the *lateral intermuscular septum,* which separates the flexor and extensor compartments of the forearm and is attached to the periosteum of the radius distal to the insertion of the pronator teres. The artery is covered proximally by the brachioradialis; it emerges distally between the brachioradialis and flexor carpi radialis to lie superficially, covered only by skin, subcutaneous tissue, and deep fascia.

Elevation of the flap is usually begun on the ulnar aspect of the flap and continued toward the radial pedicle. The antebrachial fascia is incised and elevated with the skin paddle. The flap is raised in a subfascial plane, exposing muscle bellies proximally and tendons distally, with care to preserve the paratenon for subsequent skin grafting. On the radial side of the flexor carpi radialis tendon, the dissection passes to a plane deep to the radial vessels, where it proceeds

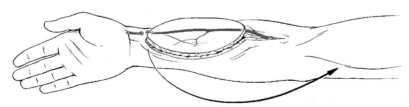

Standard arc to antecubital fossa

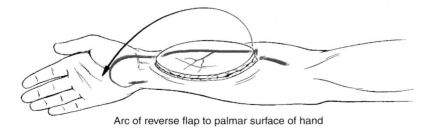

Arc of reverse flap to palmar surface of hand

Figure 128-4. Proximally and distally based radial forearm flap designs. (From Mathes S, Nahai F: Reconstructive Surgery: Principles, Anatomy, and Technique, Philadelphia, Churchill Livingstone, 1997, p 782.)

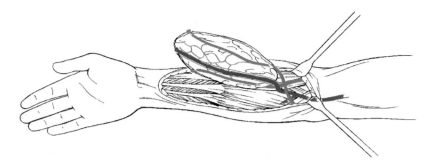

Figure 128-5. Radial forearm flap elevation. (From Mathes S, Nahai F: Reconstructive Surgery: Principles, Anatomy, and Technique, Philadelphia, Churchill Livingstone, 1997, p 789.)

to the radial side of the pedicle. The attachment of the lateral intermuscular septum to the periosteum of the radius is divided to allow elevation of the vascular pedicle and to ensure inclusion in the flap. Division of the pedicle proximally (for a distally based reverse flap) completes the dissection.

When bone is included as an osteofasciocutaneous flap, the attachment of the lateral intermuscular septum to the periosteum of the radius must be preserved. A cuff of flexor pollicis longus muscle is left attached to the radius to ensure preservation of the periosteal vessels. A keel-shaped segment of radius, not to exceed one third the thickness of the bone, is osteotomized and elevated with the flap (Fig. 128-5).

21. What is the main contraindication to use of the radial forearm free flap?

Both proximally based and reversed (distally based) radial forearm flaps require division of the radial artery. Sacrifice of the radial artery is permissible only when sufficient perfusion of the hand by the ulnar artery has been demonstrated by a normal Allen's test. In up to 15% of hands, the ulnar artery does not perfuse the radial digits because of an incomplete superficial palmar arch or prior ulnar artery injury. Reconstruction of the radial artery with a vein graft should be performed if ischemia of the hand results.

22. Can a radial forearm pedicle flap be harvested without sacrificing the radial artery?

Elevation of a radial forearm fascial flap is possible without sacrifice of the radial artery. Weinzweig et al. described a flap based on perforators from the radial artery, which form a fascial plexus extending 1.5 to 7 cm from the radial styloid. It is elevated in proximal-to-distal fashion and is based on 6 to 10 perforators found at the distal portion of the forearm. The flap easily reaches the palmar and dorsal aspects of the hand as well as the first web space.

23. What fasciocutaneous free flap can be harvested from the lateral arm?

The lateral arm flap, described by Song and popularized by Katsaros et al., is based on the posterior radial collateral artery and encompasses the posterolateral aspect of the upper arm between the insertion of the deltoid muscle and the elbow. Advantages of this flap include (1) relatively constant anatomy; (2) relatively long pedicle (up to 6 cm); (3) thin, pliable tissue; (4) use as a neurosensory flap; (5) ease of harvest in the supine position, permitting a two-team approach; and (6) direct closure of the donor site for flaps less than 6 cm wide. The only disadvantages associated with this flap are hypoesthesia in the distribution of the posterior cutaneous nerve if it is divided or harvested, and the donor site scar.

24. What is the thinnest free flap available for coverage of the dorsum of the hand?

The temporoparietal fascial flap. Described by Upton et al., this flap provides excellent coverage for defects of the hand as well as a suitable gliding surface for underlying tendons with a thin, pliable fascia that is then skin-grafted. Advantages include relative predictability of the pedicle and a concealed donor scar. Disadvantages include potential injury to the frontal branch of the facial nerve during harvest and scalp alopecia.

25. What is a functional free muscle transfer?

Free tissue transfer of muscle can be performed to restore hand function when major loss of skeletal musculature in the forearm results in a significant functional deficit that cannot be sufficiently reconstructed by a simpler procedure. Reinnervation with restoration of voluntary active muscle contraction can be accomplished by suturing a motor nerve in the recipient area to the motor nerve of the transplanted muscle. Transfer of the gracilis muscle or a segment of the latissimus muscle into the flexor compartment of the forearm with suture to the flexor digitorum profundus tendons can be performed to restore active finger flexion.

26. What is a composite free flap?

Composite defects involve multiple structures such as bone, tendon, nerve, and skin. Reconstruction of such defects can be accomplished with a composite free flap that incorporates the required structures into a single unit. A defect requiring bone, tendon, sensory nerve, and skin may be reconstructed with a radial forearm flap incorporating the palmaris longus tendon, lateral antebrachial cutaneous nerve, and a segment of radius. Another choice may be the dorsalis pedis flap with incorporation of the superficial or deep peroneal nerve, long toe extensor tendons, and metatarsal bone. A third choice may be the lateral arm flap with incorporation of the posterior cutaneous nerve, triceps tendon, and a segment of humerus.

27. What are the advantages and disadvantages of composite free flaps?

Composite free flaps permit single-stage reconstruction of defects that otherwise may require two or three stages. The main disadvantages with the use of composite free flaps are donor site morbidity, flap planning and design, and technical complexity. Common sense must dictate the planning of the reconstruction and considerations to minimize donor site morbidity. In certain situations the size, geometry, or components of a particular defect are better approached by multistage conventional procedures. An extensive soft tissue defect with a limited bone defect may be preferably managed by transfer of a skin-grafted free latissimus dorsi muscle flap and a nonvascularized iliac crest bone graft.

28. Describe the neurosensory functions of the hand.

The hand possesses a sophisticated level of sensibility with specialized neurosensory receptors on the dorsum and volar surface of the digits. Fingertips have the highest innervated density of any body surface except the tongue. Swartz has distinguished between the need for "critical sensibility" of the fingertips and "protective sensibility" of the palm and dorsum of the hand. Loss of the volar or tactile surface of the fingers requires replacement with specialized sensory cells that can be found only on the hand itself, on the toes, or on the sole of the foot—glabrous skin. Pacinian corpuscles and Meissner's corpuscles are encapsulated sensory endings found exclusively in glabrous skin. Merkel cells, which are sensory endings with expanded tips, are also found in glabrous skin. Areas of critical sensibility are covered by glabrous skin and are supported by underlying pulp tissue; they include the fingertips, palm of the hand, and sole of the foot.

29. What are the indications for the use of a sensate free flap?

The hand possesses a limited amount of sensate tissue to reconstruct defects that require sophisticated innervation crucial to tactile function. It does not possess sufficient tissue to reconstruct defects greater than those that can be covered by a Littler flap or other local innervated transposition flap. Thus, larger defects often require free transfer of a sensate flap.

30. Which sensate free flaps are commonly used?

Defects of the fingers can be reconstructed using the *toe pulp neurosensory flap,* described by Buncke and Rose, which consists of glabrous skin and underlying pulp tissue from the great or second toe. Moving two-point discrimination (2PD) of the transferred pulp tissue has been reported to range from 3 to 12 mm. The *great toe wraparound flap,* described by Morrison and MacLeod, is a composite flap of skin, nail, and pulp tissue, with or without the distal phalanx of the great toe. The great toe is partially degloved based on the dominant ulnar pedicle. The *first web flap,* described by May et al., uses the highly innervated tissue of the first web space of the foot. The flap is supplied by the first dorsal metatarsal artery and branches of the deep peroneal nerve and neighboring plantar digital nerves of both toes. A thin, pliable flap of glabrous skin and pulp measuring up to 12 cm × 8 cm can be harvested.

Several free fasciocutaneous flaps can be harvested to provide protective sensibility to a recipient site upon transfer. Examples include the *lateral arm flap* based on the posterior cutaneous nerve, the *radial forearm flap* based on the lateral antebrachial cutaneous nerve, and the *dorsalis pedis flap* based on the superficial peroneal nerve.

31. Does tissue expansion have a role in coverage of soft tissue defects of the hand?

In selected cases. Successful soft tissue resurfacing of defects involving the fingers, web spaces, and dorsum of the hand have been reported using seamless custom expanders in which the base of the expander is approximately the size of the defect to be corrected. Expanders also have been used to recruit tissue for congenital hand anomalies, such as syndactyly release, to avoid the use of skin grafts. Small elongated or rectangular expanders are used in such cases. Neurovascular compromise, implant extrusion, and infection may occur with the use of tissue expanders.

BIBLIOGRAPHY

Becker C, Gilbert A: The dorsal ulnar artery flap. In Gilbert A, Masquelet AC, Heutz VS (eds): Pedicle Flaps of the Upper Limb, 2nd ed. Boston, Little, Brown, 1992, p 129.
Cavanagh S, Pho RWH: The reverse radial forearm flap in the severely injured hand: An anatomical and clinical study. J Hand Surg 17B:501–503, 1992.
Chang J, Jones NF: Secondary soft tissue reconstruction. In Weinzweig N, Weinzweig J (eds): The Mutilated Hand. Philadelphia, Elsevier, 2005, pp 355–370.
Costa H, Soutar DS: The distally-based island posterior interosseous flap. Br J Plast Surg 41:221–227, 1988.
Daniel RK, Terzis J, Schwarz G: Neurovascular free flaps. A preliminary report. Plast Reconstr Surg 56:13, 1975.

Edstrom LE: Management of the degloved hand. In Weinzweig N, Weinzweig J (eds): The Mutilated Hand. Philadelphia, Elsevier, 2005, pp 307–321.

Ganchi PA, Pribaz JJ: Spare parts in upper extremity reconstruction. In Weinzweig N, Weinzweig J (eds): The Mutilated Hand. Philadelphia, Elsevier, 2005, pp 441–460.

Glasson DW, Lovie MJ: The ulnar island flap in hand and forearm reconstruction. Br J Plast Surg 41:349–353, 1988.

Halbert CF, Wei FC: Neurosensory free flaps: Digits and hand. Hand Clin 13:251–262, 1997.

Katsaros J, Schusterman M, Beppu M, et al: The lateral upper arm flap: Anatomy and clinical applications. Ann Plast Surg 12:489, 1984.

Lister G: Free skin and composite flaps. In Green DP (ed): Operative Hand Surgery, 3rd ed. New York, Churchill Livingstone, 1993, pp 1103–1158.

Manktelow RT, Zuker RM, McKee NH: Functioning free muscle transplantation. J Hand Surg 9A:32, 1984.

McGregor IA, Jackson IT: The groin flap. Br J Plast Surg 25:3–16, 1972.

McGregor IA, Morgan G: Axial and random pattern flaps. Br J Plast Surg 25:3–16, 1972.

Mih AD: Pedicle flaps for coverage of the wrist and hand. Hand Clin 13:217–230, 1997.

Song R, Song Y, Yu Y, Song Y: The upper arm free flap. Clin Plast Surg 9:27, 1982.

Soutar DS, Tanner NSB: The radial forearm flap in the management of soft tissue injuries of the hand. Br J Plast Surg 37:18, 1984.

Upton J, Rogers C, Durham-Smith G, Swartz WM: Clinical applications of temporoparietal flaps in hand reconstruction. J Hand Surg 11A:475, 1986.

Weinzweig J, Weinzweig N: The severely burned hand. In Weinzweig N, Weinzweig J (eds): The Mutilated Hand. Philadelphia, Elsevier, 2005, pp 323–338.

Weinzweig N, Chen L, Chen ZW: The distally-based radial forearm fasciosubcutaneous flap with preservation of the radial artery: An anatomic and clinical approach. Plast Reconstr Surg 94:675–684, 1994.

Weinzweig N, Weinzweig J: The Mutilated Hand. Philadelphia, Elsevier, 2005.

Wood MB: Composite free flaps to the hand. Hand Clin 13:231–238, 1997.

Zancolli EA, Angrigiani C: Posterior interosseous island forearm flap. J Hand Surg 13B:130–135, 1988.

INFECTIONS OF THE HAND

CHAPTER 129

Norman Weinzweig, MD, FACS, and
Mark H. Gonzalez, MD, MEng

1. Who was Allen B. Kanavel?
Allen B. Kanavel, Professor of Surgery at Northwestern University Medical School in Chicago, wrote the classic treatise, *Infections of the Hand*, in 1912 during the preantibiotic area, expounding many basic principles in hand surgery. His work served as an invaluable guide to the surgical treatment of acute and chronic suppurative processes of the fingers, hand, and forearm, including the pathways of spread of infection and placement of surgical incisions. He also promulgated the fascial-space concept.

2. What was the mortality rate associated with hand infections in the preantibiotic era?
Acute lymphangitis caused by streptococcal infections of the hand was associated with significant morbidity and mortality in the preantibiotic area. Mortality rates as high as 28% were cited in the literature. After the introduction of antibiotics, streptococcal species were found to be exquisitely sensitive to penicillin.

3. What is the most common hand infection?
Paronychia.

4. What is the most common pathogen responsible for hand infections?
Staphylococcus aureus.

5. What is the etiopathogenesis of felons?
Felons arise when a penetrating wound contaminates the fat pad of the distal phalanx, producing a closed-space abscess. The abscess is associated with progressive tenderness and throbbing pain. A vicious cycle of inflammation, congestion, venous compromise, necrosis, and abscess formation is initiated. The abscess generally points in the path of least resistance, the site of maximal tenderness. Spontaneous decompression may occur with skin necrosis. If the skin is unyielding, felons may result in osteomyelitis, tenosynovitis, or septic arthritis.

6. What are the possible consequences of untreated or inappropriately treated felons?

• Painful, unstable, insensate, unaesthetic scars	• Osteomyelitis
• Acute flexor tenosynovitis	• Deep-space infection
• Septic arthritis	• Amputation

7. What are the different types of incisions for drainage of felons?

• Fishmouth	• Volar transverse
• J or hockey stick	• Midvolar longitudinal
• Through and through	• Unilateral high midlateral

8. Describe the advantages and disadvantages of the incisions listed in Question 7.
Various incisions have been described for the treatment of felons. The fishmouth or alligator mouth incision is mentioned only to be condemned; it often results in a painful, unstable scar. The J (or hockey stick) incision and the through-and-through incision are similar to the fishmouth incision. The volar transverse incision may injure the terminal digital nerve branches at the level of the trifurcation. Popular incisions for treatment of felons include the traditional unilateral high midlateral incision and the less-known but equally acceptable midvolar longitudinal incision. The midvolar longitudinal incision must *not* be carried proximal to the distal interphalangeal joint crease to avoid problems with contracture. This incision avoids the potential problems with a high midlateral incision when the abscess points volarly, predisposing to necrosis of the intervening skin bridge.

9. What are the advantages of the midvolar longitudinal incision?

- Most direct approach: Drain an abscess where it points
- Most efficient drainage
- Minimizes injury to digital nerves
- Least amount of scarring
- Maintains stability of soft tissue pad

10. What complications may follow treatment of felons?
- Slough of the bridge of normal skin between the incision and central necrosis (high midlateral)
- Anesthesia with blind digit tips after cutting terminal digital nerve branches (transverse volar)
- Pain due to neuroma formation or cicatricial entrapment of nerve endings (transverse volar)
- Unstable pulp due to division of fibrous septae (fishmouth)
- Unsightly scars

11. What is the clinical presentation of herpetic whitlow?
This infection is common in health care workers, such as dentists and respiratory therapists, who are exposed to the herpes simplex virus. The incubation period is 2 to 14 days. It is characterized by throbbing pain, swelling, and erythema in the affected finger. Vesicles of clear fluid often coalesce to form ulcers over 10 to 14 days.

12. Is herpetic whitlow an aseptic felon?
Herpetic whitlow is often described as an aseptic felon. This is a misnomer because herpetic whitlow is a *cutaneous* disease and therefore does *not* involve the deep pulp space.

13. How is herpetic whitlow treated?
Herpetic whitlow is treated conservatively. The infection runs a self-limited course and usually resolves spontaneously within 3 weeks with normal healing. Herpes infections may be prolonged in immunocompromised patients and in patients with secondary bacterial infection. The treatment of herpes infections of the hand should be conservative with analgesics and elevation to reduce pain and swelling. Incision and drainage are to be avoided unless a secondary bacterial abscess develops. Antiviral agents such as acyclovir or foscarnet can be used in immunocompromised patients with a refractory herpetic infection.

14. Is surgical drainage ever indicated for treatment of herpetic whitlow?
No. Incision and drainage may lead to devastating complications involving the entire distal phalanx with bacterial superinfection and even ascending encephalitis that results in death. The only possible role for surgery is segmental nail removal for relief of pain over the involved portion of the nail bed.

15. What are acute paronychia?
Acute paronychia are infections of the soft tissue fold around the fingernail (nail fold). They involve disruption of the seal between the proximal nail fold and the nail plate and provide a portal of entry for bacteria.

16. What is a "runaround" infection?
Continuity of the paronychial tissue with the eponychial tissue overlying the tissue of the nail may result in extension of the infection to involve both the eponychium and paronychium. A runaround abscess usually involves the entire nail fold, spreading under the nail sulcus to the opposite side. It is most commonly seen in young children and in patients with neglected paronychia. Most often, gram-positive cocci such as staphylococci and streptococci are the culprits. In children, the infection has an increased distribution of anaerobic and mixed bacterial flora.

17. How are acute paronychia treated?
Early in their course, acute paronychia occasionally can be treated by soaks, hand elevation, splintage, and antibiotics. Once the nail fold is elevated by accumulation of pus, drainage should be performed. First the involved finger is soaked in warm suds water for 15 to 30 minutes to loosen the nail fold. A Freer elevator is used to tease gently the eponychial fold in the area of pus accumulation and thus facilitate drainage. Plain gauze 0.25-inch thick is loosely packed in the wound, the hand is splinted and elevated, and antibiotics are given. Often, no anesthetic (digital nerve block) is necessary. In rare cases, it is necessary to incise the eponychial fold longitudinally, as described by some surgeons.

18. What are chronic paronychia?
Chronic paronychia demonstrate an indurated and rounded cuticle as a result of recurring episodes of increased inflammation, drainage, and eventual thickening and longitudinal grooving of the nail plate. They are most often seen in middle-aged women as a result of prolonged occlusion of the nail fold in the presence of *Candida albicans* (cultured in 95% of cases). Mechanical separation of the undersurface of the cuticle from the upper layer of the nail plate may be due to trauma, manicure, prolonged immersion in water (dishwashers), fungal invasion of the subcuticular area, retained foreign body, and necrotic nail.

19. How are chronic paronychia similar to acute paronychia?

Chronic paronychia are a completely distinct entity from acute paronychia, with no similarities except involvement of the nail fold.

20. How are chronic paronychia treated?

Chronic paronychia are far more difficult and frustrating to eradicate than the acute form. Nonoperative treatment is universally unsuccessful. Surgical procedures include marsupialization of the eponychium, as described by Keyser and Eaton in 1976, and total onychectomy (nail plate removal) and application of antifungal steroid ointment to the nail bed (3% Bio-form in Mycolog), as described in Kilgore and Graham in 1977.

21. How many cardinal signs did Kanavel originally describe?

Kanavel originally described only three cardinal signs. Although he mentioned in his treatise that "the whole of the finger is uniformly swollen," this observation was not a cardinal sign.

22. What are Kanavel's four cardinal signs of flexor tenosynovitis?

1. Exquisite tenderness that affects the entire tendon sheath and is limited to the sheath
2. Intense pain with passive extension of the finger, most marked at the proximal end
3. Semiflexed finger
4. Fusiform or symmetric swelling of the entire finger

23. How is acute flexor tenosynovitis treated?

Acute flexor tenosynovitis is treated by tendon sheath irrigation. The patient is taken to the operating room, and either the open or closed approach is used.

24. What are the open and closed approaches to tendon sheath irrigation for acute flexor tenosynovitis?

The *closed approach* to tendon sheath irrigation involves limited incisions for drainage of the involved tendon sheath. Placement of the incisions varies, but usually they are located distal to the A4/A5 pulley at the level of the distal interphalangeal (DIP) joint and just proximal to the A1 pulley at the level of the distal palmar crease. Vigorous intraoperative irrigation of the tendon sheath is key to the treatment of this hand emergency. Although some surgeons prefer 10% antibiotic solutions for irrigation, the mechanical action of the irrigant appears to be more important than the nature of the irrigant. Many surgeons set up an irrigating system postoperatively, with two catheters situated proximal and distal to the ends of the flexor sheath, but it is most likely that intraoperative irrigation plays the critical role in treating the tenosynovitis. The closed approach allows primary wound healing with less scarring, less risk of desiccation and tendon necrosis, shorter hospitalization (<72 hours), active flexion and extension exercises within 48 to 72 hours, rapid and complete functional recovery with minimal morbidity usually within 7 to 10 days, greater patient compliance with less pain on exercise, and a smaller primary wound.

The *open approach,* which uses midaxial or volar zigzag incisions, exposes delicate structures to infection with subsequent fibrosis and loss of function. Other problems include increased risk of tendon necrosis, greater scarring, and significant morbidity. The open approach essentially involves filleting the volar aspect of the involved finger with direct drainage of any purulent material. Treatment may require secondary procedures and prolonged hospitalization and rehabilitation and yield a less desirable functional result.

25. How is gonococcal flexor tenosynovitis treated?

Gonococcal flexor tenosynovitis most commonly arises by hematogenous spread from a genitourinary focus. It is often the only manifestation of disseminated gonorrhea. The clinical picture is acute flexor tenosynovitis. Treatment is by closed sheath irrigation and intravenous penicillin G, 1 million units every 4 hours, or a third-generation cephalosporin. Good functional recovery is the rule.

26. Which pathogens are most commonly responsible for acute flexor tenosynovitis?

Most cultures are sterile because of the initiation of antibiotic therapy before culture. The most common pathogens are gram-positive cocci.

27. What are the complications of untreated or inappropriately treated acute flexor tenosynovitis?

• Skin necrosis	• Septic arthritis
• Tendon adhesions	• Osteomyelitis
• Tendon necrosis and rupture	• Deep-space abscess
• Joint ankylosis	• Amputation

28. What are the fascial spaces in the hand?

The fascial spaces are potential spaces located throughout the hand that swell after implantation of bacteria, such as by penetrating injuries.

29. Name the fascial spaces of the hand.

• Thenar space	• Dorsal subaponeurotic space
• Middle palmar space	• Dorsal subcutaneous space
• Hypothenar space	• Radial bursa
• Subfascial web space in the palm and interdigital area ("collar button")	• Ulna bursa
	• Parona's space

30. Why are the fascial spaces pertinent to hand infections?

Pus from an infection in the flexor tendon sheath of the ring or middle finger may rupture into the middle palmar space. Similarly, pus from an infection in the index flexor tendon sheath may rupture into the thenar space. Infection in the hypothenar space is rarely described. The dorsal subcutaneous space is a large potential space overlying the entire dorsum of the hand and may contain large volumes of pus. The dorsal subaponeurotic space lies deep to the aponeurosis of the extensor tendons.

31. What is a "collar button" abscess?

A collar button abscess is an infection of the subfascial palmar space, which is contiguous with the dorsal subcutaneous space between the fingers. The subfascial palmar space and the dorsal subcutaneous space are the two most superficial of the deep spaces in the hand. Collar button abscesses begin as blisters, which become infected with intracutaneous and subcutaneous pus in the palm. Tethering of the skin to the palmar fascia makes it difficult for a subcutaneous infection in this area to track superficially beneath the space or between the skin and fascia. Consequently, instead of spreading peripherally, the abscess extends dorsally to the palmar fascia. Contiguity with the dorsal subcutaneous tissues causes a great deal of dorsal swelling with abduction of the fingers because of purulence between the digits palmarly and dorsally. Treatment requires incision and drainage of the subcutaneous blister with excision of the palmar fascia. Exposure of the superficial dorsal extension allows complete unroofing of the subfascial infection. Great care must be taken to identify the bifurcation of the digital arteries to the adjacent sides of the fingers. Local wound care and early motion usually result in full functional recovery.

32. What are the causes of dorsal hand swelling?

(1) Lymphatic drainage to the dorsum of the hand from either palmar or dorsal infection sites, (2) dorsal subcutaneous abscess, and (3) dorsal subaponeurotic abscess.

33. Describe the treatment of a dorsal hand abscess.

The dorsal subaponeurotic space in the hand is a potential space that usually becomes secondarily infected from a local penetration injury. It is often difficult to differentiate this infection from a dorsal subcutaneous abscess. The problem should be approached as the worst case scenario—a subaponeurotic infection. Two linear incisions should be made on the dorsum of the hand, one over the second metacarpal and one between the fourth and fifth metacarpal. This technique permits differentiation of the infection, drainage, and satisfactory coverage of the tendons. A dorsal midline incision in the case of a subaponeurotic abscess may result in extensor tendon loss due to desiccation, infection, and ischemia. Early motion is mandatory after drainage and should involve all three digital joints plus the wrist joint to maintain extensor tendon gliding.

34. What are the boundaries of the thenar space?

- *Dorsal:* Musculature of the adductor pollicis
- *Volar:* Fascia overlying adductor pollicis
- *Radial:* Fusion of adductor pollicis and adductor fascia at their insertion into the proximal phalanx of the thumb
- *Ulnar:* Midpalmar space or oblique septum extending from the palmar fascia to the volar ridge of the third metacarpal

The thenar space is contiguous with the flexor tendons of the index finger. It is exposed to local penetrating injury.

35. What is the position of the thumb in thenar space infections?

The thumb is held in marked abduction because this maneuver reduces pressure within the abscess cavity. Progressive infection within the thenar space usually tracks dorsally over the adductor pollicis and first dorsal interosseous muscles. This progression produces a dumbbell effect with extension of the abscess from its origin deep to the flexor tendons of the index finger over the adductor pollicis and first dorsal interosseous to its site of presentation superficial to the first dorsal interosseous.

36. What incisions are used for drainage of thenar space abscesses?

Adequate drainage of a thenar space infection must permit exposure to the dumbbell abscess with care to protect the digital nerve and artery to the radial aspect of the index finger as well as the nerve and volar blood supply to the thumb (ulnar digital nerve and princeps pollicis artery or only the ulnar digital artery to the thumb). The recommended incisions are perpendicular to the web space approximately 1 cm proximal to the thenar crease and extend proximally on the dorsum or palm toward the convergence of the index and thumb metacarpals. The fascia overlying the adductor muscle and first dorsal interosseous can be excised widely. Incisions parallel to the web space either volarly or dorsally result in a contracture web space between the thumb and index finger.

37. What are the boundaries of the midpalmar space?

Midpalmar space infections are located ulnar to the oblique septum. They may result from either indirect inoculation by a penetrating injury or rupture of flexor tenosynovitis involving the middle or ring fingers. They occur less commonly than thenar space infections, probably because of the relatively protective nature of the midpalmar space compared with the dorsum of the thumb–index web. Flexor tenosynovitis involving the little finger tracks proximally through the ulna bursa and does not enter the midpalmar space. Infection results in dorsal swelling (as in a thenar abscess). It is the only infection resulting in loss of palmar concavity. The infection is located deep (dorsal) to the flexor tendons and volar to the metacarpals.

38. What incisions are used for drainage of a midpalmar space abscess?

An oblique or transverse palmar incision should allow wide exposure of the palmar fascia with identification and protection of the neurovascular bundles of the adjacent fingers as well as the deep palmar arch and ulnar motor nerve.

39. What structures are connected to form a "horseshoe" abscess?

The sheath of the flexor pollicis communicates with the radial bursa. Likewise, the sheath of the little finger communicates with the ulnar bursae. The two bursae communicate with the deep space just superficial to the pronator quadratus, termed *Parona's space*. An infection of the tendon sheath of the thumb or little finger may progress through Parona's space into the other side, forming a horseshoe abscess.

40. What factors lead to the development of osteomyelitis after a human bite?

Delayed treatment, inadequate initial débridement, and initial suturing of the wound.

41. What organisms are encountered in a human bite infection? What is appropriate initial antibiotic therapy?

The organisms are microbes commonly found on the skin or in the mouth. Examples include gram-positive aerobic organisms *(S. aureus, Staphylococcus epidermidis, Streptococcus* species) and anaerobes (*Peptococcus* species, *Peptostreptococcus* species, *Bacteroides* species, and *Eikenella corrodens*, a facultative anaerobe). Antibiotic coverage must cover gram-positive and anaerobic organisms. A first-generation cephalosporin in combination with penicillin or ampicillin in combination with clavulanic acid fosters adequate coverage. In penicillin-sensitive patients, clindamycin may be used, but *Eikenella corrodens* is resistant to clindamycin, and an additional antibiotic may be added based on culture and sensitivity.

42. What organisms are associated with wounds contaminated with river or sea water? What antibiotic therapy is appropriate?

Vibrio vulnificus occurs in coastal and brackish water and commonly infects cuts acquired while cleaning or shelling crabs. The organism is sensitive to tetracycline and chloramphenicol. *Mycobacterium marinum* infection, termed "swimming pool granuloma," is a cutaneous infection acquired in fresh water. Appropriate antibiotics are rifampin and ethambutol or trimethoprim-sulfamethoxazole. *Aeromonas hydrophila* is also commonly found in fresh water and may infect open cuts in swimmers. Appropriate antibiotics are ciprofloxacin, trimethoprim-sulfamethoxazole, and tetracycline.

43. What factors predispose to the development of necrotizing fasciitis? What are the etiologic organisms? Describe the pathologic process.

Necrotizing fasciitis is most frequently seen in intravenous drug abusers, diabetics, and alcoholics. The organisms most frequently noted are beta-hemolytic streptococci and mixed aerobic–anaerobic organisms. The infection causes liquefaction necrosis of the fascia with selective spread along fascial planes. Involvement of the skin and muscle occurs at later stages with bullae formation, skin slough, and myonecrosis.

44. What organisms are frequently seen in dog and cat bites?

- Dog bites: *S. aureus, Streptococcus viridans, Pasteurella multocida,* and *Bacteroides* species
- Cat bites: *P. multocida*

45. Describe the clinical presentation of sporotrichosis in the upper extremity. How is it treated?

Sporotrichosis is a chronic granulomatous infection caused by the saprophytic fungus *Sporothrix schenckii*. After inoculation through a skin abrasion or thorn puncture, a local ulceration develops. The disease then spreads through the lymphatic channels with red, hard nodules and ulcerations along the path of lymphatic spread in the arm. On rare occasions, the disease presents with inflammatory arthritis of the joints of the hand or wrist. Treatment is a long course of oral potassium iodide. Refractory disease and extracutaneous disease respond to intravenous amphotericin B.

46. What factors predispose to the development of gas gangrene? How is it treated?

Gas gangrene is caused by *Clostridium* species or other gas-forming organisms. The condition is frequently seen in grossly contaminated wounds with crushed or anoxic tissue. Suturing of a contaminated and inadequately débrided wound also may predispose to this condition. Treatment requires emergent débridement and appropriate antibiotics.

47. What organisms are frequently cultured from abscesses due to intravenous drug abuse?

The cultured organisms are common skin or oral flora. Saliva contamination is common because of the practice of licking needles. The drugs are not sterile and may harbor organisms. The most commonly cultured organisms are streptococci, *S. aureus, E. corrodens,* and *Bacteroides* species. Antibiotic coverage must include gram-positive organisms and anaerobes. A combination of cephalosporin and penicillin or ampicillin and clavulanic acid provides adequate initial coverage pending culture results.

48. In diabetic hand infections, what factors correlate with an increased risk of amputation?

The risk factors are infections involving structures below the subcutaneous tissue, concomitant renal failure, and infections with gram-negative, anaerobic, or polymicrobial organisms.

BIBLIOGRAPHY

Bolton H, Fowler P, Jepson R: Natural history and treatment of pulp space infection and osteomyelitis of the distal phalanx. J Bone Joint Surg 31B:499–504, 1949.

Brown P, Kinman PB: Gas gangrene in a metropolitan community. J Bone Joint Surg 56A:1445–1451, 1974.

Gonzalez MH, Papierski P, Hall RF Jr: Osteomyelitis of the hand after a human bite. J Hand Surg 18A:520–522, 1993.

Gonzalez MH, Kay T, Weinzweig N, et al: Necrotizing fasciitis of the upper extremity. J Hand Surg 21A:689–692, 1996.

Gonzalez MH, Garst J, Nourbash P, et al: Abscesses of the upper extremity from drug abuse by injection. J Hand Surg 18A:868–870, 1993.

Gonzalez MH, Bochar S, Novotny J, et al: Upper extremity infections in patients with diabetes mellitus. J Hand Surg [Am] 24:682–686, 1999.

Freeland AE, Burkhalter WE, Mann RJ: Functional treatment of acute suppurative digital tenosynovitis. Orthop Trans 5:113–114, 1981.

Kanavel A: Infections of the Hand. Philadelphia, Lea & Febiger, 1912.

Keyser J, Eaton RG: Surgical cure of chronic paronychia by eponychial marsupialization. Plast Reconstr Surg 58:66–70, 1976.

Kilgore E, Brown L, Newmeyer W, et al: Treatment of felons. Am J Surg 130:194–198, 1975.

Mann RJ (ed): Hand infections. Hand Clin 5:515–667, 1989.

Mann RJ: Infections of the Hand. Philadelphia, Lea & Febiger, 1988.

Nevaiser RJ: Closed tendon sheath irrigation for pyogenic flexor tenosynovitis. J Hand Surg 3:462–466, 1978.

Polayes I, Arons M: The treatment of herpetic whitlow—A new surgical concept. Plast Reconstr Surg 65:811–817, 1980.

Stone O, Mullins J: Chronic paronychia. Arch Dermatol 86:324–327, 1962.

REPLANTATION AND REVASCULARIZATION

Rudolf Buntic, MD, and
Harry J. Buncke, MD

CHAPTER 130

1. What is the goal of replantation surgery?

The goal of replantation surgery is successful restoration of function. Revascularization of an amputated part does not necessarily mean success. If the revascularized part will not go on to have useful function or it will interfere with normal activity, then proceeding with replantation must be questioned. The surgeon needs to decide whether the patient will be served better by replantation or by completing the amputation. Multiple factors such as the nature of the affected part(s), other injuries, mechanism of injury, age, work status, and motivation of the patient are part of the decision to replant.

2. What important factors affect outcome in extremity replants?

Multiple factors affect outcome in replantation. Certainly patient age and general health are factors. Factors that are specific to the amputation and not related to the patient's general health include the following:

- The level and complexity of the injury are crucial. The more distal the injury, the greater the chance for success. An exception is very distal replants beyond the trifurcation and distal interphalangeal (DIP) joints, where establishing circulation may be more difficult.
- Ischemia time is a crucial factor. The longer the ischemia, especially warm ischemia, the worse the prognosis.
- Upper extremity replants tend to do better than lower extremity replants.
- Sharp injuries tend to do better than crush or avulsion injuries.
- Multiple-level injuries do not do as well as single-level injuries.

3. What are the indications for replantation?

Each patient needs to be evaluated on an individual basis, taking into account all aspects of the patient's history and needs. The following factors are strong indications for replantation:

- Multiple finger amputations
- Thumb amputations
- Hand amputations at the palm or wrist
- Childhood amputations

The following types of replants have less absolute indications and are considered controversial by some. However, in appropriately selected cases, with motivated patients, results can be excellent.

- Loss of a single digit, excluding the thumb
- Ring finger avulsion injuries

4. What are the contraindications to replantation?

- Upper extremity amputation proximal to the midforearm with ischemia time greater than 6 hours
- Concomitant life-threatening injuries
- Multiple-level injuries
- Severe crush or avulsion injuries
- Extreme contamination
- Systemic illness or surgical history precluding replantation
- Self-mutilation cases, psychotic patients

5. How do you store an amputated part?

Wrap the amputated part in moist gauze and place it on top of ice, with enough of a gauze barrier that the part is kept cool but does not freeze. Submerging the part in ice can result in it freezing, which will doom the replant to failure if it is attempted.

6. What do you evaluate first in an amputation patient?

You treat the amputation patient like every other trauma patient and use the *ABC*s—*A*irway, *B*reathing, *C*irculation. Only after you have determined there are no life-threatening issues do you address the amputation in more detail.

7. Is an operating microscope required to perform a replant?

Although some surgeons report success using loupe magnification when performing free flaps, this is not the case for replantation. This is especially true in digital replantation when the vessels can be quite small and a good microscope is essential for adequate visualization and precise technique. Digital replants, especially in children, often have vessel diameters less than 1 millimeter. Loupe magnification usually is used to examine and dissect the amputated part in preparation for vessel and nerve repair.

8. What closing pressure in a microvascular clamp can result in intimal injury?

Clamp closing pressures in excess of 30 g tend to cause intimal damage. The clamp size is not as relevant as are closing pressures. Precise atraumatic technique is essential to minimize the chance of thrombosis.

9. Describe the operative sequence in finger or hand replantation.

Bone shortening and osteosynthesis usually are performed first. By shortening bone, tension-free anastomosis is facilitated. The flexor and extensor repairs usually are done next. The arterial repair is then performed, followed by nerve coaptations. The hand can then be turned over, and the dorsal vein is repaired next. The skin is then closed. Sometimes skin grafting is necessary to complete the closure. Of course, circumstances are variable, and this order can be changed to suit the particular circumstances of an amputation. A skin graft for an open wound, even if placed over an anastomosis, is safer than a tight closure. Operative sequence can change with surgeon preference, although the bone usually is done first.

In a hand replant, you may want to shunt to establish some arterial inflow to reduce the muscle ischemia time (see Question 10).

10. In what situation is bone fixation postponed?

Usually the bony alignment and fixation are performed first because they can be quite traumatic and can disrupt vessel, nerve, and tendon repairs. However, in proximal injuries where muscle ischemia is a factor, a temporary vascular shunt can be performed first to perfuse the part. With a large part that is especially susceptible to warm ischemia, immediate perfusion with a temporary synthetic tube in the artery will bring ischemia time back down to zero. Toxic metabolites that collect in the ischemic part will be washed out. The part and proximal structures can be dissected without the urgency of ongoing ischemia. Bone fixation can be done while shunting continues, or the shunting can be temporarily stopped.

11. What do you do if you cannot repair digital nerves primarily?

Digital nerves can be grafted with synthetic conduits or vein grafts in small defects.

12. How about the median and ulnar nerves? What if primary repair is not possible?

If you cannot primarily repair both the median and ulnar nerves, then consideration should be given to not performing replantation. The answer to this is not straightforward, however, because you can graft median and ulnar nerves in the same hospital stay or even later.

13. What is the treatment of arterial insufficiency after replantation?

A finger that turns white after successful revascularization usually means inflow has been interrupted. Signs of compromised inflow are a pale digit that has poor capillary refill and does not bleed if stuck with a needle. This may indicate vasospasm, extrinsic pressure on the vessel, or clotting. Vasospasm can be prevented by maintaining a warm environment, administering analgesics, and possibly performing regional blocks. The dressing may be too tight and should be removed or replaced as a first step. Another cause of ischemia may be pressure on the artery from swelling, tight closure, or hematoma. A few key sutures that may be causing tension can be removed. If this fails, operative exploration and repair are indicated if the part is believed to be salvageable.

14. Why do most replants fail?

Venous insufficiency usually is responsible for replant failure because venous structures are the most difficult structures to repair.

15. How many arteries need to be repaired to successfully revascularize a finger?

Usually only one artery repair needs to be performed. If there is a distal obstruction or an unrecognized distal arterial injury, then a second artery may need to be repaired.

16. How many veins need to be repaired?

One vein can be enough to establish adequate venous drainage. Some surgeons advocate two or three vein repairs, but this is time consuming and may not be feasible in very distal amputations or in small children.

17. What is the treatment of venous insufficiency after replantation?

A finger that turns blue and lacks venous drainage will fail just as miserably as one without arterial inflow. Capillary refill is immediate, and the part often swells. Bleeding from the digit usually is quite dark, indicating poor oxygenation. Removing the dressing and possibly removing some sutures should be considered first. The nail can be removed and the nail bed scrubbed or abraded and soaked with heparin sponges to allow continuous bleeding of the finger. Leeches can be used as well. Leeches secrete the powerful anticoagulant hirudin, which will result in bleeding of the leech bite site for several hours after the leech has filled its intestines and fallen off. The continuous oozing of blood from the replanted part allows inflow and outflow to continue until neovascularization occurs, and blood can drain via capillaries. Leeching can result in significant blood loss over time, so blood counts need to be measured at least daily. The possibility of blood transfusion should be discussed with the patient beforehand.

18. How do you sacrifice a leech after it has been used?

Leeches are only used once and then sacrificed. They cannot be reused. Sacrificing usually is performed by placing the leech in pure rubbing alcohol or by placing them in the freezer and freezing them.

19. What kind of infection is associated with leeches?

Leeches are colonized with *Aeromonas hydrophila,* which can cause serious soft tissue infections in replants. For this reason all patients who undergo leech treatment should be covered for *A. hydrophila* with prophylactic cefotaxime or ciprofloxacin.

20. Which vessels are used in ear replantation?

Ear replantation can be one of the most difficult challenges for a microsurgeon. Commonly the injury is an avulsion type with a crush component. Motor vehicle accidents and human bite injuries are frequent causes. Good vessels can be difficult to find, with venous congestion common postoperatively. Branches from the superficial temporal vessels or posterior auricular vessels can be used, if present. However, because these injuries usually have a crush avulsion component, these vessels often are too severely damaged for microsurgical repair. The superficial temporal vessels can be used directly, with or without vein grafting. The disadvantage is loss of a pedicle for the temperoparietal fascial flap if required later.

21. Which vessels are used in scalp replantation?

Although scalp replantation using a single artery and vein has been reported, multiple arterial and venous anastomoses usually are performed to provide adequate flow for the scalp. Vein grafting is often required. Any arteries or veins that are present are candidates for use. This includes the supraorbital, temporal, postauricular, and occipital vessels. If the part is small enough and does appear to adequately perfuse on one inflow and one outflow vessel, then that is enough.

22. How do you perform a penis replant?

After induction of anesthesia, the procedure requires a suprapubic cystostomy and placement of a Foley catheter through the urethra of the amputated part and proximal stump and into the bladder. Of course, the part is prepped before this. The urethra is repaired with absorbable suture under loupe magnification. The corpora are repaired with absorbable suture. After the proximal stump has been dissected and an inflow artery and outflow vein identified, the arterial repair is performed under magnification. A venous repair follows, and each of the dorsal nerves must be repaired. Mutilation of the part at the site of amputation may require shortening or vein grafting.

If suture line pressure from edema is present and potentially obstructs venous or arterial drainage, a skin graft can be placed over the vascular and nerve repairs. Vascular insufficiency may require leeching.

23. A man presents to the emergency room with a four-finger saw amputation. The thumb was not amputated. The fingers are replantable. The small and long fingers are easy to identify, but the index and ring fingers are difficult to tell apart because they are the same length. How do you tell them apart?

The index finger does not usually have hair on the dorsal midphalangeal skin, whereas the ring finger does. In the long run, this may not be important, but the patient certainly might be able to tell the difference later and wonder why you put his fingers back on the wrong way!

24. What methods are used to monitor replants?

Early recognition of circulatory compromise in a replanted part is essential if salvage is to be performed. Many types of monitoring systems with variable results have been reported. The ideal system is one that provides continuous and accurate information in a noninvasive fashion. To date, the ideal system has not been created. Clinical evaluation of the replanted part by experienced physicians and nurses is the best method of monitoring. This includes evaluation of color, capillary refill, temperature, and edema. Other more objective methods are used as well. Quantitative fluorimetry has proved successful as an objective form of measuring perfusion. Other methods such as surface temperature recordings and Doppler measurements have been described.

25. Should isolated ulnar artery or radial artery injuries be repaired if hand perfusion is judged to be good?

Repairs of ulnar and radial arteries have previously had poor results. Patency has improved with microvascular technique. Single-vessel patency rates without vein grafting have been reported at 100% in one series, as measured by Doppler ultrasound imaging. There is evidence of cold intolerance after radial artery sacrifice, making the argument for primary repair of damaged radial and ulnar arteries.

CONTROVERSIES

26. What type of postoperative anticoagulation is required after replantation?

Thrombosis of small vessels continues to be a problem after microsurgical repair. To decrease failure rates, multiple pharmacologic agents have been used in the laboratory and clinically to prevent thrombosis. No single regimen has been proven to be most successful and practice varies. Daily aspirin is commonly used as a suppressor of platelet aggregation. Low-molecular-weight dextran is often added to the regimen and usually started before the microvascular clamps are removed. It is normally used for approximately 5 days postoperatively. Dextran is believed to have both antiplatelet and antifibrin properties. It also appears to act as a volume expander. Heparin binds to antithrombin III and inactivates thrombin and other enzymes in the clotting cascade. As with other anticoagulants, administration of heparin can increase the hematoma and bleeding rate. It is commonly used as a vessel irrigant before anastomosis and systemically when postoperative thrombosis develops. If used systemically, on rare occasion some patients require short-term warfarin (Coumadin) treatment.

27. What is heterotopic replantation? Ectopic replantation?

In *heterotopic replantation,* an amputated part is replaced in an area different from where it originated. With multiple amputations, for instance, a crushed thumb may be replaced with a less injured digit, or a digit may be moved to an ulnar position to improve grip. With bilateral upper or lower extremity amputations, one limb might be replanted on the opposite side to maintain length or function.

In *ectopic replantation,* an amputated part is stored in a distant uninjured area to be retransplanted later when the recipient area and patient are stabilized. It is conceivable that a critical part could be stored in a surrogate host who is temporarily immunosuppressed while the injured victim is being treated and stabilized. Ectopic replantation is occasionally performed in major multiple trauma cases.

28. Should complete ring avulsions be replanted?

There have been some reports of poor results with complete avulsions of fingers due to rings. Usually the ring is caught on a ledge or hard object as the patient falls backward. A classification system for ring avulsion (Urbaniak) has been developed, but it has been modified and modified again and can be confusing. Even though some authors report poor results, if you can achieve nerve coaptation and sensation, ring avulsion replants can be some of the most rewarding and best results in replantation.

BIBLIOGRAPHY

Buncke, HJ (ed): Microsurgery: Transplantation-Replantation. An Atlas Text. Philadelphia, Lea & Febiger, 1991.
Colwell AS, Buntic RF, Brooks D, Wright L, Buncke GM, Buncke HJ: Detection of perfusion disturbances in digit replantation using near-infrared spectroscopy and serial quantitative fluoroscopy. J Hand Surg [Am] 31:456–462, 2006.
Davies DM: A world survey of anticoagulation practice in clinical microvascular surgery. Br J Plast Surg 35:96–99, 1982.
Partington MT, Lineaweaver WC, O'Hara M, et al: Unrecognized injuries in patients referred for emergency microsurgery. J Trauma 34:238–241, 1993.
Rothkopf DM, Chy B, Gonzalez F, et al: Radial and ulnar artery repairs: Assessing patency rates with color Doppler ultrasonographic imaging. J Hand Surg 18A:626–628, 1993.

THUMB RECONSTRUCTION

Raymond Tse, MD, FRCSC; Donald R. Laub, Jr., MS, MD, FACS; and
Vincent R. Hentz, MD

CHAPTER **131**

1. When was the first toe-to-thumb transfer performed for thumb reconstruction?
Chung-Wei and associates reported the first successful replantation involving a severed hand in 1963. The first thumb replantation was reported by Komatsu and Tamai of Japan in 1965. The first successful toe-to-thumb transfer in a monkey was performed by Buncke in 1965, and the first toe-to-thumb transfer in a human was reported by Cobbett in 1968.

2. What are the goals of thumb reconstruction?
- Functional reconstruction
  - Adequate length
  - Adequate motion
  - Appropriate position for opposition
  - Stability
  - Sensation
  - Freedom from pain
  - Durable cover
- Cosmetically acceptable thumb
- Minimal donor site morbidity

3. What is adequate thumb length for useful function?
The thumb is important for opposing fingers when grasping and pinching. When placed beside the index finger, the thumb should reach beyond the proximal third of the index proximal phalanx. Significant functional deficits occur when the thumb is shortened beyond the neck of its proximal phalanx.

4. What methods are available for thumb reconstruction?
The available surgical methods are osteoplastic reconstruction, finger pollicization (usually of the index finger), and microsurgical toe transfer. Prosthetic replacement is also a consideration.

5. In the era of microsurgery, why even consider prosthetics?
The patient may not be a surgical candidate. A prosthesis may lengthen and make useful a shortened digital stump. It also may give a more esthetic appearance to the hand. Even after successful reconstruction, patients may request an aesthetic prosthesis.

6. Is the child with a congenitally missing part an "amputee"?
No. It is a mistake to think of a child with congenital hand differences as an amputee. Children with congenital hand anomalies view themselves as normal, and the vast majority function well by using their own techniques. They are disabled only in comparison with others. To imagine what it would be like to have their deformity, we imagine an amputation.

7. Should you fit a prosthesis on a child?
If the child has a functional pinch, no. The prosthesis will be more of an encumbrance. Children with congenitally absent thumbs usually develop a pinch between the index and long finger.

8. How and why does the reconstructive approach differ in congenital and acquired thumb deficiencies?
Congenital thumb deficiencies result from a failure of formation of anatomic structures. As a result, the available recipient nerves, blood vessels, tendons, and muscles for tissue transfer are unpredictable and often unavailable. Therefore microsurgical toe transfer is not considered the most appropriate treatment.

Congenital thumb deficiencies requiring major reconstructive efforts involve the carpometacarpal (CMC) joint, whereas acquired deficiencies range from defects involving the distal phalanx to the base of the metacarpal.

Reconstruction of the congenitally deficient thumb requires consideration of the critical motor development that occurs within the first few years of life as well as future growth.

9. **What syndromes are associated with thumb hypoplasia, and what associated systemic disorders must be considered?**
   Holt-Oram syndrome is associated with cardiovascular malformations. Thrombocytopenia–absent radius (TAR) syndrome is associated with thrombocytopenia. Fanconi's anemia is associated with pancytopenia (surgery is contraindicated). VATER involves *v*ertebral defects, imperforate *a*nus, *t*racheo*e*sophageal fistula, and *r*adial and *r*enal dysplasia.

10. **What is the timing of reconstruction of the congenitally deficient thumb?**
    The main reason for early surgical reconstruction is to provide children with a functional hand and allow for cortical development during critical times. Grip and grasp functions develop between 4 and 7 months of age, thumb and index finger function develops at 1 year, and specific functional patterns develop at 2 to 3 years of age. Therefore surgeons have undertaken reconstruction as early as within 1 year of age. However, earlier surgery is made technically more difficult due to the small sizes of involved structures.

11. **How are congenital thumb deficiencies classified?**
    Blauth described five types of hypoplasia of the thumb (Table 131-1).

12. **What types of thumb deficiencies should be reconstructed?**
    Types II and IIIA are candidates for reconstruction. Types IIIB, IV, and V are best served by index finger pollicization.

13. **Why not a toe-to-thumb transfer?**
    Usually absence of a thumb is part of a more significant longitudinal deficiency with lack of recipient structures. Even in cases of hypoplasia, if the child has a functioning pinch between the index and middle fingers, existing function should be enhanced by pollicization rather than by toe transplantation.

14. **What techniques can be used for less severe hypoplasia of the thumb?**
    - Deepening of the first web space by transposition flaps
      - Four-flap Z-plasty is used for moderate gains
      - Dorsal rotation flap is used to provide a greater web space
    - Stabilization of the metacarpophalangeal (MCP) joint
      - Flexor digitorum superficialis (FDS) tendon can be wrapped around the MCP joint and inserted into the ulnar side of the joint if an FDS opponensplasty is used
      - Tendon graft reconstruction of the ulnar collateral ligament
      - Ulnar capsule reefing
    - Correction of extrinsic tendon abnormalities
      - Extensor indicis proprius or extensor digitorum communis for extension
      - FDS for flexion
    - Opponensplasty (thumb abduction and circumduction)
      - Ring finger FDS transfer
      - Abductor digiti minimi transfer (Huber technique)

Table 131-1. Classification of Hypoplasia of the Thumb	
Type I	Minimal shortening or narrowing
Type II	Narrow first web space Intrinsic thenar muscle hypoplasia Metacarpophalangeal joint instability
Type IIIA	All features of type II Extrinsic tendon abnormalities Metacarpal hypoplasia with *stable CMC joint*
Type IIIB	Same as type IIIA with *unstable CMC joint*
Type IV	As called pouce flottant (French for floating thumb) Rudimentary phalanges Thumb attached by skin bridge
Type V	Complete absence of thumb

CMC, Carpometacarpal.

15. How is the index finger pollicized?

The digit is shortened by removing almost the entire metacarpal, save the metacarpal head, which assumes the function of the trapezium. The finger is dissected as an island flap on the flexor and extensor tendons, the two neurovascular pedicles, and dorsal veins and nerves. The finger is pronated 140° to 160° and fixated into the correct axis of the thumb. Hyperextension of the index MCP joint is prevented by fixing the metacarpal head in palmar rotation.

16. Why is the metacarpal head palmarly rotated?

The MCP joint of the index finger is a condylar joint that can be hyperextended some 45°, whereas the CMC joint of the thumb is a saddle joint that circumducts but resists hyperextension. To allow the transposed index finger to generate the forceful pinch needed, it is fixed with the joint extended to full passive range. The palmar capsule and volar plate then resist further hyperextension.

17. Which muscles of the index finger assume the function of which muscles of the thumb?

See Table 131-2 and Fig. 131-1.

18. What are the options for reconstruction of the distal third of the thumb?

The distal third of the thumb involves everything distal to and including the interphalangeal (IP) joint. Local options for small defects include V-Y advancement flaps, a Moberg palmar advancement flap, and a cross-finger flap. Distant options for larger defects include groin, arm, and submammary flaps. Free tissue options include free toe pulp and composite tissue transfers (Fig. 131-2).

19. What are the options for reconstruction of the middle third of the thumb?

The middle third of the thumb involves the distal third of the metacarpal to the IP joint. Options for defects from midproximal phalanx and distal include first web space deepening ("phalangization") with a four-flap Z-plasty or a dorsal rotation flap. Options for defects proximal to the midproximal phalanx include a "cocked hat" flap, osteoplastic reconstruction (distant flap coverage of a bone graft to extend the length of the thumb), composite osteofasciocutaneous radial forearm flap, pollicization of an injured digit, and distraction osteogenesis. Toe-to-thumb transfer is an option in both proximal and distal portions of the middle third of the thumb.

Table 131-2. Index Finger Muscles that Assume the Function of Thumb Muscles

INDEX FINGER MUSCLE	THUMB MUSCLE
First dorsal interosseus	Abductor pollicis brevis
First palmar interosseus	Adductor pollicis
Extensor digitorum to the index	Abductor pollicis longus
Extensor indicis proprius	Extensor pollicis longus

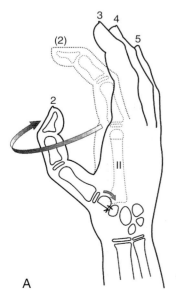
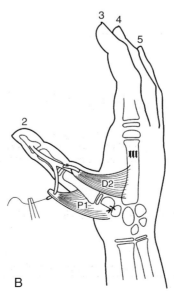

A   B

Figure 131-1. A, Pollicization of index finger, with shortening and pronation of the index ray and hyperextension of the metacarpophalangeal joint. **B,** Index interosseus muscles are used to supply function of thenar muscles.

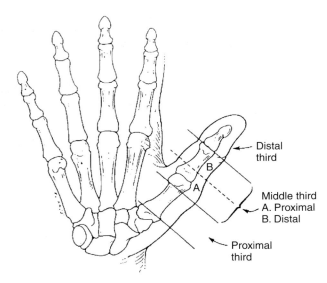

Figure 131-2. Classification of thumb amputations based on dividing the thumb into thirds. (From Strickland JW, Kleinman WB: Thumb reconstruction. In Green DP [ed]: Operative Hand Surgery, 3rd ed. 1993, p 2073.)

20. What are the options for reconstruction of the proximal third of the thumb?
The proximal third of the thumb involves amputations proximal to the distal third of the metacarpal. If adequate metacarpal base remains, a second toe transfer can be used to reconstruct the metacarpal and phalanges. If the metacarpal base is absent or inadequate, a pollicization with either an injured or uninjured digit can be used. In this case the index MCP joint is used to reconstruct the CMC joint.

21. What is osteoplastic reconstruction?
It is a multistage reconstructive technique that uses bone grafting or lengthening osteotomies, covered with skin flaps, on the remaining thumb stump to add length and to provide opposition. No joints are reconstructed. Sensation can be provided in the form of a neurovascular island flap, transferred from a finger (the usual donor is the ulnar side of the middle or ring). Most experts believe that microvascular toe transfer provides a better reconstruction with more similar tissue and joints for partial amputation of the thumb.

22. Does loss of the first toe cause gait disturbance?
Gait studies show shifting of weight distribution away from the first metatarsal head, but if the metatarsal head is preserved, the disturbance in gait is minimal.

23. What is the vascular pedicle of the transferred first toe?
The first dorsal intermetatarsal artery, which arises in most cases from the dorsalis pedis artery but occasionally from the deep planter system. The origin may be determined at the time of operation. If the deep system is dominant, a reversed vein graft extension may be needed. The more important question concerns the recipient blood vessels in the hand. In patients with any degree of injury to the hand, an arteriogram should be obtained to determine the residual vascular anatomy.

24. Can parts of toes be used?
Yes. Neurovascular island flaps can be used to provide innervated pulp to the oppositional surfaces. This technique is especially useful in the multiply traumatized hand, to which traditional neurovascular island flap techniques would add further debility. Transfer of vascularized joints from the foot to the thumb in severe isolated joint trauma has been reported.

25. Describe the different options for toe-to-thumb transfer.
Great toe transfer can be used for amputations distal to the metacarpal and provides a strong reconstruction. It is based on the first dorsal metatarsal artery (from the dorsalis pedis) and the deep plantar artery. The great toe plays a major role in normal gait. Donor site morbidity and gait disturbance are major disadvantages. The cosmetic results can be inferior to other options due to the size and bulk of the great toe.

The *trimmed toe flap* involves trimming the great toe to the dimensions of a normal thumb improving cosmesis, but this makes the operation technically more difficult.

The *wraparound flap* involves transferring only the soft tissues of the great toe in combination with a bone graft. The great toe is preserved and the donor site is skin grafted to prevent gait disturbances. The advantages include better cosmesis and prevention of donor site morbidity; however, the operation is considerably more complex.

The *second toe transfer* uses a toe other than the great toe, thereby minimizing donor site morbidity and gait disturbance. The head of the metatarsal may also be harvested to provide an additional joint and length if necessary. The second toe transfer is also based on the first dorsal metatarsal artery. Disadvantages include a small appearance and a potential mallet deformity of the IP joint.

26. When is pollicization preferable to toe transfer for reconstruction of a traumatically amputated thumb? What are the advantages and disadvantages compared with a toe-to-thumb transfer?
When the metacarpal is completely absent a pollicization is required because there is no way to reconstruct an adequate basilar joint with a toe. Compared with a toe-to-thumb transfer, a pollicization provides better sensation and finer motor control. A toe-to-thumb transfer provides a better cosmetic result and greater strength.

27. Summarize the surgical options for thumb reconstruction.
- Surgical Options for Congenital Thumb Deficiency
  - Blauth I–IIIA: First web space deepening
  - Blauth IIIB–V: Pollicization
- Surgical Options for Acquired Thumb Deficiency
  - Distal third: Local flap closure or composite tissue transfer
  - Middle third: Osteoplastic reconstruction or toe-to-thumb transfer
  - Proximal third: Toe-to-thumb transfer of pollicization
- Surgical Options for Toe-to-Thumb Transfer
  - Great toe
  - Trimmed toe
  - Wraparound
  - Second toe

CONTROVERSY

28. Which toe is preferred for thumb reconstruction?
- *The great toe.* In the United States, generally the great toe is preferred because it provides a stronger and more stable thumb for a pincer grip. The great toe is more like the thumb in appearance, although it is a bit broader. The transplanted toe atrophies and thins after time, and usually the difference is apparent only in side-by-side comparison.
- *The second toe.* In Asian cultures in which Zori-type sandals are worn, the loss of a first web space in the foot is a disability; therefore the second toe is preferred. Women who wear open-toe footwear also may find loss of the great toe disturbing. In addition, the second toe can provide greater metatarsal length for transfer, so in cases where less than one third of the first metacarpal remains, the second toe is preferred.

BIBLIOGRAPHY

Buck-Grancko D: Pollicization. In Blair WF: Techniques in Hand Surgery. Baltimore, Williams & Wilkins, 1996.
Buncke HJ: Great toe transplantation and digital reconstruction by second-toe transplantation. In Buncke HJ: Microsurgery: Transplantation-Replantation. Philadelphia, Lea & Febiger, 1991.
Pillet J, Mackin EJ: Aesthetic hand prosthesis: Its psychological and functional potential. In Hunter IM, Schneider LH, Mackin EJ, Callahan AD (eds): Rehabilitation of the Hand, 3rd ed. St. Louis, Mosby, 1990.
Wei FC, el-Gammal TA: Toe-to-hand transfer. Current concepts, techniques and research. Clin Plast Surg 23:103–116, 1996.

THE MUTILATED HAND

Jeffrey Weinzweig, MD, FACS, and
Norman Weinzweig, MD, FACS

1. What is a mutilated hand?

A mutilated hand results from a complex injury with composite tissue loss and significant functional compromise (usually impaired prehension) and often requires bone, soft tissue, and microneurovascular reconstruction. Without surgical intervention, a mutilated hand remains virtually functionless. Even with surgical intervention, the hand usually functions in an assist fashion. In addition to the loss of function, patients often complain of intractable pain and psychological stress.

2. What is prehension?

The functional hand possesses prehension—the ability to oppose the fingers to grip or grasp. According to Tubiana, "prehension is a complex function of the hand that gives it mechanical precision combined with a standard sensory pattern."

3. What are the main objectives in the treatment of a mutilated hand?

The main goals in management of a mutilated hand are restoration of form and function. Ideally, the injured parts are restored to their pretraumatic state. Although replantation of sharply severed parts may approach the ideal from an aesthetic point of view, function rarely can be restored to the preinjury level.

4. Outline a treatment plan for the management of mutilating injuries of the hand.

1. Initial assessment must include the following:
   - Accurate history, including age, handedness, occupation, avocations, mechanism of injury, time of injury, general health
   - Physical examination, including evaluation of perfusion, motor and sensory function, contamination, severity of tissue damage, and other life-threatening injuries
   - Radiographs of the hand and any amputated part
   - Angiography, when indicated.
2. Tetanus prophylaxis
3. Broad-spectrum intravenous antibiotics
4. High-pressure jet lavage and aggressive débridement of devitalized tissues (except in electrical burns)
5. Reduction and immobilization of fractures and dislocations
6. Revascularization of ischemic tissues
7. Immediate or delayed reconstruction of nerve, tendon, bone, and soft tissue
8. Early wound closure by skin grafts and/or flaps
9. Secondary procedures such as pollicization and toe-to-thumb transfer
10. Postreconstruction physical rehabilitation (uninjured or minimally injured structures must be appropriately splinted or undergo occupational therapy to prevent stiffness or instability, especially when other parts of the hand are absent or functionless)

5. How are mutilating injuries of the hand classified?

Because mutilated hands assume a myriad of forms, they should be precisely described. The goals of a classification system should be (1) accurate description of any mutilating injury, (2) user-friendliness, (3) progression of injury complexity, and (4) facilitation of communication between clinicians. Furthermore, a classification system should ideally (5) direct treatment, (6) predict functional outcome, and (7) allow derivation of a staging system based on functional outcome. This system should allow the examining surgeon to describe accurately and reproducibly any mutilating injury of the hand.

Several classifications of mutilating hand injuries have been reported in the literature; unfortunately, injuries are grouped arbitrarily according to the part of the hand predominantly involved. The Reid classification groups mutilating injuries into six categories: dorsal injuries, palmar injuries, radial hemiamputations, ulnar hemiamputations, distal amputations, and degloving injuries. The modified Pulvertaft classification groups mutilating injuries into five categories: radial, ulnar, central, transverse, and other. The Wei classification groups mutilating injuries into two categories: type I (all fingers are amputated proximal to the proximal interphalangeal joint but the thumb is intact) and type II (at least three fingers are

Box 132-1. Tic-Tac-Toe Classification System

Injury Types
  I.   Dorsal mutilation
  II. Palmar mutilation
  III. Ulnar mutilation
  IV. Radial mutilation
  V.   Transverse amputation
  VI. Degloving injury
  VII. Combined injury

Injury Subtypes
  A. Soft tissue loss
  B. Bony loss
  C. Combined tissue loss

Vascular Status (Subscript)
  0. Vascularity intact
  1. Devascularization

amputated proximal to the proximal interphalangeal joint, and the thumb is amputated proximal to the interphalangeal joint so that opposition is impossible).

6. **What is the "tic-tac-toe" classification system for mutilating injuries of the hand?**
A devascularized hand with radial hemiamputation and ulnar degloving cannot be accurately described by any of the classifications discussed in Question 5. Because a mutilated hand may have sustained several different types of complex injuries, a comprehensive classification must incorporate the degree and precise location of soft tissue and/or bony destruction and vascular integrity, in addition to the predominantly involved part of the hand. Weinzweig and Weinzweig have devised a classification system for mutilating injuries of the hand that categorizes them into seven types and three subtypes, with subscript notation indicating vascular status (Box 132-1).

The hand is then systematically divided into nine numerical zones in tic-tac-toe fashion with radial, central, and ulnar columns and proximal, central, and distal rows. The "tic-tac-toe" classification system allows the examining surgeon to describe precisely any mutilating injury of the hand. It permits accurate assessment of each hand injury by assignment of the appropriate classification type, subtype, vascular status, and zone involvement in a user-friendly and practical fashion (Figs. 132-1 and 132-2).

7. **What are dorsal mutilation injuries (type I)?**
Dorsal mutilation injuries involve the dorsal skin, extensor tendons, and bones. The tactile surface (palmar skin) of the hand is preserved. Vascularization is intact. Type I injuries are usually the least severe of the mutilating injuries but often require soft tissue coverage of the dorsum of the hand and immediate or staged extensor tendon repairs and/or reconstructions. The most common mechanism is crush–avulsion, in which the loose, mobile dorsal soft tissue is avulsed along with the extensor tendons. Occasionally, bony injury is associated with a crush component. In both cases, volar tissues such as the flexor tendons, neurovascular structures, and tactile soft tissue are preserved, thus minimizing functional losses. Functional outcome is relatively favorable and directly related to the extent of bony injury and the need for prolonged immobilization (Box 132-2).

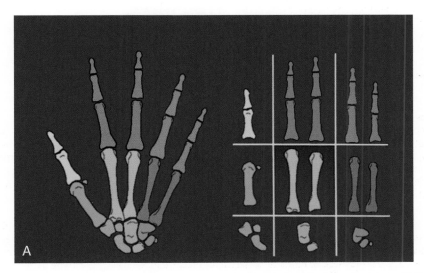

Figure 132-1. "Tic-tac-toe" classification zones. **(A** from Weinzweig J, Weinzweig N. Classification systems for multilating injuries. In: Weinzweig N, Weinzweig J [eds]: The Mutilated Hand. Philadelphia, Mosby, 2005, p 32;

COLUMNS

		RADIAL	CENTRAL	ULNAR
R O W S	D I S T A L	Zone 1	Zone 2	Zone 3
	C E N T R A L	Zone 4	Zone 5	Zone 6
	P R O X	Zone 7	Zone 8	Zone 9

B

Figure 132-1—cont'd, B from Weinzweig J, Weinzweig N: The "Tic-Tac-Toe" classification system for mutilating injuries of the hand. Plast Reconstr Surg 100:1200–1211, 1997, p 1210, with permission.)

Box 132-2. Clinical Case: Dorsal Mutilation: Type I A_0, Zones 4 to 9 (Proximal and Central Rows)

A 41-year-old woman sustained a severe crush–avulsion injury to the dorsum of the left hand when her car overturned. There was significant dorsal soft tissue loss, avulsion of the extensor digitorum communis tendons, shear and loss of the dorsal metacarpal cortices, and exposed carpus (Fig. 132-2).

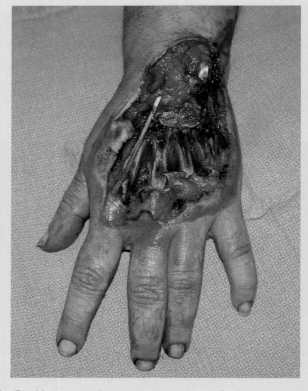

Figure 132-2. Dorsal mutilation. Type I A_0, zones 4 to 9 (proximal and central rows). (From Weinzweig J, Weinzweig N. Classification systems for mutilating injuries. In: Weinzweig N, Weinzweig J [eds]: The Mutilated Hand. Philadelphia, Mosby, 2005, p 33.)

Box 132-3. Clinical Case: Palmar Mutilation: Type II A_0, Zones 1 to 9 (Distal, Central, and Proximal Rows)

A 38-year-old man sustained a devastating volar soft tissue injury to his right hand when it was caught in an industrial slicing machine. Injury to multiple tendons, articular surfaces, and common and proper digital nerves occurred. Despite the extensiveness of this palmar injury, neither devascularization nor fracture accompanied the soft tissue injury (Fig. 132-3).

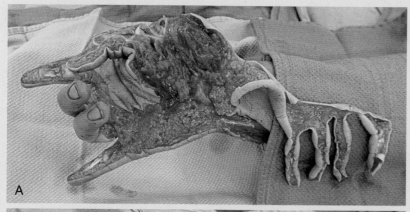

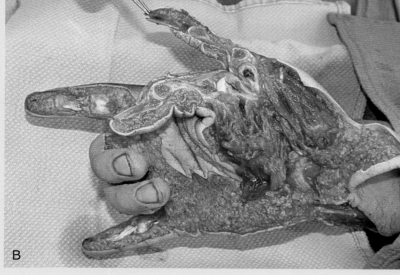

Figure 132-3. Palmar mutilation. Type II A_0, zones 1 to 9 (proximal, central, and distal rows). (From Weinzweig J, Weinzweig N. Classification systems for mutilating injuries. In: Weinzweig N, Weinzweig J [eds]: The Mutilated Hand. Philadelphia, Mosby, 2005, p 34.)

8. What are palmar mutilation injuries (type II)?

Palmar mutilation injuries involve the palmar skin (tactile surface), flexor tendons, and bones. They often involve the radial and ulnar arteries, deep and superficial palmar arches, and common and proper digital arteries with possible devascularization of one or more fingers. The median and ulnar nerves and common and proper digital nerves also may be involved. Type II injuries are generally more severe and complex than dorsal injuries. They disrupt the tactile surface of the hand, often necessitating resurfacing with regional or distant flaps. In addition, they may require open or closed reduction internal fixation of fractures and/or flexor tendon repair with or without staged reconstruction. Neurovascular compromise to one or more fingers is occasionally seen (Box 132-3).

9. What are ulnar mutilation injuries (type III)?

Ulnar mutilation injuries involve loss of the ulnar digits, destruction of the ulnar column (phalanges, metacarpals, and/or carpus), and interference with grasp or power grip mechanisms. Type III injuries involve bone, tendon, soft tissue, and neurovascular structures along the ulnar aspect of the hand, resulting in significant functional disability due to interference with grip mechanisms. An objective of reconstructive surgery is to maintain the breadth of the hand (Box 132-4).

Box 132-4. Clinical Case: Ulnar Mutilation: Type III C_0, Zones 5 and 6 (Central Row)

A 35-year-old man sustained a shotgun injury resulting in a through-and-through soft tissue and bony defect of the ulnar aspect of his hand. There was destruction of the ring and little finger metacarpals and a midshaft metacarpal fracture of the middle finger (Fig. 132-4).

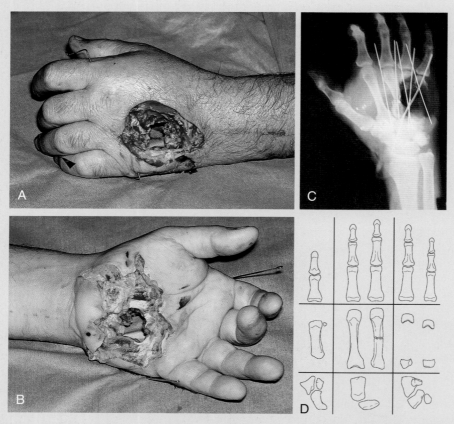

Figure 132-4. Ulnar mutilation. Type III C_0, zones 5 and 6 (central row). (From Weinzweig J, Weinzweig N. Classification systems for mutilating injuries. In: Weinzweig N, Weinzweig J [eds]: The Mutilated Hand. Philadelphia, Mosby, 2005, p 35.)

10. What are radial mutilation injuries (type IV)?

Radial mutilation injuries involve loss of the thumb, destruction of the radial column, and loss of opposition or pinch mechanisms. Type IV injuries are serious and may involve total or subtotal loss of the thumb and thenar musculature. Without restoration, they result in severe disability with loss of 50% or more of total hand function. Damage to the remainder of the hand plays a role in the choice of reconstructive options, such as pollicization of the index finger or remnants of other injured fingers, osteoplasty, or toe-to-thumb transfer. When replantation or revascularization is successful, functional results are generally good, depending on the status of the remainder of the hand (Box 132-5).

11. What are transverse amputations (type V)?

Transverse amputations result in loss of the hand or digits at different levels with corresponding functional losses. Restoration of functional pinch depends on the level of loss. Amputations distal to the metacarpophalangeal (MCP) joint level may result in a phalangeal hand (Fig. 132-7), whereas amputations proximal to the MCP joint level may result in a metacarpal hand (see Question 13). Complete hand amputation also may occur. Type V transmetacarpal injuries occur at or proximal to the MCP joint of the fingers and involve at least three fingers, with possible involvement of the thumb. They often result in significant functional losses, depending on the success of replantation or revascularization of the amputated part(s), including the fingers as a metacarpal unit and possibly the thumb (Box 132-6). Involvement of the thumb adds the component of radial mutilation to the equation, making this a combined injury (type VII, see Question 10).

Box 132-5. Clinical Case: Radial Mutilation: Type IV C$_{1(thumb)}$, Zone 1

A 22-year-old man sustained an avulsion injury of his right thumb distal to the interphalangeal joint when his hand was caught in an auger. His entire flexor pollicis longus tendon was avulsed from its muscular origin (Fig. 132-5).

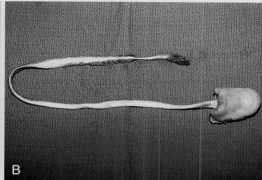

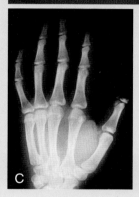

Figure 132-5. Radial mutilation. Type IV C$_{1(thumb)}$, zone 1. (From Weinzweig J, Weinzweig N. Classification systems for mutilating injuries. In: Weinzweig N, Weinzweig J [eds]: The Mutilated Hand. Philadelphia, Mosby, 2005, p 37.)

Box 132-6. Clinical Case: Transverse Amputation: Type V C$_{1(I,M,R,S)}$, Zones 2 and 3 (Distal Row)

A 28-year-old man sustained a table saw injury to his left hand resulting in amputation of the four fingers just distal to the proximal interphalangeal joints, sparing the thumb (Fig. 132-6).

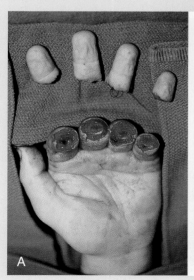

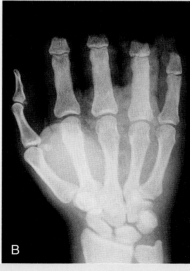

Figure 132-6. Transverse amputation. Type V C$_{1(I,M,R,S)}$, zones 2 and 3 (distal row). (From Weinzweig J, Weinzweig N. Classification systems for multilating injuries. In: Weinzweig N, Weinzweig J [eds]: The Mutilated Hand. Philadelphia, Mosby, 2005, p 38.)

Continued

Box 132-6. Clinical case: Transverse Amputation: Type V C$_{1(I,M,R,S)}$, Zones 2 and 3 (Distal Row)—cont'd

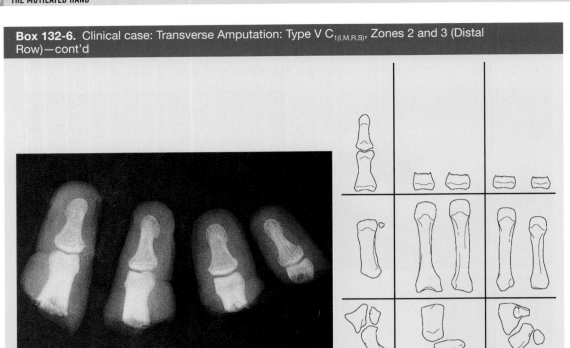

C   D

Figure 132-6—cont'd.

Box 132-7. Clinical Case: Transverse Amputation: Type V C$_1$, Zones 1 to 9

A 42-year-old psychotic man sustained a self-inflicted hack saw injury to his left hand resulting in complete amputation through the carpus. Note the *hesitation cut* across the dorsal wrist just distal to the level of amputation, indicating his initial attempt and hesitation before completing the intended self-inflicted injury (Fig. 132-7).

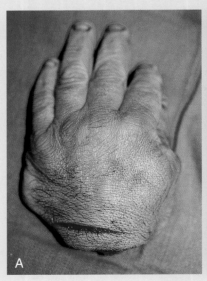

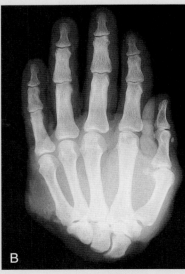

A   B

Figure 132-7. Transverse amputation. Type V C$_1$, zones 1 to 9. (From Weinzweig J, Weinzweig N. Classification systems for mutilating injuries. In: Weinzweig N, Weinzweig J [eds]: The Mutilated Hand. Philadelphia, Mosby, 2005, p 40.)

Successful replantation and revascularization at the transmetacarpal level generally result in fair-to-poor functional results, even with guillotine-type amputations. The main reason is probably ischemic insult to the interosseous and lumbrical muscles as a result of direct muscle injury or interruption of the delicate blood supply to these tiny muscles. The zone of injury is often extensive, with destruction of the intrinsic muscles, flexor and extensor tendons, MCP joints, and neurovascular structures. Multiple reconstructive procedures are required in staged fashion. Bilateral mutilations present a special circumstance with respect to functional outcome.

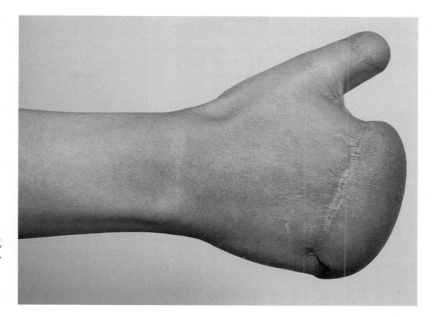

Figure 132-8. Type I metacarpal hand. (From Jain V, Wei F-C. The metacarpal hand. In: Weinzweig N, Weinzweig J [eds]: The Mutilated Hand. Philadelphia, Mosby, 2005, p 280.)

Complete hand replantations have a better prognosis than transmetacarpal replantations. The flexor tendons are injured in zone 5, and the intrinsic muscles of the hand are spared (Box 132-6, 132-7).

12. What is a phalangeal hand?

A phalangeal hand is one in which multiple fingers have been amputated at, or distal to, the middle of the proximal phalanx, with or without involvement of the thumb at, or distal to, the interphalangeal joint. Although some basic functional capacity of the hand is preserved, significant functional, aesthetic, and psychological deficits must be addressed (see Fig. 132-6).

13. What is a metacarpal hand?

A metacarpal hand is one that has lost its prehensile ability due to amputation of all fingers with or without amputation of the thumb. Functional restoration can be achieved by various microvascular toe transfer techniques. The choice of procedure depends on the level of amputation of the fingers and the functional status of the thumb. Based on their extensive experience with metacarpal hands reconstructed with toe-to-hand transfers, Wei et al. described a classification system that served as a guide to their treatment philosophy. They identified two major types of metacarpal hand based on whether the thumb is injured. The type I metacarpal hand is one in which all four fingers have been amputated proximal to the middle of the proximal phalanx with either an intact thumb or a thumb amputated distal to the interphalangeal joint. The type II metacarpal hand is one in which all four fingers have been amputated proximal to the middle of the proximal phalanx and the thumb has been amputated proximal to the interphalangeal joint (Fig. 132-8).

14. What is the Krukenberg procedure?

Originally described by Krukenberg in 1917, this operation was mainly used in Germany during World War I. The forearm is fashioned into an active pincer with the arms covered by innervated sensate soft tissue. It is indicated in cases of congenital or traumatic amputations of the hand. In unilateral amputations, a prosthesis is preferred except in patients whose occupation demands sensibility of both upper limbs. However, when both hands have been amputated, the Krukenberg operation is cited as the best approach, performed either bilaterally or unilaterally with a prosthesis on the other side. It helps bilateral amputees to regain total independence. A sensate pincer is especially necessary in blind patients. This operation is particularly indicated when both hands and both eyes have been damaged.

15. What are degloving injuries (type VI)?

Degloving injuries involve circumferential loss of innervated skin and tactile surface(s) of the hand. They are often associated with nerve, vessel, or tendon avulsion. Degloving injuries are serious injuries usually caused by avulsion of soft tissue by a roller-type mechanism. No local innervated skin is available to resurface important tactile areas of the hand. Soft tissue coverage occasionally can be achieved by harvesting a skin graft from the degloved part. Often, a groin flap or emergency free flap is required. Reconstruction is especially difficult for simultaneous provision of skin on both aspects of the hand (Box 132-8).

Box 132-8. Clinical Case: Degloving Injury: Type VI A$_1$, Zones 3 and 6 (Ulnar Column)

A 45-year-old man sustained a roller press injury to his left hand with complete degloving of the ring and little fingers and avulsion of the distal pulp and nail of the thumb. Note the avulsed neurovascular bundle to the little finger (Fig. 132-9).

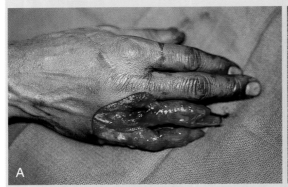
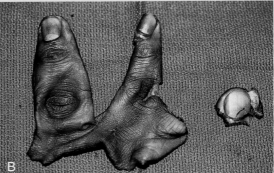
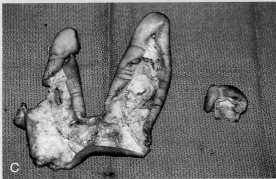

Figure 132-9. Degloving injury. Type VI A$_1$, zones 3 and 6 (ulnar column). (From Weinzweig J, Weinzweig N. Classification systems for mutilating injuries. In: Weinzweig N, Weinzweig J [eds]: The Mutilated Hand. Philadelphia, Mosby, 2005, p 41.)

Box 132-9. Clinical Case: Combination Injury: Type VII C$_{1(I,M,R,S)}$, Zones 5 to 9 (Proximal and Central Rows)

A 21-year-old man sustained a punch press injury to his left hand resulting in devascularization of the four fingers, destruction of the ulnar metacarpals and carpal bones, and palmar soft tissue loss (Fig. 132-10).

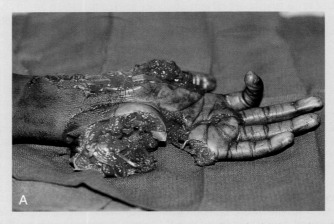

Figure 132-10. Combination injury (punch press). Type VII C$_{1(I,M,R,S)}$, zones 5 to 9 (proximal and central rows). (From Weinzweig J, Weinzweig N. Classification systems for mutilating injuries. In: Weinzweig N, Weinzweig J [eds]: The Mutilated Hand. Philadelphia, Mosby, 2005, p 42.)

Box 132-9. Clinical Case: Combination Injury: Type VII $C_{1(I,M,R,S)}$, Zones 5 to 9 (Proximal and Central Rows)—cont'd

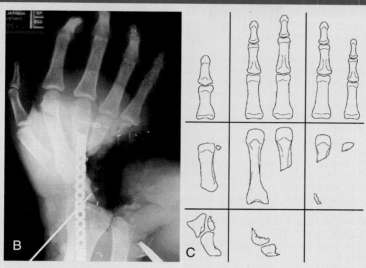

Figure 132-10—cont'd.

16. What are combination injuries (type VII)?

Type VII injuries usually involve a combination of types I through VI as well as other injuries that do not fit the more rigid definitions of injury types. Type VII injuries usually are the most severe, often caused by extreme forces such as punch presses and thermal or electrical burns (Box 132-9).

17. What is an emergency free flap?

Based on Godina's work with early microsurgical reconstruction of complex trauma to the limb, Lister and Scheker defined the emergency free flap as one performed after primary débridement or within 24 hours of surgery and reported a success rate of 93.5% (29/31 flaps). Ninkovic et al. reported their experience with 29 patients who underwent 27 emergency free flaps and three emergency toe-to-hand transfers without flap failure, infections, or wound-healing complications. Long-term follow-up demonstrates successful functional and aesthetic results with reduced rates of free flap failure, postoperative infection, and secondary operative procedures as well as reduced hospital stay and medical costs.

18. What is spare parts surgery?

Amputated parts that are not suitable for replantation can be salvaged for use as possible donors, such as pliable dorsal skin for coverage, nail bed for split- or full-thickness nail bed grafts, tendons for interpolated grafts, pulley reconstruction, or soft tissue arthroplasty, nerve grafts from nonreplantable digits, or bone grafts to bridge bony defects. Mutilating injuries usually demonstrate devastating involvement of bone and soft tissue structures. You must carefully examine the remaining extremity and amputated parts in an attempt to maximize function. Every amputated part should be considered a possible spare part before it is discarded.

19. What is ectopic parts surgery?

Ectopic parts surgery involves transfer of an amputated part to a different location where it may serve a more useful function. Short stumps of fingers (index, middle, or ring) with little function often can be pollicized to provide a useful and sensate thumb reconstruction. In addition, an amputated part can be banked ectopically in a more favorable location until the site from which it came is ready for anatomic replantation.

20. When is amputation indicated?

Realistic assessment of potential function may indicate that the revascularized part will be insensate, painful, immobile, or nonfunctional with possible decreased function of the adjacent normal digits. Amputation is not failure; instead, it often serves a patient better than multiple complex operations that restore little function.

21. What is the role of prostheses in the management of the mutilated hand?

Cable-operated or myeloelectric prostheses help to restore useful function to an otherwise functionless hand.

BIBLIOGRAPHY

Adani R, Castagnetti C, Landi A: Degloving injuries of the hand and fingers. Clin Orthop Rel Res 314:19–25, 1995.

Brown HC, Williams HB, Woodhouse FM: Principles of salvage in mutilating hand injuries. J Trauma 8:319–332, 1968.

Godina M: Early microsurgical reconstruction of complex trauma of the extremities. Plast Reconstr Surg 78:285–292, 1986.

Harris GD, Nagle DJ, Bell JL: Mutilating injuries. In Jupiter JB (ed): Flynn's Hand Surgery. Baltimore, Williams & Wilkins, 1991, pp 103–114.

Joshi BB: Sensory flaps for the degloved mutilated hand. Hand 6:247–254, 1974.

Kleinman WB, Dustman JA: Preservation of function following complete degloving injuries to the hand: Use of simultaneous groin flap, random abdominal flap, and partial-thickness skin graft. J Hand Surg 6A:82–89, 1981.

Lister G, Scheker L: Emergency free flaps to the upper extremity. J Hand Surg 13A:22–28, 1988.

Midgler RD, Entin MA: Management of mutilating injuries of the hand. Clin Plast Surg 3:99–109, 1976.

Nicolle FV, Woodhouse FM: Restoration of sensory function in severe degloving injuries of the hand. J Bone Joint Surg 48A:1511–1518, 1966.

Ninkovic M, Deetjen H, Ohler K, Anderl H: Emergency free tissue transfer for severe upper extremity injuries. J Hand Surg 20B:53–58, 1995.

Pribaz JJ, Pelham FR: Upper extremity reconstruction using spare parts. Prob Plast Reconstr Surg 3:373–390, 1993.

Reid DAC, Tubiana R: Mutilating Injuries of the Hand. Edinburgh, Churchill Livingstone, 1984.

Scheker LR: Salvage of a mutilated hand. In Cohen M (ed): Mastery of Plastic Surgery. Boston, Little, Brown, 1994, pp 1658–1681.

Sundine M, Scheker LR: A comparison of immediate and staged reconstruction of the dorsum of the hand. J Hand Surg 21B:216–221, 1996.

Tsai T-M, Jupiter JB, Wolff TW, Atasoy E: Reconstruction of severe transmetacarpal mutilating hand injuries by combined second and third toe transfer. J Hand Surg 6:319–328, 1981.

Tubiana R: Prehension in the Mutilated Hand. In Reid DAC and Tubiana R (eds): Mutilating Injuries of the Hand. Edinburgh, Churchill Livingstone, 1984, p 61.

Tubiana R, Stack HG, Hakstian RW: Restoration of prehension after severe mutilations of the hand. J Bone Joint Surg 48B:455–473, 1966.

Tubiana R: Reconstruction after traumatic mutilations of the hand. Injury 2:127–142, 1970.

Wei F-C, El-Gammal TA, Lin C-H, et al: Metacarpal hand: Classification and guidelines for microsurgical reconstruction with toe transfers. Plast Reconstr Surg 99:122–128, 1997.

Weinzweig N, Chen L, Chen Z-W: Pollicization in the severely injured hand by transposition of middle and ring finger remnants. Ann Plast Surg 34:523–529, 1995.

Weinzweig N, Sharzer L, Starker I: Replantation and revascularization at the transmetacarpal level: Long-term functional results. J Hand Surg [Am] 21:877–883, 1996.

Weinzweig N, Starker I, Sharzer LA, Fleegler EJ: Vascular supply to the lumbrical and interosseous muscles. Plast Reconstr Surg 99:785–790, 1997.

Weinzweig J, Weinzweig N: The "Tic-Tac-Toe" classification system for mutilating injuries of the hand. Plast Reconstr Surg 100:1200–1211, 1997.

Weinzweig J, Weinzweig N (eds): The Mutilated Hand. Philadelphia, Elsevier, 2005.

VASCULAR DISORDERS OF THE UPPER EXTREMITY

Nada Berry, MD, and
Michael W. Neumeister, MD, FACS, FRCS

CHAPTER 133

1. What is Raynaud's phenomenon? What is the difference between Raynaud's disease and Raynaud's phenomenon?

Raynaud's phenomenon is a vasospastic state characterized by intermittent acral color change during exposure to cold or stress. Sympathetic hyperactivity stimulates an intense arterial vasospasm leading to hypoperfusion of the digits and associated pain, triphasic color change (white, blue, red), and possible fingertip ulceration.

Raynaud's disease is a clinical entity caused by vasospasm and autonomic dysfunction without a secondary cause, such as collagen vascular disease, vaso-occlusive disease, or history of trauma.

Patients with primary vasospasm are predominantly female, experience symptoms at a younger age, have normal results of laboratory tests and angiography, normal Allen's test, rarely have ulcerations or gangrene, and are more likely to respond favorably to nonoperative treatment.

Unlike Raynaud's disease, Raynaud's phenomenon is a symptom of a preexisting disorder.

2. What is the Wake Forest classification of occlusive/vasospastic disease?

Group I and IIA patients respond well to nonoperative treatment, including smoking cessation, avoidance of cold environments, limitation of precipitating activities, and pharmacologic management (calcium channel blockers, selective serotonin reuptake inhibitors, and tricyclic antidepressants). Those with inadequate circulation may require operative treatment. Group IV patients seldom benefit from vascular or sympathetic nerve manipulation (Table 133-1).

3. What are the surgical options for treatment of Raynaud's disease? How can you preoperatively evaluate response to a sympathectomy?

Alteration of sympathetic tone and arterial reconstruction are the two main surgical approaches to vasospastic disease. Proximal (cervicothoracic) sympathectomy provides good short-term results. However, the symptoms may return or even become more severe after 6 to 12 weeks. Reversible phenol injection under computed tomographic guidance, rather than ablative sympathectomy, can provide relief of symptoms. Peripheral sympathectomy can be performed by excising the segment of the thrombosed vessel along with the periarterial sympathetic nerves and allowing maturation of collaterals *(Leriche sympathectomy). Palmar sympathectomy* involves dividing the sympathetic fibers surrounding the radial, ulnar, deep, and superficial arches and the common digital arteries through volar wrist and palmar incisions. *Digital sympathectomy* is performed through the Brunner incision extending from the distal palmar crease to midproximal phalanx. The neuronal fibers between the digital nerve and digital artery are transected. Peripheral sympathectomy requires meticulous stripping of the arterial adventitial under microscopic visualization.

Table 133-1. Wake Forrest Classification

GROUP	DISORDER	ETIOLOGY
I	Raynaud's disease	Idiopathic

II
IIA
IIB
	Raynaud's phenomenon
	    Adequate circulation
	    Inadequate circulation
		Collagen vascular disease

III
IIIA
IIIB
	Secondary vasospasm/occlusive disease
	    Adequate collateral circulation
	    Inadequate collateral circulation
		Vascular injury/occlusion/embolus

IV	Secondary vasospasm	Nonvascular (nerve, bone, soft tissue) injury

Data from Troum SJ, Smith TL, Koman LA, Ruch DS: Management of vasospastic disorders of the hand. Clin Plast Surg 24:121–133, 1997.

Improvement in symptoms, increase in digit temperature, and decrease in peripheral vascular resistance after injection of lidocaine via a digital or wrist block is often a valuable prediction of a good response to sympathectomy.

4. What is Buerger's disease?

Buerger's disease, or thromboangiitis obliterans (TAO), is an inflammatory occlusive disease of small- and medium-size vessels, predominantly seen in younger male smokers. The thrombotic disease with neutrophil infiltration and microabscess formation is found in the distal vessels and may involve the surrounding vein and nerve. Vascular insufficiency can lead to significant ischemic pain and eventual gangrene. Smoking cessation decreases disease progression and need for amputation.

5. What is the difference between a true and a false aneurysm?

A *true aneurysm* is a uniform dilation of the vessel that contains all but attenuated layers of the vessel wall (intima, media, adventitia). It is the result of chronic disease and turbulent flow and presents as a nontender pulsatile mass. A *false aneurysm*, or a *pseudoaneurysm,* usually is the result of a penetrating trauma leading to a hematoma that fibroses and recanalizes. Hence, a pseudoaneurysm does not contain the endothelial lining. Common complications of aneurysms of the upper extremity include thrombosis, embolic events, and compression of surrounding tissues. The treatment of either a true or a false aneurysm is the same: excision and ligation of proximal and distal ends, or arterial reconstruction in the case of a crucial blood supply. Arteries can be reconstructed with an end-end anastomosis, patching the vessel, or using a reversed vein interposition or bypass graft.

6. What is "steal phenomenon"?

Arteriovenous fistulas are created after trauma or infection, or iatrogenically during hemodialysis access. Diversion of blood flow from the distal arteries to the vein can lead to ischemic and neurologic sequelae, called *steal phenomenon.* In the radiocephalic fistula, the circulation is diverted from the radial artery and occasionally retrograde from the palmar arch and the ulnar artery. To increase the fistular resistance and decrease the steal, the lumen must be drastically reduced (Poiseuille's law: Resistance is inversely proportional to the radius to the fourth power). If the steal involves retrograde flow from the palmar arch, ligation of the radial artery distal to the anastomotic site may improve the symptoms. Occasionally, a bypassing graft or complete ligation of the fistula is required.

7. What is the treatment of an embolic event of the upper extremity?

Arterial emboli usually originate in the heart, subclavian artery, or palmar arch. The larger emboli, which occlude the brachial artery, are formed in the heart. Smaller thrombi usually are formed in the wrist and affect the digital arteries. The findings include petechiae, sudden onset of pain, cyanotic fingers, and possibly lack of pulses. Segmental pressures and arteriography can help localize the site of occlusion. Anticoagulation and thrombectomy for larger emboli are indicated, followed by 3 months of oral anticoagulation. Correction of the underlying cause (e.g., atrial fibrillation) is undertaken. In the case of a possible reperfusion injury, fasciotomies are imperative.

8. How does a typical hemangioma compare to a vascular malformation in a newborn?

Incidence of *hemangiomas* in a white infant is 4% to 10%, is lower in a baby with darker skin, and is as high as 23% in a premature low-birth-weight child. Only 30% of hemangiomas are noted at birth. The remainder appear as a premonitory spot and develop by the fourth week of life. They are true vascular tumors, having excessive endothelial proliferation on pathology. They are found in female/male infants in 3:1 ratio. Fifteen percent of these tumors are found in extremities. Hemangiomas undergo rapid growth early on, followed by spontaneous involution. Eighty percent are solitary tumors. If multiple, chance of internal organ involvement is greater.

Vascular malformations result from embryogenic error, not from cellular proliferation. They are congenital clusters and channels of arteries, veins, capillaries, or lymphatics. The lesions are present at birth, although they may not be clinically evident. The incidence is equal in male and female infants. Malformations grow in proportion to a child's size and may become more pronounced later in life rather than involute.

9. What are the phases of a developing hemangioma?

- *Proliferating phase* is characterized by a bright red warm mass increasing in size. This phase usually is completed by the first year of life. Endothelial cells are ample and rapidly form vascular channels in culture. Increases in numerous vascular growth factors, including vascular endothelial growth factor (VEGF) and basic fibroblast growth factor (bFGF), are noted, although multiple factors are implicated. Urine levels of bFGF can be used to monitor tumor proliferation.
- *Involuting phase* usually occurs between 1 to 7 years of age. During this phase, the growth of the tumor is slower than the growth of the child. The lesion fades into a purple, then a bluish, and finally a gray color. Endothelial cells flatten. Sinusoids dilate and are replaced by fibrous tissue. Mast cells and macrophages produce metalloproteinases, inhibiting angiogenesis. Levels of interferon-β are normalized, leading to skin keratinization.
- *Involuted phase* is characterized by vessels that have been replaced by fibrofatty tissue. Deep hemangiomas will not have cutaneous manifestations, but remnants of a superficial tumor may persist as redundant skin.

10. What is the treatment of hemangiomas of the upper extremity?

Observation continues to be the mainstay of hemangioma treatment. This may be a great challenge with anxious parents. Hemangiomas of the upper extremity can bleed easily due to the child's activity, thumb sucking, or scratching. The ulcerations can be easily treated with compression and elevation. Wound care, topical antibiotics, and limb protection help ulcer healing. Cellulitis may require systemic antibiotics.

Extensive tumors that can be life threatening usually involve the axilla and ipsilateral chest wall. These lesions may require medical or procedural treatment. Several options are available.

Intralesional steroid injection (3 to 5 mg/kg) is as effective as systemic therapy (2 to 3 mg/kg per day for 2 weeks, followed by a taper). The complications include subcutaneous tissue atrophy and hypopigmentation for local injections, and typical growth retardation, weight gain, and cushingoid changes for systemic therapy.

Interferon-α can be given to patients with complex hemangiomas who do not respond to corticosteroid therapy. It is injected subcutaneously daily. The most serious side effect is spastic diplegia, which usually appears in patients younger than 12 months. Other side effects include anemia, neutropenia, and transaminase elevation. All complications are reversible by drug discontinuation.

Surgery is rarely indicated but may be required for ulcerating, nonhealing hemangiomas. Ideally, resection, if indicated, is postponed until regression is complete.

Pulsed-dye laser photocoagulation of the premonitory spot before hemangioma development has led to very good results.

11. What is Maffucci syndrome?

This rare syndrome consists of cavernous hemangiomas and enchondromas of the long bones. Hemangiomas usually appear as blue asymmetric nodules between 4 and 5 years of age. Enchondromas are found on the hands in 89% of patients. They present with bony deformities, length discrepancies, pathologic fractures, and malunions. Approximately one third of enchondromas will differentiate into chondrosarcomas. Close monitoring and bone needle biopsies are required for pathologic evidence of neoplastic changes.

12. What are pyogenic granulomas? How are they treated?

Pyogenic granulomas are benign vascular lesions presenting as fleshy polypoid papules, usually less than 1cm in size. Their name is a misnomer; they are not related to infection or granulomatous disease. Histologically, they are composed of collagen and vascular proliferative tissue. They tend to ulcerate and bleed, but only 7% is associated with prior trauma. Treatment options include silver nitrate or electrocauterization, shave excision, laser treatment, and full-thickness excision with primary closure for larger or recurrent lesions.

13. What is a glomus tumor?

Glomus tumor is a benign tumor of the arterial portion of the glomus body, a dermal arteriovenous shunt surrounded by smooth muscle cells that contributes to the body's temperature regulation. They present in the distal extremities, especially in the subungual region, with symptoms of paroxysmal pain and cold sensitivity. Distal to the eponychium, they appear as purple nodules less than 5mm in size and can be easily identified with high-resolution magnetic resonance imaging (MR)I. Surgical excision is recommended for symptomatic lesions. Extremely rare malignant glomus tumors, glomangiosarcomas, usually are larger than 1cm, grow rapidly, and involve deeper tissues. Wide excision is curative for the malignant transformations, although they have potential for metastasis.

14. What are "Hildreth's sign" and the "Love test"?

Application of a tourniquet proximal to a glomus tumor will decrease the blood flow through the lesion and remit the pain. This is a positive *Hildreth's sign* and confirms the vascular element of the glomus tumor. The *Love test* is positive when the tip of a pencil elicits pain over the precise area overlying the lesion. The two maneuvers can be helpful in diagnosis of these tumors.

15. What is Kasabach-Merritt syndrome?

Kaposiform hemangioendothelioma or tufted angioma is a low-grade invasive vascular tumor that usually appears in infancy and involves large areas of the body. The trunk usually is involved along with the upper extremity. The tumor traps platelets, releasing platelet-derived growth factor and generating thrombin. Resulting thrombocytopenia and potential disseminated intravascular coagulopathy (DIC) is termed *Kasabach-Merritt syndrome*. The treatment usually is medical, including steroids, interferon-α, and vincristine. Sclerotherapy and surgery are used less frequently. Overall mortality rates range from 10% to 39%.

16. Why do arteriovenous malformations expand and involve surrounding tissues?

These high-flow, high-pressure anomalies dilate the vessels, forming new fistulas and recruiting surrounding tissues. Creation of steal phenomenon leads to local ischemia and neoangiogenesis. Hence, ligation of proximal arteriovenous malformations (AVMs) can lead to further lesion expansion. Finally, cells cultured from AVMs have higher proliferation rates and reduced apoptosis.

17. What are the indications for amputation?

Arteriography and embolization are first-line treatment of AVMs. Selective amputation can be therapeutic after all other management therapies have failed. These include patients with unrelenting pain, tissue necrosis, life-threatening infection, progressive congestive heart failure, and retarded growth and development. Some patients will request an amputation after prolonged treatment and poor outcomes.

18. How does a port-wine stain of the upper extremity compare to those of the head and neck?

Capillary malformations or port-wine stains of the upper extremity are less likely to develop nodularity, cobblestoning, or ulceration as they mature. Their response to a pulsed-dye laser is diminished compared with the response of malformations of the head and neck. Extensive involvement may be associated with both axial and circumferential hypertrophy of the upper extremity.

19. What are Klippel-Trenaunay syndrome and Parkes-Weber syndrome?

Klippel-Trenaunay syndrome consists of a triad of port-wine stain, varicosities, and extremity hypertrophy. *Parkes-Weber syndrome* involves the three findings of Klippel-Trenaunay syndrome as well as AVM; it has higher rates of morbidity and mortality. Radiologic imaging evaluates for limb size discrepancy. Compression garments are used for venous insufficiency, lymphedema, cellulitis, and bleeding but will increase venous stasis in extremities with anomalous deep veins. Antibiotics, analgesics, and steroids may be indicated in cellulitis or thrombophlebitis. Notable limb discrepancy is treated with osteotomies or epiphysial stapling. Because debulking may increase lymphedema, surgical intervention for soft tissue hypertrophy is reserved for patients with significant cosmetic deformity, pain, and recurrent bleeding and infection.

20. How are venous malformations evaluated?

Venous malformations (VMs) are low-flow venous lesions presenting with a mass, swelling, and skin discoloration. Compression of the mass and limb elevation will improve the lesion's appearance. They usually are found in the subcutaneous plane but may extend into the muscle. Pain and paresthesias from mass effect and phlebothrombosis are uncommon but known sequelae. In the upper extremity, VMs are equally distributed within the flexor and extensor compartments. In the hand, they are more frequent in the dorsal interossei, thenar, and hypothenar muscles than in the palmar interossei and lumbricals. Plain radiographs show calcified phleboliths. Ultrasonography shows a low-flow, compressible lesion. MRI provides thorough images of the lesions and delineate tissue involvement. Invasive techniques (e.g., phlebography and angiography) may be helpful in preoperative evaluation.

21. What are the complications of VM treatment?

Observation is the mainstay therapy for small lesions. Daily aspirin is prescribed to prevent and treat thrombosis, along with compression garments for bulk control.

Sclerotherapy is used frequently in the upper extremity with VMs. A tourniquet and 100% alcohol are used, avoiding the areas around the brachial plexus, the antecubital fossa, and the hand. Complications include skin damage and necrosis, surrounding tissue injury, compartment syndrome, and rhabdomyolysis. Systemic injection may lead to pulmonary, cardiac, and cerebral injury and potentially death.

Surgical treatment can be very challenging. Immaculate hemostasis and the surgeon's experience are imperative. In case of localized muscle involvement in the arm, complete excision and reconstruction may provide a better outcome. Care should be taken not to injure the arteries and nerves. The complication rate is 10%, and complications include hematomas, functional loss, soft tissue defect, contractures, and need for multiple procedures.

22. What is blue rubber bleb nevus syndrome?

Blue rubber bleb nevus syndrome presents with chronic gastrointestinal bleeding and small cutaneous lesions secondary to VMs. Skin lesions usually are found on the trunk, palms, and soles. They are soft and nodular. Hundreds of gastrointestinal lesions can be present. Other systems, including joints, can be involved, leading to functional difficulty.

23. What are lymphatic malformations?

Lymphatic malformations are composed of microscopic or macroscopic, multiloculated, cyst-like collections of proteinaceous fluid. They usually are seen at birth and are noncompressible. Microscopic lesions usually are found in a distal extremity and are not amenable to sclerotherapy. Lymphatic malformations usually do not penetrate the fascial planes but may track along them. They are painful if intralesional bleeding occurs. If the skin is involved, peau d'orange appearance may be present, with continuous weeping, ulceration, and an excellent pathway for bacterial invasion and chronic infections.

24. What is a cystic hygroma?

Cystic hygroma is a term for thin-walled, macroscopic lymphatic malformation usually found in the neck and axilla. MRI is required to evaluate depth and neurovascular invasion. Surgery is the mainstay treatment, ensuring near-complete excision to prevent recurrence. Airway compression requires urgent intervention.

BIBLIOGRAPHY

Arneja JS, Gosain AK: An approach to the management of common vascular malformations of the trunk. J Craniofac Surg 17:761–766, 2006.

Balogh B, Mayer W, Vesely M, Mayer S, Partsch H, Piza-Katzer H: Adventitial stripping of the radial and ulnar arteries in Raynaud's disease. J Hand Surg [Am] 27:1073–1080, 2002.

Bhaskaranand K, Navadgi BC: Glomus tumour of the hand. J Hand Surg 27:229–231, 2002.

Capraro PA, Fisher J, Hammond DC, Grossman JA: Klippel-Trenaunay syndrome. Plast Reconstr Surg 109:2052–2062, May 2002.

Cooke JP, Marshall JM: Mechanisms of Raynaud's disease. Vasc Med 10:293–307, 2005.

Olin JW: Current concepts: Thromboangiitis obliterans (Buerger's disease). N Engl J Med 343:864–869, 2000.

Sarkar M, Mulliken JB, Kozakewich HPW, Robertson RL, Burrows PE: Thrombocytopenic coagulopathy (Kasabach-Merritt phenomenon) is associated with kaposiform hemangioendothelioma and not with common infantile hemangioma. Plast Reconstr Surg 100: 1377–1386, 1997.

van Aalst JA, Bhuller A, Sadove AM: Pediatric vascular lesions. J Craniofac Surg 14:566–583, 2003.

COMPARTMENT SYNDROME AND ISCHEMIC CONTRACTURE IN THE UPPER EXTREMITY

Brian S. Coan, MD, and
L. Scott Levin, MD, FACS

COMPARTMENT SYNDROME

1. What are the compartments of the forearm, and what structures do they contain?
The compartments of the forearm are less completely separated than are those in the distal leg. However, there are three main compartments with superficial and deep subdivisions in the volar and dorsal compartments (Table 134-1). The volar and dorsal compartments are separated by the interosseus membrane. Some authors have stated that the pronator quadratus lies in its own deep compartment.

2. What are the most common causes of upper extremity compartment syndrome?
- *Increased Volume in a Muscular Compartment:* Hemorrhage, ischemia from arterial occlusion, venous obstruction, edema, electrical burns, reperfusion injury, intravenous extravasation of toxic substance, snakebite, crush injury, and supracondylar humerus fractures in children
- *External Compression:* Tight casts, extended tourniquet duration, nonexpandable burn eschar, laying on limb (altered mental status and inability to self-protect)

3. What is the physiologic cause of ischemia in the upper extremity?
Ischemia is defined as an insufficient supply of oxygen to the tissue to meet demands. In compartment syndrome this results when the driving pressure of blood in the capillary system defined as pressure arterial minus pressure venous (Pa – Pv) is less than the pressure in the surrounding tissues. As the pressure in the interstitium increases the capillaries collapse preventing flow. A lack of flow increases tissue ischemia and damage, leading to further swelling and pressure in the compartment causing a vicious cycle.

Table 134-1. Compartments of the Forearm and Their Contents

MAIN COMPARTMENT	SUBDIVISION	MUSCLES	PERFUSION AND INNERVATION
Volar	Superficial	Pronator teres, palmaris longus, flexor digitorum superficialis, flexor carpi radialis, flexor carpi ulnaris	Perfusion from anterior interosseus artery. Innervated by median and anterior interosseus nerves
	Deep	Flexor digitorum profundis, flexor pollicis longus, pronator quadratus	Same as superficial
Dorsal	Superficial	Extensor digitorum communis, extensor carpi ulnaris, extensor digiti minimi	Perfusion from radial, posterior interosseous, and anterior interosseous arteries. Innervated by posterior interosseous nerve
	Deep	Abductor pollicis longus, extensor pollicis brevis, extensor pollicis longus, extensor indicis proprius, supinator, anconeus	Same as superficial
Lateral (mobile wad)		Brachioradialis, extensor carpi radialis brevis, extensor carpi radialis longus	Perfusion from radial, recurrent radial, inferior ulnar arteries, and collaterals of profundi brachii. Innervated by radial nerve

From Ronel DN, Mtui E, Nolan WB: Forearm compartment syndrome: Anatomical analysis of surgical approaches to the deep space. Plast Reconstr Surg 114:697–705, 2004.

4. **How does elevation paradoxically worsen the compartment syndrome?**
Usually edema is reduced with limb elevation, improving pain and swelling. However, in compartment syndrome the decreased hydrostatic force of limb elevation leads to a decreased driving pressure in the capillary bed. Because the pressure in the compartment does not go down with elevation and the driving perfusion pressure is *decreased,* the result is worsening ischemia.

5. **What are the signs and symptoms of compartment syndrome?**
Common findings with compartment syndrome (the "*Ps*"):
   - Pain
   - Pallor
   - Pain with passive flexion
   - Paresthesias
   - Poikilothermy
   - Pressure *(tight compartment)*
   - Pulselessness *(very late finding)*
   - Paresis

6. **What is usually the first finding and the last?**
Extreme pain with passive extension and loss of fine touch sensation should increase clinical concern early. Because pulselessness is a very late finding, its presence should *not* be required for the diagnosis.

7. **What tests can be used if the diagnosis is uncertain, and when should they be used?**
The diagnosis is *primarily clinical.* Whenever a patient has pain out of proportion to examination, the diagnosis should be entertained. In patients who have a mechanism for compartment syndrome (e.g., crush, fracture, burn) and are unable to provide a good history, further diagnostic testing should be performed. The most common test is percutaneous compartment pressure measurement. This is usually done with a Stryker STIC device or simply an A-line setup with a needle inserted directly into the compartment of concern.

8. **At what compartment pressure does ischemia ensue?**
Although there are no firm numbers, the generally accepted threshold is 30 mm Hg (which is approximately capillary occlusion pressure). However, with a low diastolic blood pressure or inability to clearly evaluate a patient's symptoms, anything above 20 mm Hg, or within 30 mm Hg of the diastolic blood pressure, should be concerning.

9. **What is the best way to improve outcome in forearm compartment syndrome?**
Early intervention with fasciotomy before permanent muscle necrosis or nerve injury occurs is critical to achieving a favorable outcome. Tissue injury can be prevented in the first 3 to 4 hours, and permanent necrosis results after a delay of more than 4 to 5 hours, but nerve injury begins after as few as 30 minutes.

10. **Describe the technique of upper extremity compartment fasciotomy and the important structures that should be released.**
Release of forearm compartments (Fig. 134-1):
   - Skin incision
   - Avoid palmar cutaneous branch of median nerve
   - Release median nerve in carpal tunnel
   - Preserve cutaneous veins when possible
   - Release superficial and deep compartments and lacertus fibrosis at the elbow
   - Observe muscle reperfusion and perform epimysiotomy if necessary
   - Brachial artery can be exposed through proximal extension of the incision

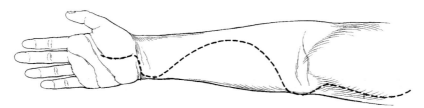

Figure 134-1. Suggested skin incision for forearm fasciotomy.

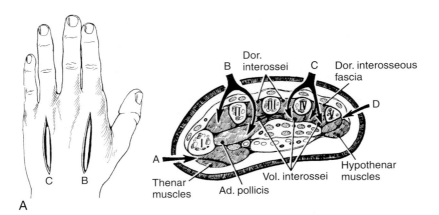

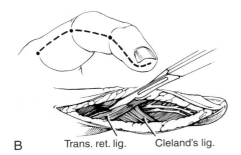

Figure 134-2. Suggested skin incision for hand **(A)** and finger **(B)** fasciotomies.

11. Are there any other treatments of acute compartment syndrome?

The mainstay of treatment is early recognition of symptoms and prompt treatment with fasciotomy. Only as an adjunct should other therapies be used to try and rescue borderline tissue. These include hyperbaric oxygen, corticosteroids, antibiotics, and oxygen-radical scavengers such as mannitol. Splinting and elevation can help reduce edema and foster earlier closure.

12. What situations might mandate an exploration of the deep compartments?

High-voltage injury preferentially affects deep compartments because bone has a high resistance and generates significant heat and tissue damage. Crush injuries and an extended period of local pressure should elicit concern.

13. What is the most common cause of hand compartment syndrome, and how is it treated?

First described by Bunnell in 1948, hand compartment syndrome is much less common than is compartment syndrome of the forearm. It usually is iatrogenic from extravasated intravenous medicines but also occurs after crush injuries and fractures. The hand has 10 compartments and usually can be decompressed adequately through dorsal incisions over the interosseus compartments (Fig. 134-2). Occasionally, additional incisions over the thenar compartments are required. A decompression of the median nerve should always be performed. Intrinsic-minus hand position (extended metacarpophalangeal joint and flexed interphalangeal joint) should be a clue to the diagnosis and increase clinical suspicion.

ISCHEMIC CONTRACTURES

14. Who first described the long term sequelae of upper extremity ischemia?

Dr. Richard von Volkmann published initial cases in 1869 and then subsequently in 1881 recognized that multiple causes of ischemia all led to similar forearm contractures.

15. When was the pathophysiology leading to contracture and effective treatment outlined?

Not until the 1970s was the connection between local tissue ischemia leading to myonecrosis, infarct, and ultimately fibrosis and contracture fully elucidated.

16. What is the most common cause of Volkmann's contractures in developing countries?

Bandages that are too tight!

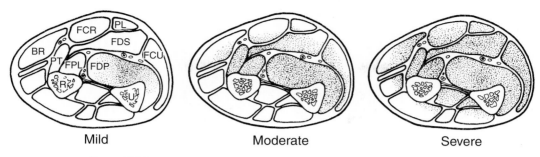

Figure 134-3. Forearm cross-sections showing injury patterns in Volkmann's contracture.

17. What injury in children is most commonly associated with Volkmann's contracture, and how does it occur?

Supracondylar humerus fractures in children have a propensity for brachial artery injury, resulting in ischemia. The fractured bone can lacerate the median nerve or brachial vein. When a supracondylar fracture is diagnosed, the arm should be carefully splinted and the fracture stabilized urgently. Frequent assessments of the forearm compartments and sensation should be performed, and if there is any suspicion of increased pressure, fasciotomies should be performed with possible exploration of the brachial vessels as indicated.

18. Which compartment is most commonly affected by compartment syndrome and why?

The deep flexor compartment of the forearm lies in direct opposition to the radius, ulna, and nondistensible interosseous membrane. It is also surrounded by a tight layer of fascia. Small changes in volume in this compartment rapidly increase the internal pressure, leading to compartment syndrome.

19. Describe three levels of severity in established Volkmann's contracture and their treatment options (Fig. 134-3).

- *Mild:* Flexion contractures of only two or three fingers with limited or no neurologic damage. Usually the middle and ring fingers are affected because they have the deepest muscle bellies and are furthest from the arterial blood supply. For these injuries conservative nonoperative management usually results in good function. Therapies include splinting and physical therapy without surgery.
- *Moderate:* All fingers have flexion contractures including the thumb, which may be locked into the palm. There is usually associated sensory loss. If initial hand function remains good, conservative treatment, as with minor contractures, should be attempted. Tendon lengthening procedures performed in the past have poor outcomes and are not recommended. When progression of the contractures is noted, treatment includes excision of the fibrotic muscle bellies, tenolysis, neurolysis, and tendon transfers (most commonly brachioradialis to flexor pollicis longus and extensor carpi radialis to flexor digitorum profundus).
- *Severe:* All forearm musculature is affected, including the flexors and extensors. Children will often have forearm length discrepancy as they grow. These patients usually require multiple operations but have better outcome with at least early débridement followed by free muscle transfer.

BIBLIOGRAPHY

Bardenheuer L: Die entstehung und behandlung der ischaemischen muskellontractur und gangran. Dtsch Z F Chir 108:44, 1911.
Botte MJ, Gelberman RH: Acute compartment syndrome of the forearm. Hand Clin 14:391–403, 1998.
Bunnell S, Doherty EW, Curtis RM: Ischemic contracture, local, in the hand. Plast Reconstr Surg 3:424–433, 1948.
D'Amato TA, Kaplan IB, Britt LD: High voltage electrical injury: A role for mandatory exploration of the deep muscle compartments. J Natl Med Assoc 86:535–537, 1994.
Dellaero DT, Levin LS: Compartment syndrome of the hand: Etiology, diagnosis and treatment. Am J Orthop 25:404–408, 1996.
Gelberman RH: Upper extremity compartment syndromes: Treatment. In Mubarak SJ, Hargens AR (eds): Compartment Syndrome and Volkmann's Contracture. Philadelphia, WB Saunders, 1981, pp 133–146.
Gelberman RH, Szabo RM, Williamson RV, et al: Tissue pressure threshold for peripheral nerve viability. Clin Orthop 178:285–291, 1983.
Gelberman RH, et al: Decompression of forearm compartment syndromes. Clin Orthop 134:225–229, 1978.
Gulgonen A: Compartment syndrome. In Green DP, Hotchkiss RN, Pederson WC, Wolfe SW (eds): Green's Operative Hand Surgery. Philadelphia, Elsevier, 2005.
Matsen FA III: Compartmental Syndromes. Orlando, FL, Grune & Stratton, 1980.
Ouellette EA, Robert K: Compartment syndromes of the hand. J Bone Joint Surg 78A:1515–1522, 1996.
Seddon HJ: Volkmann's contracture: Treatment by excision of the infarct. J Bone Joint Surg 38B:152–174, 1956.
Ultee J, Hovius SR: Functional results after treatment of Volkmann's ischemic contracture: A long-term follow up study. Clin Orthop Relat Res 431:42–49, 2005.
Volkmann RV: Die ischaemischen muskellahmungen und kontrakturen. Centralbl f Chir Leipz viii:801–803, 1881.

PERIPHERAL NERVE INJURIES

Renata V. Weber, MD, and
Susan E. Mackinnon, MD

1. Describe the functional anatomy of peripheral nerves.

Peripheral nerves are basically composed of four components (Fig. 135-1):

1. *Neurons,* the primary functional units of peripheral nerve, are composed of cell bodies and axons. The cell bodies of motor axons are found in the anterior horn area of the spinal cord, and sensory cell bodies are found in the dorsal root ganglia of the spinal cord.
2. *Connective tissues* of the nerve are arranged in three layers: *endoneurial* connective tissue, which is found around individual axons; *perineurial* connective tissue, which surrounds fascicles; and *epineurial* connective tissue, which runs between fascicles and around the outside of the nerve and constitutes the main support structure of the nerve itself.
3. *Schwann cells* supply myelin for efficient electrical nerve conduction. In addition, they appear to influence maturation and resting metabolism of axons.
4. *End organs,* including the motor endplates, sensory receptors, and autonomic receptors, transduce electrical activity into function.

Motor recovery appears to become refractory to reinnervation after approximately 15 to 18 months of denervation. Sensory recovery has been described up to 20 years after initial denervation. Autonomic function and possible reinnervation after denervation have not been well studied.

2. How are nerve injures classified? What is the clinical importance of classification?

Seddon's original classification, proposed in 1943, described three types of nerve injury:

1. *Neurapraxia* involves a local conduction block at a discrete area along the course of the nerve; subsequent wallerian degeneration does not occur.
2. *Axonotmesis* refers to direct axonal damage; wallerian degeneration occurs distal to the site of injury.
3. *Neurotmesis* constitutes transection of a peripheral nerve.

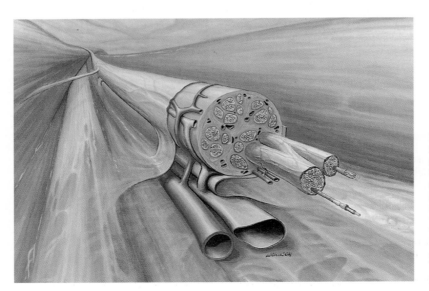

Figure 135-1. The primary unit of the peripheral nerve is the nerve fiber. The segmental extrinsic blood supply and the mesoneurium are emphasized. In the extreme lower right, a single nerve fiber is shown protruding from a nerve fascicle. Plexus formation between two fascicles is shown. (From Mackinnon SE, Dellon AL: Surgery of the Peripheral Nerve. New York, Thieme, 1988, p 21, with permission.)

Table 135-1. Classification of Nerve Injury

	DEGREE OF INJURY	TINEL'S SIGN/ PROGRESSES DAILY	RECOVERY PATTERN	RATE OF RECOVERY	SURGICAL PROCEDURE
I	Neurapraxia	No Tinel's sign	Complete	Fast (days to 12 weeks)	None
II	Axonotmesis	+/+	Complete	Slow (1 inch/ month)	None
III		+/+	Great variation*	Slow (1 inch/ month)	None or neurolysis†
IV		+/−	None	No recovery	Nerve repair or nerve graft
V	Neurotmesis	+/−	None	No recovery	Nerve repair or nerve graft
VI	Neuroma in continuity (combination of grade I–V and normal)	Varies by fascicle, depending on injury	Varies by fascicle	Varies by fascicle	Varies by fascicle

*Recovery is at least as good as nerve repair but varies from excellent to poor, depending on the degree of endoneurial scarring and the amount of sensory and motor axonal misdirection within the injured fascicle.
†If injury localizes at a known anatomic site of nerve compression, nerve decompression may enhance recovery.

Sunderland expanded Seddon's classification with grades of nerve injury from I to V. Mackinnon described a mixed injury that she called a grade VI injury. The Sunderland classification describes injury to peripheral nerves in relation to axon and connective tissue anatomy. Clinical prognosis is proportional to the level of injury (Table 135-1).

3. What is meant by wallerian degeneration?

The distal segment in a complete nerve injury undergoes a series of degenerative changes collectively known as *wallerian degeneration*. In 1850, Waller described the gross changes of turbidity or coagulation seen even at the distal most end of the neural tube after transaction. This ground-glass appearance represents the remnants of degenerated myelin and axonal material after loss of axonal continuity. The initial breakdown products of the axon and myelin are phagocytosed by macrophages and Schwann cells. Eventually, the space originally occupied by myelinated axons is filled with columns of Schwann cell nuclei and their basement membranes.

4. What are the bands of Büngner?

The collapsed columns of Schwann cells filling the distal segment of a complete nerve injury have a characteristic band-like appearance under electron microscopy; these columns are known as the bands of Büngner.

5. What are the bands of Fontana?

In 1779, Felice Fontana first described what appeared to be spiral bands surrounding the peripheral nerve. The irregular light and dark strips crossing the surface of unstretched nerves are due to the underlying undulations of the individual nerve fibers within the epineural–perineural sheaths. It has been suggested that these are nerve bands keeping the proper fascicular structure, providing the elasticity of the perineurium and tolerating stretching deformation.

6. What is Tinel's sign?

Percussion over the site of a nerve injury or nerve repair elicits a tingling or electric shock-like sensation in the distribution of the injured nerve. This sensation represents the leading edge of nerve regeneration. An advancing Tinel's sign after nerve repair implies successful nerve regeneration toward the target organ. A Tinel's sign that does not advance with time may be due to extra-epineurial growth cones that have become misdirected outside the epineurial boundary at the level of the nerve repair. Although sensory in nature, Tinel's sign is also found in regenerating motor nerve, probably because of the presence of proprioceptive afferent fibers within all motor nerves.

7. How fast do nerves regenerate?

As a general rule, regenerating nerves advance at the rate of approximately 1 mm/day or 1 inch/month. However, several clinical studies based on advancing Tinel's sign after nerve repair have reported a rate of recovery up to 2 mm/ day. There is some evidence that the immunosuppressant agent Prograf (tacrolimus [FK506]) increases the rate of axonal regeneration.

8. **If nerves regenerate at the rate of 1 inch/month and the tip of the ulnar two fingers is approximately 30 inches from the axilla, does this mean that a complete ulnar nerve injury at the level of the axilla will take 2.5 years to restore sensibility to the ulnar two fingers in the hand?**

   Yes. The time course of nerve regeneration is relatively predictable, based on the distance from the most proximal extent of injury to the end organ supplied by the nerve.

9. **In the same situation as described in Question 8, will the ulnar-innervated hand intrinsic muscles regain function 2.5 years after injury?**

   No. Like most voluntary skeletal muscle that becomes denervated and unlike sensory receptors, the intrinsic muscles of the hand become functionally refractory to reinnervation after a finite period. The absolute time is not known, but with muscle reinnervation the sooner the reconstruction the better. In closed injury, reconstruction should be performed 3 months after injury if recovery is not forthcoming. With open nerve injuries, repair should be performed as soon as clinically feasible. Intrinsic muscles in the hand do not regain function after an injury in the axilla because the prolonged denervation time precludes recovery of motor function.

10. **Do all proximal motor nerve injuries result in permanent loss of function?**

    No. Excellent recovery is possible across long distances under certain circumstances. Early primary repair of sharp transections that maintain motor and sensory topography by excellent coaptation along anatomic landmarks on the epineurium results in good recovery of function. Similarly, because of enhanced nerve regenerative capacity, shorter distances, and possibly greater central plasticity, nerve repairs in children tend to have good outcomes even with long nerve grafts. Protective sensibility and improved muscle function are possible after long nerve grafts when meticulous microtechnique is used and sensory/motor topography is correct.

11. **What are nerve transfers?**

    A nerve transfer uses an uninjured proximal nerve to "power" an injured distal nerve and may restore motor function or sensory function. Motor nerve transfers are designed by selecting donor nerves that supply nonessential muscles or muscles with redundant fiber innervation and that hopefully are synergistic with the recipient motor nerve. An example is transfer of the redundant flexor carpi radialis fascicles of the medial nerve and redundant flexor carpi ulnaris fascicles of the ulnar nerve to the biceps brachii and brachialis branches of the musculocutaneous nerve for elbow flexion recovery.

12. **Is a motor nerve transfer better than a tendon transfer?**

    Not always. Nerve injuries occurring more than 12 months earlier or that need to regenerate over long distances will have poor results and should be treated with tendon transfers. The advantage of tendon transfers is the immediate results seen soon after surgery.

    Injuries that are amenable to nerve transfers do better because (1) a nerve transfer can restore motor and sensory function, (2) multiple muscle groups can be restored with a single nerve transfer, and (3) the insertion and attachments of the muscle(s) in question are not disrupted, so the original muscle function and tension is maintained.

13. **When should a motor nerve transfer be used instead of a nerve graft?**

    A significant advantage to nerve transfers over nerve grafting or primary repair is the ability to convert a proximal high-level nerve injury to a low-level nerve injury.

    Situations in which nerve transfers are indicated include the following:
    - Brachial plexus injuries in which only very proximal or no nerve is available for grafting
    - High proximal injuries that require a long distance for regeneration
    - To avoid scarred areas where there is a high likelihood that critical structures may be injured
    - Major limb trauma with segmental loss of nerve tissue
    - As an alternative to nerve grafting when time from injury to reconstruction is prolonged
    - In partial nerve injuries with a defined functional loss
    - Spinal cord root avulsion injuries
    - Nerve injuries in which the level of injury is uncertain, such as with idiopathic neuritides or radiation trauma and nerve injuries with multiple levels of injury

14. **Should all open wounds be explored?**

    In general, nerve injuries associated with open wounds require immediate exploration. The classic case is a sharp laceration causing nerve injury that can be repaired primarily. One exception is a gunshot wound, which, although open, causes injury by indirect heat and shock effects. Such injuries more closely resemble closed or blunt traumas and should be treated as such.

15. How long should you wait before operating on a closed nerve injury?

In closed injuries such as a direct blow or traction injury, the clinical course is followed closely. If complete recovery does not occur by 6 to 8 weeks, nerve conduction and electromyographic studies are obtained for baseline evaluation. The clinical course is followed up to 12 weeks, and repeat electrical studies are obtained. If improvement in the clinical course by 12 weeks or electrical evidence of reinnervation is seen, continue with conservative management. If no sign of recovery is seen by either clinical examination or electrodiagnostic testing, operative intervention is warranted. The exact surgical procedure varies from neurolysis to nerve grafting or nerve transfer, depending on the grade of the injury and the distance of the injury from the end organ. (See Figs. 135-2 and 135-3.)

16. What is the best way to treat peripheral nerve injuries resulting in segmental loss of continuity?

Many different solutions have been proposed for the problem of nerve gaps. For a motor nerve gap that cannot be primarily repaired, the gold standard is use of autogenous nerve grafts harvested from appropriate donor sites. Recently, cadaveric nerves have become commercially available for use in place of autogenous nerves. The limits are up to 7 cm in length. Anything longer will need an autograft. For small sensory defects, as in cutaneous nerve defects up to 3 cm in length, vein grafts and artificial conduits are successfully used. Experimentally, motor defects as long as 6 cm have been repaired with vein or other conduits in motor nerves; however, they are still investigational and not being used clinically.

For long nerve gaps, nerve transfer may be a better alternative. Nerve grafts even longer than 15 cm have been used successfully; however, the success rate of nerve grafting is inversely proportional to the length of graft required.

With massive loss of nerve segments, transplanted nerves can be used for grafting. This is especially useful when large amounts of long nerve grafts are needed and in whom the amount of autogenous nerve available for grafting may be limited, such as children and amputees. Harvested donor nerves are preserved in cold University of Wisconsin solution for 7 days

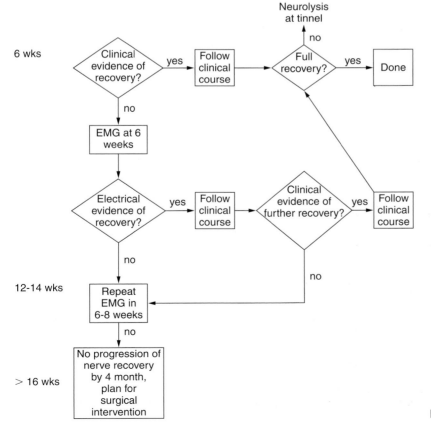

Figure 135-2.

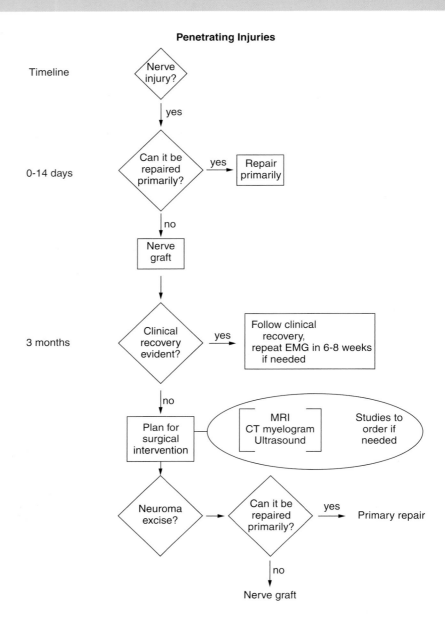

Penetrating Injuries

Timeline — Nerve injury?

yes

0-14 days — Can it be repaired primarily? — yes → Repair primarily

no

Nerve graft

3 months — Clinical recovery evident? — yes → Follow clinical recovery, repeat EMG in 6-8 weeks if needed

no

Plan for surgical intervention — MRI, CT myelogram, Ultrasound — Studies to order if needed

Neuroma excise? → Can it be repaired primarily? — yes → Primary repair

no

Nerve graft

Figure 135-3.

before transplantation to reduce antigenicity. Recipients and donors must be blood-type compatible, but human leukocyte antigen (HLA) compatibility is not necessary. Immunosuppression with Prograft, steroids, and cyclosporin A is required until there is evidence of regeneration across the graft into native distal nerve, at which point immunosuppression is stopped. Clinical success with this management in a small series of patients has been good.

17. What is the best method for surgical nerve repair?

Surgical repair of nerve injuries is best performed with several interrupted 9-0 or 10-0 nylon stitches through the epineurium. Other techniques, including fibrin glue and laser energy for epineurial coaptation, have been investigated. However, fibrin glue carries a small but possible risk of transmission of blood-borne diseases, and lasers produce heat that damages nerve tissue and results in unacceptably decreased tensile strength at the repair site. The gold standard remains microsuture applied under microscope control. Attempts at fascicular and grouped fascicular repair have shown no advantage over simple epineurial repair.

18. How are nerve repairs classified?

Primary repair occurs when the nerve is repaired within the first few days. *Delayed primary repair* occurs when the nerve is repaired between 2 to 7 days. In both cases, the proximal and distal ends are freshened and an end-to-end coaptation created. After the first week, *secondary repair* occurs. The longer the wait from time of injury, the less likely that an end-to-end coaptation can be achieved, even with significant mobilization of the proximal and distal nerve ends.

19. Is primary repair always better than secondary repair?
In most cases, yes. If the nerve has a significant crush injury, if the wound bed is highly contaminated, if viability of the nerve is questionable because of vascular supply, or if infection is present, it may be better to delay the nerve repair until the wound is clean. While committing to a nerve graft in most cases, which will necessitate two coaptation sites, thereby reducing the number of axons crossing the repair at two sites instead of one, the overall functional outcome remains high.

20. How do you know which repair should be used in which situation?
As long as the nerve is injured by a sharp or a limited crush mechanism, the wound bed is clean, and the two ends are easily juxtaposed, a primary repair should be performed. A large gap needs to be repaired with nerve grafts. Some have suggested that a nerve gap of 4 to 5 cm in the upper arm, or a 1-cm gap in a digital nerve, requires a nerve graft. A vascularized nerve graft can help ensure the survival of the graft and may hasten regeneration in situations such as a burn or irradiated tissue with poor vascularity. Conduits are indicated in patients in whom a small nerve gap is present but no autologous nerve is available or a donor defect is not warranted. Nerve transfers have specific indications when the aforementioned options are not available (Table 135-2).

21. Which quick intraoperative landmarks can be used to match fascicles during an end-to-end neurorrhaphy?
The vascular markings within the epineurium are the easiest landmark to assist with alignment of the proximal and distal stumps during surgical repair. The size and grouping of fascicles, especially at a more distal location of a nerve, where the motor and sensory fibers are more likely to be distinct, can also help align the nerve ends.

22. Describe the clinical tests for nerve function in the hand.
A simple and comprehensive way to diagnose nerve injuries in the upper extremity is to test three functions of each nerve: extrinsic motor function, intrinsic motor function, and sensibility in autonomous areas (Table 135-3).

23. What is a Martin-Gruber communication or Martin-Gruber anastomosis? Why is it important in nerve injuries of the hand?
Martin (1763) and, much later, Gruber (1870) described a crossover of median nerve fibers to the ulnar nerve. The incidence ranges from 5% to 34% in cadaveric studies and as high as 57% in electrophysiologic examinations. Anatomically, the crossing fibers come from the anterior interosseous nerve or from the median nerve to join the ulnar nerve in the proximal forearm. By electrophysiologic recording, the Martin-Gruber communication is classified into three groups: the crossing median fibers can supply the hypothenar muscles (type I); the first dorsal interosseus muscle (type

Table 135-2. Selection of Operative Procedure

SURGERY	ENDS WILL APPROXIMATE	VASCULARIZED BED	GRAFT POSSIBLE	PROXIMAL PORTION INTACT	DISTAL PORTION INTACT
Primary repair	Yes	Yes	-	Yes	Yes
Nerve graft	No	Yes	Yes	Yes	Yes
Conduit	No	Yes	Yes	Yes	Yes
Vascularized nerve graft	No	No	Yes*	Yes	Yes
Nerve transfer	No	No	No	No	Yes

*Usually reserved for longer distances (>10 cm).

Table 135-3. Clinical Tests for Nerve Function

FUNCTION	RADIAL NERVE	MEDIAN NERVE	ULNAR NERVE
Extrinsic motor	Wrist extension	Profundus index finger	Profundus small finger
Intrinsic motor	None	Abductor pollicis brevis	First dorsal interosseous
Sensory	Dorsal first web space	Pulp of index finger	Pulp of small finger

II), which is the most common; or the thenar muscles (type III). Intrinsic muscles that are normally innervated by the ulnar nerve may be innervated by the median nerve, or intrinsic muscles normally supplied by the median nerve may still receive median nerve innervation but via the median to ulnar nerve crossover. This variation requires an additional crossover in the palm from the ulnar nerve to the thenar musculature.

Martin-Gruber anastomoses are important in understanding certain clinical patterns in high injury to the ulnar nerve. For example, a complete injury to the ulnar nerve, if it occurs above a Martin-Gruber anastomosis, may present with numbness in the ulnar nerve distribution of the hand but intact function of hand intrinsic muscles.

24. What other anomalous motor nerve connections exist in the upper extremity?
- *Riche-Cannieu Anastomosis:* In 1897, Riche and Cannieu independently described the ulnar motor nerve to median nerve communication in the hand. Up to 77% of cadaver studies show this variation exists.
- *Marinacci Communication:* From 5% to 17% percent of patients have a reverse Martin-Gruber communication or Marinacci communication in which ulnar nerve fibers cross over to the median nerve.

CONTROVERSIES

25. Does end-to-side neurorrhaphy work?
Sometimes. Animal studies show effective muscle reinnervation using end-to-end or end-to-side repair. Retrograde staining for sensory fibers shows small amounts of stain pick up at the level of the dorsal root ganglion of the intact nerve. However, when retrograde tracers are used in motor nerves with end-to-side repair, no evidence of tracer at the level of the anterior horn cells has been found. Therefore, provision of motor function with this approach cannot be expected. Clinically, results have been inconsistent. In facial paralysis, hemi-hypoglossal nerve transfer, or brachial plexus injury such as a spinal accessory to supra scapular nerve transfer, motor end-to-side neurorrhaphies are performed. A crush proximal to the epineurotomy, or invasion into the perineurium, is thought to increase axonal sprouting. Less controversial is the use of end-to-side neurorrhaphy for sensory nerve transfers to achieve protective sensation.

26. Are all nerve grafts the same?
The sural nerve, a sensory nerve, is the most commonly used nerve graft. Other common nerve grafts include medial and lateral antebrachial cutaneous nerves, the distal sensory end of the posterior interosseous nerve, and the dorsal radial sensory nerve. Some experimental studies show that sensory nerves are inhibitory to motor nerve growth, thus leading to the belief that sensory nerve grafts are suboptimal to repair gaps in motor and mix nerve injuries. Experimental studies comparing motor, mixed, and sensory nerve grafts support the idea that motor or mixed nerve grafts achieve better regeneration across the repair when a pure motor or mixed nerve is used.

BIBLIOGRAPHY

Clark D: Jules Tinel and Tinel's sign. Clin Plast Surg 10:627–428, 1983, pp. 627–628.
Clarke E, Bearn JG: The spinal nerve bands of Fontana. Brain 95:1–20, 1972.
Kimura I, Ayyar DR, Lippmann SM: Electrophysiological verification of the ulnar to median nerve communications in the hand and forearm. Tohoku J Exp Med 141:269–274, 1983.
Mackinnon SE: New directions in peripheral nerve surgery. Ann Plast Surg 22:257–273, 1989.
Mackinnon SE, Dellon AL: Surgery of the Peripheral Nerve. New York, Thieme, 1988.
Mackinnon SE: Nerve allotransplantation following severe tibial nerve injury. J Neurosurg 84:671–476, 1996, pp. 671–676.
Meenakshi-Sundaram S, Sundar B, Arunkumar MJ: Marinacci communication: An electrophysiological study. Clin Neurophysiol 114:2334–2337, 2003.
Nath RK, Mackinnon SE, Jensen JN, Parks WC: Spatial pattern of type I collagen expression in injured peripheral nerve. J Neurosurg 86:866–870, 1997.
Nichols CM, Brenner MJ, Fox IK, et al: Effects of motor versus sensory nerve grafts on peripheral nerve regeneration. Exp Neurol 190:347–355, 2004.
Pourmand R, Ochs S, Jersild RA Jr: The relation of the beading of myelinated nerve fibers to the bands of Fontana. Neuroscience 61:373–380, 1994.
Rovak JM, Cederna PS, Kuzon WM Jr: Terminolateral neurorrhaphy: A review of the literature. J Reconstr Microsurg 17:615–624, 2001.
Sarikcioglu L, Sindel M, Ozkaynak S, Aydin H: Median and ulnar nerve communication in the forearm: An anatomical and electrophysiological study. Med Sci Monit 9:BR351–BR356, 2003.
Seddon H: Surgical Disorders of the Peripheral Nerve. New York, Churchill Livingstone, 1975.
Sunderland S: The intraneural topography of the radial, median and ulnar nerves. Brain 68:243–249, 1945.
Sunderland S: Nerve and Nerve Injuries. Edinburg, Churchill Livingstone, 1978.
Weber RV, Mackinnon S: Nerve transfers in the upper extremity. J Am Soc Surg Hand 4:200–213, 2004.

NERVE COMPRESSION SYNDROMES

CHAPTER 136

A. Lee Dellon, MD, PhD

1. Which nerve compression syndromes affect the upper extremity?
- *Carpal tunnel syndrome* (compression of the median nerve at the wrist)
- *Brachial plexus compression* in the thoracic inlet ("thoracic outlet syndrome")
- *Quadrilateral space syndrome* (entrapment of the axillary nerve)
- *Cubital tunnel syndrome* (compression of the ulnar nerve at the elbow)
- *Pronator syndrome* (proximal median nerve compression)
- *Anterior interosseous nerve syndrome* (proximal median nerve compression)
- *Radial tunnel syndrome* (radial nerve compression at the elbow)
- *Cheiralgia paresthetica* (radial sensory nerve compression in the forearm)
- *Compression of the lateral antebrachial cutaneous nerve* at the elbow
- *Compression of the palmar cutaneous branch of median nerve* at the wrist
- *Guyon's canal syndrome* (compression of the ulnar nerve at the wrist)

2. What area of sensibility is abnormal with pronator syndrome but not with carpal tunnel syndrome?
The thenar eminence. The palmar cutaneous branch of the median nerve arises 5 to 7 cm proximal to the carpal tunnel and, therefore, is not compressed with the median nerve in the carpal tunnel. Compression of the proximal median nerve will give decreased sensibility in the thenar eminence, which can be identified by neurosensory testing. Traditional electrodiagnostic testing rarely identifies proximal median nerve compression unless the anterior interosseous nerve is involved, and then the profundus to the index finger and the flexor pollicis longus may show electromyographic changes.

3. What surgical technique used to treat cubital tunnel syndrome has been demonstrated to reduce intraneural pressure in the ulnar nerve in all degrees of elbow flexion and has the lowest published recurrence rate?
A cadaver study comparing in situ decompression, subcutaneous anterior transposition, medial epicondylectomy, intramuscular anterior transposition, and submuscular transposition of the ulnar nerve by the musculofascial lengthening technique demonstrated that only the musculofascial lengthening technique decreased intraneural pressure along the ulnar nerve and at all degrees of elbow flexion. Long-term results (mean 4.5 years) demonstrated an approximately 1% recurrence rate with this technique.

4. What is the common name given to brachial plexus compression in the thoracic inlet? How can you make the diagnosis?
The thoracic outlet is the diaphragm, but, nevertheless, "thoracic outlet syndrome" has come to indicate problems with the subclavian artery and/or vein between the clavicle and the first rib and the anterior scalene muscle, and compression of the brachial plexus by congenital bands, a cervical rib, or posttraumatic in origin. The brachial plexus is actually between the second rib and the clavicle, and the pressure is most often caused by adherence of the anterior scalene and the anomalous structures to the plexus. Traditional electrodiagnosis cannot help here because the actual distances involved between the spinal cord and the site of compression and the variability of the thickness of the thoracic wall confound the measurements. Provocative neurosensory testing, using the index pulp to represent the upper trunk and the little finger pulp to represent the lower trunk, can identify and stage the degree of brachial plexus compression.

5. How do you distinguish de Quervain's tenosynovitis from radial sensory nerve compression?
The Finkelstein test (pain with ulnar deviation of the wrist when the thumb is adducted and flexed) is positive for both conditions. Pain with resisted thumb extension and abduction, when the wrist is motionless, is present with tendonitis of the first dorsal extensor compartment but absent with nerve compression. Tenderness over the radial styloid is present with tendonitis but not with nerve compression. Decreased sensation to touch and a positive Tinel's sign are present with radial sensory nerve compression but not with tendonitis. Tinel's sign is located where the radial sensory nerve exits from beneath the brachioradialis muscle.

6. **How do you distinguish tennis elbow from radial tunnel syndrome?**

Tennis elbow may be due to stretch/traction/inflammation of the extensors of the wrist and the fingers at their origin from the lateral humeral epicondyle. Swelling and tenderness are found directly over the lateral humeral epicondyle. Pain with resisted radial wrist extension or resisted extension of all fingers suggests tennis elbow (lateral humeral epicondylitis). Tenderness to palpation approximately 1 cm anterior or volar to the lateral humeral epicondyle suggests radial nerve compression in the radial tunnel. The radial nerve may become compressed by the fibrous edge of the extensor carpi radialis, which inserts into the base of the third metacarpal. Pain referred to the elbow region with resisted middle finger extension is a sign of radial tunnel syndrome. The counterforce brace worn around the forearm to treat tennis elbow can be a cause of radial tunnel syndrome so that both clinical conditions can exist in the same patient.

7. **What are the earliest physical findings of chronic peripheral nerve compression?**

Patients with reversible ischemic changes have symptoms without signs. With increasing duration of chronic compression, the large myelinated nerve fibers begin to change by demyelination. These fibers are related to motor function and perception touch/vibration. Manual muscle testing detects weakness, and pinch and grip strength can be measured directly. The qualitatively altered perception of vibration can be evaluated with a tuning fork applied to the target territory of the peripheral nerve, but recall that this stimulus is a wave and for the thumb will stimulate both the radial sensory and the median nerve. The best neurosensory test is evaluation of the cutaneous pressure threshold, which can identify that the pressure to discriminate one from two static stimuli is elevated while the distance between the two points is still normal.

8. **Describe the pathophysiology of chronic nerve compression.**
   - Intraneural edema occurs first, before any symptoms appear.
   - Increased intraneural pressure causes relative ischemia.
   - Neural ischemia causes paresthesia.
   - After 6 months of chronic compression, demyelination begins.
   - The earliest physical findings will be a positive Tinel's sign at the site of compression.
   - The next physical finding will be an increased cutaneous pressure threshold with a normal static two-point discrimination distance.
   - With sufficient demyelination of axons, electrodiagnostic testing will demonstrate increased distal latency.
   - After approximately 1 year of chronic compression, axonal loss begins.
   - The physical finding related to axonal loss is a decrease in static two-point discrimination.
   - With sufficient loss of axons, the amplitude of the electrical response decreases.
   - For the motor nerve, weakness precedes atrophy.
   - Weakness is to pressure threshold what abnormal two-point discrimination is to atrophy, when the sensory nerve is compared with the motor nerve.

9. **Which nerve compression syndromes affect the lower extremity?**
   - *Meralgia paresthetica* (compression of the lateral femoral cutaneous nerve at the hip)
   - *Piriformis syndrome* (compression of the sciatic nerve at the hip)
   - *Obturator syndrome* (compression of the obturator nerve at the obturator foramen)
   - *Femoral nerve compression syndrome* (compression at the inguinal ligament)
   - *Adductor canal syndrome* (compression of the saphenous nerve in the mid-thigh)
   - *Fibular tunnel syndrome* (compression of the common peroneal nerve at the fibular neck)
   - *Exertional compartment syndrome* (compression of the superficial peroneal nerve in the distal third of the leg)
   - *Anterior tarsal tunnel syndrome* (compression of the deep peroneal nerve over the anterior ankle)
   - *Entrapment of the deep peroneal nerve* (compression by the extensor hallucis brevis tendon at the junction of the first metatarsal and cuneiform bones)
   - *Tarsal tunnel syndrome* (entrapment of the tibial nerve in the tarsal tunnel, the medial plantar nerve in the medial plantar tunnel, the lateral plantar nerve in the lateral plantar tunnel, and the calcaneal nerve in the calcaneal tunnel)

10. **What are the analogous peripheral nerves that become entrapped at the wrist compared with at the ankle (carpal tunnel vs tarsal tunnel)?**

When the tarsal tunnel syndrome was described in 1962, it was the concept that the posterior tibial nerve was compressed by the flexor retinaculum that went from the medial malleolus to the calcaneus, similar to the compression of the median nerve by the transverse carpal tunnel ligament. This analogy is fallacious. The tarsal tunnel is analogous to the forearm, and the flexor retinaculum (laciniate ligament) is analogous to the antebrachial fascia. The medial plantar nerve in the medial plantar tunnel is analogous to the median nerve in the carpal tunnel. The lateral plantar nerve in the lateral plantar tunnel is analogous to the ulnar nerve in Guyon's canal. The medial calcaneal nerve in the calcaneal tunnel is analogous to the palmar cutaneous branch of the median nerve in its own tunnel alongside the flexor carpi radialis tendon.

11. Is Morton's neuroma a true neuroma?

This relatively common condition, a painful condition of the fourth toe, was described in 1875 by Morton, who thought it was related to the metatarsophalangeal joint. Yet he resected the joint and, in one patient, amputated the fourth toe along with the interdigital nerve. Subsequently, the condition was termed a "neuroma" despite the fact that light and electron microscopy documented chronic nerve compression. Compression of the interdigital nerve by the ligament joining the metatarsal heads is appropriately treated by neurolysis, not nerve resection. Recurrence of pain after resection of a "Morton's neuroma" is due to a true neuroma.

12. Describe the sequence of recovery of sensory touch submodalities.

- After a nerve repair, or after decompression of a peripheral nerve, the first perceptions to recover are those of the small myelinated and nonmyelinated fibers—pain and temperature perception.
- The large myelinated nerve fibers related to touch/pressure perception then recover in the following sequence:
  - Perception of one-point moving touch and low-frequency vibration (Meissner corpuscles)
  - Perception of one-point static touch (Merkel cell–neurite complex)
  - Perception of high-frequency vibration (pacinian corpuscle)
  - Perception of two-point moving touch
  - Perception of two-point static touch

13. What are the structures that must be released when treating the fibular canal syndrome (compression of the common peroneal nerve at the knee)?

The common peroneal nerve does not have a known site of compression proximal to the knee. As the common peroneal nerve approaches the fibular neck, it divides into the deep and superficial peroneal nerves, increasing its amount of connective tissue. At this juncture, the fascia of the peroneus longus muscle, which lies superficial to the nerve, is the first site to decompress. When this muscle is retracted, as in 80% of patients, a deep fascia to the muscle is observed to cause direct compression of the nerve. After dividing this fascia, the common peroneal nerve is elevated to determine if deep to it there is thickened fascia of the lateral gastrocnemius muscle to divide. Finally, the opening into the compartments of the leg is checked because there can be a high origin to the soleus muscle that narrows this entranceway. The immediate innervation of the overlying muscles within the fibular tunnel limits excursion of the peroneal nerve, making it susceptible to compression and stretch/traction.

14. What is the most common nerve compression occurring in the face?

The infraorbital nerve exits from the infraorbital foramen. This nerve is at risk in orbital floor fractures, in fractures of the zygoma, and during cosmetic surgery, such as malar augmentation with implants. Symptoms include numbness, paresthesias, and pain in the upper lip and cheek. This branch of the trigeminal nerve can be directly measured to determine its degree of entrapment by neurosensory testing. Treatment by neurolysis is theoretically possible.

15. Which nerve compressions masquerade as "failed carpal tunnel syndrome decompression"?

Carpal tunnel syndrome symptoms are numbness and tingling in the thumb, index, and middle fingers. Following carpal tunnel decompression, the patient may return to the surgeon complaining of these same symptoms in the thumb and index finger. The differential diagnosis of "failed carpal tunnel syndrome decompression" must include failure of the first surgery to achieve complete nerve release. However, compression of the radial sensory nerve in the forearm, proximal median nerve compression in the forearm (pronator syndrome), or a C6 nerve root entrapment (radiculopathy) can cause these same symptoms.

16. What causes "meralgia paresthetica"?

Compression of the lateral femoral cutaneous nerve at the hip was termed "meralgia paresthetica" in 1874 by Roth. This syndrome was recognized more commonly when women wore girdles. Anatomy books demonstrate this nerve, which originates from L1 and L2, to be located deep to the inguinal ligament, but at surgery it is most commonly identified within the inguinal ligament, adjacent to the anterior superior iliac crest. It is in this location in more than one third of cadavers. Today, this compression is seen after harvesting bone from the iliac crest, after seat belt injuries, and after abdominal surgery that tightens the abdominal wall; it can be associated with wearing a heavy tool belt. Treatment is a neurolysis of this nerve, extending proximally to release the nerve in the internal oblique fascia and distally into the thigh.

17. Where is the nerve entrapment site that causes scapular winging?

Winging of the scapula is known to occur after injury to the long thoracic nerve, which innervates the serratus anterior muscle. Although other shoulder girdle muscles can cause imbalance of the scapula, the classic winging is due to a problem with the long thoracic nerve. Entrapment of this nerve between the posterior and medial scalene muscles has been demonstrated to occur after blunt shoulder/neck trauma or stretch/traction injury to the brachial plexus. After anterior scalenectomy, a neurolysis posterior the upper trunk of the plexus, within the posterior and medial scalene muscles, will identify the long thoracic nerve adherent within the muscles. Neurolysis at this location is effective.

18. Describe some of the limitations to classic electrodiagnostic testing.

Electrodiagnostic testing includes both nerve conduction studies and electromyography. These studies are done by neurologists and physiatrists and require the patient to endure a usually painful electrical investigation of combinations of various peripheral nerves and muscles to arrive at a diagnosis for the patient's complaints. Often described as the "gold standard" because it is objective, electrodiagnosis is limited by low sensitivity, high cost, inability to test certain critical nerves, and failure of patients to have repeated testing for clinical follow-up. The testing evaluates only the faster conducting nerve fibers, and sufficient numbers of these may not undergo either demyelination or axonal loss to document a positive test until far along in the patient's symptomatology.

Because a decompressed or regenerating peripheral nerve does not remyelinate normally, these traditional tests may always show abnormalities postoperatively. Where the testing is best, for the median nerve at the carpal tunnel, meta-analysis demonstrates a false-negative rate of 33%. At the elbow this probably is 50% for the cubital tunnel. It is almost never positive for pronator syndrome, radial sensory nerve entrapment. It is impossible to determine entrapment of the brachial plexus except for the rare isolated entrapment of the lower trunk. The testing is even less successful in the lower extremity, where it cannot detect problems with the distal deep peroneal nerve or the calcaneal nerve. The false-negative rate for the tarsal tunnel is approximately 50%.

19. What is the difference between neuropathy and nerve compression?

Nerve compression, which is sometimes called a *mononeuropathy,* is a problem affecting a single peripheral nerve. Neuropathy implies a systemic problem with bilateral distribution of symptoms, usually occurring in the feet and legs first and then, in some forms of neuropathy, in the hands. A patient with a neuropathy may be susceptible to chronic nerve compression. For example, in diabetic neuropathy, a diffuse, distal, sensorimotor neuropathy with axonal loss, approximately one third of patients also have a chronic nerve compression. Electrodiagnosis cannot identify the patient with superimposed nerve compression in the presence of a peripheral neuropathy. The surgeon must rely on physical examination techniques, such as Tinel's sign.

20. Can the arcade of Struthers cause compression of the ulnar nerve?

There is no arcade described by Struthers. Struthers described a ligament arising from a supracondylar bone spur that compresses the median nerve proximal to the elbow. The radial artery may accompany the median nerve through this site of compression. This ligament is very rare. The ulnar nerve proximal to the cubital tunnel can fail to improve or can recur in compression due to failure to divide the brachial fascia, from the medial head of the triceps to the medial intermuscular septum, at a sufficiently proximal level. This region can look like a ligament. Also, a portion of the medial head of the triceps can arise from the medial intermuscular septum in this location.

21. Can decompression of peripheral nerves in the patient with diabetic neuropathy relieve pain, restore sensation, and prevent ulcer/amputation?

Yes. In 1988, a new optimism was suggested for patients with symptoms of diabetic neuropathy based on the hypothesis that the increased endoneurial edema from conversion of glucose to sorbitol would make the peripheral nerve susceptible to chronic compression. In a series of basic science studies, this was demonstrated in the streptozotocin-induced diabetic rat model. The first clinical series of patients to have decompression of multiple peripheral nerves was published in 1992. These results have been duplicated in many prospective cohort studies. A randomized prospective study has not been done yet. However, long-term outcomes in terms of ulcer and amputation have demonstrated that the natural history of diabetic neuropathy can be changed by this approach, and that the presence of a positive Tinel's sign over the site of known anatomic narrowing has a positive predictive value of 90%.

22. What are the cutaneous nerves that can contribute to a painful incision after decompression of the four medial ankle tunnels (tarsal tunnel surgery)?

Just as the palmar cutaneous branch of the median nerve can cause a painful carpal tunnel scar, the posterior branch of the distal saphenous nerve innervates the proximal portion of the tarsal tunnel incision, and the medial calcaneal nerve arising from the medial plantar nerve can cause a painful distal portion of the incision.

23. What nerve compression is associated with chemotherapy-induced neuropathy from cisplatin or taxol?

These active chemotherapeutic agents bind to tubulin in the axoplasm and decrease the slow component of axoplasmic transport, rendering the peripheral nerves susceptible to chronic nerve compression, similar to that found in diabetic neuropathy. In a rat model of chemotherapy-induced neuropathy with cisplatin, tarsal tunnel decompression restored the neuropathic walking track pattern to normal. This concept has now been applied to a small series of patients who obtained relief from decompression of upper and lower extremity nerve entrapments, including the median and ulnar nerves, the common peroneal nerve, and the tibial nerve and its branches in the four medial ankle tunnels.

24. After nerve decompression surgery, how long should the patient be immobilized?

During the first week after surgery, collagen is not being produced in the wound. The fibrin that is in the wound will not cause permanent fibrosis of the nerve. However, from postoperative days 7 through 21, collagen is produced and will begin cross-linking. Therefore, for patient comfort, the wound can be splinted for the first week; thereafter, it is critical that the nerve be permitted unrestricted gliding through the entire operative area, or fibrosis of the nerve will occur, and the decompression surgery or neurolysis will fail. This has been proven in an ulnar nerve/nonhuman primate model.

For carpal tunnel decompression, the wrist is splinted in neutral for 1 week, but full range of motion of the fingers permits median nerve movement within the carpal canal. After ulnar nerve transposition, the patient is permitted full range of motion of the elbow immediately after surgery, which is possible if the musculofascial lengthening technique is used. After tarsal tunnel decompression, the patient is permitted immediate full weight-bearing in a modified Robert Jones bulky supportive ankle dressing.

BIBLIOGRAPHY

Aszmann OC, Tassler PL, Dellon AL: Changing the natural history of diabetic neuropathy: Incidence of ulcer/amputation in the contralateral limb of patients with a unilateral nerve decompression procedure. Ann Plast Surg, 53:517–522, 2004.

Aszmann OC, Dellon ES, Dellon AL: The anatomic course of the lateral femoral cutaneous nerve and its susceptibility to compression and injury. Plast Reconstr Surg 100:600–604, 1997.

Boulton AJM, Arezzo JC, Malik RA, Sosenko JM: Diabetic somatic neuropathies. Diabetes Care 27:1458–1486, 2004.

Brushart TM, Gerber J, Kessens P, et al: Contributions of pathway and neuron to preferential motor reinnervation. J Neurosci 18: 8674–8681, 1998.

Coert JH, Connolly J, Dellon AL: Documenting compressive neuropathy of the lateral femoral cutaneous nerve. Ann Plast Surg 50: 373–377, 2003.

De Jesus R, Dellon AL: Historic description of the "Arcade of Struthers." J Hand Surg 28A:528–531, 2003.

Dellon AL: Clinical use of vibratory stimuli to evaluate peripheral nerve injury and compression neuropathy. Plastic Reconstr Surg 65:466–476, 1980.

Dellon AL, Keller KM: Computer-assisted quantitative sensory testing in patients with carpal and cubital tunnel syndrome. Ann Plast Surg 38:493–502, 1997.

Dellon AL, Chang E, Coert JH, Campbell KR: Intraneural ulnar nerve pressure changes related to operative techniques for cubital tunnel decompression. J Hand Surg 19A:923–930, 1994.

Dellon AL: Treatment of Morton's neuroma as a nerve compression: The role for neurolysis. J Am Podiatr Med Assoc 82:399–402, 1992.

Dellon AL, Kim J, Spaulding CM: Variations in the origin of the medial calcaneal nerve. J Am Podiatr Med Assoc 92:97–101, 2002.

Dellon AL, Mackinnon SE: Radial sensory nerve entrapment. Arch Neurol 43:833–837, 1986.

Dellon AL, Ebmer J, Swier P: Anatomic variations related to decompression of the common peroneal nerve at the fibular head. Ann Plast Surg 48:30–34, 2002.

Dellon AL, Mackinnon SE, Hudson AR, Hunter DA: Effect of submuscular versus intramuscular placement of ulnar nerve: Experimental model in the primate. J Hand Surg 11B:117–119, 1986.

Dellon AL: Wound healing in nerve. Clin Plast Surg 17:545–570, 1990.

Dellon AL, Swier P, Levingood M, Maloney CT: Cisplatin/taxol neuropathy: Treatment by decompression of peripheral nerve. Plast Reconstr Surg 114:478–483, 2004.

Dellon AL: Measuring peripheral nerve function: Neurosensory testing versus electrodiagnostic testing. In Slutsky D (ed): Atlas of the Hand Clinics: Nerve Repair and Reconstruction. Philadelphia, Elsevier, 2005, pp 1–31.

Dellon AL, Coert JH: Results of the musculofascial lengthening technique for submuscular transposition of the ulnar nerve at the elbow. J Bone Joint Surg 85A:1314–1320, 2003.

Disa J, Wang B, Dellon AL: Correction of scapular winging by neurolysis of the long thoracic nerve. J Reconstr Microsurg 17:79–84, 2001.

Fogaçç W, Ferreira MC, Dellon AL: Neurosensory testing in evaluation of infraorbital nerve injuries associated with zygoma fracture. Plast Reconstr Surg 113:834–838, 2004.

Howard M, Lee C, Dellon AL: Documentation of brachial plexus compression in the thoracic inlet utilizing provocation with neurosensory and motor testing. J Reconstr Microsurg 19:303–312, 2003.

Kim J, Dellon AL: Tarsal tunnel incisional pain due to neuroma of the posterior branch of saphenous nerve. J Am Podiatr Med Assoc 91:109–113, 2001.

Kim J, Dellon AL: Calcaneal neuroma: Diagnosis and treatment. Foot Ankle Int 22:890–894, 2001.

Larson EE, Barrett SL, Maloney CT Jr, Battiston B, Dellon AL: Accurate nomenclature of forefoot nerve entrapment: A historical perspective. J Am Podiatr Med Assoc 95:298–306, 2005.

Lee C, Dellon AL: Prognostic ability of Tinel sign in determining outcome for decompression surgery decompression surgery in diabetic and non-diabetic neuropathy. Ann Plast Surg 53:523–527, 2004.

Lee CH, Dellon AL: Surgical management for groin pain of neural origin. J Am Coll Surg 191:137–142, 2000.

Lister GD, Belsoe RB, Kleinert H.E.: The radial tunnel syndrome. J Hand Surg 4A:52–59, 1979.

Mackinnon SE, Dellon AL: Homologies between the tarsal and carpal tunnels: Implications for treatment of the tarsal tunnel syndrome. Contemp Orthop 14:75–79, 1987.

Mackinnon SE, Dellon AL: Peripheral Nerve Surgery. New York Thieme Medical Publishers, 1988.

Perkins B, Olaleye D, Bril V: Carpal tunnel syndrome in patients with diabetic polyneuropathy. Diabetes Care 25:565–569, 2002.

Rosenberg D, Conolley J, Dellon AL: Thenar eminence quantitative sensory testing in diagnosis of proximal median nerve compression. J Hand Ther 14:258–265, 2001.

Rosenberg D, Dellon AL: Results of decompression of median nerve entrapment in the forearm. Clin Exp Plast Surg 36:13–18, 2004.

Rosson G, Dellon AL: Surgical approach to multiple interdigital nerve compressions. J Foot Ankle Surg 44:70–73, 2005.

Saplys R, Mackinnon SE, Dellon AL: The relationship between nerve entrapment verus neuroma complications and the misdiagnosis of de Quervain's disease. Contemp Orthop 15:51–57, 1987.

Tassler PL, Dellon AL, Lesser G, Grossman S: Utility of decompressive surgery in the prophylaxis and treatment of cisplatin neuropathy in adult rats. J Reconstr Surg 16:457–463, 2000.

Vinik AI, Mehrabyan A, Colen L, Boulton A: Focal entrapment neuropathies in diabetes. Diabetes Care 27:1783–1788, 2004.

BRACHIAL PLEXUS

Adam J. Vernadakis, MD, and
Mark H. Gonzalez, MD, MEng

CHAPTER 137

1. Which nerve roots supply the brachial plexus?

The brachial plexus is most frequently supplied by the fifth through eighth cervical (C) and first thoracic (T) nerve roots (Fig. 137-1).

2. What is a prefixed plexus? A postfixed plexus?

A *prefixed plexus* has a contribution from the fourth cervical nerve root. A *postfixed plexus* has a contribution from the second thoracic nerve root.

3. Which nerves form the trunks of the brachial plexus?

Most frequently, the upper trunk is formed by the C5 and C6 nerve roots, the middle trunk is formed by the C7 nerve root, and the lower trunk is formed by the C8 and T1 nerve roots.

4. Which nerves form the cords of the brachial plexus?

The cords are named in relation to the axillary artery and form as each trunk divides into an anterior and a posterior division. The anterior divisions of the upper and middle trunks unite to form the lateral cord, the anterior division of the lower trunk forms the medial cord, and the posterior divisions of the three trunks form the posterior cord.

5. How are the peripheral nerves formed in the brachial plexus?

The musculocutaneous nerve arises from the lateral cord and the ulnar nerve from the medial cord. The median nerve is formed by contributions from the medial and lateral cords. The radial, axillary, and thoracodorsal nerves arise from the posterior cord.

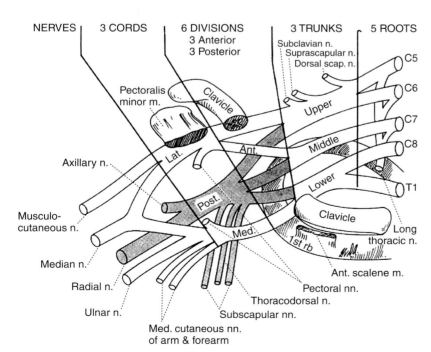

Figure 137-1. The brachial plexus. (From Lister GL: The brachial plexus. In: The Hand. Edinburgh, Churchill Livingstone, 1993, pp 243–246.)

6. **Where are lateral and medial pectoral nerves found in relation to each other? What is the clinical significance?**

The pectoral nerves are named in reference to their cord of origin from the brachial plexus. The medial pectoral nerve arises from the medial cord, whereas the lateral pectoral nerve arises from the lateral cord. Anatomically, the medial pectoral nerve lies lateral to the lateral pectoral nerve on the chest wall. The sternocostal head of the pectoralis major is innervated by both the medial and lateral pectoral nerves. This redundant innervation makes the medial pectoral nerve an excellent choice for a donor nerve during a nerve transfer.

7. **What is the common mechanism of closed brachial plexus injury in adults?**

Three basic mechanisms of injury may occur alone or in combination: traction, crush, and compression. Downward (caudal) traction to the shoulder usually causes upper trunk injuries. Traction to the abducted arm (cephalad) causes lower trunk injuries, and front-to-back force applied to the shoulder has been associated with an isolated C7 injury. Anterior dislocation of the shoulder and proximal humerus fracture have been associated with suprascapular and axillary nerve injury. Crush injuries usually result in a direct trauma as the plexus passes in the costoclavicular space between the clavicle and the first rib. Compression may result from surrounding soft tissue edema, bone fragments, hematoma, and pseudoaneurysms. The majority (approximately 90%) of plexus injuries occur in young male patients. Approximately 75% of all injuries result from motorcycle accidents, and 15% of plexus injuries will be associated with multiple trauma and shock.

8. **What is the best method to determine the level and severity of a brachial plexus injury?**

Although electrodiagnostic (nerve conduction studies [NCS], electromyography [EMG]) and radiographic studies (cervical spine and chest x-ray, computed tomographic [CT] myelogram, magnetic resonance imaging [MRI] and angiography) all are useful adjuncts, the best diagnostic tool is a thorough history and physical examination. A detailed history includes a description of the mechanism and the force involved as well as associated injuries. This will allow a focused and detailed physical examination that will both localize the injury and determine which muscle groups are spared and can be used as donor nerves for subsequent nerve transfers. Table 137-1 lists information useful in localizing the injury.

9. **What are the common clinical patterns of closed brachial plexus injury in adults?**

Proximal injuries of the brachial plexus are termed *supraclavicular injuries,* and distal injuries are termed *infraclavicular injuries.* The most common patterns of supraclavicular injury are *Erb's palsy* and *whole plexus injury.* Erb's palsy involves damage to the C5 and C6 nerve roots. Supraspinatus, infraspinatus (suprascapular nerve), deltoid (axillary nerve), brachialis, and biceps (musculocutaneous nerve) function is lost. Clinically the arm is internally rotated and adducted, and the elbow is extended in the "waiter's tip" position. The C7 nerve root also may be damaged, causing loss or weakness of elbow, wrist, and finger extension. The whole plexus injury causes complete or nearly-complete loss of arm function (flail arm). Isolated involvement of the C8 and T1 nerve roots (Klumpke's paralysis) is extremely uncommon and shows loss of hand function with sparing of the elbow and shoulder. Infraclavicular injuries commonly show loss of shoulder abduction and flexion but also may be associated with loss of hand, wrist, and elbow function.

10. **What are the indications for an arteriogram after an injury to the brachial plexus?**
- Advanced Trauma Life Support (ATLS) protocol indications on trauma evaluation including widened mediastinum, scapular fracture, and first rib fracture
- Penetrating trauma to the region of the brachial plexus
- Abnormal pulses associated with blunt or penetrating trauma
- Normal initial examination followed by subsequent brachial plexus neurologic deficit that may be due to an expanding hematoma.

The risk of arterial injury after brachial plexus injury is 10%, and some authors recommend arteriography for all brachial plexus injuries.

11. **What is the significance of a preganglionic and postganglionic lesion of the brachial plexus? What findings suggest a preganglionic lesion?**

A preganglionic lesion of the nerve root is within the intervertebral foramen proximal to the sensory root ganglion and is also termed a *root avulsion.* A postganglionic lesion is distal to the sensory root ganglion. Preganglionic lesions are not reconstructable by nerve graft, and regeneration is not possible. A postganglionic lesion can be grafted and has regenerative potential. During electrodiagnostic evaluation, the findings on nerve conduction studies are useful in determining the pattern of injury. As the motor ganglion is within the substance of the ventral horn, the compound motor action potentials (CMAPs) will be blunted in both types of lesions and motor function will be absent. As the dorsal root ganglion is peripheral to the spinal column, the cell body is preserved and the sensory axons will not undergo wallerian degeneration. Sensory nerve action potentials (SNAPs) will be preserved, whereas sensation is diminished or absent.

Table 137-1. Localizing a Brachial Plexus Injury

MUSCLE	NERVE	ROOTS	PLEXUS ORIGIN	ACTIONS
Trapezius	Spinal accessory	CN XI, C3,4	Cranial nerve, roots	Elevate, adduct, depress scapula
Rhomboids	Dorsal scapular	C4,5	Roots	Retract, stabilize, depress scapula
Serratus anterior	Long thoracic	C5,6,7	Roots	Protract, stabilize scapula
Supraspinatus	Suprascapular	C5, C6	Superior trunk	Humerus abduction
Infraspinatus	Suprascapular	C5, C6	Superior trunk	External rotation of humerus
Pectoralis major (clavicular head)	Lateral pectoral	C5, C6	Lateral cord	Transverse flexion/ adduction of humerus
Pectoralis major (sternocostal head)	Medial, lateral pectoral	C6, C7, C8	Lateral and medial cords	Adduct, internally rotate humerus
Teres major	Subscapular	C5, C6, C7	Posterior cord	Adduct, extend, internally rotate humerus
Latissimus dorsi	Thoracodorsal	C6, C7, C8	Posterior cord	Adduct, extend, internally rotate humerus
Deltoid	Axillary	C5, C6	Terminal branch	Abduct, flex, externally rotate humerus
Biceps brachii	Musculocutaneous	C5, C6	Terminal branch	Flex elbow, supinate forearm
Triceps brachii	Radial	C6, C7, C8	Terminal branch	Extend, adduct shoulder, flex elbow
Brachioradialis	Radial	C5, C6	Terminal branch	Flex elbow
Extensor pollicis longus	Posterior interosseous	C7, C8	Terminal branch (radial nerve)	Extend thumb interphalangeal
Flexor carpi ulnaris	Ulnar	C7, C8, T1	Terminal branch	Flex wrist
Flexor digitorum profundus (ulnar)	Ulnar	C7, C8	Terminal branch	Flex distal interphalangeal (ulnar digits)
Adductor pollicis	Ulnar	C8, T1	Terminal branch	Adduct thumb at carpometacarpal
Flexor carpi radialis	Median	C6, C7	Terminal branch	Flex wrist
Flexor digitorum superficialis	Median	C7, C8, T1	Terminal branch	Flex proximal interphalangeal
Abductor pollicis brevis	Median	C8, T1	Terminal branch	Abduct thumb (perpendicular to palm)
Flexor pollicis longus	Anterior interosseus	C7, C8	Terminal branch (median nerve)	Flex thumb interphalangeal

12. What is the histamine triple response?

Histamine is injected into the skin, and the triple response is vasodilation followed by a wheal and flair. The response is an axonal reflex involving the sympathetic ganglion and dorsal root ganglion. Skin denervation with an intact triple response implies a preganglionic lesion.

13. What findings are associated with root avulsions? What is the significance of a root avulsion?

Horner syndrome consists of ipsilateral ptosis (drooping eyelid), miosis (small pupil), enopthalmos (sunken eyeball), and anhidrosis (absence of sweat secretion) of the affected side of the face. The presence of Horner syndrome implies interruption of the sympathetic fibers to the face that arise in the cervicothoracic ganglion. This interruption is due to a proximal lesion to the C8 and T1 roots that frequently is preganglionic, implying a root avulsion. Denervation of the serratus or rhomboids, an intact histamine response, paralysis of the hemidiaphragm (phrenic nerve C 3,4,5), and absence of any recovery in the distribution of a nerve root may imply a root avulsion. Transverse process fractures of the cervical spine may be seen on x-ray and may be useful in localizing the level of root avulsion. Traumatic meningocoeles on CT myelogram and proximal nerve lesions on MRI suggest a preganglionic lesion. Root avulsions will not recover spontaneously and are not reconstructable with nerve grafts. Nerve transfers can be used to reconstruct the resulting deficit.

14. What are the goals of brachial plexus reconstruction?

It is mandatory to establish realistic expectations in brachial plexus surgery because the reconstructive goals are modest at best. The goals of reconstruction are restoration of the following (in order of priority):

- Elbow flexion
- Shoulder abduction
- Hand sensibility
- Wrist extension, finger flexion
- Wrist flexion, finger extension
- Intrinsic hand function

15. What techniques are used in reconstruction of the brachial plexus? What are some of the limitations of each?

The brachial plexus can be reconstructed using a number of techniques, either alone or in combination.

Nerve transfers from adjacent, intact nerves can be used to restore function to nerves that are of higher priority, with limited to no loss of function in the donor nerve. The dominant fascicle to a muscle is localized, sparing the secondary fascicles. The nerve is transferred as close to the recipient motor end plate as possible, significantly shortening the time to recovery. Donor nerves should be adjacent to the recipient, redundant and preferably synergistic. Common transfers include flexor carpi ulnaris to musculocutaneous nerve to biceps (Oberlin), distal or end-to-side spinal accessory to suprascapular nerve, and radial nerve long head of triceps branch to axillary nerve. More remote donor nerves can be used with *nerve grafts,* but axons may be lost ("drop out") in the grafting process. *Direct repair* is rarely possible but can be used. However, distal recovery may be delayed or absent as the axons must regenerate proximal to the level of injury at a rate of 1 inch/month or 1 mm/day.

Neurotized free muscle transfers can be used to reconstruct distal muscle groups following nerve regeneration through a donor nerve, but the process must be staged. Excision of the injured segment and reconstruction with *cable grafts* is a time-honored technique, but the dissection through scarred tissue often is difficult, tedious, and time consuming. There are also a limited number of nerves that can be used as graft material. Excision and cable grafting are further limited as distal recovery is poor and the technique may downgrade function by sacrificing intact nerves.

Shoulder fusion may be useful as an adjunct because 70° of abduction may be obtained from scapulothoracic motion. Donor nerve availability may be increased using this technique, but it requires intact scapular stabilizers.

16. What nerves can be used as donor nerves for nerve grafting?

The most commonly used and "gold standard" donor is the sural nerve from the lateral and posterior calf, which may provide 25 to 30 cm of graft. The medial antebrachial cutaneous nerve in the medial upper arm may provide an addition 15 to 20 cm of graft material. The sensory nerve to the third web space, which is located on the ulnarmost portion of the median nerve, and the sensory component of the radial nerve also serve as potential expendable donor nerves when needed.

17. What are the degrees of nerve injury? Why are they significant in brachial plexus reconstruction?

Seddon and Sunderland both described nerve injuries. Seddon's initial description described neuropraxia, axonotmesis, and neurotmesis, and Sunderland expanded this classification into five degrees of nerve injury.

A *first-degree injury (neuropraxia)* is a demyelination injury resulting in a temporary block at the site of the nerve injury. Recovery is spontaneous and complete in a matter of weeks to months once remyelination occurs. There is no Tinel's sign as axonal regeneration does not occur and electrodiagnostic studies are normal.

A *second-degree injury (axonotmesis)* is a nerve fiber injury in which the distal fibers undergo wallerian degeneration, but the endoneurial tubes remain open and in continuity. Recovery is complete, occurs at a rate of 1 mm/day, and may be followed by an advancing Tinel's sign.

A *third-degree injury* also undergoes wallerian degeneration distally, but the endoneurial tubes are scarred. Recovery is slow and variable.

A *fourth-degree injury* will not recover because the endoneurial tubes are completely blocked by scar and must be surgically reconstructed.

A *fifth-degree injury (neurotmesis)* is the transection of a nerve trunk, and surgical repair is indicated.

Mackinnon introduced a *sixth-degree injury,* which is a combination of the five degrees of injury. Intervention is dictated by the deficits that are present, and recovery is variable.

18. Describe the optimal timing of exploration of an adult traction injury of the brachial plexus.

After injury, a motor nerve may continue to be stimulated intraoperatively for up to 72 hours until the neurotransmitters are depleted. The neurotransmitters are completely depleted by 1 week. Wallerian degeneration of the distal nerve segment occurs over the next 3 to 6 weeks. Electrodiagnostic findings are not synchronous with nerve injury. CMAP nadir occurs at 7 days, and the SNAP nadir is seen after approximately 11 days. Fibrillations, which are markers of motor nerve injury, are seen on EMG after 3 to 5 weeks, so the inital EMG in a closed brachial plexus should be performed during the sixth week after injury.

Markers of recovery include volitional motor unit action potentials, and expectant management and observation are indicated because recovery is expected to a certain degree. If no recovery is seen after 12 weeks, intervention and reconstruction are indicated. If a root injury is suspected, CT myelogram is used for confirmation and early intervention is indicated because no recovery is expected. Timing of reconstruction is crucial. Premature intervention may downgrade the function of a nerve that may have recovered spontaneously. Late intervention may lead to successful reinnervation of a functionless muscle. Muscle atrophy begins within 1 week after denervation, and progressive interstitial fibrosis occurs after 3 months. At 18 to 24 months, the motor endplates deteriorate and there is no functional recovery. A guide to functional motor recovery is Mackinnon's "rule of 18," which notes the sum of the distance from the injury to the target muscle in inches and the time elapsed in months cannot exceed 18. As with any injury, passive range of motion must be maintained with physical therapy while recovery is progressing.

19. What causes obstetric palsy?

Obstetric palsy is believed to be due to a traumatic lesion at birth and occurs in 1:10,000 births. The injury is 175 times more common in breech delivery. Two situations may predispose to obstetric palsy. Large infants with cephalic presentation and shoulder dystocia are at risk during delivery, as are small infants born with a breech presentation. Obstetric palsy may occur after a seemingly normal delivery and has been documented even after a cesarean section.

20. What are the indications and timing for exploration of obstetric palsy?

The absence of any return of biceps or deltoid function by 3 months of age is a strong indication for brachial plexus exploration. Other criteria include the absence of elbow flexion/extension, wrist extension, or thumb/finger extension by 9 months of age. Most surgeons recommend exploration before 6 to 9 months of age.

21. What symptoms are associated with thoracic outlet syndrome?

Neurologic symptoms are most commonly associated with thoracic outlet syndrome. Burning pain involving the shoulder occurs with radiation into the inner arm and the hand, and tingling and numbness of the C8 and T1 nerve root distribution, including the ulnar two fingers, are common. Weakness and wasting of the intrinsic hand muscles, including the thenar eminence, are less common. Vascular changes of the arm and hand are infrequent but may cause venous congestion, cold intolerance, color changes, and cold sensitivity.

22. What is the anatomy of the thoracic outlet?

The thoracic outlet is a triangular space bounded anteriorly by the scalenus anticus, posteriorly by the scalenus medius, and inferiorly by the first rib. The brachial plexus and subclavian artery pass through the outlet.

23. What is the cause of thoracic outlet syndrome?

Any structure that narrows the thoracic outlet may cause thoracic outlet syndrome. A cervical rib, fibrous bands, or a mass effect (tumor) may cause nerve compression. Postural changes such as the military brace position or stooped shoulders also may contribute to development of thoracic outlet syndrome. When not associated with a structural abnormality, thoracic outlet syndrome may arise from a muscle imbalance from overused and foreshortened neck flexors and weakend scapular stabilizers leading to neck flexion and hunched, rolled shoulders (the "turtle position").

24. **Which physical examination techniques are useful in evaluation of thoracic outlet syndrome?**

In the *Roo's test,* the patient is seated with the arms abducted 90° and the elbows flexed 90°. The patient is asked to open and close the hands repeatedly for 3 minutes. The patient with thoracic outlet syndrome experiences an exacerbation of symptoms and is unable to complete the test.

During the *Adson* or *scalene maneuver,* the patient's arm is held in abduction and the radial pulse is palpated. The patient rotates the head toward the affected side and up to the ceiling and then to the opposite side. Absent or diminishing pulses may indicate scalene impingement or the presence of a cervical rib.

The *costoclavicular maneuver* is performed with the patient's scapulae adducted and retracted and the chin touching the chest while palpating the radial pulse. Changes in the vascular examination may indicate neurovascular compression between the clavicle and the first rib and may be due to subclavius or scalene tightness.

During *Wright's test,* the patients arm is abducted above the head. A diminishing or absent pulse may indicate compression by the coracoid process or the pectoralis minor.

During the *traction test,* firm traction is applied to the arm for several seconds while the pulse is examined. A diminished pulse may indicate the presence of a cervical rib.

25. **What is the treatment of thoracic outlet syndrome?**

The initial therapy of thoracic outlet syndrome is conservative, including physical therapy, weight loss when appropriate, and avoidance of conditions that exacerbate the condition, such as carrying heavy weights on the shoulder. Therapy involves postural exercises that target the muscle imbalance described in Question 23. Stretching of the foreshortened muscles including the scalenes, sternocleidomastoids, pectoralis minor, and levator scapulae must precede strengthening exercises to prevent exacerbation of symptoms of thoracic outlet syndrome. Once satisfactory length has been restored, therapy should proceed with strengthening of the weakened middle and lower trapezius, rhomboids, and serratus anterior muscles. Refractory symptoms may be amenable to surgical therapy. The thoracic outlet may be decompressed through a supraclavicular or axillary approach. The supraclavicular approach allows release of fibrous bands and the scalene muscles. The first rib or a cervical rib, when present, can be excised through either approach.

26. **What is Parsonage Turner syndrome? What is the recommended treatment?**

Parsonage Turner syndrome is also called *neuralgic amyotrophy* and *acute brachial neuritis.* Acute pain involving the shoulder with radiation into the arm is the initial symptom, with subsequent partial or complete paralysis of the arm. The paralysis is a lower motor neuron type with flaccidity. Surgical intervention is not recommended; most patients regain complete function.

CONTROVERSIES

27. **What is the indication for neurolysis of the brachial plexus?**

Neurolysis removes scar surrounding intact nerve fibers. Posttraumatic scarring of the brachial plexus can arrest nerve regeneration or cause loss of regenerated function. In this setting, neurolysis is indicated to release scar that surrounds functioning fascicles and to determine which fascicles are discontinuous and require grafting. Intraoperative nerve stimulation may be useful in identifying and protecting intact fascicles.

28. **What is the clinical significance of the suprascapular nerve?**

The suprascapular nerve innervates the supraspinatus and infraspinatus muscles and is the only root level nerve that is amenable to reconstruction. Reconstruction can be accomplished by end-to-end or end-to-side nerve transfer from the adjacent spinal accessory nerve. The supraspinatus muscle adducts the shoulder, which is redundant to the function of the deltoid muscle and one of the main priorities of brachial plexus reconstruction. Some surgeons preferentially reconstruct the suprascapular nerve in lieu of axillary nerve reconstruction due to its more accessible location.

BIBLIOGRAPHY

Boome RS (ed): The Brachial Plexus. New York, Churchill Livingstone, 1997.
Brandt KE: Nerve repair: In Evans GRD (ed): Operative Plastic Surgery, New York, McGraw-Hill, 2000, pp 809–907.
Dvali L, Mackinnon SE: Nerve Repair, Grafting and Nerve Transfers. Clin Plast Surg 30:203–221, 2003.
Exercise & Kinesiology. Available at: http://www.exrx.net/Exercise.html.
Gallen J, Wiss D, Cantelmo N, Menzoin J: Traumatic pseudoaneurysm of the axillary artery: Report of three cases and literature review. J Trauma 24:350–354, 1984.

Gilbert A, Whitaker I: Obstetrical brachial plexus lesions. J Hand Surg 16B:489–491, 1991.

Leffert RD: Brachial Plexus Injuries. New York, Churchill Livingstone, 1985.

Lister GL: The Hand. Edinburgh, Churchill Livingstone, 1993.

Michelow BJ, Clarke HM, Curtis CG, et al: The natural history of obstetrical brachial palsy. Plast Reconstr Surg 93:675–681, 1994.

Millesi H: Brachial plexus injury in adults: Operative repair. In Gelberman RH (ed): Operative Nerve Repair and Reconstruction. Philadelphia, WB Saunders, 1991, pp 1285–1301.

Novak CB: Thoracic outlet syndrome. Clin Plast Surg 30:175–188, 2003.

Novak CB: Evaluation of the nerve-injured patient. Clin Plast Surg 30:127–138, 2003.

O'Brien MD (ed): Aids to the Examination of the Peripheral Nervous System, 4th ed. New York, WB Saunders, 2000.

Roos DB: New concepts of thoracic outlet syndrome that explain etiology, symptoms, diagnosis, and treatment. Vasc Surg 13:313–321, 1974.

Sturm J, Perry J: Brachial plexus injuries from blunt trauma—A harbinger of vascular and thoracic injury. Ann Emerg Med 16:404–406, 1987.

Trumble TE: Brachial plexus. In: Principles of Hand Surgery and Therapy. Philadelphia, WB Saunders, 2000, pp. 297–312.

Tung TH, Mackinnon SE: Brachial plexus injuries. Clin Plast Surg 30:269–287, 2003.

Waters PM: Obstetrical brachial plexus palsy injuries: Evaluation and management. J Am Acad Orthop Surg 5:205–214, 1997.

Wilbourn AJ: The electrodiagnostic examination with peripheral nerve injuries. Clin Plast Surg 30:139–154, 2003.

CHAPTER 138

RHEUMATOID ARTHRITIS

Ronit Wollstein, MD; Nabil A. Barakat, MD; and
W.P. Andrew Lee, MD

1. What is the presentation of rheumatoid arthritis?

Rheumatoid arthritis (RA) is a systemic, chronic multisystem disease characterized by inflammation of synovial tissue. The presentation can be quite variable, but cartilage destruction and subsequent deformity in a symmetrical distribution are the hallmarks of the disease. Onset is most frequent during the fourth and fifth decades of life. Women are affected three times as often as men.

2. How is the diagnosis of RA made?

The diagnosis is made based on both clinical and laboratory criteria. Clinical criteria include symmetrical joint involvement and rheumatoid nodules. Laboratory criteria include the presence of rheumatoid factor (antibody to the Fc portion of immunoglobulin G [IgG]).

3. What is the pathophysiology of RA?

The precise cause is unknown, but an autoimmune reaction to an unidentified agent within the synovial tissue causes chronic inflammation. Leukocytes release inflammatory mediators causing synovitis. There are two dominant theories regarding the cell type responsible for the pathology. The first holds that the T cell is the primary cell responsible for initiating the disease as well as for driving the chronic inflammatory process. The second holds that, although T cells may be important in initiating the disease, chronic inflammation is self-perpetuated by macrophages and fibroblasts in a T-cell–independent manner. There is a genetic predisposition to the disease.

4. What are the radiographic features of RA?

A uniform joint space narrowing with characteristic erosions. These are present on both sides of the joint, correlating with the area in which normal synovium is anchored to bone. The hypertrophied rheumatoid synovium begins its invasion of bone at these sites, and this is an early radiologic sign. There is generalized osteoporosis without the subchondral sclerosis and osteophytes that are typical of osteoarthritis.

5. What are the clinical features of RA?

Characteristically this is a chronic polyarthritis, usually symmetrical. The arthritis often leads first to swelling, then to deformity with loss of function. Morning stiffness that lasts over an hour is typical of inflammatory arthritis.

Inflammation of the synovium surrounding the tendons leads to areas of tenderness and tendon ruptures. Triggering and various nerve compressions are also noted subsequent to the inflammation. Muscle wasting secondary to all of the above may result. Extraarticular manifestations include eye, lung, heart, blood vessel, muscle, and neurologic signs as well as associated autoimmune diseases.

6. What are the most common expressions of RA in the hand and upper extremity?

Synovitis of the elbow joints is common with stiffness and deformity. Wrist involvement is very common with a tendency toward ulnar translocation. Involvement of the metacarpophalangeal (MP) and proximal interphalangeal (PIP) joints are typical as opposed to involvement of the distal interphalangeal (DIP) joints in osteoarthritis. Characteristic deformities in the hand include ulnar deviation and dislocation of the MP joints and boutonnière and swan neck deformities of the fingers and thumb.

7. What is the caput ulnae syndrome?

Destructive changes following synovitis of the distal radioulnar joint (DRUJ) with attenuation of the ulnocarpal ligaments cause the caput ulnae syndrome. The caput ulnae syndrome may include dorsal dislocation of the distal ulna, supination of the carpus, and volar subluxation of the extensor carpi ulnaris. It is seen in up to one third of patients and may cause weakness and pain that are aggravated by forearm rotation. On examination the distal ulna usually is prominent. This area and its osteophytes cause attrition ruptures of the extensor tendons starting from the ulnar finger extensors.

8. What are the causes of tendon ruptures in RA?

Both extensor and flexor tendon ruptures occur in RA. These tears usually are attritional tears: over-prominent and sharp bony prominences, direct invasion by inflammatory synovium, which infiltrates the tendon, and ischemic necrosis from proliferation of the synovium in tight spaces. Ruptures from osteophytes over the distal ulna and DRUJ are called *Vaughn-Jackson lesions*. The extensor pollicis longus (EPL) tears over Lister's tubercle; this is the most common tendon tear in RA. On the flexor side, the flexor pollicis longus (FPL) is the most commonly ruptured, usually from osteophytes on the trapezium or scaphoid—the Mannerfelt syndrome.

9. What is the differential diagnosis for inability to extend the MP joints in RA?

- Extensor tendon rupture
- MP joint dislocation
- MP joint flexion contracture secondary to intrinsic tightness (rare)
- Extensor subluxation secondary to attenuation of the hood; in this case, if the finger is extended by the examiner, the patient will be able to hold the finger in extension because the tendon has been passively reduced
- PIN (posterior interosseous nerve) palsy with paralysis of the extensors; this usually is secondary to synovitis at the elbow

10. What is the medical treatment of RA?

The medical treatment of RA consists of pharmaceutical treatment, steroid injections, hand therapy, and splinting.

In pharmacologic therapy, three general classes of drugs are commonly used for treatment of RA: nonsteroidal antiinflammatory drugs (NSAIDs), corticosteroids, and remitting agents or disease-modifying antirheumatic drugs (DMARDs). NSAIDs and corticosteroids have a short onset of action, whereas DMARDs can take several weeks or months before a measurable clinical effect is seen. DMARDs include methotrexate, antimalarials, gold salts, sulfasalazine, D-penicillamine, cyclosporin A, cyclophosphamide, and azathioprine. Relatively new drugs also in use include leflunomide (Arava), etanercept (Enbrel), infliximab (Remicade), adalimumab (Humira), and anakinra (Kineret). The classic pyramid of treatment starting with NSAIDs, then moving on to corticosteroids as second-line treatment and so on is not always adhered to. The idea behind this approach is not to necessarily wait for the damage to take place but to try and prevent it. Local steroid injections occasionally give transient relief of symptoms, as do joint protection and splinting.

11. What are the four objectives of surgical treatment in the rheumatoid hand?

- To relieve pain and its debilitating effects
- To improve/restore function
- To prevent destruction and deformity
- To correct cosmetic deformity

12. How do you approach the rheumatoid hand?

Deformity without pain or functional loss is not an indication for surgery. Many deformed hands are painless, and the deformity bears no functional significance. Functional loss and effects on activities of daily living should be assessed specifically. It is very important to question the patient as to what bothers him/her most and to address those issues first. In evaluating a hand with multiple deformities, you should try to assess the cause of a certain deformity to treat it correctly. It usually is best to start with simple and more predictable procedures.

13. What are the general categories of surgical procedures performed for the rheumatoid hand and wrist?

- Preventive procedures, such as tenosynovectomy/synovectomy, removal of bone spurs, and radiolunate fusion (Chamay et al.)
- Reconstructive procedures, such as tendon transfers, arthroplasty
- Salvage procedures, such as arthrodesis.

14. What are the indications for an extensor tenosynovectomy?

There are no clear-cut guidelines for the timing of tenosynovectomy. It is best done prior to tendon rupture and in cases in which medical treatment has not controlled the synovitis. The timing is often dependent on the referring rheumatologist. This is probably the most significant preventive surgery for rheumatoid hand and can be augmented with excision of osteophytes from the DRUJ area.

15. What is the preferred treatment of extensor tendon ruptures?

The extensor tendons usually rupture in RA over the arthritic DRUJ. Therefore the ulnar extensors usually are ruptured first and sequentially the radial ones. Because these are attrition ruptures, true reconstruction is rarely attempted, and the distal ends of the torn extensors are transferred to the intact adjacent tendons. At the same time, removal of any sharp prominences should be undertaken. If there are no intact tendons to transfer to, an extensor indicis proprius tendon or an flexor digitorum profundus to the extensor side can be transferred. Rupture of the EPL can be treated by transfer of the EIP.

16. What are the typical deformities in the radiocarpal and intercarpal joints in RA?
The following are typical wrist deformities:

- Ulnar and volar translation with supination relative to the radius (this occurs secondary to synovitis and attenuation of the radiocarpal ligaments).
- Arthritis and stiffness of the radiocarpal joints. Usually the radiolunate joint is involved as opposed to degenerative arthritis of the wrist, in which this joint is relatively spared, although often the changes resemble severe osteoarthritis of the wrist.
- In juvenile RA because of premature closure of the epiphyses, the wrist is smaller and tends to be stiff and not unstable.

The indications for surgical treatment remain functional: arthrodesis (partial and total wrist) and arthroplasty. Wrist synovectomy is indicated in patients with minimal bony destruction.

17. What are the indications for MP joint arthroplasty?
The indications are pain, loss of function, and ulnar drift, along with radiographic evidence of advanced destruction of the joint. Absence of pain with a functional hand is a contraindication to surgical treatment. MP joint arthrodesis usually is avoided in view of the significant limitation that it imposes on motion. MP joint arthroplasty with silicone or pyrocarbon implants is most often used.

18. What are the common finger deformities in the rheumatoid hand?
A *swan neck deformity* with hyperextension of the PIP joint and flexion of the DIP joint and the *boutonnière deformity* with hyperextension of the DIP joint and flexion of the PIP joint are most common. Both deformities are secondary to imbalances in the extensor mechanism caused by synovitis within the joint spaces. Flexion contractures, mostly of the PIP joints, are common.

19. What is the surgical approach to correction of the swan neck deformity?
The treatment depends on the mobility of the PIP joint. If the PIP joint is flexible in all positions, DIP joint arthrodesis or dermodesis, sublimis sling/tenodesis, and Littler spiral oblique retinacular ligament (SORL) reconstruction are indicated. If PIP joint flexion is limited, intrinsic release, PIP joint manipulation, or lateral band mobilization is indicated. A stiff PIP joint with radiographic evidence of advanced intraarticular changes requires either PIP joint arthroplasty or fusion. PIP joint arthroplasty in the setting of RA has generally met with poor long-term results.

20. What is the mechanism leading to boutonnière deformity?
Inflammation within the PIP joint attenuates the extensor mechanism over the PIP joint. This causes the lateral bands to displace volarly and become fixed. They then act as flexors of the PIP joint (being volar to the axis of rotation of the joint) and become the sole extensors of the DIP joint, leading to hyperextension of the DIP joint. Surgical correction of boutonnière deformity is often associated with limited functional improvement and a high recurrence rate. Soft tissue correction is indicated only if passive extension of the PIP joint is possible and the joint is preserved. Plication or reinsertion of the central tendon and relocation of the lateral bands dorsally may be performed. If the PIP joint cannot be extended passively or if it is painful, an arthrodesis is indicated.

21. What are the indications for thumb fusion in RA?
Fusion of the MP or IP joints of the thumb may be very functional if the carpometacarpal joint has a good range of motion. They allow for stability during grasp and pinch as well as improved cosmetics.

BIBLIOGRAPHY

American College of Rheumatology Ad Hoc Committee on Clinical Guidelines: Guidelines for the management of rheumatoid arthritis. Arthritis Rheum 39:713, 1996.
Chamay A, Della Santa D, Vilaseca A: Radiolunate arthrodesis: Factor of stability for the rheumatoid wrist. Ann Chir Main 2:5–17, 1983.
Feldon P, Terrono AL, Nalebuff EA, Millender LH: Rheumatoid arthritis and other connective tissue diseases. In Green DP, Hotchkiss RN, Pederson WC (eds): Operative Hand Surgery, 4th ed. New York, Churchill Livingstone, 1999, pp. 1651–1739.
Friedman R: Rheumatoid arthritis. Select Read Plast Surg 7:9–17, 1995.
O'Brien E: Surgical principles and planning for the treatment of the rheumatoid hand and wrist. Clin Plast Surg 23:407–420, 1996.
Tomaino MM: Distal interphalangeal joint arthrodesis with screw fixation: Why and how. Hand Clin 22:207–210, 2006.

CHAPTER 139

DUPUYTREN'S DISEASE

Robert M. McFarlane, MD, FRCSC, and
Douglas C. Ross, MD, MEd, FRCSC

1. What is the cause of Dupuytren's disease?

Dupuytren's disease (DD) is a familial disease and until recently was considered to be a genetic disease due to a single dominant gene of variable penetrance. The cause probably is multifactorial, involving more than one gene as well as environmental factors.

2. What diseases are associated with DD?

- *Diabetes Mellitus.* Approximately 5% of people with DD are diabetic (type 1 or 2). The frequency of DD in diabetic patients increases with age and duration of diabetes. For instance, at 20 years' duration, 67% of diabetic patients have DD, although the disease is mild and rarely requires treatment. Patients also have a type of finger joint contracture called *limited joint mobility,* which prevents them from fully extending the fingers. The explanation for the association between DD and diabetes is unknown.
- *Seizure Disorders.* The incidence of epilepsy is 1.5% in the general population and 3% in people with DD. There are two conflicting explanations: (1) genetic linkage and (2) the theory that DD is caused by long-term barbiturate medication.
- *Chronic Alcoholism.* The prevalence of DD varies, but severe alcoholics often have severe DD. Despite frequent statements to the contrary, DD is not due to liver disease. The association is related to the volume of alcohol consumed and the age of the patient. There also may be a genetic predisposition.

3. Is DD related to work or injury?

Despite many attempts to answer this question, no study is conclusive. Patients often attribute their disease to some work pattern, whether they are manual or sedentary workers. Some studies report an increase of DD in heavy manual workers, whereas several others have found no greater incidence. Reports suggest an association with vibration injury, but the figures are not significant. The association of DD with acute injury is a separate problem. Several reports, most of which are anecdotal and involve one or two cases, relate the onset of DD to a fracture, penetrating wound, or laceration of the hand. The suggested causes are swelling and immobilization in a genetically predisposed person.

4. What are the risk factors for developing DD?

Because DD is a familial disease, the chance that a child will develop DD depends on the clinical features possessed by the parent, which were described by Hueston as "diathesis factors." The presence of one or more of these factors increases the chance that other members of the family may develop DD:

- Positive history in first- or second-degree relative
- Presence of ectopic deposits—Dupuytren's tissue that appears beyond the palmar surface of the hand; the usual sites are knuckle pads over the dorsum of the proximal interphalangeal (PIP) joints, plantar fibromatosis, and penile fibromatosis (Peyronie's disease)
- Early age of onset of disease (before age 40 years)
- Presence of severe bilateral disease, especially involving the radial side of the hand

The examiner should determine the presence or absence of each factor in every patient. Diathesis factors not only are of prognostic value; they also are essential in planning treatment.

5. Does the diseased tissue exhibit specific patterns?

Yes. The diseased fascia is not laid down haphazardly but in certain components of the normal palmar fascia (Fig. 139-1):

- The pretendinous bands of the palmar aponeurosis become the pretendinous cords (normal fascia is bandlike, whereas diseased fascia is cordlike).
- The natatory ligament becomes the natatory cord.
- The termination of the transverse fibers of the palmar aponeurosis attach to the skin at the metaphalangeal (MCP) joint of the thumb. In the fingers, the subcutaneous tissue between the neurovascular bundles becomes the central cord; the spiral, lateral, and retrovascular bands also become cords.

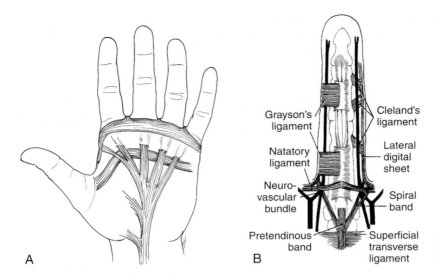

Grayson's ligament

Cleland's ligament

Natatory ligament

Lateral digital sheet

Neuro-vascular bundle

Spiral band

Pretendinous band

Superficial transverse ligament

A

B

Figure 139-1. Normal parts of the palmar **(A)** and digital **(B)** fascia that become diseased.

6. Which fascia causes the various flexion contractures in the hand?

- MP joint contracture is caused only by the pretendinous cord, which attaches to the skin and tendon sheath distal to the MP joint.
- The PIP joint is contracted most often by the central cord, followed, in descending order, by the spiral cord and lateral cord. All three cords attach to the base of the middle phalanx and may be involved alone or together.
- Contracture of the distal interphalangeal (DIP) joint is uncommon. It is caused by the retrovascular and, to some extent, the lateral cord because both cords attach to the distal phalanx.
- The natatory cord contracts the web space from side to side and prevents the fingers from separating.
- The MP joint of the thumb is contracted by the pretendinous cord but usually by no more than 30° because the cord is not well developed. The disabling deformity of the thumb is an adduction contracture caused by the natatory cord and termination of the transverse fibers of the palmar aponeurosis.

7. By what mechanism is the neurovascular bundle displaced?

An understanding of the mechanism is important to avoid digital nerve injury during surgery. The spiral cord passes deep to the neurovascular bundle to reach the side of the finger. It then passes superficial to the bundle to reach the base of the middle phalanx, where it attaches. In other words, it spirals around the neurovascular bundle. As the spiral cord shortens, the bundle is drawn toward the midline of the finger, where it may be cut inadvertently (Fig. 139-2).

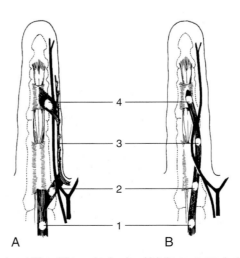

A   B

Figure 139-2. Components of the spiral cord **(A)** and the mechanism by which the neurovascular bundle is displaced toward the midline of the finger **(B)**. *1,* Pretendinous band; *2,* spiral band; *3,* lateral digital sheet; *4,* Grayson's ligament.

8. To which group of diseases does DD belong? How are they classified?

DD is one of the fibromatoses, a group of nonmetastasizing tumors that tend to invade locally and to recur after surgical excision. According to Allen (1977) and Enziger and Weiss (1983), they are classified as follows:

- *Infantile*—11 types
- *Adult*

Superficial (Fascial): Dupuytren's Disease	Deep (Musculoaponeurotic): Desmoid Tumors
Palmar fibromatosis	Extraabdominal
Knuckle pads	Abdominal
Plantar fibromatosis	Intra-abdominal: Pelvic, mesenteric, Gardner
Penile fibromatosis	syndrome

9. What are the histologic features of the nodules of DD?

The clinically apparent nodule is composed of a number of smaller nodules that are nonencapsulated but surrounded by connective tissue and collagen bundles. The predominant cell is the fibroblast. Early in the disease the cells are spindle-shaped perivascular fibroblasts. Later, when contracture is apparent, the cells are more closely packed and collagen production is evident. Ultrastructurally, the predominant cell is the myofibroblast, which contains myofibrils (actomyosin) in the cytoplasm; cell-to-cell attachments are apparent. The nuclei have deep indentations that indicate contracture. Special stains show many new blood vessels. In the late stages of the disease, the nodules disappear, and the few cells in the cords are inactive fibroblasts or fibrocytes.

10. What is the role of the myofibroblast?

Because of its electron microscopic appearance, contractile properties in tissue culture, and the presence of alpha-smooth muscle actin in the cytoplasm, the myofibroblast is assumed to have a contractile function as well as the ability to produce collagen. As new collagen is produced, the tissue is shortened by action of the myofibroblast. The result is joint contracture.

11. What is different about the collagen of normal fascia and Dupuytren's tissue?

Almost all of the collagen in normal fascia is type 1, whereas approximately 25% of the collagen in Dupuytren's specimens is type 3.

12. Where are nodules usually located?

Nodules usually are just distal or just proximal to the distal crease of the palm, in line with the ring and/or small finger. They also appear at the base of the small finger and the MP crease of the thumb. However, they may occur anywhere on the volar surface of the palm or digits.

13. What clinical features and other conditions should be considered in the differential diagnosis of DD?

The location of the nodule is almost diagnostic. It is firm and adherent to skin. It does not move with finger flexion or extension, and the skin over the proximal segment of the finger will blanch on hyperextension of the MP joint. Examine the other hand for nodules, the dorsum of the fingers for knuckle pads, and the feet for plantar nodules. All of these findings are signs of DD.

Other lumps should be easily differentiated. A *ganglion* at the base of the finger is small, spherical, mobile, and tender to palpation. An *inclusion cyst* or *benign tumor* is mobile and not adherent to the skin. *Epithelioid sarcoma* is a rare condition that mimics the nodule of DD. If the diagnosis is in doubt, a biopsy is indicated after further consultation. PIP joint contractures are commonly misdiagnosed as DD. *Camptodactyly* is usually noted by the age of 12 years in one or both small fingers. No nodules or cords are present, although the skin on the ulnar side of the proximal segment of the finger becomes tight with PIP extension. The PIP joint contracture may be fixed or passively correctable. In some cases of *trigger finger,* the patient cannot correct the PIP joint flexion. Prior triggering and pain should rule out DD. Other flexion contractures that can be differentiated by the absence of nodules are the lack of PIP joint extension often seen in diabetic patients, called *limited joint mobility,* and contractures due to *trauma* or *arthritis. Finger contractures in the elderly* simulate DD. All fingers are involved and flexed at both MP and PIP joints. The flexor tendons in the palm are prominent, and the contractures are not correctable. Finally, nodular thickening in the palm is a feature of *reflex sympathetic dystrophy.* The nodules are neither as discrete nor as large as DD nodules, but they often are diagnosed as DD. Histologically they are fibrosis rather than fibromatosis.

14. Is there a role for nonoperative treatment?

Yes, but at present it is limited. The only modality that has persisted over the years is steroid injections into the nodule. Ketchum believes that repeated injections will relieve pain and delay or sometimes stop the progress of the disease. He also advocates steroid injections for painful knuckle pads and plantar nodules. To date, attempts to weaken or disrupt contracted cords with collagenolytic agents, various drugs, stretching, ultrasound, and x-rays have not been successful. Future efforts are likely to include interferon and substances that affect growth factors.

15. What are the indications for operative treatment?

There are no absolute or urgent indications for surgery, but 30° of flexion contraction at the MP or PIP joint is a nuisance and indicates the extent of disease and the likelihood of progression. Many patients are seen soon after they notice a nodule in the palm because it is painful or patients are concerned that it may be malignant. An explanation of the nature of DD usually allays their concern. If the pain persists, one or two steroid injections may help. Excision of a nodule is not satisfactory because thickening of the fascia and scarring of the operation may worsen the condition. If excision of a nodule is necessary for diagnosis or because of pain, a generous excision of the surrounding fascia is advised.

16. What are the goals of surgery?

The goals are different at each joint. At the MP joint the surgeon should be able to completely correct the contracture regardless of its severity and assure the patient that the contracture will not recur. At the PIP joint the surgeon should forewarn the patient that joint contracture may not be fully corrected. The residual contracture may be as much as 40°, depending on the severity of the original contracture. There is also the likelihood that the residual contracture will worsen.

17. What are the options in designing an operation for DD?

By considering the three following steps separately, the operation can be individualized:

- *Skin Incision.* Exposure may be longitudinal (linear, zigzag, lazy S) or transverse. If a single ray is involved, a longitudinal incision from the proximal palm to beyond the diseased fascia in the finger permits exposure of both the fascia and the neurovascular bundles. If the disease is more widespread in the palm, a transverse incision provides good exposure. Separate longitudinal incisions may be made in the involved fingers to join the palmar incision if necessary.
- *Management of the Diseased Fascia.* The diseased fascia may be incised (fasciotomy) or excised locally or widely (regional or extensive fasciectomy). Subcutaneous or open fasciotomy has been advocated for old and debilitated patients, but it is an incomplete operation that either fails to correct the contracture or results in temporary improvement. A more definitive operation is a regional fasciectomy in which only the diseased fascia is removed. It is the usual procedure in the palm to correct MP joint contracture. However, because as many as four cords may be involved in a PIP joint contracture, a more extensive operation is often required in the finger. The diseased as well as the potentially diseased tissue is excised by extensive fasciectomy.
- *Treatment of the Wound.* The wound may be sutured, left open, or skin-grafted. Usually the wound is closed in both palm and finger procedures. In the finger, longitudinal incisions are lengthened and appropriately oriented by the use of Z-plasty. Closure of a transverse wound in the palm creates a dead space where the fascia was excised, and a hematoma is likely. A hematoma can be avoided to some extent by suction drainage, but a more reliable method is to leave the wound open and let it heal by second intention (McCash technique). Healing requires 4 to 6 weeks, depending on the width of the wound. This procedure is contrary to surgical principles, but it is a justifiable exception.

18. What is the rationale for using skin grafts? What are the indications?

Hueston made the empirical observation that Dupuytren's tissue does not grow under a full-thickness skin graft. Therefore, full-thickness skin grafts are recommended for patients in whom recurrence is likely, including (1) patients with an increased diathesis, (2) patients with recurrent PIP joint contracture, and (3) patients with primary, severe PIP joint contracture. The procedure is called a *dermofasciectomy.* The diseased fascia is excised, after which areas of skin are excised, usually near the PIP joint, and the defects are covered by full-thickness skin grafts.

19. What is the difference between extension and recurrence?

Extension refers to postoperative appearance of disease in an area of the hand not involved in the surgery. Recurrence refers to the postoperative appearance of disease in the area of previous surgery. If follow-up is long enough (10 to 20 years), virtually all patients have one or both. However, no more than 10% to 15% will have enough joint contracture to justify reoperation.

20. What are the complications of surgery?

- During surgery, division of digital arteries and nerves and inadequate excision of fascia are often due to poor planning of incisions, inadequate hemostasis, and failure to use magnification.
- Hematoma, skin necrosis, and infection usually occur in sequence and are due to inappropriate undermining of skin and lack of hemostasis.
- Joint stiffness is due primarily to the complications mentioned and is worsened by inappropriate splinting and therapy.

- Reflex sympathetic dystrophy usually is idiopathic, but statistically it occurs more frequently after an extensive operation or after one of the complications mentioned. It occurs after 3% of operations in men and 7% of operations in women.
- Uncorrected or early recurrent joint contracture (seen more frequently at the PIP joint) is due to inadequate fascial excision.

21. How are patients managed postoperatively?

The affected fingers usually are splinted in extension in the operating room. The surgeon is responsible for wound care, but ideally a therapist should see the patient within the first week to begin exercises and to fashion an appropriate splint. Splinting techniques vary, depending on whether surgical release involved the MP or PIP joint or whether an open palm technique was used. MP joint contractures do not require splinting if full extension is maintained with therapy alone. However, with an open palm procedure, the MP joint should be splinted in extension until the wound is closed. PIP joints require 6 weeks of full-time splinting and at least 3 months of nighttime splinting to prevent flexion contractures secondary to scar tissue.

BIBLIOGRAPHY

Baird KS, Alwin WH, Crossan JF, Wojciak B: T-cell mediated response in Dupuytren's disease. Lancet 341:1622–1623, 1993.
Berger A, Delbruck A, Brenner P, Hinzmann R (eds): Dupuytren's Disease: Pathobiochemistry and Clinical Management. New York, Springer-Verlag, 1994.
Burge P, Hoy G, Regan P, Milne R: Smoking, alcohol, and the risk of Dupuytren's contracture. J Bone Joint Surg 79B:206–210, 1997.
Chiu HF, McFarlane RM: Pathogenesis of Dupuytren's contracture: A correlative clinical-pathological study. J Hand Surg 3:1–10, 1978.
Darby I, Skalli O, Gabbiani G: Alpha-smooth muscle actin is transiently expressed by myofibroblasts during experimental wound healing. Lab Invest 63:21–29, 1990.
Gabbiani G, Majno G: Dupuytren's contracture: Fibroblast contraction? An ultrastructural study. Am J Pathol 66:131–146, 1972.
Hueston JT: Dermofasciectomy for Dupuytren's disease. Bull Hosp Joint Dis 44:224–232, 1984.
McCash CR: The open palm technique in Dupuytren's contracture. Br J Plast Surg 17:271–280, 1964.
McFarlane RM: Dupuytren's disease. In Georgiade GS, Riefkohl R, Levin LS (eds): Plastic, Maxillofacial and Reconstructive Surgery. Baltimore, Williams & Wilkins, 1996, pp 1038–1045.
McFarlane RM: Patterns of the diseased fascia in the fingers in Dupuytren's contracture. Plast Reconstr Surg 54:31–44, 1974.
McFarlane RM, McGrouther DA, Flint MH (eds): Dupuytren's Disease. New York, Churchill Livingstone, 1990.
Wurster-Hill DH, Brown F, Park JP, Gibson SH: Cytogenetic studies in Dupuytren's contracture. Am J Hum Genet 43:285–292, 1988.

CHAPTER 140

STENOSING TENOSYNOVITIS

Simon H. Chin, MD, and
Nicholas B. Vedder, MD, FACS

1. What is stenosing tenosynovitis?

Stenosing tenosynovitis (ST) is fibrosis and hypertrophy of the *pulley* or *sheath* overlying a gliding tendon. This leads to narrowing of the tendon passage and the characteristic pain, locking, swelling and, rarely, rupture that may be seen in ST. The tenosynovitis aspect of ST is somewhat of a misnomer as inflammation of the tendon synovium is variable. *Tendovaginitis* is a more accurate term, which describes the reactive changes that are thought to occur from repetitive motion and irritation of the overlying sheath.

2. Which tendons can be affected by ST?

ST can affect the extensor retinaculum overlying any of the six dorsal compartments. The flexor carpi radialis tendon glides under a fibrous sheath that starts at the trapezium and extends to the second metacarpal. This sheath can also undergo ST. Finally, the A1 pulleys overlying the flexor tendons are commonly involved in ST and can lead to trigger fingers (Fig. 140-1).

3. What causes ST?

Fritz de Quervain described the pathophysiology of first dorsal compartment ST due to *"friction and direct damage to the tendovaginal chamber...from trauma."* This tenet holds true today, and most authors ascribe the symptoms of ST due to overuse of the tendons.

4. What are some of the risk factors for developing ST?

Female sex, diabetes, rheumatoid arthritis, hypothyroidism, end-stage renal disease, and pregnancy are risk factors.

5. What is the initial treatment of ST, and how successful is nonsurgical management?

Splinting and steroid injection into the A1 pulley are the mainstays of initial treatment of trigger fingers. Most studies report 60% to 80% resolution of symptoms with one to three injections in nondiabetics and an approximately 50% chance of success in diabetics. Although most hand surgeons believe that the injection is most effective when placed within the flexor sheath, the importance of intrasheath placement has been questioned in a randomized trial.

6. Who was de Quervain?

Fritz de Quervain was a Swiss surgeon who first described in 1895 the nature of ST of the first dorsal compartment that now bears his name. He was a protégé of Dr. Theodore Kocher, who won the Nobel Prize in Medicine for his work in thyroid surgery.

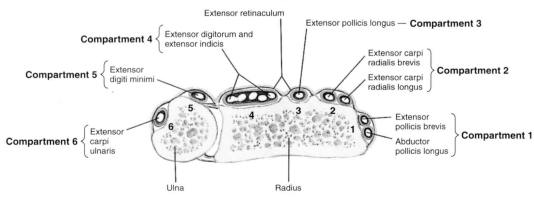

Figure 140-1. Compartments beneath the dorsal carpal ligament. (From Netter FH: Atlas of Human Anatomy. Summit, NJ, Ciba-Geigy Corporation, 1989.)

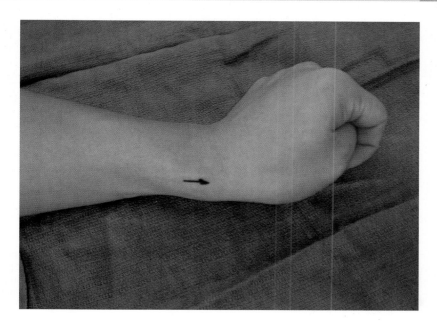

Figure 140-2. First dorsal compartment *(arrow)* where pain is elicited during the Finkelstein maneuver.

7. What is the Finkelstein maneuver?

By flexing the thumb palmarly and holding it with flexion of the other fingers, you deviate the wrist ulnarly. Pain elicited by this maneuver is caused by narrowing and irritation of the stenosed first dorsal compartment in patients with de Quervain's disease (Fig. 140-2).

8. What features distinguish de Quervain's disease from basal joint arthritis?

Although both diagnoses include pain at the radial wrist, patients with carpometacarpal (CMC) arthritis generally display a negative Finkelstein test. Patients with basal joint arthritis have a positive CMC grind test and characteristic metacarpophalangeal (MCP) hyperextension when the disease is advanced. Most significantly, patients with basal joint osteoarthritis have arthritic changes on radiographs. Patients with de Quervain's disease have normal radiographs unless a concomitant pathologic process is present.

9. What anatomic structures and variations must be remembered during de Quervain's surgical release?

- One or two branches of the radial sensory nerve lie superficial to the first dorsal compartment and must be protected during surgery.
- In 20% to 30% of cases, the compartment is divided into two tunnels: one ulnar for the extensor pollicis brevis (EPB) and one more radial for one or more slips of the abductor pollicis longus (APL). Failure to divide the separate tunnel of the EPB, when present, will result in incomplete release.
- After division of the extensor retinaculum, the surgeon must remember that the APL may have up to four tendinous slips, which often have a separate subsheath overlying them. These must be divided to provide complete release.
- The radial artery will be deep to the floor of the first compartment, and care must be taken to avoid injury.

10. What is intersection syndrome?

Classically, intersection syndrome was thought to arise from friction and irritation of the second dorsal compartment tendons as they cross over the contents of the first compartment, 4 cm proximal to the radial styloid. However, hand surgeons now have identified that the etiology is entrapment of the second compartment tendons by its overlying sheath. Further support was generated by Costa et al., who found fluid-filled compartments on magnetic resonance imaging in three patients suffering from intersection syndrome without any changes in the tendon (Fig. 140-3).

11. What is the most common digit affected in trigger finger?

The thumb is the most common digit affected, followed by the ring, long, little, and index fingers.

12. What is the etiology of trigger finger?

The A1 pulley undergoes stenosing tenosynovitis and swells, as do the tendon and synovium in that area. The tight canal prevents extension when the swollen tendon "locks" and is trapped in flexion.

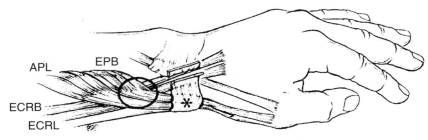

Figure 140-3. Area *(circled)* where the extensor pollicis brevis (EPB) and abductor pollicis longus (APL) cross the common radial wrist extensors. The location of the first dorsal compartment where de Quervain's disease occurs is indicated with an *asterisk*. The second dorsal compartment has been released in the manner recommended for treatment of intersection syndrome. *ECRB*, Extensor carpi radialis brevis; *ECRL*, extensor carpi radialis longus. (From Froimson AI: Tenosynovitis and tennis elbow. In Green DP [ed]: Operative Hand Surgery, 3rd ed. New York, Churchill Livingstone, 1993, p 1193.)

13. Where are the typical incisions placed for trigger finger release?

A variety of incisions offer access to the A1 pulley, and surgeons often make use of the distal and palmar creases. The thumb A1 pulley is approached through the MP crease. The index finger incision typically is within the proximal palmar crease. The middle finger A1 pulley is accessed by an incision between the proximal and distal palmar creases. Finally, the ring and small fingers use the distal palmar crease (Fig. 140-4).

14. What anatomic relationship is critical in trigger thumb release?

The radial digital nerve of the thumb crosses radially across the metacarpal near the A1 pulley and is very superficial. It must be protected during division of the A1 pulley in trigger thumb.

15. How should rheumatoid trigger finger be treated?

Medical management with pharmacologic therapy is the mainstay of initial treatment. In an acute episode of triggering, corticosteroid injection can be considered, but the rate of tendon rupture is significant. Operative exploration and tenosynovectomy is the recommended course of treatment. Pulley release should be avoided in rheumatoid patients because it may accentuate ulnar drift of the digits at the MP level.

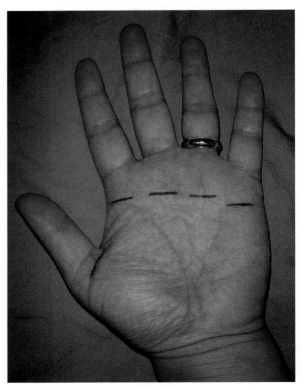

Figure 140-4. Incision placement for trigger finger release for each digit.

16. How should an infant who presents with triggering be managed?

This condition must be first diagnosed properly and differentiated from congenital clasped thumb in which there is absence or hypoplasia of the extensor apparatus. In several studies resolution of the trigger thumb was not achieved with conservative management, but other surgeons achieved success with splinting. Most authors recommend release by the age of 1 year if symptoms have not resolved. If the patient manifests severe triggering, Cardon et al. recommend searching for a flexor tendon nodule or abnormal flexor digitorum superficialis slip during surgery.

BIBLIOGRAPHY

Cardon LJ, Ezaki M, Carter PR: Trigger finger in children. J Hand Surg [Am] 24:156–1161, 1999.

Costa CR, Morrison WB, Carrino JA: MRI features of intersection syndrome of the forearm. AJR Am J Roentgenol 181:1245–1249, 2003.

De Quervain F: On the nature and treatment of stenosing tendovaginitis on the styloid process of the radius. J Hand Surg [Br] 30: 392–394, 2005.

Finkelstein H: Stenosing tendovaginitis at the radial styloid process. J Bone Joint Surg 12:509–540, 1930.

Taras JS, Raphael JS, Pan WT, Movagharnia F, Sotereanos DG: Corticosteroid injections for trigger digits: Is intrasheath injection necessary? J Hand Surg [Am] 23:717–722, 1998.

Trumble TE: Tendinitis and epicondylitis. In Trumble TE (ed): Principles of Hand Surgery and Therapy. Philadelphia, WB Saunders, 2001, pp 391–400.

Turowski GA, Zdankiewicz PD, Thomson JG: The results of surgical treatment of trigger finger. J Hand Surg [Am] 22:145–149, 1997.

Wassermann RJ, Greenwald DP: Stenosing tenosynovitis. In Weinzweig J (ed): Plastic Surgery Secrets. Philadelphia, Hanley & Belfus, 1999, pp 559–561.

Wolfe SW: Tenosynovitis. In Green DP, Hotchkiss RN, Peterson WC, Wolfe SW (eds): Green's Operative Hand Surgery, 5th ed. New York, Elsevier, 2005, pp 2137–2158.

TUMORS

Justin M. Sacks, MD, and
Kodi K. Azari, MD, FACS

1. What is the definition of a tumor?

A tumor is defined as swelling of a part of the body. More specifically, the swelling is secondary to an abnormal growth or multiplication of cells, which are either benign or malignant.

2. What types of tissues form hand tumors?

Most tumors of the hand are benign; they are recognized early and treated by excision. Typically, a favorable prognosis is rendered. These tumors can arise from any cell type, including skin, adipose, synovium, tendon, cartilage, bone, muscle, fibrous tissue, nerve, and blood vessels.

Masses such as inclusion cysts and ganglions can masquerade as tumors but are not true neoplasms; they are considered pseudotumors. Premalignant lesions such as actinic keratosis or atypical nevus can exist in the hand.

3. Are most tumors of the hand benign or malignant?

Ninety-five percent of hand tumors are benign, excluding cancerous skin lesions. However, malignant tumors do occur and can form from any type of tissue. Diagnosis based solely on physical examination alone becomes a challenging endeavor.

Malignant tumors of the hand exist and can be divided into two categories: primary and metastatic. Primary tumors can be soft tissue in nature (e.g., melanoma, basal cell carcinoma, and squamous cell carcinoma) or derived from bone (e.g., osteogenic sarcoma). Metastatic disease most commonly originates from the breast, kidney, thyroid, lung, or colon.

4. What are the basic tenets of hand tumor surgery?
- Biopsy all infections and culture all masses (Fig. 141-1)
- Beware of uncommon malignant tumors
- When in doubt, perform a biopsy

5. Are laboratory tests helpful in the diagnosis of hand tumors?

Rarely. However, increased erythrocyte sedimentation rates can be seen in Ewing's sarcoma, lymphoma, or even a myeloma. Increased serum calcium can be indicative of metastatic tumor, and an increased alkaline phosphatase can indicate osteosarcoma. In men older than 50 years with radiographs revealing blastic bone lesions, it is prudent to analyze blood prostate-specific antigen (PSA) levels to rule out a prostate malignancy.

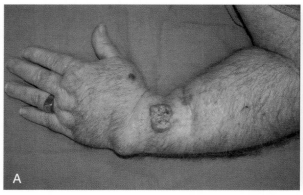
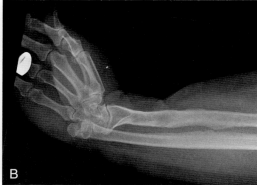

Figure 141-1. Patient with forearm mass resembling osteomyelitis over a distal radius malunion. Biopsy revealed squamous cell carcinoma, illustrating the adage "biopsy all infections and culture all masses."

6. Describe the evaluation, workup, and treatment plan for a suspicious hand mass.

Concise strategies to evaluate, diagnose, and treat tumors of the hand are required for optimal patient care. A careful history and physical examination will rapidly focus the investigation of a suspicious mass found in the hand. For example, with a history of rheumatoid arthritis or gout, search for rheumatoid nodules or evidence of tophi, respectively. An x-ray of the hand is a mandatory test. Additional use of diagnostic tools such as computed tomographic (CT) scan and magnetic resonance imaging (MRI) are required to evaluate potential bony involvement. MRI has become the "gold standard" to evaluate soft tissue masses for malignancy, and CT scans are best suited for osseous lesions. Ultrasound is a quick and inexpensive way to differentiate cystic from solid masses. If the suspected mass is a malignancy, chest radiograph, CT scan, and total body scintigraphy can help identify metastatic spread.

Ultimately, surgical excision using incisional or excisional biopsy techniques will be the final arbiter for diagnosis. Accuracy of the pathologic assessment is dependent on specimen type. Frozen pathologic section is accurate 80% of the time, whereas permanent pathologic section is 96% accurate. Immunohistochemical staining can improve the accuracy of these biopsies. Core needle biopsy has intermediate accuracy of 83% to 93% accurate but may not supply adequate tissue supply.

Surgical incisions must be planned carefully with definitive surgery in mind, using a longitudinal incision in line with or parallel to a potential limb salvage procedure. If a tourniquet is used, exsanguination is not performed to prevent potential spread of tumor cells into the lymphatic system. Proper hemostasis must be obtained, and adjacent compartments must not be violated unless a radical excision is required. Obtain biopsy samples of all infections and culture all masses. Chronic infections can masquerade as malignancies, and masses can be subclinical infections.

7. What is the most common soft tissue mass in the hand? How is it treated?

Ganglion cysts are the most common soft tissue mass found in the hand. These cysts are mucinous filled structures associated with joint capsules, tendons, and tendon sheaths caused by synovial herniation. The most common locations for this mass are the dorsal carpal region (60% to 70%) originating from the scapholunate interosseous ligament, the volar carpal region (20%) originating from the scaphotrapeziotrapezoid ligament, and the volar retinaculum (10% to 20%). Ganglions associated with the distal interphalangeal joint and osteoarthritis are termed *mucous cysts* (Fig. 141-2). Treatment is excision of the cyst along with excision of the associated osteophyte.

A key point is clarifying the benign nature of these lesions for patients who often seek reassurance when confronted with this lesion. Volar retinaculum lesions undergo spontaneous resolution in almost two thirds of patients. Aspiration techniques commonly result in recurrence. Definitive management of the ganglion cyst is surgical excision and a small cuff of retinaculum. For larger ganglions in the volar and dorsal regions of the hand, removal of the ganglion with its stalk and a portion of the joint capsule are required. A dime-sized joint capsule segment is removed to disrupt the one-way valve that has formed, allowing synovial fluid to exit but not reenter the joint space. Arthroscopic removal of ganglion cysts in the dorsal region of the wrist is currently being performed. Success rates have been favorable with limited long-term follow-up.

8. Biopsy of a hand mass reveals an orange-brown tumor with multinucleated giant and xanthoma cells on histologic analysis. What is the most probable diagnosis? Will definitive treatment require an amputation?

This patient has a giant cell tumor (pigmented villonodular synovitis), the second most common soft tissue mass found in the hand. Multinucleated giant cells and xanthoma cells reside in this benign tumor, which is found in synovial fluid-producing sites such as joints, capsular ligaments, and tendon sheaths. It is a slow-growing tumor and potentially can be associated with a mass effect on adjacent structures, at times indenting cortical bone. Clinically they are firm, nodular, and nontender (Fig. 141-3). Commonly, they are located in the radial three digits of the hand in the volar aspect. Treatment for this tumor is careful and complete excision; amputation is not required. Recurrence can be an issue if the mass is not completely excised, with an incidence ranging from 5% to 50% in some series.

9. What is the most likely diagnosis of a painful hand mass relieved only by nonsteroidal antiinflammatory drugs? What is the workup and management of this mass?

Osteoid osteoma, a benign bone-forming lesion that typically affects the distal radius, carpus, and phalanges. These bone tumors form in the hand (<1%), most commonly the scaphoid, presenting during the first 2 decades of life. Radiograph of the hand reveals sclerosis of bone around a central lucency in the carpus. CT scan is more effective than is radiograph for localizing this mass. Patients typically complain of persistent pain relieved by nonsteroidal antiinflammatory drugs (NSAIDs). Definitive treatment can be either curettage or resection. Incomplete nidus excision has been associated with recurrence. Conservative management consists of observation and NSAIDs until the disease becomes quiescent. You can reassure the patient that this is a benign lytic lesion of the bone. Histologic slides from a similar patient will demonstrate a vascular nidus surrounded by benign-appearing osteoblasts from a previously excised osteoid osteoma.

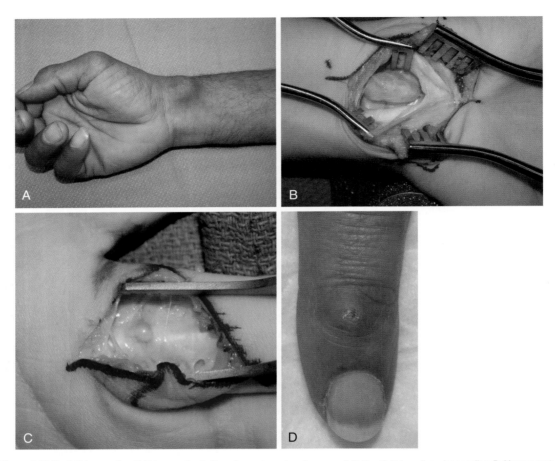

Figure 141-2. **A**, Volar ganglion. **B**, Volar ganglion in Guyon's canal causing ulnar nerve irritation. **C**, Volar retinacular ganglion. **D**, Mucous cyst.

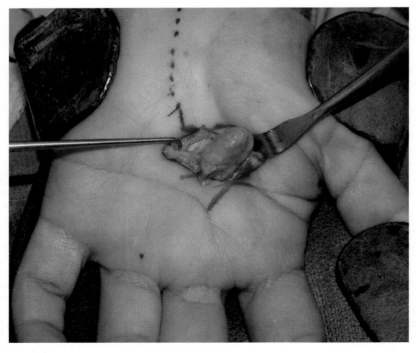

Figure 141-3. Giant cell tumor of the palm.

10. What different types of surgical margins can be used for tumors found in the hand?
The four types of surgical margins possible in removing tumors of the hand are as follow:

1. *Intralesional:* Resection through the plane of the tumor leaving gross tumor behind
2. *Marginal:* Resection through the tumor "reactive zone," which potentially misses microscopic tumor cells
3. *Wide:* Dissection plane involves removal of the mass with normal tissue but still remains within the relative tissue compartment
4. *Radical:* Resection of tumor involves removing the entire intracompartment and extracompartment of involved and uninvolved tissue.

11. Name the most common malignant bone-forming tumor found in the hand. Describe its clinical and radiographic features along with its treatment.
This tumor is an osteogenic sarcoma. It presents as a firm and rapidly enlarging painful mass. In the hand, it is commonly found in the metacarpals and proximal phalanges. Radiographs reveal a sclerotic and expansive lesion that can be blastic or lytic. The typical appearance is termed a *sunburst pattern.* Treatment initially is an incisional biopsy with concurrent local and systemic staging. Wide excision including possible finger or ray amputation is the appropriate surgical resection. Neoadjuvant therapy is used to decrease the lesion size. Wide excision and adjuvant chemotherapy are used to treat high-grade lesions of the hand.

12. A patient has exquisite point tenderness in her finger when she puts her hand in the refrigerator. What is the diagnosis?
This patient has a glomus tumor, which is a benign tumor of the neuromyoarterial apparatus, responsible for controlling skin circulation. It is a neoplasm of smooth muscle cells frequently presenting in a subungual location in the hand. The classic triad of symptoms is cold hypersensitivity, intermittent severe pain, and point tenderness. Diagnostic workup for this lesion can be performed initially using a radiograph, which reveals a "scalloped" osteolytic defect. MRI with gadolinium contrast typically reveals a high-signal-intensity lesion in the subungual region (Fig. 141-4). Excisional biopsy usually is curative, but multiple tumors can occur in up to 25% of patients and are a source for recurrent symptoms.

13. What is a pyogenic granuloma? What are treatment options?
A pyogenic granuloma is a rapidly progressing vascular lesion related to a disorder of angiogenesis. Commonly found on the fingers, it begins as a solitary "red" nodule and progresses to a chronically inflamed vascular lesion (Fig. 141-5). The exact etiology is unknown; however, an association with trauma followed by a subsequent subclinical infection has been speculated.

Conservative modalities for treatment of this lesion include simple excision, electrocautery, and silver nitrate application. However, these have proved to be unreliable. Surgical excision with a small rim of healthy tissue is the most definitive treatment, although recurrences have been documented.

14. Describe the clinical course of a keratoacanthoma. Why is an excisional biopsy recommended? If a patient presents with multiple keratoacanthomas, what other diagnostic modalities should be performed?
The lesion begins as a small red papule and typically progresses to a large ulcerated mass. This mass is "volcano shaped" with a large central crater. The natural course of the lesion is regression following a latent phase of varied

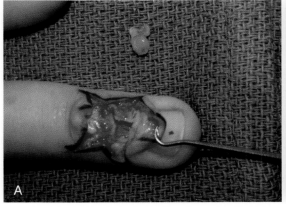
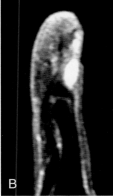

Figure 141-4. A, Glomus tumor of the distal phalanx. **B,** Magnetic resonance image showing high signal intensity.

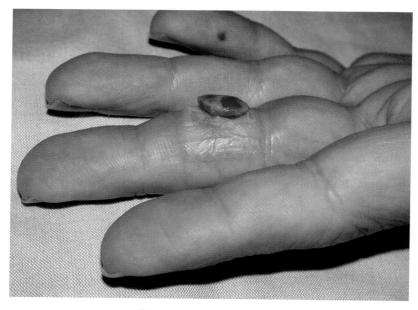

Figure 141-5. Pyogenic granuloma.

duration, which ranges from 6 months to several years. An excisional biopsy of this lesion currently is recommended. This lesion is thought to be derived from the epithelium of hair follicles typically found on hair-bearing regions within the upper extremity. Excisional biopsy is recommended to rule out a malignant neoplasm, most commonly squamous cell carcinoma. Treatment can include curettage if a benign lesion is considered. The natural history of these lesions is involution, and treatment has remained conservative. However, poor cosmetic outcomes can result from this approach. Muir-Torre syndrome is an autosomal dominant disorder associated with multiple keratoacanthomas. This syndrome is associated with visceral malignancies; therefore workup should include colonoscopy and abdominal CT scan.

15. **What are the most likely causes of carpal tunnel syndrome in a child?**
The most likely causes are ganglion, lipoma, accessory muscles, and hamartoma. A child with a lipofibromatous hamartoma typically presents with a mass in the carpal tunnel with fibrofatty infiltration within the epineurium, most commonly the median nerve. In a child who presents with carpal tunnel syndrome, this should be considered part of the differential diagnosis (Fig. 141-6). Exploration of the mass reveals fusiform swelling of the nerve without invasion into perineural tissue. Interfascicular resection is not possible and is contraindicated for treatment of this lesion. Simple decompression is recommended. Gradual deterioration of nerve function can occur, and only then should resection and nerve grafting be considered. This condition can be associated with macrodactyly.

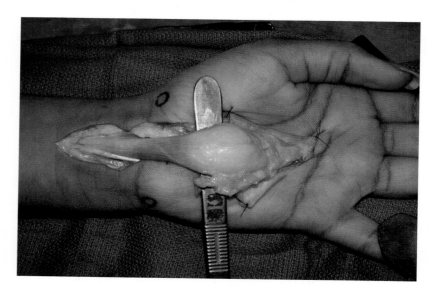

Figure 141-6. Twelve-year-old child with carpal tunnel syndrome from a median nerve hamartoma.

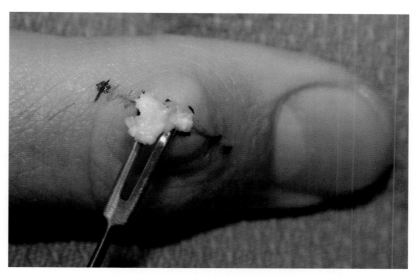

Figure 141-7. Posttraumatic inclusion cyst.

16. What is an epidermal inclusion cyst? What is the most appropriate treatment for removal of this mass?

This mass, which originates from an invagination of epithelium, can follow trauma, injection, or an incision (Fig. 141-7). The epithelium is internalized, resulting in subcutaneous keratin deposition. These lesions typically are painless and most commonly occur in the digits. Treatment involves a complete marginal excision including the cyst wall. Recurrence is extremely low.

17. A 70-year-old man presents to your clinic with a firm, nontender, nodular mass on the *volar* aspect of his right index finger that has slowly been enlarging. The mass does not transilluminate. He states, "Will you please take this sebaceous cyst out of me!" Why is his diagnosis most probably incorrect?

Sebaceous cysts are pseudotumors arising from an obstructed apocrine gland, which produces sebum as opposed to keratin. When they occur in the hand, they are found on the dorsal aspect. Volar skin does not contain sebaceous glands; therefore, they do not typically appear there. This mass most probably is a giant cell tumor or quite possibly an inclusion cyst. Either way, tumor excision is recommended for appropriate pathologic diagnosis.

18. What is the most common skeletal tumor of the hand?

Enchondroma is the most common primary bone tumor found in the hand. Only 5% of all primary bone tumors occur in the hand and the wrist. The tumor is a benign cartilaginous growth, and when it occurs in the hand it most commonly originates from within the medullary canal of the metacarpals or the proximal and distal phalanges. The tumor most commonly presents in the fourth decade of life and is associated with a clinical presentation of pain and edema occurring secondary to pathologic fractures. However, these tumors typically remain asymptomatic and present incidentally. Radiograph reveals a radiolucent and expansive lesion associated with cortical thinning and calcifications (Fig. 141-8). The most appropriate treatment of this lesion is immobilization to allow the fracture to heal. This is followed by meticulous tumor removal by aggressive curettage and possible bone autograft or allografting of the cavity.

19. What is the most common benign bone tumor?

An osteochondroma is the most common benign tumor of the bone. These benign tumors are characterized as cartilage-capped bony growths that project near the epiphysis of the involved bone. Growth typically ceases when the growth plate closes. They are painless and, when found in the hand, are located in the metacarpals and phalanges. These tumors can grow with a stalk (pedunculated), or they can have a broad base (sessile). Malignant degeneration to chondrosarcoma can occur in 0.5% to 1% of patients. This degeneration is higher in the clinical setting of a strong family history and multiple osteochondromas.

20. What is the potential for malignant transformation of a solitary enchondroma? What is Ollier disease? What is Maffucci disease? Is there a potential for malignant transformation among these disease processes?

In solitary lesions, there is a 5% potential for malignant transformation typically resulting in a chondrosarcoma, the most common primary malignant bone tumor found in the hand. A healing fracture can resemble a chondrosarcoma, so it is important to follow up these lesions with a radiograph. This is precisely the reason why enchondromas

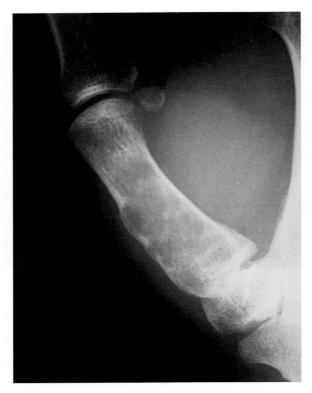

Figure 141-8. Radiographic image of an enchondroma showing a radiolucent lesion with cortical thinning and "popcorn" calcifications.

with pathologic fractures are allowed to heal and tumor excision is addressed thereafter. A chest CT is required to rule out lung metastasis, which is common. Ollier disease is characterized by multiple enchondromas. There is no hereditary propensity with these lesions. Pain is uncommon unless there is a fracture. There is a 30% to 50% risk of malignant transformation to chondrosarcoma. Maffucci disease is a nonhereditary disease characterized by multiple enchondromas and hemangiomas. The risk of malignant transformation to chondrosarcoma typically is 100%. Based on the malignant potential of an enchondroma, clinical and radiographic follow-up are required.

21. What is most important prognostic indicator based on histology in melanoma? What is the treatment of this lesion?

Complete and final pathologic diagnosis is critical to determine the depth of invasion. The Breslow system, most commonly used, reports the depth of invasion in millimeters. Prognosis is directly related to the depth of invasion and is used to correlate the rate of lymphatic spread and metastasis. Treatment planning is based on the depth of invasion of the tumor. The primary treatment of subungual melanoma is amputation. Wide resection (0.5 to 1.0 cm) has been applied to in situ melanoma. Efforts are aimed at maximizing function while decreasing the potential for recurrence. For lesions occurring in the thumb, amputations are performed to the level of the interphalangeal joint and in the fingers to the level of the distal interphalangeal joint.

22. What is the differential diagnosis of hyperpigmentation found in the eponychial fold of the finger? What is Hutchinson's sign? Is this diagnostic of a melanoma?

The differential diagnosis of this lesion includes a subungual hematoma secondary to trauma, onychomycosis, benign pigmented nevi, and melanoma. Certain medications can predispose to pigmented lesions, and being of a race with dark skin has been associated with benign pigmented lesions of the nail fold. Hutchinson's sign is the periungual extension of brown-black pigmentation from longitudinal melanonychia into the nail fold. This lesion is potentially an important but not absolute indicator of subungual melanoma. Periungual pigmentation can be found in many benign disorders and therefore is not diagnostic of subungual melanoma. Clinical observation is paramount, with excisional biopsy being diagnostic (Fig. 141-9).

23. What physical findings in a pigmented skin lesion potentially make the lesion suspicious for a malignancy? What is the appropriate workup for a skin lesion of the hand that is diagnosed as a melanoma?

Physical examination of the skin lesion follows the mnemonic ABCD: *A*symmetry of the lesion, *B*order irregularity, *C*olor dishomogeneity, and *D*iameter greater than 6 mm. A complete examination of epitrochlear and axillary lymph nodes is

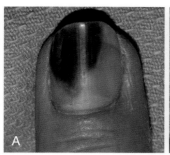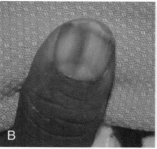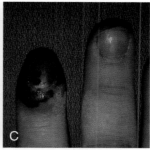

Figure 141-9. A, Onychomycosis. **B**, Benign pigmented nail streak. **C**, Subungual melanoma.

necessary. If biopsy determines the skin lesion to be a melanoma, radiologic examinations are warranted. Examination for metastasis to the head, neck, chest, abdomen, and pelvis are evaluated using CT scan. Once the thickness and depth of invasion of the lesion are determined, sentinel lymph node biopsy can be considered to evaluate metastatic spread of the tumor and to guide therapeutic modalities. Positron emission tomography (PET) scanning is frequently used for evaluation of the spread of melanoma more commonly than for evaluation of recurrence.

24. What is an actinic keratosis?
Actinic keratosis is the most common precancerous skin condition. Treatment can be continued observation or ablation. It presents as a rough, scaly, erythematous plaque found in areas of chronic sun exposure commonly tender to palpation. These lesions are also the direct result of chronic sun exposure commonly found in fair-skinned persons. Potential malignant conversion to squamous cell carcinoma ranges from 0.25% to 1 % per year. Regression can be spontaneous if sun exposure is limited.

25. A previously diagnosed actinic keratosis starts to ulcerate and bleed. What is this lesion now, and how does it spread?
This skin lesion represents a squamous cell carcinoma, the most common malignant skin lesion of the hand and upper extremity, which has converted from a previously existing benign skin lesion. Squamous cell carcinoma has a high metastatic potential and typically metastasizes through the lymphatics. This lesion commonly occurs among the elderly in sun-exposed areas.

26. What is a basal cell carcinoma? Which lesion has a higher potential to spread through the lymphatics: basal cell carcinoma or squamous cell carcinoma?
Basal cell carcinoma is the second most common skin malignancy in the upper extremity and is the most common form of skin cancer. Clinically the lesion is observed as ulcerated skin with pearly elevated edges. These lesions are malignant neoplasms of the basal epithelium. Five major types of basal cell carcinoma exist: fibroepithelioma, morpheaform, noduloulcerative, pigmented, and superficial. Squamous cell carcinoma commonly spreads through the lymphatic system. Basal cell carcinomas form insidiously but rarely metastasize.

27. A 12-year-old girl presents with a deep and painful mass in the hand located over the thenar eminence. A history of rapid enlargement is elicited from the patient and her parents. An excisional biopsy reveals a rhabdomyosarcoma. How common is this mass in children, what is it, and how do you treat it?
Rhabdomyosarcoma is the most common soft tissue sarcoma found in children and teens. It is a primary malignant tumor of muscle stem cells and typically is found in the upper extremity in the thenar eminence or between the metacarpals. Treatment is wide resection or amputation. These lesions commonly metastasize (20%), and lymph node dissection usually is necessary. Lung is the most common site of metastasis. Adjuvant radiotherapy and chemotherapy are recommended.

28. A mass similar to that described in Question 27 is found in a 40-year-old patient. However, the mass has recently ulcerated and drained fluid. Biopsy is consistent with a sarcoma, revealing epithelial cells with a central area of necrosis. What is this mass, and how common is it relative to other types of sarcomas?
This mass represents an epithelioid sarcoma. These masses can ulcerate and drain, resulting in a misdiagnosis of infection. Epithelioid sarcoma is the most common soft tissue sarcoma of the hand and wrist. It commonly presents in adolescence and young adulthood as a firm and slow growing mass. It can affect the digits and palm with proximal spread along tendon sheaths. It can be misdiagnosed as a wart or an ulcer. Treatment of this mass is wide or radical excision. Nodal status needs to be evaluated because metastasis typically occurs to regional lymph nodes. Synovial cell sarcoma, clear cell sarcoma, liposarcoma, and malignant fibrous histiocytoma also occur in the hand and wrist.

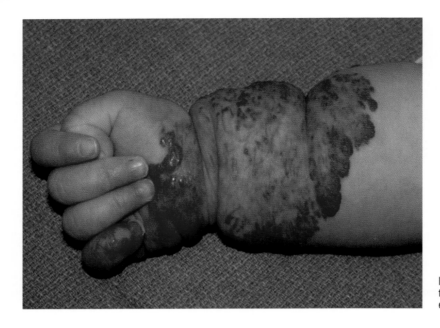

Figure 141-10. Hand and forearm hemangioma showing evidence of involution.

29. What is a hemangioma? Where does it occur in the upper extremity? What is the treatment of this lesion?

Hemangiomas are capillary malformations representing benign vascular neoplasms and are the most common vascular tumor of the hand. They can present as superficial in the cutaneous form, deep (which represents cavernous lesions), or a mixture of both. They appear during the first month of life and are not present at birth. They are characterized by a rapid growth phase during the first year. Typical involution is 50% by 5 years of age and 70% by 7 years of age (Fig. 141-10). They can appear anywhere in the upper extremity. Treatment typically is observation, as most will resolve spontaneously. However, laser therapy, systemic steroids, intralesional steroids, and interferon all have shown beneficial effects. When the lesions become symptomatic in adults, they require a marginal resection. However, these lesions can recur.

30. What is Kasabach-Merritt syndrome?

Kasabach-Merritt syndrome is the combination of infantile hemangioma, thrombocytopenia, and coagulopathy (Fig. 141-11). The hemangioma can cause consumptive coagulopathy secondary to platelet trapping. High-dose steroids and vincristine have been used to treat this syndrome.

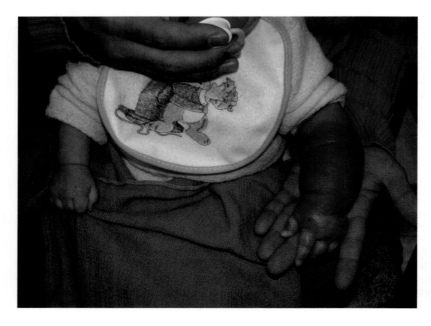

Figure 141-11. Seven-month-old boy with Kasabach-Merritt syndrome presents with rapid enlargement of the forearm and severe thrombocytopenia.

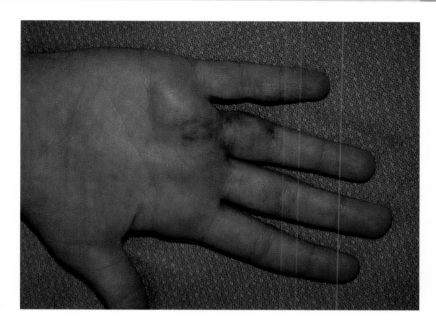

Figure 141-12. Venous malformation of the digit and palm.

31. What are vascular malformations? Are they present at birth?

Vascular malformations typically are present at birth, in contrast to hemangiomas, and represent malformed vascular channels. They are described by their location as capillary, venous, or lymphatic lesions, or as mixed venous-lymphatic malformations (Fig. 141-12). These vascular malformations are considered "low-flow" tumors. Treatment consists of observation, laser therapy, sclerosing agents, or excision. "High-flow" vascular malformations are composed of arterial or arteriovenous components. These masses potentially can undergo rapid expansion. Treatment of these tumors involves preoperative embolization followed by excision. They most probably will grow with the child unless treated.

32. A mass in the hand is extremely suspicious for a malignancy. Do you exsanguinate the hand prior to removing the mass?

It is not appropriate to exsanguinate the hand prior to removal of the hand mass. Exsanguination with an elastic bandage can increase the risk for tumor cells infiltrating the lymphatic system. Dissection of the hand and upper extremity is efficiently performed using pneumatic tourniquet control. However, in situations in which the mass being excised is potentially malignant, the optimal technique when inflating the tourniquet is to hold pressure on the brachial artery while elevating the arm and hand.

33. Name five common primary cancers that can metastasize to the hand. Which one is the most common? Which bone is commonly affected, and what does x-ray show?

The most common primary cancers that metastasize to the hand are breast, kidney, thyroid, lung, and colon cancer. Lung cancer is the most common primary cancer to metastasize to the hand, with the distal phalanx being the most common site (see Fig. 141-5). Symptoms and signs are pain, edema, and erythema. Radiographic examination reveals destructive lytic lesions. The diagnosis is confirmed by an incisional biopsy of the mass.

34. Describe a neurofibroma. What is Von Recklinghausen disease? Is malignant transformation possible?

A neurofibroma is a benign slow-growing tumor arising within a nerve fascicle histologically represented by diffuse growth of Schwann cells, fibrous tissue, and axons. Von Recklinghausen disease (neurofibromatosis 1) is associated with multiple neurofibromas. In patients with neurofibromatosis, malignant degeneration into malignant peripheral nerve sheath tumors can occur.

35. Are neurofibromas and neurilemomas the same? Does their treatment differ? Is a neurilemoma common in the hand?

No. Neurilemomas are slow-growing tumors that arise from Schwann cells; they are also known as *schwannomas*. These lesions can be "shelled" from adjacent nerve fascicles, and neurologic deficits are rare. Treatment of a neurofibroma is different because normal nerve fascicles are incorporated into the tumor. Treatment of neurofibroma is excision, but this potentially can require segmental nerve resection and nerve grafting. A neurilemoma is the most common benign nerve tumor found in the hand (Fig. 141-13).

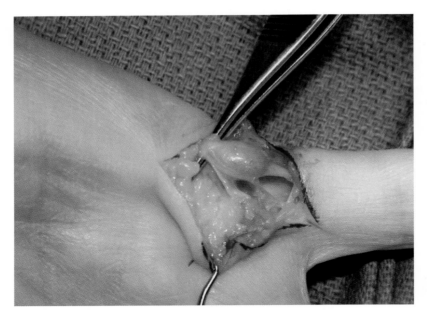

Figure 141-13. Neurilemoma of the small finger digital nerve.

Table 141-1. Enneking Classification System of Musculoskeletal Sarcomas

STAGE	GRADE (G)	SITE (T)	METASTASIS (M)
IA	G1	T1	M0
IB	G2	T2	M0
IIA	G1	T1	M0
IIB	G2	T2	M0
IIIA	G1–G2	T1	M1
IIIB	G1–G2	T2	M1

Grade (G): G1, low; G2, high.
Site (T): T1, intracompartmental; T2, extracompartmental.
Metastasis (M): M0, no regional or distant metastasis; M1, regional or distant metastasis present.

36. Describe the classification system developed by Enneking for staging of musculoskeletal tumors.

This classification system of three stages is based on grade (G), site (T), and metastasis (M) using histologic, radiologic, and clinical criteria. Grade 0 refers to benign lesions, G1 to low-grade lesions, and G2 to high-grade lesions. T0 represents a benign intracapsular and intracompartmental lesion, T1 is an intracapsular lesion, and T2 an intracompartmental lesion. M0 represents no regional or distant metastasis, and M1 represents regional or distant metastasis. Stage I represents a low-grade lesion without metastasis, stage II represents a high-grade lesion without metastasis, and stage III represents a metastatic lesion regardless of tumor grade. The Enneking classification correlates the tumor stage with the excision margins depending on whether the mass is benign or malignant (Table 141-1).

37. Who should biopsy a mass in the hand?

The physician who is both qualified and prepared to carry out definitive surgery should perform the initial biopsy. Management of tumors of the hand may require the surgeon to function dually as surgical oncologist and reconstructive surgeon. A complete understanding of both oncologic and reconstructive principles is required to achieve an optimal outcome.

BIBLIOGRAPHY

Achauer BM, Chang CJ, Vander Kam VM: Management of hemangioma of infancy: Review of 245 patients. Plast Reconstr Surg 99: 1301–1308, 1997.
Chakrabarti I, Watson JD, Dorrance H: Skin tumours of the hand: A 10-year review. J Hand Surg [Br] 18:484–486, 1993.

Daecke W, Bielack S, Martini AK, et al: Osteosarcoma of the hand and forearm: Experience of the Cooperative Osteosarcoma Study Group. Ann Surg Oncol 12:322–331, 2005.

Enneking WF, Spanier SS, Goodman MA: A system for the surgical staging of musculoskeletal sarcoma. 1980. Clin Orthop Relat Res 415:4–18, 2003.

Essner R, Belhocine T, Scott AM, Even-Sapir E: Novel imaging techniques in melanoma. Surg Oncol Clin N Am 15:253–283, 2006.

Kabisch H, Kevric M, Bernd L: Osteosarcoma of the hand and forearm: Experience of the Cooperative Osteosarcoma Study Group. Ann Surg Oncol 12:322–331, 2005.

Kerin R: The hand in metastatic disease. J Hand Surg [Am] 12:77–83, 1987.

Maguiness S, Guenther L: Kasabach-Merritt syndrome. J Cutan Med Surg 6:335–339, 2002.

McDermott EM, Weiss AP: Glomus tumors. J Hand Surg [Am] 31:1397–1400, 2006.

Murray PM: Soft tissue sarcoma of the upper extremity. Hand Clin 20:325–333, vii, 2004.

O'Connor MI, Bancroft LW: Benign and malignant cartilage tumors of the hand. Hand Clin 20: 317–323, 2004.

O'Leary JA, Berend KR, Johnson JL, Levin LS, Siegler HF: Subungual melanoma: A review of 93 cases with identification of prognostic variables. Clin Orthop Relat Res 378:206–212, 2000.

Plate AM, Steiner G, Posner MA: Malignant tumors of the hand and wrist. J Am Acad Orthop Surg 14:680–692, 2006.

Ponti G, Ponz de Leon M: Muir-Torre syndrome. Lancet Oncol 6:980–987, 2005.

Schwartz HS, Zimmerman NB, Simon MA, et al: The malignant potential of enchondromatosis. J Bone Joint Surg Am 69:269–274, 1987.

Thornburg LE: Ganglions of the hand and wrist. J Am Acad Orthop Surg 7:231–238, 1999.

Walsh EF, Mechrefe A, Akelman E, Schiller AL: Giant cell tumor of tendon sheath. Am J Orthop 34:116–121, 2005.

COMPLEX REGIONAL PAIN SYNDROME

Renata V. Weber, MD, and
Susan E. Mackinnon, MD

1. What is complex regional pain syndrome?

Since 1993, the constellation of regional pain symptoms and associated physical changes has been classified as *complex regional pain syndrome* (CRPS). All patients have the following criteria:

- Pain disproportionate to the inciting event, which may include allodynia (painful response to a stimulus that is not usually painful) and/or hyperalgesia (exaggerated response to a stimulus that is usually only mildly painful)
- Regional pain that is not limited to a single peripheral nerve distribution
- Autonomic dysregulation (edema, hyper/hypoesthesia, skin discoloration, sweating/dryness, osteoporosis)
- Functional impairment (weakness, tremor, muscle spasm, dystonia)
- Diagnosis is excluded if another condition can account for the degree of pain and dysfunction (Raynaud disease, scleroderma)

2. What are the differences among reflex sympathetic dystrophy, sympathetically maintained pain syndrome, and CRPS I?

They all refer to a similar condition. The names are often intermixed and often confusing when used incorrectly. *CRPS* is divided into two major categories and three subtypes, with the primary difference being the identification of a definable nerve injury and response to regional blocks (Table 142-1).

- *Sympathetically maintained pain syndrome (SMPS)* includes the cases previously described as reflex sympathetic dystrophy (RSD) and causalgia. RSD (CRPS I) may occur after various initiating factors other than direct nerve injury. Patients with RSD (CRPS I) have a variable response to sympathetic nerve blocks, whereas patients with causalgia (CRPS II) respond much better to sympathetic nerve blocks.
- *Sympathetically independent pain syndrome (SIPS; also known as CRPS III)* is associated with disproportionate pain and sensory changes that do not respond to sympathetic block.

3. Does experimental evidence suggest the involvement of sympathetic nerves in some chronic pain syndromes?

Yes. Electrical stimulation of sympathetic nerves in patients with clinical signs of RSD (CRPS I) results in exacerbation of pain. In 1946, Evans used the term RSD, believing that sympathetic hyperactivity is involved somehow in the abnormal activity in the periphery. Similar stimulation of sympathetic fibers in patients who are undergoing sympathectomy for vascular disease does not produce pain. Other studies have shown that injection of norepinephrine into the skin of normal patients does not cause pain but that norepinephrine injection into the skin of postsympathectomy patients recapitulates the pain present before sympathectomy. Animal studies support these clinical data. Despite all we know about RSD (CRPS I), there is still no general agreement on what to call it, what causes it, or how best to treat it.

Table 142-1. Complex Regional Pain Syndrome

CRPS CATEGORY	INTERNATIONAL PAIN NOMENCLATURE GROUP	HISTORICAL NAME	DIRECT NERVE INJURY	RESPONDS TO SYMPATHETIC BLOCKS
Sympathetically maintained pain syndrome (SMPS)	CRPS I	Reflex sympathetic dystrophy (RSD)	No	Yes, but variable results
	CRPS II	Causalgia	Yes	Yes
Sympathetically independent pain syndrome (SIPS)	CRPS III		Either	No

CRPS, Complex regional pain syndrome.

4. Describe the functional anatomy of the sympathetic nervous system.

Sympathetic nerve fibers originate in the hypothalamus. Somatic sympathetic axons descend through the posterior columns of the spinal cord and synapse at the level of spinal sympathetic chain ganglia. Postsynaptic fibers travel to end organs intimately associated with coterminous blood vessels. Peripheral terminals release norepinephrine, which acts on $alpha_1$, $beta_1$, and $beta_2$ receptors. $Alpha_2$ receptors at the sympathetic end terminals prevent release of norepinephrine. $Alpha_1$ receptors are responsible for vasoconstriction of peripheral blood vessels in the normal setting.

5. What is the relevance of the sympathetic nervous system to pain?

The exact mechanism of sympathetic involvement in chronic pain is not known. The presumed anatomic basis for SMPS is the formation of abnormal short circuits between nociceptive and mechanoreceptor afferents and sympathetic efferents at the tissue level of the spinal cord. Tissue trauma leads to inappropriate release of terminal norepinephrine. The nociceptive terminals innervating the damaged area and the central pain-projecting nerves of the dorsal horn undergo changes in physiologic function as a result of intracellular enzyme cascades, receptor modifications, and novel gene expressions. The modulation results in central sensitization that amplifies the pain response of the central nervous system (CNS). The edema is thought to be a manifestation of neurogenic inflammation in which C fibers that innervate blood vessels in the affected area release vasoactive neuropeptides that cause vasodilation and increased permeability, with consequent transudation of fluid and protein.

6. What is (or was) causalgia?

The word *causalgia* derives from the Greek for *burning pain*. In 1864, Silas Weir Mitchell coined the term causalgia to describe persistent symptoms following gunshot wounds to the extremity involving the peripheral nerve during the American Civil War. It now is referred to as CRPS II.

7. Which is more common, CRPS I or CRPS II?

It is estimated that only 10% of all patients diagnosed with CRPS have RSD (CRPS I); the majority of patients have causalgia (CRPS II). The actual incidence of CRPS is estimated at 5% after an inciting event. In up to 10% to 30% of cases there is no precipitating cause or condition.

8. What is the most common triggering event for RSD (CRPS I)?

A fracture preceded the development of CRPS I in 46% of cases. A study reported that 65% of cases occurred after trauma (mostly a fracture), 19% after an operation, and 2% after an inflammatory process (e.g., herpes zoster infection). The remaining 4% of cases included neurologic disorders (e.g., stroke, tumor, syringomyelia), ischemia, myocardial infarction, musculoskeletal disorder (e.g., shoulder rotator cuff injury), injection, intravenous infusion, cerebrovascular accident, or malignancy. In 10% to 30% of cases, no precipitant could be identified.

9. Who is more likely to be diagnosed with CRPS?

RSD (CRPS I) has a 4:1 female/male ratio with an age range of 30 to 60 years and a mean age of onset in the late 40s. CRPS is less common in children younger than 10 years, although it may reflect misdiagnosis from a milder clinical course or lower index of suspicion by the treating physicians.

10. Is CRPS overdiagnosed?

CRPS is often misdiagnosed in order to provide a diagnosis for patients with chronic pain with complex problems that defy easy categorization. Both CRPS I and CRPS II are often resistant to treatment, and diagnosing patients with sympathetically maintained pain categorizes them as difficult to manage; therefore management failures can be rationalized. Although CRPS is often overdiagnosed, delay to time of diagnosis often is 2 to 5 years from the time of onset, most often because treating physicians are unfamiliar with the entity or have the tendency to attribute the pain to psychological and social related issues.

11. Does CRPS occur only in the extremities?

The original descriptions of RSD (CRPS I) were in the extremities. The extremities are the most common locations for development of CRPS I, with the upper limbs affected twice as often as the lower limbs. Symptoms may occur in any area of the body, such as the head and neck, chest, breast, and penis, and the new CRPS classification includes regionality as an important diagnostic feature of the pain syndrome. Diagnosis and management are similar regardless of the region.

12. What is orofacial RSD, and why is it different?

Although most RSD (CRPS I) conditions are found in the extremities, orofacial RSD is reported after maxillofacial trauma, surgery, head injury, dental procedures, and neck procedures (neck dissection, vascular surgery, soft tissue biopsy, lymph node biopsy). These patients do not develop the dystrophic changes commonly seen in the extremities.

13. What are the stages of CRPS?

- *Acute stage (stage 1, early)* usually lasts a few weeks to 3 months. Nonfocal pain is more severe than would be expected from the injury, and the pain has a burning or aching quality. The affected area becomes edematous with associated joint stiffness and decreased range of motion. The skin may be hyperthermic or hypothermic, and the patient may show increased nail and hair growth and pigmentation. Radiographs may show early bony changes.
- *Dystrophic stage (stage 2, intermediate)* can last from 3 to 12 months. Pain remains the dominant feature. It usually is constant and is increased by any stimulus to the affected area. Edema progresses to dermis and fascia thickening and induration. Skin becomes cool and hyperhidrotic with livedo reticularis or cyanosis. Brawny edema changes occur, hair may be lost, and nails become ridged, cracked, and brittle. Hand dryness becomes prominent, and atrophy of skin and subcutaneous tissues becomes noticeable, especially at the fingertips. Radiographs may show diffuse osteoporosis. Triple-phase (three-stage) bone scan usually is positive.
- *Atrophic stage (stage 3, late)* is chronic. Pain continues, spreads proximally, and remains a prominent feature, even if the pain diminishes in intensity. Irreversible tissue damage occurs. Skin is thin and shiny. Edema is absent. Muscle atrophy is exacerbated, and decreased range of motion and increased joint stiffness may lead to joint contractures. The extremity is cooler with decreased vascularity. The patient is chronically depressed and may contemplate suicide. X-ray films indicate marked demineralization.

14. How can you accurately diagnose SMPS?

A given patient's pain syndrome may have components of both sympathetic and nonsympathetic pain. A structured, logical approach using objective diagnostic criteria improves the chances of managing the pain syndrome correctly. One approach is first to define the proportion of pain caused by sympathetic activity and then to look for the nonsympathetic maintaining causes, if any. The diagnosis is primarily clinical, but the following four diagnostic tests may help to confirm the diagnosis:

1. *Cold Testing:* Patients with SMPS are hypersensitive to minor cold stimulation, such as with acetone, ice or ethyl chloride. This test can be used to differentiate SMPS from SIPS.
2. *Temporary Sympatholysis:* Blockade of alpha$_1$-adrenergic receptors blocks the component of pain resulting from abnormal sympathetic connections. Alpha-adrenergic blockade protocols using intravenous phentolamine compared with placebo helps classify patients as SMPS versus SIPS. The proportion of pain reduction that occurs during phentolamine flow but not during placebo administration represents pain related to abnormal sympathetic connections.
3. *X-ray films* may show patchy periarticular demineralization within 3 to 6 weeks. The extent of osteoporosis is more than expected from disuse alone, and it is a common abnormality revealed on radiographs; however, it is sensitive only 60% of the time.
4. *Triple-Phase Bone Scan:* The delayed phase of testing reveals diffuse periarticular radionuclide uptake in cases of sympathetically maintained pain. This test has shown greater than 95% sensitivity and specificity when correlated with strong clinical signs of sympathetic overactivity in chronic pain syndromes.

15. What are the principles of management of SMPS?

Early diagnosis before the onset of permanent soft tissue changes is important. Aggressive physical therapy to prevent disuse stiffness is crucial. In addition to these ancillary measures, active treatments are designed and implemented based on anatomic and pharmacologic principles. However, truly permanent relief of all pain and associated symptoms is unusual. The first principle of management after diagnosis of SMPS is to define and treat any underlying causes of the pain, such as nerve compression. If this is not possible, sympatholysis or interruption of the sympathetic effector pathway is considered. Several possible levels of intervention in the sympathetic pathway are possible. Medical therapy targets the alpha$_1$ receptor via intravenous phentolamine (primary for diagnosis) and bretylium (for treatment). Phenoxybenzamine is orally efficacious but unfortunately is limited by side effects. Interruption of sympathetic flow at the level of the ganglion is possible as a temporary (blockade with local anesthetic injection) or permanent treatment (transection of sympathetic chain).

16. How does physical therapy help?

Patients are often reluctant to participate in physical therapy because of intense pain; however, beginning with gentle gliding exercises and progressing to weight-bearing exercises helps to increase strength and flexibility. Gradual desensitization to increasing sensory stimuli also plays an important role. Gradual increase in normalized sensation tends to reset the altered processing in the CNS.

17. What complications may develop with CRPS?

- Chronic edema or lymphedema
- Chronic relapsing infections and ulcers resistant to treatment
- Hyperpigmentation and brawny skin changes related to long-standing edema
- Dystonia, tremor, other movement disorders
- Clubbing of fingers or toes, hourglass nails

- Recurrent unexplained spontaneous hematomas
- Depression and other psychiatric disorders

18. Which invasive therapies for SMPS are most effective?

The answer is not clear. Ganglion blocks, both diagnostic and therapeutic, continue to be used with a large variability in effectiveness. For the upper extremity, a stellate (cervicothoracic) ganglion block with bupivacaine is preferred over lidocaine because of its longer half-life. Not all patients experience pain relief after blocks. If a sympathetic block produces significant pain relief twice, denervation with radiofrequency or cryoprobe could provide long-term relief. In 1974, the concept of Bier block (intravenous regional block) with guanethidine was introduced. Blocks using guanethidine may last for 2–3 days. Blocks with bretylium or reserpine have less profound effects.

Sympathectomy remains useful in the patient with CRPS II but is less effective in those with RSD (CRPS I). Surgical sympathectomy appears to be more effective than intravenous sympathetic blockade, which in turn appears to provide better relief than ganglion blockade. In recent years, use of transcutaneous electrical nerve stimulation (TENS), implantable peripheral nerve stimulation, and dorsal column stimulators have provided long-term good to fair relief in approximately 60% of patients who had RSD (CRPS I) with pain limited to one major nerve distribution. A spinal cord stimulator is especially effective for refractory pain related to RSD (CRPS I), which suggests that the spinal cord stimulator is superior to ablative sympathectomy in the management of RSD (CRPS I).

19. How does cigarette smoking affect RSD (CRPS I)?

Smoking causes increased plasma levels of epinephrine and norepinephrine by stimulating the sympathetic nervous system centrally. Peripherally, it causes vasoconstriction and decreases blood flow and ultimately may lead to ischemia. Both effects will exacerbate existing RSD (CRPS I) and may place patients at risk for developing RSD (CRPS I).

CONTROVERSIES

20. Are certain people more prone to developing SMPS?

Eighty percent of patients with CRPS were noted to have had a social stressor either less than 2 months before or 1 month after an inciting event. When time has passed and the pain has not been treated adequately, psychological factors clearly become more important in the clinical syndrome. Depression is common, and personality disorders are often seen.

It has often been suggested that certain personality traits predispose a person to develop sympathetically related pain syndromes. A review of the literature reveals no valid evidence substantiating this claim.

21. Can you prevent RSD (CRPS I)?

RSD (CRPS I) is still poorly understood, but several measures can be taken to minimize the risk for RSD (CRPS I), such as early active motion, removal of painful casts and frequent cast changes if necessary, and avoidance of painful therapy that increases inflammation. For patients with a history of RSD (CRPS I) who need surgery, long-acting block of the operative field should be administered before an incision. Keep the CNS unaware of the procedure to prevent recurrence of the pain cycle. In one study specifically of patients with Colles' fractures, vitamin C may have been effective in preventing RSD after wrist fractures. Improvements in pain and bone density following intravenous pamidronate, alendronate, or clodronate also have been described in few patients.

22. Are patients with CRPS depressed?

Much of the literature suggests a predisposing personality of depression; however, many more studies demonstrate that, although most patients are depressed, they are depressed because of their pain. Many patients with CRPS exhibit some type of movement disorder, ranging from strength reduction (78%) to tremor (25% to 60%) to myoclonus and dystonia. Although some authors believe these findings are pain induced, others believe they are primary abnormalities. Tricyclic antidepressants have been used to decrease burning pain. Gabapentin (Neurontin) and more recently pregabalin (Lyrica) as well as systemic steroids have been used with varying degrees of success. Other agents include the alpha$_1$-adrenoreceptor antagonists terazosin and phenoxybenzamine; the alpha$_2$-adrenoreceptor agonist clonidine; and the N-methyl-D-aspartate (NMDA) receptor antagonists ketamine, dextromethorphan, and calcitonin. When treatment reaches a plateau, invasive interventions to be considered include tunneled epidural catheters and neuroaugmentation.

23. Is RSD (CRPS I) an autoimmune disease?

A study reported that 40% of patients with CRPS had autoantibodies against nervous system structures in their serum, which may indicate that CRPS can result from an autoimmune process against the sympathetic nervous system. The Sudeck concept of an exaggerated regional inflammatory response is supported by new data indicating that, in patients with acute RSD, immunoglobulin G labeled with indium 111 is concentrated in the affected extremity. At this time, this concept is still in the investigational phase.

BIBLIOGRAPHY

Allen G, Galer BS, Schwartz L: Epidemiology of complex regional pain syndrome: A retrospective chart review of 134 patients. Pain 80:539–544, 1999.

Amadio PC, Mackinnon SE, Merritt WH, Brody GS, Terzis JK: Reflex sympathetic dystrophy syndrome: Consensus report of an ad hoc committee of the American Association for Hand Surgery on the definition of reflex sympathetic dystrophy syndrome. Plast Reconstr Surg 87:371–375, 1991.

Baluk P: Neurogenic inflammation in skin and airways. J Investig Dermatol Symp Proc 2:76–81, 1997.

Baron R, Janig W: Complex regional pain syndromes: How do we escape the diagnostic trap? Lancet 364:1739–1741, 2004.

Blaes F, Schmitz K, Tschernatsch M, et al: Autoimmune etiology of complex regional pain syndrome (M. Sudeck). Neurology 63:1734–1736, 2004.

Campbell JN, Meyer RA, Raja SN: Is nociceptor activation by alpha-1 adrenoreceptors the culprit in sympathetically maintained pain? Am Pain Soc J 1:3–8, 1992.

Harris J, Fallat L, Schwartz S: Characteristic trends of lower-extremity complex regional pain syndrome. J Foot Ankle Surg 43:296–301, 2004.

Hassenbusch SJ, Stanton-Hicks M, Schoppa D: Long-term results of peripheral nerve stimulation for reflex sympathetic dystrophy. J Neurosurg 84:415–423, 1996.

Kumar K, Nath RK, Toth C: Spinal cord stimulation is effective in the management of reflex sympathetic dystrophy. Neurosurgery 40:503–508, 1997.

Lynch ME: Psychological aspects of reflex sympathetic dystrophy: A review of the adult and paediatric literature. Pain 49:337–347, 1992.

Mackinnon SE, Dellon AL: Painful sequelae of peripheral nerve injury. In Mackinnon SE, Dellon AL (eds): Surgery of the Peripheral Nerve. New York, Thieme, 1988, pp 492–504.

Merritt WH: The challenge to manage reflex sympathetic dystrophy/complex regional pain syndrome. Clin Plast Surg 32:575–604, 2005.

Nath RK, Mackinnon SE, Stelnicki E: Reflex sympathetic dystrophy. The controversy continues. Clin Plast Surg 23:435–446, 1996.

Ochoa JL, Verdugo RJ: Reflex sympathetic dystrophy: A common clinical avenue for somatoform expression. Neurol Clin 13:351–363, 1995.

Paice E: Reflex sympathetic dystrophy. BMJ 310:1645–1648, 1995.

Rosenthal AK, Wortmann RL: Diagnosis, pathogenesis, and management of reflex sympathetic dystrophy syndrome. Compr Ther 17:46–50, 1991.

Sandroni P, Benrud-Larson LM, McClelland RL, Low PA: Complex regional pain syndrome type I: Incidence and prevalence in Olmsted county, a population-based study. Pain 103:199–207, 2003.

Schwartzman RJ, McLellan TL: Reflex sympathetic dystrophy. Arch Neurol 44:555–561, 1987.

Stanton-Hicks M, Janig W, Hassenbusch S, Haddox JD, Boas R, Wilson P: Reflex sympathetic dystrophy: Changing concepts and taxonomy. Pain 63:127–133, 1995.

Veldman PH, Reynen HM, Arntz IE, Goris RJ: Signs and symptoms of reflex sympathetic dystrophy: Prospective study of 829 patients. Lancet 342:1012–1016, 1993.

Woolf CJ, Salter MW: Neuronal plasticity: Increasing the gain in pain. Science 288:1765–1769, 2000.

Zollinger PE, Tuinebreijer WE, Kreis RW: Effect of vitamin C on frequency of reflex sympathetic dystrophy in wrist fractures: A randomized trial. Lancet 354:2025–2058, 1999.

REHABILITATION OF THE INJURED HAND

Lois Carlson, OTR/L, CHT, and
Lynn Breglio, MS, PT, CHT

CHAPTER 143

1. What are the physiologic effects of early motion programs after tendon repair?
Experimental studies have demonstrated that early motion favors intrinsic versus extrinsic healing. Positive results of early motion after tendon repair include improved tendon excursion, increased tensile strength, and decreased edema and joint stiffness.

2. Describe early passive mobilization after flexor tendon repair in the hand.
This technique mobilizes the repaired tendon using passive flexion and limited active or passive extension. The repair is immobilized using a forearm-based dorsal block splint, which limits extension of the wrist and metacarpophalangeal (MCP) joints. Current therapy protocols are based on one or both of the following approaches:

- *Kleinert Traction*. Rubber band traction provides passive flexion and allows active extension to the limits of the splint. The traction is secured distally to the fingernail using a nail hook and attached proximally to the forearm portion of the splint. Use of a palmar pulley increases flexion at the distal interphalangeal joint (DIP) (Fig. 143-1).
- *Duran Method*. The repaired tendon is mobilized using isolated passive extension of proximal interphalangeal (PIP) and DIP joints. The protocol is based on the need for 3 to 5 mm of tendon excursion to prevent adhesions.

Active motion is generally started by 3 to 6 weeks. Progression of treatment for individual patients varies with the level of scar formation and demonstrated active motion.

3. When are early active mobilization protocols used after flexor tendon repair?
Early active mobilization may be used if the repair is sufficiently strong to withstand early motion, if the patient is reliable, and if the protocol is guided by an experienced therapist. The repaired tendon still is protected using splinting, and elements of passive mobilization are generally incorporated into the rehabilitation program. The active part of the program may involve gentle active muscle contraction in a limited range or use of a "place-and-hold" technique. A method popularized by Strickland and Cannon includes use of a tenodesis splint (hinged wrist splint limiting wrist extension and MP extension) combined with "place-and-hold" exercises.

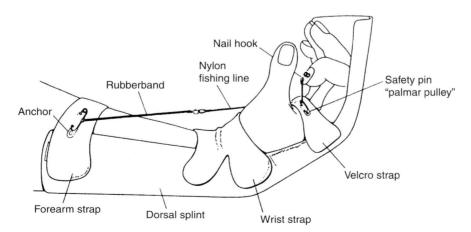

Figure 143-1. Modification of Kleinert dynamic traction splint using palmar pulley. (From Chow JA, Thomes LJ, Dovelle S, et al: Controlled motion rehabilitation after flexor tendon repair and grafting. J Bone Joint Surg 70B:591–595, 1988, with permission.)

4. Describe early passive mobilization protocols used for extensor tendons in zones V, VI, and VII.

Early passive mobilization protocols use a reverse Kleinert approach. The splint maintains the wrist in approximately 45° of extension, with dynamic traction positioning the MCP (and interphalangeal [IP]) joints in 0° of extension. Active flexion in the splint is allowed to a predetermined level, depending on the protocol and the quality of the repair. Evans recommends splinting initially to provide MCP flexion equal to approximately 30° for the index and middle fingers and 40° for the ring and little fingers to achieve 5 mm of passive tendon glide for adhesion prevention.

5. What is the short arc motion protocol for zone III and IV extensor tendon repairs?

The short arc motion (SAM) protocol, developed by Evans, is an example of an early active motion protocol for zone III and IV extensor tendon repairs. Early active motion is initiated for the repaired tendon, using volar static splints as templates. The patient flexes and extends the joints, using minimal active muscle tendon tension (MAMTT). During exercise, the wrist is positioned in 30° of flexion and the MCP joint at neutral to slight flexion. The IP joints are maintained in an extension splint between exercises.

- The patient actively flexes to 30° at the PIP joint and 20° to 25° at the DIP joint. If no extensor lag develops after 2 weeks, flexion is gradually increased by 10° each week over the next several weeks.
- With the PIP joint positioned in extension, the patient actively flexes and extends the DIP joint. Full flexion is allowed unless the lateral bands have been repaired, in which case flexion is limited to 30° to 35°.

6. What are flexor tendon gliding exercises?

Tendon gliding exercises are used to obtain maximal total and differential flexor tendon glide: flexor digitorum superficialis (FDS), straight fist; flexor digitorum profundus (FDP), full fist; and hook (or claw) position, maximal differential glide.

7. Describe splinting after MCP implant arthroplasty.

The patient is splinted with the MCP joints in the position of extension and neutral to slight radial deviation. Two splints are commonly used:

- *Dynamic Splint.* This splint is used during the day to maintain joint alignment, assist extension, and provide controlled flexion for 3 to 4 weeks after surgery. The splint helps to train the capsule to be adequately loose in the flexion/extension plane and relatively tight in the mediolateral plane. Active and passive flexion exercises are done initially within the splint. Components of the splint may include a supinator strap to the index and taping of the little finger to the ring finger to provide a flexor assist. A thumb outrigger may be needed to avoid excessive radial deviation force (Fig. 143-2).
- *Static Splint.* A volar splint is fabricated with the wrist in 15° to 20° of extension and MCP joints at 0° extension and 0° to 10° radial deviation. Thermoplastic or soft materials may be used to position the fingers. The splint is worn at night for up to 3 months or longer as needed.

Additional splinting for flexion may be required, including splints to block IP flexion during MCP flexion exercise and dynamic splinting, most commonly for the little finger.

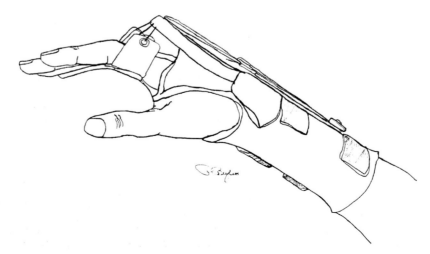

Figure 143-2. Dynamic thermoplastic splint used to position the metacarpophalangeal joints in extension and provide controlled active flexion after metacarpophalangeal implant arthroplasty.

8. **Name three possible long-term postoperative complications of MCP implant arthroplasty.**

   1. Loss of flexion or extension. In general, the goal is to achieve 0° extension and 70° flexion. According to Swanson, flexion of index and middle fingers is less critical and should be limited to 45° to 60° of flexion for stability.
   2. Ulnar drift.
   3. Fracture/dislocation of implant.

9. **Describe examples of joint protection techniques for patients with arthritis.**

   These techniques minimize stress to joints during daily activities and are appropriate for patients with arthritis in general as well as for patients who have undergone surgery such as implant arthroplasty. Examples include (1) use of larger, stronger joints; (2) three-point pinch (preferable to lateral pinch); (3) avoidance of deforming forces, such as twisting and ulnar deviation; and (4) balance of work and rest.

10. **What factors must be evaluated to determine the cause of limited passive motion?**

    Restricted motion may be due to soft tissue and/or joint restrictions. In evaluating limited flexion at the PIP joint, for example, the following factors should be considered:

    - *Extrinsic Extensor Tightness.* Flexion is affected by the position of the MCP joint. Flexion is decreased if the MCP joint is flexed.
    - *Intrinsic Extensor Tightness.* Flexion is affected by the position of the MCP joint. Flexion is decreased if the MCP joint is extended (intrinsic stretch position).
    - *Joint Restrictions.* Flexion is unaffected by the position of the MCP joint.

11. **When is it appropriate to initiate active motion after an intraarticular fracture of the PIP joint?**

    The initiation of active motion depends on the stability of the fracture. Early active motion is possible if rigid fixation is achieved, with protective splinting between exercise sessions. If less rigid fixation is used, active motion generally can be started at 3 weeks and passive motion at 6 weeks.

12. **What important principles must be followed in planning a treatment program after limited wrist arthrodesis to correct wrist instability?**

    Rehabilitation must be guided by the need for a stable, pain-free wrist with functional mobility. Keys to successful management after surgery include adequate immobilization, early active motion of uninvolved joints, a focus on regaining finger and thumb motion as soon as possible, and allowing the wrist to adapt gradually to its new kinematics through active exercise and use.

13. **Why should a patient be referred for hand therapy after a nerve injury?**

    Before regeneration it is important to prevent deformity and improve function through the use of splinting and to educate the patient about methods of compensation for loss of sensibility and autonomic function.

    During regeneration goals of therapy may include sensory desensitization and reeducation, muscle reeducation and strengthening, and restoration of functional patterns of use.

14. **What are the potential deformities and splinting needs for radial nerve injuries?**

    The major problem is wrist drop from loss of wrist extensors (radial wrist extensors are spared with posterior interosseous nerve injury). Finger extension and thumb extension/radial abduction also are affected. Splinting options include wrist extension (dynamic or static), with or without finger and thumb outriggers to provide dynamic extension force, and the tenodesis splint, as described by Colditz (static outrigger from forearm-based splint to proximal phalanges reproduces tenodesis effect).

15. **What are the potential deformities and splinting needs for ulnar nerve injuries?**

    Ulnar nerve injuries may be high (affecting half of FDP, flexor carpi ulnaris [FCU], and ulnar intrinsics) or low (affecting adductor pollicis, half of flexor pollicis brevis [FPB], interossei, half of the lumbricals, abductor digiti minimi [ADM], flexor digiti minimi [FDM], and opponens digiti minimi [ODM]). The major deformity at both levels is claw deformity, caused by loss of all intrinsics to the ring and little fingers. The claw worsens as high ulnar palsy improves (increased flexion by FDP). A splint that prevents MCP hyperextension allows substitution by the long extensors to extend the IP joints. The simplest design is a figure-of-eight splint molded to the patient with thermoplastic material, which allows full flexion and permits functional use (Fig. 143-3).

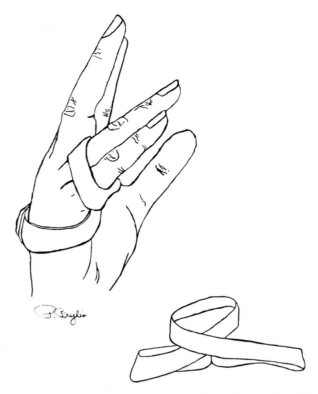

Figure 143-3. Static figure-of-eight thermoplastic splint used to correct claw deformity.

16. What are the potential deformities and splinting needs for median nerve injuries?

Median nerve injuries may be high (affecting all forearm flexor/pronator muscles except half of FDP and FCU) or low (affecting half of the lumbricals, opponens pollicis [OP], abductor pollicis brevis [APB], and half of FPB). The major deformity requiring splinting at both levels is "ape hand" or loss of opposition. An opposition splint places the thumb in the corrected position to prevent deformity and improve function.

17. What readily available tests are used for determining early changes in sensibility due to nerve compression?

Semmes-Weinstein monofilaments and vibrometry (threshold tests) have been shown to be more sensitive than innervation density tests such as two-point testing in identifying early changes due to nerve compression.

18. What are the most common postural faults noted in patients with thoracic outlet syndrome that can be improved with therapy?

Rounded shoulders with a forward head posture; tight pectoral muscles (major and minor), with weak middle and lower trapezius muscles secondary to the slumped position; and tight neck flexors and scalenes with overstretched levator scapulae and upper trapezius muscles, which cause the forward head position.

19. Describe the benefits of hand therapy for patients with carpal tunnel syndrome or other forms of cumulative trauma.

Splinting is appropriate for relative rest. Splints should be used judiciously to avoid problems such as disuse or development of abnormal compensatory patterns. Night splinting is recommended for carpal tunnel syndrome to prevent wrist flexion during sleep and median nerve compression. *Exercises* include active nerve and tendon gliding, stretching of overused tight muscles, and strengthening of opposing weak muscles, as indicated from evaluation. *Postural assessment and training* focus on the areas of malalignment, muscle tightness, or weakness. *Work-related evaluation and modification* address factors related to repetition, force, and posture, including the work station, work style assessment, and work requirements (e.g., production incentives and breaks). Finally, *biofeedback training and relaxation* can be used to relax muscle groups typically used in a state of sustained contraction.

20. What are the key issues in conservative treatment of cubital tunnel syndrome?

Patients with cubital tunnel syndrome need to avoid compression or stretching of the ulnar nerve at the elbow. The two key elements are to avoid direct pressure (leaning on elbows) and flexion greater than 90°. "Relative rest" can be achieved through the use of cushioned elbow sleeves or splints that prevent flexion. Ulnar nerve gliding exercises should be done only in a symptom-free range. As with other forms of cumulative trauma, work/activity modification is critical to long-term success.

21. What are upper limb tension tests?

Upper limb tension tests assess neural tension in the upper extremity by bringing the patient through sequential motions designed to place the neural tissues on stretch. A positive test reproduces the patient's symptoms and/or demonstrates resistance or limitations in movement. Test results are assessed in reference to expected normal responses. Butler describes four basic tests for the upper extremity, with different movement patterns for the median, radial, and ulnar nerves.

22. What general principle can be used to activate a muscle after tendon transfer?

The patient is instructed to perform the original function of the transferred muscle or to combine the original function with the new function. For example, after an opponensplasty using the ring FDS, the thumb is opposed to the tip of the ring finger.

23. What are some conservative interventions specific to treating musicians with cumulative trauma?

Conservative interventions for musicians may include postural retraining, minimalist splinting, manual techniques, and instrument modifications to avoid interference with instrument mechanics or fingering requirements. Air playing, visual review of musical scores, and a gradual increase in duration and intensity of practice/performing times may assist in reducing symptoms.

24. What are some common problems that require treatment after a crush injury?

Soft tissue injury, with associated edema and scarring, may result in restriction of the intrinsic muscles of the hand, leading to intrinsic tightness. Exercise and splinting focuses on stretching the intrinsics (IP flexion with MCP extension). Another common problem secondary to edema is decreased MCP flexion. Serial splinting (thermoplastic or plaster) is an effective way to correct this problem.

25. During the first 48 to 72 hours status post burn, what is the appropriate position for splinting the hand with dorsal thermal injuries?

The wrist should be positioned in 15° to 20° of extension, the MCP joints should be flexed to 60° to 70°, the IP joints should be fully extended, and the thumb should be positioned with slight IP flexion and palmar abduction. This position discourages edema-induced MCP hyperextension and IP flexion posturing.

26. Name three methods for preventing hypertrophic scarring after a burn to the hand.

1. Compression, which includes Jobst garments, Isotoner gloves, and Tubigrip. In addition, inserts under compression garments or in conjunction with splints can be made using elastomer, other silicone-based products, or padding materials.
2. Silicone gel pads.
3. Massage.

27. Describe examples of splints used after surgery for Dupuytren's contracture.

Splinting to maintain extension is critical after surgery. Depending on the extent of involvement, options include the following:

- Thermoplastic extension pan splint for extension of all fingers
- Joint spring splint for extension of all joints of one finger
- Joint jack splint for PIP extension

Serial casting can be used to increase extension at the PIP joint if it remains unresponsive to other forms of splinting.

28. What are tests of maximal voluntary effort?

As part of functional testing or formal functional capacities evaluation, a battery of tests is used to determine whether a patient is giving maximal effort. Such testing may be necessary to help validate findings in patients who have the potential for secondary gain from their disability. Static strength tests are performed using the Jamar dynamometer and Baltimore Therapeutic Equipment (BTE) work simulator (passing scores based on coefficients of variation of 10% to 15% or less as well as correlation of grip test results), position of dynamometer handle test (skewed bell-shaped curve is anticipated with maximal effort), and the rapid exchange test using the dynamometer (increased speed of performance results in decreased ability to control force at submaximal level). No single individual test has been conclusively shown to be an adequate measure of maximum voluntary effort. Professional judgment must be used in interpreting the results of multiple tests and observations.

29. What are some of the advantages and disadvantages of whirlpool treatment versus direct application of heat, such as a hot pack or paraffin bath?

The whirlpool can be a modality of heat or neutrality because of the adjustability of temperature, thus not compromising vascularity or damaging insensitive parts. In addition, it can be used with chemical additives to decrease bacterial count in a small open wound, and the turbulence may assist in tissue débridement. The buoyancy of the water allows the patient to exercise during treatment. The primary disadvantage of whirlpool treatments is that the extremity is placed in a position of dependency, potentially increasing edema. Paraffin and hot packs have the advantage of being able to position the hand in elevation and place the hand in a position of stretch. In addition, the oil in the paraffin provides lubrication to dry tissues. When used for treatment of the hand, paraffin and hot packs can provide vigorous heating, which increases tissue extensibility, and are useful adjuncts before exercise or splinting of the stiff hand. Ultasound can be an effective and more direct heating agent for tissues with high protein and collagen content, requiring less heating time than more superficial applications of heat.

30. How can edema in the hand be measured?

Edema can be evaluated using circumferential measurements and/or a volumeter (measures total volume of the hand using water displacement). Values are compared with the values from the unaffected side as well as sequentially over time for the involved hand.

31. How should the edematous hand be treated?

The answer depends on the stage of wound healing. If seen acutely, the standard treatment is rest, ice, compression, and elevation. However, approximately 48 hours after injury or surgery, the best way to control edema is through active exercise and functional activity. Manual techniques to reduce edema can be used in preparation for exercise.

32. Define categories of splints used to gain joint motion.

- Serial static casts or splints provide a static force at end range. This method is based on the principle that tissue lengthens and grows in response to gentle constant tension at the end of its elastic limit. Changes are made as gains in motion are achieved by remolding or refabricating the cast or splint. This type of splinting is most effective in more chronic joint contractures or joints with a hard end feel that require steady, gentle pressure over a prolonged period. Additional benefits include total contact and even pressure distribution, which assist in edema reduction and increase wearing tolerance. Unfortunately, this type of splinting may not be removable.
- Static progressive splints apply a steady, nonelastic force that can be progressed during each splinting session to accommodate improvements in motion. This type of splinting has the advantage of being removable and allows reciprocal splinting into flexion and extension if required.
- Dynamic splints provide a dynamic force (e.g., from a rubber band or spring) and are most effective with joints that have a soft end feel.

33. Why is it important to start therapy early, even while still casted, for example?

Patients benefit from early exercise of uninvolved joints to prevent stiffness and decrease edema and pain. The therapist can assist the patient in the use of adaptive devices or with modifications of the environment or of a task to increase functional independence. Examples of adaptive principles include increasing the diameter and/or friction of the item to be grasped to decrease the required force.

CONTROVERSY

34. Describe a course of treatment of reflex sympathetic dystrophy (complex regional pain syndrome type I).

There is lack of consensus about almost everything related to reflex sympathetic dystrophy (RSD; also known as complex regional pain syndrome type I [CRPS I]), including its definition, etiology, and most effective treatment approach. Our approach focuses on use of specific active loading exercises. Other approaches use gentle exercise as well as a wide array of other modalities, with or without sympathetic blocks.

Stress loading is defined as active, sustained exercise requiring forceful use of the entire extremity with minimal motion of painful joints. Clinically, two simple exercises actively load the affected arm—scrubbing and carrying. The stress-loading program follows basic principles of exercise physiology. The body adapts in response to demand. Exercise places a demand on the neural, vascular, and sensorimotor systems, all of which may play a role in initiating and/or perpetuating RSD. An overload is needed to achieve a training effect. Exercise must be of sufficient intensity, duration, and frequency to achieve this training effect. Theoretically, training may be due to the effect of stress-loading exercise on central processing abnormalities and neurovascular control mechanisms.

Keys to the success of the program include maximal load, compliance, structure, and emotional support, and separation of treatment of RSD from that of fibrosis. Passive exercise, splinting, and other forms of therapy are used only after RSD is under control. During the acute stage, symptoms generally resolve within days or weeks. If the patient is first seen during the dystrophic stage, the time required for resolution of RSD is generally longer, and treatment of fibrosis inevitably will be required through conservative measures. If treatment begins in the atrophic stage, motion gains with stress loading may be minimal, although improvement in function and a decrease in pain still can be achieved. Surgical intervention may include capsuloplasty of the MCP joints, check rein release (PIP joints), and intrinsic release.

BIBLIOGRAPHY

Bell-Krotoski JA, Figarola JH: Biomechanics of soft-tissue growth and remodeling with plaster casting. J Hand Ther 8:131–137, 1995.

Butler DS: Mobilisation of the Nervous System. New York, Churchill Livingstone, 1991.

Carlson L, Stannard J: Therapeutic management of the wrist. In Watson HK, Weinzweig J (eds): The Wrist. Philadelphia: Lippincott Williams & Wilkins, 2000.

Carlson LK, Watson HK: Treatment of reflex sympathetic dystrophy using the stress loading program. J Hand Ther I:I49–I54, I988.

Chow JA, Thomes LJ, Dovelle S, et al: Controlled motion rehabilitation after flexor tendon repair and grafting. J Bone Joint Surg 70B: 591–595, 1988.

Colditz JC: Splinting for radial nerve palsy. J Hand Ther 1:18–23, 1987.

Evans RB: Immediate active short arc motion following extensor tendon repair. Hand Clin 11:483–512, 1995.

Hunter JM, Mackin EJ, Callahan AD (eds): Rehabilitation of the Hand: Surgery and Therapy. St. Louis, Mosby, 1995.

King JW, Berryhill BH: Assessing maximum effort in upper-extremity functional testing. Work 1:65–76, 1991.

Mackin EJ, Callahan AD, Skirven TM, Schneider LH, Osterman AL: Rehabilitation of the Hand and Upper Extremity. St. Louis, Mosby, 2002.

Michlovitz SL (ed): Thermal Agents in Rehabilitation. Philadelphia, FA Davis, 1996.

Pettengill KM. The evolution of early mobilization of the repaired flexor tendon. J Hand Ther 18:157–168, 2005.

Sanders MJ: Management of Cumulative Trauma Disorders. Boston, Butterworth-Heinemann, 1997.

Wehbe MA (ed): Early motion in hand and wrist surgery. Hand Clin 12, 1996, pp. 1–184.

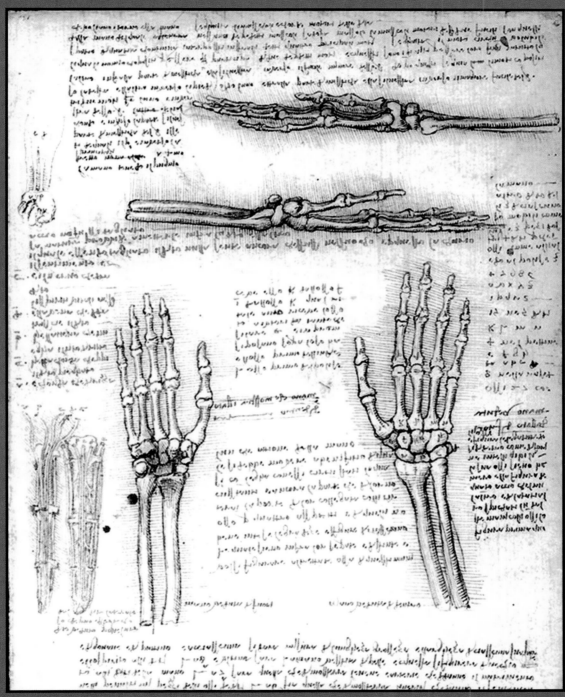

The Bones of the Hand and Wrist. Leonardo da Vinci, ca. 1510–1511. Pen and ink with wash over traces of black chalk. The Royal Library at Windsor Castle, Windsor. The Royal Collection. © 2008 Her Majesty Queen Elizabeth II.

ANATOMY OF THE WRIST

Richard A. Berger, MD, PhD

1. **What is the normal blood supply pattern of the scaphoid? The capitate? The lunate? The hamate?**

   The *scaphoid* receives its blood supply through small branches, primarily from the radial artery, that enter the bone through two channels. The distal pole is supplied by the palmar scaphoid branch, which enters the scaphoid through the palmar cortex. The dorsal scaphoid branch enters the scaphoid along the dorsal ridge of the scaphoid near the waist region. No consistent nutrient vessels enter the scaphoid proximally, and internally the nutrient vessels do not anastomose. Because the proximal pole is supplied solely by vessels entering distally and coursing proximally, the proximal pole is at particularly high risk for avascular necrosis with fractures proximal to the waist of the scaphoid.

   The *capitate* is supplied by multiple nutrient vessels entering the palmar and dorsal cortices of the body of the capitate. Because there are no soft tissue attachments proximal to the neck, the head of the capitate depends on retrograde flow from the more distal nutrient vessels and is vulnerable to avascular necrosis in the case of a fracture through the neck.

   The *lunate* has consistent nutrient vessels entering through the palmar and dorsal cortices, although there may be some dominance of the palmar nutrient vessels. The intraosseous anastomosis patterns have been described as forming X, Y, and I patterns.

   The *hamate* has three general areas of nutrient vessel penetration: dorsal cortex, palmar cortex, and hamulus. The dorsal and palmar vessels have been shown to anastomose in approximately 50% of specimens. The pole of the hamate is without direct soft tissue attachments and therefore relies on retrograde flow from the more distal palmar and dorsal nutrient vessels. Thus the pole is at risk for avascular necrosis (although it is rare) in the event of a fracture. The hamulus typically has a rich blood supply but rarely anastomoses with the vessels entering the body of the hamate. This pattern may contribute to the nonunion rate in fractures of the hamulus.

2. **What is the normal percentage of force or load transmission through the ulnocarpal joint?**

   Under normal conditions, approximately 20% of the entire longitudinal force or load is transmitted through the ulnocarpal articulation; the remaining 80% is transmitted through the radiocarpal articulation. Factors that increase ulnocarpal load transmission include wrist ulnar deviation, positive ulnar variance, and pronation of the forearm.

3. **Describe the ligaments that interconnect the bones of the proximal carpal row.**

   The ligaments that connect the bones of the proximal carpal row are the *scapholunate* and *lunotriquetral interosseous*. They are similar to each other in that both are C-shaped, connecting the palmar, proximal, and dorsal regions but leaving the distal surfaces of the joints without direct ligamentous connections. This pattern explains why in a normal midcarpal arthrogram contrast material passes proximally into the clefts of the scapholunate and lunotriquetral joints. A normal radiocarpal arthrogram shows no passage of contrast material into the scapholunate and lunotriquetral joint clefts because of the intact scapholunate and lunotriquetral interosseous ligaments. In both ligaments, the palmar and dorsal regions are composed of true ligaments with collagen fascicles, blood vessels, and nerves, whereas the proximal regions are composed of fibrocartilage without blood vessels, nerves, or distinct collagen fascicle orientations. The differences between the two ligaments are limited primarily to the relative thickness of the dorsal and palmar regions and to the merging of the radioscapholunate ligament with the scapholunate interosseous ligament between the palmar and proximal regions. The dorsal region of the scapholunate ligament and the palmar region of the lunotriquetral ligament are the thickest, whereas the palmar region of the scapholunate interosseous ligament and the dorsal region of the lunotriquetral ligament are the thinnest.

4. **How much of the proximal surface of the lunate normally articulates with the distal articular surface of the radius in the neutral wrist position?**

   Under normal circumstances, in a frontal radiographic projection at least 50% of the proximal articular surface of the lunate articulates with the lunate fossa; the average is 60%. If less than 50% of the proximal articular surface of the lunate articulates with the lunate fossa of the radius, ulnar translocation of the lunate is diagnosed. Generally, this translocation results from substantial disruption of the long and short radiolunate ligaments. In posteroanterior (PA) radiographs, substantial information can be gained about the position and orientation of the lunate simply by identifying the shape of the lunate. If the outline of the lunate is quadrangular, the lunate is dorsiflexed; if triangular in shape, the lunate is palmarflexed.

5. What are the normal radiolunate and scapholunate angles as measured on a lateral radiograph?

Before attempting to determine intercarpal or radiocarpal angles, it is imperative to ensure that a standardized quality lateral radiograph of the wrist is obtained. The ulnar margin of the wrist is placed on the x-ray cassette with the shoulder adducted to the side, the elbow flexed 90°, and the forearm positioned in neutral rotation. The wrist is positioned in neutral extension, whereby the axis of the third metacarpal is within 10° of the axis of the diaphysis of the radius. Confirmation of a true lateral radiograph of the wrist can be made by identifying the palmar cortices of the scaphoid tubercle, the body of the capitate, and the pisiform. If the palmar cortex of the pisiform falls between the palmar cortices of the scaphoid tubercle and the body of the capitate, the wrist has been positioned within 5° of a true lateral projection and is within acceptable limits. If the palmar cortex of the pisiform is seen palmar to the scaphoid tubercle, the forearm is in supination; conversely, if the palmar cortex of the pisiform is dorsal to the palmar cortex of the capitate body, the forearm is pronated.

The axis of the radius is defined by bisecting the diaphysis in two locations and connecting the bisection points. The axis of the scaphoid can be determined in several manners. First, the midpoint of the proximal and distal articular surfaces can be estimated, and a line can be drawn between the two points. Second, a tangent to the palmar cortex of the waist of the scaphoid can be drawn. The axis of the lunate is best determined by drawing a cord between the distalmost tips of the palmar and dorsal horns of the lunate. A perpendicular line to this cord defines the axis of the lunate.

Under normal circumstances, the radiolunate angle should measure ±10° (Fig. 144-1). A positive angle indicates dorsiflexion of the lunate, and any value greater than +10° is labeled as dorsiflexion intercalated segment instability (DISI). A negative angle indicates palmarflexion of the lunate, and any value less than −10° is labeled as volarflexion intercalated segment instability (VISI). The normal scapholunate angle is 46°, but it has a rather wide range of variance from 30° to 60°. A scapholunate angle greater than 70° indicates carpal instability. A study of intraobserver and interobserver variability in making such measurements determined that the overall estimated error of measurement averaged 7.4°.

6. How does the relative length of the radius and ulna, termed *ulnar variance,* change with forearm rotation?

The axis of rotation of the forearm passes through the radial head proximally and the ulnar head distally. The obliquity of orientation of this axis changes the orientation of the radius and ulna during pronation and supination, whereby the two bones are relatively parallel in supination and essentially crossed in pronation. This "crossing" generates a relative change in the distal projections of the two bones, whereby the radius projects less distally in forearm pronation. This change has implications in determining ulnar variance, which is a radiographic measurement of the relative lengths of the radius and ulna. This determination must be made with a PA radiograph taken with the forearm in neutral rotation. A pronated forearm may give the impression of positive ulnar variance (ulna projecting more distally than the radius), and supination may give the impression of a negative ulnar variance (ulna projecting less distally than the radius). Neutral forearm rotation is best ensured by taking the radiograph with the hand and wrist placed flat on the x-ray cassette with no wrist deviation, the shoulder in 90° abduction, and the elbow in 90° flexion.

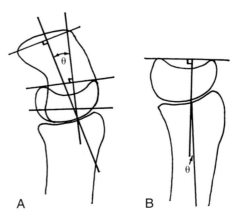

Figure 144-1. Lines for determining the scapholunate angle *(A)* and radiolunate angle *(B).*

7. The proximal carpal row moves in what general motion during wrist radial and ulnar deviation? During wrist flexion and extension?

Although there are measurable motions among the scaphoid, lunate, and triquetrum, the proximal row bones move, in general, in the same overall direction as the wrist. During wrist flexion and extension the proximal row bones also move synchronously with the distal row bones in flexion and extension, respectively. During wrist radial deviation the proximal row bones move primarily in flexion, whereas during wrist ulnar deviation the proximal row bones move primarily in extension. A simplified method for remembering these motion patterns is to realize that the proximal row bones move in the same *flexion* direction during *wrist flexion and radial deviation* and in the same *extension* direction during *wrist extension and ulnar deviation*.

8. Why is the radioscapholunate ligament no longer believed to be a significant mechanical stabilizer of the scaphoid and lunate?

The radioscapholunate ligament was postulated early to behave as an important stabilizer of the scaphoid and lunate, based largely on its position and orientation. It is located between the long and short radiolunate ligaments and appears to pierce the palmar radiocarpal joint capsule. It is grossly oriented vertically and appears to attach to the proximal surfaces of the scaphoid and lunate. There have even been isolated reports of disruption of this ligament associated with scapholunate dissociation.

However, studies have defined the histology of the radioscapholunate ligament and have shown that it is highly atypical, composed of a large number of blood vessels and nerve fibers, with a minimal content of poorly organized collagen that is covered by a thick layer of synovial tissue. Furthermore, it has been demonstrated that the radioscapholunate ligament is a termination of an anastomosis of the anterior interosseous artery and palmar radial arch of the radial artery and branches from the anterior interosseous nerve. Material property studies have shown that the radioscapholunate ligament fails at significantly lower load levels and has a much higher strain level than do contiguous ligaments. Therefore, the radioscapholunate ligament behaves more as a mesocapsule than a ligament and should not be considered a stabilizing structure of the wrist.

9. What are the normal anteroposterior and lateral intrascaphoid angles?

The normal PA intrascaphoid angle is less than 35°, and the normal lateral intrascaphoid angle is less than 35°. Patients with scaphoid malunions or nonunions with an intrascaphoid angle greater than 45° are considered at statistically increased risk for development of degenerative changes and show radiographic signs of carpal collapse. It has been found that either trispiral tomograms or computed axial tomograms may enhance the ability to measure these angles. The method used for determining the intrascaphoid angle in either plane measures the angle of intersection of perpendiculars drawn from the cords of the proximal and distal articular surface curves (Fig. 144-2).

10. Describe the normal arterial blood supply of the distal radius.

Recent descriptions of the arterial blood supply of the radius have prompted the use of vascularized pedicled bone grafts in the treatment of scaphoid nonunions, avascular necrosis of the scaphoid proximal pole, and Kienböck disease. The nutrient blood vessels entering the distal radius have a consistent pattern that makes identification and isolation relatively easy.

The longitudinally oriented vessels arise from the radial artery, ulnar artery, or posterior division of the anterior interosseous artery. Three major transverse arches interconnect the longitudinal vessels and are named from proximal to distal: dorsal supraretinacular arch (found on the extensor retinaculum), dorsal radiocarpal arch, and dorsal intercarpal arch (both found in the joint capsule proper).

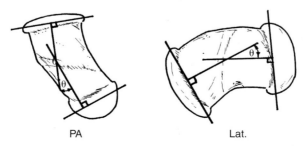

PA   Lat.

Figure 144-2. Lines for determining posteroanterior *(PA)* and lateral intrascaphoid *(Lat)* angles.

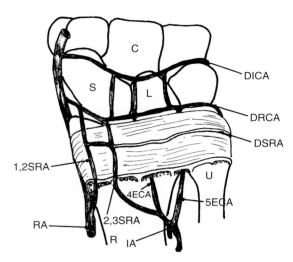

Figure 144-3. Dorsal view of carpal region illustrating the arterial blood supply. The supraretinacular arteries are found between the first and second extensor compartments *(1,2SRA)* and between the second and third extensor compartments *(2,3SRA)*. Arteries are consistently found within the fourth *(4ECA)* and fifth *(5ECA)* extensor compartments. *C,* Capitate; *DICA,* dorsal intercarpal arch; *DRCA,* dorsal radiocarpal arch; *DSRA,* dorsal supraretinacular arch; *IA,* posterior division of anterior interosseous artery; *L,* lunate; *R,* radius; *RA,* radial artery; *S,* scaphoid; *U,* ulna.

The two distinct types of nutrient vessels are the supraretinacular (SRA; between the extensor compartments) and compartmental (ECA; within the extensor compartments). The SRAs are numbered to reflect the compartments between which they are found. The ECAs are numbered according to the compartment within which they are found.

The identified nutrient vessels are, beginning radially, 1,2 SRA; 2,3 SRA; and 4 ECA. A consistent vessel found within the fifth extensor compartment is called the 5 ECA, but it has no direct penetration into the radius; rather, it is useful as a retrograde conduit to extend the length of a 4 ECA graft pedicled to the dorsal radiocarpal or intercarpal arches, through the proximal anastomosis of the 4 ECA, 5 ECA, and posterior division of the anterior interosseous artery (Fig. 144-3).

11. Name the four principal ligaments of the first carpometacarpal joint.
On the palmar surface of the joint is the anterior oblique ligament, also called the "beak ligament." Near the ulnar extreme of the joint is the ulnar collateral ligament. Dorsally, the ulnar half of the joint is covered by the posterior oblique ligament, whereas the radial half is covered by the dorsoradial ligament. There are no true ligament fibers near the radial extent of the joint, deep to the abductor pollicis longus tendon. The base of the first metacarpal is stabilized to the base of the second metacarpal by the intermetacarpal ligament, which is extracapsular and is not considered a proper carpometacarpal joint ligament.

12. Describe the anatomy of the triangular fibrocartilage complex.
The triangular fibrocartilage complex is based around the triangle-shaped articular disc, which is interposed between the ulnar head and carpal bones. This articular disc is composed of fibrocartilage; its base is attached to the radius along the distal edge of the sigmoid notch. Along the dorsal margin of the articular disc is the dorsal radioulnar ligament, which connects the dorsal aspect of the sigmoid notch of the radius to the styloid process of the ulna. Extending from the dorsal radioulnar ligament in a distal direction are fibers called the *extensor carpi ulnaris tendon subsheath,* which variably extends to the base of the fifth metacarpal. Along the palmar edge of the articular disc is the palmar radioulnar ligament, which connects the palmar edge of the sigmoid notch to the area at the base of the ulnar styloid process, called the *fovea.* Emanating from the palmar radioulnar ligament are the ulnolunate and ulnotriquetral ligaments. Near the ulnar apex of the articular disc is a depression called the *prestyloid recess,* which is generally filled with synovial villi and variably communicates with the tip of the ulnar styloid process. Between the ulnar attachments of the dorsal and palmar radioulnar ligaments is a region of small blood vessels called the *ligamentum subcruentum.* The meniscus homologue is the edge of the articular disc distal to the prestyloid recess, which in selected coronal sections resembles the profile of a knee meniscus (Fig. 144-4).

13. Where is the center of rotation of the wrist?
The center of rotation of the wrist is somewhat controversial because of the complex compound motion of all of the carpal bones. If taken as a unit, wrist movements have been labeled as dorsiflexion (extension), palmarflexion (flexion), radial deviation (abduction), ulnar deviation (adduction), axial rotation (pronation/supination), and circumduction. Any combination of these motions is possible, but the classic axes of rotation of the wrist have been identified as the flexion–extension axis and radial–ulnar deviation axis. Kinematic studies have identified the head of the capitate as the

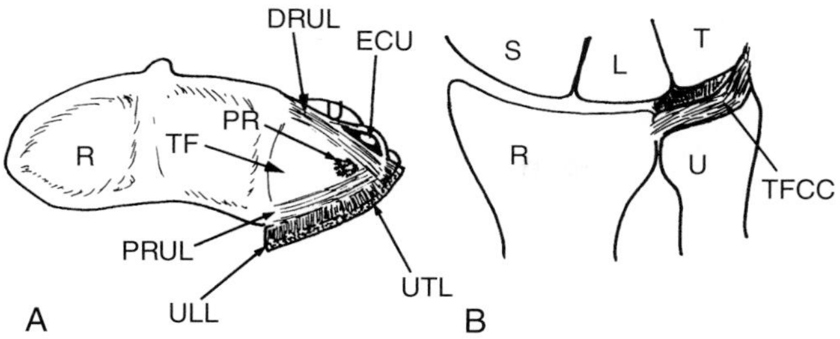

Figure 144-4. Transverse **(A)** and dorsal **(B)** views of the triangular fibrocartilage complex (TFCC). *DRUL,* Dorsal radioulnar ligament; *ECU,* extensor carpi ulnaris tendon subsheath; *L,* lunate; *PR,* prestyloid recess; *PRUL,* palmar radioulnar ligament; *R,* radius; *S,* scaphoid; *T,* triquetrum; *TF,* triangular fibrocartilage; *U,* ulna; *ULL,* ulnolunate ligament; *UTL,* ulnotriquetral ligament.

anatomic location at which these axes intersect the wrist. A functional axis, called the *"dart-throw" axis*, also passes through the capitate but represents the motion created by throwing a dart from wrist extension and radial deviation to flexion and ulnar deviation. It is important to recognize that the axes of rotation are mere approximations, and that each individual carpal bone is considered a rigid body, displaying its own kinematics, which, when summed with the remaining carpal bones, creates the overall motion that we perceive as wrist motion.

14. The midcarpal joint normally communicates with which carpometacarpal joints?
The midcarpal joint is in direct communication with the second, third, fourth, and fifth carpometacarpal joints. Only the first carpometacarpal joint is isolated from the midcarpal joint.

15. Is it normal for the radiocarpal joint to communicate with the pisotriquetral joint? With the distal radioulnar joint?
It is estimated that in 90% of normal adults the radiocarpal joint communicates with the pisotriquetral joint, as evidenced by arthrography. It is considered abnormal for the radiocarpal joint to communicate with the distal radioulnar joint, although such communications do not necessarily imply mechanical instability. Such communications, usually identified with arthrography, imply a defect in the triangular fibrocartilage complex, particularly the articular disc, which normally isolates the two joints from communication. Degenerative changes may occur in the central aspect of the articular disc as early as the third decade and increase in incidence with age thereafter.

16. Are there any normal direct tendinous insertions to any of the carpal bones?
Under normal circumstances only the pisiform has a tendinous attachment, which serves as the insertion of the flexor carpi ulnaris tendon. Anomalous insertions of the abductor pollicis longus and flexor carpi radialis tendons into the trapezium have been reported. The abductor and flexor pollicis brevis originate from the trapezium, whereas the abductor and flexor digiti minimi originate from the pisiform. The origin of the opponens digiti minimi from the hook of the hamate is variable.

17. Is there normally substantial motion between the bones of the distal carpal row?
Kinematic studies, which define motions without reference to force, have demonstrated negligible motion between the bones of the distal row because of the heavy investment of interconnecting ligaments. Between each bone are strong, transversely oriented palmar and dorsal interosseous ligaments. In addition, deep interosseous ligaments connect the trapezoid to the capitate and the capitate to the hamate. Disruptions of these ligaments result from high-energy trauma, typically with substantial additional soft tissue disruption, and are termed *axial instabilities.*

18. Is it normally possible for the lunate to articulate with the hamate?
Viegas demonstrated two broad categories of architecture of the distal surface of the lunate. The type I lunate, which occurs in two-thirds of normal wrists, has no appreciable articulation with the hamate. Rather, the distal surface of the lunate articulates solely with the head of the capitate. The type II lunate, which occurs in the remaining one-third of normal wrists, has a distinct sagittal ridge with an ulnar-sided fossa for articulation with the proximal surface of the hamate. Type II lunates have a distinct predilection to develop degenerative changes in the hamate fossa as well as to accompany degenerative changes on the proximal surface of the hamate.

19. Describe the dorsal capsular ligaments of the wrist.
The dorsal capsule of the wrist is reinforced with two major ligaments, the dorsal radiocarpal (DRC) and the dorsal intercarpal (DIC; Fig. 144-5). In the regions between the two ligaments, the joint capsule is devoid of ligament tissue. The DIC ligament connects the trapezoid and scaphoid with the triquetrum, whereas the DRC ligament connects the radius, lunate, and triquetrum. The DIC and DRC ligaments share an insertion on the dorsal cortex of the triquetrum. Proximally, the dorsal radioulnar (DRU) ligament originates adjacent to the radial attachment of the DRC but is not considered a wrist ligament per se. The anatomic arrangement of the dorsal ligaments has been put to use by introducing a fiber-splitting capsulotomy, based on their orientation. This concept promises several advantages, including minimizing scar and stiffness, enhancing visualization and accuracy in orientation, and maintaining stability

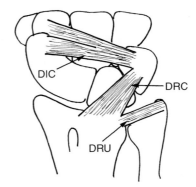

Figure 144-5. Dorsal view of the wrist illustrating the dorsal capsule ligaments. *DIC,* Dorsal intercarpal ligament; *DRC,* dorsal radiocarpal ligament; *DRU,* dorsal radioulnar ligament.

when entering the wrist from the dorsal side is necessary. The DIC and DRC ligaments can be safely bisected, creating a radially based flap that can be extended even further by dividing the radiocarpal joint capsule from the radius to the level of the radial styloid process. This exposes the radial two thirds of the radiocarpal joint and virtually the entire midcarpal joint. To expose the ulnar third of the ulnocarpal joint, the DRC ligament can be bisected and connected to a capsular incision paralleling the fifth extensor compartment creating a proximally based flap.

20. What is carpal height ratio? How is it determined?

Carpal height refers to the longitudinal length of the carpus from the distal articular surface of the radius to the distal articular surface of the capitate. It is a useful concept clinically because malrotation of the proximal carpal row bones, from problems such as rheumatoid arthritis, scapholunate dissociation, and scaphoid nonunions, may result in shortening of the carpal height. Detection of such shortening helps to classify the severity of the wrist abnormality. The problem with carpal height as a dimensional measure lies in the variability of wrist sizes, which presumably are proportionate to the size of the individual. In an attempt to bypass this variability, the concept of *carpal height ratio* nondimensionalizes the carpal height. In the classic method, the length of the carpus is defined along the projected axis of the third metacarpal, measured from the base of the third metacarpal to the point at which the projected third metacarpal axis intersects the distal surface of the radius. This measurement is divided by the length of the third metacarpal, also defined along the axis of the third metacarpal. The normal values for the carpal height ratio are 0.054 ± 0.03. This measurement must be made from a standard PA radiograph with the wrist in a neutral position and the entire length of the third metacarpal visible.

Because the third metacarpal is not consistently imaged on standard wrist radiographs, an alternative method for determining the carpal height ratio was developed. The denominator is the greatest length of the capitate, as determined from a standard PA radiograph. The carpal height measurement is made in the same manner as the standard carpal height ratio. Using the alternative method, the normal range of the revised carpal height ratio is 1.57 ± 0.05.

BIBLIOGRAPHY

Amadio PC, Berquist TH, Smith DK, et al: Scaphoid malunion. J Hand Surg 14A:679–687, 1989.
Berger RA, Crowninshield RD, Flatt AE: The three-dimensional rotational behaviors of the carpal bones. Clin Orthop 167:303–310, 1982.
Berger RA, Kauer JMG, Landsmeer JMF: The radioscapholunate ligament: A gross anatomic and histologic study of fetal and adult wrists. J Hand Surg 16A:350–355, 1991.
Berger RA: The anatomy of the ligaments of the wrist and distal radioulnar joints. Clin Orthop Relat Res 383:32–40, 2001.
Berger RA: The gross and histologic anatomy of the scapholunate interosseous ligament. J Hand Surg 21A:170–178, 1996.
Berger RA, Bishop AT, Bettinger PC: A new dorsal capsulotomy for the surgical exposure of the wrist. Ann Plast Surg 35:54–59, 1995.
Cooney WP, Linscheid RL, Dobyns JH (eds): The Wrist: Diagnosis and Operative Treatment. St. Louis, Mosby, 1998.
Garcia-Elias M: Anatomy of the wrist. In Watson HK, Weinzweig J (eds): The Wrist. Philadelphia, Lippincott Williams & Wilkins, 2001, pp 7–20.
Gelberman RH, Bauman TD, Menon J: The vascularity of the lunate bone and Kienböck's disease. J Hand Surg 5:272–278, 1980.
Gelberman RH, Menon J: The vascularity of the scaphoid bone. J Hand Surg 5:508–513, 1980.
Jiranek WA, Ruby LK, Millender LB, et al: Long-term results after Russe bone-grafting: The effect of malunion of the scaphoid. J Bone Joint Surg 74A:1217–1228, 1992.
Linscheid RL, Dobyns JH, Beabout JW, Bryan RS: Traumatic instability of the wrist: Diagnosis, classification and pathomechanics. J Bone Joint Surg 54A:1612–1632, 1972.
Nattrass GR, King GJ, McMurtry RY, Brant RF: An alternative method for determination of the carpal height ratio. J Bone Joint Surg 76A:88–94, 1994.
Palmer AK, Werner FW: The triangular fibrocartilage complex of the wrist: Anatomy and function. J Hand Surg 6:153–161, 1981.
Palmer AK, Werner FW: Biomechanics of the distal radioulnar joint. Clin Orthop 187:26–34, 1984.

Panagis JS, Gelberman RH, Taleisnik J, Baumgaertner M: The arterial anatomy of the human carpus. Part II: The intraosseous vascularity. J Hand Surg 8:375–382, 1983.

Sheetz KK, Bishop AT, Berger RA: The arterial blood supply of the distal radius and ulna and its potential use in vascularized pedicled bone grafts. J Hand Surg 20A:902–914, 1995.

Tountas CP, Bergman RA: Anatomic Variations of the Upper Extremity. New York, Churchill Livingstone, 1993.

Viegas SF, Wagner K, Patterson RM, Patterson R: Medial (hamate) facet of the lunate. J Hand Surg 15A:564–571, 1990.

Youm Y, McMurtry RY, Flatt AE, Gillespie TE: Kinematics of the wrist. I: An experimental study of radio-ulnar deviation and flexion-extension. J Bone Joint Surg 60A:423–431, 1978.

145 CHAPTER

PHYSICAL EXAMINATION OF THE WRIST

Jeffrey Weinzweig, MD, FACS, and
H. Kirk Watson, MD

1. What constitutes the first part of every thorough physical examination?

A thorough history. Information about the patient's age, handedness, chief complaint, occupation, avocational activities, previous wrist injury or surgery, exact onset of symptoms and their relationship to specific activities, frequency and duration of postactivity ache, factors that exacerbate or improve symptoms, subjective loss of wrist motion, current work status, and, certainly, workers compensation status complement findings noted during the physical examination and aid in deriving a diagnosis.

2. Is it necessary to assess the range of motion of the wrist?

Absolutely. Every examination should begin with an evaluation of passive and active range of motion of both wrists. With the patient's elbows resting on the examination table, an assessment of flexion and extension is performed. Any loss of passive motion compared with the contralateral, asymptomatic wrist usually is a sign of underlying carpal pathology. A bilateral assessment of pronation and supination is made with the examiner's hands rotating the patient's wrists from the midforearm level. Full forced pronosupination without pain eliminates the distal radioulnar joint (DRUJ) and triangular fibrocartilage complex (TFCC) as potential sources of the patient's symptoms. Degenerative joint disease, dislocation of the DRUJ, or a substantial tear of the TFCC results in pain and diminished pronosupination.

RADIAL WRIST EXAMINATION

3. Which carpal bone is involved in more than 95% of all cases of degenerative joint disease of the wrist?

The scaphoid. Periscaphoid arthritic changes involve the scapholunate advanced collapse (SLAC) pattern in 57%, the triscaphe (scaphotrapeziotrapezoid) joint in 27%, and a combination of these in 14%. The scaphoid is also involved in the etiopathogenesis of more than 90% of all ganglia.

4. Which aspect of the wrist, radial or ulnar, is involved in the majority of carpal pathology?

The majority of carpal pathology involves the radial aspect of the wrist. Although ulnar wrist pain often presents a more complex diagnostic problem than radial wrist pathology, it is less common in the typical practice.

5. How many maneuvers does the radial wrist exam include? Name them.

The examination of the radial wrist consists of five maneuvers:

1. Dorsal wrist syndrome (DWS) test
2. Finger extension test (FET)
3. Articular/nonarticular (ANA) maneuver
4. Scaphotrapeziotrapezoid (STT) test
5. Scaphoid shift maneuver (SSM)

None of these maneuvers is necessarily diagnostic by itself, nor is it intended to be. However, a diagnosis usually can be derived by assimilating the entire picture of wrist mechanics and pathomechanics with the history, symptoms, and appropriate radiographic examination.

6. Which maneuver directly examines the scapholunate joint?

The dorsal wrist syndrome (DWS) test (Fig. 145-1). Identification of the scapholunate (SL) joint is facilitated by following the course of the third metacarpal proximally until the examiner's thumb falls into a recess that lies over the capitate. SL articulation is readily palpable just proximal between the extensor carpi radialis brevis and the extensors of the fourth compartment. A normal joint produces no pain with palpation. SL dissociation, Kienböck disease, dorsal wrist syndrome (i.e., SL joint overloading with wrist pain secondary to SL ligamentous synovitis and/or tear preceding evidence of rotary subluxation of the scaphoid), or other pathology involving the SL or radiolunate joints or the lunate itself elicits pain with direct palpation.

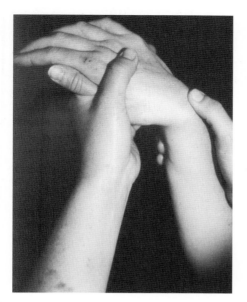

Figure 145-1. Dorsal wrist syndrome of the scapholunate (SL) joint. Identification of the SL joint is facilitated by following the course of the third metacarpal proximally until the examiner's thumb falls into a recess. SL articulation is readily palpable between the carpi radialis brevis and the extensors of the fourth compartment. (From Watson HK, Weinzweig J: Physical examination of the wrist. Hand Clin 13:20, 1997, with permission.)

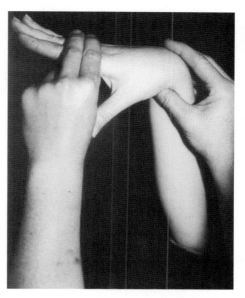

Figure 145-2. Finger extension test. With the patient's wrist held passively in flexion, the examiner resists active finger extension. (From Watson HK, Weinzweig J: Physical examination of the wrist. Hand Clin 13:24, 1997, with permission.)

7. Which maneuver indirectly examines the wrist with exceptional sensitivity?
The finger extension test (FET) (Fig. 145-2). The increased mechanical advantage on carpal loading during the FET produces a reliable indicator of carpal pathology. With the patient's wrist held passively in flexion, the examiner resists active finger extension. In patients with significant periscaphoid inflammatory change, radiocarpal or midcarpal instability, symptomatic rotary subluxation of the scaphoid, or Kienböck disease, the combined radiocarpal loading and pressure of the extensor tendons cause considerable discomfort. In our experience, such patients always demonstrate a positive FET. The FET has become a highly reliable indicator of problems at the SL joint. Full-power finger extension against resistance (i.e., a negative FET) eliminates the common dorsal wrist syndrome diagnosis as well as rotary subluxation of the scaphoid, Kienböck disease, and SLAC wrist.

8. Which maneuver specifically assesses synovitis of the scaphoid?
The articular/nonarticular (ANA) maneuver (Fig. 145-3). The proximal pole of the scaphoid articulates with the radius at the radiocarpal joint. The articular surface of the proximal scaphoid continues distally toward a junctional point along the radial aspect, where the surface changes from articular to nonarticular. With the wrist in radial deviation, the ANA junction is obscured by the radial styloid. With the wrist in ulnar deviation, the ANA junction is easily palpated just distal to the radial styloid. The ANA maneuver is performed with the examiner's index finger firmly palpating the radial aspect of the patient's wrist just distal to the radial styloid with the wrist initially in radial deviation. Pressure is maintained as the patient's wrist is brought into ulnar deviation with the examiner's other hand. The normal asymptomatic wrist demonstrates mild to moderate tenderness and discomfort at the ANA junction with direct palpation in almost every person. However, the patient with periscaphoid synovitis, scaphoid instability, or SLAC changes at the styloid experiences severe pain with this maneuver. For purposes of comparison, it is necessary to perform the maneuver bilaterally.

9. Which maneuver directly assesses the STT joint?
The scaphotrapeziotrapezoid (STT) test (Fig. 145-4). Identification of the STT or triscaphe joint is facilitated by following the course of the second metacarpal proximally until the examiner's thumb falls into a recess. That recess is the triscaphe joint. A normal joint produces no pain with palpation. Triscaphe synovitis, degenerative disease, or other pathology involving the joint or scaphoid elicits pain with direct palpation.

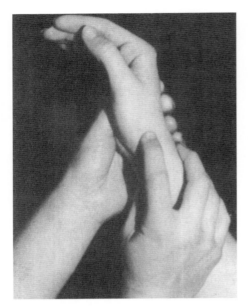

Figure 145-3. Articular/nonarticular (ANA) junction of the scaphoid. With the wrist in ulnar deviation, the ANA junction is easily palpated just distal to the radial styloid. The ANA maneuver is performed with the examiner's index finger firmly palpating the radial aspect of the patient's wrist just distal to the radial styloid with the wrist initially in radial deviation. Pressure is maintained as the patient's wrist is brought into ulnar deviation with the examiner's other hand. (From Watson HK, Weinzweig J: Physical examination of the wrist. Hand Clin 13:19, 1997, with permission.)

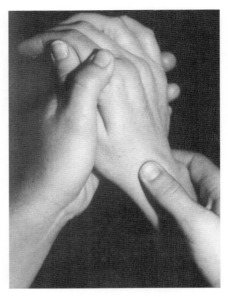

Figure 145-4. Scaphotrapeziotrapezoid or triscaphe joint. Identification of the triscaphe joint is facilitated by following the course of the second metacarpal proximally until the examiner's thumb falls into a recess, just ulnar to the anatomic snuffbox. (From Watson HK, Weinzweig J: Physical examination of the wrist. Hand Clin 13:20, 1997, with permission.)

10. Which maneuver assesses the pathomechanics of the scaphoid?

The scaphoid shift maneuver (SSM), which provides qualitative assessment of scaphoid stability and periscaphoid synovitis compared with the contralateral asymptomatic wrist. We do not refer to the SSM as a "test" or to the findings of increased pain or ligamentous laxity as a "positive scaphoid shift." Instead, laxity or discomfort with the SSM does not necessarily indicate pathology; however, asymmetrical laxity that reproduces the patient's characteristic pain is indicative of pathology. This examination, therefore, is meaningful only when performed bilaterally.

11. How is the SSM performed?

With the patient's forearm slightly pronated, the examiner grasps the patient's wrist from the radial side with the examiner's same-sided hand (e.g., the examiner's right hand is used to examine the patient's right hand) and places the thumb on the palmar prominence of the patient's scaphoid while wrapping the fingers around the patient's distal radius. This position enables the thumb to push on the scaphoid with counterpressure provided by the fingers. The examiner's other hand grasps the patient's hand at the metacarpal level to control wrist position. Starting in ulnar deviation and slight extension, the wrist is moved radially and slightly flexed with constant thumb pressure on the scaphoid (Fig. 145-5).

12. Explain the biomechanical mechanism of the scaphoid shift maneuver.

When the wrist is in ulnar deviation, the scaphoid axis is extended and lies nearly in line with the long axis of the forearm. As the wrist deviates radially and flexes, the scaphoid also flexes and rotates to an orientation more nearly perpendicular to the forearm, and its distal pole becomes prominent on the palmar side of the wrist. The examiner's thumb pressure opposes this normal rotation and creates a subluxation stress, causing the scaphoid to shift dorsally in relation to the other bones of the carpus (Fig. 145-6). This scaphoid shift may be subtle or dramatic. In patients with rigid periscaphoid ligamentous support, only minimal shift is tolerated before the scaphoid continues to rotate normally, pushing the examiner's thumb out of the way. In patients with ligamentous laxity, the combined stresses of thumb pressure and normal motion of adjacent carpus may be sufficient to force the scaphoid out of its elliptical fossa and onto the dorsal rim of the radius. As thumb pressure is withdrawn, the scaphoid returns abruptly to its normal position, sometimes with a resounding thunk.

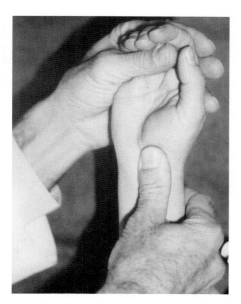

Figure 145-5. Scaphoid shift maneuver. The examiner grasps the patient's wrist from the radial side and places the thumb on the palmar prominence of the patient's scaphoid while wrapping the fingers around the patient's distal radius. This position enables the thumb to push on the scaphoid with counterpressure provided by the fingers. The examiner's other hand grasps the patient's hand at the metacarpal level to control wrist position. Starting in ulnar deviation and slight extension, the wrist is moved radially and slightly flexed with constant thumb pressure on the scaphoid. (From Watson HK, Weinzweig J: Physical examination of the wrist. Hand Clin 13:21, 1997, with permission.)

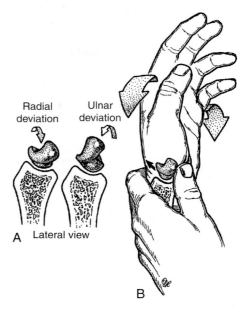

Figure 145-6. Mechanism of scaphoid shift. **A,** Relationship of the scaphoid and radius as seen in a lateral view. In ulnar deviation the scaphoid dorsiflexes, and its long axis lies nearly in line with the axis of the radius. In radial deviation the scaphoid volar flexes; its long axis lies nearly perpendicular to the axis of the wrist, and its distal pole becomes prominent on the palmar side of the wrist. **B,** During the scaphoid shift maneuver, the examiner's thumb prevents the normal palmar tilt of the scaphoid. (From Watson HK, Weinzweig J: Intercarpal arthrodesis. In Green DP [ed]: Operative Hand Surgery, 4th ed. New York, Churchill Livingstone, 1999, pp. 108–130.)

13. What is the clinical significance of the scaphoid shift maneuver?

The scaphoid may shift smoothly and painlessly or with a gritty sensation or clicking, accompanied by pain. Grittiness suggests chondromalacia or loss of articular cartilage, and clicking may indicate bony change sufficient to produce impingement. Pain is a significant finding, especially when it reproduces the patient's symptoms. Pain associated with unilateral hypermobility of the scaphoid is virtually diagnostic of rotary subluxation. A less well-localized pain associated with normal or decreased mobility is encountered in patients with periscaphoid arthritis, whether of triscaphe or SLAC pattern.

14. What percentage of normal asymptomatic people have an abnormal scaphoid shift?

Of 1000 normal asymptomatic people, 209 demonstrated a unilateral abnormal scaphoid shift maneuver with hypermobility of the scaphoid and/or pain. This finding, which represents 21% of examined people and 10% of examined wrists, stresses the importance of performing the maneuver bilaterally.

ULNAR WRIST PAIN

15. How do you examine a patient with ulnar wrist pain?

Ulnar wrist pain is a complex problem requiring a keen understanding of both intraarticular and extraarticular anatomy of the region. Distinguishing between abnormalities involving the DRUJ, TFCC, and ulnar carpus necessitates discerning soft tissue problems from bony ones. Each region of the ulnar wrist must be systematically addressed during a thorough physical examination.

16. How can you rule out pathology involving the DRUJ?

An abnormality of the DRUJ, such as degenerative disease or subluxation, should be immediately suspected on the basis of decreased or painful pronosupination. With the patient's hand in full ulnar deviation, significant pain elicited by pressing on the ulnar head by the examiner's thumb is suggestive of DRUJ pathology. Pain produced during pronosupination while the ulnar head is pressed volarward and the pisiform pressed dorsally often is indicative of an ulnar impingement or impaction syndrome.

17. How can you diagnose a TFCC injury or tear on physical examination?

The diagnosis of a TFCC tear or injury is by exclusion. It is difficult, if not impossible, to confirm the diagnosis on the basis of physical examination alone. Other more common causes of ulnar wrist pain, such as degenerative joint disease and carpal instability, must first be excluded. Examination may demonstrate loss of forearm pronosupination and wrist motion, tenderness over the TFCC dorsally, and a palpable and/or audible click with forearm rotation or radioulnar deviation of the wrist. Suspicion of TFCC pathology requires evaluation by three-compartment wrist arthrography. The presence of a radiocarpal–DRUJ arthrographic communication is pathognomonic of a TFCC perforation. However, perforations are common and do not necessarily indicate pathology.

18. What is the ulnar snuffbox?

The ulnar snuffbox is the depression palpated immediately beyond the ulnar styloid. This space is circumscribed by the extensor carpi ulnaris (ECU) and flexor carpi ulnaris (FCU) tendons, which run posteriorly and anteriorly, respectively, over the ulna at the wrist. In radial deviation, the floor of the depression is formed by the triquetrum. In ulnar deviation, the floor is formed by the joint between the triquetrum and hamate.

19. What is the lunotriquetral compression test?

The lunotriquetral (LT) compression test directs load across the LT joint along an ulnoradial axis by palpating within the ulnar snuffbox. Direct pressure in this area elicits pain from a patient with LT joint instability, synovitis, degenerative disease, or partial synchondrosis.

20. What are ballottement tests? How can they assess LT instability?

Ballottement tests, or shear tests, demonstrate joint instability by exerting pressure in opposite directions on adjacent carpal bones. Instability of the LT joint can be demonstrated by the *Reagan test.* The examiner's thumb is used to apply pressure on the patient's lunate dorsally while the examiner's index finger applies pressure on the triquetrum volarly. The *Masquelet test* is another ballottement test of the LT joint in which the examiner uses both hands to apply shear force across the articulation. The examiner's thumbs are used to apply dorsal pressure to the lunate and triquetrum while counterpressure is applied to these bones volarly by the examiner's index fingers (Fig. 145-7).

21. What is triquetral impingement ligament tear? How can it be diagnosed?

A new etiology for ulnar wrist pain that specifically involves the triquetrum has been described. The triad of localized triquetral pain along the proximal ulnar slope of the bone, a history of a hyperflexion injury, and normal radiographs is diagnostic of triquetral impingement ligament tear (TILT). The mechanism of TILT involves a cuff of fibrous tissue that has become detached from the ulnar sling mechanism and chronically impinges on the triquetrum, resulting in synovitis, bony eburnation, and pain. Point tenderness can be appreciated by palpating the ulnar aspect of the triquetrum just distal to the ulnar styloid.

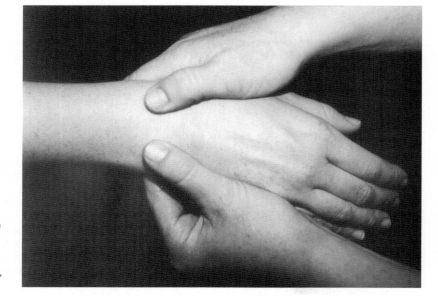

Figure 145-7. Masquelet's test of lunotriquetral (LT) instability. The examiner uses both hands to apply shear force across the LT joint. The examiner's thumbs are used to apply dorsal pressure to the lunate and triquetrum while counterpressure is applied to these bones volarly by the examiner's index fingers. (From Watson HK, Weinzweig J: Physical examination of the wrist. Hand Clin 13:25, 1997, with permission.)

RADIOCARPAL AND MIDCARPAL JOINTS

22. How can instability of the radiocarpal or midcarpal joint be evaluated?

The *anteroposterior drawer test* can be used to evaluate instability of either the radiocarpal or midcarpal joint. One of the examiner's hands holds the patient's hand by the metacarpals to apply axial traction while the other hand stabilizes the patient's forearm. While traction is maintained, anteroposterior force is applied and a drawer is elicited first at the radiocarpal and then at the midcarpal joint (Fig. 145-8).

23. What is the pivot shift test?

The pivot shift test of the midcarpal joint consists of supinating and volar subluxing the distal row of the carpus. With the patient's elbow at 90°, the hand is placed in a fully supinated position while the distal forearm is held firmly. The wrist is maintained in a neutral position while the hand is moved into full radial deviation. The ulnar side of the carpus is forced into further supination and a volar subluxed position. At this point, the hand is moved from radial to full ulnar deviation. Midcarpal instability secondary to excessive ligamentous laxity or rupture allows the capitate to sublux volarly from the lunocapitate fossa during this maneuver (Fig. 145-9).

CARPOMETACARPAL JOINT

24. Do all five carpometacarpal joints demonstrate equal motion?

Absolutely not. The carpometacarpal (CMC) joints link the digital rays with the carpus. The normal hand has no clinically detectable mobility at the second and third CMC joints and only several degrees of motion at the fourth CMC joint, which are functionally negligible. The fifth CMC joint has approximately 20° of motion, which permits functional adaptation to the transverse arch of the palm.

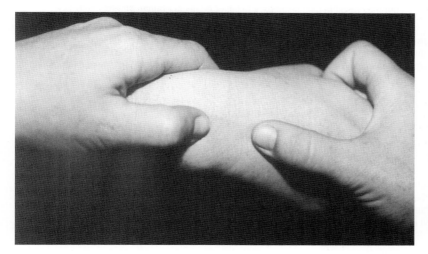

Figure 145-8. The anteroposterior drawer test of radiocarpal or midcarpal instability. One of the examiner's hands holds the patient's hand by the metacarpals to apply axial traction while the other hand stabilizes the patient's forearm. While maintaining traction, anteroposterior force is applied and a drawer is elicited at the radiocarpal and then the midcarpal joint. (From Watson HK, Weinzweig J: Physical examination of the wrist. Hand Clin 13:27, 1997, with permission.)

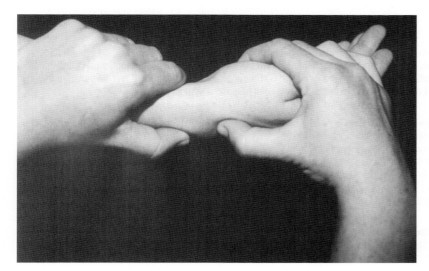

Figure 145-9. The pivot shift test of midcarpal instability. This maneuver consists of supinating and subluxing volarly the distal row of the carpus. With the patient's elbow at 90°, the hand is placed in a fully supinated position while the distal forearm is held firmly. The wrist is maintained in a neutral position while the hand is moved into full radial deviation. The ulnar side of the carpus is forced into further supination and a volarly subluxed position. (From Watson HK, Weinzweig J: Physical examination of the wrist. Hand Clin 13:27, 1997, with permission.)

25. Which is the most important of the CMC joints?

The first CMC (trapeziometacarpal) joint is functionally the most important joint of the thumb ray because it allows movement of the entire column of the thumb. Movements of this joint are quite complex, involving multiplanar motion that includes anteposition, retroposition, adduction, and abduction.

26. Degenerative joint disease most commonly involves which CMC joint?

Although degenerative disease may involve any of the five CMC joints secondary to arthritis or trauma, the first CMC joint of the thumb is most commonly involved.

27. What three tests are used to examine the first CMC joint?

1. *Grind Test.* The examiner places the thumb and index finger of one hand on either side of the patient's CMC joint. While the metacarpal is held with the examiner's other hand, the CMC joint is axially loaded. The examiner's first hand then moves the metacarpal base laterally in several directions. Symptoms are exacerbated, grating and chondromalacia are palpated, and the quality of cartilage is determined.
2. *Adduction Test.* The examiner's thumb is placed on the midportion of the patient's first metacarpal while the fingers are placed along the length of the fifth metacarpal. The first and fifth metacarpals are then passively adducted toward each other with gentle pressure.
3. *Abduction Test.* The patient's hand is positioned flat with the palm facing upward. The examiner's index and middle fingers are placed on the volar aspect of the phalanges or metacarpal of the patient's thumb as the thumb metacarpal is passively abducted into the plane of the finger metacarpals.

28. What is the carpal boss?

The carpal boss represents a partial or complete coalition or synchondrosis of the second and third CMC joints. This anomaly usually is asymptomatic but may result in pain secondary to localized degenerative arthritis.

29. How can you diagnose a carpal boss on examination?

Examination involves malalignment of the second and third metacarpals. The examiner grasps the heads of these bones with the thumb and index fingers of each hand and simultaneously shifts one metacarpal head volarly and the other dorsally. Pain with this maneuver is highly suggestive of a carpal boss.

EXTRAARTICULAR CAUSES OF WRIST PAIN

30. What is the Finkelstein test?

Stenosing tenosynovitis of the first dorsal compartment, also known as de Quervain's disease, is a common cause of wrist and hand pain, involving the abductor pollicis longus (APL) and extensor pollicis brevis (EPB) sheaths at the radial styloid process. The findings of local tenderness and moderate swelling of the extensor retinaculum of the wrist over the first dorsal compartment and a positive Finkelstein test confirm the diagnosis. This test is performed by having the patient grasp his/her own thumb within the ipsilateral palm. Moderate to severe pain is elicited as the patient's wrist is brought from radial deviation into extreme ulnar deviation.

31. What is a "wet leather" sign?

Crepitus with tendon movement, suggestive of an inflammation-induced change in the synovium or synovitis, is known as a wet leather sign.

32. How can you evaluate a problem involving the sheath of the ECU?

The ECU sheath extends from the ECU groove on the ulnar head to the dorsal base of the fifth metacarpal. Conditions such as ECU synovitis or tendinitis, subluxation, stenosis, and partial rupture result in pain on direct palpation of the tendon at the level of, or just distal to, the ulnar head with the wrist in ulnar deviation.

33. How can you diagnose a fracture or degenerative disease of the pisiform?

Pisiform fractures are uncommon, representing approximately 1% of all carpal bone fractures. Diagnosis is often overlooked because approximately 50% of all pisiform fractures are associated with more severe upper extremity injuries. In addition, pisiform fractures are missed because they are difficult to see on routine radiographs of the wrist. Subpisiform degenerative joint disease, usually secondary to delayed diagnosis of pisiform fractures or untreated injuries, is another infrequent etiology of ulnar wrist pain. Examination of the pisiform is performed quite easily by loading the subpisiform joint laterally as with the thumb CMC joint.

34. How can you diagnose an injury or fracture of the hook of the hamate?

Pain secondary to an acute fracture or nonunion of the hook of the hamate may be an elusive cause of wrist pain. Examination of the hook of the hamate is performed by deep palpation over the tip of the hamular process in the palm by the examiner's thumb and by pressure on the dorsal ulnar aspect of the same bone with the examiner's index and middle fingers. The hook is easily located by first placing the examiner's thumb on the volar pisiform. Movement approximately 2 cm along a line connecting the pisiform to the head of the second metacarpal (45° angle) locates the hamular process.

35. How can you diagnose flexor carpi radialis tendinitis?

Flexor carpi radialis (FCR) tendinitis, often seen in laborers who perform repetitive wrist motions, may cause pain over the flexor aspect of the wrist. On examination, pain is elicited by palpating over the osteofibrous FCR tunnel, which begins approximately 3 cm proximal to the wrist and extends to the main insertion of the FCR on the base of the second metacarpal. In our experience, the region of greatest acute tenderness is an area less than 1 cm in diameter centered where the FCR tendon enters the trapezium tunnel at the level of the wrist crease. Pain usually increases with resisted wrist flexion and resisted radial deviation of the wrist.

36. What is intersection syndrome? How can it be diagnosed on examination?

Pain and swelling of the muscle bellies of the APL and EPB in the area where they cross the common radial wrist extensors are characteristic of intersection syndrome. This area is approximately 4 cm proximal to the radiocarpal joint. With severe cases, swelling, redness, and crepitus may be found. Examination of the region with gentle palpation elicits marked tenderness. Tenosynovitis of the second dorsal compartment is the cause of this disorder, which occurs less commonly than de Quervain's disease and must be differentiated from it.

37. What are substitution maneuvers?

Fictitious complaints presented for secondary gain can be difficult to distinguish from actual symptoms. To do so, a number of substitution or distraction maneuvers must be incorporated into the physical examination. These maneuvers take advantage of the clinician's knowledge of wrist anatomy and biomechanics as well as the patient's ignorance. Two of our own substitution maneuvers are discussed here. However, even more important than any of these maneuvers is understanding why they are so useful. With that understanding, a myriad of additional substitution maneuvers can be devised.

- *ANA Substitution Maneuver.* With the wrist in radial deviation, the ANA junction is obscured by the radial styloid, and no amount of thumb pressure in this region results in pain. With the patient distracted, the wrist is gradually brought into ulnar deviation while the pressure is constantly applied. Only in ulnar deviation, with the ANA junction exposed to thumb pressure, should pain be elicited. Pain described while the wrist is in radial deviation should be noted as a positive substitution maneuver.
- *Flexor Pollicis Longus (FPL) Substitution Maneuver.* A patient attempting to feign hand or wrist weakness will do so without knowledge of muscular innervation patterns. This becomes extremely important during examination for carpal tunnel syndrome, in which application of a substitution maneuver can be used to assess weakness of the thenar muscles. Such thenar weakness is secondary to compression of the motor branch of the median nerve. The FPL, which is innervated by the anterior interosseous branch of the median nerve, is completely unaffected in the worst case of carpal tunnel syndrome or virtually any wrist disorder. In the cooperative patient it is all but impossible to overcome a fully flexed FPL. Thus, FPL weakness in any patient, other than one with anterior interosseous syndrome, should alert the examiner.

BIBLIOGRAPHY

Bottke CA, Louis DS, Braunstein EM: Diagnosis and treatment of obscure ulnar-sided wrist pain. Orthopedics 12:1075–1079, 1989.
Brown DE, Lichtman DM: The evaluation of chronic wrist pain. Orthop Clin North Am 15:183–192, 1984.
Cuono CB, Watson HK, Masquelet AC: The carpal boss: Surgical treatment and etiological considerations. Plast Reconstr Surg 63:88–93, 1979.
Kleinman W: The ballottement test. ASSH Correspondence Newsletter, No. 51. 1985.
Pin PG, Young VL, Gilula LA, Weeks PM: Wrist pain: A systemic approach to diagnosis. Plast Reconstr Surg 85:42–46, 1990.
Reagan DS, Linscheid RL, Dobyns JH: Lunotriquetral sprains. J Hand Surg 9A:502–514, 1984.
Stark HH, Jobe FW, Boyes JH, et al: Fracture of the hook of the hamate in athletes. J Bone Joint Surg 59A:575–582, 1977.
Tubiana R, Thomine JM, Mackin E: Examination of the Hand and Wrist. St. Louis, Mosby, 1995.
Watson HK, Ashmead D, Makhlouf MV: Examination of the scaphoid. J Hand Surg 13A:657–660, 1988.
Watson HK, Ottoni L, Pitts EC, et al: Rotary subluxation of the scaphoid: A spectrum of instability. J Hand Surg 18B:62–63, 1993.
Watson HK, Weinzweig J: Physical examination of the wrist. Hand Clin 13:17–34, 1997.
Watson HK, Weinzweig J, Zeppieri J: The natural progression of scaphoid instability. Hand Clin 13:39–50, 1997.
Watson HK, Weinzweig J: Intercarpal arthrodesis. In Green DP (ed): Operative Hand Surgery, 4th ed. New York, Churchill Livingstone, 1999, pp 108–130.
Weinzweig J, Watson HK: Triquetral impingement ligament tear [TILT] syndrome. J Hand Surg 21B:36, 1996.
Weinzweig J, Watson HK: Examination of the wrist. In Watson HK, Weinzweig J (eds): The Wrist. Philadelphia, Lippincott Williams & Wilkins, 2000, pp 47–59.

146 — CHAPTER — RADIOGRAPHIC EXAMINATION OF THE WRIST

Punita Gupta, MD, and
Louis A. Gilula, MD, ABR, FACR

1. How should the standard posteroanterior roentgenogram for examination of the wrist be obtained?

The standard posteroanterior (PA) view should be obtained with the elbow flexed 90° and the shoulder abducted 90°. The hand (not the wrist) is placed palm flat on the cassette (without any flexion, extension, or deviation). The central beam is perpendicular to the cassette and is centered to the capitate head (Fig. 146-1).

2. What criteria identify an adequate PA view?

- The third metacarpal shaft has collinear alignment with the midaxis of the radius (indicating the absence of radial or ulnar deviation).
- The extensor carpi ulnaris groove projects radial to the midpoint of the ulnar styloid (indicating that the elbow is at shoulder height).
- The second through fifth carpometacarpal joints should be evident by recognizing parallel articular cortices at these joints. Lack of profile of these joints is caused by extension of the wrist or flexion at the metacarpophalangeal joints.

3. Why is it important to obtain adequate PA views of the wrist?

Ulnar variance measurements should not be made on a PA view of the wrist that does not meet the criteria listed in Question 2 because adducting the elbow toward the patient's side usually makes the ulna more positive (longer in length than the adjacent radius).

4. How should the standard lateral view of the wrist be obtained?

The standard lateral view should be obtained with the elbow flexed 90° and adducted against the trunk. The central beam is perpendicular to the cassette and is centered over the head of the capitate. If the lateral view is performed correctly, the palmar surface of the pisiform bone is located between the ventral cortex of the head of the capitate and the ventral cortex of the distal pole of the scaphoid. This is termed the *scaphopisocapitate relationship* (Fig. 146-2).

5. How can the lateral view be evaluated to see that the elbow was adducted to the patient's side?

The ulnar styloid moves volar to the dorsal rim of the distal ulna. The distal ulnar extensor carpi ulnaris groove should not be seen. The ulnar styloid relationship to the distal ulna on the lateral view should be definitely different than that on the PA view.

6. What does the scaphoid bone do on a PA view obtained in ulnar deviation?

The scaphoid elongates because it tilts dorsally. In this view the long axis of the scaphoid is seen much better than in the neutral PA view. This view is particularly helpful for detection of scaphoid fractures because the scaphoid waist is more in profile.

7. What are the pronator quadratus and the scaphoid fat pads? What is their importance?

The pronator quadratus fat pad, seen on the lateral radiograph in Fig. 146-2, lies between the pronator quadratus muscle and the volar flexor tendon sheaths. The scaphoid fat pad (see Fig. 146-1) lies between the radial collateral ligament and the abductor pollicis longus tendon. These fat pats are disturbed in trauma and may suggest occult fractures. The fat pads are abnormal when they are bowed (convex) away from the adjacent bones.

8. What is a Colles fracture?

A Colles fracture is a fracture of the distal radial epiphyseal or metaphyseal area with the distal fracture fragment displaced or angulated in the dorsal direction. The fracture may occur with or without intraarticular involvement. It is the most common fracture of the distal radius and occurs most often in older patients. The mechanism of injury is a fall on the dorsiflexed hand (Fig. 146-3).

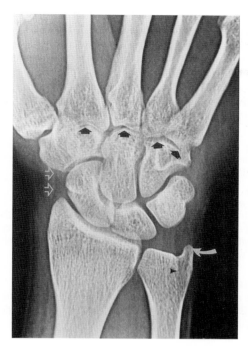

Figure 146-1. Standard neutral posteroanterior (PA) view of the wrist showing collinear alignment of the axis of the third metacarpal shaft with the mid axis of the radius. The ulnar styloid process *(curved white arrow)* is projected most ulnar. The extensor carpi ulnaris groove *(black arrowhead)* is radial to the base of the ulnar styloid. There is parallelism of the articular surfaces of the second through the fifth carpometacarpal joints *(thick black arrows),* indicating that the palm is flat on the x-ray cassette. The scaphoid fat pad *(open arrows)* is evident on this PA view.

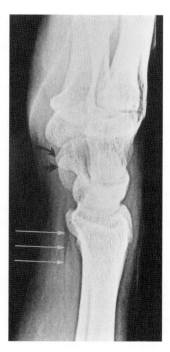

Figure 146-2. Standard lateral radiograph of the wrist. The palmar surface of the pisiform bone *(straight black arrow)* is projected 2 mm dorsal to the distal ventral pole of the scaphoid *(curved black arrow).* The pronator quadratus fat pad *(long white arrows)* is seen on the lateral view and is straight.

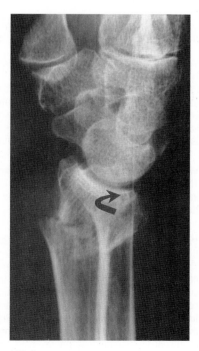

Figure 146-3. Typical Colles fracture of the distal radius with the distal fracture fragment angulated in the dorsal direction *(arrow).*

9. How are Colles fractures classified?

There are several different classification schemes for distal radius fractures. The classification of Colles fractures by Frykman has gained wide acceptance in some areas of the world. Frykman divides the fractures into eight types based on the presence of intraarticular involvement of either the radiocarpal or the distal radioulnar joint and the presence or absence of an associated fracture of the ulnar styloid.

10. How can ulnar styloid fractures be classified?

A fracture may be at the tip, the midportion, or the base of the ulnar styloid.

11. What is the importance of recognizing the various sites of ulnar styloid fractures?

When a fracture involves the base of the ulnar styloid, you may suspect that the entire triangular fibrocartilage complex (TFCC) has been avulsed, indicating probable instability of the distal ulna.

12. What is a Smith fracture?

A Smith fracture is a fracture of the distal radial epiphyseal or metaphyseal area with the distal fracture fragment displaced or angulated in the volar direction. Like a Colles fracture, a Smith fracture may occur with or without intraarticular involvement, and with or without an associated fracture of the ulnar styloid. The common mechanism of injury is a fall on the volarflexed wrist.

13. What is the definition of a Barton fracture?

The Barton fracture is defined as an intraarticular fracture of the posterior or anterior (reverse Barton fracture) rim of the distal radius with (in contrast to Smith and Colles fractures) accompanying palmar or dorsal displacement of the carpus with the radius fragment, respectively.

14. What is a fracture of the radial styloid process called?

A fracture of the radial styloid process is called a chauffeur's fracture (Hutchinson fracture). It is an intraarticular fracture in which the fracture line usually runs through the junction of the scaphoid and lunate fossae of the radius and courses radially in an oblique direction. The mechanism of injury is axial compression of the scaphoid bone against the radial styloid.

15. When a fracture line passes into the ulnar aspect of the scaphoid fossa or especially at the junction between the scaphoid and lunate fossae, what associated carpal abnormality should be questioned?

Look for scapholunate disruption. The force fracturing the radius in this site may propagate into the scapholunate area with rupture of this ligament.

16. What is the fastest and most economical way to evaluate for scapholunate joint disruption?

Perform fluoroscopic evaluation of the wrist with palm flat, as in Question 1, and move the wrist in radial, neutral, and ulnar deviation profiling the scapholunate joint. Fist compression views are then obtained in supination view with the carpometacarpal joints in profile (wrist not extended) with wrist in neutral, radial, and ulnar deviation. If the scapholunate joint is wider (especially twice as wide) than the capitolunate joint, abnormal scapholunate joint width can be diagnosed (see Questions 21 and 22). This wrist should be compared with the opposite wrist as well.

17. What is the most frequently fractured carpal bone?

The most frequently fractured carpal bone is the scaphoid. Scaphoid fractures account for 60% to 70% of all carpal injuries; 70% are located in the waist of the scaphoid, 20% are located in the proximal pole, and 10% involve the distal pole.

18. What are the complications of scaphoid fractures?

Complications of scaphoid fractures include delayed union, nonunion, malunion, and avascular (ischemic) necrosis. The tendency for these complications depends on the fracture site. In general, the prognosis is best in cases of fractures of the distal third and worst in fractures of the proximal third because proximal fractures invariably compromise the blood supply of the proximal fracture fragment. Increased density of the fracture fragment is commonly seen in the healing scaphoid fracture, especially when examined with computed tomography (CT). This finding is due to decreased vascularity of the proximal pole; as a result, the proximal pole does not demineralize as much as the distal pole. Usually with healing, revascularization of the proximal pole occurs and density differences disappear. Less commonly, true necrosis, identified by fragmentation or bone volume loss, may occur. Therefore increased density does not indicate avascular necrosis but relatively decreased vascularity, which commonly disappears with time (Fig. 146-4).

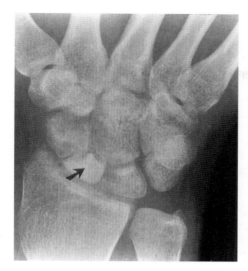

Figure 146-4. Posteroanterior radiograph of a patient who suffered a scaphoid fracture, treated with a plaster cast. Clear evidence of increased density of the proximal fracture fragment *(arrow)* indicates decreased vascularity of this proximal pole. Increased density is not synonymous with avascular necrosis. Avascular (ischemic) necrosis with fragmentation and collapse may or may not develop.

19. What is the difference between static instability and dynamic instability of the wrist?
In general, the term *carpal instability* describes abnormalities in the alignment of carpal bones. *Static instabilities* are constantly present and can be diagnosed on a routine (static) radiographic examination (PA and lateral views). *Dynamic instabilities* are not always seen on routine static radiographs. Dynamic instabilities need stress or motion to produce the instability and therefore can be diagnosed by obtaining instability series or stress maneuvers recorded with videotape, fluoroscopic spots, or overhead views with applied stress.

20. Are carpal instability patterns always unstable?
No. With major dislocations that were not treated for whatever reason, a gross instability appearance is present. However, with time, scarring will take place in the wrist. The scarring may cause the wrist lose its motion, but the wrist will be very stable due to severe scarring.

21. What is rotary subluxation of the scaphoid?
Rotary subluxation of the scaphoid (RSS; or scapholunate dissociation) is the most frequent type of wrist instability. The scapholunate joint space is of abnormal width because of rupture of the scapholunate and adjacent ligaments and capsule. In patients with an associated rupture of the volar radiocarpal ligaments, the scaphoid bone tilts volarly. This condition is RSS. Because of its volar tilting the scaphoid foreshortens and displays a signet-ring shape on the PA neutral view. The signet ring is so called because of the appearance of a stone in the middle of a ring. The shape results from the distal half of the scaphoid overlapping the proximal part of the scaphoid at its waist (Fig. 146-5).

22. Are all communicating defects or holes in the scapholunate ligament, as can be seen on arthrography, magnetic resonance imaging, magnetic resonance imaging arthrography, arthroscopy, or arthrotomy, believed to be symptomatic?
No. Incidental findings of communicating defects of the scapholunate ligament unilaterally or even bilaterally are common. Defects of the dorsal portion of the ligament usually are more important than those of the proximal (mid) or volar scapholunate ligament.

23. What are the two major types of carpal dislocations?
Carpal dislocations can be divided into two major types: lunate and perilunate. Under normal conditions on the lateral radiograph, the lunate is centered over the distal radius concavity, and the capitate is centered over the distal lunate concavity. In general, whichever bone is centered over the radius (lunate or the capitate) is the bone considered to be in normal anatomic alignment. In lunate dislocation the lunate is displaced ventrally or dorsally, and the head of the capitate is centered over the radius. In perilunate instability the lunate remains in anatomic position, and the capitate is displaced from the lunate and the radius. If neither the lunate nor the capitate is centered over the radius, the condition can be called a *midcarpal dislocation* because both the lunate and capitate are separated from each other. However, a true midcarpal dislocation is a transverse dislocation between all the bones in the proximal and distal carpal rows, a condition that has not been seen by the senior author (Fig. 146-6).

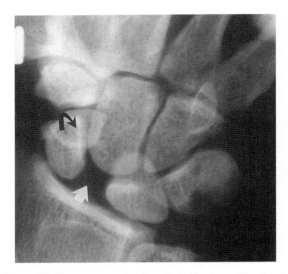

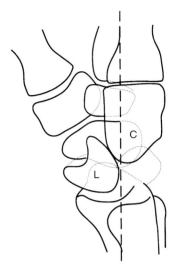

Figure 146-5. View of the wrist of a patient with rotary subluxation of the scaphoid. The scapholunate joint space *(white arrow)* is abnormally wide because of rupture of the scapholunate ligament. A signet-ring shape of the scaphoid *(curved black arrow)* is evident because of its volar tilting due to rupture of adjacent extrinsic ligaments.

Figure 146-6. Midcarpal dislocation. The lunate *(L)* is displaced ventrally, whereas the capitate head *(C)* is centered over the dorsal portion of the radius. This condition is between a perilunate and lunate dislocation. Often a perilunate dislocation precedes or is the first stage of lunate dislocation.

24. What is the role of CT in carpal trauma?

In selected cases where routine roentgenograms are inconclusive, CT has become increasingly popular for diagnosing traumatic wrist disorders. CT is useful for evaluating complex carpal trauma, detecting intraarticular osteocartilaginous bodies, visualizing bone graft material, and determining the degree of fracture healing (Fig. 146-7).

25. What are the advantages of magnetic resonance imaging for diagnosis of wrist disorders?

Magnetic resonance imaging (MRI) is the only imaging technique that allows simultaneous and direct visualization of bony, cartilaginous, and ligamentous structures of the wrist. Because of improvement in examination techniques and development of special wrist surface coils, MRI has become an important imaging technique. It is useful for direct visualization of the intrinsic and extrinsic wrist ligaments and their disorders and is extremely sensitive and specific for detection of early stages of avascular necrosis of carpal bones. In addition, MRI has become an important imaging technique for detection of occult wrist fractures (Fig. 146-8).

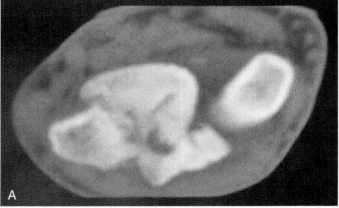

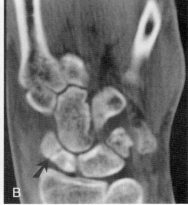

Figure 146-7. A, Axial computed tomographic (CT) scan of the distal radius and ulna. With CT, intraarticular involvement of a fracture and the degree of fracture fragment displacement are better demonstrated than with conventional radiographs. This example shows an extensively comminuted fracture of the distal radius with involvement of and displacement at the distal radioulnar joint. The *top* of the image is the volar surface of the wrist. **B,** Coronal CT scan of the wrist shows a scaphoid waist fracture. Sclerotic margins of the fracture fragments and no evidence of bony bridging of the fragments indicate nonunion of the fracture *(arrow).*

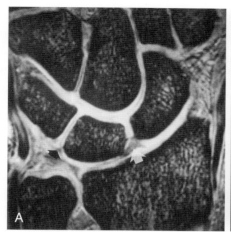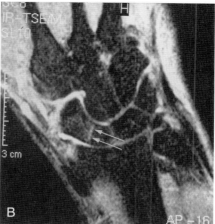

Figure 146-8. **A,** Coronal magnetic resonance imaging (MRI) of the wrist allows precise and direct visualization of the intrinsic interosseous scapholunate and lunotriquetral ligaments *(arrows)* as triangular structures of low signal intensity. **B,** On coronal MRI of the wrist in a patient with a clinically suspected scaphoid fracture, a fracture through the proximal third of the scaphoid is evident *(arrows).* The fracture was not seen on radiographs.

26. What are the most common indications for MR arthrography of the wrist rather than nonarthrographic MR of the wrist?

One well-accepted indication for MR arthrography is evaluation of wrist instability or pain when the etiology is thought to be related to the intrinsic ligaments. When routine MR of the wrist is equivocal, MR arthrography can be of great value. In our institution, we believe that MR arthrography is more sensitive than routine MR in detecting ulnar-sided TFC and TFCC tears, evaluating the intrinsic ligaments (scapholunate and lunotriquetral), evaluating for cartilage abnormalities, and detecting a new tear or a re-tear in a postoperative TFC.

However, even with today's high-resolution MR scanners and improved protocols, opinions regarding the value of MR arthrography for detecting partial tears of the TFC and for detecting tears of the lunotriquetral and scapholunate intrinsic ligaments and extrinsic ligaments tears are conflicting.

27. What are the three compartments of the wrist that have been most commonly injected for imaging?

Radiocarpal, midcarpal, and distal radioulnar joints.

28. Which of the three compartments listed in Question 27 is most commonly injected for wrist MR arthrography?

Radiocarpal.

29. What is a potential pitfall with injecting only the radiocarpal joint?

Proximal noncommunicating tears or defects of the TFC and TFCC and distal noncommunicating defects of the scapholunate and lunatotriquetral structures may be missed.

BIBLIOGRAPHY

Braun H, Kenn W, Schneider S, et al: Direct MR arthrography of the wrist: Value in detecting complete and partial defects of intrinsic ligaments and the TFCC in comparison with arthroscopy. Rofo 175:1515–1524, 2003.

Breitenseher MJ, Metz VM, Gilula LA, et al: Radiographically occult scaphoid fractures: Value of MR imaging in detection. Radiology 203:245–250, 1997.

Carrino JA, Smith DK, Schweitzer ME: MR arthrography of the elbow and wrist. Semin Musculoskelet Radiol 2:397–414, 1998.

Cerezal L, Abascal F, Garcia-Valtuille R, Del Piña F: Wrist MR arthrography: How, why, when. Radiol Clin North Am 43:709–731, 2005.

Frykman G: Fracture of the distal radius including sequelae-shoulder-hand-finger syndrome, disturbance in the distal radioulnar joint and impairment of nerve function: A clinical and experimental study. Acta Orthop Scand 108(Suppl):1–55, 1967.

Gilula LA, Mann FA, Dobyns JH, Yin Y, et al: Wrist: Terminology and definitions. J Bone Joint Surg 84A(Suppl 1):1–73, 2002.

Gilula LA, Yin Y (eds): Imaging of the Hand and Wrist. Philadelphia, WB Saunders, 1996.

Gilula LA (ed): The Traumatized Hand and Wrist: Radiographic and Anatomic Correlation. Philadelphia, WB Saunders, 1992.

Grainger AJ, Elliott JM, Campbell RSD, et al: Direct MR arthrography: A review of current use. Clin Radiol 55:163–176, 2000.

Hardy TH, Totty WG, Reinus WR, Gilula LA: Posteroanterior wrist radiography: Importance of arm positioning. J Hand Surg 12A:504–508, 1987.

Levis CM, Yang Z, Gilula LA: Validation of the extensor carpi ulnaris groove (ECUG) as predictor for the recognition of standard posteroanterior radiographs of the wrist. J Hand Surg 27A:252–257, 2002.

Scheck RJ, Romagnolo A, Hierner R, et al: The carpal ligaments in MR arthrography of the wrist: Correlation with standard MRI and wrist arthroscopy. J Magn Reson Imaging 9:468–474, 1999.

Stewart NR, Gilula LA: CT of the wrist: A tailored approach. Radiology 183:13–20, 1992.

Yin YM, Evanoff B, Gilula LA, Pilgram TK: Evaluation of selective wrist arthrography of contralateral asymptomatic wrists for symmetric ligamentous defects. AJR 166:1067–1073, 1996.

Zanetti M, Linkous MD, Gilula LA, Hodler J: Characteristics of triangular fibrocartilage defects in symptomatic and contralateral asymptomatic wrists. Radiology 216:840–845, 2000.

BIOMECHANICS OF THE WRIST

CHAPTER 147

Jaiyoung Ryu, MD, and
Jon Kline, MS, ATS, PA-C

1. Why are multiple carpal bones present in the wrist?
The function of the wrist is to position the hand optimally for specific tasks. To do so, the wrist is required to have a large arc of motion while maintaining its stability. Hip and shoulder joints have large arcs of motion, which are permitted by their fundamental design as ball and socket joints; their stability is maintained by the large muscles surrounding them. The wrist would become too bulky to function properly if it were surrounded by large muscles. Thus the wrist is designed in another way to maintain both mobility and stability—it has multilinked rows. Each link has a small range of motion but good stability. When assembled, the wrist combines the motions of the multiple links. The links, however, decrease wrist stability somewhat. To overcome this, the wrist is designed not only in multilinked rows but also in columns of these rows.

2. What is meant by the term *kinematics*? What is the difference between kinematics and kinetics?
Kinematics is the description of motion, including the pattern and speed of movement sequencing by the body segments, that often translates to the degree of coordination an individual displays. Whereas kinematics describes the appearance of motion, *kinetics* is the study of the forces and the associated motion.

3. From a kinematic standpoint, what is the difference between rotational and translational movements?
Rotation is the movement around an axis (center of rotation), whereas *translation* is the movement along an axis. Any motion between two free bodies without any restraint between them can be described by three rotations around the x, y, and z axes and three translations along the x, y, and z axes. Therefore the maximum degrees of freedom between two free bodies is six. If a joint has only pure flexion/extension (a rotation; one degree of freedom), then the joint has five restraining forces, such as collateral ligaments, joint architectural design, etc. In other words, the summation of the degree(s) of freedom and restraint force(s) is always six.

4. In what planes do the three basic wrist movements occur?
Flexion/extension occurs in the sagittal plane with the axis of rotation occurring in the coronal plane. Radial/ulnar deviation occurs in the coronal plane with the axis of rotation in the sagittal plane. Pronosupination occurs in the transverse plane. All these are rotational movements. Translational movement in the wrist is negligible.

5. What is the normal range of motion of the wrist?
The average normal range of motion in the wrist joint is 75° to 90° of flexion, 75° to 90° of extension, 15° to 20° of radial deviation, and 25° to 40° of ulnar deviation.

6. What is the functional range of motion of the wrist?
Although different ranges of motion have been described as functional for the wrist, the most widely accepted functional range of motion of the wrist is 40° of flexion, 40° of extension, 10° of radial deviation, and 30 degrees of ulnar deviation, with which a person can perform most of the activities of daily living in a normal fashion.

7. What is the physiologic motion of the wrist?
The wrist is radially deviated when it is extended and ulnarly deviated when it is flexed, as in a dart throwing motion. As the wrist is radially deviated, it flexes slightly, and vice versa.

8. What is the columnar theory of carpal kinematics?
The column theory was first proposed by Navarro in 1935. This theory divides the carpal bones into three columns. The radial column consists of the scaphoid, trapezium, and trapezoid. The central column consists of the lunate and capitate. The ulnar column consists of the triquetrum and hamate. This theory was later modified by Taleisnik in 1976. This modification moved the trapezium and trapezoid to the central column. This theory explains the load transfer patterns through the wrist, but it does not explain movement between the proximal and distal rows.

9. What is the row theory of carpal kinematics?

The row theory divides the proximal row and the distal rows into two separate functional units. Although the rows are convenient in communication, because the scaphoid does not belong to one of the two rows but bridges the two and because the so-called midcarpal joint has multiple levels of joints, the theory has limitations in describing carpal kinematics.

10. What is the ring theory of carpal kinematics?

Proposed by Lichtman in 1981, the ring theory connects the proximal and distal rows with a radial link, the scaphotrapezial joint, and an ulnar link composed of the triquetrohamate joint.

11. What is the four-unit concept of carpal kinematics?

The four-unit concept was derived from a carpal kinematic study that showed the distal carpal bones moved as a single unit while the scaphoid, lunate, and triquetrum moved independently. Use of this concept in describing normal or pathologic kinematics of the wrist as well as stability and instability of the wrist has been proposed (Fig. 147-1).

12. Which portion of the scapholunate interosseous ligament is strongest and most important for scapholunate stability?

The dorsal region of the scapholunate ligament is the strongest, requiring more than 250 N to fail, followed by the palmar region, failing at approximately 125 N. A reversed pattern was observed in the lunotriquetral ligament.

13. Which are stronger, intrinsic carpal ligaments or extrinsic carpal ligaments?

The extrinsic ligaments of the wrist, such as the palmar capsular radiocarpal ligaments, are viscoelastic structures, exhibiting stiffness behavior proportional to strain rate with failure at approximately 100 N. The scapholunate and lunotriquetrial interosseous ligaments have been identified as the strongest ligaments in the wrist, requiring force applications greater than 300 N to fail.

14. What is force coupling?

Force coupling is a mechanical condition where two forces that are not colinear and originate from opposing directions cause the object to rotate.

Because the scaphoid is aligned approximately 45° from the longitudinal axis of the forearm and wrist, the forces coming to it form force coupling. In other words, whenever there is compressive force through the wrist, the scaphoid always tries to flex.

The triquetrum, on the other side, always tries to extend because of its unique spiral articulation with the hamate.

The rotations of the scaphoid and triquetrum in opposite direction are resisted and regulated by their connection to the lunate at the middle via the scapholunate and lunotriquetral interosseous ligaments (Fig. 147-2).

15. How does rotary subluxation of the scaphoid affect carpal kinematics?

Disruption or instability of the scapholunate interosseous ligament (SLIL), through either traumatic disruption or chronic overuse forces, will result in rotary subluxation of the scaphoid. When the SLIL is disrupted or stretched, the

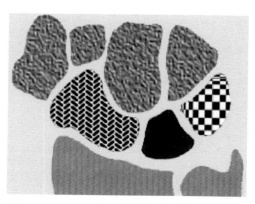

Figure 147-1. Four-unit concept of carpal kinematics.

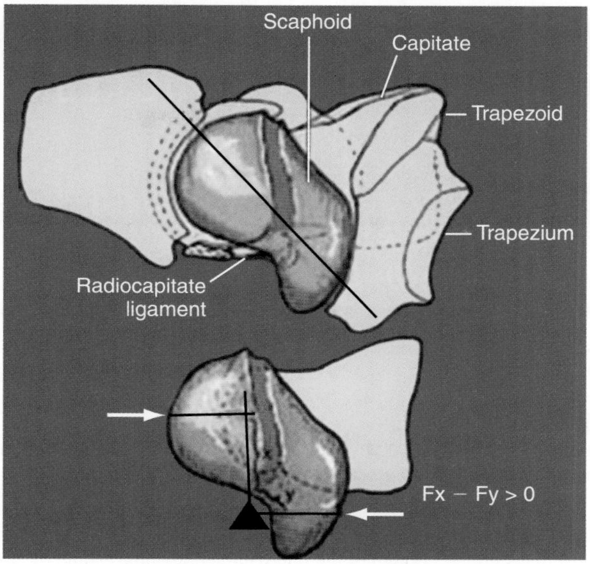

Figure 147-2. Force coupling of the scaphoid.

scaphoid will flex abnormally while the lunate and triquetrum will extend significantly during movement of the wrist. The capitate will flex abnormally relative to the lunate. Because the lunate, a representative of the intercalated segment, is dorsiflexed, this instability is referred to as a *dorsiflexion intercalated segmental instability* (DISI).

16. What is a DISI deformity?

DISI is a condition in which the lunate abnormally extends relative to the radius. This instability results from disruption or attenuation of the scapholunate interosseous ligament.

17. What is a volarflexion intercalated segmental instability deformity?

Volarflexion intercalated segmental instability (VISI) is a condition in which the lunate abnormally flexes relative to the radius. This instability results from disruption or attenuation of the lunotriquetral interosseous ligament.

BIBLIOGRAPHY

Berger RA: The gross and histologic anatomy of the scapholunate interosseous ligament. J Hand Surg [Am] 21:170–178, 1996.
Berger RA, Crowninshield RD, Flatt AE: The three-dimensional rotational behavior of the carpal bones. Clin Orthop 167:303–310, 1982.
Kobayashi M, Berger RA, Linscheid RL, et al: Intercarpal kinematics during wrist motion. Hand Clin 13:143–149, 1997.
Ruby LK, Cooney WP, An KN, et al: Relative motion of selected carpal bones. A kinematic analysis of the normal wrist. J Hand Surg [Am] 13:1–10, 1988.
Ryu J, Cooney WP, Askew LJ, An KN, Chao EY: Functional ranges of motion of the wrist joint. J Hand Surg [Am] 16:409–419, 1991.
Ryu J: Biomechanics of the wrist. In Watson HK, Weinzweig J (eds): The Wrist. Lippincott Williams & Wilkins, Philadelphia 2001, pp 27–45.
Short WH, Werner FW, Forrino MD, et al: A dynamic biomechanical study of scapholunate ligament sectioning. J Hand Surg [Am] 20:986–999, 1995.
Viegas SF, Patterson RM, Peterson PD, et al: Load mechanics in the midcarpal joint. J Hand Surg [Am] 18:14–18, 1993.

THE PEDIATRIC WRIST

Jaiyoung Ryu, MD, and
Matthew S. Loos, MD

1. By what gestational age does the carpus develop into eight distinct entities?
By the tenth gestational week. Carpal bones generally undergo membranous ossification in a predictable pattern (Table 148-1).

2. What is the carpal boss?
First described as "carpe bossu" by the French physician Foille, the carpal boss is a protuberance between the base of either the second or third metacarpal and the articulating trapezoid and/or capitate.

3. Describe the typical presentation of a carpal boss?
A carpal boss presents as a mass on the dorsum of the hand. It may be either painful or painless. Diagnostic evaluation should include a metacarpal stress test.

4. What constitutes a metacarpal stress test?
Inducing pain by distorting the quadrangular joint. This is accomplished by pronosupination of the index and long finger metacarpals with the metacarpophalangeal joints flexed.

5. What is the etiology of a carpal boss?
The cause is unclear but likely is related to repetitive trauma or periostitis near the insertion of the extensor carpi radialis brevis.

6. How is a carpal boss treated?
Carpal boss can be treated conservatively with simple analgesics, immobilization, and joint injections of corticosteroids. Operative therapy involves complete excision of the protuberance.

7. What is the Madelung deformity?
A congenital deformity of the wrist most often seen in girls ages 8 to 9 years. It is commonly bilateral in nature. It is caused by the premature arrest of the distal radial physis.

8. With which syndrome is the Madelung deformity most associated?
Leri-Weill syndrome.

9. Describe Leri-Weill syndrome.
Dyschondrosteosis. A mild mesomelic shortening of the long bones and short stature.

Table 148-1. Carpal Bone Ossification

CARPAL BONE	AGE AT OSSIFICATION
Capitate, hamate	Fourth to fifth months of life
Triquetrum	Second year of life
Lunate	Fourth year of life
Scaphoid	Fourth to fifth years of life (ossification begins distally and progresses proximally)
Trapezium, trapezoid	Fifth year of life
Pisiform	Ninth year of life or later

10. What are the two forms of Madelung's deformity?
- *Typical*: Shortened, bowed, distal radius with prominent dorsal ulnar head
- *Atypical*: Distal head of radius bends dorsally and results in volar subluxation of the ulnar head; known as "reverse Madelung deformity"

11. What is the treatment of Madelung deformity?
If the deformity is mild, surgical intervention usually is unnecessary. However, surgery is important in patients with more severe forms as a means to relieve pain and maintain functionality of the wrist. Surgery typically is avoided until the ages of 11 to 13 years, but there is some controversy about whether to perform the repair before or after closure of the physis. The surgery typically consists of a combination of ulnar shortening and radial osteotomy or radiocarpal arthrodesis.

12. What is most important to preserve in the wrist abnormality associated with cerebral palsy and arthrogryposis?
Functionality. The wrists in patients with cerebral palsy and arthrogryposis often present as flexion contractures at the wrist and metacarpophalangeal joints, ulnar deviation of the wrist and adduction of the thumb.

13. What is gymnast's wrist?
A combination of wrist pain, fractures, and joint instability.

14. Why does gymnast's wrist develop?
The wrist in a gymnast is changed from a specialized joint designed for elegant motor control to a weight-bearing joint. The repetitive trauma exerted on the joint during training damages the triangular fibrocartilage complex, can lead to dysfunctional ossification of the distal radius and ulna, and fractures.

15. What is "grip lock"?
During rotational exercises (i.e., high bars), the gymnast wears a specialized grip that contains a small dowel or crease to aid in holding onto the equipment. Occasionally, during rotation, this dowel or crease becomes locked on the apparatus, freezing the hand while the gymnast is still in motion. This "lock" can cause serious injuries ranging from open fractures to dislocations to ligamentous instability.

16. Describe the stages and treatment of gymnast's wrist.
- *Stage I*: Symptomatic wrist injuries without radiographic evidence of damage. Treatment is expectant and requires avoidance of trauma to the wrist until the patient is pain-free (usually in approximately 1 month).
- *Stage II*: Symptomatic with radiographic evidence of physeal stress injury. Treatment typically requires immobilization up to 3 months before returning to pain-free activity.
- *Stage III*: Symptomatic with radiographic evidence of damage to the physis and secondary positive ulnar variance. Typically requires surgical intervention to repair the damage.

17. What is the most common carpal bone fracture in the pediatric population?
Fracture of the scaphoid.

18. How is the diagnosis complicated in children?
The fracture pattern in children differs than that of an adult scaphoid fracture. In children, the fracture tends to be in the distal third of the bone. Diagnosis involves high clinical suspicion and evidence of soft tissue damage, dorsal swelling, and the fat stripe sign, and radiographs. Treatment requires immobilization even if the fracture is not seen radiographically. Delay in treatment may lead to nonunion, avascular necrosis, instability, and arthrosis.

19. What is the scaphoid "fat stripe" sign? What is its significance?
The scaphoid *fat stripe sign* involves loss of the small triangular fat density normally found between the radial collateral ligament and the first dorsal wrist extensor compartment. Obliteration or radial displacement of the fat stripe indicates a fracture of the scaphoid, radial styloid, or base of the thumb metacarpal. However, this sign usually is unreliable or absent in children younger than age 12 years.

20. What are the most common fractures in children?
Distal forearm fractures. Typically due to a fall onto an outstretched hand and often associated with distal radioulnar joint (DRUJ) instability.

21. What is a Galeazzi fracture?

In adults, a Galeazzi fracture is the combination of a radius fracture with a disruption of the DRUJ. In children, a Galeazzi fracture is the combination of a distal radius fracture and Salter I damage to the ulnar physis resulting in DRUJ incompetence. Thus reduction and immobilization of the arm is all that is required as the DRUJ is not disrupted.

22. What is a ganglion?

A ganglion is a benign, mucinous cyst of the joint capsule, tendon, or tendon sheath.

23. What are the etiology, location, and therapy for ganglia?

- The etiology is unclear; however, it likely is a degeneration of the fibrous tissue secondary to repetitive use.
- Typical location for the ganglia are the scapholunate joint dorsally and the scaphotrapezial or radiocarpal joint volarly.
- Conservative therapy in children is treatment of choice. Persistent pain may force surgical excision. The old axiom of crushing the ganglion with a heavy book or injection often leads to recurrence.

24. What is the most common connective tissue disorder in children?

Juvenile arthritis.

25. Describe pauciarticular, polyarticular, and systemic-onset juvenile arthritis.

- *Pauciarticular Juvenile Arthritis*: Four or fewer joints involved, with the ankles and knees the most typically afflicted. Chronic eye inflammation is common and can lead to irreversible damage if not treated. Girls are most often affected by the early form between the ages of 1 and 5 years. Fifty percent of these girls are antinuclear antibody positive. The late form typically affects boys in their large joints.
- *Polyarticular Juvenile Arthritis*: Usually involves five or more joints. The large joints are mostly affected and are associated with rheumatoid factor. Patients with rheumatoid factor positivity are almost always female and have a worse functional prognosis in the long term.
- *Systemic-Onset (Still's Disease) Juvenile Arthritis*: Found in children associated with high fevers and rheumatoid rash. Can be associated with growth delay, organomegaly, osteopenia, anemia, leukocytosis, and thrombocytosis.

26. What are the most common initial and long-term manifestations of juvenile arthritis?

Early on, patients experience stiffness, synovitis, and tenosynovitis. As the disease progresses, a flexion/ulnar deviation deformity can develop.

27. Describe the therapeutic options for juvenile arthritis.

All patients with juvenile arthritis require an ophthalmologic evaluation. Treatment consists of maintaining functionality through physical and occupational therapy. Nonsteroidal antiinflammatory drugs and other medications are used initially, and as many as 50% to 75% of children respond to this therapy within the first 3 months. If the conservative approach fails, synovectomy, tenosynovectomy, contracture release, and even osteotomies often are necessary to relieve pain and improve motion.

BIBLIOGRAPHY

Buck-Gramcko D: Congenital Malformations of the Hand and Forearm. New York, Churchill Livingstone, 1998.

Buck-Gramcko D: Congenital anomalies of the wrist. In Watson W, Weinzweig J (eds): The Wrist. Philadelphia, Lippincott Williams & Wilkins, 2001, pp 123–148.

Cuono CB, Watson HK: The carpal boss: Surgical treatment and etiological considerations. Plast Reconstr Surg 3:886–888, 1979.

Fusi S, Watson HK, Cuono CB: The carpal boss. J Hand Surg 20B:405–408, 1995.

Dobyns JH, Gabel GT: Gymnast's wrist. Hand Clin 6:493–505, 1990.

Light TR: Injury to the immature carpus. Hand Clin 4:415–424, 1988.

Ryu J, Gomberg BFC: Pediatric problems involving the wrist. In Watson W, Weinzweig J (eds): The Wrist. Philadelphia, Lippincott Williams & Wilkins, 2001, pp 149–172.

Tachdjian MO: Madelung's deformity, In Tachdjian MO (ed): Pediatric Orthopedics, 2nd ed. Philadelphia, WB Saunders, 1990, pp 210–222.

Watson HK, Pitts EC, Herber S: Madelung's deformity. J Hand Surg 18B:601–605, 1993.

Weinzweig J, Watson HK, Herbert TJ, Shaer J: Congenital synchondrosis of the scaphotrapezio-trapezoid joint. J Hand Surg 22A:74–77, 1997.

James Lilley, MD; Mark N. Halikis, MD; and Julio Taleisnik, MD

1. What is the relative incidence of carpal fractures?
- Scaphoid: 79%
- Triquetrum: 14%
- Trapezium: 2.3 %
- Hamate: 1.5%
- Lunate: 1%
- Pisiform: 1%
- Capitate: 1%
- Trapezoid: 0.2%

2. What is the blood supply to the scaphoid? Why is it important ?
The superficial palmar branch and the dorsal carpal branch of the radial artery feed the distal pole of the scaphoid. Intraosseous vessels flow retrograde to supply the proximal pole. Fractures through the scaphoid waist can sever the blood supply to the proximal pole, leading to avascular necrosis (AVN) of the proximal fragment in as many as one third of cases. An even higher incidence of AVN is found in more proximal fractures. AVN is associated with nonunion and persistent symptoms of pain or instability of the wrist (Fig. 149-1).

3. What is the typical presentation of a scaphoid fracture?
The typical patient is a young man who has fallen on an outstretched palm and extended wrist. He presents with pain and swelling of the radial wrist. Tenderness in the anatomic snuffbox should lead to a presumptive diagnosis of fracture until radiographic examination proves conclusively negative.

4. What is the anatomic snuffbox?
It is a small triangular depression just distal and dorsal to the radial styloid. The extensor pollicis brevis (EPB) and abductor pollicis longus (APL) form its volar border as they run together in the first dorsal compartment of the wrist. The extensor pollicis longus (EPL) forms the dorsal border. Extension of the thumb demonstrates the borders best. With ulnar deviation the scaphoid is uncovered by the radial styloid and is palpable at the floor of the snuffbox.

5. What radiographic views should be included in the initial workup of a scaphoid fracture?
Four views have been found to identify 97% of scaphoid fractures: one posteroanterior (PA), one lateral, and two oblique projections (supinated oblique and pronated oblique). The clenched fist position or active ulnar deviation in the PA view

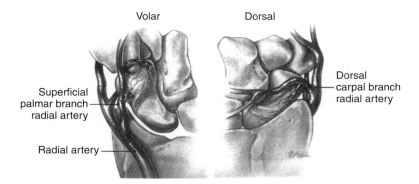

Volar   Dorsal

Superficial palmar branch radial artery

Dorsal carpal branch radial artery

Radial artery

Figure 149-1. The dorsal blood supply to the scaphoid via the dorsal carpal branch of the radial artery and the volar blood supply via the superficial palmar branch of the radial artery enter the distal pole of the scaphoid. Blood supply to the proximal pole is intraosseous and retrograde. Fractures to the waist of the scaphoid disrupt this intraosseous supply and may lead to avascular necrosis of the proximal pole. (From Amadio PC, Taleisnik J: Fractures of the carpal bones. In Green DP [ed]: Operative Hand Surgery, 3rd ed. New York, Churchill Livingstone, 1993, p 801.)

places the scaphoid more parallel to the film and improves visualization of the fracture. Several authors favor the ulnar deviation PA view in lieu of the supinated oblique. The lateral view helps to visualize fractures in the coronal plane and to assess the degree of scaphoid fracture angulation.

6. What is an occult scaphoid fracture?

A completely nondisplaced fracture or occult fracture may not appear on plain films initially. A period of 10 to 14 days may be required for resorption to occur at the fracture site before the fracture is visible radiographically. Alternatively, a bone scan may provide this information sooner. A negative scan excludes a fracture; a positive scan may warrant trispiral or computed tomographic (CT) studies to confirm the presence of fracture and define its anatomy.

7. What is the navicular fat stripe sign?

It is a small radiolucent line in the soft tissues radial to the carpus as seen on the PA view. A preserved fat stripe or fat pad is evidence that the scaphoid is intact. Fracture leads to radial displacement or (usually) obliteration of the fat stripe.

8. What are the important classification systems of scaphoid fractures?

The middle third or waist of the scaphoid is the most common location of injury. Most treatment recommendations are directed to waist fractures, which Russe subclassifies by the anatomy of the fracture. The plane of the fracture is defined in relation to the long axis of the scaphoid. *Horizontal oblique fractures*, the most frequent of the wrist fractures, are perpendicular to the long axis of the limb but oblique in relation to the longitudinal axis of the scaphoid. They are stable and should heal with 6 to 8 weeks of immobilization. *Transverse fractures* are less common and less stable. They are perpendicular to the long axis of the scaphoid but oblique in relation to the long axis of the limb. Healing occurs in 6 to 12 weeks. The rare *vertical oblique pattern* is less stable and requires even longer immobilization because it is more subject to shear forces along the long axis of the limb.

Cooney and others have recognized the importance of fracture displacement and angulation in predicting stability. For patients with displacement greater than 1 mm found on any radiographic view, nonunion rates climb 10- to 20-fold. Angulation, which is suggestive of carpal instability, also contributes to nonunion. Examples include scapholunate angle greater than 60° or radiolunate angle greater than 15°. Herbert reported an alphanumeric classification scheme that incorporates fracture anatomy, chronicity, and stability factors. Unstable or type B fractures include distal oblique, complete waist, proximal pole, and transscaphoid perilunate fracture dislocations. Prognostic information based on this system is being developed as the system is adopted by other authors (Fig. 149-2).

9. How does a scaphoid fracture contribute to wrist instability?

The wrist can be envisioned as a three-bar linkage with the distal carpal row, the proximal row, and the radius forming links in a chain. Like a chain, this construct is stable in tension but unstable in compression. It requires a stabilizing bar to support compression. The scaphoid provides this stability by its connection distally to the capitate and proximally to the lunate. Disruption of the scaphoid renders the carpus unstable and subject to collapse. The radius, lunate, and capitate then no longer are colinear. Most frequently, the lunate tilts dorsally with the attached proximal pole of the scaphoid. Loading of the distal fragment by the trapezium and trapezoid favors axial compression, causing the distal fragment to flex while the proximal fragment extends, thus creating a volar flexed "humpback" position of the scaphoid. This deformity contributes to delayed healing of the fracture because it maintains malalignment across the scaphoid waist (Fig. 149-3).

10. What are the essentials of closed treatment of scaphoid fractures?

In most cases, unstable scaphoid fractures are treated with open reduction internal fixation (ORIF). Stable or nondisplaced fractures can be treated by closed methods. Use of short or long arm casting is controversial. Although reports show a statistically significant decrement in healing time with inclusion of the elbow, short arm casting of stable scaphoid fractures yields a 95% union rate in an average of 11 weeks. Therefore stable fractures can be treated in a short arm thumb spica cast. However, inclusion of the elbow is recommended by several authors for initial immobilization followed by short arm casting until radiographic union. Electrical stimulators have been used to promote healing of the scaphoid, but prospective double-blind studies demonstrating efficacy are lacking. This type of therapy is much more costly than is casting alone.

11. What are the indications for operation on a fracture of the scaphoid?

Displacement greater than 1 mm or angulation demonstrated by a scapholunate angle greater than 60° or a radiolunate angle greater than 15° is considered significant. Displaced or angulated fractures, fractures that demonstrate no healing at 6 to 12 weeks, and nonunions that have failed closed treatment after 6 months are best treated surgically. Very proximal fractures, which are at higher risk for nonunion and AVN, also are good candidates for surgical treatment. Indeed, routine internal fixation is recommended for these proximal fractures.

TYPE A:
Stable acute fractures

A1
Fracture of
tubercle

A2
Incomplete fracture
through waist

TYPE B:
Unstable acute fractures

B1
Distal oblique
fracture

B2
Complete fracture
of waist

B3
Proximal pole
fracture

B4
Trans-scaphoid-
perilunate
fracture dislocation
of carpus

TYPE C:
Delayed union

C
Delayed union

TYPE D:
Established nonunion

D1
Fibrous union

D2
Pseudarthrosis

Figure 149-2. The Herbert alphanumeric classification system of scaphoid fractures. (From Amadio PC, Taleisnik J: Fractures of the carpal bones. In Green DP [ed]: Operative Hand Surgery, 3rd ed. New York, Churchill Livingstone, 1993, p 805.)

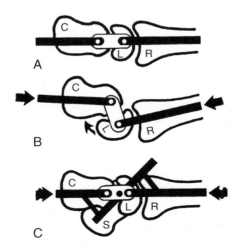

Figure 149-3. The three-bar linkage model of the wrist predicts stability in tension **(A)** and collapse in compression **(B)** unless an additional stabilizing link is added to the construct **(C)**. *C*, Capitate; *L*, lunate; *R*, radius; *S*, scaphoid, the stabilizing link. (From Amadio PC, Taleisnik J: Fractures of the carpal bones. In Green DP [ed]: Operative Hand Surgery, 3rd ed. New York, Churchill Livingstone, 1993, p 863.)

12. What surgical options are available?

Internal fixation with K-wires is indicated for fractures associated with dislocation or ligamentous instability. Smooth wires are useful for fixing an avascular fragment; a minimum of three wires is needed. The Herbert screw is a proven method for osteosynthesis of the scaphoid. The larger pitch of the leading threads compared with the trailing threads is designed to provide compression across the fracture. The screw is countersunk below the articular surface and generally is not removed. The internal fixation provided by the screw allows more rapid mobilization of the wrist. Russe described using iliac crest strips alone for fixation to improve healing potential. Healing rates are comparable to those of the Herbert screw plus bone graft. Recognizing the problems associated with the flexion or "humpback" deformity, Fisk and Fernandez described the use of a volar-placed wedge of bone to reduce the deformity. This corticocancellous graft can be fixed with wires or a screw at the nonunion site. Use of a vascularized bone graft swung on a pedicle has been described for failed grafts. Several techniques are described, including osteotomy of a portion of the pronator quadratus insertion, which is rotated distally with a strip of muscle attached.

13. What differences are seen in pediatric scaphoid fractures?

Most commonly they are located in the distal third (59%) and tubercle (33%). Few are displaced. They can and should be treated by closed technique until skeletal maturity unless they are grossly displaced.

14. Describe the surgical approaches to the scaphoid.

The key landmarks of the volar or Russe approach are the tuberosity of the scaphoid and the tendon of the flexor carpi radialis (FCR). A curvilinear skin incision that crosses the wrist crease obliquely should allow access to both landmarks. Longitudinal division of the deep fascia radial to the FCR allows radial retraction of the radial artery and ulnar retraction of the FCR and palmar cutaneous branch of the median nerve. The volar radiocarpal joint capsule can be incised to expose the scaphoid. The exposure is extended by division of the thenar origin distally and the pronator quadratus proximally.

The dorsolateral approach to the scaphoid has the disadvantage of crossing the branches of the superficial radial nerve as well as endangering the blood supply to the scaphoid; however, it provides better access to the proximal pole. The nerve is retracted in a dorsal or volar direction as needed. The extensor fascia is divided longitudinally, and the artery is exposed and retracted volarly with care to preserve the dorsal carpal branch. The proximal pole is then well demonstrated by ulnar deviation of the wrist.

15. Can the scaphoid be fixed arthroscopically?

Patients with nondisplaced scaphoid fractures who cannot commit to 8 to 12 weeks of immobilization are candidates for arthroscopically assisted fixation using the Herbert-Whipple screw, a cannulated modification of the Herbert screw. A guidewire is placed under arthroscopic guidance across the fracture, and a second, parallel wire is used for derotation. The screw is introduced volarly through a small incision and passed over the guidewire.

16. What is Kienböck's disease? How is it related to fractures of the lunate?

Fractures of the lunate are rare when distinguished from Kienböck's disease or AVN of the lunate. The etiology of Kienböck's disease is uncertain. It is possible that in some cases a fracture predisposes the bone to AVN, which leads to later collapse. Alternatively, other factors may impair blood flow to the bone, causing the necrosis, which, in turn, leads to collapse and fracture (see Chapter 150).

17. What is the typical presentation and workup of a triquetral fracture?

Isolated triquetral fractures commonly are avulsion or shear fractures from a hyperextension injury with ulnar wrist pain, swelling, and tenderness. Wrist hyperextension may cause the hamate or ulnar styloid to impinge on the triquetrum, causing a dorsal shear fracture. Acute wrist palmar flexion may lead to an avulsion fracture by the dorsal radiotriquetral ligament. Oblique radiographs are the most helpful. Treatment in a splint is adequate. Triquetral fractures are also associated with perilunate fracture dislocation. Simple fractures are treated with splint immobilization.

18. How are pisiform fractures best diagnosed and treated?

Pisiform fractures, which typically result from a direct blow, present with ulnar and volar wrist pain and unmistakable tenderness. Supinated oblique and carpal tunnel radiographic views are most helpful. Cast treatment has not proved to alter the natural history of the injury, but several authors recommend it over splinting. Symptomatic nonunions do well with excision of the pisiform.

19. What rare carpal fracture is associated with cyclists?

Trapezial fractures, which are seen best with a Bett's oblique view of the trapezium, can be treated by closed technique in a short arm thumb spica cast if nondisplaced. Displacement is often intraarticular and requires ORIF. Nonunion is treated with partial or total excision, fusion, or interposition arthroplasty.

20. Which carpal fracture is associated with golf and racquet sports?

Fractures of the hook of the hamate. A dull ache in the ulnar wrist (even dorsally) or hypothenar eminence may be associated with chronic and acute trauma to the area, especially in golf, baseball, or racquet sports. The symptoms are aggravated by lateral movement or flexion of the little finger. Diagnosis requires radiographic evaluation that includes oblique and carpal tunnel views. Standard or computed tomography of the wrist may be needed to clarify the plain film images. Immobilization reduces the risk of nonunion. Excision provides reliable relief for patients who fail conservative therapy for symptomatic nonunion.

21. What is scaphocapitate syndrome?

Scaphocapitate syndrome is caused by fractures through the waist of the capitate and scaphoid waist with rotation of the proximal capitate fragment 90° to 180°. If recognized early (3 to 4 weeks), both fractures can be treated with ORIF. Injuries recognized late can be treated expectantly, with arthrodesis reserved for persistent symptoms. AVN is a sequel to chronic or acute injury of the capitate because the blood supply to the proximal pole is tenuous.

22. How do scaphoid fractures contribute to wrist arthritis?

Patients with a symptomatic nonunion of the scaphoid have been shown to undergo a predictable pattern of wrist arthritis. Because the distal fragment is unrestrained after fracture, it tends to rotate. This rotation makes the distal articulations incongruous and promotes degenerative change. The proximal articulations are spared because they are spherical and because the proximal fragment remains stabilized by the radioscaphoid and scapholunate ligaments. The pattern of degeneration is similar to that seen in cases of rotatory subluxation of the scaphoid, also known as scapholunate advanced collapse (SLAC) wrist. This refers to a pattern of progressive joint space and cartilage loss that begins at the radial styloid and progresses down the radioscaphoid articulation. The capitolunate and scaphocapitate articulations are later involved. Still further progression leads to hamatolunate degeneration and scapholunate dissociation as the capitate migrates proximally. The radiolunate articulation is always spared (see Chapter 155).

BIBLIOGRAPHY

Amadio PC, Taleisnik J: Fractures of the carpal bones. In Green DP (ed): Operative Hand Surgery, 3rd ed. New York, Churchill Livingstone, 1993, pp 799–842.
Cheung GC, Lever CJ, Morris AD: X-ray diagnosis of acute scaphoid fractures. J Hand Surg [Br] 31:104–109, 2006.
Failla JM, Amadio PC: Recognition and treatment of uncommon carpal fractures. Hand Clin 4:469–476, 1988.
Garcia-Elias M: Carpal bone fractures (excluding scaphoid fractures). In Watson W, Weinzweig J (eds): The Wrist. Philadelphia, Lippincott Williams & Wilkins, 2001, pp 173–186.
Haisman JM, Rohde RS, Weiland AJ: Acute fractures of the scaphoid. J Bone Joint Surg Am 88:2750–2758, 2006.
Herbert TJ: The Fractured Scaphoid. St Louis, Quality Medical Publishing, 1990.
Hoppenfeld S, deBoer P: Surgical Exposures in Orthopaedics: The Anatomic Approach, 2nd ed. Philadelphia, JB Lippincott, 1994.
Jupiter J: Scaphoid fractures. In Manske PR (ed): 1994 Hand Surgery Update. Englewood, IL, American Society for Surgery of the Hand, 1994, pp 81–85.
Kalainov DM, Osterman AL: Diagnosis and management of scaphoid fractures. In Watson W, Weinzweig J (eds): The Wrist. Philadelphia, Lippincott Williams & Wilkins, 2001, pp 187–202.
Papp S: Carpal bone fractures. Orthop Clin North Am 38:251–260, 2007.
Ruby L: Fractures and dislocations of the carpus. In Browner BD, Jupiter JB, Levine AM Trafton PG (eds): Skeletal Trauma. Philadelphia, WB Saunders, 1992, pp 1025–1027.
Szabo RM, Manske D: Displaced fractures of the scaphoid. Clin Orthop Relat Res 230:30–38, 1988.
Taleisnik J: The Wrist. New York, Churchill Livingstone, 1985.
Vigler M, Aviles A, Lee SK: Carpal fractures excluding the scaphoid. Hand Clin 22:501–516, 2006.
Waitayawinyu T, Pfaeffle HJ, McCallister WV, Nemechek NM, Trumble TE: Management of scaphoid nonunions. Orthop Clin North Am 38:237–249, 2007.
Watson HK, Ryu J: Evolution of wrist arthritis. Clin Orthop Relat Res 202:61, 1986.
Whipple TL: Arthroscopic Surgery: The Wrist. Philadelphia, JB Lippincott, 1992.

1. What is Kienböck's disease?

Avascular necrosis (AVN) of the lunate. To varying degrees, collapse of the lunate is associated with avascular changes. This pathologic process may progress to carpal collapse and ultimately result is pancarpal arthritis.

2. What age-group and sex are most commonly affected?

The most common age-group affected is 20 to 40 years old. The male-to-female ratio is 2:1.

3. What is the cause?

Theories related to the etiology of Kienböck's disease are numerous and varied. In 1843, before the advent of radiographs, Peste described lunate collapse in anatomic specimens. He attributed this finding to an acute, traumatic event. In 1910, Robert Kienböck noted collapse and sclerosis of the lunate on radiographs and attributed them to progressive vascular compromise resulting from repetitive wrist sprains and contusions. Based on the radiographic association of identifiable fracture lines and lunate collapse, some authors believe that the characteristic lesions result from failure of lunate fractures to unite. Intrinsic factors such as ulnar variance, lunate vascularity, and intraosseous pressure gradients also have been implicated as etiologic agents of Kienböck's disease.

4. What is ulnar variance?

Ulnar variance is the relationship between the distal articular surfaces of the radius and the distal ulna. Zero variance refers to level articular surfaces. Ulnar-minus variance is a relatively short ulna with respect to the radius or an ulna with a more proximal articular surface. Ulnar-plus variance refers to a long ulna relative to the distal radius.

5. What is the significance of ulnar variance to Kienböck's disease?

Data indicate a higher incidence of ulnar-minus variance in patients with Kienböck's disease compared with the general population. Laboratory studies confirm that shortening the ulna results in increased shear stress across the lunate. These forces are translated across the lunate, particularly in dorsiflexion and ulnar deviation. However, not all authors agree that ulnar variance is a clinical factor. For example, certain Asian populations show less correlation between variance and Kienböck's disease.

6. Does lunate vascular anatomy influence AVN?

The extraosseous blood supply to the majority of lunates consists of contributions from the radial, ulnar, anterior intraosseous, and deep palmar arch arteries. These arteries coalesce to form a rich vascular plexus on the dorsal and palmar lunate surfaces. Furthermore, most lunates have a complex intraosseous network of anastomoses between the dorsal and palmar vessels. However, some lunates have only a single palmar vessel with minimal internal branching, especially to the proximal surface. These are the lunates that may develop AVN after traumatic arterial disruption. Data demonstrate that, in Kienböck's disease, intraosseous pressure in the lunate is higher than measurements obtained from the radial styloid, capitate, and normal lunates. This finding may imply that venous congestion rather than primary arterial insufficiency is the precipitating event.

7. What are the symptoms of Kienböck's disease?

The sine qua non of Kienböck's disease is wrist pain. Although the patient may relate a precipitating traumatic event, the symptoms usually are insidious in onset. In early stages, pain is localized to the area of the lunate and is associated with symptoms of inflammation such as swelling and pain with motion. As the disease progresses, patients report stiffness, clicking or grinding, and a concomitant crescendo in pain. Late-stage symptoms are consistent clinically with carpal degenerative arthritis.

8. What are the physical findings?

Varying degrees of swelling may be found along the dorsum of the wrist, particularly in comparison with the contralateral side. Palpation demonstrates tenderness dorsally about the lunate. Depending on the severity of the disease, grip strength may be decreased and range of motion may be painful. Later in the disease, the range of motion decreases, and grinding and crepitus with motion may be present.

9. **What are the radiographic findings?**

Although the radiographs initially may be normal, later they typically demonstrate increased density of the lunate accompanied by fracture lines, fragmentation, and progressive collapse. Advanced collapse is associated with proximal migration of the capitate, increased intercarpal widening of the proximal row, and permanent flexion of the scaphoid. The latter exhibits the characteristic ring sign on anteroposterior view.

10. **What features are found on magnetic resonance imaging?**

AVN typically involves the lunate in a diffuse pattern. The hallmark finding of AVN is a uniformly decreased signal intensity on both T1- and T2-weighted images.

11. **What role does magnetic resonance imaging serve in managing Kienböck's disease?**

The sensitivity and specificity of magnetic resonance imaging (MRI) for carpal AVN are well suited for the diagnosis of Kienböck's disease. MRI is particularly useful is early stages when clinical findings are suggestive but radiographs are negative. Diagnosis in the early stage provides the basis for instituting the appropriate treatment. Early increased signals on T2 images imply revascularization and a good prognosis.

12. **What is the differential diagnosis?**

The differential diagnosis most typically includes rheumatoid arthritis, posttraumatic arthritis, synovial-based inflammatory diseases, fractures, carpal instability, and ulnar abutment syndromes.

13. **Can children develop Kienböck's disease?**

There are a number of case reports of Kienböck's disease in the pediatric age-group. To date the youngest child diagnosed with Kienböck's disease is 8 years old.

14. **What are the clinical differences between Kienböck's disease in adults and in children?**

Symptoms, physical findings, and radiographic studies are essentially the same in adults and children.

15. **Is treatment the same for Kienböck's disease in adults and in children?**

Data suggest that children younger than 12 years respond to conservative treatment alone. Children older than 12 years respond favorably to surgery, similar to adults.

16. **What are the stages of Kienböck's disease?**

The Lichtman classification is used to evaluate Kienböck's disease and to decide the most appropriate treatment:

Stage I: Radiographs are normal. Technetium bone scans are characteristically "hot," and MRI demonstrates diffuse decreased signals on T1- and T2-weighted images. Physical findings are indistinguishable from a wrist sprain (Fig. 150-1).

Stage II: Density changes isolated to the lunate as indicated by sclerosis. The lunate may demonstrate fracture lines or minimal collapse on its radial border. However, its overall size, shape, and relationship to the carpal bones are not significantly altered. Clinically stage II is represented by recurrent pain, swelling, and wrist tenderness (Fig. 150-2).

Stage III: Collapse of the lunate. Anteroposterior views show a shortened lunate and elongation in the sagittal plane, accompanied by proximal migration of the capitate. *Stage IIIA* is characterized by no fixed carpal derangements or instability. *Stage IIIB* involves fixed rotation of the scaphoid, decreased carpal height, and ulnar migration of the triquetrum. Clinically stage III is characterized by progressive weakness, stiffness, and pain. Clicking and clunking are also noted (Figs. 150-3 and 150-4). Stage III B is now defined by a radioscaphoid angle greater than 60°.

Stage IV: In addition to the radiographic findings of stage IIIB, stage IV is associated with generalized degenerative changes in the carpus. Clinically this stage is indistinguishable from degenerative arthritis of the wrist (Fig. 150-5).

17. **How are the various stages of Kienböck's disease treated?**

See Fig. 150-6.

18. **Does immobilization have a role in the treatment of Kienböck's disease?**

In stage I, immobilization in a well-fitted short cast for up to 3 months is recommended. Although immobilization may not eliminate all axial loads encountered during routine activities of daily living, it may provide an opportunity for the lunate to heal (revascularize). A trial of 3 months immobilization should be done in children, especially if the T2-weighted MRI shows increased uptake.

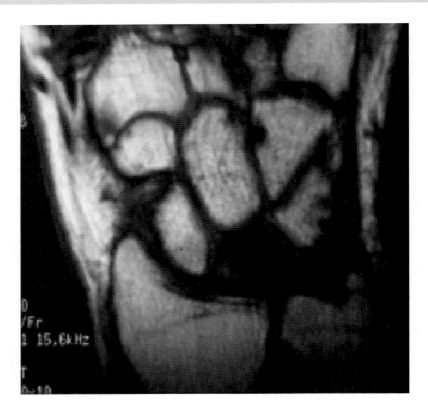

Figure 150-1. Stage I. T1-weighted magnetic resonance image shows marked signal reduction in the lunate, compatible with loss of blood supply.

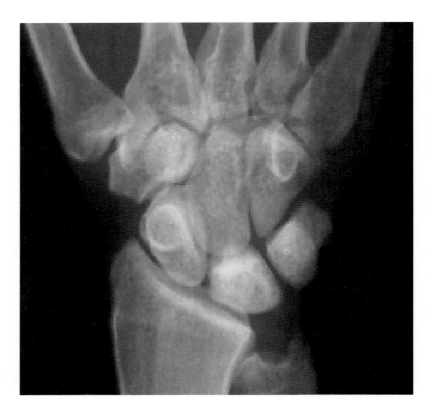

Figure 150-2. Stage II. Density changes in the lunate as indicated by sclerosis. Note ulnar-minus variance.

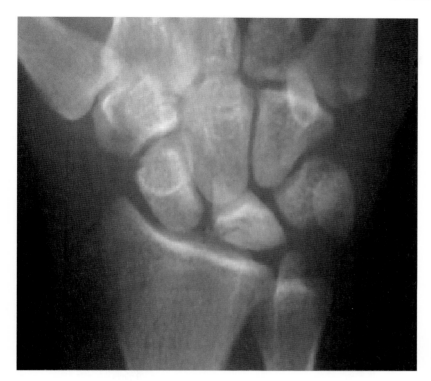

Figure 150-3. Stage IIIA. Collapse of the lunate. There are no fixed carpal derangements.

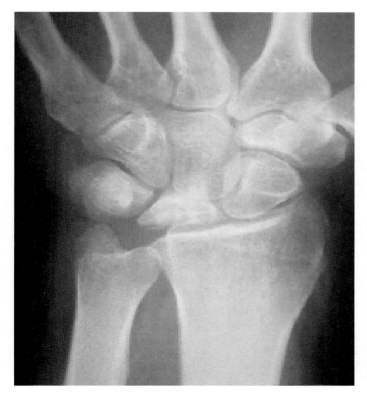

Figure 150-4. Stage IIIB. Decreased carpal height and proximal migration of the capitate. The lateral radiograph demonstrates a radioscaphoid angle greater than 60°.

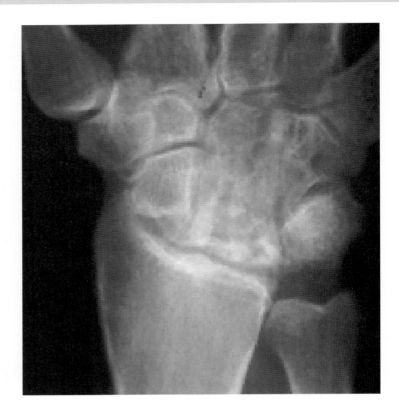

Figure 150-5. Stage IV. Generalized degenerative changes in the carpus.

19. How about simply excising the lunate?

Excising the lunate alone does not prevent proximal migration of the capitate and carpal instability secondary to disruption of perilunate ligaments.

20. What about lunate excision arthroplasty?

Historically both autogenous and synthetic "spacers" have been used for lunate excision arthroplasty. Spacers are rarely used today because placement of an anchovy tendon graft, such as a coiled palmaris longus tendon, precludes direct or indirect lunate revascularization procedures used for early stages of Kienböck's disease. Furthermore, in advanced stages, spacers alone may not provide enough support to inhibit carpal collapse. Artificial spacers such as silicon implants are no longer recommended because of the incidence of complications such as particulate synovitis and cyst formation in adjacent bones.

21. Does altering ulnar variance affect revascularization?

Both clinical and biomechanical studies support the benefit of joint-leveling procedures, either radial shortening or ulnar lengthening. Such operations significantly decompress the lunate by redistributing the axial load from the lunate to the radioscaphoid and ulnocarpal joints. The lunate then presumably will revascularize spontaneously (indirect revascularization). We recommend radial shortening for stage II or IIIA disease before significant lunate collapse occurs. This procedure is indicated only for the typical ulnar-minus case.

22. Can a lunate be revascularized by direct vessel reimplantation?

In the early stages of Kienböck's disease, various direct revascularization techniques have been successful in reversing the process of lunate collapse. Operations such as vascular bundle transfer of the second dorsal intermetacarpal artery and vein, pronator quadratus pedicled bone grafts, and pedunculated pisiform transfers have demonstrated restoration of the lunate viability. However, the success of direct revascularization is predicated on performing the procedures before significant collapse occurs. We use these procedures for stage II to IIIA disease in ulnar-plus cases (in which additional radius shortening is contraindicated).

23. When should intercarpal arthrodesis be considered?

Intercarpal arthrodesis for stage IIIB Kienböck's disease (carpal instability) provides a number of advantages. Although arthrodesis biomechanically unloads the lunate and encourages indirect revascularization, the premise of these procedures in stage IIIB is to address the carpal instability, that is, proximal migration of the capitate and scaphoid flexion. Furthermore, limited fusions are durable and maintain functional wrist mobility. A necrotic or fragmented lunate should be excised.

Treatment Algorithm for Kienböck's Disease

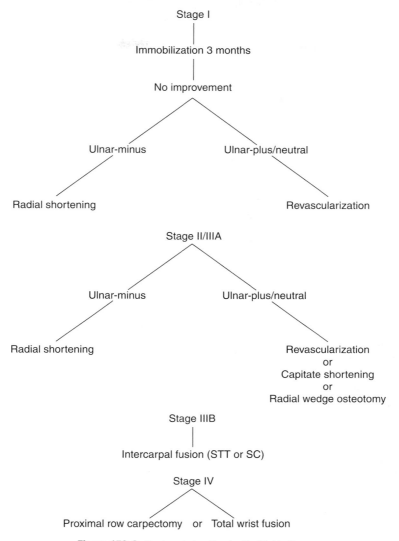

Figure 150-6. Treatment algorithm for Kienböck's disease.

24. Which intercarpal arthrodesis is most appropriate?

A triscaphe (scaphotrapeziotrapezoid [STT]) or scaphocapitate (SC) fusion is recommended in stage IIIB. Both procedures place the scaphoid in its anatomic position in reference to the scaphoid fossa and provide stability to the midcarpal joint. Other intercarpal fusions (e.g., triquetrohamate fusion) have been investigated but do not unload the lunate biomechanically.

25. What salvage procedures are preformed for advance disease?

In the presence of pancarpal arthrosis (stage IV Kienböck's disease), either a proximal row carpectomy (PRC) or total wrist fusion is recommended. Factors such as the patient's physical demands, occupation, preexisting conditions, and the articular integrity of the proximal capitate and lunate fossa of the radius are considered in choosing between the two procedures.

CONTROVERSIES

26. Are radial wedge osteotomies (closing or opening) effective procedures for Kienböck's disease?

Laboratory studies yield conflicting data about the effect of radial wedge osteotomy procedures. Increasing radial angle inclination by an opening wedge osteotomy and decreasing angle inclination by closing wedge osteotomy result in lunate decompression biomechanically. Although it is difficult to understand how both of these procedures can achieve the same biomechanical results, clinical studies to date report good results with closing radial wedge osteotomies.

27. How about vascularized radial bone grafts?

There are several reports of success with reverse-flow vascularized metaphyseal bone grafts for scaphoid nonunions. Described by Zaidemberg, the technique uses a dorsal radius graft based on an ascending branch of the radial artery, the 1,2-intercompartmental supraretinacular artery. Preliminary data about similar techniques for stage IIIA Kienböck's disease as an adjunct to prevent lunate collapse, relieve wrist pain, and improve grip strength appear promising. More data and long-term follow-up are needed before the technique is accepted in the armamentarium for treatment of lunate AVN.

28. What procedure is best suited for patients with ulnar-positive variance?

For obvious reasons, radial shortening or ulnar lengthening is contraindicated. We currently recommend direct lunate revascularization for early stages (I to IIIA). Alternatively, a radial wedge osteotomy or capitate shortening may be considered. STT or capitohamate fusion is best reserved for stage IIIB, regardless of variance.

BIBLIOGRAPHY

Alexander CE, Alexander AH, Lichtman DM: Kienböck's disease. In Lichtman DM, Alexander AH (eds): The Wrist and Its Disorders. Philadelphia, WB Saunders, 1997.

Ferlic RJ, Lee DH, Lopez-Ben RR: Pediatric Kienböck's disease: Case report and review of the literature. Clin Orthop Relat Res 408: 237–244, 2003.

Gelberman RH, Bauman TD, Menon J, et al: The vascularity of the lunate bone and Kienböck's disease. J Hand Surg 5:272–278, 1980.

Jensen CH: Intraosseous pressures in Kienböck's disease. J Hand Surg 18A:355–359, 1993.

Miura H, Uchida Y, Sagioka Y: Radial closing wedge for Kienböck's disease. J Hand Surg 21A:1029–1034, 1996.

Naksmura R, Horii E, Imaeda T, et al: Current concepts of radial osteotomy for Kienbock's disease. In Vastumaki M (ed): Current Trends in Hand Surgery. Amsterdam, Elsevier Science, 1995, pp 109–112.

Zaidemberg C, Siebert JW, Agrigiani C: A new vascularized bone graft for scaphoid nonunion. J Hand Surg 16A:474–478,1991.

CARPAL DISLOCATIONS AND INSTABILITY

CHAPTER 151

Ryan P. Calfee, MD; Amar Patel, MD; and
Edward Akelman, MD

1. How do carpal dislocations typically occur?

Most carpal dislocations result from extreme hyperextension injuries with intercarpal supination. This mechanism of injury usually is violent trauma, such as a fall from a height or a motor vehicle accident.

2. How do patients with carpal dislocations typically present?

Patients usually describe a high-energy mechanism. However, initial physical examination findings may not be particularly dramatic. Patients usually have diffuse mild to moderate swelling when seen early, but swelling is likely to increase significantly with time. Tenderness is diffuse, and range of motion is decreased significantly because of pain. Be aware of possible median nerve injury from direct contusion at the moment of impact, compression of the nerve by the lunate, and swelling within the carpal tunnel.

3. What is the difference between a perilunate dislocation and a lunate dislocation?

In a perilunate dislocation the lunate remains aligned with the radius while the rest of the carpus is displaced, usually dorsally. In a lunate dislocation the capitate remains aligned with the radius while the lunate is volarly extruded from the carpus (Table 151-1 and Fig. 151-1).

4. What is the "spilled teacup" sign? What does it signify?

Seen on a lateral wrist radiograph, the spilled teacup refers to the lunate and signifies a lunate dislocation. Normally the lunate, which is shaped like a kidney bean on lateral radiograph, lies with its convex surface against the distal radial articular surface and its concave surface holding the head of the capitate. In a lunate dislocation, the lunate has flipped volarly on its volar radiolunate ligament hinge so that the concavity (opening of the cup) faces into the carpal tunnel.

5. Where is the space of Poirier, and why is it clinically important?

The space of Poirier is located volarly over the capitolunate joint, which is left uncovered by the surrounding thick palmar carpal ligaments. This is critical in allowing for lunate dislocations to occur through capsule in this area.

6. How can a dorsal perilunate dislocation be reduced?

The technique described by Tavernier is useful. Complete muscle relaxation is essential for an atraumatic reduction. This technique entails an initial period of 5 to 10 minutes of continuous longitudinal traction in finger traps with 10 to 15 lb of weight to allow relaxation of muscle forces. Next, manual traction is maintained by the surgeon. The thumb of one hand applies gentle pressure to the volar aspect of the wrist to stabilize the lunate. With the other hand, the patient's wrist is extended while longitudinal traction is maintained. Gradually, the wrist is flexed, allowing the capitate to snap back into the concavity of the lunate.

Table 151-1. Stages of Progressive Perilunar Instability

STAGE	LIGAMENTS AFFECTED
I	Scapholunate instability with tearing of scapholunate interosseous and volar radioscaphoid ligaments
II	Midcarpal capsule disruption allows dorsal capitate dislocation
III	Lunotriquetral dissociation resulting in perilunate dislocation
IV	Lunate dislocation with disruption of the dorsal radiocarpal ligament

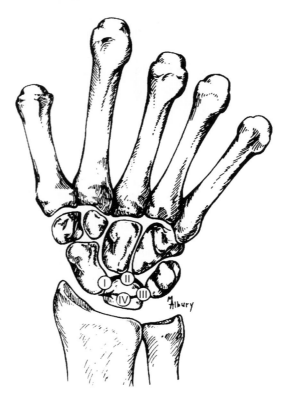

Figure 151-1. Progressive perilunar instability (PLI). According to Mayfield's sequence of ligamentous injury patterns, the four stages of PLI result in carpal instability and, eventually, carpal dislocation. (From Green DP: Carpal dislocations and instabilities. In Green DP [ed]: Operative Hand Surgery, Vol 1, 3rd ed. New York, Churchill Livingston, 1993, p 869.)

7. What is the best method for treatment of an acute perilunate/lunate dislocation or fracture/dislocation?

In general, nonoperative management with closed reduction and casting rarely is satisfactory. Some authors favor closed reduction followed by percutaneous pinning of the scaphoid to the capitate and lunate, but only if anatomic reduction of each bone can be achieved. A critical determinant of successful reduction is the position of the scaphoid. A scapholunate angle greater than 80° with a scapholunate gap greater than 3 mm indicates significant residual scaphoid rotatory subluxation and often a poor long-term outcome. Most authors now advocate open reduction, ligament repair, and internal fixation of these high-energy injuries. Many authors favor the combine dorsal and volar approach of Dobyns and Swanson to allow assessment and repair of ligamentous and bony structures on both sides of the wrist.

8. Define lesser and greater arc injuries of the carpus.

Lesser arc injuries are propagated around the lunate through purely soft tissue structures (scapholunate ligament, capitolunate ligament, lunotriquetral ligament). Greater arc injuries violate the bony structures around the lunate. These arcs are important in describing perilunate dislocations that may be purely ligamentous or may also involve fractures. For example, a perilunate dislocation with an associated scaphoid and capitate fracture is described as a transscaphoid, transcapitate perilunate fracture/dislocation.

9. Why are chauffeur's or radial styloid fractures especially concerning?

A fracture through the radial styloid may be a harbinger of a more serious ligamentous injury to the carpus. The energy that produced the radial styloid fracture may propagate through the lesser arc, producing a scapholunate disruption or more significant progressive perilunate instability.

10. Define the abbreviations CID, CIND, and CIC and describe their corresponding conditions.

- *CID (carpal instability dissociative)* is instability between bones within the same row (i.e., scapholunate dissociation).
- *CIND (carpal instability nondissociative)* is an injury occurring through either the radiocarpal or the midcarpal joint, thereby leaving each row intact.
- *CIC (carpal instability complex)* is an injury with elements of CID and CIND.

11. What are Gilula arcs, and what do their disruptions indicate?

Dr. Gilula is a radiologist who described three carpal arcs based on normal posteroanterior radiographs of the wrist.
- *Arc 1* follows the carpal side of the radiocarpal joint consisting of the proximal scaphoid, lunate, and triquetrum.
- *Arc 2* outlines the midcarpal joint following the distal border of the same bones.
- *Arc 3* follows along the proximal borders of the capitate and hamate.

Any break in an arc indicates ligamentous disruption at the joint.

12. Explain the midcarpal shift test for midcarpal instability.

Originally described by Lichtman, this test involves holding the patient's wrist pronated with the surgeon using his/her right hand to examine a right hand with a thumb over the dorsal capitate pressing palmarly. The wrist is then ulnarly deviated under this pressure looking for a painful clunk. Normally, moving into ulnar deviation involves the proximal carpal row extending, which allows the distal row to move from a palmar to dorsal position. However, in the face of midcarpal dissociation, the proximal row remains flexed until eventually it is forced into sudden extension as noted by the "clunk."

13. What is the role of arthroscopy in evaluating carpal instability?

Multiple sources now support arthroscopy as the gold standard in assessing carpal instability. Arthroscopy is more accurate than magnetic resonance imaging or arthrography (40% and 60% as sensitive, respectively) and its findings correlate well with those obtained during arthrotomy. Investigation also indicates that although radiocarpal evaluation is universally performed, midcarpal arthroscopy is a necessity that adds significantly to the operative assessment of the injured wrist.

14. What is a DISI deformity? A VISI deformity?

- *DISI (dorsiflexion intercalated segmental instability)* often occurs when scapholunate ligament disruption results in volar flexion of the scaphoid and dorsal angulation of the lunate.
- *VISI (volarflexion intercalated segmental instability)* often signifies a lunotriquetral ligament disruption with volar angulation of the lunate compared with a normally aligned scaphoid.

15. Which conditions can lead to dorsal intercalated instability? To volar intercalated instability?

- DISI deformity is a structural abnormality that can be caused by a variety of conditions. It is most often attributed to scapholunate dissociation, but reduced perilunate dislocations, acute displaced scaphoid fractures, scaphoid malunions, and fractures of the distal radius also may lead to a DISI pattern.
- VISI deformity often results from lunotriquetral dissociation, but it may occur with distal radius malunions, rheumatoid arthritis, and systemic ligamentous laxity (Fig. 151-2).

16. What is the Watson test?

The Watson test, or the "*scaphoid shift maneuver*" as Dr. Watson prefers, is a provocative maneuver used to evaluate scaphoid stability and periscaphoid synovitis. The thumb of one hand is placed on the scaphoid tuberosity (distal pole on volar surface) while the four fingers of the same hand are placed behind the radius. With the patient's wrist initially in ulnar deviation and slight extension, the examiner's opposite hand is used to deviate radially and to flex slightly the patient's wrist. Pressure on the tuberosity prevents the scaphoid from palmarflexing with scaphoid instability or rotary subluxation. The scaphoid thus is "pushed" dorsally out of the radial fossa, producing pain and/or a palpable clunk. A comparison test on the opposite wrist should always be performed.

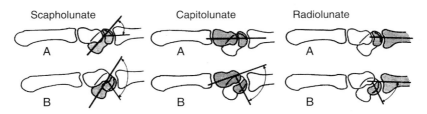

Figure 151-2. Carpal bone angles. In each case the normal angle is shown *(A)* in comparison with the abnormal angle seen with a dorsiflexion intercalated segmental instability deformity *(B)*. The average scapholunate angle is 47°; an angle greater than 80° is indicative of scapholunate dissociation or rotary subluxation of the scaphoid. The capitolunate angle should be 0° with the wrist in neutral; the normal range is 0° to 15°. The radiolunate angle is abnormal if it is greater than 15°. (From Green DP: Carpal dislocations and instabilities. In Green DP [ed]: Operative Hand Surgery, Vol 1, 3rd ed. New York, Churchill Livingstone, 1993, p 874.)

17. What is the signet ring sign?

On an anteroposterior (AP) x-ray film with scapholunate dissociation the distal pole of the scaphoid is seen as a sclerotic ring. This is due to volar flexion of the scaphoid and represents an axial view of the distal scaphoid.

18. Who was Terry Thomas? What is the significance of his name?

Terry Thomas was a famous English film comedian with a wide gap in his front teeth. The "Terry Thomas" sign, seen on an AP image of the wrist, indicates a widened scapholunate gap and signifies a scapholunate dissociation. A scapholunate gap greater than 3 mm is considered diagnostic of a scapholunate dissociation.

19. What is a normal scapholunate angle? When is a scapholunate angle considered pathologic?

On a lateral view, with the wrist in neutral, a line is drawn through the long axis of the lunate. A second line is drawn through the long axis of the scaphoid. The angle formed by the intersection of the two lines is the scapholunate angle. Normal values range from 30° to 60° with an average of 47°, as described by Linscheid. An angle greater than 80° should be considered a definite indication of scapholunate dissociation or rotary subluxation of the scaphoid.

20. Which radiographs help to make the diagnosis of scapholunate dissociation?

A typical scaphoid series includes the following:

- True lateral view with the wrist in neutral. Useful for evaluation of overall alignment and measurement of carpal angles.
- Posteroanterior (palm down) view in maximal ulnar deviation–profile view of the scaphoid. Helpful for seeing scaphoid fractures.
- AP view with clenched fist. Accentuates a dynamic scapholunate dissociation.

21. Differentiate between static and dynamic scapholunate dissociation.

Static scapholunate dissociation is associated with a fixed deformity between the scaphoid and lunate as seen on AP and lateral views. In dynamic dissociation, an abnormal scapholunate relationship is identified only on stress radiographs, such as a clenched fist AP view.

22. What are the radiographic signs of scapholunate dissociation?

- Foreshortened scaphoid/signet ring sign on AP x-ray
- Scapholunate angle greater than 60°
- Scapholunate gap greater than 3 mm
- Loss of parallelism between scaphoid and lunate articular surfaces
- Increased capitolunate angle (normally 0°, range 0° to 15°).

23. How are dorsal wrist ganglia associated with carpal instability?

The dorsal wrist ganglion, which often arises from the scapholunate ligament, has been associated with dynamic scapholunate instability. In a study by Whitman et al., dynamic scapholunate instability with an associated ganglion was treated by excision of the ganglion to the level of the ligament with 2 weeks of postoperative immobilization. After 1 year, the majority of patients continued to have a stable nontender wrist.

24. What is a SLAC wrist, and what are its characteristics?

SLAC wrist, a term coined by Watson, refers to *scapholunate advanced collapse* wrist or the pattern of arthritic degeneration following chronic scapholunate dissociation. It progresses in a sequential pattern of three stages: (1) radiostyloid–scaphoid arthritis, (2) radioscaphoid fossa degeneration, and (3) capitolunate involvement. Of note, the radiolunate joint is generally spared in this progression of arthritis.

25. What are treatment options for chronic scapholunate instability?

For scapholunate dissociation more than 3 months old, many procedures have been proposed. Options include limited tenodesis, arthrodesis, capsulodesis, direct ligament repair (with/without capsulodesis), and ligament reconstruction. Although no single procedure has prevailed, research suggests that capsulodesis may provide decreased pain but does not provide lasting preservation of carpal alignment.

26. Describe the typical history and examination of a patient with a lunotriquetral ligament tear.

The history is variable, but many patients recall a specific dorsiflexion injury even. Patients may describe a painful palpable or audible click or clunk on the ulnar aspect of the wrist, particularly with ulnar deviation. Complaints also may include weakness and decreased range of motion. Physical findings may demonstrate synovitis or arthritis with periarticular inflammation and swelling. Palpation over the lunotriquetral joint may produce local tenderness. Provocative testing that loads the ulnar carpus may demonstrate increased or pathologic motion compared with the other side. Radiographic examination ranges from completely normal to VISI deformity depending on the extent of associated injury to adjacent intercarpal ligaments.

27. Describe a shear or ballottement test of the lunotriquetral joint.

The shear test attempts to demonstrate increased lunotriquetral motion. The examiner places one thumb on the dorsum of the lunate to push volarly and the other thumb on the volar palm at the pisiform, pushing dorsally. Pain, with or without crepitance, is a positive test. Comparison should be made with the unaffected side.

28. How can lunotriquetral instabilities be graded?

Viegas has described three stages of increasing severity:

- *Stage I*: Partial or complete disruption of the lunotriquetral interosseous ligament (LTIL) with no clinical or radiographic evidence of dynamic or static VISI.
- *Stage II*: Complete disruption of the LTIL and palmar lunotriquetral ligaments with clinical and/or radiographic evidence of dynamic VISI.
- *Stage III*: Complete disruption of the LTIL and palmar lunotriquetral ligaments, including disruption of the scaphoid and lunate portion of the dorsal radiocarpal ligament, with clinical or radiographic evidence of static VISI.

29. Briefly list the key intercarpal ligaments.

- *Intrinsic*: The two most important intrinsic ligaments are the *dorsal scapholunate ligament* and the *palmar lunotriquetral ligament*, which are the strongest areas of those ligaments.
- *Palmar Extrinsic*: The key volar ligaments are the *radioscaphocapitate*, the *long radiolunate*, and the *short radiolunate*. The space of Poirier is located between the radioscaphocapitate ligament and the long and short radiolunate ligaments.
- *Dorsal Extrinsic*: The two main dorsal ligaments are the *dorsal intercarpal ligament* and the *dorsal radiocarpal ligament*.

BIBLIOGRAPHY

Feinstein WK, Lichtman DM, Noble PC, Alexander JW, Hipp JA: Quantitative assessment of the midcarpal shift. J Hand Surg 24:977–983, 1999.

Hofmeister EP, Dao KD, Glowacki KA, Shin AY: The role of midcarpal arthroscopy in the diagnosis of disorders of the wrist. J Hand Surg 26:407–414, 2001.

Idler RS: Carpal dislocations and instability. In Watson HK, Weinzweig J (eds): The Wrist. Philadelphia, Lippincott Williams & Wilkins, 2001, pp 203–230.

Johnson RP: The acutely injured wrist and its residuals. Clin Orthop 149:33–44, 1980.

Kozin SH: Perilunate Injuries: Diagnosis and treatment. J Am Acad Orthop Surg 6:114–120, 1998.

Linsheid RL, Dobyns JH, Beabout JW, Byran RS: Traumatic instability of the wrist: Diagnosis, classification, and pathomechanics. J Bone Joint Surg 54:1612–1632, 1972.

Mayfield JK, Johnson RP, Kilcoyne RK: Carpal dislocations: Pathomechanics and progressive perilunar instability. J Hand Surg 5:226–241, 1980.

Moran SL, Cooney WP, Berger RA, Strickland J: Capsulodesis for the treatment of chronic scapholunate instability. J Hand Surg 30:16–23, 2005.

Peh WCG, Gilula LA: Normal disruption of carpal arcs. J Hand Surg 21:561–566, 1996.

Ruby LK, Cassidy C: Fractures and dislocations of the carpus. In Browner BD, Jupiter JB, Levine AM, Trafton PG (eds): Skeletal Trauma, 3rd ed. Philadelphia, WB Saunders, 2003, pp 1267–1314.

Saffar PH, Pigeau Isabelle: Radiographic imaging of the hand, wrist, and forearm. In Berger RA, Weiss APC (eds): Hand Surgery. Philadelphia, Lippincott Williams & Wilkins, 2004, pp 81–104.

Viegas S, Patterson R, Peterson P, et al: Ulnar-sided perilunate instability: An anatomic and biomechanic study. J Hand Surg 15A:268–278, 1990.

Walsh JJ, Berger RA, Cooney WP: Current status of scapholunate interosseous ligament injuries. J Am Acad Orthop Surg 10:32–42, 2002.

Wheeless' Textbook of Orthopaedics. Available at: www.wheelessonline.com

Whitman B, Gelberman R, et al: Dynamic scapholunate instability: Results of operative treatment with dorsal capsulodesis. J Hand Surg Am 20:971–979, 1995.

ULNAR WRIST PAIN

Craig M. Rodner, MD, and
Arnold-Peter C. Weiss, MD

1. What five carpal bones make up the ulnar side of the wrist?
The ulnar carpus encompasses the lunate, triquetrum, pisiform, hamate, and capitate.

2. Name 10 possible entities to be considered in a broad differential diagnosis of ulnar-sided wrist pain?
1. Triangular fibrocartilage complex (TFCC) injury
2. Lunotriquetral interosseous ligament injury
3. Chondral lesion of the ulnar aspect of the lunate
4. Triquetral avulsion fracture
5. Hook of the hamate fracture
6. Pisotriquetral arthritis
7. Subluxation of the extensor carpi ulnaris tendon
8. Ulnar artery thrombosis
9. Ulnar neuropathy at Guyon's canal
10. Neuritis of the dorsal sensory branch of the ulnar nerve.

3. What structure on the ulnar side of the wrist is frequently injured yet not seen on radiographs?
The TFCC, which is made up of the ulnar carpal ligaments, ulnar wrist capsule, and triangular fibrocartilage meniscus (Fig. 152-1).

4. Tears of the TFCC are most frequently caused by what mechanism?
Tears of the TFCC are caused most commonly by a fall on an outstretched hand that results in a combination of extension, pronation, and axial loading to the wrist.

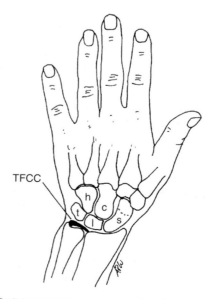

Figure 152-1. Main structures of the wrist. *c,* Capitate; *h,* hamate; *l,* lunate; *s,* scaphoid; *t,* triquetrum; *TFCC,* triangular fibrocartilage complex.

5. **What intercarpal ligament is frequently injured along with the TFCC?**
The lunotriquetral ligament is commonly injured along with the TFCC. These two structures are soft tissue elements of the ulnar wrist the most likely to cause pain.

6. **Ulnar wrist pain in the hypothenar eminence in golfers is commonly caused by what type of fracture?**
A fracture of the hook of the hamate. These fractures are frequently not seen on anteroposterior and lateral radiographs of the hand or a carpal tunnel view. They are commonly missed but can be documented by computed tomography of the wrist. Treatment involves cast immobilization, excision of the nonunion fragment if healing does not occur, or open reduction internal fixation of the hook.

7. **What does tenderness to palpation over the pisiform bone often indicate?**
Tenderness to palpation over the pisiform bone usually indicates the presence of pisotriquetral degenerative arthritis. A lidocaine injection into this joint may help make the diagnosis. If conservative measures fail to relieve the pain, a surgical excision of the pisiform bone may be necessary.

8. **What structure on the ulnar side of the wrist is prone to age-related changes?**
The TFCC is prone to degenerative tears that are directly proportional to the patient's age.

9. **What is ulnar variance?**
Ulnar variance is the length of the distal ulna compared with the lunate fossa of the distal radius. Patients are described as ulnar-plus, ulnar-neutral, or ulnar-minus. An ulnar-minus variance is associated with the development of Kienböck disease (avascular necrosis of the lunate), which can cause wrist pain. An ulnar-plus variance is associated with ulnar carpal abutment syndrome, in which the ulna is longer than the radius and is pushed into the underside of the TFCC, causing degenerative changes and ulnar-sided wrist pain.

10. **What diagnostic tests help in differentiating causes of ulnar-sided wrist pain?**
Wrist arthrography and magnetic resonance imaging (MRI). Wrist arthrography involves injection of dye into the wrist to visualize the TFCC and intercarpal ligaments. Abnormal leaks of the dye between areas where the structures are supposed to be intact indicate disruption. MRI can also define tears of the TFCC and, to a lesser degree, the intercarpal ligaments.

11. **What technique has the best sensitivity, specificity, and accuracy for defining ulnar-sided wrist pain due to soft tissue injuries?**
Wrist arthroscopy is more sensitive, specific, and accurate than other diagnostic techniques for defining soft tissue disruption of both the intercarpal ligaments and the TFCC.

12. **During arthroscopy, loss of what finding may indicate tearing of the peripheral TFCC?**
During arthroscopy a probe is used to ballot the TFCC cartilage disc. Normally the cartilage disc is taut and demonstrates a trampoline effect. If the cartilage disc does not rebound to forces provided by the probe, a tear of the peripheral TFCC should be suspected.

13. **What is the vascular anatomy of the TFCC?**
The TFCC has a rich vascular supply to the peripheral portion, whereas the central portion and the attachment to the distal radius are relatively avascular. Therefore tears located in the peripheral TFCC have a high propensity to heal if treated by débridement and/or repair, whereas tears of the central component are unlikely to heal with repair alone.

14. **What is the main form of treatment of central TFCC tears?**
Because this portion of the TFCC is relatively avascular, the redundant portions (i.e., any flaps that may be present) of the meniscal disc itself are débrided. Débridement decompresses the tear itself and does not alter the structural anatomy of the ulnar wrist.

15. **In patients who have undergone TFCC débridement but still have ulnar-sided wrist pain, what procedure can be used as an initial salvage procedure for relief of pain?**
In patients who have TFCC pain and ulnar-plus variance, an ulnar shortening osteotomy that takes pressure off the underside of the TFCC may be useful after failed TFCC débridements. This procedure also is effective in some patients who have concomitant lunotriquetral ligament and TFCC tears.

16. **What procedure may be considered as an alternative to an ulnar shortening osteotomy to reduce TFCC loading in patients with minimal ulnar-plus variance?**
In patients who have minimal ulnar-plus variance, a partial resection of the ulnar head (wafer procedure), either open or arthroscopically, may be a reasonable alternative to a diaphyseal shortening of the ulna.

17. **What vascular anatomy can be associated with patients who use their hypothenar eminence as a hammer and have ulnar-sided wrist pain?**
"Hypothenar hammer syndrome" is described in patients who use their hypothenar eminence as a hammer (e.g., jackhammer operators) and develop a clot in the ulnar artery. Thrombosis causes localized pain, and occasionally a mass is felt in the hypothenar region. The diagnosis can be made by performing an Allen's test, in which loss of refill of the ulnar digits may be noted.

18. **What physical tests are used to examine for lunotriquetral ligament tears?**
The lunotriquetral shear test (Kleinman or Reagan) and lunotriquetral compression test (Linscheid) are useful for evaluating the lunotriquetral ligament. During either test, pain or a click centered at the lunotriquetral joint may indicate disruption of this ligament.

19. **What is the most common diagnostic and therapeutic procedure for lunotriquetral ligament tears?**
Wrist arthroscopy (using the 4/5 or 6-R portals) is the best way to identify lunotriquetral ligament tears. Partial tears often can be treated by débridement alone; complete tears also occasionally can be made asymptomatic by débridement of the ligament edges. For patients who have persistent pain, lunotriquetral fusion and four-corner fusion (fusion of the capitate, hamate, lunate, and triquetrum) have been advocated.

20. **Why do some authors advocate a four-corner fusion rather than a lunotriquetral fusion for documented lunotriquetral ligament tearing?**
The fusion rate obtained with a four-corner fusion is substantially higher than that obtained with a lunotriquetral fusion. Approximately 50% of lunotriquetral fusions result in nonunion.

21. **If pain is elicited by the lunotriquetral shear test, what other condition must be ruled out?**
Pisotriquetral arthritis. Because the lunotriquetral shear test is performed by putting the thumb over the pisiform and pushing dorsally to provide shear between the lunate and triquetrum, pisotriquetral arthritis rather than any problem at the lunotriquetral ligament may cause pain by compression of this joint. For this reason, testing for pain isolated to the pisotriquetral joint by "shucking" the pisiform against the triquetrum alone should be done.

22. **What are the two classes of TFCC tears, and how are they usually treated?**
Traumatic and degenerative. In 1989, Palmer developed a classification system for injuries to the TFCC. Acute traumatic injuries were defined as class I injuries, and degenerative injuries were defined as class II injuries. Class I tears usually are linear and occur at the edges of the TFCC at either the soft tissue attachments or the attachment to the distal radius. Peripheral lesions with the capacity to heal are treated with repair. Class II degenerative tears usually represent an ulnar impaction process and often occur in older people in the midportion of the fibrocartilage meniscus. Arthroscopic débridement is the mainstay of treatment of degenerative tears. If débridement alone fails to provide relief in an ulnar-plus patient, procedures that address the mechanical overload on the ulnar side of the wrist (i.e., wafer resection or ulnar shortening osteotomy) should be considered.

BIBLIOGRAPHY

Adams BD: Distal radioulnar joint. In: American Society for Surgery of the Hand: Hand Surgery Update 3. Rosemont, IL, American Academy of Orthopaedic Surgeons, 2003, pp 147–155.

Boulas HJ, Milek MA: Ulnar shortening for tears of the triangular fibrocartilage complex. J Hand Surg 15A:415–420, 1990.

Buterbaugh GA: Triangular fibrocartilage complex injury and ulnar wrist pain. In: American Society for Surgery of the Hand: Hand Surgery Update. Rosemont, IL, American Academy of Orthopaedic Surgeons, 1996, pp 105–115.

Hornbach EE, Osterman AL: Partial excision of the triangular fibrocartilage complex. In Gleberman RH (ed): Master Techniques in Orthopaedic Surgery: The Wrist. Philadelphia, Lippincott Williams & Wilkins, 2002, pp 279–290.

Osterman AL: Arthroscopic debridement of triangular fibrocartilage complex tears. Arthroscopy 6:1220–1224, 1990.

Paley D, McMurty RY, Cruickshank B: Pathologic conditions of the pisiform and pisotriquetral joint. J Hand Surg 12A:110–119, 1987.

Palmer AK: Triangular fibrocartilage complex lesions: A classification. J Hand Surg 14A:594–606, 1989.

Palmer AK, Glisson RR, Werner FW: Ulnar variance determination. J Hand Surg 7A:376–379, 1982.

Palmer AK, Short WH, Toivonen DA. Ulnar impaction syndrome. In Watson W, Weinzweig J (eds): The Wrist. Philadelphia, Lippincott Williams & Wilkins, 2001, pp 615–632.

Palmer AK, Werner FW: The triangular fibrocartilage complex of the wrist anatomy and function. J Hand Surg 6A:153–162, 1981.

Pin PG, Young VL, Gilula LA, Weeks PM: Management of chronic lunotriquetral ligament tears. J Hand Surg 14A:77–83, 1989.

Sagerman SD, Palmer AK, Short WH: Triangular fibrocartilage complex injury and repair. In Watson W, Weinzweig J (eds): The Wrist. Philadelphia, Lippincott Williams & Wilkins, 2001, pp 607–614.

Watson HK, Weinzweig J: Triquetral impingement ligament tear [TILT] syndrome. J Hand Surg 24B:350–358, 1999.

Weiss APC, Akelman E: Diagnostic imaging and arthroscopy for chronic wrist pain. Orthop Clin North Am 26:759–767, 1995.

Weiss APC, Akelman E, Lambiase R: Comparison of the findings of triple-injection cinearthrography of the wrist with those of arthroscopy. J Bone Joint Surg 78A:348–356, 1996.

RHEUMATOID ARTHRITIS OF THE WRIST

Alarick Yung, MD, and
Leonard K. Ruby, MD

1. In patients with rheumatoid arthritis, how often is the wrist affected?

After 3 years, 70% of patients with rheumatoid arthritis (RA) have wrist involvement. After 11 years, 95% have wrist involvement.

2. How does RA affect the wrist?

RA is characterized by a destructive synovitis that affects the synovial lining of both joints and tendon sheaths. This results in joint deformity, wrist dysfunction (weakness, pain, or limited motion), joint synovitis, tenosynovitis, and tendon rupture.

3. List the criteria necessary to make a diagnosis of RA.

Four of the seven criteria listed in Table 153-1 must be met.

4. What are rheumatoid nodules?

Nodules are composed of a fibrous center and collagenous capsule. With time they become surrounded by chronic inflammatory cells. Their centers may necrose due to ischemia, and the nodule may erode through the overlying skin to form a draining sinus. They are located subcutaneously, often over bony prominences. They can be excised but often recur.

5. What is the utility of checking for serum rheumatoid factor?

As many as 70% to 80% of patients with RA will test positive for rheumatoid factor (RF). However, 20% of patients with RA remain seronegative. Of the healthy general population, 1% to 2% tests positive for RF. Additionally, elevated serum RF may be caused by other conditions such as increased age (5% to 20% of people older than 65 years become seropositive), other autoimmune diseases, connective tissue disorders, viral infections, chronic inflammatory diseases, and neoplasms. Specificity for RA increases with increasing levels of RF. Lower levels of RF often reflect milder instances of RA.

6. What is RF?

RF is an immunoglobulin (immunoglobulin M) antibody directed against the Fc portion of immunoglobulin G.

Table 153-1. Diagnosis of Rheumatoid Arthritis

CRITERION	DEFINITION
Morning stiffness	Located periarticularly, lasting 1 hour or more, for at least 6 weeks
Arthritis of three or more joint areas	Simultaneously, at least three joint areas have soft tissue swelling or fluid, for at least 6 weeks
Arthritis of hand joints	Wrist, metacarpophalangeal or proximal phalangeal joints, for at least 6 weeks
Symmetrical arthritis	Same joint areas on both sides of the body, simultaneously, for at least 6 weeks
Rheumatoid nodules	Subcutaneous nodules, over bony prominences or extensor surfaces, or in periarticular regions
Rheumatoid factor	Elevated amounts of serum rheumatoid factor
Radiographic changes	Erosive changes or decalcification adjacent to involved joint, on hand and wrist radiographs

7. What other laboratory values may be elevated in RA?

Because RA is an inflammatory arthropathy, nonspecific indicators of generalized inflammation such as serum erythrocyte sedimentation rate and C-reactive protein may be elevated. Antinuclear antibody levels may be elevated in 40% of people with RA. None of these indicators are specific enough to be diagnostic for RA.

8. Is there any utility to checking wrist joint synovial fluid in RA?

The presence of RF in synovial fluid is of uncertain importance. Still, synovial fluid analysis can be used to look for infection or crystal-induced arthritis (either gout or calcium pyrophosphate disease) as well as to help categorize the arthritic process as inflammatory, noninflammatory, or hemorrhagic.

9. Describe what a biopsy specimen of rheumatoid synovium might show.

Synovial inflammation, proliferation of synovial lining cells, lymphocytic infiltration, angiogenesis, and noncaseating granulomas.

10. What diagnostic imaging of the wrist should be obtained in RA?

Radiographs of three views (posteroanterior, lateral, oblique) should be obtained. The distal radioulnar joint (DRUJ) has the highest level of early involvement compared with all surrounding joints. The most common late finding in RA is ulnar–palmar translation of the carpus. Carpal erosion and autofusion also may be present.

11. What is a scallop sign?

Scallop sign occurs when the sigmoid notch of the DRUJ is hollowed out in a concave scalloped form on the distal radius. This may lead to extensor tendon rupture (Fig. 153-1).

12. Describe the classic pattern of deformity of the radiocarpal joint and DRUJ.

Ulnar–palmar translation and supination of the wrist characterize the radiocarpal joint. Extrinsic wrist ligaments become attenuated and bony integrity erodes away. Because ligaments have no active excursion, even a few millimeters of laxity renders them ineffective. In the destabilized carpus, strong flexor and ulnar-sided muscles assume a deforming force. The radial inclination and palmar tilt of the distal radius articular surface further favor ulnar–palmar translation. In the DRUJ, the ulnar head subluxes dorsally as the sigmoid notch erodes, and ligamentous and muscular stabilizers (e.g., triangular fibrocartilage complex [TFCC] and extensor carpi ulnaris [ECU], respectively) lose their integrity.

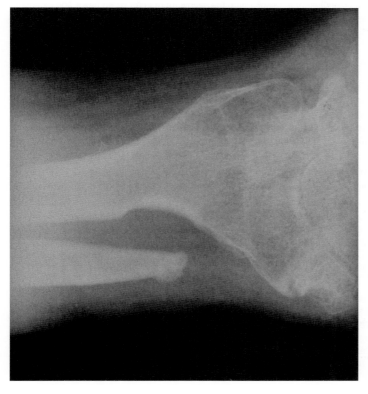

Figure 153-1. Scallop sign affecting the sigmoid notch of the distal radius.

13. What are the other characteristic deformities in the rheumatoid hand?

Metacarpals deviate radially. Metacarpophalangeal (MCP) joints are characterized by ulnar drift and palmar subluxation. MCP flexion contractures also can occur. Fingers may demonstrate swan neck or boutonnière deformities. The thumb may exhibit swan neck or boutonnière (Z-shaped) deformities as well as ulnar collateral ligament instability.

Any attempt to correct rheumatoid wrist pathology must take into account the associated deformities and disabilities of the fingers, thumb, and hand as well. The reverse also is true; correction of finger deformities must consider wrist pathology.

14. What are the three major pathophysiologic factors in RA that result in joint destruction?

- Cartilage destruction caused by lytic cytochemical effects.
- Synovial expansion causing bony erosion.
- Ligamentous laxity secondary to lytic cytochemicals and synovial expansion resulting in joint capsules and ligaments that become stretched out. Because ligaments have no active excursion, even a few millimeters of laxity renders them ineffective.

15. What is the natural course of rheumatoid disease in the wrist?

There are three stages of rheumatoid disease: proliferative, destructive, and reparative.

- In the *proliferative stage,* synovial swelling leads to pain and diminished range of motion of the wrist joint. Nerve compression may occur.
- In the *destructive stage,* synovial erosion causes bony erosion, capsular incompetence, joint subluxation, and tendon rupture.
- The *reparative stage* is characterized by fibrosis of joints and intrinsic musculature as well as tendon adhesions.

16. How does the pattern of wrist destruction in RA differ from that in an osteoarthritic scapholunate advanced collapse wrist?

In RA, the radiolunate joint degenerates first, followed by the radioscaphoid articulation. In a scapholunate advanced collapse (SLAC) wrist, typically the radioscaphoid joint degenerates the most, followed by the midcarpal joint.

17. How does tenosynovitis affect the wrist?

In RA, the synovial lining of tendon sheaths may be affected similarly to the synovium of joints. Both flexor and extensor tendon sheaths may be involved. Symptoms include limited range of motion, swelling (either painful or nonpainful), tendon ruptures, finger triggering, and compressive neuropathies such as carpal tunnel syndrome.

18. What are the treatment options for wrist synovitis?

Nonsurgical management may be useful if started early enough. Such management includes pharmacologic therapy, rest, splinting, and local steroid injection. A multidisciplinary team consisting of rheumatologists, hand therapists, and hand surgeons is most effective. The benefit of steroid injections must be balanced against their potentially weakening effects on already compromised tendon structures. If symptoms persist after 4 to 6 months despite pharmacologic intervention, then surgical synovectomy may be indicated. An exception to this time frame is the occurrence of tendon rupture, in which case immediate attention should be paid to preventing further ruptures.

19. What are the benefits of arthroscopic synovectomy?

Less morbidity and better exposure/visibility compared with open techniques. This has proved to be an excellent procedure in the right patient.

20. What pharmacologic options exist for treatment of RA?

Significant gains have been made in pharmacologic therapy in the last decade. A rheumatologist can manage use of *disease-modifying antirheumatic drugs* (DMARDs), which include methotrexate, leflunomide, etanercept, and infliximab. They function to reduce rheumatoid synovial proliferation and tissue destruction.

21. What is caput ulnae syndrome?

First described by Backdahl in 1963 and seen in up to on third of patients with RA, caput ulnae syndrome occurs when the ulnar head subluxes dorsally, the carpus supinates relative to the radius, and the ECU subluxes palmarly. This is as much a result of the ulnar head subluxing dorsally as it is the carpus and hand dislocating palmarly off the forearm. It occurs due to ulnar wrist and DRUJ ligamentous destruction. Clinically, a patient may present with dorsal ulnar head prominence, dorsal wrist swelling, ulnar-sided wrist pain, weakness, and diminished pronosupination. Backdahl recommended surgical resection of the ulnar head and tenosynovectomy of wrist extensor tendons.

22. What is a piano keyboard sign?

Because of ligamentous instability (as in caput ulnae syndrome), the ulnar head is prominent dorsally. The prominent ulnar head can be depressed palmarly, and it then rebounds dorsally as pressure is released. Balloting the ulnar head may be met with painful crepitus.

23. Why is dorsal ulnar prominence at the wrist a problem?

It can cause attrition ruptures of extensor digitorum communis (EDC) tendons. This is known as Vaughan-Jackson syndrome.

24. What are the causes of tendon rupture in RA?

- Attrition over bony prominences
- Nutrient deprivation and ischemia due to compression from synovial expansion
- Synovial infiltration into tendons

Although mechanical abrasion plays an important role, the true etiology for tendon rupture probably is multifactorial. Tendons may be compressed by synovial expansion, thereby causing tendinous nutrient restriction and ischemia. Tendons also may be attenuated and weakened through synovial infiltration.

25. Which flexor tendons commonly rupture in RA of the wrist?

The most common flexor tendon to rupture is the flexor pollicis longus tendon *(Mannerfelt lesion),* often due to a volar bony scaphoid spur. The flexor digitorum profundus to the index finger also may rupture via a similar mechanism.

26. Which extensor tendons commonly rupture in RA of the wrist?

Extensor tendons often rupture due to prominence of the ulnar head *(Vaughan-Jackson lesion).* The most common tendon to rupture is the EDC of the small finger, with progression occurring in an ulnar to radial direction. Dorsal metacarpal head spurs also may cause extensor tendon ruptures. The extensor pollicis longus may rupture on Lister's tubercle. Extensor tendon rupture is more common than is flexor tendon rupture in RA.

27. Why do patients with RA lose the ability to extend their fingers?

Extensor tendon rupture is a common etiology. Tendon subluxation at the MCP joints also can be responsible. As the sagittal bands attenuate and rupture, EDC tendons sublux ulnarly and volarly along with volar phalangeal subluxation, thereby upsetting their mechanical advantage. Posterior interosseous nerve (PIN) palsy due to compressive radiocapitellar synovitis at the elbow is a less common cause of failed finger extension.

28. How can you determine the cause of loss of finger extension?

To determine the etiology of failure of finger extension, extend and radially deviate (back to normal anatomic alignment) the MCP joints passively. If the patient can maintain the extended position, then the extensor tendons are intact, and the problem probably is due to tendon subluxation. If the patient cannot maintain the MCP joints in extension, then the EDC tendons are less likely to be functioning. The tenodesis effect can be used to differentiate between tendon rupture and PIN palsy. With maximal wrist flexion, the fingers should extend if the tendons are intact.

29. What are the surgical indications in RA of the wrist?

Disabling pain and extremity dysfunction are appropriate indications for surgical intervention. Deformity, by itself, is not an indication. Patients may have significant deformity but may maintain surprisingly adequate function. Normally, most surgeons will wait for 4 to 6 months before considering nonoperative management to have failed. In general, outcomes are best when surgical intervention is done prior to severe joint destruction, fixed contractures, subluxation, or dislocation. Tendon rupture is an indication for immediate surgical intervention.

30. What should be done during preoperative evaluation of a patient with RA?

RA may also involve the cervical spine in 60% to 90% of patients. A patient may suffer from atlantoaxial or other cervical instability. This is important for anesthetic considerations. A detailed history and thorough physical examination should include evaluation for this symptomatology. Cervical plain films (anteroposterior, lateral, odontoid, flexion, and extension views) should be obtained.

31. What are surgical options in managing DRUJ involvement in RA of the wrist?

- Darrach procedure
- Suave-Kapandji procedure
- Resection hemiarthroplasty (Bowers procedure)
- Distal ulna prosthesis.

32. What is the Darrach procedure?

Among the many variations of this procedure in use today, essentially all involve resection of the distal ulna. The Darrach procedure possibly is the most common procedure used to treat caput ulnae syndrome. Pain relief is often reported in 60% to 95% of patients. Whether the Darrach procedure halts or increases ulnar translation in RA is controversial.

33. Describe the Suave-Kapandji procedure.

This procedure involves removal of a segment of the distal ulnar shaft while preserving the ulnar head, which is then fused to the distal radius through the DRUJ. This permits forearm rotation. However, despite this procedure, ulnar shift and radial deviation may continue.

34. What does resection hemiarthroplasty involve?

Resection of just the DRUJ while preserving the full length of the ulna. This prevents contact between the radius and ulna through the arc of pronosupination. However, the TFCC attachments to the ulnar styloid are maintained, as is the joint capsule. This procedure is less commonly done today because an intact TFCC is necessary for its success, and often this structure is no longer intact in this patient population. Furthermore, ulnar styloid impaction may follow resection hemiarthroplasty.

35. What is a distal ulna prosthesis reconstruction?

This involves replacing the distal ulna either alone or along with a sigmoid component. Insufficient evidence exists for this relatively new technique, so long-term recommendations cannot yet be made.

36. What are the surgical options for treating radiocarpal involvement in RA?

- Tenosynovectomy
- Intraarticular wrist synovectomy
- Ulnar head resection
- Arthroplasty
- Arthrodesis

37. What are the indications for tenosynovectomy?

The main objectives are to prevent progression of RA (e.g., extensor tendon rupture) and reduce painful joint synovitis. Because isolated tenosynovitis is painless, patients may ignore it until complications occur. Thus there may be benefit to early intervention via tenosynovectomy, such as after 4 to 6 months of medical management.

38. How can intraarticular wrist synovectomy be performed?

There are two methods of wrist synovectomy: open and arthroscopic. With an open approach, reaching all recesses of the synovium often is difficult. Usually this approach is used in conjunction with other open procedures. Since the early 1990s, arthroscopic synovectomy has become more popular. It is indicated in patients in whom pharmacologic therapy has been inadequate or has not been tolerated. Symptoms should be present for at least 6 months and an attempt at intraarticular steroid injection made prior to arthroscopic consideration. Studies suggest that a marked reduction in pain and increased function can result. However, some authors believe that arthritic changes may be significantly hastened after arthroscopic synovectomy in patients with preexisting advanced arthritis and thus limit this technique to patients with early stages of radiographic changes. Similar to tenosynovectomy, performance of isolated synovectomy is rare unless a patient is symptomatic without radiographic joint pathology.

39. Describe the role of ulnar head resection.

Along with concomitant extensor tenosynovectomy, ulnar head resection originally was recommended by Backdahl for treatment of caput ulnae syndrome. It is performed as prophylaxis against extensor tendon rupture. However, the procedure does not address progression of disease, such as continued carpal collapse and translation. Additionally, the ulnar stump can still provide a surface against which tendons may abrade and rupture.

40. Why isn't wrist arthroplasty more popular in treating RA?

Originally, implants were made of silicone and acted as a flexible spacer. Initially they were successful in relieving pain while preserving some motion. However, implant breakage and silicone particulate synovitis curtailed their popularity. More recently, articulated wrist prostheses have been developed. However, their use has been limited by problems with instability, imbalance, loosening, metacarpal erosion with implant penetration, and periprosthetic bone resorption. Newer generations of prostheses that address these issues are being developed.

41. What are the types of wrist arthrodesis available in RA?

Wrist arthrodeses can be grouped into partial or total fusions. This concept originated with Stack and Vaughan-Jackson's report in 1971 of a patient with RA and spontaneous radiolunate fusion that exhibited halting of ulnar drift. Partial arthrodeses include radiolunate, radioscapholunate, and radiolunotriquetral fusions. In total arthrodesis, wrist pain and swelling may be better controlled, but wrist motion and grip strength are diminished when measured against partial arthrodesis. Total fusion is the most commonly performed bony procedure in RA. Often synovectomy and resection of the ulnar head are performed at the same time. Major complications of wrist arthrodesis include nonfusion, deep wound infection, DRUJ arthrosis, ulnar impaction syndrome, carpal tunnel syndrome, neuroma formation, and painful retained hardware.

42. How effective is wrist arthrodesis?

Generally, regardless of the method used, wrist fusion fairly reliably reduces wrist pain (approximately 70% of the time) and provides for wrist stability, but at the expense of wrist motion. In complete fusions, patients often are willing to accept the tradeoff of absent motion at the carpus for the pain relief and wrist stability they receive. For partial arthrodeses, this loss of motion is generally most significant in the direction of wrist flexion. However, in other directions, approximately half to two thirds of preoperative motion can be preserved. If distal ulnar resection is included in the course of the operative procedure, pronosupination often improves dramatically.

43. Is there a role for midcarpal fusion in RA?

Midcarpal fusions typically are not advocated for patients with RA because ligamentous instability and radiocarpal joint subluxation are not focused at that level. For similar reasons, proximal row carpectomy (PRC) is not commonly performed.

44. How should tendon ruptures be managed?

Although direct tendon repair is possible in the acute setting, it often is difficult and may be prone to recurrent rupture due to the underlying disease state. Tendon transfers are commonly used. Bridging tendon grafts are an alternative and are preferred by some authors. Adhesions may limit their usefulness. Regardless of the surgical method selected, tenosynovectomy and bony prominence removal should be performed at the same time to prevent future tendon ruptures.

45. What can be done if both wrist and finger extensors have ruptured?

The wrist must be fused to allow tendon reconstructions to the fingers to work.

BIBLIOGRAPHY

Adolfsson L: Arthroscopic synovectomy in wrist arthritis. Hand Clin 21:527–530, 2005.
American College of Rheumatology. Available at: www.rheumatology.org. Accessed October 27, 2009.
Anderson MC, Adams BD: Total wrist arthroplasty. Hand Clin 21:621–630, 2005.
Feldon P, Terrono AL, Nalebuff EA, Millender LH: Rheumatoid arthritis and other connective tissue diseases. In Green DP, Hotchkiss RN, Pederson WC, Wolfe SW (eds): Green's Operative Hand Surgery, 5th ed. Philadelphia, Elsevier, 2005, pp 2049–2136.
Ferlic DC: Repair of ruptured finger extensors in rheumatoid arthritis. In Strickland JW, Graham TJ (eds): The Hand, 2nd ed. Philadelphia, Lippincott Williams & Wilkins, 2005, pp 457–462.
Herren DB, Ishikawa H: Partial arthrodesis for the rheumatoid wrist. Hand Clin 21:545–552, 2005.
Lee SK, Hausmann MR: Management of the distal radioulnar joint in rheumatoid arthritis. Hand Clin 21:577–590, 2005.
Massarotti EM: Medical aspects of rheumatoid arthritis: diagnosis and treatment. Hand Clin 12:463–475, 1996.
Moore JR, Weiland AJ, Valdata L: Tendon ruptures in the rheumatoid hand: Analysis of treatment and functional results in 60 patients. J Hand Surg [Am] 12:9–14, 1987.
Rindfleisch JA, Muller D: Diagnosis and management of rheumatoid arthritis. Am Fam Physician 72:1037–1047, 2005.
Ruby LK, Cassidy C: Evaluation and treatment of the rheumatoid wrist. In Watson HK, Weinzweig J (eds): The Wrist. Philadelphia, Lippincott Williams & Wilkins, 2001, pp 645–657.
Salzman BE, Nevin JE, Newman JH: A primary care approach to the use and interpretation of common rheumatologic tests. Clin Fam Pract 7:335–358, 2005.
Smith P: Rheumatoid: Its variants and osteoarthritis. In: Lister's the Hand: Diagnosis and Indications, 4th ed. London, Churchill Livingstone, 2002, pp 331–397.
Trumble TE, Gardner GC: Arthritis. In Trumble TE (ed): Principles of Hand Therapy and Surgery. Philadelphia, WB Saunders, 2000, pp 401–435.
Watson HK, Weinzweig J: Principles of rheumatoid arthritis. In Watson HK, Weinzweig J (eds): The Wrist. Philadelphia, Lippincott Williams & Wilkins, 2001, pp 639–644.

DISTAL RADIUS FRACTURES

Chaitanya S. Mudgal, MD, MS(Orth), MCh(Orth), and
Jesse B. Jupiter, MD

1. Do fractures of the distal radius occur in all age-groups? What are the common mechanisms of injury?

Distal radial fractures have a bimodal distribution in the population. Osteopenic females in their sixth or seventh decade of life represent the most predominant group sustaining these fractures after a fall from a standing height. These fractures are considered low-energy injuries. Younger males (second and third decades of life) with denser bone compose the second major group that sustains distal radius fractures. Mechanisms of injury in this group vary from falls to sports injuries to high-speed vehicular injuries. Most of these fractures are considered high-energy injuries. Injuries sustained in the second decade before skeletal maturity are treated as pediatric injuries.

2. Is it correct to label all fractures of the distal radius as Colles fractures?

No. Eponymous associations of fractures in this anatomic region can be confusing and tricky. Knowing commonly used eponyms is prudent. However, fractures of the distal radius can be classified into various subtypes according to a plethora of existing classification systems. A description of a fracture pattern must convey the following important features to be effective and consistently reproducible:

- Is the fracture extraarticular or intraarticular?
- If intraarticular, does the fracture involve the radiocarpal joint, distal radioulnar joint (DRUJ), or both?
- Is the fracture displaced or undisplaced?
- Is the fracture shortened or impacted?
- Is there any angular deformity, and, if so, is the apex volar or dorsal?
- Is there comminution, and, if so, in which location?
- Is the distal ulna involved?

3. What are the commonly used eponyms to describe fractures of the distal radius?

An extraarticular fracture of the distal radius with apex volar angulation may be referred to as a *Colles fracture*. A similar fracture in which the angulation is apex–dorsal is known as a *Smith fracture*. An intraarticular fracture, in which the volar lip of the articular surface of the distal radius is sheared off, is known as a *volar Barton fracture*. A similar shearing injury to the dorsal rim of the distal radius is referred to as the *dorsal Barton fracture*.

4. What is the most comprehensive classification system used to classify fractures of the distal radius?

The most versatile and detailed classification system perhaps is that established by Muller et al. in 1990. The basis of this method is the division of all fractures of a bone segment into three types with further subdivision into three groups, each with subgroups based on the number of fragments. This system has an ascending order of severity defined by the morphologic findings, difficulties of treatment, and prognosis related to the fracture.

- *Type A:* Distal radial fractures not involving the articular surface (Colles and Smith fractures) (Fig. 154-1).
- *Type B:* Distal radial fractures involving part of the articular surface. These shearing fractures are subdivided into three groups (Figs. 154-2 and 154-3):
  - *B1:* Fractures in the sagittal plane such as radial styloid fractures
  - *B2:* Fractures in the coronal plane involving the dorsal rim (Barton fracture)
  - *B3:* Fractures in the coronal plane of the ventral rim or reverse Barton fracture
- *Type C:* Distal radial fractures involving a complete articular surface injury. These are classified as follows (Fig. 154-4):
  - *C1:* Two-fragment intraarticular fracture without metaphyseal fragmentation
  - *C2:* Two-fragment intraarticular fracture with multifragmented metaphysis
  - *C3:* Fractures with comminution of the articular surface; *comminution* is defined as involvement of greater than 50% of the metaphysis as seen on any radiographic view, comminution of at least two cortices of the metaphysis or shortening of the radius in excess of 2 mm

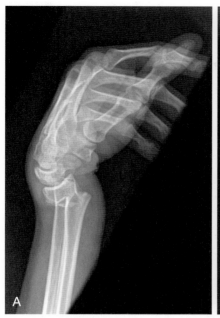
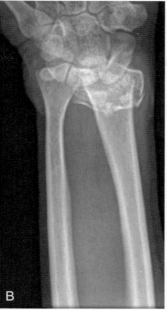

Figure 154-1. Type A distal radius fracture. This extraarticular fracture with apex–volar angulation is a classic Colles fracture.

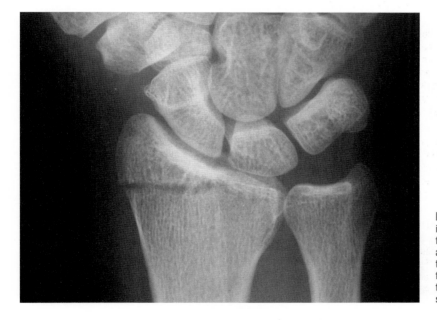

Figure 154-2. Type B fracture involving the radial styloid. Such fractures have also been referred to as "chauffeur's fractures" because they were caused by the kickback from an automobile engine in the days when automobiles were started by external crank handles.

5. What are the other common wrist injuries associated with fractures of the distal radius?

Injuries of the carpus and carpal ligaments can be seen with fractures of the distal radius and must be assessed for on radiographs. The most common carpal ligament injury is a tear of the scapholunate interosseous ligament (SLIL). Injuries to the triangular fibrocartilage complex are also well described. Although injury to the SLIL may occur with any fracture pattern, it appears that fracture lines exiting on the scapholunate crest of the distal radial articular surface have a higher chance of SLIL injury. The most commonly fractured carpal bone in association with distal radius fractures is the scaphoid, and this combination of injuries has been reported to be seen in 5% of all distal radius fractures (Fig. 154-5).

6. What are the radiographic projections used in imaging a distal radius fracture?

Standard initial radiographs must include the posteroanterior (PA), lateral, and oblique views to reveal the fracture pattern as well as the extent and direction of the initial displacement. Oblique projections can be useful in identifying displacement of fractures that involve the articular surface. The PA projection will help to define whether a fracture involves the articular surface and to identify the presence of associated carpal ligament injuries. Associated SLIL injury

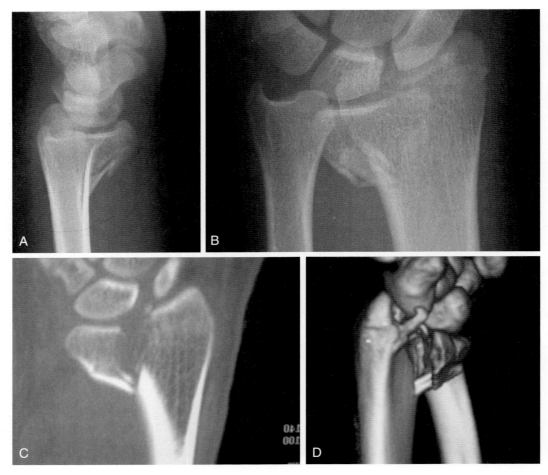

Figure 154-3. A, B, Type B fracture involving the volar articular margin, also called a reverse Barton fracture or volar Barton fracture. **C, D,** Fracture geometry is often better appreciated in intraarticular fractures with computed tomographic scans as seen in this sagittal section and three-dimensional reconstruction.

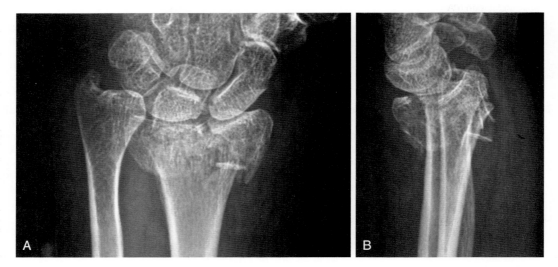

Figure 154-4. Type C distal radius fracture involving the entire articular surface and accompanied by extraarticular comminution.

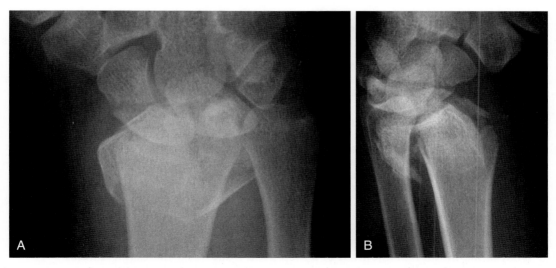

Figure 154-5. Comminuted fracture of the distal radius accompanied by a displaced fracture of the waist of the scaphoid.

may be suspected if any of the following are found: scapholunate distance on PA projection greater than 2 to 3 mm ("Terry Thomas sign"); loss of symmetry of the articular surface of the proximal carpal row (disrupted Gilula lines); or foreshortening or translation of the carpus.

7. **What are some of the cardinal measurements on radiographs of a distal radius?**
   Cardinal measurements in the PA projection include radial height (normal average 12 mm), radial inclination or ulnar tilt of the radius (average 23°), radial width (usually within 1 mm of that of the contralateral side), and alignment of the DRUJ. On the lateral view, volar tilt is the most important measurement. It is always important that the lateral projection be a "true" lateral view. A true lateral view is one in which the palmar cortices of the pisiform, lunate, and capitate are arranged from volar to dorsal with respect to the radius (Table 154-1).

Table 154-1. Radiographic Measurements

MEASUREMENT	DESCRIPTION	NORMAL VALUES
Radial inclination (PA projection)	Angle between the following two lines: A line drawn from the tip of the radial styloid to the most distal ulnar aspect of the lunate facet and a line perpendicular to the longitudinal axis of the radius	22° ± 3°
Radial length (PA projection)	Distance between a line perpendicular to the long axis of the radius drawn at the radial styloid and another line tangential to the distal articular surface of the ulna	11 ± 3 mm

Ulnar variance (PA projection)	Draw a line perpendicular to the long axis of the radius at the distal edge of the lunate facet; the amount of the ulnar head distal to that line measures ulnar variance	Axial Shortening:
		  Grade 0: <3 mm
		  Grade 1: 3–5 mm
		  Grade 2: >5 mm

Radial tilt (lateral projection)	Angle between a line through the volar and dorsal margins of the distal radius and a line perpendicular to the long axis of the radial shaft	11° ± 3°
Radial shift (PA projection)	Distance between the longitudinal axis of the radius and a line drawn tangential to the radial styloid	Compare to contralateral side PA radiograph

PA, Posteroanterior.

8. **If plain radiographs of the wrist do not provide adequate information regarding the injury, what other investigations may be indicated?**

Fracture geometry is better assessed on postreduction radiographs than on prereduction radiographs. In some fractures with severe comminution, intraarticular extension, or both, this assessment may be difficult. In such situations, computed tomography of the wrist provides information about fragment geometry, size, and location as well as the degree of comminution, its location, and intraarticular involvement. Three-dimensional reconstruction can be invaluable in determining fracture geometry and planning surgical tactics (see Figs. 154-3, *C* and *D).*

9. **What should be included in the initial clinical examination of a patient with a fractured distal radius?**

- The entire upper limb, not just the wrist.
- The volar surface of the wrist, because small open wounds usually are located here and can be easily missed.
- A complete neurologic evaluation is mandatory, with particular emphasis on the median and ulnar nerves.
- The forearm must be assessed for evidence of compartment syndrome, especially in patients with high-energy injuries with significant displacement, patients with concomitant injuries of the same upper limb, and patients whose clinical examination may be unreliable due to associated head injuries.
- Examine the elbow clinically and rule out any fractures. If in doubt, obtain radiographs of the elbow.

10. **What is the initial management of a displaced fracture of the distal radius?**

Upon completion of the initial clinical and radiographic examination, adequate pain control and splinting are the priorities. Narcotic medication may be required and should be used only after a neurologic examination has been completed. The affected limb then is elevated and can be provisionally splinted while arrangements are made for an expeditious closed reduction of the fracture or arrangements are made to bring the patient to the operating room for management of an open fracture, compartment syndrome, or median nerve compression.

11. **How is a "hematoma block" performed for a closed reduction of a distal radius fracture?**

A hematoma block consists of instillation of a local anesthetic within the fracture hematoma; 1% or 2% lidocaine usually is adequate. In most adults, 10 to 15 mL of anesthetic is instilled via one or two injections placed dorsally with a 25-gauge needle at the level of the fracture. The anesthetic is instilled toward the radial styloid as well as toward the distal radioulnar joint. If available, a portable mini-image intensifier can aid in accurate placement of the anesthetic. In the presence of an ulnar styloid fracture, a separate injection in this location is necessary. Diffusion of the anesthetic volarly around the median and ulnar nerves may occur, and patients should be reassured that digital numbness is to be expected. Therefore a thorough neurologic exam prior to anesthetic instillation is important. Hematoma blocks, by definition, work only within a fresh hematoma, usually within the first 12 to 24 hours. Thereafter, early organization of the hematoma prevents adequate diffusion of the anesthetic and usually provides inadequate anesthesia to perform a satisfactory closed reduction.

12. **How is a closed reduction of a distal radius fracture performed?**

After the hematoma block is performed, it is advisable to wait for a few minutes for it to act. The patient is placed supine at the edge of the stretcher. The shoulder is abducted, and the elbow is flexed to 90°. Commonly, the patient's thumb, index, and middle fingers are placed in finger-trap traction devices, which may be connected to an intravenous drip stand. A countertraction weight of 10 to 15 lb is applied via a padded sling to the patient's arm. The patient is then placed in this position for a few minutes for the traction–countertraction system to overcome the displacement and muscle spasm that accompanies a fracture. Manipulation starts with gentle extension of the wrist and then flexion while the surgeon's thumbs mold the distal radius by pressing it over the dorsal and radial surfaces. The fracture is reduced by applying dorsal pressure to the distal fragment, and it is "milked" back into position.

During this maneuver it is critical to be mindful of the thin skin in this area, because injudicious application of a milking maneuver can result in shearing off the skin in this area. Adequate reduction is verified by palpation for step-offs along the dorsal and radial surfaces. A well-padded sugar-tong splint is applied to the extremity. It extends from the level of the metacarpal necks volarly, goes around the elbow, and ends at the level of the metacarpal necks dorsally. As the splint is setting, it is molded into mild flexion and ulnar deviation at the wrist to restore the normal contours of the distal radius. It is important not to flex the wrist greater than 10° to 15° to avoid causing median nerve compression at the proximal edge of the carpal tunnel. After completing reduction and immobilization, postreduction radiographs are obtained to confirm the quality and stability of the reduction. The patient should receive instructions regarding cast care and the importance of elevation and early judicious finger motion.

13. **What is the management of undisplaced intraarticular and extraarticular stable fractures of the distal radius?**

Short arm casts usually are adequate for these injuries unless the fracture is associated with significant soft tissue swelling. Treatment consists of temporary immobilization in a sugar-tong splint. Clinical and radiographic follow-up is performed on a weekly basis. If the position is maintained, a short arm cast is applied within 2 to 3 weeks. The position of the wrist is maintained in 10° to 15° flexion and mild ulnar deviation. The cast is removed after 4 to 6 weeks, and rehabilitation is commenced.

14. What are the features of the initial clinical assessment that indicate the need for surgical fixation of a distal radius fracture?
Clinically, presence of an open fracture as well as symptoms of median nerve compression that do not resolve after a satisfactory closed reduction and immobilization necessitate emergent surgical treatment. Presence of a compartment syndrome also requires emergent decompression of the forearm as well as the carpal tunnel and is accompanied by stable internal or external fixation of the fracture.

15. What are the radiographic features that indicate the need for surgical treatment?
- Excessive comminution (usually dorsal)
- Initial loss of radial length in excess of 15 mm
- An initial angulation apex–volar of 20° or more
- Fracture extension into the metaphysis
- Concomitant injuries to the bones or ligaments within the carpus

16. What are some of the common forms of fixation of distal radius fractures?
Fractures of the distal radius can be fixed in a variety of ways. Current data have not proved the clear superiority of one method of fixation over the other. Percutaneous pin fixation, percutaneous screw fixation, external fixation with or without concomitant percutaneous pin fixation, and open reduction internal fixation with plates placed volarly or dorsally are some of the common forms of fixation used for distal radius fractures. Contemporary trends favor the use of volar fixed-angle plate fixation for most distal radius fractures (Figs. 154-6 and 154-7).

17. Which fractures are suitable for percutaneous pin fixation?
Extraarticular fractures that may have displaced while being treated in a cast or splint or extraarticular fractures with initial loss of radial length in excess of 15 mm, angulation in excess of 20 °, or associated with dorsal comminution are suitable for percutaneous pin fixation. This method is more suitable for young patients with adequate bone stock. In addition, grade I or II open fractures may be suitable for percutaneous pin fixation after the open wound has been débrided and irrigated (see Fig. 154-6).

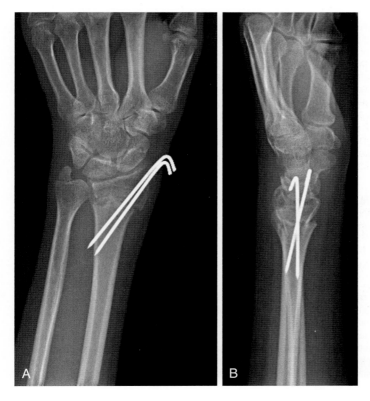

Figure 154-6. Postoperative radiographs after placement of percutaneous pins for the extraarticular fracture shown in Fig. 154-1.

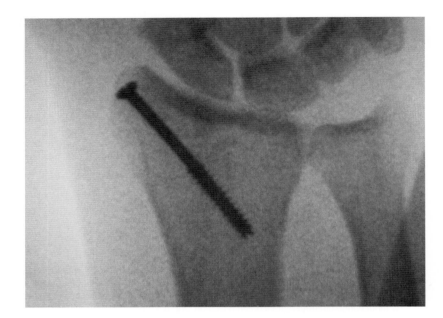

Figure 154-7. Percutaneous screw fixation of the radial styloid fracture shown in Fig. 154-2. Cannulated screws, which can be inserted over a guidewire, are commonly used.

18. How is percutaneous pin fixation performed?

Once alignment is achieved and reduction is completed, stabilization is achieved with the help of Kirschner wires. Small incisions are used. After the skin is incised, all further dissection is in a blunt spreading manner down to the bone. A drill sleeve is highly recommended because the terminal branches of the radial sensory nerve are in close proximity and can be injured. A minimum of two 0.062-inch Kirschner wires are used. The first one is inserted through the radial styloid and driven across the fracture to engage the proximal metaphysis. The second one can be placed ulnarly over the dorsal radial cortex and driven perpendicular to the former, exiting in the volar radial metaphysis. Additional wires might be required to achieve stability. Casting is necessary to augment and maintain the reduction after percutaneous pin fixation. If the fracture involves an open wound, an external fixator is better suited to augment pin fixation because it allows for easier wound care.

19. Is plate fixation for distal radius fractures performed volarly or dorsally?

There is no right or wrong answer to this question. Most contemporary plating systems rely on a fixed-angle device principle and the principle of subchondral support. This means that the screws in the distal fragment are placed in a subchondral location and are locked into the plate, making the plate a fixed-angle device. Such a plate construct is extremely stable, allowing early rehabilitation to commence. Plate fixation is performed as dictated by the fracture geometry. Dorsally applied low-profile plates are as effective as volarly applied plates. Plates applied on the dorsal surface rely on the columnar concept of fixation. This means that individual plates address major individual fragments (also known as *fragment specific fixation*), namely, the styloid or radial column and the lunate facet of the radius or the intermediate column. There is a greater tendency to develop symptoms of extensor tenosynovitis with dorsally applied plates because they can be in very close proximity to the extensor tendons. Plates applied to the volar surface of the distal radius rarely cause tendon irritation, although tenosynovitis of the flexor pollicis longus has been reported (Fig. 154-8).

20. What are the common complications of distal radius fractures?

- Inadequate reduction or loss of reduction leading to malunion
- Posttraumatic stiffness affecting the hand, particularly the metacarpophalangeal joints if a splint is applied incorrectly
- Median nerve compression
- Instability of the distal radioulnar joint
- Complex regional pain syndrome (CRPS)

21. What are the characteristics of CRPS, and how is it treated?

CRPS is now also known as sympathetically maintained pain syndrome and formerly was referred to by a plethora of names, including Sudeck atrophy/osteodystrophy, causalgia, algodystrophy, and reflex sympathetic dystrophy. It is characterized by pain that appears to be out of proportion to the injury and usually manifests within the first few weeks after the fracture. It usually is accompanied by stiffness and signs of sympathetic dysfunction, including swelling, color changes, temperature changes, and changes in patterns of hair and nail growth. Patients with this condition are often best managed in conjunction with the pain management service. Aggressive physical therapy, tricyclic antidepressants, and stellate ganglion blocks are some options for treatment.

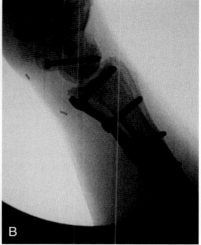

Figure 154-8. Postoperative radiographs after open reduction internal fixation of fractures of the distal radius and scaphoid shown in Fig. 154-5. The distal radius was fixed with a volar plate. The distal row of screws lock into the plate, providing a fixed-angle construct, and at the same time are placed in a subchondral location to maximize support to the articular surface and maintain its anatomic inclination.

BIBLIOGRAPHY

Jupiter JB: Complex articular fractures of the distal radius: Classification and management. J Am Acad Orthop Surg 5:119–129, 1997.

Jupiter JB, Fernandez DL, Whipple T, et al: Intra-articular fractures of the distal radius: Contemporary perspectives. Instr Course Lect 47: 191–202, 1998.

Jupiter JB, Fernandez DL: Complications following distal radial fractures. J Bone Joint Surg 83A:1244–1265, 2001.

Jupiter JB, Masem M: Reconstruction of post-traumatic deformity of the distal radius and ulna. Hand Clin 4:377–390, 1988.

Lipton HA, Jupiter JB: Open reduction and internal fixation of distal radius fractures. In Watson W, Weinzweig J (eds): The Wrist. Philadelphia, Lippincott Williams & Wilkins, 2001, pp 311–340.

Melone CP: Articular fractures of the distal radius. Orthop Clin North Am 15:217–236, 1984.

Mudgal CS, Hastings H: Scapholunate diastasis in fractures of the distal radius: Pathomechanics and treatment options. J Hand Surg [Br] 18:725–729, 1993.

Mudgal CS, Jones WA: Scapholunate diastasis: A component of fractures of the distal radius. J Hand Surg [Br] 15:503–505, 1990.

Pruitt DL, Gilula LA, Manske PR, et al: Computed tomography scanning with image reconstruction in evaluation of distal radius fractures. J Hand Surg [Am] 19:720–727, 1994.

Rettig ME, Raskin KB, Melone CP: External fixation of distal radius fractures. In Watson W, Weinzweig J (eds): The Wrist. Philadelphia, Lippincott Williams & Wilkins, 2001, pp 299–300.

LIMITED WRIST ARTHRODESIS

Jeffrey Weinzweig, MD, FACS, and
H. Kirk Watson, MD

1. What is an intercarpal arthrodesis?

Intercarpal arthrodesis, also referred to as *limited wrist arthrodesis*, is the selective fusion of adjacent carpal bones within the wrist. It is a proven method for treating specific carpal pathology that maximizes postoperative wrist motion, function, and strength while eliminating pain and instability.

2. Which wrist joints are responsible for flexion and extension?

Both the radiocarpal and midcarpal joints contribute to all phases of flexion and extension motion of the wrist. Two thirds of flexion occurs at the radiocarpal joint; one third occurs at the midcarpal joint. Slightly more extension occurs at the radiocarpal joint than at the midcarpal joint.

3. What is the functional range of wrist motion?

The functional range of wrist motion is 5° flexion, 30° extension, 10° radial deviation, and 15° ulnar deviation. Almost all activities of daily living are completed within these ranges of motion, all of which usually are surpassed with limited wrist arthrodeses. Radioulnar deviation after radiocarpal fusions is the only exception.

4. Is wrist motion lost after intercarpal arthrodesis? If so, how does the loss compare with motion lost after a total wrist arthrodesis?

In the normal wrist, adjacent carpal bones demonstrate motion limitations specific to a given intercarpal joint. Fusion of intercarpal joints results in some degree of motion loss; the extent depends on the joint(s) involved in the limited wrist arthrodesis. Fusions crossing the radiocarpal joint (e.g., radiolunate arthrodesis) result in the greatest loss of motion; fusions crossing the proximal and distal rows of the carpus or midcarpal joint (e.g., capitate–lunate–hamate–triquetral arthrodesis or scapholunate advanced collapse [SLAC] reconstruction; see Question 18) result in an intermediate loss of motion; and fusions within a single carpal row (e.g., lunotriquetral arthrodesis) result in the least loss of motion (see Question 26). When multiple carpal bones undergo fusion, a compensatory increase in motion occurs at the unfused joints, thereby maximizing total wrist motion. This adaptation of the carpus is not usually fully achieved until 9 to 12 months after intercarpal arthrodesis. Total wrist arthrodesis, however, results in complete loss of all wrist motion.

5. What are the indications for an intercarpal arthrodesis?

Intercarpal arthrodesis addresses a diverse group of wrist disorders, including degenerative disease, rotary subluxation of the scaphoid, midcarpal instability, scaphoid nonunion, Kienböck disease, carpal osteonecrosis, and congenital synchondrosis or partial fusion of various intercarpal joints.

6. Why is it critical that unaffected intercarpal joints be left unfused? Are there any exceptions?

Unaffected intercarpal joints must be left unfused if motion is to be maintained postoperatively, hence the conceptual basis for selective limited wrist fusion. An exception to this principle is the inclusion of the hamate and triquetrum in SLAC wrist reconstruction to maximize the surface area for bone graft consolidation.

7. Why must the normal external dimensions of the carpal bones included in a limited arthrodesis be preserved? Are there any exceptions?

Preservation is essential to maintain normal articulations with adjacent bones. Preservation of the external dimension of the triscaphe (scaphotrapeziotrapezoid [STT]) joint during arthrodesis is accomplished with a temporary spacer that is removed after pin placement. In lunotriquetral arthrodesis, the distal rim of cartilage on the adjacent surface of each bone is left intact. This cartilage is an important guide in maintaining reduction and alignment of the bones before fixation. SLAC wrist reconstruction (see Question 18), with fusion of the capitate, lunate, hamate, and triquetrum, is an exception to this principle. Whereas reduction of the lunate and correction of any dorsiflexion intercalated segment instability (DISI) is essential, maintenance of the original external dimensions of the four carpal bones is not. No other intercarpal joints remain to be affected. Some collapse of the capitate and hamate on the lunate and triquetrum is tolerated because all loads pass directly through the single fused unit and subsequently through the preserved radiolunate joint.

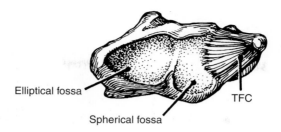

Elliptical fossa

Spherical fossa

TFC

Figure 155-1. Distal radius and ulna anatomy. An end-on view of the distal radius and ulna shows the elliptical scaphoid fossa and the spherical lunate fossa. The radial portion of the triangular fibrocartilage *(TFC)* contributes to the support mechanism for the lunate.

8. Why must pin fixation include only bones involved in the arthrodesis?

This technique permits any encountered stresses or loads to be dissipated by motion in the adjacent local joints. Inadvertent inclusion of adjoining bones during fixation inhibits the motion of adjacent joints, thus increasing the amount of load transferred through the healing arthrodesis and potentially disrupting the fusion site.

9. Why is the scaphoid susceptible to degenerative arthritic change?

The susceptibility of the scaphoid to degenerative arthritic change is attributable to its anatomy and position within the wrist (Fig. 155-1). The articular surface of the distal radius is composed of two articular fossae, a radial fossa for the scaphoid and an ulnar fossa for the lunate. The fossa for the scaphoid is ovoid or elliptical, whereas the fossa for the lunate is spherical. Part of the sphere is composed of the most radial portion of the triangular fibrocartilage. The proximal articular surface of the scaphoid resembles a simple teaspoon with its handle immediately dorsal and radial to the position of the relaxed thumb. Flexion and extension occur with full articular contact of the spoon (scaphoid) in the elliptical fossa of the radius. If the spoon handle is brought in front of the little finger and flexed so that the handle is perpendicular to the long axis of the forearm, the contact surface of the spoon in the elliptical fossa is disrupted. When this occurs, the proximal spoon surface (scaphoid) lies on the radial edges of the elliptical fossa, and fairly rapid destruction between the scaphoid and radius occurs in these regions.

10. What is a triscaphe arthrodesis?

Triscaphe arthrodesis is a fusion of the scaphoid, trapezium, and trapezoid bones and is often referred to as an *STT fusion*. A single bony unit is created with external dimensions identical to those of the three carpal bones before fusion. Preservation of the external bony dimensions is necessary to prevent carpal collapse and excessive loading of the capitate, which ultimately result in degenerative change and instability of the lunocapitate column followed by SLAC wrist (see Question 15).

Indications for triscaphe arthrodesis include symptomatic rotary subluxation of the scaphoid, degenerative disease of the triscaphe joint, nonunion of the scaphoid, Kienböck disease, scapholunate (SL) dissociation, traumatic dislocations, midcarpal instability, and congenital synchondrosis of the triscaphe joint. Triscaphe arthrodesis provides a stable radial column for load transfer across the wrist to the radius and permits the unloading of carpal units no longer capable of bearing load, such as the lunate in Kienböck disease. In addition, it provides stability and strength to a wrist affected by the pathomechanics of rotary subluxation of the scaphoid or midcarpal instability.

11. What is rotary subluxation of the scaphoid? How is it treated?

Rotary subluxation of the scaphoid (RSS) is a well-recognized entity in which the SL articulation is disrupted and the wrist develops a pattern of instability with loading. It is classically described as a diastasis between the scaphoid and lunate with dorsal displacement and rotation of the proximal pole of the scaphoid. Disruption of the ligamentous support of the proximal pole permits it to rotate dorsally while the distal pole rotates volarly, producing an increased SL angle on lateral radiographic examination with the scaphoid lying more perpendicular to the long axis of the forearm. This deformity produces a scaphoid with abnormal motion that may subject the radioscaphoid joint to abnormal loading stresses, eventually resulting in destruction of the joint.

Patients with RSS present with various combinations of five consistent complaints: (1) activity pain, (2) postactivity pain, (3) activity modification, (4) carpal tunnel syndrome symptoms, and (5) wrist ganglions. All patients present with at least three of these historical findings; many patients present with all five. Radiographic findings on the neutral posteroanterior (PA) view may include foreshortening of the scaphoid, a positive ring sign, and an increased SL gap. Radiographic findings on the neutral lateral view may include a SL angle greater than 70° and a DISI deformity of the lunate (Fig. 155-2). RSS is best treated with a triscaphe arthrodesis to stabilize the scaphoid and radial column of the carpus.

12. How is a triscaphe arthrodesis performed?

The triscaphe joint is approached through a transverse dorsal wrist incision just distal to the radial styloid. The radial styloid is exposed, and the distal 5 mm of the styloid is resected. The triscaphe joint is approached through a transverse

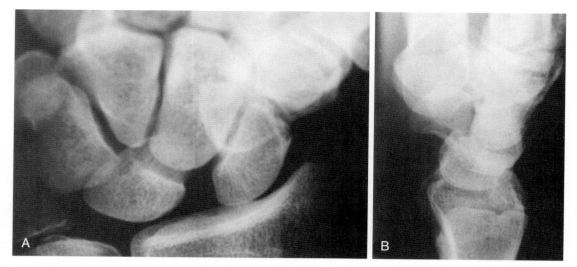

Figure 155-2. Rotary subluxation of the scaphoid. **A,** Neutral posteroanterior view shows foreshortening of the scaphoid, a positive ring sign, and an increased scapholunate gap. **B,** Neutral lateral view shows a scapholunate angle of 90° and a dorsiflexion intercalated segment instability deformity of the lunate.

capsular incision between the extensor carpi radialis longus and brevis tendons. The articular surfaces and the subchondral hard cancellous bone of the scaphoid, trapezium, and trapezoid are removed with a rongeur. The cortex dorsal to the articular cartilage on the trapezium and trapezoid also is removed to broaden the surface area for grafting.

Two 0.045-inch Kirschner wires (K-wires) are passed percutaneously and preset through the trapezoid up to the fusion site to be driven into the scaphoid. The scaphoid is reduced, and a 5-mm spacer, usually the handle of a small hook, is placed into the scaphotrapezoid space to maintain the original external dimensions of the triscaphe joint. The preset pins are driven from the trapezoid into the scaphoid, avoiding placement into the radioscaphoid joint or radius, and the spacer is removed.

Cancellous bone graft, harvested from the distal radius, is densely packed into the spaces between the scaphoid, trapezium, and trapezoid. The pins are cut beneath the skin level, and the skin incisions are closed with a single-layer subcuticular monofilament suture. The wrist capsule and extensor retinaculum are simply realigned without suturing. The postoperative dressing consists of a bulky noncompressive wrap incorporating a long arm plaster splint. The hand is placed in a protected position with the wrist in slight extension and radial deviation, the forearm neutral, and the elbow at 90° (Fig. 155-3).

13. What is the key to performing a successful triscaphe arthrodesis?

The most important step in triscaphe arthrodesis is reduction of the scaphoid. The normal SL angle is approximately 47° to the long axis of the forearm. Scaphoid reduction is accomplished by placing the wrist in full radial deviation and 45°

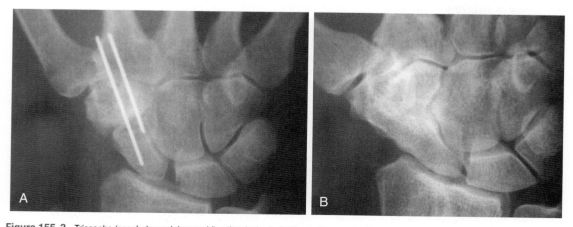

Figure 155-3. Triscaphe (scaphotrapeziotrapezoid) arthrodesis. **A,** Radiographic examination 6 weeks after triscaphe arthrodesis shows typical pin placement and adequate bony consolidation. **B,** Three months after fusion, the arthrodesis is radiographically solid.

of dorsiflexion. The scaphoid tuberosity is reduced by the surgeon's thumb to prevent scaphoid overcorrection. Pinning is performed as described, after which the scaphoid should lie at approximately 55° to 60° of palmar flexion relative to the long axis of the radius when seen from the lateral view. This position ensures optimal radioscaphoid congruity and maximizes postoperative range of motion. It is not necessary to correct abnormal rotation of the lunate.

14. Are there any absolute contraindications to a triscaphe arthrodesis?

Triscaphe arthrodesis is contraindicated if significant degenerative change is found at the radioscaphoid joint.

15. What is SLAC wrist?

SLAC wrist is the most common pattern of degenerative disease of the wrist, accounting for 57% of all periscaphoid arthritis. The scaphoid is the weak link in the wrist with regard to degenerative disease, and the specialized radioscaphoid joint is particularly susceptible. Rotation, fracture nonunion, or necrosis of the scaphoid may produce a collapse pattern on the radial side of the wrist, ultimately leading to degenerative disease or SLAC destruction, which occurs first between the radial styloid and the scaphoid (stage IA). With progressive degenerative disease, complete destruction of the radioscaphoid joint occurs with collapse of the articular space (stage IB). Once this collapse has occurred, whether it is secondary to scaphoid instability or scaphoradial in nature, the capitate–lunate joint is unable to bear loads normally. The capitate drives off the radial or dorsal radial portion of the distal lunate articular surface, causing cartilage shear stress with eventual destruction of the capitate–lunate joint and resultant midcarpal SLAC (stage II) (Fig. 155-4).

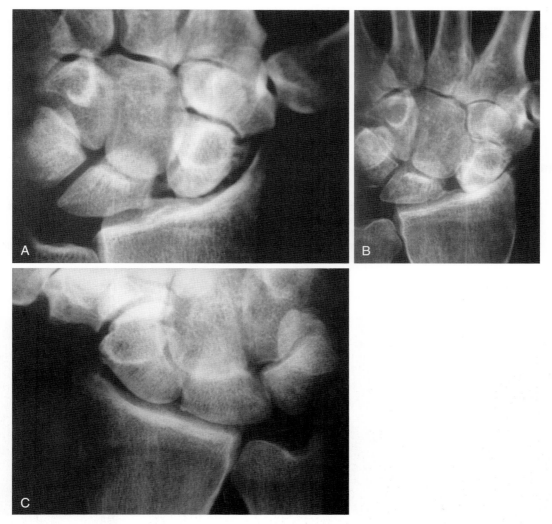

Figure 155-4. Stages of scapholunate advanced collapse (SLAC) wrist. **A,** SLAC changes are seen earliest at the radial aspect of the radioscaphoid joint beginning at the radial styloid (stage IA). **B,** Subsequently, the remainder of the radioscaphoid joint is involved (stage IB). **C,** Finally, destruction of the capitate–lunate joint occurs (stage II). Isolated involvement of the capitate–lunate joint also may be seen and is referred to as midcarpal SLAC.

16. Which conditions predispose to the development of SLAC wrist?

The most common cause of SLAC wrist is rotary subluxation of the scaphoid followed by scaphoid nonunion. Other conditions that produce SLAC degeneration include Preiser disease, midcarpal instability, intraarticular fractures involving the radioscaphoid or capitate–lunate joints, and Kienböck disease (tertiary to the secondary RSS).

17. Which joint in the wrist is virtually never involved in degenerative disease? Why not?

The key to reconstruction of the SLAC wrist lies in the radiolunate joint, which is highly resistant to degenerative change and is preserved at all stages of the SLAC sequence. The articulation of the lunate with the radius is spherical; thus the lunate can be moved volarly or dorsally, radially or ulnarly, and the proximal articular surface of the lunate will still be perpendicularly loaded. Even with significant displacement of the lunate into volarflexion intercalated segment instability (VISI) or DISI, the radiolunate joint usually is preserved.

18. How is SLAC wrist reconstruction performed?

SLAC wrist reconstruction involves excision of the scaphoid and arthrodesis of the capitate, lunate, hamate, and triquetrum. This procedure, also referred to as a *four-corner fusion*, is performed with two parallel dorsal incisions: one over the radiocarpal joint and one proximally over the distal radial aspect of the radius for bone graft harvest (same incisions as for the triscaphe arthrodesis). After incising the extensor retinaculum along the third compartment, a transverse incision is made through the wrist capsule at the level of the capitate–lunate joint. The scaphoid is approached in the interval between the extensor carpi radialis longus and brevis and removed in piecemeal fashion with a rongeur.

Longitudinal traction on the fingers permits exposure of the radiolunate joint and confirmation that it is well preserved. Articular cartilage and subchondral bone are removed from the adjacent surfaces of the capitate, lunate, hamate, and triquetrum. Cancellous bone is harvested from the distal radius. Three 0.045-inch Kirschner wires are passed percutaneously and preset through the capitate, hamate, and triquetrum up to the fusion site to be driven into the lunate. A fourth wire is preset into the triquetrum to be driven into the capitate. Part of the cancellous graft is packed in the deep interval between the capitate and lunate. After correction of any DISI deformity of the lunate (see Question 19), the preset pins are driven into the lunate from the capitate, hamate, and triquetrum and from the triquetrum into the capitate. Bone grafting, closure, and postoperative dressings are the same as for the triscaphe arthrodesis (Fig. 155-5).

19. What is the key to performing a successful SLAC wrist reconstruction?

The most important step in SLAC wrist reconstruction is correction of the commonly associated DISI deformity of the lunate. The capitate must be volarly and ulnarly displaced on the lunate to prevent the DISI position and to align the hand over the radius–lunate joint. A buttress pin running dorsally into the lunate abutting the dorsal edge of the radius can be used to maintain the lunate in a slight VISI position. A joker (similar to a Freer) placed across the distal lunate surface and used as a lever will suffice for position control. It is important to bring the capitate ulnarly and to align it centered on the lunate. Inadequate reduction of the DISI deformity of the lunate at the time of arthrodesis not only leads to loss of carpal height but also limits the available arc of radiolunate motion.

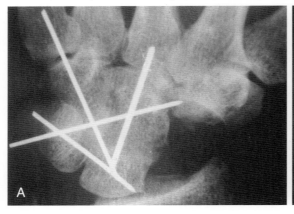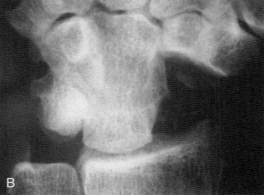

Figure 155-5. Scapholunate advanced collapse (SLAC) wrist reconstruction. **A,** Radiographic examination 6 weeks after SLAC reconstruction with limited wrist arthrodesis and scaphoid excision shows typical pin placement and adequate bony consolidation. **B,** Six months after SLAC reconstruction, the arthrodesis is radiographically solid and the radiolunate joint well preserved. Note the ulnar displacement of the capitate on the lunate, which tightens the radioscaphocapitate ligament and prevents ulnar translation.

20. Are there any absolute contraindications to SLAC wrist reconstruction?

Patients who present with SLAC wrist in conjunction with lunate or radiolunate pathology are *not* candidates for this type of reconstruction. Significant ulnar translation, which disrupts the concentric congruity of the radiolunate articulation and predictably leads to joint destruction, osteonecrosis of the lunate (as in Kienböck disease), and preexisting radiolunate degenerative change, are absolute contraindications to SLAC wrist reconstruction. The salvage procedures under these conditions include proximal row carpectomy and wrist arthrodesis.

21. What are the most common patterns of degenerative disease of the wrist?

In its normal anatomic position, the scaphoid articulates with the radius at the radiocarpal joint and with the trapezium and trapezoid at the triscaphe joint. Therefore it is not surprising that approximately 95% of all degenerative disease of the wrist is periscaphoid in origin. Review of more than 4000 radiographs of the wrist yielded 210 films demonstrating degenerative arthritic change. The SLAC pattern of degenerative change was seen in 57%, triscaphe joint arthritis in 27%, and a combination of both in 15%.

22. What is a congenital carpal synchondrosis? Which intercarpal joint is most commonly involved?

Cavitation of a common cartilaginous precursor during the fourth to eighth weeks of intrauterine life results in the formation of individual carpal bones. Incomplete cavitation results in congenital carpal synchondrosis or incomplete separation of the carpal bones, which becomes radiographically apparent as the carpus ossifies. This occurs most commonly at the lunotriquetral joint, where the joint has the pathognomonic appearance of a fluted champagne glass. The distal portion of the joint usually has normal cartilage development, whereas proximally normal joint development has been arrested, predisposing it to degenerative joint disease. The capitate–hamate joint is the next most commonly involved. Such anomalies occur rarely, are generally believed to be asymptomatic, and usually are discovered as incidental findings during radiographic evaluations for minor trauma.

23. Why might a congenitally fused intercarpal joint require subsequent arthrodesis?

Congenital synchondrosis of a joint can be recognized radiographically by the presence of bone where articular cartilage should be found. This unique radiographic finding is diagnostic of this interesting anomaly. In degenerative arthritis, on the other hand, the articular cartilage has developed and subsequently been worn away; as a result, the normal bony surfaces approach one another. The spectrum of synchondrosis ranges from partial to complete fusion, depending on the degree of formation of the articular cartilaginous elements. Degenerative disease may result from motion within a partially fused intercarpal joint that possesses inadequate cartilage to tolerate loading, necessitating a limited wrist arthrodesis.

24. What are the indications for limited wrist arthrodesis of the lunotriquetral joint?

Pathology arising from the lunotriquetral (LT) joint is a known cause of ulnar wrist pain. Indications for limited wrist arthrodesis of this articulation include LT joint instability, degenerative arthritis, and symptomatic congenital synchondrosis or incomplete separation of the lunate and triquetrum. Patients with LT pathology usually experience pain by palpation directly over the LT joint or by shear loading of the joint while performing an LT ballottement test.

25. How is an LT arthrodesis performed?

The LT joint is exposed through a transverse dorsal ulnar incision centered over the joint, and the adjacent articular surfaces are removed with a dental rongeur. The distal margins of cartilage are left intact to preserve the relationship of the two bones and to help maintain alignment during fixation. During removal of the articular surfaces, a biconcave space is created to centralize any loads and to aid in preventing displacement of grafted bone. Two 0.045-inch Kirschner wires (K-wire) are preset into the triquetrum in parallel fashion. The joint is reduced using the preserved margins as guides, maintaining the normal external dimensions of the bones, and the K-wires are driven into the lunate. The biconcave space is densely packed with cancellous bone graft. A long arm dressing incorporating a dorsal splint is applied.

26. Which intercarpal arthrodesis results in the greatest loss of wrist motion? Which results in the least loss of motion?

Of the intercarpal arthrodeses, the four-bone SLAC wrist reconstruction results in the greatest loss of wrist motion. This fusion crosses the midcarpal joint and involves four intercarpal joints (lunate–capitate, triquetrum–hamate, lunate–triquetrum, capitate–hamate). The average range of motion after SLAC reconstruction is approximately 60% of the contralateral normal wrist. The average range of motion after triscaphe arthrodesis is approximately 80% of the contralateral normal wrist. Arthrodesis of the LT joint, typically regarded as the tightest joint in the wrist, results in the least loss of carpal motion.

27. What is the optimal bone graft donor site for intercarpal arthrodesis?

The distal radius provides an ample supply of cancellous bone in the same operative field, with minimal morbidity.

28. How is bone graft harvested from the distal radius? The identification of which structure is helpful during graft harvest?

A 3-cm transverse incision is made approximately 3 cm proximal to the radial styloid, extending from the site of Lister's tubercle dorsally to a point just volar to the first dorsal compartment. A flat periosteal surface is exposed between the first and second extensor compartments; this surface is identified by a constant periosteal artery that runs longitudinally in the region. The periosteum is incised longitudinally along this small, dispensable artery and elevated to permit removal of a teardrop-shaped cortical window approximately 2 cm long × 1.5 cm wide with a narrow, straight osteotome. Harvest of the cortical window begins distally on the radial tuberosity. Adequate cancellous bone graft is harvested with an 8-mm curette, and the cortical window is replaced. The cortical window is held securely in place simply by repositioning the overlying periosteum and extensor tendons.

29. Can SL dissociation be treated with a SL limited wrist arthrodesis?

Absolutely not. SL limited wrist arthrodesis may seem an ideal approach to the management of SL dissociation, but there are several important reasons why this is not so. Perhaps the most obvious is the difficulty of achieving union by fusion of the relatively small articular surfaces of the two bones. Cancellous contact areas are inadequate; therefore nonunion rates are predictably high. However, there are two other compelling reasons to avoid this procedure. The first reason is that any limited wrist arthrodesis requires sufficient bone to carry the load of the carpus. The banana-shaped SL combination provides inadequate bony volume to carry the loads that this fusion would be required to bear and would result in carpal symptoms. The second reason is based on the fact that the scaphoid and lunate reside in two different fossae on the same bone. A ridge is typically found between the fossae on the radius and is occasionally substantial. Fusing the scaphoid to the lunate would remove the small but necessary degree of motion between the bones and result in decreased range of motion compared with the SLAC reconstruction and degenerative change of the radiocarpal joint.

30. Both scaphoid–capitate arthrodesis and triscaphe arthrodesis are used to treat scaphoid instability. How do the procedures differ biomechanically?

Scaphoid–capitate arthrodesis and triscaphe arthrodesis are two distinct operations. The scaphoid–capitate fusion transmits load directly across the fusion site from the capitate to the scaphoid and then to the radius. With triscaphe arthrodesis, the loads are not transmitted primarily through the fusion site. In fact, most of the load passes from the capitate across normal cartilage to the scaphoid and again across normal cartilage to the radius. Arthrodesis of the triscaphe joint prevents the proximal pole of the scaphoid from displacing beneath the capitate under load, but the fusion does not carry the load. The normally small amount of motion between the capitate and scaphoid gradually increases and provides a significant difference in wrist motion between the two types of limited wrist arthrodesis.

31. What are the indications for a radiolunate arthrodesis in nonrheumatoid patients?

Destruction of the radiolunate joint and ulnar carpal translation are the only indications for radiolunate arthrodesis in nonrheumatoid patients. Destruction usually results from dye-punch fractures involving the spherical lunate fossa on the distal radius. This type of limited wrist arthrodesis also may be indicated for wrist stabilization in the management of ulnar translation. The procedure requires sufficient distal radius bone graft to elevate the lunate and thereby prevent loss of carpal height. Overcorrection of the position of the lunate on the radius by slightly excessive elevation is well tolerated by the wrist and, in fact, is preferred. Undercorrection of the lunate position with loss of carpal height results in decreased wrist motion and wrist instability.

32. What is an absolute contraindication to radiolunate arthrodesis?

Destruction of the capitate–lunate joint is an absolute contraindication to this procedure because wrist motion depends on this midcarpal joint after radiolunate arthrodesis.

33. How is the wrist managed after intercarpal arthrodesis?

Our postoperative management is similar for most intercarpal arthrodeses, including triscaphe fusions and SLAC reconstructions. Maximal initial immobilization is mandatory for these small bone fusions. Three to five days after surgery, the bulky intraoperative dressing is removed, and a long arm, thumb spica cast is applied (short arm cast is used after LT arthrodesis). The proximal carpal row is easily immobilized by casting the forearm and arm, but it is difficult to maintain adequately the position of the distal carpal row. Therefore the metaphalangeal joints of the index and middle fingers are flexed to 80° to 90° and are included in the long arm cast, whereas the interphalangeal joints are left free. The index and middle metacarpals are mortised into the carpals as the "fixed unit" of the hand. Thus their immobilization tends to maintain the position of the distal carpal row. Because there is relatively free motion at the base of the ring and little metacarpals, they are not included in the cast. As with any thumb spica cast, the thumb is immobilized to the tip. We refer to this type of immobilization as a "Groucho Marx" cast because it is reminiscent of the comedian's classic pose holding a cigar.

Four weeks after limited wrist arthrodesis, the long arm cast and intracuticular sutures are removed. A short arm, thumb spica cast is applied for an additional 2 to 3 weeks. Only the thumb is included in the cast. Six weeks postoperatively, the short arm cast is removed, and radiographs are obtained. If radiographic evidence of union is seen, the pins are removed and the wrist is mobilized.

34. What is the incidence of complications after intercarpal arthrodesis?

Triscaphe arthrodesis has been an extremely reliable procedure, and complications are relatively few (approximately 1000 procedures have been performed). Nonunion has been extremely uncommon with a rate of 1% to 3%, depending on the indication for limited wrist arthrodesis. Infection, hematoma, and transient neurapraxias have been rare in our experience. Degenerative change at the radioscaphoid joint, consistent with SLAC wrist, occurred in 1.5% of cases, necessitating subsequent SLAC reconstruction. However, radiolunate degenerative change was not observed in any case.

Complications after almost 300 SLAC wrist reconstructions include nonunion in 1% of cases, wound infection in 1%, and reflex sympathetic dystrophy in 1.5%. Dorsal impingement between the capitate and radius after SLAC reconstruction required revision arthroplasty in 13% of patients. Inadequate reduction of the DISI deformity of the lunate at the time of arthrodesis not only leads to loss of carpal height but also limits the available arc of radiolunate motion. During wrist extension the capitate approaches the dorsal lip of the radius, where impingement may occur with associated pain. Coaxial alignment of the lunate with the capitate is essential for optimal outcome.

Complications after performing 26 LT limited wrist arthrodeses using the cancellous biconcave technique include reflex sympathetic dystrophy in one patient and pin migration, necessitating early removal of the K-wires, in one patient. There were no nonunions in this series.

BIBLIOGRAPHY

Ashmead D, Watson HK, Damon C, et al: Scapholunate advanced collapse wrist salvage. J Hand Surg 19A:741–750, 1994.
Ashmead D, Watson HK: SLAC wrist reconstruction. In Gelberman R (ed): The Wrist. New York, Raven Press, 1994, pp 319–330.
Ashmead D, Watson HK, Weinzweig J, Zeppieri J: One thousand intercarpal arthrodeses. J Hand Surg 21B:10, 1996.
Garcia-Elias M, Cooney WP, An KN, et al: Wrist kinematics after limited intercarpal arthrodesis. J Hand Surg 14A:791–799, 1989.
Kirschenbaum D, Schneider LH, Kirkpatrick WH, et al: Scaphoid excision and capitolunate arthrodesis for radioscaphoid arthritis. J Hand Surg 18A:780–785, 1993.
McGrath MH, Watson HK. Late results with local bone graft donor sites in hand surgery. J Hand Surg 6:234–237, 1981.
Palmer AK, Werner FW, Murphy D, Glisson R: Functional wrist motion: A biomechanical study. J Hand Surg 10A:39–46, 1985.
Trumble T, Bour C, Smith R, Edwards G: Intercarpal arthrodesis for static and dynamic volar intercalated segment instability. J Hand Surg 13A:396–402, 1988.
Viegas SF, Patterson RM, Peterson PD, et al: Evaluation of the biomechanical efficacy of limited intercarpal fusions for the treatment of scapholunate dissociation. J Hand Surg 15A:120–128, 1990.
Watson HK, Ballet FL: The SLAC wrist: Scapholunate advanced collapse pattern of degenerative arthritis. J Hand Surg 9A:358–365, 1984.
Watson HK, Fink JA, Monacelli DM: Use of triscaphe fusion in the treatment of Kienböck's disease. Hand Clin 9:493–499, 1993.
Watson HK, Goodman ML, Johnson TR: Limited wrist arthrodesis. Part II: Intercarpal and radiocarpal combinations. J Hand Surg 6:223–232, 1981.
Watson HK, Hempton RE: Limited wrist arthrodesis. Part I: The triscaphoid joint. J Hand Surg 5:320–327, 1980.
Watson HK, Ryu J, Akelman E: Limited triscaphoid intercarpal arthrodesis for rotary subluxation of the scaphoid. J Bone Joint Surg 68A:345–349, 1986.
Watson HK, Ryu J, DiBella A: An approach to Kienböck's disease: Triscaphe arthrodesis. J Hand Surg 10A:179–187, 1985.
Watson HK, Weinzweig J: Physical examination of the wrist. Hand Clin 13:17–34, 1997.
Watson HK, Weinzweig J: Intercarpal arthrodesis. In Green DP (ed): Operative Hand Surgery, 4th ed. New York, Churchill Livingstone, 1999, pp 108–130.
Watson HK, Weinzweig J: Limited wrist arthrodesis. In Watson HK, Weinzweig J (eds): The Wrist. Philadelphia, Lippincott Williams & Wilkins, 2000, pp 521–543.
Watson HK, Weinzweig J: Treatment of Kienböck's disease with triscaphe arthrodesis. In Vastamaki M, Vilkki S, Goransson H, et al. (eds): Proceedings of the Sixth Congress of the International Federation of Societies for Surgery of the Hand. Bologna, Monduzzi Editore, 1995, pp 347–349.
Watson HK, Weinzweig J, Zeppieri J: The natural progression of scaphoid instability. Hand Clin 13:39–50, 1997.
Weinzweig J, Watson HK: Wrist sprain to SLAC wrist: A spectrum of carpal instability. In Vastamaki M (ed): Current Trends in Hand Surgery. Amsterdam, Elsevier Science, 1995, pp 47–55.
Weinzweig J, Watson HK, Herbert TJ, Shaer J: Congenital synchondrosis of the scaphotrapezio-trapezoid joint. J Hand Surg 22A:74–77, 1997.
Weiss KE, Rodner CM. Osteoarthritis of the wrist. J Hand Surg 32:725–746, 2007.

INDEX

Page numbers followed by *b*, indicate boxes; *f*, figures; *t*, tables.

PLASTIC SURGERY SECRETS